KT-441-537

Chronicle of the Cinema

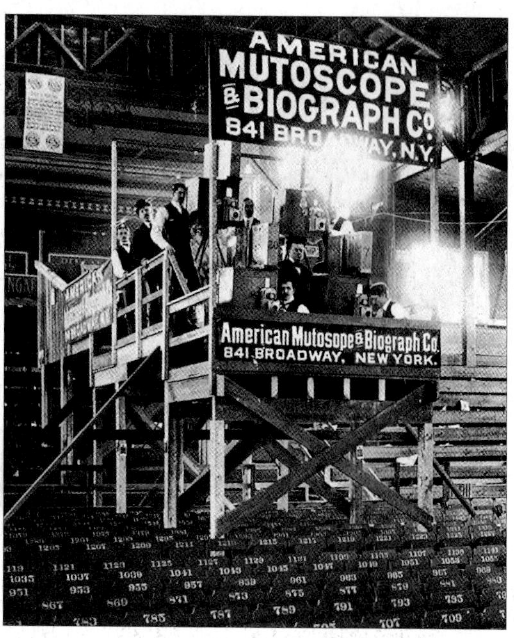
AMERICAN
MUTOSCOPE
& BIOGRAPH Co
841 BROADWAY, N.Y.
American Mutoscope & Biograph Co.
841 BROADWAY, NEW YORK.

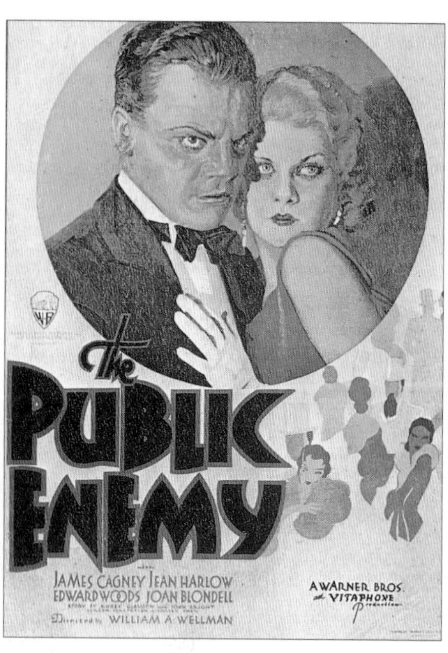
The PUBLIC ENEMY
JAMES CAGNEY JEAN HARLOW
EDWARD WOODS JOAN BLONDELL
A WARNER BROS. VITAPHONE
WILLIAM A. WELLMAN

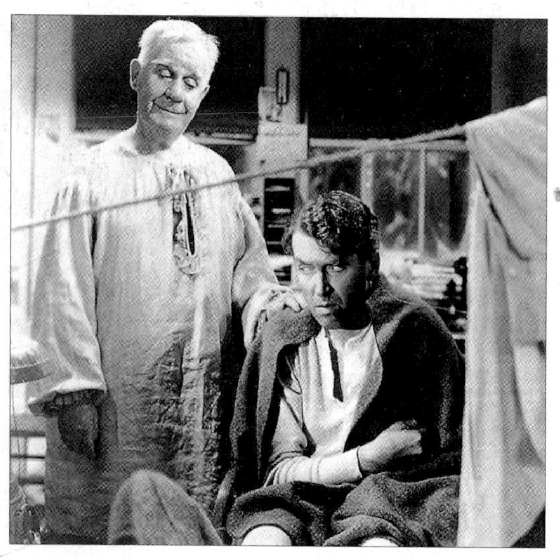

AUDREY HEPBURN
PLAYS HOLLY GOLIGHTLY, THE CRAZIEST HEROINE WHO EVER CREPT BETWEEN THE PAGES OF A BEST-SELLING NOVEL!
BREAKFAST AT TIFFANY'S
A JUROW-SHEPHERD PRODUCTION
GEORGE PEPPARD
MICKEY ROONEY
TECHNICOLOR
A PARAMOUNT RELEASE

HARRY SALTZMAN and
ALBERT R. BROCCOLI PRESENT
THE FIRST JAMES BOND FILM!
IAN FLEMING'S
DR. NO
TECHNICOLOR
SEAN CONNERY AS 007
ANDRESS · WISEMAN · LORD
DAWSON · MARSHALL
KITZMILLER · GAYSON
LEE
MAIBAUM HARWOOD MATHER YOUNG SALTZMAN BROCCOLI...EON PRODUCTIONS

A STEVEN SPIELBERG FILM
E.T.
THE EXTRA-TERRESTRIAL
IN HIS ADVENTURE ON EARTH
A STEVEN SPIELBERG FILM E.T. THE EXTRA-TERRESTRIAL
DEE WALLACE · PETER COYOTE · HENRY THOMAS AS ELLIOTT · MUSIC BY JOHN WILLIAMS
WRITTEN BY MELISSA MATHISON · PRODUCED BY STEVEN SPIELBERG & KATHLEEN KENNEDY
DIRECTED BY STEVEN SPIELBERG · A UNIVERSAL PICTURE

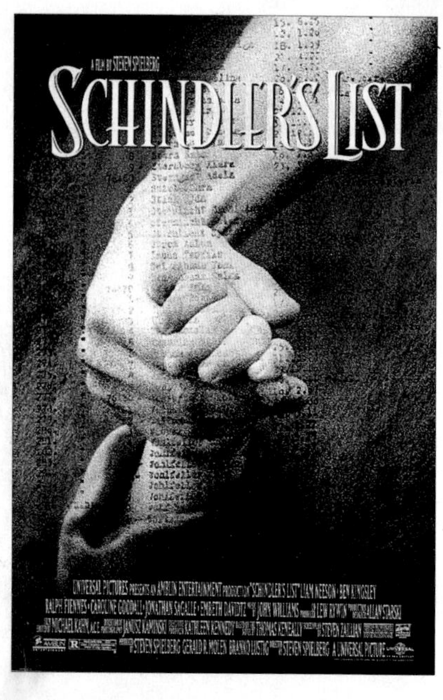
SCHINDLER'S LIST

Chronicle of the CINEMA

Dorling Kindersley

LONDON • NEW YORK • STUTTGART • MOSCOW

Directed by Catherine Legrand

Editor in chief Robyn Karney
Associate editor Joel W. Finler
Contributors Ronald Bergan, Josephine Carter, Robin Cross, Angie Errigo, Joel W. Finler, Clive Hirschhorn, Robyn Karney
Editorial assistant Ingrid Shohet
Editorial staff Josephine Carter, Nadège Guy, David Oppedisano, Irina Zarb
Index Irina Zarb
Chief researcher David Oppedisano
Picture research Anne-Marie Ehrlich *(E.T. Archives, London),* Richard Allen *(USA),* Simon Danger *(France)*
Designer Henri Marganne
E.D.P. Catherine Balouet
Software engineer Dominique Klutz

First published in 1995 by Dorling Kindersley
9 Henrietta Street, London WC2E 8PS

ISBN 0 7513 3001 9

Printed in Belgium by Brepols

Acknowledgments

Everybody who has contributed to this monumental project, not least my writers, researchers and editorial assistants, deserves special thanks for working under pressure and beyond the call of duty. Without the cooperation and generosity of various film companies, agents and public relations personnel, the task could not have been accomplished. It is impossible to list the many individuals concerned, but I would like to record my appreciation of the efforts of the wonderful staff at the Kobal Collection and the British Film Institute Stills Library, as well as those at Artificial Eye, CIBY Sales, Consolidated Pictures, Electric Pictures, Entertainment Film Distributors, ICA Projects, MacDonald and Rutter, Mainline Pictures and Metro Tartan Pictures. A special mention is due to Sue Hockey, to the British Film Institute Reference Library — particularly Bob Phillips, Erinna Laffey, Luke McKernan, David Sharp and Olwen Terris; to Philip Rose and Lucy Darwin at Columbia Pictures, and Monda Meachin at Walt Disney. To Richard Allen in New Jersey, for his immense hard work, enthusiasm and generosity in making the Carson Collection of posters available. To Jim Watters in New York, Jean-Louis Capitaine and Toby Rose in Paris, Jonathon Romney, Howard Mandelbaum and his staff at Photofest, New York, the same applies.

I must record my admiration of and gratitude to Catherine Legrand for masterminding the assembly of my pages with taste and skill.

ROBYN KARNEY, 1995

Contents

He's survived the most hostile and primitive land known to man.
Now all he's got to do is make it through a week in New York.
PAUL HOGAN IS
"Crocodile"
DUNDEE
There's a little of him in all of us.

Foreword

By Alexander Walker

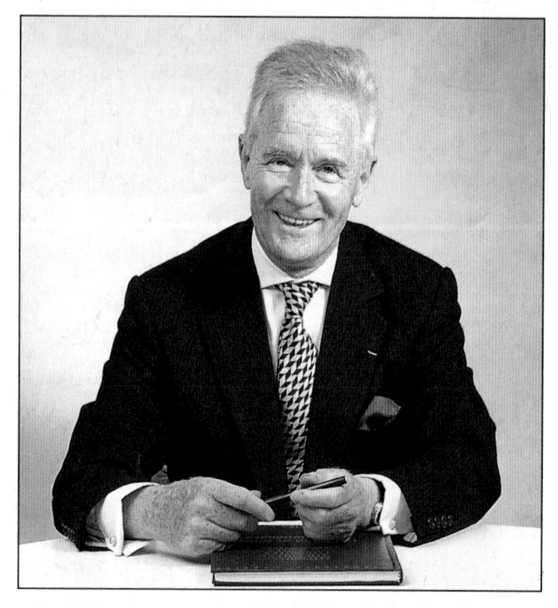

This is a timely book. Cinema is 100 years old. It's the world's youngest, yet most influential entertainment and art form. Certainly, it is the most profitable ever invented: in the USA, the movie business ranks second only to the aeronautics industry. It is also the most controversial. Democrats as well as dictators regard movies with suspicion. They have been condemned, censored, suppressed and demonised. In addition, the blame for all society's ills has often been put squarely on the power of the moving image to seduce and, allegedly, corrupt. But when the worst has been said about them, and sometimes done to them, movies not only help us endure life, they even enhance it. Movies give us the myths we worship and the metaphors that simplify our existence. Stars' faces, fashions and life-styles assume an iconic hold over us on screen and off.

I could tell you more about a country's development — past and future — by watching its movies than I could by reading its statesmen's speeches. Television may be in everybody's home: but movies are in everyone's head, and they are vastly more influential in shaping our expectations of life. This is the social change you see as you turn the pages of this book. What makes this inventory so special is the emphasis it puts on the chronological connections that have shaped cinema. It arranges events in meaningful order. If there's one lesson to be learned, it is that cinema is an entertainment whose progress lies in the constant refinement of primitive emotions and techniques. If these raw emotions appear more sophisticated today, it's only because the technology that serves them has become so sophisticated.

Near panic was the emotion registered by the first filmgoers, for all their civilised veneer, who saw the train that the Lumière brothers had filmed apparently heading straight for them out of the screen at that historic premiere of the Cinematograph in Paris in 1895. But audiences soon discovered how enjoyable alarm could be in the cinema when mediated by suspense. Likewise, the first screen kiss to be seen in close-up shocked those accustomed to the public proprieties — and distancing perspective — of love scenes in the live theatre. But before long, they too were seeking hot tips from Rudolph Valentino on how to captivate a woman. And it wasn't long, either, before the dangers of big cities everywhere were rendered curiously exhilarating when presented on the screen. Thus, the basic pattern of cinema was established early and enduringly: as the first American film critic Pauline Kael said, it boiled down to "kiss, bang, bang," otherwise known as "sex and violence". The history of cinema, as many of this book's 3,000 illustrations show, is the story of the way that the inexhaustible demand for these staple commodities has been served down the decades and in all kinds of mutations, from the flagrantly erotic to the romantically escapist, from comic knockabout to sadistic overkill.

This book also illustrates how economics as well as emotions initiate change. The sensation of talking pictures, for instance, came along at the very moment the box-office was showing its first ominous dip as the novelty of silent pictures wore off. Inside three years — the fastest technological revolution in history — the movies were talking their heads off. Sound in turn ushered in a more realistic depiction of the world, if not exactly a truer one, and a more naturalistic style of acting. Hard times in 1930s America encouraged Hollywood to console the poor, the huddled masses, with upbeat musicals, escapist romances and screwball comedies that showed the way in which the movies could mediate between the haves and the have-nots and take the latter's minds off violence on the streets by offering them cheap and potent consolation in the comfort of picture palaces: in this way, movies can subvert revolutions as well as start them. CinemaScope (and all the letter-box formats) that suddenly appeared in the mid 1950s revolutionised aesthetics as well as reviving audiences, even though it was only intended as Hollywood's answer to the threat of television. And the busting of the Hollywood morality code in the late 1960s by movies like *Bonnie and Clyde*, which showed that although crime might still not pay in the end, it could be murderous fun along the way, began the current non-stop era of "anything goes" (or very nearly). The result is a contemporary cinema with the power to panic the moralists, bring out the censors, and summon the libertarians to man freedom barricades. What's more, it spills over out of the review columns into editorials that solemnly debate where we may all be headed, and conclude that movies like *Natural Born Killers* signify the end of "civilisation as we know it." Then along comes a *Four Weddings and a Funeral,* and suddenly the air is pure again.

Much of this *Chronicle* deals with Hollywood movies. That's inevitable, given the fascination that the American life-style, for good or ill or a bit of both, possesses for the rest of the world. But it is also a realistic acknowledgment of the muscle that Hollywood unsentimentally flexes at every foreign box-office its movies now colonise. Hollywood is America's overseas empire. This is another reason why this book is timely. For the truth is, we may be seeing the death of many a national cinema in countries where it's lost its economic basis, or its audiences, as Hollywood movies monopolise the screens and capture the young generations of Europe or the Far East, who have been suckled on television serials like *Dynasty* or blockbusters like *Jurassic Park.* The multitude of national cultures that the cinema once reflected is fighting a losing battle against the American take-over.

Soon, I fear, there will be only one cinema culture: Hollywood's. But for Hollywood, too, dangers lie ahead. The movie capital itself is undergoing change, far faster than maybe even it can control. New technologies are once more altering the balance of power in screen entertainment. In the future, there will still be films, but, as they say in that cliché beloved by the science fiction epics, they may not be films as we know them. "If Midas were a moviemaker out here," one of Hollywood's cynical young "instant moguls" told me recently, "he'd want everything he touched to turn into video." Movies are already mutating faster than you can watch them. The ever-shortening attention spans of audiences reared on pop videos and TV sound-bites means that films are cut to an impatient rhythm that's often hostile to any meditative rhythm of life. Box-office safety doesn't any longer lie in numbers — did it ever? — but in formula. Sequels are given priority over originals on the production roster. And while video games strive to achieve the look of movies, the plots of movies come to resemble video games: and who wins then, except the makers?

In such unsettled times, when we don't know what the future will bring, but have good reason to fear it won't favour creative people with the freedoms their predecessors pioneered, a book like this is more welcome than ever. It shows us the unbelievable diversity that cinema has achieved in little more than an average lifetime. It should also teach us (if it is not too late) to protect our cinematic heritage: there are plenty of forces around that would recycle it or junk it. *Chronicle of the Cinema* is a celebration: it would be a tragedy if it turned into a wake.

Alexander Walker has been the film critic for the London Evening Standard *since 1960, and is the author of more than 20 books on the cinema and filmmakers.*

The editorial team, l to r: Robin Cross, Angie Errigo, Robyn Karney, Joel W. Finler, David Oppedisano, Ronald Bergan, Clive Hirschhorn

Editor's Preface

Moving pictures, or movies, as we fondly call them, have been around for a very long time in one form or another. Indeed their origins can be traced to the first magic lantern and slide shows way back in the seventeenth century.

The cinema is, without a doubt, the major art form of the twentieth century. At its highest level of achievement it can be judged alongside great literature, great music and great painting, with filmmakers creating enduring masterpieces; at the lowest level it provokes disgust and encourages censorship.

Since the 1930s, with the coming of sound to the cinema, films have utilized an amalgam of all creative forms: words and music, light and colour, the drama of the theatre, the lure of adventure, the art of the actor, the animator. They have stretched the limits of the creative imagination, feeding our common need for escape into fantastical worlds.

The first fantastical worlds were created by Georges Méliès in France at the beginning of the century. The French Lumière brothers, and a dozen or so others in France, Germany, Britain and, to a lesser extent, the United States, were exploring technical possibilities as early as the 1890s, inventing cameras and projectors and screens that, crude though they may seem now, made it possible for Méliès and his successors to work the first movie magic.

The French were the major pioneers and the moving force behind the creation of the film industry as we know it today. They were soon joined, however, by the British, the Scandinavians, the Italians (who pioneered historical epics such as *Quo Vadis?*), the Russians, the Germans, the Indians and the Japanese and, of course, the Americans.

By the late 1920s, the Americans were beginning to lead the field: with the growth of Hollywood and the coming of the moguls and their studios, the development of sound and the birth of the American musical, the United States became, and has remained, the acknowledged leader in the field of popular film, exporting her products to the rest of the world. And with the films came the cult of the star personality, and the creation of styles and fashions inspired by these stars that have been slavishly copied by millions of men and women.

The history of the cinema is endlessly fascinating, and the films themselves are a record of our rapidly changing world. The movies have something for everyone — romance, comedy, thrills, adventure, horror, war, patriotism, dance, history, and the lure of the Old West. Films can delight or enchant; they can frighten, shock or appall. They transport us into fantasy worlds; they make us laugh and cry. They provide food for thought — educating and informing us — and teaching us about other cultures. Above all, though, a successful movie ENTERTAINS.

Literally thousands of books have been produced about the movies and the people who make them. Many are popular picture books with little to say; a number are comprehensive histories, or intellectual analyses — invaluable to the specialist, hard work for average fans.

Then, too, most books tend to deal in the films of only one country, thereby depriving us of any sense of a wider, richer world. And reference books are more often than not visually dull, while picture books are frequently short on facts.

With this book, in the format of the highly successful Chronicle series, we take a journey through one hundred years of cinema history and films, analysing events as they happen, in accessible journalistic style. *Chronicle of the Cinema* is, in fact, a lavishly illustrated and extended "newspaper", which aims both to inform and delight moviegoers and to provide a unique reference book for the buff or student. It is, we hope, a treasure trove into which you can dip at random, and find something fascinating on every page. While the major focus becomes the United States, in line with its premier place in the film industry, the reader will find entertaining and informative pieces about international cinema in every year.

ROBYN KARNEY

1894

New York, 5 February
Jean Acme LeRoy has organized the first projection of Thomas Edison's films with his Marvelous Cinematograph. The private session took place in the back room of the two Riley brothers' optics and magic lantern shop at 16 Beekman Street.

Paris, 14 May
Among those present at the Robert Houdin Theatre today were magicians Georges Méliès and Félicien Trewey, photographer Antoine Lumière and his assistant Clément-Maurice Gratioulet. The latter, who is more usually known as Clément Maurice, spoke at quite some length about the Kinetoscope, Edison's latest cinematic invention. Méliès and Lumière were particularly interested by the news.

Berlin, May
Max Skladanowsky has recorded a few scenes on film using his Bioskop.

Washington, 17 July
Senator Bradley has forbidden the projection of one of Edison's films made by W.K. Laurie Dickson in the West Orange studios. In the film, which is entitled *The Serpentine Dance*, the dancer Carmencita dares to show her undergarments. It is the first case of censorship in the moving picture industry.

France, 9 September
Charles Pathé has given a demonstration of the Edison-perfected phonograph at the Montéty fairground. He has just acquired the machine from the Werner brothers, Edison's agents in Paris. Pathé intends to take the machine, which is fitted with 12 acoustic tubes to allow 12 people to listen simultaneously, on a tour through France.

West Orange, 16 October
W.K. Laurie Dickson has used the Kinetograph to film an open air rodeo scene. This event was organized by Buffalo Bill's troupe of cowboys who happened to be in the region.

Paris, 22 October
Etienne Marey has projected a chronophotographic film for the Academy of Science. It shows pictures of a cat falling from a height of one-and-a-half metres. This gave rise to a polemic: the cat's fall was studied using Delaunay's calculations. As Alphonse Allais afterwards remarked: "Life at the Academy is never boring."

Paris, October
The Werner brothers have opened a Kinetoscope Parlor in their shop at 20 boulevard Poissonnière. Viewing tickets cost 25 cents. The machine itself sells for 6,000 francs.

London, October
The optician Robert William Paul has visited the Kinetoscope Parlor recently opened by the Greeks Georgiades and Tragedes Papastakyotenipoulos. He has decided to make and exploit the Kinetoscope.

Paris, 15 November
The German inventor Ottomar Anschütz has obtained a patent for his "stroboscopic projection procedure for images".

New York, 21 November
Herman Casler has invented the Mutoscope, a box for viewing a rotating reel of photographs.

Berlin, 25 November
Ottomar Anschütz has given a projection session with his Tachyscope. Derived from the Phenakistiscope, this machine has two lenses and can project 24 pictures.

Washington, 12 December
Charles Francis Jenkins has patented a camera with a rotating lens (a disc that has 14 lenses) and a mobile film, which will enable him to take approximately 215 images per second.

Paris, 14 December
The Lumière brothers have obtained a patent for a procedure which "synthesizes color by a rapid succession of monochrome images", using a type of Praxinoscope.

New York, 31 December
Burns have published the first book specifically about the techniques for taking moving pictures. The book, *History of the Kinetograph, Kinetoscope and Kineto-Phonograph*, is written by Laurie Dickson and his daughter Antonia.

Paris, December
The editor Masson has published *le Mouvement* (*Movement*) by Etienne-Jules Marey, a synthesis of his research in chronophotography.

New York, December
Eugène Lauste, Jean Acme LeRoy's collaborator, has been hired by the brothers Otway and Grew Latham and their father, Major Woodville Latham, to turn the Kinetoscope into a projector.

Kinetoscope a success

New York, 7 November
First he gave us the Phonograph, and now he has come up with the Kinetoscope. Thomas Alva Edison's latest invention is all the rage, and not just in the States. In the main capital cities of the world, establishments called Kinetoscope Parlors built to showcase this machine are popping up like mushrooms. A constant stream of people arrives daily at the doors of these unusual places. Within the walls an even stranger sight greets the uninitiated visitor; dignified gentlemen, frequently elbow to elbow, solemnly await their turn to approach the coveted object – a very simple object to all outward appearances – a wooden case fitted with an eyepiece at easy viewing height. For the price of a small coin those interested can watch a short series of animated pictures mounted on an endless belt and lasting about a minute. Each Kinetoscope offers a completely different vision to the enthralled spectator. The subjects vary from fashionable dances, music-hall scenes, comic sketches and historical reconstructions to the highly popular boxing matches. The new Edison factories in West Orange are filming around the clock under the masterly supervision of Edison's young assistant William Kennedy Laurie Dickson to keep up with the exhibitors' demands for new material. A special film studio has been built for this purpose, nicknamed Black Maria by the employees due to its resemblance to a police lockup van. All the top stars of the moment are being filmed by Edison: Frederick Cody alias Buffalo Bill, Annie Oakley, Mae Lucas and the dancer Annabelle Whitford Moore. Some of the films, such as the saucy *Fatima's Belly Dance*, are even shrouded with a hint of prurience; the censors insisted that the dancer cover the two "offensive parts" of her body.

The machine, with its endless strip.

One can buy this for $300.

EDISON KINETOSCOPE
OFFICE

On 14 April, Raff and Gammon opened their first venue, at 1155 Broadway.

for the American inventor Thomas Alva Edison

COPYRIGHT
W.K.L.DICKSON
'93

Edison in his studio, as seen by his assistant W.K. Laurie Dickson.

But how did the famous inventor of the microphone, the incandescent lamp and the Phonograph succeed in making animated pictures? The first research in this field took place in early 1887 in Edison's newly-founded Laboratorium situated in West Orange, New Jersey. It was an enormous structure teeming with activity, and inventions of all kinds were soon underway. Edison was already very taken with the idea of inventing a machine to produce moving pictures. He had in mind something that would be to the eye that which the Phonograph was to the ear, and he set up a special film laboratory to this end that is known as "Room 5". He gave his assistant Dickson free rein to develop the research. After a number of setbacks, the two men produced a prototype called the Kinetograph in 1889. This device, which used the flexible celluloid film conceived by Eastman several years previously, had lateral perforations to ensure that the film moved smoothly on past the shutter. However, the quality of the picture obtained was not good enough to be projected on a screen, so Edison opted for the idea of individual viewing and arrived at the Kinetoscope. This machine's wooden exterior hid a fairly simple mechanism: a film approximately 17 metres in length attached to an endless belt which turned continuously, thanks to a dynamo. Right from the start the invention was a success, and the first Kinetoscope Parlor opened its doors on 14 April 1894, at 1155 Broadway in New York, with others soon following. For the spectator a whole new world of exciting images has now opened up – by simply looking through the eyepiece he can contemplate the world's most beautiful women or admire the prowess of the stars of the ring or music hall.

Edison's studio, affectionately called the Black Maria by his employees.

Boxing cats, an unexpected duo of actors for a Kinetoscope film.

A sneeze is registered for copyright

Washington, 9 January

The Edison laboratories are starting to produce their own films in readiness for the new projection equipment, which is soon to come on the market. One of the very first films, shot on 7 January and called *Edison Kinetoscope Record Of A Sneeze*, has just been lodged for copyright at the Library of Congress. In the film somebody named Fred Ott sneezes straight at the camera, to astonishingly realistic effect; the only thing missing is the sound. One almost wishes to call out, "Bless you!"

1895

Paris, 1 January
Emile Reynaud is presenting two wonderful new illuminated pantomimes at the Grévin Museum, *A Dream Beside the Fire* and *Around a Hut*.

Paris, 14 January
Charles Pathé has opened a phonograph shop at 72 cours de Vincennes.

Paris, 13 February
The Lumière brothers, Auguste and Louis, have patented a machine "to film and view chronophotographic proofs." The machine comes fitted with a driving device, which was perfected in December, for rotating the negative film. The machine can also be used to record, develop and project films.

Paris, February
Charles Pathé has returned from London where he bought one of Robert William Paul's copies of the Edison Kinetoscope.

Lyon, 19 March
Louis Lumière has begun making his first film, *la Sortie des usines Lumière* (*Leaving the Lumière factory*), using the camera he patented last month.

Paris, 22 March
The Lumière brothers have held their first public film projection. They showed *la Sortie des usines Lumière* to a gathering at the National Society for Industrial Encouragement in rue de Rennes.

Washington, 25 March
Charles Francis Jenkins and Thomas Armat have formed a partnership to manufacture film projectors.

Paris, 30 March
The Lumière brothers have lodged a new addition to their registered patent N° 245032: a triangular camshaft to drive the film holder.

West Orange, 2 April
Laurie Dickson has left the West Orange laboratories after a difference of opinion with Edison.

Paris, 17 April
The Lumière brothers have held their second public projection. This time the film was shown at the Sorbonne for the Learned Society's National Conference.

New York, 21 April
Eugène Augustin Lauste has made the projector commissioned by the Latham brothers. He has called it the Pantoptikon.

New York, 20 May
The Latham brothers and Eugène Lauste have organized their first public projection with the Pantoptikon, now called the Eidoloscope.

Lyon, 10 June
The Lumière brothers showed eight films including *The Waterer Watered* and *Baby's Teatime* for the opening of the Photographic Society's Conference.

Lyon, 12 June
The Lumière brothers have projected 10 films for restaurant owners Berrier and Millet at their premises in Bellecour Square. One of the films showed the arrival of the members of the Photographic Society at the conference.

Paris, 11 July
Today marks the Lumières' fifth public projection, using a lamp designed by Alfred Molteni. The 500 guests who attended the session run by the French *Journal of Pure and Applied Science* were highly impressed by the films.

Paris, 12 August
The Photography Syndicate has now become Léon Gaumont and Co. It is a limited partnership in joint names, with its headquarters at 57 rue Saint-Roch. Léon Gaumont himself is the director of the new company.

Paris, 26 August
Charles Pathé and Henri Joly, who have been in partnership since 13 August, have lodged a patent for a chronophotographic machine. The camera will be used to make French films for the Edison Kinetoscope which Pathé intends to sell to fairground exhibitors.

Paris, 8 November
Henri Joly has perfected a new machine for Charles Pathé. The Photozootrope is a Kinetoscope with four lenses. It should bring fair exhibitors 36 francs per hour.

Paris, 16 November
On the occasion of the opening of Gabriel Lippman's lectures at the Sorbonne, the Lumière brothers held another projection session of their films.

Jersey City, 27 December
Laurie Dickson, Elias Koopman, Herman Casler and Harry Marvin have founded The American Mutoscope Company. The company has been set up to market the Mutoscope invented by Casler, who was formerly with Edison.

LeRoy improves on Edison's Kinetoscope

New York, 22 February
A hushed murmur of admiration rose from the audience at the Opera House as, before their very eyes, a fluttering dance of trembling images, produced by the Marvelous Cinematograph, filled the screen. Never before has such a wondrous event been seen in New York. The inventor of this incredible device is Jean Acme LeRoy, an American of French descent whose interest in the problems posed by animated pictures dates back to 1893; as early as that he tried converting an Edison Kinetoscope into a projector. His first public demonstration in 1894 was far from perfect: available images filed past in a jerky, irregular fashion. As a result, LeRoy decided to produce his own film material. He found a keen collaborator in Eugène-Augustin Lauste, and the two men soon came up with convincing results by reducing the speed to 20 images per second. He modeled his projector on the cam system developed by Frenchman Georges Demenÿ. There is a risk that Kinetoscope Parlors may be superseded by this novelty.

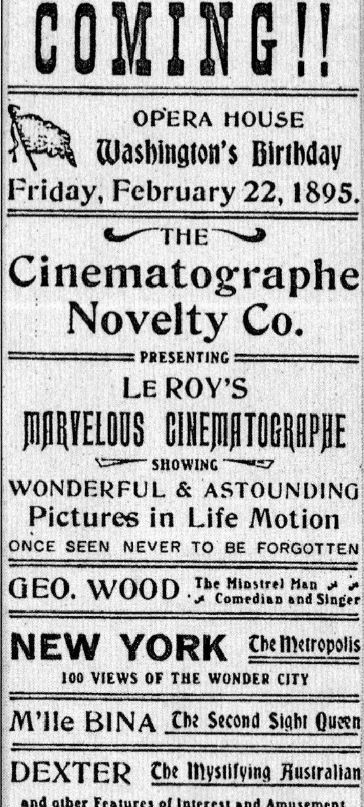
COMING!!
OPERA HOUSE
Washington's Birthday
Friday, February 22, 1895.
THE
Cinematographe
Novelty Co.
PRESENTING
LE ROY'S
MARVELOUS CINEMATOGRAPHE
SHOWING
WONDERFUL & ASTOUNDING
Pictures in Life Motion
ONCE SEEN NEVER TO BE FORGOTTEN
GEO. WOOD The Minstrel Man Comedian and Singer
NEW YORK The Metropolis
100 VIEWS OF THE WONDER CITY
M'lle BINA The Second Sight Queen
DEXTER The Mystifying Australian
and other Features of Interest and Amusement.
Prices: 15c., 25c. and 35c.

Max Skladanowsky unveils the Bioskop

Berlin, 1 November
Today marked a crucial moment in the careers of two famous magic lantern operators, Max and Emil Skladanowsky. This morning Max applied for an inventor's patent in his name only for the Bioskop, his projection device for celluloid films with metal-reinforced perforations.

Max Skladanowsky and the Bioskop.

The Bioskop is designed to project two films simultaneously but with a slight discrepancy in the movements, thanks to a double objective fitted with a mobile disc. Max uses a chronophotograph he invented himself to film the scenes. This evening's session at the Wintergarten was the first time the public has paid to watch a show produced by the Bioskop. Included among the nine films projected were a sparring match between a kangaroo and a man named Delaware, *The Boxing Kangaroo*; a dance executed by Miss Ancion, *Dance Serpentine*; an *Italian Folk Dance*; and the brothers Tcherpanoff's *Kammarintsky Russian National Dance* to name but a few. The show is under contract to the Wintergarten until the end of November, and it appears to be set for a successful run judging by tonight's reaction. Apparently, the Parisian brothers Auguste and Louis Lumière, who have also been developing the animated picture business, were troubled by news of this unexpected competition.

The Lumières enter the Cinematograph market

Inventor Louis Lumière at age 31.

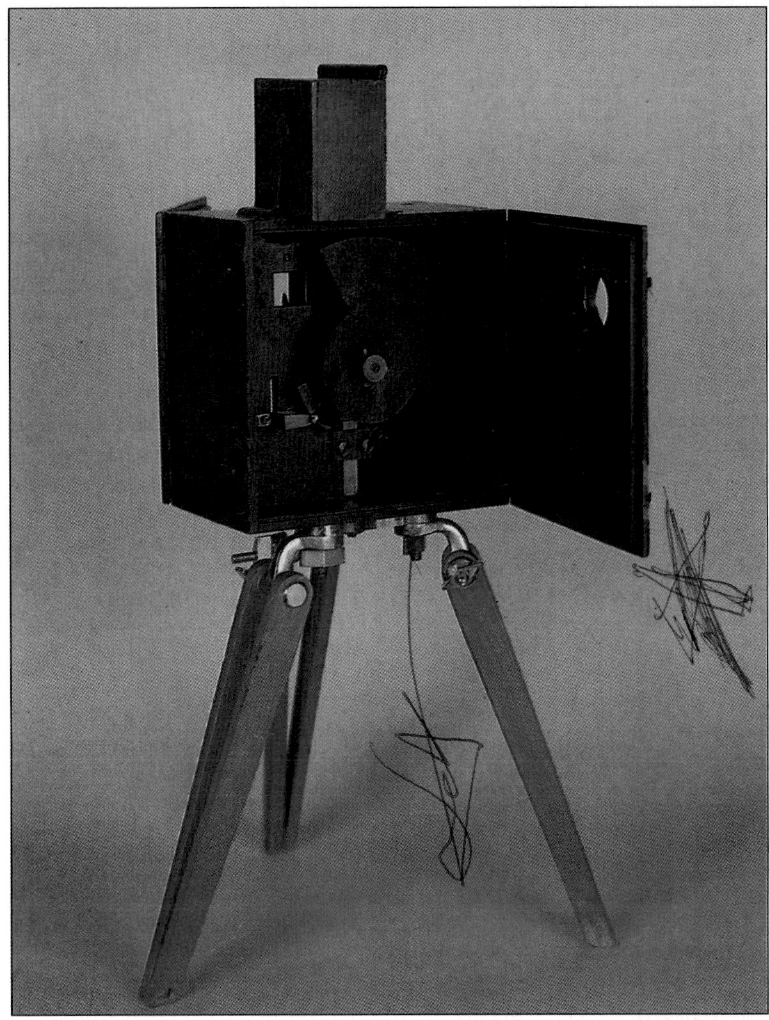
The first Lumière Cinematograph, manufactured by the engineer Carpentier.

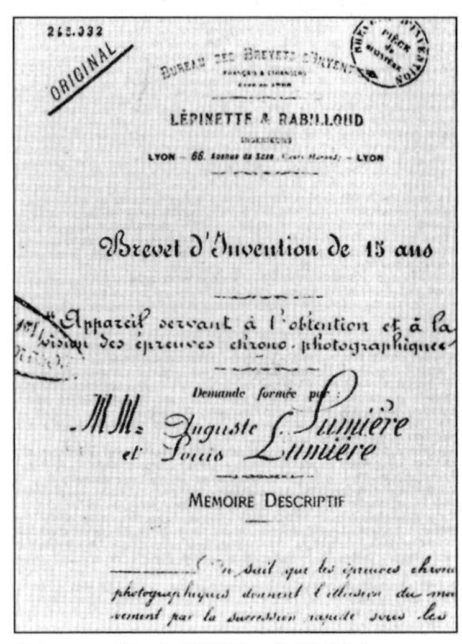
ORIGINAL

LÉPINETTE & RABILLOUD

LYON

Brevet d'Invention de 15 ans

"Appareil servant à l'obtention et à la vision des épreuves chrono-photographiques"

Demande formée par :

MM. Auguste Lumière et Louis Lumière

MEMOIRE DESCRIPTIF

License N° 245032 of 13 February.

Lyon, 20 December
The Lumière brothers are impatiently awaiting the arrival of their Lumière Cinematograph N° 1. The machine has just been sent off from Paris after undergoing two months of final adjustments by Jules Carpentier, the engineer contracted to develop a series of 25 of Lumière's machines. Negotiations took several months before an agreement was finally reached six months after their initial meeting on 22 March of this year. It was an important date for the Lumières as it marked Louis' very first public appearance in the capital, where he had agreed to speak in front of the Society For Industrial Advancement. The title of his lecture was "The Photography Industry," but Louis moved quickly and almost imperceptibly on to talk about the topic which had been uppermost in his mind for some time: the projection of animated pictures. Louis followed up his speech to the audience of 200 or so photographers, industrialists and researchers who had come to hear his ideas by showing a short film entitled *Leaving the Lumière Factory* (*Sortie des usines Lumière*), in which the dumbfounded gathering was able to watch the factory workers in action as they prepared to leave their workshops for the midday meal. This animated picture session, without precedent, left its mark on all those present, including the head of the Commercial Photography Syndicate Léon Gaumont. With the patent securely in hand, the inventors settled on the Cinematograph as a name for their projector – it seems they were totally unaware that the name had already been used in 1893 by one Léon Bouly. The brothers even went so far as to oppose their father who, influenced by a friend and no doubt Latinist, wanted to call the machine Domitor, in his opinion an easier name to protect legally than one so readily accessible, etymologically speaking. But, regardless, Auguste and Louis stood firm: it would be the Cinematograph.

In June, Louis Lumière filmed the delegates at the photography congress.

With ***Leaving the Lumière Factory****, the Cinematograph came into being.*

On 28 December, in Paris, the Cinematograph

Paris, 28 December
Antoine Lumière, the industrial photographer from Lyon, has just opened a new show in the Indian Exhibition at the Grand Café at 14 boulevard des Capucines. The press and public were invited to attend tonight's inauguration. Antoine, who has every confidence in Louis' invention, obtained a year's lease on a basement room. However, the owner of the property Mr. Volpini has so little confidence in the undertaking that he refused an offer of 20 percent of the takings, preferring a fixed figure of 30 francs a day. A man has been standing outside the building all day handing out programs to passers-by. Unfortunately, today's cold weather prevented people from stopping, and most rushed past the entry of the Exhibition to the Grand Café next door, with only a distracted glance at the notice "Lumière's Cinematograph – Entry Fr 1." As a result only 33 tickets were sold for the first show, but luckily there were several invited guests. On arrival, spectators are shown to the lavish basement hall with its oriental decor, at the far end of which two turnstiles protect the entrance to the Exhibition. Here, Clément Maurice, a photographer hired by Antoine Lumière for the occasion, welcomes the audiences. To the right of the entrance there is a compressed air ventilator.

The room seats 100 people, and as soon as the audience has settled in comfortably, the lights go out. A hushed silence falls as the white backdrop lights up with a photographic projection depicting the doors of the Lumière factory in Lyon. At the first showing, a disappointed murmur went up: "Why, it's only the old magic lantern!" Then, without warning, the picture started to move. The factory doors were flung open letting out a stream of workers, dogs ran hither and thither, a carriage rolled by... Everything moved; it was an astonishing vision of reality – of life caught in full swing. Confronted for the first time by these animated pictures, the audience must have wondered if they were hallucinating. Ten different eventful scenes followed, each reel roughly 17 metres in length. In *The Photographical Congress Arrives in Lyon*, one recognized the inventor of the shoulder-held movie camera, Jules Janssen. *Cordeliers Square in Lyon* was so realistic that a young woman in the audience leaped to her feet on seeing a horse-cab rushing toward her. *Baby's Dinner* shows Auguste Lumière and his wife trying vainly to get their baby to eat his gruel. In the background trees sway gently in the wind, leaving the audience with the impression they can hear the rustling of the leaves. *The Sea* appears calm at first then slowly builds up. Towering waves come crashing around a young man who is swimming close to the shore. However, judging by the general hilarity, *The Waterer Watered* was no doubt the most comical film.

HOTEL SCRIBE
HOTEL SCRIBE
SCRIBE
HOTEL
The historic showing was held in the Indian Salon, in the basement of the Grand Café. A seat costs one franc.

The rise of Auguste and Louis Lumière

In 1860 Antoine Lumière left his hometown in the Haute-Saône to set up a photography business in Besançon. His first son Auguste was born in 1862, and the second, Louis, arrived two years later. In 1870 Antoine moved to Lyon with his family and opened a new workshop. Over the next 10 years he gradually built up an industrial manufacturing plant for photographic plates. The factory was taken over by Auguste and Louis in 1893 and has since become a flourishing business, thanks to the Lumière brothers' technical innovations; they had both trained as research scientists before becoming industrialists. As a rule, all patents are lodged in joint names, despite the fact that the individuals are not always involved in the same research. By 1894, when Edison's Kinetoscope arrived on the scene in France, the Lumière Company, with a capital of 3 million francs, already had a work force of 300 people and was producing 15 million photographic plates a year.

Life on the boulevard des Capucines, outside the Grand Café.

makes its debut in front of thirty-three spectators

The organizer Antoine Lumière.

The technician Clément Maurice.

And lastly, in *The Blacksmith*, the rising swirl of smoke from the forge served as a fitting closing image. Each film lasted scarcely more than a minute.

When the lights came back on, the organizer of the evening's entertainment, Antoine Lumière, was given a well-deserved round of applause. Those who were interested in the Cinematograph managed to catch a glimpse of it hidden away in a velvet-lined box. The arc lamp for the lantern, made in Paris by Alfred Molteni, was adjusted by Jacques Ducom, an expert in photography. Strangely enough, the old magic lantern is still essential, even for such a modern invention. It is this bright light source that is projected through the small walnut box, with its seemingly complicated internal machinery, known as the Cinematograph. Charles Moisson, who manufactured the first prototype from a registered patent dated 13 February, was given the job of turning the handle. The model used this evening had just come out of Jules Carpentier's workshops. It is fixed to a stand so that the film drops straight into a bag placed below the machine and is then rewound onto the reel by a small hand-driven spool designed by Louis Lumière. Lastly, on the wall there is an electricity board so that the intensity of the incandescent carbons for the arc lamp can be checked regularly. Some of the audience were openly envious of this brand-new projection equipment. One of the guests, the famous illusionist Georges Méliès, owner of the Robert Houdin Theatre, asked Antoine Lumière the price of his new machine. The answer was quick and to the point: "The invention is not for sale. It would be the ruin of you. It can be exhibited for a while due to its scientific interest, but apart from that the machine has no future." However, Méliès and several other guests, unconvinced by his reply, were already wondering how they could make animated pictures without Lumière. Moreover, rumor has it that Antoine had brought forward the date for this evening's projection to avoid the possibility of someone else organizing the first paying projection. As early on as 2 November, Louis Lumière had asked Carpentier to speed up the production of the first Cinematographs because, in his own words, "We are being hounded from all sides." Nevertheless, for the time being the Lumières have carried off a triumph: their rivals have been crushed. The small easy-to-handle Cinematograph produces excellent projections, even if the picture does jerk or oscillate from time to time. Those journalists with foresight, who took the trouble to attend the show, were delighted to notice the absence of their colleagues from the big dailies. For once, the first to go to print would not be *Figaro* or *Le Matin,* but *La Poste* and *Progrès*. Despite the small number of people who attended the show, Antoine Lumière is happy in the knowledge that he has won the invention race.

Arrival of the Train in the Ciotat Station.

The Waterer Watered.

The Blacksmiths.

1896

New York, 15 January
Charles Raff and Frank Gammon have bought the Phantascope projector from Thomas Armat on behalf of Edison. It is to be called the Vitascope and is hailed by the press as Edison's latest invention.

Paris, 1 February
The Lumières' projections at the Indian Exhibition are proving highly successful; over 2,000 tickets are being sold daily. Sessions are almost continuous as the auditorium seats only 120 people.

Brussels, 1 March
The first paying session of the Lumière brothers' Cinématograph was held at 7 galerie du Roi. Tickets cost one franc.

Paris, 5 March
Raoul Grimoin-Sanson has taken out a patent for his Phototachygraph, a projector fitted with a mobile tetragonal cross.

London, 24 March
Robert William Paul has given his first public projections with his Theatrograph. He created this projector with Birt Acres.

Paris, 30 March
The Grévin Museum is advertising Emile Reynaud's animated pictures. The latter has given up his hand-painted magic lantern shows.

Paris, 4 April
Auguste Blaise Baron is patenting a new machine for "recording and reproducing sound and images simultaneously." However, the results obtained with this procedure, an electrical device connected to a phonograph, remain an approximate synchronization.

Paris, 6 April
Méliès is holding projection sessions in his Robert Houdin Theatre using Paul's Theatrograph (now known as the Animatograph) and moving pictures from Edison's Kinescope.

Paris, 30 April
Three establishments in the capital are holding projections of the Lumières' Cinematograph: the Eldorado, a cafe on the boulevard de Strasbourg, which has been holding afternoon viewing sessions on a daily basis since 16 April; the first floor of the Olympia, where projections started two days ago; and, lastly, in the Dufayel Stores on boulevard Barbès, the Cinematograph has been set up in what was previously the boardroom.

Berlin, 15 June
Oskar Messter has opened the city's first cinema at 21 Unter den Linden.

Russia, 4 July
Maxim Gorky has published an article about the recent demonstration of the Lumières' Cinematograph at Nijni Novgorod. According to him, "Everything went on in a ghostly silence... The greyness and silence of the images finishes by making one nervous and depressed."

St. Petersburg, 7 July
The French cameraman Eugène Promio gave the Czar and his family a private projection session of several films, using the Lumières' Cinematograph.

Paris, 2 September
Georges Méliès, Lucien Reulos and the technician Korsten have patented the Kinetograph, a small camera fitted with a helicoid screw which winds the film forward a notch after each shot. However, it is difficult to use.

Paris, 20 September
Henri Joly has stopped collaborating with Charles Pathé and is now working with Ernest Normandin on the commercialization of his reversible Chronophotograph. This very practical camera was patented on 17 March 1896.

Paris, 1 October
Charles and Emile Pathé have founded a company called Pathé Frères, with a capital of 40,000 francs.

Paris, 21 October
The photographer Eugène Pirou is holding projection sessions at the Café de la Paix in the boulevard des Capucines. The images are of the Czar Alexander III's recent visit to Paris. They were filmed with the camera perfected by Joly and Normandin.

Paris, 14 November
Victor Continsouza and René Bünzli have taken out a second patent (the first was registered on 28 April) for their system for feeding perforated film past the lens using a Maltese cross.

Nice, 30 December
In the winter garden at the casino, Eugène Pirou's projections of short scenes, such as *le Coucher de la mariée*, *Lever de Mlle Willy* and *Deshabillé d'un modèle*, are enjoying a certain success.

English pioneers make their presence felt

Acres, who created the Kineoptikon.

Paul, technician and industrialist.

London, 14 January
Birt Acres, a regular lanternist at The Royal Photographic Society, is back tonight with his first animated projections. The audience warmly applauded the lively series of moving pictures: *Three Burlesque Dancers, A Boxing Match, A Kangaroo Boxing its Master,* and *The German Emperor Reviews His Regiment*. The films are the end result of several months' work. Last summer Acres joined forces with Robert William Paul, a manufacturer of scientific devices who also specializes in animated pictures. In fact, Paul had himself been manufacturing and selling copies of Edison's Kinetoscope from his London shop since the end of 1894; a legal operation as Edison's invention is not patented in Great Britain. However, the main problem they faced was not how to produce the machine but how to find new films. Together with Acres, Paul perfected a type of camera that has the capability to produce quality shots. And seeing the queues outside his fairground Kinetoscopes, he then decided on animated projections – judging by today's show, they have a future.

When a kiss creates a major scandal!

New York, 15 June
Scandalous is the only word for the Edison Manufacturing Company's latest film *The Kiss Between May Irwin and John Rice*. The two stars of *Widow Jones* show a brazen lack of morality by kissing greedily in front of the camera. Reactions are strong. Today's issue of *The Chap Book*, has this to say: "The life-size view, bestial enough in itself, was nothing compared with this. Their unbridled kissing, magnified to gargantuan proportions and repeated thrice, is absolutely loathsome." In fact, from the very beginning the Kinetoscope has displayed very little delicacy: films include innumerable enticing dances, vulgar playlets and other lewd exhibitions. According to an increasing number of citizens, censorship could be the answer.

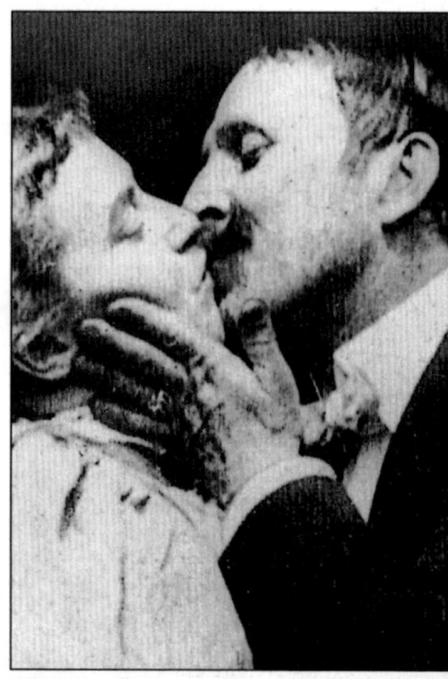

The Kiss between May Irvin and John C. Rice *is the first of its kind ever seen on the screen.*

Edison attempts to monopolize projections under French threat

Thomas Armat's invention is being developed by the West Orange firm.

New York, 29 June
The arrival of the French brothers Louis and Auguste Lumière in New York has dealt Thomas Alva Edison a hard blow. Their first show with the Cinematograph at Keith's Theater, the famous music hall in Union Square, has taken New York by storm. At the opening session, Félix Mesguich projected all the greatest successes from the Grand Café in Paris. For the first time the American public has been able to see the impressive *Arrival of a Train in Ciotat Station* and the comic gem *l'Arroseur arrosé* (*The Waterer Watered*), both highly appreciated by the audience. Unfortunately for Edison, the French equipment is technically far superior and is better adapted to collective viewing than the American Vitascope. Until now Edison has enjoyed a position of relative supremacy in the field of animated pictures, but the quality of the pictures produced by the Cinematograph poses a serious threat to the future of the Vitascope. Naturally, Edison was well aware of his rivals' progress on the other side of the Atlantic.

It must be remembered that quite some time ago Edison, having been warned in advance of this serious competition, hastened to acquire the manufacturing and operating rights to the Phantascope, a projector designed in 1895 by Thomas Armat and Charles Francis Jenkins. The inventor renamed it the Vitascope, and mass production started last April. The first public projection took place on 23 April at Koster & Bial's New York Music Hall. On that auspicious occasion two beautiful hand-colored films were shown: *Annabelle Butterfly Dance* and *Annabelle Serpentine Dance*. The projection was an immense triumph, and, during the period of nationalist euphoria that followed, Edison was hailed by one and all as the inventor of animated projections. This was a rather exaggerated view, given that he had only bought up and manufactured an existing machine and that the Cinematograph was already in service in most major European cities. It has now been exposed. Any honest comparison of the two machines is uncompromisingly damaging to the Vitascope. Not only do the pictures from this machine appear flat and dull, but the constant vibrations and oscillation are all the more irritating now that the public has proof that they can be largely overcome. And the Lumière brothers have certainly managed to alleviate most of these unsettling defects with the Cinematograph. Moreover, the French brothers' catalogue offers a far more interesting variety of material than does the American. The films range from comic sketches to panoramic views and aesthetically pleasing scenes. The audience at the opening show was particularly impressed with *The 96th Infantry Regiment on Parade* and cheered enthusiastically as the men went through their maneuvers. From now on Thomas Edison is going to have a serious competitor, and it looks as if it may be a tough struggle.

KOSTER & BIAL'S MUSIC HALL
Thirty-fourth Street, Herald Square.
KOSTER, BIAL & CO., Proprietors
Week Commencing Monday Evening, April 20, 1896
Evenings, 8:15 Saturday Matinee, 2:15
THIS PROGRAMME is subject to alterations at the discretion of the management.
1 OVERTURE, "Masaniello," Auber
2 WM. OLSCHANSKY
3 CORA CASELLI
4 THE THREE DELEVINES
5 PAULINETTI and PICO
The Athletic Gymnast and Gymnastic Comedian.
6 MONS. and MME. DUCREUX-CERALDUC
French Duettists.
7 THE BROTHERS HORN
"London Life."
THOMAS A. EDISON'S LATEST MARVEL
8 THE VITASCOPE,
Presenting selections from the following:
"Kaiser Wilhelm, reviewing his troops,"
"Cuba Libre."
INTERMISSION 10 MINUTES
IN THE GRAND PROMENADE
Dr. Leo Sommer's Blue Hungarian Band.
Programme continued on next page.

The first public showing on 23 April.

Successful launch of the Biograph

New York, 12 October
The closely packed audience in the Hammerstein Theater rose to its feet cheering the moment William McKinley, the Republican presidential candidate, appeared before them. However, the object of their enthusiasm had not even left his home in Ohio. His address for New York's Republican supporters had been filmed with a Biograph camera well before the show. American Mutoscope has reason to be proud of this new projector for animated pictures. The company was founded in 1895 by Herman Casler, Harry Marvin, Elias Koopman and W.K. Laurie Dickson. The New York Biograph program was exemplary. In addition to McKinley, the audience was able to admire Niagara Falls, a train – the Empire State Express at 60 mph – and a scene from *Trilby*. Mutoscope has passed its first test with flying colors.

Jehanne d'Alcy in *The Conjuring of a Woman at the House of Robert Houdin*, Georges Méliès' first film based on a trick of substitution.

The scope offered by the Cinematograph receives

Paris, 30 May
"A dazzling conquest! Never before has a new form of entertainment so rapidly become a vogue. Are you interested in the Cinematograph? Naturally! They are everywhere – in the basement of all the boulevard cafes, in music-hall outbuildings, in theaters where projections are often fitted into variety shows, even in private homes – guests are offered viewing sessions of this fashionable amusement." This distinctive journalistic style leaves little room for doubt: the success of the Cinematograph is assured. The above article from the pen of Dr. Félix Regnault appeared in today's issue of *L'Illustration*, a Parisian weekly. Not content to simply sing the praises of the Cinematograph, he is distinguishing himself from his colleagues by offering readers a precise history from Joseph Plateau's Phenakistiscope to Lumière's latest invention. And a great deal has been written on the subject. Since the first projections in the Grand Café's Indian Exhibition last December, Lumière's invention has been examined from every angle: sometimes scientifically, sometimes amateurishly. Journalists have shamelessly copied each other without even bothering to cite the source, as seen by a great many repeated passages written by the polytechnician A. Ray and published in the scientific journal *la Revue générale des sciences pures et appliquées*. This work contained an extremely lucid explanation of how the Cinematograph works. All the articles are marked by the same feeling of surprise and emotion in the face of what seems to be the event of the century. One detects a vague uneasiness on reading in the *Courier de Champagne*: "All these scenes seem totally detached from the realities of life." Or elsewhere: "The whole thing is strangely silent. Life goes on before us, yet we are unable to hear the din of passing wheels or footfalls or even a few words. Not a sound; not a single note of the complex symphony of sound which always accompanies the crowds' movement." And Henri Parville adds: "What about colored moving projections? When that happens, the illusion will be complete. We shall see objects in their true colors. How shall we distinguish illusion from reality?" The Cinematograph resembles the magic lantern but with an indefinable something extra. For Henri Béraud from *la Dépêche de l'Ouest*, the most extraordinary aspect is to find oneself looking into the eyes of these ghosts: "Suddenly, the magic backdrop lit up and moved, a striking image, singular because familiar to everyone: Cordeliers' Square in Lyon... A passerby stops, turns his head, and starts walking toward us, his eyes fixed on the darkness surrounding us. He could see us! He must have been able to see us." This wonderful film, *Cordeliers' Square in Lyon*,

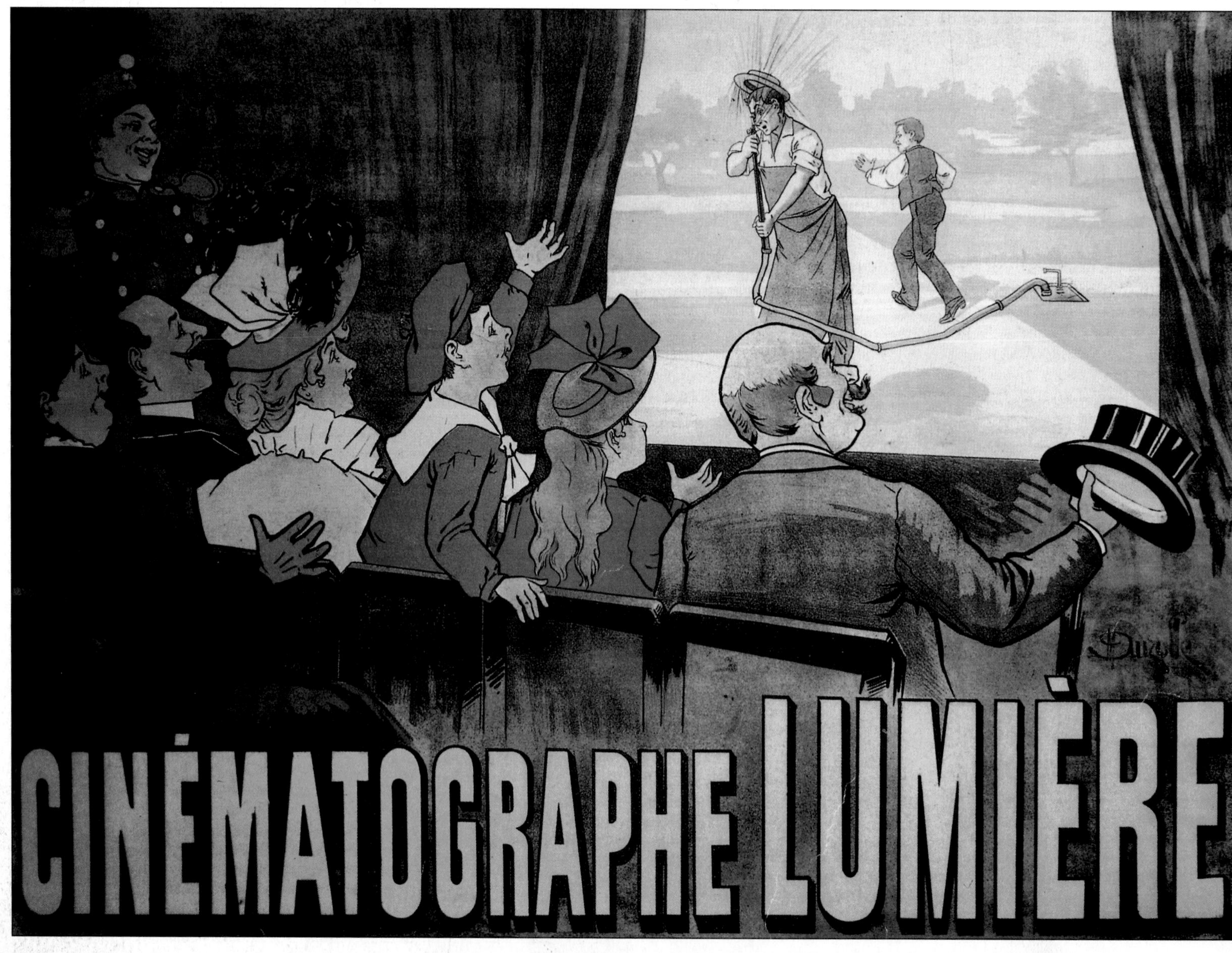
CINÉMATOGRAPHE LUMIÈRE

an enthusiastic welcome from French journalists

has received special attention from the press. *L'Univers illustré* underlines the "breathtaking realism of a tram overtaking numerous vehicles, all racing by at top speed." The paper concludes with: "These experiences, which are simply too marvelous for words, can only hint at what the future has in store and are a credit to Messrs. Auguste and Louis Lumière, Mr. Clément Maurice and their ingenious collaborators." However, this well-meaning article drew a polite correction from Maurice: "Sir, I am afraid your article of 4 January was mistaken in saying I had a part in the invention of Messrs. Lumières' Cinematograph. We owe this marvelous invention exclusively to the efforts of these two gentlemen. For my part, I simply operate the machine."

Some writers grow lyrical when confronted by the possibilities of the machine: "What deeply poignant emotions we shall experience on seeing before us those we have loved speaking and moving. Departed parents or loved ones, suddenly brought back to life, reappearing with their familiar gestures, their soft voices, all those memories that, alas, without this new invention fade further and further into the misty corners of our minds. Why, if this continues we could almost overcome memory loss, almost put an end to separations, almost abolish death itself." This from *Le Courier de Paris*. In Marseille, *Le Bavard* has announced that the lively scenes taken in the rue de Noailles "are going to disappear to be replaced by a new series of marvels which will captivate, to the point of anguish, all those who decide to contemplate them. It is said to be a show of such extraordinary dimensions that it surpasses anything one could possibly imagine." But the Lumières are no longer the only ones to make the columns of the newspapers. For example, the *Intransigeant* published a long article in their 25 February issue about Raoul Grimoin-Sanson's Phototachygraphe: "This new machine appears to be superior to Lumières' Cinematograph. Gone are those interruptions, so irritating and painful to the eye." Nevertheless, those who attended the very noisy demonstration of the Phototachygraphe remain in favor of Louis and Auguste Lumières' machine, which already has a great number of rivals. *La Science française* sums up the general opinion by stating that the Cinematograph is a "hallucinatory phantasmagoria," and "the show borders on the most unbelievably wonderful sorcery that has ever been dreamed of."

CINÉMATOGRAPHE
LUMIÈRE

Two posters for the showings at the Grand Café, in 1896. The publicity used the success of ***The Waterer Watered*** *to attract visitors.*

1897

Cuba, 7 February
The cameraman Gabriel Veyre, who is in Havana to demonstrate the Lumière Cinematograph, has made the first film to be actually filmed in Cuba, *Simulacre d'un incendie* (*Enactment of a Fire*).

Belgrade, 6 March
The French cameraman André Carré has shot the first film to be made in Yugoslavia, *Départ du roi Alexandre Obrenovic de la cour pour la cathédrale* (*King Alexander's Departure for the Cathedral*).

Paris, 12 March
The cafe-concert Bataclan is projecting Georges Méliès' films featuring Paulus. Paulus himself produces the sound by singing, behind the screen, songs such as *En revenant de la revue* (*Coming Home from the Theater*).

Paris, March
A Lumière Cinematograph has opened at 6 boulevard Saint Denis. The building was formerly a theater for magicians. Entry costs 50 cents. It is the fifth Lumière auditorium to open up since 28 December 1895, and the first establishment to specialize in projections.

New York, 31 March
The caricaturist J. Stuart Blackton and the ventriloquist Albert Smith have founded the Vitagraph Company. They intend to project Edison's films in theaters.

Paris, April
Léon Gaumont has started shooting films in his studios in rue des Alouettes near the Buttes Chaumont. Gaumont's secretary, Alice Guy, is in charge of production.

England, April
The Cinematograph is creating increasing interest here. While James Williamson and George Albert Smith have commenced making their first films, the inventor Robert William Paul has founded the Paul Animatograph Company.

Stockholm, 15 May
The cameraman Eugène Promio has filmed the jubilee celebrations of King Oscar II of Sweden. The King was able to watch the film on the same day.

France, May
The Lumière Establishment in Lyon has put the Cinematograph on the market. The machine complete with all its accessories sells for 1,650 francs. The projector alone costs 300 francs.

Brussels, May
A special exhibition of optics has opened for the World's Fair, which is being held in the parc du Cinquantenaire. The exhibition, which is run by the Belgian Optique company, a branch of the French Optique company directed by François Deloncle, is offering sessions of cinematographic projections.

Paris, 1 July
Berthon, Dussaud and Jaubert have patented a system which "combines a microphone with a camera to enable filmmakers to reproduce living scenes and sounds." The words are recorded then mimed by the actors in front of the camera.

Paris, 15 July
The film *Premier cigare* (*First Cigar*), made by Emile Reynaud for the Optic Theatre at the Grévin Museum, has just been projected for the public. The film took a year longer than expected to complete. The Museum has announced its intention to turn further toward the Cinematograph.

Shanghai, July
The American James Ricalton is projecting Edison films in tea rooms and amusement parks.

Paris, 1 August
After the accident at the Charity Bazaar, A. Delille has suggested using a water tank to protect films from the heat of the rayons produced by the condenser. It is to be hoped that this will help in avoiding further fires.

Washington, 5 August
Admiral Cigarette, produced by Edison, is the first advertising film to be lodged for copyright at the Congress Library.

Paris, 25 November
Raoul Grimoin-Sanson has obtained a patent for the Cinécosmorama. This innovative procedure can be used to film and project panoramic animated pictures on a circular screen, using 12 inter-connected projectors.

Paris, 30 November
Léon Gaumont has given up the Demenÿ 60mm "Chrono" format. He is increasing his production output using 35mm film. His films, which sell for 35 to 75 francs and cover a variety of subjects, including news items, street scenes and comic acts such as *Chez le barbier* (*At the Barber's*), *Une nuit agitée* (*A Disturbed Night*), are filmed by Alice Guy.

Cinematograph blamed

Paris, 4 May
A horrifying fire ravaged the Charity Bazaar last night, killing 121 people – 110 women and six men. A meticulous inquiry led by the Prefect of Police Mr. Lépine, has enabled the authorities to reconstruct events leading up to the disaster. The Charity Bazaar, founded in 1885 by members of Catholic high society and presided over by Baron de Mackau, opened yesterday and seemed set for success. The cream of Parisian society crowded in to the long wooden building in rue Jean-Goujon, where charity stalls divided by sheets of pasteboard lined the long hall, leaving a central passage six to seven metres wide. Overhead, an enormous canopy of white canvas, lined with a tarred material, formed a fake ceiling.

On this Tuesday, 4 May, 4,000 people were crowded into the building. At 3 p.m. Ernest Normandin, a concessionaire for the Cinematograph perfected by Henri Joli in 1895, decided to open the first session in the small nine-by-four projection room. The previous show had had to be canceled due to a technical hitch with the lamp. As a replacement, Albert Molteni, the magic-lantern manufacturer, had sent an oxyetheric lamp. A mixture of oxygen and ether fueled a flame which heated a small piece of lime to incandescence. Ironically, the lamp was called Securitas. At 10 minutes past 4 p.m., after the fourth session, the room was plunged into darkness, and the projectionist Bellac called for a pause to refuel the lamp. Brushing aside advice from the Baron's secretary to do it outside, he returned to his canvas projection box and started filling the reservoir with ether. His assistant, Grégoire Bagrachow, having asked where the matches were, proceeded to strike one – Bellac shouted in horror as soon as he realized his intention – too late... In a split second a flame spurted out of the lamp followed by a terrifying noise as the lamp and celluloid films exploded. In a few

The fire shocked France and caused attendances for film showings to drop.

for the loss of 121 lives at Charity Bazaar fire

At the moment of reckoning, survivors and the curious discovered the fragility of the building constructed for the occasion.

seconds the fire had spread to the canopy, and a general panic seized the public, turning the Bazaar into a deadly trap. Burning tar from the roof ignited the fleeing women's billowing skirts, turning them into human torches. Bagrachow was able to save more than 100 people by smashing down one of the wooden walls. Dozens of women died trampled underfoot as men, all trace of chivalry forgotten, pushed and beat their way out through the ensuing melee. Two other emergency exits were opened: a fireman's ladder and a window into an adjacent hotel. Firemen and locals worked miracles, but by 6 p.m. it was over. All that remained was a mass of charred wood and ashes over which hung a pall of dreadful smelling smoke. The bodies were taken to the Palais de l'Industrie for identification. For many, this catastrophe was an act of God: a punishment for the proud, whose acts of charity required no real sacrifice. The Cinematograph has also come under attack, accused of being a scientific conquest that thought it could outshine God.

The Molteni ether lamp, considered directly responsible for the blaze.

Legal consequences of the catastrophe

Paris, 24 August

Three people involved in the terrible fire at the Charity Bazaar appeared in court today on charges of negligence: Baron Mackau, the organizer; Bellac, Ernest Normandin's projectionist; and Bellac's friend and helper for the occasion, Grégoire Bagrachow. The verdict can only be described as controversial. Baron Mackau, who was in charge of the building and therefore the sole person in a position to ensure proper safety measures for the public, only received a 500-franc fine. Bellac, whose carelessness had inadvertently caused the fire, was given a one-year prison sentence as well as a 500-franc fine. But Bagrachow, who, though also responsible, had saved dozens of lives by his courage, has been condemned to eight months imprisonment and fined 200 francs. The public still find it difficult to understand why, once the fire had broken out, so few people were able to escape. On whom should responsibility for the disaster rest? Should the Cinematograph which, according to a deputy, "creates danger wherever it is used," be banned forever? No such decision has as yet been taken. Moreover, the Cinematograph has become so firmly established that nobody seriously believes it can be stopped.

How the decor for the occasion appeared before the conflagration.

An hour after the opening of the fete, the charity stalls were in ruins.

Georges Méliès opens a studio for moving pictures

Montreuil-sous-Bois, 22 March
Famous illusionist Georges Méliès, a recent Cinematograph convert, is thrilled. His first studio for animated pictures, built in the garden of his property in Montreuil, was inaugurated today. Since last October he has been recording films outside in his garden, in the streets nearby or in his laboratory right next to the Opéra in Paris, but bad weather and insufficient light have often prevented him from working. As a result, he decided to have a studio built. It was to be 17 metres long by seven metres wide, with an overall height of six metres. To ensure a maximum exposure to natural light he decided on a north-south orientation and to cover it entirely with glass like a photographic studio. Inside he planned a small set with a depth of five metres for actors to play out their scenes; the rest of the space was set aside for the camera and workshop. The studio floor is laid with parquet, and all sides and the roof are covered with frosted glass, except for the three spans in front of the set which are equipped with single-thickness clear panes to allow the sun's rays to light up the actors. Frames fitted with tracing-cloth are available to soften the sunlight if necessary. In fact it was Méliès himself who drew up the plans for the studio himself, but the glazier was far from impressed when he came to fit the glass roof. His first reaction was, "Who is the idiot that designed this?" Somewhat put out, Méliès, nevertheless, was forced to admit that the middle supports were leaning over in a worrying fashion. The construction underwent urgent modifications for an overall cost of 90,000 francs! However, not even this could spoil Méliès' pleasure. Ideas for films are already taking flight in his imagination; the new studio is going to open up a whole new world. Méliès is intending to begin his first projects using reconstructed news films, and the recently started Greek-Turkish War should make an excellent subject.

The building constructed on the Méliès property in Montreuil.

Méliès' films shown in his own theater

Paris, 30 October
The Robert Houdin Theatre at 8 boulevard des Italiens, is presenting the latest animated pictures produced by its owner Georges Méliès in his studio in Montreuil. For the last six months the Cinematograph has been filling the house every evening. Sessions last three quarters of an hour. For 50 cents a seat, the audience is treated to wonderfully imaginative scenes. In *L'Auberge ensorcelée* (*The Bewitched Inn*), a man chases his boots, which walk unaided. A truly astonishing sight.

Georges Méliès and his associate Lucien Reulos inaugurate Star Film.

*With **After the Ball, the Bath**, played by Jehanne d'Alcy and Jeanne Brady, Georges Méliès dared to present nudity on the screen!*

Pathé and Gaumont have begun production

Paris, 28 December
The brothers Charles and Emile Pathé have organized and founded the General Company of Cinematographs, Phonographs and Film, with strong financial backing from banker Jean Neyret and industrialist Claude Grivolas. The new company, with a capital of 1 million francs, takes over from the Pathé Brothers' establishment. Emile Pathé will deal with the phonography branch and run the factory in Chatou. Charles Pathé will be supervising both sections but intends to devote more time to the smaller cinematography branch with an eye to increasing film production. The head office and phonograph shop are situated at 98 rue de Richelieu. The same district is also home to the General Photography Syndicate (Comptoir Générale de Photography) which was acquired by Léon Gaumont on 11 September 1895. The Syndicate started out with the modest capital of 300,000 francs at the beginning of this year. But this extremely active little company not only manufactures excellent quality cameras and projectors, made to Georges Demeny's patents, but has produced a few greatly appreciated films: *At The Barber, Transformation of a Hat, Negros Bathing, Arrival of a Train in Auteuil Station...* Gaumont offers over 80 different films and also sells the Lumière collection. Nonetheless, Charles Pathé looks set to take over the still-modest animated picture market, thanks largely to his backers' support.

America embargoes Lumière material

New York, 28 July
It all happened at dawn off the Hudson Estuary. A dinghy rocked gently on the calm morning swell. On board were two Frenchmen – Monsieur Lafont, the representative in America for the French Lumière Company, and his favorite cameraman Félix Mesguich. After waiting a considerable time, a transatlantic ship flying the French flag approached, took Lafont on board and immediately set sail for France. Thus ended the Cinematograph's short-lived American epic. Congress had pulled the rug from underneath the French company four days earlier by voting in the Dingley Bill. This new law, aimed at protecting American manufacturers, hits foreign technical material with prohibitive import taxes, ranging from 25 to 65 percent of their value. American Mutoscope and the Biograph Company, whose links with the new President William McKinley are common knowledge, quickly took advantage of the situation by lodging a complaint against the Lumière Company for a supposed violation of customs regulations viz that its material, and in particular the Cinematographs, were brought into the United States without the necessary authorization. Perhaps, faced with the threat of arrest, Lafont preferred to leave the country. However, for him and a number of his colleagues the American dream is well and truly over.

Edison goes into battle over patents

Thomas Edison is happy to demonstrate the Vitascope, the machine invented by Thomas Armat.

New York, 7 December
A warning shot has been fired in the seething world of animated pictures. The International Film Company has just been ordered to cease all its business activities by Dyer & Dyer, the well-known legal firm in charge of Thomas Alva Edison's interests. The company, which was founded in November 1896 by Charles H. Webster and Edward Kuhn, specializes in the importation of foreign films and is marketing a projector, the Projectorscope, an exact copy of existent models. Charles Webster, no stranger to the world of images, was charged with the promotion of the Vitascope over in England. Impressed by the photographic superiority of European films, he worked to facilitate their arrival on the American market as soon as he returned. Kuhn was one of the filmmakers responsible for the first Kinetoscopic films. Like W.K. Laurie Dickson, he left his job, and, accompanied by his cameraman Edwin S. Porter, joined forces with Webster. In order to justify this move against his former collaborators, Edison put forward the definitive registration of his patent to August of this year. By this legal artifice, the Wizard from West Orange has become *de facto* the sole inventor of animated projections, and, therefore, has the right to bring proceedings against his rivals under the shadowy pretext of unauthorized imitations. Furthermore, the prosecutions look set to continue. Apparently, the Maguire and Baucus Company has also been summoned to appear before the courts, and other similar injunctions could be underway. Who will be the next to go? Biograph, Cinematograph, Magniscope, Polyscope and Projectorscope: could all these deliciously repetitive names be doomed to soon disappear from our vocabulary?

A Lumière cameraman in the United States, as seen by the American press.

A San Francisco Kinetoscope parlor, modeled on a West Orange hall.

1898

Naples, 18 January
The whimsical transformist Leopoldo Fregoli has presented several short films at the Gran Circo delle Varietà. The films were made with a camera called the Fregoligraph.

New York, 16 February
Theater producers Mark Klaw and Abraham Erlanger, who have imported the Lumières' film *Passion*, have received a visit from Edison's legal representatives, Dyer & Dyer. The lawyers warned them against exhibiting foreign films in America.

Spain, 28 February
Fructuoso Gelabert Badellia is in Barcelona to film the first Spanish newsreels.

France, 25 March
Clément Maurice has won the first cinematographic prize in the history of the cinema. The competition was organized by the Bain de Mer company in Monaco. The jury included well-known personalities such as Léon Gaumont, Frederic Dillaye and Georges Mareschal. Contestants were required to make a 15-minute film of "a subject with movement filmed in Monaco."

Paris, 25 March
The Pole Boleslaw Matuszewski has published a brochure entitled *Une nouvelle source d'histoire* (*A New Source of History*), where the idea of gathering, saving and stocking films is suggested for the first time.

Paris, 4 April
Auguste Baron has obtained a patent for a new sound system for the cinema. It consists of a phonograph driven by an electrical mechanism which in turn receives its impulse from the rotational movement of the camera. This results in a fairly satisfactory synchronization of sound and image. Baron has already started making sound films in a purpose-built studio.

Paris, 26 April
The first projection of Georges Méliès' new film, *Quais de La Havane et Explosion du cuirassé Le Maine* (*The Explosion of the Battleship Maine in Havana Harbor*), a reconstructed news film about the American intervention in Cuba. This is the first film in a series of five 20-metre reels dealing with the same subject. Méliès re-created the wreck in his studio in Montreuil and filmed the actors through an aquarium filled with fish.

London, 5 May
The American Charles Urban is in London to set up a branch for Edison. The new firm is called Warwick Trading Company.

New York, 19 May
Vitagraph has started making its own films. One of the first, *The Battle of Manila Bay*, about the American victory in Cuba on 1 May, was filmed using models and photographs.

Prague, 19 June
Jan Krizenecky has presented his footage of filmed news showing the river-boat which exploded on the Moldau yesterday.

Paris, 22 June
Emile Reynaud has suffered yet another disappointment. The Grévin Museum has insisted that he include in his show, Gaumont's "chronophotographic experiences", filmed with the Demenÿ camera.

New York, 13 July
J. Stuart Blackton, one of the founders of the Vitagraph Company, has settled out of court in the case brought against him by Edison. The director of the Edison Manufacturing Company, William Gilmore, dealt with the negotiations. From now on, Blackton and his associate Smith will be working under license to Edison.

Prague, 1 October
Jan Krizenecky has released three reels of fiction played by the actor Joseph Svab-Malostransky. One of them, *Smiles and Tears*, is made up of close-up shots of the actor's face.

Italy, 18 October
The cameraman Vittorio Calcina, the Lumière agent in Italy, is in Monza to present the Cinematograph to the royal family.

Paris, 18 October
The Lumière brothers and cameraman Félix Mesguich have set up an outdoor screen, at 5 boulevard Montmartre, to project a film on the merits of Ripolin's paintings.

Paris, 29 October
Lucien Reulos, Méliès' former associate, has patented his Mirograph. This machine is the first in France to use a film with the reduced width of 21mm.

Denmark, 31 December
Arnold Poulson has perfected a magnetic procedure for recording sound on bands of steel.

New developments in the patents war

New York, 13 May
There seems little chance of an end to Thomas Alva Edison's offensive, launched last December to protect his interests. Armed with the fact that he owns the first registered patent, the inventor continues to plague his rivals by instituting proceedings against them. Having attacked Webster and Kuhn, Maguire and Baucus, Sigmund Lubin, William S. Selig, Klaw and Erlanger and many others, his lawyers have now turned their attention to the American Mutoscope and Biograph Company. Biograph has received an order to cease all activity. The company's directors, especially William Kennedy Laurie Dickson who formerly worked on the Kinetoscope with Edison, are accused of fraudulent imitations and threatened with blacklisting. According to his lawyer, Edison hopes to settle out of court. The idea of a financial agreement has been mentioned, but it seems doubtful that Biograph will accept without a fight.

EDISON'S
Copyrighted Production of
All Moving Pictures.
True to Life.
THOS. A. EDISON, Inventor.
THE PASSION PLAY

The Passion inspires many filmmakers

New York, 30 January
The Cinematograph is at last reconciled with the Church, due to the popularity of Passion films. New versions are constantly appearing on the scene. Richard Hollaman's Eden Museum is presenting *The Oberammergau Passion Play*, by Henry C. Vincent. Though a huge success, the film was made on the roof of the Grand Central Palace in New York and not in Bavaria, as the bills lead one to believe. In France the Passion is also drawing in the crowds with Lumière's *Life and Passion of Christ* by Georges Hatot. Gaumont are planning their *Life of Christ*, and the Catholic *Maison de la bonne presse* is distributing Albert Kirchner's version of the story.

Medical science films are pioneered by Dr. Eugène-Louis Doyen

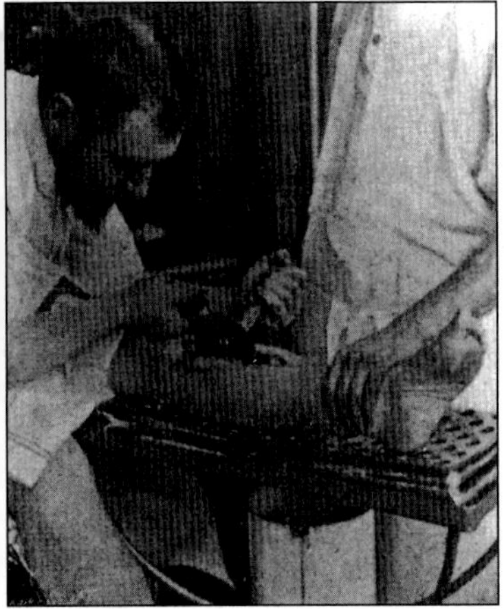
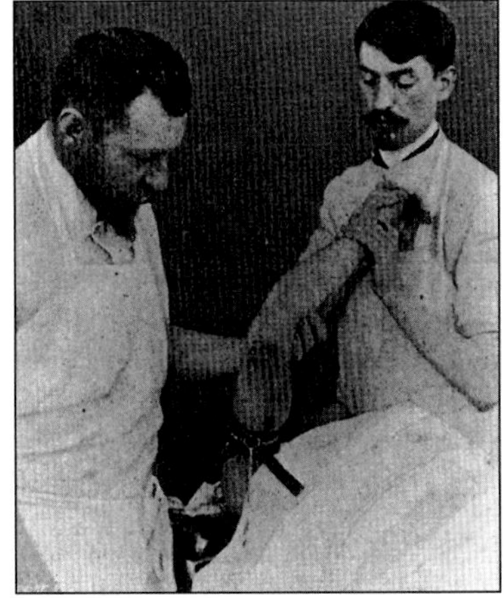
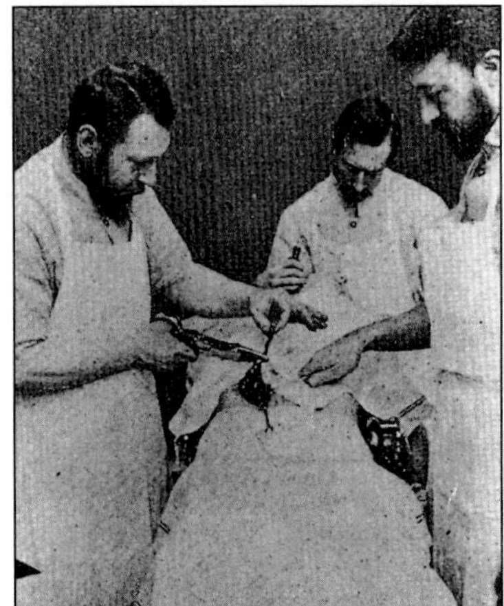

The surgeon, who has a reputation for novel and audacious methods, has been quick to use the resources of film.

Paris, 21 October
The renowned surgeon Eugène-Louis Doyen has organized, at his own expense, a projection session of medical films at the Learned Societies building. Dr. Doyen's passion for photography goes back several years. In 1890 he built up a collection of glass plates to use in similar sessions for medical students. With the invention of the Cinematograph, Doyen immediately thought about making scientific films. In 1897 this became a reality, thanks to Clément Maurice's brilliant technical assistance; the cameraman from the Grand Café has a complete mastery of the Lumière Cinematograph. Finally, a third man joined the team, Ambroise-François Parnaland, the owner of an animated-picture camera with central perforations. The two experts first made a trial film of a craniectomy in Dr. Doyen's operating room on avenue d'Iéna. Then, at the beginning of this year they started filming again, this time in a new clinic on rue Piccini equipped with powerful electric reflectors. This time the results obtained were excellent. At this point, Dr. Doyen left for England, and on 28 July he projected the films of his operations, a hysterectomy and a craniectomy, for the English Medical Association. This first film demonstration was received with enthusiasm. But in France it has been a different story. Since Dr. Doyen's return he has had to face up to a veritable cabal of scientists who feel that the Cinematograph has no role to play in the operating theater. One after another, doors have shut in his face. The Medical Academy turned down a paper he was scheduled to give, and the Surgical Congress in Paris has refused to allow him to project his films. Luckily, Dr. Doyen's films are a great success at the Learned Society.

Pathé opens film studio at Vincennes

Vincennes, June
Charles Pathé is constructing a film studio at 1 rue Polygone, though not as elaborate as Georges Méliès' Montreuil studio. It consists of a small room in a former bistro with several upstairs bedrooms which have been converted into a laboratory and workshops for developing films. Pathé leased the premises from a wine merchant, the widow Hervillard. Filming takes place, weather permitting, in the courtyard on a wooden stage measuring six by eight metres, with a naively-painted canvas as a backdrop. The wind often shakes the backcloth, and when it rains the scenery is ruined. A wooden hut serves as a storage space for the costumes, backcloths and accessories. Pathé has no real reason to invest too much money in making animated pictures, apart from a personal desire to increase film production. The powerful General Company of Cinematographs, Phonographs and Film, run jointly with his brother Emile and Claude Grivolas, makes its major profit from the sale of phonographs and cylinders. Meanwhile, Gaumont, Méliès and other artisans are taking over the market.

Lumière cameraman expelled from Russia

St. Petersburg, 27 September
Félix Mesguich, one of the Lumière brothers' best cameramen, has been escorted to the border by the Russian police. This unfortunate incident puts an end to his, until now, triumphantly-successful tour of this country with the Lumière Cinematograph. Everything had started out so well. Mesguich was first sent to Odessa on 13 November 1897 by Arthur Grunewald, the Lumière agent in Russia. After Odessa, he continued on to Yalta to show the Cinematograph to Czar Nicholas II who appeared to find the films most interesting. From there the "image hunter" journeyed throughout Russia. After a short stay in Moscow, he set up the projector in a large hall at the annual fair in Nijni-Novgorod. The audience was completely stupefied, looking behind the screen to find out how the diabolical mystery worked. The Coronation of Nicholas II was screened next. It was too much; some made the sign of the cross, others muttered angrily. A few nights later the Lumière Establishment was burned to the ground by a group of fanatics. In St. Petersburg, a final catastrophe awaited Mesguich. The Frenchman filmed the beautiful Caroline Otéro in an "explosive waltz" with stunning results. Unfortunately, her closely-held partner was a Russian officer. The following day when the film was projected at the Aquarium Theater in front of the Russian aristocracy, the entire audience rose to its feet, and in the ensuing uproar, Mesguich, himself at a complete loss, was brutally seized. The explanation given was that he had seriously offended the Russian army by turning one of its officers into a "music-hall dancer." Poor Mesguich! What an ignominious end to what had been such a wonderful journey.

CASINO DE
PARIS
THE
AMERICAN
HERMAN-CASLER de NEW-YORK.
INVENTEUR.
BIOGR
La Bataille des Oreillers
Ateliers Choubrac & Colombes Seine. imp.

Presented for the first time at the Casino de Paris, in September 1897, the films produced in New York by the American Biograph Company have been enjoying a great success there. The managers are continuing to capitalize on the exclusivity of these programs, which are presented by Eugène Lauste. The films have proved to be a choice addition to their own cabaret program. Each film lasts a quarter of an hour.

1899

Paris, 6 January
Léon Gaumont has demonstrated a Chronophotograph projector capable of screening over 600 metres of film, thanks to a system of spools, at a meeting of the French Photographic Society.

Paris, January
Young actor Ferdinand Zecca, originally from Corsica, has been taken on in the phonographic section of the Pathé brothers' establishment, directed by Emile Pathé. Zecca, who has a wonderful speaking voice, will be reading the official speeches given by politicians so that they can be engraved on sound cylinders.

Paris, 23 February
Georges Méliès was present with his camera to film President of the Republic Félix Faure's funeral. For once, Méliès has decided not to make a reconstructed news film.

Paris, 31 March
Léon Gaumont has brought out two new films in the Elgé Collection: *Panorama pris d'un train en marche* (*Scenery from a Passing Train*) and *Arrivée en gare d'un train* (*A Train Arriving at the Station*).

Vincennes, April
Ferdinand Zecca has taken part in the filmed fiction stories made by Pathé for the Galeries Dufayel. He supervised and acted alongside the comedian Charlus in *le Muet mélomane* (*The Mute Music-Lover*), a burlesque film directed by cameraman Maurice Caussade, with synchronized sound provided by a phonograph.

France, 4 May
A fire broke out at a fairground show in Cognac which was presenting the American Vitagraph. The film burst into flames and in eight terrifying minutes the entire fair was burned to the ground. The 40-metre long Vitagraph, run by fairground exhibitors Dane and Oger, is beyond repair. The damages are estimated at over 50,000 francs.

Paris, 24 May
Etienne Jules Marey has patented a device "to adjust the movement of positive film in the chrono-photographic projector."

Paris, 13 July
The Pathé brothers' General Cinematograph, Phonograph and Film Company is a thriving concern. At the annual general meeting, profits were estimated at nearly 360,000 francs.

Paris, 14 July
The shares in the Pathé brothers' General Cinematograph, Phonograph and Film Company have risen considerably in a very short time; they are now being negotiated by the bank for between 235 and 255 francs.

Prague, 30 August
Eduard Tichy, from the Variety Theater, asked the cameraman Otto Ditto to make a film for him on the Emperor François Joseph's recent visit to the capital.

France, August
Georges Méliès is in Granville to film footage of the sea. He intends to combine the views with studio scenes for his new fiction film, *le Christ marchant sur les eaux* (*Christ Walking over Water*).

Paris, 16 October
The Grévin Museum board has terminated Emile Reynaud's contract. The father of the Praxinoscope and the Optic Theatre is to be replaced by a puppeteer named Saint-Genois.

Paris, 1 November
A fight broke out today at the Lumière Cinematograph in the boulevard des Capucines. A certain Mrs. King, unable to see the screen, sat on the arm of her seat, but this obstructed the projection. When a policeman grabbed her arm to remove her, some of the audience sprung to her defense, causing a general upheaval. Seats were ripped apart and paintings were damaged... Mr. Lafont, the owner of the property has filed a complaint.

Paris, 21 November
Victor Continsouza and René Bünzli are registering their "stereoscopic animator" for patent.

Paris, 1 December
Charles Pathé has brought out a new series of animated scenes "particularly aimed at schools and youth movements."

Paris, 15 December
The Pathé productions rely heavily on dramatization but show very little artistic improvement. Charles Pathé has brought out three films all entitled *Un incendie* (*A Fire*), where one of the firemen is seriously hurt. The catalogue also lists *Arrivée d'un train* (*The Arrival of a Train*), a humorous sketch in which a cyclist falls off his bicycle, knocking over a station hand on the platform, and a host of other films very much in the same vein as the Lumières' films.

Clandestine filming of championship fight

Coney Island, 3 November
"Winner on points: Jim Jeffries!" At the referees' decision the spectators rose to give a standing ovation to the well-deserved champion and his unhappy rival Thomas Sharkey. The fight had been superb – no less than 33 brisk rounds. As the audience started to make its way out of the hall, the 400 arc lights suddenly went out, throwing the ring into shadow. However, a group of men busy with their cameras paid little heed to the general exodus; the camera crew from the American Mutoscope and Bioscope Company still had work to do. During the match they had filmed almost 1,800 metres of footage, equivalent to 30-minutes viewing time. It should be remembered that the enterprising company recently acquired film rights to the Jeffries-Sharkey boxing match from the impresario William Brady. However, it would appear that this completely new type of contract has been knowingly sabotaged by Thomas Alva Edison, who views the whole business with a very jaundiced eye. The facts are as follows: Albert E. Smith, the joint founder of Vitagraph, was caught in the act of filming the match with his camera, which was hidden under a tangle of umbrellas near the cloakroom. The deception discovered, Smith and his rival cameraman almost came to fisticuffs, just like the pugilists whose match was at stake in the conflict. In the end, Albert Smith packed up and ran, escaping with his precious negatives. When questioned later on, the daring offender confessed that his company's financial difficulties as well as pressure from the Edison Company were responsible. Smith claims that James White, the manager of the West Orange studios, had contacted Smith for the job, threatening him with legal action should he refuse. Resigned, Smith, in collusion with several people placed around the ring, had managed to elude the vigilance of Biograph's police contingent. The rival companies certainly seem set for an all-out fight between their leaders.

AMERICAN MUTOSCOPE & BIOGRAPH Co
841 BROADWAY, N.Y.
American Mutoscope & Biograph Co.
841 BROADWAY, NEW YORK.

For the Jeffries-Sharkey fight, Biograph used artificial light for the first time.

The cinema takes on the scandalous Dreyfus affair

Journalists fighting over the Dreyfus affair, filmed by Méliès after the court verdict was delivered in Rennes.

Paris, November

Everyone in France has been following the Dreyfus affair with passionate interest. The Cinematograph has taken up this sensational subject, and even fairground exhibitors are screening reconstructed newsreels (presented as genuine) showing the misfortunes of ex-officer Alfred Dreyfus. Moreover, the wave of pro-Dreyfus feeling, which has swept the country since the beginning of the year, was so strong that the new government led by Emile Loubet decided to re-open the trial. And not without reason: falsified documents were located in the dossier, and Colonel Henry, who was strongly suspected of having lied, killed himself. In August the new trial opened in Rennes amid feverish speculation from the public. On 9 September, Dreyfus was once more condemned but was immediately granted a pardon by President Loubet. This decision did little to calm the situation. In fairgrounds and cinemas Georges Méliès' series of films has met with incredible success and with feelings running so high that audiences often fight among themselves. Some regions have preferred to ban all pro-Dreyfus projections. Méliès filmed the whole affair in his Montreuil studio. The 11 films (10 20-metre films and one 40 metres in length) that he produced for sale are astonishingly realistic. The role of Laborie, the lawyer hired to defend Dreyfus, is interpreted by Méliès himself, and the owner of a local hardware store who bears an uncanny resemblance to the unfortunate defendant, plays Dreyfus. The films, which are also distributed in England by Charles Urban, the head of Warwick Trading Company, show Dreyfus' arrest, his imprisonment on Devil's Island, Colonel Henry's suicide, the trial in Rennes, the attempt on Laborie's life, Dreyfus leaving for prison after the trial... The copies sold so well that Charles Pathé decided to produce his own *Affaire Dreyfus*. The eight films, which have just been released for sale, also have a pro-Dreyfus slant. Jean Liezer, an actor from the Ambigue-Comique troupe, plays Dreyfus. This film series depicts Colonel Henry's arrest and avowal, his suicide, Dreyfus in his cell in Rennes, the court-martial, General Mercier's deposition... Pathé's series is also sold overseas, but Méliès' films have achieved a far greater success. Who can forget the dramatic *Attempt on Mr. Laborie* or *A Brawl between Journalists* in which Méliès' actors battle it out with such conviction that one honestly believes the magician slipped his camera into the courtroom in Rennes.

Pathé made their own ***Dreyfus Affair*** *with the actor Liezer.*

Images of war from Cuba to Africa

New York, 1 November

The latest offer from the American Mutoscope and Biograph Company and W.K. Laurie Dickson: war from the comfort of your chair! Dickson, a British subject, and his cameraman William Cox, have just returned from covering their compatriots' war with the Boers in the Transvaal. The news footage from Pretoria is genuine. Because of this, the faraway conflict on African soil appears closer and more tangible, a far cry from the faked images produced of the Hispano-American Conflict. In 1898 Edward Hill Amet reconstructed a *Naval Battle in Cuba* in his garden for Magniscope. Built around a large pond representing Santiago Bay with numerous model ships controlled to move in front of the camera by an electric device, his creative decor completely duped the public. Reality or fiction? The cinema's power of persuasion is surely without equal.

British films build a studio

New Southgate, 1 September
Robert William Paul, the well-known manufacturer of movie cameras and projectors, has had his own film studio built on Sydney Road. The studio, which adjoins his Theatrograph and Animatograph factory, is available to clients for all types of films, from advertising to fiction. Paul has been producing films since 1895 and is the only filmmaker in the country with such a mastery of photographic techniques, thanks to his extensive collection of theatrical props. Nothing has been left to chance in the new studio: trapdoors, pulleys, a drawbridge, a painting workshop for sets and a stock of 50 painted backcloths ready to provide any imaginable background. The building itself, built to Paul's own plans, is raised approximately two metres from the ground to allow actors to disappear through the trapdoors when special effects are required. The camera is mounted outside on a raised platform set on rails. This ingenious idea allows Paul to move the camera quickly and smoothly to produce magnified or reduced images. The results speak for themselves: the spectator feels he is actually approaching the action in scenes with "close-ups". The set measures roughly 8.5 metres by 4.25 metres and is protected by an iron structure fitted with sliding walls and a glass roof that faces north. Preparations for filming sessions are simple; it is just a matter of sliding back the walls and placing the camera at the desired distance. Paul's studio is without a doubt the most modern in Europe. Even his friend Georges Méliès is overwhelmed by such amazingly advanced techniques, but Paul has had more experience than Méliès in animated pictures. Moreover, the cinematograph has become a lucrative business for him since April 1897 when he founded Paul's Animatograph Ltd., with an initial capital of 60,000 pounds. His ambitions are artistic as well as commercial: "The public has seen too many trains, trams and buses. We have not as yet explored the possibilities of animated pictures to make people laugh, cry or simply astonish." Paul intends to change that and has begun work on a series of both comic and dramatic films.

Auguste Baron makes the cinema talk

Paris, 16 November
Just how far can the cinema go? On learning of the latest developments in the animated picture business, one might well ask this question. The engineer Auguste Baron has just applied for a patent for an outstanding new invention: a system for producing circular panoramic animated projections, with both color and sound. The Talking Cinematorama – for such is the name given to this incredible machine – consists of 10 movie cameras fitted to a circular platform and all connected to phonographs. Each camera films a section of the chosen landscape or set and records all its corresponding sounds. For projections, 10 projectors connected to loudspeakers are used instead of the cameras. Baron envisages a circular panorama with a diameter of 32 metres and a 100-metre-long screen. He has been a specialist in the talking film field for a long time; his first patent dealing with this speciality was lodged in April 1896 – an electric commutator which resulted in a very approximate synchronization. Within two years, the inventor had perfected a much more innovative procedure. The phonograph was connected to the camera by a commutator which was synchronized by the driving wheel on the camera and ensured that the two machines ran at the same speed. The principle has also been applied to projections. With this set-up, Baron is able to make talking films in a specially constructed studio in his garden in Asnières. There, inside the glass-paned studio, the camera, hooked up to the phonograph by cables, travels back and forth on rails. On the set, Guillier, a musician from the Lamoureux Concerts, poses in front of the objective, a cornet to his lips, the music flows out and is captured. The next act shows Lagrange from the Parisian Theatres – he takes a dramatic stance and declaims *The Dream of Athalie*... What more can one possibly ask for?

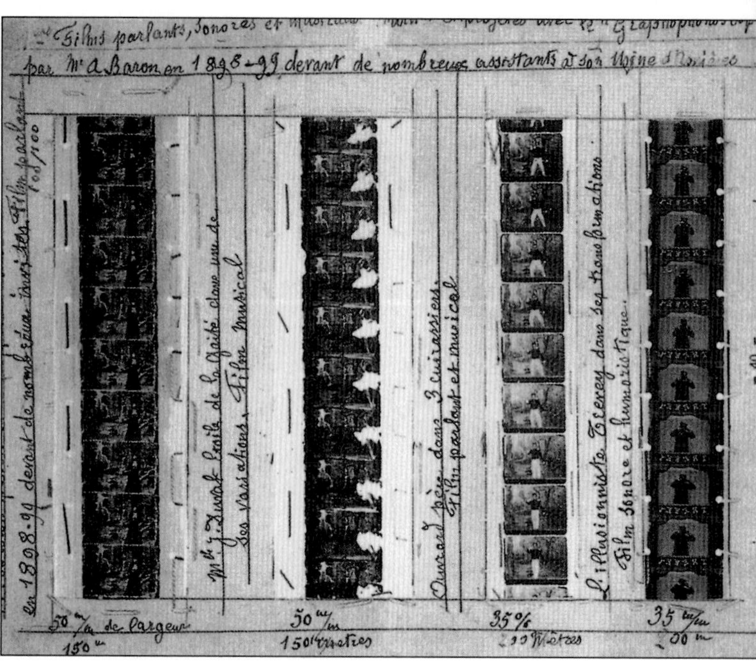

The different tests carried out by the inventor with his Graphonoscope.

Twenty-six-year-old secretary heads production at Gaumont

Paris, 30 November
Her name is Alice Guy, she is only 26-years-old, and her latest film, *L'Angelus*, has just been released for sale. She is now head of production for the General Photography Syndicate. Initially, her director Léon Gaumont was hesitant about confiding such an important position to a woman... but Guy, who has a deep passion for the Cinematograph, showed herself such a capable and original filmmaker that the Gaumont film catalogue sales soon increased noticeably. It all started in 1895 when she turned up at 57 rue Saint-Roch and knocked timidly on the door to Gaumont's office. He was looking for a simple secretary, but when he caught sight of her he exclaimed, "I'm afraid that you are too young for the job." "Sir, that won't last for long," retorted the young girl, taking the rather stern Gaumont so thoroughly off guard that he hired her. In the beginning, Alice Guy often ran into Gustave Eiffel, a company stockholder, and Georges Demenÿ, who had sold his patents to Gaumont. She became friends with them and also with the company's cameraman Anatole Thiberville, who initiated her in filming techniques. Early in 1897 Guy asked her employer's permission to try her hand at filming a few scenes. With Thiberville's help she directed several scenes at Belleville on a glassed-in terrace. Some were comic such as *le Planton du colonel* (*The Colonel's Orderly*) and *Une nuit agitée* (*An Agitated Night*), and some were light-hearted such as *le Coucher d'Yvette* (*Yvette's Bedtime*). The films sold quite well; fairground exhibitors appreciated the humor of "Mademoiselle Alice Guy." Since then her style has become more refined, and her last film, inspired by Millet's famous painting *The Angelus*, depicts an old farmer and his wife at prayer while the Angelus (on loudspeakers) rings out.

Mademoiselle Alice Guy at home.

Cinema artists born in the pioneering days

Paris, 4 January 1857
Emile Cohl (Emile Courtet)

Germany, 17 January 1867
Carl Laemmle

Hungary, 11 January 1873
Adolph Zukor

France, 19 February 1873
Louis Feuillade

Kentucky, 22 January 1875
David Wark Griffith

Paris, 2 February 1878
Maurice Tourneur (M. Thomas)

Canada, 17 January 1880
Mack Sennett
(Michael Sinnott)

San Francisco, 13 September 1880
Jesse L. Lasky

Massachusetts, 12 August 1881
Cecil Blount DeMille

Poland, 12 December 1881
Harry M. Warner

Philadelphia, 15 February 1882
John Barrymore (John Blythe)

France, 18 November 1882
Germaine Dulac
(Germaine Saisset-Schneider)

Denver, 23 May 1883
Douglas Fairbanks
(Douglas Elton Ullman)

Bordeaux, 16 December 1883
Max Linder
(Gabriel-Maximilien Leuvielle)

France, 17 December 1883
Raimu (Jules Muraire)

Michigan, 16 February 1884
Robert Flaherty

Switzerland, 26 July 1884
Emil Jannings
(Theodor Emil Janenz)

Warsaw, 27 August 1884
Samuel Goldwyn (Goldfish)

St. Petersburg, 21 February 1885
Sacha Guitry
(Alexandre-Georges Guitry)

Minsk, 4 July 1885
Louis B. Mayer
(Eliezer Mayer)

Brussels, 21 July 1885
Jacques Feyder
(Jacques Frédérix)

Vienna, 22 September 1885
Erich von Stroheim
(Erich Oswald Stroheim)

France, 5 March 1886
Léon Mathot

France, 24 December 1887
Louis Jouvet

Paris, 23 April 1888
Marcel L'Herbier

Paris, 12 September 1888
Maurice Chevalier

Budapest, 14 December 1888
Michael Curtiz
(Mihaly Kertesz)

Germany, 28 December 1888
Friedrich Wilhelm Murnau
(F.W. Plumpe)

Copenhagen, 3 February 1889
Carl Theodor Dreyer

Paris, 23 February 1889
Musidora (Jeanne Roques)

Pennsylvania, 4 March 1889
Pearl White

London, 16 April 1889
Charles Chaplin

France, 5 July 1889
Jean Cocteau

Russia, 26 September 1889
Ivan Mosjoukine

Paris, 25 October 1889
Abel Gance

England, 16 June 1890
Stan Laurel
(Arthur Stanley Jefferson)

France, 14 October 1890
Louis Delluc

Vienna, 5 December 1890
Fritz Lang

Paris, 19 April 1891
Françoise Rosay
(Francoise Bandy de Nalèche)

Georgia, 18 January 1892
Oliver Hardy

Berlin, 28 January 1892
Ernst Lubitsch

New York, 11 March 1892
Raoul Walsh
(Albert Edward Walsh)

New York, 17 August 1892
Mae West

France, 21 August 1892
Charles Vanel

Russia, 16 February 1893
Vsevolod Pudovkin

Toronto, 8 April 1893
Mary Pickford (Gladys Smith)

Nebraska, 20 April 1893
Harold Lloyd

Vienna, 29 May 1894
Josef von Sternberg
(Jonas Sternberg)

Paris, 15 September 1894
Jean Renoir

Poland, 31 December 1894
Pola Negri
(Barbara Apolonia Chalupiec)

Maine, 1 February 1895
John Ford
(Sean Aloysius O'Feeney)

France, 28 February 1895
Marcel Pagnol

Geneva, 9 April 1895
Michel Simon

Italy, 6 May 1895
Rudolph Valentino
(Rodolfo Alphonso
Raffaelle Guglielmi)

Kansas, 4 October 1895
Buster Keaton
(Joseph Francis Keaton)

Los Angeles, 29 November 1895
Busby Berkeley
(William Berkeley Enos)

Poland, 12 January 1896
Dziga Vertov
(Denis Kaufman)

Texas, 8 February 1896(?)
King Vidor

Indiana, 30 May 1896
Howard Hawks

France, 8 October 1896
Julien Duvivier

Ohio, 14 October 1896
Lillian Gish
(Lillian de Guiche)

Warsaw, 26 March 1897
Jean Epstein

Sicily, 18 May 1897
Frank Capra

Latvia, 23 January 1898
Sergei Mikhailovitch
Eisenstein

France, 15 May 1898
Arletty
(Leonie Bathiat)

Tokyo, 16 May 1898
Kenji Mizoguchi

Paris, 11 November 1898
René Clair
(René Chomette)

Netherlands, 18 November 1898
Joris Ivens

Chicago, 27 March 1899
Gloria Swanson

Nebraska, 10 May 1899
Fred Astaire
(Frederick Austerlitz)

New York, 30 May 1899
Irving Thalberg

England, 1 July 1899
Charles Laughton

New York, 7 July 1899
Georges Cukor

London, 13 August 1899
Alfred Hitchcock

New York, 25 December 1899
Humphrey Bogart

1900

Paris, 1 January
Pathé has released a reconstructed news film, *Episodes of the Transvaal War*, filmed by Lucien Nonguet in the bois de Vincennes.

New York, 20 January
Thomas Edison has terminated Vitagraph's license in reply to a lawsuit threat over Edison's alleged failure to acknowledge Vitagraph's royalties on print sales.

Paris, 15 February
Léon Gaumont has opened show rooms at 41 avenue de l'Opéra and is marketing the Kinora, a viewing machine invented by Louis Lumière in 1896 that can transform photos into moving pictures.

Paris, 15 March
The Dufayel stores at 24 rue de Clignancourt are organizing sessions of sound film, using Charles Pathé's phonograph.

Paris, 8 April
François Parnaland, inventor of the Photothéagraph, patented in 1896, is trying to compete with the two giants, Gaumont and Pathé. He is offering films in both historical and comic genres, which he prints in all sizes of perforation.

Paris, 13 May
The Hippodrome in rue Caulaincourt, a huge edifice planned by Louis Gaillot for the World's Fair and able to seat 3,945, has opened with an equestrian pantomime, *Vercingétorix*, produced by Victorin-Hippolyte Jasset, former theater wardrobe master.

Peking, 14 June
Japanese cameramen T. Shibata and K. Fukaya have made a film of the Boxer uprising against the Western powers in China.

Nîmes, 17 June
The newspaper *Torero* has published the first article by a young aficionado named Louis Feuillade.

Berlin, 30 June
Oskar Messter has formed his own production company, Messter Projections. Cameramen shot their first footage from an airship.

Paris, 10 September
Pathé has taken over Victor Continsouza and René Bünzli's precision camera factory. The new company (General Company of phonographs, cinematographs and precision machines) is making the Maltese Cross camera devised by Bünzli.

London, 28 September
According to the *British Journal*, the longest cinematographic footage to date was filmed here during the boxing match between Sharkey and Jeffries. Cameramen used four movie cameras and 400 arc lights to make the half-hour film.

Paris, 30 September
Léon Gaumont has launched a new machine, the pocket Chrono, which takes and projects films with central perforation.

Paris, 10 November
Clément Maurice and Henri Loiret's Phono-Cinéma-Théâtre, one of the central attractions at the World's Fair, has re-opened its doors on a permanent basis at 42 boulevard de Bonne-Nouvelle near the Gymnase. Overseas tours are also planned.

Montreuil, 1 December
Méliès' latest extravaganza, *Rêve de Noël*, a "full-length film" that is comprised of 160 metres with a running time of nine minutes, is selling for 435 francs.

BIRTHS

Paris, 7 January
Robert Le Vigan (R. Coquillaud)

France, 4 February
Jacques Prévert

Spain, 22 February
Luis Buñuel

Germany, 2 March
Kurt Weill

Paris, 6 March
Henri Jeanson

Milwaukee, 5 April
Spencer Tracy

Hamburg, 26 April
Douglas Sirk (H. Detlef Sierck)

Rome, 3 July
Alessandro Blasetti

Paris, 17 July
Marcel Dalio

Memphis, 8 August
Robert Siodmak

Montreal, 10 August
Norma Shearer

Paris, 14 September
Robert Florey

Switzerland, 22 December
Marc Allégret

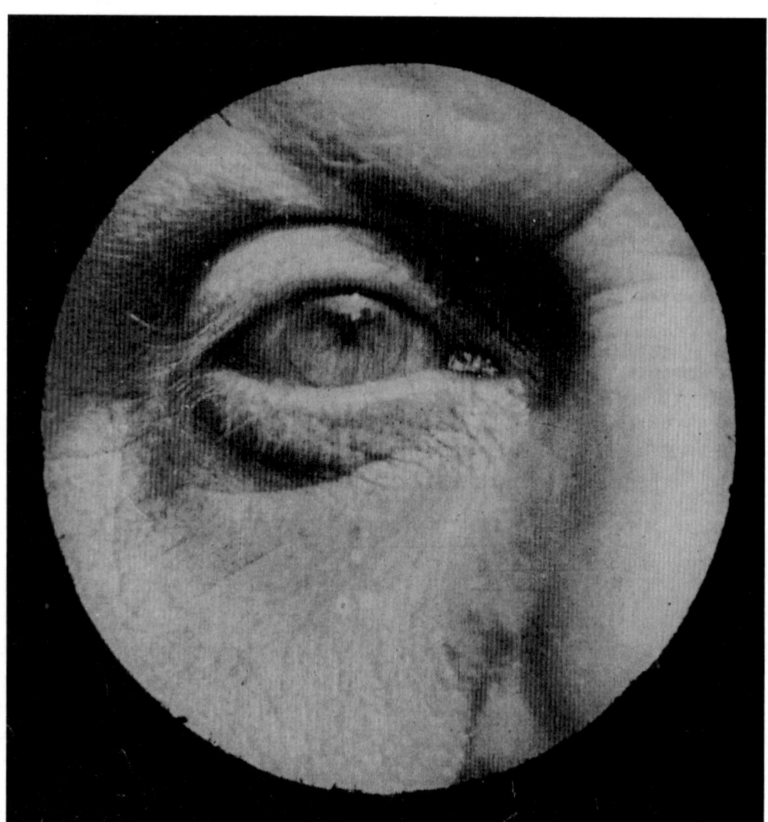

Grandma's eye as seen by her grandson through her magnifying glass. A striking image from G.A. Smith's ***Grandma's Reading Glass.***

LA GRANDE ATTRACTION NOUVELLE
DE
L'EXPOSITION
BALLON
CINÉORAMA
PROJECTIONS PANORAMIQUES
ANIMÉES
DE
GRIMOIN-SANSON
RESTAURANT KAMMERZELL & BALLON CINÉORAMA
Près la TOUR EIFFEL

Grimoin-Sanson's Cinéorama programs, cleverly filmed from a balloon, are attracting very large crowds at the World's Fair.

Vast audiences at the World's Fair are favorably

The Lumière Brothers provide one of the surprises of the fair

Louis Lumière personally directed the installation of this giant screen, 25 by 15 metres, visible to an audience of 25,000.

Paris, 15 May
One of the major events of the Exhibition was the first performance of the giant Lumière Cinematograph, which took place today in the vast Machine gallery. The overall supervisor Alfred Picard requested that Lumière undertake the projection on an enormous screen. They obviously didn't take the easy option in erecting an immense 400-square-metre white canvas in the center of the gallery that, nightly, has to be taken down to a large water storage tank. Just prior to the showing, the canvas is erected by a winch installed above the glass roof. Thus, the dampened material absorbs the light and remains sufficiently transparent to be seen from both sides. The program lasted 25 minutes and was comprised of 15 films. Originally, the Lumières wanted to use a film format in a 75-mm size. A camera was even manufactured to do this, but the projector failed to turn up on time, so they were forced to use the normal 35-mm one. Yet another Lumière project consisted of the projection of their films on a huge screen set up outside in front of the Eiffel Tower. However, the wind threatened to blow the screen down, and it was considered wiser to return to the safety of the Machine gallery. Despite these technical difficulties, the first showing was a triumph. The Lumière brothers had carried it off.

A serious crisis appears to be over

Paris, 12 November
The Universal Exhibition is over. The Cinematograph, which was unveiled five years ago, has been officially rehabilitated after the catastrophe at the Charity Bazaar on 4 May 1897. Since this fatal occurrence, moving images have been considered disreputable. Their purpose and even their morality were thought suspect. However, the Exhibition provided suitable space for a diversity of cinematographic experiments. Seventeen projection sites as well as 12 stands of cinematographic material were open to the public to mark one of the greatest inventions of the century. It's true that all the attractions devoted to moving pictures didn't enjoy as much good fortune. The panoramas attracted many more people than the Phonorama, Theatroscope and Phono-Cinema-Theatre as well as the Algerian Cinematograph. And it's better to forget the Cinéorama of Grimoin-Sanson, which was a disaster because the creator himself couldn't make it work. On the other hand, the Lumière brothers were wonderfully successful. Over one million spectators went to see their giant Cinematograph. The Lumière Company also received the Grand Prize from an international jury, who also awarded an equivalent prize to the firm of Léon Gaumont.

Brothers Auguste and Louis Lumière, close associates in all their ventures.

The new Photorama process was also presented at the Exposition.

impressed with the brilliance of the cinema

A risky undertaking by Grimoin-Sanson

The audience watches the screen from seats in the gondola of an air balloon.

Paris, 18 August

The French firm of Cinéorama, founded on 8 July 1899, has just been declared bankrupt. Eleven 70-mm cameras, 11 projectors and 119 spools of film – all the property of Raoul Grimoin-Sanson – had to be sold off at the famous Paris auction house, the Hôtel Drouot, in order to reimburse the shareholders. Grimoin-Sanson, who has claimed with self-assurance to have invented the cinematograph at the same time as the more celebrated Lumière brothers, really has had very little luck. He had triumphantly announced the opening of Cinéorama for May, when the Exhibition was in full swing. Having picked up an idea expounded in 1896 by Auguste Baron, Grimoin-Sanson patented a machine he called Cinécosmorama the following year, which later became known as Cosmorama. It consisted of moving projections across a panoramic screen. Ten cameras firmly mounted on a 2.5-metres-high wooden platform secured the steady taking of shots. The method of moving the cameras was synchronized with one large hand crank, operated by three assistants, that started the simultaneous unreeling of the films in the 10 cameras. With the financial backing of the company's shareholders, Grimoin-Sanson was able to shoot various films in many different European countries,

Device for a bank of ten cameras.

despite his odd working methods. He even shot one of these films from an air balloon he had installed in the Champs-de-Mars to mark the occasion of Cinéorama's christening. Why then this failure? At the moment, in the Cinéorama building constructed near the Eiffel Tower, there happen to be 10 projectors placed side by side which cannot operate because they release too much heat, thus putting the nitrate films in danger of catching fire. In other words, Cinéorama is just too risky to be used. Therefore, sadly, no showing took place.

PHONO-CINÉMA-THÉATRE
VISIONS ANIMÉES DES ARTISTES CÉLÈBRES
Mme SARAH BERNHARDT
Mr COQUELIN AINÉ
Mr VICTOR MAUREL
Mlle ROSITA MAURI
Mme REICHENBERG
Mlle FÉLICIA MALLET
Mlle J. CHASLES
Mlle ZAMBELLI
Mr COQUELIN CADET
Mr DE FÉRAUDY
Mr JEAN COQUELIN
Mlle MILY MEYER
Mlle MARIETTE SULLY
Mlles MANTE
Mlle CLÉO DE MERODE
Mr POLIN
LOUIS MAUREL
JULES MOY
Mme RÉJANE
EXPOSITION DE 1900
RUE DE PARIS PORTE 43 -PONT DES INVALIDES-

Clément Maurice and Henri Lioret attract the crowds to their Phono-Cinema-Théatre with the Phonorama, developed by Berton, Dussaud and Jaubert, at the pavilion set aside for the first demonstrations of sound cinema. The films boast great names from the theater and music halls.

1901

Trieste, January
Alexandre Lifka and his brother Karel, who came originally from Czechoslovakia, have fitted out the Electro-cinematographic Theatre for the Gaumont company. It is a large traveling cinema under a big top, with seating for 460.

Vincennes, January
Charles Pathé has decided he will increase production and plans to film one to two reels a day.

Montreuil, April
Georges Méliès has begun work on his new film, *Little Red Riding Hood*, described as a "full-length film" in 12 scenes.

Paris, 20 May
Claude Grivolas, one of Pathé's main shareholders, has invented a projector that produces three-dimensional pictures.

Paris, 27 July
Georges Mendel, the camera manufacturer, situated at 10 boulevard Bonne-Nouvelle, has launched a Parisian Cinematograph. He also produces comic and transformation scenes aimed at fairground shows.

London, 5 August
The Royal Animated and Singing Picture Co. today opens a cinema in the Mohawks' Hall, Upper Street, Islington. Admissions are the highest to date, with a top price of three shillings, but the inaugural program is packed with a variety of items.

Stockholm, 1 September
As part of his European tour, the talented French cameraman Clément Maurice is presenting a session of the Phono-Cinéma-Théâtre at the Olympia.

New York, 14 September
Edwin Stanton Porter has just been promoted to chief cameraman and film-director of the New York based Edison studios.

Paris, 21 September
Pathé has released *The Czar in France*, a newsreel about Nicholas II's recent visit to Paris, and the fairground shows are snapping it up. Meanwhile, the Lumière company's Paris agent H. Chevrier is trying to compete with Pathé and has brought out two new films: *les Fêtes franco-russes* and *Le tsar et le Président à Dunkerque*.

Belgium, 28 September
The fairground showman, Salsman, has put his Great Cinematograph up for sale. It consists of a 22-metre-long stall, "with gas and paraffin motors, a dynamo, lights, machinery, films and caravans."

London, October
Release of director James Williamson's *The Big Swallow*, *Stop Thief!* and *Fire*.

Paris, 15 November
Hugues Eugène Frey, the Opéra's décor designer, has just perfected a triple projector that is capable of producing still and moving projections specially intended for use in the theater or opera.

Washington, 16 December
Edison has lodged a copyright for *The Mysterious Cafe* from Edwin Porter at the Library of Congress.

Vincennes, 31 December
This year Pathé has produced 70 films (totaling 3,000 metres) in its rue du Polygone studio. Almost two-thirds of the films were directed by Ferdinand Zecca, Lucien Nonguet and Georges Hatot.

BIRTHS

Ohio, 1 February
Clark Gable

New York, 25 February
Zeppo Marx (Herbert Marx)

Georgia, 5 April
Melvyn Douglas (Hesselberg)

Montana, 7 May
Gary Cooper
(Frank James Cooper)

Philadelphia, 18 June
Jeanette MacDonald

Italy, 7 July
Vittorio De Sica

France, 3 October
Jean Grémillon

Paris, 3 November
André Malraux

Chicago, 5 December
Walt Disney

Berlin, 27 December
Marlene Dietrich
(Maria Magdalena von Losch)

Drame au fond de la mer *(Drama at the Bottom of the Sea), directed by Ferdinand Zecca, was inspired by* ***Cuirassé Maine*** *(Battleship Maine) of Georges Méliès.*

FEND L'AIR

*Ferdinand Zecca in **The Conquest of the Air**, one of his first films as a director after joining the creative team at Charles Pathé's company.*

Law rules on licensing rights

New York, 12 January
The break between Edison and the Vitagraph company is complete. Vitagraph, controlled by Albert E. Smith and J. Stuart Blackton, has been notified of the cancellation of its film license. Its commercial operations have been placed under court supervision and its films sequestered, pending an appeal. This is the latest episode in the legal dispute which began on 12 July 1898 when Edison initiated his lawsuit against the newly formed Vitagraph Company in New York. The latter had made its own films dealing with the Spanish-American War which imitated those already produced by Edison, such as *Transport Whitney Leaving Dock*. Vitagraph was accused of having infringed on the rights of Edison's Kinematograph Company, and Blackton and Smith subsequently found themselves in serious trouble. It was necessary for them to come to some new arrangement to resolve the dispute, and Edison granted a special license to his rivals. This permission was subsequently withdrawn, and a new trial, not yet concluded, began in October 1900.

Film cameras document the final journey of a great monarch

Crowds follow the new King Edward VII and Queen Victoria's cortège.

London, 4 February
Film cameras are out to record the funeral of Queen Victoria. At Victoria Station Cecil Hepworth films the cortège and the principal mourners lining up. As the procession moves off, King Edward VII, the Kaiser and the Duke of Connaught pass right in front of the camera. The King reins up for a moment to allow Hepworth to get a better shot. Later Hepworth's camera obtains a spectacular shot of the procession from the vantage point of the Canadian arch on Whitehall. However, the noise of the cameras disturbs the solemn silence of the occasion, and an embarrassed Hepworth confesses that he wished that the earth could have swallowed both him and the camera up.

Clever tricks and unpleasant surprises from the house of Méliès

Paris, 22 September
Georges Méliès was present, on crutches, at the inauguration of his new theater the Robert Houdin. The old one was burned down last January. Méliès actually broke his femur during the shooting of his latest film *Bluebeard* in Montreuil. He was showing an extra how to die, when he fell backwards. *The Man of a Thousand Tricks*, also shot by Méliès this year, clearly revealed his creative ability. It's not for nothing that his films are imitated worldwide, particularly in the U.S. In his *The One-Man Orchestra*, made in 1900, Méliès himself audaciously portrays seven men, each with a different musical instrument, who form a whole orchestra. Then the seven musicians merge into a single person – the conductor. In *The Mysterious Dislocation*, a Pierrot's arms, legs and head get detached from his body. The creator of these weird spectacles also demonstrated several astonishing conjuring tricks.

Cinematograph in city store

Paris, 6 July
Dufayel, the large department store situated near Barbès-Rochechouart, has announced that it has obtained the exclusive rights to the film of the Paris-Berlin automobile race, shot by Gaumont. The most spectacular images are those of the vehicles crossing the French/Belgian border. The film, almost 500 metres long, which represents 10 to 15 minutes of continuous projection, has already attracted a large audience. Dufayel, unhappy to be solely the marble temple of good taste, opened a hall of side shows in the spring of 1896. There, the department store offered alternating magic shows and cinematography. It brought happiness to children, as well as to people passing through. Today, the Cinematograph Dufayel is as famous as the facade of the store, which was designed by Falguière.

*Made in the studio, the two-minute long **The Chrysalis and the Butterfly** is available in a color version.*

The irresistible rise of Monsieur Ferdinand Zecca

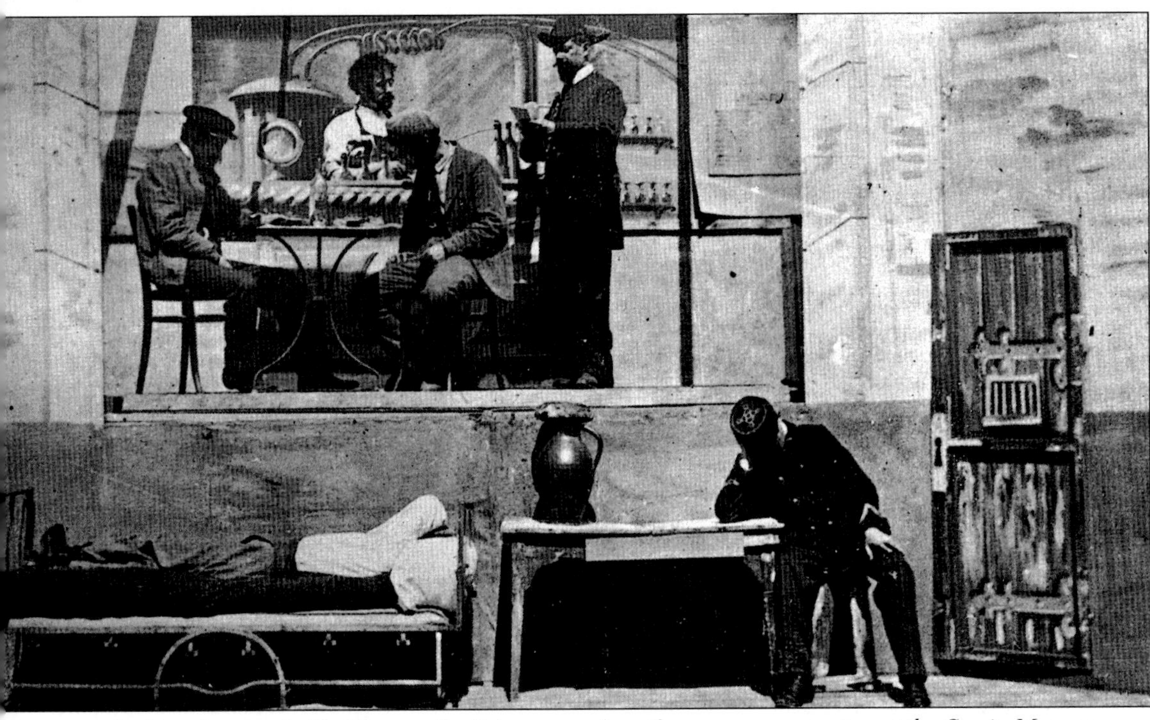

Inspiration for Zecca's remarkable ***History of a Crime*** *came from famous scenes on view at the Grevin Museum.*

Paris, 19 October

Charles Pathé's *eminence grise*, a young man called Ferdinand Zecca, has doubled the takings of the Vincennes company since his arrival at the cinematographic workshop in the rue Polygone. The second son of a theater concierge, Zecca knows a lot about the entertainment world. Pathé noticed the young employee during the Universal Exhibition, where Zecca had been assigned to the Pathé stand. After a few days, Pathé asked Zecca if he would like to work in cinematography. Zecca immediately accepted the offer and has rapidly become Pathé's right-hand man and head of production. Under his management, production has increased and so have the profits. Theater managers appreciate his simple style, which corresponds to the expectations of the public. He clearly has no second thoughts when it comes to copying Méliès and Gaumont. For example, Pathé sold a large number of copies of *The Seven Castles of the Devil* because Zecca saw a great demand. This ambitious film, containing 40 tableaux, attempts to compete with that specialist of fantastic tales, Georges Méliès. However, Zecca's triumph is *The Story of a Crime*. The success of Grévin's waxwork museum has been transposed to the screen with unprecedented realism. In this tale, a bank clerk arrested for murder dreams about his past. When women and children are in attendance in the auditorium, the film is stopped before the last scene – the terrifying fall of the guillotine's blade.

A former cafe-concert entertainer.

Britain's James Williamson delivers a hat trick to audiences

Hove, 15 October

In the backyard of a spacious house in the southern coastal resort of Hove, Englishman James Williamson is running a flourishing film business. Williamson is a former chemist for whom photography was both a hobby and a sideline to his chemist's shop. In 1896 he took up cinematography to enliven his magic lantern shows. He did not start selling films until 1898. In the same year he wound up the chemist's side of his business in Church Road, Hove, and concentrated solely on the photographic side, moving to the premises in Western Road. With the help of his family Williamson writes, produces, develops, prints and often acts in his own films. His output includes *Two Naughty Boys Upsetting the Spoons*, which was made in 1898, and *Attack on a Chinese Mission Station* (1900), in which he employs parallel action and cross-cutting techniques which are advanced for the time. His latest offerings include three lively chase films: *Fire!*, *Stop Thief!* and *The Big Swallow*.The last has an ingenious climax. The film opens with a gentleman objecting to having his photograph taken. Seen from the point of view of a still photographer, the man bears down on the camera until his head fills the screen. At this point his mouth yawns open across almost the entire width of the screen. Then there is a cut to a shot of the photographer and his camera – invisible up until now – spinning around in a black void. Finally, we leave the hungry gentleman walking happily along munching his photographic snack. This imaginative work places Williamson in the front rank of technical innovators.

This close-up is from James Williamson's ***The Big Swallow****.*

1902

Paris, 15 January
The Lumière brothers have opened a Photorama at 18 rue de Clichy. The panoramic cinema has replaced the old Pole Nord cinema.

Poland, January
Kazimerz Proszynski has used his sophisticated Pleograph to shoot some short films.

Paris, 9 April
The Medical Tribune has expressed indignation at fairground showmen for their apparent commercialization of "sensational scenes" from films of surgeries performed by Dr. Eugène-Louis Doyen. On 9 April, Clément Maurice filmed him during an operation separating the Siamese twins Radica and Doodica.

Los Angeles, 16 April
The opening of the Electric Theater, the first venue in the city to be entirely dedicated to cinematographic projections (200 seats).

Vincennes, April
Charles Pathé has had a new film studio built. Situated in rue du Bois, the glass building includes a workshop for film sets.

New York, 2 May
Vitagraph has won its court case against Edison. Stuart Blackton and Albert Smith will now be able to recommence film production.

Paris, 31 May
Pathé has released two newsreels, *The President in Russia* and *The King of Spain's Coronation*, an animated film *la Poupée merveilleuse* (*The Marvellous Doll*) and a realistic drama by Ferdinand Zecca *les Victimes de l'alcoolisme* (*The Victims of Alcoholism*) based on the seventh of Zola's Rougon-Macquart novels, *L'Assommoir.*

Paris, 4 August
One of the Gaumont cameramen, Léo Lefèvre, has become the only holder of the royal warrant, filmmaker by appointment to the Royal Spanish household. He has made a series of films about King Alphonse XIII's visits to France.

London, August
The American-born Charles Urban has just resigned from the Warwick Trading Company to form his own production company, The Charles Urban Trading Company.

Paris, 16 October
Emile Reynaud has invented the Stereo-praxinoscope. With this machine a double series of photographs can be viewed, showing the different sequences of a movement and giving the illusion of three-dimensions.

Paris, 18 October
Georges Mendel has put a newsreel on the market, *les Obsèques de Zola* (*Zola's Funeral*), and two fiction films *The Magic Table or the Talking Heads*, a plagiary of a Méliès' film, and *les Mousquetaires au couvent* (*The Musketeers at the Convent*). The films are sold with a cylinder that allows synchronized sound.

Paris, October
Warned by the American corporate magazines that his films are being copied in the United States by both Edison and Sigmund Lubin, Méliès has decided to open a New York branch. His brother Gaston is to be the general manager.

Paris, 27 December
One week after Thérèse Humbert's arrest, Georges Mendel has edited *l'Affaire Humbert*, a film about the much publicized swindle.

Japan, 31 December
One of the first Japanese films *Monijigari*, springs from the Kabuki theatrical tradition.

BIRTHS

Paris, 3 April
Henri Garat (H. Garascu)

Germany, 6 May
Max Ophuls (Max Oppenheimer)

Pittsburgh, 10 May
David O. Selznick

Moscow, 16 June
Boris Barnet

France, 1 July
William Wyler

Berlin, 22 August
Leni Riefenstahl

Nebraska, 5 September
Darryl Zanuck

Italy, 20 September
Cesare Zavattini

England, 19 December
Ralph Richardson

The refinement of Méliès' special effects is seen in ***La danseuse microscopique (The Microscopic Dancer)****; the dancer appears in place of an egg.*

*The imagination of Méliès goes even further with **Voyage to the Moon**, a 13-minute film with 30 sets, filmed between May and July.*

The new King of England is crowned in advance!

London, 9 August
At Westminster Abbey the coronation of King Edward VII unfolds without incident. The ceremony, originally set for 26 June, was postponed after the King fell ill. This evening at the Alhambra Theatre in Leicester Square, the British public is queuing to watch *The Coronation of King Edward VII,* a film directed in Montreuil by Georges Méliès and produced by the American Charles Urban, who is a London resident. It was impossible to film the ceremony in Westminster Abbey; the cameras make too much noise, and the lights are too weak. Méliès has, therefore, carefully re-staged the coronation in his own studio. Over 150 performers took part in the film, which does not last as long as the original five-and-a-half-hour ceremony. The interior of Westminster Abbey has been re-created using a painted backdrop and cardboard. Méliès' edited version of the coronation was ready by 26 June, the date originally set for the ceremony. The "magician" of Montreuil experienced great difficulty in finding a double to play Edward VII. Happily, he eventually located a man who fit the bill working in a laundry at Kremlin-Bicètre. Edward's consort Queen Alexandra is portrayed by a dancer from the Châtelet Theatre. This ambitious reconstruction of one of the great British occasions of state has been launched amid a blaze of publicity by Charles Urban, the owner of the Warwick Trading Company and Star Film's agent in Britain. With commendable honesty, the publicity makes it clear that the re-creation of the ceremony is not accurate in every detail. Nevertheless, in spite of Urban's frankness, many French journalists have accused the film-makers of deceiving the English public. But, in addition to crying "God Save the King," the British should give three cheers for Méliès.

The Coronation of King Edward VII, produced by Charles Urban and made in a few days at Montreuil.

Sound cinema according to Léon Gaumont

Paris, 7 November
The French Photographic Society welcomes the engineer and industrialist Léon Gaumont, who is delivering a lecture on sound cinema and his new Chronophone system. To the succesful manufacture of motion picture apparatus, Gaumont has added a flourishing film production business. The process that he and his technicians, Georges Laudet and René Decaux, have devised is similar to that of Auguste Baron. It uses an electric motor to synchronize a phonograph and cinematograph. Filming and recording are simultaneous; the actors' gestures are fixed on film at the same time as their words are inscribed on the wax of a phonographic cylinder. A signal engraved on the cylinder – a whistle or a bell which sounds a few seconds before the beginning of the sound accompaniment to the film – alerts the projectionist to start the cinematograph running. The two devices then operate in tandem to the end of the film with the motor synchronizing sound and image. Three films are shown. In the first, Léon Gaumont himself introduces the Block Note photographic system. The two other films show a gypsy dance and a gavotte accompanied by appropriate music. The problem with the system remains the sound. The audience had great difficulty in hearing Gaumont's explanation of the process. Gaumont has a surprise in store for his audience at the end of the evening. He announces his intention to overcome the problem of sound amplification by using compressed air.

A little fairy found in a cabbage patch

Paris, 11 October
A new version of *The Cabbage Patch Fairy*, a film originally shot in 1900 by Alice Guy and Anatole Thiberville in a garden adjoining the Gaumont development laboratories in Belleville, has been put on sale. This 20-metre-long film, interpreted by the actress Yvonne Mugnier-Sérand and emanating from Alice Guy's imagination, tells the story of a fairy who emerges from a cabbage to present a childless, young married couple with a living baby. The copies of this film have sold so rapidly to the fairground public that Guy, at the request of Léon Gaumont, has since turned out *The First Class Midwife*, or *The Birth of Children*, which follows a similar outline to the earlier film of 1900. However, the new version, which is 100 metres long and costs 200 francs, could be sold colorized.

*A scene from **The Cabbage Fairy**.*

A wonderful work from Méliès enriches the cinema

'aris, 1 September
ieorge Méliès' latest film, *Voyage) the Moon*, is an unprecedented iumph. The public at the fair-round where it was shown, unre-ervedly applauded this fantastic ıle, which contains 30 tableaux and ısts 13 minutes. Méliès has again ıanipulated the marvels of science 'ith impressive dexterity. One won-ers whether the Cinematograph /ill take the place of the large shows t the Châtelet Theatre. With Méliès nything is possible.

Completed in July, the 260-metre ilm has broken all records. It re-uired three months shooting, a ırge cast, and cost 10,000 francs. Méliès got his inspiration from two ules Verne novels – *From the Earth ɔ the Moon* and *Around the Moon*. But there are episodes in the film which Verne himself would never ave dared depict. The fantastic tale egins at the Congress of Astro-auts presided over by Professor Barbenfouillis, who is played by Méliès himself. He and five other offins take off for the moon in a iant shell fired by a cannon. The hell lands in "the eye of the moon" s the title of the ninth tableau ex-lains. Subsequent to the moon anding, the group of intellectuals xplore the place and come across ome strange creatures called the Sélénites, who scarcely appreciate uch an intrusion, and take the xplorers prisoner. Professor Bar-enfouillis then organizes their escape after finding out that the Sélénites have a fatal weakness – they explode when they are struck. When the shell returns to earth amidst panic, it falls into the sea, and the heroes are fished out. The last two tableaux show the public rejoicing and the inauguration of a statue to Professor Barbenfouillis. This amazing film has earned Méliès international popularity. However, a sole shadow was cast over *Voyage to the Moon* when, unfortunately, it was systematically pirated in the United States by the Thomas Edison and Sigmund Lubin companies. As it turned out, Edison's London representative Al Abadie secretly made a copy of the film to send to the U.S., and the result was that many counterfeits were made. These fakes deleted the Star Film trademark that Georges Méliès had taken great care to imprint on all of his films.

Méliès' most remarkable film to date, ***Voyage to the Moon*** *consists of 10 scenes played out on 30 sets.*

This extraordinary fantasy is already being imitated by others.

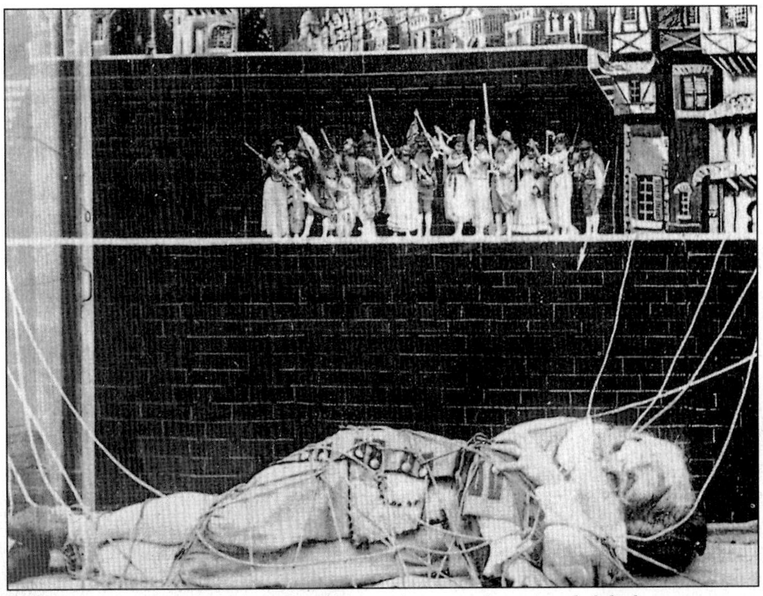

Gulliver's Travels*, based on Swift's novel, is another visual delight.*

1903

Lyon, 18 January
The Lumière firm has launched new footage of phantasmagorical, genre and transformation scenes.

Washington, 21 January
The Life of an American Fireman, Edwin Porter's first film using several different sets, has been lodged for copyright.

New York, January
Gaston Méliès has been sent to the United States by the Star Film production company to open offices at 204 East 38th Street. His son Paul is working with him.

Delhi, 8 February
Gaumont, Pathé, Georges Mendel and Warwick have all released films simultaneously about Edward VII's coronation.

New York, February
A Hungarian immigrant and furrier, Adolph Zukor, has opened a penny arcade called "The Bazaar".

Paris, 1 March
The first copy of *le Fascinateur*, a specialist publication for film lovers, is now available.

Vincennes, 5 April
Pathé has just released Ferdinand Zecca's *la Vie d'un Joueur*, a film in the same vein as *les Victimes de l'alcoolisme*.

London, May
Gaumont Ltd has been set up and is to be headed by Colonel Bromhead.

New York, 22 August
Gaston Méliès has made his producing debut with *Reliance – Shamrock III*, a film of a yacht race.

Berlin, 29 August
Oskar Messter is presenting the Biophon, his method of producing talking films, as the star attraction at the Apollo Theatre.

Paris, 12 September
The Lumière brothers have applied for a patent for Autochrome, their new trichromatic method to process color photographs.

Montreuil, October
Méliès has started shooting *Faust aux enfers*, adapted from the opera by Hector Berlioz. The film is to have 15 scenes and Méliès himself is to play the leading role.

Paris, 10 November
Léon Gaumont continues demonstrating his Chronophone to various photographic societies.

New York, November
Marcus Loew, the son of an immigrant family, has opened in New York and Cincinatti several penny arcades, which are also known as peep shows here.

Copenhagen, 31 December
Peter Elfelt has made Denmark's first fiction film, *Capital Execution* (*Henrettelson*).

Peking, 31 December
Lin Zhusan has returned to China from the U.S. with a projector and films. He is the first Chinese promoter of the cinematograph and has held several projections for his compatriots at the popular Tien Lo tea house.

BIRTHS

Alabama, 31 January
Tallulah Bankhead

Belgium, 12 February
Georges Simenon

Paris, 21 February
Madeleine Renaud

Marseilles, 8 May
Fernandel
(Fernand Contandin)

England, 12 May
Wilfrid Hyde White

Brussels, 25 May
Charles Spaak

England, 29 May
Bob Hope (Leslie Townes Hope)

Stockholm, 21 June
Alf Sjöberg

France, 23 June
Louis Seigner

France, 5 August
Claude Autant-Lara

France, 19 August
Claude Dauphin (C. Legrand)

Austria, 11 November
Sam Spiegel

Tokyo, 12 December
Yasujiro Ozu

„Das leben e Bild"
Kino-Theater
Bilder
Wöchentlich Zwei mal neues Programm
Bilder

This cinema, opened by Karl Knubbel on Germany's Frankfurter Allee (Station), is one of many such establishments that are springing up all over Europe.

LE BIOPHONOGRAPHE
MARQUE DÉPOSÉE
PHOTOGRAPHIE ANIMÉE & PARLANTE
RÉVOLUTION SCIENTIFIQUE!!!
COMÉDIE-OPÉRA-DRAME.etc.
LE SEUL APPAREIL AU MONDE PERMETTANT DE
PRENDRE ET DE REPRODUIRE A LA FOIS LES GESTES ET LES PAROLES
NE PAS CONFONDRE AVEC LES GROSSIERS ESSAIS
TENTÉS DANS LE MÊME BUT.
LE BIOPHONOGRAPHE EST UN APPAREIL SCIENTIFIQUE BREVETÉ EN FRANCE. ALLEMAGNE ET PRINCIPAUX PAYS.
KOSSUTH & Cie
PARIS

One of many attempts to achieve sound on film, the Biophonograph has enjoyed some degree of success without managing to resolve all the problems.

The enterprising Charles Urban

London, 2 November
Charles Urban, the American producer and distributor, is personally in charge of his new firm, the Urban Trading Company. He has sent cameramen out all over the world to discover and to cover sensational events. Charles Rider Noble, his photographer in Macedonia, even shot the Ilindon uprising. Earlier this year Noble filmed the Moroccan revolution and the proclamation in Delhi, India of the coronation of Edward VII. Urban's films have been selling extremely well recently. Georges Méliès' output has been included in Urban's catalogue, some of which deals with other topical events, notably Edward VII's journey to Paris; a tremendous fire in London; the automobile race in Ireland for the Gordon Bennett cup, etc. Also well presented have been both comic and dramatic productions. *Burglary in Action* gave rise to enormous and enthusiastic applause as did *Attack on a Stage Coach Last Century*, comprising 11 tableaux. *Scientific Topics* was shot by Professor Martin G. Barker as part of a series concerning the way of life of bees, which has since been copied everywhere. In addition to his films, Urban also happens to be a manufacturer of cameras. His little Bioka, an apparatus that can be operated easily by amateurs, uses the 17.5-mm format, and the results are extraordinarily accurate.

The young American who wants to 'open all eyes to the universe'.

A new field of action for Ferdinand Zecca in Vincennes studios

*Filming of **William Tell** has just been completed at Pathé's second studio, opened at Vincennes in 1902.*

Vincennes, 10 October
The ill-equipped and tiny rue du Bois workshop and theater was unworthy of the large firm of Charles Pathé. Therefore, the latter destroyed it to build a far larger theater. As production could not be halted, Pathé rented a house located at 1 rue de Paris where Ferdinand Zecca, in charge of Pathé productions, works while waiting for the opening of yet another temporary workshop in Montreuil, at 52 rue du Sergent-Bobillot. Zecca – designer, scenarist, cinematographer and actor – has enjoyed so much success in a few months that he is credited with the reputation Pathé now enjoys in the fairground world. Today there were two films shown – *William Tell*, copied from the English picture by Robert William Paul, and also *Don Quixote*, a great comic piece which Zecca and his associate Lucien Nonguet had to cut down. Originally it was 430 metres, but the fairground stall-owners protested that it was far too long. The new version has been drastically reduced to 255 metres. In truth, this is not the first time that Zecca has plagiarized the films of his colleagues, particularly those of Robert William Paul, Charles Urban, James Williamson and even Georges Méliès, all of whose work he has found useful as models. This is considered proof of his own good taste. After every success of a rival company, Zecca borrows the theme and special effects, and when he releases his own version, he adds a few details or variations of his own. Nobody can prevent him. But Zecca also possesses flair, imagination and know-how. The 1901 broad comedy *What Is Seen of My Sixth Sense*, *The Victims of Alcoholism*, a ve realistic drama in five acts, we both instigated by Zecca. And som times his style reaches unequal scatological heights, much to the j of the fairground public. In *Th Wrong Door*, shot this year, a pea ant loses his way and sits himse down on a telephone seat, mimi his satisfaction.

*With **The Victims of Alcoholism**, Ferdinand Zecca returns to the Zola-esq realism which marked his successful **History of a Crime**.*

dwin S. Porter provides a model for the 'western'

shington, 1 December
outlaw chief turns toward the nera, takes a bead with his Colt olver and then fires repeatedly at audience at point-blank range, ereupon the screen turns red! is is the major talking point of *Great Train Robbery*, the latest produced by the Edison Manufacturing Company, a copy of which just been deposited in the Library of Congress. *The Great Train bbery* has a Western setting, but st of its scenes were filmed on ation at Paterson, New Jersey, in fall of 1903. Director Edwin S. rter, who is the head of production at the Edison Manufacturing mpany, filmed much of the exciting action in the actual woods that round the infamous Lackawanna nworks, and the accent is on real-. In this story, a train is held up d the passengers are forced by the ndits to descend from their carge and form a line by the track, ir hands in the air. The robbers n make their getaway on horseck. In the meantime, the telegraph erator, who had been both bound d gagged, succeeds in raising the rm at what the Edison catalogue scribes as being a "typical Westn dance hall." A posse is raised, d the outlaws are hunted down d killed. The 10-minute running ne of *The Great Train Robbery* has en divided into 10 "tableaux" plus dramatic medium close-up of the n-toting outlaw, played by George Barnes, which exhibitors can choose to place either at the beginning or end of the film. Action keeps briskly on the move; in addition to the robbery itself there are fisticuffs, horseback pursuit and gunplay. From a technical point of view there is an interesting use of double exposure plus a clever bit of jump-cutting when a dummy is substituted for one of the trainmen and hurled off the engine after a frenzied fist fight. Porter, who not only directed but also photographed *The Great Train Robbery*, maintains a high degree of both suspense and action by intercutting between the outlaws and the posse. At times, however, the long shots used in the tableaux make it somewhat difficult to identify the individual characters. Many Western vignettes have preceded *The Great Train Robbery*, and there have even been Western films with story lines of sorts, but Porter's film has established a formula which many producers are already rushing to imitate. Thus it is clear that the Western has well and truly arrived as a staple of cinema.

Filmed for Edison, Porter's ***The Great Train Robbery*** *creates an exciting new genre for the cinema.*

typical western', according to the producer. The film opens new horizons.

Shooting at actual locations gives the film its realistic atmosphere.

1904

New York, 13 January
Wallace McCutcheon has filmed *Photographing a Female Crook* for the American Mutoscope and Biograph Co. Included in the 40-second film is an interesting sequence of tracking in for a close-up of one of the characters.

Rome, 20 January
Filoteo Alberini has opened the Cinema Moderno, the first purpose-built cinema here. He had already opened a film theater in Florence in 1899. To date, the Italian cinema has only produced newsreels.

France, 6 February
The daisy stamped in the middle of the abbreviation "Elgé", the initials of Léon Gaumont, has appeared for the first time in the corporate newspaper *l'Industriel forain*.

Montreuil, 1 March
Charles Pathé has had a new studio built at 52 rue Sergent-Bobillot. Ferdinand Zecca is working there on a news reconstruction film called *l'Incendie du théâtre de Chicago* (*Fire in the Chicago Theater*) about the fire that destroyed the Chicago Theater on 1 January.

Paris, 24 March
Lucien Bull, director of the Marey Institute in the Bois de Boulogne, has photographed the path taken by a bullet through various objects, using an electrical procedure.

Paris, 2 April
Georges Mendel has opened the Cinéma-Grapho-Théâtre.

Helsinki, 4 April
Emil Stahlberg has inaugurated the town's first cinema with the film *Mailman Ympäri.*

Paris, 30 April
Léon Gaumont has released his film *l'Attaque d'une diligence*, shot in the open air by Alice Guy, a plagiarism of Charles Urban's *l'Attaque d'une diligence au siècle dernier*, which came out in Paris last November.

St. Louis, May
George Hale, head of the Kansas City fire brigade, is presenting a new attraction at the St. Louis Fair, Hale's Touring Car. The audience, seated in the replica of a train carriage, watches the passing scenery, supplied by films from all over the world, projected onto a screen.

Paris, 11 June
After the filming of *la Valse de Barnum* at Montreuil, Pathé has released a new Gaston Velle film for sale. The film, *Métamorphoses d'un papillon*, shows a woman turning into a butterfly. A former conjurer, Velle specializes in trick effects.

St. Louis, 10 July
For the occasion of the Olympic Games, German producer Oskar Messter used his Biophon to shoot his first films with synchronized soundtrack for the export market. *The Whistling Boy* is one of them.

Paris, 27 August
Léon Gaumont has released for sale *les Petits coupeurs de bois vert*, a realistic drama on the theme of poverty, produced by Alice Guy in collaboration with Henri Gallet.

Washington, 11 November
Biograph has lodged W. McCutcheon's *The Suburbanite* for copyright.

BIRTHS

England, 18 January
Cary Grant
(Alexander Archibald Leach)

Texas, 23 March
Joan Crawford
(Lucille Fay LeSueur)

London, 14 April
John Gielgud

Washington, 2 May
Bing Crosby
(Harry L. Crosby)

Paris, 17 May
Jean Gabin (Alexis Moncorgé)

Hungary, 26 June
Peter Lorre (Laszlo Löwenstein)

Paris, 4 August
Christian-Jaques (C. Maudet)

Algeria, 18 September
Orane Demazis

Paris, 12 November
Jacques Tourneur

DEATHS

England, 8 May
Eadweard J. Muybridge

Paris, 16 May
Etienne Jules Marey

LA GREVE
MANUFACTUR

The poster advertising the release of ***The Strike****. Ferdinand Zecca was inspired by Emile Zola's title* ***Germinal*** *for this film about social conditions.*

UN ROMAN D'AMOUR

◀ *Love Story, directed by Lucien Nonguet for Pathé, is the first film with a sentimental theme to become a popular success with the public.* ▷

New initiatives in sound films

Paris, 2 April

Georges Mendel, the producer and distributor of many different kinds of films, has developed a new interest in sound and the talking films. He has published the first announcement about his experiments linking the phonograph with the cinema at his Cinema-Grapho-Theatre. It is apparent, however, that Mendel has not really invented anything himself. Henri Joly, another well-known pioneer and technical innovator who worked for Charles Pathé in 1895, has sold Mendel his original sound-film patents. The system utilizes a small electrical box to link the phonograph needle with the projector shutter and specially amplified sound. As George Mendel explains it, the bringing together of these two inventions "is designed to give the complete illusion of real life and a more satisfactory blending of gestures and words than has previously been achieved."

Cinema owner-exhibitors are now on the increase in the USA

New York, 19 June

This year has seen a rapid growth in the number of exhibition venues throughout the U.S., with new enterprises springing up almost daily. Clearly, a major stimulus has been the amazing success of *The Great Train Robbery* as well as *Hale's Tours and Scenes of the World*, which was one of the big attractions at the 1903 St. Louis Exposition. Typical of the new breed of entrepreneurs is the Warner family of Youngstown, Ohio. They have just opened the Cascade, their first small picture theater, in New Castle, Pa. However, the greatest activity can be seen in the larger cities such as New York where William Fox, who prospered in the garment trade, has just purchased the "Automat" on 14th Street. Similarly, the furrier Adolph Zukor joined Mitchell Mark earlier this year to form the Automatic Vaudeville Co. Business is so good at the Automatic One-Cent Vaudeville, they're planning more arcades in the coming months.

ADMISSION 5¢
CASCADE THEATRE
REFINED ENTERTAINMENT
LADIES
GENTLEMEN
CHILDREN

The Cascade cinema in Pennsylvania is owned by the Warner brothers.

Zecca the wanderer returns to Vincennes

Paris, 1 March

Ferdinand Zecca is well known at Pathé for his spontaneity and for the amusing ideas which augment his films. However, he also has a reputation for hypersensitivity. After a memorable quarrel with his superior, the eminent Charles Pathé, he slammed the door on the Vincennes offices and was employed by Léon Gaumont on Alice Guy's recommendation. He stayed two weeks at Gaumont and once again left discontented. Had he squabbled with Alice Guy? In the end, Pathé, who found he couldn't get by without his collaborator, re-employed him. Today, Zecca is shooting *The Chicago Theater Fire*, a reconstruction of a real event.

An actor-director's vision of himself as both the painter and the model.

An amorous chase in the heart of New York

New York, 8 August

A wild chase around the statue of General Grant on Riverside Drive: a man, clearly alarmed by the results of a personal advertisement he has placed for a bride, attempts to escape from a pursuing pack of women, all of whom are eager to marry him. This is the subject of a new picture, produced by the American Mutoscope and Biograph Company and entitled *Personal*. Besides its furious pace, the film is marked by its outdoor locations and an absence of painted backcloths. In their frantic rush the characters vault fence and hurdles, race across bridges negotiate ditches and streams, causing chaos as they pass. As they leap over obstacles separating them and their prey, the young women lift their skirts and saucily reveal their ankles, to the great delight of audiences. Exhausted, the young man admits defeat and gives his heart to the first comer. Directed by Wallace McCutcheon, this is a new kind of comedy film, full of breezy visual flair and destined for success on both sides of the Atlantic.

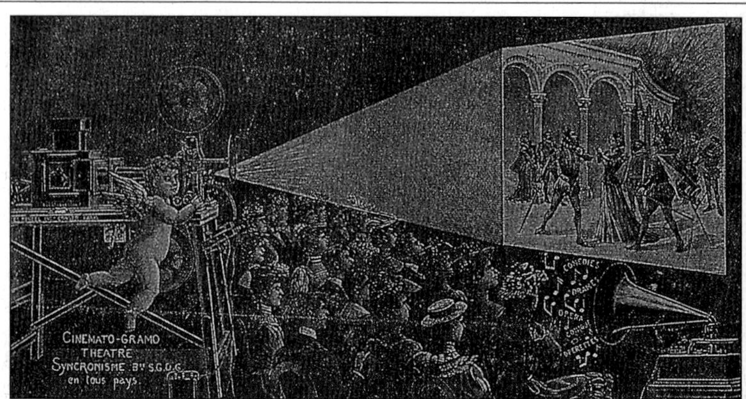
CINEMATO-GRAMO
THEATRE
SYNCROMISME BY S.G.D.G.
en tous pays

Henri Joly's Cinemato-Gramo-Theatre, demonstrated by Georges Mendel.

he international ambitions of M. Charles Pathé

ew York, 31 July
he Pathé brothers are expanding proad. They are opening a sales utlet for their phonographic and lm equipment in New York, have tablished a factory in Bound rook and set up a film studio in rsey City. The brothers are bid-ing to create a worldwide empire. February they opened a branch in loscow. Pathé's aim is to control cal production and to produce rints of their films on the spot. harles Pathé wants to make his ockerel trademark an internation-lly-recognized symbol. Revenue om Pathé's films far outstrips that om phonographs, and the compa-y is now the most important film roduction outfit in France. The ost recent Pathé catalogue, pub-shed in August, contains over ,000 titles of all kinds, some which an be enjoyed with sound provided y Pathé's Ciné-Phono. Among the ompany's specialities are bawdy cenes unsuitable for children.

PATHE FRERES
MOVING PICTURES
The Bound Brook studio, near New York, is the jewel in Pathé's ever-expanding international crown.

Georges Méliès surpasses his own best efforts

lontreuil, 31 December
fter the international success of *'oyage to the Moon*, the creator ieorges Méliès continues his astro-omic fantasies. In his glass theater t Montreuil, he has shot *Voyage eyond the Possible*, an exceptional lm of 43 tableaux with a running me of about 20 minutes. Méliès once again takes the role of a slightly crazed professor. This time he is called Mabouloff, president of the Institute of Incoherent Geography, who maintains that he can reach the sun by means of the Automabouloff, a vehicle of his own invention. The journey fails at first, but with a steam-propelled locomotive which takes off from the summit of the Jungfrau, Mabouloff and his team arrive on the sun. A refrigerator keeps them alive in the 3,000-degree temperature. As in *Voyage to the Moon*, the film concludes with the descent to earth, this time by means of a sort of submarine. Crowds cheer as they return to the Institute. Méliès has taken great care with the decor and the special effects, and certain scenes are extremely poetic. A ravishing 18-year-old actress, May de Lavergne, plays the part of a nurse. Méliès is once more in love but has nonetheless remained faithful to former loves – Jehanne d'Alcy is also in the cast.

*'he **Voyage Beyond the Possible** follows **Voyage to the Moon**.*

*A sketch by the prolific Méliès for a scene in **The Damnation of Faust**.*

1905

St. Petersburg, 6 January
Félix Mesguich, who has moved from the Urban Trading Co. to the Warwick, has filmed *The Attack Against the Czar*.

Paris, 7 January
The English firm, Warwick Trading Company, has edited four newsreels of the Russo-Japanese war. They are guaranteed genuine compared to the faked scenes in the films made by Méliès and Pathé.

London, January
Release of two action films: *The Life of Charles Peace* by the showman William Haggar, and *Rescued by Rover* by Cecil Hepworth.

Paris, 16 February
Charles Pathé has opened a display room at 31 boulevard des Italiens, to present his films to showmen and cinema owners.

Paris, 15 April
Pathé has released its first film with chase sequences, *Dix femmes pour un mari* (*Ten Women for One Husband*) by André Heuzé, a copy of the Gaumont Company's English film *Personal* by Alfred Collins.

Copenhagen, 23 April
Former circus impresario Ole Olsen has opened the city's first cinema, The Biograph Theatre.

New York, 1 June
Adolph Zukor has opened a Hale's Tour in Union Square.

Paris, 5 August
Pathé has released a film by Louis Gasnier, *A Schoolboy's First Day Out*, with Gabriel Leuvielle, an actor from the burlesque theater, now calling himself Max Linder.

Switzerland, 25 August
Félix Mesguich has filmed the traditional wine growers' festival using a long-focus lens. He sent the reel to Paris immediately, beating the cameraman for the Urban Trading Co. who had the exclusive rights.

Rome, 20 September
Release of the first Italian fiction film *La Presa di Roma*, made by Filoteo Alberini.

Paris, 1 October
The review *Phono-Gazette*, started by Edmond Benoît-Lévy, has become the *Phono-Ciné-Gazette*.

Rome, 31 October
Filoteo Alberini and Dante Santoni have set up a film studio, said to be Italy's first such establishment.

Paris, 15 December
Méliès has announced his new film, *la Légende de Rip Van Winkle*, to be filmed in 17 settings and played by himself and his son André.

Peking, December
The Feng Tai photographic studio is making its first Chinese film *The Tingchun Mountains*. Tan Xinpei, a popular singer from the Peking opera, is playing the leading role.

BIRTHS

France, 23 March
Paul Grimault

Paris, 26 April
Jean Vigo

Nebraska, 16 May
Henry Fonda

Paris, 29 July
Pierre Braunberger

Montana, 2 August
Myrna Loy

Mexico, 3 August
Dolores Del Rio (Lolita D. Martinez Asunsolo Lopez Negrette)

Tokyo, 20 August
Mikio Naruse

New York, 25 August
Clara Bow

Paris, 17 September
Claudette Colbert (Chauchoin)

Stockholm, 18 September
Greta Garbo (Gustafsson)

England, 30 September
Michael Powell

New York, 17 October
Jean Arthur (Gladys Greene)

New York, 22 October
Constance Bennett

Paris, 22 December
Pierre Brasseur (Espinasse)

Brussels, 25 December
Fernand Gravey (Mertens)

*A Pathé film, **The Apaches of Paris**, continues the tradition of **The History of a Crime**.*

L'AMANT DE LA LUNE
CINEMATOGRAPHES & FILMS
PATHÉ FRÈRES PARIS

A new success for Pathé, ***The Moon Lover*** *is directed by Gaston Velle who is a key member of Ferdinand Zecca's talented creative team.*

The cinema makes a court appearance

Narbonne, 4 March
To the all-round satisfaction of the professionals, the town court delivered a verdict exonerating the Cinematograph in a case which has been the talk of the town and in the news nationally. The Aerogyne Theatre, a fairground establishment run by the Dulaar family, had installed a cinematograph apparatus in front of the Church of Saint Just, at the time when people were coming out of mass. Jérôme Dulaar himself directed the cameraman, who had taken up a position on top of a stepladder. At the same time, a banner carrying the words "Cinematograph of the Aerogyne Theatre" was unfurled. Thus forewarned, the parishioners allowed themselves to be filmed without objection. Yet there were a few who, having seen themselves on the screen during the projection, believed they had been filmed without their consent and consequently took legal action. However, the judge decided that the filming had been done in a public place and the persons filmed had been informed. This decision came over a month after a judgment given by the civil court of the Seine. It concerned the renowned Dr. Doyen in his case against the cameraman François Parnaland. The latter, who had made educative films of the surgeon, was charged with profiting from them for commercial purposes without the physician's prior consent. The Parisian magistrates considered that the doctor could legitimately oppose all screenings.

Man's best friend is star of new filn

*Cecil Hepworth, the producer of **Rescued by Rover**, also appears in the film which is directed by Lewis Fitzhamon.*

London, 3 July
The Hepworth Manufacturing Company Ltd. was registered just over one year ago, on 25 April 1904. As befits the head of a successful business, Cecil Hepworth has become currently more of a supervisor or producer and is less involved in the actual filmmaking process. The film most recently released by the Hepworth company is a truly delightful adventure story. Entitled *Rescued By Rover*, it is sure to be enormously popular with British audiences. In the case of this film, however, not only did Hepworth take charge of the production, but his entire family pitched in on the project. The story and scenario was written by Mrs. Hepworth, who also plays the role of the distressed mother in the film, Hepworth himself appears as the harassed father, and the couple's eight-month-old baby daughter has a cameo appearance as the infant abducted by gypsies in the story. And Rover, the faithful pet and undispu ed star of the film, is the family own collie. Two actors were hire for supporting roles. Each receive a fee of half-a-guinea, which inclu ed the cost of fares from London t Walton-on-Thames, where the He worth company is based. Accordin to Hepworth, the seven-minute lon film cost exactly 7 pounds, 13 shi lings and ninepence to make, b with prints on sale for 10 pounds, 1 shillings and sixpence, the produc expects to earn a good profit. Cec Hepworth first became involved i the industry in 1897 when, at age 2 he began to put on his own fil shows with a projector which he ha adapted. The first film he made wa of the Oxford and Cambridge bo race for the Warwick company i 1898. The following year he exten ed his interests from developing an printing to the actual production o films. He constructed a small studi in his garden and soon built up catalogue of films for sale. His late pictures are longer and more sophi ticated, and include a version o *Alice in Wonderland* that is done i 16 scenes. His newest *Rover* seem to represent a fitting culmination t his recent efforts.

Notorious criminal makes gripping film subject in Great Britain

London, 1 October
One of Britain's most notorious criminals, the cat burglar and murderer Charles Peace, has now been immortalized on film by William Hagger in *The Life of Charles Peace*. The making of this film was something of a family affair. Hagger directs and takes the role of Peace, his four brothers appear in the film, and one of his daughters portrays Peace's mistress. Another daughter, age 12, has been dressed as a boy and cast as the burglar's assistant. Peace was executed in February 1879 after a 20-year career of crime. Stunted, gargoyle-faced and web-fingered, Peace was a master of the silent art of cat burglary – strong and agile and the designer of a range of sophisticated housebreaking tools of the trade. His predilection for exotic disguises and his love of the violin, which he played incessantly and extremely badly, helped turn him into a criminal legend. Often the violin case served as the container for Peace's burglary implements as he went about his nocturnal business. Eventually, Peace was condemned to death for the murder of one Arthur Dyson, the husband of a woman with whom Peace had had an affair. While awaiting execution, Peace confessed to another killing for which an innocent man had been sentenced to life imprisonment. In *The Life of Charles Peace*, Hagger plays Peace posing as a clergyman to avoid capture by the police. The film reconstructs Peace's real-life leap from a train on his way to trial for the murder of Arthur Dyson and his execution. And for the final dose of realistic effect, Hagger returned to the scene of Dyson's murder, at Banner Cross in Sheffield, to film the fatal shooting.

'inting of films is lone by stencil

'aris, 31 August
;eorges Méliès' new film *The Paris-Ionte Carlo Rally in Two Hours*, vhich pokes gentle fun at the nuierous automobile accidents sufered by the King of Belgium, is ntirely in color. This kind of film is ery popular with the public, reninding audiences of the magic antern's colored slides. However, olored films remain a luxury as the mages must be painted one at a ime by hand. Since 1896 people ave been preoccupied with paintng film images. Artists in the Méliès tudio used a very fine paintbrush to pply colors to clothing or countryide, but the results were inconsisent. During projection the colors eemed to run across the screen. Now, thanks to a stencil recently sed by Pathé and Gaumont, the ilm images have been given dazling colors. But the amount of work nvolved is daunting. First a master as to be cut out over a copy of ositive film. Next each area of film o be colored is removed with a fine lade. The stripped film is then laced on a second positive copy, ver the corresponding images. It emains only to superimpose the tencil using several different colors. There are four specialists in this ield, all of them women. Mademoielle Thullier is in charge of all the oloring for Méliès.

Nonguet tackles the Passion for Pathé

Begun in 1902, Nonguet's ***The Life and Passion of Jesus Christ*** *depicts the story of Jesus in 32 scenes.*

Vincennes, 28 July
Since 1902 Ferdinand Zecca has been supervizing the shooting of *The Life and Passion of Jesus Christ*, directed by Lucien Nonguet. Zecca and Nonguet set out to film 18 of the most well-known episodes in the life of Christ, but the success of the series prompted them to add additional tableaux. The colored prints make up an extremely attractive body of work, in spite of the disparity between the entries made in 1902 and those filmed three years later. Organizations which cater especially to young people are keen customers of Nonguet's film, either in its entirety or in individual tableaux. Although the scenes can be purchased separately, Pathé insists that the 20 tableaux are "indispensable for a representation of the sacred drama," most notably *The Entry into Jerusalem*, *The Kiss of Judas*, *Jesus' Death on the Cross* and *The Ascension*. Pathé warns exhibitors that they will ignore this series at their own peril, emphasizing its novelty "which has the power to touch the hearts of even the most profane." The exhibitors, however, are displaying a distinctly profane interest in other items in the catalogue, in which the religious scenes occupy a modest place near the back. Clearly, Pathé is reluctant to abandon the films which have been instrumental in the foundation of its fortune, for example, *Disheveled Woman* and *Love in All Its Stages,* both likely to horrify Catholic institutions seeking to buy religious films.

Pathé publishes its first catalogue

The Pathé Brothers' new summer catalogue of films available to customers gives ample evidence of the vitality of the company. According to founder Charles Pathé, the Pathé Brothers "suffused with the belief in themselves, necessary to every undertaking, possess a highly-educated personnel, consisting of the most competent people in every field. This has placed them in the top rank of cinematography in the world." Pathé believes in the wonderful possibilities of the Cinematograph, stating, "It's the theater, the school and the newspaper of tomorrow."

Harris and Davis open their first Nickelodeon in Pittsburgh

Pittsburgh, 6 November
"Nickelodeon" is the new name for the latest type of motion picture theater which John P. Harris and his brother-in-law Harry Davis have just opened at the storefront which they occupy on Smithfield Street. A variety of pictures, such as the Edison production of *The Great Train Robbery*, are shown each and every day for a full eight hours until midnight. This is the first purpose-built movie theater of its kind to be opened in the U.S., and, in order to gain admission, customers must pay an entrance fee of five cents – or a nickel – hence the name. Another innovation is that the screenings are accompanied by music from a pianist. It is a big success, with all 100 seats usually occupied.

NICKELODEON

The new Nickelodeon's takings for the first day was $23.

1906

Germany, 21 February
The founding of the Union Theatre (UT) cinema chain. The first cinema to open is in Frankfurt-on-Main.

Chicago, 25 February
Carl Laemmle, a German immigrant who arrived in the U.S. in 1884 at the age of 14, has opened the city's first nickelodeon.

Paris, 24 February
Méliès has dropped the price of all films made before number 640 in his catalogue. Showmen are rushing in to buy up his greatest hits.

Paris, 1 March
The former lawyer Edmond Benoît-Lévy, who published *Phono-Gazette* last year, has founded a trade union for the cinema industry.

New York, March
Adolph Zukor is turning his Hale's Tours into nickelodeons. Marcus Loew is doing the same thing with his penny arcades.

New York, May
William Fox, the son of Hungarian immigrants, has opened a projection room at 700 Broadway.

Copenhagen, 11 July
Ole Olsen, owner of the Biograph Theater cinema, has recently founded a production company, Nordisk Film, in partnership with Arnold Nielsen. Film director Vigo Larsen has already started shooting footage on a variety subjects for the new venture.

Chicago, 23 July
Harry Aitken and John R. Freuler, former real estate agents, have just founded a distribution outlet, the Western Film Exchange.

Paris, 15 August
Pathé has released *la Course à la perruque*, a highly imaginative film full of comic scenes, which includes a wonderful chase sequence, from the producer Georges Hatot with a scenario by André Heuzé.

Paris, 30 August
Charles Urban, G.R. Roger and the financier Ernest May have created the Société générale des cinématographes Eclipse which takes over from the Urban Company in Paris. Two Gaumont producers, Georges Hatot and Victorin Jasset, have been taken on.

Paris, 4 October
Henri Joly, Leopold Lobel, Georges Akar and the financier Dubois de Niermont have founded the new Société des photographes et cinématographes Lux.

Chicago, October
Creation of the Carl Laemmle Film Service, a distribution company.

New York, October
James Stuart Blackton has perfected a single-frame technique which creates some interesting effects in two animated films he has completed: *Humorous Phases of a Funny Face* and *The Haunted Hotel.*

Paris, 2 November
Gaumont's latest innovation is the Elgéphone. It is an amplifier for phonographs which functions on compressed air. Sales are aimed at fairground showmen and cinemas.

BIRTHS

Japan, 3 January
Shiro Toyoda

Rome, 8 May
Roberto Rossellini

Paris, 26 May
Pierre Prévert

Vienna, 22 June
Billy Wilder (Samuel Wilder)

St. Petersburg, 5 July
George Sanders

Missouri, 5 August
John Huston

Budapest, 3 September
Alexander Trauner

Paris, 15 September
Jacques Becker

Philadelphia, 6 October
Janet Gaynor
(Laura Gainor)

Milan, 2 November
Luchino Visconti

Kansas, 10 November
Louise Brooks

Vienna, 5 December
Otto Preminger

Massachusetts, 6 December
Agnes Moorehead

COPYRIGHTED

One of the gloriously extravagant scenes representing Georges Méliès' vision of how life looks ***20,000 Leagues Under the Sea.***

he Birth, the Life and the Death of Christ, a popular subject this time from Gaumont, is the pinnacle of director Alice Guy's career to date.

Italians enter the production field

Rome, 2 May
The Italian film pioneer Filoteo Alberini has opened a small film theater here called the Cinema Moderno. It is the first in the capital. Having patented an original device, the Kinetografo Alberini, as long ago as 1895, Alberini finally formed his own production company last year and last September presented his first film, *La Presa di Roma* (also known as *La Brescia di Porta Pia*). Soon afterwards he opened his first production studio in the Via Appia Nuova. More recently, the firm of Alberini and Santoni has become a joint French-Italian stock company. Known as Cines, it is headed by Baron Alberto Frassini as secretary, the French engineer Pouchain as chairman and Alberini himself as technical director. With many ambitious projects planned for the near future, the company is set to spearhead a rapid advance in Italian production which has lagged behind until now.

Méliès the diabolical magician and his four hundred blows

The apocalyptic horse and astral carriage from Méliès magical spectacle.

The author (r) plays the title role.

Paris, 31 August
Georges Méliès has placed on sale *The 400 Blows of the Devil!!!*, a fantastic tale in 35 tableaux. It is, in fact, a lengthened version of the film that Méliès shot in 1905 for the Châtelet Theatre. Victor de Cottens, the author of the play of the same name, had actually requested the master of Montreuil to film a supernatural tale with the intention of screening the film during silent moments of the play. Méliès therefore prepared two films, one entitled *The Cyclone* and the other *Journey into Space*, which were well received during their 500 performances at Châtelet. The audience was amazed by the technical boldness of these pictures in which "an apocalyptic horse" and "an astral chariot" make their appearance. The new version lasts approximately 20 minutes, with Georges Méliès playing his favorite role, that of Satan. Here, he buys the soul of the English engineer William Crackford. In exchange, Satan mus procure for him the pleasures c speed, because Crackford has a pas sion for breaking records. It is the that the famous apocalyptic hors appears, pulling a devilish coac carved in wood. There is a wonde fully effective descent into Hell, an the film ends with a diabolic balle Crackford is placed on a spit an roasted over a glowing fire, whil demons and female devils danc around him. Méliès has really com to excel in the artistic expression o weird and wonderful images. A usual, he is credited with the scen ario and the direction, as well a with all the special effects and deco of this incredible film.

New York becomes filmmaking center

New York, 25 August
According to the latest issue of *Views and Film Index*, the Vitagraph Company has opened a new film studio in the Flatbush area of Brooklyn, and has begun signing up a number of new players. In June, Biograph completed construction of a new stage for filming on East 14th Street, while Edison continues to make good use of his 21st Street studio. Filmmaking is flourishing in New York which, in recent months, has emerged more clearly than ever before as the undisputed center of filmmaking in the country.

Edison's new premises in the Bronx are designed to use natural light.

Jules Verne's imagination continues to influence Méliès' productions.

A love story in Provence for Alice Guy

The Birth, the Life and the Death of Christ by Alice Guy and Victorin Jasset.

Paris, 24 June
There was a sad return to Paris for Alice Guy's team after they finished shooting an adaptation of Frédéric Mistral's poem *Mireille* in the Camargues. Louis Feuillade, a fairly new Gaumont employee and a great aficionado of the bullfight, had the idea of filming out of doors. After a few days at Nîmes where Alice was disgusted by the corrida, they had planned to show the film to Mistral, but catastrophe intervened: the negative was completely destroyed by electric discharges. Nevertheless, Alice got to know Herbert Blaché, a young employee of the Gaumont company in London. The failed expedition brought them together, and there is already talk of marriage.

The cinema has arrived on the boulevards

CINEMA PATHE
CINÉMA
PATHÉ Frès
CINEMATOGRAPHE PATHE FRERES
L'ARMOIRE NORMANDE

The attractive Omnia is the first cinema venue opened by Pathé.

Paris, 15 December
Since the beginning of the year cinemas have mushroomed on the main boulevards of the French capital. There is the Cinématographe Bonne-Nouvelle, the Select Saint-Denis and another on boulevard Poisonnière. Today sees the opening of Cinématographe Pathé at 5 boulevard Montmartre. On 2 November a new company was formed by Edmond Bénoît-Levy, Charles Dussaud, Maurice Guegan and Emile Maugras to launch this theater, which will show only Pathé films. Another luxurious, well-appointed cinema called the Kinéma-Théâtre, owned by Gabriel Kaizer, is opening its doors on the boulevard des Italiens. Grand cinemas are now truly with us.

Ned Kelly and his gang immortalized on celluloid

Melbourne, 24 December
Australian director Charles Tait has broken new ground with *The Story of Ned Kelly*, a biopic of Australia's most famous outlaw which, measuring 4,000 feet, has a running time of about 70 minutes. Premiered at the Athenaeum Hall last night, the film was shot over a period of about six months, much of it on location on Tait's farm. The body armor actually worn by Kelly, including a bullet-proof helmet and jerkin made from ploughshares, was borrowed from Victoria's state museum and worn by the actor playing Kelly. But the actor, a Canadian touring player, disappeared before filming was finished and had to be replaced by an extra who was filmed in long shot. Produced by the theatrical company J. & N. Tait of Melbourne, *The Story of Ned Kelly* recouped its cost within a week and looks set to earn a handsome profit at home and back in the United Kingdom.

DEATH OF DAN KELLY & STEVE HART

A dramatic shoot-out from Charles Tait's ground-breaking Australian film about the notorious Ned Kelly.

1907

Paris, 1 January
Pathé has released *Aladdin and his Magic Lamp*, Albert Capellani's 250-metre film and Méliès' 364-metre *Robert, Macaire et Bertrand.*

Paris 15 January
Georges Hatot's most recent film, *les Débuts d'un chauffeur*, starring André Deed, has been released for sale by Pathé.

Paris, 26 January
Pathé has just organized the Compagnie des cinématographes Théophile Pathé with a starting capital of 2 million francs. This new company intends to produce low-budget films for fairground shows.

Berlin, 1 February
The newspaper *Der Komet* has attributed the invention of the cinema to photographer Max Skladanowsky whose first sessions of Bioskop were held on 1 November 1895 in the Wintergarten. The claim has been refuted by French journalists, thus starting a controversy about who invented the cinema.

Sweden, 16 February
N.H. Nylander, a cycle repairman, sets up the AB Svenska Biografteatern cinema chain in Kristianstad.

London, 22 February
Former magic-lantern showman Joshua Duckworth has opened the first purpose-built cinema in Britain. Central Hall, in Colne, Lancashire, cost 2,000 pounds to build.

Copenhagen, 12 March
Following on the success of *The White Slave*, in which he starred with Gerda Jenson, Nordisk's accredited producer Vigo Larsen has filmed *Roverens Brud* with Robert Storm and Clara Nebelong.

Chicago, March
The creation of the Bell & Howell Company, the first manufacturer of cameras and lenses in America.

Turin, April
Arturo Ambrosio's production firm has become a stock company with backing from the Commercial Bank of Turin. Carlo Rossi, who founded his own firm, has taken on Charles Lépine, former director at Pathé, as well as an accountant named Giovanni Pastrone.

Paris, 1 April
Zecca's *The Life and Passion of Christ* has been released for sale by Pathé. This is a new version of the 1902 film.

Paris, 11 May
The magazine *Photo-Ciné-Gazette* is organizing a big festival at the Elysée-Montmartre. An audience of 2,000 will be treated to a session of "talking pictures with the Chronomegaphone." The projection of the films combined with the Elgéphone is going to produce a "powerful, new sound," according to the manufacturer Léon Gaumont.

Paris, 20 May
There are now 15 cinemas in the capital, and 15 new cinematographs have opened since last week.

Helsinki, 29 May
The first fiction film to be produced in Finland, *Salaviinan Polttajat*, by Louis Sparre and Teuvo Puro, is now showing.

Paris, 1 June
Pathé has released *La Lutte pour la Vie* (*Struggle for Life*), the story of a railwayman who makes good, written by André Herzé.

Paris, 16 June
The Variety Theatre is showing a filmed play, *The Prodigal Child*, by the director Michel Carré with performances from George Wague and Christiane Mendelys.

Paris, 1 July
Méliès has released a burlesque fantasy called *Le Tunnel sous la Manche ou le Cauchemar franco-anglais* (*The Tunnel under the English Channel or the Anglo-French Nightmare*).

Paris, 18 July
Creation of the French Union of Directors. Léon Brézillon has been elected president.

Paris, 1 August
As a follow-up to the comic, *Cul-de-jatte emballé*, Gaumont has released Roméo Bosetti's *L'homme aimanté.*

St. Petersburg, August
Alexander O. Drankov, who opened the first Russian film studio, has filmed extracts from Pushkin's play *Boris Godounov*, directed by Ivan Chouvalov.

Singapore, August
Charles Pathé has opened his eighteenth overseas branch. He began with subsidiaries in Moscow, New York and Brussels in 1904, added Berlin, Vienna and St. Petersburg in 1905, and in 1906, Amsterdam, Barcelona, Milan, Odessa and London. This year, offices have opened in Rostov, Kiev, Budapest, Calcutta and Warsaw.

Paris, 21 October
In his report on the cinema industry for the administration at Orsay, Edmond Benoît-Lévy stated: Gaumont employs 650 workmen in its 12,000-square-metre factory and turns out 15,000 metres of film a day. But Pathé, with factories in Vincennes, Joinville-le-Pont and in New York, turns out 100,000 metres of film a day, has studios in Vincennes and Montreuil and had a turnover of 4 million francs for 1906–1907.

New York, October
Jeremiah Kennedy, a consultant engineer, has taken over as director of Biograph. He will handle the reorganization of the company under the supervision of the Empire trust company, on whom Biograph is financially dependant.

Paris, 1 December
Gaumont's newest *Le Médecin de campagne* (*The Country Doctor*), directed by Etienne Arnaud, and the comic film *Le Lit à Roulette* (*The Bed on Wheels*), made by Roméo Bosetti are now on the market.

Paris, 15 December
Gaumont has released *Bluebeard*, produced by Etienne Arnaud. The film, judged too cruel, has undergone "a few changes." His other recent releases include *The Future Revealed by the Sole of the Foot*, *La Poudre Rigolo* (*Funny Powder*) and *The Sewer Worker's Fiancee.*

Paris, 24 December
A permanent cinematograph that was designed by the architect Malo was opened at the Winter Circus today in the presence of the owner Charles Pathé, Max Linder, Gaston Velle and Albert Capellani.

Paris, 31 December
The young German, Erich Pommer, has started a career in the cinema with Léon Gaumont.

Calcutta, 31 December
The cinema Elphinstone Palace has been opened here by J.F. Maden.

BIRTHS

England, 19 January
Lilian Harvey
(Helen L. Pape)

Sweden, 15 March
Zarah Leander
(Sarah Hedberg)

England, 22 May
Laurence Olivier

Iowa, 26 May
John Wayne
(Marion Michael Morrison)

London, 3 June
Paul Rotha

New York, 16 July
Barbara Stanwyck
(Ruby Stevens)

Ukraine, 11 August
George Wakhevitch

France, 25 September
Robert Bresson

France, 13 October
Yves Allégret

France, 29 October
Edwige Feuillère
(Caroline Cunati)

France, 7 November
Jean Mitry
(Jean René Goetgheluck)

Connecticut, 8 November
Katharine Hepburn

France, 16 November
Renée Saint-Cyr
(Raymonde Renée Vittore)

France, 20 November
Henri-Georges Clouzot

Italy, 10 December
Amedeo Nazzari
(Salvatore Amedeo Buffa)

Charles Pathé is the man of the year. In 10 years, he has built his business and his reputation from nothing, and now heads a filmmaking empire that is unique in the world.

Stuart Blackton is heir to Emile Reynaud

Paris, 1 March
Today the new Vitagraph film *The Haunted Hotel* is going on sale to French exhibitors. It's a novelty animated film in which furniture moves mysteriously about as if by its own agency. The man who dreamed this up is an Englishman, John Stuart Blackton, who went to America at the age of 10 in 1885. It was Blackton's good fortune as a young journalist to interview Thomas Edison in 1895 and to convince the great inventor of his own talent as a designer. Two years later, in conjunction with William T. Rock and Albert E. Smith, Blackton founded the Vitagraph Company. In 1906 Blackton produced *Humorous Phases of Funny Faces*, which uses the technique of showing an artist drawing a still picture which then magically comes alive and moves. The effect was created using cardboard cutouts, but some genuinely animated sequences can be seen at the beginning of the film – notably a man sporting a bowler hat and umbrella seemingly drawing himself, and a man and a woman rolling their eyes. Blackton refers to this widely-used technique as the "American movement".

The Magic Pen *is the third animated film made by J. Stuart Blackton.*

Brussels won over by new art form

Brussels, 22 March
The Belgian capital has been swept up in the vogue of the Cinematograph, a trend coming mainly from Paris. Since 1905, Louis Van Goitsenhoven, the director of the Theatre of the Cinematograph, has also been running the Eden Theatre. He claims it is equipped for the presentation of "all the latest cinematographic productions from all over the world." In the autumn of 1900, the Pathé Brothers were the first to present animated films. The last few years have seen the rise of many competitors, but, on the other hand, the Molière Theatre has proudly made it known that it is "the only theater that the Cinematograph has not yet invaded."

World record beaten in Montreal

Montreal, 31 August
The largest luxury theater for the screening of animated pictures in North America, curiously named Ouimetoscope, has just opened its doors at the corner of Montcalm and Sainte-Catherine. Its 1,200 seats constitutes a world record. Léo-Ernest Ouimet, the owner, began his career as a stage electrician at the National Theatre and at the Sohmer Park, among others. In January 1906, he bought the former Poiré Hall and transformed it into a projection theater. Despite its success, the first Ouimetoscope was pulled down during the summer of 1907; since then an army of workers has rebuilt the hall of gigantic proportions on its ruins.

Louis Feuillade, new artistic director

Paris, 1 April
There have been quite a number of upheavals at Gaumont. Louis Feuillade, who came in as scenarist in 1905 under Alice Guy's direction, has replaced her as head of the department of theaters and production. Alice, who took charge of cinematographic production in 1899, got married a short while ago to the Belgian Herbert Blaché. Gaumont has appointed Blaché to the job of sales agent for the Chronophone, the projection apparatus of sound films, in Cleveland, Ohio in the U.S. Facing such a major relocation has been very sad for Alice. With great reluctance, she has been forced to quit the Buttes-Chaumont Theatre, which she managed with so much talent. In fact she herself had recommended Feuillade to the post when Gaumont made his decision known.

Feuillade and daughter Isabelle.

Vitagraph has a pretty new leading lady

New York, 7 June
The Vitagraph Company's most popular leading lady is diminutive, demure Florence Turner, star of *How to Cure a Cold*. The 20-year-old Turner, quite a successful stage performer, has been in the acting profession since the age of three. She was spotted in a crowd watching a Vitagraph production and was immediately taken on by the company as a wardrobe mistress at a salary of $18 a week with an extra five whenever she acted in a film. Like everyone in films, Turner is expected to combine several jobs in a production, but she is attracting more attention than other Vitagraph players. As yet her name has not been revealed to the public, and she is known simply as "The Vitagraph Girl." Film companies are still reluctant to name their most popular players. After all, these new stars might take the opportunity to ask for more money!

The former stage actress Florence Turner has switched to film.

Edmond Benoît-Lévy, the 'éminence grise'

Paris, 12 July
Who is Edmond Benoît-Lévy? He signed an exclusive contract today with Chares Pathé which will allow him the monopoly of Pathé films in nine French provinces as well as in Switzerland. Benoît-Lévy has gradually become the confidant of Pathé, being involved in every decision made by the Vincennes master. A former trial lawyer, he practiced law for 20 years before branching out into other activities, one of which was a lecture position at the Popular Society of Fine Arts. In 1905 Benoît-Lévy published the Phono-Gazette, which at the end of the year became known as the Phono-Ciné-Gazette. After organizing the Union of Cinematograph Exhibitors, on 2 November 1906, he went on to found a company for the showing of the Pathé Cinematograph, at 5 boulevard Montmartre, the headquarters of his paper and of the Ciné Club founded in April this year. This newspaper supported Pathé invaluably at the time that it was decided to hire the films out. Benoît-Lévy, whose firm has just changed its name to Omnia, has Pathé's permission to establish a network of Cinematographs – permanent halls or traveling stalls – which would project only Pathé films. With a capital of up to 1.2 million francs, Benoît-Lévy has managed to consolidate the cinematographic industry, although remaining in the constant shadow of Charles Pathé.

PHONO-CINÉ
GAZETTE

A secret meeting after a decisive ruling

Chicago, 30 November
The American film industry is once again in ferment. Some of the most important producers have just met in secret. Among them were George Kleine of Kalem Pictures, John Stuart Blackton and Albert E. Smith from Vitagraph, Essanay's George Spoor, and William N. Selig and Sigmund Lubin of, respectively, Selig and Lubin. A French presence is provided by Gaston Méliès, who represents Star Films, and Jacques-Emile Berst of Pathé. The meeting originally had been called to study a proposal put forth by the Edison Manufacturing Company. Edison has been proposing to award producers a license in return for a payment of a levy of half-a-cent for each foot of film printed or sold. The levy would be collected by the Eastman-Kodak foundation, which would then discount any excess profit in their accounts with the Edison company. In exchange for signing up with the scheme, Edison will undertake to protect the licensees and to take vigorous legal action on their behalf against any pirated prints, unauthorized screenings or other activities prejudicial to their interests. This is clearly an attempt to form a motion picture cartel. Edison's proposal was favorably received by the producers present, uniting bitter rivals in agreement. What lies behind this sudden change of heart? Since its birth 10 years ago the motion picture business has been characterized by endless legal disputes. William Selig, founder in 1896 of the Selig Polyscope Company, has the dubious distinction of being on the receiving end of the largest number of writs. Only last October he was found guilty by a Chicago judge, Christian Kahlseat, of using cameras which infringed upon patents taken out by Thomas Edison. This ruling had important consequences. It looked as if motion pictures would, by the same token, become the exclusive property of the wizard of West Orange. The possibility of this precedent being enforced sent a wave of alarm through the ranks of film producers. George Kleine was delegated to thrash out some common ground with the Edison Company. As a result, Kleine and Edison's business manager, Mr. Gilmore, met and agreed on the proposals which have just been considered in secret conclave by the most important figures in the industry. Observers are predicting that after several years of legal wrangling the end of the tunnel might be in sight. The resolution of these problems is welcome as an important financial shot in the arm.

Rescued from an Eagle's Nest, 'a fantastical vision' on a very popular theme, about small children captured and restored to their parents.

Key developments in the Chicago cinema

Chicago, 4 November
Recent developments in the Windy City suggest that Chicago is set to rival New York as the leading film-making center in the U.S. In fact, this city is already ahead of New York in one respect: censorship. The authorities have passed the first local censorship ordinance in the country "prohibiting the exhibition of obscene and immoral pictures commonly shown in Mutoscopes, Kinetoscopes, Cinematographs and penny arcades." Earlier this year, projectionist Donald Bell and camera repairman Albert Howell founded the Bell & Howell Camera Co. which hopes to play an important role if the industry continues to grow at the same rapid pace as during recent years. But most important of all has been the formation of the Essanay Company in February by George K. Spoor and actor-producer G.M. Anderson, who is best-known for the Westerns he has made for Selig since 1904 (the company name is derived from the two founders' initials, "S" and "A"). Wasting no time, Essanay is already filming in its studio at 501 Wells Street, having announced their first production, *An Awful Skate* or *The Hobo on Rollers*, on 27 July in *The Moving Picture World.* Not to be outdone, local entrepreneur Selig has just moved into his new plant on Western Avenue.

Essanay co-founder G.M. Anderson.

1908

Paris, 1 January
The Ciné-voiture Omnia is on display at the Motor Show. Aimed at fairground exhibitions, it contains a generator which can be used either to run a car or project films.

France, 31 January
The Eclair Company has increased its capital from 150,000 to 500,000 francs and has purchased a 14-acre building site for a studio. Georges Hatot and Victorin Jasset have been hired as film directors.

France, 4 February
Louis Feuillade has started filming three historical stories for Gaumont: *le Retour du Croisé* (*The Return of the Crusader*), *le Serment des fiançailles* (*The Betrothal Pledge*) and *la Guitare enchantée* (*The Magic Guitar*).

New York, 5 February
In the ongoing struggle against Edison's monopoly, Biograph's Vice President Henry Marvin has bought up patents to which the Edison Co. claimed it held exclusive rights.

Paris, 8 February
Creation of the first cinematographic advertising business, the Publicité Animée.

New York, 20 February
Frank L. Dyer, Edison's lawyer, has replaced Stuart Gilmore as the company's vice president. On 15 February, he informed film distributors that they would be charged an annual license fee of $5,000.

Paris, 1 March
Gaumont has released *la Course aux potirons* (*The Pumpkin Race*), a film with trick effects by the newly recruited Emile Cohl.

Paris, 9 March
European producers gathered at the Continental hotel to unite against Edison's protectionism. But Charles Pathé refused to take part in the meeting, claiming that such an effort will "only defer the inevitable ruin of certain companies."

Turin, 15 March
Giovanni Pastrone and the engineer Sciamengo have bought up Carlo Rossi's production company, which was in liquidation, and have founded their own company, Itala Film.

Paris, 15 May
Photo-Ciné-Gazette has vaunted the benefits of the "Mallet protective case", which separates the reel of film from the arc light. It should be made compulsory for all projectors in order to prevent fires.

Buenos Aires, 24 May
Showing of Argentina's first fiction film *El Fusilamiento de Dorrego* (*The Execution of Dorrego*), directed by an Italian, Mario Gallo.

Rome, 31 May
Adapted from *Hamlet* and directed by Mario Caserini for Cines, the new film *Ameleto* has been shown.

New York, 18 June
D.W. Griffith, formerly the actor Laurence Griffith, has directed his first film, *The Adventures of Dollie*, for Biograph. His wife Linda Arvidson is in the cast.

Paris, 4 July
At the Fourth of July party held for Pathé's personnel at the Winter Circus, Max Linder caused a sensation – first on screen and then by leaping in person onto the stage. He made the burlesque film *les Débuts d'un patineur* (*A Skater's Debut*) last winter under Louis Gasnier's direction.

London, 4 July
The Gem in Great Yarmouth opens today under the management of C.B. Cochran. With its 1,200-seat auditorium, it is the first purpose-built cinema in Britain to hold over 1,000 people.

Chicago, 3 August
Gaston Méliès has set up a branch here of the Georges Méliès Manufacturing Company, with a capital of $75,000, to distribute Star films and to produce films under the supervision of Lincoln J. Carter.

Paris, 10 August
A police order has just been issued to control security in cinemas. It stipulates that the projection booth has to be fire proof and that the projectionist must have a five-litre fire extinguisher and two bottles of Seltzer water within reach.

Paris, 15 August
The weekly *Ciné-Journal*, run by George Dureau, has published its first number.

New York, 17 August
D.W. Griffith has signed a contract at $50 per week with the Biograph company and has become the firm's main director due to the departure of Wallace McCutcheon.

Paris, 25 August
Roméo Bosetti has created a relief fund for cinema actors.

Rome, August
Carlo Rossi has taken over as head of Cines. Mario Caserini and Enrico Guazzoni are to be his principal film directors.

Paris, 8 September
Eclair has released the first film in the "Nick Carter" series called *le Guet-apens* (*The Trap*), directed by Victorin Jasset.

New York, 9 September
Jeremiah Kennedy, the manager of Biograph, has threatened to obtain his own licenses if Edison refuses to allow him to use his movie cameras.

Paris, 9 September
Jean Durand, who was taken on by Pathé last June to film some trick effects with an unknown actor, Maurice Chevalier, has left for Lux.

Paris, 19 September
The technician André Debrie has submitted his camera, Le Parvo, for patent. It takes 120 metres of film.

St. Petersburg, 15 October
Stenka Razine, directed by Vladimir Romachkov and produced by A. Drankov, is the first significant film produced by the fledgling Russian cinema industry.

Fort Lee, New Jersey, 16 October
D.W. Griffith is filming *The Curtain Pole* with Linda Arvidson and a young actor named Mack Sennett.

Berlin, 13 November
The International Convention of Authors' Rights has extended the legal protection defined in Berne for artistic works to include films "having a personal and original form."

Paris, 15 November
Pathé has released, *Un Monsieur qui suit les Dames* (*A Man who Follows Women*), with the performance of an actor from the Charles Petit-Demange Variety Theatre.

Paris, 10 December
The first episode from the new Victorin Jasset series entitled *Riffle, le roi de la prairie* (*Riffle, the King of the Fields*) is now screening.

Pittsburgh, 31 December
The Warner brothers have opened a film distribution company called Duquesne Amusement.

Tokyo, 31 December
The first film studio has opened in the Meguro district.

BIRTHS

France, 12 January
Jean Delannoy

Texas, 26 February
Tex Avery
(Fred Avery)

England, 5 March
Rex Harrison

Alexandria, 7 March
Anna Magnani

Berlin, 17 March
Brigitte Helm
(Eva Gisela Schittenhelm)

England, 25 March
David Lean

Massachusetts, 5 April
Bette Davis
(Ruth Elisabeth Davis)

Pennsylvania, 20 May
James Stewart

England, 26 May
Robert Morley

Wisconsin, 31 May
Don Ameche (Dominic Amici)

France, 12 July
Alain Cuny

Indiana, 6 October
Carole Lombard

Portugal, 12 December
Manoel de Oliveira

***The Assassination of the Duc de Guise**, directed by André Calmettes of the Comédie Française has been filmed at least twice before. This version is the best and most successful.*

Le Film d'Art
L'ASSASSINAT DU DUC DE GUISE
de Mr Henri Lavedan de l'Académie Française
Pièce Cinématographique
Interprètes :
MMrs. Le Bargy de la Comédie Française
Albert Lambert de la Comédie Française
Dieudonné du Théâtre de la Renaissance
MMes. Robinne de la Comédie Française
Berthe Bovy de la Comédie Française
Décors de Bertin – Meubles de Leonardi

Dumas' classic filmed in California

New York, 2 February
Southern California, with its sunshine and spectacular scenery, is beginning to attract filmmakers. The Selig Company, Edison's biggest rival, has recently filmed Alexander Dumas' *The Count of Monte Cristo* in Santa Monica. The film's interior scenes had been shot in Selig's Chicago studio, but director Francis Boggs felt that more authentic settings were required. Consequently, Boggs and another Selig employee, Thomas Persons, who leads a busy life as a cameraman, property manager, business manager and assistant director, settled on sunny California. The change of location then required a change of cast. A new Count of Monte Cristo was found in the form of an impoverished hypnotist who bore a passing resemblance to the actor who had played the role in Chicago. The hypnotist had never heard of the cinema but was only too happy to sign for Selig. Boggs set up a studio on a rooftop on Main Steet in downtown Los Angeles and also filmed on location on Santa Monica beach. Now on release, the one-reel version of Dumas' classic suggests that it will not be long before other companies follow Selig. California's benign climate, varied topography and availability of cheap labor are certain to encourage people to travel to Los Angeles, at present a sleepy town whose orange groves provide its citizens with their main source of income. And it definitely seems like the filmmakers are heading West.

The intransigent Pathé brothers make a few grand concessions

Tous y mènent leurs enfants!
CINEMA Pathé

This advertisement bears witness to the growing popularity of cinema halls, such as this venue at Vincennes.

Paris, 15 April
Edmond Benoît-Lévy's Phono-Ciné-Gazette has published the list of concessionary firms who will have the monopoly of Pathé Brothers films. These firms, which have gradually been put in place since July 1907, have been permanently set up to hire out the films. Cinema-Omnia and Cinema-Theatre, both at boulevard Montmartre, are responsible for the Northwest, Central-West, Corsica, Switzerland and Algeria. Benoît-Lévy and Serge Sandberg, the director of the Cinema-Theatre, sit on the administrative council. The lending out of Pathé films for Paris is done by the intermediary of Cinema Exploitation, whose offices can be found at Pathé, 8 rue Saint-Augustin. The Central-East and the Southeast are represented by a firm called Cinema-Monopole located in Lyons at 6 rue Grôlée and presided over by Baron Gabet. In Bordeaux, Cinema National, situated at 5 Intendance Court, is in control of the Southwest. Finally, the Belgian cinema has its headquarters in Brussels at 40 place de Brouckère and covers Belgium, the Netherlands and Luxembourg. All in all, an extremely thorough job.

CINÉMATOGRAPHE AUTOMOBILE

A typical fairground cinema of the kind in which Pathé has participated.

From now on a studio is reserved for the scientific films of Dr. Comandon.

The judicial spotlight is turned on Ben Hur

New York, 5 May
Ben Hur is condemned again! Not to the slave galley this time, but rather to pay damages totaling $25,000. The culprit is the Kalem Picture Company which was founded in Chicago in March 1907 by George Kleine, Samuel Long and Frank Marion (the company's name is derived from the initials of its three directors). One of Kalem's ambitious ideas has turned sour. In November 1907 the company made a one-reel version of Lew Wallace's best-selling novel of Ancient Rome, *Ben Hur.* Directors Sydney Olcott and Frank Oakes Rose rented background scenery left over from a summer exhibition staged by the well-known Pains Firework Company on the racetrack at Sheepshead Bay, New York and hired the Brooklyn Fire Department to stage the novel's climactic chariot race. Since Kalem had no indoor studios on any of its three lots, much of its output was shot on location. The script was written by Gene Gautier, Kalem's most popular leading lady dubbed the "Kalem Girl" and one of the busiest screenwriters in the business. The film's running time was about 15 minutes and the result, according to Kalem's publicity, was "16 magnificent scenes with illustrated titles." There was one small snag, however. Kalem had neglected to acquire any rights to the story, a not uncommon practice but one which incurred the wrath of Harper and Brothers, the book's publishers, Abraham Erlanger, the producer of the spectacular stage adaptation of *Ben Hur* and Henry Wallace, the administrator of the estate of Lew Wallace who died in 1905. Immediately after the first public showing of the Kalem version of *Ben Hur* in January, the aggrieved parties decided to take legal action, the first of its kind. The decision went against Kalem, thereby ensuring that film companies, which have previously played fast and loose with the law of copyright, will in the future have to respect the rights of authors. As a result, the posters for the Kalem version of *Ben Hur* disappeared overnight and the film was withdrawn. It was then seized by the court until Kalem came up with a surety. The film company is set to appeal the decision, and the battle might go to the Supreme Court.

Sound and color along the river Thames

London, 31 August
England is becoming the most audacious country as far as cinematography is concerned. Various pioneers are building on the work of Frenchman Eugène-Augustin Lauste who designed "a new method for the simultaneous reproduction of movement and sound." Lauste, who worked with William Kennedy Laurie Dickson some years ago, has been fascinated for a very long time by the problems of the synchronization of image and sound. Since 1904, he has dreamt of a system where the sound modulations would be etched directly onto the edge of the reel of film. One interesting experiment showed how sound managed to alter the intensity of a flame, the variations of which were subsequently recorded on film. The technique has been much improved upon since then, and the apparatus now seems to be completely satisfactory. The Englishman George Albert Smith, who made his reputation directing films in Brighton at the turn of the century, has founded Kinemacolor Ltd. together with Charles Urban. Although the company was established five months previously, the first films, which are documentary rather than fiction, have only recently started to appear on the screens. Kinemacolor is a two-toned process inspired by research carried out by the great French scientists Gabriel Lippmann and Louis-Arthur Ducos du Hauron. Patented in June 1907, this new technique, designed by Smith, has perfectly reflected the variegated and contrasting colors of the English landscape. The first public demonstration took place on 26 February last at the Palace Theatre in London, followed by other showings elsewhere before it was demonstrated in the hall of Civil Engineers in Paris a month later. Kinemacolor has been an undoubted success, and it will probably not be long before this new system is shown on European screens, where it would bring more visual variation to the programs.

Emile Cohl and the arrival of the puppets

A Drama of the Puppets*, the beginning of animated drawings in France.*

Paris, 12 November
A Drama in Fantoche's House is the third animated film to be produced by Gaumont in the last four months, which follows hard on the heels of *Phantasmagoria* and also *Fantoche's Nightmare*. They are all the work of a single man, Emile Courtet, whose *nom de plume* is Emile Cohl. Born in Paris in January 1857, Cohl was apprenticed as a jeweler and began drawing caricatures during his military service. He went on to become a political cartoonist for numerous publications, wrote for the theater, acted, dabbled in conjuring and took up photography. He also designed some of the flip books which anticipated the arrival of animated film. The story goes that one day Cohl stormed into the Gaumont offices to protest that the company had plagiarized one of his cartoons in a film poster. Cohl's reward was the offer of a job at Gaumont from Louis Feuillade, then the head of production at the studio. Cohl started at Gaumont as an ideas man and writer, graduating to the direction of animated films which exploit the relatively recent American invention of stop-go photography. One of Cohl's most popular creations is Fantoche, the engaging little man who makes regular appearances in his films. These animated frolics have all the freshness and innocent vigor of children's drawings, which is a most remarkable achievement for a man in his fifties.

The Pumpkin Race*, which blends poetry and fantasy with realism.*

The cinema is caught in the grip of respectability

The Kiss of Judas, directed by Armand Bour, with Mounet-Sully as Judas and Albert Lambert as Christ.

The Comédie-Française and the Academy give backing to Film Art

Paris, 17 November

The Film d'Art company, which was founded on 14 February by businessman Paul Lafitte, the academician Henri Lavedan, the architect Jean-Camille Formigé, and actor Charles Le Bargy of the Comédie-Française, is showing its first program tonight at the Charras Hall. All the films were shot at the Film d'Art studios in Neuilly. It is expected that an elegant crowd will be present at this event, which will mean the coming together for the first time of the French elite and members of the Academie Française with the world of the Cinematograph, that stunted offspring so criticized by high society. Film d'Art will show *Myrto's Secret*, acted by Régina Badet; *The Impression*, a mime drama with Max Dearly and Mistinguett, who dances the famous swaying waltz; and the most eagerly-awaited film, *The Assassination of the Duc de Guise*. The latter was directed by Charles Le Bargy and André Calmettes, from a scenario by Henri Lavedan, with an original music score by Camille Saint-Saëns. Charles Le Bargy, Albert Lambert, Gabrielle Robinne and Bertha Bovy perform in this film of astonishing restraint, with a skillful and tragic scenario, and polished decor. Compared with the historic scenes produced by Pathé or Gaumont, this interpretation appears to be a masterpiece. Nevertheless, there are those who are wary: the theater risks stifling the cinema, which usually tries to avoid copying its rival. But with the success of Film d'Art, the cinema has come of age.

The Assassination of the Duc de Guise *dramatizes an episode of history.*

The men of letters turn to Daudet

Paris, 1 October

The Pathé company has put on sale *l'Arlésienne*, a picture based on Alphonse Daudet, and filmed by Albert Capellani in Arles. It is the first big production following some more, and some less, successful experiments, from the company made up of composers and men of letters. This company (SCAGL), founded on 23 June by the bankers Saul and Georges Merzbach, has the popular novelist Pierre Decourcelle and the playwright Eugène Gugenheim on staff. They took their inspiration and aims from Film d'Art, which attempts to bring plays and novels to the screen starring famous actors. Their leanings are toward populist works. The Bank of Industry and Commerce is giving financial support to the business, in which one discovers once again the hand of Charles Pathé. He is one of the principal shareholders and has assisted SCAGL by lending them his cameramen and putting at their disposal his building materials and his hiring service. He has even provided them with the blueprint for a photographic studio that the new firm will build in Vincennes. Thus Pathé has gained control over the activities of SCAGL, as he does with Film d'Art which was rapidly obliged to give up its freedom by signing a contract with Pathé, the ogre whose appetite never seems to be satisfied.

Artistic director Albert Capellani.

Europeans await George Eastman

Paris, 10 December
Twenty representatives of the most important European film companies have arrived at the Paris offices of the Eclair company to meet George Eastman, the American inventor and businessman on a visit here. As he is the leading manufacturer of film stock, they hope that Eastman might be able to influence the Edison company in their favor. After waging a patents war for many years to protect his rights, Thomas Edison created the Film Service Association earlier this year – a cartel which brings together the leading American companies. Although Pathé was invited to join, all the other European producers were excluded. For them this has proved disastrous, since fully three-quarters of their income is generated in the United States. In response to Edison, they formed their own association in Paris on 9 March but have been far from united in their views. Some of the leading companies in France, including Gaumont, Urban and Cines, even tried to join the cartel, but found that their way was barred by Pathé, the company that continues to pull the strings in Europe.

Building of world's biggest studios

SOCIETE DES ETABLISSEMENTS GAUMONT
The Gaumont company, with its financial position strengthened, is now proving to be a worthy rival to Pathé.

Paris, 31 December
At Buttes-Chaumont there is a vast assemblage of offices, workshops, laboratories and also photo studios, which has now been christened the Cité Elgé, after the initials of Léon Gaumont. Since 1905, these buildings have been spread out over more than 10,000 square metres. "It's the largest studio in the world," the advertisements proclaim. Louis Feuillade is still directing productions with help from an unrivaled team: Roméo Bosetti, Etienne Arnaud, Léonce Perret and a newcomer, the designer Emile Cohl, all of whom juggle with camera technique. The basement of the glass-topped studio has been converted into artists' dressing rooms, and a second workshop has been constructed exclusively for the shooting of sound films. The warehouses for props have been enlarged and so have the workshops for the building of decor. Gaumont presides ruthlessly over his domain. The gates are closed firmly at 8 a.m. sharp each morning. Members of the staff must be punctual if they want to keep their jobs.

Edison's maneuvers cause disturbance

New York, 24 December
A serious crisis has hit the film exhibitors of New York City: pending the decision of the mayor George McClellan, as many as 500 nickelodeons may be forced to close as the result of an unprecedented citywide inspection. In an operation beginning at dawn and continuing throughout the day, a large number of inspectors were instructed to call on virtually every film hall in the city, without warning, to assess their current safety precautions. It is, of course, well-known to all that reels of film are highly inflammable, and there is always a risk of fire. Only last June, the Police Commissioner Bingham raised the possibility of revoking the nickelodeons' licenses, both for reasons of morality and public safety; fortunately for the film business, this suggestion was not taken up by the mayor. It is worth noting that the date of the current operation comes just a week or so after the formation of the Motion Picture Patents Company, or MPPC, a kind of film industry cartel set up by the Edison Co. in league with Biograph. In addition to these two leading companies, the other members of the trust include Vitagraph, Selig, Kalem, Essanay, Lubin, George Kleine, and the two largest French companies, Pathé Frères and Méliès Star Films. Aside from these signatories, no one else is allowed either to produce or to sell a single foot of film in the U.S. without the special authorization of the trust, which also asserts the right to impose its own fees and other conditions on all film renters, exchanges and exhibitors. On top of that, the trust has also drafted an exclusive agreement with the Eastman Kodak Company for the supply of new, less inflammable film, and Edison is able to use this to control the activities of exhibitors countrywide. No wonder they are ready to rebel.

A special Marguerite

Gaumont
On 14 January, the clerk of the Commercial Court of the Seine registered the Gaumont emblem, a daisy with the name Gaumont through the center. Inspiration came from the first name of Léon Gaumont's mother.

1909

Russia, 1 January
Cameramen from Pathé and Edison have filmed Leo Tolstoy at his home in Jasnia Polonia.

Turin, January
The Itala Film Company is producing the first films in a comic series played by André Deed, a French actor who was formerly a star with the Pathé company.

Paris, 1 February
Georges Demenÿ has delivered his version of "the origins of the cinematograph." He has put forward a defense of his own research and has sharply attacked the memory of his former master Etienne Marey.

USA, 8 February
Release of D.W. Griffith's *Edgar Allan Poe*, with Linda Arvison.

Rome, 2 March
The newly created Film d'Arte Italiano, a joint stock company, is a branch of Pathé's French firm.

Paris, 4 March
Eclair has released *les Dragonnades sous Louis XIV* (*The Dragonnade under Louis XIV*), made by Jasset.

Paris, 5 March
Representatives from 32 European production companies are meeting at Méliès' Robert Houdin Theatre. The participants, particularly the fairground showmen, were unable to agree on terms for film hire.

Paris, 11 March
Eclair has released *les Nouveaux exploits de Nick Carter* (*The Latest Exploits of Nick Carter*), in three episodes, by Victorin Jasset. The king of the detectives is played by Pierre Brussol.

Paris, 11 March
Albert Kahn, founder of Archives of the Planet, and his cameraman Alfred Dutertre are back from a film trip during which they visited many countries in the world, including China and Japan.

New York, 12 March
Cinema owner and distributor Carl Laemmle and film director William Rainous have founded a breakaway company from Vitagraph, Independent Motion Pictures (IMP). The imp has been chosen as its emblem.

Paris, 15 March
The measures taken by the International Congress of Film Producers concerning film hire have come into force. Films are to be rented out for a period of four months and then returned to the original production company for destruction.

New York, 14 April
The distributors Adam Kessel and Charles Baumann have founded the new Bison Life Films with the aim of producing Westerns.

Boston, April
Louis B. Mayer, formerly a scrap metal dealer turned cinema owner, founds The Gordon-Mayer Circuit with Nat Gordon.

Paris, 6 May
Maury, the owner of a franchise, has put the Ciné Multiphone Rousselot on the market, a type of piano used to produce sound effects for films.

Paris, 4 June
American Vitagraph is distributing *Napoleon – The Man of Destiny*, produced by James Stuart Blackton, the first American producer to move toward the "art film".

New York, 10 June
Following her debut screen in *The Violin Maker of Cremona* for D.W. Griffith, 16-year-old Mary Pickford is starring in the same director's *The Lonely Villa*. She had been a triumph on Broadway for two years, in a play by William De Mille, when Griffith took her on at the beginning of the year for a part in his new film *Her First Biscuits*.

New York, 15 June
Independent American film producers have made a secret agreement with the Eastman-Kodak company for supplies of safety film.

New York, 1 August
Edwin S. Porter has resigned his position as the head of Edison productions. He has now founded Rex Motion Pictures, in partnership with William H. Swanson.

Paris, 9 August
Gaumont has just released a tinted version of Louis Feuillade's *The Death of Mozart* and Etienne Arnaud's *Trait de bonté de Napoléon I* (*Napoleon I's Act of Goodness*).

Paris, 24 August
The Hippodrome in the place de Clichy has been turned into a skating rink by its new owners, Crawford and Wilkins Ltd of Liverpool, England. Henri Iclès, who already runs the Moulin Rouge and Luna Park, is the director.

Berlin, 4 September
The UT circuit has opened a giant cinema with seating for 1,000 in Alexanderplatz.

London, 19 September
The British weekly paper *The Kinematograph and Lantern Weekly* has launched the idea of film stories.

New York, 10 October
Pippa Passes, by the prolific director D.W. Griffith and starring Mary Pickford, is the very first film to rate a notice in the *New York Times*, thanks to its technical innovations.

St. Petersburg, 6 October
The Death of Ivan the Terrible, a film by Vassili Goncharov and produced by Pathé's Russian branch, has had a public screening.

Paris, 7 November
Emile Cohl has released his *les Lunettes féériques* (*The Magic Eyeglasses*), that was made by adapting the principle of the Chromatrope, or magic lantern, for the cinema.

Paris, 14 November
Harry Baur, a young actor from the Odéon Theatre, makes his screen debut in the new Eclair release *la Légende du bon chevalier* (*The Legend of the Good Knight*).

Paris, 19 December
Gaumont has released two films, which have been toned and tinted under the supervisorial eye of Louis Feuillade: *Noël d'artiste* (*The Artist's Christmas*), and *Noël du chiffonier* (*The Ragman's Christmas*).

New York, 23 December
After the success of his two-reel *Napoléon*, J. Stuart Blackton has released the first part of *The Life of Moses* a five-reeler (50 minutes), to be shown in five separate parts.

Vienna, 31 December
Erich Pommer has been named the general manager of Gaumont for the whole of central Europe.

Hong Kong, 31 December
The American Benjamin Polaski has founded The Asia Film Company. He is filming *The Pot's Revelation* and *To Steal a Roast Duck*.

Stockholm, 31 December
Charles Magnusson and Julius Jaenzon, directors of Svenska, have released a film by Carl Engdhal, *The People of the Värmland*.

BIRTHS

Wisconsin, 14 January
Joseph Losey

France, 3 February
André Cayatte

Paris, 10 February
Henri Alekan

Pennsylvania, 11 February
Joseph Mankiewicz

Egypt, 24 February
Riccardo Freda

Scotland, 1 March
David Niven

England, 15 May
James Mason

Austria, 17 May
Magda Schneider

Tasmania, 20 June
Errol Flynn

France, 23 June
Georges Rouquier

Milan, 5 July
Isa Miranda

Paris, 18 August
Marcel Carné

Istanbul, 7 September
Elia Kazan (Elia Kazanjoglou)

Stockholm, 13 November
Gunnar Björnstrand

New York, 9 December
Douglas Fairbanks Jr.

The six films in the popular police series **Nick Carter**, *made by Victorin Jasset, stars André Liabel in the title role, and Marise Dauvray. The films have made a fortune for Eclair.*

CINÉMA Eclair
NICK
CARTER
R.CHAPELET

▷

Extravagant congress of international executives

This group photograph, taken after the closing banquet, disguises the deep conflict between the various parties. In the front row, left to right: George Rogers, Charles Pathé, George Eastman, Georges Méliès and Charles Urban.

Paris, 4 February
"The Dupes' Congress" was how Georges Dureau, a journalist attached to *Ciné Journal*, described the International Congress of Film Producers, which has just finished after two days of debates. George Eastman has managed to come to France after the establishment by the Edison Trust in the U.S. of the Motion Pictures Patents Company, which has amalgamated nine new companies, including those of Pathé and Georges Méliès. In future, only the films of the MPPC can be shown in America. The founding of the company, with strong, authoritarian ambitions, has met with resistance from small and large operators within certain firms. Last October, both Nordisk in Denmark and Vitagraph, the business rival of Edison managed by Stuart Blackton, proposed the convening of a new international congress in Paris. This idea was welcomed enthusiastically because the European companies were not happy about the MPPC decisions. The stakes are high since the American market constitutes an inexhaustible outlet for all the companies. If this market is closed to certain firms, it might spell ruin for many of them. Thus, the idea of setting up a partnership of producers, a sort of rival trust, copying the American model. George Eastman has encouraged this plan, because he sees Europe as an excellent market. A skilled diplomat, he is trying to reconcile all the parties involved. His presence at the Congress was as much an event as that of Charles Pathé, the king of the cinema world. Pathé had originally cynically refused to collaborate in the Association of Filmmakers. The crisis in the industry, according to him, "will not be resolved by catastrophes and by the inevitable ruin of certain firms which are more financial than industrial." Clearly, the more bankruptcies the better! George Eastman had been persuaded to participate at th Congress. Eastman and Pathé wer there together with some 200 signif cant, and less significant, people c European cinema: Léon Gaumon Georges Méliès, Charles Jourjo and Marcel Vandal of Eclair, th American-born pioneer of Britis cinema Charles Urban, as well a the representatives of Vitagraph Lux, Cines, Ambrosio, Hepworth Warwick, Nordisk, Messter, th Russian company Drankoff, etc. A the start of the meeting preside over by Méliès, the creation of th International Committee of Film makers (CIDEF) was proposed an agreed. Therefore, a new consor tium was born, bringing together 3 different firms. The main decisio was that producers will rent ou films only to members who hav committed themselves in writing t returning their copies after fou months. The fairground-stall owner are up in arms again. The Congres not only wishes to monopolize th hiring out of films, but also wants t eliminate those who arrange the hir ing, the intermediaries between th producers and the stall owners. I fact, the Congress ended in grea confusion. Despite the agreement signed, interests diverged totally Even a decision on a just tariff fo rentals could not be reached. Ir tended to avert a serious cinem crisis, the Congress resolved noth ing. It set up a trust which can stifl the small operators. In reality th only winner of the day was Eastman who now becomes the sole supplie of the Congress members.

George Eastman is formidable as a industrialist and technician.

Georges Méliès savors his day of glory

Paris, 4 February
George Méliès, president of the International Congress of Film Producers, proudly poses for a photograph. He is seated among a group of 50 well-known figures from the cinematographic world. On his right are George Eastman and Charles Pathé; on his left Léon Gaumont. Méliès the independent amidst the three giants of the industry! During the two days of the Congress, he performed his duties perfectly with good humor and his celebrated cordiality. This exceptional honor was the crowning achievement for him. Nevertheless, certain decisions taken by the Congress risked destroying Star Film, whose finances are increasingly troubled. The industrialization of cinematograph production on a vast scale could crush the modest firm in Montreuil, which functions on a small scale. Méliès is a brilliant artist but not a good businessman. Although very happy to have presided over the Congress, Georges Méliès has no doubt of the dangers that lie in store for him. For the moment, however, he can savor his glory, smiling with his friends of the day.

he independents tand up to Edison

ew York, 20 March
ne long-running dispute between homas Edison and the smaller, in-ependent companies has suddenly ken on a new twist. Apparently, all ose companies excluded from his ust, the Motion Picture Patents ompany (or MPPC) have orga-zed themselves into a powerful rtel of independents. And, in or-er to operate with maximum effec-veness, this new cartel has taken any precautions. The most notable to make use of the special patents eld by P.A. "Pat" Powers, which ill protect them against the multi-e threats made by Edison and his wyers. By far the most important the non-patent-infringing camera eveloped by Joseph Bianchi, a re-ording expert with the Columbia honograph Company. If the small-companies continue to make use f this camera, there is no way that dison will be able to stop them om filming. In addition to this, the rench Lumière company has of-red to supply the members of this anti-trust" with a new type of less flammable film stock as an alter-ative to the highly publicized new lm from the Eastman Kodak Co. hich has been specially reserved or the members of Edison's trust. It highly likely that this new associa-on will also be able to do a thriving usiness with all those film halls that ave been excluded by Edison – an nexpected new lease on life here or the many small renters left out in ne cold by the restrictive practices f the cartel.

'Pathé faits divers' marks the launching of a weekly newsreel

A LA CONQUETE DU MONDE
scène vécue
par
PATHÉ FRÈRES
1894-19...

Barrère's view of Emile and Charles.

Paris, 31 March
Encouraged by the public's insatiable curiosity about the details of daily life in far-flung parts of the world, Pathé has launched a weekly newsreel, with exciting documentary footage provided by an army of cameramen dispatched to the four corners of the globe. From now on the company's film cameras will venture into savage and unexplored regions. Always on the lookout for the sensational, Pathé's cameramen also follow the important events of the week: disasters, murders, trials and sporting events. The newsreel, entitled *Pathé faits divers* and edited by Albert Gaveau, aims to act as an historical witness to contemporary events. *Pathé faits divers* is the first newsreel produced for general distribution. A British daily predecessor called *Day by Day* was shown only at London's Empire Theatre in Leicester Square.

One of the film news cameramen at work, sketched by a journalist.

harles Pathé defies George Eastman

New York, 16 March
merging from the recent interna-onal congress held by film industry xecutives, Charles Pathé has decid-d on the course which he must ollow in the future. He will chal-enge the virtual monopoly currently njoyed by George Eastman and the merican Eastman Kodak Compa-y. Pathé is determined to produce is own supply of film stock to eplace that of Eastman who has, up ntil now, provided most of the film sed by European companies as well s by those in the United States. Having convinced the board members of his company of the value of investing in this new area – the expensive stock supplied by Kodak has clearly eaten into profits – he has already purchased the small Blair factory in England for this purpose. He has also been exploring the possibility of recycling or reusing old reels of discarded film by peeling off the layer of sensitive emulsion. Although the results thus far have not been of the very best quality, Pathé is determined to pursue his new course, come what may, effectively declaring war on the monopolistic practices of Eastman.

Film Art finds itself at the center of a storm

Paris, 15 June
In spite of having produced many remarkable films, the Film d'Art company founded by Paul Lafitte has run into serious financial difficulties. Since the last annual meeting, debts of about 80,000 francs have been declared and the outlook is extremely grave. (Charles Pathé's position is not clear, and he has not yet offered to bail out the company.) Film d'Art will have produced the impressive total of 26 films by the end of this year, but Paul Lafitte has now been replaced by dramatist Paul Gavault as company head.

"Le Film d'Art"
LA TOSCA
Interprètes:
Mme CÉCILE SOREL, de la Comédie Française
MM. LE BARGY, de la Comédie Française
ALEXANDRE, de la Comédie Française
MOSNIER, de l'Odéon

Wilbur Wright links flying to the cinema

Pau, 22 March
The Radios Society, founded in August 1907 by Clément Maurice and Félix Mesguich, has signed a contract with the famous aviator Wilbur Wright, whose heavier-than-air machine *Flyer* made the very first powered flight in December 1903. Last September Mesguich exclusively filmed Wright's flights from a race course near Le Mans, which created quite a sensation in France. Wright was also filmed receiving the Aviation Commission's prize for having stayed airborne for over an hour and a half. At Pau, on the little airfield at Pont-Long, Mesguich has just completed an astonishing film. After giving a demonstration flight for King Edward VII, Wright suggested that he take Mesguich aloft. The intrepid cameraman accepted the invitation and strapped the camera to one of the flying machine's wings, ensuring that the crank was within reach of his hand. Wright shouted, "Let's go!" and the motor burst into life while Mesguich hung on to his camera. The ground fell away. On the horizon the Pyrenees seemed to pitch and roll. With a thumping heart Mesguich cranked the camera. After a three-minute flight Wright gently landed and skidded to a halt. The numbed Mesguich had shot over 100 feet of film. He is the first to film from an aeroplane in flight.

The machine used by the famous American aviator to break several records.

Important film company opens in New York

New York, 14 April
Thomas Edison's formation of his film industry cartel toward the end of last year does not appear to have frightened off the independents. On the contrary, the independent sector continues to grow, its most important new addition being the New York Motion Picture Company. Founded by Adam Kessel Jr. and Charles Baumann, who had previously run the Empire Film Exchange, together with cameraman Fred Balshofer, the new company's offices are located at 426 Sixth Avenue. They have already begun shooting their first film, *Disinherited Son's Loyalty*, which is due to be released next month. Apparently, when the three men met over dinner to set up their new business, they had not yet decided on a name or trademark for their production arm. Then Kessel spotted an American buffalo on the $10 bill, and Bison Films was born. Also known as "Bison" Life Motion Pictures, the new logo fits in well with plans to include many Westerns among their future productions.

New York Motion Picture Corporation

Hollywood gives a welcome to filmmakin

Open Californian spaces bathed in sunlight on the road to Hollywood.

Los Angeles, 1 November
The sleepy town surrounded by orange groves in the northern suburbs of Los Angeles seems likely to become a more lively place if an assumption can be made by the interest shown in it by filmmakers. They have already been spotted in the area, and many popular films have been shot here by crews from New York. So far the most famous is Kalem's *The Count of Monte Cristo*, adapted from Dumas' famous novel, in which director Francis Boggs cast a hypnotist found in a local fairground as the count. The film was released in New York and then around the country at the beginning of 1908 and has been such a popular and critical success that producer William Selig has decided to return to California to make more films. This will also have the happy by-product of putting a great deal of distance between Kalem and Edison, whose demands are becoming increasingly unbearable. Last May Francis Boggs and his team once again traveled to Hollywood for the filming of the new *In the Sultan's Power*. This time the leading role has been entrusted to a well-known actor, Hobart Bosworth, a Broadway star who was forced to leave the stage after temporarily losing his voice. Initially a bit reluctant to cast his lot with the cinema, Bosworth is now extremely happy with the new medium. He has reconciled himself to working conditions far removed from those he enjoyed on Broadway. Compromises include improvised sets, inexperienced leading ladies, few if any creature comforts.

Nevertheless, Selig sees a great f ture for filmmaking in Californi Now in his forties, Selig, who like to be called Colonel, is a vetera showman. A former magician, h toured with a successful minstr show before moving into the fledg ling movie business in 1896. Selig' base is in Chicago, but today see the opening of a new Selig studi and California's first, on the site of Chinese laundry in Hollywoo Meanwhile, Colonel Selig can bas in the runaway success of hi studio's recent *Hunting Big Game i Africa*, an exploitation of Theodor Roosevelt's safari. The ingeniou Selig re-created the African jungl on his Chicago lot, using a mang hired lion, some local blacks wh played natives and an actor wh impersonated Roosevelt.

Hobart Bosworth, former stage acto and producer, is one of the screen' new popular breed, the cowboy.

he rise and rise of Broncho Billy Anderson

characteristically tense moment for tough cowboy Broncho Billy Anderson.

iles, 30 December
inema's cowboy hero G.M. Anrson is about to assume a new ersona in the name of of Broncho illy, based on the character in a eter B. Kyne story, *Broncho Billy id the Baby*. The film will be called *roncho Billy's Redemption.* The urly Anderson is already one of nema's bright new stars. Born lax Aronson in Little Rock, Arkans, in March 1882, he was briefly a aveling salesman before trying his ck as an actor in New York using e stage name Gilbert M. Andern. While working as a male model 1902, he was hired by the Edison udio to play the lead in a one-reeler irected by Edwin S. Porter, *The lesssenger Boy's Mistake.* A year ter Anderson played several parts Porter's trail-blazing Western, *he Great Train Robbery*. He was originally cast as the outlaw leader but was disqualified by the fact that he could not ride. On the first day of filming he parted company with his horse – and the role of the outlaw leader! In 1907, after stints of writing, directing and acting at Vitagraph and Selig, Anderson went into partnership with George K. Spoor, the operator of a big nickelodeon chain. Together they formed the Essanay Company (after the first letters of their last names) which was originally based in Chicago. However, at this point Anderson was now more comfortable in the saddle, and he soon began filming Westerns in Colorado and comedy shorts with Ben Turpin in California. He is currently based in California, at Niles. Appropriately for a producer of Westerns, Essanay's trademark is an Indian in a war bonnet.

roncho Billy displays the gentler side of his nature with the fair sex.

A great comic talent for the French cinema

One of Max Linder's successes, in Louis Gasnier's ***The Life of Punch***.

Vincennes, 31 December
Following a difficult debut, Max Linder has become one of the most flourishing stars of the French comedy school and is now one of the best known performers in Pathé's troupe. Born in 1883, Linder, who was mad about theater, left high school to study drama and was soon acting on the Bordeaux stage. He then left his native Gironde to tackle the Paris Conservatoire, where he failed three successive exams. But thanks to his friend Adrien Caillard, the young and ambitious comedian was hired by the Ambigu Theatre, under his real name of Gabriel-Maximilien Leuvielle, playing supporting parts in melodramas. The Ambigu has provided Pathé studios with a great number of its actors over the years.

Max Linder was then taken on by Ferdinand Zecca and paid 20 francs a day on his debut. It was in July, 1905 that Linder appeared for the first time in front of the cameras, in *A Schoolboy's First Day Out*, directed by Louis Gasnier. The film attracted attention, as did *The Life of Punch* two years later, yet they still failed to launch Linder. Thus he continued to work on stage for three years, using his real name in the theater and his pseudonym for the screen. Eventually, at the end of 1907, one of Pathé's comic actors, René Gréhan, decided to go over to Eclair. Max Linder replaced him and put on the costume of a dandy which Gréhan had worn. The little comedian had finally found his personal style. With his striped trousers and morning coat, his top hat, his gloves and cane, Linder appeared in *A Skater's Debut* directed by Louis Gasnier. Ferdinand Zecca judged the film so mediocre that he preferred to postpone its release. However, the films that followed, directed by Gasnier and also by Georges Monca, found favor with the public at the beginning of the year. Linder played leading roles in all of them, dressed in diverse garb: an old man in *The Duel of a Shortsighted Man*, a Parisian tough in *A Cinematographic Show*, and even a young girl in *A Romantic Mademoiselle*. It was then that the actor adopted his permanent image – the elegant and worldly, idle dandy and woman chaser. *Don't Kiss Your Maid*, *The Mother-in-Law's False Teeth* and *The Barometer of Faithfulness* were great successes. Linder, small and delicate in spite of his athletic torso, has at last gained glory.

Dandy Max in search of a character.

Birth of an Industry

In 1895 the Lumière brothers held the first exhibitions of films to paying customers in the Indian Room at the Grand Café in Paris. Audiences, unprepared for the illusion of cinema, fled in panic as the screen was slowly filled by a train trundling into a station. *Arrival of the Train in the Ciotat Station* was baldly titled, but its locomotive was pulling behind it the infant film industry.

Five years later, at the Paris Exhibition of 1900, the industry was entering its adolescence. On display were color films tinted by hand; sound films in which the great actor Coquelin declaimed from *Cyrano de Bergerac*, his voice haphazardly synchronized on a cylindrical phonograph record; a screen 53-feet high and 70-feet wide on to which were projected spectacular scenes; and a Cinéorama that used 11 projectors to show a 360-degree image photographed from a balloon. The audience, who were standing on the roof of the drum which housed the projectors, must have felt as if they themselves were being transported in a giant balloon whose canopy swelled above them.

These modern marvels were harbingers of things to come: Technicolor, the talkies and wide-screen cinema. But in 1900, ambition outran technical development. The big screen came down in a storm, and the Cinéorama's 11 projectors generated so much heat that they violated fire regulations.

Until the outbreak of World War I in August 1914, the French led the way in film. The early 1900s saw the industrialization of filmmaking and, in 1898, Georges Méliès, the former magician and great pioneer, opened the first truly professional film studio at Montreuil near Paris. Here, in a large glasshouse, he created his cinema of illusion, displaying amazing special effects and trick photography in such films as *Voyage to the Moon* and *The Conquest of the Pole*. Gaumont studios in Paris arose around another great glasshouse, expanded by 1912 into a complex of offices, laboratories and factories, producing everything needed to make film. Even more lavish were the Pathé studios at Vincennes, run by Ferdinand Zecca.

Charles Pathé, a shrewd French businessman who had made his first fortune charging fairground crowds a fee to listen to early phonograph records, understood instinctively the dynamics and potential of the film business. He created a monopoly of production, distribution and exhibition at home, while simultaneously opening branches in every part of the world where films were shown. By 1908 Pathé was an international empire, distributing twice as much film in the U.S. as the entire American film industry. Pathé introduced the serial 'cliffhanger' to American audiences, combining the release of the weekly episode with syndicated publication in the local press. French performers had, in fact, an important impact on American film. The short films of the diffident and dandified comedian Max Linder prompted American producers to tap their native music-hall and vaudeville talent and influenced the early career of Charles Chaplin.

French pre-eminence was undermined by the outbreak of the Great War. Export markets in Europe were suddenly closed, with materials and manpower diverted into the war effort. As the French retreated, the film industry in the United States, uninvolved in the bloodletting until 1917, moved in to fill the vacuum.

Until about 1900, American motion pictures were mostly straightforward records of stage acts of the day, usually screened in vaudeville theaters. In 1902 America's first true movie house was opened on South Main Street in Los Angeles by Thomas Talley, a former cowboy. His Electric Theater promised 'An Hour's Amusement and Genuine Fun for 10 Cents Admission.' The Electric Theater was then followed by thousands of 'nickelodeons', a term first used in 1905 which stemmed from the five-cent price of admission. The nickelodeons sprang up in small stores, ballrooms and disused halls all over America. By 1908 there were about 9,000 of them providing escapist fare for millions of working-class Americans, particularly immigrants from Southern and Central Europe whose lack of English naturally discouraged them from theatergoing.

The mushrooming of these nickelodeons revolutionized the organization of the American film industry. Previously, exhibitors bought films outright from the manufacturers on the East Coast, or from local agents, at a standard price of about 10 cents a foot. Audiences, however, tired of the films long before the prints wore out. The answer was the 'film exchange', the first of which was opened in San Francisco in 1902 by Herbert and Harry Miles. The new film rental business, full of fly-by-night operators, was no place for the commercially squeamish. And it was in the typically American rough and tumble of this world that many of the industry's future moguls cut their teeth.

Carl Laemmle at Universal with a group of his actors and directors.

They were immigrants, too, most of them Jews from the ghettos of Central Europe. Above all, they were entrepreneurs searching f ground-floor entry into a busin which required little initial inve ment. Motion pictures present them with a perfect opportunity.

The most durable of them all w Adolph Zukor, who died in 1976 the ripe old age of 103. Zukor car to America from Hungary when was 16 years old, with $40 sewn in the lining of his waistcoat. As wi many Jewish immigrants, he we into the garment business, learni English while selling furs. In 1903 went into the amusement arca business, a diminutive man in a fu collared coat. Later Zukor formed partnership with another furri Marcus Loew, but struck out on h own as a showman and distribut in 1912. Zukor had long ponder how best to entice into the ciner the middle classes to whom he ha once sold furs. The one and two-re films churned out on breakne shooting schedules by compani like Biograph and Vitagraph we seen as shoddy products, profitabl but fit only for the amusement of t masses. Zukor had other ideas. 1912 he distributed the hour-lo French Film d'Art production *Queen Elizabeth*, starring Sara Bernhardt. The film was leased on States Rights basis, and the middl class audiences it drew provided t clinching argument in the battle convince the movie business that t American public would accept 'fe ture' films of far greater length tha the standard one and two-reelers.

The Film d'Art re-creations French classical theater were ine entertainments doomed to early e tinction, but the success of *Quee Elizabeth* encouraged Zukor to for a production company to film 'F mous Players in Famous Plays'. H hired Edwin S. Porter to duplica the Film d'Art approach by bringir Broadway stars to the screen in film such as *The Prisoner of Zenda*, sta ring James Hackett, and *The Cou of Monte Cristo*, with James O'Nei The resulting feature-length film were stilted and stagy, but the ne audiences they attracted led to th construction of more lavishly a pointed theaters to accommoda them. It was left to D.W. Griffit enthused by spectacular Italia epics like *Quo Vadis?* (1912) an *Cabiria* (1913), to exploit fully *he Birth of a Nation* (1915), the ossibilities opened up by the mass-ıdience appeal of the feature-ngth film.

In 1903 the four young Warner rothers opened a 99-seat store cin-na in Newcastle, Pennsylvania. arry Warner had been born in oland and his brothers in a succes-on of American cities as the family ɔllowed their traveling-salesman ather. The Warner brothers moved ext into distribution and by 1912 ere making their own films. Carl aemmle was already 40 when he ent into the picture business. Born ito a middle-class Jewish family Germany in 1867, he came to merica when he was 17. In antici-ation of a quick profit, in 1906 e opened a nickelodeon, the White 'ront Theater, on Chicago's West ide. Thereafter, he made up for lost me, expanding rapidly into distri-ution to service the Midwest chain e created. This brought him into onflict with the Motion Pictures 'atent Company (popularly known s the Edison Trust), an association f the leading American production ompanies and the U.S. branches of ıe French majors. By pooling their atents claims and assigning them to dison, and by declaring that no one /as entitled to produce, distribute r exhibit films in the U.S. without heir license, these companies aimed ɔ sew up the film business and drive ut the independents who chal-enged their monopoly.

Laemmle was one of the leaders f the crusade against the Trust. Vrits flew in all directions, smear ampaigns were waged and violence lared. Amid the tumult Laemmle egan to produce his own pictures nder the banner of the Indepen-lent Motion Picture Company of merica (IMP), founded in 1909. oon, an amalgamation with a few maller companies meant that he /as presiding over his own little film mpire. In large part that empire vas created by the emergence of the tar system, in which Laemmle layed a crucial role. In the early lays of cinema the corporation awyers and businessmen who fi-anced the film companies aimed o produce a cheap, standardized roduct. Preserving the anonymity of film actors was a simple way of eeping salaries, and overheads, lown. In this they were helped by he actors, many of whom regarded ilm work as a last resort. When the 'oung Mary Pickford expressed horror at working in 'the flickers', her mother reassured her that "It's only to tide us over."

This attitude changed as the public grew ever more fascinated with film. Exhibitors, and the entrepreneurs who ran the film exchanges, quickly grasped that the familiarity of popular players was an asset. In April 1909, in *The Moving Picture World*, an early trade magazine, Ben Turpin appeared under his own name in an article describing the life of a 'Moving Picture Comedian'. The corpulent comic John Bunny and the ersatz cowboy Broncho Billy Anderson starred in their own films. (Bunny was already an established stage performer, and Anderson owned his own production company). However, the most popular actress at Biograph, Florence Lawrence, was billed simply as 'The Biograph Girl'.

& S.L.
11488
8920

Helen Holmes in ***The Hazards of Helen*** *(1914), made for the Kalem Co.*

In 1910 Lawrence fell out with Biograph and into the welcoming arms of Laemmle's IMP. He then planted a fictitious news story that Lawrence had been killed in a streetcar accident in St. Louis. This was immediately followed by an advertisement in the trade press – headlined WE NAIL A LIE – in which the blame for the story was laid at the door of IMP's competitors. Lawrence was triumphantly produced in St. Louis to make the first personal appearance by a film star. She was mobbed by a huge crowd of fans, who tore the buttons off her coat. A star was born.

The stars rapidly moved center stage. In 1913 Adolph Zukor told Mary Pickford's mother, "if feature pictures succeed, we expect to pay according to the drawing power of the box office." By 1915 Pickford was on a salary of $10,000 a week and her drawing power was the foundation of the evolving Zukor empire which, in a series of complex deals, became Paramount studios. Stars like Pickford and Chaplin became the collateral on which the film companies could borrow huge sums of money. If you could not find a star, you created one. William Fox was another German-Jewish immigrant who had made a fortune in the film exchange business, beaten off the Edison Trust, and gone into film production in 1915 as head of the Fox Film Corporation. It was Fox who transformed a dumpy stage actress named Theodosia de Coppet, born Goodman, into the screen's first 'vamp' and million-dollar star, Theda Bara.

The growth of the star system was accompanied by the shift of filmmaking from the East Coast to California. Films had been made in and around Los Angeles from 1907, when the Selig company of Chicago shot *The Count of Monte Cristo* on Santa Monica Beach and in an improvised studio in the back of a Chinese laundry. The attractions for filmmakers were twofold: the pleasant climate and varied scenery, and California's considerable distance from the reach of the Edison Trust. Many films were shot in Hollywood, a sleepy suburb of Los Angeles surrounded by orange groves. In 1913 an ambitious young director arrived in Hollywood to shoot a film version of a popular Western novel, *The Squaw Man*. Named Cecil B. DeMille, he was a stage actor and playwright who had formed a partnership with Jesse L. Lasky and Lasky's brother-in-law Samuel Goldfish (later Goldwyn). Disappointed with the locations that had been chosen out in Arizona, DeMille and his company boarded a train and rode to the end of the line, where they stumbled on to Hollywood. There, they shot *The Squaw Man*, the picture that helped to put Hollywood on the map.

In 1912 Carl Laemmle's IMP had metamorphosed into the Universal Film Manufacturing Company, later known simply as Universal. On 15 March 1915, amid a blaze of publicity, Laemmle used a golden key to open the new Universal studios built at a cost of $165,000 on the north side of the Hollywood Hills.

Hollywood was now a factory town producing dreams for sale. The money stayed on the East Coast but the films were made on the West Coast. In 1915 alone over 250 pictures, most of them two-reelers and serials, poured out of the studios at Universal City. Later this same year, after a long legal battle, the Edison Trust bit the dust. Meanwhile the power of the stars continued to grow apace. The Famous Players were now more important than the Famous Plays. Mary Pickford's status was such that she was able to force Zukor to set up a subsidiary, Artcraft, initially for her own productions, and triple the rates he charged exhibitors for her films. In 1915, alarmed by this trend, the industry's three leading independent producer-directors, Mack Sennett, Thomas Ince and D.W. Griffith, formed Triangle, which offered them the opportunity to make films free from what they saw as the tyranny of the stars.

The Triangle company proved the forerunner of United Artists, which was founded in 1919 by Mary Pickford, Douglas Fairbanks, Charlie Chaplin and D.W. Griffith, with the object of making and distributing their own films (and the quality product of others). This move reflected its founders' suspicion of the growing corporate control of the film business pioneered by Zukor. Under his aggressive leadership, Paramount became a force in the three branches of motion pictures – production, distribution and exhibition – consolidating the vertical integration of the studio system which would emerge in the 1920s.

ROBIN CROSS

1910

London, 1 January
The Cinematograph Act of Great Britain comes into force today. Designed to protect cinemas from fire resulting from the inflammable nature of film, the Act demands the provision of a separate, fire-resistant projection box and buckets of sand in auditoriums.

Paris, 16 January
Edison has released *Faust*, adapted from Goethe, and directed by J. Searle Dawley. Copies of the 302-metre film are to be sold at 1.25 francs per metre.

Los Angeles, 20 January
D.W. Griffith has arrived in California with the Biograph troupe. He is here to complete the filming of *The Newlyweds*, a comedy he started shooting in New York.

Paris, 30 January
Gaumont have completed editing of a toned and tinted copy of *André Chénier*, "the life of a poet who died during the Revolution," made by Louis Feuillade.

Paris, 1 February
An auction sale of Pathé Frères cameras and 500 films is being held at the Hotel Drouot.

New York, 10 February
In an attempt to counter the Independents, the MPPC is trying to control regional distributors by creating its own distribution company, The General Film Company.

Paris, 12 February
Vitagraph are distributing *A Midsummer Night's Dream*, a 303-metre film adapted from the works of Shakespeare by J. Stuart Blackton.

Paris, 12 February
The firm Raleigh and Robert are distributing a new series done in six episodes, *Dr. Phantom*, directed by Victorin Jasset for Eclair.

Paris, 19 February
Louis Feuillade has undertaken a series of biblical films for Gaumont. The first of these, *Balthazar's Feast*, is now showing.

Paris, 28 February
Gaumont, like Pathé, has stopped selling films. From now on, they are only to be available for rent.

Rome, 7 March
El Cid, adapted from the play by Corneille and produced by Mario Caserini, Cines' specialist in period films, has had a public screening.

Neuilly, 27 March
Henri Pouctal is currently filming an adaptation of Goethe's *Werther*, at the Film d'Art studios. André Brulé plays the title role.

Paris, 2 April
George Eastman has put the Eclair Company in charge of his main continental warehouse. The unexposed Eastman films will be stored at the Epinay factory.

Paris, 23 April
From now on, all films supplied to France by Vitagraph will be on the new film from Eastman-Kodak that is non-inflammable.

Paris, 30 April
Eclair has created the Actors' and Writers' Association to compete with Film d'Art. It has released *Barberine*, by Emile Chautard, a former actor from the Odéon and artistic director of the Association.

New York, 16 May
Charles Pathé is making films here for the local market, under the production banner Pathé-American. The first of these, *The Girl from Montana*, starring a young blonde named Pearl White, opens today.

London, 20 May
Cameramen from Pathé, Gaumont, Eclipse, Raleigh and Robert were in the capital to film King Edward VII's funeral today.

Marienbad, 1 June
Count Alexander Kollovrath has created the Sasha-Film company, at Horni Plana, near Marienbad.

Paris, June
Franchise owners for the Enterprise Optical Company from Chicago are launching the Motiograph projector. The advertisements claim that it produces a perfectly steady picture and has 40 percent more luminosity than all other machines.

Berlin, 3 June
City cinema owners are protesting against the performance tax being considered by the mayor.

France, 18 June
The American film company Bat Films, whose emblem reflects the name, has set up business in Lyon.

Paris, 18 June
Gaumont is launching a series of art films to compete with Film d'Art. The first work is *Le Pater*, produced by Louis Feuillade.

New York, 2 July
A fire has devastated Vitagraph's studios. Numerous negatives have been destroyed.

Paris, July
The Optique Company here has launched Multicolor, a new process which adds color to films during projection.

Paris, 15 August
The 19-year-old journalist Louis Delluc is contributing articles to *Comœdia Illustré*, a glossy weekly of Parisian life, run by Maurice de Brunoff. His personal love of the theater is reflected in his articles.

Berlin, 20 August
The UT network has just opened its second cinema on the Unter den Linden, Berlin's main thoroughfare.

St. Petersburg, 21 August
Release of *The Life and Death of Pushkin* filmed by Vassili Goncharov and produced by Gaumont.

Paris, 27 August
Release of *The Samouraï's Punishment*, which presents actors from the Imperial Theatre, produced by Pathé's Japanese branch as part of the Japanese Art Film series.

Paris, 1 October
Pathé has edited a film in its "art series", *la Tragique aventure de Robert le Taciturne, duc d'Aquitaine* (*The Tragic Adventure of Robert the Taciturn, Duke of Aquitaine*), directed by Ferdinand Zecca and Henri Andréani.

Paris, 29 October
Pathé has launched a big advertising campaign for its new comic character Rigadin who is played by Charles Petit-Demange, known in the theater as Prince. The film, *Rigadin va dans le grand monde* (*Rigadin goes into the Wide World*), directed by Georges Monca, is now available.

France, 10 November
The press has announced tha Pathé's star Max Linder has unde gone an emergency operation fo appendicitis. The actor is reporte to have said to his surgeon, "I'm no afraid... After all, I'm used to bein under lights!"

Meudon, 12 November
Screening of No. 4 of Gaumont' weekly "Newsreel" series which wa started last month. The sculpto August Rodin, who has just cele brated his 70th birthday and agree to be filmed at home, is featured i the newsreel.

Paris, 26 November
Opening of the Cinérama-Théâtre a 83 avenue de la Grande-Armée, ru by a pioneer of the cinema industry Gabriel Kayser. The screening of Gaumont newsreel was followed b Pathé's *l'Inventeur* (*The Inventor*) directed by Michel Carré.

Korea, 31 December
Opening of Seoul's first cinema.

BIRTHS

Chicago, 28 February
Vincente Minnelli

Tokyo, 23 March
Akira Kurosawa

Bordeaux, 23 June
Jean Anouilh

France, 14 July
Annabella (Suzanne Charpentier)

Tokyo, 15 July
Satsuo Yamamoto

France, 8 September
Jean-Louis Barrault

Belgium, 24 September
Jean Servais

Japan, 28 November
Kinuyo Tanaka

Italy, 11 December
Carlo Ponti

The popular 'Biograph girl' has been revealed by producer Carl Laemml to be Florence Lawrence. She ha been lured away by Laemmle to join his production company IMP.

Bousum
S.F.

Biblical epic shown in four parts

New York, 2 February
In recent years Vitagraph has produced a number of split-reelers with Biblical subjects, but it has taken a great commercial gamble with a new film, *The Life of Moses*. It is reported that the company has lavished $50,000 on a five-reel epic, shown in four parts, which advance publicity proclaims is a "reverent and dignified portrayal of the Wonderful Story of Moses revealed by the Greatest Triumph of Photographic and Mechanical Art ever achieved." And lovers of spectacle are promised "The Miracle of the Red Sea. A $10,000 Water Scene." To ensure the film's religious and historical accuracy, Vitagraph engaged a clerical celebrity, the Reverend Madison C. Peters, to write the script for the first reel and advise on the authenticity of the entire project. Although various clergymen have expressed their doubts about cinematic representations of Bible stories, *Moving Picture World* comments that *The Life of Moses* is "a graphic reproduction of the main events in the life of Moses, corresponding closely to the conception which has been inculcated in those who have attended church and Sunday school."

Sound scenes are making the screen sing

Paris, 5 March
"Toreador, on guard, a dark eye scrutinizes you!" At the moment, Gaumont phonoscènes are showing *Carmen*, a sound film projected by the Chronomégaphone, the apparatus on which Léon Gaumont has been working since 1902. It contains the toreador's aria that's just 83 metres long. Not only *Carmen*, but also *Faust, Mireille, la Traviata* and *The Barber of Seville* have been adapted by Gaumont. His catalogue caters to all tastes: *la Tonkinoise, la Marseillaise, O Sole Mio, The Crucifix, le Rire du nègre* and the most celebrated songs by Mayol (*Viens Poupoule*), by Dranem (*le Trou de mon quai*) and by Polin (*le Frotteur de la colonelle*). Since 1906, the volume of sound has been improved by Elgéphone on the air as well as on phonograph records by amplifying the sound using compressed air. People at the fairs are now singing: "The newest attraction – I'll take you there Bobonne – is the Chronomégaphone!"

Bizet's Carmen is the tragic heroine of this phonoscène by Alice Guy.

Plans to preserve early French films

Paris, 27 February
What has become of the thousan of films which have been made the last 15 years? For the most pa they have been mutilated, disperse lost and melted down. The week *Ciné Journal* has urgently demand the establishment of a Cinemat graphothèque – a copyright registr tion and storage place for films ju like the one for books at the Natio al Library. "What can one say abo the negligence of our contemp raries? They are not concerned th the most thrilling spectacles of the lives have disappeared without trace." It's not a new idea. In 18 the Pole, Boleslaw Matuszewsk requested the foundation of a "historic cinematographic library" but it failed to catch on. Manufa turers and cameramen continue massacre their old films; the larg companies are content to depos scenarios, with only a sample of dozen stills in the National Librar In the United States, by contrast, storehouse for films exists in th Library of Congress where the d posited copies are printed on pape to avoid risks of fire. The pape prints also serve a legal purpose i case of counterfeit.

Frankenstein's monster comes to life

New York, 18 March
The Edison studio has produced a remarkable adaptation of Mary Shelley's macabre tale, *Frankenstein or the Modern Prometheus*. Written and directed by J. Searle Dawley, the film reinterprets rather than condenses the original, and the makers claim that they have attempted to "eliminate all the actually repulsive situations and to concentrate on the mystic and psychological problems that are to be found in this weird tale." Augustus Phillips plays Frankenstein, a young medical student whose chemical attempts to create a perfect human being produce a hideous monster, played with great relish by Charles Ogle. A veteran of the stage, Ogle has created his own makeup for the part which echoes Shelley's monstrous creation, with a ghastly chalk-white face under a wild mass of wispy hair and hands that clutch like talons. While the monster struggles with Frankenstein, he catches his reflection in a mirror and, sickened by the sight, stumbles into the night. The film reaches a terrifying climax when the monster returns to attack Frankenstein's bride-to-be, played by Mary Fuller, in her bedroom. Her agonized screams bring Frankenstein running to the rescue, only for him to find his own image in the mirror replaced by that of the horrible creature he has created. But the power of love ensures that the monster's image fades away to restore the chastened scientist to the arms of his beloved, so ending the film with an embrace. This movie is crammed with clever special effects, particularly the scene in which the half-formed monster rises from a bubbling cauldron in Frankenstein's laboratory, growing ever larger as it acquires its crude flailing arms and its ghostly face.

Actor Charles Ogle is transformed into the monster by brilliant makeup.

.W. Griffith assured a place in the sun

·iffith, now a celebrated director.

ew York, 14 April

avid Wark Griffith and his famous ım of actors and technicians have turned today from filming in sun-enched California to the studios ˙ American Mutoscope and Bio-aph Company in New York. Dur-g this four-month working vaca-ɔn, Griffith's ensemble shot 25 ms in a list of locations that gives se to dreams: Los Angeles, Santa Ionica, Pasadena, Glendale and e Sierra Madre, to name but a few. he group traveled in train coaches arked "Biograph Special", and ey each had $3 a day to spend in e dining car. The original back-ounds inspired the actors who ere invited on the trip. Mary Pick-rd and her brother Jack, Marion eonard, Linda Arvidson (Griffith's ife), Blanche Sweet and Mack ennett, to mention only the most famous. It was a happy company en route and a happy company once all had settled down in Los Angeles. There they rented a studio at the corner of Grand Avenue and Washington Street, which contained two small dressing rooms for the men and similar facilities for the women across the lot. When large numbers of extras were required, they were provided with a tent for dressing. A loft nearby was rented for laboratory space. At Santa Monica and at Port Los Angeles, they made *The Unchanging Sea*, a variation on the Enoch Arden story, featuring Linda Arvidson Griffith. The penultimate film on this first Californian trip was a version of Helen Hunt Jackson's *Ramona*, in which Mary Pickford portrayed the Indian maiden. *Over Silent Paths*, about a lone miner and his daughter making the trip to California by prairie schooner, was shot in the San Fernando Valley. All the members of the company enjoyed the Californian stay and expressed their hopes that they could return. It is nearly two years since Griffith first presided over the artistic fortunes of the celebrated New York company. Biograph had fallen on hard times when Griffith joined the ranks as scenarist, but his energy and initiative gave it a new lease on life, and it earned him the chance to direct his first motion picture, *The Adventures of Dollie*. Made in 1908, it was an immediate success. Since then Griffith has directed more than 200 films, and his Californian experience seems to have motivated him even further.

An exquisite detail from *Romance of a Butterfly*, which has been made by the English pioneer of stop-motion photography, Percy Smith.

A personal vision of the French Revolution

A scene from De Morlhon's colorful film about France's ill-fated queen.

Paris, 10 June

Charles Pathé's company has been on location shooting its new film, *The Secret Adventure of Marie Antoinette*, directed by Camille de Morlhon. This comedy-drama is almost entirely colored by stencil, and represents the aristocratic De Morlhon's personal view of the French Revolution. Introduced to the cinema by Edmond Benoît-Lévy, De Morlhon has quickly carved out an important niche at Pathé under the wing of Ferdinand Zecca. He handles all the different genres with ease and brings a characteristic vigor to each new project.

ANDRÉ CHÉNIER
JOUÉ PAR:
MM. R. ALEXANDRE, DE LA COMÉDIE FRANÇAISE
ET LE MIME GEORGES WAGUE
Gaumont

A new lease of life for German production

Berlin, 1 May

The German cinema is struggling to wake from a long sleep. In recent years it has been dominated by foreign imports, mostly from America, France and Italy. Now Paul Davidson has announced the formation of the Projection Aktien Gesellschaft Union (PAGU), the aim of which is to gather together all of the small production companies which are hostile to the monopolistic ambitions of the German industrialist Von Schack. Last April Von Schack founded FIAG (Film Industrie Anonym Gesellschaft) with the aim of uniting all the German exhibitors in a single organization. This move is likely to increase the number of foreign films flooding the German market, and Von Schack's plans have met with widespread opposition from the industry whose spokesman, Davidson, recently took over the UT circuit as well as a big cinema in Berlin's Alexanderplatz which holds 1,000 spectators. PAGU has now been given the unconditional support of the Bayerische Anilin Aktien Gesellschaft fur Anilin Fabrikation (AGFA), which is also fighting hard against American opposition in the form of the powerful Kodak company.

The house of Pathé bids for autonomy

Vincennes, 31 August
The George Eastman company in America has lost its monopoly on the production of celluloid film stock. In France, Charles Pathé, the head of the company that bears his name, is constructing a giant factory which will occupy 30,000 square metres and will be equipped to produce and process raw film stock, both positive and negative. Once it is completed, the factory, situated in Vincennes, intends to have the ability to meet the whole world's demand for raw film – certainly a victory for Pathé's famous cockerel to crow about.

Young stage actor Abel Gance makes his screen debut as Molièr

Paris, 10 September
The young man interpreting the part of the writer-actor in Léonce Perret's *Molière* is called Abel Gance. He made his theatrical debut in Brussels in 1908, and on his return to Paris, played small parts at the Ambigu and at the Athénée, without ever achieving a breakthrough. One of the means of putting an end to his poverty occurred as follows: Gaumont and Pathé are always on the lookout for original scenarios. So Gance sold ideas to both companies and to Film d'Art, and even agreed to pose in front of the camera. "The cinema really interests me. In addition, one can earn money," Gance noted ironically.

Abel Gance (standing, background right) plays the title role in Perret's film.

Pathé's life of Christ enhanced by color

Paris, 28 August
The growth of the Pathé Company has been astonishing. From its first ventures into production, the company has expanded its film activities worldwide. Not only is it involved in production, distribution and exhibition, with major investments in the manufacture of raw film stock and technical equipment, it is the largest motion picture corporation in the world, and still growing. Earlier this year Pathé released its first picture made in America and filmed at its newly-completed and extremely well equipped studio at Bound Brook, New Jersey. Thus it is no surprise to learn that it is in the forefront of introducing color into films. In the years prior to 1908, Pathé experimented with hand-tinted coloring of its films but thereafter concentrated on developing its own newly improved *Pathécolor* process. As carried out at the factory at Vincennes, where over 100 young women are employed as colorists, the technique involves the use of positive prints, one for each color. The area to be tinted is then cut from each, forming a series of stencils for every frame in the film. When the dyes are applied, the results are quite stunning, as can be seen in Pathé's new, colored version of an ever-popular subject, that of the life of Christ.

Raw power from Denmark's Asta Nielsen

Copenhagen, 12 September
The Danish film industry has a stunning new leading lady in the form of Asta Nielsen, star of *The Abyss*, which has been produced by the Kosmorama Company and directed by Nielsen's husband Peter Urban Gad. In her screen debut, Nielsen plays a piano teacher whose impetuous decision to abandon her fiance for a circus cowboy leads to heartbreak, murder and a descent into the moral abyss of the film's title. The daughter of a washerwoman, Nielsen first attended the children's school at the Royal Theatre in Copenhagen before making her stage debut at the age of 18. Her pallid beauty and blazing dark ey lend her an unusual emotional pov er in *The Abyss*, which has made big impression on the leading ligh of Danish theater. They had prev ously considered films merely lov class entertainment, but thanks t Nielsen's moving performance as fallen woman they have been co vinced of the artistic possibilities the new medium. When shown th film, Denmark's greatest comic a tor Olaf Poulsen began by makin jokes. He soon fell silent and, at th tragic conclusion, when Nielsen led away by the police after stabbin her lover to death, he was heard t mutter, "I'll be damned!"

An example of the effective tinted color used in this latest life of Christ.

Poul Reumert with Asta Nielsen, making her screen debut in ***The Abyss****.*

illy the Tomboy is good news for Alma

lma Taylor (right) and Chrissie White in ***Tilly the Tomboy Goes Boating.***

ondon, 19 September
he latest entry in the delightful Tilly" series, *Tilly the Tomboy Goes oating*, has just been released by e Hepworth Co. and depicts the rther comedic adventures of two ischievous schoolgirls who have a pecial knack for getting into – and ut of – trouble. Handled by director Lewis Fitzhamon, who obviously as a special gift both for comedy nd for working with young players, is series, first begun in 1908, has een tremendously successful. It has rned the young actresses who play e lead roles, Alma Taylor and hrissie White, into veritable stars f the British screen. The attractive nd talented Miss Taylor, in particur, must surely have a promising ture ahead of her. Appropriately nough, this comes in the same year that, across the Atlantic, a young Mary Pickford has emerged as the new leading actress for D.W. Griffith at Biograph, where she is known simply as "Little Mary", or as the "Biograph Girl". Meanwhile, in April producer Carl Laemmle succeeded in hiring the previous Biograph Girl Florence Lawrence to join his new Independent Motion Picture Company (IMP) and publicizing her name for the first time. It is clear that as the cinema develops and increases in poularity, new stars will emerge with special appeal to audiences. As Laemmle has recognized, moviegoers will want to know the names of their favorites, and the narrow-minded attitude of Edison's trust in concealing their names as far as possible, is obviously doomed to failure.

Méliès' Star Film company in difficulties

Montreuil, 30 November
Since the International Congress of Film Producers, Georges Méliès's Star Film company has gradually collapsed. Méliès, who had accepted the Congress presidency with such joy, found himself trapped by the decisions taken. He stopped the direct selling of his films and adopted the hiring-out system. The result has been total failure. His films no longer get distributed, and Méliès has had to slow down production little by little. In May last year, he was forced to sack some of his personnel. The Montreuil theater has fallen still. Not only have Méliès's productions suffered from a distribution problem, but also, thanks to the efforts of both Film d'Art and SCAGL, from a change in public taste. Fantasy films no longer sell. Méliès already belongs to the past with his papier maché decors and tricks. His style appears obsolete compared with what they are doing in the U.S. There, Méliès's brother Gaston has also given him cause to worry. The G. Méliès Manufacturing Company is spending no further money. With the profits, Gaston Méliès has decided to enlarge his company and will build a studio in Texas. Trouble between the two brothers has never been very far off. Incapable of remaining inactive, Georges is again touring with his magic shows and will perform at the Alhambra before leaving to shoot new films in Belgium and in Italy.

Little star twinkles for Louis Feuillade

Little Anatole Clément Mary in another 'Bébé' film, ***Bébé's Find.***

Paris, 24 December
Gaumont is launching a series of "Bébé" comedy films directed by Louis Feuillade. The first, *Bébé Apache*, is already delighting cinema audiences and three more are being filmed. The title role is taken by little Anatole Clément Mary, who was born in 1905. This cheeky Parisian mite was discovered by Feuillade in the Gaumont studio on the rue des Alouettes. Bébé's father is one of Gaumont's stock company of actors. In the new series Bébé's mother is played by Renée Carl, one of Feuillade's stars, and his father is played by Paul Manson. Gaumont's precocious little find is proving a hit with French filmgoers and the series looks set for a long run.

Bébé Apache*, the first of the series.*

Gaumont melts the ice at the Hippodrome

Paris, 31 December
he Gaumont company has just acuired a huge theater, the Hipporome, on the place Clichy. Built in 900, the Hippodrome has been the nancial ruin of a succession of roprietors. The Société de Cinémas-Ialls, which attempted to transform he Hippodrome into a cinema, oon went bankrupt. It was then old to a company which opened a oller and ice skating rink in August 909. Gaumont was then brought in o provide regular film shows, a nove akin to inviting a wolf into the heepfold. Gaumont has now taken ver the Hippodrome.

HIPPODROME
HIPPO-PALACE

A hall beset by several misfortunes.

1911

Chicago, 12 January
Creation of the Majestic Motion Picture Company by Harry Aitken and John Freuler.

New York, 16 January
His Trust, part one of a film by D.W. Griffith, is now screening. Part two, *His Trust Fulfilled*, should come out in three days time. Griffith wanted them shown simultaneously, but Henry Marvin, the manager of Biograph, was against the idea.

Los Angeles, 31 January
Vitagraph has opened a film studio in California.

St. Petersburg, 16 January
Alexander Khanjonkov has released *The Kreutzer Sonata*, adapted from the novella by Leo Tolstoy. Ivan Mosjoukine takes the leading role.

Istanbul, 1 February
Léon Gaumont has opened a new branch of Comptoir-Ciné-Location, a rental firm for films produced and distributed by Gaumont. He already owns branches in Paris, Brussels and Cairo.

St. Petersburg, 2 February
The Demon, an adaptation by the Italian filmmaker Giovanni Vitrotti of Lermontov's work, produced by the Gloria company, is currently screening. Filming took place in the Tiflis studios in Georgia.

Paris, 4 February
Gaumont has released Léonce Perret's *Dans la vie* (*In the Midst of Life*). The film, a "poignantly emotional story," stars Perret himself, and Yvette Andreyor.

Paris, 17 February
Léon Gaumont has once more demonstrated the Chronophone to the Photographic Society. A film was projected during the session, and Mr. d'Arsonval explained how the invention worked, while a rooster let out a loud cock-a-doodle-do through the powerful Elgéphone.

New York, 25 February
The Vitagraph company has just released *A Tale of Two Cities*, adapted from the Charles Dickens novel and produced by J. Stuart Blackton and William Humphrey. The first three-reeler made by Vitagraph, each reel will be shown separately.

Paris, 4 March
Pathé, who is the French distributor for the Russian Drankov company's documentary about Tolstoy, has just released *Anna Karenina*. The film was produced by Pathé's Russian branch and used Russian actors who worked under the direction of Maurice André Maître.

France, 11 March
The Anti-Pornography League in Lille, La Maison de la Bonne Press, and Cardinal Coullié, the archbishop of Lyon, are leading a vigorous campaign against the cinema. In Paris, the league against licentiousness has asked audiences to whistle their disapproval during immoral films and to deface posters of a questionable nature.

Paris, 16 March
Cinema Rochechouart is presently screening Guiseppe De Liguoro's adaptation of Dante's *Inferno*.

Paris, 16 March
Gaumont's new talking film, *la Vie reconstituée*, is currently showing at the Olympia.

Paris, 18 March
The Geographical Society has presented the Alfred Molteni prize to Martel, the cameraman from Lion Films, for his shots of Abyssinia.

Paris, 1 April
The Jougla Company, manufacturers of film negative, has merged with the Lumière establishment.

Paris, 7 April
Itala Films is now distributing its major production, *The Fall of Troy*, by Giovanni Pastrone.

Prague, 1 May
The producer Antonin Pech has founded the Kinofa company.

Paris, 6 May
Italian films are flooding French screens. *La Jérusalem delivrée* by Enrico Guazzoni, adapted from Le Tasse, is now screening at La Cinès.

Paris, 20 May
Pathé has released a "social drama", *les Victimes de l'alcool* (*The Victims of Alcohol*) by Ferdinand Zecca (adapted from Zola's novel *l'Assommoir*) to compete with Gaumont's "Life as it really is" series.

New York, 14 June
Enoch Arden, a two-reel film from D.W. Griffith is now screening. The Biograph company has decided to show both parts at the same session.

Paris, 17 June
Ciné-Journal has disclosed that old films are sold off to boot makers. After a treatment with celluloid they are used to glaze high quality boots.

China, 30 June
The Imperial Government here has brought in regulations concerning the cinema industry: authorization must be obtained to open a theater, men and women must be seated apart, immoral films are forbidden and the last session has to finish before midnight.

Paris, 14 July
Film d'Art has released *Camille Desmoulins*, a color-tinted film produced by Henri Pouctal.

Paris, 1 August
Gaumont has launched its 35mm, metal, X series "projection box", equipped with all the latest technology and selling for 900 francs. Pathé is selling a similar machine, the No. 4 projection box, for 876 francs.

Paris, 19 August
Gaumont has released *la Fin de Paganini* (*The End of Paganini*), the script for which was purchased by Louis Feuillade from Abel Gance.

Copenhagen, 28 August
The new Danish company Kinografen has released *De Fire Djaevle* (*The Four Devils*) by Alfred Lind and Robert Dineson, two renegades from Nordisk.

New York, 30 August
The French production company Eclair has set up its first American branch here.

Hollywood, 2 October
David Horsley, the head of a New Jersey production company, has begun building a film studio here. The Nestor will be situated at the intersection of Sunset Boulevard and Gower Street.

Rome, 27 October
Release of Luggi Maggi's *Nozze d'oro* (*The Golden Wedding*), a gold medal winner at the World's Fair.

Paris, 10 November
First release of the 810-metre lon *Notre Dame de Paris*, a SCAGI Pathé production, an adaptatio from Victor Hugo's novel by Albe Capellani, with Stacia de Napie kowska and Henry Krauss playin the main parts.

Paris, 27 December
Abel Gance has signed a contra with the Alter Ego company for th making of four films in a small st dio in Neuilly.

Paris, 29 December
Pathé has released its *Little Morit chasse les grands fauves* (*Litt Moritz Hunts Big Game*), part of th "Comica" series directed by Romé Bosetti, with the music hall acto Maurice Schwartz.

Berlin, 31 December
The production company Deutsch Bioskop has built a glass studio i Babelsberg on a block measurin 40,000 square metres.

BIRTHS

Illinois, 6 February
Ronald Reagan

Missouri, 3 March
Jean Harlow (Harlean Carpenter)

New York, 3 June
Paulette Goddard (Marion Levy)

Missouri, 16 June
Ginger Rogers
(Virginia Katherine McMath)

Paris, 13 July
Jean-Pierre Aumont

Monte Carlo, 20 July
Mireille Balin

Wisconsin, 7 August
Nicholas Ray (Raymond Kienzle)

Mexico, 12 August
Cantinflas (Mario Moreno Reyes)

Milan, 3 December
Nino Rota

Publicized under the name of its mos famous character, director Gerolam Lo Salvio's film version of Shake speare's ***The Merchant of Venice*** *is Franco-Italian co-production.*

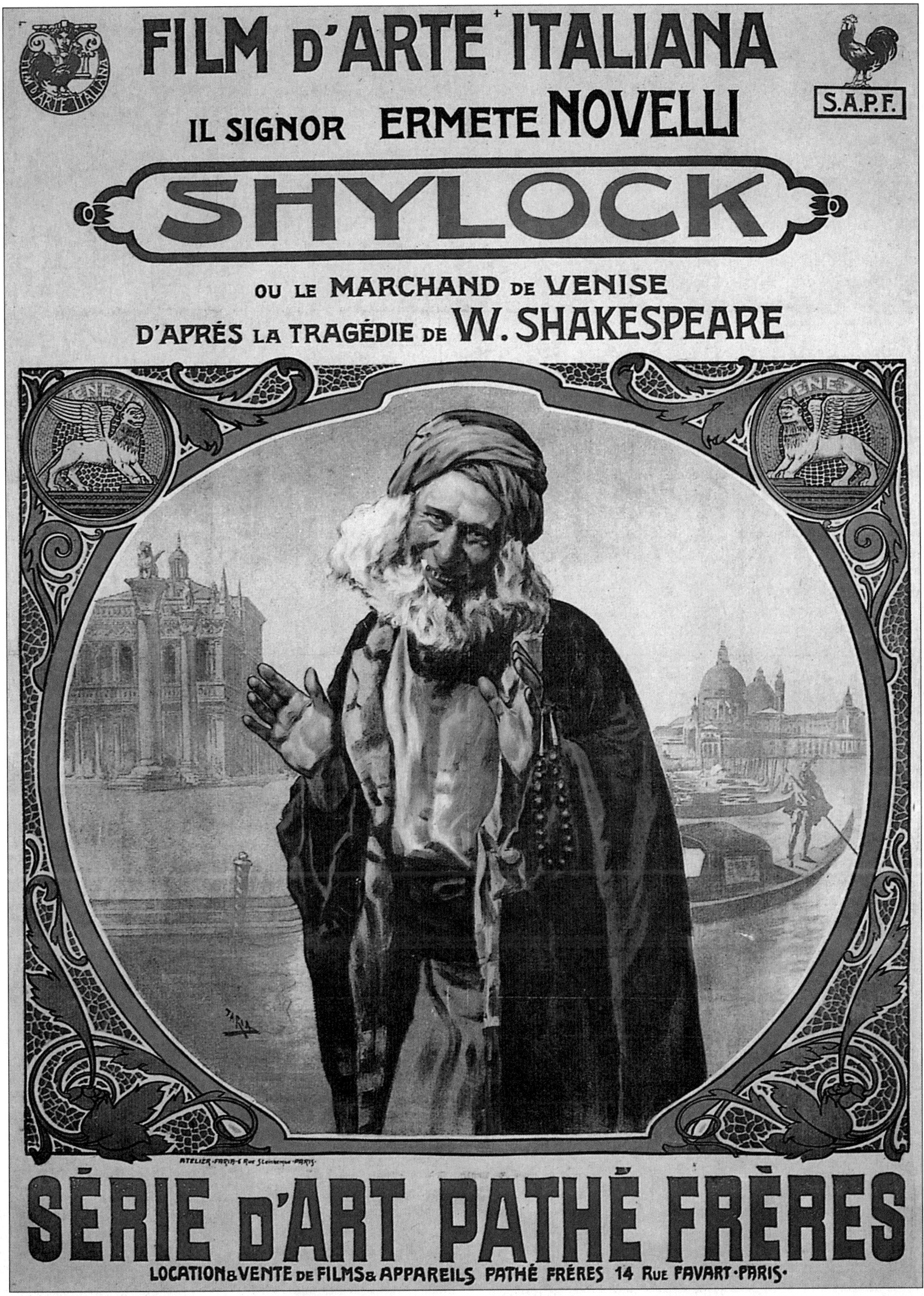

FILM D'ARTE ITALIANA

FILM D'ARTE ITALIANA

S.A.P.F.

IL SIGNOR ERMETE NOVELLI

SHYLOCK

OU LE MARCHAND DE VENISE

D'APRÉS LA TRAGÉDIE DE W. SHAKESPEARE

FARIA

SÉRIE D'ART PATHÉ FRÈRES

LOCATION & VENTE DE FILMS & APPAREILS PATHÉ FRÈRES 14 RUE FAVART · PARIS ·

Leading man Maurice Costello loses his head!

New York, 25 February
Vitagraph has just released *A Tale of Two Cities* in three parts. According to *The Motion Picture World*, "It seems safe to say that this production of one of the most famous stories will go down in motion picture history as one of the most notable of photoplay productions." Maurice Costello takes the role of Sydney Carton, Charles Dickens' hero who goes to the guillotine in his friend's place. "The Dimpled Darling", as the matinee-idol Costello is known, gives one of his finest performances in what must be his greatest triumph on screen. When Costello joined the Vitagraph company two years ago, part of his agreement was that he would not be required to perform the other production tasks expected of actors. "I am an actor, and I will act, but I will not build sets and paint scenery," he declared. With portrayals such that of Sydney Carton, Vitagraph has no cause for complaint. Costello's partner in the film is the "Vitagraph Girl" herself, Florence Turner, in the poignant role of Lucie Manette. They had appeared together previously in another classic, *The Merchant of Venice*, but this film is far superior.

'This is a far, far better thing I do...' Sidney Carton (Costello) on the scaffold awaiting his death by guillotine.

Winsor McCay animates his comic-strip

New York, 12 April
Since 1905 readers of the *New York Herald* have delighted in the magical world of the *Little Nemo in Slumberland* strip drawn by Winsor McCay. Now the strip has come to life in an animated film which is being shown tonight at the Colonial Theater as part of McCay's celebrated vaudeville act in which he sketches "The Seven Ages of Man." McCay has been experimenting with animation for almost as long as he has been drawing Little Nemo, the youthful Everyman who travels throughout space and time. The origins of his animated film, entitled *Little Nemo and the Princess*, lie in a wager the prolific McCay made with fellow cartoonists that he could not produce enough drawings to sustain a five-minute animated cartoon. The 4,000 hand-tinted drawings for the cartoon were made on transparent rice paper, mounted on thin cardboard and then photographed on to one reel at the Vitagraph studios in Brooklyn. The cartoon is preceded by a live action sequence, directed by James Stuart Blackton, in which McCay appears with Vitagraph's star comedian, John Bunny, in a fanciful re-creation of the famous wager in a saloon under the Brooklyn Bridge. In an equally humorous vein, it also provides a brief glimpse of the painstaking methods the cartoonist used to make the film. As a result, McCay's characters, Little Nemo, Flip, Impy and Dr. Pill, go through their paces with an almost uncanny smoothness. Little Nemo himself is formed by lines which resemble steel filings drawn on to a magnet. He sketches the Princess and presents her with a rose which grows just in time to be plucked. They are then carried off to Slumberland in a splendid dragon chariot. The film ends with another live action sequence which shows the happy McCay collecting his bet.

Allan Dwan and Co. take off with 'Flying A

Chicago, 5 June
"Flying A" is flying high. Although the formation of this new company was first announced in *The Moving Picture World* just eight months ago, it has been quick to make its mark. Formally known as the American Film Manufacturing Company of Chicago, it has assembled a talented production team and roster of players, some of them poached from Essanay. Three different stock companies have been operating simultaneously, filming comedies, dramas and Westerns, with two one-reelers a week released under the Flying A banner since November. Most interesting of those three is the company which headed west to film, first in Tucson, Arizona and then in Southern California. Scenario writer Allan Dwan has become the director since the departure of Frank Beal, while the leading players of note are J. Warren Kerrigan and Pauline Bush. Some idea of the range of recent releases can be gleaned fro the titles alone, included amo which are *Rattlesnakes and Gu powder*, *The Sheepman's Daught* and – on a split reel with *The Elop ments on Double L Ranch* – *T Sagebrush Phrenologist*.

PAULINE BUSH
AND
WARREN KERRIGAN
PICTURES

Max and Rigadin struggle for the top spot

aris, 17 June
ax Linder's new film *Max and his other-in-Law* has given rise to owls of laughter. Always elegant, ax is married to a charming wom- n, but his enormous mother-in-law there to ruin the honeymoon trip. he doesn't know how to skate or i. With distaste, Max must always rop her up. Finally, Max pushes his other-in-law down a snow-covered ope. Alas, the hardy creature sur- ives! The film, nevertheless, ends in l-round reconciliation. Max's films ave been very successful for a year, nd he is now known throughout urope. The dandy he impersonates ven appeals to working-class audi- nces, because he doesn't hesitate to ffect variations on risqué subjects. Pathé pays him 1,000 francs per film, and directors include Linder himself, Lucien Nonguet and Armand Massart. Rigadin, another Pathé actor, has sometimes stolen Max's limelight. Already popular in the theater under the name of Prince, he also directs spicy comedies. Rigadin, like Linder, shoots 150 to 200-metre films and deals with complicated situations. In *Rigolade and his Sons*, he plays three different characters simultaneously, thanks to special effects. Linder has an undeniable superiority over rival Rigadin in being handsome, smart and pleasing to women. Rigadin is frankly ugly, but his gags have more imagination. Who will win the title of King of Laughter?

MAX ET SA BELLE-MER
IAX LINDER
PATHÉ FRÈRES Éditeurs

The celebrated music-hall star, Mistinguett, here plays second fiddle to Rigadin.

'New' Gaumont Palace seats 3,400 people

aris, 30 September
Gaumont is growing increasingly nore powerful. In addition to stu- lios and laboratories, it has now noved aggressively into film exhibi- ion. Today Léon Gaumont opens he doors of the biggest cinema in he world. The former Hippodrome, on the place Clichy, has become the Gaumont Palace. The distinguished rchitect Auguste Bahrmann has ompletely transformed the theater, which can seat up to 3,400. Films will be accompanied from behind he screen by a 30-piece orchestra and choir under the musical direc- ion of Paul Fosse. There are two projectors, which will allow reels to be changed without any interruption o the program. Air conditioning maintains a constant temperature in the theater. The heating system, which must work overtime in such a vast space, gobbles up a daily diet of five tons of coal. During the interval the cinema's patrons can meet and eat in the Gaumont Palace's buffet, which has been placed at the center of a spacious, circular walkway. Lighting is provided by 10,000 incandescent lights and 50 arc lamps. This Saturday's program runs to over 2,000 feet of film, including tinted and sound films, the latter utilizing Gaumont's Chronophone device, newsreels and comic and dramatic scenes – in short the cream of Gaumont's output. Screened in three sessions, the Gaumont's program compares favorably with those offered by the city's other leading music halls.

Pathé releases its answer to Nick Carter

Paris, 5 August
Pathé continues to expand into new areas. It is now shooting *Nick Winter contre Nick Winter*, a comic film directed by Gerard Bourgeois and featuring Georges Winter, a leading actor from the Châtelet Theatre. The inspiration for *Nick Winter* is the *Nick Carter* series directed by Victorin Jasset for Eclair, which has been running for the last three years and stars Pierre Bressol as the debonair turn-of-the-century sleuth. The Nick Winter adventures for Pathé are comedy-thrillers with a detective background. Pathé's attempts to exploit the success of Jasset's series is a tribute to the successful formula developed by the former sculptor and stage designer who has been making films since 1905.

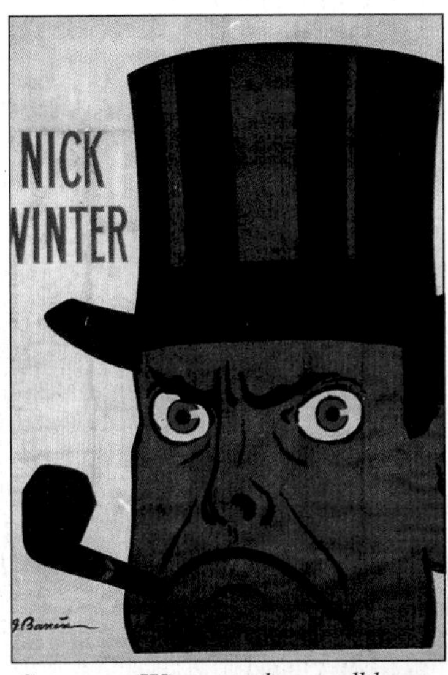
NICK
VINTER
Georges Winter, the well-known stage actor plays Nick Winter.

The cinema causes tumult amid the orange grove

Los Angeles, 1 October
Thomas Harper Ince, one of the most enterprising and dynamic of the new breed of independent producers, has been stirring things up in California. He was initially hired by Bison Pictures (the New York Motion Picture Company) to direct Westerns at their Edenvale studios, and arrived in California just a few months ago with his actress wife Alice Kershaw. However, it was not long before Ince was making some basic changes. Dissatisfied with the simply plotted and cheaply made Westerns which are currently being turned out, he made a deal with the Miller Brothers whose 101 Ranch Wild West Show had just arrived in California for the winter. At a stroke he acquired the services of a large number of authentic cowboys and cowgirls, Indians and their squaws, trained horses, oxen and buffalo, along with wagons, stagecoaches, prairie schooners, and other invaluable accessories. He also bought almost 20,000 acres of land on which to film his Westerns so as to give them a more authentic and convincing appearance. Already, Thomas Ince's first two-reeler, entitled *War on the Plains*, has set a new standard for all Western productions of the future.

Blanche Sweet in ***The Lonedale Operator****, the ninth film to be made by D.W. Griffith in California during January.*

Thomas Ince has come a long way in just a few short years. An actor on the stage from an early age like his younger brother Ralph, he first became attracted to films when he realized that he would never make a real success of the theater. Having played a few small movie roles around 1908-1909, Ince was signed up by Biograph in 1910 and appeared in a number of films. But he soon grew discontented with merely being an actor. With the help of his actress wife, he was hired by Carl Laemmle's IMP Co. to write and direct films featuring the company's newest star, Mary Pickford. He quickly turned out a number of one-reelers, including *Her Darkest Hour* and *In Old Madrid*, before he received his most recent (and best) offer from Bison. It is quite clear that much can still be expected of this man who has not yet reached his thirtieth birthday.

Florence La Badie and Lionel Barrymore in Griffith's ***Fighting Blood****.*

Striking out: Thomas Harper Ince.

Live news footage of Scott expedition

London, 1 November
For several days cinema audiences in the British capital have been watching film reports of Captain Robert Scott's expedition to the South Pole. The screening of this fascinating documentary footage has coincided with the news that Captain Scott has set off in his assault on the South Pole from his base camp on the coast of Antarctica, where he has been wintering for several months. Now that news events are being reported with greater frequency and in greater detail, the British public has become familiar with these heroic explorers and their techniques in conquering the Pole. The film was shot between the end of May 1910 and January of this year by cameraman Herbert G Ponting, who has been with the expedition since it set sail. He has brought the remote figure of Scott close to the public.

eorges Méliès
›ses independence

ris, 11 November
›orges Méliès' new film *The Hal-inations of Baron Münchhausen* is ›w available to customers. This 5-metre work of special effects is ›tributed by Charles Pathé. The ›edy producer, who invested in › film which was shot at the Mon-uil studio, is not really happy to exploiting it. In truth, Pathé has ›ked little, because poor Méliès s given Pathé his property and his ›dio at Montreuil as a guarantee. his films fail to make a profit, ›thé will be able to sell the whole .. Alas, Pathé has reason to be ›utious, because Méliès' work is no ›nger fashionable. Between 1896 ›d 1909, he directed nearly 500 ›ms, but in 1910 his marvelous ›oductions totally ceased. As a re-›t, the magician has returned to his ›rmer love, the old Robert Houdin ›eatre. At the beginning of the ›ar, Méliès received a visit from ›aude Grivolas, one of the various ›anciers backing Pathé. Grivolas s a great passion for magic and ›preciates Méliès' works, so it was rhaps he who convinced Pathé to ›t his trust in Star Film. Méliès cepted Grivolas' offer, the latter ›questing him to direct a film at ›thé's expense.

The workshop at Montreuil has ›w restarted its familiar activities. *›e Hallucinations of Baron Münch-›usen*, which began shooting in ›ay, launches the legendary Ger-›an baron into a fantastic world, by ›rns comic and frightening. The ›urce of all the phantasmagoria is a ›rge mirror. Méliès was responsible ›r the excellent special effects and ›e decor. The final result, colored › stencil, was shown to Ferdinand ›ecca and Charles Pathé, but only ›ad silence followed the screening. ›ithout a doubt, Zecca sees a rival Méliès. After burying his head in s hands, Zecca eventually said that › thought the film was too short ›d that Méliès could improve it. ›athé kept quiet but was visibly in ›reement with his artistic director. ›riticized and humiliated, Méliès ›as furious. *The Hallucinations of ›aron Münchhausen* will be hired ›ut to theaters, but if the film fails to ›eet with success, it seems clear that ›léliès' future as a director and ›roprietor will be at stake.

Feuillade gives us 'life as it really is'

Paris, 23 December
A new Gaumont film directed by the immensely prolific Louis Feuillade, *The Destiny of Mothers*, is attracting attention. It tells the story of a widow, played by Renée Carl, who initially gives up all thought of remarrying for the sake of her daughter, the beautiful Suzanne Grandais. She relents, however, and her new husband, played by the sombre René Navarre, destroys all her hopes of happiness. *The Destiny of Mothers* is the tenth film in a series which introduces cinemagoers to scenes from "Life as It Really Is". Launched in April with *The Vipers*, it is a satire against vicious gossip. Feuillade has gone on record saying that the aim of his new series is to bring to the cinema screen the kind of realism that has long been associated with literature, theater and painting. However, Feuillade's first tentative steps fall somewhat short of the work of Zola or Maupassant; the prudish Gaumont insists on maintaining a high moral tone in his films. Nevertheless, the press has affirmed that one of the films in the series, *The White Mouse*, is clearly leaning toward the pornographic: "One sees here two devout old girls flirting with two old paillards in a house de luxe to which morals object, but which the police tolerate." Louis Feuillade is in his element with this series. Films Esthétiques was launched in May 1910 to compete with the quality output of both Film d'Art and SCAGL, while at the same time avoiding long and boring Biblical or historical scenes.

Renée Carl and Suzanne Grandais, partners in ***The Destiny of Mothers.***

Newly liberated Film Art ventures into production with Réjane

"Le Film d'Art"
MADAME SANS-GÊNE
De M.M. Victorien SARDOU, de l'Académie Française, et Emile MOREAU

Gabrielle Réjane's first film appearance, opposite Edmond Duquesne.

Paris, 10 November
The General Cinematic Agency, which distributes Film d'Art productions, has just released *Madame Sans-Gêne*, an excellent 940-metre comedy in color, directed by André Calmettes and inspired by the famous play by Victorien Sardou and Emile Moreau. The celebrated actress Gabrielle Réjane plays the title role with Edmond Duquesne as Napoleon, and Georges Dorival as Lefebvre. Since 30 December 1909, Film d'Art has been freed from Pathé's stifling surveillance. Paul Gavault succeeded Paul Lafitte, but the account books continued to look extremely unhealthy. The 1908-1909 financial trading ended in failure with a deficit of 283,000 francs. Le Bargy was also dismissed, to be replaced by André Calmettes and the former actor Henri Pouctal, who arrived at the Neuilly studios in 1910. And in spite of the release of *Madame Sans-Gêne*, the year ended badly for Film d'Art, and Paul Gavault was forced to withdraw. Charles Delac now presides over the new administrative council.

1912

Paris, 5 January
Eclipse has released the film *Dans la solitude*, which was produced by Méliès' American Wild West Films.

Norway, 16 January
H. Nobel Roede has released a documentary, *All for Norway*. Strangely enough, despite the rich theatrical tradition in this country, fiction films are non-existent.

Paris, 19 January
Eclair has released *Au pays des ténèbres*, made by Victorin Jasset and based on Zola's novel *Germinal*.

St. Petersburg, 24 January
The producer Yakov Protazanov has filmed *Anfissa*, an adaptation of Leonid Andreyev's play.

Paris, 27 January
Gaumont has released a Western, *Cent dollars mort ou vif*, filmed in the Camargue by Jean Durand.

Budapest, 1 February
The Hunnia company has opened the first studio in Hungary.

Paris, 8 March
After the failure of *Tosca*, Sarah Bernhardt, aged 60, is making a comeback with her *la Dame aux camélias*, filmed by Henri Pouctal and Paul Capellani.

Paris, 9 March
From now on, Abel Gance is devoting himself to the cinema. He has published his first article in *Ciné-Journal* under the title "What is the cinema? A sixth art form!"

Monaco, 1 April
Maess and Richmann, cameramen from *Pathé-Journal*, have succeeded in filming a hydroplane race. They filmed aboard the flying machine of Eugene Renaux at an altitude of 50 metres.

Paris, 13 April
Eclair has released a new series *les Bandits en automobile*, inspired by the misdeeds of the "Bonnot band".

Denmark, 30 April
Nordisk's director Urban Gad has married his favorite actress, Asta Nielsen, the woman he brought from stage to screen. They are leaving for Germany to make several films for producers there.

Paris, 3 May
Bison Life is distributing a new Western from Thomas H. Ince, *The Battle of the Redskins*, a follow-up to *Indian Mother*.

Paris, 4 May
Gaumont has released a newsreel, which boasts that it tells *The Whole Story of the Tragic Capture of the Bonnot and Dubois bandits*.

Paris, 11 May
SCAGL-Pathé have released *Tragique amour de Mona Lisa*, written by Abel Gance.

Berlin , 15 May
A municipal by-law has been passed forbidding smoking in cinemas. It also forbids entry to children.

USA, 17 May
Carl Laemmle has organized the merger of several independant production companies to form the Universal Manufacturing Company.

Bombay, 18 May
The first Indian fiction film entitled *Pundalik*, by R.G. Torney and N.G. Chitre, is showing in the city.

Lyon, 14 June
Criminality on the screen is causing anxiety. Mayor Edouard Herriot has forbidden the screening of films depicting criminal acts.

Paris, 28 June
SCAGL-Pathé have released *les Mystères de Paris* (*The Mysteries of Paris*), by Albert Capellani, adapted from Eugène Sue.

Paris, 12 July
In competion with *Pathé-Journal*, Eclair has brought out the very first issue of its own weekly newspaper, *Eclair-Journal*.

San Francisco, 24 July
Gaston Méliès, with his wife and the team from the Gaston Méliès Manufacturing Company, are aboard the *Manuka* en route for Tahiti – part of a world film tour.

Los Angeles, 28 August
Mack Sennett and his troupe have started filming the first Keystone comedies. Some of the team, Fred Mace, Ford Sterling and Mabel Normand, left Biograph to work with Sennett.

New York, 1 September
Adolph Zukor, who presented the French film *Queen Elizabeth* with Sarah Bernhardt, has founded a new company called Famous Players.

Paris, 6 September
The music-hall stars Mistinguett and Maurice Chevalier are sharing the top billing in Pathé's film, *la Valse renversante* (*The Amazing Waltz*).

New York, 9 September
Biograph has released *An Unseen Enemy*. Directed by D.W. Griffith, it stars 16-year-old Lillian Gish and her 14-year-old sister Dorothy.

Budapest, 14 September
Release of Odon Uher's *The Sisters* (*Noverek*). It is the first full-length fiction film to be made in Hungary.

Hungary, 1 October
Sandor Korda, a young journalist, has founded a magazine here called *le Cinéma de Pest*.

Los Angeles, 1 October
Thomas H. Ince has created Kay Bee Motion Pictures with Adam Kessel and Charles Baumann.

Budapest, 14 October
The young actor Mihaly Kertesz has directed his first film, *Today and Tomorrow* (*Ma es Holnap*).

New York, 1 November
D.W. Griffith has used a panning technique to produce a panoramic effect in *The Massacre*. The film is showing here today.

Spain, 15 November
Pathé's stars Max Linder, André Deed and Stacia Napierkowska are touring the country. Max, dressed as a matador, drove the public wild at the arena in Barcelona by fighting a calf with fake horns. The memorable scene was filmed.

New York, 5 December
The New York Hat is now showing. It was made by D.W. Griffith with Mary Pickford and a relative newcomer to films, Lionel Barrymore.

London, 24 December
Despite a downturn in British production, quality films *are* being made. The latest of these is *Oliver Twist*, a film version of Dickens' novel released by Cecil Hepworth.

Paris, 27 December
The Swedish firm Svenska has r leased Mauritz Stiller's *The Bla Masks*, starring Victor Sjöström.

New York, 31 December
Charlie Chaplin has been offered contract by Keystone but has had refuse owing to his stage comm ments with the Fred Karno troup

Peking, 31 December
Benjamin Polaski has set up here branch of the Asia Film Compan

Prague, 31 December
The architect Max Urban and h wife, the actress Anna Sedlackov have founded the Asum company

Warsaw, 31 December
Several actors, including Apolon Chalupiec, have gotten together u der the direction of the filmmak Alexander Hertz to form their ow production company, Sfinks.

Berlin, 31 December
Paul Davidson's production comp ny, Projection-AG Union (Pagu has transferred its offices to Berli Work has started on the Tempelh studios.

BIRTHS

Oslo, 8 April
Sonja Henie

France, 12 April
Georges Franju

Mexico, 9 May
Pedro Armendariz

France, 4 July
Viviane Romance
(Pauline Ortmans)

England, 23 July
Michael Wilding

Pittsburgh, 23 August
Gene Kelly
(Eugene Joseph Curran Kelly)

Italy, 29 September
Michelangelo Antonioni

Having completed his ambitious ne film in color, ***The Conquest of th Pole****, Georges Méliès has been force to halt production at his Montreu studio.*

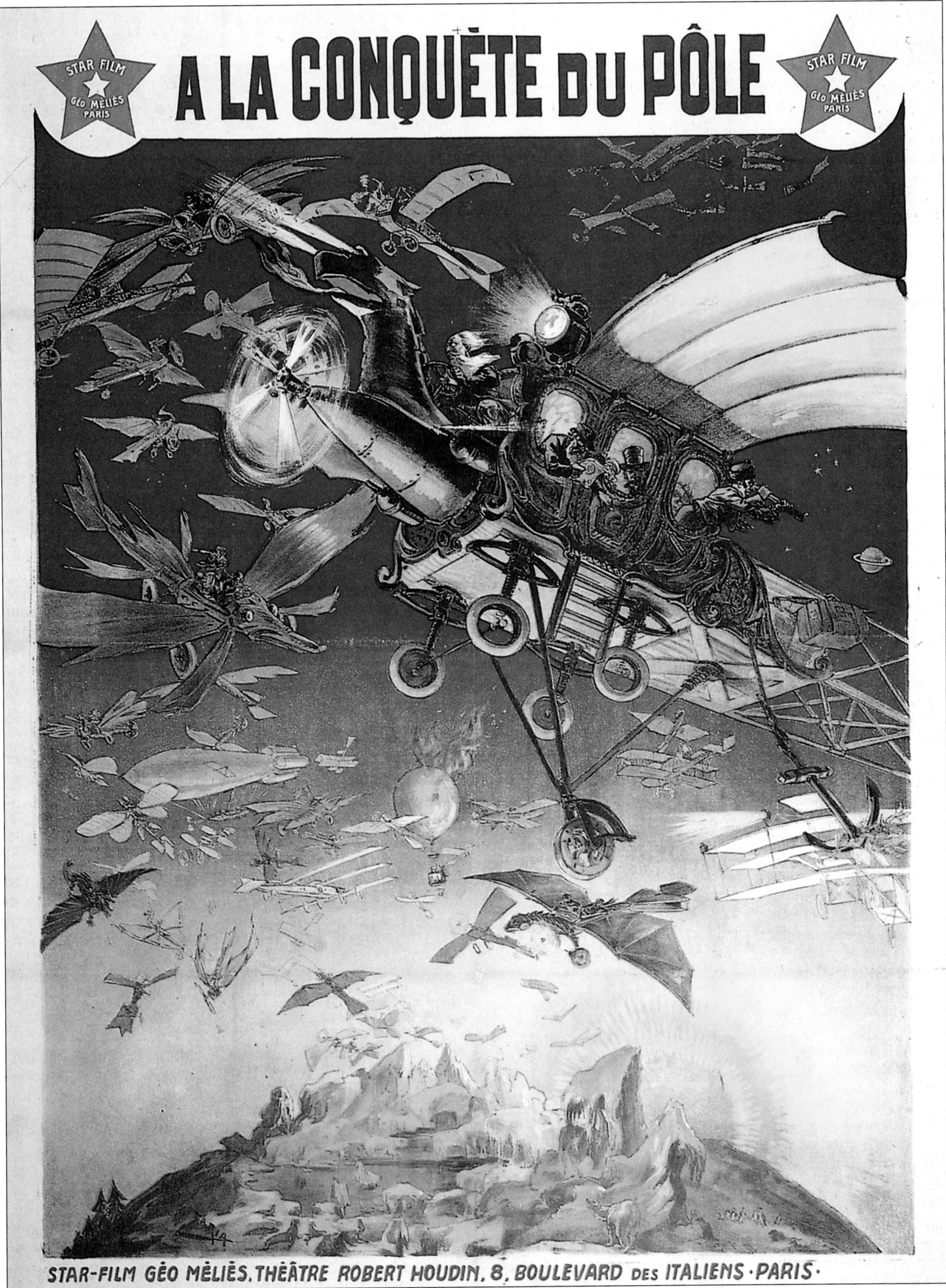
A LA CONQUÊTE DU PÔLE
STAR FILM
GÉO MÉLIÈS
PARIS
STAR FILM
GÉO MÉLIÈS
PARIS
STAR-FILM GÉO MÉLIÈS. THÉÂTRE ROBERT HOUDIN. 8, BOULEVARD DES ITALIENS · PARIS ·

Pornography poses a moral problem

Paris, 18 March
The Congress of the Federation of Businesses Against Pornography, presided over by Senator René Bérenger, opened its doors for two days. The cinema was one of the subjects discussed. Members of the church and the bourgeoisie complained about the popular pastime being a "stratagem used by the devil" which "competes with alcohol for the ruin of the public." Risqué films of "piquant interest" as well as comic scenes unleashed much anger. "Immodesty is spread shamelessly everywhere, religion is ridiculed in a manner that is most odious. It attacks the church's history, its sacraments and its ministers." The spicy films produced by Pathé or Mendel are nothing compared with the type of pornography which circulates undercover. On 7 March last, Valet, the head of the mobile brigade of Paris, accompanied by six inspectors, threw 25 kilometres of licentious films into the Seine. Unwarned, a policeman of the river brigade decided to bring a court action against them for "the throwing of refuse" into the Seine.

Zigomar's triumph, or the extraordinary luck of an adventurer

Josette Andriot, Alexandre Arquillière and Camille Bardou in Victorin Jasset's ***Zigomar Against Nick Carter.***

Paris, 22 March
Who said that Zigomar was dead and buried in the ruins after the release of the first title of the series in September 1911? The next episode in the adventures of the Master of Crime, the wicked Zigomar played by Alexandre Arquillière, has just been released by the Eclair and Victorin Jasset film company. *Zigomar against Nick Carter*, with the king of detectives played by Henry Krauss, is a large cinematographic novel [in] four parts. The first chapter, *Zig[o]mar Succeeds*, is being released t[o]day and is already in great dema[nd] by theater owners. Its success seem[s] to be assured.

From Mutual to Universal, turmoil reigns in the American cinema

Los Angeles, 17 May
It appears to be the case that a total reorganization of the American film industry has been taking place during the past few months. Most important of all, the leading independents have regrouped themselves into two powerful consortia. The rivalry between them seems likely to set the pace for future developments within the industry, with Edison's monolithic trust the Motion Picture Patents Company, left behind. First of the key developments was the formation of the Mutual Film Corporation in March, headed by Harry Aitken (president) and John R. Freuler (vice president) and backed by a number of leading financiers. As an independent film exchange, it now handles pictures from a large number of companies that include Thanhouser, Reliance, American, Majestic, Great Northern, Eclair, Lux and Comet. But at this very moment, Carl Laemmle is putting the final touches to his own new and formidable company, set to rival Mutual in the independent sector. Known as the Universal Film Manufacturing Company, it will merge Laemmle's IMP with Pat Powers' Picture Plays, Bison Life and Rex, along with Nestor and Champion. The independents are obviously flourishing, and Edison's domination has been broken.

Mary Pickford has now left the Biograph company and plans to return to the theater after completing her last film, ***The New York Hat****, for D.W. Griffith.*

Abel Gance moves behind the camera

Paris, 24 May
The young actor and scenarist Ab[el] Gance has signed a contract wi[th] the firm of Alter Ego for the shoo[t]ing of four films. The latest, *Th[e] Mask of Horror*, will be screene[d] tonight. It features the celebrate[d] actor Edouard de Max, a friend [of] Gance's. Everything is strange an[d] bold about this film. The scenario [is] unlike anything audiences have see[n] before. A mad sculptor, searchin[g] for the perfect realization of "th[e] mask of horror," places himself [in] front of a mirror after smearin[g] blood over himself with the glass [of] an oil lamp. He then swallows a vi[r]ulent poison to observe the effects [of] pain. Gance, using multiple varia[tions] of color, changes the scree[n] from blue to blood red as the terro[r-]stricken face of the actor move[s] menacingly toward the spectato[r.] An avant-garde, intense, frightenin[g] and spectacular work.

American audiences pay homage to Queen Sarah

New York, 12 July
There was a gala evening last night at the Lyceum Theater here in New York. The new organization called the Famous Players Film Company and founded last April by Daniel Frohman, Adolph Zukor and Edwin Porter, presented to a select public *Queen Elizabeth*, Sarah Bernhardt's latest film, a year after *la Dame aux Camélias*. The four-reel spectacle, produced by the Franco-German firm Eclipse and directed by Louis Mercanton in London, is the longest cinematographic work presented in the United States to date. The scenario, based on a play by Emile Moreau, retraces the last moments of the life of Elizabeth, Queen of England and Ireland from 1558 to 1603. The re-creation is brilliantly done, with the tints and color evoking the tonalities of certain paintings by Rembrandt. The film has helped give artistic dignity to the cinema. An appropriate musical accompaniment, composed by Joseph Carl Breil and interpreted by the Lyceum Theater Orchestra, added solemnity to the proceedings. One can judge the French tragedienne's enormous popularity in this country from the public's reaction. The spectators only have eyes for Sarah Bernhardt, although her partners, Lou Tellegen, Max H. Maxoudian and Marie-Louise Dorval, among others, reveal their worth. The new administrator of the Famous Players Film Company, Adolph Zukor, fought tooth and nail for the acquisition of this sensational film. He obtained, for a certain fee, the exclusive film rights for the world premiere. The work was therefore presented here for the first time before both London and Paris, where the film will not been seen until August. After lengthy negotiations, *Queen Elizabeth* received the visa of the Motion Pictures Patent Company with a license to operate. Zukor, who had wanted to do something sensational, has proven the interest of the American public in long films, provided that they are as attractive as this one. The showman has also given proof that the cinema can leave the nickelodeons behind and survive in large theaters before discerning audiences. The latter are ready to hand over more than the habitual 25 cents to see a film – something which evidently doesn't seem to spoil their pleasure.

Bernhardt originally created her role as Queen Elizabeth I for the theater.

England's mighty Queen Elizabeth (Sarah Bernhardt) exhorts her loyal and valiant troops to courage before battle.

Cinema rediscovers art of movement

Turin, 5 August
Giovanni Pastrone is not only the enlightened administrator of Itala Film as well as a talented director who has already offered us the spectacular *The Fall of Troy* – notable for its skilled handling of crowds – but he is also an unrivaled engineer. The proof is his latest invention, the Carello, which he recently patented. The Carello is a platform mounted on wheels constructed to hold the camera, permitting it to be moved around the set of a film without jolting it. Therefore, the movement of the apparatus, if manipulated by a vigilant cameraman, can give rise to stereoscopic effects of extraordinary originality. The image obtained, when projected on a screen, gains in depth and scope. Giovanni Pastrone, who has a practical mind, is to put his invention to work in his next film, provisionally entitled *The Flaming Roman*. ▷

Magical mirth from Mack and Mabel

Hollywood, 23 September

The newly-formed Keystone Pictures Corporation has released its first two films, *Cohen Collects a Debt* and *The Water Nymph*. The driving force behind this newcomer, which will specialize in comedies, is a refugee from Biograph, Mack Sennett, born Michael Sinnott in Canada in 1880. As a youth Sennett had ambitions to be an opera singer, but his search for fame and fortune in New York brought him only modest work as a chorus boy in Broadway musicals and a performer in burlesque. But his luck changed in the summer of 1908 when he began working at the Biograph studios in Manhattan. He was soon taking lead roles in one-reelers directed by D.W. Griffith, contributing scripts and eagerly absorbing all the technical aspects of the new medium of cinema from men like cameraman Billy Bitzer. By the winter of 1910 Sennett was directing as well as acting in Biograph films.

When Sennett decided to strike out on his own this year, he had gained the experience to gather around him a stable of remarkable performers who had cut their comic teeth at Biograph: Ford Sterling, Fred Mace and, above all, the enchanting Mabel Normand, whom Sennett had directed in many films at Biograph and whose vibrant personality has already turned her into a big favorite with cinema audiences. Sennett has a particularly soft spot for Normand, whom he has described as being "as beautiful as a spring morning." On 4 July, Independence Day, the die was cast for the troupe of comedians to gain their own independence. It was on that day that Sennett finalized his business agreement with two former bookmakers, Charles Baumann and Adam Kessel, to form the Keystone production company with a working capital of $2,500, and the Keystone cameras are set to roll in California, in the old Bison Life studio in the Edendale district of Hollywood. In the meantime, profiting from sunny weather, Sennett's team have been filming a project at Coney Island. *Cohen Collects a Debt* is set in the make-believe world of Luna Park and much use is made of its scenic railway. In a side-splitting comic chase, an unfaithful man is relentlessly pursued by a jealous woman. *The Water Nymph* has a similar premise, with Mabel Normand cast as a bathing beauty harassed by a group of old satyrs. Max Linder's influence can be detected in these early Sennett offerings, but they also have a frenzied energy that owes much to the vaudeville experience of the director and his talented troupe.

KEYSTONE FILMS
A QUARTET OF POPULAR FUN MAKERS
MACK SENNETT
MABEL NORMAND
FRED MACE
FORD STERLING
SUPPORTED BY AN
ALL STAR COMPANY
IN SPLIT REEL COMEDIES
A KEYSTONE
EVERY MONDAY
MABEL NORMAND
FIRST RELEASE SEPTEMBER 23
"Cohen Collects a Debt" and
"The Water Nymph"
Featuring MABEL NORMAND, the beautiful Diving Venus
MONDAY, SEPTEMBER 30
"Riley and Schultze" and
"The New Neighbor"
Amusing subjects, cleverly acted by world-famous actors
KEYSTONE FILM COMPANY

For Keystone's brilliant comic duo of Mabel Normand and Mack Sennett, any time and any place will do in which to raise a few laughs.

Famous actors for proven subjects

New York, 9 December

"Famous Actors In Famous Plays" is the new publicity slogan for the Famous Players Film Company which is busy preparing to make *The Prisoner of Zenda*, based on the celebrated romantic novel and play by Anthony Hope. The star of the film will be the great stage actor James Hackett, who triumphed in the double role of Rudolph and the King of Ruritania at the Lyceum Theater in 1895 and then toured the United States. The director Edwin S. Porter, who has just sold his interest in the Rex Film Company, which was in dire straits, was approached to undertake this ambitious project. Porter (who will co-direct with Hugh Ford) should certainly benefit from the excellent working conditions provided by Famous Players. *The Prisoner of Zenda* will be filmed in a specially converted studio at the top of the Ninth Regiment Armory situated on 26th Street. There is sufficient space and the advantage of being able to shoot, whatever the weather, under the immense glass roof. All the details have already been planned, including the many decor changes.

The Famous Players Company, which became known to the public by releasing *Queen Elizabeth* last July, has profited from its audacity. Founded earlier this year with an initial capital of $250,000, Daniel Frohman and Adolph Zukor's company gained $80,000 in profits from being the sole distributors of the highly-successful Sarah Bernhardt film. The company benefited primarily because the promotion had been entrusted to a real businessman, Al Lichtman. All the big U.S. cities snapped up the French film and Zukor, the first active partner, has largely regained his investment. From now on, the Famous Players Company has decided to produce its own films and to present the great actors of the American theater in the roles which have brought them glory and fame. It is an experiment modeled on Film d'Art in France. James Hackett, the first actor to be hired, seems delighted to be starring in his favorite role. Even if he fears the realism of the cinema, he is willing to dive into water if the scene requires it.

olette Willy falls for the cinematograph

ris, 18 October
ou would like my impressions of cinema? They are extremely fa-·able. Lack of time has prevented from making any films, but I pe that I will soon be able to rec- this." The charming young writ-of these sentiments, relayed in the umns of the weekly *Cinema* mag-ne, is called Colette Willy. In ne 1910 she divorced her hus-nd, the writer Willy, and now lives h Henry de Jouvenel. The multi-ented Colette is famous not only her *Claudine* books but also for h works as *l'Ingenue libertine* and *Vagabonde*. Since 25 April, she s been appearing at the Ba-Ta-an in *la Chatte amoureuse* (*The norous Cat*), a mime show devised by Roger Guttinger and directed by Georges Wague, a talented mime who has learned all the tricks of his art at the hands of Colette Willy. Wague also has his foot in the door of cinema having appeared in a number of films, notably *l'Enfant prodigue* (*The Infant Prodigy*) made for Film d'Art in 1907. Will Colette allow herself to be seduced by the siren song of cinema? She is always on the lookout for money-making propositions, and her friend and co-star in *la Chatte amoureuse*, the comedienne Musidora, has already received an intriguing offer from some producers, said to be anarchists, to make a film with them next year. Will Colette decide to follow in Musidora's footsteps?

ouis Feuillade has had enough of Bébé

BÉBÉ ADOPTE UN PETIT FRÈRE
e meeting between Bébé and Bout--Zan has had fatal consequences.

aris, 12 December
big internal struggle has blown up Gaumont. Louis Feuillade has rminated the contract of little natole Clément Mary, the pint-zed star of the *Bébé* series! Feuil-de loves children but his patience s reached breaking point. Anatole ément Mary has played Bébé in films, appearing in turn as an ache, a Negro, a moralist, a mil-naire, an insurance agent, a social-t and a sleepwalker. But in spite of ébé's vast popularity, he remains a ere employee of the studio. His rents have decided to take matters to their own hands, presenting aumont with their own assessment Bébé's commercial value and pestering Feuillade with repeated demands for a salary increase for their son. However, Gaumont's artistic director is cunning; to speed the painless removal of Bébé's name from the Gaumont catalogue, he has acquired the services of yet another child, four-year-old René Poyen. As Bout-de-Zan (Licorice Stick) Poyen made his debut alongside Bébé in *Bébé Adopts a Little Brother* and *Bébé, Bout-de-Zan and the Thief*. The undermining of Bébé went ahead smoothly because his parents were unaware of Feuillade's scheming. Once Bout-de-Zan had proved his worth, Feuillade was free to kiss Bébé goodbye. His departure has caused Feuillade some regret as Anatole Mary possesses genuine talent. He can continue his career, nonetheless, but only under another name, as that of Bébé has been copyrighted by Gaumont. Mary now has to cede supremacy at the Gaumont studio to his four-year-old rival, for whom stardom is now beckoning.

Bout-de-Zan is a charming little scrap, swathed in clothes several sizes too big for him. With his battered top hat or enormous bowler and his gigantic dilapidated shoes, he is the incarnation of the paupers of Paris – a combination of misery, malice and mischief. Ironically it was Bébé himself who coined his name. When they met for the first time, he cried out on seeing his rival's grubby face, "Oh, how black he is, like a licorice stick!"

The magician from Montreuil in dire straits

As in all his work, the fantastic is present but the magic no longer works.

Montreuil, 31 December
It has been a black end to the year for Georges Méliès. The films financed by Pathé did not meet with the hoped-for success. Nevertheless, *The Conquest of the Pole*, a color film of 650 metres released on 3 May last, attempted to revive the popularity of his famous and inventive earlier films. It contains a Giant of the Snows, an immense animated figure, built of papier mâché. But this is not enough to give Méliès' reputation new life. His films cut a poor figure next to those of Jasset, Feuillade or the Americans. Méliès has also given *Cinderella* and *The Knight of the Snows* to Pathé, but both have been complete failures. Theater managers have refused to show them, and Zecca has become increasingly critical of his rival. Now Méliès is currently preparing *The Journey of the Bourrichon Family*, based on Eugène Labiche's comedy. However, he is too distracted at the moment and is leaving the direction to his assistant Manuel, who really doesn't have his boss's imagination. The result risks being disastrous. Poor Méliès's mind is elsewhere – his wife Eugènie has just died, and his brother in the U.S. is on the verge of bankruptcy.

Méliès, as always, is both creator and actor in ***The Conquest of the Pole****.*

1913

Paris, 17 January
The Bébé-Cinema (380 seats) was opened today by M. Mary whose son Clément stars in the *Bébé* series.

Rome, 7 February
A cinema reserved for the clergy has opened at the Vatican. The Pope has forbidden Catholic priests to attend public cinemas.

France, 15 February
The Catholic paper *la Croix du Pas-de-Calais* has published an article criticizing the film *Notre Dame de Paris* and reminding readers that Hugo's book is blacklisted.

New York, 18 February
Opening of *The Prisoner of Zenda*. This film of Anthony Hope's popular novel has been made by Edwin S. Porter for Adolph Zukor's new Famous Players company.

Santa Monica, 1 March
Vitagraph has made a permanent move from New York and is setting up its studios in California.

Brussels, 4 March
Isidore Moray, the producer and cameraman who created the *Journal belge d'actualité*, filmed a house in rue de la Montagne being destroyed by a gas explosion. The film was on the screen five hours after shooting.

New York, 5 March
Thomas H. Ince has produced *The Scourge of the Desert*, directed by Reginald Barker. It is the first Western in a series with William S. Hart.

Vincennes, 17 March
Louis Lépine, the prefect of police in Paris, today visited Pathé's factories to watch the inflammability tests of celluloid-based "safety" film.

London, 31 March
At the instigation of the Minister of the Interior, the cinema profession has created the British Board of Film Censors to classify films into two classifications: U for suitable for all ages and A for adults.

London, March
Release of H.G. Ponting's second film on *Scott's Expedition to the South Pole*. The reels were found last December next to the frozen bodies of Captain Scott and his companions, nine months after their deaths.

Berlin, March
Erich Pommer, the managing director of Deutsche Eclair (Decla), a joint venture with Eclair, has bought up the majority of the capital from the mother company.

Paris, 19 April
The Minister of the Interior has forbidden the screening of all films depicting recently commited crimes or capital punishment.

Bombay, 3 May
A film inspired by the epic Mahabharata *King Harishchandra* and produced by Dhundiraj Govind Phalke is screening. It is the first full-length (four reels) Indian fiction film.

California, 1 June
D.W. Griffith has started filming his first four-reeler for Biograph, *Judith of Bethulia*. The film has a budget of $36,000, his highest to date.

Paris, 26 June
Eclair and Pathé have published their annual reports for 1912. Both companies show a healthy profit: 943,590 francs for Eclair and 7.3 million francs for Pathé.

Cologne, 1 August
Dekage (Deutsche Kinematograph Gesellschaft) which has extended its cinema circuit interests and become a production company is offering a fortune to actors to sign up. It has already won over the Dane Vigo Larsen and two promising French actresses, Suzanne Grandais and Yvette Andreyor.

Havana, 6 August
Producer Enrique Diaz Quesada has made Cuba's first feature film, *Manuel Garcia or the King of the Cuban Fields*, the story of a national hero in the war of independence.

Berlin, 22 August
Opening of Stellen Rye's film *The Student from Prague* starring Paul Wegener and adapted from Hans Heinz Ewers' book. The cameraman is Guido Seeber.

New York, 10 September
The Famous Players Film Company has released *In the Bishop's Carriage* by Edwin S. Porter and J. Searle Dawley. Mary Pickford who stars in the film was signed on by Adolph Zukor for $2,000 per week.

Rochester, 15 September
Eastman-Kodak have released the first panchromatic film, with sensitivity to the whole tonal range. But it is expensive and has several faults: it lacks stability, and processing takes longer than for orthochromatic film.

New York, 1 October
D.W. Griffith, who recently left Biograph, has signed a contract with Reliance-Majestic, a branch of the Mutual Film Corporation. He will be taking over the artistic direction and will be able to devote himself to full-length films, directing two to three projects a year.

Berlin, 3 October
The avant-garde producer and director of the Deutsches Theatre Max Reinhardt has made his first film since accepting Projeektion-AG Union's fabulous contract. The big-budget film *The Island of Happiness*, was shot in Corfu with an original film script.

Prague, 10 October
The Asum company has released Max Urban's *The Bartered Bride*, based on Smetana's opera, the first full-length Czechoslovakian film.

Stockholm, 3 November
Svenska has just released Victor Sjöström's eighth film, *Ingeborg Holm*, which stars Hilda Borgström. Sjöström's sensitivity and talent as a filmmaker are revealed against a background of social criticism.

New York, 24 November
One of America's first full-length films (2,000 metres) *Traffic in Souls*, by George Loane Tucker is a smash hit. It has been programmed in 28 cinemas in the country's main cities.

Paris, 25 November
Gaumont has released the first film in its "Vaudeville Comedies" series, *les Millions de la bonne* (*The Housemaid's Millions*), with the actresses Marguerite Lavigne and Madeleine Guitty. Louis Feuillade directed.

New York, 1 December
Gaston Méliès has returned from his extremely costly Pacific expedition ($50,000) to find his firm on the edge of bankruptcy. The documentaries filmed in Oceania have met with little success and many of the reels were destroyed by the heat.

Paris, 5 December
The Gaumont Palace cinema is cu rently screening Gaumont's fi Chronochrome films, one of the fi trichromatic processes to be dev oped in France.

Paris, 13 December
The Lux Company has been d solved. Its film lab in Gentilly, whi used to process 10,000 metres film per day, is up for sale.

USA, 29 December
Release of the first episode of F Grandon's *The Adventures of Ka lyn*, a 13-part serial starring Kathl Williams and produced by Selig.

Peking, 31 December
Asia Film Company has released t first full-length Chinese film *An I Fated Couple*, a satire on arrang marriages from producers Zha Shichuan and Zheng Zhengqiu. the course of this last year, As Film was taken over from Benjam Polaski by the Americans, Essl and Lehrman.

BIRTHS

Brooklyn, 18 January
Danny Kaye
(David Daniel Kaminsky)

Germany, 25 February
Gert Froebe

New York, 4 March
John Garfield
(Julius Garfinkel)

Bordeaux, 18 March
René Clément

London, 6 May
Stewart Granger (James Stewart)

New York, 2 November
Burt Lancaster

India, 5 November
Vivien Leigh
(Vivian Mary Hartley)

Cherbourg, 12 December
Jean Marais

The great British actor, Sir Johnsto Forbes-Robertson, now gives his a claimed Hamlet to posterity. The ta of Shakespeare's prince has bee filmed by E. Hay Plumb.

'Quo Vadis?' brings ancient Rome to Broadway

New York, 21 April
An Italian film entitled *Quo Vadis?* is being shown from today to an enthusiastic public at the Astor Theater on Broadway. It runs for no less than nine reels, making it the longest film ever presented in the United States. Reflecting the importance of the event, the cost of the seats is $1 instead of the usual 25 cents. *Quo Vadis?*, the adaptation from the novel by the Polish writer Henryk Sienkiewicz, needed many months shooting and an enormous investment, estimated at around 80,000 lira, on the part of the Cines production company. The first set of scenes was recorded last July and, among the many rather unusual expenses, it was necessary to get a hold of 20 lions for the arena sequences. The New York spectators have been particularly impressed by the crowd scenes, where innumerable extras have been used. The results do justice to the director, Enrico Guazzoni, who also designed the sets and the costumes.

Lia Orlandini and Gustavo Serena in a meticulous reconstruction by Guazzoni, who holds the rights to the book.

Impressive Indian film hits the jackpot

Bombay, 5 May
The infant Indian cinema industry has produced an epic to rival those made in Hollywood. At four reels, *Raja Harishchandra*, directed by D.G. Phalke, marks the beginning of feature film production on the subcontinent. Based on a Hindu legend surrounding the trials of the righteous King Harishchandra – a story resembling that of Job in the Old Testament – the film contains many spectacular scenes, including a forest fire and the apparition of the God Siva. It is now playing at the Coronation Theatre as part of a one-and-a-half-hour variety program of dancers, jugglers and comedians.

The king (center) and his small son in Phalke's enthralling Indian film.

LE PLUS
GRAND
CINEMA
DU
MONDE
DES
SALLES
AUJOURD'HUI

The Gaumont Palace and the daisy emblem have been together for two years. The building, again renovated, reopens on 5 September.

arisians tremble before Fantômas

ris, 9 May
e whole capital is fascinated by new posters which have just ap-ared on the boulevards. They rtray an elegantly-dressed Fantô-as, the Master of Crime, rendered pular by the detective novels of rre Souvestre and Marcel Allain. around Paris his sinister, masked e can be seen. These posters are marked with the name of the oks' publishers, Arthème Fayard, with the Gaumont symbol. The n company acquired the rights to successful first novel for the sum 6,000 francs, and got Louis uillade to direct the adventures of s dark, mysterious character. *Fan-nas*, a drama in three episodes ntaining over 30 scenes, was re-sed today, and it has already cap-ated the public. Contained in its 46 metres are murders, attempt- murders, robberies, blackmail d kidnappings. The three episodes e entitled *The Robbery at the Roy- Palace Hotel, The Disappearance Lord Beltham* and *Around the affold*. The 33 chapters of the ok have been condensed with eat skill by Feuillade himself, ough Gaumont, always the puri-n, asked the director not to bring e most terrifying scenes to the reen. Despite that, Feuillade has anaged to create an eerier atmo-here than that in the book. Fantô-as is interpreted by the disturbing ené Navarre, with his eagle's pro-e, who continues to baffle the poor lice inspector Juve, portrayed by éon. Young actor Georges Mel-ior impersonates Jérôme Fandor, journalist and sleuth, in association with Juve, and Renée Carl is Lady Beltham. The adventures of the arch criminal and genius of disguise in a labyrinthine Paris are unforgettable. There are powerful poetic images such as the rooftop chase on the Gaumont Palace against a background of gray sky, roads with wet stones, collapsing walls and billboards behind which ruffians in black hoods are concealed. The end of the film is distressing: Juve believes he has finally arrested Fantômas, but an innocent man is substituted for the real criminal and has to mount the guillotine. Juve catches sight of the unfortunate one in time, and he is saved. But the Master of Crime has escaped. The last shot shows the miserable Juve, sitting at his desk, promising to find Fantômas. Suddenly he jumps. A superimposed image of Fantômas laughing appears before him. The policeman moves toward it quickly, but the image disappears. The story continues in the next episode.

*René Navarre in **Juve Against Fantômas**, the second instalment of the series.*

ilming of 'The Glue' places Mistinguett in sticky situation

lbert Capellani found his inspiration here in a work by Jean Richepin.

Paris, 19 July
There has been some eventful filming in Vincennes at the SCAGL studios. Albert Capellani has adapted Jean Richepin's story *la Glu* as a vehicle for Mistinguett. The legendary music-hall star has been lured into films with a fat fee of 2,500 francs. Her money has been well earned; in one scene another actress was supposed to knock her out with a prop hammer wrapped in cotton wool. Was the blow a little too strong? Mistinguett, blood running down her face, fainted dead away in front of an astonished crew.

A weighty recruit for Mack Sennett

New York, 5 June
Two new Keystone comedies *Help! Help! Hydrophobia!* and *Passions He Had Three* feature bulky, baby-faced comic Roscoe "Fatty" Arbuckle, who has recently been signed to the studio by Mack Sennett. The 26-year-old Arbuckle is a vaudeville veteran who has tried just about everything possible during his show business career, from singing ballads in a nickelodeon to performing in a blackface act. But the breakthrough to the big-time has proved elusive. He made an early start in films in 1907 when he made some one and two-reelers for Selig. After another stint treading the boards, Arbuckle approached Sennett for a job at Keystone. Apparently Sennett was not overly impressed with the moon-faced comic but was nevertheless shrewd enough to spot that the public might find a fat policeman funny. So Arbuckle became a Keystone Cop at the princely sum of $3 a day. Impressed with Roscoe's performance in *The Gangsters*, directed by Henry "Pathé" Lehrman and starring Fred Mace, Sennett has moved the Fat Man up into featured roles. Fatty's contract looks likely to finally catapult him out of obscurity and into the limelight. Cinemagoers are warming to the nimble way so big a man negotiates the non-stop slapstick of Sennett's films. Arbuckle's combination of truculence and breezy good humor, which audiences find particularly appealing, marks him out as a man to watch. The Fat Man is a heavyweight addition to Sennett's stable of comedy stars, skillfully brought together on his Edendale lot.

French film industry mourns loss of Jasset

Paris, 5 September
Victorin Jasset's final film *Protéa* has received a warm welcome from the public since it was released, but with a certain sadness. The great director of the Eclair company died prematurely last 22 June. For the film, Jasset took advantage of the tense situation in the Balkans to shoot a spy film, which has an atmosphere that comes very close to reality. The role of the spy, Protéa, is played by Josette Andriot, who must get hold of a secret treaty between Celtia and Slavonia. With the assistance of Anguille, alias Lucienne Bataille, the beautiful heroine manages to steal the document, after having been disguised as a cat burglar, as a society woman, an aide-de-camp, an ambassador of Albania, a gypsy and a wild-animal tamer. Jasset's Dr. Phantom, Zigomar and the disturbing image of Protéa in a black leotard, will be long remembered by the public.

History and romance comes Italian style

Turin, 31 October
The Italian cinema continues to grow steadily stronger and is currently profiting from the problems of the film industry in other parts of the world. Last August, Ambrosio of Turin released *The Last Days of Pompeii*, a particularly careful and impressive adaptation from the historical novel by Bulwer-Lytton, and one of many Italian motion pictures that has found inspiration in ancient Roman history. Today, it is the turn of Gloria, also situated in Turin. This company has produced a sentimental drama entitled *But My Love Does Not Die*. The star, the elegant and sophisticated diva Lydia Borelli, has succeeded to perfection in her transition from stage to screen. Unlike the historical panoramas, which were based mainly on novels, this film was derived from a boulevard stage play. Surprisingly, these two very differently conceived films were made by the same director, Mario Caserini. Celebrated for his historical pageants such as *Joan of Arc, Beatrice Cenci, Lucretia Borgia* and *The Last Days of Pompeii*, Caserini has proven himself equally at home with romantic melodrama. A former painter, Mario Caserini entered films as an actor in 1905 before turning to directing. *But My Love Does Not Die* is a good example of a film of passion, which should thrive alongside the costume epics. The mixture of genres has been a success in Italy, where Turin, not Rome, continues to be the most important film production center in Italy. It was Arturo Ambrosio who led the way when he built a glass-roofed studio there and commenced production in 1906. The biggest competitor for Ambrosio in Turin is Giovanni Pastrone's Itala-Film.

A scene from Caserini's version of ***The Last Days of Pompeii.***

Literary classics enrich the English cinema

London, 29 October
The release this month of *Hamlet*, with Johnston Forbes-Robertson as the Prince of Denmark, is another example of the English cinema's passion for adapting literary classics. Last year we saw *Oliver Twist*, produced by Cecil Hepworth and directed by Thomas Bentley, the self-styled "great Dickens impersonator and scholar." This year the same team has repeated their success with *David Copperfield*, a film in six reels. Architectural and natural exteriors, said to be the actual places "immortalized by Dickens," were chosen for their pictorial as well as their period atmosphere. A few months ago, Mrs. Henry Wood's sentimental novel *East Lynne* was also shown to acclaim. William Barker's ambitious two-hour production has many scenes, lavish decor and sweeping photography. Now Cecil Hepworth has topped all the previous literary adaptations with his production of *Hamlet*. It cost 10,000 pounds to make and marks the final appearance of Johnston Forbes-Robertson before the great romantic actor retires at the age of 60. The film was shot mainly at Hepworth's studio at Walton-on-Thames, though considerable use was made of outdoor locations both at Hartsbourne Manor in Hertfordshire and at Lulworth

David Copperfield with Dora.

Cove in Dorset, where structur
representing Elsinore Castle we
built. Despite his age, Forbe
Robertson's lean face is still han
some and very expressive, and h
appearance on screen will be a
invaluable record of his perfo
mance in the role he first played
the Lyceum Theatre in 1897. Direc
ed by E. Hay Plumb, it is based
Forbes-Robertson's celebrated pr
duction, now in repertory at Dru
Lane. Ophelia is played by th
actor's wife Gertrude Elliott, wh
acts her mad scene in a garden. Th
film was enthusiastically receive
and should lead to more film ve
sions of the classics.

Hamlet berates his mother, Gertrude. A famous scene from a famous play.

niversal depicts horrors of white slave traffic

ew York, 24 November
his afternoon a huge crowd laid ege to Weber's Theatre on Broad-ay in the frantic rush to see *Traffic Souls*, a sensational release from e recently formed Universal Film anufacturing Company. Ticket rices for the show have been raised an exhorbitant 25 cents. This m's theme, the sinister menace to merican womanhood from gangs white slavers, is currently the bject of what the *New York World* as called "popular hysteria". Lurid age plays like *The Lure* have dealt ith the subject, and public debate as been further inflamed by the ine publication of the long-awaited ockefeller Report on Commercial-ed Prostitution in New York City. he talented director of *Traffic in ouls*, George Loane Tucker, has rawn on this report and a similar robe launched by New York dis-ict attorney Charles S. Whitman. he result is a powerful six-reel dra-a in which plucky Jane Gail and er policeman-fiance Matt Moore ave her sister from the clutches of a hite slave trader masquerading as a moral reformer. Tucker's original proposal for the film, and request for a budget of $5,000, had been turned down by Universal chief Carl Laemmle. Undeterred, Tucker then raised the money from friends and was able to make *Traffic in Souls* surreptitiously, working around his regular shooting schedule. Then the director suddenly left the studio after quarreling over another matter. There was a huge battle at Universal when Laemmle discovered the existence of *Traffic in Souls*, but, nevertheless, the film is a hit.

Ethel Grandin (left) and Matt Moore star as victim and rescuer respectively, in ***Traffic in Souls***.

ecil B. DeMille and Jesse L. Lasky join the Hollywood brigade

ollywood, 29 December
Vith Oscar Apfel as his co-director nd Al Gandolfi behind the camera, ecil B. DeMille has begun shooting *he Squaw Man* in a converted barn located at Selma and Vine in Hollywood, California. Dustin Farnum is the star and the film is based on the well-known play by Edwin Milton Royle. It is the tale of an Indian girl who saves the life of a British aristocrat in the old West, and bears him a child before committing suicide. Since most of the story takes place outdoors, *The Squaw Man* was selected as being the easiest subject to film without the use of full studio facilities. In fact, the small film company was already headed for Flagstaff, Arizona, but after one look at the built-up city, they decided to get back on the train and continue on to California instead. This is the first film to be produced by the Jesse L. Lasky Feature Play Company, founded by Lasky, his brother-in-law Samuel Goldfish, Cecil B. DeMille, and Arthur Friend earlier this year. DeMille and Lasky are both new arrivals in the film industry, having previously been involved in the theater and vaudeville respectively, but they seem to know what they are doing. Since the rights to the film have already been sold to a number of regional distributors for a substantial sum, reputedly $40,000, it is likely that the newcomers will earn themselves a good profit.

From left: DeMille, Oscar Apfel, Dustin Farnum, Lasky, Edmund Breese.

Keystone seduces hesitant Chaplin

New York, 29 December
The Keystone Picture Corporation has signed a young British comedian, Charles Chaplin. About a year ago Mack Sennett and Mabel Normand were impressed with Chaplin's comic virtuosity when they saw him playing a gentlemanly drunk in *A Night in an English Music Hall*, one of the highlights of the touring Karno Company's revue showing at the American Music Hall on New York's 42nd Street. Fellow Keystone director Adam Kessel also claims to have seen the 24-year-old Chaplin and spotted his potential, and the result was an offer to join the Keystone company as a "moving picture actor" at a salary of $150 a week. The contract was signed on 25 September and Chaplin officially left the Karno troupe, with whom he has appeared for seven years, at the end of November. Early in December he arrived in Los Angeles and has been settled in to a room at the Great Northern Hotel.

1914

Paris, 2 January
Eclair has released the first film directed by former actor Maurice Tourneur, *le Système du Dr. Goudron et du Professeur Plume*.

California, 10 January
Filming has commenced at Venice Beach of *Kid Auto Races at Venice*. Directed by Henry Lehrman, the film is a vehicule for the British comedian Charlie Chaplin, who completed his first film *Making a Living* last week.

Paris, 17 January
Charles Pathé, who has just received the Legion of Honor, has released *Napoléon: du sacre à Sainte-Hélène*. The film, directed by the Belgian Alfred Machin, was made with the participation of the Russian and Belgian armies.

Paris, 24 January
The Italian firm Celio Films is distributing a film with music, *Histoire d'un Pierrot*, starring Francesca Bertini and from the producer Count Baldassare Negroni, who is better known for his high society films.

Berlin, 31 January
The Little Angel, produced in Germany by Urban Gad and starring his wife, Asta Nielsen, is now on view to the public.

London, 2 February
Opening of *The World, the Flesh and the Devil*, a film in Kinemacolor made by Lawrence Cowen with Frank Esmond and Rupert Harvey.

New York, 10 February
The Famous Players Film Co. has released the first of its films to be made in California, *Hearts Adrift*, directed by Edwin S. Porter and starring Mary Pickford.

Paris, 27 February
The first issue of *le Film*, by André Heuzé and Georges Quellien, is now on sale.

St. Petersburg, 5 March
Screening of *The Child from the Big City* by Evgeni Bauer, with Ivan Mosjoukine.

Copenhagen, 23 March
Benjamin Christensen has produced his first film *The Mysterious X*, with himself in the leading role.

Paris, 29 March
Sarah Bernhardt has refused a role in Abel Gance's play *la Victoire de Samothrace*. Her film *Adrienne Lecouvreur*, directed by Louis Mercanton, has just been released.

New York, 11 April
The Spoilers, a Selig production by the director Colin Campbell, was screened for the opening of the new Strand Theater here. The first purpose-built cinema for new releases, it is able to seat 2,900 people.

France, 18 April
Various cinema organizations have published pamphlets attacking the cinema tax voted in by the Chamber of Deputies on 23 March.

Paris, 24 April
Louis Aubert has released the Danish film *Opium Dreams*, by Forest Holger-Madsen.

California, 4 May
Release of Charlie Chaplin's *Caught in the Rain*. This is the first film entirely written and directed by him.

Los Angeles, 4 May
Home Sweet Home has been released by Reliance-Majestic, with the Gish sisters, Mae Marsh and Henry B. Walthall. The film was directed by D.W. Griffith in the company's Hollywood studios.

Paris, 22 May
In *le Film*, Rémy de Gourmont criticizes film versions of literature: he feels "it is a shame to see the classics reduced to trembling shadows."

Paris, 23 May
Pathé has just brought out *Maudit soit la guerre!* (*A Curse on War*). The courageous though quite brutal film, made in Belgium by Alfred Machin, has been finished since 1913; however, Pathé held back its release fearing that the underlying pacificist message might offend.

Paris, 30 May
Gaumont has released Louis Feuillade's *le Calvaire*, with Musidora, a dancer from the Folies-Bergère.

New York, May
The French director Maurice Tourneur has arrived in Fort Lee to take up his position as director of Eclair's American production.

Paris, 3 June
Raymond Poincaré unveiled a monument in memory of Etienne-Jules Marey at the Parc des Princes. According to Charles Richet, winner of the Nobel Prize in medicine, Marey invented the cinematograph.

USA, 8 June
Opening of the Ebbets Field Theater, the first drive-in cinema.

Paris, 1 July
The director André Antoine has been signed up by Pathé.

California, 4 July
After months of preparation and having raised a budget of $40,000, D.W. Griffith has started filming *The Clansman*.

Austria, 16 August
The Government is worrying about the impact of the cinema on public opinion. From now on, only patriotic films may be shown. Films from enemy countries are banned.

France, 25 August
Abel Gance, who is serving as a stretcher-bearer, is horrified by the sight of the first wounded arriving from the Front. He was exempted from active military service for health reasons.

California, 5 September
Having exceeded his budget, D.W. Griffith has temporarily stopped production on *The Clansman*.

New York, 15 September
Winsor McCay has released *Gertie the Dinosaur*. The 10-minute cartoon is made up of 10,000 drawings.

Austria-Hungary, 30 September
Rival film companies are engaged in a ruthless battle for the sale of news-footage of the war.

St. Petersburg, 7 October
Vladimir Gardine has released *Anna Karenina*, adapted from Tolstoy.

New York, 31 October
Pathé America is now a production and distribution company under the new name Pathé Exchange. Charles Pathé, who is retaining 60 percent of the capital, was in the States last month to reorganize the branch, which had been put in financial difficulty by the Edison Trust.

Belgium, 14 November
The German director Stellan Ry[e], who was wounded in the fighting [at] Ypres, has died in a French hospit[al] at Flanders.

Washington, 19 December
Cartoonist Earl Hurd has registere[d] his animated cartoon technique [of] superimposing figures drawn o[n] "cellulos" over a background.

New York, 20 December
Among this year's output of motio[n] pictures was the first ever America[n] film to be directed by a woman[:] Lois Weber's screen version of *Th[e] Merchant of Venice* for the Rex C[o].

Berlin, 31 December
An actor from the Deutsches Theatre, Emil Jannings has made hi[s] screen debut in *In the Trenches*. H[e] was motivated to find film work b[y] financial need.

Paris, 31 December
Parisian cinemas have been patronized by 788,000 spectators sinc[e] they reopened in November.

BIRTHS

London, 2 April
Alec Guinness

Scotland, 11 April
Norman McLaren

Marseilles, 23 April
Simone Simon

France, 31 July
Louis de Funès
(Louis de Funès de Galarza)

Italy, 14 September
Pietro Germi

Vienna, 9 November
Hedy Lamarr
(Hedwig Eva Maria Kiesler)

Turkey, 13 November
Henri Langlois

Milan, 13 November
Alberto Lattuada

***The Battle of Elderbush Gulch** is a[n] ambitious film from Griffith about a[n] Indian attack on a settlement. In th[e] cast are Mae Marsh, Lillian Gish[,] Robert Harron and Henry Walthall.*

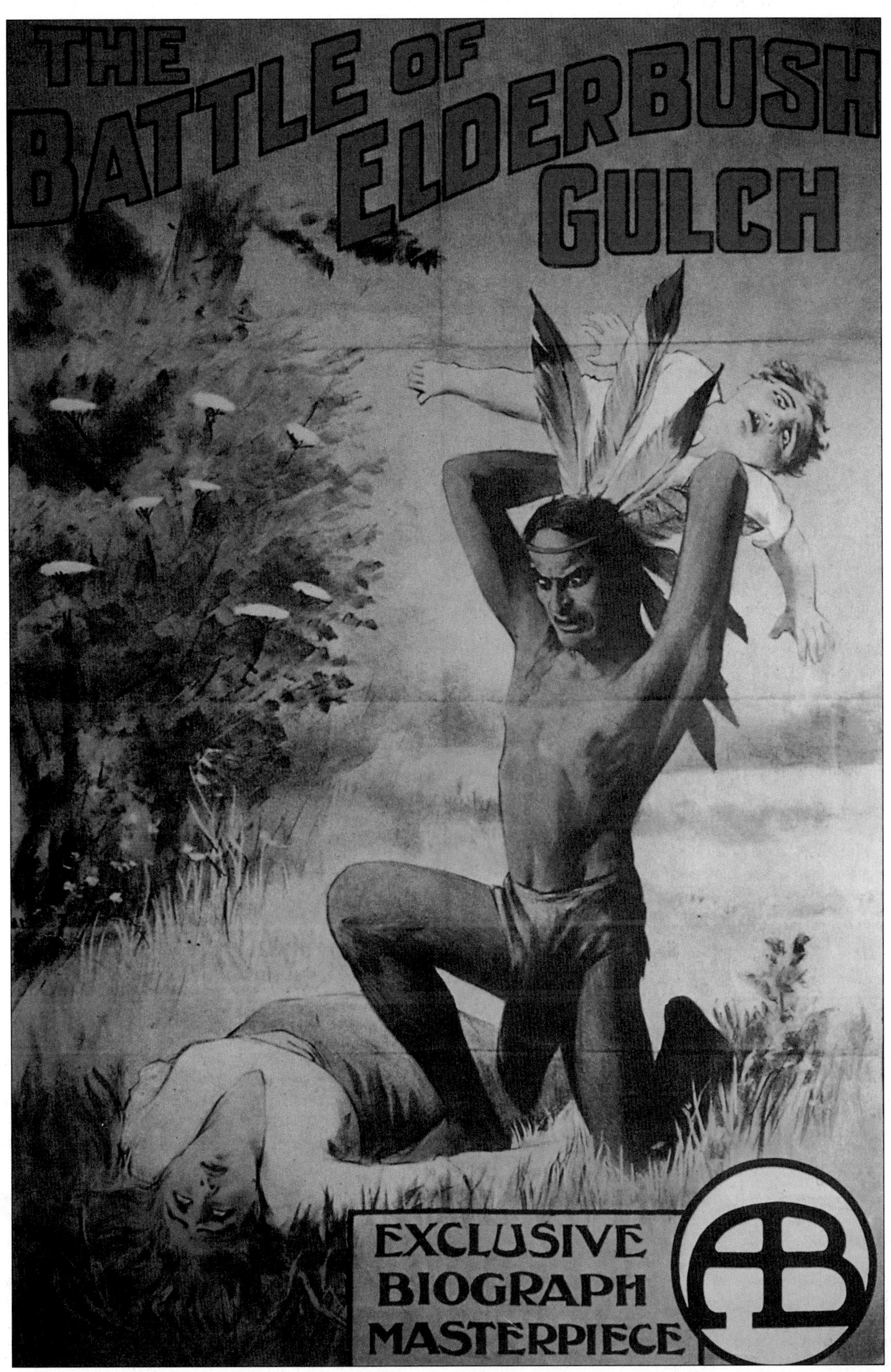
THE
BATTLE OF
ELDERBUSH
GULCH
EXCLUSIVE
BIOGRAPH
MASTERPIECE
AB

Stupendous Biblical epic in four reels from Griffith

Blanche Sweet plays the title role, with Henry B. Walthall as Holofernes.

New York, 8 March
D.W. Griffith's most ambitious film yet, *Judith of Bethulia*, has opened today at the Fifth Avenue Theater. Based on Thomas Bailey Aldrich's play, in turn derived from the Biblical Apocrypha, it marks Griffith's first venture into the longer, four-reel format. (It was, in fact, cut down from six reels.) The film tells of a respectable young widow, anxious to contribute to the defense of her surrounded and starving city, willing to undertake the mission her elders impose on her – namely, to offer herself to the Assyrian commander Holofernes in order to obtain the opportunity to kill him and thus disorganize his army so that he can be defeated by the Bethulians. Blanche Sweet brilliantly portrays the terrible inner conflict of Judith, with excellent performances from Henry B. Walthall as Holofernes, Robert Harron and Mae Marsh as the young lovers, and Lillian Gish as a mother desperately attempting to find food for her baby as the 40-day siege wears on. But it is the heroic spectacle that creates the most excitement: the attack on the walls of the city with battering rams and ladders, and the Assyrian army in full flight. *Judith of Bethulia* cost $36,000, about twice the figure at which Griffith had originally budgeted the film. The exteriors were shot in Chatsworth Park, California, and the interiors at the Biograph Studios in New York. The former were filmed in tremendously high temperatures, so that many of the extras suffered painful sunburn. So did Blanche Sweet, whose costume in a scene that required her to ride a horse, was made of crepe paper. Before filming Judith's arrival at Holofernes' camp, Griffith spent a great deal of time on an orgy scene featuring semi-nude dancing girls. The director also insisted that the well at which the young lovers meet should contain real water. As the well was a fake, Griffith had a new tank of water delivered at a cost of $80. However, this splendid, tragic love story is bound to make a profit for Biograph.

Charlie Chaplin 'makes a living'

Hollywood, 5 January
Charlie Chaplin has taken his first steps in front of the film camera. Keystone's new recruit has made his debut in a one-reel comedy directed by Mack Sennett's right-hand man Henry Lehrman. Chaplin is monocled, moustached and fraudulently elegant as an amorous cad attempting to scoop an eager-beaver reporter played by Lehrman. Entitled *Making a Living*, the film ends with a chase, followed by a mix-up in a lady's bedroom, and a grand finale on the cowcatcher of a moving train. Chaplin has spent several weeks familiarizing himself with filmmaking, getting to know his new colleagues and making a small number of "test" films. However, it seems that his first collaboration with Lehrman has not been a happy one. Chaplin did not hit it off with the director and has complained that Lehrman ignored most of his suggestions and sabotaged his best bits of comic business. Certainly the frantic pace of the Keystone films is a world apart from Chaplin's highly polished music-hall routines. Will the brilliant young comic adapt to working in a new medium?

Rival press magnates are locked in battle over serial heroines

THE TRAP
THE ECLECTIC FILM COMPANY'S
GREAT $25,000 PRIZE PHOTO-PLAY
THE PERILS of PAULINE
5TH EPISODE IN 2 PARTS

*Kathlyn Williams in **The Adventures of Kathlyn** produced by the Selig Co.*

Chicago, 31 March
Today sees the release of the first episode of a serial entitled *The Perils of Pauline* starring the vivacious blonde Pearl White, a popular star who has frequently appeared in films opposite Henry B. Walthall and Paul Panzer. A simultaneous serialization of White's cliffhanging adventures is being published by a number of the Hearst newspapers. This collaboration between newspapers and cinema is new, but it could become widespread, thus inevitably exacerbating the already shrill rivalry between two of the biggest press barons, William Randolph Hearst and Rufus McCormick. The latter dramatically boosted readership at the *Chicago Tribune* last December by publishing an abridged version of a serial produced by Selig, *The Adventures of Kathlyn*. Each week a new episode of the serial hit the screens while the daily newspaper tracked the story in its pages. The promotion increased the paper's circulation by 50,000. Determined to trump his rival, Hearst then turned to Pathé, whose Stateside subsidiary has been filming *The Perils of Pauline* since the beginning of the year. The director is Louis Gasnier, credited with discovering Max Linder and directing the comedian's early films, who has been heading Pathé's operations in America since 1912. Great success is predicted for this new venture.

Cabiria' rolls back the frontiers of Italian cinema

rin, 18 April
ith *Cabiria*, the new film by the la Film company and director d administrator Giovanni Pasne, the Turin public is witnessing e birth of a new cinematographic le. The project dates from the ginning of last year. Pastrone had cided to make a long film, an epic the Punic wars, and to display a *se-en-scène* of unrivaled magnide. All the technical means were at s disposal: sophisticated lighting, erhead cranes – a decidedly modn concept – cameras mounted on lleys, special effects, etc. *Cabiria* ok more than six months to shoot. e director had the assistance of abriele d'Annunzio, the most faous living Italian writer, who was id a generous fee for his services. though the novelist was limited to e writing of intertitles, the publici- for the film is centered on this ceptional collaboration. In addin, d'Annunzio conceived some ry curious names for the characs in the story: Cabiria (which eans "born of fire"), Croessa and aciste. The latter is a good giant r whom the audience feels great mpathy. The part is played by artolomeo Pagano, an ex-docker from Genoa. Hard up for money, this 36-year-old man took part in Itala's recruitment competition and won hands down, thanks to his powerful muscular physique. His first appearance in the film is significant – camped on a rock, with his arms crossed in such a posture as to show off his biceps, he resembles an antique statue. The adventures of Cabiria, the Sicilian slave girl, and Maciste, her strongman companion, include Hannibal's army crossing the Alps, and Archimedes firing on ships with his burning glass.

Famous writer Gabriele d'Annunzio gave financial backing to Piero Fosco, alias Pastrone, for his monumental film.

ith 'Atlantis', the 'Titanic' goes down for the second time

aris, 20 March
e very last film of the Danish ordisk company is being released Parisian screens today. Entitled *lantis*, it concerns a full adaptation of the celebrated German play by Gerhardt Hauptman, directly inspired by the recent sinking of the *Titanic*. For the reconstruction of the tragedy, the Danish production company has not stinted. A wreck was built for the incredible sum of 10,000 marks, the shooting lasted more than three months, and it required 80 first-class actors and no less than 500 extras. Unfortunately, director August Blom envisaged it on too grand a scale. According to Blom, at first, the film was to have been between 4,000 and 5,000 metres long, representing four or more hours of projection, which is obviously unacceptable to most exhibitors. At the time of the Danish release on 26 December last, not more than 2,450 metres remained, but it was still too long. The public in Copenhagen and its surroundings wanted nothing to do with this superproduction. The Italian film version measured only 1,600 metres, the French version 1,500 metres and the English 1,000. It has been a patent failure, and one wonders if Nordisk has come to grief because of this over-ambitious undertaking.

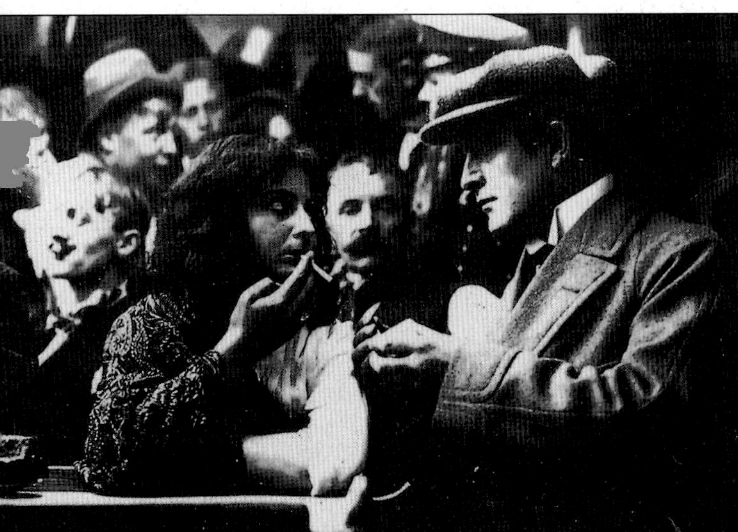

ugust Blom has made his most ambitious film to date for Nordisk.

Scenes of murder in the heart of Paris

Paris, 5 July
Despite the many regulations imposed by the Commissioner of Police, it frequently happens that technicians, actors and directors find themselves in the streets of the capital in order to shoot the exteriors for a film. Victor Méric, in the magazine *Le Bonnet Rouge*, has expressed concern about the "curious scenes" which cinema troupes have provoked when they take to the streets. Murder, kidnapping and fights in the middle of Paris have frightened pedestrians, who are terrified by the spectacle of gangs of ruffians battling with one another or of Inspector Juve firing at the fleeing Fantômas. From now on, one can easily loot a shop, pillage a house or attack an innocent passerby, while a policeman yells, "Come on, come on. Keep moving. You can see it all next Sunday at the Ciné-Folies."

▷

England warmly embraces her native son

*Charlie's tramp emerges during filming of **Kid Auto Races at Venice**.*

London, 30 June
Charlie Chaplin's first films for Mack Sennett's Keystone company have definitely been a hit with the British public. There is no bitterness that he has yielded to the temptations of the New World. In the United States Chaplin has already become a star, although his film career is barely six months old. Within a month of his screen debut in *Making a Living*, Chaplin developed a distinctive screen character – the engaging little outcast in baggy pants, oversize shoes and battered derby hat whose jaunty cane signals his pretensions to the status of a swell. The effect is completed with a small black crepe moustache which, like his cane, seems to have a life of its own. This original little personality has already captured American hearts and looks certain to conquer Europe in turn.

Paramount intends to reach the summit

New York, 15 July
A giant new distribution company has just been born, under the name of Paramount Pictures. The brainchild of W.W. Hodgkinson, it intends to operate as a nationwide distribution network with a central office located in New York City. The venture brings together a number of well-known independents, grouped under the Paramount logo of a snow-capped mountaintop surrounded by stars. Members include Adolph Zukor's Famous Players and Lasky, also Oliver Morosco, Bosworth and Pallas. Hodgkinson arrived in New York earlier this year where, drawing on his experience in operating film exchanges in the far West, he was soon involved in negotiations which led to the formation of Paramount. Not only is this new company designed to challenge such rival distribution combines as Mutual and Universal, but also to institute a new, more efficient and profitable system of exploitation and distribution to replace the current "states rights" arrangement. This latter refers to the leasing of exclusive film rights exchanges operating in the different regions of the U.S. It is then the responsibility of each exchange to promote the film in its own area and to rent it out to individual exhibitors in order to earn a profit. However, in the case of Paramount, Hodgkinson has created a system with the member companies whereby an advance of around $30,000 would be paid for the rights to each feature film handled by the company, with the rental earnings received from exhibitors to be divided with 65 percent to the original producer and 35 percent to Paramount. If this new arrangement proves successful, it will have a major influence on all future film deals in America.

DeMille and Lasky excel with the Westerr

Hollywood, 10 August
With the release of the latest Lasky production *The Call of the North*, the continuing success of his company is assured. This entertaining and dramatic adventure Western stars Robert Edeson, Winifrid Kingston and Theodore Roberts and was directed by Cecil B. DeMille. As its name implies, the Jesse Lasky Feature Play Co. has made its mark by concentrating its efforts on feature-length films of real quality, especially Westerns. Set up less than one year ago, the company got off to a good start earlier this year with the highly successful Western called *The Squaw Man*, co-directed by DeMille and Oscar Apfel. Then each director was given his own project. Apfel did well with a lively comedy subject, *Brewster's Millions*, while DeMille opted to produce another Western, *The Virginian*, adapted from the well-known novel by Owen Wister and re-teaming the two lead players from *The Squaw Man*, Dustin Farnum and Winifred Kingston. Apparently, *The Virginian* has turned out so well that the company has held back its release until early next month to take advantage of its new distribution deal with Paramount, and prefers to screen first DeMille's most recently completed feature (*The Call of the North*). Although DeMille enjoys filming Westerns on location in California, as director-general of the Lasky company h too, obviously wishes to avoid beir typecast and consequently has a ready begun shooting his first come dy subject, *What's His Name* adapted from the novel by Georg Barr McCutcheon. Having prev ously announced a policy of con pleting one film per month, Lask has already contracted to delive double this amount for Paramour release – a tall order for a ne company, but it has come such long way in so short a time th anything seems to be possible.

*Farnum (right) in **The Squaw Man**.*

*DeMille directing **The Call of the North**, his third for Jesse L. Lasky.*

riffith completes mammoth task of filming 'The Birth of a Nation'

asadena, 31 October
. W. Griffith has now finished *The irth of a Nation*, a film unlike any her. The scenario, based on two of homas Dixon's stories, *The Clans-an* and *The Leopard's Spots*, con-rns the history of two different milies, the northern Stonemans d the southern Camerons. Grif-th's intention was to recount the hole truth regarding the War of ecession in order to rehabilitate the utherners. This was an ambitious d expensive project, financed by e Mutual Film Corporation and s head Harry E. Aitkin. The final st was over $100,000, but the film ad gone over budget, and only ans from friends permitted its mpletion. The shooting of the film as done mainly at the Reliance-lajestic studio in Pasadena, Cali-rnia and lasted nine weeks. The umber of war scenes, for which riffith needed approximately 500 xtras, often take place where the ctual battles occurred. Perched on 10-metre high tower, Griffith gave ut his orders like a great military rategist. When the noise of the avalry and the booming of cannons rew louder, the instructions were tally inaudible. Extras placed at ore than three kilometres from the amera were directed with the aid of mirrors and luminous signs. During the shooting, Griffith made constant use of Mathew Brady's Civil War photographs for historical reference. For example, the surrender of General Lee at Appomatox, the signing of the proclamation freeing the slaves, and Sherman's march to the sea have been very faithfully reconstructed from some of the negatives. He also had to recreate the interior of Ford's Theater where President Abraham Lincoln was assassinated. Lincoln is played by a near-perfect double, Joseph Henabery, while Raoul Walsh with a revolver in hand, is the reincarnated personification of the murderer, John Wilkes Booth. One of the most spectacular scenes is the uprising of the riders of the Ku Klux Klan towards the climax of the film. For this sequence, Griffith had a hole dug under the place where the horses passed by, so that he could film the clamoring hoofs at ground level.

Mae Marsh (left) and Lillian Gish are the two main heroines of the film.

Keystone loses Chaplin to Essanay

Hollywood, 30 November
Charlie Chaplin has just signed a contract with Gilbert M. Anderson and George K. Spoor, directors of the Essanay company. The 24-year-old actor is bidding farewell to Keystone, where he enjoyed his first success in the movies. When his contract with Keystone's boss Mack Sennett came up for renewal, Chaplin demanded a raise from $175 to $1,000 a week. Sennett replied with a counteroffer of a three-year contract at $500 in the first year, rising to $1,500 in the third, but Chaplin had already decided that it was time to move on. Essanay, which up till now has thrived on a diet of Anderson's Broncho Billy Westerns, has offered him $1,250 a week plus a $10,000 bonus. In addition Anderson and Spoor have promised Chaplin complete artistic control of his films, of which he will be the star. Chaplin has truly come a long way in a year. With 35 Keystone films behind him, 23 of which he directed himself, he has already created his own comic universe. Now he will be exchanging the balmy climate of sunny California for breezy Chicago where Essanay are still making films in their original studio.

lew Yorkers are delighted by McCay's 'Gertie the Dinosaur'

ew York, 28 December
Vinsor McCay has created a new artoon heroine, Gertie the Dino-aur, whose adventures are the toast f the town. The inspiration sprung om an approach made to the artist y the American Historical Society o draw pictures of prehistoric ani-als. This is the first of McCay's nimated films to have a detailed ackground, all of which has been reated by the hand of John Fitzsim-ons. Gertie makes a shy debut, eering from behind some boulders. ut she soon asserts herself as she evours trees, rocks and fruit, then rinks a lake dry, tosses a mammoth ver her shoulder and dances. When he is admonished for her boisterous ehavior, she bursts into tears, melt-ng the stoniest of hearts. The car-oon is accompanied by a live action equence in which McCay and some f his cronies visit New York's Mu-eum of Natural History and prowl through the dinosaur exhibits. Later, resplendent in tuxedoes, they visit a restaurant where McCay bets that he can make a dinosaur movie and sets to work drawing. Gertie has also become part of McCay's stage act. He invites Gertie to eat an apple which he holds up. She lowers her neck and swallows the fruit to the delight of the audience.

Already popular as a comic strip, Gertie comes to life on the cinema screen.

China suffers from lack of film stock

Peking, 31 December
Cinema is just one of the victims in a country that is becoming increasingly isolated internationally. Because of the war in Europe, the young republic of Sun Yat-sen has for some time experienced ever greater difficulties in obtaining the most basic materials from the West. Unused film stock has become an extremely rare commodity because of the fact that the ingredients that constitute film, and also the money needed to then manufacture it, have ceased to arrive in Peking. As a result local production, still in its infancy, has sadly diminished. Unfortunately, in this context, the pioneer Chinese works such as the films of the Spanish cameraman Antonio Ramos or of Ling Shao Po or the Li brothers might well become relegated to the secret dungeons of cinema history.

1915

Chicago, 10 January
Charlie Chaplin's first film for Essanay titled *His New Job* is receiving a spectacular advertising campaign.

New York, 12 January
Theda Bara has made an explosive debut in *A Fool There Was*, directed by Frank Powell, an adaptation of Rudyard Kipling's *Vampire*. America's first vamp is born, helped by a publicity campaign which owes a great deal of its exoticism to the imagination of both the press and advertising agencies.

Paris, 28 January
The French branch of the German optical manufacturer Karl Zeiss has been officially impounded.

Los Angeles, 1 February
The producer, distributor and businessman William Fox has founded the new Fox Film Corporation with Winfield Sheehan.

Los Angeles, 8 February
D,W. Griffith and Harry Aitken have created the Epoch Producing Corporation on the same day as the world premiere of *The Birth of a Nation*.

Paris, 20 February
Abel Gance has accepted a proposition, by Louis Nalpas from Film d'Art, to film *Un drame au château d'Acre* in five days with a budget of 5,000 francs.

Rome, 28 February
Screening of the first film in a detective series based on the Za la Mort character, *Nellie the Gigolette*. The film is produced by Emilio Ghione and stars the diva Francesca Bertini.

Paris, 1 March
The prefect of police has banned the screening of all films depicting the scenes of desolation created by the enemy in certain regions.

Washington, 15 April
The Supreme Court has delivered a final blow to Thomas Edison by canceling all the Motion Picture Patent Corporation's patents.

Paris, 17 April
In protest against censorship, the Union of Cinematograph Directors has organized a private screening of banned films at the Palais des Fêtes.

Boston, 21 May
As a result of the campaign against *The Birth of a Nation*, the State of Massachusetts has voted in favor of creating a board of censors.

Berlin, 21 May
Ernst Lubitsch, who has already acted on stage (with Max Reinhardt) and on the screen in Carl Wilhelm's comedies for Union-Film, has gotten behind the camera to make *On the Slippery Slope*.

Paris, May
Charles Pathé has returned from a trip to the United States where he opened 22 new distribution agencies in as many states. Pathé-Exchange is now the leading firm for exporting American films to France.

Boston, 2 June
Black organizations have presented the Mayor with a petition bearing 6,000 signatures asking him to ban *The Birth of a Nation*.

California, 6 June
Harold Lloyd has completed the first film in a series of short comedies made by his friend Hal Roach. Here he portrays a character named Lonesome Luke, clearly drawing inspiration from Chaplin, and likely to displace the previous character of the Lloyd-Roach collaboration, "Willie Work".

Paris, 21 July
Abel Gance has signed up with Louis Nalpas for Film d'Art. Under the terms of his contract he has to produce nine films a year, based on senarios written by himself. Nalpas was won over by Gance's ideas and spirit in his *Un drame au château d'Acre* (*A Drama at the Château of Acre*) and *la Folie du Dr. Tube* (*The Madness of Dr. Tube*).

Paris, 30 July
Louis Feuillade has been discharged from active service due to a heart problem. He can now return to the Buttes-Chaumont studios.

Rome, 31 July
Opening of *Maciste*, directed by Vincent Denizot and Luigi Romano Borgnetto and with Bartolomeo Pagano who created the role. The film was inspired by Giovanni Pastrone's internationally acclaimed epic *Cabiria*.

Montreuil, 8 August
Gaston Méliès has turned part of his old film studio into a theater in aid of the Montreuil hospital. *The Arlesienne*, by Alphonse Daudet is playing at the moment.

France, 19 August
The Gaumont Palace in Paris and the Majestic Cinema in Lyon have reopened.

Copenhagen, 18 September
Forest Holger-Madsen's *Put Down Your Arms* is screening today in Denmark.

Paris, 1 October
French cinema production is slowly picking up after the interruption caused by the outbreak of war. As René Navarre has been called up for duty, the *Fantômas* series has been dropped. However, Louis Feuillade has started filming a new series, *les Vampires*, with Edouard Mathé, Marcel Lévesque and Jean Ayme, in the hope of forestalling the probable success in France of the highly popular *Mysteries of New York*.

Boston, 1 October
The Philarmonic Hall is screening Cecil B. DeMille's *Carmen*, with Wallace Reed and Geraldine Farrar. The prima donna, who was taken on for a fabulous sum, is making her screen debut, but... the famous voice is silent.

New York, 15 October
Release of J. Stuart Blackton's *The Battle Cry of Peace*. Financed with silent backing from the arms manufacturer Hudson Maxim, it is the first propaganda film for America's participation in the war.

New York, 31 October
Douglas Fairbanks has been signed up by D.W. Griffith. Fairbanks has just finished making *The Lamb* under Griffith's supervision at Triangle for a salary of $2,000 a week.

Paris, 12 November
Gaumont has released the first two episodes of *Vampires* from Louis Feuillade: *la Tête coupée* (*The Decapitated Head*) and *la Bague qui tue* (*The Ring that Kills*).

Paris, 25 November
First release of Giovanni Pastrone's *Cabiria* at the Vaudeville Theatre.

London, 20 December
Abel Gance is extremely impress by D.W. Griffith's highly controve sial *The Birth of a Nation*, which h not as yet been screened in Franc

Paris, 23 December
The Chamber of Deputies has vote a resolution to form a committee encourage the use of films in th education system.

Paris, 25 December
AGC is distributing Charlie Cha lin's film *Work*.

Poland, 31 December
Alexander Hertz has directed Po Negri, formerly known as Apolon Chalupiec, in *The Woman* and *Th Little Black Book*.

Prague, 31 December
Vaclav Havel has taken over A tonin Pech's Kinofa assets and h formed the Lucerna company.

BIRTHS

Wisconsin, 6 May
Orson Welles

Rome, 15 May
Mario Monicelli

Siberia, 12 July
Yul Brynner (Julius Brynner)

Paris, 31 July
Henri Decaë

Stockholm, 15 August
Signe Hasso

Stockholm, 29 August
Ingrid Bergman

Stockholm, 10 September
Gösta Ekman

New Jersey, 12 December
Frank Sinatra

Munich, 13 December
Curt Jurgens

Paris, 19 December
Edith Piaf

Four months in the making, the fir American movie epic, about the W between the States, is a testament t the ambition and genius of direct D.W. Griffith.

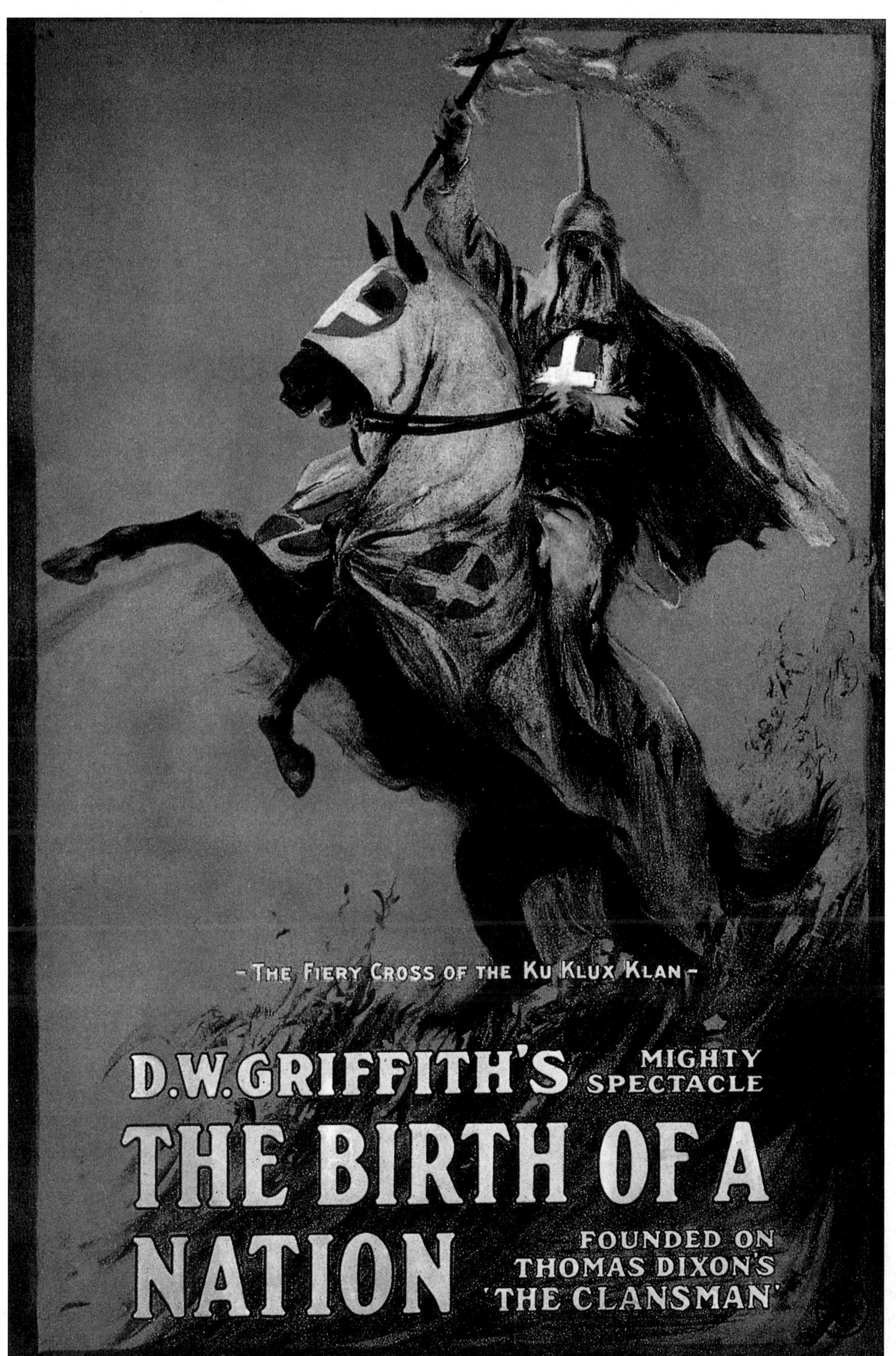
- THE FIERY CROSS OF THE KU KLUX KLAN -
D.W. GRIFFITH'S
MIGHTY SPECTACLE
THE BIRTH OF A NATION
FOUNDED ON THOMAS DIXON'S 'THE CLANSMAN'

A huge and exciting studio rises from the desert

San Fernando Valley, 21 March
Carl Laemmle, the president of Universal Manufacturing Corporation, is today a very happy man. He has just inaugurated an ensemble of prestigious studios in the San Fernando Valley in Southern California, which he has named Universal City. More precisely, these studios are situated on the 230-acre Taylor ranch across the Cahuenga Pass. Laemmle was presented with an outsize gold key by actress Laura Oakley, "chief of police" designate of the only city in the world built exclusively for the purpose of motion picture production. After announcing that there would be no long drawn-out speeches or "meaningless ceremony", Laemmle unlocked the front gates to the main entrance and pronounced the studio, and its two days' festivities, open. As he did so, the thousands of spectators marched onto the impressive new premises, gaily singing "The Star-Spangled Banner" as they went. By the afternoon the crowd had swelled to 20,000, and still they flooded in. Carl Laemmle's dream had at last become a reality. It is a tremendous triumph for this immigrant, who left Laupheim in Germany 30 years ago at age 17, and who had never previously given motion pictures a thought. The large complex employs several hundred people, and the equipment, such as revolving sets, is in the forefront of modern innovation. Among other things, the truly exceptional location of this cinema city facilitates the shooting of exteriors. This is largely thanks to the extraordinarily temperate climate which makes it "the greatest outdoor stage in the world." With the opening of Universal City, the cinema business has taken on new dimensions, though it is not clear whether Laemmle plans to expand and upgrade his productions, too. The new studio is prepared to commence a full production schedule immediately. Some stars under contract include Pauline Bush, J. Warren Kerrigan, Francis Ford, Lon Chaney, Grace Cunard, William Clifford and Gertrude Selby. Robert Cochrane is Laemmle's vice president and Pat Powell, treasurer.

WE ARE ON OUR WAY TO
Universal City Calif.
UNIVERSAL
MOVING PICTURES
ARE MADE
A flamboyant sightseeing tour of the new studio on its opening day.

Happy Mr. and Mrs. Carl Laemmle

'The Lady with the Lamp' brightens up the screens of London

London, 11 March
With British soldiers fighting in the trenches in Flanders and Gallipoli, it is hard to imagine a more inspiring subject for a film than the story of Florence Nightingale, who did so much for the efficiency of military hospitals during the Crimean War. The B. and C. Company have risen to the occasion with their production *Florence Nightingale*, starring Elizabeth Risdon as the Lady with the Lamp. Starting with the earliest stories of Florence Nightingale's childhood – we are even shown the infant heroine in her mother's arms in 1820 – the film documents her philanthropic and social work in England as well as her heroic efforts during the Crimean War. There are harrowing scenes of the appalling conditions she encountered in the Army's hospital at Scutari when she arrived in the Crimea, and a moving account of how she brought order out of chaos. The film ends with a scene in which the aged Florence Nightingale receives the Order of Merit from King Edward VII. This has been hailed not only as a triumph of makeup but also as testimony to Risdon's sympathetic interpretation. Director Maurice Elvey's careful attention to detail and skillful handling of light and shade mark him out as one to watch.

A grateful army pays homage to Florence Nightingale (Elizabeth Risdon).

The exotic allure of a new star

Hollywood, 12 March
With the opening of *A Fool There Was*, directed by J. Gordon Edwards for producer William Fox, the film community offers the public a new star of very unusual allure. The sultry Theda Bara, it is said, was "born in the shadow of the Sphinx" and purports to be the daughter of a desert princess and an Italian sculptor. However, those more enlightened know that Miss Bara was born Theodosia Goodman, the daughter of a Cincinnati tailor. Be that as it may, with her air of a predatory tigress and her exaggerated and exotic makeup, she has already been dubbed "The Vamp", a dangerous temptress who is bound to attract hordes of paying male customers to the theaters where her films are shown. Plans are already afoot for several more to follow her first sensational appearance.

Feelings run high over 'The Birth of a Nation'

).W. Griffith, from now on one of 'ie 'greats' of the world cinema.

The dramatic and exciting ride to the rescue by the Ku Klux Klan provides a suitably rousing climax to this film.

Boston, 10 April
). W. Griffith's controversial film *'he Birth of a Nation* has just been eleased at the Tremont Theater. 'housands of black activists opposed to the film marched on the apital, where clashes occurred beause of a counter-demonstration by /hite supporters of the film. The olice proceeded to make numerous rrests. This hullabaloo came as the esult of the decision by the mayor o allow the film to be shown, whatver the cost, and despite a petition f some 6,000 signatures gathered y the Boston section of the National Association for the Advancement f Colored People (NAACP). Since March, the date of the New York remiere of the film at the Liberty 'heater, the dispute continues to rage on. Oswald Garrison Villard, the grandson of the famous abolitionist and New York *Post* editor, even accused the film of being "a deliberate attempt to humiliate millions of American citizens by portraying them as complete animals." In addition, the NAACP alluded to numerous scenes where white actors, blacked up, committed the worst atrocities. The leader of the protest was William Monroe Trotter, the Harvard-educated editor-publisher of a strong-minded Negro paper, *The Guardian.* Nevertheless, everything started well for this undoubtedly magnificent 180-minute work. Simultaneously with its release, *The Birth of a Nation* was shown at the White House to President Woodrow Wilson, who stated, "It is like writing history with lightning. And my only regret is that it is all so terribly true." The next day another screening was held for 300 selected guests, including the chief Supreme Court magistrate Edward D. White and Thomas Dixon, on whose work this film was based. Their reaction was particularly enthusiastic. Despite, or because of, the vocal opposition, Griffith's film today is still drawing crowds. For the first time, millions of spectators are ready to pay $2 for their cinema seat. The movie, which cost over $100,000, including shooting, advertising and distribution, should rapidly see a substantial profit.

'Ienry B. Walthall and Lillian Gish, two lovers separated by circumstance.

Joseph Henabery (right) as Lincoln, America's controversial president.

▷

Charlie's partner is young typist

Los Angeles, 21 June

Charlie Chaplin's eighth film for Essanay, *Work*, has been released. Filmed at the Bradbury Mansion studio at 147 North Hill Street in San Francisco, it features Chaplin as a down-trodden decorator whose attempt to refurbish peppery Billy Armstrong's house ends in a huge explosion which buries everyone under a mountain of rubble. Co-starring once again with Charlie is an attractive 22-year-old blonde, Edna Purviance, who first joined forces with Chaplin last February in *His New Job*, appropriately the comedian's first film for Essanay. She had originally been recommended to Chaplin by one of Broncho Billy Anderson's cowboy actors, Carl Strauss, who had spotted her at a restaurant in San Francisco. She was located working as a secretary and Chaplin was instantly captivated by her and her ebullient sense of humor. At a party the night before she made her debut in front of the cameras, she bet Chaplin $10 that he could not hypnotize her. She then played along with him, pretending to fall under his hypnotic spell. There is little doubt, however, that it is Chaplin who has fallen under the spell of the petite beauty with the sensual mouth. In addition to his lovely new leading lady, Charlie is assembling a talented stock company to work with him at the Essanay studios at Niles, outside San Francisco. They include cross-eyed Ben Turpin, former Karno comic Billy Armstrong and another Englishman, Fred Goodwins, a former journalist and stage actor.

*With Edna Purviance in **Work**.*

Mack Sennett's 'Bathing Beauties' revive the art of burlesque

These lovely 'Bathing Beauties', revealing themselves in swimsuits are now inseparable from the Keystone image.

Los Angeles, 31 July

Keystone's Mack Sennett has created a curious *corps de ballet*. Christened his "Bathing Beauties", they are pretty young women dressed in an increasingly extravagant range of swimsuits. Always pictured in a group, they will from now on grace Keystone comedies, popping up in the most unlikely situations something like the hilariously incompetent Keystone Cops, of whom Ford Sterling and Chester Conklin are the most famous. With the advent of the "Bathing Beauties", cinemagoers are promised a treat for the eyes. The flood of Keystone films on the market has left both audiences and the studio somewhat breathless of late. But audiences will nonetheless welcome the comic reinforcement this new group is certain to add to performances of Keystone's leading lights, Mabel Normand and Roscoe "Fatty" Arbuckle, both now established as international stars.

Ford Sterling is the police chief (left) taking the call, while Fatty Arbuckle is far right in the line of Keystone Cops ready to spring into action.

Deathblow at last for Edison's trust

New York, 15 October

The U.S. Supreme Court reached a decision today on the anti-trust case brought against the Motion Picture Patents Company has sealed the fate of Edison's trust. In fact, this decision has merely confirmed what everyone already knows, since the power of the trust has been declining for many years. The members of the trust have been unable (or unwilling) to adapt to changing conditions in the production, distribution and exhibition of films. Their business has been declining during a period when the total size of the industry has been increasing, led by such independents as Paramount, Fox and Universal. In fact, a number of its own members, such as Pathé and Kleine, have already begun to distance themselves from the trust. Both Kalem and Biograph have substantially reduced their filmmaking activities, while earlier this year Vitagraph, Lubin, Selig and Essanay joined together to form the new V-L-S-E Co. to release features made by its member companies.

acha Guitry films his famous compatriots

acha Guitry and Sarah Bernhardt, mutual admirers and now close friends.

aris, 22 November
he film that the young playwright acha Guitry is presenting at the ariétés Theatre, stars a dazzling ast. In *Ceux de chez nous*, we see e sculptor Auguste Rodin; the omposer Camille Saint-Saëns; the riters Edmond Rostand, Anatole France and Octave Mirbeau; the actors Sarah Bernhardt, Lucien Guitry (Sacha's father) and André Antoine; and the painters Claude Monet, Edgar Degas and old Auguste Renoir. Afflicted by arthritis, Renoir holds his paintbrush with the help of his son Jean, at his side.

A jewel of a heroine gleams in a serial

OFFERT GRATUITEMENT PAR
Le Matin
LES MYSTÈRES DE NEW-YORK
Gd ROMAN CINÉMA AMÉRICAIN
PIERRE DECOURCELLE

Mysteries of New York *adapt the exploits of Elaine to French tastes.*

Paris, 3 December
Cinemas in Paris are now screening the first episode of *Mysteries of New York*, an American film produced in the United States by Donald Mackenzie and Louis Gasnier for Pathé-Exchange, the U.S. subsidiary of the French Pathé company. It has been eagerly awaited, and the press has been full of stories of the American infatuation with Pearl White, the serial's heroine. For several days now the daily newspaper *le Matin* has been publishing its own serialization of the film, adapted by Pierre Decourcelle. For the French market they have compiled edited versions of three original Pearl White serials, *The Perils of Pauline*, *The Iron Claw* and *The Exploits of Elaine*, 36 episodes in all. The French version runs to 22 episodes, each of which is about 1,800-feet long. In the story, Pearl White plays Elaine Dodge, a ravishing young heiress menaced by Wu Fang, the leader of a Chinese underworld gang. However, at the moments of greatest danger she is invariably rescued by Arnold Daly and Creighton Hale. Elaine's father is played by Lionel Barrymore, a talented actor of stage and screen, already well-known for his projects with the director D.W. Griffith. In America Pearl White has become a star, and the serials have been smash-hits. Their appeal lies primarily in the vibrant personality of the young actress, for it has to be said that the version produced by Mackenzie and Gasnier shows signs of haste. Meanwhile, Elaine Dodge's millions of fans are impatiently waiting for the second episode entitled *le Sommeil sans souvenir.* Blonde and lithe, our plucky, tender-hearted heroine suffers the ordeal of clutching hands, mysterious voices, threatening rays and deadly kisses, always surviving unscathed to rejoin the fray in the next episode.

ecil B. DeMille achieves stylistic refinement with 'The Cheat'

ew York, 12 December
wo men and a woman are the lead haracters in Cecil B. DeMille's new lm, a refreshing change from the normous casts and extras that toay's cinema now takes for granted. he title is *The Cheat*, and it heralds he paring down of *mise-en-scène*. his story is a melodrama involving exuality and perversion. A foolish young society woman borrows a considerable sum of money from a rich Japanese collector on the condition that she give herself to him. The promise is not kept. Furious, the man brands the young woman with a hot iron. The woman hides the exact circumstances from her husband, and he is accused of the crime. The trial which follows is going against the couple until the victim, in a display of heroism, bares her shoulder and shows the horrified jury the mark of a cheat. This Jesse L. Lasky Feature Play Company production has been a great success and has confirmed the talent of the young director Cecil B. DeMille, who shot *The Cheat* in a few weeks, at the same time as another long feature entitled *The Golden Chance*. While *The Cheat* was shot from nine to five during the day, *The Golden Chance* was filmed at night, sometimes till dawn. In such conditions, one cannot fail to be astonished by the aesthetic quality of *The Cheat* – the lighting and the framing of the images. The tragic scene of the red-hot branding iron was filmed in chiaroscuro, using close-ups and exciting editing. The young woman who attempts to deceive both men, and the lecherous Japanese villain are played respectively by the pretty Fannie Ward and the enigmatic Sessue Hayakawa. The excellence of their interpretation, especially a restrained one by the latter, should soon place them both in the firmament of stars.

he Cheat *has brought stardom to Sessue Hayakawa and Fannie Ward.*

1916

Paris, 8 January
The Italian film version of *The Lady of the Camelias*, by Gustavo Serena and starring Francesca Bertini, is to be distributed in France.

Paris, 22 January
Jacques Feyder, a young Belgian actor, has been taken on as a director by Léon Gaumont on the recommendation of Gaston Ravel.

France, 18 February
Several business magazines have remarked on the number of foreign films invading the French market at a time when French production is suffering from a lack of work.

New York, 25 February
The first cartoon in the "Krazy Kat" series, *Krazy Kat and Ignatz Mouse Discuss the Letter G*, is being shown. It was produced by Frank Moser from an adaptation of George Herriman's comic strip.

Los Angeles, 26 February
Charlie Chaplin has signed a year's contract with the Mutual Film Corporation. He is to receive $10,000 a week plus the lump sum of $150,000 on signing.

New York, 12 March
Release of *The Habit of Happiness*, directed by Allan Dwan and starring Douglas Fairbanks, an attractive newcomer to the screen.

Chicago, 27 March
The young actress Gloria Swanson has married Wallace Beery, who is always cast in brutish roles due to his rough-hewn features.

Los Angeles, 27 March
The Lone Star studios have been equipped by Mutual to make Chaplin films.

Paris, 29 March
The committee formed to study the use of films for educational purposes has been appointed by decree.

England, 31 March
The American firm Triangle has taken control of 882 cinemas within the block booking system.

Rome, 1 April
Actress Pina Menichelli is setting the screen ablaze in Giovanni Pastrone's *Il Fuoco*.

Paris, 7 April
The French Union of Cinematographers has published its first official journal, *l'Ecran*.

Paris, 22 April
Two young girls, who are appearing in court for attempted murder, have stated that their crime was inspired by a film.

Paris, 13 May
The German-owned cinema Palais Rochechouart has now reopened its doors under the management of Alphonse Frank.

New York, 15 May
Screening of Charlie Chaplin's first film for Mutual, *The Floorwalker* with Edna Purviance and Eric Campbell.

Paris, 18 May
Gaumont has released *le Pied qui étreint* (*The Grasping Foot*). The film is a parody of *Vampires*, directed by Jacques Feyder, which starred André Roanne, Georges Biscot and Musidora.

Paris, 29 May
The National Cinema Board has met to decide on import duties for foreign films. French film producers want to be protected but need to avoid a heavy tax on the importation of unexposed film.

Paris, 16 June
Gaumont has presented *Têtes de femmes, femme de têtes* from the director Jacques Feyder. The cast includes the young Françoise Rosay, Kitty Hott and André Roanne.

New York, 16 June
The Jesse Lasky Feature Play Co. and Famous Players have merged to form the Famous Players-Lasky Corporation. Adolph Zukor takes the post of president.

Paris, 1 July
Georges-Michel Coissac has published an article in *Cine-Journal* "moralizing about the cinema and calling for the banning of vulgarity on the screen."

California, 6 August
A selected public was invited to the preview of *Intolerance* (originally entitled *The Mother and the Law*), directed by D.W. Grifffith.

Paris, 11 August
Pathé is screening the two first episodes of Louis Gasnier's new American serial, *The Exploits of Elaine*, once again starring Pearl White. A Pathé-Exchange production, it has been made as a follow-up to *Mysteries of New York*.

Stockholm, 14 August
With the release of his latest film, *Karlek och Journalistic* (*Love and Journalism*), interpreted by Jenny Tschernichin-Larsson and Richard Lund, the prolific director Mauritz Stiller has created a new genre of film: domestic comedy.

Los Angeles, 15 August
Creation of The Artcraft Pictures Corporation at Paramount. This new distribution company is to devote its main energies to distributing Mary Pickford films.

Rome, 11 September
Filippo Tommaso Marinetti has published a manifesto labeled *The Futuristic Cinema*.

Los Angeles, 14 September
Samuel Goldfish has resigned his position as administrative president of Famous Players-Lasky due to a series of disagreements with the new president Adolph Zukor.

Paris, 15 September
André Antoine is filming the street scenes for *Coupable* (*Guilty*) in the place du Tertre in an attempt "to catch life in full flight."

Prague, 20 October
Lucerna has released *A Little Heart of Gold*, produced by the playwright and actor Antonin Fencl.

Berlin, 31 October
Gustav Streseman, a deputy, has asked for a parliamentary debate on the importation of foreign films.

USA, 9 December
Charlie Chaplin has won his case to prevent publication of an unauthorized biography, *Charlie Chaplin's Own Story*. He instigated proceedings in October.

Paris, 16 December
The press has had a preview of the first episodes of Louis Feuillade's *Judex*, with Musidora, Yvette Andreyor and René Cresté.

Los Angeles, 16 December
Samuel Goldfish has formed a ne production company, Goldwyn Pi tures Corporation, in associatio with Edgar and Arch Selwyn, th Broadway producers.

Johannesburg, 31 December
Harold Shaw is making *The Voo trekkers: Winning a Continent* f African Film Productions. The fil is a historical fresco recording th history of South Africa's "Afrikaa ers", as the settlers of Dutch desce became known.

BIRTHS

Buenos Aires, 11 January
Bernard Blier

Japan, 4 February
Masaki Kobayashi

California, 5 April
Gregory Peck
(Eldred G. Peck)

Quebec, 1 May
Glenn Ford
(Gwyllin Samuel Newton)

Italy, 8 June
Luigi Comencini

India, 15 September
Margaret Lockwood

England, 26 September
Trevor Howard

London, 28 September
Peter Finch
(William Mitchell)

Paris, 5 November
Madeleine Robinson
(Madeleine Svoboda)

New York, 9 December
Kirk Douglas
(Issur Danielovitch Demsky)

Milan, 23 December
Dino Risi

Paris, 31 December
Suzy Delair

---

*D.W. Griffith's **Intolerance**, boastir spectacular settings and spannir four epochs, is the filmmaker's rep to those who criticized **The Birth of Nation** as racist and bigoted.*

D·W·GRIFFITH'S
COLOSSAL SPECTACLE
THE CRUEL HAND OF INTOLERANCE
INTOLERANCE
- A SUN PLAY OF THE AGES -
MR GRIFFITH'S FIRST PRODUCTION SINCE
"THE BIRTH OF A NATION"

'Civilization': a passionate plea for peace

New York, 17 April
Thomas Ince has released his most ambitious picture to date. Produced by the Triangle Corporation and symbolically entitled *Civilization*, it draws its inspiration from *The Battle Cry of Peace*, a James Stuart Blackton film adapted from the Hudson Maxim book *Defenseless America*. The message of this ten-reel film is determinedly pacifist. A portrait of Woodrow Wilson, who has just been re-elected to the U.S. presidency on a non-interventionist ticket, makes a significant appearance at the beginning of the film. In one of the most effective scenes in *Civilization*, the commander of one of the warring powers' submarines refuses to sink a passenger ship. Clearly, this is a barely-veiled allusion to last year's torpedoing of the liner *Lusitania* in which 124 Americans died. The first half of the film is superbly controlled, depicting war sweeping over the landscape by using a succession of striking images: the silhouetted troops, ranks of charging cavalry, guns strewn over the hillside – all seem to sink through a pall of smoke as though descending into a pit of hell. At the climax of the picture, Christ returns as a submarine engineer to preach peace at the head of an army of pacifist women. Equally memorable are the less rhetorical images, such as the old woman who stares in grief as the men are taken off to war, and a shepherd boy trying to release a dove.

PEACE
THE BATTLE CRY OF
"CIVILIZATION"
INCE'S MASTERPIECE
An Epic Of Humanity
Dedicated to that vast army whose tears have girdled the universe - The Mothers of the Dead.
AMERICAN TRADING ASSN. 729 SEVENTH AVE., NEW YORK

Actor William S. Hart directs 'The Aryan'

Seventeen-year-old newcomer Bessie Love co-stars with Hart in his new film.

New York, 13 April
Today sees the release of a new William S. Hart film. Entitled *The Aryan*, it has been written by the Triangle Corporation's celebrated cowboy star. Steve Denton, better known to the public as Rio Jim, is a renegade who scorns law and morality until the day when he is redeemed by the love of a young woman, in the beautiful form of Bessie Love. The "good bad man" character is a role which Hart has turned into his own. Now in his fifties, Hart's image of a Man of the West was honed by 20 years of stage experience before entering films in 1914, at which time he began working for his friend Thomas H. Ince. Hart made an immediate impression in his first season of two-reelers and has since moved on to feature-length films which he directs himself. In 1915 he followed Ince to Triangle, where his popularity now rivals that of Broncho Billy Anderson.

Censors are hot on the murderers' trail

Paris, 17 May
With the appearance of Zigomar, Fantômas and the vampires, has the cinematograph become a school for crime? Several gangsters recently caught by the police have confessed that the latest episodes of *Mysteries of New York* had influenced them in their criminal activities. Brenier, the member of parliament for Isère, climbed onto the rostrum of the Chamber and demanded that the government prohibit the screening of "cinematographic performances which, in the guise of fantastic adventures, teach the most skillful means of killing and robbing." The Minister of the Interior, Louis Malvy, agreed and is currently in charge of setting up a special commission charged with the examination and control of films. Film censorship is not a new phenomenon. For quite some time, mayors and departmental police chiefs have made the decision, independently of Paris, to ban the showing of *The Adventures of Bonnot* or *The Grasping Hand* in their districts. From now on, the officials at the Place Beauvau will be responsible for the morality in films, even to the extent of cutting them. Many have given hypocritical reasons for their decisions. It is said that the chief commissioner requested the cutting of a suicide scene, declaring, "No violent deaths must be shown while there is a war on."

Chaplin loses case over 'Carmen'

Washington, 24 June
Charles Chaplin's long legal battle against Essanay has ended in defeat. The case has gone all the way to the Supreme Court, which has ruled in Essanay's favor. The litigation was caused by a film entitled *Charlie Chaplin's Burlesque on Carmen*, a send-up of Cecil B. DeMille's *Carmen*, with Charlie capering around as "Darn Hosiery" and playing a realistic death scene with Edna Purviance before showing the audience how it was done with a prop dagger. After the comedian's departure to Mutual, Essanay decided to turn the squib into a four-reeler, inserting new scenes directed by Leo White and featuring Ben Turpin as well as salvaging material discarded by Chaplin. When the film was released in April, Chaplin immediately went to the courts to seek a remedy. In May his attorney Nathan Burkan appealed for an injunction to prevent Essanay from distributing the film, claiming that it was a fraud on the public and that Chaplin's rights as an author had been infringed. The application for an injunction was dismissed by Justice Hotchkiss of the Supreme Court of the State of New York, and Essanay launched a counter-suit against Chaplin for an estimated half-a-million dollars in lost profits on films which they claimed he still owed them. Now the Supreme Court in Washington has upheld Hotchkiss' decision, and Chaplin has emerged from the experience a sadder but wiser man. In the future the comedian's contracts will stipulate that there will be no modification or mutilation of his movies after they have been made.

Chaplin and Edna in ***Carmen***.

The poisonous charms of Musidora

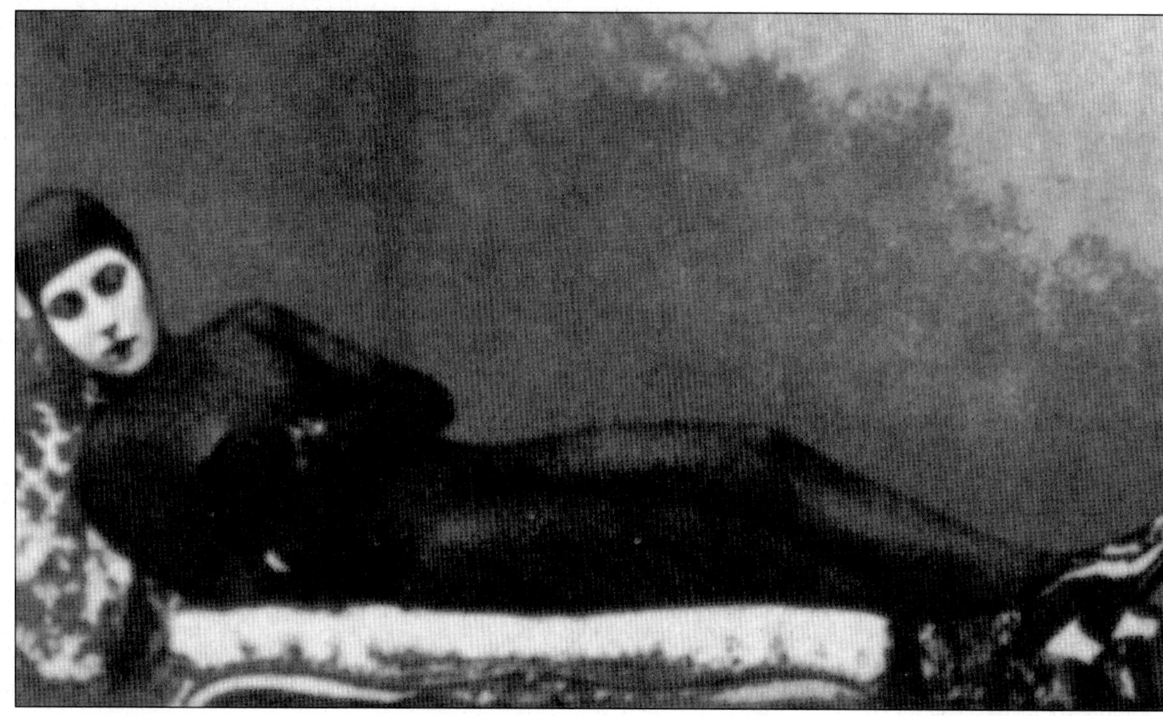

Discovered by Feuillade in 1913, the beautiful Musidora brings a totally modern sensuality to the 'Vampires' series.

Paris, 30 June
The tenth and final episode of *The Vampires*, entitled *Nights of Blood*, directed by Louis Feuillade, is now to be seen on our screens. Since the release of *The Red Code*, the third episode in the series, the whole of France has passionately followed the misdeeds of the splendid Irma Vep, a brown-eyed brunette whose name is an anagram of vampire. Musidora plays the evil-doing character, who is under the orders of the Grand Vampire, interpreted by Fernand Hermann. Dressed as a simple maid, shorthand typist or as a man, Musidora has, above all, stirred audiences in the part of the female cat burglar, because "her black tights cling to her ivory body," as the song goes. Musidora has been endowed with a provocative figure, which allows Irma Vep to glide swiftly through the shadows to steal and murder, the exact opposite of the sweet and docile Elaine Dodge. At the climax of the film, morality triumphs, because the vampire is killed by a revolver shot. Louis Feuillade has moderated the tone of the serial, primarily because the commissioner of police, Lépine, did not appreciate the failure of justice in the previous episodes. Musidora herself has been vigorously active in trying to persuade the authorities not to ban *The Vampires*. She has been successful. How can one possibly resist the charms of Irma Vep?

'Cheat' disparaged

Paris, 21 July
Critics and public alike have been knocked sideways by the latest Cecil B. DeMille film, *The Cheat*. Some have vigorously condemned the now notorious scene in which the rich and evil Japanese, played by Sessue Hayakawa, brutally bares the shoulder of a young American woman, the fragile Fannie Ward, to brand her with a red-hot iron. And one either loves or hates the director's tricks with light and shadow, enhanced in tinted copies of the film. Among *The Cheat*'s most fervent admirers is the writer Louis Delluc, who claims that the film is not only a revelation but also proof that cinema is an art form.

Jean Ayme in one of the demonic incarnations of the 'Great Vampire'.

Artistic control for Fatty Arbuckle

Atlantic City, 1 August
Roly-poly comedian Roscoe "Fatty" Arbuckle has just signed a truly unprecedented contract. Powerful producer Joseph Schenck has effectively offered Arbuckle a film company over which the comedian will maintain complete artistic control. Called The Comique Film Corporation, it will be financed and distributed by Paramount. As writer, director and star, Arbuckle will be earning $7,000 a week plus 25 percent of the profits. This deal will secure him a yearly income of over $1 million. Life is sweet for the Fat Man. After years in the wilderness he has at last been transformed into a big star.

The chubby comedian with Phyllis Allen and Minta Durfee at Keystone.

Abel Gance to make ten new films

Paris, 5 September
Abel Gance has just completed *The Right to Life*, a psychological drama shot in nine days on a small budget for Film d'Art. Relations are tense between Abel Gance and Louis Nalpas, the head of Film d'Art, who often refers to the young director's "disordered and odd" imagination. Nevertheless, Nalpas has faith in Gance: he has just signed a year's renewable contract with him. Gance is to provide him with 10 films for which the director will be paid 1,500 francs each.

'Intolerance' is a monument to love

*Even more ambitious than the controversial **The Birth of a Nation**, Griffith's new film is a highly complex work.*

New York, 5 September
The title of D.W. Griffith's new film, *Intolerance*, resounds as a response to the polemics aroused a year and a half ago by the release of *The Birth of a Nation*. Curiously, this work mixes four historical periods: The Mother and the Law, set in the present; The Nazarene, which recounts the crucifixion of Christ; The Medieval Story, which tells of the massacre of protestants on Saint Bartholomew's Day, 1572; and The Fall of Babylon, about the betrayal of Prince Belshazzar to the Persians. Punctuating the film is the symbolic image of a woman (Lillian Gish) rocking a cradle; the intention here is to help unite the various episodes. These dissimilar events have only one point in common – love. The film cost about $400,000 to make and evolved over a period of almost two years, beginning as a short feature called *The Mother and the Law*. The gigantic decor erected for the Babylonian period required several months work from the craftsmen who built it, supervised by the brilliant production designer Walter L. Hall and his assistant Huck Wortman, while the photography was in the capable hands of Billy Bitzer, assisted by Karl Brown. In the program notes for the premiere at the Liberty Theater, Griffith explained that "the purpose of the production is to trace a universal theme through various periods of the race's (*sic*) history – ancient, sacred, medieval and modern..." At the conclusion of the screening, the audience gave this ambitious work its due when both the director and the film were heartily applauded.

Walter Hall designed the spectacular and elaborate sets for the film.

lax Linder answers he call of America

aris, 30 September
lax Linder is leaving France and ie exceptional state of affairs used by the war. The star has just nbarked on the liner *Espagne* for a ng and daring crossing to the U.S. he journey is the result of his new ontract which binds him for a year Essanay, the famous Chicago film ompany. A few weeks ago, George . Spoor was at Max's bedside in a wiss military hospital. At that time lax was suffering abysmally from neumonia, which he had contract-l two years previously during the attle of the Marne. In addition, arlier in the war, Linder had been a ctim of gas poisoning and suffered serious breakdown. Spoor gave m the golden opportunity to re-lace Charles Chaplin who had left ssanay to go to Mutual. Once in merica, the French comedian will arn $5,000 per week and should be ble to direct 12 films. His health ill benefit from the sea voyage, and e hopes to be able to shoot the first cenes of his new film, *Max In merica*, on arrival.

'Daughter of the Gods' born from a wave

Australian swimmer Annette Kellerman's nude appearance caused a sensation.

New York, 30 October
There is a siren among the stars: Annette Kellerman, the fish-woman of *A Daughter of the Gods*, has met with unprecedented screen success. Directed by Herbert Brenon in Jamaica, the film features 10,000 extras, 2,000 horses and... 20 camels! Producer William Fox had to build a small town there to accommodate all those involved in this remarkable and daring spectacle.

An exploit in the name of an emperor

Vienna, 30 November
The pomp and circumstance surrounding the funeral of Emperor Franz Joseph, who died on 21 November in Schönbrunn Castle, has already been shown in the majority of the cinema theaters around Austria. It was Alexander Kollovrath and Sacha-Film which succeeded in filming the event. In the record time of three days, they made 255 copies, immediately distributing them all over the country. Sacha-Film was founded in 1910 by Count Alexander Kollovrath, the former parliamentarian. A big fan of cinema, Kollovrath is attached to the cinematographic archives of the War Ministry. His official duties have included facilitating the acquisition of material and film stock necessary for production. Sacha-Film is the first large production company in Austro-Hungary. There is also Lucerna, which presented *A Little Heart of Gold (Zlate Sredeck)* on the 20 October, directed by playwright Antonin Fend and played by Antoinie Nedosinska.

he more Charlie falls, the higher he rises

ollywood, 4 December
harlie Chaplin, happily, never fails astonish us. His eighth film for lutual, *The Rink*, is a madcap omedy set in a skating rink, around hich Charlie glides with almost balletic ease. Embroiled in Chaplin's antics are the delightful Edna Purviance and the hulking Eric Campbell, instantly recognizable by his beetling eyebrows, bristling beard and a forbidding moustache.

*harlie Chaplin on ice, with Edna Purviance and Mack Swain, in **The Rink**.*

Farrar, from Met stage to burning stake

Hollywood, 25 December
Geraldine Farrar has become very successful in the cinema. The ebullient opera singer is the star of a new super-production by Cecil B. DeMille, *Joan the Woman*, a sumptuous reconstruction inspired by the life of the French heroine. Last year, around the same time period, she triumphed in *Carmen*, a powerful adaptation of the Prosper Merimée novel, also directed by DeMille. At that time, her employment contract with Jesse L. Lasky created quite a brouhaha because she was paid an exhorbitant salary, had numerous material advantages and was offered a large percentage of the profits. This famous prima donna of New York's Metropolitan Opera was under contract to appear in up to three films per year, during her summer vacations. Deprived of her beautiful voice because of the limitations of the cinema, Farrar, nevertheless, has gained a huge following. Since 1 November last at the Boston Symphony Hall, where the unforgettable presentation of *Carmen* marked her screen debut, the success of the films has been boundless. At the present, Geraldine Farrar is known worldwide and her reputation as an attraction has grown almost to rival that of Sarah Bernhardt.

FULLER OPERA HOUSE
6 DAYS COM., MON.
OCT. 22
JESSE L. LASKY PRESENTS
GERALDINE FARRAR
CECIL B. DeMILLE'S
JOAN THE WOMAN

1917

China, 1 January
Supplies of unexposed film are once more available. The producer Zang Sichuan has founded the Huei Hsi production company.

Germany, 1 January
The Deulig (Deutsche Lichtbild Gesellschaft) production company has set itself the following goal: to act whenever possible in defense of German economy and culture throughout the world.

Paris, 5 January
A psychological drama *le Droit à la vie* (*The Right to Life*), made by Abel Gance, the director of *les Gaz mortels* and *le Périscope*, with Paul Vermoyal, Léon Mathot and Andrée Brabant, is now screening.

New York, 6 January
Joseph M. Schenck has released *Panthea*, with his wife Norma Talmadge playing the lead and directed by Allan Dwan.

Los Angeles, 8 January
Maurice Tourneur has directed Mary Pickford in *Pride of the Clan*, produced by Artcraft.

New York, 28 January
Douglas Fairbanks' last film for the Triangle Corporation *The Americano*, directed by John Emerson, is now showing.

Stockholm, 29 January
Director Victor Sjöström explores the hidden language of film in *Terje Vigen* (*A Man There Was*), a cinematographic adaptation of Henrik Ibsen's poem. This dramatic film captures the unleashed elements with superb lyricism.

Italy, 27 February
Gioacchino Mecheri, the director of Tiber Film and Celio Film has just bought out Itala Film. Giovanni Pastrone has decided to retire from the cinema.

India, 1 March
J.F. Maden has given a preview of the first Bengali fiction film, *Satyawadi Raja Harishchandra.*

California, 3 March
Release of *The Tornado* directed by Jack Ford, a relative newcomer to the cinema, who wrote the script and also played a role in the film.

France, 29 March
Emile Reynaud, the pioneer and inventor of cartoons, is without means and seriously ill. He has been confined to a hospice for the incurable at Ivry-sur-Seine.

St. Petersburg, 30 March
The union of patriotic filmmakers has released *The Great Days of the Russian Revolution*, by Vyatcheslav Viskovsky and Boutch Tovmarchersky, a film about the events leading up to the Czar's abdication. Evgeni Bauer has already released an anticzarist film, *The Revolutionary*.

Paris, 5 April
Creation of the French League for the Cinema, by Tristan Bernard, Edmond Benoît-Levy and Léon Gaumont. Its aims are to develop the cinema industry and to define its interests before Parliament.

Los Angeles, 14 April
Twenty-seven regional distributors, with over 2,000 cinemas under their control, have grouped together in an attempt to rival Adolph Zukor's Famous Players-Lasky and Artcraft company. They have formed a new production company: First National Exhibitor's Circuit.

New York, 23 April
The Butcher Boy is the first film Roscoe Arbuckle has made for his own Comique Film company. The film features a talented newcomer, Buster Keaton.

Los Angeles, 25 April
Samuel Goldfish, who from now on wishes to be known as Goldwyn, and his partners have created the Goldwyn Distribution Corporation.

New York, 30 April
Now that the United States has entered into the war, D.W. Griffith's film *Intolerance* has been withdrawn from distribution. It was already misunderstood by the public and is considered to be undesirable under the present circumstances. This move has resulted in enormous losses for the producer and distributor, Harry E. Aitken.

Los Angeles, 14 May
Cecil B. DeMille has co-written, directed and edited *A Romance of the Redwoods* for Artcraft, with Mary Pickford.

Paris, 15 June
The actor who created Fantômas, René Navarre, has now founded his own production company and has released *The Adventures of Clémentine*, a series of cartoons by Benjamin Rabier.

France, 22 June
An article has been published recently in *le Cinéma* criticizing the distracting background noises on sound tracks.

Indochina, 1 July
The governor-general, Albert Sarraut, has brought back numerous films from his recent visit to France, in order to show locals the "genius of the French nation."

Paris, 6 July
The first series of cartoons by Emile Cohl called *les Aventures des Pieds-Nickelés* has been produced by the Eclair film company.

Los Angeles, 12 July
Screening of *The Little American*, by Cecil B. DeMille with Mary Pickford and two newcomers, Wallace Beery and Ramon Novarro.

France, 26 July
Director Jacques Feyder has married actress Françoise Rosay.

Los Angeles, September
The Chaplin-First National contract has been made public. The total amounts to the sum of $1,075,000. Chaplin is to be paid $125,000 for each of the eight films that he is contracted to supply to the company over a period of 18 months, from January 1918.

New York, 16 October
D.W. Griffith is back from Europe with his film crew and numerous scenes for his new film *Hearts of the World*. The sequences were shot in England and on the French Front. The remaining scenes will be filmed in California.

Prague, 19 October
Lucarna has released *les Adamites de Prague*, by Antonin Fencl, with the actor Josef Vosalik.

New York, 20 October
Release of Charlie Chaplin's last film for Mutual *The Adventurer*, with Edna Purviance.

Shanghai, 31 October
The publishers of *The Commerci[al] Press*, run by Pao Ching-chia ha[ve] created a cinema section.

Paris, 14 November
Marcel L'Herbier has made his d[e]but as a scriptwriter with a film f[or] Eclipse, *le Torrent*, produced b[y] Jean Mercanton and René Hervil.

Berlin, 16 November
Ernst Lubitsch has written and di[-]rected a comedy *Wenn Vier d[as] selbe machen* (*When Four do th[e] Same Thing*), with his faithful par[t]ner Ossi Oswalda.

Budapest, 31 December
Sandor Korda and Miklos Pas[z]toory have bought up the Corvi[n] production company from Jen[ö] Janovicz. The company is bein[g] transferred to Budapest where [a] studio is already under constructio[n].

BIRTHS

Stockholm, 3 February
Arne Sucksdorff

Bordeaux, 1 May
Danielle Darrieux

Paris, 31 May
Jean Rouch

France, 27 July
Bourvil (André Raimbourg)

Connecticut, 6 August
Robert Mitchum

Prague, 11 September
Herbert Lom

Paris, 20 October
Jean-Pierre Melville (Grumbach)

Tokyo, 22 October
Joan Fontaine (Joan de Beauvoir de Havilland)

DEATHS

Paris, 20 December
Georges Demenÿ

Theda Bara is Cleopatra for Willia[m] Fox. Born Theodosia Goodman [in] 1890 and now famous as 'Th[e] Vamp', her debut in ***A Fool The[re] Was*** *(1915) caused a sensation.*

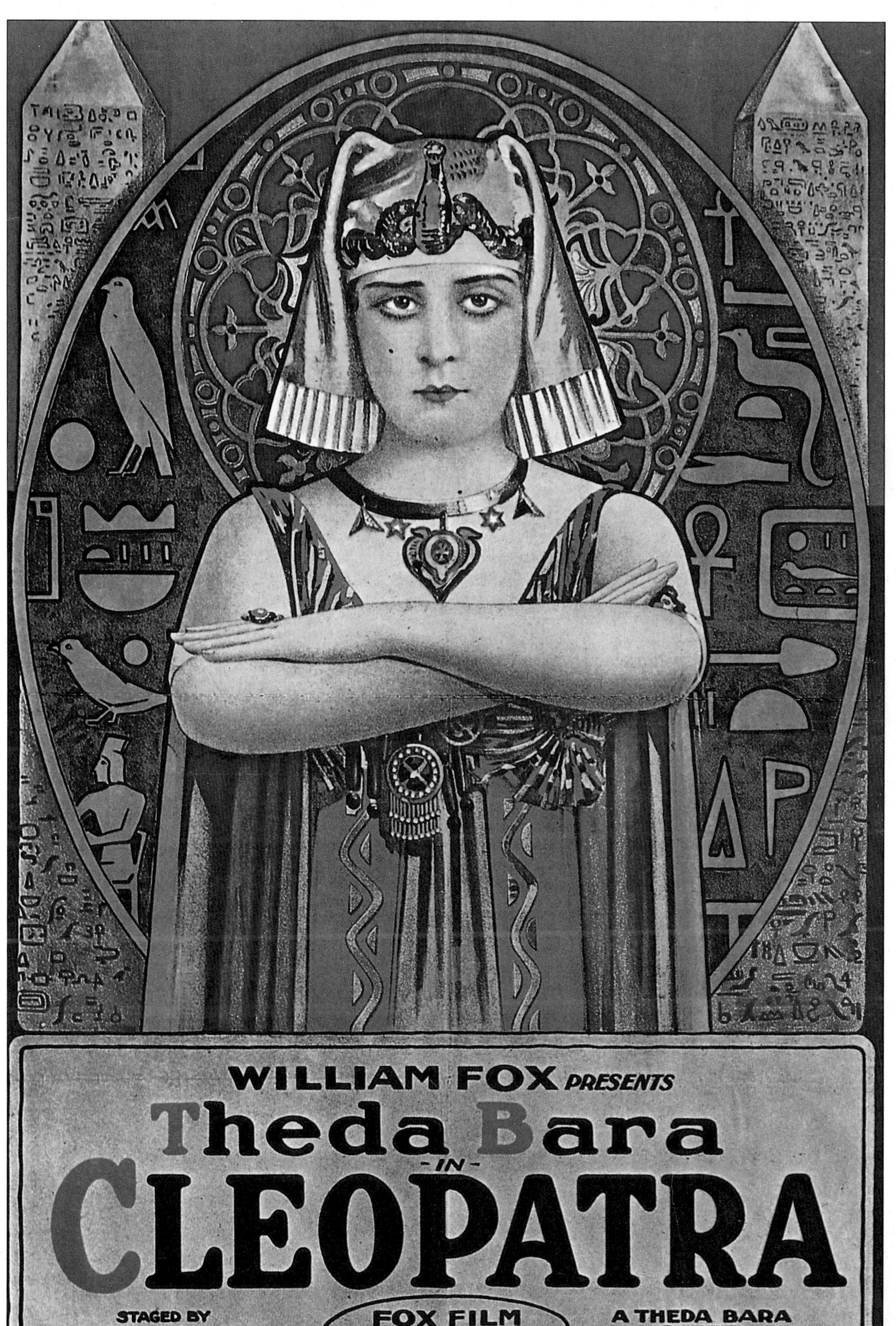
WILLIAM FOX PRESENTS
Theda Bara
-IN-
CLEOPATRA
STAGED BY
J. GORDON EDWARDS
FOX FILM
CORPORATION
A THEDA BARA
SUPER
PRODUCTION

▷

Douglas Fairbanks, an international star

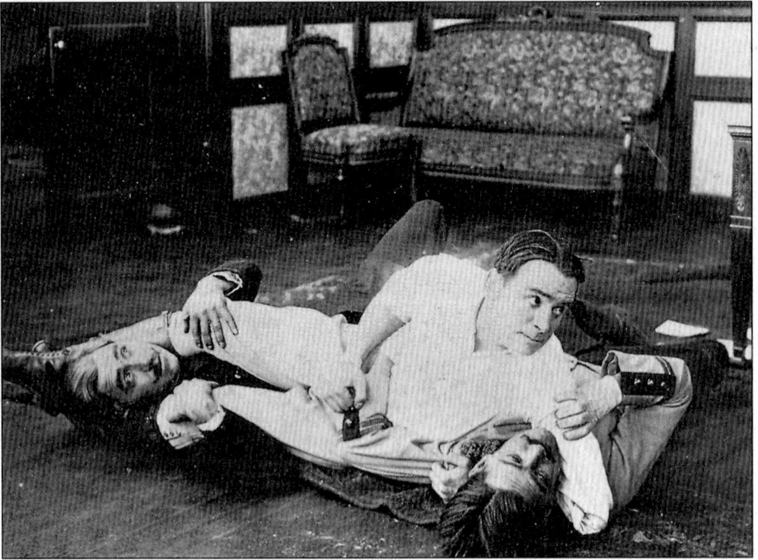

The Americano, directed by John Emerson, is a huge success for Fairbanks.

Hollywood, 1 February
Happy Douglas Fairbanks will keep on smiling for a long time. He has just signed a fabulous contract with Walter E. Greene, the president of the distributing company Artcraft, and his associate Al Lichtman. They have given total autonomy to the Douglas Fairbanks Pictures Corporation, created precisely for this purpose. The acrobatic comedy star is going to be paid a weekly salary of $10,000 as well as a percentage of the company profits.

An inglorious birthday for Thomas Edison

New Jersey, 11 February
For Thomas Alva Edison, who is today celebrating his seventieth birthday, it is clear that his personal dream of the cinema will never be realized. This world-famous inventor and entrepreneur, whose company played so important a role in the early growth of the motion picture industry, particularly through the development and exploitation of the Kinetoscope, has finally called it a day. Edison is currently involved in winding up his film production company, while the trust he set up in 1908, the Motion Picture Patents Co. and its sister organization, the General Film Co., carry on business with little of their former power or influence. Without blaming Edison himself for the failure of his companies, it is obvious that he was instrumental in determining the overall shape of their policies. In various important respects he appears never to have recognized the artistic or commercial potential of the cinema. Rather than providing leadership for the industry as a whole, Thomas

A disillusioned industrialist.

Edison will be best remembered as conservative, even repressive, pov er, more concerned with enforcin his patent rights and controlling th shape of the industry than wi encouraging innovative and ente prising new companies.

British cinema draws up its balance sheet

London, 31 March
The British film industry is currently going through one of its periodic crises, except that this time it appears to be more serious than usual. Many companies have been cutting back on production, including some of the largest established firms such as Hepworth and the London Film Co., the largest British studio. It is estimated that there are about 4,500 cinemas in Britain, and they have recently been getting larger and more luxurious. Average weekly attendance numbers about 20 million people, reflecting the great popularity of the cinema, but, unfortunately, audiences seem to prefer American films to the home-grown product. The war has, of course, played a part in bringing on the current problems, but this is only part of the explanation. Most of these problems are not new and reflect trends which have been developing over many years. Consider, for example, the current popularity of the new feature-length pictures, many of which have been arriving from the U.S. Whereas the British film industry has functioned in the past like a kind of "cottage industry" – with many small companies turning out one or two-reelers relatively cheaply and quickly – it is far more difficult, if not impossible, to produce feature films in this way. The major problem here is a lack of capital, a serious shortage of the kind of investment necessary for the construction of new and thoroughly-equipped studios, for example, or for hiring top-quality writers, directors and actors, and for training technical personnel. Writers are especially badly paid here, so it is not too surprising to discover that the scripts are generally of poor quality. Comparatively few British films are made from original scripts, but are far more likely to be adapted from plays or novels. Similarly, British companies have been very slow to invest in acting talent and to make the effort to develop and promote new stars. Undoubtedly, one of the big attractions of American movies is the large number and variety of their stars. If the short-term outlook in Britain is bleak, it is to be hoped that once the war is over the situation will improve.

Rich crop of forbidden fruit delights censor

Paris, 12 April
A conference proudly reports significant progress in the field of censorship. In the last year, 198 films have been banned or cut by the Commission of Censors. Monsieur Vendrin's approach to the problem has made it possible to levy a tax o crime films. Measures like this cr ate resentment in the film industr The banning of *Bain du préfet* (*Th Official's Bath*), for example, whe personal taste has overriden hono able intentions, seems excessive.

*The success of **Vampires** was one of the direct causes of censorship.*

·udex works in the shadows to see that good triumphs over evil

'aris, 7 April
'he hearts of hundreds of young irls are breaking on account of the ıysterious and fragile René Cresté, ıe hero of Louis Feuillade's new lm *Judex*. Every young man, too, reams of becoming Judex, able to ırow that majestic cape over his houlder in a noble gesture, and to ·ee kidnapped women. Gaumont ıunched this 12-episode adventure /ith great ceremony: posters in the treets, advertisements in magaines, stamps for schoolchildren, nd a serial written by the populist ovelist Arthur Bernède. *Le Pardon 'Amour* (*Love's Pardon*), the twelfth nd last episode of the film, has been eleased today. Throughout its long nd thrilling adventures, *Judex* has een an enormous success, more so

Louis Leubas, René Cresté and Musidora in one of the **Judex** episodes.

Tous les Jeudis
Les Romans Cinéma
JUDEX
Par ARTHUR BERNÈDE et LOUIS FEUILLADE
SIXIÈME ÉPISODE
LE MÔME RÉGLISSE
M. LOUIS FEUILLADE

'euillade, in touch with popular taste.

han Louis Feuillade's astonishing *'he Vampires*. What is the explanaion for this? There are a number of easons. Enlivening the screen is the eductive screen presence of René 'resté; the beautiful Musidora in a ouble role; little Bout-de-Zan, who lays the child Réglisse, and the irreistible Marcel Lévesque, with his ırge nose and bald head. Finally, fter the Minister of the Interior had riticized *The Vampires* for its imıoral heroes, the director has creatd the adventures of a handsome ighter of wrongs. *Judex* is a wiser, ealthier and more moral story than ither *Fantômas* or *The Vampires*. ·nd consequently, this time there has been no problem with the censors nor with the Catholic league. The scenario does not reek of sulphur, eroticism or anarchism. The hero Judex, a mysterious, cloaked crusader, battles against evil forces in order to destroy the empire of an arch criminal. *Judex* is more carefully structured and less frightening than Feuillade's previous serials, but it is highly entertaining and thrilling. Thanks to his latest film, Louis Feuillade can now be considered at the top of his profession.

The 'Great Charlot' under lock and key

Nantes, 15 August
Charlie Chaplin has been arrested by the French army! The military authorities have decided to release him but have banned him from the area. On further investigation it has emerged that Charlot was an imposter. For a month the false Chaplin, "accompanied by his closest collaborators," has been making a morale-boosting tour of the Front. What has really stuck in people's craws is that no attempt was made by the group to explain that this Chaplin was just an impressionist. Charlie has inspired many imitators. In France Antoine Bonaz is the distributor of the films of Billy Ritchie, who shamelessly copies the famous vagabond in every detail, down to even the moustache and the tramp's clothes. In the United States, Chaplin imitators abound. Among the cleverest are Billy West and Stan Jefferson, the latter a former colleague of Chaplin in his days with the Karno Company.

The cinema brings some light relief to lonely boys at the Front

France, 10 August
At the Front, in a small regulating station, a film projector has been installed in a wooden shed. It is packed with soldiers scarcely out of the trenches. The projectionist lights his arc lamps, and the film begins. At first there are patriotic scenes put out by the Gaumont company intended to raise the morale of the troops – "Unity is sacred!", "Watch out, France!" This is greeted with feeble applause. On the other hand, after the news, a new comedian from the U.S., a tramp called Charlot, is cheered. The soldiers, who had been trembling before bombs yesterday, are now doubled up with laughter. This is the miracle of the cinema. "You state that the happiness of soldiers is impossible," writes a French soldier. "It's like a smile, a magic smile that the screen gives, which brings back to us soldiers the faraway memory of happy times passed in the cinema when we were civilians." Since 5 August this year, the Ministry of War has established 125 cinematographic stations with the intention of giving performances in the camps and other places where troops are billetted. It is not the first time that the cinema has been taken to the Front. Two years ago, Georges Christy and Léon Gaumont organized a special evening of films in the Vosges sector. There were some 2,000 soldiers present at the showing which was comprised of artistic films, documentaries and comedies. It was a joyful moment just prior to the men's departing once again to confront death. Perhaps the memory of the cinema brought them comfort.

Mack Sennett, Charlie Chaplin and Edna Purviance in ***Behind the Screen****. Chaplin's films are a favorite with soldiers on active service.*

King of the Cowboys joins Queen of the Vamps

Company founder William Fox.

Gordon Edwards directed Theda Bara in the role of Egypt's sultry queen.

Hollywood, 17 October
The Fox Film Corporation, headed by the former penny arcade owner, exhibitor and distributor William Fox, continues to grow and prosper. Its latest feature *Cleopatra* has just opened, the newest vehicle for the studio's most famous and glamorous female star Theda Bara, following on her success in such roles as *Carmen*, *The Eternal Sappho*, *The Vixen*, and *The Tiger Woman*. The titles say it all! In addition, the company has just signed up popular Western star Tom Mix, formerly at Selig and now added to the Fox roster of stars headed by William Farnum, Valeska Suratt and George Walsh. Fox has succeeded in consi tently increasing the number of h feature releases every year since h first ventured into production late i 1914. Having produced almost 4 features during his first year, Fo has continued to sign up new sta and directors. In the early days h studio was located on Staten Islan before moving to New York Cit and many of the scripts were writte by Fox's wife. Last year alone th company released 50 features an opened a larger and newly improve Hollywood studio at the corner o Western Avenue and Sunset Boul vard. With the shift in productio from the East Coast to the wel equipped West Coast facility, th company appears well on course t complete over 60 films during th current year, while the 1918 outpu will obviously be bolstered by a se lection of Westerns starring Fox new acquisition, Tom Mix. Fox hardly short on directing talent e ther. Oscar Apfel, Frank Powell an British director Herbert Breno have shared the directing hono during the early years with J. Go don Edwards, who has himself ha dled most of the Theda Bara pro ductions. There is also Raoul Walsh older brother of George Walsh whose creative output ranges fro drama and social comment films t comedy and Westerns.

Top Western star Tom Mix is a valu able acquisition for Fox.

Very important year for Abel Gance

Gance, an established filmmaker.

Emmy Lynn and Firmin Gémier, the principals in ***Mater Dolorosa*****.**

Paris, 12 October
Abel Gance's new film *la Zone de la mort* (*Death Zone*), has just been released today. This year has been decisive for the director. He met Charles Pathé in Nice on 21 January last. At a private screening, the great industrialist saw *Mater Dolorosa*, the film which Gance shot for Film d'Art. Pathé was very impressed by the direction and promised his moral and financial support. When it was released it aroused great enthusiasm. Gance and his cameraman Léonce Burel had taken an immense amount of care with the editing, lighting and interpretation, intensifying the tragedy of this social drama. Afterwards, he shot *Death Zone* and *The Tenth Symphony*, two very original works. During a second meeting on 8 July, Gance expounded his ideas to Pathé. He dreams of a film called *The Scars* and also a trilogy – a huge spectacle which would denounce the horrors of war and would be called *J'accuse*. Pathé is almost as enthusiastic as the young director and has agreed to finance the project.

Newly powerful Paramount has raised the stakes

Hollywood, 30 November
Whether the company is now referred to as Famous Players-Lasky or Paramount Pictures, it is clear that this large and growing film corporation is setting the pace for the rest of the movie industry. And it is the new company president, the small and quiet-spoken but shrewd Adolph Zukor, who masterminded it all. It was only 16 months ago that Zukor first arranged the key merger between his Famous Players Co. and Lasky, then organized Artcraft Pictures for the release of the prestigious Mary Pickford features, and finally succeeded in integrating the production and distribution sides of the business under the brand-new Paramount company logo. With the departure of W.W. Hodgkinson and Chairman Sam Goldwyn not long after, Zukor's consolidation of power was complete, which left Jesse Lasky in place as vice president in charge of production and Cecil B. DeMille as director-general. During the past year the company has taken advantage of the decline of a number of other studios, Triangle in particular, and has acquired several new stars to bolster its already strong lineup. Among the most notable recent arrivals are comedian Fatty Arbuckle, cowboy William S. Hart, Charles Ray and Douglas Fairbanks. In addition, Zukor has succeeded in strengthening Paramount's position even further, at the expense of other, smaller companies, through his use of the practice of block booking, i.e. forcing exhibitors to commit themselves to the whole Paramount package – in other words, requiring them to take the less desirable films in order to get the Mary Pickford or DeMille features which they want most. But perhaps most important of all is the way in which Zukor has succeeded in opening up new sources of capital. By turning to Wall Street for help in financing his plans for the studio, which include a major increase in film production, he has recently convinced his bankers and especially Otto Kahn, head of the leading New York financial firm of Kahn, Loeb and Company, that Paramount, as Zukor has reorganized it and as the spearhead of a rapidly growing industry, is an excellent financial risk. The result is a stock issue of $10 million dollars.

L to r: Lasky, Adolph Zukor, Samuel Goldfish, DeMille and Albert Kaufman.

German cinema in the hands of the State

Berlin, 18 December
The German cinema is anticipating the end of the war. A trust has been set up to unify the different elements in an industry which is coming to a boil. It is to be called the Universum Film Aktien Gesellschaft (UFA). The new organization will regroup in the bosom of Mester and Pagu, with the support of the Deutsch Bank and powerful chemical, steel and power combines. The driving force behind this important development is General Erich Ludendorff, the German Army's Chief of Staff. Ludendorff has grasped the importance of the new medium, not only as a means of entertainment but also as a weapon of propaganda and social control. In a letter to the Minister of War, dated 4 July, Ludendorff urged that the state should move swiftly to take a controlling interest in the German film industry. "The extraordinary power of cinema", he wrote, "has been demonstrated during the war. It is now logical to centralize and control this power exercised over the masses." Several months earlier, under heavy pressure from the armed forces, the German high command had formed a picture and film bureau entitled BUFA, similar in form to the Service Cinématographique provided by the French Army. The troops at the Front will be given regular film shows. Nearly 500 cinema halls will be opened on the Western Front and about 300 on the Eastern Front. Feeding this new circuit with a diet of educational and entertainment films will present BUFA with a formidable challenge. On 29 October a top-level conference was held in Berlin between the German high command, the directors of BUFA and the Deutsch Bank. It was there that the decision was made to implement Ludendorff's recommendations without delay. State control of cinema is effectively a *fait accompli* and the German film industry a vital part of the war effort.

The end of Rebecca's circus career.
MARY PICKFORD
IN
REBECCA OF
SUNNYBROOK FARM
FROM THE PLAY BY KATE DOUGLAS WIGGIN and CHARLOTTE THOMPSON
SCENARIO BY FRANCIS MARION... DIRECTED BY MARSHALL NEILAN
PRESENTED BY
ARTCRAFT PICTURES CORPORATION
ARTCRAFT PICTURES

1918

Paris, 1 January
Gaumont's film-hire service called the Comptoir, has signed a contract with Paramount Pictures regarding exclusive rights to the American company's productions.

Paris, 4 January
The film that Albert Capellani made in the United States, *Scènes de la vie de Bohème* (*Scenes of Bohemian Life*), adapted from Murger with Paul Capellani, Alice Brady and Juliette Clarens, is now released here.

Hollywood, 21 January
Opening of the new Charles Chaplin Film Company's studios on the corner of La Brea Avenue and Sunset Boulevard.

California, 18 February
Rio Jim alias William S. Hart has cast himself in *Blue Blazes Rawden*, with Maude George and Robert McKim as his partners.

Copenhagen, 22 February
Screening of *400 Million Leagues under the Earth* by Forest Holger-Madsen, with Nicolai Neiiendam and Gunnar Tolnaes for Nordisk. However, the company is suffering financially due to competition from the rapidly expanding German film company UFA.

Paris, 3 March
Les Travailleurs de la mer (*The Sea Workers*), a Pathé-SCAGL project, adapted from Victor Hugo's work by André Antoine, with Romuald Joubé and Andrée Brabant, was screened for the Maritime League's Charity Gala at the Trocadero.

Paris, 22 March
Musidora, who stars in the film version of her great friend Colette's *The Vagabond*, also collaborated on the script and direction.

Paris, 22 March
Eclipse has released *Un roman d'amour*, by Louis Mercanton and René Hervil, with Sacha Guitry (in front of the camera), Yvonne Printemps and Fred Wright.

Los Angeles, 2 April
The king of the jungle is brought to life by Elmo Lincoln in *Tarzan of the Apes* adapted from Edgar Rice Burroughs' book, which was published in 1912.

Paris, 20 April
French producers have decided to strike from today until 23 May in protest against the difficulties they experienced with importations of unexposed reels and foreign films.

New York, 26 May
D.W. Griffith has been elected president of the Motion Picture War Service Association, which is in charge of increasing the United States' war effort by selling bonds.

Moscow, 1 June
Dziga Vertov, working under the supervision of Lev Kuleshov, is the chief editor of *Kino-Nedelia* (*Cinema Weekly*), a filmed news periodical on various aspects of Soviet life.

Berlin, 30 June
The UFA, which took over Pagu and Messter Film last year, has now taken control of the cinemas previously held by the Danish film company Nordisk.

Paris, 12 July
Clubs are Trump, one of several American films made last year by Hal Roach with Harold Lloyd is now released here by Pathé.

Moscow, 27 July
The Soviet Cinema Committee is undertaking the first state produced fiction film, *The Signal*, directed by Alexander Arkatov.

Paris, 9 August
Press magnate William Randolph Hearst's favorite, the actress and former dancer Marion Davies, has made her screen debut in *Runaway Romany*, from the director George Lederer. The film has just been released in France.

Nice, 25 August
Abel Gance, with the backing of Pathé, has started filming *J'accuse*, the first film in his trilogy about war and peace, with Romuald Joubé and Séverin-Mars. The poet Blaise Cendrars is the assistant director.

Marseilles, 31 August
The aviator Rouit has been killed during the filming of *Twenty Thousand Leagues under the Sea*, for the Jules Verne film company. He had to throw himself into a river but was caught in a whirlpool and did not reappear on the surface.

Paris, 6 September
Poor Little Rich Girl, directed in the United States by Maurice Tourneur and starring Mary Pickford, is being distributed in France.

Paris, 22 September
A gala evening has been held at the Trocadero for the opening of the Franco-American propaganda film *Lest We Forget*, directed by Léonce Perret, with Norma Talmadge.

Paris, 27 September
Charles Pathé has suggested to the Cinema Employers' Federation that a percentage of the takings replace the present film hire system. He also called for the imposition of heavy import taxes on foreign films.

Germany, 30 September
The Decla Company, which was founded by Erich Pommer with financial backing from the French company Eclair, has become 100 percent German after buying up all stock held by the mother company.

New York, 13 October
Release of *The Romance of Tarzan*, by Wilfred Lucas and starring Elmo Lincon, Cleo Madison and Enid Markey. It is a sequel to *Tarzan of the Apes*, with a prologue showing scenes from the first film.

New York, 9 November
After appearing in 34 films for Adolph Zukor, Mary Pickford has signed a contract with First National for three films to be made before 31 July 1919. She is to be paid an advance of $150,000 and then will receive $250,000 for each film. The Mary Pickford Company, which is producing the films, will select the directors and actors.

France, 11 November
According to the latest issue of *le Cinéma*, André Antoine is leaving France for Italy, where he is to film an adaptation of Henry Bernstein's play, *Israel*, for Tiber Film.

France, 30 November
The release of *The Tenth Symphony*, a new film made by Abel Gance, with Jean Toulot, Emmy Lynn and Séverin-Mars, has received a mixed reception. It has been showered with praise by some and criticized by others for its grandiloquence and visual artifices.

Paris, 30 November
The Pathé company has split in the Sound Reproduction Machi company to be run by Emile, an Pathé-Cinema Company, under th direction of his brother Charles.

Czechoslovakia, 4 December
Suzanne Marwille has made h screen debut in the film *Demo Rodu Halkenu*, produced and d rected by Vaclav Binovec.

California, 15 December
Cecil B. DeMille has finished film ing his latest production, a remak of his first film, *The Squaw Ma* starring Elliot Dexter and Katherin McDonald.

Berlin, 20 December
Release of Ernst Lubitsch's adapt tion of Merimée's *Carmen*, wi Pola Negri. This is their first fil together since making *The Eyes o the Mummy*.

Hollywood, 31 December
An increasing number of talente filmmakers from France have com to the United States. Some, such a Maurice Tourneur, Emile Chautar from Film d'Art, Léonce Perr from Gaumont (who has been bus making various propaganda films and Louis Gasnier, have alread met with success here.

BIRTHS

London, 4 February
Ida Lupino

Denmark, 8 April
Gabriel Axel

France, 18 April
André Bazin

Italy, 18 May
Massimo Girotti

Sweden, 14 July
Ingmar Bergman

New York, 17 October
Rita Hayworth
(Margarita Carmen Cansino)

---

*Elmo Lincoln is the first scree Tarzan. Weighing 200 pounds, h brings Edgar Rice Burroughs' jung hero to life in **Tarzan of the Apes** an **The Romance of Tarzan**.*

Tragedy played out in Iceland's mountains

The Outlaw and His Wife stars director Victor Sjöström and Edith Erastoff.

Stockholm, 1 January
Victor Sjöström's impressive new film, *The Outlaw and His Wife*, has just been released here. It is an adaptation from a play by the Icelandic writer Johann Sigurjonsson, and the action takes place in 19th-century Iceland. The story centers on Berg-Ejvind (Sjöström), wanted for stealing sheep to feed his starving family, and who falls in love with Halla, a rich land-owning widow (Edith Erastoff, the director's third wife). She abandons her estate and they flee to the mountains, pursued by the law. After spending an idyllic summer together, the lovers perish in a snowstorm. Most impressive are the superb landscapes, a primitive setting for this tempestuous, passionately performed melodrama. The film was shot in the mountains of Lapland, close to the Norwegian border. An expedition to the actual locale of the tale proved to be too dangerous because of the German submarines relentlessly tracking the Atlantic Ocean and the North Sea. One of the most impressive scenes in the long film has Edith Erastoff, driven back by the posse, throwing her baby from the cliff top. It is the most ambitious and impressive of the 34 films made by the 38-year-old actor-director, whose debut behind the camera was in 1912.

Feuillade renews the contract for Judex

René Cresté, who created the role of Judex, is every woman's dream.

Paris, 18 January
After the triumph of *Judex*, Gaumont and Louis Feuillade have begun their sequel to the adventures of the handsome heartthrob René Cresté, *le Mystère d'une nuit d'été* (*The Mystery of a Summer Night*). The first episode of Judex's "new mission", a romantic adventure in 12 parts, has been launched in a blaze of publicity. The screenplay is once more by Arthur Bernède and Feuillade, but, sadly, it is inferior to the original. Perhaps this is due to the absence of the captivating Musidora. The film is beautiful but lacks pace and is hampered by a combination of moralizing and melodrama. Feuillade seems to have abandone the lyricism he gave his first serial Yvette Andreyor is in tears fro start to finish and René Cres spends far too much time flashin his romantic profile. The only savir grace is the comic relief provided b Marcel Lévesque. The critics hav not minced their words. Louis De luc has called the production a "abomination", adding for goc measure that "Judex's latest adve ture perpetrates a crime greater the those regularly condemned by th council of war." Warming to h task, Delluc claims that he was take to see the film by "some friends c mine." What friends?

Emile Reynaud dies in a hospice

Ivry-sur-Seine, 9 January
Emile Reynaud (born 1844), pioneer of animated film, has just died in a hospice on the banks of the Seine, where he had been cared for since 29 March 1917. His last years were little short of tragic, from the day in 1910 when, crushed by the Cinematograph and dejected and penniless, he threw the greater part of his irreplaceable work and unique equipment into the Seine. By then the public had deserted the showings he gave of his poetic work at the "Théâtre Optique", which had been a celebrated attraction at the Musée Grevin between 1892 and 1900.

'The Count of Monte Cristo' remains seductive and disturbing

Paris, 1 March
In Paris two spectacular productions are competing for audiences: Judex's latest adventure and a new adaptation of *The Count of Monte Cristo*, an eight-part serial produced by Louis Nalpas' Film d'Art and directed by Henri Pouctal. The seventh episode of the Judex serial, *la Main morte* (*The Dead Hand*), is released today, as is the last episode of the adventures of the Count of Monte Cristo, a role played by Léon Mathot. The public has delivered its verdict. The Count has won hands down and Gaumont is now licking its wounds. Pouctal, the artistic director at Film d'Art, has delighted the public with an ambitious and brilliantly photographed film. But it helps having Alexandre Dumas provide the scenario.

Léon Mathot is Edmond Dantes in Henri Pouctal's **Monte Cristo**.

.W. Griffith plunges America into the heart of Europe's conflict

D·W·GRIFFITH'S
SUPREME TRIUMPH
HEARTS OF THE WORLD
A LOVE STORY OF THE GREAT WAR
18 MONTHS IN THE MAKING
BATTLE SCENES ON THE BATTLEFIELDS OF FRANCE

*The director of **Hearts of the World** also turns actor for the occasion.*

os Angeles, 12 March
Do you want to go to France?" hat is the slogan of D.W. Griffith's ew film *Hearts of the World*, which as just been shown at Clune's. This nti-German propaganda film, shot England, France and California, as bowled the public over and has roused great waves of sympathy for ne Allies. The action unfolds in a nall French village, before and uring the war. Douglas and Marie, layed respectively by Robert Haron and Lillian Gish, are separated y the war. The couple are reunited fter a long period, and are saved in xtremis by the intervention of the llied troops. Griffith has had no qualms about presenting the Germans as cynical and brutal, almost to the point of caricature. Erich von Stroheim has found a dream role as a Horrible Hun. Poor Lillian Gish has to suffer from bombardments throughout, as she tries to guide her confused grandfather to safety, and then later wanders dazed through the landscape carrying her wedding dress carefully in her arms. Her sister, Dorothy Gish, has a comic role as The Little Disturber, a street-singer, which she makes truly amusing with her elastic face and jaunty movements. Audiences have been particularly impressed by the realistic images of the Front. Certain scenes were shot by Captain Kleinschmidt and Billy Bitzer, with the aid of the cinematographic department of the French army, near the Front, amidst the ruins and shelling. For the few months spent in France, Griffith filmed all types of arms and military equipment used in the conflict. For a director of his caliber, it was a golden opportunity to film history as it was being made. In October 1917, Griffith brought his company back to the U.S. to finish the film in California. *Hearts of the World* is Griffith's first film for Adolph Zukor's Artcraft company, but he continues to retain artistic control of his work.

he Russian cinema is flourishing amid post-revolution chaos

Ioscow, 31 May
ver since their first days in power, ne Bolsheviks have been aware of ne importance of cinema, mainly or propaganda purposes. Almost ll the early films dealt with the reent revolutionary struggle, or with istorical events seen in a revoluionary context. But the titles of ome of the most recent and forthoming films indicate a wider subect matter: *The Young Lady and the Iooligan*, *The Woman Who Invented Love*, *Maids of the Mountain*, *enny the Maid* and *Creation Can't e Bought*, an adaptation of Jack ondon's *Martin Eden*. This month, *ather Sergius*, based on a story by eo Tolstoy, has been released. The ilm's anti-clerical stance profited rom the decree in January this year, which officially broke the connection between church and state. Another new film, *Still, Sadness... Still*, a spectacular drama in two parts, recounts the history of the cinema's birth. *The Last Tango* also opened this month, a melodrama that is set in Argentina. Both the latter films are enhanced by the presence of the Soviet cinema's most popular star, Vera Kholodnaya.

*Yakov Protazanov's seven-reel **Father Sergius** is adapted from Tolstoy.*

Russian films boast a glorious star

Moscow, 27 April
Vera Kholodnaya, the "queen of the Soviet screen", will be starring in two films opening in Moscow next month – *Still Sadness... Still* and *The Last Tango*. She alone among Russian motion picture actresses can guarantee the success of a film. Because of her appeal, she is paid a salary of 25,000 rubles ($12,500) for each production. It was in the early spring of 1915 that Vera Kholodnaya, the wife of a poorly paid officer, applied to work at the Khanzhonkov studios as an extra. Her outstanding beauty caught the attention of director Evgeni Bauer, who gave her the leading role of Valeriya in *Song of Triumphant Love*, based on Turgenev. It was a triumphant debut, and the actress went on to make five more films under Bauer's direction, the most notable being *Children of the Age* (1915), *Beauty Should Rule The World* and *A Life for a Life* (both 1916). Because she usually plays poor girls who have managed, by good fortune, to rise up the social ladder, Kholodnaya has become an ideal for many young girls who see, in her grace, style and beauty, someone to emulate. "My eyes are my bread," she has said. As if to prove to those who believed she could not act without the direction of her mentor, Evgeni Bauer, Kholodnaya gave a moving performance last year in *Tormented Souls*, directed by Vladimir Kas'yanov. Who can forget the moment when she reads the telegram from her lover, informing her that he will not return? Kholodnaya falls helplessly onto the piano, her shoulders shaking from her wracking sobs.

Kholodnaya, beautiful and talented.

'Hell Bent' comes heaven sent for Jack Ford and Harry Carey

*Harry Carey (center) in **Hell Bent** from the Ford partnership.*

Hollywood, 6 July
Hell Bent, the latest Western from the director-star team of Jack Ford and Harry Carey at Universal, has just opened and has already been well received. A writer in the *Motion Picture News* noted last week, "few directors put such sustained punch in their pictures as does this Mr. Ford." In fact, Jack started out in the movies acting in two-reelers directed by his older brother, Francis, in 1915 and 1916 before teaming up with Harry just over a year ago. This is their ninth feature together in which Carey plays the by now familiar role of "Cheyenne Harry", an easygoing Western character who is more of a saddle tramp than a typical movie hero. Audiences, however, don't seem to mind that at all.

Russian prodigy

Lev Kuleshov, born in 1899 has completed his first film, *The Project of Engineer Prite.*

Lenin enlists help of cinema for Revolution

Moscow, 13 August
Communism is off to war and so is the cinema. Today, Lenin is sending off the first propaganda train. Its carriages are covered with allegorical frescoes to the glory of the worker and Bolshevik soldiers. Inside, there is a conference hall, a school, a library stocked with some 7,000 books, an autonomous printworks and a cinematic installation, consisting of projector equipment, darkrooms, printing and editing rooms, as well as a significant stock of film. The experimental train is leaving for the Kazan region to capture the struggles of the civil war. The government of the Federal Republic of Soviet Russia and its head, Vladimir Ilyich Ulyanov, known as Lenin, think that they can rally the population who have been misled by counter-revolutionary propaganda to the Bolshevik cause. During the journey, the mobile studio will produce a weekly newspaper to be run by director of photography Edouard Tissé and his young editor Denis Arkadievitch Kaufman, known as Dziga Vertov. This original undertaking reflects a growing interest in the power of the cinema. An Institute of Photography, the first in the world, is also being set up.

The Lady and The Ruffian, made by Mayakovsky and Slavinsky.

Buster Keaton to act with Fatty Arbuckle

The two skilled comedians and a lady, at work for Comique Films.

Long Beach, 15 September
Roscoe "Fatty" Arbuckle's newest film, distributed by Paramount, is entitled *The Cook*. In the swirl of slapstick around the Fat Man is a curious little newcomer to films, Buster Keaton. This latest addition to the Arbuckle stock company began performing as a toddler in his parents' vaudeville act. Billed as "The Human Mop", he spent much of the time being tossed around the stage, acquiring in the process a remarkable physical elasticity. As befits a trouper and exponent of daredevil falls, he was given the name Buster by no less a person than Harry Houdini. In March last year, the 21-year-old Keaton wa[s] introduced to Arbuckle while th[e] latter was filming his first Comiqu[e] Film comedy, the two-reeler *Th[e] Butcher Boy*. Arbuckle co-opted hi[m] on to the film and, without any re[-]hearsal, Keaton appeared as a kin[d] of village idiot. In one scene h[e] demonstrated his remarkable fla[ir] for physical comedy by absorbin[g] the shock of a flying sack of flou[r] without even a flicker of effort. H[e] was immediately snapped up by pro[-]ducer Joseph Schenck at the modes[t] salary of $40 a week, a fraction o[f] what he could earn on Broadwa[y]. Keaton is in love with films, and *Th[e] Cook* is his twelfth for Arbuckle.

Mauritz Stiller brings 'Thomas Graal' back to Swedish cinema

Thomas Graal's Best Film.

Karin Molander in Stiller's 1916 hit ***Love and Journalism.***

Stockholm, 21 October
Thomas Graal's Best Film was such a great success last year that the director, Mauritz Stiller, has reassembled the same brilliant cast and production team for an equally entertaining sequel, *Thomas Graal's Best Child.* Both films revolve around the hero's various domestic difficulties. The best scene in the more recent picture has Thomas Graal (portrayed by Victor Sjöström) overdressing for his wedding, then having to undress in front of a shocked congregation in order to find the ring. Another amusing episode takes place when he and his bride (Karin Molander) argue on the way home from the church about whether their first child should be a boy or a girl. With the two Thomas Graal films, and the sparkling comedy *Love and Journalism* that also stars vivacious Karin Molander, the 35-year-old Stiller has established himself, together with Sjöström, as the most popular director in Sweden. Of course, both men benefited greatly from the growth of a national cinema due to the dearth of foreign imports during the war. Mauritz Stiller was born in Helsinki to Jewish Russian-Polish parents, who died when he was only four. He was trained by his adoptive parents to be a haberdasher, but entered the cinema in 1912 after fleeing to Sweden to avoid conscription in the Russian Czar's army. One of his earliest films was *Song of the Scarlet Flower*, a pastoral drama adapted from a Finnish source, and his other films were undistinguished thrillers, but it is Mauritz Stiller's comedies that have brought him fame at home and recognition abroad.

A sixteen-year-old wife for Chaplin

Hollywood, 1 November
Charlie Chaplin has returned from his honeymoon. His wife is 16-year-old Mildred Harris, who passes herself off as 18 and who Chaplin met at a party held by producer Sam Goldwyn. At the time Mildred was just another little actress on the make in Hollywood. The two were married at a simple ceremony on 23 October. Since that happy event, Mrs. Chaplin has been bombarded with offers. Louis B. Mayer came up with a contract for six films worth $50,000, something that could have only before been in the dreams of this young woman. The news of the marriage has inevitably caused a stir, not least because Charlie seems to be at the summit of his career. In June 1917 he signed a million-dollar contract with First National for eight two-reel films in 18 months. Already made are *A Dog's Life* and *Shoulder Arms.* The latter, an answer to criticism about Chaplin's lack of involvement in the war effort, took the Tramp to the Western Front, where he bombarded the enemy with grenades made from foul-smelling Limburger cheese. In between, Chaplin made a propaganda short, *The Bond*, for the Liberty Loan Committee. It has produced a flood of subscriptions, testimony to Charlie's popularity and drawing power as the greatest screen comedian of the day.

Tempestuous Pola is Ernst Lubitsch's answer to Theda Bara

Negri, with Harry Liedtke as Don Jose in Lubitsch's version of ***Carmen.***

Berlin, 17 December
Ernst Lubitsch's new film version of *Carmen*, recently completed at the UFA studios here, has just opened to great acclaim. This is only the director's second feature-length production, after *Die Augen der Mumie Ma* (*The Eyes of the Mummy*) which was released earlier this year. Both films paired the young Polish actress Pola Negri with Harry Liedtke, who appears here in the role of Don Jose. But this is Miss Negri's picture and she makes the most of it. The stylish handling by director Lubitsch is worth noting, but it is the superb performance of Pola Negri, by turns darkly intense then passionate and lively, that excites the viewer and makes this a film to remember.

Enjoying a cruise with Mildred.

1919

Czechoslovakia, 31 January
Gustav Machaty has directed his first short film at the age of 18. He wrote the burlesque-style scenario for *Teddy Wants to Smoke* in collaboration with Jean S. Kolar.

Paris, 26 February
The Cinema Director's Union has decided to ban the screening of all German and Austrian films for a period of 15 years.

Paris, 15 March
Marcel L'Herbier's first film for Gaumont, *Rose-France*, has been receiving severe criticism. The journal *la Cinématographie française* describes it as "feeble, limp, long-winded and maudlin."

Paris, 24 March
Release here of *The Turn in the Road*, American King Vidor's first full-length film, produced by the Brentwood Film Co. which was created for its production.

Berlin, 3 April
Halbblut (*The Half-Breed*), the first film directed by Fritz Lang is now screening. Until now, Lang has been writing film scenarios for Decla, but dissatisfied with the treatment given to his scripts he decided to turn to directing them himself.

Germany, 17 April
The engineers Hans Vogt, Joe Engl and Joseph Massolle are patenting their sound-recording system, the Tri-Ergon, which makes use of Lee de Forest's electrode tubes.

Paris, 20 April
Charlie Chaplin's *Shoulder Arms* is screening at the Gaumont-Palace and 10 other cinemas.

Paris, 15 June
Pierre Henry, a friend of Louis Delluc's, has started up a bi-monthly magazine *Ciné pour tous.*

Paris, 15 June
A cinema bank with a capital of 3 million francs has been created to rebuild the cinemas that were destroyed by the war.

France, 20 June
André Antoine is filming an adaptation of Emile Zola's novel *la Terre* (*The Earth*). He is assisted by Julien Duvivier.

France, 26 June
The mayor of Lyon, Edouard Herriot, is bringing into force the decree ordering all that all cinematographs, including fairground shows, are to use inflammable film.

Versailles, 28 June
The only cameraman allowed to enter the Gallery of Mirrors to film the signing of the peace treaty was corporal André A. Danton, the Armed Services cinematographic attaché. He placed his camera eight metres from the table and caught the historical occasion on 360 metres of film.

Los Angeles, 1 July
The 17-year-old Mary Miles Minter has signed a contract with Adolph Zukor. The head of Paramount intends to build her up as a rival to Mary Pickford.

Los Angeles, 1 July
Charlie Chaplin has started work on his first full-length film, *The Kid*, with 4-year-old Jackie Coogan.

Budapest, 1 August
With the fall of the Communes and the subsequent repression of its partisans, many actors and filmmakers are emigrating, among them Sandor Korda and Mihaly Kertesz.

Nice, 18 August
Germaine Dulac is directing Eve Francis in *la Fête espagnole* (*Spanish Holiday*). Louis Delluc wrote the scenario for this Nalpas independent production.

Moscow, 1 September
The State School of Cinematography has opened here to train film directors, actors, cameramen and lighting technicians. It is believed to be the first such institution founded anywhere.

California, 7 September
Release of *Back Stage* directed by Fatty Arbuckle and starring himself, Molly Malone and Buster Keaton.

France, 20 September
Jacques de Baroncelli is filming *The Secret of Lone Star*, with the American star Fanny Ward, Rex MacDougall and Gabriel Signoret. With this type of film, Delac and Vandal from Film d'Art are hoping to gain a bigger slice of the American cinema market.

Paris, 30 September
Bernard Grasset has edited *Cinéma et Cie*, a collection of articles by Louis Delluc from *le Film*. It is the first book of a critical nature to be published about the French cinema.

Hollywood, 30 September
Charlie Chaplin and Douglas Fairbanks, partners in the new United Artists Company, are planning a film in South America. They hope to work on location in Santiago, Chile for several months.

New York, 18 October
Marcus Loew, who has been at the head of an extensive cinema circuit since 1912, has now set up Loew's Incorporated, with a capital of $27 million. Negotiations are under way for the new outfit to take control of Metro Pictures.

Nice, 25 October
René Navarre has created a production company for "ciné-romans", popular films adapted from the serialized novels published simultaneously in all the main daily papers. The first film is already planned from a story by Gaston Leroux.

Stockholm, 8 November
Mauritz Stiller's latest comedy titled *Erotikon* is proving highly popular. The film, starring Karin Molander, draws its inspiration from a play by Hungarian writer Ferenc Herczeg.

Milan, 25 November
The beautiful Italian star, Francesca Bertini has been signed to a contract by Richard A. Rowland, a producer and the president of Metro Pictures, for a series of films to be made in Italy for the American market. If they are a success Francesca will be leaving for Hollywood.

Prague, 1 December
Sixteen-year-old Anny Ondra has made her silver screen debut in *The Woman with Small Feet*, directed by Jean S. Kolar from a scenario by Gustav Machaty.

New York, 7 December
Screening of *Blind Husbands* at the Capitol Theater. It is the first film to be written and directed by Erich von Stroheim, who also takes a leading role. Universal went against Stroheim's advice and changed the original title, *The Pinnacle*.

Hollywood, 15 December
Gloria Swanson, divorced from Wallace Beery, has married Herbert Somborn. Her last two films, made with Cecil B. DeMille, are *After the Rain, the Sunshine* and *The Admirable Crichton.*

Nice, 15 December
Having come here to make *Ecce Homo*, Abel Gance has given up the idea and is working on the scenario of *la Rose du rail.* But his companion, Ida Danis, who had a relapse of Spanish influenza, is now suffering from galloping consumption.

Stockholm, 27 December
Svenska Biografteatern has merged with Skandia. The new trust is to be known as the Svensk Filmindustri.

Seoul, 31 December
The premiere has taken place of the first film to be made in Korea. Directed by Do-San Kim, *Euricho Koutou* is 3,280 metres in length.

USA, 31 December
The Famous Players-Lasky have released the first issue of *Paramount Magazine*, a filmed news weekly.

BIRTHS

Paris, 29 April
Gérard Oury
(Max Gérard Houry)

Rome, 15 June
Alberto Sordi

Marseilles, 19 June
Louis Jourdan
(Louis Gendre)

Italy, 14 July
Lino Ventura
(Angelo Borrini)

Paris, 10 November
François Périer (Pilu)

Italy, 19 November
Gillo Pontecorvo

Sweden, 12 December
Arne Mattson

The Viennese actor, Erich von Stroheim (left), with Sam de Grasse in ***Blind Husbands****, his impressive directorial debut, made 10 years after his arrival in America.*

The Italian cinema is in a ferment

Rome, 9 January
The Italian cinema is attempting to recover from the damage to the industry caused by the war and increased competition from the many available American films. To this end two Italian lawyers, Gioacchino Mecheri and Giuseppe Barattolo, have recently formed a new organization, the Union Cinematografica Italiana (or UCI), bringing together all the leading Italian producers. Unfortunately, the two organizers had a falling out after only a few months. Mecheri, the head of Tiber, has taken over first Celio and then Itala, while Barattolo, managing director of Caesar, has gained control of Cines, then Ambrosio and finally Film d'Arte Italiana (FAI). Each one of these rival "holding companies" has been given substantial financial backing from banks and each has big plans for the future. It will be interesting to see if they succeed in giving a much needed boost to Italian production.

With United Artists, four great reputations are put on the line

Hollywood, 17 April
A new cinematographic company has been established in the USA: The United Artists Corporation, whose management has been entrusted to Hiram Abrams, a former member of the board at Paramount. The firm originated with four of the great names of Hollywood who are active partners – Mary Pickford, Douglas Fairbanks, Charles Chaplin and D.W. Griffith. They knew it was their personalities that had made the major film companies rich. Although they had retained considerable control over their productions, they were still subject to the will of distributors, who also took a large slice of the profits. Therefore, toward the end of 1918, the four decided to found their own company. In their opinion, it was the only way to oppose the all-powerful producers, who had monopolist ambitions. At the time, there were rumors of large mergers and salary reductions. Pickford, Fairbanks, Chaplin and Griffith met at Fairbanks' home in Beverly Hills in January. At their side was a particularly well-considered man, William Gibbs McAdoo, the son-in-law of President Wilson, who is former Secretary of the Treasury, and President of the Federal Railway Board. United Artists, on this occasion, could be established as a distribution company, with the five personaliti owning shares. Assured of sizab financial support, the company, st in its infancy, is seeking to reorg nize itself. McAdoo has given up h place to Hiram Abrams, but th three stars and D.W. Griffith r main United Artists' greatest asse

l to r: Douglas Fairbanks, Mary Pickford, Charles Chaplin and D.W. Griffi

Pacifist Abel Gance wants to see arms laid down once and for all

Paris, 31 March
The press has been enthusiastically praising Abel Gance after the showing of *J'accuse*, a tragedy of modern times in three episodes, financed by Charles Pathé and by the cinematographic department of the army. This immense work, Gance's biggest budget film to date, begun prior to the Armistice, is an anti-war indictment. A patriotic film, where the love of France is lyrically extolled, *J'accuse* is also a poignant melodrama. It begins in happiness and peace, but step by step Gance leads the audience into a bloody drama: war in all its horror. The director shows the separation of two human beings who love each other, villages in ruin, the dead, the charge of soldiers in the mud and under fire. The hero, the poet Jean Diaz played by Romuald Joubé, returns from the Front to see his dying mother. Diaz, delirious, protests, "I accuse!" Then he sees a crowd of mothers mourning and in despair. The vision is even more strongly repeated in the last part; this time Diaz the visionary, the Christ of the trenches, as Gance names him, resurrects the war dead in the film's most powerful scene. Here corpses leave their tombs and march toward the villages to find out if their deaths served a purpose. Those who benefited from the war by getting rich, flee terrified. Jean Diaz dies amidst the general madness. The sober and pacifist film has shocked chauvinists, who have accused Gance of defeatism and antimilitarism. But the critics have been unanimous in declaring *J'accuse* a masterpiece. Gance calls it "a human cry against the bellicose din of armies." One discerns the influence of the American school, notably Thomas Ince. The photography by Léonce Burel is admirable as is Gance's editing, helped by the poet Blaise Cendrars.

*The director considers **J'accuse** to be a tragedy of modern times.*

A chaste heroine for Louis Feuillade

OISEAUX
DE NUIT
Tih-Minh
CINÉ-ROMAN
Film
Le Petit Parisien

Paris, 25 April
Louis Feuillade has recovered h inspiration and his audience wi *Tih Minh*, a serial in 12 episod which is coming to the end of successful run today. The title ro of the fragile and innocent you Annamite is played by an Engli actress, Mary Harald. A gang criminals plans to kidnap her, b René Cresté intervenes...

irst National revels in the possession of Pickford

ary Pickford (center) sparkles in First National's film version of the popular bestseller **Daddy Long Legs**.

Hollywood, 18 May
With the opening of *Daddy Long Legs*, a delightful new feature produced by her own company, and with the creation of United Artists just a few weeks ago, it's been a good year so far for Mary Pickford. By far the most important female star in Hollywood, Miss Pickford has become increasingly involved in the production of her films. She has looked forward to gaining full independence and, late last year, accepted a lucrative new offer from First National that Zukor at Paramount was unable (or unwilling?) to match. Thus, she started off in 1919 starring in a characteristically charming, real "Little Mary" role as the orphan who finds happiness with her benefactor in *Daddy Long Legs*, from Jean Webster's novel. Marshall Neilan directed, with Charles Rosher as cameraman in this first film for the Mary Pickford Corporation. At the same time, Mary has been one of the prime movers in the formation of UA, a new style of distribution company for the independents.

Intolerance' freed, ut it's mutilated

aris, 12 May
tolerance, considered the major ork by D. W. Griffith, has finally ached Parisian screens. The film, ade in the United States nearly ree years ago, was at the time nned by the French military cenrs. The reason given was that the presentation of French history as seriously one-sided and bigoted, particular the dramatizing of the aint Bartholomew Day massacre. a period of the Sacred Union, the cturalization of the murder of the uguenots by Catholics would have pened old wounds. However, since e Armistice was signed, Griffith's eatness has become universally cognized, and the French authories have relented. Nevertheless, any scenes have still been cut from *ntolerance*. In an article today from e journal *Paris-Midi*, the young m critic Louis Delluc rails against e arbitrary cuts, which he claims ave distorted the director's work nd have rendered the film more or ss incomprehensible.

Lillian Gish moves America to tears with her sensitive acting

New York, 1 June
The latest Griffith film, *True Heart Susie*, is the story of a naive country girl, too shy to find herself a husband. In the starring role, Lillian Gish confirms her exceptional talent. She personifies a sort of Cinderella, wearing a shapeless long dress, an apron and a ridiculous little hat. Rarely has there been a more convincing and simple presence. Her skillful acting makes the sentimental story genuinely moving, and the character grows in stature from a funny, happy adolescent to become a dignified woman. And, a little more than two weeks ago, Gish had an even greater triumph in *Broken Blossoms*, another admirable melodrama directed by Griffith. In this, she played a little girl battered to death by her alcoholic father. The distinguished director seems to be the young actress' Pygmalion, and she has never left him since their joint debut with *An Unseen Enemy* in 1912 at Biograph.

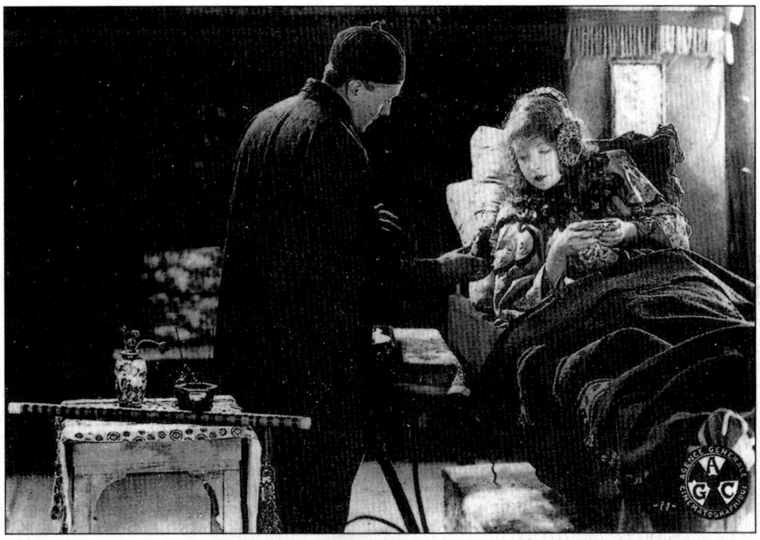

Gish with Robert Harron in **True Heart Susie** (left), and with Richard Barthelmess in **Broken Blossoms**.

Lenin nationalizes the Russian cinema

Moscow, 27 August
The decree regarding "the attachment of the photographic and cinematographic industries to the people's commissariat for the education of the public" has today been signed in the Kremlin. In other words this is the beginning of the nationalization of the cinema. From now on, the government of the Federal Republic of Soviet Russia can claim the right to "requisition materials and apparatus used in photo-ciné from large firms and small businesses" to control and regulate the photographic industry, including both stills and moving images. One can question the consequences of this decree while the civil war is raging and counter-revolutionary troops are preparing to march on St. Petersburg. Yet, because conditions for filming have deteriorated rapidly (equipment has been scarce) in the last few years, this initiative needed to be taken. It also confirms Lenin's growing interest in the intellectual and cultural virtues of the cinema.

New York's Capitol cinema opens with United Artists' first film

Douglas Fairbanks and Marjorie Daw enjoying a 'royal' love affair.

New York, 1 September
The world's largest theater, the newly constructed Capitol in New York, has finally opened its doors with the showing of the first United Artists picture *His Majesty, The American*. A tumultuous reception for both the theater and the film has meant a well-publicized beginning for the fledgling company. Douglas Fairbanks, whose public populari is growing steadily, produced a starred in this Ruritanian comed romance. The likable and live Fairbanks plays a New York ma about-town who is heir to the thro of a small European kingdom. Arri ing there to take up his new positio he uses his All-American know-ho (and his renowned gymnastics) overcome political conspirators a win the hand of the princess, play by Marjorie Daw. The picture w directed by Joseph Henabery, wh portrayed Lincoln in D.W. Gr fith's *The Birth of a Nation*, and wh has already directed Fairbanks in couple of previous pictures. As us al, Doug smiles throughout, as w he might, because *His Majesty, Th American*, made for about $300,00 is sure to recoup more than a mo est profit. United Artists hopes th there will soon be films from th three other founders of the comp ny, but presently only Fairbanks free from previous contractual co mitments. In any case, a luxurio new theater and a new movie stud bode well for the film industry.

Polish Pola fashioned as 'femme fatale' by German Lubitsch

Berlin, 18 September
This month has seen the opening of the UFA Palatz, a superb cinema built in the center of Berlin by the all-powerful film trust. For this occasion, Ernst Lubitsch, director of *The Oyster Princess*, presents his new film *Madame Dubarry*, inspired by the tragic story of the celebrated French courtesan. Filming took several months and boasts numerous sets designed by Karl Malchus and Kurt Richter. In the starring role Pola Negri has scored a brilliant success. Born Barbara Apolonia Chalupiec in the Polish town of Janowa in 1894, Negri studied ballet in St. Petersburg before making her stage debut in Warsaw in 1913. In 1917, after appearing in a few Polish films, she came to Berlin at the invitation of Max Reinhardt. Now her beautiful eyes are setting German pulses racing.

*Pola Negri in **Madame Dubarry**, German director Lubitsch's very personal view of the French Revolution.*

A joint memorial to the World War

Paris, 18 October
The Théâtre des Champs Elysées showing an American productio *The Heritage of France*, co-directe by the American artist Harry Lac man, who has lived and worked France since 1911, and the Frenc man Firmin Gémier. This is a fil with a message, shot in one of th most terrible places of the war, th Chemin des Dames, with the full c operation of the local populatio and without a single profession actor in the cast. The film will b shown in America on 11 Novembe Armistice Day, as part of a progra to raise funds to contribute to th relief of areas of France devastate by the war. Several other films als reflect the current patriotic moo *Lest We Forget*, a co-productio with the United States directed b Léonce Perret; and *Rose-Franc* directed by Marcel L'Herbier an financed by the Ministry for Prop ganda. The latter work, howeve has attracted the scorn of acerbi critic André de Russe.

eputations enhanced by 'The Miracle Man'

ɔn Chaney (left), Thomas Meighan and Betty Compson: a terrific trio.

ew York, 14 September
n unlikely candidate for stardom, ıaracter actor Lon Chaney has tracted attention in Paramount's *he Miracle Man*. He has caused a nsation with the grotesque make-ɔ he devised for his role as "The rog", a partially paralyzed beggar. he 36-year-old Chaney has a curious past. The son of deaf-mute parents, he developed his pantomimic skills as a youngster, mimicking all the day's events for his bed-ridden mother. He served his apprenticeship in touring stock companies and joined Universal in 1912 as a utility player. Seven years later, he has taken his chance with both hands.

Harold Lloyd victim of a gag that misfired

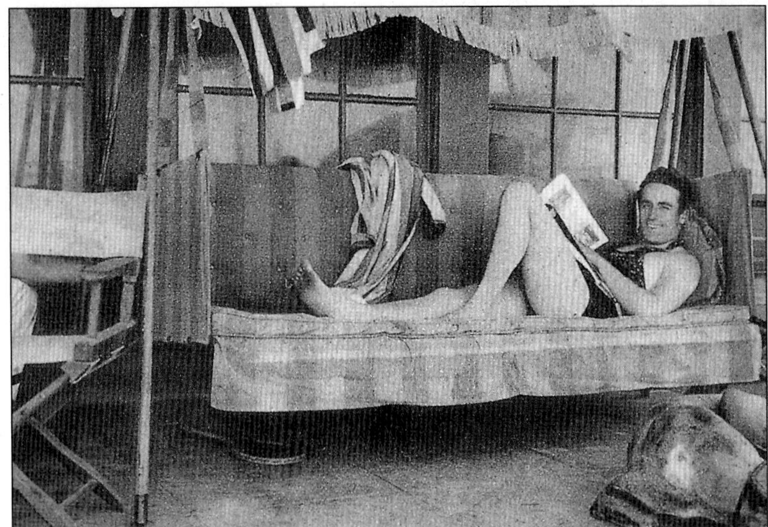

A moment of relaxation for the chief rival to Chaplin and Arbuckle.

Hollywood, 30 September
Harold Lloyd, the comedian whose trademark is his horn-rimmed spectacles, has suffered a dramatic and damaging accident. He was holding what he thought was a papier-mâché prop bomb in a publicity shot for *Haunted Spooks* when it exploded. He was rushed to hospital where the thumb and forefinger on his right hand were amputated. This misfortune threatens to end a promising career in film comedy. It began in 1915 when Lloyd teamed up with director Hal Roach to make over 100 "Lonesome Luke" films before developing a new character, the breezy, bespectacled college boy.

tupendous directorial debut for 'the man you love to hate'

ew York, 7 December
he latest production from Carl aemmle's Universal studios, *Blind 'usbands*, has just opened at the apitol Theater. Originally preıewed and screened to the press nder writer-director Stroheim's wn title, *The Pinnacle*, advance ord on the picture was that it was a ɛry special release from Universal, studio better known for cheaply ıade Westerns and action movies, ıther than intelligent drama. The lm marks a memorable writing and irecting debut for the Austrianorn Erich von Stroheim, previously nown as an actor in such films as *'he Unbeliever*, *The Hun Within* and *'he Heart of Humanity*, with Stroeim often playing a brute, which as earned him the soubriquet, "The ıan you love to hate!" The new film ɛvolves around an American coule on holiday in the Dolomites, and ıe efforts of an Austrian officer Stroheim) to seduce the young wife. Remarkably subtle and sophisticatd in its treatment of characters and ɛlationships, this exceptional work ., quite simply, a masterpiece.

Francelia Billington, the unfortunate wife, with Erich von Stroheim.

Musidora, woman in a man's world

Paris, 10 December
The celebrated Irma Vep, alias Musidora, the first "vamp" of French films, has founded her own production company, la Société des films Musidora. As a producer, director and star she is a remarkable phenomenon. Having previously worked for Gaumont, Musidora is now independent. The actress took her first steps as a director in the park at Louveciennes, shooting scenes for her film *Vicenta*, a somber melodrama to which the public gave an emphatic thumbs down. The result was a loss of 45,000 francs. Undeterred, she has come up with a new scheme. Musidora has commissioned from her friend Colette, the celebrated novelist, an original screenplay entitled *la Flamme cachée* (*The Hidden Flame*). The eagerly awaited film tells the story of the passionate affairs of a young female student that finally engulf her in tragedy. The press has welcomed the news, and, no doubt, Musidora hopes it will restore her financial fortunes.

VITAGRAPH
BLUE RIBBON FEATURE
J. STUART BLACKTON AND ALBERT E. SMITH PRESENT
Americas Daintiest Actress
ANITA STEWART
"CLOVER'S REBELLION"
BY JAMES OLIVER CURWOOD
DIRECTED BY WILFRID NORTH

Anita Stewart, star of this film, under contract to Vitagraph since 1911.

KEYSTONE
COMEDIES
WESTERN IMPORT C° L^TD
WESFILM HOVSE GERRARD STREET LONDON

1914. At the start of his career, Chaplin's face was advertised by this poster.

LE FILM FRANÇAIS
Directeur ABEL GANCE
M^r DE MAX
du Théâtre SARAH BERNHARDT dans
LE MASQUE D'HORREU

Made by French-Belgian Abel Ganc in 1912, this film was never release

Gaumont
Bout de Zan

Bout-de-Zan (1912) replaced Bébé.

TRIANGLE-KEYSTONE
"There ain't gonna be no core!"
ROSCOE ARBUCKLE
with Keystone Players in
THE OTHER MAN
MACK SENNETT PRODUCTION

1918. One of eight films directed b Roscoe Arbuckle that year.

MISTINGUETT et CHEVALIER
dans
LA VALSE RENVERSANTE
les danseurs obsédants
S.C.A.G.L.
S.C.A.G.L.

Adrien Barère's poster for George Monca's 1911 film starred Chevalier.

AMERICAN ENTERTAINMENT CO.

By 1910, Nickelodeons were giving way to cinema theaters, and production companies such as this one were mushrooming across the U.S.

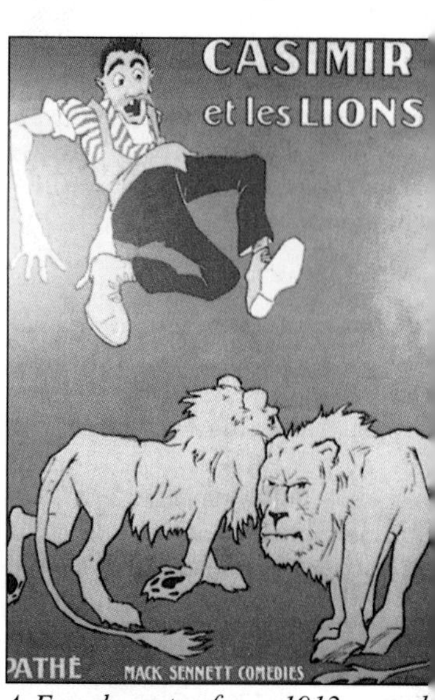
CASIMIR
et les LIONS
PATHÉ
MACK SENNETT COMEDIES

A French poster for a 1912 comed made by the prolific Mack Sennett.

ESSE L. LASKY
PRESENTS
ALICE MALE - CLEO RIDGLEY
WALLACE REID
AND
CLEO RIDGLEY
IN
THE SELFISH
WOMAN
BY HECTOR TURNBULL
Paramount

16. Cleo wed Wallace for money.

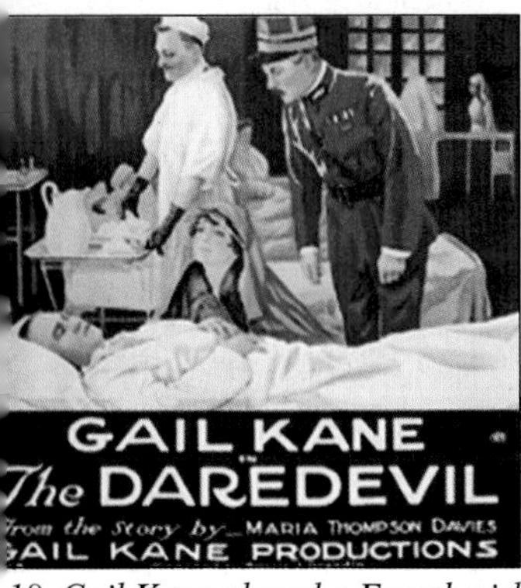
GAIL KANE
The DAREDEVIL
From the Story by MARIA THOMPSON DAVIES
GAIL KANE PRODUCTIONS

18. Gail Kane played a French girl
ced to live as a boy in the U.S.

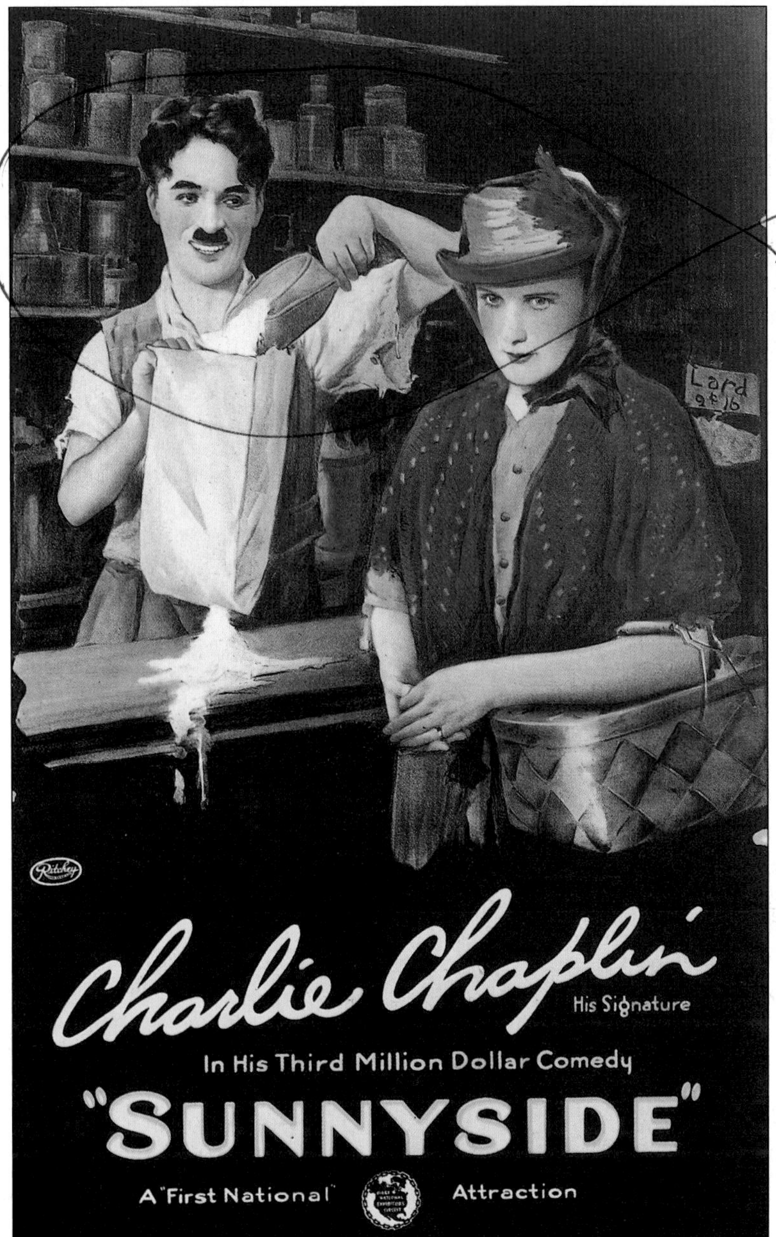
Lard
Charlie Chaplin
His Signature
In His Third Million Dollar Comedy
"SUNNYSIDE"
A "First National" Attraction

1919. Chaplin was a hotel odd-jobs man, with Edna Purviance as his co-star.

WESTERN IMPORT CO.
PRESENTS
MABEL
NORMAND
IN
"MICKEY"
SEVEN PARTS. PRODUCED BY MACK SENNETT
THE PICTURE YOU WILL NEVER FORGET

1918. The first film from star Mabel Normand's new company.

"Have We Killed Him?"
NORMA TALMADGE
IN
GOING STRAIGHT
WITH
RALPH LEWIS
RELEASED BY
S.A. LYNCH ENTERPRISES, INC.

1916. Two reformed crooks...

PARAMOUNT PICTURES
JOHNSON BECOMES A PROMISING PUPIL
JESSE L. LASKY
PRESENTS
THE FAVORITE COMEDIAN
EDWARD ABELES
IN
THE MAKING OF BOBBY BURNIT
FOUR PARTS
BY WINCHELL SMITH
AUTHOR OF
BREWSTER'S MILLIONS
350 SCENES

14. Bobby inherited $300,000...

WORLD PICTURES
WORLD PICTURES
PRESENT
MADGE EVANS
IN
"HOME WANTED"
Directed by TEFFT JOHNSON · Story by LUCY SARVER

1919. Madge Evans as an orphan.

ESSANAY
PHOTOPLAY
COMEDY
THE GIRL, THE COP,
THE BURGLAR
CONTROLLED BY THE ESSANAY FILM MFG. CO. CHICAGO, ILL.

1914. Wally Beery, Ruth Hennessy.

RASTUS
A PERDU SON ÉLÉPHANT
LOCATION, VENTE de FILMS et APPAREILS PATHÉ FRÈRES 14, Rue Favart, PARIS

1910. Allouetteau's poster for Pathé.

The Silent Era

The American film industry grew out of the rivalry of a handful of streetwise immigrants. Like small boys squabbling in a sandpit, they staked out their territory, and in the process transformed a turn-of-the-century novelty into a multi-million-dollar business. By the early 1920s motion pictures were America's fifth-ranking industry.

For the next 25 years the movies were dominated by the studio system which had evolved during the years of the First World War. While European and, later, American troops were locked in the trench warfare of the Western Front, Adolph Zukor, Carl Laemmle and William Fox consolidated their grip on the motion picture business. When the U.S. emerged from the conflict, physically unscathed and economically buoyant, the movie moguls were able to draw on, and reflect the feeling of, a country on the move. Douglas Fairbanks' ebullient go-getters had caught the confident mood of America in the war years. Soon Clara Bow's Jazz Age flappers, Tom Mix's daredevil chases and Harold Lloyd's cliff-hanging encounters with skyscrapers would celebrate the rapidly changing social and physical landscape of America in the 1920s.

A key moment came in 1924 with the merger of Marcus Loew's Metro Picture Corporation with the Goldwyn Company and Mayer Pictures, (in both of which Loew had a controlling interest) to form Metro-Goldwyn-Mayer, or MGM as it became universally known. The head of Mayer Pictures was Louis B. Mayer, a Russian-Jewish immigrant who in 1907 had moved from scrap-dealing into motion pictures, turning base metal into gold. He made his money distributing D.W. Griffith's landmark film, *The Birth of a Nation*, on the Northeastern seaboard and then moved into production, displaying an early interest in leading actresses in romantic melodramas, handled by director John M. Stahl. Mayer was appointed as vice president and general manager of MGM. As part of a financial empire with powerful banking connections and a ready-made market in the form of Marcus Loew's extensive chain of movie theaters, MGM was well placed to challenge the supremacy of Adolph Zukor's creation called the Paramount Pictures Corporation.

At MGM, Mayer's right-hand man and production supervisor was a 25-year-old graduate of business studies, Irving Thalberg. Six years earlier Thalberg had so impressed Carl Laemmle, head of Universal, that he had become Laemmle's private secretary. A year later he accompanied Laemmle to California and, at the age of 20, was appointed studio manager at Universal City. When Laemmle was away in New York, Thalberg was effectively in charge. The upward trajectory of Thalberg's career shows how the studios developed in the early 1920s as the expanding scope of their activities demanded ever-increasing supervision and control. At Universal, Thalberg locked horns with the *enfant terrible* of Hollywood, Erich von Stroheim, when the costs of *Foolish Wives* climbed over $1 million in 1920. Similarly, when costs began escalating on *Merry-Go-Round* (1923), Thalberg replaced Von Stroheim with the less interesting but more pliable Rupert Julian. Shortly afterwards Mayer poached Thalberg from Universal, reportedly after the latter declined to marry Laemmle's daughter Rosabelle. In the newly created MGM, Thalberg found himself toe-to-toe with his old sparring partner Von Stroheim, whose 42-reel epic *Greed* he ordered to be cut to a manageable length.

Another problem inherited by Thalberg was that of the spiraling cost of the Goldwyn Company's *Ben-Hur*, which was being shot on location in Italy. Thalberg moved swiftly to replace its leading man, George Walsh, with Ramon Novarro, and director Charles Brabin with Fred Niblo. Then he brought the unit back home and filmed the chariot race sequences in California before closely supervising the editing. The strain on Thalberg's weak constitution (he had been sickly since childhood) was so great that he watched the rushes from a hospital bed. The $4 million *Ben-Hur* made no money but it attracted huge audiences, and the prestige won by its production values rubbed off on MGM and set its future tone.

***Gold Diggers of Broadway** (Warner Bros., 1929) directed by Roy del Ruth.*

Thalberg's tact and discretion, and his tidy accountant's mind, contrasted with Mayer's vulgar bluster, enhancing the status of an industry which craved respectability. It was as if Mayer and Thalberg were playing a variation on the old interrogation theme – that of the nice and the nasty policeman. Those who were appalled by Mayer's bullying and crassness were sure to be disarmed by Thalberg's apparent rapport with MGM's creative personnel. But 'The Boy Wonder', as Thalberg was nicknamed, could not singlehandedly shoulder this burden. Control was exercised by a system of producers. At MGM production values would always remain high, if slightly hollow, so that beneath the studio's gloss lay an underlying blandness.

Despite his intimate involveme Thalberg's name rarely appeared screen. He once observed, "Cre you give yourself isn't worth ha ing." The names that filmgoe looked for were those of the stars, whom MGM boasted that they h 'more than there are in heave In 1927 Thalberg married one the brightest of them all, Norm Shearer, MGM's 'First Lady of t Screen'. The studios were sustain by the star system, and enormo care was taken to package and pr sent stars as fabulous creatures w inhabited a world far removed fro the daily lives of their fans. T public wanted its idols to be diff ent, and many of them were, thou image and reality were often hop lessly confused. The remarkab wedding which independent pr ducer Sam Goldwyn arranged 1927 for two of his stars, Viln Banky and Rod La Roque, w stage-managed as if it were the c max of one of the romantic mel dramas in which Banky shared to billing with Ronald Colman. Eve the wedding cake, rivaling a sma baroque church, turned out to be papier maché prop. Indeed, whe asked by a journalist what nam she favored for her first child, Bank replied, apparently without iron "I don't know, you'll have to as Mr. Goldwyn."

The rewards for such complian included huge and virtually untaxe salaries. Mary Pickford, of who Adolph Zukor remarked that sh had a mind like a cash register, b gan her movie career at Biograp in 1909 at a salary of $5. When, 1919, she left First National to c found United Artists, she was earn ing $350,000 a picture. Her nego ating skills, and those of Chapli not only paved the way for oth high salary earners but also enable stars to become independent pr ducers. In 1926 Gloria Swanso turned down Paramount's offer renew her contract at $18,000 week and went to United Artists produce her own films at a salary $20,000 a week, bankrolled by h then-lover Joseph Kennedy.

Dreams of independence coul also lead to disaster. Charles Ra was, in the early 1920s, the archet pal 'Country Boy' star of pictur ch celebrated the rustic innoce of America. Success went to y's head. He formed his own npany and went spectacularly ıkrupt after the failure of the lion-dollar epic, *The Courtship Miles Standish*. Threatened with ı, he threw a lavish party. When ed how he was going to pay for it, y replied, "Credit."

Credit was seldom extended to en stars, but the studios happily couraged them to overspend. By tting themselves in debt, they eftively mortgaged any prospect of ependence. In the early years of llywood, the movie colony lived unpretentious hotels. Now these re forsaken for the comic opera ateaux and mock baronial manns which their owners considered propriate to their elevated status. Night life arrived in Hollywood to er to celebrities and would-be ebrities. In May 1921 the Conut Grove opened at the Ambaslor Hotel, decorated with palm es left over from *The Sheik*, but ndal was bubbling away beneath glittering surface. Anita Loos ote of the early 1920s, "To place the limelight a great number of ople who ordinarily would be ambermaids and chauffeurs, and e them unlimited power and alth, is bound to produce lively ults." Successive scandals rocked llywood: the manslaughter trial Roscoe 'Fatty' Arbuckle; the ug addiction which killed Wallace id; and the unsolved murder of ector William Desmond Taylor, name but three. In the wake of the buckle affair, Will Hays, Presint Harding's Postmaster General, s appointed as a kind of moral tchdog over Hollywood, and stuos introduced 'morality clauses' o their contracts. It was left to inor Glyn to supply a tart assessent of the underlying Hollywood namic. After Arbuckle's fall from ace, she was asked what would ppen next. Miss Glyn replied, Whatever makes most money."

Hollywood money enabled the ajor studios to raid Europe for ent, particularly Germany, where ostwar angst had fueled a 'golden e' of Expressionist film whose vironments of stylized sets, lightg and performances were wellited to silent cinema. At Paraount the heavyweight German ar Emil Jannings hovered over the udio like a giant Zeppelin. Other aramount imports included the exotic Pola Negri, the first big European star to be lured to California; art directors Hans Dreier and Ernst Fegte and, finally, director Ernst Lubitsch of the legendary lightness of touch, who worked at Warners but naturally gravitated to Paramount, where he found his true home. The marriage between Berlin and Hollywood reached its apogee at Fox in 1927 with *Sunrise*, directed by F.W. Murnau, adapted from a Hermann Sudermann novel by Carl Mayer, designed by Rochus Gliese, and played by a typical American cast led by Janet Gaynor. The result was a remarkable combination of American optimism and German pessimism, in which Murnau's mobile camera moved majestically through exquisitely lit sets.

Sunrise was one of the last great peaks of silent cinema. In 1926 a John Barrymore vehicle, *Don Juan*, was the first feature film to be released with sound effects and music, but no dialogue, synchronized on disc. In October 1927 the sound barrier was finally broken by the Warner brothers and Al Jolson informing ecstatic audiences that "you ain't heard nothin' yet!" in *The Jazz Singer*. It was essentially a silent film tricked out with a few dialogue and musical sequences, but its success encouraged Warners to release their first all-talking film, *Lights of New York*. Reluctantly, the other studios followed suit, and within a matter of months silent cinema was virtually a thing of the past.

Laurel (right) and Hardy in ***Early to Bed*** *(1928), supervised by Leo McCarey.*

In the early days of cinema the insensitive, orthochromatic film stock, requiring strong light, had mercilessly exposed every line and wrinkle in the faces of the middle-aged stage stars who tried their hand in the movies. The intimacy of the medium, and its punishing schedules, demanded the fresh faces, youthful energy and well-defined personalities of the young hopefuls assembled by Griffith at Biograph. The arrival of the microphone created a new friction between the stars and the technology which brought them to the screen. When Douglas Fairbanks recorded a spoken prologue for his last silent feature, *The Iron Mask* (1929), his stentorian delivery drove the microphone back 10 yards. Clara Bow's habit of restlessly dashing about the set posed acute problems for the crude new apparatus. Above all, survival or a ticket to oblivion depended on the marriage of voice and screen personality. Norma Talmadge was betrayed by her Brooklyn twang in the 18th-century setting of *Du Barry, Woman of Passion* (1930). John Gilbert's intense style – so electrifying opposite Garbo in *Flesh and the Devil* (1928) – seemed absurd when he wooed a wooden Catherine Dale Owen in his first talking feature, *His Glorious Night* (1929). His voice, light but by no means the laughable squeak of legend, was simply not the voice that Gilbert's silent fans had heard in their minds when he had melted into the arms of Garbo. His acting, choreographed to the rhythms of the universal language of silent cinema, now seemed like so much posturing.

Gilbert succumbed to the ravages of disappointment and alcohol in 1936. Fairbanks, Pickford, Bow and Swanson made a handful of talkies, but they were now too closely associated with a cinema of the past to survive the arrival of sound. Swanson's subsequent comeback as the crazed silent movie queen Norma Desmond in *Sunset Boulevard* (1950) was ripe with irony. Nevertheless, there were far more survivors than casualties of sound. Among the stars who made the transition were John Barrymore, Laurel and Hardy, Ronald Colman, Gary Cooper, Mary Astor, William Powell, Norma Shearer, Adolphe Menjou and, after an agonizing wait, Greta Garbo. (Chaplin was by some years the last).

In the 1920s, France recovered from the ravages of World War I to foster a cinema which accommodated the extravagant technical ambitions of Abel Gance, the whimsical comedy of René Clair and the surrealist experiments of the avant-garde, the first people to recognize film as an art form – the most notable product of which was the collaboration between Spaniards Salvador Dali and Luis Buñuel on the film *Un chien andalou* (1928).

In 1920 a copy of *The Birth of a Nation* reached Moscow. Three years later Griffith was invited to take charge of film production in the Soviet Union. He declined this intriguing offer, but his work exercised a profound influence on another great director, Sergei M. Eisenstein. Like Griffith, Eisenstein was a man of the theater who turned to films in 1924, at a time when Russian cinema was at a very low ebb. However, the decision in 1925 to permit non-naturalistic and avant-garde expression in the arts in the Soviet Union paved the way for a burst of creative energy in Soviet film led by the stirring propagandist Eisenstein, the fiercely theoretical V.I. Pudovkin, the intensely lyrical Dovzhenko and the bustling Bolshevik idealist and pioneer of *cinéma vérité*, Dziga Vertov. Sadly, by 1928 the dead hand of socialist realism was starting to exert a stifling grip on Soviet cinema. The last masterpiece of the silent era was Alexander Dovzhenko's *Earth*, made in the Soviet Union in 1930. In America preparations were being made to show Eisenstein's *October*, which had already met a hostile reception from the Party hierarchy. But the talkies were now all the rage, and *October* was not screened in the U.S. until years later. A new era in cinema was about to begin.

ROBIN CROSS

1920

France, 24 January
Jean Renoir has married Andrée Heuschling, known as Dédée. She was formerly the model for the filmmaker's famous artist-father, Auguste Renoir.

London, 25 January
Doctor Elias, who is renowned for his research in optics, has developed Colorama, a new process for the cinema using natural colors.

New York, January
Loew's Incorporated have taken over the five-year-old company, Metro Pictures. Marcus Loew is to continue as president.

Paris, 1 February
After the referendum by the daily *Comœdia* for the five best films – Cecil B. DeMille's *The Cheat* and Charlie Chaplin's *Shoulder Arms* topped the list – *Filma* magazine has given up the idea of an opinion poll for the five worst films: there are too many of them.

Washington, 5 February
The undersecretary of state for the interior, F.K. Lane, has suggested to the heads of film companies that they help their country by making anti-Bolshevik propaganda films.

Copenhagen, 9 February
Carl Dreyer has released his film *President* (*Praesidenten*), which stars Halvard Hoff and Elith Pio.

Paris, 10 February
Cinema professionals gathered at the Palais d'Orsay in order to celebrate Louis Lumière's election to the Académie des Sciences on 15 December. But Auguste Lumière declined the invitation, acknowledging his brother as the inventor of the Cinematograph.

Rome, 9 March
Giuseppe Barattolo and his UCI group have signed an agreement with German counterpart UFA with the goal of eventually controlling the European market.

Hollywood, 16 March
The release of Maurice Tourneur's screen adaptation of Robert Louis Stevenson's novel, *Treasure Island*. This has been made into a 55-minute film starring Lon Chaney, Shirley Mason and Charles Ogle.

California, 31 March
The celebrated Belgian-born writer Maurice Maeterlinck, author of *Pelléas and Mélisande*, has been invited to Hollywood under contract to producer Samuel Goldwyn.

Paris, 5 April
In his editorial in the daily *Paris-Midi*, Maurice de Waleffe is severely critical of the American invasion of French screens. He suggests these films be banned.

Brussels, 20 April
In *la Libre Belgique*, the journalist Vendabole qualifies cinema lovers as "clods" and concludes that "the cinema is harmful because it renders people mindless."

Pennsylvania, 30 April
The first trains containing cinema carriages have been put into service by the Pittsburgh Harmony Butler Rail Company.

Cairo, 7 May
The Egyptian financier Talat Harb Pacha has created the Misr Bank and has announced plans to develop the cinema industry here.

New York, 31 May
Louis B. Mayer has set up Louis B. Mayer Productions Incorporated with a capital of $5 million.

Hollywood, 15 June
Max Linder has sold his car and mortgaged various personal effects to finance his new film, *Seven Years' Bad Luck*. Filming has started at Universal City.

Shanghai, 30 June
The opera singer Mei Lanfang is playing a servant in *The Fragrance of Spring Makes it Difficult to Study*, produced by the Commercial Press company from an adaptation of the play *The Pavillion of Peonies*.

New York, 13 July
D.W. Griffith has floated 500,000 shares in the new D.W. Griffith Corporation to order to finance his new studios at Mamaroneck, near New York.

Paris, 18 July
The market porters from Les Halles have invited Mary Pickford and Douglas Fairbanks to come visit the "stomach of Paris".

London, 31 July
According to a competition planned by *The Picture Show* magazine, Mary Pickford and Douglas Fairbanks are Britain's favorite stars.

Berlin, 1 September
Ernst Lubitsch's *Sumurun*, adapted from an oriental pantomime by the producer Max Reinhardt, with Pola Negri, Jenny Hasselquist and Paul Wegener, with Lubitsch himself in the role of the little hunchback, is currently showing.

Paris, 5 September
The young American star, Olive Stone, has been found dead from bichloride poisoning in her hotel room at the Ritz. She was on vacation in Paris with her husband Jack Pickford, Mary's brother. It is still not known whether it was suicide or an accident.

London, 10 September
During his visit to London, the American producer Jesse L. Lasky signed up a number of well-known writers such as Sir James Barrie, the author of *Peter Pan*, and H.G. Wells to work with future film projects for Paramount. He is even attempting to persuade George Bernard Shaw to come into the fold.

Paris, 10 September
The philosopher Henri Bergson has been quoted in *le Cinema*: "The cinematograph interests me, as do all inventions. It is capable of suggesting new thoughts to the philosopher. It could help in the synthesis of memory or thought."

Hollywood, 25 October
Film director Rex Ingram has started shooting the super-production entitled *The Four Horsemen of the Apocalypse*, at Metro studios. His wife Alice Terry is playing the lead with Wallace Beery and a young unknown, Rudolph Valentino.

Berlin, 29 October
Paul Wegener has brought out his second adaptation of Meyrenk's novel of the fantastic, *The Golem*.

France, 30 October
Abel Gance has continued filming on *la Rose du rail* at Arcachon. The film continues to be made under a cloud – Gance's companion Ida Danis is dying.

Paris, 30 November
Fatty Arbuckle, the American c median was given a warm welcor by his fans at Saint-Lazare static But they decided against carryi him in triumph: he weighs 120 k

New York, 28 December
The cinema, one of America's lea ing industries, is in a crisis due tc lack of overseas markets. Produ tion has been reduced by 50 perce putting 5,000 people out of work

China, 31 December
To date, China has produced 35 fu length films (33 in Shanghai and tw in Hong Kong), numerous sho films and documentaries.

BIRTHS

Italy, 20 January
Federico Fellini

Sweden, 28 February
Alf Kjellin

France, 29 February
Michèle Morgan (Simone Rousse

France, 21 March
Eric Rohmer (Maurice Scherer)

China, 1 April
Toshiro Mifune

Paris, 15 May
Michel Audiard

Paris, 24 August
Jean Desailly

New York, 23 September
Mickey Rooney (Joe Yule Jr.)

Nebraska, 17 October
Montgomery Clift

New York, 20 November
Gene Tierney

Sweden, 29 December
Viveca Lindfors

DEATHS

Mario Caserini

***The Cabinet of Dr. Caligari**, directe by Robert Wiene, has been receiv with enthusiastic acclaim. Its imag native narrative and visual effects r flect German Expressionism.*

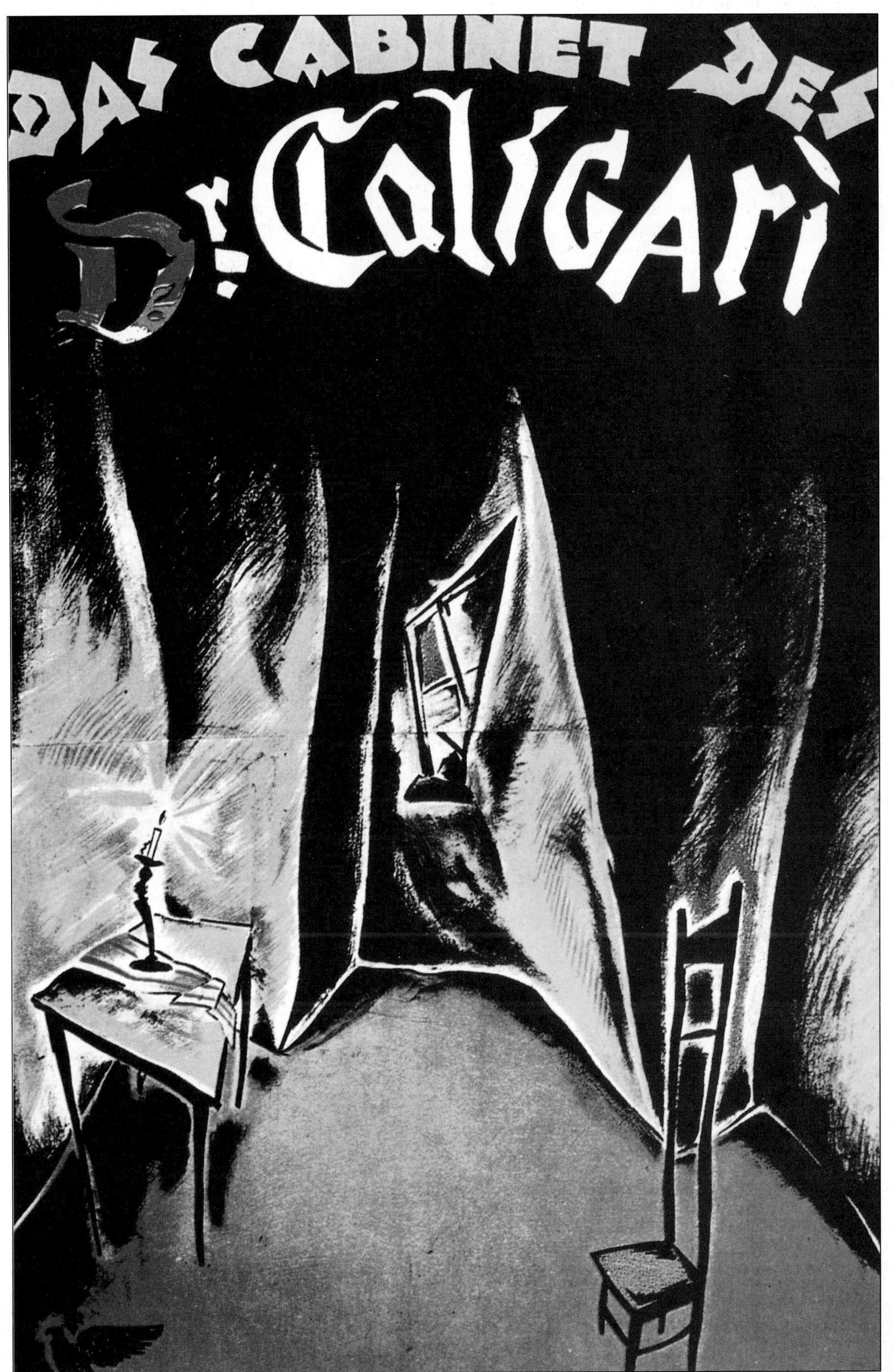
DAS CABINET DES
Dr. Caligari

▷

Robert Wiene reveals Germany's weird fantasie

Werner Krauss as the sinister Doctor Caligari, with Lil Dagover.

Conrad Veidt as the mad doctor's unfortunate servant, made to murder.

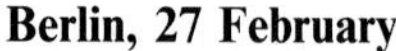

Berlin, 27 February

An extraordinary film, *The Cabinet of Dr. Caligari*, has opened in Germany. Following the recent successes of Ernst Lubitsch and Pola Negri and of new director Fritz Lang, it appears that the German cinema is making a remarkable and rapid postwar recovery. *Caligari*, produced by Erich Pommer, written by Hans Janowitz and Carl Mayer, and directed by Robert Wiene, is an astonishing attempt to translate the imagery of German Expressionist painting and design to the cinema screen. Most impressive of all are the stylized and painted canvas sets. Designers Herman Warm, Walter Reimann and Walter Röhrig collaborated closely on the production, in which they make remarkable use of deliberately distorted perspective narrow slanting streets that sl across each other at unexpected a gles – that are matched by the m merizingly strange performances Werner Krauss as Caligari and Co rad Veidt as the somnambulist.

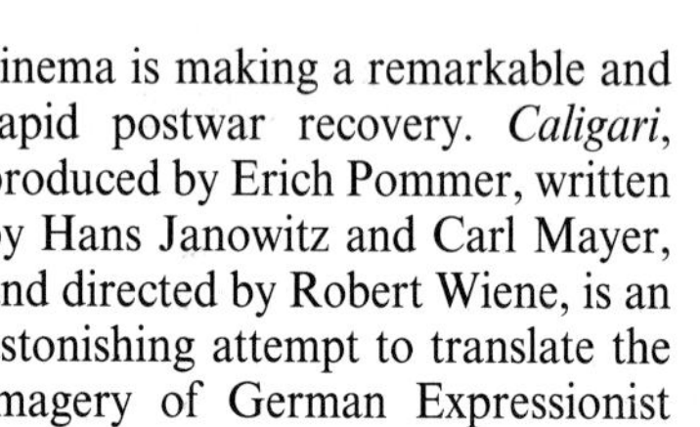

The 1001 nights of Louis Nalpas

Paris, 2 January

The Sultan of Love, a tale from *A Thousand and One Nights*, directed by René Le Somptier and Charles Burguet, has been one of the great successes of French cinema since its release last December. The producer, Louis Nalpas, invested a great deal of money in this film including inviting 50 artists to stencil-color all the images to render it even more sumptuous. It will be an enormous task, which should be completed in one to two years. For the moment, *The Sultan of Love* continues to seduce the public. Nalpas has managed to compete with Hollywood.

Charlie Chaplin and Max Linder, each a student, both masters

Los Angeles, 16 February

At the airport, while they waited to catch an airplane together, Charlie Chaplin and Max Linder were interviewed by the American correspondent of the French weekly magazine *Comœdia* about the recent poll on the world's five best films. Asked about their personal favorites, the two famous comedians paid each other diplomatic homage. Chaplin opined that the five most notable films were, naturally, made by Max Linder. His traveling companion averred that, on the contrary, the best ones could only be films featuring Charles Chaplin. At the end of this whimsical exchange, Chaplin and Linder talked about the close friendship they have enjoyed sin 1917, which began when the Fren actor-director put in a brief stint Essanay where Charlie was at wo Linder's wartime sojourn in Ame ca came to an abrupt end in m 1917. He had completed only thr films when, sadly, he contract double pneumonia and was forc to spend nearly a year convalesci in a sanitarium in Switzerland. H health has never fully recover from gas poisoning sustained duri war service. Now Max Linder h crossed the Atlantic again in a fre attempt to reconquer the Americ market – no easy task and one which he might benefit from Char Chaplin's counsel.

Their mutual professional admiration has grown into friendship.

ohn Barrymore delivers an awesome incarnation of pure evil

w York, 2 April
ın Barrymore, sweet prince of oadway's leading family, has been obbling in films since 1913 when he ıde his screen debut in Famous ıyers' *An American Citizen.* He s saved his serious energies for the ge, but now, with his twelfth film *. Jekyll and Mr. Hyde*, he has me into his own. The 38-year-old rrymore makes a handsome Dr. :yll, but when he downs the doc- 's fatal potion he turns into a nstrous vision of pure evil before r very eyes. The chilling effect is mpleted with some skillful screen ckery. The sight of Jekyll's fingers solving into claws is followed by a se-up of Barrymore's Hyde in rifying makeup. This Hyde is a leous spider-like creature who uttles on crooked legs. Soon, the nsformation begins to take place aided by the evil elixir. While Dr. kyll sleeps, an enormous phantom ider crawls across the floor of his droom, settles on top of him and elts into his body. Jekyll wakes om feverish sleep as Hyde. In a ong supporting cast, sultry Nita aldi is outstanding as the sexual mptation placed in Jekyll's way by andon Hurst's cynical Sir George Carewe. At Hyde's hands she becomes, quite literally, a shadow of her former self. *Dr. Jekyll and Mr. Hyde* will cement Barrymore's popularity with cinemagoers, although his theatrical posturing throughout the film has attracted some adverse comment. The reviewer in *Variety* observed that, for all the makeup, Hyde "was always Jack Barrymore", adding somewhat carpingly that "in one instance of alteration of personality, the director and/or star found it necessary to change the star's clothes as well as his individuality with the aid of drugs."

Louis Wolheim (left) in the clutches of Barrymore's hideous Mr. Hyde.

merica's favorite little sweetheart could be guilty of bigamy

ollywood, 14 April
ıere has been another Hollywood andal. The Attorney General of alifornia has decided to prosecute ary Pickford, whom he accuses of rjury and bigamy. This odd cir- ımstance has followed the actress's cent marriage to Douglas Fair- nks on 28 March. For some years, e extramarital liaison between the o stars, both among the highest id of the American cinema, has led the gossip columns of newspa- rs. Pickord had been married to e charming actor Owen Moore, hom she met on the set at Bio- aph in 1913. Their divorce, an- ounced in Minden, Nevada last arch, upset the innumerable ad- irers of "America's Sweetheart". t the time, she declared that she d not envisage any remarriage in e immediate future. Nevertheless, ss than a month later, the two co- unders of United Artists were arried secretly in a small Holly- ood church. Fairbanks himself had just divorced Ann Beth Sully. To those who were astonished to see the star's recent statement contradicted, she replied, "Yes, I've changed my mind! Isn't that a woman's prerogative?" These light-hearted comments were badly timed, as the law is taking an even greater interest in the escapades of Hollywood. Ignoring the controversy, the young couple are getting ready to pay an extended visit to Europe.

The two stars have regularized a liaison which was the talk of the town.

Harold impaired but not disabled

Hollywood, 10 July
Comedian Harold Lloyd, who suffered a serious accident one year ago, has been making a remarkable recovery, and his latest two-reeler, *High and Dizzy*, co-starring Mildred Davis and directed by Hal Roach, has just opened. While Lloyd posed for a gag photo at the Witzel studio in downtown L.A. last August, a prop bomb exploded and almost killed him. Forced to spend a long period in the hospital and convalescing thereafter, the actor has made a complete recovery but has lost the thumb and forefinger of his right hand. Since Lloyd had finished four two-reelers prior to his accident, Pathé was able to spread their release to meet the growing demand for his comedies during his absence. By last autumn Harold was already back at work at the newly constructed Roach studio in Culver City, completing *Haunted Spooks*, the comedy he was filming at the time of his accident. In fact he had only graduated to two-reelers early in 1919, the first of which, the appropriately named *Bumping into Broadway*, had a special New York opening in November. At that time Lloyd made a rare trip back East to meet Charles Pathé and to celebrate the signing of a new contract with producer Hal Roach – and beheld his name in lights for the first time on the marquees of two of the largest movie theaters, the Strand and the Rialto. He can now only move forward on the road to success.

Harold Lloyd with Bebe Daniels.

Gish sisters on both sides of the camera

Dorothy Gish remodeling her husband, James Rennie, for director Lillian.

Hollywood, 13 July
Lillian Gish, that wonderful star of so many D.W. Griffith films, has taken to directing. Although there is little evidence in *Remodeling Her Husband* that she will become a rival to her master and mentor, she has managed to demonstrate her imagination and competence. Admittedly, most of the laughter is provoked by the brilliant comic performance given by her sister Dorothy Gish in the main role as the vivacious heroine who, in a series of amusing episodes, teaches her smug husband (James Rennie) to appreciate her. She dominates the picture with her gift for pantomime.

Erich von Stroheim unlocks another door

Hollywood, 20 August
Stroheim has done it again! If there were ever any doubts regarding the quality of his talent as a director, they can now be set to rest. His latest film, *The Devil's Pass Key*, has just opened here to rave reviews and enthusiastic applause following the New York premiere earlier this month. According to the correspondent of *Billboard* magazine, who was present at that event, "Despite sweltering heat an SRO audience was held rapt with the enthralling interest, realism and charm so admirably pictured." Based on a story by the Baroness de Meyer entitled *Clothes and Treachery*, the new film is set in Paris immediately after the Great War and continues Stroheim's Universal studio formula of sophisticated sex, seduction and intrigue within a Continental setting. Stroheim himself does not appear as an actor in this one, however, as in *Blind Husbands*, the heroine is a dissatisfied wife (played by Una Trevelyan) who gets herself into trouble, and her well-meaning husband is played by Sam De Grasse, the husband from the previous film. Although the picture was completed and even previewed earlier this year, the Universal publicity department has been so eager to get the greatest possible mileage out of Stroheim's name that the release was delayed until now. The director has, in fact, signed a new and lucrative contract with the studio.

Fillmore, George and Busch.

Maurice Tourneur attacked by French pres[s]

Shirley Mason and Charles Ogle in Maurice Tourneur's ***Treasure Island****.*

Paris, 16 July
Louis Delluc is furious. Using his *Paris-Midi* column, he has clearly lambasted those who, in their profession as journalists, have been challenging the right of the director Maurice Tourneur to return to the U.S. On 21 April, Jean-Louis Croze, in his contribution to *Comœdia*, reproached Tourneur for having spent the war years in America, and for having thus "saved his life, while so many of his compatriots lost theirs." Delluc believes that there is an arbitrary smear campaign motivated by "a treacherous chorus of bitter, sick, jealous and rancorous failures." In 1914, because he spoke English well, Maurice Tourneur (real name Maurice Thomas) was sent to the United States to direct the American productions of Eclair at its Fort Lee, New Jersey, studios. He had been an assistant director with the company since 1911. The following year, he graduated to director and quickly gained a reputation for the pictorial quality of his work. During the last six years, he has become one of Hollywood's most respected directors, ranking only behind Griffith and Thomas Ince in popularity. The films of Tourneur (formerly a book illustrator and poster designer) are remarkable for their decors and composition. This is well-suited to fantasies such as *The Wishing Ring* (1914), *Trilby* (1915) and *The Blue Bird* (1920), outstanding examples of his ability to create a fairy-tale world. His latest picture is an adaptation of Stevenson's *Treasure Island*. As a young man, Tourne[ur] served with the French artillery [i]n North Africa, afterwards working [a]s an assistant at the atelier of th[e] sculptor Rodin. Instead of critici[z]ing Tourneur's decision to work [i]n the United States, the French shou[ld] feel proud to have a compatriot [o]f such stature.

The tragic death of Suzanne Grandais

One of France's best-loved stars.

Paris, 1 September
The funeral of Suzanne Granda[is] was held this morning at the cem[e]tery in Montmartre. A large crow[d] of mourners came to pay their la[st] respects. On 28 August the popula[r] young actress was tragically killed [i]n a car accident while returning wit[h] director Charles Burguet from shoo[t]ing her last film, *l'Essor*. She wa[s] born Suzanne Gueudret in Paris o[n] 14 June 1893.

reat loss for Griffith as Gish goes

w York, 20 September
'ew days after the release of the hly praised film, *Way Down East*, W. Griffith temporarily broke lian Gish's contract. Gish, conered to be too independent, reed the Frohman Amusement mpany on a three-year contract. is thought that because of Griffith's financial difficulties, he can no longer afford her salary. The director's decision, whatever the reasons, could have dire results. Lillian Gish is shocked, because she has always regarded their association as sacrosanct. Together, Gish and Griffith have made dozens of successful films. The triumph of *Way Down East*, for example, owed much to the charismatic actress, overpowering in her role as an unmarried young mother, pushed to despair. To try and fill the gap left by her absence, Griffith has now returned to Carol Dempster, whom he first directed in *The Girl Who Stayed At Home* and in two films since.

llian Gish and Richard Barthelmess in the poignant **Way Down East**.

D.W. GRIFFITH
PRESENTS
WAY DOWN EAST

Gabrielle Réjane is, sadly, no more

Paris, 29 October
The last film made by the great actress Gabrielle Réjane, who died on 14 June, has been released. In *Miarka, la fille à l'ours*, which is directed by Louis Mercanton, Desdemona Mazza plays Miarka, a little gypsy raised by the sorcerer Vougne who sees the future with the aid of her magic books. Réjane is Vougne and handles the part with her usual skill. Born Gabrielle Réju, she had a glittering theatrical career, covering half a century, and many compared her with Sarah Bernhardt. She was able to move easily between a comedy like *Madame Sans-Gêne* (which was also adapted for the screen) and tragedy such as *Germinie Lacerteux*. The public loved her cheeky banter, and the Parisian accent which she could drop at will. Sadly, heart trouble has meant that she has not been seen in public since 1919. In *Miarka*, which was shot in the South of France, the famous writer Jean Richepin, author of the book on which the film was based, takes on the role of the lord of the manor.

'ife trouble turns Charlie into kidnapper

s Angeles, 19 November
ildred Harris can draw grim satisction from the fact that the dirce proceedings which she opened ainst Charlie Chaplin last August ve come to a conclusion. She has en awarded $100,000 and a share of the community property acquired since their marriage in October 1918. The ruling is the outcome of protracted wrangling between Chaplin and his wife's lawyers. From the outset, her lawyers threatened to attach the negatives of Chaplin's latest film, *The Kid*, as part of the settlement. Chaplin made his own arrangements. At the beginning of August he left California in conditions of the greatest secrecy, taking with him over 200,000 feet of the completed film. Holed up with two assistants in a hotel in Salt Lake City, Chaplin set to work editing the film. Mildred's lawyers eventually relented, waiving all claim to *The Kid* and leaving Chaplin in sole possession of the rights to the film. *The Kid*, in which Charlie co-stars with four-year-old Jackie Coogan, has cost Chaplin $300,000 and taken 18 months to film. The emotional cost of the divorce has been as high, to which must be added a public brawl between Chaplin and producer Louis B. Mayer, who has been promoting Harris' career.

'ith six-year-old Jackie Coogan.

United Artists makes its mark with 'Zorro'

Los Angeles, 5 December
Crowds are already forming to see *The Mark of Zorro*, the latest film starring Douglas Fairbanks. The energetic actor has taken a risk by breaking the embargo on costume pictures. It has been a common belief in the motion picture industry that period pieces play to empty theaters. In case his new venture failed, Fairbanks decided to make it quickly and cheaply. He need not have worried. The story tells of Don Diego Vega, an effete nobleman in 19th-century California, who disguises himself as the dashing masked Zorro, protector of the weak and innocent. Doug is at his bouncy best, and the director, Fred Niblo has kept the pace lively.

Douglas Fairbanks protects Marguerite de la Motte from Robert McKim.

1921

Stockholm, 1 January
Victor Sjöström has released his film version of Selma Lagerlöf's popular novel, *Körkärlen* (*The Phantom Carriage*), starring himself and Hilda Borgström.

Paris, 10 January
Daniel Bompard's film *Une brute* (*A Beast*), with André Noix, has been banned by the censors.

Paris, 9 March
A Gaumont documentary on the transformation of engines of war into tractors was shown to deputies at the Palais-Bourbon.

Paris, 26 March
The opening session (by invitation) of the Madeleine cinema took place yesterday evening. Two American films were screened: *Wolves of the Night* with William Farnum and a Mary Pickford offering, *Little Lord Fauntleroy*.

France, 25 April
To the delight of all the inhabitants of Pérouges, Henri Diamant-Berger and his film team have arrived at the town's medieval site to continue filming *The Three Musketeers*.

Montceau-les-Mines, 1 May
René Leprince seized the occasion of the local Labor Day parade to take shots for his film *l'Empereur des pauvres* (*Emperor of the Poor*).

New York, 10 May
Abel Gance has held a preview of the American version of his film *J'accuse* (*I Accuse*), for the press and cinema owners at the Ritz. The title is already well known because of the acclaim it received from critics after its London release.

Paris, 15 May
There has been an alarming drop in cinema attendance in the capital due to the current heat wave. Very few cinemas are equiped with adequate ventilation.

Pompeii, 24 May
Luitz-Morat, the French filmmaker, received special permission from the Italian Minister for Fine Arts to shoot scenes for *la Terre du diable* among the famous ruins. The stars are Gaston Modot and Yvonne Aurel, and even Vesuvius played its role by erupting.

Pyrenees, 7 June
Pearl White has been found safe. The famous American star lost her way during an excursion on horseback in the mountains. After finding a rough shelter, she slept for 16 hours before being rescued by a local shepherd.

Paris, 10 June
A memorable quote appears in the latest issue of Louis Delluc's magazine, *Cinéa*. "There is", it says, "a great actor in *l'Atlantide* made by Jacques Feyder: it is the sand."

Paris, 15 June
According to *Ciné-Journal*, the biggest cinema in the world is the 8,000-seat Capitol in New York.

Hollywood, 1 July
Douglas Fairbanks has vowed "never to put a foot in France again." The reason is that his interpretation of D'Artagnan, in the American version of *The Three Musketeers*, directed by Fred Niblo, received bad press from the French.

Berlin, 14 July
The actress Henny Porten has married Dr. Wilhelm von Kaufmann, who has finally decided to give up his medical practice to devote himself to producing his wife's films.

France, 17 July
Séverin-Mars, the well-known star of Abel Gance's *J'accuse* (*I Accuse*) and the yet to be released *la Roue* (*The Wheel*), has died unexpectedly while vacationing on the banks of the Seine. He just made his debut as a filmmaker with *le Cœur magnifique* (*The Magnificent Heart*).

Paris, 22 July
The French public may never see the boxing match between Frenchman Georges Carpentier and the American Jack Dempsey which finished in the latter's favor. French distributors are refusing to pay Fox, who hold the rights to the match, the asking price of 700,000 francs.

New York, 31 August
D.W. Griffith has spent $150,000 building a replica of an 18th-century French village at the Mamaroneck studios for his film *Orphans of the Storm*, based on a popular French melodrama. The set is to be burned as soon as filming is over.

Paris, 5 September
Aimé Simon-Girard, D'Artagnan in Henri Diamant-Berger's film *The Three Musketeers*, has bought the horse he rode in the film. They can be seen together in the Bois.

Moscow, 15 September
S.M. Eisenstein has been admitted to the GVIRM (State Filmmakers Institute of Higher Education), headed by V.E. Meyerhold.

Nice, 19 September
The prefect of the Alpes-Maritimes, Armand Bernard, has decided to ban all films with scenes of crime, theft or murder from his region.

Paris, 20 September
Louis Delluc's criticisms and notes on Chaplin's work have been published under the title *Charlot*.

Paris, 15 October
Sirène have published *Bonjour Cinéma*, the first book by Jean Epstein. Epstein has also just made his debut in films as director Louis Delluc's assistant director on *le Tonnerre*.

Moscow, 18 November
Lenin has published his *Thesis on Propaganda and Production*: the cinema must be used in the service of ideological development.

Paris, 2 December
Abel Gance is still editing *la Roue* (*The Wheel*). Shooting finished last year, but cutting is a long process. The filmmaker is said to have exposed 277,863 metres of negative.

New York, 6 December
Release of *Be My Wife*, produced and directed by Max Linder, who also stars alongside Alta Allen and Caroline Rankin.

Paris, 16 December
The film *Pour Don Carlos* (*For Don Carlos*), co-directed by Musidora and Jacques Lasseyne, is still not having much success with the public, despite having been cut by a fifth of its original length.

Berlin, 22 December
Hintertreppe (*Backstairs*), an allegorical and Expressionist work that is directed by Leopold Jessner and Paul Leni and stars Henny Porten, Wilhelm Dieterle and Fritz Kortner, opens today.

Paris, 27 December
A gala evening to help War Wido and Orphans was held at the Opé de Paris with a screening of *l'Agon des aigles* (*The Agony of Eagle* from director Dominique Berna Deschamps. The date was carefu chosen by the organizers to coinci with the centenary of Napoleon death.

Berlin, 31 December
The number of films made by Ge man production companies duri the year was 600.

Hollywood, 31 December
Paramount Pictures has announc that it made a total of 101 featu length films during the year. This the highest output to date achiev by a single studio.

BIRTHS

London, 1 March
Dirk Bogarde

London, 4 March
Joan Greenwood

Germany, 25 March
Simone Signoret
(Simone Kaminker)

France, 25 April
Jean Carmet

Calcutta, 2 May
Satyajit Ray

France, 19 May
Daniel Gélin

Italy, 31 May
Alida Valli
(Alida Maria Altenburger)

Minnesota, 21 June
Jane Russell

Italy, 13 October
Yves Montand
(Ivo Livi)

Scotland, 20 October
Deborah Kerr
(Deborah Kerr-Trimmer)

Henri Diamant-Berger has met th high hopes of his producers, Path Consortium, with the success of ***Th Three Musketeers*** *in a year when has been filmed by the Americans.*

Ecstatic reception for little Jackie Coogan

This is the great picture upon which the famous comedian has worked a whole year.
6 reels of Joy.
Charles Chaplin
IN
"THE KID"
Written and directed by Charles Chaplin
A First National Attraction

"LE GOSSE"
(THE KID)

*Since its New York opening, **The Kid** has proved to be a major success.*

New York, 6 January
Charlie Chaplin's first feature film, *The Kid*, has opened in New York to instant and resounding success. For once Chaplin has found a foil worthy of his mettle, the bewitching little Jackie Coogan, whom he had spotted parodying his father's tap-dance routine at an Annette Kellerman revue. After meeting Jackie two days later, Chaplin declared, "This is the most amazing person I ever met in my life." As Chaplin watched the child, the idea for the six-reel film sprung into his mind. After testing the little boy in a two-reeler called *A Day's Pleasure*, he cast Coogan as the bright-eyed ragamuffin in battered cap and oversized trousers who is reared, lost and then finally regained by the Tramp. Coogan provides a miniature version of the Tramp's pathos and artfulness and at times it seems as if the "Little Fellow", as Chaplin calls the Tramp, is walking hand-in-hand with his infant self. For his own part, Chaplin has suggested that the orphaned Coogan represents all those children orphaned by the Great War. While watching the film, it is hard not to be struck by the remarkable rapport between Chaplin and his small co-star. Jackie Coogan Sr. has also played his part in the production, appearing in several roles including a bum who picks the Tramp's pocket and the Devil in a dream sequence.

The Kid has placed Chaplin in a very strong financial position. Already confident that he had a winner on his hands after giving the film a trial showing in Salt Lake City, he asked First National for an advance of $1.5 million plus 50 percent of the net after the company had recovered the advance. First National stalled, and displayed a studied lack of enthusiasm even after seeing the film. But Chaplin stuck to his guns, and the stubborn executives were forced to acknowledge that *The Kid* had given him an unbeatable hand. *The Kid* is also certain to make a worldwide star of Jackie Coogan, and Chaplin has stated that though they will not work together again, he will not hold Coogan back.

Jackie Coogan, a real heartbreaker.

Filmmakers proclaim the 'seventh art'

Paris, 27 May
The cinema has given rise to unprecedented debates on aesthetics, and the writings of the Italian poet Riccioto Canudo have only added fuel to the discussions. However, since 6 May, a new weekly magazine, *Cinéa*, has entered the fray. Louis Delluc, the editor, is a theoretician of the Impressionist school and an opponent of Canudo's somewhat woolly writing. Canudo has coined the word "screenist" to describe film directors. Delluc prefers the better-sounding "cinéaste", and expresses the hope that "the seventh art" (Canudo's expression) will be capable of giving an "accurate impression of truth and a study of mankind." The more abstract and lyrical Canudo speaks about the "rhythm of light" that the camera must provide. The Italian poet has brought a worldly air to the discussions, and has attracted an elegant and refined following to Poccardi's restaurant as well as to his residence at 12 rue du Quatre-Septembre. Last March, Canudo founded *Le Casa*, a club for the friends of "the seventh art". At the club, one can encounter the intellectual set: Léon Moussina Jean Cocteau, Blaise Cendrars, F nand Léger, Robert Mallet-Stever Jean Epstein, Abel Gance, Marc L'Herbier, Germaine Dulac a even "screenists", that is, comme cial filmmakers, such as René Pou tal and Léonce Perret, among t social elite.

Riccioto Canudo, sketched after t war by his friend Pablo Picasso.

Darkness shrouds Pathé Consortium studi

At Vincennes, artificial light is systematically and effectively used in filming

Vincennes, 14 June
Pathé Consortium, the production company spawned by the break-up of the Pathé empire, is opening a new film studio on the rue du Cinématographe. One of the most arresting features of the studio is the artificial light provided by banks of extremely powerful lamps. To mark the opening, several scenes from *The Three Musketeers* were filmed i front of an audience of notables an members of the press. The versati producer-director of this expensi 12-part serial is Henri Diaman Berger. The new company has yet establish itself, and its manageme allege that the rival Pathé-Ciném has done all in its power to unde mine its launch.

Fairbanks plays the leading Musketeer

'Musketeer' Doug has found his new role made to measure.

Hollywood, 28 August
America's idol, Douglas Fairbanks, was born to play D'Artagnan, "the best swordsman in France", and does so in Fred Niblo's new film *The Three Musketeers* which is based on Alexandre Dumas' novel. This second historical legend, following *The Mark of Zorro*, is confirmation of the recent change that has come over the energetic actor. Turning his back on contemporary comedies, Fairbanks has decided to project his American dynamism into distant times and places. As a triumphant and optimistic D'Artagnan – in his plumed headgear, long curly wig and moustache – Fairbanks has given an American flavor to Richelieu's France. And as proof of how popular the actor has become in the U.S., a mountain peak in Yosemite National Park in the Sierra Nevada has been named after him. Now that's certainly what's known as reaching the heights!

Lovely Musidora is not just a pretty face!

Paris, 8 July
Thanks to *Judex* and Louis Feuillade, Musidora is now a big star. But she is not just another run-of-the-mill actress. She has the talent to both amuse and shock, as is demonstrated by this photograph that appeared in *Cinéma* magazine. She supplied a caption which is worthy of a long article: "It is vital to be photogenic from head to foot. After that you are allowed to display some measure of talent." Musidora has plenty of both qualities.

Musidora, the complete artist, believes in intelligence as well as beauty.

England welcomes back its prodigal son

An enthusiastic welcome for his first visit to the land of his birth since 1912.

London, 15 September
Charles Chaplin's visit to Britain has proved an even bigger event than the Armistice! He decided to go on a sudden impulse several weeks before the American release of *The Idle Class*. The return to his native land of this "prodigal son" has generated a huge wave of enthusiasm. From the moment of his arrival at Waterloo Station on 10 September, the King of Comedy was engulfed by wildly excited crowds surging through the police cordons which vainly tried to hold them back. It was little short of a miracle that no one was trampled in the ensuing crush. Accompanied by actor Donald Crisp, Chaplin made a sentimental pilgrimage to the scenes of his deprived childhood. He was followed everywhere, at a respectful distance, by curious crowds. Installed in the agreeable surroundings of the elegant Ritz Hotel, he has held court to a never-ending stream of journalists and personalities come to pay homage. The great and the good have extended their hospitality. At the invitation of E.V. Lucas, he dined at the Garrick Club where he sat next to Sir James Barrie, who told Chaplin that he would like him to play Peter Pan. His encounter with the writer H.G. Wells has also been widely reported. The two men watched a new film of Wells' novel *Kipps* and dined afterwards with Rebecca West. Chaplin is now an immortal among immortals.

Fatty indicted on culpable homicide charge

San Francisco, 10 September
Grave charges have been leveled against comedian Roscoe "Fatty" Arbuckle after the death under suspicious circumstances of a young actress, Virginia Rappe. She died yesterday in the hospital where she was admitted after becoming ill at a wild 48-hour party thrown by Arbuckle in three adjoining suites at the Saint Francis Hotel. The party was held to celebrate Arbuckle's three-million-dollar move to Paramount to make full-length features. Now the deal, and Fatty's future, are imperiled by Rappe's death. The doctors diagnosed acute peritonitis caused by a ruptured bladder, but one of Virginia's friends, Maude Delmont, who was also at the party, has told police that Arbuckle raped Miss Rappe, or at least attempted to do so. On the basis of these serious allegations, Arbuckle was arrested on a homicide charge. Throughout his interrogation by the police, the comedian has vigorously protested his innocence, but a large black cloud threatens the career of the film industry's favorite Fat Man. The press has not been supportive. A Hearst newspaper has already written that Rappe, once voted the Best-Dressed Girl in the Movies, "today wears the oldest garment in the world. It is a shroud."

Reid and Swanson shock with Schnitzler

New York, 18 September
The Austrian playwright Arthur Schnitzler's first play *Anatol*, performed in 1890, was pretty shocking at the time. This was not only because of its risqué subject matter – the amorous adventures of a young Viennese man-about-town – but also because of its impressionistic technique and psychological insights. Now Cecil B. DeMille has brought it to the screen under the title *The Affairs of Anatol*, with Wallace Reid as the irresponsible gallant. Though still able to send shock waves out to audiences, the director has tried to play down the risqué elements by giving the story a moral lift. DeMille has achieved this by devoting a great deal of the footage to Anatol's wife, played by Gloria Swanson, to whom the philanderer keeps returning. Who could complain! Gorgeously dressed, Miss Swanson is once again more sinned against than sinning. Particularly pleasing are the lavish sets that create the ambiance for the teasing boudoir tale to be told.

*Wallace Reid and Gloria Swanson in DeMille's **The Affairs of Anatol**.*

Feyder's risk with 'Atlantide' pays off

Jean Angelo, Stacia Napierkowska, and Manuel Orazi's striking decor.

Paris, 30 September
At the moment, *l'Atlantide*, directed by Jacques Feyder and based on Pierre Benoit's novel, is showing here in the large auditorium of the Gaumont Palace. "A Man Who Dared..." is how the advertisers are characterizing Feyder, who did not hesitate to shoot the film in the middle of the Sahara, against the advice of all and sundry, and under extremely difficult conditions. It was worth it, because the magnificently photographed Hoggar desert is the real star of the film, more so tha the mysterious Antinéa, played b Stacia Napierkowska. Screen acto Jean Angelo and Georges Melchio in the roles of Captain Morhang and Lieutenant Saint-Avit, hav been swift to capture female heart Jacques Feyder and Louis Auber who financed the picture on a bu get of 2 million francs – making the most expensive French film t date – have carried it off. The exoti *l'Atlantide* has already become great popular success.

Richard Barthelmess and Henry King find inspiration in the hills

Los Angeles, 21 September
Richard Barthelmess has formed his own film production company, Inspiration Pictures, in partnership with the director Henry King. D.W. Griffith had acquired the rights of Joseph Hergesheimer's novel of small-town life, *Tol'able David*, for Barthelmess but, on the advice of Lillian Gish, he abandoned it to make *Orphans of the Storm* instead. Because there was no role in the latter suitable for him, Barthelmess bought the rights from Griffith for $7,500 and produced it himself. With Henry King directing his first important film, from a scenario by Edmund Goulding, *Tol'able David* is extremely successful. Richard Barthelmess is perfectly cast in the title role of a plucky and good-natured mountain boy, suspected of cowardice, who triumphs over three bullying brothers, saves the U.S. mail and becomes a man of character and strength. The film delivers a splendid evocation of rural America, with a nostalgic love of the landscape. Before the premiere this week, this star of many Griffith films showed it to his former mentor. Griffith embraced and kissed Barthelmess at the end, such was his unbegrudging admiration for the film.

Barthelmess, already a star, formed Inspiration Pictures to make this film.

Critical triumph for Fritz Lang

Berlin, 7 October
After the success of *The Spiders* las year, the 30-year-old Viennese filn director Fritz Lang has triumphe once again with a dark and mystica three-episode allegory entitled *Destiny (Der Mude Tod)*. The story, cc written with Thea von Harbou, tel of a honeymoon destroyed when th husband disappears with a siniste stranger who turns out to be Death (The German title literally mean The Tired Death.) The wife plead with Death for her husband's life and he strikes a series of bargain with her, until love finally wins out The film is even more impressive fo its mastery of visual compositio than some of the director's previou work, and confirms Lang as one o the most exciting directors workin in Germany today.

America's fair sex seduced by Italy's Latin lover

s Angeles, 30 October
most the entire female population America has fallen in love with udolph Valentino, the dashingly mantic star of Metro's *The Four orsemen of the Apocalypse*. In Rex gram's adaptation of the novel by asco Ibañez, Valentino plays a astrel who becomes a war hero. hen he swoops across the screen a sensual tango, women in the dience are seen to faint dead away the aisles.

The object of all this adulation as born Rodolfo Guglielmi in Italy May 1895, the son of a veterinary rgeon. He arrrived in America, aveling steerage, in 1913. After a ell as a gardener in New York's entral Park, he became a nightclub ncer, briefly replacing Clifton 'ebb as the partner of exhibition ancer Bonnie Glass. At this time alentino was moving in fast comany, and New York became a little o hot for him when he found himlf involved in a scandalous society ivorce. He made his way west to an Francisco with a touring the-rical company and then finally on Los Angeles and the world of the ovies. Mae Murray, an old friend, found Valentino work in *Alimony* (1918), and he soon carved a niche for himself playing oily heavies. In *Eyes of Youth*, he was cast as a professional co-respondent hired to romance Clara Kimball Young. Then shortly afterwards, his marriage to actress Jean Acker collapsed on their wedding night. Valentino's big break came earlier this year when June Mathis, chief of Metro's script department and a powerful figure at the studio, suggested him for the second lead in Rex Ingram's *The Four Horsemen of the Apocalypse*. By the end of shooting, Valentino's part had been built up into the starring role. Success, however, has only soured relations between Metro and their new star. While playing Armand opposite Nazimova in the film *Camille* he was refused a salary increase from $350 to $450 a week. The studio's stinginess could cost it dear, as both Valentino and the valued June Mathis are now contemplating a move.

Valentino: a classic pose.

The dangerously mesmeric gaze of Rudolph Valentino's seductive sheik.

our Horsemen still galloping at box office

ew York, 21 November
ox-office tills are still ringing for Ietro's *The Four Horsemen of the pocalypse* months after its sensaonal premiere in New York. Origially Rudolph Valentino had only atured billing, but all prints were recalled after the hoopla that surrounding its opening, and the credits altered to make him the star. There is general agreement in the movie world that the huge audience the film has reached will help to make picture-going respectable.

ensationally dancing the tango with Alice Terry in ***Four Horsemen*****.**

Rudy takes talent to Paramount

Hollywood, 27 November
The love affair between Rudolph Valentino and Metro has ended. Disenchanted with the studio's reluctance to reward his huge drawing power at the box office with a commensurate salary, the biggest new star in Hollywood took himself to Paramount, who secured his services at the bargain price of $500 a week. They already had the perfect property for him, *The Sheik*, adapted from the lurid bestseller by E.M. Hull. Valentino plays the prince of the desert, Ahmed Ben Hassan, and Agnes Ayres is the object of his erotic emoting. The Latin's flashing eyes and magnificently flared nostrils are sending shock waves of "Sheik mania" racing across America. Paramount has rewarded him by more than doubling his salary to $1,250 a week. His next project is *Moran of the Lady Letty*, co-starring Dorothy Dalton.

Director Lubitsch crosses the Atlantic

New York, 24 December
Ernst Lubitsch, the brilliant German director of *Carmen*, *Madame Dubarry*, *Anna Boleyn* (known here as *Deception*) and many other notable films, has arrived on his first visit to the U.S. He has just completed his latest screen epic, *The Loves of Pharaoh*, and he hopes to be around long enough to help promote it. During the course of his visit, Lubitsch also plans to make important contacts within the film industry and to familiarize himself with the latest American production techniques. It appears that he has already received offers from a number of Hollywood producers, including Mary Pickford, but he has not yet committed himself. Clearly, this young man, who has not yet reached his thirtieth birthday, has a bright future ahead, while it is likely that his favorite star, Pola Negri, will also soon be lured here.

1922

Paris, 1 January
Henri Diamant-Berger's *The Three Musketeers* has proved to be a boon for the Pathé Cinéma Consortium, despite its enormous budget. A few weeks ago, the company showed its appreciation by throwing a banquet to celebrate reaching the grand total of 1,000 copies rented to exhibitors.

Paris, 10 January
Louis Delluc has written his final critique for *Paris-Midi*. He is going to devote himself to *Cinéa* and the filming of *la Femme de nulle part* (*The Woman From Nowhere*) in the Gaumont studios at la Villette.

Paris, 13 January
First release of *la Vie et l'œuvre de Molière* for the 300th anniversary of Molière's birth. The production was made by Jacques de Féraudy on the orders of the Minister for Public Education.

Los Angeles, 2 February
Inauguration of a new series of cartoons, "Laugh-O-Grams" by Walt Disney, with *Four Musicians of Bremen*, a parody of the fable.

Copenhagen, 7 February
World premier of *Die Gezeichneten* (*Love One Another*), filmed in Germany by Carl Theodor Dreyer and starring Polina Piekovska and Vladimir Gadjarov.

Paris, 28 February
The court case of André Legrand versus Marcel L'Herbier has drawn to a close in favor of L'Herbier. The jury decided that his film *Villa Destin* was not based on Oscar Wilde's work *The Crime Of Lord Arthur Saville*, to which Legrand has the exclusive rights.

Marseilles, 31 March
The Cabinet of Dr. Caligari, the Expressionist film directed by Robert Wiene which was banned by the prefecture only three days after its release due to complaints from exhibitors, can once more be shown provided that certain scenes are cut.

Shanghai, 31 March
The filmmaker Zhang Shichuan has recently created the Mingxing Company. Production has already started on three comic films, two of them inspired by Charlie Chaplin and Harold Lloyd.

Hollywood, 1 April
Douglas Fairbanks has started work on *Robin Hood* under the direction of Allan Dwan.

Prague, 7 April
Release of Karl Anton's first film *Cikani* (*The Bohemians*), inspired by the romantic poet Karel H. Macha.

Paris, 4 May
The Cocorico Cinéma has opened in the Bellville district. The artistic director is actor René Cresté, who is best known for his roles in films by Léonce Perret and as Louis Feuillade's *Judex*.

Paris, 16 May
The news that Berthe Dagmar was seriously wounded by a panther during filming of *Marie chez les fauves*, was only made public today, when the director Jean Durand presented the film to the public.

Paris, 17 May
Baron Gabet, who chaired Pathé Cinéma's annual board meeting, has announced that the profits for the year 1921–1922 amounted to a net profit of 16,153,203 francs.

Moscow, 21 May
Kino-Pravda, still edited by Dziga Vertov has replaced *Kino-Nedelia*.

Marseilles, 31 May
Inhabitants watched in astonishment as a naval battle between 18th-century ships took place just off the coast. It had been organized by Louis Feuillade for a scene in *Fils de flibustier* (*The Buccaneer's Son*).

Paris, 6 June
It was decided at the French Entertainment Industry's annual meeting that all cinemas in France will shut on 15 February 1923 if nothing is done to reduce the crippling charges imposed on the profession.

Rome, 1 September
Release of *A noi* (*Ours*), a fascist propaganda film from the director Umberto Paradisi.

Paris, 5 September
Presentation of *l'Ouragan sur la montagne* (*Storm on the Mountain*), by Julien Duvivier, with Gaston Jacquet and Lotte Loring. This film marks the first Franco-German co-production since the Great War.

Berlin, 7 September
Marlene Dietrich is playing the lead in the revival of the play *Pandora's Box*, by Franz Wedekind, a major exponent of expressionism.

Stockholm, 18 September
Häxan (*Witchcraft Through the Ages*), directed by Benjamin Christensen with himself and Elisabeth Christensen, is now screening in the Swedish capital.

Germany, 22 September
The government is suffering a loss of 2 million marks a day because of the cinema industry's general strike against taxes.

Hollywood, 5 November
The Headless Horseman, by Edward Venturini, is the first film in the U.S. that has been shot entirely on panchromatic film.

Paris, 15 November
At the annual Cinema Festival that is organized by the Cinema Lovers' Club, Léon Moussinac gave a warmly applauded speech followed by excerpts from the most outstanding films of the year.

Paris, 2 December
In an editorial entitled "Theatre and Truth" for *Ciné-Journal*, written following the immense success of the film *Nanook of the North*, Georges Dureau remarked on "the over-all weakness of theatrical style films, and the obvious need felt by the public to see real life on the screen."

Paris, 11 December
The Chamber of Deputies is the scene of heated debates after the decision made by the president of the Censorship Board to ban Ernst Lubitsch's *Madame Dubarry*.

New York, 22 December
According to the editorial in today's *New York Times*, "Arbuckle has become a symbol of the vices indulged in by the world of cinema."

Sofia, 22 December
The first full-length Bulgarian film *Pod staroto nebe*, by Nikolai Larine, was shown at the Theatre Moderne.

Paris, 27 December
Jean Epstein's film *Pasteur*, was shown at the Sorbonne to commemorate the scientist's 100th birthday.

Germany, 31 December
Sixty-four percent of films show during the past year were hom grown productions.

Germany, 31 December
The number of production comp nies has now reached the 300 mar

Paris, 31 December
There are now 207 cinemas in t French capital and 2,959 in the e tire country, including Morocco a Algeria.

BIRTHS

England, 21 January
Paul Scofield

Italy, 22 February
Giulietta Masina

Italy, 5 March
Pier Paolo Pasolini

Italy, 5 March
Serge Reggiani

Italy, 22 March
Ugo Tognazzi

France, 16 May
Martine Carol
(Marie-Louise Mourer)

France, 3 June
Alain Resnais

Minnesota, 10 June
Judy Garland
(Frances Gumm)

Paris, 22 August
Micheline Presle
(Micheline Chassagne)

Italy, 1 September
Vittorio Gassman

Italy, 15 November
Francesco Rosi

Cannes, 4 December
Gérard Philipe

North Carolina, 24 December
Ava Gardner

Valentino went largely unnoticed i several films before reaching sta dom. This year sees him in four film of which ***Blood and Sand*** *is the mo successful.*

455-175

Stroheim's new film disturbs and seduces

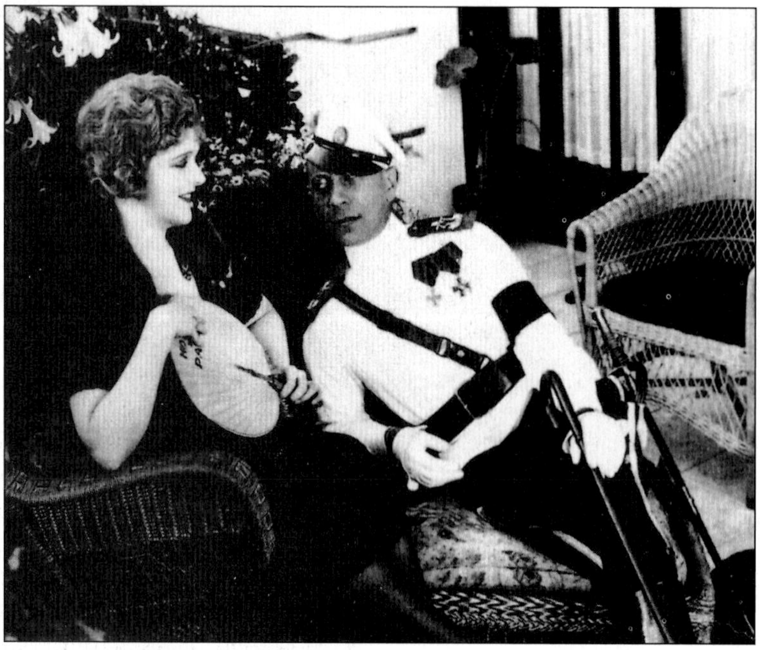

Patsy Hannen is the actress co-starred with Stroheim in ***Foolish Wives.***

New York, 11 January
The latest film written and directed by Erich von Stroheim, who also plays the lead, is *Foolish Wives*. It has just opened here at the Central Theater and is his most ambitious production by far. The film looks great with its convincing re-creation of the Monte Carlo setting and use of atmospheric photography, while the plot represents a natural culmination of the theme of the naive American wife deceived by an unscrupulous adventurer, as explored in Stroheim's previous film projects. Here, he gives his most sustained performance as the leading character, a bogus count, a seducer and a swindler, who is aided in his nefarious schemes by two cynical young ladies who pose as his cousins. Unfortunately, the film was beset by problems from the beginning and went far over budget. Worst of all, Stroheim's completed version, running 18 reels or more, was considered too long and was severely cut by the studio to its present length of 14 reels. Nonetheless, Universal's publicists have been working overtime, erecting giant billboards in New York with such advertising slogans as "He's going to make you *hate him* even if it takes a *million dollars* of our money to do it!" Undoubtedly, this is by far the most expensive film that Laemmle's Universal studio has yet made.

America gets first look at Lubitsch's Egypt

New York, 22 February
Americans have been fortunate to see the German film *The Loves of Pharaoh*, by the director Ernst Lubitsch, before it has been released in Germany. It is true, however, that the film was partly financed by an American company, the Famous Players-Lasky Corporation and that Lubitsch's previous films have all been great successes in the U.S. A grandiose epic, with vast decors and impressive crowd scenes – it used 126,000 extras and took 10 months to shoot – *The Loves of Pharaoh* is also a personal work of immense charm and sensitivity. Actor Emil Jannings, the larger-than-life Titan of the German cinema, has created a tyrannical yet pathetic Pharaoh Amenes, unhappy in love. By not neglecting any detail of the luxury and debauchery of the period, Lubitsch has succeeded in reaching the apotheosis of the historical film. I refining his style, the director *Anna Boleyn* and *Madame Dubarr* has managed to circumvent, in virtuoso manner, the traps inhere in this type of production. Here, h has confirmed his reputation fc being able to bring a human dime sion into a historical tale, sustainin the atmosphere throughout. And t lighten a rather somber story, Lu bitsch has treated certain scenes a comedy, a genre in which he is master. Participating in the achieve ment of the film were the camera men, Theodor Sparkuhl and Alfre Hansen, and the decorators, Erns Stern and Kurt Richter. Apart fro Jannings, there are also good pe formances by Dagny Servaes (wh replaced Pola Negri) as a slave wit whom the Pharaoh falls in love, an Harry Liedtke as the young ma whom the slave prefers.

The Loves of Pharaoh*, a German film made in the grand American style.*

Art the most important weapon for Lenin

Moscow, 1 February
In order to emerge from the chaos of a Russia hungry and in ruins, newspapers and novels are seeking to mobilize the population, but the vast country is 80 percent illiterate. How then can one explain, convince and educate them? How does one forge men and women anew, to create a new society? Thankfully, the cinema is accessible to all. Lenin told Lunatcharski, the people's commissar of education, an intellectual and highly-considered screen writer, "Of all the arts, the cinema is for us the most important." Indeed, he can and must relay the propaganda as widely as possible. Now that the creators of bourgeois melodramas and their clientele have left for Europe, the cinema has ceased to be a way of passing the time, and has become more a tool of social and moral progress – an art to be put to use for the benefit of the masses. The dilapidated state of the studios is an obstacle, but this ambitious task will be tackled.

Hollywood is embroiled in another scanda

Hollywood, 2 February
With the last rites being read over Fatty Arbuckle's career, another scandal has erupted at the accident-prone Paramount studio. This time it looks like murder. The victim is top Paramount director William Desmond Taylor, whose lifeless body police have discovered at his luxurious Westlake bungalow. They arrived to find the place a hive of activity. Two Paramount executives were burning papers in the fireplace while the instantly recognizable figure of lovely comedienne Mabel Normand, a close friend of Taylor, was feverishly ransacking the dea man's bureau for compromisin documents. The circumstances o Taylor's life and death are bizarre Taylor had claimed to be an Englisl gentleman, but he was in fact o Irish descent, born William Deane Tanner in 1877, who abandoned hi family in New York in 1908 an resurfaced in Hollywood. The polic have found his closets cramme with pornographic material and als lingerie that bears the monogran "M.M.M.", the initials of actres Mary Miles Minter. There are mor questions than answers to the affair

Vampire Dracula reinvented as Nosferatu

*Max Schreck (left) and Max Nemetz in Murnau's **Nosferatu, the Vampire**.*

Berlin, 5 March
Having left his sinister castle in the Carpathian mountains, in a coffin filled with earth, the vampire Nosferatu is now throwing his menacing shadow across the cinema screens of the world, and frightening audiences. Freely adapted from Bram Stoker's 1897 novel *Dracula*, the film entitled *Nosferatu, the Vampire*, was made by the great German director, Friedrich Wilhelm Murnau. Although it was shot for the most part in actual locations instead of in the usual stylized studio sets, and has used realistic interiors, the film is marked by the influence of German Expressionism. This is notable in the choice of the strange camera angles and eerie images in the photography of Fritz Arno Wagner and Gunther Krampf, as well as in the expressive decor of Albin Grau. All this makes *Nosferatu*, a "strange symphony of terror", which is the German subtitle of the work. It also uses the special effects of negative film and speeded-up motion to suggest a ghostly ride. The disturbing and fascinating vampire is brilliantly interpreted by Max Schreck. His spectral gaunt figure – shaven head, pointed ears sticking out, cavernous eyes and sharply-pointed finger nails – is unforgettable. Besides its capacity to shock, the supernatural tale is a work of poetry and immense plastic beauty.

American film industry under surveillance

Hollywood, 10 March
For some time, various voices raised against the film industry have called for some form of film censorship and industry regulation. This has escalated since the recent scandals concerning comedian Fatty Arbuckle and director William Desmond Taylor. In order to forestall such pressures, the leading studios have decided to institute a system of self-regulation, to be administered by a new organization, the Motion Picture Producers and Distributors of America (MPPDA), which will also serve as a liaison between the industry and the public. Will H. Hays, the former postmaster general, will head the organization, and has stated its aims as follows: "To foster the common interest of those engaged in the industry by establishing and maintaining the highest possible moral and artistic standards in motion picture production, by developing the education as well as the entertainment value and general usefulness of the motion picture... and by reforming abuses relative to the industry..." It seems that from now on, the industry's morals will be under close scrutiny.

Dwan and Doug dazzle in Sherwood Forest

Hollywood, 1 April
Douglas Fairbanks' new film, *Robin Hood*, has turned out to be as exciting as United Artists promised it would be... and more. The movie bowls one over with its sheer exuberance and technical wizardry. Almost entirely financed by Fairbanks himself, it cost over $1.5 million to make. Inside a new studio located on Santa Monica Boulevard, art director William Buckland built the biggest sets ever conceived for a motion picture, including a gigantic castle with 90-foot-high walls, which needed 500 workmen to construct. It seems even more immense on the screen because the top of the castle was painted onto glass before being photographed by Art Edison. Many of the action scenes surpass any Fairbanks has done before, with hidden trampolines being used to give more lift to his leaps, particularly one across a 15-foot moat. There is plenty of bounce in Alan Dwan's direction as well. Dwan agreed to work for 5 percent of the profits, which was a shrewd move when one considers the public acclaim the film has already received. Ironically, Fairbanks first refused to play the hero of Sherwood Forest, who robs the rich to give to the poor. "I don't want to play a flat-footed Englishman," he said when the project was first brought to him. Fortunately, his entourage were not afraid to argue, and they pointed out the romantic ingredients: the Merrie Men, the wicked sheriff, the evil prince and, of course, Maid Marian (Enid Bennett). Doug, at 39, seems stronger and more agile than ever, his heels hardly ever touching the ground. Fairbanks couldn't be flat-footed if he tried. *Robin Hood* is the best Fairbanks picture yet, and one wonders what further heights he will be able to scale.

Fairbanks, the perfect folk-hero.

Fatty is cleared but remains blacklisted

Hollywood, 18 April
It has taken three trials, stretching over four months, to clear Roscoe Arbuckle of the charges brought against him after the death of Virginia Rappe last September. At the first trial in December, the judge reduced the main charge to that of involuntary homicide, but the jury was unable to reach a unanimous decision. A new jury remained hung at the retrial in February. Third time around, on 12 April, it took the jury only five minutes to clear the Fat Man of all blame. They put it on record that, "We feel that a great injustice has been done to him... Roscoe Arbuckle is entirely innocent..." However, Arbuckle's acquittal has not rescued his career. He has sold his house and cars to pay his lawyers' fees. Paramount has withdrawn his movies from circulation and consigned two others recently completed to the vaults. It has reportedly cost them $1 million. Reviled by both press and public, Fatty can no longer find work in the world where he briefly reigned as one of the Kings of Comedy. ▷

Fatty Arbuckle, now disgraced.

One marriage too many for Valentino

With Nita Naldi, a classic vamp, in the torrid ***Blood and Sand****.*

Los Angeles, 21 April
Rudolph Valentino's colorful private life is once more in the news. He has been arrested and imprisoned on a bigamy charge. Last May he married for the second time, tying the knot in Mexico with the exotic costume designer Natasha Rambova (born Winifred Shaunessy in Salt Lake City). Valentino had been divorced from his first wife, actress Jean Acker, since January. That marriage was not consummated and did not last beyond their wedding night in November 1919. Nevertheless, they perforce had to stay married for the three months necessary for their divorce to go through. Unfortunately, Californian law requires a year to elapse before a new marriage can be entered into. Valentino has spent several uncomfortable hours with the police, but has convinced them of his good faith and is once more a free man. He is now reunited with Rambova, an intimate friend of the actress Alla Nazimova, Valentino's co-star in *Camille*. After the emotional turmoil he has undergone in recent years, Valentino is confident that he will find true happiness with his new wife, who will in future be designing the star's costumes.

Snowy wastes bring a breath of fresh air

Something completely different.

New York, 11 June
Nanook of the North, the extraordinary documentary by the director and explorer Robert Flaherty, has been a triumph at the Capitol, the largest movie theater in the city. With the perception of a poet, the humility of a great humanist, and the passion of an ethnologist, Flaherty shows the daily life of an Eskimo family with whom he formed a friendship during a sojourn of 15 months in the north of Canada. Benefiting from the financial support of the Revillon brothers, wholesalers and retailers of fur, Flaherty has directed a film in which the Eskimos are shown from their own point of view, and not from the perceptions of an outsider. This rapport between the people and the man behind the camera gives this document a universal quality.

Actor René Clair wants to change his role

Paris, 8 July
The 24-year-old actor and journalist René Clair, whose given name is René Chomette, made his film debut last year in *le Lys de la vie*. The talented young man has made several subsequent appearances, notably in two Feuillade serials, *L'Orphelin* and *Parisette*, but he would like t exchange acting for directing. I Brussels he has been offered a pos as assistant director to the prolifi French filmmaker Jacques de Baron celli. René Clair is on his way.

The new filmmaker, seen above in ***Parisette****, for director Louis Feuillade.*

Max Linder prefers Nice to California

Paris, 31 July
Disappointed by his three years in California, Max Linder has now returned to France and made public his wish to live in Nice, as well as to work there. Thus ends the second American phase in the career of "the man in the silk top hat". Linder's first sojourn in America, between 1916 and 1917, turned out to be disastrous because his employers at Essanay made the absurd mistake of trying to thrust him upon the American public as a "cleaner" rival of Charlie Chaplin, whom they dubbed a "dirty and sordid" comedian. Continuous ill-health had also hampered his work there. Having learned a lesson from this unhappy experience, Linder then returned to America in 1919, this time as actor, director and independent producer. But the films he directed and appeared in over there were considered by the American administration as foreign productions and, as a result, their distribution was seriously limited. However, this did not prevent him from shooting three motion pictures in California, which have been recognized as considerable successes: *Seven Years' Ba Luck*, *Be My Wife* and, above all *The Three Must-Get-Theres* (a parody of Douglas Fairbanks' recent *Th Three Musketeers*). Despite the triumphant premiere of the latter a Ocean Park, the dapper Frenc comic was not dissuaded from re turning to Europe several days later

Seven Years' Bad Luck *has brough glorious good fortune.*

Dark satanic deeds from Denmark

enjamin Christensen's startling film parades a powerful succession of images to create audacious visual effects.

openhagen, 18 September
Danish director Benjamin Christensen spent a considerable amount of time in Sweden making his latest film *Witchcraft Through The Ages* (*Häxan*), and it is his most impressive to date. Christensen conducts a documentary-style investigation into the practice of witchcraft, from medieval times to the present day, using etchings, carefully reconstructed tableaux reminiscent of paintings by Brueghel and Bosch, old manuscripts, and re-enacted episodes in which the director himself plays the Devil. The film, which was three years in the making, regards the witch as a victim of a repressive and superstitious Church – nothing more, in fact, than a harmless hysteric. An array of cinematic devices has created a film that is at once illuminating, frightening and amusing. It also presents cruelty and nudity, which are part of the diabolic and satanic practices depicted. These might find disfavor in more puritanical places outside Scandinavia. Benjamin Christensen, a former opera singer, writer and actor, made his debut as a director in 1913 with *The Mysterious X*, immediately revealing his preoccupation with the macabre. This was then followed by *Night of Vengeance*, essentially another melodrama of escape, revenge and retribution, but which was invested by Christensen with great plastic beauty. Both of those films were greatly admired by Christensen's compatriot Carl Dreyer, another master of the horror genre, whose film *Leaves from Satan's Book* appeared here to acclaim a few years ago. Because of the extraordinary length of time it took Christensen to research the subject and shoot it, *Witchcraft Through The Ages* is only the Danish director's third picture. Although made in Sweden, this remarkable film is a product of someone from Denmark, probably one of the most advanced cinematic milieus in Europe.

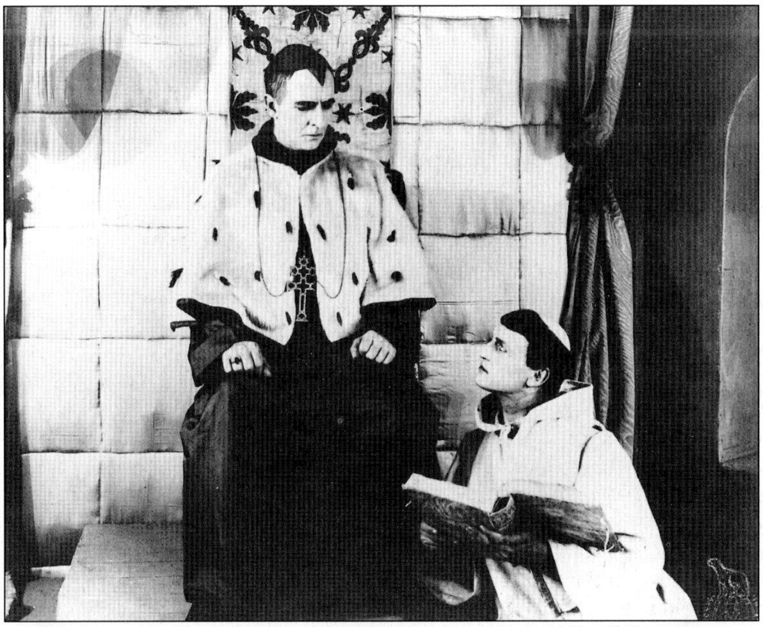

Helge Nissen (left) in Carl Dreyer's ***Leaves from Satan's Book*** (1919).

Lubitsch and Griffith anger the French

Paris, 23 December
The police have had to intervene at the Artistic Cinema in order to separate spectators when a fight broke out during the screening of *Madame Dubarry*, a German film directed by Ernst Lubitsch. For several months, a campaign has been orchestrated by an extreme right-wing newspaper, which has been denouncing, with violence and hatred, "foreign films" whose scenarios treat the history of France. A royalist group and members of *Action Française* have not hesitated to stop the projection of Lubitsch's film, as well as *Orphans of the Storm*, by D.W. Griffith, whose action takes place in Paris during the Revolution. (Griffith has "defamed the history of France in an odious manner.") The great American director has responded to these pathetic accusations with explicit historical references from the works of Guizot and Taine: "It is a very sad thing to see a group of French people condemn my little story." The followers of Léon Daudet have reproached Lubitsch and Griffith for having dared to represent the aristocrats as depraved, Louis XVI as fat and sleepy, etc. These xenophobes have invaded theaters and attacked members of the audience, thereby placing liberty of expression in jeopardy. It must be said that these films have been very successful in America.

Pola Negri as Madame Dubarry.

1923

Paris, 3 January
The chemist Berthon has demonstrated a new color film process. The negative is covered with thousands of microscopic flecks and is made sensitive by panchromatization: a screening process which filters the three primary colors.

Paris, 20 January
The Chamber of Deputies has voted to adopt an amendment, reducing taxes on those cinemas which devote at least 25 percent (in footage) of their total program to French films.

Paris, 26 January
Max Linder is presenting the first release of his latest American-made film at the cinema named after him. The film is titled *The Three Must-Get-Theres* and is a parody of *The Three Musketeers*.

Brussels, 31 January
Belgian authorities have banned Jacques Feyder's latest screen project *Crainquebille*, on the grounds that it demonstrates a lack of respect for the country's laws.

New York, 3 February
The production of *Salome* with Alla Nazimova has just been released. The costumes by Natasha Rambova were inspired by the drawings of English artist, Aubrey Beardsley.

Paris, 14 February
The Railway Union has demanded that certain scenes be cut from Abel Gance's *la Roue* (*The Wheel*) as they paint an unfavorable picture of railway workers. However, Gance has vigorously refused to comply.

Tokyo, 20 February
Kenji Mizoguchi's directorial debut *Furutaso* (*Homeland*) is now showing. The film deals with the differences between rural and urban life.

Paris, 20 February
Paramount President Adolph Zukor has told the press that his company will no longer be making films with Fatty Arbuckle.

Paris, 27 February
The committee against the danger of venereal disease has released a film *Syphilis, A Social Disease: How To Make It Disappear*, made by Gaumont, Pathé-Consortium and Dr. Comandon.

San Francisco, 13 March
Erich von Stroheim has started filming *Greed* on location.

Paris, 26 March
The great actress Sarah Bernhardt has died. She made a total of eight films including *The Clairvoyant*, which remains unfinished.

Switzerland, 30 March
Premiere of *The Call of the Mountain*, directed by the pioneer Arthur Porchet and starring Emile Crettex and Ernette Tamm.

Moscow, 25 April
In the middle of his adaptation of Ostrovsky's play *The Wise Man*, Eisenstein has inserted a film sequence of the *Journal du Gloumov*, a parody of detective films.

Nice, 30 April
Max Linder lost control of his car at high speed on a bend of the prommenade des Anglais and overturned. He was thrown clear of the vehicle and only suffered minor bruising.

Paris, 30 April
Robert Florey's book *Filmland* has now been published in France.

Paris, 1 June
The young writer Louis Aragon has written in the magazine *Théâtre et Comœdia illustré* that he would like to see the creation of "real films without hypocrisy. The perfecting of techniques are of no interest to me." The ironic reply from filmmakers: "Let's get together to offer the youngster a magic lantern."

Berlin, 12 June
The actress Marlene Dietrich has made her screen debut in *Der Mensche am Wege* (*A Man on the Path*), written and directed by Wilhelm Dieterle, who also acts in it.

Paris, 30 June
The Committee for the Protection of Entertainment is worried about the growing success of a new device, the wireless telegraph. The question they are asking their members to consider is this: does the arrival of radiotelephony pose a threat to the entertainment industry?

Cairo, 12 June
Authorities have promulgated the first law on film censorship.

Paris, 1 August
In the latest issue of *Crapouillot*, M. Lebedinsky has let his irritation show. Here he writes that "there are moments when one wishes one were deaf, so as to avoid hearing the orchestra relentlessly playing *Do You Know the Country Where Orange Trees Blossom?* while the dogs in *Nanook* are freezing to death in a snow storm!"

Paris, 2 August
Forty-year old Max Linder has wed for the first time. His young bride, the 20-year-old Hélène Peters, has known Linder since her childhood.

France, 11 August
Gaumont has obtained the exclusive rights for the distribution of Buster Keaton's film projects throughout the French Territories.

Japan, 1 September
All film studios, including that of Shochiku, have been destroyed in the earthquake which has ravaged the Tokyo and Yokohama regions. Film companies have grouped together to make use of Nikkatsu's old studios in Kyoto.

Berlin, 11 September
The last film Ernst Lubitsch directed in Germany called *Die Flamme* (*The Flame*) with Pola Negri, has been released here. Lubitsch is at present pursuing his career in Hollywood.

Paris, 20 October
The Birth of a Nation, which has been showing at the Marivaux since 17 August, has been banned by the prefect of police due to its racist scenes. Police fear they might result in disturbances of the peace.

Rome, 24 October
A new statutory order increases the Fascist Government's powers of censorship. From now on they have the right to intervene both before filming and once the film is finished.

Soviet Union, 25 October
The cinema section of the Georgian Education Board screened a film by Ivan Perestiani, *Citeli Esmakudeni* (*The Little Red Devils*).

New York, 21 December
The grand opening of Cecil B. DeMille's epic spectacular, *The Ten Commandments*.

Paris, 27 December
Alexandre Volkoff has released h latest film *Kean, désordre et gén* (*Kean, Dissoluteness and Genius*), a adaptation of Alexander Dumas' book produced by the compan Albatros Films,–which stars Iva Mosjoukine, Nathalie Lissenko an Nicolas Koline.

Paris, 28 December
Release of *Légende de sœur Béatri* (*The Legend of Sister Beatrix*), wit Sandra Milowanoff and Suzann Bianchetti, directed by Jacques d Baroncelli with the assistance c René Clair, who joined him afte giving up his project for *Genevièv de Brabant*.

La Paz, 31 December
The first Bolivian fiction film to b made here was banned by the cer sors the day after its release due t the scandal caused by the plot. Th scenario, which centers on a lov affair between an important lanc owner and an Indian servant, wa based on real events.

BIRTHS

Senegal, 1 January
Ousmane Sembene

Italy, 23 February
Franco Zeffirelli

Texas, 8 March
Cyd Charisse
(Tula Ellice Finklea)

India, 4 May
Mrinal Sen

England, 29 August
Richard Attenborough

Italy, 29 September
Marcello Mastroianni

New York, 1 October
Walter Matthau
(Matuschanskavasky)

Illinois, 4 October
Charlton Heston
(Charles Carter)

***The Ten Commandments**, a monu mental achievement, confirms tha Cecil B. DeMille is a master of spec tacle, inspired variously by religion history and legend.*

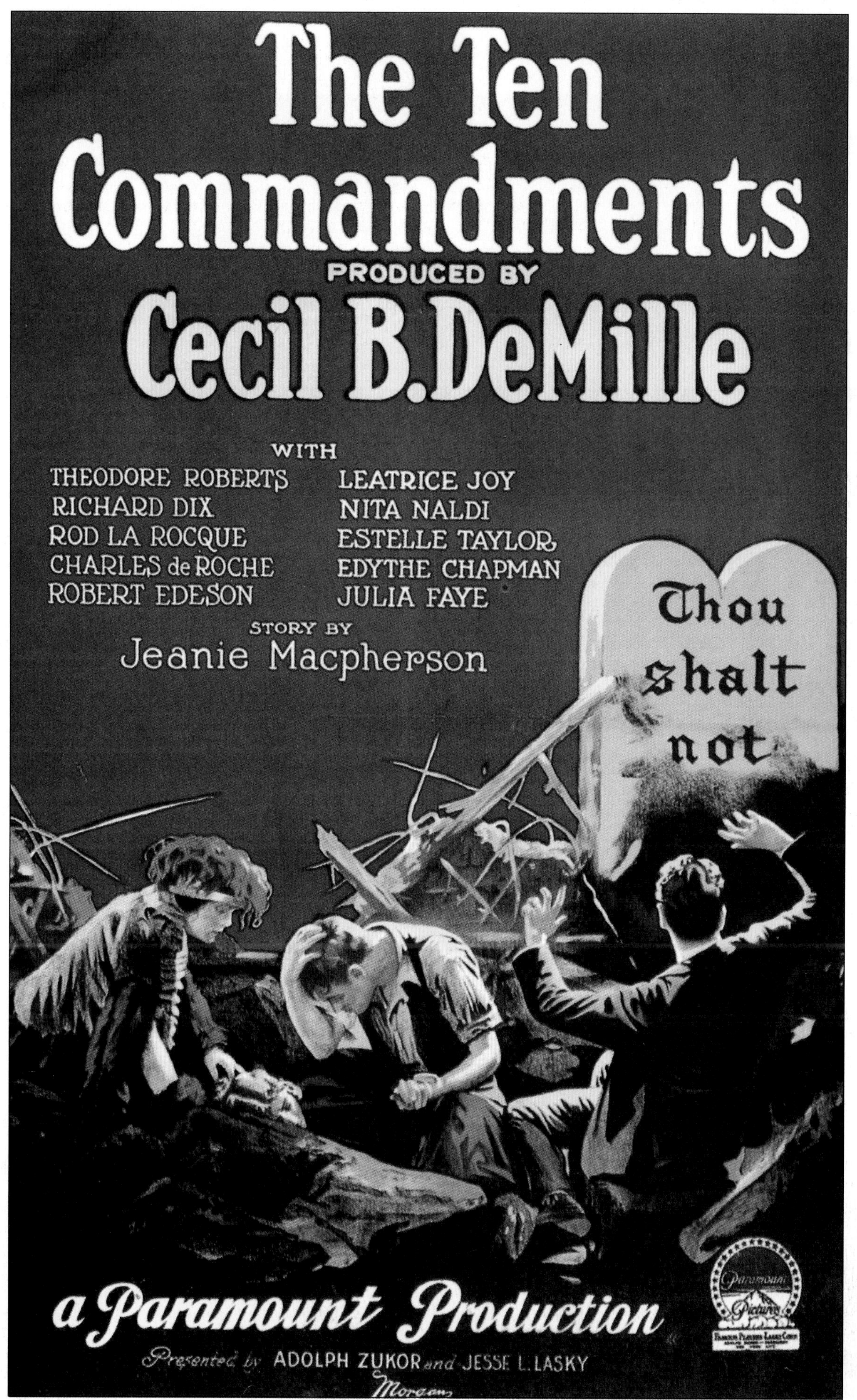
The Ten Commandments
PRODUCED BY
Cecil B. DeMille
WITH
THEODORE ROBERTS
RICHARD DIX
ROD LA ROCQUE
CHARLES de ROCHE
ROBERT EDESON
LEATRICE JOY
NITA NALDI
ESTELLE TAYLOR
EDYTHE CHAPMAN
JULIA FAYE
STORY BY
Jeanie Macpherson
Thou shalt not
a Paramount Production
Presented by ADOLPH ZUKOR and JESSE L. LASKY
Morgan

Drugs kill gorgeous Wallace Reid

Hollywood, 19 January
Wallace Reid, the handsome and popular Paramount star who specialized in breezy all-American types, has died of drug addiction at the age of 32. No one typified the clean-cut collar-ad go-getter better than Wally, which makes the circumstances of his death all the more tragic. The genial Reid began his film career as a stuntman with the Selig company. Bit parts and directing assignments followed, and in 1912 he secured his first big role in *His Only Son*. In 1913 he married Dorothy Davenport, his co-star in many films. After playing the small but memorable part of a fighting blacksmith in D.W. Griffith's *The Birth of a Nation*, he was signed by Lasky and starred in a string of action-packed comedy thrillers. The hectic pace of his working life helped to kill Reid. In 1919, while filming *The Valley of the Giants* in the High Sierra, he was given morphine to relieve the pain of a back injury sustained in a train crash. The treatment continued and Reid became an addict, a condition exacerbated by heavy drinking. For a while Wally was able to keep up appearances, but by the time he made *Thirty Days* he was wasting away and could hardly stand. He spent his last days in a sanitarium and died in agony in his wife's arms. Coming so soon after both the Arbuckle and Desmond Taylor scandals, Reid's death has given the press another field day.

A tragic waste of looks and talent.

Gance's tragedy of modern times

Gabriel de Gavrone, Ivy Close and Séverin-Mars in ***The Wheel (La Roue)****.*

Paris, 17 February
The release of *la Roue* (*The Wheel*), directed by Abel Gance, is being given a warm reception by the public at the Gaumont Palace. This modern tragedy in a prologue and six episodes, originally called *The Rose of the Railway*, runs for two-and-a-half hours, the preparation and shooting having taken nearly five years. Produced by Abel Gance Films and financed by Pathé, the film cost the colossal sum of 3 million franc However, if *la Roue* has attracte attention, it is because of its nume ous artistic qualities rather than i cost. While evoking Aeschylus an Sophocles, among others, the fil recounts the drama of a railway en ployee called Sisif, in love with h adopted daughter, and a rival to h own son. Like Oedipus, he ends u blind and crushed by Destiny. Th first part was shot in Nice, on th railway lines near Saint-Roch st tion. Filming was continued at Ch monix in order to use the scenic rai way at Mont Blanc. Gance, a pe fectionist, shot some scenes mor than 20 times. The actor Séverin Mars, remarkable in the role of Sisi was already ill during the shootin and died in 1921, shortly thereafte There is another excellent performe in *la Roue*: the locomotive. Ganc filmed this as a real character and i presence serves as a leitmotif of th film. Gance uses a rapid cuttin technique when Sisif drives the loco motive at full speed.

The Western moves forward in Cruze's 'The Covered Wagon'

Hollywood, 25 March
Up to now the Western has been regarded as one of the cheaper "bread-and-butter" genres of the American cinema, the films generally being shot quickly and on low budgets, and with an emphasis on rip-roaring action. This attitude is likely to change now that Paramount has released *The Covered Wagon*, a truly epic Western, produced and directed by James Cruze. Apparently, considerable historic research was undertaken to make this film look as authentic as possible, with Colonel Tim McCoy serving as technical advisor. Most of the footage was filmed under difficult and hazardous conditions at locations which included Milford, Utah, Snake Valley, Nevada, and Antelope Island in the Great Salt Lake for the spectacular buffalo hunt. In fact, the photography is especially impressive, particularly the wagon encampment at night, the staging of the Indian attack, the fording of the river, and the vast, panoramic vistas of the wagons winding across the barren plains. Telling the story of the perilous, 200-mile journey of the early wagon trains around 1849 from Kansas City to Oregon, the film, unfortunately, is let down by a weak and unoriginal script, adapted from the novel by Emerson Hough. The stereotyped hero, played by J. Warren Kerrigan, is an ex-army office with a troubled past, now leader c the wagon train. Lois Wilson is th girl who loves him and Alan Ha portrays the scheming villain. Bu best of all are a pair of tough India scouts, authentic and off-beat.

Young John Fox is Ted Wingate, traveling in ***The Covered Wagon****.*

Great comic Harold Lloyd has no reason to worry

BRAUN BLDG.
CLOTHES ON CREDIT
DESIGNERS & MFRS. OF SMART HATS FOR SMART LADIES

Harold in **Safety Last** *finds himself in a different kind of trouble from that courted by his rival, Charlie Chaplin.*

New York, 2 September
Harold Lloyd's second feature film of the year, *Why Worry?*, has been released. Directed by Fred Newmeyer and Sam Taylor, it throws the bespectacled comedian and his leading lady, Jobyna Ralston, into the middle of a South American revolution. This follows hard on the heels of *Safety Last*, in which Lloyd's brand of "thrill comedy" reached new heights, quite literally, as he dangled 12 stories up from the sagging hand of a clock. These films have confirmed the success of the actor's move from two-reelers to feature-length films, the first of which was the four-reel *Sailor-Made Man* (1921). The 184 short films he made between 1915 and 1919 enabled him to hone his comic technique, which has made a smooth transition to the different pace of the feature film. Lloyd also has effective collaborators in Taylor and Newmeyer. Taylor directs the comedy scenes and Newmeyer handles the hair-raising action sequences.

A heartrending hunchback from Chaney

New York, 2 September
That remarkable movie actor, Lon Chaney, has finally achieved the acclaim he deserves. It has come to him for his most recent performance as Quasimodo in *The Hunchback of Notre Dame*. Universal's most lavish production since *Foolish Wives* almost two years ago, the movie recreates medieval Paris, especially the central square dominated by the giant cathedral, in convincing sets accomplished by the studio's art department headed by Charles D. ("Danny") Hall. The cast includes Norman Kerry and Patsy Ruth Miller, but the film is totally dominated by Chaney, with his grotesque make-up and a remarkable use of his body with extraordinary, ape-like agility as the horribly ugly, but heartbreaking bell-ringer.

Bebe Daniels

Beautiful and talented, Bebe Daniels was signed to a long-term contract at Paramount in 1919 and now rivals Swanson and Negri for popularity. One of Hollywood's most versatile stars, equally effective as a charming light comedienne or a purveyor of dramatic roles, Bebe has been acting since the age of four, making her screen debut when she was seven. In her teens, she made some 200 episodes of the *Lonesome Luke* series with Harold Lloyd.

'A Woman of Paris' reveals sober side of Chaplin

Newcomer Carl Miller (center) co-stars with lovely Edna Purviance and Adolphe Menjou in Chaplin's unusual film.

Chaplin with his regular leading lady Edna Purviance in ***Police*** *(1916).*

New York, 1 October
Having discharged his contractual obligations to First National, Charlie Chaplin at last has directed his first film for United Artists. His new independence has given him the opportunity to make a serious dramatic film, *A Woman of Paris*, first conceived during his visit to the French capital in 1921. Premiered today in New York, the picture stars Edna Purviance as a country girl caught between love and money who becomes the mistress of sophisticated man-about-town, Adolphe Menjou. Chaplin does not appear on the cast list, but keen-eyed filmgoers might catch a glimpse of him as a clumsy porter in a scene at a railway station. This movie took seven months to make, with Chaplin taking infinite pains over the smallest details. Ninety takes, spread over two days, were needed to capture exactly the effect Chaplin required in a small scene in which a bored Purviance throws away a cigarette and refuses to go out. *A Woman of Paris* eventually ran to 3,862 takes amounting to 130,115 feet of film. Chaplin has reduced this to 7,557 feet in the final version. In a special program note for the premiere, the director declares: "In my first serious drama... I've striven for realism true to life. What you will see is life as I personally see it – the beauty – the sadness – the touches – the gaiety, all of which are necessary to make life interesting."

Producer-star Mary Pickford hires Lubitsch

New York, 3 September
Rosita is being premiered at the Lyric Theater. It is the first American film directed by Ernst Lubitsch and it has been produced by Mary Pickford. When the celebrated German director arrived in America last December, Miss Pickford invited him to direct *Dorothy Vernon of Haddon Hall*. However, after much discussion, director and actress decided on *Rosita* as their final choice.

A new swashbuckling rival for Valentino

New York, 30 September
There is enough room for two dashing "Latin Lovers" in Hollywood at the moment, if Ramon Novarro has anything to say about it. While Rudolph Valentino has not been seen since *Blood and Sand* last year, Novarro is now swashbuckling his way through Valentino director Rex Ingram's *Scaramouche,* following his appearance as Rupert of Hentzau in Ingram's *The Prisoner of Zenda*.

Mary Pickford, Ernst Lubitsch and Holbrook Blinn during filming of ***Rosita***.

Valentino's former co-star Alice Terry with Ramon Novarro in ***Scaramouche***.

'yrano de Bergerac plays out his sad destiny in romantic Italy

.inda Moglia and Pierre Magnier incarnate Rostand's legendary couple.

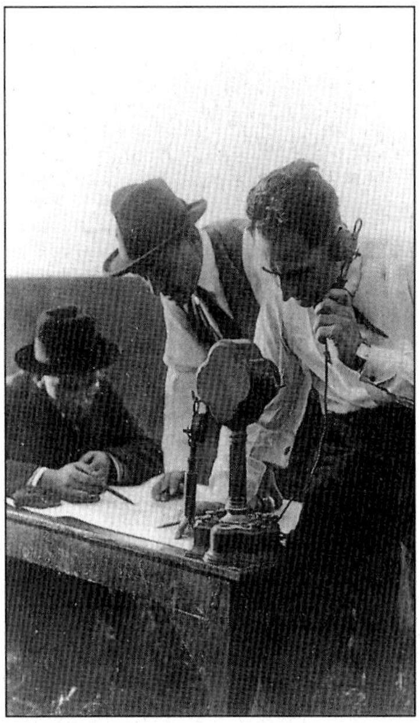

The director Augusto Genina during filming in the Roman countryside.

'aris, 16 October
'or the last few years, the young talian director Augusto Genina has een in love with France, and it ap- ears that it is because the feeling is nutual. The French press are not lways terribly kind to Italian cine- na, but they have been generous to Genino's recent films, *Bel Ami, Mademoiselle Cyclone* and *Lucretia Borgia*. Colette, the novelist and journalist, has expressed her appreciation of his humorous qualities, his sensitivity and vivacity, and she does not think he is capable of making a bad film. His *Cyrano de Bergerac*, shot in Rome and outlying districts, has many wonderful qualities, not least of which are its leading players: Linda Moglia playing Roxanne, and Pierre Magnier, an actor from the Porte-Saint-Martin Theatre, who delivers a fine performance in the title role. It was courageous of Augusto Genina to tackle Edmond Rostand's 19th-century French classic, but he has pulled it off.

A great cowboy is on the wane

Los Angeles, 2 December
The popularity of stone-faced cowboy star William S. Hart is fading quickly. Audiences, tiring of Hart's austere style, are turning instead to the flamboyant, action-packed films made by Tom Mix for the Fox Corporation. Hart's latest film is *Wild Bill Hickok*, which is prefaced by a title in which he apologizes to the audience for looking more like Hart than Hickok. The film also covers the period during which Hickok had to conceal his growing blindness.

William S. Hart, still in the saddle.

Mosjoukine makes new film in France

'aris, 2 November
'assions have been stirred by the howing of *Brasier Ardent*, written, irected and produced by Ivan Mosjoukine. The picture has se- uced the critics with its delirious omanticism and avant-garde style. However, confused by its episodic tory, the public in general has not ked it. But everyone has praised he performance of Mosjoukine, the ctor. He portrays several charac- ers: an officer, a Don Juan, a bish- p, a beggar, etc. This man of many aces is known for his extravagant ersonality and was one of the lead- ng lights of Russian cinema. After he 1917 Revolution, he and his vife, the actress Nathalie Kovanco, ke a number of their compatriots, hose to live in France. Mosjoukine as become popular here, thanks to is appearances in films like *House of Mystery*.

DeMille scores ten out of ten for impressive commandments

New York, 21 December
Earlier this year, producer-director Cecil B. DeMille embarked on the most ambitious project he had ever attempted, an elaborate version of *The Ten Commandments* that combines two stories – an extended "prologue" set in Biblical times, with Theodore Roberts in the role of Moses, and a modern story taking place in a contemporary American setting, starring Richard Dix, Rod La Rocque, Leatrice Joy and Nita Naldi. The completed film has just premiered at the George M. Cohan Theater in New York, and quite a spectacular achievement it turns out to be. Although almost certain to do well at the box office, judging from the enthusiastic audience response, the reaction from the critics has been somewhat less favorable. According to the *New York World*, for example, "In its earlier episodes the film has moments of grandeur... (but) when the story hurtles the centuries and settles into a present day symbolization of what has gone before, it is ordinary movie melodrama of the commonest type... " The Biblical sequences, occupying the opening hour of this two-and-a-half hour epic, are certainly the most memorable, and in fact should be as they alone account for two-thirds of the final $1.5 million cost, a sum which far exceeded DeMille's original budget.

Moses about to be whipped by the Pharaoh's son in DeMille's biblical epic.

1924

Los Angeles, 10 January
The producer Harry Cohn and his brother Jack, in association with Joe Brandt, have founded Columbia Pictures. The studios are situated at 6070 Sunset Boulevard, Hollywood.

Paris, 15 January
Release of a short puppet film *la Petite chanteuse des rues*, directed by Ladislas Starewitch, with his daughter Nina.

Paris, 25 January
For Pierre Gilles of the *Matin*, "the cinema is an industrial commodity that the silent partner can manipulate with impunity." But the Film Authors' Society has replied that "the artistic qualities of a film remain the property of the director."

Rome, 30 January
Due to the crisis in the Italian film industry, the producer Giuseppe Barattolo has withdrawn his financial participation in Abel Gance's *Napoleon*. If Gance wants to continue with the project he will have to find a new backer.

Canton, 1 February
Lin Minwei, who specializes in political documentaries, has finished filming Sun Yat-sen's first Kuomintang congress.

Hollywood, 3 February
The eminent Swedish director, Victor Sjöström, signed to a contract by the Goldwyn Co., has completed his first American film. *Name The Man* stars Mae Busch and Conrad Nagel, and its director is now to be known here as Victor Seastrom.

Hollywood, 4 February
The comic actor Harry Langdon has made his film debut in a Mack Sennett film, *Picking Peaches*. He intends to make 10 more films in the coming year.

Paris, 8 February
Louis Delluc, who has been ill since filming *l'Inondation* (*The Flood*), has submitted his latest article to the daily *Bonsoir*.

Hollywood, 1 March
Walt Disney has released *Alice's Day At The Sea*, the first in the series called "Alice in Cartoonland". The films are a mixture of cartoons and live action scenes.

Moscow, 1 April
Sergei Eisenstein and Pletniev have convinced the Prolekult to tackle the cinema with a cycle of films under the title of *Towards Dictatorship*. Eisenstein will be directing the first episode called *Strike*.

Paris, 15 April
The actor Camille Bardou has left for Marseilles to make *le Lion des Mogols* (*The Lion of the Mogols*). Jean Epstein is directing for Albatros, with Ivan Mosjoukine and Nathalie Lissenko.

Paris, April
Under the terms of their five-year agreement, Gaumont have formed a partnership with the American film company Loew's-Metro and will distribute their works in France. The new entity will, among other things, be taking charge of the Gaumont cinema circuit.

New York, 10 May
Reports show there are now 578 cinemas in the city with seating for 428,926 people.

Los Angeles, 28 May
Louis B. Mayer has offered Erich von Stroheim a bonus of $10,000 if he completes shooting of *The Merry Widow* in less than six weeks. Shooting has not started as yet.

Paris, 5 June
The Cinema Club has organized a special showing, at the Colisée, of an unreleased film made by André Antoine in 1920. The film, *l'Hirondelle et la mésange* (*The Sparrow and the Tit*), is based on a scenario by Gustave Gillet and was filmed entirely in the open air.

Los Angeles, 10 June
Worried by the length of time the filming of *Ben-Hur* is taking in Italy and by the mediocrity of the scenes that are already done, the directors of Metro-Goldwyn-Mayer have decided to employ radical means: the dismissal of the entire film crew.

Versailles, 7 July
Police interrupted the shooting of an Austrian-directed production in the park. Artists from the Paris Casino were being filmed in the nude in orgiastic scenes of the most liberal kind. The film's directors have been imprisoned.

Paris, 19 August
Charles Desvaux of the town council has asked the prefect to ban the Danish film *Hamlet* by Sven Gade, with Asta Nielsen. According to him it is "a vulgar melodrama with a pathetic scenario." Apparently the director made the mistake of imagining a feminine Hamlet.

New York, 9 September
Release of *The Iron Horse*, a historical fresco by John Ford with George O'Brien and Madge Bellamy.

Moscow, 25 October
The extravagant sets designed for Yakov Protazanov's *Aelita*, based on Tolstoy, have caused a sensation.

Berlin, 26 October
The Danish filmmaker Carl Dreyer has unveiled his latest film, *Michael*. It was filmed in Germany with Benjamin Christensen, Nora Gregor and Walter Slezak in the cast.

Paris, 31 October
Screening of Léon Abrams' film *la Voyante* (*The Clairvoyant*), starring Sarah Bernhardt, Harry Baur, Mary Marquet and Georges Melchior – the last one made by the great star.

Paris, 12 November
Max Linder is taking a stand against the invasion of American films in France. His attitude is exacerbated by United Artist's opposition to the American release of his last film, *Au Secours* directed by Abel Gance.

Berlin, 13 November
Release of *Das Wachsfigurenkabinett* (*Waxworks*) by Paul Leni, with Werner Krauss, Emil Jannings, Conrad Veidt and Lupu Pick.

Paris, 15 November
American actress Gloria Swanson has arrived in France to star in *Madame Sans-Gêne*, for director Léonce Perret.

Paris, 28 November
Preview of Raymond Bernard's historical fresco *The Miracle of the Wolves*, featuring 20 savage wolves.

New York, 4 December
Louis B. Mayer and Irving Thalberg have refused to release the initial 20-reel version of *Greed*. Instead, a 10-reel version disowned by Erich von Stroheim was shown at the preview.

Moscow, 10 December
The centralization of the Soviet film industry has finally been achieve with the creation of Sovkino. Th move is planned to give new impetu to flagging film production by at tracting increased financial backin from the government.

Hollywood, 13 December
The young actor Clark Gable ha gotten married to his drama teache Josephine Dillon. She is 14 years hi senior.

Berlin, 23 December
Release of *Der Letzte Mann* (*Th Last Laugh*), directed by F.W. Mu nau and starring Emil Jannings a the proud doorman.

New York, 31 December
The most successful films of the yea are: *The Sea Hawk*, *Secrets*, *Th Thief of Bagdad* and *Girl Shy*.

Italy, 31 December
This entire year's output of film production does not exceed 20 title (as compared to 921 films in 191 and 220 in 1920): the Italian cinem is dying.

Zurich, December
A production company, Praesen Film, has been set up by Lazar Wechsler, an engineer and aviatio pioneer of Polish origin.

BIRTHS

Nebraska, 3 April
Marlon Brando

Paris, 22 May
Charles Aznavour
(Shanoun Aznavourian)

New York, 16 September
Lauren Bacall
(Betty Joan Perske)

Illinois, 17 November
Rock Hudson
(Roy Fitzgerald)

Morocco, 27 November
Michel Galabru

Mae Murray, 'The Girl with th Beestung Lips', is one of the screen most popular glamour figures. Th year sees her in ***Mademoiselle Mid night*** *and* ***Circe the Enchantress****.*

A BREWSTER PUBLICATION
MOTION PICTURE
THE QUALITY MAGAZINE OF THE SCREEN
MARCH
MAGAZINE
25 CTS
Mae Murray
THE CONFESSIONS of an INTERVIEWER
In This Issue

Greta Garbo's Gösta Berling captivates Swedish audiences

Stockholm, 10 March
The premiere of Mauritz Stiller's new film *The Atonement of Gösta Berling* has attracted a big audience. This sumptuous production of Selma Lagerlöff's novel has launched a new Swedish screen star, Stiller's 18-year-old protégée, Greta Garbo. The daughter of a laborer, Garbo had an unhappy childhood and appeared to be in a dead-end job as a salesgirl in a Stockholm department store when she was chosen to appear in a publicity film, *How Not to Dress*. After another publicity short, this time for a bakery, she was cast as the leading lady in a slapstick comedy, *Peter the Tramp*. Next, she applied for, and won, a scholarship to Sweden's Royal Dramatic Theatre training school and was soon playing small parts on stage. While still at the school she was spotted by Mauritz Stiller, an accomplished director of both epic drama and social comedy who, in 1920, scored a big international success with *Erotikon*, a handsomely mounted sex drama. He is now Garbo's mentor and inseparable companion.

The 18-year-old Swedish newcomer has reached star status almost overnight.

Louis Delluc, victim of consumption

Paris, 22 March
The announcement of the death c writer and director Louis Dellu will, sadly, come as no surprise t fellow filmmakers and members c the press. Delluc never recovere from the illness which overtook hir last autumn when he was filmin *l'Inondation*. His doctors have de clared that the cause of death wa tuberculosis, but the truth is tha Delluc killed himself with overwork Author, journalist, man of the the ater and cinema, he produced in hi short working life 15 novels, a hos of poems, essays and reviews, si books on cinema plus hundreds c articles and, last but not least, eigh completed films and many unrea ized scenarios.

Actor Douglas Fairbanks makes magic in 'The Thief of Bagdad'

New York, 18 March
The first showing of *The Thief of Bagdad* took place this evening at the Liberty Theater in New York. At the end of the projection, Douglas Fairbanks, the star and producer of the film, a follow-up to his superb *Robin Hood* (1922), jumped onto the stage to tremendous applause. The director, Raoul Walsh, joined him an instant later to share in the honors. *The Thief of Bagdad* is the most ambitious and opulent film made by United Artists since being founded five years ago by Mary Pickford, Charles Chaplin, D.W. Griffith and Fairbanks. The film cost almost $2 million and took five weeks to shoot. The fabulous sets, including impressive towering minarets and Moorish buildings by William Cameron Menzies, were constructed on a six-and-a-half acre location at the Pickford-Fairbanks studio. And the sparkling costumes were designed by Mitchell Leisen. In order to create the Magic Carpet effect, an ordinary carpet was hung on piano wires from a 22-metre-high crane that swung it high over the sets, making it look as though it were actually moving between heaven and earth. The final sequence shows the hero Fairbanks and his beautiful princess (Julanne Johnston) sailing over the rooftops on the Magic Carpet, while the stars in the sky spell out "Happiness Must Be Earned."

Douglas
Fairbanks
"THE THIEF OF BAGDAD"

MGM takes lead in majors' league

New York, 26 April
The American film industry ha been transformed by the latest, an most important, merger since th formation of the Famous Players Lasky/Paramount company almos eight years ago. This new conglom erate called Metro-Goldwyn-Maye (MGM), has joined three medium sized Hollywood studios to form new "super studio" that may be in position to challenge, and compet on equal terms with, Paramount, th current industry leader. The nev amalgamation has come into bein through the partnership of two pow erful men, Marcus Loew, head o Loew's Inc. and Metro Pictures and Louis B. Mayer. Loew will con tinue to head the parent compan with its headquarters in New York while Mayer will be in charge of th filmmaking operation at the Culve City studios near Los Angeles, for merly owned by the Goldwyn Co. with Irving Thalberg as his produc tion chief. The new company ha already inherited a number of com pleted films, as well as such forth coming projects as *Ben-Hur* and *Th Merry Widow*, along with an impres sive lineup of stars which includes among others, Lon Chaney, Norm Shearer, John Gilbert, Ramon No varro, Buster Keaton, Mae Murra and Alice Terry.

{riemhild completes Lang's diptych

'agen the Hunter (Hans von Schlettow), the personification of evil, glowers in his strikingly decorated quarters.

erlin, 26 April
ritz Lang has offered us the very :st of his extraordinary talent in resenting *Kriemhild's Revenge*, the :quel to the equally magnificent *iegfried*, seen here last February. his Scandinavian legend, taken up y the 13th-century German bards, and again by Richard Wagner, has allowed Lang entrance into cinematic legend. In just seven years, the 34-year-old director and scenarist has worked on 20 films. With *Between Two Worlds, Dr. Mabuse, The Spiders* and now *The Nibelungen*, in two parts comprising 249 absorbing minutes, Fritz Lang has become a director with few rivals. His wife, Thea von Harbou, has adapted this story of terrible vengeance, which concludes with the massacre of the Huns in a massively staged battle. It is a superb example of the craftsmanship at the UFA studios.

A new studio built for Napoleon

Paris, 3 August
The studios at Billancourt are a hive of activity. Painters, carpenters and plasterers are preparing the sets for *Napoleon*, the spectacular production which director Abel Gance is planning to shoot in a few months. Several important scenes will be filmed in these studios, which have just been acquired for the purpose by the film's producers. Several different studios will be involved in this ambitious project, the cost of which is estimated at 7 million francs. The plan is to release the finished work as six separate films. Audiences will be able to follow Napoleon Bonaparte from his birth in Corsica to his exile in Saint Helena, a story which encompasses the history of France through the Revolution, the Directory, the Consulate, the Empire and the Restoration. Gance has established his name with the dramatic pacifist message of *J'accuse* (1919) and the melodrama *la Roue* (1923). Of the latter Jean Cocteau declared: "There is cinema before and after *la Roue* as there is painting before and after Picasso."

{in-Tin-Tin proves himself a wonder dog

os Angeles, 1 September
he screen has a new star, and it's a og. The canine in question is Rin-in-Tin, a German Shepherd found the trenches during the war by a J.S. Army Lieutenant named Lee)uncan. The dog accompanied his ew master back to America where Duncan trained him for a film career. Rinty made his debut in Warner Brothers' *The Man from Hell's River* and is currently starring in *Find Your Man*, written by 22-year-old Darryl F. Zanuck. Many feel that Rinty is a better actor than many of the studio's human stars.

Ford's 'Iron Horse' takes epic direction

Hollywood, 9 September
In response to Paramount's success with *The Covered Wagon* last year, Fox has come up with its own epic Western, *The Iron Horse*, depicting the construction of the transcontinental railroad in the late 1860s. George O'Brien plays the young hero who has a job on the railroad while seeking to avenge his father's murder, while Madge Bellamy provides the love interest. But the real star of the film is director John (formerly Jack) Ford, whose accomplished work has brought the story dramatically to life.

{in-Tin-Tin peeks at the script for his latest Warner picture, **Find Your Man!**

Ford (2nd left) directing **The Iron Horse** with Charles Edward Bull as Lincoln.

Buster Keaton navigates his way to further glory

New York, 13 October
Buster Keaton has come a long way since his 1917 debut alongside Fatty Arbuckle. Two years after that he formed a partnership with Joseph M. Schenck, distributing his films through MGM. In 1920 he made his first feature, *The Saphead*, and in 1921 he married into the Hollywood aristocracy when Natalie Talmadge, Joseph Schenck's sister-in-law, became his wife. Keaton's comic personality is doggedly unsentimental. Not even the slightest hint of a smile creases his face. The preoccupied little heroes in his films encounter a series of perils but react to each reversal with an exquisite economy of expression. Keaton can express passion with the subtlest droop of the eyelids or the slow tossing of his hat in the air. Since 1920 the complete artistic control he has been able to exercise over his films has resulted in a series of inventive and superbly photographed shorts and features. Last year he scored a hit with *Our Hospitality*. This year the rich vein has continued with the charming fantasy of *Sherlock Jr.* and now his latest film release, *The Navigator*. Keaton has always been fascinated by machinery, and in *The Navigator* he has fashioned a brilliant range of comic situations from a huge single prop, an abandoned schooner. This time Keaton plays Rollo, an id young millionaire whose dream gi Kathryn McGuire, turns down h marriage proposal. Disappointe he embarks on an ocean cruise, on to wake up one morning to find t ship adrift at sea with himself see ingly the only passenger aboard, e cept, of course, for McGuire. T director of *The Navigator* is Dona Crisp, but the genius in control Buster Keaton.

K23-80-
Brilliant Buster, as the navigator, is assisted by pretty Kathryn McGuire.

Cordially Mary Pickford
NEXT WEEK
REX INGRAM'S
Starstruck Buster in ***Sherlock Jr.****, gazing up adoringly at Mary Pickford.*

Rumors surround the death at sea of Thomas Harper Ince

Hollywood, 21 November
The leading figures in Hollywood, including Charlie Chaplin, Douglas Fairbanks, Mary Pickford, Harold Lloyd and Marion Davies, gathered today for the funeral of producer and director Thomas Harper Ince. Ince's body was cremated without an autopsy, which makes the circumstances surrounding his death two days ago all the more mysterious. Ince was among the party that included Chaplin, aboard the yacht owned by news tycoon William Randolph Hearst. He was taken ashore, supposedly suffering from "indigestion", and died at his Hollywood home. Rumors are circulating that the indigestion was caused by a bullet fired by Hearst, who had mistaken Ince for Chaplin whom he has suspected of having an affair with his mistress, Marion Davies.

Ince disappeared during a party on board William Randolph Hearst's yacht.

L'Herbier's sets are part of the act

Paris, 12 December
Marcel L'Herbier's impressive ne film, *L'Inhumaine*, is an absolut catalogue of French contemporar art. Written in collaboration wit Pierre Mac Orlan, the picture wa financed in part by the opera singe Georgette Leblanc, the wife c Maurice Maeterlinck. The princip interest of the film is its audaciou decor, each set being created by different designer: Fernand Lége Claude Autant-Lara, Alberto Cava canti, Mallet-Stevens. As a result, is an avant-garde work of pure art fice. The inventive L'Herbier ha succeeded in giving a visual rhyth to each bravura sequence with th music of the composer Darius Mi haud, and featuring dancers fror the Ballet Suédois.

Star trio for new MGM's 'He Who Gets Slapped'

Iollywood, 9 November
'he first film entirely prepared and roduced by the new motion picture tudio, Metro-Goldwyn-Mayer, has ıst opened in Hollywood. *He Who Gets Slapped*, based on a 1914 Rus-ian play by Leonid Andreyev, may eem to be a risky choice for the tudio's debut feature, but the ex-eptional talents involved have car-ied off a cinematic coup. Studio hief Louis B. Mayer and supervisor f production Irving Thalberg were etermined to demonstrate the new tudio's powers by casting two stars John Gilbert and Lon Chaney – as vell as new Thalberg-find Norma hearer, and employing the cele-rated Swedish director Victor Sea-trom (Victor Sjöström). The story ells of a scientist (Chaney) who ıughs in hysterical disbelief when e realizes that his benefactor has tolen not only his research but also is wife, and whose face is frozen by hat moment of shock into a fixed rin. He can go on living only as a ircus clown, an object of mockery nd abuse. Literally wearing his eart on his sleeve, he falls hopeless-y in love with Consuela (Shearer), he bareback rider. In his second Iollywood picture, Seastrom dem-nstrates his continuing mastery of ubtle lighting effects and Expres-ionist devices. He created this work for Metro-Goldwyn-Mayer, a studio born from the amalgamation of the Metro Picture Corporation, Gold-wyn Picture Corporation and Louis B. Mayer Pictures, under the corpo-rate control of Loew's Inc. As part of a financial empire with powerful banking affiliations and a ready-made market in the form of Marcus Loew's extensive chain of motion picture theaters, MGM looks likely to prosper. And if future produc-tions are of the same caliber of *He Who Gets Slapped*, the company's future looks rosy.

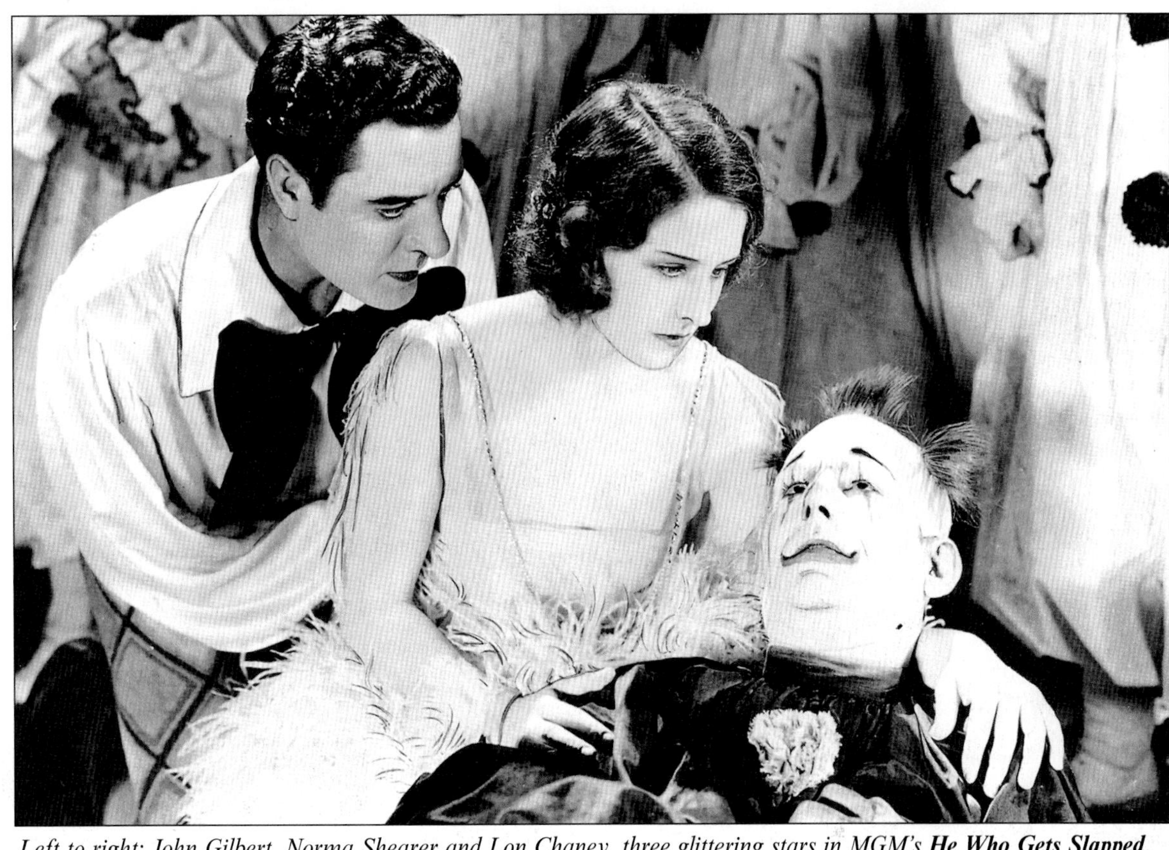
Left to right: John Gilbert, Norma Shearer and Lon Chaney, three glittering stars in MGM's ***He Who Gets Slapped****.*

ola Negri is paradise for Paramount

New York, 24 November
The rich vein of absurdity which Pola Negri struck in 1923 with her irst American film, *Bella Donna*, ontinues in *Forbidden Fruit*. Re-nited with director Ernst Lubitsch, vith whom she made *Madame Du-arry* in Germany (retitled *Passion* n America), she now stars as Cather-ne the Great in *Forbidden Paradise*. Her co-stars are Rod La Rocque nd Adolphe Menjou. Paramount's ublicity department, however, is aving to work very hard to main-ain the popularity of their Polish-orn star. To date they have built er up as a vamp and concocted a hony feud with the queen of the Paramount lot, Gloria Swanson. Now they are running the risk of ainting Negri as an over-exotic oreign interloper who is taking her ultry talents far too seriously.

Director instructs his star on the set.

Emil Jannings packs power for Murnau

Berlin, 23 December
The Berlin public now has the chance to see *The Last Laugh* (*Der Letzte Mann*), F.W. Murnau's finest film since *Nosferatu*, two years ago. This moving drama is very different from the earlier horror film. Although Expressionist in manner, *The Last Laugh* is nearer to the *Kammerspielfilm* (chamber film), which focuses on ordinary people and events and while containing an element of social criticism. The entire story, of an old hotel doorman reduced to working as a lavatory attendant, is told without any titles. As the role is played by that imposing and expressive star, Emil Jannings, no words on the screen seem necessary. After various larger-than-life characters such as Peter the Great and Nero, it is good to see this great actor playing a pathetic figure.

Emil Jannings, lonely and haunted.

1925

Los Angles, 9 January
After having a serious difference of opinion, Paramount chief Adolph Zukor has terminated the producer-director Cecil B. DeMille's contract.

Hollywood, 10 January
A compromise has been reached between D.W. Griffith and United Artists: in exchange for his freedom, the director is to provide the company with a final film, and the shares he owns in the company are to be placed in a fiduciary deposit.

Berlin, 31 January
Release of *Orlacs Hände* (*The Hands of Orlac*) by Robert Wiene, adapted from Maurice Renard, with Fritz Kortner and Conrad Veidt.

Hollywood, 31 January
A struggle between Erich von Stroheim and actress Mae Murray, has caused problems on the set of *The Merry Widow*. Louis B. Mayer fired and then re-hired the director.

New York, 7 February
Release of *The Salvation Hunters*, directed by Josef von Sternberg.

Rome, 16 March
Gabriellino d'Annunzio and Georg Jacoby's remake of *Quo Vadis?* has been badly received here. Despite the presence of Emil Jannings as Nero and financial backing from UFA, who co-produced the film, it is a pale copy of the 1913 version.

Paris, 31 March
Launching of the book *Two Years in the Studios of America*, written by Robert Florey, French director and Hollywood correspondent for the weekly *Cine-Magazine*.

Paris, 15 May
Judgment was passed today on the director and actresses arrested during an orgy at Versailles on 7 July 1924. The Austrian impresario was condemned to a month's imprisonment and was also fined 22 francs. The actresses Lucienne Schwartz, Yvonne Savaille and Lucienne Legrand received suspended sentences and were fined 16 francs each.

Berlin, 22 May
Fritz Lang has commenced filming *Metropolis* in the UFA studios. The scenario was written by the director and his wife Thea von Harbou.

Paris, 15 July
L'Histoire du cinématographe (*The History of the Cinematograph*), written by Georges-Michel Coissac, is the first historical study to be made on the origins of the cinema.

Paris, 22 July
Max Linder has been elected president of the Filmwriters Society in the place of Michel Carré who has resigned. It seems Linder's position in defense of the cinema industry in France last November explains this unexpected election.

Paris, 29 July
Release of *Feu Mathias Pascal*, a film version of the work by Pirandello, directed by Marcel L'Herbier, and starring Ivan Mosjoukine. The latter, who is under contract to Ciné-France Film, is at the moment on location in Lettonia with Victor Tourjansky for *Michael Strogoff*.

Los Angeles, 2 August
Adolph Zukor has given the go-ahead to United Artists to distribute the film directed and produced by D.W. Griffith for Paramount, *Sally of the Sawdust*, starring the popular comic actor W.C. Fields and Carol Dempster.

New York, 16 August
MGM has released *The Unholy Three*, an unusual thriller with some amazing scenes of the fantastic, directed by Tod Browning with Lon Chaney and Mae Busch.

New York, 29 August
Samuel Goldwyn has signed a contract with United Artists: he is to supply from two to four films a year and in return will receive 75 percent of the gross takings.

Paris, 22 September
The release of *The Phantom of the Opera*, directed by Rupert Julian, adapted from the novel by Gaston Leroux and starring Lon Chaney. For this lavishly produced historical drama, a replica of the entire Paris Opera was constructed at Universal Studios near Hollywood.

Copenhagen, 5 October
Carl Dreyer has made *Master of the House*, with Johannes Mayer and Astrid Holm. This film, made in Dreyer's native Denmark, is in the German *Kammerspiel* tradition.

Geneva, 9 October
Michel Simon, a photographer and actor with the Pitoeff troupe, is causing a sensation with his performance in *The Vocation of André Carrel*. From director Jean Choux, and with Blanche Montel and Camille Bert, it is Simon's first screen role.

Paris, 30 October
Max Linder, who was obsessed by death, first killed his wife Hélène and then committed suicide today.

New York, 1 November
As of today, Warner Bros. owns Vitagraph, the company created in 1896 by J. Stuart Blackton and Albert E. Smith. Under the agreement that was signed in February, Warners inherits all research undertaken by Vitagraph in the field of sound.

Paris, 3 November
Max Linder's will was read today in the Seine Civil Court. The star has bequeathed all the films produced by him to the president of the Cinema Press Association, J.L. Croze.

Paris, 4 November
Backing for Abel Gance's project *Napoleon* has been taken up by the General Film company, which was set up for this purpose. Filming was interrupted on 21 June after the main backers, the German group Stinnes, were declared bankrupt.

Rome, 5 November
Luce Institute (Educational Cinematographic Union) has been nationalized by the Facist government.

Hollywood, 7 November
The independent producer B.P. Schulberg has joined Paramount. He brings with him Clara Bow, John Gilbert and the director William Wellman.

Moscow, 21 November
Release of *Chess Fever*, the first film directed by Vsevolod Pudovkin, an actor who has previously assisted in the making of several films.

New York, 29 November
The young actress Louise Brooks has spoken to the *Daily Mail* about a series of nude photos taken of her two years ago. She wants to prevent their publication. She also alluded to her relationship with Charlie Chaplin whom she met last summer.

Paris, 25 December
Release of Henri Fescourt's versio of *les Misérables*, filmed in fou episodes with Gabriel Gabrio an Sandra Milowanoff.

Berlin, 31 December
UFA has signed a reciprocal agre ment with Paramount and MGM for the importation of films betwee the two countries. A 'progressive company has been created to di tribute Soviet documentaries.

BIRTHS

Ohio, 26 January
Paul Newman

France, 12 March
Georges Delerue

Sweden, 24 May
Mai Zetterling

New York, 3 June
Tony Curtis
(Bernard Schwartz)

France, 31 August
Maurice Pialat

England, 8 September
Peter Sellers
(Richard Henry Sellers)

France, 23 September
Jean-Charles Tacchella

Athens, 18 October
Melina Mercouri

Algiers, 20 October
Roger Hanin (R. Lévy)

Paris, 6 November
Michel Bouquet

Wales, 10 November
Richard Burton
(R. Jenkins)

Paris, 27 December
Michel Piccoli

Germany, 28 December
Hildegard Knef
(aka Hildegarde Neff)

The highly popular Richard Dix plays the lead in ***The Vanishing American****. This Western epic, from Zane Grey's novel on a theme of racial injustice was directed by George B. Seitz.*

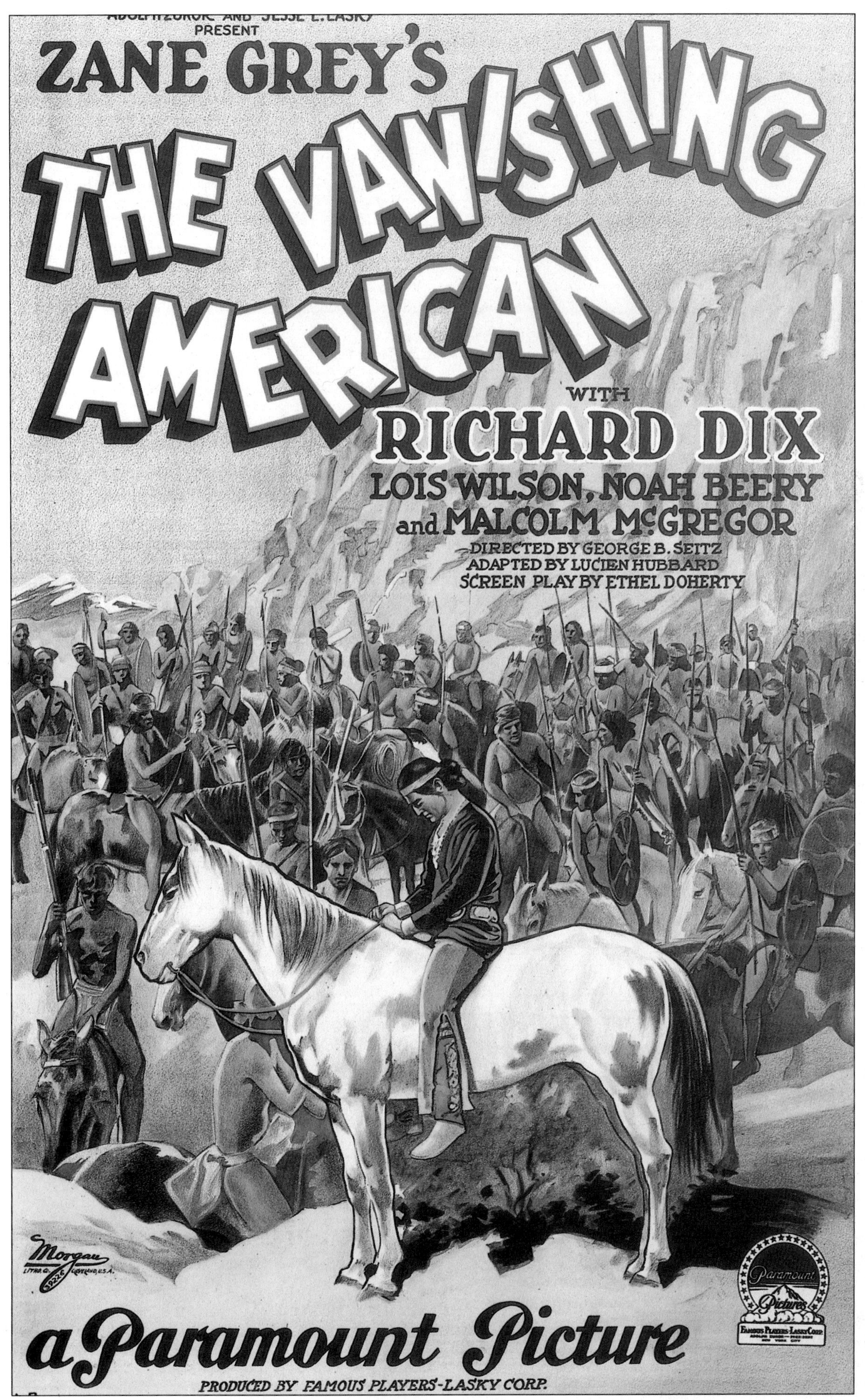
PRESENT
ZANE GREY'S
THE VANISHING AMERICAN
WITH
RICHARD DIX
LOIS WILSON, NOAH BEERY
and MALCOLM McGREGOR
DIRECTED BY GEORGE B. SEITZ
ADAPTED BY LUCIEN HUBBARD
SCREEN PLAY BY ETHEL DOHERTY
Morgan
Paramount Pictures
a Paramount Picture
PRODUCED BY FAMOUS PLAYERS-LASKY CORP.

Stroheim refuses to recognize massacred version of 'Greed'

Gibson Gowland and ZaSu Pitts.

Gowland (left) and Jean Hersholt in the climactic desert scene from ***Greed*****.**

New York, 26 January
A powerful new film from director Erich von Stroheim has just opened. It is his long-awaited production of *Greed* which he first began filming almost two years ago, in March 1923. Its release was unfortunately held up by the merger of the Goldwyn Co. into MGM last year, and the insistence of the new studio that the film be drastically reduced in length. Yet even in this mutilated form, the picture appears to be a quite remarkable and original work. For Stroheim there has been a long gap between films. It is exactly three years since his last feature, *Foolish Wives*, had its premiere. After the problems he experienced on that production, his days at Universal were obviously numbered, and he was replaced on his next film, *Merry-Go-Round*, midway through production, by the studio's new young production chief, Irving Thalberg. However, Stroheim was immediately signed up by the Goldwyn Co. and, for his first production, he turned to one of his favorite projects, a film version of *McTeague*, the best-known novel by the American naturalist writer of the 19th century, Frank Norris. The filming, almost entirely on location in San Francisco and at Death Valley, lasted for almost six months in 1923. Stroheim spent almost as much time again reducing the massive quantity of footage to his own final cut of about 22 reels, running for five-and-a-half hours and meant to be shown in two parts. However, MGM would have none of this and insisted on further cuts, reducing the film to 10 reels, less than half the original length. Despite this massacre that was then disowned by the director, much of his conception survives. The film gives the feeling of an entire milieu brought to life, with outstanding performances from Gibson Gowland and ZaSu Pitts as the simple-minded dentist and his avaricious wife, who appear less like actors than real characters existing within a real world. Although their central relationship has been cut, the most drastic pruning has affected mainly the various subplots and the extended prologue, while the amazing final climax in Death Valley has to be seen to be believed.

Death of Feuillade paralyzes Gaumont

France, 26 February
Louis Feuillade, the father of *Fant[o]mas*, has died of peritonitis. He ha[s] just finished filming the final scene of *le Stigmate*, which he was c[o-] directing with his son-in-law Mau[r]ice Champreux. Feuillade's deat[h] has caused a crisis at Gaumon[t] where he has long been a pillar [o]f strength. He arrived there as [a] screenwriter and eventually becam[e] the studio's star director. Born i[n] Lunel on 19 February 1873, Feuil[l]ade was a prolific filmmaker, turn[-]ing out hundreds of films, amon[g] them dreamlike serials such as *Le[s] Vampires* and *Judex*, which hav[e] been the cornerstones of Gaumont'[s] fame and fortune.

His last days in the sun at Nice.

Louis B. Mayer brings his epic chariot race back to Culver City

Culver City, 31 January
The chariot race in *Ben-Hur* will not be filmed in Italy as was originally planned, but in the studios of Culver City, not far from Hollywood. This change is the decision of the management at Metro-Goldwyn-Mayer, in particular Louis B. Mayer and Irving Thalberg. The shooting of the film, planned as the Goldwyn Company's most ambitious productio[n] ever, began in 1923 in Rome unde[r] the direction of Charles Brabin, wit[h] George Walsh in the title role and [a] script by June Mathis. But by th[e] time that the new MGM was found[-]ed, only part of the filming had bee[n] completed. Appalled by the continu[-]ing production problems and poo[r] quality footage, MGM replaced Bra[-]bin and Walsh with director Fre[d] Niblo and Ramon Novarro, wit[h] Bess Meredyth and Carey Wilso[n] providing the necessary script re[-]write. Filming continued in Italy fo[r] another few months before the *Ben-Hur* company was ordered back t[o] Hollywood where Thalberg coul[d] keep a sharper eye on the project. After a year's work and $2 millio[n] spent, only half the film has bee[n] completed. But if the new studio ca[n] meet this challenge, of turning a po[-]tential disaster into a triumph, the[y] will have demonstrated, better tha[n] any new project of their own coul[d] do, how effectively their new pro[-]ducer-oriented system can work.

Leading players Ramon Novarro, May McAvoy and Francis X. Bushman lend a helping hand on the site of the future arena for the ***Ben-Hur*** *chariot race.*

wo acts and an interval from René Clair

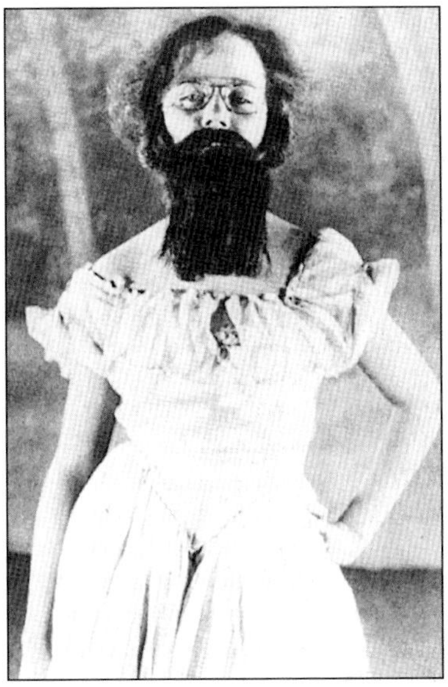

As the bearded dancer in ***Entr'acte***.

ris, 13 March
ossing successfully from the ca-
er of actor to that of director, the
ung René Clair has now made
ee movies, the latest being *The
antom of the Moulin Rouge*. With
he has returned to the formula of
first picture, *Paris qui dort*, that
etic evocation of Paris, in which a
ntastic tale is told in the French
le. Between these two films, Clair
ected *Entr'acte*, a Dadaist sketch
itten by Francis Picabia and fearing, among others, Man Ray,
arcel Achard, Marcel Duchamps
d Erik Satie, who composed the
usical accompaniment. The short
m was conceived to be shown be-
een acts of the ballet *Relâche*,
eated for Rolf de Maré's Swedish
llet company.

ené Clair surveys the scene during the filming of ***Paris qui dort (Paris Sleeps)***.

Madame Sans-Gêne' becomes American

loria Swanson in Perret's film, ade partly on location in France.

New York, 20 April
The American public has given an enthusiastic reception to *Madame Sans-Gêne*. A Paramount production directed in France by Léonce Perret, *Madame Sans-Gêne* starring Gloria Swanson, who considers Perret to be the best director she has ever worked with. Adapted from the Sardou play about Napoleon's laundress, much of the film was shot at Versailles. It is the first in a series of productions which Paramount plans to film in France. This expansionist policy will not find unanimous favor in Paris. La Société des Auteurs de Films, for example, sees this as a bridgehead toward eventual American domination of the film market in France.

Greta a brave heroine in 'Joyless Street'

Berlin, 18 May
Scarcely a year after the release in Sweden of *The Legend of Gösta Berling*, Greta Garbo has consolidated her talent as an actress in *Joyless Street*, made by the talented German director G.W. Pabst. In the leading role, she plays the daughter of a middle-class father ruined by inflation, who is faced with the terrible dilemma of entering a brothel. This truly somber (yet poetic) picture of Viennese life in the early 1920s has presented us with a new image of Garbo. Slimmer and more sensuous, she imbues the character with intense emotion. Her successful debut in German cinema has not, however, altered her plans to continue working with her Swedish mentor, Mauritz Stiller.

Greta Garbo (left) with Valeska Gert.

Hollywood beckons Garbo and Stiller

New York, 6 July
This summer, although the city has been suffering from an unprecedented heat wave, the press has still not been prevented from seizing the most minor event. Accordingly, the *Herald Tribune* has announced the arrival, on the ocean liner *Drottningholm*, of "a pleasing visitor to our country, one of the most beautiful of Swedish stars, who has signed contracts to make American films." This refers to Greta Garbo, who has arrived here with her mentor Mauritz Stiller. But New York is only a stopping place on their way to Hollywood. Some months before the shooting of *Joyless Street*, directed by G.W. Pabst, Greta Garbo became acquainted with Louis B. Mayer, the vice president of Metro-Goldwyn-Mayer. Extremely impressed by *The Legend of Gösta Berling*, he wanted to sign a contract with Stiller immediately. However, Stiller insisted that he would only accept it if Garbo were offered a contract as well. Mayer agreed, though he warned Stiller that "American men do not like fat women." That wasn't going to discourage Greta. She has since lost weight, and now knows how to exploit her mysterious beauty.

DROTTNINGHOLM
GÖTEBORG

Garbo and Mauritz Stiller on board ship during their voyage to the USA.

Comedy and pathos combine in 'The Gold Rush'

Chaplin takes time over 'Gold Rush'

Hollywood, 26 June
Charles Chaplin is taking longer and longer to make his films. Shooting *The Gold Rush* has taken him over a year, though Chaplin copyrighted his screenplay back on 29 December 1923. The inspiration for the film was a photograph of prospectors in the Klondike in 1898, which he had seen at the home of Douglas Fairbanks and Mary Pickford. *The Gold Rush* was filmed in difficult conditions at Truckee near Lake Tahoe, high in the Sierra Nevada, and then wrapped up at Chaplin's La Brea Avenue studio in Los Angeles.

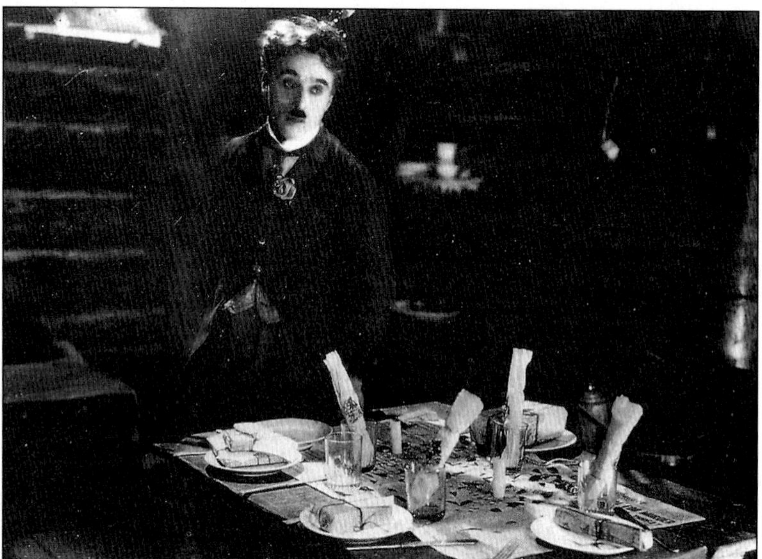
Charlie longingly contemplates a festive table, but where is the food... ?

Outcast from life rescued by love

Hollywood, 26 June
Today sees the spectacular premie of Chaplin's *The Gold Rush* Grauman's Egyptian Theater. T film is preceded by a show whi includes live seals and a troupe Eskimo dancing girls. *The Go Rush* is a great film and a great lo story. Here the Little Tramp tur prospector in the Frozen North. H only friend is the hulking Big Ji McKay, portrayed by Mack Swai Theirs is a volatile relationship th swings wildly from the happy to t homicidal, particularly when, in delirium of starvation, Big Jim ha lucinates that Charlie has turne into a chicken. The two friends a cheated by the swindling Black La son (Tom Murray). Seeking refu in the town, the Tramp falls hop lessly in love with enchanting sing Georgia Hale. Using his meag savings, he prepares a New Year party for her, but she forgets a about him and fails to turn up. H falls asleep and dreams that th party is a huge success. It is durin this sequence that the Tramp impr vises a "Dance of the Rolls", crea ing a sad little ballet with two fork and two buns. All ends happil however. Charlie strikes gold an becomes a millionaire, then on th boat back to California he is reuni ed with Georgia. Chaplin believe that this is his finest film.

Lita's pregnancy benefits Georgia Hale

Hollywood, 26 June
In March 1924, shortly before location shooting for *The Gold Rush* began in the Sierra Nevada, Chaplin chose Lillita McMurray, of the tender age of 15 years and 10 months, as his new leading lady. He also changed her name to Lita Grey. Three years previously, Lillita had appeared in Chaplin's *The Kid* as the 12-year-old "Angel of Temptation". It seems, however, that she has tempted Chaplin once again. On 26 November, Charlie married Lita in Guaymas, Mexico, making a fruitless attempt to dodge the press when he tried to sneak back into the United States with his new young bride. Amid these alarums and excursions, Chaplin replaced the by-now pregnant Lita Grey with a new leading lady for *The Gold Rush*. It was, perhaps, something of a relief for the filmmaker, since it quickly had become clear that Lita's acting skills were not equal to the task of co-starring with her husband. The role of the dance-hall girl who becomes the object of The Tramp's fantasies was therefore given to 21-year-old Georgia Hale, a recent discovery of director Josef von Sternberg, and the star of his first film, *The Salvation Hunters*.

Georgia Hale, replacing Lita Grey as the light in the Tramp's lonely life.

The actor-director, photographed on location in the Sierra Nevada mountains.

His boot and its laces become steak and spaghetti for the starving Tramp.

King Vidor glorifies the pacifist ideal

Renée Adorée, Vidor, John Gilbert.

New York, 5 November
Irving Thalberg, head of production at MGM, can rub his hands with pride, thanks to the triumph of King Vidor's *The Big Parade*. Written by Laurence Stallings, this moving tale unfolds in France during the 1914-1918 war. It is both a film about war and a tender love story centering on an American soldier and a beautiful French peasant woman, interpreted by John Gilbert and Renée Adorée. The director seems to be more interested in the rapport between the characters and in their emotions than in the battle scenes. Nevertheless, these sequences are an example of brilliant editing, and the panoramic shots of the army on the move are impressive. The result is a moving, and clearly anti-war, film.

ng Vidor's
PICTURIZATION
LAURENCE STALLINGS'
GREAT STORY
The
BIG PARADE
STARRING
JOHN GILBERT
RENEE ADOREE
A Metro-Goldwyn-Mayer Production

Gaston Leroux's famous Phantom given the Chaney treatment

Boston, 15 November
The movies' master of macabre makeup, Lon Chaney, has scored another triumph in Universal's spectacular adaptation of the Gaston Leroux warhorse, *The Phantom of the Opera*. Chaney stars as the hideously disfigured composer who haunts the sewers beneath the Paris Opera. His makeup was kept secret during shooting, thus ensuring the shock when he appears toward the end of the film, unmasked in his underground lair by lovely young Mary Philbin. Chaney's Phantom suggests a living skull. Apparently he has designed a device which, when inserted into his nose, tilts the tip and spreads the nostrils. Prongs attached to protruding false teeth pull his mouth back at the corners. Inside Chaney's mouth celluloid discs push out his cheekbones. On top of his head he wears a domed wig, stranded with lank, greasy hair. Director Rupert Julian indulges in a wry joke at the end of the film when the Phantom's coach drives furiously past the huge set of Notre Dame cathedral, built two years ago for use in another enormously successful Lon Chaney vehicle, *The Hunchback of Notre Dame*.

Lon Chaney's Phantom observes the lovers, Norman Kerry and Mary Philbin.

Against all the odds, MGM's 'Ben-Hur' is a thrilling success

New York, 30 December
MGM has finally completed production on *Ben-Hur*, the inordinately expensive undertaking which has required nearly a year to shoot, at a cost of $4 million. The long-awaited film has now opened at the George M. Cohan Theater to an enthusiastic reception. The already celebrated chariot race was filmed in a replica of the Antioch Coliseum, a larger set even than that of Babylon in Griffith's *Intolerance*. Thousands of extras were hired and more than 40 cameras filmed the scene from all possible angles, some of them in automobiles overtaking the galloping horses. The result is a great moment of cinema, which contrasts with the more conventional remainder of the film. In spite of its obvious faults, this cinematic version of the 1880 novel by Lew Wallace should become a great favorite with the public, as should the Latin Ramon Novarro, who is noticeably becoming a rival of Rudolph Valentino.

A moment of intimacy for Ramon Novarro and May McAvoy in **Ben-Hur**.

1926

New York, 7 January
Paramount has released *Moana*, shot by Robert Flaherty in the South Seas, using panchromatic film.

Paris, 9 January
The writer Pierre Mac Orlan gave a lecture on humor and the fantastic in the cinema, at the Vieux-Colombier Theatre.

Berlin, 25 January
A film version of Molière's *Tartuffe*, made by F.W. Murnau, was screened for the opening of the Gloria Palast cinema.

Hollywood, 6 February
Distributors and cinema exhibitors have signed a contract to establish a new standard of business practices which will provide a framework in case of lawsuits.

Tokyo, 28 February
Kenji Mizoguchi has finished work on his latest film, *A Paper Doll's Whisper of Spring*.

London, 1 March
A new director, Alfred Hitchcock, has been hailed by the press as "a young man with the vision of a master" after the release of his first film *The Pleasure Garden*.

Paris, 2 March
A newsreel of Citroën's expedition in Central Africa, called *The Black Crossing* and filmed by Léon Poirier, was screened at the Opera in the presence of the President of the Republic, Gaston Doumergue.

Rome, 9 March
Carmine Gallone has finished making *The Last Days Of Pompeii* for UCI, a film started but then abandoned by Amleto Palermi.

Hollywood, 28 March
Josef von Sternberg has disowned his work *The Exquisite Sinner*, in rebellion against the methods employed by the studios. But despite his decision, the film has been remade by Philip Rosen under Metro-Goldwyn-Mayer's orders.

California, March
Josef von Sternberg is making *The Sea Gull*, a film from a scenario written by himself and starring Edna Purviance. Charlie Chaplin commissioned the film from Sternberg.

Rome, 3 April
Henceforth, by decree, all cinemas have to screen Luce newsreels.

Washington, 20 April
President Coolidge has pronounced himself opposed to the idea of a federal institution for film censorship. He considers that "the producers themselves have undertaken to reform their industry," by the creation of the MPPDA.

Berlin, 26 April
Sergei Eisenstein's study trip is over. He worked on the musical score for *The Battleship Potemkin* and met directors Friedrich Wilhelm Murnau and Fritz Lang, the actor Emil Jannings, and cameraman Karl Freund while he was here.

New York, April
Warner Bros., in equal partnership with Electrical Research Products Inc. (ERPI), have set up the Vitagraph Corporation. The aim of the company is to continue research in the field of sound in close collaboration with Western Electric.

Cairo, 17 May
Youssef Wahby has caused a storm of protest by revealing his plans to make a film on the life of Mahomet.

Paris, 8 June
Release of *Tramp, Tramp, Tramp*, the first feature-length comedy directed by Frank Capra and Harry Edwards, starring Harry Langdon who is also the film's producer, with screen newcomer Joan Crawford.

Paris, 19 June
Release of *Mare Nostrum*, with Alice Terry and Antonio Moreno. It is the first film to be directed by Rex Ingram at the Victorine studios in Nice since they were taken over by Metro-Goldwyn-Mayer last year.

Hollywood, 4 July
The Hungarian film-director Mihaly Kertesz has arrived from Europe to take up his new contract with the studio Warner Bros. He is to be known as Michael Curtiz.

Moscow, 21 July
Sergei Eisenstein has received a visit from Douglas Fairbanks and Mary Pickford, who have promised to invite him to Hollywood to direct a film for United Artists.

New York, 21 July
Louise Brooks has married Edward Sutherland, the director of *It's The Old Army Game*, in which she stars with W.C. Fields.

New York, 31 July
Ernst Lubitsch's last film for Warner Bros., *So This Is Paris*, has been hailed as a success by the critics.

Hollywood, 5 August
Will H. Hays' three-year contract with the MPPDA has been extended to five years with an increase in his salary and powers.

Paris, 14 August
Jean Renoir's film *Nana*, from Zola's novel, has begun its eighth week at the Aubert Palace, which has the exclusive screening rights. The film has already beaten this year's record for box-office takings.

Hollywood, 16 August
Young New York-born star Clara Bow has signed a five-year contract with Paramount. But she is refusing to accept the traditional morality clause, which enables the studio to cancel an employee's contract if they become involved in a scandal.

Paris, 3 September
The Gaumont Palace has reopened after being renovated under the direction of Tommy Dowd from the Capitol Theater in New York. The orchestra pit is tiered and the organ rises up mechanically.

Moscow, 4 October
The Mother, by Vsevolod Pudovkin, adapted from the work by Maxim Gorki, is being hailed as a masterpiece of the silent cinema.

Los Angeles, 14 October
Gary Cooper stars in Henry King's *The Winning of Barbara Worth*.

Paris, 19 October
Release of *Mauprat*, based on the work by George Sand, produced and directed by Jean Epstein. The young Spanish journalist Louis Buñuel was Epstein's assistant during filming.

Moscow, 26 October
Projection of *Miss Mend*, by Fedor Ozep and Boris Barnet, who studied cinema at Lev Kulachev's experimental laboratory.

Berlin, 30 October
Fritz Lang has finished shooting h futuristic allegory *Metropolis*. A ne special effects process combinin life-size action with models was use during filming. With its 30,000 e tras and 750 actors the film is said have cost 5 million marks.

Paris, 31 October
Gaumont-Metro-Goldwyn have ju bought the French, Belgian an Swiss rights to Abel Gance's epi historical work *Napoleon*.

New York, 7 December
The actor, Ivan Mosjoukine, ha arrived from France on his way t Hollywood to take up his five-yea contract with Universal.

Hollywood, 31 December
Josef von Sternberg's *The Sea Gu* will not be distributed, despite tw successive versions and a new titl *A Woman of the Sea*.

BIRTHS

Egypt, 25 January
Youssef Chahine

Poland, 6 March
Andrzej Wajda

New Jersey, 16 March
Jerry Lewis
(Joseph Levitch)

Italy, 19 March
Valerio Zurlini

Los Angeles, 1 June
Marilyn Monroe
(Norma Jean Baker)

Greece, 3 September
Irene Papas

Tokyo, 15 September
Shohei Imamura

France, 9 October
Danièle Delorme
(D. Girard)

Germany, 18 October
Klaus Kinski

***The Battleship Potemkin**, directed b Sergei Eisenstein, is a landmark i the cinema. Aside from its ideologica content, it is memorable for th beauty of its construction.*

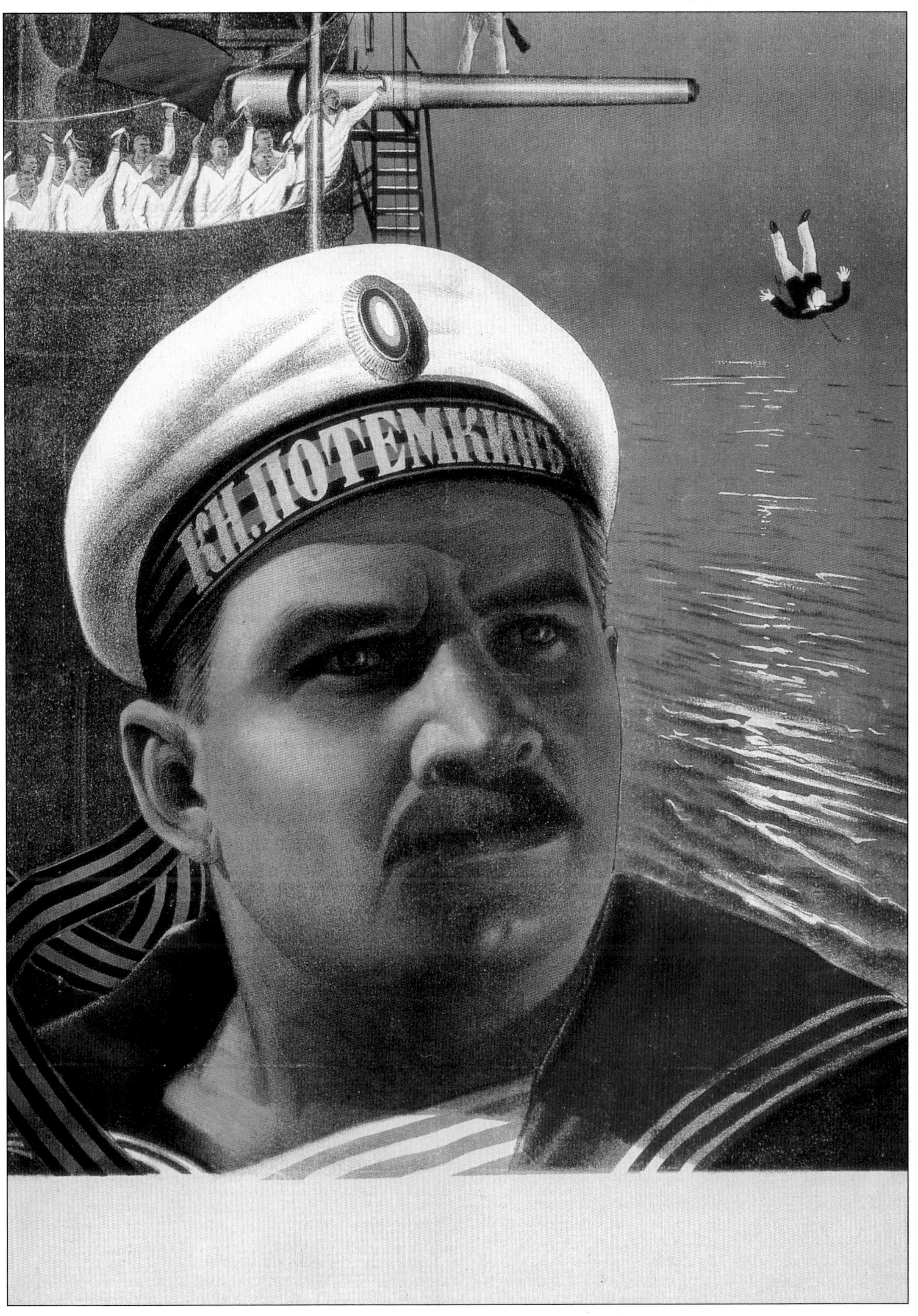
КН.ПОТЕМКИНЪ

Armand Tallier at Studio des Ursulines

*Greta Garbo in **Joyless Street**, one of the two inaugural films shown.*

Paris, 21 January
A new cinema has opened its doors in the Latin Quarter, on the site of the old Ursuline convent of Sainte-Geneviève. However, it is not a new location, since a cinema was in operation before the war at the same address, 10 rue des Ursulines, and Charles Dullin used it as a theater in 1921. Armand Tallier, one of the great stars of the French cinema for the last 10 years, is the new owner of the premises. At the Studio des Ursulines, with his friend and close associate, the well-known actress Laurence Myrga, he wishes to project "films unlike others." In other words, Tallier and Myrga wish to specialize in screening avant-garde films to an eager Parisian public. This follows the successful opening last year of the Vieux Colombier, a similar venture launched by Jean Tedesco. G.W. Pabst's *Joyless Street* and René Clair's *Entr'acte* were part of the exciting inaugural evening's program at the Studio des Ursulines. And the presence of the two famous owners attracted many celebrated and important people who came to lend their support to the experiment. Some of them came from the world of cinema – René Clair, Henri Chomette and Philippe Heriat – but there were also writers and artists such as André Breton, Philippe Soupault, Fernand Léger and Man Ray. But, for most of those present, it was the appearance of the revered Swedish actresses Greta Garbo and Asta Nielsen, the leading players in the Pabst film, that made the event an unforgettable one.

'Potemkin' joins victory and defeat

Moscow, 18 January
The official premiere of *The Battleship Potemkin*, the film commissioned to celebrate the 20th anniversary of the uprising of 1905, finally took place at the Bolshoi Theatre on 21 December last. The direction was entrusted to the 26-year-old Sergei Eisenstein, and it was written, shot and edited in four months. Taking a single obscure episode of that memorable year for its subject – the mutiny on a ship in the North Sea – Eisenstein has created a memorable film moment of recent history. The crew on board the battleship *Prince Potemkin* refuse to eat rotten meat, and the leaders of the mutiny are shot. When the civilian population of Odessa demonstrate their support for the sailors, they are mowed down by government troops. The massacre on the Odessa Steps is an extremely exciting sequence: down a seemingly endless flight of steps march soldiers advancing on the fleeing citizens. A nurse is shot, and the baby and its carriage bounce down the steps to destruction, a child lies dead in its mother's arms, and a pince-nez is caught in the tangle of ropes when the doctor's body is thrown into the water. The effects were achieved by using a trolley and a camera strapped to the waist of an acrobat. In this masterpiece, Eisenstein's theories of "the montage of attractions", which he expounded in 1923 and applied in *Strike* last yea[r] have blossomed. For example, thre[e] statues of lions express the awake[n]ing of the people by roaring wit[h] rage. At the end, a red flag is u[n]furled as the people cry, "Brothers"

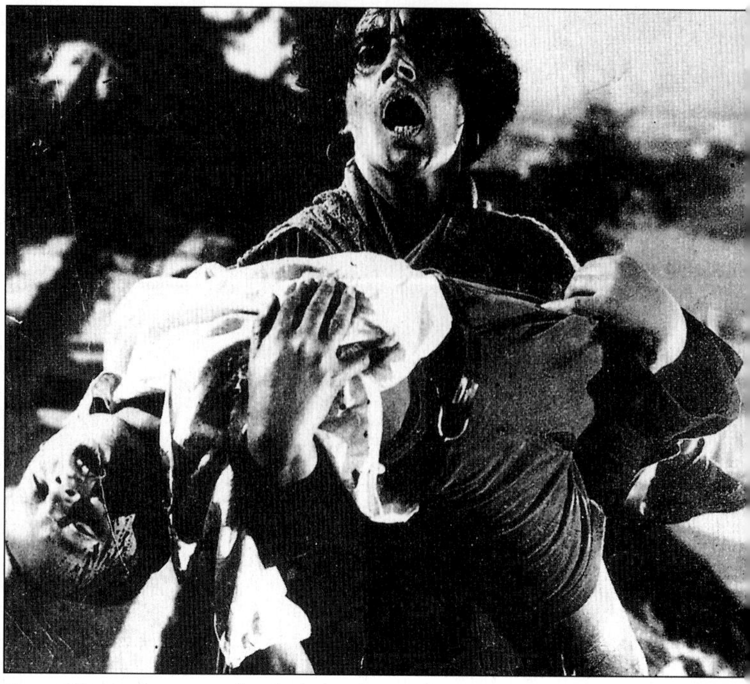

***Potemkin**, strikes a perfect balance between the literary and the visual arts.*

Matinée idol Ivor Novello stars in gripping Hitchcock thriller

London, 14 February
Ivor Novello, the handsome leading man from London's West End theater, stars as a suspected murderer, a real modern-day Jack the Ripper, in Gainsborough's *The Lodger* – a heart-stopping thriller helmed by the promising 25-year-old director Alfred Hitchcock, who was formerly the head of the titles department at the London branch of Paramount. The casting of matinee idol Novello in the part of the gentlemanly and mysterious lodger caused much comment when it was announced, but it has now been hailed as a masterstroke, with Novello giving a superb performance. The *Bioscope* has also praised the film, which is full of daring touches, as possibly "the finest British production ever made." The young director appears for a fleeting moment in one of the scenes in *The Lodger*, filling in for an extra who failed to turn up. Will he make a habit of stepping in front of the camera in his future films?

Stage star and composer Ivor Novello, an unlikely but successful choice.

pectacular action stunts in two-tone Technicolor

w York, 8 March
ouglas Fairbanks' latest film, *The ck Pirate*, is the first full-length otion picture in two-tone Techni-'or to be widely distributed. How-er, the pleasing color is only of s boisterous pirate picture's many ractions. Outstanding is a spec-ular stunt when, in order to cap-e a ship, Doug climbs up a mast d descends to the deck by piercing wide sail with his sword, ripping canvas as he goes. Other stunts lude 50 pirates swimming under ter, and the hero leaping onto the le of the ship. The director, Albert rker, an old friend of Fairbanks, eps all the elements satisfactorily oat. As for the color, the producer-r managed to obtain and use four the 11 Technicolor cameras cur-ntly in existence to considerable fect. Invented by Herbert T. Kal-us and Daniel F. Comstock, Tech-color is a two-color system which s already been used for sequences such films as *Ben-Hur* and *The antom of the Opera*. The studio nited Artists hope to use the sys-m again in the near future.

DOUGLAS FAIRBANKS in The BLACK PIRATE

reud collaborates vith G.W. Pabst

erlin, 24 March
enowned German film director .W. Pabst has been exploring the ychological theories of Dr. Sig-und Freud in his latest screen proj-t, *Secrets of a Soul*. It is the story a professor who is a victim of range torments, such as his mur-rous thoughts when innocently tting a lock of hair from his wife's ad. He therefore consults a psy-oanalyst because he associates ime with his own sexuality, and s nightmares whenever he sees or inks of a knife, a phobia which ads to an attempt to stab his wife. e depiction of the dreams is a fine ample of German Expressionist nema. The effects were achieved means of multi-layer superimpo-ions, cut-out figures against blank ckgrounds, and menacing images razors and knives. Pabst was as-sted with the script by two of reud's collaborators, the famous iennese doctor having dealt with almost identical case.

Warner Bros. risks investment in sound despite cash crisis

New York, 6 August
Warner Bros. has had a tremendous reception for its Vitaphone sound film presentation at the Warner Theater here. This two-and-a-half hour program consisted of a number of musical shorts, followed by the feature-length *Don Juan*, starring John Barrymore and Mary Astor. The film has a backing track including sound effects and a full-length score composed by William Axt and recorded by the New York Philharmonic Orchestra, but with no spoken dialogue. However, the feature project, directed by Alan Crosland, was overshadowed by the Vitaphone concert attractions, that include singers Giovanni Martinelli and Marion Tally, Mischa Elman on the violin, and a short introductory speech, recorded by Will H. Hays, the president of MPPDA. According to Mordaunt Hall, writing in the *New York Times*, the Vitaphone presentation "stirred a distinguished audience to unusual enthusiasm... The natural reproduction of voices, the tonal quality of musical instruments and the timing of the sound to the lips of singers and actions of musicians was almost uncanny." In fact during the past year, Warners has invested almost \$3 million in its experiments with sound, and is only now beginning to reap the benefits. But, if all goes well, this relatively small studio may soon become one of the major players.

WARNER BROS. present
John Barrymore
in "Don Juan"
***Don Juan**, directed by Alan Crosland, is the first film to use Vitaphone sound.*

Valentino struck down at the pinnacle of his glor

The road from Castellaneta to California

Valentino in an unexpected guise as ***Monsieur Beaucaire****, an 18th-century gallant, here with Doris Kenyon. It was a complete change of pace.*

New York, 23 August

Rudolph Valentino, adored by millions of women around the world, and derisively referred to as "The Pink Powder Puff" by some less enamored male moviegoers, has died of peritonitis at the age of 31. Death has come at a time when Valentino was $200,000 in debt and still struggling to recover from the baleful influence of his wife Natasha Rambova. After his triumph as the bullfighting hero in the 1922 *Blood and Sand*, Valentino surrendered himself to Rambova's bizarre, artistic pretensions, appearing swathed in pearls the size of tennis balls in *The Young Rajah* and demanding that Paramount give him complete control of his films. While the studio wrangled, he embarked on a nationwide tour, giving tango exhibitions. He got his way with Paramount, and under Rambova's strict tutelage his screen personality became increasingly effeminate. Moving to UA, where he made *The Eagle* and *The Son of the Sheik* with Vilma Banky, restored some of his slipping popularity, but earlier this month he was hospitalized with a perforated ulcer. The world held its breath and huge crowds gathered outside the hospital. When he died, a rumor spread that he had been poisoned by a discarded mistress, a fitting if fanciful end for the romantic Latin Lover.

As the toreador in ***Blood and Sand****.*

Multitude of admirers wracked with grief

Douglas Fairbanks, Marcus Loew, Joseph Schenck and Adolph Zukor we among the cinema's dignitaries who acted as the late star's pallbearers.

New York, 30 August

The death of Rudolph Valentino has resulted in an unprecedented outpouring of emotion. Forty thousand people turned out for his spectacular funeral in New York. Since the announcement of his death just a week ago, there have been numerous demonstrations of private despair across the United States and around the world. The American police have reported at least a dozen suicides by distraught female fans while, throughout the week, thousands filed past Valentino's coffin as he lay in state. All of America has been plunged into a veritable orgy of mourning. Even at the funeral, carried aloft by his Hollywood peers, Douglas Fairbanks, Marcus Loe Paramount chief Adolph Zuck and the chairman of United Artis Joseph Schenck, Rudy's coffin w followed by a huge crowd whi surrendered itself to collective hys ria. The funeral service almost tu ed into a riot, and dozens were jured in the crush. At the gravesic amid all of flowers, one derang female admirer attempted to slit h wrists. Only recently, Valentino c clared that, "Women are not in lo with me but with the picture of r on the screen. I am merely the ca vas on which women paint th dreams." The untimely death of t object of their obsession will n stop the fair sex from dreaming.

In one of his greatest successes, ***The Sheik****, with a swooning Agnes Ayres.*

Son of the Sheik *with Vilma Bank*

gony and madness make a masterpiece

harrowing scene of anguished women in Kinugasa's ***A Page of Madness.***

ɔkyo, 24 September
he Japanese director Teinosuke inugasa has just presented a film the German Expressionist style, ough, surprisingly, without ever aving seen any examples of the enre. *A Page of Madness* is a re- arkable work of concentrated emo- onal power, attempting to under- and the nature of insanity while ffering a straight narrative in flash- ack. This story, told with every vailable camera device, surrounds an elderly man who works voluntarily in a lunatic asylum where his wife is confined (having attempted to drown her baby son in a fit of madness many years earlier), and harbors hopes of setting her free. The 30-year-old Kinugasa had been a child actor and leading oyama (female impersonator), who turned to direction when actresses were employed in films in 1922. On the evidence of *A Page of Madness*, it can only be the cinema's gain.

MGM claims Sweden's Garbo for its own

Garbo and John Gilbert in Clarence Brown's erotic ***Flesh and the Devil.***

Los Angeles, 25 December
The opening of *Flesh and the Devil* was a premiere in more than one sense: it is the first film directed by Clarence Brown for MGM, it is the first time he has directed Greta Garbo, and it is the first pairing of John Gilbert with the Swedish star. But, however important the others are, the film belongs, without doubt, to Miss Garbo. She exudes sensuality and passion in her scenes with John Gilbert. Since arriving in Hollywood with her mentor, Mauritz Stiller, a year and a half ago, she has become a markedly better actress, and she is now consecrated as a truly American star in her third picture. Stiller, on the other hand, has had nothing but failures since his arrival. On Greta Garbo's first film, *The Torrent*, he functioned merely as assistant director and interpreter, and he was taken off *The Temptress* after only a week of shooting, to be replaced by Fred Niblo.

Buster Keaton finds humor in the tragedy of the Civil War

os Angeles, 22 December
uster Keaton's latest feature, *The eneral*, combines comedy with the ue story of a train stolen during the merican Civil War. The train is the lm's real star, reflecting Keaton's quisitive interest in machinery, nd the gags flow with an almost echanical precision. Filmed on lo- ation in Oregon, the budget gob- ed up nearly half-a-million dollars, large part of which was spent on aging a spectacular crash using a al locomotive. Many of the stunts uster performs in the film's climac- c chase are both hilarious and azardous. Perhaps the most memo- able, and equally dangerous, mo- ent in the movie comes in a period f repose when the lovelorn Buster, iling to notice the growing motion f the drive shaft on top of which he perched, describes a series of elancholy parabolas.

Keaton in ***The General,*** *a film inspired by authentic events of the Civil War.*

Russia also loves 'General' Keaton

БЕСТЕР КИТОН
ГЕНЕРАЛ

Popular even in Russia, the country which produced this poster.

1927

Paris, 1 January
A prefectorial order provides for a ban on the production of films made of inflammable material.

Paris, 18 January
New studios have been inaugurated by the producer Bernard Natan in rue Francœur, and Henri Diamant-Berger is there to direct a new film, *The Education of the Prince*, with Edna Purviance.

Paris, 25 January
Marcel L'Herbier has commenced work again on *le Diable au cœur* in Gaumont's Buttes-Chaumont studios. Filming was interrupted by Betty Balfour's illness and the death of the actor Mévisto.

Prague, 31 January
The Czechoslovakian League has proposed a program of action to protect national creativity.

Hollywood, 31 January
Eastman-Kodak held a meeting for professionals to promote the use of panchromatic film.

New York, 8 February
King Vidor has been shooting *The Crowd* here, with Eleanor Boardman. The film is in a similar realist vein to *The Big Parade*.

Paris, 11 March
Inauguration of the Museum of Photography and Cinematography at the National Conservatory of Arts and Crafts.

Paris, 12 March
Bernard Natan and Louis Albert have started work on the production of *The Life of Joan of Arc*, to be filmed by Marco de Gastyne. For the lead role, they are looking for "a young brunette of good height with equestrian experience."

Ukraine, 23 March
Alexander Dovzhenko's first full-length film, *The Diplomatic Pouch*, has been filmed here for Odessa productions.

Paris, 31 March
The young filmmaker Marc Allégret has finished the cutting on his short documentary, *Voyage to the Congo*. André Gide assisted on the Jean Renoir production in which a Parvo Debrie movie camera was used.

New York, 25 April
The German actor Emil Jannings has made his first film in America *The Way of All Flesh*, directed by Victor Fleming.

Alexandria, 5 May
Screening in this city of *A Kiss from Alexandria*, directed, acted in and produced by Bader Ibrahim and his brother Lama.

New York, 11 May
Founding of the Academy of Motion Pictures Arts and Sciences at the instigation of Louis B. Mayer.

France, 16 May
Maurice Tourneur is on location at Le Bourget to film the flying scenes for *l'Equipage* (*The Crew*), adapted from the book by Joseph Kessel.

Paris, 16 May
Adolph Zukor has named the new cinema being built on the boulevard des Italiens, the Paramount.

France, 31 May
Director Jean Renoir was lucky to escape from a nasty accident in the forest of Fontainebleau. The car was driven by his friend, actor Pierre Champagne, who was killed on impact. He had failed to take a difficult bend in the road. Poachers, who happened to be on the scene, took the director to a hospital.

Hollywood, 28 June
Louis B. Mayer has renewed Greta Garbo's MGM contract at a salary of $5,000 per week.

Paris, 30 June
Germaine Dulac is making *la Coquille et le clergyman* (*The Seashell and the Clergyman*), with Antonin Artaud, who also wrote the script.

Paris, 6 July
Gaumont has brought out an aluminum camera with variable speed intended for use by news reporters.

Hollywood, 23 August
Josef von Sternberg has at last won out after a series of humiliations. His film *Underworld* is an enormous success. He was asked to make the film by Paramount's production chief B.P. Schulberg from a script written by Ben Hecht, a journalist who has inside knowledge of the film's criminal milieu.

Geneva, 23 August
Thousands of demonstrators, who were protesting against the execution of the Italian anarchists Nicola Sacco and Bartolomeo Vanzetti in Boston, have vandalized cinemas advertising American films.

London, 23 August
Rudolph Valentino fans have created an association to help circulate his films and to do good deeds "in memory of the period when he was without friends or money."

Hollywood, 28 August
Projection of *Three's a Crowd*, the directorial debut of Harry Langdon.

Washington, 9 September
As the result of a six-year inquiry into the block-booking system, the Federal Trades Commission has ordered the Famous Players-Lasky production company to stop the practice, which they believe to be restrictive and monopolistic.

Los Angeles, 21 September
Release of *Wings*, the first Hollywood film dealing with the subject of military aviation. The ace flyer William Wellman directed.

Berlin, 23 September
Release of *Berlin – Symphony of a Big City*, by Walter Ruttman, based on an idea by Karl Freund.

Nice, 30 September
Franco-Film have bought out the Victorine Studios.

Tokyo, 14 October
Yasujiro Ozu's first film, *The Sword of Penitence*, is now screening.

Hollywood, 22 October
Howard Hughes, the Texan industrialist, continues his involvement with the cinema industry with the production of *Two Arabian Nights*. Lewis Milestone is the director.

Paris, 9 November
La Vie sans joie (aka *Catherine*), filmed by Albert Dieudonné in 1924 with Catherine Hessling and based on a scenario by Jean Renoir, has been released at last.

Cairo, 16 November
Aziza Amir and Wedad Orfy have released *Laila*, the first film from their new production company.

Paris, 19 November
MGM's *Ben-Hur*, directed by Fr Niblo, has moved into the 32 week of an exclusive run at t Madeleine Opera. Ticket sales ready exceed 4 million francs.

New York, 29 November
Gala premiere of F.W. Murnau *Sunrise*, with Janet Gaynor ar George O'Brien.

Montreal, 4 December
A parish letter from 17 archbisho and bishops from the provinces Quebec forbids Catholics to go the cinema on Sundays.

New York, 31 December
Due to its investment in talking pi tures and the triumph of *The Ja Singer*, Warner Bros. is out of t red for the first time in two years

Poland, 31 December
Léon Trystan, a virulent your theater critic and a disciple of th theories of Abel Gance and Jea Epstein, has filmed *The Revolt Blood and Iron*.

Paris, December
The journalist Jean-Placide Ma claire has opened a cinema for avan garde films, Studio 28, on the Butt Montmartre.

BIRTHS

Italy, 4 July
Gina Lollobrigida

New York, 16 September
Peter Falk

New York, 31 October
Lee Grant (Lyova Rosenthal)

Paris, 30 December
Robert Hossein

DEATHS

New York, 6 September
Marcus Loew

Hollywood, 5 October
Samuel Warner

Janet Gaynor and Charles Farre star in ***Seventh Heaven****. Directed b Frank Borzage, their performance are outstanding in a poignant fil which is immensely successful.*

WILLIAM FOX PRESENTS
THE MOTION PICTURE
7th HEAVEN
by AUSTIN STRONG
with
JANET GAYNOR
CHARLES FARRELL
BASED ON JOHN GOLDEN'S STAGE SUCCESS · FRANK BORZAGE PRODUCTION

'Metropolis', a startling voyage into the future

Berlin, 10 January
Fritz Lang's eagerly-awaited new film *Metropolis* was shown at the UFA Palast in the presence of 2,500 guests, among them the Chancellor Wilhelm Marx, the ministers Gustav Streseman and Otto Gessler and the head of the Reichsbank Hjalmar Schacht. This long (three-and-a-half hours) movie cost nearly 5 million marks and required 11 months to complete – a record for a German production. It is a work of science fiction, which takes place in the year 2000 in a gigantic city that is called Metropolis. Exploited by the factory owner who treats them like slaves, the down-trodden workers prepare for a rebellion. Only the charisma of one young woman (Brigitte Helm) prevents it. However, opposing her is a mad scientist (Rudolph Klein-Rogge), who has created a robot, a perfect replica of young Maria. The robot, or 'false Maria' succeeds in stirring up the workers and in pushing the people to revolt. Happily all ends out well: the robot is destroyed, the workers recover their freedom, and the young woman is married to the industrialist's son. The scenario, both ambitious and also surprisingly naive, was inspired by New York and its skyscrapers, which Fritz Lang remembered from a visit to the U.S. in November 1924. After the success of *The Niebelungen*, the director, with his wife Thea von Harbou, started work on the futuristic story. Filming began in May 1925 in the UFA studios in Neubabelsberg. From the start, the plan to build huge, cumbersome sets gave way to the use of miniatures, thanks to the Schüfftan process. Developed by the cameraman Eugen Schüfftan, it is a means of combining live action with models or artwork. A mirror mounted in front of the camera at an angle of 45 degrees to the optical axis both reflects light and allows light to pass through. Beyond the mirror, in line with the camera axis, is placed a full-size detail of the set a 90 degrees to the camera so that it reflected into the camera lens by th mirror. A mask is then put on th back of the mirror over that are from which only the reflected imag is required; the rest of the mod remains visible through the mirro By using this method, a great deal o money was saved. But, in order t show the huge cast to best advan tage, Erich Pommer, the artistic d rector of UFA, agreed that parts o the city had to be constructed. Un fortunately, these turned out to b extremely costly to build, and proba bly led to his falling out of favo The Tower of Babel scene, shot a Rehbergen, alone needed severa weeks filming, sometimes taking 1 hours a day, and the flooding of th basements required many months o hard labor. It is hoped that the likel success of the film will help kee UFA afloat, because its shares hav been declining recently.

METROPOLIS
EIN FILM VON FRITZ LANG
IN DEN HAUPTROLLEN:
BRIGITTE HELM · GUSTAV FRÖHLICH
AN DER KAMERA: KARL FREUND, GÜNTHER RITTAU

A futuristic vision of life with a machine playing the dominant role.

The revolt of the workers paves the way to a new and harmonious world.

Fritz Lang, the 'deus ex machina'.

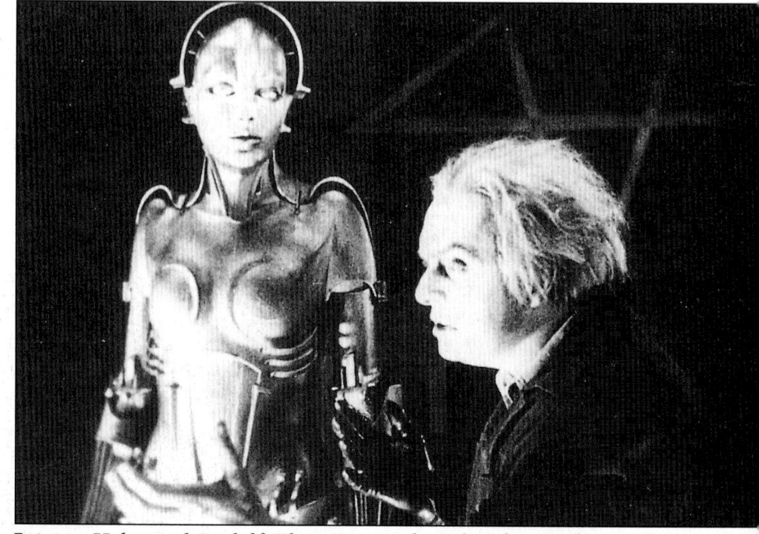
Brigitte Helm and Rudolf Klein-Rogge: the robot face to face with its master

ara Bow, the beautiful girl who has 'It'

ıra Bow (left), the 'It' girl, with writer Elinor Glyn who first used the term.

·w York, 5 February
e director Clarence Badger's new n carries the shortest of titles, *It.* actly what "It" is remains a mat- of lively debate, but Elinor Glyn, romantic novelist who has coin- the expression, affirms that it's a gnetic quality that is found in ıancipated women. And as far as yn is concerned, Clara Bow is the y actress capable of capturing s elusive attribute on the screen. ost male filmgoers have a notion t "It" is just another word for od old-fashioned sex appeal, an ribute which the ripe-bodied, sau- -eyed Bow has got in abundance. ara, a former beauty queen, has me a long way fast since breaking o films in 1923 in *Down to the Sea Ships*, after director Elmer Clifton otted her photograph in a fan ıgazine. She was taken up by inde- ndent producer B.P Schulberg, o cast her in over a dozen films in 25, including *The Plastic Age*, in ich she was billed as "The Hottest zz Baby in Films". Clara then companied Schulberg to Para- ount where she scored a big hit th *Mantrap*, as a bored housewife ntemplating an affair with lawyer rcy Marmont. By now Bow was a g enough star for *It* to be built ound her vibrant sexuality. It's no ore than a flimsy vehicle, featuring st a walk-on part for Miss Glyn, in ich Bow races around energeti- lly as a shopgirl who sets her eye on handsome store-owner Antonio Moreno, but it has established her as the queen of the Paramount lot. Barreling down Wilshire Boulevard in her red roadster, Jazz Baby Bow is the embodiment of the frantic spirit of the age. Indeed, her private *amours* are causing comment!

Harry Langdon confirms his comic genius

Los Angeles, 10 April
Whey-faced little Harry Langdon is emerging as a serious rival to Charlie Chaplin, Buster Keaton and Harold Lloyd. In his third feature film, *Long Pants*, Langdon demonstrates an original comic genius as a meek weightlifter's assistant cleaning up a modern Sodom. Langdon first went into films with Mack Sennett in 1923 after over 20 years as an entertainer, best known for an act in which a baby-faced man presides over the collapse of his automobile. At the Sennett studio, director Harry Edwards and gagmen Arthur Ripley and Frank Capra developed the character for the screen, "just a crumb from the sponge cake of life", as he was introduced in a Sennett short, *Saturday Afternoon*. But then Langdon left Sennett for a six-picture deal with First National, taking his three collaborators with him. Edwards directed his first feature, *Tramp, Tramp, Tramp*, a big hit co-starring Joan Crawford, and Capra took over for *The Strong Man* and *Long Pants*. Now Langdon has fired Capra and will direct himself.

Harry Langdon plays the leading role in ***Long Pants****, which he also produced.*

Cecil B. DeMille, maker of films and propagator of the faith

New York, 19 April
Cecil B. DeMille's new film *King of Kings* has just opened here at the Gaiety Theater. Coming three-and-a-half years after his triumph with *The Ten Commandments*, the director turned to the Bible once again and has produced yet another large-scale epic of ancient times. During the intervening years a lot has happened to Mr. DeMille. His continuing difficulties with the management of Famous Players-Lasky (or Paramount) finally led to a break with this giant studio which he himself had helped found in the mid-teens. He left the company early in 1925, at a time when the trend in Hollywood was firmly pointing to a greater concentration of power in the large companies. However, once he had decided to buck the system, DeMille quickly succeeded in establishing himself as a leading independent producer and director. Aided by his friends on Wall Street, he purchased the old Ince studios and began releasing his films through the then newly-reorganized Producers Distributing Corporation (PDC). As production head of the studio, he helped plan and supervise the work of other directors in addition to turning out his own films. The lavish execution of his latest project, *King of Kings*, reflects the success he has made of his independence.

The impressive Last Supper scene from Cecil B. DeMille's ***King of Kings****.*

Abel Gance's 'Napoleon' is a lyrical apotheosis

Damia embodies the 'Marseillaise'.

The Italian army's departure provides a grandiose climax to the film.

Abel Gance in the role of Saint-Ju

Artistic creation and financial backing

Paris, 7 April
Abel Gance's big historical fresco, *Napoleon*, opened triumphantly last night at the Opéra. The copy shown, which runs for a lengthy three-and-a-quarter hours, was specially produced for the occasion. French cinema alone could not have undertaken the financing of a work of this size, thus Gance began by knocking on numerous foreign doors. Unfortunately, the financial aid he obtained, notably from the Italian producer Guiseppe Barattolo, turned out to be insufficient. Then a miracle occurred. Two international financiers offered their assistance: the Russian emigré Vladimir Wengeroff and the German Hugo Stinnes. They were joined by investors from Czechoslovakia, Sweden, Spain, Great Britain and, of course, France – in the form of Pathé Cinéma. On 19 May 1924, the co-producers created an association of members to subscribe part of the necessary capital (140 shares at 50,000 francs each). Nevertheless, bankruptcy of the Stinnes Group, following the sudden death of Hugo Stinnes, disrupted this new financial scheme. Gance had to exert a great deal of time and effort during four months in order to keep the massive project afloat, but it was taken up again in November with the aid of Société Générale de Films.

"Qu'on délivre
ces deux hommes.
Ils sont libres!
Je puis bien leur
pardonner,
mais oublier
c'est autre chose."
(Hist.-d'Abrantès)

Technical advance at the service of an idea

Paris, 14 November
Great crowds gathered this evening at the Marivaux Theatre for the first showing to the general public of Abel Gance's *Napoleon*, in its full-length version consisting of around 15,000 metres. The film contains six episodes, which depict the life of Napoleon (Albert Dieudonné): his childhood, his military schooling, and his rise to power. The idea for the film came to Gance in 1921 after he had seen, and been immensely impressed by, D.W. Griffith's *Birth of a Nation*. In addition, the French director wanted to create a natior fresco. In the year of the centena of the death of Napoleon, his choi of subject could not have been mo appropriate. This important page French history lends itself perfec to visual evocation, displaying the resources of the cinema. Wh the choice of subject was mad Gance, by the curious phenomen of mimicry, transformed hims into a leader of men, exercising extraordinary influence over his c laborators and interpreters. Aft years of preparation, shooting b gan in January 1925 and finish the following August. At the en nearly 450,000 metres of film h been exposed by 18 cameras. The were used in countless ways: carri at arms length, attached to swing strapped to a horse's back, and se into the air in balloons. Given t immense quantity of film used, t editing alone required almost a yea The results show that Gance h extended the limits of the cinem thanks to the many inventions ar technical innovations. On occasio three scenes are juxtaposed on screen simultaneously. This proce has given unequaled scope to s quences such as the departure f the Italian campaign. And the mo impressive symbolic set-piece se Bonaparte sailing back from Cors ca in a storm while the storm in t Convention rages.

Albert Dieudonné gives a superbly convincing performance as Napoleon.

rauman's Chinese Theater: a palace of fantasy and dreams

MGMP-12045

rowds gather outside Grauman's Chinese Theater, which opened with DeMille's spectacular **King of Kings**.

ollywood, 19 May
oday sees the formal opening of per-showman Sid Grauman's Chi-se Theater. Just over a year ago e ground for the theater was bro-n with a gold-plated shovel by orma Talmadge. Now, its green bronze pagoda roof towers above a spectacular forecourt in which two large stone dogs stand guard at the entrance to this temple of cinema. In front of the stone dogs a bronze statue symbolizes the human genius of poetry and drama. Last night the theater was the venue for a special premiere of director Cecil B. DeMille's *King of Kings* before a select audience of 2,000. Outside, a crowd of 50,000 gathered. There was equal billing for Grauman, DeMille and Christ, in that order.

harlie Chaplin's marital setbacks arouse strong reactions

ita Grey during the difficult divorce oceedings which she instigated.

Fresh upheavals in his private life have disturbed work on ***The Circus.***

ollywood, 22 August
harlie Chaplin has just concluded e messiest of divorces from Lita rey, whom he married in 1924. he settlement requires Chaplin to ay Lita a lump sum of $600,000 nd set up trust funds of $100,000 r each of his sons, one-year-old ydney Earle and the two-year-old harles Spencer. The long and bit-r divorce case which followed Lita Grey's departure from the Chaplin home with her children last November has attracted lurid headlines and much prurient public attention. The complaint filed by Lita ran to 52 pages in length, and much of its grubbing detail was aimed at destroying Chaplin's reputation in the eyes of a public still shocked by both the Arbuckle and William Desmond Taylor scandals. Pirated copies of the complaint have been widely circulated. Earlier this month Lita threatened to name five "prominent women" with whom her husband had affairs during their marriage. This threat precipitated the cash settlement, the largest thus far in American legal history. Chaplin's hair turned white during the ordeal and now has to be dyed for filming. But his public remain loyal.

Greta Garbo strikes a lucrative blow

Hollywood, 1 July
Greta Garbo has established herself as a star, playing the dangerous seductress of *Flesh and the Devil.* This is her first film with John Gilbert, with whom she is now romantically linked. Garbo has demanded that MGM reconsider her contract as it has remained unchanged at $600 a week since her first film for the studio, *The Torrent*, released in 1925. Much has changed since her arrival in Hollywood with her mentor, the Swedish director Mauritz Stiller, only to be greeted by a skeptical Louis B. Mayer, who said to her, "American men don't like fat women." MGM had no plans for Stiller, and he returned to Europe after being taken off Garbo's second film, *The Temptress.* In the meantime Garbo has lost weight and created the sophisticated, scornful screen personality which Stiller intended for her from the moment he spotted the young actress at the beginning of her career. Having refused all new projects at MGM, she has emerged triumphant from the battle of wills with a chastened Mayer. Her reward is a salary of $5,000 a week.

Ivan Mosjoukine plays Casanova

Paris, 13 September
The numerous French admirers of Ivan Mosjoukine, the actor of Russian origin, will be delighted to welcome him in the title role of *Casanova.* The film, released today, is a sumptuous Franco-German production directed by Alexander Volkoff. The latter emigrated to France along with Mosjoukine and other compatriots such as the producers Ermoliev, the founder of Albatros Films, and Alexander Kamenka and Noé Bloch, who bought the company in 1922. As in *Kean*, which was considered a self-portrait, the versatile Mosjoukine has found, in Casanova, a role which has allowed him to express his delirious romanticism and powerful temperament. The remarkable performance of the celebrated Venetian seducer has been warmly received, even if the film has been greeted in a churlish manner by certain commentators.

'The Jazz Singer' heralds end of silent cinema

The rabbi's son a hit in blackface

New York, 6 October

Wild excitement has greeted the premiere of Warner Brothers' *The Jazz Singer*, the first motion picture in which spoken dialogue is heard. The studio had been in serious financial difficulties for some time. But, emboldened by the success of their John Barrymore vehicle, *Don Juan*, released last summer and the first feature film to use Warners' Vitaphone sound-on-disc system for sound effects and synchronized score, they staked everything on *The Jazz Singer*. The story of a cantor's son torn between the synagogue and show business, *The Jazz Singer* was originally a stage hit for George Jessel, who had already appeared for the studio in a 1926 silent picture entitled *Izzy Murphy*. Jessel wanted too much money to move into the uncharted territory of the "talkers", and comedian Eddie Cantor proved to be equally unwilling. Consequently, Warners turned to the greatest entertainer in the world, Al Jolson, who agreed to play the role of Jakie Rabinowitz for a fee of $75,000. It was inspired casting because Jolson brings all of his legendary attack to a piece of undiluted *schmaltz*, which remains a silent film on to which certain songs and snatches of dialogue, most of the latter improvised, have been none too subtly grafted. However, the moment that Jolson launched himself into "Toot, Toot, Tootsie Goodbye" and the show-stopping blackface "Mammy" routine, the audience went wild. And when he told them, "You ain't heard nothin' yet!" pandemonium broke out in the theater. It's unfortunate that none of the four Warner brothers was able to attend this successful premiere. Tragically, Sam Warner, the driving force behind the Vitaphone experiment, died of a sinus infection just 24 hours earlier. Harry, Albert and Jack Warner traveled immediately by train to Los Angeles for the funeral, missing a historic, and clearly defining, moment in a new era of cinema.

WARNER BROS. SUPREME TRIUMPH
AL JOLSON
IN
The JAZZ SINGER

Al Jolson and May McAvoy star in a film that marks a successful first attempt at sound for the Warner brothers.

WARNER Supreme Triumph
AL JOLSON IN THE JAZZ SINGER
WITH VITAPHONE
2.30 TWICE DAILY 8.45
Sunday Matinees 3. P.M.
WARNERS
WARNERS' THEATRE
WARNERS' AL JOLSON "THE JAZZ SINGER"
WORLD SER
MATINEE T
FLETCHER

New Yorkers throng ten-deep to purchase tickets outside the most famous marquee in American cinema history.

Bittersweet night for the Warners

New York, 6 October

The death of Sam Warner from sinus infection resulting from an c broken nose injury has deprived t Warner brothers of their moment triumph with *The Jazz Singer*. T sons of Polish immigrant paren the Warner brothers took their fi steps in the movie business in 19 when their father acquired a nic elodeon in Newcastle, Pennsylvan Eleven-year-old Jack, the young of 12 children, sang to the audien during intermissions. Two years l er, he joined his brothers Har Albert and Sam in a film distrib tion venture which was soon forc to sell out to the Patents Compa They returned to exhibition and a moved into production, but wi little success until 1918, when th released their first feature film, *A Four Years in Germany*. In 19 they established Warner Brothe West Coast Studio in Burbank, Ca fornia. By the spring of 1923, t studio was fully incorporated Warner Brothers and big enough f the simultaneous shooting of films. In 1925 they absorbed Vi graph with its New York studio, a then in 1926 formed a subsidia called Vitaphone, in associati with Western Electric, to develop sound-on-disc system for motio pictures. This gamble has produc *The Jazz Singer*.

new stage for Murnau in the glowing splendor of his 'Sunrise'

ʳnau, wearing a white cap, filming a scene for his first American movie.

w York, 29 November
h the quality of films such as *feratu* and *The Last Laugh*, F.W. rnau established himself as one he great German directors. Now he is being placed on an equal footing with the most talented of his American colleagues. Seduced by *The Last Laugh*, William Fox did not wait long to invite the brilliant young cinéaste to come and work for his company. The "German Genius" arrived here together with two of his habitual collaborators, scenarist Carl Mayer and set designer and costumer Rochus Gliese. Side by side, the trio worked on their first American film, *Sunrise*, which the Carthay Circle Theater is showing at a gala premiere. Despite the fact that Fox imposed certain scenes and a happy ending against the director's will, as well as cutting the film by 20 minutes, it remains a splendid work. *Sunrise* is a poetic melodrama, adapted from the German writer Hermann Sudermann, about a farmer's wife (Janet Gaynor) whose husband, played by actor George O'Brien, is urged to drown her by a city woman. But the husband thinks better of it, and the couple go on a second honeymoon to the metropolis. The most impressive sequence is the trip to the big city by trolley car, where she sits transfixed while the scenery whizzes by.

A rich crop from USSR this year

Moscow, 13 December
The vitality of the Soviet cinema has been very much in evidence this year with the release of a number of excellent films: some experimental, some naturalistic, some more traditional, and some all three. One of the first of the films commissioned to celebrate the tenth anniversary of the Revolution is Pudovkin's *The End of St. Petersburg*, which includes spectacular scenes showing the storming of the Winter Palace. Another truly splendid film that pays homage to Russian revolutionary history is Yacov Protazanov's *The Forty First*, about a woman serving in the Red army who takes prisoner a soldier of the retreating White army. In contrast, films such as Abram Room's *Bed and Sofa* and Boris Barnet's *Girl with the Hatbox* concentrate on the housing shortage in Moscow and the devastating effect it has on relationships.

net Gaynor and George O'Brien, the sad and tender married couple.

Wonderful 'Wings' flies higher and higher

WINGS
a Paramount Picture
LUCIEN HUBBARD PRODUCTION
Story by JOHN MONK SAUNDERS
Directed by WILLIAM A. WELLMAN

Los Angeles, 23 December
Since its premiere in August, *Wings*, with its spectacular and unfaked aerial sequences, has had a rapturous reception whenever it is shown, and is now set for a nationwide general release early next month. Paramount executives, who took a $2 million chance on young director and ace flying man William Wellman, are rubbing their hands in glee at the box-office lines. The cast, too, have reason to be delighted. Small-part player Gary Cooper, following his success in *The Winning of Barbara Worth*, excels in his one scene and has been signed to a contract, while Charles 'Buddy' Rogers and Richard Arlen are no longer up-and-coming but have arrived.

1928

Great Britain, 1 January
The Quota Act has been put into practice. This Act stipulates that domestic production must make up a minimum of 7.5 percent of films screened.

Hollywood, 21 January
The success of *Underworld* has given Josef von Stenberg the opportunity to make *The Last Command* with Emil Jannings.

Los Angeles, 13 February
Release of *Four Sons*, the first sound (but not talking) film directed by John Ford.

Moscow, 5 March
Release of *The Sold Appetite*, by Nicolas Okhlopkov, based on a short story by French writer Paul Lafargue, Karl Marx's son-in-law.

Berlin, 22 March
Release of *Spione* (*Spies*), directed by Fritz Lang for UFA, with Rudolph Klein-Rogge, Gerda Maurus and Willy Fritsch.

Paris, 23 March
Abel Gance has filed a complaint against Gaumont-Metro-Goldwyn for screening a revised version of his film *Napoleon* at the Gaumont Palace without his consent.

Ukraine, 13 April
With the release of *Zvenigora*, a lyrical hymn to his native country, Alexander Dovzhenko proves himself equal to Eisenstein and Pudovkin, the two greats of Soviet cinema.

Moscow, 12 May
Sergei Eisenstein has been appointed to a professorial chair at the GTK Institute of Cinema.

Los Angeles, 15 May
Mickey Mouse takes his first steps in Walt Disney's *Plane Crazy*.

Copenhagen, 11 June
Axel Petersen and Arnold Poulsen have demonstrated their new sound and talking film system at the Grand Theatre.

Paris, 15 June
The Bruno Rahn film with Asta Nielsen, *The Tragedy of the Streets*, which has been running for four months at the Studio des Ursulines, is now showing at the Corso Opera.

New York, 6 July
Preview of the first 'real talking' film, *Lights of New York*. Directed by Brian Foy, with Helene Costello and Cullen Landis, the film features dialogue in 22 of its 244 sequences.

Moscow, 1 August
Sergei Eisenstein has been invited to Hollywood by Joseph Schenck, the president of United Artists.

Berlin, 31 August
Release of *Zuflucht* (*The Refuge*), directed by Carl Froelich and starring Henny Porten. It addresses the human consequences of war.

Paris, 14 September
Charles Dullin is the producer for Jean Grémillon's first full-length film, *Maldone*.

Hollywood, 22 September
Buster Keaton has made his first silent film for MGM, *The Cameraman*. Edward Sedgwick directs.

New York, 22 September
Paramount has released a its part-talking film, *Beggars of Life*. It is directed by William Wellman, with Richard Arlen and Louise Brooks.

Paris, 25 September
General Films have decided not to go ahead with *The Fall of Eagles*, as a sequel to Abel Gance's *Napoleon*. Gance has passed the script to German producer Peter Ostermayer.

Paris, September
By mutual agreement, Gaumont and MGM dissolved the partnership they set up in April 1924. Both parties prefer to be independent.

New York, 1 October
Warner Bros. has bought a majority stake in First National Pictures. Henceforth it controls its studios, distribution network and cinemas.

Paris, 5 October
Studio 28 has released *The Fall of the House of Usher*, adapted from Edgar Allan Poe, and directed by Jean Epstein with the assistance of Luis Buñuel.

New York, 28 October
A recently-created weekly newsreel, *Movietone News*, will be distributed regularly to cinemas throughout the U.S. beginning 3 December.

Berlin, 30 October
The UFA circuit has inaugurated the Universum cinema, which seats 1,791 and is equipped with impressive Oskalyd organs.

Paris, 31 October
The Société des Cinéromans has constructed a studio to make films in "natural colors" using the method invented by the Frenchmen Keller-Dorian and Berthon. Jacques de Baroncelli is already there to film *la Femme et le pantin* (*The Woman and the Puppet*), with André Roanne and Dolly Davis.

Prague, 2 November
Release of *Mountain Village*, made by Miroslav Josef Kransky, and based on the novel by Bozena Nemcova, one of the great classics of Czech literature.

Hollywood, 5 November
Maurice Chevalier, who arrived here on 26 October for a Paramount project, has started making his first film, *Innocents of Paris*, under the direction of Richard Wallace.

Moscow, 5 November
Release of *Storm over Asia* directed by Vsevolod Pudovkin.

Los Angeles, 18 November
In his third film, Walt Disney's *Steamboat Willie*, Mickey Mouse speaks for the first time. It follows on the first all-talking cartoon, Paul Terry's *Dinner Time*, which premiered in New York in September.

Hollywood, 23 November
Victor Seastrom (Sjöström), who made *The Scarlet Letter* under contract to MGM has reached the peak of his art with *The Wind* for the same studio.

Berlin, 6 December
A fire broke out in the UFA buildings, destroying all the films in the laboratories. These included a print of Carl Dreyer's *The Passion of Joan of Arc*.

Los Angeles, 18 December
Metro-Goldwyn-Mayer has filmed an opening logo in its Culver City studios. It consists of a superb roaring lion enclosed in a scroll-like frame, accompanied by the firm's new motto, *Ars gratia artis* (Art for arts sake). The lion is known as Leo.

Rome, 20 December
The journalist Alessandro Blas has created a production coop tive with a group of aspiring fi makers. He has called it Augus and is presently starting work on first film as a director, *Sole*.

Hollywood, 31 December
Fox has released Howard Haw first aviation film *The Air Circus*

BIRTHS

Rome, 1 January
Ennio Morricone

Paris, 23 January
Jeanne Moreau

France, 24 January
Michel Serrault

Paris, 26 January
Roger Vadim
(Rivi Plemiannikov)

Germany, 16 March
Hardy Kruger

Paris, 2 April
Serge Gainsbourg
(Lucien Ginsburg)

California, 23 April
Shirley Temple

Milan, 11 May
Marco Ferreri

Rome, 14 July
Lina Wertmuller

New York, 26 July
Stanley Kubrick

Lithuania, 1 October
Laurence Harvey
(Lerushka Skikne)

Brazil, 22 October
Nelson Pereira Dos Santos

Havana, 11 December
Tomas Gutierrez Alea

France, 23 December
Pierre Etaix

Despite trouble with the Hays offi over its steamy subject matter, So erset Maugham's ***Rain*** *has be filmed as* ***Sadie Thompson*** *with G ria Swanson and Lionel Barrymor*

GLORIA SWANSON
in
"Sadie Thompson"
Based on the Story by W. SOMERSET MAUGHAM
Directed by RAOUL WALSH
-UNITED ARTISTS PICTURE-

Alfred Hugenberg named head of UFA

Berlin, 2 January
The new year has begun with some major changes in the German film industry. The largest studio of all, the giant Universum Film Aktien Gesellschaft, or UFA, is in serious financial trouble after the box-office failure of two of its most prestigious recent productions, F.W. Murnau's version of *Faust* and, more notably, the extremely costly *Metropolis* directed by Fritz Lang. Last May the company revealed that *Metropolis* had cost an unbelievable 5 million marks, and Lang was blamed for the company's growing financial problems. He protested, but found little support among the management or from producer Erich Pommer. In fact, Pommer himself was dislodged from his position as the head of the company, while Alfred Hugenberg has emerged as the new man of the moment. An independent producer who had previously founded Deulig, a company specializing in propaganda films since 1912, Hugenberg is also an active member of the right-wing National Socialist Party. He has managed to save the debt-ridden UFA from bankruptcy by organizing a new controlling trust, however, unfortunately, under his influence UFA is becoming an outlet for nationalist propaganda.

Charlie the clown finds his natural element in 'The Circus'

Los Angeles, 27 January
Charlie Chaplin's new film, *The Circus*, which premiered in New York on 6 January, has just opened in California at Grauman's Chinese Theater. The production has occupied Chaplin for a little over two years, not least because of his marital problems with Lita Grey and the subsequent complications of their divorce. At several points during the divorce proceedings, possession of the film itself was fought over by the two sides' lawyers. Production on the nearly-completed film was suspended early in December 1926 and not resumed until October 1927. The filming itself also had its fraught moments, particularly the 200 takes Chaplin made in a cage with real lions. Now this is almost forgotten in the excitement surrounding the film's release. *The Circus* contains some vintage Chaplin, but the public response has been less enthusiastic than the ecstatic reception given *The Gold Rush*. The filmmaker's obs sive pursuit of perfection has or again resulted in colossal quantit of discarded film – the final 6,5 foot version was edited down fr 211,000 feet. Reportedly, Chap did hundreds of takes before bei satisfied with a particularly tric tightrope scene, in which the Tra is beset by both monkeys and falli trousers. The result reflects the fluence of Harold Lloyd's "th comedy" while betraying some Chaplin's feelings about his rece marital woes.

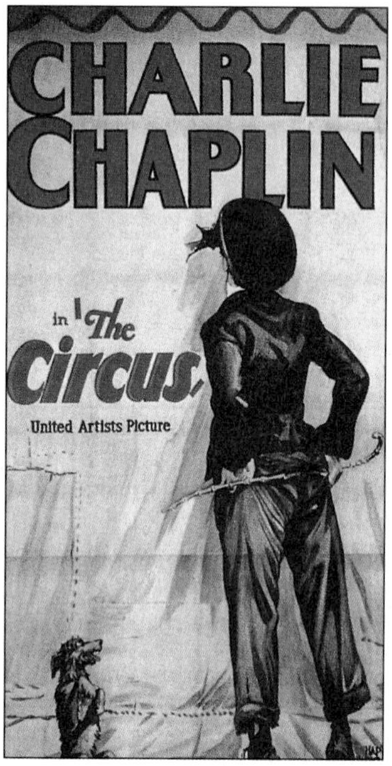
CHARLIE
CHAPLIN
in The Circus
United Artists Picture

Charlie Chaplin's co-star is Merna Kennedy, Lita Grey's childhood friend.

Artaud and the surrealists provoke a riot at the Ursulines

Paris, 9 February
The history of the cinematographic avant-garde will remain, without a doubt, indebted to Madame Germaine Dulac for a night to remember, and for a film that lasts barely 25 minutes. The director of *The Smiling Madame Beudet* unintentionally caused a riot when she presented her latest film, *The Seashell and the Clergyman*, in a program of experimental films at the Studio des Ursulines. It is based on a scenario by the poet Antonin Artaud, who intended to direct it and play the lead. He later withdrew, and claims that the film has betrayed his intentions by using the device of a dream as an alibi for his eroticism. Determined to demonstrate his opposition, Artaud alerted his friends who comprise the group of surrealists and who arrived in full force at the Studio des Ursulines to sabotage the performance. Robert Desnos got the rebellion started by shouting, "Madame Dulac is a cow!" Armand Tallier, the owner of the theater and organizer of the evening, protested that he would not tolerate such an outrage. Other spectators then started to attack the protestors. It very quickly got out of hand in the auditorium, and in the adjoining bar where René Clair, Philippe Hériat, Alexandre Arnoux and several others tried in vain to intervene. Confronted with this disaster, Armand Tallier nevertheless refused to call the police. This attitude earned him the heartfelt congratulations of the surrealists, little accustomed to such good-hearted indulgence. The writer André Breton decided to take it upon himself to report the proceedings to other surrealists.

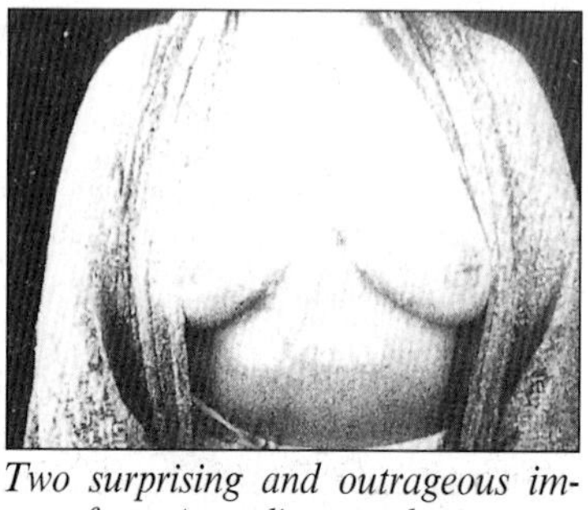

Two surprising and outrageous images from Artaud's surreal excursion.

Chaplin the mute will now talk

Hollywood, 30 June
It seems certain that *The Circus* i going to be Charlie Chaplin's las silent film. He has just decided t shoot his latest production, *Cit Lights*, in sound. He began wor on *City Lights* as a silent pictur in March, but the success of *Th Jazz Singer* has thrown the movi business into turmoil. Chapli has called a halt to production but none of this has changed hi instinctive hostility toward talk ing pictures and his convictio that the Tramp's actions spea louder than words. Sound, h claims, will destroy the beauty o silent cinema, which for Chapli perfectly represents the oldest ar in the world, that of pantomime

nil Jannings under Sternberg's command

Emil Jannings
THE LAST COMMAND
Paramount Picture

perb German import Emil Jannings and Evelyn Brent: ***The Last Command.***

w York, 28 February
.e great German actor Emil Jannings, who is the lead in F.W. Mur-u's *The Last Laugh* in Germany, s finished his second Hollywood n. Fresh from being directed by ctor Fleming in *The Way of All* *'sh*, Jannings submitted himself to instructions of the Austrian-born sef von Sternberg for *The Last* *mmand*. In it, he plays an exiled :arist general who winds up in ollywood reduced to playing ex-s in motion pictures. Flash back the year 1917, when a young man Villiam Powell), an actor serving in e army, is captured, beaten and miliated by that same general. His tress-fiancee (Evelyn Brent) then seduces his tormentor, gains his confidence, and betrays him when the Revolution triumphs. Ten years later, the young revolutionary has become a film director, and employs the former general to take part in a film about the war in Russia and the Revolution. The general, confusing reality and fiction, is meticulous in the role before dying on the set. The scenario, written by Sternberg himself, deals with the "irony of fate" as well as the distortion of memory. Echoing the subject of *The Last Command*, the director experienced great difficulties with Jannings, even though he has managed to extract a truly moving performance out of the capricious German star.

Eisenstein celebrates October Revolution

Moscow, 14 March
A number of films have been commissioned by the Soviet government to celebrate the tenth anniversary of the Revolution. Among them is Sergei Eisenstein's *October*, which is based on John Reed's *Ten Days That Shook The World*. (Others were directed by Pudovkin, Boris Barnet and Esther Shub.) However, both the shooting of Eisenstein's film and the editing ran into difficulties, and the director was obliged to reduce 49,000 metres of footage to 2,000, mainly due to the intervention of politics and censorship. For example, Trotsky had originally figured prominently in the film, but then had to be expunged from it altogether. Eisenstein's ambition was to evoke Petrograd's history between February and October 1917, from the fall of the Czar to the capture of the Winter Palace at the time when the Bolsheviks brought down the Kerensky government. But this film tends toward fiction rather than truth, and must be considered as a lyrical and heroic epic about the very beginnings of a new nation. The only real participants identified in the Revolution are Lenin and Kerensky, the head of the bourgeois government. The former, played by a worker, makes a fleeting but impressive appearance. The latter, on the contrary, is a leading character, who allows Eisenstein to display all his satiric verve. *October* reveals the chaos of the epoch by the use of dynamic montage, constantly contrasting images and visual metaphors, such as Kerensky pictured as a strutting mechanical peacock. Some of the most striking emotional and rhythmic scenes include the dismantling of the statue of Alexander III, Kerensky climbing an unending stairway, the excited crowds converging on the Winter Palace, and the opening of a drawbridge from which a dead horse is suspended.

Russia's politics on view in ***October.***

The Jazz Singer' omes to Paris

aris, 30 June
ie Jazz Singer, the film from 'arner Bros. which has revolution-ed the American film industry, has en given a press showing in Paris d will be seen across the capital xt month. Clearly, the arrival of e "talkers" will have a big impact the European film industry. With eye on the future of talking films, aramount has recently signed a al with the French music-hall star aurice Chevalier. The celebrated ulevardier had already made a reen test for MGM, but when it oved fruitless he was snapped up Paramount's Jesse Lasky.

Soviet filmmakers are demanding a bigger role for sound

Moscow, 19 July
War has been declared on talking pictures! In a spirited manifesto entitled *The Advent of Sound Film*, the distinguished Soviet directors Eisenstein, Pudovkin and Alexandrov argue that sound effects and dialogue will turn cinema into bad theater. Merely to copy reality will impoverish cinema. However, they concede that not all progress is negative. Cinema can escape from the cul-de-sac of titles if filmmakers employ a "brutal discordance of sound and image." And sound and music can become new elements in the art of montage in that they offer counterpoints and fresh perspectives to the image on the screen.

Eisenstein and his friends favor an orchestral counterpoint to their images.

Sternberg explores New York's waterfront

Betty Compson and George Bancroft star in Sternberg's atmospheric film.

New York, 29 September
Director Josef von Sternberg has brought his remarkable visual artistry to full flower in *The Docks of New York*. Light and darkness, mist and shadows, make the camerawork almost as compelling as the story. A drama of love and death, it tells of a ship's stoker (George Bancroft) who falls in love with and marries a girl (Betty Compson), whom he rescues from suicide on the waterfront. He promptly deserts her, but jumps ship in order to save her from a false murder charge, and serves a prison sentence to clear her of a further charge of theft. The girl is understandably grateful. Both leads are tremendously touching – though most surprising is "good" tough guy Bancroft, who previously played a gangster in Sternberg's earlier film *Underworld*. There is also a lot of pleasure to be had from the balance between the contrasting personalities of the tender Betty Compson and the sharp Olga Baclanova. The simple story can give no clue to its masterly execution. Like *The Salvation Hunters*, Sternberg's first film in 1925, made on location at the docks of San Pedro Bay and considered a failure; and the subsequent *Underworld* (a success), the director has approached urban squalor with poetic realism. Pictorial compositions are used in *The Docks of New York* to illuminate the characters and express their motivations.

Stroheim's discordant 'Wedding March'

New York, 2 October
The ongoing saga of the brilliant Erich von Stroheim's problems with his producers continues with the long-delayed release of his latest production, *The Wedding March*. The writer-director-star has again returned to the Vienna of his youth, and to themes that he first began exploring in his abortive production of *Merry-Go-Round* in 1922. In the new film, Stroheim himself plays the lead, the aristocratic officer Prince Nikki, with a new young discovery, Fay Wray, as the girl he loves, and ZaSu Pitts, the rich businessman's daughter whom he is forced to marry. Conceived on an epic scale, the film required the construction of three dozen elaborate sets and a replica of St. Stephen's Cathedral. After a number of disappointingly unsuccessful previews, and other delays over the past year with the growing interest in sound, the fi has at least now been issued wit synchronized music and sound fects score which, it is hoped, w bring *The Wedding March* so added public appeal.

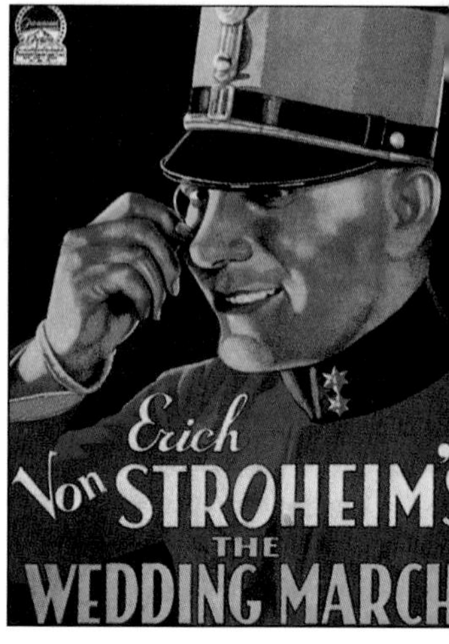
Erich
Von STROHEIM'
THE
WEDDING MARCH

Carl Dreyer's austere, powerful and passionate Joan of Arc

Striking newcomer Renée Falconetti, a brilliant Saint Joan who identifies closely with her intense and historic role.

Paris, 25 October
Directed by the Dane Carl Theodor Dreyer, the new French movie, *The Passion of Joan of Arc*, is being released in an atmosphere of polemic. Although the Archbishop of Paris was consulted in advance, he was displeased with it, and the film being shown to the public is his own censored version. Among other problems, when the film was announced nationalists protested about a foreigner daring to make a film about the Maid of Orleans, a symbol of French heroism. After having created a strong impression in France with *Master of the House*, shown in April 1926, Dreyer was offered the chance to direct his own choice of subject and was allowed a free hand in the treatment by his producers, the Société Générale de Films. The filming took place from May to October 1927 against the austere sets constructed by Herman Warm, a German designer whose name is linked with two of the great successes of German Expressionist cinema: *The Cabinet of Dr. Caligari* and *The Three Lights*. In the course of filming, which chronologically follows the actual records of the trial, Dreyer told his interpreters, Michel S mon, Antonin Artaud and Euge Silvain, to speak the exact phras which appear in the subtitles. In t name of realism, the director ask the young actress Renée Falconet who plays Joan, to crop her beau ful hair and to strip her face of makeup. Filmed mostly in close-u the agonized face of the actress, fr of all cosmetic artifice, appears eve more moving and human. The ph tography of Rudolph Maté has al conferred on the film a power ar rigor that makes *The Passion of Jo of Arc* a universal work.

jöström's sea-change produces a masterpiece

w York, 23 November
edish-born director Victor Sjös-m (who is known in America as strom) has scored a triumph with *Wind*, starring Lillian Gish and ow-Swede Lars Hanson. This un-npromising melodrama contrasts rkly with the director's recent laboration with Gish, in which gave a superb performance as ster Prynne in *The Scarlet Letter*. *The Wind* Gish plays a delicate ginia girl who comes to live with cousin and his wife on a desert ıch. The wind howls unrelentingly ound the cabin until the young man's jangling nerves are stretch-to the breaking point. Sand gets everywhere, coating the carcass a steer which swings ominously in center of the shack. She is forced o marriage and, in Seastrom's ginal version, finally wanders off o the desert, driven insane after ling a rancher. However, distribu-s refused to run a picture with ch a bleak ending, and MGM's oduction supervisor Irving Thal-rg insisted on shooting a "happi-" conclusion in which the sad roine accepts her fate.

Interior scenes for *The Wind* were ot at the MGM studios in Culver ty, and the exteriors were filmed location in the Mojave Desert. In e sandstorm scenes Lillian Gish s blasted by sand, cinders and wdust hurled at her by an enor-ous nine-propellor wind machine. noke pots increased the murk as Gish, unprotected against the scouring blast, buried the body of Montagu Love (the villain) in the drifting sand. A great actress used to grueling location work, she found this one of her toughest assignments.

Seastrom is an interesting man. Born in Sweden but brought up in America, he returned to his native country where he became a successful actor and then a leading director in the burgeoning Swedish film industry. He is a close friend and colleague of Mauritz Stiller who recently died. In 1923 he accepted an offer from Goldwyn and when it merged into MGM, he was asked to direct the new studio's first production, *He Who Gets Slapped* in 1924.

Lillian Gish and Swedish actor Lars Hanson: a sad little wedding.

Gish, the brave and tragic heroine, battling against the violent desert storm outside the primitive log cabin.

reta Garbo shocked by the death of her mentor Mauritz Stiller

ollywood, 8 November
reta Garbo was making her eighth merican film, and shooting an inti-ate love scene with leading man ils Asther, when she received a ble from Stockholm. Mauritz Stil-r had died in the hospital, a photo Garbo by his bedside. White with ock, she left the set and locked rself away in her dressing room. aiting for her there was a small ottle of brandy and a note from ouis B. Mayer: "Dear Greta, I feel r your grief but the show must go n." Garbo laughed before surren-ering herself to tears. Stiller had ever recovered from his failure in merica and the resulting separa-on from his brilliant protégée.

Victor Seastrom, Garbo and Lowell Sherman rehearse for ***The Divine Woman.***

Tragedy at Verdun ten years later

Paris, 8 November
Three days away from the tenth anniversary of the end of the Great War, there is a gala showing of a fascinating film, *Verdun, Visions of History*, directed by Léon Poirier. This is one of the rare films since Abel Gance's *J'accuse* which evokes the heroism and the horror of the war without resorting to propagandistic hindsight. Poirier has brought his own unique vision to his *Verdun* film. His reconstruction of the battle uses official war footage intercut with restaged scenes, a technique which has previously been used in documentary films by Gaumont.

★ ★ ★ ★ ★ ★ ★ ★ ★ 1929 ★

1927/8 Academy Awards, Hollywood Roosevelt, 16 May

Best Film: *Wings* (dir: William A. Wellman)
Best Director: Frank Borzage *(Seventh Heaven)*
Best Actor: Emil Jannings *(The Last Command* and *The Way of All Flesh)*
Best Actress: Janet Gaynor *(Seventh Heaven, Street Angel* and *Sunrise)*

China, 1 January
The Kuomintang has set down the first rules for film censorship.

Hollywood, 2 January
According to an article in *Variety*, the investment required to equip cinemas with sound systems will be close to $3 million.

Berlin, 17 January
An experimental screening of two short sound films was held at the Tauentzienpalast.

Portugal, 23 January
Release of J. Leitao de Barros' film *Nazare, Fishermen's Beach*.

Hollywood, 1 February
Erich von Stroheim has run into problems with his latest film, *Queen Kelly*. Both of the producers, Joseph Kennedy and Gloria Swanson, are shocked by the content of the film, which portrays the seduction of a young convent girl by a libertine prince, and as a consequence have withdrawn their financial backing.

Prague, 1 March
Release of *Father Vojtech*, the first film directed by the actor and scriptwriter Martin Fric – Karel Lamac's disciple and collaborator.

New York, 3 March
William Fox, the film producer, has announced his plans to acquire a majority shareholding in Loew's Incorporated at a cost of $50 million. Marcus Loew's company currently holds the controlling interest in Metro-Goldwyn-Mayer, whose head Louis B. Mayer is reported to be outraged at the idea of MGM being absorbed by Fox.

Moscow, 9 April
Dziga Vertov's experimental film *Man With a Movie Camera* (aka *Russia Today*) has been released here. Despite the clues given in the advertising, this documentary style view of Odessa is full of surprises.

Sao Paolo, 13 April
The Patriot, directed by Ernst Lubitsch with Emil Jannings, is the first sound film to be screened in Brazil. It was filmed, in fact, without sound and partially post-synchronized.

Berlin, 29 April
Release of *Die Frau nach der man sich sehnt* (*The Woman that Men Yearn For*), directed by the theatrical producer Kurt Bernhardt and starring Marlene Dietrich.

New York, 27 May
Release of *Broadway*, made by Paul Fejos. It is one of the first sound films to introduce a mobile camera and the use of a special crane, built for Universal at a cost of $75,000.

Hollywood, 1 June
Equity, the actors' union, has called for a strike against the studios. The union is demanding the exclusion of non-union actors, a 48-hour work week, and the guarantee that no dubbing will be undertaken without the actors' permission.

Mexico, 7 June
A decree has been passed that all foreign films must be subtitled in Spanish. However, the public, who are mostly illiterate, are demanding the integral dubbing of films.

New York, 22 June
Release of Josef von Sternberg's first talking film, *Thunderbolt*.

London, 30 June
Alfred Hitchcock's *Blackmail*, the first talking film made in England, establishes him as a master of the obsessional thriller.

France, 30 June
V. Ivanoff, the head of the Ecran d'Art company, has announced the filming of *The End of the World*, by Abel Gance. The film, based on a novel by Camille Flammarion, will be using the Gaumont-Petersen-Poulsen sound process.

Paris, 3 July
Bernard Natan, whose company Rapid Film merged with Pathé in a takeover last February, has become the new head of the Pathé empire. Charles Pathé was forced to yield his position due to pressure from his financiers. He is, however, to remain on the board of directors.

Berlin 30 July
UFA is currently building Europe's most modern sound-film studios in Neubabelsberg. The cost is estimated at 6 million marks.

USA, 3 August
Release of *The Cockeyed World*, a sequel to *What Price Glory*, both directed by Raoul Walsh with Victor McLaglen and Edmund Lowe.

Paris, 31 August
The French cinema industry has moved out of its period of stupor and seems determined to catch up with its American counterpart in the area of sound films. Léon Gaumont is rebuilding the studios at La Villette to incorporate sound studios. Tobis have re-equipped their studios in Epinay and Pathé Natan are fitting out a studio in rue Francœur.

Berlin, 5 September
Josef von Sternberg, who is looking for actors for his new film *The Blue Angel*, noticed Marlene Dietrich on stage in *Zwei Kravatten*. He was at the theater on Erich Pommer's recommendation to consider the actor Hans Albers for the film, but his visit has resulted in the casting of Miss Dietrich in the title role.

USA, 28 September
Lionel Barrymore's passionate outbursts in his first talking film *His Glorious Night*, provoke laughter: it marks the end of the road for one of the greatest stars of silent films.

Paris, 2 October
The Franco Film company run by Robert Hurel, which controls the Victorine studios and the Gaumont cinema chain, has taken over the Louis Aubert establishment through a merger. The new company is to be known as Aubert-Franco Film.

New York, 6 October
The newly-created RKO company has released the first screen version of a Broadway musical, *Rio Rita*.

Moscow, 7 October
Premiere of *The General Line*, ma
by S.M. Eisenstein in 1926 and o
ginally titled *The Old and the Ne*

Berlin, 15 October
Premiere of *Das Tagebuch ei*
Verlorenen (*Diary of a Lost Girl*),
new film from G.W. Pabst.

Rome, 24 October
Release of Alessandro Blasetti's fi
Sole, an avant-garde documentar

New York, 4 November
Warner Bros. has completed its ta
over of the First National compa

London, 10 November
Eisenstein, who is traveling w
Grigori Alexandrov and Edoua
Tissé, has met John Grierson, B
nard Shaw, Paul Rotha and Ba
Wright while in Britain.

Paris, 15 November
The federation of ciné-clubs h
been set up with Germaine Dulac
its first president.

Hollywood, 29 December
Universal has released the fi
sound film to be shot on locatio
Hell's Heroes, filmed in Death V
ley by William Wyler.

BIRTHS

Rome, 3 January
Sergio Leone

Rome, 29 January
Elio Petri

Brussels, 4 May
Audrey Hepburn

Nice, 6 July
Jean-Pierre Mocky

Italy, 20 September
Vittorio Taviani

Philadelphia, 12 November
Grace Kelly

New York, 9 December
John Cassavetes

Eminent stage actor George Arli
made his first film at age 52. Aft
playing the famous British statesm
Disraeli in a 1921 silent, he remade
in sound and won the Oscar.

WARNER BROS. present
GEORGE ARLISS
IN
"DISRAELI"
WITH
JOAN BENNETT
Based on play by Louis N. Parker
Screen Play by Julian Josephson
DIRECTED BY
ALFRED E.
GREEN
A WARNER BROS. PRODUCTION

Broadway Melody makes sweet music for Metro

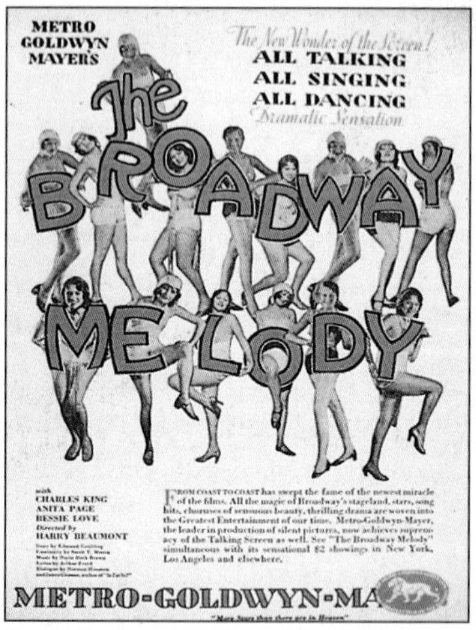
METRO
GOLDWYN
MAYER'S
ALL TALKING
ALL SINGING
ALL DANCING
The BROADWAY MELODY
CHARLES KING
ANITA PAGE
BESSIE LOVE
HARRY BEAUMONT
METRO-GOLDWYN-MA

MGM's poster speaks for itself.

New York, 2 February
"MGM has stolen the march on all their competitors in the talkie production field by being the first on the market with a combination drama and musical revue that will knock the audiences for a goal," trumpeted *Motion Picture News* a few days ago, before the premiere of *The Broadway Melody*. That prediction is right on target because audiences *have* been knocked "for a goal." Not so much by the slight story involving two small-town vaudevillian sisters (Bessie Love and Anita Page) who fall for the same Broadway song 'n' dance man (Charles King), but by the musical numbers. One of them, *The Wedding of the Painted Doll*, was filmed in two-strip Technicolor. It is part of the impresario character Francis Zanfield's most recent e travaganza, which contains a stri of hits by Nacio Herb Brown a Arthur Freed, including the ti track and the song *You Were Mea For Me*. In order to create fluenc the sound engineer Douglas Shear pre-recorded music then played through loudspeakers on the set f the performers, so the film cou later be married to the recording.

MELODY
SPEAR
SALLY CLUB

The chorus lineup here characterizes the 'all-dancing' aspect of the movie.

l to r: Page, King and Love.

It's RKO – Let's Go

With the advertising slogan "It's RKO – Let's Go", a new motion picture company has kicked off with a musical picture entitled *Street Girl*. RKO, which stands for Radio-Keith-Orpheum, came into being with the amalgamation of American Pathé, Joseph P. Kennedy's Film Booking Office of America, the Keith, Albee and Orpheum theater chain and Radio Corporation of America. To reinforce its birth coinciding with the coming of sound, RKO has adopted as its logograph the image of a giant radio tower perched atop the world, beeping out its signal of "A Radio Picture". The wide-ranging enterprise, containing production, exhibition and distribution arms, has committed itself to 12 "all-talking" pictures in its first year. The new studio has amassed a substantial contingent of talent to spearhead its quest for greatness that includes Betty Compson and John Harron, stars of *Street Girl*.

Moscow honors the Paris Commune with 'The New Babylon'

Moscow, 18 February
The Commune, cited by Marx and Lenin as an event that influenced their philosophy and eventually the Revolution, has now been used as a subject for a new Russian film. *The New Babylon* is directed by Grigori Kozintsev and Leonid Trauberg, two young cinéastes, age 24 and 27, respectively. It was they, with a few others, who founded FEKS (Factory of the Eccentric Actor) in Petrograd in 1922. They claim to be influenced by music-hall, the circus and Guignol, ignoring psychology a rhetorical gestures. One witness this in *The Overcoat*, a strange fant sy based on Gogol, and in *The Ch of the Big Deed*, a revolutiona drama. Zola would not have repu ated the story of *The New Babylo* which tells of Louise (Elena Kuzn na), a sales clerk working in the lu ury department store carrying t same name as the film, whose life changed by external events. H social situation enables her to li disparate elements – the worke with whom she lives, the rich who she serves. She sees the effects of t German advance on Paris on bo the cowardly bourgeoisie and t patriotic working class. The film climax is the collapse of the Cor mune, though a degree of optimis is provided by the social awarene which Louise's boyfriend discove in the event. One must salute t camerawork of André Moskvin which recalls the masterpieces Renoir, Manet and Daumier, a the brilliant music composed b Dmitri Shostakovich.

Elena Kouzmina in the film by Grigori Kozintsev and Leonid Trauberg.

ouise Brooks makes a fascinating Lulu

erlin, 28 February
irector G.W. Pabst is never afraid surprise or to shock. Well before ooting had finished on *Pandora's ɔx*, controversy was raging over ɛ picture. In 1922 Leopold Jessner d adapted the Franz Wedekind ay *Lulu* for the screen, with Asta ielsen in the role of the nymphoaniac who leaves havoc in her ake. Both the play and the film ovoked fury among self-appointed oral guardians. Pabst's film, based the same source, makes no conssions. He boldly presents the ostitute Lulu as a creature who mbines amorality and innocence, ithely unaware of the tragedies at mark her passage. This is no orality tale. Instead Pabst fixes his mera on the extraordinary young merican actress portraying Lulu. ouise Brooks is a 22-year-old with Hollywood films behind her and reputation as a rebel. A distinctive eauty, she has made the part of ulu her own, portraying her sexualy with a directness which has left itics and public arguing whether e performance is one of great actg or remarkable instinct.

A perfect realization of the character imagined by writer Wedekind.

A wild success for woman director Arzner

New York, 6 April
Clara Bow has made the transition to sound. The "It" girl, revealing a Brooklyn accent that perfectly suits her uninhibited personality, stars in *The Wild Party* for Paramount, in which she gives a wild and wonderful performance as a college student who falls for a handsome professor (Fredric March). It is not, however, merely Clara's powerful appeal that renders this admittedly frivolous piece worthy of our attention. *The Wild Party* is directed with zest and pace by Dorothy Arzner who, with her fifth assignment behind the camera, proves once and for all that she is equal to the task that seems otherwise exclusively entrusted to men. The Californian-born Arzner began in the film industry in 1919 as a humble stenographer in the script department of Famous Players. She was promoted to script clerk and then trained as a film cutter, graduating to the job of editor. Arzner was responsible for the imaginative editing of the exciting bullfight sequences in Valentino's *Blood and Sand*, an achievement which so impressed director James Cruze that in 1923 he entrusted her with the task of editing his now famous breakthrough Western entitled *The Covered Wagon*. Paramount finally gave her her first directing assignment with *Fashions for Women* two years ago. It is to be hoped that her latest success will allow her to bring the "woman's touch" to increasingly interesting material.

Fredric March and Clara Bow, lovers in Arzner's ***The Wild Party****.*

ailure to scandalize disappoints Luis Buñuel and Salvador Dali

aris, 1 April
is name is Luis Buñuel, he is Spanh, and he has just made a striking ntry into the closed club of the surɛalists by means of a strange film alled *Un chien andalou*. Surprisgly, the performance at the Studio des Ursulines failed to create the expected riot. Man Ray as well as the other surrealists in attendance acknowledged Buñuel and Salvador Dali, the co-author of the scenario, as being on their wavelength. However, the surrealists are shocked by the fact that many of the audiences who like the film are, in their own eyes, "bourgeois". Luis Buñuel himself was disappointed that he was not able to use the pebbles he had in his pocket in the event of any violent reactions to his film.

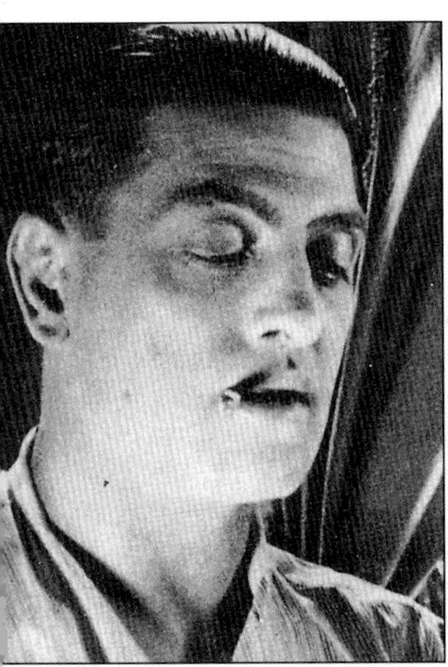

uis Buñuel, co-author with Salvador)ali of ***Un chien andalou****, appears n the screen in their bizarre film.*

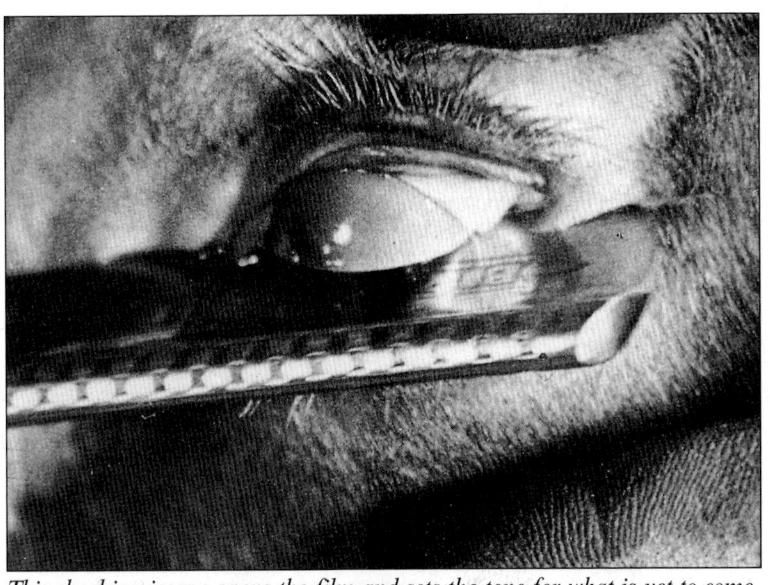

This shocking image opens the film and sets the tone for what is yet to come.

New censor laws, same old restraints

Paris, 5 April
After being banned by the authorities for four months, the new film from director Jacques Feyder, *Les Nouveaux Messieurs (The New Gentlemen)* from an original script by Feyder and Charles Spaak, has finally opened here at the Paramount, though with a few discreet cuts. The ban was actually initiated by a few members of Parliament, in spite of the support given the film by the press as well as a favorable response from most of the critics. The film, which pokes fun at rival politicians, was officially felt to go too far in undermining the "dignity of Parliament and its ministers," a decision more farcical than anything that could have been dreamed up in the screenplay. As of 11 March, the film censorship commission's decision to lift the ban was intended to allay any further criticism by the press while, at the same time, imposing certain cuts which would make the film more acceptable to Parliament. ▷

Hollywood selects first Academy Award winners

Clara Bow and Richard Arlen in William Wellman's ***Wings***.

Left to right: Best Actress Janet Gaynor, George E. Stone, Charles Farrell and Albert Gran in Best Director Frank Borzage's acclaimed ***Seventh Heaven***.

Best Actor Emil Jannings in Josef v Sternberg's ***The Last Command***.

A great gathering of professionals

Hollywood, 16 May
For the first time, representatives of the American cinema have decided to honor the best among them. The idea for the awards was born during a dinner held at Louis B. Mayer's villa in Santa Monica in January 1927, at which the actor Conrad Nagel, the director Fred Niblo and the producer Fred Beetson were present. During a second dinner, the four men invited members of other creative branches of the movie industry. In February, the Academy of Motion Picture Arts and Sciences was founded in order to "raise the cultural, educational and scientific standards" of film, in the hope that it would lend respectability to the movie industry. Thirty-six charter members were elected: producers, actors, directors, screenwriters and technicians. The first meeting of the Academy took place at the Ambassador Hotel in Los Angeles, under the chairmanship of Douglas Fairbanks. One of the first functions of the Academy, which includes Fairbanks, Mary Pickford, Cecil B. DeMille, Irving Thalberg and Raoul Walsh, was to organize the annual achievement awards. It is hoped that the Academy will be able to resolve the numerous problems that beset the movie industry.

UNDERWORLD
CLIVE BROOK, EVELYN BRENT, GEORGE BANCROFT and LARRY SEMON
A HECTOR TURNBULL PRODUCTION
a Paramount Picture

Thirty-five nominations for thirteen honors

Hollywood, 16 May
At a banquet at the Roosevelt Hotel, representatives of the film industry gathered to honor the most brilliant actors, actresses, directors and technicians of the year. William C. De Mille, elder brother of producer-director Cecil B., acted as chairman, and Douglas Fairbanks, president of the Academy of Motion Picture Arts and Sciences, handed out 13 statuettes in front of 200 members of the movie industry. The 13-and-a-half-inch tall, gold-plated eight-pound figure of a man wielding a crusader's sword standing on a reel of film, was designed in a few minutes on a tablecloth at Hollywood's Biltmore Hotel by MGM art dire tor Cedric Gibbons. Among the wi ners, who were decided upon thr months ago, was the German st Emil Jannings, Best Actor for h efforts in his first two Hollywo films, *The Way Of All Flesh* and *T Last Command*. Janet Gaynor w the Best Actress award for her co bined work in three pictures: o directed by F.W. Murnau, *Sunris* and the other two, *Seventh Heav* and *Street Angel*, by Frank Borza (who was named Best Director *Sunrise* was recognized for its Arti tic Quality of Production. The Be Picture was *Wings*, William We man's tribute to the "young warrio of the sky" during the last war. B sides being a worthy Best Pictur *Wings* also gained an award for th Engineering Effects of Roy Pom roy. The Best Original Story no went to *Underworld*. Two speci prizes were presented to Charl Chaplin for his "versatility and g nius in writing, acting, directing an producing *The Circus*", and t Warner Brothers "for producin *The Jazz Singer*, the pioneer ou standing talking picture, which ha revolutionized the industry." Th biggest sensation of the banquet wa the screening of a short talker i which Douglas Fairbanks was see and heard in a conversation wi *Wings* producer Adolph Zukor.

At the ceremony: Academy President Douglas Fairbanks (center) with Janet Gaynor, Karl Struss, Frank Borzage (right) and Richard Arlen (left).

aurel and Hardy disrobe Jean Harlow

ew York, 18 May
whiff of scandal hangs over the lease of Laurel and Hardy's latest m, *Double Whoopee*, directed by ewis R. Foster. Leo McCarey's reenplay gives blonde newcomer an Harlow ample opportunity to splay her physical charms. Hope-ss hotel porter, played by Stan aurel, contrives to shut a taxi door n the glamorous young woman's vening dress. The taxi moves off, aving Harlow on the sidewalk in er underwear. Blithely unaware of er state of *déshabillée*, she strides urposefully into the crowded hotel bby, creating a sensation among the guests. In another scene there is a wickedly funny burlesque of Erich von Stroheim which was praised by no less a movie fan than the turbulent Austrian actor-director himself. *Double Whoopee* is a triumph for Laurel and Hardy and a step on the way to stardom for Harlow. The 18-year-old Harlow was born in Kansas City, Missouri. She eloped at the age of 16, but the marriage didn't last. Eventually, she gravitated to Los Angeles where she got by with work as an extra, and featured roles in a number of two-reel Christie comedies before making her mark alongside Stan and Ollie.

ean Harlow with the terrible twosome in Lewis R. Foster's ***Double Whoopee****.*

The Marx Brothers' irresistible whirlwind

PARAMOUNT'S ALL TALKING MUSICOMEDY SENSATION
THE MARX BROTHERS
OSCAR SHAW
MARY EATON
The COCOANUTS

A splashy, effervescent color poster announces the riotous Marx Brothers.

New York, 3 August
Audiences are rolling in the aisles over Paramount's *The Cocoanuts*, the Marx Brothers' madcap movie debut. No one can make any sense of the story, written by George S. Kaufman, and the stale musical subplot, with songs by Irving Berlin, drags more than a little. But when the four Marx brothers are on the screen, it's a riot. There's Groucho, complete with his greasepaint moustache, loping walk, ready leer and lion's share of the wisecracks; Harpo, a demented little mime; Chico, caught in between the insanity of Groucho and Harpo with a pixie hat and ice-cream Italian voice; and Zeppo, the handsome but dogged straight man with all the charisma of an enamel washstand. Kay Francis and Margaret Dumont bring up the rear and attempt to maintain their battered dignity amid the non-stop craziness. The director Robert Florey is a Frenchman, former journalist and publicity man, who now lives and works in Hollywood.

idor's all-black 'Hallelujah' proves an exhilarating experience

New York, 20 August
he new all-talking, all-singing, all-ancing film by King Vidor entitled *Iallelujah*, has just been released on ur screens. It is the first sound feature film interpreted exclusively by lacks. The leading roles are taken y Daniel Haynes, who sings "Old Man River" from *Showboat*, and Nina Mae McKinney, who has been raised on Broadway, in particular n the musical revue *Black Birds*. The shooting of the film took place n Memphis, Tennessee, without any ound equipment, and the silent film vas then post-synchronized in a studio in Hollywood. The result surpasses all expectations. *Hallelujah* xplores the soul of the black people s never before, and certain scenes, ike the baptism in the Mississippi, stound with their authenticity.

In the foreground, hero and heroine Daniel Haynes and Victoria Spivey.

No Louise Brooks for René Clair

Paris, 24 August
On 25 April, the American star Louise Brooks arrived in Paris from New York to make a new film, *Prix de Beauté*, a melodrama about a shop girl who finds tragedy when she wins a beauty contest. The project was developed by G.W. Pabst, the director who drew such an extraordinary performance out of Brooks in *Pandora's Box*. However, other commitments forced Pabst to turn the film over to René Clair. Now, Clair himself has bowed out after a series of disagreements with producer Romain Pinès, and the prolific and craftsmanlike Italian director Augusto Genina has stepped into Clair's shoes following his recently completed *Quartier Latin*.

'Rio Rita' confirms a bumper first year for RKO

Bebe Daniels and John Boles, a stunningly attractive duo and stars of ***Rio Rita****.*

Sally Blane with crooner Rudy Vallee in another success, ***The Vagabond Love***

New York, 6 October
The RKO Radio studio (short for Radio-Keith-Orpheum) is celebrating its first busy year of production. Marching under the banner "It's RKO – Let's Go" are actors Bebe Daniels, Betty Compson, Richard Dix and Rudy Vallee, and directors Luther Reed, Wesley Ruggles and Malcolm St. Clair. Underlining the studio's preference for motion pictures with a high musical content, crooner Rudy Vallee has scored a solid box-office success with *The Vagabond Lover*, in which he plays a stage-struck hick who poses as America's "Saxophone King". But the studio's biggest hit of the year has been *Rio Rita*, a spectacular musical Western brought to the screen after a year's run on Broadway. Bebe Daniels, in her first talking picture, and John Boles, on loan from Universal, star as the warbling riders of the purple sage, and Wheeler an Wolsey provide comic relief. Th lavish sets and costumes were designed by Max Ree, and produce William LeBaron's determination t spare no expense has resulted in a eye-catching river barge finale, sho in two-strip Technicolor.

Doug and Mary co-star (and talk!) in 'The Taming of the Shrew'

Hollywood, 26 October
The eagerly-awaited co-starring of the King and Queen of Hollywood, Douglas Fairbanks and Mary Pickford, has finally come about in *The Taming of the Shrew*. It was Sam Taylor, the young phenomenon who recently directed Mary in *Coquette*, who urged the couple to film one of the Shakespearean plays. Douglas went along with this idea, and, by elimination as much as anything else, decided on *The Taming of the Shrew*. Some purists might object to the liberties taken with the Bard of Avon, but the adaptation and direction by Taylor is highly effective. Whereas Shakespeare takes some time to get the plot underway, the film opens with Katherina the hellcat displaying her temper. In the scene when Petruchio soliloquizes on how he is going to break Katherina's spirit and make her a dutiful wife, we see Mary eavesdropping. Audiences realize then that Mary is in complete control of the situation, and, just in case we miss the point, she gives us a big wink in the closing scene. The main interest, however, is in the performances of the two stars. Mary, smashing windows and mirrors and wielding a whip, provides a great deal of fun. And Doug, as her tamer, is as virile as ever, even characteristically leaping on horses. Their voices, too, are up to the task.

Co-stars for the first time as Kate and Petruchio in ***The Taming of the Shrew****.*

The independents hold a conference

Lausanne, 7 September
For the last five days Hélène d Mandrot, owner of the château a La Sarraz, has been playing host t the Congrès Internationale du Cinéma Independant, the first of its kind Organized by Robert Aron and Janine Bouissounouse who, along wit Jean-George Auriol, run the Paris based *Revue du cinéma*, its aim is t coordinate the activities of independent filmmakers and film societies Among those attending have bee the Russian directors Alexandrov and Eisenstein and the latter's cameraman Edouard Tissé. Eisenstei has improvised a short film aroun the conference called *Tempête su La Sarraz*, plundering the armory for costumes and props. The conference has wound up today with th decision to establish a network o cinema clubs, run from Geneva, an a Paris-based cooperative for independent filmmakers.

he great Georges Méliès lost, and found again

CONFISERIE
ET JOUETS
VOS BAGAGES

1928, Leon Druhot discovered an elderly Méliès working in a candy and toy shop at Montparnasse station.

Paris, 16 December

In the course of an exceptional gala organized in his honor by Studio 28 and the newspapers *Le Figaro* and *L'Ami du Peuple*, Georges Méliès has come into his own again. Two thousand five hundred spectators were present at the Salle Pleyel to witness his miraculous return to the limelight. A committee of honor, consisting of numerous personalities including Abel Gance, were responsible for paying this moving homage to Méliès the Magician: the creator of cinematographic spectacle. The evening climaxed with the showing of Cecil B. DeMille's *The Cheat*, and a selection of the fantasy films of Méliès, among them *The Conquest of the Pole* and *The Hallucinations of Baron Münchhausen*. These remarkable films, recently recovered from the Château Dufayel by Jean Mauclaire, founder of Studio 28, were colored by hand especially for showing at the gala. Méliès, who has not been heard from for many years, was found by chance by the editor of the weekly *Ciné-Journal*, Léon Druhot, running a modest candy and toy shop on the first floor of Gare Montparnasse. The shop belongs to Méliès' wife, Charlotte Faës, who formerly performed in his films under the name of Jehanne d'Alcy. Druhot rapidly informed several journalists, among whom were Paul Gilson and Jean-George Auriol who actually conceived the idea of the gala.

George Méliès directed his last two films in 1913. Since that time, his existence has been difficult. The problems started in 1913 with the loss of a lawsuit brought against him by Pathé Film. The war of 1914 caused him to close down the Robert Houdin Theatre. He then transformed one of his Montreuil studios into the Théâtre des Variétés. In 1923, he was totally ruined and declared bankrupt. At the request of his creditors, he was ordered by the tribunal to sell all his property, and many of his films were melted down into a substance used in the manufacture of footwear. From then on, Méliès and his family survived by giving concerts in the provinces. Widowed in 1913, he married Jehanne d'Alcy in 1925. Since then, the couple have lived very simply on the proceeds from the shop. ▷

lfred Hitchcock graduates to sound with his new thriller

ndon, 25 November

idely advertised as "The First Full ngth All Talkie Film Made in eat Britain", Alfred Hitchcock's *ackmail* has just opened here to eat acclaim. "*Blackmail* is perhaps e most intelligent mixture of si-nce and sound we have yet seen," ote the critic in *Close Up*, and the *oscope* agrees: "By this masterly oduction, Hitchcock amply fulfills e promise shown in his earlier forts." In fact, the film was not nceived as a talkie, but the pro-ction company, BIP, recognized at the sound revolution was in ogress across the Atlantic and rmitted the director to re-shoot any of the silent sequences, using e new sound equipment. The re-lting film thus retains the visual alities, pace and use of locations sociated with the silents, success-lly blended with the recorded dia-gue and sound effects of a talkie. fascinating and complex thriller, *ackmail* is notable for its sophisticated and original exploration of the triangular relationship which develops between the attractive young heroine who is implicated in a murder, her policeman boyfriend, and a sleazy character who is aware of the situation and tries to blackmail the girl. In this last role, Donald Calthrop gives a superb performance as a memorable villain.

28-72.

John Longden (left), Anny Ondra, Donald Calthrop: a tense scene in ***Blackmail***.

HAL ROACH
presents
THE CALL OF THE WILD
FROM THE FAMOUS DOG STORY
BY
JACK LONDON
DIRECTED BY FRED JACKMAN
Pathépicture

Jack London's novel, filmed in 1923 for Hal Roach, with Jack Mulhall.

A JAMES CRUZE Production
MERTON
OF THE MOVIES
STARRING
GLENN HUNTER
with VIOLA DANA
a Paramount Pictur

1924. Comedy-drama about a sma town boy in Hollywood.

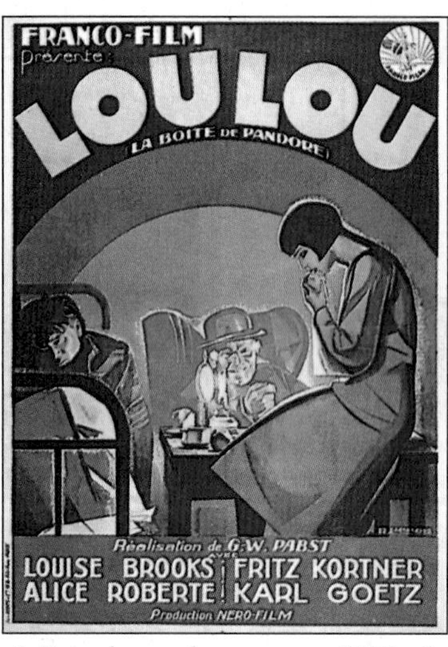
FRANCO-FILM
présente
LOULOU
LA BOITE DE PANDORE
Réalisation de G.W. PABST
LOUISE BROOKS FRITZ KORTNER
ALICE ROBERTE KARL GOETZ
Production NERO-FILM

A French art deco poster, 1928, for G.W. Pabst's ***Pandora's Box****.*

HENRY CLIVE
JESSE L. LASKY Presents
GLORIA SWANSON
IN
"HER HUSBAND'S TRADEMARK"
by CLARA BERANGER
SCENARIO BY LORNA MOON
DIRECTED BY SAM WOOD
It's a Paramount Picture
Morgan

Sam Wood directed this 1922 five-reel drama for Famous Players-Lasky.

Samuel Goldwyn presents
THE HENRY KING PRODUCTION
"The WINNING of BARBARA WORTH"
RONALD COLMAN and VILMA BANKY
RELEASED BY UNITED ARTISTS CORP.

1926. Actor Gary Cooper impresse

Love sought them out on a tenement roof.
JESSE L. LASKY
presents
May McAvoy
IN
THE TOP
OF NEW YORK
a Paramount Picture

1922. Melodrama of self-sacrifice.

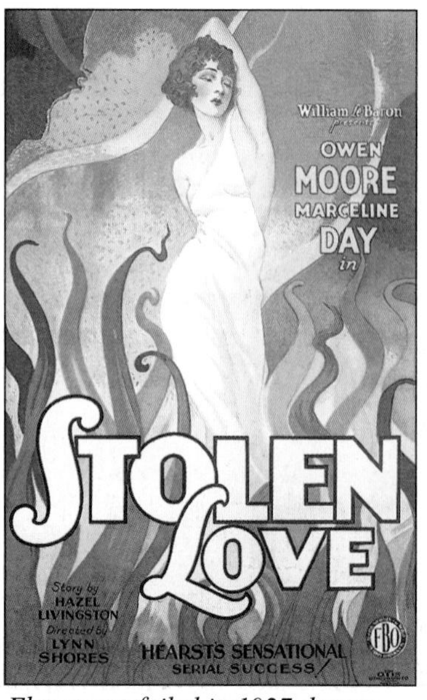
William Le Baron
presents
OWEN MOORE
MARCELINE DAY
in
STOLEN LOVE
Story by
HAZEL LIVINGSTON
Directed by
LYNN SHORES
HEARSTS SENSATIONAL
SERIAL SUCCESS
FBO

Elopement failed in 1927 drama.

JOHN GRETA
GILBERT GARBO
CLARENCE BROWN'S
PRODUCTION
A WOMAN of AFFAIRS
with
LEWIS STONE
JOHN MACK BROWN
DOUGLAS FAIRBANKS JR.
A Metro-Goldwyn-Mayer PICTURE

1928. Garbo's top billing over Gilbert.

UNIVERSAL
JEWEL
CARL LAEMMLE offers
Priscilla Dean
LON CHANEY
in "Outside The Law"
TOD BROWNING

Universal's 1921 crime melodrama

WARNER BROS. present
JOHN
BARRYMORE
in
"General Crack"
SCENES in
NATURAL
COLOR
TECHNICOLOR
DIRECTED BY
ALAN CROSLAND
WARNER BROS. PRODUCTION

929. John Barrymore's first talkie.

WILLIAM FOX
presents
JOHN GILBERT
in
"THE WOLF MAN"
SCENARIO BY FREDERICK AND FANNY HATTON
DIRECTED BY

ohn Gilbert, alcoholic in a 1924 film.

Madame
X
with
RUTH CHATTERTON
LEWIS STONE · RAYMOND HACKETT
From the play by Alexandre Bisson · Dialogue by Willard Mack · Directed by Lionel Barrymore
A Metro-Goldwyn-Mayer
ALL TALKING
Picture

In this 1929 third film version, Ruth Chatterton played the tragic heroine.

John McCormick
presents
COLLEEN
MOORE
IN
HER
WILD
OAT
Adapted from Story by
Howard Irving Young
A MARSHALL
NEILAN
PRODUCTION
A FIRST NATIONAL PICTURE

Colleen Moore is social climber Mary Brown in this First National comedy.

WARNER BROS.
present
AN ERNST LUBITSCH
PRODUCTION
"SO THIS
IS PARIS"
MONTE BLUE
PATSY RUTH MILLER
LILYAN TASHMAN
ANDRE BERANGER
Directed by ERNST
LUBITSCH

1926 Warner-Lubitsch moneymaker.

In 1927 Georges Scott composed a fresco illustrating Abel Gance's **Napoleon**.

NAZIMOVA
in Oscar Wilde's
"Salomé"
CHARLES BRYANT

1923. In the style of English artist Aubrey Beardsley, this poster highlighted Russian beauty Nazimova.

JACKIE
COOGAN
in
OLD CLOTHES
by WILLARD MACK
Directed by
EDDIE CLINE
JACK COOGAN, SR.
Metro-Goldwyn-Mayer
PICTURE

The 1925 sequel to ***The Rag Man***.

Asta Nielsen (Denmark).

Léon Mathot (France).

Norma Talmadge (USA).

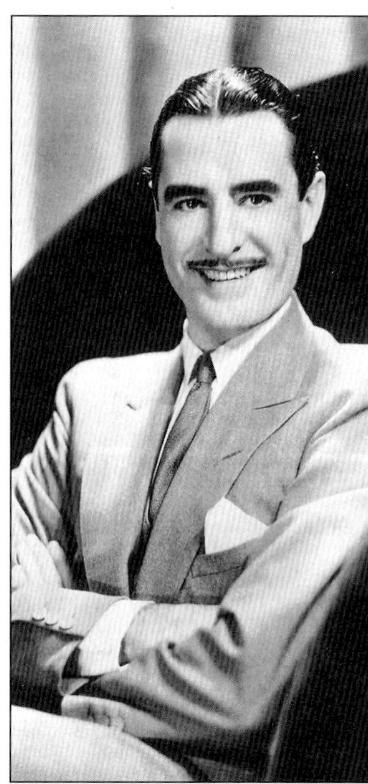
John Gilbert (USA).

Lon Chaney (USA).

Alla Nazimova (Russia/USA).

Harold Lloyd (USA).

Henny Porten (Germany).

Louise Brooks (USA).

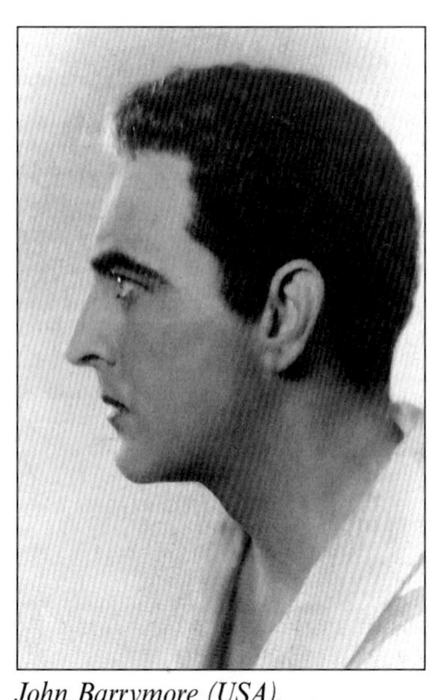
John Barrymore (USA).

Vilma Banky (USA).

Lillian Gish (USA).

The Development of Sound

The photo-electric process, which allows sound to register directly on film, was generally preferred to the prior sound-on-disc system.

Warner Bros.' Burbank studios, 1938: composer Erich Wolfgang Korngold listens as the sound mixer regulates the music volume for ***Juarez****.*

During the earliest years of the cinema, filmmakers in many countries, notably France, the U.S. and Britain, experimented with adding sound to motion pictures. At the Edison company, for example, much work was done over a long period on developing the Kinetophone, a combination of a cylinder phonograph and the Kinetoscope film viewing machine, while the best-known early French system was known as the 'Chronophone'. Many experimental screenings took place, and D.W. Griffith, who even tried adding sound effects to parts of *The Birth of a Nation* in 1915, used synchronized phonograph records to provide a few minutes of singing and dialogue in his 1921 feature, *Dream Street*.

Also during the early years, there were a number of inventors in several countries who worked on the possibility of recording sound directly on film. Most important of these was the German Tri-Ergon system, first demonstrated in Berlin in 1922, while in the United States Lee De Forest was successful in developing his voice-on-film Phonofilm system around the same time. The first public screening took place at the Rivoli Theater in New York, but De Forest continued to adjust and improve his system.

By the mid-1920s two of the leading American film studios began to develop an interest in sound. Best known (thanks largely to *The Jazz Singer*) are the early experiments carried out by Warner Bros. in New York during 1925 and 1926, but not far behind was Fox with its rival sound-on-film system – Movietone.

Sam Warner was the brother most actively involved in the company's new partnership with the Western Electric Co., formed for the purpose of developing a viable sound-on-disc system by which electric signals picked up by the microphones on the film set or sound stage were transferred to 17-inch discs by disc-cutting machines that were locked into synch with the film cameras. Each disc would play for 10 minutes, the same length of time as a 1,000-foot reel of film. Popularly known as Vitaphone (it had been perfected at the old Vitagraph studio in Brooklyn), the first screening of shorts and the feature *Don Juan* took place at the Warner Theater in New York in August 1926 and was a big success.

Around that same time period, William Fox purchased the rights to De Forest's Phonofilm, as well as acquiring the patents for the German Tri-Ergon system for his use. By early in 1927 Fox was presenting the first of its Movietone shorts, which lead to a regular Fox Movietone newsreel later that same year. Here, the electric signals from the microphone were registered by a photo-electric cell, the sound vibrations thus transformed into varying intensities or quantities of light which reacted with the sensitized emulsion on the strip of film to create the optical soundtrack. However, despite the great success of Warners' *The Jazz Singer* (1927), followed by *The Singing Fool* (1928, which also starred Al Jolson), there were too many problems associated with the sound-on-disc system and it was eventually discarded in favor of sound-on-film systems which continue to be used today.

The Trial of Mary Dugan *(1929): Norma Shearer's first sound film.*

Vitaphone's post-projection equipment. Disc and film are synchronized by the motor.

Movies Find a Voice

There is a certain irony in the fact that while America was dominated by the Depression and its aftermath, and there were serious economic crises throughout the industrial world, the 1930s was one of the richest decades, both creatively and financially, in the eventful history of motion pictures.

In Hollywood at the start of the 30s the Wall Street crash had hit many people, and most of the movie giants were in the red. The euphoria that followed the prosperity of the early talkie days diminished as the new era brought problems that ruined many. Numerous stars, foreign and American, whose faces had fitted silent films, found their voices unsuitable for the talkies. However, sound was no barrier to the many directors, set designers and cameramen who flooded in from Europe. Also making the pilgrimage to Hollywood were New York playwrights and Broadway actors, and new stars were emerging. Prominent among them were Bette Davis, Clark Gable, Gary Cooper, Barbara Stanwyck, Cary Grant, Errol Flynn, Henry Fonda, Katharine Hepburn, Robert Taylor and Joan Crawford.

Due mainly to the 'star system', and thanks to the further infusion of investment funds, filmmaking survived the crisis almost intact. By 1935, movie attendances were averaging a healthy eight million a week, and the industry was on the threshold of a glorious period that many have dubbed 'the golden age'.

The star system could not have existed without the studio system, and the key to Hollywood films in the 30s was the studio. Each of the majors developed its own characteristic style, with its own roster of directors, stars, designers and technicians who dictated the look and sound of the films.

MGM, with its huge financial resources, was the most glamorous, boasting 'More Stars Than There Are In Heaven'. Under the leadership of Louis B. Mayer and Irving Thalberg, the studio specialized in family entertainment, only rarely venturing into controversial themes. Until his premature death in 1936, Thalberg oversaw prestigious productions such as *The Merry Widow* (1934), *Mutiny on the Bounty* (1935) and *Romeo and Juliet* (1936). His policy was continued after his death, a period that reached its apogee in 1939 with *The Wizard of Oz*, *Ninotchka* and *The Women*.

If MGM encapsulated middle-class values, then Paramount, with its decorative opulence, was the studio with aristocratic pretensions. The most European of the studios, it used brilliant foreign-born directors. Josef von Sternberg made seven sensuous and exotic films featuring his discovery Marlene Dietrich; Ernst Lubitsch was noted for the sophistication of his comedies and a number of boudoir musicals; Rouben Mamoulian used sound and visual innovations in films like *City Streets* (1931) and *Dr. Jekyll and Mr. Hyde* (1932). Among the leading American directors at Paramount was one of its founder members, Cecil B. DeMille, who moved from the enjoyably Shavian *Cleopatra* (1934) to *The Plainsman* (1937), a patriotic celebration of the frontiersmen of America.

In sharp contrast to MGM's *nouveau riche* glitter and Paramount's aristocratic sheen was Warner Bros., more in tune with the working class. Notorious for frugality, no studio better evoked the Depression, both in the content and look of its films. Their memorable cycle of gangster movies, beginning with *Little Caesar* (1930) and *Public Enemy* (1931), brought stardom to Edward G. Robinson and James Cagney respectively. The studio's social dramas reflected the mood of the period even more directly – a criticism of the penal system (*I Am a Fugitive in a Chain Gang*, 1932), the iniquities of the gutter press (*Five Star Final*, 1931) and racial prejudice (*They Won't Forget*, 1937). Also prominent were a number of biopics – *The Story of Louis Pasteur* (1936), *The Life of Emile Zola* (1937) and *Juarez* (1939) – which mostly starred Paul Muni and carried a strong moral message. Even Warners' musicals, with their spectacular kaleidoscopic dance numbers by Busby Berkeley, were hard-edged, set in a seedy show business milieu peopled with gold-digging chorus girls and middle-aged sugar daddies.

Universal Pictures, who started the decade with Lewis Milestone's award-winning *All Quiet on the Western Front*, became associated in the public's mind with horror films. This was due to the impact of Tod Browning's *Dracula* (1931), *Frankenstein* and *The Bride of Frankenstein* (1935) made by his rival James Whale, Karl Freund's *The Mummy* (1932), and their vivid monsters, played by Bela Lugosi and Boris Karloff. But over-expenditure led Laemmle's Universal to the verge of bankruptcy in 1935. Rescue came in the shape of a fresh-faced, sunny-natured 15-year-old soprano named Deanna Durbin, whose string of popular, and exceedingly profitable, musicals began with *Three Smart Girls* in 1936.

Among the smaller studios was Columbia, which grew from a Poverty Row company into a major contender, thanks to the dynamic leadership of the tyrannical Harry Cohn and the creative talent of Frank Capra. It was the films directed by the latter, *It Happened One Night* (1934), *Mr. Deeds Goes to Town* (1936), and *Mr. Smith Goes to Washington* (1939) that really put Columbia on the map.

The policy of RKO Radio Pictures, born on the eve of the decade was to produce films capitalizing on its contract stars. The most popular were Fred Astaire and Ginger Rogers, whose seductive harmony of movement was given expression in nine musicals between 1933 and 1939. Katharine Hepburn made her screen debut in *A Bill of Divorcement* (1932) at RKO, starred in *Morning Glory* and *Little Women* (both in 1933), and partnered another RKO star, Cary Grant, in *Bringing Up Baby* (1938). But RKO's greatest success of the decade was *King Kong* (1933) which, despite the Depression, earned almost $2 million.

A latecomer to the majors, 20th Century-Fox was formed in 1935 by the merger of Twentieth Century Pictures with the Fox Film Corporation. The man most responsible for their particular formula was production chief Darryl F. Zanuck. The new studio immediately launched into an ambitious program that emphasized technical polish and visual gloss. As Shirley Temple was their only big name, Zanuck signed up Norwegian ice-skating champion Sonja Henie, Loretta Young, Don Ameche, Tyrone Power and Alice Faye. The studio made most of its money from light-hearted musicals as well as folksy re-creations of America's recent past, the most profitable being those directed by Henry King – *In Old Chicago* (1937) and *Alexander's Ragtime Band* (1938) – and John Ford's *Drums Along the Mohawk* (1939).

By the late 30s, Hollywood had fully recovered from the jitters of the Depression. The implementation of the rigid self-regulating body the Production Code Administration, set up in 1934 to placate the

20th
CENTURY
FOX

WARNER BROS. PICTURES INC
JACK L. WARNER
EXECUTIVE PRODUCER
PRESENTS

WARNER BROS. PICTURES
Presents

Metro Goldwyn Mayer
ARS GRATIA ARTIS
TRADE
MARK

itics of Hollywood's morals, ough inhibiting the realistic treat- ent of serious topics, helped to sure a regular family audience hich could depend on high-quality, offensive entertainment.

This kind of entertainment was uilt on the foundation of various nres – musicals, thrillers, West- ns – each conforming to a strict rmula, narrative and structure, lculated to assure commercial ccess. From then on, audiences on ve continents would associate Hol- wood with the supreme technical ills and polished productions that utdid most foreign rivals.

The industry that came closest to ollywood's approach, though not s resources, was that of Great ritain. Following the first British lkie, Alfred Hitchcock's *Blackmail* 929), which made intelligent use the new possibilities, were *Tell ngland* (*Battle of Gallipoli*, 1931), om Anthony Asquith, and Victor aville's musical *Evergreen* (1934)

COLUMBIA

ith Jessie Matthews, one of the rightest stars in Britain.

Hitchcock, however, remained e outstanding British director of e 30s with thrillers such as *The lan Who Knew Too Much* (1934), *he Thirty-Nine Steps* (1935) and *he Lady Vanishes* (1938). Despite ich players as Laurence Olivier, ivien Leigh and Anna Neagle, the ost popular stars came from the usic hall, notably George Formby, racie Fields and Will Hay.

The decade's dominant figure in ritain was Alexander Korda, a ungarian emigré who produced nd directed *The Private Life of enry VIII* (1933), with Charles aughton playing the much-married onarch. After its unprecedented ccess on both sides of the Atlantic, ith Laughton the first actor to win n Oscar in a British film, Korda ecided to take on Hollywood. A an of immense persuasiveness, he btained a loan from the Prudential ssurance Co. and built expensive udios at Denham. There, his London Films produced *Things to Come* (1936), based on the prophetic novel by H.G. Wells; *Rembrandt* with Laughton; and *Elephant Boy* with the young Sabu, all of them big-budget features.

More than 200 features were produced in Britain in 1937, but due to waste and inefficiency few companies finished the year in the black. By 1938, production dropped to half of the previous year, but there was a brief period of American activity in British studios when MGM set up production in England, successfully teaming English and American stars – Robert Taylor and Vivien Leigh in *A Yank at Oxford* (1937), Robert Donat and Rosalind Russell in *The Citadel* (1938) and Donat together with Greer Garson in *Goodbye Mr. Chips* (1939). However, for more personal, provocative and individual artistic expression, one must look outside the English-speaking world.

For the French cinema, the 30s was one of its most prolific and cre-

WALT DISNEY

ative eras. The decade saw some 1,300 films, beginning with René Clair's joyful experiments in sound, *le Million* and *A nous la liberté*, Jean Renoir's innovative *la Chienne*, shot in the noisy streets of Montmartre using direct sound, and Marcel Pagnol's realist-style *Angèle* (1934).

In 1936, the celebrated Cinémathèque Française was founded by Henri Langlois, Jean Mitry and Georges Franju. Its original purpose was to save silent classics threatened by the coming of sound, but Langlois began acquiring a huge collection, embracing almost any film that came his way.

French cinema of the late 30s was characterized by poetic realism, a profoundly pessimistic yet romantic style, embodied in the screen personality of Jean Gabin. This tragic hero made an impact in many films, among them Julien Duvivier's *Pépé-le-Moko* (1937), Marcel Carné's *Quai des Brumes* (1938) and Jean Renoir's *la Grande illusion* (1937). These works, and those by Jacques Feyder, Jean Grémillon and Jean Vigo placed France in the forefront of world cinema, until the shattering impact of World War II.

Italy and Germany, under fascist regimes, were subject to strict censorship, particularly since the authorities considered the cinema as an important medium for propaganda. Mussolini's dictatorship encouraged the expansion of Italy's film industry for the service of the State. Thus, in 1935, the government established the famed film school, Centro Sperimentale di Cinematografia, and two years later the enormous Cinecittà studios were opened near Rome, boasting Europe's most advanced production facilities.

When Hitler rose to power in Germany in 1933, Propaganda Minister Josef Goebbels took charge of all forms of public expression. Jews were purged from the industry, and liberals and independent-minded filmmakers were more subtly dis-

A
Paramount
Picture

couraged. Consequently Germany's best directors, such as Fritz Lang and G.W. Pabst, left the country. Before he went, Lang made two masterly sound films, *M* (1931), with a hypnotic Peter Lorre, and *The Testament of Dr. Mabuse* (1933).

G.W. Pabst's *Westfront 1918* (1930) and *Kameradschaft* (1931) pleaded the cause of international brotherhood, a message that would make him *persona non grata* with the Nazis. Leontine Sagan's anti-authoritarian *Maidens in Uniform* (1931) courageously, albeit discreetly, treated a lesbian relationship. Naturally, films of this sort were absent from the German cinema during the Hitler years, when audiences were fed innocuous musicals, anti-Semitic tracts, and self-glorifying documentaries such as Leni Riefenstahl's powerful hymn to the Third Reich, *Triumph of the Will* (1934).

The spirit of creative liberty, experimentation and vitality in the Soviet cinema of the 1920s was stifled before it could extend into the sound era. The derogatory term 'formalism' was current with Stalin's increasing stranglehold on the Party. Sergei Eisenstein was one of the first to feel the effects of change, and, after a fruitless trip to America and several aborted projects, the great director's only completed film of the 30s was *Alexander Nevsky* (1938), the best of several that extolled heroic figures from Russia's past. Among the many escapist musicals and stolid literary adaptations, a few stood out: Mark Donskoi's *Gorky Trilogy* (begun in 1938) and Kozintsev and Trauberg's *The Maxim Trilogy* (begun in 1935).

It was during the 1930s that Japanese cinema developed into a thriving industry. Annual feature output grew to 500 by the end of the decade, though few reached foreign screens. Despite the increasing militarism of the society, reflected in historical costume dramas, there were a number of films in which gentle humanism was expressed,

UNITED
ARTISTS

notably by Kenji Mizoguchi (*Sisters of the Gion*, 1936; *The Story of the Late Chrysanthemums*, 1939), and Yasujiro Ozu (*The Only Son*, 1936).

Of all the periods in the history of the cinema, none was more important to its growth and aesthetic perfection than the 1930s. In the decade between the Depression and World War II, American society suffered its most sweeping changes since the Civil War, which were reflected and distorted by the popular arts, especially by the cinema. European countries were wrung by shifts in their social fabric, though their film industries continued unabated. But it was Hollywood's combination of talent, capital and expertise that developed the world's largest, most powerful system for the production and distribution of motion pictures. Many greater films were being made elsewhere during that period, but for sheer concentration of imagination and enterprise, Hollywood remained unequaled.

RONALD BERGAN

1930

1928/9 Academy Awards, Ambassador Hotel, 3 April

Best Film: *Broadway Melody* (dir: Harry Beaumont)
Best Director: Frank Lloyd *(The Divine Lady)*
Best Actor: Warner Baxter *(In Old Arizona)*
Best Actress: Mary Pickford *(Coquette)*

1929/30 Academy Awards, Ambassador Hotel, 5 Nov.

Best Film: *All Quiet on the Western Front* (dir: Lewis Milestone)
Best Director: Lewis Milestone
Best Actor: George Arliss *(Disraeli)*
Best Actress: Norma Shearer *(The Divorcee)*

Paris, 10 January
René Clair has taken on the young journalist Marcel Carné as assistant director for his film *Sous les toits de Paris* (*Under the Roofs of Paris*).

Vienna, 15 January
The National Austrian Library has decided to set up film archives to store copies of the best films – documentary, fiction and educational.

Geneva, 31 January
According to the International Trade Organization, capital investment in cinema is at $4 billion. Half of this is accounted for by the U.S. where there are 225,000 workmen, 30,000 extras and several thousand actors working in the industry.

Berlin, 4 February
Menschen am Sonntag (*People on Sunday*), made by Robert Siodmak in collaboration with Billy Wilder, Edgar G. Ulmer and Fred Zinnemann, has been well-received here.

New York, 15 February
The president of the MPPDA, Will H. Hays, gave a preliminary review of sound cinema at the city's Trade Organization banquet. According to him, the new technique has attracted 10 million more spectators to American cinemas than in 1929. This success reflects the enormous effort and investment spent: $500 million in two years to install the equipment necessary to make talkies.

Hollywood, 10 March
John Gilbert's career, unlike his partner Greta Garbo's, appears to be seriously jeopardized by talking pictures: his voice tests are reported to be disastrous.

Paris, 21 March
The critics are protesting over the toning down of the French version of G.W. Pabst's German-made film *Pandora's Box*.

New York, 5 April
The board of directors has dismissed William Fox as president of the company he founded in 1915. This move is the consequence of months of costly though unsuccessful attempts to take control of MGM.

Moscow, 8 April
Release of *Zemlya* (*Earth*), Alexander Dovzhenko's eagerly awaited film, produced by the Kiev studios.

Paris, 10 April
The young director Luis Buñuel has returned from Spain where he has just finished shooting his second film *l'Age d'or* (*The Golden Age*). It was supposed to be a sequel to *Un chien andalou* (*An Andalusian Dog*), but the quarrel between Buñuel and Salvador Dali led to changes in the original project.

Paris, 29 April
The painter Marc Chagall is hostile to color films, which "will take away the charm of the cinema, for, by getting closer to reality, the cinema moves away from life. It thus becomes but artifice."

Hollywood, 15 May
Irene Mayer, the daughter of Louis B. Mayer, has married David O. Selznick, the son of producer Lewis Selznick, who is himself a producer at Paramount.

Hollywood, 15 June
The success being enjoyed by *The Virginian*, directed by Victor Fleming with Gary Cooper in the lead, marks the return to popularity of cowboy films.

Le Havre, 5 August
Erich von Stroheim has returned to Europe with the filmmaker William Wyler on board the steamer *Ile-de France*. This is his first visit since he left for the U.S. in 1909. He intends to visit his homeland Austria.

New York, 25 August
Release of *Abraham Lincoln*, D.W. Griffith's first talking film.

France, 7 October
The engineer René Barthélemy has just given a demonstration at Montrouge of his research in the field of television. For the first time an acted scene has been filmed, transmitted at a distance and projected onto a screen in front of an audience.

Paris, 25 October
The writer Jean Cocteau's first experimental film, *The Blood of the Poet* (originally *The Life of a Poet*), has been given a private screening.

New York, 31 October
MGM's new Western, *Billy The Kid*, starring John Mack Brown and filmed in the new "Realife" widescreen process, has been exhibited for the first time. However, the result has met with little enthusiasm from audiences.

Paris, 10 November
Jean Choux has begun filming *Jean de la lune* (*John of the Moon*) at the Epinay studios. The film is an adaptation of the play by Marcel Achard and stars Madeleine Renaud and Michel Simon.

Portugal, 15 November
The filmmaker José Leitao de Barros, who became known this year with *Maria Do Mar*, is making the first Portuguese talking film entitled *A Severa*, produced by the German company Tobis.

Hollywood, 15 November
Darryl F. Zanuck has been named the head of production for Warner Bros.-First National.

China, 30 November
The censorship law aimed at "protecting the national industry" and also "preventing any attacks on the dignity of the Chinese" has been promulgated.

Tokyo, 12 December
Release of *Ojosan* (*Young Miss*), directed by Yasujiro Ozu.

France, 31 December
Four hundred eighty-four full-length films have been shown this year in the 4,221 cinemas here: 100 French, 113 German and 231 American.

Paris, December
Well-known director and archivist Jean Painlevé has founded the Institute of Scientific Film in association with the School of Applied Arts and Crafts.

BIRTHS

Detroit, 10 February
Robert Wagner

New York, 19 February
John Frankenheimer

Georgia, 27 February
Joanne Woodward

Indianapolis, 24 March
Steve McQueen
(Terence Steven McQueen)

Rome, 21 April
Silvana Mangano

Paris, 29 April
Jean Rochefort

Iowa, 30 April
Cloris Leachman

San Francisco, 31 May
Clint Eastwood
(Clinton Eastwood Jr.)

Paris, 24 June
Claude Chabrol

Edinburgh, 25 August
Sean Connery
(Thomas Connery)

New York, 28 August
Ben Gazzara

Paris, 3 December
Jean-Luc Godard

France, 11 December
Jean-Louis Trintignant

DEATHS

Los Angeles, 23 February
Mabel Normand

Hollywood, 25 August
Lon Chaney

***The Blue Angel** establishes Josef von Sternberg as a filmmaker of true stature and reveals a potentially huge star in Marlene Dietrich. Their international success is assured.*

MARLENE DIETRICH
EMIL JANNINGS
DER blaue ENGEL
PLAKAT · SIEBENFARBIG · DIN A1 60x84 cm · ENTWURF BONNÉ

▷

America under the Gallic spell of dashing Maurice Chevalier

Chevalier with Jeanette MacDonald in ***The Love Parade****, directed by Lubitsch.*

New York, 19 January
Maurice Chevalier has seduced the United States with his Gallic charm, Parisian accent and his mischievous smile. *The Love Parade*, directed by Ernst Lubitsch, the French singer's second Hollywood film after *Innocents of Paris*, is currently playing in 200 theaters. Paramount, who was looking for a "young singing star", signed him to a contract last March to make 10 films in three years. Thus Maurice Chevalier entered talking films after having already appeared in 13 silents since his screen debut in 1908 in Jean Durand's production *Trop crédule*. Born on 12 September 1888, at 29 rue du Retrait, Ménilmontant, Chevalier left school when he was only 10 years old, and worked in a drawing-pin factory to help support his mother. Performing as a singer at a cafe in the boulevard Strasbourg from the age of 12, he went on to the Folies-Bergère in 1908, becoming Mistinguett's partner four years later. When he returned from a POW camp in 1918, he resumed his top position at the side of "La Miss" on the stage of the Casino de Paris. It was here that he wore his famous straw hat and carried a cane for the first time. These props have become part of his personality, which is brilliantly on display in *The Love Parade*, Lubitsch's first sound film.

French talkies made in Berlin

Paris, 1 February
The first French talking picture, *La nuit est à nous* (*The Night is Ours*), has been filmed in the UFA studios in Berlin, and the result is a worthy tribute to the French and German technicians who have mastered the techniques of sound. Presently 23 prints are ready for distribution. This Franco-German co-production has been filmed in two versions: a French one directed by Henry Roussel, and a German version handled by Carl Froelich, who established his name in newsreels in the early days of cinema and now has his own production company. This German version was presented in Berlin last December, where it was warmly received by the critics and public alike.

Marie Bell: ***The Night is Ours****.*

The police do not share in the acclaim for Sergei Eisenstein

Paris, 17 February
There was a lively evening at the Sorbonne, where a large audience had gathered to see Sergei Eisenstein's latest film, *The General Line*, in the presence of the director. But the Police Commissioner, Chiappe, fearing disturbances, banned the projection of the film just as it was about to start. The expected uproar did not, however, take place. Eisenstein, who gave a lecture on Soviet cinema, was heartily applauded. But what is he doing in Paris? It all began six months ago. On 19 August 1929, Sergei Eisenstein and his close collaborators – his assistant Grigori Alexandrov and his camera expert Edouard Tissé – left Moscow to familiarize themselves with sound techniques abroad. On the way to Hollywood, they visited various European countries, where the director gave lectures to help them with their finances. During these wanderings, Eisenstein was able to meet, among others, Josef von Sternberg, George Bernard Shaw, Jean Cocteau, Luigi Pirandello and Albert Einstein. But the Sorbonne incident has placed in doubt the continued presence of the three Soviets in France, and in fact, they risk expulsion.

Eisenstein photographed in 1925, during filming of ***The Battleship Potemkin****.*

Film producers accept a production code

Hollywood, 17 February
The leading American film studios, as represented by Will H. Hays, president of the Motion Picture Producers and Distributors of America (MPPDA), have now apparently accepted in principle a new Code of Production. This is actually a form of self-censorship, which has been proposed by Martin Quigley, editor of the *Motion Picture Herald* and the Reverend Daniel A. Lord, the well-known Catholic priest who also edits a prominent religious publication. This new decision is meant to silence, once and for all, those many vociferous critics of the film industry, making it clear that producers plan to turn over a new leaf after the kind of excesses and sagging moral standards seen on the screen in recent years, not to mention the personal scandals of the 1920s. The wide-ranging provisions of the new Code refer not only to crime, brutality and sex as portrayed in the cinema, but also deals with such contentious subjects as vulgarity, obscenity, blasphemy and profanity, in addition to the handling of national feelings, race, religion, and the treatment of animals.

'ternberg's 'Blue Angel' makes Marlene a star

arlene Dietrich is Lola, the destructive temptress in **The Blue Angel**.

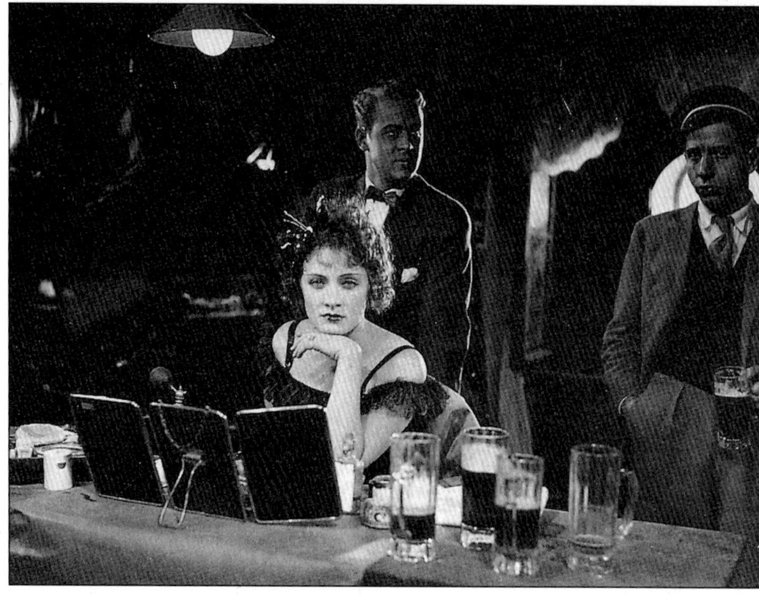

Germany's sensational new star during the filming at the studios of UFA.

rlin, 1 April
FA's first talking picture is *The ue Angel*, directed by Josef von ernberg. He returned from Holly- ood to handle the picture, adapted m the Heinrich Mann novel *Pro- ssor Unrath*, at the request of UFA d *The Blue Angel's* star, actor nil Jannings. So far so good, but ernberg immediately ran into a problem over his choice of leading lady to play Lola Lola, the promiscuous dance-hall singer who first enslaves then destroys Jannings' stuffy schoolmaster. Jannings and producer Erich Pommer had their own candidates for the role, but Sternberg insisted on casting the 28-year-old Marlene Dietrich, whom he had spotted in a Berlin revue, "Two Neckties". To just about everybody else involved in the film, Dietrich's screen test appeared quite unexceptionable, however Sternberg saw in Dietrich, already a familiar figure in German films, the quality of cheap but overpowering sexuality which makes Lola Lola so compelling a figure. Sternberg's judgment was proved correct as soon as the cameras began to roll. Dietrich's performance is a masterpiece of indolent, sluttish sensuality. As she sings in the film, she is "made for love from head to foot". Jannings, however, was less impressed during filming. Enraged that Dietrich was stealing the film from him, he nearly throttled his co-star on the set when the script called for him to attack her.

ragedy-struck film finally reaches screen

e of the happier moments.

New York, 9 March
Such Men Are Dangerous, a William Fox presentation which opens today, is a dark drama which manages to steer itself toward a satisfactorily happy ending. The making of this movie, however, ended in appalling tragedy, with the loss of 10 lives. On 2 January at Santa Monica, with filming already completed, director Kenneth Hawks (brother of Howard) embarked on a series of retakes for a flying scene with which he was dissatisfied. Two airplanes, carrying the film crew to photograph a third which features in the movie, collided in the air, burst into flame and hurtled into the Pacific Ocean below. Director Hawks was killed, together with his two cameramen, the property man, the grip, and several assistants. It is hard to conceive that the producers or leading players Warner Baxter and Catherine Dale Owen will be able to take pleasure in viewing the finished product.

'Gimme a Visky, Baby' orders Garbo

New York, 14 March
The build-up to Greta Garbo's long-delayed debut in the talkie from Eugene O'Neill's *Anna Christie* has been dominated by the main slogan "Garbo Talks!", but audiences have to sit through 34 minutes of the picture before Garbo says in seductive contralto tones, "Gimme a visky with a ginger ale on the side – and don't be stingy baby". Her fans can breathe again.

Garbo as Eugene O'Neill's unhappy Anna Christie, with Charles Bickford. ▷

Dovzhenko's new masterpiece is censored

A peasant urinates in the fields in this superbly executed film from the USSR.

Moscow, 8 April

The Soviet authorities have censored a number of scenes in Alexander Dovzhenko's latest film *Earth*. In this story of collectivization in the Ukraine in the face of opposition from the Kulaks (landowners), there were particular episodes that displeased the powers that be: when a dead man's betrothed mourns him, naked and hysterical, and when the peasants urinate in the radiator of a tractor. Nevertheless, even in this truncated version, the film's poetic images make an enormous impact. Dovzhenko has created an indelible picture of a rural paradise earned by the blood of the peasants.

Stylish René Clair conquers talking films

Pola Illery, Albert Préjean, and the song from ***Sous les toits de Paris****.*

Paris, 25 April

René Clair's first sound film, *Sous les toits de Paris (Under the Roofs of Paris)*, has just opened at the Moulin Rouge. As nothing has been heard from the director of *The Italian Straw Hat* in regard to the talkies, his debut in this new field has been awaited with impatience. Produced by the French subsidiary Tobis, a shot last January and February the Epinay studio using sets c signed by Lazare Meerson, the fi has immediately become a succe Billboards announce it as "one hu dred percent French singing a speaking." The scenario tells of t adventures of a street singer (Alb Préjean) in love with a very pre Romanian girl (Pola Illery), wh he protects from her lecherous lov (Gaston Modot), but he is accus of theft. The cast is filled out some typically French characte The use of sound and Clair's atm pheric direction, allows one to f get the slightness of the subject. T catchy title song is rendered by va ous Parisians, with the camera m ing from singer to singer and fr house to house.

The German defeat has given rise to two major war films

Berlin, 23 May

It is in the time of peace that pacifism is most expressed. The memory of the war that tore people apart is still vivid and painful. For G.W. Pabst and Lewis Milestone, there is neither a just war nor heroes – nothing but victims. *Westfront 1918*, adapted from a novel by Ernst Johannsen, depicts the daily life of German soldiers in the last months of the war against France. Pabst reveals the horror and futility of life in the trenches by concentrating on four soldiers, and the ignorance at home of the reality at the Front. *All Quiet on the Western Front*, from a novel by Erich Maria Remarque, contains a message that can only be displeasing to warmongers. Lewis Milestone denounces the tragedy of the Great War, but also the blind fanaticism of the military hierarchy. Particularly effective are the tracking shots of soldiers attacking enemy lines, and the counter-attacks with deaths on both sides.

Lew Ayres (left) and Louis Wolheim in ***All Quiet on the Western Front****.*

G.W. Pabst's ***Westfront 1918****: another film from the German viewpoint.*

The director absorbed in his work.

'aramount in Paris empted by Europe

aris, 30 June
'ill Paris develop into the new cen-r of filmmaking in Europe? The nance of this happening appears ore likely now that Paramount, e giant American studio, has be-ome involved in a new type of multi-ngual film production here. Over a ear ago, in May 1929, production nief Jesse Lasky came to France ith a plan to increase the produc-on of talkies in Europe, as well as ith proposals for the formation of Franco-American company that ould exploit the sound patents held y Western Electric. Within eight onths, the new company had been t up. It has acquired the studios at oinville that were previously owned y Ciné-Romans, and has built six ew sound stages installed with the test sound equipment. Here, the chnicians will be able to shoot in a ultiplicity of languages including rench, of course, but also German, alian and Russian.

Heroics from Hawks in 'The Dawn Patrol'

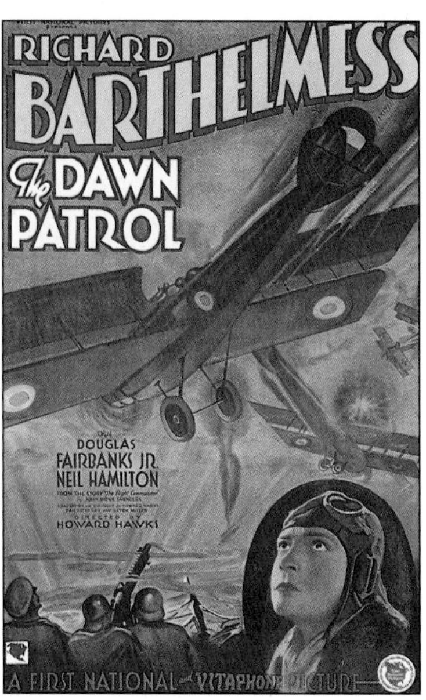
RICHARD
BARTHELMESS
The DAWN PATROL
DOUGLAS FAIRBANKS JR.
NEIL HAMILTON
DIRECTED BY HOWARD HAWKS
A FIRST NATIONAL & VITAPHONE PICTURE

A moving tale of bravery.

New York, 10 July
Director Howard Hawks' first talking picture, *The Dawn Patrol*, tells the story of a beleaguered fighter squadron in the Great War, whose leader (Richard Barthelmess) is hated by his officers because of the high death rate in his unit. Hawks is still coming to terms with the technical demands of the talkies. The film soars when aircraft are dueling over the trenches, but comes to earth with a bump on the ground, mainly because of the stilted script written by the director, with Dan Totheroh and Seton I. Miller. Nevertheless, Hawks' message that war is a synonym for waste comes over loud and clear. But legal trouble is brewing over the picture. Writer R.C. Sherriff is to sue Warner Brothers for shoehorning "substantial portions" of his play *Journey's End* into *The Dawn Patrol*. And Howard Hughes, the producer-director of another aerial saga called *Hell's Angels*, is also threatening to take Warners to court, claiming that entire sections of his film appear in *The Dawn Patrol*. Things are shaping up for a legal battle over *The Dawn Patrol* every bit as lively as its spectacularly choreographed dogfights.

Whoopee for two newcomers

Pop-eyed Eddie Cantor and friend!

Hollywood, 7 September
Saucer-eyed singing comic Eddie Cantor, along with the rest of the cast of *Whoopee!*, come direct from Florenz Ziegfeld's Broadway hit. Ziegfeld sold the rights to Samuel Goldwyn, who then produced this Technicolor musical. Goldwyn also brought in Broadway dance director Busby Berkeley to choreograph the musical numbers. Aside from Cantor's hilarious clowning, the inventive dance routines stand out, especially the opening number.

irst UFA operetta

erlin, 15 September
JFA has filmed its first operetta, nd it is directed by William Thiele. 'he theme of *Three Men and Lillian* hardly new, but audiences have een charmed by its sprightly tunes, s lavish sets and the romantic pair-g of English-born songbird Lilian Iarvey and Willy Fritsch. In the 'rench version Henri Garat takes ver from Fritsch.

ilian Harvey and Henri Garat.

Fox director Raoul Walsh makes an epic American Western

Hollywood, 24 October
Everything about director Raoul Walsh's Western, *The Big Trail*, is on an epic scale which befits this tale of a pioneering wagon train in Oregon. It has been shot in a 70-mm wide-screen process by 14 cameramen. There are a staggering 80 featured players and 2,000 Indians. The Fox studio, which has been financially ailing of late, has been pouring money into the production in an attempt to repeat the huge sucess scored seven years ago by James Cruze's *The Covered Wagon*. Hopes are high for the star of *The Big Trail*, a 23-year-old actor by the name of John Wayne. Born Marion Michael Morrison in Iowa in 1907, Wayne moved out West as a child. After he attended college at USC on a football scholarship, cowboy star Tom Mix found him a job in the Fox property department. There he met and befriended director John Ford, and even worked as a set decorator on Ford's *Mother Machree*. Ford gave him a bit part in that film and then used him again in three more pictures. People began to take notice of this husky young man whose physique is perfectly suited to action pictures. It was Ford who suggested to Walsh that he cast Wayne, known to all his friends as "Duke", as the lead in *The Big Trail*. Walsh, who had originally intended to play the lead himself, seized the opportunity. Most of the picture's budget was earmarked for location shooting, the large cast and expensive new equipment, and he couldn't afford a big-name star. Anyway, as Walsh has observed, "Duke sits better on a horse than anyone I've ever seen, knows how to handle a gun and isn't spooked by Indians or buffaloes." Among the set-piece perils he faces in *The Big Trail*, as the trapper leading a wagon train of settlers through Indian-infested territory, are Indian attacks, blizzards, raging rivers and mountains. Will Fox's investment pay off?

A scene from ***The Big Trail****, directed by Raoul Walsh with John Wayne (right).* ▷

Chaplin's view of talking pictures

Paris, 1 November
Charles Chaplin is the last great star to hold out against the arrival of sound, and it is perhaps a measure of his greatness that he can still defy the march of progress. Chaplin continues to believe that the talkies are only a passing fad, and one of which he clearly disapproves. In an interview for the American magazine *Silver Screen*, he predicts the imminent disappearance of pictures which are "100 percent talking." Remaining an implacable opponent of the films with sound he adds, "There is nothing that I could tell you about the talking pictures that would be more eloquent than my silence." In his latest film *City Lights*, which he has just completed, he has made only limited use of the technical resources of sound. *City Lights* is a silent film with explanatory titles. Synchronized music and simplistic sound effects accompany the action, leaving Chaplin vigorously unrepentant: "The talkies! You can say that I detest them!"

Second year of the Academy Awards

*Universal's **All Quiet on the Western Front** won two major Awards.*

*Norma Shearer, the Best Actress, with Conrad Nagel in **The Divorcee**.*

Los Angeles, 5 November
For the second consecutive year, the Academy Awards ceremony has taken place at the Ambassador Hotel. As was expected, the Best Picture for 1929/1930 was *All Quiet on the Western Front*, with its director, Lewis Milestone, receiving the Best Director award. This year, a new award had to be designated to honor Sound Recording. The first winner is Douglas Shearer for his work on the prison drama *The Big House*. Norma Shearer, Douglas' sister, was the winner of the Best Actress award for her performance in *The Divorcee*. It is a role that Gret Garbo turned down because she wa offended by the story of a liberate woman who seeks vengeance on he philandering husband by taking tw lovers. Norma Shearer was give the role because she begged he husband, Irving Thalberg, to let he play something more daring tha usual. The Best Actor was Georg Arliss, making his sound debut i the lead of *Disraeli* at the age of 6 Arliss has been rather dismissive c the movies, but sound has now give him a chance to use his excellen voice. The winners for 1928/192 were given their Academy Award last April. *Broadway Melody* wa named Best Picture while Warne Baxter and Mary Pickford receive the acting award for *In Old Arizon* and *Coquette*, respectively.

Paramount builds up Marlene Dietrich to rival the great Garbo

Hollywood, 4 November
Paramount's film *Morocco* brings the second collaboration between director Josef von Sternberg and his sensational German protégée, Marlene Dietrich. Before the premiere of *The Blue Angel*, Sternberg had shown a rough cut to Paramount, for whom he had worked in Hollywood, and the studio agreed to sign Dietrich for one film. To nobody's surprise she is again cast as a cabaret singer, this time playing merry hell with the Foreign Legion, giving up commanding officer Adolphe Menjou for the handsome young Gary Cooper, and tottering after him into the desert in her evening dress. *Morocco* has been premiered in New York on the same day as the English-language version of *The Blue Angel*, and the colossal public excitement this has generated has made Paramount determined to keep their new star at any price. The studio is also sinking millions of dollars into a feverish publicity campaign to build up Dietrich as the newest rival to MGM's biggest imported star, Garbo. Battle royal has been joined.

*Marlene, the new star, in her first Hollywood film, **Morocco**, co-starring Gary Cooper and directed by Sternberg.*

George Arliss was voted Best Acto for his strong portrayal of Disraeli.

ergei Eisenstein out of luck in Hollywood

e Soviet director and his cameraman Edouard Tissé, who accompanied him.

llywood, 18 November
tumn has started in a somber
nner for Sergei Eisenstein and his
o compatriots, Grigori Alexan-
ov and Edouard Tissé, now that
State Department is refusing to
olong the visas of the Soviet trio.
seems that the authorities have
en in to the pressure of the anti-
mmunist campaign to have them
ported. It is little more than a year
ce they left Moscow. One remem-
rs how they traveled to various
ropean countries, where Eisen-
in gave numerous lectures. Some-
es their presence was judged to
inopportune, as in Paris. They
Cherbourg on 8 April last on the
ropa bound for New York, and
ived in Hollywood at the invita-
n of Paramount. Since their trip
Moscow in 1926, Douglas Fairnks and Mary Pickford have had
thing but praise for the Soviet
ster. On the basis of this flatter-
report, Paramount hired Eisen-
in "to direct several films at the
nvenience of the contractee." Ei-
stein was full of hope on arrival
Hollywood with his colleagues
d the English writer Ivor Mon-
u. He was given the full-scale
dio publicity treatment but, alas,
the projects the director pro-
sed were rejected, among them
G. Wells' *The War of the Worlds,*
ld by Blaise Cendrars, and *An*
erican Tragedy from Theodore
eiser. As might have been antici-
ted, his scripts for *Gold* (retitled
tter's Gold) and *An American Trag-*
y were regarded as unsuitable by the executives at Paramount – too long, too socially conscious, not commercial enough, too expensive, etc. Clearly, the brilliant Russian director and the giant Hollywood studio have been unable to find a common ground, and Eisenstein's contract has now been canceled.

Jean Gabin is a star in spite of himself

Gabin in **Chacun sa chance**, with his wife Gaby Basset. They married in 1925.

Paris, 19 December
Mistinguett's leading man, the 26-year-old Jean Gabin, has made his screen debut in *Chacun sa chance*, a musical directed by René Pujol and Hans Steinhoff. Starring alongside Gabin is his wife Gaby Basset. The son of a cafe entertainer, Gabin began his working life as a laborer, but at the age of 19 was persuaded by his father to launch his stage career as a dancer at the Folies-Bergère. Still enjoying live theater, the busy Gabin is currently appearing on stage with Simone Simon and Edwige Feuillère.

Luis Buñuel and 'L'Age d'or' move from scandal to censorship

Paris, 12 December
The police commissioner Jean Chiappe yesterday banned showings of the surrealist Luis Buñuel's *L'Age d'or* after the screen was splattered with ink by a fascist group. Copies were seized this morning. This film, made thanks to the patronage of the Viscount Charles de Noailles, was released on 2 October last at Studio 28, and has undergone many cuts since. Because of its originality of form, the violence of subject, the condemnation of bougeois morality, and also the fierce anti-clericalism, the film created a sensation. Members of the Anti-Jewish League interrupted a showing nine days ago with the cry, "Death to the Jews!" There could be more than 8,000 francs worth of damage done by demonstrators who destroyed the paintings on exhibition in the theater, among them works by Salvador Dali, Juan Miro, Max Ernst and Man Ray. Capitalizing on the incident, *Le Figaro* and *L'Ami du Peuple* demanded the banning of the film, and Chiappe has been more than happy to oblige them.

Lya Lys, the leading lady of a film which celebrates obsessional passion.

L'AGE D'OR
de luis bunuel

The shock waves sent out make the film a veritable surrealist manifesto.

Chapter 3
"THE HORROR IN THE DARK"
Nat Levine presents
TOM TYLER IN
"The PHANTOM OF THE WEST"
with a
Great Supporting Cast including
WILLIAM DESMOND · TOM SANTSCHI · DOROTHY GULLIVER
JOE BONOMO · TOM DUGAN AND OTHERS
An ALL-TALKING SERIAL IN 10 THRILLING CHAPTERS
Directed by ROSS LEDERMAN
MASCOT SERIALS

Handsome, athletic Tom Tyler began his career in 1924, first as a stunt man.

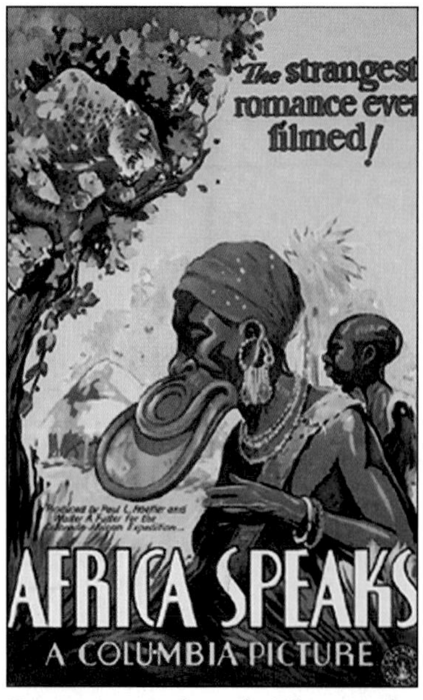
The strangest romance ever filmed!
AFRICA SPEAKS
A COLUMBIA PICTURE

Documentary about the Ubangi tribe.

WILLIAM FOX presents
HOT FOR PARIS
LOUDER AND FUNNIER THAN THE COCK EYED WORLD
VICTOR McLAGLEN
RAOUL WALSH
ALL TALKING MOVIETONE RIOT of LAUG

Raoul Walsh directed this music comedy-drama for William Fox.

Nat Levine presents
KING OF THE WILD
ALL TALKING SERIAL
WALTER MILLER · NORA LANE · DOROTHY CHRISTY · TOM SANTSCHI
BORIS KARLOFF · VICTOR POTEL and ARTHUR McLAGLEN
MASCOT SERIAL
CHAPTER 2
The Tiger of Destiny

Villains, chases and a prison escape enlivened this popular action serial from director Richard Thorpe.

A Lady's Morals
GRACE MOORE
Metro Goldwyn Mayer ALL TALKING PICTURE
REGINALD DENNY
WALLACE BEERY
JOBYNA HOWLAND

The Metropolitan Opera soprano and Broadway star Grace Moore makes her silver screen debut.

CARL LAEMMLE presents
ALL QUIET ON THE WESTERN FRONT
Produced by CARL LAEMMLE JR. Directed by Lewis Milestone
UNIVERSAL PICTURE

Universal's biggest and most serious film to date, and a landmark war movi

NANCY
CARROLL
IN
Dangerous
Paradise
WITH
RICHARD ARLEN
and WARNER OLAND
a Paramount ALL TALKING Picture

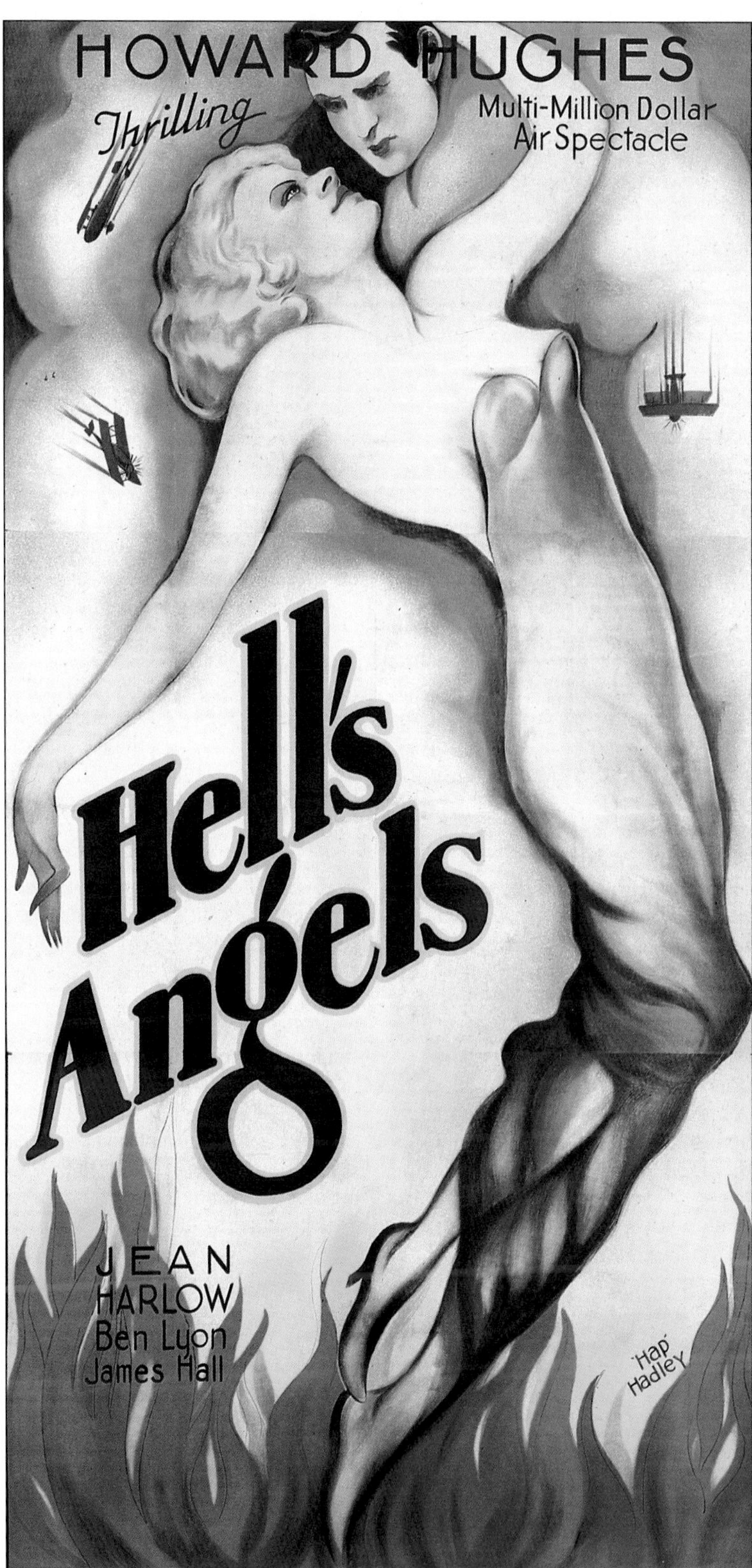
HOWARD HUGHES
Thrilling
Multi-Million Dollar
Air Spectacle
Hell's
Angels
JEAN
HARLOW
Ben Lyon
James Hall
'Hap' Hadley

THÉ presents
HOLIDAY
with
ANN HARDING
MARY ASTOR
Edward Everett HORTON
ROBERT AMES
HEDDA HOPPER
An astonishing
drama of double life
and double love!..
PATHÉ PICTURE

Inspiration Pictures Inc. presents
Henry
King's
Dramatic
Success!
"Hell Harbor"
with
LUPE VELEZ
Jean
Hersholt
and
John
Holland
Distributed by
ATLANTIC
PICTURES, Inc.

Top left: Richard Arlen rescued Nancy Carroll from villains in a South Seas island hotel in this blood-and-thunder movie, whose plot was suggested by Joseph Conrad's novel ***Victory***.

Above: Spectacular aerial sequences and the presence of 19-year-old Jean Harlow were among the major attractions of this $3 million movie.

Far left: This barbed romantic comedy, based on a stage hit, had a young lawyer switching his affections to his fiancee's more sympathetic sister.

The tempestuous Lupe Velez, known as the 'Mexican Spitfire' (and who was educated in a convent), starred in her seventh feature film.

1931

1930/1 Academy Awards, Bilmore Hotel, 10 Nov.

Best Film: *Cimarron* (dir: Wesley Ruggles)
Best Director: Norman Taurog *(Skippy)*
Best Actor: Lionel Barrymore *(A Free Soul)*
Best Actress: Marie Dressler *(Min and Bill)*

Moscow, 5 January
Director Vsevolod Pudovkin has disconcerted audiences with his first sound film *la Vie est belle* (*Life is Beautiful*), due to his exaggerated use of slow motion and an overly extravagant scenario.

Los Angeles, 30 January
Charlie Chaplin's latest film *City Lights*, with himself, Virginia Cherrill and Harry Myers, has been given a triumphant reception. The sound track was added after shooting was completed on the film with an over $1.5 million budget.

Paris, 25 February
The newly fitted out Pagoda cinema has opened in the Chinese Pavilion, rue de Babylone. A Spanish film, *The Price of a Kiss*, was scheduled for the opening.

Hollywood, 5 March
Carl Laemmle, founder and president of Universal has just celebrated his 25th anniversary in the movie business. He opened his first nickelodeon 25 years ago in 1906.

Marseilles, 10 March
A group of cinemagoers is offering to teach audiences how to whistle down bad films. The initiative is worrying local advertising agencies.

Toyko, 25 March
The Nippon Gekkyo, with its three screens, immense organs and 4,000 seats, is advertised as being more modern than the Gaumont Palace.

Algiers, 20 April
Charlie Chaplin has arrived from Nice to join his older brother Sydney. This is his first visit to North Africa and he intends among other things to visit the Casbah.

London, 30 April
French director René Clair is fast becoming one of Britain's favorite filmmakers. His film *le Million* is a triumphant success.

Paris, 30 April
The press has echoed rumors about the international crisis in the cinema industry. The problem seems to be an apparent lack of availablity of new releases in proportion to the cinema network's needs, exacerbated by the increase in costs incurred by the use of sound equipment.

Hollywood, 20 May
Mary Pickford has bought up all her silent films. She feels that the recent technical advances in the cinema industry has made actors in old films look ridiculous.

New York, 22 May
Premiere of *The Smiling Lieutenant*, directed by Ernst Lubitsch and starring Maurice Chevalier.

Berlin, 30 June
All Quiet on the Western Front has finally been passed by the censors here, despite violent protests from Hitlerian youth groups and the disapproval of the Reichstag. Special precautions have been taken in the cinema where it is being screened to avoid incidents.

New York, 21 August
Release of *Pardon Us*, the first short feature starring the comic actors Laurel and Hardy. It was directed by James Parrott and photographed by George Stevens.

Stockholm, 14 September
Release of *En Natt* (*One Night*), by Gustav Molander, with Uno Henning and Bjorn Berglund. The quality of the soundtrack is proof that Molander has made the transition to talking films without a hitch.

France, 15 September
Film director G.W. Pabst is deep in the coalmines in the Pas-de-Calais region where he is completing the last shots for *Kameradschaft* with the participation of local miners. The film is based on the 1906 mining catastrophe in Courrières.

Hollywood, 19 September
Release of the Marx Brothers' *Monkey Business*, by Norman McLeod.

USA, 20 September
At a recent congress, cinema managers united against the abundance of gangster films, which according to them, irritate the public. They also stated that the exhorbitant salaries paid to film stars are to blame for the high cost of film hire.

France, 30 September
The wet summer has been catastrophic for film production. Several films being shot on location had to be postponed or canceled.

New York, 8 October
Mrs. Josef von Sternberg has initiated proceedings against the actress Marlene Dietrich, wife of Rudolph Sieber, for the "alienation of her husband's affection."

Paris, 17 October
Release of Alexander Korda's film *Marius*, adapted from Marcel Pagnol's play. The Paramount-Pagnol production stars Pierre Fresnay, Raimu and Orane Demazis.

New Jersey, 18 October
Death of the inventor and cinema pioneer Thomas Alva Edison, at the age of 84.

Hollywood, 20 October
Douglas Fairbanks is putting the finishing touches on the film he made during a recent voyage. It is to be released under the title *Around The World in 80 Minutes*.

Lisbon, 20 October
The 23-year-old filmmaker Manuel de Oliveira has released his first film *Duoro, Faina Fluvial*. This project is a cut above the run-of-the-mill and mediocre documentaries which have proliferated since a new law in their favor was passed.

New York, 10 December
The Struggle, directed by D.W. Griffith, has been a serious failure both financially and in the eyes of the critics.

Berlin, 31 December
This year, UFA has experimented with a new color process for a film called *The Many-Colored World of Animals*.

BIRTHS

California, 5 January
Robert Duvall

Mississippi, 17 January
James Earl Jones

Milan, 28 January
Lucia Bosé

Los Angeles, 30 January
Gene Hackman
(Eugene Alden Hackman)

Indiana, 8 February
James Dean
(James Byron Dean)

London, 15 February
Claire Bloom

Boston, 26 March
Leonard Nimoy

Italy, 10 May
Ettore Scola

Pennsylvania, 28 May
Carroll Baker

France, 5 June
Jacques Demy

Paris, 1 July
Leslie Caron

New York, 17 September
Anne Bancroft

Sweden, 29 September
Anita Ekberg

North Dakota, 30 September
Angie Dickinson

France, 1 October
Philippe Noiret

Paris, 25 October
Annie Girardot

Berlin, 6 November
Mike Nichols
(Michael Igor Peschkowsky)

Italy, 8 November
Paolo Taviani

*The tough, dramatic William W[ellman] movie, **The Public Enemy**, is a[n]other success for Warners' 'crimin[al-]versus-society' subjects. It has crea[ted] a major new star in James Cagne[y].*

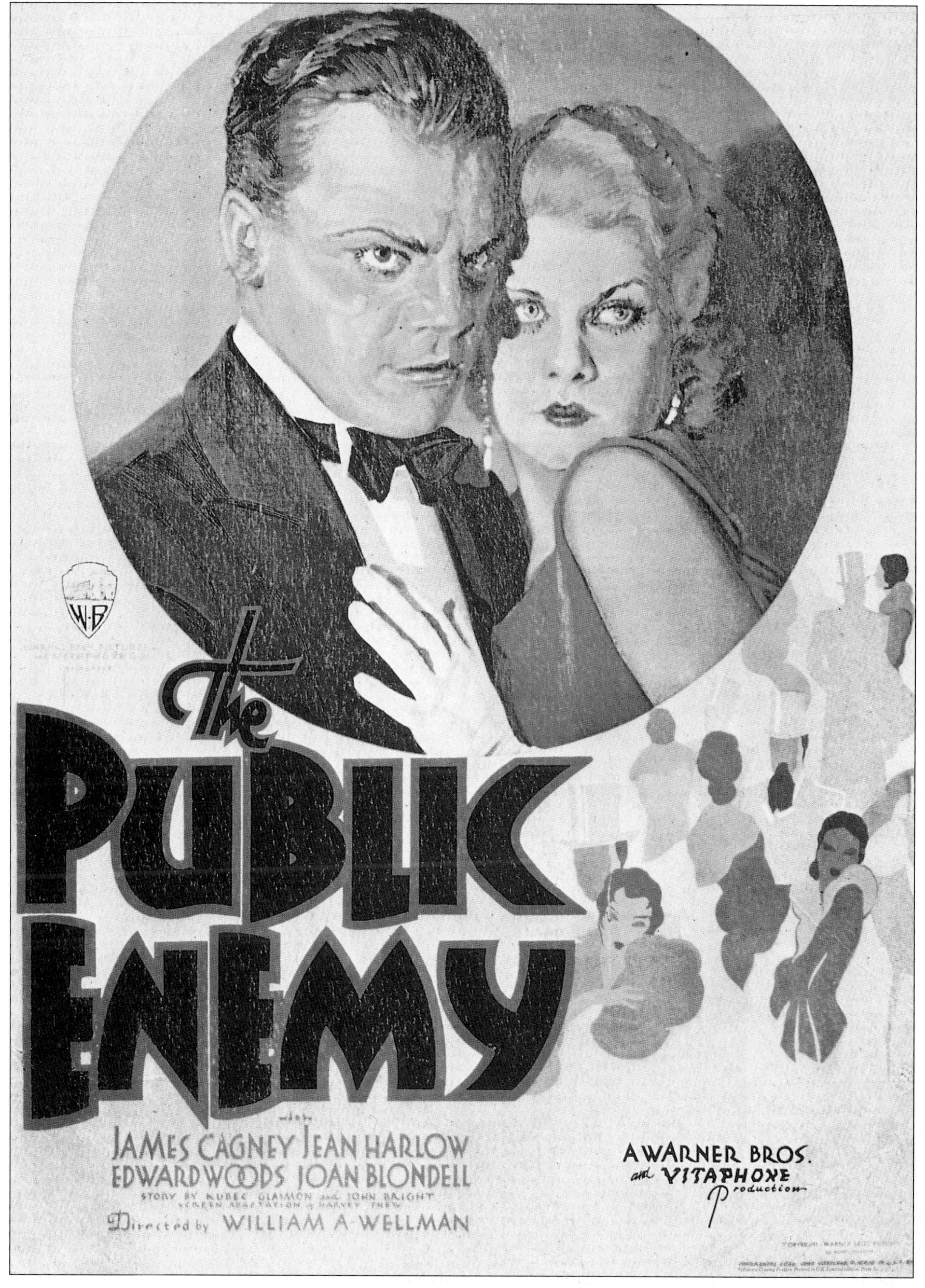

the PUBLIC ENEMY
JAMES CAGNEY JEAN HARLOW
EDWARD WOODS JOAN BLONDELL
STORY BY KUBEC GLASMON and JOHN BRIGHT
Directed by WILLIAM A. WELLMAN
A WARNER BROS. and VITAPHONE Production

The great disaster for Abel Gance

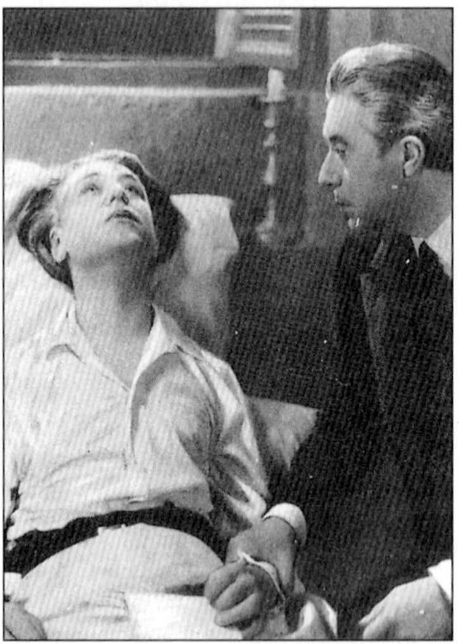

Gance at Colette Darfeuil's bedside.

Paris, 24 January
Never has a film by Abel Gance been so badly received as *The End of the World*, which was shown at a gala evening at Olympia. Featuring Gance himself in the role of Christ, and actor Victor Francen, the film confused the public, who found it incomprehensible. Opinion has also been scandalized by the manner in which Gance's first talkie was modified and cut by half on the orders of the distributor Jacques Haik, who had acquired full rights. *The End of the World* was originally meant to run more than three hours. The director was absent from the performance as a protest at the "distorted version" on display. Among other things, the sound quality was poor. Only a minority of critics remained, sensitive to the visionary aspect of this sadly missed opportunity.

Abel Gance, the film's director, also plays a leading part as Christ.

'The Threepenny Opera': too strong for the producers

216F

Left: Florelle with Albert Préjean in the French version. Right: Margo Lion in the role of the rebellious prostitute.

Berlin, 19 February
With his *The Threepenny Opera*, an adaptation from the Brecht-Weill work, G.W. Pabst has returned to the realism of his previous films. Set in 19th-century London, Mack the Knife, the King of the Underworld, kidnaps and marries Polly Peachum, daughter of the King of Beggars. Furious, the latter sends his gang to pursue the undesirable son-in-law. But all ends well when beggars and rogues are reconciled and make their fortunes with the involuntary complicity of the forces of law and order. Brecht and Weill were to do the screenplay, but the desire to give it even more an bourgeois bite than the stage versic proved too strong for the film pr ducers. Yet the performances, pa ticularly from Lotte Lenya (Weill wife), and the wonderful songs, r tain much of the original pungenc

F.W. Murnau's life is tragically ended at the age of forty-two

Hollywood, 18 March
The new film by F. W. Murnau and Robert Flaherty, *Tabu*, has just been released in American theaters. Unhappily, it will be a posthumous work for Murnau, because the famous German director (born on 28 Dec. 1888) was killed in a car accident on the Santa Barbara highway scarcely a week ago. In February 1929, the admired director of *Sunrise* broke his contract with Fox, which had obliged him to supply them with three films. He and Flaherty then formed their own company and took off for the South Seas to make *Tabu*. Murnau then proceeded to develop his own version of the film. He used the people and setting of the shimmering paradise of Tahiti to tell a fictional story – a young fisherman falls in love with a virgin dedicated to the gods. "When our yacht entered port in Bora-Bora," Murnau stated recently, "the indigenous population had never even seen a Kodak." The film was left silent and unfinished, forcing Paramount to post-synchronize it with a score by Dr. Hugo Riesenfeld.

A tender and tragic swan song, co-directed by Murnau and Robert Flaherty.

mes Cagney another recruit for Warner Bros. underworld

tle Caesar: Edward G. Robinson.

James Cagney, the 'Public Enemy' (center), with Edward Woods (left).

llywood, 15 May
llowing Edward G. Robinson's cess in *Little Caesar*, Warner s. have now another hard-edged gster movie and a new star in nes Cagney, whose dynamic permance as an underworld king in *blic Enemy* has caused a sensation. Pint-sized Cagney was originally cast as second lead to Edward Woods, but director William A. Wellman soon had second thoughts and swapped the roles. And Cagney plays hoodlum Tom Powers with gleeful relish, mashing a grapefruit in Mae Clark's face, and finally being delivered dead and bound up on his mother's doorstep. Cagney, a former vaudeville song-and-dance man, was co-starring alongside Joan Blondell in *Penny Arcade*, when Warners bought the show, turned it into *Sinner's Holiday*, and took an option on him at $400 a week.

Columbia
PICTURE
PLATINUM
BLONDE
ORETTA YOUNG
OBERT WILLIAMS
EAN HARLOW
RANK
APRA

ith her starring role in *Platinum londe* for director Capra, lovely ean Harlow has not only collect- a soubriquet but has inconstably demonstrated that she is actress of considerable talent.

The shadow of Nazism hovers above 'M'

Berlin, 11 May
M, director Fritz Lang's first talking picture, was originally entitled *The Murderers Are Among Us*, but the Nazi Party, suspecting that the title is in some way aimed at them, has turned menacing pressure on Lang. Inspired by grim real-life events in the city of Dusseldorf, where a child-killer conducted a reign of terror, Lang has created an extraordinary portrait of a psychopath. In the role of the murderer, Peter Lorre, a little-known stage actor, gives a stunning performance. Squat and corpulent, with melancholy eyes alternately beseeching or bulging with terror as he is hunted down by both the police and the underworld, Lorre creates a killer who is both pitiable and deeply disturbing, a victim himself of a diseased society. Lang has placed his monster in the context of a Germany gripped by an economic and moral crisis in which the sickness which drives the child-killer is paralleled by the uncontrollable impulses of evil political forces lurking in the shadows. The horribly plausible split personality of Lorre's killer is a metaphor for the forces which divide Germany today. Though Lang may have changed the title, the meaning remains the same. He has successfully captured the atmosphere of a city besieged by fear and torn between order and mob violence.

10000

Little Inge Landgut and the silhouette of Peter Lorre, the murderer.

Clara Bow assailed by fresh scandals

Hollywood, 9 June
Clara Bow is to be released from the contract she signed with Paramount in August 1926. Clara's fall from grace has been sad and sudden. Only two years ago the "It" girl was voted America's most popular female star, but now she is adrift on a sea of scandal. It seems that her colorful private life bears more than a passing resemblance to her first talkie, *The Wild Party*. Last year the vivacious star disclosed that she had paid off a doctor's wife for "alienation of affections." Then the dizzy girl ran up a debt of $14,000 in a Lake Tahoe gambling joint without realizing what she was doing. But worse was to come. Earlier this year Clara accused her former secretary Daisy de Voe of embezzlement and took her to court. Daisy hit back with hard evidence of the actress's predilection for booze, drugs and gigolos. Daisy was convicted on only one of 37 charges of larceny she faced, and was sentenced to a year's imprisonment, but emerged from the trial ahead on points. When Bow signed with Paramount she demanded and secured the removal of the get-out clause which allowed the studio to release her in the event of scandal. The studio also agreed to pay Bow a lump sum when the contract was dissolved, but only if no scandal attached to her departure. With Bow's popularity plummeting by the week, Paramount has decided to release her, but is hanging on to the payoff dough.

A successful star but very fragile.

▷

Sternberg and Dreiser in disagreement

*Phillips Holmes and Sylvia Sidney, the doomed lovers of **An American Tragedy**.*

Hollywood, 22 August
Josef von Sternberg's latest film, *An American Tragedy* starring Sylvia Sidney and Phillips Holmes, has just been released. Freely adapted from the novel of the same title written by Theodore Dreiser, the picture has had a troubled production history, during which Dreiser hauled Sternberg before the courts for taking too many liberties with the original. Sternberg has been obliged to restore so many scenes that in themselves they constitute a kind of premiere. As a result, the director has disowned the picture.

Danielle Darrieux at the Gaumont Palace

Paris, 11 September
A 14-year-old girl named Danielle Darrieux takes the leading role in Wilhelm Thiele's *le Bal*, now being shown on a giant screen at the huge, newly-renovated Gaumont Palace. Born in Bordeaux on 1 May 1917, Darrieux was chosen by the director, from hundreds of candidates, after a competition and a series of auditions. In this comedy-drama, opposite André Lefaur and Germaine Demoz, she plays a neglected daughter who destroys the invitations to a ball given by her parents, as revenge for their indifference. This film re-opened the famous cinema built by Leon Gaumont in 1911.

*At age 14, Danielle in **le Bal** with André Lefaur and Germaine Dermoz.*

Best actress Dressler is a surprise winner

Left to right: George Arliss, Marie Dressler, Norma Shearer, Lionel Barrymore

Hollywood, 10 November
Glamour was very much on display among the Best Actress nominees at the fourth annual Academy Award banquet that was held in the Biltmore Hotel and attended by Vice President Charles Curtis. At the gala were German star Marlene Dietrich, who made her sensational Hollywood debut in *Morocco*, cool blonde Ann Harding for *Holiday*, patrician beauty Irene Dunne for *Cimarron* and Norma Shearer, last year's winner for *A Free Soul*. But all lost to overweight, frumpish, 61-year-old Marie Dressler for her performance in *Min and Bill*. Shearer presented the statuette to her with the words, "to the grandest trouper of them all – the grand old firehorse of the screen." Dressler was a popular winner even with her younger more attractive rivals, who might have been jealous had any of their contemporaries won. In the Best Actor category 51-year-old Lionel Barrymore swooped the Oscar for *A Free Soul* from under the noses of his juniors. *A Free Soul*'s director Clarence Brown, Garbo's favorite, was up for the Best Director prize in the company of Josef Von Sternberg (*Morocco*), Lewis Milestone (*The Front Page*) and Wesley Ruggles (*Cimarron*). Surprisingly, it was Norman Taurog who got the judges' nod for his direction of *Skippy*, pleasant family entertainment with a cast of mostly children. However, Ruggles was compensated by the spectacular Western *Cimarron* winning the Best Picture award.

*Best Actor Lionel Barrymore with Norma Shearer in **A Free Soul**.*

rt imitates life for te Janie Marèze

ris, 19 November
o months after her death in a car :ident, Janie Marèze, the young r of *Mam'zelle Nitouche*, has died ain, this time on screen in Jean noir's latest film *la Chienne*. In she plays a prostitute who winds being killed by an amateur paint- whom she had been exploiting. apted from a novel by Georges la Fouchardière, *la Chienne* is astonishingly realistic work. The onstruction of Montmartre is mirable, as are the sound effects :d to recreate the ambiance of this pular and bohemian district. The formances of Marèze, Michel non (the client) and Georges Fla- nt (the pimp) are remarkable.

nie Marèze and Georges Flamant.

e actress was imposed on Renoir the co-producers, Roger Richebé d Pierre Braunberger. The direc- had wanted his wife, Catherine essling, or Florelle, for the role. t Janie Marèze knew how to get ound the producers as much as e does the two men in the film. it if the film imitated life, so life itated the film. During the shoot- , Simon became infatuated with arèze who fell for Flamant. The n completed, Flamant was driv- the fair Marèze along the Rivi- in his new Cadillac, when he lost ntrol of the car and it crashed, ling his passenger. Michel Simon is so distraught during the funeral t he fainted, and later had to be strained from attacking Flamant.

Lugosi's Dracula and Karloff's Frankenstein, rivals in horror

Hollywood, 21 November
Thanks to Universal, Hollywood is enjoying a horror boom. With Bela Lugosi in the title role, Tod Browning's *Dracula* was an immediate hit when it was released last February, and now it's the turn of director James Whale's *Frankenstein* to pull in big audiences. Adapted from a play by Peggy Webling, which in turn drew on Mary Shelley's celebrated Gothic novel, the film stars Colin Clive as the scientist who creates an uncontrollable monster. But it is the monster, played by Boris Karloff, who carries off the honors. Brilliantly made up by Jack Pierce, who made him a 18 inches taller and a full 65 pounds heavier, Karloff excites both horror and pity. The studio now has two new stars.

THE ORIGINAL HORROR SHOW!
FRANKENSTEIN
THE MAN WHO MADE A MONSTER
COLIN CLIVE·MAE CLARKE
JOHN BOLES·BORIS KARLOFF

Boris Karloff is a marvelous monster.

DRACULA
BELA LUGOSI
HELEN CHANDLER
ABRAHAM STOKER

Tod Browning, the brilliant director of ***Dracula****, now has stiff competition from Universal's James Whale.*

Sagan's 'children' prove disturbing

Berlin, 28 November
For her big screen directing debut, Leontine Sagan has chosen a previously unexplored theme: the relations between young women living in a highly authoritarian boarding school. Manuela, played by Hertha Thiele, reacts badly to the school's aggressive form of discipline, finding her only solace in the company of a sympathetic teacher, played by Dorothea Wieck. But this "forbidden passion" leads to Manuela's attempted suicide. This all-female production treats a difficult subject with tact and delicate eroticism.

Hertha Thiele is the central figure.

A glorious achievement for René Clair

Paris, 18 December
René Clair's third talkie, *A nous la liberté* has just been shown to the public. Great praise was heaped upon his previous film, *le Million*, released last April, though it had a rather antiquated plot and was a commission by Tobis. What elevated that operetta was its remarkable soundtrack and *mise en scène*. This time, Clair has been able to put his brilliant technique at the service of a wonderful subject and a scenario which he wrote himself. The story tells of a friendship which unites Louis (Raymond Cordy) and Emile (Henri Marchand), two escapees from prison. Separated by the years, chance brings them together again, when Louis becomes a worker in Emile's gramophone factory. After Emile is threatened with blackmail, he decides to give his factory to the workers, and the two buddies take to the road as tramps. By making clever use of songs, sound effects, rhythmic dialogue and accurately choreographed movements, Clair has created a musical comedy satire on the work ethic and the dehumanizing effects of mass-production techniques. In a light-hearted manner, an analogy is made between the prison and the factory, underlined by Lazare Meerson's striking sets, dwarfing the workers.

1524

The significance of the title only becomes clear at the end of the film.

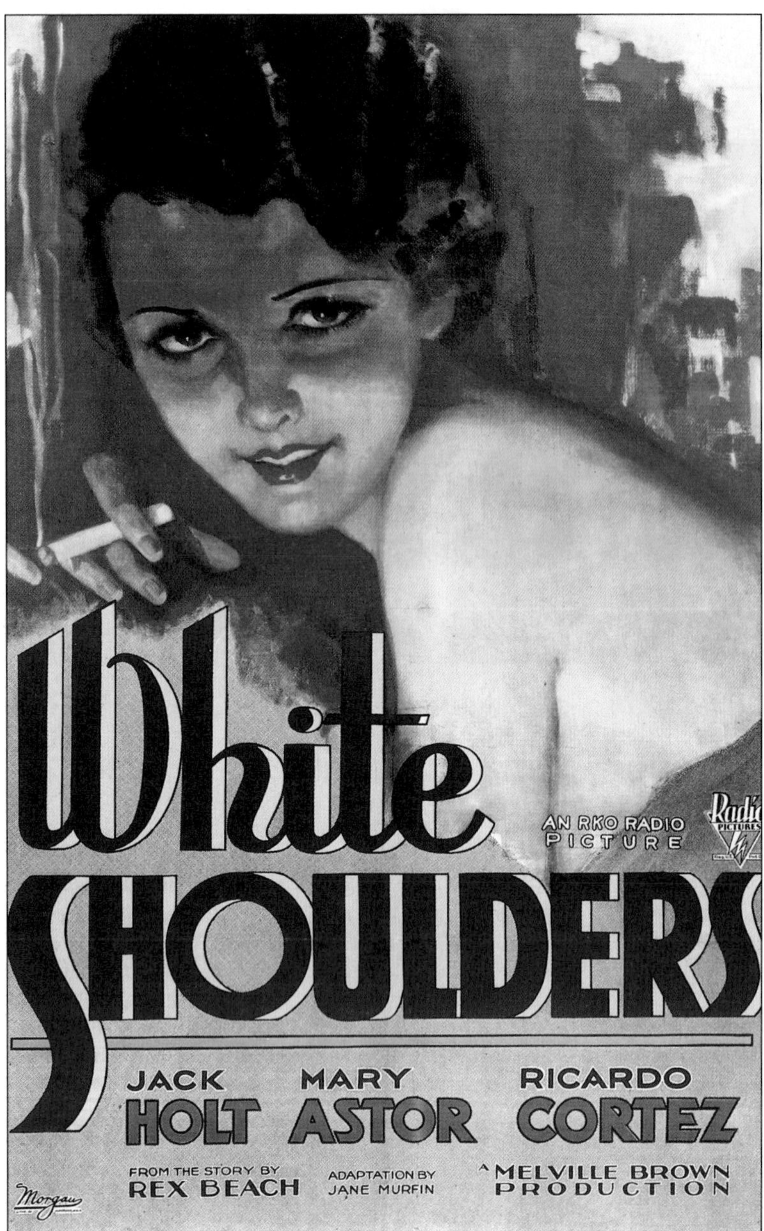
White
SHOULDERS
AN RKO RADIO PICTURE
JACK HOLT
MARY ASTOR
RICARDO CORTEZ
FROM THE STORY BY REX BEACH
ADAPTATION BY JANE MURFIN
A MELVILLE BROWN PRODUCTION

Based on a Rex Beach novel, this was a remake of the 1924 film ***Recoil***.

Gable and Garbo in ***Susan Lennox***.

Jean Harlow in ***The Iron Man***.

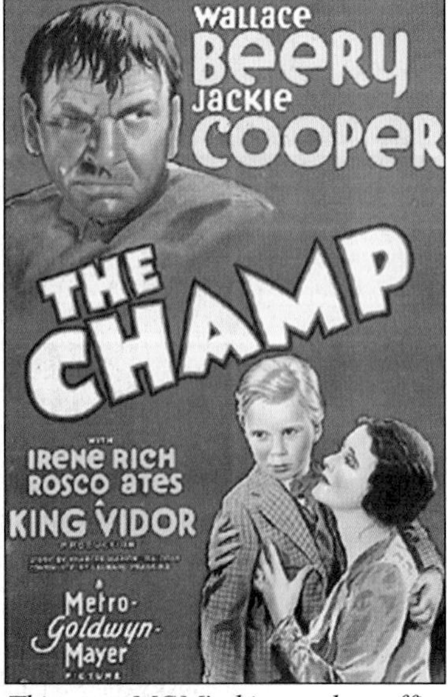
Wallace
Beery
Jackie
Cooper
THE
CHAMP
Irene Rich
Rosco Ates
King Vidor
Metro-Goldwyn-Mayer

This was MGM's biggest box-office success in 1931.

JOE E.
BROWN
in
LOCAL
BOY
MAKES
GOOD
with
DOROTHY
LEE
DIRECTED BY
MERVYN LE ROY
A FIRST NATIONAL
PICTURE

Brown as botanist in campus capers.

Janet
GAYNOR
Charles
FARRELL
in
Delicious
George Gershwin's Mu
with EL BRENDEL · RAUL ROUL
directed by David Butler

This was an insipid poor gal-rich guy romance with a great Gershwin score.

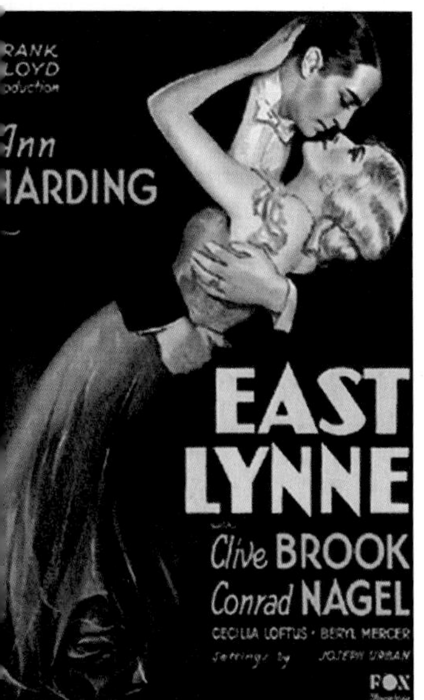
Ann
HARDING
EAST
LYNNE
Clive BROOK
Conrad NAGEL
CECILIA LOFTUS · BERYL MERCER
FOX

e cast included Cecilia Loftus, an tress considered 'one of the greatest imics the stage has ever known'.

THE
BIG
ROAR
BERT WHEELER
ROBT. WOOLSEY
DOROTHY LEE
CAUGHT PLASTERED
RKO-RADIO PICTURE

One of three 1931 films with Wheeler & Woolsey, a successful partnership since ***Rio Rita*** *(1929).*

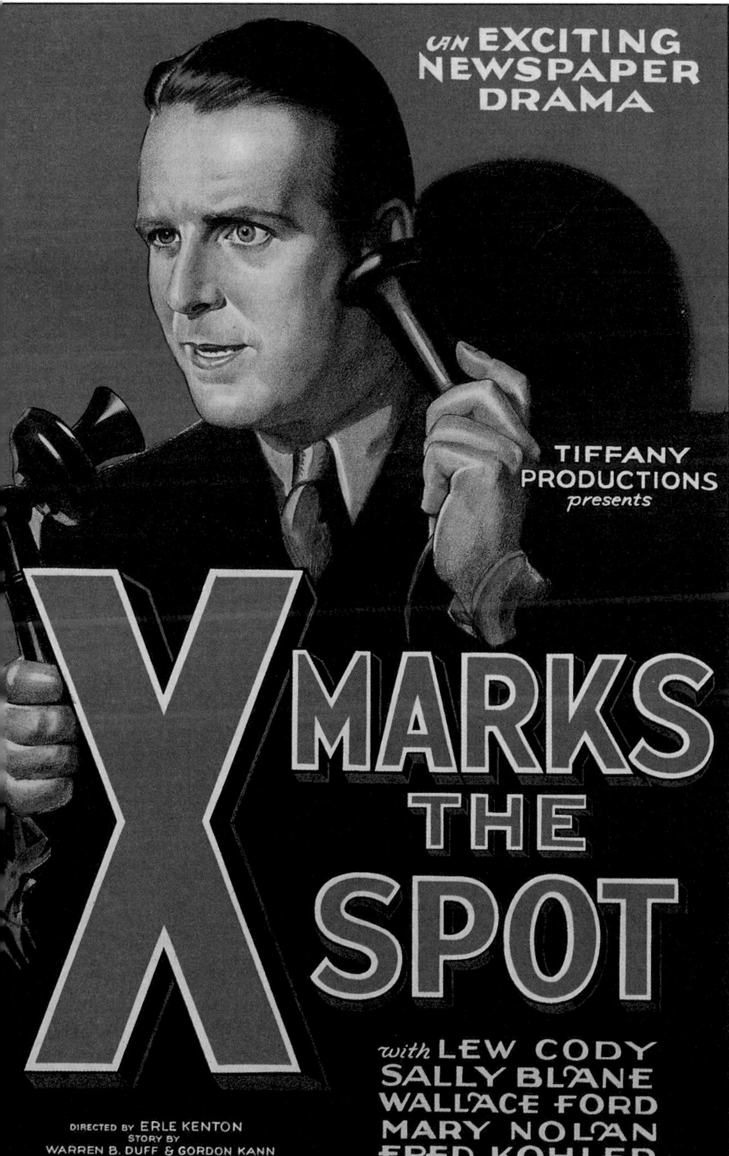
AN EXCITING
NEWSPAPER
DRAMA
TIFFANY
PRODUCTIONS
presents
X
MARKS
THE
SPOT
with LEW CODY
SALLY BLANE
WALLACE FORD
MARY NOLAN
FRED KOHLER
DIRECTED BY ERLE KENTON
STORY BY
WARREN B. DUFF & GORDON KANN
PRODUCED BY SAMUEL BISCHOFF

-Keystone Cop Erle C. Kenton directs Lew Cody (Mabel Normand's hubby).

TERRIFIC AS ALL CREATION
Edna Ferber's
COLOSSAL
CIMARRON
WESLEY RUGGLES
PRODUCTION
Distributed by
RKO DISTRIBUTING CORP.
with
RICHARD DIX
IRENE DUNNE
ESTELLE TAYLOR · WILLIAM COLLIER, JR.
NANCE O'NEIL · EDNA MAY OLIVER

Spanning 1889 to 1929, this sweeping Western cost RKO over $1.4 million.

HOOT GIBSON
PETER B. KYNE'S
"WILD HORSE"
ALBERTA VAUGHN · STEPIN FETCHIT
GOLDEN STATE RODEO
ALLIED PICTURES CORP. LTD.

Gibson is a popular B-Western cowboy, fondly known as 'The Hooter'.

LE MILLION
UN FILM DE
RENÉ
CLAIR

French René Clair's charming operetta was influencing screen musicals.

1932

1931/2 Academy Awards, Ambassador Hotel, 18 Nov.

Best Film: *Grand Hotel* (dir: Edmund Goulding)
Best Director: Frank Borzage *(Bad Girl)*
Best Actor: Wallace Beery *(The Champ)*
Fredric March *(Dr. Jekyll and Mr. Hyde)*
Best Actress: Helen Hayes *(The Sin of Madelon Claudet)*

New York, 20 January
Hiram S. Brown has resigned as president of RKO. He will be replaced by the president of the NBC radio network, Merlin Aylesworth.

Hollywood, 2 February
Joe Brandt, Columbia's president, has sold his interest in the company to Jack Cohn and his brother Harry Cohn, who is now both head of the studio and the company president.

Los Angeles, 17 February
Release of *Shanghai Express*, directed by Josef von Sternberg, with Marlene Dietrich and Clive Brook.

Berlin, 24 February
Premiere of *Das Blaue Licht* (*The Blue Light*), made by and starring Leni Riefenstahl.

Hollywood, 28 February
Cecil B. DeMille has left MGM to return to Paramount, the company he helped found. Paramount will be financing and distributing all of his future screen projects.

London, February
The film director of Hungarian origin, Alexander Korda, has been made Paramount's representative in Great Britain and has created a production firm, London Films.

Shanghai, 3 March
Japanese bombs have destroyed numerous cinemas and studios. Thirty companies have ceased production.

Paris, 10 March
Abel Gance in association with André Debrie, the inventor of the Parvo movie camera, has lodged a new application to the patent office for his Perspective Sound process.

Rochester, 14 March
Death of the industrialist George Eastman, founder and president of Eastman Kodak as well as the inventor of flexible film with celluloid-reinforced perforations.

Paris, 17 March
The president of the republic Paul Doumer attended the premiere of Raymond Bernard's film *les Croix de bois* (*The Wooden Crosses*), based on the novel by Roland Dorgelès about the Great War.

Germany, 21 April
In response to public protest, authorities have lifted the ban on Slatan Dudow's film *Kuhle Wampe*, based on a scenario by Bertolt Brecht.

New York, 19 May
Release of Howard Hawks' *Scarface*, with Paul Muni. Hawks played a role and produced the film.

Tokyo, 27 May
Because of the success of *Mushibameru haru* (*Lost Springtime*), Mikio Naruse can be considered one of the most talented Japanese directors.

Hamburg, 1 June
The negatives of Eisenstein's *Que Viva Mexico!*, which were on the way from America to Moscow, have been intercepted in transit on novelist Upton Sinclair's orders and sent back to Hollywood.

Hollywood, 28 June
The Movietone City studios, built by Fox on West Pico Boulevard, have been inaugurated. They consist of 10 huge movie sets and numerous large outbuildings.

Munich, 18 August
Premiere of *Die verkaufte Braut* (*The Bartered Bride*), adapted from Smetana's comic opera by Max Ophuls, with Jarmila Novotna and Karl Valentin.

Berlin, 14 September
Release of *Der träumende Mund* (*Melo*), by Paul Czinner, based on French author Henry Bernstein's play, with Elisabeth Bergner and Rudolph Forster. In the French version the roles are played by Gaby Morlay and Pierre Blanchar.

Berlin, 15 September
Fritz Lang has started filming *The Testament of Dr. Mabuse* in UFA's studios in Neubabelsberg.

Hollywood, 2 November
The stage actress Katharine Hepburn is making her screen debut in George Cukor's *A Bill of Divorcement*, alongside John Barrymore and Billie Burke.

Los Angeles, 8 November
Release of Lubitsch's *Trouble In Paradise*, starring Miriam Hopkins, Kay Francis and Herbert Marshall.

New York, 10 November
Mervyn LeRoy's film, *I Am a Fugitive From a Chain Gang*, with Paul Muni and Glenda Farrell has received enthusiastic press. The plot is about the inhuman treatment of a condemned but innocent man.

Paris, 11 November
Release of *Boudu sauvé des eaux* (*Boudu Saved from Drowning*) by Jean Renoir, produced and interpreted by Michel Simon, adapted from the play by René Fauchois.

Moscow, 3 December
Vsevolod Pudovkin's latest film, *A Simple Case*, is a disappointment. The script by Alexander Rjechevski is lyrical but lacks structure.

Budapest, 3 December
Release of the Franco-Hungarian co-production, *Tavaski Zapor* (*Spring Shower*), starring Annabella, in the absence of its director Paul Fejos, who has had to leave the country for political reasons.

Paris, 7 December
The release of *Poil-de-carotte* (*Redhead*), a film by Julien Duvivier, based on the book by Jules Renard, with Harry Baur and 11-year-old Robert Lynen.

Paris, 8 December
A new cinema, the Rex, has opened on the boulevard Poissonnière. Its tasteful decor and luxurious fittings make it an essential port of call for all cinema lovers.

London 20 December
The young actress Vivian Mary Hartley, who is only 19, and the lawyer Herbert Leigh Holman were married in Saint James church.

Berlin, 31 December
Under Alfred Hugenberg's manag ment, the UFA trust has recover from its financial crisis and is nc employing 5,000 people.

BIRTHS

Philadelphia, 19 January
Richard Lester

Detroit, 22 January
Piper Laurie (Rosetta Jacobs)

France, 6 February
François Truffaut

London, 27 February
Elizabeth Taylor

Japan, 31 March
Nagisa Oshima

Texas, 1 April
Debbie Reynolds
(Mary Francis Reynolds)

Spain, 4 April
Carlos Saura

New York, 4 April
Anthony Perkins

Beirut, 10 April
Delphine Seyrig

Egypt, 10 April
Omar Sharif (Michel Shahoub)

Philadelphia, 21 April
Elaine May

Paris, 27 April
Anouk Aimée
(Françoise Dreyfus)

Algeria, 10 May
Françoise Fabian (Michèle Cort de Leone y Fabianera)

Ireland, 2 August
Peter O'Toole

France, 10 October
Louis Malle

Detroit, 7 December
Ellen Burstyn (Edna Rae Gillooly

At the Academy Awards, Walt D ney was crowned king of animat film for his achievements in creati Mickey Mouse and his wonder 'silly symphony', ***Flowers and Tree***

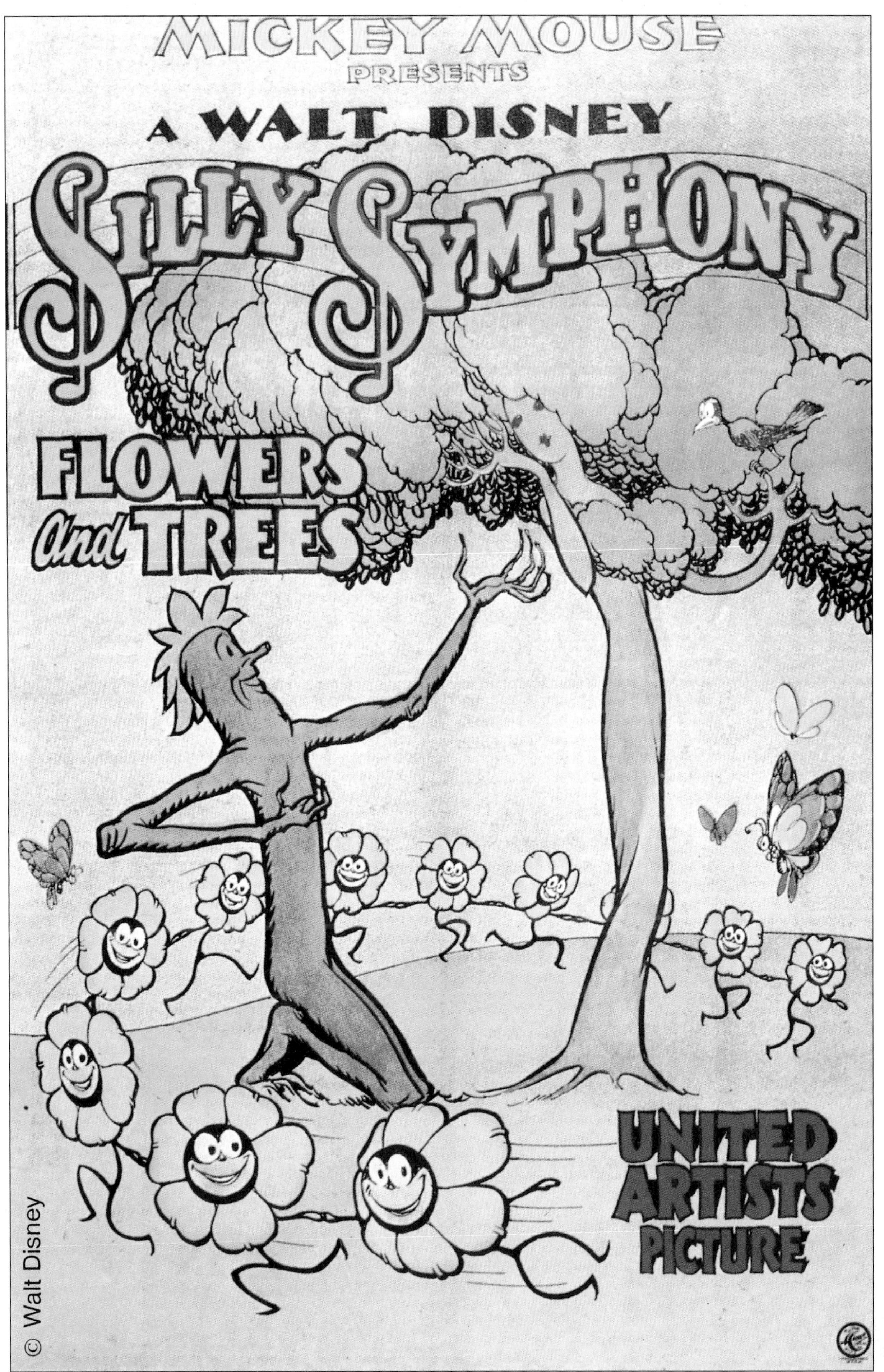
MICKEY MOUSE
PRESENTS
A WALT DISNEY
SILLY SYMPHONY
FLOWERS And TREES
UNITED
ARTISTS
PICTURE

The life of a poet according to Cocteau

Paris, 20 January

The debut film by the poet and novelist Jean Cocteau was shown to the public for the first time at a gala evening held at Vieux-Colombier. Originally titled *The Life of a Poet*, this medium-length movie is now called *The Blood of the Poet*. It was financed by the Viscount Charles de Noailles, Cocteau's friend, and was shot between April and September 1930. It is a poetic reverie in four episodes, in which a young poet passes through a mirror into another world where he finds his muse. Enrique Rivero plays the poet with Lee Miller as his muse. It is already referred to as "salon surrealism".

***The Blood of the Poet**: Lee Miller.*

Eisenstein's Mexican adventure turns into a nasty nightmare

Mexico, 16 March

Finally, after a month of waiting at the Mexican border, exit visas have been issued to Sergei Eisenstein and his two comrades, photographer Edouard Tissé and assistant Grigori Alexandrov. Thus an unhappy escapade has come to an end. After the 1930 rupture with Paramount, Eisenstein joyfully accepted the offer of the left-wing novelist Upton Sinclair to finance a documentary to be shot in Mexico called *Que Viva Mexico!*, destined to tell the thousand-year history of the country divided into four thematically related episodes: The Aztec and Maya Empire, the Spanish Conquest, Colonialization and Revolution. Eisenstein had long wanted to make a film in Mexico, and so approached the novelist on the advice of Charles Chaplin. In fact, it was Sinclair's wife who backed the project, appointing her brother Hunter Kimbrough as producer. But things began badly when, upon their arrival on 8 December 1930, the trio was imprisoned for one day. Eventually, the film got under way, but as time passed they got bogged down, and Sinclair had to put pressure on them to finish. Eisenstein's project was far more grandiose than the Sinclairs had envisaged, and he greatly exceeded his schedule and modest budget. In November 1931, the novelist even received a telegram from Stalin saying that Eisenstein "is considered as a deserter, who has broken with his fatherland." Unfortunately, Sinclair was forced to w draw his finances at the beginnin this year, owing to lack of resour Therefore, after two and a half ye absence, Eisenstein is returning Moscow. His situation looks bl after having failed to make any fi in Hollywood and leaving the M can film unfinished.

It took a year's work and 35,000 metres of negative to make this film.

'Mountain-movie' actress turns to directing

Berlin, 24 March

Leni Riefenstahl, the leading actress in four of Arnold Fanck's *mountain* films, has turned to directing. Her first venture, *The Blue Light*, is of a similar romantic vein, shot on location and emphasizing a Germanic mystical union with nature. Riefenstahl herself plays a young woman who is thought to be a witch because she alone in the Dolomite village can reach the top of a dangerous peak. A painter falls in love with her, but when he discovers her secret route to the summit, she jumps to her death. The film's strongest point is the magnificent alpine photography by Hans Schneeberger.

*Riefenstahl, also the star of **The Blue Light**, her first film as director.*

Johnny Weissmuller is the new jungle kin

New York, 25 March

Cinema's sixth and latest Tarzan is former Olympic swimming champion Johnny Weissmuller, the man who scooped a total of five gold medals at the 1924 and 1928 games. In 1929, undefeated and acknowledged as the world's finest swimmer, Johnny turned professional, appearing in a series of aquatic extravaganzas and a number of short swimming films. MGM sat up and took notice then quickly moved in to screen-test the brawnily handsome Olympian when the actor they had signed for a new Tarzan adventure fell ill. Everything went swimmingly, and Metro signed Weissmuller at $250 a week to star as Edgar Rice Burroughs' jungle hero in *Tarzan the Ape Man*. Co-starring as Jane is the sparky Maureen O'Sullivan, and the directing is capably handled by W.S. "Woody" Van Dyke, known throughout the film world as "One-Shot Woody". Weissmuller's back-projected exploits in the studio jungle play fast and loose with Edgar Rice Burroughs' original creati whose novels portrayed the ape m as the cultivated Lord Greystoke. contrast, Weissmuller's dialogue confined to grunts and monosy bles. But Johnny's blithe ability let his athletic torso do the talk has made the film a hit. MGM signed him for seven more films.

Maureen O'Sullivan, Weissmuller.

rand Hotel' hosts an assembly of stars

ector Edmund Goulding, his cast and the crew during the filming.

w York, 12 April
GM's *Grand Hotel*, directed by mund Goulding, is premiered to- at the Astor Theater. Adapted m Vicki Baum's novel of a luxuri- Berlin hotel, where "nothing r happens", the film and its un-cedented roster of stars set out to ve precisely the opposite as the racters tangle with each other. eta Garbo is a lonely ballerina; n Barrymore is her jewel-thief er; Lionel Barrymore a harassed e pen pusher; Joan Crawford a ssily ambitious stenographer; llace Beery a ruthless business-n; and, observing all the comings l goings, Lewis Stone. This gal- of stars gave the studio some lish problems. By all accounts n Crawford declined to be a m player, delaying filming by ying records of Dietrich (supposedly Garbo's great rival). Billing also required some extremely careful handling. Garbo's contract stipulates that she alone has top billing in her films. As a means of honoring this clause while at the same time not upsetting her co-stars, MGM suggested that "Garbo" should appear alone at the top of the bill and be followed by the full names of the others. Few can remember a film so excitedly anticipated as the *Grand Hotel*. It seems to have won an instant place in film history. The *New York Times* has called it "the most important film since the arrival of talking pictures," and a *Morning Post* headline claims that the film is "Screen Art at its Highest". Some are less impressed. Sydney Carroll thinks the film "only worth seeing as a drum-beating exhibition of stars... each and all of them miscast."

allace Beery and Joan Crawford, two of ***Grand Hotel***'s distinguished stars.

Carl Dreyer's vampire is given a voice

A compelling image from Carl Dreyer's atmospheric treatment of a vampire.

Copenhagen, 6 May
Denmark's Carl Dreyer has ventured into sound cinema. A perfectionist who is well-known for falling out with his backers, he has endured idleness through lack of funds since his brilliant *The Passion of Joan of Arc* was released four years ago. Now comes *Vampyr*, a horror film whose atmospheric treatment of the supernatural, aided by magnificent photography and spare but effective dialogue, surpasses most of its predecessors. Financed by Nicolas De Gunzberg, a Dutch baron and amateur actor who insisted on playing the leading role under the pseudonym Julian West, *Vampyr* was made entirely on location near Paris in French, German and English.

Ozu elevates domestic drama with his skill

Tokyo, 3 June
The 29-year-old Japanese film director Yasujiro Ozu, has produced his finest movie to date. *I Was Born, But...*, is a fine example of *shomingeki*, or lower-middle-class domestic drama. The story tells of two boys, ages 10 and eight, who watch their beloved father kowtowing to his boss and playing the fool in order to ingratiate himself. Disgusted, the boys go on hunger strike until things become clearer to them. Although *I Was Born, But...* reflects the melancholy theme of tainted innocence, it is also wonderfuly humorous, and the children (Hideo Sugahara and Tokkankozo) are a delight. Ozu has been directing for five years, and this is the third of his films with a similar qualified title, following *I Graduated, But...*, and *I Flunked, But...*, all of which center on the concerns of young students. Ozu's many films about college life might be accounted for by the fact that he himself never had one. However, his interest in the Japanese family derives from his own experience of a close-knit domestic unit. Not very strong on plot, Ozu prefers to focus on a narrow area, using a simple but affecting style.

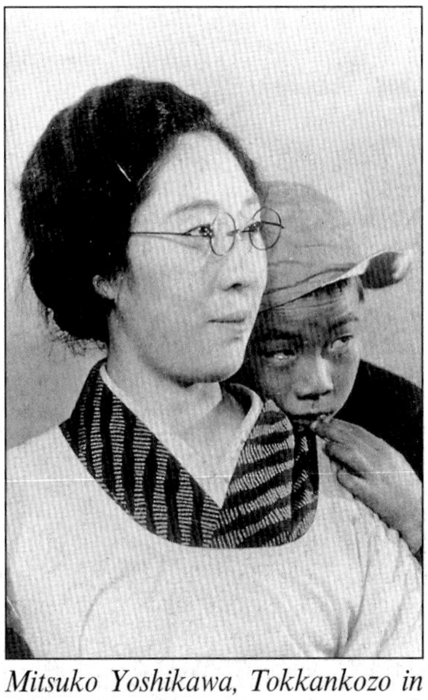

*Mitsuko Yoshikawa, Tokkankozo in Ozu's **I Was Born, But ...***

Venice launches international festival

A scene from award-winning director Nikolai Ekk's **The Road to Life**.

America's Fredric March, honored for ***Dr. Jekyll and Mr. Hyde****.*

Venice, 21 August

For two years there has been the American International Film Festival, and now Italy has decided to stage its own film festival – the International Exhibition of Cinematographic Art (or Mostra) – in Venice. The Biennale of Art in Venice has displayed the artistic trends in Europe, revealing that the public is avid for novelty. The idea of inviting film to play its part emanated from the sculptor Antonio Mariani. The Mostra opened its doors on 6 August on the Lido, and presented 29 films from many different countries. Through the festival, the Italian public has been able to discover world cinema such as *The Road to Life*, a Soviet film directed by Nikolai Ekk. The movie deals with the problems of thousands of vagrant children, orphaned in the Civil War in the 1920s. At a children's collective, they are rehabilitated and then taught a trade. No awards are given at Venice, but audiences are able to vote for their favorites, and they considered the young director of *The Road to Life* the best. They were also enthusiastic about René Clair's *A Nous la Liberté*, and Rouben Mamoulian's *Dr. Jekyll and Mr. Hyde*, for which Fredric March was particularly praised. And Helen Hayes' sensitive performance in *The Sin of Madelon Claudet* outshone all the other actresses on view. Two Italian films, Baldassare Negroni's *Two Happy Hearts* and Mario Camerini's *What Brutes Men Are* were noted for their brio and charm.

France's ***A nous la liberté*** *was judged the most entertaining film.*

Recently wed star becomes a widow

The Platinum Blonde, in mournin

Hollywood, 4 September

The producer Paul Bern has co mitted suicide at his Benedict C yon home, leaving his wife of thr months, Jean Harlow, widowed the age of 21. After an early m riage to Charles F. McGrew, wh ended in divorce, Harlow marri Bern at the end of May this ye The dead man has left no explar tion for taking his own life.

MGM executives horrified by the monstrous lovers in 'Freaks'

Hollywood, 31 August

MGM, smarting at Universal's success with *Dracula* and *Frankenstein*, has entered the horror race with *Freaks*, directed by Tod Browning. However, in their letting Browning loose, the studio has got rather more than it bargained for. Browning, who was Lon Chaney's favorite director, has fashioned a carnival of horrors among the cripples who eke a miserable living in a circus sideshow. A midget, played by Harry Earles, inherits a fortune and marries the circus' beautiful trapeze artist Cleopatra (Olga Baclanova). Included among the guests at the wedding banquet are Raudian the Living Torso, Coo-Koo the Bird Woman and Robinson the Living Skeleton. But these characters owe nothing to makeup – they are the real thing. When Cleopatra cheats on her tiny husband, his friends take terrible revenge, transforming her into a human chicken. Irving Thalberg, the studio's head of production, was horrified when he saw the result, ordering it to be cut to just over an hour in the belief that audiences would not be able to handle any more. He also inserted an introduction which stated that the fi was offered with "humility" to those who have suffered. *Freaks* b been banned in Britain and in ma states in America.

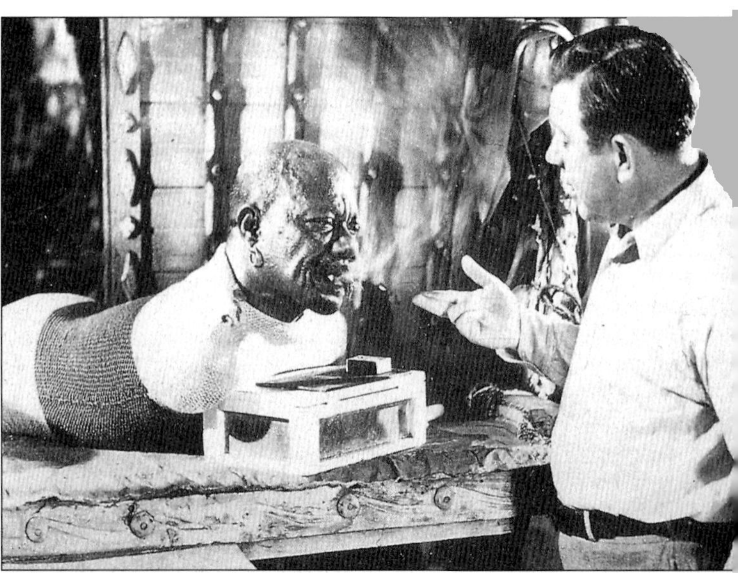

Browning (right) has created a frightening blend of realism and horror.

aul Muni moves from the brute to the brutalized

RST WARD
LETIC CLUB
HN LOVO
PRESIDENT

ul Muni (right) as the Capone-style thug with George Raft as his sidekick.

Power of another sort is exuded by Muni as the persecuted fugitive.

llywood, 11 October
ving delivered a powerful per-mance earlier this year as the pone-like gangster in Howard wks' much talked about *Scarface*, ul Muni has scored another tri-ph for Warner Bros. in *I Am a gitive from a Chain Gang*. This e, however, he is not dishing out violence but finds himself on the eiving end as a war veteran who is framed for a crime he didn't commit. Directed by Mervyn LeRoy and based on Robert E. Burns' autobiographical account of his own experiences in prison, the film charts the downward spiral described by Muni as he is betrayed by the justice system. Denied promised parole, he escapes to live out his life as a broken and desperate fugitive. This harrowing tale is not one with obvious box-office potential, but audiences have given overwhelming support to LeRoy's searing indictment of the brutal conditions of prison farms in the Deep South, thereby validating Warners' policy of making "social conscience" films. Paul Muni is the child of Austrian immigrant actors who played in Yiddish stock for many years, only essaying a role in English in 1926. In 1929 he made his film debut for Fox in *The Valiant*, and in the same year proved that he was a master of makeup in *Seven Faces*, in which he carried seven parts, including Napoleon and Don Juan. Fox let him go and it was only after a hit on Broadway *Counselor-at-Law* that Howard Hawks cast Muni as Scarface. His new contract with Warners is unique, giving him the right to approve his material.

ed Dust' blows handsome Clark Gable to the top of the ladder

llywood, 22 October
sing MGM star Clark Gable's ca-r has been given a big boost by *d Dust*, a robust romance set in Far East, in which he plays a bber planter dallying with two mes, floozie Jean Harlow and per-class vamp Mary Astor. It's a e handmade for Gable's relaxed, rthy masculinity and cements 12 onths of steady progress in which has risen from the ranks to be-me one of the studio's hottest operties. Gable had a variety of os, including those of extra and ge actor, before Lionel Barry-ore got him a screen test at MGM. e test was a flop, but after he at-cted attention in his debut film, *e Painted Desert*, MGM offered ble a contract and then rushed n through no fewer than 10 films 1931, in which he benefited from aying opposite some of the strong- leading ladies in Hollywood, nong them Greta Garbo, Norma earer and Joan Crawford.

Clark Gable and Jean Harlow, a chemically explosive couple in ***Red Dust****.*

Chaplin wants to protect his sons

Hollywood, 26 October
Charles Chaplin has just emerged victorious from a two-month legal battle with his ex-wife Lita Grey over their two sons, seven-year-old Charles and six-year-old Sydney. Their upbringing has largely been in the hands of Lita's mother while Lita tries to carve out a career as a singer. While Chaplin was traveling abroad, Lita signed a film contract with director David Butler to appear with her sons in *The Little Teacher*. On 25 August Chaplin's lawyer filed a petition objecting to the boys working in motion pictures. Battle was joined, with Chaplin protesting that he wanted the boys to lead a normal life. Chaplin himself has sad memories of his own childhood, which was anything but normal. The courts have finally ruled in the father's favor, and a happy by-product of the wrangle is that he has seen much more of his charming sons.

He Always "gets" his man!
Buck JONES in
"McKENNA OF THE MOUNTED"
with GRETA GRANSTEDT
DIRECTED BY D. ROSS LEDERMAN
A COLUMBIA PICTURE
With his horse Silver, Buck joined an outlaw gang to bring them to justice.

MAURICE CHEVALIER
IN AN
ERNST LUBITSCH PRODUCTION
"ONE HOUR WITH YOU"
Jeanette MacDONALD
GENEVIEVE TOBIN
This risqué comedy was a hit for producer-director Ernst Lubitsch.

THE 4 MARX BROTHERS
IN
HORSE FEATHER
a Paramount Pictu
Groucho was a college dean a Zeppo his son in this crazy outing

JOE E. BROWN
"YOU SAID A MOUTHFUL"
GINGER ROGERS
PRESTON FOSTER
SHEILA TERRY
FARINA
LLOYD BACON
A FIRST NATIONAL PICTURE
Inventor Joe hoped to make a fortune with a 'non-sinkable' swimsuit fabric.

Marion DAVIES AND ROBERT MONTGOMERY IN
BLONDIE OF THE FOLLIES
A MARION DAVIES PRODUCTION
BILLIE DOVE
JIMMY DURANTE
EDMUND GOULDING
Metro-Goldwyn-Mayer PICTURE
Friendly rivalry in backstage yarn about two ex-Ziegfeld girls.

SYLVIA SIDNEY
AND
FREDRIC MARCH
IN
"MERRILY WE GO TO HELL"
WITH Adrianne ALLEN
Directed by DOROTHY ARZNER
a Paramount Picture
In this drama, March's drinking and womanizing drove Sydney to despair.

) members of the all-star cast in MGM's **Grand Hotel**, Greta Garbo and n Barrymore played an unhappy ballerina and her lover.

l McCrea (left), here with Leslie Banks in **The Most Dangerous Game**.

bert Z. Leonard directed Norma Shearer and Clark Gable in **Strange Inter-'e**, a 110-minute film version of Eugene O'Neill's five-hour play.

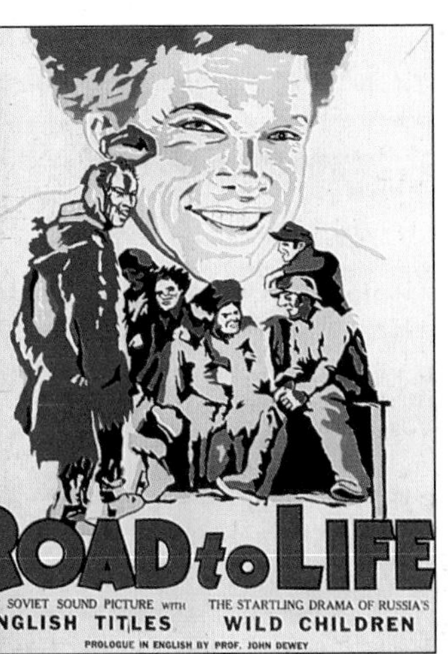
ROAD to LIFE
SOVIET SOUND PICTURE WITH ENGLISH TITLES
THE STARTLING DRAMA OF RUSSIA'S WILD CHILDREN
PROLOGUE IN ENGLISH BY PROF. JOHN DEWEY

31. First Russian film that was cially created for sound.

George Arliss was a concert pi-ist deafened by anarchist's bomb.

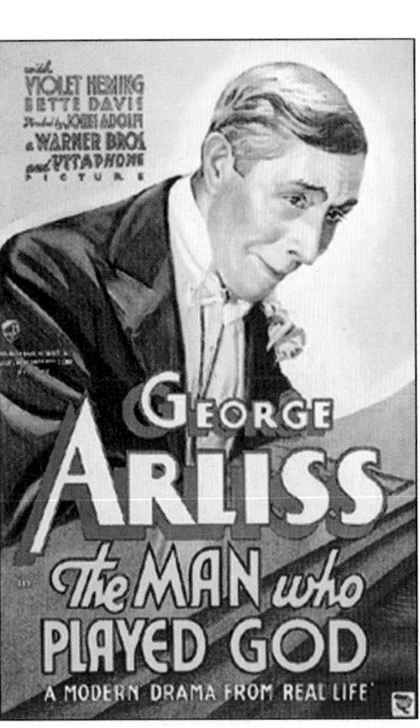
with VIOLET HEMING BETTE DAVIS
A WARNER BROS. and VITAPHONE PICTURE
GEORGE
ARLISS
The MAN who PLAYED GOD
A MODERN DRAMA FROM REAL LIFE

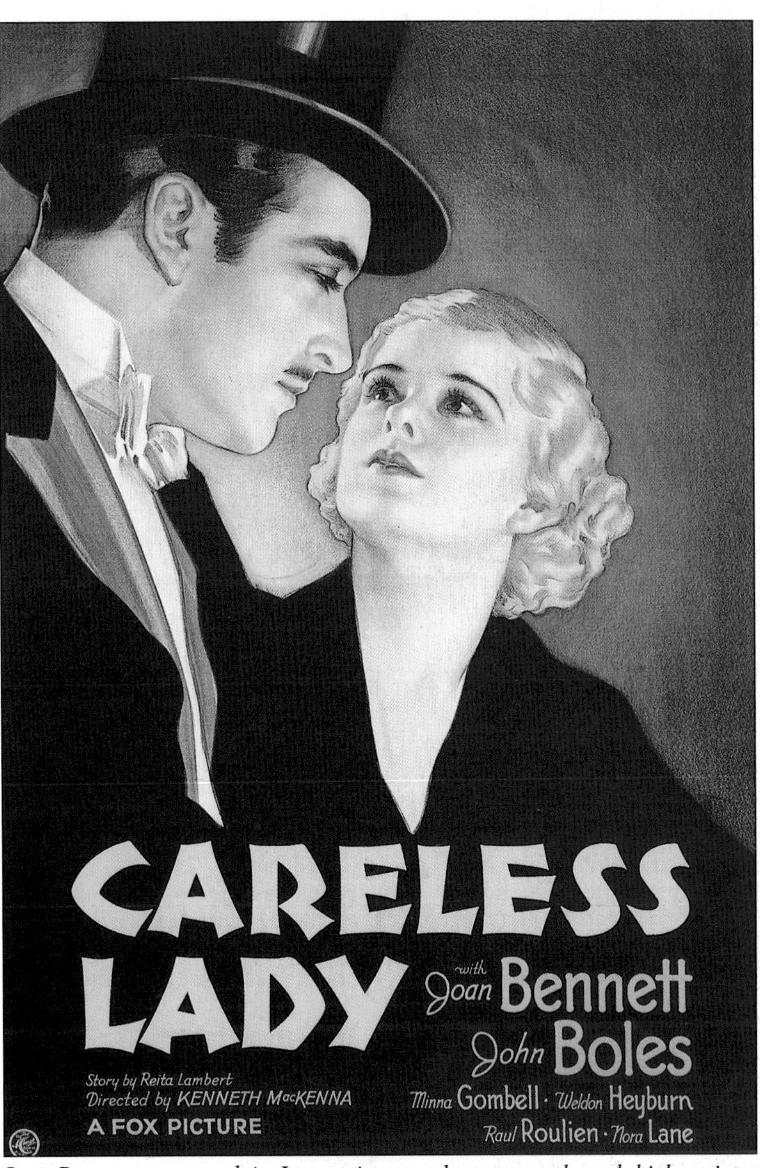
CARELESS
LADY
with Joan Bennett
John Boles
Story by Reita Lambert
Directed by KENNETH MacKENNA
A FOX PICTURE
Minna Gombell · Weldon Heyburn
Raul Roulien · Nora Lane

Joan Bennett great as plain Jane trying to nab a man and reach high society.

AVE
CÆSAR

Charles Laughton, Claudette Colbert, Fredric March in **The Sign of the Cross**.

1933

Paris, 14 January
Release of René Clair's latest film *Quatorze Juillet* (*July 14th*), which stars Annabella, Georges Rigaud, Pola Illery, Paul Olivier and Raymond Cordy.

France, 22 January
Jean Vigo has finished the location shots for *Zéro de conduite* (*Zero for Conduct*). Filming was started in the studios on 24 December but was interrupted by bad weather and the director's poor health.

Los Angeles, 23 January
RKO has declared itself bankrupt and has been placed under judicial supervision, resulting in drastic cutbacks in spending and the dismissal of a large number of employees.

Hollywood, 2 February
Louis B. Mayer, the president of MGM, has canceled actor Buster Keaton's contract for "a valid and sufficient reason." Keaton has just completed the filming of *What! No Beer?* for the studios.

Los Angeles, 1 March
The release of *Thunder Over Mexico*, presented as being Russian director Eisenstein's "American" film, has caused a violent international campaign to be waged against Upton Sinclair. The novelist, who initially backed the director's ill-fated undertaking, *Que Viva Mexico!*, is being accused of improperly using the negatives he recovered from that unfinished film.

Berlin, 3 March
Release of Max Ophuls' latest production for UFA *Liebelei*. Magda Schneider's wonderful performance and Ophuls' subtle direction transcend the plot in this film version of Arthur Schnitzler's play.

Shanghai, 5 March
There have been stormy reactions to the release of Cheng Bugao's *Wild Torrent*. It is the first Chinese revolutionary film with the peasants as the central point of interest.

California, 6 March
Under the increasing pressure of public opinion, the heads of all the major studios have undertaken to ensure that the clauses set down in the 1930 Production Code will be adhered to in the future.

USA, 9 March
Release of Lloyd Bacon's musical, *42nd Street*, with Warner Baxter, Dick Powell and Ginger Rogers.

Berlin, 23 March
The premiere of Fritz Lang's film *Das Testament des Dr. Mabuse* (*The Testament of Dr. Mabuse*) has been canceled on the orders of the government's censors.

Berlin, 29 March
After the hasty departure of Fritz Lang from Germany, Goebbels' spokesman has explained that the director's *Dr. Mabuse* was banned because of its subversive nature, which is likely to "incite people to anti-social behavior and terrorism against the State."

Paris, 4 May
Release of MGM's *Red Dust*, directed by Victor Fleming, and starring Jean Harlow and Clark Gable.

Rio de Janeiro, 23 May
Humberto Mauro, who has been making films since 1925, is presenting *Ganga Bruta*, his latest work filmed in the Cinedia studios.

Washington, 1 June
According to statistics published by the Ministry of Commerce, American cinema attendance has dropped by 56 percent since 1928.

Los Angeles, 31 July
In accordance with the directives of the National Recovery Act, the MPPDA has instituted the 40-hour week for cinema employees, a measure designed to create more jobs.

Los Angeles, 8 August
Professionals in the cinema industry have launched a series of debates and consultations to decide on the enforcement of the Motion Picture Code, in accordance with the provisions of NRA.

New York, 9 September
Release of Frank Capra's *Lady for a Day*, with Warren William and May Robson.

Sofia, 2 October
The Modern Theatre is screening the first Bulgarian sound film, *The Slaves' Revolt*, by Vassili Guendov. The film evokes the struggle for national freedom in the 19th century.

Hollywood, 4 October
20th Century, the new company owned by Darryl F. Zanuck and Joseph Schenck has released its first film *The Bowery*, directed by Raoul Walsh, with Wallace Beery and George Raft.

Prague, 13 October
Actor and director Josef Rovensky has released his second film, *Rekka*, a story of adolescent love.

Hollywood, 31 October
On signing his contract with MGM, Joseph Yule Jr. has become Mickey Rooney.

Paris, 8 November
Release of Louis Jouvet's new film *Dr. Knock*, a screen version of Jules Romain's satirical play, with Jouvet himself as Dr. Knock.

New York, 11 November
Release of *Little Women*, the film version of Louisa May Alcott's popular novel about the March family. George Cukor directed with the role of Jo played by Katharine Hepburn.

Shanghai, 12 November
As if the Japanese bombings and political disorder were not enough, a commando from the blue shirts, a fascist group, has sacked the Yi-Hua studios, which were founded by the film director Tian-Han.

Paris, 15 November
Jean Vigo has filmed the first scenes for *l'Atalante*, with Dita Parlo, Jean Dasté and Michel Simon, at Conflans-Sainte-Honorine for producers Nounez-Gaumont.

Moscow, 17 November
Release of *Velikii uteshitel* (*The Great Consoler*), by Lev Kuleshov, adapted from the novel by O'Henry.

Paris, 23 November
Jean Gabin has married Jeanne Mauchain, a dancer at the Paris Casino and the Apollo under the name Doriane.

Hollywood, 30 November
Charlie Chaplin has started work on the scenario for *Modern Times*. While on board the yacht belonging to the president of 20th Century, Joseph Schenck, he met the actress Paulette Goddard and decided to sign her up for the film.

New York, November
A committee of archbishops, pre
ed over by the papal legate Am
Cicognani, has founded the Nati
al Legion of Decency, with the
of stopping all forms of "incitem
to moral depravity."

Paris, 15 December
Director Fritz Lang is now shoot
Liliom for Fox-Europa, a comp
run by the former production c
for UFA, Erich Pommer, who
also left Germany.

Hollywood, 22 December
Dancers Fred Astaire and Gin
Rogers are partners in *Flying Do
to Rio*, directed by Thornton F
land for RKO.

Palestine, 31 December
British censors have banned the f
full-length Yiddish sound film ca
Sabra, made in Palestine by you
Polish director Aleksander Fo
They consider it a "left-wing
anti-Arab" work of propaganda.

BIRTHS

England, 18 January
John Boorman

Chicago, 13 February
Kim Novak
(Marilyn Pauline Novak)

London, 14 March
Michael Caine
(Maurice Micklewhite)

Algeria, 30 March
Jean-Claude Brialy

Paris, 9 April
Jean-Paul Belmondo

Pennsylvania, 19 April
Jayne Mansfield
(Vera Jayne Palmer)

Paris, 18 July
Jean Yanne
(Jean Gouyé)

Paris, 18 August
Roman Polanski

***King Kong**, made by Merian
Cooper and Ernest B. Schoedsa
has revealed to a fascinated pu
the scope of creative and techni
achievements possible in the cinem*

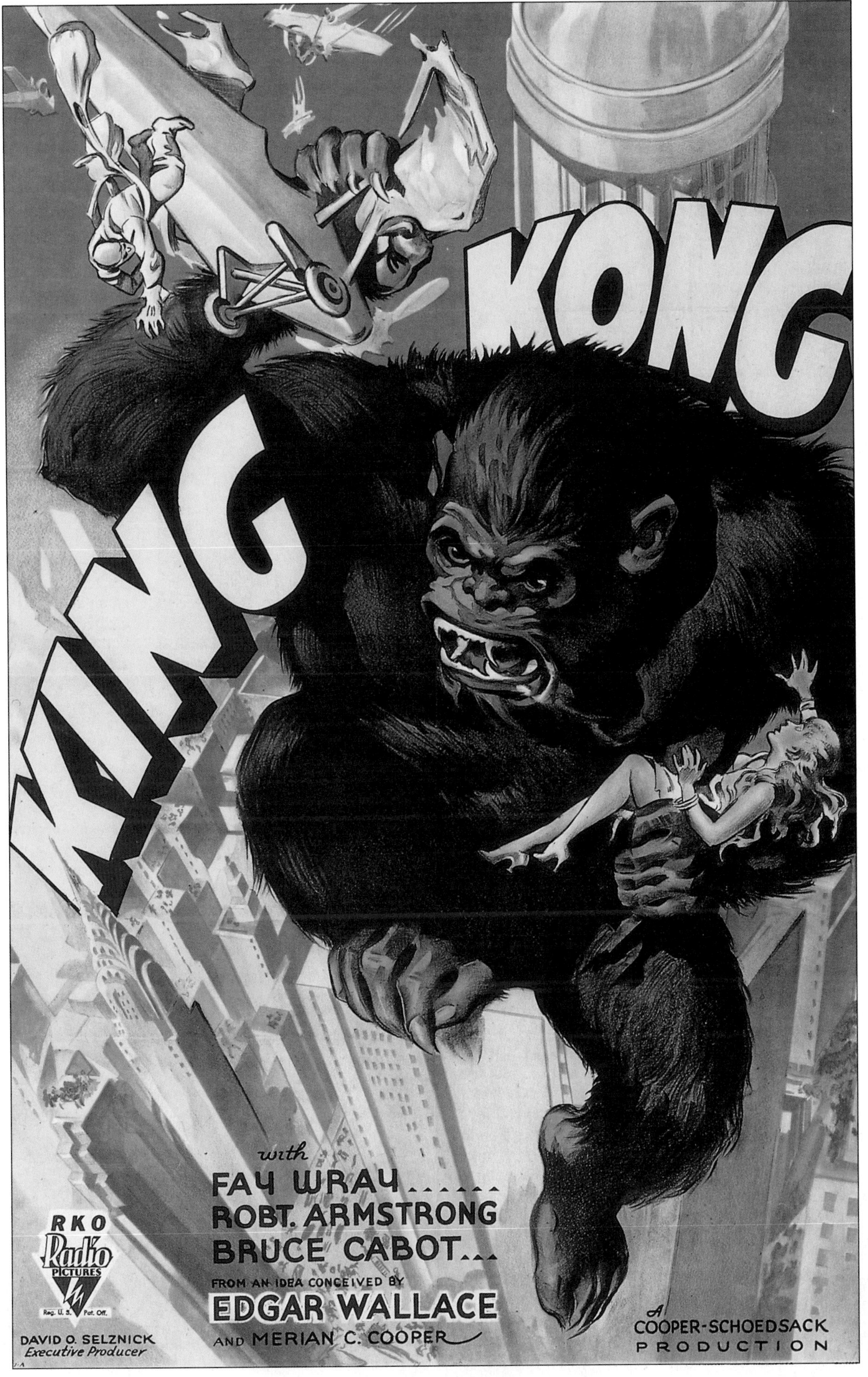
KING KONG
with
FAY WRAY ....
ROBT. ARMSTRONG
BRUCE CABOT...
FROM AN IDEA CONCEIVED BY
EDGAR WALLACE
AND MERIAN C. COOPER
RKO
Radio
PICTURES
DAVID O. SELZNICK
Executive Producer
A
COOPER-SCHOEDSACK
PRODUCTION

David O. Selznick departs from RKO

Hollywood, 2 January
The latest news about David O. Selznick, until recently the production chief at RKO Radio, is that he has been hired to produce pictures for MGM by studio boss Louis B. Mayer – who also just happens to be Selznick's father-in-law. Selznick's appointment will help MGM fill the serious gap in the production schedule caused by the recent illness of Irving Thalberg. David O. Selznick first made his name as a producer and assistant to B.P. Schulberg at Paramount from 1928 to 1931. He then hoped to establish himself as an independent producer, but found this to be extremely difficult in a Hollywood dominated by the giant studios. David Sarnoff, president of RCA, which itself was owned by RKO, was not himself a part of the movie establishment and hired Selznick in October 1931 to head the RKO studio. Selznick succeeded in turning RKO into a more efficient operation, but a contract dispute led to his resignation last month.

Eroticism on the loose with 'Ecstasy

Body and soul, Hedy Kiesler is perfect as the bride in search of satisfaction.

Prague, 20 January
The Czech film *Ecstasy*, from d tor Gustav Machaty, is evidenc great success that flirts with scan The audience will not soon fo the 10-minute scene where the h ine bathes totally nude at nigh the moonlight, clearly revealing superb figure of the 19-year-old tress Hedy Kiesler. She plays a c bride whose husband is impo and who gives herself to a stran a roadway engineer. After sh granted a divorce, she refuses to away with her lover when her husband commits suicide. Sho three versions, Czech, French German, *Ecstasy* is more tha melodrama, and the bold natur scenes are not the only ones wo of comment. The film, shot pa on location, is a beautifully vi poem to nature, which awakens sensuality of the heroine and rev the ecstasy of physical love. Ma ty, an actor turned director, alre created a sensation in 1929 wit film full of eroticism – the appro ately named *Erotikon.*

Radio City bests the Gaumont Palace

New York, 11 January
The recently opened Radio City Music Hall, situated in Rockefeller Center and the most spectacularly lavish place of entertainment in the world, is now functioning as a cinema. The inaugural film was Frank Capra's *The Bitter Tea of General Yen*, a Columbia production starring Barbara Stanwyck and Nils Asther. With its 6,200 seats, Radio City Music Hall has now overtaken the 6,000-seat Gaumont Palace in Paris as the biggest movie theater in the world.

A stunning 6,200-seat auditorium.

A scent of scandal wafts through cinemas screening Mae's film

New York, 9 February
A rescuer has come to the aid of debt-ridden Paramount in the extravagantly curved form of Mae West, whose *She Done Him Wrong* is convulsing audiences from coast to coast. Mae's first starring vehicle has been adapted from her Broadway play, *Diamond Lil*, and allows her to sashay seductively around handsome young Cary Grant, effortlessly deflate her equally pneumatic rival Rafaela Ottiano, and spray steamy one-liners all over the set. The double meanings Mae wrings out of songs such as "I Like a Guy What Takes His Time" and "I Wonder Where My Easy Rider's Gone?" have outraged certain self-appointed moral guardians but work wonders at the box office. Mae West started on stage at the age of six. By 1914 she was a vaudeville star billed as "The original Brinkley Girl" and inventor of the "shimmy" dance. In the 1920s she began to write, produce and direct her own plays. The first of them, *Sex*, earned her a 10-day jail sentence on charges of obscenity, but did not deter her from sardonically parading all the absurd delights of the aforementioned subject. She made her movie debut in 1932 in Paramount's *Night After Night*, only fourth-billed but on a salary of $5,000 per week for 10 weeks' work and writing her c lines. Paramount has increased salary to $8,500 a week, but will stay out of trouble and one s ahead of the censors she holds such contempt?

Mae West with her handsome English-born leading man, Cary Grant.

e awesome 'King Kong' offers a parable for man and beast

e magic of cinematic illusion transforms a 45-centimetre model into a giant.

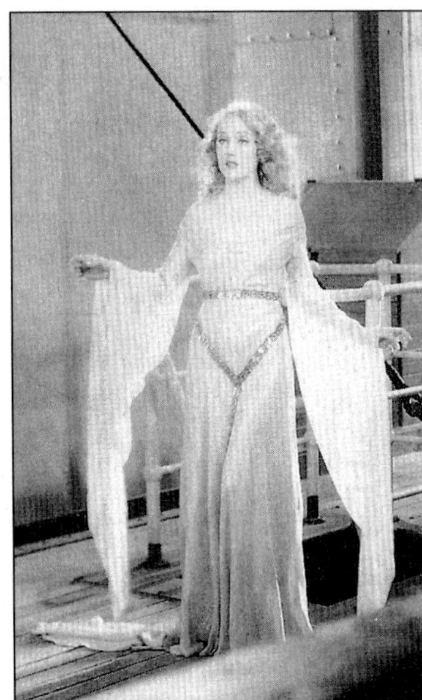
Fay Wray, suitably vulnerable.

w York, 2 March
uncharted skull-shaped island on ich the inhabitants are held in all by a giant ape; a bombastic n producer intent on bringing n back alive; a swooning blonde, pless captive of the monster as he npages through New York City; a lsating climax at the very top of Empire State Building as the ape is machine-gunned to death by a swarm of U.S. Army warplanes. These are the ingredients of *King Kong*, now astonishing audiences at Radio City Music Hall. Ernest B. Schoedsack and Merian C. Cooper have produced this epic adventure for RKO. Fay Wray is the Beauty with whom the Beast falls fatally in love, but the real star is Kong himself, the creation of brilliant animator Willis O'Brien. The giant gorilla was brought to life on the screen by the animation of six 18-inch-high models, each with a metal skeleton, sponge-rubber muscles and a skin made of rabbit fur. A giant bust of Kong, operated from inside by three men, was used for close-up work. This is film fantasy at its finest.

itz Lang rejects the poisoned chalice offered by Joseph Goebbels

rlin, 28 March
itz Lang has vanished from the pital, and for good reason. Since January, events have moved rap- y with Adolph Hitler's nomina- n to the Chancellery. Josef Goeb- s became the head of the Ministry Information and Propaganda on March. He immediately demon- ated his power over the cinema by nceling the premiere of Lang's m *The Testament of Dr. Mabuse* 23 March. Two days later, Lang is rather surprised to receive a call go to Goebbels' office. Feeling ill ease in his striped suit and stiff- llared shirt, Lang went to the Min- ry of Propaganda and wandered rough the long corridors filled th armed men. Goebbels received m amiably and explained his ver- on of the situation. The film was nfiscated because he found the ding displeasing; this was when all e Nazi slogans are put into the outh of a criminal. Eventually, oebbels came to the reason for the chat. He offered the director the job of becoming supervisor of production at UFA. A film on William Tell could be made first. Lang tried to put Goebbels off by saying to him, "My mother had Jewish parents." "We'll decide who's Jewish," retorted Goebbels. Lang asked for a few hours to consider. That evening, he took a train to Paris.

Oskar Beregi as Lang's Dr. Mabuse (with the shadow of Rudolf Klein-Rogge).

Studios must obey production code

Los Angeles, 6 March
It is exactly three years since the American film companies agreed to a new code of self-censorship. They have now recognized that a stricter enforcement of its provisions has become necessary, although it is not yet certain at precisely what date in the near future this will come into effect. It is likely that new rules will have an adverse effect on movie-making, and there is very little doubt which films and stars the crackdown is aiming at. The release of *Scarface* a year ago had been delayed many months due to a censorship dispute, and during the past several months there have been a few raised eyebrows over MGM's *Red Dust*. Jean Harlow has developed into that studio's sexiest star, while Mae West has had a spectacular success with her first starring film, *She Done Him Wrong*, which opened a month ago. Even that delightful cartoon character, Betty Boop, who singlehandedly introduced "sex" into the animated film, may not be spared by the new and stricter monitoring. *Film Daily* recently published a letter from a film theater owner in Georgia complaining about "smut in cartoons", and it is not difficult to guess who he had in mind. At this rate, even *King Kong* may not be spared censor's cuts over his provocative pawing of Fay Wray...

INKWELL
Betty Boop, censored for indecency!

Darryl F. Zanuck founds 20th Century

Hollywood, 27 April
Producer Darryl F. Zanuck has just set up his own independent production company called 20th Century Pictures, in partnership with producer Joseph Schenck. Zanuck, first as a scriptwriter, then production executive and, finally, head of production at Warner Bros. during the 1920s and early 1930s, has played a major role in the transformation of this small company into one of the leading Hollywood studios. However, a dispute over studio policy led to his recent resignation. It was not long before Zanuck, known as one of the most talented young producers in Hollywood, was able to set up his new company with Schenck, the president of United Artists. Not surprisingly, the 20th Century Pictures will be distributed through UA. Since UA has been suffering from a shortage of quality productions, the combination of Zanuck's expertise, his own stars under contract as well as access to those at MGM (which has backed this new company) may be the boost needed to remedy this situation.

'Zero for Conduct' gets nought out of ten from the censors

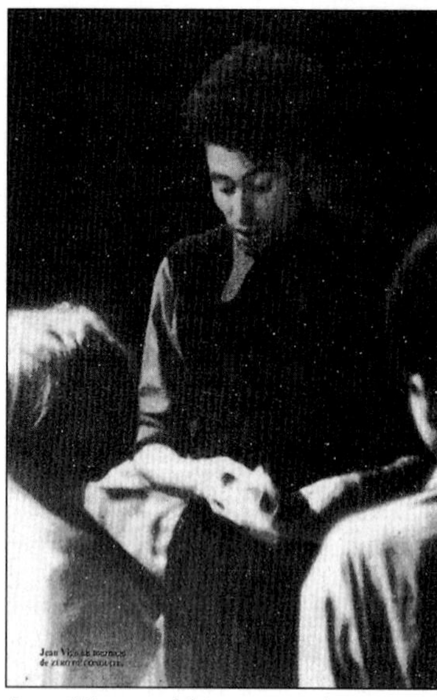
Jean Vigo and his young players.

As directed by Vigo, a pillow fight propels the film into a world of dreams.

Paris, 30 April
Under pressure from the government, the board of censors has refused to allow an exhibition license for the release of *Zero for Conduct*, the film by the young director Jean Vigo. This medium-length project, produced by Jacques Louis-Nounez, had already undergone problems during shooting. It was not finished at the Buttes-Chaumont studios until 22 January, two weeks behind schedule. When shown to the press at the beginning of this month, it was very badly received. Both the subject and its treatment are clearly of a subversive nature. Drawing on his own memories of school, Vigo tells of an uprising at a dreadful boarding school in a Paris suburb, organized by four pupils because the petty restrictions imposed them. Lively and poetic, Vigo's f openly exalts the spirit of rebelli and makes fun of the teaching p fession, things which the censor not tolerate. The headmaster, wh played by a long-bearded dwarf, both literally and figuratively look down on by the boys.

'The Sea Gull' killed by Chaplin for taxes

Hollywood, 21 June
As part of an exercise to write off taxes, Charles Chaplin, who has recently been under heavy pressure from the Internal Revenue, has destroyed the original negative of *The Sea Gull* before a number of witnesses. Chaplin produced and Josef von Sternberg directed this film in 1926. It starred Edna Purviance, once Chaplin's favorite leading lady, in a melodrama set in a Californian fishing community. The film never saw release, possibly because Chaplin was dismayed by the poor quality of Edna's performance. *The Sea Gull* disappeared into Chaplin's vault, never to be seen again. It is said that *The Sea Gull* contained the longest "traveling shot" ever made, in which the young Russian-born cameraman Paul Ivano, who was one of the small army of cameramen who shot the thrilling chariot race in *Ben-Hur*, kept the camera on the move for more than 10 minutes.

Fatty Arbuckle, the end of a wasted life

New York, 29 June
Roscoe "Fatty" Arbuckle, one of the kings of early silent comedy, has died penniless and forgotten. His career foundered in 1921 after he was tried for the manslaughter of actress Virginia Rappe, who died after being taken ill at a debauched party thrown by Arbuckle in a San Francisco hotel. It was alleged that Arbuckle had tried to rape her. After three trials Arbuckle was acquitted, but the resulting storm turned up even more skeletons. Four years earlier Arbuckle and a number of top movie executives had been involved in another scandalous party which had been hushed up thanks to some generous bribes. The studio bosses' own hypocrisy had been revealed and this could not be forgiven. So Arbuckle was tossed to the wolves. Ditched by Paramount, with whom he had recently signed a lucrative contract, and no longer able to appear in front of the camera, Arbuckle took to directing under the ironic pseudonym William B. Goodrich. Seeking to make a vaudeville comeback in Paris, he was cruelly heckled, and ended his career directing two-reelers. Sadly, the Fat Man just wasn't funny anymore.

C'est un Film Paramount
JESSE L. LASKY Présente
ROSCOE "FATTY"
ARBUCKLE
DANS
Fatty

Henri Bernstein loses in 'Melo' tri

Paris, 27 July
Unhappy with a film adaptation his work, the writer Henri Bernst has launched and lost a legal acti against the producers of *Melo*. N ertheless, the film is very capal directed by Paul Czinner and grac with charming performances fr leading players Gaby Morlay, V tor Francen and Pierre Blanchar

Bernstein's heroine is Gaby Morla

‑nry VIII revitalizes the British cinema

‑ghton's Henry with his real-life wife Elsa Lanchester as Anne of Cleves.

‑don, 17 August
‑ducer Alexander Korda has per‑ ‑ally directed his most recent film, ‑ *Private Life of Henry VIII*. In ‑ition to starring Charles Laugh‑, whose performance in the title ‑ is a tour de force, the remark‑ ‑e cast includes Elsa Lanchester, ‑bert Donat, Merle Oberon and ‑nie Barnes. Very well-made, with memorable contributions from the scriptwriter Arthur Wimperis and cameraman Georges Périnal, the film's success suggests that it will help put Britain back on the world cinema map. Indeed, the first indication of this is that United Artists has added Korda and his company, London Films, to its roster of production companies.

Grierson promotes documentary films

London, 15 September
Due to an acute budgetary crisis, the British government has been forced to discontinue its funding of the Empire Marketing Board – the organization which has served as the main center of documentary filmmaking in England during the past four years. Fortunately, the entire unit, originally formed and headed by John Grierson, has been able to find a new home and new government sponsor in the GPO (General Post Office), and will be referred to from on as the GPO Film Unit. It is hoped that this group will be able to continue its film work undiminished during the coming years. As the single most important figure connected with the British documentary movement, John Grierson has been involved in a wide range of activities in recent years. The 50-minute long *Drifters*, made in 1929 and his first outing as producer, director and scriptwriter, was a true landmark in documentary production. Although strongly influenced by American filmmaker Robert Flaherty, this particular film also demonstrated the use of a Soviet style of editing, while reflecting Grierson's personal commitment to social themes. At the EMB, Grierson succeeded in assembling, and helping to train, a group of filmmakers who have since then emerged as the mainstay of the British documentary, with Grierson producing most of their films. This notable group of directors includes Basil Wright, Arthur Elton, Stuart Legg, Edgar Anstey, Harry Watt and Paul Rotha. Grierson has put a lot of effort into getting their work widely shown, not only in commercial cinemas but also to audiences at schools, clubs and film societies, even setting up a free film-loan library at the EMB and organizing his own free screenings.

***Drifters**, directed by John Grierson in 1929 for the EMB Film Unit.*

‑n institute of film ‑pens in London

‑ondon, 1 September
‑he British Film Institute, which ‑as just been established, will ‑rve "to encourage the develop‑ ‑ent of the art of the film" and ‑o testify to life and its mores." ‑ other words, the BFI hopes to ‑nserve and disseminate cinema‑ ‑graphic culture. The necessity ‑r such an institute was under‑ ‑ned last year by the British Insti‑ ‑te of Adult Education in its re‑ ‑ort "The Film in National Life". ‑he first president is the Duke of ‑utherland, while noted novelist ‑ohn Buchan has been nominated ‑resident of the advisory board. ‑he British Film Institute will ‑raw its funds from government ‑ources and members' subscrip‑ ‑ons. The new institute has also ‑nnounced that they will soon ‑dit and publish a magazine of ‑rticles and reviews called "The ‑Monthly Film Bulletin".

'Cavalcade' is a stylish and poignant pageant of patriotism

London, 9 October
Hollywood, in the form of the Fox studio, has produced a stylish adaptation of *Cavalcade*, the play by Noel Coward which has been a huge success in the West End. Fox has filmed the stage production quite faithfully, reproducing as accurately as possible the story of one British family (and their servants) from the Boer War to the present, taking in along the way the sinking of the *Titanic*, the Great War and the Jazz Age. The director is Frank Lloyd, a Scot resident in America since 1913 and in films from the following year. The all-British cast is headed up by Clive Brook, suave epitome of the English gentleman, and also Diana Wynyard, whose graceful performance Noel Coward has found "entirely entrancing... To her I am immensely grateful... I again repeat, I find her performance magnificent." His own involvement with films began in England in 1917, when he played two bit parts in D.W. Griffith's *Hearts of the World*. Fox have poured a small fortune into his *Cavalcade*, written off by cynics as a certain flop since it hadn't even been produced on Broadway. But the doubters have been proved wrong, as this handsomely mounted production is doing brisk business at the box office. Underneath the glossy surface there is pointed criticism of the waste of war and a poignant picture of the privileged world to which it brought an end.

l to r: Herbert Mundin, Diana Wynyard, Clive Brook and Una O'Connor.

The German cinema under the control of the Nazi

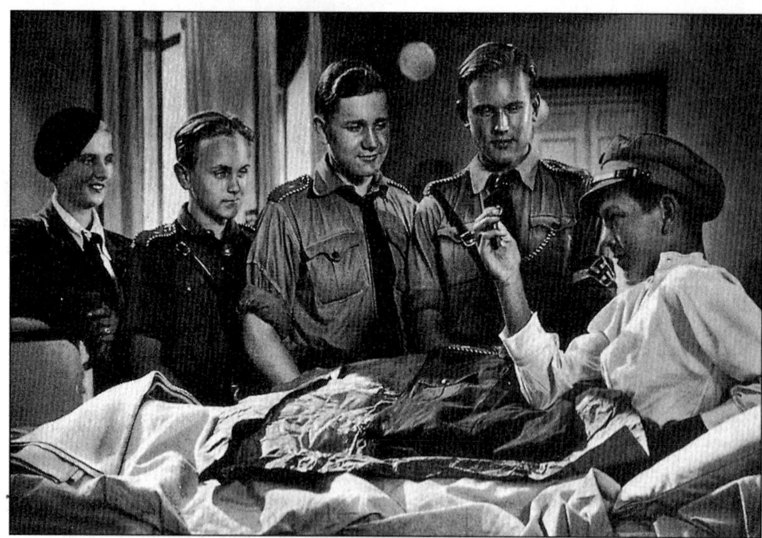

Hans Steinhoff's ***Hitler Junge Quex*** *provides a frame of Nazi reference.*

'Horst Wessel', hastily renamed ***Hans Westmar*** *by its maker, Franz Wenz*

Filmmakers constrained by strict rules

Berlin, 22 September

On 30 January last, with the arrival of the Third Reich, Germany was turned into a totalitarian state. And now cinema has been put under the control of the Nazis. On 14 July, new legislation unequivocally proclaimed that "The National Socialist Party of German Workers constitutes the only political party in Germany," with the threat of arrest, prison and other forms of punishment for those who do not comply. With Josef Goebbels as Minister of Information and Propaganda since March, the Nazification of institutions has continued unabated. The promulgation of 6 June already excluded Jews and foreigners from the cinematographic industry. To practice a profession, German citizenship has to be proven and so must Aryan origin. At the head of this Ministry is Dr. Goebbels, age 36, who has become "the agent for the Fuhrer and chancellor for everything that is concerned with the cultural and artistic life of Germany." In his opinion, the crisis prevailing in the country has been intellectual as well as material and economic. "This will continue until we have the courage to reform the German cinema right to its roots." Equally, since June, with the creation of the Filmkreditbank, the financing of productions has been placed under strict control of the state. Most recently the Third Reich has instituted the National Chamber of Culture which is presided over by Goebbels himself. It has many goals: "The promotion of German culture in the spirit of the people and of the Reich, to settle economic and social affairs of the cultural sector, and to balance the efforts of groups it controls." In it there are seven departments dependent on the National Chamber, which share all the spheres of intellectual and artistic life. Thus, the Chamber of the Cinema of the Reich has set out all aspects of the profession – administrative, commercial, distributive and ideological. It can truly be said that Nazi cinema has been born.

Cinema production promotes Nazi ideolog

Berlin, 13 December

Hans Westmar has revealed the new face of German cinema, exactly as did *Hitler Junge Quex*, released on 19 September. The films' directors, Hans Steinhoff and Franz Wenzler, have propagated Nazi ideology by inflaming youth with a vision of a better life and political responsibility. The Third Reich is very demanding, and films must be irreproachable. Thus a film by Franz Wenzler, *Horst Wessel*, was seen once and promptly banned. According to the official communiqué, the film did not do sufficient justice to the national movement; the real Horst Wessel was more of a hooligan than a hero. The director reworked film, and Horst became Hans W man, an ideal martyr. Although film does not lack lyricism, the le ing character remains lifeless. T is not the case with Heïni Völke *Hitler Junge Quex*. Steinhoff preserved his youthful freshn right to his nickname, Quex, wh means quicksilver. He also becor a hero and martyr when he is fat stabbed by Communists while tributing election leaflets in Ber Franz Seitz, who directed *SA-M Brand*, also praises Hitler You However, none of these films are "Nazi *The Battleship Potemkin*" t Josef Goebbels had wished for.

The artists reply with a massive exodus of creative talent

Berlin, 31 December

The Third Reich has moved rapidly to "purify" Germany's artistic life. In May, 20,000 books, foreign or otherwise, were publicly burnt. All the writings were judged by Josef Goebbels to be poisonous to the German mind and had to disappear. Many professionals working in the cinema, opposed to the regime or terrorized by it, have chosen to leave. Some did not wait for the arrival of Hitler. Fritz Lang hastily fled the "honors" that would be bestowed upon him, leaving behind his wife and co-screenwriter Thea von Harbou, who was sympathetic to the aims of the Third Reich. He chose exile in France, where he was reunited with the producer Erich Pommer, who had been frightened out of Germany despite his glorious career at UFA. Leontine Sagan, director of *Girls in Uniform*, emigrated to the United Kingdom at the time of the initial persecutions in 1932. Max Ophuls spent no time basking in the success of *Liebelei*. He went to Paris after the Reichstag fire. No category of artist, especially those who are Jewish, has bee able to escape the shadow of t umphant Nazism: scenarists a cameramen (Karl Freund, Ca Mayer, Eugene Schuftan, Bil Wilder), performers (Elisabe Bergner, Peter Lorre, Conr Veidt) or directors (Henry Ko ter, Robert Siodmak, Paul Czi ner, Robert Wiene and Ewal André Dupont). On New Year Eve, Berlin can claim to be rid its creative minds. To the gre satisfaction of Germany's ne masters, the country is now fr of its "most subversive" element

usby's 'Footlight Parade' provides a spectacle

e spectacular 'By a Waterfall' number by Berkeley from **Footlight Parade**.

Los Angeles, 27 November
When Samuel Goldwyn brought Broadway choreographer Busby Berkeley to Hollywood to do the numbers for the Eddie Cantor musical *Whoopee!* three years ago, few could have imagined how much he would change the concept of the Goldwyn and Warner Bros. musicals with his inventive and spectacular dance routines. His last film on his Goldwyn contract and his fourth with Cantor, *Roman Scandals*, has just opened. The movie contains a couple of Berkeley numbers to make anyone's eyes goggle. The setting of "No More Love" is a slave market in which nude girls, wearing long blonde wigs that reach almost down to their knees, are chained to pedestals. Beautiful, smiling chorus girls are also arrayed in a Roman bathhouse where Cantor exhorts them to "Stay Young and Beautiful". However, at Warner Bros., Berkeley has displayed far more than just girls. Recently in *42nd Street* and *Gold Diggers of 1933*, audiences gasped at his kaleidoscopic effects with high overhead shots. Now, in his latest film, *Footlight Parade*, he even tells a story in song and dance. A sailor (James Cagney) is searching the local bars for Shanghai Lil (Ruby Keeler). They meet in a dive, and after tap dancing on top of the bar, he leaves her to rejoin his ship, but she dons a sailor suit and goes along with him. The sailors go through a complicated military-drill routine, eventually holding up huge cards that make up the Stars and Stripes. Berkeley's choreographic genius is also in evidence in "By a Waterfall", sung by Dick Powell to a group of water nymphs.

Berkeley, Cantor (**Roman Scandals**).

e's no angel and rance loves her

ris, 6 October
ae West's huge American success, n *No Angel*, is now captivating ance. Mae, adorning the French ster in a glitzy Schiaparelli gown, ays outrageous carnival entertain- Sister Honky Tonk, again oppo- e handsome Cary Grant.

MAE WEST
"JE NE /UI/ PA/ UN ANGE"
CARY GRANT
C'est un Film Paramount

The Marx Brothers wreak fresh, frenzied and funny havoc

Hollywood, 7 November
Duck Soup, the latest from the Marx Brothers, casts Groucho as the egregious Rufus T. Firefly, president of the banana republic of Freedonia, whose decision to declare war on neighboring Sylvania (just for the hell of it) allows Harpo and Chico to go into the espionage business. The scatterbrained script penned by Bert Kalmar, Harry Ruby, Nat Perrin and Arthur Sheekman, lobs a barrage of satirical grenades at war, politics and patriotism, and the stately figure of Margaret Dumont, once again surviving an avalanche of indignities with her dignity intact. Leo McCarey, who cut his comic teeth with Laurel and Hardy, handles the accumulating anarchy with great skill, particularly in the crazy war sequences. At the end of filming, Zeppo announced that he was retiring from the movies.

Leo McCarey's hilarious **Duck Soup**. Harpo Marx (left); right: Groucho behind Zeppo (left) and Chico.

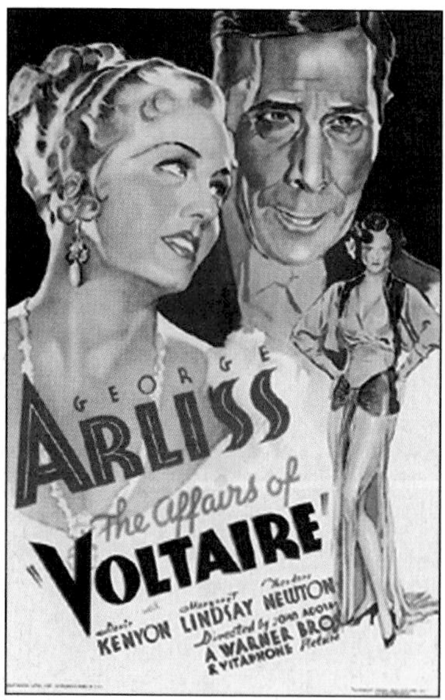
GEORGE
ARLISS
The Affairs of
VOLTAIRE
KENYON LINDSAY NEWTON
A WARNER BROS

Another biopic triumph for Arliss.

Takes its place among the greatest pictures ever made!
Lady
FOR A DAY
WITH
WARREN WILLIAM
MAY ROBSON · GUY KIBBEE
GLENDA FARRELL · NED SPARKS · JEAN PARKER
WALTER CONNOLLY · BARRY NORTON · HOBART BOSWORTH
From the story by Damon Runyon · Screen play by Robert Riskin
a FRANK CAPRA production
A COLUMBIA PICTURE

May Robson, aged 75, starred as Apple Annie in this delightful fantasy.

Nils Asther and Barbara Stanwyc
The Bitter Tea of General Yen.

JOSEPH M. SCHENCK and
DARRYL F. ZANUCK present
WALLACE
BEERY
GEORGE
RAFT
JACKIE
COOPER
and FAY WRAY
PERT KELTON
IN
THE
BOWERY
20 CENTURY
DIRECTED BY RAOUL WALSH

New York in the gay 90s, a big hit.

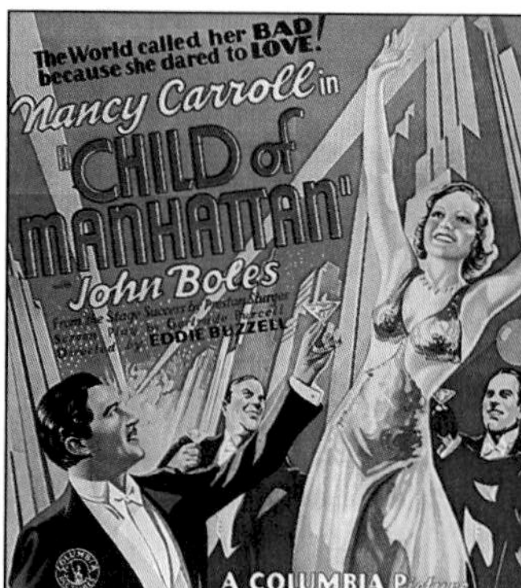
The World called her BAD! because she dared to LOVE!
Nancy Carroll in
"CHILD of MANHATTAN"
John Boles
EDDIE BUZZELL
A COLUMBIA

Nancy Carroll was wasted on t nonsense about a dance-hall girl love with a millionaire (John Bole

They found a love they dared not touch!
BARBARA
Stanwyck
in "THE BITTER TEA OF GENERAL YEN"
with Nils Asther – Walter Connolly
a FRANK CAPRA PRODUCTION
A COLUMBIA PICTURE

This Capra film opened at the new Radio City Music Hall in New York.

Noel Coward's
"design for Living"
WITH
FREDRIC
MARCH
GARY
COOPER
MIRIAM
HOPKINS
EDWARD EVERETT
HORTON
a Paramount Picture
AN Ernst
LUBITSCH
PRODUCTION

Watered-down version of a ménage à trois play was still thought shocking.

RUTH
CHATTERTON
Frisco
Jenny
DIRECTED BY WILLIAM A. WELLMAN
A FIRST NATIONAL and VITAPHONE picture

Chatterton as daughter of a Barbary Coast saloon keeper in tearful melo.

Will
ROGERS
Janet
GAYNOR
in
STATE
FAIR
with
Lew Sally
AYRES · EILERS
Norman Louise Frank Victor
FOSTER · DRESSER · CRAVEN · JORY
Story by PHIL STONG
A HENRY KING Production

A joyous day at the fair for a farm family in a delightful movie.

CHRISTOPHER STRONG
with Katharine
HEPBURN
COLIN CLIVE · BILLIE BURKE
RKO

striking star performance from tharine Hepburn as a lady flyer.

THE DOG HERO OF YOUNG AMERICA!
NAT LEVINE
RIN-TIN-TIN JR.
A MASCOT SERIAL IN 12 THRILLING CHAPTERS
IN
The WOLF DOG
with FRANKIE DARRO
DIRECTED BY HARRY FRAZER & COLBERT CLARK

This 12-part Mascot serial starred the original Rinty's replacement.

Constance
BENNETT
"OUR BETTERS"
with
ANITA LOUISE
GILBERT ROLAND
CHARLES STARRETT
From the play by W. SOMERSET MAUGHAM
Directed by GEORGE CUKOR
RKO Radio Pictures
DAVID O. SELZNICK Executive Producer

A brittle and sarcastic film from Somerset Maugham's tale of social pretension.

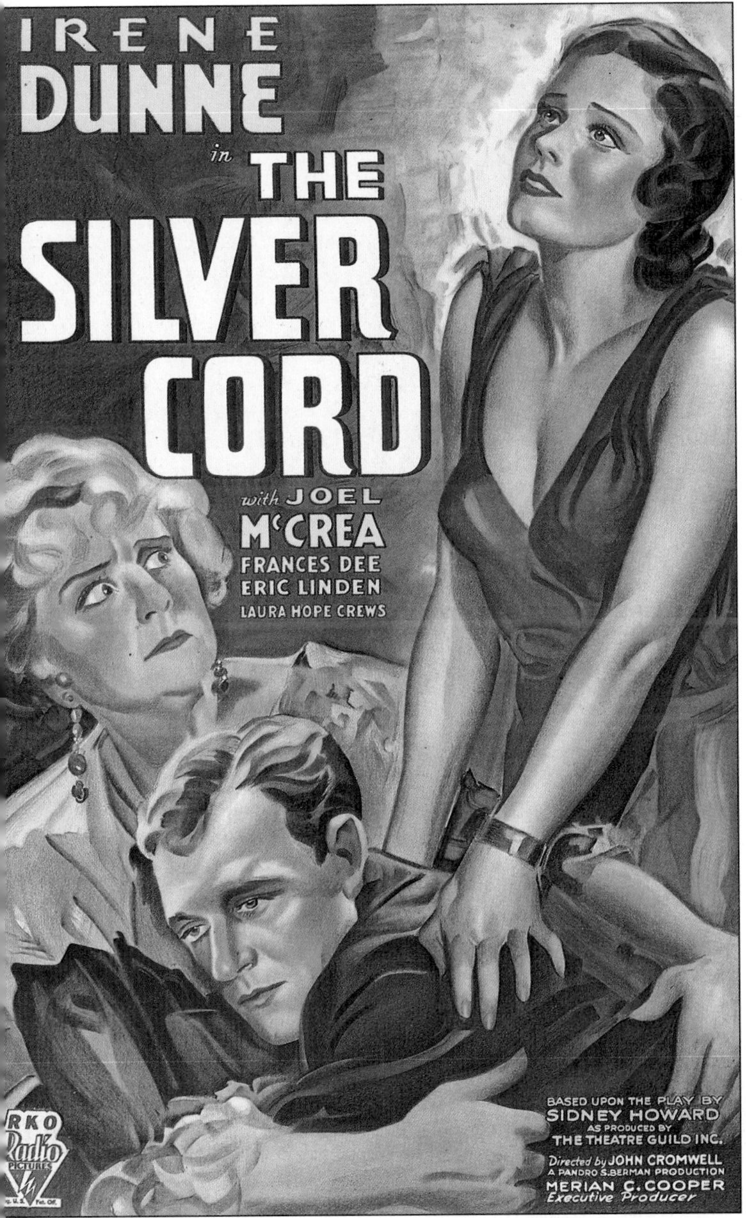
IRENE
DUNNE
in THE
SILVER
CORD
with JOEL
McCREA
FRANCES DEE
ERIC LINDEN
LAURA HOPE CREWS
BASED UPON THE PLAY BY
SIDNEY HOWARD
AS PRODUCED BY
THE THEATRE GUILD INC.
Directed by JOHN CROMWELL
A PANDRO S. BERMAN PRODUCTION
MERIAN C. COOPER
Executive Producer
RKO Radio Pictures

unne star-billed but Laura Hope Crews stole film as a dominating mother.

Gary Cooper and Joan Crawford in **Today We Live**, a film with a wartime love triangle that wasted an all-star cast on a poor script.

Dancing Lady is chiefly memorable for introducing dancer Fred Astaire (above, with star Joan Crawford) to the silver screen.

1934

1932/3 Academy Awards, Ambassador Hotel, 16 Mar.

Best Film: *Cavalcade* (dir: Frank Lloyd)
Best Director: Frank Lloyd
Best Actor: Charles Laughton *(The Private Life of Henry VIII)*
Best Actress: Katharine Hepburn *(Morning Glory)*

Prague, 1 January
Gustav Machaty, who has decided to leave the country, has held a preview of his film *Nocturne*. Shooting was done in Austria with photography by Jan Stallich.

Paris, 4 January
Premiere of Jean Renoir's new film *Madame Bovary* at the Ciné-Opéra. The film stars Valentine Tessier and the director's brother Pierre Renoir.

Berlin, 16 January
Minister Josef Goebbels has instituted an official prize, the Film Of The Nation, for works of merit, with propaganda as the obvious theme. He quoted the film *The Battleship Potemkin* as an example.

London, 10 February
Cary Grant has married the actress Virginia Cherrill at Caxton Hall.

Berlin, 16 February
Promulgation of the cinema law prepared by Goebbels' staff. The law gives the government the power to intervene in all phases of film production and absolute control over the choice of subject matter, authors and directors.

Paris, 26 February
The French version of *Liebelei*, made by Max Ophuls with Magda Schneider, has been released here under the title *Une histoire d'amour* (*A Love Story*).

London, 30 April
Robert Flaherty was invited to make *The Man of Aran* by John Grierson, the leader of the English documentary school. The film was released a couple of weeks ago and is proving very successful.

Los Angeles, 3 May
Release of *Twentieth Century*, based on the play by Ben Hecht and Charles MacArthur, and directed by Howard Hawks. John Barrymore and Carole Lombard are the stars.

Paris, 15 May
The first film directed by Fritz Lang since he left Germany, has been released today. *Liliom* was adapted from the play by Hungarian writer Ferenc Molnar and stars Madeleine Ozeray and Charles Boyer.

Switzerland, 29 May
Filming has started in St. Moritz on *The Man Who Knew Too Much*, the English director Alfred Hitchcock's latest film, which stars Peter Lorre, Leslie Banks and Edna Best.

New York, 9 June
Release of W.S. Van Dyke's new film *The Thin Man*, based on the novel by Dashiell Hammett, starring William Powell and Myrna Loy as the amateur detectives Nick and Nora Charles.

Los Angeles, 13 June
A new code has been introduced to set down production guidelines in regards to censorship and morality. Cinema owners are authorized to refuse all films produced prior to the code which they consider to be in contravention of it.

Los Angeles, 12 July
The president of the MPPDA, William H. Hays, has announced that a fine of $25,000 will be the penalty for any changes made to screenplays once they have been passed by the Commission.

Berlin, 22 July
The censors have banned *Nana*, filmed by the French director Jean Renoir from the novel by Zola. The film stars Catherine Hessling in the title role, with the Germans Werner Krauss and Valeska Gert also cast. Jewish actress Gert had to emigrate to America last year.

Hollywood, 24 July
Release of Cecil B. DeMille's work *Cleopatra*, with Claudette Colbert as the legendary beauty, Warren William and Henry Wilcoxon.

Shanghai, 31 July
The film now showing at the Jingcheng cinema, *Yu Guang Qu* (*The Song of the Fisherman*), written and directed by Caï Chusheng, has been an instant success. The exquisitely beautiful song of the title is on its way to becoming one of the most popular melodies in China.

Cairo, 15 September
The cinematographic branch of the Misr Bank, which at the moment is already involved in film production, is now building new studios.

Moscow, 15 September
The Moskino-Kombinat studio has released Mikhaïl Romm's first feature, *Pyshka*, a silent film based on Maupassant's *Boule-de-suif.*

Los Angeles, 2 October
Release of *Our Daily Bread*, by King Vidor, tells of the vicissitudes of an agricultural cooperative during the Great Depression.

Moscow, 5 October
German thespian Erwin Piscator has made his first film *The Revolt of the Fishermen*, in the Soviet Union.

Hollywood, 13 October
Ernst Lubitsch has released his screen adaptation of the famous operetta *The Merry Widow*, by Franz Lehar, with Maurice Chevalier and Jeanette MacDonald.

Prague, 26 October
Release of *Hej Rup!*, a satirical film by Martin Fric, which takes a long and bitter look at the problems caused by unemployment.

Moscow, 7 November
Lenfilm has released *Chapayev*, by Sergei and Georgi Vasiliev, a patriotic epic set during the civil war.

Tokyo, 23 November
Premiere of Yasujiro Ozu's *Ukigusa Monogatari* (*A Story of Floating Weeds*). The film deals with the difficult relationship between a father and son in a traveling troupe.

Los Angeles, 28 November
Members of the board of directors for Paramount-Publix (undergoing bankruptcy) have resigned, and a new Board has been elected. The Company has submitted its recovery plan to the courts.

Paris, 19 December
Julien Duvivier's *Maria Chap[…] laine*, with Jean Gabin and Ma[…]laine Renaud, has been awarded […] major French film prize.

Hollywood, 28 December
Charlie Chaplin has shot seve[…] scenes with dialogue between hi[…]self and Paulette Goddard for *M[…]ern Times*, a film he has been wo[…]ing on since 1933. However, none […] these sequences have been retain[…]

BIRTHS

New York, 13 February
George Segal

England, 17 February
Alan Bates

Algeria, 26 February
Mohamed Lakhdar Hamina

New York, 26 March
Alan Arkin

Virginia, 24 April
Shirley MacLaine
(Shirley MacLean Beaty)

Italy, 1 May
Laura Betti

Wisconsin, 19 June
Gena Rowlands

Paris, 1 July
Claude Berri (Claude Langman)

Canada, 17 July
Donald Sutherland

Ohio, 16 September
George Chakiris

Rome, 20 September
Sophia Loren
(Sofia Sciccolone)

Paris, 28 September
Brigitte Bardot

DEATHS

California, 28 July
Marie Dressler

The runaway success of ***It Happen[…] One Night*** *has proved the jewel in t[…] crown of the director Frank Capr[…] career as the creator of a truly uniq[…] brand of American comedy.*

TOGETHER FOR
THE FIRST TIME!
CLARK CLAUDETTE
GABLE and COLBERT
IN
"It Happened One Night"
with WALTER CONNOLLY • ROSCOE KARNS
From the Cosmopolitan Magazine story by SAMUEL HOPKINS ADAMS • Screen play by ROBERT RISKIN
COLUMBIA PICTURES
a FRANK CAPRA PRODUCTION
A
COLUMBIA
PICTURE

▷

The screen a witness to yesterday's riots

Paris, 7 February
Despite the censorship imposed by the Prefecture of Police and the Ministry of the Interior, Reginald Ford's Cinéac Theatre is showing newsreels of yesterday's Paris riots. Deciding to capitalize on the discredited actions of politicians since the scandalous Stavisky affair, Action Française, the Royalists and war veterans associations assembled in massive numbers to demonstrate against the Daladier government. As one could have easily predicted, the demonstration quickly turned into a riot, which resulted in 17 dead and 116 injured among the demonstrators as well as the police who had charged the angry crowd. This tragic event had been observed, photographed and reported on by the many journalists present, French and foreign. Thus the multitude of newsreel cameras filmed the militants of the far right, in their berets, breaking into pieces the wrought-iron grids around the trees along the Boulevard Saint-Germain, and using them as missiles to throw at the rows of police that were stationed outside the National Assembly, all the while threatening to hurl the members of the Chamber of Deputies into the Seine.

Columbia's happy hike to box office

Clark Gable and Claudette Colbert, initially reluctant stars now benefiting from the success of **It Happened One Nig**

Hollywood, 22 February
A few months after the triumph of *Lady for a Day*, Frank Capra has continued to win over the public with *It Happened One Night*. His new film for Columbia is a ravishing comedy about a capricious heiress and a sensationalist journalist who start on a cross-country journey by squabbling and end by falling head-over-heels in love with one another. She is on the run after her marriage to a fortune hunter was annulled by her father. She loses her money on a bus trip to New York, and he agrees to help her in return for an exclusive story. During the trip, the couple are forced to hitchhike, sleep in a haystack, and share a motel room while pretending to be husband and wife. Based on a story by Samuel Hopkins Adams called *Night Bus*, the film almost didn't happen. Every star under contract – Robert Montgomery for the journalist, and Margaret Sullavan, Miriam Hopkins, Myrna Loy, Constance Bennett for the heiress – turned down the screenplay. Finally, MGM lent Colum Clark Gable in exchange for Fra Capra directing a picture for the Claudette Colbert accepted the p on condition that the shooting l no more than four weeks, and t her salary be doubled. Capra acce ed the challenge, and concluded film in record time. His rapid, ha edged direction, and the light a engaging playing of the two lea has provided the Depression-we American public with just the sort tonic they need.

Victor Hugo and Gustave Flaubert in demand by filmmakers

Paris, 3 February
The great classics of French literature are lending inspiration to more film directors than ever before. Just a month after the release at the Ciné-Opéra of Jean Renoir's *Madame Bovary*, a new version of *les Misérables*, directed by Raymond Bernard, was shown at a gala evening at the Cinéma Marignan. Renoir's film brings to mind much of the beauty of his father's paintings while benefiting from excellent performances by Valentine Tessier in the title role and Pierre Renoir, the director's brother, as her husband. This has not prevented the public from displaying their indifference toward the film, though, admittedly, *Madame Bovary* was shown by the distributors in a cut and distorted version. Presented in a single evening, the three episodes of *les Misérables* were more fortunate. The public appreciated it, and the critics hailed the film and its director, whom they praised for turning Victor Hugo's immense novel into a workable and lucid scenario. With his huge talent and an imposing physique, Harry Bauer makes an unforgettable Jean Valjean, heading an equally remarkable cast that includes Charles Vanel and Orane Demazis.

Pierre Renoir and Valentine Tessier.

Harry Baur is Hugo's Jean Valjean.

Paul Czinner victim of propaganda

Berlin, 11 March
Josef Goebbels does not lack power to impose a ban on films which the Nazi Party disapprov Sometimes the methods he emplc are insidious. It would have be clumsy to prevent outright the G man release of the first film made England by director Paul Czinner Jew who left the country with actress wife, Elisabeth Bergn when the Nazis came to power l year. *Catherine the Great*, starri Bergner and Douglas Fairbanks J could not just be ignored. Goebbe tactic has been to let the Nazi pr fulminate against a foreign fil "produced by and starring Jews supported by the menacing presen of storm troopers at each showi Thus, the film has been withdra as a threat to public order.

atharine Hepburn takes home the Venice awards for Hollywood

Lowell Sherman's **Morning Glory** (left), and with Joan Bennett in George Cukor's screen version of **Little Women**.

ice, 1 August
second Venice Film Festival has led on a note of triumph for Kathe Hepburn, winner of the best ress award for her performance Jo in *Little Women*, directed by orge Cukor. Hepburn is riding crest of a wave at the moment, ing won the Best Actress Oscar March for *Morning Glory*, in ich she plays a stagestruck girl o becomes a star. The Academy ard for Best Actor in 1933 went Charles Laughton for his rumbusis performance as Henry VIII in xander Korda's *The Private Life Henry VIII*, the first British film enjoy wide international success. nk Lloyd won the Best Director car for the screen version of Noel ward's *Cavalcade* (also voted the st Picture). For Hepburn, success film has recently been accompad by the failure of her marriage to sinessman Ludlow Ogden Smith, om she divorced on 9 May. Hepn is the most atypical of Hollyod stars, striding through the vie capital in slacks, declining to e interviews and fleeing from ograph hunters. Nonplussed by novel style, movie execs are not ite sure how to handle the angu-, spirited young woman with the roughbred features and Bryn awr accent. But from the moment made her debut opposite John rrymore in *A Bill of Divorcement*, as been clear that Katharine Hepn is a star of unique qualities, termined to make her own way in movie jungle.

Wallace Beery, the best actor at Venice for ***Viva Villa*** *directed by Jack Conway.*

The triumph of Leni Riefenstahl

Nuremberg, 4 September
Triumph of the Will is the title given by the Fuhrer to a documentary film to be made on the Nazi Party's Nuremberg Rally, and the preparations for it. It will be directed by Leni Riefenstahl, a young actress until now known for her roles in mountain pictures. She has been given a contract by UFA and considerable means to carry out her mission. She will direct a team of 120 people, of which there will be 32 technicians with 32 cameras. To be able to shoot all aspects of the event, 130,000 metres of film will be at her disposal. With *Triumph of the Will*, Leni Riefenstahl has become the Egeria of the Nazi Party.

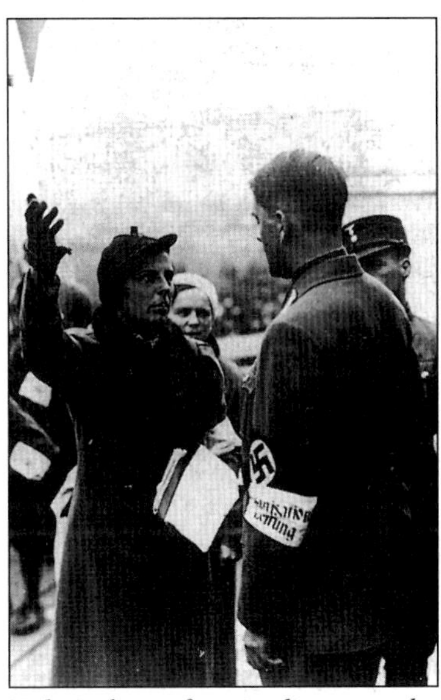

Hitler's chosen favorite director at the National Socialist Congress.

Delightfully vivacious Jessie Matthews seems younger than ever

The lovely Jessie Matthews, with Barry Mackay in Victor Saville's film.

London, 10 September
Jessie Matthews, Britain's favorite singing star, has scored her biggest film hit with *Evergreen*, a charming piece of froth about an Edwardian music-hall star blackmailed into retirement and the daughter who steps into her shoes to win stardom. Matthews' own progress from chorus girl to toast of London has taken some 10 years. Her first successful foray into films came in 1931 with *Out of the Blue*, and her current contract with Michael Balcon, head of British Gaumont, gives her script and director approval.

Another dazzling eyeful from Berkeley

Ruby Keeler, the centerpiece of the 'I Only Have Eyes For You' number.

Hollywood, 10 September
Busby Berkeley, the fantastic dance director, has continued to astonish with the routines in his latest film, *Dames*, which opened here last week. In the title number, hundreds of chorus girls in white blouses and black tights are seen waking, bathing, dressing and hurrying to the theater where they become part of a series of optical mazes. It ends with the girls reclining on different levels of a scaffold structure, but as the camera pulls back, they become tiny figures, and with an imperceptible cut, Dick Powell's head suddenly bursts through the picture in close-up. Almost as good is the "I Only Have Eyes For You" number, in which a multitude of girls all have Ruby Keeler's face, until they come together to form one huge portrait.

Sternberg's vision of 'The Scarlet Empres

The grand finale of ***The Scarlet Empress*** *with Dietrich in the title role.*

Hollywood, 14 September
Marlene Dietrich's sixth collaboration with Josef von Sternberg has produced *The Scarlet Empress*, in which the star plays the nymphomaniac Catherine the Great, stalking through an extravagantly designed and lit fantasy of 18th-century Russia. Dietrich, never more sensually photographed than this, achieves the transition from gauche child-hood to disillusioned womanho with extraordinary understandin while cameraman Bert Glenno caressing close-ups, in candle-lig and veils, are truly sumptuous. Ev the grotesque gargoyles, with whi art director Hans Dreier has dec rated the rococo sets, melt into t background as Sternberg's love leading lady makes her royal a glamorous progress.

Pagnol's 'Angèle' back in Marseilles

Marseilles, 28 September
The inhabitants of this Mediterranean port doubtless deserve the gift that a child of the area has offered them: Marcel Pagnol has just given the world premiere in Marseilles of his new film, *Angèle*, which he shot in the region. It was shown in a tinted color version, blue for the night scenes, pink for the day shots, and multicolored for the dramatic scenes. By installing his troupe on a farm, and by using direct sound, Pagnol has created a realistic Provençal background and written a beautifully crafted scenario that transcends the slightly melodramatic plot. Based on a short novel by Jean Giono, the film is admirably interpreted by Orane Demazis – in the role of the young, naive peasant girl, seduced and abandoned, who goes to Marseilles, where she has a child and becomes a prostitute – and by Fernandel who, in portraying the simple-minded farm hand Saturnin, emerges as a great tragi-comic actor.

The turbulent river of life has stopped flowing for Jean Vigo

Paris, 5 October
Jean Vigo has died of septicemia at the age of 29. His illness disrupted the making of his last film, *l'Atalante*, the shooting of which took place last winter on location in appalling weather conditions. Vigo's health had already deteriorated to such a point that Louis Chavance had to undertake the editing alone. Confined to bed, the director could not see his finished film, although it was released a few weeks ago at the Colisée. At least Vigo was spared the pain of disappointment at the result, because numerous cuts were imposed on it by Gaumont-FFA. The distributors were responding to the negative reaction the film received when it was shown to exhibitors last April. Gaumont then added a popular song by Bixio, sung by Lys Gauty, to the musical score by Maurice Jaubert, and changed the title from *l'Atalante* to the name of the song, *le Chaland qui passe*. These changes did not make for a warmer welcome by the public and critics, and the movie soon disappeared from view. The fate of the director and the film has given a slightly bitter edge to Vigo's recent utterance: "I am killing myself with *l'Atalante*." It's a pity, because the simple love story of a young barge captain (Jean Dasté), who takes his bride (Dita Parlo) to live aboard his boat, has many magical momen such as the young man searching f his sweetheart under water. Mich Simon is superb as the mate telli fantastic stories of his travels. Pe haps, one day, the film will be show in its original form, thus respecti the wishes of the late Jean Vigo.

GAUMONT-FRANCO-FILM-AUBERT présente une production J.L. NOUNEZ
L'ATALANTE
MICHEL SIMON et DITA PARLO
DANS
LE
CHALAND QUI PASSE
GFFA
JEAN DASTÉ
JEAN VIGO
Scénario de JEAN GUINÉE _ Musique de MAURICE JAUBERT

Henri Cerruti's poster designed for a film fraught with difficulties.

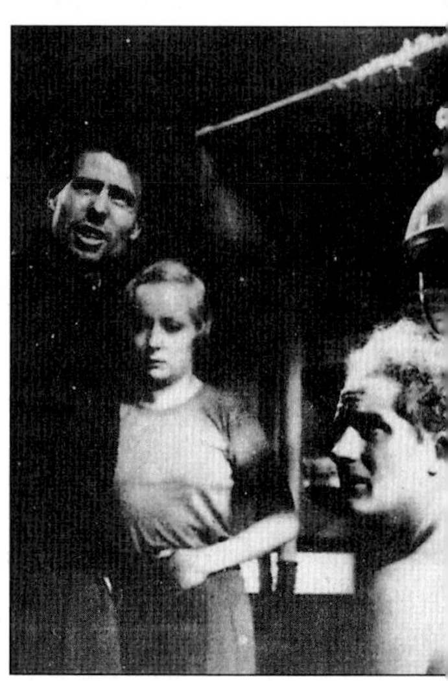

Vigo photographed during filmi with Dita Parlo and Jean Dasté.

ıe gift-wrapped Fields delights his fans

ıe well-known child-hater in **It's a Gift**, with young Tommy Bupp.

ollywood, 30 November
ɔmedy's great curmudgeon, W. C. elds, rejoins battle with his infant arring partner Baby LeRoy in ıramount's hilarious *It's a Gift*, a w production directed by Noran Z. McLeod. Fields is Harold ssonette (pronounced "Bisson-y" he dutifully writes on a placard the behest of his battleaxe of a ife), a harassed husband and store-eper whose premises are wrecked anks to the flailing white stick of a umpy blind and deaf customer, fore being inundated by a flood of olasses released by Baby LeRoy. Spreadingest stuff I ever saw," ruinates Fields sadly, before fixing a ɔtice to the front door which reads Closed on Account of Molasses". 's been a busy year for Fields. He ade a cameo appearance in *Six of Kind*; played an unsuccesful invenr in *You're Telling Me*, a virtual make of his silent feature *So's ɔur Old Man*; appeared as ZaSu tts' mail-order hubby in the third ovie version of *Mrs. Wiggs of the abbage Patch*; and scored a big hit ith *The Old Fashioned Way* as the reat McGonigle, a magnificently audulent turn-of-the-century actor-anager and self-styled "greatest agedian in the world". In *The Old ıshioned Way*, Fields recalls his ıst career as a juggler and as an tor in touring melodramas. Born 'illiam Claude Dukenfield in Philalphia on 10 February 1879, he ran vay from his poor and unhappy ɔme at the age of 11. His early enage years, spent living on his wits in the seedier streets of Philadelphia, gave him a deeply suspicious view of the world, which he frankly acknowledges and which serves as the basis of his comedy of misanthropy. Whatever it is, Fields is against it, particularly wives, dogs, small children and all forms of pompous authority. By the time he was 21, Fields had become an international juggling star. He joined the "Ziegfeld Follies" in 1914 and in 1915 made his very first film, *Pool Sharks*, based on one of his most famous acts. After an erratic career in silent films, he came into his own with the arrival of sound. His rasping voice has rounded out his comic personality, the bleary-eyed, bottle-nosed observer of the absurdity and pettiness of life. The private and public Fields are inseparable.

With ZaSu Pitts in **Mrs Wiggs**.

A sensuous portrait of faraway Ceylon

A characteristic scene from Basil Wright's **Song of Ceylon**.

London, 16 December
The last three years have seen the expansion of a British documentary movement, whose presiding genius has been John Grierson, head of the Empire Marketing Board Film Unit from 1928 and currently head of the GPO Film Unit. One of his recruits at the E.M.B., Basil Wright, taken on as an editor in 1929 before graduating to directing in 1931, has now written, directed and photographed a notable documentary called *Song of Ceylon*. In four parts, "The Buddha", "The Virgin Island", "The Voices of Commerce" and "The Apparel of a God", it is sensuous and pictorially elegant.

New Moscow musical in American mode

Moscow, 25 December
The long sojourn of Sergei Eisenstein in America between 1930 and 1932 did bear some fruit indirectly. His former assistant director, scenarist and actor, Grigori Alexandrov, who had been with him in the U.S., has just made *Jolly Fellows*, a Hollywood-style musical comedy. Alexandrov has perfectly assimilated the rules of the genre, while adapting it to the country of Socialism. It tells of a shepherd, who takes up a career in jazz, finally giving a concert at the Bolshoi. Leonid Outessov, a singer from Odessa, plays the shepherd, and the ravishing Liubov Orlova is his sweetheart.

The Soviet public adores Grigori Alexandrov's light-hearted musical romp.

Adolph Zukor presents
CECIL B. DeMILLE'S
CLEOPATRA
with CLAUDETTE COLBERT
WARREN WILLIAM
HENRY WILCOXON
JOSEPH SCHILDKRAUT
A PARAMOUNT PICTURE
A LOVE AFFAIR THAT SHOOK THE WORLD
• SET IN A SPECTACLE OF •
• THRILLING MAGNIFICENCE! •

Another airing for the Queen of the Nile, with a top-notch cast and Cecil B. DeMille's customary panache.

Françoise Rosay, the wife of director Jacques Feyder, in ***le Grand jeu****.*

His dancing partners
were but stepping
stones to fame!
George
RAFT
IN
BOLERO
WITH
CAROLE
LOMBARD
AND
SALLY
RAND
"THE FAN DANCER"
DIRECTED BY WESLEY RUGGLES
a Paramount Picture

Raft and Lombard's dance, plus Ravel's music, was a sizzler for Paramount.

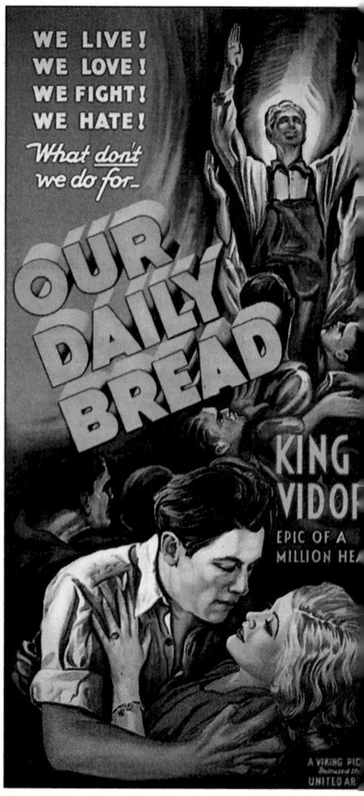
WE LIVE!
WE LOVE!
WE FIGHT!
WE HATE!
What don't
we do for...
OUR DAILY BREAD
KING
VIDOR
EPIC OF A
MILLION HE

This well-meant social drama was box-office failure.

THE KING AND QUEEN of CARIOC
FRED ASTAIRE
GINGER ROGER
THE GAY DIVORCEE
ALICE BRADY
HORTON

A memorable musical with Fre Ginger and a Cole Porter score.

You can
Judge for
Yourself – but –
Will Rogers
says –
"JUDGE PRIEST"
is My best!
FOX

A slice of small-town Americana.

GAUMONT BRITISH
Presents
"CHU CHIN CHOW"
with
ANNA MAY WONG
GEORGE ROBEY
FRITZ KORTNER
Directed by
WALTER FORDE
By
OSCAR ASCHE

Theatrical hit came to the screen.

A Ben Hecht Charles MacArthur Picture
CRIME
WITHOUT
PASSION
with
CLAUDE RAINS
WHITNEY BOURNE
MARGO
A PARAMOUNT RELEASE

Moody melo of jealousy and murder.

WILLIAM
POWELL AND MYRNA
LOY
DASHIELL HAMMETT'S
MASTER MYSTERY
The THIN
MAN
with MAUREEN
O'SULLIVA
NAT PENDLETON · MINNA GOMBEL
A Cosmopolitan Production
Metro-Goldwyn-Maye

Miraculous Powell-Loy chemistry.

ter Lorre (left), Leslie Banks in Hitchcock's **The Man Who Knew Too Much**.

) r: J.M. Kerrigan, Victor McLaglen and Reginald Denny in **The Lost Patrol**.

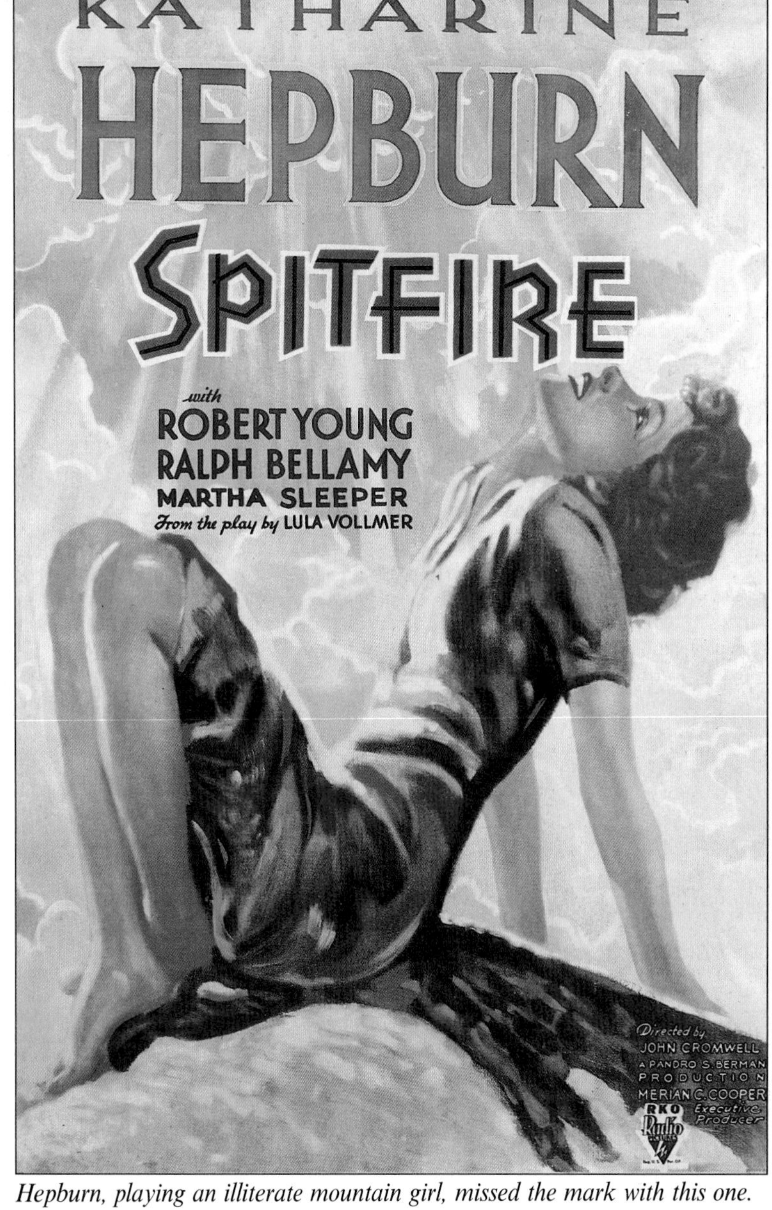
KATHARINE
HEPBURN
SPITFIRE
with
ROBERT YOUNG
RALPH BELLAMY
MARTHA SLEEPER
From the play by LULA VOLLMER
Directed by
JOHN CROMWELL
A PANDRO S. BERMAN
PRODUCTION
MERIAN C. COOPER
Executive Producer
RKO Radio
Hepburn, playing an illiterate mountain girl, missed the mark with this one.

FOX FILM presents
WAS
A SPY
deleine
ARROLL
rbert
ARSHALL
nrad
EIDT
Directed by
VICTOR SAVILLE
p British director Victor Saville
d a great cast for this WWI drama.

ANNA STEN
in the
SAMUEL GOLDWYN
production
"Nana"
with
LIONEL ATWILL
RICHARD BENNETT
MAE CLARKE
PHILLIPS HOLMES
MURIEL KIRKLAND
Released thru
UNITED ARTISTS
Sam Goldwyn's new Russian-born star failed to make an impression.

MARLENE DIETRICH
IN
THE SCARLET EMPRESS
WITH
JOHN LODGE
SAM JAFFE
LOUISE DRESSER
DIRECTED BY
JOSEF VON STERNBERG
a Paramount Picture
Catherine the Great: the luxurious sixth collaboration.

Claudette Colbert
in FANNIE HURST'S
IMITATION of LIFE
with WARREN WILLIAM
ROCHELLE HUDSON
NED SPARKS
HENRY ARMETTA
A JOHN M. STAHL production
Audiences wept buckets over this tale of mother love and racism.

1935

1934 Academy Awards, Biltmore Hotel, 27 Feb.

Best Film: *It Happened One Night* (dir: Frank Capra)
Best Director: Frank Capra
Best Actor: Clark Gable *(It Happened One Night)*
Best Actress: Claudette Colbert *(It Happened One Night)*

Washington, 12 January
RKO, Warner Bros. and Paramount have been summoned to appear before a grand jury on charges of monopolistic practices.

Hollywood, 28 February
Douglas Fairbanks and Mary Pickford's divorce is now final.

Moscow, 28 February
The Chinese film, *The Song of the Fisherman*, by Caï Chusheng has taken the prize of honor at the Moscow Festival.

Hollywood, 2 March
Friz Freleng has directed *I Haven't Got a Hat*, a short cartoon for Leon Schlesinger's "Merrie Melodies", featuring a wonderful new character called Porky Pig.

USA, 24 April
Release of Richard Boleslawski's *les Misérables*, with Fredric March, Charles Laughton, Florence Eldridge and Rochelle Hudson. This film is the third American adaptation of Victor Hugo's novel.

New York, 3 May
Release of *The Devil is a Woman*, Josef von Sternberg's adaptation of the novel by Pierre Louys, with Marlene Dietrich, Lionel Atwill and Cesar Romero.

Hollywood, 10 May
Who is Frankenstein's promised one? Those who are interested can find out in James Whale's *The Bride of Frankenstein*, which is being released today. Boris Karloff again stars as the poor creature, with Colin Clive and Elsa Lanchester.

Paris, 11 May
Abel Gance has released a sound version, with a few extra scenes, of his 1927 silent film *Napoleon*. Paramount helped bring out this new version using the Perspective sound process for the first time. The result is sensational.

Hollywood, 27 May
Joseph M. Schenck and Darryl F. Zanuck have bought a controlling interest in the Fox Film Corporation which has merged with their own company; this new company has been named 20th Century-Fox.

Hollywood, 17 June
Paramount-Publix has finished its financial reorganization. Having been bought up by its own circuit's Cinema Union, it emerges under the name of Paramount Pictures Inc.

Berlin, 2 July
A ministerial order decrees that all silent or sound films made before 30 January 1933 must once more be submitted to the censorship Commission before 31 December 1935.

London, 14 August
The actress Vivien Leigh has signed a contract with Alexander Korda, the most influential producer in Great Britain. He has granted her the privilege of being able to act on the stage for six months each year.

Tokyo, 15 August
Release of a sentimental comedy, directed by Mikio Naruse *Tsuma Yo Bara No Yo Ni* (*Wife, Be Like a Rose*), starring Sachiko Chiba, the director's companion.

New York, 13 September
Mark Sandrich's musical comedy *Top Hat*, starring Fred Astaire and Ginger Rogers, has beaten box-office records for Radio City Music Hall. Takings reached $245,000 in the first two weeks.

Paris, 20 September
Release of Julien Duvivier's *La Bandera*, which stars Jean Gabin, Annabella and Robert Le Vigan.

Copenhagen, 28 September
Paul Fejos describes the torments of an admired actress' conscience in *Det gyldne Smil* (*The Golden Smile*), which is being released today.

Tokyo, 30 September
Nikkatsu, the oldest of the major Japanese production firms, has fallen victim to a stock-market crash. Henceforth, the firm is giving up the production side of its business to concentrate on distribution.

Cairo, 10 October
All the most important people in Cairo attended the inauguration of the final stage of Misr's studios in Giza. Egyptian cinema has now become a full-fledged industry.

New Jersey, 11 October
Joan Crawford has married the actor Franchot Tone at Englewood. The star was previously married to Douglas Fairbanks Jr.

Moscow, 6 November
The production companies Ukrainfilm and Mosfilm have released Alexander Dovzhenko's latest film, *Aerograd*.

Hollywood, 7 November
Paramount has released *Peter Ibbetson*, inspired by the novel by George Du Maurier, with Gary Cooper, Ann Harding and Ida Lupino. The film is Henry Hathaway's second for 1935, the first being *The Lives of a Bengal Lancer*.

Hollywood, 8 November
Release of *Mutiny on the Bounty*, directed by Frank Lloyd, with Clark Gable as the bare-chested Fletcher Christian and Charles Laughton as the unyielding Captain Bligh.

Rome, 9 November
The Italian authorities have drawn up the constitution for the ENIC (National Board for the Cinema Industry). This new organization is in charge of film production, distribution and cinema management.

Hollywood, 15 November
The Marx Brothers have starred in their first film for MGM, *A Night at the Opera* directed by Sam Wood. Their films were previously produced by Paramount.

London, 17 December
René Clair's first English film, *The Ghost Goes West*, with Robert Donat and Jean Parker, was screened during a gala evening attended by Queen Mary. The guests were completely won over by the film.

Los Angeles, 26 December
Release of *Captain Blood* with Er Flynn in his first starring role a Olivia De Havilland. Michael Cur directed.

Berlin, 31 December
Average production costs in G many have doubled since 1933. T is mainly due to the inflated salar paid to actors and directors.

BIRTHS

Hollywood, 5 March
Dean Stockwell

Los Angeles, 31 March
Richard Chamberlain

London, 19 April
Dudley Moore

Pennsylvania, 21 April
Charles Grodin

Athens, 27 April
Theo Angelopoulos

Wisconsin, 11 June
Gene Wilder
(Jerry Silberman)

Paris, 25 June
Laurent Terzieff

England, 1 October
Julie Andrews
(Julie Elizabeth Wells)

France, 8 November
Alain Delon

Stockholm, 11 November
Bibi Andersson
(Brigitta Andersson)

New York, 1 December
Woody Allen
(Allen Stewart Koenigsberg)

Massachusetts, 14 December
Lee Remick

DEATHS

Alaska, 15 August
Will Rogers

***The Devil is a Woman** marks anoth exotic and successful collaborati between Josef von Sternberg a Marlene Dietrich. It is a romantic ta of love, jealousy and betrayal.*

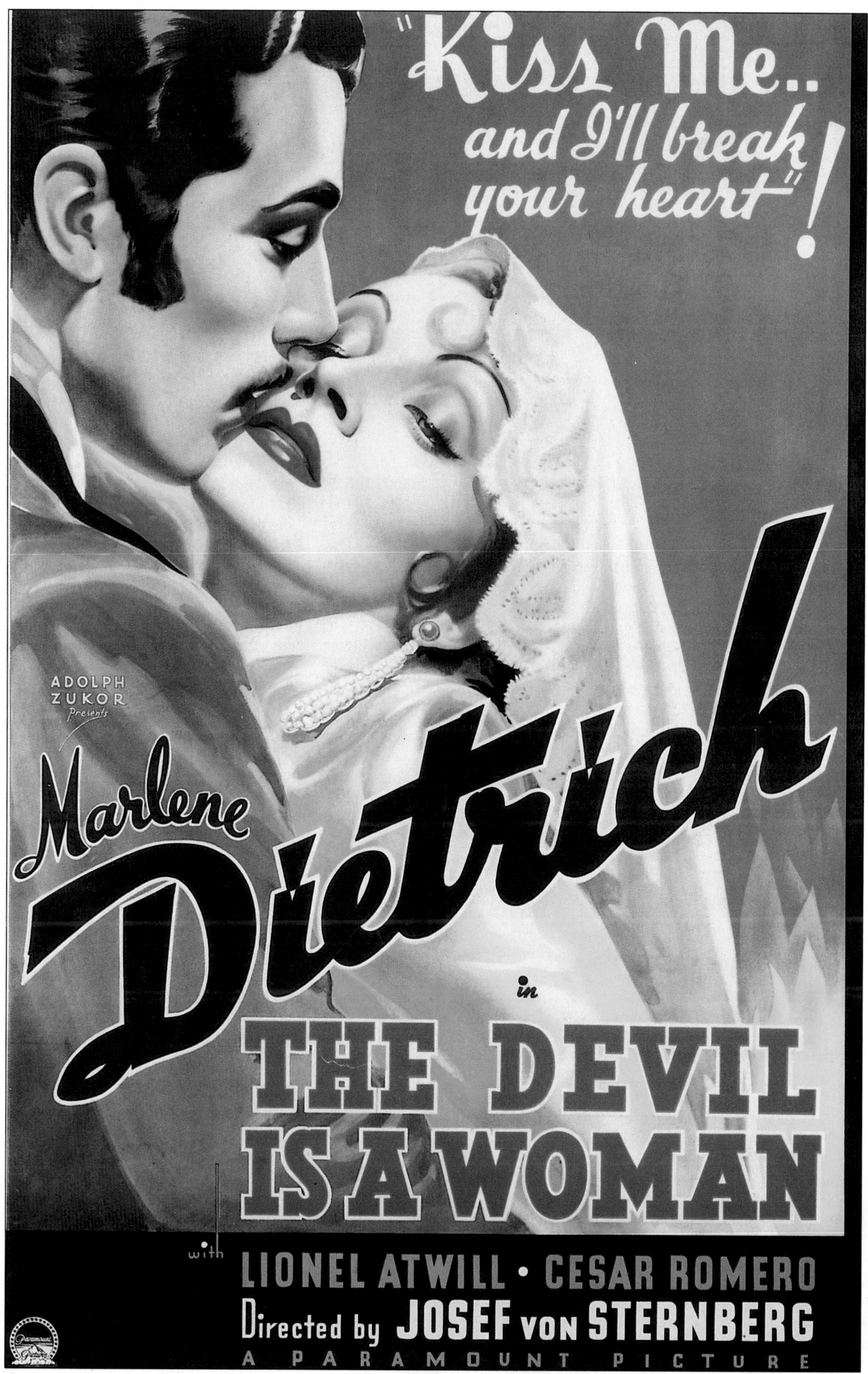
"Kiss Me..
and I'll break
your heart"!
ADOLPH
ZUKOR
Presents
Marlene
Dietrich
in
THE DEVIL
IS A WOMAN
with
LIONEL ATWILL • CESAR ROMERO
Directed by JOSEF VON STERNBERG
A PARAMOUNT PICTURE

W.C. Fields in the world of Charles Dickens

Frank Lawton (left) as David Copperfield, W.C. Fields and Roland Young.

Hollywood, 18 January
In a piece of inspired casting, MGM decided to borrow W.C. Fields from Paramount to play Wilkins Micawber in *David Copperfield*. The film's director, George Cukor, had great difficulty in persuading Fields that he could not remedy Dickens' unaccountable omission of any juggling in his novel with a few choice routines of his own. In the end, audiences have been denied the sight of a juggling Micawber – however, as the genially feckless spendthrift, Fields remains true to his own unique comic personality. When he assures us that something will turn up, we are left in no doubt that he foresees some fresh calamity looming, as bizarre and unpredictable as some of the outrageous names he habitually chooses for the characters in his films. In a splendidly cast film, Edna May Oliver plays Betsy Trotwood, Basil Rathbone and Violet Kemble Cooper play the Murdstones, Lennox Pawle is Mr. Dick, and Roland Young the slimy Uriah Heep. Luckily, these salty performances more than compensate for the anodyne David Copperfield: prissy, proper little Freddie Bartholomew as the boy, and bland Frank Lawton as the young man.

Lubitsch now Paramount's production chie

Herbert Marshall and Miriam Hopkins, the co-stars of ***Trouble in Paradise.***

DEPT

The amazing Ernst Lubitsch.

Hollywood, 5 February
The latest change to be announc by the much troubled Paramou movie empire is the appointment the leading producer-director Er Lubitsch as studio production chi Like most of the other major Hol wood studios, Paramount did w during 1929 and 1930, the first yea of sound, but by 1931 the impact the Depression was beginning to felt. Deep in the red by 1932, t company underwent a major shal up in management for the first tir since its initial formation in 191 As a result, studio head Jesse Lasky was forced out, along wi production chief B.P. Schulbe while even the powerful figure Adolph Zukor, the company pre dent, emerged from the boardroo battles with his authority severe curtailed. In spite of cost-cutting forts, the company was forced to f for bankruptcy in 1933. The ne production executive, Manny C hen, failed to match up to expec tions and thus, in a surprise mo the top executives have turned to filmmaker of stature to put the s dio back on the road to recovery

Since his arrival from Germa some 12 years ago, Lubitsch h more than repeated the success his European career. Popular wi actors and fellow-directors alike, has been closely associated wi Paramount throughout the sou era. It is likely, however, that appointment is a stop-gap measu until a suitable permanent candid can be found.

The Academy Awards now have the blessing of 'Uncle Oscar'

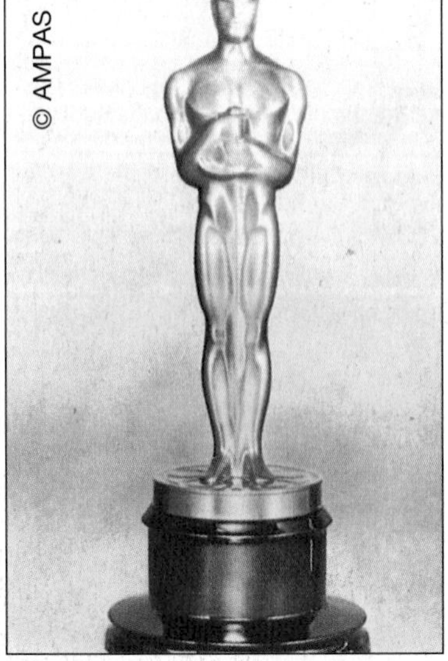
© AMPAS

The gold trophy, now called Oscar.

Hollywood, 27 February
There is some controversy about how the gold statuette presented at the Academy Award ceremony got its nickname of Oscar. Whether it came from a music-hall joke, "Will you have a cigar, Oscar?", as Sidney Skolsky the columnist claims, or was named after Bette Davis' husband, Harmon Oscar Nelson Jr., or indeed whether it derived from the Academy executive and librarian Margaret Herrick, who was supposed to have exclaimed, "Why, he resembles my Uncle Oscar!", the cognomen has been taken up by the members of the Academy and the public. The movie *It Happened One Night*, its stars Clark Gable and Claudette Colbert and the director, Frank Capra, were all recipients of Oscars. A miniature version of the statue was given to Shirley Temple "in grateful recognition of her outstanding contribution to screen entertainment during the year 1934."

Special award for little Shirley.

iefenstahl glorifies Nazi regime on film

n image of German might in this close-up from **Triumph of the Will.**

erlin, 28 March
significant cinematographic event the form of Adolf Hitler's comissioned *Triumph of the Will* preiered today at the UFA Palast am oo. Directed by Leni Riefenstahl, is enormous production has final- reached German screens after six onths editing, which entailed the lection of about three percent of e material shot in order to provide film of two hours in length. The sult has proven satisfactory to the hird Reich. This impressive documentary shows the preparations, the arches and the speeches at the uremberg Rally, held by the Nazi Party. Leni Riefenstahl has shaped the rally into a great mythic spectacle, with the Fuhrer appearing as a Wagnerian hero descending on the medieval town to save *das volk*. Ecstatic faces stare up at him as the sun catches his head like a halo. Other key sequences exalt healthy youth, family life, the virile harmony of the military, and the enthusiasm of the workers. *Triumph of the Will* concludes with the Nazi Anthem "Horst Wessel Lied". The film sets out to reveal "the order, unity and ambition of the National-Socialist Movement." As such it has been faithful to the message.

All of America is talking about John Ford

New York, 9 May
Director John Ford has triumphed with his latest film, an RKO production of *The Informer*, the second screen version of Liam O'Flaherty's novel. The story unfolds in Ireland in 1922. Gypo Nolan, played by the British star Victor McLaglen, sells out his best friend, a Sinn Fein man, for a few pounds. The dull-witted Judas is then overwhelmed by the consequences of his treachery, taken prisoner by his former comrades, tried in secret and executed.

Shot in three weeks on a relatively low budget of $243,000, *The Informer* is a powerful evocation of the fog-shrouded streets of Dublin during the days of the Black and Tans. Its psychologically insightful script by Dudley Nichols has also elicited widespread praise from the critics. John Ford, an Irish-American and keen student of Irish history, is currently riding the crest of a wave of critical approval. This latest success will cement the reputation he has gained with last year's *The Lost Patrol* and the more recent comedy *The Whole Town's Talking*. The prolific Ford, like his brother Francis, was trained at the school of Thomas Ince and became a masterly director of silent Westerns, before widening his range with the coming of sound. The burly McLaglen, one of his favorite actors, had a picaresque career before entering films, as an under-age volunteer in the Life Guards, a laborer and prizefighter in America, a goldminer in Australia and an army officer in the Great War. He made his debut in 1920 as a prizefighter in a British film, *The Call of the Road*, and established himself as an amiable roughneck in Hollywood after starring in a 1925 Vitagraph feature *The Beloved Brute*.

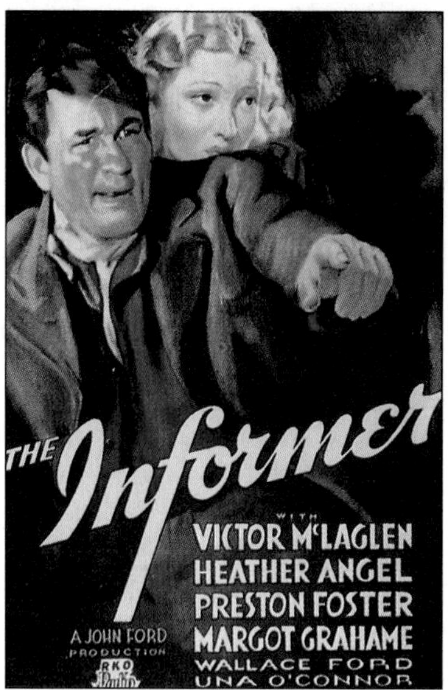
THE Informer
WITH
VICTOR McLAGLEN
HEATHER ANGEL
PRESTON FOSTER
MARGOT GRAHAME
WALLACE FORD
UNA O'CONNOR
A JOHN FORD PRODUCTION
RKO

The Informer: *a return to Ireland.*

oscow is endowed with a film festival

oscow, 1 March
he first International Film Festival Eastern Europe, held in Moscow, hich began on 21 February, has st ended. The major prize given by the jury comprising Sergei Eisenstein, Alexander Dovzhenko and Vsevolod Pudovkin, was awarded to Leningrad's Lenfilm Studios. Of the homegrown productions, the jury greatly appreciated *Chapayev* by the Vasiliev brothers, *The Youth of Maxim*, directed by Grigori Kozintzev and Leonid Trauberg, and Friedrich Ermler's *Peasants*. The best was undoubtedly *Chapayev*, which had been greeted in an editorial in *Pravda* in November 1934. An honorary prize was given to Tsai Chu-sheng's Chinese film, *The Song of the Fisherman*, which takes up the cause of Yangtze boatmen. Among the other foreign motion pictures to win prizes were René Clair's *The Last Millionaire* and King Vidor's *Our Daily Bread*.

. Chirkov (Maxim), V. Kibardina.

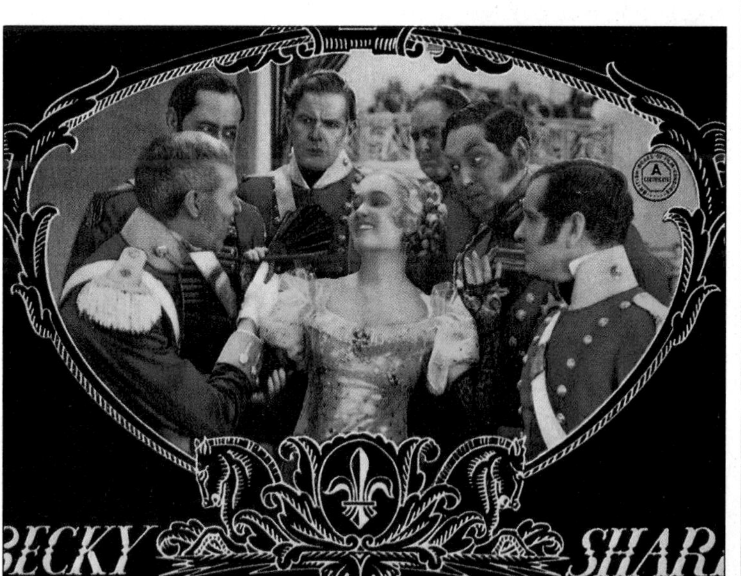
ECKY
SHAR

***Becky Sharp*, directed by Rouben Mamoulian, was released in America on 3 June. It is the first full-length film to use the trichrome Technicolor method perfected by Herbert T. Kalmus. His efforts were rewarded at the end of August when the film won the color prize at the third Venice Film Festival. Among other award winners were *Casta Diva* made by Carmine Gallone, and Clarence Brown's *Anna Karenina*, starring Garbo.**

Universal's latest horror is the 'Werewolf'

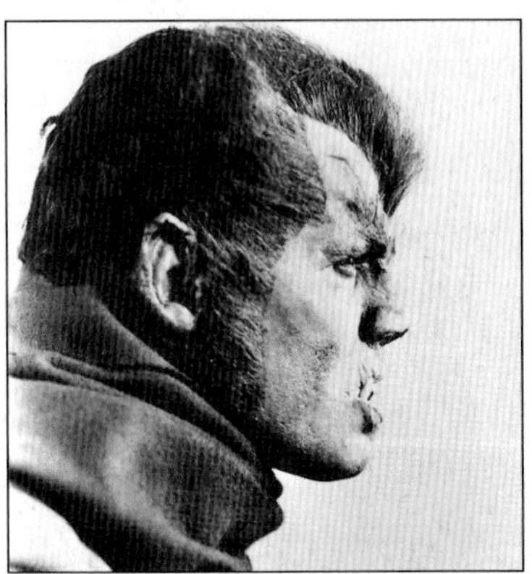

Henry Hull, ***The Werewolf of London.***

Claude Rains, ***The Invisible Man.***

Karloff, Frankenstein's monster.

Elsa Lanchester, the monster's bride.

Hollywood, 13 May

Henry Hull undergoes a remarkable transformation in Universal's *The Werewolf of London*, turning from English botanist to rampaging wolf man, thanks to a bite on the neck from fellow lycanthrope Warner Oland, some impressive makeup from Jack Pierce and the expert special effects photography of John P. Fulton. Hull's makeup took four hours to put on and two to take off, but it takes just one bullet, fired by the head of Scotland Yard, to stop him from mauling his wife (Valerie Hobson) at the picture's climax.

Since 1931 Universal has been treating audiences to a rich cycle of horror movies. *Dracula* was the first, a vehicle originally intended for Universal's famous horror star of the silent era, Lon Chaney. When throat cancer took the life of Chaney, the role of the vampire was filled by the Hungarian Bela Lugosi, complete with deathly-pallor, jet-black opera cape and hissing, hypnotic accent. There were no makeup tricks in *Dracula*, only a pair of pencil spotlights shone into Lugosi's eyes to increase the chilling effect of his baleful stare. *Dracula*'s director was Tod Browning, Lon Chaney's long-time collaborator, but British director James Whale has provided the most distinguished contributions to the genre and made a star of the studio's second great ghoul, fellow-Englishman Boris Karloff, in *Frankenstein*. Together, Whale and Karloff fashioned an almost lyrically conceived monster whose fear of fire is, perhaps, the most compelling "horror" of the film, and whose pathetic yearning for light attains a spiritual quality. Whale has followed *Frankenstein* with *The Old Dark House*, a tongue-in-cheek Gothic piece in which Karloff plays a memorably brutish butler; *The Invisible Man*, a celebration of trick photography and the silky voice of another accomplished English actor, Claude Rains; and *The Bride of Frankenstein*, in which actress Elsa Lanchester plays both Mary Shelley and the monster's mate. The film is an elegant parody of conventional Hollywood romance, with Whale ever attentive to his monster's emotional lives. But there is no happy ending. "We belong dead," intones Karloff's monster as he presses the lever which blows up the laboratory.

A master of suspense named Hitchcock

Robert Donat (left), Peggy Ashcroft and John Laurie in ***The Thirty-Nine Step***

London, 6 June

The premiere of the *The Thirty-Nine Steps*, the latest film from Alfred Hitchcock, has just taken place at the New Gallery Theatre. Loosely based on the novel by John Buchan, this by turns witty, suspenseful, romantic and always entertaining new thriller confirms Hitchcock's position as the "master of suspense", and perhaps the leading British director of his generation. However, for a time in the early 1930s Hitchcock appeared to have lost his way. His films were a mixture of play adaptations, comedies, and off-beat thrillers, none of them especially successful. Then, in 1933, when he was completing work on the romantic comedy, *Waltzes of Vienna*, he was contacted by producer Micha Balcon. This was the beginning of new and fruitful stage in the dire tor's career, starting with last year fast-moving and tense spy thrill *The Man Who Knew Too Much*, th starred Leslie Banks, Peter Lor and Nova Pilbeam, and now fo lowed by this newest productio Both films come from the team producer Balcon and associate pr ducer Ivor Montagu for the Ga mont British studio, with Charl Bennett as scriptwriter. Among t several improvements to the Bucha novel is the addition of a beautif and sophisticated heroine, played b the lovely Madeleine Carroll, opp site dashing, young Robert Dona A film to remember.

PUBLIC ENEMY NO.1
OF ALL THE WORLD
NOVA PILBEAM
PETER LORRE
LESLIE BANKS
EDNA BEST
THE MAN WHO
KNEW TOO MUCH
A GB PRODUCTION

ROBERT
DONAT
MADELEINE
CARROLL
THE 39 STEPS
with
LUCIE MANNHE
GODFREY TEAR
PEGGY ASHCRO
ALFRED HITCHCO
A GB PRODUCTIO

Two contrasting thrillers, each a brilliant achievement for Alfred Hitchcock.

:horeographer up or manslaughter

os Angeles, 21 September
he motion picture industry has een shocked to learn that the re- arkably talented Hollywood chore- grapher Busby Berkeley is to be ied on charges of manslaughter. At preliminary hearing today, the Los .ngeles Municipal Court ordered at he face two counts of second- egree murder in connection with a ree-car collision. Arraignment has een set for the morning of 7 Octo- er in Superior Court. The back- round to the trial is as follows: on e evening of 8 September, Busby ttended a party in Pacific Palisades iven by William Koenig, the pro- uction manager at Warners. But he ad to leave early to keep an ap- ointment with bandleader Gus Arn- eim in Santa Monica. As he was riving along the twisting Pacific 'oast Highway, the left front tire of is roadster blew out, and he ca- eened into the path of oncoming 'affic. In the resulting head-on colli- on, two people were killed instant- /, and a third died later. Busby was ragged unconscious from his burn- g car. His lawyer, Jerry Giesler, e well-known Hollywood attorney ho has defended many celebrities, ill try to convince the jury of the ifficulty of driving that stretch of e highway and that a blown-out re on a small roadster would make e car impossible to control. With estimony from guests at the party, iesler hopes to prove that Berkeley as not drunk when he set out.

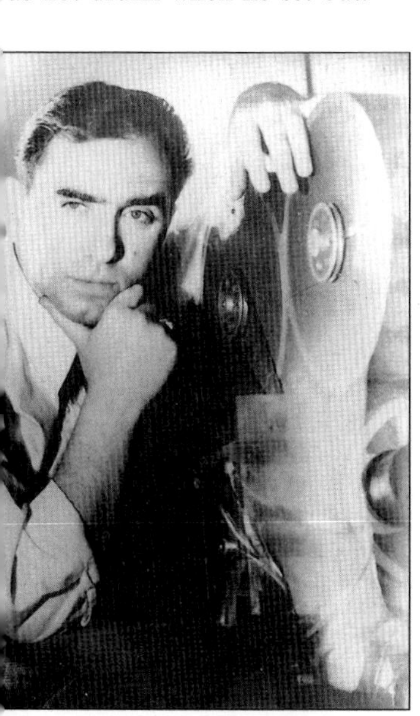

usby Berkeley: in deep trouble.

The blonde moppet delights us again

*Enchanting Shirley in **Curly Top**.*

*In her previous outing with Bill 'Bojangles' Robinson, **The Little Colonel**.*

Hollywood, 19 December
Shirley Temple, the bright-eyed, curly-topped, dimpled cherub, has scored another triumph in *The Littlest Rebel*, after *The Little Colonel* and *Curly Top* this year. Recently, President Franklin D. Roosevelt paid tribute to the talented seven-year-old: "During this Depression, when the spirit of the people is lower than at any other time, it is a splendid thing that for just 15 cents, an American can go to a movie, look at the smiling face of a baby and forget his troubles." *The Littlest Rebel*, features a different President, Abe Lincoln, on whom the tiny Shirley uses her charms to gain the release of her Southern-general father. *The Little Colonel*, where Shirley played Cupid to her sister, was also set during the Civil War, but *Curly Top*, where she sang "Animal Crackers", was more up to date.

Gentlemanly heroics from Leslie Howard's 'Scarlet Pimpernel'

London, 23 September
The British star Leslie Howard has returned from the Warner Brothers lot to make *The Scarlet Pimpernel* for Alexander Korda. Howard's quizzical style is perfectly suited to the role of Sir Percy Blakeney, the seemingly languid nobleman who saves French aristocrats from the guillotine during the French Revolution. To filmgoers Howard is the epitome of the charming Englishman. He is, in fact, the son of Hungarian Jewish immigrants who settled in England not long before he was born in 1893. Director Korda is a peripatetic Hungarian who settled in England in 1931. Korda had instantly grasped that the English have a seemingly unlimited appetite for comforting versions of their island history, and in *The Private Life of Henry VIII* (1933) he fed it with extravagant costumes and the bravura acting of Charles Laughton. With his brothers, director Zoltan and art director Vincent, Korda has taken the British movie industry by the scruff of the neck, importing a dazzling range of international talent, that included Hungarian screenwriter Lajos Biro, French cameraman Georges Périnal and the American director Harold Young, and built an ambitious studio complex outside London at Denham, which he wants to turn into a British Hollywood.

*Sir Percy Blakeney, **The Scarlet Pimpernel**: Howard with Merle Oberon.*

JEAN
WILLIAM
Harlow
Powell
IN
RECKLESS
FRANCHOT TONE
MAY ROBSON
TED HEALY
NAT PENDLETON
ROBERT LIGHT
Produced by
DAVID O. SELZNICK
Directed by
VICTOR FLEMING
METRO-GOLDWYN-MAYER'S
MAMMOTH
MUSICAL
MELODRAMA

This chorus-girl story mirrored its star Harlow's own unhappy off-screen life.

Clark Gable, Rosalind Russell, C. Aubrey Smith and Jean Harlow: **China Seas**

Groucho, Chico, Allan Jones, Harpo in Marx brothers' ***A Night at the Opera***

Victor McLaglen appeared in John Ford's powerful ***The Informer****.*
Rt: Peter Lorre in sinister ***The Hands of Orlac*** *about a dead concert pianist.*

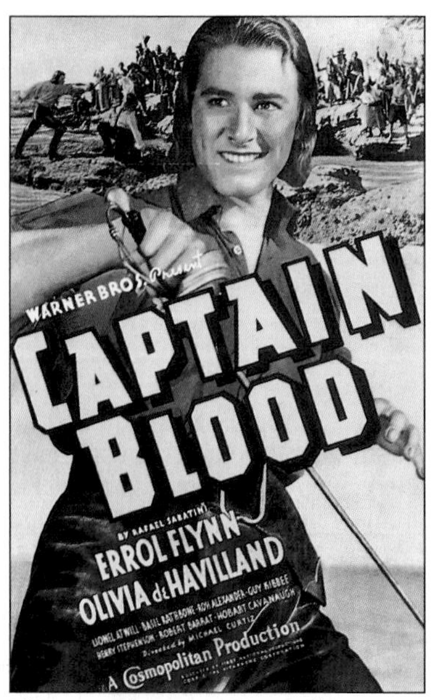
WARNER BROS. Present
CAPTAIN
BLOOD
ERROL FLYNN
OLIVIA de HAVILLAND
A Cosmopolitan Production

Flynn, and a great Korngold score.

A Notable Novel -- NOW A Great Motion Picture
IRENE DUNNE
ROBERT TAYLOR
IN
MAGNIFICENT
OBSESSION
CHARLES BUTTERWORTH
BETTY FURNESS
A UNIVERSAL PICTURE
A JOHN M. STAHL PRODUCTION

A superb, big box-office melodrama

"G MEN"
JAMES CAGNEY
ANN DVORAK
MARGARET LINDSAY
ROBERT ARMSTRONG
A FIRST NATIONAL PICTURE
gney on the right side of the law.

harlie Ruggles, Charles Laughton ***Ruggles of Red Gap*.**

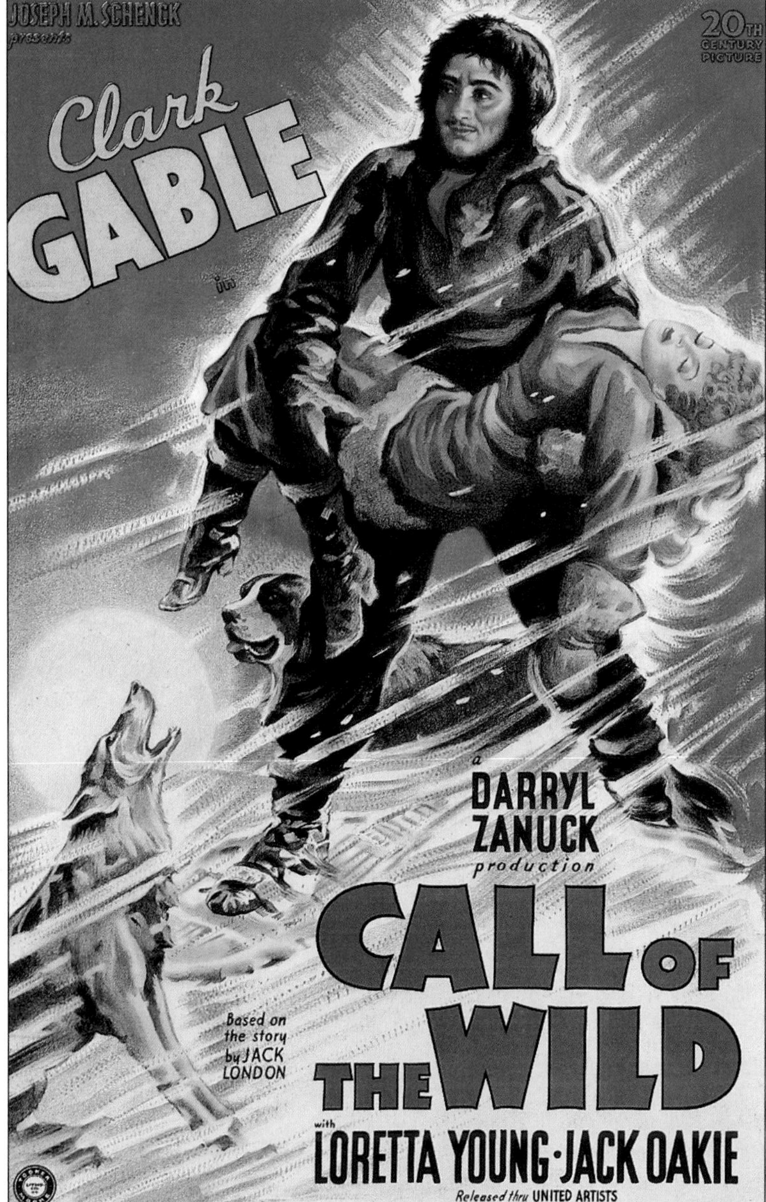
JOSEPH M. SCHENCK
presents
20TH CENTURY PICTURE
Clark
GABLE
a
DARRYL
ZANUCK
production
CALL OF THE WILD
Based on the story by JACK LONDON
with
LORETTA YOUNG · JACK OAKIE
Released thru UNITED ARTISTS
A Yukon adventure directed by William Wellman from Jack London's novel.

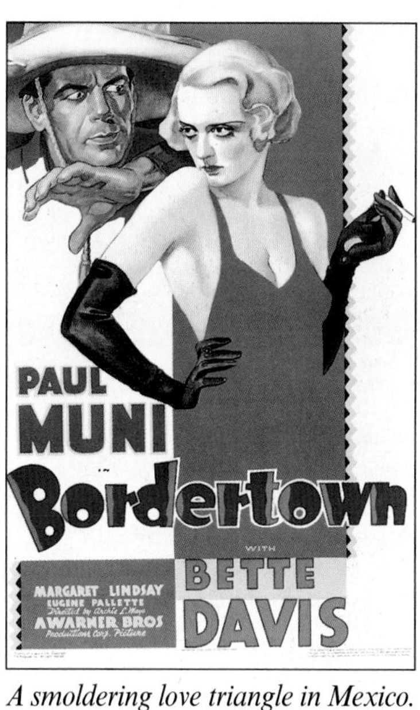
PAUL
MUNI
in
Bordertown
WITH
BETTE
DAVIS
MARGARET LINDSAY
EUGENE PALLETTE
A WARNER BROS
A smoldering love triangle in Mexico.

LONDON FILMS PRESENT
Paul ROBESON
Leslie BANKS
in
EDGAR WALLACE'S
SANDERS
of the RIVER
with
Nina Mae
McKINNEY
DIRECTED BY
ZOLTAN KORDA
AN
ALEXANDER KORDA
PRODUCTION
Distributed by London Films International Ltd.
146, Piccadilly, London W.1.
The Kordas went to Africa for this.

ADOLPH ZUKOR
"The LIVES of a
BENGAL LANCER"
ARY COOPER · FRANCHOT TONE
ICHARD CROMWELL · Sir GUY STANDING
A PARAMOUNT PICTURE
smash-hit action adventure, both morous and exciting, set in India.

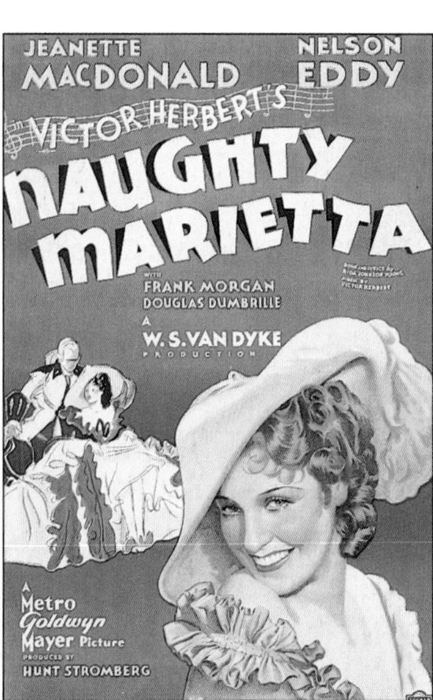
JEANETTE
MACDONALD
NELSON
EDDY
VICTOR HERBERT'S
NAUGHTY
MARIETTA
with
FRANK MORGAN
DOUGLAS DUMBRILLE
A
W.S. VAN DYKE
PRODUCTION
A
Metro
Goldwyn
Mayer Picture
PRODUCED BY
HUNT STROMBERG
The first, warmly applauded pairing of songbirds MacDonald and Eddy.

JOSEPH M. SCHENCK PRESENTS
CLIVE OF
INDIA
STARRING
Ronald
COLMAN
WITH
LORETTA YOUNG
20th CENTURY
DARRYL F. ZANUCK
PRODUCTION
This account of the famous Empire-builder was more fiction than fact!

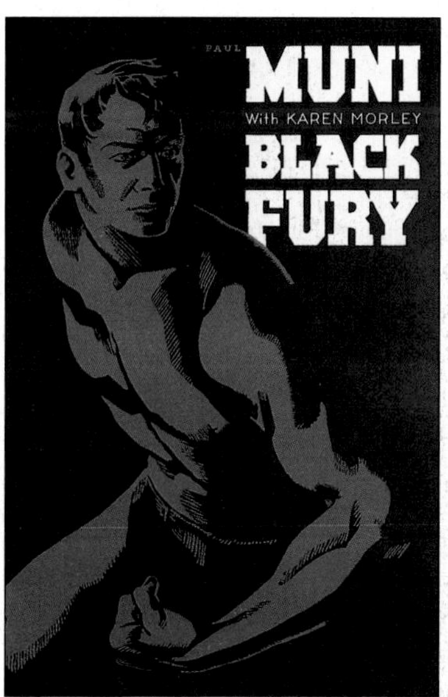
MUNI
with KAREN MORLEY
BLACK
FURY
Coalminer Muni battled for better conditions in this controversial film.

1936

1935 Academy Awards, Biltmore Hotel, 5 Mar.

Best Film: *Mutiny on the Bounty* (dir: Frank Lloyd)
Best Director: John Ford *(The Informer)*
Best Actor: Victor McLaglen *(The Informer)*
Best Actress: Bette Davis *(Dangerous)*

Prague, 1 January
The Barrandov studios have had two new sound stages built, making them the biggest and most modern studios in Europe. Even foreign film crews are coming to work here.

Warsaw, 2 January
Aleksander Ford's documentary *Street of the Young*, about the plight of impoverished Jewish and Polish orphans in a sanitarium, has been banned as being "a vehicle for communist propaganda."

Rome, 29 January
Benito Mussolini laid the first stone of the Cinecittà studios today. It is hoped that the new facilities will help in boosting Italian production.

Berlin, 1 February
Three years after the Nazi party's arrival in power, the German cinema finds itself in a serious crisis. This is primarily due to a growing rejection of German films in other countries because they are so loaded with German propaganda.

Cairo, 10 February
Release of *Wedad*, the first film to come out of the new Misr studios. It is also the singer Oum Kalsoum's first screen role.

Paris, 12 February
First screening of *Mayerling*, adapted from Claude Anet's novel by Joseph Kessel, and directed by Anatole Litvak with Charles Boyer and Danielle Darrieux.

Paris, 17 February
The Pathé-Natan company has been pronounced bankrupt by the courts.

Paris, 31 March
Marcel Carné has started shooting *Jenny*, his first full-length film, in the Billancourt Studios. It stars Françoise Rosay, Lisette Lanvin, Albert Préjean and Charles Vanel. Director Jacques Feyder is on hand to advise his former assistant.

Berlin, 31 March
Dr. Alfred Hugenberg, who has been under a cloud since he resigned from the Ministry of Economy, has now been ousted as head of the UFA trust. Goebbels has replaced him with a committee presided over by filmmaker Carl Froelich.

Hollywood, 12 April
Release of *Desire* for Paramount, supervised and produced by Ernst Lubitsch, and directed by Frank Borzage with Marlene Dietrich and Gary Cooper.

Paris, 15 May
The Mogador marks its debut as a first-run cinema with the Parisian premiere of George Cukor's *Sylvia Scarlett* with Katharine Hepburn.

Paris, 6 June
Striking workmen in Joinville are organizing free screenings in the studios to help pass the time.

Berlin, 30 June
Carl Froelich is in the UFA studios to direct *Das Schonheitsfleckchen*, based on a short story by Alfred de Musset. It is the first German fiction film to be shot in color using the Siemen's Opti-color process.

Tokyo, 1 July
Creation of the Toho studios with a capital of 500,000 yen.

Moscow, 17 July
Release of a Lenfilm production *Syn Monglii* (*Son of Mongolia*), directed by Ilya Trauberg. The film, a mixture of fact and fiction, tells of a young horseman's quest for love.

Le Havre, 20 July
The actress Marlene Dietrich has arrived in France. After spending a few days in Paris, she will go to London for the filming of *Knight Without Armor*, directed by Jacques Feyder, a spy drama set against a backdrop of the Great War, and co-starring Robert Donat.

London, 20 July
After several months of effort, 20th Century-Fox's attempts to gain financial control of British Gaumont have failed. Fox has had to relinquish half of the already acquired shares to MGM.

Hollywood, 22 July
Dashiell Hammett's novel *The Maltese Falcon*, is a source of inspiration for scriptwriters: the second film version, *Satan Met a Lady*, directed by William Dieterle, was released here today.

Mexico, 25 July
The young filmmaker of Austrian origin, Fred Zinnemann, has presented his documentary, *The Wave*, co-directed and produced by Paul Strand. The influence of the Soviet cinema is omnipresent in both the content and artistic style of the film.

Venice, 2 September
Jacques Feyder's *Carnival in Flanders* was voted best foreign film at the Festival here. Paul Muni was best actor for *The Story of Louis Pasteur*, and Annabella the best actress for *Veille d'armes*.

Tokyo, 15 October
Kenji Mizoguchi continues to examine the destiny of Japanese women. In his new work *Gion No Shimai* (*Sisters of the Gion*), he depicts the unhappy life of two geishas whose fate depends on the desires of men.

Los Angeles, 1 November
Release of *Charge of the Light Brigade*, made by Michael Curtiz and starring the popular Errol Flynn and Olivia De Havilland.

Paris, 5 November
Since its release in October, *le Roi* (*The King*), by Pierre Colombier, with Victor Francen, Gaby Morlay, Raimu and Elvira Popesco, has beaten all box-office records at the Marivaux Cinema.

Rome, 17 November
The president of the MPPDA, Will Hays, has received an audience with Pope Pius XI.

Paris, 7 December
Erich von Stroheim is in the capital to appear in *Marthe Richard*, under the direction of Raymond Bernard, with Edwige Feuillère.

Paris, 7 December
A gala showing of the uncut versi[on] of Abel Gance's *Un grand amour [de] Beethoven* (*The Life and Loves [of] Beethoven*), with Harry Baur, Ann[ie] Ducaux and Janny Holt. Musi[c] lovers were reserved in their opini[on] of the film but it was applauded [by] the critics.

New York, 29 December
The National Board of Review h[as] selected Jacques Feyder's *Carni[val] in Flanders* as its film of the ye[ar]. The French film even beat Fra[nk] Capra's *Mr. Deeds Goes to Town*.

BIRTHS

New York, 28 January
Alan Alda

Georgia, 11 February
Burt Reynolds

Argentina, 16 February
Fernando Solanas

England, 9 May
Albert Finney

England, 9 May
Glenda Jackson

Kansas, 17 May
Dennis Hopper

London, 23 May
Joan Collins

New York, 27 May
Louis (Lou) Gossett Jr.

Chicago, 4 June
Bruce Dern

Texas, 22 June
Kris Kristofferson

Paris, 15 June
Claude Brasseur
(Claude Espinasse)

Texas, 23 December
Frederic Forrest

New York, 29 December
Mary Tyler Moore

Gary Cooper stars in ***The Gene[ral] Died at Dawn****, from director Le[wis] Milestone. The screenplay by Cliff[ord] Odets tells of a mercenary who ov[er]comes an evil warlord in China.*

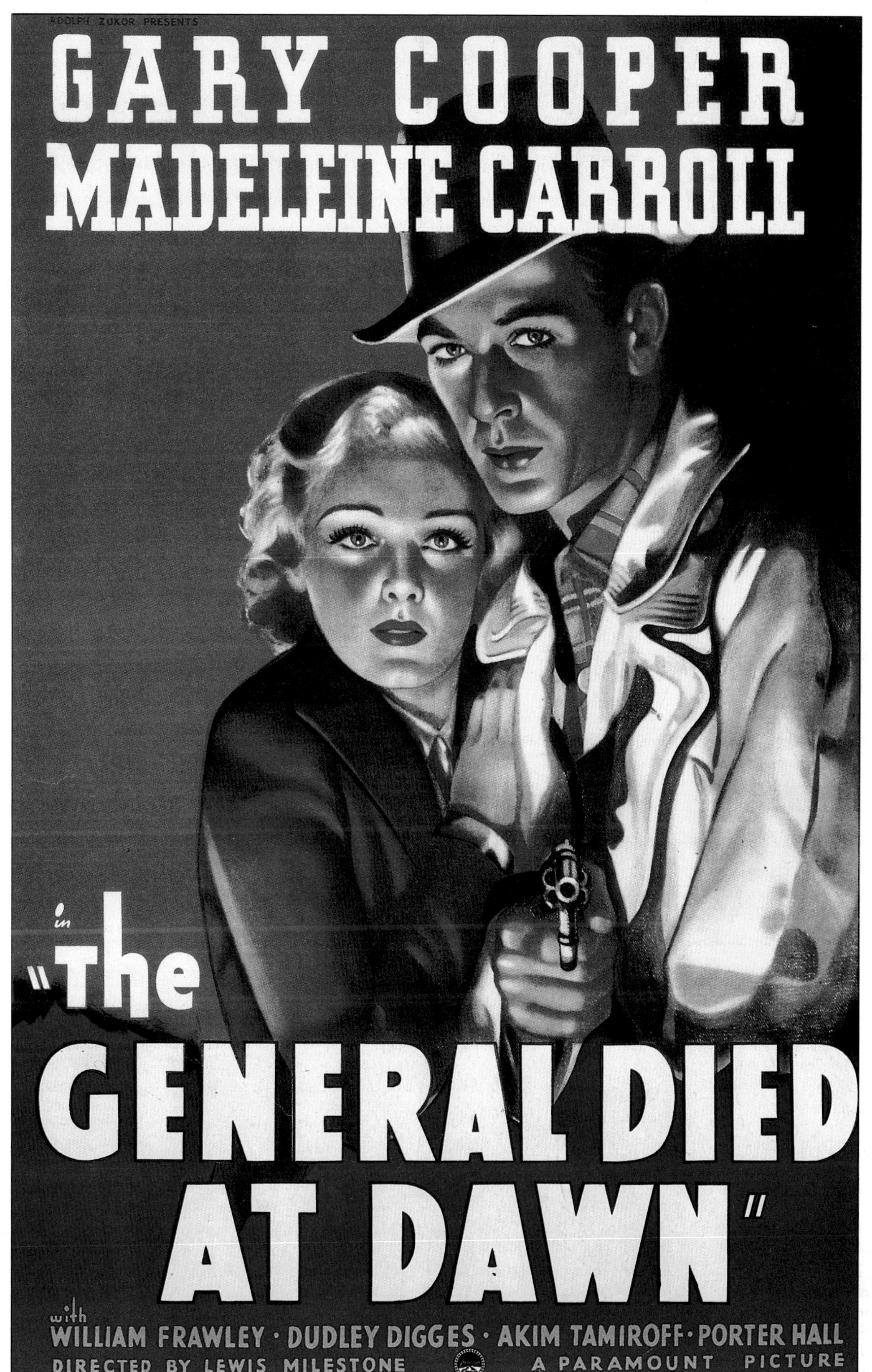
ADOLPH ZUKOR PRESENTS
GARY COOPER
MADELEINE CARROLL
in
"The
GENERAL DIED
AT DAWN"
with
WILLIAM FRAWLEY · DUDLEY DIGGES · AKIM TAMIROFF · PORTER HALL
DIRECTED BY LEWIS MILESTONE
A PARAMOUNT PICTURE

▷

End without glory for a fallen star

Los Angeles, 11 January
John Gilbert is being buried today. He has died of a heart attack at his Hollywood home at the age of 40. After the death of Valentino, Gilbert became the silent screen's most popular leading man. The sexual electricity which crackled in his screen romances with Garbo in *Love*, *Flesh and the Devil* and *A Woman of Affairs*, led to a celebrated romance, which prompted columnist Walter Winchell to coin the phrase "Garbo-Gilberting" as shorthand for torrid affairs. Gilbert's career was killed by the talkies, not so much because of his squeaky voice, as some alleged, but because his acting style was too intense to bear the weight of words. Valentino's successor as the Great Lover drank himself to death.

Garbo and John Gilbert in ***Queen Christina****, from director Rouben Mamoulian, and their last together.*

Chaplin and the contemporary age

Charlie is still in the business of exposing injustice and in ***Modern Times*** *the dangers of the assembly line.*

New York, 5 February
Modern Times, Charlie Chaplin's first film since the 1931 *City Lights*, has opened at the Rivoli Theater to capacity business. The gestation of the film followed a by-now familiar pattern. He spent a year preparing the story and then 11 months shooting. When filming finally began, at the beginning of October last year, Chaplin was still undecided about making a sound film in which the Tramp would speak for the first time. Dialogue had been written by Chaplin but, in the end, all we hear from him is a strange little nonsense song performed in a language of Charlie's own invention. In *Modern Times* the Tramp finds himself one of the millions trying to cope in a modern world that is dominated by machines. Working on a factory conveyer belt, Charlie is caught in the cogs of a malevolent machine, is used to test an automatic feeder and finally runs amok. His further adventures include a spell in prison acccused of being a Red agitator (after considerately picking up a red flag which has fallen off a truck), but things pick up when he encounters the Gamin, a gutsy young woman on the lam from juvenile office[rs]. She is played by Paulette Goddar[d], Chaplin's companion since 1933, [al]though neither will confirm wheth[er] or not they are married. Goddard, [a] former Goldwyn Girl whom Cha[p]lin met while on the yacht of Jose[ph] Schenck, is a revelation in the ro[le]. In a tattered dress and innocent makeup, she nevertheless radiat[es] sensuality as well as an underlyi[ng] strength and stubborness. At t[he] end of the picture the Tramp and t[he] Gamin toddle off hand in hand, [re]treating into a rural sunset remin[is]cent of Chaplin's days at Mutual.

New film from Renoir and Prévert is more than propaganda

Paris, 24 January
By taking a story of a crooked boss and a workers' cooperative, Jean Renoir has succeeded in his latest film, *The Crime of Monsieur Lange*, in trenchantly dealing with contemporary issues. Shot in 25 days, the film reflects the optimism of the Popular Front, but is delivered in the language of black comedy. The scenario, co-written by poet Jacques Prévert, tells of a group of workers who take over a publishing house when their boss absconds, making them believe he is dead. When he returns to gain control, Lange, a writer of Westerns, kills him. The two contrasting central actors – the evil Jules Berry and the good René Lefèvre – are superb.

Jules Berry, René Lefèvre and Florelle in ***The Crime of Monsieur Lange****.*

Musketeer marries his English mistres[s]

Los Angeles, 7 March
Douglas Fairbanks has remarrie[d]. His bride is his former mistress, t[he] English Sylvia Hawkes, former Lady Ashley. The couple have ma[de] their home in Fairbanks' ranch ne[ar] Santa Monica on the Pacific coa[st]. Fairbanks' fabulous film career [fi]nally seems to be winding down. [He] has been inactive since 1934, wh[en] he made *The Private Life of D[on] Juan* in England. He still keeps fer[o]ciously fit, but the domestic joys [of] his new marriage can be no subs[ti]tute for the years of adulation in t[he] 1920s, when his appearance wi[th] Mary Pickford would stop traffic [in] any city in the world.

ord and Lloyd ompete for 'Oscar'

'tte Davis was voted Best Actress r her performance as an alcoholic 'tress in **Dangerous**.

ollywood, 5 March
ıe ninth annual presentation of the cademy Award trophies, that are ɔw known as Oscars, took place at e Biltmore Hotel this evening. lthough the Best Picture winner as Frank Lloyd's *Mutiny on the ounty*, John Ford got the nod over oyd as Best Director for *The Inrmer*. The latter film also trumped film rival because its star, Victor cLaglen, won over Clark Gable in *utiny on the Bounty*. As for the est Actress, Bette Davis was the cipient of the "holdover award" r *Dangerous*. This refers to the andalous oversight of last year, hen she was not even nominated r *Of Human Bondage*.

harles Laughton is Bligh in Lloyd's *lutiny on the Bounty*, the Best Film.

Hathaway's Technicolored outdoors

"THE TRAIL OF THE LONESOME PINE"
STARRING FRED MacMURRAY · SYLVIA SIDNEY
HENRY FONDA
COLOR BY TECHNICOLOR

On location for **The Trail of the Lonesome Pine**, ground-breaking in its use of exteriors and Technicolor.

Hollywood, 13 March
Based on the novel by John Fox Jr., *The Trail of the Lonesome Pine* is an old-fashioned story of feuding hillbilly families. It has been filmed twice before by Paramount, the first version in 1915 being one of Cecil B. DeMille's early features. This time, the story has been given a big boost – not only by a starry cast headed by Henry Fonda, Sylvia Sidney and Fred MacMurray, but by the addition of the new, three-strip Technicolor. Whereas the first pictures shot in this process, such as *Becky Sharp* and *La Cucuracha*, were studio-bound productions, here director Henry Hathaway and producer Walter Wanger have opted for substantial location shooting, and the natural outdoor settings look no less than stunning. From shots of the simple views of mountains, sky and forest, to the picturesque wooden houses and large waterwheel, the feel of this rough and primitive country is superbly captured. Unfortunately, the plot, dialogue and characterization are so weak that the fine actors make little impression.

Cooper's 'Mr. Deeds' is an eloquent mouthpiece for Frank Capra

Hollywood, 4 May
Frank Capra is currently the hottest director in Hollywood, and his latest picture, *Mr. Deeds Goes to Town*, has had an ecstatic reception. Here Capra and screenwriter Robert Riskin have fashioned a winning tale of the young hick Longfellow Deeds, a kind of grown-up version of Tom Sawyer played by Gary Cooper, who inherits $20 million and wants to give it all to the poor. Graham Greene has written that Cooper's performance is "subtle and pliable... something of which other directors have only dreamed." There are few, if any, more "natural" actors working in pictures today. And providing sterling support to Cooper is Jean Arthur, who plays the smart big-city reporter who tries to figure out what makes this unusual philanthropist tick. This is a populist film, hymning the innate decency of the common man at a time when the New Deal introduced by President Franklin D. Roosevelt, of whom Capra is a great admirer, is grappling with the problems of the Depression. Whether the tide of cynicism and corruption so clearly seen by Capra can be turned back by the simple-minded sincerity of a wide-eyed hero is another matter altogether, but the director is determined that his films should have a "message".

Gary Cooper co-stars with Jean Arthur in **Mr. Deeds Goes to Town**.

Fritz Lang, Germany's great filmmaker, joins Hollywood's ranks

*In **Fury**, Spencer Tracy portrays the innocent man, unjustly hunted down by a crazed mob in search of vengeance.*

New York, 5 June
The first American film by the great German director Fritz Lang, *Fury*, has been successfully released. It stars Spencer Tracy and Sylvia Sidney in a somber tale of a lynching. In 1933, following the banning of *The Testament of Dr. Mabuse* in Germany and Goebbels' suggestion that he become head of the new Nazi cinema, Lang fled to Paris. After a brief sojourn in France, where he shot *Liliom* with Charles Boyer, the director accepted David O. Selznick's invitation to come to the U.S. Under contract to MGM, the monocle-wearing Lang familiarized himself with the local mores, learned English by talking to cab drivers, waitresses and gas station attendants, and lived for almost eight weeks with the Navajos. Many of his script suggestions were turned down until his adaptation of a four-page synopsis by Norman Krasna called *Mob Rule* was finally given the go-ahead by the studio. The shooting of *Fury* took place under some difficulties. Lang had to adapt to American methods of filming that were so different from German practices. Used to absolute control at the UFA studios, he had no idea that union rules demanded that food and rest breaks were called for in his unrelenting schedule. Even Tracy sided with the hordes of extras who felt they were being exploited. Producer Joseph L. Mankiewicz rewrote some of the dialogue, and MGM, imposing a happy ending on the film, prevented Lang from editing it. (Scenes showing blacks victimized by a gang of whites were cut.) Nevertheless, *Fury* is a powerful statement about an innocent man arrested as a suspected kidnapper, who escapes lynching, but returns to prove his innocence.

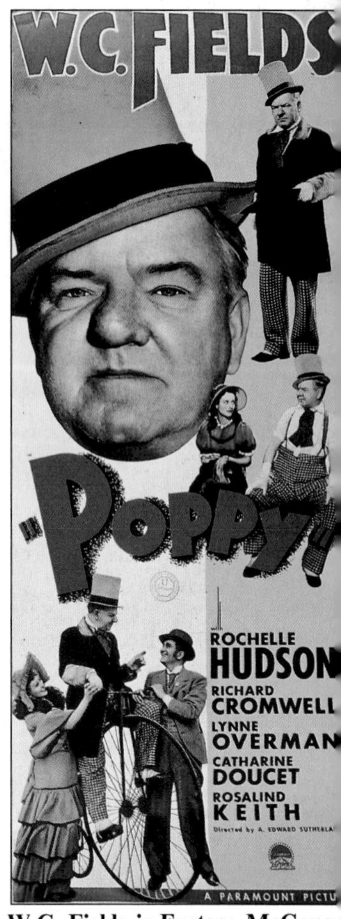
W.C.FIELDS
POPPY
ROCHELLE
HUDSON
RICHARD
CROMWELL
LYNNE
OVERMAN
CATHARINE
DOUCET
ROSALIND
KEITH
A PARAMOUNT PICTU

W.C. Fields is Eustace McGonagle, carnival man extraordinaire again! Fields first played the role on stage in *Poppy*, then again in a silent movie version, *Sally of the Sawdust*, in 1925. This time is indisputably the funniest.

San Francisco collapses in smoking ruins for our entertainment

Hollywood, 26 June
MGM has a habit of hitting the screen with spectacular entertainment, and there's spectacle aplenty in the second half of the studio's *San Francisco*, which features the earthquake that devastated the city in 1906. The first half is some fluff about nightclub czar Clark Gable, one of his "chantoosies" Jeanette MacDonald and his boyhood chum, a priest played by Spencer Tracy. For the climactic quake in the second half, MGM special effects men Arnold Gillespie and James Basevi constructed full-size buildings on top of hydraulically operated rocker platforms. During filming the set shook and disintegrated, panicking the extras when the first tremors hit, but injuring no one as walls collapsed and bricks rained down.

GABLE
MACDONALD
San Francisco
TRAC

Pius XI calls for moral standards

Rome, 15 July
The church is worried about the ba moral influence which the cinem can have on a worldwide scale. Th Pontifical Encyclical *Vigilanti Cur* sent to American bishops, recom mended the boycotting of indecen films and congratulated the Legic of Decency on their activities. Pop Pius XI is particularly concerne about the influences on youth, an has expressed his desire for a rigo ous classification system. The d mands of the Pope coincide wi those of the Fascist censors, who a leaning toward a more edifying cin ma. Above all else, the portrayal women must be circumscribed. heroine in a melodrama has to be virgin, or faithful wife and mothe

͏eni Riefenstahl and ͏e Berlin Olympics

͏e official chronicler of the Games.

͏rlin, 17 August
͏rlin's Olympic Games have fin͏ied. It was an occasion for Ger͏any to show the world the power Hitler's regime. Leni Riefenstahl ͏s commissioned by the Fuhrer to ͏m the Games "as a song of praise the ideals of National Socialism." ͏ capture the great event, she had ͏er 30 cameramen, as well as many ͏anes and airships at her disposal. will be edited into two parts – the ͏stival of Nations and the Festival Beauty – and will be, in the direc͏r's words, "a hymn to the power ͏d beauty of Man."

͏anglois creates ͏he Cinémathèque

͏aris, 2 September
͏renchman Henri Langlois is fight͏g to prevent the destruction of ͏ent films, along with ensuring the ͏istence of future safeguards of this ͏untry's rich cinematographic her͏ge. Thus he has just registered the ͏nstitution of a non-profit French ͏inémathèque whose headquarters ͏e located at the premises of Paul-͏uguste Harlé's *La Cinématograph͏ue Française*. More than a year has ͏ssed since Harlé backed young ͏anglois' efforts. Now the Ciném͏a͏èque has become a vital link with ͏e Cinema Circle film club founded ͏ Langlois and Georges Franju last ͏ar. Harlé has been appointed pres͏ent and Langlois and Franju are ͏int secretary generals.

Jean Renoir abandons country pleasures for the slums of the city

France, 20 August
What should have been a sunny rural idyll for Jean Renoir and his cast and team of friends, filming *A Day in the Country* beside the river Loing in the Ile de France, was dampened by the one of the wettest summers for years. As a result, this screen adaptation of a Guy de Maupassant short story had to be abandoned, with only two sequences left to be shot. The director had been happy to make a film in the sort of location dear to the Impressionists, and to compose images worthy of his father's paintings. Reluctantly, Renoir has had to desert the countryside to take up work on *The Lower Depths*, for which he has been contracted. A story of urban squalor, it is based on the play by Maxim Gorky.

Jane Marken is charmed by Jacques Brunius in Renoir's ***A Day in the Country****.*

Astaire and Rogers fly on wings of dance for the sixth time

Hollywood, 27 August
Fred Astaire and Ginger Rogers have attained the summit of their terpsichorean talents in *Swing Time*, which marks their sixth pairing since *Flying Down to Rio* three years ago. More than ever have the dancing duo of RKO musicals demonstrated their virtuosity. The number "Never Gonna Dance" has Fred trying to win Ginger over in dance. They hold each other closely, but she achingly spins away from him and the dance ends in separation. Their numbers are not merely the gems that stud rather simple stories, but, far more than dialogue, also trace the emotional development of the two characters and even advance the plot. For example, in order to get to meet dancing teacher Ginger, Fred pretends he can't dance a step. Blaming her for her pupil's two left feet, her boss fires her. Fred gets her job back by demonstrating the skills she has taught him in one lesson. The music is by Jerome Kern, a favorite composer of the two stars who have both danced, separately, in Kern shows on Broadway.

FRED
ASTAIRE
Ginger
ROGERS
IN
TOP HAT
MUSIC and LYRICS by
IRVING
BERLIN
with
EDWARD EVERETT HORTON
HELEN BRODERICK
Erik RHODES Eric BLORE
DIRECTED BY
PANDRO S. BERMAN

The twinkle-toed partners in ***Swing Time****, directed by George Stevens.*

'Boy Wonder' of MGM dies at thirty-seven

Irving Thalberg: taste and brilliance.

Los Angeles, 15 September
"The Boy Wonder" of Hollywood, Irving Thalberg, has died of pneumonia. The son of German-Jewish immigrants, he suffered ill-health from childhood and had a severe heart attack toward the end of 1932, which forced him to take off several months from MGM where he was production chief. Thalberg began his career as a humble secretary at Universal, but his exceptional qualities of judgment and organization led to a meteoric rise which prompted Carl Laemmle to appoint him to head of production before he was much past age 20. At Universal, the toughness beneath his frail exterior was evidenced in his stormy confrontations with Von Stroheim over *Foolish Wives* and *Merry-Go-Round*, a situation which later repeated itself at MGM over the editing of *Greed*. Thalberg and Laemmle fell out early in 1923 when the former refused to marry the latter's daughter. The young tyro joined Louis B. Mayer and, with the formation of MGM in 1924, he became the new studio's production chief, marrying actress Norma Shearer in 1927. He wielded immense power as a brilliant hands-on producer and his loss will be keenly felt. He leaves behind a fortune estimated in millions.

Chilling view of future from Korda's stabl

H.G. WELLS'
THINGS TO COME
ALEXANDER KORDA Production
RAYMOND MASSEY · RALPH RICHARDSON
CEDRIC HARDWICKE · MARGARETTA SCOTT
JOHN CLEMENTS
Directed by
WILLIAM CAMERON MENZIES

London, 14 September
The celebrated writer H.G. Wells has adapted his novel, *The Shape of Things to Come*, for the screen. The result is a visually superb science fiction film, *Things to Come*, direc ed by William Cameron Menzie which takes a sobering look at t future and climaxes with humani venturing into space.

Françoise Rosay helps Carné to success

*Vanel, Barrault, Préjean and Toutain with Françoise Rosay in Carné's **Jenny**.*

Paris, 16 September
The first full-length film by Marcel Carné, *Jenny*, has been released. During the shooting of *Carnival in Flanders* last year, Carné was merely an assistant to Jacques Feyder. The film's star, Feyder's wife Françoise Rosay, offered the young man her services free of charge for his first film, an agreement that was decisive in helping him realize the project. *Jenny* has had a rather cool reception, some judging it as no more than a conventional melodrama, but thanks to the superior dialogue by Jacques Prévert, and an excellent use of locations, the film is an auspicious debut for Carné.

Sacha Guitry and the morality of a cheat

Actor-director Sacha Guitry, here in his role as the cheat, his fourth film.

Paris, 19 September
For having stolen a few francs, a young lad is deprived of mushrooms for dinner, and thus escapes from the poisoning which destroys his whole family: so begins *le Roman d'un tricheur (The Story of a Cheat)*, Sacha Guitry's new film, which can be seen at the Marignon. Adapted by the director himself from his ow novel published in 1934, the film is stylish and witty comedy about t art of cheating, which neverthele ends on a moral note. The story narrated in the first person by Gu ry himself, who portrays the chara ter of a repentant conman in his ow inimitable way.

ıe Prix Louis Delluc gives its first nod to 'The Lower Depths'

AN RENOIR
ES BAS-FONDS
MAXIME GORKI

*Jean Gabin, Louis Jouvet and Vladimir Sokoloff in **The Lower Depths**.*

ıris, 22 December
ıe first ever winner of the Prix ıuis Delluc, created on the initia- e of the group of Young Indepen- nt Critics in homage to the critic d director who died recently, is an Renoir's *The Lower Depths*. ıe film won by three votes over arcel Carné's *Jenny*. Among the nel of judges present were Marcel hard, Maurice Bessy, Claude Ave- ıe, Pierre Bost, Henri Jeanson and eorges Altman. In one sense, the ize is meant to counterbalance the ademicism of the Grand Prix du Cinéma Français. The Prix Louis Delluc will try to reflect the tastes of the man who first coined the word "cinéaste" (meaning filmmaker), and one of the first critics to consider film as an art form and work out a theory. Delluc would certainly have approved of *The Lower Depths* with its flowing camerawork, superb sets and locations, and splendid performances, particularly those from Louis Jouvet and Jean Gabin. Although ostensibly situated in Moscow, the movie is very French in flavor. According to Renoir, "I was not trying to make a Russian film. I wanted to make a human drama based on Gorky's play."

o Roach, but a double dose of comedy from Laurel and Hardy

ew York, 10 November
nhappy with *The Bohemian Girl*, eir last film made for Hal Roach, an Laurel and Oliver Hardy de- ded to break out on their own. It as Stan who wanted more control over their pictures, and set up Stan Laurel Productions. The first one released under this banner, *Our Relations*, is also one of their best. In it, Stan and Olly play themselves and their twin brothers, Alfie Laurel and Bert Hardy, causing double trouble when they turn up at different times at Denkers' Beer Garden. It is impossible to describe the twists and turns of this comedy of errors, but, needless to say, it is hilarious.

*ıe comic duo in **Our Relations**.*

*The fat man and the thin, spying on Mae Busch in **The Bohemian Girl**.*

A few surprises in new popularity poll

London, 31 December
The year ends with some revealing polls as to who are the most popular stars. And from the studios' point of view, of course, this means WHO equals Big Bucks at the Box Office! Especially interesting is the fact that America's favorites are not necessarily tops with the rest of the world. The major Quigley poll, whose results were published in *Variety* last week, list the U.S. Top Ten, starting from No. 1 as follows: juvenile curly-top Shirley Temple, dashing he-man Clark Gable, dancing duo Fred Astaire and Ginger Rogers, handsome Robert Taylor, jug-faced comedian Joe E. Brown, somber Dick Powell, glamorous Joan Crawford, sparkling Claudette Colbert, songbird Jeanette MacDonald and perennial favorite Gary Cooper. Precocious moppet Temple supersedes glamour and sex appeal outside the U.S. as well, but gorgeous Gary Cooper moves in to No. 2 elsewhere while Robert Taylor drops down to 10, with Charlie Chaplin, Garbo, Dietrich, diva Grace Moore and the Fat man and the Thin man – Laurel and Hardy – joining the world popularity list from No. 5 to No. 9. The top international box-office film for the year was Chaplin's *Modern Times*, MGM's W.S. Van Dyke is the director who brought in the most dollars for his combined output (which included both *San Francisco* and *Rose-Marie*), and finally the New York Film Critics voted *Frank Capra's Mr. Deeds Goes to Town* as the year's best film.

*French-born Claudette Colbert, the effervescent star of **It Happened One Night**, in at No. 9.*

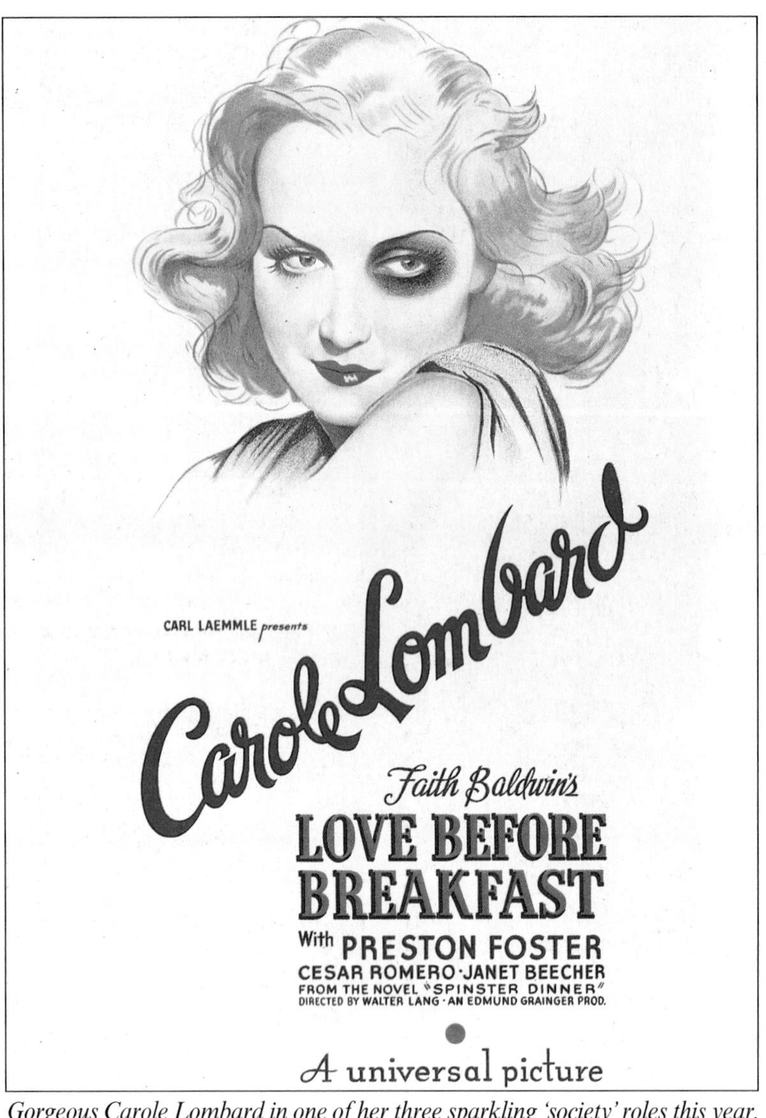
CARL LAEMMLE presents
Carole Lombard
Faith Baldwin's
LOVE BEFORE BREAKFAST
With PRESTON FOSTER
CESAR ROMERO · JANET BEECHER
FROM THE NOVEL "SPINSTER DINNER"
DIRECTED BY WALTER LANG · AN EDMUND GRAINGER PROD.
A universal picture

Gorgeous Carole Lombard in one of her three sparkling 'society' roles this year.

Jean Gabin, Louis Jouvet and Vladimir Sokoloff in Renoir's ***The Lower Depth***

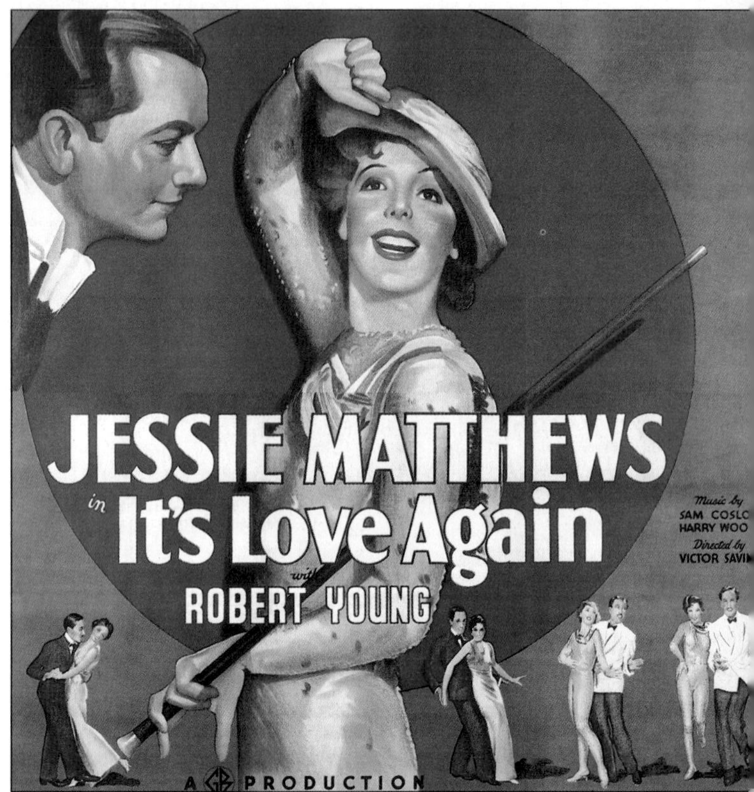
JESSIE MATTHEWS
in It's Love Again
with ROBERT YOUNG
A PRODUCTION

Director Saville and star Matthews teamed again for British musical charme

Olivia De Havilland and Errol Flynn in ***The Charge of the Light Brigade.***

Charles Laughton was Rembrandt.

Marlene Dietrich and Basil Rathbo in ***The Garden of Allah.***

HE GREAT
ZIEGFELD
The Sensation of the Century!
POWELL
LOY
RAINER
FRANK MORGAN · FANNIE BRICE · VIRGINIA BRUCE
REGINALD OWEN · RAY BOLGER · ERNEST COSSART
NAT PENDLETON · HARRIET HOCTOR · JOSEPH CAWTHORNE
A Metro-Goldwyn-Mayer PICTURE

instant winner: MGM spared no pense to make this dazzling, lavish pic of the Broadway impresario.

ARY
JEAN
OOPER · ARTHUR
CECIL B. DeMILLE'S
HE PLAINSMAN

imaginary romance between Wild ll Hickok and Calamity Jane.

NDER TWO FLAGS
Ronald
Claudette
COLMAN · COLBERT
Victor
Rosalind
cLAGLEN
RUSSELL
and a cast of 10,000

uida's tale filmed for the third time.

The FIRST
DANCING
MUSICAL
IN
100% NEW
TECHNICOLOR
PIONEER
PICTURES
PRESENTS
DANCING
PIRATE
DIRECTED BY
LLOYD CORRIGAN
DESIGNED IN COLOR BY
ROBERT EDMOND
JONES
PRODUCED BY
JOHN SPEAKS
EXECUTIVE PRODUCER
MERIAN C. COOPER
DISTRIBUTED BY
RKO-RADIO PICT., Inc.
WITH A CAST OF HUNDREDS Introducing
CHARLES COLLINS
(THE SCREEN'S NEW DANCE SENSATION)
FRANK MORGAN
STEFFI DUNA
LUIS ALBERNI · VICTOR VARCONI · JACK LA RUE

Technicolor was the real star of this largely disappointing costume musical.

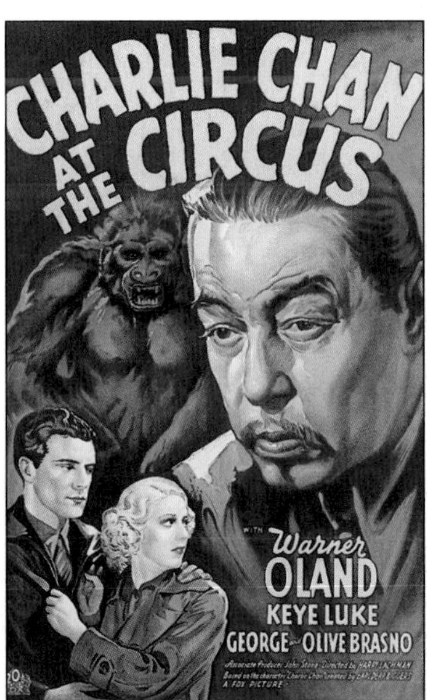
CHARLIE CHAN
AT THE
CIRCUS
Warner
OLAND
KEYE LUKE
GEORGE · OLIVE BRASNO

Detective Chan, based on real-life sleuth Chang Apada, in one of four filmed outings this year.

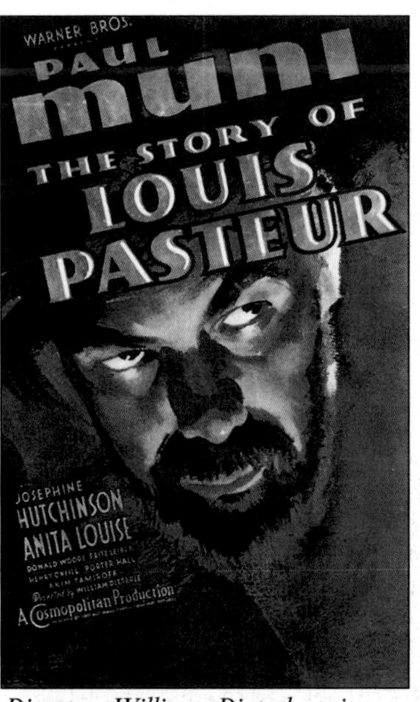
WARNER BROS.
PAUL
muni
THE STORY OF
LOUIS
PASTEUR
JOSEPHINE
HUTCHINSON
ANITA LOUISE
A Cosmopolitan Production

Director William Dieterle, given a scant budget, created a prestigious biopic of the famous scientist.

John WAYNE
The OREGON TRAIL
A REPUBLIC PICTURE

The aggressive pioneer John Wayne opened up the frontier in one of seven films he made this year.

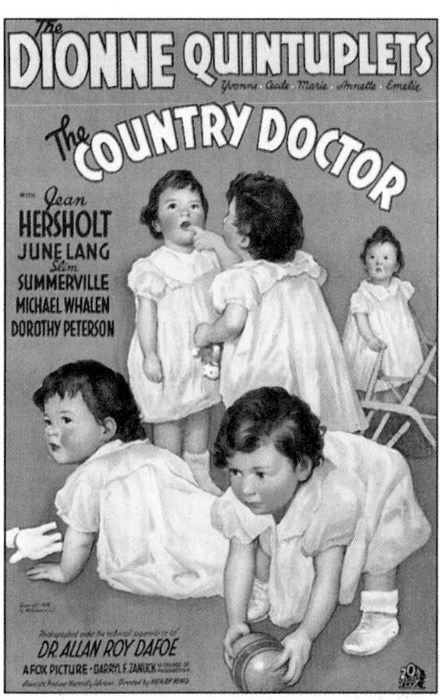
The
DIONNE QUINTUPLETS
Yvonne · Cecile · Marie · Annette · Emilie
The COUNTRY DOCTOR
with
Jean
HERSHOLT
JUNE LANG
Slim
SUMMERVILLE
MICHAEL WHALEN
DOROTHY PETERSON
DR. ALLAN ROY DAFOE

'Dr.' Jean Hersholt delivered quins!

LLOYDS OF
LONDON
Freddie
BARTHOLOMEW
Madeleine
CARROLL
Sir GUY STANDING
TYRONE POWER
SMITH · FIELD
AND A MAMMOTH CAST

Founding of the great insurance co.

1937

1936 Academy Awards, Biltmore Hotel, 4 Mar.

Best Film:	*The Great Ziegfeld* (dir: Robert Z. Leonard)
Best Director:	Frank Capra *(Mr. Deeds Goes to Town)*
Best Actor:	Paul Muni *(The Story of Louis Pasteur)*
Best Actress:	Luise Rainer *(The Great Ziegfeld)*
Best Supp. Actor:	Walter Brennan *(Come and Get It)*
Best Supp. Actress:	Gale Sondergaard *(Anthony Adverse)*

Paris, 15 January
Abel Gance has been forced to accept the release of an entirely altered version of his film *The Life and Loves of Beethoven*. Despite the court decision allowing cuts to 55 sequences, the film has been given a highly favorable reception. Harry Baur is memorable as Beethoven.

France, 31 January
Jean Renoir has begun filming *The Grand illusion*, in the town of Colmar's barracks. Pierre Fresnay has accepted to play the role of Captain de Boëldieu.

Moscow, 2 February
The Mosfilm production company held a preview of *The Last Night*, by the filmmaker Yuli Raizman.

Paris, 8 February
The CGT has announced that Jean Renoir is to make a new film about the French Revolution. The project, already supported by the Union, *Ciné-Liberté* magazine and the Popular Front government, will be financed by a national subscription.

Hollywood, 9 March
Captain Dreyfus' son, Pierre Dreyfus, has approved the script inspired by the Dreyfus case that Warner Bros. want to produce under the title *The Life of Emile Zola*. Paul Muni will play Zola, and William Dieterle will direct.

London, 21 March
Alexander Korda has abandoned *I, Claudius* with only 20 minutes of expensive filming completed. Adapted from Robert Graves' bestseller, this major production, directed by Josef von Sternberg with Charles Laughton in the title role and Merle Oberon playing Messalina, has been dogged by both dispute and disaster. Sternberg's obsessive perfection upset Laughton, and his disregard for the budget alarmed Korda. To top it all, Miss Oberon has received serious injuries in a car crash.

Hollywood, 17 April
Release of *Porky's Duck Hunt*, a Tex Avery cartoon for Warner Bros.' "Looney Tunes", introducing the character of Daffy Duck.

Paris, 8 June
Premiere of Marc Allégret's *Gribouille*, with Michèle Morgan, Jean Worms, Raimu and Julien Carette.

Hollywood, 30 June
Rita Cansino, who married the millionaire Edward Judson just three months ago, has adopted the screen name Rita Hayworth during the shooting of her 13th film *Criminals of the Air*.

Hollywood, 30 June
Actor Ronald Reagan has signed a seven-year contract with Warner Bros. for $200 per week.

Shanghai, 10 July
For the first time, scriptwriter Tian Han's name has appeared officially in the credit titles. The film, *The Youth March*, was directed by Shi Dongshan. Until now Tian Han has been under suspicion due to his left-wing sympathies and has been forced to work under a pseudonym.

Prague, 30 July
Release of *Svet patri nam*, by Martin Fric. The film appeals for a mobilization against Nazism.

New York, 22 August
Alfred Hitchcock has arrived on board the *Queen Mary*. According to news reports he is on holiday in the United States.

Munich, 1 September
Jacques Feyder is undertaking the filming of *les Gens du voyage* (*Wanderers*) for Tobis, with Françoise Rosay and André Brulé.

London, 10 September
René Clair is filming *Break the News* at Pinewood studios, with Jack Buchanan and Maurice Chevalier.

France, 25 September
Popular French actress Danielle Darrieux has embarked for Hollywood to make a film for Universal, while director Julien Duvivier has been taken on by MGM for a trial period of six months.

New York, 30 September
Hedy Kiesler, who fled to America to escape the Nazi regime and her husband – the arms manufacturer Friedrich Mandl – has decided to take Hedy Lamarr as her new stage name, in memory of Barbara La Marr, the star of silent films.

Paris, 22 October
Release of Max Ophuls' film *Yoshiwara*, with Pierre Richard-Willm and Sessue Hayakawa.

Paris, 25 October
Censorship has been tightened up. From now on, visas from the censorship commission will be refused to all films which make the army look ridiculous or could upset the national feelings of foreigners. The latest changes are directly aimed at war and spy films.

Washington, 11 November
President Roosevelt has enjoyed a private view of *The Grand Illusion*, screened at the White House, and has declared that in his opinion "every democratic person in the world should see this film".

California, 30 November
The French film *Club de femmes* (*Women's Club*), by Jacques Deval, has been accused of immorality by the American censors who have demanded several cuts. The film has already been banned by the censors in Great Britain. Other films under attack are: *Faisons un rêve* (*Let's Dream a Dream*), by Sacha Guitry and *Lucretia Borgia*, a historical drama by Abel Gance.

Los Angeles, 24 December
After seeing the new Swedish film *Intermezzo*, from director Gustav Molander, David O. Selznick is reported to be very taken with the young actress Ingrid Bergman.

Los Angeles, 24 December
Premiere of Walt Disney's wonderful cartoon *Snow White*. The film is the first full-length cartoon in the history of the cinema.

Mexico, 31 December
Among the 38 films produced Mexico during the year, 20 we based on the "rancheros", a mixtu of folklore and country life. T success of these films in all Lat American countries puts the Me can cinema on the top rung of t Spanish-speaking cinema industry

BIRTHS

London, 30 January
Vanessa Redgrave

England, 25 February
Tom Courtenay

Virginia, 30 March
Warren Beatty (Henry W. Beaty)

New Jersey, 22 April
Jack Nicholson

Nebraska, 27 April
Sandy Dennis

France, 28 July
Francis Veber

Los Angeles, 8 August
Dustin Hoffman

California, 18 August
Robert Redford

Moscow, 20 August
Andrei Mikhalkov-Konchalovsky

Paris, 13 October
Sami Frey (Samuel Frei)

Paris, 30 October
Claude Lelouch

New York, 21 December
Jane Fonda

Wales, 31 December
Anthony Hopkins

DEATHS

Hollywood, 7 June
Jean Harlow

Hollywood, 11 July
George Gershwin

---

*Walt Disney's **Snow White and t Seven Dwarfs**, made at vast expen over a three-year period, is the fi full-length animated feature. It h received a rapturous welcome.*

HIS FIRST FULL LENGTH FEATURE PRODUCTION
Walt Disney's
Snow White
and the Seven Dwarfs
in the Marvelous
MULTIPLANE TECHNICOLOR
©WDP
Distributed by RKO Radio Pictures, Inc.

© Walt Disney

Garbo a luminous Lady of the Camelias

Greta Garbo and Robert Taylor are Marguerite Gauthier and Armand Duval.

New York, 22 January
Greta Garbo has given her most intensely moving performance as Dumas' consumptive courtesan in the movie *Camille*, which co-stars Robert Taylor, who made his first big impression in 1935 with *Magnificent Obsession*. In his piece in the *New York Herald Tribune*, writer Howard Barnes says, "With her fine intelligence and unerring instinct, she has made her characterization completely credible, while giving it an added poignancy that, to me, is utterly irresistible." Seeing Camille's death scene, it is hard to imagine the difficulty skilled director George Cukor had in shooting it. His leading lady required several takes, as she repeatedly burst into uncontrollable fits of nervous laughter the moment the cameras began to roll.

Inventive gags for seedy stationmaster

London, 3 January
Gainsborough Pictures bring the music-hall magic of comedian Will Hay to the screen in the comedy film *Oh, Mr. Porter!* Directed by Marcel Varnel, Hay plays a bungling station master sent to remote Northern Ireland, where gun-running with the Free state is rife. Sterling support comes from crazed Moore Marriott and, joining Hay for the first time, cheeky fat boy Graham Moffatt.

Will Hay observes Moore Marriott's efforts to milk a cow in ***Oh! Mr. Porter****.*

César joins Marius and Fanny in trilogy

A card game worthy of record played by friendly but argumentative compa ions. L to r: Raimu, Charpin, Paul Dullac and Robert Vattier (back view).

Nice, 23 January
The Escuriel and the Rialto, who have been simultaneously showing Marcel Pagnol's *César*, the last part of his Marseilles trilogy, have netted their largest box-office takings since *Ben-Hur* – a total of 315,000 francs. All of the 58 copies that Pagnol made of the film in his Marseilles laboratories are circulating throughout Provence, gaining huge success everywhere. The Trilogy, begun six years ago with *Marius*, was an adaptation of Pagnol's play, with no real thought to any sequel. But the popularity of the film, directed by Alexander Korda, encouraged the author to do a follow-up by transposing *Fanny* to the screen, directed by Marc Allégret. Pagnol decided to direct *César* himself, which is the only one of the three to have be written directly for the cinema. Th transformation of a single work in a diptych and then a triptych h been justified because Pagnol's cha acters are so alive, and the acto who embody them so brilliant, th the public demanded more of the. Who could forget Raimu as Cés the crabby but lovable proprietor the Marine Bar, whose son Mari (Pierre Fresnay) runs away to s leaving a pregnant Fanny (Ora Demazis). Poor Fanny then marri Panisse (Charpin), a kindly widow who then dies, leaving the way f reconciliation all around. The thr films are fictionalized portraits Marseilles life described by a wo derful storyteller who creates path without sentimentality.

l to r: Charpin, Alida Rouffe, Orane Demazis and Raimu in ***Fanny****.*

André Fouché with Raimu in ***Cés*** *which completes the trilogy.*

abin in the skin of 'Pépé-le-Moko'

ris, 29 January
ın Gabin and Mireille Balin have ɜn brought together again in *Pépé-Moko*, Julien Duvivier's new film. ıbin, who was seen recently in ın Renoir's *The Lower Depths* and Duvivier's *la Belle équipe*, is appearing in his twenty-fifth film in s than five years. He is now the ;hest paid actor in France, getting ·s of 100,000 francs per film. With ılogue by Henri Jeanson, adapted ·m the novel by Roger D'Ashelbé, *pé-le-Moko* is an exotic tale set in giers. Gabin plays Pépé, a high-wered jewel thief and bank rob- r forced to flee from his beloved ris and live in the Algerian Cas- h as his only means of avoiding ·est. When he falls in love with a autiful visiting Parisienne (Balin), leaves the Casbah to seek her and caught. Gabin, at his most attrac- ely roguish, brilliantly portrays ː quintessential loner in a film that ·ms with life, romance, suspense and humor. The studio-constructed Casbah, under Duvivier's expert direction, is beautifully lit and photographed (by Jules Kruger), with songs sung by Fréhel, who herself plays an old singer in the film. *Pépé-le-Moko* is the fourth motion picture on which Gabin and Duvivier have worked, and they obviously make a perfect team.

Jean Gabin with Mireille Balin and Lucas Gridoux, two faces of treason.

Sergei Eisenstein admits his 'errors'

Moscow, 25 April
No one will ever see Sergei Eisenstein's first sound feature, *Bezhin Meadow*. Inspired by a Turgenev tale, it tells of the youthful organizer of a village Young Pioneer group who is killed by his own *kulak* father while guarding the collective harvest against sabotage. The film's troubled production began in the spring of 1935 but has been constantly interrupted by Eisenstein's ill health and orchestrated political interference. And drastic revisions in the screenplay to conform to the Soviet doctrine of Socialist Realism have proved unavailing. All work on the film was stopped in March, followed by a vicious attack on Eisenstein in *Pravda*. The director has now been forced to make a public admission of his "errors" and to disown his film. The state-sponsored campaign to humiliate Eisenstein has reached new and shameful heights.

ocu-drama makes star of young Indian

ndon, 9 April
ı intriguing collaboration between ıltan Korda and celebrated docu- ɜntary filmmaker Robert Flaherty s thrown up a new star, Sabu, an chanting 13-year-old Indian boy. aherty discovered Sabu, a former ıble boy at the court of an Indian aharajah, and immediately cast n in the title role of *Elephant Boy* play the native lad who claims he ows the location of a mythical elephant herd. The movie is loosely based on a Kipling story. Flaherty filmed the exterior scenes on location in India, and the interiors were shot by Zoltan Korda. Flaherty has given the film the required authenticity, the Kordas have provided the polish and Sabu has supplied bags of unforced charm. Director Zoltan Korda, younger brother of Alexander Korda and also a product of the vanished Austro-Hungarian empire, has played an enthusiastic part in the celebration of the slowly vanishing British empire. His *Sanders of the River*, adapted from an Edgar Wallace story, cast Paul Robeson as an African chief, but was fashioned into a hymn for British imperialism which so upset the black American star that he walked out of the London premiere when asked to make a speech. One suspects, however, that Korda is more interested in picturesque adventure than the politics of empire. But the more pliable Sabu proves the perfect centerpiece for *Elephant Boy*'s romantic view of India. He was paid a living wage during filming, and was grateful for it, but fame and fortune beckon, and it seems unlikely that he will return to the maharajah's stable.

ung Sabu scrubs his elephant.

On 4 March *The Great Ziegfeld*, directed by Robert Z. Leonard, was awarded the Best Film Oscar and its female star, Luise Rainer, the Best Actress award. Frank Capra won the Best Director Oscar for *Mr. Deeds Goes to Town*, and Paul Muni was named Best Actor for *The Story of Louis Pasteur*.

Jean Renoir and the illusion of peace

Commanding officer Von Stroheim.

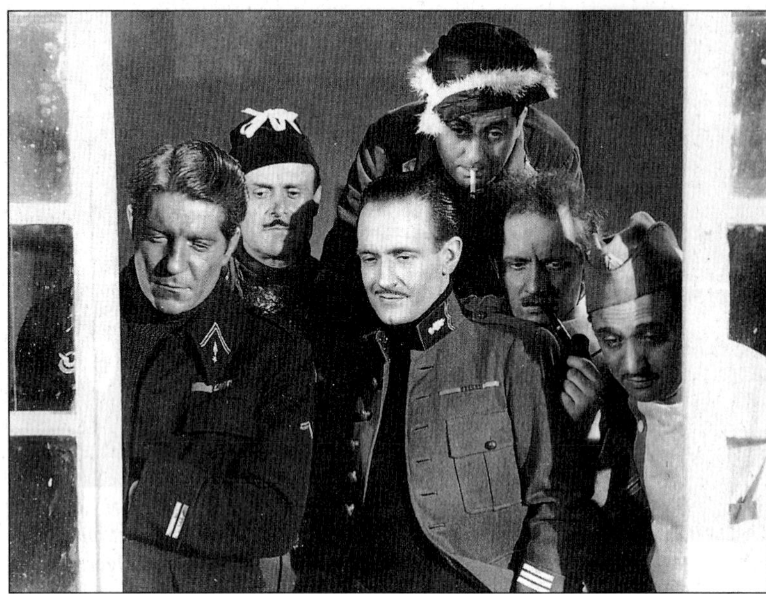

Gabin, Fresnay and Dalio represent differing classes united in War.

Paris, 8 June
Jean Renoir's latest film, *la Grande illusion*, has just opened to a warm reception from the public and critics alike. After his *The Lower Depths*, Renoir has returned to a more personal subject and created an anti-war masterpiece in the process. The story was inspired by the adventures of General Pinsard, whom Renoir met in 1916 when they served in the same squadron. The director also added many of his own memories of the war. For him, "the Frenchmen in the film are good Frenchmen, and the Germans are good Germans. It is not possible for me to take the side of any of my characters." A wonderful cast has been assembled to play these characters: Jean Gabin, Marcel Dalio and Pierre Fresnay are three French prisoners of war, and Erich von Stroheim is the sympathetic German Commandant.

Cinecittà biggest studio in Europe

Rome, 28 April
Italy has just opened its own "dre
factory" called Cinecittà. It has be
set up in the Roman countryside,
kilometres from the via Tuscola
and covers 60 hectares filled w
workshops, auditoria, laboratori
nine sound stages, and villas to ac
modate the casts, crews and dir
tors. Just like Hollywood, Cineci
enjoys a mild climate and an exc
tional quality of light. All of it to
over a year to construct, making
the largest cinematographic co
plex in Europe. Mussolini laid
first stone at 9 a.m. on the morni
of 29 January 1936. The studio h
been created with the intention
breathing new life into Italian fi
production, because the cinema h
recently been recognized as an i
portant means of propaganda.
prestigious workplace was needed
entice the filmmakers, and Il Du
hopes it will become an internatic
al attraction, an ambitious Fasc
Hollywood. Above the gates of
studio, an aggressive motto has be
inscribed: "The Cinematograph
the Strongest Weapon."

Sacha Guitry finds riches in stolen jewels

Paris, 11 May
Sacha Guitry's new film, *The Pearls of the Crown*, is a trilingual story – French, English and Italian – about seven pearls given to a range of famous personages over the ages, and a number of contemporary people of different nationalities who search for them. As usual, Guitry has provided a film of style and wit, with most of the pearls in the dialogue, rather than in the plot.

Filming of ***The Pearls of the Crown****, with Arletty as the Queen of Ethiopia.*

Jean Harlow cut off in the prime of life

Los Angeles, 7 June
Jean Harlow has died in the hospital of a cerebral edema. She became seriously ill during the filming of *Saratoga* and had been treated for uremic poisoning. Some blame her mother, a Christian Scientist,
preventing Harlow from receivi
the treatment that might have sav
her. Anita Loos claims that Harl
was severely depressed by the end
her affair with William Powell.

Harlow with Clark Gable in ***Saratoga****, her last film made just before she di*

ɪinese cinema is inspired by Hollywood

:th *Malu Tianshi*, *Yuan Muzhi has made a recognizable Chinese classic.*

king, 24 July
new Chinese film, *Malu Tianshi* *reet Angel*), is a highly original ·rk, even if it's been influenced by ank Borzage's 1928 Hollywood ɪma of the same title. Its 28-year-ɪ director, Yuan Muzhi, had a tinguished career on stage before entering films as an actor and writer. The movie captures the atmosphere of one of Shanghai's poorest areas, where a young man is in a chaste affair with a woman pressed into prostitution. The tragi-comic film is firmly rooted in reality, and explicit in its criticism of Chinese society.

ean Gabin proves capable of vulnerability

ris, 29 September
his latest film, *Gueule d'amour*, ɪn Gabin assumes his habitual .e of pessimistic anti-hero, playing army officer who is betrayed by woman he loves. But this time he allows himself to suggest vulnerability in his screen persona which has previously been concealed from cinema audiences. Nevertheless, he remains cinema's quintessential loner, doomed in life and love.

ɪbin's seducer who becomes a melancholy victim is a departure for the actor.

Search for memories in 'Un carnet de bal'

Marie Bell finds Louis Jouvet during her search for her lost dance partners.

Paris, 7 September
The scenario of Julien Duvivier's new film, *Un carnet de bal* (*Dance Card*), focuses on a rather original idea. A wealthy, middle-aged widow (Marie Bell) finds an old dance card dating back to her sixteenth year, and decides to find out what has happened to the men whose names are on it. She discovers an epileptic doctor (Pierre Blanchar), a monk (Harry Baur), a hairdresser (Fernandel), a crooked nightclub owner (Louis Jouvet), a skiing instructor (Pierre Richard-Willm) and a small-town mayor (Raimu). Her quest reveals the indifference and pettiness of the world, and she finds her existence meaningless. However, when she adopts an orphan boy, her life takes on new meaning. The optimistic ending does not efface the pessimism that precedes it. This elegant film allows a galaxy of French stars to do short turns, doubtless contributing to its great success.

Françoise Rosay and Marie Bell.

On 3 September, Italy's *Scipione the African*, directed by Carmine Gallone, was voted best film at Venice. Duvivier's *Dance Card (Un carnet de bal)* was best foreign film and, despite protests from the Italian government, Renoir's *The Grand Illusion* was chosen as best film for overall artistic quality.

Carné and Prévert, victims of the 'bizarre'

Jouvet and Michel Simon in ***Drôle de drame****, aptly known as* ***Bizarre, Bizarre****.*

Paris, 20 October
The new film from Marcel Carné, *Bizarre, Bizarre* (*Drôle de drame*), was greeted with whistles and boos when it opened at the Colisée. The public failed to appreciate the craziness of the humor which recalls *It's in the Bag* (*l'Affaire est dans le sac*) by the Prévert brothers. This connection is not accidental because *Bizarre, Bizarre* is Jacques Prévert's second collaboration with Carné. The film, set in Edwardian London, tells what happens when a mystery writer (Michel Simon) has to pretend to a visiting Bishop (Louis Jouvet) that his wife (Françoise Rosay) has been called away. The failure of this witty and anarchic farce is even more bitter for Carné because it was shot in an unpleasant atmosphere. Jouvet and Simon didn't think much of it, and spent their time making nasty comments on the set.

Ruined village gets a face-lift from Pagn

Fernandel and Orane Demazis in ***Regain****, from the novel by Jean Giono.*

Paris, 28 October
Audiences who go to see Marcel Pagnol's *Harvest* (*Regain*) will be astonished to learn that the ruined village, in which the action of the film unfolds, was built entirely from scratch in Provence by Marius Broquier, the art director. Drawn from a novel by Jean Giono, the film tells the story of a poacher (Gabriel Gabrio), longing for fatherhood, who coaxes an itinerant girl (Orane Demazis) away from her simple kn grinder companion (Fernandel). sets up house with her in a deser village, which they bring back to l The film contains superb panthei images, and atmospheric music Arthur Honegger. *Harvest* will given a gala showing tonight at Marignan cinema, for the benefit the country's war orphans, and be attended by the President of Republic, Albert Lebrun.

First award given of new acting prize

Paris, 31 October
The first winner of the new Suzanne Bianchetti Prize is a young actress from Marseilles, Junie Astor. She has won the award for her performances in Raymond Bernard's film *Coupable*, Jean Renoir's *The Lower Depths*, and Jean de Limur's work *la Garçonne*. Junie made her screen debut three years ago, sparring with Noël Noël's gloriously befuddled soldier in *Ademai aviateur*. This prize has been set up by the critic René Jeanne as a memorial to his wife, Suzanne Bianchetti, who tragically disappeared without trace in November 1936 at age 47. A star of the silent screen she appeared in many films, including Jacques de Baroncelli's *le Père Goriot* in 1921, Léonce Perret's *Madame Sans-Gêne* in 1925 and finally in Abel Gance's *Napoleon* in 1927.

A sweet, light soufflé of American comedy from Leo McCarey

Hollywood, 4 November
Director Leo McCarey has scored a tremendous success with an hilarious Columbia comedy, *The Awful Truth*, which stars Cary Grant and Irene Dunne. They play a married couple whose decision to divorce leads to innumerable romantic complications. A graduate of the Hal Roach studio and the man responsible for pairing Stan Laurel with Oliver Hardy, McCarey has found in Grant and Dunne the perf combination of warmth and come technique. If proof is required th for the moment at least, Colum need not rely solely on Frank Cap then McCarey has demonstrated

IRENE DUNNE
CARY GRANT
AVEC
RALPH BELLAMY
ALEXANDER D'ARCY
CECIL CUNNINGHAM
DANS
CETTE SACRÉE VÉRITÉ
THE AWFUL TRUTH

Sophisticated banter between Cary Grant and Irene Dunne in ***The Awful Tru***

elznick goes from strength to strength

lznick: a force to reckon with.

A Star is Born: *March and Gaynor.*

ollywood, 26 September
is has been a good year for procer David O. Selznick. Two years er leaving MGM to form his own lependent production company, lznick International Pictures, he s begun to fulfill his promise. Two tstanding new films have already ened, *A Star is Born* with Janet ynor and Fredric March, and *e Prisoner of Zenda*, based on the vel by Anthony Hope and with an -star cast headed by Ronald Colan, Douglas Fairbanks Jr., Rayond Massey, Madeleine Carroll d Mary Astor. In addition, a third oject, *Nothing Sacred*, has been ished for a November premiere. is last is from the same team as *A ar is Born*: director William Wellman, art director Lyle Wheeler, actor Fredric March starring (with Carole Lombard), and color specialist W. Howard Greene behind the camera. Both pictures were filmed in Technicolor and demonstrate that it can enhance the look of a modern drama or comedy, and need not be restricted to costume pictures, musicals or exotic subjects. Most of all, these films reflect Selznick's commitment to top quality stories and scripts – not only published works such as *Zenda* or *The Adventures of Tom Sawyer* (currently filming), but to film originals like *Nothing Sacred* from Ben Hecht, and *A Star is Born* from Wellman and Robert Carson, and scripted by Dorothy Parker and Alan Campbell.

arole Lombard, Walter Connolly and Fredric March in ***Nothing Sacred****.*

Disney's Snow White even silences Grumpy

© Walt Disney

Hollywood, 21 December
Judy Garland, Marlene Dietrich and Charles Laughton are among the stars attending the premiere, at the Cathay Circle Theater, of Walt Disney's *Snow White and the Seven Dwarfs*, the first feature-length animated film in three-strip Technicolor. Disney, who hit the road to fame and fortune in 1928 when he created Mickey Mouse, has taken an enormous artistic and financial risk in the creation of *Snow White*, which has been four years in the making at a cost of $1.5 million. In addition to the pioneering animation techniques employed by the Disney studio, under the supervision of David Hand, music plays an important part in the production, and tunes like "Whistle While You Work" and "Some Day My Prince Will Come" look like they will become immediate big hits with the public.

© Walt Disney

MICKEY MOUSE
MICKEY MOUSE

Walt Disney has published a comic book of his 1928 creation, Mickey Mouse.

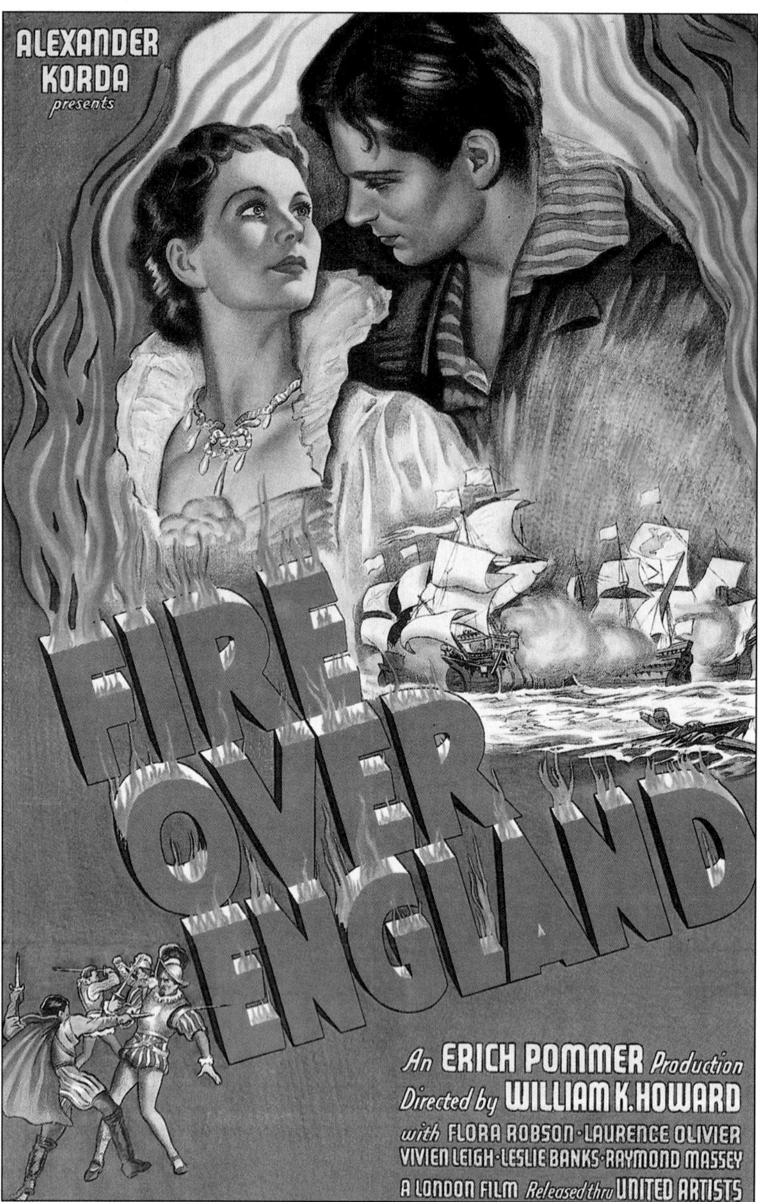
ALEXANDER KORDA presents
FIRE OVER ENGLAND
An ERICH POMMER Production
Directed by WILLIAM K. HOWARD
with FLORA ROBSON · LAURENCE OLIVIER
VIVIEN LEIGH · LESLIE BANKS · RAYMOND MASSEY
A LONDON FILM Released thru UNITED ARTISTS

Flora Robson was Elizabeth I, but Laurence Olivier and Vivien Leigh got raves.

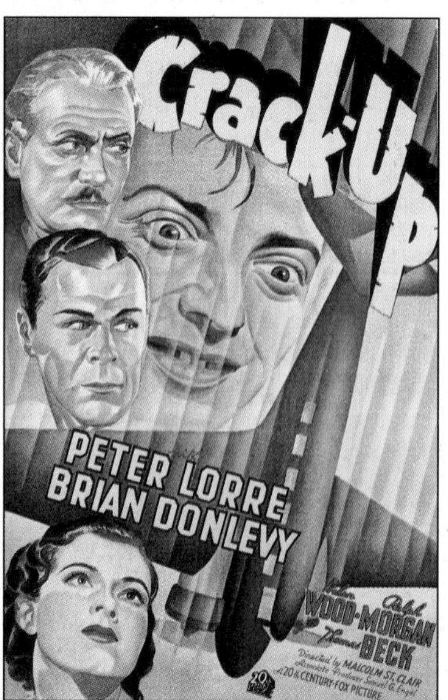
Crack-Up
PETER LORRE
BRIAN DONLEVY
WOOD-MORGAN
BECK

The inimitable Peter Lorre played a spy, out to secure secret documents in this successful thriller.

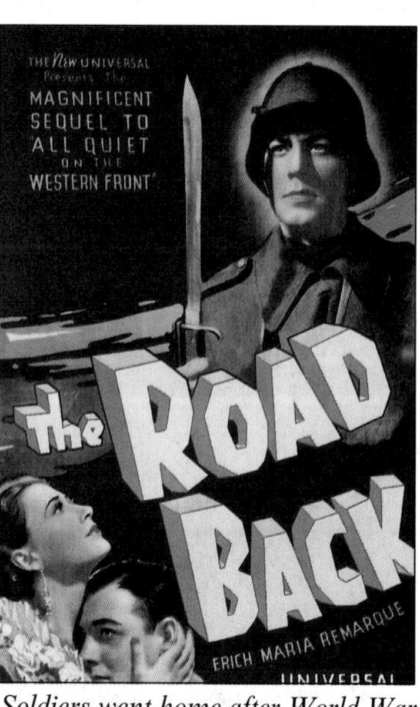
MAGNIFICENT SEQUEL TO 'ALL QUIET ON THE WESTERN FRONT'
the ROAD BACK
ERICH MARIA REMARQUE
UNIVERSAL

Soldiers went home after World War I to problems and disillusion. This time they were German.

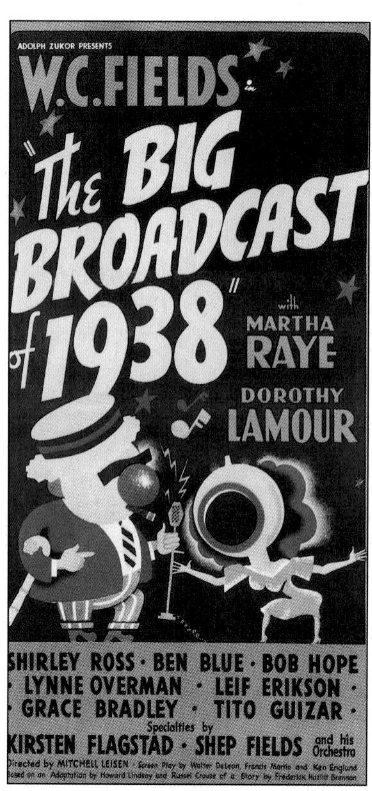
ADOLPH ZUKOR PRESENTS
W.C. FIELDS in
"The BIG BROADCAST of 1938"
with MARTHA RAYE
DOROTHY LAMOUR
SHIRLEY ROSS · BEN BLUE · BOB HOPE
· LYNNE OVERMAN · LEIF ERIKSON ·
· GRACE BRADLEY · TITO GUIZAR ·
Specialties by
KIRSTEN FLAGSTAD · SHEP FIELDS and his Orchestra
Directed by MITCHELL LEISEN

Empty-headed excuse for star turns.

AS GREAT AS "MUTINY ON THE BOUNTY"
Rudyard Kipling's
CAPTAINS COURAGEOUS
DIRECTED BY VICTOR FLEMING
Freddie BARTHOLOMEW
SPENCER TRACY
Lionel BARRYMORE
MELVYN DOUGLAS
A Metro-Goldwyn-Mayer PICTURE

Exciting, emotional whaling yarn.

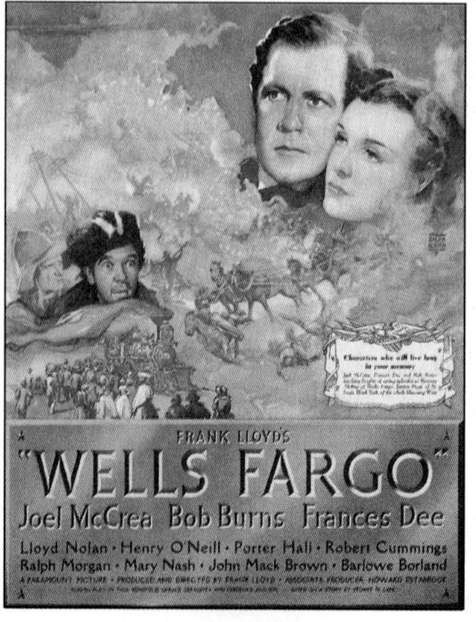
FRANK LLOYD'S
"WELLS FARGO"
Joel McCrea Bob Burns Frances Dee
Lloyd Nolan · Henry O'Neill · Porter Hall · Robert Cummings
Ralph Morgan · Mary Nash · John Mack Brown · Barlowe Borland

JESSIE
MATTHEWS
in
GANGWAY
with NAT PENDLETON
BARRY MACKAY
NOEL MADISON
DIRECTED BY SONNIE HALE

Vehicle for a much-loved British s

ADOLPH ZUKOR presents
JACK BENNY in
ARTISTS and MODEL
IDA LUPINO
RICHARD ARLEN
GAIL PATRICK
· BEN BLUE ·
JUDY CANOVA
YACHT CLUB BOYS
LOUIS ARMSTRONG
MARTHA RA
ANDRE KOSTELAN
RUSSELL PATTERSO
"PERSONETTE
CONNIE BOSW

Paramount's amusing and zippy m sical had Ida Lupino pretending to a socialite, and then soliciting Ja Benny's assistance to become Que of the Ball. Raoul Walsh directed.

Wells Fargo was a fictionalized count of the famous coach compa of the same name. Joel McCrea w a Unionist, married to a Confedera She was played by his real-life w Frances Dee.

harine Hepburn, Franchot Tone in ***Quality Street*** *from J.M. Barrie's play.*

trich, Herbert Marshall in ***Angel****.*

FRED ASTAIRE
GEORGE BURNS and GRACIE ALLEN
in "A Damsel in Distress"
JOAN FONTAINE
REGINALD GARDINER · RAY NOBLE
Music by GEORGE GERSHWIN · Lyrics by IRA GERSHWIN
A PANDRO S. BERMAN Production
Directed by GEORGE STEVENS

Fred, no Ginger, but Gershwin score.

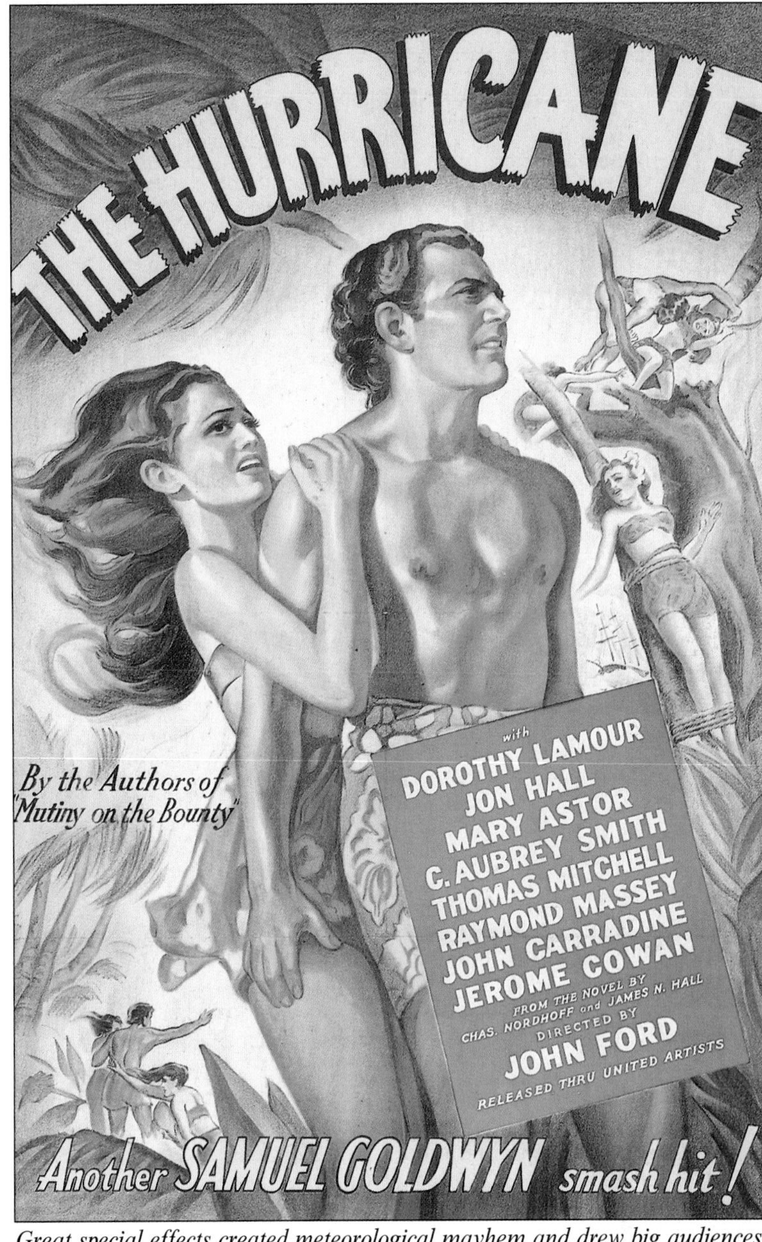
THE HURRICANE
By the Authors of "Mutiny on the Bounty"
with
DOROTHY LAMOUR
JON HALL
MARY ASTOR
C. AUBREY SMITH
THOMAS MITCHELL
RAYMOND MASSEY
JOHN CARRADINE
JEROME COWAN
FROM THE NOVEL BY CHAS. NORDHOFF and JAMES N. HALL
DIRECTED BY
JOHN FORD
RELEASED THRU UNITED ARTISTS
Another SAMUEL GOLDWYN smash hit!

Great special effects created meteorological mayhem and drew big audiences.

e Marx brothers scored another comedy success in ***A Day at the Races****.*

AMAZING! DIFFERENT! UNIQUE!
ROBERT MONTGOMERY
ROSALIND RUSSELL
NIGHT MUST FALL
with
Dame May WHITTY
Alan MARSHAL
Merle TOTTENHAM
Kathleen HARRISON
Richard THORPE
METRO-GOLDWYN-MAYER
HUNT STROMBERG

Taut adaptation of Emlyn Williams' play about a psychopath.

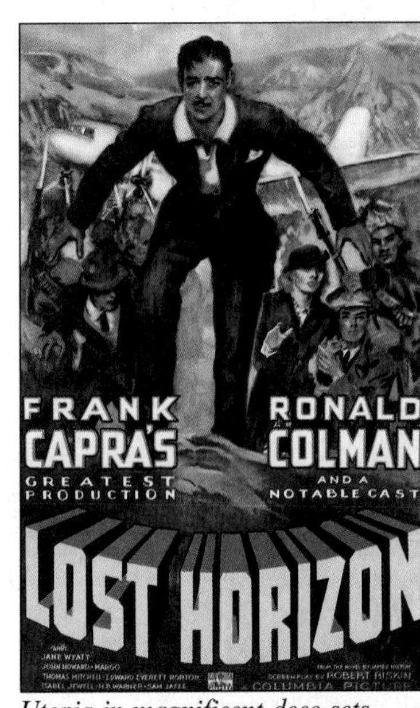
FRANK CAPRA'S
GREATEST PRODUCTION
RONALD COLMAN
AND A NOTABLE CAST
LOST HORIZON

Utopia in magnificent deco sets.

1938

1937 Academy Awards, Biltmore Hotel, 10 Mar.

Best Film:	*The Life of Emile Zola* (William Dieterle)
Best Director:	Leo McCarey *(The Awful Truth)*
Best Actor:	Spencer Tracy *(Captains Courageous)*
Best Actress:	Luise Rainer *(The Good Earth)*
Best Supp. Actor:	Joseph Schildkraut *(The Life of Emile Zola)*
Best Supp. Actress:	Alice Brady *(In Old Chicago)*

France, 4 January
Marcel Carné has started work on *Quai des brumes*. After UFA's refusal to produce the film, the subject had to be modified and transferred to France.

Paris, 9 February
Inauguration of the Olympia cinema on the boulevard des Capucines. The facade has been transformed by 25,000 lights and 1,500 metres of neon lighting.

Hollywood, 24 February
MGM has bought the rights for the famous children's book, *The Wizard of Oz* by Frank Baum.

New York, 3 March
Release of Howard Hawks' *Bringing Up Baby*, with Cary Grant and Katharine Hepburn.

Marseilles, 15 March
Marcel Pagnol is supervising the construction of his new studios, which are to include three sound stages, at the same time as finishing filming *The Schpountz*. He has no doubts about his future success, and is convinced that: "Marseilles will become the French Hollywood."

New York, 7 April
Release of *The Adventures of Marco Polo* with Gary Cooper in the title role, and Basil Rathbone.

Paris, 13 April
The Marivaux cinema is now screening Christian-Jaque's film *les Disparus de Saint-Agil* (*Boys' School*), starring Erich von Stroheim, Michel Simon, Armande Bernard, Robert Le Vigan and three young actors, Serge Grave, Jean Claudio and Marcel Mouloudji.

Paris, 13 May
Release of *l'Etrange Monsieur Victor* (*The Strange Mr. Victor*), by Jean Grémillon, with Raimu, Madeleine Renaud, Pierre Blanchar and Viviane Romance.

Paris, 23 May
Saint-Lazare station was thronging with crowds of well-wishers as Danielle Darrieux, back from America, stepped off the train with her husband, the director Henri Decoin. She announced that she is looking forward to returning to work in French studios.

New York, 2 June
Release of *Three Comrades*. Adapted from the novel by Erich Maria Remarque, with Robert Taylor, Margaret Sullavan, Franchot Tone and Robert Young. Scott Fitzgerald is credited as co-scriptwriter and Frank Borzage directed.

Moscow, 18 June
The director Mark Donskoi has just released *The Childhood of Maxim Gorky*, the first of a trilogy, based on Maxim Gorky's autobiography. This film about childhood and the realities of Russian peasant life is produced by Soyezdetfilm studios.

Paris, 23 June
Over 150,000 people have seen the Walt Disney cartoon *Snow White and the Seven Dwarfs*, which has been screening for seven weeks at the Marignan cinema.

Hollywood, 23 June
According to the press, Norma Shearer has been chosen to play the role of Scarlett O'Hara in *Gone With the Wind*.

Washington, 20 July
The Justice Department has begun instituting proceedings against eight influential studios and 25 of their branches for violation of the anti-monopoly laws.

Paris, 1 August
Abel Gance has obtained a patent for the Pictographe, in association with cameraman Roger Hubert and the engineer Pierre Angénieux. The device improves the quality of shots requiring depth of field.

Paris, 10 August
Julien Duvivier is back after shooting *The Great Waltz* in Hollywood with Fernand Gravey: "A huge whatsit with music, I hope everyone will be satisfied with it," he said.

Washington, 15 August
Senator Sullivan declared in front of the House Committe on Un-American Activities, which has been in action since 10 August, that he believes "Hollywood is becoming a breeding ground for communist propaganda."

Venice, 20 August
A dark cloud hangs over this year's awards, where the jury's political affinities were obvious. The Mussolini award was shared by Leni Riefenstahl for *Olympia* and Goffredo Alessandrini for *Luciano Serra, Pilot*. However, nobody contested the crowning of Marcel Carné for *Quai des brumes*, nor Norma Shearer and Leslie Howard's best acting awards in W.S. Van Dyke's *Marie Antoinette* and Anthony Asquith's *Pygmalion*, respectively, while Disney's *Snow White and the Seven Dwafs* was deemed a worthy winner of the art award.

Hollywood, 25 August
David O. Selznick has signed an agreement with MGM whereby the studio will loan out Clark Gable to Selznick for *Gone With the Wind* in exchange for the film's distribution rights and 50 percent of its profits.

London, 1 September
Release of Alfred Hitchcock's latest film, *The Lady Vanishes*.

Paris, 19 September
Marcel Carné has started shooting *Hôtel du Nord* in the Billancourt studios. The film sets, designed by Alexander Trauner, are already being talked about.

China, 30 September
The Cinema Group of Yenan has been set up. It is to be managed by the great actor-director Yuan Muzhi under the political supervision of the Eighth Communist Army.

Paris, 5 October
Release of Marc Allégret's new project *Entrée des artistes* (*The Curtain Rises*), starring Louis Jouvet and Odette Joyeux.

New York, 14 October
The Roxy Theater is holding premiere of *Suez*, directed by A Dwan, with Tyrone Power in role of Ferdinand de Lesseps, etta Young and the French act Annabella. Persistent rumors going around about a romance tween the handsome young leac man and Annabella.

Great Britain, 31 October
Four hundred cinemas are simu neously screening Sacha Guit *The Story of a Cheat* (*le Roman c tricheur*), which was released Paris two years ago. This is the French movie to enjoy such w spread distribution in Great Brit

Paris, 7 December
The César cinema is currently sh ing *Werther*, Max Ophuls' new f based on the work by Goethe, v Pierre Richard-Willm and Ar Vernay. It was photographed black and white but the exte shots are being projected in blu

BIRTHS

New York, 1 April
Ali MacGraw

Paris, 10 May
Marina Vlady
(Marina de Poliakoff Baidaroff)

San Francisco, 20 July
Natalie Wood (Natasha Gurdin)

Vienna, 23 September
Romy Schneider
(Rosemarie Albach-Retty)

Iowa, 13 November
Jean Seberg

New York, 29 December
Jon Voight

DEATHS

Paris, 4 August
Pearl White

California, 27 December
Florence Lawrence

Betty Davis is triumphant as a spoi Southern belle, brought to her sen by her love for Henry Fonda. T prize role is her consolation for be denied the part of Scarlett O'Har

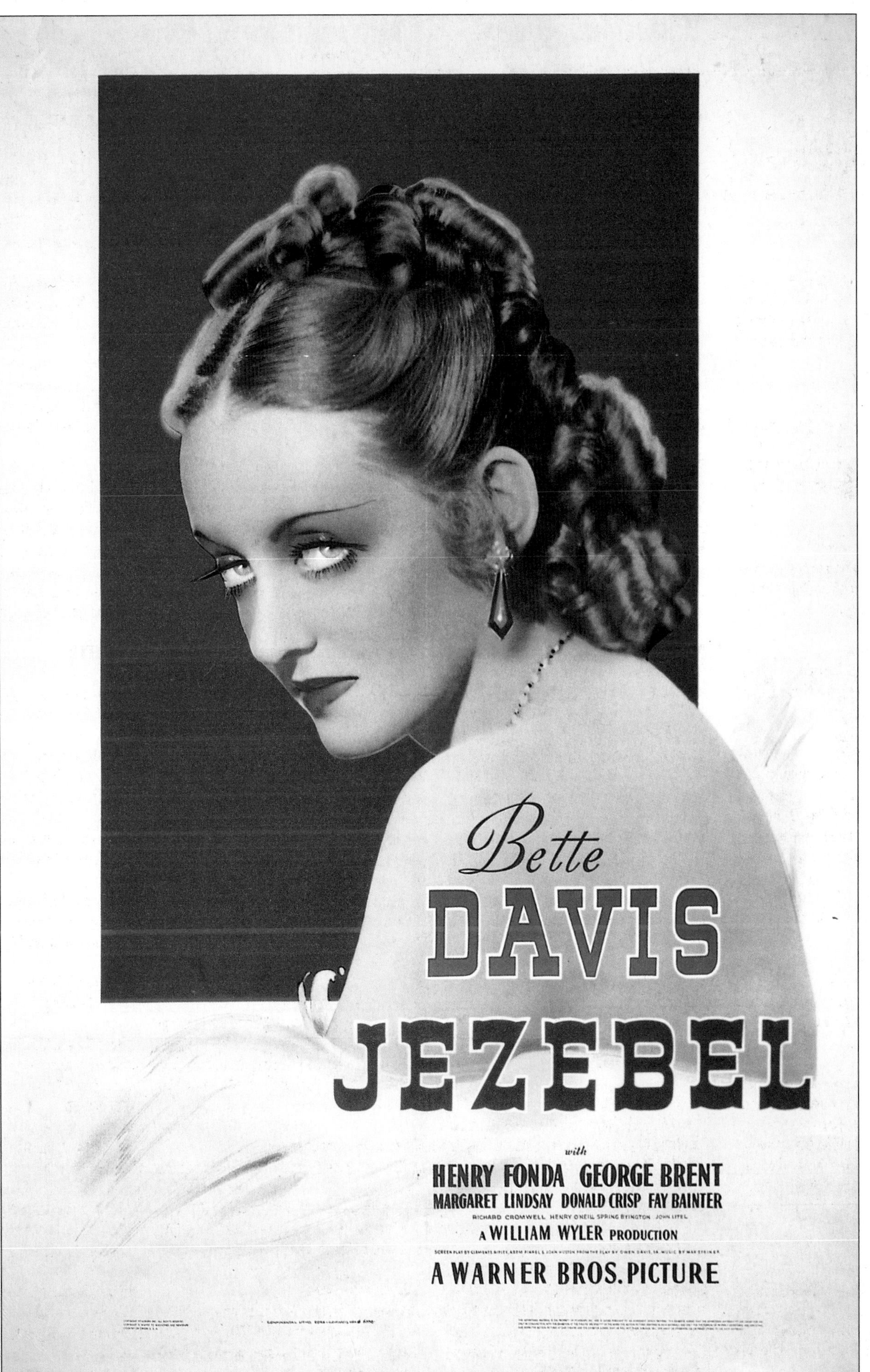
Bette
DAVIS
JEZEBEL
with
HENRY FONDA GEORGE BRENT
MARGARET LINDSAY DONALD CRISP FAY BAINTER
A WILLIAM WYLER PRODUCTION
A WARNER BROS. PICTURE

Méliès and Cohl: two magicians gone

Paris, 25 January
Among the mourners who accompanied Georges Méliès to his final resting place at Père Lachaise cemetery, were the two young founders of the French Cinémathèque, Georges Franju and Henri Langlois. There were also many other admirers of Méliès, most of whom have only recently rediscovered this pioneer of cinematographic art. This fervent group had paid homage to the modest and forgotten magician in his old age after he had been found in a little toy shop at the Gare Montparnasse. Méliès died at the age of 78 on 21 January. Ironically, the day before, Emile Cohl died tragically at an old people's home at Villejuif, a candle having set his beard on fire. Thus, by an astonishing accident, he was reunited in death, after an interval of a only few hours, with another early enchanter of the cinema, two sprites with white goatee-beards and sparkling eyes.

Delluc prize goes to 'The Puritan'

Paris, 16 February
After having impressed the public and critics on its release last December, *The Puritan*, Jeff Musso's first film, has become the second recipient of the Prix Louis Delluc. Adapted from a story by the Irish writer Liam O'Flaherty, it tells of Francis Ferriter, a journalist who belongs to a secret society dedicated to cleansing the country of moral impurities. When a fellow member refuses to denounce his own son's affair with Molly, a woman of easy virtue, Ferriter murders her, only realizing much later that he was motivated by his own sexual desire. There is a superb performance by Jean-Louis Barrault in the title role, leading a fine cast that includes Viviane Romance as Molly and Pierre Fresnay as the probing and perceptive police chief. The re-creation of the atmosphere of Dublin also, quite obviously, influenced the panel of judges in their choice.

Mark Twain's Tom Sawyer is back again

Hollywood, 11 February
The producer David O. Selznick has brought Tom Sawyer back to the silver screen in *The Adventures of Tom Sawyer*, starring Tommy Kelly in the title role. There is, perhaps, a little more slapstick in this handsome production than Mark Twain would have liked, but the cave sequence with evil-eyed Victor Jory as Injun Joe captures the chilling mood of the original. Photographed in Technicolor by James Wong Howe and designed by Lyle Wheeler and William Cameron Menzies, the film presents a highly romanticized view of life in the American South from the producer who is about to embark on his production of *Gone With the Wind*. Norman Taurog directed.

Tommy Kelly, here with May Robson, is Twain's irrepressible Tom Sawyer.

'Marseillaise': a modern-day revolution

A film born of a trade union initiative and partly financed by public mone

Paris, 9 February
The Parisian public are at last able to enjoy *la Marseillaise*, the great film about the French Revolution that Jean Renoir has promised for a year. The originality of the screenplay lies in the events of 10 August 1792, and not those of 1789. There must have been a tremendous temptation to deal with the leading figures of the epoch. Instead, Renoir has preferred to cast his eye over the ordinary people who made up the Marseilles Batallion, the group of volunteers who marched to Paris. Pierre Renoir plays Louis XVI and Lise Delamare is Marie-Antoinette, but the real heroes of the popular fresco are a peasant, a customs official, a mason and a house painter.

The collective production, finan by the French trade unions is " film of the union of the French tion against a minority of exploite the film of the rights of man and the citizen." In commemorating 150th anniversary of the Revo tion, Renoir is celebrating, at same time, the Popular Front. O should ask, however, if this idea arrived too late, as the enthusia for the Popular Front is not wha was in 1936. Originally, the idea w to finance the film by issuing pub subscriptions at two francs apie however, it fell short of the total quired. In addition, financial su port was lost when Léon Blu government fell last year. Nevert less, Renoir's film is a triumph.

Louis XVI (Pierre Renoir, center) with the Royal family in the Tuileries.

tte Davis sizzles as rebellious 'Jezebel'

›y Fonda (right) is an appropriately distinguished co-star for Bette Davis.

ywwod, 10 March
bitter contractual battles with ner Brothers behind her, Bette ıs has hit her stride with *Jezebel*, ›ted by William Wyler. She de-s a magnetic performance as ɔestuous Southern belle Julie ston, "half-angel, half-siren, all woman!" as the posters shriek, who goes a tad too far in attempting to arouse fiance Henry Fonda's jealousy. Davis' extraordinary conviction ensures that the red dress she wears to scandalize New Orleans society loses none of its impact in a black-and-white picture.

Luise Rainer pulls off an Oscar double

Tracy and Bartholomew in **Captains Courageous**; Rainer in **The Good Earth**.

Hollywood, 10 March
Luise Rainer was content to stay at home on the evening of the tenth annual Academy Awards ceremony held at the Biltmore in front of over 1,000 guests. After all, although she had been nominated for her role in *The Good Earth*, she had already won the Best Actress Oscar last year for *The Great Ziegfeld*. And on top of that, her rivals this time around were Greta Garbo (*Camille*), Barbara Stanwyck (*Stella Dallas*), Janet Gaynor (*A Star is Born*) and Irene Dunne (*The Awful Truth*). However, at 8:35 p.m., the names of the winners were given to the press, and Rainer was telephoned at home and told she had won. Quickly changing into an evening dress, she dashed downtown to receive her second statuette. She therefore becomes the first star to win two Oscars in succession. The evening's other big winners were Spencer Tracy (*Captains Courageous*), director Leo McCarey (*The Awful Truth*) and *The Life of Emile Zola*, voted the Best Picture.

onid Moguy has warm regard for his 'Prisoners without Bars'

s, 16 February
former news cameraman and sian emigré, Leonide Moguy, is emely content with the enthusi- which has greeted his second ıre, and second French film, ɔn *Without Bars*, at the Max ler cinema. This social drama takes place in a woman's prison, and relies heavily on its brilliant female cast. It includes Annie Ducaux of the Comédie Française; rising star Ginette Leclerc, who portrays a depraved prisoner, and also Corinne Luchaire, a young 17-year-old actress with a strange beauty who is the daughter of the journalist Jean Luchaire. Among this group of talented women, the male lead, Roger Duchesne, has some difficulty getting himself noticed. *Prison Without Bars* should enable the director, who came to France in 1929, to continue to make a successful career here.

inne Luchaire (left) and Ginette Leclerc (center) play the two principal roles in Moguy's **Prison Without Bars**.

Best Film: Henry O'Neill (right), Paul Muni in **The Life of Emile Zola**.

World of cinema demonstrated by Pagnol

Fernandel and Orane Demazis in ***The Schpountz****, from an original screenplay.*

Paris, 15 April
The curious title of Marcel Pagnol's new film playing at the Olympia, *The Schpountz*, was borrowed from Slavonic slang that means a simple or screwy person, and was originally suggested by Pagnol's photographer Willy Faktorovitch. In this case it refers to Fernandel as a cinema-mad grocer, who becomes the victim of a practical joke played on him by a cynical film crew touring his district of Provence. He arrives at the studio in Paris on their false promises, but reveals himself as a successful comedian. Apparently, this ironic, very amusing, self-mocking and acerbic satire was based on a true story. Fernandel in the title role is wonderfully "schpountzy" and is encircled by a rich gathering of characters, among them the Pagnol favorites Charpin and Orane Demazis, the Panisse and Fanny of his trilogy.

'Olympia' celebrates German athleticis

Goebbels (left) and Leni Riefenstahl at a press reception for the Olympic

Berlin, 20 April
For those who could not attend the Berlin Olympics, the event has been stunningly captured on film by Leni Riefenstahl, chronicler of the Nazi rallies at Nuremberg in *Triumph of the Will*. Her *Olympia*, backed by all the resources of the State, is a virtually delirious celebration of the postures of German physical vitality, divided into two parts: the Fest de Völker is an evocation of Ancient Greece utilizing a combinatio "strength through joy" and Isa Duncan; the Fest der Schönhei ebrates the games itself, emph ing athletic shape rather than details of competition. How this hymn to glistening muscle been marred by the demand of ideology that the minimum of a tion be paid to the highlight o Olympics, the triumphs of the b American sprinter Jesse Owens

Abel Gance looks to Latin America

Paris, 6 May
Abel Gance, director of *Napoleon*, has never concealed his preference for screenplays of vast historic frescoes. Unfortunately for him, there are not many producers capable of financing his unbounded ambitions. However, it seems as though this state of affairs may be on the verge of change. Following an announcement in the press today, Gance is preparing to make three large films for the Sud company. The trio will highlight three significant historical figures: Christopher Columbus, the Genoese who discovered America; Ignatius Loyola, the Spanish theologian who founded the Jesuit order, and finally the Cid Campeador, the eleventh-century Castilian knight, already the hero of a great many literary works, of which Corneille's play is the most famous. According to the director, the films will be a huge "Latin Gesture".

A dashing, daring Errol Flynn follows in Fairbanks' footsteps

Hollywood, 12 May
Already this looks like Errol Flynn's year. Warner Brothers' swashbuckling star has stepped into the shoes of Douglas Fairbanks in *The Adventures of Robin Hood*, a high, wide and handsome story of Sherwood Forest shot in glorious three-strip Technicolor and directed with immense panache by Michael Curtiz, who took over the director's c from William Keighley after film began. The legendary medieval law was originally supposed t played by James Cagney, but project was shelved after one o feisty star's disputes with the stu However, after Flynn's triump the 1935 *Captain Blood*, it was o matter of time before Jack Wa dusted off the property for his letic new star. Flynn is backed superb supporting cast, inclu Olivia De Havilland as a melti lovely Maid Marian, Alan Hale rumbustious Little John, and a line Basil Rathbone as the si villainous Sir Guy of Gisbou perishing at the sharp end of Fly sword after an epic battle to death. Erich Wolfgang Korngo stirring score spurs the action al and Carl Jules Weyl's magnifi sets provide the perfect backdro a $2 million extravaganza which boast of sufficient stunts for at l six adventure yarns.

Errol Flynn as the legendary Robin Hood in a film of superb color quality.

ean Gabin on the 'Quai des brumes'

ı Gabin and Michèle Morgan are threatened with destruction by the violent jealousy of Michel Simon-Zabel.

great filmmaking team surrounds the stars, left to right, Alexander uner, Jacques Prévert, Carné, Eugen Schüfftan and Simon Schiffrin.

Paris, 18 May

Marcel Carné's third feature, *Quai des brumes*, is now showing at the Marivaux. This story, adapted by Jacques Prévert from the novel by Pierre Mac Orlan, tells of an army deserter (Jean Gabin), who is driven to murder by evil forces and flees to Le Havre. It is there that he meets and falls in love with Nelly (Michèle Morgan), but their plan to escape together is foiled by her guardian (Michel Simon). In the end, he is shot and killed by a gangster (Pierre Brasseur) whom he had humiliated. When Gabin tells the 18-year-old Morgan, in trench coat and beret, that she has beautiful eyes, nobody in the audience could disagree. The doomed and poetic atmosphere of the film is created by muted lighting and the somber, fog-bound sets designed by Alexander Trauner. All the characters give the impression of living in suspense, in a world where corruption has triumphed. Perhaps it is this quality which has annoyed some of the critics. Both those on the left and right have reproached *Quai des brumes* for being totally pessimistic. In his column in the Communist newspaper *l'Humanité*, Georges Sadoul referred to "the politics of deadly nightshade running downstream". Jean Renoir felt antipathy toward the film, seeing it as "Fascist propaganda", and believing that the immoral characters were "fascist at heart", who would happily shake the hand of a dictator. Prévert, who considers himself violently anti-fascist, was incensed by his friend's remarks.

ımous set designer Lazare Meerson dies

ıdon, 30 June

celebrated art director Lazare erson has died at the age of 38. n in a part of Poland long domi- ed by Russia, he left Eastern Eu- e after the Bolshevik revolution, nding several years in Germany ore settling in France in 1924. m working for directors such as ques Feyder amd Marcel l'Her- , Meerson revolutionized the k of French films, moving away m the pervasive expressionism to ieve a "poetic realism" which dominated the French cinema in ent years. The huge studio-built scapes Meerson created for such vies as René Clair's *Sous les toits de Paris* have influenced art directors in Europe and Hollywood. His career ended on a high note, working for Alexander Korda on *The Citadel* in England.

Meerson (right) photographed with Georges Auric (left) and René Clair during the filming of ***le Million****.*

The 'Rage of Paris' is rage of Hollywood

Paris, 1 July

The young French film star Danielle Darrieux, known in France simply as "D.D.", has recently returned from Hollywood, which she set out to conquer last autumn. Accompanied by her husband, director Henri Decoin, she intends to resume her career in Europe. Her return coincides with the French release of her first American film, *The Rage of Paris*, a fast-moving comedy that co-stars Douglas Fairbanks Jr. and has been smoothly tailored by Universal to introduce the charming star to the American public. Director Henry Koster heads the same team who shot Deanna Durbin to stardom.

With Douglas Fairbanks in ***The Rage of Paris****, directed by Henry Koster.*

Film archives united

Paris, 15 July

This month sees the establishment of the Fédération internationale des archives du film (FIAF). The driving force behind this new organization has been Henri Langlois, a film archivist who founded the Cinémathèque Française along with George Franju in 1936. Langlois believes most passionately that the true key to safeguarding the heritage of the world cinema lies in establishing close links between national film libraries. Outside France there are film archives in Britain, the United States and Germany. FIAF's headquarters will be in Paris, but its first congress will be held in New York. ▷

Raimu makes a colorful and moving baker

With Ginette Leclerc in ***The Baker's Wife*** *based on a story by Jean Giono.*

Paris, 8 September
Filmgoers have been flocking to see Marcel Pagnol's new film, *la Femme du boulanger* (*The Baker's Wife*). Inspired by an episode in the Jean Giono novel *Jean le Bleu*, the film received its first public showings in Marseilles, in a theater rented by Pagnol and renamed Le César for the occasion. Thanks mainly to its star, Raimu, this acutely observed drama dealing with infidelity has been an instant popular and critical success. Having played the irascible César in Pagnol's Marseilles trilogy, Raimu is cast as a baker bewitched, bothered and bewildered when his young wife (Ginette Leclerc) leaves him for the handsome shepherd Charles Moulin.

'Alexander Nevsky' is an epic film-oper

БОЛЬШОЙ ЗВУКОВОЙ ИСТОРИЧЕСКИЙ ХУДОЖЕСТВЕННЫЙ ФИЛЬМ

Moscow, 1 December
After years of failure and fruitless projects, Sergei Eisenstein has finally succeeded in creating his first sound film. The action of *Alexander Nevsky* takes place in 1242, when Holy Russia was invaded by the armies of Teutonic knights. Prince Alexander Nevsky (Nikolai Cherkassov) forms a people's army to drive the brutal invaders from t land. Eisenstein, combining aest ic demands with a popular the has placed his ideas about mus counterpoint and sound at the vice of a patriotic epic. The re offers stirring images and a "s phonic structure" (with the drar ic music of Prokofiev), particul during the Battle of the Ice.

Rumors of film festival in Cannes

Paris, 19 September
It was while on the train headed to Venice, where they would attend the Mostra film festival, that Emile Vuillermoz and René Jean, two journalists, had the idea for an international film festival to be held in France. When put to Jean Zay, the Minister of Education and Arts, he was very interested. And in fact, the transformation of the Mostra of Venice into a highly politicized event has necessitated the creation of another film festival. That is why the Americans and the British have let it be known that they would encourage the setting up of an international festival in France. Already, many towns have put forward their candidature, notably Vichy, Biarritz and Algiers. Nevertheless, it looks as if the town of Cannes has won this race. Its sunny Mediterranean climate and its refined atmosphere would be an excellent shop-window for France and her cinema.

Classic Shaw play looks to be a 'bloody likely' hit in the USA

New York, 2 December
Audiences at Radio City Music Hall give thumbs up to Leslie Howard's production of the Bernard Shaw play *Pygmalion*. Howard is perfectly cast as the unworldly philologist, Professor Higgins with the delightful Wendy Hiller co-starring as the Cockney flower girl he turns into a lady. Bernard Shaw's original screenplay was adapted by Ian Dalrymple, Cecil Lewis and W.P. Lipscomb. Three men have had a hand in the direction of *Pygmalion*, Howard, Anthony Asquith and the volatile central European, Gabriel Pascal, whom Shaw has entrusted with the filming of his plays. Shaw had previously rejected various Hollywood suitors, including Sam Goldwyn, to whom he personally delivered the tart observation,"The trouble, Mr. Goldwyn, is that you are only interested in art, and I am only interested in money." Little love was lost between Howard and Pascal during filming, but none of this can be discerned in the final product. Indeed, after completing the film, Howard and Pascal announced their plan for Howard to play two real-life British heroes, Nelson and also Lawrence of Arabia. Howard's co-star Wendy Hiller has been on stage since age of 18, and in 1935 scored a sonal triumph in London and York in the Depression drama ti *Love on the Dole*.

Professor Higgins (Leslie Howard) picks up Eliza Doolittle (Wendy Hiller)

acDonald and Eddy romance in triple color

lywood, 26 December
;M has chosen *Sweethearts* for first three-tone Technicolor pic-. Starring Nelson Eddy and Jean- MacDonald, the film is based Victor Herbert's 1913 operetta not only introduces the singing birds in color, but also places m into a contemporary setting for the first time. MacDonald has bright red hair and green eyes, and is dressed throughout by Adrian in pale pink shades. In the title number, the fair-haired Eddy wears a bright uniform, and she is in a gold sequined gown. Of course, the stars' voices make the film as much of a joy to the ears as to the eyes.

MacDONALD
Nelson EDDY
Frank MORGAN
Ray BOLGER
Florence RICE
Mischa AUER
BING
GARDINER
Photographed in Technicolor
Sweethearts
Directed by W.S. VAN DYKE II
Produced by HUNT STROMBERG

Carné's brilliant cast shines in poetic drama

*Louis Jouvet and Arletty in the striking 'atmosphere' scene in **Hotel du Nord**.*

Paris, 16 December
"Atmosphere, atmosphere... I've had a gutsful of atmosphere!" so says Arletty in Marcel Carné's "atmospheric" new film *Hôtel du Nord*. Although this time Carné has used a screenplay penned by Henri Jeanson and Jean Aurenche instead of Jacques Prévert, the dialogue is as eloquent and incisive as in *Quai des brumes*. The writers have given the director ample opportunity to create a poetic bittersweet drama, and the splendid cast the chance to shine. Adapted from the populist novel by Eugène Dabit, the film focuses on the residents of a rundown hotel on the Canal Saint-Martin in Paris. They include a young couple (Jean-Pierre Aumont and Annabella) who make a suicide pact, and a cynical murderer on the run (Louis Jouvet) with his lively mistress (Arletty). In order to create the atmosphere required, Carné got his art director Alexander Trauner to construct the hotel and the Quai in the studio. The subtly-lit and perfectly designed sets are well photographed by Armand Thirard, except when a bus, passing a scaled-down hotel facade, reaches up to the first-floor windows.

ean Renoir returns to Emile Zola twelve years on from 'Nana'

ris, 21 December
n Renoir's new project entitled *e Human Beast* (*la Bête humaine*) ne about because Jean Gabin nted to work with Renoir again, d because of the star's love of omotives. Like *Nana*, which Ren- directed for his wife Catherine Hessling 12 years ago, *The Human Beast* originates from Emile Zola's Rougon-Macquart series of novels, though the style of the film is vastly different. While *Nana* was close to German Expressionism, the recent film is full of the fatalistic mood of French realism. Renoir's beautifully crafted screenplay that has been updated to contemporary France, does remain faithful to the 1890 novel and provides opportunities for the powerful, brooding presence of Gabin and the enchanting Simone Simon, and allows Gabin to actually drive a train from Paris to Le Havre.

n Gabin with his iron friend.

Jean GABIN
Simone SIMON
DANS UN FILM DE
JEAN RENOIR
LA BÊTE HUMAINE
D'APRÈS LE CHEF-D'ŒUVRE
d'EMILE ZOLA
avec LEDOUX
et CARETTE

Prix Louis Delluc

Paris, 23 December
A bit in advance of the customary award date, the jury for the Prix Louis Delluc, currently in its third year, has named Marcel Carné's *Quai des brumes* as the winner of its award. Carné's film was chosen from a prestigious selection of pictures that include: *les Disparus de Saint-Agil*, *l'Etrange Monsieur Victor*, *Entrée des artistes*, *Hôtel du Nord* and *la Bête humaine*. Meanwhile, *Alerte en Mediterranée* from director Leo Joannon has won the Grand French prize.

Margaret Lockwood, Paul Lukas, Philip Leaver, Michael Redgrave and Mary Clare in Hitchcock's splendid **The Lady Vanishes**.

Charles Boyer and Hedy Lamarr in **Algiers**, based on the classic **Pépé-le-Moko**.

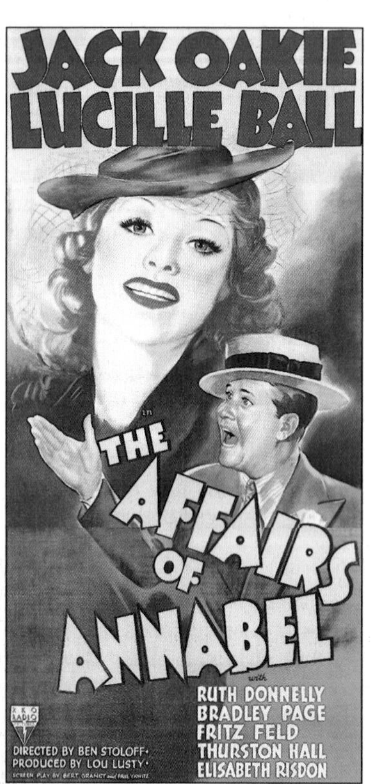
JACK OAKIE
LUCILLE BALL
in
THE AFFAIRS OF ANNABEL
with
RUTH DONNELLY
BRADLEY PAGE
FRITZ FELD
THURSTON HALL
ELISABETH RISDON
DIRECTED BY BEN STOLOFF
PRODUCED BY LOU LUSTY

This wonderfully well-acted screwball comedy was actually an affectionate satire on Hollywood.

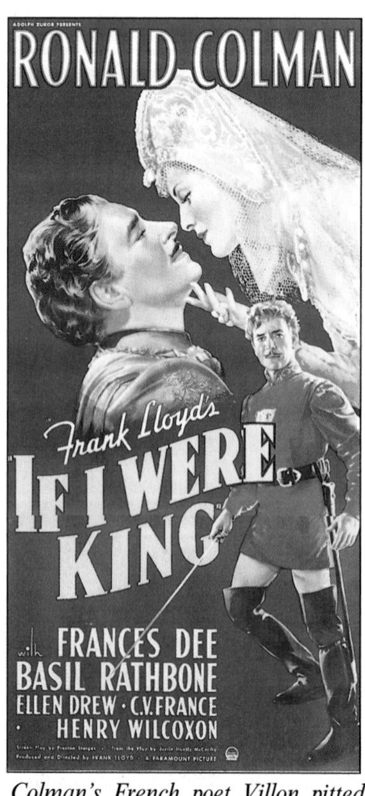
RONALD COLMAN
Frank Lloyd's
IF I WERE KING
with FRANCES DEE
BASIL RATHBONE
ELLEN DREW · C.V. FRANCE
HENRY WILCOXON

Colman's French poet Villon pitted his wits against, and was outacted by, Rathbone's King Louis XI.

DARRYL F. ZANUCK'S Production of
IN OLD CHICAGO
The Great American Motion Picture!
with Tyrone POWER Alice FAYE Don AMECH
Alice BRADY Andy DEVINE Brian DONLE
Phyllis BROOKS Tom BROWN Sidney BLACKM
Berton CHURCHILL June STOREY Paul HU
DIRECTED BY HENRY KING
ASSOCIATE PRODUCER ~ Kenneth Macgowan
A 20th Century Fox Picture

This popular period melodrama was a $2 million **San Francisco** lookalike.

Alexander Nevsky, directed by Eisenstein, used music instead of natural sou

ECIL B.
MILLE
FREDRIC
MARCH
UCCANEER
with FRANCISKA GAAL and
TAMIROFF · MARGOT GRAHAME · WALTER BRENNAN
ITH ANTHONY QUINN · BEULAH BONDI · ROBERT BARRAT
ASS DUMBRILLE · DIRECTED BY CECIL B. DeMILLE
A PARAMOUNT PICTURE

pite critical indifference, strong lic enthusiasm greeted this swash-kling movie.

Tyrone Power, with Norma Shearer as ***Marie Antoinette****, in the lavish film of that name.*

LPH ZUKOR PRESENTS
MAE WEST
"Every Day's a Holiday"
with
EDMUND LOWE
CHARLES BUTTERWORTH
CHARLES WINNINGER
WALTER CATLETT
LLOYD NOLAN
HERMAN BING CHESTER CONKLIN and LOUIS ARMSTRONG
Screen Play by Mae West An EMANUEL COHEN Production Directed by A. EDWARD SUTHERLAND A Paramount Picture

e doubled as both a blonde and a brunette, and wore seventeen gowns!

Clark GABLE
Myrna LOY
Spencer TRACY
IN VICTOR FLEMING'S
Production of
TEST PILOT
WITH Lionel BARRYMORE
SCREEN PLAY BY VINCENT LAWRENCE AND
WALDEMAR YOUNG—ORIGINAL STORY BY FRANK WEAD
Directed by VICTOR FLEMING
PRODUCED BY LOUIS D. LIGHTON
A Metro-Goldwyn-Mayer PICTURE

Aerobatics and romance made this one of the year's top ten moneymakers.

David Niven, Claudette Colbert, Tommy Ricketts in ***Bluebeard's Eighth Wife****.*

TARZAN'S
REVENGE
STARRING Glenn
MORRIS
Eleanor
HOLM
BARBIER · GORDON
HOPPER
A
PRINCIPAL
PRODUCTION
Released by

Morris, a real-life Olympic medalist.

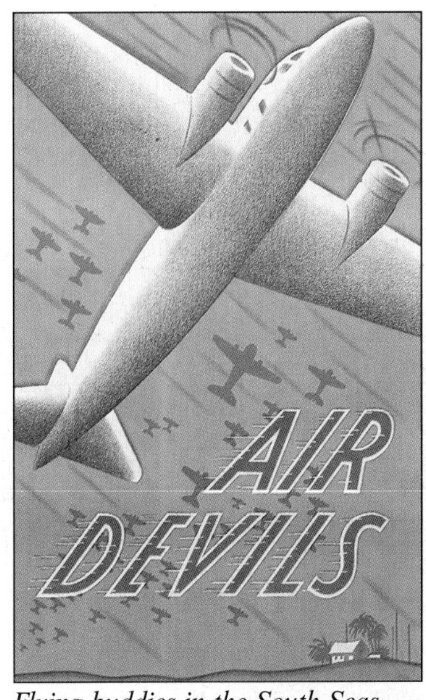
AIR
DEVILS

Flying buddies in the South Seas.

1939

1938 Academy Awards, Biltmore Hotel, 23 Feb.

Best Film:	*You Can't Take It With You* (dir: Frank Capra)
Best Director:	Frank Capra
Best Actor:	Spencer Tracy *(Boys Town)*
Best Actress:	Bette Davis *(Jezebel)*
Best Supp. Actor:	Walter Brennan *(Kentucky)*
Best Supp. Actress:	Fay Bainter *(Jezebel)*

Paris, 25 January
First screening of *Trois de Saint-Cyr*, directed by Jean-Paul Paulin. Love becomes inextricably tangled up with heroism in Paulin's version of the archetypal colonial-cum-military adventure so greatly appreciated by the French public.

Moscow, 2 February
Release of *The Vyborg Side*, by Grigori Kozintsev and Leonid Trauberg, the last part of the trilogy which started in 1935 with *The Youth of Maxim*.

Billancourt, 6 February
Marcel Carné has started shooting the studio footage for *le Jour se lève* (*Daybreak*). Carné is back working in collaboration with Jacques Prévert on this film.

Madrid, 15 February
The producer G. Renault-Decker has obtained permission from Franco's government to film *Christopher Columbus* in Granada. Abel Gance will be directing the film in several languages.

Villars-de-Lans, 27 February
Jacques Feyder is on location in the Vercors for the film *la Loi du nord*. The action is actually supposed to take place in the far North of Canada in the world of the trappers.

Moscow, 7 March
Release of the second part of *Peter the Great*, by Vladimir Petrov, and with Nikolas Simonov and Nikolai Cherkassov.

Warsaw, 8 March
Opening of *Trois valses* at the Napoléon, a cinema reserved exclusively for French productions. The film was made by the German Ludwig Berger now working in Paris.

Los Angeles, 17 March
Release of *Love Affair*, by Leo McCarey, starring Charles Boyer, Irene Dunne and Maria Ouspenskaya.

Epinay, 22 March
Claude Autant-Lara and Maurice Lehmann have started shooting *Fric-frac* in the Eclair studios. Arletty and Michel Simon are once again playing the roles that made them famous in the theater.

Paris, 21 April
Premiere of Marcel L'Herbier's *Entente cordiale* at the Marivaux. The film is based on André Maurois' book *Edward VII and His Time*. Gaby Morlay interprets the role of Queen Victoria.

New York, 11 May
Release of *Only Angels Have Wings*, directed by Howard Hawks, with Jean Arthur, Cary Grant, Richard Barthelmess and Rita Hayworth heading the cast.

Hollywood, 19 May
The cameras had scarcely started turning for *Ninotchka*, when Greta Garbo, who usually has a very good relationship with the director Ernst Lubitsch, suddenly decided he was speaking too loudly. She snapped at him, in German, "Could you be so kind as to speak more softly when you address me." Lubitsch was apparently quite taken aback.

Soviet Union, 1 June
Sergei Eisenstein and his cameraman Edouard Tissé have just started shooting the short documentary *The Grand Canal of Fergana*.

Washington, 9 June
German actress, Marlene Dietrich, who came to work for Paramount in 1930, has now officially become an American citizen.

Paris, 20 June
A special evening was held at the university in honor of Charlie Chaplin on his 50th birthday. It was organized by Laure Albin-Guillot from the National Cinema Archives and Henri Langlois from the French Cinematèque.

Brussels, 31 July
The History of the Cinematic Art, written by Carl Vincent, has been published by Trident. The book is one of the first attempts at a general history of the cinema.

Cannes, 1 August
Preparations for the International Film Festival are actively underway. The supplementary funding has been voted by the municipal council to finish equipping the casino. The opening is planned for 1 September.

Los Angeles, 14 August
Janet Gaynor, who was the winner of the first-ever Academy Award for Best Actress in 1929, today married top designer Adrian.

Paris, 24 August
The Paramount cinema has released *Louise*, by Abel Gance, based on the opera by Charpentier, with the American soprano Grace Moore, tenor Georges Thill, André Pernet and Robert Le Vigan in the cast.

Paris, 28 August
With the threat of war approaching, a censorship law has been passed to control all printed matter, written work, radio transmissions and film projections. This law is aimed at titles such as *le Déserteur*.

New York, 1 September
Release of *The Women*, by George Cukor. This adaptation of Claire Booth Luce's hit play stars Norma Shearer, Joan Crawford, Rosalind Russell, Joan Fontaine and Paulette Goddard plus a host of other actresses from the MGM stable.

Washington, 20 October
Frank Capra's newly released political satire, starring James Stewart, *Mr. Smith Goes to Washington* has been given a hostile reception by certain politicians.

New York, 21 December
The film critic for the *Daily Worker* has been dismissed because editors thought he wasn't harsh enough in his review of *Gone With the Wind*. The paper considers the film to be an apology for slavery.

Paris, 29 December
The Cinematographic Service for the army is to hold recreational film sessions for soldiers on campaign.

Hollywood, 31 December
At year's end, the top three office grossers in America are *B in Arms*, Ford's *Drums Along Mohawk* and *Goodbye, Mr. Ch*

England, 31 December
This year's production is down t films compared to 228 in 1937.

BIRTHS

Brazil, 14 February
Glauber Rocha

New York, 23 February
Peter Fonda

Oklahoma, 10 March
Chuck Norris

New York, 26 March
James Caan

Germany, 31 March
Volker Schlöndorff

Detroit, 7 April
Francis Ford Coppola

Tunis, 15 April
Claudia Cardinale

London, 19 May
James Fox

London, 23 July
Terence Stamp

New York, 30 July
Peter Bogdanovich

France, 9 August
Bulle Ogier

Detroit, 1 September
Lily Tomlin

Boston, 28 October
Jane Alexander

Tokyo, 16 December
Liv Ullman

DEATHS

New York, 28 October
Alice Brady

After many problems, including search for Scarlett', and a chang director (Victor Fleming repla George Cukor), ***Gone With the W*** *is a monumental success.*

GONE WITH
THE WIND

André Malraux returns from Spain

Paris, January
Anti-fascist writer André Malraux has just returned from Spain. At the start of the Spanish Civil War, three years ago, he placed himself at the service of the Republican government. He has brought back with him the footage of a film made in the last few months that is entitled *Sierra de Teruel*. The storyline is drawn from a chapter in Malraux's novel called *l'Espoir*, and unfolds during the bitter fighting around the Aragonese town of Teruel. Shooting of the film, which was undertaken in extremely difficult conditions, was abandoned after the fall of Barcelona to the Nationalists. It was then that Malraux decided to return to France.

*A scene from **Sierra de Teruel**.*

The Hollywood Western comes of age with Ford's 'Stagecoach'

...THE STRANGEST ADVENTURE in FRONTIER HISTORY!
A WILD RIDE PACKED WITH THRILLS!
STAGECOACH
Claire TREVOR with John WAYNE
GEO. BANCROFT
ANDY DEVINE
JOHN CARRADINE
DONALD MEEK

*John Wayne, with George Bancroft and Louise Platt, in a typical scene from Ford's beautifully composed **Stagecoa***

Hollywood, 2 March
The fortunes of the big-budget Western, at a low ebb for several years, have been boosted by John Ford's impressive and absorbing new film *Stagecoach*, produced for United Artists by Walter Wanger. Adapted from an Ernest Haycox story, *Stagecoach* stars John Wayne as the outlawed Ringo Kid, who joins a mixed bunch of passengers for an eventful trip West. The picture's stunning exteriors, shot on location in Utah's Monument Valley, with its vast skies and its weathered sandstone bluffs, lends a new scenic grandeur to the Western and provides a spectacular backdrop to a thrilling sequence in which the stagecoach careers across salt flats pursued by an Indian war party. Sharing screen honors v Wayne, who has recently been c signed to humdrum B-Westerns, Claire Trevor as a golden-hear whore, Thomas Mitchell playin whisky-sodden sawbones, John C radine as a doomed gambler Andy Devine as the fat, cowa stagecoach driver, squawking v panic as the Indians close in.

Frank Capra, Bette Davis and Spencer Tracy share 1938 Oscars

Hollywood, 23 February
The Academy Award ceremony is entering its second decade, and this year, the Academy's 12,000 members have voted Bette Davis Best Actress for her performance in *Jezebel*. Spencer Tracy scooped the Best Actor prize for his role as the crusading Father Flanagan in *Boys Town*. Frank Capra's *You Can't Take it With You* won two Awards, Best Picture and the Best Director prize for Capra. The Best Supporting Actor and Actress awards went, respectively, to Walter Brennan for his work in *Kentucky* and to Fay Bainter for her sterling performance as Aunt Belle in *Jezebel*.

*Frank Capra (center) with James Stewart and Jean Arthur, two of the stars of **You Can't Take It With You**.*

*Spencer Tracy with the young and talented Mickey Rooney in **Boys Town**.*

Jean Zay's view of cinema's future

Paris, 17 March
Replying to the ever-increasing mands of professionals who w with the cinema, the Daladier g ernment has recently completed drafting of a law concerning the organization of the cinematograp industry. Signed by President Al Lebrun and prepared under the thority of Jean Zay, the Minister Public Education, the text is be presented today to the Chamber Deputies. It is the most import effort to date by the governmen constitute a legal statute pertain to the French film. Relatively c prepehsive in scope, the text of law deals with and defines cens ship, the ownership of films, conditions of work in the cinema graph industry, the importation distribution of foreign films, ad tising, financial arrangements, c tracts and also the activities of c involved in the field.

'Vuthering Heights' comes to the screen

"I am Heathcliff
I love a woman who belongs to another by law . . . My love was fierce . . . My hate is burning . . . I will have vengeance!"
SAMUEL GOLDWYN presents
WUTHERING HEIGHTS
A Story of Vengeful, Thwarted Love
co-starring MERLE OBERON · LAURENCE OLIVIER · DAVID NIVEN
with Flora Robson · Donald Crisp · Geraldine Fitzgerald · Released thru United Artists · Directed by WILLIAM WYLER
Screenplay by Ben Hecht and Charles MacArthur

w York, 13 April
n Goldwyn's production of Emi- Bronte's *Wuthering Heights* has tten off to a slow start at the box ice. Goldwyn made sure that the n had a turbulent time reaching screen, suggesting innumerable w titles, including *Bring Me the orld* and *The Wild Heart*, all the ile referring to Bronte's original as "Withering Heights"! He also insisted on adding an up-beat ending. Two Britons, Laurence Olivier and Merle Oberon, star as Bronte's pair of doomed lovers Cathy and Heathcliffe. Director William Wyler has coaxed a superb performance from Olivier, previously unhappy in Hollywood and over-theatrical in his approach to filming.

Warners first into the propaganda field

Francis Lederer (left) and Edward G. Robinson in ***Confessions of a Nazi Spy****.*

Hollywood, 6 May
With the war clouds gathering in Europe, Warner Brothers have taken the bold step of producing a film with an explicitly anti-Nazi message. *Confessions of a Nazi Spy*, starring Edward G. Robinson, is based on the real-life exploits of former FBI agent Leon G. Turrou, who infiltrated a German spy network operating in America. During filming, Robinson, Jack Warner and many others connected with the picture received threatening letters. The premiere was attended by almost as many G-men as moviegoers. Warners have good reason to loathe the Nazis. They closed their Berlin office after the studio's local representative was murdered by fascist thugs.

ıe professionals ıoose favorites

ris, 19 April
poll on the commercial value of ovie stars, organized by theater anagers, has placed Jean Gabin at top of the list. He is followed by rnandel, Louis Jouvet, Raimu, erre Fresnay, Charles Boyer, Sa- a Guitry and lastly Erich von Stro- im. For the actresses, Viviane Ro- nce heads the list. Coming on her els is Danielle Darrieux, followed Yvonne Printemps, Michèle Mor- n, Corinne Luchaire, Annabella, vira Popesco and Greta Garbo. eanwhile, the Film Academy has 'arded the Méliès prize to Jean noir's *The Human Beast* (*la Bête maine*) and to Marcel Carné's *ai des brumes*. Carné shares the w Jean Vigo prize with the direc- r Christian-Jaque (*les Disparus de int-Agil*), for which Michel Simon is given the Pierre Batcheff prize. letty was presented with the Janie arèze prize for *Hôtel du Nord*.

Marriages between stars liven up Hollywood gossip columns

Los Angeles, 23 April
Following hard on the heels of long-time companions Clark Gable and Carole Lombard, who tied the knot in the tiny town of Kingman, Arizona on 29 March, Tyrone Power has just married the French actress Annabella. Unlike Gable and Lombard, for three years a fixture on the Hollywood scene, Power and Annabella have known each other only a few months. They met in the summer of 1938 during the filming of *Suez*, in which Power played Ferdinand de Lesseps, the French engineer who built the canal of the title. At 34 the divorced Annabella is nine years older than Power.

Annabella and Tyrone Power in Allan Dwan's ***Suez*** *(1938).*

Carole Lombard and Clark Gable at their wedding reception given by MGM.

Marcel Carné fashions an intriguing drama from a workaday idea

Gabin and Arletty in ***le Jour se lève (Daybreak)****, a tragedy played out in everyday surroundings designed by Trauner.*

Paris, 9 June
Marcel Carné's new film, *Daybreak* (*le Jour se lève*), is a rather commonplace story of tragic love, but its treatment has drawn a lot of attention. The scenario came about after Carné received a visit from his neighbor Jacques Viot. Viot suggested the plot and wrote the synopsis, which Jacques Prévert then adapted for the screen. It tells of a worker (Jean Gabin) who gets involved with the mistress (Arletty) of a shady showman (Jules Berry), and kills him in a jealous confrontation over an innocent flower seller (Jacqueline Laurent). He then barricades himself in his small room during the night as the police and crowds wait below. Most of the film is told by flashing back and forth between the past and the present. Memorable atmospheric use is made of the dark tenement set designed by Alexander Trauner, and Gabin's tragic stature is almost matched by the hypnotically suave villainy of Berry.

A new film from René Clair

Paris, 17 July
René Clair's first French film si
le Dernier milliardaire in 1934 is
new *Air pur*. The director came b
to France last November and ad
ted that he was rather disappoin
by his experience in England, wh
he made *Break the News* starr
Maurice Chevalier and Jack Buch
an. Clair worked hard over the w
ter creating the scenario of *Air p*
searching for new inspiration an
new style. This film centers aroun
young welfare officer who has de
cated his life to sending children
the poor people of Paris to the co
tryside in order to improve th
health. It is a departure for the
rector of *Sous les toits de Paris*
that most of the film takes place
natural surroundings in the Ma
Central, the mountainous region
central France. Also, the fact t
the performers in the film are re
tively unknown, or are playing the
selves, including 15 children, a
that he uses a hand-held camera
the first time, points to Clair's n
interest in realism.

Cool reception for 'The Rules of the Game'

Paris, 22 July
After Jean Renoir's new film, *The Rules of the Game*, was loudly booed at its gala showing at the Colisée two weeks ago, it has been withdrawn. With a budget of 2.5 million francs, much of it from the director's own pocket, the film was eagerly awaited. Even if the critics were not unanimous, the public seems to be totally against it, despite Renoir having reduced the film by a sizable 23 minutes. Because of the poor reception of this bitter social satire, Renoir has even thought about quitting the cinema. In the meantime, however, he has departed for Italy, where he is to make *La Tosca*.

Director Jean Renoir appears in his new film. Here, with Nora Grégor.

'Beau Geste' looks set for socko box-offi

Hollywood, 24 July
One of Paramount Pictures' greatest box-office successes in the silent era was *Beau geste*, filmed in 1926 and starring Ronald Colman in the title role. Now the same studio looks as though it will even surpass that hit of yesteryear with its spectacular remake of the P.C. Wren colonial adventure story, directed by William Wellman. It closely follows the earlier picture's flashback format, with its memorable opening scene of a desert fort manned by corpses. The three well-born English Geste brothers, who join the Foreign Legion to escape disgrace, are played by Gary Cooper, Ray Milland and Robert Preston. Although they seem unlikely siblings, and even more unlikely Englishmen, these three stars have made the trio of heroes believable and spirited. Brian Donlevy makes a splendidly sadistic sergeant. Only one of the brothers (Cooper) survives the sergeant, an abortive mutiny and an attack by Arab tribesmen. After again demonstrating his comic talents in his last two films, Ernst
Lubitsch's *Bluebeard's Eighth W*
and H.C. Potter's *The Cowboy a*
the Lady, it is good to finally s
Gary Cooper back in a full-blood
adventure yarn again. *Beau ge*
was filmed on location in Butterc
Valley, west of Yuma in Arizona
landscape that stands in perfec
for the Arabian desert.

Gary Cooper and Ray Milland.

Iagic trip with Judy down the yellow brick road

llywood, 17 August
e gala premiere of *The Wizard of* will take place tonight at Grau-n's Chinese Theater. MGM has ated a magical Technicolor musi- fantasy, based on the famous ildren's story by L. Frank Baum. is also a wonderful vehicle for a ght new star, Judy Garland. But s most expensive production in studio's history was not made thout many difficulties. Producer ervyn LeRoy started with Richard orpe directing, but he stopped ooting after a few weeks, scrap-g all the footage. It restarted un- George Cukor, who stayed three ys. Victor Fleming then took over h a new script. King Vidor com-ted the project, when Fleming ved on to direct *Gone With the ind*. In addition, there were sever- problems before the right cast was osen. MGM initially tried to get irley Temple to play Dorothy, but h Century-Fox would not loan r out. Then Universal refused to rt with Deanna Durbin for one ture. Hence Judy Garland, who gan her work in a fancy blonde wig, wearing heavy cherubic make-up. It was Cukor, during his brief stint on the picture, who insisted Judy look like a real Kansas farm girl. Buddy Ebsen was originally cast as the Tin Woodman, but the aluminium dust he was covered in coated his lungs, and he had to be hospitalized. His replacement, Jack Haley, had to wear a painful costume, and was in agony throughout. Then, too, the crowd of Munchkins, played by midgets and Lilliputians, were up to all sorts of tricks, drinking and gambling on the set.

The story follows the dream adventures of Dorothy who, after being knocked unconscious during a tornado, makes her way, with her dog Toto and some bizarre companions she meets on the Yellow Brick Road, to the Emerald City to find the Wizard of Oz. The song, *Over the Rainbow*, that Judy sings at the beginning, was supposed to be cut, but producer Arthur Freed argued vehemently for it to remain. We should be grateful, because it is a charming melody, touchingly delivered. A treat for all ages.

Scarecrow (Ray Bolger), Tin Man (Jack Haley) and Dorothy (Judy Garland).

KO studios engage n 'Infant Prodigy'

llywood, 21 August
the conclusion of a long and de-led series of negotiations, George haefer, the president of RKO, has nounced that he has now signed son Welles to a film contract. is talented young man, who has y little prior film experience, has en offered the most remarkable ms to work for RKO as a produc- director, actor and scriptwriter film projects of his own choos-g. Although this may appear quite ceptional, Welles has already, in t, proved the range of his abilities rough his previous work in the ater and on the radio. He has, for ample, shown an impressive grasp the relatively new medium of ra-, and an ability to use sound and alogue creatively as demonstrated erhaps all too well – in his famous oadcast version of H.G. Wells' *ar of the Worlds* which turned this elles into a celebrity overnight, stly increased his radio audience d has led to his RKO contract.

Formidable lineup of MGM's distaff side

New York, 1 September
MGM have assembled an all-star female cast for *The Women*, directed by George Cukor. In this adaptation of Clare Boothe's successful stage celebration of bitchery, Joan Crawford, as hairdresser Crystal, leaves rivals Norma Shearer (the tear-stained socialite) and Rosalind Russell out in the cold.

Norma Shearer (second right) heads the lineup of MGM ladies in ***The Women.***

The war puts an end to illusions

Paris, 3 September
The currently general mobilization of all troops and reserves, and the sudden declaration of war by the French government, has taken by surprise many of France's leading producers and directors. About 20 feature films are currently in mid-production and will be adversely affected. Director Max Ophüls, for example, was just in the process of shooting the exteriors for his newest film, *From Mayerling to Sarajevo*, when he lost the actor, Gilbert Gil, who was cast to play the assassin, Prinzip. In the meanwhile, the director himself has been called up to rejoin his army unit. Others affected include Jean Grémillon, currently filming *Remorques*, Marcel Pagnol, who is in the midst of *la Fille du puisatier*, Marc Allégret with his *le Corsaire* and Christian-Jaque with *Tourelle 3*. Even the celebrated René Clair, back filming in France for the first time in five years, has not been spared these circumstances. ▷

Rathbone brings Sherlock Holmes to life

Basil Rathbone, the perfect Holmes.

London, 11 September
Sir Arthur Conan Doyle's great creation, Sherlock Holmes, has a cinema history stretching back to 1903. Now Holmes returns to the screen in 20th Century-Fox's handsome new version of *The Hound of the Baskervilles*. Basil Rathbone, whose gimlet profile usually dispenses deadly villainy in Warner Brothers' costumers, is cast as the master detective and Nigel Bruce plays the bluff Dr. Watson, courageous to a fault but usually about three steps behind the fast-moving plot. Two more Britons head the cast list: handsome Richard Greene plays Sir Henry Baskerville, heir to a dangerous inheritance; and Lionel Atwill, heavily bearded and bespectacled in a sinister red herring role. The film is briskly paced by director Sidney Lanfield, a specialist in comedies rather than period thrillers, and the fog machine works overtime to disguise the fact that much of the outdoor action takes place on a single master set. When the production was announced, fans were alarmed by Lanfield's stated aim to "pep up the story" and make Holmes more "up to date". In fact, *The Hound of the Baskervilles* is a respectful version of the original. And, in Rathbone, Fox has discovered such an incisive Holmes that a sequel is inevitable.

Selznick unveils his new Swedish find

With Leslie Howard in the remake of her Swedish success, ***Intermezzo****.*

Hollywood, 5 October
After protracted negotiations with David O. Selznick, the Swedish actress Ingrid Bergman left her doctor husband and baby daughter at home in Stockholm, and arrived in New York aboard the *Queen Mary* on 6 May. At Selznick's behest, little fanfare attended her coming, but her first American film opens toda Entitled *Intermezzo: A Love Stor* co-starring Leslie Howard and c rected by Gregory Ratoff, it is t emotional tale of a concert violin who falls in love with a young pia teacher and runs away with her – remake of the film that made Mi Bergman a star in her native land

'Comrade' Garbo laughs for Lubitsch

Hollywood, 3 November
The posters for MGM's *Ninotchka* bear the slogan "Garbo Laughs!" Seeking to restore Garbo's sagging popularity, the studio has cast her in a romantic comedy which guys her solemn image. The ploy has worked. Garbo plays a high-minded Soviet official charmingly won over to Western ways by debonair Melvyn Douglas. It's by no means the first time that Garbo has laughed on screen, but MGM's accountants are laughing all the way to the bank.

Any moment now, Melvyn Douglas will have Garbo laughing at his silly jokes!

Deanna Durbin has grown up at last...

Hollywood, 10 November
Universal's lovely, youthful singing star and most bankable asset, Deanna Durbin, has slowly but surely blossomed into young womanhood in *First Love*, in which she receives her first screen kiss. The lucky man is Robert Stack, making his screen debut, and that kiss has created headlines throughout the country. The major box-office star is coming up to her eighteenth birthday, and Universal Pictures decided that Deanna should be allowed to grow up. *First Love* is a Cinderella story in which she plays an orphan adopted by a rich, uncaring family. Snubbed by relatives, and prevented from going to the gala ball, she gets to meet her Prince Charming, with the help of servants. It is now three years since Durbin started on her career in *Three Smart Girls*. She has continued to wow audiences with her bell-like voice and Pollyanna personality. Whether their loyalty will follow her into adulthood remains to be seen.

Deanna Durbin and Robert Stack.

avish treatment given to 'Gone With the Wind'

rlett O'Hara (Vivien Leigh) in the gardens of her beloved mansion, Tara.

The spectacular burning of Atlanta was the first scene of the film to be shot.

th Rhett Butler (Clark Gable).

Atlanta, 14 December
The most eagerly-awaited film of the year, *Gone With the Wind* has just been given its world premiere in the city where a great deal of the story unfolds. This was the culmination of the most intensely publicized production ever. It was introduced by the producer David O. Selznick, in the presence of the principal cast members and the author Margaret Mitchell who wrote the bestseller from which this super-production was adapted. The credited director, Victor Fleming, who considered himself neglected, was absent. It is true that Selznick appears to be the film's real creator. Since June 1936, when he bought the rights to the novel for $50,000, about 15 screenwriters and four directors have been employed on it at various times. The original scenario, written by Sidney Howard who, sadly, died last June, was reworked by Ben Hecht and Scott Fitzgerald, among others, each of them working on a different colored script.

Production began in January and ended on 1 July. The first director, George Cukor, was fired scarcely two weeks into shooting after several disagreements with Clark Gable, the male lead. Fleming worked on the film until May when he left ill and exhausted, handing on the baton to Sam Wood who completed it. As for the stars, the choice of Gable as Rhett Butler was automatic, due to a poll held among the public. Casting Scarlett O'Hara proved far more problematic. Some of the biggest female stars who wanted the role had screen tests: Bette Davis, Katharine Hepburn, Paulette Goddard, Susan Hayward and Loretta Young, among dozens of others, as well as 1,400 unknowns. Selznick was still undecided until his brother Myron introduced him to Vivien Leigh, an English actress who had had a brilliant stage career prior to appearing in a number of British films before the war. Selznick immediately fell under her charm, and courageously decided to cast her in the much sought-after role. For the sequence depicting the burning of Atlanta, Selznick ordered more than 30 acres of the old Pathé backlot of tinderbox sets to be put to the torch. Every Technicolor camera in Hollywood, all seven of them, were used to record the conflagration from different angles. All in all, *Gone With the Wind*, which runs three hours and 42 minutes plus an intermission, and cost over $4 million, is a magnificent achievement. What lifts the film into the highest category is not only its spectacular depiction of the American Civil War, but also its range of strongly drawn characters, seen especially in the central relationship between Rhett and Scarlett – a monument to devouring passion.

Leslie Howard, Olivia De Havilland. ▷

ashbuckler Doug lays down his sword

nta Monica, 13 December
e legendary screen star Douglas rbanks died yesterday at his Calinia home at the age of 56. After king his last film, the 1934 *The vate Life of Don Juan*, Fairbanks tanced himself from the movies. s burial was an intimate ceremony ended by members of the family l a few faithful friends. Among m were Charles Chaplin, who sed his studio to attend, Doug's e and son, Douglas Fairbanks born in 1909 during Fairbanks' rriage to Ann Beth Sully. Fairnks was born Douglas Ullman in nver, Colorado on 23 May 1883. en he was signed by the Triangle rporation in 1915 he was already a successful juvenile lead on Broadway. Fairbanks quickly established himself in a series of fast-paced satirical comedies, artfully scripted by Anita Loos, which crystallized the impulses and daydreams of American moviegoers. By 1917 he had his own production company, and two years later joined Chaplin, Griffith and Mary Pickford to form United Artists. His marriage to Pickford followed, along with a string of classic roles, all of them infused with Doug's athletic grace and abundant good humor: Zorro, Robin Hood, the Black Pirate and the Thief of Bagdad. No one exemplified better than Doug the maxim that motion pictures are all about movement.

Edgar Wallace's
GREATEST THRILLER
The PHANTOM STRIKES
SONNIE HALE · WILFRID LAWSON
LOUISE HENRY
A MONOGRAM RELEASE

Vengeful killer, gripping suspense.

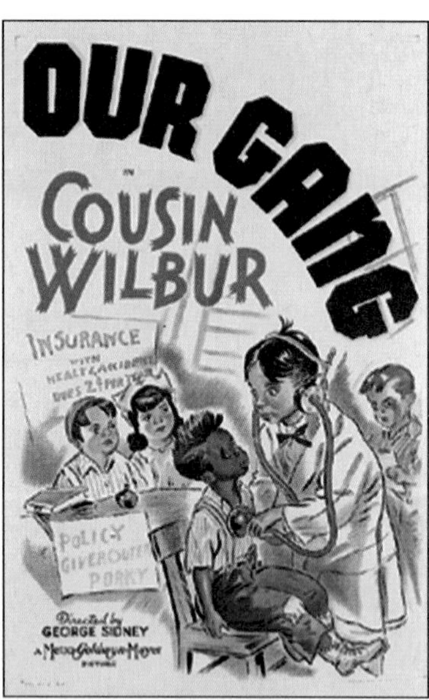
OUR GANG
in
COUSIN WILBUR
Directed by GEORGE SIDNEY

MGM's much-loved gang in another mischievous caper.

GULLIVER'S TRAVELS
in TECHNICOLOR
Produced by
MAX FLEISCHER
Based on Jonathan Swift's Immortal Tale
Directed by
DAVE FLEISCHER
A PARAMOUNT PICTURE

Dave and Max Fleischer created their first full-length challenge to Disney.

*l to r: Michel Simon, Arletty and Fernandel in Autant-Lara's **Fric-Frac**.*

*Fred Astaire (2nd left), Ginger Rogers in **The Story of Vernon and Irene Castle**.*

Robert DONAT
"The Best Picture of Any Year"
Goodbye Mr. Chips
with Greer GARSON
A SAM WOOD Production
A Metro-Goldwyn-Mayer PICTURE

MGM's British unit scored with this poignant film adaptation of James Hilton's bestseller.

SAMUEL GOLDWYN
RAFFLES
DAVID NIVEN · OLIVIA de HAVILLAN
Directed by SAM WOOD

A fourth, and less successful, outi for the charming and gentlema English society thief.

photographed in TECHNICOLOR
The Epic Story of the most Colourful Outlaw who ever lived
JESSE JAMES
TYRONE POWER · HENRY FONDA
NANCY KELLY · RANDOLPH SCOTT
HENRY HULL · SLIM SUMMERVILLE · J. EDWARD BROMBERG · BRIAN DONLEVY
JOHN CARRADINE · DONALD MEEK · JOHN RUSSELL · JANE DARWELL
Directed by HENRY KING

npathetic outlaw wows audiences.

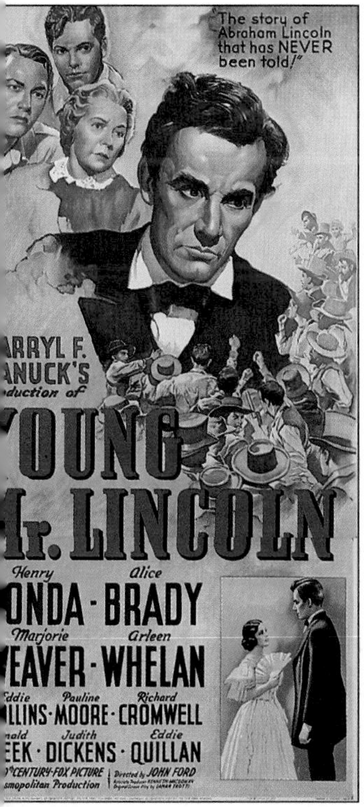
"The story of Abraham Lincoln that has NEVER been told!"
Mr. LINCOLN
Alice BRADY
Arleen WHELAN
Richard CROMWELL
Eddie QUILLAN
Directed by JOHN FORD

piring view of a historical giant.

UNION PACIFIC
is coming!

McCrea built first transcontinental track in DeMille's tribute to rail pioneers.

DRUMS ALONG THE MOHAWK
IN TECHNICOLOR
Claudette COLBERT
Henry FONDA
OLIVER · COLLINS
CARRADINE · BOWDON
RALPH · SHIELDS
LOWERY · IMHOF
20th CENTURY-FOX PICTURE
JOHN FORD

Rich depiction of settler life in upstate New York proved to be one of the year's biggest successes.

CLAUDETTE COLBERT
DON AMECHE
MIDNIGHT
JOHN BARRYMORE · FRANCIS LEDERER
MARY ASTOR ELAINE BARRIE

Billy Wilder scripted this deliciously witty film about a penniless American girl in Paris.

Tarzan: O'Sullivan and Weissmuller.

*Mireille Balin and Sessue Hayakawa in **Macao, l'enfer du jeu**.*

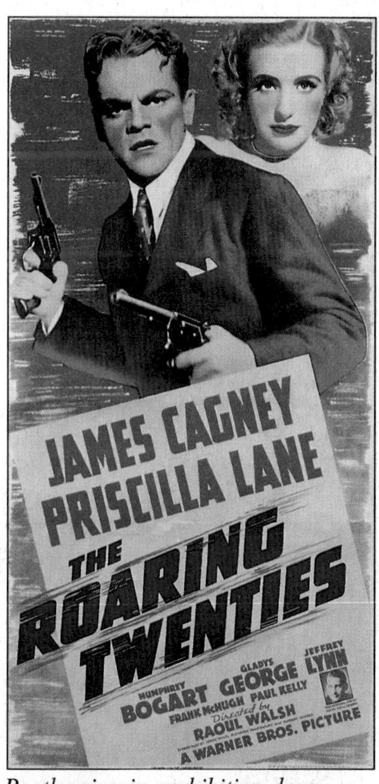
JAMES CAGNEY
PRISCILLA LANE
THE ROARING TWENTIES
HUMPHREY BOGART · GLADYS GEORGE · JEFFREY LYNN
FRANK McHUGH · PAUL KELLY
Directed by RAOUL WALSH
A WARNER BROS. PICTURE

Bootlegging in prohibition days.

War and After

The decade opened with the outbreak of the Second World War and closed with the onset of the Cold War. In Europe the war was already three months old when, on 15 December 1939, David O. Selznick's *Gone With the Wind* was spectacularly premiered in Atlanta, Georgia. The city's population swelled from 300,000 to one-and-a-half million as huge crowds lined the streets to see the stars parade in 50 flower-bedecked automobiles. *Gone With the Wind* remains the definitive Hollywood blockbuster and, though not apparent then, it rang down the curtain on Hollywood's Golden Age. Ten years later the dismemberment of the studio system, and the challenge posed by the growing popularity of television, propelled the American film industry into a new age of uncertainty.

In the intervening years, cinema had borne witness to a world in turbulent change, and in the process underwent its own transformation. The sensation of 1940 was Carmen Miranda, the extravagant 'Brazilian Bombshell', whose preferred headgear usually included several pounds of tropical fruit. In 1950 the most striking newcomer was a young graduate of the Actors Studio, Marlon Brando, who brought the Method style to his portrayal of an embittered paraplegic in *The Men*.

At the beginning of the war the United States remained neutral, but events on the other side of the Atlantic had a serious effect on the Hollywood majors. By the summer of 1940 Hitler's conquests in Eastern and Western Europe had closed 11 countries to American films. At the end of 1940, with the exception of Sweden, Switzerland and Portugal, the whole of continental Europe was closed to American films. In large measure this explains the elevation of Carmen Miranda to star status, as she elbowed Betty Grable and Don Ameche aside to hijack Fox's *Down Argentine Way*. With the disappearance of the European market, Latin America was now Hollywood's only strong foreign outlet. The ebullient Miranda thus found herself in the vanguard of a concerted export drive.

Initially, the major studios were somewhat less vigorous in taking a stand on events in Europe. In part, they were tracking public opinion, which remained overwhelmingly isolationist. The honorable exception was Warner Brothers, who had made the one explicitly anti-Nazi picture of the prewar period, *Confessions of a Nazi Spy* (1939). Nevertheless, it is significant that, after its release, the U.S. government unofficially leaned on Warners to abandon any similar projects.

The reluctance to commit box-office suicide by offending the strong isolationist sentiment in America was eventually overtaken by a cautious commitment to the Allied cause. At MGM Louis B. Mayer gingerly dipped his toe into the water with *The Mortal Storm* (1940), set in Germany in the early 1930s and tackling the persecution of Jewish academic Frank Morgan. The barriers were coming down. In UA's *So Ends Our Night* (1941), adapted from an Erich Maria Remarque novel, Glenn Ford, Margaret Sullavan and Fredric March were refugees fleeing the Nazis.

No one could ignore Charles Chaplin's *The Great Dictator* (1940), in which he delivered a comic broadside against fascism and ventured fully into sound for the first time. Alfred Hitchcock sounded a rallying cry for the beleaguered British in *Foreign Correspondent* (1940), at the end of which newsman Joel McCrea warns the audience, "The lights are going out in Europe. Ring yourself around with steel, America!" More tributes to the British were paid in films like *A Yank in the RAF* (1941), while the military preparedness urged by McCrea was celebrated in *I Wanted Wings* and *Dive Bomber* (both 1941). Isolationism was implicitly criticized in *Sergeant York* (1941), and in the same year *Buck Privates* and *Caught in the Draft* initiated a long line of service comedies which became staples of wartime cinema.

After the Japanese attack on Pearl Harbor on 7 December 1941, the Hollywood majors threw themselves into the war effort, discovering with some relief that patriotism could be highly profitable. In 1942 Paramount's profits leapt to $13 million, closely followed by MGM with $12 million, Fox with $10.5 million and Warners with $8.5 million. The U.S. government recognized the importance of cinema as an arm of national policy, and the movie industry remained relatively unaffected by wartime shortages. In turn the majors were happy to submit to the Office of War Information's guidelines on many issues. Of all the American war industries, the movie production lines were the easiest to convert to wartime needs. All the stock genres could be manipulated to accommodate war-related themes. Nazi villains even rode the ranges of the B-Western. Throughout the war the enemy was routinely portrayed in stereotypes. Nazis came in three styles: reptilian, most memorably in the form of Conr Veidt's Major Strasser in *Casabl ca* (1942); bullet-headed, as perso fied by Otto Preminger in *The P Piper* (1942); or hopelessly bu bling, like Sig Ruman's Gesta man in Ernst Lubitsch's biting sa *To Be or Not To Be* (1942). T Japanese were uniformly portray as buck-toothed subhumans. Ho wood's attitude towards them w caught in George Tobias' exult shriek, "One fried Jap going dow in Howard Hawks' film *Air Fo* (1943). There were few attempts explore the moral complexit which affected all the combatan Cedric Hardwicke played a thoug ful German commander in *T Moon is Down* (1943); and in *T Seventh Cross* (1944) there was acknowledgment of the existence 'good Germans'.

Lewis Milestone's fine war film, ***A Walk in the Sun*** *(1946): Dana Andrews (second left), John Ireland, Lloyd Bridges and Richard Conte (standing right).*

In 1943 the number of films de ing either directly or indirectly w the war reached a peak. There wa more frank approach to the realit of battle in pictures like *Guadalca Diary*, *Bataan* and *The Immor Sergeant*. Women war workers their bit in *Swing Shift Maisie*; w widows suffered pluckily in *Ten Comrade*; and Washington's w time housing shortage was the s ject of the sprightly comedy *T More the Merrier*. In *The Miracle Morgan's Creek* (made in 194 Preston Sturges satirized the heavals – principally sexual – t the war visited on small-town Am ca. Sturges' films of this period w notably out of step with the er escapist musicals, gung-ho action and the studio-bound dreamwor confected in films like *Casablan* The most impressive treatment men in battle came in 1945, wh the war was won: William W man's *The Story of GI Joe*, ba on the exploits of the war corresp dent Ernie Pyle, followed the bloo progress of an infantry compa as it slogged its way up the Ital peninsula; and Lewis Milestone's *Walk in the Sun*, rhythmically scri ed by Robert Rossen, focused a short, bloody action – one thousands – that was fought in same theater of war.

By 1944, however, the number war films made in Hollywood w falling. The war was clearly w and the majors began plough oney into more popular escapist ıtertainment. The film musical ›urished, freeing itself from the age and reaching a triumphant gh point in 1949 with *On the Town* which Gene Kelly starred and co- rected with Stanley Donen. Uni- :rsal revived its horror cycle, and ·ovided gloriously cockeyed ad- ·nture in the Technicolor 'East- ns' starring Maria Montez, one of e more engagingly camp icons of e Forties. The studios catered to e massive wartime audience of omen separated from their men- lk with the throbbing melodramas which Greer Garson, Bette Davis ıd, above all, Joan Crawford, suf- red mightily and usually in mink. his tear-sodden motherlode was :ver mined more skillfully than in lichael Curtiz's *Mildred Pierce* 945), Miss Crawford's triumphant ›meback for Warners after her de- ırture from MGM in 1943.

In the Forties the art of making ms in the studio reached a peak, ·fined by technical advances which cluded the development of more nsitive, fine-grained film stock, ›rtable power units and improved ·und recording and mixing. These ayed an important part in the low- :y lighting and virtuoso camera- ›rk of the *noir* cycle of films of the id- and late-1940s, in which double- :aling *femmes fatales* prowled ıadow-drenched sets in pursuit of ıe *film noir*'s compromised heroes: arbara Stanwyck ensnaring the zily philandering Fred MacMur- y in *Double Indemnity* (1944); ›an Bennett picking Edward G. obinson apart in *The Woman in* ·e *Window* (1944); and Jane Greer ıckering Robert Mitchum, laconic ‹iom of the *film noir*, in *Out of* ·e *Past* (1947).

Seen as immediate audience fod- :r when they were released, the cy- e of *noir* films, with their fatalistic ›ice-overs and doomed obsessions, :vertheless touched on the feeling ' unease which descended on post- ar America. In 1946 cinemagoing ·ached a peak with audiences of) million a week. But the ground as shifting underneath the feet of ıe Hollywood majors. Changing isure patterns caused a decline in nema audiences, and this problem as compounded by the arrival of levision as a serious competitor. In ›46, TV was a tiny cloud on the ›rizon, but by 1950 its steady ıtput of domestic comedies, cop rillers and Westerns had killed off the B-movie, for nearly 20 years the forcing ground for new talent and the pasture on which fading stars were put out to graze.

The Hollywood majors were further weakened by the increased artistic freedom accorded to producer-directors such as Alfred Hitchcock and William Wyler and writer-directors such as John Huston and Joseph L. Mankiewicz. Following Olivia De Havilland's landmark legal victory over Warners in 1945, the studios were no longer able to discipline willful stars with restrictive and punitive clauses in their contracts. In the immediate postwar period, a succession of bitter labor disputes in Hollywood prompted the House Un-American Activities Committee to launch an investigation of alleged Communist subversion in the film industry. The onset of the Cold War brought with it a debilitating witch hunt for Communists which spread its ugly tentacles throughout Hollywood. The final blow was delivered in 1948 with the Consent Decree, when the Supreme Court ruled that the Hollywood majors had to split their theater organizations from the production-distribution side of the business and abandon such practices as 'block booking', which obliged exhibitors to take movies they did not want. The eventual implementation of this ruling spelled the end of the vertically integrated studio system which had guaranteed the profitability of most films, including the mediocre. In 1949 MGM celebrated its silver jubilee amid a blaze of publicity which served only to illuminate the changing landscape.

Singer Lena Horne, a rare black star, in MGM's ***Broadway Rhythm*** *(1943).*

In Britain the outbreak of World War II coincided with one of the British film industry's recurring periods of crisis. After a faltering start, which mirrored the nation's uncertain progress through the Phony War, British filmmakers began to address the major themes of a People's War with growing confidence. A profound influence on wartime cinema was exercised by the documentary school of filmmaking fostered at the GPO Film Unit in the 1930s by John Grierson. Under the auspices of the wartime Crown Film Unit, it found an outlet in a stream of impressive documentary and propaganda films, including *Listen to Britain* (1942) and *Fires Were Started* (1943), both directed by Humphrey Jennings, and Pat Jackson's *Western Approaches* (1944). The impact of the documentary school worked its way into the mainstream of the feature film in *San Demetrio, London* (1943), *Millions Like Us* (1943), *Waterloo Road* (1944) and *The Way Ahead* (1945), all of which focused on the experiences of ordinary soldiers and civilians. Swimming against the documentary tide was the writer-director team of Emeric Pressburger and Michael Powell. This distinguished partnership offered a more complex and romantic picture of 'Englishness' in their masterly *The Life and Death of Colonel Blimp* (1943).

The British film industry entered the postwar period in a mood of high optimism. The success on both sides of the Atlantic of films like *In Which We Serve* (1942) and *Henry V* (1944) convinced the industry's most important figure, J. Arthur Rank, that he could take on the Hollywood majors in America. In this he came badly unstuck, but the years from 1945 to 1950 were to be one of the most fertile periods in British cinema, culminating in Ealing Studios' *annus mirabilis* in 1949 when it produced the three great comedies with which it is most closely associated, *Whisky Galore!*, *Kind Hearts and Coronets*, and *Passport to Pimlico*.

Wartime filmmakers in Germany and occupied Europe were inhibited rather than liberated by the war. German cinema consisted of a mixture of hymns to national history and military strength, anti-Semitic tracts and frothy escapism. French cinema was badly hit by the flight of many of its top talents to Hollywood. To avoid the heavy hand of German censorship, filmmakers developed a strain of 'poetic romanticism' whose political messages were couched in terms of oblique allegory in films such as Marcel Carné's *les Visiteurs du soir* (1942). In 1945, as France was liberated, Carné reached his artistic peak with *les Enfants du paradis*, a sprawling masterpiece set in the romantic theater of 19th-century Paris and two years in the making.

Italian wartime cinema continued to be dominated by smooth, empty entertainments dubbed 'white telephone films'. The reaction against them was signaled by Luchino Visconti's *Ossessione* (1942), a coolly observed melodrama based on James M. Cain's novel *The Postman Always Rings Twice*, and a harbinger of the neo-realist cycle of films launched by Roberto Rossellini's *Rome, Open City* (1945), in a semi-documentary style shot under very difficult conditions which aimed to capture the experience of ordinary people caught up in political events. The intensity and immediacy of neo-realist films, which made a virtue of the difficulties of filmmaking in postwar Italy, had a worldwide influence. By the end of the decade it could be seen at work in films as diverse as the Japanese *Drunken Angel* (1948) and *Stray Dog* (1949) and hard-nosed American urban thrillers like *The Naked City* (1948) and *He Walked by Night* (1948), which took the cameras out of the studio and into the city streets as Hollywood extended the range of its filmmaking just prior to the takeover of color, which began in the early 1950s.

ROBIN CROSS

1940

1939 Academy Awards, Ambassador Hotel, 29 Feb.

Best Film:	*Gone With the Wind* (dir: Victor Fleming)
Best Director:	Victor Fleming
Best Actor:	Robert Donat *(Goodbye, Mr. Chips)*
Best Actress:	Vivien Leigh *(Gone With the Wind)*
Best Supp. Actor:	Thomas Mitchell *(Stagecoach)*
Best Supp. Actress:	Hattie McDaniel *(Gone With the Wind)*

Paris, 10 January
Max Ophuls has finished shooting *From Mayerling to Sarajevo*, in the Billancourt studios. The film, which traces the life of François-Ferdinand Hapsburg was interrupted by the declaration of war. Ophuls received permission to leave his sector on the Front to finish the film.

Hollywood, 11 January
Release of *His Girl Friday*, directed by Howard Hawks, from Ben Hecht and Charles MacArthur's play *The Front Page*, with Cary Grant, Ralph Bellamy and Rosalind Russell.

Warsaw, 20 January
German authorities in all the newly occupied countries want to re-open the cinemas so that German propaganda films can be screened in aid of the war effort.

New York, 25 January
Release of Ernst Lubitsch's *The Shop Around the Corner*, with James Stewart and Margaret Sullavan.

London, 5 February
Producer-director Alexander Korda has announced his intention to join his brother, the film director Zoltan Korda, in the United States, where he plans to continue working with his actress wife Merle Oberon.

Rome, 14 February
Fire ravaged Cinecittà this morning destroying two sound studios and jeopardizing the work of Mario Bonnard and Vittorio De Sica.

Lyon, 20 February
The reopening of the Normandy cinema after undergoing a complete transformation. The interior decor (starry sky, guardrails) represents a liner in the middle of the ocean.

Los Angeles, 13 March
Release of Victor Schertzinger's latest musical, *Road to Singapore*, starring Bing Crosby, Bob Hope, and Dorothy Lamour.

Madrid, 16 March
The French ambassador, Marshal Philippe Pétain, has organized a screening of Guitry's film *les Perles de la couronne* (*The Pearls of the Crown*), for the diplomatic corps.

Billancourt, 23 March
Filmmaker Maurice Tourneur has resumed production on *Volpone*, with Harry Baur, Louis Jouvet and Charles Dullin.

Madrid, 2 April
A recently published circular forbids any reference to the names of American cinema personalities, such as Charlie Chaplin, Joan Crawford and Bette Davis, who gave support to the Spanish Republic.

New York, 10 April
The French film *la Femme du boulanger* (*The Baker's Wife*), by Marcel Pagnol, has been given an enthusiastic reception by the critics.

Paris, 25 April
Henri Decoin's *Battements de cœur* (*Heartbeats*), starring his wife Danielle Darrieux and Claude Dauphin has reached its 14th week at the Madeleine Cinema.

Los Angeles, 28 April
The Laurel and Hardy film released today, *Saps at Sea*, from director Gordon Douglas is the troublesome two's last film for Hal Roach. They have decided not to renew the contract which has bound them to the producer since 1926.

Hollywood, 18 June
Writer Herman J. Mankiewicz has decided on the final version of the script for Orson Welles' film *The American*, and has now changed the title to *Citizen Kane*.

Hollywood, 14 August
Release of the first film to be directed by scriptwriter Preston Sturges, *The Great McGinty*, with Brian Donlevy and Akim Tamiroff.

Moscow, 25 August
The Kiev Studios have presented the latest film by Alexander Dovzhenko and Julia Solntseva, *Osvobojdeniye (Liberation)*.

Paris, 5 September
Jean-Louis Barrault and Madeleine Renaud, both actors at the Comédie-Française, have married. They first met in 1936 on the set of *Hélène*, by Jean Benoît-Lévy.

Hollywood, 6 September
After watching the preview of his new film *The Great Dictator*, Charlie Chaplin has decided to cut and reshoot certain scenes.

Paris, 30 October
The distributor Henri Beauvais has presented a reconstructed version of the film *l'Atalante* to the Ursuline studios, in honor of the late Jean Vigo, who directed the original film in the early 1930s.

Hollywood, 1 November
Walter Lantz has released his new cartoon *Knock, Knock*, presenting Woody Woodpecker.

Paris, 2 November
The *Journal officiel* has published a decree to reorganize the cinema industry. One of the measures is an identity card for all professionals, with the exception of Jews, who are not entitled to be card-holders.

Prague, 15 November
The release of *Babicka* (*Grandmother*), by Frantisek Cap, has caused many patriotic anti-Nazi demonstrations. The film has been banned in numerous towns in Bohemia.

Berlin, 21 November
All filmed news produced by UFA, Tobis and Deulig has been placed under Goebbels' personal control.

Los Angeles, 19 December
Bud Abbott and Lou Costello, the comic duo who are better known simply as Abbott and Costello, have starred in their first film, *One Night in the Tropics*.

Bordeaux, 20 December
Jean Renoir and his companion Dido Freire have boarded the ship *Siboney*, for the U.S. Renoir is sharing a cabin with Antoine de Saint-Exupéry.

Berlin, 31 December
The Agfa company is experimenti[ng] with a trichrome color process f[or] the cinema by making a series [of] short documentary films.

BIRTHS

England, 22 January
John Hurt

Philippines, 3 April
Lino Brocka

Sudan, 21 April
Souleymane Cissé

New York, 25 April
Al Pacino

Los Angeles, 19 August
Jill St. John
(Jill Oppenheim)

Nice, 28 August
Philippe Léotard

Chicago, 5 September
Raquel Welch
(Raquel Tejada)

New Jersey, 11 September
Brian de Palma

Copenhagen, 22 September
Anna Karina
(Ann Karin Bayer)

Berlin, 5 November
Elke Sommer
(Elke Schletz)

Massachusetts, 15 November
Sam Waterston

San Francisco, 27 November
Bruce Lee

Illinois, 1 December
Richard Pryor

DEATHS

Hollywood, 1 July
Ben Turpin

Arizona, 12 October
Tom Mix

Banned in Germany, ***The Great Di[c]tator****, with its barely disguised po[r]trait of Hitler, is a courageous a[nd] brilliant achievement for Chaplin, [the] master of laughter through tears.*

'The Grapes of Wrath' presents the bitter harvest of the thirties

The suffering Joad family, Jane Darwell, Henry Fonda and Russell Simpson.

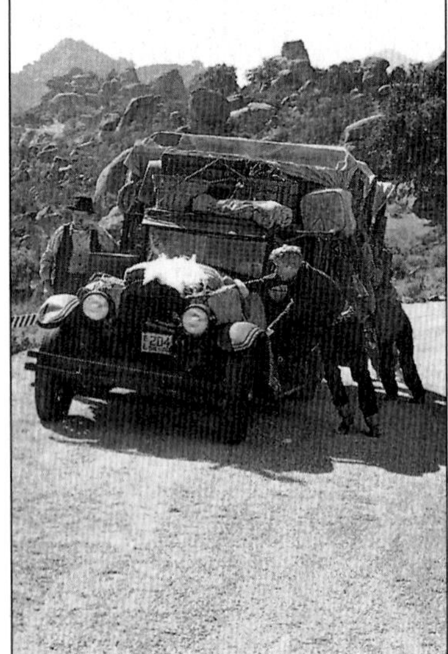

An arduous cross-country journey.

Hollywood, 24 January
John Ford's *The Grapes of Wrath* is a triumph. Rigorously adapted (by Nunnally Johnson) from the celebrated reportage novel by John Steinbeck, the picture follows the poignant journey of the Joad family of Oklahoma farmers to California during the Great Depression. These "Okies" have joined the mass exodus from the Dust Bowl to cross the country in an old automobile, hoping for a better life. But when they get to the "Promised Land", they come across only miserable campsites, and the horrors of exploited farm labor. Despite its harsh subject, Ford has still evoked a nostalgic poetry in the beautifully lit studio exteriors (photographed by Gregg Toland) and in the composed shots of poverty. Yet there were scenes shot in the actual migrant camps around Los Angeles, and the film's romanticism does not prevent it from also being a trenchant social statement in which the cast, and in particular Henry Fonda and Jane Darwell, become representatives of ordinary, suffering humanity.

Fields and West: a devilish paring

Hollywood, 9 February
Universal has paired two com heavyweights, Mae West and W. Fields, in *My Little Chickadee*. Ta ing its cue from the success of t comedy-Western film *Destry Rid Again*, the studio has sent them we to Greasewood City in the roles two competing con-artists, Cuthbe J. Twillie and Flowerbelle Lee, wh contract, but perhaps fortunately not consummate, a phony marriag When an amorous Fields then fin himself barred from the marital be chamber, he bellows through t keyhole, "I have certain very de nite pear-shaped ideas to discu with you." The collaboration b tween the two idiosyncratic sta was, by all accounts, a stormy on West, who hones her lines to perfe tion, did not appreciate Fields' a libbing, or his drinking. Indeed, s told the press,"There is no one qu like Bill... My only doubts about hi come in bottles." However, Fiel sneaked the last laugh, ad-libbi West's immortal line, "Come and see me some time", and th adding, "in Philadelphia."

A great game of cat and mouse

Hollywood, 10 February
A terrific new cartoon cat and mouse team has been created by Joe Barbera and William Hanna for a short film called *Puss Gets the Boot*. The wicked cat is continually frustrated in his pursuit of the wily mouse. This might prove to be the start of a new series for the MGM cartoon department, headed by producer Fred Quimby. Up to now, this studio's animated section has been outshone by Walt Disney and the Fleischer brothers' cartoon shorts, such as Popeye.

TOM
and
JERRY

Puss Gets The Boot!

Selznick and Fleming's 'GWTW' sweeps the board at the Academ

Hollywood, 29 February
David O. Selznick's *Gone With the Wind* has swept all before it at the Academy Awards ceremony, held at the Cocoanut Grove of Hollywood's Ambassador Hotel. Master of ceremonies Bob Hope quipped that the whole thing had turned into a benefit night for the triumphant Selznick. *Gone With the Wind* won nine Oscars, including Best Picture, Best Director (Victor Fleming), Best Actress (Vivien Leigh) and Best Supporting Actress (Hattie McDaniel). There was a particularly warm welcome for McDaniel's award, for her heartwarming performance as the eternal black mammy, but special permission was needed to enable her to sit at Selznick's table during the ceremony. Leigh's Oscar seemed inevitable from the moment she was chosen to play Scarlett O'Hara, but the strongly favored Clark Gable was edged out for the Best Actor prize by Robert Donat in *Goodbye, Mr. Chips.* Rumors are circulating that Gable is furious, convinced that his strained relations with Selznick led to a trade-off that ultimately got Donat the award. Thomas Mitchell was voted Best Supporting Actor for his performance as the drunken doctor in *Stagecoach*, a special mini-Oscar was presented to Judy Garland, and a posthumous award w made to Douglas Fairbanks, t first president of the Academy. separate posthumous award went Sidney Howard for the screenpl of the year's all-conquering *Go With the Wind.*

James Stewart in Capra's ***Mr. Smith Goes to Washington****, a close contende*

onskoi completes his life of Maxim Gorky

y Universities, the final film of Donskoi's trilogy based on Gorky's life.

oscow, 27 March
e director Mark Donskoi has fi-
lly completed his movie trilogy,
rted in 1938, based on Maxim
orky's autobiography. *The Child-
od of Maxim Gorky* deals with the
y's early joys and sorrows, and
e way he learns to love the people
his country, suffering under the
ar. *My Apprenticeship* sees the teenage Gorky working at various menial jobs, while observing the hardships of the society around him. *My Universities*, which has just opened, ends symbolically with the great Russian writer-to-be seeing the coming of a better future. The trilogy is rich in incident, character and period detail, making it one of the best Soviet works for some time.

Stunning film version of best-selling novel

Laurence Olivier and Joan Fontaine as Max De Winter and his second wife.

Hollywood, 28 March
After the extraordinary success of *Gone With the Wind*, David O. Selznick has pulled off another remarkable coup with *Rebecca*, the first Hollywood film handled by the immensely talented British director Alfred Hitchcock. The screen version of Daphne du Maurier's Gothic bestseller went into production three months before the release of *Gone With the Wind*. Selznick, determined to evoke a genuine British atmosphere with *Rebecca*, hired Hitchcock, whom he had been trying to lure to Hollywood since 1937. The role of Maxim de Winter, the brooding master of Manderley – the house haunted by his first wife Rebecca – went to Laurence Olivier, who established his star credentials in Sam Goldwyn's film *Wuthering Heights*. In contrast, the casting of Maxim's timid, mousy second wife, through whose eyes the story unfolds, was a long drawn-out affair. Vivien Leigh was tested for the role, as were Margaret Sullavan, Loretta Young, Anne Baxter and also Anita Louise, all of them unsuccessfully. Finally, Hitchcock decided on Joan Fontaine, a choice urged by fellow-director George Cukor. This was against Selznick's wishes, but it was part of manipulative Hitchcock's plans to ensure that Fontaine, until now very much in the shadow of her older sister Olivia De Havilland, came to the part with all the anxiety and self-doubt which afflicts the character she plays. The supporting cast is superb: Judith Anderson as sinister housekeeper Mrs. Danvers, guardian of Rebecca's flame; and George Sanders as the Savile-Row suited blackmailer Jack Favell, his insinuating drawl lingering in Manderley's paneled rooms long after he has left them. But, in an impeccable production, the acting honors go to Fontaine, previously considered a beautiful but wooden performer.

atriotism comes boxed as a thriller from Alfred Hitchcock

w York, 16 August
fred Hitchcock's second Ameri-
n feature, *Foreign Correspondent*,
s just opened here, and is very
ferent indeed from *Rebecca*, his
st. Whereas that was a solidly
afted and well acted Selznick pro-
ction, here the director has taken
e opportunity to demonstrate the
her side of his filmmaking perso-
. This one is a faster-moving film
iginal, an exciting spy thriller in
e tradition of his 1930s British
ctures, using a mixed British and
nerican cast. It tells the story of a
eable but naive American news-
per correspondent, played by Joel
cCrea, who is sent abroad to cov-
events taking place in August
39 just before the outbreak of
r. However, for the highly dramat-
ending, there is a leap in time to
e summer of 1940 when McCrea
oadcasts an impassioned plea to
nerica asking for support of the
itish cause, and during which the
und of bombs dropping on Lon-
n outside the radio studio can be heard. For the English-born Hitchcock it was important to present the British viewpoint to the American public in this highly effective way. His film is but one of a number of pro-British or anti-German productions that have come out of U.S. studios during the past year, beginning with *Confessions of a Nazi Spy* from Warner Bros., while Chaplin's just completed *The Great Dictator* is due to open shortly. Meanwhile, the official American government policy remains one of neutrality.

Joel McCrea, left, Laraine Day and George Sanders in ***Foreign Correspondent****.*

Scarlett says yes to Heathcliff

New York, 30 August
Two British stars who have made their mark on Hollywood, Laurence Olivier and Vivien Leigh, are getting married and will have their wedding here in the U.S. The couple met in England in 1936 when they played the young lovers for Alexander Korda in his historical Elizabethan film, *Fire Over England*, and have been closely involved ever since. But it hasn't been easy. Miss Leigh (born Mary Hartley in India), whose Oscar-winning Scarlett O'Hara has brought her worldwide fame, was divorced from her first husband Herbert Leigh five years ago. However, the handsome Olivier, who made *his* mark as Heathcliff in *Wuthering Heights*, has only just been freed from his marriage to Jill Esmond. Larry and Viv, as they are known in their profession, had hoped to co-star in *Wuthering Heights*, but Merle Oberon won over Leigh.

Ferocious satire from Charles Chaplin

Hynkel becomes the Great Dictator.

The little Jewish barber courts the pretty Hannah (Paulette Goddard).

New York, 15 October
With much of Western Europe under German domination, Charles Chaplin has delivered his damning verdict on fascism and his first dialogue film, *The Great Dictator*. It's also the first Chaplin picture to start with a completed script, which originally ran to 300 pages, and the first in which Chaplin has assembled a talented and well-balanced cast to work alongside him. The story goes that *The Great Dictator* was initially prompted by the British film magnate Alexander Korda's observation of the physical similarity between the Tramp and Adolf Hitler. Chaplin has cast himself in the dual role of Adenoid Hynkel, the ranting dictator of Tomania, and his doppelganger, a downtrodden little Jewish barber. However, their identities are confused, and it is the barber who delivers the picture's lengthy final speech in which he pleads for an end to tyranny in the world. Strong support is provided by lovely Paulet Goddard (presently estranged fro Chaplin), Henry Daniell, playi Hynkel's henchman Garbitsch, a portly Jack Oakie, blustering ma nificently as Hynkel's rival dictat the Mussolini-like Benzino Nap loni, the ruler of Bacteria. Chap relished the upstaging battle wi Oakie. On set he joked, "If you rea want to steal a scene from me, y son-of-a-bitch, just look straight the camera." Some of *The Gre Dictator*'s impact is muffled by clumsy construction and Chapli tendency to resort to sentimentali but it is full of his inspired pan mime, not least a ballet, both de cate and macabre, in which the i capering Hynkel dances with a hu balloon globe of the world.

Veit Harlan extols Hitler's racial ideology

Berlin, 24 September
With his *Jew Süss*, Veit Harlan has directed a work of allegiance to the Third Reich, though he has already glorified Nazi ideology in his two previous films. With the personal encouragement of Josef Goebbels, Harlan has made an anti-Jewish film from the famous 1925 pro-Jewish novel by Lion Feuchtwanger. As the plot goes, in the 18th century Süss Oppenheimer, financial advisor and tax collector for the Duke of Wurtemberg, uses evil methods to gain power for himself and his people. Rejected by the Duke's daughter, Oppenheimer rapes her. He is then hanged for the crime, and the Jews are exiled. The title role, played by Ferdinand Marian, is a crude caricature, and the climax of the film seems to condone all the pogroms, deportations and genocide of the Jewish people.

*Heinrich George and Ferdinand Marian in **Jew Süss**, archetypal Nazi cinema.*

Jack Oakie, right of Chaplin, is the flamboyant Napaloni (Mussolini!).

he French cinema nder Vichy rules

ıris, 4 November
 the *Journal officiel*, the Vichy ›vernment has published a decree at will allow for the creation of a m authority called the Comité organisation de l'industrie cinéma-graphique (COIC). Charged with gulating the production of French ms, this body is to be headed by a rector and a 20-member consulta-/e commission, the latter divided to five sub-committees overseeing e five major areas of the industry: e manufacture of filmmaking and hibiting equipment, all the pre-oduction activities (such as script-riting), film production, publicity ıd exhibition (including exports). OIC's brief covers all technical, onomic and social issues relating the film business. It will control e professional organizations in the dustry and represent their inter-ts when dealing with other govern-ent bodies and foreign markets.

'Pinocchio' and 'Fantasia' spell great year for Walt Disney

Walt Disney's
TECHNICOLOR FEATURE TRIUMPH
FANTASIA
with
Stokowski
© Walt Disney

© Walt Disney

After the success of his first full-length cartoons, Disney takes up the challenge of transposing music into visuals.

Los Angeles, 13 November
In the last few years, Walt Disney has been working simultaneously on various projects in preparation for the transfer of his studios to Burbank. The result of all this impressive activity has been the release of two full-length cartoon films within nine months of each other. Last February, *Pinocchio* was released following the enormous success of his first animated feature, *Snow White and the Seven Dwarfs*. Based on the story by Collodi, *Pinocchio* is a technical advance on the earlier film, giving audiences even more of a feeling of depth of vision. For the characters, the designers were inspired by clay and wooden models, as well as actors filmed in their costumes. Now Walt Disney is offering us *Fantasia*, an even more audacious and original work. It was first conceived as a short film, featuring Mickey Mouse acting out *The Sorcerer's Apprentice* by Paul Dukas, conducted by Leopold Stokowski. This grew into a full-length musical feature of an experimental nature. Divided into eight parts, including the Dukas bit, the film also finds visual equivalents to the music of Tchaikovsky, Stravinsky, Schubert, Beethoven, Mussorgsky, Ponchielli and Bach. Leopold Stokowski collaborated with Disney at each stage of the production, and was the one responsible for the experiment in stereophonic sound which makes the music swoop across the screen in synchronization with the drawings.

© Walt Disney

*The well-loved tale of **Pinocchio** is told in Disney's second full-length feature.*

A sparkling comedy of wedding nerves

ew York, 27 December
he picture breaking all records at ıe Radio City Music Hall since its remiere last month is *The Philadel-ıia Story*, splendidly directed by eorge Cukor. Who would believe ıat its star, Katharine Hepburn, ıd been put on the infamous "Box-ffice Poison" list only last year? But after her triumph in the stage version of *The Philadelphia Story*, she convinced MGM to give her a chance in this sophisticated romantic comedy. As society girl Tracy Lord, almost lured away from marriage to stuffed-shirt Cary Grant by the antics of James Stewart, Hepburn is terrific. How could it miss?

*ımes Stewart (left), Cary Grant, Katharine Hepburn: **The Philadelphia Story**.*

A DRAMA OF INHUMAN CRUELTY!
Devil's ISLAND
Starring BORIS KARLOFF
with A GREAT SUPPORTING CAST

Controversial exposé offended the French, who delayed its release for a year.

Outrageous pairing: W.C. Fields and Mae West in ***My Little Chickadee****.*

Margaret SULLAVAN • James STEWART
The ERNST LUBITSCH Production
The SHOP AROUND THE CORNER
with FRANK MORGAN
JOSEPH SCHILDKRAUT

Lubitsch charmer reunited the stars.

WOMEN IN WAR
THE EMOTIONAL BI
PARADE OF TODAY
ELSIE JANIS
WENDY BARRIE
PATRIC KNOWLE

By Hungarian director John H. Au

KEYE LUKE IN
PHANTOM OF CHINATOWN
WITH
LOTUS LON
GRANT WITHE
Produced by PAUL MALVEF
Directed by PHIL ROSE
Screenplay by JOSEPH WES
Original Story by RALPH BETTI
Based on the COLLIER'S MA
Stories by HUGH WIL
A MONOGRAM PICTURE

Keye Luke replaced Boris Karloff in this sixth film of the 'Wong' series.

IN TECHNICOLOR
NORTHWEST PASSAGE
BOOK I - ROGERS' RANGERS
Starring
pencer
RACY
with
ROBERT YOUNG
WALTER BRENNAN
RUTH HUSSEY
NAT PENDLETON
Produced by HUNT STROMBERG
Directed by KING VIDOR

pular, costly adventure lost money.

yrone Power in **The Mark of Zorro**.

Darryl F. Zanuck's
PRODUCTION OF
LILLIAN RUSSELL
Alice
FAYE
Henry
FONDA
Don
AMECHE
Edward ARNOLD
Warren WILLIAM
Leo CARRILLO
A 20th CENTURY-FOX PICTURE

avish showcase for Alice Faye.

Vivien
LEIGH
Robert
TAYLOR
HER FIRST
PICTURE SINCE
"GONE WITH
THE WIND"
WATERLOO
BRIDGE
with
LUCILE WATSON
VIRGINIA FIELD
MARIA OUSPENSKAYA
C. AUBREY SMITH
A MERVYN LE ROY Production
SCREEN PLAY BY S. N. BEHRMAN, HANS RAMEAU AND GEORGE FROESCHEL
BASED ON THE PLAY "WATERLOO BRIDGE" BY ROBERT E. SHERWOOD
Directed by MERVYN LE ROY
Produced by SIDNEY FRANKLIN
A METRO-GOLDWYN-MAYER
PICTURE

Leigh in tear-jerking wartime melodrama of superb quality, set in London.

Henry Daniell and Errol Flynn dueled in Michael Curtiz's **The Sea Hawk**.

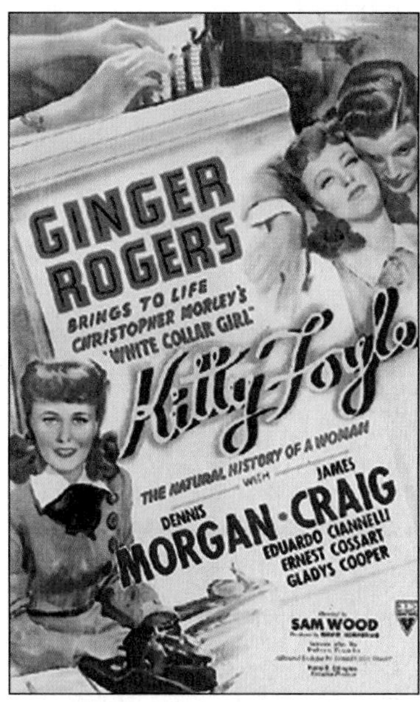
GINGER
ROGERS
BRINGS TO LIFE
CHRISTOPHER MORLEY'S
"WHITE COLLAR GIRL"
Kitty Foyle
THE NATURAL HISTORY OF A WOMAN
with
DENNIS
MORGAN
JAMES
CRAIG
EDUARDO CIANNELLI
ERNEST COSSART
GLADYS COOPER
SAM WOOD

Rogers a hit in straight dramatic role.

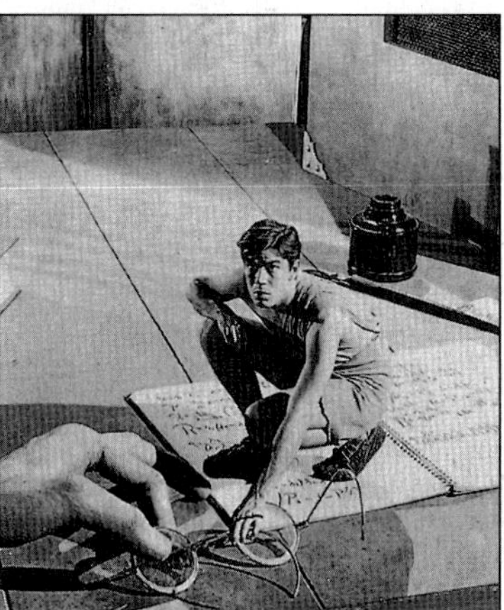

Charles Halton in **Dr. Cyclops**.

in Technicolor
TYPHOON
with
DOROTHY LAMOUR
ROBERT PRESTON
LYNNE OVERMAN
J. CARROL NAISH
A PARAMOUNT PICTURE

Island tale blew up box-office storm.

1941

1940 Academy Awards, Biltmore Hotel, 27 Feb.

Best Film:	*Rebecca* (dir: Alfred Hitchcock)
Best Director:	John Ford *(The Grapes of Wrath)*
Best Actor:	James Stewart *(The Philadelphia Story)*
Best Actress:	Ginger Rogers *(Kitty Foyle)*
Best Supp. Actor:	Walter Brennan *(The Westerner)*
Best Supp. Actress:	Jane Darwell *(The Grapes of Wrath)*

New York, 10 January
The Hearst press has been forbidden to publish any mention of the film *Citizen Kane* or any other RKO work. Proprietor William Randolph Hearst considers the film defamatory and has doubled his threats of a court case.

Hollywood, 15 January
Jean Renoir, who has signed a year's contract with 20th Century-Fox, has this comment to make about the company's vice president Darryl F. Zanuck: "He is a producer who even goes so far as to choose the color of his actors' ties."

New York, 31 January
Release of *Mr. and Mrs. Smith*, by Alfred Hitchcock. Carole Lombard, the star of the film, had asked to work with Hitchcock, who obliged with a piece that is not a thriller.

Paris, 14 February
Release of the German propaganda film *Jew Süss*, by Veit Harlan, which has met with very positive reactions.

Hollywood, 21 February
Rita Hayworth has a starring role for the first time in Raoul Walsh's newly released, saucy comedy, *The Strawberry Blonde*, with Olivia De Havilland and James Cagney.

Hollywood, 27 February
At the Academy Awards ceremony here last night, Ginger Rogers was named Best Actress for *Kitty Foyle*. The dramatic role was a departure for a star usually associated with the tapping feet of Fred Astaire. John Ford's highly acclaimed film, *The Grapes of Wrath*, received an impressive 14 nominations.

Washington, 8 March
The government has made public the salaries earned by heads of well-known companies. Louis B. Mayer (MGM) is the highest paid executive in the country with an annual salary of approximately $700,000.

Moscow, 15 March
Sergei Eisenstein has been awarded the Stalin prize for his historical epic *Alexander Nevsky*.

Los Angeles, 13 June
The American Federation of Labor (AFL) has called for a boycott of all Disney productions in support of strikers at Disney, who have been battling in vain for higher wages and the recognition of their union.

Hollywood, 14 June
Scriptwriter John Huston has started filming *The Maltese Falcon*. It is his first project as a director.

Berlin, 24 June
A circular handed down from the Ministry of Propaganda and Information has ordered the press to "immediately cease all debate on American films" and goes on to say that "the German public is only interested in German films."

Paris, 30 June
Abel Gance, who has been accused of being Jewish, is required by the Vichy Government to prove his "Aryan" origins to the head of the cinema industry.

Hollywood, 1 August
Orson Welles is working on a scenario for *Journey Into Fear*, based on the novel by Eric Ambler. His friend, the actor Joseph Cotten, is involved with the project.

Hollywood, August
As his latest contribution to the British war effort, Alfred Hitchcock has come up with an idea for a new film about fifth columnists sabotaging American defense plans.

Hollywood, 31 August
Ava Gardner, a young beauty who was spotted in a photograph, has signed a seven-year contract with MGM. She thus joins other budding stars as a member of the coveted MGM "seraglio".

Berlin, 5 September
After six years of exile in France, G.W. Pabst has at last returned to Germany in response to Goebbels' insistent demands. He is making *Komodianten* (*The Actors*), with Henny Porten and Hilde Krahl.

Washington, 21 September
Harry M. Warner, the president of Warner Bros., has given evidence to the Commision of Inquiry about "cinematographic propaganda". He is having to defend his productions against accusations of "militarism and incitement to war."

Hollywood, 30 September
Walt Disney has given the press a preview of his latest cartoon feature *Dumbo*, about a flying elephant.

Rome, 4 October
Release of Roberto Rossellini's first full-length feature film entitled *La Nave Bianca* (*The White Ship*). Originally planned as a documentary with a non-professional cast, it then developed into a dramatic and uncompromising study of war at sea.

Soviet Union, 14 October
Eisenstein and his personnel have been transferred to Alma-Alta in Kazakhstan because of the German army's advance.

Los Angeles, 28 October
Release of Jean Renoir's first American film *Swamp Water*, starring Walter Brennan, Anne Baxter and Dana Andrews.

Tokyo, 1 December
Kenji Mizoguchi, who has been working for the Shochiku company since the bankruptcy of Nikkatsu, has returned to historical films (known as sabre-films or jidai-geki) with *The Loyal 47 Ronin – Part I.*

Hollywood, 12 December
Filmmaker Frank Capra has announced his intention to join the Cinema Services section of the armed forces. He is hoping to use his knowledge to further democracy.

New York, 26 December
Release of *The Shanghai Gesture*, by Josef von Sternberg, which stars Gene Tierney, Victor Mature, Walter Huston and Ona Munson. This is Sternberg's first major film since his separation from Marlene Dietrich.

China, 28 December
The Wan Brothers have released *T[ie] Shan Gongzhu* (*The Iron Fan*), t[he] first full-length Chinese carto[on]. The film's success is in part due [to] its resolutely anti-Japanese tone.

Hollywood, 31 December
Producer Hal Wallis has sent [a] memo to all departments at Warn[er] Bros. regarding the recently [ac]quired story *Everybody Comes [to] Rick's*. The title has been changed [to] *Casablanca*.

BIRTHS

London, 9 January
Susannah York
(Susannah Yolande Fletcher)

Florida, 14 January
Faye Dunaway

Italy, 16 March
Bernardo Bertolucci

Zurich, 22 March
Bruno Ganz

India, 14 April
Julie Christie

Los Angeles, 20 April
Ryan O'Neal

Sweden, 28 April
Ann-Margret
(Ann-Margaret Olsson)

England, 20 June
Stephen Frears

Paris, 13 July
Jacques Perrin (Jacques Simonet)

Chile, 25 July
Raul Ruiz

Havana, 4 December
Humberto Solas

Hollywood, 19 December
Beau Bridges
(Lloyd V. Bridges III)

England, 31 December
Sarah Miles

***Citizen Kane** establishes Ors[on] Welles as a genius of the mode[rn] cinema. Innovatively photograph[ed] by Gregg Toland, the film's for[m] matches its imaginative content.*

EVERYBODY'S TALKING ABOUT IT!
It's Terrific!
ORSON
WELLES
CITIZEN
KANE
The Mercury Actors
JOSEPH COTTEN
DOROTHY COMINGORE
EVERETT SLOANE
RAY COLLINS
GEORGE COULOURIS
AGNES MOOREHEAD
PAUL STEWART
RUTH WARRICK
ERSKINE SANFORD
WILLIAM ALLAND

Welles' 'Citizen Kane' sets Hearst against RKO

Orson Welles as the young Kane, a powerful press baron seemingly inspired by the life of William Randolph Hears

New York, 1 May

The first film directed by Orson Welles, *Citizen Kane*, has at last opened in New York. Its release was planned for 14 February, but it was postponed because of the press campaign that was organized by the newspaper magnate William Randolph Hearst. It was Hearst, among others, who had inspired the scriptwriter Herman J. Mankiewicz to create the megalomaniac character. RKO, who produced the picture, refused to give in to pressure and organized various private screenings before showing it to the press on 9 April. This incurred the wrath of Hollywood's unofficial arbiters of taste, Hedda Hopper and Louella Parsons, the latter being a Hearst employee. For his first incursion into cinema, Orson Welles, only 25, has shown a perfect mastery of the medium. This brilliant actor and director of the Mercury Theater, had already acquired notoriety from his radio adaptation of H.G. Wells' *The War of the Worlds* aired on 30 October 1938. So realistic was it, that listeners in their thousands believed an invasion from Mars had taken place, and fled the cities. Because of his reputation, Welles was offered a contract by RKO Radio studios president George Shaefer. The contract tied him to make two films, both of which he would produce, direct, write and appear in for a fee of over $100,000 a picture. *Citizen Kane* was not, however, the multi-talented Welles' first choice. He proposed a version of Joseph Conrad's *The Heart of Darkness*, then Nicholas Blake's *The Smiler with the Knife*, before he was attracted to the story of a press baron, seeing in it a terrific role for himself. The official shooting began on 29 June and finished on 23 October 1940. For all of Welles' fears of a law suit from Hearst, *Citizen Kane* opened spectacularly at the Palace Theater today, with crowds lining the streets. Some audiences might be confused by a film that seems to break all the rules. Charles Foster Kane is seen from many viewpoints, which goes against chronological narrative conventions. Of the many memorable sequences is one wh we see the growing gulf between tycoon and his wife through a ser of vignettes, in which the cou move further and further away fr each other at the breakfast tab Cameraman Gregg Toland's use wide-angle and deep focus lens the innovative deployment of sou narration and overlapping dialog Bernard Herrmann's music, all pursuit of the meaning of the w Rosebud, make this one of the m audacious jigsaw puzzles of a fi ever produced. It is a remarka debut by the "Boy Wonder".

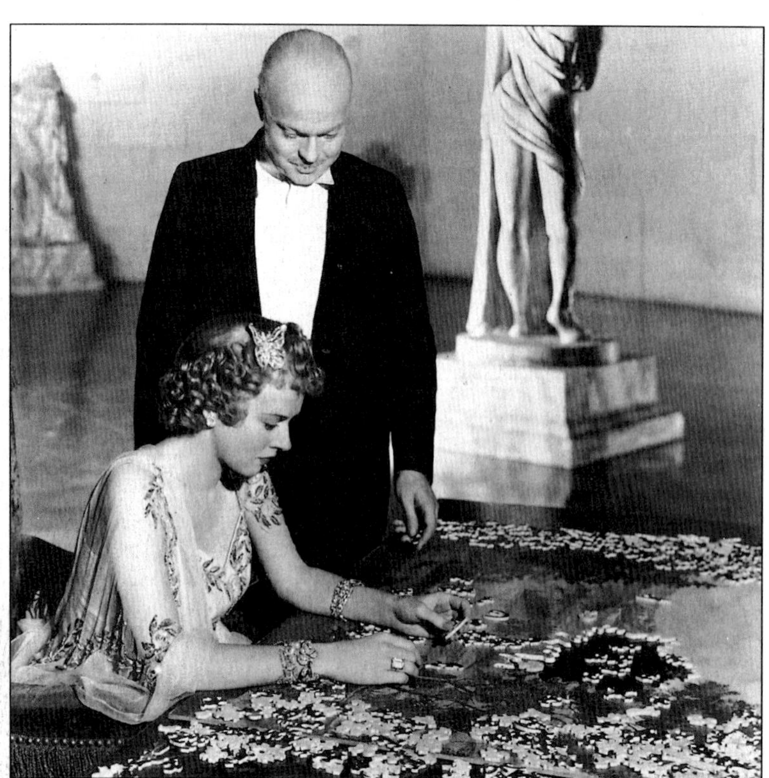

Dorothy Comingore is Kane's mistress, Susan, based on Marion Davies.

BOARDING H

Kane, briefly seen as a small child (Buddy Swan) with Agnes Moorehead.

lorious blend of color, action and magic

n eye-catching moment in Alexander Korda's remake of ***The Thief of Bagdad.***

ondon, 10 March
monster eye on the prow of a ship ides into view during the opening oments of Alexander Korda's new he *Thief of Bagdad*, a spellbinding rabian Nights fantasy, full of stunng special effects, in which Sabu oes battle with Conrad Veidt's evil rand Vizier, and Rex Ingram tows over the rest of the cast as a mischievous outsize genie. Three directors, Ludwig Berger, Michael Powell and Tim Whelan, had a hand in the production, which began in England and was finally completed in Hollywood. The screenplay is by Lajos Biro, and the stunning Technicolor photography has been masterminded by the brilliant French cameraman Georges Périnal.

Stanwyck's chancy Eve wins Fonda's heart

Charles Coburn (left), Barbara Stanwyck and Henry Fonda in ***The Lady Eve.***

Los Angeles, 25 March
The supremely professional Barbara Stanwyck stars in what promises to be one of the year's sparkiest comedies, written and directed by Preston Sturges, who found his feet last year with *The Great McGinty*. Stanwyck is the lady of the title, a ruthless cardsharp who preys on the smart set with her father Charles Coburn. Working the trans-Atlantic luxury liner beat, she sets her sights on tangle-footed brewery heir Henry Fonda, whose only passion is rare snakes, until he encounters Stanwyck over a marked deck of cards. Stanwyck is superb, alternately pugnacious and melting, while Fonda's bashful deliberation provides her with the perfect comic foil.

rosby, Hope and Lamour back on the road

ollywood, 11 April
ollowing the enormous success of st year's *Road to Singapore*, Paraount decided to send the same am of Bing Crosby, Bob Hope and orothy Lamour on another exotic journey, this time on the *Road to Zanzibar*. This romp is even funnier than the previous film, and looks like it will be an even bigger hit. If so, the studio might consider sending the trio on more comic trips.

Gary Cooper is magnificent as pacifist York

Hollywood, 2 September
In the title role of Howard Hawks' new film *Sergeant York*, Gary Cooper delivers a magnificent performance. He gradually changes from a simple farmer into a hero, having to adapt his beliefs to the circumstances of the Great War. The film is an ideal frame for the star's underplaying, and he exudes the goodness and piety of the real-life man on whom York is based.

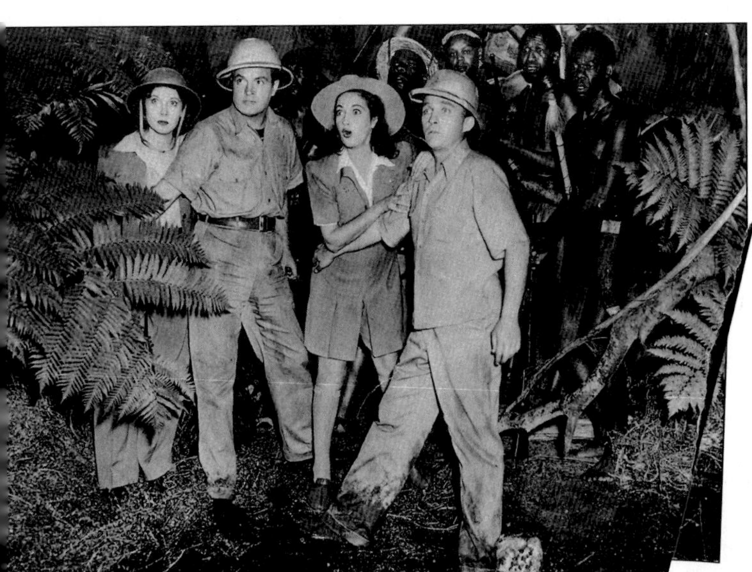

na Merkel with star trio Hope, Lamour and Crosby in ***Road to Zanzibar.***

Gary Cooper as the reluctant soldier-hero of Howard Hawks' ***Sergeant York.***

Despite discord, Davis-Wyler film a winner

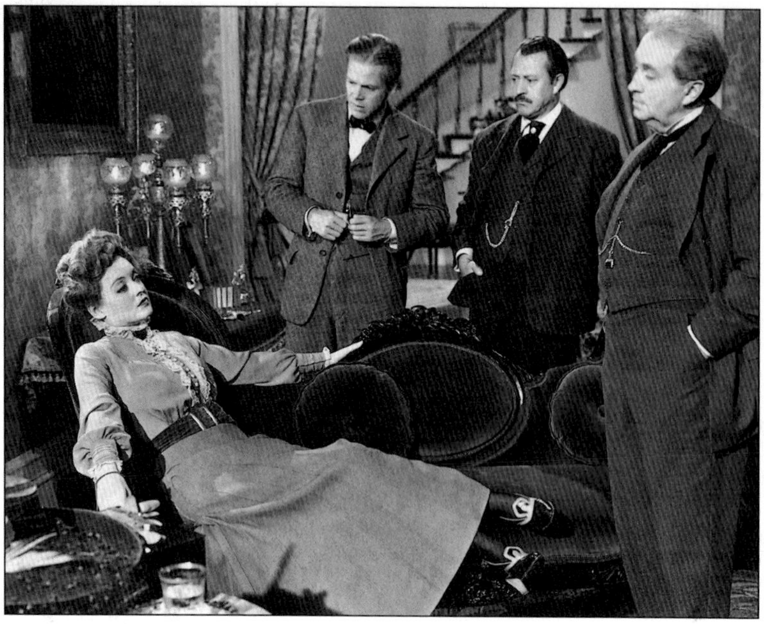

Bette Davis gives a chilling performance as Regina in ***The Little Foxes****.*

New York, 8 August
The privileged audience at the premiere of William Wyler's new film, *The Little Foxes*, unanimously hailed the performance of Bette Davis. As in Lillian Hellman's original play, the action takes place at the beginning of the century in Louisiana. Davis plays the odious Regina Giddens, who would allow her banker husband to die so that she can inherit his fortune. An excellent role for an actress who has come out on top in a poll organized by the *Motion Picture Herald*. Yet *The Little Foxes* marks a break between the star and her favorite director. Wyler and Davis were in disagreement over her interpretation of the role, which Wyler thought lacked subtlety.

'That woman' becomes a 'lady' in Britain

Laurence Olivier and Vivien Leigh as Horatio Nelson and Emma Hamilton.

London, 29 September
Laurence Olivier and Vivien Leigh make a handsome couple in Alexander Korda's *Lady Hamilton*, released in America as *That Hamilton Woman*. Produced and directed by Korda in Hollywood for United Artists, the picture stars the glamorous husband-and-wife team as Admiral Lord Nelson and his famously flamboyant mistress, Mis Emma Hamilton. Their romanc set against the background of th Napoleonic Wars, is cut short b Nelson's death in 1805 at the Batt of Trafalgar. The parallel betwee Napoleon and Hitler has clearly d lighted the British Prime Ministe Winston Churchill, who says *Lad Hamilton* is his favorite film.

John Huston displays master touch in debut

New York, 18 October
John Huston, the son of the actor Walter Huston, has made a magnificent debut as a film director with *The Maltese Falcon*. Huston, who has been a screenwriter at Universal and Warner Bros., chose to make a third adaptation of the crime novel. Providing a strong cast and a sharp script, he has rendered Dashiell Hammett's prose style into film terms. The title refers to a precious statuette which various crooks and the private eye, Sam Spade, want to get hold of. For the role of the detective, Huston originally wanted to cast George Raft, but when the star refused, the director got the idea of using Humphrey Bogart, an actor who has specialized in portraying gangsters but rarely had a leading role. This decision has contributed greatly to the film's success. By the force of his talent, Bogart has made Sam Spade into a hard-boiled man without illusions.

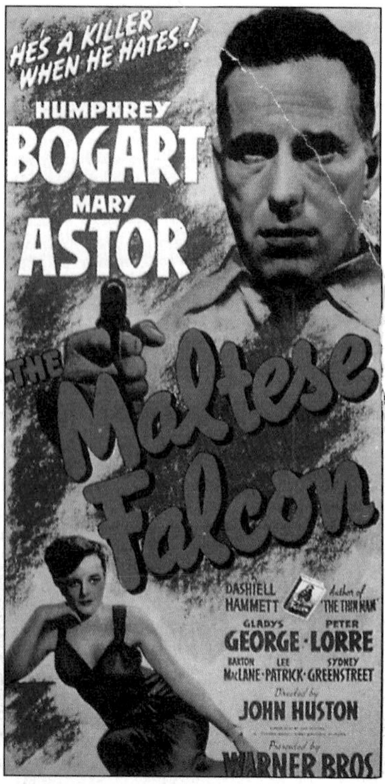
HE'S A KILLER WHEN HE HATES!
HUMPHREY
BOGART
MARY
ASTOR
THE Maltese Falcon
DASHIELL HAMMETT
Author of "THE THIN MAN"
GLADYS GEORGE · PETER LORRE
BARTON MacLANE · LEE PATRICK · SYDNEY GREENSTREET
Directed by JOHN HUSTON
Presented by WARNER BROS

Famous mining drama filmed by Ford

New York, 28 October
20th Century-Fox created a little bit of Wales in California when they made the screen version of Richard Llewellyn's best-selling novel, *How Green Was My Valley*, from Philip Dunne's evocative script adaptation. The studio built a Welsh mining village in the hills north of Los Angeles, and filled it with as many Welsh singers as it could find on the West Coast. The picture tells the tory of the Morgan family, headed y stern paterfamilias Donald Crisp Scotsman) and kindly Sarah All- od (of Irish extraction). Their ngest son, played by English war uee Roddy McDowall, narrates tory of this mining family in ack. American-Irish director Ford bathes the novel's turn- -century world in a richly rhap- s glow, photographed by Arthur M , which Welsh miners in the ha conditions of today might find a lit hard to recognize. However, protests from critics on the othe side of the Atlantic have been mu fled by the sound of ringing cas registers as the box-office returr pay testimony to John Ford's co summate skill as a storyteller.

itchcock's new film suspiciously amoral

'tchcock with Grant and Fontaine.

ollywood, 16 November
fred Hitchcock's latest movie, *spicion*, has just opened. A well-afted, beautifully acted suspense ama, set in England and based on *fore the Fact*, a successful novel author Francis Iles in the tradi-n of *Rebecca*, the film reunites itchcock with Joan Fontaine, who on an Oscar for her performance the earlier film. Since the comple-n of *Rebecca* early in 1940, the rector has found himself in the mewhat strange position of being under contract to a producer, David O. Selznick, who has in fact given up producing films. As a result, Hitchcock has been "loaned out" to other producers and studios for a variety of projects, all carefully selected for him. He has apparently also been able to function more or less as a producer-director who has a large degree of creative freedom, however with *Suspicion*, he had to cope with meddling studio executives for the first time. This particular project, sophisticated and ambiguous, casts the plausible, handsome and very charming Cary Grant as Fontaine's husband who may, or may not, be planning to murder her. RKO attempted to take the film away from Hitch and re-cut it to excise all hints of such intention – a step that would have eliminated the superbly developed suspense and tension of the piece. Fortunately, the picture has been released in its maker's version and looks likely to be a big success. Hitchcock has already moved on to his next film, for yet another studio, Universal. An anti-Nazi spy thriller called *Saboteur* and starring Robert Cummings and Priscilla Lane, it is part of his personal contribution to the war effort and is based on his own story idea.

'King's Row' an enthralling melodrama

Ann Sheridan, Ronald Reagan and Robert Cummings in ***King's Row***.

Hollywood, 24 December
King's Row, based on the bestseller by Henry Bellamann, takes a look at life in small-town America and delivers a community touched by murder, madness and sadism. Directed by Sam Wood, photographed by James Wong Howe, designed by William Cameron Menzies, with a score by Erich Korngold, *King's Row* could not fail to be entertainment of the highest quality. The acting in this enthralling 127-minute long melodrama also comes up to scratch, particularly in the performances of Ronald Reagan and Ann Sheridan, who have confounded those cynics who had assumed they would be too lightweight for their respective roles.

ivine Garbo bids farewell to the screen

ew York, 31 December
aving successfully gotten Garbo to ugh in last year's *Ninotchka*, GM has over-extended itself with *vo-Faced Woman*, whose selling e is "Garbo is Twins!" Appearing in her second comedy vehicle, directed by George Cukor, Garbo plays a woman who marries New York businessman Melvyn Douglas and then turns vamp to thwart his old flame, Constance Bennett, by seducing him for a second time in the guise of her predatory sister. But the comedy never catches fire, and the film has been given a mauling by the critics. Increasingly disillusioned with filmmaking and suspicious that *Two-Faced Woman* was part of an MGM plot to "kill her off", Garbo has therefore chosen this moment to announce her retirement from the screen. After 27 films she has no wish to disappoint her admirers by growing old on the screen. For its part, the studio which brought her to Hollywood in 1925 is happy to bid her goodbye. In recent years Garbo has been more popular in Europe than in America, but most of the overseas market is now closed to the Hollywood majors.

Two-Faced Woman*, her last film.*

French cinema victim of insidious controls

Paris, 31 December
Six statutes have been enacted today by the Propaganda Division, the regulating body for the cinematographic profession. They include the exclusion of Jews, a measure Vichy has applied with alacrity. Last September, German censorship came into force over film distribution in the occupied zone. The German High Command alone is empowered to authorize films being made in French studios. With the creation of Continental, a new subsidiary of UFA, the occupying powers have a total grip on French cinema.

PHARM
Raimu in Continental's ***l'Assassinat du Père Noël*** *directed b*

THE 3 MESQUITEERS
PRAIRIE PIONEERS
A REPUBLIC PICTURE
ROBERT
LIVINGSTON
Bob STEELE • Rufe DAVIS
Livingston mounts again as Western hero Stoney Brooke in popular series.

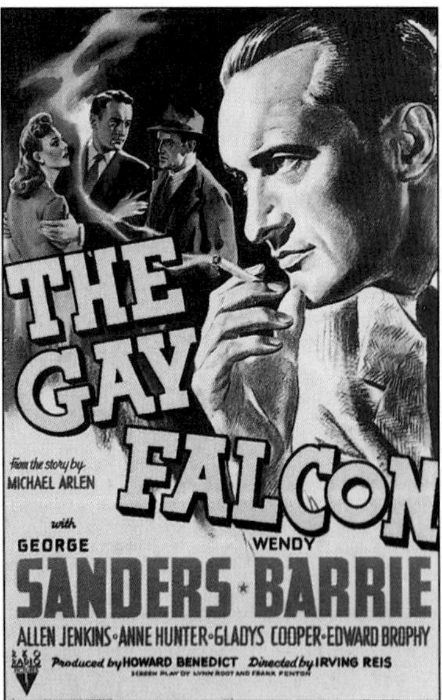
THE
GAY
FALCON
From the story by
MICHAEL ARLEN
with
GEORGE
SANDERS
WENDY
BARRIE
ALLEN JENKINS • ANNE HUNTER • GLADYS COOPER • EDWARD BROPHY
Produced by HOWARD BENEDICT Directed by IRVING REIS
Sanders' stylish copy of his 'Saint' persona landed RKO with a lawsuit.

The
WOLF MAN
with
CLAUDE RAINS
WARREN WILLIAM
RALPH BELLAMY
PATRIC KNOWLES
BELA LUGOSI
MARIA OUSPENSKAYA
EVELYN ANKERS
and
LON CHANEY
as "The Wolf Man"
Lupine chiller showcased the talent of brilliant makeup artist Jack Pierce.

l to r: Jean-Louis Barrault, Edith Piaf, Roger Duchesne: ***Montmartre-sur-Seine****.*

JAMES CAGNEY
OLIVIA
DeHAVILLAND
Strawberry
Blonde
RITA
HAYWORTH
ALAN HALE • JACK CARSON • GEORGE TOBIAS
Directed by
RAOUL WALSH
WARNER BROS.
' delightful 1910 Sunday afternoon with a perfect cast, sharply ·hed by James Wong Howe.

NEW TRIUMPH BY THE AUTHOR OF
"Goodbye, Mr. Chips!"
Robert
MONTGOMERY
Ingrid
BERGMAN
RAGE IN HEAVEN
GEORGE SANDERS
LUCILE WATSON
OSCAR HOMOLKA
Despite the casting, and a plot from James Hilton's novel, this was a stilted and disappointing melodrama.

Judy Garland and Mickey Rooney were effervescent in ***Babes on Broadway***

ırles Boyer and Olivia De Havilland in **Hold Back the Dawn**, an affecting ıance directed by Mitchell Leisen.

ı Hayworth and Tyrone Power in Mamoulian's drama **Blood and Sand**.

in Technicolor
MOON
OVER
MIAMI
A 20th CENTURY-FOX PICTU
with
DON AMECHE
BETTY GRABLE
Robert
CUMMINGS
Charlotte GREENWOOD Jack HALEY
Carole LANDIS Cobina WRIGHT JR.
Produced By
HARRY JOE BROWN
Directed by Walter Lang

Breezy musical was one of three 1941 films with soldiers' sweetheart Grable.

ack Benny in
HARLEY'S AUNT
with
KAY FRANCIS
JAMES ELLISON
ARCHIE MAYO
WILLIAM PERLBERG
BELLE STARR
The Bandit Queen
IN TECHNICOLOR
Randolph Gene
SCOTT ★ TIERNEY
Dana John
ANDREWS · SHEPPERD
IRVING CUMMINGS
Elizabeth PATTERSON · CHILL WILLS
A 20th CENTURY-FOX PICTURE

ıpteenth version of this well-loved torian farce gloriously showcased ·-clad Jack Benny.

The svelte Gene Tierney found herself miscast as the most notorious female outlaw.

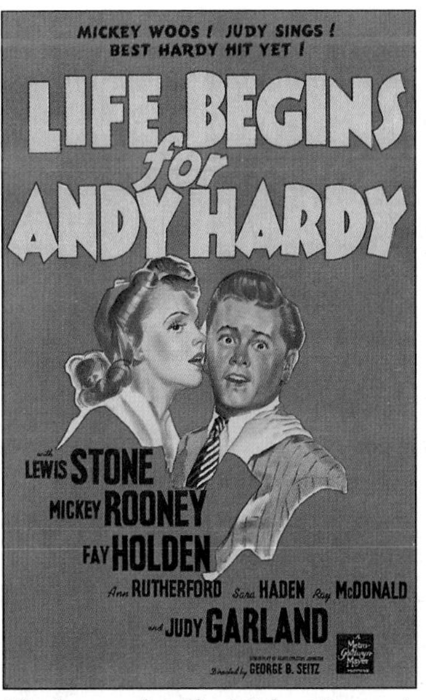
MICKEY WOOS! JUDY SINGS!
BEST HARDY HIT YET!
LIFE BEGINS
for
ANDY HARDY
with LEWIS STONE
MICKEY ROONEY
FAY HOLDEN
Ann RUTHERFORD Sara HADEN Ray McDONALD
and JUDY GARLAND
Directed by GEORGE B. SEITZ

The best to date for Mickey Rooney's small-town wisecracker.

HE KILLED...
and there on the crest of Sierra's highest crag...
HE MUST BE KILLED!
HIGH
SIERRA
IDA
LUPINO
HUMPHREY
BOGART
RAOUL WALSH
WARNER BROS.

Bogart as the sympathetic fugitive in a high-class gangster drama.

1942

1941 Academy Awards, Biltmore Hotel-Banquet, 26 Feb.

Best Film:	*How Green Was My Valley* (dir: John Ford)
Best Director:	John Ford
Best Actor:	Gary Cooper *(Sergeant York)*
Best Actress:	Joan Fontaine *(Suspicion)*
Best Supp. Actor:	Donald Crisp *(How Green Was My Valley)*
Best Supp. Actress:	Mary Astor *(The Great Lie)*

Lyon, 1 January
The Lumière factories have been forced to close down due to the coal shortage. This puts an end to the manufacture of negative film in the unoccupied zone.

Hollywood, 24 January
David O. Selznick signed up the young actress Phyllis Walker. She is to be known as Jennifer Jones.

Paris, 31 January
Cinema takings in the French capital have increased 68 percent in comparison with January 1941.

Los Angeles, 4 February
Orson Welles has left to join his film crew in Rio de Janeiro, where he is to film the Carnival for one of the semi-documentary episodes of the Pan-American project for RKO, *It's All True*.

Vichy, 10 February
From now on, Jews and foreigners are forbidden by law to use a pseudonym in the cinema.

Algiers, 16 February
Because of the coal shortage, all weekday film matinees are canceled.

Hollywood, 17 February
Ernst Lubitsch has presented his latest comedy, *To Be or Not to Be*, with Carole Lombard (her last film before her tragic death), Jack Benny and Robert Stack. The heroes of the film are a group of Polish actors confronted by the Nazis.

Copenhagen, 19 February
The critics applauded at the preview of *Afsporet* (*Distraction*), by Bodil Ipsen and Lau Lauritsen.

Paris, 1 March
French cartoon films are making a comeback. There are at present four films underway, including *le Marchand de notes* (*The Note Seller*), by Paul Grimault, produced by one of the UFA branches, Continental.

Hollywood, 24 April
Ingrid Bergman, who is under contract to producer David O. Selznick, has been loaned out to Warners for the co-lead in *Casablanca*. In return, Warners have put Olivia De Havilland at Selznick's disposal for eight weeks.

New York, 7 May
Premiere at Radio City Music Hall of *Saboteur*, a taut espionage thriller from Alfred Hitchcock, with Robert Cummings and Priscilla Lane.

Hollywood, 22 May
Rita Hayworth has decided to divorce her multi-millionaire husband, Edward Judson. She is reported to be in love with Victor Mature, whom she met during the filming of *My Gal Sal*.

New York, 29 May
Release of *Yankee Doodle Dandy*, directed by Michael Curtiz, with James Cagney, Walter Huston and Joan Leslie.

Paris, 8 July
Sacha Guitry donated a painting by Utrillo, worth 650,000 francs, at the Union of Artists' gala. A great number of artists attended the evening's entertainment.

Moscow, 9 July
A documentary, *Leningrad Takes Up Arms*, made from footage taken by four cameramen during the siege of the city, has been released by the Leningrad studios.

Paris, 19 July
Germaine Dulac, the avant-garde director and cinema theorist, died unexpectedly during the night.

Paris, 7 August
The release of screenwriter Henri-Georges Clouzot's first full-length film as director *l'Assassin habite au 21* (*The Murderer Lives at No. 21*) starring the delightful Suzy Delair and Pierre Fresnay.

Hollywood, 31 August
Darryl F. Zanuck has resigned as head of production at 20th Century-Fox to join the armed forces. He is to serve as a colonel in the cinema section of the Signal Corps.

Vichy, 15 October
Effective immediately, no English or American films may be screened in France. Any already extant copies have to be handed in to the Ministry of Information.

Hollywood, 31 October
Charlie Chaplin has started work on a screenplay about the life of the notorious Landru. He has paid Orson Welles $5,000 for having suggested the idea.

Paris, 13 November
The actress Gina Manès has been seriously wounded by a tiger while taking part in a performance at the Médrano circus.

New York, 16 November
An article in the *New York Times* has announced that the producer David O. Selznick has lent most of his contracted actors to Fox. These include Dorothy McGuire, Joan Fontaine, Gregory Peck and the producer-directer Alfred Hitchcock.

Los Angeles, 19 November
Release of *I Married a Witch*, directed by René Clair, with the charming Fredric March beautifully paired with Veronica Lake.

Berlin, 24 November
Release of *Die Goldene Stadt* (*The Golden Town*), filmed in Agfacolor by Veit Harlan.

Hollywood, 26 November
The producers of *Casablanca* have taken out a $100,000 insurance policy to cover the company in the event of the death of the leading player Humphrey Bogart. In fact, his wife Mayo Methot, convinced that he is having an affair with co-star Ingrid Bergman, has been threatening to kill him.

New York, 6 December
Producer Val Lewton, who always wanted to make horror films with a difference, has released his first production, *Cat People*. Directed by Jacques Tourneur, it stars Simone Simon and Kent Smith.

Hollywood, 7 December
In the last year American stud have produced 150 free films for armed forces' training programs.

Paris, 16 December
Release of Jean Delannoy's *Mac l'enfer du jeu*, which stars Sess Hayakawa and Pierre Renoir.

Beverly Hills, 23 December
The young actress Joan Bar whose contract had been cance by Charlie Chaplin, burst into home and threatened to kill hers

BIRTHS

France, 16 January
Richard Bohringer

Paris, 21 March
Françoise Dorléac

England, 23 March
Michael York

New York, 24 April
Barbra Streisand

Montreal, 1 July
Geneviève Bujold

Chicago, 13 July
Harrison Ford

Stockholm, 29 September
Britt Ekland

England, 26 October
Bob Hoskins

New York, 17 November
Martin Scorsese

England, 18 November
David Hemmings

DEATHS

Nevada, 16 January
Carole Lombard

Hollywood, 29 May
John Barrymore

Hollywood, 4 August
James Cruze

*A superior wartime romance, set in studio-created Britain, **This Above** stars Joan Fontaine and Tyrone Po er. He is a conscientious objector, s is a surgeon's daughter.*

Tyrone
POWER
Joan
FONTAINE
THIS
ABOVE
ALL
by ERIC
KNIGHT
Produced by
DARRYL F. ZANUCK
Directed by
Anatole Litvak
SCREEN PLAY BY R.C. SHERRIFF
A 20th CENTURY-FOX PICTURE
LET'S GO! U.S.A.
KEEP 'EM FLYING!
A
LITHO. IN U.S.A. #7113
THIS POSTER IS THE PROPERTY OF TWENTIETH CENTURY-FOX FILM CORP.
IT IS LEASED - NOT SOLD
COPYRIGHT BY TWENTIETH CENTURY-FOX FILM CORP. MCMXLII
TOOKER LITHO. CO., N.Y.

The tragic loss of Carole Lombard

Los Angeles, 17 January
Witty, glamorous, tough, notoriously outspoken and a splendidly versatile actress, Carole Lombard is dead at the age of 34. The much-loved star of *Bolero*, *Twentieth Century*, *Now and Forever*, *Nothing Sacred* and *Made For Each Other*, among other films, was killed last night on her return from a highly successful War Bonds tour, when the airplane crashed in the mountains of the Sierra Nevada. All 19 passengers aboard the DC-3 from Indianapolis, including the star's mother and her press agent, met their deaths. Carole Lombard was born Jane Alice Peters in Fort Wayne, Indiana, on 6 October 1908, but moved to Los Angeles at the age of six when her parents separated. At age 16, she signed with Fox and changed her name, but shortly thereafter a serious car accident laid her off for 18 months. After short stints with both Mack Sennett and Pathé, in 1930 she landed a seven-year contract with Paramount. By 1937, Academy Award-nominated for her wonderfully screwball performance opposite ex-husband William Powell in *My Man Godfrey*, Lombard was Hollywood's highest paid actress and then decided to freelance. Her last film, *To Be or Not To Be*, an anti-Nazi satire for Lubitsch, was completed just two weeks after the bombing of Pearl Harbor and is awaiting release. In 1939, after a long and complicated courtship, Lombard married Clark Gable, who is now reported to be in a grief-stricken state at the couple's Encino ranch.

The lovely Carole Lombard.

A romantic fable from Preston Sturges

New York, 28 January
In *Sullivan's Travels*, the latest film from Preston Sturges, Joel McCrea plays a successful director of film comedies, who goes off to live the life of a tramp in order to have first-hand experience of social deprivation for a drama he wishes to make. Things turn nasty and he ends up in a chain gang. One night, the sullen prisoners shuffle in to see a movie, but they are soon laughing uncontrollably at a Mickey Mouse cartoon. This convinces Sullivan that to make people laugh is the finest achievement. The credo of this tragicomic romantic fable can be taken as writer-director Sturges' own. His mission has been to make people laugh since he started his career.

In the guise of a tramp, Joel McCrea takes to the road in ***Sullivan's Travels****.*

Oscar ceremony defers to war

Hollywood, 26 February
The annual Academy Award p[illegible] sentation ceremony took place [illegible] evening at the Biltmore Hotel, [illegible] months after the bombing of P[illegible] Harbor and the American entry i[illegible] the war. Academy President B[illegible] Davis asked that the event be hel[illegible] a large auditorium and be open[illegible] the public for the price of a tic[illegible] the proceeds of which would g[illegible] the Red Cross. When her req[illegible] was rejected, Davis resigned. H[illegible]ever, in keeping with the som[illegible] spirit of our times, formal attire [illegible] banned, there were no searchlig[illegible] playing outside the venue, and [illegible] banquet was downgraded to a [illegible]ner. Donald Crisp, Best Support[illegible] Actor winner for John Ford's *H[illegible] Green Was My Valley* and a vete[illegible] of the Boer War and the Great W[illegible] presented himself in uniform. Ja[illegible] Stewart, last year's Best Actor, [illegible] in his Air Corps Lieutenant's [illegible]form as he handed over the statu[illegible] to Gary Cooper, the star of *Serge[illegible] York*. Joan Fontaine was Best A[illegible]ress for *Suspicion*, and *How Gr[illegible] Was My Valley* carried off the B[illegible] Director and Best Picture award[illegible]

The late Carole Lombard shines in Lubitsch's anti-Nazi satire

Hollywood, 6 March
The critics are divided about Ernst Lubitsch's latest picture, United Artists' *To Be or Not To Be*, a biting satire set in Nazi-occupied Warsaw. Jack Benny and Carole Lombard portray a husband-and-wife acting team, Joseph and Maria Tura, who use their thespian skills in a running battle with the Gestapo. Lubitsch's flair for cynically urbane comedy has not prepared some critics for this excursion into the dark side of events in Europe. *Life* thunders, "In years to come, the fact that Hollywood could convert part of the world crisis into such a cops and robbers charade will certainly be regarded as a remarkable phenomenon." However, the movie's most remarkable phenomenon is Benny's performance as the self-infatuated Joseph Tura, the most succulent of classical hams. When, in disguise, he asks buffoonish Gestapo man Sig Ruman what he thinks of Joseph Tura, Ruman replies, "Ah, yes, I saw him once before the war. Believe me, what he did to Shakespeare we are now doing to Poland." Playing way beyond his normal range, Benny, supported by a luminous Lombard in her last film, [illegible]veals a far greater acting talent th[illegible] usual, while Lubitsch demonstra[illegible] that this is his funniest film to da[illegible] because it is his most serious.

l to r: Charles Halton, Tom Dugan, Lionel Atwill, Benny, Lombard, Stack.

ean-Louis Barrault impersonates Berlioz

ris, 1 April
n-Louis Barrault portrays Hec- Berlioz as a romantic and pas- nate character in *la Symphonie tastique*, the title borrowed from of the French composer's most ous works. The movie, directed by Christian-Jaque, is an evocation of Berlioz's tumultuous life, during which he climbs from obscurity to fame. It also provides a feast of musical extracts "conducted" by Barrault. Other parts are played by Renée Saint-Cyr and Jules Berry.

n-Louis Barrault with Renée Saint-Cyr in Christian-Jaque's biopic.

Cagney sings and dances his way to glory

Hollywood, 28 May
Yankee Doodle Dandy begins in 1937 with James Cagney taking the complex role of composer-singer-playwright-actor-dancer and producer George M. Cohan recounting his life story to President Franklin D. Roosevelt. Afterwards, the president decorates him for his services to the American Musical Theater, a medal that the multi-talented Cagney has convinced us is merited. Cagney emotes, sings and hoofs his way into the hearts of millions with his portrayal of the pint-sized showman. When Cohan sold Warner Bros. the rights to his life story, he had insisted that James Cagney play him. In fact, Cagney, with his head forward and bottom sticking up in the "Cohan Strut", even outdoes its originator. His exuberant singing and dancing is best exhibited in a lengthy extract from Cohan's hit show *Little Johnny Jones*, containing two of its most successful ditties, the title song and "Give My Regards To Broadway". Although the screenplay of this warm and witty biopic has taken some liberties (for example Cohan was not born on 4 July, but the day before), *Yankee Doodle Dandy* remains as true an account of the Cohan story as Hollywood is capable of. Thus we see Cohan in his early years as part of a family vaudeville act called the Four Cohans, and then his big break in *Peck's Bad Boy*. We follow his successful association with producer Sam Harris and also watch his relationship with Mary, the woman who would become his wife. The film, directed by Michael Curtiz, is going over as a treat with audiences, because it is not only a nostalgic extravaganza but also a patriotic pageant featuring songs like "You're a Grand Old Flag". ▷

l to r: Jeanne Cagney, James Cagney, Rosemary de Camp, Walter Huston.

irector George Stevens' matchmaking brings happy alliance

s Angeles, 15 April
oman of the Year, now showing at auman's Chinese Theater in Holvood, has brought Spencer Tracy d Katharine Hepburn together the first time. Though both have eady won Oscars, Tracy is at the ight of his fame, while Hepburn's reer has been flagging from the lure of many of her films over the t few years. But thanks to the eat success of *The Philadelphia ory*, she was given a long-term GM contract and her choice of co- r, her director George Stevens, o had made some of her RKO ovies, as well as two little-known iters, Ring Lardner Jr. and Mi- ael Kanin. The chemistry of the rs is the real triumph of the pic- re, and rumor has it that they have len in love. When Hepburn was st introduced to Tracy by Herman ankiewicz in a corridor at MGM, said, "I'm afraid I'm a little too l for you, Mr. Tracy." Mankie- cz then responded, "Don't worry, ate, he'll soon cut you down to e," referring to Tracy's rather ll-known strong-willed personali- Soon afterwards, Hepburn realized that he was the man she really understood. She declared, "I'm dull, nervous and sometimes I'm a real nuisance. However, he is so manly that for him I'm an easy target. He can put me down, but not offend me." She was divorced in 1934, but she can become Tracy's wife only in a screenplay, because he has been married to Louise Treadwell since 1923 and has two children, John (born in 1924) and Louise (born in 1932). In the film, Kate plays an international columnist on a New York newspaper, while Spencer is a sportswriter on the same paper.

Spencer
Katharine
TRACY·HEPBURN
THE PICTURE OF THE YEAR!
Woman of the Year
A GEORGE STEVENS Production
FAY BAINTER · REGINALD OWEN
Metro-Goldwyn-Mayer

London's Blitz evoked by William Wyler

Greer Garson and Walter Pidgeon, splendid as Mr. and Mrs. Miniver.

Hollywood, 6 June
MGM has lent its considerable weight to the British war effort with William Wyler's film *Mrs. Miniver*. Greer Garson stars as the plucky middle-class British housewife of the title, reading *Alice in Wonderland* to her children in the air raid shelter and capturing the downed German flier Helmut Dantine in her garden. Co-star Walter Pidgeon plays her tweedily reliable husband in a glossily photographed Hollywood version of Britain at war, which ends in a bombed church to the strains of "Land of Hope and Glory".

'Magnificent Ambersons' create bad blo

Dolores Costello as Isabel Amberson Minafer with Tim Holt as her wayw son George Amberson Minafer, who finally gets his come-uppance.

Hollywood, 1 July
RKO took unfair advantage of Orson Welles' absence in South America by editing down *The Magnificent Ambersons* from 131 minutes to 88. Because *Citizen Kane* failed at the box office, the studio hoped that his second attempt would appeal to a wider public, but they were pleased at the rushes and decided edit it themselves. Although the fi remains a haunting and ironic p trait of Booth Tarkington's dec ing aristocratic 19th-century fam the director was furious at the lib ties taken with his work.

For Bette Davis, love is a shared cigarette

Hollywood, 31 October
A plain, drab, gauche and unhappy spinster, driven to a breakdown, re-emerges as a poised, glamorous and charming woman who finds romance... Thus does Bette Davis, star of the irresistible new three-hankie tear-jerker *Now, Voyager*, prove that no challenge is beyond her formidable gifts. Directed by Irving Rapper for Warners, the movie could start a new fashion for lovers, certain to copy Bette's co-star, Paul Henreid, in lighting two cigarettes simultaneously and handing one to his *amour*. Seductive stuff!

Paul Henreid and Bette Davis in ***Now, Voyager*** *directed by Irving Rapper.*

Lovely reunion for Astaire and Hayworth

Los Angeles, 19 November
Fred Astaire and Rita Hayworth are dancing up a storm in Columbia's *You Were Never Lovelier*, a musical romance with the currently fashionable Latin-American background, deftly directed by William A. Seiter. Fred pursues the lovely Rita with the aid of her matchmaking fath Adolphe Menjou and a delicio score by Jerome Kern and John Mercer. The title is an apt descr tion of Hayworth as she dream duets with Astaire on a moon terrace, proving once again h sensational skills as a dancer.

Grace, elegance and charm: Rita Hayworth and Fred Astaire.

yrone's red-blooded power packs punch

ollywood, 4 December
ery pirate film cliché is paraded in orious Technicolor in Fox's *The ack Swan*, directed with immense ive by Henry King. Tyrone Power a swashbuckling sea gypsy who ams up with burly Laird Cregar's enry Morgan to sail the Spanish ain in search of booty and busty aureen O'Hara. She persuades wer to end his pirate ways, which ads to a climactic showdown with old rival Redbeard, played with arling relish by George Sanders. fred Newman's throbbing score, agnificent cinematography from on Shamroy, bravura acting and series of excitingly staged action quences employing full-size gal-ons and blazing broadsides add up a thundering screen spectacle.

Tyrone Power, a handsome 'pirate'.

TYRONE POWER
MAUREEN O'HARA
FAEL SABATINI'S
THE BLACK SWAN
COLOUR BY TECHNICOLOR
WITH LAIRD CREGAR
THOMAS MITCHELL
GEORGE SANDERS
ANTHONY QUINN
GEORGE ZUCCO
DIRECTED BY HENRY KING
PRODUCED BY ROBERT BASSLER

Devil's envoy finds romance in escapist tale

Arletty and Alain Cuny (foreground right) struggle against evil forces.

Paris, 5 December
Marcel Carné's new film, *les Visiteurs du soir* (*The Devil's Envoy*), is a medieval fable in which two minstrels (Alain Cuny and Arletty), actually servants of the Devil (Jules Berry), arrive at a castle during the betrothal feast of a baron's daughter and a knight. When Cuny falls in love with the bride-to-be, the Devil turns them into stone, though their hearts continue to beat. Audiences are interpreting it as an allegory of the Occupation, with the Devil representing the occupiers, and the lovers the indomitable French spirit.

'Random Harvest' set for gigantic success

New York, 17 December
Velvet-voiced Ronald Colman and glamorous Greer Garson co-star in *Random Harvest*, based on James Hilton's novel and directed for MGM by Mervyn LeRoy. Set in England in a very convincing re-creation, this is the tale of a wartime amnesia victim who, in a clever twist, suffers a double memory loss. Though somewhat hard to believe and with a focus on the grief suffered by the woman who loves this man, a crack team has produced a highly romantic film from a painful subject. The audiences are left tear-sodden but happy, and box-office tills are working overtime.

Marlene and Gabin neighbors at Universal

ollywood, 31 December
aving officially acquired Ameri-an nationality in June 1939, Mar-ne Dietrich has now been totally jected by the Nazi regime. The ewspaper *Der Sturmer* has pub-hed a photo of the star posing in ont of the Star-Spangled Banner ith the caption: "Born in Ger-any, Dietrich has become totally -Germanized by consorting with e Jews of Hollywood." This has ad no effect on her, and she contin-es to use a large part of her fortune help her friends in Germany to cape to the U.S. or Great Britain. he sees very little of her husband Rudolph Sieber, though he is employed in the foreign department of Universal. However, Marlene is often with Jean Gabin, with whom she is in love. At the moment, the French star is busy shooting *The Imposter*, for director Julien Duvivier, which is an account of the activities of the Free French forces and the Resistance movement. The film is a testimony to the political commitment of both the actor and director. On a neighboring sound stage, Marlene is completing *The Spoilers*, co-starring John Wayne and Randolph Scott, in between continuing her humanitarian work.

Greer Garson and Ronald Colman, caught in heartbreak and happiness.

CLARA CALAMAI
MASSIMO GIROTTI
JUAN DE LANDA
Regia: LUCHINO VISCONTI
PRODUZIONE E DISTRIBUZIONE
Ossessione

Original Italian poster for Luchino Visconti's neo-realist drama.

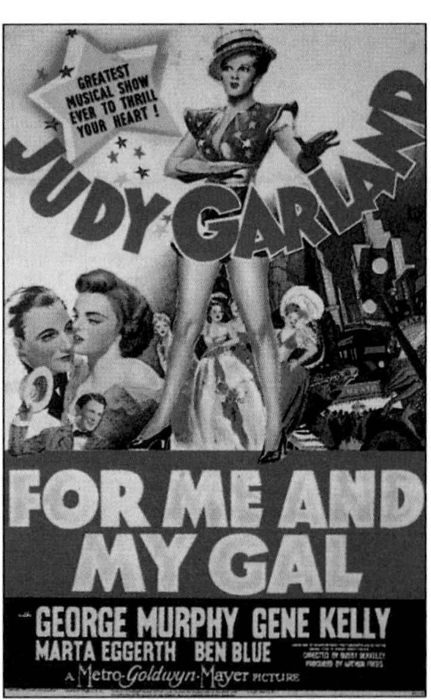
GREATEST MUSICAL SHOW EVER TO THRILL YOUR HEART!
JUDY GARLAND
FOR ME AND MY GAL
GEORGE MURPHY GENE KELLY
MARTA EGGERTH BEN BLUE
A Metro-Goldwyn-Mayer PICTURE

Garland got Kelly as a dance partner.

NO MAN CAN RESIST HER!
"I married a Witch"
...and I'm not complaining would you?
Starring
FREDRIC MARCH
VERONICA LAKE
with
ROBERT BENCHLEY · SUSAN HAYWARD
CECIL KELLAWAY · A Cinema Guild presentation
A RENE CLAIR Production
Directed by RENE CLAIR
Released thru United Artists
THE PASSIONATE WITCH

Frenchman René Clair's delightful Hollywood film showcased Veronica Lak

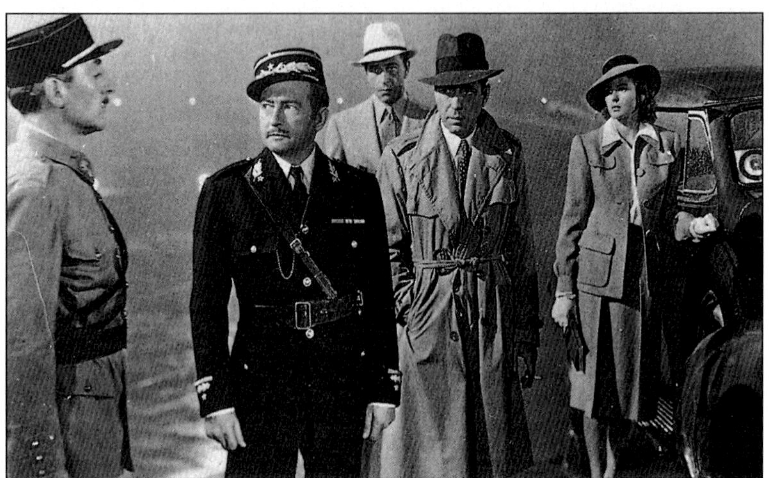

Claude Rains (2nd left), Paul Henreid, Bogart, Bergman: ***Casablanca****.*

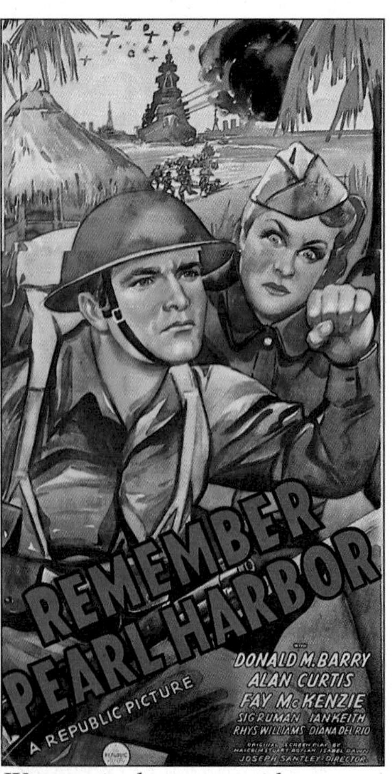
REMEMBER PEARL HARBOR
DONALD M. BARRY
ALAN CURTIS
FAY McKENZIE
SIG RUMAN IAN KEITH
RHYS WILLIAMS DIANA DEL RIO
A REPUBLIC PICTURE
JOSEPH SANTLEY DIRECTOR

War movies kept pace with events.

Hitler's Children
Based on
GREGOR ZIEMER'S
"EDUCATION FOR DEATH"
The book that Shocked the World... and as told to millions in...
READER'S DIGEST

Anticipated, but released in 1943.

Dona Drake, Bob Hope, Bing Crosby in ***Road to Morocco*** *(third in the serie*

Gene
George
ERNEY·MONTGOMERY
Lynn
BARI
CHINA
GIRL
Victor
McLAGLEN
Alan
BAXTER·RUMANN
Sig
THAWAY BEN HECHT
ENTURY-FOX PICTURE

e and adventure in the Orient.

JEAN
IDA
GABIN·LUPINO
Moontide
Thomas MITCHELL Claude RAINS
ARCHIE MAYO·Mark Hellinger·A 20th CENTURY-FOX PICTURE

Jean Gabin's first Hollywood movie.

ne Tierney (left), Ona Munson in Von Sternberg's **The Shanghai Gesture**.

America will never forget
WAKE ISLAND
RIAN DONLEVY·MACDONALD CAREY·ROBERT PRESTON
BERT DEKKER·WILLIAM BENDIX·WALTER ABEL
DIRECTED BY JOHN FARROW
Screen Play by W. R. Burnett and Frank Butler
A PARAMOUNT PICTURE

cumentary-style realism of this South Pacific war film was well-received.

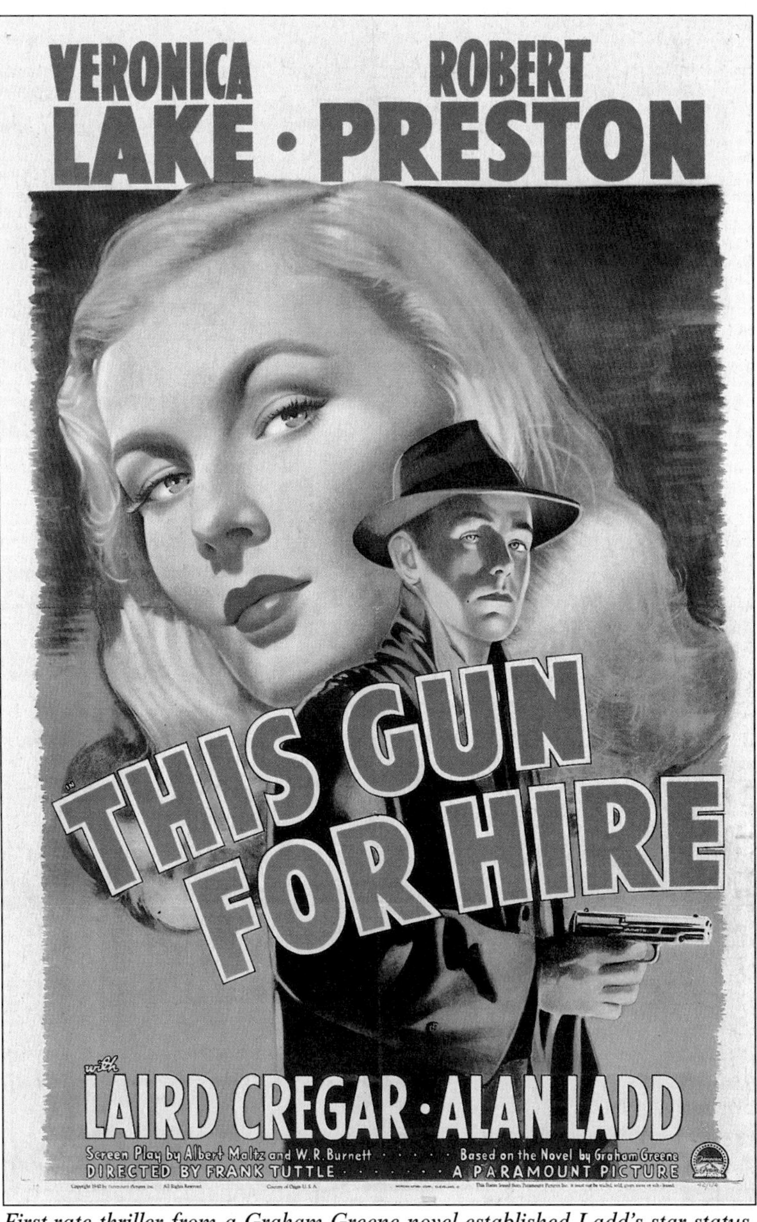
VERONICA
LAKE
ROBERT
PRESTON
THIS GUN
FOR HIRE
with
LAIRD CREGAR·ALAN LADD
Screen Play by Albert Maltz and W. R. Burnett
Based on the Novel by Graham Greene
DIRECTED BY FRANK TUTTLE
A PARAMOUNT PICTURE

First-rate thriller from a Graham Greene novel established Ladd's star status.

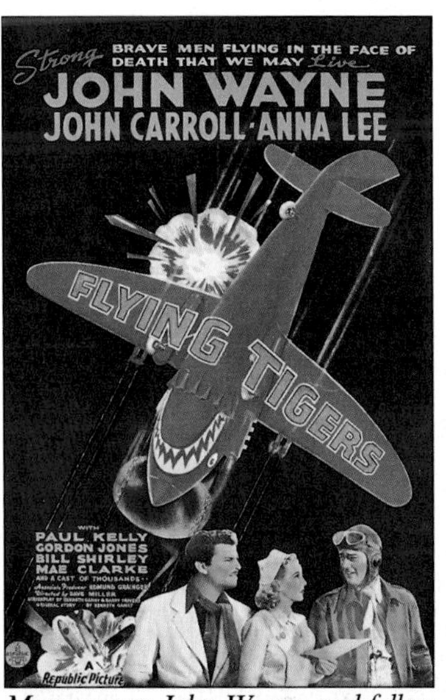
Strong
BRAVE MEN FLYING IN THE FACE OF DEATH THAT WE MAY Live
JOHN WAYNE
JOHN CARROLL·ANNA LEE
FLYING TIGERS
PAUL KELLY
GORDON JONES
BILL SHIRLEY
MAE CLARKE
A Republic Picture

More war as John Wayne and fellow airmen fought with the Japanese over World War II China.

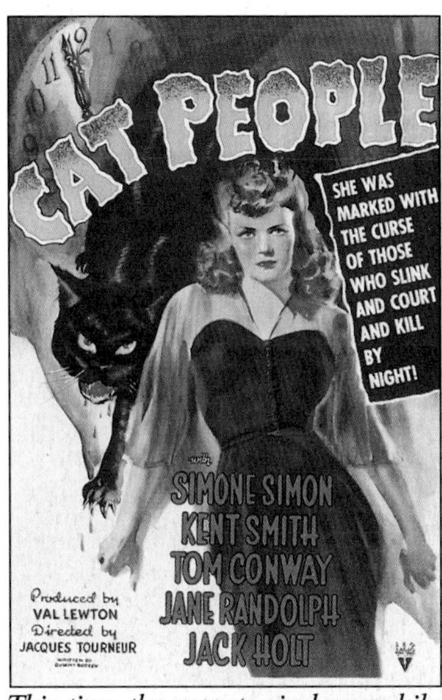
CAT PEOPLE
SHE WAS MARKED WITH THE CURSE OF THOSE WHO SLINK AND COURT AND KILL BY NIGHT!
SIMONE SIMON
KENT SMITH
TOM CONWAY
JANE RANDOLPH
JACK HOLT
Produced by
VAL LEWTON
Directed by
JACQUES TOURNEUR

This time the monster in horrorphile Val Lewton's film lurked in the darkness of the mind.

1943

1942 Academy Awards, Ambassador Hotel, 4 Mar.

Best Film:	*Mrs. Miniver* (dir: William Wyler)
Best Director:	William Wyler
Best Actor:	James Cagney *(Yankee Doodle Dandy)*
Best Actress:	Greer Garson *(Mrs. Miniver)*
Best Supp. Actor:	Van Heflin *(Johnny Eager)*
Best Supp. Actress:	Teresa Wright *(Mrs. Miniver)*

Moscow, 1 January
The exiled Polish filmmakers Jerzy Bossak and Aleksander Ford have created the Avant-Garde Cinema company with the goal of making filmed reports on the Polish struggle and the work of the partisans.

Hollywood, 1 January
At the request of the American Government, Warner Bros. have given up plans to make a biographical film of Charles de Gaulle. The tension between De Gaulle and Roosevelt appears to be the reason for this change of mind.

Paris, 12 January
Cinemas now have to close on Tuesdays to economize on electricity, and studios are ordered to cease all activity for two days a week.

Paris, 3 February
Release of a brilliantly executed comedy *l'Honorable Catherine*, from director Marcel L'Herbier and starring Edwige Feuillère.

France, 3 February
For a period of a week, a percentage of all cinema takings throughout the country will be sent to the National Aid organization for war victims.

Los Angeles, 6 February
Errol Flynn has been found not guilty of the accusation of corruption of a minor, after a trial which lasted 21 days. The charge was made by two adolescents.

France, 7 February
A member of a group of resistants, Robert Lynen, the young actor who played Poil-de-Carotte at age 11, has been arrested by the Germans. He has been imprisoned in Marseilles.

Paris, 8 February
Gilles Grangier has made *Ademai, bandit d'honneur*, produced by the Associated Prisoners' film company, a new company created by recently released prisoners.

Los Angeles, 18 March
Premiere of George Cukor's *Keeper of the Flame*, starring Katharine Hepburn and Spencer Tracy.

New York, 19 March
Eight of Al Capone's accomplices have been charged with extorting $2.5 million from the Cinema Technicians Union.

Tokyo, 25 March
Release of director Akira Kurosawa's first film *Sugata Sanshiro* (*Judo Saga*), with Susumu Fujita and Takashi Shimura.

Vichy, 15 April
A decree requires distributors and cinemas to give priority to short films of "national interest".

Italy, 16 April
Fascist authorities have seized all copies of Luchino Visconti's earthy film, *Ossessione*.

Hollywood, 21 April
Release of *I Walked With a Zombie*, directed by Jacques Tourneur for Val Lewton at RKO.

Hollywood, 10 May
An opinion poll carried out by the *Motion Picture Herald* has shown that the public is saturated with war films and is demanding movies that distract and entertain.

Los Angeles, 27 May
RKO has released Jean Renoir's *This Land is Mine*, a film about the French Resistance shot entirely on studio sets, starring Charles Laughton, Maureen O'Hara and George Sanders.

New York, 27 May
Billy Wilder has made a film about Rommel's exploits in North Africa. *Five Graves to Cairo* stars Franchot Tone, Anne Baxter, Akim Tamiroff and Erich von Stroheim. Wilder also wrote the screenplay for the film which is being released today.

Paris, 31 May
Jean Grémillon is on location at the airport in Le Bourget for his latest film *le Ciel est à vous* (*The Woman Who Dared*).

Paris, 21 June
A devastating fire has destroyed the France-Actualités' film library and all the cutting studios at the Buttes-Chaumont.

New Delhi, 17 July
As the British sources of supply are uncertain due to the war in Europe, the government is now rationing unexposed negative. All advertising films are forbidden.

Paris, 3 August
The Commercial court for the Seine has endorsed the Pathé-Cinéma company's recovery by certifying the payment of their debts.

Los Angeles, 11 August
Release of Ernst Lubitsch's *Heaven Can Wait* with Gene Tierney, Don Ameche and Charles Coburn.

France, 12 August
German authorities have forbidden all filming in the coastal zones.

Hollywood, 22 August
The studios are dubbing their recent films in French and Italian with the plan to distribute them in Europe after the war.

Nice, 9 September
Fighting in Italy has forced studios to close. The shooting of two films has been interrupted: *la Boite aux rêves*, by Yves Allégret, and *les Enfants du paradis* (*Children of Paradise*), by Marcel Carné.

Washington, 30 September
Clark Gable, who signed up as a lieutenant in the air force, has been awarded the Distinguished Flying Cross and the Air Medal.

Lisbon, 12 October
Antonio Lopes Ribeiro, generally considered to be the "official" filmmaker for the Salazar regime, has released, *Amor de perdiçao*.

Rome, 30 October
Young scriptwriter Federico Fellini has married the actress Giulietta Masina. The newlyweds are both 23 years old.

Moscow, 1 November
Release of *Jdi menya* (*Wait for M*
by Alexander Stolper and B
Ivanov. It is the first film about l
rather than heroic deeds of war t
made since the fighting began.

Los Angeles, 27 December
Henry King has made *The Song*
Bernadette, based on Franz Werf
book, with Jennifer Jones, Cha
Bickford, and Vincent Price.

BIRTHS

Texas, 6 February
Gayle Hunnicut

New York, 21 March
Christopher Walken

Paris, 28 April
Jacques Dutronc

England, 13 June
Malcolm McDowell

New York, 17 August
Robert De Niro

New York, 27 August
Tuesday Weld

Paris, 22 October
Catherine Deneuve (C. Dorléac)

Algiers, 4 November
Marlène Jobert

Illinois, 5 November
Sam Shepard

South Carolina, 17 November
Lauren Hutton

Poland, 25 December
Hanna Schygulla

England, 31 December
Ben Kingsley

DEATHS

Hollywood, 3 April
Conrad Veidt

Near Lisbon, 1 June
Leslie Howard

Named for the servicemen's club
New York where stars entertain
boys on leave, this film boasts a b
of United Artists' best, from He
Hayes to Johnny Weissmuller.

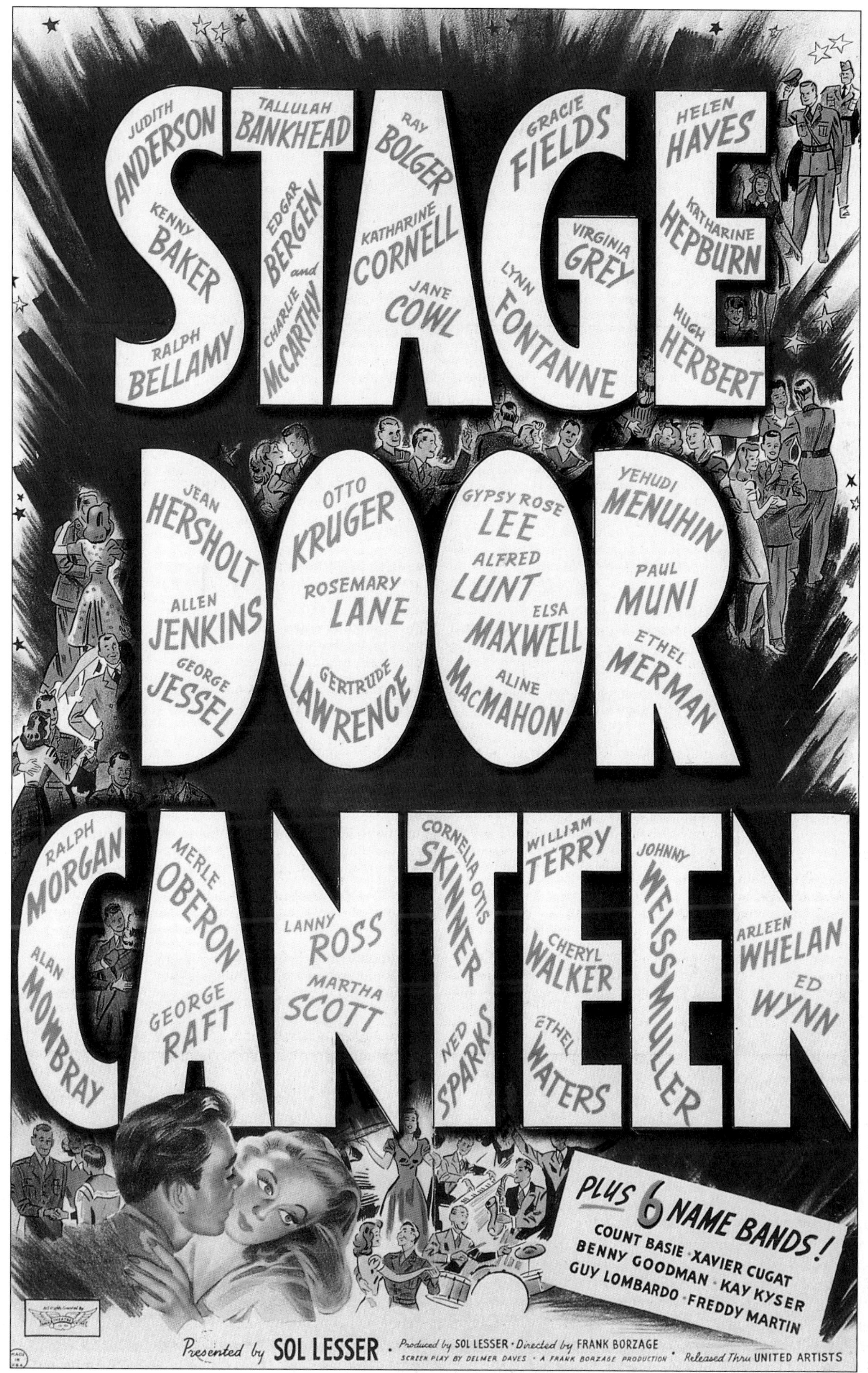
STAGE DOOR CANTEEN
JUDITH ANDERSON
TALLULAH BANKHEAD
RAY BOLGER
GRACIE FIELDS
HELEN HAYES
KENNY BAKER
EDGAR BERGEN and CHARLIE McCARTHY
KATHARINE CORNELL
VIRGINIA GREY
KATHARINE HEPBURN
JANE COWL
LYNN FONTANNE
HUGH HERBERT
RALPH BELLAMY
JEAN HERSHOLT
OTTO KRUGER
GYPSY ROSE LEE
YEHUDI MENUHIN
ALFRED LUNT
ALLEN JENKINS
ROSEMARY LANE
PAUL MUNI
ELSA MAXWELL
GEORGE JESSEL
GERTRUDE LAWRENCE
ALINE MacMAHON
ETHEL MERMAN
RALPH MORGAN
MERLE OBERON
CORNELIA OTIS SKINNER
WILLIAM TERRY
JOHNNY WEISSMULLER
LANNY ROSS
ARLEEN WHELAN
ALAN MOWBRAY
CHERYL WALKER
GEORGE RAFT
MARTHA SCOTT
ED WYNN
NED SPARKS
ETHEL WATERS
PLUS 6 NAME BANDS!
COUNT BASIE · XAVIER CUGAT
BENNY GOODMAN · KAY KYSER
GUY LOMBARDO · FREDDY MARTIN
Presented by SOL LESSER · Produced by SOL LESSER · Directed by FRANK BORZAGE
SCREEN PLAY BY DELMER DAVES · A FRANK BORZAGE PRODUCTION · Released Thru UNITED ARTISTS

Love lost and war won in Casablanca

New York, 23 January
With considerable commercial acumen, Warner Brothers have delayed the release of their espionage melodrama *Casablanca* to coincide with the big Allied conference in the same North African city. The screen Casablanca is not the thriving modern metropolis but an exotic hotbed of spies, black marketeers, refugees and Gestapo men where "everybody goes to Rick's." And presiding over Rick's Café Americain is Humphrey Bogart's disillusioned gun-runner Richard Blaine, a bruised idealist haunted by the bittersweet memory of a fleeting Paris romance with Ingrid Bergman. Her sudden reappearance at Rick's, and request for pianist Dooley Wilson to play "As Time Goes By", tests the tortured Rick's loyalty to the limit. Director Michael Curtiz handles a swirl of subplots and salty supporting players with great aplomb: twitchy little black marketeer Peter Lorre; Sydney Greenstreet's massively amiable fixer; Claude Rains as an elegantly amoral Vichy chief of police, "rounding up the usual suspects"; and Conrad Veidt's reptilian Nazi. This is hokum of the very highest class, set in a chiaroscuro never-never land which grips from the movie's opening montage. As director Curtiz has told Jack Warner, "The scenario isn't the exact truth, but we have the facts to prove it."

Humphrey Bogart as Rick the cafe owner and Ingrid Bergman as Ilse.

Hitch casts doubt on Main Street USA

Hollywood, 20 January
Director Alfred Hitchcock's lat thriller, *Shadow of a Doubt*, mark quite radical departure from previous Hollywood productio An intimate, low-keyed drama, i most remarkable for its highly ori nal and slightly off-beat evocation life in a back-water American tow achieved by shooting much of t film on location in a real Califor podunk far from the studio back-l Hitchcock said, "I am extrem anxious to avoid the conventio small-town American scene and t stock figures that have been seen so many films." The director coll orated closely with writer Thornt Wilder on the brilliant script tha about a charming and handso man (Joseph Cotten), arriving town to visit his relatives, who tu out to be a murderer on the r Tension mounts to a hair-raising max as his niece (Teresa Wrig grows increasingly suspicious of h and fears for her own life...

Captain Coward's courage serves British

New York, 4 January
Clinching proof that the war has regenerated British cinema is provided by a superb new picture, *In Which We Serve*, written and produced by Noel Coward, who also stars and co-directs with former film editor David Lean. Coward plays Captain Kinross, the commander of the warship HMS *Torrin*, a part closely modeled on his friend Louis Mountbatten, whose own ship *Kelly* was sunk off Crete in 1941. The story of the *Torrin* and her crew is told in flashback, after her own sinking, and is notable for giving even-handed treatment to the ship's officers and men.

Luchino Visconti unveils 'neo-realism'

Rome, 31 January
Ossessione has annoyed the intellectual and social elite of Rome. For many months a sense of mystery has surrounded Luchino Visconti's first feature film. The 36-year-old Milanese aristocrat is known for his affiliations with young anti-fascists, has worked at the *Centro Sperimentale di Cinematografia* and on the ma zine *Cinema*. It was Jean Ren who had advised Visconti to ada James Cain's novel *The Postm Always Rings Twice* for the scre Visconti has pulled no punches the telling of this tragic story, a st which the critic Antonio Pietrang has labeled "neo-realist".

Noel Coward, captain of the war ship, tends an injured crew member.

Massimo Girotti and Clara Calamai in ***Ossessione*** *from James M. Cain's nov*

oward Hughes shocks with 'The Outlaw'

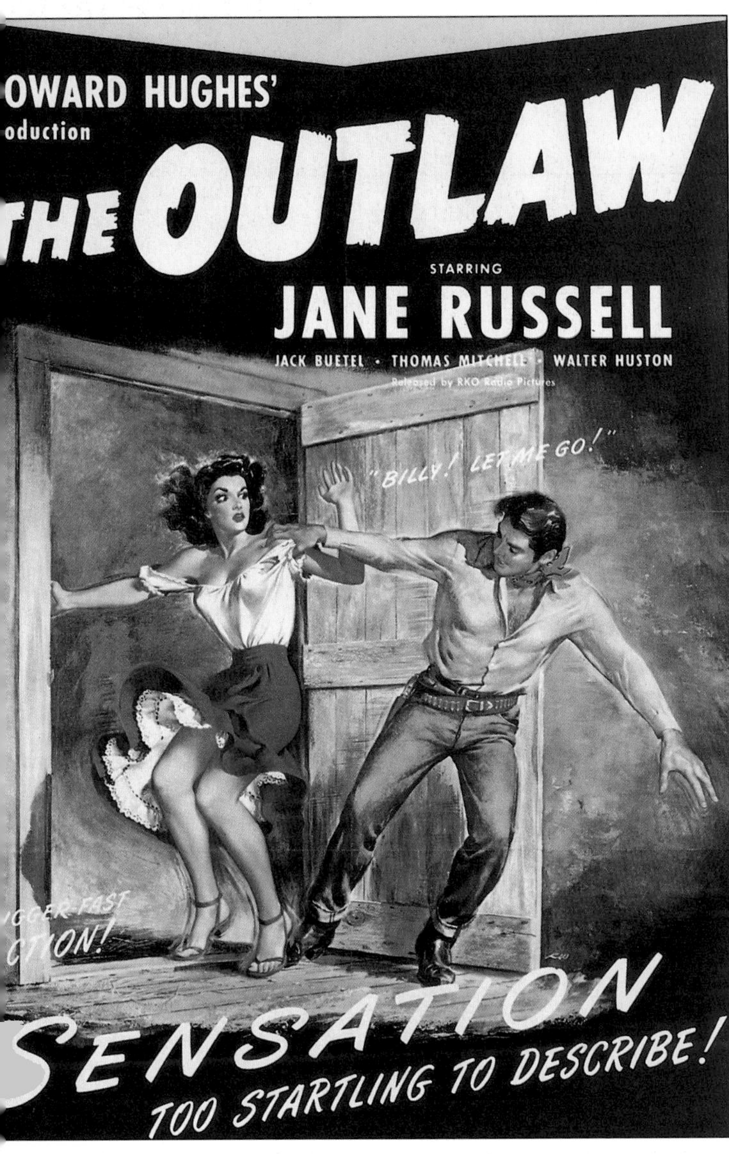
OWARD HUGHES'
oduction
THE OUTLAW
STARRING
JANE RUSSELL
JACK BUETEL · THOMAS MITCHELL · WALTER HUSTON
"BILLY! LET ME GO!"
SENSATION
TOO STARTLING TO DESCRIBE!

s Angeles, 5 February
huge uproar has broken out over premiere of RKO's *The Outlaw*, bizarre Western that was designed launch Jane Russell, the most recent "discovery" of the millionaire ovie dilettante and all round oddball Howard Hughes. He built the entire production around Russell's magnificent breasts, even designing a special brassiere to enhance her dizzying cleavage. The censors and the Catholic League of Decency have forced the film's withdrawal.

Münchhausen' marvelous in Agfacolor

rlin, 5 March
ron Münchhausen, a delightful, tertaining new fantasy and adventure film, starring Hans Albers in e title role, has taken three years to ach the screen. The project was st set in motion by Nazi propaganda minister Josef Goebbels, who nted to celebrate UFA's 25th anniversary with a suitably spectacular gfacolor production. The public is ing to love it.

Jennings pays his tribute to firefighters

A characteristic moment from ***Fires Were Started****, a document of quiet heroism.*

London, 12 April
The British documentary filmmaker Humphrey Jennings, a graduate of the influential GPO Film Unit, has paid poetic tribute to the efforts of London's Auxiliary Fire Service at the time of the Blitz in *Fires Were Started*. The film follows the integration of a new volunteer (played by novelist William Sansom) into a fire team during the night of a heavy raid. Jennings evokes the dirt and danger of their work with a stream of striking images as the firemen fight to stop a docklands blaze from spreading to a munitions ship.

Billy Wilder's fight against the Desert Fox

New York, 26 May
Director Billy Wilder has cast bullet-headed Erich von Stroheim as the dashing Desert Fox, General Erwin Rommel, in Paramount's new *Five Graves to Cairo*. The film is a reworking of the 1939 *Hotel Imperial*. Here British agent Franchot Tone infiltrates Akim Tamiroff's German-occupied desert inn to uncover the secrets of Rommel's supply dumps before the Battle of El Alamein.

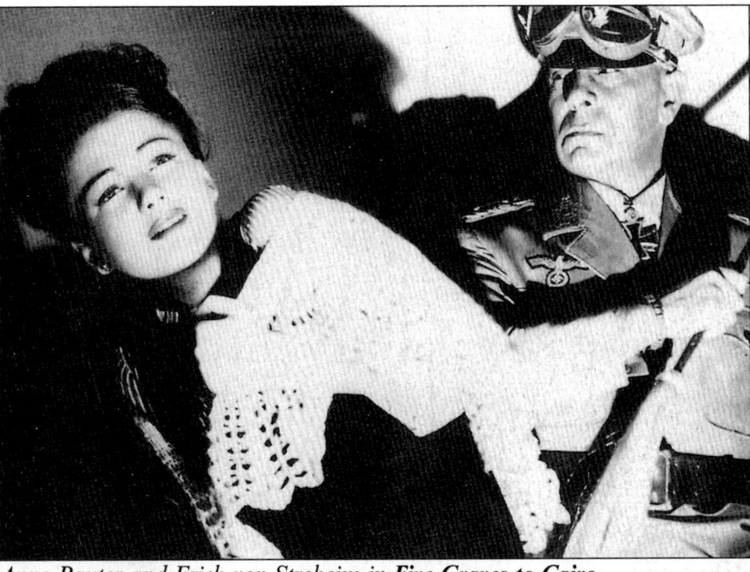

Anne Baxter and Erich von Stroheim in ***Five Graves to Cairo****.*

Renoir follows Lang in American war effort

This Land is Mine: *George Sanders, left, Maureen O'Hara, Walter Slezak.*

New York, 27 May
Since America's declaration of war against Germany, Hollywood has felt free to produce various anti-German films. A few months after Fritz Lang brought out *Hangmen Also Die*, based on a story by Bertolt Brecht, and set in Czechoslovakia after the assassination of Heydrich, a new film by Jean Renoir is now contributing to the anti-Nazi cause. *This Land Is Mine* tells of a cowardly, mother-dominated schoolteacher (Charles Laughton) who is secretly in love with a colleague (Maureen O'Hara). She is engaged to a railway superintendent (George Sanders), who betrays her brother and resistance fighter (Kent Smith) to a Nazi major (Walter Slezak). Laughton finally gets up enough backbone to speak out against the enemy and is arrested. Such phrases as "sabotage is the only weapon left to a free people" as well as the film's condemnation of collaboration are extremely effective and necessary in the propaganda war.

Donlevy, Anna Lee in Lang's film.

Robert Bresson films a passionate sacrifi

Silvia Montfort and Renée Faure in Bresson's ***les Anges du péché.***

Paris, 23 June
Robert Bresson's first full-length film, *les Anges du péché*, has a very original tone. Using a screenplay by Father Raymond-Leopold Bruckberger and Jean Giraudoux, the film succeeds in being religious without falling into religiosity. It tells of a young novice (Renée Fauré) w devotes herself to the redemption an ex-prisoner and murderer (Ja Holt) even though it means sacri ing herself. The rigor and intens of the direction and acting ov comes some of the more melod matic aspects of the plot.

Bell still tolls for Spanish Republicans

New York, 14 July
The publicity for *For Whom The Bell Tolls* promises audiences "168 Minutes of Romance and Suspense that will leave you Breathless!" It was Ernest Hemingway who suggested that the part of the American adventurer from his Spanish Civil war novel be taken by Gary Cooper. T role of the woman with whom falls in love initially went to Ve Zorina who, fortunately, was placed by Ingrid Bergman. The l ter has created a sensation by r plucking her eyebrows and havi her hair cut very short.

Charlie Chaplin marries Oona O'Neill

California, 16 June
At a quiet ceremony in south Burbank, 54-year-old Charlie Chaplin has married for the fourth time. His bride is 18-year-old Oona O'Neill, the daughter of playwright Eugene O'Neill. The couple met at a dinner party in Hollywood in the spring of 1942 at a time when Oona was trying to launch her acting career. The delicately beautiful young woman had already tested for a part in an Anna Sten vehicle. Chaplin, who was then considering filming Paul Vincent Carroll's play *Shadow and Substance*, offered the gazelle-like O'Neill a contract. By the time the project was shelved at the end of the year, Chaplin was passionately in love with O'Neill, captivated by her beauty, intelligence and reticence. They decided to get married as soon as Oona turned 18. The ceremon y, news of which was broken exclusively by the columnist Louella Parsons, was conducted in great secrecy. The only hitch came when the elderly minister registered Chaplin's name as Chapman, a mistake which was quickly rectified. The couple are now incommunicado somewhere in Santa Barbara, hunted by a pack of reporters. However Eugene O'Neill, who strongly disapproves of this marriage, has cut communications with his daughter.

Gary Cooper (center) and Ingrid Bergman in ***For Whom the Bell Tolls.***

vesey and Powell's superb 'Blimp'

orah Kerr and Roger Livesey in **The Life and Death of Colonel Blimp**.

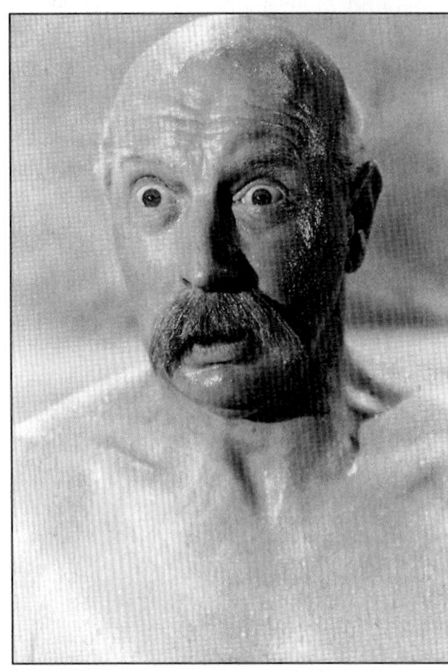
Livesey as the old Colonel Blimp.

don, 26 July
writer-director team of Emeric sburger and Michael Powell e now brought cartoonist David 's Colonel Blimp to the screen *he Life and Death of Colonel ıp*. The screen Blimp is Major-eral Clive Wynne-Candy, the ghty old tusker whose life we w from impetuous youth to tering old age. Powell had wanted Laurence Olivier, now serving in the Fleet Air Arm, to play the title role, but he was not available. He was replaced by Roger Livesey, who gives a brilliantly observed portrait of a hidebound but good-hearted old bumbler. Strong support is provided by Anton Walbrook as Livesey's German friend and Deborah Kerr, red-haired and ravishing as the three different women in Wynne-Candy's life. However, this densely layered and intensely personal national epic has been attacked by critics for being out of touch with the mood of wartime Britain. And Prime Minister Winston Churchill has made an unsuccessful bid to have the film banned for export on the grounds that so sympathetic a portrait of such a reactionary character would be bad for morale.

Rita Hayworth is Mrs. Orson Welles

Santa Monica, 7 September
"Orson Welles has shot into my life like a comet trailing fire," says Rita Hayworth, who has just become the Boy Wonder's second wife (he divorced his first, Virginia Nicholson, in 1939). Rita met the brilliant young director at a private film showing last spring, and they have been inseparable ever since. In July and August they entertained troops on a morale-boosting tour. Rita has taken a stimulating route on the way to her rendezvous with Welles, much to the exasperation of Columbia boss Harry Cohn, who has tried, without a great deal of success, to direct her personal affairs. After the collapse of her marriage to businessman Ed Judson, she has been successively "engaged" to Victor Mature, her co-star in *My Gal Sal*, Gilbert Roland, Howard Hughes, Tony Martin and, last but not least, British star David Niven. The wedding, as befits two of Hollywood's most glamorous figures, was a glittering affair, and Hayworth, at her most sumptuous, drew an eight-column headline trumpeting "The Marriage of Beauty and the Brain."

galaxy of stars lighten the wartime load

lywood, 25 September
nk Your Lucky Stars is a bumper kage of star turns designed to g entertainment into the lives of liers overseas as well as the fami- they have left behind. On the k of a slender plot, featuring Dennis Morgan as a singer trying to get Eddie Cantor to put him on his show, are hung appearances by Bette Davis, Errol Flynn, John Garfield, Ida Lupino and Olivia De Havilland, among a host of other Warner Bros. stars.

'ie Cantor and girls do a turn for the boys in **Thank Your Lucky Stars**.

Director Clouzot wields a poisoned pen

Paris, 28 September
The second feature film from Henri-Georges Clouzot, *le Corbeau*, is a vitriolic look at French provincial life. It tells of a spate of poison-pen letters from someone ("the raven" of the title) who knows the secrets of the recipients, and the effect it has on those small-town inhabitants. Produced with German capital, the film has avoided Vichy censorship, though rumors regarding its showing in Germany under the title of *A Small French Town* are unfounded.

Ginette Leclerc, at the center of scandal, in Clouzot's **The Raven (le Corbeau)**.

The
OX-BOW
INCIDENT
starring
HENRY FONDA
Dana ANDREWS ★ Mary Beth HUGHES
WILLIAM A. WELLMAN ★ LAMAR TROTTI
20th CENTURY-FOX PICTURE

No real heroes in solemn, impressive, unromantic reinterpretation of the West.

*The musical **Cabin in the Sky** was Vincente Minnelli's film directing debut.*

Richard Tregaskis'
GUADALCANAL
DIARY
PRESTON FOSTER · LLOYD NOLAN · WILLIAM BENDIX · RICHARD CONTE · ANTHONY QUINN
LEW SEILER
BRYAN FOY
ISLIN AUSTER
20th

Overheated World War II action picture of Marines fighting for Pacific base was blatant propaganda.

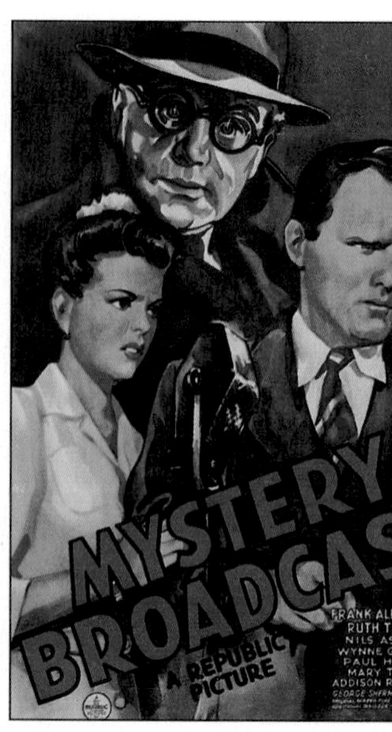
MYSTERY
BROADCAS
A REPUBLIC PICTURE

This was a departure for Ge Sherman, a prolific director kn for low-budget Republic Western

Metro-Goldwyn-Mayer presents
MICKEY ROONEY
JUDY GARLAND
THE BIG MUSICAL WITH BROADWAY FLAIR AND A WESTERN AIR!
GERSHWIN'S
GIRL CRAZY
with GIL STRATTON · ROBERT E. STRICKLA
"RAGS" RAGLAND · JUNE ALLYS
NANCY WALKER · GUY KIBB
TOMMY DORSEY AND HI ORCHEST
DIRECTED BY NORMAN TAUROG · PRODUCED BY ARTHUR F

One of the year's musical highs with gorgeous George and Ira Gershwin sc

Orson Welles'
MERCURY PRODUCTION
OURNEY
NTO FEAR
Starring
JOSEPH COTTEN
DOLORES DEL RIO
RUTH WARRICK
ORSON WELLES

lles scripted this enjoyable melo, ' co-directed with Norman Foster.

Betty
GRABLE
George
MONTGOMERY
Cesar
ROMERO
CONEY
ISLAND
in TECHNICOLOR
20th
Charles WINNINGER Phil SILVERS
WALTER LANG
WILLIAM PERLBERG

Two fairground showmen vied for singer's affections in big hit.

Paramount Presents
FOR WHOM
THE BELL TOLLS
From the celebrated novel by Ernest Hemingway
Starring
GARY
COOPER
INGRID
BERGMAN
PRODUCED AND
DIRECTED BY
SAM WOOD
B.G. DeSYLVA
EXECUTIVE PRODUCER
AKIM TAMIROFF · ARTURO de CORDOVA
JOSEPH CALLEIA and KATINA PAXINOU
Screen Play by Dudley Nichols
IN TECHNICOLOR
A Paramount Picture

Paramount paid $150,000 for the rights to Ernest Hemingway's famous novel.

AN
Ernst
LUBITSCH
PRODUCTION
Heaven Can Wait
TECHNICOLOR
20th
CENTURY-FOX
PICTURE
WITH
GENE
TIERNEY
DON
AMECHE
AND
Charles COBURN · Marjorie MAIN · Laird CREGAR · Spring BYINGTON · Allyn JOSLYN
SCREEN PLAY BY SAMSON RAPHAELSON — BASED UPON THE PLAY "BIRTHDAY" BY LAZLO BUS-FEKETE
PRODUCED AND DIRECTED by ERNST LUBITSCH

' 'Lubitsch Touch' was much in evidence in this charming period fantasy.

TODAY'S GREATEST
DRAMA!
John Steinbeck's
The
MOON
IS
DOWN
20th
CENTURY-FOX
PICTURE
with
SIR CEDRIC
HARDWICKE
HENRY
TRAVERS
LEE J.
COBB
DORRIS
BOWDON
MARGARET
WYCHERLY
IRVING PICHEL
NUNNALLY JOHNSON

Nazi-resistance tale set in Norway.

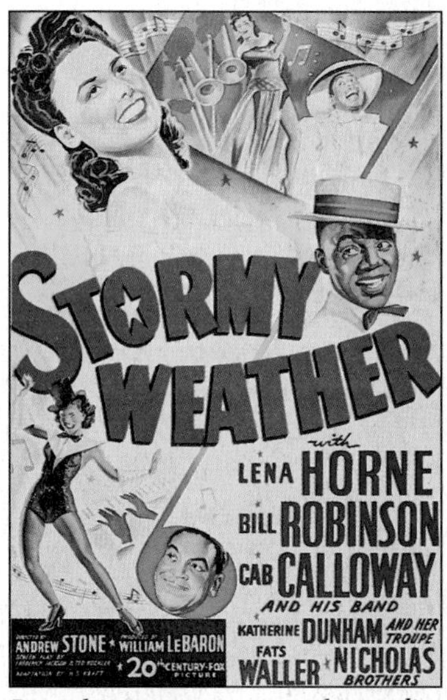
STORMY
WEATHER
with
LENA HORNE
BILL ROBINSON
CAB CALLOWAY
AND HIS BAND
KATHERINE DUNHAM AND HER TROUPE
FATS WALLER
NICHOLAS BROTHERS
ANDREW STONE
WILLIAM LeBARON
20th CENTURY-FOX

Big talent overcame a weak storyline in this all-black revue.

1944

1943 Academy Awards, Grauman's Chinese Theater, 2 Mar.

Best Film:	*Casablanca* (dir: Michael Curtiz)
Best Director:	Michael Curtiz
Best Actor:	Paul Lukas *(Watch on the Rhine)*
Best Actress:	Jennifer Jones *(The Song of Bernadette)*
Best Supp. Actor:	Charles Coburn *(The More the Merrier)*

Poland, 1 January
Filmmaker Aleksander Ford is shooting *Majdanek,* a documentary on the Nazi extermination camp, which has just been liberated by the Soviet army.

New York, 12 January
Release of Alfred Hitchcock's film *Lifeboat*, with William Bendix, Tallulah Bankhead, John Hodiak and Walter Slezak in the cast.

Paris, 15 January
After the release of Pierre Billon's *Vautrin* (*Vautrin the Thief*), with Michel Simon, a newspaper published the following: "The cinema has condemned us to seeing the base, disgusting, revolting face that Michel Simon gives to Vautrin." Denounced by *le Pilori* as a Jew, his photo is on view at the anti-Semite exhibition at the Berlitz Palace.

Rome, 17 January
With the liberation of the capital, Roberto Rossellini has started filming *Roma Città Aperta* (Rome, Open City), starring Anna Magnani and Aldo Fabrizi.

Moscow, 24 January
Release of director Mark Donskoi's *Radouga*, which portrays life in a Ukrainian village subjected to atrocities by the German troops during the Occupation.

Paris, 31 January
Death of Jean Giraudoux – author, playwright, scriptwriter and the former Commissioner of Information.

Los Angeles, 4 February
Little 11-year-old Elizabeth Taylor is making *National Velvet* for MGM's Clarence Brown.

Los Angeles, 6 February
Jean Renoir has married Dido Freire. One of the witnesses was Charles Laughton, who stars in Renoir's latest film about the French Resistance, *This Land is Mine.*

California, 14 April
Marlene Dietrich has undertaken a tour of the American bases in Italy and North Africa.

Los Angeles, 2 May
Release of *Going My Way*, a musical comedy about the conflict between a priest (Barry Fitzgerald) and his young replacement (Bing Crosby). Leo McCarey directs.

New York, 4 May
Premiere at the Capitol Theater of George Cukor's *Gaslight*, starring Charles Boyer and Ingrid Bergman.

Italy, 3 June
Partisans have managed to free director Luchino Visconti from the prison in San Gregorio where he had been transferred for acts of resistance. His political connections have made him a popular target for the fascist regime.

Hollywood, 29 June
Otto Preminger has finished filming *Laura* with Gene Tierney in the title role and Dana Andrews. Laura's portrait in the film is in fact a photograph done over with oil paint.

Hollywood, 1 July
Leon Schlesinger, the producer of "Merry Melodies" and "Looney Tunes", has decided to retire. He has sold his studio to Warner Bros.

Paris, 22 August
Henri Langlois, under the aegis of the French Cinemathèque, has just screened Victor Fleming's *Gone With the Wind* before the cinemas have even had time to reopen. It is the first American film to be shown in Paris since the Liberation.

Paris, 25 August
The actor Charles Dauphin, a colonel with the Leclerc division, took part in the liberation of Paris. Having served in London and in the U.S., he arrived in France with the Allied forces on 14 July.

New York, 1 September
Warner Bros. have finally released *Arsenic and Old Lace*, directed by Frank Capra before he offered his services to the U.S. Government to supervise the production of a series of propaganda films to explain the America's war commitment.

Paris, 24 September
Fred Astaire is giving a show for the allied forces at the Olympia Theatre. It is the first time the famous dancer and actor has appeared on stage in France, but unfortunately, the show is not open to the public.

Paris, 27 September
The actor Roger Duchesne has been arrested in the 18th arrondissement, where he has been in hiding since the Liberation. He is accused of having worked for the Gestapo.

Stockholm, 2 October
Release of *Hets* (*Torment*), by Alf Sjöberg, who is considered to be Sweden's leading filmmaker, with Stig Jarrel, Alf Kjellin and Mai Zetterling. Ingmar Bergman wrote the impressive screenplay.

Paris, 4 October
Marlene Dietrich has arrived in the capital to take part in a show at the Olympia for the allied forces.

Paris, 13 October
Actress Odette Joyeux, who was arrested at home yesterday following a denunciation, has been released. The charges proved groundless.

New York, 16 October
Release of *Spies on the Thames* (aka *Ministry of Fear*), by Fritz Lang, adapted from a Graham Greene novel. The film stars Ray Milland, Marjorie Reynolds and Dan Duryea.

Paris, 24 October
Charles Vanel's appearance in Paris has put an end to the rumors about his disappearance.

Paris, 6 December
After a long four-year break, the activities of the Cercle du Cinéma, organized by Henri Langlois, have started up again. A screening will take place at 8:15 p.m. in the Studio de l'Etoile, with a program of films by Méliès, Emile Cohl, René Clair, Luis Buñuel and Jean Vigo.

Madrid, 20 December
Due to financial problems enco tered by the producers, Abel Ga has had to stop work on the film started two weeks ago, starring famous matador Manolete.

Germany, 31 December
In a country ruined by the war, ducers, nevertheless, managed turn out 75 full-length films du the past year.

BIRTHS

California, 1 January
George Lucas
(George Walton Lucas Jr.)

Netherlands, 23 January
Rutger Hauer

New York, 13 February
Stockard Channing
(Susan Stockard)

England, 14 February
Alan Parker

Paris, 5 May
Jean-Pierre Léaud

Indochina, 10 May
Marie-France Pisier

California, 31 July
Geraldine Chaplin

Australia, 21 August
Peter Weir

England, 13 September
Jacqueline Bisset

New York, 25 September
Michael Douglas

New York, 8 October
Chevy Chase
(Cornelius Crane Chase)

New Jersey, 17 November
Danny DeVito

DEATHS

Los Angeles, 22 December
Harry Langdon

Laurence Olivier as Shakespea ***Henry V*** *in the stirring and visu magnificent film version of the p with which this compelling actor also made his directing debut.*

Mexico delivers Del Rio in scorching drama

Dolores Del Rio and Pedro Armendariz, the leads in **Maria Candelaria**.

Mexico, 20 January
The same day as the Mexican director Emilio Fernandez commenced shooting *The Pearl*, based on John Steinbeck's novella, his latest film *Maria Candelaria* has opened to acclaim. Both the exquisite Dolores Del Rio, showing few signs of age at 38 (she had been a star of Hollywood silents), in the title role as an Indian peasant girl, and Pedro Armendariz as her poverty-stricken fiance, are excellent. Particularly impressive is Gabriel Figueroa's photography of the Mexican settings. This violent and flamboyant melodrama tells of how Maria's mother had been stoned to death by the members of a primitive community after she had posed nude for an artist. When her lover is jailed for stealing quinine for her malaria, Maria poses, head only, for the same artist to obtain funds. The locals make assumptions and history repeats itself. Although often verbose and solemn, the film has surprising flashes of humor embedded in its sad tale. The two great stars of the Mexican cinema had already worked together under Fernandez last year in *Flor Silvestre*.

Gene Kelly (left), Phil Silvers and Rita Hayworth in the exuberant 'Make Way For Tomorrow' number from *Cover Girl*. This first-rate musical about struggling showbiz folk, has a score by Jerome Kern and Ira Gershwin.

Warners' 'Casablanca' makes more wav

Best Actress Jennifer Jones, with Vincent Price, in **The Song of Bernadette**.

Hollywood, 2 March
This year the Academy Awards ceremony has been held in new surroundings, Grauman's Chinese Theater, with Jack Benny presiding as master of ceremonies. The proceedings are carried live by radio across the United States and to troops fighting in Europe and the Pacific. The Best Actress Oscar has been won by Jennifer Jones for performance in *Song of Bernade* while Paul Lukas scooped the B Actor Oscar for *Watch on the Rhi* Jack Warner elbowed producer H Wallis aside to pick up the Best P ture award for *Casablanca*, whi also garnered the awards for bo Best Director (Michael Curtiz) a Best Screenplay.

Sensational satire benefits Paramount

Hollywood, 7 June
Having very recently aimed his darts at motherhood in *The Miracle of Morgan's Creek*, the director-writer Preston Sturges has turned his satiric eye toward flag-waving patriotism in *Hail the Conquering Hero*. It hilariously tells of how asthmatic mild-mannered Woodrow, beautifully played by Eddie Bracken, is unwillingly set up as a war hero in hometown, a situation created a maintained by the sentimental ar sergeant (William Demarest). T fast-paced comedy, which also tak cracks at parochial politics, sm town America and apple-pie fam life, is attracting large audienc perhaps wearied by too much se ous military screen heroism.

Conquering hero Bracken, center, Franklin Pangborn, left, William Demare

ays of Glory' reveals new leading man

gory Peck and Tamara Toumanova (right) in a scene from **Days of Glory**.

Angeles, 16 June
O's *Days of Glory*, another Hol- ood tub-thumper for our Soviet s, has launched the film career andsome 28-year-old newcomer gory Peck. He co-stars with nara Toumanova, the wife of the ure's writer and producer Casey oinson, as an uncommonly good- king pair of partisans, prettily bing Molotov cocktails at Ger- n tanks. Born in La Jolla, Cali- nia, in April 1916, former medical student Peck began his acting career in 1939 with New York's Neighborhood Playhouse, modeling shirts in his spare time. He made his Broadway debut in Emlyn Williams' *The Morning Star*, following which he was tested, and turned down, by David O. Selznick. But after scoring a big stage hit in a dual role in *The Willow and I*, his chiseled good looks caught the attention of RKO. *Days of Glory* has had a cool reception, but Peck is a hot property.

Billy Wilder launches a brilliant 'film noir'

Barbara Stanwyck and Fred MacMurray, the deadly duo in **Double Indemnity**.

Hollywood, 6 September
When George Raft, a notoriously poor judge of scripts, turned down the male lead in Billy Wilder's latest picture, *Double Indemnity*, the director knew he had a hit on his hands. And instead, easy-going Fred MacMurray proves perfect in the part of the idly philandering insurance salesman ensnared by *femme fatale* Barbara Stanwyck in a plot to kill her husband, take the money, and run. Stanwyck plays the cold-blooded killer in a blonde wig and ankle bangles because Wilder wanted to make her look "as sleazy as possible." The result is a tautly orchestrated melodrama, which both Wilder and thriller writer Raymond Chandler adapted from James M. Cain's novel, in which the oppressive tension mounts as the homicidal couple's nemesis – MacMurray's cigar-chomping boss Edward G. Robinson – uncovers the truth of their "perfect murder".

ench cinema industry plays significant part in the Liberation

is, 25 August
Committee for the Liberation he Cinema remains active in the istance movement and is thwart- the Germans wherever possible. th *l'Ecran français*, its clandestine lerground newspaper plus the usands of leaflets it distributes r the city, the Committee has s managed to sabotage many of hy's directives. And just six days , the patriotic militia arm of the mmittee took over occupation of group of buildings held by the rmans, including the premises of HEC (the Institute of Cinematic dies), the General Administra- n of the Cinema, laboratories and dios at the Buttes-Chaumont, as l as companies set up and man- d by Germans: the production npany Continental Film, the dis- oution company Tobis and the nmercial channels of Sogec. This ies of insurrections has the sup- t of various cinematographic ups that comprise this Committee which has not ceased its acts of resistance since its creation early this year. Its aim is to defend the interests of the workers, to fight against deportation and to assist resistants, escaped prisoners and the families of victims. In response to orders given by the Committee, numerous professionals in the industry have continued to be active, but the skirmishes at Batignolles have given rise, tragically, to casualties.

The Resistance, mainly filmed in the Vercors by clandestine news cameramen.

Towards a cinema with clean hands

Paris, 18 July
According to an article headlined "The Cinema with Clean Hands", just published in *l'Ecran français*, there will be no place in the French cinema of tomorrow for those who collaborated with the enemy. The first edition of the clandestine newspaper was published in December 1943. Managed by René Blech, the editorial board is comprised of Pierre Blanchar, the president of the Committee, Louis Daquin, Jean Delannoy, André Luguet and André Zwobada. Only this edition has been printed bearing the name *l'Ecran Français*; the others were incorporated in *les Lettres française*. Two additional newspapers have been published in the last months: *la Cinématographie française*, put out by the Film Trade Unions (C.G.T.), and *Opera*, supported by the Resistance Committee of the Cinematographic Industry.

Fritz Lang delivers suspense noir-style

Joan Bennett and Edward G. Robinson in Fritz Lang's ***Woman in the Window****.*

New York, 10 October
Fritz Lang has returned to a favorite theme, the ruinous effect of a man's lust for a woman, in *Woman in the Window*. This powerful *film noir* traces the descent of a middle-aged professor (Edward G. Robinson) from his uneventful life into a nightmare world of deception and murder, after he meets a woman (Joan Bennett) whose portrait in a store window has hypnotized him. The performances of the leads could not have been better, and the strong supporting cast includes Raymond Massey and Dan Duryea. Certain critics have attacked the surprise ending, but it offers a Freudian explanation, implying a deeper and darker side to surface respectability.

Betty and Bogey seem to be inseparabl

MYSTY
REPERTOIR
MONTMARTROI

Newcomer Lauren Bacall with Humphrey Bogart in ***To Have and Have N***

New York, 11 October
Howard Hawks, producer-director of Ernest Hemingway's *To Have and Have Not*, has found a stunning new leading lady for the film's star Humphrey Bogart. Last autumn, Hawks' wife spotted the 18-year-old model Betty Perske on the cover of *Harper's Bazaar*. Within a month Hawks had signed her to a seven-year contract. Under her new na Lauren Bacall, she makes a se tional debut opposite Bogart as insolently independent young dri who teaches him how to whistl the sexiest possible way – "You put your lips together and blo The couple's crackling on-sc chemistry has sparked an off-scr romance, provoking the fury of 45-year-old Bogart's present Mayo Methot. However, Ha was delighted, sitting up at n with screenwriter Jules Furthma work the intimacy between Bo and Bacall into the script. Bac husky voice, carefully coached Hawks, lowered eyelids and taw tumbling hair have wowed Warn who have dubbed her offbeat bea "The Look". Money alone can create such magic.

Gene Tierney alluring as mysterious Laura in Preminger's film

New York, 11 October
Femmes fatales are all the rage at the moment, and beautiful Gene Tierney is the mystery dame in the title role of Fox's *Laura*. She's the enigmatic career girl, supposedly dead, whose life-size portrait begins to obsess dogged detective Dana Andrews. Director Rouben Mamoulian prepared the project, but after only a few days shooting he was replaced by Otto Preminger, the film's producer. Preminger fought with studio boss Darryl F. Zanuck throughout the production, but the final product looks like it will be a critical and commercial hit. In a superb supporting cast, Clifton Webb gives an outstanding performance, making his talking picture debut as the epicene columnist and murder suspect Waldo Lydecker. "I'm not kind, I'm vicious," says Waldo. "It's the secret of my charm."

l to r: Clifton Webb, Vincent Price, Judith Anderson and Dana Andrews.

Gene Tierney, the mysterious Laura.

Bogey filming ***Passage to Marsei*** *with Michèle Morgan shortly be he met Betty Perske, now Bacall.*

Minnelli, the magic master of color

ther (Garland) tries to cheer up sister Tootie (Margaret O'Brien) by singing 'Have Yourself a Merry Little Christmas'.

ew York, 28 November
remarkable new Technicolor mu-al has opened here. Undoubtedly e most stylish color picture yet eased by the giant MGM studio, *eet Me in St. Louis* is based on the stories by Sally Benson, first published in the *New Yorker*, about her life in St. Louis at the turn of the century. Producer Arthur Freed was quick to recognize the potential of this charming family chronicle, especially as a vehicle for MGM's leading young musical star, Judy Garland, and the studio's gifted new director, Vincente Minnelli. Sparing no expense, MGM has assembled a fine cast, including Mary Astor and Leon Ames as the parents, and newcomer Lucille Bremer as Judy's elder sister, along with an outstanding production team headed by cameraman George Folsey, art directors Lemuel Ayres and Jack Martin Smith, and a delightful score by Hugh Martin and Ralph Blane. The songs and dances, choreographed by Charles Walters, are seamlessly integrated into the story, while Minnelli, known as a fine director of actors, proves to be a remarkable color stylist as well. Most memorable of all is the acting of little Margaret O'Brien and, of course, Judy Garland, whose sensitive singing and acting is a sheer delight.

n board for the 'Trolley Song'.

A happy gathering of the Smith family, left to right, Henry Daniels Jr., O'Brien, Garland, Leon Ames, Joan Carroll, Mary Astor and Lucille Bremer.

Olivier's battle cry for England

London, 30 November
While Hitler's V-2 rockets fall on London, the renaissance of British cinema during the war years has been confirmed by the release of Laurence Olivier's *Henry V*, a brilliant adaptation of Shakespeare's war play. Olivier has fought his own private war to get the film to the screen, and critics are unanimous in their praise. Olivier stars and directs in one of the first British Technicolor productions, filmed in County Wicklow, Ireland, where there are none of the signs of war left which still disfigure the English landscape. *Henry V* reaches a stirring climax in the Battle of Agincourt sequence, whose sweeping style owes much to Sergei Eisenstein's *Alexander Nevsky*. Olivier did all his own stunt work, and at one point he was hobbling around with a crutch under his right arm, his left arm in a sling and a plaster bandage around his face. The final cost of *Henry V* has come in at around half a million pounds, a record for a British picture, and it was completed only with the financial help of J. Arthur Rank, who came to the rescue of producer Filippo Del Giudice when he looked to be running out of cash. The brilliant color photography is from Robert Krasker and the stirring score has been composed by William Walton. With its bold combination of stylized and naturalistic sequences, and superb supporting cast of distinguished Shakespeareans, this is a film fit to greet the end of the war.

Henry delivers the Agincourt speech.

Eric Porter in **A Canterbury Tale**.

Paramount's
Lady in the Dark
In Technicolor
Starring
GINGER ROGERS · RAY MILLAND
WARNER BAXTER · JON HALL
with MISCHA AUER
A MITCHELL LEISEN Production
Lush, funny psychoanalytic musical.

HUMPHREY
BOGART
...with his kind of woman in a powerful adaptation of
Ernest Hemingway's most daring man-woman story!
Ernest Hemingway's
"TO HAVE AND HAVE NOT"
WALTER BRENNAN · LAUREN BACALL · DOLORES MORAN
HOAGY CARMICHAEL · A HOWARD HAWKS PRODUCTION
PRESENTED BY
WARNER BROS.
In first film, Bogart and Bacall were an explosive combo on-screen and off.

Spencer Tracy and Signe Hass
The Seventh Cross.

LI'L ABNER
COLOR CARTOON
SADIE
HAWKINS
DAY
A COLUMB
SHORT-SUBJ
PRESENTAT
Li'l Abner frolicked with Daisy M

Mary Anderson and William Bendix, all at sea in Hitchcock's unusual **Lifeboat**.

Ingrid Bergman and Charles Boyer in George Cukor's remake of **Gaslight**

OR THEIR CRIMES...WE SHALL
JUDGE THEM!
ONE SHALL
ESCAPE
(The Trial of the War Criminals!)
A COLUMBIA PICTURE

ːi officer's career in flashback.

ce Behind Every Shadow... Suspense in Every Move!
INISTRY OF
FEAR
BY THE AUTHOR OF
"THIS GUN FOR HIRE"
AY MILLAND
MARJORIE REYNOLDS
CARL ESMOND · HILLARY BROOKE
PERCY WARAM · Directed by FRITZ LANG
A PARAMOUNT PICTURE

tz Lang tried out Graham Greene.

ly Garland and Lucile Bremer in **et Me in St. Louis**.

ANN
SHERIDAN
DENNIS
MORGAN
JACK
CARSON
IRENE
MANNING
"SHINE ON HARVEST MOON"
Presented by
WARNER BROS.
with
S.Z.SAKALL
Directed by
DAVID BUTLER

Pleasant backstage musical purporting to be biopic of vaudevillian Nora Bayes.

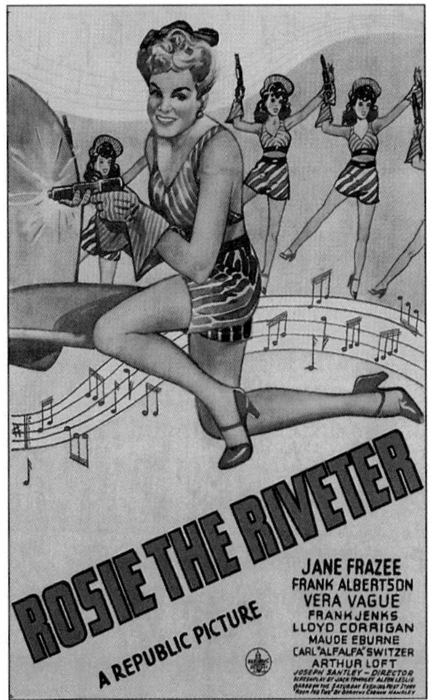
ROSIE THE RIVETER
A REPUBLIC PICTURE
JANE FRAZEE
FRANK ALBERTSON
VERA VAGUE
FRANK JENKS
LLOYD CORRIGAN
MAUDE EBURNE
CARL "ALFALFA" SWITZER
ARTHUR LOFT
JOSEPH SANTLEY - DIRECTOR

Jane Frazee did many B-musicals.

*Captive **Wild Woman**'s weak sequel.*

JUNGLE WOMAN
with
EVELYN ANKERS
J. CARROL NAISH
LOIS COLLIER
MILBURN STONE
DOUGLASS DUMBRILLE
and
ACQUANETTA
as The JUNGLE WOMAN
A UNIVERSAL PICTURE

*Robert Young (left) in Jules Dassin's **The Canterville Ghost**.*

*Critical raves greeted Alexander Knox's portrayal of U.S. President **Wilson**.*

1945

1944 Academy Awards, Grauman's Chinese Theater, 15 Mar.

Best Film:	*Going My Way* (dir: Leo McCarey)
Best Director:	Leo McCarey
Best Actor:	Bing Crosby *(Going My Way)*
Best Actress:	Ingrid Bergman *(Gaslight)*
Best Supp. Actor:	Barry Fitzgerald *(Going My Way)*
Best Supp. Actress:	Ethel Barrymore *(None but the Lonely Heart)*

London, 18 January
The Rank Organisation has created a production company, J. Arthur Rank Productions Ltd., with its base at Pinewood. This is an impressive addition to the number of studios, laboratories and cinema companies already set up by the organization since 1935.

Los Angeles, 3 February
Walt Disney gave a preview of his new cartoon feature, *The Three Caballeros*, with Donald Duck, Pablo Penguin, José Carioca and the bird Aracua, "the clown of the jungle".

Paris, 11 February
Louis Jouvet and his troupe are once more on French soil after an absence of four years in South America. Jacques Feyder has already approached him for a role in the film *Talleyrand*.

California, 15 February
Olivia De Havilland has won a landmark decision in her case against Warner Bros. The studios were trying to bind the actress, whom they had earlier suspended for rebellious behaviour, to an extra six months. The Supreme Court has now set the outside limit of a studio-player contract at seven years, including *periods of suspension*.

New York, 1 March
Release of *The Picture of Dorian Gray*, directed by Albert Lewin. This adaptation of Oscar Wilde's famous novel stars Hurd Hatfield, as the tormented anti-hero, with George Sanders, Donna Reed and Angela Lansbury in support.

Hollywood, 13 March
The strike by 15,000 machinists and technicians has paralyzed all activity in the studios.

Copenhagen, 23 March
Carl Dreyer has given a preview of a film he made in Sweden *Tva Manniskor* (*Two People*).

Los Angeles, 24 March
Friz Freleng has finished making his latest cartoon *Life With Feathers* for Warner Bros.' "Merrie Melodies" series, which features a new loveable cartoon character called Sylvester the cat.

Paris, 4 April
The Clichy Palace cinema, which specializes in American films for the Allied forces, is screening a copy of Marcel Carné's *les Visiteurs du soir*, with English subtitles and retitled *The Devil's Envoy*.

Paris, 14 April
All city cinemas and other places of entertainment will be shut today as a mark of respect for the American President, Franklin D. Roosevelt. His funeral takes place today in Washington.

Berlin, 17 April
In the middle of the last desperate days of fighting, Goebbels is reported to have said at a conference with the Propaganda Ministry that: "Gentlemen, a hundred years from now, a wonderful color film will be shown about these terrible days we are going through. Stand firm today, so that the audience does not whistle you down when you appear on the screen in a hundred years' time."

Paris, 25 April
Actress Micheline Presle has interrupted the shooting of Christian-Jaque's film *Boule-de-suif* to marry Michel Lefort, the tennis champion and Bordeaux wine merchant.

Grasse, 28 April
An extra was killed by a bullet wound in the chest during takes for Jeff Musso's film *Vive la liberté* (a stroke of irony: the film's original title was *We Killed a Man*).

Prague, 12 May
Jiri Trnka and several collaborators have created an animation unit, "Trick Brothers" (Batri v Triku).

Paris, 18 May
Premiere of Max Ophuls' *From Mayerling to Sarajevo*, with Edwige Feuillère. Work on the film began in 1939, was interrupted by the war, then finished in the spring of 1940, only to be banned by the Germans.

Italy, 23 May
The actress Corinne Luchaire has been arrested in the company of her mother and father, the journalist and collaborator Jean Luchaire, who had become a minister in the exiled Laval Government.

Los Angeles, 6 June
A two-year legal battle has ended for Charlie Chaplin. The court has ordered him to pay $100 a week for the maintenance of the small daughter of 26-year-old actress Joan Barry, who was briefly under contract to Chaplin in 1942. In June 1943 Joan Barry had filed a paternity suit against Charlie Chaplin. In February 1944 blood tests proved conclusively that Chaplin could not be the father of Barry's child, but after two paternity trials the court defied logic and ruled that Chaplin had to pay. Chaplin's motion for retrial has been denied.

Los Angeles, 15 June
Singer-actress Judy Garland, who divorced David Rose in 1944, has married the film director Vincente Minnelli. They have just made *The Clock* together in New York.

Prague, 11 August
The National Union government has decreed the nationalization of the country's film production. From today, all film companies have become State property under the name Statny Film.

Hollywood, 1 November
Alfred Hitchcock has presented his latest thriller, the psychoanalytical melodrama *Spellbound*, from the novel by Francis Beeding, with actor Gregory Peck showing a darker side of his persona, and Ingrid Bergman. Salvadore Dali has designed a striking dream sequence.

Paris, 14 November
On Abel Gance's return from Spain, the film magazine *Paris-Cinéma* published the following warning: "Silent partners beware! – lock up your deposit boxes."

Paris, 19 December
Pathé-Cinéma are celebrating 52nd week of exclusive screening Marcel Carné's *les Enfants du adis* (*Children of Paradise*).

France, 22 December
Georges Rouquier has finis shooting *Farrebique* in the Avey district. The family chronicle t almost a year to film.

Copenhagen, 26 December
Release of *De Rode Enge* (*The Earth*), directed by Bodil Ipsen Lau Lauritzen Jr., with Lisbeth M in and Paul Reichhardt. A gripp account of the Danish resistanc

Los Angeles, 30 December
Film critics have hailed Fr Borzage's newly released film *Spanish Main*, which stars Maur O'Hara and Paul Henreid, as a w derful adventure film. It was sho Technicolor.

BIRTHS

Switzerland, 28 January
Marthe Keller

Detroit, 29 January
Tom Selleck

Los Angeles, 9 April
Mia Farrow

Chicago, 28 February
Mimsy Farmer
(Merle Farmer)

Germany, 31 May
Rainer Werner Fassbinder

Texas, 1 August
Steve Martin

Washington D.C., 21 November
Goldie Hawn

Honolulu, 1 December
Bette Midler

DEATHS

Los Angeles, 12 July
Alla Nazimova

Marcel Carné's ***les Enfants du pa dis (Children of Paradise)****, a supe tive dramatic and visual achievem of the French cinema, realizes its high ambition.*

PATHÉ CONSORTIUM CINÉMA
PRÉSENTE

LE ROUGE GORGE
BAL

b. Lancy

ARLETTY . JEAN-LOUIS BARRAULT . PIERRE BRASSEUR . PIERRE RENOIR
DANS
UN FILM DE
MARCEL CARNÉ

LES ENFANTS DU PARADIS

SCÉNARIO ET DIALOGUES DE JACQUES PRÉVERT
AVEC
LOUIS SALOU . MARIA CASARÈS
ET
MARCEL HERRAND

1ère ÉPOQUE
LE BOULEVARD
DU CRIME

PRODUCTION
S.N.
PATHÉ-CINÉMA

IMAGES DE ROGER HUBERT DIRECTEUR DE PRODUCTION FRED ORAIN

'Ivan the Terrible' the crowning glory of Eisenstein's achievement

Moscow, 16 January
Sergei Eisenstein has already directed many great films, but *Ivan the Terrible* is an immediate masterpiece. After the German attack of 22 June 1941, the Mosfilm Studio was evacuated to Alma-Ata in Central Asia. There the filmmakers improvised in precarious conditions with courage and imagination. Because of the resounding success of *Alexander Nevsky*, Eisenstein was trusted to make another historical drama, this time about the 16th-century Czar Ivan IV, who created a unified Russia from a collection of feudal holdings. Eisenstein began shooting the first part of the three-part epic after more than two years of research, making sketches of every scene of the film.

Ivan the Terrible is a spectacular fresco about the seizure of power by Prince Ivan. While still a child, Ivan hears of the assassination of his mother and understands that he is in the hands of the ambitious boyars. Finally reaching his majority, he has himself crowned Czar. By this action, he shows his will to reign single-handedly and enlarge Russia. He achieves this in winning various rebellions and taking the town of Kazan from the Tartars. But his aunt Euphrosyne conspires against him and poisons his beloved wife Anastasia, and his best friend betrays him. He leaves Moscow in disgust, but the people find him and bring him back. The film ends with crowds on their knees. It is difficult to know what to admire most: the strength of the dialogue, the beauty of Prokofiev's music, the majestic images created by the photography of both Andrei Moskvin and Eduard Tissé, or the magnificent performance by Nikolai Cherkassov (who had played Alexander Nevsky) as the fierce Czar. Now back in Moscow, Eisenstein is preparing the second part of *Ivan the Terrible*.

Part II of the film, which is still being edited, will be released at a later date.

Last Nazi film fron[...] behind the lines

La Rochelle, 30 January
Kolberg, probably the last ciner[...]tographic venture of Veit Harl[...] Josef Goebbels' favorite director[...] being shown simultaneously in B[...]lin and in La Rochelle, the Fre[...] port still occupied by the Germa[...] In fact, it was necessary to send [...] reels by parachute. The film to[...] two years to make, during wh[...] time the defeat of Germany beca[...] inevitable. Goebbels, who had wa[...]ed the director to make a mor[...] raising film that would galvanize [...] population, finally chose the hist[...] of Kolberg, a small Baltic port t[...] resisted Napoleon's troops after [...] victory of Iéna. For this purpo[...] Harlan was given every means at [...] disposal – an unprecedented [...] million marks (making it eight tim[...] more costly than a normal prod[...]tion), 6,000 horses, 10,000 costum[...] and more soldiers than, in reali[...] were actually available on bo[...] sides. Filmed in color, *Kolberg* [...] more spectacular than convinci[...] Is not this work praising the G[...]man soul, the last shot fired by [...] Nazi cinema 12 years after the r[...] of Hitler?

'Going My Way' is showered with Oscars

Hollywood, 15 March
Bing Crosby (Best Actor), Barry Fitzgerald (Best Supporting Actor), Leo McCarey (Best Director, Best Original Story), and Frank Butler and Frank Cavett (Best Screenwriter) received Oscars for *Going [...] Way*, which won the Best Pict[...] award. This heart-warming st[...] about a Catholic priest is a po[...]lar winner, as is Ingrid Bergm[...] the Best Actress for *Gaslight*.

Czar (Nikolai Cherkassov, left), and his small son (right) on set with Eisenstein.

Holding their prized statuettes are Ingrid Bergman, Best Actress for ***Gaslig[...]*** *with* ***Going My Way*** *winners Barry Fitzgerald (left) and Bing Crosby.*

'Children of Paradise' weaves a dazzling spell

‧rre Brasseur plays Lemaître.

Jean-Louis Barrault as the great artist of mime, Baptiste Deburau, performing a dramatic scene in the theater.

ris, 9 March

e premiere of *Children of Para-e (les Enfants du paradis)* was ‧en at a gala evening at the Palais Chaillot. Marcel Carné's uncom-ɔnly long film (almost three hours) :eived a lukewarm welcome, no ubt on account of the terrible ɔustics in the hall as well as the xiety of many in the audience, ɪo did not want to miss the last :tro. Both parts of the film – *le ulevard du crime* and *l'Homme ɪnc* – will be released exclusively the Madeleine and the Colisée d shown at a single performance. ven the dearth of quality enter-ɪnment, it seems certain that the blic will take to it heartily. It is, in :t, an exceptional film: a richly tertaining and intensely romantic ɔcation of an epoch. The tale unfolds against a meticulously reconstructed setting of mid-19th-century Paris, in the milieu of the popular theater. It tells of the doomed love between the famous mime Deburau and the beautiful courtesan named Garance, unforgettably played by Jean-Louis Barrault and Arletty, respectively. And the cast around this couple is prestigious: Pierre Brasseur as the classical actor Frederick Lemaître, Marcel Herrand as the poet-assassin Lacenaire, Louis Salou as the aristocrat Comte Montray, and also Pierre Renoir, Marcel Pérès and Gaston Modot, as well as the young Maria Casarès, making her screen debut. All their fates are intertwined among the crowds that throng the boulevards. Naturally, the brilliant and ironic scenario and dialogue is by Jacques Prévert. As was the case in *les Visiteurs du soir*, Alexander Trauner (the vivid sets) and Joseph Kosma (the haunting music) were uncredited, because of their Jewish origin. After the success of the previous film, the producer André Paulvé gave director Carné carte blanche to compose his vast fresco. After many months of preparation, the shooting was ready to begin in mid-August 1943 at the Victorine studios in Nice. But the American landings in Sicily interrupted work because the team was ordered by authorities to return to Paris. The project was purchased by Pathé who controlled it well. The larger-than-life characters, narrative skill and the sweep of the production should make it a triumph.

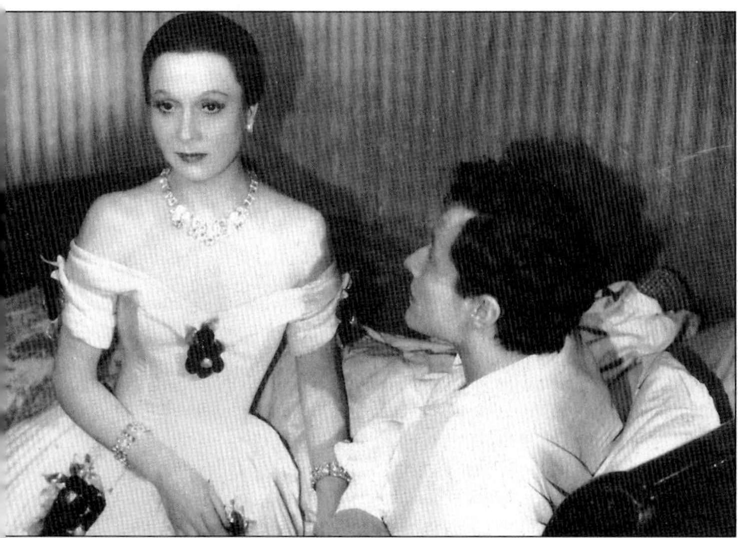

‧burau and Garance (Arletty) are the lovers doomed to separation.

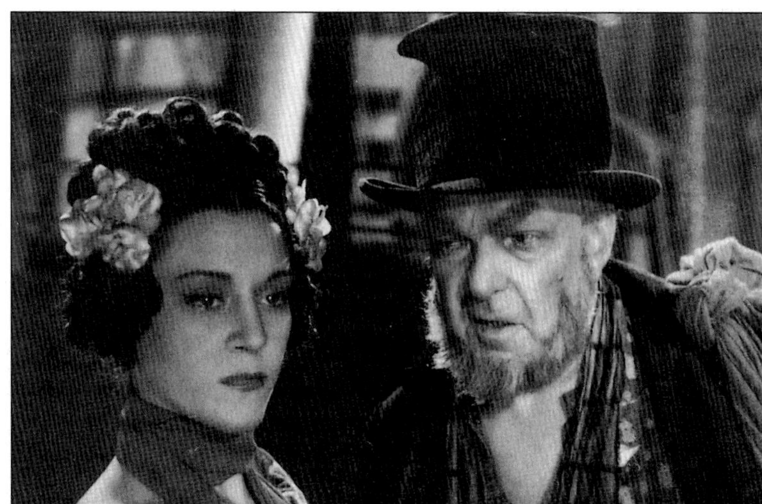

Maria Casarès plays Nathalie, the wife cast aside by Deburau, and Pierre Renoir is Jericho, a character who personifies the idea of fate.

▷

No songs for Garland in wartime romance

Robert Walker and Judy Garland, the tender lovers in the shadow of war.

New York, 3 May
Following on last year's string of musical successes for MGM, Judy Garland is reunited with *Meet Me in St. Louis* director Vincente Minnelli for *The Clock*. This small-scale and poignant film tells of a girl and a soldier who meet for the first time in New York City, fall in love, and marry – all in the space of the GI's 48-hour leave. Playing opposite a well-cast Robert Walker, 23-year-old Judy moves and beguiles the audience with a thoroughly sincere and convincing performance. What is really noteworthy, however, is that she does it without singing a note. It seems that this exceptional musical star is now likely to develop into a straight dramatic actress.

Micheline Presle is France's star of the year

BOULE DE SUIF

Paris, 17 October
The singular charm of Micheline Presle has given her top billing since she appeared in Abel Gance's *Paradise Lost* in 1939. But only now has she managed to shake off the label of the frivolous Parisian that categorized her. Four months ago we discovered her as a passionate woman in Jacques Becker's *Falbalas* opposite Raymond Rouleau, from whom she had learned much about acting. Now she is playing a very different part – that of the good-hearted prostitute – in *Boule-de-suif*, directed by Christian-Jaque, and based on Guy de Maupassant's story.

Roberto Rossellini enters neo-realist fiel

Anna Magnani and Aldo Fabrizi in Rossellini's searing ***Rome, Open City***.

Rome, 24 September
Scarcely six months have passed since the war ended, so perhaps it is too soon to show the public such a neo-realistic narrative as that of *Rome, Open City*. The preview of Roberto Rossellini's film was greeted coldly. Romans could not tolerate seeing again so soon the events of the winter of 1944. This story centers around the last days of the German occupation of Italy when a Resistance leader, Manfredi (Ma cel Pagliero), fleeing the Gestapo, given refuge by the pregnant Pi (Anna Magnani). When she is sh he takes shelter with a good-time g (Maria Michi), who betrays hi Manfredi and a priest (Aldo Fa rizi) are arrested and executed. his use of a documentary approa filming in the streets and apartme of Rome, Rossellini has achieved immediacy seldom seen before.

Joan Crawford scales new dramatic height

Joan Crawford, Ann Blyth, troubled mother and daughter in ***Mildred Pier***

Hollywood, 25 October
Since leaving MGM for Warner Brothers in 1943, Joan Crawford has been absent from the screen, save for a brief appearance in the 1944 *Hollywood Canteen*. Now she returns with her blistering performance in *Mildred Pierce*, directed Michael Curtiz. She takes the ti role of a relentlessly over-achievi career woman, suffering as o Crawford can at the hands of liza like Zachary Scott and her pois ous brat of a daughter Ann Blyt

ncompromising study of alcoholism

spite the barman's pleas, the tormented Milland is unable to resist one more.

llywood, 16 November
pper Paramount leading man y Milland has stepped out of racter to play failed alcoholic ter Don Birnam in Billy Wilder's *e Lost Weekend.* Adapted from arles Jackson's harrowing novel, aints an uncompromising picture self-destruction, with the haggard, unshaven Milland lurching up New York's Third Avenue trying to hock his typewriter, unaware that all the pawnshops are closed for Yom Kippur. This scene was shot on location one Sunday, with Milland staggering from 55th Street to 110th Street while Wilder's camera filmed from inside of a bakery truck. Whether shrinking from imaginary bats as he succumbs to the horrors of delirium tremens, or slyly finding new places to hide bottles from girlfriend Jane Wyman, Milland is a revelation as a man trapped by the hazy romance of booze. Telling support is provided by Howard da Silva as a world-weary bartender and Frank Faylen as a sadistic nurse in the alcoholic ward in Bellevue hospital. Even the somewhat glib "happy ending", in which Milland is hauled back from the brink by Wyman, cannot dent the impact of this powerful picture. During its Santa Barbara previews, *The Lost Weekend* was greeted with laughter and cards which said that it was tasteless. The studio considered shelving the film, and there was even an alleged report that the mobster Frank Costello, acting on behalf of the liquor industry, had offered Paramount $5 million for the negative so that it could be destroyed. But Paramount President Barney Balaban, figuring that it was futile to make expensive movies and then shelve them, gave the go-ahead to release the picture.

Box-office bells ring for Ingrid and Bing

Hollywood, 28 December
Bing Crosby's career continues to sail "straight down the middle". In his new *The Bells of St. Mary's*, Leo McCarey's smash-hit sequel to *Going My Way* – made for contractual reasons at RKO – we can follow the further adventures of Bing's Father O'Malley, here saving a school with the help of Sister Superior Ingrid Bergman and warbling a few songs in between. As he tells Ingrid, "If you're ever in trouble, dial O for O'Malley."

Bing Crosby and Ingrid Bergman.

Brief Encounter' an 'ordinary' love story

ndon, 26 November
e latest collaboration between el Coward and David Lean has oduced *Brief Encounter*, which is sed on one of Coward's prewar e-act plays. It's a tender suburban e story in which a speck of dirt in eye leads to a doomed romance ween housewife Celia Johnson d married doctor Trevor Howard. Much of the affair is played out in the steamy fog of a railway station buffet, where the couple snatch fretful hours away from their respective spouses, their middle-class reticence counterpointed by Lean's use of Rachmaninov's lush Second Piano Concerto. Critics have drawn comparisons with French cinema, but *Brief Encounter* is very English.

Suave James Mason pulls off the double

London, 22 November
Sardonic, sexy James Mason is currently the hottest property in British cinema. Mason's powerful brand of sadistic charm was given full rein in Gainsborough's *The Seventh Veil*, in which he played the crippled guardian of concert pianist Ann Todd, bringing his cane crashing down on her fingers in a frenzy of impotent rage. In *The Wicked Lady*, he is Captain Terry Jackson, a dashing 17th-century highwayman who acquires a stimulating partner in the form of adventuress Margaret Lockwood. This racy example of "Gainsborough Gothic" proved too much for U.S. censors, and Lockwood's plunging cleavage had to be adjusted for American audiences.

vistful parting ends a brief encounter for Celia Johnson and Trevor Howard.

Margaret Lockwood and James Mason, period glamour in ***The Wicked Lady***.

Dick
POWELL
Claire
TREVOR
Anne
SHIRLEY
Murder, My Sweet
OTTO KRUGER · MIKE MAZURKI
MILES MANDER · DOUGLAS WALTON
DON DOUGLAS

This film from Raymond Chandler's ***Farewell, My Lovely***, with Powell as Philip Marlowe was an RKO success.

LES FILMS RAOUL PLOQUIN
PAUL BERNARD
MARIA CASARES
ELINA LABOURDETTE
LES DAMES DU BOIS DE BOULOGNE
Un film de ROBERT BRESSON
LUCIENNE BOGAERT et JEAN MARCHAT

Bernard Lancy's original poster for Bresson's symbolic melodrama.

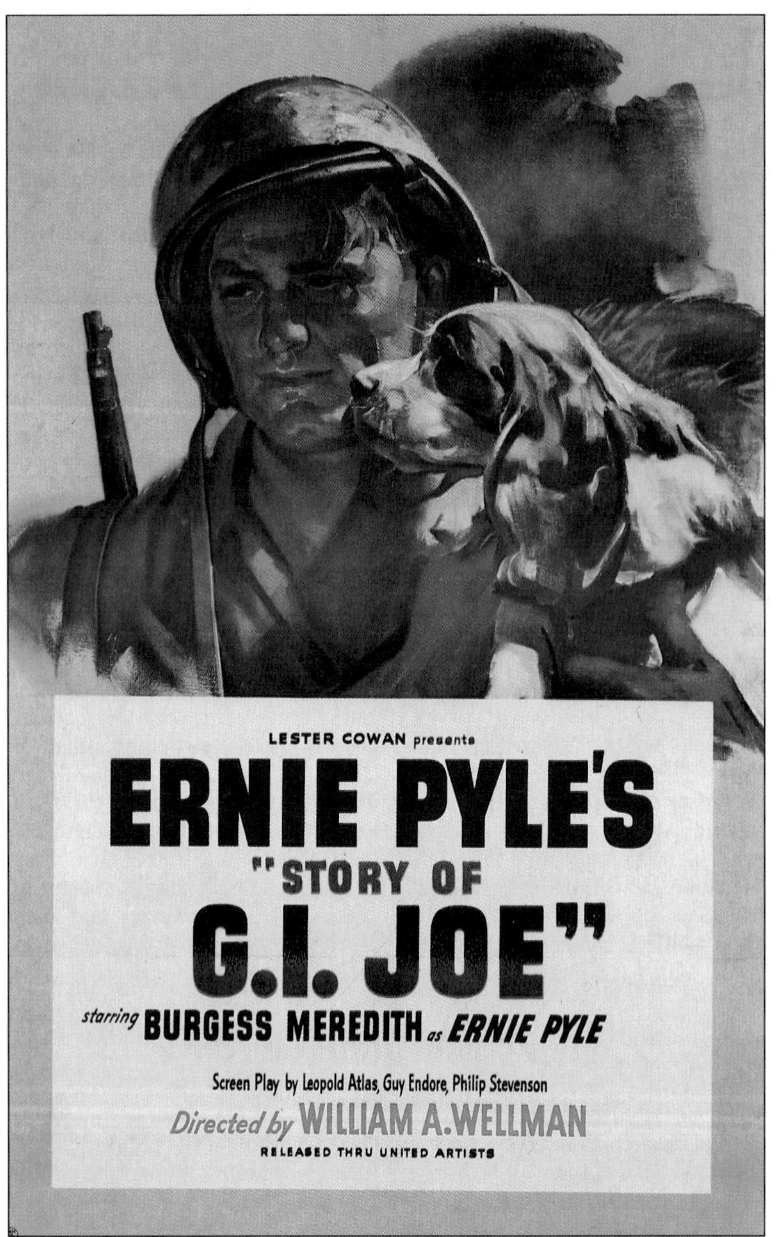
LESTER COWAN presents
ERNIE PYLE'S
"STORY OF
G.I. JOE"
starring BURGESS MEREDITH as ERNIE PYLE
Screen Play by Leopold Atlas, Guy Endore, Philip Stevenson
Directed by WILLIAM A.WELLMAN
RELEASED THRU UNITED ARTISTS

Meredith was real-life correspondent Ernie Pyle, in one of the best war films.

THE HOUSE ON
92nd STREET
William
EYTHE
Lloyd
NOLAN
Signe
HASSO
20th CENTURY FOX
LOCKHART · CARROLL
ST.CLAIR · POST
HATHAWAY · de ROCHEMONT

FBI foiled Nazi spies in New York.

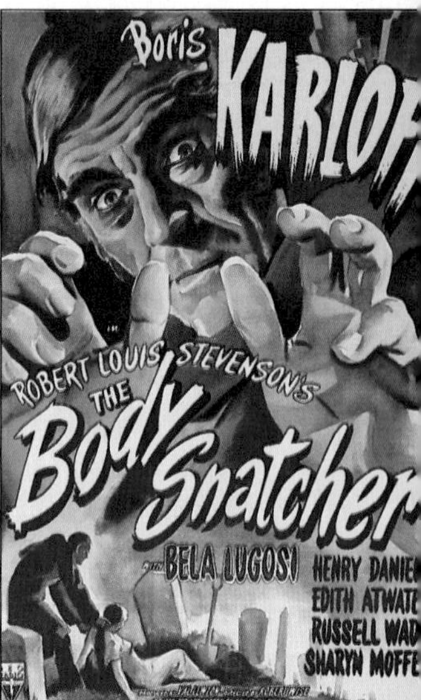
Boris KARLOFF
ROBERT LOUIS STEVENSON'S
THE
Body Snatcher
BELA LUGOSI
HENRY DANIELL
EDITH ATWATER
RUSSELL WADE
SHARYN MOFFETT

Karloff and Lugosi in classic thriller about grave-robbers.

Frank Morgan with Fred Astaire in MGM's ***Yolanda and the Thief***.

ROY ROGERS
King of the Cowboys
TRIGGER
SMARTEST HORSE IN THE MOVIES
UTAH
A REPUBLIC PICTURE
GEORGE (Gabby) HAYES
and DALE EVANS
BOB NOLAN and
The SONS of THE PIONEERS
DIRECTED BY JOHN ENGLISH

Another from King of the Cowboys.

Vaudevillians June Haver (left) and Betty Grable shone in ***The Dolly Sisters***.

hn Wayne, Donna Reed and Robert Montgomery in **They Were Expendable**.

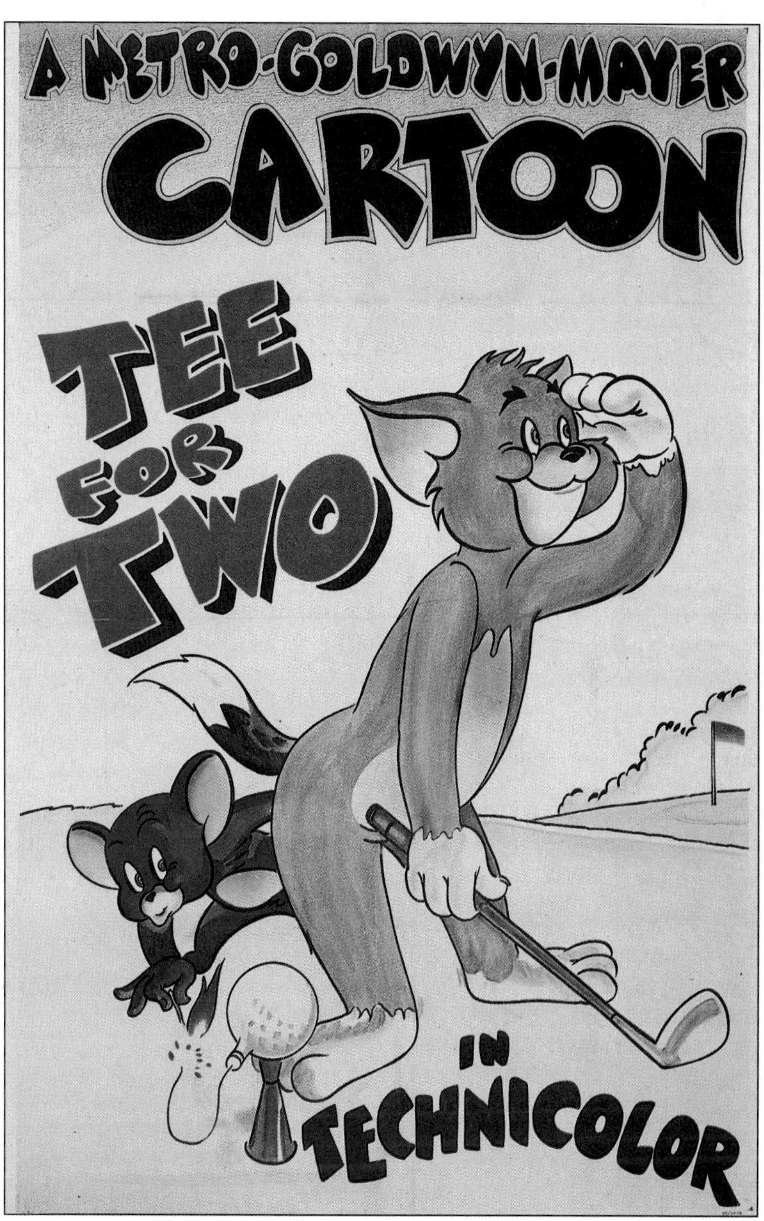
A METRO-GOLDWYN-MAYER
CARTOON
TEE FOR TWO
IN
TECHNICOLOR

Hilarity and hi-jinx on the golf course with MGM's much-loved cat and mouse.

grid Bergman and Gregory Peck in Hitchcock's psychodrama **Spellbound**.

mes Dunn and Peggy Ann Garner in Elia Kazan's **A Tree Grows in Brooklyn**.

Ann Todd and James Mason: concert pianist and guardian in **The Seventh Veil**.

1946

1945 Academy Awards, Grauman's Chinese Theater, 7 Mar.

Best Film:	*The Lost Weekend* (dir: Billy Wilder)
Best Director:	Billy Wilder
Best Actor:	Ray Milland *(The Lost Weekend)*
Best Actress:	Joan Crawford *(Mildred Pierce)*
Best Supp. Actor:	James Dunn *(A Tree Grows in Brooklyn)*
Best Supp. Actress:	Anne Revere *(National Velvet)*

Switzerland, 15 January
Jean Delannoy has started filming *The Pastoral Symphony*, based on André Gide's novel, with Michèle Morgan and Pierre Blanchar.

Paris, 15 February
Jean Vigo's *Zéro de conduite* has finally been passed by the film control commission. The work was banned on its release in 1933.

London, 23 February
Jean Delannoy's *l'Eternel retour* (*Love Eternal*) has had a negative reception from British film critics. They find the blond hero, played by Jean Marais, "too Aryan".

Paris, 27 February
The first full-length film by director René Clément *la Bataille du rail*, has been greeted with enthusiasm. The project, which was originally begun as a clandestine documentary of work being carried out by the Resistance, gradually developed into a full-scale film accurately dramatizing wartime events.

New York, 15 March
Release of the film *Ziegfeld Follies*. This musical extravaganza, directed by Vincent Minnelli, has William Powell as impresario Florenz Ziegfeld, with guest appearances from a huge all-star cast that includes Fred Astaire, Esther Williams, Lucille Bremer, Lena Horne, Judy Garland and Gene Kelly.

Hollywood, 23 April
Shirley Temple, who won an Academy Award when she was only six, has given a party for her 18th birthday. As a symbolic gesture to the passing of her famous childhood, she burned a red school tunic in front of the 100 guests.

Marseilles, 1 May
The Capitole cinema has reopened its doors to the public. It had been requisitioned, first by the Germans and then by the Americans.

Shanghai, 23 May
Audiences at *One Night's Kiss* will see the first screen kiss in the history of Chinese cinema. But, out of respect for the public's sense of propriety, the couple in Yasuki Chiba's film do so behind an open parasol.

Paris, 23 May
The actors Daniel Gélin and Danièle Delorme have married. They met while attending René Simon's acting classes.

Atlantic City, 3 July
Jerry Lewis, who is doing a music hall number at Club 500, has come across a new singer with talent in Dean Martin.

France, 8 July
Servicemen on leave are no longer entitled to free cinema tickets.

Paris, 13 July
The professional weekly *la Cinématographie française* has devoted an article to the French cinema's rising stars: Simone Signoret, Gérard Philipe, Martine Carol, Yves Montand and Daniel Gélin.

Hollywood, 16 July
Fox has signed up the 20-year-old photographic model Norma Jean Baker at a salary of $75 a week. She will now be known professionally as Marilyn Monroe.

Rome, 9 August
Premiere of *Desiderio*, co-directed by Roberto Rossellini and Marcello Pagliero, starring Elli Parvo and Massimo Girotti and filmed before the making of *Roma Città Aperta* (*Rome, Open City*). The shooting, which started in Rome in 1943, was interrupted by the fall of Mussolini, then restarted at the end of 1945.

France, 10 August
The producer and distributor Léon Gaumont, a major pioneer of the cinema industry, has died at his property in the Var.

New York, 22 August
Alfred Hitchcock's *Notorious* is being advertised as the film with the "longest screen kiss in the history of the cinema." Two-and-a-half minutes of passion between Cary Grant and Ingrid Bergman, broken here and there by the words necessary to satisfy the 30-second contact limit imposed by the censors.

Paris, 20 September
The French film world is in mourning for Raimu, the wonderful character actor of the Pagnol trilogy.

Hollywood, 30 September
In the opinion of the vice president of the American Federation of Labor, Matthew Woll, Hollywood is the "third largest Communist center in the United States." He has also warned studios that the unions will not countenance actors and scriptwriters "guilty of treason."

New York, 24 October
Ava Gardner has been granted a dihvorce from the musician Artie Shaw on grounds of mental cruelty.

Paris, 6 November
The release of Walt Disney's new cartoon *Fantasia* has given rise here, just as in the U.S., to a debate on the cinematographic interpretation of musical works.

Paris, 16 November
Actor Robert Vigan has received a 10 year sentence with hard labor for open collaboration with the enemy and their program of anti-Semitic propaganda on Radio Paris. All the actor's belongings have also been confiscated.

Hollywood, 3 December
Release of John Ford's *My Darling Clementine*, starring Henry Fonda, Linda Darnell, Victor Mature and Walter Brennan.

Tokyo, 17 December
Kenji Mizoguchi's film *Five Women Around Utamaro* is a stylized portrayal of the legendary 18th-century artist Edo that is now screening.

Paris, 22 December
French gala premiere at the Palais de Chaillot of Vittorio De Sica's *Sciuscia* (*Shoeshine*), with Rinaldo Smordoni and Franco Interlengi as the two enterprising shoeshine boys.

Los Angeles, 31 December
At a staggering $120 million, combined profits of the eight bigg studios have almost doubled in co parison with the already record f ures for 1945.

BIRTHS

Los Angeles, 5 January
Diane Keaton (Diane Hall)

Missouri, 20 January
David Lynch

London, 5 February
Charlotte Rampling

France, 17 February
André Dussollier

Los Angeles, 12 March
Liza Minnelli

Algiers, 22 April
Nicole Garcia

Los Angeles, 9 May
Candice Bergen

California, 20 May
Cher (Cherilyn Sarkisian)

New York, 6 July
Sylvester Stallone

New York, 15 September
Oliver Stone

New York, 4 October
Susan Sarandon (Susan Tomalin

California, 6 November
Sally Field

DEATHS

London, 5 February
George Arliss

California, 19 April
Mae Busch

Los Angeles, 23 June
William S. Hart

Los Angeles, 25 December
W.C. Fields

Columbia has a hit with ***Gilda****, due no small measure to Rita Haywor in the title role as a nightclub owne wife and her tangled relationsl with his manager (Glenn Ford).*

There NEVER was a woman like Gilda!
COLUMBIA PICTURES presents
Rita HAYWORTH
as
Gilda
with
Glenn FORD
GEORGE MACREADY · JOSEPH CALLEIA
SCREENPLAY BY MARION PARSONNET
Produced by
Directed by
VIRGINIA VAN UPP · CHARLES VIDOR

David Lean fulfills expectations, it's great!

Finlay Currie as the convict Magwitch and Anthony Wager as young Pip.

London, 27 January
David Lean has produced a masterful screen version of Charles Dickens' *Great Expectations*, an object lesson in compression, definition and narrative drive. The accomplished cast brings Dickens' characters to vibrant life: Finlay Currie as the convict Magwitch, who erupts from the clay of a remote graveyard like a force of Nature; John Mills as a delightful Pip; Alec Guinness, making his screen debut as the whimsical Herbert Pocket; and Martita Hunt's Miss Havisham, brooding over the cobweb-clogged remains of her wedding feast. The picture's success has convinced British film mogul J. Arthur Rank that he can conquer the American market.

The postman rings for Turner and Garfiel

Turner and Garfield, the unhappy lovers in ***The Postman Always Rings Twic***

Hollywood, 2 May
In 1939 the French called it *The Last Bend*, with stars Fernand Gravey and Corinne Luchaire; in 1942, Visconti unleashed the Italian neo-realist movement with it, under the apt title, *Ossessione*, with Massimo Girotti and Clara Calamai. Now, with Tay Garnett at the helm, it's Hollywood's turn to film James M. Cain's tale of lust, murder and ret bution. Lana Turner and John Ga field are the stars of *The Postm Always Rings Twice*, and, with r spect to the European versions, th make the most sizzling pair to da as the unhappy wife and her love who plot to kill her boorish husban Certainly a departure for MGM, t studio of family entertainment.

The 1945 Oscars reward Billy Wilder

Hollywood, 7 March
With the war over, searchlights were illuminated once again outside of Grauman's Chinese Theater where Billy Wilder's *The Lost Weekend* came out tops at the Oscar ceremony. It won Best Picture, Best Actor (Ray Milland), Best Director and Best Screenplay (Charles Brackett and Wilder). Yet, *The Lost Weekend* was very nearly a lost film. When it was first previewed, audiences reacted negatively to the realistic and down-beat story of an alcoholic, and the film's release was postponed. However, after some private screenings, its image improved, and it became one of the year's top money-spinners. The Best Actress award went to Joan Crawford for her no holds barred performance in *Mildred Pierce*. It couldn't have happened at a better time for the 41-year-old star, who had come to be regarded as "box-office poison".

De Sica and Zavattini bear witness to the lost children of the wa

Rome, 10 May
Although *Shoeshine*, Vittorio De Sica's latest film, is a powerful and touching semi-documentary of poverty in postwar Italy, Italian audiences have preferred to flock to the more frivolous American offerings. Director De Sica and his scenarist Cesare Zavattini already showed their concern for children suffering from the separation of parents *The Children Are Watching Us* thr years ago. With *Shoeshine* the to has become more scathing and a cusatory, yet it remains human Since the war, bands of childre have been forced to live in t streets, many of them becomir shoe-shine boys to survive. De Si concentrates on two in particula Giuseppe and Pasquale, who drea of buying a horse with the little ext money they make out of dealing t black market goods, but they end u in reform school instead. They e cape, but in a fit of bitter rag Pasquale kills his friend. The situ tion, according to the film, is t result of fascism and not the fault the children. The astonishingly nat ralistic performances by the you non-actors, and the shooting in re locations, create an unforgettab impression. It is to be hoped th eventually Italian audiences w want to see films that reflect the own society.

With ***Shoeshine****, De Sica joins Rossellini and Visconti as a great Italian director.*

ʀrson Welles gives ʗhaplin subject

ᴏs Angeles, 1 May
fter the emotional highs and lows ː has experienced during the last ʋo years, Charles Chaplin has beɹn production on a project which, . characteristic style, he has been ːveloping since the winter of 1942. s origins lay in a suggestion by rson Welles that he would like to rect a documentary reconstrucɔn of the career of the French wifeurderer Landru, with Chaplin in e leading role. This provided Chapı with the germ of an idea for his ːw film, *Monsieur Verdoux*, a title hich he adopted in June 1946. In larch, Edna Purviance, Chaplin's ading lady in many of his greatest lent films but absent from the reen since 1926, was tested for a ıpporting role in the picture. There as an emotional reunion at Chapı's studio, which Purviance had ɔt visited for 20 years, but it seems at she will be seen only as an extra. haplin has reportedly had enorɒus difficulty getting the film's ript past the censors at the Breen ffice, and many scenes have been .ed. Sharing direction with Chapı is Robert Florey.

Ingrid, Cary give glamour to notoriety

Cary Grant and Ingrid Bergman, teamed to beguiling effect by Hitchcock.

New York, 22 July
In RKO's *Notorious*, a scintillating espionage thriller with a South American setting, Alfred Hitchcock drives a coach and horses through the Production Code, maneuvering Cary Grant and Ingrid Bergman through the longest embrace in screen history in a small masterpiece of impish eroticism. Ingrid Bergman plays the daughter of a convicted spy manipulated by U.S. intelligence into marrying mother-fixated Nazi villain Claude Rains. Most of the manipulating is done by Cary Grant at his most charmingly calculating. Rains is also superb as the sympathetic heavy, and Hitchcock delivers another directing tour de force at one of the film's most suspenseful moments: with a little help from the cameraman Ted Tetzlaff, Hitchcock pulls off an extraordinary crane shot which begins at the top of a lengthy staircase and then swoops down to the floor below, where a party is in progress, finally to focus in close-up on a key clutched in the hand of Bergman. Evidently, Tetzlaff ribbed Hitchcock on the set with the playful remark, "Getting a bit technical, aren't you, Pop?"

ꟾewcomer Kirk Douglas is a rising star

ollywood, 24 July
ritten by Robert Rossen and diɛcted by Lewis Milestone, *The range Love of Martha Ivers* is one the most uncompromisingly nasty elodramas to hit the screen. Barɪra Stanwyck is twice the viper of *ɔuble Indemnity*, well-matched by Van Heflin as a diabolical counterpart. Playing the supporting role of the weakling husband, cleft-chinned Kirk Douglas has to fight to be noticed – and noticed he is. It is quite evident that with his looks, presence and control, he will not be relegated to the background for long.

ɪrbara Stanwyck and Kirk Douglas in ***The Strange Love of Martha Ivers****.*

Canine Lassie co-stars with Elizabeth Taylor

New York, 24 July
Having co-starred with a horse in *National Velvet* in 1944, Elizabeth Taylor now shares top billing with a dog in *The Courage of Lassie*, directed by Fred M. Wilcox. The two of them are old friends, having first met in *Lassie Come Home* in 1943, although this time around a different dog has taken over the role of the Greer Garson of the canine world. Now a ripening teenager of lustrous beauty, Taylor rehabilitates a mixed-up Lassie, suffering from combat stress after war service as a killer dog.

Young Elizabeth Taylor with courageous dog Lassie, and Frank Morgan.

Bombshell Hayworth, the gorgeous Gilda, explodes on Bikini

Bikini, 27 July
Rita Hayworth was not pleased to see her image gracing the side of the atomic bomb tested on the Pacific atoll of Bikini. She made her feelings known at a press conference she gave yesterday. Nevertheless, last March she made her own atomic impact in *Gilda*, directed by Charles Vidor. As the *femme fatale* of the title, she played a sexy woman of the world, sheathed in shining black, her hair tumbling over one eye and teeth bared under glistening lips as she taunted Glenn Ford with "Put the Blame on Mame" (dubbed by Anita Ellis) in her husband George Macready's Buenos Aires casino. The posters for the picture proclaimed "There Never was a Woman like Gilda!", prompting British film critic C.A. Lejeune to say "Blimey! There Never Was!" *Gilda* has now established Hayworth as the sleekest of sexual animals, the dream mistress of men the world over and one of Hollywood's brightest stars.

Voted the GI's favorite, Rita Hayworth here with Glenn Ford in Vidor's ***Gilda.***

Gilda: an archetypal sex image.

'Ivan the Terrible' stands accused

Moscow, 16 August
One would have thought that t
problems that weighed Sergei Eise
stein down before the war belong
to the past – the re-cutting impos
upon *The General Line* and t
banning of *Bezhin Meadow*, t
negative of which disappeared in t
bombing of Moscow in 1942. T
critical and public acclaim of *Iv*
the Terrible last year seemed to off
the director a brighter future, b
the first warning of trouble came
February when Eisenstein was ho
pitalized with heart trouble aft
Part II of *Ivan the Terrible* was pr
sented. The magazine *Soviet A*
severely criticized him for gross e
rors in judgment by reducing t
work of a great progressive Czar
sordid palace intrigues and tran
forming Ivan into "a man lacking
will and in character, resembling t
irresolute Hamlet, and his court in
a den of the Ku Klux Klan." T
release of the second part of *Ivan t*
Terrible seems in jeopardy, and it
said that Stalin, who approved
Part I, has turned against Part II.

Bogart captures essence of Philip Marlowe

Hollywood, 23 August
Raymond Chandler has given the seal of approval to Humphrey Bogart's portrayal of his cynical shamus Philip Marlowe in Warners' *The Big Sleep*. Chandler believes that "Bogart can be tough without a gun." Bogey, co-starring opposite his new wife Lauren Bacall, eases his way through Howard Hawks' powerhouse thriller, which is notably stronger on atmosphere than plot, the convolutions of which defeated the combined efforts of screenwriters William Faulkner, Leigh Brackett and Jules Furthman.

Humphrey Bogart and Lauren Bacall in Howard Hawks' ***The Big Sleep.***

Stunning 'film noir' recruits a new star

New York, 28 August
Robert Siodmak's latest *film noir*, *The Killers*, based on Ernest Hemingway, has revealed a striking new star. It is the first screen appearance of ex-acrobat Burt Lancaster, who plays Pete Lunn, the unfortunate hunted hero known as "Swede". His imposing stature and his toot
smile have gained much praise. O
posite Lancaster is the statuesq
Ava Gardner, who makes an i
pression as a tart with a heart. D
covered four years ago by MG
she is certain to become, like h
partner, a top ranking star.

Newcomer Burt Lancaster with Ava Gardner in Robert Siodmak's ***The Kille***

The International Film Festival returns to Cannes

annes, 7 October
he dark years of the war, which aralyzed international film production, are now behind us. To confirm is, the French cinema invited the orld's professionals to a sumptuus feast of films at the first International Film Festival at Cannes. ranted, there had been one prior, it it had been more of a meeting ace than a competition. With the ception of France, the U.S., Great ritain and the USSR, who were articipating on a large scale, many her countries were represented by ort films. No matter, since the estival was held in an atmosphere tolerance and elegance. It has en, above all, a fraternal and apoical window on the latest motion ctures from around the world. Financed by the French government d the town of Cannes, the Festival s no intention of rivaling that of enice. As Italy and France are now ends, it is intended to hold the estival biannually, one year in annes, the next in Venice. The estival was inaugurated with a slip the tongue from the new Minister Commerce and Industry, who, viously moved, declared "the first estival of Agriculture" open. The ry was composed of members om the participating countries, nscious that no nation should be nitted from the awards. Two films om France won top prizes: Jean elannoy's *The Pastoral Symphony*, hich gained the Grand Prix, and r which Michèle Morgan, as the ind orphan girl, won the best actress award, and *Battle of the Rails* which walked off with the best director (René Clément) and Special Jury prizes. The Americans were also there in force, no doubt hoping for more awards than they obtained. Nevertheless, Ray Milland won the best actor prize for his remarkable performance as the alcoholic in Billy Wilder's *The Lost Weekend*. Other directors who shared various prizes were the Englishman David Lean (*Great Expectations*), the Italian Roberto Rossellini (*Rome, Open City*), the Soviet Frederic Ermler (*The Turning Point*), the Swede Alf Sjöberg (*Iris and the Lieutenant*), and the Mexican Emilio Fernandez (*The Pearl*). George Huisman, the president of the Festival, can be proud of an illuminating film week.

Grace Moore sings 'La Marseillaise'.

Actress Michèle Morgan with Georges Huisman, the president of the Festival.

Michèle Morgan, here with Pierre Blanchar in ***The Pastoral Symphony****.*

uch of ***Battle of the Rails*** *was made in secret with railway Resistance fighters.*

The Turning Point*, from Frederic Ermler of the USSR, won two awards.*

The world's filmmakers are back at Venice

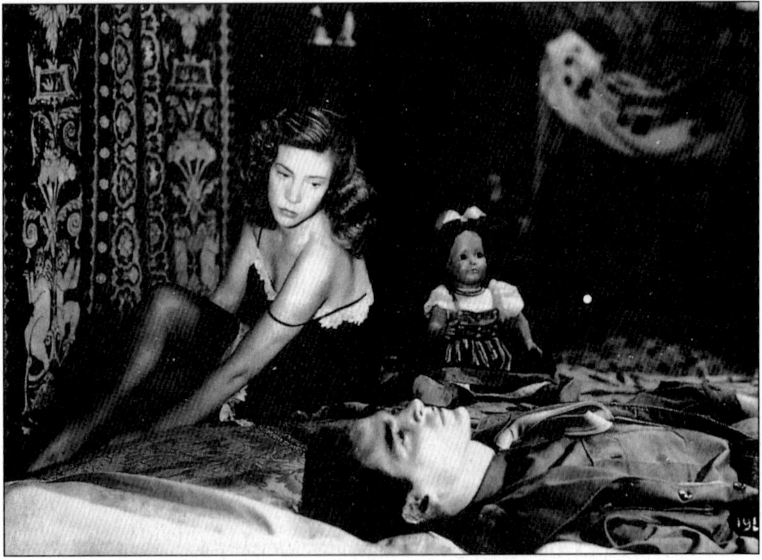
*Maria Michi in Roberto Rossellini's **Païsa**, much lauded at the Festival.*

Venice, 1 September
The Allies continue to occupy the Lido at Venice, but the Mostra (the Venice Film Festival) has been reborn. *The Southerner*, directed by Jean Renoir in America, which sensitively describes the existence of poor farmers, was judged the best film. Other works of exceptional quality were Fritz Lang's *Hangmen Also Die*, that was inspired by the Nazi "butcher of Prague"; Laurence Olivier's *Henry V*, an astonishing directorial debut by the great Shakespearean actor; Roberto Rossellini's *Païsa*; Marcel Carné's *Children of Paradise*; and Julien Duvivier's atmospheric *Panic*, all of which made the Mostra a festival of welcome homecomings and rediscoveries.

Zachary Scott in Jean Renoir's film.

Germany's cinema rises from its ashes

Berlin, 15 October
Defa, the East German-Soviet film company established some months ago in the splendid Neubabelsberg studios, has presented its first production. This world premiere of *Murderers Among Us* is of symbolic value, being the first postwar German film. Its director, Wolfgang Staudte, is not unknown. He was born in Saarbrucken in 1906, and started his career very young as a stage actor and then in the cinema. In 1943 he made his first feature film, *Akrobal Schö-ö-ön*, inspired by the life of the Rivels, a celebrated family of clowns. It was not a propaganda film, being one of the many in that epoch that were made for pure entertainment. But with *Murderers Among Us*, Staudte has painted a moral and physical portrait of country emerging from disaster. Th action takes place in Berlin in 194 where Mertens, a young doctor, b comes an alcoholic while trying forget the horrors of the war, duri which Bruckner, his military supe or, was responsible for wiping o an entire Polish village. Though could not prevent the massacre, is now determined to kill Bruckn and is only prevented from doing by Susan, a young Jewish girl wh loves him. Encouraged by her, denounces the man to the war crin investigators. The movie, admirab directed in an expressionist manne reveals the talent of Hildegard Kn as Susan, and faces the question responsibility for the crimes of t Nazi era.

*Hildegard Knef and Ernst Borchert in Staudte's **Murderers Among Us**.*

*Fritz Lang's **Hangmen Also Die**, is a harrowing portrayal of Nazism.*

Entertainer Al Jolson and the 'Jazz Singer' return as Larry Park

New York, 10 October
Columbia has struck gold with *The Jolson Story*, its tribute to the legendary vaudevillian who introduced talk to the movies with the immortal words, "You ain't heard nothin' yet!" The studio had to restrain the aging but irrepressible Jolson from playing himself, eventually confining him to dubbing the songs for contract player Larry Parks in his first big screen role. The movie avoids some of the more colorful aspects of Jolson's life, including his messy 1940 divorce from Ruby Keeler, but Parks makes a game stab at conveying Al's foghorning style, a one-man showbiz Blitzkrieg.

Larry Parks (right) re-creates the spirit of Al Jolson in a 'Blackface' number

itter homecoming from war with William Wyler

w York, 20 November
e major movie theme of the year been postwar readjustment, as lions of returning servicemen rn how to deal with the stresses d strains of a civilian world which moved on since they went away war. In Goldwyn's *The Best Years Our Lives* this experience has en brilliantly distilled by director William Wyler, who saw combat himself while filming a memorable documentary about an Eighth Air Force B-17 bomber, *The Memphis Belle*. Here three veterans huddle together in the plexiglass nose of the aircraft flying them home. Back in their Midwestern town of Boone City, former bank executive Fredric March, ex-soda jerk Dana Andrews and maimed sailor Harold Russell (a real veteran who lost both his arms in combat) attempt to pick up the threads of their lives. March discovers that he has grown apart from his wife Myrna Loy and is a stranger to his daughter Teresa Wright. Andrews, reduced again to the rank of soda jerk after serving as an officer, is disillusioned with the wife (played by Virginia Mayo) he had known for only 20 days before he went away to fight. And Russell, giving an exceptionally moving performance, rejects his fiancee Cathy O'Donnell because he fears her pity. With its screenplay by Robert E. Sherwood adapted from the book by MacKinlay Kantor, and the superb deep-focus photography of master lighting cameraman Gregg Toland, *The Best Years of Our Lives* combines laughter, tears, romance and social comment in a powerful package which will strike a chord with audiences nationwide.

rold Russell and Cathy O'Donnell.

l to r: Russell, Teresa Wright, Andrews, Loy, Hoagy Carmichael, March.

ean Cocteau's extraordinary 'beast' wins Louis Delluc prize

ris, 13 December
e fifth presentation of the Louis lluc Prize has gone to Jean Cocu's *Beauty and the Beast*, released t October. For his first featuregth film, Cocteau has drawn on a ry story by Madame Leprince de aumont, dating from 1757. The n was shot last winter at the Saintaurice studios, and most of the eriors were filmed in the semid park of the Raray Château in Oise region. The decor and cosnes by Christian Bérard, and the otography by Henri Alekan have eated a magic world. Cocteau ted that he discouraged both rard and Alekan from virtuosity order to show unreality in realistic ms. But thankfully, virtuosity is dent in the scenes in the Beast's stle. Jean Marais, behind extraorlary makeup, is touching, and auty (Josette Day) seems rather appointed when he turns into his mantic self. However, in the magine *Christian Witness*, Michel de int-Pierre thought Cocteau's style s "surrealism which would have emed audacious around 1916." vertheless, most critics believe it be a fairy tale for children and elligent adults.

Josette Day and Jean Marais in Cocteau's lyrical masterpiece, a key work.

Creation of CNC

Paris, 5 October
Since the promulgation of 26 April last, when a law dissolved many professional organizations, it became urgent to create a new institution concerned with the running of French cinema. That is why the Assembly has set up the Centre National du Cinéma Français (CNC) in Paris to be a watchdog over the fortunes of the French movie industry. In controlling financing of authorized films as well as the receipts of all films shown in France, the Centre will wield disciplinary powers useful in its attempts at coordinating various branches of the industry. The Cinémathèque Française and the Institut Des Hautes Etudes Cinématographiques (IDHEC) are also to be under its wing. The budget of the CNC will originate from the state, certain financial organizations and diverse firms connected with the movie industry. The director-general of the CNC will be assisted by ministers of state from the ministries of Information, Foreign Affairs, Education, Economy, Industry, Colonies and Agriculture.

Martita Hunt as Miss Havisham and Anthony Wager as the boy Pip in David Lean's superb Dickens adaptation, ***Great Expectations***.

Their Love was a Flame that Destroyed!
MGM presents
LANA TURNER
JOHN GARFIELD
THE Postman Always Rings Twice
CECIL KELLAWAY
HUME CRONYN · LEON AMES
AUDREY TOTTER · ALAN REED
DIRECTED BY TAY GARNETT
PRODUCED BY CAREY WILSON
The Book that Blazed to Best-Seller Fame!

John Garfield and Joan Crawford had an ill-fated affair in ***Humoresque***.

Turner and Garfield were a combustible duo in third version of Cain's nov

WONDERFUL!
WONDERFUL!
WONDERFUL!
HOW COULD IT BE ANYTHING ELSE!
LIBERTY FILMS INC
Presents
Frank CAPRA'S
"IT'S A WONDERFUL LIFE"
Starring
James STEWART
and Donna REED
Produced and Directed by
FRANK CAPRA
LIONEL BARRYMORE · THOMAS MITCHELL
HENRY TRAVERS · BEULAH BONDI · WARD BOND
FRANK FAYLEN · GLORIA GRAHAME

Frank Capra's mix of comedy, drama and fantasy lit up the movie year.

Katharine Hepburn and Robert Taylor in Vincente Minnelli's suspense movie, ***Undercurrent***.

CLUNY BROWN
BY Margery Sh

Charles Boyer and Jennifer Jones Lubitsch's ***Cluny Brown***, a roman comedy for 20th Century-Fox.

DARRYL F. ZANUCK
Presents
JEANNE
CRAIN
ARGIE
in Technicolor
GLENN LANGAN · LYNN BARI · ALAN YOUNG
20th CENTURY-FOX
Produced by WALTER MOROSCO · DIRECTED BY HENRY KING

e title song of this pleasing piece of stalgia became a popular hit.

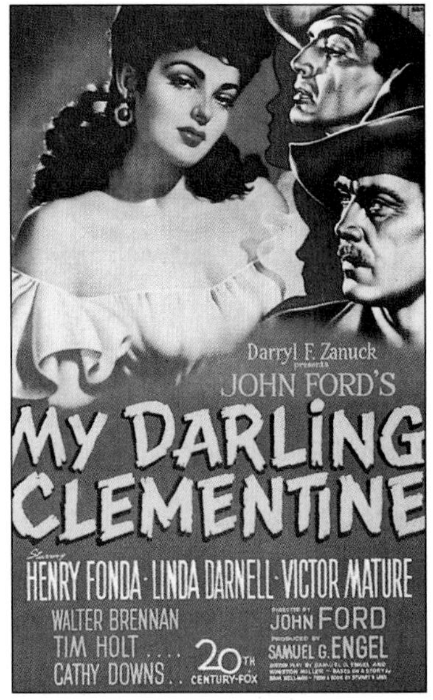
Darryl F. Zanuck
presents
JOHN FORD'S
MY DARLING CLEMENTINE
HENRY FONDA · LINDA DARNELL · VICTOR MATURE
WALTER BRENNAN
TIM HOLT ....
CATHY DOWNS ..
20th CENTURY-FOX
JOHN FORD
SAMUEL G. ENGEL

Henry Fonda was Wyatt Earp in this poetic, gripping Ford Western.

LLIP MARLOW
The Star-Sentinel
NEW CLEWS FOUND IN
"LADY IN LAKE" MURDER

e Lady in the Lake: After Dick Powell, Robert Montgomery was Marlowe.

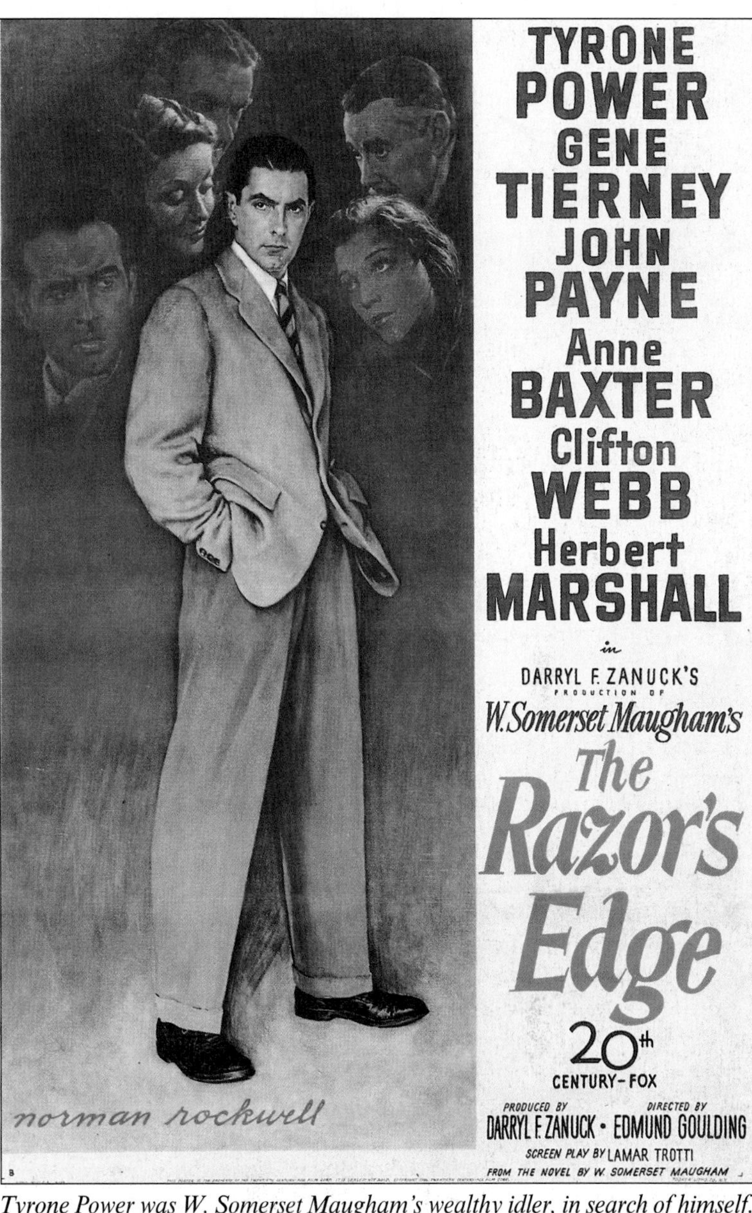
TYRONE POWER
GENE TIERNEY
JOHN PAYNE
Anne BAXTER
Clifton WEBB
Herbert MARSHALL
in
DARRYL F. ZANUCK'S
PRODUCTION OF
W. Somerset Maugham's
The Razor's Edge
20th CENTURY-FOX
PRODUCED BY DARRYL F. ZANUCK · DIRECTED BY EDMUND GOULDING
SCREEN PLAY BY LAMAR TROTTI
FROM THE NOVEL BY W. SOMERSET MAUGHAM
norman rockwell

Tyrone Power was W. Somerset Maugham's wealthy idler, in search of himself.

JEAN MARAIS
JOSETTE DAY
UNE SUPERPRODUCTION ANDRÉ PAULVÉ

un Cocteau's reworking of **Beauty d the Beast** *was a magnificent and aching piece of visual art.*

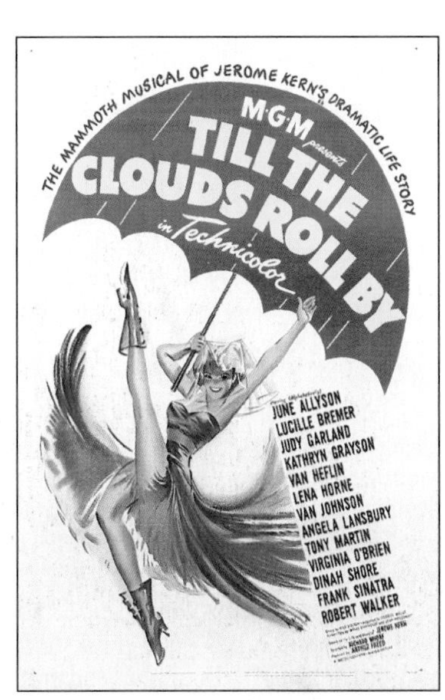
THE MAMMOTH MUSICAL OF JEROME KERN'S DRAMATIC LIFE STORY
M·G·M presents
TILL THE CLOUDS ROLL BY
in Technicolor
JUNE ALLYSON
LUCILLE BREMER
JUDY GARLAND
KATHRYN GRAYSON
VAN HEFLIN
LENA HORNE
VAN JOHNSON
ANGELA LANSBURY
TONY MARTIN
VIRGINIA O'BRIEN
DINAH SHORE
FRANK SINATRA
ROBERT WALKER

Song-filled biopic of Jerome Kern.

Michèle Morgan and Pierre Blanchar in **The Pastoral Symphony**.

Hepburn, Tracy in **The Sea of Grass**.

1947

1946 Academy Awards, Shrine Auditorium, 13 Mar.

Best Film:	*The Best Years of Our Lives* (dir: William Wyler)
Best Director:	William Wyler
Best Actor:	Fredric March *(The Best Years of Our Lives)*
Best Actress:	Olivia De Havilland *(To Each His Own)*
Best Supp. Actor:	Harold Russell *(The Best Years of Our Lives)*
Best Supp. Actress:	Anne Baxter *(The Razor's Edge)*

Nice, 4 January
René Clément is shooting the final scenes of *les Maudits* (*The Damned*) in the Victorine studios. The film stars Michel Auclair, Florence Marly and Henri Vidal.

Paris, 29 January
Release of *Scarlet Street* by Fritz Lang, a remake of the Jean Renoir classic *la Chienne*.

Paris, 18 February
Christian-Jaque and Renée Faure, whom he directed in *la Chartreuse de Parme* (*The Charterhouse of Parma*), are to marry.

Moscow, 26 February
The actor Nikolai Cherkassov has been made "an artist of the people." His letter of thanks to Stalin starts: "Dear Comrade Stalin, thank you for everything..."

Prague, 14 March
The release of *Uloupena Hranice* (*The Stolen Frontier*), marks the rebirth of national Czech cinema. The film, Jiri Weiss' first attempt at fiction, is based on the events in 1939.

New York, 12 April
Charlie Chaplin's alleged lack of patriotism was the focus of a violent verbal attack on the filmmaker at a recent press conference.

Paris, 21 May
Danielle Darrieux has been granted a divorce from the South American diplomat Porfirio Rubirosa.

Mexico, 12 June
Release of *Gran Casino*, Luis Buñuel's first Mexican film, from producer Oscar Dancigers, with Jorge Negrete and the Argentinian star Libertad Lamarque.

Moscow, 19 June
Eisenstein has been made head of the cinematographic section of the History and Art Institute at the Soviet Union Science Academy.

Brussels, 19 June
Jean Dréville's *Copie conforme* (*Confessions of a Rogue*), starring Louis Jouvet in a double role, is the French entry for the World Festival of Film and Fine Arts in Belgium. The film also stars Jean Carmet in his first big role.

Paris, 28 June
Rita Hayworth, in France for the release of *Gilda*, attended a gala exhibition of stylish automobiles in the gardens at the Trocadero.

Hollywood, 23 July
Edward Dmytryk, who is suspected of communist sympathies by the House Un-American Activities Committee (HUAC), has completed his latest film *Crossfire*. The film stars Robert Young, Robert Mitchum and Robert Ryan and deals with the subject of anti-Semitism.

Paris, 28 July
Danielle Darrieux and Pierre Louis have broken off their engagement, citing incompatibility of temperament of their respective mothers.

Le Bourget, 3 September
Three bronze reproductions of the sculpture *la Victoire de Samothrace* have flown off to the U.S. They are meant for Bette Davis, Gary Cooper and William Wyler, who were selected by the French public as the most popular Americans in films.

Hollywood, 5 September
Release of *Dark Passage*, directed by Delmer Daves and based on David Goodis' novel. This marks the third co-starring venture for Humphrey Bogart and Lauren Bacall.

Cannes, 12 September
The city's cinemas went on strike for two hours to add weight to their demands for compensation in order to counter the effects of the film festival. According to managements the occasion results in a dramatic loss of takings.

Stockholm, 16 September
Gustav Molander has completed *Kvinna utan Ansikte* (*Woman Without a Face*), with Alf Kjellin and Anita Björk. The film marks Molander's first joint effort with Ingmar Bergman, who wrote the script.

Paris, 8 October
Yves Allégret has started shooting *Dédée d'Anvers* (*Dedee*), which stars Simone Signoret and Bernard Blier.

France, 14 October
Jean Cocteau has arrived at Vizelle, the ancient capital of the Dauphiné for the first scenes of his new film starring Jean Marais, *l'Aigle à deux têtes* (*The Eagle Has Two Heads*).

Paris, 26 October
The Gaumont Palace has organized a special session of Jacques Becker's film *Antoine and Antoinette*, with free admission for those with either of the title names. The film is a tender chronicle of the lives of a young working class couple in Paris.

Moscow, 30 October
The Soyezdetfilm studios have released *Selskaya outchitelnitsa* (*The Village Teacher*), by Mark Donskoi.

Los Angeles, 10 November
Release of *Body And Soul*, directed by Robert Rossen. This film, costarrring John Garfield and Lilli Palmer, deals with an ambitious young boxer's rise to fame.

New York, 24 November
The 50 most influential studio chiefs and producers have decided to dismiss any of their employees who refuse to cooperate with the HUAC, or whom they suspect of harboring Communist sympathies.

Los Angeles, 25 November
Release of Jacques Tourneur's *Out of the Past*, with Robert Mitchum, Jane Greer and Kirk Douglas.

Hollywood, 3 December
The production code has been even further tightened by a recent amendment which is banning all scenarios describing the life of "notorious criminals" unless the character is seen to pay the price of his crime. A list of previous films which fall short of this principle has been published and cinemas have been advised not to screen them.

Hollywood, 4 December
Fox has added an edifying prolog and epilogue to Otto Preminge *Forever Amber* after accusations immorality by Cardinal Spellmar

BIRTHS

France, 16 January
Juliet Berto

France, 26 January
Patrick Dewaere (Patrick Maurin)

Los Angeles, 14 March
Billy Crystal

Connecticut, 19 March
Glenn Close

Utah, 18 April
James Woods

France, 18 June
Bernard Giraudeau

Austria, 30 July
Arnold Schwarzenegger

St. Louis, 24 October
Kevin Kline

New York, 29 October
Richard Dreyfuss

Paris, 12 November
Patrice Leconte

London, 14 December
Jane Birkin

Cincinnati, 18 December
Steven Spielberg

Arizona, 29 December
Ted Danson

DEATHS

Copenhagen, 26 January
Grace Moore

Paris, 23 March
Ferdinand Zecca

California, 21 September
Harry Carey

Charles Chaplin's ***Monsieur Verdo*** *is inspired by the life of Bluebea the murderer Landru. The film te its gory and horrible tale in a tone once funny, cynical and bitter.*

LES ARTISTES ASSOCIÉS présentent
CHARLES
CHAPLIN
dans son
CHEF d'OEUVRE
"MONSIEUR
VERDOUX"
avec MARTHA RAYE
MARILYN NASH
ISOBEL ELSOM
ROBERT LEWIS
UNITED ARTISTS
Production & Mise en Scène CHARLES CHAPLIN · Assistant ROBERT FLOREY

▷

Jimmy Stewart rescued by an angel's vision

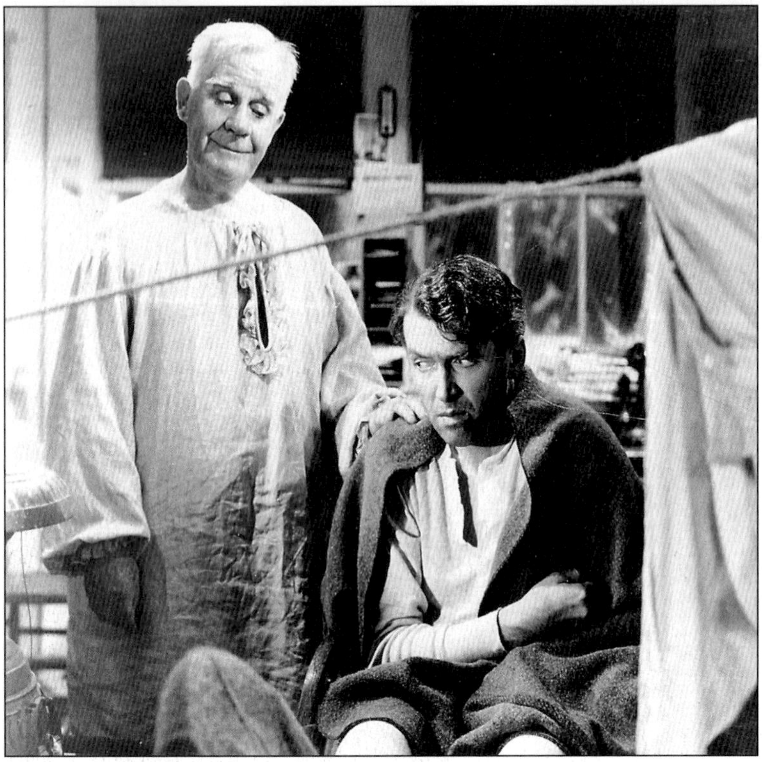

Henry Travers (left) as the angel, reclaiming James Stewart from despair.

Los Angeles, 7 January
Director Frank Capra has taken the title of his latest film, *It's a Wonderful Life*, from a Christmas card, which hints at the sentimental treatment he has given an engaging fantasy about the basic decency of small-town America. James Stewart, in his first film since returning from war service, stars here as a suicidal bank manager who is persuaded not to kill himself by Angel (2nd Class) Henry Travers. His heavenly friend shows him a vision of his hometown as it would have been had he not been born, a Middle-American idyll transformed into a sleazy hell. All ends happily, but some critics are finding this charming fairy tale too sugary for current taste.

Gunman on the run makes superb drama

*James Mason is the IRA **Odd Man Out** in Carol Reed's impressive film.*

London, 6 February
Director Carol Reed's first postwar film, made for Alexander Korda, is *Odd Man Out*. Adapted from F.L. Green's novel by R.C. Sherriff, it follows the final hours of an idealistic IRA gunman (James Mason), on the run in Belfast after being fatally wounded during a raid on a factory. Unfortunately, Mason takes an unconscionable amount of time to di[e] and some of his encounters, notab[ly] with pop-eyed artist Robert Ne[w]ton, verge on the bizarre. Howeve[r] director Reed's fascination with th[e] theme of a man doing the wron[g] thing for the right reason togeth[er] with Mason's richly romantic pe[r]formance as the doomed gunma[n] strike a powerful, dramatic chord.

Russia's distinguished director Eisenstein received by Stalin

Moscow, 24 February
The release of Part II of *Ivan the Terrible* has prompted Stalin, Molotov and Zhdanov to meet Eisenstein and the leading actor Nikolai Cherkassov to discuss the film. The atmosphere in Moscow has become more and more repressive. Last August the Central Committee of the Party took a stand against certain magazines which published "anti-Soviet" authors. Then came the attacks on various films, many of which were subsequently banned or re-edited. It seems as if the cinema here is having to undergo a purge. The second part of Eisenstein's fresco on the life of the Czar has aroused Stalin's anger because the film has become a meditation on the exercise of power and its abuse.

*Nikolai Cherkassov (left) in the color sequence for **Ivan The Terrible, Part II**.*

Reagan is elected president of Guild

Hollywood, 13 March
The 36-year-old actor Ronald Re[a]gan has launched himself into pol[i]tics. Reagan has been involved i[n] film industry affairs since his retur[n] from war service as a captain in th[e] USAAF assigned to the productio[n] of training films. Today sees h[is] election to the presidency of th[e] Screen Actors Guild. Reagan's vi[ce] president is Gene Kelly. They su[c]ceed, respectively, Robert Mon[t]gomery and Franchot Tone, wh[o] resigned because of their productio[n] interests, as have committee mem[]bers Dick Powell, John Garfiel[d], Harpo Marx and James Cagne[y]. Reagan resumes a screen care[er] with Warners after a five-year ga[p].

azan displays his brand of neo-realism

llywood, 5 March
th *Boomerang*, his third feature n, Elia Kazan has gained the reptation of being among the best film ectors in America. Born in Istan- in 1909 to Armenian parents o emigrated to the U.S. when he s five years old, Kazan acquired ne directing and acting on Broady. In 1933, he joined the radical oup Theater run by Lee Stras-g, Cheryl Crawford and Harold Clurman, who practised Stanislavsky's acting method as instituted at the Moscow Arts Theatre. Revealing more of the influence of Italian neo-realism, *Boomerang* relates the story of the arrest of an innocent man charged with the murder of a clergyman. Presented as the objective facts of a police statement, the film, nevertheless, becomes a critique of weaknesses in the American judicial system.

Chaplin's 'Verdoux', a departure of genre

New York, 11 April
Charlie Chaplin's long-awaited film *Monsieur Verdoux* that premiered today at the Broadway Theater, sees him turn from the Tramp into the dapper anti-hero of the title, murdering a string of wealthy women to support his crippled wife. It's hard work, particularly when the intended victim is murder-proof Martha Raye. Before the guillotine catches up with him, Verdoux explains that he is merely practising, on a small scale, what is sometimes sanctioned by the state on an infinitely greater scale. As a businessman, he kills for profit. War, and the death of millions, is simply bigger business. The film's message has convinced many hostile critics that Chaplin is feeding the American public Communist propaganda. There were hisses as well as laughter from the audience at the movie's premiere.

B TEST BULLET
A... MURDER BULLET

na Andrews is the state prosecutor who believes in justice in ***Boomerang****.*

Chaplin as Verdoux the suave killer, here in a scene with Martha Raye.

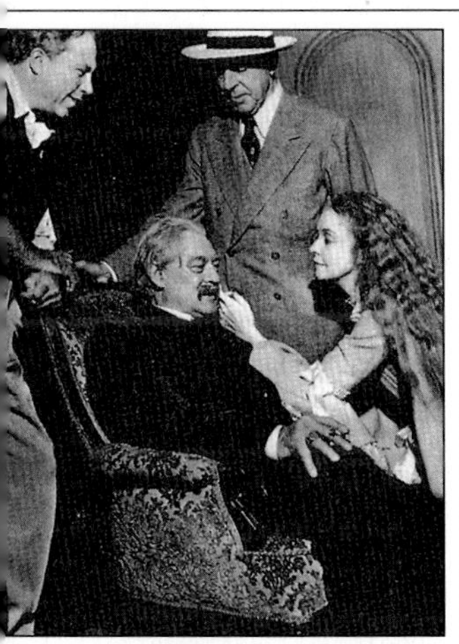

)uring the filming of *Duel in the 'un*, which opened on 31 December, the director King Vidor was isited on the set by the great).W. Griffith (standing right). ;riffith found himself reunited ith his old friends and colleagues, ionel Barrymore and Lillian ;ish (pictured here), who play imortant supporting roles in the lm to lead stars Jennifer Jones nd Gregory Peck.

Awards triumph for William Wyler

Hollywood, 13 March
Hosted by Mervyn LeRoy and presented by Jack Benny, the 19th Academy Awards ceremony was dominated by William Wyler's film *The Best Years of Our Lives*. It walked away with seven Oscars: Best Picture, Best Director (Wyler), Best Actor (Fredric March), Best Supporting Actor (Harold Russell), Screenplay (Robert Sherwood), Editing (Daniel Mandell) and Scoring (Hugo Friedhofer). Thwarting what was nearly a clean sweep was the Best Actress award won by Olivia De Havilland for her performance in *To Each His Own* as the unwed mother who must remain "aunt" to her son John Lund. And the Best Supporting Actress award went to Anne Baxter for her portrayal of the alcoholic whom Tyrone Power romances on the rebound from Gene Tierney in *The Razor's Edge*.

Martine Carole attempts suicide in Paris

Paris, 10 April
The French film actress Martine Carol threw herself off the Alma bridge into the Seine at 5:15 a.m. this morning. She was fished out and taken rapidly to the hospital where her condition is judged to be satisfactory. It seems most likely that it was a suicide attempt caused by depression related to personal problems and to the profession she chose when she was an adolescent. Born Maryse Mourer in Biarritz on 16 May 1922, she attended the dramatic classes of René Simon and Robert Manuel, before her screen debut in 1941 in *le Dernier des six*, directed by Georges Lacombe. Six years and eight films later, she has still not made much of an impression on the public, and has failed to either win fame or a man's love. Extremely lonely, she chose to end her life at the beginning of spring. In fact, it is possible that this bungled suicide attempt might gain her some much-needed publicity and bring her the recognition that her acting talent has failed to do. It will be interesting to see whether the box-office takings for her latest film, *Carré de valets*, will increase because of her melodramatic gesture.

Martine Carol, beautiful but sad.

Censure and diplomacy conflict in Brussels

Brussels, 29 June
The organizers of the World Festival of Film and Fine Arts probably never expected anything like the sight of the French ambassador to Belgium leaving the hall in protest against a French picture! The movie in question was none other than Claude Autant-Lara's *Devil in the Flesh* (*le Diable au corps*), adapted from Raymond Radiguet's novel, which created a scandal when it was originally published in 1923. The ambassador's reaction subsequently deprived the film of the Grand Prix for which it was a candidate. A far less controversial French film, René Clair's *Silence is Golden* (*le Silence est d'or*), was presented with the statue of St. Michel awarded to the best feature. Nevertheless, the jury still wanted to acknowledge *Devil in the Flesh*, doing so via the best actor prize, which was handed to Gérard Philipe, whose performance as an adolescent in love with a married woman impressed everybody. The International Critics proved their independence by presenting their prize to the Autant-Lara film. As for the 17 other participating countries, those that stood out were England, which garnered the Grand Prix of the Belgian Government for Carol Reed's *Odd Man Out*; the United States, awarded the best screenplay prize for William Wyler's *The Best Years of Our Lives*, and for Myrna Loy's performance in the same film. Finally, Italy was rewarded with the Special Grand Prize for Roberto Rossellini's *Païsa*.

Marcelle Derrien, François Périer.

Best actor winner Gérard Philipe with Micheline Presle in ***Devil in the Flesh****.*

Maurice Chevalier (right) in René Clair's ***Silence is Golden****, the main winner.*

Emotion and stunning visuals from Powe

Jean Simmons, whose frustration leads to madness in ***Black Narcissus****.*

London, 26 May
Michael Powell has re-created the Himalayas in the studios at Pinewood in his remarkable screen version of Rumer Godden's novel titled *Black Narcissus*. A group of nuns, led by Deborah Kerr, move into a remote Nepalese palace, at one tir the home of the ruler's concubin They stir the sexual static of t "House of Women". The movi pulsing colors and feverish clima scored by Brian Easdale, strength the film's disturbing erotic charg

A sad interruption at Belle-Ile-en-Mer

Belle-Ile-en-Mer, 20 July
The shooting of *la Fleur de l'âge*, begun last May, has been interrupted, probably permanently. Directed by Marcel Carné and written by Jacques Prévert, the film describes a tragic revolt in a children's prison. After having mobilized all the inhabitants of the town and shaved the heads of 200 boys, the director seems to have lost control of the film. The producers reproached him for over-spending and not keeping to previous commitments. But negotiations have failed, and the crew and actors, including Nicole Dreyfus, whom Carné has since renamed Anouk Aimée, are stranded.

Anouk Aimée and Claude Romain

he multiple faces of Kaye's genius

w York, 14 August
: fourth film of singer-dancer-nedian Danny Kaye, *The Secret e of Walter Mitty*, is also his best 'ar, as it gives him the opportuni-o play several characters and use full range of his talents and per-ality. Though James Thurber, o wrote the original short story out a day-dreaming henpecked band, offered to give producer nuel Goldwyn $10,000 *not* to n it, the picture has turned out cessful on almost all fronts. To w for romance, the screenplay made the timid Walter Mitty a helor, though dominated by his ther (Fay Bainter) and his pushy ncee (Ann Rutherford). Mitty's aginary adventures punctuate the n, which culminates in his taking t in a real adventure. Among the racters hilariously impersonated Kaye are a fast-drawing cowboy, Mississippi riverboat gambler, a lliant surgeon, a dashing RAF ot and lastly "Anatole of Paris", a ench fashion designer. In Mitty's eams, the same glamorous blonde oine always appears, played by ginia Mayo. As she was in his previous films – *Wonder Man* d *The Kid from Brooklyn* – Mayo Kaye's ideal woman. But here in e *Secret Life of Walter Mitty*, the eam girl finally enters his real life, cing the confused Kaye to help escape an evil character who's en following her.

Samuel Goldwyn spent more than million to make this sumptuously oduced Technicolor Danny Kaye owcase. So far, on each occasion ce his manic debut in *Up in Arms* three years ago, Goldwyn's discovery has delivered the goods. This latest extravaganza, which also features Boris Karloff and the Goldwyn Girls, should keep box offices humming for a long time to come. Danny Kaye, born David Daniel Kaminski on 18 January 1913 in Brooklyn, began his clowning career on the "Borscht Circuit", playing various resorts in New York's Catskill Mountains, before making his Broadway debut opposite Imogen Coca in *The Straw Hat Revue*. But it was his appearance in Kurt Weill's *Lady in the Dark* on Broadway, during which he stopped the show with his tongue-twisting rendition of "Tchaikovsky", that brought him to the attention of Goldwyn, who astutely signed him up, and got him to dye his hair bright reddish-blond. Not only was a star born, it exploded across the screen.

Pilot Walter Mitty: Virginia Mayo with Danny Kaye in one of his many guises.

e meek and mild milkman turns prizefighter in ***The Kid from Brooklyn.***

Ninety killed in horrifying accident

Rueil, 3 September
It was just another Saturday night at the Select cinema in the suburbs of Paris. Nearly 800 filmgoers were packed together in the auditorium, hoping for a brief release from the drudgery of daily life in the darkness of the theater. Then catastrophe struck. An electrical fault sparked a conflagration. Ninety people died in the blaze and many more were seriously injured. This is the worst tragedy to occur in a theater since the fire at the Charity Bazaar in 1897, an incident which marred the early days of film and threatened to turn audiences away at a time when its popularity was growing.

Screen lovers continue to scandalize public

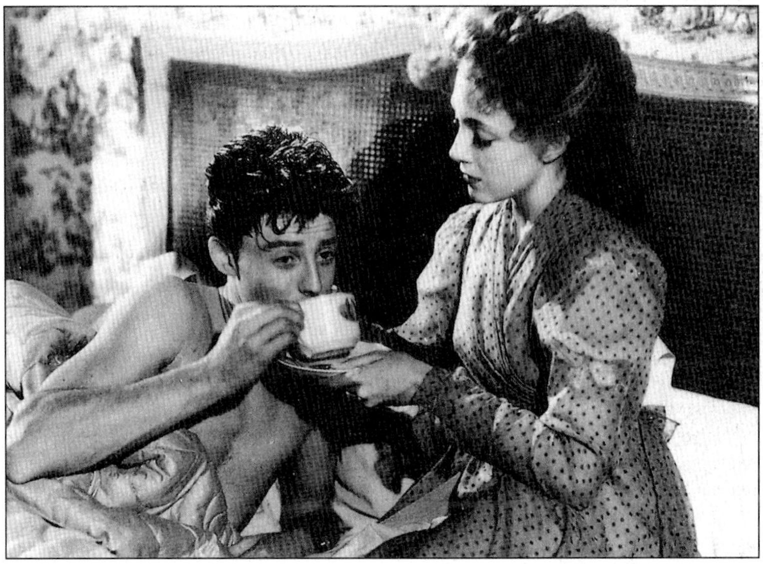

Gérard Philipe and Micheline Presle give strikingly truthful performances.

Paris, 12 September
At its publication in 1923, five years after the armistice, *Devil in the Flesh* (*le Diable au corps*), the novel by Raymond Radiguet, shocked patriots and created a scandal because, in the context of the Great War, it was sympathetic to the guilty liaison between a young student and a married woman whose husband was at the Front. A quarter of a century later, and two years after the end of the last war, the scandal has resurfaced. But this time it concerns the film, adapted from the novel by Jean Aurenche and Pierre Bost and directed by Claude Autant-Lara. After the premiere of the film in Bordeaux, the local press described it as "vile", "ignoble" and a "stream of filth", and asked that it be removed from the screens on the grounds that it exalted adultery and ridiculed the Family, the Red Cross and also the Army. Now in Paris some critics have joined the "scandalized" camp, not hesitating to describe the movie as "repugnant". Paradoxically, the publicity surrounding the release of the film has been excellent for the box office. But if it deserves success, it is due to its artistic qualities and the performances of Gérard Philipe and Micheline Presle, who portray the two lovers with so much sensitivity and honesty.

Eccentric 'Life with Father' provides a filmic delight for all ages

Dunne, Powell (center) with Jimmy Lydon, Heather Wilde, Martin Milner.

Hollywood, 14 September
Broadway audiences have had 3,224 opportunities to delight in the long-running comedy, *Life With Father.* Now the whole country can enjoy this heartwarming piece, which is brought to the screen in a sumptuous, Technicolored re-creation of 1880s New York. This is the charming tale of an eccentric, irascible father – with a heart of gold underneath, of course – who upsets his family by refusing to be baptized. It is directed with a light touch by Michael Curtiz, who is usually associated with tougher fare, and it is acted in fine style by William Powell as father, enchanting Irene Dunne as mother, and a first-class supporting cast. Warner Bros. is clearly in for a box-office bonanza.

From Venice to Cannes, festivals compete for international films

Cannes, 25 September
At the moment, while the Cannes Film Festival is drawing to a close, the increasingly numerous commentators are busy deploring the fact that many international festivals are concentrated around the same time each year. No fewer than three festivals have taken place during just the past four months: Lugano (Switzerland), Venice (Italy) and Cannes (France). And the latter two practically overlap, casting a shadow over each other – Cannes opens before Venice has finished. One can easily imagine the problems that the organizers of both festivals are faced with in order to procure rare cinematographic gems before the other does. Is it then for this reason that the Cannes Festival has lost some of its international flavor this year? Besides its exclusively French jury, the winning works came only from France and the United States. The prizes went to Jacques Becker's film *Antoine and Antoinette*, René Clément's *The Damned*, *Crossfire* from Edward Dmytryk, Walt Disney's cartoon feature *Dumbo* and Metro-Goldwyn-Mayer's all-star showcase *Ziegfeld Follies.*

The international jury of the Mostra at Venice has shown itself to be far more open to world cinema by awarding the Golden Lion to the Czechoslovakian film *The Strike* (*Sirena*), directed by Karel Stekly, which has given that country's revived industry a shot in the arm. The prize for best director and best actor both went to Frenchmen: Henri-Georges Clouzot, who had not been permitted to direct a film for four years, for his atmospheric thriller *Quai des Orfèvres*, and Pierre Fresnay for his portrayal of the 17th-century saint, Vincent de Paul, in *Monsieur Vincent*, directed by Maurice Cloche. Fresnay, growing from a young man into old age manages to evoke saintliness without sermonizing and sanctimoniousness. As for the best actress prize, there were few complaints when Anna Magnani won for the title role in *Angelina* (*l'Onorevole Angelina*). In this Italian-made comedy-drama, directed by Luigi Zampa, Magnani plays a housewife, fighting heroically to improve the living conditions of her family and neighbors in postwar Italy. The magnificent Italian actress makes the most of this star vehicle, exploiting her earthiness, humor and passion. What is significant about the Venice Film Festival in contrast to that of Cannes, is that all the winners are associated with films that were important socially, politically or carried a moral message. Cannes, on the other hand, was quite content to acknowledge more commercial motion pictures made purely for entertainment.

LUIGI ZAMPA
Anna
MAGNANI
AVE NINCHI
AGNESE DUBBINI
E. ALMIRANTE
A. MIGLIARI
l'onorevole
ANGELINA
Anna Magnani was crowned the best actress for ***Angelina.***

Fred Astaire in ***Ziegfeld Follies.***

Louis Jouvet reinstates Clouzot

Louis Jouvet and Robert Dalban.

Paris, 3 October
For having made *le Corbeau* 1943, a film produced by the G man company Continental and th judged at the time of Liberation a piece of anti-French propagan the director Henri-Georges Clouz had difficulties working in Fran again. Louis Jouvet, an admirer Clouzot's work, invited him to ta up his career again. The result *Quai des Orfèvres*, a thriller in whi Jouvet plays an ambiguous poli inspector investigating a murder the milieu of a music hall. Clouzo observation of human frailty, pressed with a mixture of wit a compassion, and filmed with a fi sense of composition and atm spheric lighting, and the memoral performance of Jouvet, part cyn part sentimentalist, makes *Quai d Orfèvres* a great comeback.

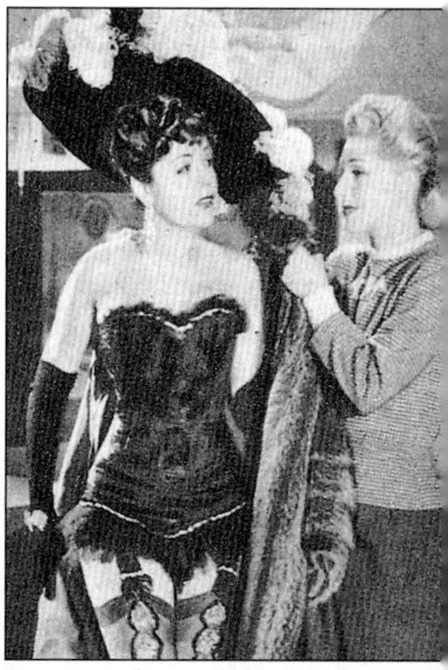
Suzy Delair (left) and Simo Renant in ***Quai des Orfèvres.***

ox points finger at anti-Semitism

w York, 11 November
·h, God, I've got it. It's the only y. I'll *be* Jewish!" With these ring- words, magazine journalist Greg- Peck launches his crusade to pose the extent of anti-Semitism in nerica in Fox's new *Gentleman's reement*, adapted from Laura Z. bson's best-selling book and di- ted by Elia Kazan. Posing as a v, Peck finds that his incognito estigation has an alarming effect himself, his family and also his nds. For example, his girlfriend rothy McGuire, the daughter of magazine's publisher, fails to derstand the baleful effect of ial intolerance, even though she convinced that she is free of big- y. Amid the agonizing and breast- ating, and bouts of bewildered cerity from Gregory Peck, it is to John Garfield as a Jewish viceman to bring a measure of cerity to a film that is admirable d absorbing, but somewhat overly nvinced of its own impeccable dentials. Written by Moss Hart, *ntleman's Agreement* bears the llmarks of the producer Darryl F. nuck's preoccupation with realis- films that explore contemporary problems from a stolidly liberal view-point. Even though Zanuck's firm commitment to these projects has been hailed as daring in some quarters, others, including critic James Agee, regard them as a profitable form of "safe fearlessness". After a preview of the movie, writer Ring Lardner Jr. quipped, "The movie's moral is that you should never be mean to a Jew, because he might turn out to be Gentile."

Dorothy McGuire, Gregory Peck, Albert Dekker in ***Gentleman's Agreement.***

UAC's Communist witch hunt snares ten of Hollywood's best

ashington, 26 November
e witch hunt for Communists has read its tentacles into Hollywood. the urging of Eric Johnston, esident of the Association of Mo- n Picture Producers and also the successor to Will H. Hays, Edward Dmytryk, the director of the highly praised *Crossfire*, has been dismissed by RKO. Nine others have suffered the same fate: Adrian Scott, the producer of *Crossfire*, producer-director Herbert Biberman and screenwriters John Howard Lawson, Lester Cole, Dalton Trumbo, Alvah Bessie, Albert Maltz, Ring Lardner Jr. and Samuel Ornitz. They have been cited for "contempt of Congress", after refusing to divulge to the House Un-American Activities Committee their past and present political affiliations. The Hollywood Ten, as they are already being dubbed, refused to answer the question: "Are you now, or have you ever been, a Communist?" They regard the activities of the Committee, which has been investigating alleged Red infiltration of Hollywood since the spring, as unconstitutional. John Howard Lawson declared that "I am not on trial here... the Committee is on trial before the American people." One of the few to condemn the treatment of the Hollywood Ten has been Sam Goldwyn, no lover of Communism but a man who feels the Committee's behavior is itself un-American.

r: Robert Ryan, Robert Mitchum and Robert Young in Dmytryk's ***Crossfire.***

The 'Lubitsch Touch' is sadly no more

Hollywood, 30 November
The Hollywood director of German origin, Ernst Lubitsch, has died at the age of 55 after a long illness. The shooting of *That Lady in Ermine*, on which he worked for 35 days, has been interrupted until Otto Preminger takes over. Ernst Lubitsch was born in Berlin on 28 January 1892, the son of a wealthy tailor. He was drawn to the stage in his teens and acted in Max Reinhardt's company. Then in 1914, he began acting, writing and directing a series of short comedy films. Included among the features he did in Germany were a number of ironic historical romances such as *Madame Dubarry* (1919), *Anna Boleyn* (1920) and *The Loves of Pharaoh* (1922). He arrived in Hollywood in 1923 to direct Mary Pickford in *Rosita*. After completing five scintillating social comedies for Warner Bros. he went to Paramount where he established a style of wit and sophistication in opulent surroundings. Lubitsch's first sound film, *The Love Parade*, cast Maurice Chevalier opposite Jeanette MacDonald. He worked again with both stars in one of the most polished of screen musicals, *The Merry Widow* (1934). Other gems in the Lubitsch collection included *Trouble in Paradise* (1932) and *To Be or Not To Be* (1942). The now-famous "Lubitsch Touch" has been variously defined, but the touch is that of a master chef who knows exactly the right amount of spice or sugar to add to a dish. He will be greatly missed.

Laughing Garbo in ***Ninotchka.***

Howard Duff (left) and Burt Lancaster starred in Jules Dassin's **Brute Force**.

RKO
Robert MITCHUM · Jane GREER
Out of the Past
KIRK DOUGLAS · RHONDA FLEMING
RICHARD WEBB
WARREN DUFF
JACQUES TOURNEUR

Great film noir about a detective tangling with a homicidal woman.

BETTY GRABLE
DICK HAYMES
THE SHOCKING MISS PILGRIM
in Technicolor
GEORGE and IRA GERSHWIN
ANNE REVERE
GEORGE SEATON
WILLIAM PERLBERG
20th CENTURY FOX

Grable fought for women's rights, with her famous legs covered!

l to r: Brian Donlevy, Richard Widmark and Victor Mature in ***Kiss of Death****.*

ORSON WELLES'
DANS UNE PRÉSENTATION RÉPUBLIC PICTURES
MACBETH
PRODUCTION MERCURY

An unconventional and only partly successful version of Shakespeare's pl made in 21 days by cinema's ***enfant terrible****.*

Rex Harrison was the sea captain who haunted Gene Tierney in the unusu ***The Ghost and Mrs. Muir****, directed by Joseph L. Mankiewicz.*

Ambre
CORNEL RICHARD GEORGE
RNELL·WILDE·GREENE·SANDERS
PREMINGER
WILLIAM PERLBERG
nch poster for **Forever Amber**.

UN FILM DE
RENÉ CLAIR
MAURICE CHEVALIER
FRANÇOIS PERIER
LE SILENCE
EST D'OR
Clair's **Silence is Golden**: a delight.

an Crawford in **Daisy Kenyon**.

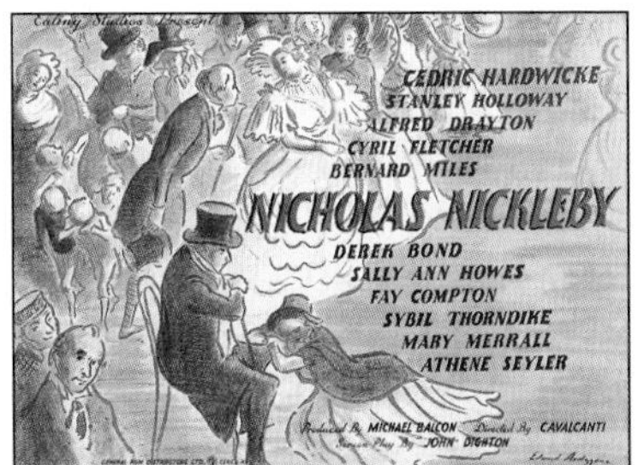
CEDRIC HARDWICKE
STANLEY HOLLOWAY
ALFRED DRAYTON
CYRIL FLETCHER
BERNARD MILES
NICHOLAS NICKLEBY
DEREK BOND
SALLY ANN HOWES
FAY COMPTON
SYBIL THORNDIKE
MARY MERRALL
ATHENE SEYLER
Another great Dickens adaptation.

Jiri Trnka's **The Czech Year**.

WALTER WANGER presents
ısan HAYWARD Lee BOWMAN
larsha HUNT Eddie ALBERT
SMASH-UP
The Story of a Woman!
with CARL ESMOND · CARLETON YOUNG · CHARLES D. BROWN
woman destroyed by alcoholism.

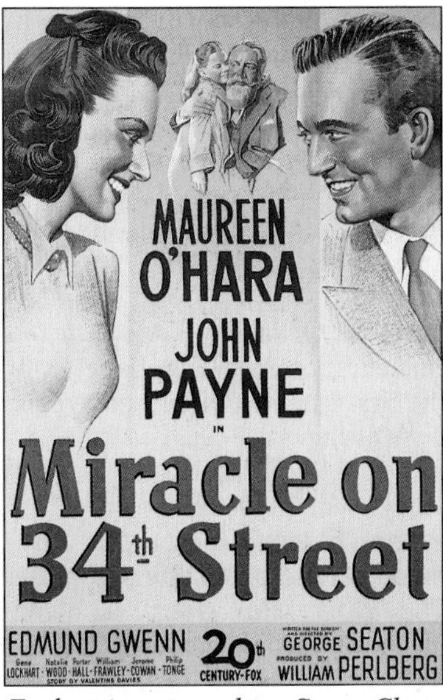
MAUREEN
O'HARA
JOHN
PAYNE
IN
Miracle on
34th Street
EDMUND GWENN
GEORGE SEATON
WILLIAM PERLBERG
20th CENTURY-FOX
Enchanting story about Santa Claus.

All for you....
BODY
and
SOUL
The ENTERPRISE STUDIOS present
JOHN GARFIELD · LILLI PALMER
Garfield played a boxer in this uncompromising drama about the fight game.

Five Women Around Utamaro.

Unconquered: Cooper and Karloff.

1948

1947 Academy Awards, Shrine Auditorium, 20 Mar.

Best Film:	*Gentleman's Agreement* (dir: Elia Kazan)
Best Director:	Elia Kazan
Best Actor:	Ronald Colman *(A Double Life)*
Best Actress:	Loretta Young *(The Farmer's Daughter)*
Best Supp. Actor:	Edmund Gwenn *(Miracle on 34th Street)*
Best Supp. Actress:	Celeste Holm *(Gentleman's Agreement)*

Paris, 4 January
Cinema professionals held a demonstration against the invasion of American films. The march was led by Simone Signoret, Jean Marais and Raymond Bussières.

Paris, 7 January
Maurice Cloche's *Monsieur Vincent* has been chosen as the well-deserved winner for the major French cinema award. The script was written by Jean Anouilh, and part of the finance came from public subscription. The film paints an admirable portrait of court life during the reign of Louis XIII. Pierre Fresnay, who gives a brilliant performance as St. Vincent, brings a depth and extraordinary presence to the role.

Paris, 13 January
Henry Verdoux, an employee of a Parisian bank has brought an action against the producers of the film *Monsieur Verdoux.*

Paris, 16 January
Marcel Pagnol has joined the ranks of France's most illustrious men of science and letters today. His entry into the hallowed sphere of the French Academy as both writer and director of such marvelous films as *César* and *The Baker's Wife* makes him the first Academy member to come from the world of cinema.

Los Angeles, 20 January
Release of *The Naked City*, directed by Jules Dassin. A new *film noir* melodrama from the director of *Brute Force*. Barry Fitzgerald stars.

London, 22 January
Release of *Anna Karenina*, a British made version of Tolstoy's novel, directed by Julien Duvivier, with Vivien Leigh, Ralph Richardson and Kieron Moore.

London, 8 February
Viviane Romance is making her first film in England, *The Woman Hater*, with director Terence Young.

Washington, 8 March
Under the terms of an agreement with the United Kingdom, American film companies are undertaking to reinvest the $60 million profit made in England. The English in return will reduce the 1947 tax on American films by 75 percent.

Paris, 24 March
Roger Leenhardt's first film *les Dernières vacances* (*The Last Vacation*) is a gentle evocation of the awakening love between two 16-year-old cousins who are spending their last holiday on the family property in the Languedoc. Young Odile Versois is outstanding in the role of Juliette.

Mexico, 25 March
Ismael Rodriguez' latest project *Nostrotros los pobres* is a typical "rancheros" melodrama and has met with the usual enthusiasm.

Mexico, 27 March
The release of John Ford's first Mexican film, *The Fugitive*, is causing controversy here. The movie, based on Graham Greene's famous novel *The Power and the Glory*, brings back unwelcome memories of Mexico's darker hours under the anti-clerical rule of Francisco Madero. Henry Fonda co-stars with Mexicans Dolorès Del Rio and Pedro Armendariz, and the filmmaker himself co-produced with Merian Cooper and RKO.

Sofia, 5 April
The production, distribution and importation of films have become state monopolies.

Hollywood, 26 April
Lana Turner, MGM's resident voluptuous blonde, has married Henry J. Topping, known as Bob.

Washington, 19 April
Scriptwriter John Howard Lawson has been convicted of contempt of Congress for refusing to give evidence in front of the HUAC.

Hollywood, 15 May
Cyd Charisse, alias "Hollywood's most beautiful legs", has married the crooner Tony Martin after divorcing Nico Charisse, her first husband and dancing instructor, who married her when she was only 15 years old.

Washington, 15 May
The Supreme Court has handed down a decision in favor of the Justice Department. The five major studios have been declared guilty of "conspiracy and discrimination" in order to secure a monopoly of the cinema circuits.

Los Angeles, 16 July
Bogart and Bacall are once again in the limelight in the latest John Huston film *Key Largo*, with Claire Trevor and Lionel Barrymore.

Hollywood, 8 August
Ginger Rogers and Fred Astaire are together again on the screen for the first time in nine years in *The Barkleys of Broadway*, directed by Charles Walters.

France, 15 September
Marcel Pagnol is in the Alpes-Maritime where he has just finished shooting *la Belle Meunière*, played by his wife Jacqueline and Tino Rossi. The film which was made in Rouxcolor – named after the Roux brothers, its inventors – is the second French color film.

Los Angeles, 30 September
Robert Mitchum has been freed from prison. He was sentenced to 21 days for the possession and use of marijuana, despite having paid a $1,000 bond.

Los Angeles, 1 October
Release of Howard Hawks' *Red River* with John Wayne, Joanne Dru and Montgomery Clift.

Paris, 26 October
Inauguration by Henri Langlois of the first cinema museum in avenue de Messine.

Hollywood, 30 October
Release of the fifth American adaptation of Alexander Dumas' novel *The Three Musketeers*, a highly inventive version made by George Sidney with dancer Gene Kelly as D'Artagnan.

Rome, 2 November
Release of Roberto Rossellini's n effort *l'Amore* (*Women* aka *Ways Love*), a film in two parts: the f taken from *The Human Voice* Jean Cocteau, and the second, *T Miracle*, based on an idea by Fed co Fellini, who also plays the m lead with Anna Magnani.

Los Angeles, 30 November
Rita Hayworth and Orson Wel have filed for divorce.

Los Angeles, 27 November
Release of *The Boy With Gre Hair*, a fable about conformity a the right to be different, directed Joseph Losey, with Dean Stockw in the title role.

New York, 31 December
Louise Brooks, who retired from t cinema in 1938 after her flaggi career failed to revive, is now wo ing as a $40-a-week salesgirl at Sa Fifth Avenue.

BIRTHS

New York, 16 January
John Carpenter

Missouri, 28 March
Dianne Wiest

France, 21 June
Philippe Sarde

England, 19 September
Jeremy Irons

France, 3 December
Diane Kurys

France, 27 December
Gérard Depardieu

DEATHS

Switzerland, 25 May
Jacques Feyder

France, 6 June
Louis Lumière

Los Angeles, 23 July
D.W. Griffith

Rita Hayworth is the disturbing a disconcerting focus of ***The Lady fr Shanghai****, made by her husband O son Welles, who also co-stars. Wei visually compelling cinema art.*

COLUMBIA FILMS S.A. présente :
RITA
HAYWORTH
ORSON
WELLES
DANS
LA DAME DE SHANGHAI
(The lady from Shanghai)
AVEC
EVERETT SLOANE et GLENN ANDERS
Scénario et Production Orson WELLES
COLUMBIA FILMS S.A. 20, Rue de Troyon . Paris.
MODÈLE B
COLUMBIA FILMS

Bogart and the Hustons search for treasure

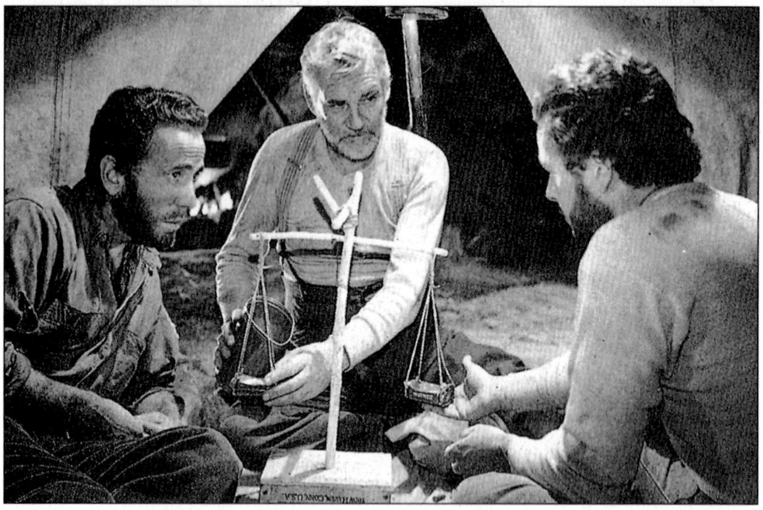

Bogart (left), Walter Huston and Tim Holt in ***The Treasure of the Sierra Madre.***

Hollywood, 23 January
Writer-director John Huston has woven a powerful parable of greed around *The Treasure of the Sierra Madre*, adapted from the novel by the mysterious writer B. Traven. Shot on location in Mexico, the film follows a trio of drifters prospecting for gold: whiskery old-timer Walter Huston; baby-faced Tim Holt, more familiar as a star of B-Westerns; and Humphrey Bogart's own three-time loser, Fred C. Dobbs. They strike it rich but not lucky, and Bogart pays with his life. Jack Warner hated the film and insisted that Bogart survive the final reel, but Huston held firm and killed him off.

Sudden death of Sergei Eisenstein

Moscow, 11 February
The great Russian film director Sergei Eisenstein has succumbed to a heart attack at the age of 50. His lonely death, on a winter's night, brings his tragic destiny to a close. Subsequent to his memorable debut films – *Strike* (1925) and *The Battleship Potemkin* (1925) – problems began to accumulate, and his trip to the U.S. and Mexico turned into a nightmare. In the Soviet Union his qualities as a director were recognized, but he was reproached for not toeing the party line. He had to suffer the humiliations of self-criticism demanded by mere functionaries of the state. What a waste of energy and intelligence! Another bitter pill he had to swallow was the destruction of a number of reels he shot for the final part of *Ivan the Terrible*. Despite all this, Sergei Eisenstein has left us with at least four towering masterpieces of the cinema.

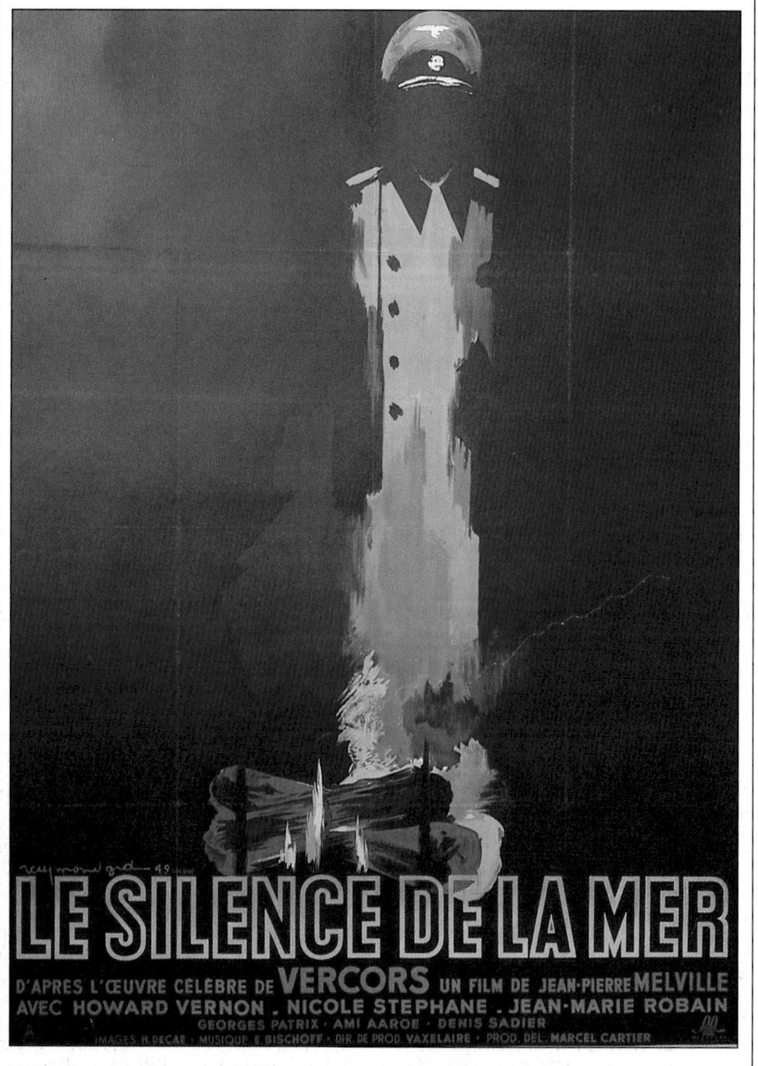
LE SILENCE DE LA MER
D'APRES L'ŒUVRE CÉLÈBRE DE VERCORS UN FILM DE JEAN-PIERRE MELVILLE
AVEC HOWARD VERNON . NICOLE STEPHANE . JEAN-MARIE ROBAIN
GEORGES PATRIX · AMI AAROE · DENIS SADIER

Elia Kazan captures the major Oscars

Shelley Winters and Best Actor Ronald Colman in Cukor's ***A Double Life.***

Hollywood, 20 March
It was no surprise that *Gentleman's Agreement*, nominated for six Oscars, should have won the Best Picture and Best Director (Elia Kazan). Celeste Holm was named Best Su porting Actress for her role as t chic but lonely fashion writer in t same film. Among the cast, Gregc Peck lost to Ronald Colman *Double Life*) and Dorothy McGu to Loretta Young (*The Farme Daughter*). In his fourth featu Kazan sensitively tackled the thor subject of anti-Semitism in the U. making the film one of the first i portant American social messa films of the postwar period.

Rossellini has conquered Bergma

Los Angeles, 15 March
A telegram sent to the residence Ingrid Bergman and her husba Dr. Peter Lindstrom read: "It with great emotion that I receiv your letter. By luck it arrived on r birthday, and it is the most beauti of my presents. Believe me, I drea of shooting a film with you, and shall do everything in my power make it come about." It was sign Roberto Rossellini. Ingrid had wr ten to the Italian director a few da earlier, expressing her admirati for his films and to suggest th work together. In the lengthy rep which followed, Rossellini sketch the outlines of a scenario, ending t letter thus: "Will it be possible f you to come to Europe? May I inv you to Italy where we can chat abo the project in a leisurely way? You enthusiastically, Roberto Rosse ni." It seems likely that Bergm will soon be packing her bags.

ta, Orson lost in a hall of broken mirrors

'les and Hayworth in the striking 'hall of mirrors' climax to the film.

York, 8 April
return of Orson Welles as direc- has not passed unnoticed. *The 'y from Shanghai* is in the best lition of the thriller genre, as well eing a star vehicle for Welles' Rita Hayworth. Having cut and ched her famous auburn locks the role, Hayworth plays a mys- ous *femme fatale* who draws Welles, portraying a tough innocent Irishman, deeper into the web she weaves. The tour-de-force climax is a shootout between Hayworth and her crippled power-hungry husband Everett Sloane in a hall of mirrors at Luna Park, hitting images of each other before finding the flesh. "It's true, I made a lot of mistakes," she says in her dying breath.

Howard Hughes is in control of RKO

Hollywood, 15 May
Howard Hughes, the eccentric Texan multimillionaire, airplane designer, aviator and business entrepreneur, who has occasionally ventured into film production in the past, has completed his purchase of the RKO Radio company, including its Hollywood studio and its chain of 124 cinemas. This troubled company has had a long history of management reshuffling and financial problems since its formation in 1929, and although it has many memorable films to its credit, from *King Kong* to *Citizen Kane*, it has enjoyed few box-office hits. Having benefited from the wartime boom, profits declined steadily from their peak in 1946 when current studio boss Floyd Odlum decided to quit. As owner of TWA and the Hughes Tool Co., the new owner was easily able to agree to the purchase price of $8.8 million. But given the past history of his dabblings in movies, most recently with *Mad Wednesday* and *Vendetta*, the outlook for RKO is bleak.

Fred and Judy a couple of swells

'Just a couple of swells'. Terrific!

New York, 30 July
After two years of retirement, Fred Astaire was called back by MGM to co-star with Judy Garland in *Easter Parade* when Gene Kelly broke his ankle. They make a swell couple, especially in the duet, "A Couple of Swells", dressed as hoboes.

ssellini amid rubble and ruin in Berlin

ne, 30 May
Germany, Year Zero, Roberto ssellini took his cameras into the astation of postwar Berlin, in or- to give the film the authenticity documentary. Against this grim kground, he unfolds the tale of a year-old boy, trying to feed his ily, who kills his sickly father to lessen the burden. Unable to live with the deed, he throws himself off a ruined building. The director's compassion shines through the tragic story, which becomes symbolic of the country as a whole. The final section when the child finds a moment to play before dying, shows Rossellini at his poignant best.

youthful protagonists confronted with the aftermath of World War II.

Zinnemann uncovers postwar heartbreak

New York, 6 August
Fred Zinnemann, filming on location in the ruins of war-torn Germany, has come up with a remarkable film in semi-documentary style. *The Search* is that of a child, on the run from a displaced persons camp, for his mother. He is cared for and helped by an American GI, played by newcomer Montgomery Clift. The truth and simplicity of the piece cannot fail to bring tears, and a new awareness in the U.S. of the plight of Europe's war orphans. Clift is surely destined for stardom, while Ivan Jandl, a nine-year-old Czech boy who lived under the Nazi occupation of Prague, is a natural.

Soldier Montgomery Clift and homeless Ivan Jandl do battle in ***The Search.***

Multiple honors go to Olivier's Hamlet

*Following on his brilliant **Henry V**, Laurence Olivier plays and directs **Hamlet**.*

Venice, 5 September
Laurence Olivier's *Hamlet* has carried away the prize for best film at the Venice Film Festival. Jean Simmons, his shimmeringly beautiful Ophelia, was voted best actress, and the film's lighting cameraman Desmond Dickinson won for best cinematography. *Hamlet* is a technical tour de force in black and white, in which Dickinson's camera roams obsessively through Roger Furse's sets and the battlements of Elsinore, capturing the players in stunning deep focus. Olivier's blond Hamlet is a sleepwalker with an Oedipus complex, and comic relief is provided by Stanley Holloway's wry performance as the gravedigger. A remarkable exercise in English expressionism, *Hamlet* is an intriguing marriage of film and theater.

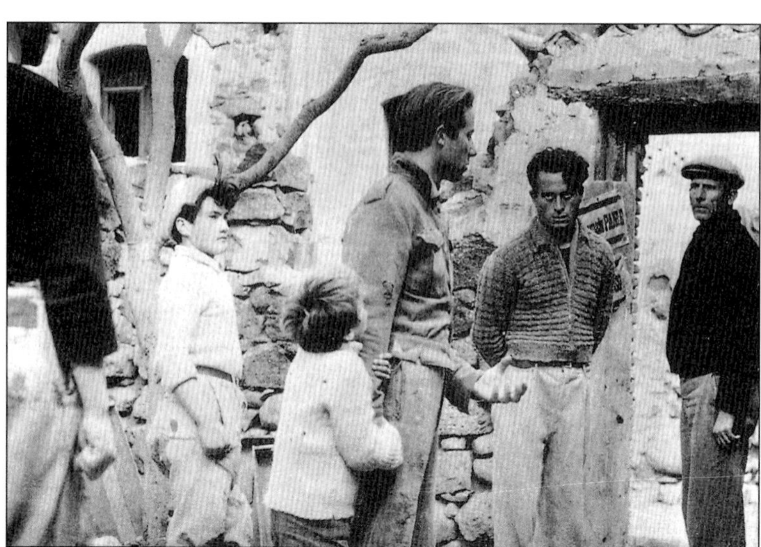
*Visconti only received a consolation prize for his powerful **La Terra Trema**.*

Conflict highlights outstanding Western

Montgomery Clift (right) with John Ireland in Hawks' magnificent Wester

New York, 20 August
Howard Hawks has reworked the *Mutiny on the Bounty* into a masterly Western, *Red River*, with martinet trail boss John Wayne driving a huge herd of cattle from Texas to the railhead at Abilene. On the way, his adopted son Montgomery Clift, in his first film role, rebels against his tyrannical behavior. Another n comer to make an impact in *R River* is John Ireland, cast as young gunslinger who tangles fat with Wayne at the end of the mov During filming, the handsome I land fell in love with the lead lady, Joanne Dru, and they w married shortly afterwards.

Hitchcock pulls a new trick with 'Rope'

Hollywood, 26 August
Alfred Hitchcock's new film, *Rope*, represents yet another departure for the "master of suspense". It is the first picture for his own new production company, Transatlantic Pictures, in partnership with British producer Sidney Bernstein. It is also his first film in color. Based on the successful play by British author Patrick Hamilton, it concerns two young men who murder for kic They conceal the corpse in a la chest in the living room of th apartment, where they entertain victim's father and friends, and p a game of cat and mouse with th former teacher (a fine performa from James Stewart). It is grippin filmed in long takes, averaging s en to eight minutes each, preservi the unity of time and space.

*Left to right: Farley Granger, James Stewart and John Dall in **Rope**.*

masterly mix of tragedy and dance

ira Shearer the tormented heroine, with Leonide Massine in **The Red Shoes**.

ndon, 6 September
ector Michael Powell's progress ard the musical choreographing a film has produced *The Red es*, a fantasy set in the world of et. The shoes are those of Hans istian Anderson's fairy tale, nsformed into a ballet danced by redheaded ballerina Moira Shearer. She is possessed by their spell and dances to her death. Drenched in color and saturated with surging emotions moving in time with the soundtrack, *The Red Shoes* ran way over budget but looks to be a hit on both sides of the Atlantic.

Sad and tender tale of man, boy and bike

Rome, 26 November
Italy is now living through extremely difficult times, with many of the country's population deprived of jobs, food and money. Vittorio De Sica's most recent film, *The Bicycle Thief* (*Ladri di Biciclette*), poignantly and powerfully reflects this turmoil through the story of Antonio Ricci, a 40-year-old worker, who has been unemployed for two years. When he is offered a job as a bill-sticker, provided he has a bicycle, he retrieves his own from the pawnbroker by having his wife pawn their only pair of sheets. However, on the first day of work the bicycle is stolen, and he spends a long day with his small son searching for it. His only comfort comes from the little boy, who holds his hand tenderly. Finally, out of desperation, Antonio decides to steal a bicycle for himself. After De Sica's success in the U.S. with *Shoeshine* (1946), David O. Selznick offered to produce his next film, suggesting Cary Grant for the lead. De Sica refused, raised the money himself, and continued his policy of shooting in real locations with non-actors. This principle has paid off, because the very un-Hollywood quality of *The Bicycle Thief* – the simplicity and underlying social criticism – is what will give the film a wide international appeal.

Lamberto Maggiorani (left), Enzo Staiola: father and son in ***The Bicycle Thief.***

ench state lps filmmakers

is, 23 September
the most part it is thanks to the ion of the Committee for the De- se of French Cinema that the ernment has decided to pass a to help the motion picture in- try. Carrying the name of the poser of the law, Géraud-Jouve, as just been adopted on a second ding in the National Assembly. law will aid producers and man- rs of theaters. In the main, it ncerns the introduction of a tax in lition to the price of tickets, and levied on a film's release at 400 ncs per metre. It is hoped that million francs will be available h year to make new films.

De Havilland's brilliant portrayal of madness in harrowing setting

Olivia De Havilland (seated on bench, right) trapped in the mental ward.

Los Angeles, 4 November
Olivia De Havilland gives a superbly judged performance in Fox's *The Snake Pit*. She portrays an intelligent woman hovering on the edge of mental disintegration in an over-crowded state mental asylum. Leo Genn and Mark Stevens provide somewhat stolid support as, respectively, a gently romantic psychiatrist and a bewildered but loyal husband, while Betsy Blair, Isabel Jewell, Jan Clayton and Beulah Bondi act up a storm as De Havilland's fellow patients. Based on an autobiographical novel by Mary Jane Ward, and directed by Anatole Litvak, *The Snake Pit* paints a harrowing picture of mental breakdown and the slow and painful process of recovery. ▷

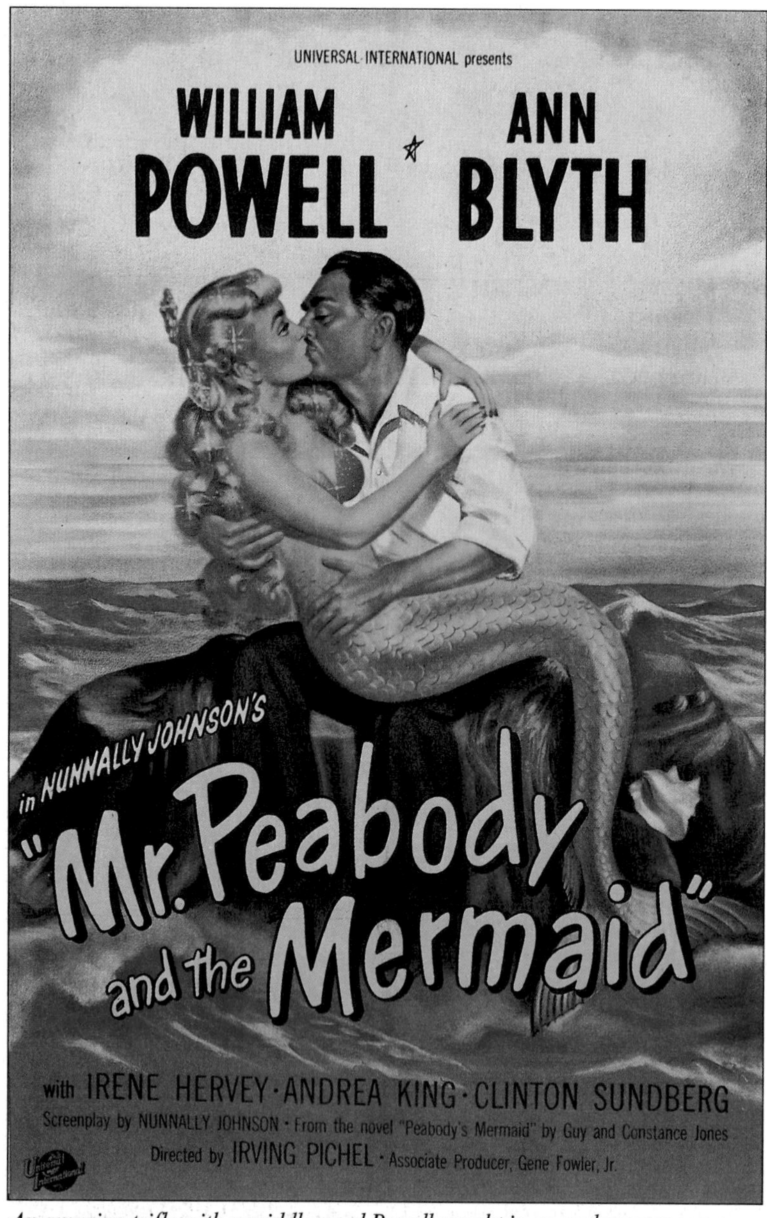
UNIVERSAL-INTERNATIONAL presents
WILLIAM POWELL ANN BLYTH
in NUNNALLY JOHNSON'S
"Mr. Peabody and the Mermaid"
with IRENE HERVEY · ANDREA KING · CLINTON SUNDBERG
Screenplay by NUNNALLY JOHNSON · From the novel "Peabody's Mermaid" by Guy and Constance Jones
Directed by IRVING PICHEL · Associate Producer, Gene Fowler, Jr.

An amusing trifle with a middle-aged Powell caught in an underwater romance.

Geoffrey Keene, Jack Hawkins, Bobby Henrey, Bernard Lee: **The Fallen Idol**.

Jean-Louis Barrault in Christian-Jaque's **D'homme à hommes (Man to M**

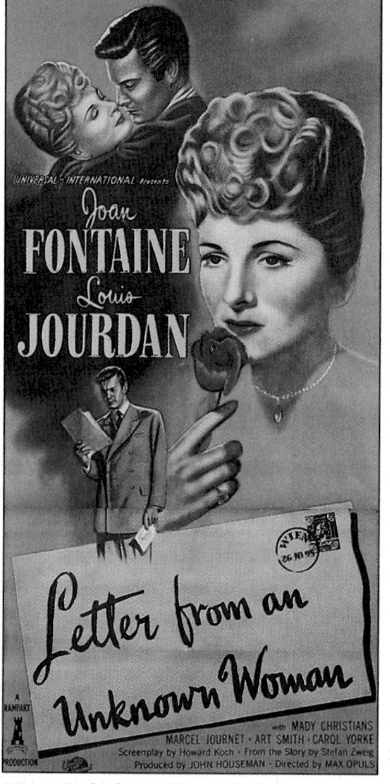
UNIVERSAL-INTERNATIONAL presents
Joan FONTAINE
Louis JOURDAN
Letter from an Unknown Woman
with MADY CHRISTIANS
MARCEL JOURNET · ART SMITH · CAROL YORKE
Screenplay by Howard Koch · From the Story by Stefan Zweig
Produced by JOHN HOUSEMAN · Directed by MAX OPULS
A RAMPART PRODUCTION

Max Ophuls at his stylish best.

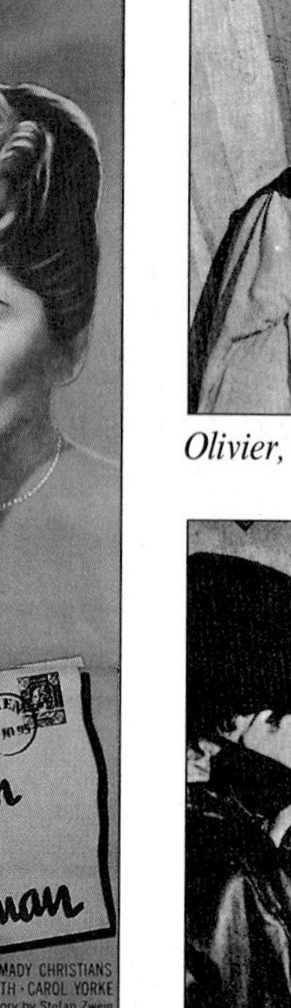

Olivier, Jean Simmons in **Hamle**

Luchino Visconti's **La Terra Trem**

Humphrey BOGART
Edward G. ROBINSON
Lauren BACALL
KEY LARGO
Lionel BARRYMORE
Claire TREVOR
JOHN HUSTON

Bogart, Bacall in the Florida Keys.

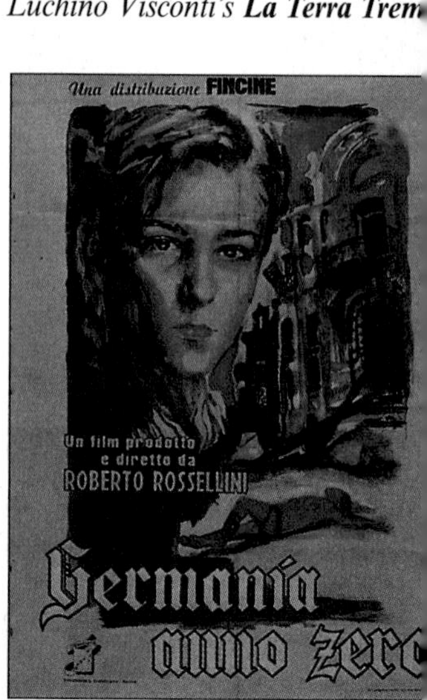
Una distribuzione FINCINE
Un film prodotto e diretto da ROBERTO ROSSELLINI
Germania anno zero

Rossellini's **Germany, Year Zero**.

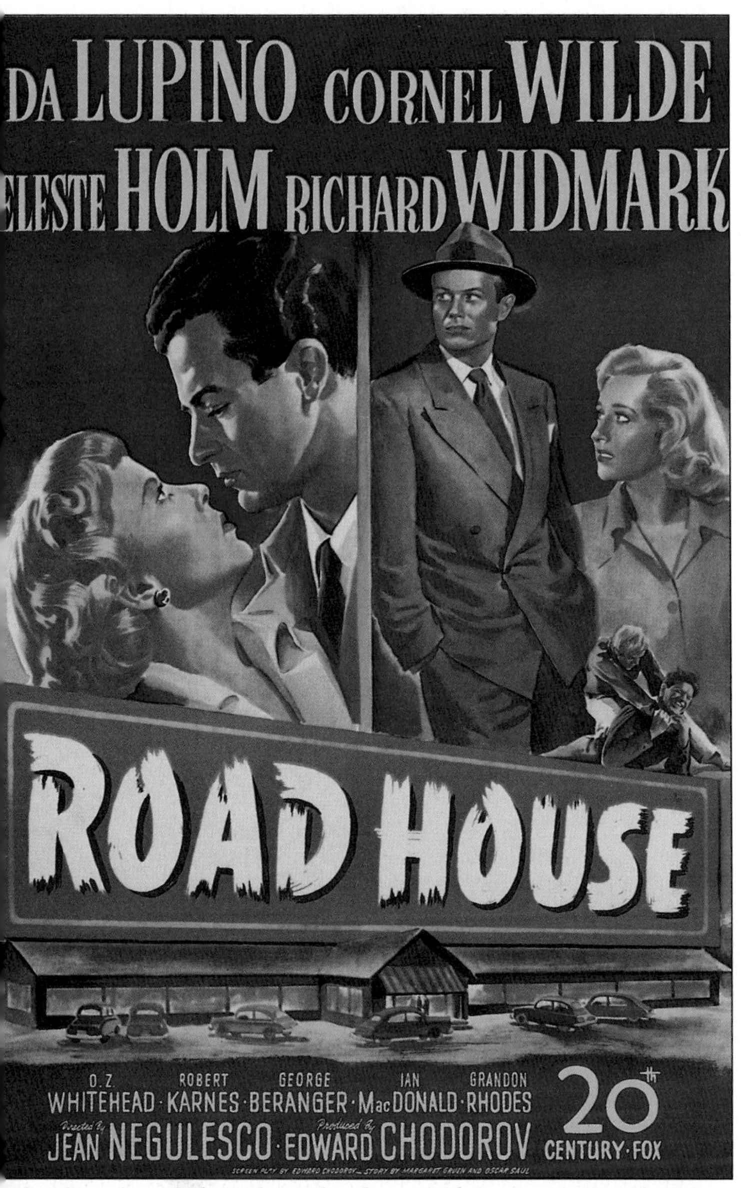
DA LUPINO CORNEL WILDE
ELESTE HOLM RICHARD WIDMARK
ROAD HOUSE
O.Z. WHITEHEAD · ROBERT KARNES · GEORGE BERANGER · IAN MacDONALD · GRANDON RHODES
Directed by JEAN NEGULESCO · Produced by EDWARD CHODOROV
20th CENTURY-FOX

absorbing drama of murder and jealousy, with Lupino singing 'Again'.

mous for Scarlett O'Hara, Vivien Leigh played Tolstoy's Anna Karenina.

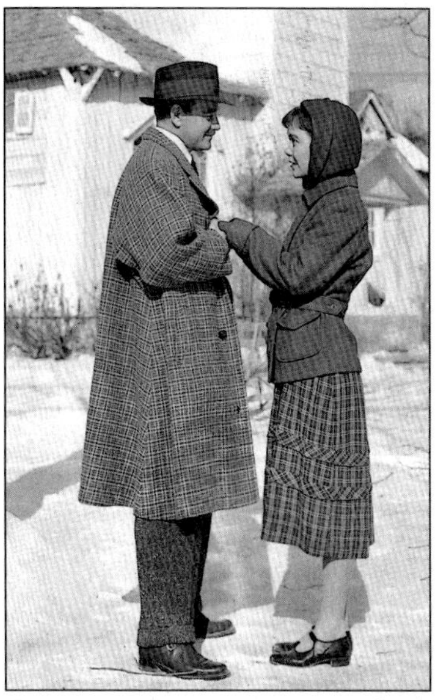

***Johnny Belinda**: Jane Wyman's back at Warners in a brilliant performance as a deaf mute, called the 'dummy'.*

*Ingrid Bergman and Charles Boyer in Milestone's **Arch of Triumph** about an unhappy love affair in Paris.*

*Gene Tierney and Dana Andrews in Preminger's **Where the Sidewalk Ends**.*

DAN DAILEY
IN
Give my Regards to Broadway
COLOR BY TECHNICOLOR
Charles Nancy Charlie Fay
WINNINGER · GUILD · RUGGLES · BAINTER
Directed by LLOYD BACON · Produced by WALTER MOROSCO
20th CENTURY-FOX

Old-timer yearned for vaudeville.

Like Merry Xmas and Happy New Year...They Belong Together!
Paramount presents
The Paleface
Color by Technicolor
Starring
BOB HOPE
JANE RUSSELL
Produced by ROBERT L. WELCH
Directed by NORMAN Z. McLEOD

Stars in top form in comedy Western.

★ ★ ★ ★ ★ ★ ★ ★ ★ 1949 ★

1948 Academy Awards, Academy Awards Theater, 24 Mar.

Best Film:	*Hamlet* (dir: Laurence Olivier)
Best Director:	John Huston *(The Treasure of the Sierra Madre)*
Best Actor:	Laurence Olivier *(Hamlet)*
Best Actress:	Jane Wyman *(Johnny Belinda)*
Best Supp. Actor:	Walter Huston *(The Treasure of the Sierra Madre)*
Best Supp. Actress:	Claire Trevor *(Key Largo)*

Hollywood, 3 January
Alfred Hitchcock has just signed a contract with Warner Bros., in which he agrees to make four films in the next six years.

Los Angeles, 6 January
Humphrey Bogart is a father. Wife Lauren Bacall has just given birth to their first child, Stephen.

Paris, 10 January
Yves Allégret has started shooting *Manèges* (*Wanton*), starring Simone Signoret and Bernard Blier.

Los Angeles, 20 January
Release of *A Letter to Three Wives*, by Joseph L. Mankiewicz, starring Jeanne Crain, Linda Darnell, Kirk Douglas and Ann Sothern.

Paris, 20 January
Premiere of *Une si jolie petite plage* (*Riptide*), by Yves Allégret, with Gérard Philipe and Madeleine Robinson. Hunted by the police for the murder of a dancer, a man returns to the scene of his childhood.

England, 26 January
Release of *The Passionate Friends*, directed by David Lean, with Ann Todd and Claude Rains.

Washington, 25 February
Paramount has signed the anti-trust agreement, aimed at separating production and distribution, whereby it will hand over its cinema network interests. The 1,450-strong cinema circuit is to be be taken over by a new company and reduced by one third to 600 cinemas by 1952.

Paris, 25 February
The Eclair company has launched the portable Camiflex 300, using André Coutant's patents.

Paris, 9 March
Release of Henri-Georges Clouzot's *Manon*, a transposition of Prévost's chivalric novel *Manon Lescaut* to the postwar years.

Paris, 28 March
Jean Gabin has married Christiane Fournier, known as Dominique. It is the great French star's third marriage, his former wives were Gaby Basset and Doriane. His new wife, one of the top models for Lanvin, was introduced to Jean at a dinner party. According to the happy couple, the meeting was a case of love at first sight. She has been seen every night, since 9 February, at the Ambassadeurs Theatre where Jean is currently playing in *la Soif*.

Peking, 31 March
A Cinema Board has been set up by the People's Liberation Army, which has been in control of the capital since January. Yuan Muzhi, the head of the army's cinematographic section since 1938, has been chosen to run the Board.

Sicily, 4 April
Roberto Rossellini is shooting on location on the volcanic island of Stromboli, just off the straits of Messina, for *Stromboli, terra di Dio*, to star Ingrid Bergman and non-actor Mario Vitale, a fisherman.

Paris, 21 April
Jean-Pierre Melville's first feature film *le Silence de la mer*, succeeds in transposing Vercor's practically unfilmable parable of the Resistance to the screen. The film is virtually a monologue by the German officer, but a great deal of what is going on beneath the surface is suggested by look and gesture. The actors, most particularly the Swiss Howard Vernon, are all excellent.

New York, 12 May
The press have attended a preview of Mark Robson's latest effort *Home of the Brave*. It is the first film to deal with the problem of racial hatred in the army.

Vallauris, 27 May
Rita Hayworth has married Prince Aly Khan.

Rome, 18 June
Abel Gance and producer Georges de la Grandière have been given a private audience by Pope Pius XII at the Vatican, where they discussed their project on the life of Christ, *The Divine Tragedy*.

Berlin, 15 July
The direct control of German film production exercised by the Allies has been replaced by a production code based on the American one.

Paris, 3 September
After a widely talked about affair, Micheline Presle has finally married the American director Bill Marshall, formerly married to another French actress, Michèle Morgan.

Hollywood, 29 September
Singer Dean Martin and comedian Jerry Lewis have made a film together, *My Friend Irma*, directed by George Marshall.

Stockholm, 17 October
In the newly released *Torst* (*Thirst*), Ingmar Bergman invites audiences to follow the tortured journey taken by a couple who are torn apart by their inability to communicate.

Padua, 26 October
Pier Paolo Pasolini has been expelled from the Italian Communist Party in disgrace for "morally and politically unacceptable behavior" after members received a police report on his homosexuality.

Los Angeles, 4 November
Director Nicholas Ray's first film *They Live by Night*, with Cathy O'Donnell and Farley Granger in the leading roles, has been released today in the U.S. Unusually, it had already been released in Europe.

Los Angeles, 8 November
Premiere of *All the King's Men*, directed by Robert Rossen, with Broderick Crawford, Joanne Dru and John Ireland. The film is based on the hard-hitting novel about corruption by Robert Penn Warren.

Washington, 9 December
Congressman J. Parnell Thomas, former chairman of the HUAC and leader in the fight against Communist influence and lax morals, has been sentenced to 10 months imprisonment for embezzlement.

Mexico, 20 December
Congress has answered the dema of professionals by voting in a law protect the cinema industry fr the importation of films. This m sure is aimed especially at Ameri productions.

New York, 25 December
Release of George Cukor's *Ada Rib*, starring Katharine Hepbu Spencer Tracy and Judy Hollida

Rome, 29 December
A new law designed to promote cinema industry has been passed the initiative of Giulio Andre The law will increase subsidies also strengthens government cont over film censorship.

BIRTHS

Chicago, 24 January
John Belushi

France, 22 March
Fanny Ardant

Minnesota, 20 April
Jessica Lange

New Jersey, 22 June
Meryl Streep (Mary Louise Stre

California, 8 August
Keith Carradine

Philadelphia, 29 August
Richard Gere

New York, 8 October
Sigourney Weaver (Susan Weave

Los Angeles, 4 December
Jeff Bridges

Texas, 25 December
Sissy Spacek
(Mary Elizabeth Spacek)

DEATHS

Hollywood, 6 January
Victor Fleming

Hollywood, 15 April
Wallace Beery

---

*Carol Reed's **The Third Man** not o splendidly pairs Joseph Cotten w Orson Welles, at the peak of his a ing talent, but raises the British ci ma to a high level of achievement.*

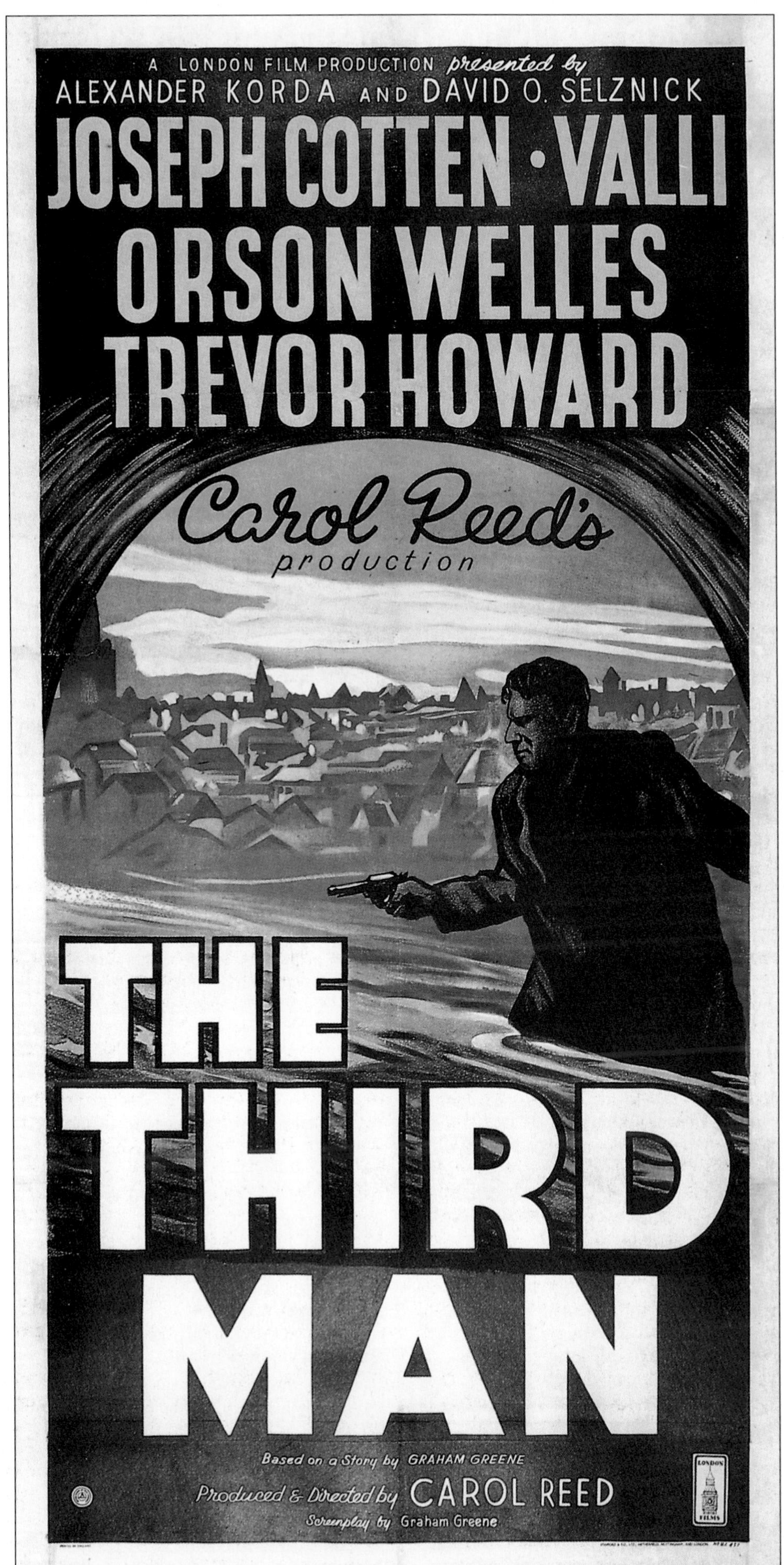
A LONDON FILM PRODUCTION presented by
ALEXANDER KORDA AND DAVID O. SELZNICK
JOSEPH COTTEN · VALLI
ORSON WELLES
TREVOR HOWARD
Carol Reed's
production
THE
THIRD
MAN
Based on a Story by GRAHAM GREENE
Produced & Directed by CAROL REED
Screenplay by Graham Greene
LONDON
FILMS

Scott adventure chills and moves

London, 7 March
In January 1945, as the war drew to a close, Michael Balcon, the head of Ealing studios, outlined a bold program for postwar British cinema: "British films must present to the world a picture of Britain as a leader in social reform, in the defeat of social injustices and a champion of civil liberties... Britain as a questing explorer, adventurer and trader... " Part of this pledge has been fulfilled in Ealing's *Scott of the Antarctic*, directed by Charles Frend. The British are curiously attached to heroic failures, and in this sad canon there are few more notable than that of Captain Robert Falcon Scott's doomed attempt to race the Norwegian explorer Amundsen to the South Pole. Scott and his party perished on the return journey, just short of a supply dump which might have saved them. The film, heavily based on Scott's diaries and shot in Technicolor on location in Switzerland and Norway, is a measured, slightly stilted account of the expedition, in which the stiff upper-lip reaction to disaster dominates, and the mood is one of wry understatement. John Mills portrays Scott, an English amateur bested by the professional Norwegians, with solid support coming from Harold Warrender, Reginald Beckwith, Derek Bond and James Robertson Justice as his doomed companions. The unrelenting drama of Scott's terrible journey across the icy wastes is underpinned by Ralph Vaughan Williams' evocative score.

John Mills as the heroic explorer.

Star-crossed love elevates young Anouk

Anouk Aimée and Serge Reggiani are the 'Romeo and Juliet' of Cayatte's film.

Paris, 7 March
During the shooting of a film version of Shakespeare's *Romeo and Juliet*, the two understudies of the leads fall in love. This is the basis for the scenario of André Cayatte's new film, *The Lovers of Verona*. Written by Jacques Prévert, it brings a fresh quality to the updating of the classic story. It was Prévert who had the idea of writing the part of the modern-day Juliet for 16-year-old Anouk Aimée. Her glowing beauty, the intensity of Serge Reggiani as her Romeo, the brilliant acting of Pierre Brasseur and Martine Carol, and the stunning location photography of Venice, should assure the film a wide success.

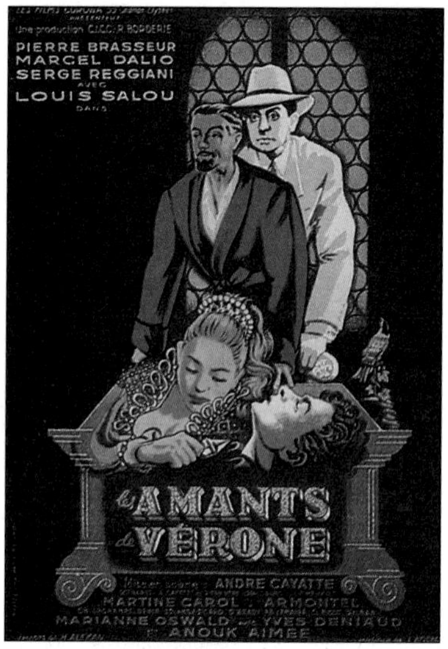
PIERRE BRASSEUR
MARCEL DALIO
SERGE REGGIANI
AVEC
LOUIS SALOU
AMANTS
VÉRONE
ANDRE CAYATTE
MARTINE CAROL
MARIANNE OSWALD
YVES DENIAUD
ANOUK AIMÉE

First time for Osca at Academy Theat

Hollywood, 24 March
This year's Academy Award pres tation ceremony turned out to b chaotically cramped affair. The cision to relocate the show from l er venues to the 950-seat Acade Theater was admirably motivate the major Hollywood studios, se tive to charges of having previo brought their influence to bear the voters, had withdrawn all di financial support of the event. B resulted in an undignified scram for places and the resignation Academy President Jean Hersh Nevertheless, during the even presented by Robert Montgom and Ava Gardner, there were li musical interludes from Doris D Gordon Macrae and Jane Rus and most of the awards were deserved. Laurence Olivier's *H let* was not only the first British, also the first non-American, film win the Best Picture prize. Tho Olivier lost out to John Huston Best Director for *The Treasure the Sierra Madre* (in which the di tor's father, Walter Huston, Best Supporting Actor), the g Shakespearean walked away the Best Actor award for his per mance in the title role of his f Jane Wyman, who used to play chorines, obtained the Best Act Oscar for her heartbreaking trayal of a deaf-mute farm gir *Johnny Belinda*.

Zany satire on British eccentricity is good-humored entertainme

London, 1 April
After four years of postwar austerity there is an atmosphere of mild anarchy in the air, perfectly caught by Ealing's *Passport to Pimlico*, directed by Henry Cornelius. In this pointed social satire, a small district in London wakes up to discover that it is part of the ancient dukedom of Burgundy. "Blimey, I'm a foreigner," gulps the local copper. So the inhabitants immediately establish their new kingdom as an independent, ration-free state, with hilarious results. This warm-hearted celebration of an embattled but united community, a metaphor for Ealing itself, keeps the spirit of the studio's wartime films burning in a Britain that's edging from austerity into affluence.

Margaret Rutherford, Stanley Holloway, Philip Dupuis in ***Passport to Pim***

rd-hitting exposé of the fight racket

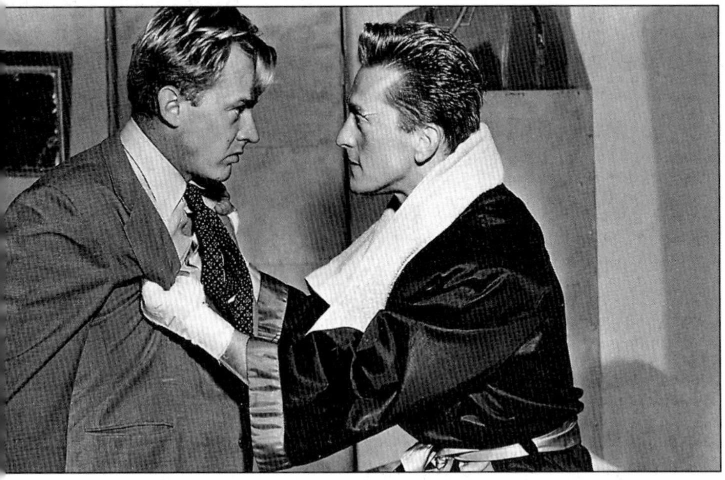

ur Kennedy and Kirk Douglas in **Champion**, a Stanley Kramer production.

York, 10 April
: Douglas takes the title role in ted Artists' *Champion*, an adap-n of Ring Lardner's story of the and fall of a cocksure boxer se savage fight scenes belie its center. Douglas, reveling in his as a heel, double-crosses his ager Paul Stewart, two-times his wife Ruth Roman for blonde floozie Marilyn Maxwell and then dumps her for Lola Albright. However, he does send money to his Mom and helps his crippled brother Arthur Kennedy. But this fails to save him from a KO come-uppance in the final reel, swiftly followed by madness and death.

Tati offers the French cinema a real feast

Guy Decomble, Jacques Tati (on cycle) and Paul Frankeur in ***Jour de fête****.*

Paris, 4 May
Made in 1947, Jacques Tati's first feature film, *Jour de fête*, has only now been released. Tati has already appeared as an actor in Claude Autant-Lara's *Sylvia and the Phantom*, and is the director/performer of several short films, one of which, *School for Postmen*, was a rough sketch for *Jour de fête*. As the postman in a French village who decides to emulate the high-speed delivery of mail in the U.S., Tati proves himself to be the true descendant of the silent movie comedians, relying as he does on sight gags. Shot with modest means, the film is packed with comic invention.

llywood blacklist ows ever longer

shington, 8 June
cartoon published in the British spaper *Reynolds News*, David gdon shows Hollywood Boule-l packed with Stalin lookalikes. e FBI is to be believed, this satir-vision is likely to come true. In middle of a spy trial, the Bureau released a confidential docu-nt which accuses a number of s of being Communist sympa-ers. Among those named are n Garfield, Paul Muni, Edward Robinson and Sylvia Sidney. In ition, a Senate committee that is stigating anti-American activi-has published an astonishing list everal hundred people alleged to e "followed the Communist Par-ne." Some of the biggest names Hollywood crop up on this list: rles Chaplin, Gregory Peck, harine Hepburn, Gene Kelly, nny Kaye, Fredric March, Frank atra and Orson Welles. Most of n are well known for their liberal progressive views, but the no-that the rich pastures of Beverly s have been colonized by hard-Bolsheviks is absurd.

Crime as practised by Dennis Price is most definitely a fine art!

Alec Guinness in six of his eight roles as members of the D'Ascoyne family.

Price: in search of wealth and title.

Guinness as Admiral D'Ascoyne.

London, 16 June
Certainly influenced by Chaplin's *Monsieur Verdoux*, Ealing director Robert Hamer has produced a brilliantly barbed comedy of murder, *Kind Hearts and Coronets*. Adapted from Roy Horniman's Wildean novel of decadence, *Israel Rank*, the film stars suave Dennis Price as a social outcast who murders his way to a dukedom through an entire family of unspeakable relatives. All eight D'Ascoynes are portrayed by Alec Guinness in a series of neatly observed cameos, from ferocious suffragette Aunt Edith, whose ballooning activities are brought to an abrupt end by a well-placed arrow, to blustering General D'Ascoyne who meets his end while digging into a booby-trapped pot of caviar. The film's feline script, by John Dighton, Hamer's elegant interplay between word and image, and the smooth visual surface provided by cameraman Douglas Slocombe, have created a masterpiece of black comedy. Above all, Dennis Price's coolly considered performance as the calculating and self-possessed murderer Louis Mazzini marks him out as an actor to watch.

'The Fountainhead' diluted but still daring

Architect Roark (Cooper), Dominique (Neal) and the New York skyline.

New York, 8 July
Ayn Rand's best-selling 1943 novel, *The Fountainhead*, has been brought to the screen by King Vidor, with a script by Rand herself. Although the film version has diluted some of the book's more extreme views, it has, nevertheless, retained much of its powerful symbolism – the phallic buildings and tools employed, the hero's climactic ascent by construction elevator to the top of the cloud-surrounded tower. The normally taciturn Gary Cooper is somewhat miscast as Howard Roark, the uncompromising architect based on Frank Lloyd Wright. Yet, Patricia Neal as the architecture critic who is sexually drawn to him, and Raymond Massey as her unscrupulous publisher, deliver the verbose dialogue with gusto. The musical score by Max Steiner perfectly underlines the drama, and Edward Carrere has provided brilliant sets and designs. Vidor wanted Lloyd Wright himself to design the film, but studio head Jack Warner vetoed the idea.

Ingrid sends shock waves through USA

Los Angeles, 6 August
Reports from the Italian newspaper, *Corriere della Sera*, confirming the details of Ingrid Bergman's liaison with Roberto Rossellini are causing a scandal in the film community and is a shock to the American people, who took the Swedish star to their hearts after the release of *Intermezzo* 10 years ago. Miss Bergman arrived in Rome on 20 March this year, prior to filming *Stromboli* for the Italian director. Their collaboration began when the actress wrote to Rossellini expressing her admiration for his film, *Rome, Open City*, and making clear her desire to work with him. They met in Paris last summer, and in January this year Rossellini came to Los Angeles for further discussions, staying with Ingrid and her husband, Dr. Peter Lindstrom. Close observers noted the growing bond between the actress and her guest, and Lindstrom was not happy about his wife's visit to Rome. Now, having completed location filming on the island of Stromboli (after which the film is named), Bergman is back in Rome. Throughout the arduous shoot, financed by Howard Hughes, rumors ran wild about the adulterous nature of the relations between Bergman and Rossell The rumors are now confirmed: couple are living together as m and wife and, worse still, the s who already has a small daughter her husband, is pregnant. The sit tion is now a "cause célèbre" h with Americans unwilling to forg a once much-loved star whose re tation has been built on an image moral purity and family values.

In Hitchcock's ***Under Capricorn****.*

Stalingrad tribute lasts nearly four hours

Vladimir Petrov's ***The Battle of Stalingrad****, 3 hours and 40 minutes of history.*

Moscow, 7 August
The war has been over for four years, but the USSR has not forgotten the high price it paid for victory. The first part of Vladimir Petrov's immensely long *The Battle of Stalingrad*, released in Moscow last May, has just won the Grand Prix at the Karlovy-Vary Festival in Czechoslovakia. Here, Petrov, a specialist in historical frescoes, has impressively re-created the heroic struggle.

James Cagney red-hot in 'White Heat'

Virginia Mayo, with gangster James Cagney in typically violent mood.

Los Angeles, 2 September
"Top of the world, Ma!" shrieks psychopathic mobster James Cagney as he goes up in flames at the end of Raoul Walsh's pulsating *White Heat*. As the mother-fixated Cody Jarrett, Cagney delivers electric performance as a helpl manic outlaw running wildly ou control. Cornered by the cops, goes out with a bang as he turn petrol tank into a colossal fireba

w headquarters for the Cannes Festival on the famous Croisette

v a few weeks ago, the Festival Palace was still a huge building site.

Third Man, voted best film, boasts brilliant atmospheric photography.

Cannes, 17 September
Since the creation of the Cannes Festival, the mayor of the city and the organizers of the festival have wanted to open the Festival Palace on the Croisette, which they had claimed to be "worthy of good taste and French art." It was with pride then that they were finally able to inaugurate the building in the presence of celebrities from around the world. But the edifice, started hastily in 1947, still resembles a building site, as it continues to be patched up. Meanwhile, sightseers could catch a glimpse of Martine Carol, Orson Welles, Joseph Cotten, Alida Valli and many other international stars, entering the unfinished Palace. This year's festival saw 80 countries participating, some with a single short film, and others such as France, the U.S., England and Italy with full-length features. It was, therefore, expected that those four countries mentioned should have shared the bulk of the awards. English director Carol Reed's *The Third Man* walked off with the Grand Prix, while the Frenchman René Clément took the best director prize for *The Walls of Malapaga*, co-produced by Italy. Isa Miranda was presented with the best actress award for her role as the lonely waitress in the latter film. America's consolation came in the form of Edward G. Robinson's best actor performance in Joseph Mankiewicz's *House of Strangers*, and also Virginia Shaler's award for her best screenplay, *Lost Boundaries*, directed by Alfred Werker, which deals with racism.

FESTIVAL INTERNATIONAL
DU
FILM
CANNES
DU 2 AU 17 SEPTEMBRE
1949

is Buñuel is now making films in Mexico

s Buñuel's second Mexican film.

Mexico, 25 November
After dropping out of sight since his departure from the United States, Luis Buñuel has been discovered living in Mexico where two films he made here have just been released. They are a musical, *Gran Casino*, and a melodrama called *El Gran Calavera*. It has been 15 years since Luis Buñuel last directed a film. Between 1944 and 1946, the Spanish emigré had worked at Warner Bros. dubbing and supervising foreign versions of Hollywood films. He had been under consideration for the assignment of director of *The Beast With Five Fingers*, but the job went to Robert Florey. After another abortive project, Buñuel was welcomed by Mexico.

A natural beauty in the rice fields

Mangano in ***Bitter Rice****, a new star.*

Rome, 1 November
New director Giuseppe De Santis, a friend of Luchino Visconti and the screenwriter on Visconti's *Ossessione*, has retained the passion he had when he was a critic for the magazine *Cinema*. His first film, *Tragic Hunt* (*Caccia Tragica*) in 1947, placed him among the leading Italian neo-realists, the movement which he had helped formulate as a critic. In *Bitter Rice* (*Riso Amaro*), De Santis has returned to the countryside of his youth in the Po Valley. The slightly melodramatic storyline deals with one of the many urban women who come each year to work in the rice fields, wading up to their waists in the water. The girl falls for a petty thief (Vittorio Gassman) who hopes to steal the rice crop. There is no doubt that *Bitter Rice* will make the 19-year-old Silvana Mangano, Miss Rome of 1946, into a star. The voluptuous Mangano in thigh-revealing shorts and torn nylons, her ample breasts thrust forward, her seductive head held high, standing in a rice paddy, is the film's most memorable image and the one that audiences will take with them. Ostensibly a neo-realist exposé of the exploitation of women workers, the steamy film in reality exposes more of Mangano than its subject. ▷

Superb evocation of greed and corruption

WILLIE!

Broderick Crawford (center), a superb performance in Robert Rossen's film.

New York, 8 November
Since returning from war service, burly Broderick Crawford, the son of thespians Lester Crawford and Helen Broderick, has been mostly confined to parts in cheap Westerns. Now Robert Rossen has cast him as the demagogic Southern politician Willie Stark in *All the King's Men*, adapted from the Pulitzer Prize-winning novel by Robert Penn Warren. Stark is closely modeled on the Louisiana "Kingfisher" Huey Long. It's a part perfectly tailored to fit Crawford's belligerent and bullying style, and provides an example of actor and character becoming completely one. There is strong support from Mercedes McCambridge, and from John Ireland as the cynical journalist who narrates this cautionary political tale.

Becker explores Saint-Germain-des-Prés

Paris, 6 December
Jacques Becker's new film, *Rendez-vous de juillet*, tells the story of a group of young people planning to make an anthropological documentary in Africa, and who attempt to find maturity and happiness through love, theater and jazz. The film presents a vivid picture of French youth marked by the war, and evokes the Saint-Germain-des-Prés jazz clubs, which they frequent. Since getting a cool reception at the Cannes Film Festival, Becker has re-edited and reduced its length. This more concise and lucid version has been sufficiently appreciated to win this year's Prix Louis Delluc.

The Lorientais jazz cellar, a perfect milieu for Jacques Becker's Parisian film.

Kelly and Sinatra, sailors on the loose

EXIT
TIMES

Frank Sinatra, Gene Kelly and Jules Munshin about to go ***On the Town***.

Hollywood, 8 December
The dancer Gene Kelly, who made *The Pirate* last year under Vincente Minnelli, has now become a director himself. Conceived balletically and co-directed by Kelly's colleague and friend, the choreographer Stanley Donen, *On the Town* is a joyous and innovative musical which follows three sailors (Kelly, Frank Sinatra and Jules Munshin) on a 24-hour leave in New York. The opening number "New York, New York" was actually filmed on location that "wonderful town". After trio has paired off with three g (Vera-Ellen, Betty Garrett and A Miller), the six go visit the Emp State building, this time a Ho wood set, more exciting and colo than the real thing. Full of dyna dance numbers and produced MGM by Arthur Freed, the f was freely adapted by Betty Co den and Adolph Green from Leonard Bernstein Broadway hi

Clark Gable remarries after seven years

Santa Barbara, 21 December
Clark Gable has never been the same man since the tragic death of Carole Lombard in 1942. Now it seems that he has rediscovered a measure of happiness with Sylvia Hawkes, former wife of Lord Ashley, Douglas Fairbanks Sr. and Baron Stanley of Alderly. Clark and Sylvia have known each other for only a few weeks. Their whirlw romance became a marriage w Gable, fortified by a bottle of ch pagne, whisked Hawkes off t quiet wedding by the sea. The nesses were Gable's secretary J Garceau and MGM publicity n Howard Strickling. Gable's sud decision to tie the knot has cau alarm among his family and frien

The Studio System

Photographed in the 1930s, the 20th Century-Fox studio complex.

ong the most famous company nes in the history of the cinema Warner Bros., MGM, Para-unt, United Artists (or UA), x (20th Century-Fox), Univer- Columbia and Disney. Indeed, history of the cinema in the ited States can be understood ough observing the ups and vns of these giant Hollywood dios. But their beginnings were y different from their present porate stature.

As with other countries, the nerican cinema started out as liverse collection of small, com-ing companies. In 1908 a num- of industry leaders, including ograph and Vitagraph, joined ether under Edison to set up restrictive Trust to control the oduction, distribution and exhi-ion of films. These companies, wever, had become set in their ys, often opposed to making ger films at a time when the n market was growing and be-ming increasingly competitive. is opened the way for a few terprising independents to risk production of feature-length tures. Thus, several famous ovie moguls first made their rk at this time, notably Carl emmle, Adolph Zukor, William x, Jesse Lasky and Cecil B. De-ille. A key event was the merger Zukor's Famous Players with sky and the Paramount Distri-tion Co. in 1916. Other compa-es such as First National (1917) and United Artists were formed to meet the threat of Paramount. However, the real challenge didn't come until 1924 with the formation of Loew's Metro-Goldwyn-Mayer, headed by Marcus Loew and Louis B. Mayer. By the end of the 20s the classic Hollywood lineup had taken shape. The costly changeover to sound had caused a shakeout among the smaller companies and led to a further consolidation of power by the large studios. Filmmaking was now concentrated more than ever within the studio walls, with stars, directors and other personnel bound by long-term contracts. The five largest companies were Paramount, MGM, Fox, Warner Bros. (who had just taken over First National) and the new RKO Radio – followed by the three mini-majors – Universal, United Artists and Columbia.

Despite the problems caused by the Depression, the studio and star system flourished in Hollywood throughout the 1930s, with MGM the clear industry leader. But the outbreak of war in 1939 marked the beginning of the end. Studios cut back on production and made changes in the restrictive contract system. During the postwar era many leading stars and directors decided to go independent, films were increasingly made on location, and the government's 1948 Consent Decree forced the majors to sell off their movie theaters and give up other monopolistic practices. RKO, headed by the eccentric Howard Hughes, was the only studio to fold, however, and, in the 1950s, the three mini-majors, along with Disney, began challenging the top group for the first time. UA in particular was revitalized by a new management team. Production continued to decline, but studios diversified into other areas such as TV and music, a process continued in the 1960s when there were a number of takeovers and mergers. Studios suffered in the late 1960s with audiences at a record low, but soon recovered with the aid of a new generation of successful directors (Francis Coppola, George Lucas, Steven Spielberg, etc.). The main casualties in the 1980s were MGM and United Artists who had merged, then collapsed after a number of complicated deals. But Disney, with a big boost from its Touchstone subsidiary, had the most remarkable success in the 1980s. The list of majors still include some of those very familiar names which go back 70 years or more: Columbia (paired with Tristar and owned by Sony), 20th Century-Fox (now owned by Rupert Murdoch), Warner Bros. (joined up with Time Magazine in Time-Warner), Universal/MCA (now owned by Matsushita) and Paramount Pictures (taken over by Viacom in 1994). Owners may change and managements reshuffle, but these Hollywood giants appear to be indestructible.

he producing team of Richard Zanuck and David Brown in 1973.

l to r: Harry Warner, Joan Crawford, Jack Warner and Michael Curtiz.

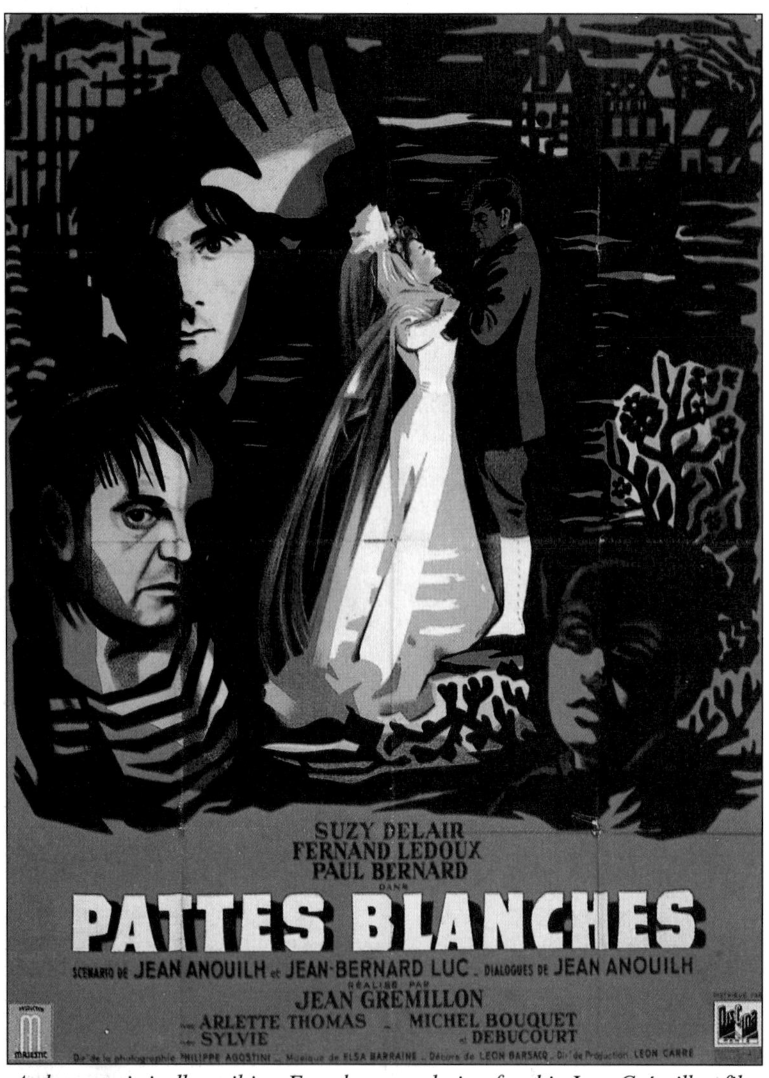
SUZY DELAIR
FERNAND LEDOUX
PAUL BERNARD
DANS
PATTES BLANCHES
SCENARIO DE JEAN ANOUILH et JEAN-BERNARD LUC . DIALOGUES DE JEAN ANOUILH
RÉALISÉ PAR
JEAN GREMILLON
ARLETTE THOMAS . MICHEL BOUQUET
SYLVIE et DEBUCOURT
MAJESTIC

A characteristically striking French poster design for this Jean Grémillon film.

Cathy O'Donnell and Farley Granger in Nicholas Ray's **They Live By Nig**

JOUR de FÊTE
JACQUES TATI

Capturing the spirit of Tati's film.

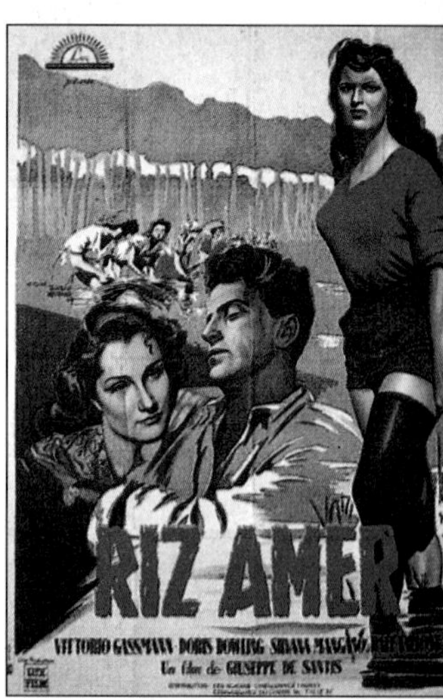
RIZ AMER

The French poster for **Bitter Rice.**

Jean Gabin and Isa Miranda in René Clément's **The Walls of Malapaga.**

Fred Astaire danced 'Shoes with Wings On' from **The Barkleys of Broadw**

ia De Havilland and Montgomery Clift co-starred in the film **The Heiress**.

MIGHTY
JOE YOUNG
RY MOORE
JOHNSON
ERT ARMSTRONG
MERIAN COOPER'S AMAZING ADVENTURE IN THE UNUSUAL!

l follow-up from **King Kong** team.

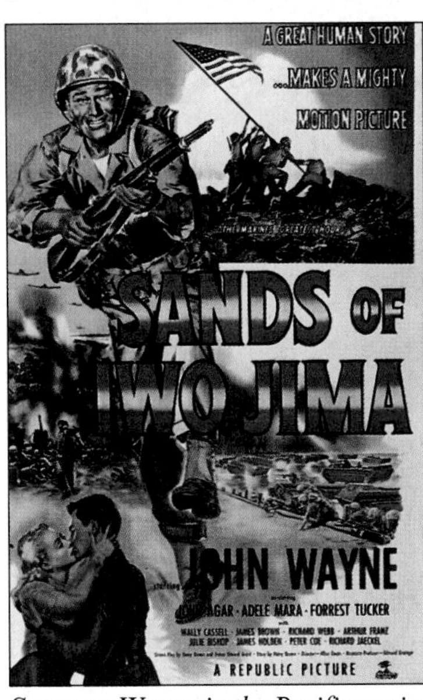

A GREAT HUMAN STORY
...MAKES A MIGHTY
MOTION PICTURE
SANDS OF
IWO JIMA
JOHN WAYNE
AGAR · ADELE MARA · FORREST TUCKER
A REPUBLIC PICTURE

Sergeant Wayne in the Pacific again.

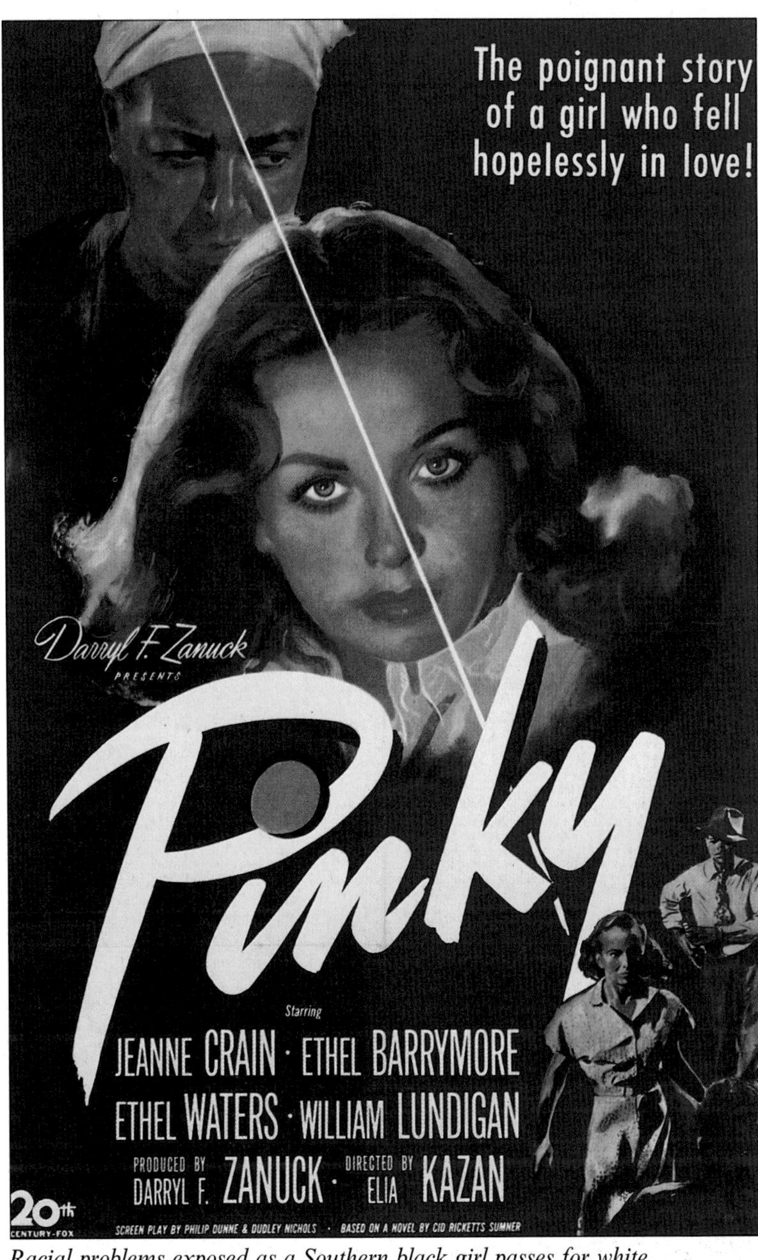

The poignant story
of a girl who fell
hopelessly in love!
Darryl F. Zanuck
PRESENTS
Pinky
Starring
JEANNE CRAIN · ETHEL BARRYMORE
ETHEL WATERS · WILLIAM LUNDIGAN
PRODUCED BY DARRYL F. ZANUCK · DIRECTED BY ELIA KAZAN
20th CENTURY-FOX
SCREEN PLAY BY PHILIP DUNNE & DUDLEY NICHOLS · BASED ON A NOVEL BY CID RICKETTS SUMNER

Racial problems exposed as a Southern black girl passes for white.

d **Hearts and Coronets**: Alec Guinness got ill to the delight of Dennis Price.

Color by TECHNICOLOR
John Ford's New and Finest Picture of the Fighting Cavalry
JOHN WAYNE
JOANNE DRU
JOHN AGAR
BEN JOHNSON
HARRY CAREY, JR.
"SHE WORE A YELLOW RIBBON"
DIRECTED BY
JOHN FORD
VICTOR McLAGLEN · MILDRED NATWICK
GEORGE O'BRIEN · ARTHUR SHIELDS

Great photography by Winton Hoch.

A STORY
OF TWELVE
MEN AS
THEIR
WOMEN
NEVER
KNEW
THEM
TWELVE
O'CLOCK HIGH
Starring
GREGORY PECK
DARRYL F. ZANUCK
HENRY KING

An immensely successful war drama with Peck losing his nerve.

The Swing of the Pendulum

It was around the time that the cinema celebrated its 50th anniversary that the most perceptible transformation in the American motion picture industry took place, both creatively and commercially, while those in many other countries remained in the doldrums.

Although audience figures in the USA had already started to decline in 1947, the main cause for the drastic decline in box-office takings was laid at the door of the one-eyed monster that was proliferating throughout the country in the early 50s. While Senator McCarthy was seeing Reds under every bed, film moguls saw the box in people's living rooms as the real enemy.

Ironically, this arch-enemy provided Hollywood with some of the best screenplays of the era, as well as the first generation of directors to come to the movies via the TV studio – John Frankenheimer, Sidney Lumet, Robert Mulligan, Delbert Mann. *Marty* (1955), directed by Mann, and based on a Paddy Chayefsky teleplay, was the 'sleeper' of the decade. As a result, other realistic television dramas such as *The Bachelor Party* and *Twelve Angry Men* (both 1957) were transmuted into feature films.

The existence of a financial competitor to Hollywood produced both good and bad effects. One of the worst was the industry's panicky reaction to the threat, which led to the belief that big is beautiful. Desperate to entice people away from the 21-inch black-and-white screen, a complex series of devices and gimmicks were offered to the public. This campaign to win back audiences began in 1952 with *Bwana Devil* in 3-D, and *This is Cinerama*, which gave spectators the sensation of riding a roller coaster.

The pictures might have 'got small', according to Gloria Swanson in the guise of forgotten silent screen star Norma Desmond in *Sunset Boulevard* (1950), but the screens certainly got bigger. In 1953, 20th Century-Fox's CinemaScope made its appearance with *The Robe*, followed by Paramount's VistaVision, used for the first time in *White Christmas* (1954). One of the most star-studded and top money-making movies to date, *Around the World in Eighty Days* (1956) was shown in the 70mm Todd-AO process. Production teams went on trips to foreign climes to capture Rome for *Three Coins in the Fountain* (1954); Hong Kong for *Love is a Many-Splendored Thing* (1955), and Japan for *Sayonara* (1957) on the wide screen.

Nevertheless, Elia Kazan's *East of Eden* (1955), Nicholas Ray's *Rebel Without a Cause* (1955), Vincente Minnelli's *Lust for Life* (1956), Otto Preminger's *River of No Return* (1954) and John Sturges' *Bad Day at Black Rock* (1955) proved that CinemaScope could be an asset rather than a hindrance. Though used far less in other countries during the decade, there were some outstanding examples of the use of the wide screen such as Max Ophuls' *Lola Montès* (1955) in France, and Julia Solntseva's *Poem of the Sea* (1958) in the USSR.

In contrast, Hollywood found a more interesting device for getting people to leave their TV sets for a movie theater. Controversial and adult subjects, deemed unsuitable for home viewing by TV's commercial sponsors, could be aired in the cinema. Thus Preminger's *The Moon is Blue* (1954), released without the Production Code's Seal of Approval, helped to create a permissiveness that wrested Hollywood from the puritan values that had long gripped it. Independent producers like Preminger began to break the stranglehold of the major studios, tackling more daring subjects, and delving into those areas from which Hollywood had previously shied away.

But it took America a little longer to emerge from the sinister shadow which was cast over the film industry in the first years of the decade by Joseph McCarthy. The Senator from Wisconsin was the prime force behind the House Un-American Activities Committee's second series of hearings which began in March 1951. As a result of those, 212 people were blacklisted. This took place in the climate of the Cold War, while the hot war in Korea demanded unconditional patriotism from United States citizens.

Although Hollywood grew jittery, liberal themes continued to be explored, and the tenets on which American society was based were questioned. The Red Indian was sympathetically treated in films like *Broken Arrow* (1950); racial intolerance was examined in *The Defiant Ones* (1958), drug addiction in *The Man With the Golden Arm* (1955), and juvenile delinquency in *The Blackboard Jungle* (1955).

***Bad Day at Black Rock** (1955), left to right: Spencer Tracy, Robert Ryan, John Ericson, Walter Brennan, Lee Marvin, Walter Sande and Dean Jagger.*

The major studios still clung to their traditions, but genres such as the Western became more complex, some of the best examples being Fred Zinnemann's *High Noon* (1952), George Stevens' *Shane* (1953), and John Ford's *The Searchers* (1956). At MGM the artistic status of the musical was raised with Minnelli's *An American in Paris* (1951) and Kelly and Donen's *Singin' in the Rain* (1952).

But whatever the size of t screen, and no matter how imp tant the subject or advances withi genre, it was the stars, above all, tl the public still paid to see. Of th of an earlier era, Bette Davis beg the 50s by playing a fading actress *All About Eve* (1950), her last gr role; Judy Garland made a sen tional comeback in *A Star is B* (1954); Ingrid Bergman returned Hollywood from exile to win an (car for *Anastasia* (1956), and Fr Astaire blithely continued to dan after having announced his reti ment in 1945.

Hollywood kept producing number of stars in the glamorc tradition: Ava Gardner, Elizab Taylor, Rock Hudson, Grace Ke Stewart Granger, Audrey Hepbu and Doris Day. Yet the predo nant iconography of the period mains Marlon Brando in leatl sitting astride a motorcycle in *T Wild One* (1954); the soulful boy features of James Dean, and Ma lyn Monroe, skirt swirling above New York subway grating in B Wilder's *The Seven Year Itch* (195 Because of the growing youth au ence, youth culture began infiltr ing the movies in the 50s, and it w possible for the first time for you people to identify with certain sta Former pin-up boy Tony Cu gradually changed his image – compromisingly loathsome in Al ander Mackendrick's *Sweet Sm of Success* (1957), and gorgeou feminine in drag in Wilder's *So Like It Hot* (1959). The skinny crooner Frank Sinatra made a s ond career for himself when he w the Best Supporting Actor Os for the role of Private Maggio *From Here to Eternity* (1953). T film also saw Deborah Kerr rescu from gentility, playing the adult ous wife making love to Burt L caster on a beach. Lancaster hims emerged, with Kirk Douglas, as most versatile and adventurous the Hollywood stars at the time. fact, they were among those w gained greater independence by ing freelance, and by becoming p ducers themselves.

By 1958, 65 percent of Ho wood movies were being made independents, a nail in the coffin the studio system. With overhea becoming impossibly high, with

:oaching, with changes in the .ıs of actors, producers and di- ors, the dissolution of the system becoming inevitable, and would omplete by the mid-1960s.

was also the era when films had ore international flavor. Because ing was cheaper in Britain, Italy Spain, and, certainly, authentic ign locations were not only e convincing but less expensive studio mock-ups, many Ameri- films were shot abroad. There- , there were successful Anglo- erican productions such as John ston's *The African Queen* (1951) *Moulin Rouge* (1952), and vid Lean's *The Bridge on the* *er Kwai* (1957), Britain's most ctacular box-office hit of the 50s. rnational co-productions made taly were *Helen of Troy* (1956) *War and Peace* (1956), and aley Kramer's *The Pride and the* *sion* (1957) was made in Spain.

uropean stars also began to n larger on the international izon. Italy contributed Sophia en, Anna Magnani and Gina lobrigida, and West Germany vided Horst Buchholz, Curt Jur- s, Romy Schneider and Maria ell. In France, Brigitte Bardot red her pretty, pouting, kittenish d in Roger Vadim's *And God* *ated Woman* (1956), which ught French films out of the art se ghetto and into mainstream ma in the U.S., where this movie ned $4 million.

3y 1950 French cinema was firm- established commercially, as di- tors of the 1940s launched them- es into big-budget period films – ques Becker's *Casque d'Or* 52), Claude Autant-Lara's *le* *ge et le Noir* (1954), and René ment's *Gervaise* (1956). Among returning wartime exiles was x Ophuls, who delivered the ele- t *la Ronde* (1950) and *le Plaisir* 52); and Jean Renoir, who made *nch Cancan* (1955) and *Eléna et* *hommes* (1956).

Many of the best directors ig- ed contemporary France, others ned out uninspired movies. Some eptions were Robert Bresson's *ry of a Country Priest* (1951) and *Man Escaped* (1956), H.-G. uzot's *The Wages of Fear* (1953) l *les Diaboliques* (1955), and ques Tati's *Mr. Hulot's Holiday* 53) and *My Uncle* (1958).

n 1951 a group of film critics hered around André Bazin and ed for change, using the magazine *Cahiers du Cinéma* as a forum for their campaign. By the end of the decade, these critics were making their feature film debuts – Claude Chabrol's *le Beau Serge* and *les Cousins*; François Truffaut's *The Four Hundred Blows*, and Alain Resnais' *Hiroshima mon amour* – bringing about the New Wave, which would come to full fruition during the 1960s. The French film industry reacted favorably to this new development and backed it financially. While there had been a decrease in film attendances in 1957, the years 1958-1959 brought a renewed interest in film, with the development of art houses being given government subsidies.

Though there was much that was pedestrian in the pre-New Wave output in France, it was more significant than the films being produced in Britain, Germany, Czechoslovakia and Italy, all of whom were marking time through a mediocre decade before their own reawakening.

In Great Britain, Ealing continued to produce a number of typical home-grown comedies such as *The Lavender Hill Mob, The Man in the White Suit* (both 1951) and, in 1955, *The Ladykillers*, while the Boulting Brothers, John and Roy, working in the same tradition though with a more satirical edge, made *Private's Progress* (1956) and *I'm All Right, Jack* (1959). But few British films dealt with contemporary society, preferring to look back on the war years in *The Cruel Sea* (1953), *The Colditz Story* (1954) and *The Dam Busters* (1955). Despite *The Tales of Hoffman* (1951), Michael Powell and Emeric Pressburger's best work was behind them, and so was Carol Reed's, while David Lean, after *The Sound Barrier* (1952) and *Hobson's Choice* (1954), would move into huge international co-productions.

It was only in 1958, with Jack Clayton's *Room at the Top*, that British films started to reflect the 'angry young men' generation which had arrived two years earlier in the theater and in literature. Tony Richardson's screen version of *Look Back in Anger* (1959) anticipated films that would deal more realistically than ever before with sexual and social issues.

By 1950, Italian neo-realism was already in decline. The public, after years of hardship, looked to more light-hearted entertainment, and were obliged with a stream of frivolous comedies, melodramas and costume films. Among the few commercial films to win an audience abroad were Luigi Comencini's *Bread, Love and Dreams* (1953) and *Bread, Love and Jealousy* (1954), both starring Gina Lollobrigida and Vittorio De Sica. As a director De Sica enjoyed success in 1950 with *Miracle in Milan*, but struggled to make an impact at the box office with his last neo-realist masterpiece, *Umberto D* (1952). Meanwhile, Roberto Rossellini continued on a doomed path with Ingrid Bergman in *Europa 51* (1952), *Journey to Italy* (1953) and *Fear* (1954), all critical and financial disasters. A bright spot was the emergence of Federico Fellini with *La Strada* (1954) and *Nights of Cabiria* (1956), the first winners in successive years of the newly-instituted Best Foreign Film Oscar, and both featuring the director's wife, the Chaplinesque Giulietta Masina.

1816-28
Lauren Bacall, Rock Hudson, Dorothy McGuire: Sirk's ***Written on the Wind.***

In the eyes of critics and audiences worldwide, Sweden, Poland and India seemed to be one-man industries, each dominated by a single giant figure: the Swede Ingmar Bergman (*Smiles of a Summer Night*, 1955; *Wild Strawberries* and *The Seventh Seal*, both 1957), the Pole Andrzej Wajda (the war trilogy, *A Generation*, 1954, *Kanal*, 1957 and *Ashes and Diamonds*, 1958), and the Bengali Satyajit Ray (the Apu trilogy, *Panther Panchali*, 1955, *The Unvanquished*, 1956 and *The World of Apu*, 1959).

In contrast to Europe, Japan enjoyed a period of unparalleled prosperity, with annual output reaching its prewar level of 500 features by the mid-Fifties. This was due, in part, to the success of Akira Kurosawa's *Rashomon*, the first Japanese film to be widely shown in the West. This intriguing murder tale opened the way for many more films by Kurosawa such as *The Seven Samurai* (1954); Kon Ichikawa's *The Burmese Harp* (1956); Kinugasa's *Gate of Hell* (1953); and remarkable films from Mizoguchi and Ozu, as well as popular science fiction movies like *Godzilla* (1954).

With a new era of relative freedom ushered in by Nikita Kruschev's speech in 1956 at the Twentieth Party Congress, the Soviet Union's film industry saw a renaissance. Grigori Chukrai was the first director to take advantage of the 'thaw' by making *The Forty-First* (1956), a barely concealed attack on the already dying cult of the hero. Chukrai followed this with *Ballad of a Soldier* (1959), a simple and unrhetorical view of everyday life in wartime Russia which continued the trickle of new Soviet films to be welcomed in the West. That same year, Mikhail Kalatozov's *The Cranes Are Flying* was acclaimed in the U.S. under an American-Soviet cultural exchange program.

This free flow of films and stars between nations, international coproductions, and authentic foreign locations, exposed people as never before to other cultures, and made them realize that Hollywood, cut off as it had been in previous decades, was not the only kind of cinema. This was a salutary lesson from which motion picture industries all over the world, including America, would greatly benefit.

RONALD BERGAN

1950

1949 Academy Awards, RKO Pantages Theater, 23 Mar.

Best Film:	*All the King's Men* (dir: Robert Rossen)
Best Director:	Joseph L. Mankiewicz *(A Letter to Three Wives)*
Best Actor:	Broderick Crawford *(All the King's Men)*
Best Actress:	Olivia De Havilland *(The Heiress)*
Best Supp. Actor:	Dean Jagger *(Twelve O'Clock High)*
Best Supp. Actress:	Mercedes McCambridge *(All the King's Men)*

London, 1 January
Release of Basil Dearden's *The Blue Lamp*, starring Dirk Bogarde and Jack Warner.

Moscow, 21 January
Mosfilm studios present Mikhail Chiaureli's two-part super production *Padeniye Berlina* (*Berlin Falls*).

Stockholm, 20 February
Premiere of Ingmar Bergman's *Till Gladje* (*To Joy*) with Maj-Britt Nilsson, Stig Olin, Victor Sjöström and, in a minor role, Erland Josephson.

Cannes, 25 February
A decision reached at the Film Producer's Conference will change the Cannes Film Festival to take place in the spring from now on, rather than in September; consequently, there will be no festival this year.

Madrid, 8 March
Franco's government has announed the creation of the National Office of Entertainment Classification to give a morality rating (on a scale of one to six) to all films.

Washington, 10 April
The Supreme Court is refusing to comment on the condemnation of screenwriters Dalton Trumbo and John Lawson for their contempt of Congress. This effectively upholds the condemnation. It also affects the eight other hostile witnesses.

Los Angeles, 12 April
After making its reputation in Cannes, the British director Carol Reed's *The Third Man* is now seeing release in the U.S. Here, too, Anton Karas' haunting zither music will no doubt captivate the public.

Buenos Aires, 13 April
The powerful influence of certain European films and a strong literary sensibility are discernible in Leopoldo Torre Nilsson's first feature film, *El Crimen de Oribe* (*Oribe's Crime*), which starts screening today.

Hollywood, 20 April
Alfred Hitchcock has bought the rights to Patricia Highsmith's first novel *Strangers on a Train.*

Peking, 30 April
Effective immediately, the Central Office of Cinematographic Control is now attached to the Ministry of Culture. Mao Tse-Tung's wife Jian Quing, who was herself an actress in prewar Shanghai, is a member of a committee set up to advise and control the film industry.

Los Angeles, 20 June
Singer Judy Garland, who has been suffering from deep depression, has attempted suicide by cutting her throat with a piece of glass. Her family raced to her aid, and she is reported to be out of danger.

Hollywood, 30 July
Mary Pickford and Charlie Chaplin have decided to sell 3,600 of their 4,000 shares in United Artists.

Prague, 4 August
Director Jiri Weiss has released his new film *Posledni vystrel* (*The Last Shot*), filmed with a cast of nonprofessional actors.

Tokyo, 25 August
Release of Akira Kurosawa's film *Rashomon.* An intriguing work with forceful performances from Toshiro Mifune and Takashi Shimura.

Paris, 26 August
With producer Georges Grandière failing to honor his commitments, and the backing for the film not yet assured, Abel Gance has canceled his contract for *The Divine Tragedy.* The film will not be made.

Tokyo, 1 September
American occupational authorities have instituted a purge among the Japanese cinema circles where numerous key figures were, and are still, very involved with militarist and ultra-nationalist movements.

Venice, 10 September
This year's awards have been given to films addressing social problems. Best Italian film goes to Leonide Moguy's work *Domani è troppo tardi* (*Tomorrow is Too Late*), and André Cayatte's handling of a euthanasia case in *Justice est faite* takes off with the Golden Lion award. Eleanor Parker receives the best actress nod for her role as the moving victim in John Cromwell's pessimistic film *Caged* and Sam Jaffe is named best actor for *The Asphalt Jungle.*

New York, 14 September
During a reception in his honor, Joseph L. Mankiewicz violently denounced the current blacklisting as well as Cecil B. DeMille's demand that members of the Screen Directors' Guild swear an oath of loyalty.

Paris, 29 September
Jean Cocteau has made a screen version of his play *Orphée.* Jean Marais and Marie Déa portray Orpheus and Eurydice. It is the second film in Cocteau's Orphic trilogy, the first being *The Blood of the Poet.*

Monaco, 31 October.
Accused of "libidinous relations" with a 17-year-old girl, actor Errol Flynn has just been acquitted by the Monaco court.

Rio de Janeiro, 1 November
The Vera Cruz company, created and run by director Alberto Cavalcanti, who has recently returned from Europe, has released its first film, Adolfo Celi's *Caiçara.*

Hollywood, 21 November
RKO has yielded to injunctions from the Ministry of Justice regarding the integration of its activities. The organization will split into two distinct companies: RKO Pictures Corporation, which takes over film production, and RKO Theaters Corporation to manage the cinemas.

Mexico, 23 November
Luis Buñuel's *The Young and the Damned* has to close after only four days. It has been widely attacked and has failed to attract the public.

Milan, 15 December
Roberto Rossellini's newest work *Flowers of St. Francis*, played by Aldo Fabrizi, is an honest portrayal of the saint's spiritual quest.

Washington, 31 December
According to the latest census th are approximately 71,500 cine in the world, a figure which inclu America's 11,300 cinemas and 4,700 drive-ins.

BIRTHS

Algiers, 24 January
Daniel Auteuil

Tennessee, 18 February
Cybill Shepherd

Paris, 22 February
Miou-Miou (Sylvette Hery)

England, 22 February
Julie Walters

Ireland, 25 February
Neil Jordan

West Virginia, 18 March
Brad Dourif

Washington D.C., 20 March
William Hurt

Chicago, 31 May
Tom Berenger

Germany, 2 August
Mathieu Carrière

Paris, 9 August
Anémone (Anne Bourguignon)

Toronto, 31 October
John Candy

Missouri, 15 December
Don Johnson

DEATHS

California, 7 April
Walter Huston

Hollywood, 22 July
Rex Ingram

San Francisco, 23 October
Al Jolson

Hollywood, 28 October
Maurice Costello

Swanson makes an amazing co back to the screen, virtually play herself and doing it brilliantly, in ly Wilder's scathing view of e Hollywood titled ***Sunset Boulevar***

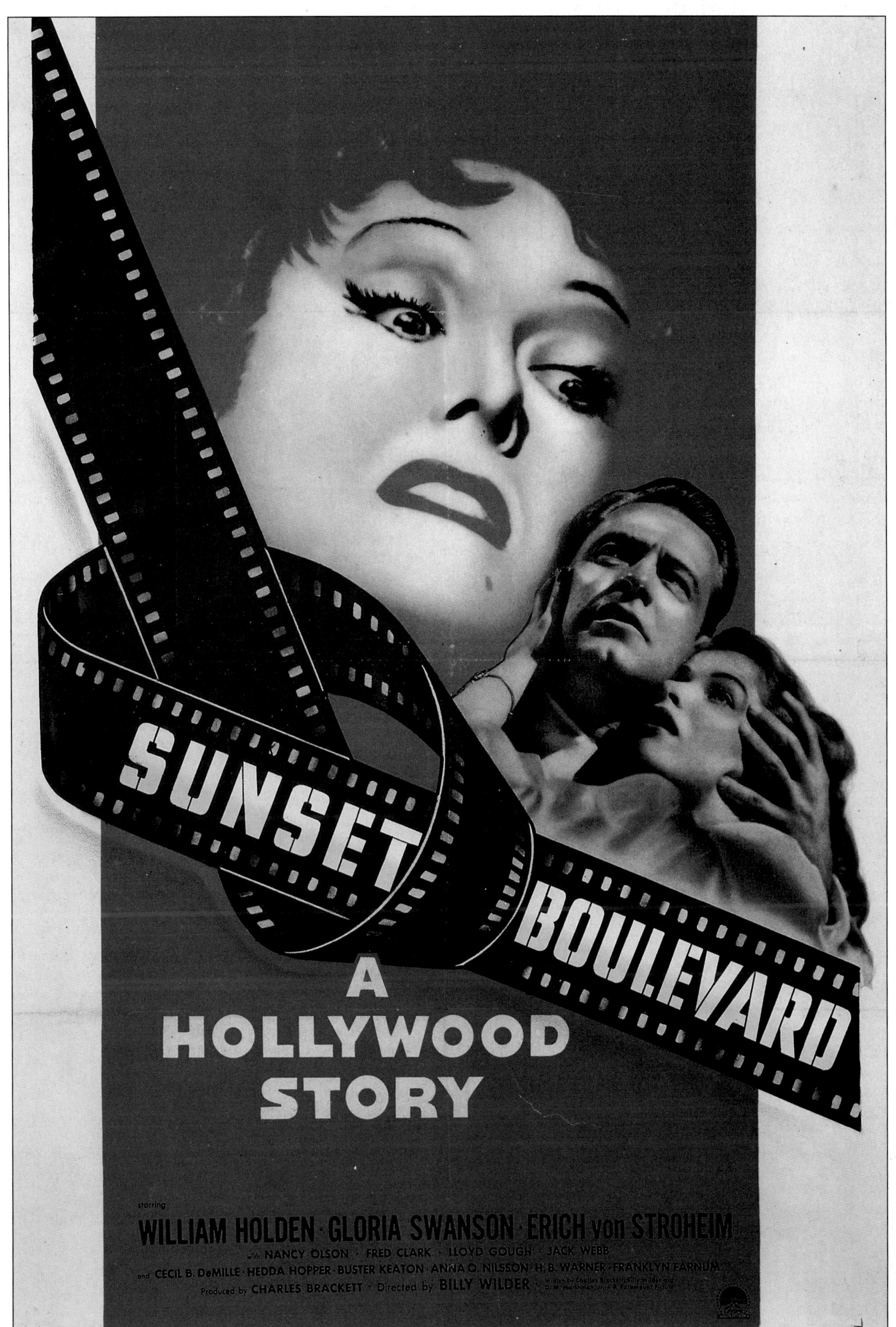
SUNSET
BOULEVARD
A
HOLLYWOOD
STORY
starring
WILLIAM HOLDEN · GLORIA SWANSON · ERICH von STROHEIM
with NANCY OLSON · FRED CLARK · LLOYD GOUGH · JACK WEBB
and CECIL B. DeMILLE · HEDDA HOPPER · BUSTER KEATON · ANNA Q. NILSSON · H. B. WARNER · FRANKLYN FARNUM
Produced by CHARLES BRACKETT · Directed by BILLY WILDER

Fourth film for Signoret-Allégret menage

Simone Signoret and Jane Marken, a deeply unpleasant mother and daughter.

Paris, 25 January
Married since 1944, Simone Signoret and the director Yves Allégret have made four films together, the latest being *Wanton* (*Manèges*), released today. Like their preceding film, *Dédée d'Anvers*, this is a dark realist drama, written by Jacques Sigurd. Signoret plays a convincing bitch, who shamelessly deceives her pathetic middle-aged husband (well portrayed by Bernard Blier), and bleeds him dry with the help of her greedy mother. This moody story is narrated in flashbacks, which are quite cleverly utilized to reveal the truth, after we initially see the wife through the eyes of her husband.

Gabin and Carné are back together again

Paris, 25 February
Having been on bad terms from the time Jean Gabin refused to appear in Marcel Carné's *les Portes de la nuit* (*Gates of the Night*) in 1946, the actor and director have finally reconciled. Gabin and Carné have just worked together again on *la Marie du port*, which is an atmospheric drama based on Georges Simenon.

Nicole Courcel and Jean Gabin, seducer and willing victim in Carné's film.

Film turns spotlight on the racist South

Left to right: Claude Jarman Jr, Will Geer, Porter Hall and David Brian.

Los Angeles, 3 February
Having tackled anti-Semitism in 1948, Hollywood turned the spotlight on the color question in 1949 in Fox's *Pinky*, directed by Elia Kazan, in which Jeanne Crain played a light-skinned colored girl passing for white and romancing William Lundigan. The casting of a white star in a colored role – thus avoiding a shock to audiences with a black-white kiss – underlined the compromises which the studio felt it had to make. Now MGM's *Intruder in the Dust*, adapted from the Willi[a] Faulkner novel, confronts the pr[o]lem of race relations. Directed Clarence Brown with an intens uncharacteristic of the studio's gl sy image, the film tells the story an elderly Southern black, play with great dignity by Juano Hern[a]dez, falsely accused of murder a then threatened with lynch law. H disdain for his bigoted accusers is intense that he declines to defe himself, and it falls to a group liberal-minded whites to save hin

'Brazilian Bombshell' livens up ocean tri

Hollywood, 10 March
Pretty and petite Jane Powell, the natural successor to actress Deanna Durbin, appears in the title role of MGM's new musical *Nancy Goes to Rio*, which is, in fact, a remake of the 1940 Durbin vehicle, *It's a Date*. The story of a mother (Ann Sothern) and teenage daughter (Powell), both coveting the same parts in a play and the same man (Barry Sullivan), is wafer thin, even though it is stuffed with musical goodies. In the film Miss Powell sings "Time and Time Again" as well as "Musetta's Waltz" from *La Bohème*. Naturally, given Nancy's destination, it comes as no surprise to discover Carmen Miranda turning up to provide a few laughs and then sing a characteristic number called "Cha Bomm Pa Pa". Unfortunately, the "Brazilian Bombshell" has been seen very little lately. She enlivened many a 20th Centu Fox musical in the early 1940s, the time when this eccentric, exc entertainer was one of the high paid in America.

The lady in the tutti-frutti hat!

ademy's twenty-second Oscar ceremony

n Sothern and Kirk Douglas, husband and wife, in **A Letter to Three Wives**.

llywood, 23 March
e most successful movie at this r's Academy Awards ceremony s Robert Rossen's *All the King's n*. It has been voted Best Picture d also won the Best Actor award Broderick Crawford's blistering formance as the corrupt South- politician Willie Stark. For the ne film, Crawford's co-star Mer- les McCambridge, a distinguish- stage actress making her motion ture debut, took the Best Sup- rting Actress Oscar. The Academy voted Olivia De Havilland the Best Actress for the second time, a just reward for her portrayal of the gauche spinster Catherine Sloper in *The Heiress*. Joseph L. Mankiewicz received both the Best Director and Best Screenplay nods for his elegant but barbed satire, *A Letter to Three Wives*. The Best Supporting Actor prize went to Dean Jagger for his work in the war drama titled *Twelve O'Clock High*. Special Awards were made to Fred Astaire, Cecil B. DeMille and child star Bobby Driscoll.

an-Pierre Melville adapts Jean Cocteau

ris, 29 March
teenage brother and sister share a ustrophobic, self-obsessed world a single cluttered room, and the rusion of others leads to tragedy. These are the ingredients of *les Enfants terribles* from Jean Cocteau's bizarre 1920s novel, brilliantly shot by Jean-Pierre Melville almost entirely on the Théâtre Pigalle stage.

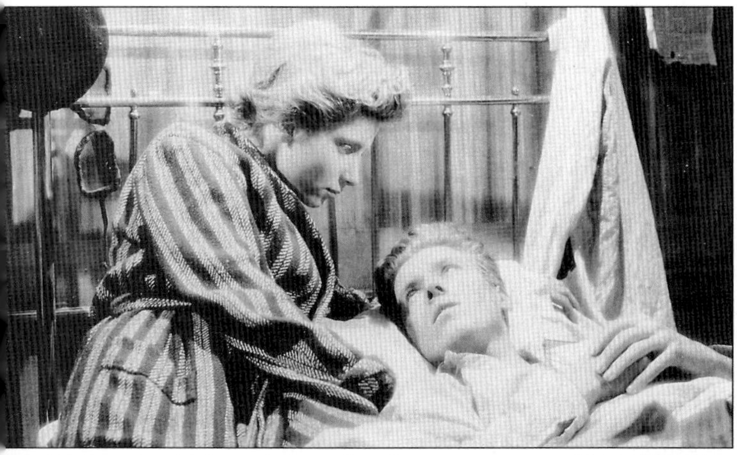

cole Stéphane and Edouard Dermithe, the 'strange ones' of Melville's film.

Bergman as Rossellini's new heroine

An exile in search of herself: Bergman with Mario Vitale in ***Stromboli****.*

Rome, 31 March
The release of Roberto Rossellini's latest film, *Stromboli*, is set to cause a stir. Ingrid Bergman stars alongside Mario Vitale as a Lithuanian woman who marries a young Italian fisherman to escape from an internment camp. However, she finds only loneliness and hostility on his barren island home. At the climax of the film, the pregnant Bergman flees in terror from the island's erupting volcano. Bergman's fans have been taken aback at seeing her stripped of the trappings of Hollywood stardom, and puritan groups in the United States are already up in arms about stories that Bergman has left her husband to live with director Roberto Rossellini.

On the volcano's harsh slopes, a long way from Hollywood's splendors.

Anna Magnani (left) with Geraldine Brooks in William Dieterle's ***Volcano****, the Italian star's retaliation against Roberto Rossellini.*

Blonde sex symbol shines in Huston's murk

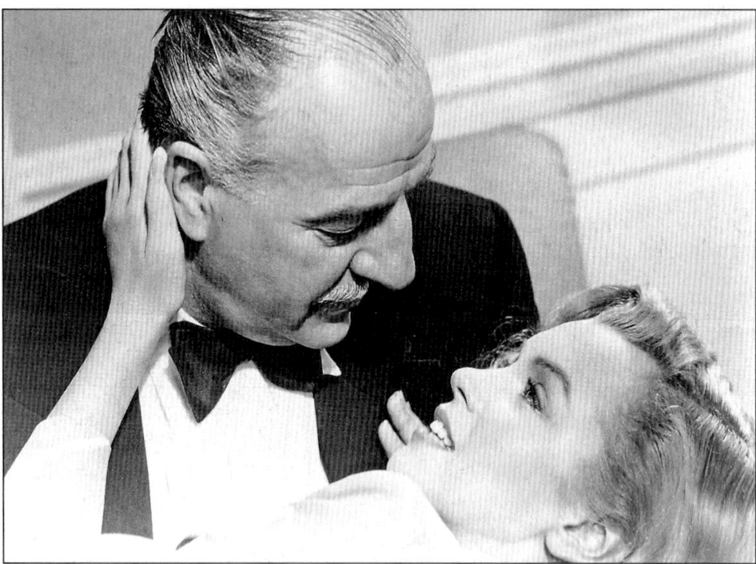

Louis Calhern and the breathtaking Marilyn Monroe in Huston's film.

Hollywood, 8 June
Hollywood is always full of young blonde hopefuls with luscious bodies but little discernible talent. One such was former model Marilyn Monroe, who made little impact in the movies until she allowed herself to be ogled by Groucho Marx in last year's film *Love Happy*. Then she got an agent, Johnny Hyde, who had her jaw remodeled and nose bob-tipped. He saw that Monroe had that special "something extra", and his lobbying of producers has secured her a small but significant part in the gripping thriller by John Huston, *The Asphalt Jungle*, as the mistress of crooked legal big-shot Louis Calhern. But Monroe has only to sprawl languorously across the sofa in their love-nest to charge the screen with crackling sexual static. Born Norma Jean Baker in Los Angeles in 1926, she had an unhappy childhood followed by marriage to her first husband at age 16 simply to forestall a spell in the county orphanage. After the war she drifted into model work and then films, making her screen debut with a small part in the 1947 film *Dangerous Years*, a B-picture about juvenile delinquents. Now, after two years of struggling to make a breakthrough, it looks as if Norma Jean's ship is about to come in.

Sterling Hayden, the shadowy hero.

'Broken Arrow' pleads justice for Indian[s]

Los Angeles, 20 July
The first Western from director Delmer Daves, *Broken Arrow*, tells the story of U.S. army scout Jefford (James Stewart), who marries a young Apache girl (Debra Paget), becomes the friend of Cochise (Jeff Chandler) and convinces him to sign a peace treaty with the whites. But Geronimo and a number of arms dealers refuse to accept peace. Then when white renegades murder his wife, Jefford rebels against those of his race. *Broken Arrow* can be considered as the first great pro Red Indian film. Based on verifiable fact, it faithfully evokes the relationship between Cochise and Jefford, marking an historic rehabilitation of Indians in the cinema. It is also one of the first Hollywood films to show a mixed race marriage. "It is said that *Broken Arrow* is the first adult Western talkie. We have tried to present the Apaches as human beings and not as savages," said Delmer Daves. "At the beginning, James Stewart's voice indicates what is in the offing. He says, 'The Indians, when they speak, will speak American, so that you'll be able to understand them.' Therein lies the main theme of the film, the necessity to understand our neighbors irrespective of race [or] skin color, to reach the only possi[ble] rational means of living, to lea[d a] peaceful life." A fine message [of] tolerance, which the quality of [the] film justifies. The director gai[ned] sympathy for the Red Indians fr[om] living among the Navaho and H[opi] tribes in his youth. It is hoped t[hat] Daves will continue on the sa[me] path of peace.

OF THIS MOTION PICTURE THE SCREEN CAN BE PROUD....
TODAY.... TOMORROW....A GENERATION FROM NOW......
JAMES STEWART
in
BROKEN
ARROW
COLOUR BY
Technicolor
WITH JEFF CHANDLER
DEBRA PAGET
Directed by DELMER DAVES
Produced by JULIAN BLAUSTEIN

One of several striking posters issu[ed]

Victim of Red scare Jules Dassin recycles 'Naked City' in Londo[n]

London, 10 June
Forced out of Hollywood last year by the anti-Red witch hunt, Jules Dassin has come to England, where he has made *Night and the City*. The plot plunges us into a London milieu of seedy nightclubs, sharks, killers, con artists and tarts – a background Dassin uses as effectively as he had used New York in *The Naked City* two years ago. Americans Richard Widmark and Gene Tierney lead a virtually all-English cast: he a hustler, whose greatest ambition is to promote wrestling matches, she [a] singer at the Silver Fox nightcl[ub]. Crooked deals and double-cros[ses] have Widmark running from ga[ng]sters. Tautly directed and strong [in] atmosphere, the film proves that [ex]ile has not diluted Dassin's talen[t].

Richard Widmark is hounded by London criminals in ***Night and the City.***

Googie Withers, an ambiguous ro[le]

)utrageous 'la Ronde' is given stylish treatment

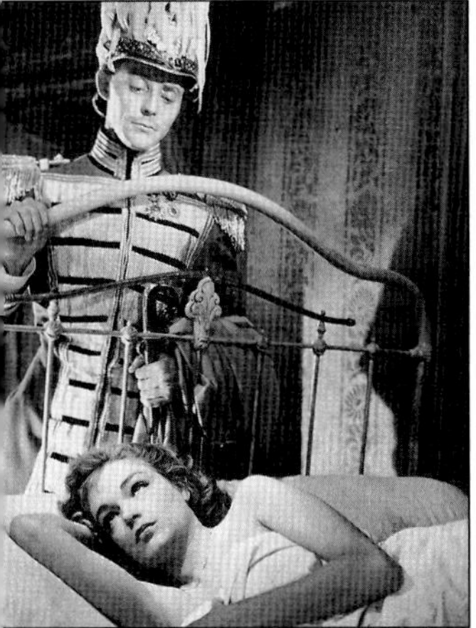
rard Philipe and Simone Signoret.

Isa Miranda and Gérard Philipe.

Danielle Darrieux and Daniel Gelin.

Simone Simon and Daniel Gelin.

ris, 17 June
ter his eight-year sojourn in Hol-
ood, Max Ophuls has marked his urn to France with a flourish. His *Ronde*, adapted from Arthur hnitzler's scandalous play, con-ts of 10 episodes, linked by a ster-of-ceremonies narrator (An-1 Walbrook), in which the protag-ists ride a sexual merry-go-round in 19th-century Vienna. The circular structure reveals one partner in one story always connecting with one in the next, such as the whore and the soldier, the soldier and the maid, the maid and the master, and so forth. To tell this tale of sexual mores and the illusion of love, Ophuls has assembled a glittering cast: Simone Signoret (whore), Serge Reggiani (soldier), Simone Simon (maid), Daniel Gélin (young man), Danielle Darrieux (married lady), Fernand Gravey (husband), Odette Joyeux (grisette), Gérard Philipe (lieutenant), Isa Miranda (actress) and Jean-Louis Barrault (poet). The picture opens with narrator Anton Walbrook giving a splendidly elegant performance, walking through a film studio onto a *fin-de-siècle* set, putting on an opera cloak and commenting on the action, providing a distancing effect. Fitting style to subject, Ophuls utilizes a mobile camera that itself acts as a kind of carousel, and with Oscar Straus' seductive waltz theme, *la Ronde* is a witty confection, lighter than the more mordant Schnitzler original.

ton Walbrook, pictured here with Simone Signoret, is the puppet master-narrator who links the ten protagonists of ***La Ronde*** *on their sexual carousel.*

Love conquers all for Martine Carol

Inconstante et fidèle.
Caroline Chérie

Paris, 7 August
Martine Carol's failed suicide attempt on 10 April 1947 seems to have given her a new lease on life, although a faction of the press continues to criticize the young actress. Nevertheless, she looks radiant and acts seductively in her latest film, *Caroline chérie*, which just opened in Paris. Exuding happiness, Martine Carol appeared on the arm of her husband Steve Crane, the ex-husband of Lana Turner, at the premiere held at the Marivaux cinema. They have been married for some months, and her private life, like her career, looks like it has improved. *Caroline chérie* is a large-scale costume production, based on the 1949 best-selling historical novel by Cecil Saint-Laurent, with a scenario by the playwright Jean Anouilh. It is directed by Richard Pottier, who had given Carol her first genuine role in *la Ferme aux loups* in 1944. Carol plays Caroline de Bièvres, a 16-year-old girl who attains womanhood in the arms of young Count Gaston de Sallanches (Jacques Dacqmine), before the two are separated by the upheavals of the French Revolution. Caroline is plunged into a series of romantic and dangerous adventures, even getting married out of spite, while searching for her lover through a France in turmoil. Naturally, they are reunited at the happy ending. We are left with little doubt that this film will rocket the voluptuous blonde Martine Carol to stardom at last.

Billy Wilder fires off a savage salvo

New York, 10 August
In Billy Wilder's *Sunset Boulevard*, the old Hollywood, in the form of Gloria Swanson's forgotten silent star Norma Desmond, comes into uncomprehending and fatal contact with the new Hollywood, represented by William Holden's washed-up screenwriter Joe Gillis. Rummaging in the dim recesses of his memory, Holden recalls that Gloria used to be big in pictures. She hisses back, "I *am* big. It's the pictures that got small!" Wilder's savage satire on Tinseltown comes at a time when Hollywood's horizons are shrinking, its nerve failing and its very future seems in question. Swanson is the ghost at this feast, in her umpteenth comeback as a mad silent movie queen haunting a decaying mansion where thousands of images of herself gather the dust of ages, and the "waxworks" of Hollywood history – Buster Keaton, H.B. Warner and Anna Q. Nilsson – gather to play interminable hands of bridge. Norma also dreams of a comeback, with her crazy script edited by gigolo Holden, and Wilder fills the picture with references to Swanson's own past in the high summer of the silents: Norma, talons clawing the air, caught in the flickering light cast by *Queen Kelly*, whose director Erich von Stroheim is cast in *Sunset Boulevard* as her former husband and director now turned sepulchral butler; Norma's visit to Swanson's old stamping ground, Paramount studios, where the real Cecil B. DeMille is directing *Samson and Delilah* and calls her "young fellow", just as he did in 1919 when th were making *Male and Female*; a Swanson's repeat of the marvel Chaplin imitation from the 19 *Manhandled*. The story goes t Mae West, Pola Negri and M Pickford turned down the part fore Swanson, who has lost none her native shrewdness, seized it w both hands and made it her own

Gloria Swanson's Norma Desmond in the grip of illusion and madness.

Joseph Mankiewicz reveals the dark secrets of the dressing roo

Hollywood, 22 October
Writer-director Joseph L. Mankiewicz's latest for Fox is *All About Eve*. The woman of the title is Anne Baxter's scheming young would-be actress who inveigles her way into the entourage of veteran Broadway star Bette Davis to launch her own career. Davis is superb in the role of Margo Channing, the aging actress ruthlessly undermined by her o protégée, as cozy as a curdled co tail, clutching an ever-present ci rette in her talons and dispensi measured venom in all directio with her corncrake voice. The m who really knows "all about Eve" waspish theater critic Addison Witt, played with suave caddishn by George Sanders, and it is voice-over which provides the e gantly barbed commentary to t saga of backstabbing among thea folk. At one point Sanders appe with rising star Marilyn Monroe his arm and languidly introduces h as "a graduate of the Copacaba school of acting." Though fac with strong opposition from a c that's on top of its collective for Sanders steals the film. According Mankiewicz *All About Eve* is bas on a similar incident in the lives Elisabeth Bergner and Paul Czin after they took an equally ambitic young actress under their wing.

Duplicitous Eve Harrington (Anne Baxter, left) with Margo Channing (Davis).

iolence of life in Mexico City's slums

ıñuel's **Los Olvidados**, his third in Mexico, about slum violence.

exico, 19 November
e release here of Luis Buñuel's test project, *The Young and the amned* (*Los Olvidados*), has proked violent reactions. The press d conservative politicians have manded it be banned because "it nstitutes an insult to the Mexican tion." Various unions and associions have asked that the Spanish nigré director be expelled from the country forthwith. The film has obviously touched a raw nerve. Shot in only 21 days in the slums of the capital, it exposes the terrible life that faces the youth, forgotten by Mexican society and often driven to delinquency. The harsh realism of many of the incidents, notably the beating up of a blind musician, is mixed with Buñuel's surrealism in the powerful dream sequences.

Effervescent Judy repeats stage triumph

Left to right: Broderick Crawford, William Holden and Judy Holliday.

New York, 26 December
Judy Holliday is ultimate "dumb broad" Billie Dawn in the film version of *Born Yesterday*, a part she played on Broadway four years ago. Ordered by her ox-like sugar daddy Broderick Crawford to pick up a little bit of culture from college-boy reporter William Holden, she finally floors brutish Brod with the immortal invocation, delivered in a piercing Bronx whine, to "Drop dead!" Holliday is a actress of great intelligence, exuberance and precision, and an accomplished stealer of pictures, as she proved last year when playing the bird-brained attempted-murder suspect in *Adam's Rib*. Incredibly, she was only Columbia's fifth choice for *Born Yesterday*, after Rita Hayworth, Jan Sterling, Gloria Grahame and Evelyn Keyes.

ichelangelo Antonioni delivers a lesson to the neo-realists

ome, 25 November
ith *Chronicle of a Love* (*Cronaca un Amore*), Michelangelo Antonii has at last taken his place among alian feature-length film directors. rn in Ferrara in 1912, he studied the University of Bologna, where spent his time between business d economics studies indulging in usic, art and tennis. After experienting with 16mm films and writg film critiques for a local paper, came to Rome in 1939 where he en became an influential critic on e magazine *Cinema*. After the war ded, he collaborated on screenays for Giuseppe De Santis and berto Rossellini. He then direct- six short documentaries before aking his first feature at age 38. *ronicle of a Love* tells of an adulrous wife (Lucia Bosé) and her imverished lover (Massimo Girotti) otting to murder her rich husband, t when he dies under mysterious cumstances, they have to live with the guilt of their intention. The director's elegant style, using long takes while remorselessly pursuing the characters, is in contrast to the neo-realist manner of many of his Italian contemporaries. The plot, however, is similar to *The Postman Always Rings Twice*, which inspired Luchino Visconti's first film, *Ossessione*, also starring Girotti.

Lucia Bosé and Massimo Girotti star in Antonioni's ***Chronicle of a Love****.*

Ingrid weds Roberto at long last

Rome, 18 November
From the time the American public learned that Ingrid Bergman, wife and mother, had become the mistress of the Italian director Roberto Rossellini, groups of moralists have raged against her. In making a reference to *Stromboli*, Bergman's first movie in Italy, Senator Edwin C. Johnson declared: "The degenerate Rossellini has deceived the American people with an idiotic story of a volcano and a pregnant woman. We must protect ourselves against such scourges." Ingrid Bergman has not tried to justify herself, but stated, "Americans do not understand that a mother might be blinded by passion to the point of sacrificing her daughter." Her divorce from her husband Peter Lindstrom having been finalized in Los Angeles on 1 November, the star is now able to marry Rossellini at last.

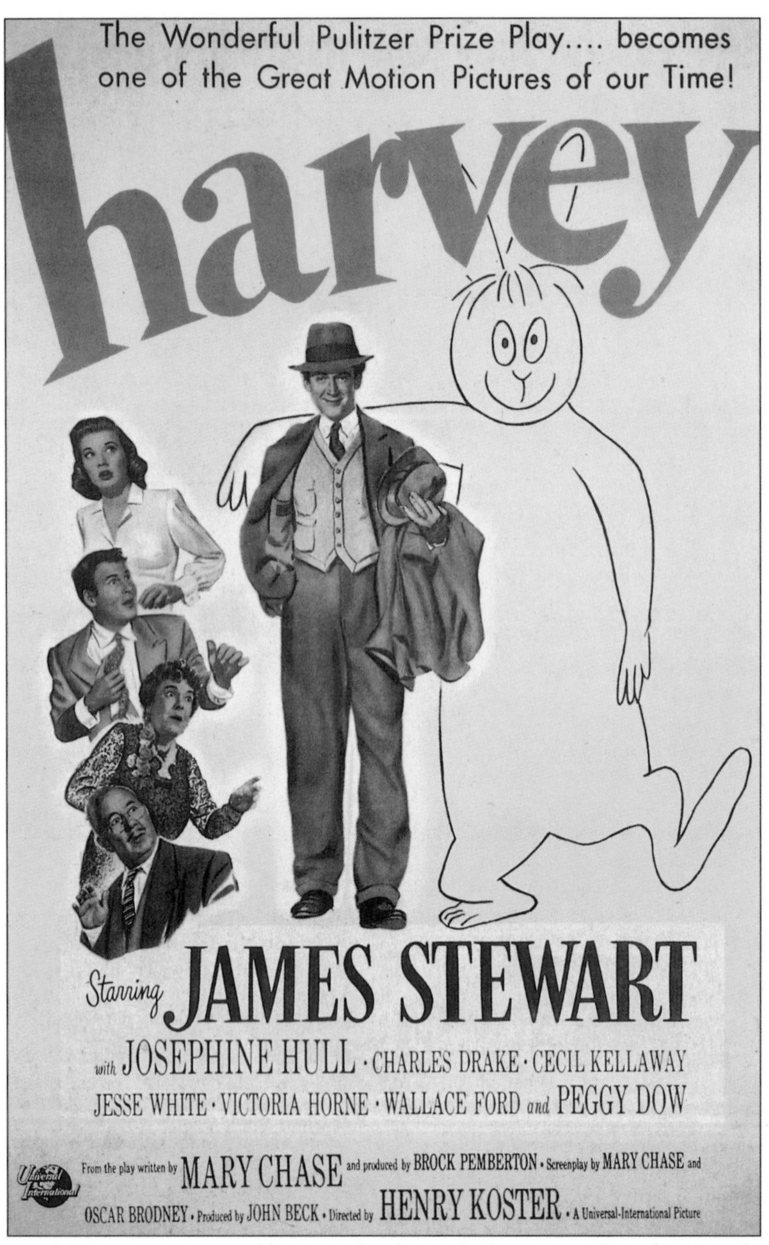
The Wonderful Pulitzer Prize Play.... becomes one of the Great Motion Pictures of our Time!
harvey
Starring JAMES STEWART
with JOSEPHINE HULL · CHARLES DRAKE · CECIL KELLAWAY
JESSE WHITE · VICTORIA HORNE · WALLACE FORD and PEGGY DOW
From the play written by MARY CHASE and produced by BROCK PEMBERTON · Screenplay by MARY CHASE and
OSCAR BRODNEY · Produced by JOHN BECK · Directed by HENRY KOSTER · A Universal-International Picture
Universal International

Faithful screen version of hit comedy play with Stewart as Elwood P. Dowd.

*Alfonso Mejia (l) and Roberto Cobo in Buñuel's **The Young and the Damne***

*Raf Vallone (left), the lead in Pietro Germi's **The Path of Hope** (Italy).*

*Toshiro Mifune and Machiko K in Akira Kurosawa's **Rashomon**.*

*James Stewart (center), Jay C. Flippen (rt) in Anthony Mann's **Winchester 73**.*

SPENCER TRACY
JOAN BENNETT
ELIZABETH TAYLOR
The Bride gets the THRILLS! Father gets the BILLS!
Father of the Bride
DON TAYLOR · BILLIE BURKE
Directed by VINCENTE MINNELLI
Produced by PANDRO S. BERMAN

Dad Tracy, daughter Taylor... bliss!

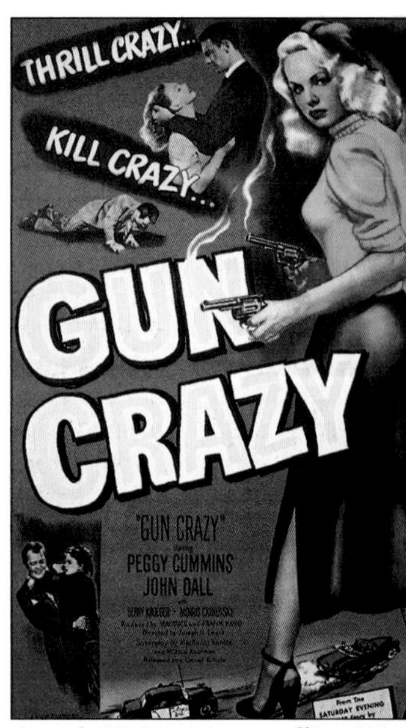
THRILL CRAZY...
KILL CRAZY...
GUN CRAZY
"GUN CRAZY"
PEGGY CUMMINS
JOHN DALL

Joseph H. Lewis' compelling 'B'.

CLIFTON WEBB
JEANNE CRAIN · MYRNA LOY
He's the New Father of His Country!
CHEAPER BY THE DOZEN
COLOR BY TECHNICOLOR
with Betty LYNN · Edgar BUCHANAN · Barbara BATES · Mildred NATWICK · Sara ALLGOOD
Directed by WALTER LANG · Produced by LAMAR TROTTI
20th CENTURY-FOX
Screen Play by LAMAR TROTTI · Based on the Novel by FRANK B. GILBRETH, Jr. and ERNESTINE GILBRETH CAREY

ebb brilliant as Frank Gilbreth, father of 12 children based on a true story.

incess of Death (Maria Casarès), Orpheus (Jean Marais): Cocteau's **Orphée**.

M-G-M PRESENTS
THE ASPHALT JUNGLE
THE CITY UNDER THE CITY
STARRING
STERLING HAYDEN
LOUIS CALHERN
WITH
JEAN HAGEN · JAMES WHITMORE
SAM JAFFE · JOHN McINTIRE
A JOHN HUSTON PRODUCTION
DIRECTED BY JOHN HUSTON
PRODUCED BY ARTHUR HORNBLOW, JR.

MGM boss Mayer hated this one.

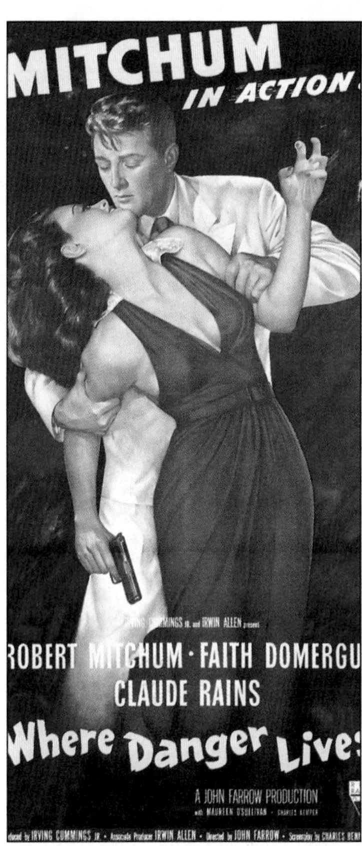
MITCHUM
IN ACTION
ROBERT MITCHUM · FAITH DOMERGU
CLAUDE RAINS
Where Danger Lives
A JOHN FARROW PRODUCTION

Mitchum finds himself in trouble.

Anne Baxter, Bette Davis, Marilyn Monroe, George Sanders: ***All About Eve***.

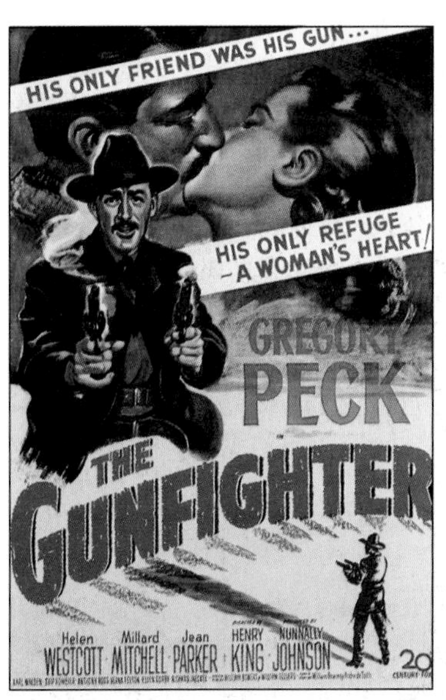
HIS ONLY FRIEND WAS HIS GUN...
HIS ONLY REFUGE – A WOMAN'S HEART!
GREGORY PECK
THE GUNFIGHTER
Helen WESTCOTT · Millard MITCHELL · Jean PARKER · HENRY KING · NUNNALLY JOHNSON

Outlaw Gregory Peck seeks reconciliation with his wife and son.

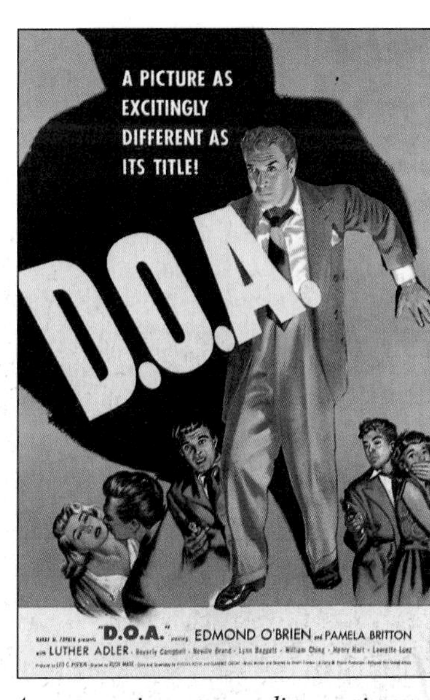
A PICTURE AS EXCITINGLY DIFFERENT AS ITS TITLE!
D.O.A.
"D.O.A." EDMOND O'BRIEN and PAMELA BRITTON
with LUTHER ADLER

A man arrives at a police station to report his own murder...

1951

1950 Academy Awards, RKO Pantages Theater, 29 Mar.

Best Film:	*All About Eve* (dir: Joseph L. Mankiewicz)
Best Director:	Joseph L. Mankiewicz
Best Actor:	Jose Ferrer *(Cyrano de Bergerac)*
Best Actress:	Judy Holliday *(Born Yesterday)*
Best Supp. Actor:	George Sanders *(All About Eve)*
Best Supp. Actress:	Josephine Hull *(Harvey)*

Chicago, 2 January
Yesterday marked a television milestone, with the first public test of phonevision, or pay-as-you-look TV, being carried out among 300 families representing a cross section of the public. They are being offered three movies a day for $1 per film. Curtains went up at 4 p.m. with *April Showers*, a musical starring Jack Carson and Ann Sothern.

Prague, 26 January
Opening of Jiri Trnka's animated feature film *Bajaja* (*The Princess Bayaya*). Trnka drew his inspiration from an old folk tale.

New York, 9 February
Actress Greta Garbo, a resident in the United States since 1925, has become an American citizen.

New York, 21 February
A revised edition of David Lean's acclaimed British film, *Oliver Twist* (1948), which had been judged "anti-Semitic", was accorded a Production Code seal of approval today by the directors of the MPAA. Eagle Lion Classics are reported to have made "extensive cuts".

Tokyo, 1 March
Filmmaker Keisuke Kinoshita has produced the first Japanese color film (filmed in Fujicolor), *Karumen Kokyo Ni Kaeru* (*Carmen Comes Home*), starring Hideko Takamine.

Washington, 21 March
Larry Parks, star of smash hits *The Jolson Story* and *Jolson Sings Again*, has admitted to the HUAC that he was a member of the Communist Party from 1941 to 1945.

Hollywood, 27 March
New restrictions are announced in the Production Code: any reference to venereal disease, abortion or drugs is forbidden. Additionally, suicide may not be shown in a favorable light, nor used by any character to escape the penalty of the law.

Paris, 2 April
The new cinema publication *Cahiers du Cinéma* is now on sale. The journal, which is financed by the owner of Cinéphone distribution, Léonid Keigel, is the work of a group of young film critics from the now defunct *Revue du Cinéma*. Well-known writers such as André Bazin, Lo Duca, Jacques Doniol-Valcroze and Edward Dmytryk are among contributors to the first issue.

Mexico, 11 April
Opening of Luis Buñuel's *Susana* aka *The Devil and the Flesh*, with Rosita Quintana and Fernando Soler. In this film, the director pushes the conventions of melodrama to their extreme limit.

Los Angeles, 30 April
Vincente Minnelli and Judy Garland, who have been married since 1945, have filed for divorce.

Tokyo, 23 May
Akira Kurosawa's *The Idiot* (*Hakuchi*), based on Dostoevsky's novel and featuring Masayuki Mori and Toshiro Mifune, opens today.

Peking, 30 June
Under personal pressure from Mao Tse Tung, the popular *People's Daily* is launching a violent campaign against Sun Yu's film *The Life of Wu Xun,* released several months ago. The cinema world fears this is only the beginning of a wave of ideological "purification".

Rome, 13 July
A group of producers has set up Italian Film Export, a company that will promote Italian films in the American market, which European filmmakers are finding increasingly difficult to break into.

New York, 20 July
Time Inc. has decided to suspend production of *The March of Time*. The famous weekly newsreel was begun in 1935.

Vermont, 23 July
Distinguished documentary filmmaker Robert J. Flaherty died today. He was planning two projects for the State Department, one about the division of Germany and another on the Hawaiian Islands.

Czechoslovakia, 29 July
First prize at the Karlovy Vary Festival went to Soviet director Yuri Raizman's *Dream of a Cossack*.

Hollywood, 14 August
The most powerful newspaper tycoon in America, William Randolph Hearst, has died. He had provided Orson Welles with his inspiration for the fascinating and enigmatic character *Citizen Kane*.

Tokyo, 14 September
Opening of Kenji Mizoguchi's film *Woman of Musashino* with Kinuyo Tanaka and Masayuki Mori.

Paris, 24 September
Jacques Becker has begun filming *Casque-d'or* (*Golden Marie*) starring Simone Signoret and singer Serge Reggiani at the Billancourt studios.

New York, 4 October
A press preview is to be held today of *An American in Paris*, Vincente Minnelli's new musical for MGM, co-starring Gene Kelly and French actress Leslie Caron.

New York, 7 October
The New York State Censor has refused a license to Max Ophuls' French film *la Ronde*. They consider the plot (from the play by Arthur Schnitzler) to be amoral and outside the boundaries established by the Production Code. In the censor's view, the film shows adultery not as a fall from grace, but as a game.

Los Angeles, 18 October
Cowboy star Roy Rogers today won a fight begun last June in the State District Court to prevent Republic from selling or licensing any of his old films for use in TV. Rogers had claimed that the advertisements shown during commercial breaks in his films would suggest he was endorsing the products. He has been granted a permanent injunction.

Hollywood, 19 November
Charlie Chaplin has commenced shooting his new film *Limelight*.

Cairo, 19 November
Egyptian director Salah Abou Sei[illegible] film *Lak yum ya zalim* (*Your D[illegible] Will Come*), which opens today, [illegible] loosely based on Emile Zola's no[illegible] *Thérèse Raquin*.

Stockholm, 26 December
Opening of *Divorced*, the latest fi[illegible] from the Swedish director Gust[illegible] Molander, with Inga Tidblad a[illegible] Alf Kjellin, from an idea suggest[illegible] by Ingmar Bergman.

France, 31 December
During the year, 411 million cine[illegible] tickets have been sold here.

BIRTHS

Massachusetts, 17 March
Kurt Russell

Paris, 11 March
Dominique Sanda

Chicago, 14 May
Robert Zemeckis

California, 9 July
Anjelica Huston

California, 8 August
Keith Carradine

Pennsylvania, 5 September
Michael Keaton
(Michael Douglas)

California, 7 September
Julie Kavner

New York, 5 October
Karen Allen

Connecticut, 1 December
Treat Williams

DEATHS

Hollywood, 7 May
Warner Baxter

Paris, 14 August
Louis Jouvet

California, 27 August
Robert Walker

*Made on location in Africa, T[illegible] **African Queen** (an old river boat) [illegible] one of the year's hits. Among [illegible] many attractions is the unexpect[illegible] pairing of Bogart and Hepburn.*

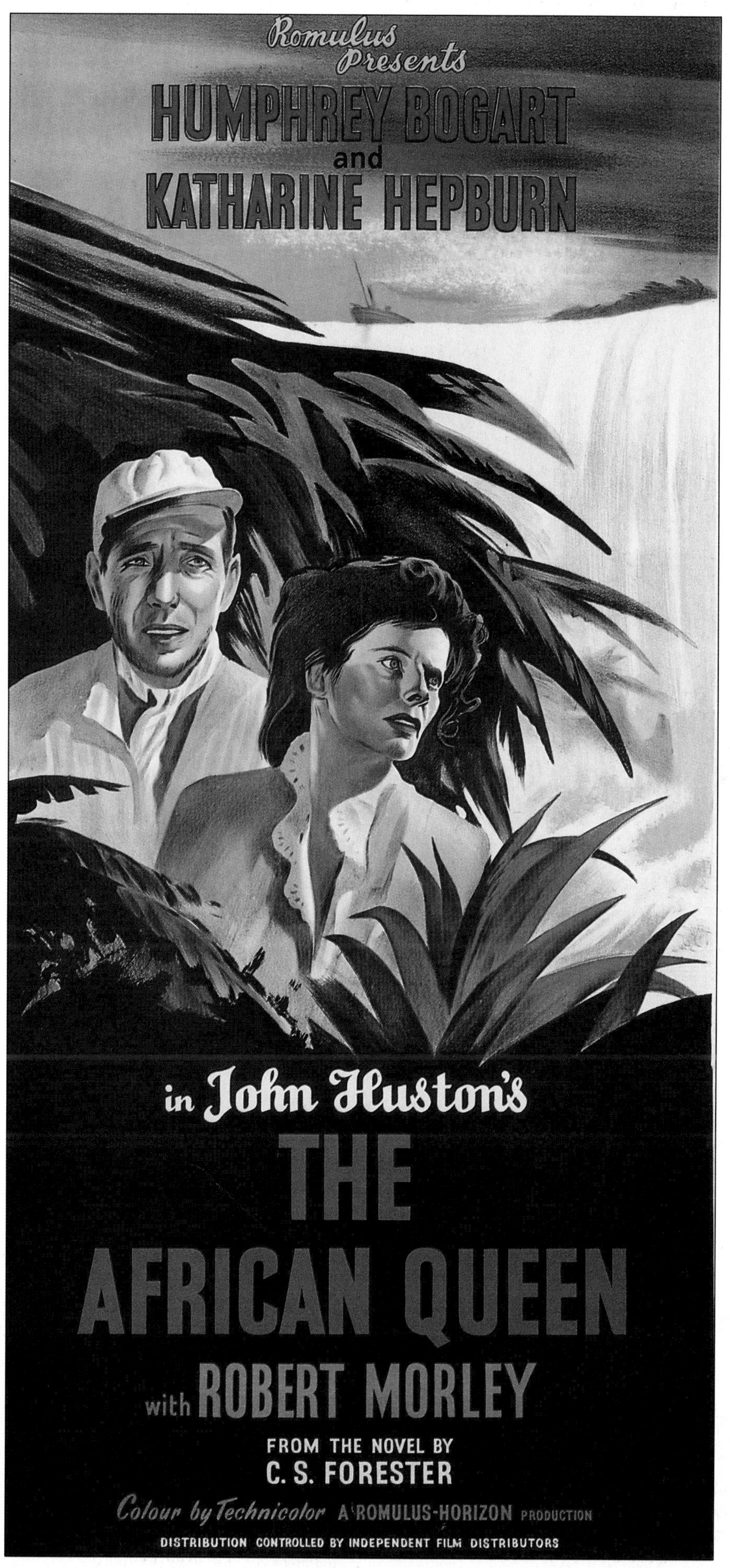
Romulus
Presents
HUMPHREY BOGART
and
KATHARINE HEPBURN
in John Huston's
THE
AFRICAN QUEEN
with ROBERT MORLEY
FROM THE NOVEL BY
C. S. FORESTER
Colour by Technicolor A ROMULUS-HORIZON PRODUCTION
DISTRIBUTION CONTROLLED BY INDEPENDENT FILM DISTRIBUTORS

▷

Bresson conveys the spiritual anguish of Bernanos' country priest

JOURNAL D'UN
CURÉ DE CAMPAGNE
PRIX LOUIS-DELLUC 1950

Claude Laydu and Nicole Ladmiral in ***Diary of a Country Priest.***

Paris, 7 February
Six years after *les Dames du bois de Boulogne*, Robert Bresson is at last presenting audiences with his new movie, *Diary of a Country Priest* (*Journal d'un curé de campagne*). Based on the 1936 novel of the same title by Georges Bernanos, the film recounts, through the pages of a diary, the daily life of a young priest (Claude Laydu), assailed by self-doubt and unable to resolve the problems of his small parish at Ambricourt in the province of the Pas-de-Calais. He ultimately dies alone, painfully of stomach cancer, murmuring "All is Grace." Bresson, who wrote the scrupulously faithful scenario himself, has pushed the austere style of his previous two films to the limit. In fact, not since the films of Carl Dreyer has there been such an uncompromising eye. Bresson's use of non-actors, natural sound, pared-down images and real locations has disconcerted a number of critics. Among them, Ado Kyrou has been the most virulent, fulminating against what he sees as "anti-cinema". Bernanos' spiritual tale seemed an unlikely subject for a motion picture, but Bresson has managed to convey the solitude and inner anguish of the characters by their external behavior and by shots of them in isolation, while using the literary device of the first person narrative or interior dialogue.

Ava Gardner to be Mrs. Frank Sinatra

Philadelphia, 7 March
Frank Sinatra, who divorced Nan Barbato last November, has nc announced that he is to marry A Gardner, whose latest film is Albe Lewin's *Pandora and the Flyi Dutchman*. Ava and Frank got know each other in December 19 and since then have conducted affair interrupted by a succession stimulating scandals. In March 19 the besotted Sinatra fired two pis shots out of the window of the Ho Hampshire in an imaginative ploy convince Ava that he was attemp ing suicide. In May, Frank hurri to Barcelona to prise Ava from t arms of her lover Mario Cab Blows were exchanged between t rivals for Pandora's favors. In Ju the two lovers descended on Lo don, where Ava was presented Queen Elizabeth, who had the go sense to ensure that the brawli singer was not on hand to shatter t calm of the proceedings. In spite these episodes, and other pub spats too numerous to mention, t couple set off today to be married Mexico at the home of theatric agent Lester Sachs.

'All About Eve' takes Oscars in quality year

Hollywood, 29 March
It was hard to say whether the art form being honored at the Oscar ceremonies held at the RKO Pantages Theater was the cinema or the stage. The Best Picture (and the recipient of a record-breaking 14 nominations) was Joseph L. Mankiewicz's brittle comedy-drama of backstage life, *All About Eve*. The film managed to garner both the Best Director and Best Screenplay Oscars (Mankiewicz), as well as Best Supporting Actor, the latter going to George Sanders as the acid-tongued theater critic Addison de Witt. But *Eve*'s star, Bette Davis, lost out to Judy Holliday for her appearance as a dumb blonde turned smart cookie in George Cukor's *Born Yesterday*, adapted from a long-running Broadway play. The film proved no less triumphant for Holliday than the play had done, which could equally apply to Josephine Hull, who was named Best Supporting Actress for her portrayal of James Stewart's dotty sister in *Harvey*. Another film adapted from the stage was *Cyrano de Bergerac* for which José Ferrer obtained the Best Actor prize. The film gave a wider audience a chance to witness his dynamic tragi-comic performance as the long-nosed poet and swordsman, whom Ferrer had played on Broadway.

José Ferrer as ***Cyrano de Bergerac.***

Dmytryk 'confesses' all to U.S. inquisitio

Washington, 25 April
Edward Dmytryk, the only well-known director among the Hollywood Ten, most of them writers who were found guilty of contempt of Congress in 1948, has now recanted and appeared before the HUAC as a "friendly witness". Having served a six-month prison sentence in 1950 and effectively blacklisted by the Hollywood studios, Dmytryk has now attempted to distance himself from the other members of the Hollywood Ten. In this way, he probably hopes to resume his career as a successful director. On his release from jail, he met on a regular basis with a "rehabilitation" committee that included Ronald Reagan and Roy Brewer (the latter representing the newly formed Motion Picture Industry Council), and his current testimony at HUAC's new round of hearings here is the result. Dmytryk, a leading RKO director during the 1940s whose successful works included *Farewell My Lovely* (1944) and *Crossfire* (1947), ironically, indictment of intolerance, went England after the 1947 HUAC he ings and continued work there. the time he returned to the U.S. f sentencing in 1950, he had alrea completed three movies, of whi *Obsession* (1948) with Robert Ne ton is the most interesting.

Edward Dmytryk studying a scrip

annes becomes the festival of springtime

lf Palme and Anita Björk in Alf Sjöberg's version of Strindberg's **Miss Julie**.

annes, 20 April
or the first time, the Cannes Film estival has been held in spring. herefore, it will no longer have to ompete with the Mostra at Venice, hich will continue to take place in e fall. The jury presented their rand Prix jointly to Vittorio De ica's fairy tale *Miracle in Milan* and *Miss Julie*, Alf Sjöberg's adapta- on of the August Strindberg play. The Special Jury Prize was given to Joseph Mankiewicz's *All About Eve*, while Bette Davis was compensated for not winning the Oscar by being named best actress for the same film. England's Michael Redgrave was awarded the best actor prize for *The Browning Version*, and Luis Buñuel was considered the best director for his *The Young and the Damned* (*Los Olvidados*).

Enrico Caruso comes back as Mario Lanza

The great tenor Enrico Caruso (Mario Lanza) giving a concert recital.

New York, 10 May
In his third film for MGM, Mario Lanza stars in *The Great Caruso*, a cliché-clogged biopic about one of opera's immortals with a noticeably portly Lanza warbling away in the title role. As an accurate portrait of Caruso the picture treads a fine line between complete fabrication and total invention, but it has all the makings of a huge box-office hit. Ann Blyth co-stars as Caruso's wife Dorothy Benjamin (his other wife had been written out of the script) and opera fans are treated to a parade of talent which includes not only the treacle-voiced Lanza but also Blanche Thebom, Teresa Celli and Guiseppe Valdengo. All in all, the picture represents a triumph for the engagingly vulgar cultural pretensions of producer Joe Pasternak.

tevens reworks 'An American Tragedy' for Clift and Taylor

ew York, 28 August
irector George Stevens' *A Place in e Sun* is a somewhat portentous make of Theodore Dreiser's *An merican Tragedy*, originally filmed 1931 by Josef von Sternberg. lontgomery Clift is the charming ut weak drifter fatally torn between nderprivileged factory drab Shelley Vinters and rich society beauty Eliz- beth Taylor, and Stevens concen- ates on the romantic aspects of the ory rather than on Dreiser's anat- my of class conflict. The result is a ipping but supremely glossy tear- rker, full of swooning embraces in hich Clift and Taylor melt into ch other in massive close-up. Ulti- ately, the picture is overwhelmed y the technical polish applied by e director, but an excessively drab helley Winters is outstanding, and harlie Chaplin has hailed *A Place the Sun* as the best movie ever to ome out of Hollywood. It already oks like a strong contender for the cademy Awards.

Elizabeth Taylor and Montgomery Clift, beautiful but damned lovers.

Robert Walker dies at age 33

Hollywood, 28 August
Troubled star Robert Walker has died during the filming of Leo McCarey's *My Son John*. Ravaged by the alcoholism which overwhelmed him after his divorce from Barbara Ford, daughter of John Ford, Walker nonetheless turned in a remarkable performance in Alfred Hitchcock's recent *Strangers on a Train*. As the playboy psychopath Bruno Anthony, casually swapping murders with Farley Granger's weak-willed tennis star, Walker painted a disturbing portrait of a demonic hero light years away from the boys next door he played at the beginning of his career. Hitchcock enabled McCarey to finish *My Son John* by turning over out-takes from the final reel of *Strangers on a Train*. So we get to see Bruno Anthony die twice on screen. Walker was married to Jennifer Jones (1939-47) by whom he had two sons.

Japan's finest hour at Venice Film Festival

*Akira Kurosawa's intriguing feudal drama, **Rashomon**, proved a revelation.*

Venice, 1 September
The Venice Film Festival has reaffirmed its international credentials by awarding its Golden Lion prize for the first time to a Japanese film, *Rashomon*, reportedly to the great amazement of its director Akira Kurosawa. His work has been coolly received in Japan but the jury at Venice was unanimous in its praise of the film's visual, narrative and erotic qualities. In *Rashomon* four people involved in a rape-murder give varying accounts of what happened. Its success will open up new markets for Japanese cinema.

Brando's combustible Kowalski on screen

Leigh and Brando unforgettable as Blanche Dubois and Stanley Kowalski.

Los Angeles, 29 September
It has cost Warner Brothers $75,000 to turn Marlon Brando into an international star. That's the fee this graduate of the Actors Studio received to play Stanley Kowalski in Elia Kazan's screen version of Tennessee Williams' play *A Streetcar Named Desire*. Brando, a leadin exponent of the Method school acting, plays the brutish, mumblir Kowalski like a Caliban in a torn shirt, smoldering with sex appeal he circles Vivien Leigh's touching faded Southern belle Blanche D bois. The screenplay, written by Wi liams, makes some concessions censorship but retains the steam atmosphere of the original, in whic Brando was directed by Kazan o Broadway. Born in Omaha, Nebra ka, in 1924, Brando was educated Shattuck Military Academy, fro which he was expelled, and the studied drama in New York. H made his Broadway debut in 194 and two years later was voted Broa way's Most Promising Actor. Aft his triumph in *Streetcar* in 1947, th movies beckoned, and he made h screen debut in 1950 as an embi tered paraplegic in *The Men*.

*Brando in Zinnemann's **The Men**.*

An American called Kelly is let loose in Paris with superb results

New York, 4 October
The inspiration for the sensational new MGM musical, *An American in Paris*, grew from producer Arthur Freed's attending a George Gershwin concert of the title music and wanting to produce a movie set in Paris starring Gene Kelly. He got Vincente Minnelli to direct, and cast French newcomer Leslie Caron. Her classical training and naive charm serves her well, especially in the "Love Is Here To Stay" number, dancing with Kelly on the banks of the Seine. Among other splendid routines is Kelly performing "I Got Rhythm" with a group of street urchins. The film culminates with an 18-minute ballet, in which the city's celebrated landmarks are depicted using the styles of various French painters. *An American in Paris* has brought the art of the film musical to a new high.

Left to right: Alex Romero, Ernie Flatt, Kelly and Dick Humphries in one of the superb dance numbers.

Quo Vadis?' an expensive epic on a grand scale

he might of the Roman Empire has been recreated in spectacular sets.

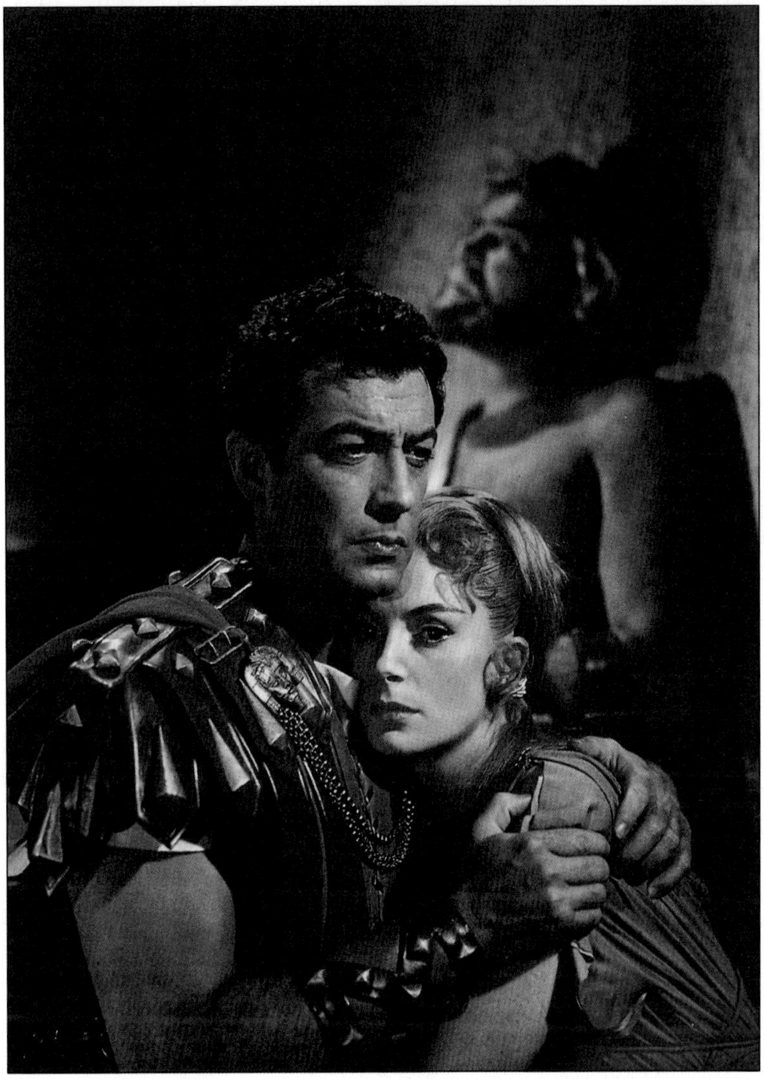

Robert Taylor and Deborah Kerr, the attractive lovers in ***Quo Vadis?***

ew York, 8 November
fter six months of filming in Rome a cost of nearly $7 million, the iggest budget Hollywood movie nce *Gone With the Wind*, the 171-inute Technicolor MGM specta- *Quo Vadis?* was completed and n now be seen on our screens. The ighlights of this picture are the gionnaires' return to the capital, e burning of Rome and the killing the Christians in the arena. There ad been several silent film adapta-ons of the Henryk Sienkiewicz nov-, but Louis B. Mayer dreamed of aking his own version with his udio's vast resources. Two years ago, a company headed by director John Huston and with stars Gregory Peck and Elizabeth Taylor went to Rome to begin shooting, but the production was shut down, with the estimated cost of the debacle set at $2 million. The present second attempt was better budgeted by producer Sam Zimbalist, under trusted director Mervyn LeRoy. This time Robert Taylor and Deborah Kerr costar as the Roman legionnaire and the Christian slave who fall in love, and Peter Ustinov is a raving Nero. *Quo Vadis?* is the first color film to be made at Cinecittà, and it has given a boost to the Italian studio.

Arne Mattsson's *One Summer of Happiness* tells of a youthful love affair that ends in tragedy. The protagonists are played by Folke Sundqvist and Ulla Jacobsson.

Humphrey Bogart and Katharine Hepburn: who would believe it!

New York, 26 December
The extremely unlikely pairing of Humphrey Bogart and Katharine Hepburn in *The African Queen* appears to have come off brilliantly. The title refers to a rusty river steamer that takes the two stars down the Congo river in German East Africa in 1914, but it is also a vehicle that carries them to new heights in what are essentially character parts. Here Bogart is Charlie Allnutt, a scruffy, profane, unshaven, gin-drinking captain of a small trading boat, and Hepburn plays Rose Sayer, a prim, temperance-espousing, scrawny, Bible-quoting spinster missionary. The twosome are thrown together after Hepburn's brother (Robert Morley) is killed by German soldiers, and Bogart persuades her to escape with him. Negotiating rapids, shallows and storms, they finally succeed in blowing up a German gunboat. The director John Huston, who co-wrote the screenplay with James Agee (an adaptation from C.S. Forester's novel), wisely concentrated on the two ripe performances, showing the characters' shared animosity gradually changing into love. Huston has transformed a somewhat improbable adventure-romance, virtually a duologue, into a convincing story of love growing out of shared endurance and delivered with endearing humor. *The African Queen* is the first Technicolor feature for Huston, Bogart and Hepburn, and was actually shot under difficult conditions in the Belgian Congo. Even though Katharine Hepburn contracted a bad case of dysentery, which held up her scenes, she gives one of her most memorable performances.

Charlie Allnutt comforts Rose Sayer.

MOIRA SHEARER · ROBERT HELPMANN · LEONIDE MASSINE
The Tales of Hoffmann
Colour by TECHNICOLOR
CO-STARRING
ROBERT ROUNSEVILLE · PAMELA BROWN
LUDMILLA TCHERINA · ANN AYARS
CONDUCTOR
SIR THOMAS BEECHAM Bart.
WITH
Superb treatment by Powell and Pressburger of Offenbach's fantastical opera.

Daniel Gélin, Anne Vernon in Becker's wicked satire, ***Edward and Caroline.***

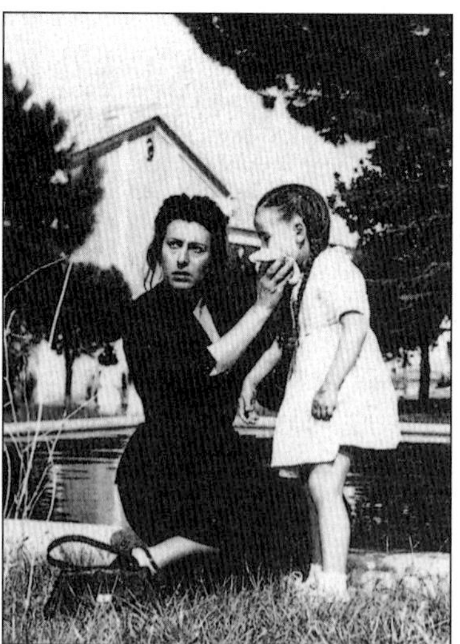
Anna Magnani and Tina Apicella in Luchino Visconti's ***Bellissima.***

FARLEY
GRANG
RUTH
ROMA
ROBERT
WALKE
L'INCONNU
DU
NORD-EXPRESS
French poster for Alfred Hitchcock ***Strangers on a Train.***

Evelyn Keyes and Van Heflin in Joseph Losey's taut thriller, ***The Prowler.***

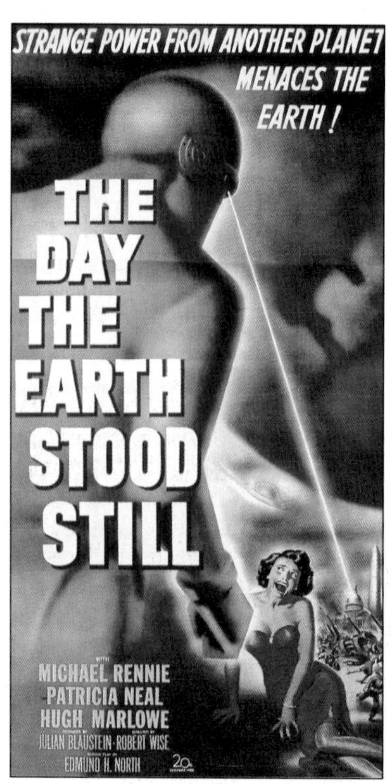
STRANGE POWER FROM ANOTHER PLANET
MENACES THE
EARTH !
THE
DAY
THE
EARTH
STOOD
STILL
MICHAEL RENNIE
PATRICIA NEAL
HUGH MARLOWE
JULIAN BLAUSTEIN · ROBERT WISE
EDMUND H. NORTH
Occupant of a flying saucer brings a dire warning to Washington D.C.

Alec Guinness (l), Stanley Hollow in ***The Lavender Hill Mob.***

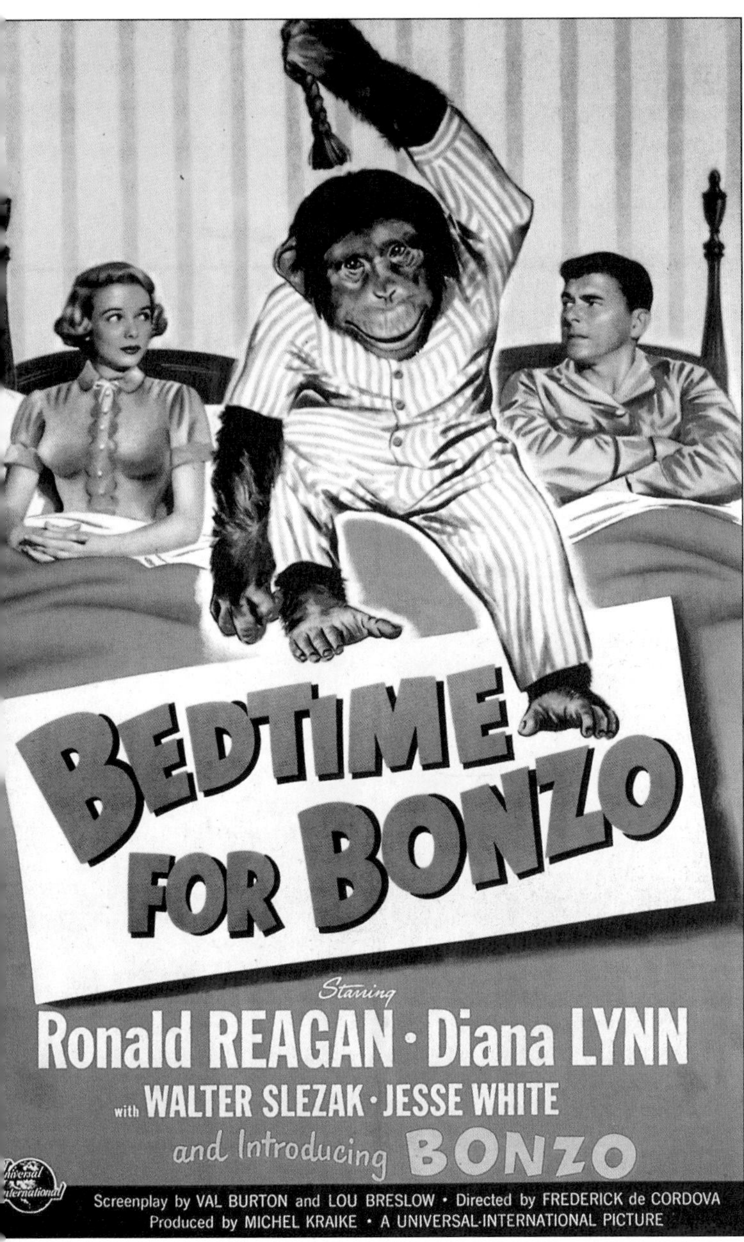
BEDTIME FOR BONZO
Starring
Ronald REAGAN · Diana LYNN
with WALTER SLEZAK · JESSE WHITE
and Introducing BONZO
Screenplay by VAL BURTON and LOU BRESLOW · Directed by FREDERICK de CORDOVA
Produced by MICHEL KRAIKE · A UNIVERSAL-INTERNATIONAL PICTURE

udiences loved Bonzo, the chimp Ronald Reagan reared as a human baby.

Kirk Douglas plays the newsman in Billy Wilder's ***Ace in the Hole*** *aka* ***The Big Carnival****.*

Vivien
LEIGH
Marlon
BRANDO
Un TRAMWAY
nommé
DESIR

The French poster for ***A Streetcar Named Desire****.*

Fredric March triumphed as tragic Willie Loman in ***Death of a Salesman****.*

larilyn Monroe, Albert Dekker in the affable comedy ***As Young as You Feel****.*

JUNE
HAVER
WILLIAM
LUNDIGAN
FRANK
FAY
MARILYN
MONROE
LOVE
NEST
PAAR · JOY
KULKY
JULES BUCK · JOSEPH NEWMAN · I.A.L. DIAMOND

Another frothy, forgettable but fun outing featuring Marilyn Monroe.

Peter Ustinov as the mad Nero and Patricia Laffan in ***Quo Vadis?***

1952

1951 Academy Awards, RKO Pantages Theater, 20 Mar.

Best Film:	*An American in Paris* (dir: Vincente Minnelli)
Best Director:	George Stevens *(A Place in the Sun)*
Best Actor:	Humphrey Bogart *(The African Queen)*
Best Actress:	Vivien Leigh *(A Streetcar Named Desire)*
Best Supp. Actor:	Karl Malden *(A Streetcar Named Desire)*
Best Supp. Actress:	Kim Hunter *(A Streetcar Named Desire)*

Bombay, 24 January
The opening of the Indian International Film Festival marks the first festival of cinema in Asia. Forty feature-length films from 21 countries will be screened.

Paris, 13 February
Jean Gabin and Danielle Darrieux share the top billing in *la Vérité sur Bébé Donge* (*The Truth About Baby Donge*). Darrieux is directed once again by her ex-husband, Henri Decoin, with whom she has made six films in the past.

Hollywood, 5 April
Howard Hughes has announced the temporary closure of RKO Studios to facilitate the dismissal of close to 100 employees suspected of having Communist sympathies.

Washington D.C., 10 April
Today Elia Kazan denounced 15 of his former colleagues to the HUAC. Earlier this year, Kazan had admitted membership of the Communist Party from 1934 to 1936, but had refused to name any of his friends. He claims that his change of heart is due to a new appreciation of the dangers inherent in the Communist doctrine. His recent picture *Viva Zapata!*, with Marlon Brando, is openly anti-Communist.

Tokyo, 24 April
Completed in August 1945, Akira Kurosawa's film, *The Men Who Tread on the Tiger's Tail*, is only now released in Japan, as the American Army censors had prohibited it because of its feudal ideology.

Washington D.C., 25 May
The Supreme Court has delivered a unanimous verdict in favor of the distributor of Rossellini's film *The Miracle*. The Court ruled that the cinema has the right to constitutional guarantees protecting freedom of expression. Until now, the law has regarded the cinema as "a purely commercial venture".

New York, 1 July
The new projection system known as Cinerama was put on display for the first time last night before an invited audience at the Broadway Theater. Thrills and scenic wonders combine to impressive effect on this sweeping wide-angle (146 degree) screen which is also higher than ordinary screens, and added impact is provided by "stereophonic" sound. The tri-panel panoramic picture is thrown from three projectors but looks like a single picture.

Mexico, 14 July
Luis Buñuel has begun shooting *Robinson Crusoe*, from the novel by Daniel Defoe, with Dan O'Herlihy. Produced by Oscar Dancigers, it is Buñuel's first feature film in color.

Quebec, 21 August
Alfred Hitchcock begins shooting for *I Confess*, starring Montgomery Clift in the role of a priest.

Venice, 1 September
At this year's festival here, the Golden Lion has been won by René Clément for *Jeux interdits* (*Forbidden Games*), while Fredric March won the Volpi award for best actor for *Death of a Salesman*. The jury's special prize went to a French cartoon by Paul Grimault, *la Bergère et le ramoneur*, from a script by Jacques Prévert. No prize was given to an actress this year.

London, 4 September
Opening of *Operation Burma*. The controversial film was accused of being a travesty of the Burma campaign by the British. It was taken off a week after its opening in 1945.

Washington D.C., 19 September
James McGranery, U.S. Attorney General, has announced that he has ordered the immigration services to refuse Charles Chaplin entry to America until the conclusions of the inquiry into his political activities are known.

London, 23 September
Charlie Chaplin has been warmly welcomed by his countrymen on his return to England with his wife and family after a 21-year absence.

London, 9 October
Gala premiere at the Empire Theatre in Leicester Square of David Lean's semi-documentary British film, *The Sound Barrier*.

Paris, 15 October
The 87-year-old actress formerly known as Jehanne d'Alcy and now Madame Charlotte Méliès, widow of Georges Méliès, appears in some scenes in Georges Franju's documentary film *le Grand Méliès* (*The Great Méliès*).

Germany, 1 November
Charlie Chaplin has refused to allow *Limelight* to be distributed here unless German audiences are first able to see *The Great Dictator*.

London, 23 November
French actress Edwige Feuillère has been elected "Star of Stars" by *The Sunday Graphic*.

Hollywood, 28 November
The Hollywood premiere of Arch Oboler's much advertised 3-D film *Bwana Devil*, which co-stars Robert Stack and Barbara Britton, brought screams from the audience as a lion appeared to leap from the screen. The audience wore polaroid glasses to obtain the full 3-D effect.

London, 1 December
Serge Reggiani, Claude Dauphin and Simone Signoret are in the British capital to dub Jacques Becker's film *Golden Marie* (*Casque d'or*) themselves.

Hollywood, 20 December
Opening of Harry Horner's anti-Communist, science fiction film called *Red Planet Mars*, in which two scientists, an American and a German, captured by the Soviets, must persuade the Martians to incite revolution in the United States.

Paris, 21 December
Eighteen-year-old actress Brigitte Bardot married director Roger Vadim in a civil ceremony yesterday. The couple will celebrate a religious ceremony in the parish church in Passy today.

BIRTHS

Paris, 27 March
Maria Schneider

Paris, 15 April
Josiane Balasko

Ireland, 7 June
Liam Neeson

France, 16 June
Michel Blanc

Rome, 18 June
Isabella Rossellini

Rome, 18 June
Ingrid Rossellini

Missouri, 20 June
John Goodman

Canada, 1 July
Dan Aykroyd

Chicago, 21 July
Robin Williams

Texas, 18 August
Patrick Swayze

New York, 27 August
Pee Wee Herman
(Paul Rubens)

New Jersey, 22 September
Paul Le Mat

New York, 25 September
Christopher Reeve

Holland, 28 September
Sylvia Kristel

Pittsburgh, 22 October
Jeff Goldblum

DEATHS

New York, 8 May
William Fox

New York, 21 May
John Garfield

Hollywood, 27 October
Hattie McDaniel

Twelve years after its launch, t… Tom and Jerry cartoons continue … delight. This year's ***Smitten Kitt…*** *uses a series of flashbacks to previo… amorous adventures enjoyed by To…*

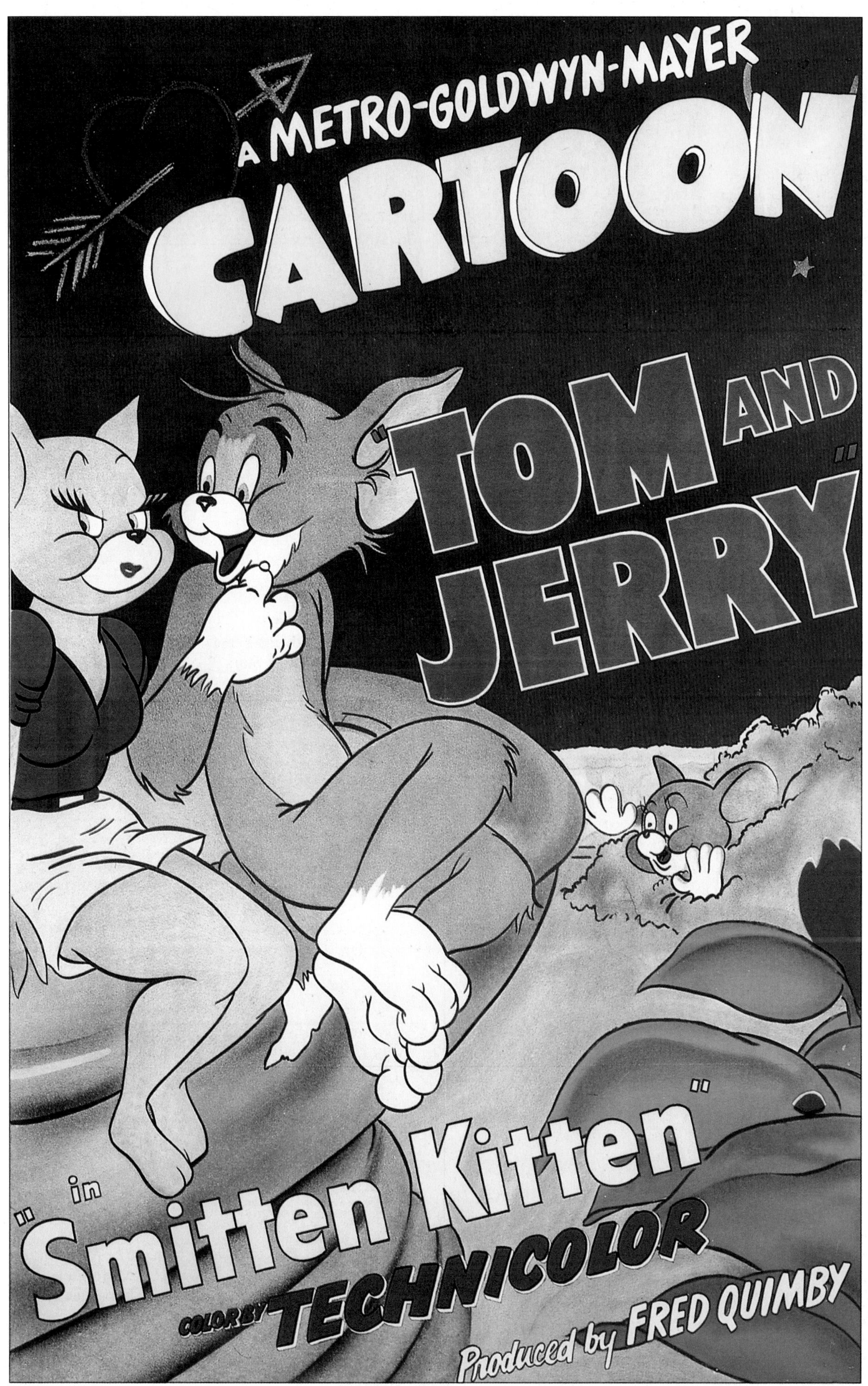
A METRO-GOLDWYN-MAYER
CARTOON
"TOM AND JERRY"
in
"Smitten Kitten"
COLOR BY TECHNICOLOR
Produced by FRED QUIMBY

Life under the big top with Cecil B. DeMille

Cornel Wilde is the male trapeze artist in **The Greatest Show on Earth**.

Hollywood, 2 January
Cecil B. DeMille has lost none of his cinematic swagger. With his latest, *The Greatest Show on Earth*, he has proved that there's still a market for 24-karat hokum. With the help of the Ringling Brothers & Barnum & Bailey Circuses, an all-star cast goes over the top in the big top. Here James Stewart plays the clown who hides his criminal past beneath several layers of makeup, Cornel Wilde is the daredevil aerialist the Great Sebastian, and Betty Hutton is the woman who loves and loses him. Newcomer Charlton Heston is the hard-driving manager. There's a spectacular train crash and surprise appearances by Dorothy Lamour, Bob Hope and Bing Crosby.

Swashbuckling Philipe is Fanfan-tastic

Italy's voluptuous Gina Lollobrigida.

GERARD PHILIPE
GINA LOLLOBRIGIDA
Fanfan la Tulipe
CHRISTIAN-JAQUE

This French poster conveys the r
mantic atmosphere of adventure.

Paris, 20 March
A mischievous, lively and seductive Gérard Philipe swashbuckles his merry way through *Fanfan the Tulip*, his third outing under director Christian-Jaque. Here Philipe, as the happy-go-lucky Fanfan, is persuaded to join the army of Louis XV by the recruiting officer's daughter (the voluptuous Gina Lollobrigida). No sooner is he made a soldier th
he rescues the king's daughter a
Madame Pompadour from coa
robbers. Almost single-handedly d
feating the Austrian army, Fanf
then realizes all his dreams. Th
satire on Douglas Fairbanks-sty
films and historical romance kee
up a rapid pace without sacrifici
characterization or wit.

Tawdry truths lurk beneath the glamorous surface of Hollywood

Hollywood, 15 January
Vincente Minnelli's *The Bad and the Beautiful* paints a dyspeptic picture of Hollywood as seen through the career of ambitious producer Kirk Douglas and his relations with fading star Lana Turner, writer Dick Powell and director Barry Sullivan. Turner's role does invite comparison with the turbulent trajectory of Diana Barrymore, daughter of the Great Profile, John Barrymore. Her puffball blonde vulnerability is ruthlessly exploited by Douglas, who predictably moves into overdrive as a prince of heels. Turner's careering car ride when she realizes that Douglas does not really love her is an explosion of emotion, full of delirious camera movement, well-judged bursts of light, deafening music and rapid editing. With this brilliantly controlled melodrama, Minnelli has temporarily abandoned the musicals so closely associated with him for a film of penetrating psychological insight in which individual stories are linked together by his fluid visual style. Outstanding in a supporting role is Gloria Grahame, who narrowly escaped being trampled to death by Lyle Bettger's elephants in *The Greatest Show on Earth* and is now cast as the irritating Southern belle, bored with the pipe-sucking screenwriter Dick Powell, and consoling herself with Gilbert Roland. A replica Oscar seen in the office of studio boss Walter Pidgeon suggests that Minnelli is slyly dropping a broad hint to the Academy.

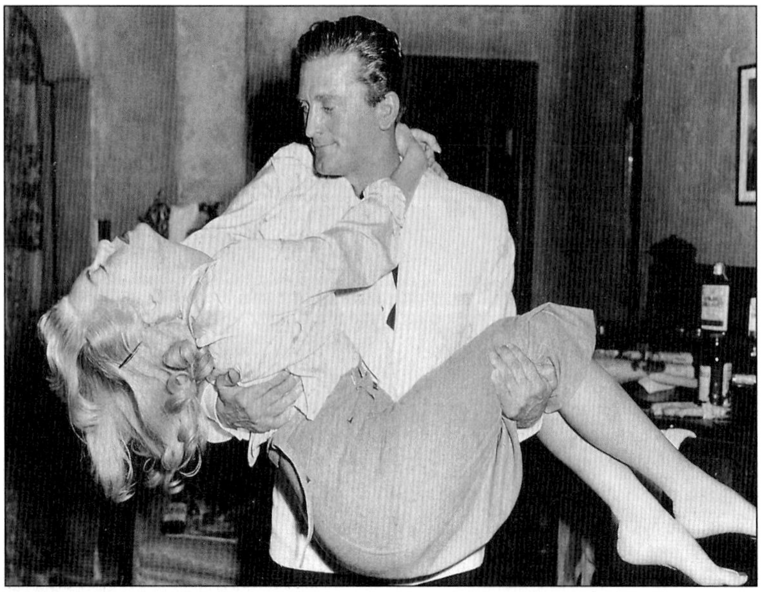

Kirk Douglas and Lana Turner in Minnelli's biting view of Hollywood.

Ronald Reagan marries Nancy Davi

Hollywood, 4 March
Ronald Reagan, who divorced Ja
Wyman in 1948, has now marri
another but less well-known actres
Nancy Davis. Reagan, who is al
known as "Dutch" to his friend
met Davis on the Warner lot. Th
fact that she was an MGM contra
player was no bar to romance, and
seems that it was a case of love
first sight for the president of t
Screen Actors Guild. But Reagan
romantic and political achievemen
have not recently been matched b
his acting career, which has bee
confined to B-pictures like his lates
She's Working Her Way Throu
College, directed by second-featu
workhorse H. Bruce Humberston
It's a musical remake of the 194
The Male Animal, that has Virgin
Mayo hogging the limelight as
burlesque queen with aspirations
be a serious actress. Reagan pla
the college professor who gets into
tangle with spouse Phyllis Thaxt
when he unwisely befriends Mayo

oyous musical journey back to early Hollywood

ne Kelly, literally singing and dancing in the rain, in the film's title number.

Gorgeous, leggy Cyd Charisse partners Kelly in the major production numbers.

ollywood, 27 March
ne dazzling new MGM musical, *ngin' in the Rain*, has everything – eat songs, splendid dances, a won-rful cast, a terrific nostalgia story d hilarious comedy routines, all cily co-directed by its star Gene elly, and Stanley Donen. Screen-iters Adolph Green and Betty omden had the ingenious idea of aking a Hollywood musical about e motion picture industry's pain- transition to sound. Months were ent in research to get the feel of e era, and the creators even use some of the original cameras and sound equipment in this picture, while Walter Plunkett's costumes wittily and accurately conjure up the flapper period. It is 1927, and Don Lockwood (Kelly) and Lina Lamont (Jean Hagen) are the greatest stars of the silent cinema, but when the talkies come in, it is discovered that Lina has a high-pitched screechy voice. The screen love team seems doomed, until along comes dancer-singer and would-be serious actress Kathy Selden (Debbie Reynolds), who agrees to dub the bitchy Lina's voice. At the finale, when the truth is finally revealed, Don and Kathy become the new stellar team at Monumental Pictures.

Singin' in the Rain cost $2.5 million, but it was worth every cent. The climactic "Broadway Rhythm" ballet, which took up a fifth of the budget, shows Kelly as a hick hoofer arriving in the big city chanting, "gotta sing, gotta dance." He does certainly get his chance in this routine, dancing with the seductive Cyd Charisse, and also in the liberating title number. As the rain pelts down, Kelly, in love, dispenses with his umbrella, and "laughing at clouds, way up in the sky" does literally the splashiest dance ever committed to film. Other high spots include Donald O'Connor's dynamic "Make 'em Laugh" number, the cheery matinal greeting "Good Morning" delivered by Kelly, Reynolds and O'Connor, and the touching lyrical duet, "You Were Meant For Me". All the songs in this affectionate spoof were written by Arthur Freed and Nacio Herb Brown, aptly dating from an earlier period.

rthur Freed and his musicals are honored

ollywood, 20 March
ne audience at the 24th Academy ward ceremony, held at the RKO ntages Theater, was taken com-etely by surprise when Ronald olman announced that the Best cture prize had been awarded to *n American in Paris*, over the clear vorites *A Streetcar Named Desire* d *A Place in the Sun*. This notable cognition of the Vincente Minnelli-rected Gene Kelly musical is due ainly to the efforts of the MGM oducer Arthur Freed. A master of e genre, Freed was honored with e Irving G. Thalberg Memorial ward for his many superb musical oductions, which include *Babes in rms*, *Cabin in the Sky*, *Meet Me in . Louis*, *Ziegfeld Follies*, *Easter rade* and *On the Town*. A great dge of talent, former songwriter reed has always managed to gather quality directors and artists around him. *An American in Paris* not only captured the biggest award of the evening, but also won five further Oscars (for Story and Screenplay, Color Cinematography, Color Art Direction, Color Costume Design and Best Score for a Musical Motion Picture). Both of the dramas beaten by the musical were compensated when George Stevens gained the Best Director prize for *A Place in the Sun*, and *A Streetcar Named Desire* won three of the four acting awards (Vivien Leigh, Karl Malden and Kim Hunter). It was Humphrey Bogart who came along on the outside to take the Best Actor Oscar for his drunken, grizzled boat captain in John Huston's *The African Queen*. *Quo Vadis?* was the big loser, having been nominated for eight Oscars and yet coming away empty-handed.

Mizoguchi elevates the suffering of women

Tokyo, 3 April
The 52-year-old Japanese film director Kenji Mizoguchi, a number of whose previous pictures had been flops, risked everything to make *The Life of O-Haru*, an adaptation from Saikaku's classic picaresque novel. It must surely be that the quality of the film will finally mark this director's recognition in the West since it tells a universal story of women's suffering. O-Haru (Kinuyo Tanaka, a great performance), the daughter of a samurai, falls in love with a man from a lower social class (Toshiro Mifune). After he is beheaded, she is forced to become the mistress of the head of a great clan in order to bear him an heir. Her duty done, she is dismissed from the palace, and then descends from marriage to a poor merchant, who is later killed, to becoming a beggar and a prostitute. Without sentimentality or moralizing, Mizoguchi watches the various moments of crisis and violence from a discreet distance, deepening our sympathy for the characters.

Kinuyo Tanaka is the tragic O-Haru.

Musical biopic a tribute to singer's courage

Susan Hayward as Jane Froman.

New York, 4 April
Susan Hayward, one of the gutsiest leading ladies in Hollywood, is in top form in Fox's new tearjerking musical biopic, *With a Song in My Heart*. Hayward stars as singer Jane Froman, whose career was nearly wrecked by a wartime air crash that left her crippled. Much of the film is devoted to Froman's courageous battle to recover, with Hayward giving the punchiest performance in a musical since James Cagney ran wild in *Yankee Doodle Dandy*. The songs, including the splendid rendition of the title number, have been dubbed by Froman, and the skillful musical direction and choreography are, respectively, by Alfred Newman and Billy Daniels. David Wayne and Rory Calhoun portray the men in Froman's life, and the gravel-voiced Thelma Ritter is fourth-billed as the woman who nursed the singer back to health, in the process becoming a lifelong friend. Also making an impression as a handsome young paratrooper suffering from shellshock is newcomer Robert Wagner, who made his screen debut in 1950 in *The Halls of Montezuma*.

Zinnemann follows new trail with Wester

Newcomer Grace Kelly and veteran Gary Cooper, man and wife in ***High Noc***

Hollywood, 24 July
Gary Cooper has brought a poor run of films to an end with his performance in Fred Zinnemann's challenging Western *High Noon*. He is Sheriff Will Kane, the retiring lawman, troubled, decent and showing his age, who has to buckle on his gunbelt one last time to deal single-handedly with the return of an old enemy, Frank Miller, and his gang. It's Kane's wedding day, and Tex Ritter's plaintive singing of the Dimitri Tiomkin-Ned Washington ballad "Do Not Forsake Me, Oh My Darling" provides a haunti background to the action, whi unfolds in "real time". Grace Ke plays his Quaker bride, and the are strong supporting performanc from Katie Jurado as an old flan and Lloyd Bridges as Kane's co ardly deputy. A debate is raging Hollywood now about the deep message of the film. Liberals clai that the picture, with its pessimis view of civic responsibility during crisis, is a metaphor for the Ame can public's failure to unite again the ravages of McCarthyism.

Children of war play forbidden games

Georges Poujouly and Brigitte Fossey in ***Jeux interdits (Forbidden Games).***

Paris, 9 May
In 1940, as refugees flee from the Germans, an orphaned five-year-old girl and the young son of a peasant family who takes her in, build a cemetery for animals, stealing crosses from the churchyard to do so. This is the basis for René Clément's new film, *Forbidden Games* (*Jeux interdits*), a moving document about the effects of war on children. At its center are wonderfully natural performances from little Brigitte Fossey and young Georges Poujouly.

Don Camillo and Peppone, tender enemie

Paris, 4 June
With his *The Little World of Don Camillo*, director Julien Duvivier provides a treat for lovers of warm-hearted comedy and of Fernandel. He plays Giovanni Guareschi's creation, the scheming country priest who conducts conversations with God as well as a running feud with the local Communist mayor, Gino Cervi. They declare a truce to help a modern Romeo and Juliet, Franco Interlenghi and Vera Talqui.

Fernandel (left) and Gino Cervi.

haplin's 'Limelight' buries laughter under tears

ith his young co-star Claire Bloom.

ndon, 23 October
arles Chaplin's *Limelight* has its rld premiere today at the Odeon ema, Leicester Square. This is a eply personal film in which Chap- slips back into the Edwardian sic hall of his youth to bring us lvero, the broken-down comedian o nurses a young, paralyzed ballerina back to health. Poignant reminders of Chaplin's past include the appearance of his one-time leading lady Edna Purviance as an extra, and a brief, brilliant double-act with his great silent rival Buster Keaton. The crippled dancer Terry is touchingly played by 21-year-old British actress Claire Bloom. The premiere has been accompanied by a political storm. Two weeks after he sailed for Britain with his wife and four children, the U.S. Attorney General, James McGranery, announced that Chaplin would be required to face a hearing if he opted to return to the United States, as he was suspected of being a member of the Communist Party who displayed a "leering, sneering" attitude toward America. Chaplin's socialist beliefs, successive scandals, and his refusal to take out U.S. citizenship, have provided his enemies with the pretext to exclude him from America.

In the character of Calvero, Charlie Chaplin finds inspiration in his own past.

rawford, Palance chill in nerve-jangler

w York, 7 August
r several years Joan Crawford s been stalking grimly into middle e, seemingly determined to play th the male and female leads in r movies. And young men have come figures of menace in her ctures, not the least of which is ck Palance in her latest, *Sudden ar*. Palance, whose strikingly taut atures are the result of wartime astic surgery, is cast as wealthy playwright Crawford's sponging husband, plotting with floozy Gloria Grahame to bump her off. Crawford stumbles on their scheme, and her attempt to use her dramatist's skills to try turning the tables on the unlovely couple lead to a crackling climax in a suspenser tightly orchestrated by the director David Miller. Palance made an impressive movie debut in 1950 as the plague-carrying criminal in *Panic in the Streets*.

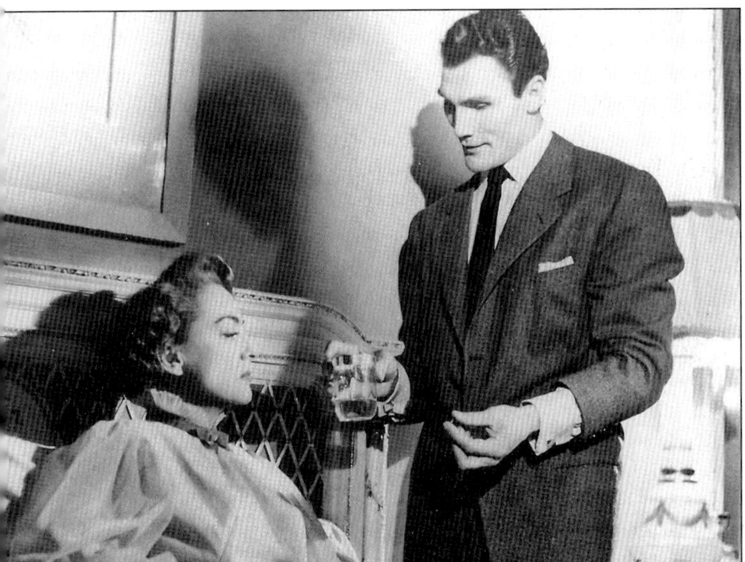

ould she trust him? Joan Crawford and Jack Palance in a tense moment.

Julie Harris a poignant wedding guest

Los Angeles, 24 December
The Member of the Wedding, Carson McCullers' tender and haunting novel about the loneliness and confusion of an adolescent girl in the Deep South, comes to the screen, using the Broadway cast from the play version. Directed with absolute fidelity to the material by Fred Zinnemann, this tale of a motherless girl, whose only companions are the family cook (Ethel Waters) and her small cousin (Brandon De Wilde), and who wants to accompany her brother on his honeymoon, marks the screen debut of Julie Harris. The 22-year-old Miss Harris, waif-like and brilliant, is memorable as 12-year-old Frankie. Filmed in Colusa, a small town in California built by Southerners, the atmosphere is authentic. Already dismissed as "art house" by certain critics, the movie is a gem for the discriminating.

Julie Harris (left) in ***The Member of the Wedding****, here with Ethel Waters.*

M·G·M's Gay TECHNICOLOR Musical!
The Belle of New York
Starring
FRED ASTAIRE
VERA-ELLEN
HEAR THE STARS SING THE HITS IN THE M-G-M RECORDS ALBUM

Memorable for Astaire and Vera-Ellen's pas de deux over New York's rooftops.

Marlon Brando (left) as the Mexican revolutionary in Kazan's **Viva Zapata**.

The Importance of Being Earnest: Edith Evans' Lady Bracknell.

Marlene
DIETRICH
Arthur
KENNEDY
Mel
FERRER
FRITZ LANG
RANCHO
NOTORIOU
TECHNICOLOR

German poster for Hollywood's Fr
Lang-directed Dietrich vehicle.

What a Glorious Feeling
SINGIN' IN THE RAIN
MGM's TECHNICOLOR MUSICAL TREASURE
Starring
GENE KELLY
DONALD O'CONNOR
DEBBIE REYNOLDS
HEAR THE STARS SING THE HITS IN THE M-G-M RECORDS ALBUM
with
JEAN HAGEN · MILLARD MITCHELL and CYD CHARISSE
Story and Screen Play by BETTY COMDEN and ADOLPH GREEN
Lyrics by ARTHUR FREED · Music by NACIO HERB BROWN · Directed by GENE KELLY and STANLEY DONEN · Produced by ARTHUR FREED

Great talent from all MGM departments made this the best musical this ye

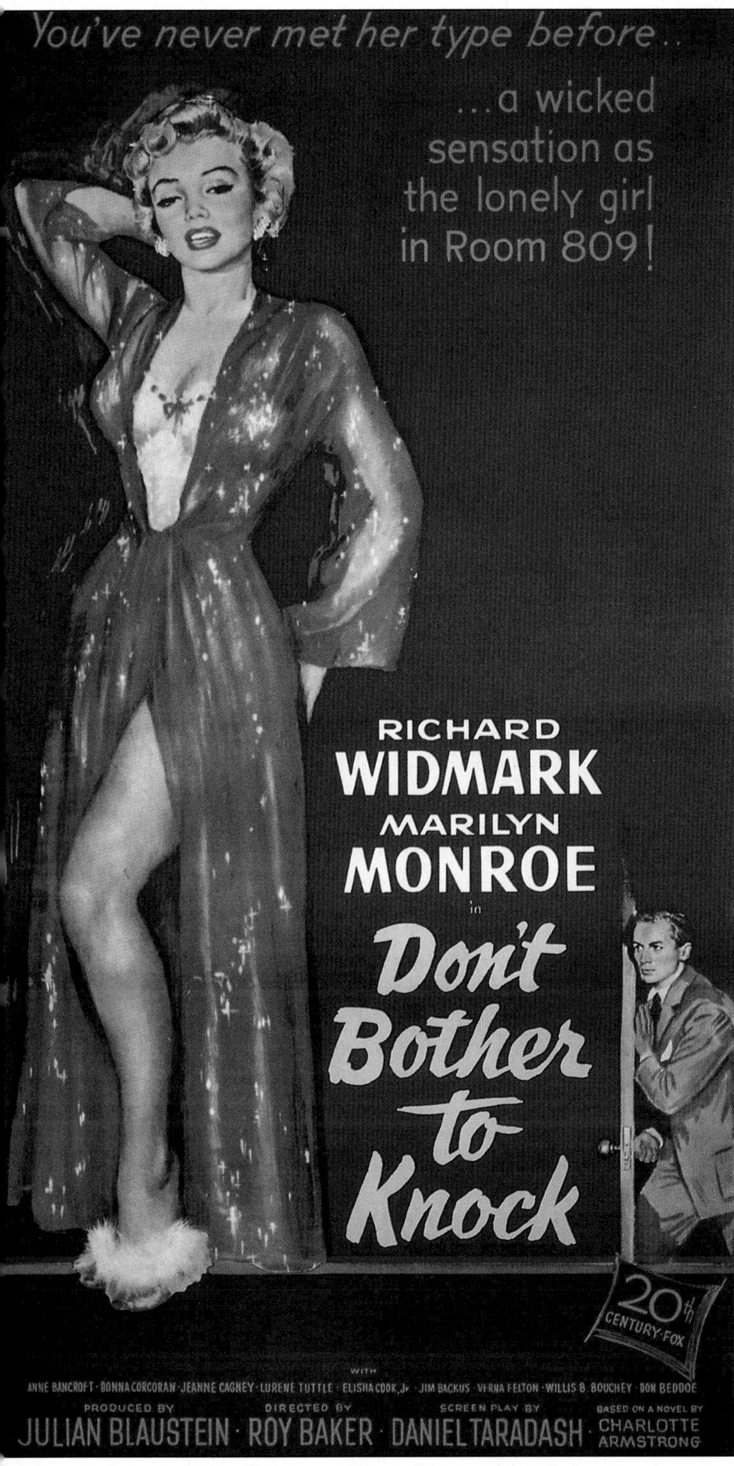
You've never met her type before...
...a wicked sensation as the lonely girl in Room 809!
RICHARD WIDMARK
MARILYN MONROE
in
Don't Bother to Knock
20th CENTURY-FOX
WITH
ANNE BANCROFT · DONNA CORCORAN · JEANNE CAGNEY · LURENE TUTTLE · ELISHA COOK, Jr. · JIM BACKUS · VERNA FELTON · WILLIS B. BOUCHEY · DON BEDDOE
PRODUCED BY JULIAN BLAUSTEIN · DIRECTED BY ROY BAKER · SCREEN PLAY BY DANIEL TARADASH · BASED ON A NOVEL BY CHARLOTTE ARMSTRONG

arilyn Monroe surprisingly cast as a sexy but psychotic baby sitter.

aniel Gélin (left) and Jean Servais in Max Ophuls' ***House of Pleasure****.*

Zsa Zsa Gabor, José Ferrer and Suzanne Flon in ***Moulin Rouge****.*

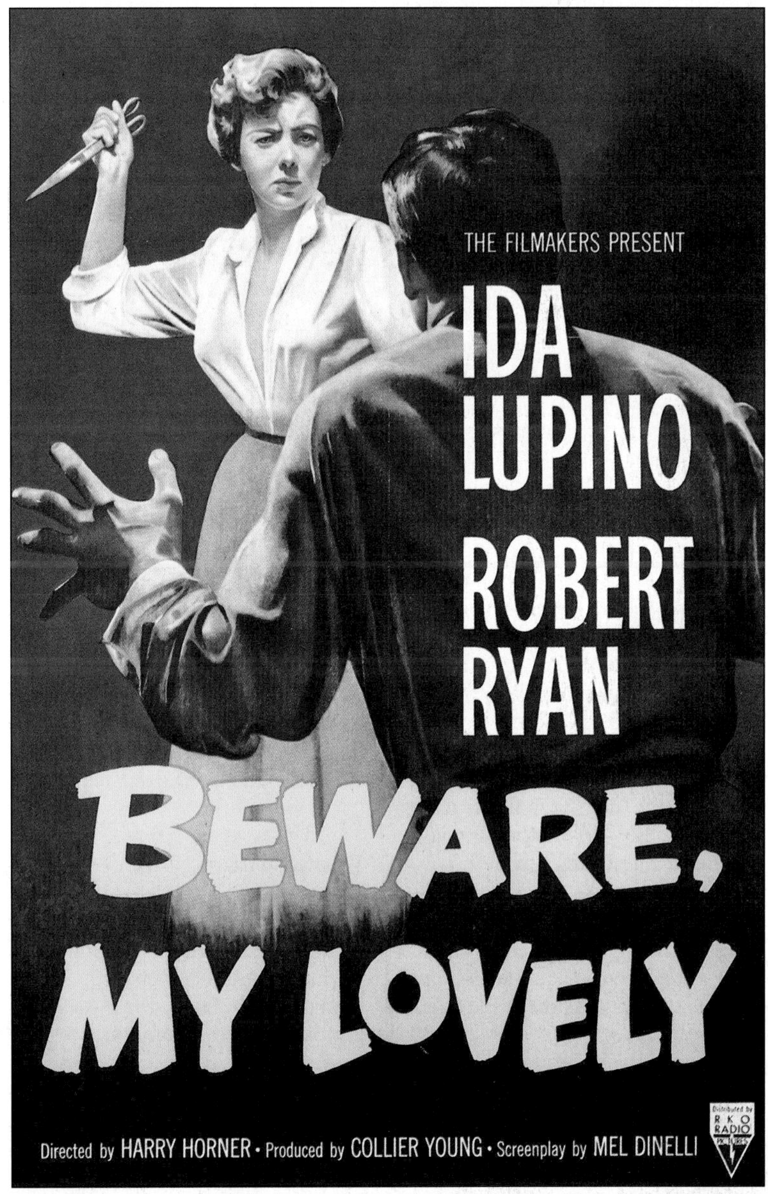
THE FILMAKERS PRESENT
IDA LUPINO
ROBERT RYAN
BEWARE, MY LOVELY
Directed by HARRY HORNER · Produced by COLLIER YOUNG · Screenplay by MEL DINELLI
RKO RADIO

Noir thriller wasted talents of Lupino and, as a deranged handyman, Ryan.

1953

1952 Academy Awards, RKO Pantages Theater, 19 March	
Best Film:	*The Greatest Show on Earth* (dir: Cecil B. DeMille)
Best Director:	John Ford *(The Quiet Man)*
Best Actor:	Gary Cooper *(High Noon)*
Best Actress:	Shirley Booth *(Come Back, Little Sheba)*
Best Supp. Actor:	Anthony Quinn *(Viva Zapata!)*
Best Supp. Actress:	Gloria Grahame *(The Bad and the Beautiful)*

Rome, 8 January
Opening of Roberto Rossellini's *Europa 51* with Ingrid Bergman, Alexander Knox and Giulietta Masina; this is the second Bergman-Rossellini collaboration.

Paris, 16 January
Marcel Pagnol's latest film *Manon des Sources*, is a wonderfully told story of fortitude and revenge. The cast is headed by Jacqueline Pagnol, Rellys and Henri Poupon.

Hollywood, 1 February
Twentieth Century-Fox has announced that all its films will now be made in CinemaScope. The studio recently bought up the rights for the wide-screen process from French inventor and optical scientist, Henri Chrétien.

London, 11 February
As part of a festival of French films here in the capital, René Clair's *les Belles de nuit* (*Night Beauties*) is to be shown in the presence of Queen Elizabeth II.

New York, 19 February
The much publicized *Bwana Devil*, made in 3-D by Arch Oboler on a shoestring budget as an experimental venture, has opened here. The film, which caused a furor at its Hollywood premiere last year, has been somewhat loosely called "the *Jazz Singer* of 3-D". However, several critics have voiced doubts as to whether this new technique really enhances the artistic or dramatic quality of motion pictures.

Hollywood, 5 March
Screenwriter Herman J. Mankiewicz, the brother of director Joseph L. Mankiewicz, has died. He wrote numerous screenplays and adaptations and was largely responsible for the Academy Award-winning screenplay of *Citizen Kane*, which he wrote in collaboration with Orson Welles. He was also an executive producer of several films in the 1930s.

Paris, 13 March
Eisenstein's *The Battleship Potemkin* is finally seeing a general release. Made in 1925, the film remained banned in France due to political censorship; until now it has only been shown in cinema clubs.

Hollywood, 18 March
MGM has decided not to develop its own system of wide-screen filming but rather to use the CinemaScope process under license from Fox.

Paris, 24 March
Orson Welles has appeared before the Board of Arbitration at the request of set designer Alexandre Trauner, who claims two million francs are owed to him for his work on the sets for Welles' *Othello*.

Mexico, 3 April
Gérard Philipe has arrived in Alvaro for the filming of Yves Allégret's *les Orgueilleux* (*The Proud Ones*). His co-star Michèle Morgan will join him there.

New York, 25 April
The press and trade were invited to a demonstration of 20th Century-Fox CinemaScope, the wide-screen projection system supplemented by stereophonic sound, in the Roxy Theater this morning. Trailers of forthcoming Fox films were shown on a screen measuring 65 by 25 feet. A tribute was paid to Henri Chrétien who perfected the anamorphic lens used for the process.

Washington D.C., 7 May
The producer Robert Rossen, who has previously refused to speak at the HUAC hearings, now admits to having been a member of the Communist Party from 1937 to 1947, and has named 57 others.

Los Angeles, 4 June
Opening of Joseph Mankiewicz's *Julius Caesar* from the Shakespeare play, with Marlon Brando, James Mason and John Gielgud.

Hollywood, 5 June
Entertainer Dooley Wilson, best known for performing "As Time Goes By" in response to Ingrid Bergman's "Play it again Sam..." in *Casablanca*, has died.

Paris, 1 July
The French-born Hollywood star, Claudette Colbert, is in Paris to make her first French film, Sacha Guitry's *Si Versailles m'était conté* (*Royal Affairs in Versailles*).

London, 8 July
René Clément is shooting *Monsieur Ripois* with Gérard Philipe. Clément and his British cameraman, Oswald Morris, are filming as much as possible in street locations here.

Paris, 14 July
Abel Gance, assisted by Argentinian journalist Nelly Kaplan, whom he met at Cannes, is filming the 14th of July celebrations in the capital in Eastmancolor using the Polyvision multiple-image process and stereophonic sound.

Paris, 9 August
American producer Samuel Goldwyn has organized a pre-release screening of his latest film, *Hans Christian Andersen*, from director Charles Vidor.

Turin, 7 September
Lana Turner has married for the fourth time. Her new husband is the former screen Tarzan, Lex Barker. Miss Turner is reported to have fainted during the wedding service.

Hollywood, 12 September
Lewis Stone died of a heart attack today. Stone, a matinee idol on Broadway, made his screen debut in 1915. He will be remembered for his portrayal of Judge Hardy in the "Andy Hardy" film series.

Stockholm, 14 September
Ingmar Bergman's *Gycklarnas Afton* (*Sawdust and Tinsel*) with Ake Grönberg and Harriet Andersson which opens today, is a sad tale set in a shabby touring circus.

Hollywood, 25 September
Alfred Hitchcock has finished filming *Dial M for Murder*, adapted from the stage success of the same name and starring Ray Milland, Grace Kelly and Robert Cummings.

New York, 9 October
John Ford's new film, *Mogamb* with Clark Gable, Ava Gardner a Grace Kelly, opens today. Kel who plays the role originally offer to Gene Tierney in this jungle r mance, confesses she made the fil for three reasons: Ford, Gable a a trip to Africa.

Hollywood, 11 November
According to a report prepared f the Screen Actors Guild, which re resents over 8,000 professional p formers, movie production is at "all-time low". The report, furthe more, states that it sees little ho for immediate improvement. T preoccupation with new, expensi film technology and an increase overseas production were blam for the slump here. Directors ha pledged to fight against inroads "runaway foreign film production and "to promote additional produ tion" in America.

Washington D.C., 25 November
The Library of Congress has issu two supplementary volumes of Catalogue of Copyright Entries. A films registered for copyright fro 1894 through 1949 is listed. T complete publication now, appa ently, runs to a daunting and im pressive 76,000 titles.

BIRTHS

Arkansas, 8 February
Mary Steenburgen

California, 10 September
Amy Irving

Wisconsin, 6 December
Tom Hulce

Georgia, 8 December
Kim Basinger

New Jersey, 9 December
John Malkovich

DEATHS

Hollywood, 5 June
William Farnum

***The Robe**, from the novel by Lloyd Douglas, marks a new advance technology: CinemaScope. The fil is directed by Henry Koster for Fo who are promoting this process.*

20th CENTURY-FOX'S
The Robe
TECHNICOLOR
The First Motion Picture In
CINEMASCOPE
The Modern Miracle You See Without Glasses!
STARRING
RICHARD BURTON · JEAN SIMMONS · VICTOR MATURE · MICHAEL RENNIE
with JAY ROBINSON · DEAN JAGGER
PRODUCED BY FRANK ROSS
SCREEN PLAY BY PHILIP DUNNE · FROM THE NOVEL BY LLOYD C. DOUGLAS
DIRECTED BY HENRY KOSTER

Steamy starring role for Marilyn Monroe

Marilyn Monroe positively sizzles with sex appeal in the dramatic ***Niagara.***

New York, 21 January
One of cinema fiction's more implausibly married couples, Joseph Cotten and Marilyn Monroe, are at the stormy center of Henry Hathaway's *Niagara*. Monroe, whose wiggling walk is attracting increasingly frenzied attention, is cast here as Rose Loomis, the nymphomaniac wife of wizened war veteran Cotten, whose plans to dispose of her husband at the honeymooners' paradise go fatally awry. First co-conspirator Richard Allan winds up in the river, and then Monroe is strangled by a vengeful Cotten before he cuts loose on a rampage with a honeymooner as a hostage. The posters promise "Marilyn Monroe and *Niagara* – a raging torrent of emotion that even nature can't control!" Monroe's ripe sexuality, already seen in flashes in *The Asphalt Jungle*, *Monkey Business* and *Clash by Night*, has now earned her top billing. Sultrily singing her way through "Kiss", or tossing teasingly on her motel bed with only a sheet to cover her naked body, she sets the screen crackling with sexual static.

A hopeless view of adolescent sexuality

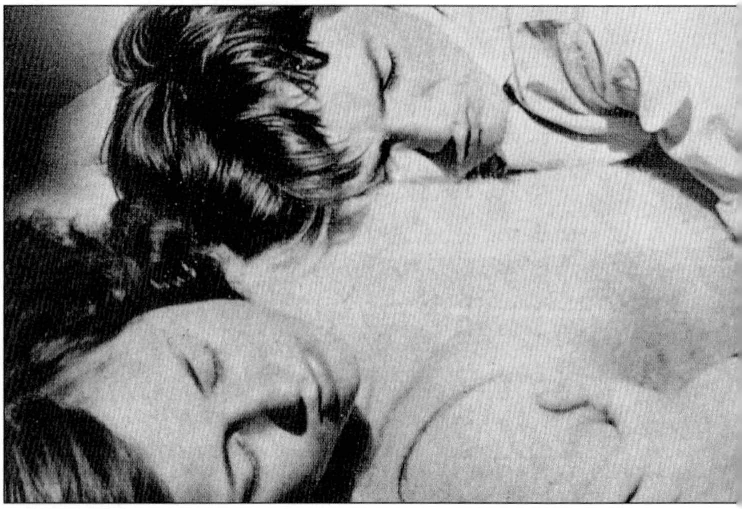

Harriet Andersson and Lars Ekborg star as Bergman's tormented couple.

Stockholm, 9 February
After the bleakness and bitterness of some of his earlier films, such as *Crisis, A Ship to India* and *Night is My Future*, the principal setting of Swedish director Ingmar Bergman's latest film, *Summer With Monika*, gives the impression that he has changed. However, like several of his previous films, this deals with adolescents struggling against an unfeeling grown-up world, and for whom the director sees little hope. But Bergman's photographer Gunnar Fischer has brilliantly captured the transient sun-soaked Swed summer days, the only period happiness for the young couple fore the encroachment of autu and reality. Monika (Harriet Ande son) is an irresponsible teenage g who spends her summer holic alone on an island with a you clerk (Lars Ekborg), sunbathi swimming and making love. S soon gets pregnant, and leaves poor boy literally holding the ba The two young leads, especially minkish Andersson, give this sim tale a remarkable veracity.

Rita and Aly now divorced

Reno, 26 January
Actress Rita Hayworth and Prince Aly Khan have just gotten divorced in Reno, Nevada. The couple had been separated for several months, and Rita had declared in an interview she gave last September that it was "impossible to continue with a marriage which has brought nothing but unhappiness. I want a divorce." To demonstrate her determination, she has agreed to start work on a new film, *Affair in Trinidad*, directed by Vincent Sherman, her first since 1948. Her co-star here will be Glenn Ford, with whom she struck sparks in *Gilda*. She married Aly Khan at Vallauris, in France, on 27 May 1949 and then gave birth to a daughter, Yasmin, the following December. She has one other child, Rebecca, born in 1944 from her marriage to Orson Welles.

The hilarious chaos of Monsieur Hulot's unforgettable holiday!

Paris, 27 February
For his second feature, *Monsieur Hulot's Holiday*, Jacques Tati refused to revive the postman hero from *Jour de fête*. Declining the many suggestions offered by producers, the actor-director preferred to create a new character, Monsieur Hulot. This amiable and bumbling bachelor was inspired by a sergeant Tati knew in the army and a clum architect called Hulot. The film to over a year to shoot, from July 19 to October 1952, at the Boulog Billancourt studios, and on locati at Saint-Marc-sur-Mer, near Sa Nazaire in Brittany. It concentra on how Monsieur Hulot, during summer vacation at a small seasi resort, inadvertently sparks off series of mishaps. Hulot, invarial wearing a hat, overcoat and rath too short trousers, smoking a pi and walking as if against a stro wind, is not only the instigator incidents but also an observer of idiosyncracies of the French mid class at the seaside. There is ve little dialogue or plot – the film i running series of comic episod climaxing with Hulot setting fire a shed full of fireworks – the gen humor resides in Jacques Ta body language and in the supert controlled soundtrack.

Tati as the accident prone M. Hulot in the film which he also wrote and directed.

...irley Booth scoops Best Actress Oscar

...llywood, 19 March
...er years of having rejected the ...vances of television, the Academy ... succumbed at last, and this ...r's Awards show was beamed to ... million viewers all across the ...ntry. They saw Shirley Booth, ...ner of the Best Actress Award ... *Come Back, Little Sheba*, as she ... up the red-carpeted stairs of the ...ernational Theater to collect her ...ze, almost tripping over her long ...wn. In her breathless acceptance ...ech, the 45-year-old stage actress ...narked, "I guess this is the peak." ...hough she has won the Oscar on ... screen debut, Booth had played ... role of the slovenly wife of an ...oholic more than 1,000 times in ...lliam Inge's play on Broadway. ... contrast, the Best Actor winner ...s the veteran movie star Gary ...oper, who took the award for his ...tured portrayal of the lone sheriff ...ced to face four outlaws on his ...dding day in Fred Zinnemann's ...*gh Noon*. The Oscars were distributed more evenly this year than most, with John Ford as the Best Director for *The Quiet Man*, and Cecil B. DeMille's circus spectacle, *The Greatest Show On Earth*, if not exactly living up to its lofty title, considered Best Picture.

Booth in ***Come Back, Little Sheba.***

A supernatural tale from Kenji Mizoguchi

Tokyo, 26 March
It is very often the case that films most deeply embedded in a national tradition and culture possess universal characteristics. Such a film is *Ugetsu Monogatari* (*Tales of the Pale and Silvery Moon After Rain*), Kenji Mizoguchi's new work. Simultaneously violent and contemplative, the film embraces four typical Japanese genres: the historic fresco, the elegiac poem, the fantastic tale and the Kabuki theater. The result is a work of captivating beauty and refinement. It is the story of a poor potter, trying to make a living in a war-torn medieval village, who is lured away from his devoted wife by a mysterious woman, who turns out to be a ghost. When he returns home repentant, his wife, too, has become a ghost. Mizoguchi recounts the tales, based on two 18th-century ghost stories by Akinari Veda, and one by Guy de Maupassant, using lyrical, haunting and intense images which never ignore the human element. His artistry is best demonstrated by the trip across the lake as the boat emerges from the mist, hinting at the supernatural; and also the final sequence when the potter sees the phantom vision of his dead wife where there was emptiness before.

Sakae Ozawa and Masayuki Mori.

...one, laconic Ladd leads haunting Western

...ey (Brandon De Wilde) with his hero Shane (Ladd) in George Stevens' film.

...s Angeles, 6 April
...ecently in contract disputes with ...ramount, Alan Ladd suddenly ...und himself back in the big league ...th *Shane*, a superb Western di...cted by George Stevens. Ladd is ...e buckskin-clad guardian angel ...otecting homesteaders from hired killer Jack Palance. Told from the viewpoint of a small boy, Brandon De Wilde, *Shane* seamlessly blends a realistic approach to the Wyoming range wars as well as a sure grasp of American history, with a distillation of many of the most potent myths that characterize the Western film.

'The Moon is Blue' defies Production Code

Maggie McNamara and William Holden in Otto Preminger's 'daring' comedy.

Hollywood, 4 June
Hollywood, in its competition with television, is currently adopting an ostensibly daring approach to subjects previously thought risqué or taboo. Sex is getting a more frank treatment, and audiences watching Otto Preminger's film version of the stage hit *The Moon is Blue*, released without a Production Code Seal of Approval, can hear words such as "virgin" and "seduce". The virgin in question is Maggie McNamara, who is circled by a predatory William Holden in a comedy which has defied the censors.

'The Wages of Fear' conquers Cannes

Charles Vanel (left), winner of the top acting prize, here with Yves Montand.

Cannes, 29 April
Since the opening of the Cannes Film Festival two weeks ago, autograph hunters, photographers and film fans have had a field day. Errol Flynn, Gary Cooper, Kirk Douglas, Yves Montand, Silvana Mangano and many others have been gently jostled by the enthusiastic crowd. Meanwhile, the jury was engaged in more serious activities, watching dozens of films from all over the world to dig out the rare pearls worthy of being awarded a prize. The selection this year has been particularly rich, with the president Jean Cocteau, and the others on the jury, being offered a veritable cornucopia of film. This explains the reason why the prizes have been awarded to seven of the 28 participating nations. However, by unanimous verdict, it was France, with Henri-Georges Clouzot's film *The Wages of Fear*, which gained the well-deserved Grand Prix.

Inspired by a novel by Georges Arnaud, Clouzot's screenplay focuses on four down-and-out adventurers (Yves Montand, Charles Vanel, Peter Van Eyck and Folco Lulli) languishing in a festering South American town. They agree to risk their lives transporting two truckloads of highly dangerous nitroglycerine over treacherous roads to an oil field 300 miles away, where it is needed to blow up a burning oil well. Only one of them survives to claim his wages. The extremely suspenseful film, which matches anything Hollywood can produce in the same genre, gripped the audience from start to finish. It's not only an action film, however, but also a powerful study of failure. Clouzot, who filmed on location in the South of France, has brilliantly created the sweaty atmosphere of the tropics where his disenchanted and greedy characters are put through the mill. The actors, too, including the director's wife Vera Clouzot, found the shooting particularly grueling, thanks to the challenging physical demands of the plot. For his performance, Charles Vanel was compensated with the best actor prize.

Le Salaire de la Peur
EXPLOSIVES
H.G. CLOUZOT

Marisa Prado and Alberto Ruschel in Brazil's ***O Cangaceiro (The Bandit)***. Lima Barreto's film earned special mention for its pulsating music.

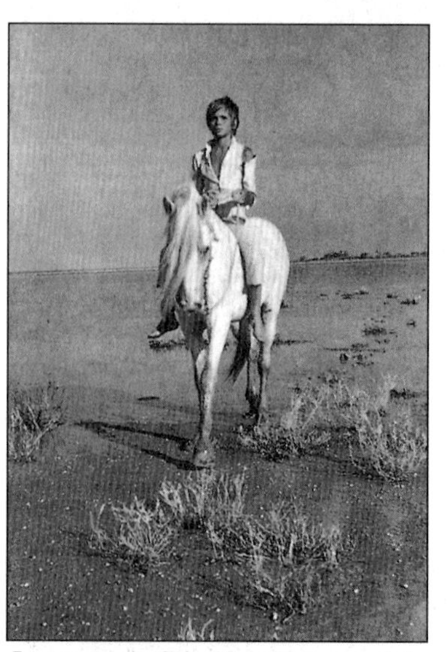
Lamorisse's ***Crin blanc*** was voted the best short film at the Festival.

Chaplins emigrate

Chaplin and wife Oona in New Y
prior to leaving the country.

Corsier-sur-Vevey, 23 August
The fifth child of Charles and Oc Chaplin, a boy who will be nam Eugene, was born today. This j ous event comes at the end of ma turbulent months for the Chapli who have now settled in Switzerla in an elegant villa, set in 37 acres parkland, which they bought from former U.S. ambassador for a ported $100,000. Chaplin will not returning to the United States. (19 September last year, after he a his family sailed for Europe, U authorities rescinded his re-ent permit. The following Novemb Oona Chaplin returned to Ameri to wind up her husband's busin affairs. Meanwhile, many cinem in America canceled showings of movie *Limelight*. It was some sm consolation that at the beginning March this year *Limelight* was vot best film by the Foreign Langua Press Critics in America. Only o month later Chaplin surrendered U.S. re-entry permit, declaring, have been the object of lies a vicious propaganda by power reactionary groups who, by th influence and with the aid of Ame ca's yellow press, have created unhealthy atmosphere in which l eral minded individuals can be s gled out and persecuted... I find virtually impossible to continue r motion picture work, and I ha therefore given up my residence the United States."

Delicate Deborah startles in sex scene

New York, 5 August
Fred Zinnemann's *From Here to Eternity* is a toned-down but still powerful film adaptation of James Jones' steamy novel of Army life in Hawaii in the days before the Japanese attack on Pearl Harbor. A high-voltage cast ensures that the robust flavor of the original is transferred to the screen. Burt Lancaster plays tough top Sergeant Milt Warden, and in the pivotal role of the victimized boxer/bugler Robert E. Prewitt, Montgomery Clift gives a superbly judged performance, one almost guaranteed to garner an Oscar nomination. Prewitt's conviction that "If a man don't go his own way, he's nothin'," bears more than a passing resemblance to the actor's own credo. Nevertheless, the revelations of this movie are Deborah Kerr and Frank Sinatra. Hollywood has always reserved a pedestal for stately British leading ladies, cool and graceful actresses under whose gentility there might lurk a streak of sensuality. Kerr, in America since 1947, has been confined mainly to decorative roles in melodramas and adventure films, but in *From Here to Eternity* she has abandoned restraint to play the nymphomaniac Karen Holmes, taking an illicit tumble in the surf with Burt Lancaster. But for actor-singer Frank Sinatra, this has been a make-or-break movie. Since 1949, when he left MGM, his career has been in a free fall. His marriage to Ava Gardner foundered, he flopped on TV, was taken up and dropped by Universal and then let go by Columbia Records. Sinatra was in dire straits when he pleaded for, and got, the part of the brow-beaten Italian GI Maggio in *From Here to Eternity* at the knock-down salary of $8,000 a week. Now he's hit the comeback trail and must be in the running for an Oscar.

English rose Deborah Kerr with Burt Lancaster in ***From Here to Eternity****.*

Gamine European 'princess' Audrey captivates New York public

New York, 27 August
William Wyler's *Roman Holiday* is a romantic, bittersweet account of 24 hours in the life of a young European princess. On a state visit to Rome, she rebels against the constraints of her royal existence and goes AWOL. Drowsy and disoriented, she is found by an American newsman who shows her the sights of the Eternal City...

The film has premiered here with the sweet smell of instant success, not least thanks to its leading lady, newcomer Audrey Hepburn. This European "gamine" captivated both Wyler and her co-star Gregory Peck during the arduous location filming in the heat of Rome, and she has received a rapturous reception from the first audiences. The daughter of a Dutch baroness and an Anglo-Irish banker, the 24-year-old Miss Hepburn spent the war years in Nazi-occupied Holland, often in near-starvation. After the war, she pursued her ambition to dance until, believing herself too tall for the world of classical ballet, she joined the chorus of a London musical. This set her on a path which culminated in her being chosen by the French novelist Colette to play the title role in *Gigi* on Broadway. Her success gave Paramount executives the confidence to cast her. Hepburn is an original: a thin child-woman with irregular teeth, wide jawbone, flaring nostrils and upswept brows. Yet she carries herself with ethereal grace, entrances with a smile both wistful and radiant, and has remarkably large and expressive eyes.

Eddie Albert, Audrey Hepburn and Gregory Peck on their ***Roman Holiday****.*

Huston's vision of Paris woos Venice

Venice, 4 September
The Venice Film Festival failed to award a Golden Lion this year, but elected instead to hand out six Silver Lions to honor a range of diverse but equally brilliant films. They are *The Little Fugitive*, a highly imaginative story of a boy in Coney Island who believes he has committed a murder, directed on a low budget by Morris Engel and his wife Ruth Orkin; Kenji Mizoguchi's magnificent *Ugetsu Monogatari*, a supernatural tale of love deceived; Alexander Ptouchko's *Sadko*, a Sovcolor version of Rimsky-Korsakov's fairy-tale opera from the Soviet Union; Federico Fellini's *I Vitelloni*, about idle youth in a resort town; Marcel Carné's Zola adaptation, *Thérèse Raquin* and John Huston's *Moulin Rouge*. Huston's re-creation of late 19th-century Paris was perhaps the most appreciated of all, with the 20-minute opening sequence especially applauded. With its kaleidoscopic color, imaginative cutting and evocative sets and costumes, we get to see the celebrated cabaret of the title through the eyes of French artist Henri Toulouse-Lautrec (José Ferrer). In a series of *tableaux vivants*, the cancan, singer Jane Avril (Zsa Zsa Gabor) and other entertainments burst onto the screen. Based on Pierre La Mure's book about the painter, it deals with his hopeless affair with a whore (Colette Marchand), his platonic relationship with his model (Suzanne Flon), and his descent into alcoholism. Ferrer, who had to play the role on his knees, is utterly convincing as the suffering, dwarf-like Lautrec.

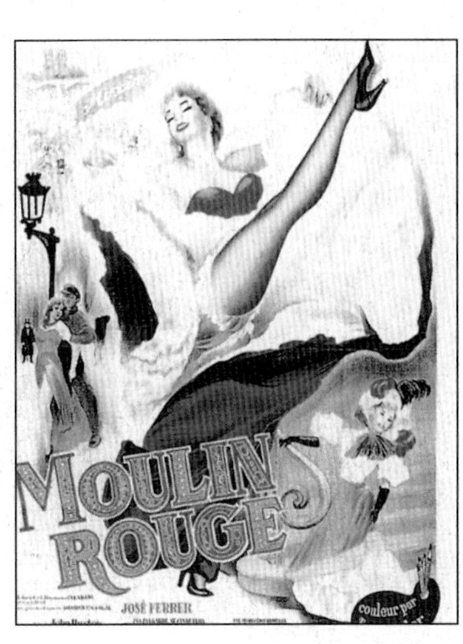
MOULIN ROUGE
JOSÉ FERRER

CinemaScope arrives with 'The Robe'

Henry Koster's film keeps a historical flavor in telling an ancient tale, while using the latest technical innovation.

New York, 16 September
Following on the launch of the first 3-D movies and Cinerama last year, the cinema has now gone in for giganticism with the opening at the Roxy of *The Robe*, the first fiction feature film in 20th Century-Fox's new process called CinemaScope. This wide-screen technique was first developed in the 1920s by French physicist Henri-Jacques Chrétien, and involves the use of a special lens that spreads the image over a larger area than the normal screen. *The Robe* itself is a rather uninspired Biblical epic, which stars Richard Burton, Victor Mature and Jean Simmons, and is directed by Henry Koster, but CinemaScope is impressive enough to hope its sweep will be used on better material.

'The Big Heat' is a scalding brew of corruption and courage

New York, 5 August
Glenn Ford, who achieved stardom opposite Rita Hayworth in *Gilda*, is one of Hollywood's most likable actors, radiating genial, relaxed sincerity. However, he is currently displaying the steel which lies under the smiling surface in Fritz Lang's *The Big Heat*, in which he plays an idealistic cop whose campaign against mobster Alexander Scourby turns into a grim personal vendetta after his wife is blown up by a car bomb. He is befriended by gangster's moll Gloria Grahame, who, for her pains, is horribly burned when the brutish hoodlum Lee Marvin throws a pot of scalding coffee in her face. She does the same to him in the film's finale, but perishes herself in the way of tarnished women who come to the aid of movie heroes. It's a remarkable and unsettling performance, that prompted *Picturegoer* magazine to comment, "If she were more synthetic, producers might not be so wary of her particular kind of explosive sex appeal. But she's very real, too real perhaps." Maybe the wide-eyed, pouting Grahame, with her small Southern-accented voice, is an actress just a little too out of the ordinary to take a conventional path to film stardom.

Lee Marvin with Gloria Grahame, for whose scarred face he is responsible.

Sinatra and Gardn
call it a day

Nebraska, 31 October
In spite of the intervention of Fra Sinatra's mother in an attempt reconcile her son to his wife of thr years, Ava Gardner, the separati of the couple has become offici The final night they spent togeth was a month ago when they met Palm Springs, California. Sinat had just wound up a series of singi engagements at the Riviera in N Jersey, and Gardner had return from Ireland where she was shoo ing *Knights of the Round Table* which she plays Guinevere. On October, MGM announced that t two stars had separated. And tod Sinatra confirmed this at a pre conference in Carson City, Nevac He seemed especially upset by t loss of their baby in November last year, even more than by t dissolution of the marriage. Av who hates to be alone for long, h left for Spain in order to join h new boyfriend, the matador Lu Miguel Dominguin. Perhaps it w give her the opportunity to make movie in Europe, something she h long expressed a desire to do. It the end of a well-publicized, storr marriage which began in 1951. Ma ters came to a head last year wh Frank accompanied Ava to Ken for the shooting of John Ford's fil *Mogambo*, during which they co tinually fought and made up. At o stage, Ava threw away a mink co Sinatra had bought her as a pea offering. It was the second marria for both of them, and those wh know them would be very surpris if it was the last for either.

Ava Gardner, a great beauty.

Blondes prefer to marry millionaires!

...rilyn Monroe ...

Los Angeles, 10 November
Gold-diggers Marilyn Monroe, Lauren Bacall and Betty Grable rent a plush Manhattan penthouse as the first move in a determined manhunt in Jean Negulesco's *How to Marry a Millionaire*. Bacall is the one who winds up with the millionaire of the title, seemingly poor working stiff Cameron Mitchell. Earlier this year Monroe and Jane Russell memorably co-starred as an equally formidable pair of floozies, the two big girls from Little Rock in Howard Hawks' entertaining adaptation of Anita Loos' smash-hit musical comedy *Gentlemen Prefer Blondes*. As the gold-digging Lorelei Lee, Monroe was superb, breathily singing "Diamonds Are a Girl's Best Friend". And Russell weighed in with an extraordinary routine in a ship's gymnasium, warbling "Ain't There Anyone Here for Love" while fondling serried ranks of compliant musclemen. All in all, it's a good cinematic year for gals who know what they want and go out to get it.

As Anita Loos' immortal Lorelei in Hawks' ***Gentlemen Prefer Blondes****.*

... and Jane Russell.

...istol-packin' Doris Day goes great guns

...ris Day as Calamity Jane.

New York, 4 November
Doris Day is at her most effervescent in the title role of *Calamity Jane*, a horse-musical which bears a striking resemblance to *Annie Get Your Gun*. She and Howard Keel, her opponent/lover in a battle of the sexes, do full justice to the breezy Sammy Fain-Paul Francis Webster songs, such as "The Deadwood Stage", "I Just Blew In From The Windy City" and "The Black Hills of Dakota". But the big hit of the picture is Doris touchingly crooning "Secret Love" – leaning against a tree, on horseback, and on top of a hill – at the top of her voice. The hugely popular blonde singing star, renowned for her freshly-scrubbed looks, remains grimy throughout, only emerging at the end from the chrysalis of tomboyhood into the butterfly of femininity in order to charm Howard Keel as "Wild Bill" Hickok, her "Secret Love".

A leather-clad Brando in insolent mood

New York, 30 December
The leather-jacketed bikers who have been terrorizing America have now invaded the screens in Laslo Benedek's *The Wild One*, starring Marlon Brando. The film was inspired by an incident in 1947 when a group of 4,000 motorcyclists decided to celebrate the Fourth of July by descending on the small Californian town of Hollister. After its brilliant opening sequence in which we see the bikers roar into town, the film concentrates on the anti-social behavior of "The Black Rebels", the most vicious of them being Johnny (Brando) and Chino (Lee Marvin). But Johnny's romantic encounter with the daughter (Mary Murphy) of the town's ineffectual cop, brings out the contradictory nature of his personality. Brando manages to express these two diverse elements – violence and sensitivity – in a tour de force performance.

Based on news reports of actual events, Benedek's film has produced, in Marlon Brando, a rebellious hero figure for youthful audiences.

GET ABOARD
The Band Wagon
m·g·m's
TOP
color by Technicolor
musical
starring
FRED ASTAIRE ★ CYD CHARISSE
OSCAR LEVANT · NANETTE FABRAY · JACK BUCHANAN
with JAMES MITCHELL Story and Screen Play by BETTY COMDEN and ADOLPH GREEN
Songs by HOWARD DIETZ And ARTHUR SCHWARTZ
Produced by ARTHUR FREED Directed by VINCENTE MINNELLI
A METRO-GOLDWYN-MAYER PICTURE

John Wayne (left), a Shane-style hero, with Rodolfo Acosta in ***Hondo****.*

Harriet Andersson, Ake Grönberg in Ingmar Bergman's ***Sawdust and Tinsel***

'Triplets': Astaire (l), Nanette Fabray, Jack Buchanan in ***The Band Wagon****.*

Esther Williams in a spectacular Busby Berkeley sequence from ***Easy to Love***

M-G-M's
TECHNICOLOR
MUSICAL of TROPICAL PASSIONS!
Latin Lovers
LANA TURNER
RICARDO MONTALBAN
JOHN LUND
LOUIS CALHERN

roy directed his discovery, Turner.

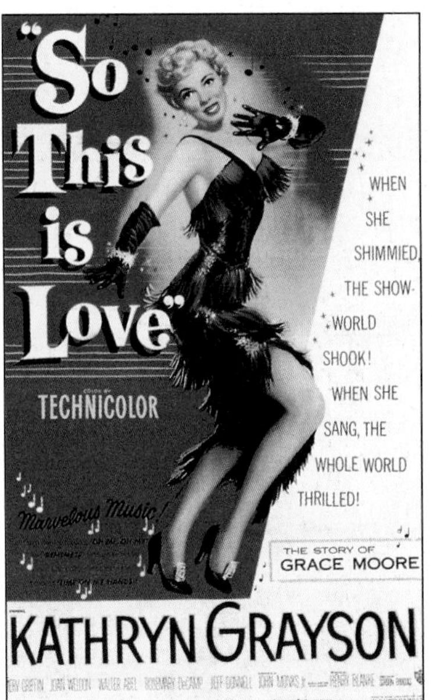
"So This is Love"
TECHNICOLOR
WHEN SHE SHIMMIED, THE SHOW-WORLD SHOOK! WHEN SHE SANG, THE WHOLE WORLD THRILLED!
THE STORY OF GRACE MOORE
KATHRYN GRAYSON

So-so biopic of soprano Grace Moore.

ft to right: Millard Mitchell, Robert Ryan, Janet Leigh, Ralph Meeker and mes Stewart in Anthony Mann's **The Naked Spur**.

THE CLOWN
RED SKELTON
JANE GREER · WITH TIM CONSIDINE
MARTIN RACKIN
ROBERT Z. LEONARD
WILLIAM H. WRIGHT
AN M-G-M PICTURE

eak replay of **The Champ** (1931).

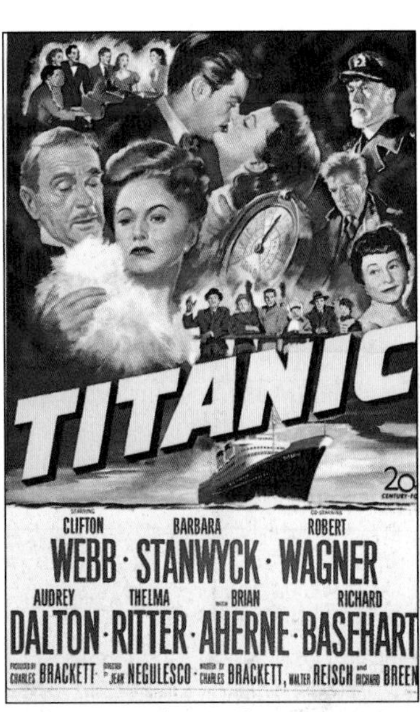
TITANIC
CLIFTON WEBB · BARBARA STANWYCK · ROBERT WAGNER
AUDREY DALTON · THELMA RITTER · BRIAN AHERNE · RICHARD BASEHART
BRACKETT · NEGULESCO · BRACKETT, REISCH · BREEN

Dull script sinks good production.

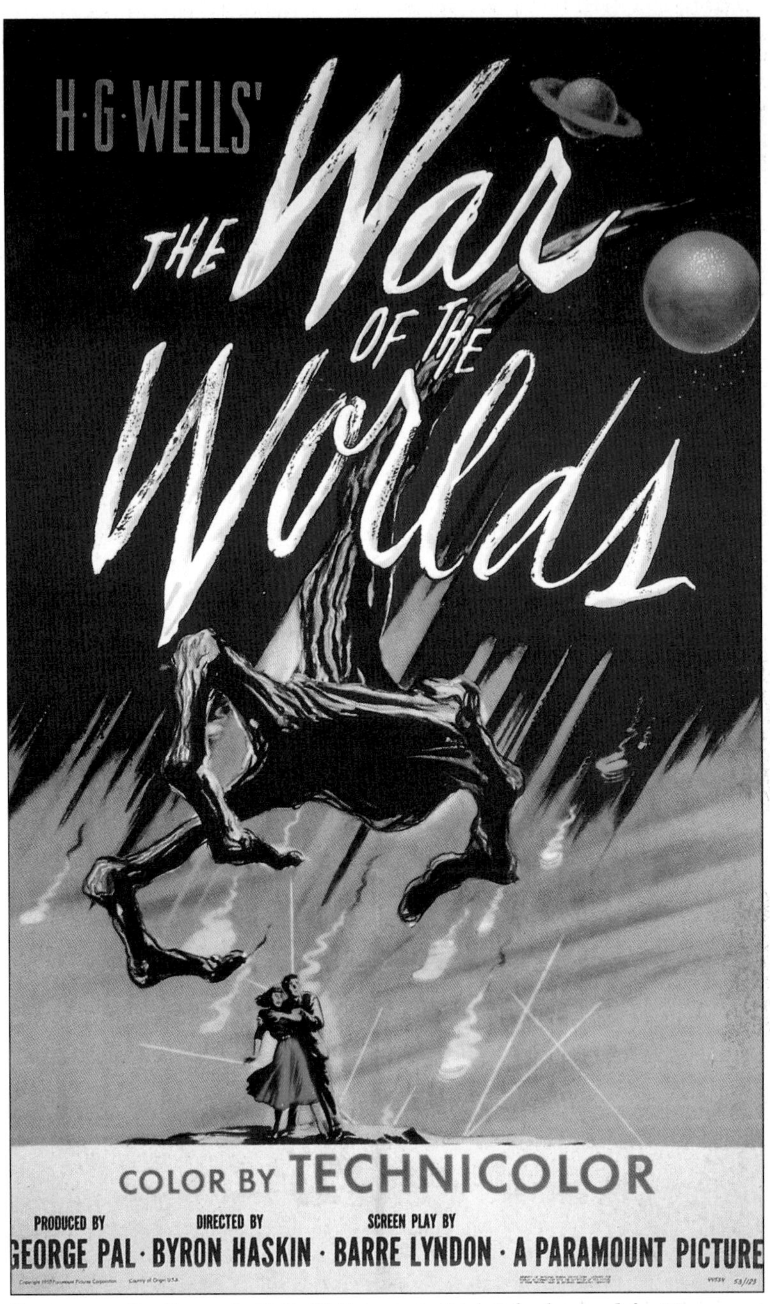
H·G·WELLS'
THE War OF THE Worlds
COLOR BY TECHNICOLOR
PRODUCED BY GEORGE PAL · DIRECTED BY BYRON HASKIN · SCREEN PLAY BY BARRE LYNDON · A PARAMOUNT PICTURE

Paramount finally made H.G. Wells' novel which it had owned for 29 years.

l to r: Louis Calhern (Caesar), Marlon Brando (Marc Antony), Greer Garson and Deborah Kerr in **Julius Caesar**, directed by Joseph L. Mankiewicz.

1954

1953 Academy Awards, RKO Pantages Theater, 25 Mar.

Best Film:	From Here to Eternity (dir: Fred Zinnemann)
Best Director:	Fred Zinnemann
Best Actor:	William Holden *(Stalag 17)*
Best Actress:	Audrey Hepburn *(Roman Holiday)*
Best Supp. Actor:	Frank Sinatra *(From Here to Eternity)*
Best Supp. Actress:	Donna Reed *(From Here to Eternity)*

Paris, 1 January
Cahiers du Cinéma has published an outspoken attack on "certain trends in French films" written by André Bazin's young protégé François Truffaut, in which Truffaut compares the rejected scenario of Pierre Bost and Jean Aurenche's *Diary of a Country Priest*, adapted from Georges Bernanos' work, with the film made by Robert Bresson. And he concludes with: "Of what value is an anti-bourgeois film made by a bourgeois for the bourgeoisie?"

Paris, 8 January
American screen comedian and filmmaker Buster Keaton, taken on by the Medrano Circus, makes his debut with the company tonight, when he will perform a sketch.

New York, 8 January
The New York critics have voted André Cayatte's French film, *Justice is done* (*Justice est faite*) as the best foreign film shown in the United States during 1953. Cayatte and Charles Spaak co-wrote the script for this ironic examination of the French legal system. Both of them are former lawyers.

New York, 26 January
The film rights to Charles A. Lindbergh's autobiography *The Spirit of St. Louis* have been acquired by director Billy Wilder and Broadway producer Leland Hayward for what is reported to be the highest price paid by Hollywood for a literary work – an estimated $1 million.

Korea, 1 February
Marilyn Monroe is on a tour of the battle front, boosting morale by entertaining the troops.

Hollywood, 16 February
David O. Selznick voiced his anger over use of a *Gone With the Wind* clip in a birthday salute to MGM on the Ed Sullivan Show. Selznick feels it is misrepresentation as the film was not an MGM production.

Hollywood, 2 March
Clark Gable has announced that he is leaving MGM after 23 years there under contract. His annual salary was $500,000. It is not yet known whether other studios have made an approach to the star.

Los Angeles, 19 March
Responding to rumors predicting an imminent breakup, Dean Martin and Jerry Lewis state: "We do indeed intend to dissolve our team... on 25 July 1996, for the 50th anniversary of our partnership."

Los Angeles, 25 March
At this year's Oscar ceremony, the Academy honored the Bausch and Lomb Optical Company with a special award for their contributions to the advancement of the motion picture industry. On the artistic side, Greta Garbo, who never won the Oscar despite her legendary success, was finally honored with a statuette for "her unforgettable screen performances", as was Danny Kaye "for his unique talents, his service to the Academy, the motion picture industry and the American people".

New York, 2 May
The *New York Times* today has published a letter from Robert Bresson protesting against the cuts made by the American distributor of his film *Diary of a Country Priest*, which, in his view, render the film incomprehensible. According to the paper the slow pace of certain foreign films is alien to American taste.

Hollywood, 28 May
Dial M for Murder, Alfred Hitchcock's last film for Warner Bros. is released today in a "flat" version although it was filmed in 3-D. Is the vogue for stereoscopic films over?

Hollywood, 20 September
Walt Disney has terminated his distribution agreement with RKO. All his films will in future be distributed by his own subsidiary, Buena Vista.

Stockholm, 4 October
Premiere of Ingmar Bergman's film *Lesson in Love*, which co-stars Eva Dahlbeck and Gunnar Björnstrand. The work is one of Bergman's rare excursions into comedy.

Los Angeles, 5 October
Opening of Otto Preminger's film *Carmen Jones*, inspired by Bizet's opera and retaining its score with a new libretto. The press revealed that the composer's heirs refuse to allow the film to be shown in France.

Paris, 18 November
Two French stars, Stéphane Audran and Jean-Louis Trintignant, were married today.

Tokyo, 23 November
Opening of Kenji Mizoguchi's film *Chikamatsu Monogatari* (*The Crucified Lovers*). Set in 17th-century Japan, the word is that it is one of the great director's best films.

Hollywood, 30 November
The Screen Actors Guild has sent a letter to the Immigration Bureau urging a "stricter application", by the United States Immigration and Naturalization Service, of regulations governing "alien actors coming into this country to take supporting or even minor roles in movies being made here." The letter stressed that the protest was aimed at "non-resident aliens" who are employed for lower salaries than American actors and not at "stars of distinguished merit and ability".

Hollywood, 1 December
Yesterday, Darryl Zanuck, the production chief at 20th Century-Fox, declared that the attitude of foreign exhibitors and producers to his company's wide-screen process was one of "eagerness and enthusiasm". To substantiate his claim he cited increases in receipts of over 50 percent in all British theaters showing CinemaScope films with similar figures from France. So far orders for CinemaScope photographic lenses have come from West Germany, Italy, England and France.

New York, 26 December
Release of *Vera Cruz*, directed by Robert Aldrich and the first film made in Superscope, a process akin to CinemaScope. Burt Lancaster and Gary Cooper head the cast.

New York, 28 December
The New York Critics have vo Marlon Brando best actor for E Kazan's *On the Waterfront*, a Grace Kelly best actress for Geo Seaton's *The Country Girl.*

BIRTHS

Ohio, 22 January
Jim Jarmusch

New Jersey, 18 February
John Travolta

Oklahoma, 1 March
Ron Howard

Houston, 9 April
Dennis Quaid

New York, 16 April
Ellen Barkin

Toronto, 18 April
Rick Moranis

Chicago, 15 May
James Belushi

Missouri, 19 June
Kathleen Turner

Canada, 16 August
James Cameron

Minnesota, 29 November
Joel Coen

England, 15 December
Alex Cox

New York, 28 December
Denzel Washington

DEATHS

Hollywood, 19 January
Sydney Greenstreet

Vienna, 4 June
Charles Vidor

Hollywood, 3 September
Eugene Pallette

California, 15 November
Lionel Barrymore

Alfred Hitchcock's ***Rear Window*** *is highly ingenious thriller with a hou. bound James Stewart relying on t gorgeous Grace Kelly for help w his amateur sleuthing efforts.*

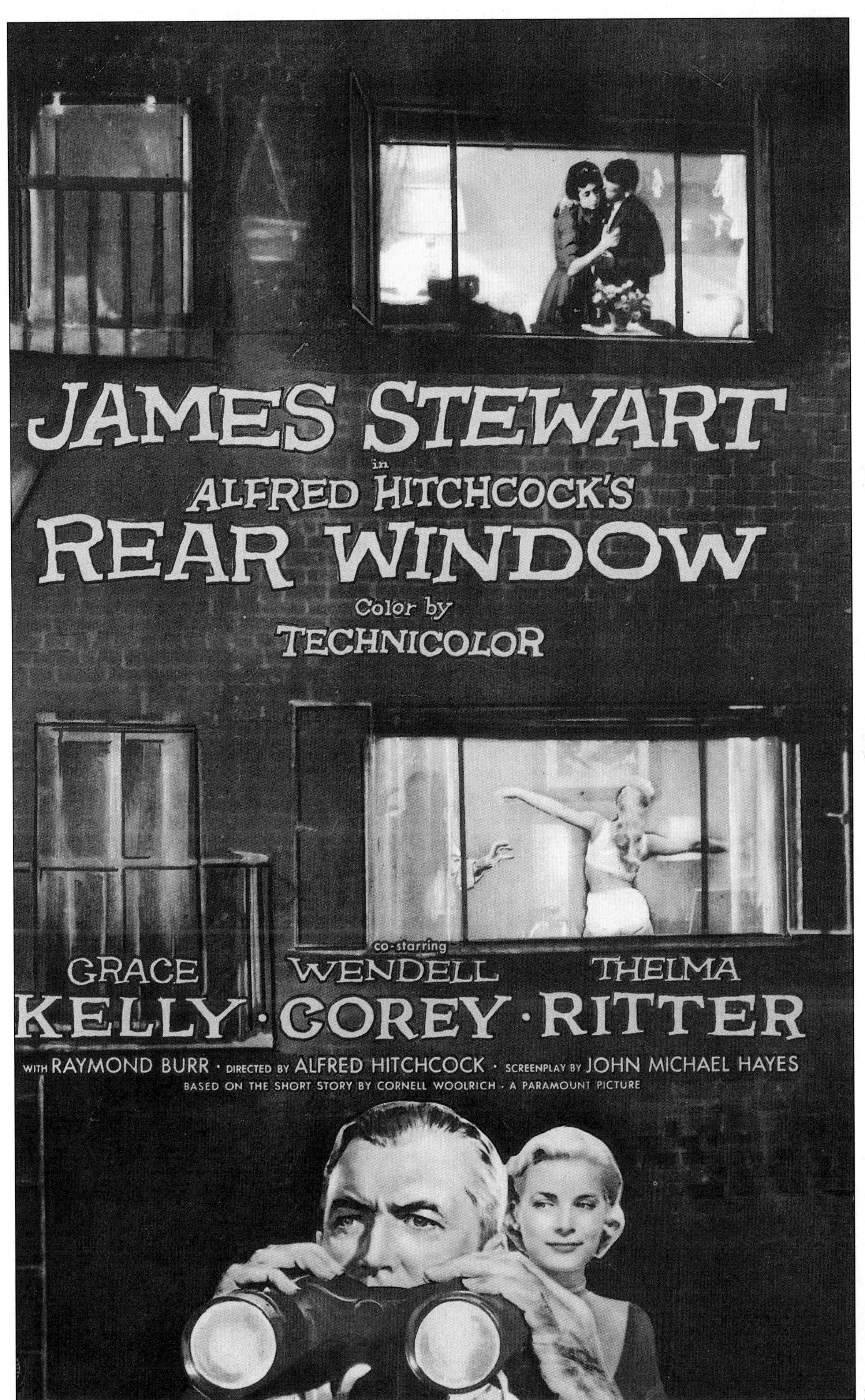
JAMES STEWART
in
ALFRED HITCHCOCK'S
REAR WINDOW
Color by
TECHNICOLOR
co-starring
GRACE KELLY · WENDELL COREY · THELMA RITTER
WITH RAYMOND BURR · DIRECTED BY ALFRED HITCHCOCK · SCREENPLAY BY JOHN MICHAEL HAYES
BASED ON THE SHORT STORY BY CORNELL WOOLRICH · A PARAMOUNT PICTURE

▷

Gabin shrugs off stereotype with 'Grisbi'

Jean Gabin in Becker's film, with Dora Doll (left) and Jeanne Moreau.

Paris, 17 March
With Jacques Becker's newest film *Touchez pas au grisbi* (*Honor Among Thieves*), Jean Gabin has finally managed to dispose of the image long-associated with him about his choice of roles – that of the good-natured working-class fellow, on whom tragic misfortune always lands. In Becker's movie, adapted from the gangster novel by Albert Simonin, Gabin paints us a poignant portrait of Max the Liar, an aging hoodlum on a search for respectability who dreams of drawing his pension in a few years. What primarily interested Becker was not the cops and robbers plot – after a bank robbery, the gang fights to the death over the loot – but rather an exploration of friendship and betrayal among the characters.

Feudal Japan the setting for sublime fil

Kyoko Kagawa, the girl sold as a slave to Sansho (Eitaro Shindo, right).

Tokyo, 31 March
Kenji Mizoguchi has consolidated the great international success of *Ugetsu Monogatari* last year with a slightly more realistic, but no less impressive, film called *Sansho the Bailiff* (*Sansho Dayu*). Set in a barbaric period, authentically recreated, Mizoguchi has transformed the ancient Japanese legend, as told by the novelist Ogai Mori, into a timeless, humanist statement of inju and suffering. It tells of how th and daughter of a noble fami feudal Japan are kidnapped sold as slaves to a tyrannical b Years later, the son escapes a reunited with his mother, now b crippled and living in abject pov Mizoguchi creates an elegiac n that is unbearably moving wit becoming sentimental.

The whole of RKO for one single man

New York, 18 March
Howard Hughes has gained total control of RKO for $23.5 million, making him the first individual ever to wholly own a motion picture company. However, RKO's prospects look bleak. Hughes is a reclusive aviation enthusiast who, in 1923 at the age of 18, inherited an industrial empire from his father. He has been involved in films since the mid-1920s. He made his name in the industry as the producer-director of *Hell's Angels* in 1930, launching the career of Jean Harlow, one of the first of dozens of starlets he has compulsively signed to long-term personal contracts. Jane Russell, busty star of *The Outlaw* is another. Hughes' behavior has become increasingly bizarre following a serious air crash in 1946. And since he acquired a controlling interest in RKO in 1948, his decisions have nearly bankrupted the studio.

'From Here to Eternity' cleans up with eight Academy Awards

Hollywood, 25 March
One movie dominated this year's Oscar ceremony: Fred Zinnemann's *From Here to Eternity*. Impressively, it has matched the record held by *Gone With the Wind* by nabbing eight Academy Awards. Included in those is that of Best Supporting Actor to Frank Sinatra, a man coming back from bankruptcy, falling popularity and divorce settlem His first dramatic role as Pri Maggio has given him a new on life. Donna Reed, Best Sup ing Actress, also took advantag having a meatier role than usu the nightclub singer-cum-prosti Other awards received were Picture, Best Director, Best Sc play, Best Cinematography, Sound Recording and Best Editing. The Best Actor and Ac nods went to an old hand (Wil Holden) and a fresh young t (Audrey Hepburn) for *Stalag* and *Roman Holiday*, respecti Holden, like Reed and Sinatra, cast against type in Billy Wil POW comedy-drama, portrayi wheeling-and-dealing sergeant. though *Roman Holiday* was Au Hepburn's seventh film, in w she portrays a princess on a spre was the first which she carrie her frail shoulders, becoming ne overnight one of Hollywood's r bewitching of stars.

Don Taylor (left) and Best Actor William Holden in Billy Wilder's ***Stalag 17****.*

ate of Hell' sees off Cannes competitors

nnes, 9 April
: jury at this year's Cannes Film tival, presided over by Jean cteau together with Luis Buñuel l André Bazin, has awarded the and Prix to the Japanese film *e of Hell* (*Jigokumon*) in prefer-e to the other strong contender, ié Clément's *Knave of Hearts.* : latter, a British production, was npensated by being given the cial Jury prize, and its leading man Gérard Philipe took the best actor award. In the role of a young French philanderer in London who confesses all his affairs to his wife, Philipe, alongside British actresses Valerie Hobson, Margaret Johnston and Joan Greenwood, is perfectly cast. *Gate of Hell*, the first Japanese movie to use a Western color process (Eastmancolor), remains within the conventions of the *Jidai-Geki*, or period film, Japan's most popular genre. It tells of a 12th-century warlord who desires a married woman, but when she kills herself rather than submit to him, he is filled with remorse and becomes a monk. The film makes a strong visual impact, as much for its camerawork and color as for its elaborate costumes, and has managed to reproduce the pictorial qualities of traditional Japanese art. Machiko Kyo gives an impressive portrayal of the ideal Japanese wife, beautifully conveying the reserves of courage and passion behind an exterior of calm submissiveness, and Kazuo Hasegawa suggests a disturbing, menacing quality as the warlord. Teinosuke Kinugasa, a former child actor and leading *oyama* (female impersonator), studied briefly with Eisenstein.

chiko Kyo (right), the tragic hero-of Kinugasa's ***Gate of Hell.***

Remake of tearjerker pulls out all the stops

Rock Hudson and Jane Wyman in Douglas Sirk's ***Magnificent Obsession.***

Los Angeles, 21 July
A good-for-nothing layabout causes an attractive woman's blindness in an accident. Stricken with remorse, he sets about becoming an eye surgeon and restores her sight, winning the Nobel Prize in the process. The magnificent hokum of *Magnificent Obsession* was successfully filmed in 1935 with Robert Taylor and Irene Dunne. Here, handsome hunk Rock Hudson, who until now attracted little attention, makes a maximum impact opposite Jane Wyman and a high-octane supporting cast. Director Douglas Sirk delivers a calculatedly overblown tearjerker with no melodramatic punches pulled, and made with consummate and effective professionalism.

ie dark shadow of McCarthyism lurks 'On the Waterfront'

llywood, 15 April
ne critics have suggested that a Kazan's latest picture *On the terfront* reflects his role as a iendly" witness before the House -American Activities Committee 1952, where he admitted past mbership in the Communist Par-and named names. The movie, tten by Budd Schulberg, who had imilar experience, is a clear para-of loyalty and betrayal. It is the ry of a docker (Marlon Brando), o denounces the corrupt and all-verful labor boss (Lee J. Cobb) to police. Thus, he is considered an ormer and has to suffer the con-uences. *On the Waterfront* is not first work to be inspired by the ent McCarthy period. Last year, adway saw *The Crucible* from hur Miller, an allegory about a n who refuses to give in to a ch-hunting tribunal. Here putting le the political analogies, Kazan ngs to the screen a brilliantly ected, written and performed production, shot entirely on location in Hoboken, New Jersey. Brando is superb as an uneducated, inarticulate, confused ex-boxer, and he gets sterling support from such Actors Studio alumni as Rod Steiger and Karl Malden. Sam Spiegel is the daring producer who took on the production after it was turned down by every major Hollywood studio.

Marlon Brando as Terry Malloy, fighting against the corrupt labor bosses.

What Jimmy sees in own backyard

New York, 4 August
Hitchcock's recently opened *Rear Window* is a highly original nail-biter. James Stewart plays a news cameraman confined to his apartment with a broken leg. What he sees in the apartment across the court as he watches through his rear window, and what he does about it, makes a gripping movie.

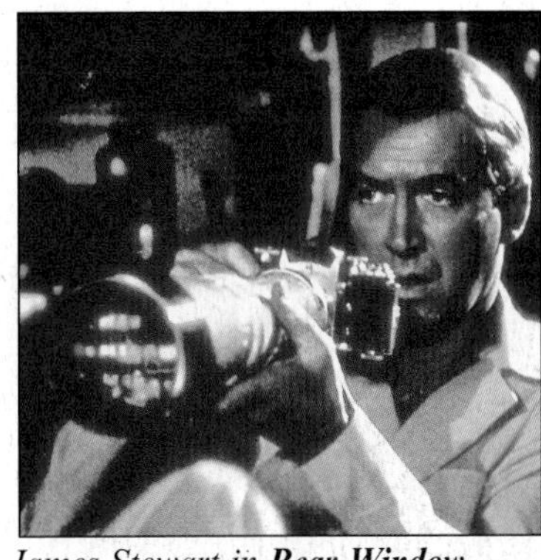

James Stewart in ***Rear Window.***

Magnificent star reborn

*Judy Garland as rising singer Esther Blodgett in Cukor's **A Star is Born**.*

New York, 5 August
The opening of *A Star is Born* today must surely represent a landmark in the screen musical, and in the troubled career of its star, Judy Garland. The film is a musical remake of the 1937 drama of the same name that starred Janet Gaynor and Fredric March. That was loosely based on the 1932 *What Price Hollywood*, directed by George Cukor. Once again, Cukor is at the helm, and with the help of a magnificent score – songs by Gershwin, Rodgers and Hart plus a host of others – and, especially, his leading lady, he has brought in a memorable film. The tried and trusted tale is of Esther Blodgett, an aspiring young singer who reaches the upper echelons of success as Vicky Lester, only to have her heart broken by her film-star husband, Norman Maine, who descends into alcoholism. It's a strong story well told, and British actor James Mason as Maine, a role that was turned down by Cary Grant and Humphrey Bogart, is superb. But the film is Garland's triumph. She gives it her all with a mixture of pluckiness and vulnerability that tugs at the heart, and in her musical numbers is nothing short of magnificent. It is almost impossible to single out the high-spots, there being so many, but the lengthy "Born In a Trunk" routine, written by Leonard Gershe, impresses, and she reveals the full range of her vocal and interpretive powers in "The Man That Got Away". Granted that a running time of 154 minutes is not inconsiderable, it is nonetheless sad to note that studio chief Jack Warner demanded the removal of almost half-an-hour of film, which included two new numbers specially written by Harold Arlen and Ira Gershwin.

ARNER BROS PRÉSENTE
Judy
GARLAND
James
MASON
TECHNICOLOR
CINEMASCOPE
Une Etoile est Née...
"A STAR IS BORN"
JACK CARSON · CHARLES BICKFORD

Venice falls for Masina

*Giulietta Masina as the cruelly treated waif, Gelsomina, in **La Strada**.*

Venice, 7 September
There was only one name on people's lips at this year's Venice Film Festival: Guilietta Masina. In *La Strada*, directed by her husband Federico Fellini, Masina plays Gelsomina, a simple-minded girl who is "bought" from her family for a few lira by Zampano (Anthony Quinn), a whoring, drunken, itinerant strongman. He puts her to work as a clown and ignores her, even though she loves him. When Zampano fights and kills Il Matto (Richard Basehart), the tightrope walker who befriended her, Gelsomina dies of a broken heart. After she is dead, Zampano realizes his need for her. Fellini, having given Masina her first starring role, uses her waif-like persona to perfection. But the di tor had problems convincing ducers to accept her, as they thou her too old at 33. However, ther something ageless about the fur touching and vulnerable chara of this female clown, described most critics here, not unjustly. Chaplinesque. Surprisingly, the decided not to award a prize to actress this year, despite Masi performance, and those of Barb Stanwyck, Alida Valli and Jea Moreau. Instead, they handed Volpi Cup for best actor to J Gabin for his appearance in Jacq Becker's *Touchez pas au grisbi*. Golden Lion was awarded to Re to Castellani's *Romeo and Juliet*. *Strada* received a Silver Lion.

*Akira Kurosawa's magnificent film **Seven Samurai** was shown at Venice.*

e frustrations of oarefoot beauty

ywood, 29 September
The Barefoot Contessa, Joseph Aankiewicz has directed one of nost personal films. Ava Gard- is Maria d'Amato, née Maria gas, a girl from the slums of drid, who becomes a Hollywood The story begins at the star's ral in the rain. Beside the grave ds Humphrey Bogart, the world- ry director who discovered her e years before. The flashback, ically narrated by Bogart, tells er rise to fame, her love affairs her marriage to aristocrat Ros- Brazzi, who turns out to be otent. Ava's physical attributes well on display, especially when kicks off her shoes, lifts her skirt dances with the gypsies, thus iting the description of her in the licity slogan accompanying the : "The World's Most Exciting mal". Unfortunately, Ava Gard- s limited acting range is more osed than her body. Some of the racters in Mankiewicz's cynical witty screenplay were based on life people – Rita Hayworth, ward Hughes and Aly Khan – ough the threat of libel resulted ertain cuts in the dialogue. Most ple in the industry would recog- Edmond O'Brien's sweating, less press agent as an amalgam uch types. For his first picture olor, Mankiewicz filmed on lo- on in Spain, Italy and on the nch Riviera, photographed ele- tly by Jack Cardiff.

Gardner in the title role.

Luchino Visconti sacrifices realism to overpowering sensual beauty

*Alida Valli and Farley Granger in Visconti's **Senso**: politics, love and betrayal.*

Rome, 1 December
When Luchino Visconti's *Senso* was shown at the Venice Film Festival last September, it was given a chilly reception. Perhaps the director had disappointed those who thought of him as the instigator of the Italian neo-realist cinema. But *Senso* could not be further from that movement. Working through the conventions of Italian grand opera – the film opens sumptuously at the opera house during a performance of Giuseppe Verdi's *Il Trovatore* – Visconti has created a lush, melodramatic historical romance. The story is situated in Venice in 1866, where a married Italian noblewoman (Alida Valli), working for the cause of independence, falls in love with an Austrian officer (Farley Granger) in the army of occupation. But she denounces him for desertion after he has been unfaithful to her. The theme of the film is proclaimed from the beginning when the operatic chorus chants *All'armi, all'armi* (to arms, to arms), and the Italians in the audience take up the chant and unfurl the Italian flag to the alarm of the Austrian officers. Director Visconti has counterpoised rebellion and romance, though the motives of the proud patriots seem as dubious as those of the selfishly lustful. The period of the *Risorgimento* has seldom been more stunningly recaptured, this being principally due to the color photography by Aldo Graziata (credited as G.R. Aldo) and Robert Krasker. (Sadly, Graziata died in a car crash during the shooting.)

Merry musical bells ring out for a sparkling 'White Christmas'

New York, 14 October
Paramount have a palpable hit on their hands with *White Christmas*. Smoothly directed by Michael Curtiz, it's perfect family fare with a score by Irving Berlin and a cast list headed by Bing Crosby and Danny Kaye. In the first movie to be filmed in VistaVision, the wide-screen process adopted by Paramount, Danny and Bing play song-and-dance men who save their wartime commander Dean Jagger's ski resort hotel from bankruptcy by putting on the inevitable show. Rosemary Clooney and Vera-Ellen provide the love interest and combine with Kaye and Crosby to sing a cute version of "Sisters".

Back row, l to r: Rosemary Clooney, Danny Kaye, Bing Crosby and Vera-Ellen.

WALT DISNEY'S MIGHTY, MAGNIFICENT, MEMORABLE
20,000
LEAGUES UNDER THE SEA
STARRING
KIRK DOUGLAS · JAMES MASON · PAUL LUKAS
PETER LORRE
Based on the famous Jules Verne novel
TECHNICOLOR · CINEMASCOPE · Directed by RICHARD FLEISCHER · Screenplay by EARL FELTON

Jules Verne's famous novel about shipwrecked scientists captured by the mysterious Captain Nemo was given its due.

James Stewart convinced in Anth… Mann's ***The Glenn Miller Story****.*

Left to right: Van Johnson, Barry Jones, Gene Kelly and Cyd Charisse in ***Brigadoon****, directed by Vincente Minnelli from the Broadway hit.*

Harry Belafonte, Dorothy Dandridge in ***Carmen Jones****.*

Ray Milland starred in Hitchcoc… ***Dial M for Murder****.*

Gina Lollobrigida and Vittorio De Sica in ***Bread, Love and Jealousy*** *(Italy).*

Gérard Philipe in ***Monsieur Ripois****.*

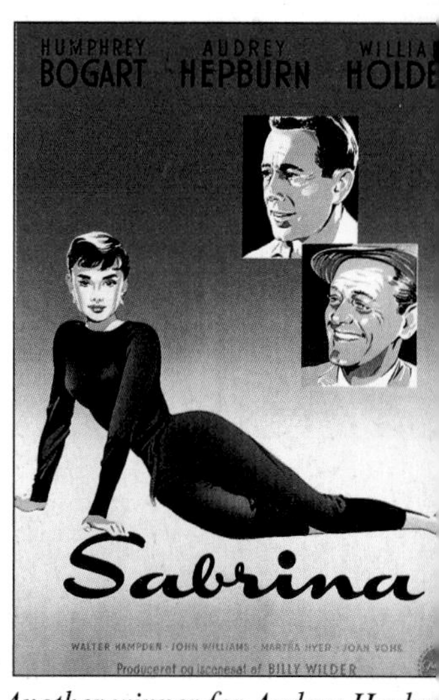
HUMPHREY BOGART
AUDREY HEPBURN
WILLIA… HOLDE…
Sabrina

Another winner for Audrey Hepbu…

CREATURE FROM THE BLACK LAGOON
Starring
RICHARD CARLSON
JULIA ADAMS

e half-man, half-fish creature was tacky, but it drew in the crowds.

bert Mitchum, Marilyn Monroe and Tommy Rettig in **River of No Return**.

It Holds You Spellbound with Suspense!
Alfred Hitchcock's
"dial M for Murder"
"is that you, darling?"
NOT SUITABLE FOR CHILDREN
PRESENTED BY WARNER BROS.
RAY MILLAND · GRACE KELLY · ROBERT CUMMINGS
WarnerColor
WARNER BROS.

A very successful movie version of the long-running play.

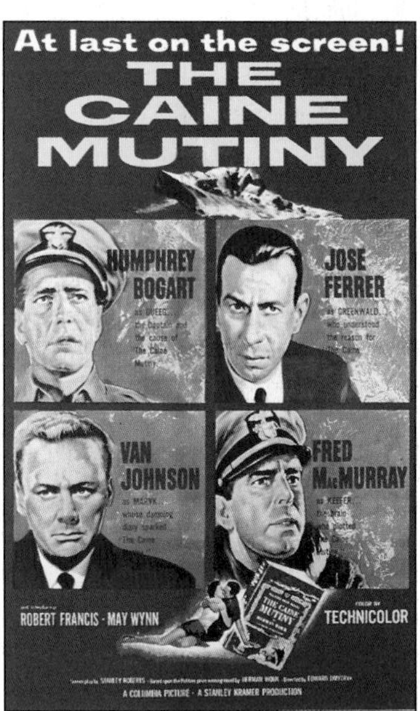
At last on the screen!
THE CAINE MUTINY
HUMPHREY BOGART
JOSE FERRER
VAN JOHNSON
FRED MacMURRAY
ROBERT FRANCIS · MAY WYNN
TECHNICOLOR
A COLUMBIA PICTURE · A STANLEY KRAMER PRODUCTION

Humphrey Bogart made Captain Queeg unnervingly his own.

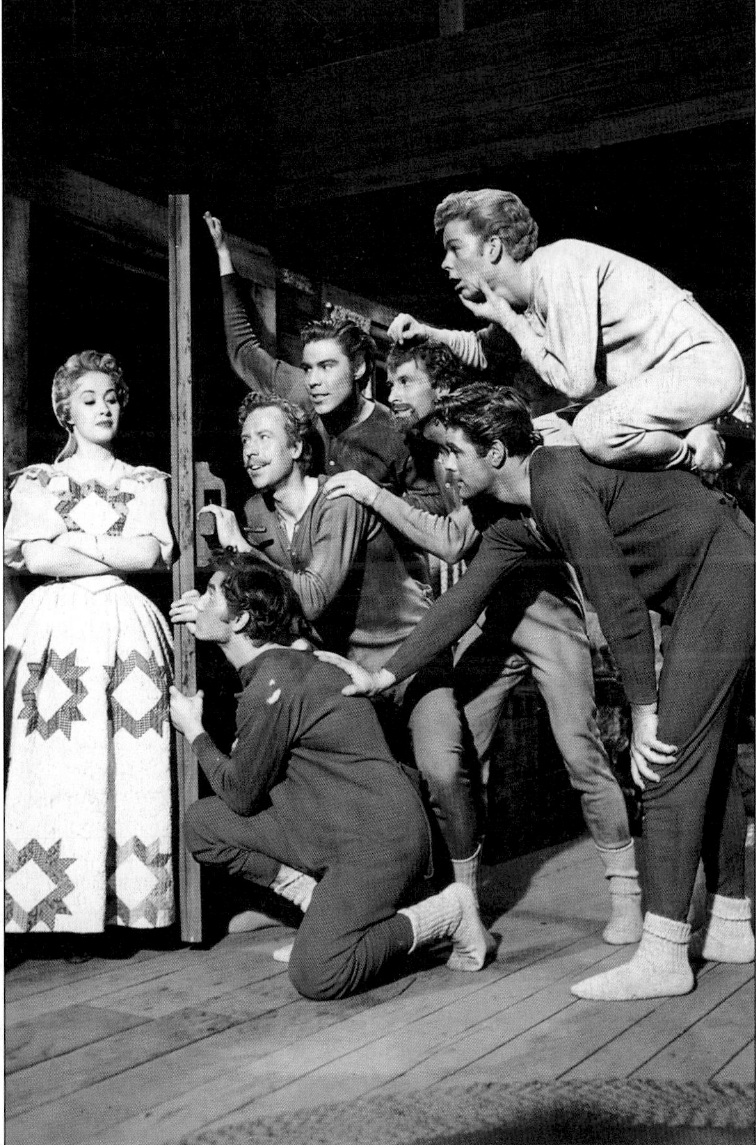

Jane Powell, one of the seven brides, with six of the seven brothers in Stanley Donen's popular MGM musical, **Seven Brides for Seven Brothers**.

1955

1954 Academy Awards, RKO Pantages Theater, 30 Mar.

Best Film:	*On the Waterfront* (dir: Elia Kazan)
Best Director:	Elia Kazan
Best Actor:	Marlon Brando *(On the Waterfront)*
Best Actress:	Grace Kelly *(The Country Girl)*
Best Supp. Actor:	Edmond O'Brien *(The Barefoot Contessa)*
Best Supp. Actress:	Eva Marie Saint *(On the Waterfront)*

New York, 31 January
Marilyn Monroe has announced the formation, with Milton Greene, of Marilyn Monroe Productions. The star also stated that she does not wish to renew her contract with Fox.

Milan, 15 February
Dubbed "The Mona Lisa of the Twentieth Century", Gina Lollobrigida is posing for 27 painters in the lounge of a hotel.

Hollywood, 23 February
Dorothy Dandrige is the first black actress to be nominated for an Oscar in the Best Actress category – for her sparkling performance as *Carmen Jones*. The other nominees are Grace Kelly, Audrey Hepburn, Judy Garland and Jane Wyman.

Mexico, 3 April
Luis Buñuel's black comedy, *Ensayo de un Crimen* (*The Criminal Life of Archibaldo de la Cruz*) with Ernesto Alonso and Miroslava Stern, has opened here.

Hollywood, 4 April
Fox having decided, for reasons of prestige, that all films in CinemaScope must be in color, has opposed the filming of *Rebel Without a Cause* in black and white by Warners. Director Nicholas Ray has been forced to interrupt shooting and begin again in Eastmancolor.

Paris, 20 April
The premises of the Cinémathèque Française in Avenue de Messine have been closed.

Hollywood, 21 April
Samuel Goldwyn acquired the old United Artists studio today with a bid of $1.92 million, outbidding his former partner, Mary Pickford, by $20,000. The sale by public auction was ordered by Judge Paul Nourse last January due to a conflict of interest between the producer and Miss Pickford. No outside bids were made at today's sale.

New York, 30 May
The giant poster of Marilyn Monroe with her skirts billowing has been removed from the facade of Loew's State Theater under pressure from the League of Decency. The poster, which had only been up for five days was to promote her latest film, Billy Wilder's *The Seven Year Itch*.

Moscow, 31 May
The American movie *Marty*, directed by Delbert Mann, the love story of a Bronx butcher, received a rave notice in the Communist Party newspaper *Pravda*. The picture was the recipient of the Palme d'Or at the Cannes Festival earlier this month.

Colorado, 15 June
On location in the Rockies for *Tribute to a Bad Man*, Spencer Tracy has complained of the altitude and is refusing to continue work. MGM has retaliated by threatening to replace him with James Cagney.

Los Angeles, 17 June
Representatives from the MPAA testifying before the Senate Committee to Investigate Juvenile Delinquency said that films remained well behind other forms of the media in a general trend towards relaxed moral standards. In their opinion, books, plays and daily newspapers are filled with a far greater degree of licentiousness, sex and violence.

Hollywood, 24 June
The director of the Advertising Code has cautioned the heads of studio publicity and advertising departments to ease off sex and violence in exploiting movies.

Kuwait City, 18 July
The first cinema in the city opens its doors today.

Paris, 1 August
Sally Marlow, Gina Lollobrigida's stunt double for filming *Trapeze* had a fall during a scene on the flying trapeze. She broke her nose.

Guyancourt, 3 September
At the airport in the Yvelines here, Lindbergh's historic and triumphant arrival in France is being re-created for Billy Wilder's film *The Spirit of St. Louis*, with James Stewart in the role of the famous aviator.

Paris, 20 October
According to a report in *France-Soir*, the film so far this fall with the best weekly receipts in France is Walt Disney's *20,000 Leagues Under the Sea*, directed by Richard Fleischer.

New York, 7 November
The British picture, *The Constant Husband*, starring Rex Harrison and Kay Kendall, was transmitted by the NBC television network last night. This was the first time ever that a feature-length film has premiered on TV in the United States before reaching the theaters.

New York, 8 November
Opening of Robert Aldrich's *The Big Knife*, based on the play by Clifford Odets, with Jack Palance, Ida Lupino, Shelley Winters and Rod Steiger.

Los Angeles, 9 November
Rock Hudson has married Phyllis Gates, his agent's secretary.

Paris, 29 November
At the Boulogne Studios, Michèle Morgan is filming the beheading sequence in *Marie-Antoinette* under Jean Delannoy's direction.

London, 20 December
Laurence Olivier presents his new adaptation of Shakespeare's work *Richard III*. He is the film's producer, director and star, with Claire Bloom as Lady Anne.

Paris, 23 December
Robert Hossein has married the young actress Marina Vlady. She is the 17-year-old sister of well-known actress Odile Versois.

Hollywood, 31 December
According to the *Motion Picture Herald*'s annual referendum among cinema staff, the most popular star at the box office is James Stewart. His films this year are *The Far Country*, *The Man From Laramie* and *Strategic Air Command*, all three directed by Anthony Mann.

BIRTHS

Kansas, 12 January
Kirstie Alley

California, 18 January
Kevin Costner

Georgia, 19 February
Jeff Daniels

Paris, 16 March
Isabelle Huppert

Germany, 19 March
Bruce Willis

Ohio, 17 May
Debra Winger

New York, 8 June
Griffin Dunne

Ohio, 15 June
Julie Hagerty

Paris, 27 June
Isabelle Adjani

France, 29 June
Jean-Hugues Anglade

Wisconsin, 22 July
Willem Dafoe

New York, 19 August
Peter Gallagher

California, 20 November
Bo Derek

New Jersey, 18 December
Ray Liotta

DEATHS

Hollywood, 12 February
S.Z. "Cuddles" Sakall (Eugene Gero Szakall)

Los Angeles, 7 April
Theda Bara

Hollywood, 5 August
Carmen Miranda

California, 30 September
James Dean

Sunny buttercup blonde Doris D successfully plays a dramatic role famous 1920s singer Ruth Etti Cagney is the racketeer who he her to the top but drives her to dri

LIFE-INSPIRED DRAMA FROM
DANCE HALL TO ZIEGFELD FOLLIES!
DORIS
DAY
as FAMED RUTH ETTING
JAMES
CAGNEY
"THE GIMP"
M·G·M presents in CINEMASCOPE and COLOR
LOVE ME
OR
LEAVE ME
Co-Starring CAMERON MITCHELL with ROBERT KEITH · TOM TULLY · Screen Play by DANIEL FUCHS and ISOBEL LENNART · Story by DANIEL FUCHS Photographed in EASTMAN COLOR
Directed by CHARLES VIDOR Produced by JOE PASTERNAK AN M-G-M PICTURE

H.G. Clouzot proves a match for Hitchcock

Vera Clouzot (left), the director's wife, and Simone Signoret, a 'diabolical pair'.

Paris, 28 January
Henri-Georges Clouzot's *les Diaboliques* is being shown in France and an air of mystery surrounds it. Nobody is allowed into theaters after the start of the picture, and there is a cautionary title at the end: "Don't be diabolical yourself. Don't spoil the ending for your friends by telling them what you've just seen. On their behalf – Thank you!" With this chilling tale of murder, set in a gruesome school, Clouzot has lived up to his nickname as the "French Hitchcock". It tells of how two women (the director's wife Vera Clouzot and Simone Signoret) join forces to kill the sadistic headmaster (Paul Meurisse), who is the husband of one and the mistress of the other.

Glenn Ford takes on juvenile delinquent

Glenn Ford in the 'blackboard jungle' with Sidney Poitier (r), Vic Morrow

New York, 20 March
Glenn Ford's brow is even more furrowed than usual in MGM's *The Blackboard Jungle*, adapted from a novel by Evan Hunter and directed by Richard Brooks. He plays Navy veteran Richard Dadier whose first teaching job pits him against a class of juvenile delinquents at a tough New York high school. His hep-talking class, led by knife-wield Brando lookalike Vic Morro christen him "Daddy-O" while battles to communicate with younger generation. The film's b gimmick comes at the start wh the soundtrack blasts out "Ro Around the Clock" by Bill Ha and the Comets. This movie sparked a rock 'n' roll revolution

'Ice-maiden' Grace Kelly wins the Oscar

Hollywood, 30 March
Grace Kelly, known for her cool, blonde beauty, has won the Best Actress Oscar this year in a role that cast her very much against type. In *The Country Girl* she appears in dowdy cardigans, spectacles, and "plain" makeup as the lonely wife of an alcoholic singer (Bing Crosby), proving that she is more than just a pretty face. There could be no greater contrast between her and Marlon Brando, the Best Actor winner for his portrayal of the has-been boxer in Elia Kazan's *On the Waterfront*. Among the eight awards won by the latter film were Best Picture and Best Director.

'Country girl' Grace Kelly with Bing Crosby (center) and William Holden.

'Marty' brings new kind of movie roman

New York, 11 April
In its on-going efforts to win back movie audiences, Hollywood is not only turning to new techniques (3-D, CinemaScope, Todd-AO) and spectacles, but continues to turn out small-scale, serious black-and-white movies as well, such as *Marty*, a Harold Hecht-Burt Lancaster production adapted from a TV film by the playwright Paddy Chayefsky. Directed by Delbert Mann, a veteran of TV drama, *Marty* stars Ernest Borgnine as a plug-ugly Bronx pork butcher sadly resigned to bachelorhood and the aimless rituals of male cameraderie. Then he meets, woos and wins sweet but plain teacher Betsy Blair, telling her "Dogs like us, we're not such dogs as we think we are." Borgnine is a revelation in the role that was originally played on television by Rod Steiger. He is best known as a bulging-eyed villain in movies like *From Here to Eternity*, where he played the sadistic stockade sergeant, and *Bad Day at Black Rock*. In *Marty* his naturalistic performance as a man unexpectedly stumbling on love has won univer praise. Because of *Marty*'s succe it seems likely it will spawn a stri of modestly budgeted TV-deriv "clothesline" dramas that explo working-class life, scripted and rected by the talented young m who have cut their creative teeth live television drama.

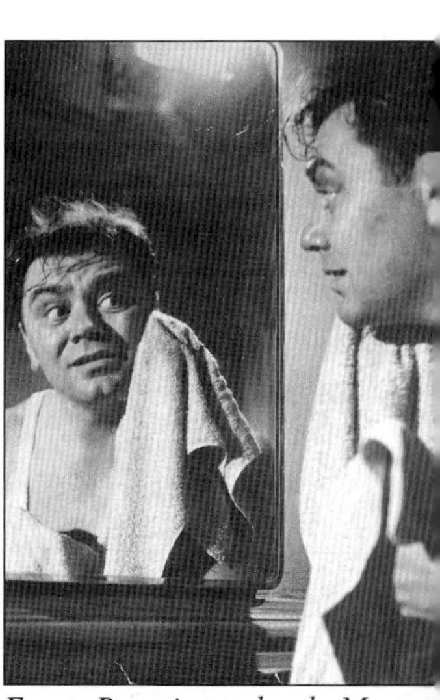

Ernest Borgnine as lonely Marty.

·illiant French thriller from Jules Dassin

r: Carl Mohner, Jean Servais and Robert Manuel in Dassin's ***Rififi***.

·is, 13 April
·erican director Jules Dassin, ·ing left the United States after ·ng targeted by HUAC in 1950, chosen to make his home in ·nce, where he has directed an ·remely effective thriller called *·ifi* (*Du rififi chez les hommes*). ·ginally assigned to the director ·n-Pierre Melville, the film con·trates on a bold burglary carried by four likeable gangsters, who ·n get themselves killed in a gun ·tle with a rival gang. If the sub· seems to lack originality, the ·lity of the screenplay by Auguste Breton (adapted from his novel), ·né Wheeler and Dassin com·ed with the skills of the director, ·ke *Rififi* a model of the genre. The sleazy Montmartre underworld is depicted in impeccable detail, peopled by convincingly portrayed criminals. The cast is headed by Jean Servais, Carl Mohner, Robert Manuel, Magali Noël and Dassin himself under the pseudonym of Perlo Vita. The highlight of the picture is the meticulously enacted and suspenseful 22-minute jewel robbery sequence played in total silence. It is five years since Dassin's last film, *Night and the City*, which he made in England. It is encouraging that the qualities of *Rififi* demonstrate that the director, who made his reputation in America in the late Forties with *films noirs*, such as *The Naked City*, is able to adapt his style to other countries and conditions.

·inster finds first-time romance in Venice

·ndon, 29 May
·tish director David Lean's latest ·, *Summer Madness*, has opened ·e. Mr. Lean, increasingly associ·d with huge epics of enormous ·ual impact, has regressed, at least ·subject matter, to the small-scale ·macy of plot which marked his early career, notably with *Brief Encounter*. However, his sense of visual beauty, captured in color, has not deserted him – indeed, Venice, the setting of the film, with its glorious buildings and canals lovingly photographed on location, is in danger of distracting attention from the plot. The story is simple: a middle-aged spinster on holiday in Venice encounters a married Italian antique dealer, they fall in love, and she ends the affair on moral grounds, going home with her memories. Slight, tender, and unbearably poignant, the film draws a magnificent performance from Katharine Hepburn, playing opposite the accurately cast Italian actor, Rossano Brazzi.

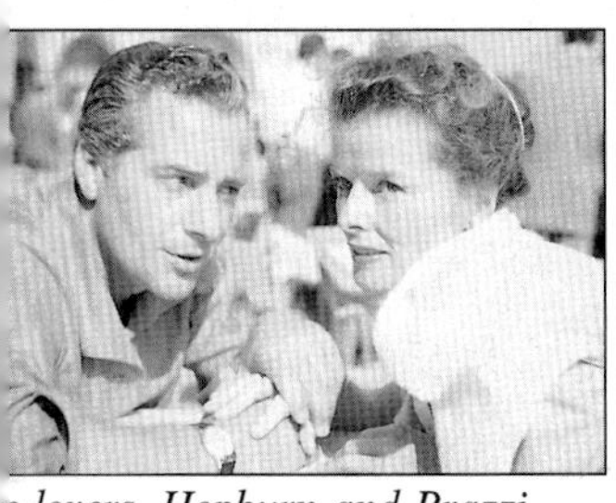

·e lovers, Hepburn and Brazzi.

Renoir celebrates return with the Cancan

Françoise Arnoul, one of the lovely women in Renoir's film, with Jean Gabin.

Paris, 27 April
For Jean Renoir's first French film in 15 years, *French Cancan*, he has chosen to go back to his roots in Montmartre, the world of his childhood and his famous painter father. Based on the life of Ziedler, the man who founded the Moulin Rouge, the film brilliantly re-creates the colorful world of *la Belle époque*, ending with the cancan, when the screen explodes with exuberant dancing. Jean Gabin, who last worked with Renoir in *la Bête humaine* before the war, gives a remarkably shaded performance, passionate and tender, as the impresario. The haunting theme song was written by Georges Van Parys, with the lyrics by Jean Renoir himself.

'Kiss Me Deadly' is savagely effective

Ralph Meeker as Spillane's 'hero', Mike Hammer, with Maxene Cooper.

Los Angeles, 18 May
Mickey Spillane's swaggering, brutal private eye Mike Hammer has been brilliantly brought to the big screen in *Kiss Me Deadly*, directed by Robert Aldrich. Ralph Meeker portrays Hammer as a swaying, strutting fascist thug in a stunning portrait of self-sufficient brutality. Lurking on the borderline between roughneck thriller and science fiction *film noir*, *Kiss Me Deadly* sends Hammer lurching in pursuit of the "great whatsit", a nuclear Pandora's box which is fatally opened at the picture's pulsating climax. By combining elements of ancient myth with the paranoia abroad in today's nuclear age, Aldrich's version of Spillane packs a deadly punch. ▷

With Wilder at the helm, Marilyn Monroe sails full-steam ahead

Marilyn Monroe in New York: 5,000 gaping onlookers watched the first takes.

New York, 6 June
Director Billy Wilder and screenwriter George Axelrod turn their mordant humor on the subject of sex in *The Seven Year Itch*. Tom Ewell is the New Yorker indulging in Walter Mittyish fantasies one long hot summer while his wife is away. They are stimulated by the arrival of curvaceous blonde neighbor Marilyn Monroe, a devastating ingenue with more physical assets than brains, who likes to keep her panties in the fridge and who can recognize classical music because "there isn't a vocal." Monroe oozes unconscious sexiness. At one point she straddles a subway grating as the uprush of air from a passing train billows her white dress while Ewell gawps lewdly. The stunt was originally shot at 52nd and Lexington Avenue in New York, but it failed to carry the remarkable erotic charge which Wilder later achieved, in one take, in the studio. The director has referred to Monroe's appeal on the screen as "flesh impact".

Howard Hughes sells off major ass

New York, 18 July
A little over a year after acquir total control over RKO, How Hughes has sold the studio and entire backlog of old movies to G eral Teleradio (a subsidiary of giant General Tire and Rubber C for $25 million. As the owner c number of TV stations, this com ny, headed by Tom O'Neil, has b especially interested in acquir the rights to old movies. O'Nei also hoping to keep RKO going an active film production ent Since Hughes appears to have d onstrated little interest in mak films during the seven years when ran the studio – indeed, it is diffi to understand why he bought it remains to be seen whether a r management team can breathe fr life into the struggling outfit. Unf tunately, the general outlook is good since cinema attendance declining and even the top stud are making only minimal profits

Dream world of Disneyland opens its gates

Los Angeles, 18 July
"Disneyland is dedicated to the ideals, dreams and struggles that made America." These words greet the visitor to a unique new city, born out of the desire of a man to make his dreams come true – Walt Disney. The five million visitors that are expected annually will get the impression that they are traveling through a cartoon universe. They can fly with Peter Pan, shake the hands of Donald Duck and Mickey Mouse, go through the mirror into Wonderland, or enter the castle of Sleeping Beauty. A half an hour from downtown Los Angeles on the highway, Disneyland was constructed on 150 acres of orange groves. Yesterday, a televised inauguration was held in the presence of 30,000 privileged people.

Over 150 acres of stucco, steel and concrete built at a cost of $17 million.

Denmark's Dreyer takes home Golden Li

Venice, 9 September
Rather like last year, when the jury of the Venice Festival could not decide on a best actress winner, this year they could not choose between Curt Jurgens in *les Héros sont fatigués* and Kenneth More in *The Deep Blue Sea* for best actor. A compromise was reached, allowing them to share the trophy. The jury was also split on the Silver Lion, giving it to no fewer than four fil Fortunately, there was unanin when it came to presenting Golden Lion to Carl Dreyer's *Or* Based on a play by Kai Munk, film is an extraordinary express of spiritual optimism. The tale a miraculous resurrection brou about by love could easily have b pious and sentimental, but Dre makes it an enriching experience

Henrik Malberg (l) and Preben Lerdorff Rye, father and visionary son in ***Or***

st for life brings cruel death to James Dean

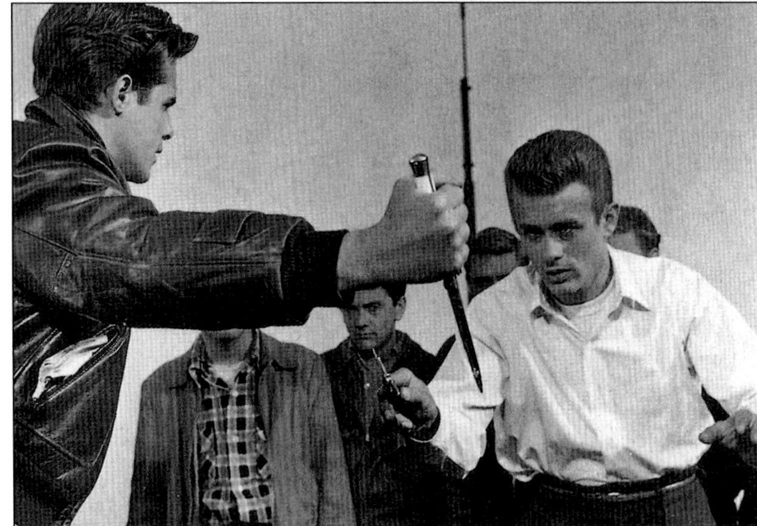

ew and powerful icon for contemporary youth: James Dean, here with Raymond Massey in **East of Eden** (left), and in **Rebel Without a Cause.**

Angeles, 1 October
nes Dean was killed yesterday in r accident while driving his silver sche 550 Spider to Salinas to ticipate in their autumn racing nt. It happened at 5:58 p.m. at intersection of Highway 41 and ute 466. He left Hollywood in the y afternoon and was stopped by ice at 3 p.m. for excess speeding. vertheless, he continued to step the gas, with the sun in his eyes. car in front, driven by a student, refused to let Dean, who was veling at 115 miles per hour, rtake it. The 24-year old actor found with his neck broken. His chanic, Ralph Weutherich, is in ous condition. A few days ago an had completed shooting on *nt* with Elizabeth Taylor and Rock Hudson, under the direction of George Stevens. Ironically, the star had recently made a short publicity film for road safety, declaring, "Drive carefully... It's perhaps my life that you will save."

James Dean was born on 8 February 1931 in a small town in Indiana, the son of a dental technician. His mother had a passion for poetry and gave him Byron as a second name. After graduating from Fairmont High, where he became interested in art and literature, he went to California where he enrolled in James Whitmore's drama classes at UCLA. In order to purchase a new Triumph, he did some TV commercials, and managed to get himself bit parts in three movies. In 1952, Dean went to New York, where he was able to watch some classes at the Actors' Studio, but after an audition he felt like "a rabbit being vivisected." He then got a part in a play called *See the Jaguar*, which ran for only six performances, but he was noticed by producer Billy Rose who cast him as the pederastic Arab boy in André Gide's *The Immoralist*. This led to a screen test at Warner Bros. followed by a seven-year contract. It was Elia Kazan who asked for Dean to play Caleb Trask in *East of Eden*, which made him an overnight sensation when it opened last February. With his animated shoulders, tortured postures, extravagant gestures, studied hesitancy and untamed animal sensitivity, he painted a perfect portrait of a disturbed and complex adolescent with whom young audiences could identify. His death has made people even more impatient to see his second starring feature, Nicholas Ray's *Rebel Without a Cause*, which will be released at the end of this month. His next movie was to have been *Somebody Up There Likes Me* with Pier Angeli, the girl he had wanted to marry. In the 24 hours since his death, James Dean has already entered Hollywood legend.

nis last film, **Giant**.

Awesome directorial debut from 55-year-old Charles Laughton

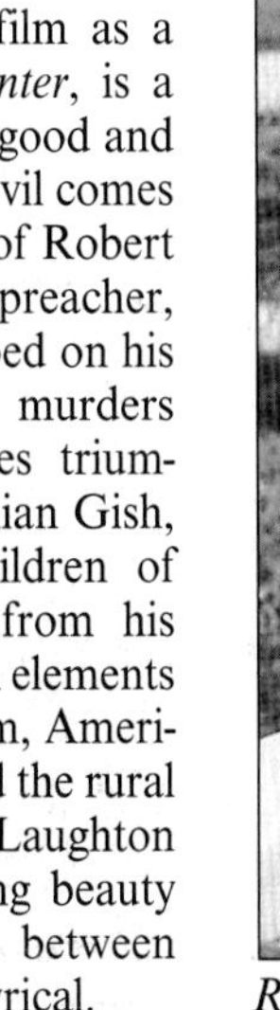

New York, 29 September
Charles Laughton's first film as a director, *Night of the Hunter*, is a remarkable parable about good and evil set in rural America. Evil comes unforgettably in the form of Robert Mitchum's psychopathic preacher, with Love and Hate tattooed on his hands, who marries and murders rich widows. Good comes triumphantly in the form of Lillian Gish, who rescues the two children of Mitchum's latest victim from his rabid clutches. Drawing on elements as diverse as Expressionism, American primitive paintings and the rural dramas of D.W. Griffith, Laughton fashions a film of haunting beauty which moves effortlessly between the nightmarish and the lyrical.

LOVE

Robert Mitchum in **The Night of the Hunter**: fake pastor, evil psychopath.

Exuberant screen transfer of 'Guys and Dolls'

Gambler Sky Masterson (Brando) 'corrupting' Salvation Army Sister Sarah Brown (Simmons) in Havana.

New York, 4 November
Producer Samuel Goldwyn pai reported $1 million for the mo rights to the great Broadway sical *Guys and Dolls*, handed direction to Joseph L. Mankiew (his first musical), and then sp another $4.5 million on the prod tion. The result? A 158-minute ro as gambler Sky Masterson (Mar Brando) sets about winning a that he can persuade buttoned Sally Army lass Sarah Brown (J Simmons) into a date; and Nat Detroit (Sinatra) tries to keep crap game afloat and his fiancee 14 years running (a brilliant Viv Blaine) at bay. Marlon croons wi pleasingly husky voice, but is cle not destined for a vocalist's care but Sinatra is in peak form. Mich Kidd's choreography is spectacu and the score, despite a couple the original songs being replac retains its exuberant fizz.

Preminger defies production code again

New York, 12 December
Because the Motion Picture Association of America has refused to give a Seal of Approval to Otto Preminger's new project, *The Man With the Golden Arm*, United Artists has resigned from the MPAA and submitted the film to local state censors, most of whom have been willing to grant it a certificate. Producer-director Preminger has again taken on the censors after *The Moon is Blue* controversy two years ago, and won. *The Man With the Golden Arm* is Hollywood's first attempt to tackle the subject of drug addiction, and does so realistically and responsibly. Audiences watching Frank Sinatra go "cold turkey" after he becomes seriously hooked on narcotics, can be in no doubt as to the movie's attitude to the problem.

Frank Sinatra and Kim Novak in Preminger's stark study of drug addiction.

Hayward perfects portrayal of alcoholism

Los Angeles, 21 December
Susan Hayward is no stranger to the bottle. In 1947, in *Smash-Up, The Story of a Woman*, she played a torch singer who gives up her husband and family for the booze. Reportedly, she researched the role by attending meetings of Alcoholics Anonymous, and even going on a binge herself. She hit the bottle again, though rather more romantically, in the 1949 *My Foolish He* This experience must have hel Hayward when she approached part of alcoholic chanteuse Lil Roth in her latest picture, anot all-stops-out weepie called *I'll Tomorrow*. Hayward, who pla crippled singer Jane Froman th years back in *With a Song in Heart*, is able to be a lush *and* a s fering entertainer in her new fil

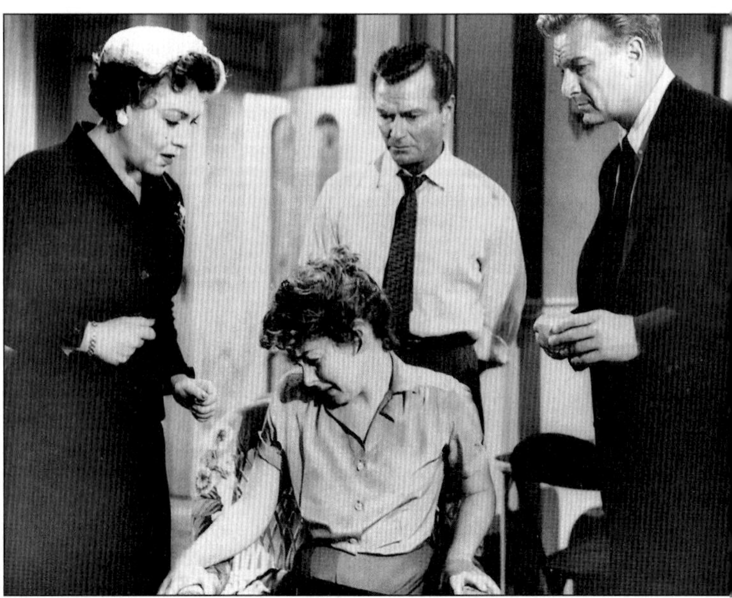

Susan Hayward (center), Jo Van Fleet (left) and Eddie Albert (right).

ita Hayworth ersus Columbia

llywood, 27 December
e ongoing love-hate relationship tween Columbia boss Harry Cohn d the studio's star discovery, Rita yworth, appears finally to have ached an acrimonious climax. hn and Columbia Pictures have tiated a court action against the ress for having refused to appear the biblical epic, *Joseph and His ethren*, which was being planned her and for which she received substantial advance payment that has not returned. Apparently studio has invested much time d effort (as well as money) in the *seph* project, the first production involve former MGM boss Louis Mayer as an independent pro-cer, with elaborate costumes and s having been designed, Lee J. bb signed to play Potiphar, and fford Odets employed as script-iter. In addition, the studio lent 0,000 to Dick Haymes, Rita's rmer husband and partner in her n producing company, who also ped to star in the movie. Miss yworth will not be in court to ntest the case. Her divorce from ymes, her fourth husband, was fact granted two weeks ago, and e has recently left the U.S. for rope with her two young daugh-s. It looks as if the star's reign as een of the Columbia lot has now ded, and a sexy, blonde, 22-year-l newcomer named Kim Novak is ing groomed by Harry Cohn to e her place.

Martine Carol makes a flamboyant and sympathetic Lola Montès

The colorful heroine of Max Ophuls' baroque spectacle was inspired by a 19th-century historical figure.

Paris, 22 December
Max Ophuls' new film, *Lola Montès*, represents the apogee of his work. The Franco-German co-production, which cost nearly 650 million francs, stars Martine Carol, astonishing in the sympathetic title role of the tragic heroine. The story begins with Lola locked in a golden cage as a circus attraction, and proceeds in a series of multiple flashbacks. The ringmaster (Peter Ustinov) tells of the celebrated courtesan's love affairs with King Ludwig I (Anton Walbrook), Franz Liszt (Will Quadflieg) and a young student (Oskar Werner). But the originality of the film's structure has furiously divided the critics and disconcerted the public. As a result, the producers intend to cut the 140-minute color film and redo the editing with the object of putting the narrative into a strict chronological order. This would be a great shame, because changes might diminish the impact of the film, which treats the space of the CinemaScope screen (utilizing masking and other devices) in a breathtaking manner, while the crane shots and camera movements (plus a 360-degree revolve) have the virtuosity of a Liszt sonata.

arilyn Monroe signs new Fox contract

*arilyn in the steamy **Niagara**, a lestone in her career.*

New York, 31 December
With her latest picture, *The Seven Year Itch*, established as one of this year's biggest hits, Fox has wisely decided to offer a new, improved contract to its biggest asset, Marilyn Monroe. Not only will she be paid $100,000 per film and a percentage of the profits, but she will also have script and director approval, along with the choice of subjects. In turn, Marilyn has agreed to star in four films for the company during the next four years, but she is free to appear in other, outside productions as well. A film version of William Inge's play, *Bus Stop*, will be her first under the new terms.

Martine Carol in a scene with Peter Ustinov who plays the ringmaster.

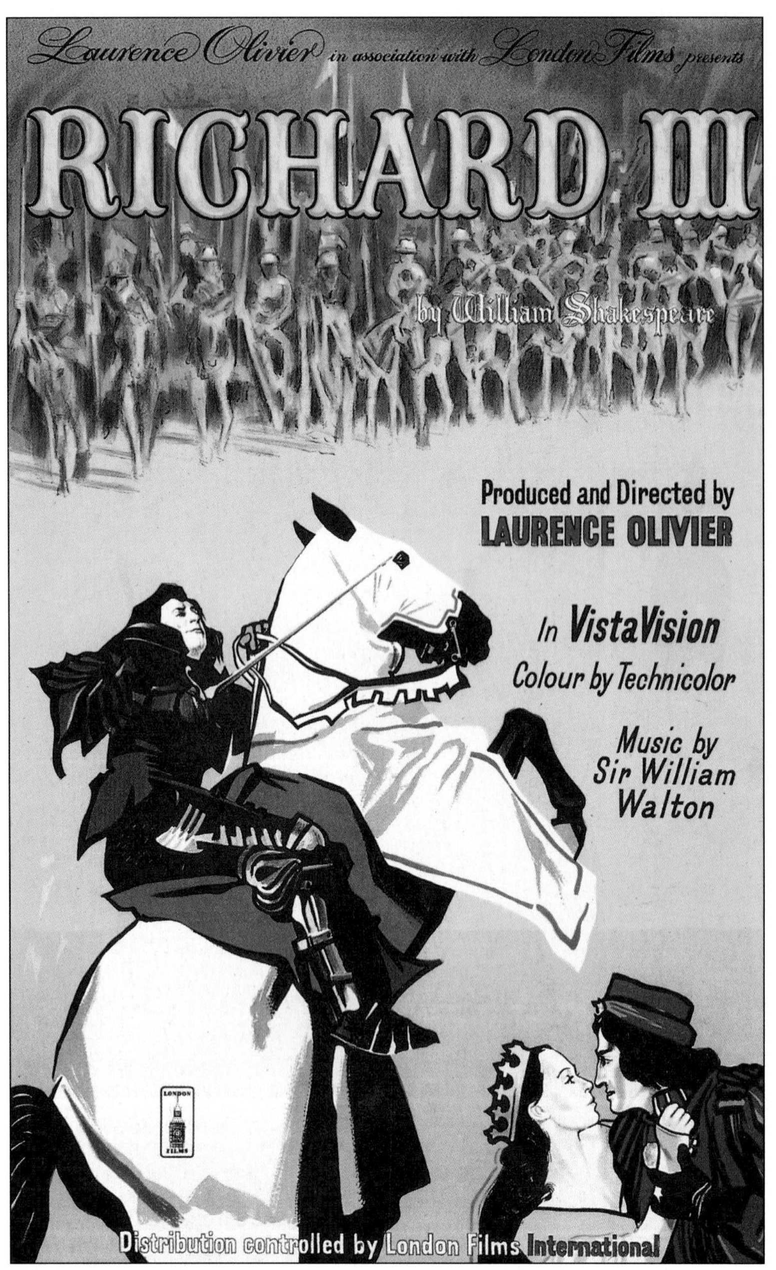
Laurence Olivier in association with London Films presents
RICHARD III
by William Shakespeare
Produced and Directed by
LAURENCE OLIVIER
In VistaVision
Colour by Technicolor
Music by
Sir William
Walton
Distribution controlled by London Films International

Memorably vile 'crook-back' in Olivier's third Shakespeare as actor-director.

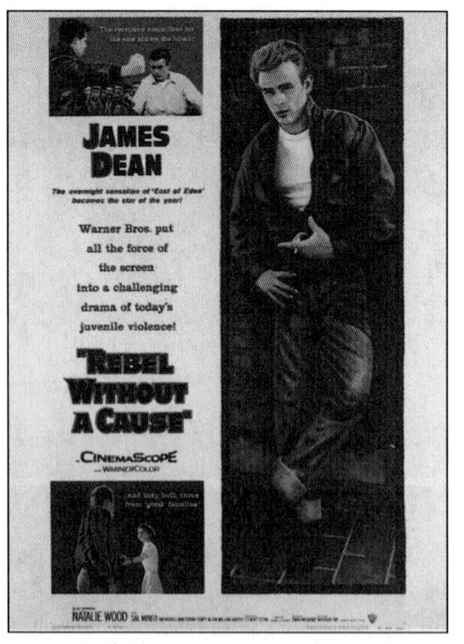
JAMES
DEAN
Warner Bros. put
all the force of
the screen
into a challenging
drama of today's
juvenile violence!
"REBEL
WITHOUT
A CAUSE"
CINEMASCOPE
NATALIE WOOD

The defiant yet vulnerable image of a new youth icon.

Czech animator Jiri Trnka's ***T Good Soldier Schweik****.*

Björn Bjelvenstam (l) and Gunnar Björnstrand in Ingmar Bergman's ***Smiles a Summer's Night****. This film is charming and sensuous yet probing.*

Clark Gable (l), Jane Russell, Robert Ryan in Raoul Walsh's ***The Tall Men****.*

Kirk Douglas (right) was ***The Man Without a Star*** *in King Vidor's Western*

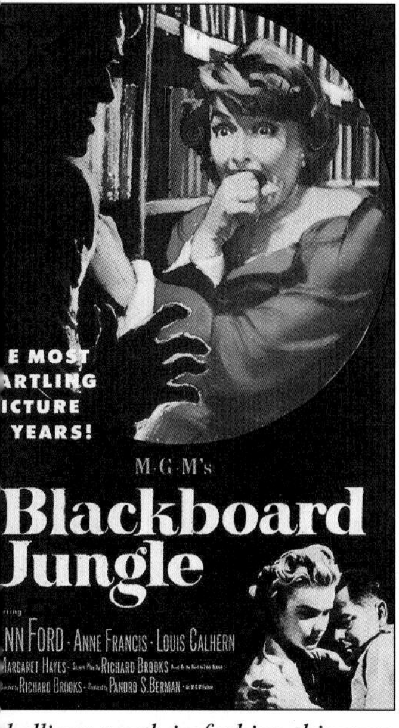
M·G·M's
Blackboard
Jungle

ʻbellious youth in fashion this year.

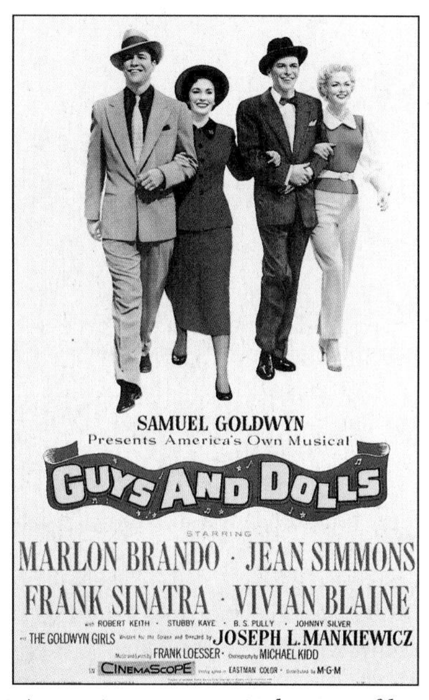
SAMUEL GOLDWYN
Presents America's Own Musical
GUYS AND DOLLS
STARRING
MARLON BRANDO · JEAN SIMMONS
FRANK SINATRA · VIVIAN BLAINE
JOSEPH L. MANKIEWICZ
FRANK LOESSER
MICHAEL KIDD
CINEMASCOPE
EASTMAN COLOR
M-G-M

A superior stage musical now on film.

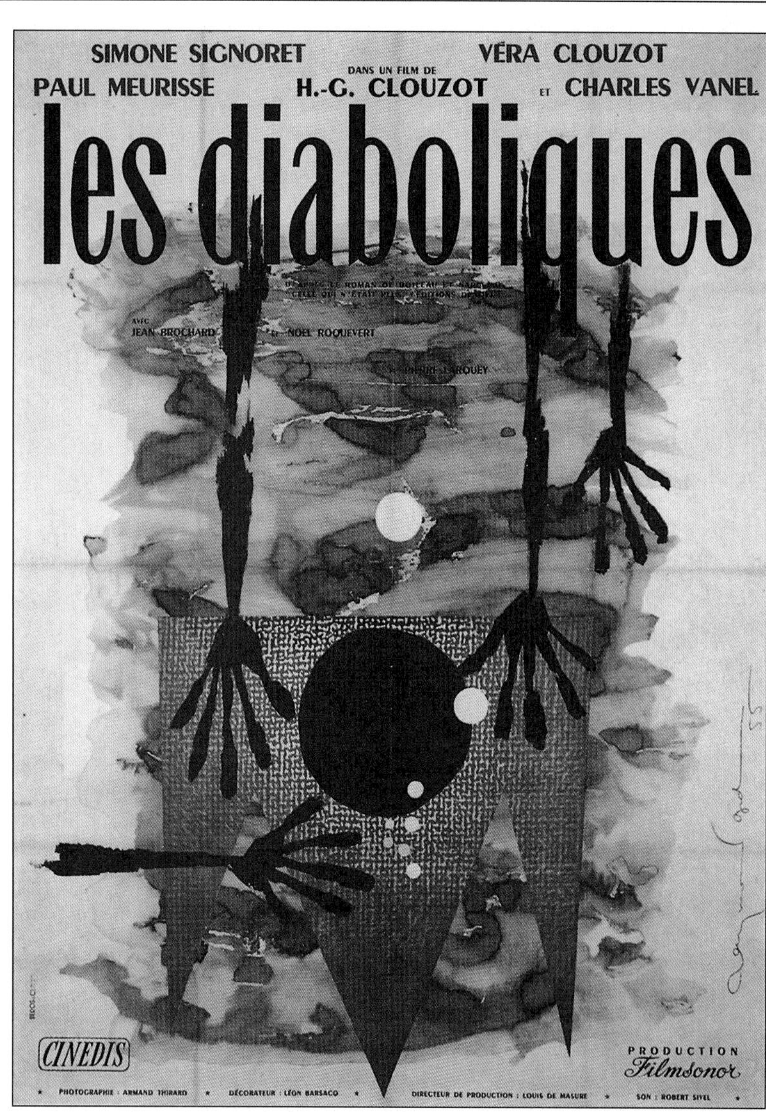
SIMONE SIGNORET
VÉRA CLOUZOT
DANS UN FILM DE
PAUL MEURISSE
H.-G. CLOUZOT
ET CHARLES VANEL
les diaboliques
CINEDIS
PRODUCTION
Filmsonor
PHOTOGRAPHIE : ARMAND THIRARD
DÉCORATEUR : LÉON BARSACQ
DIRECTEUR DE PRODUCTION : LOUIS DE MASURE
SON : ROBERT SIVEL

The French poster for a French film that found international favor.

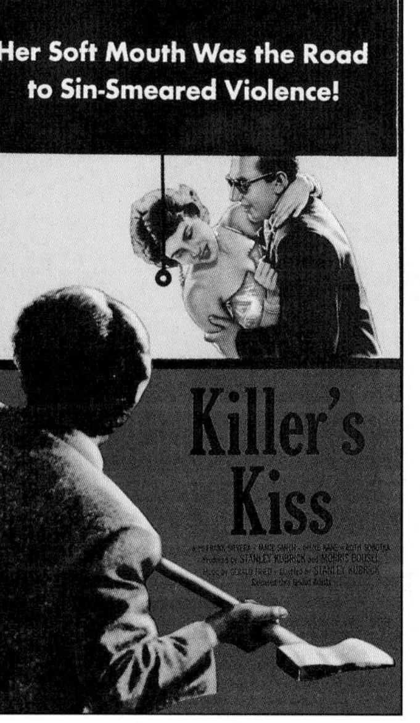
Her Soft Mouth Was the Road
to Sin-Smeared Violence!
Killer's
Kiss

om newcomer Stanley Kubrick.

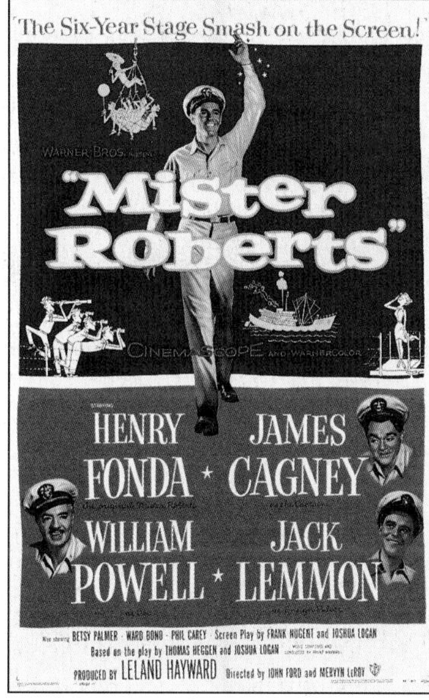
The Six-Year Stage Smash on the Screen!
"Mister
Roberts"
HENRY FONDA ★ JAMES CAGNEY
WILLIAM POWELL ★ JACK LEMMON
PRODUCED BY LELAND HAYWARD
Directed by JOHN FORD and MERVYN LeROY

Fonda repeats his Broadway role.

ʻother British comedy winner, ***The Lady Killers***. Behind Peter Sellers (left) d Alec Guinness are Danny Green, Herbert Lom and Cecil Parker.

Cyd Charisse in Stanley Donen's ***It's Always Fair Weather***.

Rock Hudson as ***Captain Lightfoot***, a Douglas Sirk film.

1956

1955 Academy Awards, RKO Pantages Theater, 21 Mar.

Best Film:	*Marty* (dir: Delbert Mann)
Best Director:	Delbert Mann
Best Actor:	Ernest Borgnine *(Marty)*
Best Actress:	Anna Magnani *(The Rose Tattoo)*
Best Supp. Actress:	Jack Lemmon *(Mister Roberts)*
Best Supp. Actress:	Jo Van Fleet *(East of Eden)*

New York, 6 January
Prince Rainier of Monaco and actress Grace Kelly have officially announced their engagement.

Hollywood, 4 February
The studios are closed today, Saturday, for the first time; the unions have won a five-day working week.

Washington, 6 February
French inventor Professor Henri Chrétien who developed Hypergonar from which CinemaScope is derived, has died.

Tokyo, 18 March
Kenji Mizoguchi, although seriously ill, is determined to be present at the press showing of his latest film *Akasen Chitai* (*Street of Shame*).

Nice, 21 March
The screening of Grace Kelly's penultimate film, *The Swan*, has been canceled. Kelly's films have been banned in Monaco since her marriage, and Nice's cinema owners do not wish to offend their royal neighbor, the Prince.

Mexico, 26 March
Luis Buñuel is filming *Evil Eden*, a Franco-Mexican co-production with Simone Signoret, Georges Marchal, Charles Vanel and Michel Piccoli. It renews Buñuel's recent links with the French cinema, recalling his beginnings as a filmmaker in France almost 30 years ago.

Hollywood, 12 April
Filming of *Bus Stop* has been halted by Marilyn Monroe's hospitalization for "exhaustion due to overwork..., and acute bronchitis."

Paris, 14 April
The American producer Otto Preminger is here for a meeting with Françoise Sagan, author of *Bonjour tristesse*. He wants to turn the best-selling novel into a film and is also searching for the ideal actress for the lead.

Hollywood, 10 May
Harry and Albert Warner are selling their holdings in the studio to a group of investors headed by the First National Bank of Boston. Jack Warner is holding on to his, however, and remains the largest individual shareholder in the company.

Los Angeles, 13 May
Montgomery Clift was injured early this morning when his car struck a power pole. The actor was returning from a party given by the actress Elizabeth Taylor. Clift, aged 35, suffered facial cuts, bruises and a broken nose.

New York, 16 May
Alfred Hitchcock proves his ongoing mastery of the thriller genre with his American remake of *The Man Who Knew Too Much*. Hitchcock first made the film in England in 1934. This time the action is transposed from Switzerland to Morocco but none of the suspense is lost. James Stewart, who worked for Hitchcock in both *Rope* and *Rear Window*, co-stars with Doris Day.

New Delhi, 19 May
The Indian Government has banned six American and two British films for presenting a "disparaging" impression of life in Africa. Last year, after a demonstration by African students over the Universal production *Tanganyika*, Prime Minister Nehru made an informal recommendation that the censors ban films depicting Africa as part of "the white man's burden." *African Queen* and *Mogambo* have been banned.

Paris, 1 July
At the announcement of the results of the Concours du Conservatoire, Jean-Paul Belmondo, who only received an honorable mention, was triumphantly carried shoulder-high by his friends who were disgusted by the list of winners. He gave a mocking salute in passing to the jury of this venerable institution.

Nice, 4 July
Gary Cooper is reported to have met Pablo Picasso while out for a walk and to have asked him for his autograph.

London, 18 August
Vivien Leigh has had a nervous breakdown, following a miscarriage.

London, 5 September
Theater managers called for police protection today to control teenage audiences during showing of an American "rock 'n' roll" movie titled *Rock Around the Clock*. Seven "Teddy boys" have been fined for rioting in a theater showing the film. According to them the music "sent them up the wall."

Hollywood, 20 September
Michael Wilson has not received screenplay credits on the release prints of William Wyler's *Friendly Persuasion*. Allied Artists, who are distributing the film, have evoked the Screen Writers Guild's amended clause to contracts with studios. The clause allows studios to deny credits to any writer revealed to be a member of the Communist Party or refusing to give evidence before the HUAC. Wilson refused to testify to the HUAC in 1951.

Los Angeles, 5 October
Opening here of Cecil B. DeMille's *The Ten Commandments*, which stars Charlton Heston, Yul Brynner, Anne Baxter, Edward G. Robinson and Yvonne De Carlo.

London, 30 October
Marilyn Monroe was among the group of international stars who were presented to the Queen at last night's Royal Command Performance. The Queen is reported to have asked her how she liked living in Windsor eliciting a nervous "What?" from the star! The film shown was Michael Powell's *The Battle of the River Plate*.

Ceylon, 8 November
Peasants fled in terror today as paratroopers descended on a village 12 miles from Ceylon. They set the temple bells ringing to signal the start of an invasion. Police were called to the village to explain that the "invaders" were actors in British director David Lean's new film, *The Bridge on the River Kwai*.

Los Angeles, 23 November
Jayne Mansfield has been serv with a writ by her husband. He a cuses her of being an unwort mother on the grounds that she living with her lover, and has pos nude for *Playboy* magazine.

New York, 18 December
Premiere of Warner Bros.' *Ba Doll*, directed by Elia Kazan, at t Victoria Theater. The film has be condemned by the Roman Catho Church and the National League Decency as "evil in concept". Pr ceeds from tonight's opening will to the Actors Studio.

Italy, 31 December
At the present time, Italy has t largest network of cinemas in t whole of Europe: 17,000. This is t highest number ever reached in t "old world".

BIRTHS

New York, 3 January
Mel Gibson

Georgia, 20 March
Spike Lee

Cuba, 12 April
Andy Garcia

California, 9 July
Tom Hanks

Los Angeles, 21 October
Carrie Fisher

DEATHS

London, 23 January
Alexander Korda

California, 26 April
Edward Arnold

Tokyo, 12 May
Louis Calhern

Beverly Hills, 2 June
Jean Hersholt

Los Angeles, 16 August
Bela Lugosi

MGM's ace color stylist Vincen Minnelli, working in CinemaSco directed ***Lust for Life****, a filmed count of the brilliant and tragic Dut born artist, Vincent Van Gogh.*

M · G · M PRESENTS IN CINEMASCOPE AND METROCOLOR
KIRK DOUGLAS
IN
LUST FOR LIFE
CO-STARRING
ANTHONY QUINN · JAMES DONALD · PAMELA BROWN
WITH EVERETT SLOANE · SCREEN PLAY BY NORMAN CORWIN · BASED ON THE NOVEL BY IRVING STONE
DIRECTED BY VINCENTE MINNELLI · PRODUCED BY JOHN HOUSEMAN
A METRO-GOLDWYN-MAYER PICTURE
LUST FOR LIFE
THE FRANK, REVEALING BOOK IS ON THE SCREEN!
© Copyright 1956 Loew's Incorporated
Property of National Screen Service Corp. Licensed for display only in connection with the exhibition of this picture at your theatre. Must be returned immediately thereafter.
Country of Origin U.S.A.

Meek and mirthful jester from Danny Kaye

Defiance disguised as a joke.

Los Angeles, 1 February
Danny Kaye's latest film, *The Court Jester*, is a return to his best hilarious form. The Robin Hoodish plot shows Kaye accidentally becoming a jester at the English court of the wicked king, played with sneering relish by Basil Rathbone. The film allows the comedian time to romance Glynis Johns, and to exploit his way with tongue-twisting words. The best comic moment comes when, as a reluctant participant in a joust, he is provided with knockout drops for his antagonist, but must remember in which cup they have been put. Thus the mnemonic: "The pellet with the poison's in the vessel with the pestle, the chalice from the palace has the brew that is true." Norman Panama and Melvin Frank take equal credit for the direction and screenplay.

'The Burmese Harp' plays melancholy tun

Shoji Yasui as the soldier-priest.

Tokyo, 21 January
The new film by Kon Ichikawa, *T. Burmese Harp*, is one of the fi Japanese films concerned with pa fist themes related to the defeat Japan in 1945. Scripted by Na Wada, the director's wife, it tells o young soldier-musician in Burma the time of the Japanese capitu tion, who takes on the role of Buddhist priest and tries to bury many bodies as he can. Ichikaw who has stated that he has attem ed to explore what he terms "t pain of the age", has created here non-naturalistic odyssey in visiona black-and-white images, throbbi with the anguish that war brings. T the director, however, the idea of t unbreakable continuity of the pa present and future, holds more i portance than a realistic reporta on a specific war.

'Pod people' arrive with sci-fi frightener

Los Angeles, 29 February
Aliens take possession of human bodies in Don Siegel's *The Invasion of the Body Snatchers*. The inhabitants of a sleepy California town are remorselessly replaced by automaton-like simulacra hatched from enormous seed pods. Local doctor Kevin McCarthy is powerless to halt the march of the "pod people". In one gruesome sequence he takes a pitchfork to an oozing pod as it is about to give birth to the image which will replace him. There's no happy ending here. McCarthy's girlfriend Dana Wynter is possessed by the alien intelligence and pods are dispatched all over America. As the film ends, he stumbles along the freeway yelling "You're next!" to the faceless drivers who flash past him. Critics are divided about the film's message. Is it a metaphor for an "enemy within", and if so, who is the enemy? Communist witch-hunters like Senator McCarthy, as some suggest, or Communists themselves, as others argue.

l to r: Dana Wynter, Carolyn Jones, Kevin McCarthy, King Donovan.

Italian firebrand is this year's Best Actres

Hollywood, 22 March
The Italian actress Anna Magnani was asleep in her apartment in Rome when she was woken up with the news that she had won the Best Actress Oscar for her first American film *The Rose Tattoo*. "If this is a joke," she shrieked over the telephone, "I will get up and kill you whoever you are." Magnani in no way conforms to the conventional conception of a movie star, being rather plump, short in stature, unkempt in appearance and having dark circles under her eyes. But she is able to express earthy, temperamental Mediterranean sensuality better than most Latin performers. In *The Rose Tattoo*, based on Tennessee Williams' play, she is perfect as a widowed housewife tempted into a love affair with a truck driver (Burt Lancaster). Even less typical of a star is Best Actor winner Ernest Borgnine for *Marty*. The former movie heavy was sympathetically cast as an ugly 34-year-old butcher from the Bronx, who forges a relationship with a plain schoolteacher. *Marty*, which has brought a new naturalism into Hollywood movies, was also honored with Best Picture, Best Director (Delbert Mann), and Best Screenplay (Paddy Chayefsky). Grace Kelly, who presented the statuette to Borgnine, had just announced her engagement to Prince Rainier of Monaco. She was offer best wishes from the film commu ty by Jerry Lewis, the evening's M Another curiosity was that Jam Dean, who was killed in a car cra six months ago, became the fi actor ever to receive a posthumo nomination for *East of Eden*. Van Fleet was the Best Supporti Actress for her role as Dea mother in the same movie, and u and-coming actor Jack Lemm was the Best Supporting Actor f *Mister Roberts*.

Earthy Magnani with her awards.

Ⅰiss Kelly is now ᵉrincess Grace

Ionaco, 19 April
. week ago Grace Kelly, accompa-ied by her parents, arrived in the rincipality aboard the liner *Consti-ıtion*. She was greeted with showers f red and white carnations dropped om a seaplane owned by Artistotle nassis. For the last seven days, elly has been preparing for her edding while over 2,000 journalists ave descended on Monaco. Today, front of an assembly of European ɔyalty, presidents, and stars of age and screen, Grace married rince Rainier in the Cathedral of e Immaculate Conception. It was wedding worthy of the hoary old escription "fairy tale", and in the rocess Kelly made the transition om the queen of the MGM lot to al-life princess.

Ⅰontgomery Clift ay be disfigured

ontgomery Clift in ***The Men***.

os Angeles, 13 May
Iontgomery Clift, who was in the idst of filming *Raintree County*, ıs had a serious car accident. He as at the wheel when he suddenly st control of the steering and ran raight into a tree. In the near-fatal cident Clift lost four teeth, broke s nose, fractured his jaw and suf-red a huge cut from his nose rough his upper lip. His face mus-es have been seriously damaged. ıe accident was the culmination of troubled period for Clift. On loca-ɔn for *Raintree County* he was ice found walking around at night ark naked and is also said to have ken an overdose of sleeping pills.

Documentary-film prizes are inaugurated at the Cannes Festival

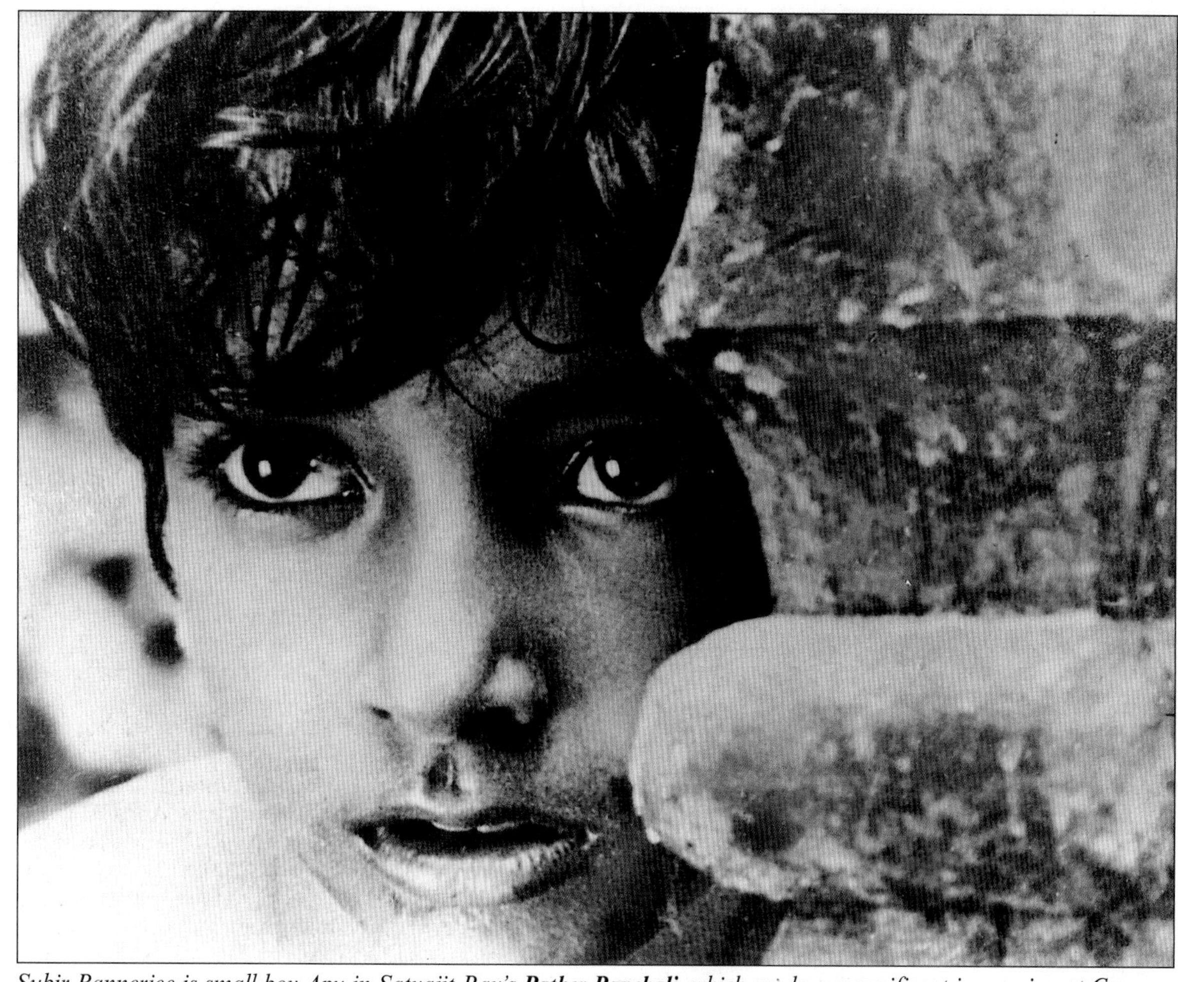

Subir Bannerjee is small boy Apu in Satyajit Ray's ***Pather Panchali****, which made a magnificent impression at Cannes.*

Cannes, 11 May
An exceptional event has taken place at this year's Cannes Film Festival – the two major prizes have been awarded for the first time ever to documentaries. The jury rather audaciously has decided to honor Jacques-Yves Cousteau's *The Silent World* with the Golden Palm, and Henri-Georges Clouzot's *The Picasso Mystery* with the Special Jury Prize. The former is a genuine odyssey of exploration of the fauna and flora of the ocean's depths by the famous French oceanographer, diver and documentary filmmaker. With his co-director, the 24-year-old Louis Malle, and two other underwater cameramen, Cousteau was able to observe the submarine life of the Red Sea, the Indian Ocean and the Persian Gulf. Thanks to technically sophisticated equipment that includes aqua lungs and underwater scooters, the team, operating from Cousteau's vessel *Calypso*, has made it possible for audiences to enter an unknown world of striking beauty. *The Picasso Mystery* introduces us to a no less fascinating world, that of artistic creation. Clouzot filmed the 75-year-old modern master at work, using special transparent canvases so that the act of painting could be shot from behind. When Picasso works in charcoal or ink, the film is in black and white, but from the moment he takes up his paints, it bursts into color. And a standing ovation was given to the delightful 36-minute fantasy *The Red Balloon*, shown out of competition.

LE MONDE
DU SILENCE

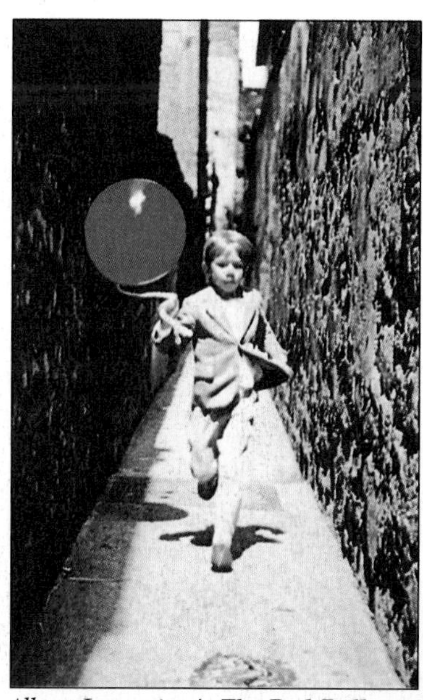

Albert Lamorisse's ***The Red Balloon***. ▷

John Ford delivers outstanding Western

John Wayne and Tab Hunter on the search in Ford's superb revenge Western.

Chicago, 22 May
The limitless vistas of Utah's Monument Valley play an integral part in John Ford's superb new Western, *The Searchers*. Here, landscape is movingly related to theme as John Wayne conducts a relentless search over several years for a niece captured by Indians. In the role of the embittered ex-Confederate Ethan Edwards, Wayne gives his finest performance, playing a stubborn man heartrendingly excluded at the last from family reunion and left as a lonely, romantic figure facing the magisterial landscape of the West.

'The King and I' a sumptuous success

Hollywood, 28 June
Yul Brynner repeats his smash-hit Broadway performance as the irascible King of Siam in Fox's lavish silver screen version of Rodgers and Hammerstein's *The King and I*, that has been loosely based on a 1946 non-musical picture, *Anna and the King of Siam*. Brynner's Broadway co-star, the late Gertrude Lawrence, is replaced here by Deborah Kerr, who whistles a happy tune as the resourceful governess of his unruly children. Kerr's vocals are dubbed by Marni Nixon, but her warm performance provides a perfect foil to the dominating style of the bald, brooding Brynner.

Deborah Kerr as Anna Leonowens, governess to the King of Siam's children.

Brilliant bird's-eye view of seedy criminal

l to r: Ted de Corsia, Joe Sawyer, Elisha Cook Jr., Sterling Hayden and Jay C Flippen plan the robbery in Kubrick's gripping third feature.

New York, 23 May
Who says the B-movie is dead? Moviegoers paying to see Robert Mitchum sleepwalking through *Foreign Intrigue* will get their money's worth from the supporting feature, *The Killing*, a cracking thriller directed by newcomer Stanley Kubrick. Based on Lionel White's book *Clean Break*, and scripted by both Kubrick and pulp writer Jim Thompson, *The Killing* stars Sterling Hayden as an ex-con who sets up a meticulously planned racetrack heist. The operation is seen from the viewpoint of the participants: twitchy little racetrack cashier Elisha Cook Jr., reformed alcoholic Jay C. Flippen, crooked cop Ted de Corsia, barma Joe Sawyer, wrestler Kola Kwaria and ultra-cool crippled gunma Timothy Carey. Everything goe like clockwork, but the gang is b trayed by Cook's wife, Marie Win sor at her flooziest, who blows th whistle on them to her gangster bo friend Vince Edwards. Although th picture's *Dragnet*-style commentar palls very quickly, its sure pace an strong ensemble playing signal th arrival of an interesting new dire tor. The 29-year-old Kubrick is former photographer who made h feature film debut in 1953 with th cheapie *Fear and Desire*, finance by family and friends.

Rocky Graziano fights on as Paul Newman

New York, 5 July
The stuttering career of Paul Newman, hailed a couple of years ago as the "new Brando", has been given a shot in the arm by MGM's new *Somebody Up There Likes Me*, the story of one of New York's favorite sons, the boxer Rocky Graziano. The film's director, Robert Wise, persuaded Metro to cast Newman as the slum kid who became middleweight champion of the world, and the result looks like it will make a star of Newman, who is still trying to live down his 1954 movie debut in Warners' clodhopping Biblical epic, *The Chalice*, in which he was cast as the Greek craftsman who made the vessel of the title for Saint Luke. Somebody up there likes Newman.

Newman, a convincing prizefighter

uscious Audrey graces lumbering 'War and Peace'

:erre (Henry Fonda) surveys the carnage on the battlefield against Napoleon.

Natasha (Hepburn) arrives at her first ball with her brother (Jeremy Brett).

'ith her seducer, Vittorio Gassman.

New York, 21 August
Veteran director King Vidor's *War and Peace* opens today. Produced by Dino De Laurentiis and shot on location in Italy at a cost of $6 million, it weighs in at 208 minutes. The money has certainly been well spent on the battle scenes, notably Napoleon's retreat from Moscow, which are epic, authentic and visually spectacular, but the film's sprawling narrative fails to gel. The intimate scenes lack bite, and a motley conglomeration of accents from a multinational cast (including Vittorio Gassman, John Mills and Anita Ekberg) strains credibility. Audiences, however, will be delighted to see Audrey Hepburn again in only her third movie since *Roman Holiday*. Playing Tolstoy's heroine Natasha, the ravishing Miss Hepburn is perfectly cast and, with her blend of innocence, vulnerability and inner strength, manages to overcome the limp screenplay (which required the input of six writers), a miscast and too-old Pierre in Henry Fonda, and a wooden Prince Andrei from her real-life husband, Mel Ferrer.

Ar. and Mrs. Miller rrive in London

ondon, 14 July
crowd of 3,000 fans gathered to ·eet Marilyn Monroe today when ·e arrived in London. She was ·companied by her husband, the ·amatist Arthur Miller, whom she arried just nine days ago in White ains, New York. None of Mon·e's family or friends attended the ·remony, which was conducted by rabbi. The news of the marriage as only made public several hours ter the wedding. The couple have)me to London for the filming of *'he Prince and the Showgirl* in which onroe will co-star with Laurence livier. In 1953 Olivier starred in e stage version of this story with s wife Vivien Leigh. Now he has lapted it for the screen. Monroe, ho is determined to establish herlf as a serious actress, has set uch store on this new film, and has ought with her, as dialogue coach, ıula Strasberg, wife of the founder ' the Actors Studio, Lee Strasberg.

Ingrid Bergman stars as a beautiful princess for Jean Renoir

Paris, 12 September
Ever since meeting Ingrid Bergman in Hollywood in the early Forties, Jean Renoir wanted to make a film with her. He initially proposed a movie called *Sarn*, adapted from Mary Webb's novel *Precious Bane*, but producer David O. Selznick rejected it because the heroine has a harelip, an unthinkable impediment to impose on a glamorous film star. Selznick, however, wanted to make *Joan of Arc* with the Swedish actress and offered it to Renoir, who refused because of memories of Carl Dreyer's masterpiece, *The Passion of Joan of Arc*. Over a decade later, Jean Renoir and Ingrid Bergman have finally gotten together for a delightful period piece called *Eléna et les hommes* (*Paris Does Strange Things*), filmed simultaneously in both French and English. In the Paris of the 1880s, Princess Eléna Sorokovska (Bergman), a merry but impoverished Polish widow, agrees to marry Martin-Michaud, an elderly but wealthy boot magnate, for money. Meanwhile, she has attracted the attentions of General Rollan (Jean Marais) and Henri de Chevincourt (Mel Ferrer), an aristocratic dilettante. At the end, she finally chooses Henri (love) over Martin-Michaud (money) and General Rollan (power). The director has said that he chose this operetta-like comedy because he wanted to see Ingrid Bergman smile again on screen. She has seldom been more ravishing and beguiling, setting a joyous tone as she flits from one man to another. ▷

The impoverished princess and one of her suitors, soldier-hero Jean Marais.

The death of Kenji Mizoguchi

Japan, 24 August
The great Japanese film director Kenji Mizoguchi, best known for *Ugetsu Monogatari* (1953), has just died of leukemia at the age of 58. The son of a carpenter, he began directing in 1922. Out of over 80 films, only about a dozen have been seen in the West, though these have been enough to establish him as a master. Despite being forced to make many films in which he had little interest, Mizoguchi gradually developed his own style and subject matter. His humanist view of the brutality of feudal Japan focuses mainly on the sufferings of women, as seen in his undisputed masterpieces, *The Life of O-Haru* (1952) and *Sansho, the Bailiff* (1954).

The torments of Vincent Van Gogh are relived by Kirk Douglas

Kirk Douglas takes the role of tormented Impressionist Vincent Van Gogh.

New York, 17 September
The tormented life of the paint Vincent Van Gogh, from his days the coal-mining region of Belgium his suicide at Auvers-sur-Oise, is t subject of a splendid new film Vincente Minnelli called *Lust f Life*. Before shooting started, t director had several battles with t MGM front office. He won his fig to shoot in actual European loc tions, and to substitute Ansco col for Eastman color, which wou better capture the paintings, but had to accept CinemaScope, a sha unsuitable to fully represent V Gogh's work on screen. The phy cal likeness of Kirk Douglas to V Gogh is hallucinatory, and his pe formance is full of passionate inte sity, as is that of Anthony Quinn fellow-artist Paul Gauguin.

Phileas Fogg's fantastic eighty-day journey around the world

Phileas Fogg (David Niven) and his devoted servant (Cantinflas) in the balloon.

Aboard a train, escorting an Eastern princess (Shirley MacLaine, right).

New York, 18 October
Depending on your point of view, Mike Todd, former carnival barker and producer of Broadway spectaculars, is a master-showman, gambler, promoter or con-man supreme. Now he has ventured into film with an extravagant screen version of Jules Verne's *Around the World in 80 Days*. David Niven stars here as Phileas Fogg, archetypal English clubman, who wagers that he can span the globe in the time specified by the title. Accompanied by his valet, played by the Mexican bullring comedian Cantinflas, he sets off, pursued by Robert Newton's Inspector Fix. Along the way he rescues Shirley MacLaine's Indian princess from a pyre and meets a host of stars in cameo roles. Among them are Ronald Colman, Noel Coward, Marlene Dietrich, Buster Keaton, Bea Lillie, Peter Lorre, Red Skelton, John Gielgud, George Raft, Fernandel and Juliette Greco. The picture was scripted by S.J. Perelman and directed by Michael Anderson after the original choice, John Farrow, had been fired by the volatile Todd. Production ground to a halt several times as Todd ran out of cash, but the result, shot on locations round the world and on a variety of Hollywood backlots, is a monument to the great showman's *chutzpah*. Sadly, a few days after filming ended, Robert Newton died.

'Elvis the pelvis' becomes an actor

New York, 15 November
Rock 'n' roll sensation Elvis Presl has made his movie debut in Fox *Love Me Tender*. It's a Western which he gets shot by Neville Bran although he reappears as a ghost the end, warbling the title song a strumming his guitar!

Elvis Presley in tough-guy mode.

resson films a esson in courage

ROBERT BRESSON
N CONDAMNÉ A MORT S'EST ÉCHAPPÉ
"LE VENT SOUFFLE OÙ IL VEUT"

aris, 11 December
obert Bresson's latest film, *A Man scaped*, recounts the harsh ordeal f Fontaine (brilliantly played by rançois Leterrier), a French Resistnce member arrested by the Gespo and imprisoned at Montluc. here, he holds on to sanity by eticulously planning every detail f a seemingly impossible escape. Vhen he is condemned to death, he ets about putting that plan into peration. Bresson was inspired by ie true-life experiences of André Devigny, who served as technical dvisor. The director's austere camra, stripping the action of all but ie bare essentials, totally involves ie audience in this testament to ourage, faith and ingenuity, all the ore authentic for the use of nonrofessional actors.

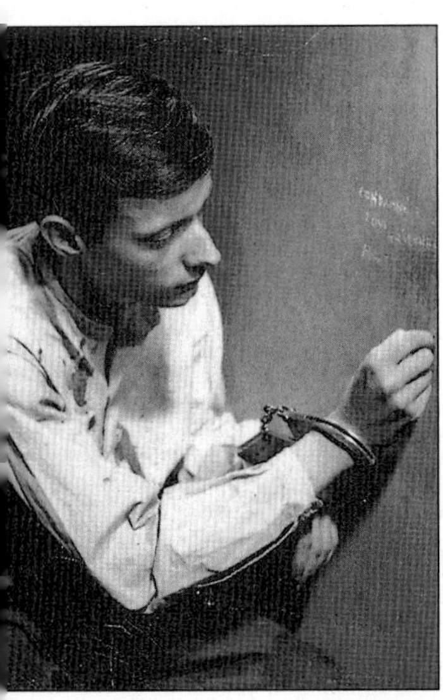
Condemned man François Leterrier.

Scandalous charms of Brigitte Bardot

Paris, 28 November
Roger Vadim has created a scandal with his first film, *And God Created Woman*, which stars his young wife Brigitte Bardot. The ruckus has been caused by the eroticism and nudity in the love scenes, and the amoral nature of the sexy 18-year-old heroine. But Vadim regrets that he could not go as far as he wished, because the censors forced him to cut many sequences. In reply to those who have criticized him for exhibiting his wife in such a manner, Vadim says, "Brigitte loves the nude scenes because she hates hypocrisy. She is a girl of her own time, liberated from all feelings of guilt and free from all taboos imposed by society." The critic François Truffaut defended the film in an article published in the magazine *Arts*, titled "B.B. is the victim of an intrigue." Apart from the kittenish charms of Bardot, the film reveals the delights of St. Tropez in color and CinemaScope.

Brigitte Bardot and Jean-Louis Trintignant in ***And God Created Woman.***

Carroll Baker is Tennessee's teenage bride for Elia Kazan

New York, 18 December
The Roman Catholic Church and the Legion of Decency have loudly condemned Elia Kazan's latest film, *Baby Doll*, the latter claiming that the movie "dwells almost without variation or relief upon carnal suggestiveness." These protests should most likely assure the picture, written by Tennessee Williams, a huge box-office success. Carroll Baker plays the backward, thumb-sucking virgin child bride of aging cotton mill owner Karl Malden. He is sexually frustrated by her refusal to allow him into her bed, even though it is a child's cot, too small for her ample proportions. Enter virile Sicilian worker Eli Wallach, who seduces her, and you have a combustible triangular situation. The black-and-white photography of Boris Kaufman brilliantly captures the steamy atmosphere of the Mississippi backwoods. Tennessee Williams' witty and trenchant screenplay, and Elia Kazan's graphic direction are as bold as the Production Code will allow. Twenty-five-year-old Carroll Baker, dressed in a short and revealing nightgown, has become the newest sensational screen sex goddess. Born in Pennsylvania in May 1931, the daughter of a traveling salesman, the blonde Carroll Baker left Junior College in order to join a dance company. After a brief marriage to a furrier, she set off for Hollywood where she had a bit part in the Esther Williams vehicle *Easy to Love* (1953). Back in New York, while appearing in TV commercials, she studied at the Actors Studio, where she met her future husband, stage director Jack Garfein. Shortly thereafter, she was cast in several parts in TV dramas and a role in Robert Sherwood's play *All Summer Long*. When she finally returned to Hollywood for the part of Elizabeth Taylor and Rock Hudson's daughter in *Giant*, released two months ago, she landed the role of *Baby Doll* at the same time. As the physically forward virgin, Carroll Baker manages simultaneously to express sensuality and innocence.

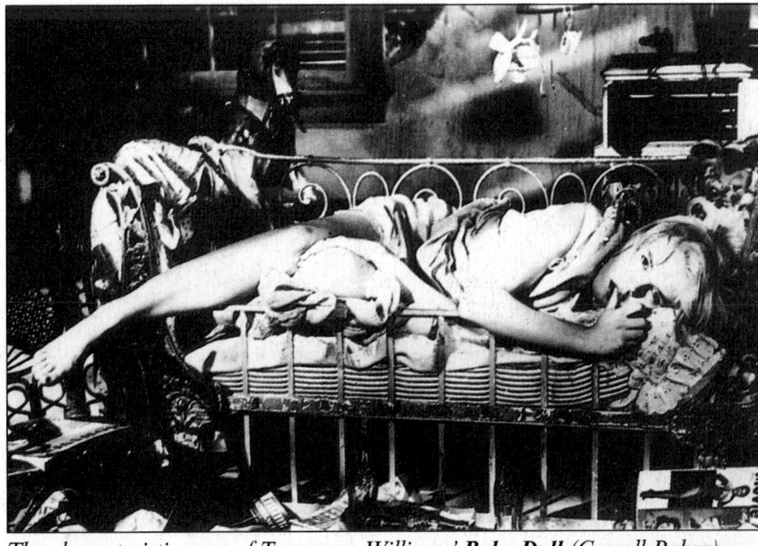
The characteristic pose of Tennessee Williams' ***Baby Doll*** *(Carroll Baker).*

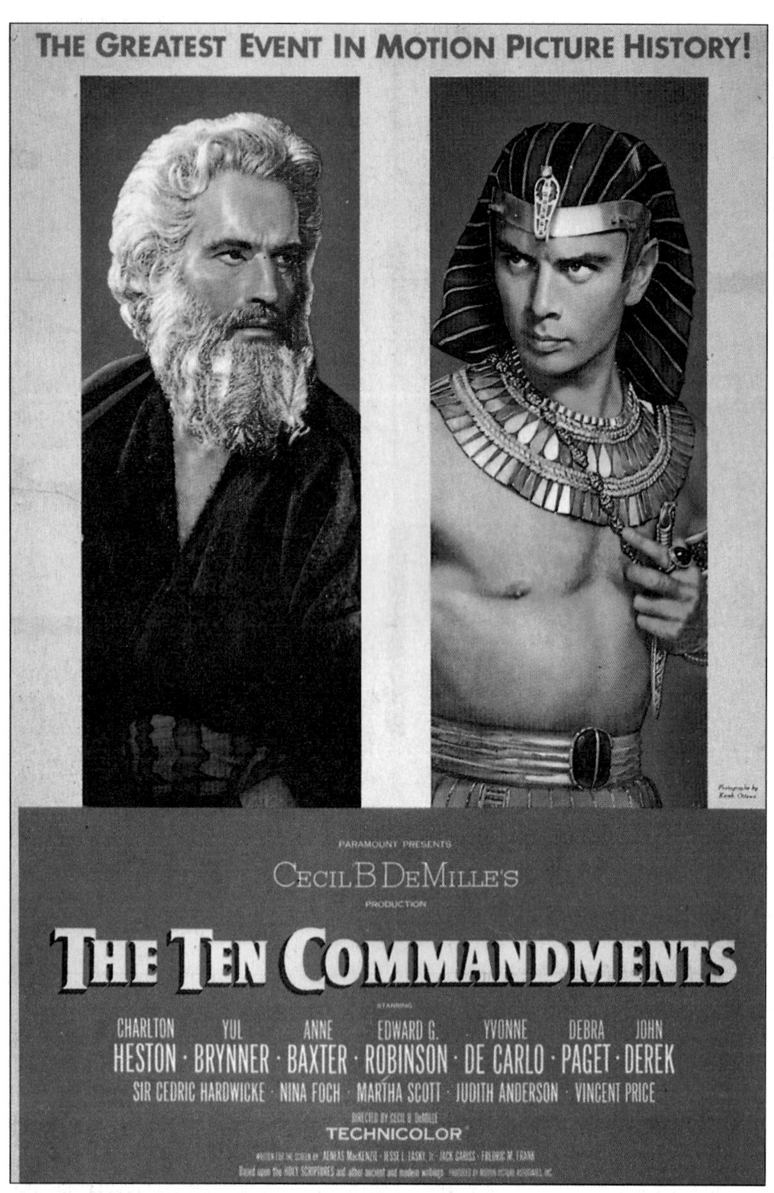
THE GREATEST EVENT IN MOTION PICTURE HISTORY!
PARAMOUNT PRESENTS
CECIL B DEMILLE'S
PRODUCTION
THE TEN COMMANDMENTS
STARRING
CHARLTON HESTON · YUL BRYNNER · ANNE BAXTER · EDWARD G. ROBINSON · YVONNE DE CARLO · DEBRA PAGET · JOHN DEREK
SIR CEDRIC HARDWICKE · NINA FOCH · MARTHA SCOTT · JUDITH ANDERSON · VINCENT PRICE
TECHNICOLOR

Cecil B. DeMille remade his 1923 biblical epic, this time with full Technicolor.

Dana Andrews and Joan Fontaine starred in the ingenious Fritz Lang thriller, ***Beyond a Reasonable Doubt*****.**

MARLON BRANDO
GLENN FORD
MACHIKO KYO
All The Riotous Fun
Of The Prize-Winning Stage Comedy!
M-G-M CINEMASCOPE METROCOLOR
The TEAHOUSE of The AUGUST MOON
EDDIE ALBERT

Marlon Brando goes Japanese.

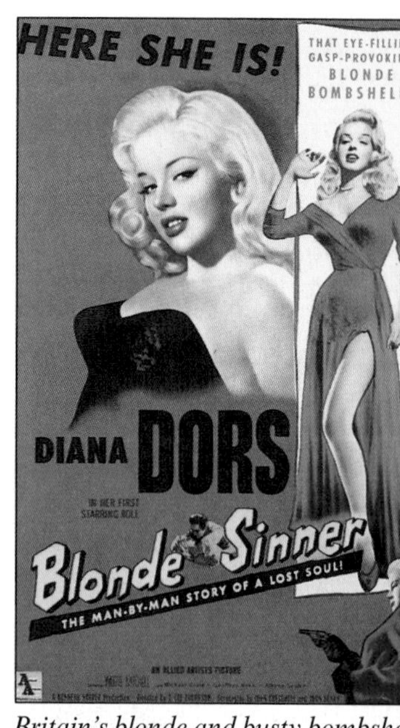
HERE SHE IS!
THAT EYE-FILLIN GASP-PROVOKIN BLONDE BOMBSHELL
DIANA DORS
Blonde Sinner
THE MAN-BY-MAN STORY OF A LOST SOUL!

Britain's blonde and busty bombshe

Brigitte Bardot and Jean-Louis Trintignant: ***And God Created Woman*****.**

George Stevens' ***Giant****: James Dea*

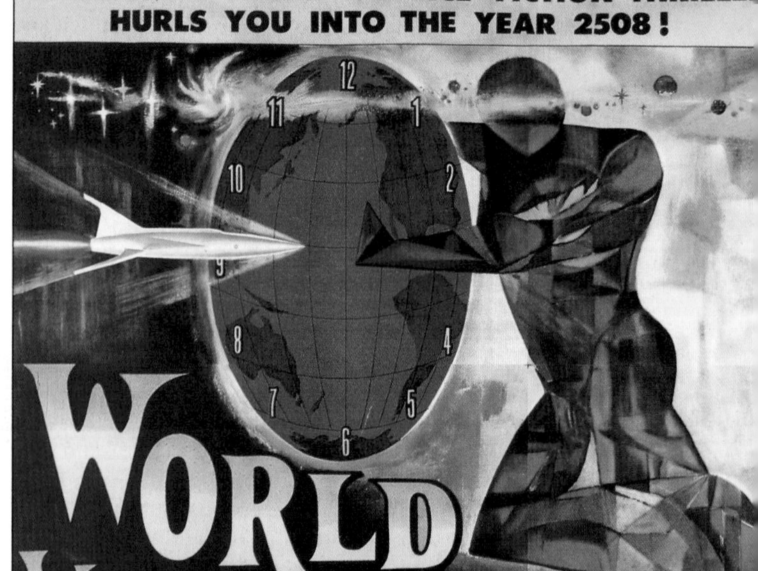
CINEMASCOPE'S FIRST SCIENCE-FICTION THRILLE
HURLS YOU INTO THE YEAR 2508!
WORLD Without END
starring
HUGH MARLOWE
NANCY GATES
Nelson Leigh · Rod Taylor · Shawn Smith · Lisa Montell
AN ALLIED ARTISTS PICTURE
PRODUCED BY RICHARD HEERMANCE
WRITTEN AND DIRECTED BY EDWARD BERN
CINEMASCOPE
TECHNICOLOR

Shades of H.G. Wells as spaceship comes to earth in the 26th century.

M·G·M PRESENTS
FORBIDDEN PLANET
AMAZING!
WALTER PIDGEON · ANNE FRANCIS · LESLIE NIELSEN
WITH
ARREN STEVENS AND INTRODUCING ROBBY, THE ROBOT
SCREEN PLAY BY CYRIL HUME
BASED ON A STORY BY IRVING BLOCK AND ALLEN ADLER
PHOTOGRAPHED IN EASTMAN COLOR
DIRECTED BY
ED McLEOD WILCOX
PRODUCED BY
NICHOLAS NAYFACK
IN CINEMASCOPE AND COLOR
A METRO-GOLDWYN-MAYER PICTURE

ci-fi suspense and rollicking humor, inspired by Shakespeare's ***The Tempest***.

WALTER WANGER
CREATES THE ULTIMATE
IN SCIENCE-FICTION!
ALLIED ARTISTS
INVASION OF THE
BODY SNATCHERS
FILMED IN
SUPERSCOPE
KEVIN McCARTHY · DANA WYNTER

First-class effort in a sci-fi year.

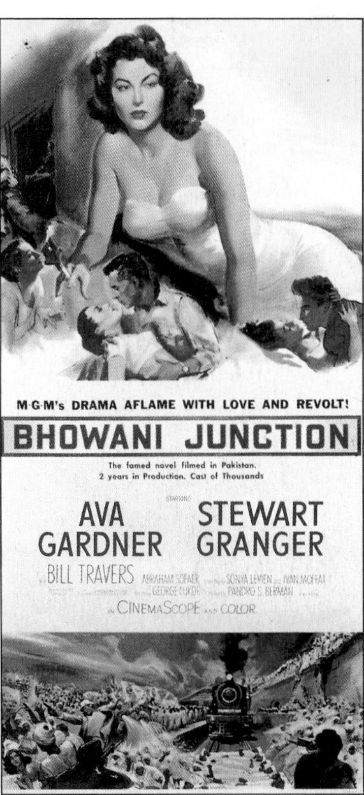
M·G·M's DRAMA AFLAME WITH LOVE AND REVOLT!
BHOWANI JUNCTION
The famed novel filmed in Pakistan.
2 years in Production. Cast of Thousands
AVA GARDNER
STEWART GRANGER
BILL TRAVERS
CINEMASCOPE AND COLOR

George Cukor directed in Pakistan.

*Deborah Kerr and John Kerr (no relation) starred in **Tea and Sympathy**.*

*obert Hirsch, Gina Lollobrigida and Jean Danet in Frenchman Jean Delanoy's **Notre-Dame de Paris**, adapted from Victor Hugo.*

JAMES
STEWART · DORIS
DAY
ALFRED HITCHCOCK'S
THE MAN WHO KNEW TOO MUCH
VISTAVISION
COLOR BY TECHNICOLOR

Hitchcock remade his own 1934 film.

INCREDIBLE, UNSTOPPABLE TITAN OF TERROR!
GODZILLA
It's Alive!
KING OF THE MONSTERS!
CIVILIZATION CRUMBLES as its death rays blast a city of 6 million from the face of the earth!
RAYMOND BURR
MIGHTIEST MONSTER!
MIGHTIEST MELODRAMA of them all!

Japan's answer to current sci-fi craze.

1957

1956 Academy Awards, RKO Pantages Theater, 27 Mar.	
Best Film:	*Around the World in 80 Days* (dir: Michael Anderson)
Best Director:	George Stevens *(Giant)*
Best Actor:	Yul Brynner *(The King and I)*
Best Actress:	Ingrid Bergman *(Anastasia)*
Best Supp. Actor:	Anthony Quinn *(Lust for Life)*
Best Supp. Actress:	Dorothy Malone *(Written on the Wind)*

New York, 2 January
The women's fashion press has just elected the best dressed women of the year. Among them are Princess Grace of Monaco, Audrey Hepburn and Marlene Dietrich.

Tokyo, 15 January
Opening of Akira Kurosawa's film *Kumonosu-Jo* (*Throne of Blood* aka *Castle of the Spider's Web*), a new version of Shakespeare's *Macbeth* set in medieval Japan, with Toshiro Mifune and Takashi Shimura.

Paris, 18 January
Actress Maria Schell has signed a contract to play the leading role in Alexandre Astruc's latest film *Une vie*, adapted from the novel by Guy de Maupassant.

Hollywood, 18 February
Orson Welles has begun filming *Touch of Evil* for Universal Studios. The cast is headed by Charlton Heston, Janet Leigh, Marlene Dietrich and the director himself. It is his first U.S. film since *Macbeth* in 1948.

Paris, 19 February
The Lutetia production company has threatened Brigitte Bardot with a lawsuit if she continues to fail to turn up on the set of *la Chatte* (*The Cat*), based on Colette's novel. The film's producers are prepared to sue her for the sum of $50 million in damages – the star's casual attitude could cost her dearly.

London, 22 February
During the shooting of Otto Preminger's *Saint Joan*, the actress Jean Seberg narrowly escaped being burnt alive while shooting the sequence where she is tied to the stake for just such a fate in the film.

Washington D.C., 26 February
James Stewart has been promoted to the rank of Brigadier General in the United States Armed Forces. President Eisenhower himself conferred this honor on the actor.

Rome, 21 March
John Huston, who had just begun filming *A Farewell to Arms* from the novel by Ernest Hemingway, has been sacked by producer David O. Selznick; the director Charles Vidor is to replace him.

Cannes, 22 April
The People's Republic of China has withdrawn from the Festival competition on learning that Taiwan is also taking part.

Paris, 18 May
At the Maison des Lettres, Claude Lelouch, a young director, is presenting *Vers une nouvelle technique* (*Towards a New Technique*), three short 16mm experimental films.

Washington D.C., 1 June
The playwright Arthur Miller has been found guilty of contempt of Congress for refusing to reveal to the HUAC the names of members of a literary circle suspected of Communist affiliations.

Paris, 7 June
At the Rex, the first escalators to be installed in a cinema were set in motion by Gary Cooper and Mylene Demongeot.

New York, 9 June
There are currently 6,000 drive-in theaters in America and operators predict this number should rise to 10,000 in two years. Many of today's drive-ins have fully-equipped children's playgrounds, supermarket-sized cafeterias and an "all weather" theater for those who prefer to sit indoors in bad weather.

New Orleans, 18 July
Robert Rossen's new film, *Island in the Sun*, opened today in spite of objections from a citizen's council chapter and an American Legion committee over the film's content – a romance between a colored man (Harry Belafonte) and a beautiful white woman (Joan Fontaine).

Rome, 7 September
After seven years of marriage, actress Ingrid Bergman and director Roberto Rossellini have decided to separate. Rossellini, who is reportedly in love with a young Indian woman, has given Ingrid custody of their three children, Roberto, Ingrid and Isabella, on the condition she stays in Europe until they are of age. The actress is leaving for Paris tomorrow to continue rehearsals for Robert Anderson's play *Tea and Sympathy* at the Théâtre de Paris.

Hollywood, 22 September
Actress Kim Novak has gone on strike. She considers her popularity to be worth more than her current salary of $1,250 per week.

Hollywood, 20 September
Lauren Bacall has formally denied rumors of a forthcoming marriage to Frank Sinatra.

Paris, 3 October
Jayne Mansfield, who is here for the opening of her film *Will Success Spoil Rock Hunter?*, directed by Frank Tashlin, happened to meet Greta Garbo at Maxims and was quick to ask for an autograph.

Hollywood, 10 October
RKO studios have been sold to Desilu, the television production company founded by Lucille Ball and Desi Arnaz, stars of the famous *I Love Lucy* series.

London, 13 October
A newspaper has disclosed that the Indian actress Anna Kashfi, whom Marlon Brando has just discreetly married, is in fact the daughter of a Welsh laborer and is named Joan O'Callaghan.

Hollywood, 29 November
Composer Erich Wolfgang Korngold, aged 60, has died. The former child prodigy from Czechoslovakia won two Oscars for film musical scores. He first came to Hollywood in 1934 to arrange the music for *A Midsummer Night's Dream*.

Paris, 4 December
Claude Chabrol, a film critic for *Cahiers du Cinéma*, has commenced shooting his first feature-length film, *Bitter Reunion* (*le Beau Serge*), starring Gérard Blain, Jean-Claude Brialy and Bernadette Lafont.

BIRTHS

Massachusetts, 21 January
Geena Davis

New York, 28 February
John Turturro

California, 20 March
Theresa Russell
(Theresa Paup)

New York, 29 March
Christopher Lambert

Swaziland, 5 May
Richard E. Grant

New York, 9 August
Melanie Griffith

Paris, 18 August
Carole Bouquet

Minnesota, 21 September
Ethan Coen

Paris, 24 November
Thierry Lhermitte

DEATHS

Hollywood, 14 January
Humphrey Bogart

California, 31 March
Gene Lockhart

Paris, 12 May
Erich von Stroheim

Hollywood, 29 July
James Whale

California, 7 August
Oliver Hardy

London, 20 October
Jack Buchanan

Los Angeles, 29 October
Louis B. Mayer

Las Vegas, 24 December
Norma Talmadge

Monte Carlo, 25 December
Charles Pathé

---

*Directed by Jack Arnold for Unive sal, **The Incredible Shrinking Man** impressive sci-fi in which Gra Williams shrinks to micro-size aft being caught in a radioactive mist.*

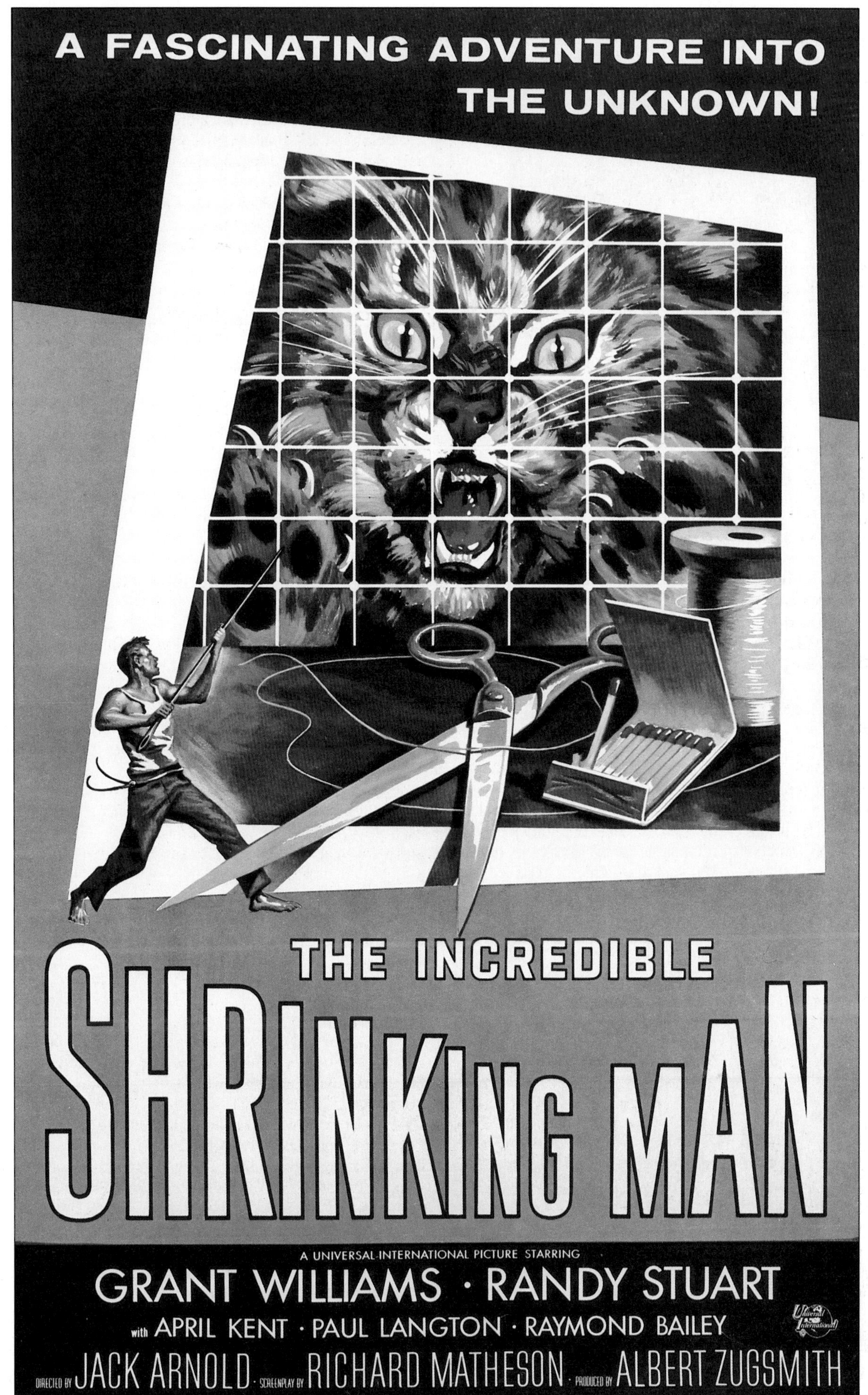
A FASCINATING ADVENTURE INTO
THE UNKNOWN!
THE INCREDIBLE
SHRINKING MAN
A UNIVERSAL-INTERNATIONAL PICTURE STARRING
GRANT WILLIAMS · RANDY STUART
with APRIL KENT · PAUL LANGTON · RAYMOND BAILEY
DIRECTED BY JACK ARNOLD · SCREENPLAY BY RICHARD MATHESON · PRODUCED BY ALBERT ZUGSMITH

▷

Humphrey Bogart succumbs to cancer

With his wife, actress Lauren Bacall, and their two children in happy times.

Los Angeles, 17 January
Three days ago Humphrey Bogart lost a long battle against throat cancer. The slide began after an operation in March last year, but Bogey, unwilling to change the habits of a lifetime, continued to smoke and drink whisky. At the end he was so weak and emaciated that a service elevator was converted to bring the wheelchair-bound star downstairs to meet friends. Today, after a short funeral service, Bogart was cremated at Forest Lawn. Beside him was a whistle as a reminder of *To Have and Have Not.*

America forgives Ingrid Bergman her sins

New York, 20 January
Ingrid Bergman has at last returned to New York and the arms of the American people. The reconciliation has been effected by the success of *Anastasia*, directed by Anatole Litvak, in which she plays an amnesiac refugee selected by Yul Brynner to impersonate the surviving daughter of Czar Nicholas II. Meanwhile, her marriage to Roberto Rossellini has hit the rocks. Bergman has been nominated for an Oscar for *Anastasia*, and has already received the New York Critics award for her performance.

At Idlewild, the star is surrounded by eager press photographers en route to a welcome from fans who have remained loyal through the years of exile.

A new busty blonde explodes on the scree

New York, 8 February
The American male's obsession with big breasts has found its perfect incarnation in the sumptuous 40-19-36 statistics of Jayne Mansfield, who shot to stardom last year in Frank Tashlin's rock 'n' roll comedy *The Girl Can't Help It*, memorably clutching two milk bottles to her ample bosom. Today sees the release another Tashlin picture titled *W Success Spoil Rock Hunter?*, in whi Tony Randall plays an ad-man tr ing to persuade movie star Jayne endorse Stay-Put lipstick. Wheth the 24-year-old former beauty que will stay put on the movie sce remains to be seen.

Jayne Mansfield in ***Will Success Spoil Rock Hunter?*** *A parody of Marilyn.*

Entrepreneur Mike Todd marries Liz Taylo

Mexico, 2 February
Although she has not officially divorced Michael Wilding, Elizabeth Taylor has pressed ahead with her marriage to Mike Todd, tying the knot in the small Mexican village of Puerto Marquez, far away from the complications of the American legal system. It is the third time around for both Liz and Mike, who was previously married to Joan Blondell. Producer and originator of the Todd-AO wide-screen process, Todd met Taylor during the filming of *Around the World in 80 Days*. He swept Liz off her feet, presenting her with a $30,000 ring, which she has pointedly worn on her left ring-finger in the presence of the hapless Wilding. Taylor's attachment to the baub became so great that she even trie surreptitiously to wear it during th shooting of *Raintree County*. Tod who is 25 years Taylor's senior, la on a characteristically opulent cer mony: over 15,000 flowers, doze of cases of champagne and a sma mountain of caviar, although the were few people present at the r ception. Those guests who wer there included Eddie Fisher, Debb Reynolds and Cantinflas, who ha the role of Passepartout in *Aroun the World in 80 Days*. The happ couple will shortly sail for Europ where they are planning to interru their honeymoon to drop in on th Cannes Film Festival.

agmar Bergman and the question of death

ax Von Sydow (left) and Bengt Ekerot play a deadly game of chess.

ockholm, 16 February
gmar Bergman's 17th film, *The venth Seal*, has definitely set him mly in the pantheon of directors. fter his bubbling comedy of man-rs, *Smiles of a Summer's Night*, hich received worldwide acclaim o years ago, Bergman has now turned to explore the darker side life. *The Seventh Seal*, shot in only days, is a medieval morality tale hich powerfully depicts the cruel-s of the time such as witch burning and flagellation, as well as the joys and aspirations of ordinary people. This movie follows, in luminous images derived from early church paintings, the journeys of a knight (Max Von Sydow) returning from the Crusades through a Sweden ravaged by plague. In his search for God, he meets a group of strolling players, suffering peasants, and Death (Bengt Ekerot) himself, with whom the knight plays a deadly game of chess.

A trip around the world worth five Oscars

Hollywood, 27 March
The fact that flamboyant showman-producer Michael Todd, whose film *Around the World in 80 Days* carried off five Oscars, had never worked in the cinema before, was only one of the oddities at this year's Academy Award ceremony. The Best Actor Oscar was awarded to the virtually unknown, bald Yul Brynner, who claims to be a gypsy born in Outer Mongolia, for his performance as the despotic King of Siam in *The King and I*; the Best Actress went to Ingrid Bergman for the title role in *Anastasia*, after she had been ostracized by Hollywood for many years; and James Dean, for the second year running, was a posthumous nominee for Best Actor in *Giant*. Although *Around the World in 80 Days* may be the most star-studded movie of all time, it failed to gain any acting honors, its Oscars being awarded for Best Picture, Best Cinematography, Best Adapted Screenplay, Best Film Editing and Best Musical Score. Much of the film was shot around the world in 70mm Todd-AO and Eastman Color, as Inspector Fix (Robert Newton) follows Phileas Fogg (David Niven) and Passepartout (Cantinflas).

Ingrid Bergman and Helen Hayes.

udrey's 'Funny Face' delights Fred Astaire

ew York, 28 March
udrey Hepburn has made her first reen musical, co-starring with the oyen of dance, 57-year-old Fred staire, who is still spry, graceful d charming. Directed by Stanley onen, the "Cinderella" story tells a Greenwich Village bluestocking (Hepburn), transformed into a top model by a fashion photographer (Astaire), in the face of opposition from his *Vogue*-type editor (Kay Thompson). Around this – and a subplot that takes a side-swipe at phony intellectuals – a spell is woven of song, dance, Paris locations and a spectacular Givenchy wardrobe for Hepburn, under the supervisory visual eye of photographer Richard Avedon, on whom Astaire's character is said to be based. From the first Paris number, "Bonjour Paree", where Astaire, Thompson and Hepburn run into each other atop the Eiffel Tower in triple split-screen, through the outdoor photo sessions, to the romantic finale ("S'Wonderful") in a churchyard, the film lovingly captures Paris – and the magic essence of Audrey. And it does so in a swirl of energy and high spirits, wonderfully orchestrated by Donen, a former dancer, choreographer and an integral member of MGM's famous Freed unit.

a left-bank club in Paris.

Depressing party makes impressive movie

New York, 9 April
The team of producer Harold Hecht, director Delbert Mann and writer Paddy Chayefsky, have followed up their success with *Marty* (1955) with *The Bachelor Party*. Set in a cheerless New York at night, the film traces the attempts of five office workers to enjoy the final moments of bachelorhood of one of their number. But instead of having a good time, their emotional problems come to the surface. Each of the relatively unknown actors gives an excellent, realistic performance in a downbeat but impressive movie.

l to r: Jack Warden, Don Murray and Carolyn Jones in Delbert Mann's film.

Andrzej Wajda magnificently revives the cinema in Poland

Warsaw, 23 April
Polish films had disappeared during the six years of the war. Technical equipment was destroyed by the Germans and the directors sought asylum in London and New York. In 1945, the cinema became nationalized, with a leaning towards Soviet ideology, and the output remained feeble and lacking in originality. But since the death of Stalin in 1953, there have been profound changes. Young directors are beginning to emerge, determined to make films with a personal stamp, something that was eclipsed by commissioned works. One of them is Andrzej Wajda (born in 1926), who launched a bitter and anti-romantic cry of hatred against war in *A Generation* three years ago. Now his second feature, *Kanal*, pays homage to the heroes of the 1944 Warsaw uprising. The son of a cavalry officer killed in World War II, Wajda joined the Polish resistance at the age of 16. Much of this claustrophobic and often depressing film takes place in the sewers of the city, into which a group of partisans has been forced. The events that take place underground reveal bravery, cowardice, fidelity and treason, with the sewers becoming a tomb. Despite some heavy-handed symbolic references to Dante's *Inferno*, the powerful theme and imagery should awaken the world to the new Polish cinema.

*Tadeusz Janczar and Teresa Izeweska, trapped wartime partisans in **Kanal**.*

Erich von Stroheim has gone forever

France, 12 May
The celebrated film director, write and actor Erich von Stroheim ha died peacefully in his sleep at th Château de Maurepas in Seine-e Oise, 30 miles outside Paris, whic he shared with the French actres Denise Vernac, his collaborator an close companion for almost 2 years. Stroheim was born, the son o a Jewish hatmaker, in Vienna on 2 September, 1885. He emigrated t the U.S. in 1909, arriving in Holly wood in 1914. After initially makin his name as an actor, he emerged a a leading director of silents from h first remarkable feature, *Blind Hu bands* (1919) to *Queen Kelly*, halte midway through filming in 1929. I the sound era he was best known a an actor, particularly for *Sunset Bou levard*, though he continued writin and developing other projects. Tw months before his death, his geniu was recognized with the award o the French Legion of Honor.

Newcomers star in savage view of TV

New York, 28 May
After their triumphant collaboration on *On the Waterfront* (1954), director Elia Kazan and writer Budd Schulberg have teamed up again for *A Face in the Crowd*, a powerful indictment of the processes through which personalities are manufactured by television to be then accepted at face value by the public at large. In addition to Patricia Neal, Anthony Franciosa and Walter Matthau, the cast includes two highly impressive screen debutants. Andy Griffith is both charming and repulsive in the role of Lonesome Rhodes, a hillbilly philosopher on a local radio station made into a star, and 21-year-old Lee Remick as a nubile sexy drum-majorette.

Wyatt Earp, Doc Holliday take on Clantons

New York, 29 May
The legendary lawman Wyatt Earp rides again, this time in the form of quietly-spoken Burt Lancaster in *Gunfight at the OK Corral* directed by John Sturges. Shooting it out at his side is the more explosive Kirk Douglas as the doomed Doc Holliday, gambler, gunman and sometime dentist. Jo Van Fleet gives a powerful performance as the Doc' woman, Kate Fisher, too smart t be fooled by his charm but too wea to break away from him. The cl mactic gunfight with the Clanto family, probably the most celebrate piece of gunplay in Western histor occupies six minutes of film time but took John Sturges 44 hours t film to his satisfaction.

*Lee Remick and Andy Griffith are the stars of **A Face in the Crowd**.*

l to r: Kirk Douglas, Burt Lancaster, John Hudson and DeForrest Kelly.

'weet Smell of Success' has bitter flavor

ırtis, left, Lancaster in Alexander Mackendrick's corrosive study of power.

s Angeles, 19 June
Match me, Sidney!" rasps Burt ncaster's ruthless New York gos- columnnist J.J. Hunsecker as his oveling gofer Sidney Falco, por- ayed by Tony Curtis, gropes for a ht. These high-voltage performan- s power *Sweet Smell of Success*, directed by Alexander Mackendrick who has returned from Britain's Ealing studios to his native America to deliver a blistering exposé of the world of press agents and columnists. And the resemblance between Hunsecker and Walter Winchell is wholly intentional.

welve good men win Berlin jury verdict

rlin, 5 July
most the whole of *Twelve Angry en* takes place in a jury room ere the jury is considering if a m kid is guilty of knifing his fa- er. It is doubtful that the jury of e Berlin Film Festival had such a ugh time reaching its decision to vard the Golden Bear to this grip- ng drama. Having directed the expertly contrived Reginald Rose play for television, Sidney Lumet, making his first feature, shot the film in 20 days, creating an intimate, sweaty, claustrophobic atmosphere. A great deal of pleasure is derived from watching each excellent actor do his turn, as Henry Fonda persuades them, one by one, to return a verdict of not guilty.

ıssionate Henry Fonda practising the art of persuasion on his fellow jury-men.

Cary and Deborah: a scintillating affair

Hollywood, 20 July
With *An Affair to Remember*, which opens here today, veteran director Leo McCarey has pulled off a unique and extraordinary career double. In 1939, he made *Love Affair*, from a story he wrote with Mildred Cram, and a screenplay by Delmer Daves and Donald Ogden Stewart. The 89-minute, black-and-white film starred Charles Boyer and Irene Dunne, and told the story of a sophisticated European man of the world, who meets and falls in love with a New York girl on board a transatlantic liner. A huge success, the film picked up five Academy Award nominations and today is considered as a jewel in the crown of 1930s Hollywood romantic comedies, treasured for the quality of the repartee, as well as its stylish tone and marvelous performances. Now, 18 years later, comes *An Affair to Remember*, the mixture as before, but brought up to date, running at 114 mins and made in CinemaScope and color. The new script is by McCarey himself with Delmer Daves, and the new stars are the serenely lovely Deborah Kerr as a very classy ex-nightclub singer, and Cary Grant as the wealthy bachelor playboy who woos, wins, and almost loses her. Congratulations are in order all around. McCarey retains all his style and assurance, and his players are an equal match for their illustrious predecessors. The lush sentimentality of the movie is nicely balanced by the witty script and the polish and sincerity of the performances, particularly that of Miss Kerr, Hollywood's treasurable "English rose".

Deborah Kerr and Cary Grant: a clandestine shipboard romance that delights.

Ingrid Bergman is reunited with Pia

Paris, 8 July
Ingrid Bergman has been reunited with her daughter, Pia Lindstrom, whom she has not seen since she left the U.S. in 1949 to work with Roberto Rossellini. When that relationship turned into an affair and marriage, Ingrid's former husband, Dr. Peter Lindstrom, refused the star access to her child. Now, at last, they are together in Paris, where Bergman is starring in a French stage production of *Tea and Sympathy*.

Sacha Guitry dies peacefully at home

Paris, 24 July
Sacha Guitry has died peacefully in his Paris apartment surrounded by his wife, Lana Marconi, his secretary, Stéphane Prince, and his faithful friend Albert Willemetz. The son of the actor Lucien Guitry, Sacha was born in St. Petersburg on 21 February 1885. An actor since the age of 14, he wrote his first play in 1902, and directed his first film in 1915. The funeral will take place at the cemetery of Montmartre.

▷

India's Ray gains the top honor over Italy's Visconti at Venice

Pinaki Sen Gupta in Satyajit Ray's superb ***Aparajito (The Unvanquished).***

Maria Schell and Marcello Mastroianni in Visconti's ***White Nights.***

Venice, 9 September
Audiences and critics were split down the middle in their reactions to this year's awards at the Venice Film Festival. Two films hotly contested the top prize: Satyajit Ray's *Aparajito* (*The Unvanquished*) and Luchino Visconti's *White Nights.* When the Golden Lion was presented to the Ray picture, there were as many jeers as cheers. Perhaps there were a number of Italian chauvinists among those against the Indian film. *Aparajito* is the sensitive sequel to *Pather Panchali*, the story of the boy Apu growing up in a small Bengali village. The film is a world away from the crass commercial Indian cinema. The Visconti picture, which won the Silver Lion, is a charming, stylized adaptation of the Dostoevsky short story, relocated to Italy and starring Maria Schell, Marcello Mastroianni and Jean Marais.

'Raintree County' reveals damage to Clift

Kentucky, 2 October
After a traumatic production history, in which Montgomery Clift was badly scarred in an automobile accident, *Raintree County* has hit the screen. It is an egregious attempt by MGM to outdo *Gone With the Wind*, starring Elizabeth Taylor in Scarlett O'Hara mode as a petulant Southern belle, and a mannered Clift portraying a man seeking his destiny. However, ghoulish cinemagoers are trying to spot the shots of Clift before the accident and after. Although his face was patched up after the auto smash, it seems that Clift has lost his special beauty, and is aware of it. It remains to be seen whether the physical and psychological scars Clift has sustained will strengthen him as an actor or undermine the intense concentration he has shown in films like *Red River* and *From Here to Eternity.*

Montgomery Clift and Elizabeth Taylor star in MGM's ***Raintree County.***

Anti-American satire from Charlie Chaplin

Paris, 24 October
Charlie Chaplin's new film, *A King in New York*, is showing at the Gaumont Palace in the French capital, six weeks after its London premiere. Filmed in Britain at Shepperton studios, *A King in New York* is a companion piece to *The Great Dictator*, that switches the satirical attack from the fascists of the 1930s to the American McCarthyites of the 1950s – the very people who sent Chaplin into exile in Switzerland. Chaplin casts himself as the exiled King Shahdov, colliding unhappily with American materialism and mania for social conformity. In the process he exacts a vicarious revenge on the House Un-American Activities Committee by drenching a bunch of fatuous American politicians with a fire hose. Critics are divided over the film, but it contains some memorable moments of slapstick, notably when the exiled king resorts to sign language to order caviar in a crowded restaurant. Perhaps Chaplin still hankers after the lost glories of silent cinema.

Sophia Loren marries Carlo Pont

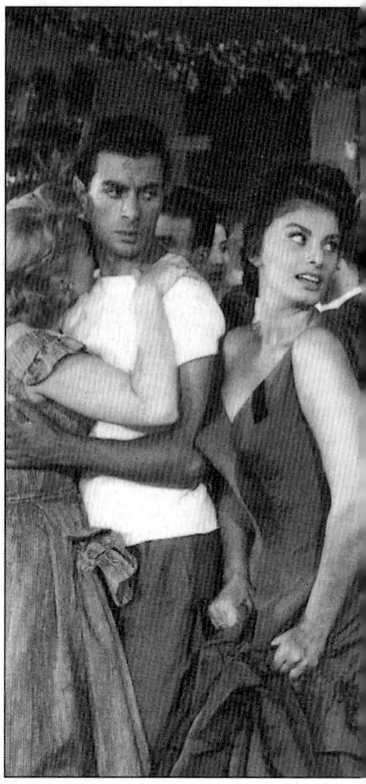

Dino Risi's ***Bread, Love, and Ame***

Mexico, 17 September
Sophia Loren, aged 23, has marri 46-year-old producer Carlo Ponti Juarez, a Mexican town just over t border from California. The you Italian star has been pursuing Hollywood career for a year wi the assistance of Ponti, who nego ated her contracts. But the coup were not themselves present for t ceremony, having delegated t power of signature to their lawye Loren is about to begin shooti her fourth American-produced fil *Desire Under the Elms.*

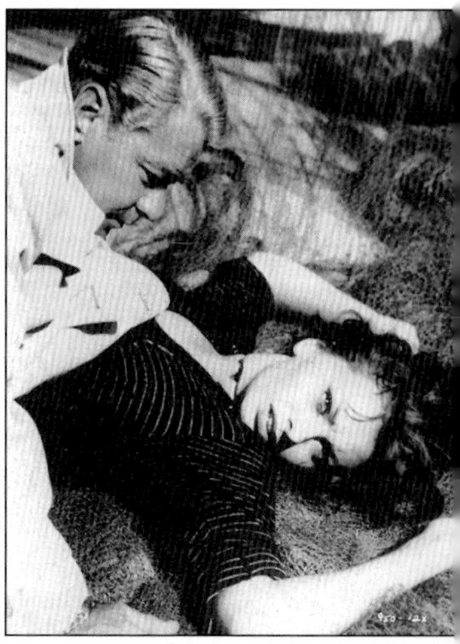

Boy on a Dolphin *with Alan Ladd.*

ourage on the banks of the Kwai

ec Guinness and Sessue Hayakawa: conflict and respect between warring protagonists in David Lean's film.

ndon, 29 November
e futility of war is the underlying eme of *The Bridge on the River vai*, Sam Spiegel's impressive new million production. Filmed on cation in the jungles and mouns of Ceylon, the 161-minute epic, sed on the novel by Pierre Boulle, ls of how badly-treated British)Ws in Burma were forced to build a massive bridge in dreadful conditions. The film, however, centers on the clash of wills between a martinet, strictly-by-the-book British colonel (Alec Guinness) and the equally duty-bound Japanese commander (Sessue Hayakawa). The latter insists that officers as well as privates take part in the construction. Guinness disagrees, refuses to acquiesce, and is punished by torture. Ironically, the completion of the bridge then becomes his obsession. Director David Lean's strong cinematic eye and his ability to tell a story with maximum impact are demonstrated to perfection. The magnificent Alec Guinness gets fine support from William Holden and Jack Hawkins, among the cast.

tanley Kubrick brings back a pacifist message from the trenches

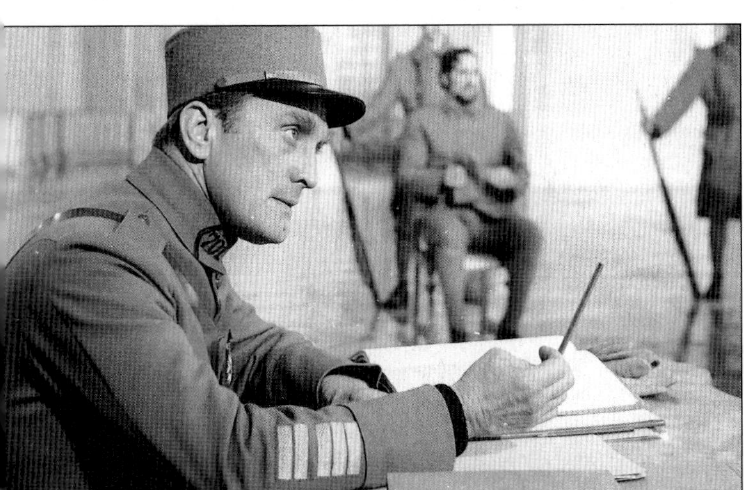

irk Douglas as the officer in Stanley Kubrick's powerful anti-war film.

New York, 27 December
The powerful anti-militarist stance of Stanley Kubrick's *Paths of Glory* has come opportunely in the aftermath of the Korean War, although the film is set in France in 1916. The story is based on an actual incident when a general ordered a captain to fire on his own troops because some of them refused to go over the top. The captain defied orders, and three men were chosen at random and executed. The affair was hushed up by the French authorities at the time. This bitterly ironic and moving film has already been banned in parts of Europe and in U.S. military movie theaters.

The double journey of Professor Borg

Stockholm, 26 December
For the leading role in his most recent film, *Wild Strawberries*, Ingmar Bergman, the great Swedish director of today, has chosen Victor Sjöström, the great Swedish director of yesterday. In fact, the older director's *The Phantom Carriage* was a powerful influence on the younger man. The 78-year-old Sjöström plays Professor Borg, who travels by car with his daughter-in-law (Ingrid Thulin) from Stockholm to Lund to receive an honorary doctorate. On the way there, a visit to the family home and various meetings inspire reminiscences, insights into his own shortcomings, and intimations of mortality. Although Bergman's previous film, *The Seventh Seal*, was set in medieval times, *Wild Strawberries* is a complementary work. Borg, like the Knight, pursues a quest, not for God but for self-understanding. The car journey functions as a pilgrimage into his own personality. The action moves between past and present, fantasy and reality, with a significant dream sequence at the beginning. The flashbacks that the old man "enters" unobserved by the people of his past, are filmed lyrically, in contrast to the harsh cutting and bleak lighting of his present. Bergman has gathered around Sjöström his brilliant repertory company, including Max Von Sydow, Bibi Andersson and Gunnar Björnstrand. Gunnar Fischer, Bergman's regular cameraman, proves himself once again a master of black-and-white imagery, particularly on the outdoor location shots.

Victor Sjöström and Ingrid Thulin.

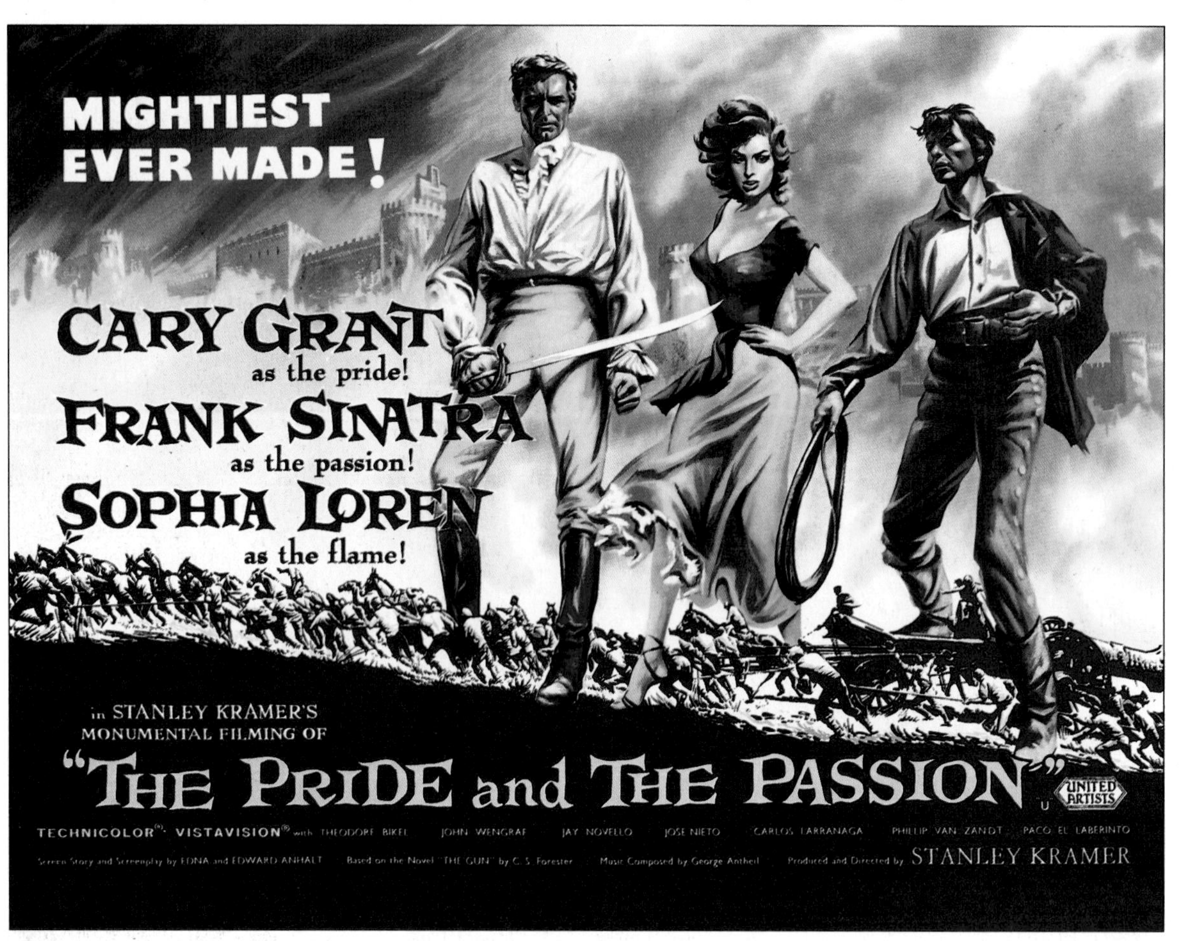
MIGHTIEST
EVER MADE!
CARY GRANT
as the pride!
FRANK SINATRA
as the passion!
SOPHIA LOREN
as the flame!
in STANLEY KRAMER'S
MONUMENTAL FILMING OF
"THE PRIDE and THE PASSION"
UNITED ARTISTS
TECHNICOLOR® · VISTAVISION® with THEODORE BIKEL JOHN WENGRAF JAY NOVELLO JOSE NIETO CARLOS LARRANAGA PHILLIP VAN ZANDT PACO EL LABERINTO
Screen Story and Screenplay by EDNA and EDWARD ANHALT Based on the Novel "THE GUN" by C. S. Forester Music Composed by George Antheil Produced and Directed by STANLEY KRAMER

This starry, over-inflated and expensive ($5 million) movie, set in Spain, was adapted from C.S. Forester's **The Gun**.

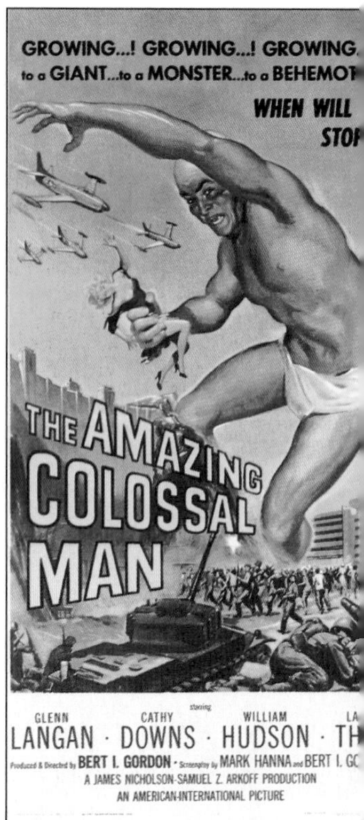
GROWING...! GROWING...! GROWING
to a GIANT...to a MONSTER...to a BEHEMOT
WHEN WILL
STOP
THE AMAZING COLOSSAL MAN
starring
GLENN LANGAN · CATHY DOWNS · WILLIAM HUDSON · TH
Produced & Directed by BERT I. GORDON · Screenplay by MARK HANNA and BERT I. GO
A JAMES NICHOLSON-SAMUEL Z. ARKOFF PRODUCTION
AN AMERICAN-INTERNATIONAL PICTURE

A U.S. Army colonel is exposed radiation after a nuclear bomb te mutates into a giant who goes on rampage and is hunted down by own men. Well written but spec effects not always up to scratch.

MONTGOMERY CLIFT
ELIZABETH TAYLOR
EVA MARIE SAINT
M·G·M PRESENTS IN MGM CAMERA 65 "WINDOW OF THE WORLD"
RAINTREE COUNTY
IN THE GREAT TRADITION OF CIVIL WAR ROMANCE

Clift had his car crash midway through filming of the $6 million production.

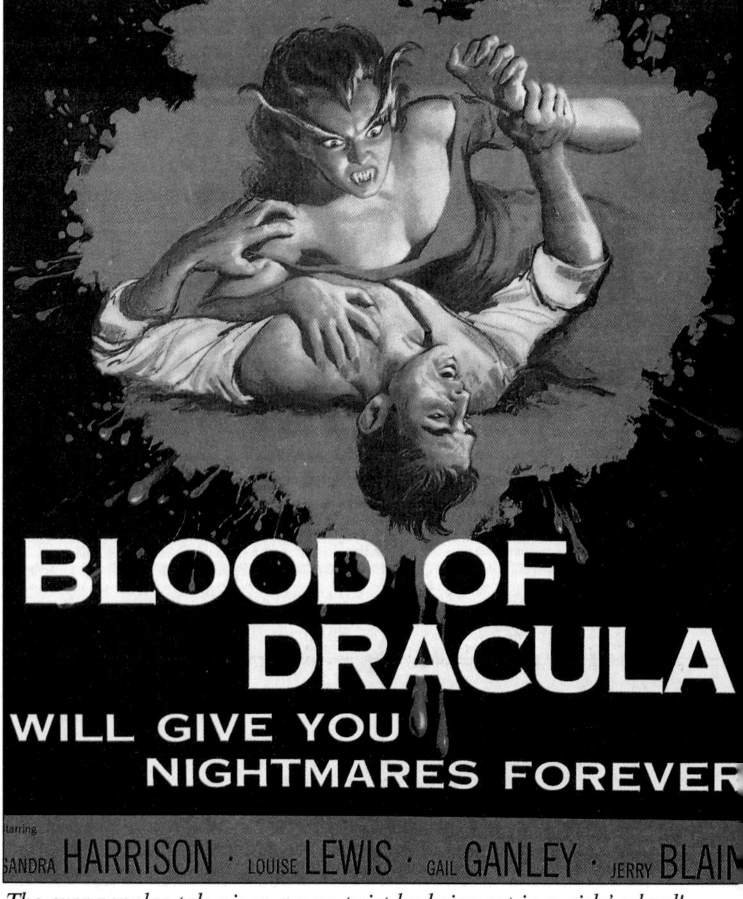
BLOOD OF DRACULA
WILL GIVE YOU
NIGHTMARES FOREVER
starring
SANDRA HARRISON · LOUISE LEWIS · GAIL GANLEY · JERRY BLAIN

The ever-popular tale given a new twist by being set in a girls' school!

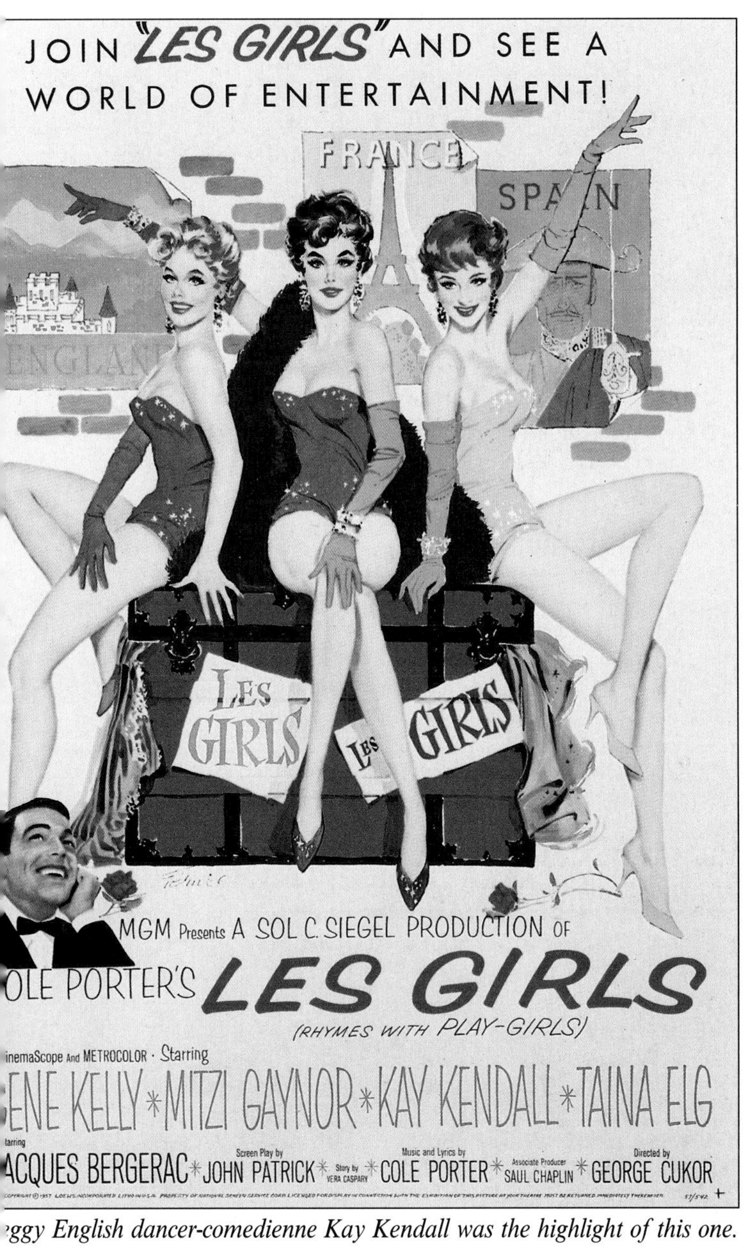
JOIN "LES GIRLS" AND SEE A WORLD OF ENTERTAINMENT!
FRANCE
SPAIN
ENGLAND
LES GIRLS
LES GIRLS
MGM Presents A SOL C. SIEGEL PRODUCTION OF
OLE PORTER'S LES GIRLS
(RHYMES WITH PLAY-GIRLS)
inemaScope And METROCOLOR · Starring
ENE KELLY * MITZI GAYNOR * KAY KENDALL * TAINA ELG
ACQUES BERGERAC * JOHN PATRICK * COLE PORTER * SAUL CHAPLIN * GEORGE CUKOR

ggy English dancer-comedienne Kay Kendall was the highlight of this one.

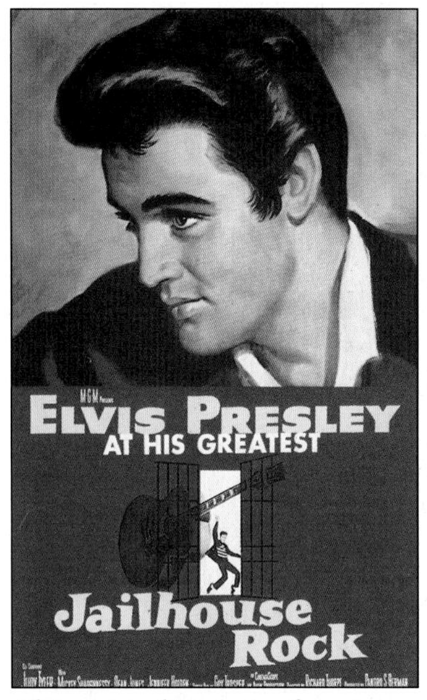
ELVIS PRESLEY
AT HIS GREATEST
Jailhouse Rock

Elvis: now a bigger star than ever.

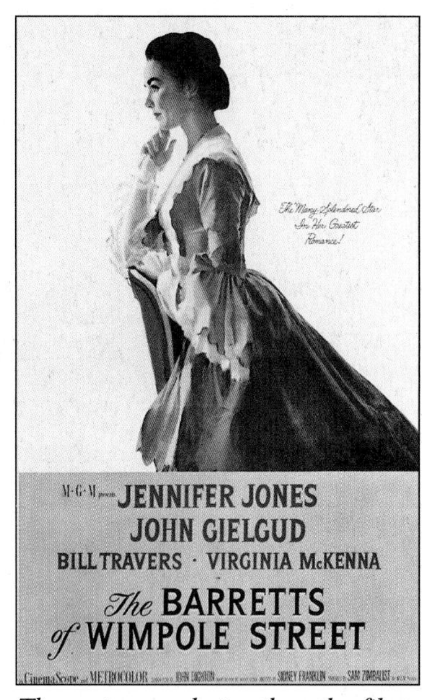
JENNIFER JONES
JOHN GIELGUD
BILL TRAVERS · VIRGINIA McKENNA
The BARRETTS of WIMPOLE STREET

The poster was better than the film.

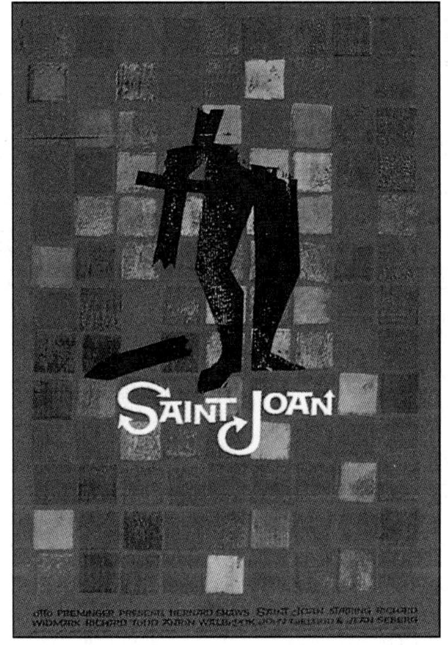
SAINT JOAN

Saul Bass designed this poster.

Nikolai Cherkassov in ***Don Quixote****, from Grigori Kozintsev (USSR).*

unning Fred Astaire in ***Silk Stockings****, a musical remake of* ***Ninotchka****.*

The Witches of Salem *was a French version of Arthur Miller's* ***The Crucible****.*

1958

1957 Academy Awards, RKO Pantages Theater, 26 Mar.

Best Film:	*The Bridge on the River Kwai* (dir: David Lean)
Best Director:	David Lean
Best Actor:	Alec Guinness *(The Bridge on the River Kwai)*
Best Actress:	Joanne Woodward *(The Three Faces of Eve)*
Best Supp. Actor:	Red Buttons *(Sayonara)*
Best Supp. Actress:	Miyoshi Umeki *(Sayonara)*

Cairo, 20 January
Premiere of Youssef Chahine's film *Cairo Station* in which the director - playing a simpleton who turns criminal – also demonstrates that he is an excellent actor.

Hollywood, 8 February
Paramount has sold the television rights of its catalogue prior to 1948 (750 films) for a total of $50 million to the Music Corporation of America (MCA). Paramount shares have skyrocketed.

Hollywood, 21 February
Ma and Pa Kettle have come to the end of their 10-year run. The popular series, starring Marjorie Main and Percy Kilbride, had its genesis in *The Egg and I* (1947). *Ma and Pa Kettle* followed in 1949, with a film a year until 1957's *The Kettles on Old MacDonald's Farm*, which, it was decided, would be their last.

Washington D.C., 3 March
The Supreme Court has returned an unfavorable verdict to the 23 victims of the blacklist who instituted proceedings against the studios which had suspended them; the decision ratifies the suspensions.

London, 6 March
Simone Signoret has received the British Academy Award for her performance in *The Witches of Salem*. Raymond Rouleau directed this adaptation of Arthur Miller's play, *The Crucible*.

New York, 10 March
At Carnegie Hall, Danny Kaye conducted the Philharmonic Orchestra with his feet! The occasion was a benefit concert.

Los Angeles, 11 April
After having heard evidence from Lana Turner for an hour, an investigating jury exonerated her daughter Cheryl of all charges in the Johnny Stompanato murder case, which they ruled as "justifiable homicide."

Cannes, 4 May
A furious Sophia Loren has left early from the Festival because the film she stars in, *Desire Under the Elms*, an adaptation of Eugene O'Neill's play directed by Delbert Mann, has not been given an evening screening as requested by the star.

Rome, 20 May
William Wyler has begun filming a new version of *Ben-Hur* with Charlton Heston in the title role.

Monaco, 16 June
Frank Sinatra appears in a documentary on Monaco for American television in which he interviews his former co-star, Grace Kelly, now Princess Grace.

Paris, 8 July
According to a recent survey published in *France Soir*, 63 percent of French men and 59 percent of French women are interested in the cinema; 25 percent prefer romantic films, 20 percent thrillers and 12 percent historical films.

Hollywood, 9 July
Marilyn Monroe has returned to the cinema capital after an absence of two years. She will be filming *Some Like It Hot* with Jack Lemmon and Tony Curtis, for Billy Wilder.

London, 9 July
At the premiere of *The Vikings*, directed by Richard Fleischer, the movie's star Kirk Douglas presented the Duke of Edinburgh with a miniature Viking ship for his son, Prince Charles.

Venice, 1 September
The number of films in competition at the Venice Film Festival has been steadily decreasing throughout the decade. For the third year in succession, only 14 films (representing 10 countries) have been entered. This is a marked contrast to the 31 titles competing in 1952 and 1953, 29 in 1954 and 31 again in 1955.

Moscow, 1 September
The second part of Eisenstein's *Ivan the Terrible*, banned since 1946, is finally being shown.

Venice, 2 September
The arrival of Brigitte Bardot on the banks of the lagoon here provoked a virtual riot. She was accompanied by Sacha Distel.

New York, 10 September
A chemical manufacturing company has announced the forthcoming completion of an Anglo-American project, endowed with a $3 million budget, which aims to bring a new dimension to cinema – smell!

Washington D.C., 17 September
Alfred Hitchcock has been given permission to use models of the faces on Mount Rushmore, which are protected by copyright, for scenes in *North by Northwest*.

Paris, 29 September
The critic François Truffaut, encouraged by the welcome given to his first short film, is going to make a feature, *The Four Hundred Blows*. He is looking for a boy of about 12 for the leading role.

New York, 15 December
The Old Man and the Sea, directed by John Sturges from the Hemingway novella and starring Spencer Tracy, has been awarded first prize by the Catholic International Office of Cinema.

London, 18 December
Boris Karloff's two young nephews aged 10 and 13 have been found with their throats cut. The children's mother is accused of the murder.

Paris, 18 December
Brigitte Bardot was at the Palais de Justice for the injunction proceedings instigated by her against Bruno Coquatrix, from the Comédie Caumartin Théâtre, over the title of his latest revue, *Ça va Bardot!*

London, 21 December
Ingrid Bergman today married producer Lars Schmidt. He is the Swedish star's third husband.

Washington D.C., 31 December
The U.S. Treasury has received $425,000 in settlement of back taxes from Charlie Chaplin.

BIRTHS

Pennsylvania, 10 March
Sharon Stone

Atlanta, 20 March
Holly Hunter

London, 21 March
Gary Oldman

New York, 3 April
Alec Baldwin

South Carolina, 21 April
Andie MacDowell

London, 29 April
Daniel Day Lewis

Kansas, 28 May
Annette Bening

Philadelphia, 8 July
Kevin Bacon

France, 3 August
Lambert Wilson

Michigan, 16 August
Madonna
(Madonna Louise Ciccone)

California, 16 October
Tim Robbins

Illinois, 17 November
Mary Elizabeth Mastrantonio

Los Angeles, 21 November
Jamie Lee Curtis

DEATHS

California, 13 January
Edna Purviance

California, 19 May
Ronald Colman

London, 9 June
Robert Donat

Madrid, 15 November
Tyrone Power

California, 21 December
H.B. Warner

Richard Brooks directs the scre version of Tennessee Williams' exp sive ***Cat on a Hot Tin Roof****. As t unhappy wife (married to Paul Ne man), Elizabeth Taylor impresses.*

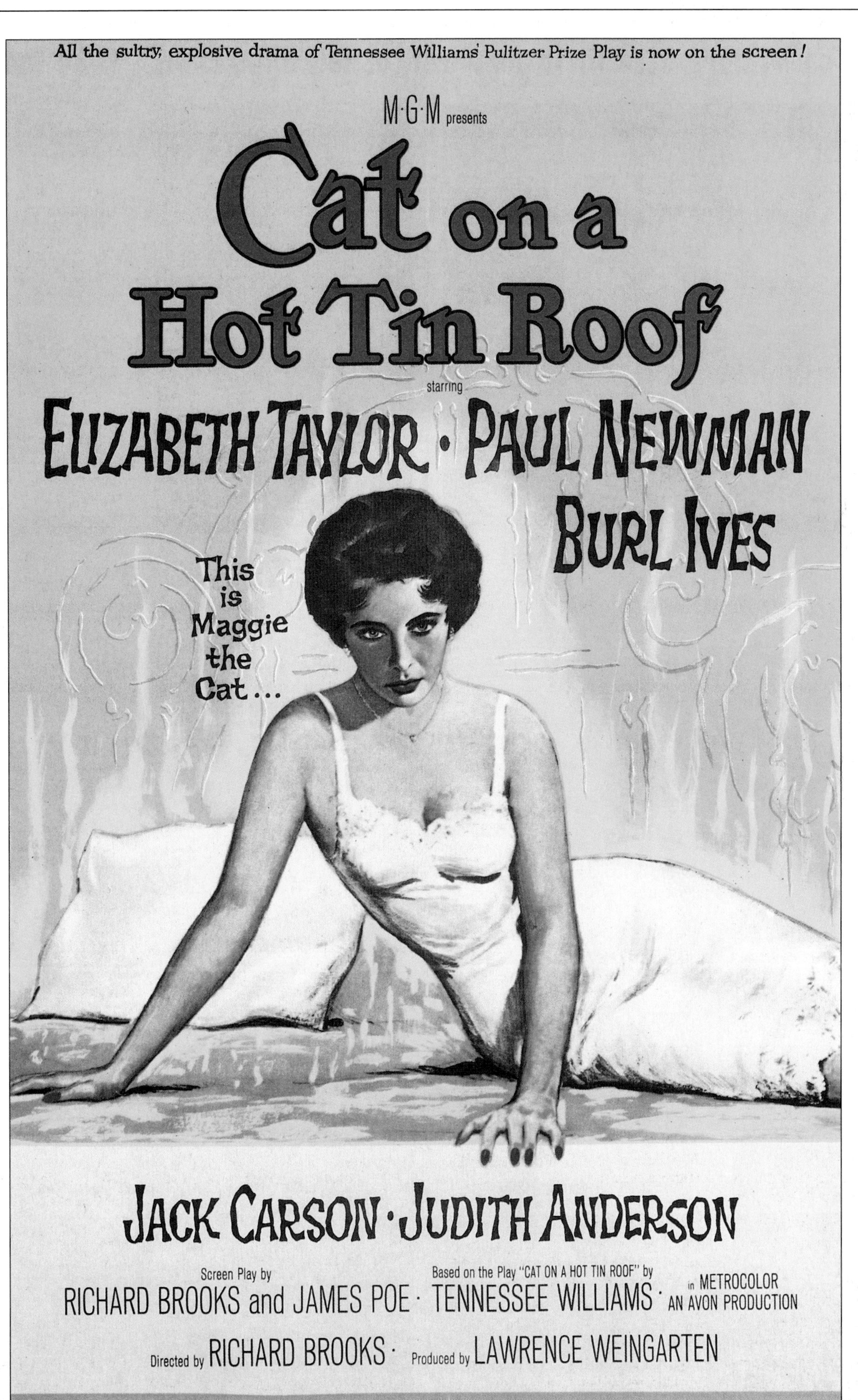
All the sultry, explosive drama of Tennessee Williams' Pulitzer Prize Play is now on the screen!
M·G·M presents
Cat on a Hot Tin Roof
starring
ELIZABETH TAYLOR · PAUL NEWMAN
BURL IVES
This is Maggie the Cat...
JACK CARSON · JUDITH ANDERSON
Screen Play by RICHARD BROOKS and JAMES POE
Based on the Play "CAT ON A HOT TIN ROOF" by TENNESSEE WILLIAMS
in METROCOLOR
AN AVON PRODUCTION
Directed by RICHARD BROOKS · Produced by LAWRENCE WEINGARTEN

Louis Malle's elevator gives a lift to popularity of new filmmakers

Maurice Ronet (left) and Lino Ventura in Louis Malle's psychological thriller.

Leading lady Jeanne Moreau.

Paris, 29 January
Recent Louis Delluc Prize-winning film titled *Frantic* (*Ascenseur pour l'échafaud*), heralds a new generation of French directors. The 26-year-old Louis Malle had tried for many months to shoot an autobiographical screenplay, but producers refused, thinking he was too young to undertake such a task. Malle, therefore, decided he would make this thriller, which he has overlaid with a dark atmosphere and psychological depth. Tension is well built up, especially in the crucial scene when the hero is stuck in an elevator. The effective jazz score was improvised by jazz man Miles Davis.

Mike Todd killed in airplane crash

Hollywood, 25 March
The movie theaters in Chicago, N
York and Los Angeles where M
Todd's *Around the World in 80 D*
is showing, have closed their do
today as a sign of mourning for
producer. The flamboyant imp
sario, born Avron Goldbogen
June 1907, was killed three days a
when his private plane, *Lucky Liz*,
which he was flying to New Yo
crashed in a storm near Albuqu
que. Elizabeth Taylor had want
to accompany her husband on t
flight but was persuaded to stay
home because of a flu virus. T
couple had been married only sev
months. On 6 August last year, th
daughter Lisa was born by Caes
ean, and both mother and ch
nearly died. Liz was advised nev
to have another baby. On heari
the news of Todd's tragic accide
Liz screamed so loudly that neig
bors a few doors away could he
her. The star had to be drugged
prevent her taking her own life.

Seven Oscars for 'Kwai' in year of contrasts

Hollywood, 26 March
This year's Academy Awards ceremony, the thirtieth, was hosted by Rosalind Russell, James Stewart, Bob Hope, David Niven and Jack Lemmon. The most successful film of the year was *The Bridge on the River Kwai*, produced by Sam Spiegel, directed by David Lean and starring Alec Guinness, William Holden, Jack Hawkins and Sessue Hayakawa. The film is a monument to the Spiegel method: the meticulous preparation of an ostensibly solemn subject, swathed in handsome production values and with its hint of radicalism kept firmly under control by the tidy impersonality of David Lean's direction. Nevertheless, the movie's eschewing of stereotyped heroics, together with its message that war is "madness", has enabled it to carry away seven Oscars: Best Picture, Director and Actor (Alec Guinness as the tragic Colonel Nicholson), Cinematography (Jack Hildyard), Editing (Peter Taylor), Score (Malcolm Arnold) and Screenplay (Pierre Boulle, who adapted it from his own book). The Best Actress Oscar went to Joanne Woodward for her gripping performance in *The Three Faces of Eve* as the young woman afflicted with multiple personalities. Red Buttons and Miyoshi Umeki were presented with the Best Supporting Actor and Actress Awards for their work in *Sayonara*. That same film also managed to scoop the Art Direction-Set Decoration award, while *Nights of Cabiria* from Italy's Federico Fellini was voted Best Foreign Film.

Woodward: ***The Three Faces of Eve.***

Brando goes blond for 'The Young Lions'

New York, 2 April
Ever the chameleon, Marlon Brando has assumed a blond hairstyle for *The Young Lions*, adapted from Irwin Shaw's novel, in which he plays a wartime Nazi officer who comes to see the error of his ways. He shares the acting honors with Mo
gomery Clift, cast as a Jew harass
with anti-Semitism by his fell
American soldiers. Their lives, a
Brando's death, are intertwined
the war in a powerful film with
stirring score by Hugo Friedhofe

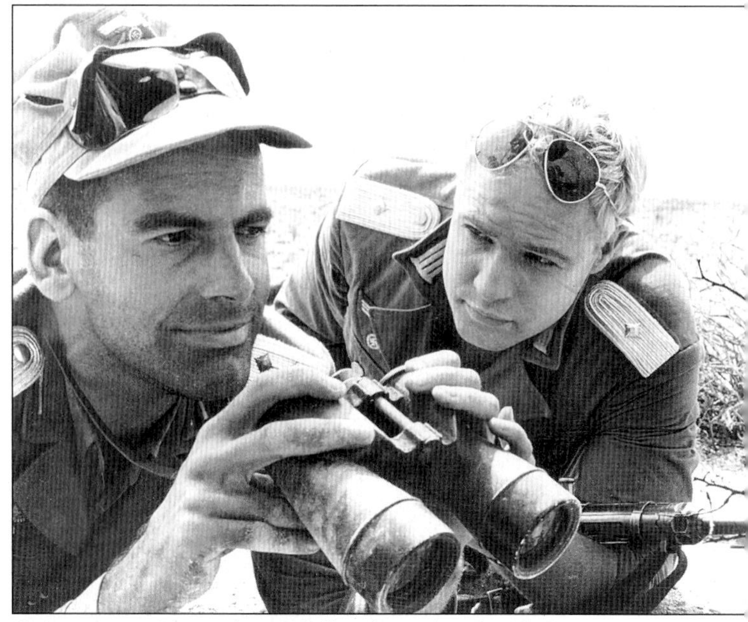
German actor Maximilian Schell with Marlon Brando in ***The Young Lions.***

érard Philipe plays the painter Modigliani for Jacques Becker

'tist Modigliani (Gérard Philipe) in his Montparnasse studio in Becker's film.*

Moreau plays Jeanne Hébuterne.

ris, 4 April
cques Becker's latest film, *Modig- ni of Montparnasse* (*Montparnasse*), is dedicated to the memory of ax Ophuls, who died in March last ar. Initially, it was meant to be directed by Ophuls, but when the German director was hospitalized with a heart attack, he suggested Becker take over. Becker provoked the ire of the screenwriter Henri Jeanson by making changes to the text, and also had to contend with Modigliani's daughter on the set. Considering the circumstances, this tale of the unfortunate painter has been effectively realized and Gérard Philipe is ideal in the lead role.

Star's daughter kills mother's lover

Hollywood, 4 April
Troubled star Lana Turner has always protested that "I find men terribly exciting", but she got more than she bargained for when she took former mobster Johnny Stompanato, alias Johnny Valentine, into her bed. Stompanato was no funny Valentine. While Turner was away filming *Another Time, Another Place* on location in England, he ran up massive gambling debts and, reportedly, sexually abused Turner's unhappy 14-year-old daughter Cheryl Crane. Lana and Johnny's stormy relationship, punctuated by violent physical altercations, reached its bloody climax today. When Stompanato threatened to take a knife to her mother, Crane plunged a nine-inch carving knife into his chest. The police arrived almost immediately, but too late to save Johnny. Cheryl has been arrested but is claiming self-defense. Her grandmother will take care of her while she awaits a juvenile court appearance.

hampagne success for a musical 'Gigi'

ollywood, 15 May
'hile *My Fair Lady* is still packing em in on Broadway, a scintillating w film musical by the same com- osers, Alan Jay Lerner and Freder- k Loewe, also designed by Cecil eaton, has opened to acclaim. Pro- uced by Arthur Freed and directed Vincente Minnelli in the best GM musical tradition, *Gigi* is a rsion of Colette's novel, already lapted as a 1948 French film, and so a Broadway play. The delightful eslie Caron takes the role of a oung girl raised by two old cocottes be a courtesan in the Paris of 00. However, when she refuses to the mistress of Gaston (Louis ourdan), a bored man-about-town, proposes marriage. Much of *Gigi* as actually shot in Paris, the princi- al sites being the Bois de Boulogne, laxim's and the Tuileries gardens. he captivating presence of Maur- e Chevalier recalls the world of s 1930s Paramount musicals as he ngs "I'm Glad I'm Not Young nymore" and "Thank Heaven For ittle Girls", plus a touching and umorous duet with Hermione Gin- old, "I Remember It Well".

Young Gigi with her aunt (Hermione Gingold), Gaston (Louis Jourdan).

Gigi, now flowering into beautiful young womanhood, with Gaston.

Hitchcock, Stewart climb to dizzy heights

San Francisco, 28 May
Alfred Hitchcock's *Vertigo* would have looked like a good commercial proposition to Paramount, but they could hardly have anticipated the strength of the final product. Based on a French novel by Pierre Boileau and Thomas Narcejac (whose *les Diaboliques* was a big success here), the picture was cast with big box-office stars James Stewart and Kim Novak, and photographed in color and VistaVision at a variety of picturesque locations in and around San Francisco, where it has just opened to acclaim. It is clear that Hitch has accomplished something original and unexpected. The movie is not at all a conventional thriller, but rather a crime drama-cum-black romantic fantasy, and Stewart's ex-police detective is hardly a conventional hero. He is a troubled and obsessive character who falls in love with a young woman half his age. Hired to tail and look after her, he is shattered when she commits suicide. He delivers his usual excellent performance, but Kim Novak is a revelation, perfectly cast in the dual role of a cool, sophisticated blonde and a young, sexy and brunette shop girl. Paramount's own VistaVision process has never been more imaginatively or effectively used (photography by Robert Burks), while other key members of the creative team include the composer Bernard Herrmann, Edith Head (clothes) and Saul Bass (titles).

James Stewart and Kim Novak.

Tatiana reduces grown men to tears

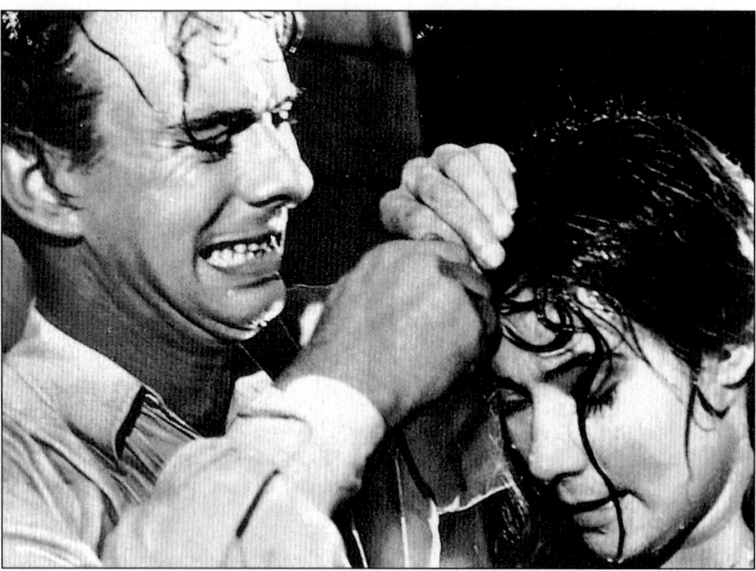

Tatiana Samoilova and Alexei Batalov in ***The Cranes Are Flying*** *(USSR).*

Cannes, 18 May
The actress Tatiana Samoïlova was chosen by the jury of the Cannes Film Festival as the recipient of a special award for her moving performance in the Soviet film *The Cranes Are Flying*. Samoilova plays a young hospital worker who hears that her fiance has been killed in the war. She refuses to believe it, yet she marries another man whom she does not love. The actress touched the jury with her beautiful eyes, which bear the look of a hunted animal. They were also impressed by the lyricism of Mikhail Kalatozov's direction, and the sweeping camerawork, and offered the picture the Golden Palm. But if the highest prize went to a story that got audiences weeping, the Special Jury award was a tribute to laughter. It was presented to *My Uncle*, Jacques Tati's hilarious satire on the middle-class' obsession with modernity. The film also reintroduced us to the engaging character that Tati created in *Monsieur Hulot's Holiday* five years ago. After *The Seventh Seal* won the Special Jury Prize last year, Ingmar Bergman returned to receive the best director award for *Brink Of Life*. This enclosed drama, set in a maternity ward, has the advantage of three brilliant actresses – Ingrid Thulin, Eva Dahlbeck and Bibi Andersson – who earned a collective best actress prize. America's Paul Newman was voted best actor for a powerful performance in *The Long Hot Summer*, a tale of family intrigue in the deep South.

Jacques Tati in his prize-winning film, ***My Uncle****, which he also directed.*

Brando and Anna are parents of a baby so

New York, 11 May
Nine months to the day after his marriage to the Indian actress Anna Kashfi, Marlon Brando has become a father. The surprise wedding had taken place at the home of his aunt in California during the shooting of *The Young Lions*, and, evidently inspired, Brando will call his son Christian Devi, the first name after the character he played in the film. The actor had wanted to get married and have children for a long time. Originally *The Young Lions* was to have been a small-budget picture, but this adaptation of Irwin Shaw's multi-layered war novel grew into a super-production when Brando, Montgomery Clift, Dean Marti Maximilian Schell, Hope Lan Barbara Rush and May Britt we cast, and Edward Dmytryk took the director's reins. Brando playec young Nazi officer whose pacif inclinations struggled with his r tions of duty, thus rendering hi a human being assailed by doub Since the movie's release in Apr the film has attracted much criticis because of the hero being a rath sympathetic Nazi. In response these attacks, Brando retorted th "passing one's time obsessively h ing is perfectly sterile." He now h only love for his son, to whom will dedicate all his leisure time.

Orson Welles returns with a 'Touch of Evi

Marlene Dietrich and Orson Welles in his Hollywood comeback ***Touch of Ev***

Brussels, 8 June
Orson Welles has made a blistering Hollywood comeback with *Touch of Evil*, which has won the main prize at the Brussels film festival, but the volatile star has already disowned the picture, claiming that it has been mutilated by Universal. Welles was set merely to co-star with Charlton Heston, but the latter insisted that he also direct, which he did for nothing. Welles sets a sizzling pace from the film's stunning opening sequence, a marathon crane and tracking shot by cameraman Russell Metty. Thereafter he dominates the film as Hank Quinlan, a crooked cop in a sleazy Texas border town. This monstrous creation, a sweat-sodden, candy bar-gobbling mountain of flesh, tangles with Mexica narcotics agent Heston over a mu der investigation, with Heston bride Janet Leigh as the pawn their struggle. An outstanding su porting cast includes Joseph Callei Akim Tamiroff and Dennis Weave and there are unbilled cameos fro Joseph Cotten, Ray Collins ar Mercedes McCambridge, the last a leather-clad harpy wielding a s ringe. The film also reunites Well with Marlene Dietrich, whom l sawed in half 14 years ago in *Follo the Boys*. And at the end of th film Marlene's Mexican madam o serves that Quinlan was "some kir of a man" as his bloated corpse bo in the shallows of the Rio Grand The same could be said of Welles

‹ing Creole' acting challenge for Presley

characteristic image of Elvis who in fact plays a dramatic part in **King Creole**.

ew York, 3 July
ıst as "a hustler out to make a fast ıck" in Paramount's *King Creole*, vis Presley is called upon to give mething resembling a dramatic rformance. Based on a Harold obbins novel, *A Stone for Danny sher*, this is a New Orleans-set elodrama in which busboy Elvis sets his sights on the nightclubs of Bourbon Street with the help of ruthless manager Walter Matthau. Veteran director Michael Curtiz skillfully summons up the seedy, sweaty milieu in which Presley rises to stardom, and the Pelvis is given every opportunity to exercise those million-dollar vocal chords.

'Porgy and Bess' finds itself in difficulties

Dorothy Dandridge and Sammy Davis Jr. in Preminger's **Porgy and Bess**.

Hollywood, 3 August
Samuel Goldwyn's new production, *Porgy and Bess*, seems to be the victim of a curse. The Screen Directors Guild has threatened to boycott the picture unless the director Rouben Mamoulian, whom Goldwyn fired a week ago, is reinstated. Mamoulian, who directed the first production of the George Gershwin opera on Broadway in 1935, had appealed to the Guild. Meanwhile, the producer has replaced Mamoulian with Otto Preminger. (Fourteen years ago, Preminger replaced Mamoulian on *Laura*.) This event follows a month after a huge fire destroyed many of the sets for the film.

ope intercedes or Rossellinis

ome, 10 July
ıanks to the intervention of the onsignor Floriot in France, Mongnor Graziadei in Italy and the ope, no less, the eight-year marage of Roberto Rossellini and grid Bergman has been annulled the Vatican. Even if they were vorced in the eyes of the world, oberto and Ingrid have remained arried in Italy because divorce oes not officially exist there. The wedish actress, a 43-year-old moth- of four children, has dreamed of marriage. She met the Swedish eater producer Lars Schmidt in rance when she was shooting Jean enoir's *Paris Does Strange Things*, vo years ago. "I live in Paris with y children, and Roberto seems ery satisfied with the arrangeent," Ingrid explained. "However, was unaware of Lars' existence. e didn't think there could be anyne else in my life." Ingrid Bergman ill now able to marry Schmidt, cause she is single again at the ope's bidding.

Grief-stricken Liz excels as Maggie the Cat

Hollywood, 18 September
Tennessee Williams' intense family drama, *Cat on a Hot Tin Roof*, directed by Richard Brooks, stars Paul Newman as Brick, and Elizabeth Taylor as Maggie, the wife he refuses to sleep with. With Burl Ives reprising his stage performance as Big Daddy, the cast is impressive, although the movie is somewhat sanitized. Taylor, however, is a revelation, demonstrating her personal courage as well as talent. Filming commenced very shortly after her husband Mike Todd was killed, and though grief-stricken, she reported for work to deliver a stunning performance, moving from seductive Southern kitten to tigerish cat in her rage and frustration.

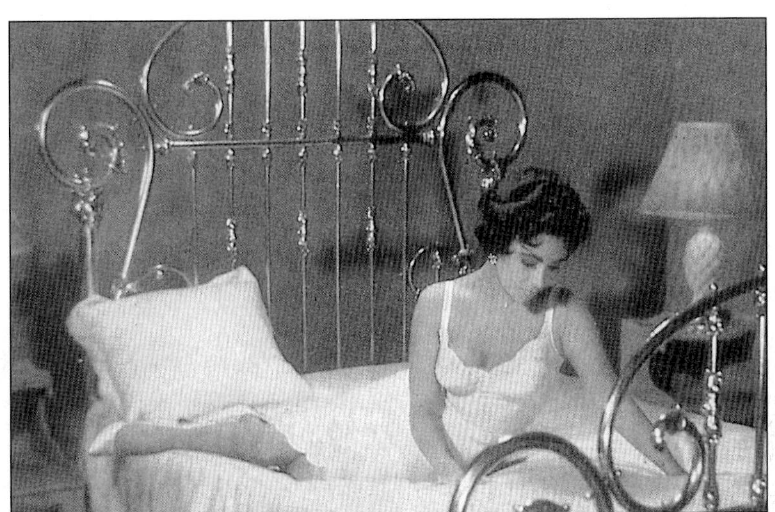

Elizabeth Taylor as neglected wife, Maggie, the 'cat' of the film's title.

Venice discovers Francesco Rosi

Venice, 8 September
The Venice Film Festival is in the habit of discovering new talent, and this year is no exception. Of the three directors whose films gained the top prizes, 35-year-old Italian Francesco Rosi is the least known. His first feature, *The Challenge* (*La Sfida*), is a corrosive condemnation of the Mafia. That picture shared the Silver Lion with Louis Malle's *The Lovers*, the latter being a brave choice by the jury because of the scandal the film has caused in Italy and France. Perhaps *The Lovers* has offended certain people because it equates love with adultery – surely pardonable when the temptress is Jeanne Moreau. The winner of the Golden Lion was Hiroshi Inagaki's *The Life of Matsu the Untamed*, a remake of a 1943 Japanese picture which shows, with great passion, the differences between the social classes in Japan. Sophia Loren for *Desire Under the Elms* and Alec Guinness for *The Horse's Mouth* received the acting laurels.

Veteran Jean Gabin seduced by youthful sex kitten Brigitte Bardot

B.B. with Franco Interlenghi (left) and Jean Gabin in ***Love is My Profession****, directed by Claude Autant-Lara.*

Paris, 17 September
A controversial rendezvous between veteran star Jean Gabin and current sensation Brigitte Bardot has been arranged in Claude Autant-Lara's *Love is My Profession*. Gabin might have had his doubts about playing a middle-aged lawyer who falls for Bardot, whom he is defending on a charge of theft. But after a long delay he was persuaded to take on the role by Edwige Feuillère, cast as his wife in the film. He was also reassured by the fact that the screenplay is adapted from a novel by Georges Simenon, of whom Gabin is an unqualified admirer. In spite of its racy English title, *Love is My Profession* is a solid melodrama, an intriguing collision of generations and attitudes, in which Gabin amusedly contemplates Bardot's sumptuous body while casually walking away with the acting honors.

World's best films assembled togeth

Brussels, 12 October
On the occasion of the Bruss World Fair, the Belgian Ciném thèque organized a poll of the b films of all time. The 12 top pictu were, in order, Eisenstein's *The B tleship Potemkin* (100 votes), Cha lin's *The Gold Rush* (85), De Sic *The Bicycle Thief* (85), Dreyer's *T Passion of Joan of Arc* (78), Renoi *la Grande illusion* (72), Strohein *Greed* (61), Griffith's *Intoleran* (61), Pudovkin's *Mother* (54), Ors Welles' *Citizen Kane* (50), Dovzhe ko's *Earth* (47), Murnau's *The La Laugh* (45) and Wiene's *The Ca net of Dr. Caligari* (43). The sele tion was made by a jury of 117 fil historians from 26 countries, amo them John Grierson, Iris Barry, A dré Bazin and Henri Langlois. It significant that the list includes or three sound films almost 30 yea after talkies came in. By combini the number of votes obtained each director for all of the film mentioned in the ballot, Chapl easily topped the list.

Wajda's trilogy comes to stunning climax

Warsaw, 3 October
More mature and ironic than *A Generation* and *Kanal*, the first two parts of Andrzej Wajda's war trilogy, *Ashes and Diamonds* brings it to a stunning climax. The action takes place on the last day of the war in 1945, when the youngest member of a Nationalist underground movement in a provincial Polish town is ordered to kill the new Communist district secretary. As he waits in a hotel during the night, he meets and falls in love with a girl and learns that there is more to life than killing. The brilliant young actor Zbigniew Cybulski creates a complex characterization of the protagonist that embodies the skeptical new generation now in Poland.

Marcel Carné examines modern youth

Paris, 10 October
Marcel Carné's new film, *Youthful Sinners (les Tricheurs)*, seems set to be the box-office success of the season. Without a single star in the cast, the film concerns existentialist youth in Saint-Germain-des-Prés. Included among them is a middle-class student (Jacques Charrier), who falls in love with a girl (Pascale Petit) among the young crowd dedicat to defying social and moral conve tions. Unfortunately, blackmail, i fidelity and group pressure sabota the relationship. Apart from t fresh young cast, one of the maj interests of the film is the jazz scor which includes recordings by St Getz, Roy Eldridge, Oscar Peterso and Dizzy Gillespie.

Zbigniew Cybulski, the brilliant Polish star of Wajda's ***Ashes and Diamonds****.*

Jacques Charrier, Andréa Parisy in Carné's ***Youthful Sinners (les Tricheurs***

ock and admiration greet Louis Malle's award-winning lovers

nne Moreau and Jean-Marc Bory in Louis Malle's **The Lovers (les Amants)**.

Moreau is the bored wife who betrays her husband (Alain Cuny) in an erotic relationship with a young man whom he has brought to their home.

ris, 5 November
ançois Truffaut has called Louis alle's *The Lovers*, "the first night love in the cinema," and Malle s awarded a Special Jury Prize the Venice Film Festival two onths ago. The Parisian public is w able to judge for themselves. The heroine is a young provincial middle-class wife (Jeanne Moreau), bored with her lover as well as her husband. She then meets an archeology student (Jean-Marc Bory), with whom she spends a night of erotic bliss at her country house, before they leave together at dawn. Many have found the boldness of the semi-nude love scenes shocking, but rarely in the cinema has the act of love been shown with such purity. This is not the opinion of the Catholic Church, who have commented that "Christian duty demands that the film should be avoided."

Tyrone Power has played his last role

Madrid, 15 November
While filming a swordfight with George Sanders for *Solomon and Sheba*, Tyrone Power suffered a massive heart attack. He was rushed to hospital but died an hour later without regaining consciousness. Born in Cincinnati in 1913, Tyrone was the son of matinée idol Tyrone Power Sr., and there was never any doubt about the career he should follow. After early work on stage and radio, he followed his father to Hollywood, and when Powell Sr. died in 1931, the son was given a bit part, his first, in *Tom Brown of Culver*. After another stint on the stage, he was signed by Fox in 1936, and remained under contract to that studio for most of his career. His first two wives were Annabella and Linda Christian, who bore him two sons. He had recently gotten married to Debbie Smith Minardos. The filming of *Solomon and Sheba*, a hopeful return to the swashbuckling successes of Power's early career, has been suspended until a replacement can be found.

rench criticism oses its model

aris, 11 November
ndré Bazin, the French critic nd theorist, has died of leukemia t the age of 40. His illness had mited his activities during the ıst few years, but he continued to e seen once a week at *Cahiers du Cinéma*, the influential magazine e co-founded in 1951. A student f the Catholic philosopher Emmanuel Mounier, and follower f the critic and director Roger eenhardt, Bazin was undoubtdly the greatest film critic of his eneration. During the Occupaion, he formed a ciné club where olitically banned movies were hown in defiance of the German uthorities. As editor of *Cahiers*, azin gradually formulated a thery of cinema in opposition to isenstein's theory of montage. mong the directors who satisied his criterion of "objective eality" were Dreyer, Stroheim, Velles, Wyler and Renoir.

North Wales subs for China as missionary Ingrid brings happiness

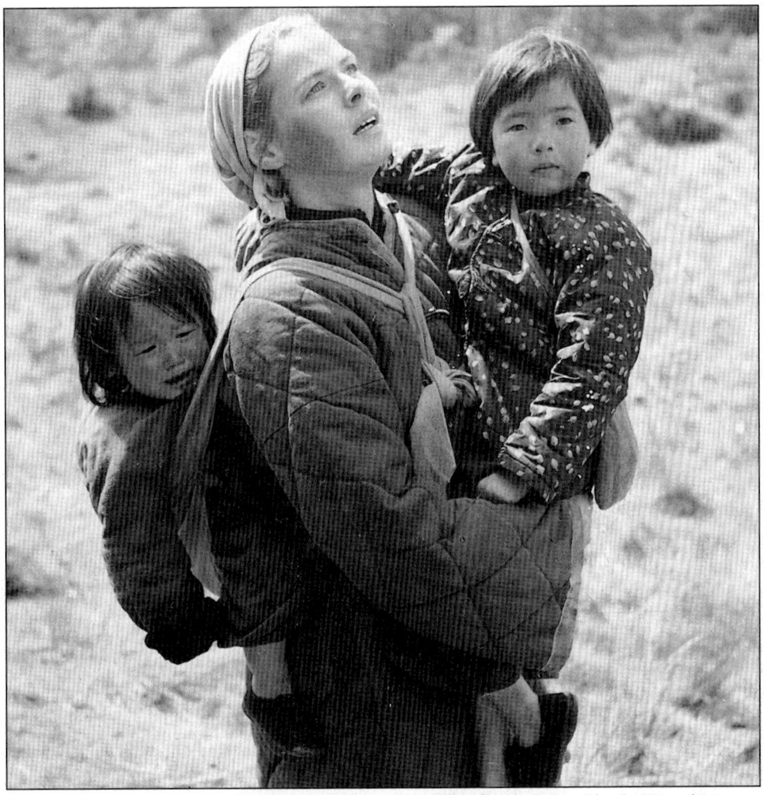

*Bergman as missionary Gladys Aylward in **The Inn of the Sixth Happiness**.*

London, 24 November
The mountains of north Wales double for China in the 1930s in 20th Century-Fox's *The Inn of the Sixth Happiness*, starring Ingrid Bergman as a missionary who carries the Christian faith to regions dominated by war lords and converts a mandarin played by Robert Donat. Curt Jurgens is cast as the Chinese soldier with whom Bergman falls in love, only to leave him when a party of children must be led to safety over the mountains. Based on the real-life story of Gladys Aylward, *The Inn of the Sixth Happiness* is a moving story which holds back from pounding the religious keys too hard. However, its release is tinged with sadness. Clearly speaking with great difficulty, Robert Donat delivers the last line of the film to a tearful Ingrid Bergman: "We shall never see each other again, I think. Farewell". The words were prophetic. Not long after filming finished, Donat died in a hospital from the chronic asthma which had dogged his career since the early 1930s.

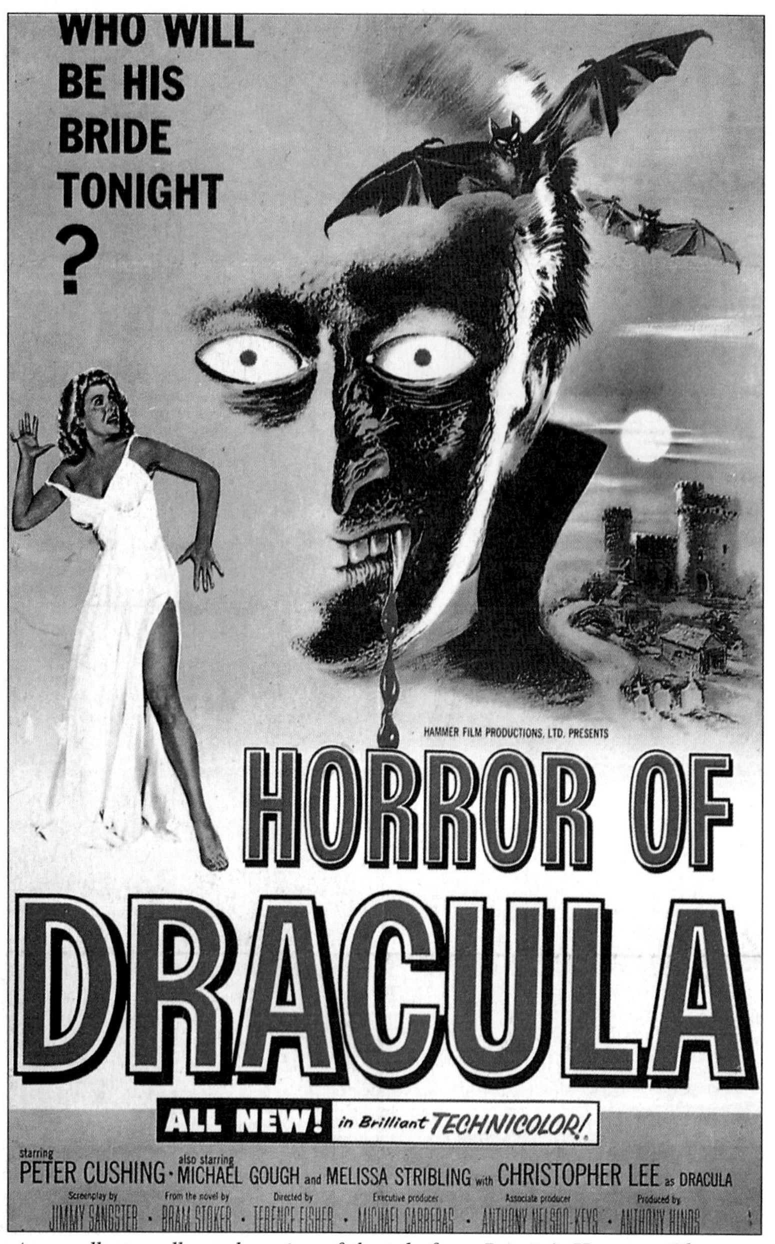
WHO WILL BE HIS BRIDE TONIGHT ?
HAMMER FILM PRODUCTIONS, LTD. PRESENTS
HORROR OF DRACULA
ALL NEW! in Brilliant TECHNICOLOR!
starring PETER CUSHING · also starring MICHAEL GOUGH and MELISSA STRIBLING with CHRISTOPHER LEE as DRACULA
Screenplay by JIMMY SANGSTER · From the novel by BRAM STOKER · Directed by TERENCE FISHER · Executive producer MICHAEL CARRERAS · Associate producer ANTHONY NELSON-KEYS · Produced by ANTHONY HINDS

An excellent, well-acted version of the tale from Britain's Hammer Films.

Max Von Sydow and Ingrid Thulin in **The Magician**, Ingmar Bergman's examination of the duality of the artist, one of his favorite themes.

THE FLY WITH THE HEAD OF A MAN...!
AND THE MAN WITH THE HEAD OF A FLY!
THE FLY
£100 TO THE FIRST PERSON WHO CAN PROVE IT CAN'T HAPPEN!
CERT. 'X'
STARRING
AL HEDISON · PATRICIA OWENS · VINCENT PRICE · HERBERT MARSHAL
A 20th CENTURY-FOX CINEMASCOPE PICTURE IN GLORIOUS TERROR COLOUR
Produced & Directed by KURT NEUMANN · Screenplay by JAMES CLAVELL

Another excursion into horror has a scientist turning into a monster fly.

Kerwin Mathews and Kathryn Grant in Nathan Juran's **The Seventh Voyage of Sinbad**. This film showcased terrific special effects.

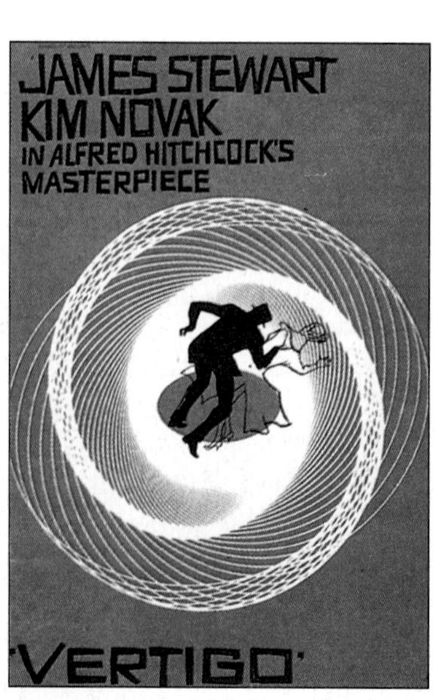
JAMES STEWART
KIM NOVAK
IN ALFRED HITCHCOCK'S MASTERPIECE
VERTIGO

Characteristic Saul Bass design for 1958's Hitchcock offering.

John Gavin in **A Time to Love and Time to Die**, made by Douglas Si

abi Biswas (left) and Padma Devi in Indian director Satyajit Ray's ***The usic Room***, *an exquisite study of a declining aristocrat.*

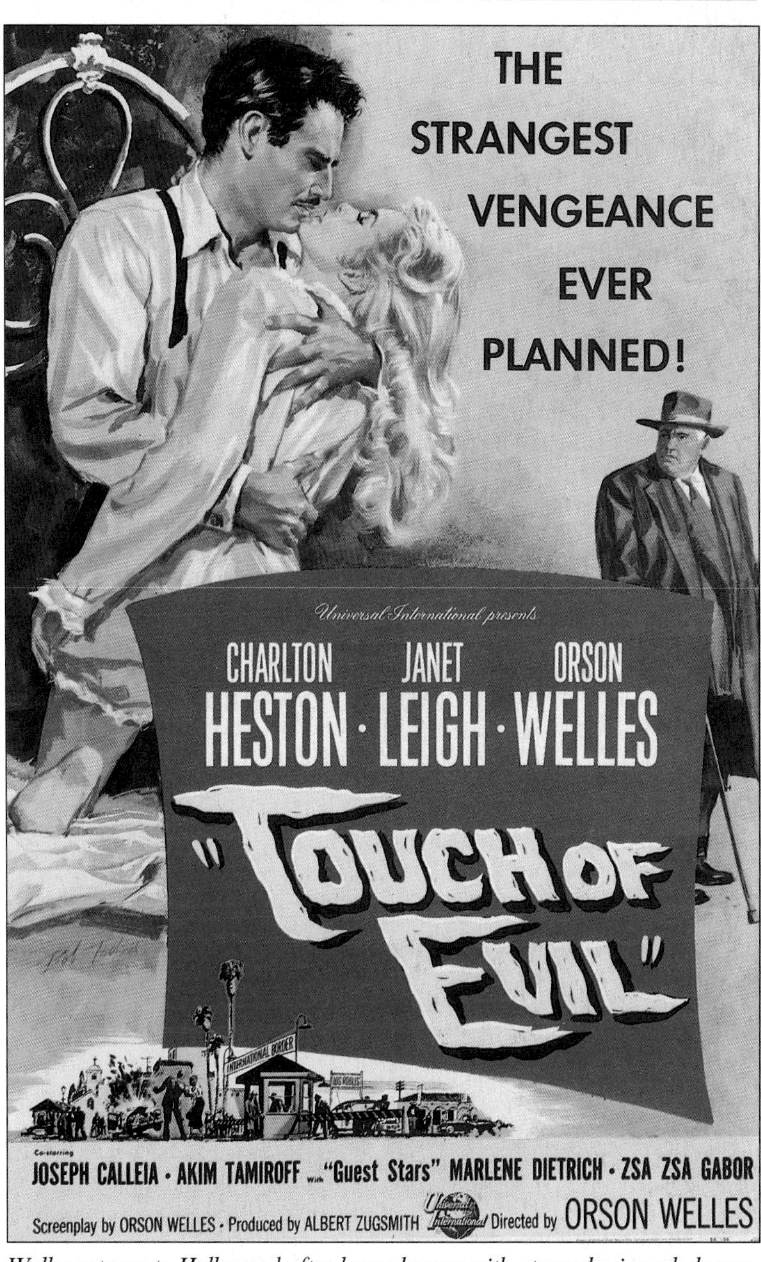
THE
STRANGEST
VENGEANCE
EVER
PLANNED!
Universal-International presents
CHARLTON HESTON · JANET LEIGH · ORSON WELLES
"TOUCH OF EVIL"
Co-starring
JOSEPH CALLEIA · AKIM TAMIROFF · With "Guest Stars" MARLENE DIETRICH · ZSA ZSA GABOR
Screenplay by ORSON WELLES · Produced by ALBERT ZUGSMITH · Directed by ORSON WELLES

Welles returns to Hollywood after long absence with atmospheric melodrama.

THE
NOTORIOUS–
PHILIP YORDAN'S
Anna Lucasta
starring
EARTHA KITT
and
SAMMY DAVIS, JR.
as "Danny"
Screenplay by PHILIP YORDAN
Directed by ARNOLD LAVEN
Produced by SIDNEY HARMON

a all-black remake of a 1949 melo, originally a popular stage play.

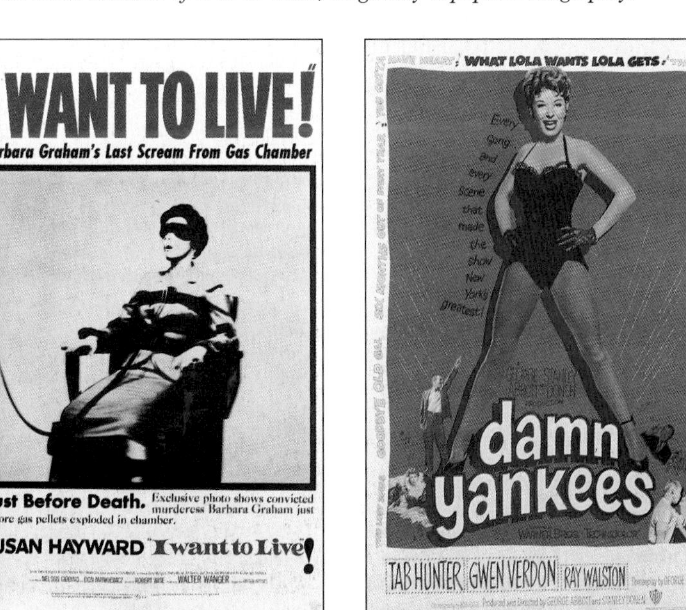
I WANT TO LIVE!"
arbara Graham's Last Scream From Gas Chamber
lust Before Death. Exclusive photo shows convicted murderess Barbara Graham just efore gas pellets exploded in chamber.
USAN HAYWARD "I want to Live!"
WALTER WANGER

arbara Graham's true, tragic story.

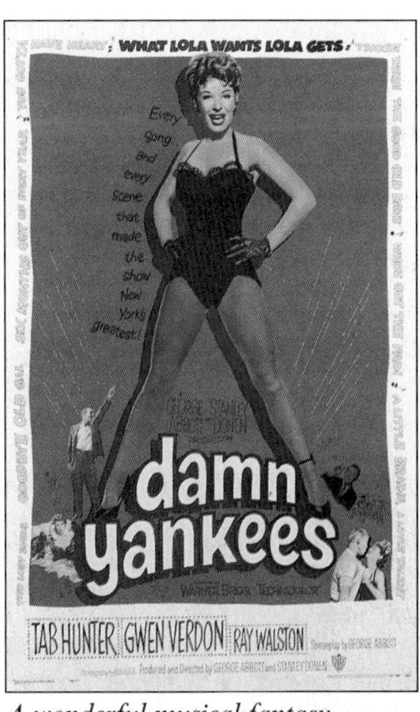
WHAT LOLA WANTS LOLA GETS
Every song and every scene that made the show New York's greatest!
damn yankees
TAB HUNTER | GWEN VERDON | RAY WALSTON

A wonderful musical fantasy.

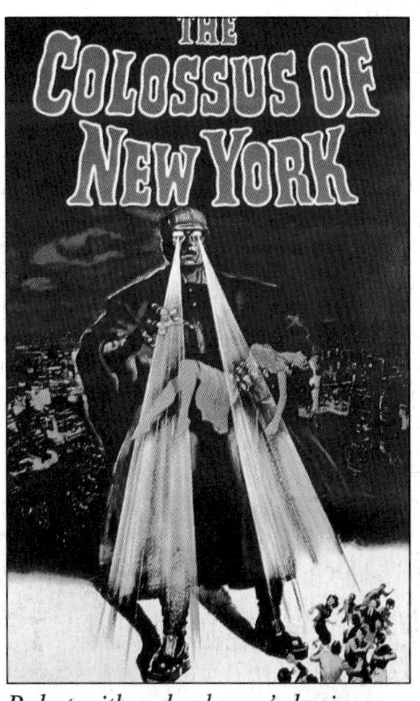
THE
COLOSSUS OF
NEW YORK

Robot with a dead man's brain.

TOHO SCOPE
文部省特選
黒沢明監督作品
山野を駈けめぐる精悍の美姫！莫大な隠し財宝を守って敵国突破を企てる猛将！勇壮豪快に描く戦国スペクタクル！

Kurosawa's ***The Hidden Fortress.***

1959

1958 Academy Awards, RKO Pantages Theater, 6 April

Best Film:	*Gigi* (dir: Vincente Minnelli)
Best Director:	Vincente Minnelli
Best Actor:	David Niven *(Separate Tables)*
Best Actress:	Susan Hayward *(I Want to Live!)*
Best Supp. Actor:	Burl Ives *(The Big Country)*
Best Supp. Actress:	Wendy Hiller *(Separate Tables)*

London, 1 January
The distinguished actor, Alec Guinness, a star of both stage and screen, has been honored with a knighthood in the Queen's New Year's List.

New York, 1 January
The MPAA has repealed a 1957 ruling that forbids persons sympathetic to communism, or those who refused to give evidence to the HUAC, from being nominated for an Academy Award.

Los Angeles, 16 January
In a television interview, the formerly blacklisted screenwriter Dalton Trumbo has revealed that he is the author, under the pseudonym of Robert Rich, of the screenplay for *The Brave One*, which won the 1956 Oscar for Best Screenplay. Nobody at the time came forward to receive the trophy.

Spain, 25 January
The filming of *Solomon and Sheba* is dogged with disaster and tragedy. Following Tyrone Power's death from a heart attack during filming, Spanish actor Luis Santana accidentally set himself on fire today by dropping an oil lamp on his clothes.

Los Angeles, 20 February
Singer Eddie Fisher has filed for divorce from his wife, actress Debbie Reynolds. Fisher and Elizabeth Taylor have apparently been inseparable since the star went to watch Eddie, the best friend of her late husband Mike Todd, perform at the Tropicana in Las Vegas.

Rome, 16 March
The Swedish actress Anita Ekberg has arrived at Cinecittà to film *La Dolce Vita* under the direction of Federico Fellini.

Cairo, 18 March
Egyptian censors have decided to ban all of Elizabeth Taylor's films as a retaliatory measure against the actress' financial support for Israel.

Hollywood, 29 March
Elizabeth Taylor, originally Protestant, has been officially converted to Judaism. The ceremony took place at a Hollywood synagogue.

France, 18 June
Brigitte Bardot and actor Jacques Charrier have disclosed that they were married in secret on 5 June. The couple, who have been hounded by journalists since making *Babette Goes to War*, left St. Tropez yesterday, hidden in two cars. The press was invited to the official ceremony at Brigitte's parents' home today.

Rome, 30 July
Fire broke out today at Cinecittà destroying the sets used for director Carmine Gallone's film *Carthage in Flames*, and injuring 20 people.

London, 5 August
Cary Grant's former chauffeur has failed in a suicide attempt. He is implicated in the divorce of the actor and his wife Betsy Drake. Grant has accused his employee of having an affair with his wife.

Moscow, 6 August
Soviet censors have banned director Christian-Jaque's *Babette s'en va en guerre* (*Babette Goes to War*), even though he is a member of the jury for the Moscow Film Festival.

New York, 6 August
The French film, *Love is My Profession*, directed by Claude Autant-Lara, is to be shown here without any cuts. The American censor has passed all Brigitte Bardot's nude scenes intact.

Rome, 8 August
Sophia Loren has just returned here with her husband Carlo Ponti, who could find himself charged with bigamy. Their marriage, which took place on 17 September 1957, is not considered valid in Italy because divorce is not recognized here. Under Italian law Ponti is still married.

Paris, 9 August
It has been reported that the French actress Jeanne Moreau intends to leave the cinema and devote herself to the stage.

Brazil, 22 August
Following Italy's lead, Brazilian authorities have banned Louis Malle's *les Amants* (*The Lovers*).

London, 6 September
Actress Kay Kendall has died of leukemia. Her dearest wish, "to marry Rex Harrison", was realized in 1957 as soon as he was separated from his previous wife, Lilli Palmer.

Paris, 9 September
The premiere of Roger Vadim's *les Liaisons dangereuses 1960* was canceled at the last moment. The 800 guests, among them Audrey Hepburn and her husband Mel Ferrer, left without having seen the film.

Hollywood, 19 September
The Soviet leader, Nikita Kruschev, seemed to appreciate the charms of capitalism on his visit to Los Angeles. Despite his recent criticism of American politics, he appeared relaxed and smiling at a dinner in his honor in Hollywood during which several stars, including Marilyn Monroe, Frank Sinatra and Gary Cooper, were presented to him.

Zagreb, 12 October
Abel Gance is making *Austerlitz*, a joint Italo-Franco-Yugoslav production. The project has a provisional budget of 48 million francs and prestigious international distribution deals are already in place.

New York, 22 October
Errol Flynn has bequeathed the major part of his immense fortune ($50 million) to his estranged third wife Patrice Wymore.

Tokyo, 3 November
Premiere of Kon Ichikawa's *Fires on the Plain*, a violent description of the wanderings of Japanese soldiers trapped in the jungle who end up eating their dead comrades.

Hollywood, 25 November
Eleanor Powell and Glenn Ford, who married in 1943, have divorced. One of Hollywood's greatest screen dancers, Miss Powell gave up her career for her marriage.

BIRTHS

St. Louis, 22 January
Linda Blair

Washington, 22 February
Kyle MacLachlan

Chicago, 8 March
Aidan Quinn

Paris, 18 March
Luc Besson

California, 22 March
Matthew Modine

London, 15 April
Emma Thompson

California, 29 April
Michelle Pfeiffer

Madrid, 4 July
Victoria Abril

New York, 10 August
Rosanna Arquette

Stockholm, 3 November
Dolph Lundgren
(Hans Lundgren)

DEATHS

Hollywood, 21 January
Cecil B. DeMille

Hollywood, 4 March
Lou Costello

Beverly Hills, 18 June
Ethel Barrymore

New York, 6 August
Preston Sturges

Rome, 7 October
Mario Lanza

Vancouver, 14 October
Errol Flynn

California, 7 November
Victor McLaglen

Paris, 25 November
Gérard Philipe

Billy Wilder's ***Some Like It Hot*** *sta ring Monroe with Jack Lemmon ar Tony Curtis, turned out to be t year's most clever, original, hilario and even poignant, comedy.*

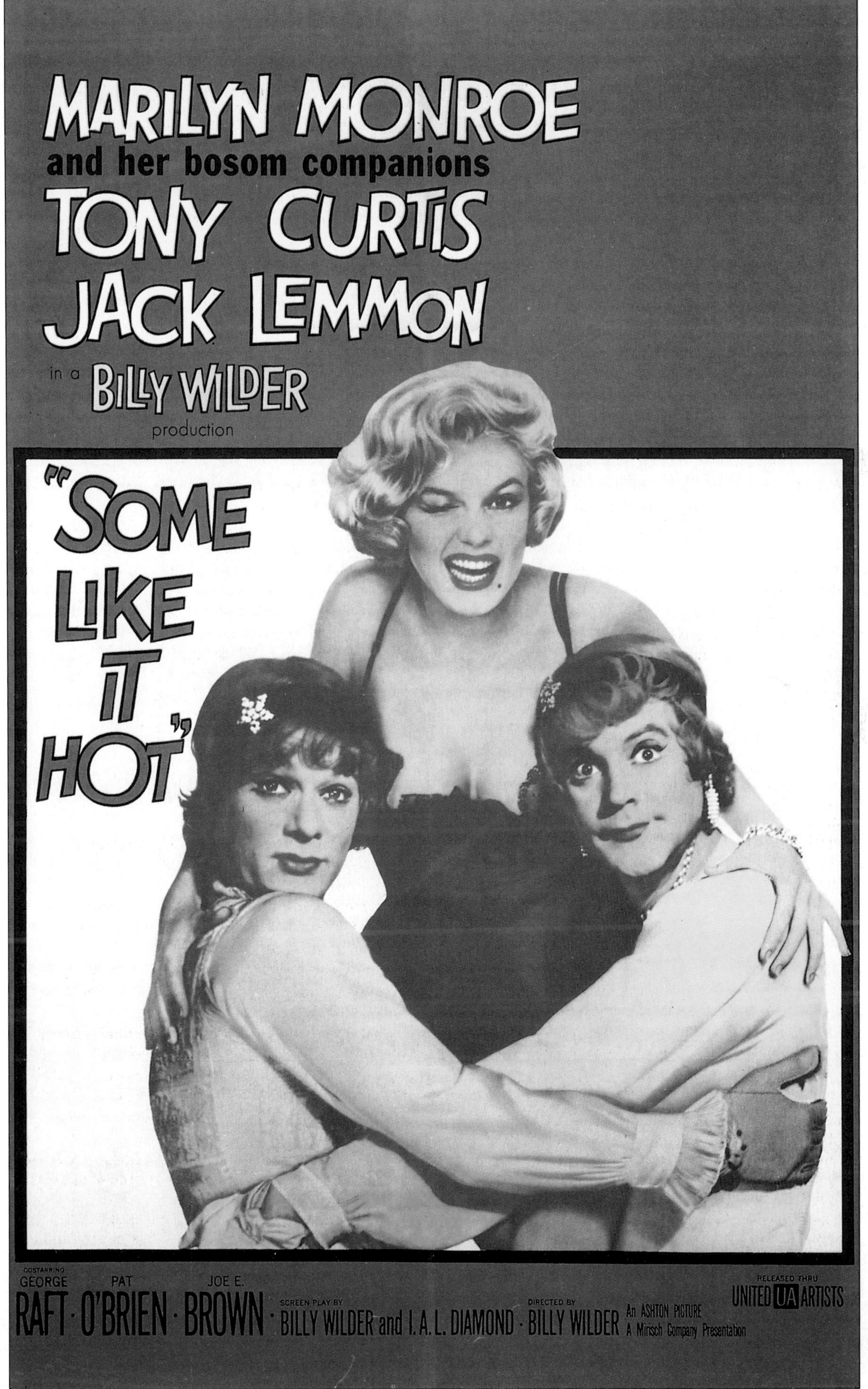
MARILYN MONROE
and her bosom companions
TONY CURTIS
JACK LEMMON
in a BILLY WILDER
production
"SOME LIKE IT HOT"
COSTARRING
GEORGE RAFT · PAT O'BRIEN · JOE E. BROWN
SCREEN PLAY BY BILLY WILDER and I. A. L. DIAMOND
DIRECTED BY BILLY WILDER
An ASHTON PICTURE
A Mirisch Company Presentation
RELEASED THRU
UNITED UA ARTISTS

Brigitte follows in Marlene's foosteps

*Bardot in **la Femme et le pantin**, the third film version of Pierre Louys' novel.*

Paris, 13 February
Concha Perez, the beautiful, seductive heroine of Pierre Louys' novel *la Femme et le pantin* (*The Woman and the Puppet*) has previously been portrayed on the screen by Conchita Montenegro in 1929, in a film directed by Jacques de Baroncelli, and unforgettably by Marlene Dietrich in Josef von Sternberg's *The Devil is a Woman* in 1935. Now it's the turn of Brigitte Bardot, today's sex goddess, to play this mythical and mysterious *femme fatale* in *la Femme et le pantin*. While retaining the Spanish location – the hot atmosphere of the Seville festival – director Julien Duvivier has now updated the story, and has transformed the film's heroine into a French girl who is raised in Spain. Bardot remains a provocative creature who drives men mad.

Tense and tragic story of Anne Frank ope

Living in hiding: Joseph Schildkraut, with Millie Perkins as Anne Frank.

New York, 18 March
The director George Stevens has brought all of his meticulous preparation and shooting method to bear on *The Diary of Anne Frank*. The result is a three-hour portrait of a Jewish family's survival in an Amsterdam attic during the wartime occupation by the Germans. It has been adapted from the Broadway production which drew heavily on the real diary kept by Anne Fran teenager whose family underw the ordeal depicted in the film ended with their discovery in 19 following which they were sent the death camps. Stevens' solem smothers Anne's remarkable gai and love of life, and his choice the inexperienced former cover Millie Perkins to play Anne wa gamble which has not paid off.

Kirk Douglas lets Anthony Mann go

Hollywood, 13 February
Less than two weeks after shooting began on *Spartacus* in Death Valley, California, Kirk Douglas, executive producer and principal actor of the film, has fired Anthony Mann as director. The star has decided to replace him with the 30-year-old Stanley Kubrick, who had directed Douglas in the brilliant anti-war movie *Paths of Glory* a couple of years ago. At the news of Anthony Mann's sacking, many in the motion picture profession have expressed their misgivings. Mann is one of the most respected of American directors, known principally for his Westerns with James Stewart. Others have expressed their doubts as to whether Kubrick, who up until now has only made films on a limited budget, will be able to handle a $12 million project like *Spartacus*, a huge star-studded epic set during the Roman Empire.

Howard Hawks has a new angle on the Old West in 'Rio Bravo'

Angie Dickinson and John Wayne: a flirtatious moment from Hawks' Western.

New York, 18 May
In *Rio Bravo*, Howard Hawks abandoned the sweeping exteri of the traditional Western for claustrophobic interiors of a fron town's bars, hotel and jail. J Wayne plays cantankerous, lo lawman John T. Chance who re tantly gathers a "family" arou him – old-timer Walter Brenn drunken deputy Dean Martin, p fessional gambler Angie Dickins and beardless youth Ricky Nelso in order to bring murderer Cla Akins to trial. Hawks claims t *Rio Bravo* is his response to *H Noon*. "Gary Cooper ran arou trying to get help and no one wo give him any. And that's a rat silly thing for a man to do. S said, we'll just do the opposit And the result is a laconic "indo Western in which Angie Dickins is outstanding as Feathers, a wa and sexy woman moving easily i man's world without ruffling of its conventions.

he heat's on Tony, Jack and Marilyn

ywood, 29 March
Wilder's new film, *Some Like ot*, is a high-water mark in screen edy. Wilder and his usual screen-er I.A.L. Diamond have created amalgam of parody, slapstick, ance and farce – modern in its al approach, nostalgic in its ute to screwball comedies and gangster movies. The clever plot ins in the Chicago of the 1920s, re Joe (Tony Curtis) and Jerry k Lemmon), two jazz musicians are on the run from gangsters, uise themselves as "Josephine" "Daphne" in order to join an all-band on its way to Florida. They ome friends with Sugar Kane, band's singer, with whom Joe in love. Wilder's speedy comic gets equal performances from three stars and a supporting cast includes Joe. E. Brown, George t and Pat O'Brien. Curtis and nmon give unparalleled drag por-als: Tony in a dark wig, high-hed voice and alluring made-up s, Jack in high-heeled shoes, a per's frock and a blonde wig. rilyn, the genuine female article, ngs sensitivity to her role, and s two zippy numbers.

Just girls together! 'Daphne' (Jack Lemmon) and Sugar Kane (Monroe).

'Gigi' breaks record but Leslie loses

Hollywood, 7 April
The record of Oscars won by a single film, held by *Gone With the Wind* and only twice matched, has finally been beaten. By the end of the evening at the RKO Pantages Theater, *Gigi* had scored a grand total of nine Oscars: Best Picture, Director (Vincente Minnelli), Screenplay (Alan Jay Lerner), Cinematography (Joseph Ruttenberg), Art Direction (William A. Horning, Henry Grace, Preston Ames, Keogh Gleason), Film Editing (Adrienne Fazan), Song (Gigi), Musical Score (André Previn) and Costume Design (Cecil Beaton). Unusually, not one of the film's cast was honored in any category; its star, Leslie Caron, lost to Susan Hayward for her all-stops-out performance as Barbara Graham, the petty criminal executed for murder in the harrowing *I Want to Live*. The Best Actor prize went to David Niven's subtle playing as a bogus major arrested for molesting women in the cinema in *Separate Tables*. Wendy Hiller gained a Best Supporting Actress Oscar for her landlady in the same movie. The burly Burl Ives was delighted to be given the Best Supporting Actor award for his role as the obstinate patriarch in *The Big Country*.

e Jean Vigo jury honors Claude Chabrol

is, 11 March
t as Claude Chabrol's second ure, *The Cousins* has been re-ed, the Jean Vigo prize jury has sen to honor his first film, *Bitter nion* (*le Beau Serge*). But that ice created certain rumblings from those in the profession who object to the young director's rapid rise. Chabrol's two films, the first set in the country, and the second in Paris, have the same excellent young actors in the leads, Gérard Blain and Jean-Claude Brialy.

ude Chabrol (3rd left) making his first film ***le Beau Serge (Bitter Reunion)****.*

Alain Delon and Romy Schneider

Switzerland, 22 March
Alain Delon and Romy Schneider got to know each other in Vienna last summer during the making of *Christine*, which was directed by Pierre Gaspard-Huit. If Delon had first described Schneider as a "little white goose", he soon fell under her spell, and enjoyed the many retakes of their screen kisses. By the time filming was completed, the couple had fallen deeply in love with each other. Romy decided not to return to Cologne but to rejoin Alain in Paris, where they are now living together in his apartment on the quai Malaquai. Magda Schneider, Romy's actress mother, expressed her disapproval of her daughter's actions, but to no avail. Romy broke all contact with her family to prove her determination and Magda has finally given in. Alain and Romy have announced their engagement, putting the affair on a legal basis.

Susan Hayward in ***I Want to Live****.*

The New Wave breaks on the shore of Cannes

Cannes, 16 May
Accompanied by their "mentor" Jean Cocteau, the hot-heads of the New Wave arrived in force for this year's Cannes Film Festival. In addition to Jean-Luc Godard, Claude Chabrol and François Truffaut, one also noticed the presence of Roger Vadim, Alain Resnais, and Marcel Camus, who could certainly be considered part of the New Wave. If Truffaut, Resnais and Camus came to speak up for their own films, others arrived to support them. It was François Truffaut, the former harsh critic for *Cahiers du Cinéma*, who carried off the Best Director prize for his first feature, *The Four Hundred Blows*. Truffaut derived the screenplay from his own deprived childhood, and follows the adventures of a 12-year-old Parisian boy, neglected by both his mother and stepfather, who plays truant and takes to petty crime. He is placed in a reform school, but escapes to the coast. The film ends with a freeze of the child's face as he runs to the sea and, perhaps, liberty. The film's freewheeling quality is refreshing, but it is the natural performance of the young Jean-Pierre Léaud that makes it outstanding. Unfortunately, Resnais' *Hiroshima mon amour*, original in concept and subject, was shown outside of competition. The Golden Palm was given to *Black Orpheus*, Marcel Camus' musical transposition of the Greek myth to the carnival in Rio.

As the 12-year-old Antoine Doinel in ***The Four Hundred Blows****, Jean-Pierre Léaud carries Truffaut's message.*

Marpessa Dawn in ***Black Orpheus****, Palme d'Or winner for Marcel Camus.*

Eiji Okada and Emanuelle Riva in Alain Resnais' ***Hiroshima mon amour****. Although presented out of competition the film won the Critics Prize.*

Simone Signoret, voted best actress for the British ***Room at the Top****.*

Where will it go?

It is far too early to specula about the arrival of the Ne Wave, which has been hailed the press, radio and television Cannes. However, one can ways question the nature of th so-called "movement". Launch last year by Françoise Giroud an article in *l'Express*, the lab New Wave now embraces dire tors that are very different fro one another, even though son of them belong to the *Cahiers Cinéma* group. Twenty of the young directors are taking pa in a symposium at La Napoul organized by the Cannes Fil Festival. This idea had originate from the communiqué they r cently published which outlin the areas of "total agreemen and those of "total disagreeme concerning details." It remains be seen whether these undoubte ly talented young people will co tribute something genuinely ne to the art of cinema. Some cor mentators have recollected tha in terms of innovation, the dire tors of the so-called New Wa are indebted to predecessors suc as Roger Leenhardt, Jean-Pier Melville, Alexandre Astruc ar Agnès Varda, who always worke alone, and never considered ther selves part of a movement. Th New Wave directors have tea spirit. That is what gives the their strength.

llini parades the sour side of the sweet life with Marcello

rcello Mastroianni, Fellini's doom-laden hero, with sensual Anita Ekberg.

New York, 19 April
Having caused scandal and division among critics, audiences and churchmen in its native Italy as well as in Catholic Europe, Federico Fellini's *La Dolce Vita* (*The Sweet Life*) has arrived in the U.S. This study of crippling boredom, leading to artistic paralysis and loose sexual morals, played out against the decadence of postwar Roman cafe society is an undoubted cinematic masterpiece. Fellini's imagination has run riot with a series of striking, brilliantly photographed images as his central character (Marcello Mastroianni), a journalist, lives out 24 hours in search of a story. Memorable scenes include a huge statue of Christ flown over Rome, Anita Ekberg drenched in the Trevi Fountain with a kitten on her head and Nadia Gray hosting an orgy at which she performs a striptease. Here is a contrived world of shoddy pleasures in a film that amazes and enthrals.

Pity and pain from Luis Buñuel

Mexico City, 4 June
Luis Buñuel's latest film, *Nazarin*, tells of how a humble and unworldly priest attempts to live by the precepts of Christianity, but is despised for his pains, finding compassion only with a prostitute. Told in the manner of a Christian parable, the film is touching, as well as being an ironic and forceful criticism of formal religion.

Francisco Rabal and Marga Lopez.

yal premiere for 'angry young man'

don, 29 May
ight sees the gala premiere of film version of John Osborne's dmark play *Look Back in Anger*. tars Richard Burton as "Angry ung Man" Jimmy Porter, the oding misogynist trapped in a ary Midlands town and raging nst the fossilized state of British ety. Mary Ure plays his put-upon wife Allison and Claire Bloom gives an icy edge to her friend Helena, the "unmarried Mother Superior" who temporarily takes over from Allison at the ironing board and in Jimmy's bed. Director Tony Richardson has opened up the play for the screen, and softened some of Jimmy's impotent rage, but the picture still packs a punch.

my Porter (Burton) with wife (Mary Ure, left) and mistress (Claire Bloom).

Fred Zinnemann's act of faith pays off

New York, 18 June
With the opening of *A Nun's Story*, director Fred Zinnemann's faith has borne fruit. His persistence and the securing of Audrey Hepburn for the role of Sister Luke convinced Jack Warner to make the film, based on the true story of former nun Marie-Louise Habets. Made in Rome, Belgium and the Congo jungle, the film, from its early sequences in the convent, through harrowing scenes in a madhouse, to the key Congo episodes rich in a sense of missionary selflessness, is majestic and moving. Its excellence is matched in every department, notably by Hepburn as the nun whose sense of individual self brings her into agonizing conflict with her vocation.

Sister Luke (Audrey Hepburn) in the Congo with missionary Niall MacGinnis.

Gripping courtroom drama from Preminger

James Stewart and Lee Remick star in Preminger's ***Anatomy of a Murder.***

New York, 6 July
Otto Preminger is code-breaking again in *Anatomy of a Murder*, a courtroom drama adapted from retired judge Robert Traver's novel and filmed in Traver's hometown in Michigan. James Stewart plays the easygoing country lawyer defending Ben Gazzara, accused of shooting the man who tried to rape his wife Lee Remick, and words such as "panties" and "contraception" are daringly bandied about. Presiding over the court is real-life Boston lawyer Joseph Welch, the man who helped expose Senator McCarthy.

A cocktail of suspense, sex and humor

A case of mistaken identity lands Cary Grant in danger ***North by Northwe***

Hollywood, 6 August
Alfred Hitchcock's latest effort is a blithely implausible chase thriller in which glibly feckless ad-man Cary Grant becomes the object of a cross-country spy hunt. It's packed with artful set pieces characteristic of Hitchcock, which include Grant being pursued across the prairie b crop-duster and a climax on Mo Rushmore, which prompted Hi to suggest the film be called "T Man Who Sneezed in Linco Nose". Eva Marie Saint smold sexily and there's a masterclass silky villainy from James Mason

'Apu' concludes Ray's humanist triptych

Paris, 14 September
Satyajit Ray's "Apu Trilogy", begun in the great Indian director's mind almost 10 years ago, has reached its climax with the release of *The World of Apu*. Taken at a less leisurely pace and more conventionally structured than either *Pather Panchali* or *The Unvanquished*, it is, nevertheless, imbued with the same keen observation, beautiful performances and memorable scenes, such as Apu (Soumitra Chatterjee) scattering the pages of his novel over a mountain at dawn. Although Apu is inconsolable when he loses his wife in childbirth, this humanist triptych ends on a note of hope.

The man Apu: Soumitra Chatterjee, Sharmila Tagore in ***The World of Apu.***

Frank and frothy comedy for Doris and Ro

Los Angeles, 14 October
Rock Hudson reveals a deft talent for comedy in *Pillow Talk*, in which he plays a philandering songwriter whose shared party phone line with career girl Doris Day leads to romantic complications. Directed by Michael Gordon, produced by Ross Hunter, and sleek as a brand-new Cadillac in Eastmancolor and Ci maScope, *Pillow Talk* features a perb supporting cast that inclu Tony Randall as one of Day's dis pointed suitors and Thelma Rit as a tipsy maid. It's a departure Day, too. As interior designer J Morrow, she swaps the suburb housewife look for *haute couture*

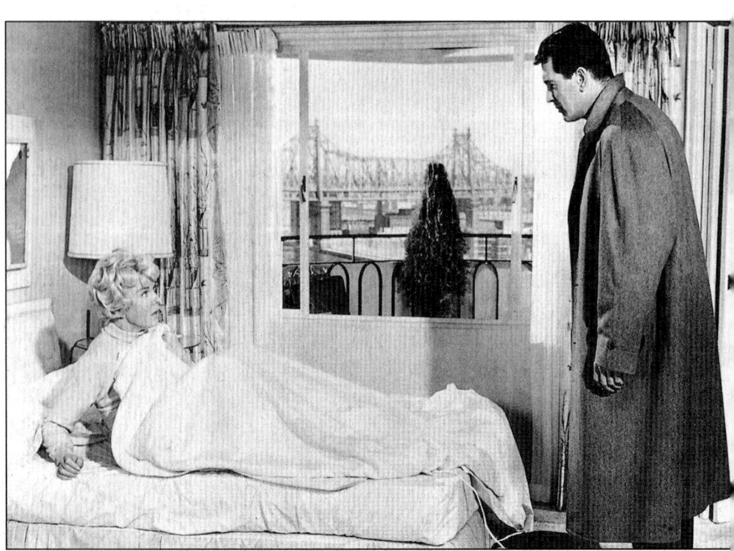

Doris Day and Rock Hudson, the couple who fall in love on a party phone li

e-man Errol Flynn ies aged 50

ncouver, 14 October
rol Flynn has died of a heart at-k at the age of 50. A life devoted dissipation has finally caught up th him. According to Jack War-r, the star had long been one of living dead, ravaged by drink d drugs, bottle-nosed, bleary-eyed d wasted. Flynn's recent films ve cast him as a drunk: a wastrel patriate in *The Sun Also Rises*; th tragic irony as his old drinking rtner John Barrymore in *Too ıch Too Soon*; and then rambling ozily among African elephants in *e Roots of Heaven*. There were ll flickers of the old charm but the hts were about to go out. Flynn's al film was a semi-documentary, *ban Rebel Girls*, featuring his last ver, the 16-year-old Beverly Aad-d. The coroner who examined ynn's body said that the most shing and athletic of all screen bin Hoods had the body of an l, sick and tired man.

Ben-Hur: even bigger, but is it better?

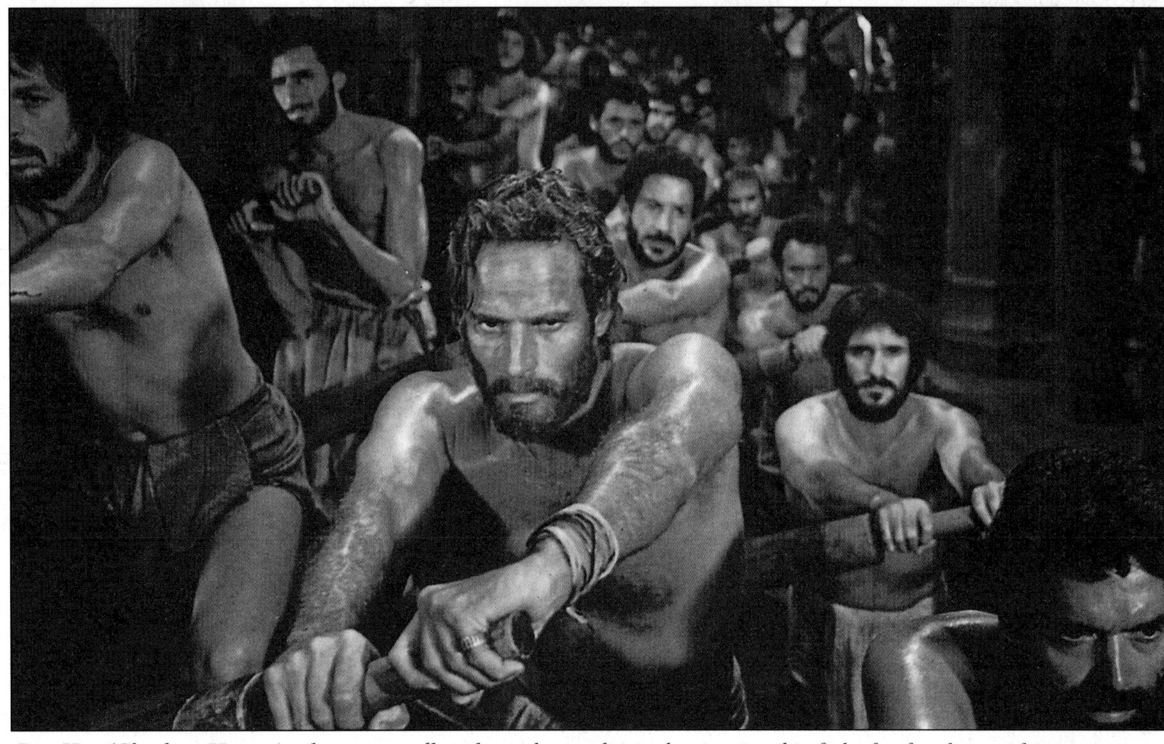

Ben-Hur (Charlton Heston) taken as a galley slave, the condition that inspires his fight for freedom and justice.

Hollywood, 18 November
Just as it was in 1925, the future of MGM is riding on a big-budget production of *Ben-Hur*. Director William Wyler, who also acted as producer after the death of Sam Zimbalist, worked as an assistant director on the chariot race in the original. This time around he has handed over the shooting of this thunderous sequence to Andrew Marton and ace stuntman Yakima Canutt. Charlton Heston's Judah Ben-Hur and Stephen Boyd's Messala battle it out to the death in the Circus Maximus, re-created at the Cinecittà studios in Rome and the largest outdoor set ever built. Everything's big about this production, and with a budget of $14.5 million it's the most expensive movie ever made. It's also a supreme test of the stamina of Charlton Heston. Will its quality justify the cost?

ffecting tale of wartime life in Russia

oscow, 18 December
ter the worldwide success of *The anes Are Flying* two years ago, the viet cinema is offering audiences other film that promises to be ually welcome abroad. Entitled *llad of a Soldier* and directed by igori Chukrai, it tells of a young ldier, on four days leave from the Front during World War II, traveling by train, truck and on foot to see his mother. En route, he meets a variety of people affected in different ways by the war, and a girl with whom he falls in love. This simple, touching and unrhetorical view of everyday life in wartime Russia, is directed with superb technical skill.

adimir Ivashev, star of ***Ballad of a Soldier****, with Antonina Maximova.*

l to r: Heston, Sam Jaffe, Martha Scott, Haya Harareet, Cathy O'Donnell.

Color and Widescreen

Impressive example of early color in French film, ***Cyrano de Bergerac*** *(1923).*

Michael Curtiz made ***Robin Hood*** *for Warners (1938) in striking Technico*

Today we take color pretty much for granted in the cinema and are occasionally pleasantly (or unpleasantly) surprised by a film made in black and white. Yet color took a long time to establish itself. The first big breakthrough came in the late 30s – after the introduction of the newly developed three-strip Technicolor process – with the success of Walt Disney's first feature-length cartoon, *Snow White and the Seven Dwarfs* (1937), Warner Bros.' lively and entertaining version of *The Adventures of Robin Hood* (1938) and David O. Selznick's *Gone With the Wind* (1939). But color filming did not entirely replace black and white until the late 60s.

Color was, in fact, first introduced at the very beginning of the cinema. As early as 1894, the Edison company began adding color by hand to such films as *Annabella's Dance*, which ran for only a few seconds and were viewed in the company's Kinetoscope machines. Ten years later, in France, Georges Méliès was adding imaginative hand-tinted color, thus providing an additional, delightfully picturesque quality to the fairy-tale fantasy and special effects (transformations, explosions, etc.) found in his short films. Also in France, around 1908, the Pathé company had initiated the first ever production and distribution of color prints on a large scale, making use of assembly-line methods of stencil tinting at its Vincennes factory where over 100 young women were employed as colorists. In England the Kinemacolor compa first introduced its two-color 'ad tive' system which involved filmi through a red-orange and blue-gre filter, then projecting the complet movie through matching filters.

Many filmmakers experiment with color processes through the silent era, but such names Polychromide, Prizma and Chro chrome merely merit a footnote cinema history. The most famil form of color from 1915 to 19 was the overall tinting or toni

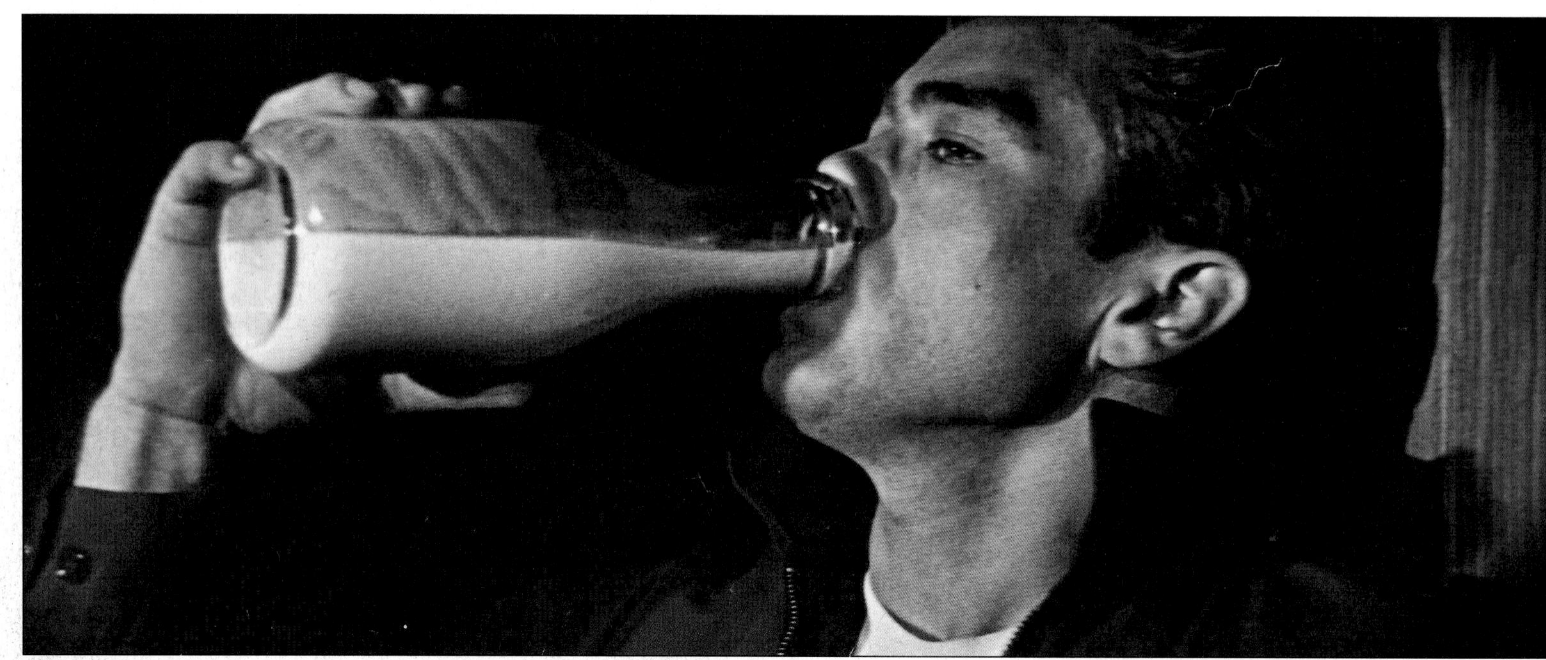

feature films, with sepia or pink · day scenes, blue for night, and so . The first widely adopted system two-color subtractive photogra-y was developed by Herbert Kal-s of the Technicolor Co. in the rly 20s. This made use of a beam-litting device behind the camera s so that red and green exposures uld be made simultaneously. It s first used for shooting special quences in a number of major llywood costume movies such as *e Ten Commandments* (1923) and *n-Hur* (1925), and for entire fea-es such as *The Black Pirate* 925), starring Douglas Fairbanks, d *The Viking* (1929), as well as for ny of the most spectacular early und musicals including *Gold Dig-s of Broadway* and *Show of Shows* 1929, *Sally, Whoopie!* and *The gabond King* in 1930.

By 1934 a new Technicolor which corded the entire color spectrum came available, but required film-g with special three-strip cameras. ocessing took place at Technicol-'s labs where the three separate gatives were used to make matrix ief films in what was known as bibition printing, and these were mbined to make the final release int. The first three-strip feature, *cky Sharp* in 1935, was followed numerous other features in the S., and in England where Techni-lor set up a lab. But the numbers ew only slowly since color filming s expensive, the special cameras quired were large and awkward to ndle and most of the leading di-ctors and (non-musical) stars preferred black and white. In the words of Bette Davis, "They gave the color to the terrible scripts as an added inducement to get the public in. My pictures brought the public in without the added expense." In the U.S. an imaginative use of color was seen mainly in the musicals where MGM was the leader, beginning with *The Wizard of Oz* (1939) and, especially, *Meet Me in St. Louis* (1944) directed by Vincente Minnelli. However, the leading creative filmmaker working in color during these years was an Englishman: Michael Powell's remarkable films, in both ideas and visual quality, included an original treatment of war themes in *The Life and Death of Colonel Blimp* (1943), *Stairway to Heaven* (aka *A Matter of Life and Death*), *Black Narcissus* (1947) and, most successful of all, *The Red Shoes* (1948). Finally, in the early and mid-50s the long overdue increase in color filming took place in the U.S. and abroad, coinciding with, and stimulated by, various new technical innovations. The Technicolor monopoly was seriously challenged for the first time by a less expensive, single-strip Eastmancolor which could be used in a standard 35mm camera, while the introduction of various new wide-screen and large format processes also put the emphasis firmly on color. The decade was characterized by great technical diversity, black and white existing side by side with color, 35mm with 70mm. However, there was a basic change in the screen format or height to width ratio, which has been maintained up to the present day. The old 1.33 or 'Academy' was replaced by 1.75, 1.85 or occasionally 1.65, with the new CinemaScope and 70mm providing a 'letterbox' shape of 2 or 2 ½ to 1. During these years many leading directors made features in color for the first time, among them Anthony Mann, George Stevens and William Wyler in the U.S., John Huston, Carol Reed and Alexander Mackendrick in England, Jean Renoir in France, Luchino Visconti in Italy, and, in Japan, two creative giants, Ozu and Mizoguchi. For some, their first in color was also in CinemaScope (Cukor, Kazan, Ophuls). By the mid-60s the 35mm Panavision (anamorphic) lenses had replaced those of CinemaScope, black and white was on the way out, and the last films were being shot in 70mm, for it was now cheaper and easier to film with the new improved 35mm equipment and fine-grain Eastman negative, then print up to 70mm. Thus, the main choice for filmmakers today is between a standard wide screen or anamorphic (letterbox) shape, with black and white rarely an option. A leading director such as Robert Altman likes the freedom which the extremely wide shape (and looser framing of shots) allows, while Martin Scorsese, Francis Ford Coppola and Woody Allen generally prefer the standard wide screen. And the choices made by Steven Spielberg are especially interesting: normal wide screen for the intimate *E.T.*, the wider Panavision for *Jaws*, *Close Encounters* and the *Indiana Jones* movies, and black and white for *Schindler's List*.

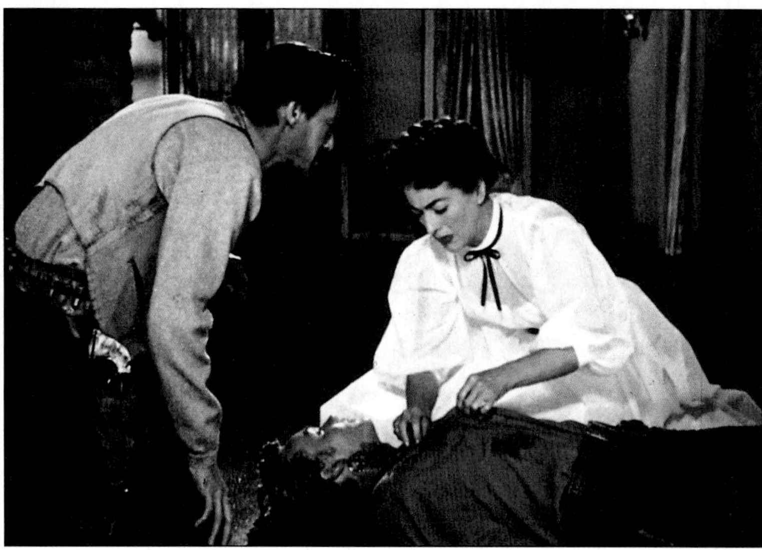

*Joan Crawford in Nicholas Ray's **Johnny Guitar**, shot in Trucolor for Republic.*

TWENTIETH CENTURY-FOX
PRESENTS
A
CINEMASCOPE
PICTURE

COCINOR présente
JEAN-PIERRE LEAUD
DANS
PRIX DE LA MEILLEURE MISE EN SCÈNE au FESTIVAL de CANNES 1959
les Quatre Cents coups
PRIX DE L'OFFICE CATHOLIQUE INTERNATIONAL DU CINÉMA
UN FILM DE
FRANÇOIS TRUFFAUT
avec CLAIRE MAURIER et ALBERT REMY
GUY DECOMBLE - GEORGES FLAMANT - PATRICK AUFFAY
scénario de FRANÇOIS TRUFFAUT adaptation de M. MOUSSY et F. TRUFFAUT
DIALOGUES DE MARCEL MOUSSY
Directeur de la photographie HENRI DECAE
DYALISCOPE
Musique de JEAN CONSTANTIN
COCINOR
Production LES FILMS DU CARROSSE - SEDIF

François Truffaut's **The Four Hundred Blows** was much praised everywhere.

From Italy, ***Big Deal on Madonna Street***, *an impeccable social comedy that spoofs* ***Rififi***, *directed by Mario Monicelli. Here, Renato Salvatore (left), Toto.*

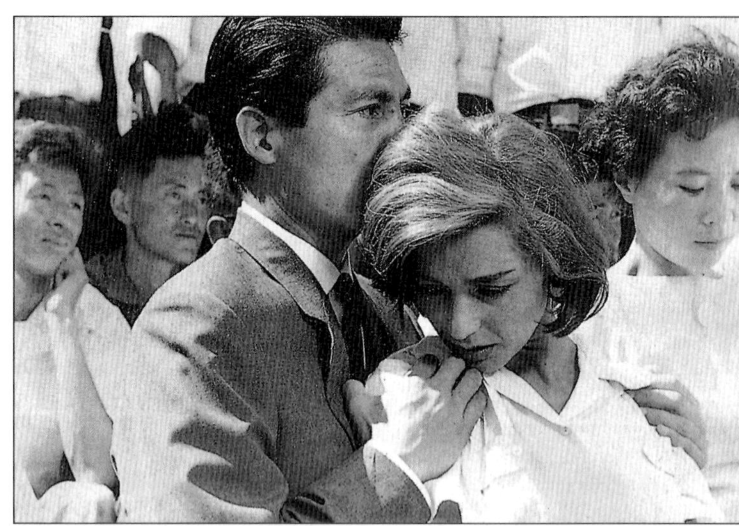

Eiji Okada and Emmanuelle Riva in Alain Resnais' ***Hiroshima, mon amo***

Eiji Funakoshi (c), Mantaro Ushio in ***Fires on the Plain*** *from Kon Ichikaw*

His TRUE, SHOCKING STORY... Filmed with BULLET FORCE!
AL CAPONE
ROD STEIGER
FAY SPAIN · JAMES GREGORY · NEHEMIAH PERSOFF

The most famous of gang bosses brought realistically to life.

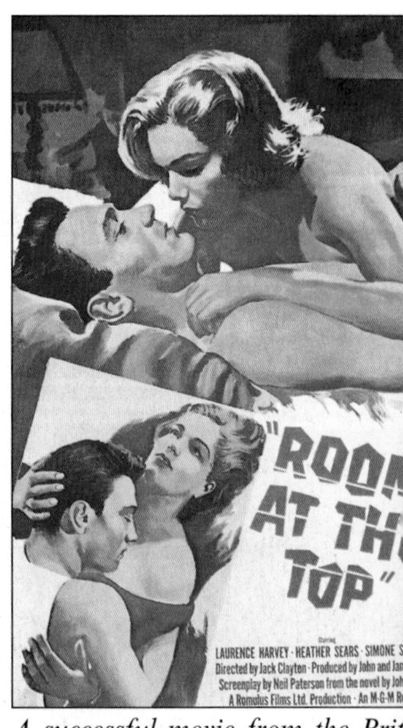
LAURENCE HARVEY · HEATHER SEARS · SIMONE S

A successful movie from the Brit bestseller by John Braine.

THE ENTERTAINMENT EXPERIENCE OF A LIFETIME!
METRO-GOLDWYN-MAYER
presents
A Tale of the Christ
by GENERAL LEW WALLACE
BEN-HUR
Directed by
WILLIAM WYLER
Starring
CHARLTON HESTON · JACK HAWKINS
HAYA HARAREET · STEPHEN BOYD
HUGH GRIFFITH · MARTHA SCOTT with CATHY O'DONNELL · SAM JAFFE
Screen Play by
Produced by
KARL TUNBERG · SAM ZIMBALIST
TECHNICOLOR
FILMED IN CAMERA 65

arlton Heston got the title role sought after by Rock Hudson and Brando.

Sugar Kane (Marilyn Monroe), Josephine (Tony Curtis): ***Some Like It Hot****.*

Richard Widmark (l), Henry Fonda (r) in Edward Dmytryk's ***Warlock****.*

inther Hoffman in Bernhard Wicki's powerful anti-war film from Germany ed ***The Bridge (Die Brücke)****.*

BRANDO
MAGNANI
WOODWARD
...and now the screen is struck by lightning!
TENNESSEE WILLIAMS'
THE FUGITIVE KIND
MAUREEN STAPLETON · VICTOR JORY
TENNESSEE WILLIAMS
MEADE ROBERTS
SIDNEY LUMET
MARTIN JUROW · RICHARD A. SHEPHERD
UNITED ARTISTS

An explosive, doom-laden trip into Tennessee Williams territory.

LANA TURNER
JOHN GAVIN
Imitation of Life
COLOR
SANDRA DEE · DAN O'HERLIHY · SUSAN KOHNER
ROBERT ALDA · JUANITA MOORE
MAHALIA JACKSON
EARL GRANT
DOUGLAS SIRK
ROSS HUNTER

Lush Technicolor remake by Douglas Sirk of the 1934 hit.

The New Wave

There was a new spirit abroad as the new decade dawned. America woke up from its sleep under President Eisenhower to a young and dynamic new leader, John F. Kennedy. The countries of Eastern Europe were gradually shaking off the shackles of Stalinism, and more and more colonized countries were on the road to freedom. Everywhere there was a battle between the old world and the new. The cinema had to move with the times and answer the aspirations of the citizens of the world. Only a violent shake-up could save the global movie industry, which was losing audiences rapidly. The first rumblings of change took place in France with the New Wave (*Nouvelle Vague*), which swept across continents, even affecting the entrenched attitudes of Hollywood.

The French New Wave came into being when several young critics on the magazine *Cahiers du Cinéma* decided to take practical action in their battle against the 'Cinéma du Papa' by making films themselves. The leading figures of the group were François Truffaut, Jean-Luc Godard, Alain Resnais, Claude Chabrol, Jacques Rivette and Louis Malle. They reacted against the hidebound, old-fashioned French cinema of boudoir comedies, facetious swashbucklers and sterile star-studded adaptations of the classics. Their idols were Americans Howard Hawks, Alfred Hitchcock, Nicholas Ray and Charles Chaplin, and, virtually alone among French directors, Jean Renoir. They viewed the great filmmaker as having an individual and spontaneous stamp to his work, using the camera as a means of personal expression.

The French New Wave directors turned their backs on conventional filming methods. They took to shooting in the streets with hand-held cameras and a very small team, using jump cuts, improvisation, deconstructed narratives, and quotes from literature or other films. Following up on the debut features, the most notable examples were Truffaut's *Shoot the Pianist* (1960) and *Jules and Jim* (1961), Godard's *Vivre sa vie* (1962) and *Pierrot-le-fou* (1965), Chabrol's *les Bonnes femmes* (1960) and Rivette's *Paris Belongs to Us* (1960). On the whole these lacked political commitment, being content merely to shock and unsettle the established order. Godard's *le Petit soldat* (1960), about the Algerian War, affronted both Left and Right opinion, and General De Gaulle objected to *A Married Woman* (1964) for its 'negative' portrayal of French womanhood. Jacques Rivette's *la Religieuse* (1965) was initially banned in France on the grounds of anticlericalism. But just as Renoir had done in the 1930s, these young directors captured the life of 1960s France, particularly in Paris, as it was lived by its young people.

In 1960 alone, some 18 directors had made their first features in France. In 1962, *Cahiers du Cinéma* devoted a whole issue to the New

***Goldfinger** (1964): Villain Gert Frobe and 007 James Bond (Sean Connery).*

Wave, and listed 162 new directors working in France. They helped restore the international prestige of French cinema during the 60s, and temporarily revived the drooping economics of the national industry.

Their methods and subject matter were taken up and adapted by young directors in other countries, especially Great Britain and Czechoslovakia. Britain's new wave, known as the Free Cinema, began in earnest with Karel Reisz's *Saturday Night and Sunday Morning* (1960), Tony Richardson's screen version of *A Taste of Honey* (1961) and *The Loneliness of the Long Distance Runner* (1962), John Schlesinger's *A Kind of Loving* (1962) and Lindsay Anderson's *This Sporting Life* (1963). All of them dealt honestly and vigorously with working-class life in industrial areas, containing an overt criticism of the 'never had it so good' philosophy of the Conservative government of the day.

The period of political relaxation in Czechoslovakia produced an upsurge of imaginative films with contemporary themes. Between 1962 and 1968, some 60 new directors made films in an atmosphere of enthusiasm. Using mostly non-actors, a *cinéma vérité* technique and minimal plots, Milos Forman's *Peter and Pavla* (aka *Black Peter*, 1963), *A Blonde in Love* (1965) and *The Firemen's Ball* (1967) revealed a comic freshness and a keen eye. Vera Chytilova's *Daisies* (1966), the most adventurous and anarchic of Czech films of the period, Ivan Passer's *Intimate Lighting* (1965) and Jiri Menzel's Oscar-winning *Closely Watched Trains* (1966) were further lively examples of films which blossomed during the 'Prague Spring'.

The liberalizing spirit abroad in the early 1960s spilled into the Soviet Union, with both veteran and young directors participating in a revitalized program of production. Among the best films were Mikhail Romm's *Nine Days of One Year* (1961), Andrei Tarkovsky's *Ivan's Childhood* (1962), Grigori Kozintsev's *Hamlet* (1964) and Sergo Paradjanov's *Shadows of Our Forgotten Ancestors* (1964).

There were short lived new waves in South America too, particularly in Brazil where a group called Cinema Novo tried to create indigenc work, free from the pervadi North American influence. Th leading member was Glaul Rocha, whose ritualistic and radi films included *Black God, Wh Devil* (1964) and *Antonio das Mor* (1969), while Nelson Pereira D Santos supplied *Barren Li* (1963), all three landmarks in La American cinema.

A resurgence in Italy began 1960, signaled by the presentation the Cannes Festival of Michelang Antonioni's *L'Avventura* and F erico Fellini's *La Dolce Vita*. An nioni's film was booed and Fellin threatened with excommunicati by Catholic Italy. Both films w making a conscious break w mainstream cinema in their rej tion of conventional narrative, th length, and their consideration what was to become a major the of the decade, social breakdown a alienation in a materialistic socie

This theme manifested itself many American movies of the pe od, when Hollywood found its with a relatively new audience creasingly drawn from the 16 to age bracket. This younger gene tion expressed a growing aversion traditional values and political a social processes, an attitude wh culminated in the anti-Vietnam W movement in 1968. Furthermo with the demise of the old Prod tion Code, the limits of langua topics and behavior were consid ably widened, almost enough to s isfy the tastes of the young. Th were catered to mainly by the lo budget youth-oriented movies Roger Corman such as *Wild Ang* (1966) and *The Trip* (1967), bo starring Peter Fonda, who produc and featured in *Easy Rider* (196 whose combination of drugs, ro music, violence and motorcyc caught the imagination of youth.

More in the mainstream w Mike Nichols' *The Graduate*, t appeal of which lay mainly amo alienated middle-class college ki anxious about the draft and t threat of nuclear war. These fe were given expression in Stan Kubrick's *Dr. Strangelove: or, Ho Learned to Stop Worrying and L the Bomb* (1963), which viewed t end of the world as the ultimate surdity, and Arthur Penn's *Alic staurant* (1969), which attracted se who identified with the hippie unter-culture.

Penn had previously directed *Bon- and Clyde* (1967), which has ained one of the most influen- movies of the later decades in amoral attitude to the 'outlaw', n from a modern social perspec- e. The much-imitated ending, en hundreds of bullets are pump- into the miscreant (and physically autiful, as portrayed by Faye naway and Warren Beatty) cou- who die in slow motion, was a p towards a generally more ac- ted level of violence in the nerican cinema. This trend was in- sified in Sam Peckinpah's bloody estern *The Wild Bunch* (1969). though there was a discernible ft of focus among a vast segment American audiences towards re sex and violence, there was o less adulation of stars and a ater appreciation of the direc- 's contribution to film, an aware- ss that was sharpened by the New ave and the French *auteur* or 'au- r' theory.

While smaller-scale, independent- produced pictures were attracting young, the major studios contin- d to target large family audiences. ce movie-going had ceased to be egular national habit, each film d to attract its own audience, and ravagant advertising campaigns companied the many million- llar spectacles that bludgeoned ir way onto the screens. Most of se blockbusters were shot in ain and Italy and further dimin- ed the significance of Hollywood a production center. Such films luded Anthony Mann's *El Cid* 61) and *The Fall of the Roman pire* (1964); Nicholas Ray's *King Kings* (1961) and *55 Days at Pe- g* (1963); and George Stevens' *e Greatest Story Ever Told* (1965). Twentieth Century-Fox came un- ck by disastrously, and infamous- investing $40 million in the Tay- -Burton *Cleopatra* (1963). But x regained its fortune with *The und of Music* (1965), one of the st commercially successful mu- als in Hollywood history. Con- ced that the 'Open Sesame' to ronomical profits lay in big- dget musicals, the studio then ured millions into *Dr. Dolittle* 67) and the biopic, *Star* (1968), h of which failed to break even. The decade had opened with a ke on 15 January by the screen section of the Writers' Guild of America, which was holding out for more equitable contracts and a share of the profits from films sold to television. In March 1960, the Screen Actors' Guild of America demanded a raise in minimum salaries as well as a share in TV residuals. Both the writers and the actors won their cases, victories that became a contributory factor in pushing Hollywood to the brink of economic disaster. A rope was thrown to Paramount by Gulf & Western, while Warner Bros. merged with the television company Seven Arts Ltd., and MGM shifted its interests into the real estate business.

Meanwhile, American investment in U.S.–British co-productions was paying off nicely, especially with the string of James Bond movies, which began modestly with *Dr. No* (1962), and was still going strong over 30 years later, despite several changes of agent 007, initially immortalized by Sean Connery. American producers were attracted to 'Swinging' London by the common language, and by the high standards of British actors and technicians. With *Lawrence of Arabia* (1962) and *Dr. Zhivago* (1966), both made with mainly British teams, David Lean became the most commercially successful English director. Curiously enough, it was an adaptation of a classic 18th-century English novel, Henry Fielding's *Tom Jones* (1963), directed by Tony Richardson, that triggered off the vogue for trendy pictures set in London. These included three films directed by the American-born Richard Lester – the Beatles' extravaganzas, *A Hard Day's Night* (1964) and *Help!* (1965), each earning a healthy $4 million, and *The Knack... And How to Get It* (1965). Even the Italian Antonioni got into the act with *Blow Up* (1966).

Folk singer Arlo Guthrie in Arthur Penn's archetypally 60s ***Alice's Restaurant.***

Apart from the big names of the New Wave in France, Luis Buñuel made a new career beginning with *Diary of a Chambermaid* (1964) and *Belle de jour* (1967), and Claude Lelouch scored a huge commercial success with the Oscar-winning *A Man and a Woman* (1966). Soon after, the political events of May 1968 had repercussions throughout the entire French motion picture industry. The Cannes Film Festival of that year was abandoned in midstream, and filmmakers of various backgrounds jointly demanded a complete reorganization of the industry, including its nationalization. Unconventional directors such as Jean-Luc Godard and Chris Marker moved towards making far more overtly political films.

Just when it seemed that the cinema of the USSR was again on the path to creative health, political events in the Soviet Union undermined its recovery. Khruschev's forced retirement in 1964 was followed by a gradual regression and the retightening of state controls over films. Tarkovsky's impressive epic *Andrei Rublev* (1966), for example, was shelved by the Soviet authorities. In Czechoslovakia, the 'Prague Spring' gave way to sudden winter, in life and art, with the Soviet invasion in 1968.

In Japan, the boom ceased in the early 60s due mainly to the growth of television which weakened the grip of the big companies on production. Nevertheless, there were a number of significant Japanese films that found audiences abroad: Kon Ichikawa's *An Actor's Revenge* (1963) and *Alone on the Pacific* (1963), both demonstrating a masterful use of the wide screen; Masaki Kobayashi's *Kwaidan* (1964), Kaneto Shindo's *The Island* (1961) and Hiroshi Teshigahara's *Woman of the Dunes* (1964). Akira Kurosawa's *Yojimbo* (1961) and *Sanjuro* (1962) were influences on the universally popular Spaghetti Westerns made in Italy in the mid and late 60s, just as *The Seven Samurai* had provided the plot for John Sturges' Western, *The Magnificent Seven* (1960).

Spaghetti Westerns became an important staple of the Italian film industry, while the great Italian directors continued to supply masterpieces: Fellini *8 ½* (1963), Antonioni *La Notte* (1961), Visconti *The Leopard* (1963) and Pier Paolo Pasolini *The Gospel According to Saint Matthew* (1964).

With the Cold War still threatening to become hot and the Vietnam War raging, films, like society, were questioning traditional certainties. Meanwhile, in the face of menacing financial disaster, the break-up of the major studios, and younger more demanding audiences, Hollywood still provided the kind of genre movies with which it has always been identified. There were splendid musicals: *West Side Story* (1961), *Gypsy* (1962), *My Fair Lady* (1964) and *Funny Girl* (1968), all derived from Broadway shows; Westerns, notably John Ford's *The Man Who Shot Liberty Valance*, Sam Peckinpah's *Ride the High Country*, David Miller's *Lonely Are the Brave* (all 1962), and Howard Hawks' *El Dorado* (1966), most of them valedictions to the old West, and romantic comedies like *Pillow Talk* in the popular Doris Day-Rock Hudson cycle of comedy romance.

Social issues were not neglected. Stanley Kramer tackled *Judgment at Nuremberg* (1961) and racism in *Guess Who's Coming to Dinner* (1967), while Sidney Poitier, the star of the latter, made further strides towards tolerance in Norman Jewison's *In the Heat of the Night* (1968). The former Hollywood may have been buried by the many changes wrought by the decade, but it refused to die, continually rising up to provide the world's most popular entertainment.

RONALD BERGAN

1960

1959 Academy Awards, RKO Pantages Theater, 4 Apr.

Best Film:	*Ben-Hur* (dir: William Wyler)
Best Director:	William Wyler
Best Actor:	Charlton Heston *(Ben-Hur)*
Best Actress:	Simone Signoret *(Room at the Top)*
Best Supp. Actor:	Hugh Giffith *(Ben-Hur)*
Best Supp. Actress:	Shelley Winters *(The Diary of Anne Frank)*

Hollywood, 16 January
The Screen Writers Guild has called for a strike. It is demanding that its members receive a percentage of the television rights for films.

Stockholm, 8 February
Jungfrukällan (*The Virgin Spring*) with Max Von Sydow opens today. Ingmar Bergman's film is another foray into the dark and primitive world of medieval Sweden.

Paris, 18 February
For his first film in 10 years Jean Cocteau has remained true to his adage, "Everything that is explained or proven is vulgar." To the exasperation of film critics, nothing is clear in Cocteau's dreamlike evocation of a poet's experiences in *The Testament of Orpheus*, with the great poet himself in the leading role.

Paris, 3 March
Release of *Yeux sans visage (Eyes Without a Face)*, starring Alida Valli and Pierre Brasseur, and directed by Georges Franju.

Hollywood, 7 April
John Huston has finished shooting his latest Western, *The Unforgiven*, with Burt Lancaster and Audrey Hepburn as the central characters and featuring Lillian Gish.

New York, 17 April
Opening of George Cukor's *Heller in Pink Tights*, which stars Sophia Loren and Anthony Quinn. It's an unusual Western about a theatrical troupe traveling through the Far West in a horse-drawn wagon.

New York, 17 April
Henry Fonda's daughter Jane has acted in her first film *Tall Story*, co-starring Anthony Perkins and directed by Joshua Logan.

Paris, 1 May
Brigitte Bardot is making *la Verité* (*The Truth*) with co-star Sami Frey for Henri-Georges Clouzot.

Paris, 26 May
Release of Peter Brook's *Moderato Cantabile*. While making the film Jean-Paul Belmondo crashed the car in which he was driving Jeanne Moreau's 10-year-old son, Jerôme. The child was seriously injured and despite his now being out of danger, the press is still critical of the actor.

Nantes, 7 June
Jacques Demy is dedicating his new film *Lola*, with Anouk Aimée, to Max Ophuls as an homage to the great director's *Lola Montès*.

Paris, 10 June
Opening of Philippe Agostini's *le Dialogue des Carmélites* (*The Carmelites*), based on the novel by Georges Bernanos, with Jeanne Moreau, Alida Valli, Madeleine Renaud and Pierre Brasseur.

Los Angeles, 11 July
A friend and staunch supporter of John F. Kennedy, Frank Sinatra with fellow singers Dean Martin and Sammy Davis Jr. opened the Democratic Party Convention by singing the national anthem.

Switzerland, 17 July
Audrey Hepburn gave birth to her first child today, a boy, by her actor-director husband, Mel Ferrer. Miss Hepburn, who had suffered several miscarriages prior to this confinement (the last being after a fall from a horse during the filming of *The Unforgiven* just over a year ago) is reported to be well. The happy couple have called the baby Sean.

Hollywood, 26 July
The well-known set designer Cedric Gibbons has died after a long illness. Starting his career at the Thomas A. Edison Studio in New York, he became head of Metro's art department in 1924. During his 32 years with the studio he created sets for over 2,000 films and was the worthy recipient of 11 of the Academy Awards, which he designed.

Los Angeles, 1 September
Yves Montand, during an interview with gossip columnist Hedda Hopper for the *Los Angeles Times*, is reported to have said in answer to questions about his relationship with Marilyn Monroe, his co-star in *Let's Make Love*, that "Nothing could destroy my marriage." His wife is actress Simone Signoret.

Los Angeles, 7 September
Ronald Reagan and his wife Nancy have resigned from the Screen Actors Guild. Neither of them has made a film since 1956 when they co-starred in *Hellcats of the Navy*.

London, 28 September
Rouben Mamoulian has begun directing the first scenes for *Cleopatra*, with Elizabeth Taylor in the title role. Miss Taylor has been hired for the fabulous sum of $1 million plus 10 percent of the profits.

New York, 7 October
Stanley Kubrick held a press preview of his latest film, *Spartacus*, with Kirk Douglas (the producer of the film) in the title role, Laurence Olivier, Jean Simmons, Charles Laughton and Peter Ustinov.

London, 8 October
At the opening of his film version of John Osborne's *The Entertainer*, director Tony Richardson said that making low-budget films for limited audiences could be the answer to Britain's "ailing film industry."

Hollywood, 2 November
Clark Gable, who has just finished his final scene for *The Misfits*, confided to director John Huston that he considered it to be one of his finest pieces of acting.

Madrid, 14 November
Anthony Mann has started filming his super-production of *El Cid*, the legendary story set in the 11th century about how the Castilian kings won Spain back. Charlton Heston and Sophia Loren co-star.

Los Angeles, 16 November
The French actress Simone Signoret has been quoted by the *Los Angeles Times* as having said, "If Marilyn Monroe is in love with my husband (Yves Montand) that only proves she has good taste, because I am also in love with him."

New York, 17 November
Release of *Butterfield 8*, directed b Daniel Mann, based on Steinbeck novel and starring Elizabeth Tayl as a disillusioned call-girl.

Tahiti, 28 November
Marlon Brando has arrived here f the filming of MGM's *Mutiny on t Bounty*, under the direction of Car Reed. Despite a year's work, t screenplay is still incomplete.

Los Angeles, 6 December
Release of Blake Edwards' late comedy, *Operation Petticoat*, wi Tony Curtis and Cary Grant.

Japan, 31 December
Production figures rose to 555 film this year compared to 370 in 195

BIRTHS

New York, 7 February
James Spader

Italy, 18 February
Greta Scacchi

Paris, 6 May
Anne Parillaud

California, 16 August
Timothy Hutton

California, 17 August
Sean Penn

New York, 18 November
Elizabeth Perkins

Belfast, 10 December
Kenneth Branagh

DEATHS

Connecticut, 1 January
Margaret Sullavan

Stockholm, 3 January
Victor Sjöström (aka Seastrom)

Hollywood, 5 November
Mack Sennett

Hollywood, 17 November
Clark Gable

---

*Otto Preminger directed **Exodus** fro the best-selling novel by Leon U about the emergence of the State Israel. The film stars Paul Newm as a Jewish freedom fighter.*

DESIGNED BY SAUL BASS
EXODUS
OTTO PREMINGER PRESENTS
PAUL NEWMAN · EVA MARIE SAINT
RALPH RICHARDSON · PETER LAWFORD
LEE J. COBB · SAL MINEO · JOHN DEREK
HUGH GRIFFITH · GREGORY RATOFF
JILL HAWORTH IN "EXODUS"
MARIUS GORING • ALEXANDRA STEWART • MICHAEL WAGER • MARTIN BENSON • PAUL STEVENS • BETTY WALKER • MARTIN MILLER
VICTOR MADDERN • GEORGE MAHARIS • JOHN CRAWFORD • SAMUEL SEGAL • SCREENPLAY BY DALTON TRUMBO • BASED ON THE
NOVEL BY LEON URIS • MUSIC BY ERNEST GOLD • PHOTOGRAPHED IN SUPER PANAVISION 70, TECHNICOLOR® BY SAM LEAVITT • TODD
AO STEREOPHONIC SOUND • ART DIRECTOR RICHARD DAY • A U.A. RELEASE • PRODUCED AND DIRECTED BY OTTO PREMINGER

Maria Félix raises temperature in El Pao

Maria Félix plays a Machiavellian widow in Buñuel's ***Republic of Sin****.*

Paris, 6 January
The Franco-Mexican co-production, *Republic of Sin* (*la Fièvre monte à El Pao*), directed by Luis Buñuel, has been released less than a month after the premature death of its star, Gérard Philipe. He had been ill during the shooting of this steamy melodrama in Mexico. Philipe plays an idealistic man, who falls under the spell of Maria Félix, the widow of the assassinated governor of a Latin-American Republic. Philipe eventually becomes governor, only to find that power corrupts. Maria Félix's sexy charms are given full rein, but Philipe makes a disappointing exit in an underwritten part.

Jacques Becker's energy was not enough

Philippe Leroy and Jean Kéraudy in ***le Trou (The Hole)****, Becker's last film.*

Paris, 21 February
Just a few days after the release of his final film, *The Hole* (*le Trou*), Jacques Becker has died at the age of 54. Becker, who was very ill during the shooting of the movie, was courageously determined to complete it. The subject, drawn from the novel by José Giovanni, deals with the attempts of four long-term pr oners to escape their cells by diggi a tunnel through the prison vaul and into the Paris sewers. Using no professional actors, natural sou and an austere camera style, Beck seemed to be taking a new directio Sadly, we shall never know where would have led him.

Montand plays with co-star Monroe

Hollywood, 18 January
Today sees the start of shooting on Fox's *Let's Make Love*, co-starring Marilyn Monroe and French import Yves Montand. The latter plays an international tycoon who falls in love with off-Broadway star Marilyn but decides not to reveal his true identity because he is the satirical subject of the show in which she is appearing. Instead he masquerades as a struggling actor, hiring the likes of Bing Crosby, Milton Berle and Gene Kelly to teach him the rudiments of their craft. It is rumored that the tycoon in Norman Krasna's original screenplay, written with Yul Brynner in mind, bore a resemblance to Howard Hughes that was a little too close for comfort. Rock Hudson, William Holden, Gregory Peck, Charlton Heston, Cary Grant and James Stewart all turned down the role before Montand was hired by Fox, on the advice of Monroe's husband Arthur Miller, and was installed in Hollywood with his wife Simone Signoret.

Belmondo and Seberg leave audiences gasping in 'Breathless'

Paris, 16 March
Jean-Luc Godard's first feature film *Breathless* has caused a sensation. Based on an idea by François Truffaut, and dedicated to Monogram Pictures (Hollywood's all B-movie studio), it tells of a young car thief (Jean-Paul Belmondo) who kills a policeman and then goes on the run with his American girlfriend (Jean Seberg). The plot is conventional, but the treatment is the opposite. By attempting to recapture the directness and economy of the American gangster movie, Godard has used a hand-held camera (often with the cameraman, Raoul Coutard, in a wheelchair), location shooting, and brutal jump cuts, which elimina the usual establishing shots. T acting of the anarchic Belmon and the sweetly seductive Sebe leave audiences breathless. Goda achieved the immediacy of the pe formances by cueing the actors, w were not permitted to learn th lines, during the takes.

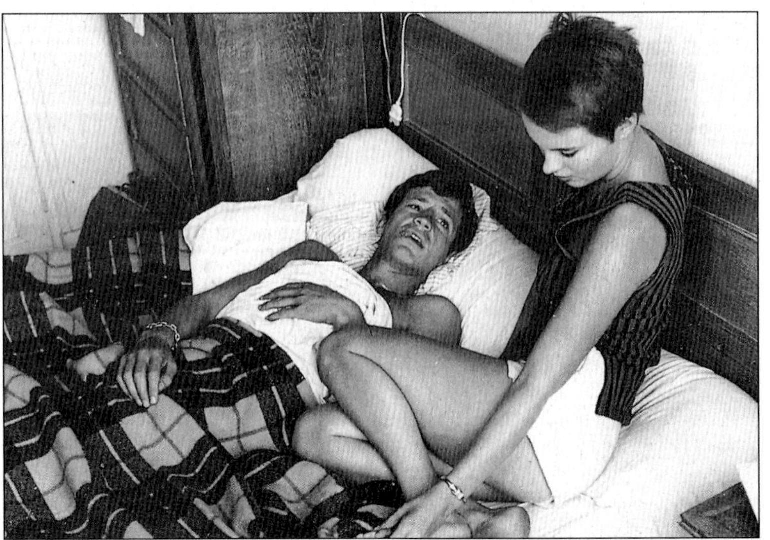

Jean Seberg and Jean-Paul Belmondo in ***Breathless (A bout de souffle)****.*

Jean Seberg with director Godard.

ené Clément carried along on the 'Wave'

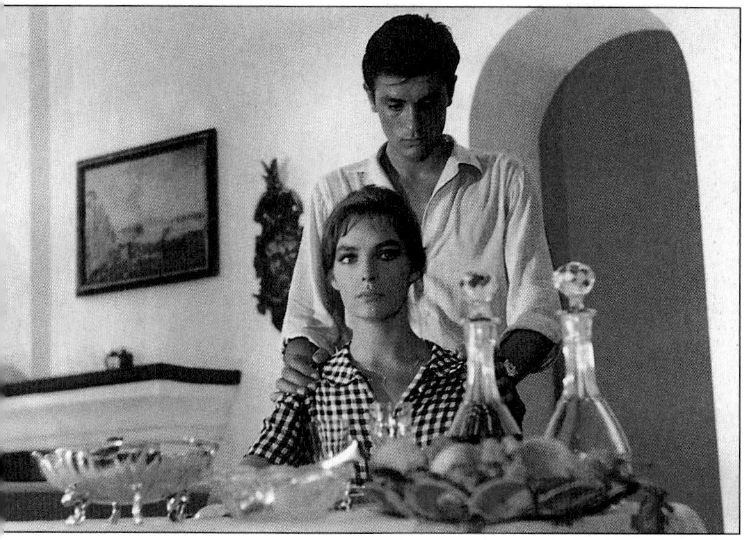

'ain Delon and Marie Laforêt in **Purple Noon**, *from Highsmith's novel.*

aris, 10 March
ıe director René Clément has cap-red the spirit of the times with his test film, *Plein soleil*, based on a atricia Highsmith novel, for which has hired the services of New 'ave screenwriter Paul Gégauff. 's a suntanned *film noir*, brilliantly ıotographed by Henri Decaë and redolent of murky Hollywood B-movies of the 1940s, in which the 24-year-old Alain Delon delivers a persuasive performance as Highsmith's charming psychopath Tom Ripley, plotting to rob his playboy friend Maurice Ronet blind, steal his girfriend Marie Laforêt and then take his life.

Chilling study of killer divides opinion

London, 16 May
Director Michael Powell has stirred up a hornets' nest with his latest picture, *Peeping Tom*, the third in a series of horror films produced by Anglo-Amalgamated. It stars Carl Boehm as a psychopathic film technician who murders women – one played by ballerina Moira Shearer – by impaling them on a spike hidden in his 16mm camera. The film is ugly, daring and brilliant, though there are many who are offended. Powell himself plays Boehm's father, a psychologist who deliberately terrified his small son and would then film his reactions. In a further twist, the child in these films within the film is played by Powell's son Columba. One outraged critic has suggested that the only way to deal with *Peeping Tom* is to flush it down the toilet. Few if any can see the dark humor of the picture or grasp the notion that *Peeping Tom* is a densely layered examination of the conflict between Life and Art, Powell's principal preoccupation, into which the controversial director has poured a lifetime in films.

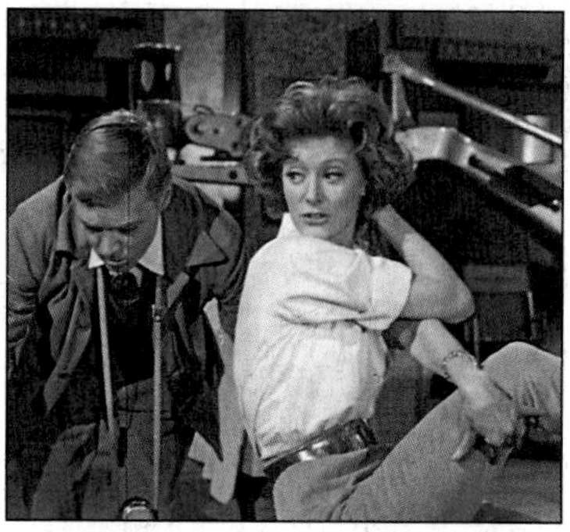

Lovely ballerina Moira Shearer plays one of Boehm's chosen targets.

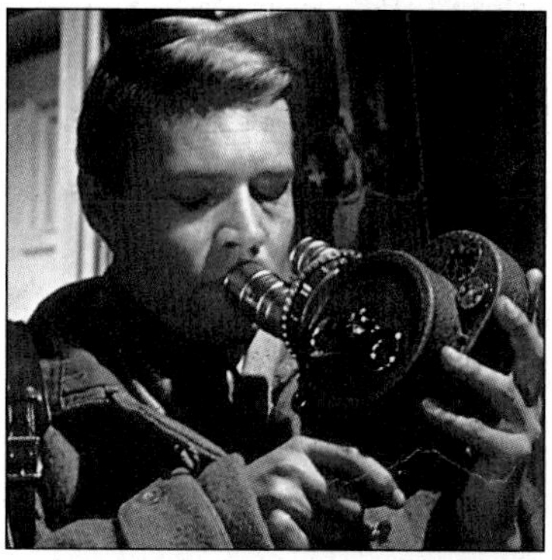

***Peeping Tom**, played by Carl Boehm, here with his great love, the camera.*

ollywood finds 'Room at the Top' for award-winning Signoret

ollywood, 5 April
ve years after Italian actress Anna agnani walked off with the Best ctress Oscar for *The Rose Tattoo*, e Academy has once again chosen bestow the honor on a foreign ar. This year's winner is French tress Simone Signoret, acclaimed r her warm, sensual and moving rformance in the British work, *oom at the Top*, directed by Jack ayton, in which she co-starred as e lonely "older woman" who is duced and then abandoned by a ung, ambitious working-class man aurence Harvey). Adapted from hn Braine's bestseller, the film so won the Best Screenplay award the category for material based on other medium. Best Supporting ctress was Shelley Winters for *The iary of Anne Frank* but, thereafter, e evening belonged to MGM's re-ake of *Ben-Hur*. This awesomely ectacular epic, which took nine onths to shoot at a cost of $15 mil-on, was amply rewarded. Apart om both the Best Picture and Best irector (William Wyler) Oscars, e film swept the board with Best Actor (Charlton Heston), Best Supporting Actor (Hugh Griffith), and the Oscars for Cinematography, Art Direction, Sound, Musical Score, Film Editing, Special Effects and Costume Design, thereby setting a new record. This bonanza denied Billy Wilder's *Some Like It Hot* its considerable due, but nobody can argue with the achievement of *Ben-Hur*. The Best Foreign Film was Marcel Camus' exotic and seductive *Black Orpheus*, making France the winner two years in a row.

Best Actress Simone Signoret with Laurence Harvey in ***Room at the Top**.*

Burden of blacklist grows lighter

Hollywood, 10 April
The start of a new decade appears to mark the beginning of the end for the notorious Hollywood blacklist of the 1950s. Whereas many of the blacklisted directors were forced to search abroad for work, while actors retired or turned to the theater, many of the scriptwriters were able to carry on working anonymously or under various aliases. Thus, it seems only just that Dalton Trumbo, one of the "Hollywood Ten", is the credited writer on two new films – *Spartacus*, produced by its star Kirk Douglas' own Bryna company for Universal, and Otto Preminger's *Exodus* for UA. It is amusing now to note that Trumbo appears to have won a 1956 Academy Award for his original story for *The Brave One* under the name "Robert Rich", while the 1957 Oscar for *The Bridge on the River Kwai*, won by French novelist Pierre Boulle, reflected yet another cover-up for two blacklisted writers, exiled in England – Carl Foreman and Michael Wilson. ▷

Proud Italian filmmakers fly their colors at the Cannes Festival

Monica Vitti the stunning Italian star of Antonioni's prize-winning ***L'Avventura.***

Anita Ekberg in ***La Dolce Vita.***

Cannes, 20 May
This year the mood at the Cannes Film Festival has changed. Four days ago, the director Michelangelo Antonioni with his leading lady, Monica Vitti, left the Grand Palace extremely upset after the screening of *L'Avventura*, which was shown in a hostile atmosphere. However, they have been well compensated by the jury's perspicacity, presided over by the author Georges Simenon. The film received the Special Jury Prize for "its remarkable contribution to the search for a new cinematographic language." In general, the jury and critics have shown approval of Italian directors this year. Federico Fellini was the unanimous winner of the Golden Palm for *La Dolce Vita*, though this did not prevent the film from being booed by sections of the audience. The baroque fresco, shot at Cinecittà, casts an ironic and scathing eye on the world of stars, pseudo-intellectuals and *paparazzi*. Perhaps, it is Fellini's very lucidity that has disturbed some people. Marcello Mastroianni, as a gossip columnist, Anouk Aimée and Anita Ekberg, among the large cast, are convincing in their roles as members of the decadent Roman society.

'Elmer Gantry': an alliance of God, Mammon and Burt Lancaster

New York, 7 July
Writer-director Richard Brooks has bucked the current Biblical trend, producing a movie about religion which is not set in the time of Christ. *Elmer Gantry*, adapted by Brooks from Sinclair Lewis' novel, stars Burt Lancaster as the silver-tongued salesman who joins evangelist Jean Simmons' barnstorming crew in the West of the 1920s. However, the group's phony mission is exposed by the skeptical journalist Arthur Kennedy while he tracks the evangelists' Bible-thumping progress through the American heartland. Shirley Jones, until now associated with virginal roles, is cast as Lulu Bains, the blowzy hooker redeemed by Lancaster. And singer Patti Page makes her screen debut as a gospel singer. Playing the ambiguous Sister Sharon, who bears more than a passing resemblance to Aimée Semple MacPherson, Jean Simmons gives a stunning performance. No wonder that Brooks considers his wife "a remarkable human being and an incredible actress."

Elmer Gantry (Burt Lancaster) exhorting the crowds to follow the faith.

Dietrich visits her 'fatherland'

Munich, 31 May
Until now, Marlene Dietrich has n returned to her homeland since sh left for the United States during th spring of 1930. For the first tim she is facing German audiences du ing her long concert tour around th country. In most of the towns h show has gone off without inciden but in some, "Marlene Go Home had been daubed on the walls, an she has been pelted with tomatoe A section of the population has n forgiven her for her exile. Yet sh was a triumph in Berlin and wa rapturously received in Munic "I'll be back," she promised.

'L'Avventura'

Cannes, 17 May
The works of Michelangelo Antonioni have often divided public opinion. The showing of *L'Avventura*, however, has been greeted with rare hostility. Naturally, this indignant outcry has provoked a rapid reaction from admirers of the film. A manifesto in support of *L'Avventura* was immediately drawn up. This states: "Aware of the exceptional importance of Michelangelo Antonioni's film and disgusted by the demonstration of hostility which it has engendered, the members of the film profession and the critics whose names are signed below also wish to express their wholehearted admiration for the maker of this film. Others who share this enthusiasm, wish to make known their approval." Included among the signatories are film directors Roberto Rossellini, Jean Baral Mario Ruspoli Di Poggio-Suasa Nelly Kaplan, Ennio Lorenzini... performers: Maurice Ronet, Alice Saprich... producers and distributors: Yvonne Decaris, Anatole Daumon... journalists and writers: Georges Sadoul, Rober Benayoun, Janine-André Bazin... and a large number of magazines *Image et Son, le Parisien Libéré Cinéma 60, la Marseillaise, Paris Match*. The statement, published by *les Bulletins du Festival*, was then handed to the director of the controversial film.

ack and Shirley, and Billy's key to happiness

ick Lemmon passes another lonely evening at home in front of the TV.

Fran Kubelik (Shirley MacLaine) about to be assailed at the office party.

ew York, 15 June
illy Wilder's latest project, *The partment*, is bound to attract large d enthusiastic audiences. Wilder, ho wrote the screenplay with his artner I.A.L. Diamond, once again emonstrates an outstanding gift r brilliant plotting and sparkling alogue, and an acute eye and ear for the idiosyncracies of the human race. More tellingly, he manages to make a hilarious comedy, combined with a touching romance, out of raw ingredients that include questionable sexual morals, loneliness in the big city and even an attempted suicide. Throbbing with the pulse of New York City, the movie concerns bachelor office clerk C.C. Baxter (Jack Lemmon) who is prevailed upon to lend the key of his apartment to his married superiors for their illicit liaisons. Returning home after one of these assignations is supposedly over, he stumbles on the inert form of Fran Kubelik (Shirley MacLaine), the office elevator girl whom he secretly fancies... What happens from that moment on is the basis for a comedic tour de force from Lemmon, a champagne performance from MacLaine and, above all, the satisfactory working out of a situation in which Wilder obliquely comments on the less appetizing side of supposed respectability.

lfred Hitchcock's latest shocker enters the realms of madness

os Angeles, 10 August
lfred Hitchcock, cinematic torturer supreme, has stepped into the orld of madness with *Psycho*. And, ith typical perversity, he disposes his leading lady, Janet Leigh, rly in the picture. Leigh plays a hoenix secretary, on the lam with 2,000 of her boss's money crammed into her bag. The theft is not r big mistake. It's her decision to eck in for the night at the seedy ates Motel – 12 cabins and 12 vancies with old Mrs. Bates' Amerin Gothic house perched above on hill. Then, after sharing a frugal eal with Mrs. Bates' twitchy son orman, Leigh decides to take a ower. That's her last mistake. In e jet-black comedy which follows e discover the true identity of Mrs. ates as well as the true nature of orman. Hitchcock is at his most asterfully manipulative in *Psycho*, t the revelation of the picture is nthony Perkins, son of the late acr Osgood Perkins, as the haunted orman Bates. Gangling, stuttering d slyly attractive with a snake-fast sh of a smile, Perkins animates Norman with a creepy life of his own. It's hard not to sympathize with him as, beneath the savage, slashing beaks of his stuffed bird collection, he shares a moment of mutual loneliness with Leigh before going on to spy on her taking a shower through a hole in the wall. The film ends with Norman's nervous chatter finally silenced as he crouches under a blanket in the asylum to which he has been confined. Hitchcock is reportedly nervous about the commercial potential of *Psycho*, which he playfully describes as "my first horror film."

Anthony Perkins is an insane and scary Norman Bates in Hitchcock's **Psycho**.

A clamor for blood and guts

New York, 28 September
It has been known for some time that the American cinema also has its "angry young men." A statement put out by the New American Cinema Group claims :"We don't want rose-colored films any more, but films the color of blood." Created by Jonas Mekas, Shirley Clarke and several other New York directors, the group has the same aims as the French New Wave and the British Free Cinema movements. They wish to shake up the old cinema and make independent films, "rough, badly-made perhaps, but alive." In the U.S., which is still the mecca of filmmaking, their pronouncements seem much bolder than those of their European confreres. Of Lithuanian origin, Mekas has made a number of experimental films in 16mm. He also founded the magazine *Film Culture* in 1956. A dancer by education, Clarke has principally filmed dancers, most notably Daniel Nagrin in *Dance in Love*, and Anna Sokolow in *Bullfight*. ▷

'Spartacus' an epic of substance as well as scale

New York, 6 October
Twelve million dollars, two years of intensive preparation and 8,000 Spanish extras have been poured into Universal's *Spartacus*, a sword and sandal blockbuster to rival *Ben-Hur*. Kirk Douglas is the star and executive producer, taking the title role of the rebellious Thracian slave hero who gave Rome the runaround in 73 B.C., leading an army of gladiators against the legions. Douglas is also up against some heavyweight British acting competition: Laurence Olivier as his nemesis, the general Crassus; Charles Laughton as the senator Gracchus; and Peter Ustinov as Batiatus, the sweatily venal dealer in gladiators. Tony Curtis plays Crassus' servant Antoninus and Jean Simmons is Varinia, the slave girl for whom Douglas falls. This is very much Douglas' production. After a week of shooting, he fired his original choice as director, Anthony Mann, and replaced him with 30-year-old Stanley Kubrick, who imparts a degree of intimacy and personal depth to the story as the epic action unfolds in Technirama 70. Dalton Trumbo's literate screenplay, adapted from Howard Fast's sprawling novel, is the first for which he has been credited since falling foul of the Hollywood blacklist. Filmed on location outside Madrid and also on the Universal backlot, *Spartacus* has prompted Douglas to observe that if it's a thrilling spectacle, $12 million "is a drop in the bucket. If not, $12 million was too much."

Kirk Douglas in the title role.

The fighting Spartacus in a characteristically epic scene from this productio

Outrageous, ebullient Mercouri beguiles

New York, 18 October
Exuberant Greek actress Melina Mercouri explodes on to the screen in *Never on Sunday*, as an unrepentant hooker happily plying her trade in the port of Piraeus and effortlessly thwarting American writer Jules Dassin's attempts to reform her. It is a case of uptight America colliding with sensual Mediterranean warmth with chain-smoking, gravel-voiced Mercouri walking away with the honors. Dassin, exiled to Europe by the Hollywood blacklist, has his work cut out as Mercouri's co-star, husband and director.

Dockside revelry in Piraeus with Melina Mercouri and her adoring 'customers'.

Zazie discovers Paris above the ground

Paris, 28 October
After filming *Frantic (Ascenseur pour l'echafaud*) and *The Lovers*, Louis Malle has changed again and taken another direction. His new work, *Zazie dans le métro*, seems to defy all classification, going against the grain of conventional comedy. Because of this, its commercial possibilities could be severely limited. Malle has tried very boldly to create visual equivalents to the eccentric syntax of Raymond Queneau's novel by using a series of cinematic tricks – speeded-up action, slow motion, quotes from other movies and silent-comedy techniques. It is a brightly-colored surreal view of Paris, including a wild scene on the Eiffel Tower. Yet the director, with the assistance of screenwriter Jean-Paul Rappeneau, has preserved the essentials of the story and much of Queneau's dialogue. This movie's burlesque style is justified because the world is perceived from the viewpoint of precocious, foul-mouthed little Zazie, marvelously interpreted by Catherine Demongeot. The chi spends 36 hours with her fema impersonator Uncle Gabriel (Pl lippe Noiret) in Paris with the sc intention of going for a ride on t metro, but a series of frenetic in dents, often instigated by Zaz conspires to prevent this.

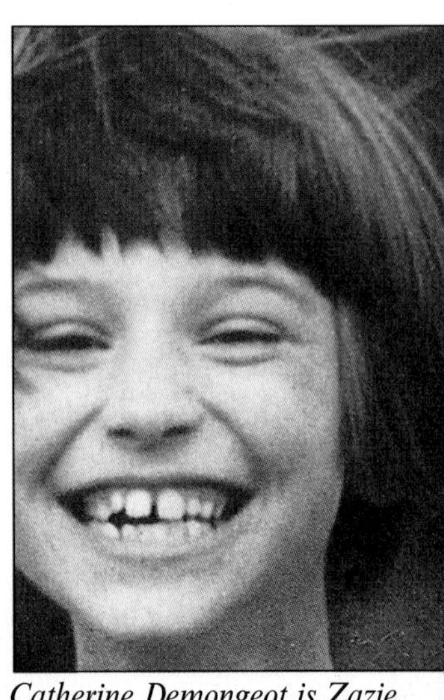

Catherine Demongeot is Zazie.

Marilyn finds herself adrift between films and between loves

larilyn Monroe with her French co-star Yves Montand in **Let's Make Love**.

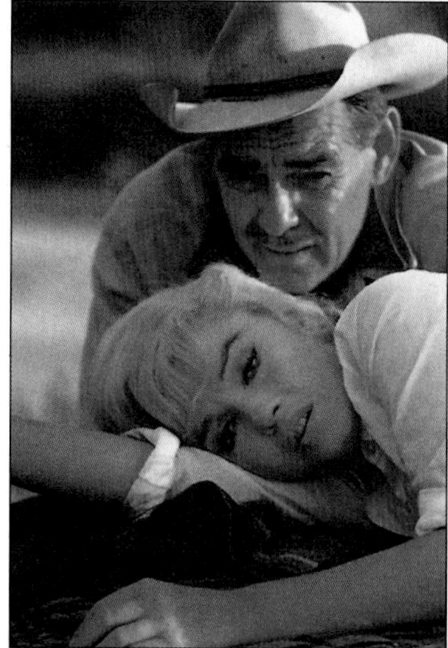

With the now, sadly, late Clark Gable in John Huston's ***The Misfits****.*

evada, 16 November
n 11 November, after shooting ad been completed on *The Misfits*, larilyn Monroe and Arthur Miller ere officially divorced. Miller had ritten the original screenplay for s wife, but their already difficult lationship deteriorated consider- ly during the troubled making of e film, directed by John Huston in the Nevada desert. Marilyn has been in a poor mental state and was never on time on the set, keeping her co-stars Clark Gable, Montgomery Clift and Eli Wallach waiting around in the high temperatures. She was sleeping badly and taking Nembutal, and therefore could not be moved in the morning. Production was suspended for a few weeks when Marilyn was hospitalized. She had tried to reach Yves Montand, with whom she had fallen in love during the making of her previous film, *Let's Make Love*, but he refused to answer her calls. It does seem unlikely that Marilyn will be well enough to appear in her new film, *Something's Got to Give*, due to start shooting next spring.

Death of Gable, 'king' of Hollywood

California, 17 November
Only a short time after finishing work on Huston's *The Misfits*, Clark Gable has died of a heart attack at his Encino home. The strain of the production, in which he insisted on performing all his own stunts, had taken its toll on the aging King of Hollywood. A few weeks ago he learned that his wife, Kay Spreckels, was pregnant and that at the age of 60 he was to be a father for the first time. "It will be a boy," Gable confidently predicted, but the child will never know its father. Commenting on *The Misfits*, producer Frank Taylor has said, "We felt that there was only one actor in the world who expressed the essence of complete masculinity and virility that we needed for the leading role – and that was Gable." Funeral services will be held at Forest Lawn, where he will be buried alongside Carole Lombard, the great love of his life, from whose death he never really recovered. He had often said, with characteristically gruff modesty, "If something happens to me, don't make a circus out of it."

estern owes a debt to 'Seven Samurai'

os Angeles, 23 November
hn Sturges' latest Western, *The agnificent Seven*, is a straight lift om the 1954 classic *The Seven umurai*. Yul Brynner leads an ill-sorted band of gunfighters against ındits terrorizing a Mexican vilge. These cynical professionals discover a moral purpose in the task, though some pay with their lives. Sturges' sure hand orchestrates the confident swagger of the seven in a movie which looks to be launching the careers of co-stars Steve McQueen, Charles Bronson, James Coburn and Eli Wallach.

e Magnificent Seven, l to r: Steve McQueen, James Coburn, Horst Buchholz, l Brynner, Brad Dexter, Robert Vaughn and Charles Bronson.

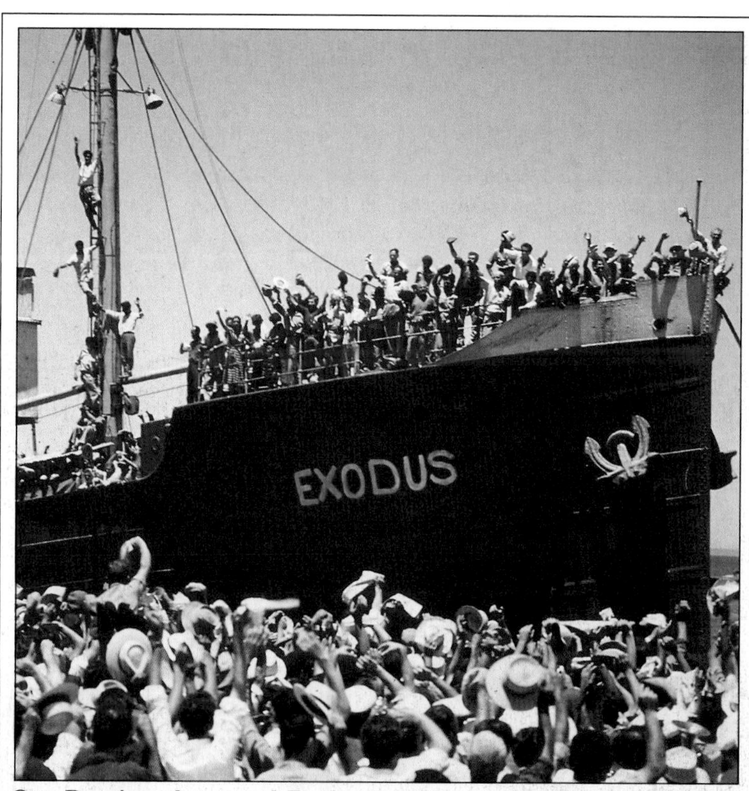
EXODUS

Otto Preminger has turned *Exodus*, the 600-page bestseller, into a sprawling, rather leaden epic, critically ill-received. But the public seems to like it, perhaps because Paul Newman plays Jewish hero Ari Ben Canaan.

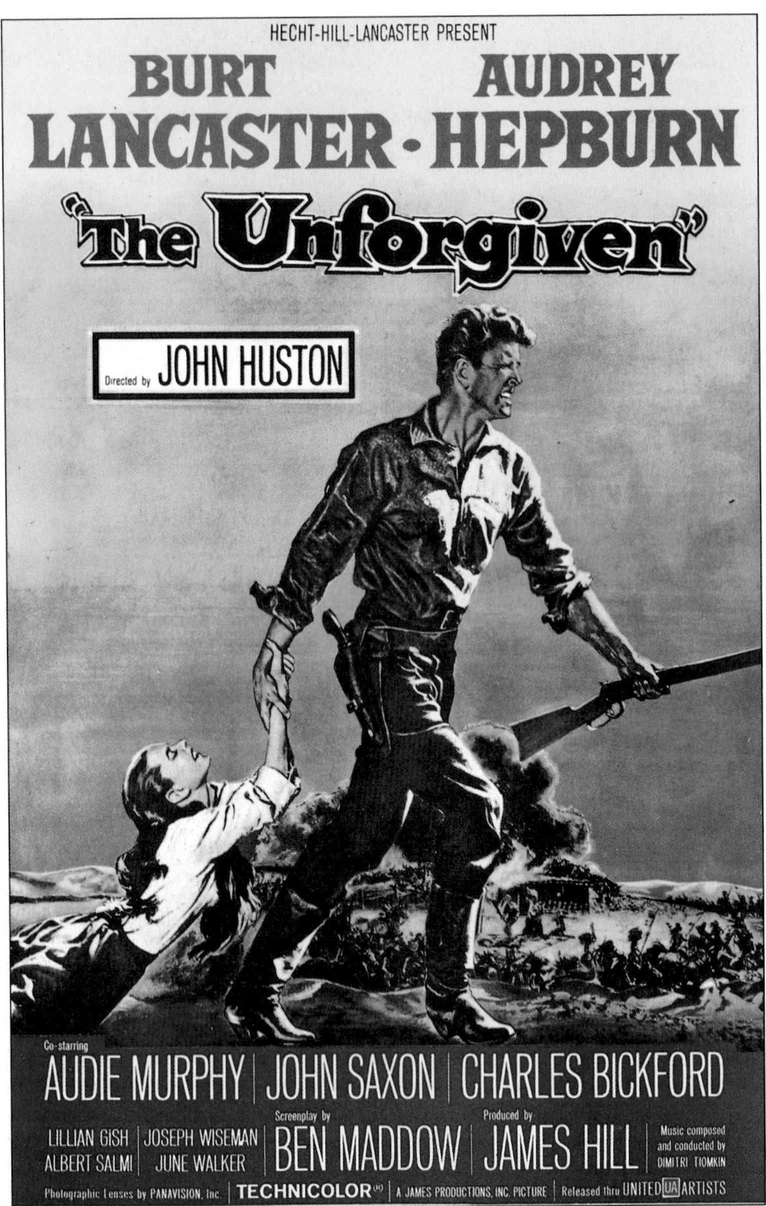
HECHT-HILL-LANCASTER PRESENT
BURT LANCASTER · AUDREY HEPBURN
"The Unforgiven"
Directed by JOHN HUSTON
Co-starring
AUDIE MURPHY | JOHN SAXON | CHARLES BICKFORD
LILLIAN GISH | JOSEPH WISEMAN
ALBERT SALMI | JUNE WALKER
Screenplay by BEN MADDOW
Produced by JAMES HILL
Music composed and conducted by DIMITRI TIOMKIN
Photographic Lenses by PANAVISION, Inc. | TECHNICOLOR® | A JAMES PRODUCTIONS, INC. PICTURE | Released thru UNITED UA ARTISTS

One of Huston's least successful films cast Audrey Hepburn as an Indian girl. She lost her own baby in a fall from a horse during shooting.

*Blue-collar hero Albert Finney in **Saturday Night and Sunday Morning**.*

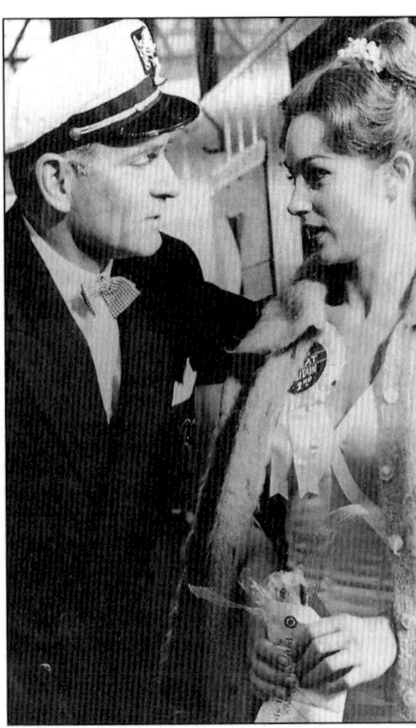

*Laurence Olivier and Shirley Ann Field in **The Entertainer**.*

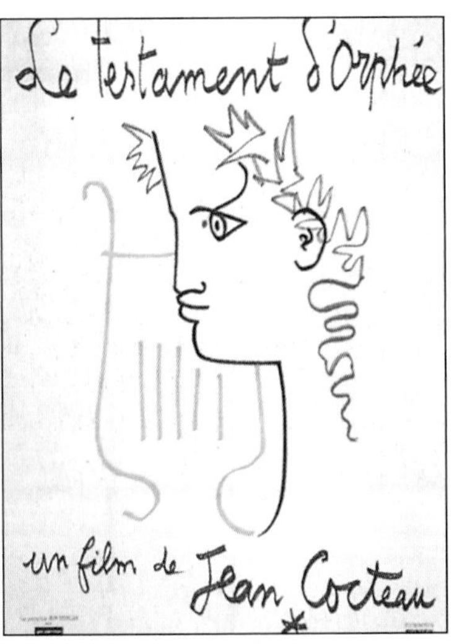
Le Testament d'Orphée
un film de Jean Cocteau

The variously gifted Cocteau's own poster design for his film.

*Doris Day and Rex Harrison in the thriller **Midnight Lace**.*

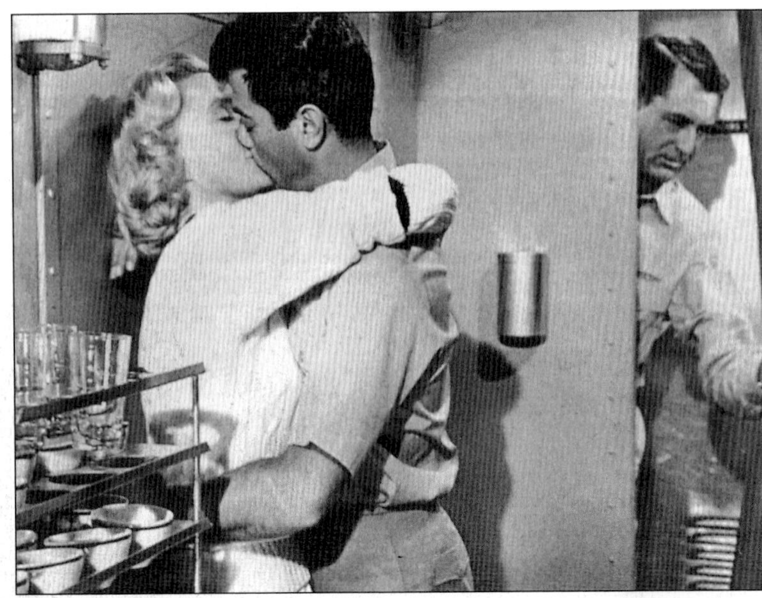

*Dina Merrill, Tony Curtis, Cary Grant: Blake Edwards' **Operation Petticoat**.*

The most evil DRACULA of all!
The BRIDES OF DRACULA
TECHNICOLOR®
Starring PETER CUSHING FREDA JACKSON · MARTITA HUNT · YVONNE MONLAUR
Screenplay by JIMMY SANGSTER, PETER BRYAN and EDWARD PERCY · Directed by TERENCE FISHER · Produced by ANTHONY HINDS
Executive Producer MICHAEL CARRERAS · A Hammer Film Production Released by Universal-International through Rank Film Distributors Ltd.

*A great variation on **Dracula**, with a disciple of the Count on the rampage.*

HERE COME "THE SUNDOWNERS"! They're real people, fun people, fervent people. They have a tremendous urge to keep breathing. Their rousing story comes roaring across six thousand miles of excitement...
DEBORAH KERR ROBERT MITCHUM PETER USTINOV
FRED ZINNEMANN'S PRODUCTION OF The SUNDOWNERS
Co-Starring GLYNIS JOHNS · DINA MERRILL · Screenplay by ISOBEL LENNART · MUSIC COMPOSED AND CONDUCTED BY DIMITRI TIOMKIN
Directed by FRED ZINNEMANN · TECHNICOLOR® · PRESENTED BY WARNER BROS

An Anglo-American cast, headed by Robert Mitchum and Deborah Kerr, in a lovingly filmed saga of a pioneering family in the Australian bush.

Judy Holliday (left) and Dean Martin (second left) in Minnelli's film of the Broadway musical ***Bells Are Ringing****.*

CHARLES AZNAVOUR
TIREZ SUR LE PIANISTE

Singer Charles Aznavour stars in Truffaut's ***Shoot the Piano Player****.*

Annie Girardot, a tragic figure in Visconti's ***Rocco and His Brothers****.*

Psycho*: Motel owner Norman Bates (Anthony Perkins) and guest Janet Leigh.*

KIRK DOUGLAS
LAURENCE OLIVIER
JEAN SIMMONS
CHARLES LAUGHTON
PETER USTINOV
JOHN GAVIN
and TONY CURTIS
SPARTACUS
TECHNICOLOR® TECHNIRAMA® LENSES BY PANAVISION
Directed by STANLEY KUBRICK Music composed and conducted by ALEX NORTH Screenplay by DALTON TRUMBO
Based on a novel by HOWARD FAST Produced by EDWARD LEWIS Executive Producer KIRK DOUGLAS
A Bryna Production Released by Universal-International

Aristocrats of the acting profession illumine this epic of Ancient Rome.

1961

1960 Academy Awards, Santa Monica Civic Auditor., 17 Apr.

Best Film:	*The Apartment* (dir: Billy Wilder)
Best Director:	Billy Wilder
Best Actor:	Burt Lancaster *(Elmer Gantry)*
Best Actress:	Elizabeth Taylor *(Butterfield 8)*
Best Supp. Actor:	Peter Ustinov *(Spartacus)*
Best Supp. Actress:	Shirley Jones *(Elmer Gantry)*

Prague, 3 January
Vera Chytilova is filming *Strop*, an innovative film dealing with the world of high fashion models and women's social conditions.

London, 8 January
Gary Cooper, who is on location for Michael Anderson's *The Naked Edge*, was received by Prince Philip.

London, 18 January
Rouben Mamoulian, the director of *Cleopatra*, has resigned after refusing Lawrence Durrell's script.

Washington D.C., 19 January
Frank Sinatra is organizing a gala evening in honor of tomorrow's investiture of President Kennedy. Harry Belafonte, Shirley MacLaine, Bette Davis and Sidney Poitier are among the personalities to be presented to the President.

London, 1 February
Joseph L. Mankiewicz has arrived from the United States to take over the direction of *Cleopatra*.

Tahiti, 25 February
The whole film crew for *Mutiny on the Bounty* has been ordered back to Hollywood after director Carol Reed's refusal of a new schedule imposed by MGM. He is to be replaced by Lewis Milestone.

Switzerland, 3 March
Danish actress Anna Karina married the director Jean-Luc Godard today. Godard has just directed her in *A Woman is a Woman.*

London, 6 March
Elizabeth Taylor has been in a coma since her operation on 4 March. She has stopped breathing several times and the six doctors in charge of her case fear for her life.

Dakar, 4 April
The newsreel *Senegalese Cinema News*, became a weekly production on the country's independence day.

Hollywood, 13 May
Of Gary Cooper, who has just died, Charles Laughton had this to say: "He had something I'll never have: he had no idea just how great an actor he was." And from John Barrymore: "He was the greatest actor in the world. He managed effortlessly to do that which we strive towards all our lives: to be natural."

Paris, 18 May
Alain Delon told Nicole Zand of the *France-Observateur* that he would like to make films which could be listened to like an opera.

Mexico, 4 July
Lauren Bacall has married the actor Jason Robards in Ensenada, a small Mexican village near the Californian border. Robards, who was a close friend of Bacall's first husband Humphrey Bogart, was a great support to the actress after Bogey's tragic death in 1957.

Paris, 5 July
In the press release for *Handsome Antonio*, Mauro Bolognini refers to the still delicate subject of masculine impotence. Marcello Mastroianni and Claudia Cardinale co-star.

Moscow, 23 July
At the International Film Festival, the main prize was awarded to the Japanese film *Hadaka no shima* (*Naked Island*), by Kaneto Shindo.

Locarno, 30 July
The top award at the festival here has gone to *Fires on the Plain* (*Nobi*), by Kon Ichikawa.

New York, 2 August
Astor Films is negotiating for U.S. and Canadian distribution rights for Roger Vadim's film version of *les Liaisons dangereuses 1960*. The film, which co-stars Jeanne Moreau and Gérard Philipe, opened in Paris in late 1959, but was then banned for export as it presented contemporary France in an unfavorable light.

Paris, 9 August
Pierre Kast, a former film critic for *Cahiers du Cinéma*, has made his second feature film *la Morte-saison des amours* (*The Season for Love*), starring Pierre Vaneck, Françoise Arnoul and Daniel Gélin.

Hollywood, 27 September
The most successful musical in Broadway history, *My Fair Lady*, is about to be sold to the movies for a record price. Warner Bros. is reportedly prepared to pay $5 million in cash plus 47.5 percent of the film's gross box-office receipts over $20 million. Herman Levin, who produced the musical, has 26 days to negotiate a better offer before the deal is made final.

Rome, 28 September
Filming of *Cleopatra* has restarted under Joseph L. Mankiewicz's direction and with a few cast changes. Rex Harrison replaces Peter Finch as Caesar, and Mark Antony will now be played by Richard Burton, not Stephen Boyd.

New York, 6 October
Henry Mancini composed the haunting music for Blake Edwards' *Breakfast at Tiffany's*, adapted from the book by Truman Capote and starring Audrey Hepburn and George Peppard. The film is being released today.

Beverly Hills, 13 October
Director Zoltan Korda, brother of Alexander Korda, has died.

Tokyo, 29 October
Release of *Kohayagawa-ke no aki* (*The End of Summer* aka *Early Autumn*), directed by Yasujiro Ozu, the tale of a dying patriarch's visit to his former mistress.

Rome, 23 November
During the premiere of Pier Paolo Pasolini's film, *Accatone*, the neo-fascist movement, Nuova-Europa, caused a violent disturbance, attacking the spectators and vandalizing the cinema.

Havana, 1 December
At the inauguration of the Cuban Film Archives in the presence of some of the leading figures in the Castro government, Fidel Castro announced the setting up of a plan to help the cinema industry.

Paris, 6 December
Release of *Tintin and the Mystery of the Golden Fleece*, by Jean-Jacques Vierne, based on an story by Hergé with Jean-Pierre Talbot in the role of Tintin, and Georges Wilson as Captain Haddock.

Paris, 20 December
Release of Walt Disney's animated *One Hundred and One Dalmations.*

BIRTHS

Berlin, 24 January
Nastassja Kinski
(Nastassja Naksynski)

New York, 3 April
Eddie Murphy

Vancouver, 9 June
Michael J. Fox

Texas, 15 July
Forest Whitaker

Illinois, 18 July
Elizabeth McGovern

Georgia, 30 July
Laurence Fishburne

California, 29 August
Rebecca De Mornay

Connecticut, 19 November
Meg Ryan

Oregon, 22 November
Mariel Hemingway

DEATHS

England, 6 March
George Formby

Paris, 4 August
Maurice Tourneur

New York, 30 August
Charles Coburn

Hollywood, 22 September
Marion Davies

Hollywood, 11 October
Chico Marx

Despite having sanitized Truman Capote's novella, Blake Edwards has scored a huge success with ***Breakfast at Tiffany's*** *due to the irresistible presence of Audrey Hepburn.*

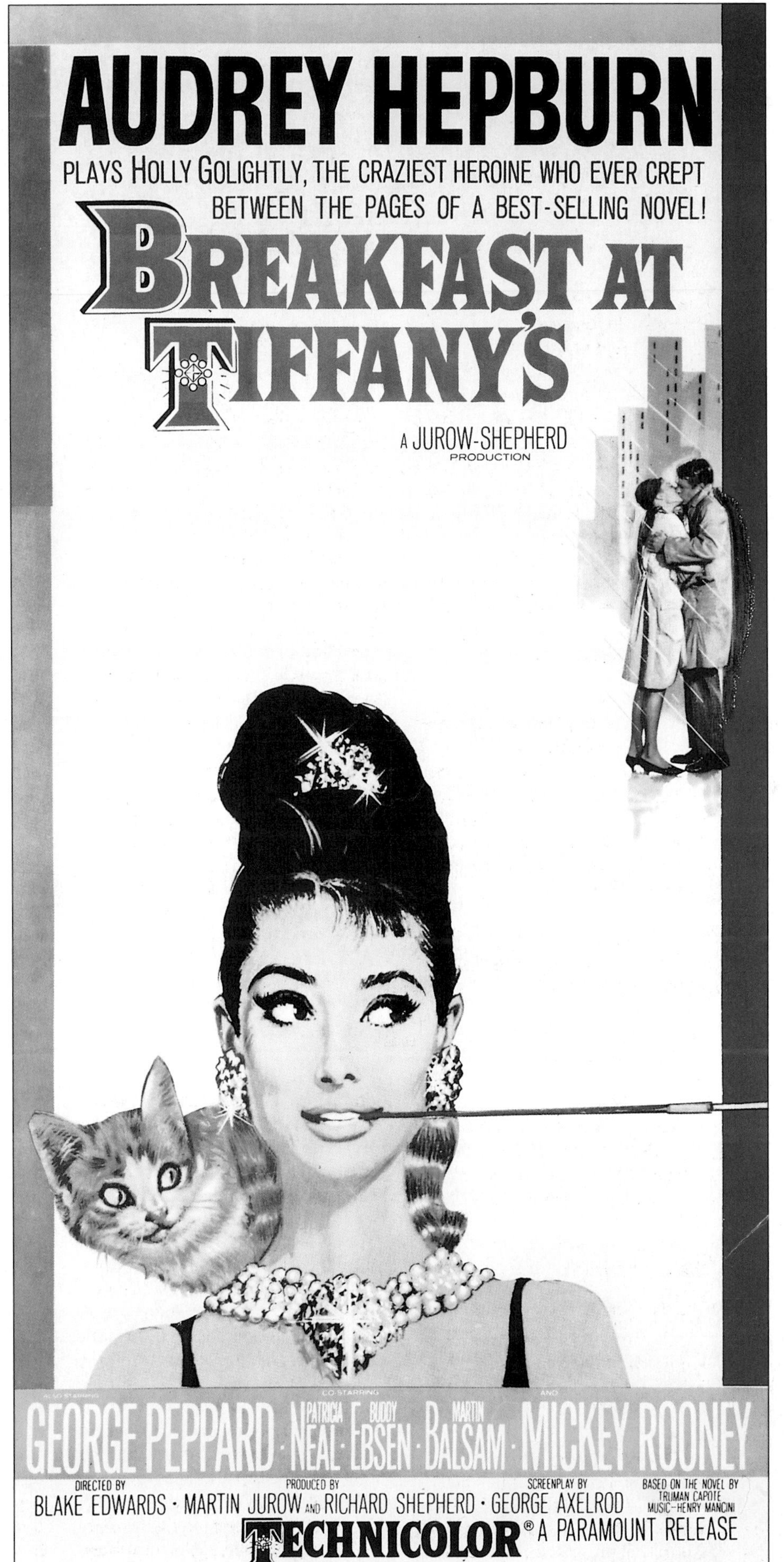
AUDREY HEPBURN
PLAYS HOLLY GOLIGHTLY, THE CRAZIEST HEROINE WHO EVER CREPT BETWEEN THE PAGES OF A BEST-SELLING NOVEL!
BREAKFAST AT TIFFANY'S
A JUROW-SHEPHERD PRODUCTION
CO STARRING
GEORGE PEPPARD · PATRICIA NEAL · BUDDY EBSEN · MARTIN BALSAM · AND MICKEY ROONEY
DIRECTED BY BLAKE EDWARDS · PRODUCED BY MARTIN JUROW AND RICHARD SHEPHERD · SCREENPLAY BY GEORGE AXELROD
BASED ON THE NOVEL BY TRUMAN CAPOTE
MUSIC–HENRY MANCINI
TECHNICOLOR® A PARAMOUNT RELEASE

The harsh life of 'misfits' in the desert

l to r: Thelma Ritter, Clark Gable and Marilyn Monroe, in a moment of calm.

New York, 1 February
Marilyn Monroe and Montgomery Clift were present at the world premiere of their new film, *The Misfits*, directed by John Huston. This gala performance was given in memory of Clark Gable, one of the stars of the film, who died of a heart attack two and a half months ago, a mere couple of weeks after shooting was completed. Gable's death is said to have been hastened by the strenuous roping of stallions demanded by his role. *The Misfits* has the smell of doom about it, not only because of Gable's death, or Marilyn's disintegrating marriage to Arthur Miller, who wrote the screenplay, but because of the disenchanted subject of the film itself. (Ironically, the film is set in and around Reno, the divorce capital.) Huston described his reaction on first reading Miller's script: "I read it like a boxer with my guard up, and suddenly I received a punch in the pit of my stomach." It tells of three failed men who come together in the Nevada desert to catch wild mustangs to be sold and slaughtered for dog food. They are an aging cowboy (Gable), a broken broncobuster (Clift) and a former wartime pilot (Eli Wallach). Their values are put into perspective by a tenderhearted divorcee (Monroe), who is repelled by the harsh cruelty of their calling. Despite the fraught conditions of filming in extremely high temperatures, the stars give among their most profound performances. Huston wisely concentrates on the famous faces, as well as providing superbly shot visual set pieces, such as the final roundup.

Montgomery Clift (left), Clark Gable (center) and Eli Wallach in ***The Misfits****.*

Elizabeth Taylor gets Best Actress Oscar

For her unhappy call-girl in ***Butterfield 8****, Elizabeth Taylor is Best Actress.*

Hollywood, 18 April
Bob Hope was this year's master of ceremonies at the Academy Awards gathering, which was produced by Arthur Freed and directed by Vincente Minnelli. Top film of the year is Billy Wilder's *The Apartment*, which has garnered five Oscars, including Best Picture and Director. The Best Actor Award has gone to Burt Lancaster for *Elmer Gan*
Elizabeth Taylor, only recently
covered from pneumonia, has w
the Best Actress award on a tide
sympathy for her role as a call gir
Butterfield 8. There was a mom
of high emotion at the end of
ceremony when Gary Cooper, t
ill to attend, was awarded a spec
Oscar for his services to film.

'Two Women' displays Sophia's mettle

New York, 8 May
American cinema never properly learned how to exploit the voluptuously earthy appeal of Italian actress Sophia Loren. In films such as *Boy on a Dolphin* (1957) and *Desire Under the Elms* (1958), she appeared almost as a caricature of herself. Now American audiences are able to judge her talents on her home ground in Vittorio De Sica's new movie, *Two Women* (*La Ciociara*). Loren plays a widowed mother of a 13-year-old daughter, fleeing south after the Allied bombing of Rome in 1943. They survive enemy attack, deprivation and, ultimately, rape by Moroccan Allied soldiers. The title of this project, based on a story by Alberto Moravia, refers to both mother and daughter; however it is Sophia Loren's powerful performance on which most attention is focused. Minus the glossy image fabricated for her in Hollywood, Loren's gutsy acting confirms Jean Cocteau's aphorism, "A bird sings best on its family tree." It is some years since De Sica made his na
with neo-realist classics such as *T*
Bicycle Thief and *Umberto D*, yet
director has not lost his ability
move us, for the film contains ma
touching and harrowing scenes.

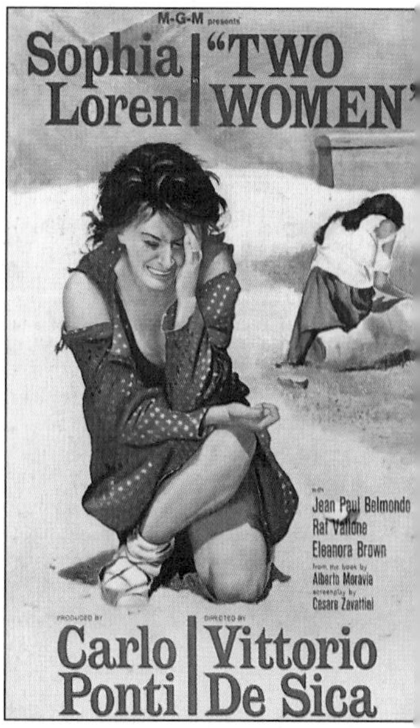
M-G-M presents
Sophia Loren
"TWO WOMEN"
Jean Paul Belmondo
Raf Vallone
Eleanora Brown
Alberto Moravia
Cesare Zavattini
Carlo Ponti
Vittorio De Sica

ary Cooper, a great star dies at age 60

'ith Deborah Kerr in his last film, Michael Anderson's **The Naked Edge**.

os Angeles, 13 May
ary Cooper has died of cancer at s Bel Air home. His career had anned 35 years and, except at its ginning and very end, he was one Hollywood's biggest stars. Be- een 1936 and 1957 he was only out of the Exhibitors' Top Ten list three times, and in 1953 he headed it. Of his own career, he once said, "Until I came along, all the leading men were handsome, but luckily they wrote a lot of stories about the fellow next door."

Marlon Brando on both sides of the camera

New York, 31 May
One-Eyed Jacks, the first film to be directed by Marlon Brando, starring himself, has just been released in 128 movie theaters across America. It was while he was working on *The Young Lions* that he announced his intention to move to the other side of the camera, explaining that it would allow him "a greater opportunity for expression." He started shooting the Western on 2 December 1958, with a budget of $2 million and a schedule of 60 days. Filming lasted six months, cost more than $6 million, and exposed more than a million feet of film, an all-time record. Originally, *One-Eyed Jacks* was to have been directed by Stanley Kubrick, with a screenplay by Sam Peckinpah and Brando in the lead. After disagreements between the director and star, Brando suggested he direct the film himself. The first version of this story of a man's quest for the fellow outlaw who betrayed him, ran four hours 42 minutes, but was cut to exactly half that length by the studio. The film is still rather long, rambling and self-indulgent, but with superb VistaVision photography by Charles Lang Jr., and a brooding Byronic performance by its star and director.

The actor-turned-director, during the filming of ***One-Eyed Jacks***.

pain hangs its head in shame over Buñuel

ladrid, 31 May
he head of the Spanish Film Ad- inistration has begun to curse the iumph of *Viridiana*, Luis Buñuel's rst film in his native land for 29 ars. The fact that this "impious, crilegious" film was awarded the olden Palm at Cannes has resulted the official being dismissed from s post. He had, unforgivably it ems, allowed the film be shown at Cannes as a result of a strange set of circumstances which worked to Buñuel's advantage. The film, edited in Paris, was not completed until five days prior to the opening of the Festival. It was too short a time for a copy to go to Madrid for inspection, and was sent directly to Cannes. On the day of the awards, the film was denounced by the Vatican and by the Spanish authorities.

'La Notte' finds favor at Berlin Festival

Berlin, 5 July
Michelangelo Antonioni's newest film, *La Notte* (*The Night*), has won the Golden Bear at the Berlin Film Festival. The film concentrates on 24 hours in the life of a Milanese novelist (Marcello Mastroianni) and his wife (Jeanne Moreau), during which they visit a dying friend in the hospital, go to a nightclub, meet a rich industrialist's daughter (Monica Vitti) at a party, and face the emptiness of their lives and marriage. Following *L'Avventura*, the director further explores an alienated couple placed in an unresponsive environment. Here, the background is the cold beauty of Milan's modern architecture, and the streets through which Moreau wanders despondently at one point – the best sequence in an impressive film.

'ernando Rey and Silvia Pinal in a scene from Luis Buñuel's **Viridiana**.

Marcello Mastroianni in the midst of severe marital crisis in Antonioni's ***La Notte****, seeks solace away from wife (Moreau) and mistress (Vitti).*

Moral issues come in the guise of a thriller

Dirk Bogarde, the barrister with a dark past, and wife Sylvia Syms, in ***Victim.***

London, 1 September
Dirk Bogarde has decided to cast aside his matinee idol image to play a homosexual barrister in *Victim*, directed by Basil Dearden. He faces ruin when a young man with whom he has been having an affair hangs himself in a police cell. His death drives Bogarde to expose a ring of blackmailers who exploit the fact that homosexuality remains a serious criminal offense. In the process Bogarde discovers that the victims range from an elderly hairdresser to an aristocratic member of his own gentleman's club. This is a brave film which draws an even braver performance from Bogarde, who has finally tired of the comedy, war and costume films he has been making for the last 10 years. He receives solid support from Sylvia Syms as the wife who has to come to terms with her husband's secret life.

Provocative love triangle in fashion worl

Marie Laforêt (left) and Françoise Prévost in ***The Girl With the Golden Ey***

Paris, 1 September
Thirty-year-old Jean-Gabriel Albicocco seems to have scored a great success with his first feature, *The Girl With the Golden Eyes*, starring his attractive wife, Marie Laforêt, in the title role. An updated adaptation of Balzac's *The Story of the Thirteen*, this stylish, stylized and provocative film is set in and around the Paris fashion houses of the 1960s. A man (Paul Guers) who is working in the world of *haute couture* falls for girl (Laforêt) of whom he know nothing, not even her name. He e lists the aid of a powerful group men known as "The Thirteen", ar soon discovers that she is the lov of a female colleague (Françoi Prévost). He becomes a threat their lesbian relationship, and t tale ends with a powerful crime passion, when one of the wome fatally stabs the other.

Ravishing Anna Karina stars in Jean-Luc Godard's ménage à trois

Paris, 6 September
Jean-Luc Godard's third picture, *A Woman is a Woman*, features his wife of a few months, the Danish actress Anna Karina, who was in Godard's previous film, *The Little Soldier*, which the French government has banned. Now most audiences will be getting a first glimpse of the ravishing Karina, who plays a nightclub stripper. She wants a baby by her lover (Jean-Claude Brialy), but when he refuses to oblige, she turns to his best friend (Jean-Paul Belmondo). Set mainly in a Paris apartment, Godard's first color film is a breezy homage to the spirit of MGM musicals. Jeanne Moreau appears briefly as herself.

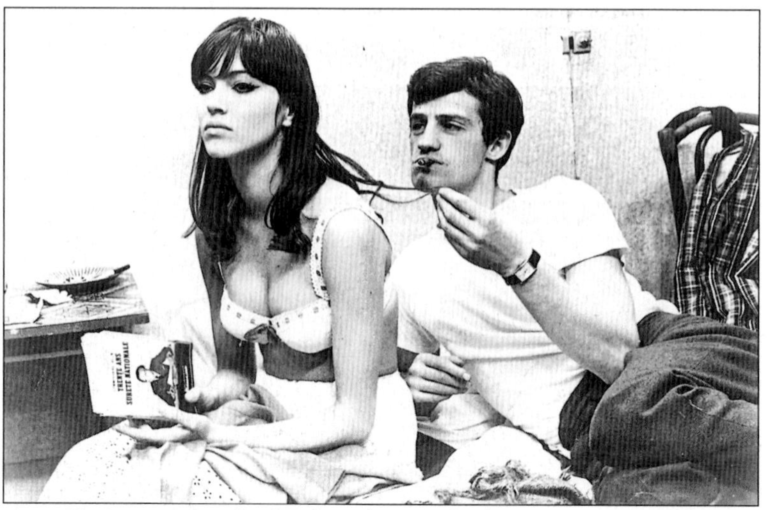

Anna Karina and Jean-Paul Belmondo in Godard's ***A Woman is a Woman.***

The contagious fait of priest Belmondo

Paris, 22 September
Jean-Pierre Melville's latest fil *Léon Morin, Priest*, originally ra over three hours, but the direct himself decided to reduce it to 1 minutes. Adapted from the novel b Béatrix Beck, the film is set in rur France during the German Occup tion, where a young atheist wido (Emmanuelle Riva) falls in love wi a priest (Jean-Paul Belmondo), wh converts her to religion. Not as p ous as it sounds, Melville's quiet polemical film explores the huma character of the priest, played in surprisingly restrained and persu sive manner by Belmondo.

aul pools winning resources with Rossen

aul Newman (2nd left) is **The Hustler** and protégé of George C. Scott (center).

ew York, 25 September
aul Newman plays Fast Eddie Felon, the disenchanted drifter and ool-hall shark in Robert Rossen's *he Hustler*, a story about winners nd losers in the tough world of arathon games for high stakes. ast Eddie has his sights set on ackie Gleason's portly maestro, linnesota Fats, with whom Eddie as already had one disastrous enounter in New York, from which he had emerged both psychologically and physically battered. Nursed back to health by crippled alcoholic Piper Laurie and then taken up by the hardbitten professional gambler George C. Scott, Fast Eddie rediscovers his will to win and heads for a gripping climactic encounter with the Fat Man. Rossen's brilliant film reeks of the smoke and sweat of the dingy pool halls in which men like Fast Eddie hunt for fast bucks.

This Holly goes lightly in Capote adaptation

Holly Golightly (Audrey Hepburn) has difficulty waking up as 'cat' looks on.

New York, 5 October
Audrey Hepburn, who spent last year recovering from a miscarriage sustained while on location for *The Unforgiven*, and has subsequently given birth to a baby son, is back on the screens from today in *Breakfast at Tiffany's*. From director Blake Edwards, this rather sanitized adaptation of Truman Capote's novella has not, reportedly, met with the writer's approval. Certainly, it is true that his off-beat heroine, Holly Golightly, was hardly the innocent she becomes in the hands of Miss Hepburn. Capote's hooker is now just a crazy kook, looking to marry a millionaire, who captivates George Peppard's struggling novelist in the upstairs apartment. That said, Audrey makes Holly her own, transcending the screenplay's bland ambiguities, and entrancing with her own special brand of vulnerabilty.

he MPAA code noves with times

ew York, 3 October
he gradual liberalizing of the proviions of the Hollywood Production ode – first spelled out in 1930 and trictly enforced since 1934 – connues apace. The MPAA has just nnounced that the strict ban on epicting sexual "perversions" such s homosexuality or lesbianism has ow been lifted to allow discreet or asteful treatment of such themes. hus, a Code seal can be granted to wo major new films which have not et been released, Otto Preminger's *dvise and Consent* and William Vyler's *The Children's Hour*, adaptd from Lillian Hellman's play.

Natalie Wood, Warren Beatty excel in drama of adolescent love

Natalie Wood and Warren Beatty, young lovers of ***Splendor in the Grass****.*

Hollywood, 11 October
Critics are already parading Warren Beatty as the new James Dean after his debut performance opposite Natalie Wood in Elia Kazan's *Splendor in the Grass*. They play a pair of teenage lovers in 1920s Kansas, torn apart by parental disapproval. For a newcomer, Beatty received the exceptionally high fee of $200,000. Born in Richmond, Virginia, in 1937, Beatty is the younger brother, by three years, of Shirley MacLaine. He made his acting way in TV before appearing on Broadway in *A Loss of Roses* by William Inge, who wrote the screenplay for *Splendor in the Grass*. Beatty now has a contract for several more films with Kazan. ▷

Music, dance and tragedy colors NY's West Side

George Chakiris (center) is Bernardo, the leader of the Puerto Rican Sharks.

Hollywood, 19 October
Leonard Bernstein's 1957 landmark Broadway musical, *West Side Story*, has now been made into a dynamic film. The director Robert Wise has transformed the essentially theatrical mixture of opera, ballet, musical comedy and social drama into cinematically pleasing entertainment that has been shot in Technicolor and Ultra Panavision 70. As in the theater, however, it is the choreography of Jerome Robbins, who receives co-director credit, and the vigorous dancing that dominate the movie. The picture opens with a helicopter shot of Manhattan, the camera zooming in on the finger-snapping American-born youths of the Jets, the sworn enemies of the Sharks, a Puerto Rican gang. They then dance balletically through the streets, actually filmed on location on West 64th Street. Maria and Tony, the star-crossed lovers from opposing factions in this updating of Shakespeare's *Romeo and Juliet*, are sympathetically played by Natalie Wood and Richard Beymer, though their singing voices are dubbed. When they meet for the first time at the gymnasium hop, the lights di and they only have eyes for ea other, just like their illustrious Ver nese models. The lyrics of Steph Sondheim come over brilliantly the two humorous numbers, "Ge Officer Krupke" and "America the latter danced and sung wi panache by Rita Moreno, Geor Chakiris and chorus on the roof a building. The melodious balcon duet, "Tonight", that is sung by t sweethearts, concludes with an u expected cut to the truculent voic

Natalie Wood and Richard Beyme

of the gang, and the lovers' idy "One Hand, One Heart", is the violently shattered by a reprise "Tonight". The "rumble" or gan battle is galvanically shot, with th fighting youngsters eventually fle ing the cops in a lightning series tilted, low-angle shots.

A great deal of the film was sh in parts of New York City current in the process of demolition, in ad dition to the 35 sets that were co structed in the studio. The shootin took six months, with no less tha five weeks for the exteriors. Interes ingly, Irene Sharaff's costumes fo the denizens of the New York slum cost a great deal. The boys' blu jeans were dyed, redyed and the "distressed" to appear worn, an specially woven with elastic threa to allow for violent movement. Th was especially necessary, becaus the dances are among the most ene getic ever seen in the cinema. *We Side Story* is also one of the fe Hollywood musicals which contain elements of social consciousnes particularly the theme of racism ending with the murder of the her as a tragic consequence.

'A Soldier's Prayer' completes nine hours of Kobayashi trilogy

Tokyo, 20 November
The Human Condition, the overall title for Masaki Kobayashi's impressive, ambitious and harrowing war trilogy, begun with *No Greater Love* in 1958, then *Road to Eternity* the following year, has come to its conclusion with *A Soldier's Prayer*. It continues the story of the pacifist Kaji (Tatsuya Nakadai) who, having been interned in a labor camp after the defeat of Japan in World War II, makes his escape in the snow to get back to his wife (Michiyo Aratama). Director Kobayashi has managed to convey the humanistic message of Jumpei Gomikawa's monumental novel through an almost documentary-like visual treatment, while not neglecting the wider symbolism of the story. The trilogy deals with Japanese war guilt, imperialism, fascism, militarism and, above all, the cruelty that human beings are capable of inflicting upon one another in the name of ideology. The nine hours of *The Human Condition* make for an unforgettable experience.

Tatsuya Nakadai and Michiyo Aratama in Kobayashi's ***The Human Condition****.*

asolini journeys beyond sordid reality

catone, with Franco Citti, Pasolini's first film adapted from his own novel.

ome, 23 November
er Paolo Pasolini, already a well-own novelist, poet, short-story iter and scenarist, has at last ade his first feature as a director the age of 39. *Accatone* is based his 1959 novel, in which he drew his intimate knowledge of sub-oletarian Rome. Accatone is a ung pimp from the slums, who takes to thieving after trying to earn an honest living. The film is a brutal and unsentimental view of disillusioned youth, with a cast of non-professionals led by Franco Citti. He plays Accatone with a mixture of lethargy and vigor, seeking no sympathy. The use of Bach on the soundtrack ironically counterpoints the sordid world the film portrays.

Cagney and Coca-Cola a potent comic mix

James Cagney and Lilo Pulver in Billy Wilder's satirical ***One, Two, Three.***

Los Angeles, 15 December
In Billy Wilder's new comedy, *One Two, Three*, James Cagney demonstrates that he has dissipated none of the demonic energy that has driven his long film career. He plays C.R. MacNamara, a Coca-Cola executive in Berlin who fizzes over when his boss' visiting daughter secretly weds a Communist. Wilder and I.A.L. Diamond's script, inspired by a one-act Molnar play, sprays satirical machine-gun bursts in all directions, lambasting Communists and capitalists alike. A hardworking supporting cast includes Horst Buchholz, Pamela Tiffin, Red Buttons and Hubert von Meyerinck as the gloriously named Count von Droste-Schattenberg, a lavatory attendant.

ilmmaker is in he news again

ome, 18 November
he accusation of delinquency is ot confined to urban small-time riminals. The writer and director ier Paolo Pasolini has just been rrested for attacking a petrol ttendant, in order to steal 2,000 ra from him. The crime cannot e excused as an error of youth. asolini is not a teenager nor is he product of a deprived environ-nent. Born in Bologna in 1922, descendant of aristocrats, he is he son of a professional soldier. Ie discovered very young that he ad a talent for writing, and his oems have gained the admira-ion of Alberto Moravia. In three lays time, Pasolini's first film as lirector, *Accatone*, will be shown o the general public. This work vill certainly attract a lot of atten-ion and has already aroused the atred of the neo-fascists. The lirector is a committed Marxist.

Epic account of 11th-century Spanish hero stars Charlton Heston

New York, 15 December
In order to make *El Cid* effective as a grandiose historic fresco, producer Samuel Bronston placed vast resources at the disposal of director Anthony Mann: more than 7,000 extras, a battle fleet of 35 sailing ships, monumental sets and a number of international stars. Bronston also lavished $150,000 on medieval objects and $40,000 on jewelry. As a result, *El Cid* is a magnificent looking spectacle, with fine photography by Robert Krasker, and superbly staged battle scenes by second unit director Yakima Canutt. To guarantee historical accuracy, the Spanish historian Don Ramon Menendez Pidal was used as consultant to the screenwriters Philip Yordan and Fredric M. Frank, and to art directors Veniero Colesanti and John Moore. Mostly shot in Spain, the epic 11th-century tale tells of the legendary Rodrigo Diaz de Bivar, known as El Cid, who drove the Moors from Spain. Charlton Heston is at his stoical heroic best in the title role, while Sophia Loren is alluring as Chimene, his fiancee. Anthony Mann chased the Italian actress all over Rome to get her to agree to portray the Spanish noblewoman, a role she had turned down twice, saying, "I just don't see myself in the part." Luckily, she was persuaded, as were Raf Vallone and Genevieve Page in supporting roles. ▷

Sophia Loren and Raf Vallone (left) with Charlton Heston (right) as El Cid.

Un film di
Michelangelo Antonioni
LA NOTTE
con
Marcello Mastroianni
Jeanne Moreau
Maria Pia Luzi
Rosy Mazzacurati
Monica Vitti
e
Bernhard Wicki
DINO DE LAURENTIIS
CINEMATOGRAFICA DISTRIBUZIONE SPA

The Italian poster for Italy's ***La Notte (The Night)****, Michelangelo Antonioni's bleak and brilliant follow-up to* ***L'Avventura****.*

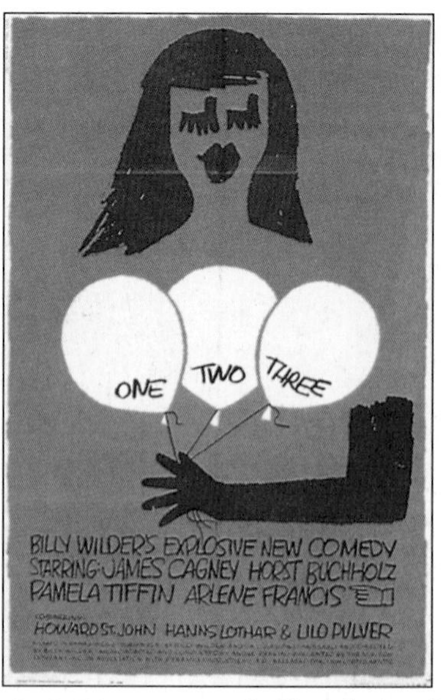
ONE TWO THREE
BILLY WILDER'S EXPLOSIVE NEW COMEDY
STARRING JAMES CAGNEY HORST BUCHHOLZ
PAMELA TIFFIN ARLENE FRANCIS
HOWARD ST. JOHN HANNS LOTHAR & LILO PULVER

Saul Bass, unmistakably, designed the witty poster for Wilder's film.

The Hustler*: 'Fast' Eddy Felson (Pa Newman) shoots; George C. Scott*

FEDERICO FELLINI'S
LA DOLCE VITA
THE SWEET LIFE
MARCELLO MASTROIANNI ✱ ANITA EKBERG
ANOUK AIMEE • YVONNE FURNEAUX • ALAIN CUNY • ANNIBALE NINCHI • WALTER SANTESSO AND MAGALI NOEL ✱ LEX BARKER
JACQUES SERNAS AND WITH NADIA GRAY
TOTALSCOPE
A COLUMBIA PICTURES RELEASE

Federico Fellini's ***La Dolce Vita*** *(aka* ***The Sweet Life****) caused outrage in Ita and a sensation in the rest of the world.*

Corinne Marchand as Cléo in director Agnes Varda's ***Cléo From 5 to 7****.*

Lucyna Winnicka, Mieczyslaw Voit: ***The Devil and the Nun*** *(Poland).*

Jerry Lewis in ***The Errand Boy****; wrote, produced and directed it.*

A CITY TERRORISED BY IT'S OWN EVIL!
Herbert LOM
John GREGSON
Sean CONNERY
THE FRIGHTENED CITY
Alfred Marks · Yvonne Romain

iminal racketeering British-style s a successful formula.

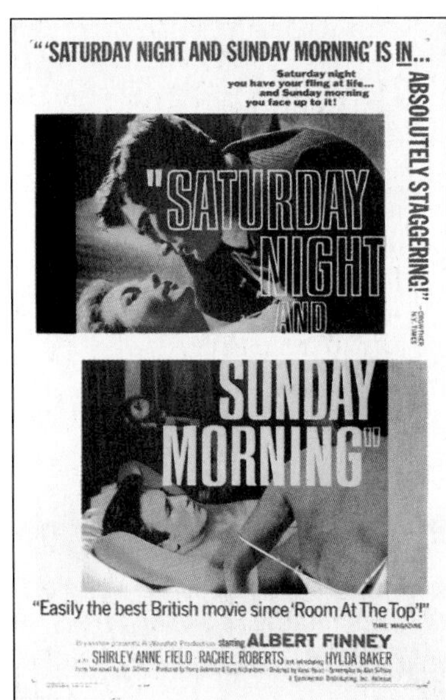
"'SATURDAY NIGHT AND SUNDAY MORNING' IS IN...
Saturday night you have your fling at life... and Sunday morning you face up to it!
ABSOLUTELY STAGGERING!"
"SATURDAY NIGHT AND SUNDAY MORNING"
"Easily the best British movie since 'Room At The Top'!"
ALBERT FINNEY
SHIRLEY ANNE FIELD RACHEL ROBERTS HYLDA BAKER

The American critics gave a seal of approval to last year's British hit.

m-m-m-m-Mylene's-m-m-m-m-Marvelous!
MYLENE
DEMONGEOT
MICHAEL
CRAIG
ANNE
HEYWOOD
JAMES ROBERTSON
JUSTICE
THE RANK ORGANIZATION presents
A BETTY E. BOX–RALPH THOMAS PRODUCTION
Upstairs and Downstairs
ALSO STARRING
SIDNEY JAMES
COLOR by DE LUXE
Screenplay by FRANK HARVEY Produced by BETTY E. BOX Directed by RALPH THOMAS

Lightweight but cheery British comedy about young marrieds and maids.

ownbeat but first-class British movie, ***A Taste of Honey****, with Murray Melvin d Rita Tushingham, again directed by Tony Richardson.*

eft to right: David Niven, Gregory Peck and Anthony Quinn in ***The Guns of avarone****, directed by J. Lee Thompson from Alistair Maclean's novel.*

From Italy this year came Pietro Germi's delightful satire, ***Divorce, Italian Style****, with Marcello Mastroianni and Daniela Rocca.*

1962

1961 Academy Awards, Santa Monica Civic Auditor., 9 Apr.	
Best Film:	*West Side Story* (dir: Robert Wise, Jerome Robbins)
Best Director:	Robert Wise and Jerome Robbins
Best Actor:	Maximilian Schell *(Judgment at Nuremberg)*
Best Actress:	Sophia Loren *(Two Women)*
Best Supp. Actor:	George Chakiris *(West Side Story)*
Best Supp. Actress:	Rita Moreno *(West Side Story)*

Prague, 2 January
Director Jiri Trnka has started filming *Kybernetika Babicka* (*Cybernetic Grandma*), a puppet film which deals with the problems associated with man's reaction to advances in technology.

Tokyo, 2 January
Release of Akira Kurosawa's film, *Tsubaki Sanjuro* (*Sanjuro*), which stars Toshiro Mifune. Eight young warriors and a wandering samurai take on a corrupt lord in this satirical historical "Eastern-Western".

Rome, 6 January
Renato Salvatori and Annie Girardot were married today. The two actors first met while filming *Rocco and his Brothers.*

Rome, 15 January
The producer Dino De Laurentiis has laid the foundation stone for the Dinocittà studio.

Los Angeles, 20 January
To allay rumors about a return to 20th Century-Fox, Darryl Zanuck has left the following memo: "I am not bitter, but I have reached the age... where I cannot spend my days with people I would not like to have dinner with..."

Paris, 27 January
In *le Monde*, François Truffaut is quoted as saying:"The thing which gives me the courage to keep going is that in the cinema industry one does not feel isolated. Solitude is one of the greatest problems facing other artists such as abstract painters and musicians."

Paris, 31 January
Opening of Louis Malle's latest film, *Vie privée* (*A Very Private Life*) co-starring Marcello Mastroianni and Brigitte Bardot. Critics have not failed to notice the similarity between Louis Malle's tragic heroine and the tribulations suffered in real life by Miss Bardot.

Paris, 5 February
The Empire cinema has reopened under the name Empire-Abel Gance, with a Cinerama film *la Grande rencontre*. Special homage was paid to Abel Gance's inventive genius during the opening speech.

Paris, 5 February
Roger Vadim is shooting the first scenes for his new film *le Repos du guerrier* in the Billancourt studios. It is his fourth film with his ex-wife, Brigitte Bardot, who is partnered by Robert Hossein, and likely to be his last as Bardot has said she intends to retire from the screen.

Milan, 22 February
Première of *Boccaccio '70*, a film of short vignettes, directed by Federico Fellini, Vittorio De Sica, Luchino Visconti and Mario Monicelli. The cast is headed by Romy Schneider, Sophia Loren, and Anita Ekberg.

Tunis, 2 March
The Tunisian Federation of ciné-clubs, which was created in 1950, has at last received official recognition. It now has the enviable status of a National Cultural Society.

Paris, 7 March
Release of *Cartouche*, directed by Philippe de Broca, with Jean-Paul Belmondo and Claudia Cardinale.

Sicily, 14 March
Burt Lancaster has hurt his leg and is unable to dance with Claudia Cardinale for the ball scene in *The Leopard* (*Il Gattopardo*). The scene, which called for 250 extras, as well as 120 wardrobe masters, makeup artists and hairdressers, has had to be postponed. Director Luchino Visconti is apparently furious.

New York, 20 March
The *New York Times* has announced that Grace Kelly, now Princess Grace of Monaco and retired from the screen, will return to star in Alfred Hitchcock's next film, *Marnie.*

Rome, 1 April
On location here for *Cleopatra*, stars Richard Burton and Elizabeth Taylor have been seen together frequently. Despite repeated denials from their agents, their liaison is now public knowledge. The press appears to be on the side of Sybil Burton and Taylor's husband, Eddie Fisher, the wronged parties.

Rome, 9 May
Federico Fellini has started filming *Eight and a Half* (*Otto e mezzo*) in the Cinecittà studios, with Marcello Mastroianni, Claudia Cardinale and Sandra Milo.

Paris, 25 May
The press has been showing a great deal of interest in the Tahitian liaison between Martine Carol and a young soldier named Jean-Marie Dallet, who is said to be one of Georges Pompidou's nephews.

Paris, 10 June
A quote from film critic Robert Benayoun in the magazine *Positif* – "Have you been abroad lately? There are two things other countries envy us for: De Gaulle and the *Nouvelle Vague* (*New Wave*)."

Paris, 13 August
Philippe Noiret has married Monique Chaumette. Both of them had worked at the National Theatre.

Los Angeles, 18 September
The Music Corporation of America (MCA) has taken over the Decca record company, the major shareholder in Universal.

Rome, 22 September
At the premiere of *Mama Roma*, in the Quattro Fontane Cinema, the film's director, Pier Paolo Pasolini, was attacked by members of fascist groups who had turned up to protest against the film.

Paris, 20 November
After three years of married life, Brigitte Bardot is divorcing Jacques Charrier. The couple's problems have been exacerbated by Brigitte's infatuation with Sammy Frey, her co-star in Henri-Georges Clouzot's *la Verité*. Charrier has been given the custody of their two-year-old son Nicholas, as Brigitte, who recently attempted suicide, feels incapable of taking on the responsibility.

Tokyo, 20 November
Yasujiro Ozu's latest film *Samma* *Aji* (*An Autumn Afternoon*) h opened in the capital.

Paris, 10 December
Issue no. 130 of *Cahiers du Ciném* is a special number devoted to t *Nouvelle Vague*, and includes a lo interview with Jean-Luc Godar According to the filmmaker: "T sincerity of the *Nouvelle Vague* essentially that it deals intelligent with things it knows about, rath than speaking badly of things knows nothing about."

California, 20 December
A real-estate firm has bought t Hal Roach studios in Culver Cit The studios were built in 1920 ar innumerable short comic films, i cluding all Laurel and Hardy's ear work, were made there.

BIRTHS

Los Angeles, 5 February
Jennifer Jason Leigh

New York, 21 March
Matthew Broderick

New York, 12 May
Emilio Estevez

New York, 3 July
Tom Cruise

New Mexico, 11 November
Demi Moore (Demi Guynes)

Los Angeles, 19 November
Jodie Foster

DEATHS

Hollywood, 10 April
Michael Curtiz

Hollywood, 19 June
Frank Borzage

Hollywood, 6 October
Tod Browning

California, 17 December
Thomas Mitchell

English director David Lean's dese epic on the life of T.E. Lawrence h revealed an unusual and charismat new star in Peter O'Toole. The film other star is undoubtedly the Sahar

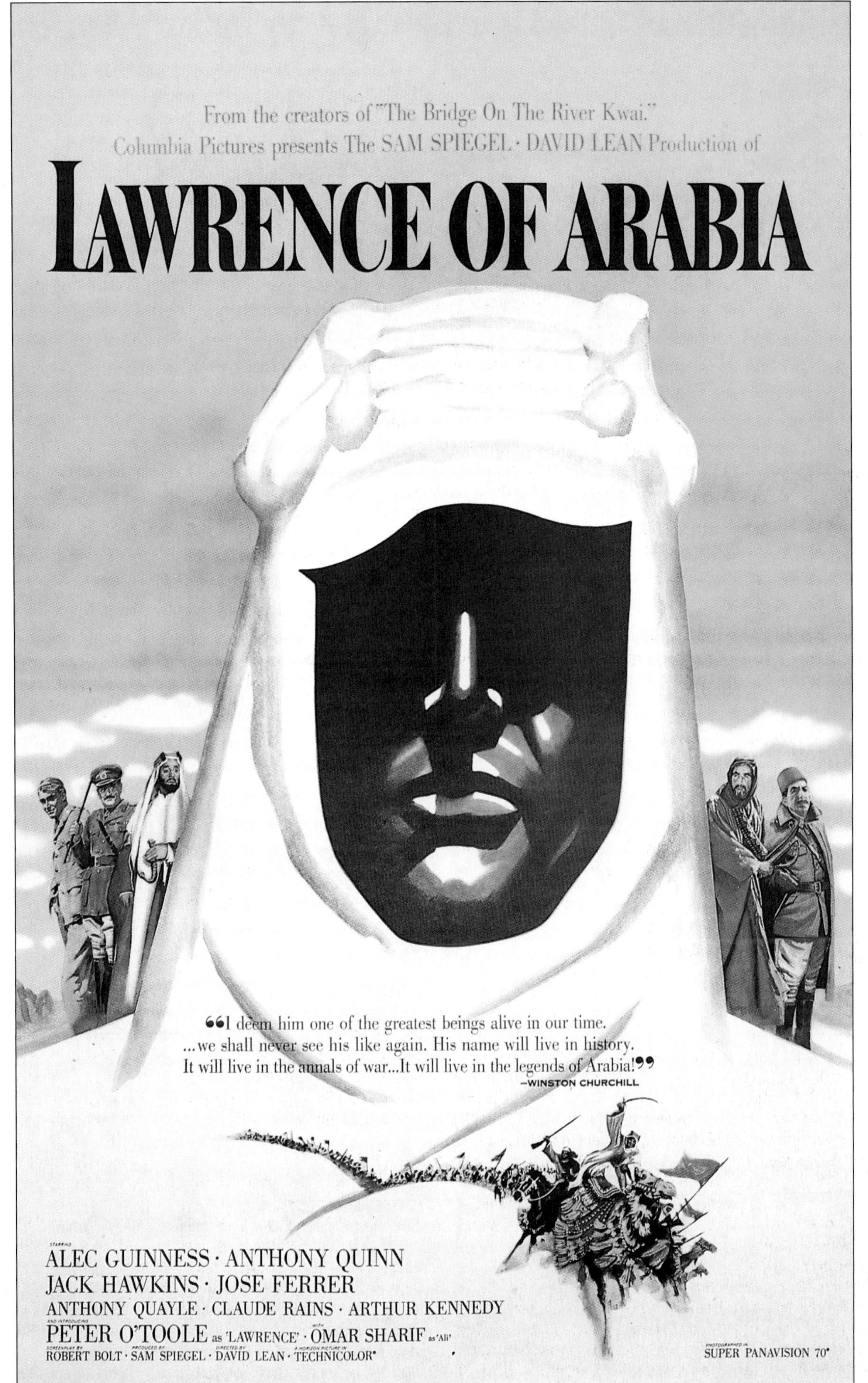
From the creators of "The Bridge On The River Kwai."
Columbia Pictures presents The SAM SPIEGEL · DAVID LEAN Production of
LAWRENCE OF ARABIA
"I deem him one of the greatest beings alive in our time.
...we shall never see his like again. His name will live in history.
It will live in the annals of war...It will live in the legends of Arabia!"
–WINSTON CHURCHILL
ALEC GUINNESS · ANTHONY QUINN
JACK HAWKINS · JOSE FERRER
ANTHONY QUAYLE · CLAUDE RAINS · ARTHUR KENNEDY
PETER O'TOOLE as 'LAWRENCE' · OMAR SHARIF as 'Ali'
ROBERT BOLT · SAM SPIEGEL · DAVID LEAN · TECHNICOLOR®
SUPER PANAVISION 70®

Jules, Jim and Catherine are bathed in a tender glow by Truffaut

Truffaut with Jeanne Moreau.

Catherine (Moreau) with Frenchman Jim (Henri Serre) in a somber moment.

Paris, 24 January
A *ménage à trois* is the subject of François Truffaut's new film, *Jules and Jim*, a story that might have been sordid in anyone else's hands. It tells of how close friends, the German Jules (Oskar Werner) and the Frenchman Jim (Henri Serre), both fall in love with Catherine (Jeanne Moreau). However, Jules marries her and takes her back to Germany. World War I separates the two friends even further, and when they meet again after hostilities, Catherine decides to change partners. Although Truffaut's invigorating tale of friendship and love is full of cinematic allusions, (one to Chaplin's *The Kid*), and is a homage to Jean Renoir, it is a unique piece of filmmaking. The director, while he remains true to Henri-Pierre Roché's first novel, employs a wide range of cinematic devices to express the shifting moods of the characters and plot, including both stills and newsreels. The three leads are delightful, and Jeanne Moreau's charming singing of "le Tourbillon" is a memorable moment. Truffaut came across the novel as long ago as 1953, and determined then to film it one day. It is a dream come true.

Germany's answer to the 'New Wave'

Oberhausen, 28 February
The annual festival of short films Oberhausen is always an exception event in the cinematographic cale dar. This year a manifesto was p sented, signed by 26 young Germ filmmakers. They are concern about the evolution of their cine and condemn its stultifying conf mity, typified by the *Sissi* series a *Heimatfilme* (rural films). Like t "angry young generation" of t British Free Cinema, and those the French New Wave, Herbert V ely, Alexander Kluge and others a trying to make themselves hea Their ambition is to create a n German cinema of full-length fil as interesting as the shorts sho here. This generation of directo has already presented many of short films to acclaim at other int national festivals. They now w to bring this "new cinematograph language" into features and are w ling to take economic risks. Herbe Vesely's *Das Brot der Fruhen Jah* (*Bread of Youth*) is representative this New German Cinema.

'West Side Story' dances off with ten Oscars

Hollywood, 9 April
The Academy Awards ceremony this year, once again presented by Bob Hope with the assistance of Ann-Margret, saw the triumph of *West Side Story*, directed by Robert Wise and Jerome Robbins. This film scooped ten Oscars, including Best Picture, Best Director and both Best Supporting Actor and Actress, the last two awards being handed, respectively, to George Chakiris and Rita Moreno. The Best Actor award went to Maximilian Schell for his strong performance as the defense attorney in *Judgment at Nuremberg*. Sophia Loren was voted Best Actress for *Two Women*.

Spencer Tracy and Marlene Dietrich in Kramer's **Judgment at Nuremberg**.

Cléo sees her life flash past in two hours

Corinne Marchand and Jose Luis de Villalonga in Varda's **Cléo From 5 to**

Paris, 11 April
Two hours in the life of a superstitious young nightclub singer (played by the beautiful ex-model Corinne Marchand) as she waits for the medical verdict on whether she will live or die, is the subject of the new film from Agnes Varda, *Cléo From 5 7*. The director has managed to ca ture Paris as seen through the ey of the heroine, where every trivi incident takes on new significanc Part of the film's originality is th the story unfolds in real time.

ayne and Stewart, old comrades-in-arms

ames Stewart (center) and John Wayne, two old-timers reunited in the West.

an Francisco, 11 April
ohn Ford's newest Western, *The Man Who Shot Liberty Valance*, explores the transformation of the frontier from wilderness to garden and the myths on which the process of civilization depend. James Stewart is Ransom Stoddart, the bookish eastern lawyer who becomes a hero, and a senator, when he confronts and kills the brutal gunslinger of the title, played by Lee Marvin. But his belated confession that Valance was shot by John Wayne's Tom Doniphon, symbol of the Old West, is dismissed by a newspaper editor who comments, "when the legend becomes fact, print the legend."

Peck and Mitchum: a fight to the death

Robert Mitchum, Gregory Peck struggle for survival in a terrifying sequence.

Florida, 12 April
Robert Mitchum is at his most powerfully malevolent as Max Cady, the vengeful, cigar-chomping ex-con stalking upright Florida attorney Gregory Peck and his family in *Cape Fear*, directed by Britain's J. Lee Thompson. Mitchum's attentions soon move from poisoning the family dog to sexually asssaulting Peck's teenage daughter Lori Martin. Finally the desperate Peck uses Martin and wife Polly Bergen as bait in a trap he sets for Mitchum in the steamy mangrove swamps of the Everglades. Not since *The Night of the Hunter* has Mitchum reveled in such rich villainy.

British realism colors 'A Kind of Loving'

ondon, 21 May
A Kind of Loving, director John Schlesinger focuses on the kind of smoky, northern industrial environment which is rapidly becoming a cliché of British cinema. The film stars Alan Bates and June Ritchie as a young couple forced to marry when Ritchie becomes pregnant. Schlesinger explores the landscape of their lives, both interior and exterior, with some sensitivity, but the feeling remains that they are representatives of a particular kind of social thinking rather than living, breathing people.

une Ritchie and Alan Bates, a bleak union in John Schlesinger's film.

Chinese women of war win coveted prize

Peking, 22 May
The magazine *Popular Cinema* has just created the One Hundred Flower prize, chosen by a poll of its readers. The first winner is *Detachment of Women*, directed by Xie Jin last year. Born in 1923, the director is already well-known, with *Basketball Player No. 5* being among his successes. His latest film takes place on the island of Hainan in 1930, where the Communist guerillas consist solely of women. The stirring story along with the engaging presence of the young Zhu Xijuan, has enchanted the public.

Zhu Xijuan in Xie Jin's award-winning Chinese film ***Detachment of Women.***

Antonioni and Bresson share in triumph

*Alain Delon, Monica Vitti in Special Jury prizewinner **The Eclipse**.*

Cannes, 25 May
Without taking into consideration the negative reactions of the public to both Robert Bresson's *The Trial of Joan of Arc* and Michelangelo Antonioni's *The Eclipse*, the films shared the Special Jury Prize. Neither could be called crowd pleasers. Bresson's austere work was drawn from the actual transcripts of the trial of Joan, played by Florence Carrez, a non-professional actress. *The Eclipse* completes Antonioni's trilogy of alienation, and dwells on the emptiness of modern life. To everybody's surprise, the Golden Palm went to *The Given Word*, a Brazilian film by Anselmo Duarte.

Political potboiler casts pall on U.S. Senate

New York, 6 June
The wheelers and dealers of Washington come under the skeptical scrutiny of Otto Preminger in his new film, *Advise and Consent*, adapted from a novel by Allen Drury. For the task he has drawn together a superb cast: Franchot Tone as the dying president; Lew Ayres as the disarmingly youthful vice president who succeeds him; Henry Fonda as a presidential candidate; and Don Murray and Charles Laughton as senators – the former tortured by his homosexuality and the latter in flamboyant form as a wily Southern fixer. Sadly it was Laughton's last performance. He died of cancer in a Hollywood hospital on 15 December last year, at the age of 63.

*Charles Laughton (left) and Walter Pidgeon appear in **Advise and Consent**.*

Teenage temptress Lolita arrives on scree

*James Mason and Sue Lyon in Kubrick's **Lolita** from the novel by Naboko*

New York, 13 June
"How Could They Make a Movie of *Lolita*?" the ads for Stanley Kubrick's latest film demand. Well, the answer must be, they have – up to a point. A significant difference between Vladimir Nabokov's screenplay and his bestselling novel is that the age of the nymphet in the book has been raised into the teens to make it more acceptable to movie audiences, thereby changing Humbert Humbert's "perverse passion" into something less shocking. This alteration, and the reduction of the American landscape's importance in the novel (the picture was shot in England) still does not diminish the impact of this acerbic tragi-comedy. Apart from the obvious differences between the novel and the film, the story is basically the same. Humbert Humbert (James Mason), a middle-aged professor of French literatu in New Hampshire, rents a roo for the summer in the house Charlotte Haze (Shelley Winters), snobbish widow whose 14-year-o daughter Lolita (Sue Lyon) he fin irresistibly attractive. He marries t mother to be closer to the daughte and Charlotte dies in a freak ac dent shortly after learning the trut Humbert takes the girl on a long c trip, but is dogged all the way mysterious writer Clare Quilty (P ter Sellers). Both Mason and Selle play their off-beat roles to perfe tion, and Shelley Winters touching and humorously suggests emotion starvation and middlebrow prete tions. Sixteen-year-old Sue Lyon, her first film, wonderfully catch Lolita's blend of gum-chewing vu garity and quivering animal tende ness and sensuality.

Jean Gabin meets his alter ego

Paris, 11 May
Two great French actors, each from a different generation, have come face to face in Henri Verneuil's film *A Monkey in Winter* (*Un singe en hiver*): Jean Gabin from the Golden Age of prewar French cinema and Jean-Paul Belmondo, the darling of the New Wave. In the course of making the film, set in Normandy in 1944, the two stars struck up a friendship. At one stage, Gabin told Belmondo, "Kid, you're me at 20."

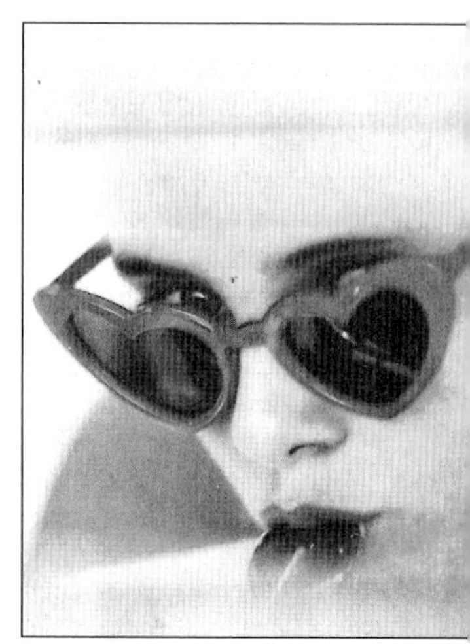

Sue Lyon: a junior femme fatale.

The final crack-up in Marilyn Monroe's life

s Angeles, 6 August
arilyn Monroe has been found ad in her bed this morning in her entwood house on the west side of s Angeles. The autopsy revealed t she had succumbed to a massive se of sleeping pills. If it was a case suicide, then numerous reasons uld be given for it: a loveless and ofoundly unhappy childhood; a entally unstable mother and an known father; three failed mar-ges; two miscarriages; a number unfulfilled romances; constant essure from the press; and profes-nal difficulties due to a loss of nfidence in herself... In fact, very le had gone well for her since bruary 1961, after her divorce m Arthur Miller. It was then that Marilyn entered a psychiatric clinic, fearful that she might suffer insanity as her mother before her.

Marilyn returned to work last April to begin shooting on her 29th movie, *Something's Got to Give*, directed by George Cukor, and with Dean Martin and Cyd Charisse as co-stars. One of her last public appearances was at Madison Square Garden in New York on 21 May. Dressed in a clinging, flesh-colored, sequined dress, she sang "Happy Birthday" to President Kennedy. Production on the film was interrupted soon after. Marilyn, who was said to be ill, seldom turned up on the set, forcing the director to shoot as much as he could around her. The studio (20th Century-Fox) began to look for a replacement, but Dean Martin, a friend of hers, threatened to quit the film if Marilyn went. She came back for a day's shooting at his instigation, but then disappeared again. This time Fox started proceedings against the star, reclaiming $750,000 from her for breach of contract. Marilyn sent a letter to the film team which read, "Please believe me, I did not do it without good cause. I would have loved to have worked with you." Just three months later, she was dead, leaving no message that would explain her final gesture. "Marilyn was the most frightened little girl," Joseph L. Mankiewicz had once commented. "And yet scared as she was, she had this strange effect when she was photographed... In fact, the camera loved her."

How to Marry a Millionaire.

Marilyn's bedroom, the scene of her tragic, premature and mysterious end.

Crowds gathered for the star's funeral held at Westwood Memorial Park.

arryl F. Zanuck takes the reins at Fox

ollywood, 29 August
arryl F. Zanuck has just been apointed as the new president of 20th entury-Fox. This comes six years ter he relinquished his post as that udio's vice president in charge of oduction in favor of a new career an independent in Europe, proucing films such as *The Sun Also ises* (1957), *The Roots of Heaven* 958) and completed this year, *The ongest Day*. Unfortunately, Fox erformed badly under departing esident Spyros P. Skouras, and s recorded huge losses during the st three years, only managing to rvive by selling off 260 acres of its back lot. The situation has become increasingly desperate during the past year, with the costs of *Cleopatra* climbing over $30 million to make it by far the most expensive movie ever made; while the Marilyn Monroe film, *Something's Got to Give*, abandoned midway through production, involved around $2 million in cost write-offs. On his taking over, Zanuck immediately shut down the studio and dismissed most employees in order to cut costs and gain some breathing space before the release of both *The Longest Day* and *Cleopatra*, films which should replenish the company offers.

Honors for Italy and the USSR at Venice

Venice, 8 September
At this year's Mostra the jury found it impossible to decide which of two films merited the Golden Lion. They resolved this problem by giving it both to Andrei Tarkovsky's *Ivan's Childhood* and to Valerio Zurlini's *Family Diary* (*Cronaca Familiare*). The choice shows that they went for emotion rather than pyrotechnics. The Soviet film tells of the adventures of 12-year-old Ivan, whose family is wiped out by the Nazis. Hell-bent on revenge, he joins a detachment of Partisans who are able to use his size and agility for intelligence purposes. It concludes that "childhood is made to love, and not for combat." The 30-year-old Tarkovsky's feature debut shows a rich pictorial sense, especially in the lyrical black-and-white landscapes. Also beautiful to look at is *Family Diary*, with Zurlini using color to evoke the Impressionists. It is a melancholy tale of two brothers, newspaperman Enrico (Marcello Mastroianni) and Lorenzo (Jacques Perrin), separated in childhood, but later brought together in a close and loving relationship. The film takes the form of flashback reminiscences of Enrico following the death of the younger Lorenzo from an incurable disease. ▷

Zanuck's all-star cast disembarks for longest da

Paris, 10 October
Producer Darryl F. Zanuck, who for several years has been operating as an independent based in France, has become a five-star general for *The Longest Day*, fighting the Normandy invasion all over again with a budget of $10 million, 50 international stars, 10,000 extras, 48 technical advisors and dozens of locations. No black-and-white movie has ever cost as much. Three directors were assigned to the picture – Ken Annakin, Andrew Marton and Bernhard Wicki – but there was never any doubt about who was in charge. Darting from location to location in a helicopter, the cigar-chewing Zanuck declared, "This is my picture. When one wants to take the credit for something one must also take the responsibility. I don't mind the hard work. There is plenty of compensation in the pride one can feel when it's all over." These are the words of a producer who had not had too much success lately as an independent. Carried along with Zanuck in this great executive assault on the events of 6 June 1944 are John Wayne, Rod Steiger, Robert Ryan, Henry Fonda, Richard Burton, Eddie Albert, Curt Jurgens, Peter Lawford, Gert Frobe, Robert Wagner, Sal Mineo, Richard Beymer, Richard Todd and a host of others. It must all seem very familiar to Todd who, as a paratrooper, actually took part in Overlord. The film has been adapted by Cornelius Ryan from his best-selling book, and looks at the titanic events of D-Day from nearly every viewpoint, including that of the Germans. And a healthy measure of authenticity h been achieved by the decision to low the characters to speak in th own languages, with subtitles. T result receives its world premi today. Zanuck has succeeded in own longest day, a triumph of ci matic logistics.

The Longest Day *happened on 6 June 1944. Robert Mitchum leads his men.*

Curt Jurgens (left), the German si

Anna Karina is Jean-Luc Godard's muse

Paris, 22 September
After winning the Special Jury Prize at the recent Venice Film Festival, Jean-Luc Godard's fourth feature, *My Life to Live* (*Vivre sa vie*), has just opened in Paris. It is the story (told in 12 chapters) of Nana S., a girl from the provinces, who gets a badly-paid job in a record shop in Paris. Then when she finds herself unable to pay the rent, she is gradually initiated into prostitution, finally becoming experienced. Using interview techniques, direct sound, long takes, texts, quotations and statistics, Godard has given this probing and dazzling examination of prostitution a documentary tone. Godard's screenplay was inspired by a survey carried out by Marcel Sacotte on the current state of prostitution in France, extracts of which are read out by Saddy Rebot, who plays a pimp. The philosopher Brice Parain also makes an appearance in which he reflects on the heroine's actions. Above all, however, the film is a passionate cinematic love letter to his wife Anna Karina, who plays Nana. Close-ups of her remind one of Louise Brooks and Lillian Gish as well as Falconetti, the latter tearfully watched by Karina in Carl Dreyer's *The Passion of Joan of Arc*. The star has become, more than ever, Godard's muse.

VARIETES
RECORD
DANNY

Anna Karina in ***My Life to Live****.*

Sean Connery a very special agent 007

London, 1 October
The current Cuban missile crisis has provided a real-life backdrop to the screen debut of Ian Fleming's secret agent James Bond in *Dr. No*, produced by Harry Saltzman and Cubby Broccoli. Sean Connery takes the part of agent 007, licensed to kill. His combination of physical gra classless Scots burr and hint sadism fleshes out the perfect fa tasy spy, thwarting the eponymo villain's dreams of world domi tion and wryly watching Ursula A dress' Honey Rider rise glisteni from the sea.

Switzerland's Ursula Andress and Scotland's Sean Connery star in ***Dr. No****.*

'The Manchurian Candidate' is, simply, brilliant

New York, 23 October
"More and more I think our society is being manipulated and controlled." These words come from director John Frankenheimer whose latest screen effort, *The Manchurian Candidate*, plunges into the world of brainwashing, political extremism and the murky machinations of the Cold War. Adapted by George Axelrod from Richard Condon's best-selling novel, this movie stars Laurence Harvey as a returning Korean War hero who is not all he seems. "Why do you always have to look as if your head were about to come to a point?" asks his mother Angela Lansbury. But his zombie-like behavior is understandable. Harvey was brainwashed while a prisoner of the Communists in North Korea. Now Lansbury and her husband, a rabidly McCarthyite senator, are using their son to carry out a series of assassinations in America for their own nefarious purposes. Total disaster is averted by wartime buddy Frank Sinatra in a stunning set piece staged at a convention in Madison Square Garden. Unfazed by Frankenheimer's feverish direction, Angela Lansbury delivers a superb performance as the most monstrous of mothers. In reality she is only three years older than her screen son, but she looks more interested in life than the pointy-headed Harvey.

Brainwashed: Laurence Harvey.

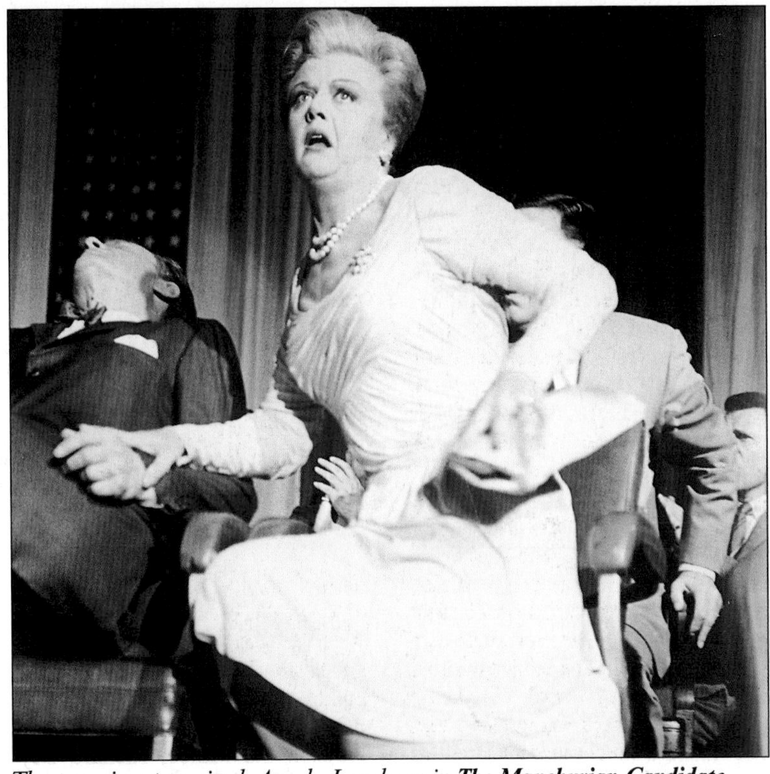
The terrorizer terrorized: Angela Lansbury in ***The Manchurian Candidate***.

See 'Gypsy' and have 'a real good time'

New York, 1 November
The long-running Broadway hit musical *Gypsy* comes to the screen with its virtues intact, despite losing the unique Ethel Merman in favor of Rosalind Russell. The memorable score by Jule Styne, with lyrics to match from Stephen Sondheim and a great libretto, lights up this enthralling real-life tale that charts the childhood, adolescence and subsequent career of stripper Gypsy Rose Lee. Natalie Wood excels in the role, as does Russell playing Rose, Gypsy's brash, dominating show-biz mom, at the center of things.

EXIT
Rose's turn: Rosalind Russell (left), and Natalie Wood in the title role in ***Gypsy***.

Three directors win the West in Cinerama

London, 1 November
The dramatic possibilities of Cinerama are showcased in *How the West Was Won*, an episodic history of the opening up of the American frontier directed by Henry Hathaway, John Ford and George Marshall. This film opens with the exploits of mountain man James Stewart and closes with a train robbery. Along the way the three-camera system, projected on to a huge screen, provides some breathtakingly spectacular action that includes a buffalo stampede, shooting the rapids and an Indian attack on a wagon train.

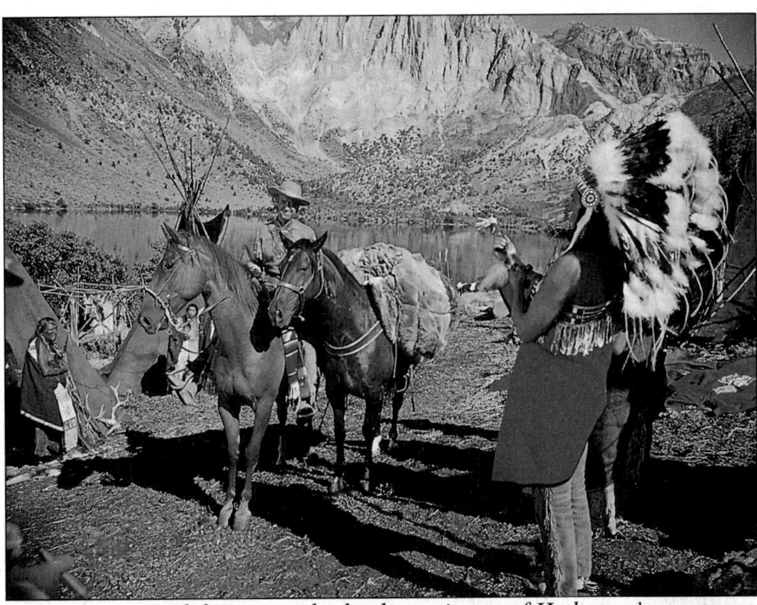
James Stewart and the spectacular landscape in one of Hathaway's sequences. ▷

Bette and Joan in gothick horror melo

New York, 6 November
Director Robert Aldrich has given Bette Davis and Joan Crawford a bizarre new lease on life in *What Ever Happened to Baby Jane?*, an extraordinary extension of the sado-masochistic elements that have been running through their film careers, in which they play two elderly sisters trapped in the past. Davis was the child star of the title until Crawford became a leading lady and elbowed her out of the spotlight. Now the studio lights have been switched off for both of them, and they occupy a shuttered mansion, Crawford in a wheelchair, drink-sodden Davis gleefully serving her rats for dinner. There's heavyweight support from 300-pound newcomer Victor Buono and Aldrich works all the organ stops on this bit of sub-Gothic horror. It's ironic that rivals Crawford and Davis should join forces at Warners, scene of their 1940s triumphs.

Joan Crawford and Bette Davis.

Marlon Brando plays Fletcher Christian

New York, 9 November
Marlon Brando has made a spirited but wayward attempt to reinvent an English version of Clark Gable in *Mutiny on the Bounty*. In the 1935 film, Gable and Charles Laughton were the mutinous Fletcher Christian and the martinet Captain Bligh; now Brando co-stars with Trevor Howard and a replica of the original *Bounty* which gobbled up a sizeable chunk of the $19.5 million budget.

Marlon Brando (left) as Fletcher Christian and Trevor Howard as Captain Bligh in Lewis Milestone's remake of ***Mutiny on the Bounty****.*

Huston, Freud and the country of the mi[nd]

Hollywood, 13 December
Among the many biopics that have come out of Hollywood over the years, the latest one, John Huston's *Freud*, is one of the most successful. Originally, the director had asked Jean-Paul Sartre to write the screenplay, but the French philosopher and writer delivered a script that would have entailed a film of 16 hours running time. Though Huston found it unusable, he went to work on it with screenwriter Charles Kaufman and producer Wolfgang Reinhardt, picking out some of Sartre's better ideas. The end result is a fascinating portrait of the father of psychoanalysis, seen from inside the profession, mixing real biographical elements with fictional ones. The picture begins with the 30-year-old Freud taking a leave of absence from his work in the General Hospital in Vienna to delve deeper into the causes of hysteria. His work with several patients, especially a woman with a father fixation, prompts him to begin writing his theories, which are derided by his peers. Montgomery Clift, though miscast in the title role, is able to suggest a world of meaning in his soulful eyes as he stumbles to formulate the Oedipus complex. Curiously enough, during the shooting, he had an operation to remove cataracts from both eyes. He was also suffering fro[m a] thyroid problem, and had difficu[lty] remembering his lines. Much [of] *Freud* was filmed in England, a[nd] Huston, with photographer Doug[las] Slocombe, has evoked the text[ure] of some of the famous painti[ngs] of the period.

Montgomery Clift plays Freud.

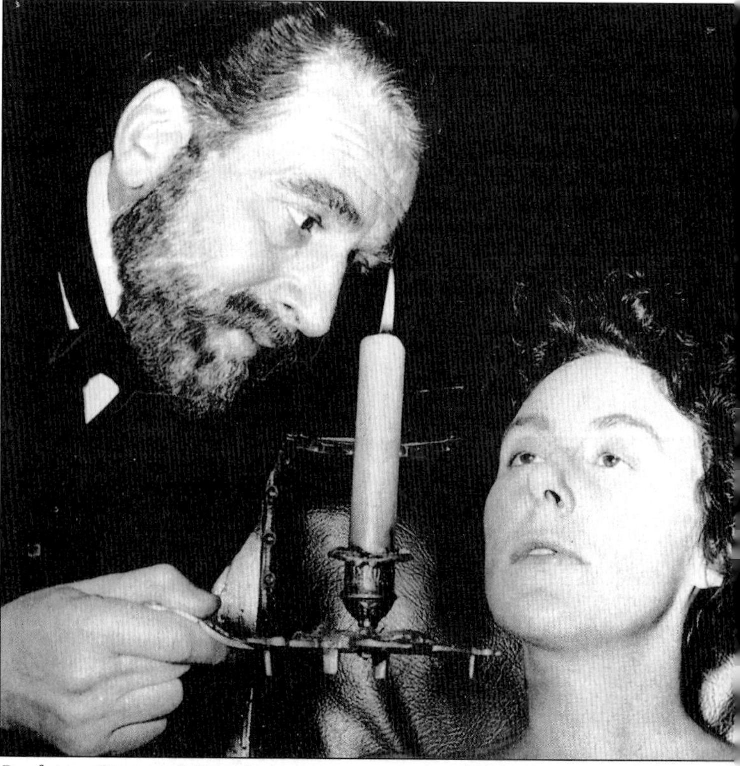
Professor Sigmund Freud attempts to uncover the dark secrets of the soul.

eter O'Toole and the Sahara compete for beauty

er O'Toole and Omar Sharif.

w York, 16 December
rector David Lean has exchanged steamy jungles of Ceylon, in ich he filmed his *The Bridge on River Kwai*, for the shimmering pty spaces of the Jordanian des-, where the subject of his latest ture fought a legendary guerrilla mpaign in the First World War. *Lawrence of Arabia*, Lean and oducer Sam Spiegel have mount- an epic examination of the am- guous war hero and writer T.E. Lawrence which is bound to spark off a controversy. In the title role Lean has cast a relatively unknown actor, 30-year-old Irish-born Peter O'Toole, whose blond hair and staring pale blue eyes give his interpretation of the compromised hero an unnerving intensity. Here, Lean orchestrates the expansive action in leisurely style, and makes a nod in the direction of the Lawrence enigma, hinting at the repressed homosexual and sado-masochistic tendencies which lay under the surface of the warrior-scholar. The $15 million picture, which has been three years in the making, also boasts a strong supporting cast that includes Alec Guinness as Prince Feisal and Jack Hawkins as General Allenby. And, riding out of the pulsing desert haze aboard a camel, is Egyptian star Omar Sharif as Lawrence's friend Sherif Ali.

O'Toole as Lawrence, a romantic figure, leads the Arabs into battle.

eck marvelous in 'To Kill a Mockingbird'

s Angeles, 25 December
itics have long contrasted Greg- y Peck's exceptional good looks th his unexceptionable acting tal- t. Now he has silenced them with s persuasive performance as the eral Southern lawyer in Robert ulligan's *To Kill a Mockingbird*, apted from the novel by Harper e. His low-key personality is ideal- suited to the part of the soft-spoken Alabama attorney who has to defend black man Brock Peters on a rape charge, while bringing up two children on his own and patiently trying to give them an insight into the proceedings. It's a performance of quiet conviction and inner strength, well balanced by Peters' measured dignity, which culminates in a long and superbly handled series of courtroom scenes.

Destruction of 'Days of Wine and Roses'

Los Angeles, 26 December
Hot on the heels of Christmas cheer comes a harrowing reminder of the destruction that can be caused by alcohol and mutual dependency. The ironically titled *Days of Wine and Roses* follows a PR man whose drinking gets out of control. By way of being supportive, his wife joins him in his binges but, sadly, while he rehabilitates himself, she becomes a hopeless alcoholic. This thought-provoking movie, directed by Blake Edwards, is a little uneasy in tone, veering between slick comedy, sentimentality and impending doom, but it grips the attention throughout. Above all, it confirms Jack Lemmon as one of the most impressively versatile and convincing of America's actors, and Lee Remick as an attractive and gifted co-star.

regory Peck, the quietly heroic lawyer, with his daughter (Mary Badham).

Lee Remick and Jack Lemmon, the unhappy couple doomed by alcoholism.

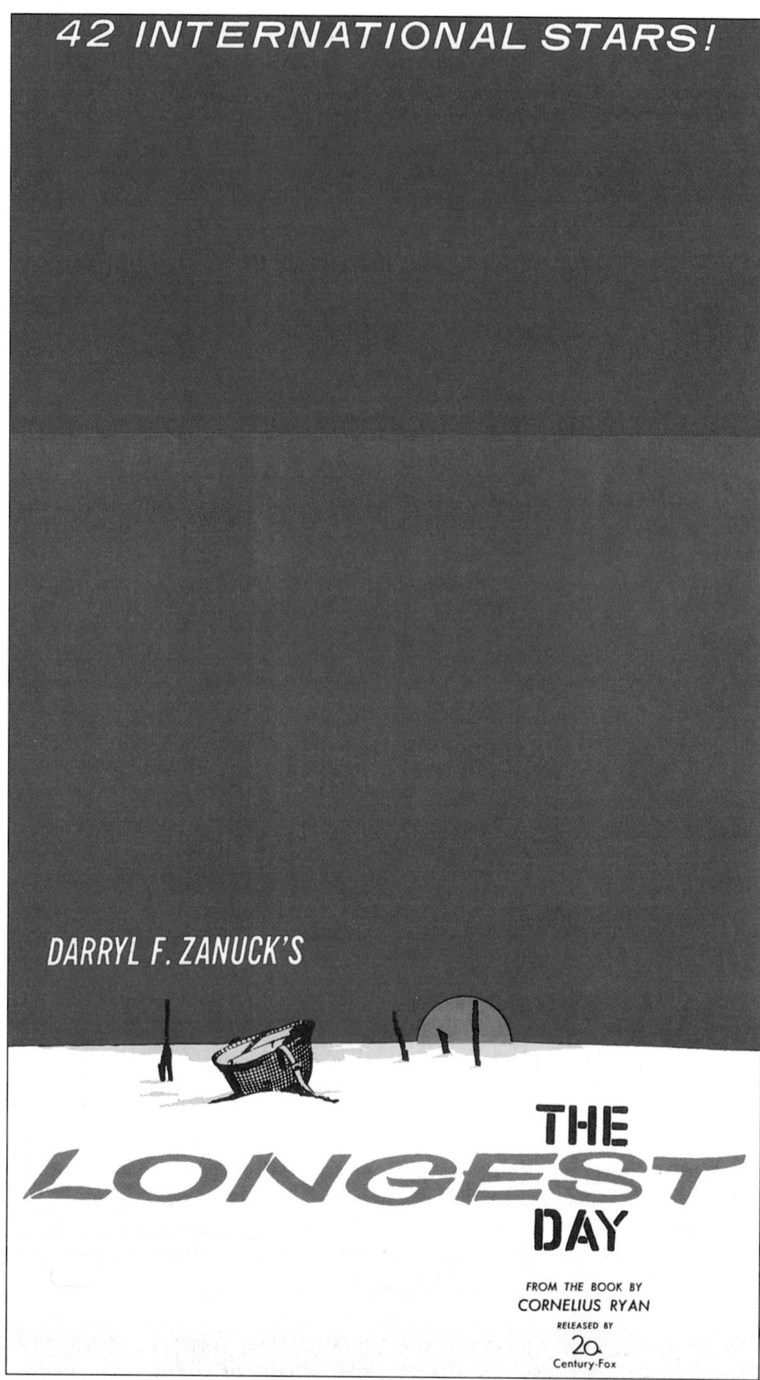
42 INTERNATIONAL STARS!
DARRYL F. ZANUCK'S
THE
LONGEST
DAY
FROM THE BOOK BY
CORNELIUS RYAN
RELEASED BY
20
Century-Fox

Like the poster says, 42 stars re-enacted D-Day landings for Darryl Zanuck.

Jean-Pierre Cassel (left), Claude Brasseur in Renoir's ***The Vanishing Corporal****.*

Luis Buñuel's surreal ***The Exterminating Angel*** *with (left to right) Jacquel Andere, Silvia Pinal and Enrique Garcia Alvarez.*

14
7

The Loneliness of the Long Distance Runner*: another from Tony Richards and the British school of realism, with Tom Courtenay, left, and James Fox*

GREGORY
PECK
ROBERT
MITCHUM
POLLY
BERGEN
CAPE
FEAR

Thriller with two heavyweight stars.

Irene Papas in the role of ***Elect*** *here with Yannis Fertis.*

BIA PICTURES PRESENTS CHARLES K. FELDMAN'S
ALK ON THE WILD SIDE
a new kind of love-story starring
LAURENCE HARVEY
CAPUCINE
JANE FONDA
ANNE BAXTER
BARBARA STANWYCK
as "JO"
IS AN ADULT PICTURE Parents Should Exercise Discretion In Permitting the Immature to See It.
A MOORE Screenplay by JOHN FANTE & EDMUND MORRIS Based on the novel by NELSON ALGREN Produced by CHARLES K. FELDMAN Directed by EDWARD DMYTRYK

lward Dmytryk directed this movie set in a New Orleans brothel but, despite anwyck's presence, the best bit was the Saul Bass title sequence.

Tom Tryon had his best part to date in Otto Preminger's **The Cardinal**.

o you've killed a lot and you've bled a lot and your guts are
racked and your nerves are mauled and an inch is a mile
nd an hour is forever.... Man, your war has just begun—
ou're one of
Merrill's Marauders
True story!
Incredible story!
How they fought those last 500 miles will remain forever in your memory!
starring
JEFF
HANDLER
TY HARDIN
PETER BROWN
WILL HUTCHINS
ANDREW DUGGAN
TECHNICOLOR
WARNER BROS.

Sam Fuller's bloody Burma war pic.

HARRY SALTZMAN and ALBERT R. BROCCOLI PRESENT
THE FIRST JAMES BOND FILM!
IAN FLEMING'S
DR. NO
TECHNICOLOR
SEAN CONNERY AS 007
URSULA ANDRESS · JOSEPH WISEMAN · JACK LORD
DAWSON · MARSHALL
KITZMILLER · GAYSON
BERNARD LEE
Screenplay by
MAIBAUM HARWOOD MATHER
Directed by YOUNG
Produced by SALTZMAN BROCCOLI...EON PRODUCTIONS

With Scotsman Sean Connery playing Ian Fleming's James Bond, Agent 007, **Dr. No** was one of the year's blockbusters.

lsa Martinelli and Michèle Girardon in ***Hatari!***, directed by Howard Hawks.

Leon Niemczyk (left) and Zygmunt Malanowicz in Polish director Roman Polanski's gripping drama, ***Knife in the Water***.

1963

1962 Academy Awards, Santa Monica Civic Auditor., 8 Apr.

Best Film:	*Lawrence of Arabia* (dir: David Lean)
Best Director:	David Lean
Best Actor:	Gregory Peck *(To Kill a Mockingbird)*
Best Actress:	Anne Bancroft *(The Miracle Worker)*
Best Supp. Actor:	Ed Begley *(Sweet Bird of Youth)*
Best Supp. Actress:	Patty Duke *(The Miracle Worker)*

Algiers, 9 January
Authorities have decided to create an office for Algerian News under the control of director Mohamed Lakhdar Hamina.

New York, 6 February
According to *Variety* magazine, Fox has received advances of $8.35 million from exhibitors for *Cleopatra*.

Paris, 1 March
Release of Jacques Demy's *la Baie des anges* (*Bay of Angels*), starring Jeanne Moreau and Claude Mann.

New York, 26 March
20th Century-Fox shares are now at $29 compared to $15 in June 1962 before Darryl Zanuck took over.

San Francisco, 4 April
The director Jean Renoir has been made Doctor *honoris causa* of the University of Southern California.

Los Angeles, 13 April
Two new categories have been created by the Academy Award Board of Governors to replace the Special Effects Award: Special Visual Effects and Sound Effects. Emil Kosa Jr. won the visual award for *Cleopatra*, while the award for sound went to Walter G. Elliott for *It's a Mad, Mad, Mad, Mad World*.

Madrid, 8 May
New censorship norms are to be introduced. To a certain extent, they will ease the restrictions which have been in force since the civil war.

Paris, 5 June
Opening of the Cinémathèque's new cinema at the Palais de Chaillot. An homage to Charlie Chaplin was followed by a retrospective on the American and Japanese cinema.

Brazil, 18 June
The filmmaker Glauber Rocha has started shooting his film, *Deus e o diabo na terra do sol* (*Black God White Devil*).

Los Angeles, 25 June
The Black civil rights organization, the NAACP, has accused film studios of racial discrimination. As an example, there is not a single black actor in the film *The Longest Day*, although 1,700 black soldiers took part in the Normandy landings.

Paris, 26 June
First day of shooting for *The Black Tulip* (*la Tulipe noire*). Christian-Jaque directs, Alain Delon stars.

New York, 8 August
Release of *The Great Escape*, a World War II film directed by John Sturges and starring Steve McQueen, James Garner, Richard Attenborough and Charles Bronson.

Hollywood, 14 August
Dramatist and screen writer Clifford Odets has died.

Hollywood, 20 August
A meeting between the representatives of the NAACP and producers, about the of employment of black actors in the cinema industry, has resulted in a quota agreement.

Rio de Janeiro, 24 August
Nelson Pereira dos Santos has held a preview of *Vidas Secas* (*Barren Lives*), adapted from the novel by Graciliano Ramos. The film evokes the plight of the poor farmers from the Northeast with a documentary style realism, and is already being hailed by the critics as the symbol of the Cinema Novo in Brazil.

New York, 10 September
For the first New York Film Festival, 31 films are being screened at the Lincoln Center and the Museum of Modern Art.

New York, 11 September
New York's first film festival opened last night at the Lincoln Center for the Performing Arts, with a screening of Luis Buñuel's *The Exterminating Angel*.

New York, 12 September
Samuel Fuller today held a preview of his film *Shock Corridor*, starring Peter Breck, Constance Towers and Gene Evans, about a journalist investigating a murder in an asylum.

Hollywood, 17 October
Under the terms of a new agreement, Frank Sinatra now owns one third of the Warner Bros. Record Company. Sinatra has announced his intention to devote himself entirely to artistic activities and to give up his questionable interests in the gambling industry.

Hollywood, 20 October
The Screen Actors Guild and other unions are accusing producers of trying to obstruct a Congressional inquiry into the recently growing trend of making films overseas.

Hollywood, 4 November
For the launching of *It's a Mad, Mad, Mad, Mad World*, producer-director Stanley Kramer and United Artists, his distributor, are organizing the most expensive press reception in the history of the cinema. Two hundred and fifty reporters from 26 countries have been invited for four days of festivities at a cost of $250,000.

Hollywood, 25 November
All film studios closed today as a mark of respect to the late President, John F. Kennedy, assassinated three days ago.

New York, 1 December
In reply to the accusations made by the unions, Eric Johnston, the president of the MPAA, has declared that the cinema industry would be unable to survive without making a percentage of its films overseas, where costs are considerably lower.

New York, 4 December
MGM has announced that its films will no longer be released under the exclusive rights system but under the Showcase system recently launched by Fox and United Artists: the film is shown simultaneously at 20 or so cinemas in each major city.

Los Angeles, 11 December
Frank Sinatra's son Frank Sinatra Jr., who was kidnapped on 9 December, has been released after the payment of a $240,000 ransom.

Prague, 20 December
Press preview of Vera Chytilov first full-length film *O Necem Jin* (*Something Else*). The film's lo framework and spontaneous st are reminiscent of the *cinéma-vér*.

Italy, 31 December
Over the last year, 32 magaz covers were devoted to Clau Cardinale, 30 to Sophia Loren a 11 to Gina Lollobrigida.

BIRTHS

Kentucky, 9 June
Johnny Depp

London, 11 May
Natasha Richardson

Florida, 30 July
Wesley Snipes

Los Angeles, 5 November
Tatum O'Neal

Oklahoma, 18 December
Brad Pitt

DEATHS

California, 2 January
Jack Carson

Hollywood, 3 January
Dick Powell

New York, 6 May
Monty Woolley

Hollywood, 7 June
ZaSu Pitts

Los Angeles, 18 June
Pedro Armendariz

New York, 17 August
Richard Barthelmess

France, 11 October
Jean Cocteau

Beverly Hills, 29 October
Adolphe Menjou

Hollywood, 2 December
Sabu

***Cleopatra** reached the screen th year. Dogged by delays, illness, sca dal, changes of director and escal ing expense, it was finally broug home by Joseph L. Mankiewicz.*

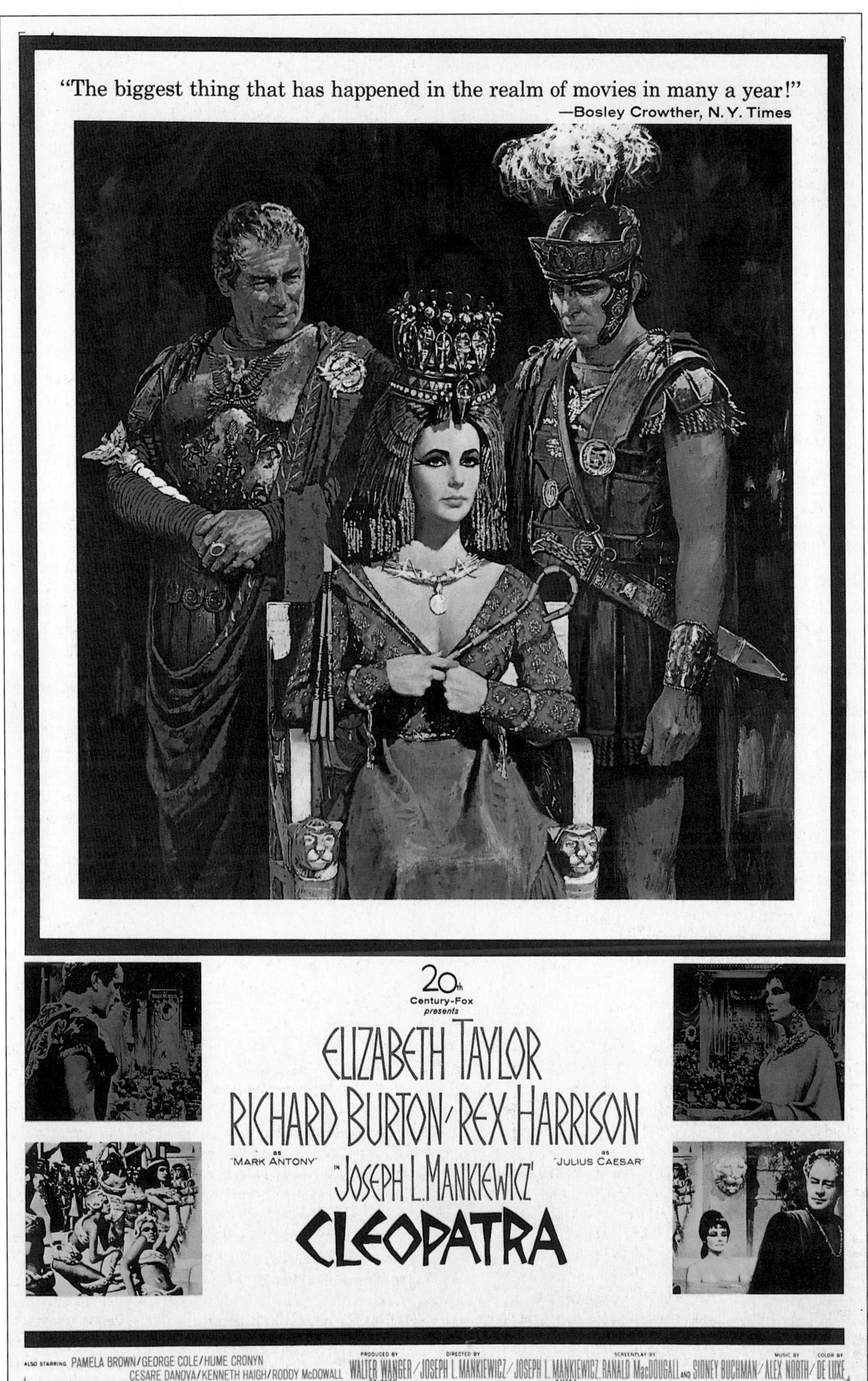
"The biggest thing that has happened in the realm of movies in many a year!"
—Bosley Crowther, N.Y. Times
20th Century-Fox presents
ELIZABETH TAYLOR
RICHARD BURTON · REX HARRISON
as "MARK ANTONY"
as "JULIUS CAESAR"
in JOSEPH L. MANKIEWICZ'
CLEOPATRA
ALSO STARRING PAMELA BROWN/GEORGE COLE/HUME CRONYN
CESARE DANOVA/KENNETH HAIGH/RODDY McDOWALL
PRODUCED BY WALTER WANGER/DIRECTED BY JOSEPH L. MANKIEWICZ/SCREENPLAY BY JOSEPH L. MANKIEWICZ, RANALD MacDOUGALL AND SIDNEY BUCHMAN/MUSIC BY ALEX NORTH/COLOR BY DE LUXE

Magic of Kabuki in 'An Actor's Revenge'

総天然色

Kazuo Hasegawa as the actor and Ganjiro Nakamura in ***An Actor's Revenge.***

Tokyo, 13 January
Kon Ichikawa, who began his career in cartoon and puppet films, uses some of these skills to conjure up the world of the Kabuki theater in his latest film, *An Actor's Revenge*. It tells of how an *onnagata* (female impersonator), during the early 19th century, takes revenge on the three men who caused the death of his parents. The veteran actor Kazuo Hasegawa not only gives an extraordinary performance as the hero-heroine, but also portrays a daring bandit in the complex subplot. The Daieiscope screen is brilliantly used in this fascinating and ambiguous study of opposites.

This Landru ignites spark of black humor

Paris, 25 January
Following the example of Charles Chaplin's work *Monsieur Verdoux*, Claude Chabrol has tackled a similar tale of a multiple murderer with cynicism and black humor. Entitled *Landru*, it recounts the true story of the notorious Henri Désiré Landru, who charmed a number of unsuspecting women, and then killed them. Charles Denner, with bald dome, bushy eyebrows and black beard, gives a strong performance in the title role, supported by a starry female cast, including Michèle Morgan, Danielle Darrieux, Hildegard Knef and Stéphane Audran. Yet critics have expressed disapproval, particularly of Françoise Sagan's awkward dialogue.

Charles Denner in the title role, with Catherine Rouvel in Chabrol's ***Landru.***

Fellini revealed in circus of life and art

Rome, 25 February
People have been puzzled by the title of Federico Fellini's new film, *8 1/2* (*Otto e Mezzo*), until it was explained by the director. As the picture is semi-autobiographical, Fellini has added up his seven solo features plus three collaborations, counting a half each, to get the title. The film attempts as few others have done to enter the mind of an artist (in this case a movie director) and explain the creative process. Marcello Mastroianni, in a thinly-veiled portrait of Fellini, is unable to find the inspiration for his next film. Having been immensely successful with his last picture, he is harried by his producer (Guido Alberti), his wife (Anouk Aimée) and his mistress (Sandra Milo) to get started on a new one. Needing rest, he goes off to a spa, where he retreats into personal recollections, dreams and fantasies. He remembers his dead mother and father, an obese hooker on a beach, his Catholic school, and has an erotic wishful fantasy that involves his controlling a horde of beautiful women with a whip. In reality, he is forced to examine his relationship with the women in his life, including an actress (Claudia Cardinale), whom he believes p sonifies every woman he has ev dreamed of. The finale has everyo in his life, living and dead, joini hands in a circus parade. In *8 1,* Fellini has not only produced a c gent statement about the nature inspiration and creativity, but h also made a sharp comment on selfish and superficial society. addition, it is visually stunning, e hilarating and constantly surprisir underlined by the evocative qualiti of the Nino Rota score.

'Film director' Mastroianni.

In this film, Federico Fellini retreats into his own fantasies and recollection.

er Paolo Pasolini taken to court

ne, 1 March
r Paolo Pasolini is not only the *noir* of the neo-fascists, but also he Church. *La Ricotta*, the sketch directed for the film *RoGoPaG*, title made up from the names he four directors involved: **Ros**ini, **Go**dard, **Pa**solini and **G**regtti), has got him into trouble for lermining the state religion. Pasi's film is a vigorous satire on contrast between the Christian ssage and those that propagate Laura Betti portrays the Virgin ry, with Orson Welles as a ditor making a religious epic, dur which a simple man dies on the ss. His death is due to overeating feast which includes ricotta, the ite cheese that gives the story its . Pasolini's only crime seems to that he has denounced those who garize religion.

son Welles in ***RoGoPaG****.*

asolini sentenced o four months

ome, 11 May
he affair of *La Ricotta*, the saric sketch in *RoGoPaG* that has en deemed blasphemous, has rned bitter for Pier Paolo Palini, who directed and wrote it. e lost the court case last month, out 12 days after the release of e collective film. The controveral director was found guilty of public defamation" and has reived a four months suspended ison sentence.

Visconti's sad reflections on the death of the Sicilian aristocracy

The Prince of Salina (Lancaster).

Alain Delon and Claudia Cardinale attend a ball as the old order collapses.

Rome, 27 March
Only Luchino Visconti's ninth film in almost 20 years, *The Leopard* seems destined to become his biggest success. Previously, each of his pictures divided opinion sharply. Some criticized the "father of neorealism" for making a period piece such as *Senso*, but when Visconti returned to his own epoch with the realistic *Rocco and His Brothers*, he unleashed a scandal. The premiere of *The Leopard* resembled a reconciliatory high mass. This gorgeous evocation of the era of the *Risorgimento*, which was faithfully adapted from Giuseppe De Lampedusa's 1958 novel, is full of set pieces, particularly the final ball which takes up to 40 minutes of screen time. In order to get 20th Century-Fox to release the film internationally, Visconti had to agree to cast Burt Lancaster in the role of the Prince of Salina, the dying 19th-century Sicilian aristocrat. Lancaster delivers a rich performance while Alain Delon and Claudia Cardinale make an attractive young couple. "We are the leopards, after us the jackals will come," comments the Prince sadly, a phrase that might express the aristocratic director's feelings.

Murderous birds share star billing with Hitchcock's latest blonde

New York, 29 March
The stuffed birds which loom over Anthony Perkins in *Psycho* have proved strangely prophetic. In Alfred Hitchcock's latest, *The Birds*, they have come alive with a vengeance, swarming in their tens of thousands to terrorize the inhabitants of a small community north of San Francisco. Says Hitch, "They are the victims of Judgment Day. I felt that after *Psycho* people would expect something to top it." Rod Taylor and Tippi Hedren are the stars battling the winged terror, which presented Hitchcock's special effects team with an enormous technical challenge. They tackled it with a combination of back projection, animation and lifelike mechanical birds. However, for the scene in which Hedren is trapped in a room by a swarm of feathered enemies, real birds were attached to her body. Hitchcock, who notoriously likes to put his "ice maiden" leading ladies through several kinds of hell, was reportedly extremely pleased with the results in this scene. Hedren was less enthusiastic about the ordeal. *The Birds* reunites Hitchcock with Daphne du Maurier 23 years after *Rebecca*: Evan Hunter's spare script has been loosely adapted from one of her stories. It daringly uses the device of a science fiction apocalypse to underline the intriguing sexual and emotional insecurity radiated by the cool leading lady.

Tippi Hedren is the central victim of Alfred Hitchcock's terrifying birds.

Epic films compete but intimate acting wins

*Anne Bancroft (left) and Patty Duke in Arthur Penn's **The Miracle Worker**.*

Hollywood, 8 April
Two blockbusters, David Lean's *Lawrence of Arabia* and Darryl F. Zanuck's *The Longest Day*, were vying for the Best Picture award at this year's Oscar ceremony. The prize went to *Lawrence of Arabia*, with Lean picking up the Best Director award. The other major awards were spread among more intimate films. Gregory Peck deservedly won the Best Actor award for his performance as a quietly spoken Southern lawyer in *To Kill a Mockingbird*. Anne Bancroft was voted Best Actress for *The Miracle Worker*, repeating her stage success as Annie Sullivan, the teacher battling with Patty Duke's blind-deaf Helen Keller. Bancroft's performance, a brilliant dramatization of the struggle between liberty and discipline, has brought her back to Hollywood after a gap of five years in which she has established herself as a formidable stage actress. Patty Duke won the Best Supporting Actress award, and Ed Begley was named Best Supporting Actor for his performance as the corrupt Southern town "boss" out to fix movie star Paul Newman in *Sweet Bird of Youth*.

Newman's 'Hud': a troublemaker in Texas

Paul Newman and Patricia Neal.

Los Angeles, 22 May
Paul Newman plays a cynical, womanizing cowboy in Martin Ritt's bleak contemporary Western, *Hud*. Newman's Hud is strictly a Cadillac cowpuncher and the despair of his father, Melvyn Douglas, a man who passionately loves the harsh Texas landscape; Brandon De Wilde plays Hud's nephew, uncertain whether to follow the uncle he worships or the old man he respects; and Patricia Neal (superb) the woman who suffers at Hud's hands. Things come to a head when Douglas' herd contracts foot and mouth disease, he dies, and De Wilde takes off for a new life, leaving an unconcerned Hud, a man of straw, presiding over a ranch that has become a physical and moral wasteland.

The Taylor-Burton show has finally opene

New York, 12 June
The long-awaited premiere of *Cleopatra* is finally taking place at the Rivoli Theater in New York. Walter Wanger's gigantic production cost 20th Century-Fox $40 million. This was due to the sumptuous sets, the 26,000 costumes... but mainly to the innumerable difficulties during its making. On 30 September 1960, Rouben Mamoulian started filming at Pinewood Studios in England with Elizabeth Taylor, Peter Finch (as Caesar) and Stephen Boyd (as Anthony). Miss Taylor was being paid $1 million against 10 percent of the gross, making her the highest paid performer in the history of Hollywood. However, she hardly appeared on set for over a month. First she was stricken with a cold, then a fever, then an infected tooth. In March 1961, Taylor was rushed to the London Clinic with lung congestion. Shooting was suspended and Mamoulian, Finch and Boyd left the film. Joseph L. Mankiewicz was hired to take over at the helm, Rex Harrison and Richard Burton joined the cast, and the entire project was shipped from the cold of England to sunny Rome. *Cleopatra* had already cost $7 million for seven minutes of film. The beautiful s arrived in Italy with a sizeable tourage consisting of one husba (Eddie Fisher), three children, dogs, two cats, various secreta and dozens of servants, and insta herself in a 14-room mansion. It w soon evident that Taylor and Bur were attracted to one another, a the studio publicists played it up all it was worth. After all, it w a multi-million dollar product about one of the world's grea love stories. Now audiences can how the love that was the talk modern Rome, compares with t of ancient Rome.

Elizabeth Taylor, Richard Burton

After two years of difficulties, a monumental visual epic has emerged.

dro Armendariz mmits suicide

Angeles, 18 June
xican actor Pedro Armendariz shot himself through the heart r learning that he had cancer. knew that he was condemned to th, and refused to simply waste y. Armendariz was born in Mex- on 9 May 1912, and studied in Antonio, Texas, and at the Cali- ia Polytechnic Institute. After king for a Mexican railroad com- y and at a hotel, he had a brief e career before making his big en debut in 1935 in his home- l. He rapidly became Mexico's film star, appearing in around motion pictures, many directed Emilio Fernandez, the most fa- us of those being *Maria Cande- a* (1943) and *The Pearl* (1946). later starred in Luis Buñuel's *Brute* (1952). Armendariz made e films with John Ford – *The itive* (1947, shot in Mexico), *Fort che* (1948) and *Three Godfathers* 49). His last appearance was in new James Bond movie, *From sia With Love.*

Hilarious 'Jekyll-and-Hyde' role for auteur and comic Jerry Lewis

Stella Stevens co-stars with zany Jerry Lewis in ***The Nutty Professor.***

Hollywood, 18 July
With *The Nutty Professor*, his fourth film as director, Jerry Lewis has become a true *auteur*; he is not only the screenwriter (with Bill Richmond) and director, but also the star, and plays a double role. This parody of Robert Louis Stevenson's *Dr. Jekyll and Mr. Hyde* takes place in an American college where Jerry is a bespectacled absent-minded professor of chemistry. Because he is unable to gain the attention of the lovely girl (Stella Stevens) to whom he is attracted, he concocts a potion in the laboratory that temporarily transforms him into a handsome, debonair, swinging playboy. In fact, Jerry Lewis/Dr. Jekyll turns himself into a man who bears a truly striking resemblance to Dean Martin/Mr. Hyde, his former screen partner. This wicked take-off of an egocentric, lazy crooner has a further edge to it, because the team had split up acrimoniously. It is also a hilarious demonstration that inside every Jerry Lewis is a Dean Martin trying to get out, and highlights Jerry's Jekyll-and-Hyde personality. Lewis also satirizes certain aspects of the American Way of Life. The film is full of visual and sound gags learned from his mentor Frank Tashlin, who directed two of the last Martin and Lewis films, as well as a couple of Jerry's early solo efforts. It was Tashlin who persuaded Lewis to direct his own films, the first of which was *The Bellboy* (1960), followed by *The Ladies' Man* and *The Errand Boy* (both 1961), sufficient to prove that he is not only a talented comedian, but a director of comic verve.

ergman's dark, elusive and erotic silence

ckholm, 23 September
mar Bergman began his angst- len, intimist trilogy with *Through lass Darkly* in 1961, followed by *nter Light* last year. It has now n completed with *The Silence*, title of which could sum up gman's bleak philosophy – "God never spoken, because He does not exist." *The Silence* centers on Ester (Ingrid Thulin) physically attracted to her sister Anna (Gunnel Lindblom), herself a sexually vibrant mother of a 10-year-old boy. This dark, passionate and elusive film, impeccably interpreted, is perhaps even better than its two impressive predecessors.

Sidney Poitier makes the flowers grow

New York, 1 October
Sidney Poitier's abundant charm and deft handling of comedy enable him to negotiate a minefield of sentimentality in *Lilies of the Field*, in which he plays the handyman who teaches English to a group of five Eastern European nuns and helps them build a chapel in the Arizona desert. Writer James Poe and producer-director Ralph Nelson, who also joins the cast of the film, expound the messages of Christian unity and racial harmony with an unselfconscious directness which looks set to pay dividends at the box office. In the era of the blockbuster, small is sometimes more profitable.

r: Gunnel Lindblom, Jörgen Lindström and Ingrid Thulin in ***The Silence.***

Sidney Poitier brings light into the lives of the nuns in ***Lilies of the Field.***

Boisterous Finney a fabulous Tom Jones

Susannah York and Albert Finney in Tony Richardson's ebullient ***Tom Jones.***

New York, 7 October
Director Tony Richardson has cast aside British cinema's recent preoccupation with gritty realism to produce a freewheeling adaptation of *Tom Jones*, Henry Fielding's picaresque 18th-century novel. Shot entirely on location, the film stars Albert Finney as the eponymous hero, whose bawdy adventures burst from the screen with all the red-faced vigor of a Hogarth cartoon. And Richardson maintains the pace with a battery of tricks from freeze-frames to speeded-up chases. Outstanding in a superb supporting cast are Hugh Griffith as the bucolic Squire Western, squatting in the mud to test the size of his prize bull's testicles; and Edith Evans playing his haughty sister who rebukes an importunate highwayman with the words, "Stand and deliver? I am no traveling midwife!"

Bond tackles the Russians in fine style

Lotte Lenye as the infamous agent Rosa Klebb in ***From Russia With Love***

London, 10 October
Bond mania is beginning to break out as Harry Saltzman and Cubby Broccoli consolidate the success of *Dr. No* with *From Russia With Love*, the 007 adventure which is one of President Kennedy's favorite books. Istanbul and Venice form the backdrop to Bond's deadly battle with the forces of SPECTRE, the Special Executive for Counter-Intelligence, Terrorism, Revenge and Extortion, who are chasing a top-secret So coding machine. Sean Connery in admirably laconic form as 0 spotting the stony-faced SPECT agent Robert Shaw as a wrong when the latter orders red wine w fish on the Orient Express. C nery's other principal adversary Lotte Lenya's ferociously frun SPECTRE operative Rosa Kle whose sensible shoes come arn with poison-tipped spikes.

Cocteau follows Piaf on final journey

Paris, 11 October
Close friends Jean Cocteau and Edith Piaf died within a few hours of each other today. A few days ago, the poet had found the strength to joke with the singer about their respective conditions. "Our doctors don't understand anything. They see us dead, and then revive us." This time, alas, the man whose light flickered at the end of *The Testament of Orpheus* will not rise again. One cannot convince oneself that he had "pretended to die" as he had at the climax of that film. He knew full well that he would never direct again. The financial difficulties he had suffered during *The Testament* convinced him to make it his last. Cocteau's farewell to the cinema was his faithful adaptation of the novel from Madame de La Fayette, *The Princess of Cleves*, for Jean Delannoy in March 1961.

Stuntmen come to the fore in Kramer's crazy star-studded farce

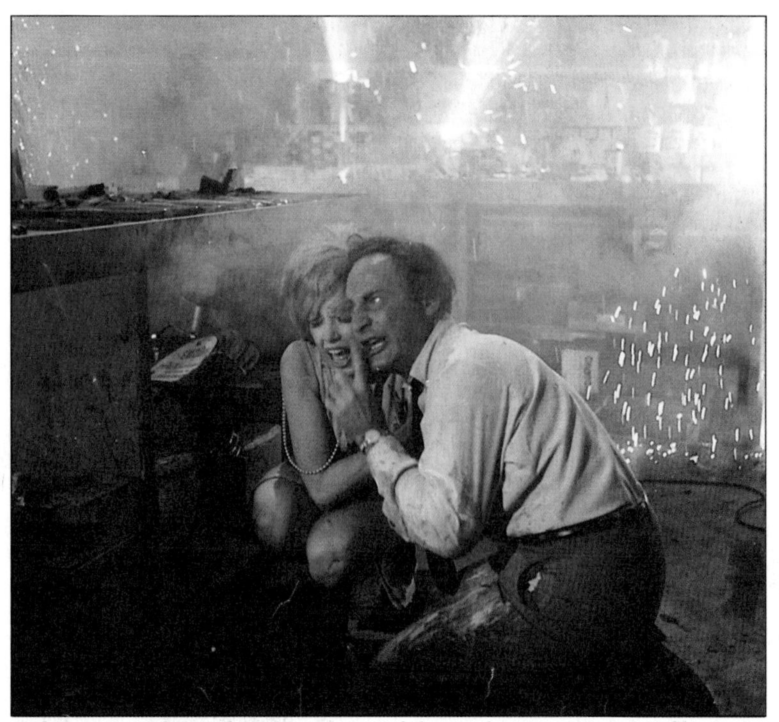
Sid Caesar and Dorothy Provine, two of the mad cast in Kramer's film.

Los Angeles, 7 November
The cinema's current obsession w size has now invaded the world comedy. Stanley Kramer's *It's Mad, Mad, Mad, Mad World*, film in Ultra Panavision for United A ists, boasts a colossal comedy ros – Milton Berle, Sid Caesar, Et Merman, Phil Silvers, Dick Shaw Terry-Thomas, William Demar Buddy Hackett, Mickey Roon Buster Keaton, the Three Stoog Joe E. Brown and Jimmy Durar When crook Durante dies, the r is on for his cache of bank loot der the watchful eye of police ch Spencer Tracy. It's an excuse for explosion of stunts which involv nearly every stuntman and wom in Hollywood. As stunt coordina Carey Loftin claims, "You nam stunt we did it – in airplanes, au mobiles, tractors, trucks, fire gines... fisticuffs, fireworks, f from fire escapes, ladders, pa trees and building tops."

epburn and Grant make a real class act

ry Grant and Audrey Hepburn , an absolutely magical pairing in **Charade**.

w York, 5 December
th *Charade*, the director Stanley nen has achieved the magic pair- that everybody wanted to see: drey Hepburn and Cary Grant. matter that (as so often with drey and her leading men) there 27-year age difference between m. Grant is a very fit and attrac- man, and a scintillating screen- y uses the age gap to advantage. de on location in Paris, with Hep- n again eye-catchingly clothed by venchy, this is a high-octane, high-definition romantic comedy-thriller. The complicated plot centers on the plight of Reggie Lampert, wife of a wealthy Paris-based businessman, who returns from a trip to find her husband mysteriously murdered. Enter a trio of richly characterized villains (James Coburn, Ned Glass, George Kennedy), the American ambassador (Walter Matthau) – and Cary Grant. The leads sparkle, she insouciant and vulnerable, he debonair and charming. A winner to close out the year.

Elia Kazan honors his debt to America

Stathis Giallelis and George Rozakis in Elia Kazan's ***America, America.***

New York, 16 December
Director Elia Kazan has returned to his immigrant roots with *America, America*, based on his 1962 novel, in which he depicts with reflective warmth the trials and tribulations of his own uncle's odyssey from Turkey to the United States. Kazan himself was born Elia Kazanjoglou in Istanbul in 1909, and was taken to America by his parents in 1913. The immigrant experience in the New World is wrapped up in this absorbing two-and-a-half hour film superbly photographed by Haskell Wexler. A graduate of the Group Theater, which he joined in 1932, Kazan directed his first movie, *A Tree Grows in Brooklyn*, in 1945 and thereafter has divided his time between Hollywood and influential theater work. Briefly a Communist in the 1930s, in 1952 he disclosed the names of fellow-Communists to the House Un-American Activities Committee. This secured his future in Hollywood, and the disrespect of his more loyal peers.

e great director Yasujiro Ozu dies on his sixtieth birthday

an, 12 December
great Japanese director Yasu- Ozu has just died of cancer on eve of his 60th birthday. His th comes shortly after the death his mother, with whom he had ays lived, never having married. rn in Tokyo, the son of a cattle d salesman, Ozu was taken on as istant cameraman at the Shochi- studios in 1922. By 1927, he had n promoted to director, his first n being *Sword of Penitence*, based an idea by Kogo Noda, who be- ne his resident screenwriter right to the end. Most of his early ns were American-style comedies sed on the Japanese way of life, h as *I Graduated But...* (1929) or ial comedies such as the delight- *I Was Born But...* As late as 1936 u made his first sound film, *The ly Son*, which also marks the be- ning of his special interest in ddle-class domestic drama, retain- few traces of the comic characterizations found in his splendid earlier comedies. In exploring Japanese family life and the relationships between the generations, Ozu continued to make use of a restrained and simple style and a static camera placed at a low angle, turning out such postwar masterpieces as *Late Spring* (1949), *Tokyo Story* (1953) and *An Autumn Afternoon* (1962).

Chichu Ryu (left), Shima Iwashita in Ozu's last film ***An Autumn Afternoon.***

Godard directs from novel by Moravia

Paris, 20 December
In his most recent film, *Contempt* (*le Mépris*), Jean-Luc Godard has slyly used Alberto Moravia's novel *Il Disprezzo* to make his own sharp comment on international filmmaking, by using color, wide-screen and a multinational cast. The first third of the movie, shot in Italy, is concerned with the breakdown of a marriage, made in a remarkable flowing sequence set in the apartment of a couple superbly played by Brigitte Bardot and Michel Piccoli. The latter is a scriptwriter increasingly despised by his wife as he tries to set up a film in Rome of *The Odyssey* with an American producer (Jack Palance) and directed by Fritz Lang (who plays himself). Godard has explained that he had wanted to make a film by Michelangelo Antonioni, in the style of Howard Hawks or Alfred Hitchcock! ▷

le nouveau Film de
Joseph Losey
DIRK BOGARDE
SARAH MILES
WENDY CRAIG
The SERVANT
JAMES FOX

Joseph Losey, a French favorite.

JAMES BOND IS BACK!
HARRY SALTZMAN & ALBERT R. BROCCOLI present IAN FLEMING'S
FROM RUSSIA WITH LOVE
STARRING
SEAN CONNERY
as
JAMES BOND 007
TECHNICOLOR
ALSO STARRING Pedro ARMENDARIZ Lotte LENYA Robert SHAW AND Bernard LEE
INTRODUCING DANIELA BIANCHI
SCREENPLAY BY Richard MAIBAUM
TITLE SONG WRITTEN BY Lionel BART
PRODUCED BY HARRY SALTZMAN AND ALBERT R. BROCCOLI
DIRECTED BY TERENCE YOUNG
EON PRODUCTIONS LTD

Sean Connery is now firmly established as the world's favorite spy with this successful return of James Bond.

Glamorous Ava Gardner in Nicholas Ray's ***55 Days at Peking****.*

B·O·A·C

English actress Margaret Rutherford in ***The V.I.P.s****, with Lance Percival.*

BRIGITTE BARDOT
dans un film de
JEAN-LUC GODARD
LE MÉPRIS
d'après le roman d'ALBERTO MORAVIA
JACK PALANCE

The English title of this is ***Contem***

Cary Grant
Audrey Hepburn
You can expect the unexpected when they play...
"Charade"
a STANLEY DONEN production
in TECHNICOLOR
Walter Matthau James Coburn Screenplay by PETER STONE
Produced and Directed by STANLEY DONEN Music HENRY MANCINI A UNIVERSAL RELEASE

Grant and Hepburn: pure magic!

Burt Lancaster, Claudia Cardin in Visconti's ***The Leopard****.*

If ever this
mad, mad, mad, mad world
needed "It's a
mad, mad, mad, mad world"
IT'S NOW!
starring
SPENCER TRACY
and starring in alphabetical order
MILTON BERLE
SID CAESAR
BUDDY HACKETT
ETHEL MERMAN
MICKEY ROONEY
DICK SHAWN
PHIL SILVERS
TERRY-THOMAS
JONATHAN WINTERS
STANLEY KRAMER
presents
"IT'S A MAD, MAD, MAD, MAD WORLD"
co-starring in alphabetical order
EDIE ADAMS
DOROTHY PROVINE
also starring in alphabetical order
EDDIE "ROCHESTER" ANDERSON
JIM BACKUS
BEN BLUE
JOE E. BROWN
ALAN CARNEY
BARRIE CHASE
WILLIAM DEMAREST
ANDY DEVINE
PETER FALK
NORMAN FELL
PAUL FORD
STERLING HOLLOWAY
EDWARD EVERETT HORTON
MARVIN KAPLAN
BUSTER KEATON
DON KNOTTS
CHARLES McGRAW
ZASU PITTS
CARL REINER
MADLYN RHUE
ARNOLD STANG
THE 3 STOOGES
JESSE WHITE
A FEW SURPRISES!
and in alphabetical order
JIMMY DURANTE
music ERNEST GOLD · story and screenplay by WILLIAM and TANIA ROSE · produced and directed by STANLEY KRAMER · filmed in ULTRA PANAVISION and TECHNICOLOR
Re-released thru
United Artists
Entertainment from Transamerica Corporation
G ALL AGES ADMITTED General Audiences

nley Kramer's ***It's a Mad, Mad, Mad, Mad World*** is well-named: even the choice mix of cast smacks of lunacy!

ANGELO RIZZOLI presenta
FEDERICO FELLIN
8 1/2
MARCELLO MASTROIANNI
CLAUDIA CARDINALE
ANOUK AIMEE
SANDRA MILO
ROSSELLA FALK · BARBARA STEELE
GUIDO ALBERTI · MADELEINE LEBEA
JEAN ROUGEUL · CATERINA BORATT
ANNIBALE NINCHI · GIUDITTA RISSO
CINERIZ

Mastroianni, Fellini's alter ego.

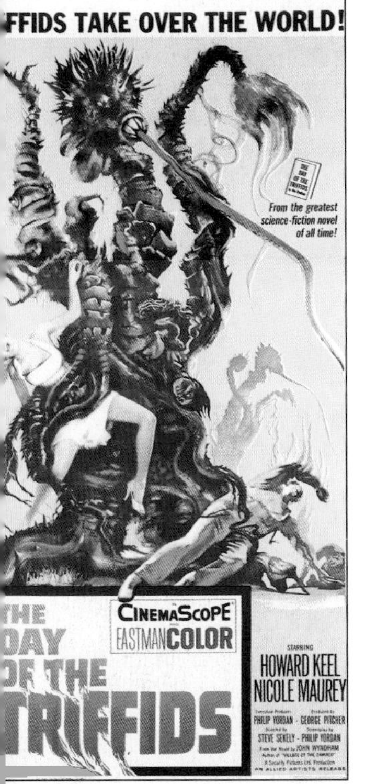
FFIDS TAKE OVER THE WORLD!
From the greatest science-fiction novel of all time!
CINEMASCOPE
EASTMANCOLOR
THE DAY OF THE TRIFFIDS
STARRING
HOWARD KEEL
NICOLE MAUREY
PHILIP YORDAN · GEORGE PITCHER
STEVE SEKELY · PHILIP YORDAN
AN ALLIED ARTISTS RELEASE

ve Sekely directed this uneven itish version of John Wyndham's nous sci-fi novel, for which he as- nbled an international cast that's ıded by Howard Keel.

Richard Harris as the miner who turns rugby player in ***This Sporting Life****, a British film directed by Lindsay Anderson.*

HOTEL CASANOVA

Shirley MacLaine in ***Irma la Douce****.*

"TAKE THY BEAK FROM OUT MY HEART, AND TAKE THY FORM FROM OFF MY DOOR!" QUOTH THE RAVEN, "NEVERMORE" —POE
american-international presents
EDGAR ALLAN POE'S
THE RAVEN
PANAVISION & PATHECOLOR
STARRING
VINCENT PRICE
PETER LORRE
BORIS KARLOFF

Corman's medieval horror hokum.

1964

1963 Academy Awards, Santa Monica Civic Auditor., 13 Apr.

Best Film:	*Tom Jones* (dir: Tony Richardson)
Best Director:	Tony Richardson
Best Actor:	Sidney Poitier *(Lilies of the Field)*
Best Actress:	Patricia Neal *(Hud)*
Best Supp. Actor:	Melvyn Douglas *(Hud)*
Best Supp. Actress:	Margaret Rutherford *(The V.I.Ps)*

Moscow, 1 January
The *Selected Works of Eisenstein*, a collection of articles and essays by the director, have been published in six volumes, under the editorship of Serge Yutkevitch.

Hollywood, 27 January
Director Norman Z. McLeod has died. McLeod started his career in 1927 as assistant director on *Wings*, but was best known for his wonderful comedies notably *The Secret Life of Walter Mitty*.

Palm Springs, 29 January
Alan Ladd, whose memorable films include *The Blue Dahlia* and *Shane*, has apparently committed suicide.

New York, 19 February
Paramount has sold to NBC the television rights of 200 full-length films made prior to 1948. The transaction cost $60 million.

New York, 12 March
Having been arrested for publicly showing Jack Smith's underground film, *Flaming Creatures*, the cinema-lover and film critic Jonas Mekas declared: "We refuse all censorship of art." He wants to found a New York League for sexual liberty.

Hollywood, 18 March
MGM producer Martin Ransohoff has called upon the MPAA to end its ban on nudity in films as part of sweeping changes being made to Hollywood's voluntary censorship code. He feels the code should not be a matter of "specific rules", but that it should "consider the intent of the producer and the content of the film." Ransohoff's latest film, *The Americanization of Emily* had to be made without the nude scenes called for in Paddy Chayefsky's script, to gain a seal of approval.

Prague, 17 April
Release of Czech filmmaker Milos Forman's first full-length feature *Cerny Petre* (*Peter and Pavla*).

Paris, 22 April
Release of Abel Gance's new film, *Cyrano and d'Artagnan*, which drew on the works by Edmond Rostand and Alexandre Dumas. The critics' reaction has been unenthusiastic.

Hollywood, 27 April
William Wyler asserted today that many of the highly acclaimed European New Wave films did little more than confuse. He pointed out that there was a difference between "the artistic and the arty, between the subtle and the incomprehensible." Federico Fellini's *La Dolce Vita* was, however, "a great, great film... it had something to say and was clearly artistic."

Rome, 30 April
Twenty-four "spaghetti westerns" have been made since the beginning of July 1963.

New York, 5 July
Charles Chaplin's *Monsieur Verdoux*, a failure 17 years ago, is a hit revival. The film opened last Friday as part of a Chaplin Festival at the Plaza Theater on East 58th Street, and grossed a total of $13,500 over the three-day holiday weekend.

London, 6 July
The premiere of Richard Lester's *A Hard Day's Night* caused a huge traffic jam in Piccadilly. Thousands of fans had turned up hoping to catch a glimpse of their idols.

New York, 21 July
The Irish playwright Samuel Beckett has started shooting a film with Buster Keaton, based on three short pieces written by himself, Harold Pinter and Eugène Ionesco.

London, 1 August
Release of *Goldfinger*, made by Guy Hamilton, and again starring Sean Connery, is the third James Bond film based on Ian Fleming's novels. The title song, recorded by Shirley Bassey, is already in the charts.

Paris, 3 August
Le Figaro has published a long interview with Alain Delon explaining why he is suing a journalist from the *Herald Tribune*. It appears the latter had twisted his words "in order to make him appear a doubly stupid cretin, a churlish boor, a fathead reeking of hollow pretentions only good enough to be locked away in the nearest padded cell."

New York, 5 August
Actress Anne Bancroft, who won the Best Actress Award last year for *The Miracle Worker*, has married comedy writer Mel Brooks.

France, 27 September
The German film about the Berlin Olympic Games, *Olympiad*, directed by Leni Riefenstahl during the Nazi era, has been shown here on television for the first time.

Paris, 13 October
British director Clive Donner has started shooting *What's New Pussycat?*, in the Billancourt studios. The stars of the film are Ursula Andress, Peter O'Toole, Peter Sellers and Romy Schneider, while its scriptwriter, the American director-actor Woody Allen, plays a character role.

Los Angeles, 16 October
Composer and lyricist Cole Porter has died. The celebrated songwriter composed numerous hits for both Broadway and Hollywood musicals including his unforgettable "Night and Day".

Paris, 30 November
In honor of the cinema, the Théâtre National Populaire (TNP) is screening a musical comedy cycle including Stanley Donen's *Singin' in the Rain*, starring Gene Kelly.

Boulogne-Billancourt, 7 December
Elizabeth Taylor gave a cocktail party here for studio personnel and friends to mark the end of filming on Vincente Minnelli's *The Sandpiper*. During the party the American star's handbag was stolen.

Paris, 15 December
Costa-Gavras, the French director of Greek descent who was formerly assistant director to René Clément and Yves Allégret, is shooting his first film *Compartiment tueurs* (*The Sleeping Car Murders*).

Stockholm, 21 December
Swedish actress Mai Zetterling directed her first film, *Alskande* (*Loving Couples*), co-starring Ha[...]et Andersson, Gunnel Lindbl[...] and Anita Björk. Three young [...]pectant mothers think over t[...] past relationships with men.

BIRTHS

California, 7 January
Nicolas Cage
(Nicolas Coppola)

New York, 18 February
Matt Dillon

Paris, 9 March
Juliette Binoche

Virginia, 17 March
Rob Lowe

Lebanon, 2 September
Keanu Reeves

France, 19 December
Béatrice Dalle

DEATHS

New York, 21 January
Joseph Schildkraut

California, 29 January
Alan Ladd

Hollywood, 23 March
Peter Lorre

New York, 18 April
Ben Hecht

London, 13 May
Diana Wynyard

Hollywood, 27 August
Gracie Allen

Hollywood, 28 September
Harpo Marx

Hollywood, 10 October
Eddie Cantor

Los Angeles, 14 December
William Bendix

---

*Lerner and Loewe's stage hit, **My F[...] Lady**, was brought to the screen [...] vast expense by Jack Warner. Dire[...]ed by George Cukor, it stars [...] Harrison and Audrey Hepburn.*

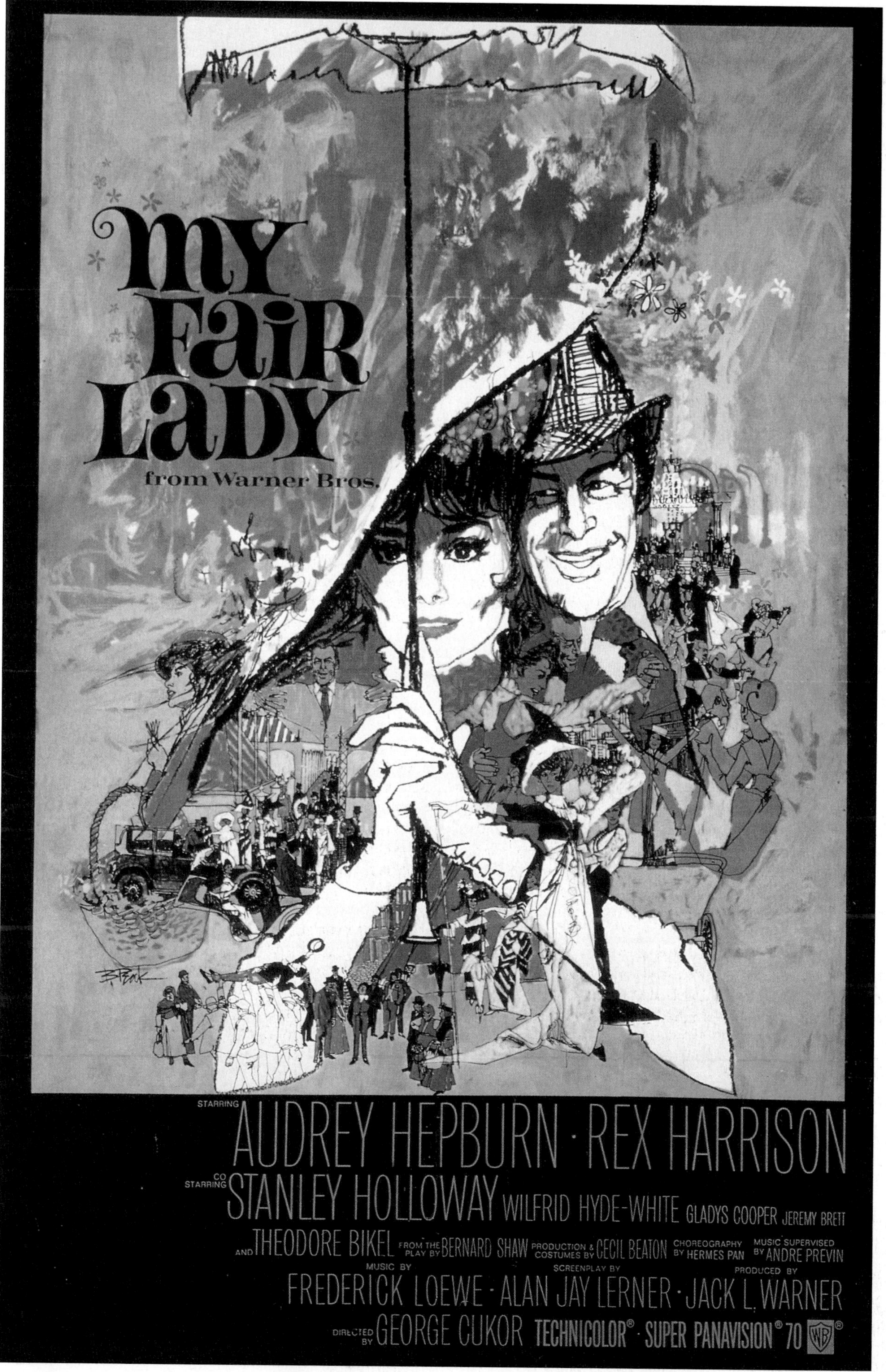
MY
FAIR
LADY
from Warner Bros.
STARRING
AUDREY HEPBURN · REX HARRISON
CO STARRING STANLEY HOLLOWAY WILFRID HYDE-WHITE GLADYS COOPER JEREMY BRETT
AND THEODORE BIKEL FROM THE PLAY BY BERNARD SHAW PRODUCTION & COSTUMES BY CECIL BEATON CHOREOGRAPHY BY HERMES PAN MUSIC SUPERVISED BY ANDRE PREVIN
MUSIC BY FREDERICK LOEWE · SCREENPLAY BY ALAN JAY LERNER · PRODUCED BY JACK L. WARNER
DIRECTED BY GEORGE CUKOR TECHNICOLOR® · SUPER PANAVISION® 70

A touch of madness threatens the planet

Peter Sellers (right) and Peter Bull in Stanley Kubrick's ***Dr. Strangelove.***

New York, 31 January
Stanley Kubrick's *Dr. Strangelove: or, How I Learned to Stop Worrying and Love the Bomb*, has a long title and a brutal message. If it is not controlled, the technology we have created will destroy us. Here, it's the Soviet Doomsday machine which, once triggered, moves relentlessly towards the meltdown of nuclear war. And it is about to be triggered by Sterling Hayden's crazed USAF General Jack D. Ripper, who has launched his own unauthorized preemptive strike against the Reds. The U.S. President, his metal-clawed, ex-Nazi scientific advisor Dr. Strangelove and a stiff-upper-lipped RAF officer (all brilliantly played by Peter Sellers) are helpless to prevent apocalypse in this savage satire on the mad logic of nuclear strategy.

The seamy side of 'Swinging London'

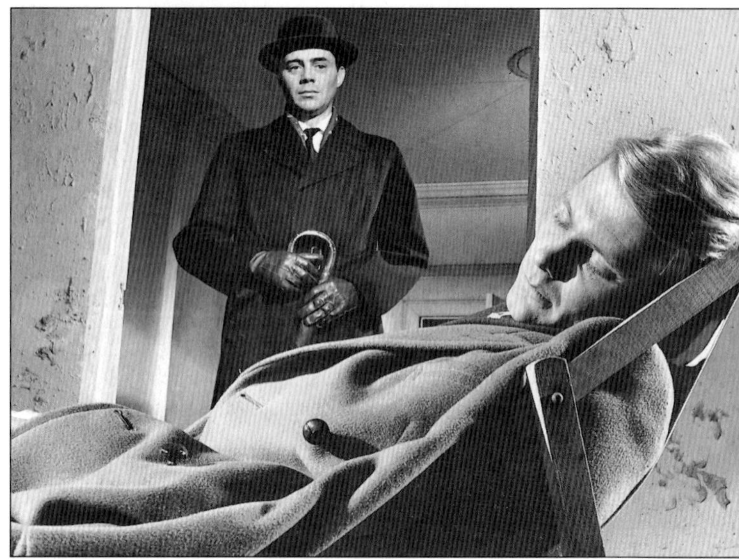

Dirk Bogarde (left) is the sinister servant to James Fox in Losey's film.

London, 10 February
In Joseph Losey's *The Servant*, Dirk Bogarde continues to refashion himself as a screen actor. He portrays Barrett, the creepily obsequious manservant hired by languid young aristocrat James Fox to run his newly acquired Chelsea home. The gentleman's gentleman undermines and then destroys his master. Adapted by Harold Pinter from a 1948 novella by Robin Maugham, *T Servant* is a superbly nuanced exa ination of the tensions, evasions a deceit which infest the British cl system. Bogarde and Fox are perbly matched protagonists, w supported by Sarah Miles as t predatory waif, infiltrated into Fo house by Bogarde as Pinter's c test of seduction and dictators moves to its bleak conclusion.

In the bedrooms of the bourgeoisie with Buñuel and Moreau

Paris, 4 March
After Jean Renoir's film version of Octave Mirbeau's novel *Diary of a Chambermaid*, made in Hollywood in 1946, Luis Buñuel has now tackled the same subject. As might be expected, given the differences between the two directors, Buñuel's adaptation is black and cynical while Renoir's is shining and optimistic. Nor is there any foot fetishism or sexual activity present in the less acid and lighter earlier film. Buñuel and his screenwriter Jean-Claude Carrière have transposed the plot to the end of the 1920s, the epoch during the Spanish director's first sojourn in France, when he made his first two films. By updating the story and making the sadistic valet Joseph (Georges Géret) a member of the French Fascist party, Buñuel has brought the social satire into sharper focus. At the end, the Fascists shout "Vivre Chiappe", referring to the Paris chief of police who had suppressed Buñuel's *l'Age d'or* in 1930. Jeanne Moreau plays Célestine, who takes up a post as chambermaid to a *bourgeois*, provincial family, and becomes the catalyst that reveals their sexual, religious and social repressions. Moreau – sexy, cruel and cool – is unscrupulous enough to be like Joseph, whose *petit bourgeois* ambitions she shares, and with whom she ends up.

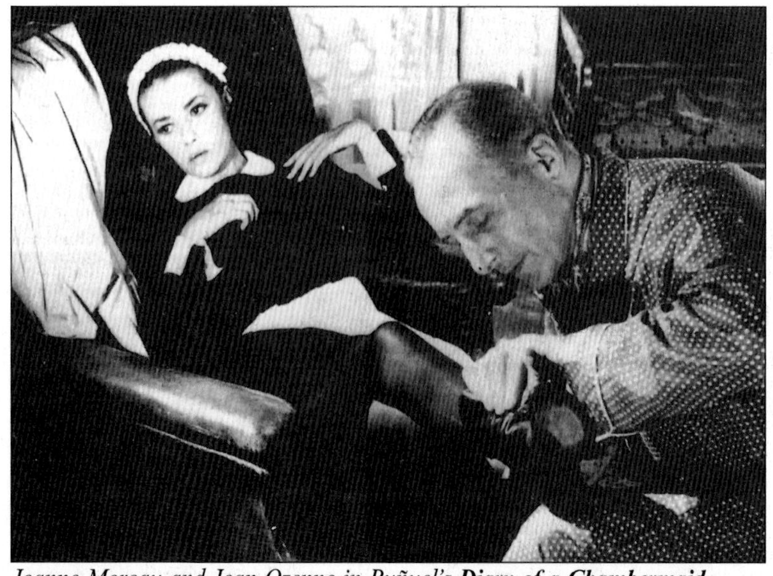

Jeanne Moreau and Jean Ozenne in Buñuel's ***Diary of a Chambermaid.***

'Tom Jones' wins four Awards

Hollywood, 13 April
Tom Jones, Tony Richardson's 18 century romp, has walked away w four Oscars: Best Picture, Direct Screenplay (John Osborne) a Score (Richard Addison). It's cl that *Tom Jones* marks a watersh in the British cinema, creating extravagant world perfectly in tu with that of "Swinging London Sidney Poitier was voted Best Ac for his performance in *Lilies of Field*. Patricia Neal scooped t Best Actress prize for *Hud*, in wh she played the overworked but i mensely sexy housekeeper on P Newman's dusty Texan ranch. T Best Supporting Actor award we to Melvyn Douglas for his perf mance as the grizzled patriarch the same film; and Margaret Ruth ford romped in as Best Supporti Actress for the *V.I.P.s*, in wh she played a charmingly querulc airline passenger.

e happy shelter of Demy's umbrellas

ıo Castelnuovo and Catherine Deneuve in ***The Umbrellas of Cherbourg.***

ınnes, 14 May
is year at the Cannes Film Festi-
l, the jury, presided over by Fritz
ng, has given the Grand Prize,
ıich replaces the Golden Palm, to
cques Demy's *The Umbrellas of*
erbourg. Demy seems to be the
ly French director interested in
king film musicals. However, he
s gone even further than the tradi-
nal musical, because the words
: sung throughout, without any
oken dialogue. Demy had hoped
start shooting in September 1962,
t due to the film's originality, he
d difficulties in getting it made. It
s worth all the effort, because he
d the composer Michel Legrand
ve carried it off with aplomb. The
ɔt tells of Geneviève (Catherine Deneuve), who works in her widowed mother's umbrella shop, in love with Guy (Nino Castelnuovo), a garage mechanic. She discovers that she is pregnant when he goes away on military service, so she marries a young diamond merchant (Marc Michel) for security. Filming in color for the first time, Demy had both the exterior and interior of houses in Cherbourg painted in an array of colors, matching the clothes of the characters. As unusual in a very different way from *The Umbrellas of Cherbourg* was the Special Jury Prize winner, Teshigahara's *Woman of the Dunes*. An audacious erotic fable, much of it takes place at the bottom of a huge sandpit where a man and a woman are trapped.

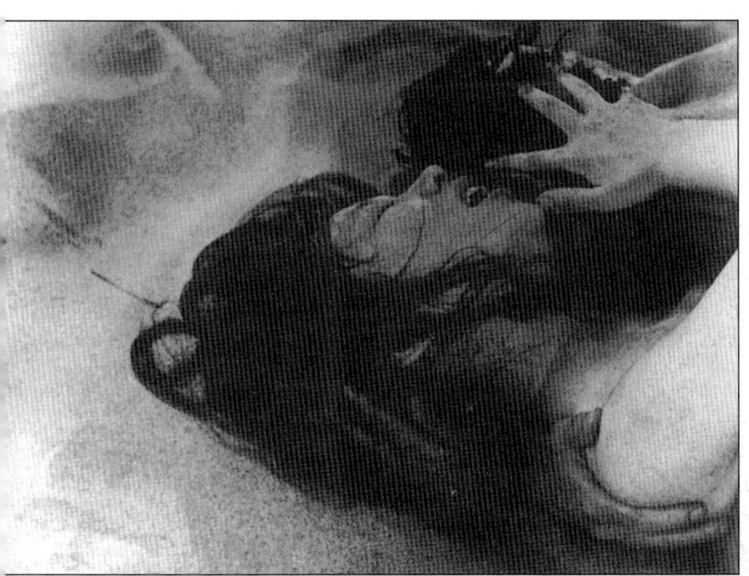

ɔoto Koshoda in Teshigahara's prize-winning ***Woman of the Dunes.***

Triangle of love and death reflects life

Paris, 20 May
After the triumph of *Jules and Jim* three years ago, François Truffaut has followed it with another triangle story, this time, as the director explained, "a violent answer to *Jules and Jim*... a truly modern love; it takes place in planes, elevators; it has all the harassments of modern life." *The Soft Skin* (*la Peau douce*, came from a newspaper report of an incident that occurred in a full restaurant when a woman entered and shot her husband with a hunting rifle. Truffaut then set about inventing a story to explain the circumstances that led to this actual event. The film tells of a married, middle-aged editor of a literary magazine (Jean Desailly), who falls in love with an air stewardess (Françoise Dorléac) while on a trip to Lisbon, and leaves his wife (Nelly Benedetti) for her. When his lover rejects him, he seeks reconciliation with his wife, who shoots him in a restaurant. The name of the male protagonist, Pierre Lachenay, is the nom-de-plume under which Truffaut wrote some of his articles for *Cahiers du Cinéma*. This is but a small indication that *The Soft Skin* is a very personal film, in which the critic Georges Sadoul rediscovered the "raw sensitivity" of *The Four Hundred Blows*, Truffaut's first feature. Truffaut has deliberately made sure that Lachenay would not win the audience's sympathy, so, like its title, the film has a brilliant surface, but, despite patches of warmth and wit, is uncharacteristically cool.

Françoise Dorléac and Jean Desailly in François Truffaut's ***The Silken Skin.***

Algeria sets up a national cinema center

Algiers, 8 June
Born in the midst of the war of liberation against the French seven years ago, the Algerian cinema is in the process of strengthening itself institutionally, thanks to a series of laws and measures taken by the government of the new Algerian Republic. After the creation of the Department of Algerian Information last year, the Center of Algerian Cinema has now been inaugurated in Algiers. The purpose of this organization is to stimulate various cinematic activities, significantly in the realms of production, distribution and presentation. A nationalized body, the Center has been conceived within a Socialist framework, the government intending to oversee all aspects of cinematographic activity. A lack of technical equipment and training facilities has been a factor in inhibiting the growth of the Algerian cinema, considered among the most healthy and promising of the young North African film industries. Among this country's best films has been *The Olives of Justice*, released in 1962. ▷

'Marnie' a beautiful blonde with problems

Sean Connery and Tippi Hedren: the husband and his traumatized wife.

New York, 1 June
After threatening Tippi Hedren with death by pecking in *The Birds*, Alfred Hitchcock has turned her into a traumatized, man-hating kleptomaniac in *Marnie*. Sean Connery, making his American debut, is the suave naturalist-cum-businessman who sets out to tame this exotic creature and unlock the secrets of her past. Hitchcock originally offered the title role to Grace Kelly, hoping to entice her out of royal retirement in Monaco, but Hedren proves to be rather more than second best, bringing insight and pathos to the sexually inhibited thief in a film which tells us much about the director's own view of his troubled heroine's psychopathology.

'A Shot in the Dark' goes home for Seller

Peter Sellers and Elke Sommer in Blake Edwards' ***A Shot in the Dark.***

New York, 24 June
The success of *The Pink Panther* has created a new comic favorite in the accident-prone form of Peter Sellers' Inspector Clouseau. A sequel was inevitable, and it has arrived in the shape of *A Shot in the Dark*, again directed by Blake Edwards, in which the magnificently maladroit Clouseau lurches towards the solution of a murder myst adapted from plays by Harry K nitz and Marcel Achard. In try to clear Elke Sommer of the crin Clouseau leaves a trail of additio bodies in his wake before findi that all is revealed in a nudist cam "Give me ten men like Clouseau a I could destroy the world," blurts bewildered boss Herbert Lom.

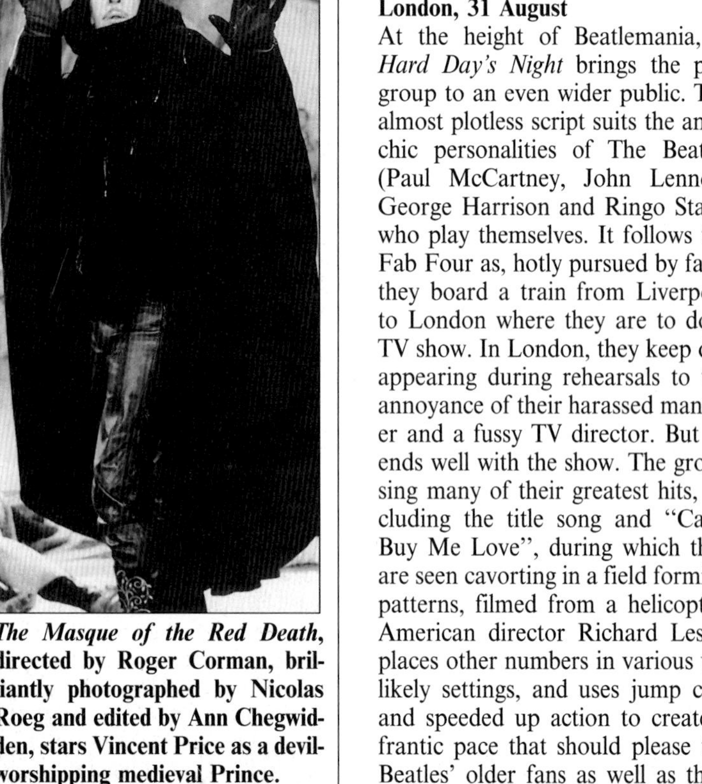

The Masque of the Red Death, **directed by Roger Corman, brilliantly photographed by Nicolas Roeg and edited by Ann Chegwidden, stars Vincent Price as a devil-worshipping medieval Prince.**

Richard Lester brings the Beatles to the screen in madcap farce

London, 31 August
At the height of Beatlemania, *A Hard Day's Night* brings the pop group to an even wider public. The almost plotless script suits the anarchic personalities of The Beatles (Paul McCartney, John Lennon, George Harrison and Ringo Starr) who play themselves. It follows the Fab Four as, hotly pursued by fans, they board a train from Liverpool to London where they are to do a TV show. In London, they keep disappearing during rehearsals to the annoyance of their harassed manager and a fussy TV director. But all ends well with the show. The group sing many of their greatest hits, including the title song and "Can't Buy Me Love", during which they are seen cavorting in a field forming patterns, filmed from a helicopter. American director Richard Lester places other numbers in various unlikely settings, and uses jump cuts and speeded up action to create a frantic pace that should please the Beatles' older fans as well as their youthful ones.

l to r: Paul McCartney, George Harrison, Ringo Starr and John Lennon.

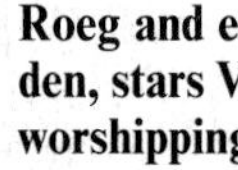

:hairman Mao jives call for order

'eking
he time seems to have come for ıe Chinese cinema to remake it-
ɔlf, as has already been achieved ı the theater under the aegis of 'hiang Qing, Mao's wife, where ıe classical repertoire has been rogressively abandoned. In De-
ɔmber 1963, Mao fumed, "In umerous fields, Socialist trans-
ɔrmation has produced only min-
nal results, those of a bygone ge continue to reign supreme." ast February, in the *People's aily*, Mao stated, "The whole ountry must be re-educated by ıe Popular Army of Liberation." 'his has now become law, and ıe meaning of culture has been ɔdefined. "Many writers, play-
rights and directors have not ɔllowed the Party line. They have id on the slippery slopes of revi-
ionism," Mao has said. From ow on, ideological changes will ffect the motion picture indus-
y, which now produces about 80 features annually.

harlie Chaplin tells e story of his life

ndon, 30 September
ɔw aged 75, Charles Chaplin has en a resident in Switzerland, at home in Corsier-sur-Vevy near usanne, since 1953. And it is in itain, the country of his birth, that has decided to publish the fasci-
ting story of his life titled *My tobiography*. The book has been ur years in preparation and runs over 500 pages. The first third, ich takes him to the beginning of 16, is especially vivid, not least en describing Chaplin's unhappy ildhood. But thereafter he seems ener to talk about his social life d the celebrities he met than to veal the secrets of his filmmaking . Many of his surviving collabora-
rs are reported to be hurt by his lure to acknowledge their roles. ıe of those, Robert Florey, who s Chaplin's associate director on *onsieur Verdoux*, has expressed disapproval in a review of the ench edition, titled *Histoire de ma* , in *Paris-Match*.

The Gospel according to Pasolini enrages Italy's neo-fascists

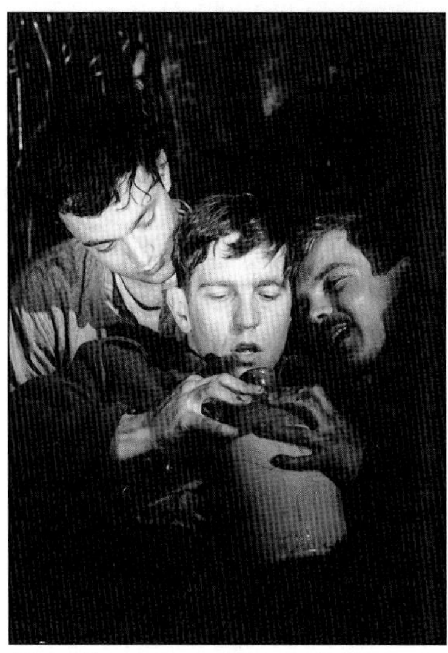

Tom Courtenay: ***King and Country.***

Pier Paolo Pasolini's second feature ***The Gospel According to St. Matthew.***

Venice, 10 September
The Venice Film Festival has often been accused of timidity in its prize-giving, but this year the jury can be congratulated for its courage. A week ago, neo-fascist organizations disturbed the showing of Pier Paolo Pasolini's *The Gospel According to Saint Matthew*. This did not prevent the film from being awarded the Special Jury Prize. Despite Pasolini's claim to have broken away from Christianity, he has treated this religious subject with respect, humanity and energy. After he had been accused of blasphemy over his sketch in *RoGoPaG* two years ago, Pasolini has now been forgiven by the Catholic Church, who helped finance the film. Applying neo-realist methods, the director shot this version of the life of Christ in Calabria, using the expressive faces of non-professionals. The Golden Lion was presented to Michelangelo Antonioni's *The Red Desert*, his first film in color. Deep reds and greens reflect the neurosis of a wife (Monica Vitti) having an affair with her husband's best friend, while brighter colors appear during her flights into fantasy. With the two Italian films gaining the most attention in Venice this year, Britain could be pleased with Tom Courtenay's best actor prize for *King and Country*.

Julie Andrews makes a dream of a governess for Walt Disney

© Walt Disney

English stage star Julie Andrews makes her screen debut as Mary Poppins.

New York, 25 September
Disney's delightful musical comedy *Mary Poppins*, directed by the ever-reliable Robert Stevenson, is calculated to appeal to children of all ages. After the disappointment of not landing the role of Eliza Doolittle in *My Fair Lady*, Julie Andrews makes a spectacular movie debut as P.L. Travers' "practically perfect" Edwardian nanny, who delights her young charges and grown-ups Glynis Johns and David Tomlinson in equal measure. Dick Van Dyke co-stars as the tuneful handyman Bert, and there's movie magic aplenty as every technical resource at Disney's disposal is used to combine live action with animation, whisking the co-stars over the rooftops of London with assorted chimneysweeps and enabling Van Dyke to cut a caper with some penguins. Other highlights include the tongue-twisting "Supercalifragilisticexpealidocious" song and Van Dyke's rendition of "Chim Chim Cheree".

Hepburn and Harrison charm in 'My Fair Lady'

Flower girl Eliza Doolittle sings up a storm in Covent Garden market.

New York, 21 October
Alan Jay Lerner and Frederick Loewe's long-running stage musical, *My Fair Lady*, finally reaches the screen, with Rex Harrison repeating his London and Broadway performance as Shaw's Professor Higgins, who, for a bet, turns a guttersnipe into a "lady". However, English rose Julie Andrews, a fine soprano but unknown to movie audiences, is replaced by one of the world's most loved film stars, Audrey Hepburn who, her tremulous and appealing delivery of "Moon River" in *Breakfast at Tiffany's* notwithstanding, can barely sing a note.

The 'lady' arrives at the ball.

Jack Warner, last of the old-style moguls, has staked much on this lavish production. Determined to acquire the rights after seeing the Broadway show at its 1956 opening, it took him several years to clinch a deal which cost a massive $5.5 million for the rights alone. Preparation was dogged with problems. Warner wanted Peter O'Toole and, when that idea foundered, Cary Grant – who, wisely, said that Harrison was the only possible choice. Then Alan Jay Lerner, unable to persuade Warner to cast Andrews, was left angry and disappointed at the choice of Hepburn, who Warner regarded as the surefire security for his investment. For her part, Hepburn was reportedly thrilled to get the role (and a $1 million paycheck) and, was confident that she could learn to sing it. She set about voice lessons with dedication, only to be told, after months of hard work and her songs already recorded, that musical director André Previn had decided to hire Marni Nixon to dub the famous numbers, thus inflicting a bitter blow to Audrey's professional pride. Warner personally took on the producer role, and chose veteran George Cukor to direct. The darling of screen actresses, Cukor's experience of the musical form has previously been limited to the essentially dramatic remake of *A Star is Born* with Judy Garland. However, the film has retained not only Harrison, but Stanley Holloway as Doolittle ("Get Me to the Church on Time" is a high point) and Cecil Beaton as designer, with the result that the clothes are stunning, particularly in the famous Ascot scene.

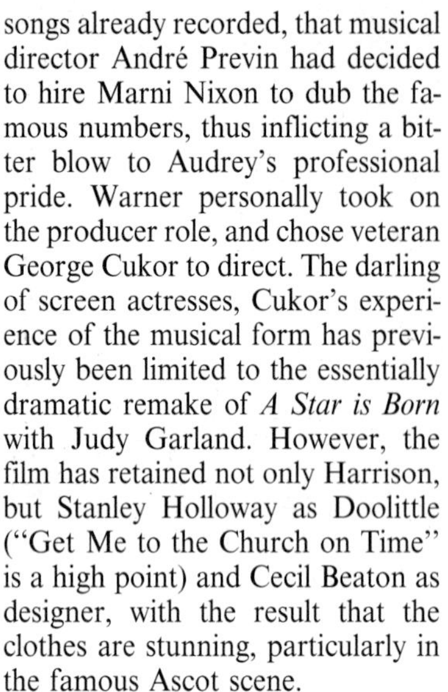

The result of this troubled history is a film which, thanks to its indestructible story, score and lyrics, cannot help but beguile. Harrison is impeccable, as is Wilfrid Hyde White as Pickering, with Jeremy Brett well-cast as luckless Freddy-Eynsford Hill. But the enterprise is marred by some obviously artificial "staginess" and an occasional disjunction between the admirable Miss Nixon's voice and Hepburn's personality. And what of Audrey Hepburn? Even the most ardent of her many fans would have to concede that as a Cockney flowersel her efforts at authenticity simply f to convince. However, from t moment of her transformation ir a lady, all the Hepburn magic intact: grace, dignity, charm, a vulnerability. Her appearance at t top of the stair in the white Beat ballgown must surely become one the iconic images of female beau in the modern cinema, and is o that, ultimately, sends audienc home happy.

'I could have danced all night...'

A posed publicity shot in her Ascot outfit designed by Cecil Beaton.

·eath of brilliant young Indian film director

new frontier in Indian cinema: Guru Dutt in his film **Paper Flowers.**

ombay, 10 October
›nsitive and tormented, resembling any of the characters he played in s own films and in those directed › others, the Indian director and ›tor Guru Dutt has committed sui-›de at the age of 39. Born in Banga-re, Dutt studied at Uday Shank-'s academy of art, before entering the cinema in 1951, the year he shot his first film, *Game*. He made seven other pictures, of which two are considered to be masterpieces, *The Thirsty* (1957) and *Paper Flowers* (1959). Dutt reconciled the traditions of popular Indian cinema with more demanding fare, thus paving the way for younger directors.

Clint Eastwood in an unusual Western

Rome, 10 November
After small parts in 10 movies and seven years acting in TV's *Rawhide* series, 34-year-old Clint Eastwood is now starring in an Italian-German co-production called *A Fistful of Dollars*, which happens to be a Western. The producers had originally wanted Henry Fonda in the lead, but they couldn't afford him. The director is a certain Bob Robertson, the American-sounding pseudonym of Sergio Leone, who made such epics as *The Last Days of Pompeii* and *The Colossus of Rhodes*. Here he has taken on a genre hitherto exclusively American, and scored a success. Other Italians involved in the picture disguised themselves behind names such as Dan Savio (the composer Ennio Morricone), Jack Dalmas (the cinematographer Massimo Dallamano) and John Welles (co-star Gian Maria Volonte). Clint Eastwood had no need to change his name, although he plays the mysterious Man With No Name. The plot, taken from Akira Kurosawa's *Yojimbo* (1961), tells of how Eastwood, as a quick-on-the-trigger mercenary, plays off two rival gangs against each other, and then faces five gunmen alone in the final protracted shootout. With a small budget of $100,000, Leone shot the exteriors in Spain, while the interiors were filmed at Cinecittà in Rome.

TV cowboy Clint Eastwood in Sergio Leone's ***A Fistful of Dollars****.*

·ary Grant marooned with a brood of kids

·ew York, 10 December
·aired with Audrey Hepburn last ·ar in *Charade*, Cary Grant is now ·-starring with Hollywood's other ·uropean gamine, the delightfully ·rench Leslie Caron, in *Father ·oose*. But the formula is not nearly · successful, thanks to a second-·te screenplay. Grant, with the aid of a beard and a sailor's cap, plays a beachcombing type forced to man a small island during World War II. Events saddle him with Caron, a schoolteacher, and half-a-dozen refugee schoolchildren. Competently directed by Ralph Nelson, the film might appeal as undemanding family viewing over the festive season.

·ry Grant and Leslie Caron, the stars of Ralph Nelson's ***Father Goose.***

U.S. studios looking financially healthier

Hollywood, 31 December
After experiencing problems during the early 1960s, the past year has marked a recovery in the fortunes of most of the leading Hollywood film companies. Their profits have been on the rise, especially at Disney, boosted by the spectacular success of *Mary Poppins*, by far the biggest hit of the year and the most popular "live action" feature in the company's history. The movie stars Julie Andrews, who was snubbed by Warner Bros. for the role of Eliza Doolittle, and, ironically, it appears that Warners' lavish production of *My Fair Lady* has flopped at the box office, with Warners as the one top studio that has failed to share in the general recovery. Most impressive of all has been the performance of United Artists with two big James Bond hits, *From Russia With Love* and *Goldfinger*, along with Blake Edwards' *The Pink Panther* starring Peter Sellers, *A Hard Day's Night* with the Beatles, and Stanley Kramer's *It's A Mad, Mad, Mad, Mad World*, released late last year. MGM has climbed back into the black after a disastrous 1963 with the help of a couple of successful musicals, *Viva Las Vegas* and *The Unsinkable Molly Brown*, while 20th Century-Fox appears to be making a comeback under Darryl Zanuck and his son Richard. Embassy and Paramount had a big hit with Joseph E. Levine's *The Carpetbaggers*, and Columbia did well with *The Cardinal* and *Dr. Strangelove*. It looks as though the long postwar fall in audiences may at last be bottoming out. Certainly, the improvement in movie company results would indicate this.

The success of the third James Bond film, ***Goldfinger****, made a major contribution to United Artists' revenue.*

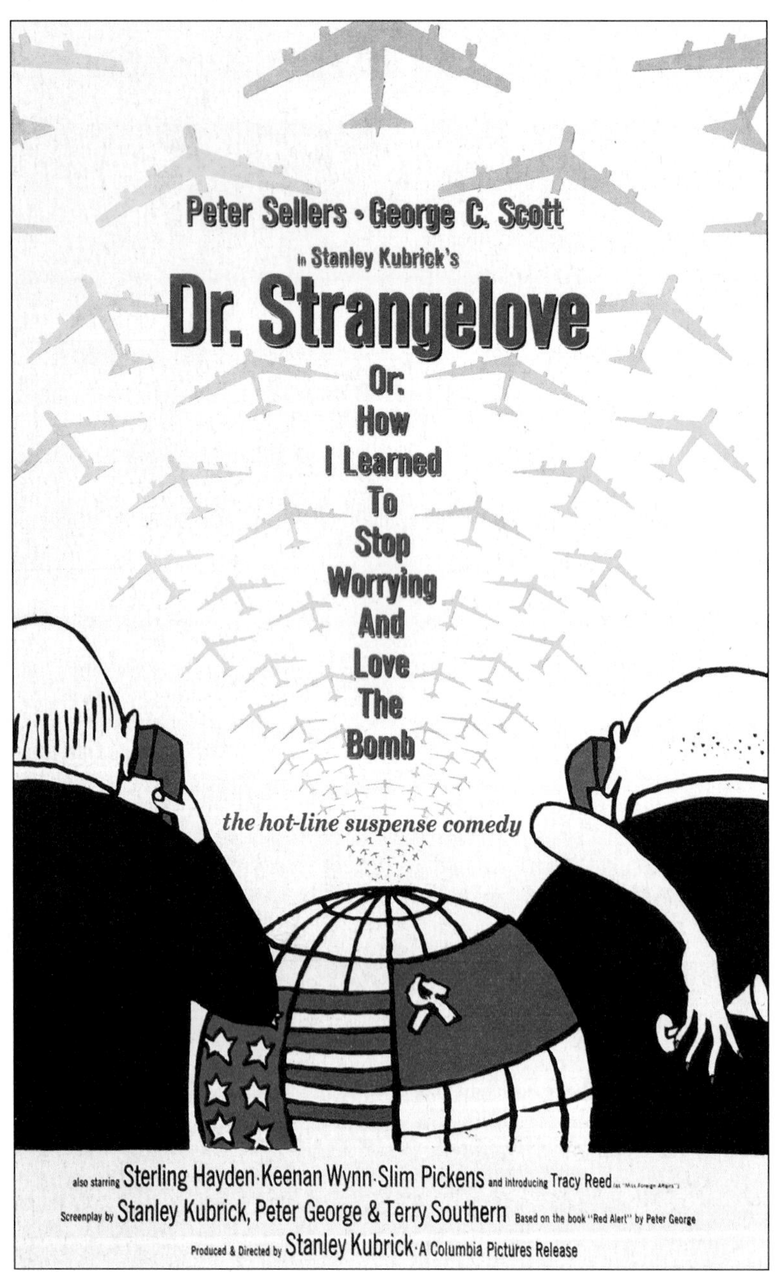
Peter Sellers · George C. Scott
in Stanley Kubrick's
Dr. Strangelove
Or: How I Learned To Stop Worrying And Love The Bomb
the hot-line suspense comedy
also starring Sterling Hayden·Keenan Wynn·Slim Pickens and introducing Tracy Reed
Screenplay by Stanley Kubrick, Peter George & Terry Southern Based on the book "Red Alert" by Peter George
Produced & Directed by Stanley Kubrick·A Columbia Pictures Release

Stanley Kubrick's film used black comedy to transmit a frightening message.

*Kyoto Koshoda in Teshigahara's erotic, bizarre **Woman of the Dunes**.*

*Jean-Paul Belmondo in **That Man From Rio**, a spoof thriller.*

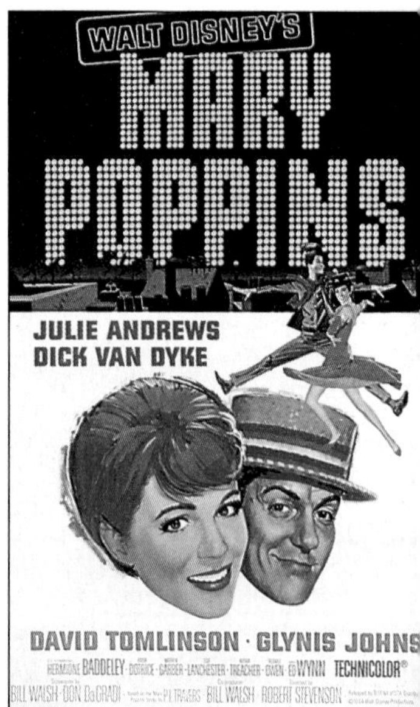
WALT DISNEY'S
MARY POPPINS
JULIE ANDREWS
DICK VAN DYKE
DAVID TOMLINSON · GLYNIS JOHNS
TECHNICOLOR®

A supercalifragilistic hit!

*Andréa Parisy and French heart-throb Jean-Paul Belmondo: **Greed in the Sun**.*

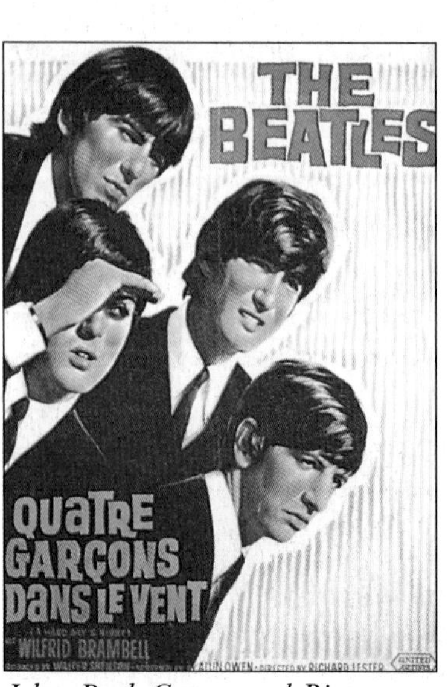
THE BEATLES
QUATRE GARÇONS DANS LE VENT
WILFRID BRAMBELL

John, Paul, George and Ringo were loved everywhere. (French poster).

VIVE L'ARMÉE

*Jeanne Moreau in **The Diary of Chambermaid** for Luis Buñuel.*

ft to right: Olivia De Havilland, Bette Davis, Agnes Moorehead: grotesquerie **Hush, Hush, Sweet Charlotte**, from director Robert Aldrich.

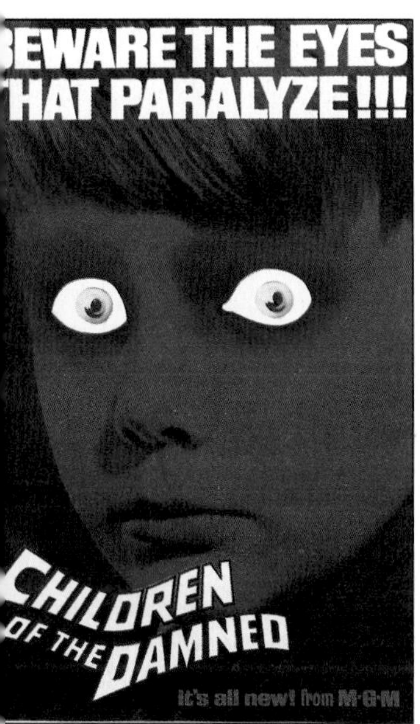
EWARE THE EYES
HAT PARALYZE!!!
CHILDREN OF THE DAMNED
it's all new! from M-G-M

i-fi from MGM's British arm.

Black God, White Devil comes from Brazil's Glauber Rocha.

e Fang and Cao Yindi were **Two Stage Sisters**, a wonderful picture from ina's Xie Jin, made just before the Cultural Revolution.

to make You dream
to make You dream to make Yo
o make You dream to make You dream to make Y
warren BEATTY
jean SEBERG
Robert Rossen's Lilith
co-starring
PETER FONDA · KIM HUNTER · with ANNE MEACHAM · JAMES PATTERSON · ROBERT REILLY
Screenplay by ROBERT ROSSEN · Based on the novel by J.R. SALAMANCA · Produced and Directed by ROBERT ROSSEN
A CENTAUR PRODUCTION · A COLUMBIA PICTURES RELEASE
ORIGINAL SOUNDTRACK LP ON COLPIX

This wistful romance deals with a therapist/patient love affair in an asylum.

Kobayashi's **Kwaidan**: five years to prepare, one to shoot and a huge budget.

1965

1964 Academy Awards, Santa Monica Civic Auditor., 5 Apr.

Best Film:	*My Fair Lady* (dir: George Cukor)
Best Director:	George Cukor
Best Actor:	Rex Harrison *(My Fair Lady)*
Best Actress:	Julie Andrews *(Mary Poppins)*
Best Supp. Actor:	Peter Ustinov *(Topkapi)*
Best Supp. Actress:	Lila Kedrova *(Zorba the Greek)*

Copenhagen, 1 January
Release of Carl Theodor Dreyer's new film, *Gertrud*, with Nina Pens Rode and Bendt Rothe.

Madrid, 4 January
The British director David Lean has just begun filming *Doctor Zhivago*, based on Boris Pasternak's Nobel Prize-winning novel.

Hong Kong, 18 January
Philippe de Broca is on location for his new film *les Tribulations d'un Chinois en Chine*, starring Jean-Paul Belmondo, Ursula Andress and Jean Rochefort.

Genoa, 27 January
During the congress on "The Third World and the World Community", Brazilian director Glauber Rocha presented his manifesto titled *The Aesthetics of Hunger*.

Paris, 2 February
The *Bulletin d'information du CNC*, has published an alarming report on cinema attendance: 273 million spectators in 1964 as compared to 423 million in 1957.

London, 15 February
Royal Command Performance of *Lord Jim* at the Odeon cinema in Leicester Square, in the presence of Queen Elizabeth, the Queen Mother and HRH the Princess Margaret. Peter O'Toole plays the title role in writer-director Richard Brooks' adaptation of the Joseph Conrad novel, a mammoth production, wonderfully photographed by Freddie Young. Proceeds from the evening will go to the Cinema and Television Benevolent Fund.

Cairo, 3 March
Henry Barakat, one of Egypt's most prolific filmmakers, has moved off the beaten track of musical comedy and melodrama with his latest film *The Sin* (*Al Haram*). Starring Faten Hamama, it is a cruel naturalist drama on the realities of rural life.

Lisbon, 15 March
Release of *The Enchanted Isles* (*As Ilhas Encantados*), by Carlos Vilardebo, with Amalia Rodrigues and Pierre Clementi.

France, 30 March
In protest against duties and taxes, exhibitors have organized a country-wide "Free entry" operation to draw the public's attention to the problems faced by the industry.

Los Angeles, 22 June
Producer David O. Selznick has died of a heart attack (his fifth) at the age of 63. His widow is actress Jennifer Jones.

Hollywood, 13 July
Columbia has announced that Jerry Lewis is to shoot *Three on a Couch*, his first film for the studio after completing 33 films for Paramount.

London, 18 August
Catherine Deneuve and the English photographer David Bailey were married today. Despite being the mother of Roger Vadim's son Christian, it is Miss Deneuve's first marriage. Vadim has recently married actress Jane Fonda.

Los Angeles, 26 October
George Stevens has started proceedings against Paramount and the NBC television network to prevent the mutilation of his film *A Place in the Sun*, which the network is scheduled to screen on 12 March 1966. He is demanding $1 million in damages if cuts are made to the film.

Rome, 30 October
Federico Fellini has just completed *Giulietta degli Spiriti* (*Juliet of the Spirits*), starring Giulietta Masina.

London, 31 October
Charlie Chaplin called a press conference to announce his plans to make a new film, *A Countess From Hong Kong*. Marlon Brando and Sophia Loren will co-star.

Paris, 1 November
The editorial staff of *Cahiers du Cinéma* has come up with some new policy decisions: firstly to distance itself from writers' political views, secondly to refuse to systematically promote American films. The film critics' new methods are to be based on structuralism and linguistics.

Paris, 10 November
Brigitte Bardot has claimed a symbolic one-franc payment of costs and damages from several publications which published photos, taken with a telescopic lens, of La Madrague, her property near St. Tropez, and its occupants.

Prague, 12 November
Release of *Lasky Jedne Plavovlasky* (*Loves of a Blonde*), director Milos Forman's second film.

Los Angeles, 15 November
Walt Disney and his brother Roy have announced their plans for a second Disneyland in Florida. Walt Disney World, which is planned to open in October 1971, will cover an area twice the size of Manhattan. The land alone cost $5 million.

Paris, 17 November
On leaving a club in rue Princesse, the actor Peter O'Toole hit the Comte Philippe de La Fayette over the head. The latter has decided to lodge a complaint.

Paris, 22 November
Roger Vadim has started shooting *la Curée*, based on the novel by Emile Zola. The film will star American actress Jane Fonda (daughter of Henry), who has agreed to appear nude on the screen for the first time. She happens to be the director's wife.

New York, 30 November
Otto Preminger is appearing in the State Supreme Court where he has brought charges against Columbia's television subsidiary, Screen Gems, for having granted transmission rights for his highly acclaimed film, *Anatomy of a Murder*, to a Chicago station which is planning 36 commercial breaks during screening.

New York, 30 November
The Legion of Decency has been re-christened the National Catholic Office of Motion Pictures.

New York, 13 December
Brigitte Bardot's arrival at Kenne airport today caused great excit ment and jostling among the crow assembled to greet her.

Hollywood, 22 December
The Screen Writers Guild signed new retrospective agreement tod with Universal Pictures for fil made during the period 1948-196 From now on, script writers are receive 1.5 percent of the studi revenue from television screeni rights for their credited films.

BIRTHS

New York, 4 April
Robert Downey Jr.

New York, 31 May
Brooke Shields

Paris, 14 August
Emmanuelle Béart

Illinois, 24 August
Marlee Matlin

New York, 3 September
Charlie Sheen (Carlos Estevez)

DEATHS

Texas, 14 January
Jeanette MacDonald

California, 23 February
Stan Laurel

Hollywood, 23 March
Margaret Dumont

Hollywood, 23 March
Mae Murray

Chicago, 10 April
Linda Darnell

New York, 7 June
Judy Holliday

Hollywood, 8 September
Dorothy Dandridge

Los Angeles, 27 September
Clara Bow

Englishman Michael Caine, w combines an earnest, bemused a with cool nonchalance and a core steel, is the perfect screen incarnati of Len Deighton's Harry Palmer.

"AN ADMIRABLE THRILLER IN EVERY RESPECT!" —THE NEW YORKER

"A THINKING MAN'S 'GOLDFINGER', FUNNIER BY FAR THAN ANY OF THE BOND FILMS AND MORE REWARDING, TOO!" —Newsweek

HARRY SALTZMAN presents

THE IPCRESS FILE

From the breathless best-seller by LEN DEIGHTON

starring

MICHAEL CAINE

also starring

NIGEL GREEN · GUY DOLEMAN · SUE LLOYD

Produced by HARRY SALTZMAN · Directed by SIDNEY J. FURIE · Executive Producer CHARLES KASHER

Screenplay by BILL CANAWAY & JAMES DORAN · Music composed and conducted by JOHN BARRY

TECHNICOLOR® TECHNISCOPE® A UNIVERSAL RELEASE

UNIVERSAL CITY STUDIOS

▷

Happy Agnes Varda wins the Prix Louis Delluc with 'le Bonheur'

Seule, une femme
pouvait oser faire ce film
MAG BODARD
le Bonheur
AGNES VARDA
JEAN-CLAUDE DROUOT
MARIE-FRANCE BOYER
Interdit aux moins de 18 ans

Marie-France Boyer and Jean-Claude Drouot in ***le Bonheur****, a film which surprises with its liberal expression of passion.*

Paris, 8 January
Agnes Varda's third film, *le Bonheur* (*Happiness*), has been awarded the 22nd Louis Delluc prize. The plot is rather unusual: François, a young carpenter, lives happily with his wife Claire and their two children, Sandrine and Olivier. One day, François falls in love with Emilie, a pretty post-office employee. He conceals nothing from his wife, hoping she will accept the fact that he can be happily married and, at the same time, love his mistress. Then when Claire drowns herself, François lives happily ever after with Emilie and the children. The use of idyllic color landscapes, advertisement-style aesthetics and Mozart's music on the soundtrack, create an ambiguity and ironic reflection on the film's title. The amorality of the ending has provoked controversy: Is it a feminist or anti-feminist statement? As if to answer, the posters proclaim: "Only a woman would have dared make this film!" Another layer is added to the film by the fact that the man, his wife and children are played by a real-life family, Jean-Claude, Claire, Sandrine and Olivier Drouot. Marie-France Boyer portrays the mistress.

The hills are alive with the supercalifragilistic sound of Julie

New York, 3 March
Julie Andrews' shining soprano rectitude soars above the saccharine sentimentality of Rodgers and Hammerstein's Broadway smash, *The Sound of Music*, directed by Robert Wise. Andrews is in her element as Maria, the postulant nun who leaves her Austrian abbey to care for the seven children of Christopher Plummer's irascible Baron von Trapp, stays with them through thick and thin and eventually becomes his wife. With her guidance the family is then transformed into a troupe of singers, and as such they elude the Nazis and escape into Switzerland. Based on a real-life story, and handsomely filmed on location in Salzburg and the Austrian Alps, *The Sound of Music* is more than two and a half hours of captivating corn. Christopher Plummer, himself a distinguished Shakespearean actor, seems glumly aware of this and his performance appears almost willfully wooden. This does nothing to prevent Andrews dispensing her special brand of wholesomeness over the entire landscape from the moment she begins to belt out the title number and Ted McCord's Todd-AO camera pans across swathes of truly breathtaking scenery. Other musical highlights include "Edelweiss", sung by Andrews, the children and Plummer (his voice was dubbed by Bill Lee), the Andrews number, "My Favorite Things" and Abbess Peggy Wood singing "Climb Every Mountain".

Julie Andrews, Christopher Plummer and the entire Von Trapp tribe.

The final curtain falls for Stan Laure

Los Angeles, 23 February
Eight years after the death of Oliv Hardy, Stan Laurel has succumb to a heart attack in his Santa Moni home. Born Arthur Stanley Jeffe son in Ulverston, England, on June 1890, he settled in the Stat in 1912, after understudying Charl Chaplin during a Fred Karno to of America. He changed his nam to Stan Laurel and began a lengtl stint in vaudeville before breaki into films in 1917. That year he a peared in a two-reel short with O ver Hardy, but it was not until 19 that they began their comic partne ship in *Putting Pants on Philip*.

Sylvie revitalized at the age of 82

Sylvie, delightfully shameless at 82

Paris, 26 February
The Shameless Old Lady, the fir feature directed by theater design René Allio, gives the octogenari actress Sylvie, the role of her li Sylvie, born Louise Sylvain, a cha acter actress in the French cinem for over 50 years, grabs her fi starring role with both hands. Bas on a story by Bertolt Brecht, it te of how a grandmother, who h lived a quiet life devoted to her larg family, decides to change her habi on becoming a widow. She buys car, joins a political group, befrien a prostitute, and goes on vacatio before dying happily.

...udrey's disappointment is Julie's reward

...o r: Rex Harrison, Audrey Hepburn, Jack Warner and George Cukor.

...os Angeles, 5 April
...his year's Academy Awards cere-...ony, hosted by Bob Hope at the ...nta Monica Civic Auditorium, ...as a bittersweet occasion: bitter for ...udrey Hepburn, sweet for Julie ...ndrews. Miss Hepburn, exquisite ... a white full-length gown with ...oves to match, found herself pre-...nting the Best Actor Oscar to her *...y Fair Lady* co-star, Rex Harrison, ...d having to stand by and watch ...e original Eliza Doolittle, Julie ...ndrews, who was passed over for ...e film in Audrey's favor, receiving ...e Best Actress Oscar for *Mary ...oppins*. The pill was particularly ...tter to swallow, since Audrey had ...iled even to be among the 12 nom-...ees for *My Fair Lady*, which went ...n to win eight Awards, including Best Picture, Best Director (George Cukor) and Color Costume Design (Cecil Beaton). It was sweet revenge for Andrews, who was cast in her winning role by Jack Warner, the very man who refused to use her for Eliza Doolittle. Non-Americans Peter Ustinov and Lila Kedrova took away the Best Supporting Oscars, the former for the heist comedy, *Topkapi* and the latter for her affecting performance in *Zorba the Greek*. *Mary Poppins* and *My Fair Lady* shared the music awards between them, making it a bonanza year for Warner Bros., while the choice for Best Foreign Film was *Yesterday, Today and Tomorrow*, a compendium of three stories from director Vittorio De Sica, past his best, and hardly a worthy contender.

...an Bates (left), Anthony Quinn in **Zorba the Greek**, cinematography winner.

Shocking death by fire of Linda Darnell

Linda Darnell with Cornel Wilde in her best-known role in **Forever Amber**.

Hollywood, 10 April
Linda Darnell has met a terrible end while staying with friends. She was burned to death when a cigarette she had been smoking set fire to the living room where she was sleeping. Apparently she had been watching one of her old movies before the fire broke out. Darnell was a dark-eyed, sultry siren at Fox during the 1940s, where she did her best work with Otto Preminger, but her career wound down rapidly in the Fifties. She had recently hit the comeback trail with an A.C. Lyles Western, *Black Spurs*, which awaits release.

Rod Steiger haunted by the Holocaust

New York, 24 April
Rod Steiger, whose career has been languishing of late, has delivered a clammily impressive performance in *The Pawnbroker*, directed by Sidney Lumet, with whom Steiger worked in television a decade ago. Steiger takes the title role, playing Sol Nazerman, a Jew living in Harlem who inhabits a private world haunted by memories of the Nazi death camps of World War II. Adapted from Edward Lewis Wallant's novel by David Friedkin and Morton Fine, the film was shot on location in New York, lending authenticity to a harrowing portrait (further embellished with a fine score by Quincy Jones).

Rod Steiger (right) with Jaime Sanchez in Sidney Lumet's **The Pawnbroker**. ▷

'The Knack' knows how to get it at Cannes

Ray Brooks and Rita Tushingham in ***The Knack... And How to Get It.***

Cannes, 12 May
Great Britain reigned at this year's Cannes Film Festival, taking the Grand Prix for Richard Lester's *The Knack... And How to Get It*, and capturing the best actor and actress awards for the co-stars of William Wyler's film *The Collector*, Terence Stamp and Samantha Eggar. *The Knack*, a tale of four young people sharing lodgings in London, has a youthful jauntiness, and fresh performances from a relatively unknown cast. In contrast, Special Jury Prize winner Masaki Kobayashi's *Kwaidan* is an eerie compendium of four ghost stories, its imagery, derived from Japanese paintings, beautifully composed on the wide screen.

Stamp and Eggar, ***The Collector.***

A murderously mad Catherine Deneuve

Psychosis: Catherine Deneuve.

London, 10 June
Roman Polanski's *Repulsion* is an inside-out *Psycho* in which cool Belgian blonde Catherine Deneuve surrenders to schizophrenia in an apartment in London's South Kensington. Her sexual fears drive her to kill her boyfriend John Fraser and slash lecherous landlord Patrick Wymark to death with a razor. We follow the descent into madness through her eyes, from the minutely observed obsession with cracks in the pavement to the terrifying hallucinations which crowd in on her. The film's sense of oppressive decay is symbolized by the image of a fetus-like skinned rabbit stuffed into Deneuve's handbag.

Ida Kaminska: a miracle not to be missed

Ida Kaminska and Jozef Kroner in Kadar's poignant heart-rending film.

Cannes, 25 May
The Czechoslovakian director Jan Kadar's *The Shop on Main Street* has been shown at Cannes, giving an opportunity to see a revelatory, indeed miraculous performance by the elderly actress, Ida Kaminska, and leaving not a dry eye in the house. Set in Nazi-occupied Czechoslovakia, the film tells the story of an old Jewish lady who owns a button shop with barely a button in it, is stone deaf, and seems not to knc that there is a war going on. A low carpenter (Jozef Kroner) is ma "Aryan controller" of the shop, a he becomes caught between se interest and growing affection f the innocent and bemused object his surveillance. Kadar captures t political climate with absolute cla ty, but it is the personal relationshi and the tragedy that comes abo that stays in the memory.

Julie Christie's high style and loose mora

New York, 3 August
As the titles roll in John Schlesinger's latest screen effort entitled *Darling*, Julie Christie's gigantic face is slapped over the images of starving children on a London advertisement billboard. She's a model, drifting opportunistically through the shallows of chic London society, her image defined by the men she is with, all of them "image-makers": Dirk Bogarde's liberal television pundit, Laurence Harvey's sleekly glib marketing mogul and Roland Curram's homosexual photographer with whom Christie competes for the same lover on a Capri holiday. Frederic Raphael's acerbic screenplay reserves an ironic fate for the blithely self-absorbed "Darling" – an empty marriage to an Italian aristocrat in which she is condemned to an endless round of hollow good works. This British production is a bleak comment on the so-called "Swinging Sixties".

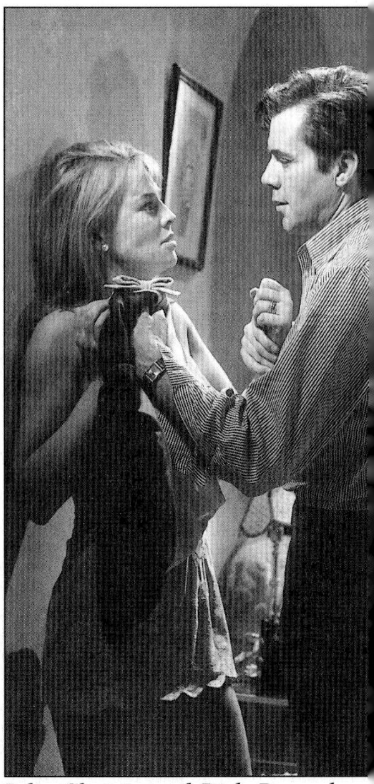

Julie Christie and Dirk Bogarde.

Truffaut has some questions for Hitchcock

Hollywood, 13 August
Today is not only Alfred Hitchcock's 66th birthday, but is also the day that he and the French director François Truffaut have agreed to meet in order to embark on a unique book project: to discuss and dissect the films and career of the "master of suspense", from his beginnings during the silent era of the 1920s up to the present day. Truffaut has already arrived in Hollywood with his friend and assistant Helen Scott, who will serve as interpreter. They hope to spend about 50 hours interviewing Hitchcock in his office at Universal Studios. First attracted to Hitchcock's films during his years as a critic on *Cahiers du Cinéma*, Truffaut hopes that this book will help to establish Hitch as one of the great figures of the world's cinema, and feels that, up to now, his achievements have been grossly underrated.

Bardot, Moreau in 'political' extravaganza

Paris, 22 November
Louis Malle has not prepared us for his new film *Viva Maria!*, which comes as a surprise in many respects. First, it is rare for a French director to attempt a Western-type picture. Shot in Eastmancolor and Panavision on location in Mexico, the movie has attempted to emulate the visual quality of the Hollywood movies, at the same time wittily sending up the kind of superproduction it is. In addition, the stars are the explosive duo of Brigitte Bardot and Jeanne Moreau as the Two Marias, a song-'n'-dance act in an unspecified Central American state. They both fall for a revolutionary leader (George Hamilton) whom they help in the struggle to overthrow the country's dictator. The gaiety of this large-scale extravaganza is in complete contrast to Louis Malle's last film, the downbeat *le Feu follet*. France's two top female stars seem to relish the zestful occasion, though some critics have deplored Malle's foray into commercial cinema.

*Brigitte Bardot and Jeanne Moreau in **Viva Maria**, politics and spectacle.*

Karina and Belmondo in 'Pierrot le fou'

Paris, 1 October
Jean-Luc Godard's new film, *Pierrot-le-fou*, shares some common ground with his first feature, *Breathless*. There is a clear similarity between the two heroes, both played by Jean-Paul Belmondo. Both are on the run, both are unable to assimilate into society, and each is betrayed by the woman he loves. Belmondo fits the role so well that it is surprising to learn that Godard originally had Michel Piccoli in mind, then tried to get Richard Burton. Nor did he originally cast his wife Anna Karina as co-star, but Sylvie Vartan, the singer, who refused the offer. The film is a stunning study of personal and global violence (there are references to Vietnam) which uses color in a dramatic and symbolic manner. Asked why there was so much blood in the film, Godard replied, "It is not blood but red." But mainly it is a tragedy about the transience of love. At the end, abandoned by Karina, Belmondo paints his face blue, places sticks of dynamite around his head and lights the fuse. He has second thoughts, but it is too late. "Damn, it's too absurd!" he says, before being blown up.

Jean-Paul Belmondo in Godard's study of personal and global violence.

Love in the time of revolution with Zhivago

New York, 22 December
Omar Sharif, who shot to international stardom in David Lean's film *Lawrence of Arabia*, has been cast in the title role of the same director's *Doctor Zhivago*, exchanging Arabian sand for Finnish snow. He is the idealistic doctor hero swept along by the epic events of the Russian Revolution in Robert Bolt's adaptation of Boris Pasternak's Nobel Prize-winning novel. Lean has explained that the Revolution provides "the canvas against which we tell a moving and highly personal love story." The lovers are Sharif's Zhivago and Julie Christie's beautiful Lara, for whom a brief happiness is tragically engulfed by the tide of history. Co-starring are Geraldine Chaplin, Rod Steiger, Tom Courtenay, Alec Guinness and Ralph Richardson, an immensely strong cast but one which fails to give the picture a specifically Russian flavor. Director Lean has approached the project with his customary deliberation and meticulous preparation. Shooting took nine months, in Finland and in Spain, where a huge exterior set representing 1917 Moscow was erected. In his youth Lean was an accountant, and something of the tidy precision of the bookkeeper has crept into the international movie packages over which he presides. It's as if the laborious preparation and then the process of editing, which Lean, a former editor, has described as "a kind of magic," mask a directing talent which has atrophied under the weight of craftsmanlike production values. Has Lean ceased to be a director and become a technician?

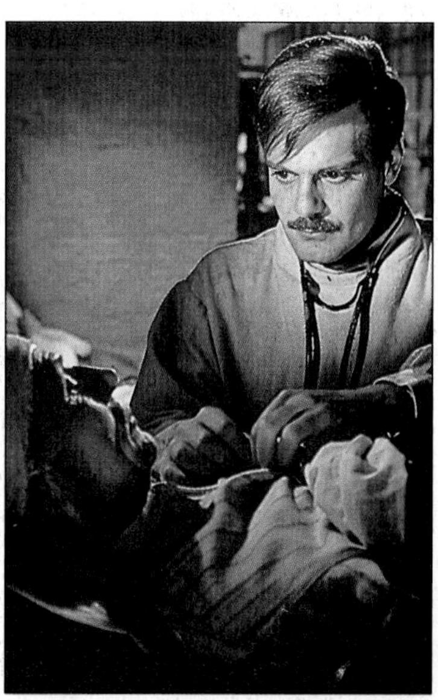

The doctor and one of his patients. ▷

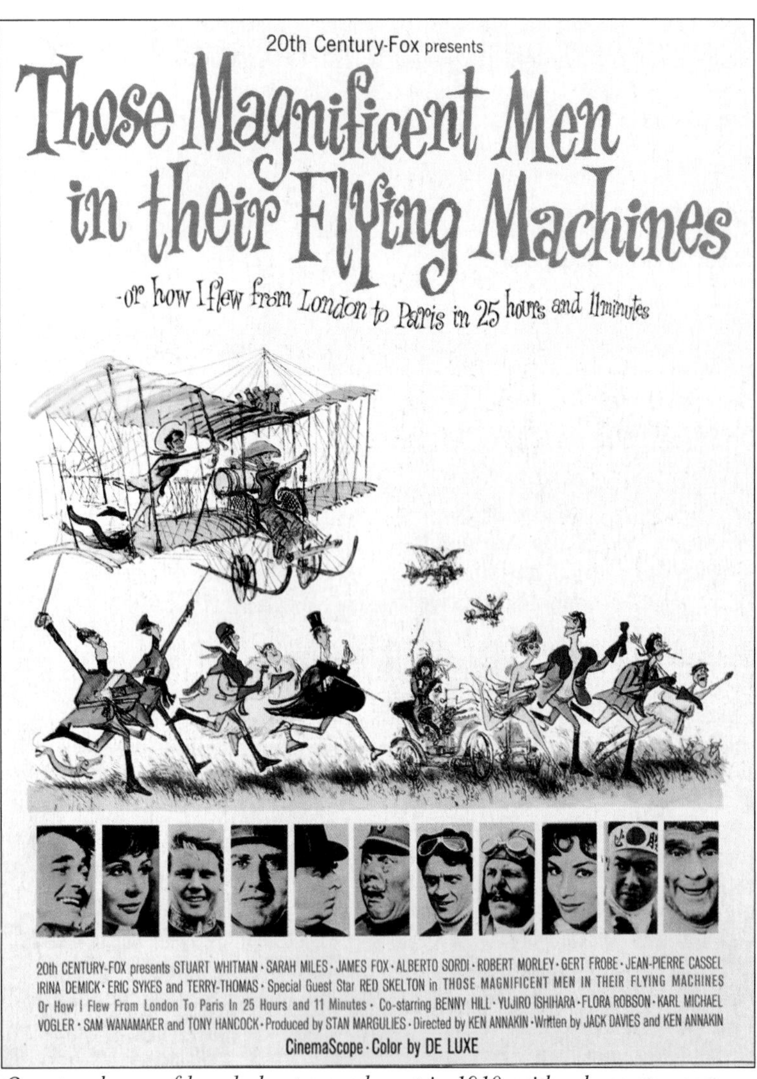

20th Century-Fox presents
Those Magnificent Men in their Flying Machines
-or how I flew from London to Paris in 25 hours and 11 minutes
20th CENTURY-FOX presents STUART WHITMAN · SARAH MILES · JAMES FOX · ALBERTO SORDI · ROBERT MORLEY · GERT FROBE · JEAN-PIERRE CASSEL IRINA DEMICK · ERIC SYKES and TERRY-THOMAS · Special Guest Star RED SKELTON in THOSE MAGNIFICENT MEN IN THEIR FLYING MACHINES Or How I Flew From London To Paris In 25 Hours and 11 Minutes · Co-starring BENNY HILL · YUJIRO ISHIHARA · FLORA ROBSON · KARL MICHAEL VOGLER · SAM WANAMAKER and TONY HANCOCK · Produced by STAN MARGULIES · Directed by KEN ANNAKIN · Written by JACK DAVIES and KEN ANNAKIN
CinemaScope · Color by DE LUXE

Over two hours of knockabout comedy, set in 1910, with a huge star cast.

Charlton Heston in ***Major Dundee****.*

Julie Andrews: ***The Sound of Music***

France's much-loved comic, Bourvil, in Gérard Oury's ***le Corniaud****.*

Larisa Kadochnilova and Ivan Nikolaychuk in Sergo Paradjanov's ***Shadows of Our Forgotten Ancestors*** *(USSR).*

604 ELC

Jane Birkin and Ray Brooks star in the prize-winning British export, ***The Knack... and How to Get It****.*

'ists in the Pocket: Lou Castel.

Julie Christie and Omar Sharif in ***Dr. Zhivago*** *from Pasternak's novel.*

ELLINI'S MASTERPIECE!
ANGELO RIZZOLI
FEDERICO FELLINI
GIULIETTA MASINA
SANDRA MILO
SYLVA KOSCINA
JULIET OF THE SPIRITS
RIZZOLI

'ontent poor, visuals superb.

JAMES STEWART
SHENANDOAH
TECHNICOLOR
DOUG McCLURE · GLENN CORBETT · PATRICK WAYNE · KATHARINE ROSS
and ROSEMARY FORSYTH

Affecting family saga in Civil War.

'ungarian Gabor Argady (left), Tibor Molnar (center) and Andras Kozak 'ight) in Miklos Jancso's hypnotic ***The Round-Up***.

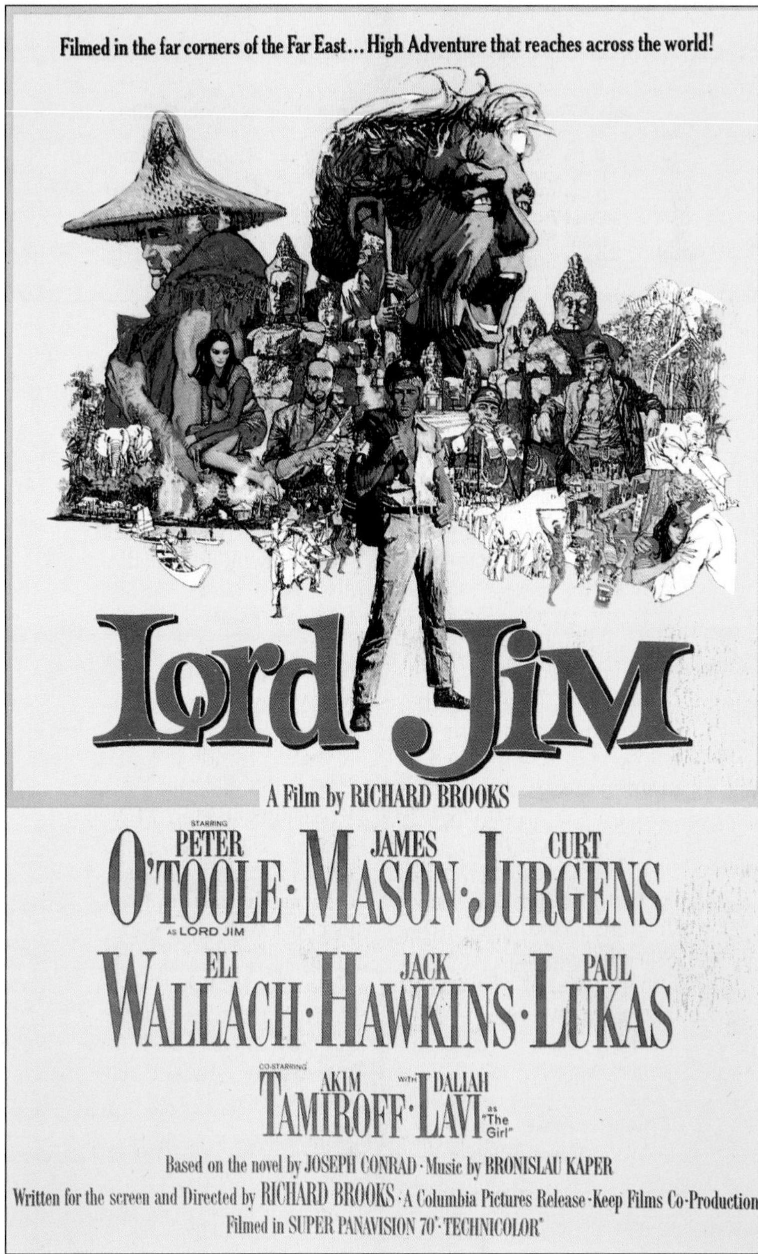

Filmed in the far corners of the Far East... High Adventure that reaches across the world!
Lord Jim
A Film by RICHARD BROOKS
STARRING
PETER O'TOOLE · JAMES MASON · CURT JURGENS
AS LORD JIM
ELI WALLACH · JACK HAWKINS · PAUL LUKAS
CO-STARRING AKIM TAMIROFF · WITH DALIAH LAVI as "The Girl"
Based on the novel by JOSEPH CONRAD · Music by BRONISLAU KAPER
Written for the screen and Directed by RICHARD BROOKS · A Columbia Pictures Release · Keep Films Co-Production
Filmed in SUPER PANAVISION 70® · TECHNICOLOR®

Lavish but tedious version of Conrad's novel which even O'Toole couldn't save.

Sailen Mukherjee (left) and Soumitra Chatterjee in Indian director Satyajit Ray's poignant ***Charulata*** *(aka* ***The Lonely Wife****).*

1966

1965 Academy Awards, Santa Monica Civic Auditor., 18 Apr.

Best Film:	*The Sound of Music* (dir: Robert Wise)
Best Director:	Robert Wise
Best Actor:	Lee Marvin *(Cat Ballou)*
Best Actress:	Julie Christie *(Darling)*
Best Supp. Actor:	Martin Balsam *(A Thousand Clowns)*
Best Supp. Actress:	Shelley Winters *(A Patch of Blue)*

London, 12 January
François Truffaut has started shooting his first film in English titled *Fahrenheit 451*, which stars Julie Christie and Oskar Werner.

New York, 20 January
Otto Preminger, the director and producer, lost his case yesterday to prevent any cuts or excessive commercial interruptions during the televised showing of his film *Anatomy of a Murder*. Justice Arthur Klein rejected Mr. Preminger's suit, which had been closely watched by the television industry.

Los Angeles, 31 January
Barbara Rooney, actor Mickey Rooney's wife, and her lover Milos Milocevic were found dead at her home. Police believe that Milocevic killed Barbara in a fit of jealousy, before taking his own life.

Hollywood, 25 March
Seymour Poe, Fox's executive vice president reported yesterday that up to 16 March, *Cleopatra*, which was considered to be the disaster of the decade, had earned $38,042,000 as the distributor's share of world box-office receipts. The film, which cost $31,115,000 to produce and a fortune in lawsuits, needs to bring in $41,358,000 for Fox to break even. Mr. Poe feels confident that the film will bring in $47 million over the next five years.

Paris, 5 April
The Film Authors Federation, the French Film Critics Association and the Writers Union for Truth are protesting about the banning of Jacques Rivette's new film, *Suzanne Simonin, la religieuse de Diderot* (*The Nun*).

Paris, 22 April
Release of Jean-Luc Godard's film *Masculin-féminin*, a sociological view of today's youth, with Jean-Pierre Léaud, Chantal Goya, and making her debut, Marlène Jobert.

Lausanne, 18 May
Greek actress Melina Mercouri has married director Jules Dassin.

Paris, 20 May
Release of the German film *Young Torless*, starring Mathieu Carrière. Volker Schlöndorff directed, and also adapted the screenplay from the work by Robert Musil.

New York, 24 May
MGM have announced that all their surviving silents are to be transferred on to non-inflammable film.

Rochefort-sur-Mer, 31 May
Jacques Demy has started shooting *les Demoiselles de Rochefort*, a musical comedy starring Françoise Dorléac and Catherine Deneuve.

Nashville, 18 July
Police have seized *Who's Afraid of Virginia Woolf?* and arrested the manager of a local cinema for contravening a municipal order that bans all entertainment of an obscene nature.

Los Angeles, 27 July
Release of Hitchcock's new film *Torn Curtain*, with Julie Andrews and Paul Newman.

New York, 12 August
Variety has published an article stating that 62 of the 136 American films underway this year are being made overseas. Among the biggest budget films are *2001: A Space Odyssey*, filmed in Great Britain, as is *The Dirty Dozen*, while *The Sand Pebbles* is being made in Taiwan.

New York, 16 August
Jack Valenti, the recently elected president of the MPAA, has sent a confidential memo to the heads of all studios recommending that "The classification of films by the government should be avoided at all costs." He feels the film industry should have its own classification system to avoid all external censorship.

Copenhagen, 19 August
Henning Carlsen has announced the release of his adaptation of Knut Hamsen's masterpiece titled *Sult* (*Hunger*), starring Per Oscarsson and Gunnel Lindblom.

Paris, 8 October
Channel One has screened ORTF's production *la Prise du pouvoir par Louis XIV* (*The Rise of Louis XIV*), directed by Roberto Rossellini from a script by Philippe Erlanger. Cinema distribution is also planned.

San Francisco, 12 October
Shirley Temple has resigned from the Festival selection board in protest against the planned screening of the Swedish film by Mai Zetterling, *Nattlek* (*Night Games*). The film deals with the question of incest.

Paris, 18 October
Director Jean-Luc Godard has stated: "Until I am paid on a par with Clouzot, Fellini and Clément, I cannot consider myself to be a success."

Stockholm, 18 October
Opening of Ingmar Bergman's film *Persona*, with his favorite actresses, Liv Ullmann and Bibi Andersson.

London, 26 October
Elizabeth Taylor and Richard Burton have founded their own production company, *Taybur*.

Washington D.C., 2 November
The Justice Department has decided that the massive acquisition of Columbia shares by the Banque de Paris et des Pays Bas to be illegal. American law forbids the ownership of television stations by foreign companies, and Columbia owns Screen Gems, a television distribution company.

Paris, 5 November
François Truffaut's much awaited biography of Alfred Hitchcock, *Le Cinéma Selon Hitchcock*, is at last available. The biography, which is based on a series of interviews between the two men last year, traces Hitchcock's life and career from his childhood up to his 50th film, *Torn Curtain*. Apart from Hitchcock's obvious sincerity, the book's greatest quality is the importance that Truffaut gives to the filmmaker's methods rather than to an analysis of the meaning of his films.

New York City, 1 December
Andy Warhol's *The Chelsea Gir* has made history as the first eve "underground" film to play in mainstream movie theater. Havir mesmerized audiences since Septer ber at the 41st Street Baseme Cinémathèque, the non-synchro ized two-screen marathon mov today transfers to the Cinema Re dezvous for a limited run only. special holiday release of *The Soun of Music* starts on 21 December.

Paris, 2 December
Release of Roman Polanski's *Cu de-sac*, The director's second Britis film after *Repulsion*.

Hollywood, 7 December
Vincente Minnelli is leaving MGM after 22 years. All his films, whic have ranged across a broad spe trum, were made at this studio.

BIRTHS

Los Angeles, 10 February
Laura Dern

Paris, 17 November
Sophie Marceau (Sophie Maupuis

London, 21 December
Kiefer Sutherland

DEATHS

Hollywood, 21 January
Herbert Marshall

Hollywood, 1 February
Hedda Hopper

Hollywood, 1 February
Buster Keaton

New York, 18 February
Robert Rossen

New York, 23 July
Montgomery Clift

Hollywood, 23 August
Francis X. Bushman

Beverly Hills, 13 October
Clifton Webb

Roger Corman produced and direc ed this unusual film which looks c California life: motorcycle gang. Mexicans, orgies, rape, death, et Peter Fonda is the wildest angel.

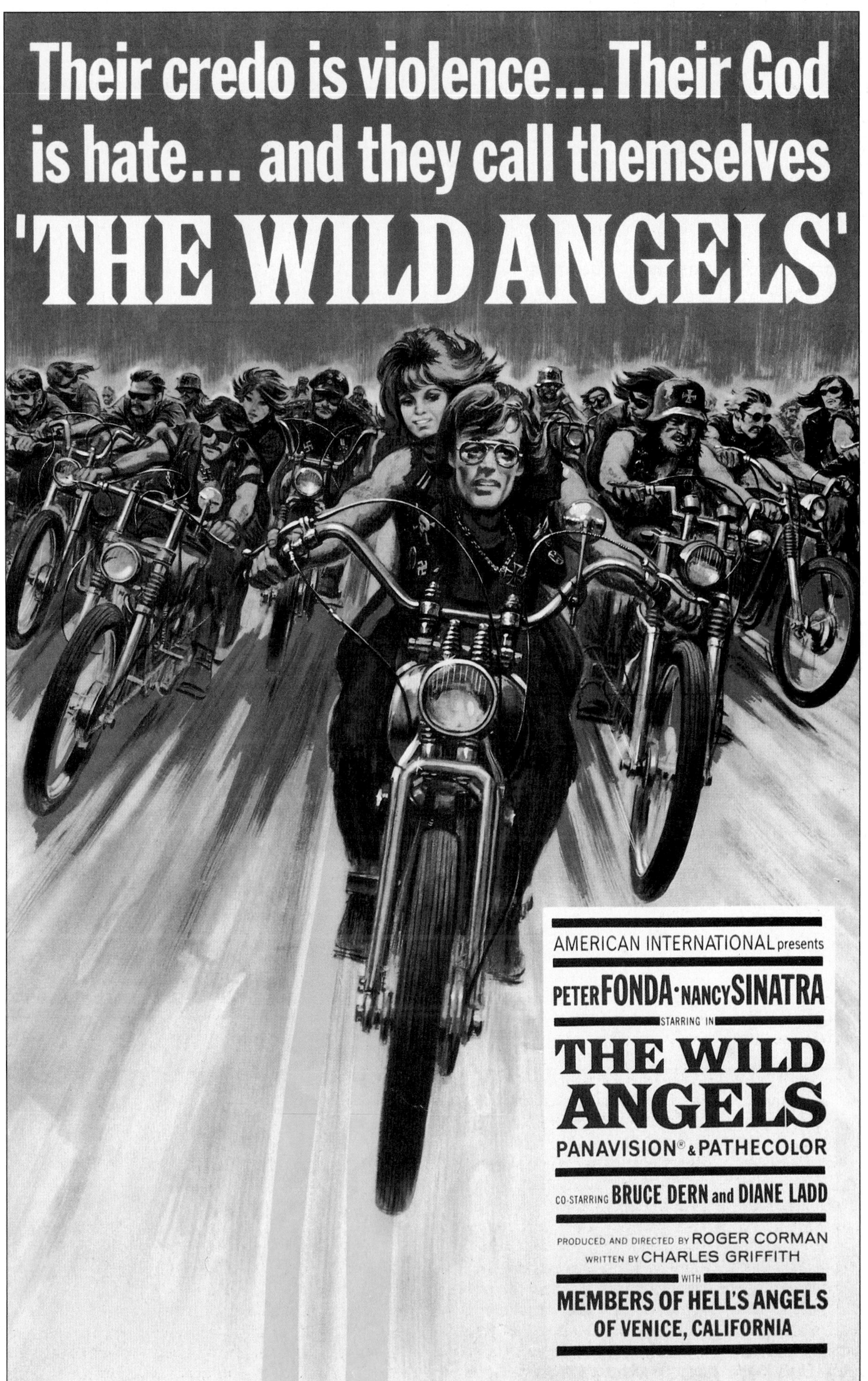
Their credo is violence... Their God is hate... and they call themselves
'THE WILD ANGELS'
AMERICAN INTERNATIONAL presents
PETER FONDA · NANCY SINATRA
STARRING IN
THE WILD ANGELS
PANAVISION® & PATHECOLOR
CO-STARRING BRUCE DERN and DIANE LADD
PRODUCED AND DIRECTED BY ROGER CORMAN
WRITTEN BY CHARLES GRIFFITH
WITH
MEMBERS OF HELL'S ANGELS
OF VENICE, CALIFORNIA

Hedy Lamarr lives out a nightmare

New York, 30 January

Fallen star Hedy Lamarr has been imprisoned for shoplifting. It's not the first time she has courted scandal. Born Hedwig Kiesler in Vienna on 9 November 1913, she was discovered by Max Reinhardt and in 1932 gained international notoriety by appearing fleetingly naked in a Czech film, *Ecstasy*. Her reputation went before her to London, from where she pursued a reluctant Louis B. Mayer to America on board the *Normandie*. Before the liner docked in New York, she had a seven-year contract and a new name. In the early Forties, Hedy was a byword for Hollywood glamour; however, although frequently cast as a woman of mystery or a *femme fatale*, she lacked the vital spark of personality. By 1949 she was virtually a back number when Cecil B. DeMille cast her to play Victor Mature's devious mate in *Samson and Delilah*, about which Groucho Marx observed that he never went to see movies where the hero's breasts were bigger than the leading lady's! By 1957, she was virtually playing herself as an aging movie star in *The Female Animal*. The much-married Lamarr has had four husbands: screenwriter Gene Markey, actor John Loder, a Texan millionaire and her own divorce lawyer. But now that she has fallen on hard times, Lamarr's private life is getting more column inches than her films.

With Mature in ***Samson and Delilah****.*

Michael Caine scores a huge success as Cockney Casanova 'Alfie'

London, 24 March

Michael Caine is the chirpy Cockney philanderer in *Alfie* directed by Lewis Gilbert and adapted from Bill Naughton's play. He plays merry hell with the women in his life, mournful Vivien Merchant, buxom Shelley Winters and waif-like Jane Asher, but he's beginning to find the competition catching up with him. Alfie's snappy flannels and bogus regimental blazer mark him out as an old-fashioned sexual predator, but losing ground to the dandified young bucks who prowl "Swinging London". His humiliation comes at the hands of Winters, whom he finds cavorting in bed with a young musician whose guitar, like a phallic symbol, is propped up by the door. There's something of Alfie in the bespectacled Caine's background. He was born Maurice Micklewhite in London in 1933, worked as a porter in Smithfield meat market and drifted into films after stage and television work. A long string of bits and walk-ons followed before he made his mark in *Zulu*, struggling with his vowels as an aristocratic officer. He then proved that girls do make passes at men wearing glasses, playing Len Deighton's hangdog hero Harry Palmer in *The Ipcress File*. Caine's Cockney accent and good-humored bewilderment at his success are perfectly attuned to the new "classless" world promoted by Britain's media. He seems like a handsome version of the guy who pulls you a pint in the pub or sells you a pound of oranges off the barrow in a street market. And his myopia makes him the first star since Harold Lloyd to wear glasses.

The reprobate Alfie (Michael Caine) with one of his 'harem' (Jane Asher).

The shadows of forgotten ancestors live on in new Soviet film

Moscow, 25 March

One of the most unusual and impressive Soviet films for a long time has just opened in Moscow. *Shadows of Our Forgotten Ancestors* is a variation on the Romeo and Juliet story set in the Carpathian mountains at the turn of the century. A young peasant falls in love with the daughter of the man responsible for the death of his father, but marries a woman who indulges in sorcery. The director, Sergo Paradjanov, reveals a remarkable talent for lyrical extravagance, placing him in the grand tradition of Alexander Dovzhenko. Using radiant Sovcolor, he brings a swirling, kaleidoscopic camera style to this rural folk tale. But who is Paradjanov? He was born Sarkis Paradjanian in Tbilisi in Georgia of Armenian parents in 1924. He was brought up in luxury, though the family went through hard times during the Stalin years. He studied music at the conservatoire at Tbilisi, before enrolling in the state film school in Moscow at the age of 22. After he graduated, he worked in Kiev, where he co-directed his first feature work, *Andriesh*, in 1955, noteworthy for its use of surrealistic elements. This was followed by several undistinguished comedies and melodramas in the socialist-realist style. *Shadows of Our Forgotten Ancestors* is a striking departure from his previous work as well as from much of postwar Soviet cinema. The intense Ukrainian nationalism of the film has granted Paradjanov the patronage of Pyotr Shelest, the Ukrainian communist party boss.

Ivan Nikolaychuk in Paradjanov's ***Shadows of Our Forgotten Ancestors****.*

A second wedding or Sophia Loren

èvres, 9 April
etween the shooting of two films, ophia Loren has once again mar- ed Carlo Ponti, with whom she has een together since 17 September 957, after a marriage in Mexico. n order not to be prosecuted for igamy in Italy, where the producer still considered married to his first ife because divorce does not exist ere, Sophia has taken French na- onality. This second marriage, held the town hall at Sèvres, has given e marriage a legal basis. After the eremony, the couple were invited dine at the Coq-Hardi restaurant Bougival. The Italian star has just ompleted *A Countess From Hong ong*, opposite Marlon Brando, un- er the direction of Charles Chaplin. he leaves in a few days for the outh of Italy, where she will co-star ith Omar Sharif in *More Than a Miracle* (*C'era una Volta*), directed y Francesco Rosi, and produced y Carlo Ponti. She has decided that fterwards she will put her career on old for a while, because, at 34 years ld, she is expecting her first child.

David Lean and 'Doctor Zhivago' lose out to 'The Sound of Music'

Best Supporting Actress Shelley Winters, Sidney Poitier, Elizabeth Hartman.

Hollywood, 18 April
At this year's Oscar ceremony, televised in color for the first time, the Best Picture award was one of the most closely contested ever. *The Sound of Music* and *Doctor Zhivago* entered the competition neck and neck with 10 nominations apiece, and it was to remain a tie at the end. Five Oscars went to David Lean's Russian epic (Best Screenplay, Cinematography, Art Direction, Original Musical Score and Costume Design) but the top prizes eluded it. The Rodgers and Hammerstein musical was considered Best Picture, and Robert Wise gained the edge on David Lean for Best Director. *The Sound of Music* also won Best Musical Score, Editing and Sound. When it came to the Best Actress award, two Julies were in the running: Andrews for *The Sound of Music* and Christie for *Darling* and *Doctor Zhivago*. In the event it was Julie Christie who triumphed for her portrayal of an ambitious young model in the cynical and modish milieu created by John Schlesinger for *Darling*. Had her rival won, she would have been the first to match a record established by Luise Rainer for two Best Actress Oscars in succession. As it was, Julie Andrews accepted defeat gracefully, hugging her tearfully overjoyed fellow Brit. Best Supporting performers were the veteran trouper Martin Balsam for *A Thousand Clowns*, and second-time winner Shelley Winters as the blowzy, overbearing mother of a blind girl in *A Patch of Blue*. Lee Marvin carried off the Best Actor statuette for his hilarious, drunken, has-been gunfighter in *Cat Ballou*.

Rivette's controversial film is banned despite initial approval

Paris, 15 April
ifteen days after the banning of acques Rivette's *la Religieuse* (*The un*), André Malraux, the Minister f Culture, has announced that he ould not oppose the showing of e film at the Cannes Festival next onth. He has therefore implicitly epudiated Yvon Bourges, the Sec- etary of State for Information. The atter has already been long drawn ut. It was in 1962 that Rivette first onceived this faithful film adapta- on of Diderot's novel of 1760. But or three years the project came p against official opposition. Last eptember, after numerous changes ere made in the screenplay, Riv- tte and his producer, Georges de eauregard, began shooting, with e title role going to Anna Karina. he plot concerns Suzanne Simon- , who is forced, through lack of a owry, to enter a convent where she ndergoes a great deal of suffering, ncluding semi-starvation, beatings, sbian attentions from the Mother uperior, and attempted rape by a riest. Even before the film was completed, and without having seen any of the rushes, the association of former nuns, and the parents of students in "free" schools demanded a banning order. At the receiving end was Yvon Bourges, who went against the Censorship Commission which had authorized the film. The banning has now set public opinion alight, and an air of scandal surrounds the film. Finally, the sole beneficiary has been Diderot. For some days copies of his novel have been selling like hot cakes.

Anna Karina and Liselotte Pulver in Jacques Rivette's ***la Religieuse.***

Top box-office for happy film

New York, 18 April
Not only has Fox's *The Sound of Music* carried off the Oscar, but, with rentals topping the $70 million mark for North America alone, it has easily surpassed the recent box-office records set by MGM's *Ben-Hur* to become the biggest hit since *Gone With the Wind*. Mainly filmed on location in Austria in the 70mm Todd-AO process, with a budget of $8 million, the picture has played a major role in re-establishing Fox as one of the most active Hollywood studios – this only four years after it faced bankruptcy due to a series of flops and the escalating costs of *Cleopatra*. Not surprisingly, the studio intends to make more musicals, and is already planning a follow-up picture for star and director of *The Sound of Music*, Julie Andrews and Robert Wise, while *Dr. Dolittle*, starring Rex Harrison, starts filming shortly.

Lelouch's prize-winning romance opens in Paris

Racing driver Jean-Louis Trintignant in Lelouch's ***A Man and a Woman***.

Anouk Aimée and Souad Amidou.

Paris, 27 May
Claude Lelouch's film *A Man and Woman*, the Jury Prize winner at th Cannes Film Festival, has opened i Paris. It's a color supplement ro mance, starring Anouk Aimée an Jean-Louis Trintignant as a wido and widower who fall in love to th catchy strains of Francis Lai's mac deningly memorable theme song Lelouch himself was a photographe for glossy magazines, and *A Ma and a Woman*'s sleek surface more of a trick of the ad-man's len than an examination of the thorn reality of loss that invades the live of real people. The pain of the prin cipals is smoothed over by the pre tiness of Lelouch's camerawork an the luxury of their lives. The film sure to be a huge hit.

The Burtons dispense on-screen vitriol

Los Angeles, 22 June
Booze and self-disgust flow in torrents in the screen version of Edward Albee's play *Who's Afraid of Virginia Woolf*? Here, Warners have cast the world's most famous married couple, Elizabeth Taylor and Richard Burton, as one of the unhappiest ever to have tied the knot. The love-hate relationship between college history professor George and his blowzy wife Martha, daughter of the college president, has been festering for years before it explodes like a boil in the faces of the young campus couple – George Segal and Sandy Dennis – whom they invite home. As the martinis mingle with mutual loathing, both couples find themselves staring into the abyss. Choreographing this lacerating encounter, and also making his screen debut, is Broadway director Mike Nichols, who found the film a tough assignment: "There was a very unpleasant aspect for all of us. We had to keep coming back to the same damn room, over and over, every day. And the poor Burtons had to spit at each other and hit each other for days." How different from the stars' own decorous home lives.

An even-handed account of recent history

Venice, 10 September
For the Golden Lion this year, the jury of the Mostra has chosen a disturbing film which has attempted to seek out the truth of an event in recent history. Gillo Pontecorvo's *The Battle of Algiers* deals with the guerrilla war for Algerian independence from the French in 1957, as seen through the eyes of the participants. Shot in the actual locations, mixing actors with those who fought in the battle, and without recourse to any newsreel footage, the film probably comes closer to the truth and the complexities of the situation than many documentaries have. Its mai strength lies in its scrupulous atte tion to the views and problems c both sides. The film, subsidized b the Algerian government, exploi the possibilities of the Casbah's bac streets, contrasted with the sma avenues of the French quarters. Th winner of the Special Jury Prize wa Alexander Kluge's *Yesterday Gi* (*Abschied von Gestern*), a debut fe ture from Germany. This tale of completely amoral and rebelliou East German girl comes as a breat of fresh air from the moribund Ge man film industry.

George and Martha (Burton and Taylor), a pair of experts in bitter invective.

Jean Martin in Gillo Pontecorvo's ***The Battle of Algiers***, *the best film.*

ruffaut's journey to Britain with Bradbury

rançois Truffaut during the filming.

Paris, 16 September
Director François Truffaut has ventured into color for the first time with *Fahrenheit 451*. Adapted from a Ray Bradbury novel, it's a science fiction parable set in a future dystopia where all books are banned. Squads of firemen incinerate those that survive (the title refers to the temperature at which they ignite). Oskar Werner is the fireman who begins to have doubts about his job, seeks solace in a secret hoard of literature and finally joins the "book people", a community of fugitives who commit classics to memory. Each one is a living book. Cameraman Nicolas Roeg's photography, particularly the close-ups of blazing books, is superb.

'he fire brigade as conceived in the world of Ray Bradbury and Truffaut.

'he Production Code is thirty-six years old

lew York, 20 September
lecognizing that many changes in nores and social standards have aken place during the 36 years since ne Production Code was first estabshed, the MPAA (The Motion Picare Association of America), headd by Jack Valenti, has announced ne formulation of a new and more exible 'code of self-regulation' to eplace the more strictly enforced ules and regulations of the Hays 'ode. In fact, the thinking behind nis new approach was suggested by draft code published last year and ollows on the controversy caused y two recent films, *The Pawnbroker* 1965) and *Who's Afraid of Virginia Voolf?* It read, in part, "Brutality, licit sex, indecent exposure, vulgar r profane words and gestures, and offensive treatment of religions and racial or national groups, are noted as subjects for restraint, but interpretation in all cases... including nudity, is left to the discretion of the administrators." However, unlike the old Code, the wording of the new one has been left deliberately vague. In addition, it does not stress the moral obligations of filmmakers, nor does it insist on certain specific standards of moral conduct. It looks likely, therefore, that a new system of classification will be set up, designating films as "suitable for children" or "for adults only", similar to the one that is already operating in Great Britain. The code will thus meet the requirements of today's world, without the necessity for government regulation.

Ursula and the tribulations of Belmondo

*Jean-Paul Belmondo and Ursula Andress met while making **Tribulations d'un Chinois en Chine (Up to His Ears)** for director Philippe de Broca.*

Paris, 29 September
Jean-Paul Belmondo met sultry star Ursula Andress for the first time when they began filming *Tribulations d'un Chinois en Chine*, directed by Philippe de Broca. The co-stars rapidly became inseparable. Now Belmondo's wife, Elodie Constante, the mother of their three children, has filed for divorce, citing her husband's "intimate relations with a well-known actress." It would seem that Belmondo has tribulations of his own.

Flames quenched by a shower of stars

Paris, 13 October
The cast of René Clément's *Is Paris Burning?* reads like a Who's Who of international stars, among them Leslie Caron, Orson Welles, Gert Froebe, Alain Delon, Kirk Douglas, Glenn Ford, Anthony Perkins, Jean-Paul Belmondo and Simone Signoret. And that would appear to be the problem. The distinguished director's account of the historic liberation of Paris in 1944 is a tedious and disappointing muddle. Adapted by Americans Francis Ford Coppola and Gore Vidal from a French book, and backed by a stirring Maurice Jarre score, the film seems more concerned with parading its dozens of cameo performances than in delivering a coherent story.

*Orson Welles (left) and Gert Froebe in René Clément's **Is Paris Burning?***

Paramount bought by Gulf & Western

New York, 19 October
At the company's recent annual meeting, the stockholders of Paramount Pictures agreed to accept an offer of $83 per share (almost $10 over the market price) from Charles Bluhdorn's Gulf & Western Industries. This essentially means that the deal will now go ahead as expected. Paramount thus becomes the first major Hollywood film company to be owned by a corporate conglomerate. (General Tire and Rubber Company's purchase of RKO in 1955 hardly qualifies, since the studio was already in its death throes at the time.) Founded by Bluhdorn in 1957, the rapidly expanding Gulf & Western encompasses a variety of financial and manufacturing interests – not to be confused with Gulf Oil, an entirely different company. This new development represents a culmination of a battle for control of Paramount which has been waging over the past year. Under attack were the policies of executive vice president George Weltner, who had been running the company ever since longtime president Barney Balaban became chairman of the board. Weltner was challenged by a dissident group headed by Broadway producers Feuer and Martin and the chemicals mogul Herbert Siegel. While this group was making plans for a proxy overthrow of the management, Bluhdorn successfully stepped in.

Ronald Reagan is elected as governor

California, 9 November
Former movie actor Ronald Reagan, best known for *King's Row* and *Bedtime for Bonzo*, has been elected Republican governor of California, with 58 percent of the vote. Previously a Democrat, he was active in SAG (Screen Actors Guild) in the 1940s, becoming a board member and gaining his first experience of elective office as SAG president for six years. In the 1950s he worked most frequently on TV, hosting the *General Electric Theater*. Reagan first registered as a Republican in 1962, supporting Goldwater in 1964 before deciding to run for governor.

Czechoslovakia's young filmmakers brave forbidden ground

Prague, 18 November
The just-released *Closely Watched Trains* has already aroused much enthusiasm from both critics and the public. In his first feature film, 28-year-old Jiri Menzel brilliantly balances the themes of war and sexuality in a story set during the German occupation of Czechoslovakia. Menzel's screenplay focuses on the life of a young trainee railway guard at a remote country station, desperately trying to lose his virginity. He finally achieves his goal with a Partisan girl, who calls herself Victoria Freie (the underground password), before he is killed because of clumsiness and excess zeal. The director wanted a happy ending, but his co-writer Bohumil Hrabal, on whose novel this film was based, persuaded him to retain the tragic conclusion. But this closely-observed, satiric, touching and humorous film is an excellent example of the Czech New Wave.

For about three years now, the Czech cinema has continued to astonish with its freshness. There are now more than 20 directors in the country, mostly graduates from FAMU, the Prague film school founded in 1946. They have reacted against the ponderous and conformist films made during the Stalin era, drawing on everyday life for their inspiration in a realistic manner. Their humor sometimes verges on the burlesque, but it allows them to tell the truth beneath a jokey surface. Milos Forman's *Peter and Pavla* and *Loves of a Blonde* places the characters in various hilarious situations, a pretext to show how ill at ease the younger generation feels under a repressive regime. In Vera Chytilova's *Daisies*, two bored adolescent girls destroy material goods and play some outrageous pranks on those who belong to the consumer-oriented society. And an existential anguish pervades Jaromil Jires' *The Cry* and Ivan Passer's *Intimate Lighting*. These recent films are planting the seeds of the new Czechoslovakian society, one which addresses the aspirations of the young.

38 1639
Jiri Menzel's *Closely Watched Trains*. The films, too, are under scrutiny.

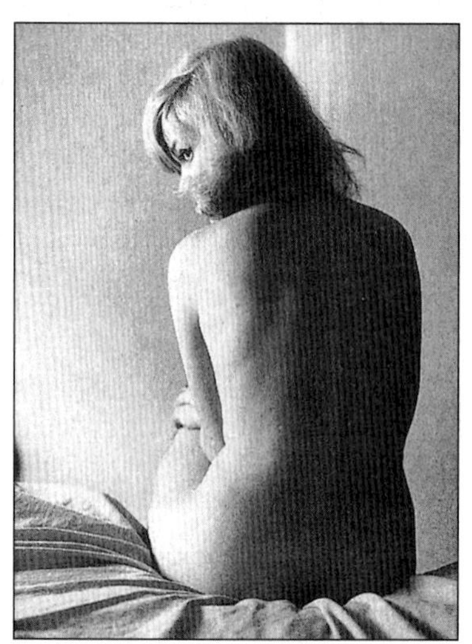
Lovely Hana Brejchova in Milos Forman's *Loves of a Blonde*.

Forman's first feature, *Peter and Pavla* (aka *Black Peter*), a key film.

***The Cry* directed by Jaromil Jires.**

he Disney kingdom oses its ruler

alifornia, 15 December
'alt Disney, one of the greatest gures of the entertainment world, as died aged 65. He suffered an cute circulatory collapse following rgery for the removal of a lung mor. "Pleasing the public is one of e most difficult tasks, because we on't really know ourselves what we ally like and what we want," he eclared in 1938. He certainly knew ow to please the public better than ost. Born in Chicago in 1901, Walt isney began work in a commercial rt studio in Kansas City, where he et Ub Iwerks, another promising oung artist. In 1923, he, Iwerks, nd Walt's older brother Roy set up eir own company to produce the artoon series, *Oswald the Rabbit*. 1 1928, the character that placed)isney on the road to fame and rtune, Mickey Mouse, was born. 'he Disney studio then grew and rew, its "stars" like Donald Duck nd Goofy, becoming international avorites. In 1934, Disney had the ovel idea of making an animated eature. *Snow White and the Seven)warfs* proved an enormous success, and it was followed by prewar lassics such as *Fantasia*, *Pinocchio*, *)umbo* and *Bambi*. Later on, the tudio branched out into live-action eatures, such as *Treasure Island*. Even though these never quite captured the perfection of the earlier lms, Walt Disney productions continued to make a vast amount of noney at the box office. Not content vith films and television programs,)isney fulfilled his dream in 1955 vhen he opened Disneyland, one of he most popular tourist attractions n the world.

Valt Disney, an original genius.

Antonioni's English film exposes the dangerous power of images

London, 18 December
The mystique of the fashion photographer in "Swinging London" has become so great that Italian director Michelangelo Antonioni has made *Blow Up*, a film about one. Former child actor David Hemmings plays the trendy, cherub-faced snapper whose photograph snatched of a couple in a park may, or may not, provide proof of a murder. His desultory sleuthing is constantly disrupted as he wanders through London's "magic village", inhabited by the beautiful people. Eventually the real and imaginary become inseparable. The body Hemmings has discovered disappears and his evidence is destroyed, with the exception of the largest "blow-up", which has become too abstract to reveal its secret. Antonioni's artful meditation on the manipulation of images has caught the mood of the moment.

*Hemmings the photographer and Redgrave the model in Antonioni's **Blow Up**.*

The director during the filming.

Tunisia holds its first film festival

Tunis, 11 December
The holding of the first Cinematographic Days at Carthage, is an important event for Arab and African cinema, which until now has been singularly lacking in international festivals. This festival, which was founded by Tahan Cheriaa, head of the cinema section of the Ministry of Culture and Information, is an ambitious project; it is hoping to become the principal meeting place for directors from Africa and Asia. Among the many films shown as part of the competition, the winner of the Grand Prix was a Senagalese film called *Black Girl*, directed by Ousmane Sembene. It tells the tragic story of a young Senegalese woman working as a maid for an affluent French family on the Riviera, concentrating on her isolation and her growing despair. Shot in a quasi-documentary style, influenced by the French New Wave, it is a remarkable first feature by Sembene, who is also a novelist of stature. Second prize went to the Kuwaiti film, *The Falcon*, by Khaled Siddiq.

Egyptian film falls foul of Nasser regime

Cairo, 30 December
Although the Egyptian film director Tewfik Saleh is the most cultivated of his generation, he has encountered nothing but hostility and incomprehension. After the commercial failure of his first two films, *Madmen's Alley* and *The Struggle of Heroes*, his third, *The Rebels*, has been censored. About a rebellion in a sanitarium, it is an allegory directed at the present Egyptian regime, and a thinly-veiled criticism of Nasserism. The Ministry of National Culture here imposes strict censorship on ideas it finds unpalatable.

*Tewfik Saleh's **les Révoltés**, the director's third attempt at gaining recognition.* ▷

The adventure, the ecstasy, the supreme suspense of a woman wronged beyond words, almost beyond revenge...
PARAMOUNT PICTURES AND KURT UNGER PRESENT
SOPHIA LOREN
IN
"JUDITH"
CO-STARRING
PETER FINCH · JACK HAWKINS
WITH HANS VERNER · TERENCE ALEXANDER · FRANK WOLFF · ARNALDO FOA · ANDRE MORELL · PRODUCED BY KURT UNGER
DIRECTED BY DANIEL MANN · SCREENPLAY BY JOHN MICHAEL HAYES · FROM A STORY BY LAWRENCE DURRELL · MUSIC SCORED BY SOL KAPLAN
TECHNICOLOR® PANAVISION®
A PARAMOUNT PICTURE

Sophia suffered in glorious makeup as the avenging wife of a Nazi. Dismal.

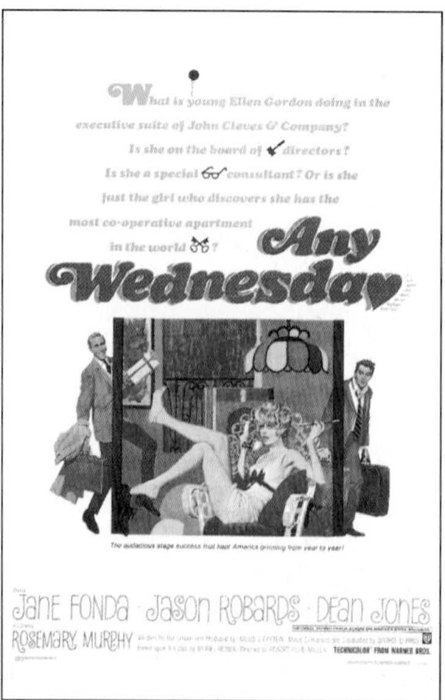
What is young Ellen Gordon doing in the executive suite of John Cleves & Company? Is she on the board of directors? Is she a special consultant? Or is she just the girl who discovers she has the most co-operative apartment in the world?
Any Wednesday
Jane Fonda · Jason Robards · Dean Jones
Rosemary Murphy
TECHNICOLOR

Millionaire and mistress a topic for farce, from a Broadway hit.

*Mike Hynson and Robert August i Bruce Brown's **The Endless Summe***

*Jeanne Moreau in **Mademoiselle**, directed by Tony Richardson.*

THEY STICK UP THE QUEEN MARY IN MID ATLANTIC
QUEEN MARY
FRANK SINATRA
VIRNA LISI
ASSAULT ON A QUEEN
Richard CONTE Errol JOHN Alf KJELLIN and
TONY FRANCIOSA
ROD SERLING · JACK FINNEY · WILLIAM GOETZ · JACK DONOHU

A caper movie that bombed.

*Andras Balint (left) and Klari Tolnay in Istvan Szabo's **Father** (Hungary).*

*Monica Vitti and Terence Stamp in **Modesty Blaise**, directed by Joseph Losey*

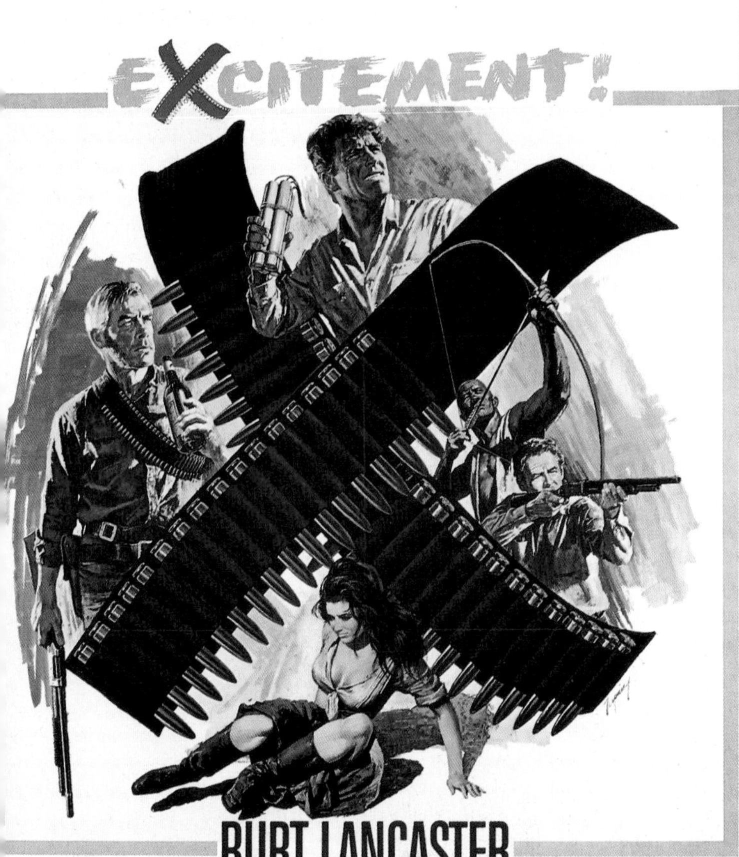
EXCITEMENT!
BURT LANCASTER
LEE MARVIN / ROBERT RYAN / JACK PALANCE
RALPH BELLAMY
with CLAUDIA CARDINALE
as Maria
THE PROFESSIONALS
PANAVISION® · TECHNICOLOR®
Based on a novel by FRANK O'ROURKE · Music by MAURICE JARRE
Written for the screen and Directed by RICHARD BROOKS · A COLUMBIA PICTURES RELEASE

KHARTOUM–WHERE THE NILE DIVIDES, THE GREAT CINERAMA ADVENTURE BEGINS!
CHARLTON HESTON · LAURENCE OLIVIER
RICHARD JOHNSON
RALPH RICHARDSON
KHARTOUM
ULTRA PANAVISION · TECHNICOLOR
UNITED ARTISTS

Five-star visuals and acting but dull account of General Gordon.

Kenneth Anger's underground film: ***Inauguration of the Pleasure Dome****.*

International Velvet stars in Andy Warhol's ***The Chelsea Girls****.*

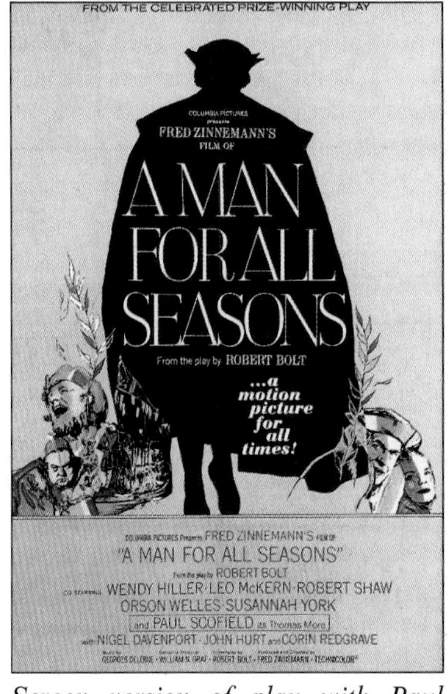
FROM THE CELEBRATED PRIZE-WINNING PLAY
FRED ZINNEMANN'S FILM OF
A MAN FOR ALL SEASONS
From the play by ROBERT BOLT
...a motion picture for all times!
"A MAN FOR ALL SEASONS"
WENDY HILLER · LEO McKERN · ROBERT SHAW
ORSON WELLES · SUSANNAH YORK
and PAUL SCOFIELD as Thomas More
NIGEL DAVENPORT · JOHN HURT and CORIN REDGRAVE

Screen version of play with Paul Scofield as Sir Thomas More.

N DE M

urt Lancaster (left), Claudia Cardinale and Lee Marvin in Richard Brooks' ***he Professionals****, a strong, suspenseful Western.*

l to r: Candice Bergen, Elizabeth Hartman, Kathleen Widdoes, Mary Robin Redd, Jessica Walter (on the couch): ***The Group****, directed by Sidney Lumet.*

1967

1966 Academy Awards, Santa Monica Civic Auditor., 10 Apr.

Best Film:	*A Man for All Seasons* (dir: Fred Zinnemann)
Best Director:	Fred Zinnemann
Best Actor:	Paul Scofield *(A Man for All Seasons)*
Best Actress:	Elizabeth Taylor *(Who's Afraid of Virginia Woolf?)*
Best Supp. Actor:	Walter Matthau *(The Fortune Cookie)*
Best Supp. Actress:	Sandy Dennis *(Who's Afraid of Virginia Woolf?)*

London, 2 January
Opening at the Carlton Theatre of Charlie Chaplin's *A Countess From Hong Kong* starring Marlon Brando and Sophia Loren. It is the second of Chaplin's films to star actors other than himself (the other was *Public Opinion*), and also the second to be made by Chaplin in Britain since his arrival from the U.S.

Paris, 20 January
The Studio des Ursulines cinema in the Latin quarter has re-opened after undergoing renovations.

New York, 20 January
MGM has published a full page announcement in several papers, pointing out that the company's shares have risen by 150 percent since Robert O'Brien took over as president in January 1963.

Hollywood, 20 February
Yakima Canutt has been awarded an honorary Oscar for his work as a stuntman and for developing safety devices to protect all stuntmen.

Paris, 22 February
Release of *le Voleur* (*The Thief of Paris*), directed by Louis Malle, with Jean-Paul Belmondo, Geneviève Bujold, Françoise Fabian, Marie Dubois and Charles Denner.

New York, 2 March
Judy Garland has announced her return to the screen in a film version of Jacqueline Susann's bestseller *The Valley of the Dolls,* which is to be filmed by Mark Robson for Fox. She made her last film in 1962.

Los Angeles, 8 March
Shirley MacLaine has won the suit she brought against 20th Century-Fox in 1966. The studio has been ordered to pay her $800,000, the total of her contract for the unmade film, *Bloomer Girl.* The star's contract stated that she was to be paid her salary whether or not the film was made.

Wilmington, 15 March
Philip Levin has begun new proceedings against MGM in the Federal court in Delaware, accusing Robert O'Brien's group of buying the votes of several shareholders in order to make sure that those supporting Levin would be in the minority at the general meeting.

San Francisco, 15 March
The Transamerica Company, an insurance and financial services giant, has made a public offer for United Artists. The company's board of directors is encouraging shareholders to accept this "friendly" offer.

Los Angeles, 10 April
At this year's Academy Awards Ceremony, both the Irving G. Thalberg Memorial Award and the Jean Hersholt Humanitarian Award, which are not always given, found worthy recipients. The Thalberg award went to Alfred Hitchcock, while actor Gregory Peck's many contributions to the film acting profession were recognized with the Hersholt award.

Lisbon, 20 April
Release of *Mudar de Vida* (*A New Life*), directed by Paulo Rocha with Isabel Ruth and Geraldo del Rei. Rocha was Jean Renoir's assistant on *The Vanishing Corporal.*

New York, 6 May
Gloria Swanson attended the first American screening of the restored version of *Queen Kelly*, directed by Erich von Stroheim, of which she was the producer and star. The uncompleted film had never been distributed in the U.S., but a short version of the film had been shown in Europe.

Los Angeles, 8 May
Robin Moore, the author of *The Green Berets*, which John Wayne intends to turn into a film, said in a radio interview that the Pentagon had done all in its power to prevent production of the film.

New York, 24 May
Release of *Cool Hand Luke*, directed by Stuart Rosenberg, starring Paul Newman.

Los Angeles, 28 May
Dyan Cannon has been granted a divorce from Cary Grant on the grounds of "brutal and inhuman treatment." Miss Cannon asserted that Grant used to lock her up and beat her, and on two occasions forced her to take LSD. The couple married in 1965.

Washington, 5 June
An official announcement has confirmed the creation of the American Film Institute. The Institute aims to train young filmmakers, to stock and conserve America's film heritage and to publish a catalogue listing all American-produced films. The $5 million annual budget will be funded jointly by the Federal Government, the MPAA, the Ford Foundation and a number of other private organizations. Headed by George Stevens Jr. the Institute has numerous filmmakers, actors and producers on its board of directors.

London, 10 June
The Queen attended the premiere of the fifth James Bond film *You Only Live Twice,* directed by Lewis Gilbert. Sean Connery stars once again as Agent 007, and the film introduces lovely newcomer Mie Hama.

England, 28 August
Britain's most prolific film director Maurice Elvey has died. During his long directorial career, which started in 1913, Elvey made over 300 feature films, including a handful in the U.S., and numerous shorts.

Paris, 13 October
Film critic and historian Georges Sadoul has died after a long illness.

London, 8 November
Roman Polanski's third English film, *The Fearless Vampire Killers,* with Sharon Tate is showing in London for the first time today.

Los Angeles, 8 December
Mike Nichols has presented his latest film, *The Graduate*, to the press. It stars Dustin Hoffman in his first major role – a role that was originally offered to Robert Redford who turned it down.

Paris, 19 September
A group of extremist right-win youths vandalized the Kinopanora ma Cinema, in the avenue de La Motte-Piquet, which was screenin *Far From Vietnam*. The manage was hurt in the attack.

Rome, 27 December
Actor Marcello Mastroianni ha been honored with the Italian Re public's Order of Merit.

BIRTHS

France, 31 May
Sandrine Bonnaire

Georgia, 28 October
Julia Roberts

DEATHS

California, 21 January
Ann Sheridan

France, 6 February
Martine Carol

Berlin, 29 April
Anthony Mann

New Hampshire, 30 May
Claude Rains

Hollywood, 10 June
Spencer Tracy

New Orleans, 29 June
Jayne Mansfield

London, 8 July
Vivien Leigh

New York, 21 July
Basil Rathbone

Germany, 9 August
Anton Walbrook

Hollywood, 13 August
Jane Darwell

California, 25 August
Paul Muni

Los Angeles, 9 November
Charles Bickford

---

*Lerner and Loewe's record-breakin stage musical, **Camelot**, comes to th screen. Directed by Joshua Loga with its glorious score intact, it co the studio a fortune to make.*

A WHOLE NEW WORLD OF MAGNIFICENT MUSICAL ENTERTAINMENT
CAMELOT
STARRING
RICHARD HARRIS · VANESSA REDGRAVE · FRANCO NERO · DAVID HEMMINGS · LIONEL JEFFRIES
ORIGINAL SOUND TRACK ALBUM ON WARNER BROS. RECORDS.
LAURENCE NAISMITH
PRODUCTION AND COSTUMES BY JOHN TRUSCOTT
BASED ON THE PLAY "CAMELOT" · BOOK AND LYRICS BY ALAN JAY LERNER · MUSIC BY FREDERICK LOEWE · DIRECTED BY MOSS HART · From "THE ONCE AND FUTURE KING" by T. H. WHITE
MUSIC SUPERVISED BY ALFRED NEWMAN
MUSIC BY FREDERICK LOEWE · SCREENPLAY AND LYRICS BY ALAN JAY LERNER · PRODUCED BY JACK L. WARNER · DIRECTED BY JOSHUA LOGAN
VANESSA REDGRAVE'S MAKEUP BY WARNER BROS. COSMETICS
TECHNICOLOR® PANAVISION® FROM WARNER BROS.

Demoiselles Deneuve and Dorléac dance for Demy

Real-life sisters Catherine Deneuve (left) and Françoise Dorléac in ***les Demoiselles de Rochefort****, a multi-colored universe.*

Paris, 8 March

The two sisters, Françoise Dorléac and Catherine Deneuve, are cast as the twins Solange and Delphine in Jacques Demy's newest film, *The Young Girls of Rochefort*. Following *Lola*, which was situated in Nantes, and *The Umbrellas of Cherbourg*, Demy has continued his exploration of the towns of the west coast of France, the area where he was born. The film was actually shot in Rochefort-sur-Mer, mainly in the Place Colbert, in the center of this charming town. Last year, Demy visited many towns along the coast looki for a square which could accomm date the vigorous choreography ar sweeping camera movements, ar his choice finally fell on Rochefo Teams of painters, under the dire tion of the designer Bernard Evei were assigned to redecorate t square, painting the facades of t houses in white, blue and pink. C 27 May last, Demy was ready shoot this colorful CinemaScop picture, a direct homage to the gre days of the MGM musical, whi Gene Kelly's presence in the ca underlines. The plot tells of two gir who run a ballet school and wh pine to meet their ideal man. Kell a concert pianist, and Jacques Pe rin, a sailor on leave, are also loo ing for their ideal woman. Mich Legrand composed the melodio songs which Dorléac and Deneu put over with enthusiasm, while th dancing, choreographed by Iris man Norman Maen, has been give a dynamic boost by Broadway hoo ers George Chakiris and Grov Dale. As for Gene Kelly, at 55 n body expected the kind of energet dancing that informed *On the Tow* to which this film pays tribute. B he lends the film an authentic imag of the Hollywood musical.

Martine Carol's sad passing

Monte Carlo, 6 February

Martine Carol has died of a heart attack, probably brought on by a mixture of alcohol and tranquilizers. Born Maryse Mourer in Biarritz on 16 May 1922, Carol made her big screen debut in 1943 in *la Ferme aux loups*. During the early 1950s she was the unchallenged sex symbol and box-office queen of French cinema before being finally overtaken by Brigitte Bardot. A voluptuous blonde whose ripe sensuality outweighed her modest acting talent, she was memorable in Richard Pottier's *Caroline chérie*, René Clair's *les Belles de nuit* and Max Ophuls' *Lola Montès*. She also appeared in a number of costume spectaculars directed by her husband Christian-Jaque. However, recent attempts to revive her flagging career met with little success.

Eric Rohmer's first feature-length 'moral tale' is set in St. Trope

Paris, 2 March

A new art cinema on the Left Bank, the Studio Gît-le-Coeur, has been inaugurated with the first showing of Eric Rohmer's second full-length feature, *la Collectionneuse*. It is the third of the director's Six Moral Tales, the first two being *The Baker of Monceau* and *Suzanne's Career*, both short films made some four years ago. *La Collectionneuse* concerns an artist (Patrick Bachau) and an antiques dealer (Daniel Pommereulle) sharing a friend's villa in St. Tropez with a bikini-clad nymphet (Haydée Politoff), who sleeps with a different boy every night. The two older men try to resist being added to her collection. "Less concerned with what people do than what is going on in their minds while they are doing it," in the words of the director, the film is witty, intellectual and analytical, as well as erotic. Rohmer establishes the theme of resistance to sexual temptation using the hedonistic, sun-soaked and undoubtedly alluring setting of St. Tropez to underline the dangers. Eric Rohmer is now hoping to complete the series with *The Girl on th Bicycle*, *Claire's Knee* and *Love the Afternoon*, titles which give som idea that the director will be conti uing to explore the same territory.

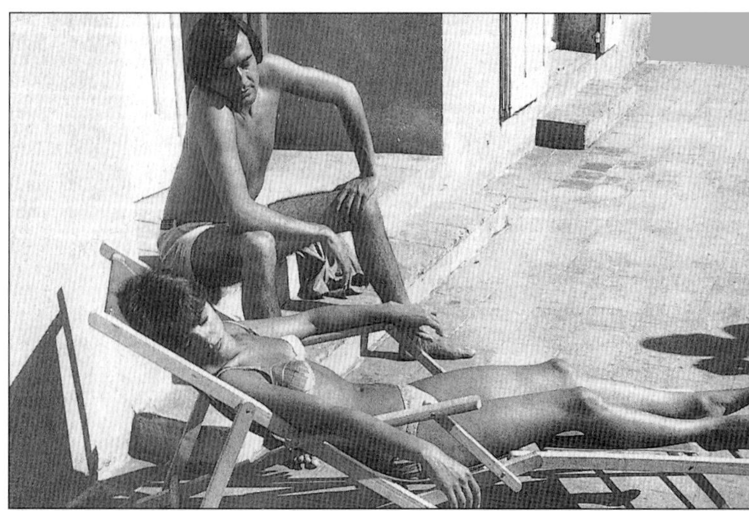

Haydée Politoff and Patrick Bachau in ***la Collectionneuse****, a 'moral' tale.*

oung boy shakes old man's prejudices

ichel Simon and Alain Cohen in Claude Berri's touching film **The Two of Us**.

aris, 11 March

he Two of Us (*le Vieil homme et nfant*), Claude Berri's first feaure, is a semi-autobiographical tale ry close to the director's heart. his work is a reconstruction of erri's own childhood experience, hich he describes as "a love affair etween a Jew and an anti-Semite." et during the Nazi occupation of aris, it tells the story of Claude (Alain Cohen), an eight-year-old Jewish boy, who is sent to stay with an elderly couple in the country. Since Pépé (Michel Simon), the old man, is a rabid anti-Semite, the boy is instructed to conceal his origins. Once there, Claude and Pépé forge a close relationship. The complex situation is handled with sensitivity and humor, seen mainly through the amused and bemused child's eyes.

Oscar ceremony almost ruined by TV strike

Los Angeles, 10 April

Only hours before the Academy Awards ceremony it was unclear whether the proceedings would be televised. The ABC network was threatened with strikes which would black out the prize-giving and leave the Academy with a financial loss of nearly a million dollars. In the end everything went ahead as planned, with Bob Hope once again acting as master of ceremonies. The most successful film was Mike Nichols' *Who's Afraid of Virginia Woolf?*, which won five Oscars, including a second Best Actress award for Elizabeth Taylor and Best Supporting Actress for Sandy Dennis, who made her screen debut six years ago in *Splendor in the Grass* but is better known as a Tony Award-winning Broadway star. Also taking home statuettes for their work on that picture were Haskell Wexler (cinematography), Richard Sylbert (art direction) and Irene Sharaff (costume). The vote for Best Picture went to *A Man for All Seasons*, directed by Fred Zinnemann, who also won the Best Director prize. His star in the picture, Paul Scofield, won the Best Actor award for his portrayal of the prickly, principled martyr Sir Thomas More. Walter Matthau, master technician of mordant comedy, was given the Best Supporting Actor Oscar for his performance as the ambulance-chasing lawyer in Billy Wilder's biting satire, *The Fortune Cookie*. And the Best Foreign Film award went to Claude Lelouch's huge international hit, *A Man and a Woman*.

Robert Shaw: ***A Man for All Seasons.***

Velles plays merry havoc with Falstaff

ew York, 19 March

rson Welles' third assault on hakespeare is *Chimes at Midnight*, ased on his own stage adaptation f the Falstaff scenes in *Henry IV, arts One and Two* and filmed in pain. His own interpretation of the le of the rascally Sir John Falstaff, hobbling on a gnarled walking stick, conjures poignant images of the tragic trajectory of Welles' own career. A bravura battle scene, filmed on a shoestring in a Madrid park, and the firelight dancing on the faces of Falstaff and Shallow remind us of the waste of this great talent.

ctor-director Orson Welles, a larger-than-life Falstaff in ***Chimes at Midnight.***

Tragic love story lyrically filmed in Sweden

Stockholm, 24 April

The director Bo Widerberg has addressed himself to a true-life tragedy for the subject of *Elvira Madigan*. It tells of a tightrope artist (Pia Degermark) and a married army officer (Thommy Berggren) who fall in love, run away together and enjoy an idyllic time in the countryside, before the outrage of 19th-century society destroys them. This affecting film is exquisitely shot with a lyrical camera and well-acted (to the strains of Mozart's Piano Concerto No. 21). One can anticipate an overseas audience for this.

Pia Degermark and Thommy Berggren in Bo Widerberg's ***Elvira Madigan.***

French film hits American jackpot

New York, 2 May
The winner of two Oscars at last month's Academy Awards ceremony – Best Foreign Language Film and Best Original Screenplay – Claude Lelouch's *A Man and a Woman* is one of the rare French pictures to make a hit in the United States. It opened modestly at a small art house in Manhattan last summer, immediately after its success at Cannes. The film did so well at the box office that it opened in other cities around the country. *Variety* has now devoted an entire article to the phenomenon: "According to Allied Artists, it is the most profitable film in their history, considering that it was made for a mere $100,000." *A Man and a Woman* has already made $2 million, a sum which could treble by the end of its showing. Its attraction seems to be its ultra-chic setting (Deauville), its attractive stars (Jean-Louis Trintignant and Anouk Aimée) and Francis Lai's catchy musical theme.

Cinema Novo director Rocha shocks Brazil with 'Land in Anguish

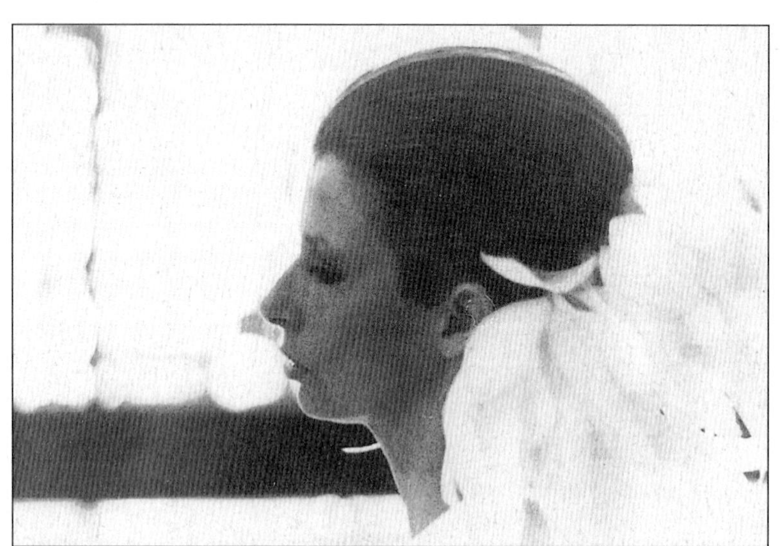
Glauce Rocha is the bereaved mistress in ***Terra em Transe (Land in Anguish).***

Black God White Devil*: his first fil*

Brazil, 2 May
Glauber Rocha is undeniably the leader of *Cinema Novo*, the radical movement of Brazilian directors. Rocha, who created a sensation three years ago with *Black God White Devil*, has now returned to similar territory with the equally lyrical *Land in Anguish* (*Terra em Transe*). The hero of the film is a journalist and poet severely beaten up by the police. On his death bed, he recalls his past and his struggle against the destructive agents of multinational companies and the Church. Rocha has here launched a vigorous attack on the "permane state of madness" that his count seems to be living in since the mi tary coup d'etat in 1964. In his d nunciation, he has called upon eve cinematic weapon at his disposal shock montage, jump cuts and t film-within-a-film technique.

Veteran star Spencer Tracy is laid to rest after a lengthy illness

Hollywood, 11 June
Spencer Tracy has died at his Hollywood home shortly after completing work on his last film, *Guess Who's Coming to Dinner*. Born in Milwaukee, Wisconsin, on 5 April 1900, he made his stage debut in 1922 as a robot in Karel Capek's *R.U.R.* He entered films in 1930, making two shorts for Vitaphone before John Ford cast him in *Up the River* and Fox gave him a contract. After four frustrating years at Fox, in which he gained a reputation for irascibility and heavy drinking, Tracy moved to MGM, where he established himself as a front-rank star in Fritz Lang's *Fury*. In 1942 he was teamed for the first time with Katharine Hepburn in *Woman of the Year*. Their remarkable partnership in nine subsequent films was matched by a lifelong romance, although Tracy never divorced his wife Louise Treadwell, whom he had married in 1923. Tracy was ill and exhausted throughout his final film, but, as Humphrey Bogart has said, "Spence was a natural, as if he didn't know a camera was there, or as if there had *always* been a camera there."

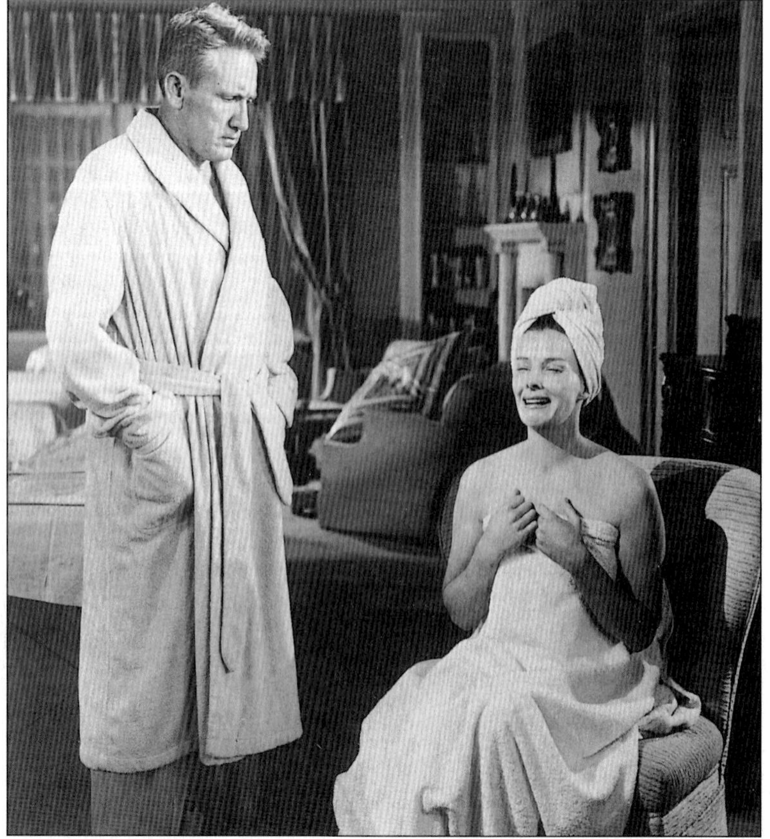
With Katharine Hepburn in George Cukor's ***Adam's Rib****, a huge hit in 1949.*

Tragedy strikes tw stars in two days

New Orleans, 29 June
Within the space of two days, t film world has lost two of its stars tragic accidents: the French actre Françoise Dorléac and the Ame can sex goddess Jayne Mansfiel Dorléac had been on vacation wi her sister Catherine Deneuve an brother-in-law David Bailey near S Tropez. She left two days ago drive to Nice in order to catch plane. But while traveling on t slippery road leading to the airpo she lost control of the car and w killed instantly. Dorléac was on 25 but had already made 15 film working with directors René Cla Roman Polanski, François Truffau Ken Russell and Jacques Dem Today, Jayne Mansfield, her lawy and chauffeur died in a car accide They were on the way to New O leans, when they ran into the back a truck which had stopped suddenl The star was found decapitate Mansfield, aged 34, had made h reputation as a busty blonde in number of comedies such as *Th Girl Can't Help It.*

e lovely Vivien Leigh dies of tuberculosis

*vien Leigh in **The Roman Spring of Mrs. Stone** (1961) with Warren Beatty.*

ndon, 8 July
ctress Vivien Leigh, forever Scar-t O'Hara in *Gone With the Wind*, is died of tuberculosis. Born Viv-n Mary Hartley in Darjeeling on November 1913, she made her reen debut in 1934. In 1939 David . Selznick chose her for *Gone With the Wind*, which brought fame and an Oscar. Marriage to Laurence Olivier followed in 1940 and lasted till 1960. She won a second Oscar in 1952 for her Blanche Dubois in *A Streetcar Named Desire*, but latterly her career had been dogged by depressive illness.

Black and white on same side of the law

*Sidney Poitier and Rod Steiger in Norman Jewison's **In the Heat of the Night**.*

New York, 2 August
The theme of racial bigotry in a small, sweltering Mississippi town is wrapped around a murder hunt in Norman Jewison's *In the Heat of the Night*. Sophisticated Philadelphia homicide expert Sidney Poitier reluctantly joins forces with the swag-bellied, manically gum-chewing red-neck local police chief Rod Steiger to solve the killing of "the most important white man in the town." In the process they strike up an uneasy but affecting relationship. The stirring theme song is delivered with feeling by Ray Charles.

La Religieuse' inally unbanned

aris, 26 July
was necessary for a change in the overnment, along with the replace-ent of Yvon Bourges by George orse as the Minister of State for formation, for the long ban on cques Rivette's *la Religieuse* to be ted. Nevertheless, Rivette has had make one slight compromise: the m will now be shown under the ti-e of *Suzanne Simonin, la religieuse Diderot*. The controversial work, ompleted in 1965, was originally nned from general release, but ndré Malraux permitted it to be own at last year's Cannes Film estival. Initially, it was a case of overnment officials giving in to rtain religious and moral pressure oups, who had objected, without aving seen the film, to its subject atter. Rivette's 140-minute color laptation from Diderot's 18th-ntury novel of the travails of a oung woman who is forced to enter convent, is far from prurient. In ct, it is directed with an austere etachment and an authentic sense f claustrophobia and pain.

'Bonnie and Clyde' is a defiant challenge to the social system

New York, 14 August
Warren Beatty has turned producer with *Bonnie and Clyde*, which stars Faye Dunaway and himself in the title roles. They're Bonnie Parker and Clyde Barrow, the publicity-hungry bank robbers whose gang blazed its way across the Midwest during the Depression years. Beatty canvassed François Truffaut and Jean-Luc Godard before securing the services of Arthur Penn as director. Penn has given his bandits a heroic quality: Dunaway's Bonnie is a touching blend of sensuality and innocence, while Beatty's impotent and shyly limping Clyde Barrow suggests a link between sexual satisfaction and outlawry. Their death, a slow-motion ballet of blood and bullets, has caused a sensation. With strong support from gang members Gene Hackman, Estelle Parsons and Michael J. Pollard, *Bonnie and Clyde* switches back and forth exhilaratingly between comedy, melodrama and barbed social comment.

Left: Clyde Barrow and Bonnie Parker in the climactic shoot-out that ends their lives. Right: How it all began...

Dark secrets of 'Belle de jour' win the prize

Catherine Deneuve in Luis Buñuel's ***Belle de jour****, winner of the Golden Lion.*

Venice, 10 September
Luis Buñuel continues to astonish. His latest film, *Belle de jour*, shot in France, is a witty and erotic exploration into the secrets of femininity. It tells of a respectable doctor's wife, who spends her afternoons working in a high-class brothel with kinky clients. Catherine Deneuve, as the part-time *bourgeois* whore, grows more beautiful with each perversion, imagined or otherwise. The film merited the Golden Lion. Coincidentally sharing the Special Jury Prize were two films reflecting the current Western interest in Maoism: Jean-Luc Godard's *la Chinoise* and Marco Bellocchio's *China is Near*.

Newman's lonely hero tough and touchin

Luke (Paul Newman) about to swallow fifty hard-boiled eggs in one session

New York, 1 November
"What we've got here is a failure to communicate," says Strother Martin's prison boss to Paul Newman's uncooperative inmate in *Cool Hand Luke*, directed by Stuart Rosenberg. Newman takes the title role of the loner, imprisoned for decapitating parking meters, who becomes the camp hero after defeating hulkir George Kennedy in a hardboil egg-eating contest guaranteed leave cinemagoers queasily eyei their popcorn. A descendant of suc 1930s melodramas as *I Was a Fug tive From a Chain Gang*, *Cool Har Luke* hands Newman one of h most powerful roles to date.

Charming swan song for Tracy and Hepburn

New York, 11 December
Stanley Kramer's *Guess Who's Coming to Dinner* at first appears to be a daring approach to romantic comedy, being about a love affair that crosses the color bar. It is, in fact, devoid of real problems, as a group of very attractive protagonists easily sort out the temporary discomfort caused by the intended engagement of an eligible middle-class black man (Sidney Poitier) to an eligible middle-class white girl (Katharine Houghton, Katharine Hepburn's real-life niece). But despite its soft center, this is a heartwarming and entertaining movie, likely to be a huge hit because it marks the final collaboration of a legendary team, Spencer Tracy and Katharine Hepburn. As the bewildered parents of the girl, both are superb. That Tracy died soon after filming was completed brings an extra lump to the throat.

Left to right: Sidney Poitier, Katharine Houghton and Katharine Hepburn.

Carryings-on at King Arthur's court

Warners have lavished no less than $15 million on *Camelot*, the screen version of Lerner and Loewe's Broadway show, which was itself adapted from the Arthurian novel by T.H. White, *The Once and Future King*. However, it's hard to see exactly where the money has gone, as the sets and costumes look decidedly tacky, and they are not enhanced by director Joshua Logan's vulgar use of color filters. It also remains to be seen whether the starry cast, none of whom can exactly be described as a scintillating singer, will ensure its success at the box office. Richard Harris, Vanessa Redgrave and Franco Nero form the Round Table ménage à trois as King Arthur, Guinevere and Lancelot, and they are supported by David Hemmings as Mordred, Lawrence Naismith as Merlin and Lionel Jeffries as King Pellinore. It will require something of Merlin's wizardry for the studio to recoup its investment. There's also some very sloppy continuity work. Lionel Jeffries' King Pellinore meets King Arthur for the first time about an hour into the picture, yet about 20 minutes earlier he can be clearly spotted at Arthur's wedding.

Harris, Redgrave and Nero.

nlikely candidate graduates to stardom

ne Bancroft as the predatory Mrs. Robinson and 'graduate' Dustin Hoffman.

w York, 21 December
the midst of a cold New York nter, there are long lines of young ople outside movie theaters, full expectation at seeing a movie at addresses them and their probns. The film is Mike Nichols' *The aduate*, and it features an unlikely w young star called Dustin Hoffman. He portrays 21-year-old Ben Braddock, who feels alienated from the shallow values of his wealthy parents and friends, and is lured into a relationship with a much older woman (Anne Bancroft). Hoffman is short and a bit of a *nebbish*. But it's the loser image that will make him a winner with the young.

i-fi and soft porn from Roger Vadim

ris, 25 December
ne Fonda has been directed for third time by her husband Roger dim in *Barbarella*, based on a ence fiction comic book. The film s created a storm, because Miss nda does a striptease during the opening credits. Although her nudity is partially hidden, this did not stop the censors from cutting some of it before releasing the film with a certificate restricted to audiences over 18. Thus critics have unfairly accused Vadim of "anti-eroticism."

ne Fonda in **Barbarella**, *a film version of Jean-Claude Forest's comic strip.*

'Weekend' opening closes Godard's year

Godard during the filming of **Weekend**, *his devastating attack on our society and the horrors of the motor car, which stars Mireille Darc and Jean Yanne.*

Paris, 29 December
With the release of *Weekend*, Jean-Luc Godard has ended a particularly prolific year, during which five of his films were shown to the public. *Made in USA* and *Two or Three Things I Know About Her* were released in January and March respectively. Godard had shot both films simultaneously during the previous summer. With these pictures, the director's style has become more elliptical, and his attitudes more militant. *Made in USA* takes place in 1969, in an Americanized Paris, where Anna Karina is searching for a man involved in the assassination of the Algerian leader Ben Barka. This is Godard continually redefining cinematic images in a spontaneous, topical, pop art manner. *Two or Three Things I Know About Her* is about a housewife (Marina Vlady) who prostitutes herself one day a week to obtain the household luxuries she wants. The film, the title of which refers to Paris, is another advance towards Godard's desire to find an equivalent to *"bourgeois* cinema". With *la Chinoise*, Godard seems to have moved towards a Maoist political commitment. It concerns five young people who set up a Maoist cell to try to put their theories into revolutionary practice. (Red is the appropriately dominant color.) And a disenchantment with French society is even stronger in *Weekend*, a devastating attack on modern life and the motor car.

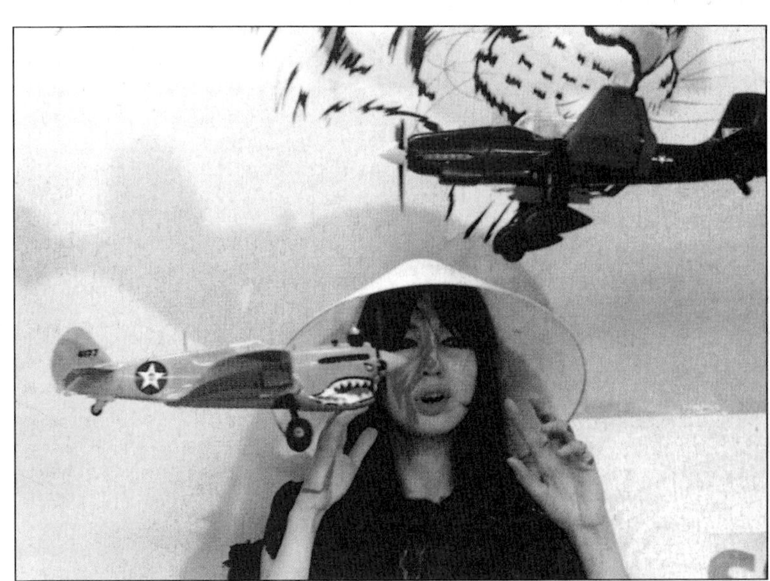

Juliet Berto in **la Chinoise** *which won the Special Jury Prize at Venice.*

Catherine Deneuve is the part-time prostitute in ***Belle de jour****, directed by Luis Buñuel, here with one of her customers (Iska Khan).*

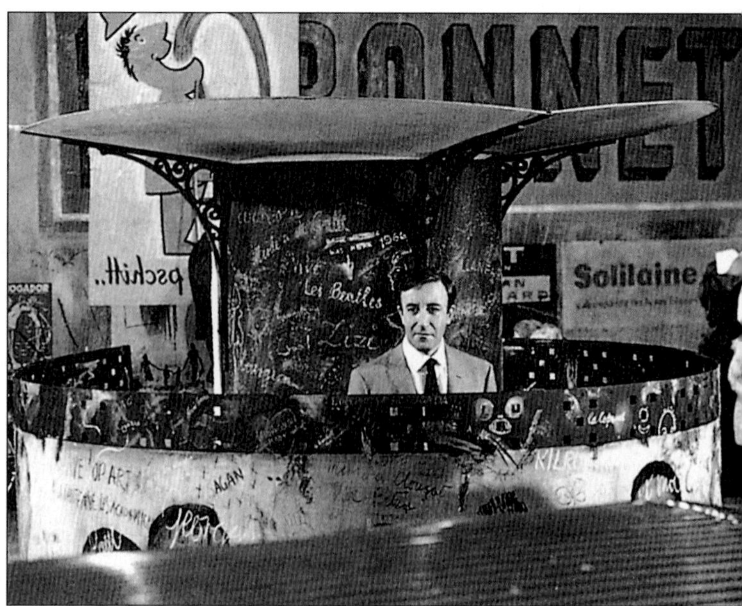
Solilaine

Peter Sellers in ***Casino Royale****, a misguided James Bond spoof with star ca*

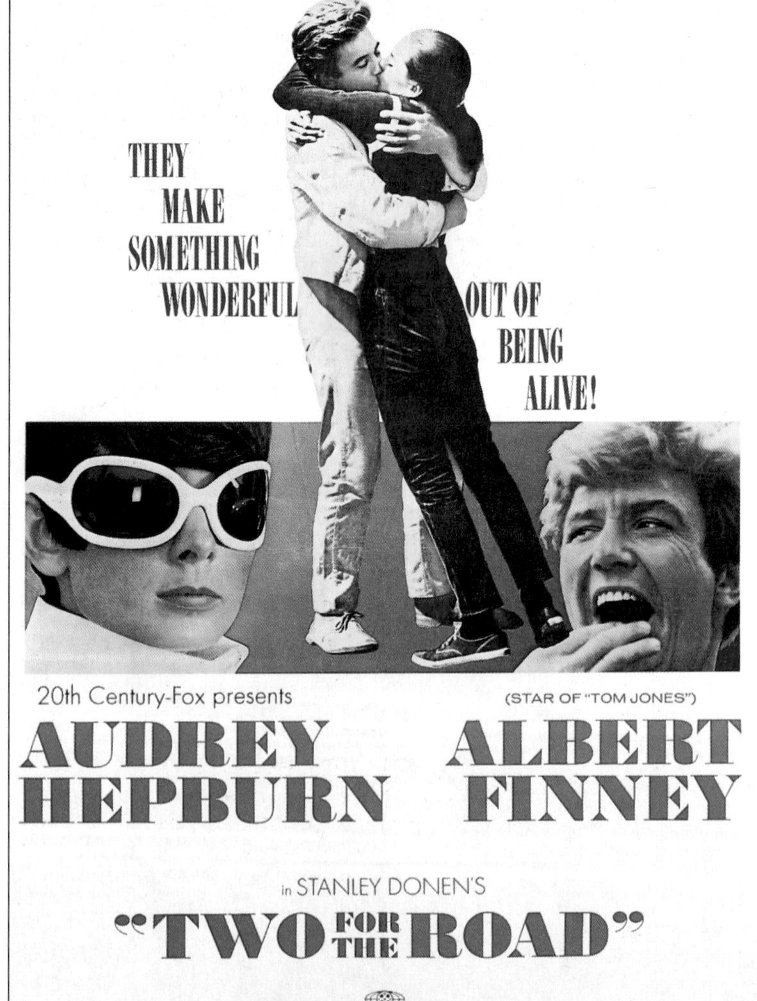
THEY MAKE SOMETHING WONDERFUL OUT OF BEING ALIVE!
20th Century-Fox presents
(STAR OF "TOM JONES")
AUDREY HEPBURN
ALBERT FINNEY
in STANLEY DONEN'S
"TWO FOR THE ROAD"
Suggested For Mature Audiences
with ELEANOR BRON · WILLIAM DANIELS · CLAUDE DAUPHIN · NADIA GRAY
produced and directed by STANLEY DONEN
written by FREDERIC RAPHAEL
music-HENRY MANCINI
Panavision® Color by DeLuxe
ORIGINAL SOUNDTRACK ALBUM AVAILABLE ON RCA VICTOR RECORDS

Chic, witty and wistful tale of marriage directed by Stanley Donen.

Mireille Darc and Jean Yanne in the nightmare of Godard's ***Weekend****.*

Elizabeth Taylor stars in ***Reflections in a Golden Eye****.*

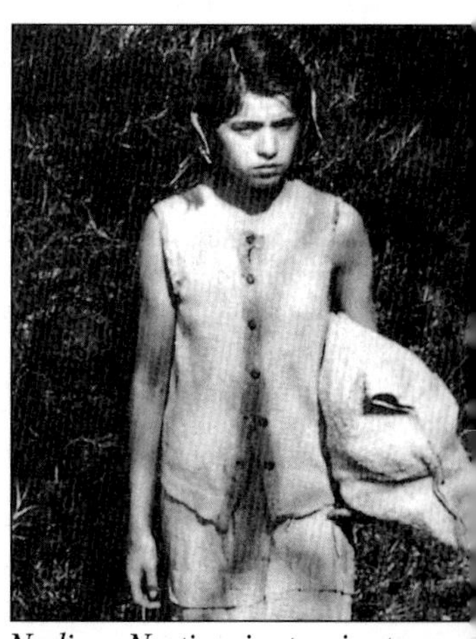

Nadine Nortier is tragic teenag ***Mouchette*** *for Robert Bresson.*

·e Marvin, Angie Dickinson in John Boorman's rough, tough **Point Blank**.

·hoolteacher Sidney Poitier (right) with Judy Geeson: **To Sir With Love**.

·eter Cook and Dudley Moore of **Beyond the Fringe** stage fame, are reunited
·n the big screen in Stanley Donen's **Bedazzled**.

*Sophia Loren and Marlon Brando in Chaplin's **A Countess From Hong Kong**.*

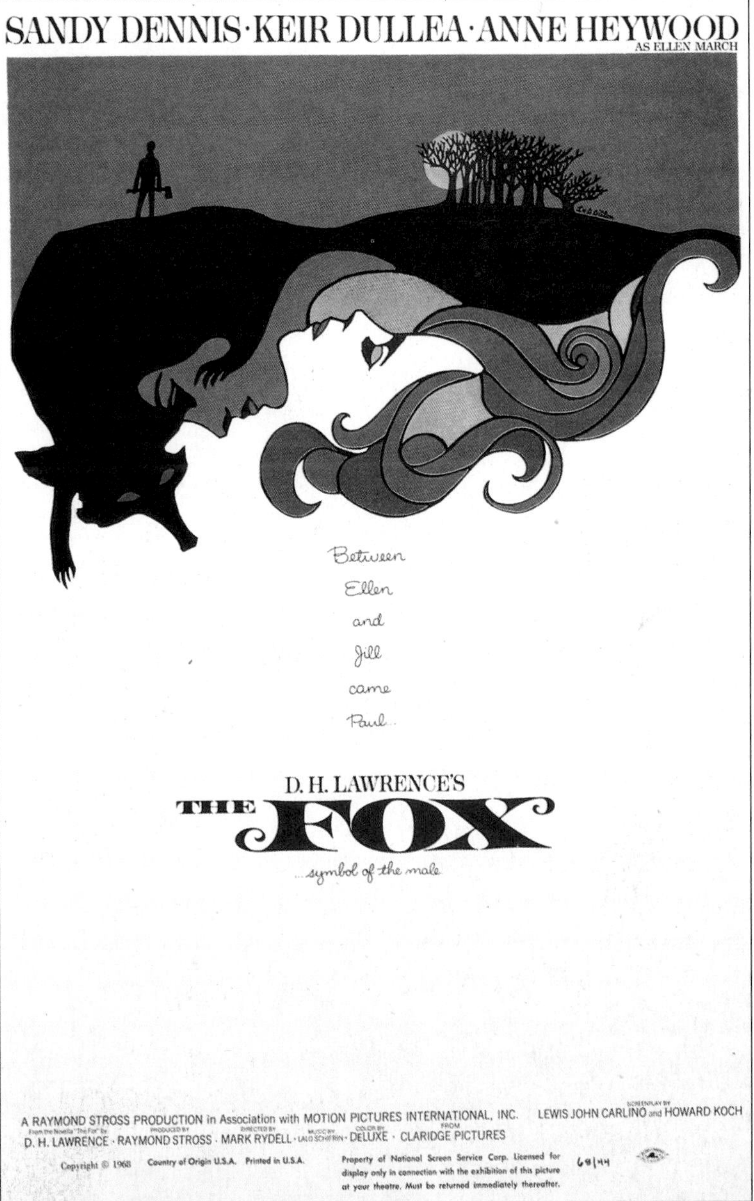
SANDY DENNIS·KEIR DULLEA·ANNE HEYWOOD
AS ELLEN MARCH
Between
Ellen
and
Jill
came
Paul.
D. H. LAWRENCE'S
THE FOX
...symbol of the male
A RAYMOND STROSS PRODUCTION in Association with MOTION PICTURES INTERNATIONAL, INC.
SCREENPLAY BY LEWIS JOHN CARLINO and HOWARD KOCH
From the Novella "The Fox" by D. H. LAWRENCE · PRODUCED BY RAYMOND STROSS · DIRECTED BY MARK RYDELL · MUSIC BY LALO SCHIFRIN · COLOR BY DELUXE · FROM CLARIDGE PICTURES
Copyright © 1968 Country of Origin U.S.A. Printed in U.S.A.
Property of National Screen Service Corp. Licensed for display only in connection with the exhibition of this picture at your theatre. Must be returned immediately thereafter.
68/44
A daring, atmospheric version of D.H. Lawrence's novel on a lesbian theme.

1968

1967 Academy Awards, Santa Monica Civic Auditor., 10 Apr.

Best Film:	*In the Heat of the Night* (dir: Norman Jewison)
Best Director:	Mike Nichols *(The Graduate)*
Best Actor:	Rod Steiger *(In the Heat of the Night)*
Best Actress:	Katharine Hepburn *(Guess Who's Coming to Dinner)*
Best Supp. Actor:	George Kennedy *(Cool Hand Luke)*
Best Supp. Actress:	Estelle Parsons *(Bonnie and Clyde)*

New Delhi, 5 January
Louis Malle has arrived in India, where he plans to make a film.

New York, 15 January
Customs have seized a copy of Jack Smith's avant-garde film *Flaming Creatures*. The picture has been declared obscene and the Justice Department is starting proceedings against its distributor.

New York, 19 January
A Swedish film directed by Vilgot Sjoman, *I am Curious - Yellow*, has been seized by the United States Customs Service here. Arthur Olick an assistant United States attorney said yesterday that the film was seized because "...it leaves nothing to the imagination, including the act of fornication."

London, 15 February
Laslo Benedek's *The Wild One*, has at last been released here. It has been banned by the British censors for 14 years due to the activities of a group of bikers in the film which were judged likely to incite violence among the youth.

New York, 21 February
Variety has reported that the 1967 release of *Gone With the Wind* earned $7.5 million in film rentals for MGM.

New York, 25 February
MGM has launched its publicity campaign for Stanley Kubrick's new film *2001: A Space Odyssey*, with a four page advertisement in the *New York Times*, the *Los Angeles Times* and the *Washington Star*.

Paris, 8 April
George Gorse, the Minister for Information, has authorized the release of Romain Gary's *les Oiseaux vont mourir au Pérou* (*The Birds Come to Die in Peru*), starring Jean Seberg and Maurice Ronet. The Cinema Control Commission had asked for a ban on the film.

New York, 17 April
Variety has announced that Frank Sinatra and Elizabeth Taylor are to co-star in *The Only Game in Town*. Filming is scheduled to start in early September.

New York, 18 April
The popularity of film study courses has soared in the last year. There are now 60,000 graduate and undergraduate students enrolled in 1,500 film courses at 120 colleges throughout the United States.

New York, 28 April
The American premiere of the Russian-made *War and Peace* will be held tonight at the DeMille Theater, Seventh Avenue and 47th Street. According to the Russians the seven-hour film is the most expensive ever produced. Screenings will be in two parts: alternate matinees and evenings. Admission prices are a record $7.50 for the best seats.

New York, 3 May
Producer Joseph E. Levine has sold his company Embassy Films to the Avco conglomerate for $40 million. Embassy first made a name for itself in the early 60s distributing foreign films, but soon moved into production. Its greatest success to date has been *The Graduate*.

Paris, 6 May
In an announcement made to the daily, *Combat*, Robert Favre Le Bret, the general organizer of the Cannes Festival, said: "This year's Festival will have sportsmen, musicians, festivities of all kinds and a truly exceptional selection of films."

Los Angeles, 1 June
Director Jacques Demy is making *The Model Shop*.

New York, 3 June
Andy Warhol was hit by several bullets fired by one of his entourage, Valerie Solanis. He is in a hospital, reported to be in a critical state.

Washington D.C., 16 July
The American Film Institute has embarked on an ambitious new publishing project to compile a complete catalogue of all films produced in the U.S. since the beginning of the cinema.

Hollywood, 5 August
Italian director Michelangelo Antonioni has started shooting his first American film, *Zabriskie Point*, with Mark Frechette and Daria Halprin.

USA, 31 August
Robert Redford has opened an ecological ski resort, Sundance, created and named by him.

Rome, 13 September
Director Pier Paolo Pasolini's film, *Theorem*, has been seized by order of the courts.

Stockholm, 29 September
Release of *Skammen* (*Shame*), by Ingmar Bergman, with Liv Ullmann and Max Von Sydow.

New York, 9 October
For the first time in the history of American motion pictures, the film industry has, of its own volition, opted to use a classification system. MPAA head Jack Valenti stated that the system will come into effect on 1 November. Classifications are as follows: G – general exhibition; M – mature audiences; R – under 17s only admitted accompanied by an adult; X – adults only (over 18). However, States may raise the ages of the last two ratings to comply with their own laws.

Paris, 30 October
Release of *la Chamade* (*Heartbeat*), directed by Alain Cavalier, with a screenplay based on the novel by Françoise Sagan. Michel Piccoli and Catherine Deneuve head the cast.

Paris, 11 November
The French director of Polish origin Walerian Borowczyk has won the art film prize for *Goto, l'Ile d'amour* (*Goto, the Island of Love*), with Pierre Brasseur, Ligia Branice, Ginette Leclerc and René Dary.

Paris, 12 November
From today the Institute of Advanced Cinema Studies (IDHEC), will hold its classes in the Raleigh Cinema building in rue des Vignes.

San Francisco, 21 November
Jane Fonda has taken up the cau of the American Indians who ha settled on Alcatraz Island.

Italy, 29 November
Romain Gary's French film, *T Birds Come to Die in Peru*, has be banned throughout the country.

London, 30 November
Premiere of Jean-Luc Godard's fi *One Plus One*, with the rock gro the Rolling Stones.

Paris, 22 December
Three Parisian cinemas specializi in sex films, the Strasbourg, Rex ar Bosphore have been closed by t police until mid-February.

Italy, 31 December
The total number of productio (including co-productions) for th year is 254 films, compared to 1 in 1965. About 40 films belong the erotic comedy genre.

BIRTHS

California, 14 February
Molly Ringwald

DEATHS

California, 13 February
Mae Marsh

Hollywood, 16 April
Fay Bainter

Italy, 4 June
Dorothy Gish

Los Angeles, 7 June
Dan Duryea

New York, 26 August
Kay Francis

New York, 18 September
Franchot Tone

Hollywood, 30 October
Ramon Novarro

New York, 12 December
Tallulah Bankhead

*Peter O'Toole and Katharine He burn in **The Lion in Winter**. Hepbur won her third Best Actress Oscar, u precedented in being a shared awa with Barbra Streisand.*

The Most Significant Reserved Seat Attraction Of The Year!

JOSEPH E. LEVINE presents
AN AVCO EMBASSY FILM
Starring PETER O'TOOLE
as Henry II, King of England

KATHARINE HEPBURN
as Eleanor of Aquitaine, His Wife
A MARTIN POLL Production
THE LION IN WINTER
with JANE MERROW as Princess Alais JOHN CASTLE as Prince Geoffrey TIM DALTON as King Philip of France
ANTHONY HOPKINS as Prince Richard the Lionhearted NIGEL STOCK as William Marshall NIGEL TERRY as Prince John
Based upon the play by JAMES GOLDMAN
Executive Producer JOSEPH E. LEVINE
Screenplay by JAMES GOLDMAN
Produced by MARTIN POLL
Directed by ANTHONY HARVEY
Music composed and conducted by JOHN BARRY
An AVCO EMBASSY PICTURES Release PANAVISION® In COLOR

Roman Polanski has married Sharon Tate

London, 20 January
Last year, the Polish-born director Roman Polanski made *The Fearless Vampire Killers, or Pardon Me But Your Teeth Are in My Neck*, in London, with a young, unknown American actress, Sharon Tate. Today, aged 33, Roman married Sharon. Polanski began his career in Poland, but has since made films abroad, one in Holland (an episode of *The Beautiful Swindlers*) and three in England, the first two being *Repulsion* and *Cul-de-Sac*. He now hopes to settle in the United States with his wife. Polanski has just signed a contract to direct his first Hollywood film, *Rosemary's Baby*, a horror story set in Manhattan.

Carl Dreyer's lasting legacy

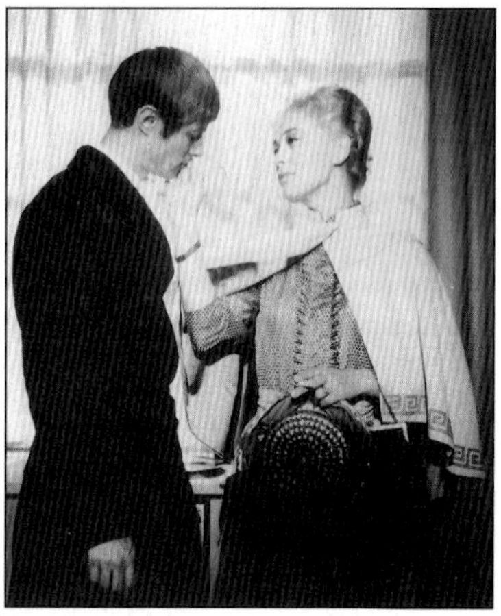

Bendt Rothe and Nina Pens Rode.

Copenhagen, 20 March
The death of Danish director Carl Dreyer, aged 79, has caused sadness and anger among his admirers, due to the negative response to his last film, *Gertrud*, released in 1965. The film, which deals with the growing awareness of a young woman (Nina Pens Rode) betrayed in love (by Bendt Rothe), has remained both unappreciated and misunderstood. Subsequent to its failure, the great director had difficulty in getting his projects realized. He never got the chance to make *Jesus Christ Jew*, which had haunted him since 1949. To quote *Gertrud*, his life was "a long, endless pursuit of dreams, one superimposed upon the other."

Charlton Heston finds himself in a strange world ruled by apes

*Charlton Heston in **Planet of the Apes**, directed by Franklin J. Schaffner.*

New York, 9 February
Franklin J. Schaffner's *Planet of the Apes* looks like it may change the course and momentum of science fiction cinema, which has been in the doldrums for most of the decade, in large part reduced to the role of a supermarket supplying decorative elements to spice up other genres. Adapted by the prolific Rod Serling and the former blacklist victim Michael Wilson from the satirical novel by Pierre Boulle titled *Monkey Planet*, *Planet of the Apes* has reworked the time travel then putting astronaut Charlton Hest through a timeslip and on to a po holocaust Earth in which intellige apes have become the defenders "humanity". Firmly controlled Schaffner, an old-fashioned craf man, and strikingly photograph in the national parks of Utah a Arizona by Leon Shamroy, *Plan of the Apes* moves at a measur pace towards a memorable clim in which Heston finds the ruine half-buried remains of the Statue Liberty and comes to the bitter re ization that he is on Earth after a The remarkably flexible ape mak up, which has enabled the acto playing the apes to create believab characters rather than stereotyp was created by John Chambe Roddy McDowall and Kim Hunt are outstanding as the sympathet ape scientists who examine Hest to discover whether he might be t "missing link" in simian develo ment, a delightful conceit whi neatly underlines the notion of rat nal ape confronting irrational ma

Zeffirelli's pair of star-crossed lovers are properly youthful

London, 4 March
At the ages of 17 and 15 respectively, Leonard Whiting and Olivia Hussey are as close to the ages of Romeo and Juliet as William Shakespeare intended. And, indeed, they make a very pretty couple of star-crossed lovers in Franco Zeffirelli's exuberant screen version of *Romeo and Juliet*. Alas, neither of them has a shred of acting ability, so that Shakespeare's verse is hopelessly garbled whenever they appear. Poetry takes second place to pictorial extravagance, with the rich Technicolor photography of Pasqualino de Santis and handsome costumes designed by Danilo Donati a treat for the eye. Some acting ballast is provided by Laurence Olivier's prologue, Michael York's athletic Tybalt and John McEnery's whimsical Mercutio. The Italian Zeffirelli began his career as an actor and later became Luchino Visconti's assistant on films like *La Terra Trema* and *Senso*. He has also enjoyed a successful career as an international opera designer and director in London, New York and Milan, with a reputation for opulent spectacle.

Olivia Hussey and Leonard Whiting as Romeo and Juliet in Zeffirelli's film

anley Kubrick ventures into space and the future

York, 4 April
ley Kubrick's *2001: A Space ssey*, loosely adapted from his story *The Sentinel* by Arthur larke, explores at greater length question taken up in *Planet of Apes* regarding the forces which rol man's evolution. *2001*, shot ngland at a cost of $10.5 million, s to restore speculative thought cience fiction film, along with imitive sense of wonder which s back to the early days of cine- The result is a technical tour force in which images of vast, plex spacecraft float infinitely ly through deep space to the ins of Strauss' "Blue Danube tz". At its heart the film con- s one of the most stunning jump in film – the moment when an nal bone hurled into the air by a historic man is transformed into owly turning spaceship. We fol- space-age man Keir Dullea in a ch for a Higher Power behind a sterious monolith discovered on moon. He outwits the homicidal sion computer HAL before tak- a hallucinogenic ride through ar gate to reemerge as a "tran- nded man". Kubrick has a clin- vision of the future in which nkind is just a cipher controlled the force embodied in the mono- . But the reclusive filmmaker nains coy about the message, ming, "The feel of the experience e important thing, not the ability erbalize or analyze it. Those who n't believe their eyes won't be e to appreciate this film."

Stanley Kubrick's ***2001: A Space Odyssey*** *searches for the origins of man across millions of years and through space.*

essed for the space adventure.

Oscars promote racial tolerance in wake of King assassination

Los Angeles, 10 April
This year the Academy Award ceremony was held under unusually somber circumstances. The assassination of Reverend Martin Luther King caused the event to be postponed for 48 hours. And for the same reason, the annual post-Oscar ball was canceled altogether. It was significant, therefore, that most of the major awards went to two films that deal with racial prejudice. The Best Picture winner, Norman Jewison's *In the Heat of the Night*, takes place in a small, steamy Mississippi town where Philadelphia's number one detective Virgil Tibbs reluctantly arrives to help the redneck police chief solve a murder. The fact that the senior visitor is black – Sidney Poitier at his most dignified and passionate – and that the local cop is a white bigot, makes for an entertaining game of dominance, with a social message. Rod Steiger, behind yellow sunglasses and incessantly chewing gum, won the Best Actor prize for managing to find nuances in his role as Poitier's adversary. Katharine Hepburn was presented with her second Best Actress Oscar for Stanley Kramer's comedy of racial coexistence, *Guess Who's Coming to Dinner*. She gave a warm and touching portrayal of an understanding woman whose daughter wishes to marry a black man (Sidney Poitier again), partnered for the last time by Spencer Tracy. Both movies won screenplay Oscars. The Best Director award went to Mike Nichols for only his second film, *The Graduate*, a movie that touched a chord among the nation's youth.

Guess Who's Coming to Dinner*: Hepburn and Tracy (his last film).*

Jeanne Moreau a vengeful black widow

Charles Denner and the image of Jeanne Moreau in ***The Bride Wore Black****.*

Paris, 17 April
François Truffaut has paid his most direct homage to his idol Alfred Hitchcock in his new film, *The Bride Wore Black*. Based, like *Rear Window*, on a novel by William Irish (Cornell Woolrich) and with a score by Bernard Herrmann, Hitch's frequent composer, it relates how the widow of a man shot dead on his wedding day, tracks down the group of men responsible, and eliminates them one by one. Jeanne Moreau is superb as the seductive avenging angel, and there are splendid cameos from the victims.

Matthau and Lemmon, hilariously odd

New York, 2 May
Jack Lemmon and Walter Matthau are paired again in the screen version of Neil Simon's Broadway smash *The Odd Couple*, in which two divorced men share an apartment. Matthau is reprising the role he played in the original, that of sloppy Oscar, while Lemmon is cast as fussy Felix. With a face which resembles a cross between a bloodhound and Yogi Bear, Matthau spent much of the early part of his screen career playing heavies. In a memorable screen debut in 1955 he took a bullwhip to Burt Lancaster in *The Kentuckian*. Now, at the age of 48, he's hit the big time.

Felix Unger (Jack Lemmon, left) and Oscar Madison (Walter Matthau).

Worldwide support pours in for Langlois

Simone Signoret and Michel Piccoli join the throngs supporting Langlois.

Paris, 30 April
The affair of the Cinémathèque has been brought to an end with the reinstatement of Henri Langlois as its head. The crisis erupted last February, but the attempt of the state to control the Cinémathèque dates back further. When André Malraux became Minister of Culture in 1959, the government demanded representatives on the administrative council. They removed control over the funds from Langlois, and appointed a deputy financial manager. Rapidly, the Treasury started quibbling, and the number of civil servants on the administrative council was increased until they had gained an absolute majority. During a meeting of the council on 9 February, Pierre Moinot was elected to the presidency of the Cinémathèque, replac the film director Marc Allég Moinot demanded Langlois' s pension and named Pierre Bar in his place. *Le Monde* publishe protest signed by 40 directors on February, which mobilized the tire profession. French as well foreign filmmakers (including J Renoir, François Truffaut, Jean-L Godard, Roberto Rossellini, Fed co Fellini and Ingmar Bergma announced they would not per the new administration to scre their films. Four days later, th were demonstrations outside Cinémathèque. Given the passic aroused, the state had no choice b to withdraw its control, but also subsidies. The Cinémathèque v now be free, but poor.

Henri Langlois, the guiding light of the Cinémathèque, back in his right place in the rue de Courcelles, holds the keys to the future.

annes Festival is caught in the eye of the storm

ged on by the recent events in Paris, young filmmakers take over the Palais.

José Lopez Vasquez, Geraldine Chaplin in Carlos Saura's ***Peppermint Frappé.***

nnes, 18 May
bert Favre le Bret, president of Cannes Film Festival, had every son to be happy. The 1968 vin- e augured well and many presti- us guests were present at the gala ening, during which *Gone With Wind* was shown in 70mm and reophonic sound. Meanwhile, in ris the students were confronting ice across the barricades erected the Latin Quarter. For some days, festival-goers seemed uncon- rned with the reverberations ema- ting from the capital. Yet today, t before the showing of the Span- film, Carlos Saura's *Peppermint appé*, an angry group of people mbed onto the stage and grabbed curtain. "In no way are we going allow the Festival to continue ile students are endangering their es on the barricades in Paris," ey shouted. Among this group re two of the young lions of the ew Wave, Jean-Luc Godard and ançois Truffaut, as well as Claude louch, Claude Berri, the critic an-Louis Bory and the actor Jean- erre Léaud. In addition to their sire to demonstrate their solidari- with the students, the rebellion as provoked by Culture Minister ndré Malraux's decision to sack enri Langlois from his post as ad of the Cinémathèque. And in annes, as in Paris, events were oving fast. A press conference was ld regarding the "Cinémathèque fair", and there were meetings in e auditorium of the Palais. Then me the news of the resignation of ur members of the jury, including Louis Malle and Roman Polanski, followed by the decision of Alain Resnais, Milos Forman and Carlos Saura to withdraw their films from the Festival.

Because of the disruptions to the Festival, many of the interesting works were not shown. The films selected bore witness to the new movements and tendencies in world cinema, particularly the emergence of a whole new generation of young directors who promise to be tomorrow's masters of the art. Among them are representatives of the young Czechoslovakian cinema. Jan Nemec's bold Kafkaesque film, *A Report on the Party and the Guests*, was made two years ago, but was denounced by the National Assembly in Prague, and has only now been released. Milos Forman, who had astonished us with *Loves of a Blonde*, was to have screened *The Firemen's Ball*, a virulent satire on Czech society. Another example of the regeneration of the film industry in Eastern Europe is the Hungarian Miklos Jancso, whose originality is well demonstrated in *The Red and the White*. He uses the possibilities of the large screen, orchestrating a large-scale drama of domination and submission, with the minimum of dialogue. The Spanish director Carlos Saura would have been one of the top contenders for a prize with his *Peppermint Frappé*, had the showing of his film not been interrupted. The director has dedicated his film to Luis Buñuel, whose influence is evident in his treatment of the dreams and memories of his hero, focusing on his repressive religious upbringing. However, the demonstrations heralded the death warrant of this year's potentially rich Cannes Film Festival.

Mia Farrow mesmerized by witchcraft in the heart of Manhattan

New York, 12 June
Waif-like beauty Mia Farrow gives monstrous birth to a child of the Devil in *Rosemary's Baby*, Roman Polanski's brilliant shocker adapted from a novel by Ira Levin. When she and her husband John Cassavetes move into a Gothic apartment block in Manhattan, they are adopted by their elderly neighbors Ruth Gordon and Sidney Blackmer. But their kindly attentions mask a sinister purpose, for they are Satanists, and Farrow has been chosen to carry the Devil's baby. Making his Hollywood debut, Polish writer-director Polanski tells the story from Farrow's point of view, so that the audience shares the growing realization on her part that there is something horribly wrong with her pregnancy, and that the twittering, vulgar Gordon and the courtly Blackmer are not all that they seem. Even Cassavetes turns out to be party to the plot as her grisly confinement draws near. Shot on location in the creepy Dakota apartment building in New York City, *Rosemary's Baby* cleverly mingles the mundane and the macabre to suspend our disbelief in witchcraft and give the film's coven a terrible plausibility.

Mia Farrow in Polanski's ***Rosemary's Baby*** *from the novel by Ira Levin.*

Steve and Faye play sexiest chess game!

Boston, 19 June
There's never been an insurance investigator like Faye Dunaway in *The Thomas Crown Affair*. With a wardrobe full of Paris fashions, some of them rather startling, she has been unleashed on Steve McQueen's Tommy Crown, a laid-back Boston playboy who has a nice line in bank heists. Now he's planning another one, with the full knowledge that he is being stalked by the sophisticated Dunaway, whose investigative methods are as unconventional as her clothes. When they lock horns over a game of chess in Crown's pad, the way they handle the pieces gives a new meaning to the notion of foreplay. Jewison's use of split-screen heightens the tension in a movie as sleek and self-satisfied as its protagonists.

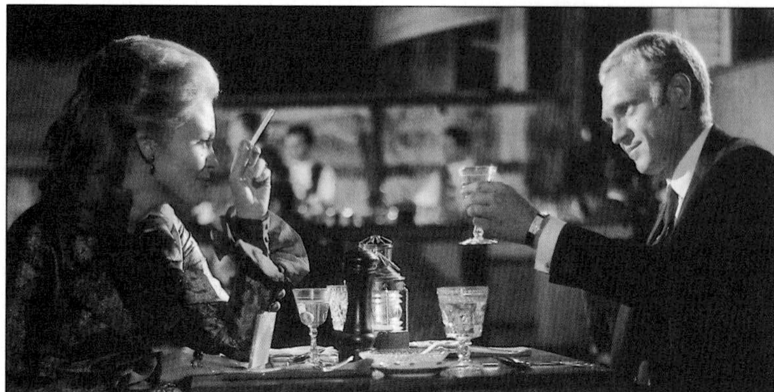

Steve McQueen, Faye Dunaway a magnetic duo in ***The Thomas Crown Affair.***

A funny girl with a truly sensational voic

New York, 19 September
Fanny Brice, born to a Jewish New York family, grew up with one burning ambition: to succeed in the theater. That Fanny was ugly, skinny and flat-chested, and yet overcame these disabilities to reach stardom, was testament to her determination. The story of Brice was told in the hit Broadway musical, *Funny Girl*, which made a star of a Jewish girl from New York, determined to succeed – Barbra Streisand. Now *Funny Girl*, directed by William Wyler, with choreography by Herb Ross, and its terrific Jule Styne-Bob Merrill score, has been filmed, bringing 151 minutes of Streisand. She has presence, humor, acting talent and, above all, a rich and powerful voice that belts its way through the songs with considerable artistry. And co-starring as Brice's no-good husband, Nicky Arnstein, is Dr. Zhivago himself, Omar Sharif, whose collaboration has, reportedly, incurred the disfavor of Egypt's government.

Streisand: a new phenomenon.

Pasolini's 'Theorem' angers all factions

Venice, 18 September
The Festival has ended today in confusion. The Grand Prix of the International Catholic Office of Cinema has been awarded to Pier Paolo Pasolini's *Theorem*, although it was seized six days ago by the public prosecutor in Rome for obscenity. The film has thus divided believers as much as the general public and critics. It has also displeased some Marxists, who see it as an implicit attack on their ideology, and has disturbed puritans with its attitude to sexual taboos. This fable of the middle-classes tells how a handsome young man (Terence Stamp) ingratiates himself into the home of a wealthy industrialist and sleeps with every member of the family – the father, the mother, the daughter, the son, and even the maid. (The latter is played by Laura Betti, who took the best actress prize.) The QED of Pasolini's theorem might be puzzling, but there is a certain mathematical beauty in his efforts to reach it.

Terence Stamp takes his turn with wife and mother Silvana Mangano.

Warhol and Morrissey focus on 'Flesh'

New York, 26 September
Flesh is the last film to come from Andy Warhol's Factory, which has closed after the attempt on Warhol's life in June of this year. It is Paul Morrissey's first full-length feature, and has all the hallmarks of the Factory, being peopled by junkies, hookers and drag queens. However, *Flesh* is narratively more ordered than Warhol's own experimental movies, and subsequently is being given a commercial showing. It is an amusing camp exercise in the best of bad taste. The plot, such as it concerns a male hustler (beefy J Dallessandro), who sells his body earn enough money to pay for wife's girlfriend's abortion. Oth members of Warhol's band, su as Geri Miller and Candy Darli make striking appearances. The characters are treated sympathe cally and directly, and Morriss films them in a simple, unfus *cinéma vérité* manner. Morriss joined Warhol in 1963 as prod tion assistant and cameraman.

Joe Dallessandro, the Warhol factory's icon of easy sex, in Morrissey's ***Fles***

daredevil chase through the tortuous streets of San Francisco

ve McQueen and new British star Jacqueline Bisset in Peter Yates' **Bullitt**.

New York, 17 October

Impressed by Britisher Peter Yates' staging of a car chase through London in *Robbery* (1967), Steve McQueen was responsible for getting Yates to direct *Bullitt*. The hero of this thriller, a police lieutenant, spends a great deal of time speeding after villains through the undulating streets of San Francisco. McQueen is not only bucked by an ambitious politician (Robert Vaughn) but by the mafia as well, as he picks his way through the knotted threads of a murder involving a grand jury witness. The memorable chase occurs about midway through the film, a chase with a difference, and probably the most thrilling ever committed to film, during most of which McQueen insisted on doing his own stunts. Jacqueline Bisset plays McQueen's attractive girlfriend. This thriller is put together with pace and style by Peter Yates, directing his first American film, and making stunning use of the locations.

Novarro murdered in his home

Hollywood, 31 October

The blood-spattered corpse of 69-year-old silent star Ramon Novarro has been found sprawled in the bedroom of his Hollywood home. It seems that he choked to death on a lead Art Deco dildo – a present from Rudolph Valentino – which had been rammed down his throat by his assailants, two young hustler brothers from Chicago, Paul and Tom Ferguson.

Novarro in 1930, a typical image.

oogan's Bluff' shows Clint ain't kidding

w York, 2 October

ector Don Siegel and Clint East-od form an explosive partnership *Coogan's Bluff*, a pacy police ma which dispatches laconic zona lawman Eastwood to New rk to extradite homicidal hippie n Stroud. When Stroud goes on lam, Eastwood tracks him down using methods more appropriate he West than the Big Apple. Lee Cobb plays the bemused city cop ng to keep him under control, oud is splendidly malevolent as Eastwood's quarry, and Tisha Sterling catches the eye as his strung-out girlfriend. Director Siegel is a durable Hollywood veteran, a montage specialist at Warners in the mid-Forties, whose features career began with *The Verdict* in 1946. Many of his films have focused on outsiders balefully at odds with society, and Clint Eastwood is the latest addition to Siegel's gallery of tough loners. The two men seem made for each other, and *Coogan's Bluff* promises an interesting partnership.

LOVE

*nt Eastwood is the toughest cop on the job in Siegel's **Coogan's Bluff**.*

Horror and beauty of 'The Living Dead'

New York, 4 December

George Romero's debut film is a Z-budget shocker, *Night of the Living Dead*, shot over several weekends in Pennsylvania. It chronicles the desperate efforts of a bunch of Middle Americans, trapped in a remote farmhouse, to beat off the attacks of an army of walking dead – zombies who have inexplicably risen from the grave or broken out of the morgue. With a skill worthy of Hitchcock, Romero undercuts the traditions of the horror movie: the apparent heroine lapses into a state of permanent catatonia early in the film; a young couple, society's hope for the future, are burned to a crisp and return as zombies; and the black hero gets all his companions killed before being mistaken for a zombie and shot by a redneck rescue party. Film freak Romero worked as a grip on *North by Northwest* when he was at college. Now his own Pittsburgh-based Latent Image Company has graduated from commercials to a drive-in smash.

George A. Romero's
Horror Masterpiece...
NIGHT
OF THE
LIVING
DEAD
X

'Truth rises from the grave'! A highly original film from George A. Romero.

JULIE CHRISTIE · GEORGE C. SCOTT
IN A RICHARD LESTER–RAYMOND WAGNER PRODUCTION
People bugged by people will do extraordinary things.
Petulia
...the uncommon movie.
RICHARD CHAMBERLAIN AS DAVID DANNER
ARTHUR HILL · SHIRLEY KNIGHT and JOSEPH COTTEN as Mr. Danner
LAWRENCE B. MARCUS · DENIS O'DELL · RAYMOND WAGNER · RICHARD LESTER
TECHNICOLOR® FROM WARNER BROS.-SEVEN ARTS

It's flashy, trendy and well-acted but still not as good as the poster!

Ava Gardner, Omar Sharif in a tedious remake of tragic romance ***Mayerl***

JANE FONDA
The space age adventuress whose sex-ploits are among the most bizarre ever seen.
SEE BARBARELLA DO HER THING!
JOHN PHILLIP LAW · MARCEL MARCEAU
DAVID HEMMINGS · UGO TOGNAZZI

The famous comic strip comes to life.

STEVE McQUEEN
ist
'BULLITT'

This has the best car chase yet.

Three of the four Monkees, from left to right, Mickey Dolenz, Peter Tork and Michael Nesmith in Bob Rafelson's ***Head****.*

Charlie Bubbles*: Liza Minnelli made her screen debut with Albert Finney.*

An epic drama of
dventure and exploration
Man's colony on the Moon... a whole new generation has been born and is living here... a quarter-million miles from Earth.
2001: a space odyssey
MGM PRESENTS A STANLEY KUBRICK PRODUCTION
CINERAMA
Super Panavision and Metrocolor

nley Kubrick ventured into space, 'tripping' on technology and symbolism.

Max Von Sydow and Liv Ullmann in Ingmar Bergman's parable, ***The Shame.***

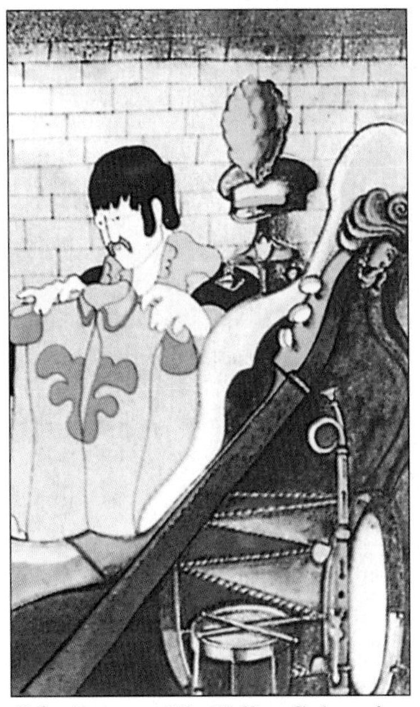

John Lennon: ***The Yellow Submarine.***

Peter Sellers stars in Blake Edwards' comedy of disaster, ***The Party.***

lward G. Robinson and Vittorio De Sica: ***The Biggest Bundle of Them All.***

David Hemmings in Tony Richardson's ***The Charge of the Light Brigade.***

1969

1968 Academy Awards, Dorothy Chandler Pavilion, 14 Apr.

Best Film:	*Oliver!* (dir: Carol Reed)
Best Director:	Carol Reed
Best Actor:	Cliff Robertson *(Charly)*
Best Actress:	Katharine Hepburn *(The Lion in Winter)* Barbra Streisand *(Funny Girl)*
Best Supp. Actor:	Jack Albertson *(The Subject Was Roses)*
Best Supp. Actress:	Ruth Gordon *(Rosemary's Baby)*

Prague, 1 January
Anxiety is growing among filmmakers here. The period of comparative freedom of expression, enjoyed during the "liberal spring", appears to be drawing to a close. Relations between the film industry and the state have become increasingly strained since troops entered the city. Milos Forman and Jiri Menzel have been warned about giving an unfavorable impression of the conditions of the working class and Forman, who is in Paris, has decided not to return to Czechoslovakia. His last film to be made there was *The Firemen's Ball* in 1967.

Hollywood, 12 January
Judy Garland, who divorced Mark Herron in 1967, has married again. Her husband is a young hairdresser named Mickey Deans.

New York, 15 January
Darryl F. Zanuck, the head of Fox, has refused to distribute Edouard Luntz's *le Grabuge,* from a scenario by Jean Duvignaud, which was produced by the American company. He is shocked by the anti-bourgeois violence in the film.

New York, 17 February
Hedy Lamarr, the star of Gustav Machaty's 1933 production *Ecstasy*, has instigated proceedings against the editor of her biography *Ecstasy and Me, My Life as a Woman*, and against all those who took part in the writing and publishing of the book, which the actress describes as being obscene and shocking. Miss Lamarr is demanding $21 million as compensation for the damage done to both her reputation and career.

Boston, 11 March
An exhibitor has been condemned to six months imprisonment and fined $1,000 for screening Robert Aldrich's film *The Killing of Sister George*. The film had been banned by the local censor due to its controversial lesbian love scenes.

Boston, 30 March
The Killing of Sister George continues to be shown after the court ruled against the seizure of the film. Judith Crist, one of the country's most respected film critics, stated during the trial that not only is the film not in the least pornographic but, in her view, it is among the 10 best films of the year.

Las Vegas, 8 May
Lana Turner has married the magician and hypnotist Michael Dante.

Hollywood, 26 May
Edgar Bronfman replaces Robert O'Brien as president and chief executive officer at MGM.

Washington D.C., 8 June
The State Department has just announced that Stanley Kubrick's film *2001: A Space Odyssey*, is the USA's official entry for the Moscow Film Festival in July. Selection was made by three representatives of the film industry: director-producer Frank Capra, producer Walter Mirisch and scriptwriter Michael Straight.

New York, 10 June
David Picker, aged 33, has been elected president of United Artists. He replaces Arthur Krim who has moved on to the board of directors with Robert Benjamin.

New York, 10 June
Warner Bros.-Seven Arts' shareholders have approved a merger with Kinney National Services. The cost is estimated at $11.5 million.

California, 10 June
Franklin J. Schaffner has finished filming *Patton* at the military base in Pendleton. Shooting started in Spain in February.

New York, 18 June
A great deal of controversy has arisen over the extreme violence of Sam Peckinpah's latest Western, *The Wild Bunch*, now on release.

Boston, 24 June
The Supreme Court has upheld the ban on Frederick Wiseman's feature-length documentary *Titicut Follies*, which was shot in the Bridgewater State hospital for mentally disturbed criminals in 1967. Permission has, however, been granted for the film to be shown non-commercially for groups of professionals.

Algiers, 1 July
The Algerian government has announced the nationalization of all film companies. The move is aimed at forcing big foreign companies with branches in Algeria, such as Paramount, MGM and Fox, to give up their interests in the country.

New York, 28 July
MGM has taken Kirk Kerkorian to court. The latter wants to buy $35 million worth of MGM shares. However, since finance for the purchase comes mainly from Transamerica, which already owns United Artists, this is regarded as unacceptable.

New York, 10 August
Despite the court descision, Kirk Kerkorian has acquired 24 percent of MGM by turning to alternative sources of finance.

Woodstock, 15 August
A vast outdoor rock music festival opened here today. Documentary filmmaker Michael Wadleigh has been chosen to film the concerts for Warner Bros., who have acquired the film rights.

Paris, 28 August
Release of Robert Bresson's new film *Une femme douce* (*A Gentle Creature*), based on the short story by Dosto evsky. The film reveals the talent of Dominique Sanda.

Paris, 5 September
Release of Jean-Pierre Melville's *l'Armée des ombres* (*The Army in the Shadows*), drama of the Resistance, adapted from Joseph Kessel's novel and starring Lino Ventura, Simone Signoret and Paul Meurisse.

New York, 29 September
Jerry Lewis held a press conference to announce the creation of his new cinema chain in association with Network Cinema Corp. He hopes to open 750 cinemas by 1974. The first is already under construction.

San Francisco, 14 November
Francis Ford Coppola and Georg Lucas have founded American Zo trope. The main aim of the compan is "to work with the most talente youngsters in all aspects of the cin ma, using the latest in technology.

New York, 18 November
Director Elia Kazan's latest wor *The Arrangement*, with Kirk Dou las, Deborah Kerr and Faye Du away, has received scathing review from the critics. The screenplay wa based on Kazan's own novel.

Paris, 31 December
Industry professionals are worrie by the number of cinema closure They blame the increasing popular ty of TV (there are now 9,378,03 sets licensed in France) and also th programming by ORTF of 327 fe ture films during 1969.

BIRTHS

New York, 18 August
Christian Slater

DEATHS

England, 2 February
Boris Karloff

New York, 5 February
Thelma Ritter

England, 7 February
Eric Portman

Texas, 27 February
John Boles

Hollywood, 8 June
Robert Taylor

London, 22 June
Judy Garland

California, 5 July
Leo McCarey

Norway, 13 October
Sonja Henie

Hollywood, 22 December
Josef von Sternberg

Italian filmmaker Sergio Leo made an international star of Cl Eastwood. He now makes his fi American epic, the impressive ***On Upon a Time in the West***.

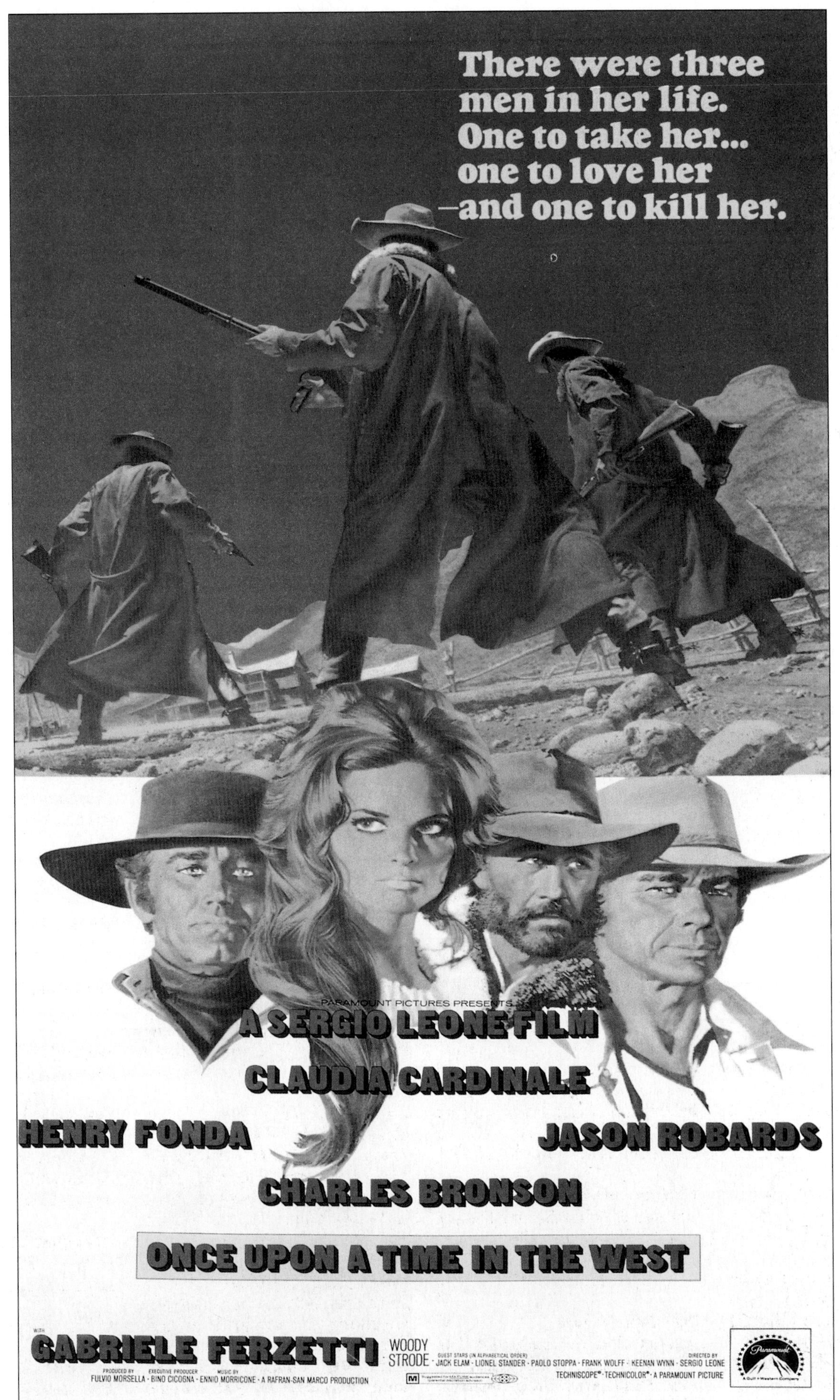
There were three men in her life. One to take her... one to love her —and one to kill her.
PARAMOUNT PICTURES PRESENTS
A SERGIO LEONE FILM
CLAUDIA CARDINALE
HENRY FONDA
JASON ROBARDS
CHARLES BRONSON
ONCE UPON A TIME IN THE WEST
WITH
GABRIELE FERZETTI · WOODY STRODE
GUEST STARS (IN ALPHABETICAL ORDER) JACK ELAM · LIONEL STANDER · PAOLO STOPPA · FRANK WOLFF · KEENAN WYNN
DIRECTED BY SERGIO LEONE
PRODUCED BY FULVIO MORSELLA · EXECUTIVE PRODUCER BINO CICOGNA · MUSIC BY ENNIO MORRICONE · A RAFRAN-SAN MARCO PRODUCTION
M
TECHNISCOPE® · TECHNICOLOR® · A PARAMOUNT PICTURE
Paramount
A Gulf + Western Company

The 'Lovely War' that both horrifies and amuses

A monument to senseless carnage.

London, 10 April
In his first project as a director, Richard Attenborough has restaged the First World War on Brighton pier. *Oh! What a Lovely War* is an ambitious attempt to translate to the screen Joan Littlewood's history of the 1914-18 conflict. Her Stratford East stage hit combined music-hall songs, diaries and contemporary commentary in a withering attack on the folly of war and the fatuity of the ruling class. Attenborough has retained the basic structure, anchored in a seaside pierrot show, and opened it out to take in the Victorian splendor of Brighton pier along with the rolling hills of Sussex Downs, which stand in for the Western Front. The film is full of small miracles of production design: John Mills' Field Marshal Haig directs the Battle of the Somme from the top of a helter-skelter while the mounting losses are posted on a cricket scoreboard; a member of the representative Smith family, Maurice Roeves, gets on the pier's miniature railway and leaves for the Front; at the end of the film the last surviving Smith boy follows a red tape from the trenches to a room where the Armistice is being signed.

'I'll make a man of every one of you': Maggie Smith entices boys to the call-u

Some of the searing quality of the original has been smothered by the scale of the production and the roster of stars in cameo roles, among them Ralph Richardson, Laurence Olivier, Dirk Bogarde, Michael and Vanessa Redgrave and, memorab Maggie Smith as the raddled c soubrette who lures young men (to the music-hall stage and straig into the welcoming arms of the r cruiting sergeant.

Maurice Pialat wins the Jean Vigo prize

Paris, 20 March
The Jean Vigo prize has been awarded to the first feature by the documentary director Maurice Pialat for *l'Enfance nue*, made two years ago, and not yet released. Pialat exhibits a superb control of his subject, an examination of childhood, which is never allowed to become sentimental. Played by non-professionals, the film tells the touching story of a 10-year-old boy, abandoned by his mother, and sent to a working-class foster family where his behavior is disturbed. He is then moved to a second family, which proves more successful, though the boy's tendency to lose control of his emotions leads to a crisis. As a distant cousin to *The Four Hundred Blows* and *The Two of Us*, it is therefore not surprising to find that François Truffaut and Claude Berri are two of the film's executive producers.

Katharine Hepburn wins her third Oscar

Los Angeles, 14 April
When Ingrid Bergman unsealed the envelope containing the name of the Best Actress winner at this year's Oscar ceremonies, she exclaimed, "It's a tie!" Barbra Streisand (for her impersonation of the vaudeville queen Fanny Brice in *Funny Girl*), and Katharine Hepburn (for her portrayal of Eleanor of Aquitaine in *The Lion in Winter*) had each obtained exactly the same number of votes. Hepburn thus becomes t first performer ever to win a tr of major Oscars, and her tally 11 nominations is the highest ev recorded in the Academy's histor The Best Actor award went to Cl Robertson for his extraordinary pe formance as the mentally retarde *Charly*. The jolly Dickens music adaptation, *Oliver!* received both t Best Picture and Best Direct (Carol Reed) statuettes.

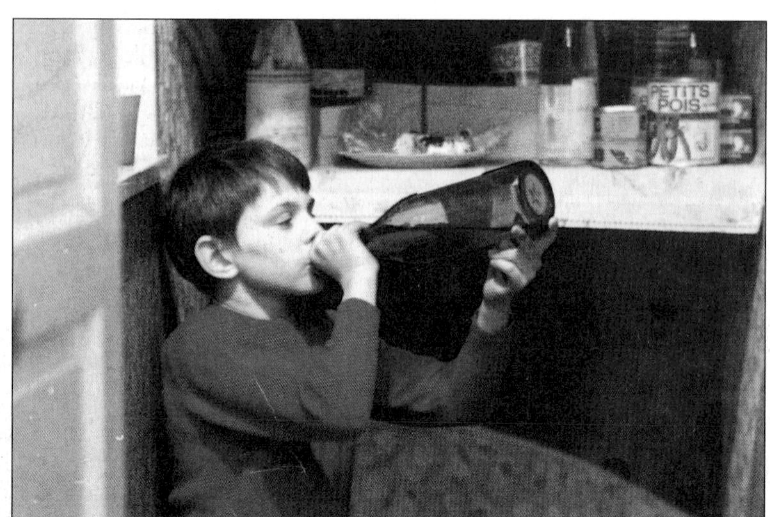
PETITS
POIS

Michel Tarrizon is the adopted child at the center of Pialat's truthful film.

Mark Lester as Oliver Twist in Best Director Carol Reed's Dickens musical.

he Soviets and the British feature at Cannes

lcolm McDowell (center) in Lindsay Anderson's ***If***, the major prizewinner.

Tarkovsky's ***Andrei Rublev*** previously banned by the Soviet authorities.

nnes, 23 May
hough the prizes at this year's nnes Film Festival were spread ong the British, French, Brazil-, Swedish and American entries, vas a Soviet film that created most erest. Completed in 1966, *Andrei blev* has been kept on the shelf by government of the USSR, who nd various pretexts to ban it, one them being that they felt it was "dark" for the 50th anniversary the October Revolution. The film, ected by Andrei Tarkovsky, con-ts of eight imaginary episodes in life of Rublev, the 15th-century n painter, as he journeys through dal Russia. Faced with the cruel- and horror of what he sees, he abandons speech and his art, until a simple act renews his faith in mankind. This slow, powerful and impressive epic, in black-and-white and CinemaScope, ends with a color sequence which does justice to the paintings.

As for those who took the prizes, the Grand Prix was awarded to Lindsay Anderson's *If*, a vitriolic attack on the British class system which owes much to Jean Vigo's *Zero for Conduct*. Karel Reisz, Anderson's colleague from the days of the Free Cinema movement in the 1950s, was represented by *Isadora*, for which Vanessa Redgrave won the prize for best actress for her role as the celebrated American dancer Isadora Duncan. Jean-Louis Trintignant was chosen as best actor for his portrayal of the honest judge in Costa-Gavras' effective political thriller, *Z*. The *Cinema Novo* from Brazil was acknowledged by the jury, headed by Luchino Visconti, with the best director award given to Glauber Rocha for his baroque *Antonio das Mortes*. The Special Jury Prize went to another film with a political theme, *Adalen 31*. Directed by Bo Widerberg, it concerns a lengthy strike at a paper mill in a small town in the north of Sweden in 1931, which ended with five workers being killed by soldiers. The actor Dennis Hopper gained the prize for a best first feature, *Easy Rider*.

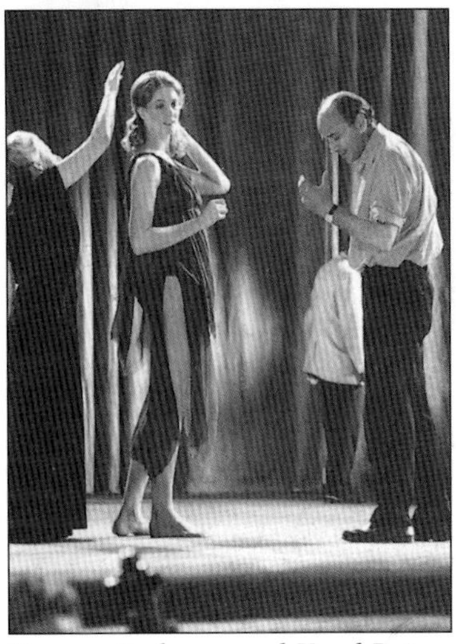
Vanessa Redgrave and Karel Reisz.

ustin Hoffman's Ratso Rizzo in 'Midnight Cowboy' is a triumph

w York, 25 May
r his role as the unattractive bum tso Rizzo in *Midnight Cowboy*, ıstin Hoffman was paid 10 times ore than he received for his part in *e Graduate* a couple of years ago. ith greasy hair, pallid complexion, d teeth and gammy leg, he bril-ntly represents a man who merges sily into the seedy and sordid at-osphere of New York as conjured by British director John Schles-ger, making his first American ovie. Opposite Hoffman is Jon oight as a would-be stud. It is the lationship between this big, blond, able dimwit and the small down-d-outer that is the impressive cen-rpiece of this comedy-drama.

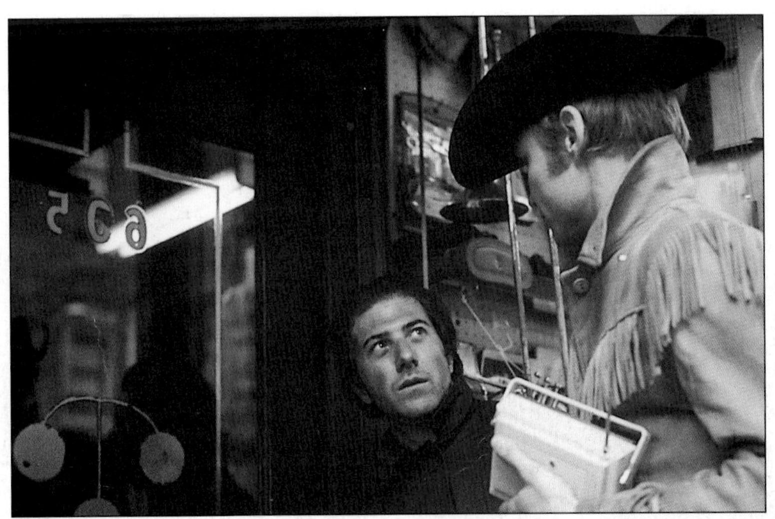

655

Ratso Rizzo (Hoffman) and Joe Buck (Jon Voight, right) in ***Midnight Cowboy***.

Michèle is favorite

Because of her series of *Angélique* films, Michèle Mercier has become one of France's most popular stars. To satisfy her admiring public, she can now be seen in yet another story of Angélique, *The Indomitable Angélique*. It all began in 1964 with *Angélique*, the first of the films based on the books by Serge and Anne Golon, recounting the adventures of a *Forever Amber*-like heroine in the France of Louis XIV. Then *Marvelous Angélique*, *Angélique and the King* and *Angélique and the Sultan* followed. Settings and costumes are colorful and Mlle Mercier pouts prettily throughout.

Sergio Leone takes on America's Old West

Charles Bronson in Sergio Leone's ***Once Upon a Time in the West.***

New York, 28 May
Henry Fonda makes a rare excursion into double-dyed villainy in Sergio Leone's *Once Upon a Time in the West*. The man who became a Western film icon as Marshal Wyatt Earp in John Ford's masterpiece *My Darling Clementine*, has been cast as a cold-eyed killer targeting Claudia Cardinale, a widow locked in battle with the railroad over water rights. Leone's follow-up to his "Dollars" trilogy, co-scripted with Dario Argento and Bernardo Bertolucci, is built around a complex series of references to classic Westerns – *High Noon*, *Shane* and *The Searchers* in the first 15 minutes alone – all of which are couched in Leone's bravura, operatic style. Leone calls this collision of Western stereotypes with the onward march of frontier history a "ballet of the dead." The Monument Valley locations also mark Leone's departure from the Cinecittà origins of his "spaghetti" Westerns. Reportedly, the set for "Flagstone" cost more than the entire budget of *A Fistful of Dollars*. *Once Upon a Time in the West* also boasts the longest credits sequence in the history of the Western. Originally, Leone wanted to say goodbye to his earlier triumphs by killing off Clint Eastwood, Eli Wallach and Lee Van Cleef, the stars of *The Good, the Bad and the Ugly*, at the beginning of the picture, but Eastwood wouldn't play ball.

Liberated woman and shameless Don Ju

Françoise Fabian and Jean-Louis Trintignant in ***My Night With Maud.***

Paris, 7 June
Just opened here is Eric Rohmer's *My Night at Maud's*, the fourth of his Six Moral Tales, and probably his best film to date. This witty, erotic and profound film proves that long intellectual discussions can be as cinematic as more obviously visual material. Set in snowy Clermont-Ferrand, it tells of an engineer a devout Catholic (Jean-Louis Tr tignant) who spends a chaste nig with the dark, seductive and fr thinking Maud (Françoise Fabia even though they are mutually tracted. She calls him "a shamel Christian pretending to be a shan less Don Juan."

A dose of decadence from 'The Damned'

New York, 28 May
In his latest film, Luchino Visconti has set out to examine the ideological link between the Nazis and the capitalist bourgeoisie. Entitled *The Damned* (*Gotterdämmerung*), this German-Italian co-production has a fine international cast that includes Ingrid Thulin (Swedish), Dirk Bogarde and Charlotte Rampling (British), Renaud Verley (French), Umberto Orsini (Italian) and Helmut Berger (German). It deals with the conflicts within a powerful family of munitions manufacturers operating in Germany during the rise of Nazism. The film is directed in a flamboyant style, typified by a scene where Berger performs in Dietrich-style drag.

Ingrid Thulin and Dirk Bogarde.

Helmut Berger in decadent drag.

Symphonic violence in 'The Wild Bunch'

Los Angeles, 18 June
Sam Peckinpah's directing career has been in the doldrums since 1965 when he fell out with the producer of *Major Dundee*. Now he has re-established himself with *The Wild Bunch* in which William Holden stars as the aging leader of a band of outlaws driven into Mexico after an unsuccessful bank raid. They are men out of their time. Involveme in the civil war raging between t Mexican army and guerrilla forc leads to a climactic battle agai impossible odds in which the ga is wiped out in a burst of sensua filmed and edited violence. It's brutal but humane film, which co fronts head-on the violence whi lies at the heart of the Western.

Ernest Borgnine in Sam Peckinpah's unusually violent ***The Wild Bunch.***

arland's star is tragically extinguished

Babes on Broadway (1941).

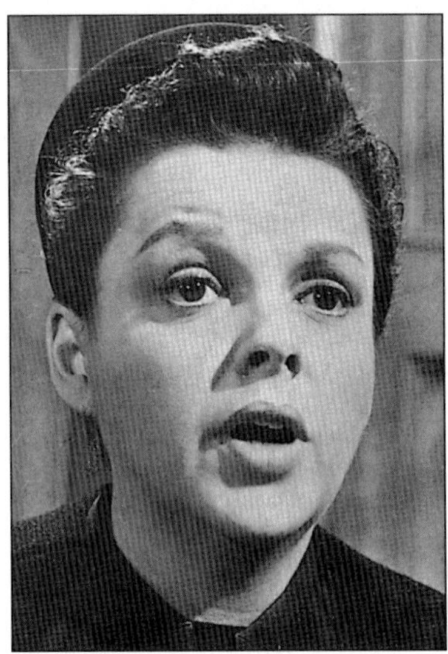

***Judgment at Nuremberg** (1961).*

ondon, 27 June
dy Garland, who died of a drug erdose in London six days ago, as buried today. Her passing at the e of 47 marks the end of a difficult e which encompassed worldwide me and adulation but was punctued by nervous breakdowns, suide attempts, studio suspensions, lawsuits, and five husbands (including Vincente Minnelli). Her fifth, Mickey Deans, was present at the funeral with her daughter, Liza Minnelli. From *The Wizard of Oz* (1939) onwards, she remained uniquely gifted, never more so than in *A Star is Born* (1954), in which she made a comeback after a long rough patch.

Hippie America howls across the screen

Peter Fonda (left) and Dennis Hopper, a defiant generation ill-at-ease.

New York, 14 July
Trailing clouds of glory from the Cannes Festival, where it won the directing prize for Dennis Hopper and Peter Fonda, is *Easy Rider*. Hopper co-stars with producer Fonda as two hippie bikers searching for the "real America" to the strains of a pounding rock soundtrack. Jack Nicholson, a graduate of Roger Corman's Z-budget movie academy, plays the boozy lawyer who comes along for the ride. Hopper's reputation for difficult behavior has, until recently, barred him from most of the studios. Now the majors are scrambling to emulate the sensational success of *Easy Rider*.

ssured debut from Swiss Alain Tanner

*rançois Simon in **Charles Dead or Alive**, a quality debut from Alain Tanner.*

witzerland, 1 August
he award of the Grand Prix of the ocarno Film Festival to *Charles ead or Alive*, the debut feature by e Swiss director Alain Tanner, is a ther late recognition of the emerence of the young Swiss cinema, nd promises to wake the national dustry out of its lethargy. Tanner, a former TV and documentary director, has been the moving spirit of the movement. *Charles Dead or Alive*, a cruel fable that questions the complacent values of Swiss society, deals with a middle-aged watchmaker (François Simon, Michel Simon's son), who abandons the rat race for a new life.

Sharon Tate killed in horrifying bloodbath

*Tate and Polanski in **The Fearless Vampire Killers** made two years ago.*

Hollywood, 9 August
With Roman Polanski in England preparing a film, his pregnant wife Sharon Tate was killed last night in a particularly shocking manner. She was in her villa in the Hollywood Hills entertaining three guests: the producer Voyteck Freykowsky, his girlfriend Abigail Folger and Jay Sebring, the hair stylist. Nobody knows exactly what happened next. When police arrived this morning they found four mutilated bodies, one of them Sharon Tate, who had been stabbed 15 times and whose breasts had been severed. On the front door, the word "Pigs" had been scrawled in blood.

▷

Newman, Redford: effervescent outlaws

Redford (left) and Newman, two outlaws exhausted from a hard day's work!

Connecticut, 23 September
George Roy Hill's *Butch Cassidy and the Sundance Kid* is not the first screen portrayal of two of the West's legendary outlaws, leaders of the "Hole in the Wall" gang, but it looks like it is the most profitable. Paul Newman and Robert Redford make an attractive Butch and Sundance (whose real name was Harry Longbaugh), laid-back outlaws for whom the West is a playground rather than the killing ground portrayed by Sam Peckinpah. The film is full of the currently fashionable nostalgia for the passing of the West – "the horse is dead," announces a bicycle salesman – and the use Hill makes of sepia-tinted photographs glows warmly with the light of other days. At the center of the film is the relationship between Newman and Redford, frozen forever in the last frame as they break cover to die at the hands of a small army of Bolivian soldiers.

Ken Russell unveils 'Women in Love'

Oliver Reed and Glenda Jackson are Lawrence's Gerald and Gudrun.

London, 13 November
Flamboyant director Ken Russell has fashioned a sexually frank and passionate version of D.H. Lawrence's *Women in Love*. This is familiar territory for Russell, who cut his teeth making arts documentaries for British television, and he is well-served by his principal players: Glenda Jackson as the strongwilled Gudrun Brangwen; Alan Bates as the D.H. Lawrence figure Rupert Birkin; and Oliver Reed, radiating bull-like potency as the mine-owner Gerald Crich. His firelit nude wrestling match with Bates is one of the highlights of the film.

'Bob and Carol and Ted and Alice'... !

New York, 8 October
Paul Mazursky has made his directing debut with *Bob & Carol & Ted & Alice*, a film which capitalizes on the new wave of permissiveness and the fashionable encounter group philosophy it has spawned. It's at such a group that sophisticated suburban swingers Robert Culp and Natalie Wood discover a philosophy of sexual freedom which they then try to sell to their uptight friends Elliott Gould and Dyan Cannon. Mazursky's sharp comedy of manners draws excellent performanc from the principals, particularly t 30-year-old Gould, who began h career in the chorus line of the sta version of *Irma la Douce*. Broadw stardom arrived when he co-starr with Barbra Streisand in *I Can G It for You Wholesale*, and he g Streisand wholesale when he ma ried her in 1963. They divorced la year as her career took off whi his seemed stalled. Now movie sta dom beckons for the agreeably se deprecating actor.

Left to right: Elliott Gould, Natalie Wood, Robert Culp and Dyan Cannon.

Costa-Gavras takes a swipe at the colonel

New York, 8 December
The military regime of the Greek colonels is the target of a new political thriller, *Z*, shot in Algeria by the Greek-born director Constantin Costa-Gavras who is now a French citizen. Yves Montand, the leader of a pacifist opposition party in an unidentified Mediterranean countr (which is clearly Greece), is knocke down by a van and dies after unde going brain surgery. Investigatin magistrate Jean-Louis Trintignan treats the case as a murder whe he uncovers a government-suppor ed conspiracy to assassinate "Z" Based on a novel by Vassili Vass likos, *Z* is a virtuoso indictment o the junta now ruling Greece and o the methods applied by totalitaria regimes throughout the world. Th son of a Greek bureaucrat, Costa Gavras left Greece at the age of 1 to pursue a degree in literature a the Sorbonne. After attending th Institut des Hautes Etudes Cinéma tographiques (IDHEC), he becam assistant director to Yves Allégre and René Clément before makin his directing debut with *The Sleep ing Car Murders*, a taut suspense starring Yves Montand. His secon film was *Shock Troops*, a harrowin tale about the French Resistance.

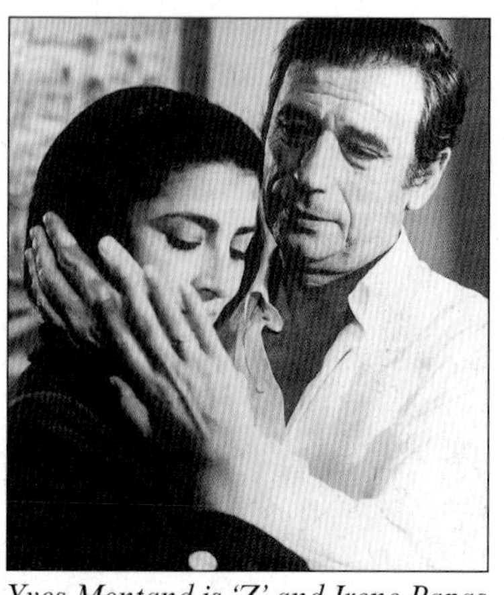

Yves Montand is 'Z' and Irene Papas his wife in Costa-Gavras' film.

'Satyricon' a procession of wild orgies

ome, 1 December
ederico Fellini has defined his new ork, *Fellini Satyricon*, based on etronius' ancient Roman fragment id other fables, as more science ctional than historical. "Decadent ome is as far from me as the

*r his **Satyricon**, Fellini's fertile imagination has turned for inspiration to a decadent period in Rome's past culture.*

oon," the director explained. The cture tells of two students in Rome *rca* A.D. 500, who go their differt ways after fighting over a pretty y. Their separate adventures inude drunken orgies, imprisonment a galley ship and a duel fought ith the Minotaur, before they meet again. The film is really *La Dolce ita* in Ancient Rome, with Fellini oking with disapproval at the imoral goings-on in a pre-Christian society, and by implication today's. He emphasizes this connection by casting two unmistakably modern young men in the leading roles: Englishman Martin Potter and American Hiram Keller as Encolpius and Ascyltus, whose sole aim is the pursuit of pleasure. Fellini employed more than 250 character actors and extras and had 90 sets built, making *Satyricon* the most expensive movie made at Cinecittà since *Ben-Hur*.

he great Italian director at work on what is a visually extraordinary film.

Josef von Sternberg dies at age 75

Hollywood, 22 December
Josef von Sternberg, one of the great pictorial stylists of the Golden Age of Hollywood, has died in a Hollywood hospital at the age of 75. He was born plain Josef Sternberg in Vienna in 1894 – the "von" was acquired later in Hollywood – and arrived in America with his parents at the age of seven. As a silent film director at Paramount, he quickly created his own artificial world of light and shade filled with strong men and mysterious women. He launched Marlene Dietrich in 1930 in *The Blue Angel*, and in six subsequent films she became the enigmatic centerpiece of Sternberg's obsession with light and composition. Known as a notoriously difficult man to work with, Sternberg once said, "The only way to succeed is to make people hate you. That way they remember you."

Dolly years too young but full of bounce

New York, 16 December
Fox have reportedly spent $24 million on filming the smash-hit stage musical, *Hello, Dolly!* They have staked the money on hot star Barbra Streisand, who delivers the goods with exuberance, vivacity, a great line in rapid-fire patter and, of course, that voice. However, it must be said that as Dolly Levi, matchmaker and self-appointed fixer, in search of a rich husband (Walter Matthau), she is at least 20 years too young for the role, which may disturb some. Terrific entertainment, though, with Gene Kelly directing a first-rate cast and handing the choreography over to Michael Kidd.

The title number: Dolly Levi is welcomed back at the Harmonia Gardens.

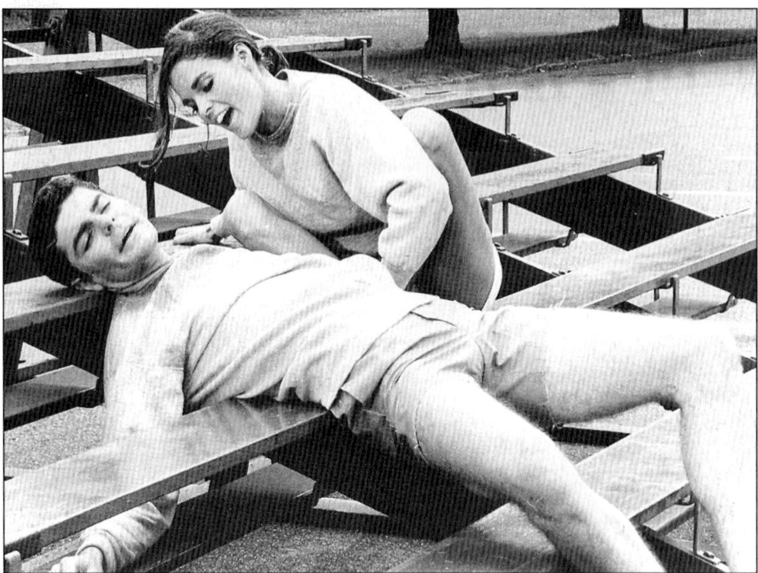

Richard Benjamin and Ali MacGraw in Larry Peerce's **Goodbye, Columbus**.

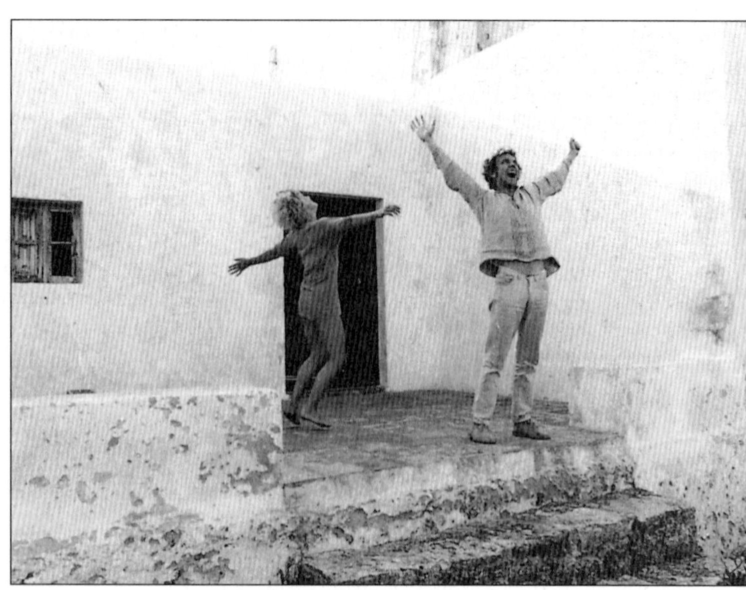

Mimsy Farmer and Klaus Grumberg in Barbet Schroeder's **More** (France).

A JEROME HELLMAN-JOHN SCHLESINGER PRODUCTION
DUSTIN HOFFMAN
JON VOIGHT
"MIDNIGHT COWBOY"
BRENDA VACCARO JOHN McGIVER RUTH WHITE SYLVIA MILES BARNARD HUGHES
COLOR by DeLuxe
United Artists

Hoffman and Voight: memorable.

A man went looking for America.
And couldn't find it anywhere...
Cannes Film Festival WINNER 'Best Film By a New Director'
PANDO COMPANY in association with RAYBERT PRODUCTIONS presents
easy Rider
starring
PETER FONDA · DENNIS HOPPER · JACK NICHOLSON
Written by PETER FONDA DENNIS HOPPER TERRY SOUTHERN
Directed by DENNIS HOPPER
Produced by PETER FONDA
Associate Producer WILLIAM HAYWARD
Executive Producer BERT SCHNEIDER · COLOR
Released by COLUMBIA PICTURES

A small-scale, big impact movie: Dennis Hopper (r) directed **Easy Rider**; Peter Fonda (l), Jack Nicholson (c) co-starre

Belmondo, mail-order bride Deneuve in Truffaut's **The Mississippi Mermaid**.

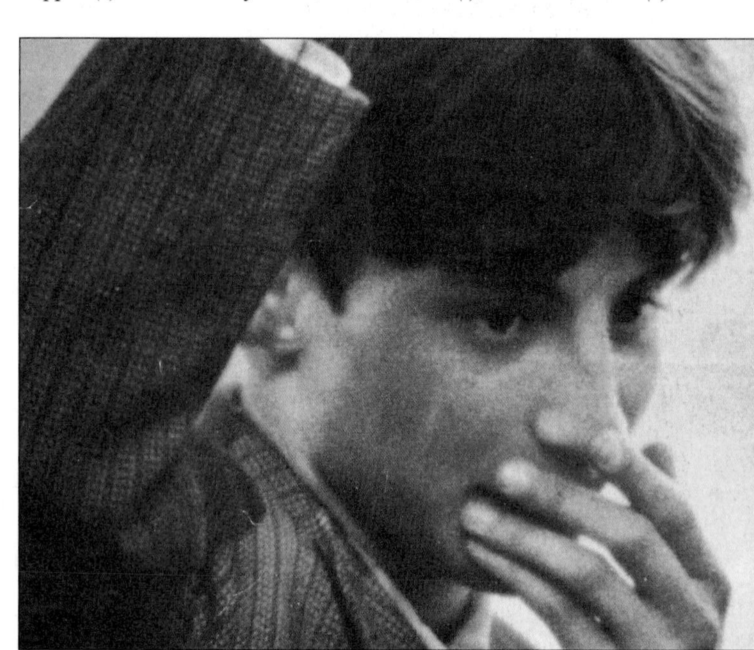

Peter Schildt in Bo Widerberg's **Adalen 31**, a strike tragedy from Sweden.

You never met
pair like Butch
nd The Kid
They're Taking Trains...
They're Taking Banks
And They're Taking
One Piece Of Baggage!
0th Century-Fox presents
PAUL NEWMAN
ROBERT REDFORD
KATHARINE ROSS
BUTCH CASSIDY AND THE SUNDANCE KID
A George Roy Hill–Paul Monash Production Co-Starring STROTHER MARTIN, JEFF COREY, HENRY JONES.
Executive Producer PAUL MONASH Produced by JOHN FOREMAN Directed by GEORGE ROY HILL Written by WILLIAM GOLDMAN
Music Composed and Conducted by BURT BACHARACH A NEWMAN-FOREMAN Presentation PANAVISION® COLOUR BY DE LUXE

irector George Roy Hill found this year's dream ticket, and 'Raindrops Keep Fallin' on My Head' topped hit parade.

Brigitte Bardot and Xavier Gélin in ***The Bear and the Doll*** *(France).*

Susannah York in Sydney Pollack's ***They Shoot Horses, Don't They?***

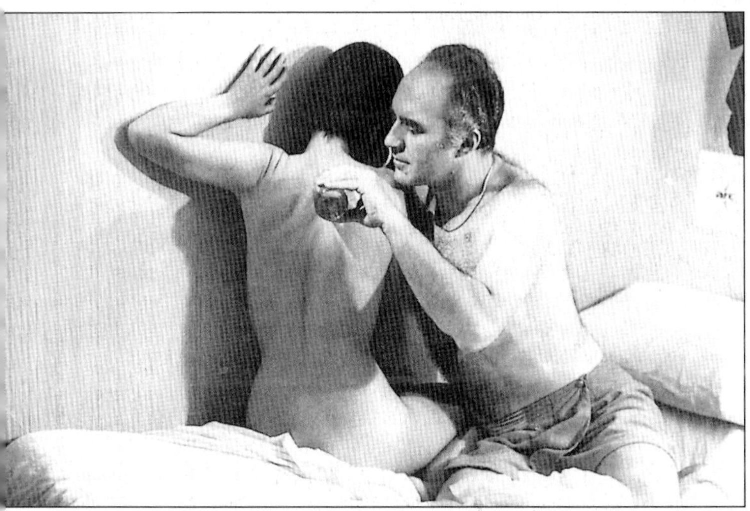

nita Pallenberg, Michel Piccoli: ***Dillinger is Dead*** *from Italy's Marco Ferreri.*

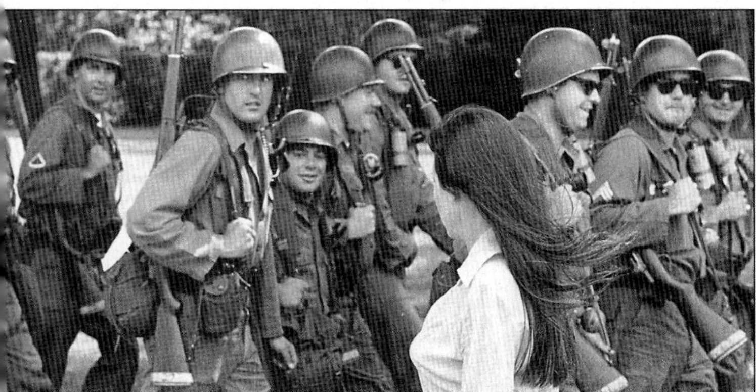

'erna Bloom in Haskell Wexler's comment on 60s America, ***Medium Cool****.*

53

Michele Lee and Buddy Hackett in, and with (!) ***The Love Bug****, from Disney.*

Strange Bedfellows

Though fewer Americans went to the cinema each week in the 1970s than they had done in the three preceding decades, when a movie was released that they really wanted to see, they turned out in greater numbers than ever before. Indeed, the 70s may have produced fewer feature films than at any time in Hollywood's history, but the handful of major hits, such as William Friedkin's *The Exorcist* (1973), George Roy Hill's *The Sting* (1973), Steven Spielberg's *Jaws* (1975) and George Lucas' *Star Wars* (1977) became blockbusters.

The latter grossed more than $164 million in only two years in the U.S. It also began movie merchandising of spin-off gadgets in earnest, with sales of *Star Wars*-related goods eventually reaching around $1.5 billion per year worldwide. Hits such as the above were able to carry a dozen or so box-office flops. The decline in worldwide audiences leveled out in the decade and, with the sharp increase in ticket prices, total dollar earnings generally kept pace with the costs of production.

As the 70s began, nervous producers, unable to predict what punters would be looking for, set out to replicate some of the trends that had been initiated in the previous decade. For example, after the extraordinary success of Dennis Hopper's seminal road movie *Easy Rider*, and Arthur Penn's Arlo Guthrie-inspired *Alice's Restaurant* (both 1969), a spate of anti-heroic, predominantly youth-oriented films bombarded the market place.

George Lucas' 'coming of age mosaic', *American Graffiti* (1973), which was set in a small town in 1962, made a star of Richard Dreyfuss, and was the best of an impact-making bunch that also included Bob Rafelson's *Five Easy Pieces* (1970), Stuart Hagman's *The Strawberry Statement* (1970), Terrence Malick's *Badlands* (1973), Michael Wadleigh's rock music documentary *Woodstock* (1973) and David and Albert Maysles and Charlotte Zwerin's *Gimme Shelter* (1970), a chilling account of the Altamont Freeway concert by the Rolling Stones that ended in murder.

The cinema's new permissiveness was also luring audiences away from the tamer, more strictly censored fare offered at home on television. Hard-hitting cop movies such as Don Siegel's *Dirty Harry* (1971), Robert Aldrich's *Hustle* (1975) and *The Choirboys* (1977), Roman Polanski's remarkable *noir*-like *Chinatown* (1974), and Friedkin's *The French Connection* (1971) were tough, efficient and uncompromising entertainments that brought out the macho best in actors like Clint Eastwood, Jack Nicholson, Gene Hackman and Burt Reynolds, building up their star status.

Violence also featured prominently (and quite startlingly) in Stanley Kubrick's frightening adaptation of Anthony Burgess' novel *A Clockwork Orange* (1971), Michael Ritchie's *Prime Cut* (1972), John Boorman's *Deliverance* (1972), Tobe Hooper's influential *The Texas Chainsaw Massacre* (1977), John Schlesinger's *Marathon Man* (1977) and Alan Parker's disturbing *Midnight Express* (1978).

For the first time in Hollywood's checkered history there was also an outspoken approach to sex, demonstrated in Mike Nichols' *Carnal Knowledge* (1971), Hal Ashby's *Shampoo* (1975) and Louis Malle's first American movie, *Pretty Baby* (1978). From Europe and elsewhere came Just Jaeckin's *Emmanuelle* (1975), Bernardo Bertolucci's *Last Tango in Paris* (1972), Pasolini's *The Decameron* (1971) and *Salo* (1975), Nicolas Roeg's *Don't Look Now* (1973) and Oshima's explicit *In the Realm of the Senses* (1976).

With the Warren Report on the assassination of President Kennedy and the murk that was Watergate, the eternal verities so deeply embodied in the American way of life came into question. If the elected representatives of the country's welfare could no longer be trusted, who could? With no satisfactory answers forthcoming, Americans during the 70s were nervous and insecure about the state of the nation, and saw their fears made manifest in a series of 'conspiracy' movies. These pitted individual integrity and vulnerability against corporate might and political corruption.

Among the best movies which reflected this near-paranoia were Sidney Lumet's *The Anderson Tapes* (1972), Francis Ford Coppola's *The Conversation* (1973), Sydney Pollack's *Three Days of the Condor* (1975), Alan J. Pakula's *The Parallax View* and *All The President's Men* (1976, directly about Watergate) and James Bridges' *The China Syndrome* (1979), which articulated the unease about the dangers of nuclear power. From Europe came Elio Petri's *Investigation of a Citizen Above Suspicion* (1970), Costa-Gavras' *State of Siege* (1974) and Francesco Rosi's *The Mattei Affair* and *Illustrious Corpses* (1975), proving that corruption was not an exclusively American preserve.

Robert De Niro (l), Harvey Keitel in Martin Scorsese's ***Mean Streets*** *(1973).*

The other major event addressed by American cinema was the Vietnam War – a subject that would prove increasingly fertile and disturbing in the 1980s. The first cro dealt either with the war itself – as Ted Post's underrated *Go Tell th Spartans* (1978), Sidney J. Furie *The Boys in Company C* (1978) ar Coppola's remarkable *Apocalyp Now* (1979) – or, as in Mart Scorsese's controversial *Taxi Driv* (1976), with the traumatic afte effects on individual soldiers.

Other movies that dealt with th domestic problems of the physical and mentally war-scarred include Jeremy Paul Kagan's *Heroes* (1977 Hal Ashby's *Coming Home* (197 and Michael Cimino's *The De Hunter* (1978). Set before, durin and after the war, and, arguably, th finest of the Vietnam movies of th period, this last film drew attentic to Meryl Streep, and confirme Robert De Niro's status as one the screen's finest actors.

The majority of those people wh went to the cinema with any regula ity in the 70s were in their teens an early twenties, and, in order to cate to their tastes, the studios turned a quartet of talented young film school graduates who would n only dominate the cinema of th decade but that of the 1980s an 90s, and whose films would b among the biggest grossers in th history of motion pictures.

The oldest was Francis For Coppola (born 1939), who, in 196 founded his own (ultimately i fated) production company, Zo trope, and whose two most notab movies in the 70s were *The Godfa ther* (1972) and *Apocalypse Now*.

George Lucas (born 1944) cam to prominence with the influenti (and profitable) *American Graffi* though its financial returns were nothing compared with the millio earned by *Star Wars*, the most fi nancially successful movie of th decade, which brought Harriso Ford to prominence, and spawne two equally successful sequels.

The third of the 'movie brats', a they came to be known, was Marti Scorsese (born 1942). After makin a handful of independent feature this NYU graduate made his break through with *Mean Streets* (1973 a critically acclaimed drama abo young men in Manhattan's Littl Italy, which turned De Niro int a star and elevated Harvey Keite Scorsese reinforced his reputatio s one of the boldest, most exciting oung directors of his generation ith his 1976 New York-based *Taxi Driver* with De Niro and featuring n adolescent Jodie Foster.

But the most successful of these *underkinder* was Steven Spielberg). 1947) whose surreal, low-budget, nade-for-TV horror picture *Duel* 1971) – in which a businessman n the freeway is terrorized by a ehemoth with an invisible driver – d the production company, Universal, to offer him his feature debut 1974 with the road movie *The Sugarland Express*. He followed this ith the phenomenally successful *aws* (1975) and, even more of a ontrast, *Close Encounters of the Third Kind* (1977), arguably the nost intelligent sci-fi film ever.

The radical change that characterized the movies of the 70s was lso reflected in the Hollywood musical. Though a large part of the ecade saw several Broadway hits – *Fiddler on the Roof* (1971), *Man of La Mancha* (1972), *1776* (1972), *esus Christ Superstar (1973), Mame 1974), The Wiz* (1979) – receiving he big screen treatment, director-horeographer Bob Fosse redefined his hitherto escapist genre. He, and creenwriter Jay Presson Allen, did his with a radical adaptation of he long-running Broadway success *Cabaret* (1972), which made a superstar of Liza Minnelli, gave birth o the "adult" musical, and was rewarded with several Oscars.

Fosse explored his own life in *All That Jazz* (1979), the first musical to leal with the subject of death; while Mark Rydell's *The Rose*, in which Bette Midler made an astonishing creen debut, also eschewed escapism for gritty realism in a story oosely based on the life of doomed inger Janis Joplin.

The most commercially successful nusicals of the decade, though, vere *Saturday Night Fever* (1977) nd *Grease* (1978), both starring a newcomer called John Travolta and rend-settingly placing the accent quarely on youth. Another discernble trend in the 70s was the big-budget "disaster" movie such as *Airport* (1970), *The Poseidon Adventure* (1972), *The Towering Inferno* 1974), *Earthquake* (1974), *The Hindenburg* (1975) and *The Swarm* 1978). Martial arts movies also abounded, their chief exponent being Bruce Lee in such actioners s *Fists of Fury* (1972) and *Enter the Dragon* (1973).

In complete contrast were actor-director Woody Allen's sophisticated and hilariously angst-ridden New York movies. The cycle took off with *Annie Hall* in 1977, introducing the most persuasive (and pervasive) strand of Jewish neurosis yet into screen comedy.

This was the decade in which it became clear that producers believed the maxim, if at first you succeed, try, try again. Hence the rash of sequels to hits, among them *The Godfather*, *Airport*, *Star Wars*, *The Exorcist* and *Rocky* (1976).

The European cinema was well represented throughout the 70s, especially by France, some of whose most notable achievements included Eric Rohmer's *Claire's Knee* (1970) and François Truffaut's *Day for Night* (1973). Also from France came Jacques Tati's inventive *Traffic* (1970), Louis Malle's *Lacombe Lucien*, Claude Chabrol's *Violette* (1977) and Bertrand Blier's *Get Out Your Handkerchiefs* (1977).

Luis Buñuel continued to contribute significantly to world cinema with *The Discreet Charm of the Bourgeoisie* (1972) and *That Obscure Object of Desire* (1977), while the decade saw in the New German Cinema. Its main exponent, Rainer Werner Fassbinder, directed such highly individual films as *The Bitter Tears of Petra von Kant* (1972), *Fear Eats the Soul* (1974), *Effie Briest* (1974) and *The Marriage of Eva Braun* (1978), which made a star of Hanna Schygulla. Also from Germany came Werner Herzog's *Aguirre, The Wrath of God* (1973), *The Mystery of Kaspar Hauser* (1974) and a striking new version of *Nosferatu* (1979); and Wim Wenders' *Kings of the Road* (1976) and *The American Friend* (1977).

Italy relied largely on its veterans to keep its seriously depressed industry from drowning in mediocrity. The most notable films of the decade were Vittorio De Sica's *The Garden of the Finzi-Continis* (1971), Fellini's *Roma* (1972), *Amarcord* (1974) and *Casanova* (1976), and Bertolucci's *The Conformist* (1970) and *1900* (1976).

Nor was this a particularly fruitful decade for British cinema which, after the boom period of the 'Swinging Sixties', found itself fighting for its life. The best of British – many of which were produced or directed by Americans – included Schlesinger's *Sunday Bloody Sunday* (1971), Kubrick's *A Clockwork Orange* and *Barry Lyndon* (1975), Melvin Frank's *A Touch of Class* (1973), Lindsay Anderson's *O Lucky Man!* (1973), Nicolas Roeg's *Don't Look Now* and *The Man Who Fell to Earth* (1976) and Richard Lester's *Robin and Marian* (1976), which brought Audrey Hepburn back to the screen after a nine-year absence.

*Donald Sutherland, a brutal fascist in Bertolucci's epic **1900** (Italy, 1976).*

Like Britain, the Swedish film industry found itself beset with problems (mainly financial). With the exception of Jan Troell's *The Emigrants* (1971) and *The New Land* (1973), it was Ingmar Bergman who, as always, dominated the scene with such complex dramas as *Cries and Whispers* (1972), *Scenes From a Marriage* (1974), his enchanting vision of Mozart's *The Magic Flute* (1975) and *Autumn Sonata* (1978). This last one brought him together, on the only occasion in both their careers, with his countrywoman and namesake Ingrid Bergman.

The two principal filmmaking countries of Eastern Europe, Poland and Czechoslovakia, were still suffering from the effects of 1968's tumultuous events – the student demonstrations in Poland and the Russian invasion of Czechoslovakia – and the political purges that followed in their wake, and produced little of cinematic value in the 70s.

For signs of renewed hope in the art of cinema, one had to look further afield, mainly to the former French colonies of Africa. Because of increased investment in the film industry, pictures from Senegal, Mali and Mauritania began to appear with success at festivals, and gradually gained an admiring international audience. Directors leading the way were the Senegalese Ousmane Sembene with *Xala* (1974) and *Ceddo* (1976), comedy-dramas that dug deeply into African society, and the Mauritanian Med Hondo, who turned a savage eye on the French colonial past beginning with *Soleil Ô* (1970). There was also a breakthrough for Algerian cinema when director Mohammed Lakhdar-Hamina's 175-minute epic *Chronicle of the Burning Years*, one of the most expensive productions ever to come from the Third World, won the Golden Palm at Cannes in 1975.

Meanwhile, back in Hollywood, Columbia, suffering the worst losses in its history, gave up its long-established Gower Street studio and, as Columbia Pictures Industries Inc., moved to Burbank where it shared facilities with Warner Bros., which had become Warner Communications Inc. Around the same time, MGM sold two of its largest back lots totaling 100 acres and, in October 1973, it ceased to exist as an individual maker and distributor of feature films.

The terminal decline of the studio system and huge diminution of output was symbolized by an event which took place in May 1970. A fabulous auction of thousands of movie props and costumes was held at MGM Studios, the once-proud giant and industry leader. It was reminiscent of the opening scene of *Citizen Kane*, when all the multi-millionaire's goods are put under a hammer. Hollywood, like Xanadu, was being sold off, but it still retained a certain grandeur and its power lingered on.

CLIVE HIRSCHHORN

1970

1969 Academy Awards, Dorothy Chandler Pavilion, 7 Apr.

Best Film:	*Midnight Cowboy* (dir: John Schlesinger)
Best Director:	John Schlesinger
Best Actor:	John Wayne *(True Grit)*
Best Actress:	Maggie Smith *(The Prime of Miss Jean Brodie)*
Best Supp. Actor:	Gig Young *(They Shoot Horses, Don't They)*
Best Supp. Actress:	Goldie Hawn *(Cactus Flower)*

New York, 11 February
The trade journal *Variety* has revealed that Walt Disney's *Song of the South* (1946) was withdrawn from circulation in 1958 due to the racist attitudes reflected in the roles played by Negroes.

New Jersey, 17 February
Frank Sinatra has been forced to give evidence at a hearing of the State of New Jersey's Commission of Inquiry into Organized Crime. Sinatra, who was questioned about his association with certain well-known members of the Mafia, has denied any contact with the organization. He insists that a misunderstanding arose due to shares he once held in a Las Vegas casino. The actor has been exonerated.

France, 1 March
Jacques Demy has started shooting *Peau-d'ane* (*Donkey Skin* aka *The Magic Donkey*), based on the tale by Charles Perrault, on location at the Château de Chambord. Shooting of this fairytale is next scheduled to move to the castles of Plessis-Bourré and Gambais.

Paris, 9 March
The Armand Tallier prize for the best film book has been won by the Swiss film critic and historian, Freddy Buache for his work *The Italian Cinema from Antonioni to Rosi*, published by The Age of Man.

New York, 23 March
CBS held a demonstration of a color video recording and announced that the first commercial distribution of videotapes would begin next fall. Darryl Zanuck has declared that 20th Century-Fox intends to sell films on videotape five years after their release in cinemas.

New Jersey, 25 March
The first Jerry Lewis cinema opened in Wayne. Lewis, who now plans only 355 cinemas instead of 750, is seeking investors.

Paris, 27 March
An article representing the views of the French "workers party", which appeared in the professional weekly *le Film français*, attacked the "unhealthy nature" of today's French films: "A small group of neurotic intellectuals and film merchants show no hesitation in corrupting our nation and, in particular, our young people."

Denver, 16 April
Jane Fonda slept outdoors and fasted for 36 hours in protest against the war in Vietnam and against John Wayne's film, *The Green Berets*, to the displeasure of her father, Henry Fonda.

Los Angeles, 26 April
The celebrated stripper and burlesque queen of the 30s, Gypsy Rose Lee (Rose Louise Hovick), has died.

Lyon, 23 May
A group of 40 conservationists from the International Federation of Film Archives (FIAF) are working on the problems related to film preservation. High on the agenda is the necessity of raising the awareness of authorities and the public to the importance of restoring and protecting art treasures hidden away in film libraries.

Los Angeles, 15 June
The trial of Charles Manson and five members of his sect opened today. They stand accused of the murder of actress Sharon Tate and four other people on 9 August in Hollywood. They confessed to the "ritual killings" when first arrested last November.

Paris, 20 June
Although François Truffaut denies being a "revolutionary", he has been selling *la Cause du peuple* (*The People's Cause*) on the streets, in the company of Jean-Paul Sartre and Simone de Beauvoir, to uphold the cause of freedom of expression.

Los Angeles, 24 June
Dennis Hopper has started proceedings against Peter Fonda and his Pandro Company. Hopper is asking for 3 percent of the profits of *Easy Rider* as payment for his contribution to the screenplay.

Pakistan, 10 July
Jean-Luc Godard's *Alphaville* has been banned in all cinemas throughout the country.

Paris, 5 August
The first drive-in cinema in the Paris region has opened in Rungis.

London, 7 August
Actor Albert Finney has married French star Anouk Aimée.

Paris, 14 August
Abel Gance has signed a contract with Claude Lelouch for a new release of his reconstructed silent film *Napoleon*, following an unsuccessful attempt in 1968.

New York, 29 August
Paramount's Vice President Stanley Jaffe has been named president, making him, at age 30, the youngest man to hold such a position in the cinema industry.

Los Angeles, 27 August
The Screen Actors Guild has promised to help Chicanos improve their image. Following a meeting between Charlton Heston, Guild president, and representatives from a group called Justice for Chicanos, the Guild resolved to review and demonstrate against films judged demeaning to Mexican-Americans, such as *Butch Cassidy and the Sundance Kid* and *El Condor*, which depict a handful of whites gunning down entire armies of Latin Americans.

Paris, 29 August
Release of *Candy*, a film directed by the actor Christian Marquand from Terry Southern's best-selling novel, with Richard Burton, Marlon Brando, Ringo Starr, Charles Aznavour and John Huston.

Hollywood, 8 September
All the major studios except Fox have started proceedings against ABC and CBS. The television stations have started making their own films, and it is alleged that this is a contravention of the anti-trust law.

Culver City, 5 October
MGM has started selling off its bac lot by auction. The third lot of 3 hectares sold for $7.25 million.

Tokyo, 31 October
Release of *Dodes' kaden*, directe Akira Kurosawa's first film sinc 1965, with Yoshitaka Zushi an Junzaburo Ban. The film runs fo four hours and is Kurosawa's fir to be made in color.

Cleveland, 9 November
Jane Fonda has appeared in cou for possession of narcotics. She wa arrested on her return from Canad on 3 November. Some see this a another anti-government ploy by th star who has been protesting again racial prejudice in the U.S., the wa in Vietnam and the invasion o Cambodia by U.S. troops.

Paris, 12 November
All cinemas are closed today as sign of respect to General de Gaul who died on 9 November.

Paris, 7 December
Henri Duchemin, an employee a the Simca factory, has demande the seizure of Claude Lelouch's fil *le Voyou* because one of the charac ters has the same name as he.

Los Angeles, 31 December
The 10 hits of the year, includin *Airport*, *M*A*S*H*, *Patton*, and *Bo & Carol & Ted & Alice*, account fo 40 percent of the distributors' tota takings for 1970.

BIRTHS

Boston, 29 April
Uma Thurman

DEATHS

Los Angeles, 14 May
Billie Burke

Indiana, 1 August
Frances Farmer

California, 29 September
Edward Everett Horton

Set in Ireland against a backgroun of magnificent seascapes, Davi Lean brought his characteristic ep sweep to what was essentially a lov story during the Irish Rebellion.

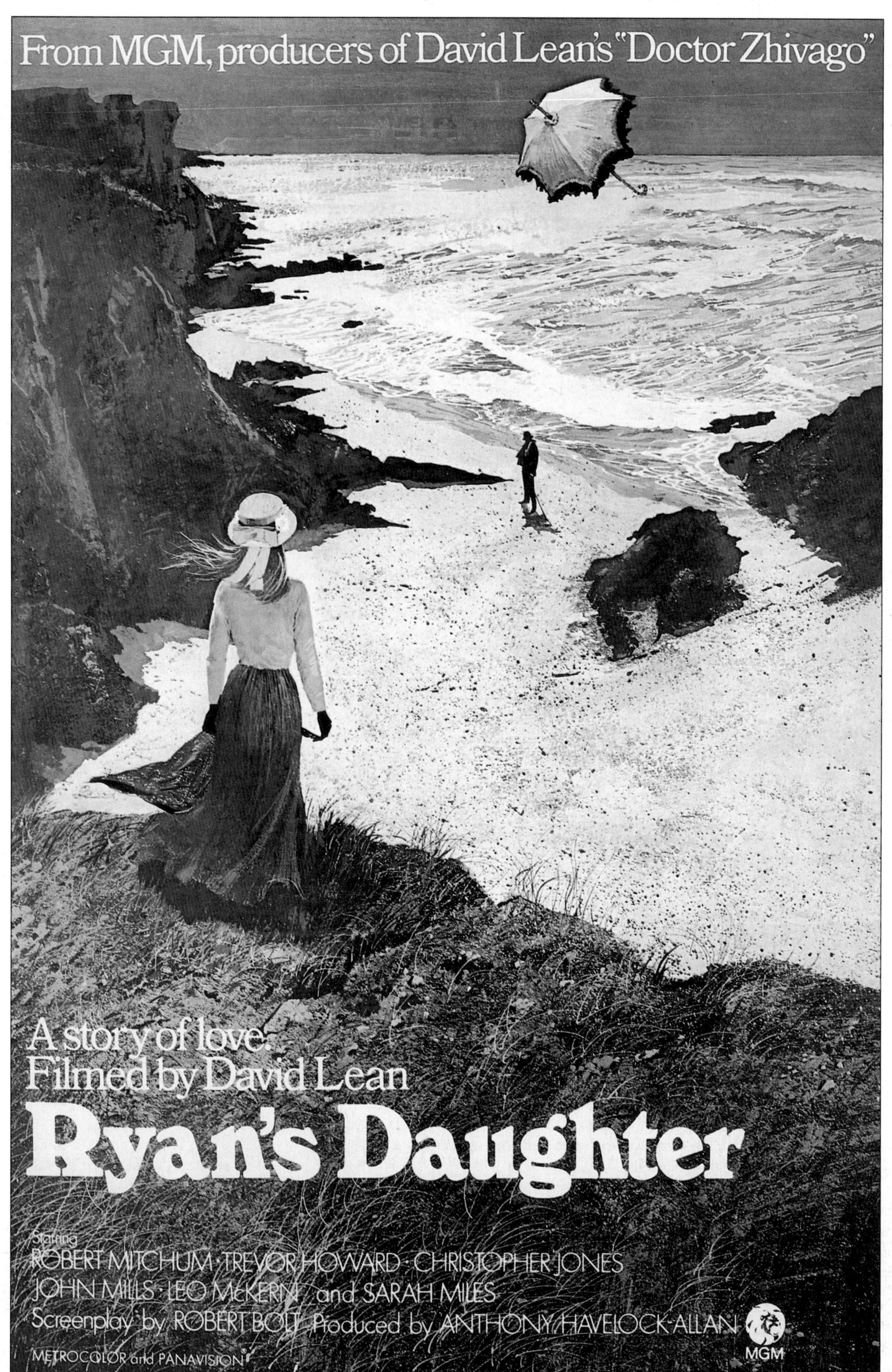
From MGM, producers of David Lean's "Doctor Zhivago"
A story of love.
Filmed by David Lean
Ryan's Daughter
Starring
ROBERT MITCHUM · TREVOR HOWARD · CHRISTOPHER JONES
JOHN MILLS · LEO McKERN and SARAH MILES
Screenplay by ROBERT BOLT Produced by ANTHONY HAVELOCK-ALLAN
METROCOLOR and PANAVISION
MGM

A final disappearing act from Jiri Trnka

Prague, 2 January
Jiri Trnka, Czechoslovakia's great master of puppet films, died two days ago at the age of 57. He had been ill for some years, but he told his friends, "I want to stay alive in order to work." Trnka, a graduate of the School of Arts and Crafts in Prague, created a puppet theater in 1936, which was disbanded at the outbreak of World War II. During the war, he designed stage sets and illustrated children's books. In 1945, he set up an animation unit at the Prague film studio, calling it Trick Brothers. It specialized in puppet animation as well as cartoons. Some of Trnka's imaginative features included *A Midsummer Night's Dream* (1958), shot in Eastmancolor and CinemaScope. Earlier films were *The Chinese Emperor's Nightingale* (1949), *Song of the Prairie* (1949), *Cybernetic Grandma* (1962) and *The Good Soldier Schweik* (1954), adapted from the Czech comic novel. His final film, *The Hand*, stands as his artistic and political testament.

Trnka with one of his characters for ***The Chinese Emperor's Nightingale.***

Three of Jiri Trnka's marionettes.

Romy Schneider and 'The Things of Life'

Romy Schneider with Michel Piccoli in Claude Sautet's ***The Things of Life.***

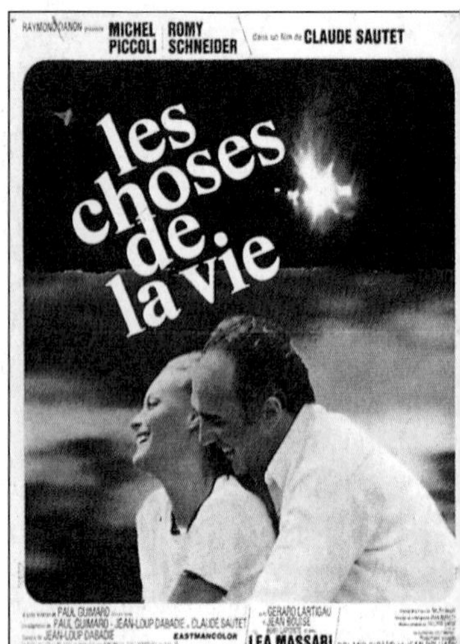
MICHEL PICCOLI ROMY SCHNEIDER
CLAUDE SAUTET
les choses de la vie
LEA MASSARI

Paris, 9 January
The Louis Delluc Prize has been awarded this year to *The Things of Life* (*les Choses de la vie*), which stars Romy Schneider and Michel Piccoli. It is directed by Claude Sautet, who is something of a discovery even though this is his fourth feature. *Bonjour sourire* (1955), *The Big Risk* (1960) and *Guns of the Dictator* (1965) were effective crime dramas which did not receive the attention from the public that they deserved. However, his new film, which moves into different territory, has hit the jackpot. It is a sharply observed study of a mid-life crisis beginning with a sequence which alerts the audience to the fact that the hero (Piccoli) is to die in a car crash. In flashback we learn that he is separated from his wife (Lea Massari), and is having an affair. But he still retains an attachment to and interest in, his wife, his son, his friends, the places he has known – in short the "things of life", and consequently finds it difficult to make a commitment to his mistress. The latter is played by the lovely Romy Schneider, who has now matured into a fine actress.

Major American studios find themselves in severe financial crisis

Hollywood, 10 February
The problems experienced by many of the leading Hollywood studios during the late 60s have worsened over the past year, forcing companies to cut back on production plans, cancel some projects outright, and dismiss large numbers of employees. According to an article in the *Hollywood Reporter*, "The film studios are continuing to trim staffs as they liquidate inventories estimated at $400 million. MCA (which owns Universal) and 20th (Fox) hit new lows for the year on the New York Stock Exchange." The report further describes the high level of redundancy at four companies in particular – Universal, MGM, Fox and Warners – where revenues and profits have fallen dramatically. Only Universal has stayed in the black, while the other three are awash in red ink, with combined total losses between them amounting to $100 million, and no end yet in sight, despite the management shake-ups that have taken place. Financier Kirk Kerkorian has taken over at MGM, and Kinney National has recently acquired a controlling interest in Warner Bros.-Seven Arts. And it doesn't look as if the Zanucks (president Darryl and his son, production chief Richard) can survive much longer at Fox. The continuing fall in movie attendance is a problem, and the studios have invested large sums in expensive productions which have flopped. The list of high-cost lossmakers includes *Camelot* (Warners, 1967), *Paint Your Wagon* (Paramount, 1969) and, from UA, *Chitty Chitty Bang Bang* (1968) and *Battle of Britain* (1969). But most disastrous of all has been the recent run of flops at Fox including *Dr Dolittle* (1967), *Staircase* and *Hello Dolly!* (both 1969). And the studio's nightmare is not over yet. Much is riding on two new productions, the $10 million *The Only Game in Town* and the $25 million *Tora! Tora! Tora!* The outlook for the Zanucks is distinctly bleak.

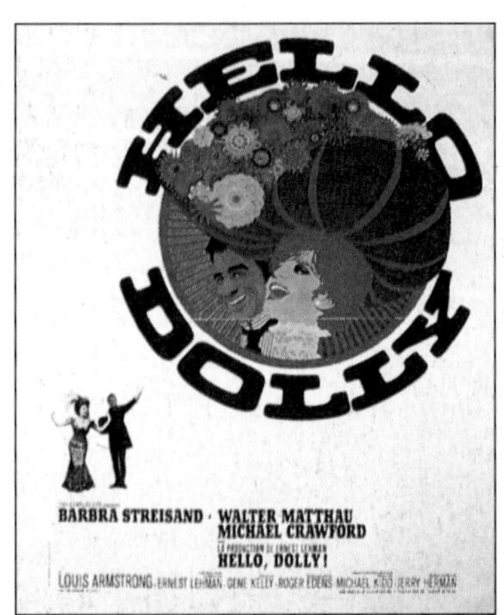
HELLO DOLLY
BARBRA STREISAND · WALTER MATTHAU
MICHAEL CRAWFORD
HELLO, DOLLY!

The disastrous failure of this musical, directed by Gene Kelly, involved considerable losses for Fox.

Truffaut and the troubled spirit of a 'wild child'

In *The Wild Child*, *François Truffaut gives himself a role for the first time.*

With young Jean-Pierre Cargol.

Paris, 26 February
After the expensive production of *Mississippi Mermaid*, shot in Cinemascope and color with two big-name French stars, Catherine Deneuve and Jean-Paul Belmondo, the director François Truffaut has returned to a far more austere and modest style. His film *The Wild Child* (*l'Enfant sauvage*) is set in 1798, and tells the true story of the discovery of a naked boy, who resembles and behaves like a wild beast, in the woods in central France. He is sent to the Institute for the Deaf and Dumb in Paris, where Dr. Jean Itard struggles to make him walk upright, wear clothes and teach him to speak. This detached, but still moving, film has a remarkable performance from Jean-Pierre Cargol, of gypsy parentage, in the title role. Truffaut cast himself as the doctor so that he could direct the boy both in front of the camera and behind it. The head to head battle between the doctor and his patient on screen reflects that of the director and actor. It is significant that *The Wild Child* is dedicated to Jean-Pierre Léaud, the brilliant young lead in Truffaut's first feature, *The Four Hundred Blows*, during which a similar relationship was formed. Constructed in the form of an academic study, the film charts each fascinating step in the boy's education, and makes an interesting comparison with *The Miracle Worker* (1962).

This butcher's knife cuts to the heart

Paris, 27 February
Against a background of bourgeois provincialism, observed with detailed precision, Claude Chabrol's new film *le Boucher* (*The Butcher*) is a provocative, challenging and compelling thriller. In a village in the Périgord, Popaul the local butcher (Jean Yanne), a fat and lonely ex-soldier, pays court to Hélène the schoolmistress (Stéphane Audran), beautiful, lonely and repressed. Hovering like a cloud over the village and its inhabitants, is the threat posed by a killer in their midst who mutilates his victims with a knife... Tension mounts on screen and in the audience with Hélène's growing suspicion that her unsuitable suitor might be the killer, counterpointed by several Hitchcockian touches from Chabrol that add to the suspense. It's a tight, taut film, superbly acted by Yanne and Audran (supported by a cast of locals playing themselves), but what sets it above others in the genre is the subtle complexity of the central relationship. *Le Boucher* evokes compassion as well as horror.

A star-studded catastrophe in the skies

New York, 5 March
Universal producer Ross Hunter has blended group jeopardy with *Grand Hotel* and has come up with *Airport*, based on Arthur Hailey's phenomenal bestseller. The blizzard-swept runways and stormy skies above an international airport are stacked with stars going through various kinds of hell. Dean Martin is the veteran Global Airlines pilot with a marriage problem and a mixed bag of passengers, including geriatric stowaway Helen Hayes and psychopathic Van Heflin, whose bomb is primed to blow them all to kingdom come. Battling to control mounting chaos on the ground, where a vital runway is blocked by a snowbound plane, is hard-driving airport manager Burt Lancaster. Lending a hand are security chief Lloyd Nolan and the cigar-chewing maintenance man George Kennedy, as Jacqueline Bisset, a curvaceous stewardess, mops Martin's fevered brow while the minutes to disaster tick away. Universal have invested $10 million in the production, and it looks like it will be a hit.

Stéphane Audran and Jean Yanne in Claude Chabrol's ***The Butcher****.*

A distressed Helen Hayes (center) during the crisis. Van Heflin is on the right.

Two heart-throbs join forces in 'Borsalino'

A return to 1930s Marseilles. Alain Delon (left) and Jean-Paul Belmondo.

Paris, 20 March

A recent popularity poll in France placed Alain Delon and Jean-Paul Belmondo in equal first place. Now, for the first time, they are appearing together in the same film, *Borsalino*. The two stars play a couple of petty crooks, who join up and rise in the underworld of 1930s Marseilles until they control all meat supplies. Delon and Belmondo got on well while making this jaunty, tongue-in-cheek gangster movie. However, their relationship has subsequently deteriorated. As Delon was also the producer of *Borsalino*, his name appears twice on the billboards, much to the chagrin of Belmondo, who intends to sue. It is doubtful we will see them on screen together again.

Theaters rock to the sounds of 'Woodstock

New York, 26 March

For three days in August 1969, a 600-acre farm in upstate New York was invaded by half a million people who flocked to the Woodstock Festival, a feast of rock music presented on an unprecedented scale. If you didn't make it to Max Yasgur's farm, you can now get something of the flavor of this remarkable event in Michael Wadleigh's documentary account of the great gathering of the tribes of youth culture. With a team of 12 cameramen using 16mm film, Wadleigh shot some 120 hours of film which has been edited down to 184 minutes. There's arresting footage of the festival's once-in-a-lifetime lineup, which included Jimi Hendrix, Joe Cocker, Joan Baez, The Who, Crosby, Stills and Nash, Arlo Guthrie, Santana, Country Joe and the Fish, and Sly and the Family Stone. But Wadleigh also turns the camera's eye on the raggle-taggle army encamped in the mud who came to watch, dance and dream the festival away amid the Purple Haze conjured up by the Jimi Hendrix Experience.

The flower children at Woodstock.

Joe Cocker: one of the top acts.

Unconventional characters win Oscar votes

Los Angeles, 7 April

This year no fewer than 17 stars hosted the Oscars ceremony. In an evening full of surprises, none of the favorites won an award. The Best Picture Oscar went to *Midnight Cowboy*, which also won the Best Director award for John Schlesinger. Maggie Smith was voted Best Actress for her superb performance as the mesmerizing schoolmarm in *The Prime of Miss Jean Brodie*. Thirty years after he played the Ringo Kid in *Stagecoach*, John Wayne received his first Academy Award, that of Best Actor for his warm performance as the boozy lawman Rooster Cogburn in *True Grit*. Costa-Gavras' *Z* was voted the Best Foreign Film.

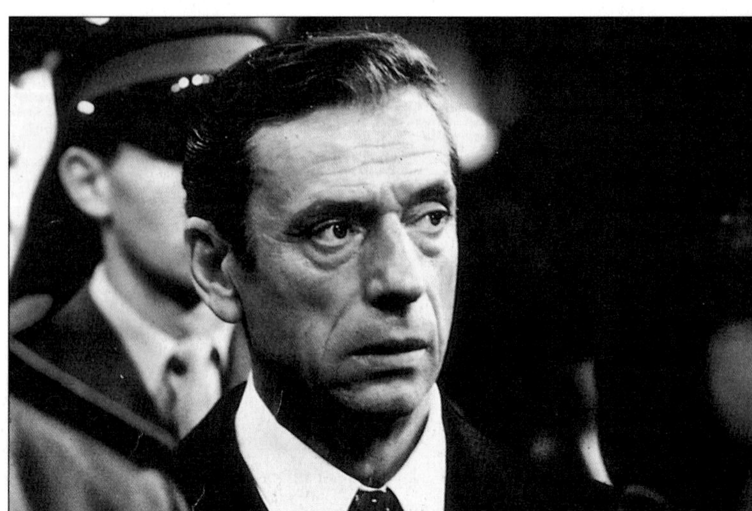

Yves Montand in the trial scene from **The Confession***, a Stalinist critique.*

Costa-Gavras attacks the Czech Stalinists

Paris, 29 April

Because he had closed his eyes to certain crimes committed by communist regimes at the time he was a member of the French Communist Party, Yves Montand has long wanted to atone for his past errors. This explains the conviction with which he threw himself into Costa-Gavras' *The Confession*. After attacking the far Right with enormous success i *Z*, the director has now turned hi attention to the Czech Stalinists Montand plays Artur London, wh was arrested, imprisoned and tortured during a political purge i 1951. The true story packs a punch especially during the interrogatio scenes which lead to the false con fession of the title.

Maggie Smith as Jean Brodie with a group of her admiring students.

Public and critics at Cannes greet Uncle Sam's medics with delight

to r: Elliott Gould, Robert Duvall and Donald Sutherland in *M*A*S*H*.

*Florinda Bolkan in Elio Petri's **Investigation of a Citizen Above Suspicion**.*

Cannes, 16 May
Can one make a comedy today out of a situation as tragic as war? The American director Robert Altman has shown it can be done with *M*A*S*H*, a hilarious, iconoclastic, anti-war satire, which has won the Grand Prix at this year's Festival. After he'd directed four forgettable movies, the 45-year-old Altman was then offered *M*A*S*H* because "14 more acceptable directors turned it down." The film has struck a responsive chord with audiences, who see the film's Korean War setting as a reference to Vietnam. It deals with two surgeons (Donald Sutherland, Elliott Gould) at a mobile hospital at the Front, who spend their time chasing women and bucking authority in order to keep themselves sane. The other Festival winners were all Italian: Elio Petri's *Investigation of a Citizen Above Suspicion* (Special Jury Prize); Marcello Mastroianni in *Drama of Jealousy*, and Ottavia Piccolo in *Metello*.

20th Century-Fox plunges to all-time low with Russ Meyer feature

Los Angeles, 17 June
In spite of its title, Fox's *Beyond the Valley of the Dolls* has nothing to do with the novel by Jacqueline Susann. It's a sexploitation movie directed by "skin flick" king Russ Meyer, a World War II combat cameraman and former *Playboy* photographer who has made millions out of drive-in fodder like *Faster, Pussycat! Kill! Kill!* featuring lots of sex and violence dealt out by Amazonian women with huge breasts. For years the cheerfully vulgar Meyer has been ridiculed by the Hollywood establishment as a peddler of schlock, but the huge success of his 1968 *Vixen*, which took $5 million in rentals on an investment of $75,000, excited the interest of profit-hungry Fox who let him loose as producer-director on *Beyond the Valley of the Dolls*, which he has co-scripted with film critic Roger Ebert. The result – decidedly less raunchy than Meyer's usual offerings – follows the bizarre adventures of a three-girl rock group called the Carrie Nations as they go in search of fame and fortune in the cynical, scheming and, it would seem, largely bisexual music world of Los Angeles. However, Meyer's particular brand of playful perversity and sense of the surreal (absolutely anything can happen in a Meyer movie and usually does) have been smothered by the size of the budget. Low-rent genius flourishes best when operating on a shoestring.

to r: Marcia McBroom, Dolly Read and Cynthia Myers in Russ Meyer's movie.

Mae goes west with Welch in 'Myra'

New York, 23 June
Mae West has not made a movie since 1943, although she has not wanted for offers – she was the first on Billy Wilder's list for *Sunset Boulevard*, but was reported to be "insulted" by the notion that she might play mad old movie star Norma Desmond. After all, Miss West was very much alive and kicking. To prove it she has made her long-delayed comeback, at the age of 78, in Fox's version of Gore Vidal's sex-change fantasy, *Myra Breckinridge*, directed by former English pop singer Mike Sarne. Raquel Welch stars as Myra, who was Myron and looked like Rex Reed in a former life, but is now a woman who looks like Marlene Dietrich in *Seven Sinners*. West is a Hollywood agent, surrounded by studs and resembling a faintly blurred version of her old self, although her legendary drawl has survived the passing of the years. Mae's fee of $335,000 for 10 days' work (in addition to writing her own dialogue) was almost certainly worth every penny in publicity to Fox, but the film has emerged as a frightful farrago, stitched together with clips from old Fox movies and torpedoed by Sarne's inexperience. Inevitably, perhaps, a feud developed between its two stars. Raquel Welch was reported to be enraged by West's top billing. But West has had the last laugh. At the New York premiere she was mobbed while the fans ignored Welch.

Mae, with Raquel Welch (Myra).

Mixed reception for film of 'Catch 22'

Left to right: Austin Pendleton, Orson Welles, Martin Balsam, Buck Henry, Bob Newhart, Norman Fell and Alan Arkin in Mike Nichols' film.

New York, 24 June
Eighteen years after it was published, Joseph Heller's *Catch-22*, a black comedy set in wartime Italy, has hit the screen. At one point it looked as if it would be filmed by Stanley Kubrick, but the man at the helm of this $10 million Paramount production is Mike Nichols. Alan Arkin heads a starry cast as Yossarian, the pacifist American bomber pilot trapped in the toils of military double-think contained in the title and personified by Orson Welles' monstrous General Dreedle. The picture represents a considerable technical triumph for Nichols, but he is only intermittently successful in transferring Heller's bleakly surreal vision to the screen.

Jack Nicholson drifting in search of himsel

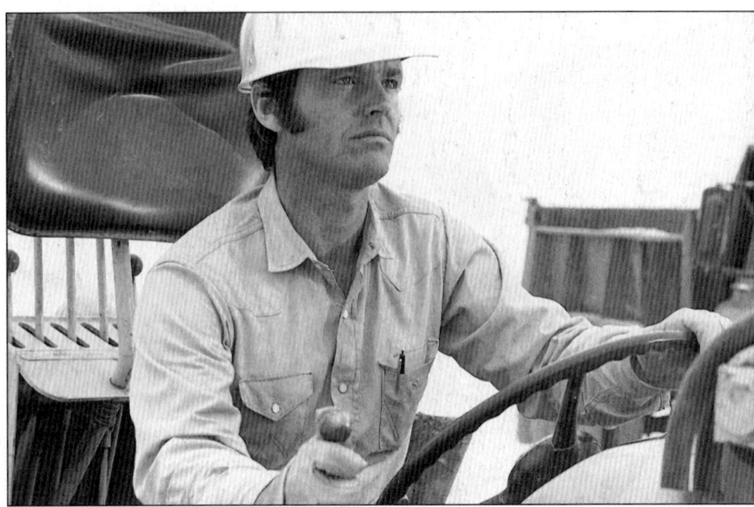

Middle-class intellectual turned truck driver: Nicholson in ***Five Easy Pieces****.*

New York, 12 September
Bob Rafelson's *Five Easy Pieces* is a road movie built around the evasive charm of Jack Nicholson. Screenwriter Adrien Joyce has partly fashioned the character around the actor's own personality. He is Bobby Dupea, a middle-class drifter who briefly abandons oil-rigging and a sluttish girlfriend (Karen Black) to return to his middle-class, musica family – the title refers to five piece by Chopin. In the end he forsake his family, the pregnant Black, an the chance of happiness with Susa Anspach, for the road to Alaska It's a poignant tale of wasted intelli gence and American restlessness and one of the few Hollywood film to explore the theme of class.

James Earl Jones explodes onto the screen

New York, 11 October
Howard Sackler's Broadway success, *The Great White Hope*, comes to the screen directed by Martin Ritt and stars the original leads, James Earl Jones and Jane Alexander. The film is a thinly disguised biopic of the great black boxer Jack Johnson, here called Jefferson. He becomes a sporting hero when, in 1910, he wins the world heavyweight championship. But fame, riches and sporting honor are insufficient to keep racism at bay, and he is cruelly hounded for his relationship with his white girlfriend. James Earl Jones' towering central performance is matched by that of striking newcomer Jane Alexander. Their tragedy is a plea for racial tolerance.

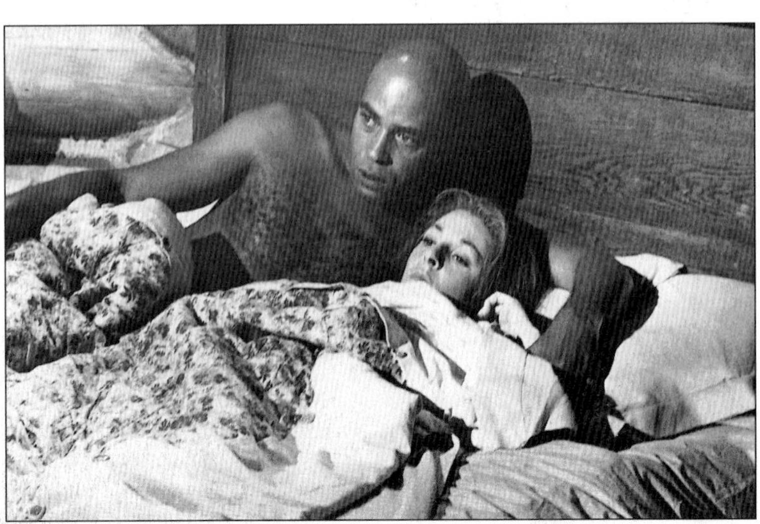

Crossing the color bar: Jones and Jane Alexander in ***The Great White Hope****.*

Festival opens with Chahine's new film

Tunis, 18 October
Most of the African and Arab filmmakers and critics gathered at the third "Days at Carthage" Festival, consider Egyptian director Youssef Chahine to be a master. So it was no surprise when loud applause greeted the announcement that the Grand Prix was to be awarded to him for the ensemble of his work. His new film, *The Choice*, which opened th Festival, is a denunciation of th failure of the intellectual elite t take on their social responsibilities Constructed like a hall of mirrors which reflects the hero's split per sonality, it is as far from commercia Egyptian cinema as one can get Second prize was given to the Syria film, *Men of the Sun*.

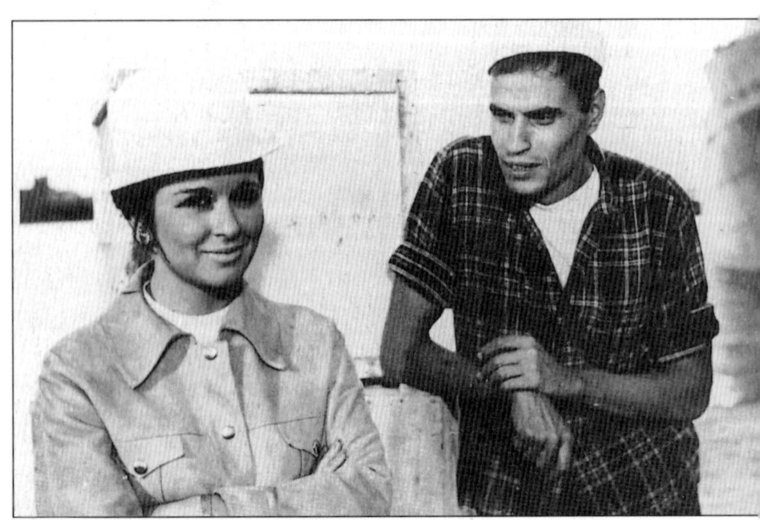

Soâd Hussny, Isat El Alâli in ***The Choice****, Chahine's impressive new film.*

'herlock Holmes given new life by Wilder

obert Stephens as Sherlock Holmes.

New York, 29 October
The Private Life of Sherlock Holmes is an amusing attempt by Billy Wilder, along with his co-writer I.A.L. Diamond, to debunk the legend of Sir Arthur Conan Doyle's famous sleuth. Holmes (played sardonically by Robert Stephens) complains that he only wears the deerstalker and cape and smokes a pipe because the public has come to expect it of him. Happier taking cocaine and playing his violin than solving mysteries, he finds that almost every one of his conclusions are inaccurate. In two unrelated plots, he and Dr. Watson (Colin Blakely) get mixed up with the Russian Ballet and a beautiful German spy (Genevieve Page).

Rural romance and rebellion from Lean

Trevor Howard, Sarah Miles and John Mills in Lean's **Ryan's Daughter**.

London, 9 December
MGM has recently been racked by crisis brought on by the abandonment of Fred Zinnemann's latest project, *Man's Fate*, and the spectacular box-office failure of Antonioni's *Zabriskie Point*. Now the studio is pinning its hopes on David Lean's film, *Ryan's Daughter* – 10 months in the writing and nearly a year in the filming on location on Ireland's Dingle peninsula. Set in 1916, in the time of the Troubles, it stars Sarah Miles as the village schoolmistress married to dull Robert Mitchum and falling for British officer Christopher Jones. The film is just as plodding as the Mitchum character. A simple love story has been swollen by Lean's cinematic elephantiasis and cannot be rescued by Freddie Young's superb photography or a wordless performance by John Mills as the village idiot.

Love Story' guarantees public a good cry

.ew York, 16 December
The death of a beautiful woman . always a poetic subject." So says aramount executive Robert Evans, 'ho encouraged writer Erich Segal) write the best-selling novel *Love 'tory* and has now brought it to the :reen. It's just an old-fashioned ıree-handkerchief weepie, with a dash of *Romeo and Juliet*, in which banker's son Ryan O'Neal woos and wins Italian immigrants' daughter Ali MacGraw in the face of parental opposition, only to lose her to a tastefully fatal illness. Everyone's repeating the picture's catchphrase, "Love means never having to say you're sorry."

li MacGraw and Ryan O'Neal as Jenny and Oliver in the hit tearjerker.

Dustin remembers 121 years on earth

New York, 14 December
If one were going to cast anyone in the title role of a movie called *Little Big Man*, there would not be many actors in Hollywood besides Dustin Hoffman who come to mind. It was also inevitable that the actor who seems to epitomize the New Hollywood should work with Arthur Penn, one of the directors most attuned to young audiences. *Little Big Man* continues Penn's preoccupation with the outsider by seeing the Cheyennes as "ethnic" hippies who contrast favorably with white civilization. Hoffman plays Jack Crabb, a 121-year-old survivor of Custer's Last Stand, who reminisces over his long and eventful life. In order to play the old man, Hoffman had to suffer under a 14-piece latex mask, which took five hours a day to apply under the hot makeup lamps. He is brilliantly convincing as the centenarian, as well as managing to look and behave like a very young man when the movie goes into flashback. The plot follows Crabb from the time when, as a 10-year-old white orphan, he is found and adopted by the Cheyenne, and is later made a brave. Penn's film has been seen as an obvious analogy between the treatment of the Indians and the Vietnam War.

Hoffman, a stunning performance.

Delphine Seyrig, Catherine Deneuve: **Donkey Skin**, Jacques Demy's fairy tale.

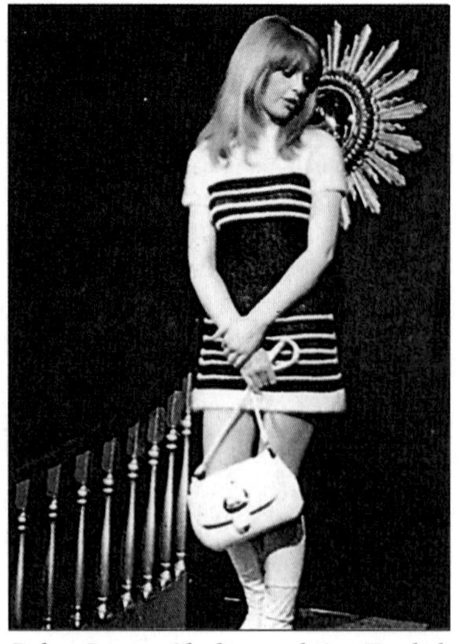

Pole Jerzy Skolimowski's English film **Deep End** stars Jane Asher.

A sad boy and his pet bird: Dav Bradley in **Kes** (Great Britain).

Barbra Streisand is the wacky hooker in **The Owl and the Pussycat**.

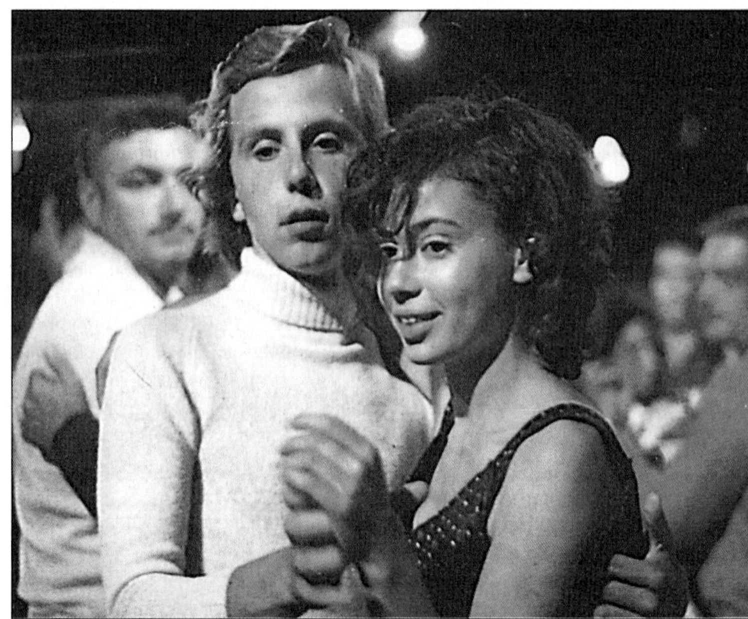

Fabrice Lucchini with Béatrice Romand (Claire's sister) in **Claire's Knee**.

Edy Williams, David Gurian in Russ Meyer's **Beyond the Valley of the Dolls**.

Cliff Gorman and his poodle attract glances in **The Boys in the Band**.

"'M·A·S·H'
IS WHAT THE NEW FREEDOM OF THE SCREEN IS ALL ABOUT!"
—Richard Schickel, Life
"A cockeyed masterpiece—see it twice."
—Joseph Morgenstern, Newsweek
"'M*A*S*H' is the best American war comedy since sound came in!"
—Pauline Kael, New Yorker
20th Century-Fox presents
M·A·S·H An Ingo Preminger Production
Starring
DONALD SUTHERLAND · ELLIOTT GOULD · TOM SKERRITT
Co-Starring SALLY KELLERMAN · ROBERT DUVALL · JO ANN PFLUG · RENE AUBERJONOIS
Produced by INGO PREMINGER
Directed by ROBERT ALTMAN
Screenplay by RING LARDNER, Jr.
From a novel by RICHARD HOOKER Music by JOHNNY MANDEL
Color by DE LUXE® PANAVISION®
R

Hilarious army antics, smash-hit.

Introducing
COFFIN ED
and
GRAVEDIGGER.
Two detectives only a mother could love.
SAMUEL GOLDWYN, JR.
presents
"COTTON COMES TO HARLEM"
starring GODFREY CAMBRIDGE · RAYMOND ST. JACQUES · CALVIN LOCKHART
JUDY PACE
REDD FOXX · JOHN ANDERSON and J.D. CANNON
ARNOLD PERL and OSSIE DAVIS
CHESTER HIMES
Music by GALT MacDERMOT
SAMUEL GOLDWYN, JR.
Directed by OSSIE DAVIS · COLOR by DeLuxe®
United Artists
ORIGINAL MOTION PICTURE SOUNDTRACK AVAILABLE ON UNITED ARTISTS RECORDS
R

An amiable, all-black caper.

TORA! TORA! TORA!
The incredible attack on Pearl Harbor as told from both the American and Japanese sides.
G
From 20th Century-Fox. The most spectacular film ever made.

Expensive, faithful but boring account of Pearl Harbor, seen from both sides.

*James Earl Jones is the beleagured champ in **The Great White Hope**.*

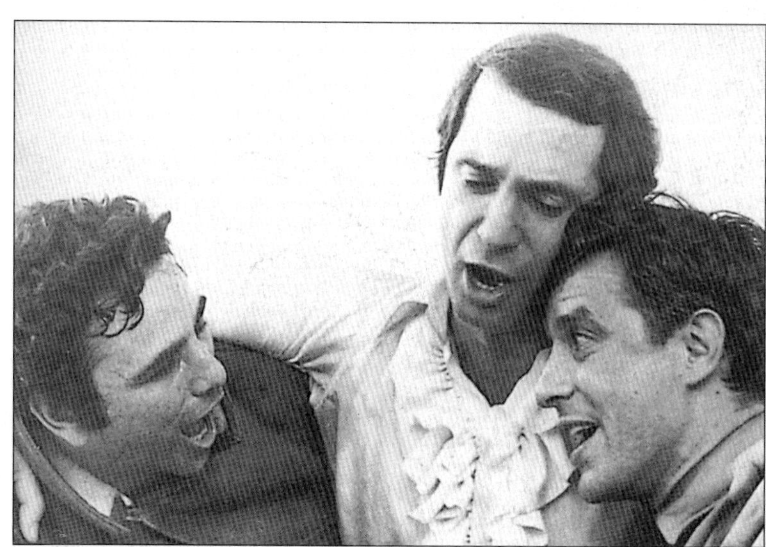

*l to r: Peter Falk, Ben Gazzara and John Cassavetes in the latter's **Husbands**.*

1971

1970 Academy Awards, Dorothy Chandler Pavilion, 15 Apr.

Best Film:	*Patton* (dir: Franklin J. Schaffner)
Best Director:	Franklin J. Schaffner
Best Actor:	George C. Scott *(Patton)*
Best Actress:	Glenda Jackson *(Women in Love)*
Best Supp. Actor:	John Mills *(Ryan's Daughter)*
Best Supp. Actress:	Helen Hayes *(Airport)*

Paris, 14 January
Eric Losfeld, editor of the film magazine *Positif* as well as numerous books on the cinema, has been fined by the courts for publishing material classified as "pornographic".

New York, 16 January
MGM and Fox have let it be known that the merger project concerning the two companies, first suggested to Darryl Zanuck by James Aubrey, the president of MGM, has now been dropped.

Washington D.C., 22 January
President Nixon has given his seal of approval to Arthur Hiller's *Love Story*. Chatting informally to newsmen this morning at the White House, he said he had enjoyed the film and added "I recommend it." But he did say that he had been mildly upset by its profanity.

Hollywood, 25 January
Charles Keating, the leader of the anti-pornographic crusade, has declared that "Darryl Zanuck and Russ Meyer should be arrested and imprisoned for daring to make *Beyond the Valley of the Dolls*." Russ Meyer had already made a name for himself as a controversial filmmaker in 1968 with *Vixen*, a $75,000 film which has, to date, grossed an impressive $5 million.

Washington D.C., 2 February
The American Film Institute has published a guide to cinema courses available in the U.S. It lists 1,679 courses taught at 300 American universities.

Cairo, 15 March
Youssef Chahine attended the opening of *The Choice* (*Al Ikhtiyar*).

New York, 23 March
John Johnson, the editor of *Ebony* magazine, has been elected to Fox's board of directors. It is the first time a black American has held an administrative job in a major studio.

Hollywood, 24 March
Francis Ford Coppola has started shooting *The Godfather*. Financing for the project was finally agreed with Paramount. At the request of the Italian-American Civil Rights League, the producer has had all references to the Mafia and Cosa Nostra eliminated from the script, based on Mario Puzo's best-selling novel about a Mafia family.

Paris, 11 May
The widow of the assassinated Greek Deputy Lambrakis has begun proceedings against the producers of the film *Z* for breach of privacy. The scenario is based on her husband's assassination.

London, 17 June
British-born director Alfred Hitchcock is back in London after 20 years to prepare a new thriller called *Frenzy*. According to him, films have changed little over the years except that some are now full of tricks for the sake of tricks, and stylistic clichés. He describes himself as a puritan – as only "a visual story teller... To me the visual is first, the oral is supplementary."

New York, 23 June
Dr. Aaron Stern has replaced Eugene Dougherty as the head of the Code and Rating Administration. Jack Valenti, president of the MPAA has admitted the need for reforms in the Code to allow for changes in moral standards.

Moscow, 20 July
The general director of the Moscow Film Festival has made it clear that Soviet authorities regard their festival differently from Western organizers of such affairs. In an article in *Iskusstvo Kino*, a cinema journal, he is reported as saying that film festivals should be seen as "serious ideological confrontations" between bourgeois and Communist views of art, and not as places for movie stars to attract publicity.

New York, 25 July
Vincent Canby, cinema critic for the *New York Times*, has written an article exposing the practice of advertising agencies which use misleadingly edited versions of film reviews to promote certain titles.

California, 27 August
Governor Ronald Reagan, himself a former screen actor, is aware of the film industry's needs. He has written to President Nixon, seeking the adoption of a more favorable tax law for the cinema business.

Hollywood, 10 September
Pier Angeli has died aged 39. The actress is reported to have taken an overdose of barbiturates.

Paris, 22 October
Cobblestones were thrown at the facade of the Saint-Séverin Cinema during a screening of *la Guerre d'Algérie*, made from news footage of the Algerian war, edited by Yves Courrières and Philippe Monnier.

Paris, 29 October
Release of Ken Russell's film, *The Devils*, inspired by the affair of the possessed nuns of Loudun in 1634. In accordance with an official order handed down from the Ministry of Cultural Affairs, cinemas have to display a sign outside warning spectators of the cruelty and sadism of certain scenes.

Los Angeles, 2 November
Richard Zanuck and David Brown, respectively former president and vice president of 20th Century-Fox, have started proceedings against the studio; they claim they were forced to resign illegally in 1970. Zanuck is demanding $14.5 million and Brown $7.5 million in damages.

Italy, 13 November
Pier Paolo Pasolini's *Decameron*, based on the tales by Boccaccio, has been seized by the police by order of the state prosecutors from Ancona and Sulmona.

Moscow, 26 December
Soviet censors have lifted a ban on the politically controversial film, *Andrei Rublev*. It was made in 1966 by the Russian director Andrei Tarkovsky, and won an award in 1970 at Cannes, but was judged too sensitive for Russian audiences.

New York, 19 December
Both the Catholic and Protestan[t] churches have criticized the MPA[A] rating system as "it is practised."

Hollywood, 28 December
The Viennese-born composer Ma[x] Steiner has died, aged 83. Durin[g] his long career, Steiner compose[d] the music for films as varied as *Gon[e] With the Wind* and *King Kong*. H[e] actually won the coveted Academ[y] Award three times.

Tokyo, 28 December
Japan's oldest production company Nikkatsu, has decided to launch [a] new series of romantic-cum-porno graphic films to avoid bankruptcy.

Paris, 31 December
During the past year, 392 featur[e] films were televised here. Of these 196 were French.

BIRTHS

Oregon, 23 August
River Phoenix

London, 29 September
Emily Lloyd

Texas, 6 November
Ethan Hawke

DEATHS

Hollywood, 8 March
Harold Lloyd

London, 16 March
Bebe Daniels

California, 21 April
Edmund Lowe

Virginia, 28 May
Audie Murphy

Hollywood, 23 July
Van Heflin

Morocco, 15 August
Paul Lukas

Hollywood, 23 September
Billy Gilbert

Malcolm McDowell plays the lead i[n] Stanley Kubrick's violent and shock[-] ing view of a world turned bleak an[d] hopeless in the near future. A majo[r] achievement for all concerned.

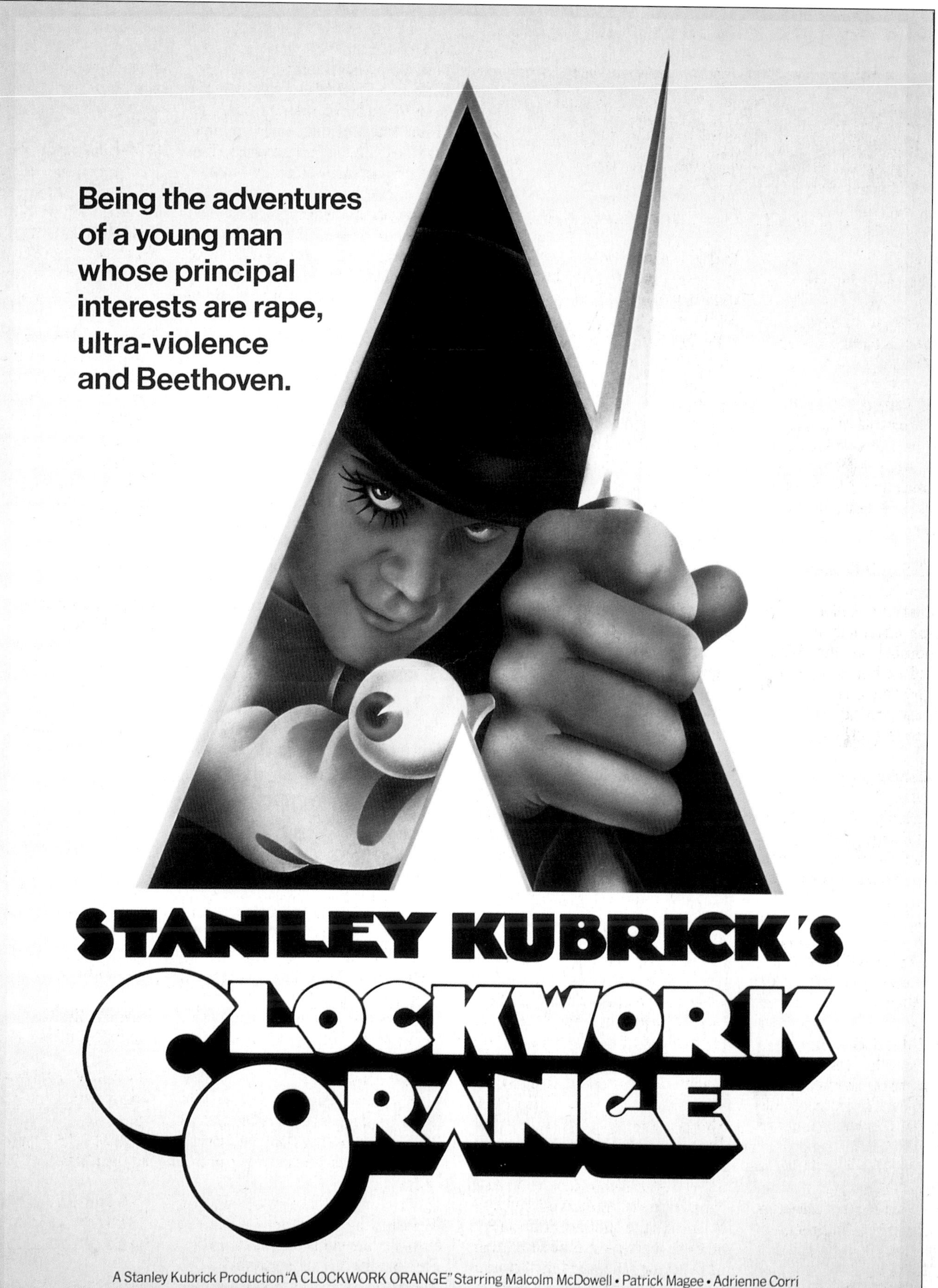
Being the adventures
of a young man
whose principal
interests are rape,
ultra-violence
and Beethoven.
STANLEY KUBRICK'S
CLOCKWORK
ORANGE
A Stanley Kubrick Production "A CLOCKWORK ORANGE" Starring Malcolm McDowell • Patrick Magee • Adrienne Corri
and Miriam Karlin • Sceenplay by Stanley Kubrick • Based on the novel by Anthony Burgess • Produced and
Directed by Stanley Kubrick • Executive Producers Max L. Raab and Si Litvinoff • WARNER BROS A WARNER COMMUNICATIONS COMPANY

Rolling stone gathers no moss, much murk

Rolling Stone Mick Jagger plays the sleazy ex-pop star turned gangster.

London, 5 January
After being "locked up" for two years by Warner Bros.-Seven Arts, the controversial work *Performance*, co-directed by screenwriter Donald Cammell and cinematographer Nicolas Roeg, has finally reached the screen in a heavily edited version. James Fox plays a gangster's enforcer, a bemused Caliban to Mick Jagger's contemporary Prospero, a washed-up rock star planning a comeback from his shuttered Notting Hill mansion. The two men meet and gradually merge personalities in a complex and fitfully brilliant parable influenced by the writings of Jorge Luis Borges.

May's 'New Leaf' blossoms after storms

New York, 11 March
Making her debut as writer-director in *A New Leaf* is the multi-talented Elaine May, former comedy partner of Mike Nichols. She co-stars, too, as the shortsighted, klutzy botanist whose inherited fortune attracts the attention of bankrupt blueblood Walter Matthau. He marries her, with murder in mind, but love blooms along the way. *A New Leaf* is a charming comedy with more than a hint of the screwball classics of the 1930s. Miss May's accident-prone heiress recalls Henry Fonda's snake-loving simpleton in *The Lady Eve*, but the marriage between Paramount and Elaine May has proved less amicable. She is suing the studio for interfering with the picture. Her partnership with Mike Nichols, one of the most successful satirical pairings in the history of American show business, ended in 1961 after their Broadway triumph with "An Evening With Mike Nichols and Elaine May". After writing and directing for the stage, Miss May made her screen debut as an actress in 1967, co-starring with Jack Lem mon in *Luv*. She now looks likel to mature into that rare Hollywoo phenomenon – a woman directo with a flair for comedy.

Elaine May and Walter Matthau.

Fernandel leaves an unfinished film

Paris, 26 February
Fernandel, the great horse-faced French comic, died today of heart failure at 4:30 p.m. in his apartment on the Avenue Foch. He suffered an attack of pleurisy a few months ago, and thus had to interrupt the shooting of the new *Don Camillo* film, directed by Christian-Jaque. Born Fernand Contandin on 8 May 1903 in Marseilles, he made 144 films in his career, among his most popular being the *Don Camillo* series, in which he played a lovable Catholic priest at war with the Communist mayor. It was Marcel Pagnol who gave Fernandel the opportunity to emerge as a wonderful tragicomic actor in *Angèle*, *Harvest* and *The Well-Digger's Daughter*. Fernandel also appeared in *Paris Holiday* opposite Bob Hope, and turned up in *Around the World in 80 Days*. His last completed film was *Happy as Ulysses*, released last year. A few hours before his death, he drank his daily glass of pastis, ate a plate of bouillabaisse, his favorite dish, and then took a nap...

Czech director Milos Forman's unusual view of America takes o

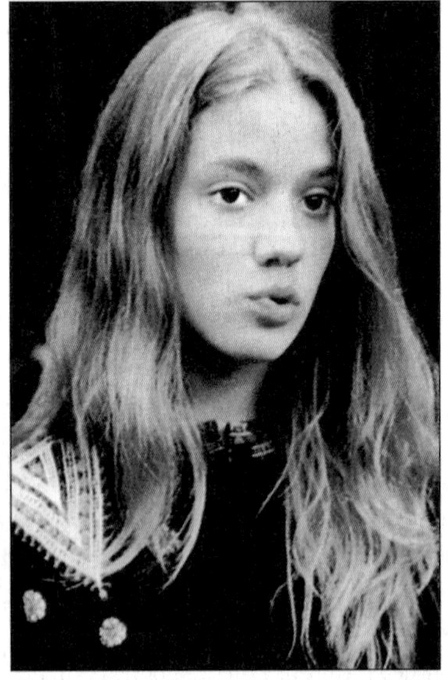

Linnea Heacock: the girl takes off.

Buck Henry and Lynn Carlin (left), the put-upon parents trying hard.

New York, 29 March
Czech director Milos Forman has made an impressive American debut with *Taking Off*, bringing his satiric European eye to bear on the contemporary American scene. The result is an affectionate comedy that examines the chasm which exists between the generations, a theme he had explored in his own country. As exploited by the keenly observant Forman, in what amounts to a series of sketches, it is an absolute delight. The film concentrates on the way the confused middle-class parents of a teenage daughter behave when the girl runs away from her Forest Hills home to live in New York's Greenwich Village. In order to get in tun with their offspring, a Society o Parents of Fugitive Children is se up, in which the adults are intro duced to marijuana, rock music, etc Forman and his little-known cast ge most comic mileage from showin the impact of the permissive societ on bourgeois respectability.

rench TV censors efuse documentary

aris, 5 April
RTF, the state-owned French television organization, has refused to roadcast Marcel Ophuls' documenry, *The Sorrow and the Pity*, subtled *A Chronicle of a French Town nder the Occupation*. It was to have een produced by French television, ut when they got cold feet it was ft to Swiss and German TV comanies to put up the money. Nevereless, it can now be seen in a umber of cinemas in Paris and sewhere around the country, and already attracting large audiences. his remarkable four-and-a-half-our film consists largely of interews with inhabitants of Clermont-errand who lived through World Var II. A probing, incisive and fluıt interviewer, as well as a brilliant accomplished documentary director, Ophuls (son of Max) ruthlessly xposes the degree of collaboration mong the French citizenry. He also lks to members of the Resistance nd some of the Nazi occupiers.

General George C. Patton marches away from his Oscar victory

George C. Scott in Franklin J. Schaffner's ***Patton****, Best Film and Best Director.*

Los Angeles, 15 April
A first-class uproar broke out at the 43rd Academy Awards ceremony when George C. Scott refused to accept the Best Actor Oscar for his performance as the controversial World War II General George S. Patton in Franklin J. Schaffner's *Patton*. Scott, who 10 years ago refused a Best Supporting Actor nomination for *The Hustler*, has denounced the Oscars ceremony as a "meat market" which degrades the acting profession. No one doubts that Scott takes the business of acting seriously, some might say too seriously at times, but in an industry which is hooked on awards his truculent stand is unlikely to win him many friends in Hollywood. *Patton* was also voted Best Picture and won the Best Director prize for Schaffner. Glenda Jackson was voted Best Actress for her portrait of a "free" woman in Ken Russell's *Women in Love*. The great surprise of the evening was the failure of *Love Story*, which had received 10 nominations, to win any of the major awards. The only Oscar that came its way was for Francis Lai's music. David Lean's ponderous film *Ryan's Daughter* picked up two statuettes, one for Freddie Young's cinematography and the other for John Mills, who was named as Best Supporting Actor. The Best Supporting Actress award went to Helen Hayes for her performance as the twittering old stowaway in *Airport*. The Best Foreign Film Oscar was won by Elio Petri's suspenseful *Investigation of a Citizen Above Suspicion*.

lew permissiveness sweetly packaged

ew York, 18 April
obert Mulligan has taken gentle dvantage of the new permissiveess that is abroad in the cinema. *ummer of '42* is set in a New Engnd beach resort at vacation time. nitially, we follow a group of adoscent boys, whose preoccupation ith sexual matters is largely conned to big talk, wish-fulfillment and the odd fumbled grope in the back row of the movies. The tenor of the piece changes, however, when the quietest of their number (Gary Grimes) has a poignant affair with a young woman (Jennifer O'Neill) whose husband is away on active service. Director Mulligan handles his situations with charm, humor and delicacy, as appropriate.

ary Grimes and Jennifer O'Neill in Robert Mulligan's poignant love story.

Cannes Festival celebrates 25th birthday

Cannes, 27 May
To celebrate the 25th anniversary of the Cannes Film Festival, the jury has killed two birds with one stone by awarding two top prizes. The traditional Grand Prix was given to Joseph Losey's *The Go-Between*, and a special 25th anniversary prize to Luchino Visconti's *Death in Venice*. The latter is a sensitive and intelligent adaptation of Thomas Mann's novel evoking *fin-de-siècle* Venice to breathtaking perfection. Also beautifully realized, and reflecting English class prejudice around the same period, *The Go-Between*, from L.P. Hartley's novel, tells the story of a 12-year-old boy who carries love letters from a tenant farmer to the daughter of the big house.

Bjorn Andresen is the young boy who obsesses Dirk Bogarde in ***Death in Venice****.* ▷

This boy's best friends are... his rats

Bruce Davison as the lonely Willard, feeding his army of trained rats.

New York, 18 June
The withdrawn Bruce Davison is a young man of many resentments, most of which are directed towards his overbearing mother Elsa Lanchester and boorish boss Ernest Borgnine, who might just have contrived his father's death to seize control of the family business. Davison finds a strange comfort among the rats which infest their rickety old mansion, eventually training them to his bidding. His furry friends become accomplices in robbery and then murder. Dominated by an old dark house and monstrous mother, Daniel Mann's *Willard* stirs memories of *Psycho*, though screenwriter Gilbert A. Ralston, sees the movie as a "rat morality play".

A tough, cool and violent private eye

Richard Roundtree stars as Shaft.

Los Angeles, 23 June
The flood of blaxploitation pictures continues with *Shaft*, in which Richard Roundtree plays the eponymous black private eye hired to find the kidnapped daughter of a big-time Harlem mobster. Former photographer Gordon Parks directs with his foot pressed firmly down on the sex and violence pedal. The 30-year-old Roundtree came to acting by way of a modeling career, joining the Negro Ensemble Company in 1967. His only previous film appearance was in a bit part in last year's *What Do You Say to a Naked Lady?*, Alan Funt's X-rated variation on the *Candid Camera* theme.

'Tec, call girl at center of quality thriller

Boston, 23 June
In Alan J. Pakula's *Klute*, Jane Fonda plays Bree Daniels, a high-class New York hooker who might hold the key to the disappearance of an out-of-towner. Doggedly trying to unravel the mystery is provincial private eye Donald Sutherland, the Klute of the title, who is drawn into Bree's world. During filming Fonda improvised a few of her scene Pakula says, "There's a scene wi her psychiatrist where Jane sudde ly explodes and starts talking abo what she is beginning to feel for th man Klute and how it frightens h because she's so used to being control – and I could feel my sk crawling up my back, it was th moving and unexpected."

Detective Donald Sutherland and call girl Jane Fonda in Pakula's ***Klute***.

Wild Warren and juicy Julie on the frontie

New York, 24 June
In Robert Altman's quirky Western *McCabe and Mrs. Miller*, Julie Christie plays an opium-addicted madam who teams up with blustering, two-bit gambler Warren Beatty. The latter dreams of turning a mud-caked frontier settlement into a bustling town, but he has hardly begun when he is gunned down by the agents of a sinister mining company. This no ordinary Western. Altman allov conversations to overlap, encou ages the actors to improvise and to cameraman Vilmos Zsigmond use yellow filters for some scen and underexpose others. Altma claims the picture is "less about th spirit of the pioneer than about th spirit of the entrepreneur."

Julie Christie and Warren Beatty: successful business partners on the frontie

he hollow art of promiscuity revealed

ew York, 30 June
ale attitudes towards sex is the ıbject of Jules Feiffer's screenplay ›r *Carnal Knowledge*, directed by 1ike Nichols. It follows Jack Nichson and Art Garfunkel from libidous adventures in college to the ardening sexual arteries of middle ge. It's a bitter morality tale which leaving audiences with a sour taste in their mouths. The surprise of the film is Ann-Margret, who displays a touching vulnerability as the blowzy bedmate who stokes Nicholson's dying sexual fires before they finally gutter out in a crabbed male menopause. Previously regarded as a teen-market sex kitten, the Swedish-born Ann-Margret reveals hitherto unsuspected depths as an actress.

rt Garfunkel, Ann-Margret in Nichols' bleak study of sexual relationships.

Ripping off the English middle-class facade

London, 1 July
Peter Finch and Glenda Jackson are put on the emotional rack by director John Schlesinger in *Sunday, Bloody Sunday*. They're both in love with the same young man, but as the object of their affections is the lumpish Murray Head, it's hard to see what all the fuss is about. There is, however, an excellent script by Penelope Gilliatt and a fine performance from Finch as the smitten homosexual Jewish doctor, a part he took over at short notice from Ian Bannen. Schlesinger's camera lingers balefully over the middle-class milieu in which the protagonists move, and will provide sociologists of the future with an anatomy of the British bourgeoisie of our times.

l to r: Murray Head, Peter Finch, Glenda Jackson: contemporary London life.

aunting heartbreak in Edwardian England

ominic Guard is the go-between.

London, 24 September
After winning the top prize at the Cannes Film Festival, Joseph Losey's film *The Go-Between*, based on L.P. Hartley's novel, sees a general release. This is the third collaboration between Losey and playwright Harold Pinter, who wrote the screenplays for *The Servant* and *Accident*. Dominic Guard plays the young messenger of the title, innocently carrying love letters between aristocratic Julie Christie and farmhand Alan Bates in the golden glow of an Edwardian summer. The inevitable tragedy which overtakes the lovers is recalled in flashback by Michael Redgrave as the boy grown old, but still numb with shock at the memory of the past. Pinter and Losey make a formidable team, outsiders who anatomize the codes and calculated circumlocutions of the class-ridden British society with a baleful eye. Losey believes that Pinter's spare dialogue "evokes the visual for me." And Pinter is quick to point out that Losey's camera "never becomes complacent."

'The Last Picture Show' is rich in detail

New York, 3 October
Peter Bogdanovich is following in the footsteps of French New Wave directors like François Truffaut and Jean-Luc Godard, who wrote about movies before they started making them. He had made his screen debut in 1968 with *Targets*, an ingenious low-budget concoction for Roger Corman which collided aging horror star Boris Karloff with an all-American killer. His second project is the elegiac *The Last Picture Show*, filmed in black and white and set in the early 1950s in a dusty Texas town whose rickety cinema is about to close. Naturally it's showing *Red River*, a Howard Hawks masterpiece about which Bogdanovich has written so eloquently as a film critic.

A painful and touching moment: Timothy Bottoms and Cloris Leachman.

Hackman makes an unpleasant connection

Gene Hackman has caused a stir as tough cop Popeye Doyle in Friedkin's film.

New York, 8 October
After having dealt with drug traffic in the United States, the American cinema has now turned its attention to the supply route from Europe in *The French Connection*. This tough crime movie, realistically directed by William Friedkin, is based on a true case, and contains an incredibly exciting train chase through New York. As "Popeye" Doyle, the cop who passionately hates all drug pushers, Gene Hackman creates a thoroughly convincing portrait of a crude and violent man, rare in its total lack of concession to audience sympathy. Roy Scheider is perfect as his sidekick.

Subtle treatment of inflammatory subject

Benoît Ferreux and Lea Massari in ***Murmur of the Heart****: forbidden love.*

New York, 17 October
French director Louis Malle's film *Murmur of the Heart* is a triumph of delicacy in dealing with the uncomfortable subject of incest. In truth, the film is about the pains of adolescence as experienced by 15-year-old Laurent (Benoît Ferreux). After an illness leaves him with a heart murmur, his mother (Lea Ma sari) takes him to a spa. There, eac meets with sexual rejection, an their mutual sympathy and love cu minates in bed. Set in the context c 1950s middle-class family life, this i a truthful, funny and affectiona work, in which Massari handles he task with exquisite finesse.

'Fiddler' introduces a new star from Israel

New York, 3 November
"If I Were a Rich Man" laments Tevye the Jewish milkman in the best-loved song from *Fiddler on the Roof*, the long-running stage hit about the trials and tribulations of a family who survive the pogroms of pre-revolutionary Russia. Topol, the Israeli actor who created the role in London, will not have to share Tevye's longings. In the film version, just opened here, he is a powerhouse of attractive charm, humor, vitality and passion. In short, a star. Norman Jewison's lumbering film cannot destroy the Jewish jokes, poignant story and appealing music of the original, nor dampen Topol.

Israeli star Topol as Tevye the milkman, dreams of being a rich man.

Clint Eastwood makes his directing debut

New York, 3 November
Clint Eastwood's fruitful collaboration with Don Siegel has produced *Play Misty for Me*, Eastwood's directing debut, in which Siegel plays a small role as a laconic barman. He is a confidant of Clint's laid-back Monterey-based late-night disc jockey who gets more than he bargained for when he has a casual fling with psychotic admirer Jessica Walter. Walter, a highly regarded Broadway actress who makes occasional forays into films, gives a riveting performance as a woman who just won't take no for answer, sliding from edgy infatuation into homicidal hysteria as she stalks her increasingly twitchy prey. Eastwood's portrayal of the beleagured hero chimes with his recent performance in Siegel's *The Beguiled* in which Geraldine Page amputated one of his legs. In *Play Misty for Me*, Walter threatens to dismember him with a meat cleaver before a well-aimed sock to the jaw sends her floating face-down out to sea to the strains of Errol Garner's title song. Since comin together in *Coogan's Bluff*, Sieg and Eastwood have enjoyed a pa ticularly productive partnership, bu it now looks as if the latter's strong commercial personality will ove whelm his mentor. Eastwood look as comfortable behind the camer as he does in front of it.

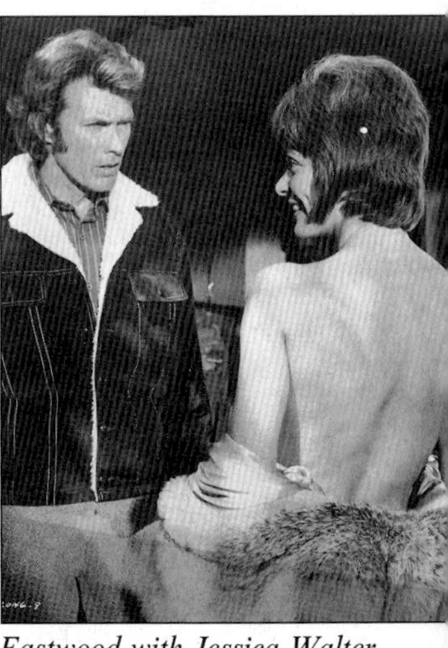
Eastwood with Jessica Walter.

he poison spreads in an Italian garden

ominique Sanda comforts grandmother Inna Alexeiff before being led away.

el Aviv, 2 December
alian director Vittorio De Sica nerged from a period in the cre- ive wilderness with *The Garden of e Finzi-Continis*, a haunting and agic testament to Italy's involve- ent in the Holocaust. Brilliantly ıst (Dominique Sanda, Lino Capo- cchio, Helmut Berger) and photographed, the film won the Foreign Film Oscar and was voted best at Berlin, before its acclaim in U.S. and European cinemas. However, its opening here has particular emotional resonances for an audience all too familiar with the fate of Jews under Fascism, whose wealth and position offered no protection.

Harold and Maude: a very bizarre affair

New York, 20 December
Safely settled ideas of taste have been disturbed by Hal Ashby's new film *Harold and Maude*, an oddball love affair between death-obsessed 20-year-old Bud Cort and speed-obsessed 80-year-old Ruth Gordon. She lives in a disused railroad car, he stages an hilarious succession of suicide attempts to ruffle the placid feathers of his unflappable mother, Vivian Pickles. Harold and Maude meet at a funeral – they both like attending the last rites of total strangers – and they get married on Ruth's 80th birthday. The screenplay is by Colin Higgins and the score is from rock troubador Cat Stevens. Thirty-five-year-old Ashby hitchhiked to California in his teens and worked his way through the movie business to be an assistant director on several William Wyler and George Stevens pictures. He won an editing Oscar for his work on Norman Jewison's *In the Heat of the Night*, then acted as associate producer on the same director's *The Thomas Crown Affair*, and it was Jewison who gave him his chance to direct. *The Landlord*, made in 1970, was a quirky comedy-drama starring Beau Bridges as the rich kid who buys a Brooklyn tenement intending to turn it into his own home and then, touched by the plight of his tenants, changes his mind.

Bud Cort and Ruth Gordon.

tanley Kubrick discomforts with a devastating look at the future

ondon, 20 December
tanley Kubrick's latest project, *Clockwork Orange*, will no doubt ıock those who believe in the reas- ıring prospect of social progress. Adapted from the novel by Anthony Burgess, it's a frightening, prophetic vision of a Britain of the future in which roaming gangs of young men have adopted violence as their only way of life. In one sequence, Alex (Malcolm McDowell), a brutal teenage hood, the head of the band of Droods, beats a woman to death with a giant phallic sculpture. Sent to prison for murder, Alex becomes a guinea pig in a rehabilitation program based on aversion therapy, and emerges having lost his soul. The film's controversial message seems to be that free will and individuality must be preserved at any cost. The violence, though explicitly shown, is given a stylized unreality, mainly through the use of music, such as the voice of Gene Kelly crooning "Singin' in the Rain" while the gang beat up an old tramp, or the choral movement from Beethoven's Ninth which becomes Alex's stimulation to sadistic pleasures. Kubrick also makes stunning use of color – harsh and glossy for the first part of the film, muted and more naturalistic after Alex has been brainwashed. Malcolm McDowell is remarkable as an inverted Candide, seemingly irredeemably amoral.

Ialcolm McDowell in Kubrick's adaptation of the Anthony Burgess novel.

Clint Eastwood is *Dirty Harry*, a tough San Francisco cop as brutal as the psycho criminals he nails – except that he's on the right side of the law. Don Siegel's film is stylish, ambiguous and violent; Eastwood is compelling.

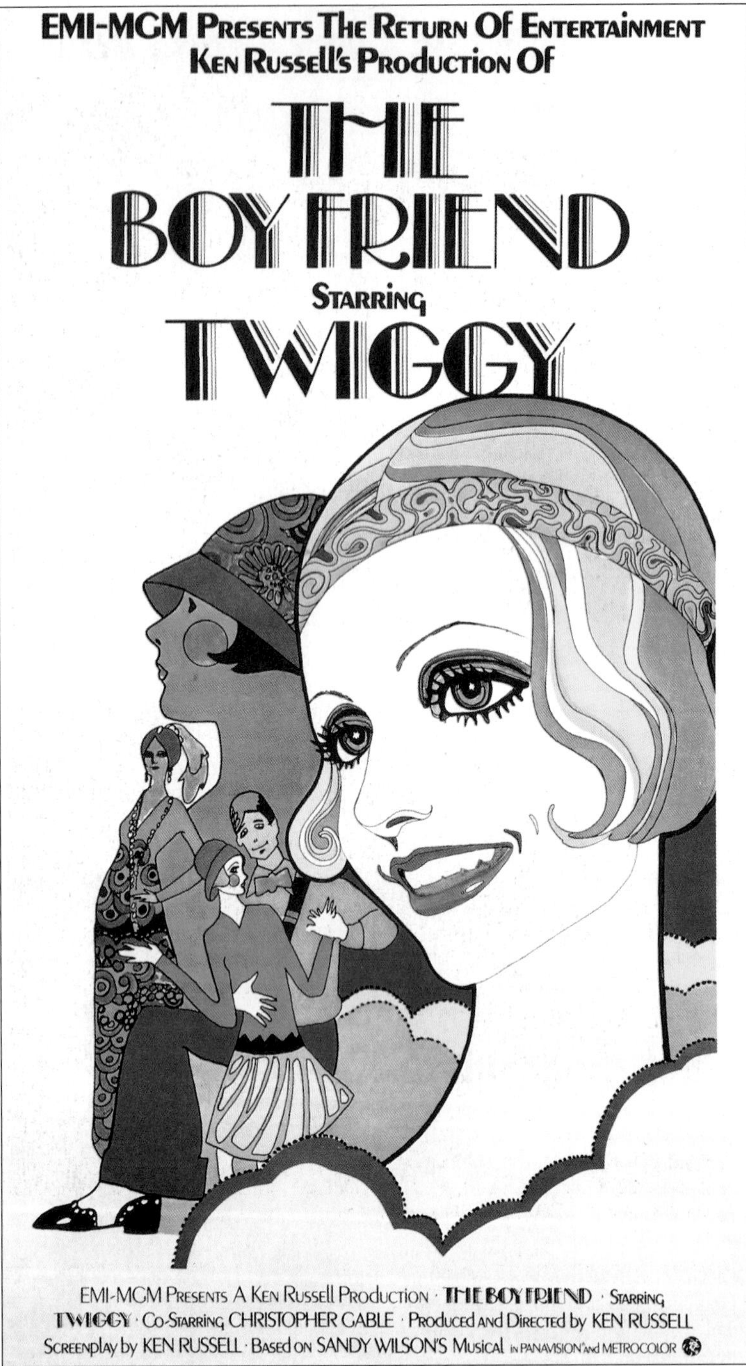
EMI-MGM Presents The Return Of Entertainment
Ken Russell's Production Of
THE BOY FRIEND
Starring
TWIGGY
EMI-MGM Presents A Ken Russell Production · THE BOY FRIEND · Starring
TWIGGY · Co-Starring CHRISTOPHER GABLE · Produced and Directed by KEN RUSSELL
Screenplay by KEN RUSSELL · Based on SANDY WILSON'S Musical in PANAVISION and METROCOLOR

This glorious 20s pastiche introduced English model Twiggy to the screen.

***Two Lane Blacktop**: Beach Boy Dennis Wilson (l), Laurie Bird, James Taylor.*

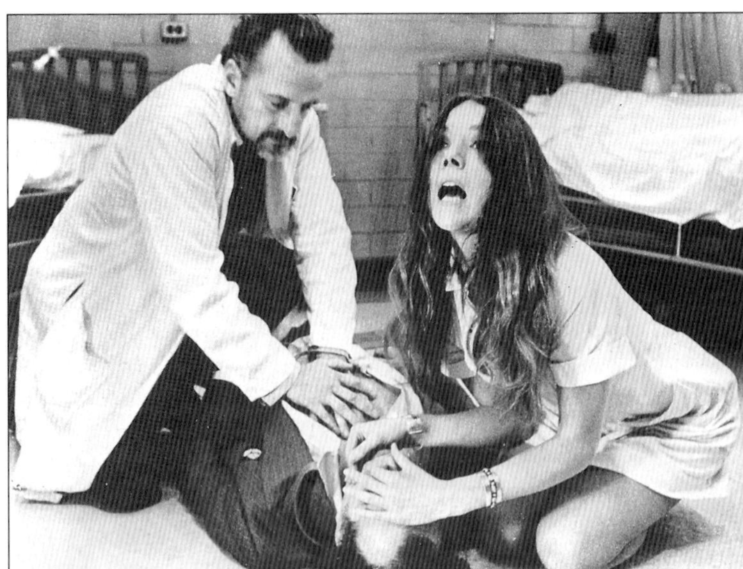

*George C. Scott, Diana Rigg in Arthur Hiller's black comedy, **The Hospital**.*

*Richard Attenborough is mass-murderer Christie and Judy Geeson is the ill fated Mrs. Timothy Evans in Richard Fleischer's **10 Rillington Place**.*

*Alain Delon, Ursula Andress, Toshiro Mifune: **Plein Soleil (Purple Noon)**.*

WARREN BEATTY
JULIE CHRISTIE
McCABE & MRS. MILLER
name your poison

tman's twist on pioneering Westerns presented brothels as big business.

ıri Yarvet is **King Lear** in Grigori ɔzintsev's film (USSR).

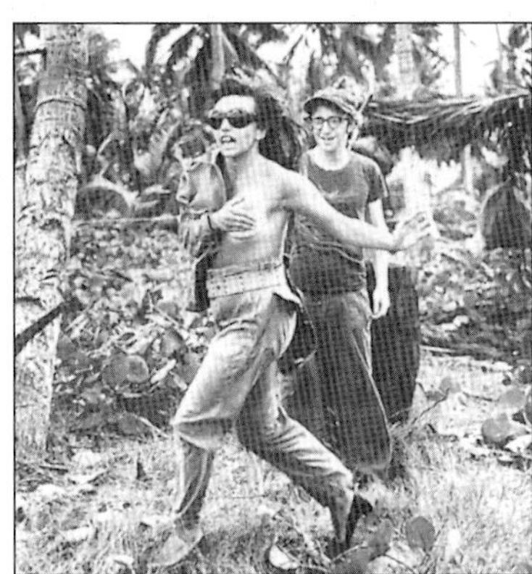

*Snake-bite woman (Princess Fatosh) and Woody Allen in **Bananas**.*

llini's Roma: *The Eternal City as seen by the great Italian director.*

*Martin Shaw (left) with Jon Finch who played **Macbeth** in Polanski's film.*

*Vincent Price is **The Abominable Dr. Phibes**, here with Virginia North.*

To Life!
A NORMAN JEWISON FILM
"FIDDLER ON THE ROOF"
TOPOL
NORMAN JEWISON
JOSEPH STEIN
JERRY BOCK
SHELDON HARNICK
HAROLD PRINCE
JEROME ROBBINS
United Artists
"Fiddler on the Roof"
on the screen

The world-famous violinist Isaac Stern did the fiddling on the roof.

1972

1971 Academy Awards, Dorothy Chandler Pavilion, 10 Apr.

Best Film:	*The French Connection* (dir: William Friedkin)
Best Director:	William Friedkin
Best Actor:	Gene Hackman *(The French Connection)*
Best Actress:	Jane Fonda *(Klute)*
Best Supp. Actor:	Ben Johnson *(The Last Picture Show)*
Best Supp. Actress:	Cloris Leachman *(The Last Picture Show)*

Prague, 2 January
Dusan Hanak's feature-length documentary *Images of the Old World* (*Obrazy stareho sveta*), has been banned by the authorities because they consider that the picture it paints of the Slovak peasantry is "too negative".

Los Angeles, 10 January
The CBS television network has stated that it intends to stop producing films for the big screen. CBS has produced 27 films, recording a total loss of $10 million.

Paris, 10 January
Actress Mia Farrow has begun filming here for Claude Chabrol. The film, *Doctor Popaul*, co-stars Jean-Paul Belmondo.

Rome, 27 January
Actor Gian Maria Volonte has refused an offer from Hollywood of 250 million lira, a sum he considers disproportionate. He reportedly has said that his "left-wing sympathies" prevent him from accepting such a high wage for his job as an actor.

Los Angeles, 3 February
A Superior Court judge has ruled that the late Bela Lugosi's identification with his movie role as Count Dracula, the Transylvanian vampire, was so pronounced that his heirs could inherit and make money from it. The actor's widow Hope L. Lugosi and her son Bela George Lugosi sued Universal Pictures after the studio began licensing producers of Dracula merchandise (games, masks, T-shirts etc.). Universal has been ordered to hand over any licensing agreements it made since 1964 to the heirs.

Hollywood, 5 February
Charlie Chaplin's nomination for a star on the 19-block Walk of Fame has been rejected by the Chamber of Commerce Executive Board here. It appears that Mr. Chaplin's Marxist views are behind this rejection.

Bordeaux, 6 February
During the screening of the Italian film *The Battle of Algiers*, by Gillo Pontecorvo, fighting broke out in the cinema and in the street between the audience and nostalgic supporters of French Algeria.

Rome, 17 February
French actor Pierre Clémenti is on trial for possession of drugs. There is a real risk that he may be sentenced to a term in prison.

New York, 27 February
Stanley Kubrick has published an article in the *New York Times* defending *A Clockwork Orange* against its critics. According to him, the film illustrates that it is man who corrupts society rather than the reverse.

Mexico, 20 March
Police have found Marlon Brando's son Christian being held by a group of people who say that his mother, Anna Kashfi, paid them to kidnap the child. Miss Kashfi, meanwhile, has been arrested and imprisoned in Los Angeles for disorderly behavior and assault.

New York, 25 March
The opening of the first Cuban Film Festival here was broken up by anti-Castro youths last night. A group of about 21 demonstrators caused a considerable uproar by releasing white mice among the audience during the screening of the feature film, Humberto Solas' *Lucia*. They then proceeded to throw stink bombs and fights broke out. Several people have been arrested.

Paris, 31 March
France's most famous cinema, the Gaumont Palace in the place Clichy, is closing today to make way for a hotel and shopping complex. The 6,000-seat cinema first opened in 1911; in 1966 seating was reduced to 2,800 when the screen was modified (advertised as the widest in Europe) for Cinerama.

New York, 1 April
Cosmopolitan magazine has published a centerfold of Burt Reynolds in the nude.

New York, 17 April
Variety has announced that *The Godfather* has taken in $26 million at the box office in the first few days of its release. No other picture has ever equaled these results.

Paris, 13 June
Over 200 international personalities from the cinema and entertainment world have published a petition in protest against the arbitrary arrest of the Turkish filmmaker Yilmaz Guney. He has been accused of aiding urban guerillas, apparently without a shred of evidence.

California, 26 June
George Lucas has started shooting *American Graffiti* for Universal, on location in San Rafael. Francis Ford Coppola is producing the film with a modest $750,000 budget, $90,000 of which has been set aside for the rights to the 25 songs on the film's soundtrack.

Colorado, 7 July
Brandon De Wilde, aged 30, was killed in a car accident yesterday. De Wilde made his Broadway debut at age seven in *The Member of the Wedding*, and took the role to the screen in 1952. He will be best remembered for his first-class performances in *Shane* and *Hud*.

Hollywood, 7 July
Richard Zanuck and David Brown have resigned from Warner Bros. where they had been in charge of production for the last 18 months. They plan to open their own independent production company, the Zanuck-Brown Company.

Hanoi, 14 July
Jane Fonda has chosen Hanoi as the point of departure for a trip to North Vietnam. During the first of 10 scheduled radio broadcasts she spoke critically of Nixon and the American government's political stance in Vietnam. Many Americans consider her attitude defeatist, and some have accused the star of treason for telling the U.S. troops that, "the men who order you to use your weapons are war criminals in the eyes of international law."

Washington D.C., 18 July
Frank Sinatra has given evidence the U.S. House of Representativ to a commission of inquiry into ganized crime.

Washington D.C., 17 August
Everybody involved in the maki of *Deep Throat* has been charg with violating the law prohibiti the movement of pornographic m terial from one state to another.

Rome, 7 October
Pier Paolo Pasolini's film, based the ribald classic by Chaucer, *T Canterbury Tales*, is under judic impoundment.

Paris, 11 November
The French Catholic Film Boa has decided to relax its ratings sy tem. The rating "not to be seer may no longer be used.

Hollywood, 9 December
Columnist Louella Parsons, t highly influential gossip writer, h died aged 91. Apart from her fr quent scoops, Miss Parsons al wrote two volumes of memoirs a appeared in several films, the la being *Starlift* in 1951.

Germany, 9 December
Director William Dieterle has die He lived and worked in Hollywoo where his films included *The Life Emile Zola* (1937).

Lisbon, 26 December
Release of *The Past and the Prese* by Manoel de Oliveira, with Ma de Saisset and Barbara Vieira.

DEATHS

Paris, 1 January
Maurice Chevalier

California, 6 April
Brian Donlevy

Spain, 25 April
George Sanders

New York, 9 October
Miriam Hopkins

John Boorman's ***Deliverance*** *p duced a clutch of superb perf mances, and a frightening insig into the hearts and minds of a gro of seemingly 'regular' guys.*

This is the weekend they didn't play golf.

Deliverance

A JOHN BOORMAN FILM Starring JON VOIGHT · BURT REYNOLDS in "DELIVERANCE"
Co-Starring NED BEATTY · RONNY COX · Screenplay by James Dickey Based on his novel · Produced and Directed by John Boorman
PANAVISION®·TECHNICOLOR®· From Warner Bros., A Warner Communications Company

Shades of Judy Garland as Liza Minnelli lights up the screen

New York, 14 February

In only her fourth feature, Liza Minnelli lights up the screen as the wild and electrifying Sally Bowles in Bob Fosse's *Cabaret*, which was shown last night before an invited audience that included the cast and director. The role was clearly tailored to suit Liza's exuberant style and warm, throaty voice, reminiscent of her mother – Judy Garland. The brashness that covers the insecurities of her character is perfectly suited to the brashness that covered the insecurities of Berlin in the 30s. Of course she is too good a singer to be found in such a sleazy dive as the Kit Kat Club, but who cares? Her songs are put over with such bite and passion, and her acting carries a moving conviction. Sally Bowles, an American stranded in Germany on the eve of Europe's cataclysm, is not as decadent as she thinks she is and, indeed, in her scenes with Michael York, the young, innocent Englishman abroad, she is both vulnerable and lovable. Bob Fosse has wisely jettisoned most of the stage musical, but has kept the cabaret itself at the center of the movie. With excellent color photography and editing, the nightclub is seen to reflect the frenetic and ugly nature of German society at that time, with the brilliantly clever songs providing a pungent commentary on the situation. Joel Grey's lewd, sexually ambivalent and anti-Semitic MC provides the right tone throughout.

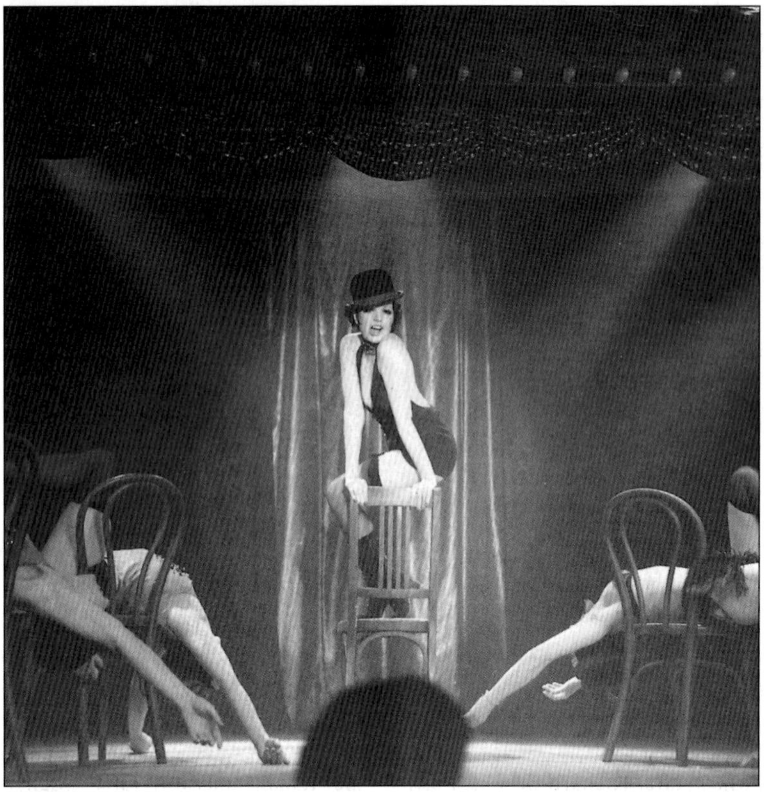

*Liza Minnelli as Sally Bowles in **Cabaret**: Nazism in song and dance.*

Joel Grey as the androgynous emcee of the Kit Kat club, with his 'chorus girls'.

New cinema desired by the Algerians

Algiers, 2 March

Carried along by the enthusiasm for the agrarian revolution launched by the Algerian authorities four months ago, those who work in television, radio and the cinema have met today to finally create a Union of the Audiovisual Arts. The participants have assessed the situation of the last 10 years and found it wanting. Among them was the director Mohamed Bouamari, who has invented the term "cinema *djidid*" (new cinema) to describe the sort of films he feels Algeria has need of from now on. Like Bouamari, many young Algerian directors have reproached their country's film industry since Independence, for dealing almost exclusively with the struggle for liberation while ignoring the many contemporary problems that the nation is facing. The newly-formed Union, therefore, sees the new cinema as a means of making people aware of Algeria's priorities, especially for its poorer classes.

Barbra, Ryan great in screwball comedy

New York, 9 March

The ghost of Howard Hawks' *Bringing Up Baby* stalks through Peter Bogdanovich's latest, *What's Up Doc?* It's a contemporary slice of screwball with Ryan O'Neal and Barbra Streisand stepping into the shoes of Cary Grant and Katharine Hepburn. Streisand is the kook who makes life miserable for stuffy musicologist Ryan and his fiancee portrayed by newcomer Madeline Kahn. It's all great fun, punctuated by bursts of hectic physical comedy, but can never match the superbly self-contained comic worlds created by the 1930s originals, nor the dark quality which Hawks gave to *Bringing Up Baby*, where a hint of madness lingers in the air.

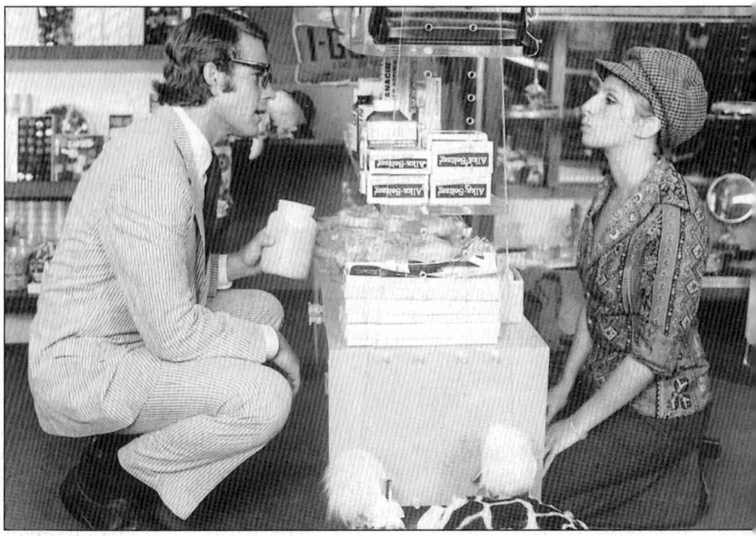

Absent-minded musicologist Ryan O'Neal and crazy kook Barbra Streisand.

nna Kashfi hides on from Brando

ew York, 13 March
nna Kashfi, who was married to arlon Brando from 1957 to 1959, uld not accept the fact that their n, Christian, was constantly with father. Kashfi accused Brando monopolizing the boy, now 13-d-a-half, and keeping him far ay from her. Because she felt that ando has not kept to the custody reement, she has abducted Chris-n, and is hiding him, threatening ver to let Brando have access to son again. The actor claims to ve the law on his side and is doing erything possible to find Christian d be reunited with him in a short ile. Brando has been in Paris for month where he has been shooting *st Tango in Paris* under the direc-n of Bernardo Bertolucci, but s had to interrupt his work in der to fly back to New York. ere, he told the press that if he is able to get his son back by legal eans, he is not averse to resorting other methods.

Coppola films the blood, sweat and tears of a Mafia 'family'

Marlon Brando as Mario Puzo's Don Corleone, with Robert Duvall (left).

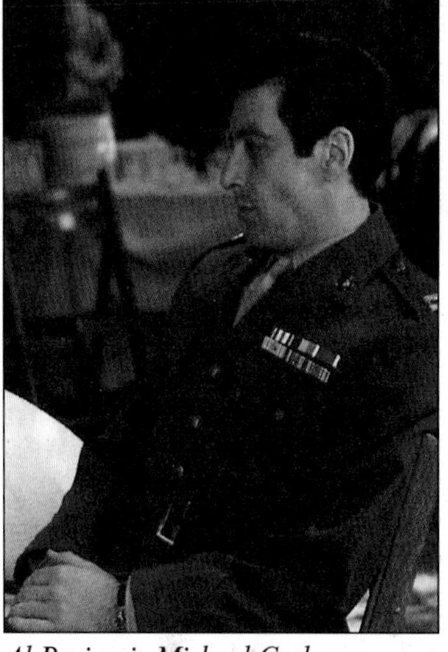
Al Pacino is Michael Corleone.

New York, 15 March
Adapted from Mario Puzo's best-selling Mafia saga, *The Godfather* has opened here to acclaim. Paramount's selection of Francis Ford Coppola to direct this expensive project, after Richard Brooks, Peter Yates and Costa-Gavras refused, was surprising, considering that his main reputation so far is as a screenwriter, and his films as director have not been commercially successful. The production was beset with difficulties. Before shooting began, the Italian-American Civil Rights League held a rally in Madison Square Garden and raised $600,000 towards attempts to stop the film which they claimed was a slur on their community. There were bomb threats, and the producer's car was fired at. Finally, Coppola agreed to eliminate the words "Mafia" and "Casa Nostra" from the screenplay, to employ some members of the League, and to donate proceeds from the movie's premiere to the League's hospital fund.

This long (175 minutes) and leisurely apotheosis of The Family marvelously builds up a rich pattern of relationships, meticulously detailing the rituals of an enclosed group. However, even though Coppola and Puzo's script seems to condemn the violence and cruelty of the Mafia, the tone of the film is laudatory and romantic. Marlon Brando in the title role, for which Edward G. Robinson and Laurence Olivier were both strongly tipped, has given his declining career a new impetus. With stuffed cheeks and an almost inaudible whisper, Brando's Don Vito Corleone is a great achievement. His barely stated movements make little concession to emotion as he dispenses life and death, though here is a giant of a man also aware of his mortality and the limitations of his heirs, among whom are his sons played by James Caan and Al Pacino. *The Godfather* contains some unforgettable set pieces such as the opening wedding celebration, a severed horse's head left in an enemy's bed, and the cold-blooded killing happening simultaneously with a baby's baptism. ▷

he murder of Leon Trotsky examined by director Joseph Losey

ris, 30 March
'or one moment, they hold history their hands. With one terrible ow, they make it," is the publicity gan for *The Assassination of otsky*, Joseph Losey's new film. owever, when political cinema ems to be in vogue, it is surprising w apolitical this Anglo-Franco-lian production is. Losey and his screenwriters, Nicholas Mosley and Masolino D'Amico, have opted to concentrate more on the psychology of the protagonists than the wider implications of their actions. It succeeds on this level because of the performances of Richard Burton, who creates a deliberately dry and pedantic figure as the exiled Russian revolutionary leader, and Alain Delon as his nemesis, the passionate Stalinist agent, who tracks down Trotsky to Mexico, and kills him with an ice pick. The latter's character is best revealed as he watches a bullfight. Shot on location in Mexico and Italy, the film, while taking some liberties, is an attempt to faithfully recapture a key moment in the history of our times.

*he killer and the victim: Alain Delon and Richard Burton in **The Assassination of Trotsky**: a detailed reconstruction.*

America makes peace with Chaplin

Los Angeles, 10 April

Nearing his 83rd birthday, Charles Chaplin has been awarded a special Oscar for his "exceptional and invaluable contribution to the art of cinema in the twentieth century." The golden statuette was presented to him by master of ceremonies Jack Lemmon and president of the Academy, screenwriter Daniel Taradash. Chaplin revelled in the emotion of the event, and delighted the audience with an old vaudeville trick involving a bowler hat. To mark Chaplin's return to Hollywood, the Academy staged a spectacle, entitled *Lights, Camera, Action*, which celebrated Chaplin's phenomenal career. Forty-three years after giving him an Oscar for *The Circus* at the very first Academy Awards ceremony, the United States has made its peace with Charlie. He arrived in New York on 2 April and the following day appeared at a gala tribute to him at the Philharmonic Hall in aid of Lincoln Center Film Society. There, the legendary filmmaker told the cheering audience, "This is my renaissance. I am being born again." Hollywood, it seems, has now forgotten the shabby way Chaplin was treated during the McCarthy era and, for his part, the talented comedian has been overwhelmed by the affection and adulation which has greeted his return.

*Chaplin directs daughter Geraldine in **The Countess From Hong Kong** (1967).*

The soul of Italy is bared under the bright sun of the Croisette

*Gian Maria Volonte in **The Mattei Affair**, directed by Francesco Rosi.*

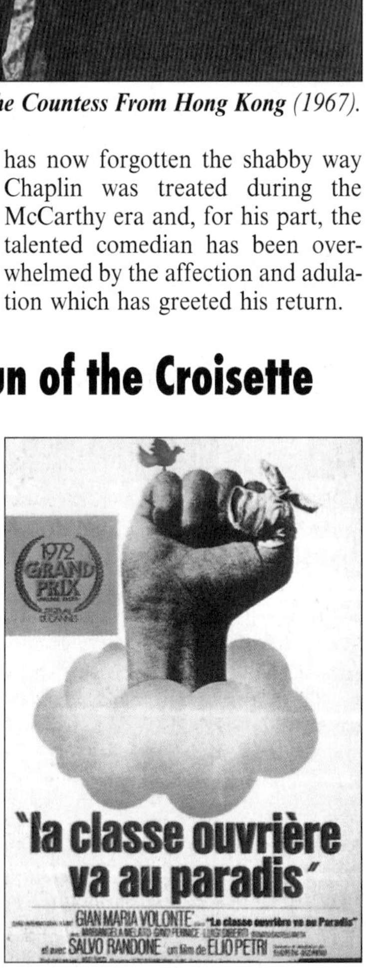
1972
GRAND
PRIX
'la classe ouvrière
va au paradis'
GIAN MARIA VOLONTE
SALVO RANDONE
un film de ELIO PETRI

Cannes, 19 May

Present-day Italian cinema seems to be particularly effective in delving into the political and social realities of the nation. The Italian selection in competition at Cannes this year is a reflection of this preoccupation, offering three films that investigate the corruption at the heart of capitalism: Lina Wertmuller's *The Seduction of Mimi* (*Mimi Metallurgico Ferito Nell'Onore*), Elio Petri's *Lulu the Tool* (*La Classe Operaia va in Paradiso*) and Francesco Rosi's *The Mattei Affair*. The latter two shared the Grand Prix, a unanimous decision reached by the jury, presided over by Joseph Losey. Petri's work deals with a factory piece-worker (Gian Maria Volonte), obsessed with achieving the highest daily output, who alienates his fellow workers, inviting exploitation by shop stewards and frustrating his mistress (Mariangela Melato). In *The Mattei Affair*, Rosi makes use of a bold, semi-documentary style to dissect the life and death of the socialist oil magnate Enrico Mattei, "the most powerful Italian since Augustus Caesar", killed in a mysterious plane crash in 1962. Volonte gives another fine performance in the title role. Two East European films were also among the winners: the visually striking science fiction allegory, *Solaris*, from Soviet Andrei Tarkovsky, which gained the Special Jury Prize, while the Hungarian Miklos Jancso was given the director's award for his highly stylized political fable, *Red Psalm*.

And then there were the Oscars!

Los Angeles, 10 April

The most succesful movie at t 44th Academy Awards was the p sating police thriller *The Fren Connection*, from director Willia Friedkin. Not only was it voted Be Picture but it also gained the Be Director prize for Friedkin and t Best Actor Oscar for his star, Ge Hackman, superb as the driven thi taker Popeye Doyle. Jane Fon was voted Best Actress for her pe formance as Bree Daniels, the pro titute in jeopardy in Alan J. Pakula *Klute*. Peter Bogdanovich's homa to American cinema past, *The La Picture Show*, has won two maj awards. Ben Johnson, a particul favorite of John Ford, was vot Best Supporting Actor for his pe formance as grizzled Sam the Lio proprietor of a moribund cinema a small Texan town. Cloris Leac man's poignant performance in t same film as a housewife edgi into despair won her the Best Su porting Actress Oscar. A runner- in the 1946 Miss America pagea Leachman is a veteran of Broadw and television but until now has r mained a relatively unknown mov personality in spite of incisive pe formances in several films, not lea Robert Aldrich's Fifties classic *K Me Deadly*. The Best Foreign Fil award was won (for the fourth tim by Vittorio De Sica, this time f *The Garden of the Finzi-Contin* an exquisitely photographed dran about an aristocratic Jewish fami in Italy during the Second Wor War who choose to ignore the cree ing shadow of the concentratio camps until it is too late.

*Best Actress Jane Fonda in **Klute**.*

oredom with life kills off George Sanders

nders as ***Bluebeard*** *in 1960.*

rcelona, 25 April
e lifeless body of George Sanders s been discovered in a hotel room Casteldefells, near Barcelona. He d committed suicide with a drug overdose, and left a note which blamed it all on boredom: "Dear World, I am leaving you because I am bored. I am leaving you with your worries in this sweet cesspool." For over 30 years Sanders had padded down a path of silky villainy and purring caddishness, dispensing sneers and disdainful dialogue with an inimitably studied weariness. In fact the pose concealed an insecure man and immensely hardworking actor whose career reached a peak in 1950 with *All About Eve*. Nature created Sanders to play Addison de Witt, the waspish theatre critic whose voice-over provides a barbed commentary to that film's backstage backstabbing. That performance won Sanders a Best Supporting Actor Oscar, but the success seemed to dismay him into a slow decline. He was married to tempestuous actress Zsa Zsa Gabor from 1949 to 1954, and briefly married to her sister Magda in 1970.

A scandalous pair in 'Last Tango in Paris'

Paris, 15 December
The cinematic event of the moment in Paris is the release of *Last Tango in Paris*, Bernardo Bertolucci's first film since *The Conformist* two years ago. This screenplay follows a simple line. Marlon Brando and Maria Schneider are strangers who meet by chance inside an empty Paris apartment, where they suddenly and passionately make love. They subsequently embark on further erotic encounters in the apartment, agreeing never to talk about their lives or reveal their names, in order to keep the relationship anonymous and exclusively physical. However, it is revealed that she is about to be married to a young TV filmmaker (Jean-Pierre Léaud), while Brando is attempting to understand the recent unexplained suicide of his wife. The main focus of this disturbing picture is the painful, joyless and loveless grappling of Brando and Schneider, most controversially using butter in a sodomy scene. And Brando, freed from the restrictions of Hollywood, delivers his most mature, powerful and committed performance.

Marlon Brando, Maria Schneider.

unning for office with Robert Redford

w York, 29 June
obert Redford looks every inch the ennedyesque venturer into politics Michael Ritchie's *The Candidate*. plays the apolitical California vyer whose self-effacing good oks ease him into a senatorial seat. ong the way he is dismayed to d that his values and lifestyle ust change to accommodate his w role. Karen Carlson is the wife cut adrift during the campaign, and Peter Boyle is superb as the campaign manager happy to toss Redford's integrity out the window. Ritchie's documentary-style direction and Jeremy Larner's pungent screenplay highlight the dirty side of politics, but their distaste for smoke-filled rooms suggests the kind of cop-out liberalism which would prefer to do without politics altogether.

litical candidate Robert Redford out and about wooing potential voters.

Disaster strikes star-filled ocean liner

Los Angeles, 16 December
In *The Poseidon Adventure* an ocean liner the size of the *Queen Mary* is capsized by a freak wave and turns upside down. Nearly all of the passengers, whooping it up in the ship's dining room, are killed, but 10 survive the disaster. Led by two-fisted priest Gene Hackman, they thread their way through the upside-down world of the liner, from top to bottom, in search of escape. The intriguing inverted sets designed by William Creber camouflage most of the movie's dramatic implausibilities, while the steadily rising water injects a healthy measure of tension. The sets were mounted on slanted tracks which were gradually lowered into water tanks while the likes of Shelley Winters, Red Buttons and Ernest Borgnine emoted furiously.

l to r: Stella Stevens, Ernest Borgnine, Jack Albertson, Shelley Winters, Red Buttons, Carol Lynley and Pamela Sue Martin in a state of shock.

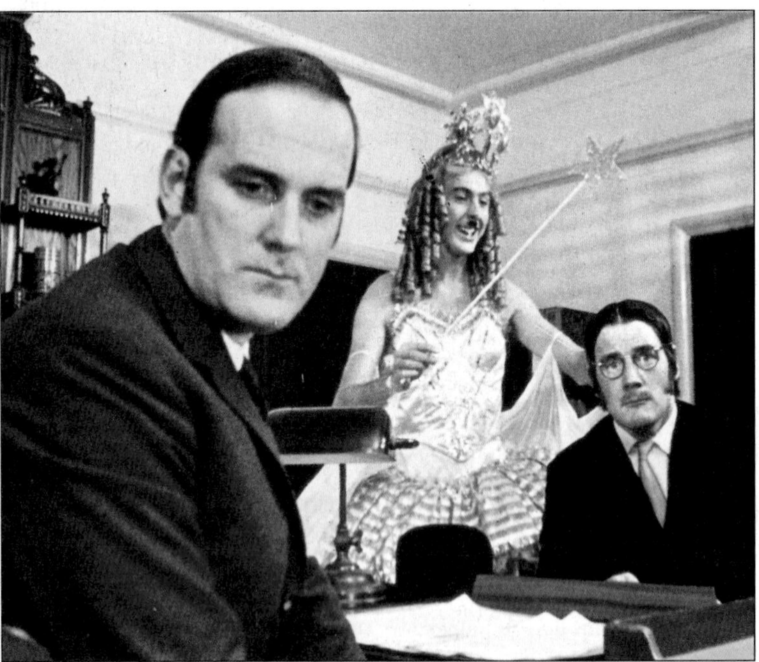

Left to right: John Cleese, Eric Idle and Graham Chapman in ***...And Now for Something Completely Different*** *(Monty Python).*

Jon Voight and Ned Beatty in John Boorman's ***Deliverance****.*

Paul Winfield, Kevin Hooks and the title hound ***Sounder****.*

Malcolm Tierney, Sandy Ratcliffe in ***Family Life****: attacking British psychiatry.*

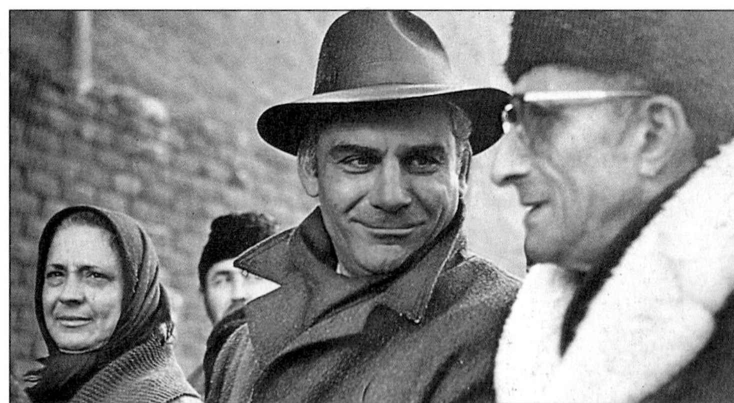

Gian Maria Volonte in Francesco Rosi's ***The Mattei Affair*** *(Italy).*

Pier Paolo Pasolini in his film of ***The Canterbury Tales****.*

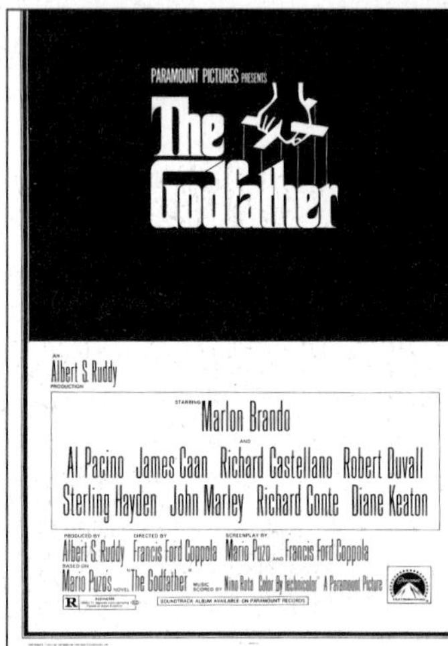
PARAMOUNT PICTURES PRESENTS
The Godfather
Albert S. Ruddy
PRODUCTION
STARRING Marlon Brando
AND
Al Pacino James Caan Richard Castellano Robert Duvall
Sterling Hayden John Marley Richard Conte Diane Keaton
PRODUCED BY Albert S. Ruddy DIRECTED BY Francis Ford Coppola SCREENPLAY BY Mario Puzo AND Francis Ford Coppola
BASED ON Mario Puzo's NOVEL "The Godfather"
SOUNDTRACK ALBUM AVAILABLE ON PARAMOUNT RECORDS
A Paramount Picture
R

A suitably stark and somber ad.

Paul Morrissey's ***Heat*** *for Andy Warhol: Sylvia Miles and Joe Dallesandro.*

'ichael Caine and Laurence Olivier in Joseph Mankiewicz's cunning **Sleuth**.

:atman Crothers (left) and Jack Nicholson in **The King of Marvin Gardens**.

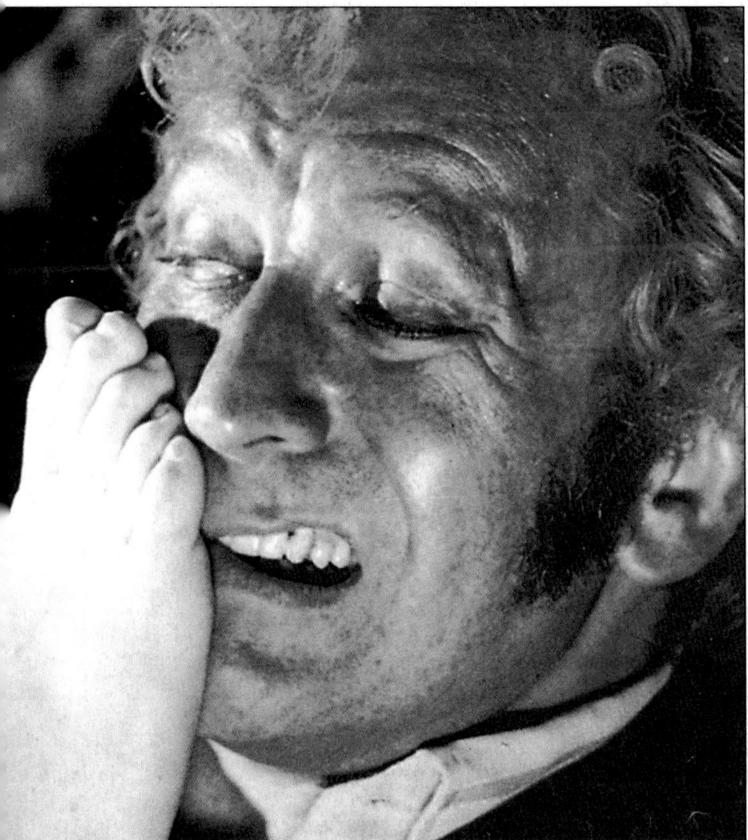

'arry Foster is the psychopath in Hitchcock's British film **Frenzy**.

MEN
2

Animator Ralph Bakshi wrote and made his first feature, **Fritz the Cat**.

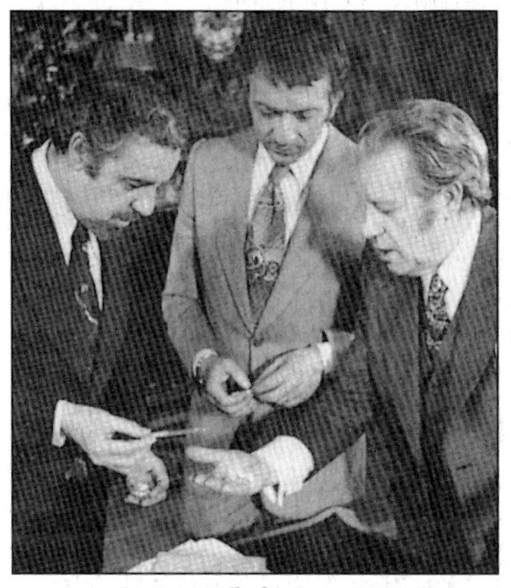

Fernando Rey (left) in **The Discreet Charm of the Bourgeoisie**.

Diana Ross is singer Billie Holliday in **Lady Sings the Blues**.

Gian Maria Volonte (l), Jean-Louis Trintignant in Boisset's **l'Attentat (Plot)**.

1973

1972 Academy Awards, Dorothy Chandler Pavilion, 27 Mar.

Best Film:	*The Godfather* (dir: Francis Ford Coppola)
Best Director:	Bob Fosse *(Cabaret)*
Best Actor:	Marlon Brando *(The Godfather)*
Best Actress:	Liza Minnelli *(Cabaret)*
Best Supp. Actor:	Joel Grey *(Cabaret)*
Best Supp. Actress:	Eileen Heckart *(Butterflies Are Free)*

Hollywood, 7 January
Paramount is celebrating its founder Adolph Zukor's 100th birthday. Over a thousand people have been invited to a party in his honor. The estimated cost of the reception is $100,000.

Paris, 14 January
The 30th Louis Delluc Prize has been awarded to Costa-Gavras for *State of Siege*, with Yves Montand, a political film dealing with CIA involvement in Latin America.

Malibu, 19 January
Jane Fonda has married political activist Tom Hayden.

Rome, 2 February
A Bologna criminal court today lifted a ban on *Last Tango in Paris*, and acquitted the director of the film, Bernardo Bertolucci, its stars Marlon Brando and Maria Schneider and two others of obscenity charges. The trial started on 15 December, and on 21 December the movie was seized throughout Italy on orders from a deputy prosecutor in Rome. Bertolucci welcomed the news not just for the film but "for the freedom of expression in Italy."

Los Angeles, 31 March
The American Film Institute has honored John Ford with its Lifetime Achievement Award. President Nixon attended the ceremony and personally handed the Liberty medal, the country's highest civil award, to the film director.

Washington D.C., 6 April
The American Institute's inaugural film festival was marred by confusion and charges of censorship. Only hours before the opening a New York distributor announced that a third of the films scheduled were to be withheld as a protest against the withdrawal of Constantin Costa-Gavras' picture *State of Siege*. New York film critics have harshly criticized the affair.

San Diego, 21 April
Pioneer Merian C. Cooper, who, with Ernest B. Schoedsack, directed exotic adventure films including the memorable *King Kong*, has died.

New York, 24 April
Jerry Lewis has removed his backing from the Network Cinema group (about 200 cinemas) due to its serious financial difficulties. He blames the failure on a lack of suitable films for general viewing.

Stockholm, 25 April
Ingmar Bergman's *Cries and Whispers* (*Viskningar och Rop*), released here last month, is set to be picked up for international release.

New York, 10 May
Abel Green, the chief editor of the weekly show-biz bible *Variety*, has died at the age of 72.

Rhode Island, 6 June
Jack Clayton has started filming *The Great Gatsby*, based on the novel by F. Scott Fitzgerald and starring Robert Redford and Mia Farrow.

New York, 12 June
Marlon Brando let fly with his fists in anger at a photographer who was annoying him, and broke his jaw. Brando himself had to be hospitalized with a swollen hand.

Washington D.C., 21 June
The Supreme Court has voted in a decision (six to three) which drastically modifies its previous attitude toward pornography. Henceforth, it will be left to the state governments to decide what constitutes obscenity and whether a film should be protected by the First Amendment of the Constitution.

Hollywood, 24 June
Seventy percent of Screen Writers Guild members have voted to end the strike which started on 7 March, bringing to an end the longest strike in the history of Hollywood.

New York, 3 July
A spokesman for Richard Burton and Elizabeth Taylor has announced that the couple have decided to separate, despite numerous attempts at a reconciliation.

Cairo, 4 July
The opening of Salah Abou Seif's film *The Baths of Malatili* (*Hammam el Malatili*), has caused a sensation because of its author's daring exploration of all forms of sexuality.

New Jersey, 4 July
Georgina Spelvin, star of the erotic film *The Devil in Miss Jones*, has been arrested. She was making a promotional visit to a cinema showing her film.

New York, 25 July
Alan Hirschfield, one of Herbert Allen's protégés, has replaced Leo Jaffe as president of Columbia Pictures Industries. Jaffe has become chairman of the company's board of directors.

Hollywood, 28 September
Metro-Goldwyn-Mayer's lion is not roaring as loudly under James T. Aubrey Jr.'s new streamlined regime as it did in the old Louis B. Mayer days. But Leo still intends to be heard from for the next 10 years under a new distribution deal with United Artists. The deal includes distribution to movie theaters and TV syndication. Distribution fees are confidential, but UA have also agreed to purchase MGM's Robbins, Feist and Miller music publishing company and its half interest in Quality Records of Canada for about $15 million.

New York, 31 October
Release of the American Film Theater's first production, *The Iceman Cometh*, a film version of Eugene O'Neill's play directed by John Frankenheimer, with Lee Marvin, Robert Ryan and Fredric March. Ely Landau founded the AFT with the idea of producing film adaptations of American theater classics.

Paris, 30 November
A tax inspector, Edouard Dega, has been accused of laxity in dealing with certain taxpayers, including the film directors Bernard Borderie and Alain Cavalier, who have been under investigation.

Las Vegas, 5 December
Inauguration of the MGM-finance MGM Grand, the biggest hotel ar casino complex in the U.S.

London, 7 December
Technicolor is reported to have so a film processing lab to Communi China for around $7 million.

New York, 19 December
American premiere of Charl Chaplin's *A King in New Yor* Chaplin had always refused to r lease the film in the U.S. (it can out in Europe in 1957) until la year's reconciliation.

DEATHS

Hollywood, 26 February
Edward G. Robinson

Switzerland, 10 March
Robert Siodmak

Jamaica, 26 March
Noel Coward

California, 2 July
Betty Grable

Vermont, 7 July
Veronica Lake

New York, 11 July
Robert Ryan

London, 18 July
Jack Hawkins

Hong Kong, 20 July
Bruce Lee

California, 31 August
John Ford

Rome, 26 September
Anna Magnani

Tokyo, 23 November
Sessue Hayakawa

London, 25 November
Laurence Harvey

Los Angeles, 20 December
Bobby Darin

Director George Roy Hill reteame the smash-hit duo of Newman ar Redford in **The Sting**. *This engagir tale of two Thirties con-men ended u walking away with seven Oscars.*

PAUL NEWMAN · ROBERT REDFORD
ROBERT SHAW

IN A BILL/PHILLIPS PRODUCTION OF
A GEORGE ROY HILL FILM

THE STING

A RICHARD D. ZANUCK/DAVID BROWN PRESENTATION

AMSEL

...all it takes is a little Confidence.

Written by DAVID S. WARD · Directed by GEORGE ROY HILL · Produced by TONY BILL, MICHAEL and JULIA PHILLIPS

Music Adapted by MARVIN HAMLISCH · A UNIVERSAL PICTURE · TECHNICOLOR® ORIGINAL SOUNDTRACK AVAILABLE EXCLUSIVELY ON MCA RECORDS AND TAPES PG PARENTAL GUIDANCE SUGGESTED

74/8

Werner Herzog in the heart of Eldorado

*Klaus Kinski in **Aguirre, the Wrath of God**, Herzog's mythic adventure.*

Paris, 5 January
With *Aguirre, Wrath of God*, the German director Werner Herzog has offered us a spectacle far from his earlier experimental films. Inspired by the insane exploits of 16th-century conquistador Don Lope de Aguirre, who led a hazardous expedition through the wilds of Peru in search of El Dorado, the film does not attempt a mere historical reconstruction. Herzog, through the delirium of his hero, wishes to reveal, not the story of conquest, but the fevered fascination of the lure of gold and of power. The final shot, an aerial view of a lone survivor on a raft, is masterly. Like his protagonist, Herzog had to overcome extremely difficult conditions during the shoot in the Peruvian Andes. He made the film in six weeks at extraordinary risk to the lives of his cast and crew. The director also had problems dealing with Klaus Kinski, whose intense performance in the title role is one of the great strengths of the film. Kinski, a temperamental man, often threatened to abandon the whole project.

The fantastic found in the snow of Avoria

Avoriaz, 11 February
The ski resort of Avoriaz in the French Alps has been invaded by a very different type of tourist from the usual. For the last 12 days, fans have been gathering for the first International Festival of Horror and Fantasy Films, initiated by journalist and publicist Lionel Chouchan. The jury, headed by director René Clément, has given the first prize to an American film, *Duel*, made for television by a talented young director named Steven Spielberg. Written by Richard Matheson, adapting his own novel, it is an immen effective man vs. machine thri about a salesman driving alon highway who gradually realizes h being chased across the country b huge and menacing truck, the dri of which is never seen. The Spe Jury Prize went to *Themroc*, an tremely strange French film direc by Claude Faraldo, in which characters communicate only i series of formless noises. It tells a factory worker, living in a squa apartment, who suddenly reb causing anarchy.

*Dennis Weaver in **Duel**, a terrifying allegory made for TV by Steven Spielbe*

Luchino Visconti completes his trilogy of 'German decadence'

Rome, 18 January
As a Marxist, Luchino Visconti should, in principle, be dedicated to the destruction of the class and culture he represents, and yet it is bourgeois European art that attracts him most – Mahler, Bruckner, Lampedusa, Thomas Mann, Wagner... He is both repelled by and drawn to the decaying society that he depicts in such impressively loving detail. Visconti's latest film, *Ludwig*, which completes his trilogy of "German decadence", following *The Damned* and *Death in Venice*, is no exception. This long (186 minutes) and unhurried look at the life and premature death of Ludwig II of Bavaria, revels in the Bavarian locations and castles, and the costumes and manners of the mid to late 19th century. Helmut Berger, who has gained the nickname Ham Berger, is excellent in the title role, and looks uncannily like the tortured king. He ages convincingly from the young Ludwig who ascends the throne to the 41-year-old madman who drowns himself. Naturally, much of the film is taken up with Ludwig's patronage of Richard Wagner (Trevor Howard), and his platonic relationship with his beautiful cousin, Elizabeth of Austria (Romy Schneider).

Romy Schneider, with Helmut Berger as King Ludwig, in Visconti's film.

Sissi exorcised

Italy, 18 January
While still in her teens, during th mid-1950s, Romy Schneider be came the most popular young sta of the German-speaking world a "Sissi", the future Empress Eliza beth, in three romantic and senti mental films about the Austro Hungarian royal family. Usuall shown cut together in the U.S. a one movie under the title *Foreve My Love*, they are part-operetta part-Hollywood style biopic. Th role of "Sissi" has haunted Rom ever since, and is one which sh has always mocked. Therefore, took some convincing on Luchi no Visconti's part to persuade th lovely star to reprise the role i *Ludwig*, this time as a more ma ture and cynical Empress, cousi to the King of Bavaria, in a ver different kind of film.

'Deep Throat' has to swallow a heavy fine

w York, 1 March
expected, a New York court has ged the sexploitation movie *Deep roat* to be obscene. A stiff fine has n imposed – twice the picture's x-office receipts. This judgment lows action taken against *Deep roat* in a number of cities, notably Miami and Toledo, Ohio, where vas seized by police on the day vas released. Directed by Gérard manio, *Deep Throat* follows the otic adventures of a young wom-, Linda Lovelace, who discovers t one of her most important erog-ous zones, her clitoris no less, is ated in her throat. This unique edical condition leads to a feast of latio. Released in New York last ne in a Times Square theater that ecializes in such fare, *Deep Throat* joyed such a phenomenal success t, like *The Devil and Miss Jones*, transferred to an East Side art house. It is, indeed, rarely that a film of a pornographic nature manages to escape from the low-rent ghettos to which such movies are normally confined.

Linda Lovelace, the protagonist.

'Godfather' Marlon's message to Indians

Los Angeles, 27 March
Francis Ford Coppola's *The Godfather* has been voted Best Picture at this year's Oscar ceremony at Los Angeles Music Center. Marlon Brando won the Best Actor award for his performance in the same movie. This was no surprise, but his reaction certainly was. The star did not attend the ceremony. In his place he sent an Indian girl called Sasheen Littlefeather (in reality an actress named Maria Cruz). Littlefeather read out a statement from Brando accusing the motion picture industry of "degrading the Indian and making a mockery of his character." It seems you can't even give Oscars away these days. This year's Best Actress was Liza Minnelli for her performance in *Cabaret*, which won seven other Oscars, including Best Supporting Actor (Joel Grey), Director (Bob Fosse) and Cinematography (Geoffrey Unsworth). Best Supporting Actress was Eileen Heckart for *Butterflies Are Free* and Best Foreign Film was *The Discreet Charm of the Bourgeoisie*.

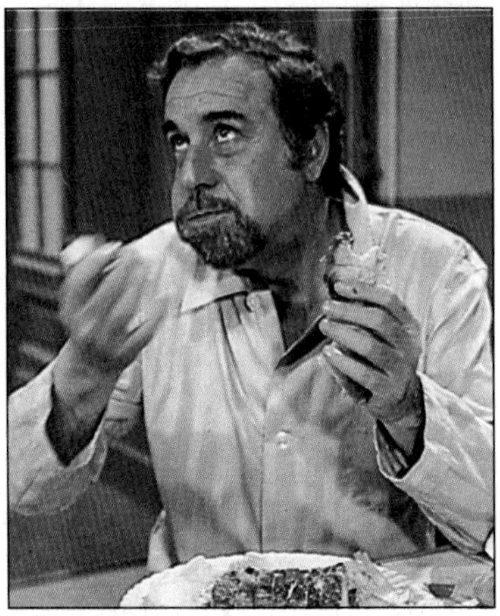

*Fernando Rey in Buñuel's **The Discreet Charm of the Bourgeoisie**.*

arriage put under Bergman's microscope

*v Ullmann and Erland Josephson are the couple in **Scenes From a Marriage**.*

tockholm, 11 April
gmar Bergman began working for levision around the mid-1960s, a edium which he found stimulated s imagination. His latest TV pro-uction is a series consisting of six)-minute episodes, collectively ti-ed *Scenes From a Marriage*. It nalyses the traumatic breakup of e 10-year marriage between Mari-nne (Liv Ullmann) and her hus-and Johan (Erland Josephson), ho is seriously involved with a ounger woman (Bibi Andersson). The rupture is painful for both, and each of them deals with it in a different way. The years pass, but they seem closer than ever since the divorce. Played largely in close-up, it creates a claustrophobic, hermetically-sealed atmosphere, while the terse exchanges and bitter silences convey a sense of bleak aridity in the beleaguered marriage. Though depressing, it is undeniably absorbing, with the director's style everywhere evident, especially in the sensitive handling of his accomplished cast.

This Ryan's daughter steals the show

New York, 16 May
Cheerfully ignoring the old theatrical warning to avoid acting with dogs or children, Ryan O'Neal has embarked on a movie which co-stars his *own* daughter Tatum. In *Paper Moon*, directed by Peter Bogdanovich, he plays a Bible-selling con man in Depression-era Kansas who falls in with a sassy, cigarette-smoking little girl who proves to be as sharp, if not sharper, than he is. It's a variation on the relationship between Charlie Chaplin and Jackie Coogan in *The Kid*, and while not quite in that class, *Paper Moon* nevertheless threatens to be a runaway hit. Inevitably, Tatum O'Neal steals the show as the self-possessed nine-year-old who succumbs to childish jealousy when grown-up girl Madeline Kahn (superb) comes along for the ride. She's already being tipped for an Oscar nomination.

*Little Tatum O'Neal practically eclipses her daddy, Ryan, in **Paper Moon**.*

The Cannes Festival is rocked by controversy

Jean-Pierre Léaud, Françoise Lebrun and Bernadette Lafont in ***The Mother and the Whore***. *Jean Eustache's film won the Special Jury Prize.*

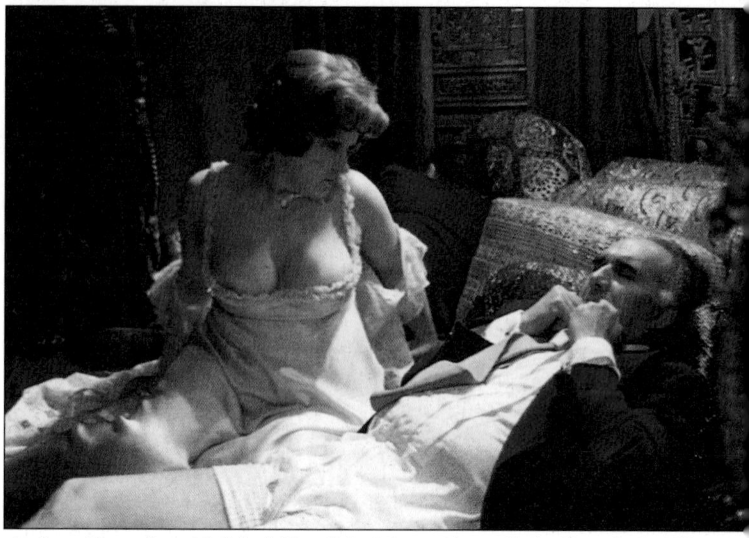

Andrea Ferreol and Michel Piccoli in Marco Ferreri's ***la Grande bouffe***.

Cannes, 25 May

When they chose Jean Eustache's film *The Mother and the Whore* and Marco Ferreri's work *Blow-Out* (*la Grande bouffe*) to represent France at this year's Cannes Festival, the selection committee could not have foreseen the furor that would ensue. Eustache's work provoked loud protests during and after the screening, primarily because of its crude dialogue. The director was almost physically assaulted when he exited the auditorium with Jeanne Moreau, who had taken his arm in friendship. The 215-minute film of a *ménage à trois* is witty, verbose and erotic, and consists mainly of monologues, conversations and confessions. The showing of *Blow-Out* was the last straw. This story of four middle-aged men literally eating themselves to death, seems to have offended the defenders of good taste, morality and national pride, and there were cries of "Nauseating! Disgusting!" during the film.

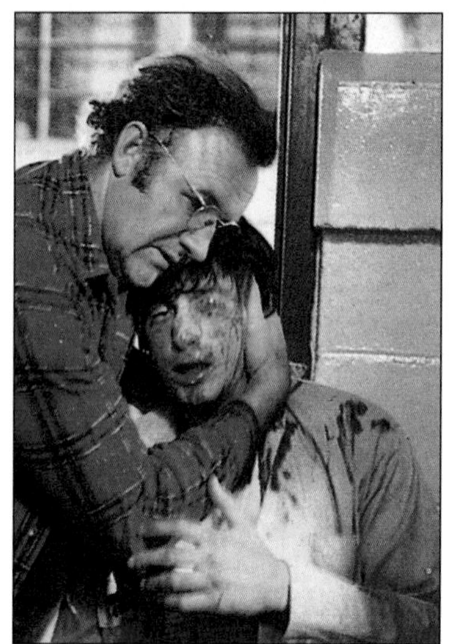

Gene Hackman and Al Pacino in Jerry Schatzberg's ***Scarecrow***.

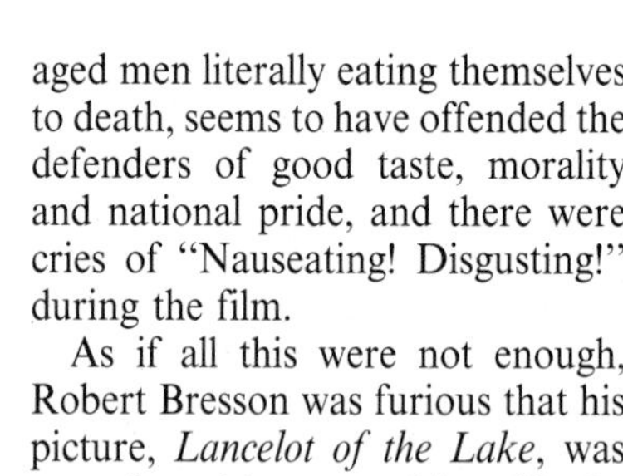

As if all this were not enough, Robert Bresson was furious that his picture, *Lancelot of the Lake*, was not selected in competition. He declared: "The Cannes Festival has sunk deep into mediocrity and error." After Bresson's film received almost as noisy a reception as those of Eustache and Ferreri, Michel Piccoli, one of the stars of *Blow-Out*, acted as spokesman for the director. "Monsieur Robert Bresson, in accord with his producers and the Society of French Directors, has decided not to show *Lancelot of the Lake* this evening. Out of respect fo the jury and the public, he woul like to reverse his decision, but h wishes to express his indignation a the conditions under which the Fe tival is taking place. The spirit th reigns over the selection and th organization of the Festival seem to him to be contrary to the be ideals of cinema." The selectors e plained that they wanted to mak the Festival an "event", and chos French films which are "daring an original". This has gone beyon their wildest dreams, because th French entries have eclipsed all ot ers, even the two films that share the Grand Prix – Jerry Schatzberg *Scarecrow* and Alan Bridges' *Th Hireling*, American and British pr ductions respectively.

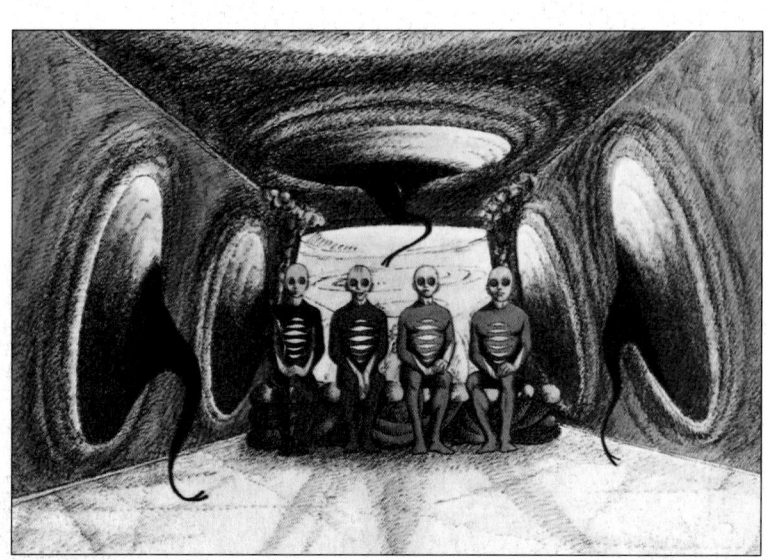

René Laloux and Roland Topor won a special prize for ***la Planète sauvage***.

The jury on the terrace of the Palais surround their president, Ingrid Bergma

nglo-American relations a real romp

›orge Segal tries to teach Glenda Jackson baseball in London's Hyde Park.

›ndon, 24 May
›eorge Segal and Glenda Jackson ›ike sparks in *A Touch of Class.* ›e's the married executive who ›hisks prim Jackson off to Spain ›r a bit of sun and sex but finds ›r more than a mite quarrelsome. *Touch of Class* harks back to many an older, and better, movie in which a meeting cute is followed by a long battle before the final clinch and fade-out. Segal dispenses lots of shaggy charm as the besotted businessman, dislocating his back in bed, but Jackson, essaying her first film comedy, is far too shrill.

ixties America revisited by George Lucas

›s Angeles, 5 August
›e second feature from 29-year-old ›eorge Lucas, *American Graffiti*, is ›dreamy vision of adolescent life in small Californian town in 1962, ›fore Vietnam and the drug scene; time of comparative innocence. ›sing the rock 'n' roll hits of the ›riod on the soundtrack and with brilliant hyper-realist photography, the movie creates a finger-lickin' golden past. It also draws on memories of teen-pix of the 1950s, on which the director grew up. The refreshing little-known cast includes Richard Dreyfuss, Ronny Howard, Paul Le Mat, Cindy Williams, Candy Clark and Harrison Ford.

›aul Le Mat (left), Cindy Williams and Ronny Howard in ***American Graffiti.***

François Truffaut's tribute to filmmaking

Paris, 24 May
It was while cutting *Two English Girls* (aka *Anne and Muriel*) at the Victorine Studios in Nice, that François Truffaut got the idea for his new film, *Day for Night.* The sight of the decor for *The Mad Woman of Chaillot*, Bryan Forbes' British film, awoke his desire to make a film about making a film. The screenplay revolves around the shooting of a melodrama called "Meet Pamela", during which the juvenile lead (Jean-Pierre Léaud) falls hopelessly in love with the married international star (Jacqueline Bisset); an Italian actress (Valentina Cortese) keeps forgetting her lines; the male lead (Jean-Pierre Aumont) is killed in an automobile crash; time and money begin to run out; and someone has a baby.

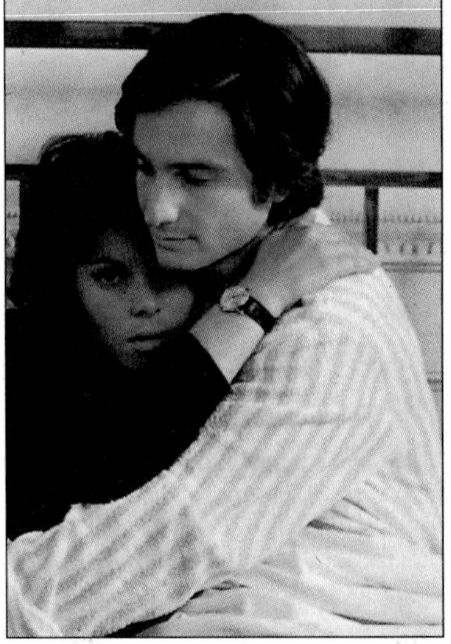

*Dani and Jean-Pierre Léaud in **Day for Night**. Truth or fiction?*

"Are films more important than life?" Léaud asks at one stage. Truffaut, himself playing the director called Ferrand, answers in the affirmative. Despite all the difficulties it reveals, *Day for Night* is an exuberant celebration of filmmaking. Never before have the atmosphere and techniques of filming been so lovingly and vividly presented. The title itself is a term for simulating night by the use of filters in daylight. We see how crowd scenes are organized, how crane and tracking shots are set up, dialogue agreed, actors and actresses encouraged and placated, props gathered and stunt work carried out. In one sequence, derived from his own *la Peau douce* (*The Soft Skin*), Truffaut shows the problems of introducing animals into a film, by using a stubborn kitten. *Day for Night* also wittily explores the relationship between the audience and the film-within-a-film. Georges Delerue's cod baroque music adds vitality to the already springy editing. The movie abounds with references to other films, directors and books (the novelist Graham Greene appears in an uncredited bit part as a money man), and special tribute is paid to Hollywood – the film is dedicated to the Gish sisters, and Truffaut-Ferrand dreams of stealing stills of *Citizen Kane* from outside a movie theater. Truffaut is at the center, soothing everyone from the stars to the continuity girl, and communicating his enthusiasm.

Director Truffaut (right) with Jean-Pierre Aumont and Jacqueline Bisset.

Bob and Barbra act out thirty years of nostalgia

New York, 17 October
Barbra Streisand and Robert Redford are an unlikely pairing in Sydney Pollack's *The Way We Were*, a romantic drama set against three decades of American political history. She's a left-wing activist and he's a Waspish literary type who meet, marry and divorce as the Second World War gives way to the Cold War and the menace of McCarthyism. The screenplay is by Arthur Laurents, who lived through the days of fear and betrayal in Hollywood in the early Fifties. However, director Pollack has been quick to reassure moviegoers that the film is a romance rather than a political tract, adding, "but I hope that audiences also ponder some of the movie's serious undertones." Redford gracefully plays second fiddle to Streisand, who apparently insisted on some of his scenes being cut. There's also a strong and haunting title song, belted out by Streisand.

Robert Redford as the screenwriter with Barbra Streisand as the girl he marrie

Barbra Streisand as the young, left-wing idealist in the early sequences.

Eight-year-old Ana Torrent as the lonely little girl in Victor Erice's impressive debut film, *The Spirit of the Beehive*. Her wide brown eyes reflect the world of her imagination, in which most of the film's events take place, especially centered on her obsession with Boris Karloff's good-bad monster in the film of *Frankenstein*.

Film colony loses major figures

California, 31 August
It has been a black summer for the film world with the announcements of the deaths of Betty Grable, Veronica Lake, Robert Ryan and Bruce Lee. Martial arts star Lee died on 15 July, aged only 33. Three weeks ago, French director Jean-Pierre Melville died in his mid-50s. Born Jean-Pierre Grumbach, he changed his name because of his fondness for the great American writer Herman Melville. But it was the American gangster novel and *film noir* that were the main influences on his films. Now today, John Ford has died of cancer at Palm Desert, his Californian ranch. Arguably the greatest American-born Hollywood director, Ford was known principally for raising the Western to artistic status, starting with *Stagecoach* (1939). But it was for non-Westerns that he won his four directing Oscars: *The Informer*, *The Grapes of Wrath*, *How Green Was My Valley* and *The Quiet Man*.

The brilliant French filmmaker, Jean-Pierre Melville: a loss.

ardot says her farewells to the screen

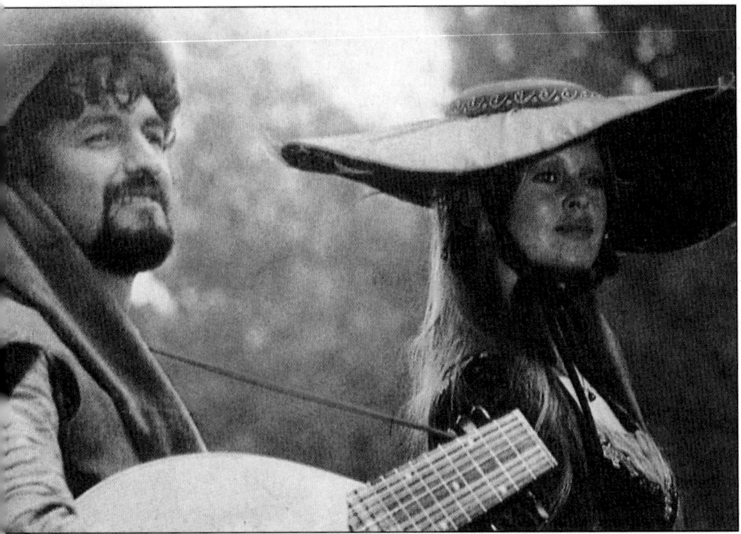

Histoire très bonne et très joyeuse de Colinot Trousse-chemise.

ris, 25 October
ı the release of her latest film, *Iistoire très bonne et très joyeuse Colinot Trousse-chemise*, Brigitte ırdot has announced her retire- ent from the screen, soon after ving celebrated her 39th birthday. e reached the decision because of e recent failure of *Don Juan 73 or Don Juan Were a Woman*, direct- by her ex-husband Roger Vadim. She told a magazine: "I've made 48 films of which only five were good. The rest are not worth anything. I will not make another, and I will never visit a plastic surgeon." One of the great beauties of the cinema, she has refused to allow herself to be seen aging on screen. In fact, Bardot never really enjoyed acting, and will now be able to devote her time to the cause of animal welfare.

Pacino superb in police corruption drama

Sidney Lumet's ***Serpico*** *stars Al Pacino, here in uniform and undercover.*

New York, 5 December
Al Pacino, recently seen to such good effect in *The Godfather*, which gained him an Oscar nomination for Best Supporting Actor, takes the title role in *Serpico*. It's based on the true story of a brave New York cop whose revelations in 1970 of institutionalized corruption rocked the police establishment to the core. In his role as the whistle-blowing cop, Pacino deftly subverts the tepid realism of director Sidney Lumet with an idiosyncratic portrait of a loner, isolated from his comrades by his incorruptibility and turning into a maddeningly modish hippie with beard, bobble hat and Old English sheepdog in tow. Man and dog survive the film, which was pacily scripted by Norman Wexler and Waldo Salt from Peter Maas' biography.

rutality of prison life on Devil's Island

ew York, 17 December
ıe semi-autobiographical best- ller by Frenchman Henri Char- re, *Papillon*, has been made into $13 million Hollywood movie di- cted by Franklin J. Schaffner. This ean of praise to survival stars Steve McQueen as the convict determined to escape from Devil's Island where he has been sentenced to life imprisonment, and Dustin Hoffman as his feeble, thickly bespectacled friend. The suffering of the prisoners is particularly well depicted.

eve McQueen and Dustin Hoffman in Franklin J. Schaffner's ***Papillon***.

Ludicrous horror pic pulls out all the stops

Los Angeles, 26 December
Twelve-year old Linda Blair is the child of every parent's nightmare in *The Exorcist*, vomiting jets of green bile over a priest and masturbating with a crucifix. William Friedkin's messy parable of demonic possession is packed with startling effects, not least the chilling moment when, almost subliminally, one realizes that Blair's head has turned around way beyond human limits. The demon's mocking voice was provided by Mercedes McCambridge.

Max Von Sydow, the exorcist of the title, with distraught mother Ellen Burstyn.

Tom Laughlin as half-breed **Billy Jack**. Huge at the box office.

Edward Fox (left) and Cyril Cusack: **The Day of the Jackal**.

Joe Don Baker (right) in **Walking Tall**, the true story of a vigilante.

From France, Roland Topor and René Laloux's animated **la Planète sauvage**.

Enter the Dragon: a new kind of actioner based on Kung Fu, with Bruce Le

Eustache's **The Mother and the Whore**: Jean-Pierre Léaud, Bernadette Lafont.

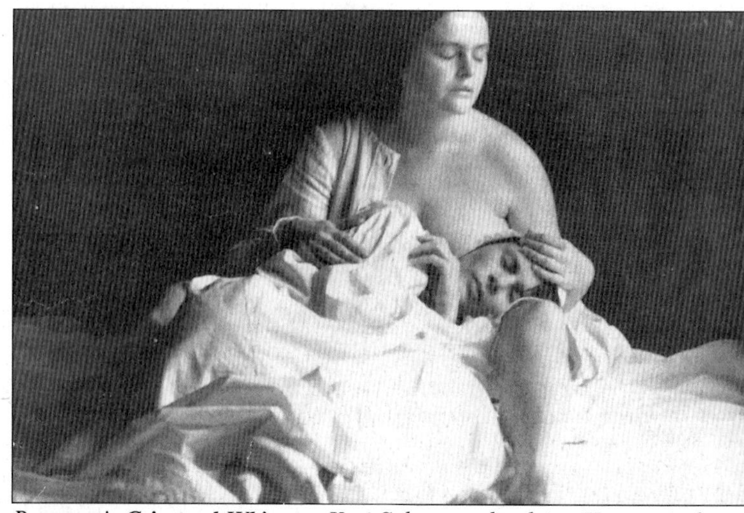
Bergman's **Cries and Whispers**: Kari Sylwan and a dying Harriet Andersso

to r: Randy Quaid, Otis Young, Jack Nicholson in Ashby's ***The Last Detail****.*

Andréa Ferreol, Marcello Mastroianni: ***la Grande bouffe (Blow Out)****.*

Marcello Mastroianni with Sophia Loren in ***The Priest's Wife****.*

ane Fonda as Nora in Joseph Losey's version of Ibsen's ***A Doll's House****.*

Helmut Berger as the mad Bavarian king, with Romy Schneider in ***Ludwig****.*

Max Von Sydow (left) and Jason Miller in William Friedkin's ***The Exorcist****.*

Robert Shaw, Robert Redford, Paul Newman in George Roy Hill's ***The Sting****.*

1974

1973 Academy Awards, Dorothy Chandler Pavilion, 2 Apr.

Best Film:	*The Sting* (dir: George Roy Hill)
Best Director:	George Roy Hill
Best Actor:	Jack Lemmon *(Save the Tiger)*
Best Actress:	Glenda Jackson *(A Touch of Class)*
Best Supp. Actor:	John Houseman *(The Paper Chase)*
Best Supp. Actress:	Tatum O'Neal *(Paper Moon)*

Paris, 10 January
The Communist Deputy Jack Ralite protested in the National Assembly about the meager share of the state budget (0.049 percent) allocated to the French film industry.

Mexico, 17 January
The Mexican Cinémathèque, which has been organized on the French Cinémathèque model, opened today with great ceremony.

Avoriaz, 28 January
The main prize at the second International Festival of Fantasy Films was awarded to Richard Fleischer's *Soylent Green.*

France, 20 February
Funds of 3.6 million francs have been allocated to the Film Archives Service to build three new special storage vaults to take 55,000 reels of highly inflammable nitrate film.

Hollywood, 7 March
Wildwood Productions, Robert Redford's company, has acquired the rights to the Carl Bernstein and Bob Woodward book, *All the President's Men*, for $450,000. About the events in the Watergate scandal, it was published in February.

Los Angeles, 13 March
The American Film Institute has honored James Cagney with its Lifetime Achievement Award. This is the second year this award has been given to reward and acknowledge exceptional careers in film.

Paris, 18 April
Marcel Pagnol has died at his home in Paris. The 69-year-old writer and filmmaker leaves us with the image of a man deeply attached to his native Provence, which he depicted with honesty and warmth in films such as *la Femme du boulanger*, *Manon des Sources* and the early classic *Topaze*. Pagnol was also the first film director to become a member of the Académie Française.

Massachusetts, 2 May
Steven Spielberg has started filming *Jaws* on location at Martha's Vineyard. The movie, based on a book by Peter Benchley, is the first independent production from Richard Zanuck and David Brown.

Hollywood, 6 May
A fire has destroyed part of the Samuel Goldwyn studios, causing $3 million worth of damage.

Cambridge, 10 May
The satirical magazine *The Harvard Lampoon* has awarded the prize for the worst actor of 1973 to Barbra Streisand for her performance in *The Way We Were.*

Washington D.C., 23 June
The Supreme Court ruled against a city ordinance as "unconstitutional interference" today. The ordinance made drive-in theaters criminally liable for showing films with nude scenes if they are visible outside the theater grounds. Justices ruled that while such films may be offensive to some, they could easily be avoided, and were no more likely to stop the traffic than scenes of violence.

Washington D.C., 24 June
The Supreme Court has ruled that the film *Carnal Knowledge* is not obscene. This ruling quashes a previous decision handed down by a court in Georgia.

Chicago, 13 July
Chicago's best-known cinema, the Biograph, has gone out quietly almost 40 years to the day after the violent death of its most famous patron John Dillinger. The flamboyant Dillinger, known as "Public Enemy No. 1" died in a gunfight with Federal agents outside the movie theater where he had been watching Clark Gable in *Manhattan Melody*. Trivia fans will remember that he sat in the middle of the 12th row handy to the exit. Sadly, the Biograph was no longer economically viable.

Paris, 27 August
The President of France, Valéry Giscard d'Estaing, said during an interview on television that film censorship would be abolished in the near future.

Paris, 2 October
A special soiree in honor of Woody Allen was held at the Chaillot Cinémathèque. The film chosen for the evening, *Sleeper*, was selected by Allen himself: "Perhaps my least successful film with the French public but the one I like the best."

London, 30 October
Charles Chaplin has compiled a companion volume to *My Autobiography* (1964). The new book, *My Life in Pictures*, comes out today.

Los Angeles, 1 November
Release of *Earthquake*, directed by Mark Robson, with Charlton Heston, Ava Gardner and Geneviève Bujold. The film is the first to be made in "Sensurround". This process works by emitting such deep sound that it is almost inaudible but at extremely powerful levels so that the vibrations are felt by the body.

New York, 8 November
Frank Yablans has surprised the film world by resigning from his position as president of Paramount Pictures. Barry Diller, who became chairman last October, now finds himself in charge of the studio.

Chile, 29 November
Actress Carmen Bueno and leading cameraman Jorge Muller have been arrested in Santiago by the DINA, Pinochet's political police.

London, 6 December
World premiere of Guy Hamilton's latest James Bond, *The Man With the Golden Gun*, with Roger Moore once again playing agent 007.

Hollywood, 11 December
MGM's profits for the year 1973-74 have risen by 190 percent compared to the previous year. This result is in large part due to its hotel-casino, the MGM Grand in Las Vegas.

Rome, 20 December
Release of Luchino Visconti's latest film, *Conversation Piece* (*Gruppo di Famiglia in un Interno*), with Burt Lancaster and Silvana Mangano.

New York, 25 December
An editorial criticizing *The Godf- ther I* and *II* has appeared in th *New York Times*. The films are d scribed as "breaking the record fo pornography and violence." The a ticle is concerned with the televisic screening of the first *Godfather* an its effect on young viewers.

New Delhi, 30 December
Opening of the fifth Indian Fil Festival, presided over by Satya Ray. From now on the festival is t be held annually. The Indian fil *Siddhartha*, is causing controvers due to a semi-nude scene.

Paris, 31 December
Four American films – *The Hustle The Exorcist*, *Robin Hood* and *Pap lon* – appear in the list of France Top Ten box-office hits for the yea

New York, 31 December
Cinema receipts, unadjusted for i flation, appear to be the highest o record, while distribution receip are up 25 percent from last year.

DEATHS

Palm Springs, 1 January
Edward Sutherland

Los Angeles, 31 January
Samuel Goldwyn

California, 24 April
Bud Abbott

Minnesota, 30 April
Agnes Moorehead

California, 21 September
Walter Brennan

Paris, 13 November
Vittorio De Sica

London, 17 November
Clive Brook

Paris, 15 December
Anatole Litvak

Beverly Hills, 26 December
Jack Benny

***The Godfather Part II** enjoyed th distinction of repeating the huge su cess of the original. Al Pacino mem rably and brilliantly stepped int Brando's shoes as the new Don.*

PARAMOUNT PICTURES PRESENTS
Francis Ford Coppola's PRODUCTION
The Godfather PART II
Al Pacino
AND
Robert Duvall Diane Keaton Robert De Niro
Talia Shire Morgana King John Cazale
Mariana Hill Lee Strasberg
SCREENPLAY BY
Francis Ford Coppola AND Mario Puzo
BASED ON THE NOVEL
'The Godfather' BY Mario Puzo
PRODUCED AND DIRECTED BY
Francis Ford Coppola
CO-PRODUCERS
Gray Frederickson AND Fred Roos
MUSIC SCORED BY
Nino Rota
Color by Technicolor®
SOUNDTRACK AVAILABLE ON ABC RECORDS
A Paramount Picture
Paramount
A Gulf+Western Company

A timely first film from Bertrand Tavernier

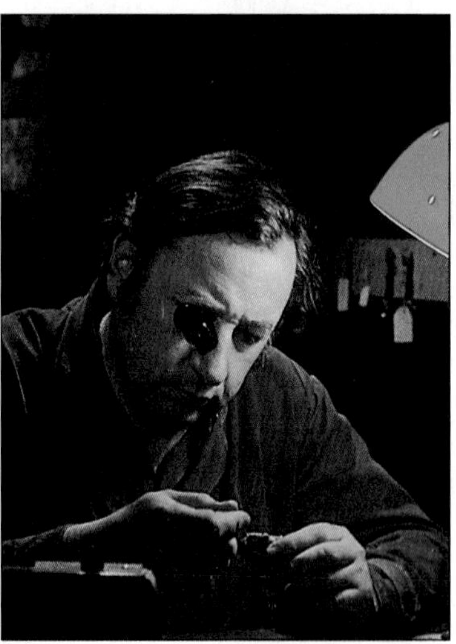

*Philippe Noiret stars as **The Watchmaker of Saint Paul** for Tavernier.*

Paris, 11 January
The Louis Delluc Prize has been awarded this year to *The Watchmaker of St. Paul*, the first feature by the former critic and press officer, 33-year-old Bertrand Tavernier. The director, an admirer of the best of pre-New Wave French cinema, employed the veteran writing team of Jean Aurenche and Pierre Bost, after 10 years of silence from them. They have come up with a well-crafted and intelligent screenplay based on the Georges Simenon novel titled *l'Horloger d'Everton* and set in Tavernier's hometown of Lyons. It concerns a watchmaker (Philippe Noiret), living a quiet life in St. Paul, a suburb of Lyons, who is stunned when he learns that his son is wanted for the murder of a factory owner. Pestered by a police inspector (Jean Rochefort), he is gradually forced to reconsider his life as a man and father. Tavernier has the controlled style and acute observation of his idol, Jacques Becker. The social detail and the almost imperceptible psychological hints, plus the interplay between Noiret and Rochefort make this an impressive debut.

Mel Brooks' crazy ride to the Wilder West

New York, 7 February
The range reverberates to the sound of flatulence in Mel Brooks' hilarious spoof Western, *Blazing Saddles*. Brooks mines every cliché of the genre with immense gusto, kicking off with an over-the-top Frankie Laine theme song and black railroad construction gang singing "I get no kick from champagne." He then turns every kind of racial stereotype upside down, casting himself as state governer and in a cameo as a Jewish Indian chief; Cleavon Little as the fashion-plate black sheriff drinking his whiskey from a wineglass; and, the star of the proceedings, Gene Wilder as the Waco Kid, Cleavon's sidekick. Villainy is supplied by Harvey Korman's crooked speculator Hedley Lamarr and glamor in the shapely form of Dietrich-like saloon singer Madeline Kahn. And the flatulence? That's caused by the campfire diet of Brooks' motley bunch of Hollywood cowpunchers.

Wilder: an over-the-hill gunfighter.

Louis Malle and the tragedy of history

Paris, 31 January
Louis Malle's new film, *Lacombe Lucien*, could be considered the first French feature to air the thorny subject of collaboration during the Occupation, already dealt with in a documentary form by Marcel Ophuls' *The Sorrow and the Pity*. It focuses on Lucien, a 17-year-old peasant of mean intelligence, who falls in with the Gestapo and moves in on a Jewish family in hiding. The director treats Lucien with cool objectivity, revealing the banality of his repellent actions. The wartime atmosphere of an occupied provincial town is authentic, and the terrifying dilemma of the family, at the mercy of their young captor, is expressed with subtlety and sympathy. The performances are brilliant, notably from Holger Löwenadler as the once fashionable Jewish tailor, and from Pierre Blaise, in the title role, a young peasant from the region, discovered by Malle.

Pierre Blaise, a boy driven to cause destruction by the Nazi authorities.

Man's inhumanity in the new Germany

Munich, 5 March
Rainer Werner Fassbinder's *Fear Eats the Soul* is a realistic portrait of particular problems that are prevailing in the working-class milieu of contemporary Germany. It tells the story of Ali, a lonely Moroccan mechanic, who is befriended by Emmi, a lonely widowed cleaning lady years older than he. Despite the hostility that surrounds them, the relationship blossoms into love and marriage, whereupon the couple are reviled and pilloried by the community. The film explores racial, and other, prejudices in a clear and accessible narrative and, as played by El Hedi Ben Salem and Brigitte Mira, is a salutary and heartbreaking experience for audiences.

Brigitte Mira and El Hedi Ben Salem in Fassbinder's painfully honest film.

Bertrand Blier takes French cinema into new field

Patrick Dewaere, Gérard Depardieu.

Dewaere, Miou-Miou and Depardieu in Blier's ***Going Places (les Valseuses).***

Paris, 20 March

Bertrand Blier's third feature, *Going Places* (*les Valseuses*), could become the film that best represents those socially, morally and sexually liberated young people who emerged from the tumultuous events of May 1968. The director (the son of the well-known roly-poly screen actor Bernard Blier) has adapted his own 1972 novel, the French title of which is slang for testicles. The movie's "heroes" are two young layabouts (Gérard Depardieu and Patrick Dewaere), who steal cars and break into houses, usually as a prelude to abducting, seducing and otherwise exploiting women. While they're on the run, they take up with a sexy but frigid hairdresser (Miou-Miou) with whom they form a strange *ménage à trois*. (Dewaere's character has had an accident that makes him impotent.) They also come across Jeanne Moreau as a just-released jailbird. Blier follows his amoral protagonists in a jaunty manner – Stéphane Grappelli's swinging score undercutting the anarchic situations – without condemnation or praise, though the charm of the actors incline to the latter. Although this is his 15th movie, 25-year-old Gérard Depardieu only now reveals himself as a star of the future, as do Dewaere, a year older, and 24-year-old Miou-Miou, who had been spotted in a cafe-theater. *Going Places* is considered to be an important breakthrough in French cinema because of the unconstrained nature of the characters, the sexual scenes and the dialogue. It is certain to be a triumph at the box office even though it is forbidden to those under 18 years of age.

'Badlands' heralds new screen talents

New York, 24 March

Terrence Malick, who impressed last year with his screenplay for Stuart Rosenberg's modern Western *Pocket Money*, has turned director with *Badlands*. The film is based on the true story of a pair of young delinquents who embarked on a killing spree in the 1950s Midwest. The great spaces of the American heartland are the backdrop to the doomed rebellion of simpleminded smalltown cheerleader Sissy Spacek and brooding, denim-clad James Dean lookalike Martin Sheen. Malick, a former Rhodes scholar and journalist, counterpoints their world of tawdry dreams with the iconography of the period in a picture of ravishing beauty and studied irony.

The Academy honors Langlois and Truffaut

Los Angeles, 2 April

It was gratifying, at this year's Oscar celebrations, to see the Academy honoring the contribution of foreigners to the film industry. The Swede Sven Nykvist won the Best Cinematography award for Ingmar Bergman's film *Cries and Whispers*, François Truffaut's *Day for Night* was the Foreign Language Film winner, and Henri Langlois, the head of the French Cinémathèque, received an honorary Oscar. Back on home ground, *The Sting* took seven awards, including Best Film and Best Director (George Roy Hill). Jack Lemmon was Best Actor for *Save the Tiger*, while Glenda Jackson won her second Best Actress prize for *A Touch of Class*.

Martin Sheen and Sissy Spacek in Terrence Malick's outstanding debut film.

Gene Kelly delivered the speech of tribute to Henri Langlois.

Paul Newman and Robert Redford, stars of George Roy Hill's ***The Sting.***

Fellini's world of memory and imagination

***Amarcord**: a trip back into childhood memories during Italy's fascist era.*

Rome, 5 April
The title of Federico Fellini's latest film, *Amarcord*, in Roman dialect means "I remember". This is related to the director's own memories of his childhood in the seaside town of Rimini, where he was born. Fellini has already dealt, more realistically, with his early days in the town in *I Vitelloni* (1953), and touched on his youth elsewhere, but *Amarcord* is his most affectionate semi-autobiographical film. It is an often dream-like vision of the past, as well as a bawdy, funny and melancholy one. The episodic screenplay revolves around one family during the fascist era in the 1930s. It consists of an irascible anti-fascist father, a domineering, long-suffering mother, her layabout brother, a petomaniac grandfather, an insane uncle and Titta, the sex-obsessed teenage son. The parade of inhabitants of the town includes Gradisca (Magali Noël), a seductive hairdresser, who dreams of marrying Gary Cooper some day. Among the inspired set pieces is the visit of an Emir and his harem to the local grand hotel, a youth rally to greet Benito Mussolini, and the vision of the *Rex*, an immense transatlantic luxury liner looming into view to the delight of the townspeople in their small boats. Nino Rota's distinctive music and Danilo Donati's impressionistic art direction add to that very special Fellini flavor.

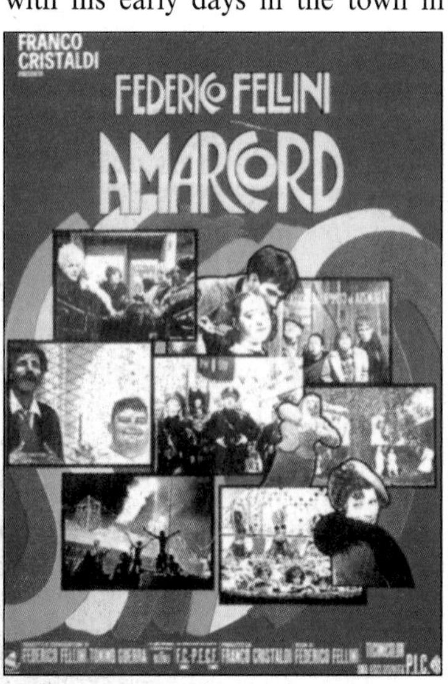
FRANCO CRISTALDI
FEDERICO FELLINI
AMARCORD

*Fellini has said that **Amarcord** is drawn from his own experiences.*

Coppola, Spielberg impress Cannes jury

*Gene Hackman stars in **The Conversation**, an insight into conspiracy.*

Cannes, 24 May
Two young American directors have figured strongly at the Cannes Festival this year, one of them already established and the other a feature film debutant. Francis Ford Coppola, whose *The Godfather* made such an impact a couple of years ago, has now offered a much smaller-scale but no less impressive work with *The Conversation*. This intriguing post-Watergate thriller, about an expert in bugging devices who investigates a murder plot, won the Grand Prix. Gene Hackman is splendid as the eavesdropper being bugged himself, and Coppola moves seamlessly from the physical to the metaphysical. After the mark he made with the made-for-TV *Duel* in 1971, the 27-year-old Steven Spielberg has come up with his first feature work, *The Sugarland Express*, for which Hal Barwood and Matthew Robbins gained the best screenplay award. Like *Duel*, it is also about a chase, this time a true story of a young couple (Goldie Hawn and William Atherton) pursued along the highways of Texas. The winner of the Special Jury Prize was Pier Paolo Pasolini's *The Arabian Nights*, the final and best segment of his trilogy of classic story cycles, following *The Decameron* (1971) and *The Canterbury Tales* (1972). Shot in Yemen, Eritrea, Iran and Nepal, the film captures the beauty (landscape and people) of those countries, retaining the magical and erotic spirit of the original tales, untramelled by European religious guilt.

*At Cannes, Alain Resnais (second right) paid special tribute to Charles Boyer (left) for **Stavisky**. Also here, Jean-Paul Belmondo and Anny Duperey.*

Burton and Taylor: the end of a legend

Burton and Taylor in Zeffirelli's film version of ***The Taming of the Shrew.***

New York, 17 June
Elizabeth Taylor and Richard Burton, who since 1964 have been the most famous married couple in the world, have divorced. Their separation was announced last autumn. At the time Taylor was living in a New York hotel and seeing a great deal of one Henry Wynberg, a former dealer in second-hand cars. The divorce will be a costly business for Burton, who will have to pay over $7.5 million to Taylor. The dubious honor of the record in this field is held by Dean Martin, who made a settlement of $8.2 million with his former wife Jeannie in 1972. Taylor will also keep the celebrated $5 million diamond which Burton gave her. The last picture Taylor and Burton made together had a prophetic title, *Divorce His, Divorce Hers*. Taylor will shortly begin work on a new film, *Ash Wednesday*.

Polanski's 'Chinatown' murky and corrupt

New York, 28 August
Like many European directors who preceded him, Roman Polanski has realized his dream of making an American *film noir* with *Chinatown*.

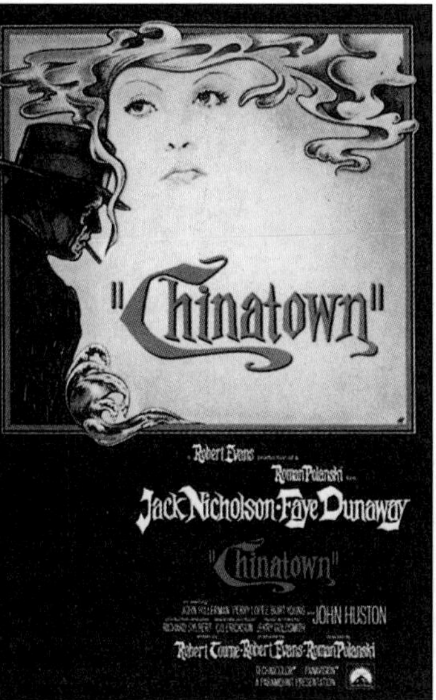
"Chinatown"
Jack Nicholson·Faye Dunaway
"Chinatown"

Set in Los Angeles in 1937, it has an extremely complicated plot, in which crimes and corruption are unpeeled like onion skins as it runs its gripping 131-minute course, with a murder on the outside and a land-grabbing fraud at the core. The film stars Jack Nicholson as Jake Gittes, a gumshoe who suspects and then protects a beautiful widow (Faye Dunaway at her most icily glamorous), whose tycoon father (John Huston) is plotting to control L.A.'s water supply. Not long into the film, Nicholson has a nostril slit by one of the villainous Huston's pint-sized henchman (portrayed by Polanski himself), and has to play the rest of the movie with a conspicuous white band-aid covering his nose. It is a visual coup which makes Nicholson's drily humorous character even more memorable. Polanski has created a murky world, haunted by the past, both of its setting and that of the cinema itself.

Beatty stars in chilling political thriller

New York, 19 June
Paranoia seems contagious these days. The latest Hollywood movie to deal with the helplessness of the individual against state or corporate power, or an unholy alliance of the two, is Alan J. Pakula's political thriller *The Parallax View*. Here, in a variation on the theme of the assassination of John F. Kennedy, investigative journalist Warren Beatty infiltrates a sinister organization only to discover that he has been set up as a patsy for another assassination, an outcome suggested in the picture's opening shot, where the camera tracks past a totem pole to reveal a tower block, and the title itself – a parallax is an apparent change in the position of an object caused by a change in the position of the observer. It seems you can't trust anybody these days.

There is no conspiracy.
Just twelve people dead.
WARREN BEATTY
"THE PARALLAX VIEW"
A superior conspiracy thriller.

Chahine, the symbol of hope for Egypt

Cairo, 26 August
Imprisoned in a cage by the Egyptian censors for more than a year, *The Sparrow*, directed by Youssef Chahine, has finally been released, thanks to a formidable mobilization of Egyptian intellectuals in favor of the film and its director. Its showing here is a cultural event of major importance. In fact, it is the first film to make reference to the Six Day War of 1967, which the Arabs lost to Israel. Several parallel stories are told through the eyes of ordinary people, their suffering, their mourning and their anger during the week that shook the Arab world. They gather in a house from where a sparrow – symbol of the Egyptian people – is released. Stylistically adventurous, the film is politically explosive in that it attempts to show how the war was lost from within the country, as well as being a cry for solidarity among the oppressed. Chahine's pleas are couched in an imaginative cinematic language that grips the attention while making its didactic points powerfully. Egyptian cinema has found its voice.

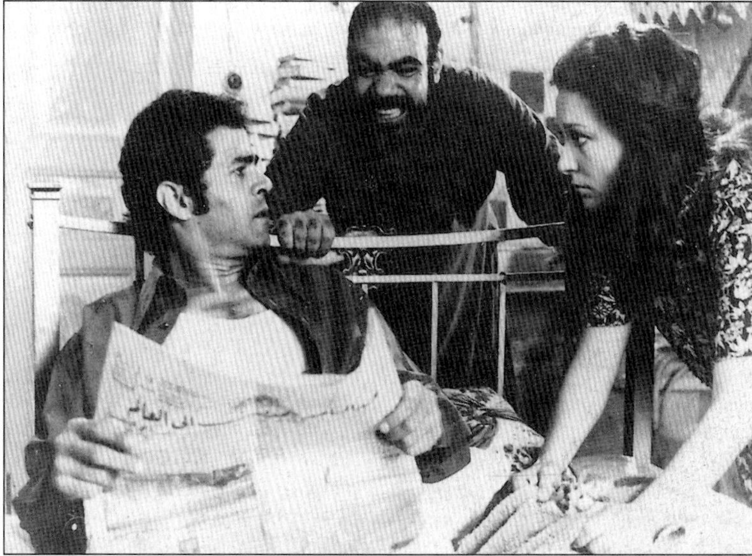
*With **The Sparrow**, Chahine has brought a new forcefulness into Arab cinema.* ▷

French screens are assailed by pornography

Paris, 28 August
The announcement yesterday by President Valéry Giscard d'Estaing of the lifting of most film censorship has particularly delighted the producers and distributors of pornographic movies, a side of the industry which is flourishing. In fact, the mode for porno has been in full swing for some time, and business has never been better. Some of the better porno movies have left the "ghetto" of specialized theaters, even making it to the prestigious picture palaces along the Champs-Elysées, as well as to those cinemas in the Latin Quarter usually designated for art movies. This has been the case with *Emmanuelle*, which is an unprecedented box-office triumph for this type of film since it was released two months ago. In addition, Sylvia Kristel, the 22-year-old Dutch actress in the title role, has become, in a matter of weeks, a real star of the screen. The phenomenal success of this soft-core picture can be attributed to the fact that the producers and the director, Just Jaeckin, chose a professional cast (including an actor of the quality of Alain Cuny), had a relatively large budget, and avoided any hard-core sex scenes. Jean-Louis Richard's screenplay deals with Emmanuelle, the bored wife of a French Embassy official in Bangkok, who is urged by her libertine husband to explore all the possibilities of sex. Thus, she finds herself in bed with, among others, a lesbian archeologist and an elderly *roué*.

A couple of other recent movies deemed soft-core, but from well respected *auteurs*, have followed in the wake of *Emmanuelle*. The latest film by the novelist Alain Robbe-Grillet, *Glissements progressifs du plaisir*, slides progressively further along the porn road than his previous ventures into erotic fantasy. And just released today is Walerian Borowczyk's *Immoral Tales*, reflecting the Polish director's fascination with the iconography of erotica and the emotions that lie beneath it. The film tells four stories, each situated in a different century. One involves Lucrezia Borgia's seduction of Pope Alexander VI, and another a virgin discovering masturbation.

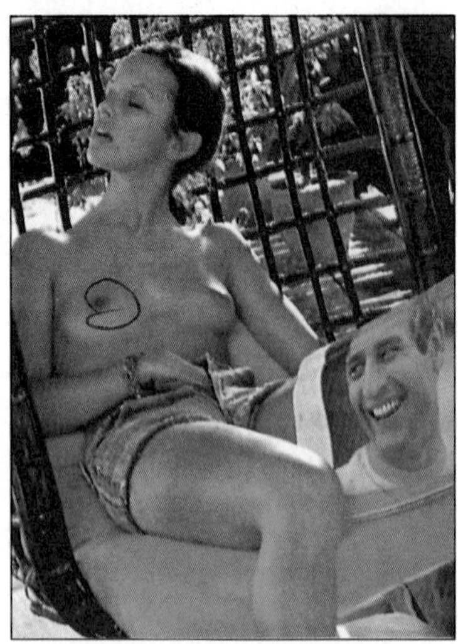

Inspired by Emmanuelle Arsan's controversial novel, ***Emmanuelle****, made by Just Jaeckin is already a genre prototype.*

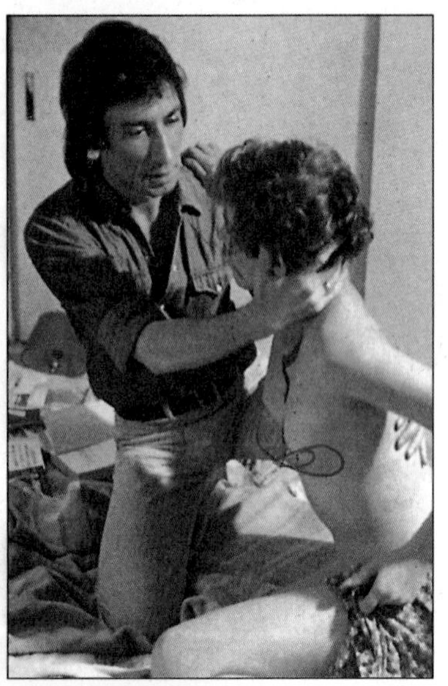

The first version of François Jouffa's **la Bonzesse** *was initially rejected by the censors. Its release has now been allowed.*

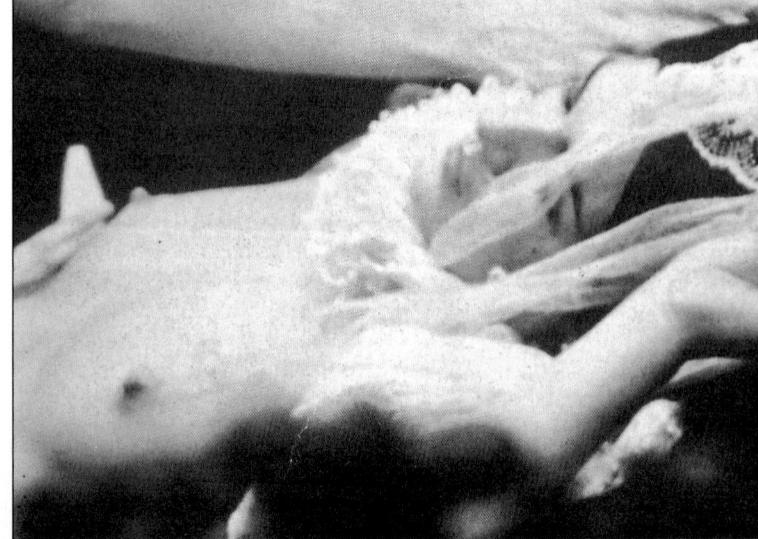

Immoral Tales*, directed by Walerian Borowczyk with Paloma Picasso, reveals the director's fascination with erotica.*

An orgy of blood and gore in Texas massacre

Philadelphia, 18 October
Director Tobe Hooper, who as a child gorged himself on films in his father's Texas cinema, serves up a bloody feast in *The Texas Chainsaw Massacre*. It's a grisly tale of travelers in rural America who fall into the clutches of a hellish inversion of the all-American family – three ghoulish brothers and their blood-sucking skeleton of a father. Like *Psycho*, the movie owes something to the real-life career of the "Wisconsin Ghoul", mass murderer Ed Gein, but it derives its considerable power from Hooper's assured camerawork and editing – the sensational title belies the fact that there is very little on-screen bloodletting – and an eerie *musique concrète* score which Hooper co-wrote with Wayne Bell. In part the film is a heavily ironic comment on the perversion of the "pioneer" ethic beloved of Americans: its deranged latter-day "frontiersmen" decorate their cabins with severed limbs and hunt humans rather than buffalo.

Marilyn Burns in Hooper's shocker about a murderous psychopathic family. The film was made for less than $200,000.

New York subway paralyzed with terror

New York, 2 October
At the best of times the New York subway is a hostile environment, but it becomes positively lethal in Joseph Sargent's pulsating thriller, *The Taking of Pelham One, Two, Three*. A gang led by ruthless Robert Shaw hijacks a subway train and holds its passengers hostage while demanding that a million dollars in cash be delivered within the hour. Can Walter Matthau's Transport Authority man thwart them? Peter Stone's cracking screenplay, adapted from John Godey's bestseller, swoops from black comedy to heart-stopping thrills while Sargent screws the tension up to breaking point.

Robert Shaw in the subway in ***The Taking of Pelham One, Two, Three.***

Disaster becoming a new Hollywood genre

New York, 18 December
Movie companies have been rediscovering a genre which was popular in the late 30s, when such titles as *San Francisco* (1936) with its 1906 earthquake climax, *The Good Earth* with its plague of locusts, and *The Rains Came* (1939) rated highly with audiences. Now, able to take advantage of the latest advances in special effects, the Hollywood studios are once again promoting disasters in a big way. Universal intitiated the new cycle with the highly successful *Airport* in 1970, and Fox followed with *The Poseidon Adventure* in 1972. Now things have been really heating up with the release of *Airport 1975* and *Earthquake*, which introduces a new sensation to movie audiences – seats equipped to shake at key moments in the film so filmgoers can share the sensations experienced by the actors on the screen. Most recently we have been treated to *The Towering Inferno* in which a starry cast, that includes William Holden, Faye Dunaway and Fred Astaire, are trapped by fire in the penthouse restaurant at the top of the world's tallest building.

Guillermin's ***The Towering Inferno.***

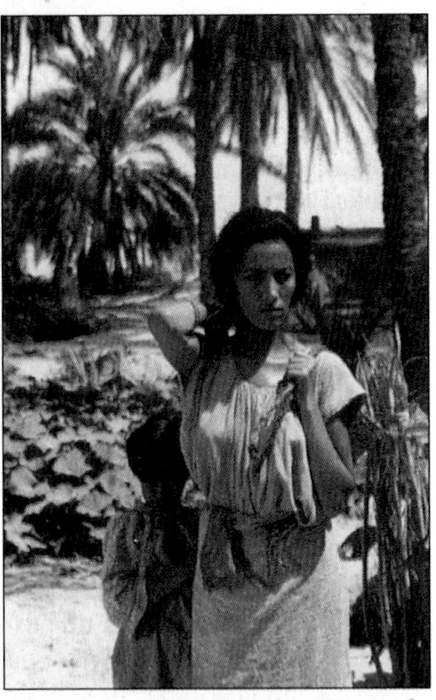

***Chronicle of the Burning Years**, by Mohammed Lakhdar-Hamina*

*Bruno S. in Werner Herzog's **The Enigma of Kaspar Hauser**.*

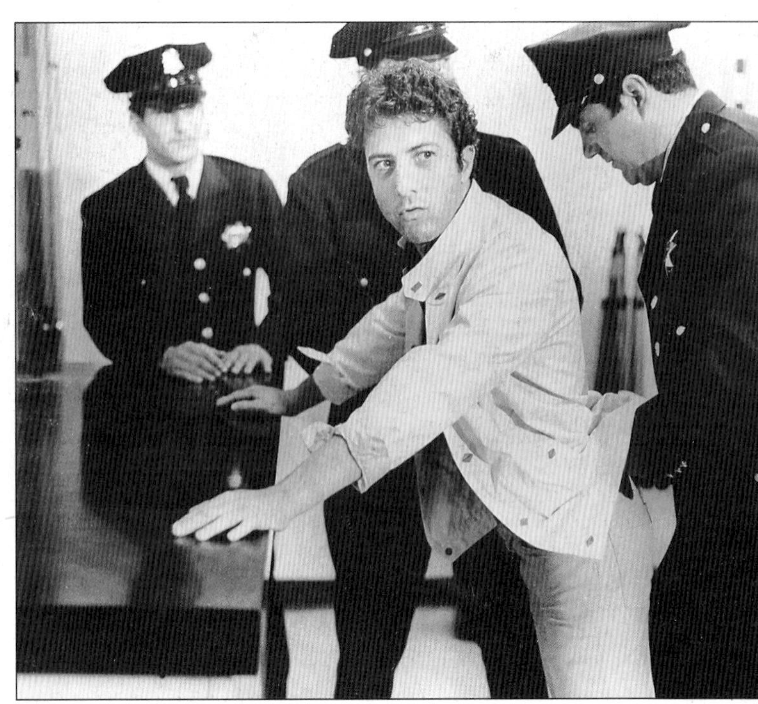

*Anarchic comedian Lenny Bruce (Dustin Hoffman) in trouble in **Lenny**.*

*Richard Dreyfuss is waiter Duddy and Micheline Lanctot is chambermaid Yvette in Ted Kotcheff's **The Apprenticeship of Duddy Kravitz**.*

*David Drach, Marie-José Nat (both right) in Michel Drach's **les Violons du ba***

*Peter Boyle (l) and Gene Hackman in Mel Brooks' spoof, **Young Frankenstein**.*

*The avant-garde French theater director Ariane Mnouchkine's **1789**.*

Elliott Gould (left) and George Segal in Robert Altman's **California Split**.

Sean Connery in Boorman's **Zardoz**.

Brian De Palma's rock/pop remake, **Phantom of the Paradise**.

Phase IV: Designer Saul Bass directed this sci-fi movie in the Arizona desert.

Gena Rowlands is **A Woman Under the Influence** for spouse John Cassavetes.

Jack Lemmon, Walter Matthau in Billy Wilder's remake of **The Front Page**.

Mrs. Hubbard (Lauren Bacall) explaining to Hercule Poirot (Albert Finney) that a knife was found in her handbag in **Murder on the Orient Express**.

1975

1974 Academy Awards, Dorothy Chandler Pavilion, 8 Apr.

Best Film:	*The Godfather Part II* (dir: Francis Ford Coppola)
Best Director:	Francis Ford Coppola
Best Actor:	Art Carney *(Harry and Tonto)*
Best Actress:	Ellen Burstyn *(Alice Doesn't Live Here Anymore)*
Best Supp. Actor:	Robert De Niro *(The Godfather Part II)*
Best Supp. Actress:	Ingrid Bergman *(Murder on the Orient Express)*

Paris, 1 January
Isabelle Adjani has left the Comédie-Française. After the success of *The Slap (la Gifle)*, the young actress is preparing to film *The Story of Adèle H.* (*l'Histoire d'Adèle H.*) with director François Truffaut.

Paris, 21 January
President Valéry Giscard d'Estaing, who was so moved by seeing Marcel Carné's *le Jour se lève* (*Daybreak*) (1939) on television, has invited the cast to lunch at his official residence, the Elysée palace. Actor Jean Gabin is the only one to have refused the invitation.

Los Angeles, 22 January
Superior Court Judge Norman R. Dowds today lifted a temporary restraining order against a segment of *Hearts and Minds*, a documentary produced by Bert Schneider and Peter Davis about the Vietnam War. Walt W. Rostow, national security advisor to President Lyndon B. Johnson, had tried to bar the use of an interview of himself, which he feels is damaging to his image.

Avoriaz, 26 January
At the closing ceremony of the third International Fantasy Film Festival, the main prize was awarded to the musical horror film, *Phantom of the Paradise*, a satirical rock opera from director Brian De Palma.

Paris, 29 January
Patrice Chéreau has released his first film *The Flesh of the Orchid (la Chair de l'orchidée)*, based on a James Hadley Chase novel, with Bruno Cremer, Simone Signoret, Edwige Feuillère and British actress Charlotte Rampling.

New York, 31 January
Lawyers for the Walt Disney Co. have filed a suit to have the "Mickey Mouse Club" song removed from the soundtrack of the pornographic film, *The Happy Hooker*. The music is played during an orgy scene.

Cairo, 3 February
Millions of fans took part in the funeral procession of Oum Kalsoum through the streets of Cairo today. The singer-actress, who is better known to her faithful following as the lady of Arab song and the star of the East, became famous through radio in the early 20s, and although she made relatively few films, those she did appear in were greatly appreciated by the public.

New York, 16 April
Variety has announced that Universal intends to run a TV advertising campaign with prime-time viewing spots for the release of *Jaws*. This method replaces the usual step-by-step approach. The studio feels that the high initial investment will prove economically worthwhile.

New York, 5 May
The Lincoln Center Film Society has paid tribute to Paul Newman and his wife Joanne Woodward for their contribution to the cinema.

Los Angeles, 25 May
The American Film Institute has organized a ceremony for the release of a new postage stamp honoring the memory of D.W. Griffith.

New York, 18 June
The American Legion has protested against, and is asking for a boycott of, the documentary about Vietnam *Introduction to the Enemy*. The film is co-directed by Haskell Wexler, Tom Hayden and Jane Fonda.

Hollywood, 7 July
Hollywood appears to have found a new gilt-edged hero to add to its long list of furry and feathered friends – a not-so-friendly, 25-foot-long killer shark. Peter Benchley's *Jaws* is helping to revive an otherwise gloomy year at the box office. According to Universal the film has grossed $25.7 million in box-office receipts around the country since its release on 21 June.

Moscow, 10 July
The absence of an American presence at the film festival here has been noticed. According to Jack Valenti, president of the MPAA, Hollywood's participation in the preceding years' festivals had not produced results worthy of further effort. The impact of American films on the Russian market remains insignificant.

Washington D.C., 13 August
D.W. Griffith's great film, *The Birth of a Nation*, has been declared out of copyright as a result of proceedings started by Epoch Productions against the Museum of Modern Art.

New York, 31 August
Benji, directed and scripted by newcomer Joe Camp, is an unexpected hit. The film has already grossed about $23 million and, judging by the long queues outside the Guild Theater in Manhattan where the picture is currently showing, it looks set to make a killing.

Hollywood, 2 September
John Milius has said that *Apocalypse Now* will be the most violent film ever produced. He has just completed the writing of the script.

Stockholm, 17 September
Ingmar Bergman has received an honory doctorate of philosophy from the University of Stockholm.

Rome, 27 September
Luchino Visconti, who has been in a wheelchair since a fall last April, has started shooting *The Innocent* (*l'Innocente*), based on a novel by Gabriele D'Annunzio, with Giancarlo Giannini and Laura Antonelli.

Botswana, 10 October
Elizabeth Taylor has remarried Richard Burton. Their divorce was made final in June 1974.

Hollywood, 28 October
Actor Charlton Heston has been re-elected chairman of the American Film Institute. George Stevens Jr.'s position as head of this prestigious body has been renewed for another three years.

Hollywood, 3 November
Kathleen Nolan is the first woman to be elected president of the Screen Actors Guild.

Rome, 5 November
The Italian Communist Party has decided to handle all the funeral arrangements for Pier Paolo Pasolini as well as the commemorative service to be held at the Campo dei Fiori. The director was brutally murdered three days ago.

Paris, 21 November
The cinema sex magazine *l'Organe* has been banned.

Paris, 1 December
Joseph Losey has completed the first day of shooting of *Monsieur Klein*, starring Alain Delon.

New York, 15 December
Twentieth Century-Fox's board of directors has decided to go ahead with the production of *Star Wars*. George Lucas has been working on his original script since May 1974 and has finally convinced Alan Ladd Jr., the head of production for the studio, to back the project.

Hollywood, 25 December
Composer Bernard Herrmann has died. He was best known for his imposing film scores for directors Orson Welles and Alfred Hitchcock.

BIRTHS

Los Angeles, 22 February
Drew Barrymore

DEATHS

Los Angeles, 8 March
George Stevens

Los Angeles, 14 March
Susan Hayward

Los Angeles, 10 April
Marjorie Main

California, 13 April
Larry Parker

Los Angeles, 14 April
Fredric March

Los Angeles, 12 December
William Wellman

The British director John Schlesinger, who turned a lethal eye on New York in ***Midnight Cowboy****, dealt perceptively with Hollywood in this film version of Nathanael West's novel.*

BY TRAIN, BY CAR, BY BUS,
THEY CAME TO HOLLYWOOD...
IN SEARCH OF A DREAM.

THE
DAY
OF THE
LOCUST

BYRD

Paramount Pictures Presents
A JEROME HELLMAN PRODUCTION
A JOHN SCHLESINGER FILM

THE DAY OF THE LOCUST

Starring DONALD SUTHERLAND · KAREN BLACK
WILLIAM ATHERTON · BURGESS MEREDITH RICHARD DYSART
JOHN HILLERMAN and GERALDINE PAGE as Big Sister · Based on the Novel by NATHANAEL WEST · Screenplay by WALDO SALT
Produced by JEROME HELLMAN · Directed by JOHN SCHLESINGER · Music Scored by JOHN BARRY · In Color–Prints by Movielab A Paramount Picture

R RESTRICTED

Hairdresser at the service of his customers

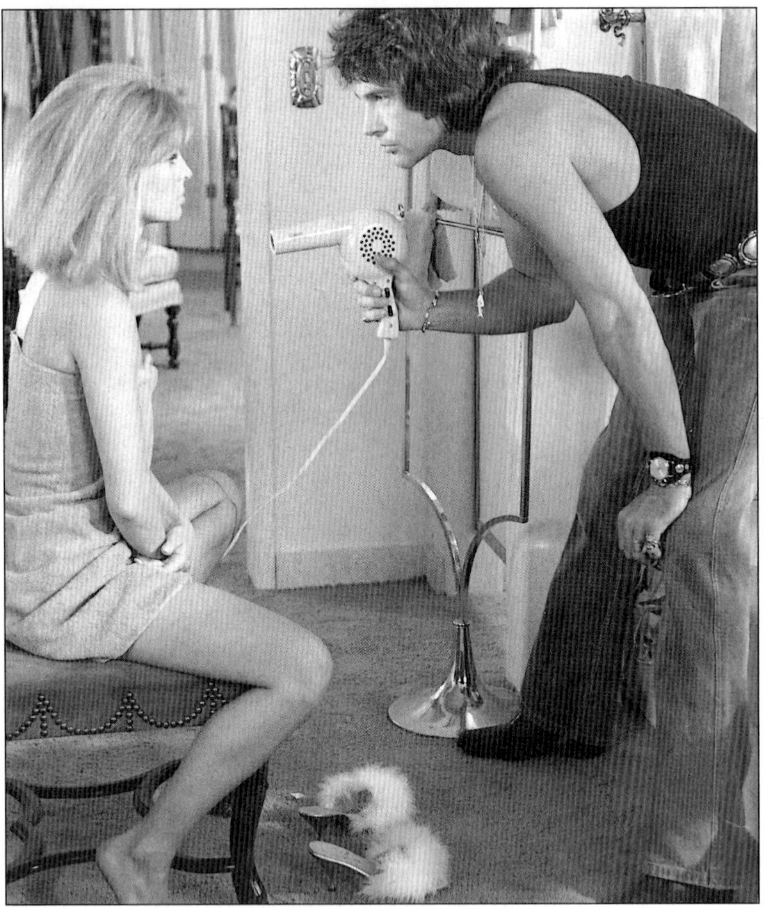

No ordinary hairdresser: Warren Beatty with Julie Christie in Ashby's movie.

New York, 11 February
Warren Beatty's fingerprints are all over his latest picture, *Shampoo*, directed by Hal Ashby. Beatty is the star, producer and, with current hot property Robert Towne, co-writer of this sweet and sour comedy with a political message. Set on the eve of the 1968 presidential election, it follows the amorous adventures of Beatty's hairstylist to the stars (he "does" Barbara Rush) as he gradually grasps the emptiness of his existence. Beatty says the film is not just about "a handful of characters but a whole country in a process of disintegration through hypocrisy and a loss of leadership and values."

The gorgeously corpulent transvestite Divine (center) as criminal nightclub owner Dawn Davenport, partnered by Cookie Mueller (left) as Concetta and Susan Walsh as Chiclett in John Waters' extravaganza of bad taste, *Female Trouble*. Thanks to Waters, Divine, born Harris Glenn Milstead, has fulfilled the dream of all drag artists by becoming a genuine movie star.

Ingmar Bergman's glorious 'Magic Flute'

Ingmar Bergman with Birgit Nordin during the filming of ***The Magic Flute.***

Stockholm, 1 January
Ingmar Bergman took two years to prepare, and nine months to shoot, his adaptation of Mozart's *The Magic Flute*, originally made for Swedish television. The entire opera was filmed in a studio reconstruction of the interior of the exquisite 18th-century Drottningholm Theatre. The production (sung entirely in Swedish) is a model of opera films, respecting the theatrical conventions yet making the experience cinematic. Bergman also demystifies the performers by showing them backstage at the interval, playing chess, reading a comic book and smoking. Despite a few perverse liberties taken with the text, it is an enchanting work, which replaces the darkness and gloom of Bergman's usual world with light and joy.

Francis Ford Coppola dominates the Oscars

Los Angeles, 8 April
The Academy Awards ceremony is now 47 years old, and this year it has been dominated by Francis Ford Coppola's *The Godfather Part II*, which has carried away six Oscars. It was chosen as Best Picture and Coppola was voted Best Director. Coppola shared the Best Screenplay prize with Mario Puzo, and Robert De Niro scooped the Best Supporting Actor Oscar. The picture also won Oscars for score and art direction. The Best Actress award deservedly went to Ellen Burstyn for her performance in *Alice Doesn't Live Here Anymore* as the widow setting off with a child in tow on a voyage of self-discovery. Although directed by Martin Scorsese, the film was very much Burstyn's project. She found the screenplay and reworked it, chose the cast and director and sold it to Warners for 10 percent of the profits. Art Carney was a surprise choice as Best Actor for *Harry and Tonto*, a bittersweet comedy directed by Paul Mazursky. Ingrid Bergman won the Best Supporting Actress award for her performance as a shy spinster in the Agatha Christie tale *Murder on the Orient Express*.

Best Actress Ellen Burstyn in ***Alice Doesn't Live Here Anymore.***

France to have its own 'Oscar'

Paris, 5 April
Three days before the annual American Academy Awards ceremony, Georges Cravenne has announced the creation of a French cousin of Oscar, to be called César after the name of the sculptor who will make the statuettes. These will be presented each year by those in the movie industry to the best French films, performers, directors and technicians. The secret vote will be based on the Academy model in order to keep up the suspense until the last moment. Cravenne has left for L.A. to "spy" on the American event.

Nicholson, Schneider, North Africa: a mesmerizing combination

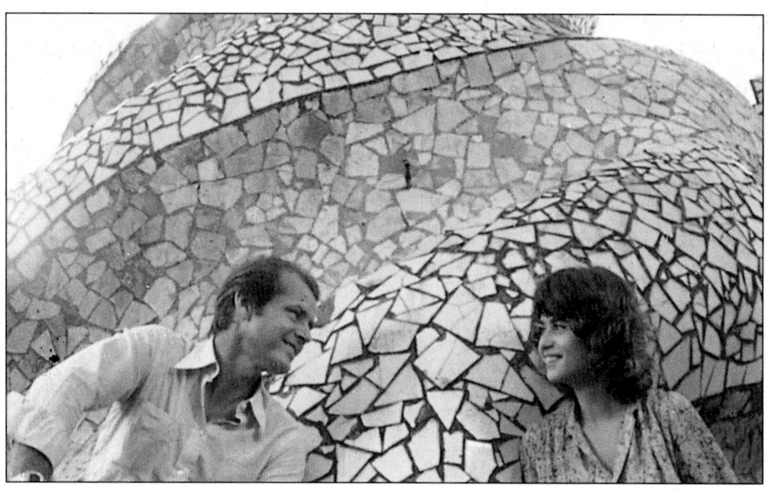
Jack Nicholson and Maria Schneider in Antonioni's odyssey, ***The Passenger.***

New York, 9 April
In *The Passenger*, Michelangelo Antonioni's first film in five years (excepting *Chung Kuo*, a documentary on China), the Italian director has returned to the theme of the search for identity. The mesmerizing and enigmatic film stars Jack Nicholson as a journalist in North Africa, who comes across a dead man bearing a striking resemblance to himself. At the end of his tether, he exchanges passports with the corpse, hoping to lead a new life. In Spain, he meets Maria Schneider, a French girl, with whom he continues his travels. The film ends with a stunning seven-minute single-shot sequence.

Algerian director acknowledged at Cannes

Vittorio Gassman, voted the best actor for ***Scent of a Woman.***

Cannes, 23 May
The winner of this year's top prize at Cannes is *Chronicle of the Burning Years*, from Algerian Mohammed Lakhdar-Hamina. This impressive 175-minute film recounts the history of Algeria from 1939 to 1954, the year the revolution began, through the lives of the inhabitants of two impoverished villages. It's one of the most ambitious and expensive productions to come out of the Third World. The Special Jury Prize was given to *Every Man for Himself and God Against All* aka *The Enigma of Kaspar Hauser*, Werner Herzog's riveting telling of the true story of the strange young man, who suddenly appeared mysteriously from nowhere one day in Nuremberg in the early 19th century.

Chronicle of the Burning Years *directed by Mohammed Lakhdar-Hamina.*

Woody fantasizes on a theme from Tolstoy

New York, 11 June
Woody Allen's new film, *Love and Death*, shows him maturing as a director. Shot mainly in Hungary, it is better constructed and more handsome to look at than his previous four movies. In addition, the film amply demonstrates his preoccupation with the two subjects of the title, albeit through his New York Jewish humor. Allen's opening voice-over, as the leading character, tells us he is about to be executed for a crime he didn't commit. "Isn't all mankind ultimately executed for a crime it never committed?" he asks, then deflates such pretentions by adding a gag line. The film is full of such duality of purpose. Allen's script, a pastiche of 19th-century Russian novels and certain Soviet films (in particular, Eisenstein's), also resembles the kind of period romp which used to feature his idol, Bob Hope. Set in the time and place of Tolstoy's *War and Peace*, Woody plays an inveterate coward called Boris Grushenko, who becomes a war hero in spite of himself in a battle against the French army. He marries his beautiful cousin Sonja (played by Diane Keaton, in her best role to date) and they go to Moscow to assassinate Napoleon. However, Boris can't go through with it because "he's probably someone's grandfather." In one of the rare occasions in comedy, the hero dies, and at the end is seen dancing away with Death, in a Bergmanesque manner.

Woody Allen in the duel scene of his parody on a great Russian novel.

Danger in a seaside resort is good fun

Richard Dreyfuss, Roy Scheider and the terrifying denizen of the deep!

New York, 21 June
In *Jaws*, an adaptation from Peter Benchley's bestseller and directed by Steven Spielberg, a peaceful little New England holiday resort is getting ready to celebrate 4 July when a Great White shark claims its first two victims. When the mayor refuses to close the beaches and lose holiday trade, local police chief Roy Scheider watches helplessly as the shark comes back for more. Enlisting the help of Richard Dreyfuss' breezy shark expert and Robert Shaw's Ahab-like shark hunter, the sea-fearing Scheider sails off to kill the monster. But the hunters soon become the hunted.

'Picnic at Hanging Rock' is unnerving

Anne Lambert is Miranda in Peter Weir's striking Australian mystery story.

Sydney, 9 August
Director Peter Weir, who made his debut last year with *The Cars That Ate Paris*, has followed it with an atmospheric and unnerving mystery, *Picnic at Hanging Rock*. On a turn-of-the-century outing to a huge rock in the Australian outback, three schoolgirls and their teacher vanish. Their disappearance is never explained but it would seem that they have been claimed by the rock itself, a phallic force of nature. Weir skillfully moves from the recognizable world of the girls' school, thrumming with emergent sexuality, to a pagan environment in which "modern" values have no meaning.

Kurosawa and a noble Siberian savage

Tokyo, 12 August
The distinguished Japanese director Akira Kurosawa has recovered from a 1971 suicide attempt to make *Derzu Uzala*, based on the journals of Vladimir Arseniev. Derzu Uzala is a young Russian scientist's guide on a topographical expedition in turn-of-the-century Siberia. In Maxim Munzuk's warm portrait, Uzala emerges as a wily expert in the art of survival, on several occasions saving his Russian employer from a sticky end. In one bravura set piece he constructs a shelter as a storm brews up, rendered magnificently on the 70mm screen with its six-track stereo sound.

Maxim Munzuk, hunter-guide Derzu Uzala, greets Yuri Solomin, the scientist.

Rocking with transvestites in Transylvania

London, 14 August
Richard O'Brien's stage hit, *The Rocky Horror Picture Show*, has been transferred on to the screen by writer-director Jim Sharman. A camp horror movie spoof larded with sex, transvestites and rock music, Richard O'Brien's monster of a musical is located somewhere between Gay Liberation and Z-movie Gothick. Tim Curry reprises his stage role of Frank 'n' Furter, whose annual convention of transvestite Transylvanian aliens is interrupted by the arrival of "straight" couple Brad and Janet, played by Susan Sarandon and Barry Bostwick. Do you want to party, Brad?

Susan Sarandon plays Janet.

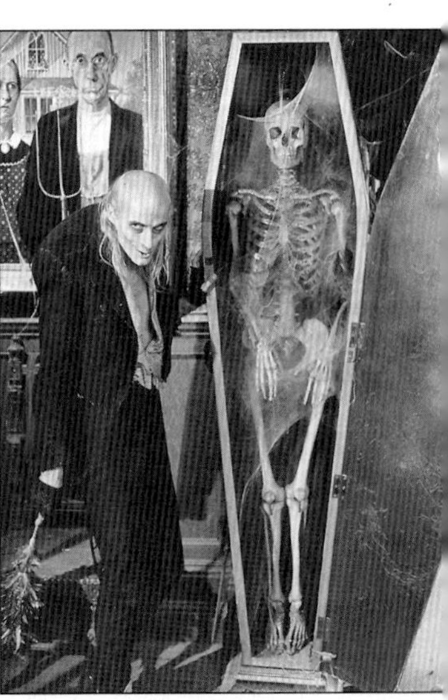

Riff-raff (Richard O'Brien) and pal.

Hollywood comes to elegant Deauville

Ronee Blakely and Henry Gibson entertain in Robert Altman's **Nashville.**

Deauville, 12 September
André Halimi and Lionel Chouchan are the driving force behind the first European festival of American film, which is being held in Deauville, the resort which provided the elegant backdrop to Claude Lelouch's *A Man and a Woman*. Henri Langlois is one of the sponsors of this festival, which declines to award prizes. At Deauville, films are shown but not judged. The program is comprised of seven categories, including works which have yet to be premiered, independent productions and films made for television. Two eagerly awaited films are Robert Altman's *Nashville*, a kaleidoscopic view of the home of American country music, and *Rollerball*, Norman Jewison's view of gladiatorial sport in a future dystopia.

Sad, absorbing chronicle of desperation

John Cazale (left) with Al Pacino, the two ill-fated would-be bank robbers.

New York, 21 September
Al Pacino is up against it in *Dog Day Afternoon*, directed by Sidney Lumet. He has a mountain of debts, an unhappy wife and a male lover who wants a sex-change operation. So he enlists the help of John Cazale to rob a Brooklyn bank. The heist goes horribly wrong and the two men wind up holding the staff and clients hostage while the incident snowballs into a city-wide ordeal. Pacino delivers a mesmeric performance as the loser who begins to relish the notoriety he wins while negotiating with the cops in the sticky heat of a New York summer. It is based on a real-life event (nothing surprises New Yorkers) and has been tautly scripted by Frank Pierson, drawing on an article by B.F. Kluge and Thomas Moore.

Pierre Blaise meets with fatal accident

France, 31 August
The young actor discovered by Louis Malle for the title role in *Lacombe Lucien*, has been killed in a car accident. He was born in 1955 in Moissac, and first worked as a woodcutter. Recently, there had been rumors in the press that he was Brigitte Bardot's new love. Sadly, *Lacombe Lucien*, in which he was so remarkable, remains his only film.

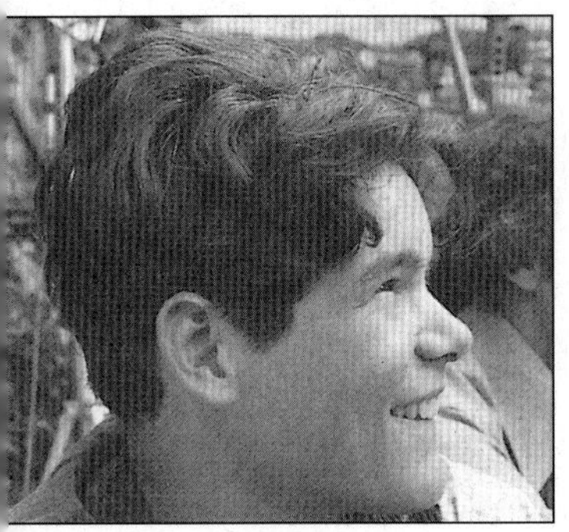

While filming ***Lacombe Lucien.***

Isabelle Adjani plays out the passionate folly of Hugo's daughter

Truffaut, during filming, with his leading lady Isabelle Adjani, who plays Adèle Hugo, in ***The Story of Adèle H.***

Paris, 8 October
François Truffaut has described his new film, *The Story of Adèle H*, as "a musical composition for one instrument." That instrument is the exquisite 19-year-old Isabelle Adjani as Victor Hugo's benighted daughter. Based on Adèle's diary, written in code and decoded in 1955, the film, shot partly in English, concentrates on Adjani in the throes of *amour fou*, as she follows a young English lieutenant from Guernsey to Nova Scotia and Barbados, despite his indifference to her.

Schlöndorff depicts a pitiless era

Munich, 10 October
Volker Schlöndorff's analytical style and a liking for parables is especially suited to social and political subjects as he has previously shown in films such as *The Sudden Fortune of the Poor People of Kombach* (1971), and *Summer Lightning* aka *A Free Woman* (1972), an ironic feminist comedy on divorce, both co-written with and featuring his wife, Margarethe von Trotta. In adapting Heinrich Böll's novel for their latest film, *The Lost Honor of Katharina Blum* (*Die Verlorene Ehre der Katharina Blum*), Schlöndorff and Von Trotta have shifted some of the emphases of the original to make a statement on modern terrorism and police methods in Germany. Nevertheless, Böll's attack on the yellow press remains powerfully intact as the principal theme of the film. Angela Winkler plays Katharina Blum, who spends a night with a young man, a new acquaintance who is, unknown to her, under police surveillance as a left-wing terrorist. The encounter has serious repercussions for her: taken in for questioning, she is released only to find herself mercilessly hounded by the press who turn her into an object of public opprobrium. *The Lost Honor of Katharina Blum* has consolidated the reputation of Volker Schlöndorff, and has added considerably to the prestige of the New German Cinema, unafraid to tackle controversial contemporary political subjects.

Pasolini, the champion of Italian low-life, has been murdered

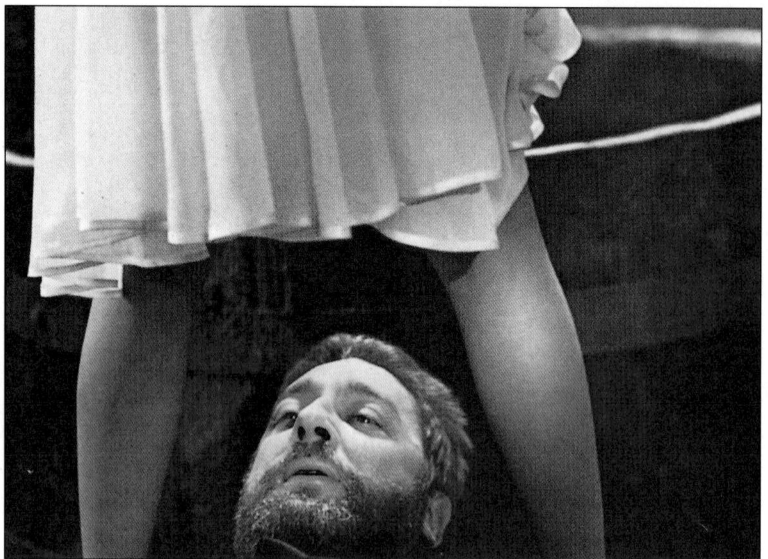

***Salo or the 120 Days of Sodom**, Pasolini's last film, to be shown in Paris.*

Controversial, unpredictable and individualistic, Pier Paolo Pasolini has imposed his ideas through his films.

Rome, 1 November
The film world is stunned by the murder last night of Pier Paolo Pasolini under particularly horrifying circumstances. The Italian director was found this morning, mutilated and disfigured, on the beach near the shantytown at Ostia. The explanation offered that it was a sexual crime seems plausible. Pier Paolo never made a secret of his homosexuality nor of his attraction to the low-life, as depicted in his first feature, *Accatone*. Certain people, however, will rejoice at his death. He was reviled by the extreme right wing, and his last film *Salo or the 120 Days of Sodom* fueled their hatred even more. Pasolini's friends Bernardo Bertolucci, Ettore Scola, Mauro Bolognini and Laura Betti have all expressed their deep sorrow at the loss of this poet of the cinema, dead at the age of 51.

French pornographic films are now a matter for the government

Paris, 5 November
The decree, adopted by the government a week ago, which has decided to exclude X-rated pictures from subsidy, has provoked much anger. According to some politicians, the plan goes against the fundamental non-preferential basis for aid to the cinema industry. A special list of movies which are considered pornographic has been drawn up. There is a risk that a number of films of quality, given an X certificate because of their eroticism, will not receive financial aid. A film such as Walerian Borowczyk's *The Beast* could be deemed pornographic. This would be a scandal, because the film is an astonishing transposition of the *Beauty and the Beast* tale. Among the other recently released erotic films which have a certain artistic ambition, one could cite Just Jaeckin's *The Story of O*.

Angela Winkler as Katharina Blum.

*Corinne Cléry in Just Jaeckin's **The Story of O** from the frank novel.*

*Walerian Borowczyk has gone further than ever in **la Bête (The Beast)**.*

Manic Jack Nicholson brilliant in 'Cuckoo's Nest'

ıcMurphy (Jack Nicholson) in one of his moments of joyful madness.

McMurphy, the hero of the asylum, keeps his fellow inmates entertained.

ɩew York, 20 November

'or his second American movie, xiled Czech director Milos Forman as brought his humor and sharp bservation to bear on *One Flew)ver the Cuckoo's Nest*, derived om Ken Kesey's 1962 counterulture bestseller. Kirk Douglas, who had starred in the dramatization on Broadway, tried for years to get a film version off the ground, but his son Michael and Saul Zaentz pulled it off as producers, at a cost of $3 million. Although the 60s setting of the state mental institution still stands as a metaphor for a conformist society, the film has replaced the novel's drug-induced subjectivity with a more realistic stance. Jack Nicholson is brilliant as the anti-hero McMurphy, fighting the system as represented by Nurse Ratched, played with chilling authority by Louise Fletcher. Nicholson organizes a basketball game, gives a baseball commentary in front of a blank TV, slips porno cards into a playing deck, takes his fellow patients on a truant excursion of deep sea fishing, and generally wakes them out of their apathy. But he is defeated in the end.

ſainted splendor of Thackeray's 'Barry Lyndon'

ɩew York, 20 November

Vith *Barry Lyndon*, director Stanley ubrick has forsaken the ugly fuıre of *A Clockwork Orange* for a)urney back into the 18th century. dapted from a minor novel by Villiam Thackeray, the film follows ıe rise and fall of the Irish adventurer of the title, played by Ryan O'Neal. Deserting the British Army, he marries wealthy widow Marisa Berenson and becomes the master of a great estate. But Barry Lyndon is eventually undone by his own greed and egotism and we leave him alone, poverty-stricken and minus one of his legs. Sadly, one can muster little sympathy for him, as a miscast Ryan O'Neal is simply not up to the task of suggesting the complexities which lie beneath his character's arrogant exterior. While the film lacks a human center it is, nevertheless, an astonishing feat of *mise en scène*, presenting the 18th century through the eyes of the 20th with a painterly precision worthy of the landscape and portrait masters of the period. The price Kubrick pays for his perfectionism is to have created a glittering ornament with a hollow center.

ı sticky moment for Lyndon.

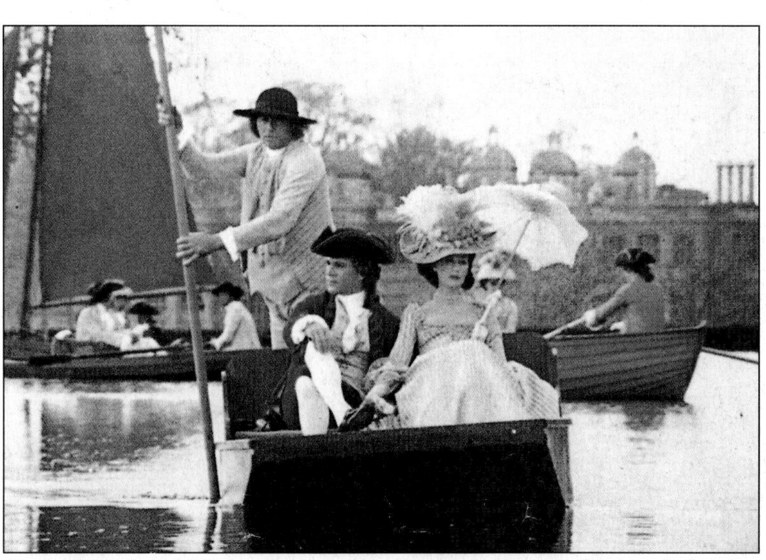

Ryan O'Neal and Marisa Berenson in the visually breathtaking period piece.

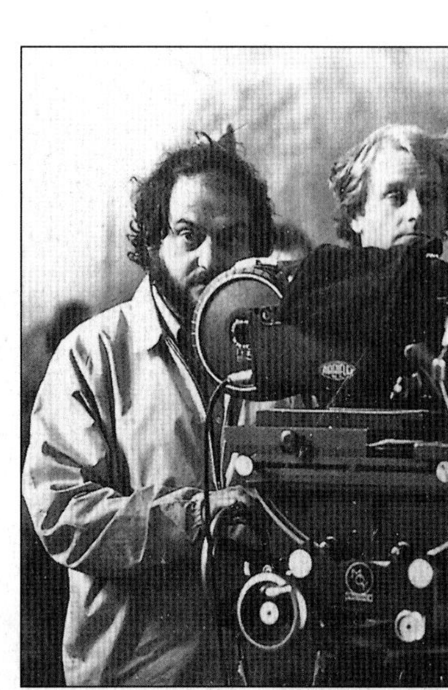

Director Stanley Kubrick at work.

Roberto Rossellini's ***The Messiah*** *with Pier Maria Rossi as Christ.*

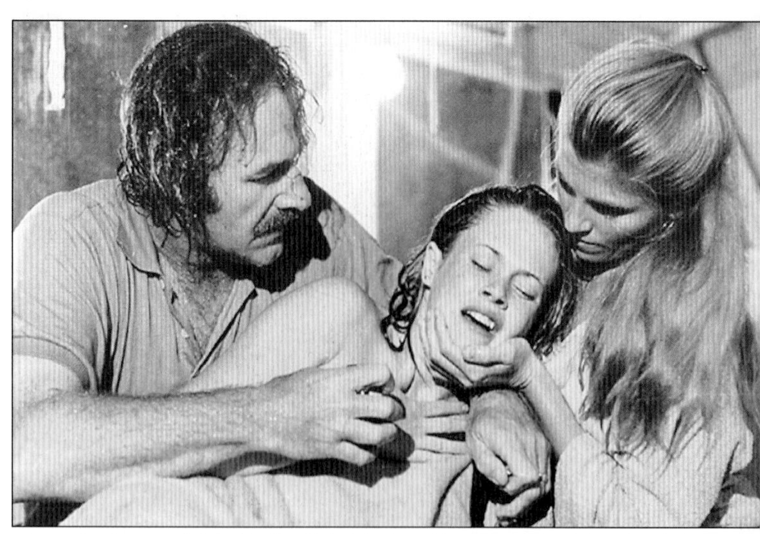

Gene Hackman, Melanie Griffith (c), Jennifer Warren in Penn's ***Night Moves***

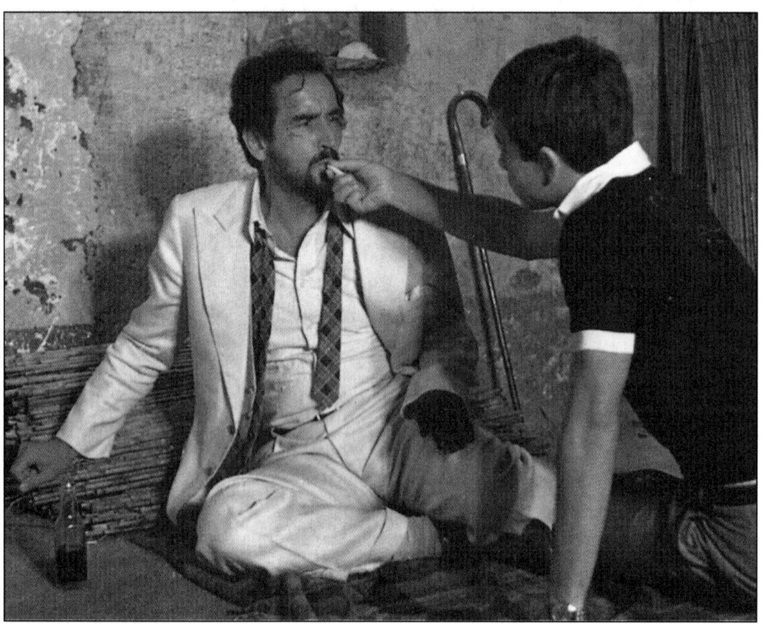

Dino Risi's ***Scent of a Woman*** *with Vittorio Gassman (l), Alessandro Momo.*

Redford as WWI flyer turned aerial stuntman, ***The Great Waldo Pepper****.*

The Lost Honor of Katharina Blum*: Mario Adorf and Angela Winkler (c).*

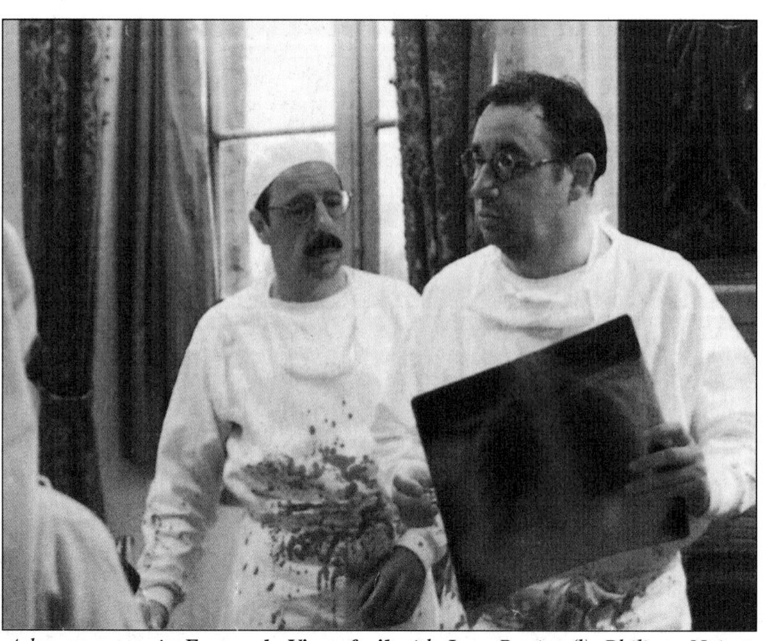

A huge success in France, ***le Vieux fusil*** *with Jean Bouise (l), Philippe Noiret.*

Kati Berek in ***Adoption****, directed by Hungary's Marta Meszaros.*

ean Connery (l) and Michael Caine
The Man Who Would Be King.

Winstanley: *British film historian Kevin Brownlow directed cast of unknowns in haunting tale of 17th-century England.*

PIN BALL LORD
CHAMP
CHAMP
CHAMP

en Russell's rock opera was written by Pete Townshend and The Who. Roger altry (left) is ***Tommy****, and Elton John is the Pinball Wizard.*

Daniel Olbrychski (center) in ***Land of Promise*** *from Poland's Andrzej Wajda.*

ajos Balazsovits (right) in Miklos Jancso's ***Private Vices and Public Virtues****.*

Ryan O'Neal is Thackeray's 18th-century gentleman of fortune, ***Barry Lyndon****.*

1976

1975 Academy Awards, Dorothy Chandler Pavilion, 29 Mar.

Best Film:	*One Flew Over the Cuckoo's Nest* (dir: Milos Forman)
Best Director:	Milos Forman
Best Actor:	Jack Nicholson *(One Flew Over the Cuckoo's Nest)*
Best Actress:	Louise Fletcher *(One Flew Over the Cuckoo's Nest)*
Best Supp. Actress:	George Burns *(The Sunshine Boys)*
Best Supp. Actress:	Lee Grant *(Shampoo)*

Manila, 2 March
Francis Ford Coppola has arrived in the Philippines to shoot the location scenes for *Apocalypse Now.*

Paris, 2 March
Release of *The Best Way to Walk* (*la Meilleure façon de marcher*), the first full-length film directed by Claude Miller, who was formerly assistant to Jean-Luc Godard and François Truffaut.

Tennessee, 3 March
The trial involving the film *Deep Throat* has started in Memphis. Eleven people are being charged with "conspiring to distribute obscene material from one state to another". In several states the film has already been the object of 11 trials; in eight of them the film was exonerated from the obscenity accusations.

Paris, 17 March
Release of François Truffaut's latest picture, *l'Argent de poche* (*Small Change*), with Virginie Thévenet, Jean-François Stévenin and numerous children and teenagers, among them the director's two teenage daughters, Eva and Laura Truffaut.

Westchester, 11 April
Frank Sinatra was photographed at a concert in the company of two notorious Mafiosi, Carlo Gambino and Paul Castellano.

Stockholm, 22 April
Ingmar Bergman announced today that due to tax problems he could no longer live in Sweden. He said that he had been harassed and humiliated by "prestige-seeking poker players" in the tax bureaucracy. He plans to continue his work abroad.

Salt Lake City, 27 April
A document purporting to be the will of Howard Hughes has been left by an unknown person at the Mormon Church's headquarters. One of Hughes' assistants has referred to it as "a very clever forgery."

Argentina, 27 May
The Argentinian film director Raymundo Gleyser has been arrested by the death squad.

Hollywood, 10 June
The American cinema magnate, Adolf Zukor, has died at the venerable age of 103. Zukor's life was a true rags-to-riches success story. Born in Hungary, he was selling rabbit skins in the streets of New York at the age of 16. By the time he was 30 he had started buying up penny arcades to transform into nickelodeons. The creator of Famous Players Pictures, he became head of Paramount in 1935.

California, 1 July
One of the most uniquely told stories of the American Bicentennial opens to the public today at the Smithsonian Institute. Filmed in IMAX, the world's largest film format, *To Fly*, the history of American aviation, is a visual and aural experience rather than an historical epic. It will be shown on a screen 75 feet wide and five stories high.

Berlin, 6 July
Robert Altman's *Buffalo Bill and the Indians* has carried off the main prize, the Golden Bear, at the Berlin Festival. Altman, who had in fact written an open letter to the head of the Festival asking that his film be ignored, refuses to acknowledge the version produced by Dino De Laurentiis for European distribution.

Paris, 16 July
Claude-Jean Philippe presented *le Roi des Champs-Elysées* during the Channel 2 program "Ciné-Club". The film, directed by Max Nosseck in 1934, was the only Buster Keaton film to be shot in France.

Karlovy-Vary, 20 July
The main prize at the 20th Festival was awarded to the Cuban director Humberto Solas for his *Cantata of Chile.*

Paris, 30 July
Simone Signoret has managed to finish her autobiography *La Nostalgie n'est plus ce qu'elle était* (*Nostalgia Is Not What It Used To Be*), despite being very busy with the television series *Madame le juge.*

Los Angeles, 23 September
A preview is being held of *Marathon Man*, directed by John Schlesinger and starring Laurence Olivier and Dustin Hoffman.

Washington D.C., 6 October
Congress has brought in a new copyright law to replace that of 1909. It will take effect on 1 January 1978. Protection now lasts for the life of the author plus 50 years. In the case of films only the producer will be recognized as the author.

New York, 14 November
The most popular movie ever shown on American television is *Gone With the Wind.* The film, shown in two parts by NBC last week, was viewed on successive nights by 33.9 and 33.7 million householders.

Jerusalem, 29 October
Simone Signoret, Michèle Morgan, Kirk Douglas and Danny Kaye were part of an honorary committee for the first Jewish Film Festival which is taking place here.

Rome, 1 November
Release of the second part of Bernardo Bertolucci's epic *Novecento (1900).* The film traces the social evolution in the Italian provinces in the early 20th century. Robert De Niro and Gérard Depardieu star.

Los Angeles, 8 November
Premiere of Elia Kazan's *The Last Tycoon*, adapted from the unfinished novel by F. Scott Fitzgerald. Robert De Niro plays the title role, said to have been based, by Fitzgerald, on producer Irving Thalberg.

Los Angeles, 11 November
Universal and Walt Disney Pictures have commenced legal proceedings against the manufacturer and distributor of videotapes, Sony-Betamax, for breach of copyright laws.

New York, 15 November
Michael Eisner, who comes from the television industry, has been appointed head of Paramount.

New York, 30 November
The French film *Cousin, Cousine*, directed by Jean-Charles Tacchella, has been enthusiastically received here by both critics and the public.

Paris, 27 December
According to the results of a survey published by *l'Express* on the subject of film censorship, 65 percent of those questioned agree that some type of control is needed.

BIRTHS

West Hollywood, 16 April
Lukas Haas

DEATHS

England, 13 January
Margaret Leighton

Philadelphia, 23 January
Paul Robeson

England, 5 February
Roger Livesey

California, 11 February
Lee J. Cobb

Hollywood, 12 February
Sal Mineo

California, 13 March
Busby Berkeley

Rome, 17 March
Luchino Visconti

Hollywood, 28 March
Richard Arlen

London, 25 April
Carol Reed

Los Angeles, 2 August
Fritz Lang

London, 19 August
Alistair Sim

France, 15 November
Jean Gabin

Los Angeles, 28 November
Rosalind Russell

Martin Scorsese's ***Taxi Driver****, a dar[k] and violent vision of New York's fa[]miliar 'mean streets', is a commen[t] on the psychological after-effects o[f] the Vietnam War. De Niro dazzles.*

COLUMBIA PICTURES presents
ROBERT DE NIRO
TAXI DRIVER
A BILL/PHILLIPS Production of a MARTIN SCORSESE Film
JODIE FOSTER ALBERT BROOKS as "Tom" HARVEY KEITEL
LEONARD HARRIS PETER BOYLE as "Wizard" and
CYBILL SHEPHERD as "Betsy"
Written by PAUL SCHRADER Music BERNARD HERRMANN Produced by MICHAEL PHILLIPS
and JULIA PHILLIPS Directed by MARTIN SCORSESE Production Services by Devon/Persky-Bright
Columbia Pictures
R RESTRICTED

Renoir receives the Legion of Honor

Paris, 2 January
Françoise Giroud, the secretary of state for culture and communication, has just returned from the U.S. where she decorated Jean Renoir with the Legion of Honor. The ceremony took place at Renoir's Hollywood home last week. Aged 81, the great director is now unwell and confined to a wheelchair. It is three years since Renoir found he could not walk any longer, following the fate of his famous father, Auguste Renoir. He did not remember that Françoise Giroud (under her real name of Gourdji) was continuity girl on *la Grande illusion*, over 40 years ago. At that time, she was taking her first steps as a writer, and claims to have contributed a few lines between Jean Gabin and Marcel Dalio in the final scene. Giroud recalls Renoir telling her, "You have talent, but it is necessary to first learn how to ruin it."

Louis Delluc Prize goes to a thoroughly modern set of cousins

The cool Marie-France Pisier.

Victor Lanoux and Marie-Christine Barrault in Jean-Charles Tacchella's film

Paris, 8 January
The box-office hit, *Cousin, Cousine*, Jean-Charles Tacchella's second picture, has been awarded the Louis Delluc Prize. This charming and polished comedy revolves around two married couples, who meet at a wedding which makes them cousins. Soon, they become entangled with each other's spouses. In the case of Marie-Christine Barrault and Victor Lanoux, they hold on to their virtue in the face of their partners' (Gu[y] Marchand and Marie-France Pisier) adultery, until they decide to g[o] away together. This work gentl[y] pokes fun at the hypocrisy of th[e] French bourgeoisie.

A leisurely and enigmatic road movie

Berlin, 4 March
For 11 weeks, young German director Wim Wenders traveled along the border between West and East Germany with his small team, consisting of his splendid cameraman Robby Muller and his two main actors, Hanns Zischler and Rudiger Vogler. The result is *Kings of the Road*, a complex, subtly comic, buddy-buddy road movie. It follows an itinerant film projector mechanic, and his friend fleeing his family, as they go around the repair circuit. Taking a gloomy view of the present state of German cinema, the film makes direct references to the silent pictures of Fritz Lang and his exile in America. Exile and borders are used both literally and metaphorically, and are conveyed in arresting black and white images.

Lisa Kreutzer and Rudiger Vogler in Wim Wenders' ***Kings of the Road.***

Touching return of an autumnal Audrey

New York, 11 March
Richard Lester's *Robin and Marian*, starring Sean Connery and Audrey Hepburn, was premiered last night at Radio City Music Hall. This elegiac reworking of the Robin Hood legend, its mythic figures in the poignant autumn of their years, was well-received by an enthusiastic audience. However, the reception of this good-looking, well-acted film (made on location in Spain) wa[s] nothing compared to the receptio[n] that met Miss Hepburn's arrival a[t] the theater. This much-loved sta[r] returning after a nine-year absenc[e] from the screen, was greeted b[y] several thousand fans, chantin[g] "We love you, Audrey." The grac[e]fully aging but still beautiful actres[s] who makes a splendid Marian, wa[s] visibly moved to the point of tears

Back with Robin (Connery), Maid Marian (Hepburn) abandoning her habit.

·ainsbourg takes to film with Jane Birkin

·erge Gainsbourg and Jane Birkin during filming of ***Je t'aime moi non plus.***

·aris, 10 March
·erge Gainsbourg has moved from ·nging to directing. The title of his ·rst film, *Je t'aime moi non plus*, ·erives from the song he recorded ·ith his companion Jane Birkin in ·969. Birkin has the starring role, that of an androgynous barmaid who falls in love with a homosexual truck driver in the middle of the desert. Gainsbourg says for him, "Film directing is the culmination of a year of architecture, 18 years of painting, and 17 years of singing."

George Burns, aged 80, gets an Oscar

Los Angeles, 29 March
The greatest delight of this year's Academy Awards ceremony has been the Best Supporting Actor Oscar won by George Burns for his performance in Neil Simon's *The Sunshine Boys*. Vaudeville veteran Burns' last movie was made 37 years ago, but he was perfectly cast in *The Sunshine Boys* as the cranky trouper teaming up with his old partner Walter Matthau for a TV special. Burns' real-life comedy partner, Gracie Allen, died in 1964, but he remains philosophical about his new movie career. Puffing on his trademark cigar, he says. "It couldn't have happened to an older guy." Lee Grant was voted Best Supporting Actress for her performance as one of Warren Beatty's lovers in *Shampoo*. Milos Forman's *One Flew Over the Cuckoo's Nest* won the Best Picture award and Forman was voted the Best Director, while Jack Nicholson took the Best Actor Oscar for his portrayal of the feisty misfit in a mental institution and Louise Fletcher won for Best Actress for her role as the hard-faced nurse who clips his wings. Laurence Hauben and Bo Goldman's Oscar-winning screenplay made *One Flew Over the Cuckoo's Nest* the first film to scoop all five major Oscars since *It Happened One Night*.

Best Supporting Actor George Burns.

·isconti, a great Italian master, is dead

·irector Visconti (right) on the set of his last film, ***The Innocent***, *with Giancarlo ·iannini (left), Jennifer O'Neill and Didier Haudepin.*

·ome, 17 March
·uchino Visconti has died aged 69 ·n his small apartment at 101 via ·leming, where he has lived for the ·st three years. Confined to bed for ·everal days with flu, he died at the ·oment of the day he most loved to ·lm – the twilight. The great Italian ·irector's death has not surprised ·ose close to him, who watched him ·adly getting weaker and weaker since he completed his last film, *The Innocent*, which he directed from a wheelchair. Visconti never fully recovered from an illness that struck him while filming *Ludwig*. Last year, a fall in which he broke a leg did not deter him from completing his swan song. Visconti, born the Duke of Modrone, was a man of contradictions, all of which are reflected in his impressive body of work.

The first César awards ceremony is held

Paris, 3 April
The César awards, the French equivalent of the Oscars, were presented for the first time at a televised ceremony. Robert Enrico, the president of the Academy of Arts and Techniques of the Cinema, asked 950 film professionals to select the best French pictures shown during 1975. Jean Gabin, honorary president for the evening, joined Michèle Morgan on stage to present the first prize to *le Vieux fusil* (*The Old Rifle*), directed by Enrico. Bertrand Tavernier was named best director for *Let Joy Reign Supreme* (*Que la fête commence*). The acting awards went to Romy Schneider in *l'Important, c'est d'aimer*, and Philippe Noiret in *le Vieux fusil*. Winners in supporting roles were Marie-France Pisier for *Cousin, Cousine* and Jean Rochefort for *Let Joy Reign Supreme*, making a total of four Césars for the latter.

Romy Schneider and Philippe Noiret in ***le Vieux fusil****, voted the best film.*

'All the President's Men' causes sensation

Washington Post

Dustin Hoffman, Robert Redford.

New York, 8 April
The political scandal that rocked the world has come to the screen. In *All the President's Men*, Robert Redford and Dustin Hoffman star as Bob Woodward and Carl Bernstein, the *Washington Post* reporters whose investigations into the Watergate break-in played a large part in the downfall of President Nixon. Redford, familiar with political skulduggery since making *The Candidate*, bought the screen rights to Woodward and Bernstein's book for $225,000, brought in Oscar-winning screenwriter William Goldman and persuaded Hoffman to play Bernstein on the strength of his script. Director Alan J. Pakula, whose "conspiracy" films include *The Parallax View*, has delivered the suspense the story demands.

Robert De Niro compelling in 'Taxi Driver'

Cannes, 28 May
The president of this year's Cannes Festival jury, the American playwright Tennessee Williams, has made it known that he considers *Taxi Driver* far too violent. Therefore, it was rather surprising that the Martin Scorsese movie was awarded the Golden Palm. Indeed, *Taxi Driver* is probably the most violent film seen at Cannes, although it is a just reflection of that which confronts America today. The main character, magnificently played by Robert De Niro, is a paranoid loner, alienated from urban society. A Vietnam vet, he sees New York as "an open sewer", stressed by the director's hellish vision of the city. The Special Jury Prize was shared between Carlos Saura's *Raise Ravens* (*Cria Cuervos*), and Eric Rohmer's *The Marquise of O*. Saura's film, a dreamlike attempt to enter the mind of an unhappy child, contains two superb performances from Ana Torrent and Geraldine Chaplin. Rohmer's picture, made in Germany, is an ironic and touching version of the classic Von Kleist novel. Ettore Scola was named best director for the hilarious satire, *Down and Dirty*.

Maria Luisa Santella and Nino Manfredi in Ettore Scola's ***Down and Dirty****.*

Ingmar Bergman's rupture with Sweden

The distinguished Swede with Liv Ullmann while making ***Face to Face****.*

Stockholm, 21 April
The great Swedish director Ingmar Bergman has just left his native land, perhaps permanently. He has good reason to complain about the way he has been treated. According to Bergman, who had been charged with tax evasion, he has been handled like a "vulgar exporter of perishables." It all started last January during the rehearsals for August Strindberg's *Dance of Death* at the Swedish National Theatre. The man who has contributed more tha anyone else to the reputation of th performing arts in Sweden, wa rudely interrupted in his work, an arrested like a cheap crook. He ha now given up his idyllic existenc on the isle of Faro and is living i Germany. In a week's time, *Face t Face*, Bergman's new four-part se ries for Swedish television, will b shown. It will be interesting to gaug its impact on the critics and publi of the country he has abandoned.

Mysterious death of Howard Hughes

California, 7 April
Howard Hughes, the eccentric aviator, oil-tool company heir, film producer and would-be movie mogul, has died at the age of 70. According to *Variety* he was taken ill while on board a chartered airplane, with a doctor in attendance, en route from Acapulco, Mexico, to the Methodist Hospital at Houston, Texas. "Death was attributed to a stroke but, as with nearly all details concerning Hughes in the past 20-odd years, was shrouded in secrecy." A familiar figure in Hollywood in his youth, the producer-director of *Hell's Angels* (1930) and *The Outlaw* (1931) and producer of *Scarface* (1932) acquired control of the RKO studios in 1948, but ran it in such an unpredictable manner that there was little left when he sold out seven years later. In the 60s he became a recluse, inaccessible to all but a chosen few.

Liz and Richard: the saga continues

Los Angeles, 30 April
Having married Richard Burton fo a second time in South Africa i October 1975, Elizabeth Taylor ha divorced him for a second time. Th couple have announced that the sec ond marriage has not fulfilled thei hopes and from now on it would b better for each of them to go thei own way. At the moment nothin seems to be going right for Taylo either romantically or professiona ly. Her latest film, *The Blue Bir* shot in the Soviet Union by Georg Cukor, has been given the thumb down by critics and public alike. I recent weeks Liz has been consolin herself in the company of Irania ambassador Ardeshir Zahed an U.S. Navy Secretary John Warne Doubtless Taylor will not remai alone for long, and the smart mone is on Warner becoming husban number eight.

Aore urban paranoia with Roman Polanski

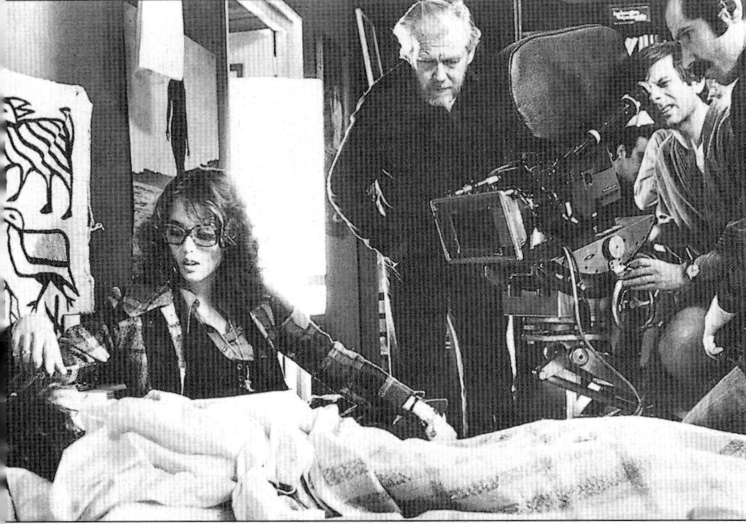

sabelle Adjani, cinematographer Sven Nykvist (center) and Polanski.

'aris, 26 May
)pening today and coming directly rom its warm reception at the 'annes Festival is Roman Polanki's *The Tenant*, with the small 'olish emigré director himself in ıe arduous title role. Indeed, he lays a displaced Pole who moves ıto an apartment in a shabby Paris uilding. He soon discovers, howevr, that the previous occupant had ırown herself out of the window nd is dying in the hospital. After isiting her and tentatively begining a romance with her best friend (Isabelle Adjani), he becomes aware of strange happenings in the house, and he descends into paranoia. Like the figure of K in Kafka's novels, Polanski's Kafkaesque character uncomprehendingly believes himself to be guilty of a crime he has not committed. The atmosphere of the film is subtly created, and the weird events are revealed by the probing camera of Sven Nykvist (Ingmar Bergman's usual cinematographer). Veterans Melvyn Douglas, Shelley Winters, Jo Van Fleet and Lila Kedrova give fine support.

Clint's Josey Wales a superb achievement

Eastwood as the intriguing and courageous hero of ***The Outlaw Josey Wales.***

Los Angeles, 23 August
Clint Eastwood took over the direction of his latest picture, *The Outlaw Josey Wales*, from its co-scenarist Philip Kaufman when the two men fell out over the character of Josey Wales. The result is Eastwood's finest film to date, both as actor and director. He plays a peaceable Missouri farmer whose family is murdered by Unionist guerrillas. He takes his revenge as a Confederate guerrilla, and when the Civil War ends sets off for Texas with a bounty on his head, reluctantly acquiring a motley bunch of companions on the way. They set up a commune which draws Wales back into the world of emotions. At the film's climax, they must defend it against Wales' pursuers. This is a superb Western of epic scope and, thanks to John Surtees' cinematography, great pictorial beauty. Eastwood is supported by some spirited playing, notably from Chief Dan George as a self-mocking Indian ancient, and John Vernon as Wales' compromised Civil War commander, condemned to hunt him down.

'ritz Lang is dead ar from Germany

.os Angeles, 2 August
'he celebrated Austrian-born direcɔr Fritz Lang has died today at the ge of 85. One of the great names 'ho put the German cinema on the ıap in the 1920s with such memoable films as *Der Mude Tod* (*Desny*, 1921) and *Metropolis* in 1927, e fled to Paris when the Nazis came ɔ power in 1933, then moved on to Iollywood where he fitted uneasily ıto the studio system. Though Lang irected a wide variety of projects uring the course of his long career, e will be best remembered for his ırillers, particularly because of his riginality in using the genre to ıake comments on the state of ɔntemporary society, from *Dr. Iabuse Der Spieler* (1922) and *M* 1931), to *You Only Live Twice* 1937) and *The Big Heat* (1953).

Oshima's frank 'In the Realm of the Senses' is badly received

Tokyo, 15 September
One would have thought that the fashion for pornography on Japanese screens was a sign of the easing of censorship in the Land of the Rising Sun. But the problems that have beset director Nagisa Oshima reveal this to be far from the truth. After having been banned, his *In the Realm of the Senses* (*Ai No Corrida*) has finally been allowed a release, but in a maimed version. For example, one sex scene has been cut in order to mask the genitals of the couple. *In the Realm of the Senses* was inspired by an actual criminal case in 30s Japan. A married man and a geisha retreat from the militarist Japan of 1936 into a world of their own where they obsessively act out their sexual fantasies. Finally, in a quest for the ultimate orgasm, she strangles and then castrates him. Although it undoubtedly enters the realm of pornography on occasion, the film treats seriously the link between eroticism and death (a theme previously dealt with a few years ago by Bertolucci in *Last Tango in Paris*). The Japanese title gives an idea of the ritualistic element – "the corrida of love".

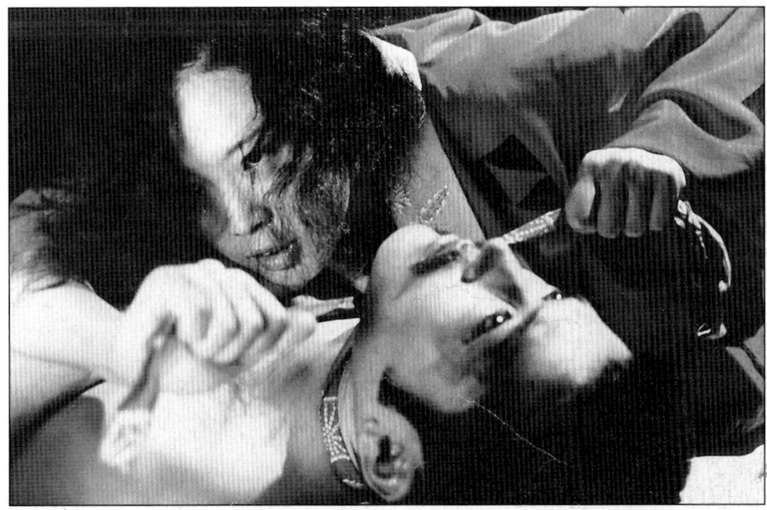

A deadly embrace in pursuit of pleasure: Eiko Matsuda strangles Tatsuya Fuji.

Ball-breaker Dunaway in power game

Peter Finch and Faye Dunaway, caught in the jungle of competitive television.

Los Angeles, 14 November
After working with her on *Chinatown*, Roman Polanski described Faye Dunaway as a "gigantic pain in the ass." With a reputation for being difficult, Dunaway also seems to relish playing the bitch on wheels, and they don't come bitchier than her ruthless TV programming executive in Sidney Lumet's *Network*. She continues to rave about the ratings while bedding understandably dispirited newsman William Holden. Dunaway's is the most incisive performance in writer Paddy Chayefsky's gleeful exposé of the cynical world of television, in which the ailing network of the title exploits newscaster Peter Finch's on-screen breakdown to boost its ratings.

The great Gabin's ashes cast in the sea

*Jean Gabin (left) in his last film **l'Année sainte**, with Jean-Claude Brialy.*

France, 19 November
Five days ago, Jean Gabin, the actor most associated with the golden age of French cinema, died at the American Hospital in Paris where he had been admitted two days earlier. Because he was shocked by the way the press and public had invaded the funeral of Fernandel, he decided not to be buried, but to have his ashes dispersed over the sea, lik those of sailors. During the wa Gabin had been in the navy and ha fond memories of his seagoing day Last Wednesday, the crematio took place at the Père Lachais cemetery, and today his ashes wi be cast into the Irish Sea in th presence of his family and clos friends, among them Alain Delon.

Inarticulate Rocky talks with his fists

New York, 21 November
The B-movie is alive and well, albeit in inflated form, in *Rocky*, the story of a washed-up boxer who gets a million-to-one shot at the world title and self-respect. The story parallels that of *Rocky*'s begetter, named Sylvester Stallone, an obscure actor who shares the pug's blue-collar background. Stallone was offered $300,000 for his script – said to have been written in three days. Although he was broke, he demanded $75,000, a percentage of the profits *and* the lead. He got all three and delivers a performance bursting with the blue-collar heroism beloved of Americans. Director John G. Avildsen captures the smell of sweat as Rocky pounds through the Philadelphia streets on the way to his rendezvous with destiny.

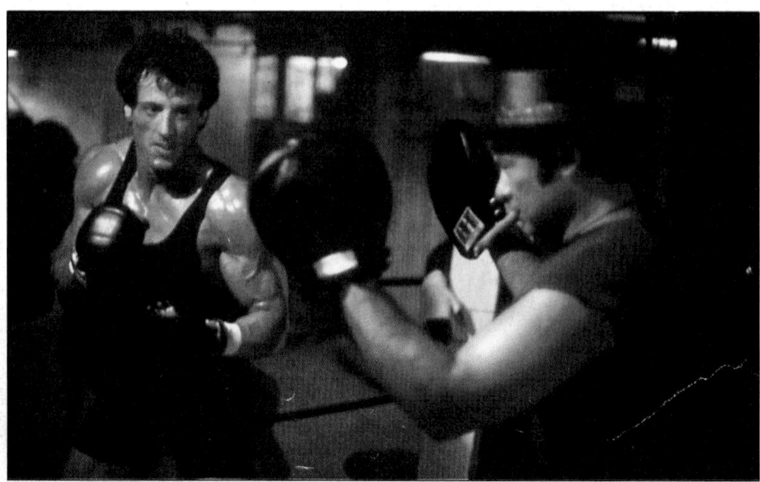

Rocky Balboa (Sylvester Stallone) works out with his trainer (Burt Young).

Hal Ashby tells the Woody Guthrie tal

New York, 5 December
David Carradine convinces as the legendary Depression-era folk singer Woody Guthrie in Hal Ashby's *Bound for Glory*. It recounts his journey from Texas to California, his political activism among fellow migrant workers and his rise to fame through the medium of radio. Ashby, with cameraman Haskell Wexler, evokes the images made famous in the 1930s by photographer Walk er Evans – soup kitchens, hob camps, dust storms and hoppin freight trains – in a film which high on sentiment but skimps o Guthrie's songs. One is reminde that David Carradine's father, Joh Carradine, made a similar gruelin journey in the film of Steinbeck' *The Grapes of Wrath* directed b John Ford.

Woody Guthrie (Carradine) argues with his wife (Melinda Dillon).

ing Kong is back four decades later

King Kong
Dino De Laurentiis presents
a John Guillermin Film
"King Kong"
Jeff Bridges Charles Grodin Introducing Jessica Lange

n tune with the 1970s, the new King Kong lands on the World Trade Center.

ew York, 18 December
am Goldwyn once said, "If they ved it once, they'll love it twice." lamming Sam would have had to at his words over producer Dino e Laurentiis' botched remake of *ing Kong*. Here, newcomer Jessica ange flounders in a feminist ver- ion of the role made famous by Fay Wray. Worse, however, was De Laurentiis's publicity blitz that *his* Kong was a 40-foot robot and a miracle of modern technology. Except for a few shots, the great ape is impersonated by a man in a gorilla suit, designed and worn by makeup man Rick Baker. Willis O'Brien must be turning in his grave.

ollowing in Fay Wray's footsteps, Jessica Lange is abducted by King Kong.

Tanner revives dreams of a better world

*The director during filming of **Jonah Who Will Be 25 in the Year 2000.***

Paris, 1 December
Alain Tanner's new film, *Jonah Who Will Be 25 in the Year 2000*, reveals once again the Swiss director's interest in Utopian possibilities of change. With the English Marxist writer John Berger, Tanner has created that rare species, a polemical comedy. It focuses on the lives of eight people in Geneva – a copy editor, a secretary, a rural worker and his factory worker wife, a farmer and his wife, a teacher and a supermarket cashier, all trying to maintain the ideals of the events of May 1968 in Paris. Far from being mere cyphers, the characters are warmly and vividly portrayed.

Barbra in third version of 'A Star is Born'

New York, 18 December
Barbra Streisand treads a well-worn path in a second remake of *A Star is Born*. This time the background is the world of rock music. Kris Kristofferson and Streisand are the ill-starred couple, her meteoric rise to fame mirrored by his vertiginous fall from grace and descent into alcoholism. A literate screenplay by John Gregory Dunne, Joan Didion and director Frank Pierson, and superlative singing from Streisand, ensure that while comparisons with the Judy Garland-James Mason predecessor are invidious, this new version should keep Streisand fans happy and the box-office busy.

Barbra Streisand and Kris Kristofferson are the unhappy couple this time.

*Underground auteur George Kuchar and Marian Eaton in **Thundercrack**.*

*Austin Stoker is a cop under siege in John Carpenter's **Assault on Precinct 13**.*

*Ana Torrent in Carlos Saura's **Cr Cuervos (Raise Ravens)** (Spain).*

*An overtly stylized ocean decor for **Fellini's Casanova**, a showy but bleak tale.*

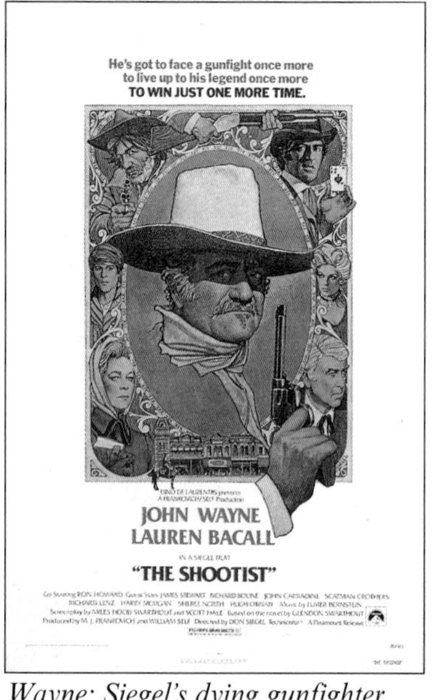
He's got to face a gunfight once more
to live up to his legend once more
TO WIN JUST ONE MORE TIME.
JOHN WAYNE
LAUREN BACALL
"THE SHOOTIST"

Wayne: Siegel's dying gunfighter.

*Cybill Shepherd and De Niro in **Ta Driver** (a Bernard Herrmann score,*

*Left to right: Guy Bedos, Jean Rochefort and Claude Brasseur in **Pardon mon affaire**, a comedy directed by Yves Robert (France).*

WASH
STAY IN CAR

*Richard Pryor (right) is about to have his shoes shined by Clarence Muse (watched by The Pointer Sisters, in Michael Schultz's **Car Wash**.*

'o r: Alec Guinness, Peter Falk and Eileen Brennan in **Murder by Death**.

*Harvey Stevens is Damien in **The Omen**, here with Gregory Peck.*

*Charles Vanel in Italian director Francesco Rosi's **Illustrious Corpses**.*

*obert De Niro as Scott Fitzgerald's **The Last Tycoon** (with Ingrid Boulting).*

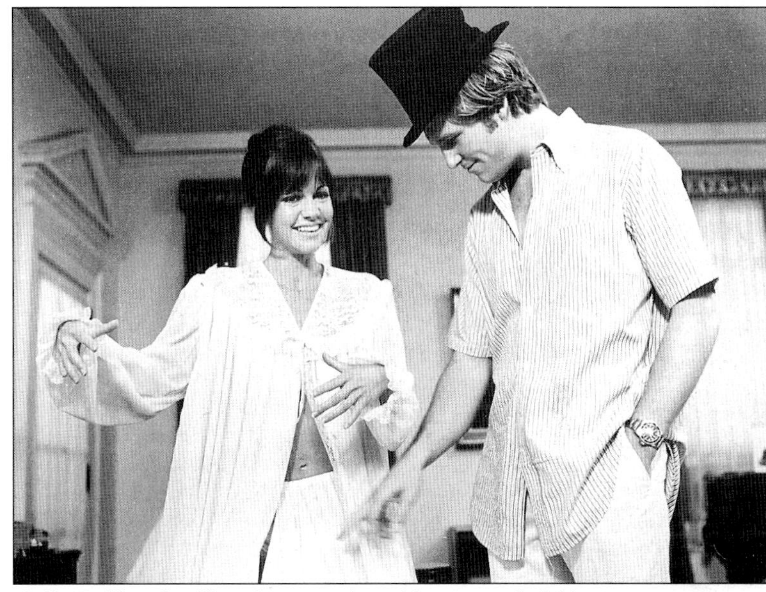

*Sally Field and Jeff Bridges in Bob Rafelson's gentle fable, **Stay Hungry**.*

*mixed reception greeted Michael Anderson's sci-fi excursion, **Logan's Run**.*

*Pop star David Bowie as the alien in Nicolas Roeg's enigmatic, unsatisfying but technically brilliant sci-fi, **The Man Who Fell to Earth**.*

1977

1976 Academy Awards, Dorothy Chandler Pavilion, 28 Mar.

Best Film:	*Rocky* (dir: John G. Avildsen)
Best Director:	John G. Avildsen
Best Actor:	Peter Finch *(Network)*
Best Actress:	Faye Dunaway *(Network)*
Best Supp. Actor:	Jason Robards *(All the President's Men)*
Best Supp. Actress:	Beatrice Straight *(Network)*

Hollywood, 30 January
The acting debut awards at last night's Golden Globe ceremony at the Beverly Hills Hilton went to Arnold Schwarzenegger and Jessica Lange for their respective performances in *Stay Hungry* and *King Kong*. Harry Belafonte hosted the live telecast for Metromedia.

Paris, 7 February
William Friedkin, American director of *The French Connection* and *The Exorcist*, has married French actress Jeanne Moreau, ex-wife of director Jean-Louis Richard.

Paris, 16 March
Release of the film made by Pier Paolo Pasolini in 1964 titled *Comizi d'Amore*. The work is made up of interviews with numerous anonymous couples as well as with famous people such as Alberto Moravia and Antonella Lualdi.

Madrid, 9 April
Sixteen years after it was made, Luis Buñuel's *Viridiana*, with Silvia Pinal and Francisco Rabal, has been released in Spain.

Paris, 25 April
René Féret's *la Communion solennelle*, the chronicle of a family, is the first film to be awarded a prize by the Philip Morris Foundation.

Prague, 2 May
Release of *The Liberation of Prague* (*Osvobozeny Prahi*), the third film in director Otokar Vavra's trilogy depicting the state of the country since the Munich agreements.

Paris, 10 May
Journalists from France Inter, Anne Gaillard and Jean-Edern Hallier said they "seriously doubted whether Simone Signoret actually wrote her own autobiography *Nostalgia Is Not What It Used To Be* (*La nostalgie n'est plus ce qu'elle était*)" (Seuil). The actress has decided to sue the journalists.

New York, 31 May
Rita Hayworth has been made a ward of her daughter, Yasmin, while being treated for alcoholism.

San Francisco, 7 June
Francis Ford Coppola mortgaged all of his personal assets (including his house) as a guarantee for the $10 million loan made to him by United Artists to complete his Vietnam War epic, *Apocalypse Now*.

Hollywood, 20 June
Warner Bros. has modified the ending of John Boorman's *Exorcist II: the Heretic*, following negative reactions from audiences. Instructions were telephoned in by the director from Ireland.

New York, 21 June
A new policy limiting the size, format and content contained in advertisements of pornographic films in the *New York Times*, will take effect on 1 July. The guidelines are as follows: only single-column displays up to an inch in length; content will be limited to the name of the film, the name and address of the theater, the session times and the label "adults only"; no illustrations or other information; no offensive theater names or film titles; no more than one advertisement from any one theater in each issue.

Tokyo, 16 August
Director Nagisa Oshima has been charged with violating the law for publishing a book containing extracts, which have been judged to be licentious, from his film *In the Realm of the Senses.*

Los Angeles, 16 September
David Begelman, the vice president of Columbia Pictures Industries, has denied forging actor Cliff Robertson's signature in order to cash a check made out to Robertson by the studio accountant. The New York head office of Columbia is gravely concerned about the matter.

Paris, 22 September
Director Claude Autant-Lara, who was interviewed for the release of his new film *Gloria*, has analyzed the drop in cinema attendance. According to him, it's Jean-Luc Godard and his New Wave friends who have emptied the cinemas.

Cannes, 1 October
The Festival Board of Directors have named Gilles Jacob as their new general representative.

Washington D.C., 22 October
Postal officials here have ordered the removal of posters depicting Al Jolson made up in blackface from 5,000 major post offices. The idea had been to use scenes from the *Jazz Singer* to promote a commemorative issue that would honor the 50th anniversary of talking pictures, but after receiving complaints that the poster was insulting to black people it was withdrawn. Officials were, however, quick to point out that the stamp does not reflect the actual Jolson image.

Cairo, 5 November
Misr Studios held a huge celebration to mark the 50th anniversary of the Egyptian cinema.

Paris, 9 November
Release of *Crabe-Tambour*, directed by Pierre Schoendoerffer from his own book, with Jacques Perrin and Jean Rochefort.

Madrid, 11 November
A Royal decree has abolished film censorship and authorized the free importation of films.

Washington D.C., 18 November
The American Film Institute last night named *Gone With the Wind* America's greatest movie. The decision was reached by a vote involving the 350,000 members of the AFI from all 50 states and 50 foreign countries. The result was announced before an audience of 2,200 directors, producers, writers, studio heads, film stars and politicians including President and Mrs. Carter. Other films voted into the select Top Ten of America's best were *Casablanca*, *Singin' in the Rain*, *One Flew Over the Cuckoo's Nest*, *The Wizard of Oz*, *2001: A Space Odyssey*, *The African Queen*, *Citizen Kane* and *The Grapes of Wrath*.

Los Angeles, 20 November
The *Los Angeles Times* has pu lished an article in praise of Stev Spielberg's UFO fantasy *Close E counters of the Third Kind*, adapt from the novel by Ray Bradbur the famous science-fiction writer: " is without doubt the most importa film of our era... A religious expe ence with a universal message f of hope."

Johannesburg, 26 December
Director Gibson Kente's music film, *How Long*, has been bann and Kente and some of his film cre have been arrested. This film is t first South African effort to be e tirely produced and directed black South Africans.

DEATHS

Los Angeles, 1 January
Groucho Marx

Paris, 12 January
Henri-Georges Clouzot

Los Angeles, 14 January
Peter Finch

California, 28 February
Eddie 'Rochester' Anderson

New York, 10 May
Joan Crawford

Rome, 3 June
Roberto Rossellini

Memphis, 16 August
Elvis Presley

California, 17 August
Delmer Daves

Los Angeles, 19 August
Stephen Boyd

Madrid, 14 October
Bing Crosby

Switzerland, 25 December
Charles Chaplin

Hollywood, 26 December
Howard Hawks

John Travolta became a new icon f 70s youth with ***Saturday Night Feve*** *The movie, bursting with life a vigor, rode in on the back of the dis craze that was sweeping America.*

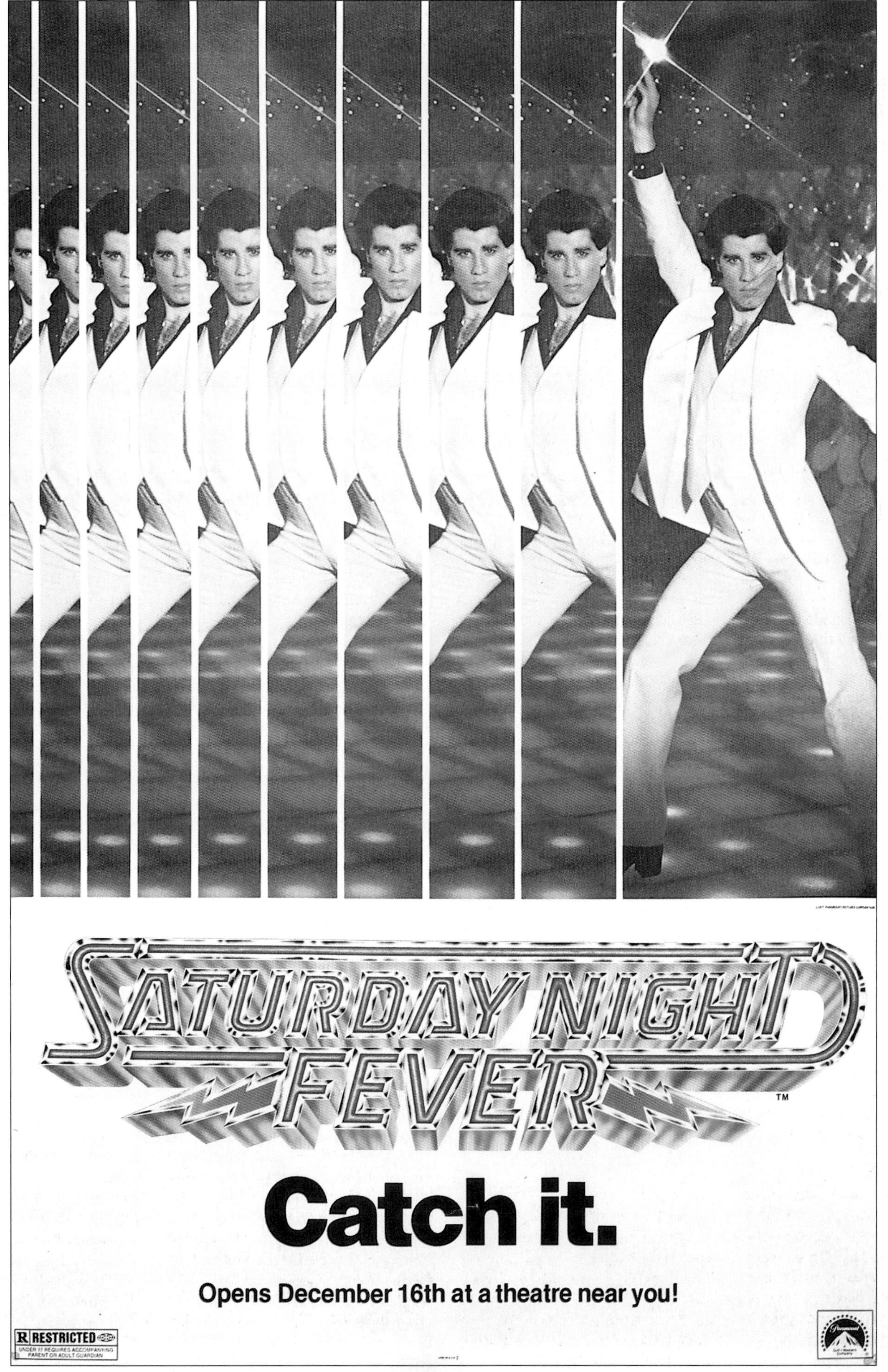
SATURDAY NIGHT FEVER
TM
Catch it.
Opens December 16th at a theatre near you!
R RESTRICTED
UNDER 17 REQUIRES ACCOMPANYING PARENT OR ADULT GUARDIAN
Paramount

Flames of De Palma's 'Carrie' melt the ice

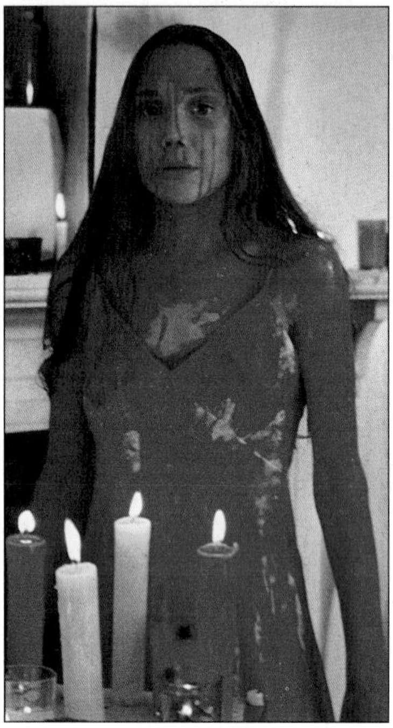
Sissy Spacek as extrasensory Carrie.

Avoriaz, 23 January
Some critics consider director Brian De Palma the natural successor to Alfred Hitchcock. It's true that De Palma has done little to discourage the comparison and has larded his work with nods towards the master of suspense. At the Festival of Fantastic Film at the winter resort of Avoriaz, his latest film, *Carrie*, adapted from a Stephen King novel, has caused such a sensation that the jury has unhesitatingly awarded him the Grand Prix. Once again De Palma has demonstrated his technical virtuosity and ability to manipulate the audience. Sissy Spacek stars as the high school ugly duckling who unleashes terrible telekinetic powers against those who have drenched her with pig's blood at the prom. The school is reduced to rubble, her religious zealot of a mother, Piper Laurie, impaled by a hail of flying implements. More shocks follow...

Haunting journey through life and death

Paris, 9 February
"Rather than a film about death, *Providence* is more a film about the desire not to die," remarked Alain Resnais on his latest work. *Providence* is basically a multi-layered nightmare dreamed by a dying novelist (John Gielgud, in one of his most audacious and testing screen roles) inhabited by four members of his family. The next morning everything is bathed in light as they all come together joyously to celebrate his birthday. The thin dividing line between fact and fiction, dream and reality, has hardly ever been better conceived. During his fight against the dying of the light, Gielgud is able to crystallize the psychological traits of his two sons and their women. The Anglo-American cast consists of Ellen Burstyn, Elaine Stritch, David Warner and Dirk Bogarde, the latter with whom Resnais had wanted to work since 1966. The British playwright David Mercer provided the complex and fascinating screenplay.

l to r: David Warner, Ellen Burstyn, John Gielgud and Dirk Bogarde.

Fellini's cold study of sexual obsession

Donald Sutherland in the title role of ***Fellini's Casanova****, a bitter view.*

Paris, 23 February
As with *Satyricon*, Federico Fellini has once again gone into the past to find analogies for the decadence which he perceives in present-day Italy. This time, the director has adapted episodes from the life of the 18th-century author, scientist and libertine, Giacomo Casanova. In order to symbolize the lovelessness of Casanova's erotic encounters, Fellini shows the hero, who has fornicated mechanically with one girl after another, finally having sex with an actual automaton. After th[e] warmth of Fellini's previous autob[i]ographical films, such as *Roma* an[d] *Amarcord*, this is a chilling study o[f] a sexual obsessive. The backgroun[d] is an artificial Venice, the sumptu[]ous sets for which were created a[t] Cinecittà by Danilo Donati. Behin[d] extraordinary makeup, Donald Suth[]erland is very impressive in the titl[e] role. Despite the coldness of th[e] character, Sutherland manages t[o] lend Casanova a certain poignanc[y] as the aging man at the end.

Dark dramas capture this year's Césars

Paris, 19 February
Neglected by award-givers for some years now, Joseph Losey was delighted to receive the two top Césars for his dark drama of the Occupation, *Mr. Klein*. It was considered the best film, and Losey the best director. Alain Delon, excellent in the title role, plays Robert Klein, a womanizing antique dealer, untouched by the German occupation and indifferent to the fate of the Jews under the Nazis – until he is confused wit[h] another Robert Klein, a wante[d] man and a Jew. This complex an[d] absorbing examination of identity i[s] a blend of Kafkaesque nightmar[e] and pacey thriller. Annie Girardo[t] was voted best actress for *Dr. Fran[]çoise Gailland*, and the best acto[r] was Michel Galabru for *The Judg[e] and the Assassin*, Bertrand Tavern[i]er's new period piece. All the film[s] honored were noticeably downbea[t].

Vajda attacks the present through its past

ʼrzy Radziwilowicz in Andrzej Wajda's ***Man of Marble***, *sequel to* ***Man of Iron***.

'arsaw, 25 February
he Stalinist period still remains boo in many East European counies, especially in Poland, so one as to admire the courage of Anzej Wajda for making *Man of Iarble*. However, the film's release as held up for four years. This old, no-holds-barred political tale Wajda's reflection on Poland's present through its immediate past. This is achieved by following a film student's investigations into the life of a bricklayer hero of the 1950s as a basis for her graduation project. But she finds obstacles in getting at the truth about the worker who stepped out of line. Most effective are the black-and-white reconstructions of the newsreels of the time.

Agnes Varda and the happiness of women

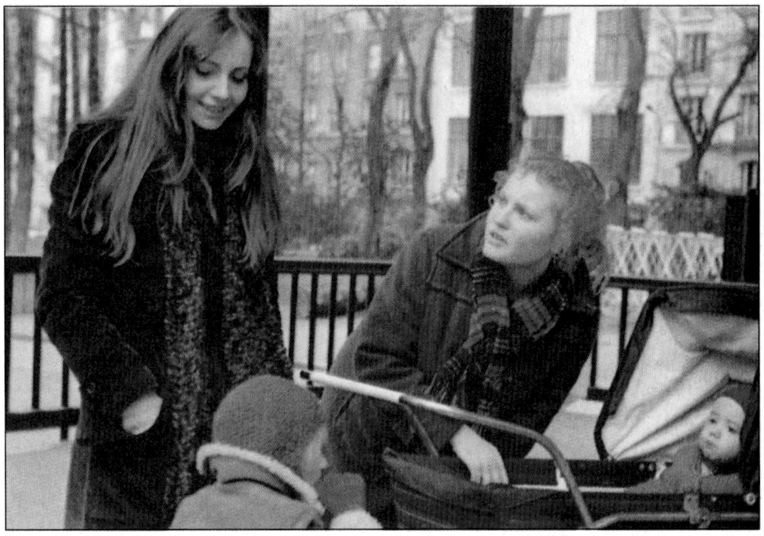

Thérèse Liotard and Valérie Mairesse in ***One Sings, the Other Doesn't***.

Paris, 9 March
After a nine-year absence from fiction films, Agnes Varda has made a triumphant return with *One Sings, the Other Doesn't*, an irrefutably feminist movie, which the director claims is about "the happiness of being a woman." Taking Simone de Beauvoir's maxim that "Women are made, not born" as her theme, Varda examines the lives of two friends (Valérie Mairesse and Thérèse Liotard) of different temperaments and backgrounds who both face adversity but finally achieve independence and fulfillment, over a number of years. One becomes a singer, travels the world and has children by her Iranian lover, the other runs a family planning clinic.

olanski dragged hrough the courts

os Angeles, 24 March
n evil curse seems to have hung ver Roman Polanski since the Polh director settled in the United ates. Thus, after the gruesome and agic death of his pregnant wife, the ctress Sharon Tate, murdered in 969 by the demonic disciples of harles Manson, Polanski is at the enter of another sordid affair, this me with himself as the unfortunate rotagonist. He was arrested two eeks ago in Beverly Hills on the omplaint of a mother who accused im of having sex with her underge daughter. He will appear before grand jury for the corruption of a inor, an extremely serious offense America, where puritanism can xpress itself with vehemence. There good reason, therefore, for the irector of *Chinatown* to be worried bout the outcome of this case, hich could have grave conseuences for his future as a film irector and his continued residence the States.

Sylvester Stallone delivers massive knock-out punch at Oscars

Los Angeles, 29 March
This year the Academy Awards ceremony was staged by William Friedkin and the Oscars presented by Jane Fonda, Ellen Burstyn, Warren Beatty and Richard Pryor. The biggest sensation has been caused by Sylvester Stallone, who was a complete unknown until a few months ago. Now *Rocky*, the project which he wrote and in which he starred, has won two major Oscars, Best Picture, and the Best Director statuette for John G. Avildsen. Stallone hardly looks like a movie star, there is something of a caricature Victor Mature about him, and he's about as articulate as his mumbling two-fisted hero. But *Rocky*'s phenomenal success has shown that the American Dream never dies. Peter Finch won a tragic posthumous Best Actor Oscar for his performance as the "mad prophet of the airwaves" in *Network*. He died of a heart attack during the picture's publicity campaign, and his wife accepted the Oscar on his behalf. His co-star in *Network*, Faye Dunaway, was voted Best Actress for her portrayal of a ruthless TV executive. Beatrice Straight won an unexpected Best Supporting Actress Oscar for her brief appearance as the neglected wife of William Holden in the same movie, and playwright Paddy Chayefsky was honored for *Network*'s screenplay. The Best Supporting Actor award went to Jason Robards for his neatly judged performance as *Washington Post* editor Ben Bradlee in Alan J. Pakula's rivetting *All the President's Men*.

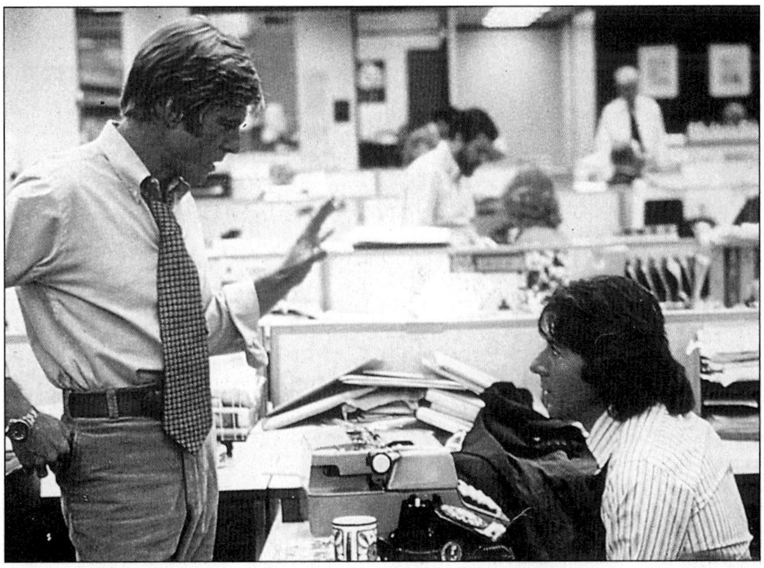

All the President's Men: *Redford (Bob Woodward), Hoffman (Carl Bernstein).*

Keaton-Allen partnership hits new high

New York, 20 April
With his latest film, *Annie Hall*, Woody Allen has hit his stride. In this semi-autobiographical "nervous romance" he plays Alvy Singer, a stand-up comic with a style not a million miles away from that of the younger Allen. Woody's partner Diane Keaton, appearing with him for the third time, is the wacky, Waspish gamine of the title, gawkily dressed in an outfit of waistcoat, baggy trousers and oversize hat which looks likely to start a fashion. They meet over a game of tennis and fall in and out of love as Allen muses over the other main character in the movie, New York City, gingerly dips his toe into the warm waters of life in California, shmoozes with Paul Simon and, gloriously, summons up Marshall McLuhan to silence a fatuous bore in an art-house cinema queue. "Boy, if life were only like this!" laments Alvy. In *Annie Hall*, Allen celebrates his love affair with New York and with Keaton (whose real name is Hall), and the middle-class Manhattan-Jewish background which informs his comedy, the basis of which is the wry one-liner. Critics have compared the film to Fellini's *8 ½*, but Allen's characteristically self-deprecating response is, "It's more like my *2 ½*."

Diane Keaton and Woody Allen.

Huppert is moving as 'The Lacemaker'

Paris, 17 May
Claude Goretta, who has directed films in his native Switzerland, has brought his talents to bear on a new French picture, *The Lacemaker*. Its main revelation is Isabelle Huppert as the guileless heroine, although she has already appeared in 14 films. Despite the passivity of the role of a reticent Parisian hairdresser, Huppert retains our sympathy throughout. This touching, well-observed tale tells how the girl meets and falls in love with a university student while on vacation in Normandy. Back in Paris, the gap in class and education causes a painful rift, and the girl's breakdown.

Burt's bandit in a crazy chase comedy

Burt Reynolds and Sally Field.

New York, 19 May
Smokey and the Bandit casts Burt Reynolds as the Bandit, an ace trucker running a 900-mile gauntlet pursued by Jackie Gleason's crackpot redneck Sheriff Burford T. Justic Making his debut as a director former stuntman Hal Needham, s the action is fast and furious a the laid-back Reynolds outpac Gleason in an action-packed mov which is about as subtle as an outin with the Three Stooges but manag to retain a madcap charm amid th mayhem of hurtling automobile Reynolds has been looking for a h to break a disapppointing run o movies: *WW and the Dixie Danc kings*, *Lucky Lady* and Peter Bo danovich's *At Long Last Love*. Bu almost succeeded in extricating hin self from the latter clinker with som engagingly amateurish hoofing, b then went down with all hands la year in Bogdanovich's *Nickelodeo* After establishing his credentials a director with last year's *Gator*, seems that, at long last, Burt has smash on his hands.

'Star Wars' is an $11 million revelation

New York, 25 May
Both Universal and United Artists turned down the chance to produce *Star Wars*, directed by 33-year-old George Lucas. Twentieth Century-Fox finally accepted, giving Lucas complete control during the four years of preparation and a relatively modest budget of $11 million, of which half went toward the sets and special effects. Shot in Guatemala, Tunisia and Death Valley, with interiors at Elstree Studios in England, the film is so spectacular that it looks as if it cost three times as much. Obviously influenced by th old Flash Gordon and Buck Roge serials, as well as tales of knights o old, it tells of how Luke Skywalk (Mark Hamill), given a sword b his mentor Ben Kenobi (Alec Gui ness), and assisted by space pil Han Solo (Harrison Ford), rescue Princess Leia (Carrie Fisher) fro the evil clutches of Darth Vade Two robots, C-3PO and R2D2, pr vide comic relief. *Star Wars* ha turned out to be one of the mo exciting, amusing and inspiring sc ence fiction movies ever made.

Isabelle Huppert as 'Pomme', the unhappy hairdresser in ***The Lacemaker****.*

Harrison Ford and 'Chewbacca' in George Lucas' phenomenon ***Star Wars****.*

ophia trapped in banality of fascism

ophia Loren plays a lonely drudge of a housewife in Scola's **A Special Day**.

ome, 1 June
ttore Scola has drawn on his own emories for his new film, *A Special ay*. He was six-and-a-half years old n 8 May 1938, when Adolf Hitler rrived in Rome to meet Benito Iussolini. He recalls the fascist ropaganda, "the apotheosis of rhetric". The buildings were empty as veryone rushed into the streets to cclaim Il Duce and the Fuhrer. 'his is the background to *A Special ay*, most of whose action takes lace in an apartment between two onely people. They are a weary other of six children and a homoexual radio announcer. They are rawn together while the populace, cluding the woman's brutish fascist husband, are out cheering their heroes. Repression, social and political, is the common bond between the two very different characters. What makes this encounter enthralling is the casting against type of the normally glamorous Sophia Loren as a frumpish housewife, and the "ladies man" Marcello Mastroianni as the homosexual. The fact that Mastroianni temporarily abandons his homosexuality to make love to Loren, though contrived, reveals the strength of their need for love and companionship. The film ends on a downbeat note when Loren's husband returns home, invigorated by the macho image of Mussolini, and forces himself upon her.

Fernando Rey caught between two women

Carole Bouquet and Fernando Rey in Buñuel's **That Obscure Object of Desire**.

Paris, 17 August
Luis Buñuel's most recent film, *That Obscure Object of Desire*, is a very free adaptation of the Pierre Louys novel, *The Woman and the Puppet*, already the basis for the Sternberg-Dietrich 1935 movie, *The Devil is a Woman*. When Maria Schneider left the project after only three weeks, Buñuel, with the surreal logic that runs through his work, decided to cast two actresses (Carole Bouquet and Angela Molina) to alternate the role of Conchita, the maid who bewitches her master. Fernando Rey, that embodiment of Buñuel's libido, delivers his most sinister, witty and sly performance as the worldly businessman, whose hopes are fed by Conchita who refuses to give herself to him. At first the dual casting is disconcerting, but it gradually becomes strangely normal – revealing two different sides of the same woman which the man fails to notice. In the background to the activities of Fernando Rey, that discreetly charming *bourgeois*, are those of a revolutionary group, attempting to undermine his life style. *That Obscure Object of Desire* is another brilliant Buñuel bomb placed under the privileged classes, revealing that the 77-year-old Spanish master has lost little of his anarchic sense of humor over the years, since his first film, *Un chien andalou*, almost half a century ago.

'he sudden death of Elvis Presley shocks millions of his fans

Iemphis, 16 August
:lvis Presley has died of a heart ttack at his Graceland mansion, here he was living with daughter isa-Marie. Since April the 42-yearld star had been having serious ealth problems caused by repeated hots of Demerol and morphine. At p.m., his companion Ginger Alden ound him unconscious on the bathoom floor. He died en route to the ospital. Tennessee-born, and nickamed "Elvis the Pelvis" and later The King", he made 33 movies, nd changed the history of popular nusic. Although his dependency on rugs and his passion for junk food ere well known, his millions of fans re in a state of shock. To them, ough, he will never die.

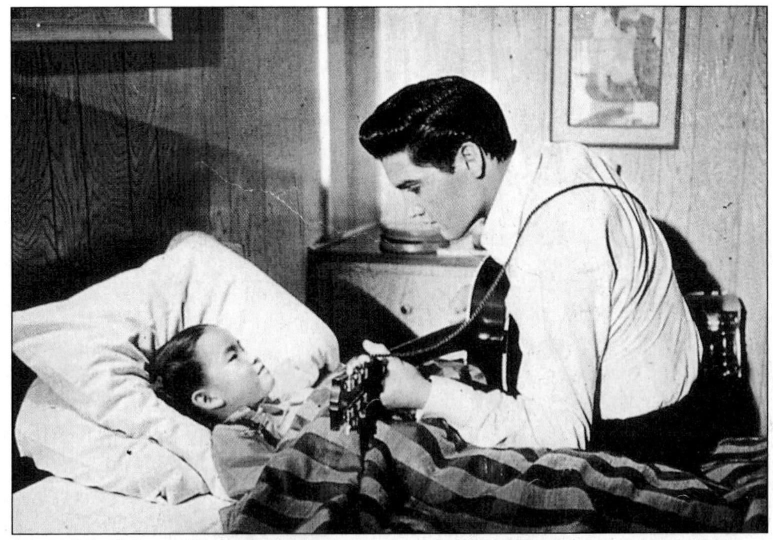

*The idol of the millions in **It Happened at the World's Fair**, made in 1963.*

Psychiatric testing for Polanski

Los Angeles, 19 September
In the ongoing scandal surrounding Roman Polanski, a grand jury has brought in a six-count indictment, remanding him to 90 days in prison with a psychiatric evaluation. The jury has determined that there is sufficient evidence supporting the allegations brought against him of corrupting a minor. The mother of a 13-year-old girl has accused the director of assaulting her daughter during a photo shoot for a French magazine. If the psychiatric evaluation indicates that Polanski suffers from a disorder, that may alleviate his sentence, the maximum of which is 50 years behind bars.

Diane Keaton's dark and disastrous quest for 'Mister Right'

Diane Keaton excels as a lonely New Yorker looking for love and finding trouble in ***Looking for Mr. Goodbar.***

New York, 19 October
To demonstrate that she is not just a charmingly kooky one-note personality, Diane Keaton has followed *Annie Hall* with a challenging role in Richard Brooks' *Looking for Mr. Goodbar*, adapted from Judith Rossner's best-selling novel. She plays a teacher of deaf children who cruises singles bars at night for high-risk sexual adventures which lead her to a violent encounter with a bisexual psychopath convincingly played by Tom Berenger. Also making an impact is Richard Gere in the role of Tony Lopanto, chilling as the self-styled "greatest fuck of your whole life", from whose sadistic treatment Keaton derives a perverse pleasure. Writer and director Brooks says of Keaton, "I wondered if Diane could handle the dark side of the character as well as the teacher side, but she's sensational."

Electrifying newcomer John Travolta sends the girls into a fever

John Travolta and Karen Lynn Gorney compete in the disco dance contest.

New York, 15 December
Male dancing on screen has been given the kiss of life by the discovery of John Travolta in *Saturday Night Fever*, a movie that should be shown in seatless cinemas, giving the kids space to dance to it. The discotheque, with its strobe-lighting and tinsel atmosphere, is the 70s equivalent of those sumptuous nightclubs of 30s musicals, sonic and scenic escapes from the drab reality outside. Travolta plays a paint-store clerk in Brooklyn, a weekday nobody, who is transformed on Saturday nights into a stunning stud in the disco where he is king. On a floor lit from below, to music by the Bee Gees, he dances dynamically in ensembles, pairs and solo. The story, originally derived from an article by Nik Cohn entitled "Tribal Rites of the New York Saturday Night", pales besides the numbers. These include "Night Fever", "Stayin' Alive", "How Deep Is Your Love?" and "Jive Talkin'". The picture, directed by John Badham, was shot in the predominantly Italian neighborhood of Bay Ridge and in Manhattan.

Powerful return to the death camps

Munich, 25 November
A West German film about the Na
concentration camps is a rare even
and Theodor Kotulla's *Death is M*
Trade (*Aus Einem Deutschen Leber*
makes a powerful impression. It i
based on the life of the notoriou
Rudolph Höss (not to be confuse
with Hess) from 1922 until 194
For some reason named Franz Lan
in the film, he is seen as a Germa
working-class patriot who joins th
Nazi Party in 1924 and distinguishe
himself by dedicated hard work an
application. Himmler appoints hir
to an important post at Dachau anc
seven years later, he is commandar
at Auschwitz, made responsible fc
carrying out the Final Solution. A
ter the war is over, he writes hi
memoirs and dies without exhibitin
a hint of remorse. He is portraye
by Götz George as a rather ordinar
man, committed to his duty. A de
tached account of events in a sem
documentary style, *Death is M*
Trade is all the more chilling for i
lack of emotion and the seemin
normality of its protagonists. Of th
German high command's skill i
securing unquestioning faith in it
ideology, the 145-minute film offer
neither comment nor apology. W
look forward to more German film
on the subject.

Götz George as Franz Lang.

riumphant confrontation with another universe

ew York, 16 November
ı *Star Wars*, George Lucas aimed : re-creating the non-stop action of ıe classic serials of the 1930s. In *'lose Encounters of the Third Kind*, teven Spielberg digs back farther ıd deeper, seeking to release in the ıdience the sense of wonder expeenced by those who saw the mirae of motion pictures for the first me. *Close Encounters* invokes the osing words of Howard Hawks' ience fiction classic *The Thing* – Watch the skies" – but with none f the hysteria of the 1950s. The npulse behind the picture is, peraps, religious, a yearning to establish contact with a race of benevont aliens rather than turn our guns n them. For the movie's central haracter Richard Dreyfuss, the ourney to Devil's Tower, Wyoning, where an alien ship will land, a pilgrimage. Like a latter-day aint his own close encounter bathes im in the glow of the vision he has ourished along the way. The miliıry men who ring the landing site ıake no attempt to remove him 'hen he joins the throng who watch 'ith upturned faces as the Mother hip descends. If Dreyfuss is Everyıan, then the Gallic charm of Franois Truffaut, cast as a UFO expert, used by Spielberg as a neat shortand for liberal humanism. Trufaut's character is based on Jacques 'allée, a real-life UFO-logist and ne-time collaborator with Allen Iynek, whose *The UFO Experiences* rovided the inspiration for the film. Iynek appears as a pipe-puffing observer in the climactic encounter with the aliens. With this material, Spielberg has wrought his own kind of magic, demonstrating that miracles – like the parting of the Red Sea in *The Ten Commandments*, glimpsed on the television in Dreyfuss' living room – can come true.

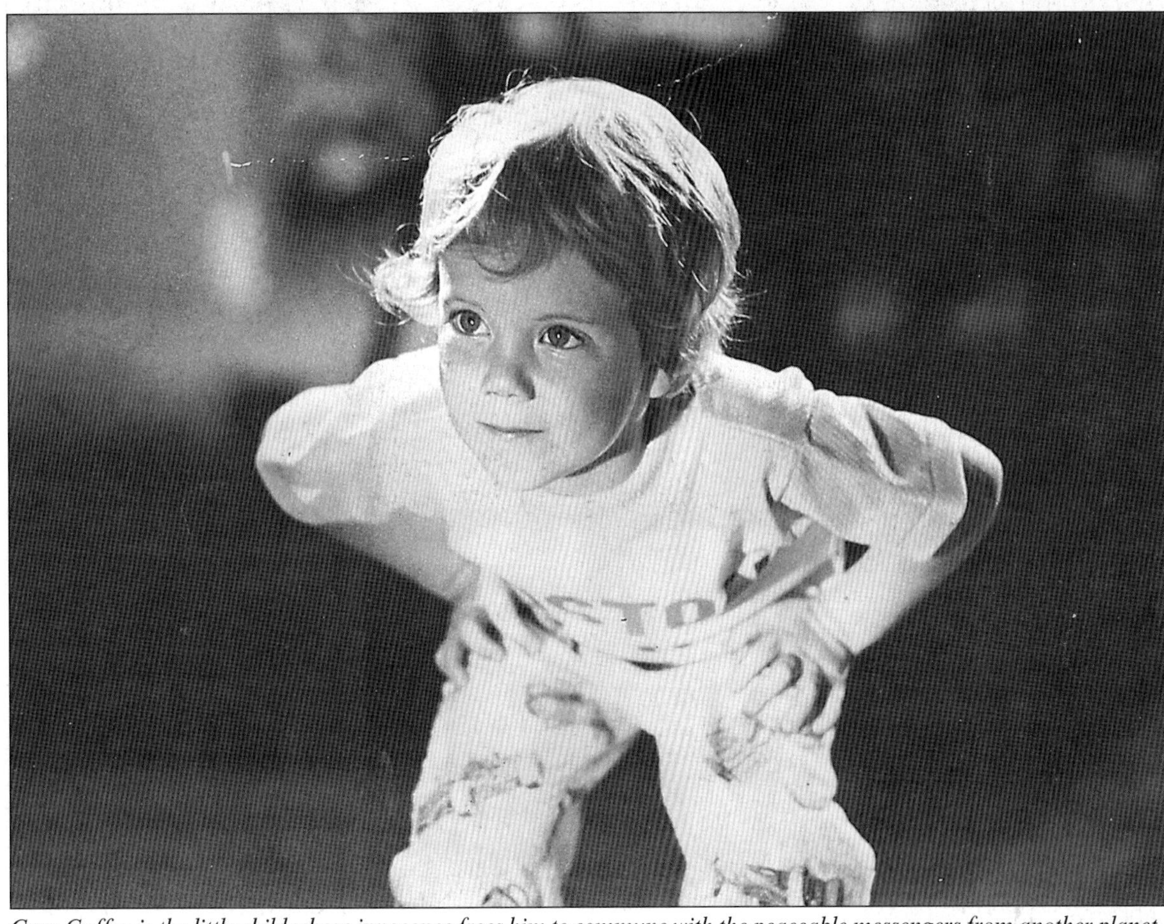

Cary Guffey is the little child whose innocence frees him to commune with the peaceable messengers from another planet.

'rançois Truffaut, Steven Spielberg.

The encounter coming closer.

The great Chaplin dies on Christmas Day

Corsier-sur-Vevey, 27 December
Two days ago Charles Chaplin died in his sleep at the age of 88. His funeral was held today at 11 a.m. in the intimate surroundings of the Anglican church in Vevey. A gentle rain was falling as the coffin, covered with a black and silver pall, was lowered into the grave. Chaplin's long journey is over.

The funeral of Chaplin was held in the small cemetery at Corsier-sur-Vevey. ▷

Robert Fortier with Sissy Spacek in Robert Altman's enigmatic **Three Women**.

Outrageous: wicked drag impersonator Craig Russell's Judy Garland.

SERGE SILBERMAN présente
UN FILM DE LUIS BUNUEL
Cet
Obscur
Objet
du
Désir

René Ferracci's surreal French poster reflects the tone of Buñuel's film.

The war was over and
the world was falling in love again.
A love story is like a song. It's beautiful while it lasts.
LIZA MINNELLI ROBERT DE NIRO
"NEW YORK, NEW YORK"

Liza Minnelli, sax player Robert De Niro in Scorsese's **New York, New York**

Philippe Noiret and veteran Fred Astaire in Yves Boisset's **The Purple Taxi**.

Coline Serreau's **Pourquoi pas? (Why Not?)**: Mario Gonzales (l), Samy Frey.

ft to right: Paul Le Mat, Candy Clark and Roberts Blossom in Jonathan mme's **Handle With Care** (aka **Citizen's Band**).

Gaumont
Stephane TCHALGADJIEFF
LE DIABLE PROBABLEMENT...
Un film de Robert BRESSON

Bresson's ***The Devil, Probably*** *was the winner of the Berlin jury prize.*

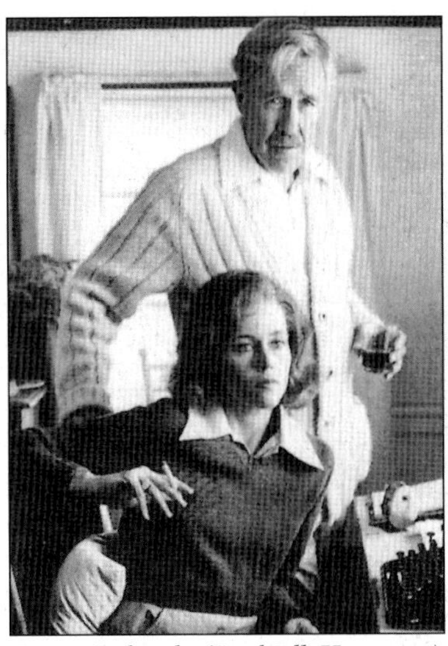

Jason Robards (Dashiell Hammett), Jane Fonda (Lillian Hellman): ***Julia.***

t Carney, the private investigator, in Robert Benton's ***The Late Show.***

Julie Christie in Donald Cammell's nasty sci-fi film, ***Demon Seed.***

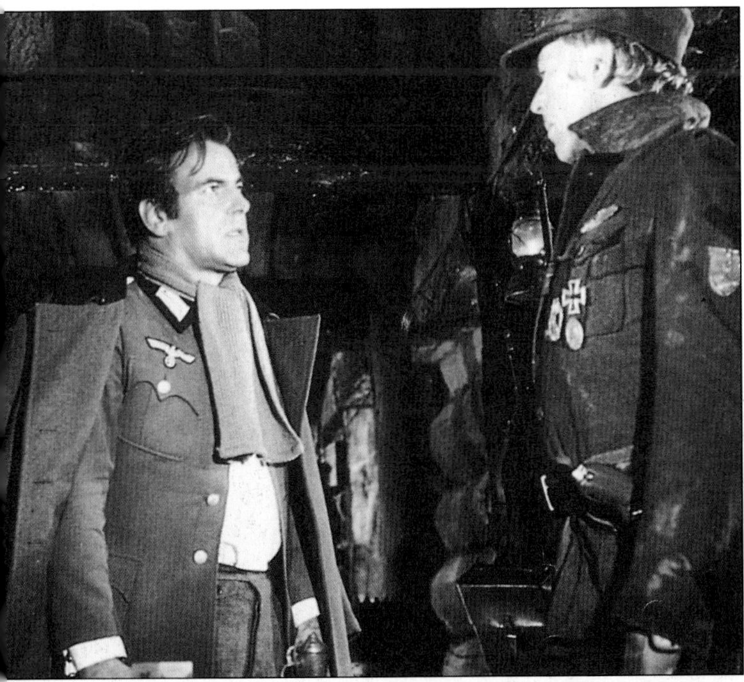

aximilian Schell and Klaus Löwitch in Sam Peckinpah's ***Cross of Iron.***

John Heard, Lindsay Crouse in Joan Micklin Silver's ***Between the Lines.***

★★★★★★★★★ 1978 ★★★★★★★★★★★★★★★★★★★★★★★★★★★★★★★

1977 Academy Awards, Dorothy Chandler Pavilion, 3 Apr.

Best Film:	*Annie Hall* (dir: Woody Allen)
Best Director:	Woody Allen
Best Actor:	Richard Dreyfuss *(The Goodbye Girl)*
Best Actress:	Diane Keaton *(Annie Hall)*
Best Supp. Actor:	Jason Robards *(Julia)*
Best Supp. Actress:	Vanessa Redgrave *(Julia)*

Cannes, 7 January
The new director of the Cannes Film Festival, Gilles Jacob, has announced that the event will run for only 11 days this year. Hoteliers and shopkeepers are protesting.

Paris, 26 January
The X-rating of Francis Giacobetti's *Emmanuelle II* has been removed by a special court decision.

Peking, 30 January
Director Yuan Muzhi has died. He was an important personality during the 1930s and one of the leaders of the Popular Liberation Army's revolutionary cinema.

Prague, 1 February
Release of *Hra o jablko* (*The Apple Game*), by Vera Chytilova, made in 1976, with director Jiri Menzel in the lead role. It is Chytilova's first fiction film since 1969.

London, 9 February
Roman Polanski, recently convicted of corruption of a minor in the United States, has announced his intention to remain outside the U.S. He left California the day before the sentence was pronounced.

Calcutta, 12 February
Indian filmmaker Satyajit Ray is bemused by the lack of interest in his latest film in his native India. Despite his popularity abroad, Mr. Ray has been unable to find a distributor in India for *The Chess Player*. The distributors who had been planning to open the movie in Calcutta and several other major towns turned it down after a private showing. The film, starring British actor Richard Attenborough, was well received by the public and film critics at the London Film Festival last month.

Cairo, 26 February
The Egyptian Film Association has proclaimed Salah Abou Seif's film *The Death of the Water-bearer* (*As saqqa mat*) the best film for 1977.

Paris, 27 February
Actress Jean Seberg has published an open "Letter to drug addicts" in the daily paper, *Libération.*

Los Angeles, 2 March
The president of the MPAA, Jack Valenti, has denied press reports that there was a huge government investigation into alleged corruption in the motion picture industry. The reports of a Hollywood inquiry followed the recent upheaval at the Columbia studios, whose president, David Begelman, resigned after admitting to embezzling studio funds.

Lebanon, 15 March
The Palestinian filmmakers Ibrahim Mustapha Nasser and Abdel-Hafeth al Asmar have been killed while filming an Israeli military operation in the region.

Los Angeles, 7 April
The Ontario Film Classification Board has banned Louis Malle's film about a 12-year-old prostitute, *Pretty Baby.*

Switzerland, 17 May
Charlie Chaplin's coffin and body have been recovered in the town of Noville, only a few kilometers from the cemetery in Vevey where his tomb was robbed. It is believed that the criminals were hoping to extort money from the Chaplin family. No arrests have been made.

Bombay, 28 May
The kiss has come to the Hindi screen, shocking some and titillating others. Shashi Kapoor, India's answer to Robert Redford, kisses his co-star several times in a new film, *Love Sublime*, directed by his brother Raj. And although they are tame by Western standards, they are the first kisses on the Hindi screen for years. In the Indian cinema industry the film is seen as a landmark and as a sign of what the Government calls greater "creative freedom", after Indira Gandhi's authoritarian rule.

Los Angeles, 15 June
The Doheny Plaza theater, which had contracted to show the allegedly anti-Israel documentary by Vanessa Redgrave titled *The Palestinian*, was bombed at 4:26 a.m. today, causing an estimated $1,000 damage. Despite this the theater said it would show the film tomorrow night as scheduled. Two suspects have been arrested. Although Miss Redgrave has resolutely denied claims that she is anti-Semitic, she recently called for members of the British actors union to boycott Israel.

Copenhagen, 21 August
Release of *Honeymoon* (*Honningmane*), by Bille August, with Claus Stranberg and Kirsten Olesen.

Hollywood, 17 September
Director Michael Cimino has had discussions with Stephen Bach at United Artists about his proposed new project, *The Johnson County War*, a Western.

Paris, 25 September
Director Eric Rohmer is shooting *Perceval le Gallois* (*Perceval*) in the Epinay studios, based on Chrétien de Troyes' epic poem, inspired by the Knights of the Round Table.

New York, 19 October
The body of actor Gig Young was found lying beside that of his bride of three weeks. He was clutching a revolver. Police think the actor killed his wife before turning the gun on himself. Young made over 50 films during his career, including his Academy Award-winning performance in Sydney Pollack's *They Shoot Horses, Don't They?*

Rio de Janeiro, 23 October
Considered as the best Brazilian film for the year at the Festival de Brasilia, *Tudo Bem* (*Everything is Fine*), directed by Arnaldo Jabor, is now on release.

Paris, 25 October
Release of Edouard Molinaro's *la Cage aux folles*, based on a play by Jean Poiret, with Michel Serrault and Ugo Tognazzi.

Biarritz, 15 November
Bernard Marie, the deputy mayor of Biarritz, has announced the creation of an annual Latin American and Spanish film festival here.

Paris, 22 November
Le Figaro magazine revealed ir latest issue that four giants of American and English screen – R ert Mitchum, Richard Burton, P O'Toole and Richard Harris – well-known to be heavy imbib have given up drinking.

France, 30 November
The Center of Research into Ad tising has revealed that 55 percen French people never go to the c ma. Audiences in the 15 to 20 group (20 percent of the populati make up 52 percent of admissio

Paris, 5 December
Opening of an exhibition at George Pompidou Center of So director Sergei Eisenstein's origi sketches and drawings.

Paris, 26 December
Between December 17 and 25 t year, the three television chanr programmed 28 movies. Some ci ma professionals are uneasy ab this profusion of films on TV.

DEATHS

California, 23 January
Jack Oakie

England, 27 January
Oscar Homolka

New York, 12 March
John Cazale

Los Angeles, 9 August
Jack L. Warner

Arizona, 26 August
Charles Boyer

Ireland, 28 August
Robert Shaw

Paris, 9 October
Jacques Brel

Los Angeles, 16 October
Dan Dailey

New York, 19 October
Gig Young

Michael Cimino's ***The Deer Hunter*** *a significant movie about the Vi nam experience. In a brilliant cast, relative newcomer named Me Streep made an impression.*

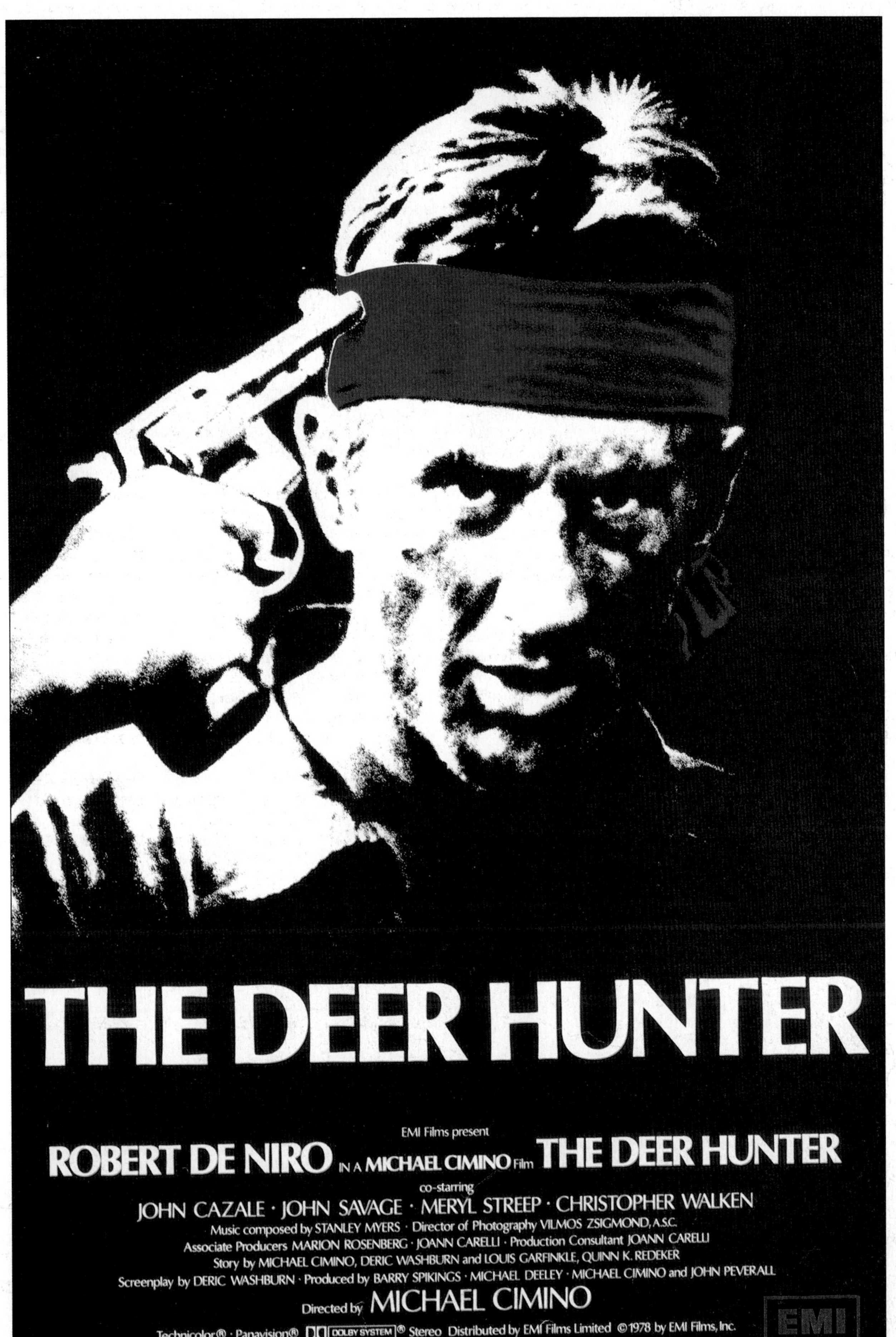
THE DEER HUNTER
EMI Films present
ROBERT DE NIRO IN A MICHAEL CIMINO Film THE DEER HUNTER
co-starring
JOHN CAZALE · JOHN SAVAGE · MERYL STREEP · CHRISTOPHER WALKEN
Music composed by STANLEY MYERS · Director of Photography VILMOS ZSIGMOND, A.S.C.
Associate Producers MARION ROSENBERG · JOANN CARELLI · Production Consultant JOANN CARELLI
Story by MICHAEL CIMINO, DERIC WASHBURN and LOUIS GARFINKLE, QUINN K. REDEKER
Screenplay by DERIC WASHBURN · Produced by BARRY SPIKINGS · MICHAEL DEELEY · MICHAEL CIMINO and JOHN PEVERALL
Directed by MICHAEL CIMINO
Technicolor® · Panavision® DOLBY SYSTEM® Stereo Distributed by EMI Films Limited ©1978 by EMI Films, Inc.
EMI

Sensitive, charming debut film wins Delluc

Eléonore Klarwein (foreground left), Odile Michel (right) in ***Peppermint Soda.***

Paris, 14 January
The Louis Delluc Prize has been awarded to *Peppermint Soda* (*Diabolo menthe*), the first feature by Diane Kurys, a former actress with the Madeleine Renaud/Jean-Louis Barrault theater company. Kurys (born 1948) has drawn her screenplay from experiences of her own adolescence, with the action taking place in 1963, from the time of Kennedy's assassination. It revolves around Anne (Eléonore Klarwein) and Frédérique (Odile Michel), the teenage daughters of a divorced Jewish couple. They live with their mother, attend an authoritarian school, and spend their vacations with their father, with whom they are ill at ease. This gentle, observant and nostalgic debut movie, has attracted large audiences of young people since it opened in Paris a month ago.

David Begelman affair, or Hollywoodgat

Cliff Robertson (here in De Palma's ***Obsession****), is at the center of the affai*

New York, 6 April
David Begelman's departure from the presidency of the film and television division of Columbia Pictures is the culmination of an extraordinary series of events. It all began last year when actor Cliff Robertson discovered that he had been credited with a payment of $10,000 which he had never received. It turned out that a check for this amount had been forged and cashed by Begelman, who subsequently admitted to e bezzling more than $60,000 fro the studio. He was suspended on September, 1977, then reinstated December when the studio, who st regarded him as an important figu who had helped in its prosperi hoped the furor had blown ov This, however, has proved to wishful thinking, and casts an int esting light on the behavior of Holl wood studios and their executives

A traumatic homecoming from Vietnam

Los Angeles, 15 February
Coming Home is very much Jane Fonda's project. She commissioned Nancy Dowd to write a story about the impact of the Vietnam War on people at home which would be implicitly critical of U.S. policy. Fonda plays an army wife married to Marine Corps action man Bruce Dern. While he is serving his tour of duty in Vietnam, she takes a job in a veteran's hospital where she meets an old high school classmate, Jon Voight, who is now paralyzed from the waist down. This condition does not prevent him from pleasuring her, however, and they embark on an affair which has a liberating effect on Fonda. When Dern returns from Vietnam, traumatized by his experiences there, she has to choose between the two men. Director Hal Ashby handles the love affair between Fonda and Voight with discretion, but the film slowly slithers into tearjerker territory while whole chunks of dialogue are lost in the din of a pounding rock soundtrack. For the moment the public have given this contemporary mixture of *Since You Went Away* and *Brief Encounter* a resounding thumbs down.

Jane Fonda and Jon Voight.

Woody beats robots to the big awards

Los Angeles, 3 April
The 50th Academy Awards ceremony saw the odds-on favorite, George Lucas' innovative, effects-packed blockbuster *Star Wars*, ousted by the intimist New York Jewish comedy angst of Woody Allen. *Annie Hall* had Woody named Best Director of the Best Picture, and winning the Best Original Screenplay Oscar, while his co-star Diane Keaton was voted Best Actress for her performance in the title role. However, Best Actor was Richard Dreyfuss for his gleefully manic performance in Neil Simon's *The Goodbye Girl* as an egocentric off-Broadway actor. At only 29, Dreyfuss is the youngest winner of this award. For the second year in a row, Jason Robards was Best Supporting Actor, taking the Oscar this time for his performance as washed-up writer Dashiell Hammett in Fred Zinnemann's adaptation of Lillian Hellman's *Julia*. The best thing in the film was Vanessa Redgrave in the title role, the mystery woman saving Jews from t Nazis. It won her a deserved Be Supporting Actress Oscar and chance to harangue the audien about Palestine.

Marsha Mason, Richard Dreyfuss.

A is threatened y ruptures

w York, 19 April
even years after the Transamerica rporation took over United Art-s, five of the film company's main ecutives – Arthur Krim, Robert njamin, Eric Pleskow, Mike Med-oy and William Bernstein – have signed. They have already an-unced their plan to form a new mpany called Orion Pictures and ake a distribution deal with War-r Bros. which will be providing bstantial financial backing for the w studio. Krim and Benjamin re responsible for revitalizing UA the 1950s and 60s and had headed e company for 26 years, during nich time it won many Oscars and rned small but steady profits. Un-rtunately, UA had a few bad years the early 1970s which strained lations between Transamerica and e UA management. Though the mpany recovered and continued do well, Krim and Benjamin were termined to regain their indepen-nce. The current Orion plan is the sult of this determination.

Strange childhood in New Orleans brothel

*Life in the brothel: Keith Carradine and Brooke Shields in **Pretty Baby**.*

New York, 4 April
Twelve-year-old Brooke Shields, already a successful model, broke into films last year with *Alice, Sweet Alice*. Now, in Louis Malle's *Pretty Baby*, she is the star attraction in a New Orleans brothel in 1917. By any standards this is dangerous territory, but as Malle explains, "I'm always interested in exposing something, a theme, a character or a situation which seems to be unacceptable. Then I try to make it work." Malle has succeeded, and avoided sensationalism, by giving Shields a matter-of-fact approach, viewing the brothel as home and the workplace of her mother, Susan Sarandon.

Columbia troubled by Hollywoodgate

New York, 20 July
The ongoing controversy and publicity caused by the Begelman affair at Columbia during the past year, and related management problems, have now led to the firing of company President and Chief Executive Officer Alan Hirschfield. In fact, a difference of opinion as to how to deal with Begelman had opened up a rift between Hirschfield and Herbert Allen Jr., the most powerful member of the board of directors, whose company Allen & Co. had bought a controlling interest in the studio in 1973. In spite of the fact that Hirschfield had played a major role in the revival of the company, he was voted out of office by the board, with Chairman Leo Jaffe as the only one who opposed the move. In a masterful piece of understatement, the board's press release read, "It has recently become apparent that for Columbia to move forward to new levels of accomplishment, fresh leadership and greater management unity are required."

low Travolta takes a trip to the Fifties

ew York, 11 June
fter drawing the crowds last year ith his galvanic dancing in *Satur-ay Night Fever*, John Travolta has nother smash with *Grease*. Based n the Broadway hit musical, it is a ostalgic trip back to the 50s, and ars Travolta and Olivia Newton-ohn as two kids at a rockin' 'n' rollin' high school. This takeoff of Beach Party movies pulsates with terrific numbers, including "Summer Nights" and "Look At Me, I'm Sandra Dee". The cast includes such veterans as Eve Arden, Joan Blondell and Sid Caesar, as well as stars of the period pastiched, Frankie Avalon and Edd "Kookie" Byrnes.

*livia Newton-John and John Travolta, co-stars in Randal Kleiser's **Grease**.*

Crude, rude and comical college caper

New York, 28 July
Is this a new trend in the making? Writer Harold Ramis and director John Landis have concocted a new kind of college campus movie with *National Lampoon's Animal House*. Set sometime around the early 60s, the story – if story it can be called – concerns the antics of a bunch of vulgar newcomers at a college who set out to disturb the stuffed-shirt order of things by their outrageous behavior. The movie, with its crude gags and anarchic set pieces, taking in everything from sexual escapades to bad table manners, is so over-the-top that it becomes quite absorbing. Watch out for gross John Belushi.

James Daughton (left) attacks John Belushi about his gross eating habits.

Harrowing ordeal in a Turkish prison relived

London, 10 August
After the "cute" violence of *Bugsy Malone*, director Alan Parker has turned to the real thing in *Midnight Express*. It's the story of the ordeal suffered by young American Billy Hayes, played by Brad Davis, while serving a sentence in Turkey for drug smuggling. The physical and emotional brutalization to which Davis is exposed has prompted accusations that Parker has painted a racist picture of the Turks, but the appalling state of the Turkish penal system represents only half of the picture's argument. The underlying theme tackles our deep-rooted fear of "otherness", which is an inescapable part of the human condition. Parker, himself a liberal-minded man, has defended himself vigorously against his critics.

The drugs that caused the trouble.

John Hurt (left) and Brad Davis, companions suffering in a Turkish prison.

Miraculous meeting of Ingmar and Ingrid

Stockholm, 8 October
Autumn Sonata is Ingrid Bergman's first Swedish film for almost 40 years, and it was her namesake Ingmar Bergman, who finally tempted her back to her native land. After some years in the kind of movies that hardly stretched her considerable talent, Ingrid has been handed one of her meatiest roles, in which she delivers a remarkable performance, displaying every aspect of her screen personality over the years – naivety, sophistication, gaiety and tragedy. Here, she plays Charlotte, a world-renowned concert pianist, who returns to Sweden to visit the two daughters she has not seen for many years, one married (Liv Ullmann) and the other severely handicapped (Lena Nyman). Charlotte has to face up to feelings of guilt for having put her career above her family, and the painful recognition that the past cannot be altered. The director, with a masterly use of close-up, and the flashback used as the subconscious, has created a work of Strindbergian intensity – a long night's journey into day.

The tragedy of an Australian half-caste

Melbourne, 21 August
The flowering of the Australian film industry, helped by constructive government funding, is continuing apace. The latest homegrown offering to open here, titled *The Chant of Jimmie Blacksmith*, received warm plaudits in competition at Cannes earlier in the year. Now, local audiences have the opportunity to see director Fred Schepisi's well-made, absorbing film, which deals with the plight of a half-caste aborigine. Jimmie Blacksmith, very movingly portrayed by non-actor Tommy Lewis, is caught in the trap of his mixe origins. Torn between the Christia teachings of his boyhood, and tl ancient aboriginal lore, Jimmie d cides to join the native life of tl city. He finds himself living in squalid shanty town, while his e forts to find work are increasing characterized by humiliation ar degradation, although he marries white servant girl. The tale ends tragedy and bloodshed, leaving a diences to face a disturbing indic ment of our destruction of anoth race's culture and dignity.

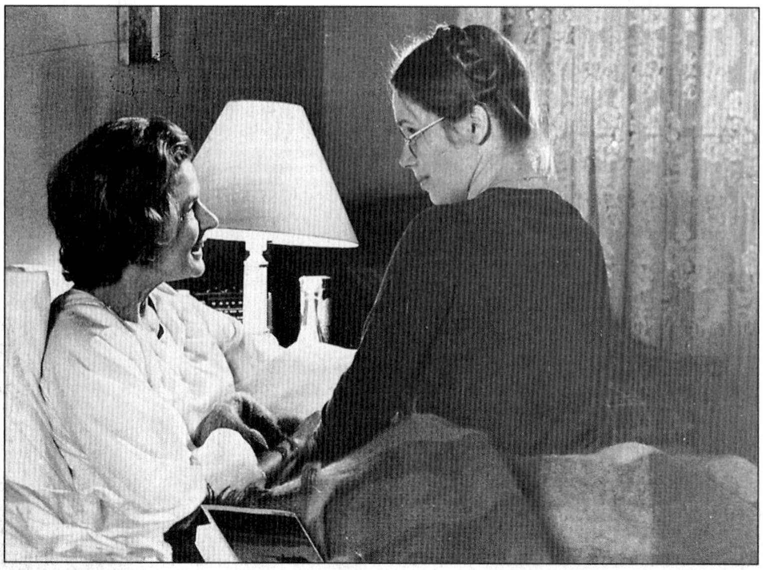
Mother and daughter share a rare moment of sympathy and understanding.

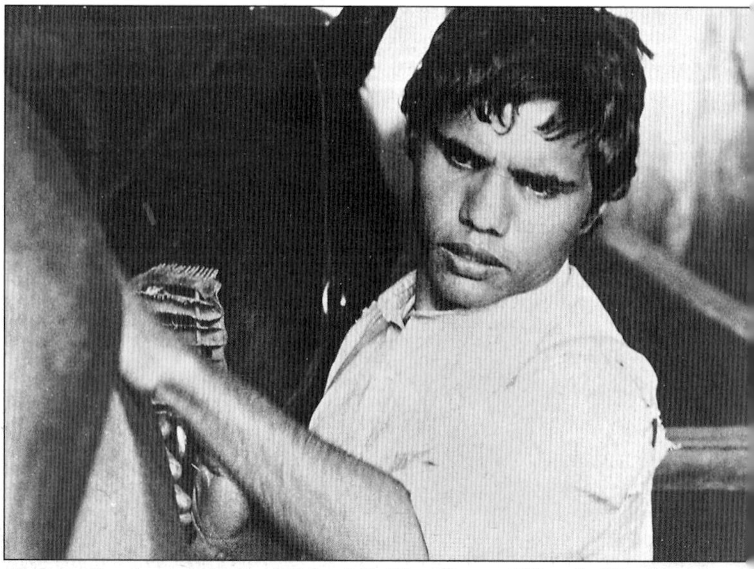
Tommy Lewis stars in Fred Schepisi's ***The Chant of Jimmie Blacksmith****.*

easonal shocker from John Carpenter

frightened Jamie Lee Curtis.

Los Angeles, 27 October
In his latest film, *Halloween*, John Carpenter appears to have been afflicted with Psycho-itis. It's a horror film peppered with Hitchcockian shock cuts in which Jamie Lee Curtis (the daughter of *Psycho*'s Janet Leigh) is pursued by a mad killer who himself seems to be unkillable. While the Bernard Herrmann-like theme (composed by the director) cranks up the tension, Carpenter's camera prowls through the night, always hinting at something horrible about to burst in from the periphery of the Panavision screen. Such plot as there is concerns an insane killer who first struck as a child on Halloween and threatens to do so again 15 years later. There are plenty of shocks along the way, and film buffs will spot the sly in-jokes Carpenter has buried in the film.

imino and war-scarred American psyche

ew York, 15 December
ichael Cimino's second feature ollowing *Thunderbolt and Light-ot* four years ago) is the epically nceived *The Deer Hunter*, which tempts to address the effect of the ietnam War on the American psy-e. The three-hour film accurately ptures the mood in America at e moment – the need to find some stification for the war. It focuses the lives of three steelworkers – obert De Niro, Christopher Walk- and John Savage, before and ter their Vietnam experiences. sing the camera as an observer, Cimino allows the narrative to unfold in an almost documentary style. In the first half, two long sequences introduce us to the characters: an elaborate wedding (practically a production number), and the deer-hunting expedition which foreshadows the horrors that await them in the jungles. In Vietnam, there is a gripping set piece when the friends are forced to play a game of Russian roulette by their Viet Cong captors, a scene which has been criticized for depicting the enemy as the incarnation of evil, without comment on the American tactics.

***he Deer Hunter**: John Savage (left) and Robert De Niro at war in Vietnam.*

Superman flies high over humdrum world

*Clark Kent (Christopher Reeve) transformed into comic-book hero **Superman**.*

New York, 15 December
Joel Schuster and Jerome Siegel's comic-strip hero Superman made his screen debut in Sam Katzman's gimcrack 1948 serial. This time, at considerably greater expense, Christopher Reeve assumes the role of the Man of Steel in *Superman – The Movie*, directed by Richard Donner. Sidestepping the camp clichés celebrated by *Batman* 12 years ago, Donner and his screenwriting team tread a fine line between gently satirizing the original character and hymning his superhuman feats of strength. Christopher Reeve, an accomplished stage actor with an academic background, brings bags of ironic charm to the role of the self-effacing Clark Kent – dispensing a stream of earnest advice to Margot Kidder's Lois Lane – and dons his alter ego's red cape and blue tights with equal aplomb. His chiseled features and formidable physique, specially built up for the role, are the perfect expression of the fantasy hero lurking in the breast of every 98-pound weakling. Gene Hackman was reportedly paid $2 million to play Superman's eccentric enemy, Lex Luthor, but he looks far less happy in the role. Marlon Brando was paid even more, at least $2.5 million, to play Superman's father in the opening sequence when the infant Superman is dispatched to Earth from the exploding planet Krypton. It was worth every cent in publicity which, in the breathless build-up to *Superman*'s release, was summed up in the slogan, "You'll believe a man can fly!" *Superman*'s special effects ensure that you will. ▷

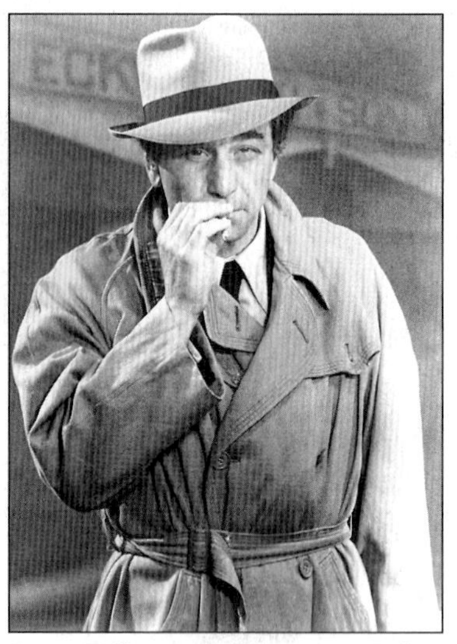
Peter Falk, a spoof Bogart in Robert Moore's **The Cheap Detective**.

Tommy Chong (left), Cheech Marin in **Up in Smoke**, directed by Lou Adler.

Gérard Depardieu in Marco Ferrer black comedy, **Bye Bye Monkey**.

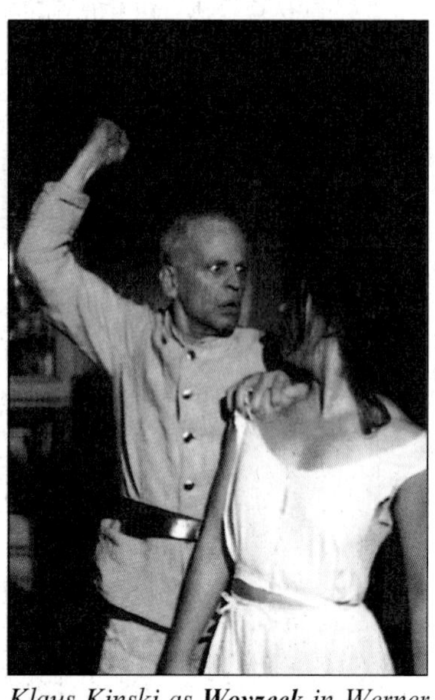
Klaus Kinski as **Woyzeck** in Werner Herzog's version of Büchner's work.

On trial: Isabelle Huppert is Claude Chabrol's **Violette Nozière**.

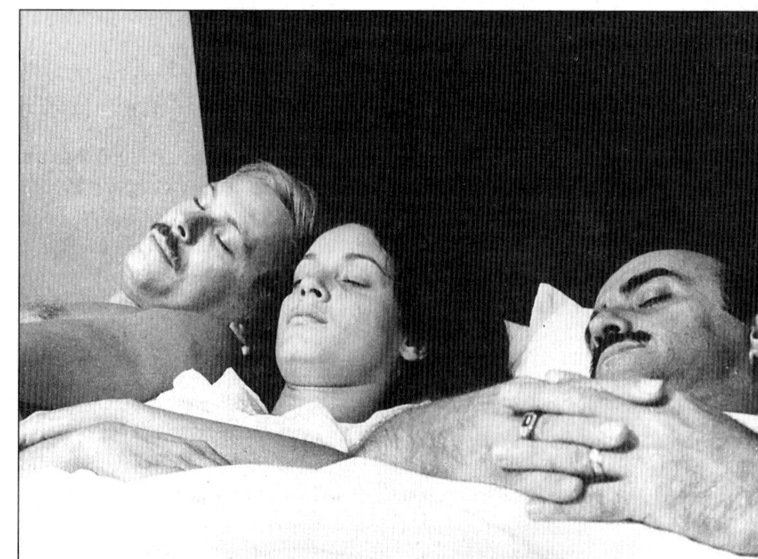
Dona Flor and her Two Husbands: Sonia Braga with José Wilker and Mau Mendonca, directed by Bruno Barreto (Brazil).

The Herd (Sürü) was scripted by the imprisoned Turkish director Yilmaz Güney and made on his behalf by Zeki Okten.

Jill Clayburgh is Mazursky's **An Unmarried Woman**, Alan Bates her lover.

inda Manz in Terrence Malick's second film, the painterly **Days of Heaven**.

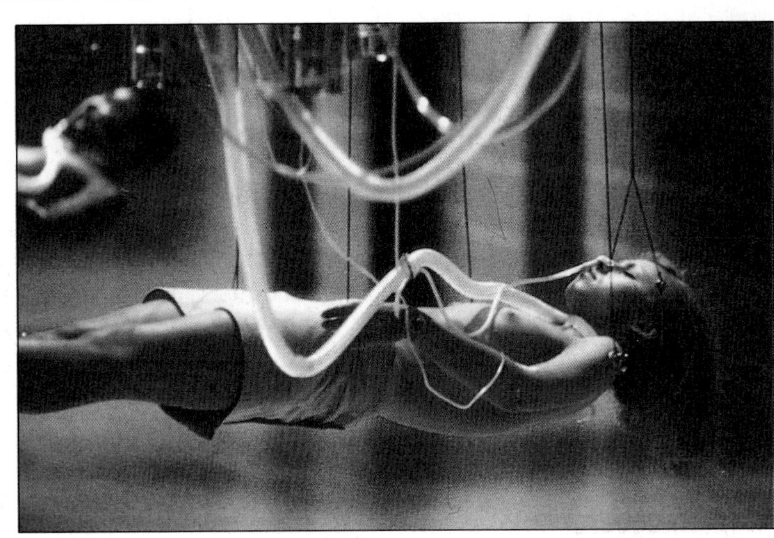

One of the year's successes, Michael Crichton's gripping, worrying **Coma**.

ick Nolte and Tuesday Weld in the hard-hitting **Who'll Stop the Rain?** (aka **og Soldiers**), directed by Karel Reisz.

KDAV

Gary Busey superb as tragic rock 'n' roll pioneer in **The Buddy Holly Story**.

ohn Cassavetes (l), Charles Durning in Brian De Palma's chiller, **The Fury**.

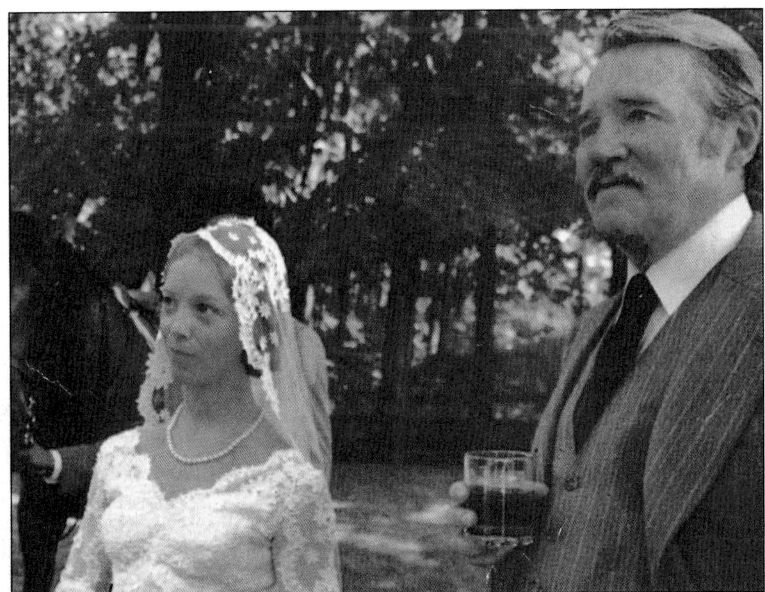

Amy Striker and Howard Duff in Robert Altman's merciless and hilarious satire on American middle-class mores, **A Wedding**.

1979

1978 Academy Awards, Dorothy Chandler Pavilion, 9 Apr.

Best Film:	*The Deer Hunter* (dir: Michael Cimino)
Best Director:	Michael Cimino
Best Actor:	Jon Voight *(Coming Home)*
Best Actress:	Jane Fonda *(Coming Home)*
Best Supp. Actor:	Christopher Walken *(The Deer Hunter)*
Best Supp. Actor:	Maggie Smith *(California Suite)*

New York, 10 January
The doyenne of Hollywood actresses, Katharine Hepburn, lives up to her reputation for bluntness. In a rare television interview for CBS, to be shown next Sunday, she lashes out at the current pervasiveness of pornography in films.

Los Angeles, 12 January
John Wayne, suffering from cancer, has undergone a serious operation in which most of his stomach had to be removed.

Rome, 23 January
Sophia Loren's husband, producer Carlo Ponti, has been charged by the Italian courts with illegal exportation of capital.

Paris, 24 January
Actress Jeanne Moreau has shown *Adolescente*, her second film as a director, with Simone Signoret and Francis Huster.

New York, 16 February
Following outbreaks of violence in several cinemas screening Walter Hill's *The Warriors*, Paramount has decided to cancel its advertising campaign and remake the trailers.

West Berlin, 22 February
The Soviet Union and other communist countries have withdrawn from the West Berlin Film Festival in protest against the showing of Michael Cimino's *The Deer Hunter*, a movie about the war in Vietnam.

Hollywood, 23 February
Despite sporadic outbursts of violence and vandalism at theaters showing *The Warriors*, a film about teen-age gang violence in New York City, Paramount Pictures has now decided to continue advertising the film. However, the company said it would release exhibitors from their contractual obligations if they felt it posed a threat either to property or persons. The film grossed over $12 million in its first two weeks.

Hollywood, 9 April
After the Oscar ceremony, actress Jane Fonda declared that Michael Cimino's Oscar winner *The Deer Hunter* "was a racist film, which presented the official version of the war in Vietnam."

Ohio, 9 April
Bob Rafelson has started shooting *Brubaker*. The cameramen's union is up in arms about the signing of Bruno Nuytten, the French director of photography, as Haskell Wexler's replacement, and are demanding the withdrawal of his work permit.

New York, 20 April
Release of Woody Allen's *Manhattan*. Allen, Diane Keaton, Michael Murphy and Mariel Hemingway star. The luminous black-and-white photography is by Gordon Willis.

Montana, 28 April
Michael Cimino, on location with *Heaven's Gate*, is 10 days behind on his shooting schedule despite the fact that he has been here since the beginning of the month. He has apparently already spent $11 million of his budget.

Hollywood, 5 August
David Field, the joint head of United Artists production, has imposed a new budget of $27.5 million and a maximum of three hours viewing time on *Heaven's Gate*.

Colorado, 31 August
As part of the Telluride Festival, the uncut original version of Abel Gance's *Napoleon*, reconstructed by historian Kevin Brownlow, with its final scene projected onto a triple screen, was shown in the open air. The director, who was present at the screening, was given a standing ovation by the public.

New York, 30 September
Lauren Bacall has published a book about her private life and career titled *Lauren Bacall, by Myself*.

Los Angeles, 2 October
Universal and Disney Pictures have lost their court case against Sony-Betamax. The court has decided that the use of a video recorder for personal use does not constitute a breach of copyright laws.

New York, 5 October
Opening of Blake Edwards' film, *10*, and the revelation of the sexy Bo Derek, who co-stars with Dudley Moore and Julie Andrews. The film looks set to make Ravel's "Bolero" the hottest music of the moment. But Edwards, who wrote, produced and directed the comedy, is reportedly furious with Orion studios over the visual advertising they chose to promote the film. The poster in question, which the director classifies as "sexist and vulgar", shows Dudley Moore swinging from a chain around the neck of an extremely well-endowed girl.

South Carolina, 23 October
Monty Python's Life of Brian, has been short lived here in Columbia. Ecclesiastical outrage over the British comedy group's satirical movie has forced a cancelation after the first evening's showing. However, the withdrawal of the film is causing an even greater upheaval as citizen groups level charges of censorship and prior restraint at Senator Thurmond, the politician instrumental in the film's suspension.

New York, 7 November
Entertainer and singer Bette Midler has her first starring role on screen in Mark Rydell's *The Rose*, which is being released today. Alan Bates, Frederic Forrest and Harry Dean Stanton co-star.

Palm Springs, 22 December
Darryl Zanuck, the last of the big-name producers in the American movie industry, has died. Zanuck started his career as a gagman for Warner Bros. before becoming a scriptwriter and, by the end of the 20s, a producer. In 1933 he created his own company, 20th Century which merged with Fox two years later to become 20th Century-Fox. Zanuck reigned as absolute master of the company until 1956 when he decided to go independent. He returned to 20th Century-Fox as head of production in 1962 and saved the studio from ruin.

Hollywood, 22 December
Disney has announced plans for first co-production. The film is *Po eye* and the co-producer Paramou

Los Angeles, 23 December
When asked which French direct they would most like to work wi 10 young actors out of 10 answer François Truffaut.

Hollywood, 31 December
The studios have announced a 5 pe cent increase in takings from U. releases this year. Richard Donne *Superman* is well in the lead wi $80 million in box-office receipts.

DEATHS

Los Angeles, 12 February
Jean Renoir

London, 24 March
Yvonne Mitchell

California, 26 May
George Brent

California, 29 May
Mary Pickford

New York, 2 June
Nicholas Ray

Los Angeles, 6 June
Jack Haley

Los Angeles, 11 June
John Wayne

Paris, 8 September
Jean Seberg

California, 26 September
John Cromwell

Capri, 27 September
Gracie Fields

California, 23 November
Merle Oberon

Paris, 26 November
Marcel L'Herbier

California, 25 December
Joan Blondell

Francis Ford Coppola broke new an terrifying ground with ***Apocalyp Now****. A major achievement, it cost fortune (Brando was paid $1 millior and was dogged by disaster.*

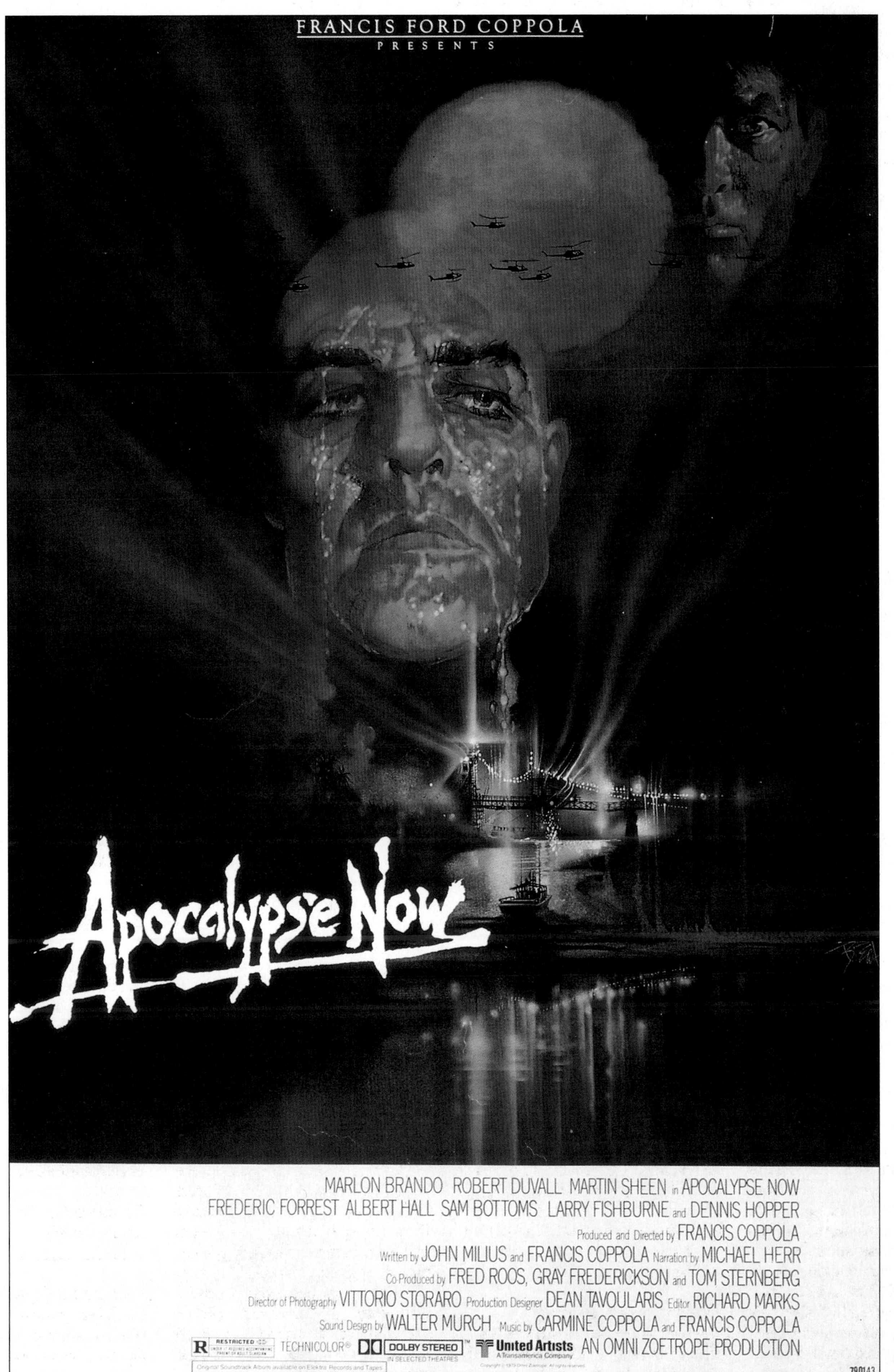
FRANCIS FORD COPPOLA
PRESENTS
Apocalypse Now
MARLON BRANDO ROBERT DUVALL MARTIN SHEEN in APOCALYPSE NOW
FREDERIC FORREST ALBERT HALL SAM BOTTOMS LARRY FISHBURNE and DENNIS HOPPER
Produced and Directed by FRANCIS COPPOLA
Written by JOHN MILIUS and FRANCIS COPPOLA Narration by MICHAEL HERR
Co-Produced by FRED ROOS, GRAY FREDERICKSON and TOM STERNBERG
Director of Photography VITTORIO STORARO Production Designer DEAN TAVOULARIS Editor RICHARD MARKS
Sound Design by WALTER MURCH Music by CARMINE COPPOLA and FRANCIS COPPOLA
R RESTRICTED
TECHNICOLOR®
DOLBY STEREO
IN SELECTED THEATRES
United Artists
A Transamerica Company
AN OMNI ZOETROPE PRODUCTION
Original Soundtrack Album available on Elektra Records and Tapes
790143

Antoine Doinel takes a look at his past

Jean-Pierre Léaud, Marie-France Pisier, Daniel Mesguish in ***Love on the Run.***

Paris, 24 January
François Truffaut's new film, *Love on the Run*, is the fifth in the series of the adventures of the director's alter ego Antoine Doinel alias Jean-Pierre Léaud. This picture is an affectionate backward look at the previous episodes, using some of the footage from them, the first being *The Four Hundred Blows* almost 20 years ago. Here, Doinel, at the age of 35, separated from his wife (Claude Jade) and young son, is involved with Sabine (Dorothée) until he meets Colette (Marie-France Pisier), a childhood sweetheart, now a lawyer. Although as lightweight as the other tales, the movie cannot hide the pain at the loss of youthful spontaneity and the difficulties of obtaining lasting love. This could be the last chapter.

Romy wins a second consecutive César

Arlette Bonnard (left) and Romy Schneider in Claude Sautet's ***A Simple Sto***

Paris, 3 February
The Césars have been in existence for only four years, but already one star has been crowned best actress twice. Romy Schneider received her second César (after *l'Important c'est d'aimer*) for Claude Sautet's film *A Simple Story*, in which she plays a divorced woman with a teenage son, trying to come to terms with reaching 40. The best actor could also have been awarded the best actre prize, because it went to Mich Serrault's outrageously successf drag queen Alban in Edouard Mo naro's *la Cage aux folles*. *L'Arge des autres* was honored with Césa for both the best film and the be director (Christian de Chalong while the Italian Ermanno Olm *The Tree of Wooden Clogs* took t best foreign language film award.

Renoir, a French genius, dies far from his beloved Montmartre

Hollywood, 13 February
One of the truly great figures of the cinema, director and writer Jean Renoir has died at his home in Beverly Hills, aged 86. The second son of the Impressionist painter Auguste Renoir, the young Jean often modeled for his father and grew up within an artistic environment which profoundly influenced his attitude to the creative process. Throughout his life he preserved his creative independence, though he regarded the cinema very much as a collaborative art and was a quite talented director of actors. Renoir thus never became part of the French film industry, and fitted even less well into the Hollywood studio system when he arrived as a refugee from Occupied France in 1940. His great period as a director was during the 1930s, when he produced one remarkable film after another, ranging from drama (*la Chienne* 1931, *Toni* 1934, *le Crime de M. Lange* 1935) to thrillers (*la Nuit du carrefour* 1932) and comedy (*Boudu sauvé des eaux* 1932). But Renoir will be best remembered for his celebrated anti-war drama, *la Grande illusion* (1937) starring Jean Gabin and Erich von Stroheim, and for his great masterpiece *la Règle du jeu* (1939) which he scripted, directed and in which he starred. Despite his antipathy to the Hollywood system, he made five interesting films in the U.S. and went on to work in India, Italy, and back in his native France in the 50s. Sadly, he found it impossible to get financing for many of his projects and turned to writing in his later years.

Renoir in his masterpiece ***The Rules of the Game****, here with Carette (right).*

Alfred Hitchcock honored by the AFI

Hollywood, 7 March
The American Film Institute h presented director Alfred Hitchco with its Life Achievement awar With the leading celebrities in H lywood in attendance, the eveni ceremony was held at the Bever Hilton Hotel and recorded by C TV for broadcast later in the wee Many of the stars of Hitchcock films, plus other associates, we there including Cary Grant, Ja Wyman and James Stewart, pr ducer Sidney Bernstein and stud head Lew Wasserman, along wi French director François Truffa and Hitch's favorite female star the 1940s, Ingrid Bergman, wl served as the evening's M.C. Unfo tunately, it was impossible to di guise the fact that this was a sa occasion. Hitchcock and his wif Alma, who had collaborated many of his projects, are both extremely poor health and, qui clearly, were unable fully to appre ate this event held in their honor.

'he hippies of 'Hair' filmed by Forman

'he Czech Milos Forman filmed **Hair**, an archetypally American subject.

'wyla Tharp was the choreographer.

New York, 14 March
After making films about adolescence in Czechoslovakia and *One Flew Over the Cuckoo's Nest*, a hymn to non-conformity, emigré Milos Forman was the logical choice to direct *Hair*, the movie version of hippiedom's hit 1967 stage musical. Although the Age of Aquarius is long over and the Flower People have withered and died, the film offers some vigorous dancing in the streets and parks of New York, some uninhibited playing from the young performers, and a touch of nostalgia for the over-25s. The episodic story follows a naive draftee (John Savage), who gets involved with a bunch of turned-on hippies at a "be-in" in Central Park.

)scar pays homage to Vietnam this year

.os Angeles, 9 April
\s Oscar enters its 51st year, films bout Vietnam are honored with ʌichael Cimino's *The Deer Hunter* 'oted Best Picture and Cimino himelf Best Director. Jon Voight and ane Fonda, who co-star in *Coming Iome*, won the Best Actor and Actress awards for their performances in that film. Christopher Walken was voted Best Supporting Actor for his harrowing performance in *The Deer Hunter* as the blue-collar boy from Pennsylvania undone by his experiences in Vietnam. Maggie Smith won her second Oscar, this time the Best Supporting Actress award, for her work in *California Suite* as, ironically, a Tinseltown actress nominated for an Oscar. The award for best foreign film went to *Préparez vos mouchoirs* (*Get Out Your Handkerchiefs*), directed by Bertrand Blier, while special awards were given to Laurence Olivier, director King Vidor and animator Walter Lantz, the man who created Woody Woodpecker.

ʌichael Caine and Maggie Smith.

'China Syndrome' comes horribly to life

Jane Fonda and Michael Douglas hot on the trail of the nuclear menace.

Pennsylvania, 28 March
The crisis which has gripped the nuclear power station at Three Mile Island has given a terrifying topicality to *The China Syndrome*, released two weeks ago. The title refers to a melt-down in a nuclear reactor triggering an uncontainable fire which, theoretically, could burn through to China. They say it couldn't happen but *The China Syndrome* entertains the possibility of a serious nuclear accident being hushed up. Jane Fonda plays the journalist on the trail of a hot story, and Michael Douglas, who also produces, is her intrepid cameraman. Jack Lemmon co-stars as the plant's chief engineer, undergoing his own emotional melt-down as disaster looms. James Bridges' intelligent direction focuses not only on the safety of nuclear power but also on the role and responsibilities of journalists.

Sober romanticism in 'The Brontë Sisters'

Paris, 9 May
André Téchiné has wanted to make *The Brontë Sisters* since 1972. Luckily, he waited until he could gather together three of the most talented young actresses in France to play the trio of celebrated Yorkshire authors: Isabelle Adjani (Emily), Marie-France Pisier (Charlotte) and Isabelle Huppert (Anne). The film, cut from three to less than two hours, centers around the sisters' somber relationship with Branwell (Pascal Greggory), their spoiled-genius brother, set in a careful re-creation of the period.

l to r: Marie-France Pisier, Isabelle Huppert and Adjani are ***The Brontë Sisters***.

Germany and America share Golden Palm

*Special Jury Prize winner **Siberiade**.*

*David Bennent (left) in Volker Schlöndorff's **The Tin Drum**.*

Cannes, 24 May
Françoise Sagan and the other members of the jury at this year's Cannes Film Festival had difficulty in choosing between Volker Schlöndorff's *The Tin Drum* and Francis Ford Coppola's *Apocalypse Now*. Therefore they decided that the two films should share the Golden Palm. In a sense, the German and the American movies have something in common since both evoke black pages in their country's history – the rise of Nazism in Germany, and the misguided Vietnam adventure. *The Tin Drum*, based on Günther Grass' complex allegorical novel, is a disturbing look at German history through the relentless gaze of a weird child. The teenage Oskar stopped growing at the age of three by an act of will. Naturally, he is a concern to his parents, because he has tantrums, constantly bangs a toy tin drum, and has a scream that shatters glass. Oskar acts as a sort of conscience to the inhabitants of Danzig when the Nazis are in power and the war rages. The remarkable performance by 12-year-old David Bennent, son of actor Heinz Bennent, effectively brings the book's character to life. War is the principal subject of *Apocalypse Now*, a film which contains some extraordinary set pieces. Coppola has explained that he wanted "to give its audience a sense of the horror, the madness, the sensuousness and the moral dilemma of the Vietnam War." This the director has certainly achieved by camera and sound techniques that assault the senses.

Cannes pays homage to Miklos Jancso

Cannes, 24 May
Discovered on the Croisette in 1965 with his film *The Round-Up*, the Hungarian director Miklos Jancso has now been honored not only with a prize given to his complete oeuvre, but with the screening of many of his films during the Festival. These include *The Round-Up*, *The Confrontation* (1969), *Winter Sirocco* (1969), *Agnus Dei* (1970), *Red Psalm* (1971) and his latest production, *Hungarian Rhapsody*. The latter marks Jancso's return to his native land after making three less successful films in Italy. There are few directors so akin to a choreographer, his films being elaborate ballets, emblematically tracing the movements in the fight for socialism and Hungarian independence – ritual dances of life and death enacted on a bleak Hungarian plain where power constantly changes hands. The camera weaves in and out like an invisible observer, sometimes dancing with the people, at others tracking them down, shooting them. A tracking shot takes on new meaning in Jancso's films.

'Alien' horror from British import Scott

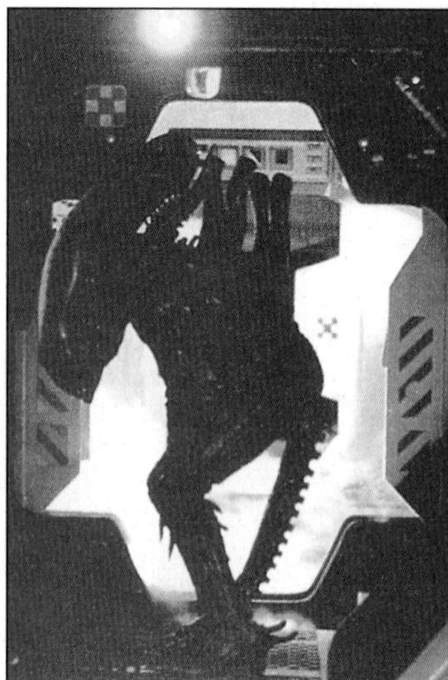
*Sigourney Weaver and a hideous space monster in Ridley Scott's **Alien**.*

New York, 24 May
Constructed as skillfully as the commercials he used to make, Ridley Scott's *Alien* is located in the pulpy, phallic world of the surrealist artist H.R. Giger. Giger's visions of a disturbing biomechanical world owe much to the tales of necromancy written in the 19th century by H.P. Lovecraft. It is on a planet full of these strange shapes that the crew of the space cruiser *Nostromo* find the derelict spacecraft that contains th ultimately terrifying alien of the titl The alien hitches a ride with th *Nostromo* and, in a manner whic recalls an old B-movie, *It! The Terrc From Beyond Space*, begins to wor its way through the crew, displayin a ferocious will to live and procreat at whatever cost to those around i In the words of *Alien*'s advertisin slogan,"In outer space no one ca hear you scream!"

Hollywood mourns the death of its 'Duke'

Hollywood, 11 June
John Wayne has lost a long and painfully fought battle with cancer. Three years ago he made his last film, *The Shootist*, playing an aging gunfighter who is dying of the same affliction. Later he appeared in TV ads for cancer research funds, using the scene from *The Shootist* in which doctor James Stewart diagnoses the disease. Wayne had been a major star since 1939, when he played the Ringo Kid in *Stagecoach*, and grew into a monolith of survival. His approach to filmmaking was characteristically straightforward: "I play John Wayne in every picture regardless of the character, and I've been doing all right, haven't I?" But he has left a number of imperishable performances, notably as abrasive and solitary men, in *Red River*, *Rio Bravo* and, unforgettably, in *The Searchers*, where the character of Ethan Edwards is mapped so closely to Wayne's own gestures that he hardly seems to be acting at all. In recent years the actor's right-win views have been known to stir cor troversy, but his death and the brav manner of his departing have move the film world.

John Wayne, defender of the faith.

oppola at the heart of darkness

lartin Sheen finds himself plunged into a dark world of almost hallucinatory horror during the Vietnam War.

Jew York, 15 August
'he making of *Apocalypse Now*, 'rancis Ford Coppola's latest film, vas almost as apocalyptic as its ubject. This work on the Vietnam Var (loosely based on Joseph Conad's *Heart of Darkness*) started hooting in March 1976 on location n the Philippines, where Coppola nd his team had planned to work or 13 weeks. They finished 238 days ter, having raised the budget from 12 million to $31 million. Much f this came out of Coppola's own ocket and from funding for which e, as an independent producer, ould be held accountable. During the course of filming, the director faced many difficulties, including a typhoon that destroyed most of the huge and expensive sets. He also had problems with top-billed, top-salaried Marlon Brando, who appears as Colonel Walter E. Kurtz very far on into the two-and-a-half-hour movie. After a week, Harvey Keitel, in the key role of Captain Benjamin Willard on the quest for Kurtz, had to be replaced by Martin Sheen, who then suffered a heart attack, which held up much of the shooting until he had recovered. To make matters worse, a civil war broke out in the Philippines, depriving Coppola of the helicopters he needed. Such were the troubles and delays on the production that the press rechristened it "Apocalypse When?" After three nightmarish years, *Apocalypse Now* has finally reached our screens, but with two different endings – one with a bang, the other with a whimper – because Coppola himself was not sure how the film should conclude. The climax that was ditched from the one version, and reinstated in the other, is an assault on Kurtz's base by both American and Viet Cong forces, a sequence whose force justifies the movie's title.

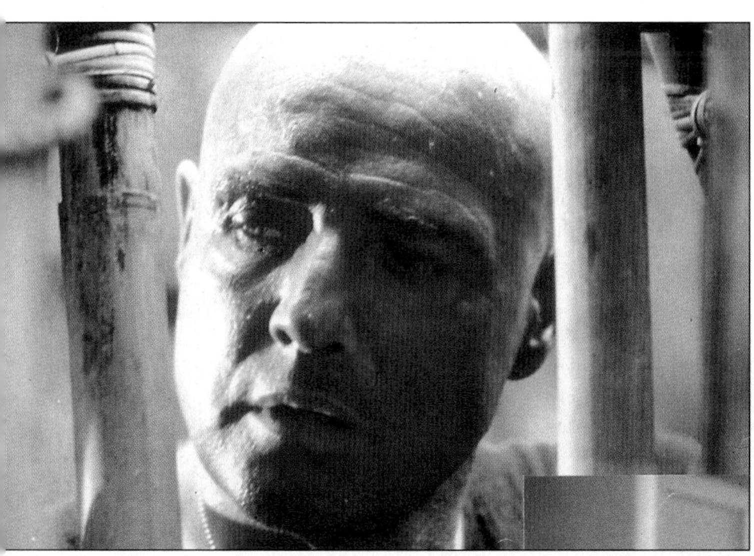

larlon Brando in the role of Colonel Kurtz, symbolic of a world gone mad.

Australia produces a star in Judy Davis

Melbourne, 17 August
Director Gillian Armstrong, the creator of several highly regarded short films, has made a sparkling feature debut with *My Brilliant Career*. Acclaimed at Cannes, and the winner of seven Australian awards, including best film and direction, it reveals Miss Armstrong's central concern with the rights of women to independence and free thought. Set in the late 19th century, the sense of period is beautifully evoked in the story of Sybylla, a headstrong young girl from a farming family who eschews the conventional life mapped out for her in order to become a writer. In this role, Judy Davis not only has presence, but also displays the kind of intelligent talent that gives notice of a star in the making. The supporting cast, especially Sam Neill, is excellent.

Co-stars Judy Davis and Sam Neill.

In Krzysztof Kieslowski's *Camera Buff*, worker Jerzy Stuhr buys a home-movie camera to film his baby. However, he becomes the official filmmaker at the factory where he works and comes into conflict with his bosses.

The revitalization of the German cinema

Hamburg, 22 September
Not since the 1920s has the German cinema known as much feverish creative activity as it has in recent years. Heading the list of top directors are Rainer Werner Fassbinder, Werner Herzog, Wim Wenders and Volker Schlöndorff. The prolific Fassbinder has delivered two films this year, *The Third Generation*, about a group of terrorists, and *The Marriage of Maria Braun*, which retraces the history of postwar Germany through the portrait of a formidable woman, played by Hanna Schygulla, star of the young German cinema. Fifty-seven years after F.W. Murnau, Herzog has resuscitated the Dracula myth with *Nosferatu the Vampire*, in which Klaus Kinski, the director's favorite actor, hypnotically plays the title role. Wenders has moved into the world of *film noir* with *The American Friend*, adapted from the Patricia Highsmith thriller *Ripley's Game*. Shot partly in English, it stars Bruno Ganz and Dennis Hopper, with appearances by Hollywood directors Nicholas Ray and Sam Fuller. The international success of many of these films, especially Fassbinder's *The Marriage of Maria Braun* and Schlöndorff's *The Tin Drum*, has undoubtedly contributed to the rebirth of the German cinema. And a dozen West German directors, including Fassbinder, Schlöndorff, Edgar Reitz and Alexander Kluge, have contributed to the recent film *Germany in Autumn*, revealing the extent of the talent available.

Director and young star (left) of ***The Tin Drum****, a ferocious portrait of Germany under the stranglehold of the Nazis.*

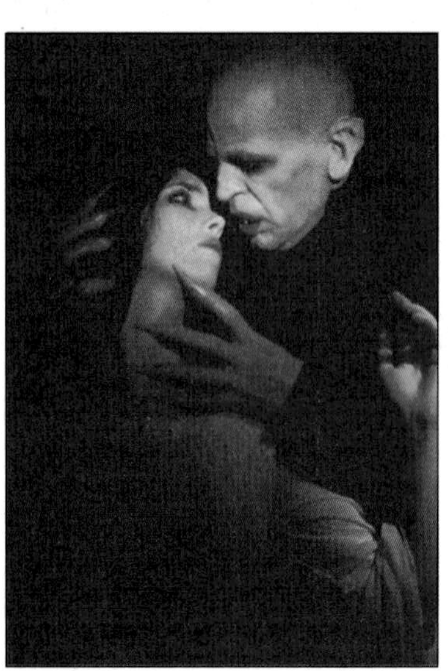

Isabelle Adjani and Klaus Kinski in Herzog's version of ***Nosferatu****.*

Dennis Hopper (left) and Bruno Ganz in Wim Wenders' ***The American Friend***

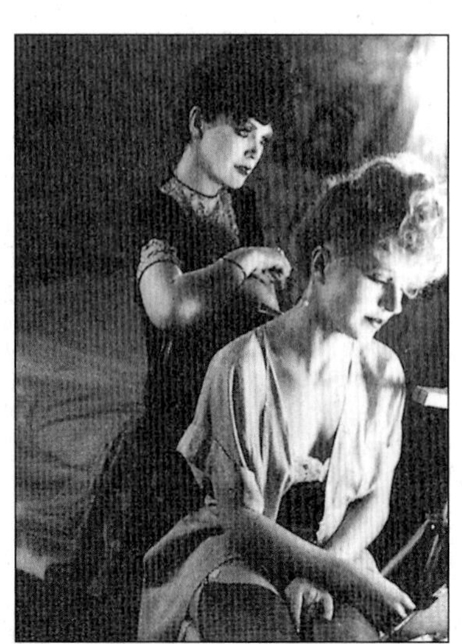

Fassbinder's ***The Marriage of Maria Braun****. On the right, Hanna Schygulla.*

The 'Declaration of Hamburg'

Hamburg, 22 September
"The German cinema of the 1980s will not submit to the decisions of commissions nor administrations, and its progress will not be determined by pressure groups," declared the 43 young German filmmakers who have gathered to assess the last few years of the industry. They have decided to take a united position in the face of the growing number of constraints put upon them by the powers-that-be. This declaration recalls the celebrated Oberhausen Manifesto of 1962 when a group of young filmmakers, working outside the commercial system, stormed the festival, criticizing "Papa's Kino" and promising to make good films at half the usual cost. Even more so than then, the directors' meeting in Hamburg has given proof of their talent and popularity, at home and abroad. To date, West Germany produces an average of 65 films a year, of which more than half derive from the so-called "Young German Cinema".

ean Seberg falls victim to despair

Paris, 8 September
This evening, in a side street of the 6th arrondissement, the corpse of ean Seberg was found in the back of a car. The American-born actress had disappeared from her home a week ago. Eleven days earlier, on returning from filming in Guyana, she attempted to commit suicide by throwing herself in front of a subway train. She succeeded on her second attempt with an overdose of sleeping pills. The 40-year-old Seberg shot to fame at the age of 7 playing the title role in Otto Preminger's *Saint Joan*. She later moved to France and for a while was married to the writer and film-maker Romain Gary.

*Seberg in Preminger's **Saint Joan**.*

Financial crisis over for Bergman

Stockholm, 29 November
It now looks likely that Ingmar Bergman, Sweden's leading director of films and theater, may be returning to his country after three-and-a-half years of self-imposed exile. The Swedish government is apparently taking steps to remedy the scandalous situation whereby Bergman, accused of owing back taxes, was treated quite disgracefully by the tax authorities. During his years in Munich, Bergman directed *The Serpent's Egg* (in English) as well as a British/Norwegian co-production *Autumn Sonata* (both 1978).

Polanski tackles English classic with 'Tess'

Paris, 31 October
Two years have passed since Roman Polanski skipped bail after being found guilty of having sex with a minor, and he remains a fugitive from American justice. His latest film, *Tess*, adapted from Thomas Hardy's Wessex novel *Tess of the D'Urbervilles*, has been filmed in France, since residency in Britain would have led to his extradition to the United States. It's a handsome production, starring the staggeringly beautiful Nastassja Kinski in the title role as the innocent country girl corrupted and discarded by polite society. The daughter of German character star Klaus Kinski, Nastassja made her film debut in 1975 with a small role as a juggler in Wim Wenders' *Wrong Movement*.

Nastassja Kinski is Hardy's heroine.

Losey's terrific excursion into filmed opera

Paris, 14 November
Joseph Losey's film adaptation of Mozart's *Don Giovanni* was the brainchild of Daniel Toscan du Plantier, a producer at Gaumont who wants to steer his company towards more cultural films. Losey, however, insisted that the film would not be merely a reproduction of a theatrical event, with static action and reduced decor. He, therefore, shot the opera in and around handsome Palladian villas in northern Italy, getting his singers to move through the settings as naturally as possible. For example, Don Ottavio's two arias have him being rowed along in a boat and walking over sleeping peasants. Then, during the "Catalogue" aria, a parade of nubile young women is displayed for Don Giovanni's delight. Losey and his co-scenarist, the well-named Frantz Salieri, have introduced a young man in black as a silent attendant on the libertine, and the climax has Giovanni tumbling into a glass-blower's vat rather than journeying to the depths of Hell. The work, conducted by Loren Maazel, is superbly sung by, among others, Ruggero Raimondi (Giovanni), Kiri Te Kanawa (Elvira), Edda Moser (Anna) and José Van Dam (Leporello).

Ruggero Raimondi sings Don Giovanni in Losey's film of Mozart's opera.

Soft-shoe shuffle of top executives

Hollywood, 18 December
The uncertainties of the movie business and the basic insecurity of the Hollywood studios lie behind the recent musical chairs played by many of the leading production executives during the past year. When, for example, a production chief is considered a "hot property", normal business considerations no longer apply. Thus, although it is not too clear to what extent David Begelman was responsible for the modest recovery at Columbia in the mid-1970s, the studio made every effort to keep him on, even after he admitted he had embezzled money from the company. And now, a relatively short time since his departure from Columbia (in February 1978), he has been hired by MGM as their new studio head. Similarly, when Alan Hirschfield was dismissed by Columbia six months after Begelman, he soon found a new home as the boss of 20th Century-Fox, replacing Alan Ladd Jr. who had resigned in June 1979 along with his two vice presidents Gareth Wigan and Jay Kanter. As the team which had been most responsible for the revival of Fox in the Seventies, they too were certain not to remain unemployed for long, and it was only a few months before they were able to announce the formation of a new independent production company. The Ladd Co., with financial backing from Warner Bros. as part of a deal to distribute their films, was obviously following in the footsteps of Arthur Krim and Robert Benjamin, who departed from United Artists to found Orion Pictures a year or so earlier.

All this activity, and the continual jockeying for position, reflects the film industry's recovery in general during the past couple of years – improved attendance and box office finally reversing the long postwar decline, and a rapid growth in the video and cable TV markets which is set to continue well into the foreseeable future. The value to film production companies and owners of a backlog of old movies is obvious. This clearly looks like a new period of opportunity for the industry, and it is not surprising that there are many who wish to be a part of this growth and to reap the benefits. ▷

TV's 'Star Trek' arrives on the big screen

Leonard Nimoy plays Spock.

New York, 8 December
Throughout the 1970s, the *Star Trek* teleseries created by Gene Roddenberry was kept alive in the form of endless repeats demanded by its fanatical fans, dubbed "Trekkies". And now their heroes have been translated from the small to the big screen in *Star Trek – The Motion Picture*, directed by Robert Wise. Captain Kirk, Mr. Spock and their colleagues on the starship *Enterprise* find themselves defending the Earth in the 23rd century against an alien which has assumed the form of new crew member Persis Khambatta, who sets some kind of film first by appearing as a bald leading lady – an interesting counterpoint to the assorted toupees worn by the aging stalwarts on the *Enterprise*'s flight deck. It is reported that Paramount has lavished $40 million on the picture, approximately eight times the original budget. For those operating on the new frontier of special effects, the cost of putting a spaceship on the screen is beginning to rival building the real thing. Some of the intimacy of the teleseries has been lost, although the thoughtful plot attempts to play on the series' great strength in dealing with ideas rather than action.

Sellers triumph in cynical satire on politics

Gardiner (Sellers) and Eve Rand (MacLaine) at a Washington D.C. party.

New York, 20 December
Peter Sellers gives a performance of unusual restraint in Hal Ashby's *Being There*, playing an innocent, childlike man catapulted by chance into the cynical world of wealth and politics. Chauncey Gardiner ("Chance") is a strange blank whose aphoristic utterances, gleaned from watching TV, earn him an extraordinary celebrity. Adapted by Jerzy Kosinski from his own short novel *Being There* is a pointed satire on the American obsession with fame.

Child a battleground for Dustin and Meryl

New York, 19 December
Kramer vs. Kramer is a small movie carrying some heavyweight casting. Dustin Hoffman is the successful Madison Avenue man whose wife walks out on him and their six-year-old son Justin Henry. Meryl Streep is the spouse in question, and in her hands the character emerges in the divorce proceedings as elegant, aloof and more than a little dangerous. The film, however, belongs to Hoffman, who has been waiting for over 10 years for a role as meaty as the one which launched his career in *The Graduate*. The tug of love is deftly handled by former screenwriter Robert Benton, who co-wrote *Bonnie and Clyde* and *What's Up Doc?* before moving behind the camera in 1977 with an oddball Western, *Bad Company*. Anticipating a hit, Columbia is rushing the picture out to qualify for the Oscars.

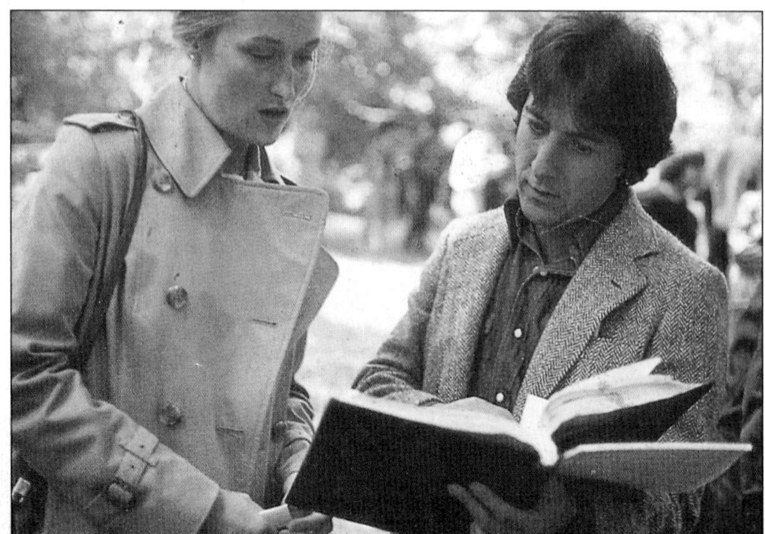
Meryl Streep and Dustin Hoffman in Robert Benton's ***Kramer vs. Kramer****.*

Autobiographical fantasia from Fosse

New York, 20 December
Bob Fosse's fourth movie, *All That Jazz* is, like its three predecessors, *Sweet Charity*, *Cabaret* and *Lenny*, set in the world of show business. However, Joe Gideon, the hero played by Roy Scheider, has a great deal in common with Fosse himself. Gideon is a workaholic womanizing director of Broadway musicals, has marital problems, and is the victim of a serious heart attack. Last year, the thrice-married Fosse was hospitalized with a heart condition. He recently declared, "Death fascinates me more than most things." *All That Jazz* is a cynical two-hour razzle dazzle production, in which Gideon does not survive his meeting with Death. However, while accepting the picture's autobiographical elements, Fosse, at 52, does not claim it as his last testament, and still has a lot more shows in him.

Joe Gideon (Roy Scheider) takes a dance rehearsal in Fosse's ***All That Jazz****.*

The Oscar Story

Each year the Oscar ceremony gives Hollywood a sense of community and a chance to honor its own. It is also the night when the rest of the world can enjoy the razzamatazz and share in Tinseltown's special glory. This glittering occasion, now seen on TV by an average 70 million Americans and 500 million people in at least 90 countries, started modestly.

The Academy of Motion Picture Arts and Sciences was dreamed up by mogul Louis B. Mayer, head of MGM, to lend respectability and status to the movie industry, the reputation of which was tarnished during the 'Roaring Twenties'. Formed on 4 May 1927, it was designed to 'raise the cultural, educational and scientific standards' of film, a statement calculated to placate those who saw the movies as having a corrupting effect on American morals and ideals.

Until 1931, the thirteen-and-a-half inch tall, eight-pound figure of a man with a crusader's sword, standing thoughtlessly on a reel of film, was known merely as The Statuette. Legend has it that the Academy librarian, Margaret Herrick, chanced to remark on studying it: "Why, he looks just like my uncle Oscar!" Just as likely is the competing claim that Bette Davis named it after her first husband, Harmon Oscar Nelson Jr. But whatever the truth behind its christening, the name has stuck, and people have always been more comfortable using the affectionate if slightly disreputable nickname of 'Oscar' to describe an Academy Award. The double Oscar-winning scriptwriter Frances Marion once described the figurine as "a perfect symbol of the picture business; a powerful athletic body clutching a gleaming sword, with half of his head, that part which held the brains, completely sliced off."

'Oscar' was designed in a few minutes on a tablecloth at Hollywood's Biltmore Hotel by MGM art director Cedric Gibbons (an 11-times recipient of his own creation), executed by sculptor George Stanley and manufactured by the Dodge Trophy Co. of Crystal Lake, Illinois. The value of the gold-plated statuette is around $250, but winners pledge never to sell it except back to the Academy – a rule that has been broken on a handful of occasions, with Oscars such as Vivien Leigh's for Scarlett O'Hara fetching large sums at auction. Oscar's value at the box office is, however, inestimable. So important is it as a means of increasing business that major studios spend in the region of $500,000 publicizing their nominated properties.

One of the first functions of the 36 Charter members of the Academy, who included Douglas Fairbanks, Mary Pickford, Cecil B. DeMille, Irving Thalberg and Raoul Walsh, was to organize the annual achievement awards. For the first nine years, only Academy members determined the awards, but in 1937 voting was extended to some 15,000 people in the movie industry, although the nominations were limited to Academy members. Later, the procedure was reversed, with the industry at large selecting the nominations and the Academy the winners. From 1957 to the present day all voting has been confined to the Academy. The latter is divided into several branches – acting, writing and so on. These decide on the five nominees for their particular category, but all branches select the Best Picture nominees. The Best Foreign Language film is selected by the entire Academy membership. Any country can submit films for competition, but only one per nation can be nominated in a particular year. (France, the first major film pioneering country, has been the most often favored winner.)

To be eligible for nomination, a film must be shown in the Los Angeles area for at least one week during the previous year. An exception to this rule is the Foreign Language movie, which only needs showing in the United States.

The winners at the first award-giving ceremony, held at Hollywood's Roosevelt Hotel on 16 May 1929, had been known for three months before the banquet. During the following years, prizes were announced a week prior to the presentations. In 1941, the policy of sealed envelopes, opened to accompanying squeals of surprise, was introduced. As the event became more prestigious, so the venue increased in size. From various hotels, it moved to Graumann's Chinese Theater in 1944, then the larger Shrine Auditorium in 1947, and on to the RKO Pantages Theater from 1950 to 1959. The Santa Monica Civic Auditorium was the site until 1969, when it moved to its present home, the Dorothy Chandler Pavilion at the L.A. County Music Center.

*Meryl Streep's first Oscar (**Kramer vs. Kramer**, 1979) from Cloris Leachman.*

Over the years there have been variations in designations of awards and increases in the categories due to changes in techniques and attitudes, but the general lines laid down for the reward of excellence have remained. The Awards came into being simultaneously with the birth of sound, so that the very first honors represented a valedictory homage to the silent cinema. By the second year, the award for Title Writing had disappeared and, the following year, a Sound Recording category was added, while Best Song and Best Score were first recognized in 1934. Despite the fact that the 30s saw the acme of fashion in Hollywood, costume designers had to wait until 1948 for inclusion, and the ceremony was in its ninth year before the important contribution of supporting players was acknowledged. Arthur Freed, the composer and producer of musicals, and the Academy's president from 1963-1967, was quoted as saying that the awards "honor artistic achievement, with little regard for popularity, box-office success or other yardsticks applied by the critics or the general public." Despite many controversial judgments, and occasional submissions to 'other yardsticks', the Academy, as a whole, has maintained those standards. At the same time, it has seldom cut itself off from public taste, and has acknowledged Hollywood's greatest strength: the manufacture of superbly crafted mass entertainment.

Mainly, however, the story of 'Uncle Oscar' reflects the development of American cinema, and the trends, tastes, and events in society as a whole. When the movies thrived as great escapist entertainment during the Depression, the annual awards were the cherry on the top. The outbreak of war in Europe in 1939 changed the character of Hollywood films and the flavor of the Awards ceremony. After Pearl Harbor, formal attire was banned from the evening event, the banquet was renamed a dinner, and searchlights that usually played outside the venue were switched off until peace returned.

Although the Academy makes financial contributions to the development of cinematic techniques and supports a substantial film library, it is Awards night that lends the institution its glamour and continues to cause excitement among fans. Oscars are as sought after as they ever were.

Nosferatu
THE VAMPYRE
TWENTIETH CENTURY-FOX presents
KLAUS KINSKI ISABELLE ADJANI
in NOSFERATU THE VAMPYRE
(English Subtitles)
with BRUNO GANZ
MICHAEL GRUSKOFF presents A WERNER HERZOG FILM
Written, Produced and Directed by WERNER HERZOG Color by EASTMAN
Now in paperback from AVON

German Werner Herzog remakes F.W. Murnau's 1921 classic vampire tale.

*Dustin Hoffman plays mother to Justin Henry in **Kramer vs. Kramer**.*

*Barbara Harris, Alan Alda in the political drama **The Seduction of Joe Tynan***

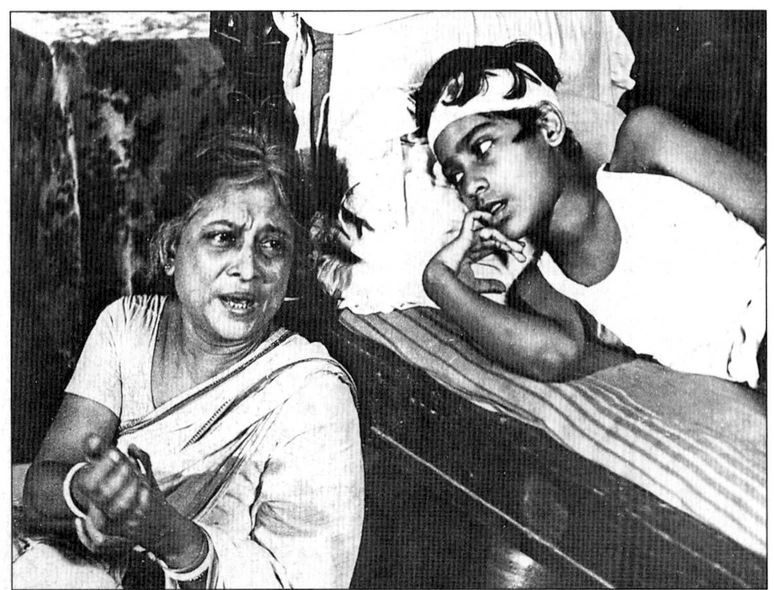

***And Quiet Rolls the Dawn** is a powerful drama from India's Mrinal Sen.*

*l to r: John Cleese, Michael Palin (Pontius Pilate), Graham Chapman in the irreverent **Monty Python's Life of Brian**, directed by Terry Jones.*

The last law in a world gone out of control. Pray that he's out there somewhere.
MFP
INTERCEPTOR
MAD MAX
Produced by BYRON KENNEDY · Directed by GEORGE MILLER · With MEL GIBSON · Music by BRIAN MAY
Written by JAMES McCAUSLAND and GEORGE MILLER
Australian George Miller's debut stars Mel Gibson as a leather-clad avenger.

CUTTERS
CUTTERS
CUTTERS
Left to right: Jackie Earle Haley, Daniel Stern, Dennis Quaid and Dennis Christopher in **Breaking Away**, this year's sleeper hit.

Miss Piggy, Kermit the Frog make their big-screen debut: **The Muppet Movie**.

Flesh-eating zombies walk the earth in George A. Romero's suspense horror flick, **Dawn of the Dead**, follow-up to **Night of the Living Dead**.

Steve Martin is **The Jerk** in Carl Reiner's movie.

James Brolin, one of the victims of **The Amityville Horror**.

The Reagan Years

The installation of a former movie actor in the highest elected office provided spectacular evidence for the argument that the film industry is not merely providing entertainment that reflects society's tastes and behavior, but is indeed a powerful vehicle for propaganda, attitudes, and politicking personalities.

The new President of the United States, Ronald Reagan, crucially, had served his apprenticeship in the hurly-burly of the Warner Bros. studio, and had honed his communication and public relations skills as president of the Screen Actors Guild during a tricky, crisis-strewn, violently anti-labor and anti-Communist period.

Now, money and power-driven Hollywood, frequently but quite erroneously characterized as a hotbed of liberalism, contributed to the nation's mood swing to a new conservatism, with mainstream commercial cinema of the 1980s elaborating on many of the ideas and ideals being expounded from the White House. Family-oriented spectacles, gung-ho action and escapism became the staples of the screen. Social comment, and themes dealing with that which was ugly, threatening or cautionary were, for the most part, left to independent filmmakers or the impressively emerging Third World cinema.

Between them, George Lucas and Steven Spielberg can be credited with improving the health of the entire industry – and probably saving Paramount and Universal in the process – by producing and/or directing an extraordinary share of the blockbusters of the decade: two sequels to 1977's *Star Wars* (*The Empire Strikes Back*, 1980 and *The Return of the Jedi*, 1983), the *Indiana Jones* adventure trilogy, and *E.T. The Extra-Terrestrial* (1982), Spielberg's fairy tale about a boy and his alien that would reign as the top-grossing film ever for more than a decade.

Youth-targeted movie merchandising to accompany these smashes boosted the coffers and grew into a multi-million-dollar industry. The eagerness to exploit the teen market also made this the era of cross-promotion: movie-TV-video-radio-record tie-ins were developed to plug movies.

Allegedly adult entertainment, too, was most likely to succeed when absurd, with the wacky disaster-movie spoof *Airplane!* (1980) spawning many imitative parodies, knucklehead comedies such as the *Police Academy* series (1984–1994), and various antics bearing the *National Lampoon* banner a permanent feature of the yearly box-office Top Tens. Sensationalist, effects-packed horror flicks also had a big following, with the five *Nightmare on Elm Street* slasher-saga entries epitomizing the teen gore genre and making a fortune. Only a handful of films with any claims to sophistication or 'wrinklies' appeal scored heavily at the box office: *Kramer vs. Kramer*, *On Golden Pond*, *Tootsie*, *Terms of Endearment* and *Rain Man* proved unexpected sensations, with three of these starring the favorite thespian of the middle-aged and the middlebrow, Dustin Hoffman.

The middle-aged and the middlebrow got their own back, dispensing Oscars largely to the earnest, the tearful, and the sumptuous: films such as *Gandhi* (1982), *Amadeus* (1984), *Out of Africa* (1985) and *The Last Emperor* (1987). A notable wild-card honoree was the angry, macho filmmaker Oliver Stone, a Vietnam veteran and blood-and-guts screenwriter, whose war parable-cum-memoir *Platoon* made him the hottest director in America.

Artistically and commercially the filmmakers to reckon with in the 70s suffered mixed fortunes in the 80s. Martin Scorsese began the decade with a landmark – some would argue the best – film of the 80s, *Raging Bull*, a compelling portrait of a boxer and a virtuoso technical display that also confirmed Robert De Niro's pre-eminence as the greatest screen actor of his generation. From there Scorsese extended his range with comedy, commercial entertainment, and the highly controversial *The Last Temptation of Christ*. After a heady 70s, Francis Ford Coppola's reversal of fortune was dispiriting. His studio, Zoetrope, foundered in ambitious failures, leaving him with crippling debt. In this he was not alone. Lemons of the 1980s include Lucas' $34-million turkey *Howard the Duck*, Warren Beatty's $40 million disaster *Ishtar* and, most infamously, Michael Cimino's $40 million catastrophe for United Artists, *Heaven's Gate*. Quietly aloof from the industry, New York auteur Woody Allen was in his prime, juggling anguish and hilarity in a film per year, with *Hannah and Her Sisters* in 1986 striking the happiest balance of popular and critical favor. Spielberg became indisputably the most successful director in history on the balance sheets, but failed to earn critical respect for his 'serious' films, *The Color Purple* (1985) and *Empire of the Sun* (1987).

There was no shortage of directorial talent. The most personal and highly individual work came from veterans who knew how to use the system, and bright sparks working outside it. The aged John Huston, the unrepentant maverick Robert Altman and the very determinedly fringe but very influential John Cassavetes did notable work.

David Lynch and David Cronenberg made their names, with the former's *Blue Velvet* creating a furor; the sibling directing-producing team of Joel and Ethan Coen, beginning with *Blood Simple* in 1984, wowed cinéastes, and from the margins of independent American filmmaking emerged Jim Jarmusch, Steven Soderbergh and the gifted black provocateur Spike Lee.

Among producers, the partnership of Don Simpson and Jerry Bruckheimer supplied *Beverly Hills Cop* (1984) and *Top Gun* (1986). Joel Silver achieved major status with *Lethal Weapon* and *Die Hard*. More quietly, Canadian-born producer-director Ivan Reitman was making an unbroken string of comedy hits such as *Ghostbusters*, many of them employing former stand-up comics who had become popular on TV's *Saturday Night Live*. Writer-director-producer John Hughes devoted his impressive energies to a series of 'clean-teen' romantic comedies set exclusively in middle-class Midwestern suburbia.

The real power in Hollywood in the 1980s lay not with studio executives, the moguls of the past having been succeeded by corporation employees whose job tenure was averaging a fleeting 18 months, but with agents. The breed long dismissed as 'Ten Percenters' became feared super-agents, none more so than CAA chief Michael Ovitz, designated Most Powerful Man In Hollywood for taking deal-making to unprecedented domination. By the end of the decade the price tag for a top star rose to a reported $15 million for the likes of Arnold Schwarzenegger. Meanwhile, actors, most notably among them Robert Redford and Warren Beatty, were following Clint Eastwood in taking up the directing reigns.

Reflecting the 'we're in the money' and 'all's right with the world' lines promulgated from Washington and the West Coast, the top stars were the funny men and the tough take-charge guys. Harrison Ford starred in five of the top grossing films, while the 21-year-old comic Eddie Murphy leaped to stardom in

Sigourney Weaver's 2nd outing as Ripley in James Cameron's ***Aliens*** *(1986).*

1983 with *48 HRS* and had the clout of a king after *Beverly Hills Cop* (1984). His profane, sassy persona carried even the flimsiest of movies to box-office success. Sylvester Stallone remained the testosterone king well into the 80s, with further outings for *Rocky* and three bloodthirsty comic-book sagas as the armed-to-the-teeth Vietnam vet and defender of freedom, John Rambo. Glamorous Mel Gibson and droll Bruce Willis presented a challenge, while former Mr. Universe, property tycoon and talk show regular Arnold Schwarzenegger was cannily masterminding his rise from Conanesque cult star to Terminator to superstar. Marrying into the Kennedy family, Arnie even hinted at political aspirations and served as head of the President's Council for Fitness for his friend and Reagan's heir, George Bush. The most acclaimed and accomplished actress of the 80s was Meryl Streep, who took the lioness' share of prestigious women's roles, but it was Sigourney Weaver who struck one of the more notable successes in the male preserve as the action heroine Ripley in *Aliens* (1986).

The sad and sensationally reported death of Rock Hudson from AIDS in 1985 shook the film community and prompted celebrities, led by Elizabeth Taylor, to make AIDS research the most emotive and urgent hip cause of the time. Entertainment circles were hard hit by subsequent devastating deaths, but nobody could raise the money to make a film dealing with the subject.

Hudson's death signified the end of an era. He had been one of the last major stars manufactured by the extinct, manipulative studio contract system. New stars were plucked from school corridors, streets, TV commercials and the loins of Hollywood's own. The more visible of the 80s young set, loosely and collectively dubbed the Brat Pack, revolved around actor Martin Sheen's sons Emilio Estevez and Charlie Sheen, Sean Penn, Matt Dillon, Rob Lowe, and 'teen princesses' Ally Sheedy, Molly Ringwald and Demi Moore. Many got their breaks and recurring work in John Hughes pictures like *The Breakfast Club* and *Pretty in Pink*. Coppola's back-to-back youth films of 1983, *The Outsiders* and *Rumble Fish*, were also a veritable Who's Who of Who Will Be Who, featuring Lowe, Dillon, Estevez, C. Thomas Howell, Ralph Macchio, Patrick Swayze, Tom Cruise and token chick Diane Lane. Cruise would leap in 1986 from teen heart-throb to bona fide movie star in the number one hit of that year, *Top Gun*, raise his stock higher in the company of Paul Newman and Dustin Hoffman and end the decade with an Oscar-nominated performance as paraplegic Viet vet Ron Kovic in Oliver Stone's second Vietnam War piece, *Born on the Fourth of July*.

For the more mature, one of the savviest career rises was that of Michael Douglas, son of Kirk, who had won the Best Picture Oscar for producing *One Flew Over the Cuckoo's Nest* (1975), years before attaining screen celebrity. Three hits teaming him with Kathleen Turner saw them dubbed the Tracy and Hepburn of the 80s, and he was atop the 1987 A-list after *Fatal Attraction* with Glenn Close and his Oscar-winning performance in Stone's *Wall Street* as the reptilian yuppie icon Gordon Gekko.

*Emmanuelle Béart was **Manon des Sources**: sequel to **Jean de Florette** (1986).*

American cinema's preoccupation with the juvenile was felt worldwide. Economically the rest of the world sank into recession well before it took hold in the U.S., the country which still dominated in the marketplace, setting the tone as European film industries lurched through crises.

A decade that had seemed so promising in the UK when *Chariots of Fire* won the Oscar for Best Picture turned out anything but. Hemdale's producing *Platoon* (1986) was one of the few profit-making coups to boast of. The warhorse Rank Organisation ceased production and the $36 million *Raise the Titanic* sank Sir Lew Grade. It was left to aggressive young production companies Palace Pictures, Working Title and Initial to cajole modest budgets from international sources and come up with *succès d'estimes* like Neil Jordan's *Mona Lisa* (1986), Stephen Frears' *My Beautiful Laundrette* (1985), Chris Menges' *A World Apart* (1988) and Alex Cox's *Sid and Nancy* (1986).

Australia yielded one phenomenal hit in comic Paul Hogan's *Crocodile Dundee*, but the celebrated Renaissance of the 70s came to grief in the 80s, by which time leading lights Peter Weir, Bruce Beresford and George Miller had decamped to Hollywood.

The French industry remained self-sufficient, able to produce profitable films for an avid domestic audience. Veterans Robert Bresson, Jacques Demy, Maurice Pialat, Erich Rohmer, Alain Resnais, Jean-Luc Godard and François Truffaut (whose death in 1984 was mourned around the world) were still forces. Jean-Jacques Annaud was foremost in mounting multinational productions like *The Name of the Rose* (1986) for an international audience, while new young lions Luc Besson, Jean-Jacques Beineix (*Diva*) and Léos Carax won cult followings with their contemporary ideas and style. Claude Berri's *Jean de Florette* (and its companion *Manon des Sources*) was a spectacular international success. The eponymous hero of that tragedy, Gérard Depardieu, was Oscar-nominated for *Cyrano de Bergerac* (1990) – a rare event for a foreign film, as was Isabelle Adjani for *Camille Claudel* (1988). Depardieu was far and away the biggest (in all senses) French personality, with foreign audiences under the impression that few films were made in France without him.

After the death of Rainer Werner Fassbinder and the 'internationalization' of Wim Wenders with *Paris, Texas* (1984), German cinema was comparatively quiet, and after *Das Boot* (1981) Wolfgang Petersen was wooed to Hollywood. In Poland Krzysztof Kieslowski inherited Andrzej Wajda's mantle as the foremost contemporary filmmaker in that country. Following Ingmar Bergman's triumphant swan song, *Fanny and Alexander* (1983), Scandinavian cinema seemed to be preoccupied with the search for the new Bergman, and hoped to have found him in Bille August, although Gabriel Axel pipped him to honors as the first Dane to receive the Best Foreign Film Oscar with 1987's *Babette's Feast*, and the Swede Lasse Hallström (*My Life as a Dog*) also soon defected West.

Italian filmmakers were dispirited by a sharp decline in native audiences who deserted them in favor of American films, but Federico Fellini, the Taviani brothers and Ettore Scola held their ground and repute, while Giuseppe Tornatore delighted international audiences with *Cinema Paradiso* (1988).

There was an explosion of talent from Africa where filmmakers like Mali's Souleymane Cissé and Burkino Faso's Idrissa Ouedraogo were exploding African culture, tradition and social issues with subtlety and, often, great beauty.

Japan's venerable Akira Kurosawa still had two masterpieces in him, *Kagemusha* (1980) and *Ran* (1985), but the most welcome development in world cinema came from China. The reopening in 1978 of the Beijing Film School (closed in the Cultural Revolution) bore fruit in the so-called "Fifth Generation" of filmmakers. The leaders of the group were Chen Kaige and Zhang Yimou, whose revelatory work began to appear abroad in 1984.

The 80s came to an end in climbing cinema attendances but worsening recession. There was no country where filmmakers could be sanguine about the social climate in which they worked. The cinema was approaching its centenary in a rapidly changing political landscape.

ANGIE ERRIGO

1980

1979 Academy Awards, Dorothy Chandler Pavilion, 14 Apr.

Best Film:	*Kramer vs. Kramer* (dir: Robert Benton)
Best Director:	Robert Benton
Best Actor:	Dustin Hoffman *(Kramer vs. Kramer)*
Best Actress:	Sally Field *(Norma Rae)*
Best Supp. Actor:	Melvyn Douglas *(Being There)*
Best Supp. Actress:	Meryl Streep *(Kramer vs. Kramer)*

New York, 3 January
Peter Yates' *Breaking Away* was awarded top film honors yesterday by the 35-member National Film Society of Film Critics. This populist story by Steve Tesich about four cycling midwestern locals who race against all odds, also took the best screenplay award. Runners-up to Peter Yates' film were Woody Allen's *Manhattan* and Robert Benton's *Kramer vs. Kramer.*

Hollywood, 3 January
The venerable Alfred Hitchcock has received a knighthood and is now Sir Alfred. The British consul here personally took the news to the director at Universal Studios.

New York, 28 January
A record high first-run admission price of $7.50 will be charged for Bob Guccione's $17 million film *Caligula*, when it has its American premiere on 1 February at the Penthouse East Theater here.

Bagdad, 7 February
The Iraqi government has created the Babylone production company by grouping together the private and public sectors of the industry.

New York, 12 February
Release of *Cruising*, directed by William Friedkin and starring Al Pacino. Shooting of the film proved difficult due to demonstrations by the gay community. Many people are demanding that an X replace the picture's R rating.

Paris, 13 February
Roman Polanski's *Tess* has won the César for best film and best director. Miou-Miou was named best actress for *la Dérobade* and Claude Brasseur best actor for Robin Davis' *la Guerre des polices*. The César for the best foreign film went to Woody Allen's *Manhattan*. Three special Césars were awarded to Louis de Funès, Kirk Douglas and producer Pierre Braunberger.

Los Angeles, 17 February
John Huston has directed a biting satire on obsessive, fundamentalist religion. *Wise Blood* is adapted from Flannery O'Connor's novel, with Brad Dourif, Harry Dean Stanton and Daniel Shor heading the cast.

Kinshasa, 21 February
General Mobutu, the head of state in Zaire, has decided to nationalize Cofilmex, a distribution company financed from Belgium.

Florida, 10 March
According to the current issue of the *National Enquirer*, actor Steve McQueen has cancer.

Hollywood, 11 March
Francis Ford Coppola has bought the Hollywood General Studios for $6.7 million after three months of negotiations. Coppola's plans for the studios, renamed Zoetrope, include the creation of a "complete, fully integrated film studio with the best features of the studios of the 1930s and 1940s."

India, 15 April
The National Film Development Corporation, a central group of film producers and exporters, has been created to promote Indian films.

Hollywood, 9 June
Actor Richard Pryor has suffered serious burns. According to a police report, he was experimenting with a mixture of cocaine and ether which caught fire as he was inhaling it. He is said to be in a critical condition.

Hollywood, 17 June
The Shining, Stanley Kubrick's adaptation of Stephen King's horror bestseller, opened 13 June across North America to blockbuster business, grossing a truly phenomenal $7,763,426 at 747 theaters in three days. The totals represent the biggest opening day and opening weekend for any film in the history of Warner Bros.

Los Angeles, 18 July
Release of *The Big Red One*, Samuel Fuller's first film since 1972, with Lee Marvin, Robert Carradine and Mark Hamill.

London, 29 July
The story of American Communist John Reed is told in *Reds*, which is moving to the completion of its filming here. Warren Beatty, starring as Reed, is also directing this ambitious project, his first solo attempt behind the camera.

Paris, 3 August
Several thousand reels of film went up in smoke in a fire which ravaged the stockpile in the Cinémathèque Française. The disaster came at the worst possible moment: the Cinémathèque has been in disarray since Henri Langlois' death in 1977. The fire raises the question of finances, since present funding is insufficient to carry contents insurance. The Minister for Culture, Jean-Philippe Lecat, has announced an emergency allocation of 4 million francs for the construction of a new building in Bois-d'Arcy.

Paris, 1 September
From today, cinema prices are no longer fixed and will be available at half-price on Mondays.

Hollywood, 17 September
Negotiations between professional unions and producers have started again after a break of 12 days.

Paris, 24 September
Italian director Ettore Scola is in Paris for the release of his film, *The Terrace* (*La Terrazza*).

New York, 26 September
Release of Woody Allen's *Stardust Memories*, his most expensive film to date, starring Allen, Charlotte Rampling, Jessica Harper, and the French actress Marie-Christine Barrault. It cost $10 million to make.

Washington D.C., 4 November
Ronald Reagan has been elected President of the United States. The former actor gave up films in 1964 after making *The Killers*. Twice elected governor of California (in 1966 and 1970) he has been working towards this moment for the last five years. He is to be sworn in at the White House on 20 January.

Los Angeles, 14 November
Release of *Raging Bull*, director Martin Scorsese's film based on the autobiography of the colorful boxer Jake La Motta. Robert De Niro plays the lead.

New York, 20 November
After fruitful negotiations with Francis Ford Coppola, Jean-Luc Godard's film, *Sauve qui peut (la Vie)*, has been released under the title *Every Man for Himself* (aka *Slow Motion*). The film is proving popular with both New York audiences and critics.

Munich, 29 December
The last 13 episodes of Rainer Werner Fassbinder's 26-episode *Berlin Alexanderplatz*, are being shown on television. The director considers this epic piece of filmmaking (drawn from a novel by Alfred Doblin and starring Gunter Lamprecht, Barbara Sukowa and Hanna Schygulla) to be his major work.

BIRTHS

New York, 26 August
Macaulay Culkin

DEATHS

Los Angeles, 29 January
Jimmy Durante

Los Angeles, 29 April
Alfred Hitchcock

London, 24 July
Peter Sellers

Mexico, 7 November
Steve McQueen

Los Angeles, 22 November
Mae West

New York, 24 November
George Raft

California, 26 November
Rachel Roberts

California, 31 December
Raoul Walsh

George Lucas responded to the unprecedented success of ***Star Wars*** *with a superb sequel,* ***The Empire Strikes Back****. The same good guy-bad guy teams fight it out in space.*

THE STAR WARS SAGA
CONTINUES

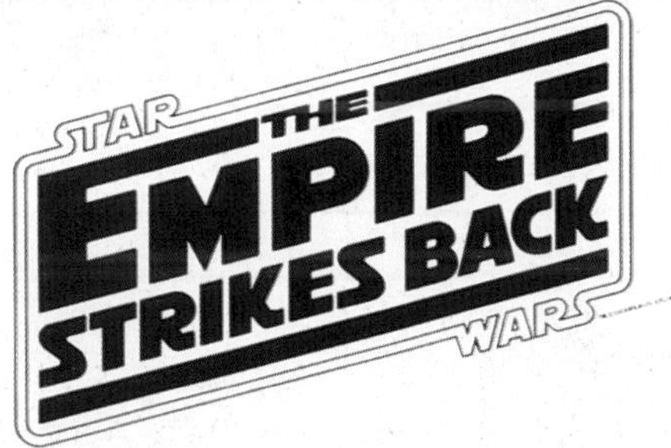
STAR
THE
EMPIRE
STRIKES BACK
WARS

Starring
MARK HAMILL · HARRISON FORD · CARRIE FISHER
BILLY DEE WILLIAMS · ANTHONY DANIELS
as C-3PO
Co-starring DAVID PROWSE as Darth Vader · KENNY BAKER as R2-D2 · PETER MAYHEW as Chewbacca · FRANK OZ as Yoda
Directed by IRVIN KERSHNER
Produced by GARY KURTZ
Screenplay by LEIGH BRACKETT and LAWRENCE KASDAN
Story by GEORGE LUCAS
Executive Producer GEORGE LUCAS
Music by JOHN WILLIAMS
DOLBY STEREO
IN SELECTED THEATRES
ORIGINAL SOUNDTRACK ON RSO RECORDS
Filmed in Panavision® — Color by Rank Film Laboratories — Prints by Deluxe®
NOVELIZATION FROM BALLANTINE BOOKS
A Lucasfilm Ltd. Production — A Twentieth Century Fox Release

A woman in Zanuck's chair

Hollywood, 1 January
The film company executive Sherry Lansing has been appointed president at 20th Century-Fox, the first time in the history of Hollywood that a woman has occupied such a position (though 60 years ago Mary Pickford was one of the founders of United Artists and played a major role in the running of the company). Miss Lansing first became involved in films as an actress in *Loving* and *Rio Lobo* (both 1970) and numerous TV shows. She worked for a time as a story editor at MGM, and then became vice president in charge of production at Columbia before she was offered her new post.

Male prostitution spells stardom for handsome Richard Gere

Richard Gere escorting a wealthy client in Paul Schrader's ***American Gigolo.***

New York, 1 February
Richard Gere has his best role to date in Paul Schrader's *American Gigolo*. He lets his brooding good looks and perfectly muscled body do the talking as Julian Kay, the high-class L.A. stud of the title who can satisfy rich women but remains unfulfilled himself until he is redeemed by Lauren Hutton. Paul Schrader has lifted the final sequence straight from Robert Bresson's *Pickpocket* (1959), but *American Gigolo* does not carry the weight of that austere masterpiece. Schrader is an interesting character, an intellectual in Hollywood whose strict Calvinist upbringing meant that he did not see a film until the age of 17. His work retains a puritanical streak.

John Gielgud is 'The Conductor' for Wajda

Berlin, 27 February
Even though Sir John Gielgud, the great English classical stage actor, has worked with some of the best film directors – Alfred Hitchcock (*The Secret Agent*, 1936), Joseph L. Mankiewicz (*Julius Caesar*, 1953) and Orson Welles (*Chimes at Midnight*, 1966) – his long but intermittent career on screen has seldom done him justice. However, he gave an unforgettable performance as the witty, bilious, dying novelist in Alain Resnais' *Providence* three years ago, and has now been given almost as good a role as *The Conductor* in Andrzej Wajda's latest film. Though Sir John is unfortunately deprived here of one of his most distinguished and distinguishing features – his mellifluous voice – through the Polish dubbing, he remains outstanding even with a borrowed voice. In this film, Gielgud plays a celebrated Polish-born conductor, who returns to his birthplace after 50 years in the U.S. Although old and dying, he is able to electrify a struggling provincial orchestra, something its own conductor has never been able to do. The younger man's feelings of inadequacy puts a strain on his marriage. The screenplay by Andrzej Kijowski hints at a deeper meaning, which suggests a parable on Polish feelings of inferiority.

Sissy Spacek sensational as Loretta Lynn

Philadelphia, 7 March
In *Coal Miner's Daughter*, Sissy Spacek's abundant talent is tested to the full as she matures from an unworldly 13-year-old to a country music star battling drug addiction and marital breakdown. The film tells the story of Loretta Lynn, the girl from Butcher's Hollow in the Appalachians, who was married at 13, a mother of three at 18 and a star of the Grand Ol' Oprey by her late 20s. Neatly negotiating the pitfalls of the standard rags-to-riches biopic, *Coal Miner's Daughter* also gives Spacek the opportunity to do her own singing, coming creditably close to capturing Lynn's trademark glottal catch. Tommy Lee Jones, an underrated actor whose intense, reflective style catches the dark side of the good ol' boy persona, provides superb support as Doolittle Lynn, Loretta's pushy but vulnerable husband. And there is good work, too, from Beverly D'Angelo as another country legend with a great voice, the tragic Patsy Cline. The film is skillfully directed by an Englishman, Michael Apted, who was called in as a last-minute replacement for Joseph Sargent, who had refused to work with Spacek. Apted claims that Appalachia is not so very different from the north of England, where he cut his teeth in television.

Krystyna Janda and Sir John Gielgud in Andrzej Wajda's ***The Conductor.***

Tommy Lee Jones and Sissy Spacek: a family scene in ***Coal Miner's Daughter***

Fellini's fantasy vision of the female

Marcello Mastroianni, caught between bizarre dreams and nightmares.

Rome, 31 March
After dealing with the eternal masculine myth in *Casanova*, Federico Fellini has now turned his attention to the emancipation of women in his latest film *City of Women*. Marcello Mastroianni finds himself in a nightmarish world completely dominated by women. Although a rather simple-minded, anti-feminist allegory, the film has the advantage of Fellini's usual visual mastery.

Hitchcock: a sixty-year career is ended

Hollywood, 29 April
The great British-born director Alfred Hitchcock died early this morning at his Bellagio Road home in Bel Air, which he had shared with his wife Alma since 1942. The last year of his life had, unfortunately, been a sad one for Hitch. In May he finally closed his office at Universal Studios, since it had been apparent for some time that he was no longer capable of directing a new picture. He had completed his last feature, *Family Plot*, in 1975 and had recently put a good deal of time and effort into a new script adaptation of the novel, *The Short Night*, based on the true story of British spy George Blake. He was briefly cheered by a visit from one of his favorite stars, Ingrid Bergman, in August, and was included in the Queen's Christmas Honors List in December. His knighthood was officially presented by the British consul at a brief ceremony at Universal on 3 January this year. It is exactly 60 years since the young Hitchcock entered the British film industry as a designer of film titles, a modest beginning for one of the most memorably original and creative careers in the history of the cinema.

During the filming of ***Family Plot****.*

Academy voters ignore the blockbusters

Los Angeles, 14 April
Although Francis Ford Coppola's *Apocalypse Now* was nominated in eight categories at this year's Oscar ceremony, this $31.5 million film about the Vietnam War was virtually ignored, as were other of the year's blockbusters. The Academy favored the smaller-scale movies, especially the tug-of-war child custody drama, *Kramer vs. Kramer*, which gathered five Oscars: Best Picture, Best Director (Robert Benton), Best Actor (Dustin Hoffman, after three previous nominations), Best Supporting Actress (Meryl Streep) and Best Screenplay (Benton). Known principally as TV's Gidget, Sally Field blossomed into a superb dramatic performer in the title role of the gutsy union organizer in Martin Ritt's *Norma Rae* to win the Best Actress award. The 79-year Melvyn Douglas gained the Best Supporting Actor prize for his dying financier in *Being There*.

Sally Field (left) was voted the Best Actress for Martin Ritt's ***Norma Rae****.*

'The Empire Strikes Back' in galactic war

New York, 21 May
According to producer Gary Kurtz, the spectacular new space epic, *The Empire Strikes Back*, should not be regarded as merely a sequel to *Star Wars*, but as the second part of a trilogy which is itself – as conceived by the creator of the series, George Lucas – the middle of three trilogies. The extraordinary success of the first one made it certain that Lucas would proceed with other films in the cycle, though this time he has stayed more in the background. He is credited with the original story and as executive producer, while the spectacular effects were created by his own Industrial Light and Magic Co. in Marin County, California. However, Lucas here has handed the directing reins to the veteran Irvin Kershner, best known for his handling of unusual contemporary subjects as in *A Fine Madness* (1966) and *Loving* (1970). Since the new film is financed by Lucasfilm with Fox serving only as distributor, the budget of $22 million is more generous (about double) than for *Star Wars* and, if it is anywhere near as successful, we shall doubtless be seeing more films in the intended cycle over the coming years.

C-3PO, voiced by Anthony Daniels.

Yoda is Luke Skywalker's ally.

Cannes jury at loggerheads over top prizes

*The spectacular **Kagemusha** shared the Golden Palm with **All That Jazz**.*

Cannes, 23 May
The top prizes at this year's Cannes Film Festival were divided among three very different films, though each displayed its director at the height of his powers. Unhappily, among those on the jury there was disagreement as to their merits. The Golden Palm was shared by Akira Kurosawa's *Kagemusha* and Bob Fosse's *All That Jazz*. A favorite for the best film award was Alain Resnais' *My American Uncle*, the cause of a dispute between Kirk Douglas, the president of the jury, and several of its members who accused him of not taking the Resnais film into consideration. A compromise was reached by awarding *My American Uncle* the Special Jury Prize. When it was presented to Resnais, it was explained that "in the spirit of the Festival, the Golden Palm and the Special Jury Prize are on the same level." Resnais' fascinating film is based on the theories of the animal behaviorist Dr. Henri Laborit, who plays himself. Resnais applies these to the lives of three people, brilliantly cutting between them. *Kagemusha*, Kurosawa's first film for years, is one of the most expensive ever made in Japan. The screen is splendidly used to frame the grandeur of this 16th-century tale of a thief employed as the double or *kagemusha* of a clan leader, in order to confuse the enemy. Unforgettable are the sunsets, vivid rainbows, the multi-colored flags of soldiers, and the dream-like battle scenes with horses and men dying in slow motion. *All That Jazz*, already acclaimed in the U.S., is an unusual Felliniesque musical on the unlikely subject of Bob Fosse's own heart operation, and his relations with his wife, mistress and daughter.

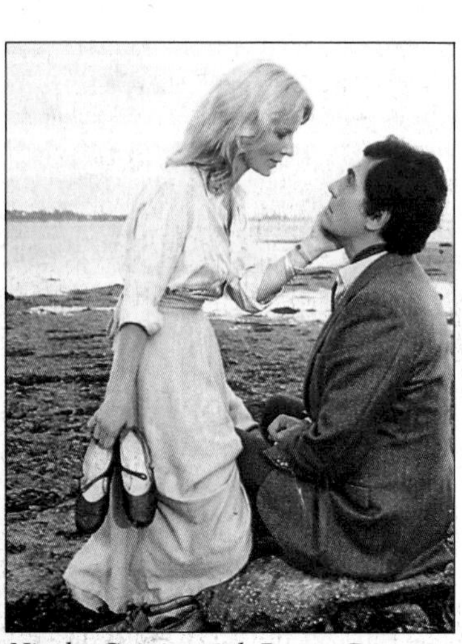

*Nicole Garcia and Roger Pierre in **My American Uncle**.*

*Best actors Anouk Aimée and Michel Piccoli in **Leap Into the Void**.*

Jack Nicholson runs amok for Kubrick

*Jack Nicholson and Shelley Duvall in Stanley Kubrick's **The Shining**.*

New York, 23 May
In *The Shining*, from the novel by Stephen King, Stanley Kubrick exchanges the outer space of *2001* for the inner space of a disintegrating mind. Jack Nicholson is blocked writer Jack Torrance who takes a job as winter caretaker in a huge hotel, the Overlook, in snowbound Colorado. Haunted by his creative failure, and the ghosts which people the Overlook's agonizingly empty spaces, Nicholson is overwhelmed by homicidal dementia, taking an axe to the hotel's only other occupants: his wife Shelley Duvall and small son Danny Lloyd. Kubrick's Steadicam camera roves through the Overlook's numbing emptiness, actually Oregon's Timberline Lodge, capturing one heart-stopping moment of horror as the elevator doors in the deserted lobby slide open to disgorge a tidal wave of blood.

Seamy side of life attracts Golden Lions

Venice, 5 September
Two American films shared this year's Golden Lion at Venice, both revealing the seamier side of life stateside. Louis Malle's third U.S. movie, *Atlantic City*, stars Burt Lancaster as a man from the gangster past, trying to survive on lies, who gets involved with present day small-time crooks. The different values of the past and the present, and the old and the young, are captured with a subtle eye for detail and lives lived in the literally crumbling and tawdry city of the title. Gena Rowlands, in her husband John Cassavetes' latest film, *Gloria*, is an ordinary woman in her 40s, suddenly having to flee the Mafia with an eight-year-old boy who has a diary of all their nefarious activities. The probing movie, with a marvelous performance from Rowlands, moves at a brisk pace. The same cannot be said of *Alexander the Great* by Theo Angelopoulos, who won the best director award. Angelopoulos takes his time to unfold this 210-minute allegory of Greek socialism. He uses numerous slow pans, pauses and long takes, but it is often intriguing and superb to look at. Ironically, the Alexander of the title is not the famous Macedonian general, but a bandit who has helped the peasants overthrow their feudal masters.

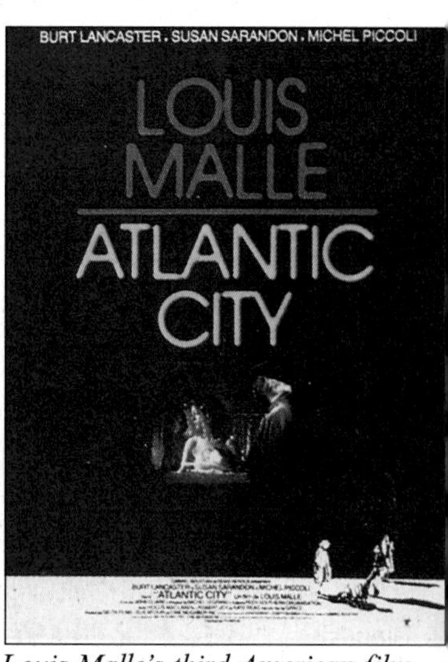
BURT LANCASTER . SUSAN SARANDON . MICHEL PICCOLI
LOUIS
MALLE
ATLANTIC
CITY

Louis Malle's third American film.

Controversial new shocker from Brian De Palma

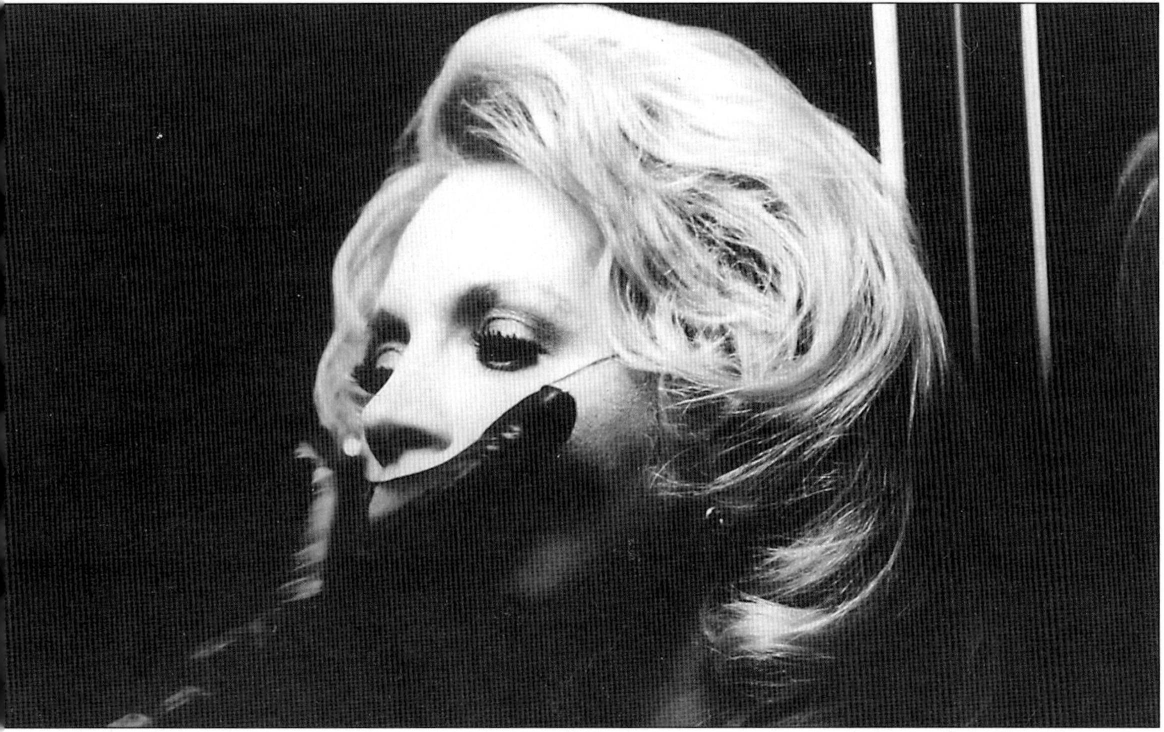

Angie Dickinson is trapped in an elevator by a psychotic killer in Brian De Palma's controversial slasher movie.

New York, 28 July
Director Brian De Palma has revealed both his skill and his taste for blood in five weird, occult-laden movies – *Sisters*, *Phantom of the Paradise*, *Obsession*, *Carrie* and, most recently, *The Fury* – which have certainly seemed to please audiences. However, his newest film, *Dressed to Kill*, is outraging feminists, who are picketing the theaters where it is showing and voicing their disapproval of the sadistic and perverted flavor of the plot, which they consider to be anti-women. Audiences in general will have to judge the issue for themselves. What nobody can argue about, however, is the expertise with which De Palma unfolds his tale of a misogynistic serial killer whose target is murdering women. This is an out-and-out slasher movie which will appeal to fans of the genre, and which boasts Michael Caine, Angie Dickinson and De Palma's wife Nancy Allen in the cast.

Torn between heroism and passion...

Paris, 17 September
François Truffaut has claimed that his new movie, *The Last Metro*, has fulfilled three of his ambitions: to recreate on film the climate of the Occupation, to show the backstage life of the theater and to provide Catherine Deneuve with the role of a responsible woman. This work achieves all three. Set in Paris in 1942, it tells of a Jewish manager of a Montmartre theater, forced into hiding in the cellar of his building while his wife (Deneuve) runs the acting company. This includes a member of the Resistance (Gérard Depardieu), who falls in love with her. Ironically, this entertaining and gripping drama, shot entirely in a studio, resembles closely the kind of "quality French film" that the young critic Truffaut despised.

Catherine Deneuve and Gérard Depardieu star in Truffaut's ***The Last Metro.***

Robert Redford steps behind the camera

New York, 19 September
With *Ordinary People*, Robert Redford has triumphantly demonstrated that there is more to him than a dazzling smile. He has made his debut as a director with an adaptation of an unpublished novel by Judith Guest, a Minnesota housewife. It's an understated family drama in which the middle-class harmony of married couple Mary Tyler Moore and Donald Sutherland is threatened by the nervous breakdown of their surviving younger son Timothy Hutton. Psychiatrist Judd Hirsch can provide no easy answers. In a film infused with Redford's humane liberalism, Hutton gives an outstanding performance as the young man haunted by his brother's death. He is the son of amiable leading man Jim Hutton, who died last year.

Robert Redford directs his young star, Timothy Hutton, for ***Ordinary People.*** ▷

Actors' long strike has now ended

Hollywood, 23 October
One of the longest and most damaging strikes in the history of Hollywood has ended. The members of the Screen Actors Guild have signed a new, three-year contract with the producers which should keep everyone satisfied for years to come. Reflecting the recent rapid growth in the video and cable television market, and the importance to the actors of so-called ancillary rights, the strike began on 21 July last year when SAG and the union representing radio and television actors found themselves in disagreement with the production companies over a new scale of salaries plus a share of valuable new ancillary rights. The shooting of 11 films and 45 TV series was immediately interrupted, although 14 other features, including Milos Forman's *Ragtime*, were able to proceed with production as planned, due to a special interim agreement with their producers.

Robert De Niro into the ring with Scorsese: a double triumph

Robert De Niro as Jake La Motta in the thick of battle (left)... and, later, grown obese in the shadow of failure.

New York, 14 November
Films about the fight game have an honorable place in the history of Hollywood, but none of them have had the crunching immediacy of Martin Scorsese's work *Raging Bull*. Robert De Niro stars as New York's Jake La Motta, one of the hardest middleweights ever to pull on the gloves and a man whose biggest opponent was himself. To play La Motta in bloated middle age, De Niro refused prosthetics and put on 55 pounds in an eating marathon in France and Italy. The scorching fight scenes, brilliantly edited by Thelma Schoonmaker with sickening sound effects by Frank Warner, capture the savage beauty of prizefighting in all its sweat-drenched, blood-spattered glory.

Hughes: a legacy from beyond the grave

New York, 26 September
Jonathan Demme takes a sideways look at the American Dream in *Melvin and Howard*. It's based on the true story of one Melvin Dummer, an all-American loser who may (or may not) have stopped on the Nevada highway one night to pick up a wild-haired tramp who may (or may not) have been eccentric billionaire Howard Hughes. When Hughes died, Melvin produced a will naming him as the heir to the Hughes fortune. Melvin never saw a cent but Demme fashions a poignant comedy around the tale, with Paul Le Mat as Melvin, Mary Steenburgen providing many laughs as his stripper wife, and Jason Robards playing "Howard Hughes". The real Melvin appears briefly as a bus depot counterman.

Paul Le Mat (left) as pathetic Melvin and Jason Robards as Howard Hughes.

Cimino faces multi-million-dollar failure

Hollywood, 19 December
After *Heaven's Gate* was lambasted by the critics on its first showing, United Artists got it reduced from 225 minutes to 148. The director Michael Cimino had originally offered the studio a film that lasted five-and-a-half hours. As the budget for this epic Western had escalated from $11 million to over $35 million, it is unlikely to recover even a fraction of this amount at the box office. Therefore, the movie threatens to be the most expensive flop of all time, and the ruin of UA. As a result of the severe cutting, the sprawling narrative on the Johnson County War between the cattlemen and the immigrant farmers, becomes confusing at times. However, there is still a virtuoso sweep to some of the panoramic ensembles.

Isabelle Huppert and Kris Kristofferson in the $36 million disaster.

Cameras

270
270

Cecil B. DeMille with the 1913 Mitchell used for filming ***The Squaw Man****.*

Shooting ***Hud*** *(1963): James Wong Howe and Mitchell (Panavision lens).*

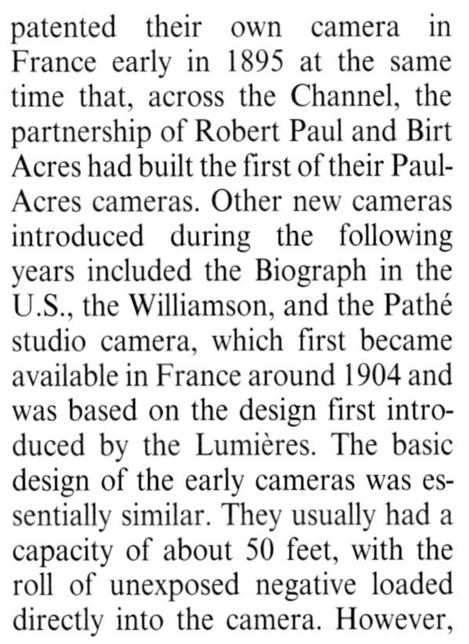

The many advances in movie technology over the years are nowhere better reflected than in the evolution of the camera itself. Yet the standard 35mm format and perforated celluloid used for most professional filming has not changed. It was first tested and used by W. K. Laurie Dickson in the Kinetograph camera which he developed for the Edison company in 1893. During the following years the increasing number and variety of cameras in use reflected the diversity of companies beginning to make films all over the world, most notably in the U.S., France and England. The Lumière brothers patented their own camera in France early in 1895 at the same time that, across the Channel, the partnership of Robert Paul and Birt Acres had built the first of their Paul-Acres cameras. Other new cameras introduced during the following years included the Biograph in the U.S., the Williamson, and the Pathé studio camera, which first became available in France around 1904 and was based on the design first introduced by the Lumières. The basic design of the early cameras was essentially similar. They usually had a capacity of about 50 feet, with the roll of unexposed negative loaded directly into the camera. However, the Pathé marked a major improvement, with two square wooden magazines mounted one behind the other on the top of the camera body, each capable of holding 400 feet of film. It was extremely popular and was used worldwide by filmmakers, including D.W. Griffith on *The Birth of a Nation* and Cecil B. DeMille. A major competitor came from France soon after with the small Debrie Parvo which came into use at about same time as the American-made Bell and Howell, the first camera to be constructed entirely of metal, and with many unique features which made it useful in filming special effects. However, at a cost of $2,000, it was pricey for its time. In 1921 the first Mitchell camera, designed by John E. Leonard, arrived on the U.S. market and became Bell and Howell's main competitor. With the coming of sound, the Mitchell, quieter and easier to handle, took over and became, with improvements and modifications, the leading studio camera in the U.S.

The new technology introduced in the 50s required special cameras: Cinerama, Todd-AO, Natural Vision (3-D) and VistaVision, among others, but the Mitchell continued in use for normal 35mm and CinemaScope filming. By the early 60s there was an increasing demand for lighter-weight cameras that could be moved about easily while filming on location, or hand-held by the cameraman. Originally developed for 16mm documentary filming ('direct cinema' or 'cinema vérité') the newly improved Arriflex and Eclair, used especially by the New Wave directors such as Godard and Truffaut, their favorite cameraman Raoul Coutard, and America's Cassavetes, influenced styles of feature filming all over the world. In the U.S. the Panavision Co., which had been developing its own 35mm cameras and lens systems, finally introduced its improved, lighter-weight Panaflex which in the 70s replaced the Mitchell and has been in widespread use ever since.

Director John Cassavetes making ***Husbands*** *(1972) with an Arriflex.*

Director Roman Polanski at work on ***Tess*** *from Hardy's novel,* ***Tess of the D'Urbervilles****. He is on location, using a Panavision Panaflex camera.*

*Jacques Dutronc and Nathalie Baye in Jean-Luc Godard's **Sauve qui peut (la vie)** aka **Slow Motion**.*

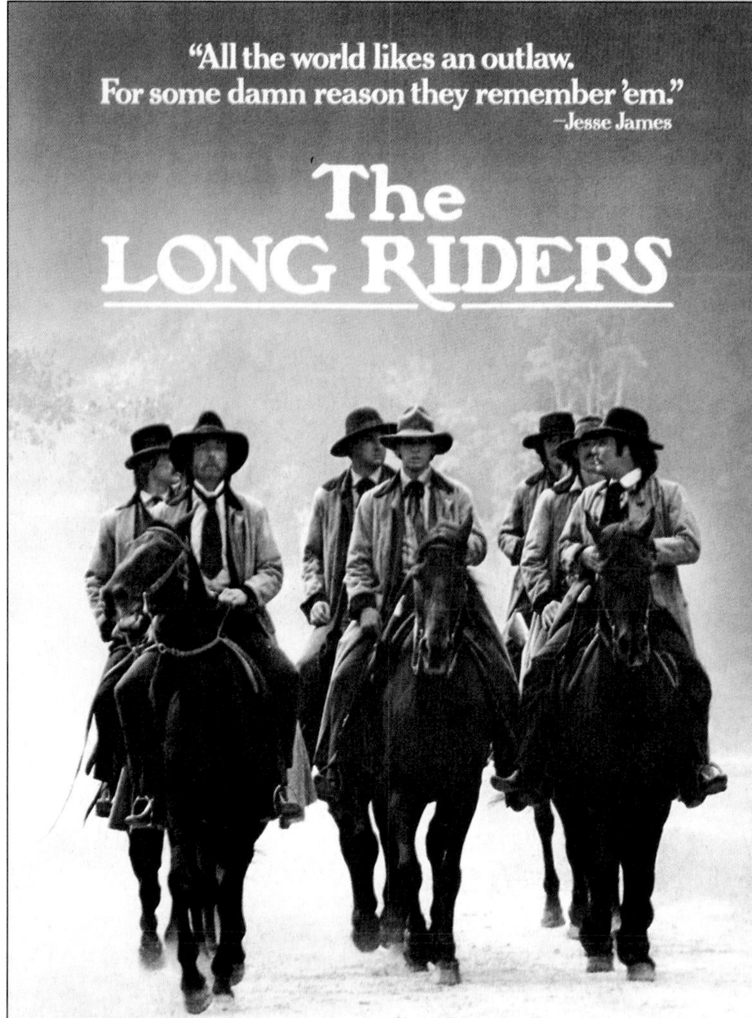
"All the world likes an outlaw.
For some damn reason they remember 'em."
–Jesse James
The LONG RIDERS
The Long Riders
David Carradine Keith Carradine Robert Carradine
James Keach Stacy Keach Dennis Quaid Randy Quaid
Christopher Guest Nicholas Guest Music composed and arranged by Ry Cooder
Produced by Tim Zinnemann Directed by Walter Hill
Written by Bill Bryden, Steven Phillip Smith, Stacy & James Keach
Executive Producers James and Stacy Keach Technicolor
United Artists
A Transamerica Company
R
Read the Avon Paperback
Original soundtrack available on Warner Bros. Records and Tapes

Three sets of real-life brothers rode to a Ry Cooder score for Walter Hill.

*Grimault's charming animation, **le Roi et l'oiseau (The King and the Bird)**.*

*Bill Murray in Harold Ramis' infantile, amusing moneymaker, **Caddyshack**.*

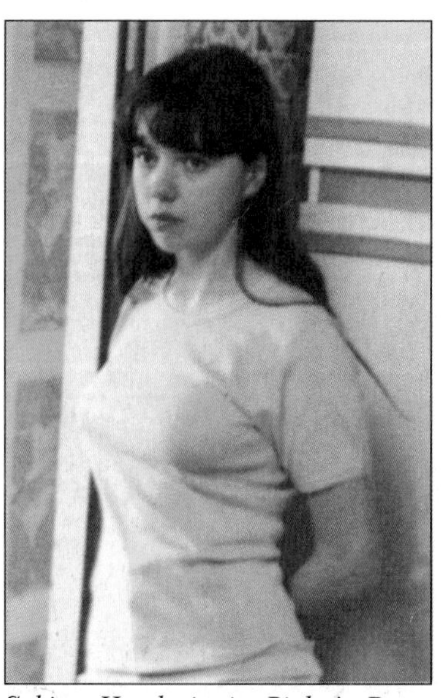

*Sabine Haudepin in Pialat's **Passe ton bac d'abord (Graduate First)**.*

*Gena Rowlands and John Adams in **Gloria**, directed by John Cassavetes.*

Left to right: Lily Tomlin, Dolly Parton and Jane Fonda, three office workers who outwit their chauvinist boss in Colin Higgins' ***Nine to Five***.

John Nance in David Lynch's finally released ***Eraserhead***.

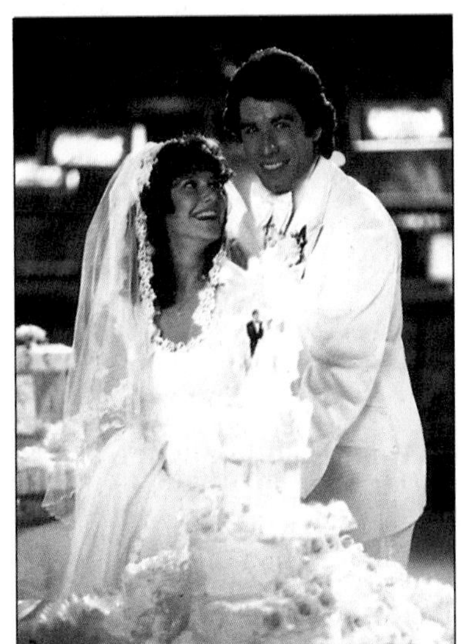

Debra Winger and John Travolta in the drama, ***Urban Cowboy***.

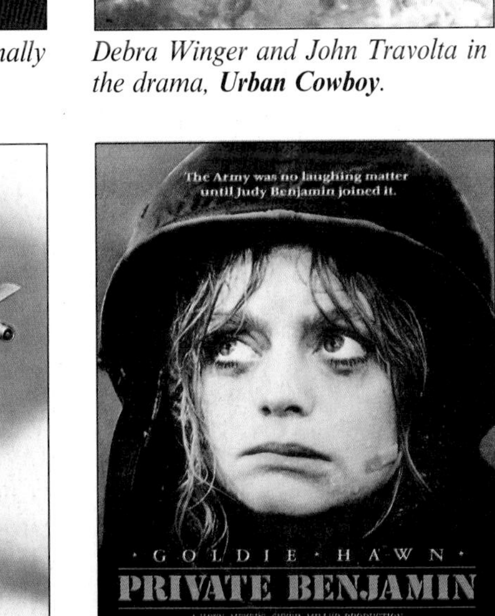
What's slower than a speeding bullet, and able to hit tall buildings at a single bound?
AIRPLANE!
Thank God it's only a motion picture!
PARAMOUNT PICTURES PRESENTS A HOWARD W. KOCH PRODUCTION AIRPLANE!
ROBERT HAYS & JULIE HAGERTY JIM ABRAHAMS DAVID ZUCKER JERRY ZUCKER
JON DAVISON JIM ABRAHAMS DAVID ZUCKER JERRY ZUCKER

Delirious parody made a fortune.

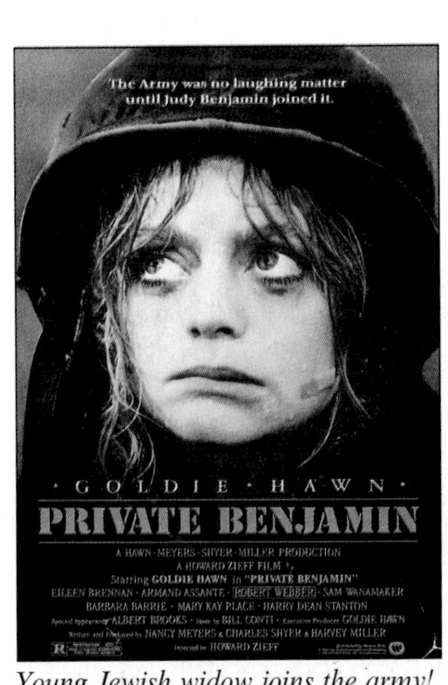
The Army was no laughing matter until Judy Benjamin joined it.
GOLDIE HAWN
PRIVATE BENJAMIN
A HAWN · MEYERS · SHYER · MILLER PRODUCTION
A HOWARD ZIEFF FILM
Starring GOLDIE HAWN in "PRIVATE BENJAMIN"
EILEEN BRENNAN · ARMAND ASSANTE · ROBERT WEBBER · SAM WANAMAKER
BARBARA BARRIE · MARY KAY PLACE · HARRY DEAN STANTON
ALBERT BROOKS · BILL CONTI · GOLDIE HAWN
NANCY MEYERS & CHARLES SHYER & HARVEY MILLER
HOWARD ZIEFF

Young Jewish widow joins the army!

What is this thing called love.
PAUL MAZURSKY'S
WILLIE & PHIL
TWENTIETH CENTURY-FOX PRESENTS "WILLIE & PHIL"
MICHAEL ONTKEAN/MARGOT KIDDER/RAY SHARKEY
PRODUCED BY PAUL MAZURSKY AND TONY RAY
DIRECTOR OF PHOTOGRAPHY SVEN NYKVIST, A.S.C.
MUSIC BY CLAUDE BOLLING
WRITTEN AND DIRECTED BY PAUL MAZURSKY
PRINTS BY DE LUXE/COLOR BY MOVIELAB

Michael Ontkean, Margot Kidder, Ray Sharkey are Mazursky's threesome.

Olive Oyl (Shelley Duvall) looks on as Popeye (Robin Williams) holds the baby in Robert Altman's film of the comic strip.

1981

1980 Academy Awards, Dorothy Chandler Pav., 31 Mar.

Best Film:	*Ordinary People* (dir: Robert Redford)
Best Director:	Robert Redford
Best Actor:	Robert De Niro *(Raging Bull)*
Best Actress:	Sissy Spacek *(Coal Miner's Daughter)*
Best Supp. Actor:	Timothy Hutton *(Ordinary People)*
Best Supp. Actress:	Mary Steenburgen *(Melvin and Howard)*

Berlin, 1 January
The Golden Bear at this year's Berlin Festival has gone to Spain. The winner was *Deprisa, Deprisa*, directed by Carlos Saura.

New York, 23 January
Radio City Music Hall is screening the uncut version, with soundtrack, of Abel Gance's *Napoleon*. The film is being presented by Francis Ford Coppola, whose father, Carmine Coppola, composed the music.

Burkino Faso, 13 February
Souleymane Cissé's film *The Wind* (*Finyé*) has won the top award at the eighth Ouagadougou Film Festival. A special prize was awarded to Gaston Kaboré for *The Gift of God* (*Wend Kuni*).

Paris, 25 February
The poster for Pascal Thomas' film *Celles qu'on n'a pas eues* (*The Girls We Never Had*), which was drawn by Topor, has been judged indecent and is banned from train and metro stations. Even the entertainment guide *l'Officiel des spectacles* has refused to include it.

Paris, 4 March
The first film in Eric Rohmer's new series entitled "Comedies and Proverbs", *la Femme de l'aviateur* (*The Aviator's Wife*), is a youthful comedy of errors with a lightness of tone not present in his previous, rather more serious cycle of "Six Moral Tales" (opening with *la Boulangère de Monceau* in 1962, and finishing with *Love in the Afternoon* in 1972).

New York, 7 March
The influential film critic Bosley Crowther has died of heart failure. The outspoken, movie-loving Crowther wrote the daily reviews as well as Sunday overview pieces for the *New York Times*. He received the first award for film criticism from the Screen Directors' Guild in 1954 and was named critic emeritus of the *New York Times* in 1967.

Hollywood, 10 March
Disney Pictures have announced the creation of Disney Channel, their own pay-cable television channel.

Paris, 15 March
The distinguished French filmmaker René Clair has died. Clair's career spanned four decades and produced such French classics as *le Million* and *Beauties of the Night*, as well as several American films including *I Married a Witch*.

Paris, 30 March
Georges Franju has resigned from his position as artistic director of the Cinemathèque due to internal problems. He was one of its founders.

Paris, 28 May
France's new Prime Minister Pierre Mauroy has formed his government and has appointed Jack Lang as Minister of Cultural Affairs.

New York, 5 July
West Coast punk rockers the Alice Big Band, Black Flag, the Circle Jerks and Catholic Discipline are documented by director Penelope Spheeris in her first feature film, *The Decline of Western Civilization*, which is being released today.

Paris, 9 September
Opening of *Pour la peau d'un flic*, Alain Delon's first film as director, with himself and Anne Parillaud.

Turkey, 1 October
Director Yilmaz Guney, imprisoned since 1972, has left Turkey. He made a secret exit from the country while out on a pass.

New York, 5 October
Character actress Gloria Grahame has died of cancer. Miss Grahame, who was the winner of the Best Supporting Actress Oscar for *The Bad and the Beautiful* (1952), and recipient of a nomination for her performance in *Crossfire* (1947), had recently returned to the stage.

Athens, 18 October
Melina Mercouri has been made Minister of Culture in Andréas Papandreou's socialist government.

Hollywood, 24 October
Edith Head, Hollywood's most celebrated costume designer, has died. During her long career Miss Head received 34 Oscar nominations and won eight times. As couturière to such stars as Marlene Dietrich and Ingrid Bergman, her styles influenced fashion trends worldwide. She became well-known to the general public through her frequent TV and radio talk-show appearances and her syndicated newspaper column on women's fashion.

Paris, 4 November
Bertrand Tavernier has transposed a novel by Jim Thompson set in the Deep South to West Africa in his latest film, *Coup de torchon* (*Clean Slate*). Philippe Noiret stars as the anti-hero, with Isabelle Huppert and Stéphane Audran. The film opens here today.

Paris, 11 November
Abel Gance, director of such legendary films as *la Roue* and *Napoleon*, has died. Gance was irresistibly drawn to the theater and left his job as a legal clerk to begin acting in 1908. He made his film debut in 1909, going on to form his own film company in 1911. His early films, however, met with little success. Gance's pacifist statement on the futility of war, *I Accuse* (1918), influenced the work of Eisenstein, Pudovkin and Dovzhenko.

Lausanne, 17 November
Claude Autant-Lara has donated his film library and objects and documents from his films (costumes, photos, etc.) to Freddy Buache's Swiss Cinémathèque.

New York, 20 November
Milos Forman has filmed *Ragtime*, based on the novel by E.L. Doctorow. James Cagney appears in his first film role for 20 years, along with Elizabeth McGovern, Mary Steenburgen and Brad Dourif.

New York, 10 December
Release of *Reds*, directed by Warren Beatty, who also produced, collaborated on the screenplay and played the lead.

Budapest, 12 December
A comprehensive exhibition of the work of set designer Alexander Trauner is being held in the city where he was born. Trauner left Hungary in the late 20s, and came to prominence with the French "poetic realism" movement of the 30s.

Paris, 16 December
Otto Preminger's screen version of *Carmen Jones* (1954), based on the stage musical which, in turn, uses Bizet's *Carmen* opera score, has at last been released in France. The composer's heirs have now agreed to its distribution here. The film stars Dorothy Dandridge and Harry Belafonte.

Hollywood, 31 December
The average production cost for a feature film made by a major studio is estimated to be around $9.75 million. The highest budgets for this year were for *Reds* ($35 million) and *Ragtime* ($32 million).

New York, 31 December
Sales of video recorders exceeded the million mark for the first time this year.

DEATHS

Italy, 4 February
Mario Camerini

Beverly Hills, 27 July
William Wyler

New York, 4 August
Melvyn Douglas

Rio de Janeiro, 22 August
Glauber Rocha

Los Angeles, 30 August
Vera-Ellen

New York, 27 September
Robert Montgomery

California, 16 October
William Holden

California, 29 November
Natalie Wood

---

*Spielberg's **Raiders of the Lost Ark** saw a return to the Saturday morning serial of old, albeit in high-tech 80s style. The film introduced a new hero, Indiana Jones (Harrison Ford).*

Indiana Jones—the new hero
from the creators of JAWS and STAR WARS.
RAIDERS
of the LOST ARK
AMSEL
PARAMOUNT PICTURES Presents A LUCASFILM LTD. Production
A STEVEN SPIELBERG Film
Starring HARRISON FORD
KAREN ALLEN · PAUL FREEMAN · RONALD LACEY · JOHN RHYS-DAVIES · DENHOLM ELLIOTT
usic by JOHN WILLIAMS · Executive Producers GEORGE LUCAS and HOWARD KAZANJIAN · Screenplay by LAWRENCE KASDAN · Story by GEORGE LUCAS and PHILIP KAUFMAN
oduced by FRANK MARSHALL · Directed by STEVEN SPIELBERG Filmed in Panavision®
DOLBY STEREO IN SELECTED THEATRES
NOVELIZATION FROM BALLANTINE BOOKS
ORIGINAL SOUNDTRACK ON COLUMBIA RECORDS & TAPES
A PARAMOUNT PICTURE
TM. Copyright © Lucasfilm Ltd. (LFL) MCMLXXXI All Rights Reserved
PG PARENTAL GUIDANCE SUGGESTED
OME MATERIAL MAY NOT BE SUITABLE FOR CHILDREN
810100
"RAIDERS OF THE LOST ARK"

Raoul Walsh, the end of an adventure

California, 1 January
Raoul Walsh, one of Hollywood's most durable and prolific directors, has died aged 93. Although best known for his Westerns, action movies and thrillers, he handled a wide variety of films during his 50-year career, from *The Life of General Villa* in 1914 to *A Distant Trumpet* in 1964. It was in the mid-1920s that Walsh first emerged as a leading talent with *The Thief of Bagdad* (1924) starring Douglas Fairbanks, the smash-hit *What Price Glory?* (1926) and *Sadie Thompson* (1928) in which he also co-starred with Gloria Swanson. (An accident in which he lost an eye ended his acting career.) Independent-minded, he did not function well within the constraints of the studio system until he joined Warner Bros. in 1939 where his career was revitalized, beginning with *The Roaring Twenties* and including *Objective Burma* (1945), the masterly *Pursued* (1947) and *White Heat* (1949). He remained active for a further 15 years until he retired.

Avoriaz audiences are seduced by a new kind of poignant horror

John Hurt in ***The Elephant Man****, an extraordinarily difficult role which conclusively demonstrated his exceptional talent.*

Avoriaz, 19 January
The young American director David Lynch, who made the cult movie *Eraserhead*, was eagerly awaited at the Festival of Fantasy and Horror at Avoriaz, where he was to present his new film, *The Elephant Man*. Lynch and the picture got a warm reception, and it was not surprising that it won the Grand Prix. Made in England and produced by Mel Brooks, this bizarre and moving story, set in Victorian London, is based on fact. It is the story of John Merrick (John Hurt), a horribly deformed young man, yet sensitive and intelligent, who lives as a circus freak until he is rescued by Dr. Frederick Treves (Anthony Hopkins), and brought to a hospital where he can be studied and helped. With superb black-and-white photography by Freddie Francis, Lynch wonderfully evokes the period. The cast is splendid, especially the suffering Hurt, hidden behind extraordinary makeup by Christopher Tucker.

'One from the Heart' is in serious trouble

Hollywood, 10 March
Francis Ford Coppola is one filmmaker who is not afraid of taking risks. Having experienced terrible problems in shooting his ambitious Vietnam movie, *Apocalypse Now*, (1979) on location in the Philippines at a cost of over $30 million – it was originally budgeted at $12 million – he appears to be having similar difficulties with his latest project, *One From the Heart*. A totally studio-bound production and, in marked contrast to the harsh realities of his previous film, a kind of musical fantasy, it started life as a relatively modest idea. However, escalating costs of elaborate sets and electronic equipment are threatening to get out of control. Coppola bought the old Hollywood General Studios one year ago, renamed it Zoetrope, and planned to make it a haven for creative filmmakers. Unfortunately, one of the very first productions, *Hammett* directed by Wim Wenders, immediately ran into trouble and was shut down before completion. Now Coppola is having teething problems with his own film. Using the latest video and computer technology, which he refers to as "The Electronic Cinema", he finds that the money is already running out, he is having trouble meeting his payroll, and will be forced to close other departments of the studio to complete *One From the Heart*. The success of the Zoetrope experiment hangs in the balance.

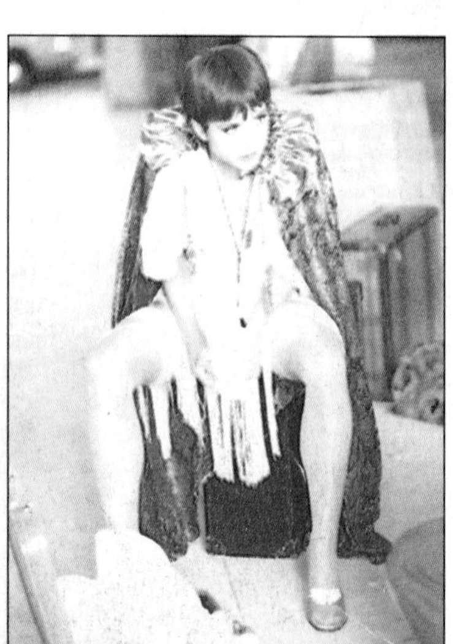

Nastassja Kinski: one from the heart.

Beineix's 'Diva': No art without artifice

Paris, 11 March
Diva, the first feature by 35-year-old Jean-Jacques Beineix, is enthusing Parisian audiences. It is not difficult to understand the reason for its success, especially among the young. The director, who has made film commercials, has brought much of the slick style of advertisements to bear on this tale of a young postal messenger's obsession with an opera singer. Mixing fact and fantasy, violence and romance, and adventurous camerawork, it is a flashy package of ultra-chic designer images and punk aesthetics. Yet beneath the surface gloss is an intriguing *film noir* plot, and a homage to the dark world of the silent Louis Feuillade serials. A striking debut.

Thuy An Luu and Frédéric Andrei in ***Diva****, directed by Jean-Jacques Beineix.*

James M. Cain's postman rings yet another door

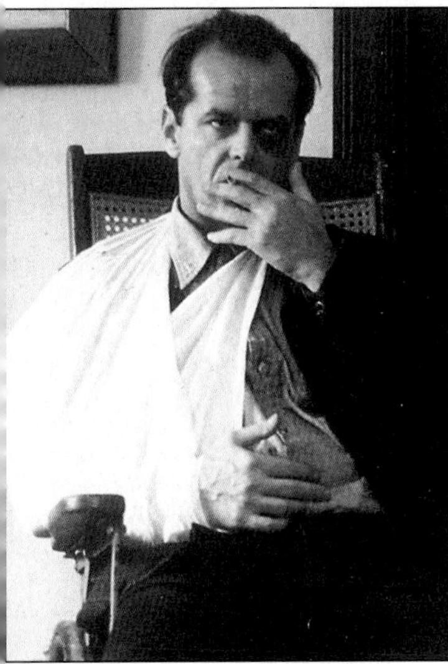
A good role for Jack Nicholson.

New York, 20 January
It's fourth time around for James M. Cain's *noir* Depression-era classic, *The Postman Always Rings Twice*. The first was the French *le Dernier tournant* (1939), the second was the Italian Luchino Visconti's version, *Ossessione* (1942) and in 1946 Hollywood made it a vehicle for Lana Turner, luring drifter John Garfield into a plot to kill her elderly husband. Swathed in dazzling white, Lana created a memorable image of low-rent carnality. Now director Bob Rafelson takes up the baton and it's the turn of Jack Nicholson and Jessica Lange to portray the doomed couple. In 1946 the steamy side of Cain's story was watered down to meet the requirements of the Hays Office, but 35 years on such restraints no longer apply and David Mamet's screenplay remains faithful to the original. Lange, who made the most inauspicious of film debuts five years ago in the remake of *King Kong*, gives a performance which crackles with sleazy sexual static. There is a story doing the rounds that Lange and Nicholson's acting was so realistically torrid that Rafelson had to leave a lot of footage on the cutting room floor.

Jessica Lange is striking as the fourth interpreter of the unhappy wife.

Oscar welcomes film from USSR

Los Angeles, 31 March
Moscow Does Not Believe in Tears is only the second Soviet film (after *War and Peace*, 1968) to win the Foreign Film Oscar. This work from Vladimir Menshov is a well-acted comedy-drama about the loves and lives of three Russian girls in 1958.

Actor-turned-director Robert Redford goes home with four Awards

Los Angeles, 31 March
One of Hollywood's most popular leading men, Robert Redford, who has never won an Oscar for acting, managed to carry off the coveted Best Director award on his first attempt for *Ordinary People*. The film, produced by Redford's Wildwood Enterprises, also won Best Picture, Best Screenplay (based on another medium) and Best Supporting Actor for Timothy Hutton, son of the lanky Jim Hutton, who died in 1979. The 19-year-old Hutton, the youngest winner of the award, plays a tormented boy struggling to come to terms with the drowning death of his brother in a sailing accident. His guilt and suicide attempts force his wealthy, middle-class parents (Donald Sutherland and Mary Tyler Moore) to confront the realities of their unhappy marriage. Country singer Loretta Lynn and boxer Jake La Motta were both in the audience to witness the stars who played them on screen collect the Best Actor and Actress Oscars – Sissy Spacek in *Coal Miner's Daughter* and Robert De Niro in *Raging Bull*.

Russian actress Vera Alentova.

Timothy Hutton and Elizabeth McGovern in Redford's ***Ordinary People**.*

Robert DeNiro in ***Raging Bull**.*

The Golden Palm pays tribute to the courage of Polish Solidarity

Cannes, 27 May
Five years ago Andrzej Wajda became spokesman for the movement for change in Poland as reflected in his film *Man of Marble*. Since then, the free trade union organization Solidarity has become a leading political force in the country. Taking account of the changing reality of Poland, Wajda has followed up on the earlier film with a sequel titled *Man of Iron*, which has received the Golden Palm. It takes the form of an investigation by a radio reporter, expected to cover the 1980 Gdansk shipyard strike from the official point of view, who meets the son of 1950s worker hero, the *Man of Marble*, now married to a dissident filmmaker. The personal story is linked with the wider struggle for the recognition of Solidarity. Filmed under enormous pressure during the actual events, it leaps off the screen like the day's headlines. The best actress award went to Isabelle Adjani for her performances in both James Ivory's *Quartet* and Andrzej Zulawski's *Possession*, while Ugo Tognazzi was considered best actor for Bernardo Bertolucci's work *The Tragedy of a Ridiculous Man*, the director's first film for many years to deal with contemporary Italy. The jury, presided over by French director Jacques Deray, presented their Special Prize to Swiss director Alain Tanner, who recently underwent heart surgery, for *Light Years Away*, his first film in English, a magical folk tale set in Ireland and starring British actor Trevor Howard.

*Wajda's **Man of Iron**, sequel to his **Man of Marble**, was voted the best film.*

Best actor Ugo Tognazzi (standing), Ricardo Tognazzi and Anouk Aimée.

Ailing United Artists merges with MGM

Hollywood, 12 June
The complete box-office failure of Michael Cimino's $40 million Western, *Heaven's Gate*, and continuing financial problems in the company, have persuaded Transamerica, United Artists' parent company, that this is a good time to sell the studio. Kirk Kerkorian at MGM has now acquired UA, along with its valuable backlog of old movies for the relatively modest sum of $370 million, far less than the $700 million recently paid by oil tycoon Marvin Davis for 20th Century-Fox. Clearly, UA never recovered from the loss of its top management team three years ago, and this sale is the result.

Spielberg and Lucas turn back the clock

New York, 12 June
Steven Spielberg and George Lucas have joined forces to re-create the thrills and spills of the Saturday-morning serial with *Raiders of the Lost Ark*. This is a no-holds-barred celebration of the stunt-packed cliff-hangers churned out by Republic, Columbia and Universal in Hollywood's heyday. But while classics like *The Green Hornet* and *Secret Agent X-9* were produced on a wing and a prayer, *Raiders of the Lost Ark* cost $22 million, much of it devoted to state-of-the-art special effects supplied by Lucas' Industrial Light and Magic. In the days of Buck Rogers, exotic locations were created in the Californian hills and deserts, but filming of *Raiders* live action has taken actors and crew to France, Tunisia, Hawaii and Britain's Elstree studios. Harrison Ford stars as Indiana Jones, the rugged 1930s archaeologist-adventurer who puts his bullwhip to good use in routing a bunch of evil Nazis searching for the Ark of the Covenant, possession of which will confer unlimited power. Apparently Tom Selleck was the first choice but was unavailable. Ford has seized his chance with both hands and director Spielberg has peppered the picture with a host of movie in-jokes that are calculated to delight the buffs.

*Isabelle Adjani was voted best actress in Andrzej Zulawski's **Possession**.*

*Harrison Ford as Indiana Jones in Spielberg's **Raiders of the Lost Ark**.*

John Gielgud walks off with comedy honors

Dudley Moore and John Gielgud.

New York, 17 July
John Gielgud has long regarded movie-making with an air of studied perplexity, making periodic forays into it with the air of an innocent happy to carry away large sacks of money. In recent years, richly rewarded cameos have outnumbered the parts which have released his powers – the dithering Lord Raglan in *The Charge of the Light Brigade* or the dying novelist in *Providence*. Now, in *Arthur*, the latest (frankly feeble) attempt to revive screwball comedy, Gielgud demonstrates his impeccable comic pedigree. Cast as spoiled millionaire Dudley Moore's profane valet, he delivers a string of expletives with a Shakespearean air and walks off with the movie.

$12 million U-Boat movie from Germany

Berlin, 15 September
Das Boot, West Germany's most expensive film to date, tells the story of a wartime submarine, *U-96*, on an eventful voyage in the autumn of 1941. The accent here is on realism, with director Wolfgang Petersen's steadicam tracking through the submarine's claustrophobic interior as its crew brave hell, high water and Allied depth charges. However, *Das Boot* slides away from confronting Nazism head-on by delivering the kind of well-crafted adventure yarn which dominated the British war films made in the 1950s.

Jürgen Prochnow, captain of the U-Boat, on a dangerous mission to Spain.

Pixote, an unhappy child of Brazil's gutter

Fernando Ramos da Silva as street urchin Pixote, with Marilia Pera.

New York, 11 September
One of Brazil's leading post-*cinema novo* directors, the Argentinian-born Hector Babenco, has gained his first international success with *Pixote*, which has just opened here. Babenco originally intended this film on the plight of Brazil's three million abandoned children to be a documentary, and had completed 200 hours of interviews with children in reform schools. But when he was refused further access, he turned to the streets and got the children to play themselves. The result is that the performances by the kids, who improvised their own lines, are impressively natural. The plot itself is a sordid one, involving the eponymous 10-year-old boy in drugs and prostitution, leading to his arrest and confinement.

An Australian view of World War I tragedy

Melbourne, 16 September
Director Peter Weir's *Gallipoli* is an engrossing drama which follows the fortunes of youthful idealists Mark Lee and Mel Gibson from their decision to join up in World War I to the horror of the trenches in the Dardanelles in 1915. Their developing friendship amid adversity is the principal theme of *Gallipoli*, which sees the war from an Australian point of view; as the third wave of young volunteers prepares to attack in the movie's meticulously realized climactic batttle, their fatherly commanding officer tells them, "Remember, you are men from Western Australia." The film's final, frozen frame is reminiscent of a photograph taken by Robert Capa during the Spanish Civil War, depicting a soldier at the moment of death.

Mel Gibson (r) and Mark Lee in Peter Weir's harrowing WWI film ***Gallipoli.*** ▷

Meryl goes 'English' for Fowles heroine

Jeremy Irons and Meryl Streep in the film-within-a-film in Pinter's screenplay.

New York, 18 September
Meryl Streep's impressive technical powers are on display in *The French Lieutenant's Woman*, Karel Reisz's film adapted by Harold Pinter from the novel by John Fowles. She has transformed herself, complete with English accent, into the raven-haired pre-Raphaelite beauty of the title, the governess in Victorian England stranded between geologist Jeremy Irons and the memory of her vanished French officer lover. It's a formidable performance in a handsome picture which falters because of Pinter's failure to translate the intricate structure of Fowles' best-seller to the screen.

Dunaway plays a monster Joan Crawford

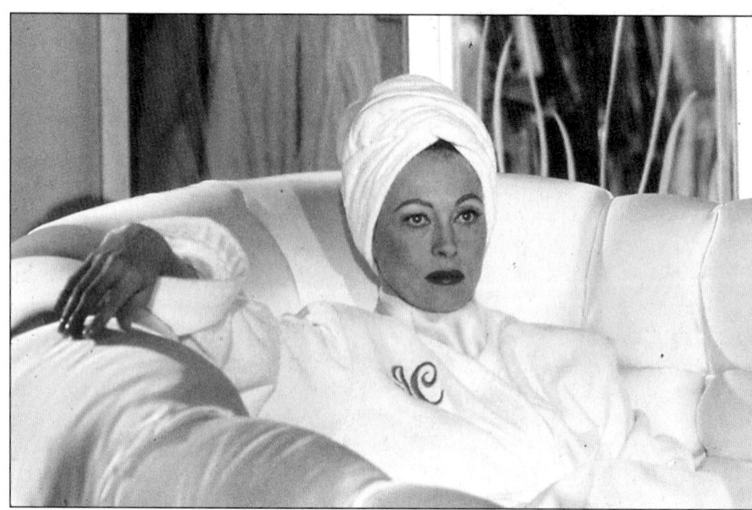

Faye Dunaway, convincing as flamboyant and legendary star Joan Crawford.

New York, 18 September
In her autobiography, Joan Crawford wrote, "of all actresses, to me Faye Dunaway has the talent and courage to make a real star." Were she alive today, she might be less flattering about Dunaway's extraordinary impersonation of her in *Mommie Dearest*, adapted from the account of the bizarre rearing of Joan's four adopted children written by one of them, Christina Crawford. In *Mommie Dearest*, Dunaway's striking physical resemblance to Crawford at her most manic, with devouring eyes and savage slash of a mouth, makes watching the movie a weirdly voyeuristic experience.

Klaus Maria Brandauer is electrifying in Nazi-era 'Mephisto'

Munich, 25 September
Hungarian director Istvan Szabo's *Mephisto* has opened here. When it reaches the U.S. and Britain, it should meet with the same acclaim it is now receiving. Apart from the fact that the screenplay, photography, direction and overall performances are of the highest order, the film offers Klaus Maria Brandauer (well-known in the theater here) a title role which invites a tour de force of acting, and gets it. English-speaking audiences are unfamiliar with Brandauer's gifts, his only foray in English being as a heavy in *The Salzburg Connection* (1972). *Mephisto* tells of a German actor, famous for his interpretation of Mephistopheles, who is a man of Left-wing leanings hoping to establish a workers' theater. When the Nazis take power, his hunger for fame silences his conscience, leading him to betray colleagues and family. Szabo's chilling study of compromise, is based on a novel by Klaus Mann, in turn drawn from the life of his uncle, actor Gustave Grundgens. In a gripping story of overweening ambition and creeping corruption, Brandauer's explosive and committed performance is unforgettable.

Klaus Maria Brandauer as Högen, the acclaimed actor, in Szabo's ***Mephisto.***

In the role that destroys him.

Louis Malle serves a dinner for two

New York, 8 October
There are few directors who could get away with filming 110 minutes of just two people having a conversation in a restaurant, but this is precisely what Louis Malle has achieved in his new American picture, *My Dinner With André*. Shown at the New York Film Festival, this unusual and absorbing film was written by the two protagonists, Wallace Shawn and André Gregory, based on conversations they have had over the years. That it was actually *written* needs to be stressed, because the natural manner in which the dinner companions chat gives the impression that the conversation is being improvised there and then before our eyes. Gregory, a tall, good-looking actor and director, seems initially more sure of himself, while Shawn, a bald and short actor and playwright, is more the uncertain listener. Gregory is the idealist, Shawn the realist. Malle's camera hovers around the table like a discreet maître d'hôtel eavesdropping on the fascinating conversation.

Mystery drowning of Natalie Wood

Hollywood, 30 November
After having had a drink in the salon of her yacht with her husband Robert Wagner and the actor Christopher Walken, Natalie Wood announced that she was going to bed. An hour later, worried when he found her cabin empty, Wagner searched the boat for his wife and found that the dinghy was missing. He sounded the alarm immediately. At 7:45 a.m., police found the body of Natalie Wood floating in the water beside the dinghy, about one and a half miles from the yacht. The tragic and mysterious death of the lovely 43-year-old star is ironic in that she had always expressed a fear of water. Shooting on her last film, *Brainstorm*, a science-fiction movie directed by Dalton Trumbo and co-starring Christopher Walken, was nearing its completion.

'On Golden Pond' reconciles Henry Fonda with daughter Jane

New York, 4 December
Since her childhood, Jane Fonda has reproached her father for neglecting her and her brother Peter. For his part, Henry Fonda found it difficult to accept his daughter's militancy vis-à-vis the Vietnam War, her position on abortion and her sympathy for the Black Panthers. Father and daughter remained distant for some time. As the years passed, and Jane saw her father enter old age, she wanted to get closer to him. Therefore, she had been looking for some time for a screenplay which would allow them to act together. She finally found it in *On Golden Pond*, based on a play by Ernest Thompson. It concerns a crusty 80-year-old former college professor (Henry Fonda), returning with his wife (Katharine Hepburn) to their beloved lakeside holiday cabin in New England, where their daughter (Jane Fonda) – on a rare visit – brings her new boyfriend and his 13-year-old son to stay. Always at odds with one another, father and daughter are reconciled in an embrace at the end. "The nature of the film made us think of time passing. My father and I were forced to seize the opportunity to get to know each other, and profit from the experience," Jane explained.

Doug McKeon (son and grandson), Jane Fonda and her father Henry.

'Reds': the epic ambition of Warren Beatty

New York, 4 December
Director-star Warren Beatty has not chosen the most propitious of political times to make *Reds*. The story of John Reed, a brilliant journalist and founder-member of the American Communist Party, is not one calculated to catch the mood of Reagan's conservative America. Thirty years ago a project like this might have attracted the baleful attention of the House Un-American Activities Committee. Now Beatty has only to face the critics and the public, and the initial verdict is that he has overstretched himself. Reed had a remarkable if short-lived career, the high point of which was his chronicling of the Russian Revolution, which he witnessed, in *Ten Days That Shook the World*. But Beatty, who also co-wrote the screenplay with Briton Trevor Griffiths, has tried to combine the sweep of this colossal upheaval with the more intimate story of Reed's passion for writer Louise Bryant, portrayed by Diane Keaton. And here the movie degenerates into a bad case of Reds-on-the-bed. Moreover, the presence in *Reds* of "witnesses" like Rebecca West and Henry Miller jars with the appearance of stars such as Jack Nicholson in cameo portraits of real people, in Nicholson's case playwright Eugene O'Neill. The one unmitigated joy of the film lies in the superb cinematography of Vittorio Storaro, who received an Academy Award for his work on *Apocalypse Now*. As producer, director, star and co-scenarist, Beatty has bitten off more than he can chew, and the result is a sprawling, confused hymn to a kind of liberal idealism which remains deeply unfashionable in contemporary America.

Jean-Jacques Annaud lights up prehistory

Paris, 16 December
Jean-Jacques Annaud's ambitious and highly original *Quest for Fire* is creating quite a stir. Freely adapted from a novel by J-H Rosny Aisné, an author of books set in prehistoric times, it tells the tale of the Ulam tribe, attempting to find the fire they have lost, and which they need in order to survive. During their quest, they encounter other tribes and must defend themselves. Set against beautifully shot landscapes that conjure up the Stone Age, the film's only dialogue is an invented language by Anthony Burgess. Financed partly by American and Canadian money and budgeted at nearly $12 million, the production, created for universal comprehension, seems perfectly suited for a worldwide market.

***Quest for Fire**: Jean-Jacques Annaud's tribute to our early ancestors.*

UN FILM DE JOHN BOORMAN
EXCALIBUR
The Arthurian legend retold.

STALKER
UN FILM d'ANDREÏ TARKOVSKI
Tedious script, amazing images.

Dee Hepburn, Gordon John Sinclair in **Gregory's Girl** (Great Britain).

Oleg Tabakov is Nikita Mikhalkov's **Oblomov**, with Yuri Bogatyryov (r).

Wallace Shawn, André Gregory conversing in Malle's **My Dinner With André**.

Left to right: Jessica Harper, Bernadette Peters and Steve Martin in **Pennies From Heaven** from Dennis Potter's British TV success.

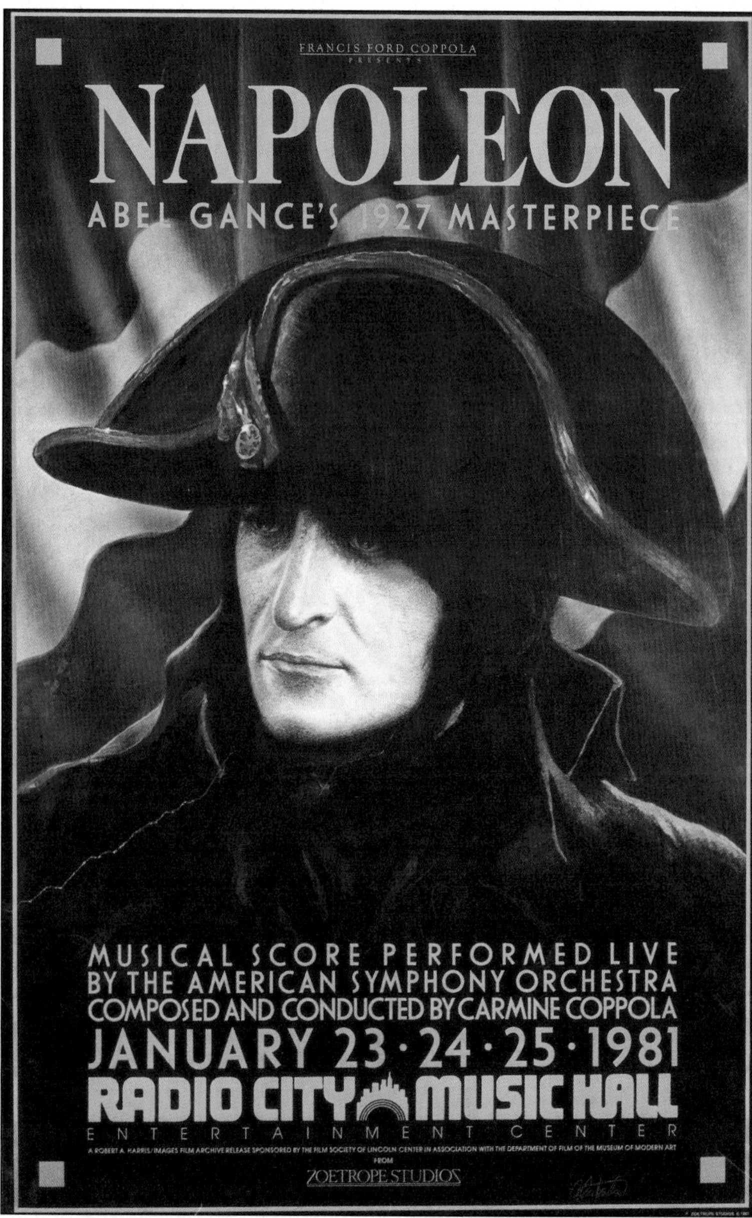
FRANCIS FORD COPPOLA
PRESENTS
NAPOLEON
ABEL GANCE'S 1927 MASTERPIECE
MUSICAL SCORE PERFORMED LIVE
BY THE AMERICAN SYMPHONY ORCHESTRA
COMPOSED AND CONDUCTED BY CARMINE COPPOLA
JANUARY 23 · 24 · 25 · 1981
RADIO CITY MUSIC HALL
ENTERTAINMENT CENTER
ZOETROPE STUDIOS
Reconstructed by Kevin Brownlow, Abel Gance's magnificent 1927 epic.

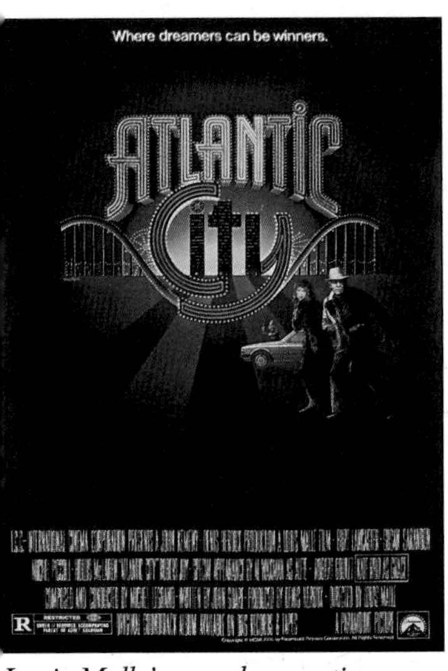
Where dreamers can be winners.
ATLANTIC
CITY
Louis Malle's superb evocation.

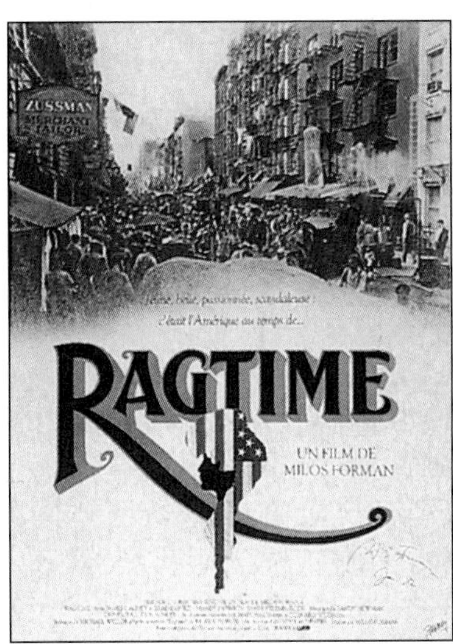
ZUSSMAN
RAGTIME
UN FILM DE
MILOS FORMAN
Forman made Doctorow's bestseller.

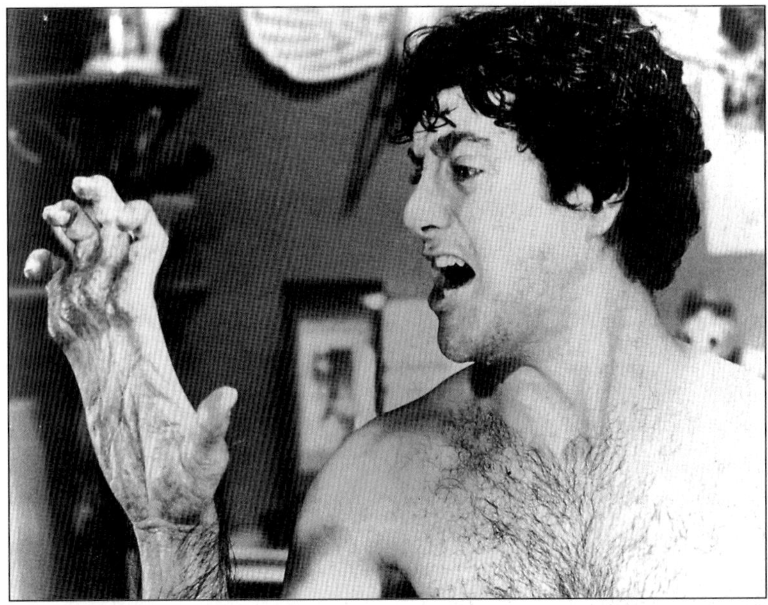
David Naughton transforming into **An American Werewolf in London**.

A characteristically mind-blowing image from David Cronenberg's **Scanners**.

Clash of the Titans, directed by Desmond Davis, was a not too successful spectacle involving Greek mythology.

David Warner in Terry Gilliam's **Time Bandits**, a mix of violence and humor.

1982

1981 Academy Awards, Dorothy Chandler Pavilion, 29 Mar.

Best Film:	*Chariots of Fire* (dir: Hugh Hudson)
Best Director:	Warren Beatty *(Reds)*
Best Actor:	Henry Fonda *(On Golden Pond)*
Best Actress:	Katharine Hepburn *(On Golden Pond)*
Best Supp. Actor:	John Gielgud *(Arthur)*
Best Supp. Actress:	Maureen Stapleton *(Reds)*

New York, 4 January
The National Society of Film Critics Awards ceremony last night (Louis Malle's *Atlantic City* took three of the major awards) was notable for the way critics called on Polish authorities to release Andrzej Wajda "and all other Polish film directors, producers, screenwriters, actors and craftsmen who are currently being detained for their political beliefs and associations."

Hollywood, 8 February
The filming of *Brainstorm*, which was interrupted last November by the death of its star, Natalie Wood, has started again. A new ending has been written for the film and Lloyd's of London have paid out $3 million so that the film can be completed.

New York, 18 February
Lee Strasberg, founder of the Actors Studio, died of a heart attack yesterday, just three days after his spirited chorus routine with former students Robert De Niro and Al Pacino at Radio City Music Hall's "Night of 100 Stars".

Paris, 24 February
Former scriptwriter Laurence Kasdan's first feature as director, *Body Heat*, opens here. A contemporary *film noir* with echoes of *Double Indemnity*, starring Kathleen Turner, it has made a substantial impression in America.

Berlin, 25 February
A homegrown film, Rainer Werner Fassbinder's *Veronika Voss*, has won the Golden Bear at the 32nd Film Festival here. The film, starring Rosel Zech as a has-been movie star, pays tribute to UFA.

Los Angeles, 4 March
Frank Capra was honored with the AFI's Life Achievement Award. Among the numerous stars of his films present for the occasion were James Stewart, Barbara Stanwyck, Claudette Colbert and Bette Davis.

Atlanta, 19 March
Columbia, the last of the majors from Hollywood's golden era to remain independent, has now been sold on the open market. The successful bidder is the Coca-Cola company, which is reported to have paid a cool $750 million for the prestigious film company.

Hollywood, 31 March
Carolco, the financing and foreign sales organization, has sold its first in-house production, *First Blood*, almost worldwide. The film, not as yet complete, has survived injuries to star Sylvester Stallone, the exit of Kirk Douglas over script disagreements, and the harsh Canadian weather. Carolco's partners blame the inflated $15 million budget on these mishaps.

Santa Fe, 27 April
Godfrey Reggio's *Koyaanisqatsi* stunned audiences last night at its Santa Fe Film Festival world premiere. The film, seven years in the making and shot across 14 states, features a minimalist musical score by Philip Glass. The title is a Hopi Indian expression meaning "life out of balance".

New York, 21 May
Release of *Annie*, John Huston's film version of the Broadway musical comedy inspired by Harold Gray's cartoon strip.

New York, 9 June
Steven Spielberg, an avid collector of cinema objects, has purchased "Rosebud", the child's sled belonging to Charles Foster Kane (Orson Welles) in the film *Citizen Kane*, for $60,500.

Hollywood, 30 June
Shooting starts today on *Psycho II*, to be directed by Anthony Perkins who will also reprise his role as the proprietor of the Bates Motel. Vera Miles, who was in the 1960 original, appears again.

Los Angeles, 8 July
Over 1,000 people are expected to turn out tonight at the Variety Arts Theater for the 6th Annual Erotic Film Awards. According to industry spokesman Dave Friedman, during 1981 over a million X-rated videocassettes were sold in America.

Hollywood, 13 July
After 16 weeks of national release *Porky's* has become only the 27th film to top the $100 million mark.

Los Angeles, 12 August
The much loved stage and movie actor, Henry Fonda, has died after several months of illness. Fonda rose to international stardom in the mid-1930s and throughout his acting career was appreciated by the public and profession alike. He got the AFI Life Achievement Award in 1978 and won his only Oscar for *On Golden Pond* earlier this year.

Los Angeles, 16 August
Rouben Mamoulian was honored last night as the 13th recipient of the Directors Guild of America D.W. Griffith Award for a lifetime of outstanding contributions to motion pictures. On this occasion of the Golden Jubilee of his 1932 film, *Love Me Tonight*, the audience was treated to clips from many of his works, including *Queen Christina*.

London, 29 August
Ingrid Bergman has died. Her last film was Ingmar Bergman's *Autumn Sonata* in 1978.

Monaco, 14 September
Princess Grace of Monaco was killed in a tragic car accident today. The former actress Grace Kelly gave up her star status to marry Prince Rainier of Monaco in 1956.

Hollywood, 6 October
Fines totalling $62,375 were levied against five people or companies for 45 safety code violations in connection with the *Twilight Zone* helicopter tragedy last July. John Landis and his company Levitsky Prods. were fined $30,955 and Western Helicopter Inc. $20,965.

Tunis, 30 October
The major prize at the ninth cinema festival here has been awarded to the Malian film *The Wind* (*Finyé*), directed by Souleymane Cissé.

Los Angeles, 1 November
King Vidor has died at the age of 88. Vidor began directing with a two-reeler on car-racing, *The Tow*, in 1914, and made his final film (another short, *The Metaphor*) 66 years later in 1980. This makes his the longest directorial career on record.

London, 2 November
A new commercial television channel, Channel Four, dedicated to transmitting quality programs and catering to special interests, goes on the air today.

Los Angeles, 30 November
After her period as a political activist, Jane Fonda has taken up a less radical cause: the body beautiful. The star's fitness book, *My Method*, has already sold 700,000 copies in the U.S. and is now being published in Europe.

Hollywood, 31 December
Universal alone accounted for over 30 percent of all box-office takings during the year, thanks to the unprecedented success of Steven Spielberg's *E.T.*. During the year the major studios have produced only 50 films in the U.S., while the number of films made abroad was up 75 percent from 1981.

DEATHS

California, 11 February
Eleanor Powell

Los Angeles, 5 March
John Belushi

England, 26 April
Celia Johnson

Munich, 10 June
Rainer Werner Fassbinder

California, 29 June
Henry King

London, 12 June
Kenneth More

Paris, 5 November
Jacques Tati

This fairy-tale image captures the heart-warming theme of ***E.T. The Extra-Terrestrial.*** *Steven Spielberg's film deservedly won the hearts and minds of children of all ages.*

A STEVEN SPIELBERG FILM
E.T.
THE EXTRA-TERRESTRIAL
IN HIS ADVENTURE ON EARTH
A STEVEN SPIELBERG FILM E.T. THE EXTRA-TERRESTRIAL
DEE WALLACE · PETER COYOTE · HENRY THOMAS AS ELLIOTT · MUSIC BY JOHN WILLIAMS
WRITTEN BY MELISSA MATHISON · PRODUCED BY STEVEN SPIELBERG & KATHLEEN KENNEDY
DIRECTED BY STEVEN SPIELBERG · A UNIVERSAL PICTURE ·
SOUNDTRACK AVAILABLE ON MCA RECORDS AND TAPES
READ THE BERKLEY BOOK ©1982 UNIVERSAL CITY STUDIOS, INC.

▷

Costa-Gavras turns his spotlight on America with 'Missing'

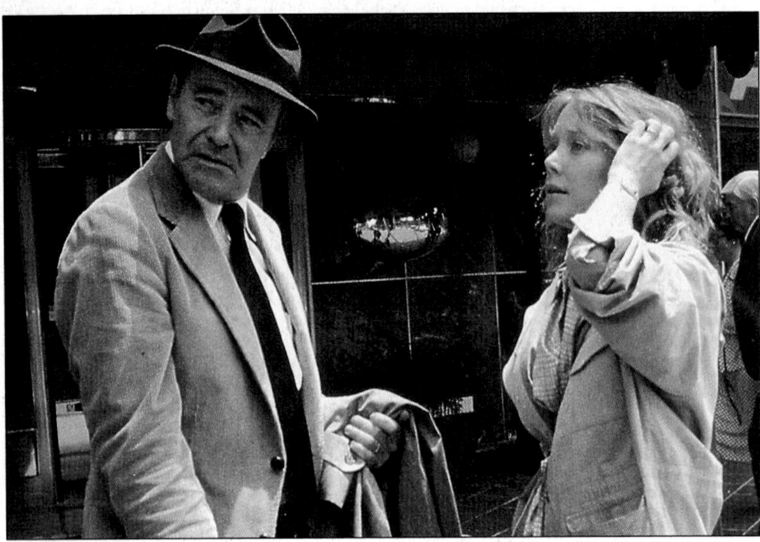

Jack Lemmon, the distraught father, and Sissy Spacek, the desperate wife.

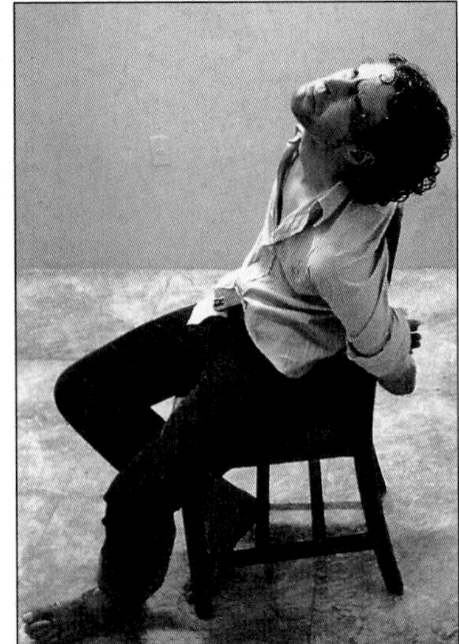

The tortured prisoner, Jack Shea.

New York, 12 February
Costa-Gavras makes his Hollywood debut with *Missing*. The French-based filmmaker, a specialist in thrillers with a strong political angle, has turned his attention to the machinations of the CIA. Jack Lemmon plays a stiffbacked American patriot whose son disappears in mysterious circumstances in Chile in 1973. On his quest to find the truth he gradually begins to realize that he is in fact the dupe of the U.S. Intelligence services. Costa-Gavras and Donald Stewart's screenplay is based on the real-life experiences of Ed Horman and confirms the director's ability to make pointedly political films which are also exciting and commercially successful. Here he combines the polemical with the domestic as Lemmon is reconciled with his liberal daughter-in-law Sissy Spacek in a shared tragedy.

The Actors Studio mourns Strasberg

New York, 18 February
Lee Strasberg, director, actor and drama teacher, died last night aged 81. He was born in Austria, and came to the United States at the age of nine. He studied acting under Richard Boleslavsky and Maria Ouspenskaya at the American Laboratory Theater, making his stage debut in 1925. He was among the founders in 1930 of the radical Group Theater in New York, for which he directed many plays. In 1948 Strasberg became the artistic director of the Actors Studio, where he influenced a new generation of performers, among them Marlon Brando, Paul Newman, Joanne Woodward, Eli Wallach, Shelley Winters and Rod Steiger. They were among the stars who, in the 1950s, popularized The Method, a realistic approach to acting derived from the teachings of Stanislavsky. Strasberg made an auspicious screen debut in *The Godfather Part II*, for which he was nominated for a Best Supporting Oscar.

A vicious gang war with a British flavor

London, 26 February
Gangsters are on the loose in London in John Mackenzie's pulsating new thriller, *The Long Good Friday*. Chief among them is the burly little bullfrog figure of Bob Hoskins' East End mobster Harold Shand, anxious to clinch a "legitimate" deal with some money-men from the Mafia but discovering that he has been targeted by the IRA, an outfit which doesn't play to the usual gangland rules. Harold gets even, but a nasty surprise is in store for him and his sultry mistress Helen Mirren at the end of the film. This is a breakthrough performance by Hoskins, an experienced character actor who first came to prominence on British TV as the tragic little Depression-era Everyman in Dennis Potter's brilliant serial *Pennies From Heaven*.

Gang boss Hoskins and his girlfriend Mirren on board their luxury yacht.

Cunning 'policier' collects three Césars

Paris, 27 February
The evening of the presentation of the Césars was enlivened by the presence of Orson Welles, who had received the Legion of Honor from the president of France a few hours earlier. The great American actor-director witnessed the award for best film and best director going to Jean-Jacques Annaud's stone-age epic, *Quest for Fire*. Claude Miller's *Garde à vue* (*The Inquisitor*) gained the best screenplay, actor (Michel Serrault) and supporting actor (Guy Marchand) prizes. This taut *policier* is confined almost entirely to the interrogation room inside a police station where the inquisitor (Lino Ventura) and the suspect (Serrault) arrested for child rape and murder, engage in an absorbing game of cat and mouse.

Left to right: Lino Ventura, director Claude Miller, Guy Marchand and Michel Serrault rehearsing a scene for ***The Inquisitor (Garde à vue)****.*

Julie Andrews delightful in drag

Julie Andrews, sparkling as 'Victor'.

New York, 19 March
Julie Andrews seems determined to dismantle her Goody-Two-Shoes image. Last year she bared her breasts in her director husband Blake Edwards' *S.O.B.* Now, in his stylish comedy *Victor/Victoria*, she is cast as a temporary "transvestite". She's a singer on the skids who masquerades as a man and becomes the toast of the cabarets in 1930s Paris, to the delight of gay mentor Robert Preston and bewilderment of American suitor James Garner. The screenplay is based on a 1933 German film, *Viktor und Viktoria*.

Britain's 'Chariots of Fire' races away with Best Picture Oscar

Los Angeles, 29 March
On receiving his Best Screenplay Oscar for *Chariots of Fire*, Colin Welland, echoing Paul Revere's warning cry to Americans of the Redcoats' advance, exclaimed, "The British are coming!" This British film, which also took Best Picture, Best Original Score and Costume Design awards, originated from producer David Puttnam, inspired by a history of the Olympic Games. It was the 1924 event that caught his attention, because of the different motivations of two of Britain's gold medalists – runners Harold Abrahams, who ran for his country to overcome the anti-Semitism of which he was conscious, and Eric Liddell, a Scottish missionary, who ran for the greater glory of God, but never on a Sunday. The contrasts and similarities between the Jew and the Scot are well delineated in the performances of Ben Cross and Ian Charleson respectively. It is a classic English tale, told in classic English terms, with a certain nostalgia for Empire, which ends with director Hugh Hudson pulling out all the stops for the final sporting triumph. Running has never looked more exhilarating. Hudson lost out as Best Director to Warren Beatty for his Russian Revolution epic, *Reds*. The Best Actor and Actress Oscars were awarded to the two veteran stars of *On Golden Pond*, Henry Fonda and Katharine Hepburn, moving and amusing as a loving couple having to face the death of one partner.

Racing to the finish line: Hugh Hudson's ***Chariots of Fire*** *was voted Best Film.*

Katharine Hepburn and Henry Fonda: her fourth Academy Award, his first.

Continuing crisis for Francis Coppola

Hollywood, 3 May
The ambitious plans of producer, director and would-be mogul Francis Ford Coppola for his Zoetrope studio have collapsed in a heap. Despite a well publicized and spectacular launch of his extravagant musical romance, starring Nastassja Kinski, *One From the Heart*, at Radio City Music Hall earlier this year, the film has flopped. Since it ended up costing about $26 million, twice the original budget, this means that Coppola is now deeply in debt and unlikely to be able to find the funds to save his studio which is currently up for sale.

Gérard Depardieu impressive in 'The Return of Martin Guerre'

Depardieu, the mysterious stranger.

Paris, 12 May
Almost 10 years since his first film, *les Hommes*, Daniel Vigne has finally delivered his second, an intriguing medieval mystery, *The Return of Martin Guerre*. Given the director's scrupulous attention to every detail of the period, it is not surprising the project took him so long to realize. Gérard Depardieu, playing with controlled power, is a man who comes to a 16th-century French village claiming to be Martin Guerre, a youth who left his child-bride pregnant eight years earlier. The question that has to be established is whether he is an imposter. The court case contains as much suspense as any modern drama.

With his bride (Nathalie Baye).

▷

Richly international lineup at 35th Festival

***Parsifal** from Germany's Hans Jürgen Syberberg, shown outside competition.*

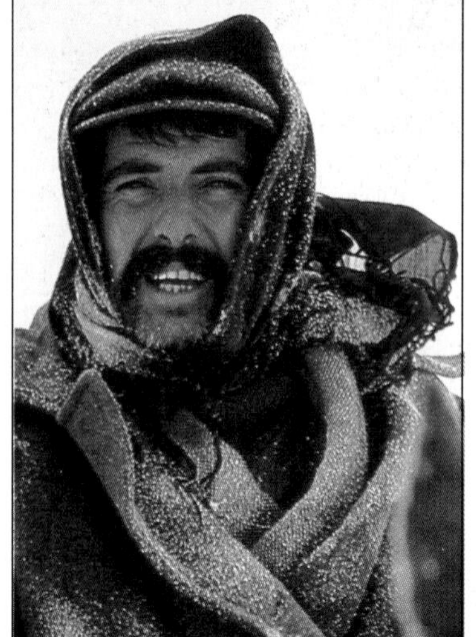
*Guney's **Yol**: sharing the Palm.*

Christine Boisson in Antonioni's film.

Cannes, 26 May
Because of the exceptional quality of this year's Festival entries, the jury, presided over by Italian stage director Giorgio Strehler, created a special award, the 35th Festival prize, as was done exactly 10 years ago for Cannes' 25th birthday. It was presented to Michelangelo Antonioni's film *Identification of a Woman*, his first in seven years, during which time he had been experimenting with video techniques. The great Italian director has returned here to familiar territory – the void at the heart of a relationship, and the difficulty of loving someone fully in our times. The joint winners of the Golden Palm were both powerful denunciations of repressive regimes. *Missing*, Costa-Gavras' first American film, follows the tortuous quest of a father (Jack Lemmon, voted best actor) for his son who has been arrested by the military junta in Chile. The film chillingly captures the atmosphere of a police state, and the political message is unequivocal. *Yol* is even more remarkable in that it was shot in Turkey by Serif Gören from a detailed script written by Yilmaz Guney when he was in jail. The negative was smuggled out to Europe where Guney, following his escape from prison last year, edited it. *Yol*, "the road of life" being the nearest translation, follows the lives of five prisoners on a week's parole to all corners of the country. It is acted with exceptional conviction, against vividly realized landscapes. And political repression, the 1956 Hungarian uprising, also forms the background to Karoly Makk's *Another Way*, featuring two brilliant actresses, one of whom (Jadwiga Jankowska-Cieslak) won the award. The Special Jury Prize went to a less contemporary but no less effective film. This was *Night of the Shooting Stars* (*La Notte di San Lorenzo*) by Paolo and Vittorio Taviani, which retells the events of August 1944 when a Tuscan town was threatened with destruction by the Nazis as the Americans advanced. It is full of bravura and inspiring sequences, as was the bizarre epic *Fitzcarraldo*, for which Werner Herzog won the best director award.

Terrific young cast makes a meal of 'Diner'

Baltimore, 14 May
Diner is a touching and funny portrait of a group of guys moving awkwardly out of their teens as the 60s are about to dawn. First-time director Barry Levinson has conjured up his own memories of hanging out with the gang at the eating place of the title in his native Baltimore. Each of the characters, played brilliantly by relative newcomers, has a different problem to resolve. Daniel Stern, the only married man, finds he has nothing much to say to his wife, Ellen Barkin; Steve Guttenberg is afraid that the same thing will happen to him; Kevin Bacon is a dropout who drinks too much, and Mickey Rourke is under pressure to settle a gambling debt. Beguiling.

Daniel Stern, Mickey Rourke, Steve Guttenberg, Kevin Bacon, Timothy Daly.

Best actress Jadwiga Jankowska-Cieslak (left) and Grazyna Szapolowska.

omy dies of broken heart

ıris, 29 May
ɔmy Schneider has been found ad from a heart attack, brought out by an excess of alcohol and ls. Since the tragic death of her n David last July, Romy declared at she felt she was living on a ıking ship. "My life is over," she ld the German magazine *Stern*. evertheless, she finished shooting film dedicated to "David and his ıther", and was hoping to return the stage. Hounded by the tabloid ess, she was forced to change her ldress several times before settling to an apartment with her new ɔyfriend Laurent Pétin. At 7:30 is morning, he found her dead on e sofa, a pen in her hand and an ıfinished letter by her side.

ossett gives lesson to Gere

ollywood, 28 July
ichard Gere has exchanged the signer suits he wore in *American igolo* for the crisp white uniform of *n Officer and a Gentleman*. He is e misfit in the middle of a grueling urse at the Naval Officer Candi- ıte School, who is challenged by ugh black drill sergeant Louis ossett Jr. to prove whether he's steer or a queer." Fortunately ebra Winger is on hand to put the sue beyond doubt in a romance hich, in spite of swear words and eamy sex scenes, follows a tried ıd trusted Hollywood formula.

ichard Gere and Lou Gossett Jr.

Another magic message from space

Henry Thomas, the little boy, with his new friend, the gentle visitor from space magnificently created by Carlo Rambaldi.

New York, 13 June
Variety has already called Steven Spielberg's latest picture, *E.T. The Extra-Terrestrial*, "the best Disney film never made", and the movie is, indeed, a remarkable celebration of the childhood innocence dear to Walt Disney's heart. A fatherless 10-year-old boy, played by Henry Thomas, befriends a creature from another planet who has been stranded on Earth. Much of the movie is shot from hip height, the point of view of small children, and in the process the charming little alien becomes the secret companion of all our childhoods as Spielberg moves from terror through comedy and death to the exhilaration of the children's climactic magic BMX bike ride. This is Spielberg's most personal film, and it is all the more powerful for being filtered through his instinctive grasp of the power of myth. Smallness never diminishes anything in a Spielberg film, not least the small protagonists in *E.T.*

Ridley's replicants show a frightening future in 'Blade Runner'

Los Angeles, 25 June
After *Alien*, Ridley Scott has stayed in the world of science fiction with *Blade Runner*, adapted from the Philip K. Dick classic, *Do Androids Dream of Electric Sheep?*. An android might be programmed with sufficiently sophisticated human responses to convince him that he is, indeed, human. This possibility hovers in the background of *Blade Runner*, in which Harrison Ford plays the hardboiled bounty hunter on the track of a band of semi-human robot replicants in the trash-littered, steam-shrouded streets of Los Angeles' Chinatown in 2019. The replicants combine instinctive animal grace with balletically explosive violence directed against their human creators. Fighting to stay the hand of the executioner, these deadly creatures engage our sympathy more than their sub-Bogartian pursuer who, ironically, might himself be a highly specialized android. With superb production design by Lawrence G. Paull, special effects by Douglas Trumbull and an arresting performance by Dutch actor Rutger Hauer in the role of the blond and piercingly blue-eyed chief android, *Blade Runner* brilliantly combines the conventions of the private eye genre with a bleak vision of a 21st-century future. It's a world in which, as the film's publicity tells us, "no one gets out of life alive."

Pris (Daryl Hannah) and Batty (Rutger Hauer), ***Blade Runner****'s 'replicants'.* ▷

Germany's leading director is dead

Munich, 10 June
Rainer Werner Fassbinder has been found dead in his Munich apartment at the age of 37, just as he was completing the cutting of his last film, *Querelle*. The cause of death was reported to be heart failure due to a mixture of sleeping pills and cocaine. Almost a one-man film industry, he made over 30 films in 12 years. It is a surprisingly consistent, entertaining and probing output. He began directing in 1969, rapidly becoming part of the new generation of directors who put German cinema on the map again after 30 years, his work revealing a heartless, avaricious, materialistic New Germany. Most of his characters are frustrated by the barrenness of urban existence, sometimes turning to violence. Although he was homosexual, women, usually played by Ingrid Caven, Hanna Schygulla or Barbara Sukowa, were at the center of his films. *The Marriage of Maria Braun* (1978), *Veronika Voss* (1979) and *Lola* (1981) show them trying to survive in an ironically evoked postwar Germany.

'Mad Max 2: The Road Warrior'

New York, 21 August
George Miller's *Mad Max 2* goes one better than the original. It's a post-holocaust Western in which embittered ex-cop Mel Gibson rides to the rescue of civilization's last representatives, who are besieged in a desert fortress by an army of freaks under the command of a giant called the Humungus. Directed at a frantic pace and exploding with stylized violence, *Mad Max 2* stays just on the right side of parody.

Mel Gibson returns in Mad Max.

A new black star is born in '48 HRS'

Los Angeles, 8 December
Black comedian Eddie Murphy, a veteran of TV's *Saturday Night Live*, has made an explosive debut in Walter Hill's fast and furious action comedy *48 HRS*. Murphy is the sassy con sprung by hulking cop Nick Nolte for the hours in question to help him track down Murphy's homicidal partner. At first the two men heartily loathe each other but, as is the way in Hollywood, they take their final leave of each other after some heavy-duty male bonding. Murphy is superb, mocking Nolte's taste in clothes and cars, punctuating the picture with his trademark hiccuping cackle, chasing every skirt in sight and terrorizing the patrons of a redneck bar.

Cop Nick Nolte and convict-helper Eddie Murphy wait for their quarry.

Gandhi an inspiration to a troubled worl

Gandhi (Ben Kingsley) flanked by his followers in Attenborough's epic.

London, 3 December
A project which Richard Attenborough has been nurturing for 20 years has finally come to fruition. *Gandhi*, a sweeping account of the life and times of Mohandas K. Gandhi, the saintly, pacifist father of modern India, is epic filmmaking in the grand tradition. Attenborough (*Young Winston*, *A Bridge Too Far*) certainly has the pedigree as a director, having a grasp of storyline, an ease at chronicling the lives of great men and a mastery of logistics. All were required in the making of *Gandhi*, which, for the productic company Goldcrest, carried a pric tag of some $20 million. At tl center of the film is Ben Kingsley riveting performance as Gandh Kingsley is an Anglo-Indian, bor Krishna Banji in 1944 in Nort ampton, England, but *Gandhi* toc him to India for the first tim Preparing for the role, he ensure that he gave his performance an e tra dimension by immersing himse in Gandhi's way of life, sitting cros legged on a mat, following his di and practising yoga.

A favorable verdict for new Newman pic

New York, 8 December
Sidney Lumet's new film should impress the critics and please the public, but is not likely to find favor with the New England legal establishment. In *The Verdict*, Paul Newman plays an attorney on the skids, spending his time at the wrong kind of bar in the absence of clients. Out of the blue, he is approached to take on a malpractice case involving a Boston hospitals board which appears impossible to win. Accepting the challenge, he gets involved with sexy Charlotte Rampling and viperous James Mason (the opposing counsel) along the way and, needless to say, comes up trumps. Lumet's picture is a gripping thriller-cum-courtroom drama with a moral message, and Newman in top form.

James Mason and Paul Newman.

leryl Streep brilliant as Polish Sophie

leryl Streep as the tragic Sophie.

lollywood, 10 December
leryl Streep has focused her great ·chnical gifts on *Sophie's Choice*, irected by Alan J. Pakula, in which ıe plays the Nazi death camp survivor of the title, haunted by her harrowing past in postwar Brooklyn. Her Polish accent is perfect, but her remarkable characterization cannot carry the weight of a film which founders on the premise of the title (the decision whether or not to surrender her child) which introduces an element of the meretricious to the tragedy of the Holocaust. Ironically, Streep struck just the right kind of note as a young Aryan German woman trying to save her husband in *Holocaust*, a 1978 televison series whose populist ambitions were not suffocated by the portentousness which clings to *Sophie's Choice*. Streep is never less than compelling in the flashbacks which take us back to Auschwitz, but Pakula's screenplay, the first he has written for one of his films, can only grope at the real horror of those times. Filmmakers have yet to find a way of directly confronting the experience of the death camps.

ustin's 'Tootsie' is a gold-plated riot!

os Angeles, 17 December
.t Mann's Chinese Theater last ight, in the presence of a starry udience that included Christopher eeve, Barbra Streisand, Michael ouglas and Tina Turner, the longwaited comedy from Dustin Hoffıan, *Tootsie*, was unveiled to loud ughter and applause. By now everyone knows that it involves Dustin laying a woman. In fact, he delivers brilliantly deft comic double – self-mocking as a pretentious, out-of-work, avant-garde actor; and instantly likable as Dorothy, whose persona he takes on in order to get an acting job in a TV "soap". It is arguably the most convincing drag portrayal in cinema history. With her large round spectacles, tailored suits, flashing smile, and soothing Southern accent (with just the right amount of prissiness), Dorothy is a wonderful creation.

ustin Hoffman as 'Dorothy' with her actress friend (Jessica Lange).

Perfect and magical evocation of childhood

Bertil Guve and Pernilla Alwin are the children in Ingmar Bergman's film.

Stockholm, 25 December
Often in the past, Ingmar Bergman has suffered from the incomprehension and even ingratitude of his country. However, he has offered Swedish audiences a wonderful Christmas present in *Fanny and Alexander*, which the director has announced as his last film for the big screen. It opens with the wealthy, loving and ebullient Ekdahl family gathered to celebrate Christmas. When the actor-father of 10-year-old Alexander and eight-year-old Fanny dies, their mother marries the city's bishop, a strict disciplinarian, who runs an extremely ascetic household. His cruelty to his two stepchildren leads Grandmother Ekdahl's Jewish friend and lover to rescue them. Happiness and balance is restored as new babies are born, and the family gathers once more to celebrate. Bergman's most optimistic film creates pure enchantment as romance, tragedy, comedy, realism and fantasy blend into a perfect evocation of childhood, the place and the period (turn-of-the-century Sweden), caught in glowing images by the ravishing color camerawork of Sven Nykvist. The wonderful cast includes three of Bergman's regulars: Gunnar Björnstrand, Erland Josephson and Harriet Andersson. Bergman has claimed the influence of two writers on the film – the storyteller E.T.A. Hoffmann and Charles Dickens. If he is true to his word, then this final film is a superlative culmination of his 37 years as one of cinema's greatest artists.

A superb culmination of a 37-year-long career from a great cinema artist.

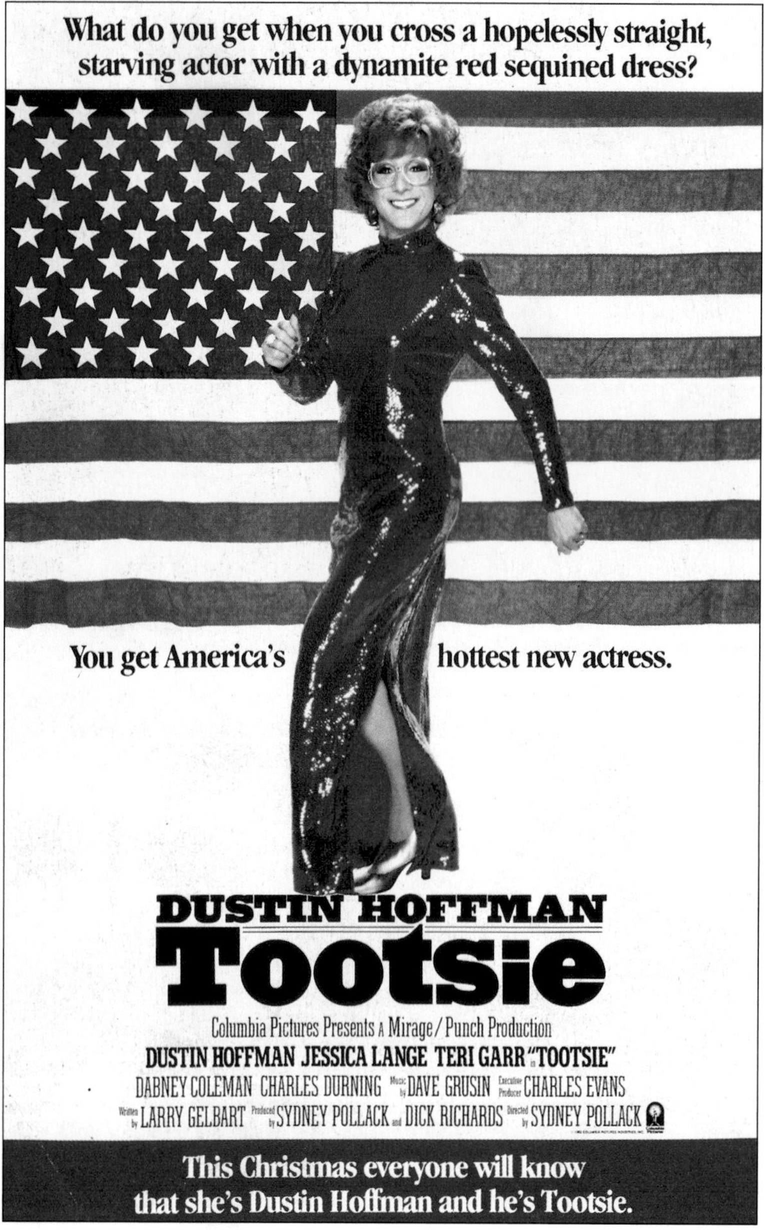
What do you get when you cross a hopelessly straight, starving actor with a dynamite red sequined dress?
You get America's hottest new actress.
DUSTIN HOFFMAN
Tootsie
Columbia Pictures Presents A Mirage/Punch Production
DUSTIN HOFFMAN JESSICA LANGE TERI GARR in "TOOTSIE"
DABNEY COLEMAN CHARLES DURNING Music by DAVE GRUSIN Executive Producer CHARLES EVANS
Written by LARRY GELBART Produced by SYDNEY POLLACK and DICK RICHARDS Directed by SYDNEY POLLACK
This Christmas everyone will know that she's Dustin Hoffman and he's Tootsie.

Sydney Pollack-Hoffman collaboration produced best-ever drag performance.

Isabelle Weingarten and Jeffrey Kime in Wim Wenders' ***The State of Things***

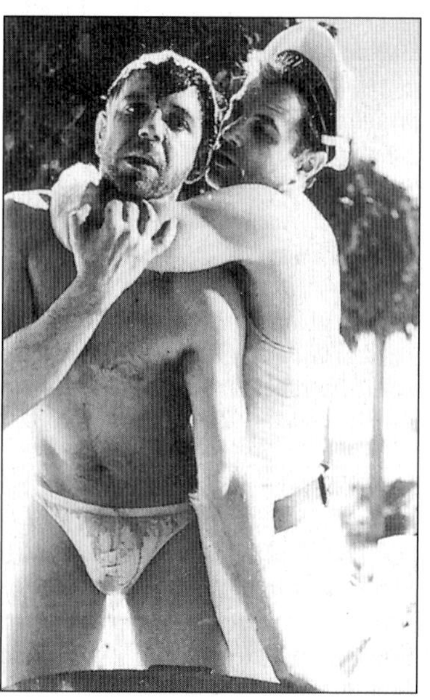

Fassbinder's ***Querelle****: Brad Davis (r) with Gunther Kaufmann.*

Jeremy Irons as a Polish builder in Jerzy Skolimowski's ***Moonlighting****.*

Paul Bartel (l), with Mary Woronov, in his own black comedy, ***Eating Raoul****.*

Dolly Parton (r), the ebullient madam of ***The Best Little Whorehouse in Texas***

VERONIKA VOSS
A Film By
RAINER WERNER FASSBINDER
Starring ROSEL ZECH · HILMAR THATE · CORNELIA FROBOESS
United Artists Classics

A striking study, in black and white, of has-been movie star evokes Nazi era.

Janet Suzman, Anthony Higgins: Greenaway's ***The Draughtsman's Contract****.*

Baby, It's You*: Vincent Spano and Rosanna Arquette in John Sayles' film.*

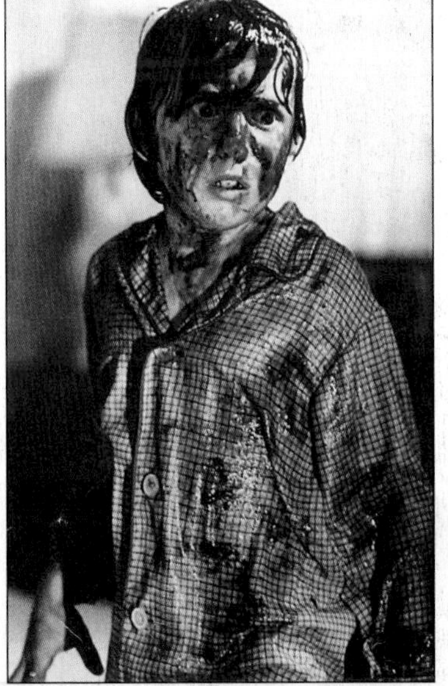

Craig T. Nelson and Jobeth Williams, the parents in Tobe Hooper's ***Poltergeist****, Oliver Robbins the child victim of evil.*

A remake of a 1933 German hit.

1983

1982 Academy Awards, Dorothy Chandler Pavilion, 11 Apr.

Best Film:	*Gandhi* (dir: Richard Attenborough)
Best Director:	Richard Attenborough
Best Actor:	Ben Kingsley *(Gandhi)*
Best Actress:	Meryl Streep *(Sophie's Choice)*
Best Supp. Actor:	Lou Gosset Jr. *(An Officer and a Gentleman)*
Best Supp. Actress:	Jessica Lange *(Tootsie)*

Lisbon, 2 January
Paulo Rocha is presenting one of the country's most extravagant cinema productions, *A ilha dos Amores*. It is an astonishing vision of Portuguese history, seen through the life of a colonial officer at the end of the 19th century.

Los Angeles, 2 January
The district attorney's report on the inquiry into the death of Marilyn Monroe 20 years ago clearly refutes the allegations that the star was murdered. It confirms the diagnosis of forensic experts at the time: Miss Monroe died of a heart attack due to an overdose of barbiturates.

Hollywood, 3 January
Sherry Lansing, who resigned from the presidency of 20th Century-Fox on 21 December, is forming an independent production company in partnership with Stanley Jaffe. They have signed a five-year exclusive rights agreement with Paramount.

London, 11 January
This year marks the British Film Institute's jubilee. Two royal performances are being planned for the occasion. The Institute not only runs a large reference library and one of the world's most comprehensive film archives, but also boasts a distribution division for hard-to-handle titles, runs a number of cinemas across the country and produces films, including this year's *The Draughtsman's Contract*.

Paris, 11 January
The Minister for Culture Jack Lang's new measures for the cinema have been hailed as the most important reforms in the history of the industry here. The main points are as follows: the creation of a financial institute to guarantee bank loans, the doubling of advances on box-office receipts, a support system for the small distributors and exhibitors, and the creation of an agency to distribute short films.

Paris, 20 January
French film stars have decided to strike in protest at a new law restricting cinema actors and technicians' right to collect unemployment.

Berlin, 1 March
The Festival's Golden Bear has gone to the British film *Ascendancy*, directed by Edward Bennett, with Julie Covington and Ian Charleson. French actress Jeanne Moreau presided over this year's ceremony.

Paris, 13 March
The first public screening of André Antoine's *l'Hirondelle et la mésange* has taken place at the Chaillot Cinémathèque. It was screened for a few people in 1924 but was never exploited commercially. The rushes which came to light in 1982 were used to restore the film.

Bombay, 11 March
Gandhi has become the hottest ever foreign film at the box office both here in Bombay and in New Delhi. It is also the first European film to prove as popular as Indian films.

Hollywood, 13 April
George Cukor's *A Star is Born* is undergoing extensive reconstruction after the discovery of approximately 20 minutes of footage, including two unseen musical numbers by Judy Garland "Lost That Long Face" and "Here's What I'm Here For". Film historian Ron Haver was instrumental in the tracking down of the missing *Star* segments, omitted when Jack Warner ordered the 1954 original to be shortened.

Hollywood, 26 April
United Artists Classics have rescued five "lost" Three Stooges films from the MGM vaults. Two of the five shorts, made at MGM prior to the duo's Columbia contract, are in two-strip technicolor. The shorts, which are being released as part of an MGM Three Stooges Festival, have not been shown since 1930s.

Hollywood, 24 May
Fay Wray has been invited to chair a special tribute to mark the 50th anniversary of the release of *King Kong* on 26 May. A screening of the film will be followed by a reception at the Hollywood Roosevelt Hotel where a collection of Kong memorabilia will be on display.

Los Angeles, 25 May
Release of George Lucas' *The Return of the Jedi*, the third film in the *Star Wars* saga, directed this time by Richard Marquand.

London, 31 May
A London court has awarded Universal Pictures $6,620,768 against a London pirate lab and distribution network. It is the highest amount awarded anywhere in the motion picture industry's five-year fight against video-piracy.

New York, 2 October
Diane Kurys' French film *Coup de foudre* (*At First Sight*) was a triumphant success at the New York Film Festival. The filmmaker was given a standing ovation.

Paris, 25 October
During a press conference, the Minister of Communication, Georges Filloud announced the creation of a new pay-channel, Canal Plus, before the end of 1984. Forty percent of viewing time is to be devoted to feature films.

Los Angeles, 9 November
Brian De Palma's *Scarface*, which was given an X-rating by the MPAA's Classification and Rating Administration on 3 November on the basis of excessive violence, has won an appeal and is now rated R.

London, 9 December
Samuel Fuller's controversial 1981 thriller, *White Dog*, has been making a lot of noise at the London Film Festival. The *Times* rave reviews have classified it "a virtuoso thriller..." and "clearly anti-racist". The British theatrical release for the movie is scheduled for March.

New York, 16 December
Showtime, the pay-cable channel which has the most subscribers after Home Box Office, has just paid $500 million for five years' exclusive rights to all Paramount productions.

Los Angeles, 20 December
20th Century-Fox has launched a advertising campaign to attract pc tential advertisers who wish to se their brand names displayed prom nently within the studio's featur films. Fox is the first big studio t openly use this method.

Moscow, 19 December
Grigori Alexandrov, longtime ass ciate of the celebrated Russian filr director Sergei Eisenstein, died t day. Alexandrov co-directed suc classic works as *October* (1928) an *The General Line* (1929) befor striking out on his own. He gaine critical acclaim abroad for films c the ilk of *Meeting on the Elbe*.

Rome, 23 December
Release here of Federico Fellini' latest film, *E la Nave va* (*And th Ship Sails On*), made with severa British actors in the cast.

India, 31 December
During the last year, 741 films wer produced in 27 different language for the domestic market. The pro duction center for popular films i the city of Bombay.

DEATHS

New York, 24 January
George Cukor

New York, 4 April
Gloria Swanson

California, 11 April
Dolores Del Rio

California, 12 June
Norma Shearer

Mexico City, 29 June
Luis Buñuel

Geneva, 29 July
David Niven

London, 10 October
Ralph Richardson

Los Angeles, 5 December
Robert Aldrich

Mike Nichols' film tells the true an terrible story of nuclear facility em ployee Karen Silkwood, who met mysterious and tragic end. She i brilliantly played by Meryl Streep.

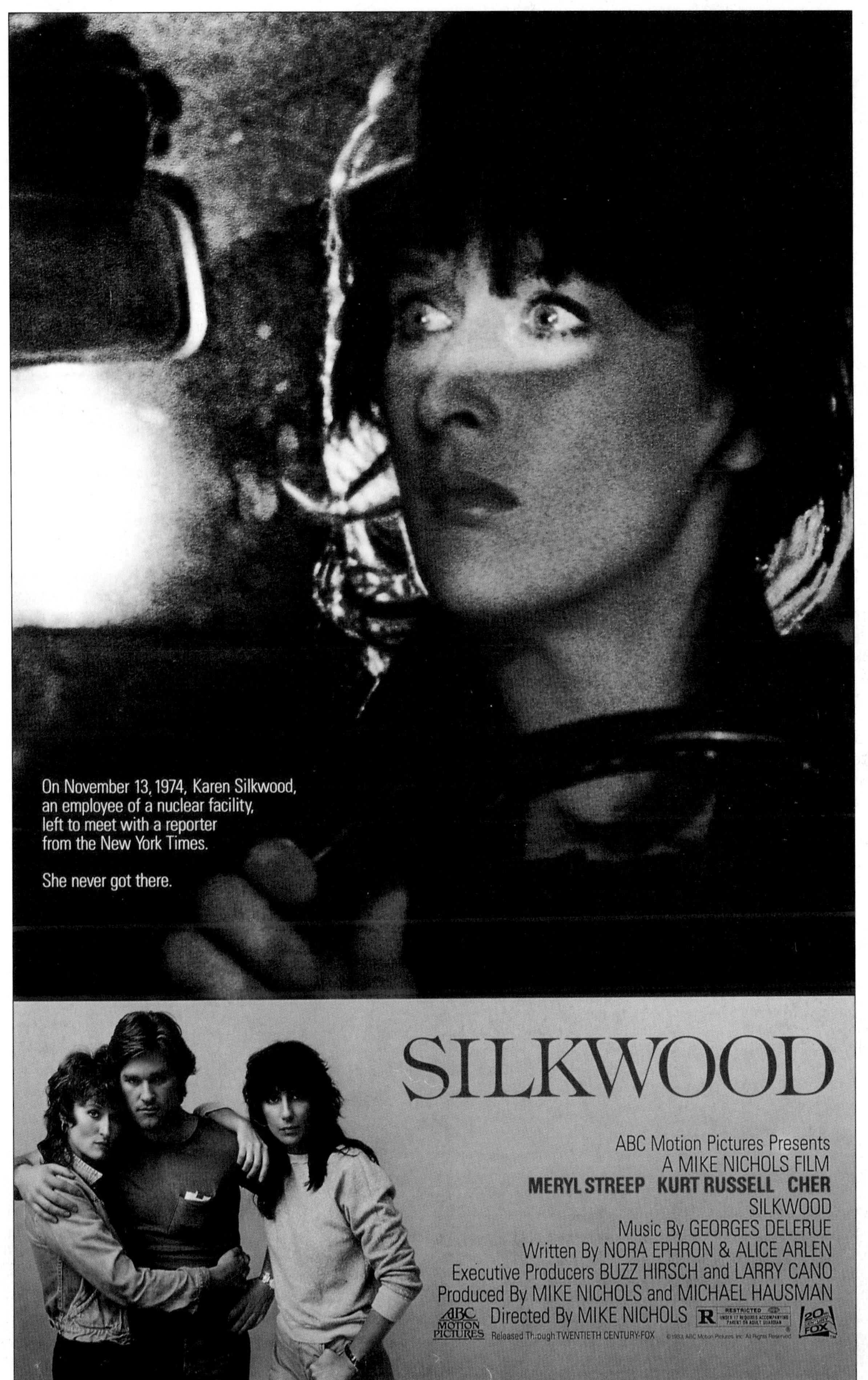
On November 13, 1974, Karen Silkwood,
an employee of a nuclear facility,
left to meet with a reporter
from the New York Times.
She never got there.
SILKWOOD
ABC Motion Pictures Presents
A MIKE NICHOLS FILM
MERYL STREEP KURT RUSSELL CHER
SILKWOOD
Music By GEORGES DELERUE
Written By NORA EPHRON & ALICE ARLEN
Executive Producers BUZZ HIRSCH and LARRY CANO
Produced By MIKE NICHOLS and MICHAEL HAUSMAN
ABC MOTION PICTURES
Directed By MIKE NICHOLS
R RESTRICTED
Released Through TWENTIETH CENTURY-FOX
20th CENTURY FOX

Conan and Rambo, new hero-avengers

Sylvester Stallone stalks through the Vietnamese jungle as John Rambo.

Arnold Schwarzenegger as Conan.

New York, 2 January
Sometimes cinema acts as a mirror, reflecting the changing mood of society. Nowhere is this more evident than in contemporary America where the success of Ted Kotcheff's *First Blood* and John Milius' *Conan the Barbarian* has created a new race of heroes for a nation drained of confidence by defeat in Vietnam, undermined by economic problems and humiliated by terrorists and drug barons. In *First Blood*, Sylvester Stallone plays John Rambo, a Vietnam veteran who goes to war with the society which has marginalized him. But instead of a martyr, Kotcheff gives us an invincible superman. In *Conan the Barbarian*, the former Mr. Universe Arnold Schwarzenegger lets his pectorals do the talking in a sword and sorcery epic in which he wields a mean broadsword and bites the head off a vulture. Rambo and Conan are latterday Hercules, who battle not for Good but simply for survival.

Poland's Wajda and the French Revolution

Danton (Depardieu), the French Revolution's idealist en route to the guillotine

Paris, 12 January
The recent Louis Delluc Prize winner, *Danton*, is the first French film to be directed by Andrzej Wajda. It takes as its subject the clash between the warmly idealistic Danton and the coldly pragmatic Robespierre over the direction the French Revolution should take, and ends with Danton on the guillotine. Most critics have made an analogy between the central ideological conflict and that of General Jaruzelski and Lech Walesa in today's Poland, although the film is based on a 1931 play by Stanislawa Przybyszewska. Gérard Depardieu does not play Danton as an opportunist, as is usually the case, but as a sincere man, one of the first to oppose the Terror.

The cinema of the fantastic is just that!

Avoriaz, 23 January
Muppet creator Jim Henson, with Frank Oz (the voice of Miss Piggy among others), has explored new territory in *Dark Crystal*, the winner of the Grand Prix at this festival of the fantastic. The film is a technically superb venture into fantasy, whose simple message – that good triumphs over evil – is imaginatively conveyed. The jury's special prize went to *The Last Battle*, a first feature by 23-year-old Luc Besson, an impressive fable of survival in stark black-and-white images, with no dialogue at all.

***Dark Crystal** made by the creators of the Muppets, Jim Henson and Frank Oz*

Comic genius Jerry Lewis held to ransom by Robert De Niro

Pupkin's great moment comes.

Jerry Langford (Lewis) and his admiring fan Rupert Pupkin (De Niro).

New York, 18 February
Jerry Lewis' career has been on the skids since his abandonment, in 1972, of *The Day the Clown Cried.* The title of his last movie, *Hardly Working*, was an ironic commentary on the backwater into which he had bobbed. But now Lewis is threatening a revival in Martin Scorsese's bleak anti-comedy *King of Comedy*. He's cast as the ferociously grumpy TV chat show host Jerry Langford, who is kidnapped by besotted fan Sandra Bernhard and Robert De Niro's would-be comic and ultimate schmuck Rupert Pupkin. But, as Rupert observes, it's better to be "a king for a night than a schmuck for a lifetime", and by the close of the film it's Rupert whose star is rising. Even when gagged and immobilized by swathes of white adhesive tape, Lewis radiates a sour malevolence which makes Jerry Langford one of the most memorably unpleasant characters in films of recent years. And there is a certain irony in the link between this storyline and Lewis' own *The Patsy*, in which he is groomed to replace a dead comic.

American Swaim tilts the balance

Paris, 27 February
The eighth César award ceremony, hosted by Catherine Deneuve, was held at the Rex on the picture palace's 50th birthday. It was *la Balance*, by Bob Swaim, an American director resident in Paris, that was voted the best picture of 1982. In addition, the two leads of this exciting police thriller, Philippe Léotard and Nathalie Baye, took the best acting awards. Léotard plays a petty crook coerced by the police to turn informer – "la balance" in underworld parlance – using his relationship with a prostitute (Baye) to nail a gang boss. Andrzej Wajda was best director for *Danton*, and Blake Edwards' popular *Victor/Victoria* with his wife Julie Andrews, was the best foreign film. Two new awards were instigated this year for the most promising actor and actress. These went to Christophe Malavoy in *Family Rock*, and to Sophie Marceau in *la Boum II*. Finally, a homage was paid to the actress Arletty, who greeted the audience on a screen from her Paris apartment.

Director Diane Kurys lovingly faces her past

Paris, 6 April
Having made a nostalgic journey to her own 60s adolescence in her first two charming films, the talented Diane Kurys reverts to the 50s with *Entre nous* (aka *At First Sight*). Green-eyed Isabelle Huppert and dark-eyed Miou-Miou take center stage as two women whose passionate friendship leads them to leave their inadequate husbands and open a dress shop together. Set in Lyons, the tender, atmospheric and well-acted tale is drawn from the experience of the director's mother (played by Huppert).

'E.T.' passed over in favor of 'Gandhi'

Los Angeles, 11 April
The most successful picture at this year's Oscar ceremony was *Gandhi*, which won eight awards, including Best Picture, Best Director for Richard Attenborough and Best Actor for Ben Kingsley in the title role. Meryl Streep was voted Best Actress for *Sophie's Choice*. Louis Gossett Jr. won the Best Supporting Actor award as the drill sergeant in *An Officer and a Gentleman* and Jessica Lange was Best Supporting Actress for *Tootsie*, all of which left the spectacularly successful *E.T.* surprisingly out in the cold.

Miou-Miou (left) and Isabelle Huppert in ***Entre nous (aka At First Sight)****.*

Happy Richard Attenborough brandishes his Best Picture and Director Oscars.

Robert Bresson causes controversy at Cannes

Monty Python, special prizewinner.

Shohei Imamura's ***The Ballad of Narayama***, winner of the Golden Palm.

ELECTION
FRANCE
ANNES
1983
L'ARGENT
DE
ROBERT
BRESSON

Cannes, 19 May
With his first picture in six years, *l'Argent*, 76-year-old Robert Bresson has divided the public at the Cannes Film Festival into two distinct camps. British director Alan Parker stated: "This is the work of an old man. It's unbearably boring." However, François Truffaut regretted that certain people failed to respond to Bresson's poetry. Another cause for chatter along the Croisette was that Caroline Lang, the daughter of the Minister of Culture Jack Lang, had an important role in the film. Whatever the reactions to *l'Argent*, Bresson has remained true to his austere vision in this updating of a Tolstoy story about a young man who passes a forged note in a photographer's shop, an action that leads him into theft and murder. The film shared the Grand Prize with *Nostalgia*, Andrei Tarkovsky's obscure, melancholy and poetic Italian-made drama. Then, some hours before the winners were announced, a Japanese journalist told his colleagues that he had been informed that the Golden Palm was to be given to Nagisa Oshima's *Furyo*. But it was another Japanese film that gained the top prize – Shohei Imamura's *The Ballad of Narayama*, a powerful remake of Kinoshita's 1958 vision of cruelty in a primitive society. Set in a remote mountain village, it tells of the custom of abandonment of anyone over 70 on the top of Mount Narayama. In contrast to the earnest films at the Festival, the Special Jury Prize was won by the British comedy *Monty Python's The Meaning of Life*.

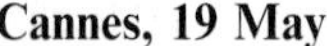

Heredity pitted against environment makes hilarious movie

New York, 8 June
Black comedian Eddie Murphy, who made an impactful debut in *48 HRS* last year, is back in *Trading Places*, made by John Landis for Paramount, who have reason to expect great things from it at the box office. The intriguing premise concerns two wealthy old codgers (veterans Don Ameche and Ralph Bellamy) locked in an argument over environment vs. heredity. Finally, they agree on a wager to put the case to the test by picking a conman beggar (Murphy) off the streets and training him to be a socially acceptable commodities broker, at the same time throwing their bright incumbent (Dan Aykroyd) onto the streets. Murphy, managing to be streetwise and charming all at once, is a delight, but the film has much more to offer. Witty and engaging, it is a welcome throwback to comedy of the past. The screwball goings-on are wrapped in satire reminiscent of Preston Sturges, though there is much of Capra's corn and good nature. The cast, including Jamie Lee Curtis as a delightful hooker, play it for all its worth. Director Landis, whose previous movies include *National Lampoon's Animal House*, *The Blues Brothers* and last year's terrific *An American Werewolf in London*, proves his versatility as well as his expertise.

Don Ameche (left), Ralph Bellamy with the object of their bet, Eddie Murphy.

Great return of Gance's 'Napoleon'

Paris, 22 July
Just 56 years after the 1927 Paris premiere of Abel Gance's *Napoleon*, the film has made a triumphant return in front of 3,700 spectators, accompanied by an orchestra conducted by Carl Davis, who assembled the new score. The saga of the film's reconstruction by English film historian and director Kevin Brownlow, began in the mid-1960s when he completed a short documentary about Gance, *The Charm of Dynamite*. Shown by the BBC in June 1968, it stimulated renewed interest in the director and his work. A reconstructed *Napoleon* was shown at London's National Film Theatre in 1970, and a more complete version with the final triptych was screened at Colorado's Telluride Film Festival nine years later. The 89-year-old Gance, present at the event, later remarked that the occasion was as good as the Paris Opera premiere.

Buñuel, scourge of the establishment, dies

Spanish cinema's greatest and most misunderstood son studied with the Jesuits.

Mexico, 30 June
Luis Buñuel, perhaps the most mordantly comic and subversive of all the great film directors, has died aged 83. Appropriately born (in Spain) with the century, he came from a cultured bourgeois family and was educated at a Jesuit school. This background and education turned Buñuel into a consistently anti-middle class and anti-clerical director. In Paris, he came under the influence of André Breton's Surrealist Manifesto, a vision from which he never wavered. With Salvador Dali, Buñuel embarked on his film career with one of the most startling images in all cinema, an open eye being slashed with a razor at the beginning of *Un chien andalou* in 1928.

Godard basks in warmth of the Golden Lion

Venice, 11 September
Whenever the films of Jean-Luc Godard are shown, they create controversy, so it was no surprise that there was grumbling from some quarters when his *First Name Carmen* won not only the Golden Lion, but also a technical award for the cinematography of Raoul Coutard. This is Godard at his most mischievous, playing wittily with a B-movie plot, Mérimée's *Carmen* and notions of cinema. Euzhan Palcy's first feature, the entrancing *Black Shack Alley* (*Rue Cases Nègres*), set in Martinique, took the Silver Lion.

Jacques Bonnaffé and Maruschka Detmers in Godard's ***First Name Carmen****.*

Australia joins the international scene

Mel Gibson and Sigourney Weaver in ***The Year of Living Dangerously****.*

Paris, 1 September
Praised by the critics at Cannes this year, the first Australian picture to be wholly financed by a major American studio (MGM), *The Year of Living Dangerously*, has had a box-office success hitherto rarely achieved by a film from that continent. The year of the title is 1965 in Indonesia (it was shot on location in the Philippines), leading up to the events of 30 September, when the dictatorial President Sukarno was deposed in a military coup. Living dangerously are Mel Gibson, a rookie Aussie foreign correspondent, Sigourney Weaver, attaché at the British embassy, with whom he falls in love, and a dwarfish Chinese-American cameraman, unusually and triumphantly played by Linda Hunt in a male role. It was directed with great virtuosity by Peter Weir, who vividly captures the tense atmosphere of the public happenings as a background to a love story in the best traditions of Hollywood romance in exotic climes. Mel Gibson, who was discovered in George Miller's *Mad Max* (1979), the only previous Australian movie to make such a commercial impact, has now become an international star. Peter Weir first came to the fore with *Picnic at Hanging Rock* (1975), the most important film of Australia's New Wave. Other directors who have made an impact are Bruce Beresford (*The Getting of Wisdom*, 1978; *Breaker Morant*, 1980); Phillip Noyce (*Newsfront*, 1978; *Heatwave*, 1981) and Paul Cox, who first gained attention with his off-beat romance *Lonely Hearts* in 1981.

Norman Kaye, Wendy Hughes in Paul Co

Humor and nostalgia warm 'The Big Chill'

Back: Glenn Close, Meg Tilly, Tom Berenger, Mary Kay Place. Front: Kevin Kline, William Hurt, Jeff Goldblum and JoBeth Williams.

New York, 29 September
In Lawrence Kasdan's *The Big Chill*, a group of Sixties radicals is reunited for the funeral of a college friend who has committed suicide. Over the course of the weekend they review the ways they have had to change, share confidences and regrets, and swap snappily cynical aphorisms. Kasdan has assembled a brilliant ensemble (William Hurt, Kevin Kline, Jeff Goldblum, Glenn Close, Tom Berenger, Meg Tilly, JoBeth Williams and Mary Kay Place) in a reflective movie which explores, with wit and warmth, similar territory to John Sayles' *The Return of the Secaucus Seven*.

More youth drama from the 'Brat Pack'

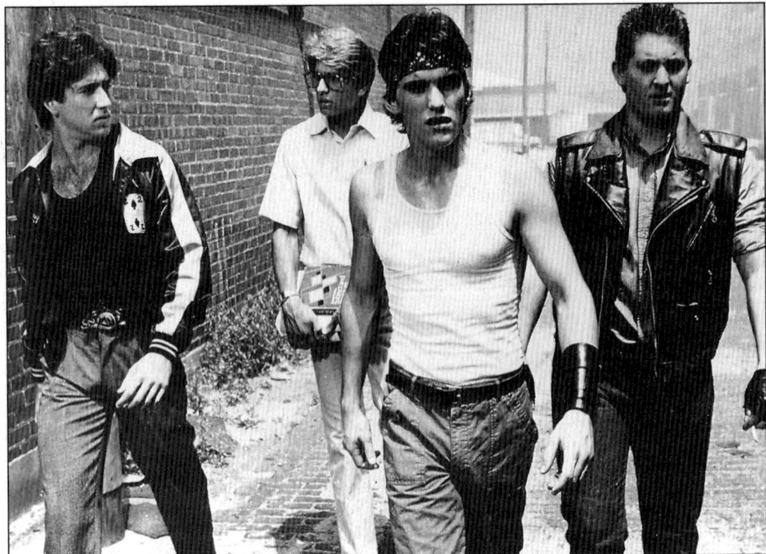

***Rumble Fish** (l to r): Nicolas Cage, Vincent Spano, Dillon, Christopher Penn.*

New York, 9 October
After the monumental failure of *One From the Heart* last year, Francis Ford Coppola has made two films on a much smaller scale. *The Outsiders* and *Rumble Fish* were shot back-to-back in Tulsa, both based on novels of adolescence by S.E. Hinton. The latter, filmed in monochrome with intermittent use of color, tells the story of a gang leader (Mickey Rourke) idolized by his kid brother (Matt Dillon), who cannot see the damage done to him by violence. *The Outsiders* is about a group of young men from the wrong side of the tracks. Both films shine with promising, new young stars.

A stirring tribute to American astronauts

New York, 21 October
Tom Wolfe's *The Right Stuff*, the best-selling account of the early days of the U.S. space program, has been turned by Philip Kaufman into an intriguingly off-beat celebration of the Mercury astronauts and laid-back, legendary test pilot Chuck Yeager, played by Sam Shepard, who blazed the trail for them. Skillfully interweaving Yeager's intensely individualistic approach with the group dynamics of the Mercury team, Kaufman vividly shows us the "right stuff" is more than just a metaphor for machismo.

l to r: Scott Glenn, Scott Paulin, Charles Frank (Scott Carpenter), Fred Ward [illegible] Dennis Quaid, Ed Harris (John Glenn).

Streisand combines ambition and schmaltz

Los Angeles, 18 November
Barbra Streisand makes an ambitious directing debut (also co-writer and producer) with *Yentl*. Filmed in Czechoslovakia and London, it came in over budget at $17.5 million. The result is questionable, but there's plenty to please Barbra's fans in Isaac Bashevis Singer's tale (turned into a musical) of a Jewish girl in Poland who masquerades as a boy so as to attend the rabbinical seminary, and finds herself married to her fellow student's fiancee! Mandy Patinkin and Amy Irving lend sterling support.

Mandy Patinkin, Amy Irving and Barbra Streisand at the Sabbath dinner.

'Terms of Endearment', an abrasive weepie, looks set for success

Hollywood, 24 November
The strong pairing of Jack Nicholson and Shirley MacLaine provides ashings of humor and heartache in *Terms of Endearment*, produced, written and directed by James L. Brooks from a novel by Larry McMurtry. In his directing debut, TV series wizard Brooks has fashioned a superior soaper which tracks the relationship between eccentric widow MacLaine and her feisty daughter Debra Winger. Nicholson plays MacLaine's ex-astronaut neighbor Garrett Breedlove, a man whose waistline is expanding as fast as his horizons seems to be receding. The movie is woven around his developing affair with MacLaine and the diagnosis of cancer in Winger, a combination of sentimentality and seriousness which, it must be said, produces its fair share of mawkish moments but also manages to draw high-definition performances from the principals which are bound to attract attention when the Oscars come around. The fact that MacLaine and Winger were barely on speaking terms during filming is not discernible in the finished product. Brooks cut his teeth in TV on hits like *The Mary Tyler Moore Show* and *Taxi* before moving into feature films as the screenwriter on *Starting Over*, a wistful comedy starring Burt Reynolds and Jill Clayburgh.

More than a match for each other: Shirley MacLaine and Jack Nicholson.

Major cinema historian dies

Paris, 25 November
The celebrated film historian Lotte H. Eisner has died aged 87. Born in Germany, where she studied the history of art and archeology, Eisner fled to Paris in 1933 at the rise of Nazism. There she worked as a correspondent for *World Film News* and other publications. In 1945, she joined the Cinémathèque Française, working closely with Henri Langlois programming festivals, lectures and exhibitions. She held the post of Head Curator of the Cinémathèque until 1975. Eisner was an expert on Expressionism in German cinema, and her 1952 book on the subject, *l'Ecran démoniaque* (translated into English as *The Haunted Screen* in 1969), was extremely influential. Aside from her contributions to film magazines, she also wrote a study of F.W. Murnau, and a large-scale work on the films of her old friend Fritz Lang.

Violence the keynote of 'Scarface' remake

Los Angeles, 9 December
Brian De Palma has remade the Howard Hawks gangster classic, *Scarface*, turning Paul Muni's Capone-like mobster into Al Pacino's Cuban cocaine dealer Tony Montana. Part of the jetsam of Castro's Cuba, Pacino moves steadily toward the center of power in the world of drug-trafficking but, like Muni, he is undone by the obsessively protective attitude he has toward his sister. Eventually he is destroyed, not by the forces of law and order, but by an even more ruthlessly efficient crime syndicate. Pacino gives a performance of hysterical malevolence in a movie which, perhaps, owes as much to *The Godfather* as to the Hawks original, and Michelle Pfeiffer is outstanding as his blonde junkie wife Elvira, symbol of the Wasp bastions of power Montana wants to annex.

'Silkwood' truthful, somber and alarming

Chicago, 14 December
Having seen his film career come to a halt eight years ago with *The Fortune*, Mike Nichols has hit the comeback trail with *Silkwood.* It's based on the real story of whistle-blowing nuclear worker Karen Silkwood, who died in 1974 under the mysterious circumstances of a "one-car accident". Here, Meryl Streep immerses herself in the part of Silkwood, a gum-chewing miniskirted working girl who finds herself on a mission to expose the dangers of nuclear power and begins to suspect that her employers are out to get her. Her involvement with the union and with union organizer Ron Silver recalls Sally Field in *Norma Rae*. There are strong supporting performances from Cher in the role of Karen's lesbian lodger and passionately devoted friend Dolly Pelliker, and Kurt Russell as her lover.

Al Pacino as the Cuban mobster losing control at the end of De Palma's film.

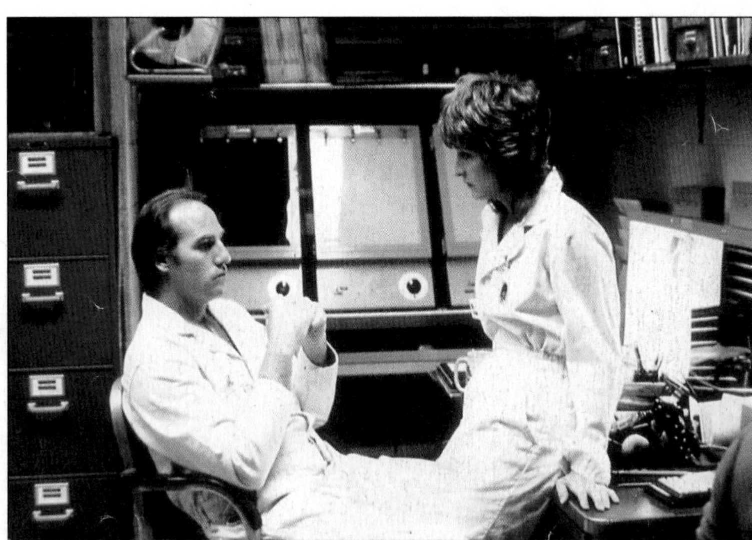
Meryl Streep (Silkwood) discussing a problem with Craig T. Nelson in the lab. ▷

JAVA, 1942—
A CLASH OF CULTURES,
A TEST
OF THE HUMAN SPIRIT.
平
和
MERRY CHRISTMAS,
MR. LAWRENCE
JEREMY THOMAS Presents A FILM BY NAGISA OSHIMA
"MERRY CHRISTMAS, MR. LAWRENCE"
DAVID BOWIE · TOM CONTI
RYUICHI SAKAMOTO · TAKESHI and JACK THOMPSON
Associate Producer: JOYCE HERLIHY · Music: RYUICHI SAKAMOTO
Screenplay by NAGISA OSHIMA with PAUL MAYERSBERG
Based on the Novel by SIR LAURENS VAN DER POST
Produced by JEREMY THOMAS · Directed by NAGISA OSHIMA
A UNIVERSAL RELEASE
R

Nagisa Oshima's star David Bowie.

There's a time
for playing it safe
and a time for...
Risky
Business
THE GEFFEN COMPANY Presents
A STEVE TISCH-JON AVNET Production
"RISKY BUSINESS"
TOM CRUISE REBECCA DE MORNAY
Produced by JON AVNET and STEVE TISCH
Written and Directed by PAUL BRICKMAN
R
A GEFFEN COMPANY RELEASE

Tom Cruise in risqué teen comedy.

Something happens
when she hears the music...
It's her freedom. It's her fire.
It's her life.
Flashdance
What a feeling.
Take your passion and make it happen!
PARAMOUNT PICTURES PRESENTS A POLYGRAM PICTURES PRODUCTION
AN ADRIAN LYNE FILM · FLASHDANCE · JENNIFER BEALS · MICHAEL NOURI
MUSIC SUPERVISED BY PHIL RAMONE · EXECUTIVE PRODUCERS—JON PETERS
AND PETER GUBER · SCREENPLAY BY TOM HEDLEY AND JOE ESZTERHAS
STORY BY TOM HEDLEY · PRODUCED BY DON SIMPSON AND JERRY BRUCKHEIMER
DIRECTED BY ADRIAN LYNE ORIGINAL SOUNDTRACK ON CASABLANCA RECORDS AND TAPES
R
A PARAMOUNT PICTURE

Jennifer Beals, a female Travolta!

Each summer one film opens
that you've never heard of...
and that you'll never forget.
NIGHTMARES
...is this year's "sleeper."

Four stories, director Joseph Sargent.

Koyaanisqatsi: non-narrative view of America with time-lapse photography.

Mia Farrow, Woody Allen in the latter's **Zelig**, about a human chameleon.

Peter Riegert (2nd right) and Burt Lancaster (r) in Bill Forsyth's **Local Hero**.

Isabelle Adjani is the deranged heroine of **One Deadly Summer** (France).

Vittorio Gassman, Geraldine Chaplin in Alain Resnais' ***Life is a Bed of Roses***.

Mel
BROOKS
Anne
BANCROFT
TO BE
OR
NOT TO BE
That's the movie!

This was a brave stab, but it doesn't match Lubitsch's 1942 masterpiece.

Psycho II*: Norman Bates and the old dark house are back after 22 years.*

Linda Griffiths (left) and Jane Hallaren are lovers in John Sayles' ***Lianna***.

Catherine Deneuve and David Bowie in vampire pic ***The Hunger***.

Richard Farnsworth as a real-life robber in ***The Grey Fox*** *(Canada).*

Matthew Broderick and Ally Sheedy in John Badham's ***War Games****: a school kid taps into the Pentagon computer, causing havoc.*

1984

1983 Academy Awards, Dorothy Chandler Pavilion, 9 Apr.

Best Film:	*Terms of Endearment* (dir: James L. Brooks)
Best Director:	James L. Brooks
Best Actor:	Robert Duvall *(Tender Mercies)*
Best Actress:	Shirley MacLaine *(Terms of Endearment)*
Best Supp. Actor:	Jack Nicholson *(Terms of Endearment)*
Best Supp. Actress:	Linda Hunt *(The Year of Living Dangerously)*

Acapulco, 20 January
Johnny Weissmuller has died at the age of 79, after suffering severe congestion of the lungs. It was an ironic end for the multiple Olympic champion, who found even greater fame as a screen Tarzan. Weissmuller made his debut in 1932 as *Tarzan the Ape Man* and continued in the role until 1948, bowing out with *Tarzan and the Mermaids*.

New York, 31 January
American film critics have voted Gérard Depardieu best foreign actor of 1983 for his performances as Danton (in Wajda's *Danton*) and in the title role of Daniel Vigne's *The Return of Martin Guerre*.

Hollywood, 20 February
Disney has announced the creation of a new production company called Touchstone to make films aimed at adult audiences.

Berlin, 26 February
Maximilian Schell presented his new work, a documentary titled *Marlene*, at the 34th International Film Festival. The film, which is based on 17 hours of interviews with Marlene Dietrich, who never appears on the screen, features only the actress' voice, evoking her life and career.

Berlin, 28 February
The Golden Bear has been awarded to *Love Streams*, made by American director John Cassavetes.

Los Angeles, 13 March
Walt Disney Pictures chose the right film, *Splash*, to launch Touchstone Films. The Ron Howard movie did just that over the weekend, marking the best ever weekend box-office results with an impressive $6.174 million in its first three days.

Hollywood, 19 March
James Cameron has begun shooting his latest film, *The Terminator*, starring Arnold Schwarzenegger and Linda Hamilton.

Paris, 24 March
The president of Walt Disney Productions, Michael Eisner, has signed a contract with the French prime minister, Laurent Fabius, for the construction of a European Disneyland. The new park is to be built in Marne-la-Vallée, just outside Paris, and is planned to open early in 1990.

Copenhagen, 14 May
Opening of Lars von Trier's *Element of Crime* (*Forbrydelsens Element*), with British actors Esmond Knight and Michael Elphick. A police inquiry gives way to madness.

Cannes, 15 May
During the Festival here Richard Attenborough unveiled a $4.5 million project bannered "A British Film Year". The aim of the project, which is backed by all sectors of the British film industry, is twofold – to revitalize movie attendance at home and to increase awareness of British talent abroad through major exhibitions of British films worldwide.

France, 17 May
According to figures published by the National Center for Cinema, attendance for 1983 was down 5.4 percent from the previous year. However, there was an increase in the number of French productions.

Hollywood, 4 June
Disney Productions has bought back 11 percent of its shares held by the financier Saul Steinberg, who was trying to gain control of the studio. The cost of the operation for Disney is estimated at $300 million.

Hollywood, 8 June
The Screen Actors Guild has a new member: Donald Duck. To fete the famous fowl's 50th birthday, Ralph Bell (SAG's vice president) and *Tap Dance Kid* stars Alfonso Ribiero and Martine Allard presented the Disney Duck with an honorary SAG membership card at a birthday brunch in the Rockefeller Plaza.

London, 22 June
One of the cinemas most intriguing directors, Joseph Losey, has died. He was blacklisted in 1951 and worked in England under pseudonyms for several years. Considered in France as one of the great auteurs of the cinema, Losey's work has at times been shunned by the public at large here and in the U.S.

Los Angeles, 27 June
The MPAA has introduced a new rating for films, PG-13, which indicates parental guidance is recommended for children under 13.

Paris, 12 August
Parisians can now see Fritz Lang's great German classic *Metropolis*, (1926) put to music and colored by Giorgio Moroder. Protesting filmlovers see it as a perversion of the filmmaker's art.

Paris, 14 September
Crowds of cinema-lovers as well as Kurds attended the funeral of the exiled director Yilmaz Guney at Père-Lachaise cemetery. He died of cancer on 9 September.

Hollywood, 1 October
Barry Diller has resigned as president of Paramount to take over from Alan Hirschfield as president of 20th Century-Fox. Diller had been head of the studio for 10 years.

New York, 25 October
Jim Jarmusch has brought out his first feature film, *Stranger Than Paradise*. The film, shot in black-and-white and in formal minimalist style, features an off-beat collection of characters.

Paris, 25 October
The sudden death of Pascale Ogier is reported. The 24-year-old actress was the daughter of Bulle Ogier.

France, 4 November
Canal Plus, the first French TV pay-channel, has started its programs with 200,000 subscribers.

Hollywood, 26 November
Robert Zemeckis is busy shooting *Back to the Future*. Filming is taking place on a closed set to ensure that the plot of the $15 million fantasy, starring young newcomer Michael J. Fox, remains secret, but audiences are promised terrific special effects.

New York, 14 December
Francis Ford Coppola's new film, *The Cotton Club*, stars Richard Gere and tap wizard Gregory Hines. The crazy years of jazz in swinging New York are magnificently reconstructed in this truly sumptuous film for producer Robert Evans.

Cannes, 14 December
Pierre Viot, former head of CNC, is to take over from Robert Favre Le Bret as Film Festival president.

Los Angeles, 31 December
Two movies have grossed more than $100 million this year. Ivan Reitman's *Ghostbusters*, starring Bill Murray, took in $120 million, and the Steven Spielberg-Harrison Ford 'prequel' to *Raiders of the Lost Ark*, *Indiana Jones and the Temple of Doom*, came in at $109 million.

DEATHS

California, 5 March
William Powell

England, 4 May
Diana Dors

Los Angeles, 26 June
Carl Foreman

Switzerland, 24 July
James Mason

Switzerland, 27 July
Richard Burton

California, 14 September
Janet Gaynor

Los Angeles 17 September
Richard Basehart

California, 26 September
Walter Pidgeon

France, 21 October
François Truffaut

Germany, 23 October
Oskar Werner

California, 28 December
Sam Peckinpah

Peter Shaffer's long-running Broadway and London hit play was filmed by Milos Forman. The sumptuous result offered a feast of Mozart music among its many other pleasures.

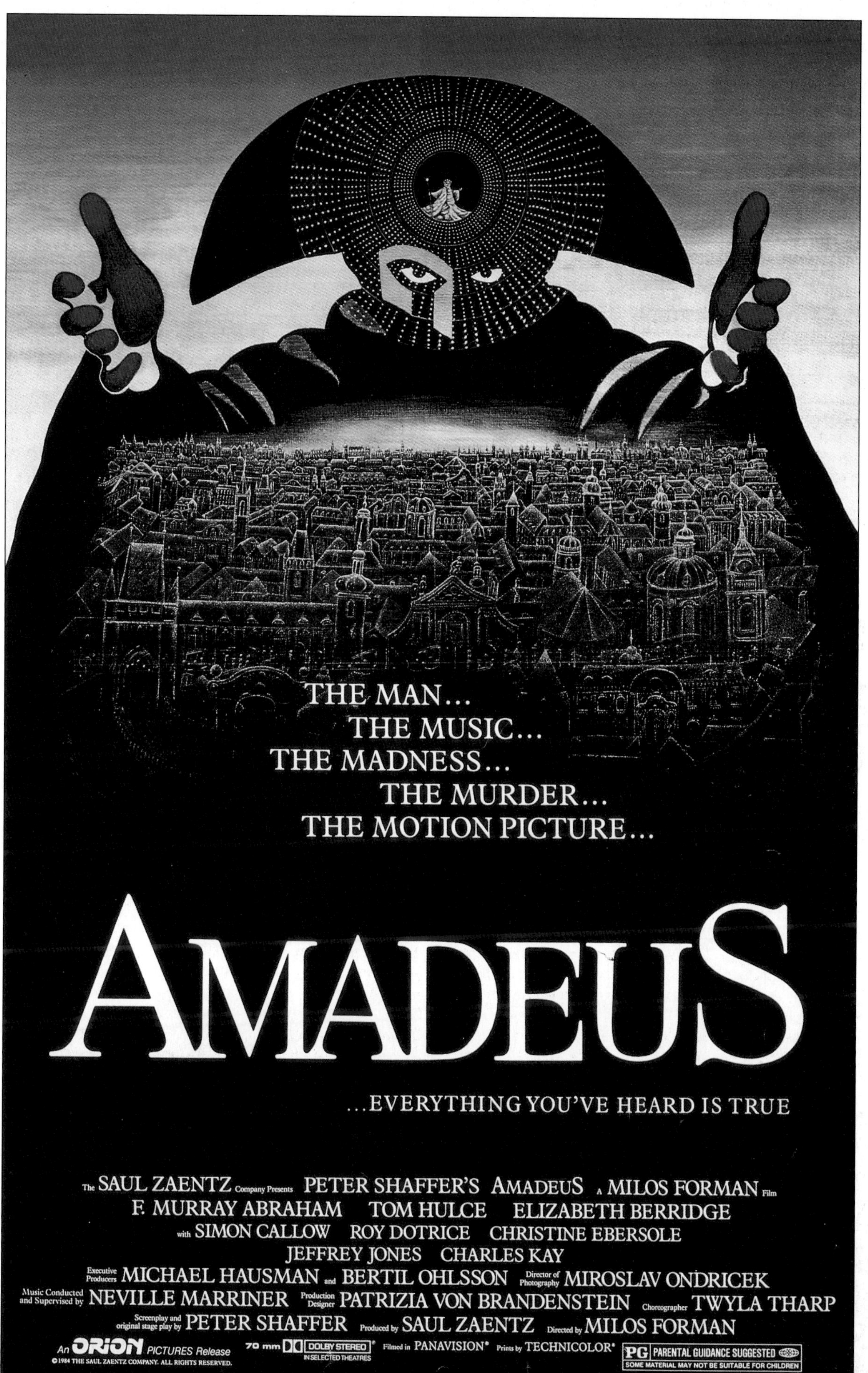
THE MAN...
THE MUSIC...
THE MADNESS...
THE MURDER...
THE MOTION PICTURE...
AMADEUS
...EVERYTHING YOU'VE HEARD IS TRUE
The SAUL ZAENTZ Company Presents PETER SHAFFER'S AMADEUS A MILOS FORMAN Film
F. MURRAY ABRAHAM TOM HULCE ELIZABETH BERRIDGE
with SIMON CALLOW ROY DOTRICE CHRISTINE EBERSOLE
JEFFREY JONES CHARLES KAY
Executive Producers MICHAEL HAUSMAN and BERTIL OHLSSON Director of Photography MIROSLAV ONDRICEK
Music Conducted and Supervised by NEVILLE MARRINER Production Designer PATRIZIA VON BRANDENSTEIN Choreographer TWYLA THARP
Screenplay and original stage play by PETER SHAFFER Produced by SAUL ZAENTZ Directed by MILOS FORMAN
An ORION PICTURES Release
70 mm DOLBY STEREO IN SELECTED THEATRES
Filmed in PANAVISION Prints by TECHNICOLOR
PG PARENTAL GUIDANCE SUGGESTED
SOME MATERIAL MAY NOT BE SUITABLE FOR CHILDREN
©1984 THE SAUL ZAENTZ COMPANY. ALL RIGHTS RESERVED.
PRINTED IN U.S.A.

Simple, small-scale Woody Allen appeals

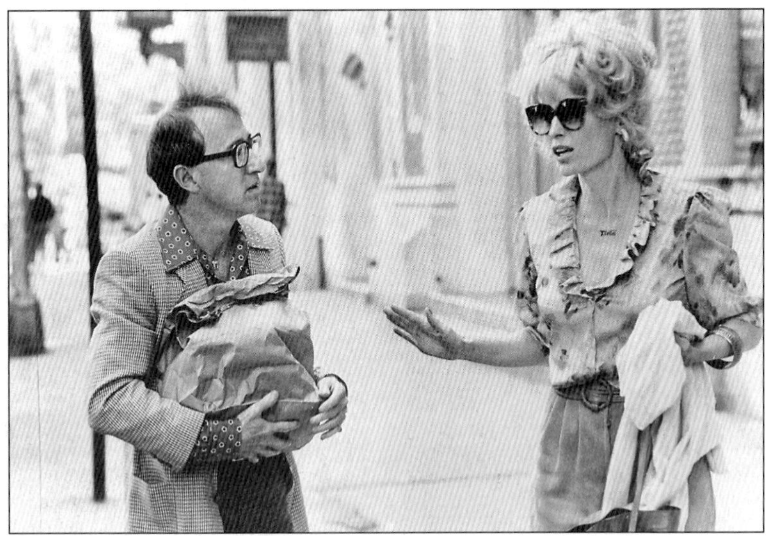
Danny Rose (Allen) and Tina Vitale (Farrow) arguing on a Manhattan street.

New York, 27 January
Although *Broadway Danny Rose* might be considered one of Woody Allen's more minor movies, it is a thoroughly charming and often extremely amusing Runyonesque moral fable. Allen himself plays the small-time showbiz agent of the title, a nebbish whose problem is that as soon as one of his clients actually makes it, they drop him in favor of a big-name agent. Danny, stuck with a washed-up Italian crooner who is attempting a comeback, unwittingly gets involved with the singer's girlfriend (Mia Farrow). The film is not only funny about the old vaudeville days, but is also touchingly nostalgic. Farrow is brilliantly cast against type as a vulgar blonde bimbo.

A brilliant study of dreams and disillusion

Frenchman Maurice Pialat has made a powerful film with ***To Our Loves****. This study of disaffected youth reveals a new star in Sandrine Bonnaire.*

Paris, 27 January
The Louis Delluc Prize this year has been awarded to *To Our Loves* (*A nos amours*), Maurice Pialat's first film since *Loulou* four years ago. The director had wanted to shoot the Arlette Langmann screenplay since 1976, but he could not get it financed, nor could he find the right female lead. But with 16-year-old Sandrine Bonnaire, making her very first screen appearance, it was worth the wait. Bonnaire brings vitality and intensity to the role of the young girl who, unable to feel love, becomes increasingly promiscuous in her search for it. The film is a painful and perceptive study of the gulf between romantic yearnings and the ability to realize them.

Ill-fated Zoetrope is auctioned off

Hollywood, 10 February
Zoetrope Studios have now been taken over by Canadian financier Jack Singer, whose involvement with producer-director Francis Ford Coppola has come to an acrimonious end. However, as Coppola pointed out when the crisis began to develop, "It's important to remember that Zoetrope Company, as opposed to Zoetrope Studios, has been alive for 13 years now, and if we sell the studio it has nothing to do with our company and all our assets." Thus, despite the unexpected box-office failure of his innovative musical *One From the Heart* in 1982, he has already produced and directed two more movies, *The Outsiders* and *Rumblefish*, both adapted from novels by S.E. Hinton, and is finishing a third, *The Cotton Club*. A lavish drama with music, set in 1930s Harlem, it is co-produced with the ex-Paramount boss Robert Evans, producer of the Godfather films with Coppola 10 years ago.

Volker Schlöndorff takes on Swann, but will Proust fans approve?

Paris, 22 February
Among the many directors who have dreamt of bringing Marcel Proust's masterpiece, *Remembrance of Things Past* (*A la recherche du temps perdu*) to the screen, have been Luchino Visconti and Joseph Losey. Harold Pinter, in fact, wrote a scenario for Losey. But they were all defeated by the problems of reducing this monumental work down to the proportions of film. German director Volker Schlöndorff, who has previously adapted works by Robert Musil and Günter Grass to the screen, has not been intimidated by the prospect. He has tackled only the first volume of the novel, *Swann's Way*, and even then the action has been reduced in the screenplay by Peter Brook and Jean-Claude Carrière to only 24 hours. *Swann in Love* concentrates on the passion that Charles Swann (Jeremy Irons) has for the beautiful demimondaine Odette (Ornella Muti), over whom he is racked with insane jealousy. It also touches on the snobbery of the aristocratic circles in which Swann, a Jew, moves. The film is elegant, refined and well-played – especially, and surprisingly, by Alain Delon as the decadent Baron Charlus. Sven Nykvist's camera has exquisitely caught the atmosphere of turn-of-the-century Paris, and Hans Werner Henze has created appropriate music. Nevertheless, Schlöndorff's film cannot begin to approach the richness of Proust's novel, and Proustians will find the elimination of the narrator only one essential dimension missing. Those who have not read Proust are likely to be more responsive.

Ornella Muti and Jeremy Irons (left) in Schlöndorff's ***Swann in Love****.*

Francesco Rosi back to Bizet for latest 'Carmen'

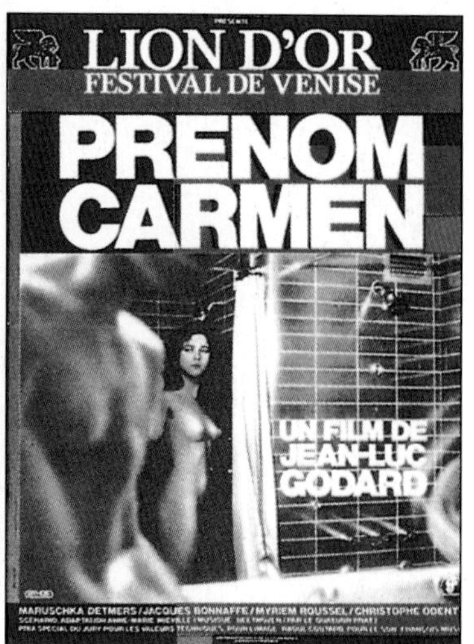
LION D'OR
FESTIVAL DE VENISE
PRENOM
CARMEN
UN FILM DE
JEAN-LUC
GODARD
Godard in mocking, comedic mode.

Carlos Saura's stunning Spanish Flamenco-dance version of the popular work.

Domingo and Migenes-Johnson.

Paris, 14 March
After the success of Joseph Losey's *Don Giovanni* (1979), Daniel Toscan du Plantier, the head of Gaumont, decided to produce Bizet's *Carmen*, the most popular of all operas, and his choice of director was the Italian Francesco Rosi. In fact, this is the fourth, and only straightforward, version of the work in the space of seven months. Last August, Carlos Saura directed a flamenco-inspired ballet film which featured the dancer Antonio Gades. Three months later, three films were made (with different casts) of Peter Brook's pared down *Carmen*, which he staged at his theater, the Bouffes du Nord. Then in January Jean-Luc Godard's singular *First Name Carmen* was released, and we can soon expect *Naked Carmen*, a soft porn adaptation by Albert Lopez. Meanwhile, there is Rosi's attractive, intelligent and entertaining film. The director opted for realism, shooting on location in Andalucia, which brings authenticity to Meilhac and Halévy's libretto. The opening sequence, using slow-motion in the bullring, followed by a dramatic Corpus Christi procession, sets the tone for the events to come, rooting them firmly in the dark mystique of Spanish ritual. Julia Migenes-Johnson delivers a smolderingly sexy Carmen, Placido Domingo is convincing as her victim, and Ruggero Raimondi is an imposing Escamillo. The orchestra is conducted by Loren Maazel.

Tarzan taken from jungle to stately home

New York, 30 March
The greatest screen Tarzan, Johnny Weissmuller, died two months ago. Now there's a new $33 million version of the evergreen Edgar Rice Burroughs potboiler, *Greystoke: The Legend of Tarzan, Lord of the Apes*, a title longer than the dialogue that carried Weissmuller through most of his jungle epics. The new Tarzan, French-American actor Christopher Lambert, is more talkative, reunited with civilization as the aristocratic English heir to Ralph Richardson. Lambert's leading lady, the former model Andie MacDowell, remains speechless; her Southern drawl is dubbed by Glenn Close.

Douglas, Turner in fun adventure caper

Hollywood, 30 March
With its combination of rousing "Raiders of the Lost Ark"-style action thrills and delicious romantic hokum, *Romancing the Stone* is a surefire bet to charm audiences. Kathleen Turner is wonderfully likeable as a wistful writer of romance novels, propelled into her own madcap high adventure in the jungles of Colombia with sexy, caddish mercenary Michael Douglas. Danny De Vito, their disaster-prone pursuer in the quest for a priceless diamond, adds to the exuberant fun, pacily directed by Robert Zemeckis. A Turner-Douglas partnership may become a trademark for the mid-80s.

Christopher Lambert as the free-spirited Tarzan with his jungle friends.

Michael Douglas and Kathleen Turner, an attractive pair of adventurers.

▷

Four top awards for 'Terms of Endearment'

Robert Duvall in ***Tender Mercies****.*

Los Angeles, 9 April
"There has been a lot said about the studios that turned it down, but I think it's more significant that a Hollywood studio [Paramount] did make it," said James L. Brooks, the director of *Terms of Endearment*, the winner of five Oscars, including Best Picture. Brooks took Best Director and Best Screenplay Adaptation for this astutely written, eccentric family comedy-drama. But the film belongs to the actors, headed by Shirley MacLaine's striking Oscar-winning performance as a middle-aged widow, all frills, flounces and hairpieces, who is forced to come to terms with the revelation that her daughter has terminal cancer. Jack Nicholson (Best Supporting Actor) gives a bravura performance as her crude, licentious and finally caring neighbor and lover. The Best Actor winner Robert Duvall was superb as an over-the-hill country-and-western singer in *Tender Mercies*.

Gripping thriller from Iranian in exile

Houshang Touzie, the reluctant assassin in Parviz Sayyad's ***The Mission****.*

New York, 2 May
Iran's Parviz Sayyad, forced into exile by the revolution, has made a film in New York co-financed by German and American money. *The Mission* concerns a young man sent to assassinate an opponent of the Ayatollah (played by Sayyad). It is a marvelous piece of work, at once tense, ironic and moving, that exposes the contradictions on both sides of the Iranian conflict.

Nasty little 'Gremlins' hugely entertaining

New York, 8 June
Joe Dante's *Gremlins* is a gleeful inversion of *E.T.* and a typically subversive dig at the film's sponsor, Steven Spielberg. Inventor Hoyt Axton's Christmas present to his son Zach Galligan is a Mogwai, a cuddly little creature he has picked up in a Chinese curio shop. However, when Gizmo, as the Mogwai is called, gets wet, he produces a number of decidedly less friendly creatures who go on the rampage in a gloriously anarchic display of unrestrained, childlike malice. In the process they trash a Capraesque small town as Dante affectionately thumbs his nose at *It's a Wonderful Life*. Also caught by Dante's scattergun are Walt Disney, the YMCA, Phil Spector's *Christmas Album* and Santa Claus. A graduate of the Roger Corman Z-movie academy, the inventive Dante gives *Gremlins* his customary trademark, a cameo by B-movie icon Dick Miller.

Zach Galligan in the clutches of a gremlin in Joe Dante's fanciful movie.

Special effects pitch for 'Ghostbusters'

New York, 8 June
The spirit of the old Bob Hope horror-comedy vehicles, *The Cat and the Canary* and *The Ghost Breakers*, is alive and well in Ivan Reitman's *Ghostbusters*. Dan Aykroyd, Harold Ramis and Bill Murray play redundant parapsychologists who form a team dedicated to dealing with spooks. Their highly specialized skills are soon required to eliminate the threat posed by a New York skyscraper, built by the worshippers of an ancient god, which is acting as a gateway to the spirit world. Crammed with sardonic one-liners and exploding with up-to-the-minute special effects, which absorbed a large part of the picture's $32 million budget, *Ghostbusters* bids fair to become this summer's box-office sensation. But it's a shame that Sigourney Weaver, looking slightly uneasy in comedy, is relegated to the role of love interest for wacky Bill Murray.

Left to right: Ghostbusters Bill Murray, Dan Aykroyd and Harold Ramis.

Wim Wenders' journey to Paris, Texas overwhelms Cannes jury

Cannes, 25 May
It is extremely rare for a Golden Palm winner at the Cannes Film Festival to be greeted with such unanimous approval as was Wim Wenders' *Paris, Texas*. This project represents the culmination of themes that have run through much of the German director's work over the years. He has always been more aware than most of his fellow German directors of the cultural influence of America on Germany. Wenders has already made a number of road movies set in Germany, so it was only natural that he should finally make one in America. In many ways, *Paris, Texas* is archetypal Wenders. A man (Harry Dean Stanton), lost in an empty landscape and speechless during the first 20 minutes, is shell-shocked by the separation from his wife (Nastassja Kinski) and wants to become a real father to his seven-year-old son. The extraordinary, calm intensity of Stanton's performance, the brilliant color photography from Robert Müller (Wenders' regular cameraman) and Ry Cooder's haunting music, give the film the mythic dimension of a Western. The jury gave their Special Prize to *Diary for My Children*, directed by the Hungarian Marta Meszaros, in which she draws on her own painful memories of the 1950s Stalinist period. Bertrand Tavernier collected the best director award for *Sunday in the Country*, a stylish, charming and nostalgic period piece (set in 1912) of a pastoral family gathering.

Nastassja Kinski, an extraordinary performance in Wenders' ***Paris, Texas****.*

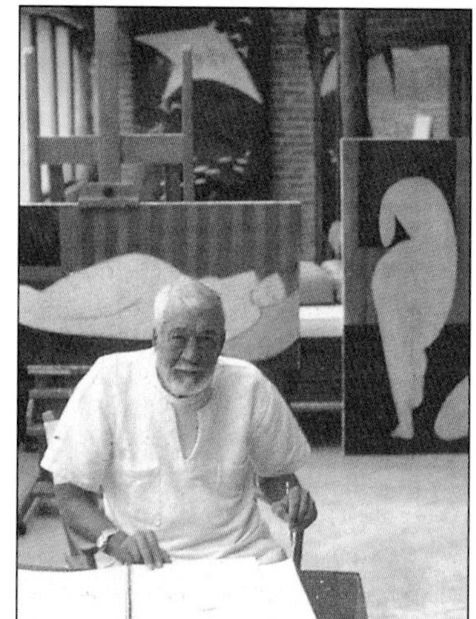

John Huston during filming of ***Under the Volcano****, shown at Cannes.*

Agreement forged at Cap d'Antibes

Antibes, 20 May
At the Eden-Roc Hotel, far from the hustle and bustle of the Cannes Film Festival, a significant meeting has been taking place between Jack Lang, the French Minister of Culture, and Jack Valenti, president of the MPAA (Motion Picture Association of America), the organization that represents the interests of the American film industry. They have reached agreement on a number of important issues, including the protection of French production from American competition, the need to combat video piracy, and the promotion of cinema showings of films ahead of any subsequent TV or video release.

Leone plunges into America's melting pot

New York, 1 June
It is 1920 and a band of adolescent Jewish thieves roam New York City's Lower East Side. The years pass and, thanks to Prohibition, the small petty thieves become grown-up mobsters. Two of them, Noodles and Max, meet in their childhood haunts in 1968 to reminisce about the past. Sergio Leone's long, fascinating homage to the gangster movie, *Once Upon a Time in America*, has been shorn of 88 of its original 277 minutes running time, to the disgust of the director, who has disowned the picture. For 13 years Leone has been working on this project, the evolution of gangster culture among the ethnic minorities which made up the American melting pot. In spite of the mutilation inflicted on the film, which renders chunks of the storyline virtually incomprehensible, *Once Upon a Time in America* remains a remarkably imaginative work, with outstanding central performances from the intense, explosive James Woods and Robert De Niro, in whom Leone has rekindled the passion which blazed in *Raging Bull*. *Once Upon a Time in America* is a fitting sequel to Leone's 1969 *Once Upon a Time in the West*.

Sunday in the Country*, Bertrand Tavernier's distinguished contribution.*

Young roughnecks, swindlers and good guys in ***Once Upon a Time in America****.*

Dutchman's black comedy impresses

New York, 27 June
Films from the Netherlands have rarely made an impact on the art cinema circuit in the United States, but Paul Verhoeven's splendidly overwrought *The Fourth Man* seems to have broken through the barrier. Obviously, the movie's mixture of homo-erotic imagery, black humor, Christian guilt and High Gothic camp appeals to sophisticated Manhattan audiences. *The Fourth Man* is based on a Dutch novel by the gay Catholic author Gerard Reve.

Jeroen Krabbe: ***The Fourth Man.***

Outrageous Mozart from Tom Hulce

New York, 19 September
Milos Forman returned to his hometown of Prague to shoot most of his new film *Amadeus*. It is a sumptuous adaptation from the Peter Shaffer play about the rivalry between Wolfgang Amadeus Mozart, the musical genius but vulgar, childish buffoon, and Antonio Salieri, the pompous and dignified but far less talented court composer. Salieri is eaten up by his jealousy of the prodigy's God-given abilities – compounded by his distaste for the man – and when he can stand it no longer he dresses up like an avenging angel in black mask and cape and gives Mozart a commission that he knows will kill him. Tom Hulce, in the title role, gives a manic bravura performance, lending the character a high-pitched giggle. A magnificent moment comes when the dying Mozart speaks of his gratitude and admiration for the man who is killing him, and of his fear that Salieri disliked him. As Salieri, F. Murray Abraham is impressive, managing to reveal an intelligence behind the malevolence, and making the crazed figure into a tragic and sympathetic one. He is especially moving when he first gazes at Mozart's sketches for the Requiem. "Here was the very voice of God," he proclaims with a mixture of admiration and envy.

Tom Hulce as the young Mozart with his wife Constanza (Elizabeth Berridge).

Steve and Lily: which is which?

Hollywood, 21 September
In Steve Martin's fourth collaboration with Carl Reiner, *All of Me*, Martin plays an idealistic lawyer, half of whose body is possessed by the spirit of Lily Tomlin's dead and unpleasantly crotchety millionairess. It's an uneven effort, but Martin provides a feast of physical comedy as he simultaneously walks and talks as half-man, half-woman.

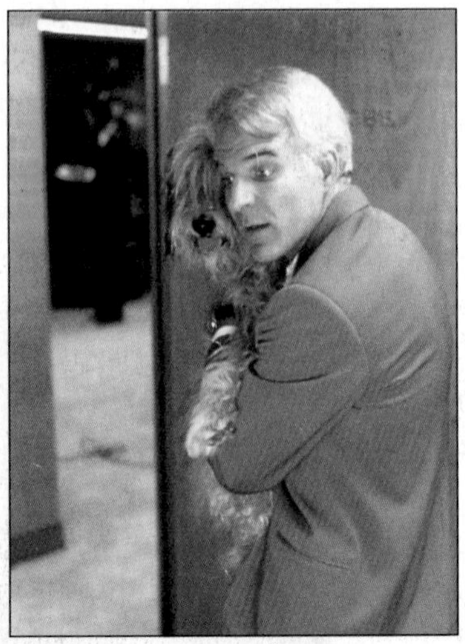

Steve Martin in a tight spot.

François Truffaut, leading light of the French New Wave, is dead

Paris, 24 October
François Truffaut, who died three days ago from a brain tumor, was buried today at the Montmartre cemetery after being cremated. The director knew the nature of his illness, but he refused to recognize its gravity. In August of last year, while he was working on the scenario of *la Petite voleuse*, he suffered a cerebral hemorrhage and had to undergo a serious operation. Since then, he had been unable to complete work on what would have been his 23rd feature film. Gérard Depardieu, while shooting *Fort Saganne*, visited Truffaut almost every day to discuss future joint projects. Truffaut was also planning to direct a new adaptation of *The Count of Monte Cristo* for American television. Death, alas, prevented these plans from coming to fruition. Truffaut's last appearance in public was on *Apostrophes*, the popular television book program, on which he discussed the definitive edition of his famous interviews with his idol Alfred Hitchcock. Truffaut once said that he wanted to film tender stories like Hitchcock and thrillers like Jean Renoir. "Are films more important than life?" asks Jean-Pierre Léaud in *Day for Night*. For Truffaut, one of the first New Wave directors, the answer was in the affirmative. The enthusiasm he felt for filmmaking communicated itself in that movie, and in a career in which he demonstrated a wide range of styles and treated a variety of subjects with immediacy, freshness, lucidity, and freedom of expression.

Isabelle Adjani with Truffaut during the filming of ***The Story of Adèle H.***

'Terminator' nasty, compelling, original

On a mission of destruction: Arnold Schwarzenegger as ***The Terminator****.*

Los Angeles, 26 October
Arnold Schwarzenegger has found a role perfectly tailored to his superb physique and limited acting talent. In *The Terminator* he plays an unstoppable android assassin who is dispatched from the future to rub out seemingly insignificant waitress Linda Hamilton and change the future. Director James Cameron, another talented graduate of Roger Corman's New World Pictures, has fashioned a relentless, hi-tech science fiction thriller, pitting man against machine in a pounding actioner which never loosens its grip.

Cambodian war film stars real-life victim

Dith Pran (Haing S. Ngor) undergoes torture during the Pol Pot regime.

New York, 2 September
Produced by David Puttnam and directed by Roland Joffe, *The Killing Fields* is a British film with an epic sweep. It tells the true story of American journalist Sidney Schanberg (Sam Waterston) who was separated from and eventually reunited with his Cambodian friend, photographer Dith Pran, during the war in Cambodia. Cast in the role of Dith Pran is Cambodian doctor Haing S. Ngor, who himself had to flee the murderous Khmer Rouge when they took over his country with the horrifying results depicted.

Wes Craven unleashes nightmare Freddy

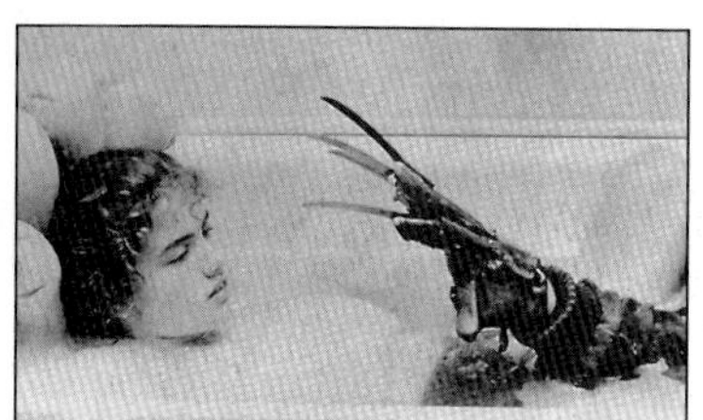

Heather Langenkamp terrorized.

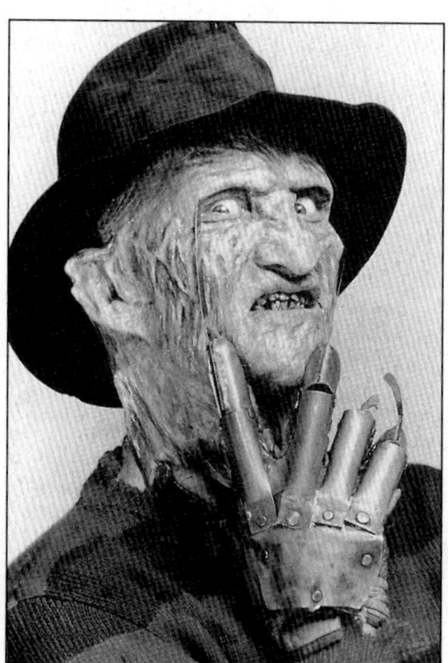

Robert Englund as Freddy Kreuger.

Hollywood, 9 November
Horror specialist Wes Craven, director of *The Last House on the Left* and *The Hills Have Eyes*, has always been fascinated by dreams, and the subconscious plays a driving role in his latest picture, *A Nightmare on Elm Street*. Craven got the idea from a news item about Laotian refugees so afflicted with horrifying nightmares that they became terrified of falling asleep. He has transplanted the theme to the realm of "teen terror" and in the process created an outrageous new bogeyman, the hamburger-faced, razor-taloned Freddy Krueger, a child murderer who was burned to death after escaping conviction and has now returned to his old stamping ground on Elm Street to haunt the dreams of its teenage inhabitants. They share common nightmares as Freddy, played by Robert Englund, stalks them in their dreams, using his claws to carve his way into their homes and their minds. Like some ghastly combination of Peter Pan and the Pied Piper, Freddy makes sure they never grow up.

Murphy makes 'Beverly Hills Cop' a riot

Los Angeles, 5 December
Paramount have closed the year with a monster hit, *Beverly Hills Cop*, starring Eddie Murphy as Axel Foley, an unorthodox Detroit cop who goes to Los Angeles to track down the killers of an old friend. In a part originally offered to Sylvester Stallone, Murphy seizes an otherwise unremarkable action caper by the scruff of the neck, trading streetwise profanity with everyone who crosses his path, including villainous art dealer Steven Berkoff. Paramount are understandably keen to hang on to Murphy and are now negotiating to keep him in golden chains with a five-picture deal.

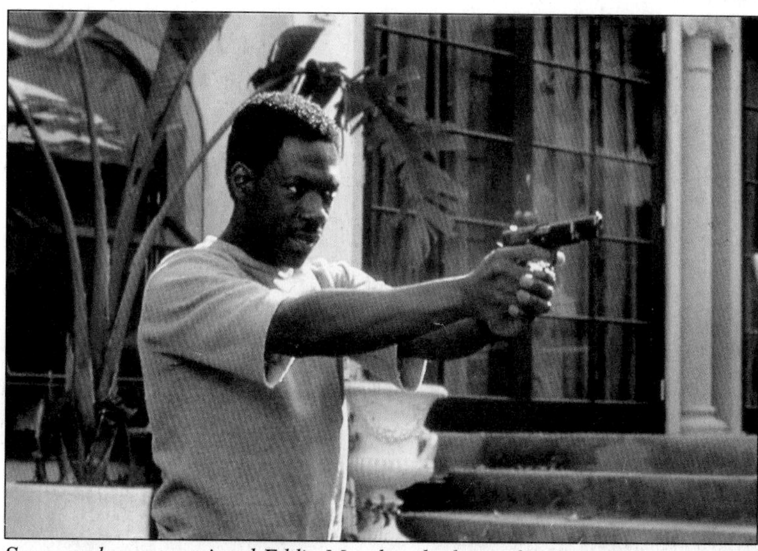

Sassy and unconventional Eddie Murphy, the hero of ***Beverly Hills Cop****.* ▷

-AND NOW GOOD-BYE
Strangers Kiss
MICHAEL WHITE presents PETER COYOTE VICTORIA TENNANT BLAINE NOVAK in STRANGERS KISS
Starring DAN SHOR and RICHARD ROMANUS Also Starring LINDA KERRIDGE CARLOS PALOMINO
Director of Photography MIKHAIL SUSLOV Editor WILLIAM CARRUTH Music Score by GATO BARBIERI
Visual Consultant MICHAEL RIVA Associate Producer SEAN FERRER Co-Producer HERCULES BELLVILLE
Screenplay by BLAINE NOVAK and MATTHEW CHAPMAN Story by BLAINE NOVAK
Executive Producer MICHAEL WHITE Producer DOUGLAS DILGE Director MATTHEW CHAPMAN
R RESTRICTED
Copyright © 1983 Orion Classics Corp. An ORION CLASSICS Release

Off-beat, original mix of thriller, romance, and comment on movie-making.

WELCOME to Florida

*Left to right: Richard Edson, Eszter Balint and John Lurie in **Stranger Than Paradise**, directed by Jim Jarmusch.*

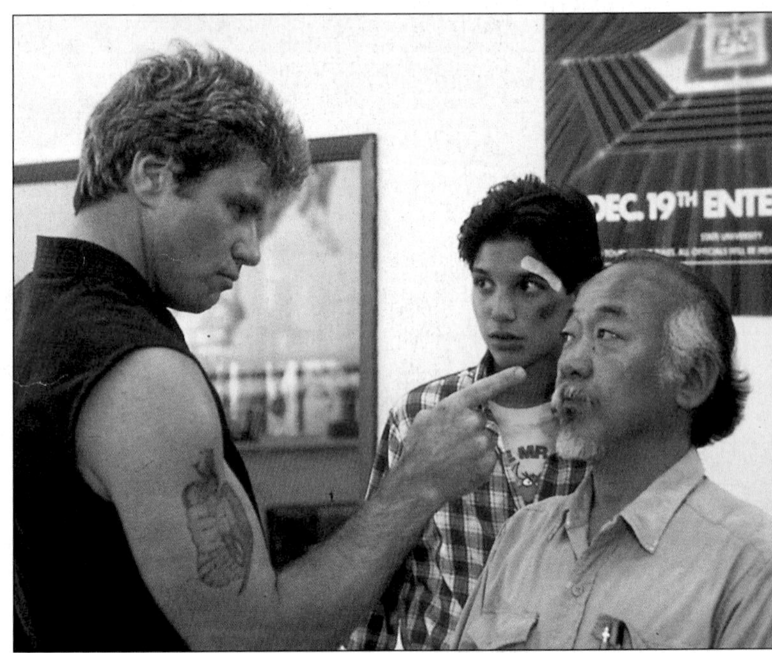
DEC. 19TH ENTE

*Martin Kove (l), trainer Pat Morita (r) and **The Karate Kid**, Ralph Macchio.*

***Greystoke**: Christopher Lambert's Tarzan in England, with Ralph Richardson.*

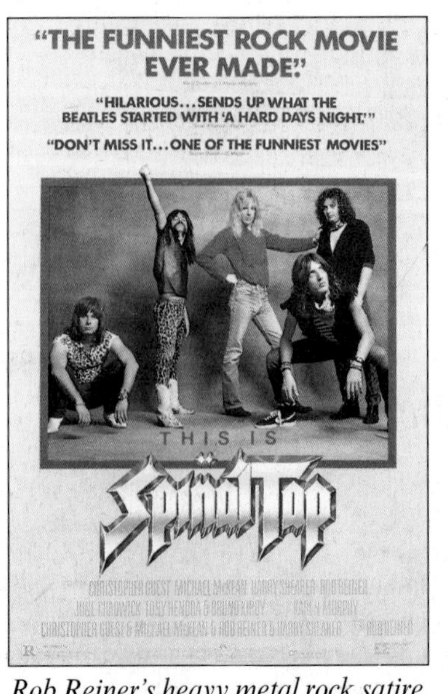
"THE FUNNIEST ROCK MOVIE EVER MADE!"
"HILARIOUS...SENDS UP WHAT THE BEATLES STARTED WITH 'A HARD DAYS NIGHT.'"
"DON'T MISS IT...ONE OF THE FUNNIEST MOVIES"
THIS IS
Spinal Tap

Rob Reiner's heavy metal rock satire.

Two days ago, this girl showed up naked at the Statue of Liberty.
For Alan Bauer, it was love at first sight.
Now, everyone is chasing her...
trying to prove she's a mermaid.
From the first laugh you'll be hooked.
Splash

Tom Hanks, Darryl Hannah starred.

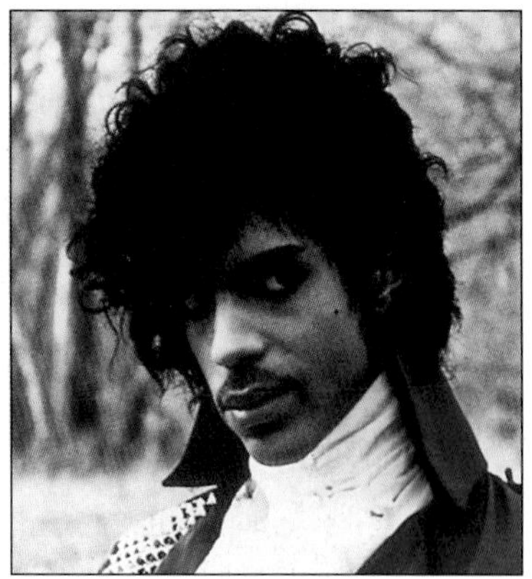

***Purple Rain**: Prince makes a film.*

*Michael Palin in **A Private Function**.*

*Emilio Estevez (left) and Harry Dean Stanton in Alex Cox's **Repo Man**.*

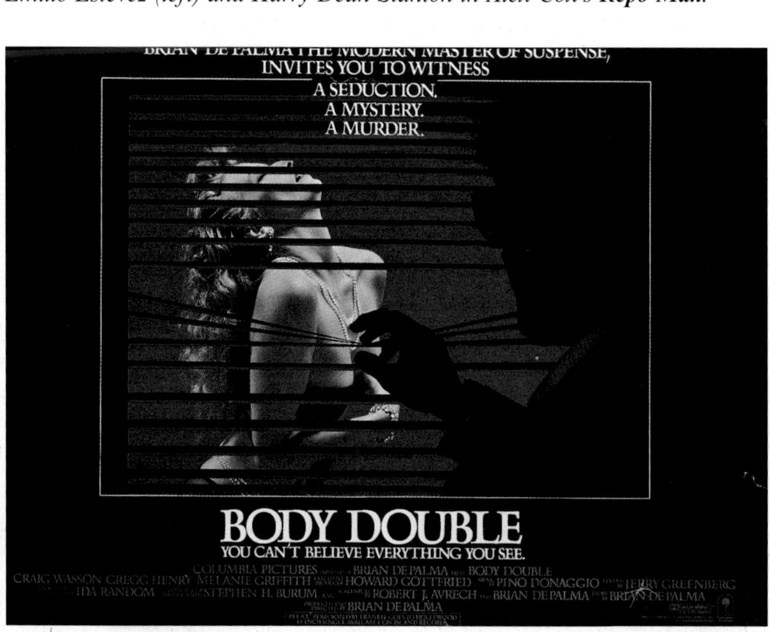

INVITES YOU TO WITNESS
A SEDUCTION.
A MYSTERY.
A MURDER.
BODY DOUBLE
YOU CAN'T BELIEVE EVERYTHING YOU SEE.
COLUMBIA PICTURES BRIAN DE PALMA BODY DOUBLE
CRAIG WASSON GREGG HENRY MELANIE GRIFFITH HOWARD GOTTFRIED PINO DONAGGIO JERRY GREENBERG
IDA RANDOM STEPHEN H. BURUM ROBERT J. AVRECH BRIAN DE PALMA BRIAN DE PALMA
BRIAN DE PALMA

Melanie Griffith, Hitchcockian elements, semi-porn and extreme violence.

ROBERT REDFORD
From an age of innocence
comes a hero for today.
The NATURAL
TRI-STAR PICTURES PRESENTS ROBERT REDFORD IN "THE NATURAL" ROBERT DUVALL · GLENN CLOSE · KIM BASINGER · WILFORD BRIMLEY · BARBARA HERSHEY · ROBERT PROSKY AND
RICHARD FARNSWORTH AS "RED" MUSIC BY RANDY NEWMAN PRODUCTION DESIGNER MEL BOURNE DIRECTOR OF PHOTOGRAPHY CALEB DESCHANEL EXECUTIVE PRODUCERS ROGER TOWNE AND PHILIP M. BREEN
A TRI-STAR PICTURES RELEASE
BASED ON THE NOVEL BY BERNARD MALAMUD SCREENPLAY BY ROGER TOWNE AND PHIL DUSENBERRY PRODUCED BY MARK JOHNSON DIRECTED BY BARRY LEVINSON

Redford as a big-league baseball star in an attractive Barry Levinson film.

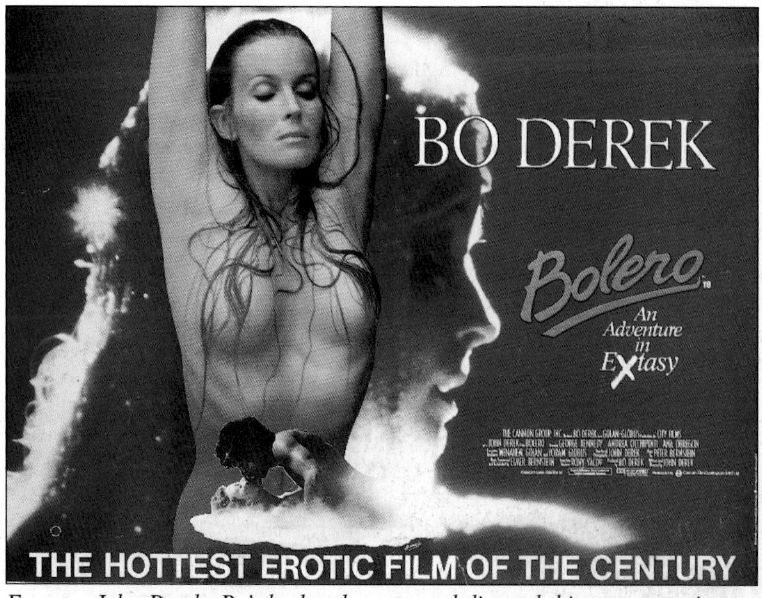

BO DEREK
Bolero
An Adventure in Extasy
THE HOTTEST EROTIC FILM OF THE CENTURY

Ex-actor John Derek, Bo's husband, wrote and directed this unsavory piece.

1985

1984 Academy Awards, Dorothy Chandler Pavilion, 25 Mar.

Best Film:	*Amadeus* (dir: Milos Forman)
Best Director:	Milos Forman
Best Actor:	F. Murray Abraham *(Amadeus)*
Best Actress:	Sally Field *(Places in the Heart)*
Best Supp. Actor:	Haing S. Ngor *(The Killing Fields)*
Best Supp. Actress:	Peggy Ashcroft *(A Passage to India)*

Hollywood, 29 January
MGM-United Artists has just announced that *Yankee Doodle Dandy* (1942) is to be colored using a new process developed by Color System Technology. The studio is planning, initially, to have 20 black-and-white films colored.

Paris, 6 February
Emmanuelle, made by Just Jaeckin with Sylvia Kristel, has finished its long run. It had been showing at the Triomphe cinema on the Champs-Elysées since its release on 26 June 1974, beating the previous record held by *West Side Story*.

Hollywood, 7 March
Gene Kelly has been honored with the American Film Institute's Life Achievement Award.

London, 18 March
Launch of British Film Year with the presentation to the Queen of David Lean's screen adaptation of E.M. Forster's *A Passage to India*.

Hollywood, 25 March
The selection of *The Times of Harvey Milk* as Best Feature Documentary at this year's Academy Awards marks a significant shift in attitude from Academy voters. The portrait of San Francisco's murdered gay city supervisor, Harvey Milk, won against strong competion from Maximilian Schell's *Marlene* and the El Salvador chronicle, *In the Name of the People*.

Hollywood, 31 March
My Mother's Keeper, an autobiographical book by Bette Davis' daughter Barbara, has caused a scandal with its unsavory revelations about the great star.

Buenos Aires, 4 April
Luis Puenzo has released his much awaited film *The Official Story (La Historia Official)*, about middle-class life under the harsh dictatorship of the junta.

Paris, 15 May
Filmmaker Youssef Chahine is in Paris to present *Adieu Bonaparte*, the Franco-Egyptian co-production which he directed. The film, an official entry at Cannes, is about the life of an Egyptian family in Alexandria during Napoleon's occupation, and stars Michel Piccoli, Mohsen Mohieine, and Patrice Chéreau as the French Emperor.

France, 9 June
At this year's International Festival of Animated Pictures (JICA – Journée Internationales du Cinéma d'Animation) in Annecy, the jury, to everyone's amusement, awarded equal first prize to *Hell* (Soviet Union) and *Paradise* (Canada).

Paris, 8 July
Jean-Jacques Annaud announced that he plans to make a film version of Umberto Eco's prize-winning bestseller *The Name of the Rose*.

New York, 23 July
Woody Allen has signed a new contract with Orion Pictures. At his request it includes a clause forbidding the marketing of his films in South Africa because of that country's color *apartheid*.

France, 25 July
Actor Rock Hudson has been admitted to the American Hospital at Neuilly where he continues his battle against AIDS.

New York, 16 August
Singer Madonna and actor Sean Penn were married in a private ceremony here today.

New York, 27 August
The Warner Bros. production, *Pee Wee's Big Adventure*, was the top box-office draw in the New York area this past weekend. The episodic comedy, by first-time director Tim Burton, features the rather surreal Pee Wee Herman in a manic search for his stolen bicycle.

Venice, 7 September
At this year's Festival, French director Agnes Varda has carried off the Golden Lion for *Sans toit ni loi* (*Vagabonde*), while the Silver Lion went to another woman director, Marion Hänsel, for *Dust*. The best actor award was won by Gérard Depardieu for his performance in Maurice Pialat's film *Police*. The jury's special prize was awarded to *Tangos, l'exile de Gardel*, directed by Fernando Solanas.

Los Angeles, 19 September
Elizabeth Taylor is organizing a gala evening to collect funds for the fight against AIDS.

New York, 7 October
Several thousand people took part in a demonstration in front of the Lincoln Center today. They were protesting, in response to an appeal by the Catholic League for Civil and Religious Rights, against the "blasphemous nature" of Jean-Luc Goddard's film *Hail Mary* (*Je vous salue Marie*). The film is currently being shown as part of the 23rd New York Film Festival.

Hollywood, 15 October
Rupert Murdoch's relentless march towards media control in the U.S. is causing concern on Wall Street. His latest acquisition, 20th Century-Fox from Marvin Davis' holding company, cost him over $500 million. Last month Murdoch gave up his Australian citizenship and became an American in order to buy up five of Metromedia's television stations. The magnate has now announced the merger of Fox with the television stations to form Fox Inc.

New York, 16 October
Yul Brynner, who lost his fight against lung cancer last week, has left a last testament to the world – a short film "clip" begging all smokers to give up cigarettes.

Los Angeles, 13 December
Paramount's *Clue*, the first film to be based on a popular board game, is releasing today with four different endings on 1,006 screens. Along with Tim Curry, Madeline Khan and Christopher Lloyd, the film features Eileen Brennan. *Clue* heralds Brennan's return to the screen following a devastating run-in with a speeding Thunderbird in late 1982.

Los Angeles, 16 December
The "unreleasable" *Brazil* has won top honors at the Los Angeles Film Critics Association's annual vote. The controversial movie, which has been the center of a heated dispute between director Terry Gilliam and MCA president Sidney Sheinberg, almost scooped the pool by winning best picture, best director and best screenplay (Gilliam, Tom Stoppard, Charles McKeown).

New York, 31 December
According to a marketing company, in 1985 cinema attendance by the adolescent population dropped by 20 percent. On the other hand, this same group rents three times more films on video than previously.

DEATHS

England, 2 March
Michael Redgrave

California, 9 May
Edmond O'Brien

Connecticut, 16 May
Margaret Hamilton

New York, 8 August
Louise Brooks

Massachusetts, 28 August
Ruth Gordon

France, 30 September
Simone Signoret

Beverly Hills, 2 October
Rock Hudson

New York, 10 October
Yul Brynner

Hollywood, 10 October
Orson Welles

California, 1 November
Phil Silvers

California, 19 November
Stepin Fetchit

New York, 4 December
Anne Baxter

***Witness** is the first American movie made by the prize-winning Australian director Peter Weir. Set largely in an Amish community near Philadelphia, it has proved immensely successful.*

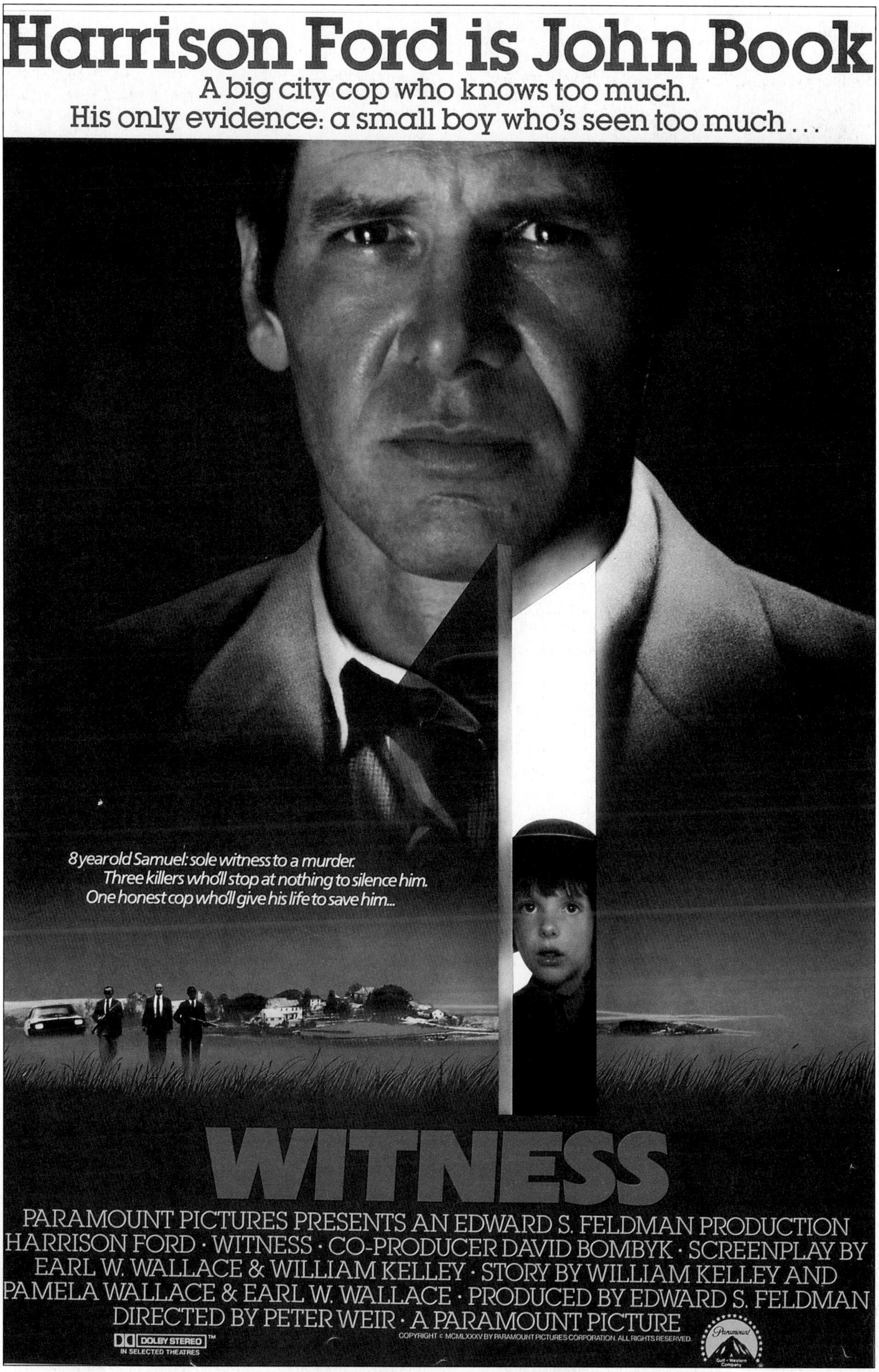

Harrison Ford is John Book

A big city cop who knows too much.
His only evidence: a small boy who's seen too much . . .

8 year old Samuel: sole witness to a murder.
Three killers who'll stop at nothing to silence him.
One honest cop who'll give his life to save him...

WITNESS

PARAMOUNT PICTURES PRESENTS AN EDWARD S. FELDMAN PRODUCTION
HARRISON FORD · WITNESS · CO-PRODUCER DAVID BOMBYK · SCREENPLAY BY
EARL W. WALLACE & WILLIAM KELLEY · STORY BY WILLIAM KELLEY AND
PAMELA WALLACE & EARL W. WALLACE · PRODUCED BY EDWARD S. FELDMAN
DIRECTED BY PETER WEIR · A PARAMOUNT PICTURE

DOLBY STEREO™ IN SELECTED THEATRES

Paramount
Gulf + Western Company

Creepy, clever first film from Coen brothers

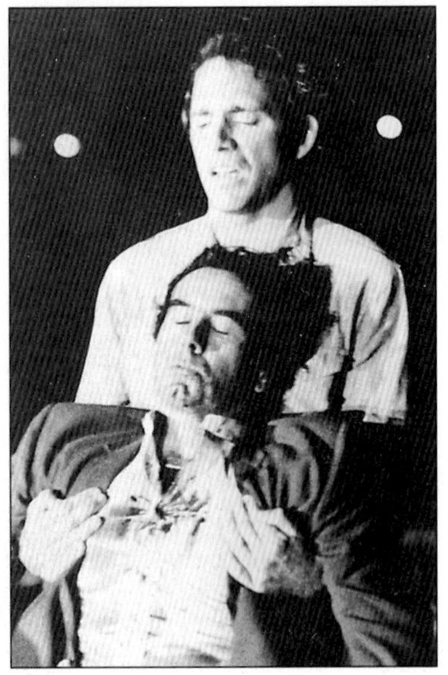
John Getz with Dan Hedaya's corpse.

New York, 18 January
The Coen brothers, a young pair of sibling screenwriters who divide producing (Ethan) and directing (Joel) chores, make their sensational debut with *Blood Simple*. Blatant, clever homage to *film noir* peppers a twisting thriller in which the hapless protagonists remain largely in the dark, while the audience is grippingly informed about who is doing what to whom. A faithless wife and her bartender boyfriend (Frances McDormand, John Getz) are the pawns in a cold, cunningly plotted tale of duplicity and murder, set in motion by her boorish husband and the sleazy 'tec (M. Emmet Walsh) he's hired. Executed on a shoestring budget with ingenuity and style, the film serves notice of two to watch.

Albert Brooks wittily demolishes rat race

Julie Hagerty, Albert Brooks enjoy temporary success in a Las Vegas casino.

Los Angeles, 15 February
Acting in his seventh movie and directing his third, comedian Albert Brooks (real name Albert Einstein) has come up with a winner, which he also co-wrote. The ironically titled *Lost in America* has Brooks as a high-flying member of the rat race who quits his job after a row, and decides that he and his wife (the fabulous Julie Hagerty) will abandon materialistic values and get back to the simple life. He sells up their worldly assets and buys a caravan equipped to the hilt with every last appurtenance of middle-class living. This is the first satirical sideswipe at the character he plays, and sets the tone for the rest of a rollickingly funny, clever and salutary tale.

Australian Weir's stunning U.S. debut

Harrison Ford questions little Lukas Haas, the young witness of the title.

Philadelphia, 8 February
Peter Weir's classy thriller *Witness* has an unusual setting, a farm in an Amish religious community whose inhabitants live lives little changed from those of the Pilgrim Fathers. One of their children has been an inadvertent witness to a murder in Philadelphia, and cop-on-the-lam Harrison Ford arrives to persuade the boy's widowed mother Kelly McGillis to allow him to testify. The killers are on Ford's trail, and he hides out with McGillis, who finds herself romantically drawn to him. Weir, who took on the assignment at short notice, skillfully handles the fish-out-of-water scenario and draws strong performances from Ford and the 27-year-old McGillis, previously seen as Tom Conti's girlfriend in the 1983 *Reuben, Reuben*. This tall, commanding actress is particularly effective and moving as a young woman who knows that her desire for Ford cannot be fulfilled.

Wild Orwellian fantasy from Terry Gilliam

London, 29 June
Terry Gilliam, the brilliant animator on the madcap Monty Python TV series of the 70s, has moved away from Pythonesque humor in his third solo-directed movie, *Brazil*. Gilliam's long battle with Universal to gain the "final cut" on the picture was justified by the result, which is a visually stunning portrayal of an Orwellian future. Jonathan Pryce plays a put-upon worker in the oppressively bureaucratic Ministry of Information, whose apartment is invaded by a guerilla engineer, none other than Robert De Niro.

l to r: Peter Vaughan, Katherine Helmond and Jonathan Pryce in ***Brazil.***

Rose-colored homage to movie magic

Mia Farrow, a Depression-weary waitress who finds happiness at the movies.

New York, 1 March
The title of Woody Allen's new film, *The Purple Rose of Cairo*, refers to the movie-within-the-movie, a sleek and sophisticated black-and-white romance, made to divert audiences during the Depression. The story focuses on Celia (Mia Farrow), a battered wife and overworked waitress, who spends most of her free time at the movies. One day, as she watches *Purple Rose* for the umpteenth time, the hero addresses her directly and comes down from the screen to enter her life. It is not the first time that Allen has played with this Pirandellian concept, or with the thin dividing line between film fantasy and fact, but never with such warmth or technical aplomb.

Hulce disappointed, Ashcroft recognized

The Best Actress: Sally Field.

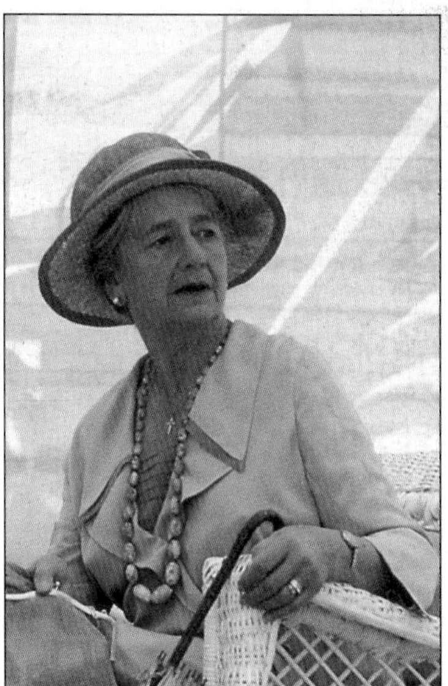
English veteran Peggy Ashcroft.

Los Angeles, 25 March
Amadeus took away eight Oscars at this year's ceremony, including Best Picture, Best Director (Milos Forman) and Best Actor. Surprisingly, the latter was given not to Tom Hulce's dazzling performance in the title role, but to the less flashy F. Murray Abraham as Mozart's rival Salieri. Sally Field collected her second Best Actress Oscar for her role as the indomitable cotton-picking widow and mother in *Places in the Heart*. The Best Supporting Actor went to Cambodian screen debutant Haing S. Ngor in *The Killing Fields*, while one of England's greatest actresses, 77-year-old Dame Peggy Ashcroft, finally won international recognition in *A Passage to India*.

Claude Zidi's rotten cops, Lhermitte and Noiret steal Césars

Paris, 2 March
At a glittering César award ceremony, where Simone Signoret, Kirk Douglas, Jeanne Moreau and Gina Lollobrigida were among the presenters, Claude Zidi's *les Ripoux* was the winner of the best film and director prizes. This amiable and amusing comedy about police corruption shows how veteran roguish cop (Philippe Noiret) initiates his prudish new partner (Thierry Lhermitte) into his wicked ways. The acting awards went to Sabine Azema in Bertrand Tavernier's *Sunday in the Country*, and to Alain Delon in Bertrand Blier's *Our Story*. On this tenth anniversary of the Césars, the public was asked to vote for the "César of Césars". Robert Enrico's *The Old Rifle* (*le Vieux fusil*) (1976) topped the poll. Danielle Darrieux and the late François Truffaut were awarded honorary Césars.

Thierry Lhermitte and Philippe Noiret, the corrupt cop team of Zidi's film.

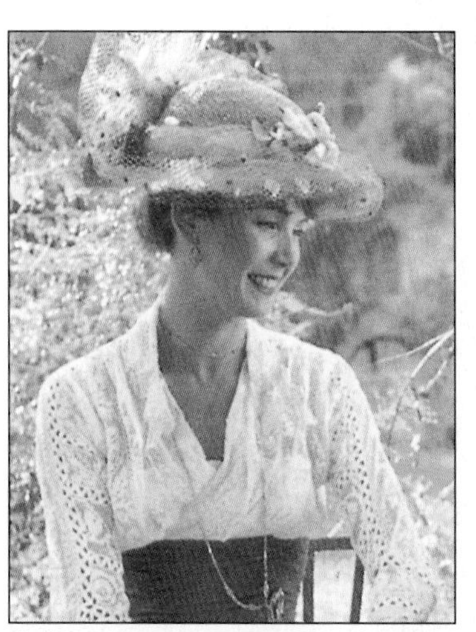
*Sabine Azema stars in Tavernier's **A Sunday in the Country**.*

Alan Ladd Jr. is new MGM chief

New York, 14 March
Ever since wealthy financier Kirk Kerkorian bought MGM in 1969, it has been unclear as to whether he had any real interest in movies or movie-making, or merely regarded the studio as just another of his many investments. In 1981 Kerkorian purchased United Artists and there was a suggestion that the new MGM/UA would become a more active player in Hollywood, but recent results have been distinctly mixed. Thus, the appointment of Alan Ladd Jr. as the studio's new head of production (the latest in a long line of executive changes) will be watched with some interest. During the past decade, Ladd has built up a reputation as one of the most highly respected of production executives, first as production chief at 20th Century-Fox in the mid-Seventies and then as the head of his own independent production outfit, The Ladd Co., during 1979-84. ▷

Redl another tour de force for Brandauer

Brandauer as Colonel Alfred Redl. The mask symbolizes the living of a lie.

Berlin, 29 March

Four years after *Mephisto*, audiences can look forward to the arrival of Klaus Maria Brandauer in another towering role and performance as *Colonel Redl*, which will shortly be on the international circuit. Directed by *Mephisto*'s Istvan Szabo with the same theatrical sweep as the previous film, this is based on Englishman John Osborne's play, *A Patriot for Me*, set in the twilight of the Austro-Hungarian Empire. Redl, of humble origins, high intelligence and massive ambition, rises to become head of military intelligence, but conceals that he is both Jewish and bisexual. His flawed nature betrays others and, ultimately, destroys him.

High-tech and low tone from 'Subway'

Isabelle Adjani and Christopher Lambert in Besson's unconventional movie.

Paris, 10 April

After his startling debut with *The Last Battle* in 1983, 26-year-old Luc Besson has fulfilled his promise as a director with a striking visual sense in his second feature, *Subway*. It is set mainly in the Paris metro, where safecracker Christopher Lambert has fled after stealing important documents from a crooked businessman whose wife, Isabelle Adjani, he has fallen for. The movie has the advantage of high-tech art work from veteran Alexandre Trauner, and a daring use of 'Scope and Dolby sound, creating a fantastic yet familiar nether world inhabited by social misfits. Adjani, in her first movie for two years, is as lovely as ever in a smallish role.

Yugoslavia's Emir Kusturica wins well-deserved Golden Palm

Cannes, 20 May

The winner of the Golden Palm at this year's Festival was an entry from Yugoslavia called *When Father Was Away on Business*, directed by Emir Kusturica. The 30-year-old director had already won the Golden Lion at Venice in 1981 with his auspicious feature film debut, *Do You Remember, Dolly Bell?* His second film is an absorbing portrait of provincial life and politics in 1950s Yugoslavia, much of it seen through the eyes of a six-year-old boy. Kusturica's observation and humor must have reminded jury president Milos Forman of some of *his* early work. Juliette Binoche was the best actress in *Rendez-vous* by André Téchiné, who won best director, while William Hurt took the best actor award for his effeminate gay prisoner in Hector Babenco's *Kiss of the Spider Woman*.

Emir Kusturica's ***When Father Was Away on Business*** *won the Golden Palm.*

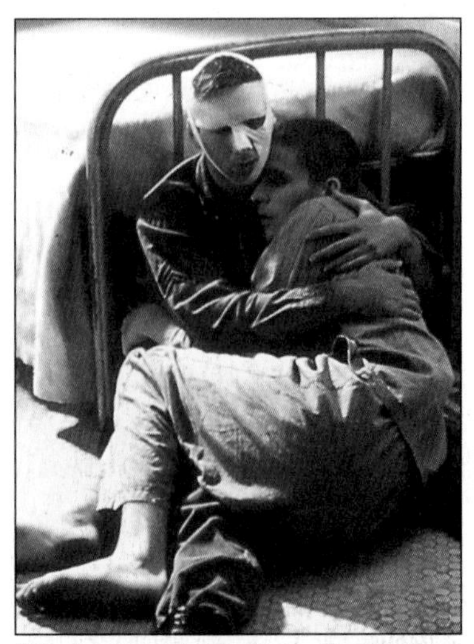

Nicolas Cage (left) and Matthew Modine in Alan Parker's ***Birdy****.*

'Rambo II' released in 2,074 cinemas

New York, 22 May

Reflecting the latest approach in movie marketing strategies in the United States, *Rambo: First Blood Part II*, the latest blockbuster release from the new TriStar studio, has opened in over 2,000 theaters across the country. It thus breaks the record set by *Star Trek III* just one year ago, which was given a blanket release in 1,966 cinemas. As devised by the marketing experts, such a "saturation" opening of a new picture, especially during the peak movie-going months from mid-May through early September, is ideal for taking advantage of nationwide media coverage and, especially, making use of advertising on national network TV. This new $25 million action adventure sequel will obviously also benefit from the fact that audiences are already familiar with the character of avenger-hero John Rambo as played by Sylvester Stallone in *First Blood*, produced by the Carolco company in 1982.

Kurosawa's 'Lear' visual and emotional stunner

Tokyo, 1 June

The most universal of Japanese filmmakers, Akira Kurosawa, has never hidden his admiration for William Shakespeare, the most universal of English playwrights. Apart from *Castle of the Spider's Web* (1957), which was based directly on *Macbeth*, many of his other epics testify to the influence of Shakespeare. *King Lear* has always been a particular favorite, especially now that the 75-year-old director feels that he is the dethroned king of Japanese cinema. *Ran*, which means "chaos" in Japanese, is its venerable maker's first film for five years, and is an adaptation of *King Lear*. Although Kurosawa has turned the daughters into sons, and transposed the action to 16th-century Japan, he has kept many of the main themes of Shakespeare's tragedy, those that have preoccupied the director over the years. Kurosawa has dealt with the theme of old age, and that of the drive for power most effectively in his past period pieces, as well as in strong contemporary tales such as *To Live* (1952) and *The Bad Sleep Well* (1960).

One of the rich, epic scenes from ***Ran****, Kurosawa's personal vision of King Lear.*

Ran begins with the aged Lord Hidetora's abdication in favor of his eldest son Taro, only to find himself driven out of his own kingdom, which is then torn apart by greed and rivalry. There are powerful performances from Tatsuya Nakadai as the Lear figure, and Mieko Harada as an evil masculine conflation of Goneril and Regan. There is also an effective rendering of the Fool by a transvestite going under the sole name of Peter. The battles are visually stunning, far more involving than in *Kagemusha*, Kurosawa's previous picture. The 162-minute Franco-Japanese production cost $11.5 million, $7 million of which was Japanese, and the rest from a French company, Greenwich Films. It is said that Kurosawa is the best known of Japanese directors in the West because he is most influenced by European and American culture. Yet however much he has been attracted to Western art, he is essentially Japanese in that he is drawn into the world of Noh drama, as well as being a man deeply affected by the ravages of World War II on his country. It is this combination of twin cultures that makes *Ran* such a fascinating experience.

Old-timers get the gift of youth in 'Cocoon'

Los Angeles, 21 June

Peter Pan meets E.T. in Ron Howard's *Cocoon* as a group of Florida senior citizens discover a fountain of youth courtesy of some obliging aliens in human form led by Brian Dennehy. Howard has borrowed elements from *E.T.*, *The Man Who Fell to Earth* and *Close Encounters of the Third Kind* in a tale which eventually succumbs to sentimentality but is sustained by the warm skills of veteran actors Wilford Brimley, Jack Gilford, Hume Cronyn, Jessica Tandy, Maureen Stapleton and Don Ameche. The theme of rejuvenation is particularly appropriate for Don Ameche, debonair Fox star of the Thirties and Forties, who has been enjoying a new lease of cinematic life after his comeback in 1983 in *Trading Places*.

Clint's new film evokes ghost of 'Shane'

New York, 28 June

A small mining community working the seams of Carbon Canyon is threatened by a grasping mine owner and his hired killers. Riding to their rescue comes a mysterious stranger, a preacher with what appears to be a pattern of fatal bullet wounds on his back. In *Pale Rider*, his first Western since *The Outlaw Josey Wales*, director-star Clint Eastwood combines elements of his own *High Plains Drifter* and George Stevens' classic *Shane*. Its impact is undercut by Eastwood's low-key performance as the miners' possibly supernatural savior – he is the soul of good sense, exemplifying the same solid values represented by the prospectors. The Gothic underpinning is provided by the lyrical cinematography of Bruce Surtees.

Joe (Hume Cronyn) revitalized!

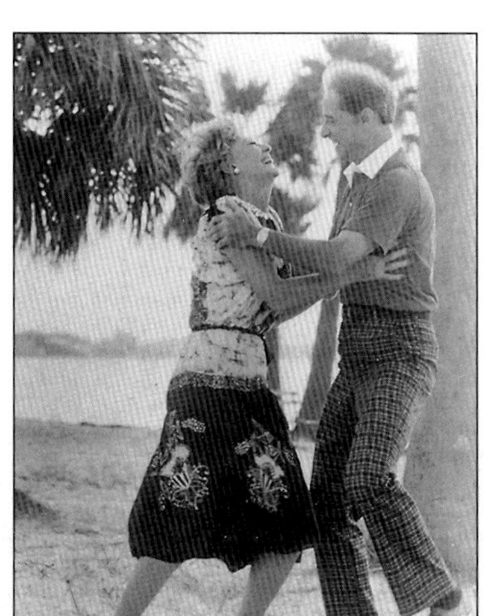
Gwen Verdon and Don Ameche.

Men of the West await their nemesis in Eastwood's richly atmospheric film.

'Brat-packers' move into the real world

Left to right: Rob Lowe, Demi Moore, Emilio Estevez, Mare Winningham, Judd Nelson, Ally Sheedy and Andrew McCarthy in ***St. Elmo's Fire.***

Hollywood, 28 June
St. Elmo's Fire is the ideal showcase for many of the young "Brat Pack", now growing up. The plot follows the lives of a batch of college graduates: Emilio Estevez as a law student in love with Jenny Wright; Rob Lowe married to a girl he made pregnant but does not love; Mare Winningham as a virgin social worker enamored with Lowe; Judd Nelson as a philanderer who is having an affair with Ally Sheedy; Demi Moore as a drug-taking high-flyer, and Andrew McCarthy as an obituary writer who longs for better things. This glossy package, which will certainly appeal to the yuppie generation, is neatly tied up by director Joel Schumacher.

'The Emerald Forest' enchants and disturbs

Charley Boorman undergoes unusual rites of passage with the Indian tribe.

New York, 3 July
Ecological concerns and a protest at man's disdain for nature and his fellow human beings, lie at the heart of John Boorman's new film, *The Emerald Forest*. As is to be expected from Boorman (*Deliverance*, *Excalibur*, etc.), the film ravishes the eye (photography by Philippe Rousselet) but sits less kindly on the ear and suffers from simplistic characterization. However, the message comes across loud and clear in a plot that holds the attention as engineer Powers Boothe searches for his lost son (Charley Boorman) in the Brazilian jungle. The boy is living with an Indian tribe, learning their rituals, and a respect for nature that so-called civilized man has lost.

'Future' looks bright for Michael J. Fox

Los Angeles, 3 July
Teen heart-throb Michael J. Fox – 24 going on 16 – takes a roller-coaster ride into the past in Robert Zemeckis' science fiction romp *Back to the Future*. Hitching a lift in mad inventor Christopher Lloyd's time-traveling De Lorean automobile, he finds himself back in the Fifties, where he must arrange for his mismatched parents to meet, or *he* won't exist. The trouble is that Mom seems more interested in him! Spielberg protégé Zemeckis pushes the picture along at a cracking pace. According to his simple philosophy, "Good directing is good writing and good casting, that's all!"

Christopher Lloyd, eccentric inventor of the time machine, with Michael J. Fox.

A crazy night in Manhattan with Scorsese

New York, 13 December
Martin Scorsese lays on a "yuppie nightmare" in *After Hours*, a black comedy set in the arty SoHo district of Manhattan. Griffin Dunne plays a word processor operator, dissatisfied with the clinical world of new technology, whose artistic and social aspirations lead to a night of spiraling disaster. A chance encounter with spaced-out Rosanna Arquette triggers an inexorable chain of Kafkaesque events which confirm his worst paranoid fears and, in an ironic climax, leave him trapped inside a plaster of Paris sculpture. Scorsese himself appears briefly as a demonic figure in a SoHo niterie.

Paul (Griffin Dunne) encounters crazy sculptress Kiki (Linda Fiorentino).

Orson Welles latest in crop of unhappy losses

Orson Welles in the 1940s.

Rock Hudson at the peak of stardom.

*Simone Signoret: **The Fiends** (1955).*

The magic Louise Brooks in the 20s.

Los Angeles, 10 October
One of the legends of cinema, Orson Welles, has died of a heart attack. His life's work, like that of Charles Foster Kane's Xanadu, remains a sprawling folly, its spoiled grandeur unfinished and undefined. Welles' last years were haunted by abandoned projects, guest appearances on comedy shows and lager commercials ringing with all the hollow promise of his "Declaration of Principles" in *Citizen Kane*. Indeed that masterpiece now seems increasingly less like a portrait of William Randolph Hearst and more like a prediction of the tragic trajectory which Welles' own career would take. His death is the latest in a sad series which has deprived cinema of some of its leading lights. On 8 August, Louise Brooks, incomparable silent star of G.W. Pabst's *Pandora's Box*, died at her home in Rochester in upstate New York. In recent years she wrote brilliantly about cinema but declined to pen her own memoirs. On 1 October Simone Signoret was buried in Paris' Père-Lachaise cemetery after a long battle with cancer, and within 24 hours Rock Hudson was carried away in Beverly Hills by AIDS, the first major star to succumb to the disease. Hudson concealed his homosexuality for years, but his decision to reveal the cause of his illness in the weeks before his death has focused widespread attention on the seriousness of the AIDS epidemic.

A look at gay love across the color bar

London, 16 November
Originally made for Channel Four television, Stephen Frears' *My Beautiful Laundrette* explores life in multiracial Britain in the context of a love affair between two youths from South London, the Asian Gordon Warnecke and the white Daniel Day Lewis, the latter a jaunty Cockney with blond-streaked hair whose connection with the racist National Front organization adds an element of tension to their relationship. Hanif Kureishi's screenplay skillfully weaves together themes of class, race and politics in an intriguing commentary on Britain, well acted by an interesting cast.

Pain and humor of a Swedish childhood

Stockholm, 13 December
One of the most delightful surprises of the year is the second feature by Lasse Hallström, *My Life as a Dog*. Avoiding cuteness and sentimentality, the director tells an enchanting tale of a resourceful and energetic 12-year-old boy who lives with his beloved dog, elder brother and sick mother in 50s Sweden. Proving too much of a handful, he's sent away to stay with relatives in a small country village, almost entirely populated by eccentrics. There he gets involved in the lives of the rural community, suffering growing pains in the process. The young hero is played unaffectedly by Anton Glanzelius.

A peroxided Daniel Day Lewis with Gordon Warnecke who plays his lover.

*Anton Glanzelius and the pet he loves in Hallström's **My Life as a Dog**.*

Nicole Garcia, seductress, in Michel Deville's ***Death in a French Garden****.*

FEDERICO FELLINI
GINGER
&FRED
GIULIETTA MASINA / MARCELLO MASTROIANNI

Old troupers Masina, Mastroianni are poignant and delightful.

Alexandra Pigg and Peter Firth in Chris Bernard's British ***Letter to Brezhnev****.*

Madonna's non-singing role in Susan Seidelman's ***Desperately Seeking Susan****.*

Alexei Kravchenko in Elem Klimov's horrifying ***Come and See*** *(USSR).*

Sequel mania gripped ***la Cage aux folles****: Michel Serrault's third time out.*

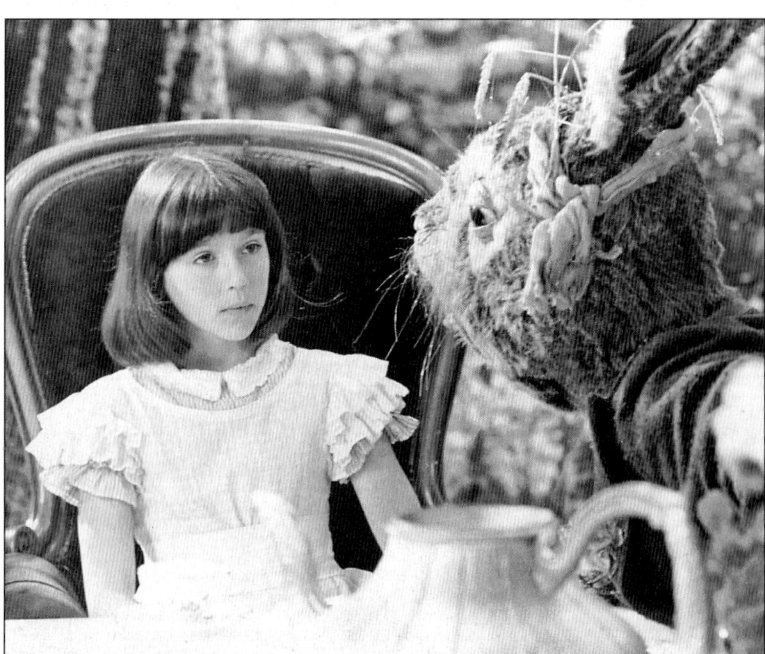

Amelia Shankley as the real-life Alice of Lewis Carroll in ***Dreamchild****.*

***Pee-Wee's Big Adventure**: Pee-Wee Herman (right) and Mark Holton.*

*Whoopi Goldberg in Spielberg's **The Color Purple** from Alice Walker's novel.*

*Lawyer Glenn Close, client Jeff Bridges in Richard Marquand's **Jagged Edge**.*

TREBLINKA

*Claude Lanzmann's epic Holocaust documentary, **Shoah**. Witness Henrik Gawkowski (above) drove trainloads of Jews to their deaths at Treblinka.*

JACK NICHOLSON
KATHLEEN TURNER
Hired killers by day. Devoted lovers by night.
Until they found out their next assignment was each other.
PRIZZI'S HONOR
ABC MOTION PICTURES Presents A JOHN FOREMAN PRODUCTION of A JOHN HUSTON FILM
Starring JACK NICHOLSON · KATHLEEN TURNER · PRIZZI'S HONOR Music ALEX NORTH Director of Photography ANDRZEJ BARTKOWIAK
Screenplay by RICHARD CONDON and JANET ROACH From the novel by RICHARD CONDON
Produced by JOHN FOREMAN Directed by JOHN HUSTON
R RESTRICTED UNDER 17 REQUIRES ACCOMPANYING PARENT OR ADULT GUARDIAN
© 1985 ABC MOTION PICTURES, INC. All Rights Reserved.
© 1985 TWENTIETH CENTURY FOX

John Huston's great cast included daughter Anjelica in black comedy-thriller.

*Jessica Lange as singer Patsy Kline in **Sweet Dreams** from Karel Reisz.*

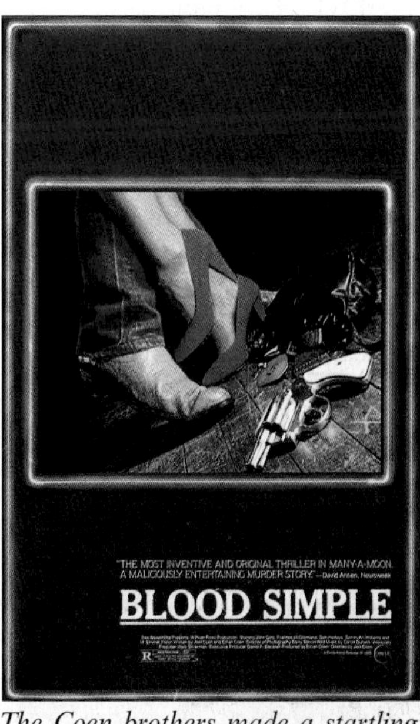
"THE MOST INVENTIVE AND ORIGINAL THRILLER IN MANY-A-MOON.
A MALICIOUSLY ENTERTAINING MURDER STORY." —David Ansen, Newsweek
BLOOD SIMPLE

The Coen brothers made a startling debut with this modern noir.

1986

1985 Academy Awards, Dorothy Chandler Pavilion, 24 Mar.

Best Film:	*Out of Africa* (dir: Sydney Pollack)
Best Director:	Sydney Pollack
Best Actor:	William Hurt *(Kiss of the Spider Woman)*
Best Actress:	Geraldine Page *(The Trip to Bountiful)*
Best Supp. Actor:	Don Ameche *(Cocoon)*
Best Supp. Actress:	Anjelica Huston *(Prizzi's Honor)*

Washington D.C., 6 February
To mark the centenary of the Statue of Liberty, which was made by the French sculptor Bartholdi, French actress Catherine Deneuve today handed President Reagan a crystal replica of the statue as a gesture of France's friendship.

Los Angeles, 25 March
Writer Oliver Stone, recognized for his screenplays for Cimino and De Palma, has made his directing debut with *Salvador*. The film is a vigorous denunciation of the State Department's role in Central America.

California, 4 April
Actor Clint Eastwood has been elected mayor of Carmel with 72 percent of the vote.

Cannes, 19 May
At this year's Film Festival, the jury's special prize was awarded to Andrei Tarkovsky's mystical *Offret* (*The Sacrifice*), while the main prize went to Alain Cavalier's *Thérèse*. The best actor award was given to Michel Blanc for his performance in *Tenue de soirée* (*Evening Dress*) and Martin Scorsese was named best director for *After Hours*.

Hollywood, 24 May
Yakima Canutt, the pioneer stuntman and actor, has died of natural causes at 90 years of age. Canutt started out as a cowboy, winning the world champion all-round cowboy title in 1917 and 1919. This led to bit parts and stunt work in silent Westerns. However, with the arrival of sound his voice put an end to his acting career and he began full time stunt work. He is credited with turning stunting into a respectable job in the film industry.

Washington D.C, 26 May
Gian Coppola, the 23-year-old son of director Francis Ford Coppola, was killed yesterday when the boat he was piloting ran into a rope on South River in Maryland.

Paris, 18 June
Release here of Marco Bellocchio's latest film *Il Diavolo in Corpo* (*The Devil in the Flesh*). The film, which includes an explicit fellatio scene, has caused a scandal.

London, 8 August
Stanley Kubrick has completed *Full Metal Jacket*, his first film since *The Shining* six years ago.

New York, 20 August
Spike Lee, a young black director, has released his first feature film *She's Gotta Have It*. His unconventional approach has been compared to that of Woody Allen by the New York critics.

Hollywood, 26 August
Claude Lelouch is in America to promote his new film which opened here Friday, *A Man and a Woman: 20 Years Later*. Anouk Aimée and Jean-Louis Trintignant reprise their roles from the original 1967 film. Lelouch said he made the film because he felt impelled "to see how people develop with time."

Los Angeles, 1 September
British producer David Puttnam has taken up his appointment as chairman of Columbia Pictures, as was announced last June. Puttnam, previously an independent, is the first British producer to hold such a post in a major American studio.

Paris, 8 September
Pierre Lescure and René Bonnell have bought the television rights to 80 films produced by Paramount and Universal for Canal Plus, the French pay-channel.

New York, 19 September
Three French films were warmly received at the International Film Festival: Bertrand Blier's *Evening Dress* (*Tenue de soirée*), Bertrand Tavernier's *'Round Midnight* (*Autour de minuit*), and Jean-Jacques Beineix's *Betty Blue* (*37°2 le matin*).

Paris, 22 September
French actresses Brigitte Bardot and Catherine Deneuve are suing Roger Vadim, ex-husband and lover respectively, for invasion of privacy. Both stars are asking 200,000 francs in compensation for the "scandalous revelations" about them in his autobiography, *D'une étoile à l'autre* (*Bardot, Deneuve, Fonda: My Life With the Three Most Beautiful Women in the World*). The book is already a bestseller.

Helsinki, 18 October
Release of Aki Kaurismäki's latest film, *Shadows in Paradise* (*Varjoja Paratiisissa*), with Matti Pellonpää and Kati Outinen. It is the third and final film of the director's so-called "working class" trilogy, and confirms him as Finland's most prominent filmmaker.

Los Angeles, 22 October
With *Something Wild*, starring Jeff Daniels and Melanie Griffith, director Jonathan Demme leads the audience into the fantastical dramatic adventures of a young executive kidnapped by an irresistibly eccentric girl. The film opens today.

Paris, 23 October
A restored copy, with added soundtrack, of Marcel L'Herbier's silent classic *l'Inhumaine* was projected in the great hall at La Villette. The film was produced in 1924.

New York, 28 October
Paul Newman has returned to the character of "Fast" Eddie Felson which he first played 25 years ago in *The Hustler* for Robert Rossen. Martin Scorsese directs the new film, *The Color of Money*.

Los Angeles, 13 November
Illness has not prevented John Huston from holding a press conference to protest about the coloring of his black-and-white film, *The Maltese Falcon*, by the WTBS television channel. This condemnation of the practice adds weight to the criticism already proffered by the Directors Guild of America and the American Film Institute over the coloring of films such as the Michael Curtiz classic *Captain Blood*.

Hollywood, 14 November
Columbia is releasing Luis Valdez's *La Bamba* in bilingual versions.

Paris, 31 December
French cinemas drew just over 1.63 million people this year while America (with only four times the population) had 10.3 million entries.

DEATHS

Los Angeles, 2 January
Una Merkel

Nebraska, 24 January
Gordon MacRae

Los Angeles, 27 January
Lilli Palmer

California, 10 March
Ray Milland

New York, 30 March
James Cagney

New York, 23 April
Otto Preminger

California, 26 April
Broderick Crawford

London, 26 April
Bessie Love

London, 12 May
Elisabeth Bergner

California, 23 May
Sterling Hayden

England, 3 June
Anna Neagle

California, 3 July
Rudy Vallee

Los Angeles, 25 July
Vincente Minnelli

New York, 6 September
Blanche Sweet

California, 5 October
Hal B. Wallis

Iowa, 29 November
Cary Grant

California, 26 December
Elsa Lanchester

Australia's favorite comedian, Paul Hogan, came to international fame on the big screen as ***Crocodile Dundee****. In Australia, the film took over $2 million in the first week.*

He's survived the most hostile and primitive land known to man.
Now all he's got to do is make it through a week in New York.

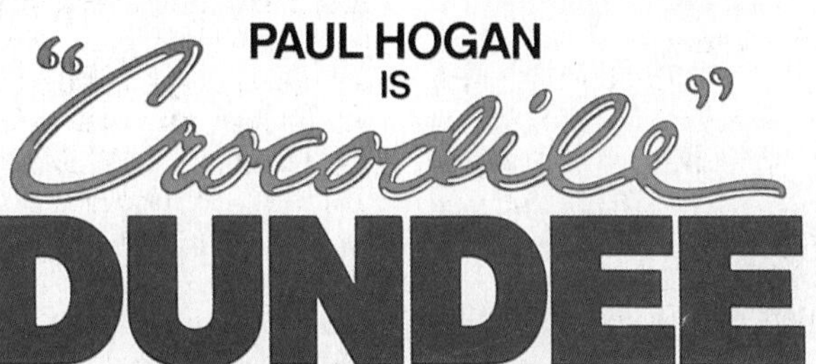
PAUL HOGAN
IS
"Crocodile"
DUNDEE

There's a little of him in all of us.

PARAMOUNT PICTURES PRESENTS "CROCODILE" DUNDEE · LINDA KOZLOWSKI · MARK BLUM · DAVID GULPILIL
MICHAEL LOMBARD AND JOHN MEILLON · ORIGINAL MUSIC SCORE BY PETER BEST · DIRECTOR OF PHOTOGRAPHY RUSSELL BOYD, A.C.S. · LINE PRODUCER JANE SCOTT
ORIGINAL STORY BY PAUL HOGAN · SCREENPLAY BY PAUL HOGAN, KEN SHADIE & JOHN CORNELL · PRODUCED BY JOHN CORNELL · DIRECTED BY PETER FAIMAN

PG-13 PARENTS STRONGLY CAUTIONED
Some Material May Be Inappropriate for Children Under 13

DOLBY STEREO
IN SELECTED THEATRES
PANAVISION

A PARAMOUNT PICTURE

Fellini's nostalgia digs the knife into crass Italian television

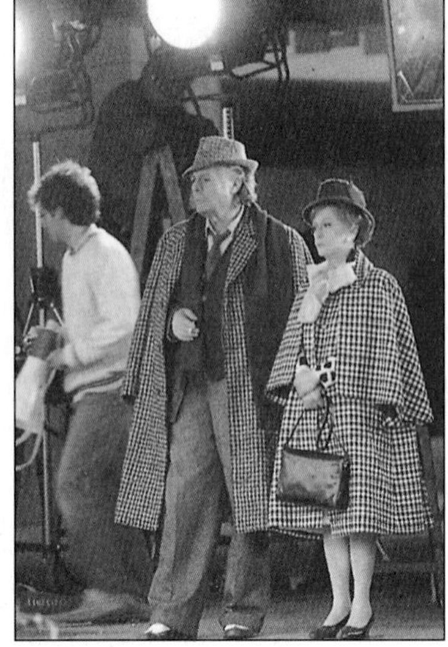

*Marcello Mastroianni and Giulietta Masina in **Ginger and Fred**, a broken-down dance team called back for TV.*

Paris, 22 January
In *Ginger and Fred*, Federico Fellini pays a nostalgic homage to old troupers, and an affectionate tribute to both his former alter ego, Marcello Mastroianni, and his wife Giulietta Masina, whom he last directed 20 years ago in *Juliet of the Spirits*. However, he also digs the knife into the crass commercialism of Italian television, at whose hands his films have been indiscriminately mangled. Mastroianni, flabby and balding, and Masina, still child-like without being coy, are a delight as has-been dancers, who performed a cabaret act as Astaire and Rogers before the war. Having gone their separate ways, they are reunited in a pathetic attempt to relive their past glory for a popular TV show.

Love, life and death with gay New York

New York, 19 February
Much of *Parting Glances* is a weepie in the tradition of Warner Bros. melodramas of the 30s about love and affliction such as *Dark Victory* starring Bette Davis. But what gives it an extra modern dimension and interest is that it is a romantic story of two male lovers parting against the backdrop of AIDS. It was directed, written and edited on a low budget by Bill Sherwood, who also composed the score and edited the sound. It is an engaging portrait of New York gay life, told and played with tenderness and humor.

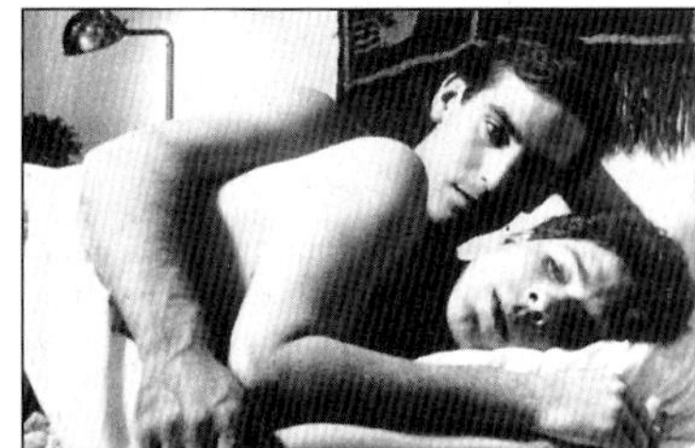

Richard Ganoung and John Bolger.

'Hannah and Her Sisters' is vintage Allen

New York, 7 February
After two films which experimented with notions of reality (*Zelig* and *The Purple Rose of Cairo*), and a minor excursion into Runyonesque comedy (*Broadway Danny Rose*), Woody Allen has returned to the territory he knows best of all – the emotional and psychological problems of middle-class Manhattan intellectuals. His latest movie, *Hannah and Her Sisters*, not only has the largest cast he has ever assembled (with a supporting role for himself), it is also one of his most accomplished. The movie is essentially a tragi-comic study of the relationship of three very different sisters, played superbly by Mia Farrow, Barbara Hershey and Dianne Wiest.

British cast in perfect Forster evocation

New York, 7 March
The producing-directing team of Ismail Merchant and James Ivory, who have been making films together since 1963, have hit the jackpot with E.M. Forster's *A Room With a View*, adapted for the screen by their long-time collaborator, novelist Ruth Prawer Jhabvala, whose Booker Prize-winning *Heat and Dust* Merchant-Ivory filmed in 1983. Literary adaptations are their specialty, and *A Room With a View*, filmed on location in Italy, boasts a superb cast which includes Maggie Smith, Denholm Elliott, Daniel Day Lewis, Judi Dench and Helena Bonham Carter. The picture, which cost less than $5 million, looks like becoming a mainstream hit.

Hannah (Mia Farrow, left) and sisters Barbara Hershey and Dianne Wiest.

*Julian Sands, Helena Bonham Carter in James Ivory's **A Room With a View**.*

Sydney Pollack bests John Huston in quality year

Anjelica Huston, a winner.

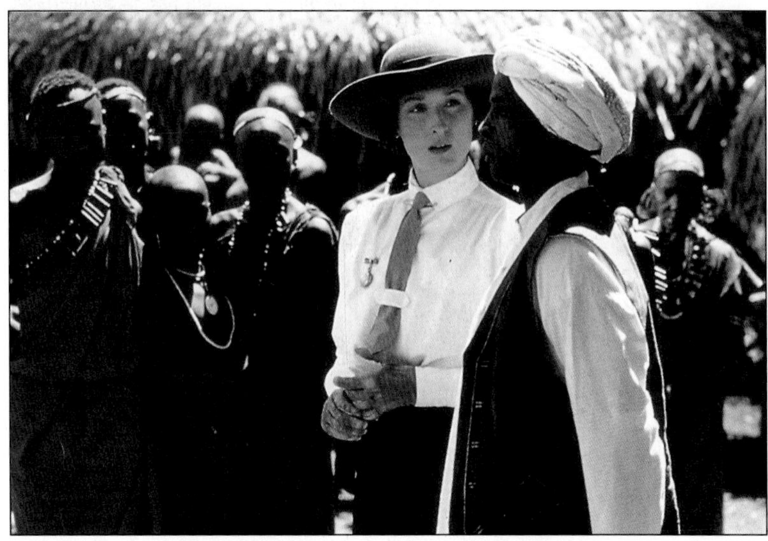
Meryl Streep as Karen Blixen surrounded by her workers in ***Out of Africa****.*

William Hurt voted Best Actor.

Hollywood, 24 March
This year's Oscar presentations will probably be remembered not for who won, but for who lost. The Academy's snubbing of Steven Spielberg, whose *The Color Purple* had 11 nominations, was the main talking point at the Dorothy Chandler Pavilion. It was only the second time (*The Turning Point*, 1977, was the first) that a movie with 10 or more nominations failed to notch up a single win. The film's main rival, also with 11 chances, *Out of Africa*, took eight Oscars, including Best Picture. Sydney Pollack was considered lucky to win Best Director in an internationally-flavored year in which John Huston (*Prizzi's Honor*), Japan's Akira Kurosawa (*Ran*), the Brazilian Hector Babenco (*Kiss of the Spider Woman*) and Australian Peter Weir (*Witness*) were in the running. There were, however, no top acting awards for *Out of Africa*, those going to William Hurt for his sensitive portrayal as the effeminate but ultimately heroic prisoner in a South American jail in *Kiss of the Spider Woman*, and 61-year-old Geraldine Page for her hymn-singing pensioner in *The Trip to Bountiful*, after eight tries at the award. Although John Huston missed out personally, he shared the triumph of his daughter Anjelica's win as Best Supporting Actress for *Prizzi's Honor*, while 77-year-old first-time nominee Don Ameche was voted Best Supporting Actor for *Cocoon*.

Tycoon Ted Turner takes over MGM-UA

Hollywood, 25 March
It appears that financier Kirk Kerkorian's purchase of United Artists in 1981 to merge it with MGM was a shrewd business move. His design was to make the company more appealing to a prospective buyer, rather than to genuinely upgrade it to viable production and distribution status once again. He has now sold the entire operation to CNN's Ted Turner. Though the full extent of their complicated deal is not yet clear, it appears that the cable TV mogul, based in Atlanta, Georgia, has bought the companies so as to acquire the rights to their valuable backlog of old movies for broadcast on his cable TV network, and is unlikely to retain the film companies and their production facilities, which include the Culver City lot and film lab. Kerkorian's behavior recalls that of Howard Hughes, who virtually destroyed RKO studios, which he unloaded 30 years ago.

Trendy Beineix raises the temperature of new French cinema

Paris, 9 April
Like a boxer who only loses or wins by knockout, Jean-Jacques Beineix, who scored a terrific hit with *Diva*, was absolutely flattened three years ago by *The Moon in the Gutter*. He has since got to his feet, and his most recent film *Betty Blue* (*37°2 le matin*) is sure to raise temperatures, mainly because of its pretty torrid love scenes, and the sensational new discovery, 22-year-old Béatrice Dalle. She plays Betty, a sensual but disgruntled waitress, who lives with her handyman boyfriend Zorg (Jean-Hugues Anglade). One day she burns down the beach shack in which they live, and they take off to Paris and then to a provincial town where, disillusioned and on drugs, she has a mental breakdown. Beineix's modish use of decor and color is an effective background to this frank depiction of *amour fou*.

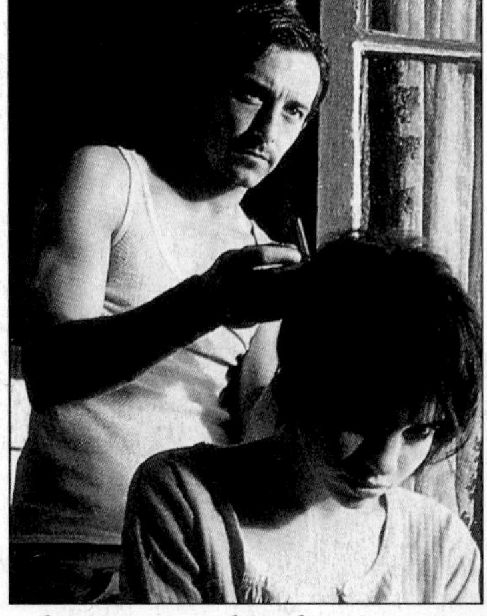
Jean-Hugues Anglade and Béatrice Dalle star in ***Betty Blue****, Beineix's tale of love, degeneracy and madness.*

Gung-ho flying saga 'Top Gun' is a sure-fire hit for Tom Cruise

Los Angeles, 16 May
Like his brother Ridley, British director Tony Scott cut his cinematic teeth making television commercials. His mastery of the 30-second attention span-style has stood him in good stead in *Top Gun*, which he has turned into a two-hour recruiting advertisement for the U.S. Navy. At the Navy's elite aviation training school young tyros compete for glory in the air and on the ground. Ceaselessly smirking behind his Ray-Bans is pint-sized Tom Cruise, a gung-ho pilot and cardboard stud making a play for coolly leggy flying instructor Kelly McGillis. McGillis looms over Cruise in much the same way that tall leading ladies used to cast their shadow over Alan Ladd and, it has to be said, theirs is a pairing which generates absolutely no sexual chemistry. Scott seems more excited by the dogfights he stages like billion-dollar video games. What acting there is in the movie is accomplished by the boyish Anthony Edwards, cast as Cruise's sidekick, who emerges as the most personable and, therefore, ill-fated, of the clean-cut wannabes in this slickly contrived entertainment which, in Scott's hands, has become its own commercial.

Tom Cruise, flying ace in the making, with instructor and lover Kelly McGillis.

Brash Bette outwits the 'Ruthless People' in a mad comedy

Hollywood, 27 June
Big, bad, brassy Bette Midler is the world's most disagreeable kidnap victim in *Ruthless People*, directed by Jim Abrahams and David and Jerry Zucker, the team responsible for *Kentucky Fried Movie*, *Airplane* and *Top Secret*. She's been snatched by suburban couple Judge Reinhold and Helen Slater, whose fashion designs have been ripped off by Midler's slimy little husband Danny De Vito. The only problem is that De Vito, while bewailing the fate of his wife for the benefit of the cops, is quite happy to see his wife disappear – he was planning to murder her anyway. Meanwhile his mistress Anita Morris, suspecting that De Vito has contrived the kidnap himself, is hatching a plot to blackmail him with the help of her slow-witted boyfriend Bill Pullman. Amid all these shenanigans, the only people who fail the ruthlessness test at the first fence are health-conscious kidnappers Slater and Reinhold, who keep lowering the ransom price. All ends happily, if such a thing is possible with so many deeply unpleasant people stalking the screen. One suspects that the real purpose of the movie, apart from allowing Midler to holler her head off, is to send up Robert Redford's po-faced hit *Ordinary People*.

Helen Slater (left) with Bette Midler as the 'prisoner' she hopes to ransom.

Gruesome, effective remake of 'The Fly'

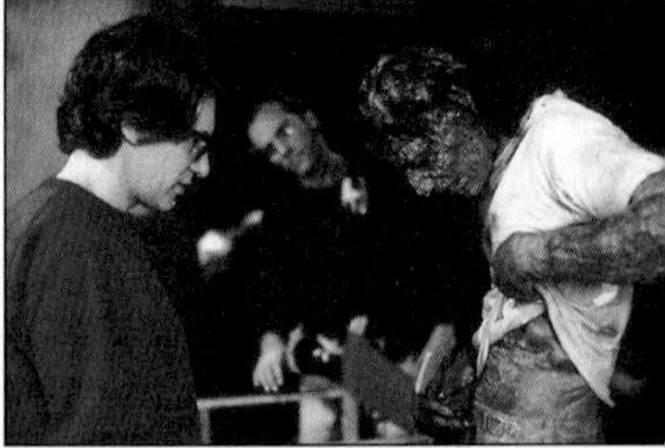

Director David Cronenberg examines Jeff Goldblum's amazing makeup.

Los Angeles, 15 August
One of the more engagingly dotty science fiction movies of the 1950s was *The Fly*, in which an unfortunate design defect in scientist Al Hedison's matter transmitter turned him into half-man, half-fly. Now David Cronenberg has remade this schlock classic, casting a frenetic Jeff Goldblum as Dr. Seth Brundle, whose teleportation experiments succeed only in fusing his genes with those of the insect of the title. The most literal-minded of horror and science fiction directors, Cronenberg piles one stomach-churning special effect on top of another as Goldblum's body is hideously distorted and his lingering humanity ebbs away. Cronenberg once observed that he could "conceive of a beauty contest for the inside of the human body where people would unzip themselves and show you the best spleen, the best heart, the best-looking viscera." *The Fly* is a truly visceral experience which the director sees as a metaphor for aging: "In time we all turn into monsters."

Before his transformation into a fly.

How much do movie stars earn today?

London, 1 August
According to a long article in *Company* magazine last month, the most highly paid actor in the world is Sylvester Stallone. Based on the tremendous success of the *Rocky* films (which he wrote and, later, directed) and the two *Rambo*s (which he co-wrote), Stallone is the first star to break the $10-million barrier. He currently commands around $12 million per film, though this was topped by Brando, who got nearly $3.5 million for 12 days shooting on *Superman* (1978). Other highly paid stars are Dustin Hoffman, Warren Beatty and Robert Redford, all around the $5.5 to $6-million mark, followed by Paul Newman and Jack Nicholson between $4 and $5 million, and Eddie Murphy the one black star able to match this. The women have earned less than the men throughout the post-studio era, and only Streisand at about $5 million and Meryl Streep ($4 million) currently earn the real top bucks.

The Lido acknowledges Eric Rohmer's 'Comedies and Proverbs'

Vincent Gauthier and Marie Rivière in Eric Rohmer's ***The Green Ray****.*

Round Midnight*: Dexter Gordon.*

Venice, 3 September
Once again the Mostra has cast its vote for a French film. The fifth chapter of Eric Rohmer's series of Comedies and Proverbs, *Summer* (*le Rayon vert*), won this year's Golden Lion at the Film Festival. Unlike Rohmer's previous films, the dialogue of this comedy of manners was entirely improvised, creating both the tedium and fascination of real speech. Marie Rivière plays a Parisian secretary, alone during the long summer vacation, who takes herself off to various places but is bored and depressed everywhere. The green ray of the French title is taken from the Jules Verne novel. It refers to the last magical ray of sunset, the green of which is supposed to make observers more aware of the feelings and perceptions of others. Eric Rohmer's films have much the same effect.

Unsavory subject given stylish treatment

London, 5 September
Busy, bustling Bob Hoskins gives his finest performance to date in Neil Jordan's dark drama *Mona Lisa*. He's superbly cast as the ex-con turned driver for beautiful, manipulative hooker Cathy Tyson. Hoskins is a hard nut with a soft heart who is finally betrayed by love and devotion. Jordan and screenwriter David Leland take Hoskins and the audience on a voyage of grim discovery through a London poisoned by vice and greed, where armies of child prostitutes and tramps camp near the homes of the rich. This moral collapse is personified in the slimy figure of Hoskins' boss, played by Michael Caine like Alfie's psychopathic twin brother.

Off-beat talents revealed in 'Down By Law'

New York, 19 September
The third feature from the independent writer-director Jim Jarmusch, whose laconic, observational style has more affinity with Europe than Hollywood, is an engaging bittersweet lark. A trio of incompatible no-hopers, played by musicians Tom Waits and John Lurie (who both contributed the soundtrack) and the Italian comic actor Roberto Benigni, share a jail cell in New Orleans, escape, and have bickering misadventures on the lam across Louisiana. Quirky and ironic, the movie is enhanced by its actors, particularly the hilarious Benigni in his English-language debut, and the arresting black-and-white cinematography of Germany's Robby Muller.

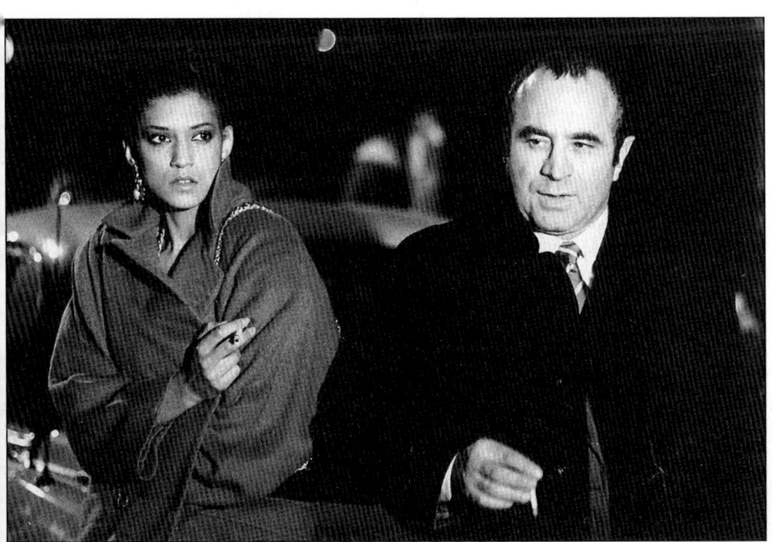

Cathy Tyson and Bob Hoskins in British director Neil Jordan's ***Mona Lisa****.*

l to r: Tom Waits, John Lurie and Roberto Benigni, three unlikely companions.

'Blue Velvet': the dark side of suburbia

*Sadistic pervert Dennis Hopper with Isabella Rossellini in **Blue Velvet**.*

Los Angeles, 19 September
Writer-director David Lynch has come up with an audacious shocker that proves itself a determinedly weird, disturbingly original and subversive take on middle America. In *Blue Velvet*, clean, sweet, small-town youngsters Kyle MacLachlan and Laura Dern get caught up in the mystery surrounding nightclub chanteuse Isabella Rossellini and discover, to their horror, what goes on behind neat picket fences. Rossellini is tormented by psychotic sadist, kidnapper and drug dealer Dennis Hopper, whose intense performance dominates and is appallingly riveting. The sexual violence and obscenities will offend those squeamish of eye and ear.

Runaway hit for bushwhacker Paul Hogan

*Paul Hogan as the appropriately nicknamed hero of **Crocodile Dundee**.*

New York, 26 September
Laid-back Australian TV comedian Paul Hogan has hit the jackpot with *Crocodile Dundee*, a vehicle tailor-made for his brand of amiable charm. He plays the adventurer of the title who shows American reporter Linda Koslowski around the outback before giving up wrestling the local animal life to tangle with the low life which infests her native Manhattan. Hogan's wry charm suggests that Dundee's legendary field-craft might hover on the fraudulent, but he certainly adapts quickly to life among the coke-snorting sophisticates of New York. Asked why he likes the Big Apple, he replies, "It's a real lunatic asylum. That's why I like it. I fit right in."

The short and horrible life of Sid Vicious

New York, 3 October
Explaining why he filmed the sordid tale of Sid Vicious and Nancy Spungeon, director Alex Cox has said, "Though a lot of people are put off by the idea of a love story between these two unsavory-seeming people, it *is* a love story..." In *Sid and Nancy*, Cox chronicles the downward spiral described by the Sex Pistols' singer and his junkie girlfriend, played by Gary Oldman and Chloe Webb. It's grim stuff, characterized by the moment when Nancy appears to Sid while he is watching *Night of the Living Dead* on TV.

Gary Oldman as Sid Vicious and Chloe Webb as girlfriend Nancy Spungeon.

'Fast' Eddie Felson, twenty-five years later

Los Angeles, 17 October
A quarter of a century after playing poolroom shark "Fast" Eddie Felson in *The Hustler*, Paul Newman reprises the role in Martin Scorsese's *The Color of Money*. Eddie is greying around the temples now and selling liquor for a living. But he returns to the world of high-stakes pool when he encounters a young version of himself in flashy cue man Tom Cruise, whom he decides to promote in another shot at the big-time. Electrifying performances by both principals compensate for the film's anti-climactic conclusion.

Paul Newman as the former pool champion with his young protégé Tom Cruise.

Debonair Cary Grant's long run is over

Still handsome in middle age.

New York, 30 November
Cary Grant, for 50 years a byword for suave good looks and the smoothest of screen talents, has died of a stroke while attending a film festival in Iowa. He was 82. His last film was the 1966 *Walk, Don't Run* but his seemingly ageless good looks never deserted him in a retirement enlivened by work as an executive for a perfume company. He was born Archibald Leach in Bristol, England, in 1904 and came to America as a teenage tumbler, making his screen debut in 1932 in *This is the Night*. The key to Grant's appeal was his ability to appear at once attractive and threatening, the animating force in films as disparate as *Only Angels Have Wings*, *Suspicion*, *His Girl Friday* and *Notorious*. There was a light and a dark side to Grant, as his fourth wife Dyan Cannon has attested. In his films, whenever one is dominant the other creeps into view. But the image that lingers is one of easy, self-deprecating sophistication and charm. When a journalist wired his agent "How old Cary Grant?", Grant himself replied, "Old Cary Grant fine. How you?"

Oliver Stone relives Vietnam experience

New York, 19 December
Platoon is the first movie about the war in Vietnam made by a veteran of that conflict. Director Oliver Stone, the son of a wealthy family, dropped out of Yale, volunteered for the infantry as a private and saw the war in Southeast Asia "from the lowest level", being twice wounded and decorated. In 1975, as Saigon was falling, Stone wrote a script about the war which has taken 11 years to bring to the screen. The movie reflects his own experience, with Charlie Sheen cast as a callow "grunt" (and Stone's alter ego) over whom two sergeants, nice Willem Dafoe and nasty Tom Berenger, fight a moral battle. Stone, who is a determined political liberal, entered films as a writer-director with the 1973 *Seizure*. He won an Oscar for the screenplay of *Midnight Express* and scored a success earlier this year with *Salvador*, a hard-hitting attack on U.S. policy in Central America.

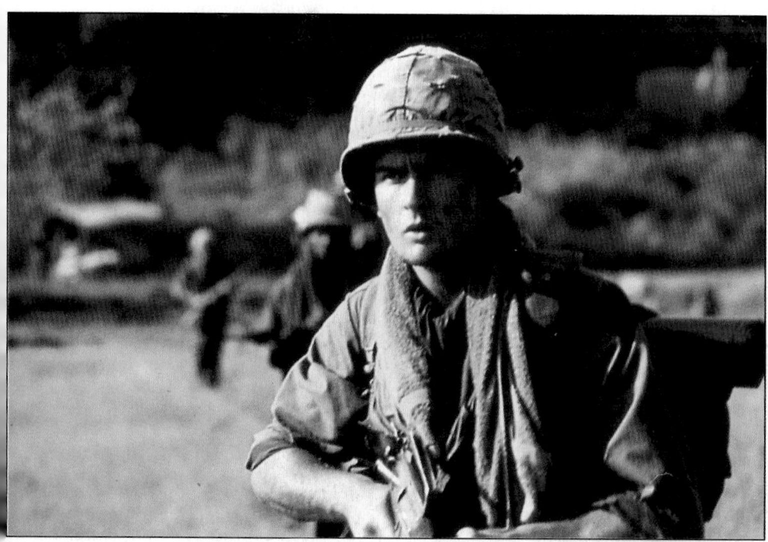

Charlie Sheen stars as the disillusioned rookie soldier in ***Platoon****.*

Annaud films Eco's 'The Name of the Rose'

Christian Slater and Feodor Chaliapine Jr. in an affecting scene from the film.

Paris, 17 December
Jean-Jacques Annaud is not a director who goes for the easy option. After having made *Quest for Fire* (1981), the Stone-Age romance with an invented language, he has now tackled Umberto Eco's complex, metaphysical, medieval detective story, *The Name of the Rose*. Despite having had to reduce the plot for cinematic reasons, Annaud has almost carried off the impossible. Most impressive are the claustrophobic sets, especially the labyrinthine library, through which move Sean Connery as William of Baskerville, a Franciscan Sherlock Holmes, and Christian Slater as his teenage apprentice, trying to solve the mystery of a series of murders in a monastery. Connery has just the right mixture of humor and gravitas to make him an ideal guide. The monks, with F. Murray Abraham as a bald-pated, bearded inquisitor and Michel Lonsdale as an ambiguous abbott, are a wonderful collection of Breughelesque grotesques.

Tarkovsky, the Soviet perfectionist, is dead

Paris, 29 December
Andrei Tarkovsky, aged 54, has just died of cancer. The Russian director had been extremely ill for several months, and was thus unable to go to the Cannes Film Festival last May, where his final film, *The Sacrifice*, won the Special Jury Prize. This Franco-Swedish production, filmed on the island of Gotland in the Baltic Sea, was his second film after *Nostalgia* (1983), during his self-imposed exile from the USSR. His career in his own country had been a long struggle against the Soviet authorities, especially with their initial interdiction of *Andrei Rublev* (1966) and *Mirror* (1974). His two science fiction films, *Solaris* (1972) and *Stalker* (1979), somehow managed to escape their disapproval. Tarkovsky's perfectionism and rich pictorial sense was already evident in his first feature, *Ivan's Childhood*, in 1962. His seven films in 24 years are among the most intensely personal and visually powerful statements to have come out of Eastern Europe during the postwar era.

During filming of ***Mirror****.*

▷

KIM
BASINGER
MICKEY
ROURKE
THEY BROKE
EVERY
RULE
9½ Weeks
PRODUCERS SALES ORGANIZATION SIDNEY KIMMEL
KEITH BARISH PRODUCTION ADRIAN LYNE
MICKEY ROURKE · KIM BASINGER '9 1/2 WEEKS' JACK NITZSCHE
ELIZABETH McNEIL PATRICIA KNOP
ZALMAN KING SARAH KERNOCHAN KEITH BARISH
FRANK KÖNIGSBERG ANTONY RUFUS ISAACS
ZALMAN KING ADRIAN LYNE JONESFILM
GALACTIC FILMS TRIPLE AJAXXX

Adrian Lyne directed the sexy duo in this sensation-causing soft porn.

*Christopher Lambert co-starred with Sean Connery in **Highlander**.*

*Writer-director-actor Spike Lee made his debut with **She's Gotta Have It**.*

*François Cluzet in Bertrand Tavernier's evocative jazz film, **Round Midnight**.*

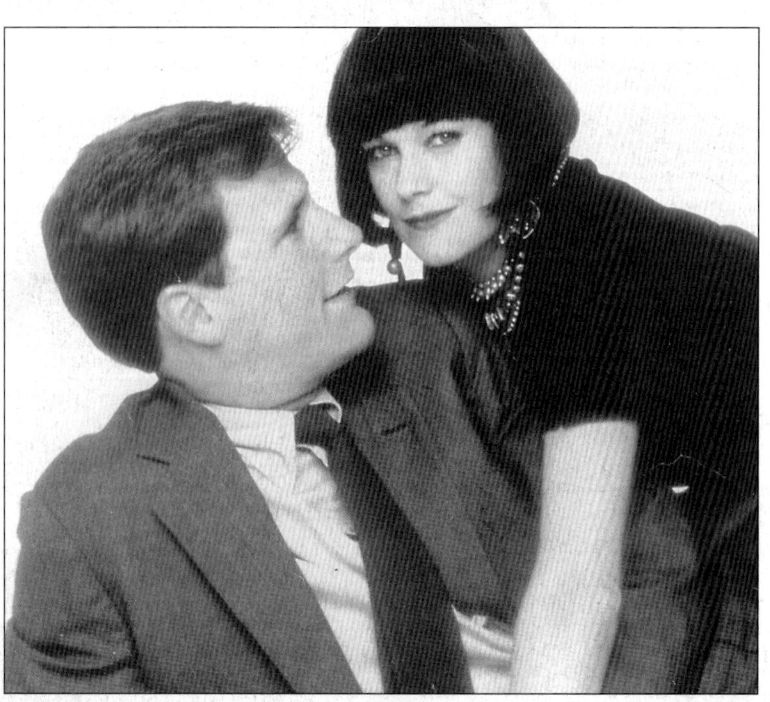

*Jeff Daniels and Melanie Griffith in Jonathan Demme's **Something Wild**.*

*Roland Joffe's **The Mission** was set in mid-18th-century South America.*

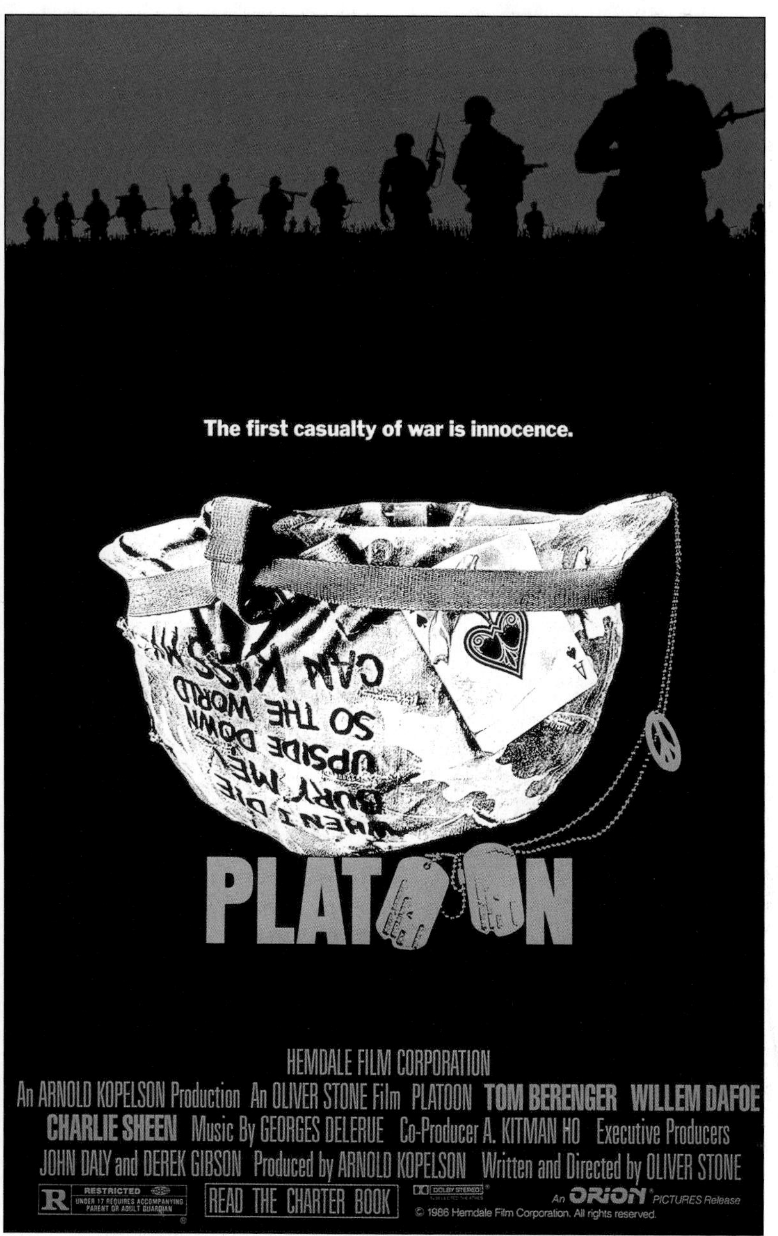
The first casualty of war is innocence.
PLATOON
HEMDALE FILM CORPORATION
An ARNOLD KOPELSON Production An OLIVER STONE Film PLATOON TOM BERENGER WILLEM DAFOE
CHARLIE SHEEN Music By GEORGES DELERUE Co-Producer A. KITMAN HO Executive Producers
JOHN DALY and DEREK GIBSON Produced by ARNOLD KOPELSON Written and Directed by OLIVER STONE
R RESTRICTED UNDER 17 REQUIRES ACCOMPANYING PARENT OR ADULT GUARDIAN
READ THE CHARTER BOOK
DOLBY STEREO
An ORION PICTURES Release
© 1986 Hemdale Film Corporation. All rights reserved.

This was a powerful return to the Vietnam War from ex-soldier Oliver Stone.

Juliette Binoche, Denis Lavant: Carax's ***The Night is Young (Mauvais sang)****.*

André Dussollier and Sabine Azema in ***Melo****, directed by Alain Resnais.*

Michael Mann's ***Manhunter****: Brian Cox as cannibal Hannibal Lecter.*

Macho wish-fulfillment with Chuck Norris in ***Delta Force****.*

Bernadette Lafont, Jean Poiret in Chabrol's 'tec thriller ***Inspecteur Lavardin****.*

★★★★★★★★★ 1987 ★★★★★★★★★★★★★★★★★★★★★★★★★★★

1986 Academy Awards, Dorothy Chandler Pavilion, 31 Mar.

Best Film:	*Platoon* (dir: Oliver Stone)
Best Director:	Oliver Stone
Best Actor:	Paul Newman *(The Color of Money)*
Best Actress:	Marlee Matlin *(Children of a Lesser God)*
Best Supp. Actor:	Michael Caine *(Hannah and Her Sisters)*
Best Supp. Actress:	Dianne Wiest *(Hannah and Her Sisters)*

Paris, 18 January
Isabelle Adjani appeared as newsreader Bruno Masure's guest on the Channel Two news at 8 p.m. this evening. The appearance was planned to put an end to rumors that the star is dying of AIDS. Miss Adjani, who appeared to be in perfect health, said she had no idea how the rumor had started but that she was finding its persistence demoralizing.

New York, 19 January
Release of *Radio Days*, Woody Allen's nostalgic evocation of his childhood and the role played by the radio in American homes.

Hollywood, 18 February
Taxi's Emmy Award-winning actor Danny De Vito will make his directorial debut with a comedy for Orion Pictures, *Throw Momma From the Train*. Filming is scheduled to start in Los Angeles in April. De Vito will co-star with Billy Crystal.

California, 27 February
Hollywood has decided to hold a centenary celebration in its own honor. For those who are confused, in 1887 an estate agent named Harvey Henderson Wilcox registered a new land subdivision as Hollywood Ranch. It soon became the greatest dream-factory in the world.

Los Angeles, 20 March
Barry Levinson exposes the world of aluminum siding salesmen in the 50s with *Tin Men*. Danny De Vito and Richard Dreyfuss star.

Paris, 25 March
Release of *le Grand chemin*, by Jean-Loup Hubert, with Anémone and Richard Bohringer.

New York, 30 March
The Coen brothers, Joel and Ethan, have released their second feature *Raising Arizona*, starring Nicolas Cage. An offbeat satire, it confirms the promise of their debut feature *Blood Simple* (1985).

Hollywood, 10 April
At last nights's AFI Life Achievement Award dinner in her honor, Barbara Stanwyck's comment after being lauded for 90 minutes by many of Hollywood's top personalities was, "Honest to God, I *can't* walk on water!"

New York, 15 May
In *Gardens of Stone*, Francis Ford Coppola depicts the war in Vietnam indirectly, through the eyes of the men who take care of the military cemetery in Arlington.

Los Angeles, 1 June
A Los Angeles Superior Court jury has found director John Landis and four co-defendants not guilty of all charges related to the fatal 1982 helicopter accident. The judge declared the deaths of Vic Morrow and two child actors on the set of *The Twilight Zone* "an unforeseeable accident".

Paris, 18 June
Brigitte Bardot held an auction sale of her dresses, make-up case, guitar and other souvenirs to raise funds for her association for the prevention of cruelty to animals.

Washington D.C., 22 June
The U.S. Copyright Office's decision on Friday to register colorized versions of black-and-white films was a blow for the detractors of the process, and a boon to those in the colorization business who believe it opens up film classics to a new generation of viewers.

Los Angeles, 18 September
David Puttnam has announced he will resign his position as chairman of Columbia Pictures. The decision follows the Columbia-Tristar merger which formed Columbia Pictures Entertainment. The new company has appointed Victor A. Kaufman as its head, thus greatly reducing Puttnam's capacity as chairman and chief executive.

Washington D.C., 24 September
Bob Fosse collapsed with a heart attack a few minutes before he was due to go on stage in *Sweet Charity* last night. Fosse's highly acclaimed, semi-autobiographical film, *All That Jazz*, takes on a prophetic quality; its choreographer suffers a similar fate.

Los Angeles, 12 October
Barfly, the German director Barbet Schroeder's newly released American movie, evokes the twilit world of writer Charles Bukowski. Mickey Rourke and Faye Dunaway star as a pair of hopeless drinkers.

Los Angeles, 14 October
Lillian Gish is celebrating her 90th birthday today. Miss Gish, whose screen career began in 1912, made her last appearance to date in 1978 in Robert Altman's *A Wedding*.

New York, 31 October
The stock market crash has affected most film companies including the most successful. The major studios' shares have dropped by 20 percent.

Copenhagen, 15 December
According to statistics, a cinema closes in Denmark every two weeks.

New York, 20 December
Opening here of *The Dead*, the last film from director John Huston. It was completed just before his death last August.

New York, 23 December
Release of Oliver Stone's *Wall Street*. The film depicts the pitiless world of the stock market and high finance, with Michael Douglas as an unscrupulous dealer and mentor to rookie Charlie Sheen.

Copenhagen, 26 December
Release of *Pelle the Conqueror* (*Pelle Erobreren*), directed by Bille August, starring Pelle Hvengaard and Max Von Sydow.

France, 31 December
The latest survey of the number of cinemas has shown a drop of 346 from last year for a total of 4,808.

Hollywood, 31 December
Paramount has accounted for 20 percent of the total distribution takings for the year, thanks to three big films: *Beverly Hills Cop II*, *Fatal Attraction* and *The Untouchables*.

New York, 31 December
The total receipts from video sales and rentals in America has reached $7.4 billion: twice the total of box office takings.

DEATHS

New York, 22 February
Andy Warhol

New York, 25 February
James Coco

Los Angeles, 2 March
Randolph Scott

Los Angeles, 3 March
Danny Kaye

Santa Barbara, 21 March
Robert Preston

New York, 14 May
Rita Hayworth

New York, 13 June
Geraldine Page

Los Angeles, 22 June
Fred Astaire

Texas, 1 August
Pola Negri

Rhode Island, 28 August
John Huston

Arizona, 29 August
Lee Marvin

Connecticut, 31 August
Joseph E. Levine

Beverly Hills, 13 September
Mervyn LeRoy

California, 25 September
Mary Astor

Spain, 2 October
Madeleine Carroll

France, 22 October
Lino Ventura

Los Angeles, 4 December
Rouben Mamoulian

Bernardo Bertolucci's ***The Last Emperor*** *is a magnificent spectacle which tells the poignant tale of the Emperor Pu Yi who ascended to the Dragon throne of China, aged three.*

He was the Lord of Ten Thousand Years,
the absolute monarch of China.

He was born to rule a world
of ancient tradition.

Nothing prepared him for our world of change.

THE LAST EMPEROR

A True Story.

HEMDALE FILM CORPORATION PRESENTS
A JEREMY THOMAS PRODUCTION A FILM BY BERNARDO BERTOLUCCI
JOHN LONE JOAN CHEN
PETER O'TOOLE AS R.J.
"THE LAST EMPEROR"
YING RUOCHENG VICTOR WONG DENNIS DUN AND RYUICHI SAKAMOTO
ASSOCIATE PRODUCER (U.K.) JOYCE HERLIHY PRODUCTION SUPERVISOR MARIO COTONE COSTUMES JAMES ACHESON PRODUCTION DESIGNER FERDINANDO SCARFIOTTI
EDITOR GABRIELLA CRISTIANI PHOTOGRAPHY BY VITTORIO STORARO (AIC) MUSIC RYUICHI SAKAMOTO DAVID BYRNE AND CONG SU
ASSOCIATE PRODUCER FRANCO GIOVALE SCREENPLAY MARK PEPLOE WITH BERNARDO BERTOLUCCI PRODUCER JEREMY THOMAS DIRECTOR BERNARDO BERTOLUCCI

PG-13 PARENTS STRONGLY CAUTIONED
Some Material May Be Inappropriate for Children Under 13

DOLBY STEREO IN SELECTED THEATRES

EASTMAN COLOR TECHNOVISION CAMERAS & LENSES TECHNICOLOR (ROME)
SOUNDTRACK ALBUM "THE LAST EMPEROR" AVAILABLE ON VIRGIN RECORDS

A COLUMBIA PICTURES RELEASE

Columbia Pictures

PRINTED IN U.S.A.

NSS 870142

A cynical and observant conversation piece from French Canada

Paris, 4 February

The French-Canadian film director Denys Arcand has finally gained an international reputation with his fifth fiction feature, *The Decline of the American Empire*. It focuses on a group of Quebecois artists and intellectuals – four men and four women preparing a gourmet dinner in a country mansion. Their sexually segregated discussions range over the subjects of sexuality, fidelity, aging, success and failure. Later, at the dinner, the wide-ranging conversation takes a different turn when one of the women announces that she has slept with two of the men, including one whose wife is present. The film, on similar lines to John Sayles' *Return of the Secaucus Seven* (1979) and Lawrence Kasdan's *The Big Chill* (1983), is a cynical and observant conversation piece in which the protagonists' attitudes to sex serve to unmask their personalities, and their deeper political concerns. From early on in his career, beginning with his full-length documentary *On est au coton* (1970), about abuses in the textile industry, Arcand has demonstrated that he is an astute chronicler of social and political life in Quebec. *The Decline of the American Empire* is informed with the same spirit, but with a sharper satirical edge.

The four women who match the men in their intellectual and sexual modernity.

American remake of French comedy

New York, 23 March

Coline Serreau's *Trois hommes et un couffin* (*Three Men and a Cradle*), one of the most popular French films for many years – it has attracted over 10 million spectators in France alone – is about to be remade by Hollywood, with the action transposed to the USA. It is to be directed by Leonard Nimoy, best known for his role as Spock in the *Star Trek* TV and film series, and not by Serreau as originally intended. She will be retained as screenwriter. The three carefree bachelors who have an abandoned baby thrust upon them are being portrayed by Tom Selleck, Steve Guttenberg and Ted Danson. The remake, called *Three Men and a Baby*, is being produced by Walt Disney's Touchstone company, with Jean-François Lepetit, the producer of the French film, as executive producer.

Gibson, Glover, a lethal box-office combo

Hollywood, 8 March

Once again Mel Gibson is cast as a man on the edge, this time playing strung-out cop Martin Riggs in *Lethal Weapon*, directed by Richard Donner. The weapon of the title is not a fearsome handgun of the type usually waved in the faces of hoods by Dirty Harry. It's Riggs himself, a veteran of the Special Forces in Vietnam who has been so traumatized by the death of his wife that he has become a pyschological time bomb, ready to explode at any moment. He teams up with middle-class black colleague Danny Glover to wreak spectacular justice on a gang of drug traffickers, led by maverick military man Mitchell Ryan and ex-Vietnam mercenary Gary Busey. This combination of cop thriller, buddy movie and vigilante picture enables Richard Donner to restage the Vietnam War – with heroin the issue at stake and, this time at least, the good guys coming out on top.

Danny Glover and Mel Gibson as the two cops with a great relationship.

Oscars make reparation for Vietnam War

Los Angeles, 30 March

After a lull of seven years since *Apocalypse Now*, the last serious film to depict the Vietnam War, Oliver Stone's *Platoon* forcefully returned the war to the Hollywood agenda, and picked up Oscars for both Best Picture and Best Director in the process. Loosely autobiographical, Stone's screenplay follows raw recruit Charlie Sheen into the hell of Vietnam, where he witnesses the torture and killing of Vietnamese peasants by American soldiers who also suffer a dependency on drugs. The Best Actor award was given to Paul Newman, reprising his role as "Fast" Eddie Felson in *The Color of Money*, Martin Scorsese's sequel to the 25-year-old *The Hustler*. In contrast to Newman, who had astonishingly never won an Oscar before, the Best Actress winner was Marlee Matlin, a partially deaf actress making her screen debut as a deaf-mute in *Children of a Lesser God*.

Marlee Matlin and William Hurt.

Tom Berenger in ***Platoon****.*

ita Hayworth's uffering is over

ew York, 15 May
ita Hayworth died last night at the New York home of her daughter Yasmin. For a number of years she had been suffering from the incurable degenerative condition known as Alzheimer's disease. Born Margarita Carmen Cansino, Hayworth was a cousin of Ginger Rogers and began her career in her father's dance act while she was in her teens. She was signed by Fox, consigned to B-pictures and found her way to Columbia, where she became Rita Hayworth in the 1937 *Girls Can Play*. Her lustrous beauty blooming in the early war years, Hayworth quickly became a forces' favorite, unforgettably gliding across a moonlit terrace with Fred Astaire in *You Were Never Lovelier*. She revealed her potent blend of casual eroticism in *Gilda*, vamping Glenn Ford while singing "Put The Blame On Mame", but her career never recovered from her marriage to Aly Khan in 1949 (her second husband had been Orson Welles). After the failure of her third and fourth (to Dick Haymes) marriages, fame, looks and confidence deserted her. Alcoholic breakdown overwhelmed her in the 70s, followed by Alzheimer's disease. In later years Hayworth said, "Every man I knew had fallen in love with Gilda and wakened with me."

Festival's special 40th anniversary prize goes to Federico Fellini

Gérard Depardieu and Sandrine Bonnaire in ***Under Satan's Sun****.*

Best actor Marcello Mastroianni with Elena Sofonova in ***Black Eyes****.*

Cannes, 19 May
This year's prize-giving ceremony at the Cannes Film Festival was broadcast live throughout the world. A special 40th anniversary prize was presented to *Intervista*, Federico Fellini's affectionate tribute to the Cinecittà studios in Rome, where he made most of his movies. In contrast to the warm reception given to the maestro, Maurice Pialat was booed by a small section of the audience when he came up to accept the Golden Palm for *Under Satan's Sun*. True to his reputation, Pialat raised his fist at his detractors, and shouted, "If you don't like me, then I can say I feel the same about you lot." This incident obscured the fact that this was the first French film to win the top prize since *A Man and a Woman* in 1966. Based on a novel by Georges Bernanos, *Under Satan's Sun*, an uncompromisingly bleak, claustrophobic and humorless film, was not destined to please the majority. Gérard Depardieu portrays a simple and devout priest who senses Satan everywhere, especially in the heart of a wild, young murderess (Sandrine Bonnaire). The German Wim Wenders was judged the best director for his fantasy *Wings of Desire*.

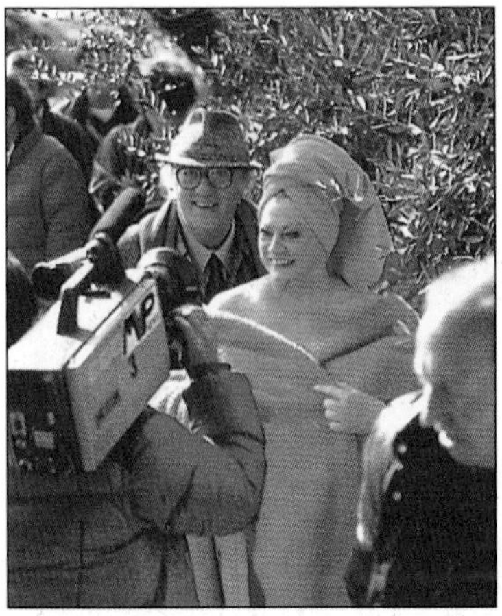

Federico Fellini and Anita Ekberg.

Nobuko Miyamoto in the title role of *Tampopo*, the widowed owner of a Japanese noodle shop. Juzo Itami's wonderful gastronomic comedy of table manners satirizes Japanese social behavior in a series of short scenes, most of which take place in the 'ramen', the Japanese term for the shop.

Fred Astaire puts away his dancing shoes

Los Angeles, 22 June
Fred Astaire has passed away in his Hollywood home as gracefully and discreetly as he lived. Born Frederick Austerlitz on 10 May 1899, Astaire made his screen debut in 1933, following a disastrous early screen test which led a studio talent scout to conclude: "Can't act. Can't sing. Slightly bald. Can dance a little." In fact he was to become the most technically exacting and ambitious of screen dancers. With Ginger Rogers he made nine musicals that are the perfect expression of self-sufficient movement, where hard heels on glossy floors beat out a rhythm of bliss. He retained his breezy elegance and his professionalism to the end. He once said, "I suppose I made it look easy, but, gee whiz, did I work and worry."

With Ginger in ***Top Hat****.*

▷

Bizarre British comedy wins audiences

Withnail (Richard E. Grant, right) and his buddy (Paul McGann).

New York, 19 June
In *Withnail and I*, British writer-director Bruce Robinson takes us on an autobiographical return journey to the Sixties. It's the fall of 1969 and two out-of-work actors, Richard E. Grant's eponymous Withnail and Paul McGann's "I", abandon their grungy London flat for a trip to a country cottage owned by Withnail's homosexual Uncle Monty, played with gloriously corpulent relish by Richard Griffiths. After various wild and comic adventures they say goodbye to each other and to the Sixties themselves.

Enthusiastic welcome for 'Jean de Florette'

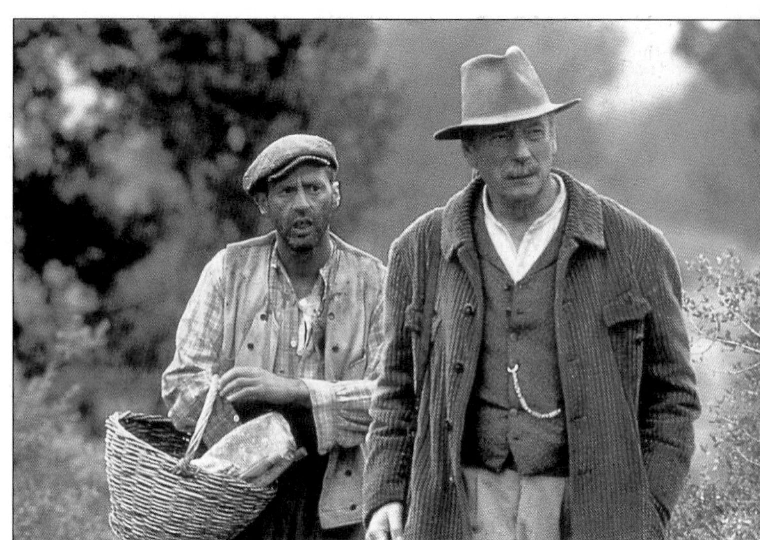

*Daniel Auteuil (left) and Yves Montand, both memorable in **Jean de Florette**.*

New York, 26 June
American audiences have given a warm welcome to *Jean de Florette*, the first of two pictures by Claude Berri based on Marcel Pagnol's 1963 novel. Faithful to Pagnol's vision, Berri has told a good yarn against gorgeous sun-bleached Provençal settings. The three male leads give towering performances: Daniel Auteuil, simple, comic and touching; Yves Montand, earthy, charming and cunning; and Gérard Depardieu, loving and tragic in the title role of the hunchback deprived of his land by the other two.

Futuristic violence from Paul Verhoeven

Los Angeles, 17 July
For his American debut with *Robocop*, Dutch director Paul Verhoeven has resurrected the Frankenstein myth in the form of the robot policeman of the title. This unstoppable composite is fashioned from the remains of mortally wounded patrolman Peter Weller and a grim carapace of computerized body armor. It's Robocop's duty to patrol the streets of a nightmarish Detroit of the near future where both police and criminals are controlled by Omni Consumer Products, the ultimate in rampant capitalism, which sees death simply as an opportunity to update its hardware. Things unravel violently when their latest example recalls his human past.

*Peter Weller is superb as the reconstructed **Robocop**, a reluctant killer.*

John Huston signs off with 'The Dead'

Rhode Island, 28 August
John Huston has died aged 81 of the emphysema that had plagued him for the last 10 years. His death has come just before his last film, *The Dead*, is to be shown at the Venice Film Festival. Huston's illness forced him to direct the picture from a wheelchair, while constantly using an oxygen mask. Nevertheless, he was seldom absent from the set, although the insurance company insisted that Karel Reisz stand by at all times to take over if necessary. *The Dead*, based on the James Joyce short story, stars the director's daughter Anjelica, and his son Tony wrote the script. "I won't retire until the last nail has been hammered into my coffin," Huston once said.

Huston's daughter Anjelica and Donal McCann in the director's final film.

Patrick Swayze takes over from Travolta

Agile heart-throb Patrick Swayze with dancing partner Jennifer Grey.

Hollywood, 21 August
Unheralded, a small-budget ($5 million) romance about a Jewish teen who gets lessons in life, love and dancing at a Catskills resort in the early 60s, is a wow. *Dirty Dancing* is a star-making showcase for hunky dancer-turned-actor Patrick Swayze, best known previously for television's *North and South*, now revealing himself as able to top Travolta. Jennifer Grey, daughter of Joel, charms as the awkward heroine and, if melodramatic clichés tend to take over from the comedy, Swayze's hot gyrations more than compensate.

Venice jury favors Malle, Olmi and Ivory

Raphael Fejto (left) is Jean Bonnet, Philippe Morier-Genoud (right) the master.

Venice, 6 September
Au revoir les enfants was based by Louis Malle on "the most dramatic experience of my childhood." Set at a French boys' boarding school during the Nazi occupation, this unsentimental but affectionate view of a boyhood spent in exceptional circumstances, deservedly won the Golden Lion at this year's festival. The Silver Lion was shared by James Ivory's *Maurice*, a view of the narrow attitude towards homosexuality in Edwardian England, and Ermanno Olmi's *Long Live the Lady!*, an allegory of greed.

Sparks ignite cop Quaid and DA Barkin

Los Angeles, 21 August
Set in New Orleans, *The Big Easy* is a flavorsome romantic thriller in which homicide detective Dennis Quaid locks horns with formidable lady DA Ellen Barkin. Competently directed by Jim McBride from a decent script, with stalwarts Ned Beatty and John Goodman among those lending local color, the film makes for smooth entertainment. But what makes it worthy of reportage is the combustible teaming of the two leads. Ellen Barkin in particular makes an impact as a woman repressed, uncompromising yet vulnerable. Playing uptight but undone by Dennis Quaid's easy charm, she and he give us one of the steamiest clothed sex scenes in memory.

Ellen Barkin and Dennis Quaid in a tender moment from ***The Big Easy****.*

'Hope and Glory' relives wartime London

London, 4 September
For *Hope and Glory*, the autobiographical wartime family saga written and directed by John Boorman, a meticulously detailed suburban street was built which was one of the largest outdoor film sets constructed in Britain since Hitchcock recreated the East End at Lime Grove for *Sabotage*. The film focuses on the early years of the war and follows the progress towards maturity of a young boy, played by Sebastian Rice-Edwards, and the experiences of his family as the Blitz brings disruption and excitement in equal measure. Rich performances and Boorman's sure feel for the deceptive intricacies of family life make *Hope and Glory* a hymn to England.

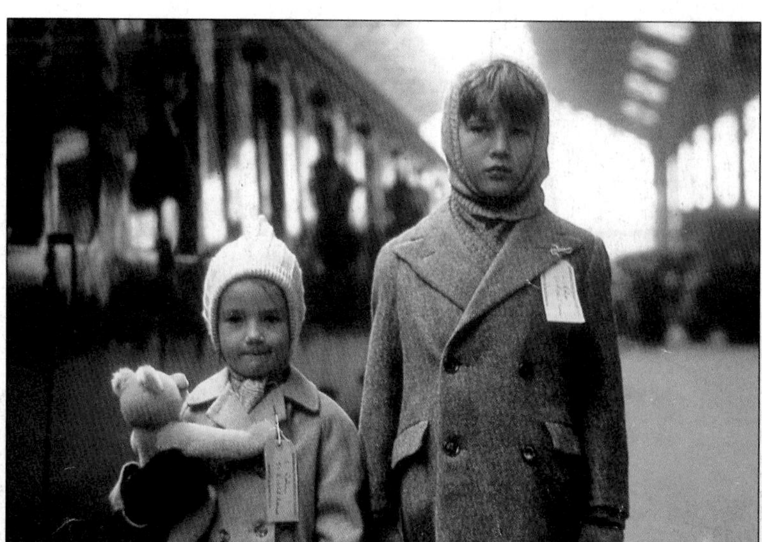

Sebastian Rice-Edwards and Geraldine Muir, children in the London Blitz.

Wenders whimsy is well-received

Paris, 16 September
Wim Wenders, winner of the best director prize at Cannes this year for *Wings of Desire*, is gratified by the film's success in Paris. The main strength of this whimsical tale of two angels descending on a modern and crumbling Berlin, is the masterful black-and-white photography of the great 75-year-old Henri Alekan.

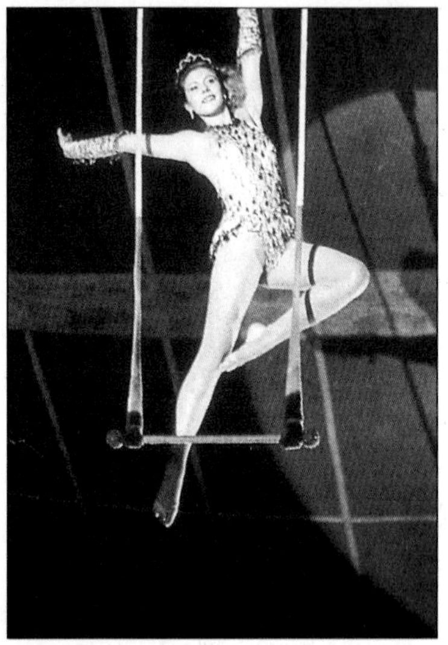

Solveig Dommartin in Wenders' film.

A mad 'Fatal Attraction' stirs controversy

New York, 18 September
Adrian Lyne's *Fatal Attraction* from producers Sherry Lansing and Stanley Jaffe is causing a huge controversy. The story is unremarkable: successful executive Michael Douglas, happily married to Anne Archer, falls into the trap of a one-night stand with sophisticated Glenn Close when his wife is away. He thinks the terms are clear, but she clings on, gradually revealing herself as some kind of dangerous lunatic. It's a terrific melodrama, expertly put together, with steamy sex, tension, and goodies and baddies nicely delineated. However, a large body of opinion believes the Close character makes the film deeply suspect, and feminists are picketing. Others see it as a metaphor for AIDS and a warning against promiscuity. What *is* clear is that box-office tills will keep ringing.

Dan Gallagher (Douglas) comforts a distraught, suicidal Alex Forrest (Close).

Berenger watches over Mimi Rogers

New York, 9 October
In *Someone to Watch Over Me*, plainclothes man Tom Berenger must protect Park Avenue heiress Mimi Rogers from sinister death threats. He is a happily-married ordinary Joe, she's single and high society. They fall in love. Ridley Scott has shaped a stylish, unusual and gripping film from this premise.

Tom Berenger and Mimi Rogers.

Attenborough salutes Biko and Woods

New York, 6 November
Richard Attenborough brings his customary epic, *Gandhi*-style treatment to *Cry Freedom*. Kevin Kline is excellent as the crusading South African journalist Donald Woods, forced to flee after the death of his black activist friend Steve Biko (Denzel Washington). The movie plays like an old-fashioned escape adventure, missing its opportunities, but at least the anti-*apartheid* message is clear. It has been banned by the South African government.

Twenty thousand mourners gather to hear the address at Steve Biko's funeral.

Spielberg, Bertolucci share Chinese spoils

New York, 9 December
By coincidence, two recent films by leading directors have dealt with 20th-century China, although they are vastly different in subject and approach. Bernardo Bertolucci's *The Last Emperor* tells the life story of the last of the Manchu dynasty, covering nearly 60 years, while Steven Spielberg's *Empire of the Sun* concentrates on the period of the Japanese invasion in World War II, and the experiences of a young boy in a prisoner-of-war camp.

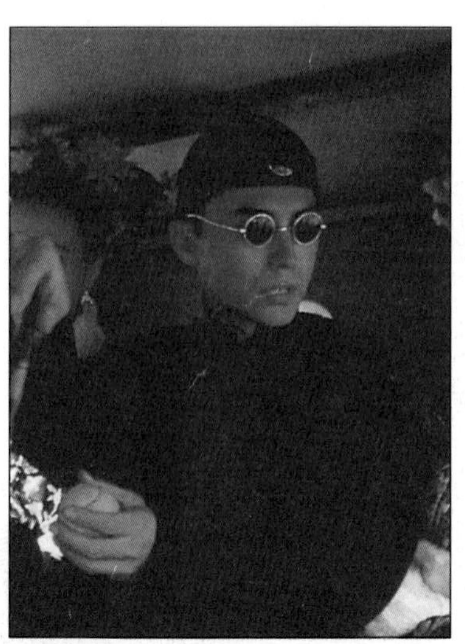

John Lone, the last emperor.

Christian Bale in ***Empire of the Sun**.*

Raucous young Emily Lloyd has star quality

An anarchic Emily Lloyd tormenting her father (Geoffrey Hutchings).

London, 2 December
Sixteen-year-old Emily Lloyd has already captivated audiences at the Cannes Film Festival with her performance in *Wish You Were Here* as a defiantly unruly and sexually precocious teenager ruffling the prim respectability of a seaside town in drab Fifties Britain. Now her clarion cry of "Up yer bum!" and determined public discussion of "willies" looks set to wow cinema audiences on both sides of the Atlantic. Based on Paul Bailey's biography of brothel-keeper Cynthia Payne and directed by David Leland, *Wish You Were Here* pokes pointed fun at the puritanical British bourgeoisie.

Moonbeams light Cher in 'Italian' comedy

Cher and Nicolas Cage are a pair of volatile, Italian-American lovers.

New York, 16 December
Director Norman Jewison has set out to make an old-fashioned fairy tale of love at first sight in the manner of Lubitsch or Capra. *Moonstruck* is set in the Italian section of New York and stars Cher as a widowed accountant who accepts a proposal of marriage from dull businessman Danny Aiello and then falls head over heels for his volatile baker brother Nicolas Cage. Cher's accent seems located more in Little Venice, California than Little Italy and the relentless emphasis on pasta and vino threaten to turn this romantic comedy into a compendium of clichés, but it charms nonetheless.

Fellini's touching reminiscences charm

Paris, 23 December
Conceived by Federico Fellini as a tribute to the 50th anniversary of the Cinecittà studios, *Intervista* is more of a self-homage from a director who has earned such a right. While in the process of making a film of Kafka's *Amerika*, the maestro, interviewed by a Japanese TV crew, reminisces about his first visit to the studio as a young reporter, lightly balancing illusion and reality. The director then takes the Japanese, and Marcello Mastroianni, on a nostalgic visit to Anita Ekberg's house in the country. Thus follows a moving reunion between the two stars of *La Dolce Vita*, changed by time, who watch a scene from the film together.

Federico Fellini appears in his own mix of fact and fantasy, ***Intervista.***

Verbal pyrotechnics from Robin Williams

Chicago, 23 December
Stand-up comedian and TV's *Mork and Mindy* star Robin Williams, in his seventh feature film, *Good Morning, Vietnam*, now has a vehicle guaranteeing him a wider audience. Director Barry Levinson has turned to Vietnam for his subject but, this time, to satirize the buffoon-like stupidity of the top brass back in the comfort of their headquarters and, while not eschewing poignancy, to raise a barrel of laughs, largely provided by his star. Williams is (real-life) forces DJ Adrian Cronauer, and dazzles with his Danny Kaye-like and irreverent verbal pyrotechnics that win the devotion of the boys on the battlefield and provoke fury among their superiors.

Robin Williams as the irreverent radio disc jockey, Adrian Cronauer.

IN VIETNAM
THE WIND
DOESN'T BLOW
IT SUCKS
BORN TO KILL
Stanley Kubrick's
FULL
METAL
JACKET

Army training and war: harsh view.

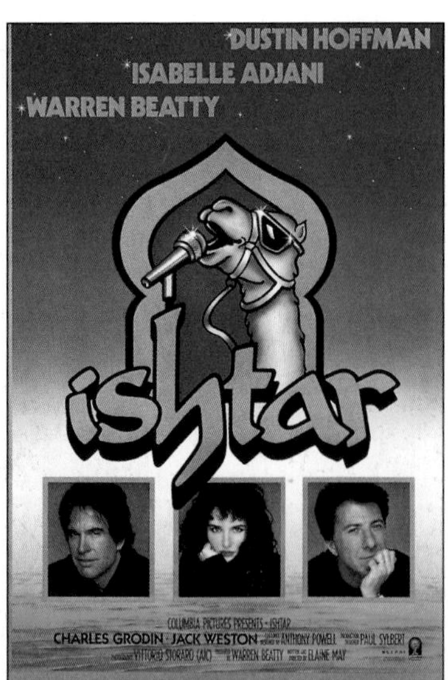
DUSTIN HOFFMAN
ISABELLE ADJANI
WARREN BEATTY
ishtar
CHARLES GRODIN · JACK WESTON

A multi-million-dollar floperoo!

*Joan Cusack (standing), Holly Hunter and Albert Brooks in **Broadcast News**.*

*Julie Walters (left), John Shrapnel, Shirley Stelfox: **Personal Services.***

*Lindsay Crouse in David Mamet's debut film, **House of Games**.*

THE
LOST BOYS
Being wild is in their Blood.

Biker-vampires Jason Patric, Corey Haim, Dianne Wiest, Kiefer Sutherland.

MOONSTRUCK
CHER · NICOLAS CAGE
METRO-GOLDWYN-MAYER PRESENTS A PATRICK PALMER-NORMAN JEWISON PRODUCTION
A NORMAN JEWISON FILM
"MOONSTRUCK" STARRING VINCENT GARDENIA OLYMPIA DUKAKIS AND DANNY AIELLO MUSIC COMPOSED AND ADAPTED BY DICK HYMAN
PRODUCTION DESIGNER PHILIP ROSENBERG COSTUME DESIGNER THEONI V. ALDREDGE DIRECTOR OF PHOTOGRAPHY DAVID WATKIN FILM EDITOR LOU LOMBARDO
ASSOCIATE PRODUCER BONNIE PALEF WRITTEN BY JOHN PATRICK SHANLEY PRODUCED BY PATRICK PALMER & NORMAN JEWISON
DIRECTED BY NORMAN JEWISON

Director Norman Jewison struck gold with this NY-based romantic comedy.

Steve Martin, a modern Cyrano de Bergerac, with Daryl Hannah in ***Roxanne****.*

Issiaka Kane, Aoua Sangare: Souleymane Cissé's ***Yeelen (Brightness)*** *(Mali).*

Forest Whitaker as the legendary Charlie Parker in Clint Eastwood's ***Bird****.*

David Hemblen, Gabrielle Rose in Atom Egoyan's ***Family Viewing*** *(Canada).*

AL CAPONE.
He ruled Chicago
with absolute power.
No one could touch him.
No one could stop him.
Until Eliot Ness
and a small force of men
swore they'd bring
him down.
THE UNTOUCHABLES
PARAMOUNT PICTURES PRESENTS AN ART LINSON PRODUCTION A BRIAN DE PALMA FILM
THE UNTOUCHABLES KEVIN COSTNER CHARLES MARTIN SMITH ANDY GARCIA
ROBERT DE NIRO as AL CAPONE and SEAN CONNERY as MALONE
Music by ENNIO MORRICONE Visual Consultant PATRIZIA VON BRANDENSTEIN Art Director WILLIAM A. ELLIOTT
Director of Photography STEPHEN H. BURUM, A.S.C. Written by DAVID MAMET Produced by ART LINSON Directed by BRIAN DE PALMA
R RESTRICTED
PANAVISION
READ THE IVY BOOK.
DOLBY STEREO
A PARAMOUNT PICTURE

De Palma's bloody but stylish feature about FBI man Eliot Ness (Costner).

1988

1987 Academy Awards, Shrine Auditorium, 11 April

Best Film:	*The Last Emperor* (dir: Bernardo Bertolucci)
Best Director:	Bernardo Bertolucci
Best Actor:	Michael Douglas *(Wall Street)*
Best Actress:	Cher *(Moonstruck)*
Best Supp. Actor:	Sean Connery *(The Untouchables)*
Best Supp. Actress:	Olympia Dukakis *(Moonstruck)*

Paris, 6 January
The Madeleine Renaud-Jean-Louis Barrault theater company is presenting a play written and directed by filmmaker Eric Rohmer.

Avoriaz, 24 January
The festival's main prize has been awarded to the American director Jack Sholder for *The Hidden*.

Paris, 7 February
Opening of the Paris Video Library. The public can now consult a databank of images on individual video screens. Films related to the capital will also be screened.

New York, 20 February
With *The Unbearable Lightness of Being*, Philip Kaufman has made an intelligent and faithful adaptation of Milan Kundera's novel. The film, which stars Daniel Day Lewis, Juliette Binoche, and Lena Olin, is now on release.

Berlin, 23 February
Chinese director Zhang Yimou's *Red Sorghum* has been awarded the Golden Bear at this year's festival.

France, 20 March
At this year's Women's Film Festival in Créteil there were over 100 films from 20 countries. A special tribute was paid to Agnes Varda, whose diptych on Jane Birkin was chosen to open and close the festival. Among festival highlights was a retrospective of nine of Dominique Sanda's films. Spectators were also able to see Anglo-American actress Ida Lupino's work as a director.

San Francisco, 19 March
A hypnotic documentary called *The Thin Blue Line* world premiered last night as part of the San Francisco Film Festival. The film, directed by Errol Morris, shows the bizarre aspects of a real-life murder case through the words of the actual participants – Randall Adams (convicted) and David Harris (suspect).

New York, 22 April
Crown publishers have just brought out a new book which they refer to as "a tour de force history of the American film industry." Titled *The Hollywood Story*, it was written by Joel Finler, an American movie historian currently living in London.

Paris, 7 June
Canal Plus has signed an agreement with cinema exhibitors restricting the screening of films before 11 p.m. (instead of 10 p.m. as previously).

Paris, 23 June
Producer Daniel Toscan du Plantier has been elected as the head of Unifrance Film, the industry organization which promotes French films.

Hollywood, 7 August
The scriptwriters' strike has come to an end after a five-month battle. Losses to the film studios are estimated at $150 million.

Los Angeles, 10 August
Francis Ford Coppola pays tribute to American business spirit and optimism with *Tucker: The Man and His Dream*. Jeff Bridges plays an independent car-builder determined to break the monopoly of the big Detroit firms in this film based on a true story.

London, 29 August
Release of Jonathan Demme's *Married to the Mob*, with Michelle Pfeiffer and Dean Stockwell. A comedy about the Mafia and its legendary bad taste.

London, 15 September
Prince Charles has opened England's new temple to the cinema, the Museum of the Moving Image (MOMI). The 3,000 square-meter museum is, like the National Film Theatre, situated under Waterloo Bridge. The MOMI offers visitors a chronological history of the cinema, illustrated by astonishing sets and machines.

Greece, 27 September
Under the aegis of the European Year of Cinema and Television, authors from the EEC have adopted the text of a European audio-visual charter. It is a real declaration of television and film authors' rights.

Los Angeles, 30 September
Bird is a departure for director Clint Eastwood. It is not a Western but a sober and sad film on the life of musician Charlie Parker (played by Forest Whitaker). Eastwood avoids the clichés so often encountered in jazz films.

Paris, 26 October
Jean-Jacques Annaud's latest film, *The Bear* (*l'Ours*), has drawn 3.5 million spectators in its first week of release here. The maker of *Quest for Fire* has told his charming and unusual tale from the bear's point of view using natural sounds and no dialogue.

New York, 29 October
Release of Woody Allen's *Another Woman*, starring Gena Rowlands, Mia Farrow and Gene Hackman, a somber drama reflecting the fears and regrets of a 50-year-old woman.

Marseilles, 31 October
Bertrand Blier has started shooting his new film, *Trop belle pour toi!* (*Too Beautiful for You*), starring Gérard Depardieu, Josiane Balasko and Carole Bouquet.

Paris, 19 November
Eric Serra's score for Luc Besson's *le Grand bleu* (*The Big Blue*) has won the prize for the best film music at the Victoires de la musique.

Berlin, 28 November
Over 300 million viewers watched last night's televised coverage of the first European Oscars from the Theatre des Westerns. Krzysztof Kieslowski's controversial entry *A Short Film About Killing* was voted Best Film. Wim Wenders won Best Director for *Wings of Desire*, while the Best Actor and Actress prizes went to Max von Sydow (*Pelle the Conqueror*) and Carmen Maura (*Women on the Verge of a Nervous Breakdown*). Louis Malle won the prize for Best Script for *Au revoir les enfants*. Ingmar Bergman was given a standing ovation as he received a special life achievement award.

Paris, 8 December
The Louis Delluc Prize has been awarded to Michel Deville's *la Lectrice*, starring Miou-Miou.

New York, 16 December
The New York Film Critics have voted Lawrence Kasdan's *Accidental Tourist* the best film of 1988.

Paris, 30 December
Le Monde has published an interview with Jean-Luc Godard which quotes him as saying, "The cinema is dead."

Hollywood, 31 December
Disney studios have reached almost 20 percent of all annual takings with three big successes: *Who Framed Roger Rabbit*, *Three Men and a Baby* and *Good Morning, Vietnam*.

Los Angeles, 31 December
Fifteen million videotapes of *E.T.* have been sold: a record number.

DEATHS

London, 7 January
Trevor Howard

Los Angeles, 7 March
Divine (Harris Glenn Milstead)

New York, 12 July
Joshua Logan

California, 5 August
Ralph Meeker

West Germany, 5 September
Gert Froebe

Spain, 20 September
Roy Kinnear

Hollywood, 1 October
Lucien Ballard

California, 31 October
John Houseman

Italy, 27 November
John Carradine

California, 27 December
Hal Ashby

Bruce Willis came to mega-stardom this year playing a cop who single-handedly outwits a gang of violent international thugs. John McTiernan directed with finesse.

Twelve terrorists. One cop.
The odds are against John McClane...
That's just the way he likes it.

BRUCE WILLIS
DIE HARD
TWENTIETH CENTURY FOX Presents A GORDON COMPANY/SILVER PICTURES Production A JOHN McTIERNAN Film BRUCE WILLIS DIE HARD
ALAN RICKMAN ALEXANDER GODUNOV BONNIE BEDELIA Music by MICHAEL KAMEN Visual Effects Produced by RICHARD EDLUND Film Editors FRANK J. URIOSTE, A.C.E.
and JOHN F. LINK Production Designer JACKSON DeGOVIA Director of Photography JAN De BONT Executive Producer CHARLES GORDON Screenplay By JEB STUART and STEVEN E. de SOUZA
Based on the novel by RODERICK THORP Produced by LAWRENCE GORDON and JOEL SILVER Directed by JOHN McTIERNAN
PANAVISION
Color by DeLuxe
Read The Fawcett Paperback.
DOLBY STEREO IN SELECTED THEATRES
20th CENTURY FOX
COMING THIS JULY

Hilarious farce strikes at the bourgeoisie

The working-class family of rogues and thieves in this wildly entertaining film.

Paris, 3 February
Etienne Chatiliez, a former director of quirky French commercials, has made a tremendous feature debut with *Life is a Long Quiet River*, one of the funniest and most incisive comedies for many a year. The plot, poking fun at class differences, involves two babies being switched at birth. One infant goes to the Le Quesnoys, middle-class, wealthy and respectable; the other is brought up by the unemployed, illiterate and semi-criminal Groseilles family. When the error is discovered, the former family wishes to buy back their son, a situation that unleashes chaos in their well-ordered household. Apart from Daniel Gélin, the excellent cast is not well-known.

Waters in world of rock and beehive hair

Velma Von Tussle (Debbie Harry, left) and Amber (Colleen Fitzpatrick).

Los Angeles, 26 February
John Waters, a camp underground favorite for years, famed for his outrageous bad taste in films such as *Pink Flamingos* (1972) and *Polyester* (1981) starring Divine, the director's drag "prima donna", has now made a mainstream movie. *Hairspray* is a crazy, good-natured, inoffensively satirical 60s musical, with lively dance numbers and a nostalgic soundtrack. Both Waters and former hairdresser Divine, who plays the plump heroine's fat mother, hail from Baltimore, which the director has characterized as "The Hairdo Capital of the World". There are certainly plenty of beehives bobbing on *The Corny Collins Show*, the teens' TV favorite.

Three daddies for one baby

Coline Serreau's French box-office smash, *Three Men and a Cradle*, remade as *Three Men and a Baby*, is proving equally popular here. Directed by Leonard Nimoy, the comedy plot concerns three bachelors (Tom Selleck, Steve Guttenberg, Ted Danson) who find a baby on their doorstep...

'The Last Emperor' matches the Oscar record set by 'Gigi'

Los Angeles, 11 April
In what could be called the year of the Chinese, *The Last Emperor* won all nine Oscars for which it was nominated – the first time this has happened since *Gigi* in 1958. Although it is the first Western film made almost entirely in the new China, and although the majority of the cast is Chinese, its Oscar-winning director (Bernardo Bertolucci), cameraman (Vittorio Storaro) and editor (Gabriella Cristiani) are Italians; the producer (Jeremy Thomas) and co-screenwriter (Mark Peploe) are British; one of the stars is an Irish-born Englishman (Peter O'Toole), and one of the composers is Japanese (Ryuichi Sakamoto). The film is a long (163 minutes), fascinating, sumptuous epic following the life of Pu Yi from the time he succeeds to the throne of China at the age of three, to his dotage as a gardener in a Peking park. *The Last Emperor* so swept the boards that the only other picture to take away more than one award was Norman Jewison's *Moonstruck*, for which Cher as a drab widow transformed into a passionate and attractive woman, and Olympia Dukakis as her warm mother, gained the Best Actress and Best Supporting Actress prizes respectively. The Best Actor was Michael Douglas for his portrayal of a ruthless stockbroker in Oliver Stone's *Wall Street*. First-time nominee and winner of the Best Supporting Actor Oscar was Sean Connery as the incorruptible Irish cop in Brian De Palma's *The Untouchables*. Denmark won the Foreign Film award with *Babette's Feast*, a superb adaptation of the Karen Blixen story about a French *cordon bleu* cook, who provides an austere remote Jutland community with a gastronomic treat. A cinematic feast directed by Gabriel Axel.

Michael Douglas in ***Wall Street.***

Stéphane Audran as Babette.

Writers' strike continues to hurt

Los Angeles, 12 April
The strike by the Writers Guild of America is now in its sixth week, and is really hitting the movie and television industries hard. Union TV writers halted their work on the script for last night's Academy Awards ceremony, and CBS had to shelve two new shows. The size of the pickets outside studios reveals a solidarity of the writers that did not exist in 1985 when the 9,000-member guild caved in after a half-hearted two-week strike. Among those walking the picket line in front of the 20th Century-Fox studios has been the actress Patty Duke, president of the Screen Actors Guild. Also out protesting were James L. Brooks and Albert Brooks, the director and star of *Broadcast News*, who stood, ironically, beneath a billboard advertising their Fox movie. The main point at issue is that producers are seeking a two-tier pay system in which first year TV writers would receive less money. They also want to define low-budget films as those costing less than $8 million. For low-budget movies, writers can be paid roughly half of the average $40,000 minimum fee for writing a movie treatment and screenplay. Both sides seemed surprised that the negotiations ended in a strike.

'The Big Blue': a dream is realized

Jean Reno, the rival diver who pushes himself beyond the limits of endurance.

Paris, 11 May
Shown out of competition this year at Cannes, *The Big Blue* was greeted coolly by the critics, but in the movie theaters where it is already playing, huge young audiences are welcoming it enthusiastically. It has always been a dream of the 29-year-old Luc Besson to make a film inspired by the life of Jacques Mayol, a man who dedicated his life to deep-sea diving without an aqua-lung. Although Besson was born in Paris, his richest experiences have been at the coast. *The Big Blue* was shot over nine months, mostly in Greece and Sicily, and is divided into two parts. The first part, in black and white, evokes the childhood of the hero diving off the coast of a Greek island; the second, in color, follows the adult Mayol attempting to beat the world diving record without oxygen. He feels at one with the creatures of the sea, and talks to dolphins. The role, which was originally refused by both Christopher Lambert and Mel Gibson, is taken by the unknown Jean-Marc Barr, his girlfriend, a New York insurance agent, is played by Rosanna Arquette, and Jean Reno is his boyhood friend and rival. The magnificent underwater photography in 'Scope is counterpointed by the music of Eric Serra.

The delightful adventures of a young boy inhabiting a man's body

I ♥ NY
OREO
*Man-boy Tom Hanks (right) with his best friend (Jared Rushton) in **Big**.*

New York, 3 June
Penny Marshall's *Big* has to be the best body-swap movie made in anyone's memory. This is fairy-tale time (though with a wry, poignant sting in the tail) as a young boy fervently asks the genie in a fairground wishing machine to make him a man. The wish is granted and he wakes up as Tom Hanks, though inside the man's body the boy remains. The movie is superbly and subtly scripted and directed to avoid the pitfalls of a plot in which the boy-man becomes, among other things, romantically involved (with Elizabeth Perkins). Hanks is an absolute and convincing delight, whether gleefully enjoying himself in the F.A.O. Schwartz toy store, or attacking a baby ear of corn at a cocktail party in some bewilderment. This has to be the summer's "big" one.

UN FILM DE CLINT EASTWOOD
BIRD
With *Bird*, Clint Eastwood ventures into new territory as a director. A long (161 min.), brooding and enthralling bio of the great jazz saxophonist, Charlie Parker (nickname: Bird), the film boasts a terrific central performance from Forest Whitaker.

The profound, political and tragic are rewarded

The lonely Molly (Johdi May) with black companions in ***A World Apart.***

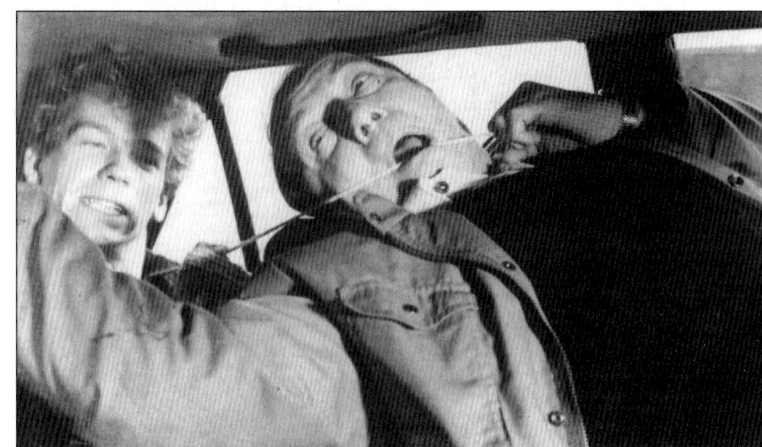
Miroslaw Baka commits a senseless murder in ***A Short Film About Killing.***

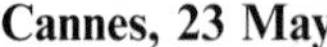
Cannes, 23 May
Three ambitious films dealing with political and ethical issues were presented with the top prizes at this year's Cannes Festival. The Golden Palm was awarded to *Pelle the Conqueror*, a moving and impressively photographed epic about the exploitation of farm workers in turn-of-the-century Denmark. Directed by the Dane Bille August, a former cinematographer, it stars Max Von Sydow. This is a sensational double for Denmark after the triumph of *Babette's Feast* at the Oscars exactly a month ago. The winner of the Special Jury Prize, Chris Menges' British film *A World Apart*, is a powerful indictment of *apartheid* in South Africa delivered through the true story of two of its brave opponents. The jury thought Krzysztof Kieslowski the best director for his *A Short Film About Killing*, the shock entry of the festival. This work presents in graphic detail the story of the senseless and brutal murder of a taxi driver by a young and aimless drifter, and the man's subsequent arrest and execution.

Pelle Hvenegaard, Max Von Sydow.

Hoskins competes with cartoon characters

Bob Hoskins and Jessica Rabbit.

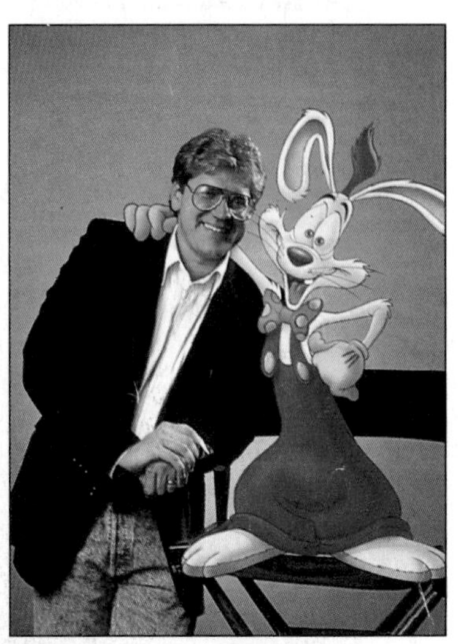
Director Zemeckis and Roger.

Hollywood, 22 June
Bob Hoskins has one of the most intriguing acting assignments of his career in *Who Framed Roger Rabbit*, playing a down-at-heel detective on the trail of a murderer with a small army of cartoon characters as his co-stars. There's nothing new about combining live action with animation – Gene Kelly capered with cartoon mouse Jerry in *Anchors Aweigh* in 1945 – but there has been nothing quite like this Spielberg-Disney production, directed by Robert Zemeckis, whose state-of-the-art integration of animated and real-life figures has cost $70 million. The picture's animation director Richard Williams has said, "We were essentially making two films – one live action and one animated – to be fused together into one film by the optical department of Industrial Light and Magic." The manic Roger Rabbit is voiced by Charles Fleischer and married to an animated seductress called Jessica with a mind-blowing figure and the sexy tones of an uncredited Kathleen Turner. As Jessica explains, "I'm not bad, I'm just drawn that way."

Macho Bruce an urban Tarzan for the 80s

Los Angeles, 15 July
Bruce Willis, who made his Hollywood debut last year in *Blind Date*, is set for stardom after his gritty performance as super-tough New York cop John McLane in *Die Hard*. In the hands of commercials king John McTiernan, *Die Hard* explodes on the screen as a cross between *Lethal Weapon* and *The Towering Inferno* as Willis does battle with a team of international terrorists holed up with a group of hostages on the upper stories of a Los Angeles high-rise. The stunts and special effects, coordinated by Robert Edlund, are non-stop as Willis plays a deadly game of cat and mouse with the chief heavy, smooth British classical actor Alan Rickman. These days in Hollywood the best villains have British accents.

Bruce Willis protecting his estranged wife (Bonnie Bedelia) from the carnage.

Chiller offers two for the price of one

Doctors Beverly and Elliot Mantle (Jeremy Irons) escort Genevieve Bujold.

New York, 23 September
David Cronenberg is not a director for the squeamish. In *Dead Ringers* he returns to his obsession with, and seeming disgust at, the human body. Jeremy Irons plays the dual role of telepathic gynecologist twin brothers whose relationship is disturbed when they encounter childless actress Genevieve Bujold, who has three cervixes. As the delicate balance between the twins is fatally frayed, she realizes that she has been making love not to one man but two. This is a deeply morbid movie, black with Cronenberg's association of sex with bodily decay and bright with the harsh light refracted from the clinical instruments on which his camera lingers with baleful relish.

Falling hook, line and sinker for Wanda

London, 14 October
The comedy hit of the year looks like being *A Fish Called Wanda*, directed by 78-year-old Ealing Studios veteran Charles Crichton. It's a caper movie in which tight-assed British barrister John Cleese becomes entangled with sexy con artist Jamie Lee Curtis and her weird boyfriend Kevin Kline, a psychopathic burglar with ludicrous intellectual pretensions and a taste for live fish. The combination of American talent with *Monty Python* graduates Cleese and Michael Palin and Crichton's deft skills (he directed the 1951 classic *The Lavender Hill Mob*) has produced an off-beat comedy with some hard edges – at one point the gang of thieves tries to give an old woman a fatal heart attack by killing her pet corgis.

Jamie Lee Curtis and John Cleese: hilarious Anglo-American cooperation.

Guttersnipe in tough tale of street life

New York, 9 October
Indian director Mira Nair's *Salaam Bombay!* arrives here already covered in awards. Deservedly so, for Miss Nair makes of her sad and terrible tale – a 12-year-old boy adrift in Bombay lives the life of the street among pimps, prostitutes, drug peddlers and poverty – a thoroughly absorbing pageant. She manages some humor and flirts attractively with melodrama, getting wonderful performances from a cast of largely amateur players. Krishna, the child at the center of the action, is remarkably played by the irresistible Shafiq Syed, literally plucked from the gutters of the city for the film.

Shafiq Syed: ***Salaam Bombay!***

Jodie Foster in controversial rape movie

KGRR
TV3

Rape victim Jodie Foster hounded by the press in Kaplan's ***The Accused.***

Boston, 14 October
Jodie Foster, one of Hollywood's most determined and talented customers, is once again courting controversy, this time as the victim of gang rape in *The Accused*, directed by Jonathan Kaplan. Public prosecutor Kelly McGillis cuts a deal with the defense – Foster was drunk, stoned and dressed like a hooker, and one of the three accused is a clean-cut college boy. But Foster rebels, and McGillis brings new charges of solicitation against the men who witnessed the rape, in the games room of a bar, and did nothing to stop it. The picture tackles the current issue of whether a woman who flirts, openly displaying her sexuality, invites rape even when she says no, as if by exhibiting active desire she relinquishes control over her body. The rape itself is not shown until near the end of the film, and then in an unblinking detail which some critics have suggested will turn the cinema audience itself into voyeurs. Nonetheless, this is a brave film in which Kaplan and producers Stanley Jaffe and Sherry Lansing (who were responsible for *Fatal Attraction*) tread a fine line between social concern, feminism and exploitation.

▷

Scorsese's 'Christ' is pilloried by the Church

*Martin Scorsese's controversial **The Last Temptation of Christ**: Willem Dafoe.*

Paris, 22 October
Wherever it has been shown, Martin Scorsese's *The Last Temptation of Christ* has caused controversy and sometimes violent demonstrations, whether in Protestant America and Great Britain, or in Catholic Italy. In America, there were pickets outside the movie theaters where it was showing, and militant religious groups threatened to use bombs. After similar protests at the Venice Film Festival, and a condemnation from the Vatican, trouble has now flared up in France. Five Catholics set fire to a Paris cinema for daring to show the film. What has caused such passions to be aroused? Principally, it is the dream-on-the-cross sequence, during which Jesus imagines himself making love to Mary Magdalene, and dreams of the companionship of marriage and a family. Scorsese wanted to show Christ as a man suffering human doubts and desires, and to present us with a Christ for the 80s. Far from being blasphemous, this portrait is reconcilable with the Bible's notion of the Son of God made man.

Adjani and Camille Claudel a perfect match

Isabelle Adjani as Camille Claudel.

Paris, 7 December
After appearing opposite Warren Beatty and Dustin Hoffman in the disastrous *Ishtar* last year, Isabelle Adjani has made a glorious return to French cinema in the title role of *Camille Claudel.* The sister of the writer Paul Claudel, Camille studied sculpture with Auguste Rodin, who recognized her remarkable artistic talent. But she became the victim of 19th-century bourgeois social codes, and descended into madness. Cinematographer Bruno Nuytten's directing debut brilliantly shows the agony and ecstasy of creation. The film, above all, has Adjani giving the performance of her life, matched by Gérard Depardieu as a powerful Rodin, her master and lover.

Ingenious thriller: avoid if claustrophobic!

Johanna Ter Steege in George Sluizer's brilliant claustrophobic thriller.

Amsterdam, 27 January
Holland's new year kicks off with a thriller from George Sluizer that guarantees 106 minutes of nail-biting. *The Vanishing*, whose theme is that of obsession, particularly the psychopathic, has one of the most truly shocking climaxes of any film, and comes with a "don't tell your friends" plea. The plot has a young Dutch couple motoring in France. At a motorway stop, in broad daylight and surrounded by people, she goes to fetch a drink and is never seen again. The rest of the film is taken up with his search for her... Brilliantly constructed and acted, it's a must-see for fans of the genre.

Alan Parker confronts ugly side of America

New York, 9 December
Feisty British director Alan Parker takes on the Ku Klux Klan in *Mississippi Burning*. Two FBI agents, tight-lipped play-it-by-the-book type Willem Dafoe and more instinctive Southern lawman Gene Hackman, head up a government probe into the disappearance of three civil rights workers in Mississippi during the summer of 1964. There's a strong period feel and a persuasive performance from Hackman as the former small-town sheriff who figures out how to crack the case. But the film's concentration on the efforts of two white men, and the marginalization of blacks in the story, has brought accusations of racism which Parker strongly denies.

Gene Hackman (right) and Willem Dafoe, investigating officers on the job.

'Rain Man' winner for Hoffman and Cruise

Raymond Babbitt (Dustin Hoffman, left) and brother Charlie (Tom Cruise).

Hollywood, 16 December
The combined salaries of the two stars of Barry Levinson's *Rain Man*, Dustin Hoffman and Tom Cruise, was around $9 million, though few doubt it was money well spent. They play contrasting brothers – unfeeling money-mad yuppie Cruise, autistic Hoffman – who get to know each other during a four-day trip from Cincinnati to L.A. in a '49 Buick sedan. The acting is a tour de force for two hands, one young and one old; Cruise skillfully manages the change from selfish to loving, and Hoffman's year-long research into autism shows in every detail of his funny and touching performance.

Audacious casting in 'Dangerous Liaisons'

Valmont (John Malkovich) seducing Madame de Tourvel (Michelle Pfeiffer).

New York, 21 December
In the aristocratic world of 18th-century France a ruthless marquise enlists the help of a like-minded count to wreak sexual havoc in the lives of those around them. Adapted from Christopher Hampton's play, itself based on the classic French epistolary novel of the period, *Dangerous Liaisons* is an elegant study of seduction, desire and control with a predominantly American cast. Glenn Close is the marquise whose schemes lead to the death of her ally, the reptilian Vicomte de Valmont, played by John Malkovich. Also prominent is Michelle Pfeiffer as the predatory Valmont's pious victim.

'Feel-good' fantasy of a working girl

New York, 21 December
Director Mike Nichols has made a Capraesque, fairy-tale comedy of modern Wall Street manners with *Working Girl*. The wish fulfillment element of the movie is a throwback to the 30s, proving that in an age of violence, audiences still welcome a comedy romance in which not a drop of ketchup is spilt. The working girl is secretary Melanie Griffith, who commutes from Staten Island daily to slave for a gorgon boss (Sigourney Weaver). When the latter goes away for a while, Melanie spots the opportunity to climb the corporate ladder by deviously taking her place, and ensnaring Harrison Ford in the process. Delightful stuff which should pay dividends for Fox.

Brainy secretary Melanie Griffith and her ally Harrison in ***Working Girl***.

Housefrau makes magic in Mojave desert

New York, 22 December
The German director Percy Adlon, whose work, covering a wide variety of subject matter, is much admired in Europe, has made his first film in America. One hopes that it won't be his last. Casting his German star, the flamboyantly overweight Marianne Sägebrecht, to lead an otherwise all-American cast, notably Jack Palance and C.C.H. Pounder, he has come up with the truly magical *Bagdad Cafe*. Sägebrecht is a Bavarian tourist, dumped in the Mojave desert by her unpleasant husband. She finds her way to the dilapidated motel of the title, settles in, and transforms the place and its no-hope inhabitants. An original, funny and tender collector's piece.

Marianne Sägebrecht and C.C.H. Pounder, together in the Mojave Desert.

In This House... If You've Seen One Ghost... You Haven't Seen Them All.
Michael Keaton is
BEETLEJUICE
The Name In Laughter From The Hereafter
The Geffen Company presents a Tim Burton film "Beetlejuice" Alec Baldwin Geena Davis Jeffrey Jones Catherine O'Hara Winona Ryder
and Michael Keaton as Beetlejuice music by Danny Elfman director of photography Thomas Ackerman story by Michael McDowell & Larry Wilson
screenplay by Michael McDowell and Warren Skaaren produced by Michael Bender, Larry Wilson and Richard Hashimoto directed by Tim Burton
PG PARENTAL GUIDANCE SUGGESTED
SOME MATERIAL MAY NOT BE SUITABLE FOR CHILDREN
Wild comedy-horror-fantasy directed by the imaginative Tim Burton.

Charlotte Gainsbourg plays Claude Miller's ***la Petite voleuse****.*

Australia's Yahoo Serious directed, played and wrote ***Young Einstein****.*

Richard Donner updated Dickens with ***Scrooged****, starring Bill Murray (above).*

l to r: Freda Dowie, Dean Williams, Angela Walsh and Lorraine Ashbourne in Terence Davies' haunting ***Distant Voices, Still Lives*** *(Great Britain).*

From Britain's Peter Greenaway: ***Drowning By Numbers****.*

EDDIE MURPHY
This summer, Prince Akeem discovers America.
COMING TO AMERICA
Murphy an African prince in NYC.

LUST. SEDUCTION. REVENGE.
THE GAME AS YOU'VE NEVER SEEN IT PLAYED BEFORE.
GLENN CLOSE
JOHN MALKOVICH
MICHELLE PFEIFFER
Dangerous
LIAISONS

Stephen Frears' splendid version.

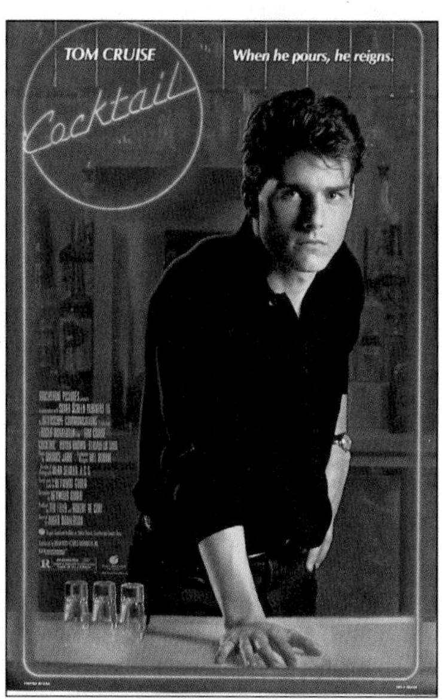
TOM CRUISE
When he pours, he reigns.
Cocktail

Strictly for Tom Cruise fans.

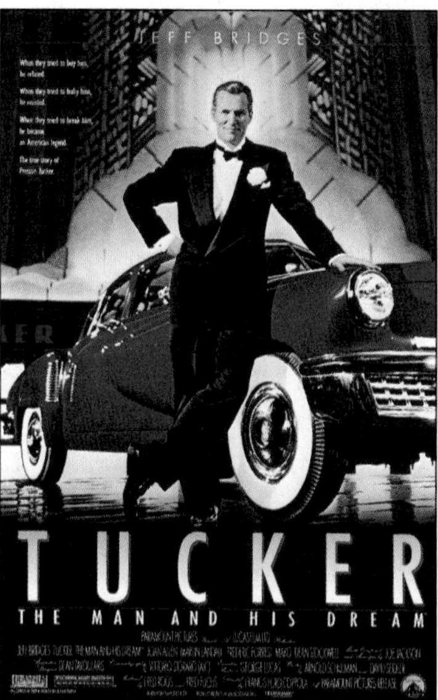
JEFF BRIDGES
TUCKER
THE MAN AND HIS DREAM

Coppola's homage to car pioneer.

KEN RUSSELL'S
LAIR
WHITE
WORM

Grotesque, crude and unpleasant!

Isabelle Adjani as sculptress ***Clamille Claudel****; Gérard Depardieu as Rodin.*

River Phoenix and Martha Plimpton in Sidney Lumet's ***Running on Empty****.*

Dan Aykroyd and Kim Basinger in ***My Stepmother is an Alien****.*

Pierre Dux with Miou-Miou, ***la Lectrice*** *of the title, in Michel Deville's film.*

Lena Olin: ***The Unbearable Lightness of Being*** *from Kundera's novel.*

1989

1988 Academy Awards, Dorothy Chandler Pavilion, 29 Mar.

Best Film:	*Rain Man* (dir: Barry Levinson)
Best Director:	Barry Levinson
Best Actor:	Dustin Hoffman *(Rain Man)*
Best Actress:	Jodie Foster *(The Accused)*
Best Supp. Actor:	Kevin Kline *(A Fish Called Wanda)*
Best Supp. Actress:	Geena Davis *(The Accidental Tourist)*

Japan, 10 January
Akira Kurosawa has begun shooting *Dreams*, an American-Japanese co-production. The movie presents a series of vignettes, one of which is played by director Martin Scorsese.

New York, 30 January
Premiere of the new print of *Gone With the Wind*, with the color completely restored.

Hollywood, 16 February
Jane Fonda has divorced Tom Hayden after 16 years of marriage. He is said to be having an affair with Morgan Fairchild, the former star of the TV series *Flamingo Road.*

Texas, 1 March
Randall Dale Adams, the central figure in *The Thin Blue Line*, saw his conviction overturned today in the Texas Court of Criminal Appeals.

Paris, 2 March
Tom Cruise, who has been in France to promote *Rain Man*, has canceled all his engagements and returned to the U.S. after a short stay in the American Hospital at Neuilly with the flu.

New York, 6 March
The Museum of Modern Art is paying tribute to French producer Marin Karmitz, head of MK2, with the screening of 10 films produced by him, including *Une affaire de femmes*, by Claude Chabrol.

London, 18 March
Terry Gilliam's startlingly innovative update of *Adventures of Baron Munchhausen*, rumored to have cost an excessive $45 million, opens today in London.

Paris, 3 April
Elizabeth Taylor was at the Automobile Club to promote "Passion", her new perfume for men. Five hundred journalists from 35 countries attended the reception which was covered by Mondovision.

Hollywood, 18 April
First day's shooting of *The Two Jakes*, directed by and starring Jack Nicholson. The film, Nicholson's third as director, is a sequel to Roman Polanski's film, *Chinatown.*

Paris, 19 May
Brigitte Bardot has agreed to return to the screen but in a very different role. She is to host a program on Channel 1 called *SOS* in defense of her four-legged friends, a cause she has espoused for the last 15 years.

Paris, 7 June
Release of *Little Vera*, a Russian film by Vassily Pitchoul, starring Natalia Negoda. It is an outspoken portrait of disaffected youth which could not have been made before the new era of *glasnost.*

Aspen, 26 June
Melanie Griffith has married Don Johnson, hero of television's *Miami Vice*, for the second time.

New York, 6 July
Errol Morris is reportedly "hurt and upset" by the case being brought against him by Randall Adams, the man he helped to release from death row. Mr. Adams, who has received six-figure offers from publishers and film companies, is trying to regain the rights to his story.

Los Angeles, 7 July
The recent run of fatal helicopter accidents on movie sets abroad is worrying industry professionals. Some say the insurance companies used by producers bear a share of the responsibility. According to a spokesman from West Coast Helicopters, pilots involved in accidents were often not stunt-qualified.

Los Angeles, 10 July
Mel Blanc, the actor-voice specialist, has died. Blanc provided the voices for over 3,000 animated cartoons during his 60-year career, including Bugs Bunny and Daffy Duck.

London, 25 July
Actor Rex Harrison was knighted today at Buckingham Palace. Asked how he felt during the investiture he replied, "It was a marvelous moment kneeling there and getting tapped on the shoulder."

Hollywood, 31 July
Allegations that actor Rob Lowe made a pornographic home-movie with an underage girl have shocked fans of the man until now considered Hollywood's hottest property.

Prague, 23 August
Former child star Shirley Temple arrived in Prague today. She appears to have already won the hearts of Czechoslovakians, who gave her a warm welcome at a party held in her honor. Miss Temple is here as the United States ambassador to Czechoslovakia.

Cannes, 5 October
Director, former critic and a cofounder of *Cahiers du Cinéma*, Jacques Doniol-Valcroze has died of a heart attack.

New York, 16 October
Release of *Crimes and Misdemeanors* directed by Woody Allen, the most pessimistic and misanthropic of all his films to date.

Paris, 8 November
Pop singer Vanessa Paradis makes her screen debut in Jean-Claude Brisseau's *Noce blanche.*

Sarasota, 19 November
Audrey Hepburn has opened the first Festival of French Films to be held in the U.S. The directors and actors of many of the films are present to introduce their work to the public. The French industry is hoping this will open new doors (at present French films represent only one percent of the market here). A special homage was paid to René Clément and Jeanne Moreau.

Hollywood, 25 November
The most holy sanctuary of American culture – film production – has fallen to the Japanese giant Sony. The corporation has acquired Columbia Pictures for $3 billion. Producers Jon Peters and Peter Guber are to head the Japanese owned studio. The industry is reeling under the shock of this news.

Paris, 6 December
Valmont, the latest film from Milos Forman, has opened here. This is the second adaptation of Choderlos de Laclos' 18th-century epistolary novel this year; the first was Steven Frears' *Dangerous Liaisons.*

Los Angeles, 10 December
Fox's blacker-than-black comedy, *The War of the Roses*, took the top spot this week, out-grossing *National Lampoon's Christmas Vacation.*

New York, 20 December
Director Costa-Gavras has turned his attention to the issue of Nazism. His newly released film *Music Box* concerns a woman lawyer who, defending her own father against charges of Nazi war crimes, must confront a dark and disturbing past. Jessica Lange plays the role.

DEATHS

Los Angeles, 3 February
John Cassavetes

Paris, 29 March
Bernard Blier

Los Angeles, 26 April
Lucille Ball

Rome, 30 April
Sergio Leone

Los Angeles, 2 July
Franklin J. Schaffner

England, 11 July
Laurence Olivier

New York, 22 September
Irving Berlin

Paris, 6 October
Bette Davis

Los Angeles, 16 October
Cornel Wilde

California, 16 December
Lee Van Cleef

Madrid, 16 December
Silvana Mangano

Phil Alden Robinson's ***Field of Dreams*** *was the year's blockbuster hit. Iowa farmer Kevin Costner's involvement with the ghosts of the Chicago White Sox made baseball tops.*

KEVIN • COSTNER
All his life, Ray Kinsella was searching for his dreams.
Then one day, his dreams came looking for him.
FIELD OF DREAMS
A GORDON COMPANY PRODUCTION A PHIL ALDEN ROBINSON FILM "FIELD OF DREAMS"
KEVIN COSTNER • AMY MADIGAN • JAMES EARL JONES • RAY LIOTTA • BURT LANCASTER BASED ON THE BOOK "SHOELESS JOE" BY W.P. KINSELLA
MUSIC BY JAMES HORNER DIRECTOR OF PHOTOGRAPHY JOHN LINDLEY PRODUCTION DESIGNER DENNIS GASSNER EXECUTIVE PRODUCER BRIAN FRANKISH
PRODUCERS LAWRENCE GORDON AND CHARLES GORDON WRITTEN FOR THE SCREEN AND DIRECTED BY PHIL ALDEN ROBINSON
PG PARENTAL GUIDANCE SUGGESTED
SOME MATERIAL MAY NOT BE SUITABLE FOR CHILDREN
ORIGINAL SOUNDTRACK ALBUM AVAILABLE ON NOVUS/RCA RECORDS LPs, CASSETTES AND CDs
A UNIVERSAL RELEASE
© 1989 UNIVERSAL CITY STUDIOS, INC.
PRINTED IN U.S.A.

Black South African ghetto could be Harlem

Thomas Mogotlane as 'Panic'.

London, 13 January
The cruel limitations placed on endeavor by South Africa's *apartheid* laws has resulted in a parochial and underdeveloped film industry. It is, therefore, quite an achievement for writer and director Oliver Schmitz (white) and writer-actor Thomas Mogotlane (black) to have made *Mapantsula* at all. Already seen at Cannes last year, it unveils a vivid picture of township life in Soweto. The main character, Panic (Mogotlane), an apolitical petty gangster, is finally forced to confront the political realities of the police state in which he lives. Low-budget but lively and revealing, the similarity in the habits and conditions of its underclass to that of Harlem is striking.

Almodóvar puts Spain on commercial map

Julieta Serrano (left), and Carmen Maura the woman on the verge...

Paris, 1 February
After having broken all box-office records in Spain, *Women on the Verge of a Nervous Breakdown* looks as though it might do the same in Paris and elsewhere. Although Pedro Almodóvar's previous picture, *Law of Desire*, did well last year, it was nothing compared to the impact of his seventh feature, which has really put Spain on the commercial map. The story focuses on Pepa (Carmen Maura), a volatile and attractive actress, pregnant by Ivan, her philandering lover who, like herself, dubs Hollywood movies. Unaware of her condition, he blithely abandons her via a farewell message on her answering machine. As all her efforts to contact him fail, Pepa grows totally distraught and hysterical, setting fire to her bed, and flinging the telephone out the window. Yet she is still able to help other women with their men problems. A series of increasingly bizarre and manic events develop, among them the spiking of gazpacho with a heavy dose of barbiturates. Almodóvar, attempting to recapture the glossy and vulgar visual style of 20th Century-Fox movies of the 50s, has delivered a rapid farce without any diminution in his affection for the characters. All the performances are splendid, especially from the smoldering Maura, who is destined to be a big star.

Individualist Cassavetes dies of cancer

Directing Gena Rowlands and Peter Falk in ***A Woman Under the Influence****.*

Los Angeles, 3 February
John Cassavetes, aged 59, has just died of lung cancer. The son of a Greek-born businessman, Cassavetes made his name as an actor on TV in the 50s, playing private eye Johnny Staccato, an apt nickname for him as both actor and director. With money earned from acting, he directed his first film *Shadows* in 1960, shot in 16mm on location in New York with a crew of four and a script evolved from the actors' improvisations. It had a raw vitality and inspired other young filmmakers to make films outside the studio system. His next two pictures, *Too Late Blues* and *A Child is Waiting*, made within the system, were not happy experiences. From 1968 he was able to work in his own way with a group of technicians, actor-friends (Peter Falk, Ben Gazzara, Seymour Cassel) and his wife, Gena Rowlands. Like the jazz which often accompanies his films, they were made in an improvisational manner and the performers had a fairly free rein. Using *cinéma vérité* techniques with vast close-ups, the characters/actors are revealed to the camera/psychoanalyst, generally depicting menopausal (male and female) emotional crises. Cassavetes seemed to be aware that such a method did not always determine Truth, and acting itself became a theme, whether acting out one's social roles as in *Faces* (1968), or in the inability to identify any longer with the role of wife and mother in *A Woman Under the Influence* (1974), or in actual stage acting in *Opening Night* (1977). As an actor, he was best known for his role as Mia Farrow's husband in *Rosemary's Baby* (1968).

A recent photo of Cassavetes and his wife, the brilliantly gifted Gena Rowlands.

Babbitt wipes out Rabbit at the Oscars

Best Supporting: Geena Davis.

Hollywood, 29 March
Dustin Hoffman was judged Best Actor for his remarkable performance as the autistic Charlie Babbitt in *Rain Man*. In fact, *Rain Man*, which also won Best Picture, Best Director (Barry Levinson) and Best Original Screenplay Oscars, overwhelmed all other contenders, including the eye-boggling blend of live action and animation, *Who Framed Roger Rabbit*, which won for Film Editing, Sound and Visual Effects. The 26-year-old Jodie Foster, already a veteran of 20 films, carried off the Best Actress prize as the rape victim in *The Accused*, while Geena Davis was voted Best Supporting Actress for her comic role in *The Accidental Tourist*.

Baseball brings Costner another diamond

***Bull Durham**: with Susan Sarandon.*

Chicago, 21 April
Despite the popularity of his baseball sex comedy, *Bull Durham*, Kevin Costner's wisdom in making back-to-back baseball movies was questioned by industry skeptics. But the magical *Field of Dreams* is a vindication of the star's faith. Director Phil Alden Robinson's fine adaptation of *Shoeless Joe* by W.P. Kinsella is an enchanting, funny fable of reconciliation and faith that is sparked when an Iowa farmer, prompted by a ghostly voice, turns his cornfield into a baseball diamond to host heavenly players. The result of a cross-country journey of self-redemption makes for a male weepie that will have even tough guys groping for Kleenex.

Baseball old-timer Burt Lancaster with loyal fan and dreamer Kevin Costner.

Canada's film industry is 50 years old

Montreal, 2 May
For filmgoers, it is a day of celebration in Montreal, as well as in other parts of the country, because the National Film Board of Canada is 50 years old today. In 1939, to counteract the prevailing dominance of Hollywood and to coordinate all government film activity, the Board was set up under John Grierson, the British documentary producer. He brought over film experts from England, Joris Ivens from Holland, and the animator Norman McLaren from Scotland via New York. The NFBC then spearheaded Canada's role as a provider of war propaganda, especially in two series, *World in Action* and *Canada Carries On*, which were shown in many parts of the world. After the war the Board not only concentrated on educational films, but also had a profound effect in the long term on the Canadian cinema in general. Through its distribution system, people even in the remotest areas were able to see films. It also had an important influence on Canadian filmmakers, most of whom have worked for the Board. In the early 60s, it became more involved with features, and gave increasing support to productions in French.

*Canada now: **Jesus of Montreal**.*

Indy looks for dad and finds Sean Connery

Hollywood, 24 June
Sean Connery is 59 and Harrison Ford is 47, but this hasn't stopped Connery from being cast as Indiana Jones' grizzled father in *Indiana Jones and the Last Crusade*, in which Indy once again tangles with a bunch of Nazis in a chase for the Holy Grail. The two stars strike sparks off each other in the third of Steven Spielberg's Indiana Jones adventures. Shot in Spain, Italy and Jordan and at Elstree Studios in Britain, the picture boasts a formidable array of sets and props, including no fewer than 7,000 rats and a replica World War I tank which cost over $150,000 to build. In the opening sequence the young Indy is played by the attractive young actor River Phoenix, who played Ford's unhappy son in *The Mosquito Coast*.

A difficult moment for Indiana Jones and his long-lost father, Sean Connery. ▷

Sex and deception compete with nostalgia

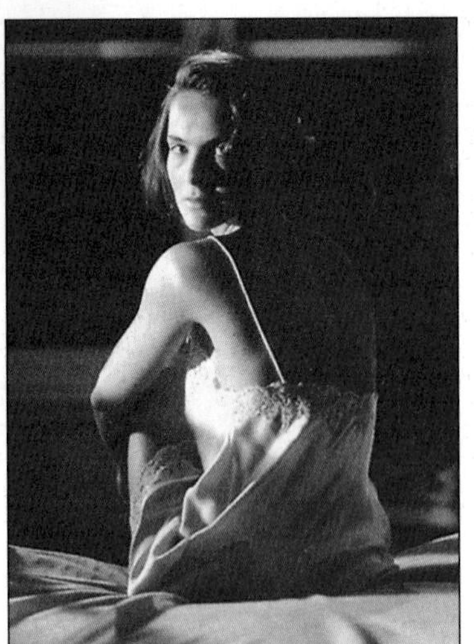

Trop belle pour toi!: *Carole Bouquet.*

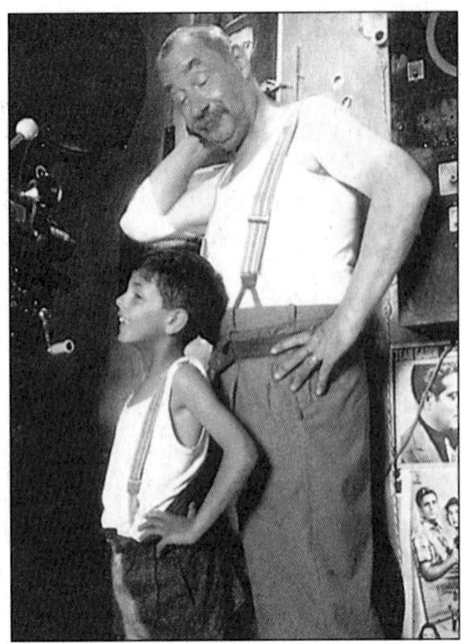

Noiret, Cascio: ***Cinema Paradiso.***

Cannes, 23 May
The jury of this year's Cannes Film Festival, presided over by Wim Wenders, expressed eagerness to reward a work that would encourage confidence in the future of cinema. Thus, they had no hesitation in handing the Golden Palm to *sex, lies and videotape*, directed by first-time filmmaker, 26-year-old Steven Soderbergh. It was written in eight days, shot in a month and edited in four weeks, on the tiny budget – by Hollywood standards – of $1.2 million. The result is a remarkably assured work, full of insight, humor and eroticism, which deals with the emotional life of four young people. Sharing the Special Jury Prize were Giuseppe Tornatore's *Cinema Paradiso*, about a touching friendship between a small boy and an old projectionist through an affection for the cinema, and *Trop belle pour toi!* (*Too Beautiful for You*), Bertrand Blier's perverse comedy in which a man with a beautiful wife falls for his plain and dowdy secretary.

Summer heat of Brooklyn sparks off Spike

New York, 30 June
Following his debut movie *She's Gotta Have It*, Spike Lee's latest, *Do the Right Thing*, is as hip, hot and accomplished a picture as is likely to be seen this year: an angry, funny, uncompromising commentary on the state of the nation seen as a slice of life in Brooklyn, where the residents of one block swirl in and out of Sal's (Danny Aiello) pizzeria that is the focal point of the street. The pace and the uneasy racial dynamics are shrewdly stepped up as the summer temperatures and tempers soar to a shocking climax, acknowledging that people, when pushed, choose sides. The talented Lee also plays the leading role.

Dodgers

Spike Lee in his own movie.

Robin Williams, a free-spirited teacher

New York, 2 June
It is three years since the Australian-born Peter Weir's last film, *The Mosquito Coast*, was greeted with less than enthusiasm. Now, 14 years after *Picnic at Hanging Rock*, he has come up with another school drama in *Dead Poets Society*. The movie is set in 1959 in Vermont, at a private boys' school whose repressive response to ideas and sensitivity is challenged by a new English master, who exhorts his students to "Seize the day" (*Carpe diem*). As the anti-conformist professor whose dedication to instilling a love of literature and poetry into overprivileged and previously uninterested boys leads to tragedy, Robin Williams brilliantly seizes his day, playing a dramatic role with passion and restraint.

James Spader, the video freak, and Andie MacDowell in ***sex, lies and videotape.***

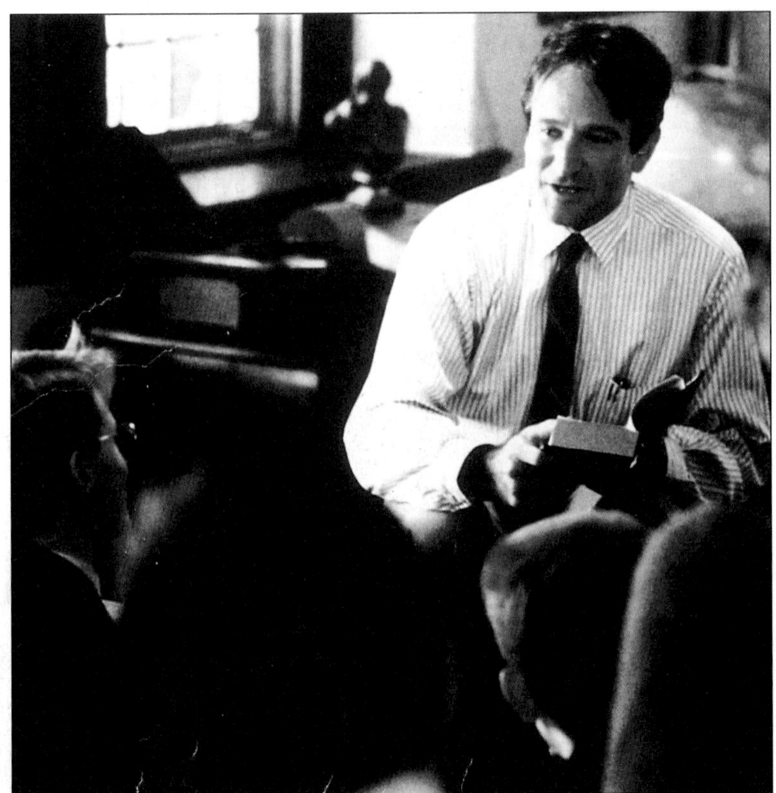

Rebel teacher Robin Williams at the head of the class in ***Dead Poets' Society.***

Billy and Meg great as Harry and Sally

Sharing a sandwich during their long on-again off-again relationship.

New York, 12 July
In Rob Reiner's new comedy, bouncy blonde Meg Ryan is the "modern" girl who believes that she and Billy Crystal can be friends without being lovers. Crystal, on the other hand, believes that men and women can't enjoy a friendship without sex getting in the way. *When Harry Met Sally* is a variation on the time-honored Hollywood theme in which the leading man and woman spend the entire film finding an excuse not to fall in love before tumbling into each other's arms in the final reel. The stand-out scene in a likeable movie occurs in a deli where Ryan demonstrates beyond a doubt that it's possible to fake an orgasm of thermonuclear proportions.

Al Pacino returns, stronger than ever

Al Pacino as the New York detective involved with prime suspect Ellen Barkin.

New York, 15 September
After being wildly miscast as a fur trapper in the disastrous *Revolution*, Al Pacino withdrew from films. He consoled himself with stage work and, he now admits, heavy drinking. Now, four years on, he's back and in great form, playing the morose middle-aged cop cast adrift on a *Sea of Love* with explosively sexy murder suspect Ellen Barkin. The movie looks to be equally notable for establishing the immensely talented Barkin, who made her screen debut in the 1982 *Diner*, as a top-rank star. For his part, Pacino has told the press, "I'm coming back, out of hibernation. It's going to be interesting to see how the audiences accept me back."

De Palma follows Stone into Vietnam

Los Angeles, 18 August
Brian De Palma's *Casualties of War* intrudes into Oliver Stone territory. It does so with some power and in spectacular locations, but has probably come too late in the spate to be taken as seriously as its maker would want. Like the war on which it focuses, the picture is uncompromisingly horrible, as soldier Michael J. Fox attempts to protect a captive Vietnamese girl from his cronies who, incited by the near-psychopathic Sean Penn, are intent on rape. Despite the usual criticisms made against De Palma, he tells his terrible tale without a trace of salaciousness.

A protective Michael J. Fox ministers to Vietnamese Thuy Thu Le.

Baker boys get more than they bargain for

Los Angeles, 13 September
Gorgeous Michelle Pfeiffer, named one of the world's 10 most beautiful women by *Harper's*, scores a bull's-eye with *The Fabulous Baker Boys*. They are real-life brothers Jeff and Beau Bridges, here playing double piano in the lower echelons of the hotel and nightclub circuit. Deciding to hire a vocalist to revive their dying act, they land themselves with Suzie Diamond (Pfeiffer), former small-time whore with a great line in wisecracks, whose sexy presence plays havoc with the brothers' relationship. Pfeiffer, ably supported and singing in an attractively off-key voice, sets the screen alight.

Jack Baker (Jeff Bridges) and Susie Diamond (Pfeiffer), a steamy duo.

Woody Allen reveals a darker side of life

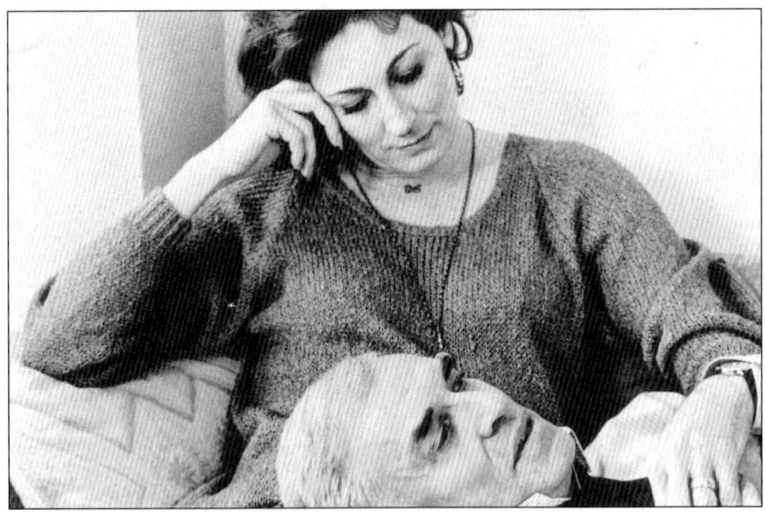

Anjelica Huston, the mistress, and Martin Landau, the troubled lover.

New York, 13 October
After two bleak dramas, *September* and *Another Woman*, both of which failed to appeal to the public or the critics, Woody Allen has come up with a more accessible but no less bleak film in *Crimes and Misdemeanors*. As the title suggests, the movie has Dostoevskian undertones with two stories running concurrently. One is serious, where adultery leads to murder; the other treats adultery in a more flippant manner. Though there is merely a tenuous link between them, Allen manages to keep them both in the air simultaneously. The film is perhaps one of the director's most pessimistic statements, where evil remains unchallenged (in the form of the tortured figure of opthalmologist Martin Landau), and mediocrity triumphs (in the form of the smarmy egocentric TV personality, Alan Alda). The cast includes Woody himself in one of his most archetypical nebbish roles, Mia Farrow, whom he lusts after, Anjelica Huston (as Landau's mistress-victim) and Sam Waterston as a rabbi going blind, whose spiritual insight is contrasted with Landau's moral murkiness.

Tom Cruise proves himself a heavyweight

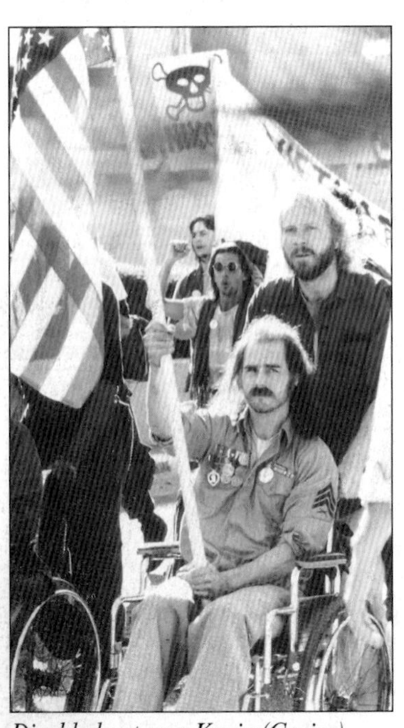

Disabled veteran Kovic (Cruise).

New York, 20 December
In Oliver Stone's *Born on the Fourth of July*, Tom Cruise has switched off his constant grin and disappeared beneath straggly hair and a mustache to play the wheelchair-bound Vietnam veteran Ron Kovic. Kovic, who was crippled in Vietnam, collaborated with Stone on the screenplay, which takes him from gung-ho patriot to anti-war activist. Cruise is superb as Kovic, banishing the sour taste left by his self-satisfied performance in the hawkish *Top Gun*. Stone claims, "It's the biggest film I've ever shot. It has about 170 speaking parts and covers about 30 years of life. It's about a boy coming of age in my generation, going to war and coming back, and what America was going through in that period... I wrote it 10 years ago, straight after *Platoon*... I never thought I'd get a chance to do it."

Branagh shoulders the mantle of Olivier

Young King Henry (Branagh) woos Catherine de Valois (Emma Thompson).

New York, 8 November
Kenneth Branagh, the Boy Wonder of English theater, steps into the seven league boots of Laurence Olivier to direct himself in the title role of Shakespeare's *Henry V*. To reclaim the play from its associations with Olivier's World War II film, he plays the victor of Agincourt as a calculating bully, and the battle itself is mounted as a mud-clogged slogging match reminiscent of World War I. It's a brave effort, but Branagh is no Olivier, and an element of strain clings to his assault on the play's great exhortatory passages before the siege of Barfleur and the moment of truth at Agincourt.

'Batman' busts 1989 box-office records

Hollywood, 31 December
The recent growth in movie attendance in the U.S. and the rise in average ticket prices – up from $4.11 last year to $4.45 – means that the total box-office receipts for 1989 have topped the $5 billion mark for the very first time. The biggest hit of the year was the Guber-Peters production of *Batman*. Released by Warner Bros. and shown simultaneously in 2,850 theaters in June, the picture, starring Michael Keaton, Jack Nicholson (as the Joker) and Kim Basinger, set several records in the first weeks of its opening, and continued strong throughout the peak summer months.

Michael Keaton as Batman.

Jack Nicholson is the Joker.

Box-Office Hits

It is perhaps unfortunate that the run of box-office hits from the major Hollywood producers during recent years have become all too predictable. Movies have long conformed to formula and genre, but, with the industry centenary approaching, technology increasingly drowns content. It has not always been that way. In fact, the list of hit movies during the first 50 years of the cinema is full of surprises, with the smaller and independent companies often outflanking the major studios. Since one and two-reelers were churned out by all the companies in vast numbers in the early years, the first big breakthrough at the box office came, not surprisingly, with the changeover to features during 1912-15. And here one can also chart the origins of the studios in the first big hits. For Adolph Zukor there was *Queen Elizabeth* (1912) starring Sarah Bernhardt; for Laemmle's Universal, *Traffic in Souls* the following year, Lasky and DeMille with *The Squaw Man* and Selig with *The Spoilers* (both 1914), and William Fox with his first Theda Bara movie, *A Fool There Was* in 1915. However, the most spectacularly successful film of all was D.W. Griffith's independently made *The Birth of a Nation*, widely shown all over the world with estimated grosses of $15-20 million. The next important cluster of popular successes is associated with the coming of sound. Ironically, the top hit was not *The Jazz Singer* (1927), perhaps because there were not enough cinemas equipped to show it, but Warner Bros.' follow-up film with the same star, Al Jolson, *The Singing Fool* (1928), while musicals topped the bill the following year headed by MGM's *The Broadway Melody*, Warners' *Golddiggers of Broadway* and RKO's *Rio Rita*. In the same way that Warners, a small enterprising company, had stolen the box-office thunder from the large studios in the late 20s, so in the 30s did Disney, with *Snow White* easily the top hit of the decade, and Goldwyn in the 40s with *The Best Years of Our Lives*. And David O'Selznick's *Gone With the Wind*, first shown in December 1939, actually straddled the two decades as the most successful movie since *The Birth of a Nation*. In the 50s, the big companies' success in attracting audiences to the new, larger and wider screen movies is reflected in the hits headed by MGM's *Ben-Hur* (1959) filmed in Camera 65, and *The Ten Commandments* (1956) from Paramount in VistaVision. Others include *Around the World in 80 Days* (1956) and *South Pacific* (1958) shot in Todd-AO, *The Robe* (1953) and *The Bridge on the River Kwai* (1957) in CinemaScope and *This is Cinerama* (1952). The surprise financial bonanza in the 60s came from two treacly films – *The Sound of Music* (1965) and *Love Story* (1970) – before a new generation of young directors arrived to take Hollywood by storm with rather stronger fare. First off the mark were Francis Ford Coppola with *The Godfather* (1972) and William Friedkin with *The French Connection* (1971) and *The Exorcist* in 1973. However, it was George Lucas and Steven Spielberg who soon established themselves as the most successful producer-director team in the history of Hollywood with *American Graffiti*, *Jaws*, *Close Encounters* and *Star Wars* in the 70s, through *E.T. the Extra-Terrestrial* and the *Indiana Jones* cycle in the 80s, up to *Jurassic Park* and *Schindler's List* in the 90s.

l to r: Cher, Susan Sarandon, Michelle Pfeiffer were ***The Witches of Eastwick*** *(1987), directed by George Miller.*

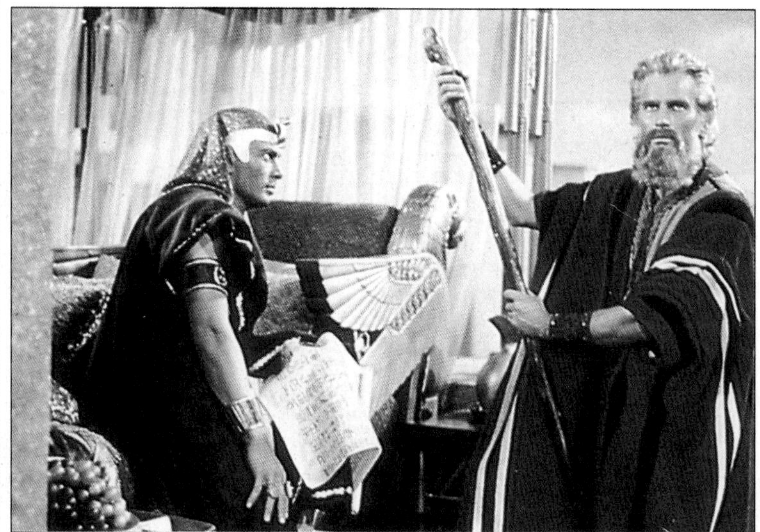

Charlton Heston (left) and Yul Brynner in ***The Ten Commandments*** *(1956), Cecil B. DeMille's hit remake of his 1923 epic success.*

Kelly Lynch and Matt Dillon in Gus Van Sant's ***Drugstore Cowboy***.

Michael Moore caused a stir with documentary ***Roger and Me***.

Hou Hsiao-Hsien's award-winning film ***A City of Sadness*** *from Taiwan.*

Heroes Alex Winter (l), Keanu Reeves: ***Bill and Ted's Excellent Adventure***.

WOODY ALLEN ROSANNA ARQUETTE MIA FARROW GIANCARLO GIANNINI JULIE KAVNER NICK NOLTE TALIA SHIRE
NEW YORK STORIES
ONE CITY. THREE STORIES TALL.
WOODY ALLEN'S
OEDIPUS WRECKS
FRANCIS COPPOLA'S
LIFE WITHOUT ZOE
MARTIN SCORSESE'S
LIFE LESSONS

Three famous directors each tell a story. Woody's was best, Coppola's worst.

Helen Mirren, Michael Gambon: ***The Cook, the Thief, his Wife and her Lover***.

Karen Colston as Kay in Jane Campion's bizarre and brilliant ***Sweetie****.*

John Travolta with Kirstie Alley and 'baby' in ***Look Who's Talking****.*

Guy Stockwell and Thelma Trixou in Jodorowsky's ***Santa Sangre****.*

Mary Elizabeth Mastrantonio underwater in James Cameron's ***The Abyss****.*

Bridget Fonda (l), Joanne Whalley as Rice-Davies and Keeler in ***Scandal****.*

Winona Ryder, Kim Walker, Lisanne Falk, Shannen Doherty in ***Heathers****.*

Fairuza Balk, Colin Firth: ***Valmont****, Milos Foreman's* ***Dangerous Liaisons****.*

Towards the Millenium

Socially, politically and economically, no one can pinpoint when the climate of the 1980s became distinctively that of the 90s. Greed, quick fortunes and Me First acquisitiveness were supposed to be out; caring, sharing New Men were proclaimed in. Disenchanted with old regimes, weary of bureaucracy and corruption, people's attitudes shifted sufficiently on national scales to see the Democrats return to the White House with Bill Clinton in 1992. Leaders from Tokyo to Rome were ousted; the far right rose in Western Europe; socio-economic upheaval took hold of the former Soviet bloc. The world was repeatedly stunned by the rapidity of events: the international effort in the Gulf War to resolve one crisis, the lack of international will to deal with another in the former Yugoslavia, the rivetting turn of the *apartheid* tide in South Africa.

In attempting to keep abreast of public moods, what was a film producer to do? On screen it was hard to detect just how much the times were changing, for to the big boys in entertainment, the answer was business as usual. If, for example, one had a multi-million-dollar package in post-production which played on Cold War paranoia, such as *The Hunt for Red October*, one simply stuck on a prefatory caption setting the action in the not-too-distant past. Or old enemies were replaced on the screen by terrorists, sinister corporations or futuristic fiends.

The highest stakes continued to be placed on escapism, thrills and family-oriented spectaculars, with sequels and comedies still showing strongly. The biggest effort and budgets went into special effects-packed action pictures planned as summertime blockbusters.

The two smash hits of 1990 around the world, however, were both surprise sleepers, released with little fanfare and indicating a lucrative vein seldom mined in the new decade: romance. The contemporary Cinderella tale of a business tycoon and a Hollywood Boulevard hooker, titled *Pretty Woman*, revived Richard Gere's career and launched the phenomenon of Julia Roberts, whose appeal carried over to feebler vehicles, even sending the thriller *Sleeping With the Enemy*, into the Top Ten of 1991. Despite the too-much-too-soon prognostications and a hiatus following her much publicized exhaustion and romantic turmoils, Roberts was back with a vengeance in 1994 with *The Pelican Brief*, the first of several major productions with which she retained her position as one of the highest paid actresses in the world.

Ghost topped even *Pretty Woman*, with audiences going back for repeat viewings of a weepy that mixed comedy, the supernatural and undying love, raised the stock of Patrick Swayze and, even more markedly, that of former Brat Pack ingenue and now Mrs. Bruce Willis, Demi Moore, as well as Whoopi Goldberg, whose Oscar-winning turn dramatically revitalized her flagging film career.

Less successful return of Leslie Nielsen's bungler in ***Naked Gun 2½*** *(1991).*

Roberts, Moore and Michelle Pfeiffer were the top trio of most wanted leading ladies, rivaled by new goddess Sharon Stone after her star-making exposure – literally – in the controversial 1992 sex thriller *Basic Instinct*, while Goldberg with her high concept antics in the Whoopie-goes-to-a-convent wheeze, *Sister Act* (also 1992) displaced Bette Midler as Disney's Queen of Comedy. Geena Davis showed strongly, while the prestige projects increasingly went to Susan Sarandon, Jodie Foster and Britain's Emma Thompson.

The junior set embraced a new idol in the John Hughes discovery Macaulay Culkin, the highest paid child star of all time after 1991's *Home Alone* became the biggest grossing comedy in history.

Intergalactic superstar status was firmly held by Arnold Schwarzenegger, whose *Terminator 2* with director James Cameron, landmark 'morphing' special effects and a budget reputedly the first to hit $100 million, ruled in 1991; though the failure of the ambitious, mistargeted *The Last Action Hero* (1993) handed him a spectacular comedown. Meanwhile, the beefcake he had dethroned, Sylvester Stallone, came back fighting in 1993 with *Cliffhanger* and *Demolition Man*.

Tom Cruise and Harrison Ford had few rivals in the realm of glamorous, A-list leading men. Cruise took *A Few Good Men* and *The Firm* to huge success and proved a controversial but, to the producers, irresistible choice to play the vampire Lestat in the long-awaited screen adaptation of Anne Rice's *Interview With the Vampire* for director Neil Jordan in 1994. Ford's outings in *The Fugitive*, and his unprecedented ten-picture deal to play novelist Tom Clancy's ex-CIA hero Jack Ryan, made him the safest bet for a hit. Among the teen heart-throbs of the early 90s, including Johnny Depp and Brad Pitt, it was Keanu Reeves who shot to major player status first, with the surprise wow of summer 1994, the Die-Hard-On-A-Bus smash, *Speed*.

Actor-directors Kevin Costner and Clint Eastwood scored notable personal triumphs. Costner's directorial debut, *Dances With Wolves*, grossed over the magic $100 million and took seven Oscars including Best Picture and Direction, while his critically-panned popcorn movies, *The Bodyguard* with chanteuse Whitney Houston and *Robin Hood: Prince of Thieves*, were nevertheless massive hits; and his central role in Oliver Stone's highly provocative *JFK* gave him another substantial credit. Eastwood won belated respect from the film community with the majestic *Unforgiven*, bringing him a fistful of Oscars, and received the best reviews of his acting career for *In the Line of Fire*. He and Costner teamed for *A Perfect World*.

While actor-directors had been at work in Hollywood since Mable Normand and Charlie Chaplin helmed their own comedies, they were everywhere in the 90s. Aside from Costner, other artists who made directorial debuts included Robert De Niro, Mel Gibson, Jodie Foster, Sean Penn, Billy Crystal, John Turturro and Tim Robbins. By the middle of the decade many more, among them Anjelica Huston, Anthony Hopkins and John Malkovich were set to follow suit.

Sequels – *Die Hard 2, The Naked Gun 2 ½, Lethal Weapon 3* – showed no signs of going away, although by *Teenage Mutant Ninja Turtles 3, Alien 3*, and *Rocky V* it was apparent that some formulae were losing their charm. More than ever, Hollywood looked to foreign language films, earlier hits and television for safe investments over original risks, and Americanized remakes from the French abounded.

Martin Scorsese, surprisingly, enjoyed his biggest commercial hit with an in-your-face, histrionic remake of *Cape Fear*; Alec Baldwin and Kim Basinger, husband and wife, got their stalled careers up and running again as the gorgeous outlaws in a remake of *The Getaway*, and Francis Ford Coppola at last made some money with his lavish psychosexual version of Bram Stoker's Dracula. Such varied fare as *The Addams Family, The Fugitive, The Flintstones, Maverick* and *The Beverly Hillbillies* were concocted from 60s television series, while teen comedy monster Wayne's World also sprang from TV, and bestselling fiction from John Grisham and Michael Crichton was filmed as fast as it could be written.

With an achievement astonishing even by his own standards, Steven Spielberg delivered an unparalleled one-two punch in 1993, going from *Jurassic Park* (which was topping an incredible $330 million at the box office in the U.S. alone) to the overwhelming Holocaust chronicle, *Schindler's List*, a film for which none of his previous work had prepared audiences or critics.

Although political correctness was much discussed in the media and made language and behavior deemed racist, sexist, ageist or any other 'ist' unacceptable in some quarters, P.C. didn't have much impact on the mainstream output. Women, with few exceptions, still figured most prominently in films as property for barter (*Indecent Proposal*), psychos (*The Hand That Rocks the Cradle*), screaming sidekicks and even lesbian psychokillers (*Basic Instinct*), although they also served as moral, maternal and even armed support (*Lethal Weapon 3*, *In the Line of Fire*). *Thelma and Louise* gave Sarandon and Davis rip-roaring roles as female buddies on the lam, *Fried Green Tomatoes at the Whistle Stop Cafe* and *A League of Their Own* provided ensembles of actresses with crowd-pleasing women-bonding stories, and roles as lawyers, doctors, scientists and journalists were added to the clichés.

African Americans, Hispanics and Asian Americans continued to be under-represented on the screen, with actors Denzel Washington, Wesley Snipes and Lawrence Fishburne most successfully battling against old stereotypes to distinguish themselves in wide ranging roles. In the wake of Spike Lee's celebrity as *the* Angry Young Black filmmaker, a new wave of black directors was dubbed the 'Black Pack', a lumping together of extremely disparate filmmakers that included veteran Bill Duke, filmmaker's son and actor Mario Van Peebles, Lee's cinematographer Ernest R. Dickerson, youngsters Matty Rich and John Singleton (whose debut with *Boyz N the Hood* at age 23 made him the youngest director ever Oscar-nominated), and former actor Carl Franklin among the most noteworthy. With few exceptions, it was from their ranks that the only realistic films addressing America's inner city crises came.

More widespread public attention was paid to the themes of sex and violence in films, reawakening a cyclical debate about censorship as pundits still struggled to prove any real link between movies and anti-social behavior. An apparent backlash in the 90s against glamorizing criminal, dark and abusive acts was supposed to herald a rise in family entertainment, as with environmentally friendly surprise hits *The Secret Garden* and *Free Willy* (the story of a boy bonding with a captive whale). But while it was briefly trendy to come down hard on the wannabe heirs to Peckinpah, Leone and Scorsese, the most talked about newcomer was Quentin Tarantino, whose clever, brutal panache was hailed in *Reservoir Dogs*, rewarded at Cannes for *Pulp Fiction*, provided the racy, shocking screenplay for *Tru Romance* and made him the hottest new kid on the block. Nor did the spectacular performance of Jonathan Demme's *The Silence of the Lambs*, and its unprecedented Oscar sweep for a psycho-thriller bear out the much-vaunted return to sweetness and light, which saw only *Sleepless in Seattle* penetrating the collective consciousness.

Much more money was poured into the return to shoot-'em-up. The success of *Dances With Wolves* and *Unforgiven* prompted a stampede of Westerns, from rival Wyatt Earp bios to a black Western, *Posse*, and a woman's Western, *Bad Girls*, most of which were inept flops. And a wave of romances aimed at the 20-somethings, who marketing analysts dubbed Generation X, generally backfired as well, with Cameron Crowe's *Singles* a rare charmer against much-hyped but blink-and-they-were-gone efforts like *Reality Bites*, *Bodies Rest and Motion* and *Threesome*. Films tailored for the 'wrinklies' such as *Grumpy Old Men* and *Wrestling Ernest Hemingway* also met mixed fortunes, while biceps and ballistics continued to hold sway. While UK film production continued to decline, the reputation of British actors and technicians grew. Daniel Day Lewis, Jeremy Irons and Anthony Hopkins took the Best Actor Oscar in consecutive years, Emma Thompson received three Oscar nominations (and one win) in two, and Miranda Richardson, Joan Plowright and Alison Steadman among others were honored abroad for their work. Neil Jordan's *The Crying Game*, the last film produced by Palace Pictures before the company went bankrupt, won international acclaim, as did Merchant-Ivory's *The Remains of the Day*, while Mike Newell's romantic comedy *Four Weddings and a Funeral* became the first British film to reach No. 1 at the U.S. box office since the 1988 smash-hit, *A Fish Called Wanda*.

Brilliant effects in ***The Lawnmower Man*** *(1992), from Stephen King's story.*

A welcome development in Italy came in the reappearance of topical social and political dramas such as Gianni Amelio's *The Stolen Children*, Rick Rognazzi's *The Escort* and Carlo Carlei's *The Flight of the Innocent*. Elsewhere, struggling with unhealthy economics and, often, social mayhem, European production was reeling, although there were interesting works reflecting the situation, such as Istvan Szabo's return to Hungary to make *Sweet Emma, Dear Bob*, a painful look at post-Communist society.

Hong Kong remained an assembly line for chop-sockey martial arts pictures, but a new line in tough, ultra-violent, ultra-stylish thrillers emerged from filmmakers such as Ringo Lam and the influential Chinese answer to Sergio Leone, John Woo, most of which starred the handsome Chinese Robert Mitchum lookalike Chow Yun Fat.

In Japan the former stand-up comic 'Beat' Takeshi Kitano rose from protégé of Oshima and ubiquitous TV personality of the 80s to attain the stature of a Japanese Clint Eastwood, directing and starring in tough, hard-hitting but thoughtful pieces like *Sonatine* and *Violent Cop* that stood apart from the body of yakuza crime flicks.

Other Asian filmmakers to make their presence felt included Taiwan's Hou Hsiao Hsien and Ang Lee (*The Wedding Banquet*), and the Vietnamese director Tran Anh Hung made an acclaimed debut with *The Scent of Green Papaya*. But it was from China that the most dazzling films were coming, with Chen Kaige's dazzling *Farewell My Concubine* the first film from China to win the Cannes Palme d'Or.

However, it was the French who were showing the rest of the world the way ahead in multi-national ventures, the surest shape of things to come. In addition to producing huge epics like Claude Berri's Zola adaptation *Germinal*, and *Indochine* starring the remarkably enduring Catherine Deneuve, there was Kieslowski's *Three Colors* trilogy, a new international leading lady in Juliette Binoche and second generation film stars in Guillaume Depardieu, Marie Trintignant and, especially, Romane Bohringer. But France's biggest contribution to the international scene went almost unremarked: the substantial and canny investment by French production-distribution and TV company Canal Plus in all manner of foreign films, from *Basic Instinct* to Australia's *The Piano*, ironically at the same time that French filmmakers and cultural watchdogs were decrying the threat by foreign films to their domestic products. In this, the French led the way to the future, far ahead of the rest of the European Community where only fitfully were joint national financing deals successfully put together.

ANGIE ERRIGO

1990

1989 Academy Awards, Dorothy Chandler Pavilion, 28 Mar.

Best Film:	*Driving Miss Daisy* (dir: Bruce Beresford)
Best Director:	Oliver Stone *(Born on the Fourth of July)*
Best Actor:	Daniel Day Lewis *(My Left Foot)*
Best Actress:	Jessica Tandy *(Driving Miss Daisy)*
Best Supp. Actor:	Denzel Washington *(Glory)*
Best Supp. Actress:	Brenda Fricker *(My Left Foot)*

London, 1 January
British actress Maggie Smith has been made a D.B.E. in the New Year's Honors List.

Paris, 20 January
Rain Man drew the highest number of paying customers to the box office in the Paris region during 1989, with 1,509,707 tickets sold.

Paris, 28 February
Release of *le Bal du gouverneur* (*The Governor's Ball*), which marks the directing debut of actress Marie-France Pisier. The talented Miss Pisier has adapted the film, shot mainly in New Caledonia, from her own novel.

France, 4 March
A preview of the versatile Serge Gainsbourg's film *Stan the Flasher*, has been shown on Canal Plus. The film is scheduled for release in three days' time.

Paris, 20 March
Brigitte Bardot's lawyer, Maître Gilles Dreyfus, has categorically denied rumors that his client is planning to play Elena Ceausescu, the wife of the powerful Romanian dictator, in a film.

Hollywood, 26 March
Thirty seconds of advertising space on television during the Oscars costs $3.5 million.

Los Angeles, 30 March
Teenage Mutant Ninja Turtles grossed a massive $25.4 million on its opening weekend in the U.S.

London, 2 April
Christies has sold 10 paintings of Alain Delon's for 2 million pounds.

Nantes, 9 April
Agnes Varda has started shooting a film about her husband Jacques Demy's childhood and adolescence in Nantes. The title of the film has as yet to be decided.

Switzerland, 23 April
Paulette Goddard, popular 40s star, has died. Among her four husbands were Charlie Chaplin, with whom she co-starred in *Modern Times*, and novelist Erich Maria Remarque. Managing to escape typecasting, she is also remembered in the title role of Renoir's *Diary of a Chambermaid* (1946).

Philadelphia, 25 April
Dexter Gordon, the famed jazz saxophonist who played the lead in Bertrand Tavernier's *'Round Midnight*, has died.

London, 2 May
Parkfield Picture's *The Krays*, an East End-thugland movie directed by Peter Medak, made a forceful first-week's entry in the capital with a box-office gross of 61,134 pounds.

Moscow, 6 June
The Confession (*l'Aveu*), an attack on Stalinism made by Costa-Gavras in 1970, is at last being shown in Moscow where, for obvious reasons, its release was withheld.

Paris, 20 June
Spanish director Pedro Almodóvar, who is in Paris to present his new film *Atame* (*Tie Me Up, Tie Me Down*) co-starring Victoria Abril and Antonio Banderas, is reportedly furious over the X-rating given to the movie by the MPAA and is seeking to have the film re-certified R.

Auckland, 10 July
New Zealand director Jane Campion has agreed to worldwide release of *An Angel at My Table*. At the outset, Miss Campion wanted to stop theatrical showings of her film, which was made as a three-part mini series for TV, as she felt it was unsuitable for cinema viewing. Favorable reactions from theatrical buyers in Cannes and the "most popular film" vote from audiences at the Sydney Film Festival are responsible for this change of heart.

Armenia, 21 July
Sergo Paradjanov, the innovative Russian director, has died. Paradjanov directed his first feature film *Andriesh* in 1955 but it was with *Shadows of our Forgotten Ancestors* (1964), which won over a dozen international awards, that he gained worldwide recognition. He earned further overseas acclaim in 1977 with the long withheld release of *Sayat Nova*. In 1974 he was imprisoned for five years for homosexuality and several trumped up charges. However, a campaign by European filmmakers led to an early release. Paradjanov made his final picture *Ashik Kerib* in 1988.

London, 10 August
Hong Kong director John Woo's melodramatic, ultra-violent thriller *The Killer* has opened at the ICA cinema today.

Hollywood, 22 August
Paramount's romantic thriller *Ghost* has overtaken the $100 million mark in only 39 days of domestic release and looks set to outdistance the summer's biggest blockbusters *Dick Tracy* and *Die Hard II*.

Sarasota, 15 November
The French Minister for Culture, Jack Lang, accompanied by Catherine Deneuve, Alain Delon and producer Daniel Toscan du Plantier, is in Florida to open the second Festival of French Films.

Moscow, 3 December
The Mir Cinema has reopened under the direction of Paris-Moscow-Media, a Franco-Soviet company. The renovated cinema, which seats 1,200, is intending to specialize in French films.

France, 10 December
The little district borough of Mériel in the Val d'Oise is creating a Jean Gabin Museum. A bust of the actor, donated by Jean Marais, is to be erected in the village square. It was here that Jean Moncorgé, the future Jean Gabin, spent the greater part of his childhood and adolescence.

Rome, 21 December
A recent poll shows that Italian art-house attendances now account for almost 10 percent of all cinemagoers. Of Italy's 1,300 screens, 200 fit into the art-house category.

DEATHS

England, 8 January
Terry-Thomas

Los Angeles, 20 January
Barbara Stanwyck

London, 25 January
Ava Gardner

England, 19 February
Michael Powell

Maine, 5 March
Gary Merrill

Switzerland, 17 March
Capucine

New York, 15 April
Greta Garbo

Los Angeles, 16 May
Sammy Davis Jr.

New York, 16 May
Jim Henson

California, 18 May
Jill Ireland

New York, 2 June
Rex Harrison

London, 15 July
Margaret Lockwood

Hollywood, 4 September
Irene Dunne

New York, 14 October
Leonard Bernstein

Paris, 15 October
Delphine Seyrig

California, 20 October
Joel McCrea

France, 27 October
Jacques Demy

New York, 7 December
Joan Bennett

California, 8 December
Martin Ritt

---

*Martin Scorsese's **GoodFellas**, based on the memoirs of Henry Hill about his experiences with the Mafia, elevates the gangster movie genre to a new level of style and realism.*

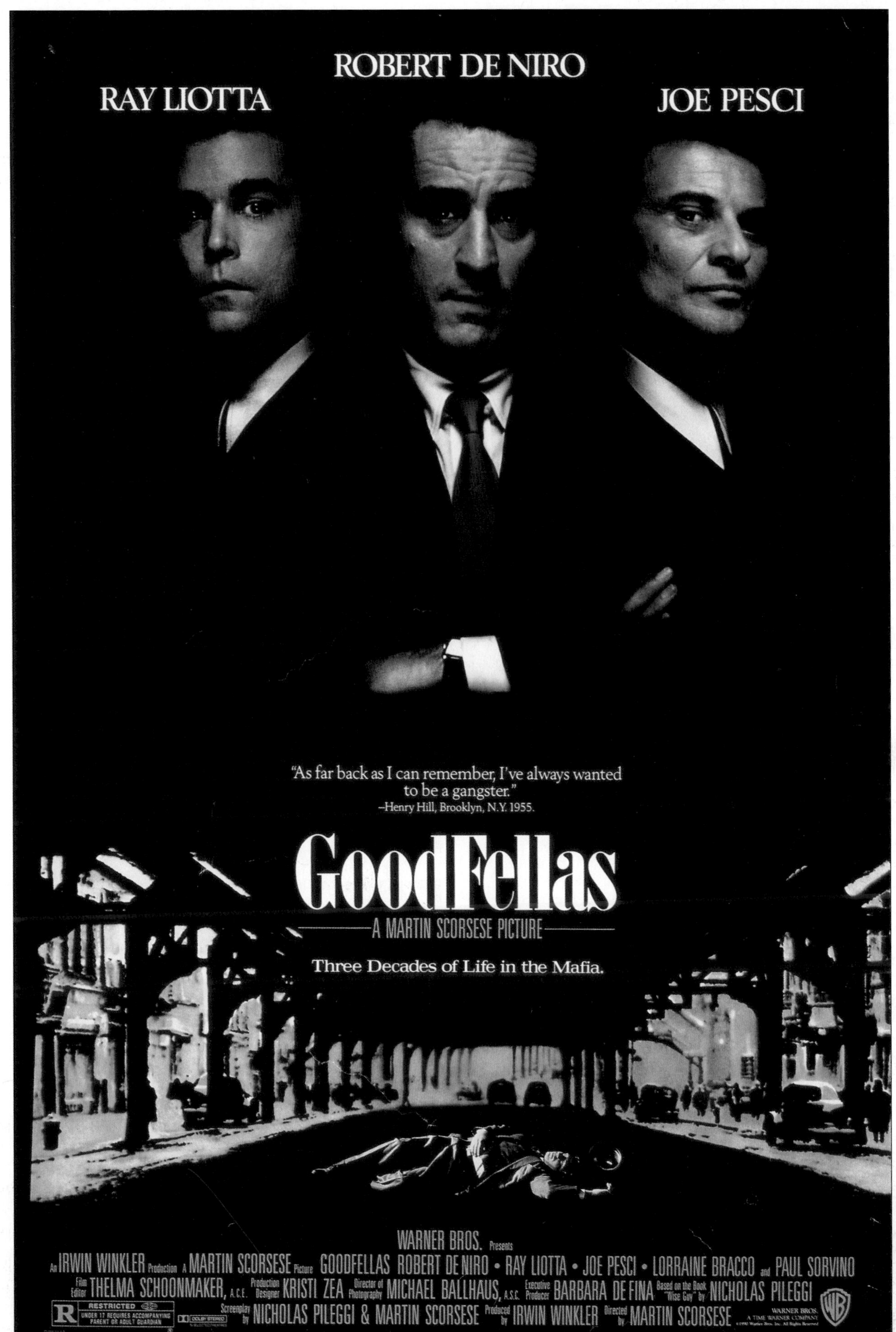
ROBERT DE NIRO
RAY LIOTTA
JOE PESCI
"As far back as I can remember, I've always wanted to be a gangster."
–Henry Hill, Brooklyn, N.Y. 1955.
GoodFellas
A MARTIN SCORSESE PICTURE
Three Decades of Life in the Mafia.
WARNER BROS. Presents
An IRWIN WINKLER Production A MARTIN SCORSESE Picture GOODFELLAS ROBERT DE NIRO • RAY LIOTTA • JOE PESCI • LORRAINE BRACCO and PAUL SORVINO
Film Editor THELMA SCHOONMAKER, A.C.E. Production Designer KRISTI ZEA Director of Photography MICHAEL BALLHAUS, A.S.C. Executive Producer BARBARA DE FINA Based on the Book "Wise Guy" by NICHOLAS PILEGGI
Screenplay by NICHOLAS PILEGGI & MARTIN SCORSESE Produced by IRWIN WINKLER Directed by MARTIN SCORSESE
R RESTRICTED
UNDER 17 REQUIRES ACCOMPANYING PARENT OR ADULT GUARDIAN
DOLBY STEREO
WARNER BROS.
A TIME WARNER COMPANY
WB

Time and Warner: the union is official

New York, 10 January
The past year has been a memorable one for the Warner Bros. studio. It led all the other companies at the box office, helped by such mega-hits as *Batman* and *Lethal Weapon 2*, and has taken part in a spectacular merger with the news magazine company, Time Inc., to form the largest communications conglomerate in the world. The original plans for a swap of stock between the two companies was disrupted by a rival offer to Time by Paramount, and ended with Time making a friendly but costly takeover of Warners. The new company name is Time Warner Inc., with Warner boss Steven J. Ross, widely regarded as the mastermind behind the new deal, taking the post of chairman and co-chief executive. Accomplished at a cost of about $14 billion, the outlook for the new company is far from rosy, given the high level of debt it will be carrying into the 1990s.

Gere and Garcia tangle over corruption

Los Angeles, 12 January
Richard Gere hasn't had a real hit since *An Officer and a Gentleman* in 1982. His career seemed to grind to a halt two years ago, beset by the law of diminishing box-office returns. Now he's bidding for the big time again with two movies shot virtually back-to-back, the first of which has opened. Directed with style and tension by Brit Mike Figgis, *Internal Affairs* has Gere as a murderously brutal, corrupt and sexually sadistic cop, under investigation by Internal Affairs officer Andy Garcia. Like its leading character, the movie is nasty and misogynistic but, for audiences who have the stomach for it, it should prove the vehicle Gere has been waiting for.

Richard Gere (l), the psychotic cop under investigation, with William Baldwin.

Francis Coppola declared bankrupt

Hollywood, 25 January
Despite the serious financial problems connected with his Zoetrope studios, which he was forced to sell, producer-writer-director Francis Ford Coppola continued fairly active through the 1980s. He was producer-director on *The Outsiders* and *Rumble Fish* (both 1983), writer and director of *The Cotton Club* (1984) and the "Life With Zoe" episode in *New York Stories* (1989), and director only on *Peggy Sue Got Married* (1986) and *Tucker: The Man and His Dream* (1988). Unfortunately, none of these movies, or others on which he served as executive producer, made much impression at the box office, failing to generate the profits needed to settle his substantial debts amounting to well over $20 million. Now the courts have finally declared him bankrupt. Typically, though, Coppola is currently in Italy, taking another crack at *The Godfather* with Part III.

Malle's 'Milou' and the events of May '68

Paris, 24 January
During the student uprising in May 1968 in Paris, Louis Malle was one of a group of directors whose protestations brought about the abandonment of the Cannes Film Festival. Twenty-two years later, Malle has reflected upon that extraordinary month from the perspective of the provinces in *May Fools* (*Milou en mai*). This delightful black comedy revolves around a bourgeois family gathered on a country estate for the funeral of a matriarch. They spend their time squabbling over her will and belongings, and playing sexual games, believing the revolution is imminent. The film provides splendid ensemble playing, headed by Michel Piccoli.

Milou (Michel Piccoli, in the hat) surrounded by his eccentric family.

Lots of brawn, little brain in Seagal actioner

Los Angeles, 9 February
Steven Seagal, former martial arts instructor to the stars, and to super-agent Mike Ovitz, actually proves impossible to kill in *Hard to Kill*, his second sadistic action extravaganza. Hyped as the new Stallone, and a suitably hulking heir to the Chuck Norris karate and kick-boxing genre, Seagal sweats it out as a tough cop battling corruption and disposing of an army of hired killers, in an absurd revenge plot targeted at his *Above the Law* admirers.

Seagal, former martial arts instructor to the stars, now takes to the screen.

Digging up the past with 'The Nasty Girl'

Lena Stoltze, the 'nasty' girl of the title, marries Robert Giggenbach.

Hamburg, 20 February
The Nasty Girl takes a novel attitude to the theme of German fascism, not only in the past, but in its present-day form, treating it in the style of a witty, satiric fable. For his plot, screenwriter and director Michael Verhoeven has taken the true story of a schoolgirl's investigations for an essay entitled "My Hometown During The Third Reich". Although she finds the inhabitants unwilling to help her, she doggedly continues in her determination to uncover the truth. The film, while scoring telling points, also has a youthful vigor and freshness, and even an attractive indiscipline in its structure.

'Pretty Woman' a Pygmalion for the 90s

A hooker transformed: Julia Roberts (dressed by Cerruti) and Richard Gere.

Los Angeles, 23 March
Following right on his bid to regain a place in the firmament with *Internal Affairs*, Richard Gere stars as an elegant millionaire asset-stripper in Garry Marshall's *Pretty Woman*. It should prove the big one. However, more notably, the movie introduces leggy, auburn-haired Julia Roberts (sister of Eric) as a hooker hired by Gere, who takes her on longer-term than intended and makes a lady of her. Not since Audrey Hepburn has there been such a stunning debut. A Cinderella-cum-Pygmalion tale for the 90s, the film is witty, romantic and delightful. And watch out for Hector Elizondo...

Besson deserts blue for red and black

Paris, 21 February
The director Luc Besson promised that after his oceanic film, *The Big Blue*, his next picture would be dark, urban and violent. *Nikita*, shot under highly secretive conditions, is everything he described. This glossy, pulsating thriller deals with the transformation of Nikita from a 19-year-old drug-addicted girl sentenced to life imprisonment for murder, into a top killer in the French secret service. The uninhibited performance from the beautiful Anne Parillaud in the title role holds the far-fetched plot together. Besson, as usual, displays a mastery of camerawork and editing to create the maximum impact. Jeanne Moreau is impressive as one of Nikita's mentors.

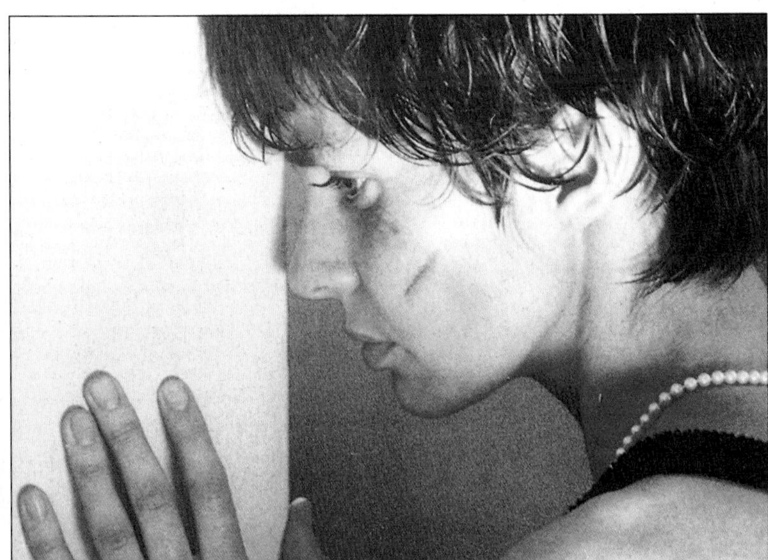

Anne Parillaud stars in Besson's ***Nikita****: rehabilitation by brainwashing.*

Panache and poetry illumine new Cyrano

Paris, 28 March
Staying close to the content and poetic form of Edmond Rostand's late 19th-century romantic classic, director Jean-Paul Rappeneau's *Cyrano de Bergerac* is impressively spectacular. His handsome film captures the atmosphere of 17th-century France in a series of rumbustious set pieces – particularly effective in the opening sequence at the theater, which introduces the audience (on and off-screen) to the long-nosed army officer, fearless swordsman and brilliant poet. Though perhaps not the ideal Cyrano, Gérard Depardieu plays him with sincerity, vigor, clarity and pathos. Anne Brochet, Vincent Perez and Jacques Weber give quality support.

Anne Brochet as the lovely Roxane, the object of Cyrano's secret passion.

Depardieu, a towering Cyrano.

Veteran Jessica Tandy drives out 'Born on the Fourth of July'

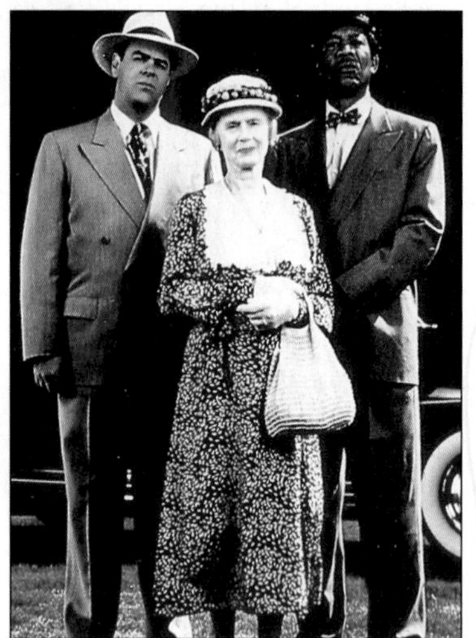

Jessica Tandy as Miss Daisy, Dan Aykroyd (l) and Morgan Freeman.

Daniel Day Lewis as crippled Christy Brown, with his mother (Brenda Fricker).

Hollywood, 26 March
Jessica Tandy in the title role of *Driving Miss Daisy* has become, at 80 years and nine months, the oldest Oscar winner ever, outstripping George Burns, who was a mere 80 years and two months old when he won his Best Supporting Actor award for *The Sunshine Boys* in 1976. Aside from the Best Actress prize, Bruce Beresford's tender film about the relationship between a wealthy Jewish widow and her black chauffeur, also carried off the Best Picture award and Best Screenplay adaptation, leaving its nearest rival, *Born on the Fourth of July*, with the Best Director (Oliver Stone) and Film Editing Oscars. In the Best Actor category, Daniel Day Lewis as the quadraplegic writer Christy Brown in *My Left Foot*, edged out Tom Cruise (the favorite) as the paralyzed Vietnam War vet Ron Kovic in *Born on the Fourth of July*. Stone struck a sour note by complaining that "There was a concerted right-wing media effort against the movie. Because it's political, it made a lot of people angry."

Garbo the legend has really gone

New York, 15 April
Garbo, perhaps the greatest of all female screen legends, is no more. The reclusive star died aged 84 in a New York hospital earlier today. It was Mauritz Stiller, the Swedish director and her mentor, who gave Greta Gustafsson the name of Garbo before he cast her in *The Atonement of Gösta Berling* (1924). In 1925 he accompanied her to Hollywood and MGM, where he realized his dream of creating a "sophisticated, scornful and superior" woman, but "warm and vulnerable" beneath the glittering surface. After stunning silent screen vehicles, the moment came when MGM trumpeted that "Garbo Talks!" in *Anna Christie* (1930). She displayed her maturing ability as tragic heroines in *Queen Christina* (1933), *Anna Karenina* (1935) and *Camille* (1937), and as a comedian in Ernst Lubitsch's *Ninotchka* (1939). A year later Garbo suddenly retired from the screen permanently, shunning publicity ever after and hiding her face from the world. The legend will live on.

Popular comic-book mutants hit the screen

Hollywood, 30 March
Dreamed up in 1983 by a fast-food chef and a freelance illustrator, the *Teenage Mutant Ninja Turtles* have become a kids' phenomenon. The four masked, pizza-munching superheroes have progressed from cult comic strip to TV cartoon series to massive screen success and spin-off goldmine. New Line's $12 million debut feature took $25.4 million in its first weekend, the biggest ever opening for an independent film. And with 250 merchandising outlets worldwide and a sequel next January, these terrapins should *run...*

*Judith Hoag with a group of the amazing **Teenage Mutant Ninja Turtles**.*

Beyond the 'Mountains of the Moon'

London, 20 April
Based on William Harrison's biographical novel, *Burton and Speke*, and on original journals by the 19th-century explorers Sir Richard Burton and John Hanning Speke, *Mountains of the Moon* is a sprawling, exciting homage to the spirit of the pioneer adventurer. It has long been a pet project of director Bob Rafelson, a filmmaker more associated with contemporary American subjects. He has crammed the historical and epic story with pertinent period detail, and Roger Deakins' exceptional photography has captured many of the places where it all took place. The film follows the rivalry (and possible homosexual relationship) between Richard Burton (Patrick Bergin) and John Hanning Speke (Iain Glen) exploring the source of the Nile in "the bleak and hopeless landscapes" of East Africa, confronting dangers such as bloodthirsty tribesmen. The adventurers are charismatically portrayed by the two leads, at the head of an excellent British cast.

Patrick Bergin (l) and Iain Glen.

Christian Brando accused of murder

Los Angeles, 16 May
Christian, the 32-year-old son of Marlon Brando and Anna Kashfi, has been arrested for murder by L.A. police. He is accused of putting a bullet through the head of Dag Drollet, a young Frenchman, the boyfriend of Christian's 20-year-old half-sister Cheyenne. She is the daughter of Tarita, Marlon's second wife. The two men had quarreled at Marlon Brando's house. Christian had wanted Dag to leave Cheyenne, who had complained of being mistreated by her lover and sought help from her half-brother. The argument turned nasty yesterday when Christian got hold of a gun and shot Dag at point-blank range. On his arrest, the shocked Christian explained that it was an accident. Brando Sr. has canceled all his commitments to give support to his son. Christian was in the news at the age of 14 when his mother abducted him and hid him away from Marlon.

The Croisette is set alight by David Lynch's sulphurous couple

*Pavel Lounguine's entry, **Taxi Blues**.*

*Laura Dern and Nicolas Cage in **Wild at Heart** directed by David Lynch.*

Cannes, 21 May
David Lynch's torrid road movie, *Wild at Heart*, sent a shock wave along the Croisette because of its provocative sexiness and the bizarre and amoral behavior of the nasty on-the-run lovers (Nicolas Cage and Laura Dern). Nevertheless, it was awarded the Golden Palm. Cage as wild, snakeskin-jacketed Sailor Ripley with an Elvis Presley voice, and Dern as the uninhibited Southern sex bunny Lula Pace Fortune, create mayhem as they take their own Yellow Brick Road to happiness. (The film is an unlikely tribute to *The Wizard of Oz*.) This is all a long way from the comparatively innocent world of the Africa of Idrissa Ouedraogo's admirable *Tilai*, which won the Special Jury Prize.

Schwarzenegger in the grip of paranoia

New York, 1 June
With his role in *Total Recall*, Arnold Schwarzenegger is back in the business of kicking butt spectacularly in a brutal, relentlessly action-packed entertainment. A clever adaptation from a Philip K. Dick (*Blade Runner*) short story, it's helmed by Paul Verhoeven with plenty of explosively, gruesomely amazing special effects. Big Arnie plays a 21st-century construction worker who's haunted by nightmares about his experiences on Mars, although he's never been to the colonized Red Planet. Or has he...? Thus he's plunged into a twisty mystery of his true past, memory erasure, mutants in rebellion and just why people keep trying to slaughter him. The sci-fi set pieces on the climactic trip to Mars will be the movie's big talking point.

Lavish comeback for ace detective Tracy

Los Angeles, 15 June
Warren Beatty's version of *Dick Tracy* has opened at last. Chester Gould's original comic strip, on which the entertaining and visually striking film is based, began life in 1931, and has already been made into four serials, four shoestring features, and both a live-action and cartoon series on TV. Martin Scorsese and Brian De Palma were among directors considered when the film option was bought in 1974, while Clint Eastwood and Harrison Ford were keen to play the jut-jawed detective. But Beatty won out to produce, direct and star, with a budget around $20 million and another $10 million for marketing and post-production. Beatty, somewhat bland in the title role, has good support from Madonna and Al Pacino.

*Arnold Schwarzenegger as the brainwashed secret agent in **Total Recall**.*

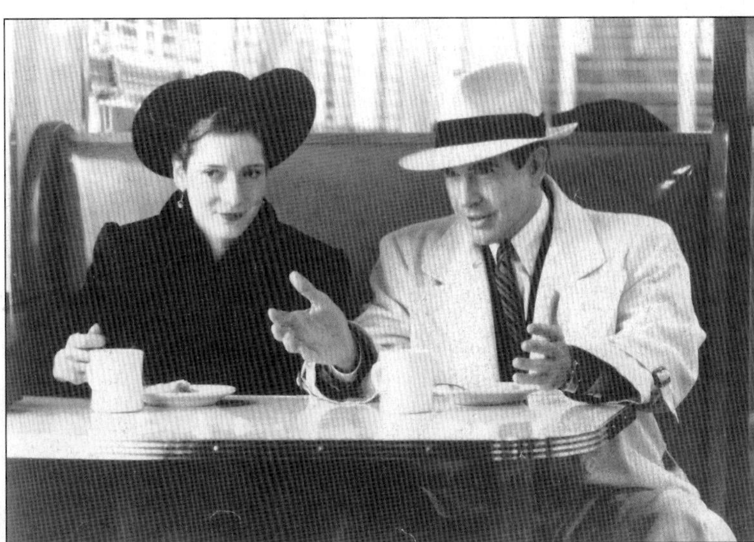
Tess Trueheart (Glenne Headly) and Dick Tracy enjoy a relaxed moment.

Death triggers off sweetly romantic movie

Unusual medium Whoopi Goldberg, with murder victim Patrick Swayze.

Hollywood, 13 July
Patrick Swayze badly needed a hit and *Ghost*, an unheralded $15 million film that has been captivating preview audiences weary of action blockbusters this summer, is it. Jerry Zucker injects a good deal of fun into his first "straight" directing solo, a supernatural romance thriller in which Swayze's hero is bumped off in reel one to get to grips with the afterlife, solve his own murder, devise a revenge sting and haunt his true love, Demi Moore. The film also revives the fortunes of Whoopi Goldberg, a comedian-actress for some time adrift on a sea of poor material, and here a delight as the phony medium getting more than she bargains for. The premise is ludicrous, but some of the special effects are inspired, the performances from Swayze and Moore are sweet, and Whoopi, firing on all cylinders, is a shamelessly entertaining smorgasbord of sex, guns, gags, and even a dance number. Patrick and Demi doing naughty things with wet clay over a potter's wheel might trigger a craze for pottery!

Life with gilded youth in 'Metropolitan'

Edward Clements and Carolyn Farina, two of the group in ***Metropolitan****.*

New York, 3 August
Set "not so long ago" among the UHB ("urban haute bourgeoisie") of New York, *Metropolitan* follows a red-haired radical in a rented tuxedo who semi-accidentally gets invited to a debutante party. He finds himself, however, thrown into the company of the "Sally Fowler Rat Pack", a group of neurotic, rich young things who get together after formal balls and stay up all night doing nothing in particular. With only a smattering of a plot, this refreshingly different and intelligent movie is far more concerned with dialogue and character. Director Whit Stillman, making an impressive debut, observes these idle young people with a keen and satiric eye, but never presents them as merely two-dimensional social parasites. So convincing are the performances by, among others, Carolyn Farina, Edward Clements and Christopher Eigerman, that it is difficult not to believe that they have inside experience of the characters. Yet this realism is placed in a fantasy-tinged vision of New York during the Christmas season.

Chills, spills and thrills with killer spiders

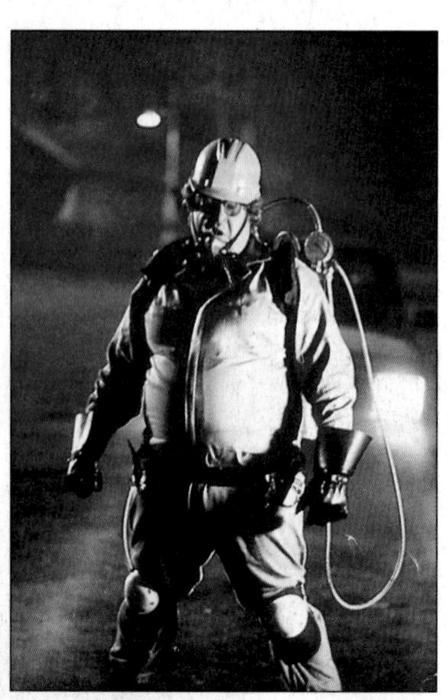

John Goodman, the exterminator!

Hollywood, 18 July
Remembering *Jaws*, it's no surprise to learn that Steven Spielberg was the executive producer for director Frank Marshall's *Arachnophobia*. Story has the always appealing Jeff Daniels as a doctor in search of a new life, who moves to the country with his wife (Harley Jane Kozak) and kids, only to be confronted by a mysterious plague of killer spiders. The movie provokes screams of real fright and shrieks of laughter in a cunning mix of entertainment. Funniest of all is John Goodman, whose cameo as a bumbling termite exterminator is truly riotous. The effects are terrific, matched by the cinematography and straight-faced acting. Even arachnophobics should have a good time.

Streep and MacLaine a knock-out combo

Los Angeles, 12 September
Carrie Fisher's comically excruciating backstage Hollywood to hell and back confessional, *Postcards From the Edge*, has been filmed by Mike Nichols. Meryl Streep finally gets a sharply witty vehicle for her hitherto undervalued comedic talents: an actress in drug rehab, struggling to rescue her career and resolve her nerve-wracking relationship with her boozy, overpowering mother, an aging but ballsy musical star played bravely and brilliantly by Shirley MacLaine. The teaming is hugely entertaining, as are a host of starry supporting turns from the men, notably Gene Hackman, as Tinseltown denizens. Both leading ladies make show-stoppers out of their musical numbers. Yes, Streep can sing!

Meryl Streep and Shirley MacLaine.

'GoodFellas' an electrifying and troubling mafia masterpiece

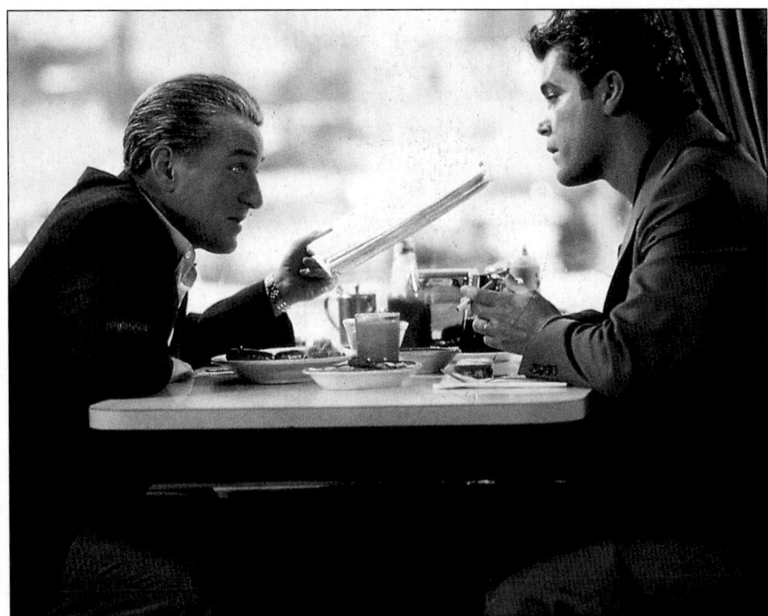
Ray Liotta (r) as Henry Hill, with his violent mentor Robert De Niro.

New York, 19 September
Martin Scorsese's *GoodFellas* is a long, violent and enthralling interweaving of biography (the real-life tale of Henry Hill, who grew to manhood in the Mafia, and eventually ratted on his former associates), social observation and black comedy. The superb cast includes some of the best of New York's character actors: Paul Sorvino, Lorraine Bracco (as Hill's JAP wife), and Joe Pesci, who turns in a remarkably realistic performance, most menacing when he feigns anger with Hill (Ray Liotta), and when he guns down a young man who has insulted him. A commendably restrained Robert De Niro, in his sixth collaboration with Scorsese, is only the second lead as Hill's mentor, but makes his usual impact. As Henry Hill, the young "hero", relative newcomer Liotta gives a mercurial portrayal of this complex character – an Irish-Italian kid who succeeds in his youthful ambition to become a wealthy gangster, only to have his position slowly eroded until it almost destroys him. Scorsese sustains the fast tempo of the tale to the exciting climax. Nevertheless, the physical impact of the movie tends to suppress the troubling issues that lie beneath it: to what extent is the graphic depiction of horrifying violence justified, and is it permissible to find these unscrupulous characters glamorous or sympathetic?

Lyrical, sensuous excursion into Marcel Pagnol's Provençal past

Paris, 26 October
Two months after the triumph of *la Gloire de mon père* (*My Father's Glory*), the second part of Marcel Pagnol's childhood memories, *le Château de ma mère* (*My Mother's Castle*), has just been released, and there is no reason to think it will not be equally successful. The excellent director of both films is Yves Robert, who demonstrated many years ago with *The War of the Buttons* (1962) that he was able to penetrate the psychology of children. In this lyrical and sensuous Pagnol diptych, Robert has managed to evoke the blissful childhood of Marcel, recapturing his summer holidays in the Provençal countryside spent with his brother Paul, his little sister, his loving parents, and Aunt Rose and Uncle Jules. The films show Marcel's discovery of the beauties of nature, country estates and gardens. Robert had long wanted to adapt the books to the screen, and approached their author in 1963. Pagnol (who died 11 years later) gave Robert the rights, despite his desire to make the films himself.

Benoît Martin (r) as the young Marcel with his peasant friend (Joris Molinas).

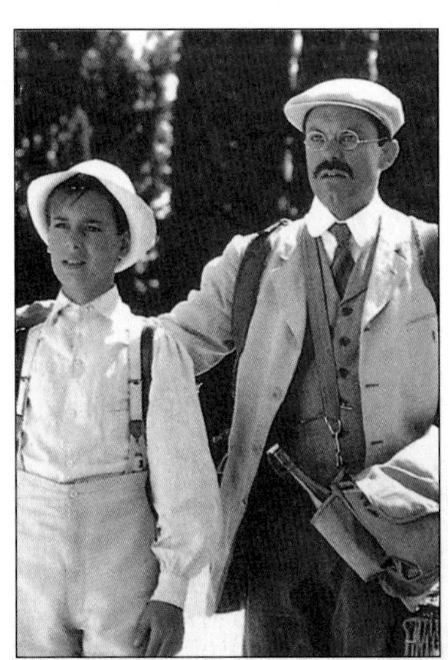
With Father (Philippe Caubère).

Parretti takes over ailing MGM/UA

Los Angeles, 1 November
The long and troubled history of Kirk Kerkorian's reign as owner of MGM has finally ended with the sale of the company to Italian financier Giancarlo Parretti for $1.3 billion. As the *Financial Times* noted, "In the 21 years since Mr. Kerkorian bought control of MGM, he has spun off, sold, rebought and generally shuffled assets with great fervor." During the past six years alone there were deals to sell all or part of the company to CNN's Ted Turner, then to Guber-Peters-Barris; rumors of negotiations with Sony and with Rupert Murdoch's News Corp., were followed by a deal with Australian entrepreneur Christopher Skase's Quintex group in 1989, which fell through. Now, with financial backing from the giant French Crédit Lyonnais, Parretti has succeeded. Two years ago he rescued the Cannon group, renaming it Pathé Communications, and, as of today, he owns MGM/UA. A glossy booklet out for the occasion says, "Three names now united in a worldwide multi-media conglomerate with the production resources, management talent and creative energy to forge the most formidable entertainment concern since the origin of Hollywood itself."

Japan's most popular comic strip, *Akira*, becomes a film about a violent futuristic Tokyo. Poor narrative, but revolutionary, brilliant and realistic animation.

'Dances With Wolves' a new ballgame for Kevin

New York, 9 November
Advance word on Kevin Costner's $18 million directorial debut, a three-hour ode to the noble Native American – some of it in Sioux with subtitles – had Hollywood wags gleefully referring to "Kevin's Gate". But *Dances With Wolves* is a personal and artistic triumph for Costner. The title is the name the Indians give to Costner (who also plays the lead), a Civil War officer, after he's posted to the frontier and goes native. The story of how he comes by his new name makes as enchanting a Western as ever was, rich, lyrical and full of exciting action, beautifully shot by Australian Dean Semler. Come Oscar night, it will be a major surprise if this evocative and enjoyable epic is not in there pitching.

Director and star Kevin Costner as the liberal-minded cavalry officer.

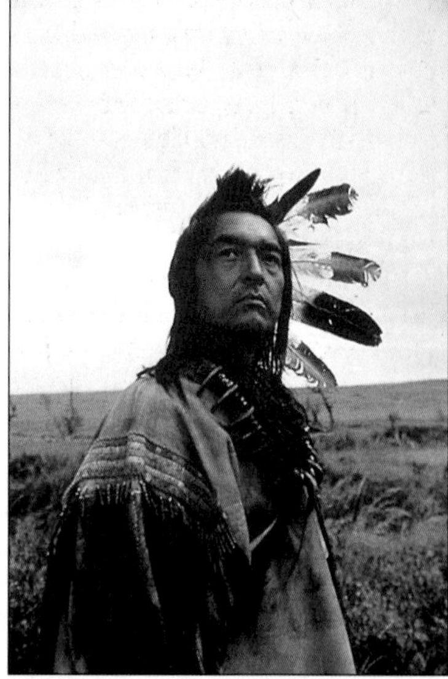

Graham Greene, a friendly Sioux.

A new hero for the under-twelves

Los Angeles, 16 November
John Hughes, who for years has tapped into the youth market, has written the script for *Home Alone*, directed by Chris Columbus. This time for children of all ages, it's a delightful romp in which Hughes' utterly engaging discovery, Macaulay Culkin, plays an eight-year-old accidentally left behind when his family goes away at Christmas, who ingeniously defends the house against criminals. Riotously funny, with Culkin set to become the biggest child star since Shirley Temple.

Johnny Depp charms in bizarre fairy tale

Los Angeles, 7 December
Tim Burton's greatest pleasure as a child was watching Vincent Price movies on TV. Price appears as a Dr. Frankenstein figure in Burton's new film, *Edward Scissorhands*, a beguiling fable about a young man with scissors for hands, which draws on fairy tale and Gothic romance. In a beautifully re-created early 60s kitsch wasteland, the good-natured hero, played by Johnny Depp with effective little-boy poignancy, falls hopelessly in love with Winona Ryder, his real-life girlfriend.

With Godfather III, the dynasty drags on

New York, 25 December
Francis Ford Coppola, after a number of relative flops such as *Gardens of Stone* and *Tucker: The Man and His Dream*, and hungry to recover his past success, has gone back to the Corleone dynasty in *Godfather Part III*. Ironically, it was not so long ago that Coppola refused to embark on another *Godfather*, saying, "I would just take the story and tell it again, which is what they do on these sequels. I'm not really interested in gangsters anymore." Yet the director has succeeded in creating a sumptuous and powerful, if uneven, coda to the family saga that began 16 years ago. There are several survivors from the original cast – Al Pacino as Michael Corleone, now the *paterfamilias*, doing deals with the Vatican; Diane Keaton, as his wife, and Talia Shire (Coppola's own sister) his sister. It would certainly not have been possible to make without Pacino, who allowed Coppola to twist his arm with $5 million plus a percentage. The younger generation is well represented by Andy Garcia, carving his way into the family by marrying the Corleone daughter, played by Coppola's daughter Sofia, disastrously replacing an ill Winona Ryder.

Macaulay Culkin, a new star.

Johnny Depp and Winona Ryder.

Diane Keaton, George Hamilton and, as the latest Godfather, Al Pacino.

Reel Music

Film music cannot make a bad film good, but it can make a good film better. At its best it enhances, at its worst it is intrusive and can interfere with one's concentration on the movie. In most critical studies of the movies, this essential area, the musical score, is often pushed to the sidelines. In any consideration of motion picture history, the music must be taken, with the imagery, acting and dialogue, as an integral part of the aesthetic whole. For, although film is regarded as primarily a visual art, it is closer to opera than any other form, or rather to Richard Wagner's definition of the ideal opera as a *Gesamtkunstwerk* – a complete work of art uniting all the arts.

For most audiences, music has become an indispensable part of their response to film, whether conscious or unconscious. This has been the case since the Lumière brothers first showed their films to the public on 28 December 1895, when a piano accompanied the flickering images. In the very early days, music not only served to counteract the noise of the projector, but added to the mood of the scenes depicted.

Music for silent films ranged from solo pianists to small instrumental ensembles to huge orchestras in the larger picture palaces. The first 'serious' composer to write for the cinema was Camille Saint-Saëns, composing for *The Assassination of the Duke de Guise*, in 1908. D.W. Griffith demonstrated the importance he placed on music by working closely with J.C. Breil on *The Birth of a Nation* (1915). Together they constructed an elaborately cued score made up of original passages and traditional American tunes.

Other directors and composers who made creative use of music in the 'silent' era were Abel Gance and Arthur Honneger on *Napoleon* (1927) in France, and Grigori Kozintsev and Leonid Trauberg, working with Dmitri Shostakovitch on *The New Babylon* (1929), in the Soviet Union.

Because of the expense, there were attempts to replace musicians with gramophone records, and in 1926 Warner Bros. issued *Don Juan* in their Vitaphone sound-on-disc process. This consisted of recorded background music played in synchronization with the film. That process signaled the end of live film music. As Hollywood went over to sound, each major studio set up its own music department with a musical director.

The influx of talented composers, many of them refugees from Europe, helped to extend the scope of film music. Among the most outstanding were Max Steiner, Dmitri Tiomkin, Franz Waxman, Miklos Rozsa, Erich Korngold and Victor Young. Steiner's emotional scores include those for *Gone With the Wind* (1939), and romantic Warner melodramas of the 40s such as *Now Voyager* (1942) and *Casablanca* (1943). Tiomkin's best work provided sweeping scores for Westerns such as *Red River* (1948) and the haunting music for *High Noon* (1952) which yielded a famous song, "Do Not Forsake Me, Oh My Darlin'". Adept at psychologically-laden music, Waxman contributed to *Rebecca* (1940) and *Sunset Boulevard* (1950) while the Hungarian-born Rozsa was good at eerie mood music – *Spellbound, The Lost Weekend*, both 1945 – and majestic scores for epics such as *Quo Vadis?* (1951), *Ben-Hur* (1959) and *El Cid* (1961). The Czech-born Korngold gave up opera and concert composition to write for films including *The Adventures of Robin Hood* (1938) and *Kings Row* (1942). Victor Young scored most of Paramount's lavish productions from the late 30s to the early 50s. His last work, composed shortly before his death, was the music for *Around the World in Eighty Days* (1956).

In France, Maurice Jaubert provided delicate music for René Clair (*The Last Millionaire*, 1934) and Jean Vigo (*Zero for Conduct*, 1933), and Joseph Kosma supplied wistful themes for many of Jean Renoir's best films. In the Soviet Union, Prokofiev collaborated closely with Eisenstein on *Alexander Nevsky* (1938), a film described by its maker as a 'symphonic structure', and in Britain, Laurence Olivier's *Henry V* (1944) benefited greatly from William Walton's stirring score.

FIRE EXIT
EXIT

Oscar-winning composer/MD Miklos Rozsa at work in the sound studio.

By the 50s, the musician's role in Hollywood was accorded greater status. Film music began to be issued on records, and the provision of a theme song helped to sell a movie. There was enormous success for the title songs of *Three Coins in a Fountain* (1954) and *Love is a Many Splendored Thing* (1955). The *Blackboard Jungle* (1955) virtually introduced rock 'n' roll to the screen with Bill Haley's "Rock Around the Clock", but it would take more than a decade for background music to be often replaced by hit pop songs as in *The Graduate* (1967) and *Easy Rider* (1969).

With the break-up of the big studios, new composers emerged: the versatile and prolific Elmer Bernstein, whose work ranges from *The Ten Commandments* (1956) to *Ghostbusters* (1984); John Barry, who made his reputation with the James Bond movies and landed his third Oscar in 1990 for *Dances With Wolves*; and Marvin Hamlisch, who wrote the score and title song for *The Way We Were* (1973). Two French musicians broke into American films: Francis Lai moved from *A Man and a Woman* (1966) to *Love Story* (1970), and Michel Legrand from *The Umbrellas of Cherbourg* (1964) to *The Thomas Crown Affair* (1968). A number of composers of the past have made a significant posthumous contribution to film music, notably Rachmaninov in David Lean's *Brief Encounter* (1945); Bach in Robert Bresson's *A Man Escaped* (1956); Mozart in *Elvira Madigan* (1967); and Mahler in Visconti's *Death in Venice*. Stanley Kubrick has been particularly adept at using the classics, most memorably Richard Strauss' "Thus Spake Zarathustra" and Johann Strauss' "The Blue Danube" in *2001* (1968), and Beethoven's 9th Symphony in *A Clockwork Orange* (1971).

The intertwining of vision and music is best illustrated by the director-composer teams. Bernard Herrmann's pulsating rhythms perfectly counterpointed the off-center world of Alfred Hitchcock; and it is almost impossible to separate the work of Federico Fellini from that of Nino Rota, who provided the jaunty, circus-like tunes for most of the films. The richly throbbing scores of Maurice Jarre fitted David Lean's epics as much as the sugar-sweet melodies of Henry Mancini suited Blake Edwards' wry comedies. There are fewer more distinctive film composers than the Italian Ennio Morricone, who came to prominence with his haunting scores – unusually using choruses, solo voices and whistling – for Sergio Leone's Spaghetti Westerns. But probably the music most familiar to audiences by the 1990s was that of John Williams, whose large-scale works have accompanied almost all Steven Spielberg's films.

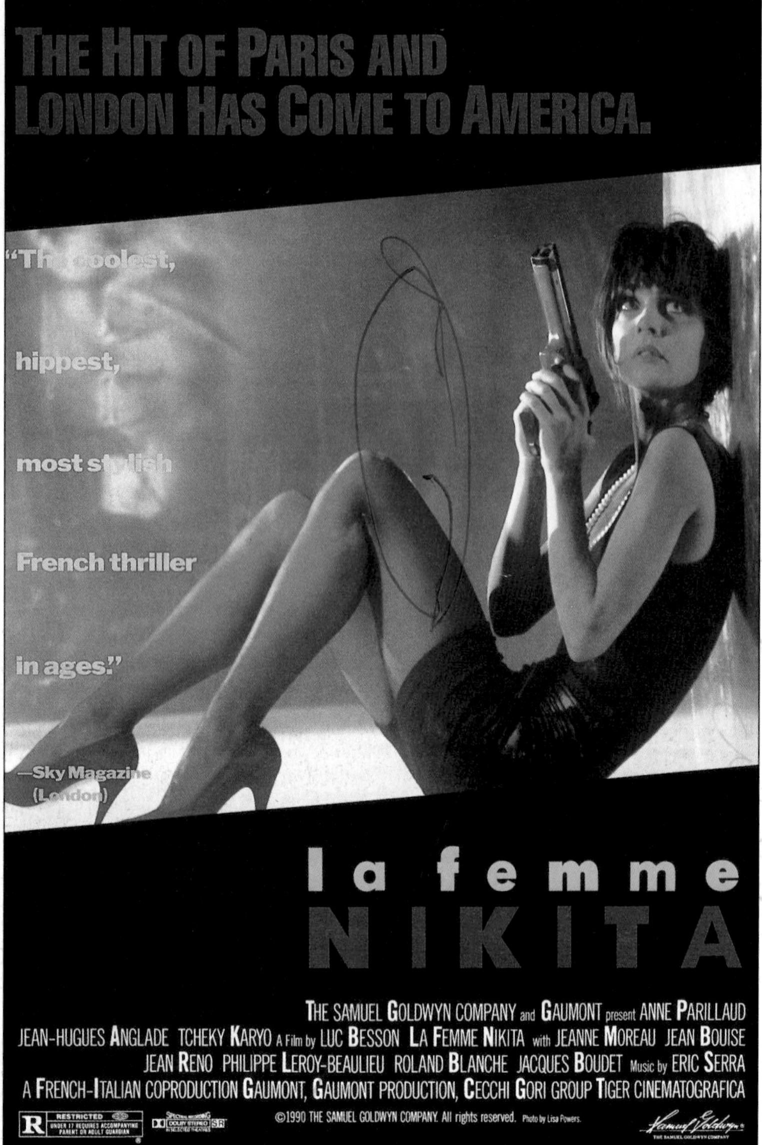
THE HIT OF PARIS AND
LONDON HAS COME TO AMERICA.
"The coolest,
hippest,
most stylish
French thriller
in ages."
—Sky Magazine
(London)
la femme
NIKITA
THE SAMUEL GOLDWYN COMPANY and GAUMONT present ANNE PARILLAUD
JEAN-HUGUES ANGLADE TCHEKY KARYO A Film by LUC BESSON LA FEMME NIKITA with JEANNE MOREAU JEAN BOUISE
JEAN RENO PHILIPPE LEROY-BEAULIEU ROLAND BLANCHE JACQUES BOUDET Music by ERIC SERRA
A FRENCH-ITALIAN COPRODUCTION GAUMONT, GAUMONT PRODUCTION, CECCHI GORI GROUP TIGER CINEMATOGRAFICA
R RESTRICTED
©1990 THE SAMUEL GOLDWYN COMPANY. All rights reserved. Photo by Lisa Powers.

Anne Parillaud in Luc Besson's internationally successful high-tech thriller.

Gérard Depardieu, Andie MacDowell in Peter Weir's ***Green Card****.*

Kathryn Bigelow's tough thriller ***Blue Steel*** *with cop Jamie Lee Curtis.*

From Hong Kong's John Woo: Danny Lee (l), Chow Yun Fat in ***The Killers****.*

Dirk Bogarde, Jane Birkin, father and daughter in ***These Foolish Things****.*

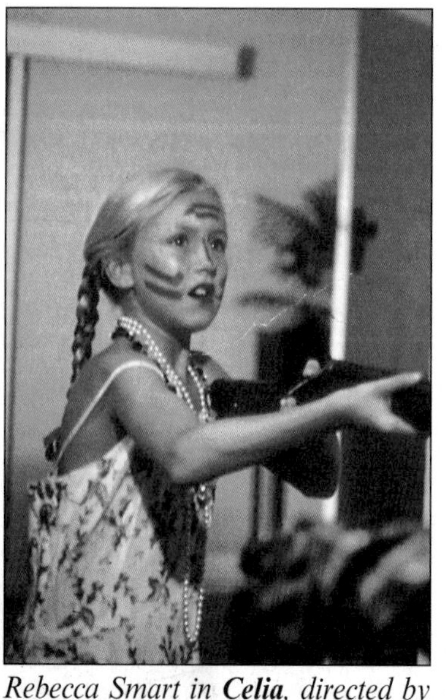

Rebecca Smart in ***Celia****, directed by Australian filmmaker Anne Turner.*

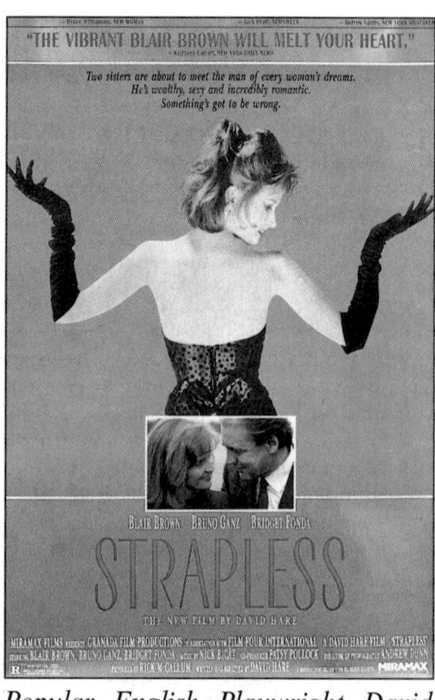
"THE VIBRANT BLAIR BROWN WILL MELT YOUR HEART."
Two sisters are about to meet the man of every woman's dreams.
He's wealthy, sexy and incredibly romantic.
Something's got to be wrong.
BLAIR BROWN BRUNO GANZ BRIDGET FONDA
STRAPLESS
THE NEW FILM BY DAVID HARE
MIRAMAX FILMS GRANADA FILM PRODUCTIONS FILM FOUR INTERNATIONAL A DAVID HARE FILM "STRAPLESS"
BLAIR BROWN, BRUNO GANZ, BRIDGET FONDA NICK BICÂT PATSY POLLOCK ANDREW DUNN
RICK McCALLUM DAVID HARE
MIRAMAX

Popular English Playwright David Hare directed his own screenplay.

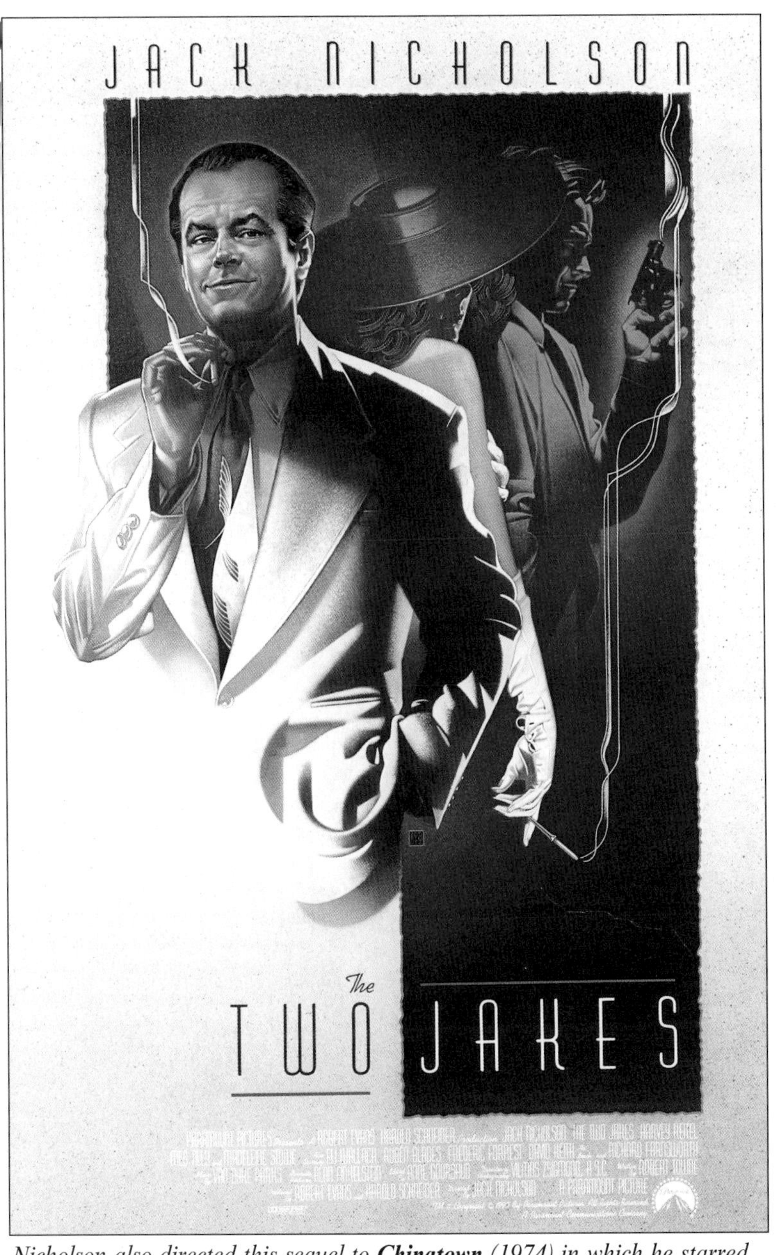
JACK NICHOLSON
The
TWO JAKES

Nicholson also directed this sequel to **Chinatown** (1974) in which he starred.

Julia McNeal (l), Adrienne Shelly in Hal Hartley's ***The Unbelievable Truth****.*

Last Exit to Brooklyn*: Tralala (Jennifer Jason Leigh) picks up a soldier.*

Marco Hofschneider and Julie Delpy in Agnieszka Holland's ***Europa, Europa****.*

Let's Get Lost*: trumpeter Chet Baker plays in a film based on his life.*

Helen Mirren and Rupert Everett in ***The Comfort of Strangers****.*

1991

1990 Academy Awards, Dorothy Chandler Pavilion, 20 Mar.

Best Film:	*Dances With Wolves* (dir: Kevin Costner)
Best Director:	Kevin Costner
Best Actor:	Jeremy Irons *(Reversal of Fortune)*
Best Actress:	Kathy Bates *(Misery)*
Best Supp. Actor:	Joe Pesci *(Goodfellas)*
Best Supp. Actress:	Whoopi Goldberg *(Ghost)*

Hollywood, 4 January
The Academy of Motion Picture Arts and Sciences has announced that a record high of 37 countries have submitted entries for the foreign film Oscar this year.

New York, 6 January
The National Critics Association today voted Martin Scorsese as best director for *GoodFellas*, which was also judged best film. Jeremy Irons was best actor for his portrayal of Claus von Bulow in Warner Bros.' *Reversal of Fortune*, while the award for best actress went to Anjelica Huston for her performances in *The Witches* and *The Grifters*, which also won best supporting actress for Annette Bening. Aki Kaurismaki's *Ariel* was voted best foreign film.

Utah, 28 January
Todd Haynes' *Poison*, an unconventional three-part drama inspired by the writings of Jean Genet, overcame divided opinion at this year's Sundance Film Festival to win the grand jury prize. Haynes first gained notoriety with his widely acclaimed film *Superstar: The Karen Carpenter Story*. The film, which employed Barbie and Ken dolls to dramatize the singer's tragic death in 1982 from anorexia nervosa, has since been withdrawn due to its illegal use of original Carpenters music.

New York, 30 January
According to the movie magazine *Premiere*, three couples paid the sum of $14,000 to have breakfast at Tiffany's with Audrey Hepburn, the allusion being to the 1961 film by Blake Edwards. The money will go to UNICEF for which Miss Hepburn is a roving ambassador and tireless fundraiser.

Burkino Faso, 2 February
The jury of the 12th Pan-African Film Festival in Ouagadougou, presided over by Malian director Souleymane Cissé, has awarded its main prize to *Tilai*, by Idrissa Ouedraogo.

New York, 7 March
Pauline Kael, the often controversial film critic, retires this month after 23 years as the regular critic for the *New Yorker*. Her last review appeared in the 11 February issue. Miss Kael, whose outspokenness caused a few difficult moments in her early days, was fired from McCalls in 1965 for calling *The Sound of Music* "The Sound of Money". Although considered a role model for a new generation of serious film critics, she could turn a phrase with the best of them. On Costner and *Dances With Wolves*, she quipped, "Costner has feathers in his hair and feathers in his head..."

Hollywood, 25 March
Popular actor and comedian Billy Crystal, this year's compere at the Oscars, threw the following at the Academy audience during the announcements: "We are very happy that there are no more American prisoners in the world... apart from those at Paramount."

Hollywood, 5 April
Ex-producer Julia Phillips, once one of Hollywood's brightest stars (she was the first woman producer to win a Best Picture Oscar) before her drug habit sent her on a downward spiral, is enjoying the sweet taste of revenge. Her autobiographical bestseller, already in its fourth printing after barely a month on the shelf, has been raising temperatures in Tinseltown with its biting disclosures of *le tout Hollywood*.

Paris, 17 April
Jean-Pierre Jeunet and Marc Caro, who have already directed numerous video clips and advertisements as well as the astonishing short film *le Bunker de la dernière rafale*, have released their first feature film *Delicatessen*. A strange story which mixes cannabalism with poetic realism, it stars Dominique Piñon and Jean-Claude Dreyfus and looks to be causing something of a sensation.

Paris, 22 April
A UNESCO report has revealed that American films are flooding African screens. In Egypt, for example, American films have captured 86 percent of the market.

Philippines, 22 May
Lino Brocka, the *bête noire* of the Marcos regime, has been killed in a car accident. His last film, *les Insoumis*, was presented as part of the official selection at the Festival of Cannes in 1989.

Toronto, 10 June
David Cronenberg has begun shooting *Naked Lunch*, adapted from William Burroughs' book about the sex and drugs culture. Until now it has been considered an impossible work to adapt for the screen.

Sarasota, 28 July
Popular actor Pee Wee Herman (Paul Rubens) was arrested here yesterday for indecent behavior in an adult movie theater. Pee Wee has been a phemonenon with children and adults alike since his wacky debut in *Pee Wee's Big Adventure* in 1985. He developed the cherry-lipped, loveable brat in shrunken grey suit and bow tie as a comedian with the Groundlings, a Los Angeles improvisational group, in 1979.

Hollywood, 12 August
Dustin Hoffman, who is at present making *Hook* with Steven Spielberg, has signed a three year contract with Columbia TriStar.

New York, 12 August
Jennie Livingston's acclaimed documentary about New York's Harlem drag balls, *Paris is Burning*, has come under harsh criticism from the Atlanta-based Christian Film and Television Commission, which seeks to promote "the moral, family-oriented, Judeo-Christian viewpoint". Prestige, the Miramax Films division distributing the film, has decided to counter the CFTC attack by handing out petitions over the weekend at the 26 theaters currently showing the film.

London, 30 August
Opening of Peter Greenaway's *Prospero's Books*, a loose adaptation of William Shakespeare's *The Tempest*. Michael Nyman has again composed the music for Greenaway.

Los Angeles, 6 October
Elizabeth Taylor has married for the eighth time. Her new husband, Larry Fortenski, is a builder whom she met while undergoing treatment for alcoholism. The wedding took place at Michael Jackson's ranch.

Los Angeles, 25 November
Anton Furst, the special effects designer who won an Academy Award for art direction on *Batman*, died yesterday. According to a Columbia spokesman he committed suicide. Furst developed and designed the holographic light show for the rock group The Who.

DEATHS

Paris, 2 March
Serge Gainsbourg

California, 27 March
Aldo Ray

London, 16 April
David Lean

California, 20 April
Don Siegel

Palm Springs, 1 May
Richard Thorpe

California, 19 June
Jean Arthur

California, 2 July
Lee Remick

Hollywood, 3 September
Frank Capra

Los Angeles, 13 September
Joe Pasternak

California, 5 November
Fred MacMurray

Texas, 6 November
Gene Tierney

France, 9 November
Yves Montand

Los Angeles, 14 November
Tony Richardson

Jodie Foster gives an extraordinary performance, matching that of Anthony Hopkins as Hannibal Lecter, in Jonathan Demme's screen version of the Thomas Harris novel.

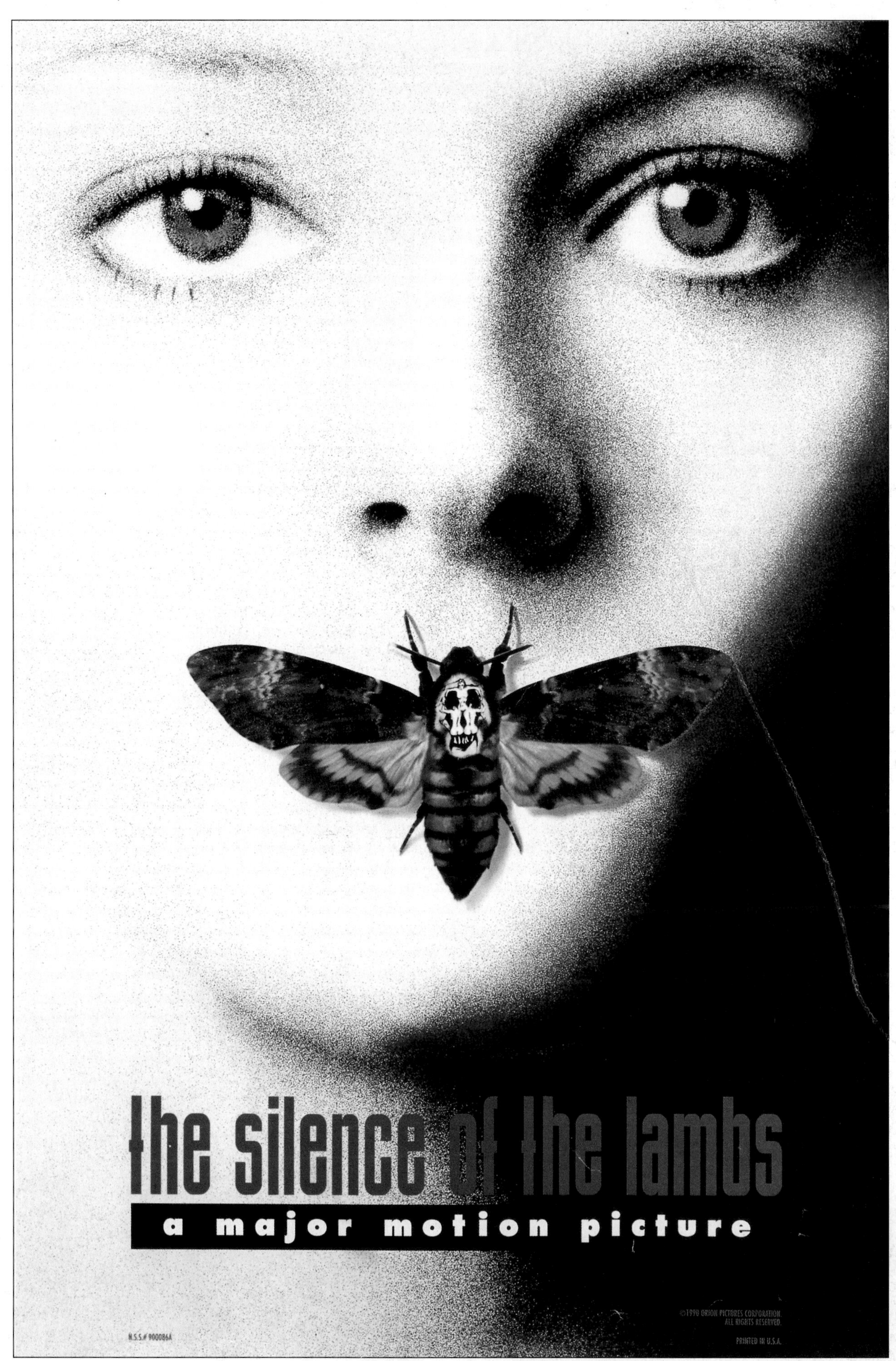
the silence of the lambs
a major motion picture
©1990 ORION PICTURES CORPORATION.
ALL RIGHTS RESERVED.
PRINTED IN U.S.A.
N.S.S.# 900086A

Andrzej Wajda wrestles with the Holocaust

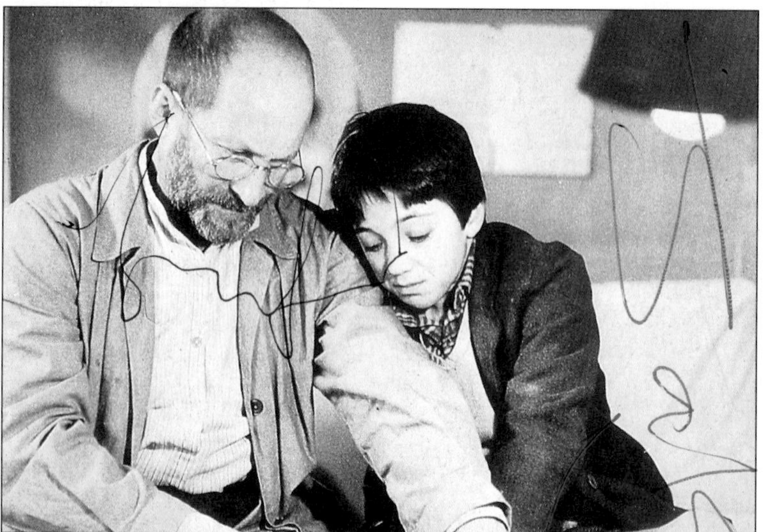

Wojtek Pszoniak as Doctor Janusz Korczak, the Jewish orphanage director.

Paris, 9 January
It is fitting that the Polish director Andrzej Wajda, himself a Resistance fighter, who made his reputation with his war trilogy, should return to his country's darkest days with *Korczak*. It tells the true story of Dr. Korczak, director of a Jewish orphanage, who is forced to transfer the home to the Warsaw ghetto when the Nazis invade Poland in 1939. Three years later, he and the children are on their way to Treblinka. But the director, admitting that he could not come to terms with the reality, imagines the children's souls being released from the train and able to romp in the countryside.

Mel Gibson gives his best shot to Hamlet

'Alas, poor Yorick... ' Mel Gibson soliloquizes in his role as Hamlet.

Boston, 18 January
Franco Zeffirelli's choice of Mel Gibson for Hamlet, the greatest role in the English language other than King Lear, is vindicated by a competent, thoughtful and attractive performance that has vigor and humor. Gibson, neither noble youth nor persuasive scholar, is a tad stolid when soliloquizing, but impressive when his blood is up or when feigning madness. An extravagantly coiffed Glenn Close looks ridiculously young to have hatched this prince and much of the direction is uninspired, but Paul Scofield's majestic Ghost brings class to a handsome but disappointing film.

'The Grifters' a terrifying trio of tryers

Los Angeles, 25 January
For his first film set in America, British director Stephen Frears chose *The Grifters*, adapted from a relentlessly cynical, downbeat and fascinating thriller by Jim Thompson. Set in a stylized Southern California (drifting between the 1950s and the 1980s), this is a subtle and stylish *film noir* about three con artists or "grifters". They are played to perfection by Annette Bening, a queen spider attracting men into her web; a blonde Anjelica Huston, the tough and fatalistic old hand; and John Cusack as her son, caught between them, hostile to mother, but following in her footsteps.

Steve Martin tells an off-the-wall LA story

Los Angeles, 8 February
"Romance does exist deep in the heart of L.A.," says nutty television weather forecaster Steve Martin in *L.A. Story*, a romantic comedy set in the city with no heart. Martin, who wrote the script, does a series of amusing comic turns, including a balletic glide through the County Museum, as he pursues visiting English journalist Victoria Tennant. But despite some satiric cracks at the modish eccentricities of L.A., both British director Mick Jackson and the star cannot resist adding a confusing dose of whimsy, such as a talking freeway information sign which plays cupid to the hero.

Anjelica Huston, confidence trickster extraordinaire, in ***The Grifters****.*

Steve Martin with Sarah Jessica Parker in ***L.A. Story****, from the script he wrote.*

'Silence of the Lambs' a tour de force

New York, 14 February
"Believe me, you don't want Hannibal Lecter inside your head," rookie FBI agent Jodie Foster is warned in *The Silence of the Lambs*. But Dr. Hannibal "the Cannibal", a once eminent psychiatrist turned serial killer, as brilliantly portrayed by Anthony Hopkins, is bound to stay inside audiences' heads. Tautly directed by Jonathan Demme, this gripping and eerie psychological thriller largely manages to avoid sensationalism. The best scenes are the confrontations between the caged Hopkins and Foster, she regarding him with morbid fascination as he unblinkingly plays an intricate game of cat and mouse with her.

Anthony Hopkins and Jodie Foster.

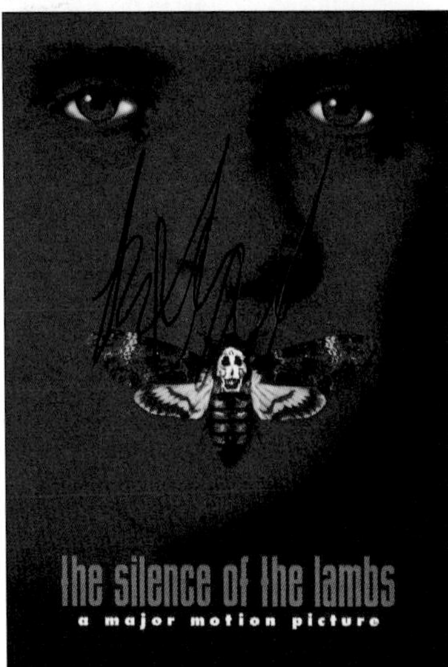
the silence of the lambs
a major motion picture

Blier mixes an audacious cocktail

Paris, 13 March
It is obviously too soon to expect 55-year-old Bertrand Blier to have settled down and renounced the style which has contributed to his originality – a poetic disenchantment with life, derision and insolence, which always prevents his films from being gratuitously vulgar. Thus Blier's latest film, *Merci la vie* – in the spirit of his youthful works like *Going Places* (*les Valseuses*) – is probably his most anti-conformist film in attitude as well as form. It follows two very different young girls on a testing voyage of discovery. Both Charlotte Gainsbourg and Anouk Grinberg are remarkable.

Christian Brando guilty of murder

Los Angeles, 28 February
Christian Brando, aged 33, has been convicted of the murder of Dag Drollet, the boyfriend of his half-sister, Cheyenne. Through William Kunstler, his lawyer, Marlon Brando's son by his first wife Anna Kashfi, pleaded not guilty. He has always maintained that the killing, which took place at his father's Californian home on 16 May last year, was an accident, and that there was no criminal intent on his part. He explained that the gun that killed Drollet had been fired involuntarily during a struggle after Christian had demanded that Drollet, who had been mistreating Cheyenne, leave the house. Marlon Brando, who took the witness stand, defended his son passionately, with tears in his eyes. The jury, however, remained unmoved by the famous actor's words, and Christian was condemned to 10 years in prison.

Christian Brando and his father at the conclusion of the trial.

Academy salutes Costner's directing debut

Glenn Close, Jeremy Irons as Sunny and Claus Von Bulow in happier times.

Hollywood, 25 March
Kevin Costner, a good-looking, dependable and amiable 35-year-old actor, astonished everybody by producing, directing and starring in *Dances With Wolves*, the film that cleaned up on most of this year's Oscars. Costner himself played Lieutenant John J. Dunbar, an army officer who asks to be posted to the western frontier. Living alone at "the furthest outpost of the realm", he gradually earns the trust of the Sioux Indians. Renamed Dances with Wolves, he joins their tribe, but is brutally treated by a newly arrived cavalry detail. As a debut director, Costner displayed extraordinary confidence, handling the big scenes of this three-hour epic, and the more intimate ones, with real feeling for the medium. It also comes closer than most commercial movies to an accurate re-creation of the Native American way of life. *Dances With Wolves* won the best film, director, writing, cinematography, editing, sound and music awards, but the acting Oscars went to Jeremy Irons (Best Actor, *Reversal of Fortune*), Kathy Bates (Best Actress, *Misery*), Joe Pesci, (Best Supporting Actor, *GoodFellas*), and Whoopi Goldberg (Best Supporting Actress, *Ghost*).

Cyrano de Bergerac sets César record

Paris, 13 March
The record for the number of Césars obtained by one film has been broken by *Cyrano de Bergerac*, which won 10 awards. These included best director (Jean-Paul Rappeneau), best actor (Gérard Depardieu), best cinematographer (Pierre Lhomme), best supporting actor (Jacques Weber) and, naturally, best film. At the ceremony, actor Richard Bohringer presented the César for best actress to Anne Parillaud for her exciting performance in the title role of Luc Besson's *Nikita*. The recipient burst into tears, which were wiped away discreetly by Besson.

Carole Bouquet (l), Anne Parillaud.

▷

Life-enhancing trip to Canadian countryside

Cissy Meddings (left) and Alice Diablo in Cynthia Scott's lyrical film.

New York, 10 May

From Canada comes filmmaker Cynthia Scott's award-winning *The Company of Strangers*, a semi-documentary that brings unalloyed, life-enhancing delight. Seven elderly women, on a day trip in the lovely countryside outside Quebec, are stranded when their bus breaks down. They take refuge in a derelict farm, where they must live off their wits and courage, and pass the time telling the stories of their own lives. Improvised from the raw material of the real-life, non-acting cast, this is not a talking heads picture, but a warm, optimistic tribute to the human spirit and old age.

Varda's magic tribute to husband Demy

RÉPARATIONS
ENTRETIEN
GARAGE AU MOIS

Agnes Varda with Demy (right) and her young players during the filming.

Paris, 15 May

Jacques Demy was nine years old at the outbreak of the Second World War. Brought up in Nantes, the young boy occupied his spare time making puppets. Soon after, he discovered the cinema, and began to make films with a little camera. These childood memories of the director of *Lola* and *The Umbrellas of Cherbourg*, have been re-created in a magical manner by his widow, Agnes Varda, for a film that's called *Jacquot de Nantes*. Varda has also included a series of moving interviews with her ailing husband, who died last November, a short while after the film was completed.

'Barton Fink' breaks records at Cannes

Cannes, 20 May

By carrying off the Golden Palm, the director's prize and the best actor award, *Barton Fink* has succeeded in doing what no other film has ever done in the history of the Cannes Festival. However, admired as Joel and Ethan Coen's American movie was, a number of critics considered that making it a triple winner was going a bit too far, especially as it was in competition with Jacques Rivette's *la Belle Noiseuse* and Krzysztof Kieslowski's *The Double Life of Véronique*. Nevertheless, the former gained the Grand Prix, and the latter the best actress award for Irene Jacob in the double title role. But *Barton Fink* impressed the jury, under Roman Polanski, with its skillful mixture of the sordid and the poetic, the real and the unreal, in a Kafkaesque vision of 1940s Hollywood. Thirty-four-year-old John Turturro, remembered as the racist pizza man in Spike Lee's *Do the Right Thing*, deserved his best actor award for the role of a serious playwright hired by a big movie studio to write a screenplay, and finding himself being drawn deeper and deeper into a nightmarish situation. It's the fourth and best feature by the Coen brothers, Ethan (producer) and Joel (director).

John Turturro as Barton Fink.

Susan and Geena a great pair in road movie

New York, 24 May

Ridley Scott's *Thelma and Louise*, scripted by Callie Khouri as a right-on variation of *Butch and Sundance*, may or may not be a feminist manifesto for the 90s. But it *is* an opportunity, brilliantly seized, for Susan Sarandon and Geena Davis to exchange a beguiling mix of womanly wisecracks and emotion as bosom buddies, on the lam from abusive men and the law in a liberating misadventure of crime and self-discovery. Few men who wish to be well thought of will dare to demur as angry women around them cheer on Thelma and Louise, violently, hilariously, and movingly take charge.

Close friends Thelma and Louise (Susan Sarandon, left, and Geena Davis).

All-star cast takes new stab at Robin Hood

Costner, the prince of thieves.

New York, 14 June
Having seen off the dreary competition from a more modestly budgeted version of the Robin Hood legend, starring Patrick Bergin, Kevin Costner, sounding more like the outlaw of Malibu than of Sherwood Forest, arrives in *Robin Hood: Prince of Thieves*. This is lavish piffle, in which Kevin – with Morgan Freeman curiously in tow – takes on Alan Rickman's scene-stealing, dementedly camp Sheriff of Nottingham, wins Mary Elizabeth Mastrantonio's feisty Maid Marian, and coaches a rag-tag group, including Christian Slater, into a lean, mean, arrow-shooting machine for some rousing rebellion and action. Some may sneer at the period and accent gaffes, and lament the lack of Errol Flynn romanticism, but this is a fun swashbuckler for the 90s.

Abel Ferrara comes into the mainstream

London, 21 June
Abel Ferrara, an independent New York filmmaker whose rough, tough forays into sleazy backstreets and their even sleazier inhabitants have a weirdly baroque immediacy reminiscent of certain underground styles, is famed as the perpetrator of the notorious *Driller Killer*. The movie is banned in Britain, where Ferrara is otherwise not well known, though he began nibbling at the mainstream with the reasonably well-received *Cat Chaser* (1989). Now, leaving his unknown actors (e.g. the wonderfully named Zoe Tamerlis played *MS 45 – Angel of Vengeance*, a particularly crude and brutal story) and his hand-held camera behind him, he has made *King of New York*, which is having a mixed reception here. A charismatic Christopher Walken, the "king" of the title, is a thoroughly rotten apple, bent on controlling the city's drug market by any means, including murder. It's nasty, hollow and overblown, but stylish and glossy. For Ferrara followers, it leaves the suspicion that, in going big-budget, this unique chronicler of the Manhattan underbelly has lost his unique vision.

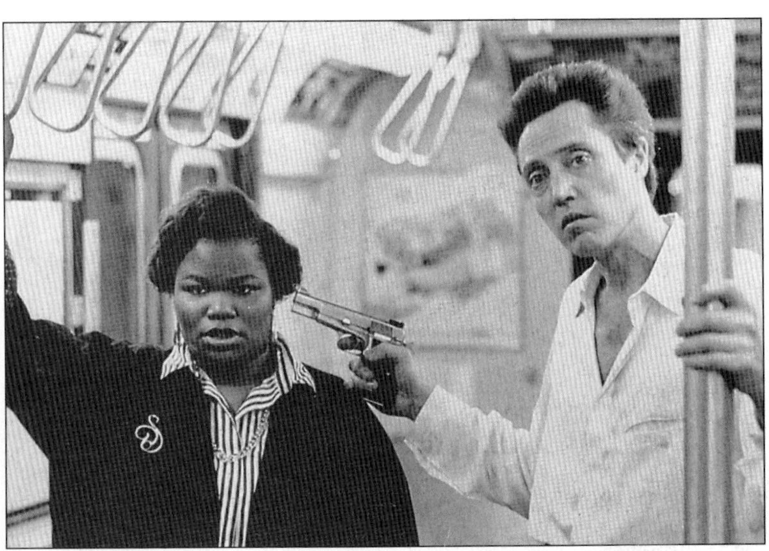
Christopher Walken as drug lord Frank White, in typically threatening mode.

The vengeful dreams of 'Toto the Hero'

An image of childhood from Dormael's mixture of fantasy and black comedy.

Paris, 19 June
Winner of the Caméra d'Or prize at Cannes this year, *Toto the Hero* is a strangely poetic, humorous and melancholy film. Its young director, the Belgian Jaco Van Dormael, has constructed a fascinating puzzle of a plot, which follows the lives of two men, Thomas and Albert, born on the same day. The former, dissatisfied with his mournful existence, and envying the latter's secure and happy life, is convinced that they were given to the wrong parents at birth, and is determined to revenge himself upon Albert.

An insider's view of L.A.'s street gangs

Los Angeles, 12 July
John Singleton describes his impressive directorial debut, *Boyz N the Hood*, as a film about "boys becoming men", which pleads for "African American men to take more responsibility for raising their children, especially the boys." Directed with bold certainty, it is as much a portrayal of urban gang warfare in South Central L.A. as a romantic elegy to the stable patriarchal unit. Singleton addresses his film mainly to young black men, urging them (in an unpreachy tone) to become the better fathers of the future. The director-screenwriter is wonderfully served by a fine cast who do justice to an intelligent script. Larry Fishburne has the central role of Furious Styles, the father of Tre Styles, played by Cuba Gooding Jr., who is drawn into a black gang. The real surprise, however, is the performance of the rapper Ice Cube, who plays Doughboy, a doleful, heavy-set tearaway, who avenges his friend Ricky's (Morris Chestnut) death by shooting his three killers. As can be expected, the boisterous movie has equally boisterous music on the soundtrack, including a few tracks by Ice Cube himself.

Cuba Gooding Jr., the protagonist.

'Truly, Madly, Deeply' a reply to 'Ghost'

*Juliet Stevenson and Alan Rickman 'reunited' in **Truly, Madly, Deeply**.*

London, 16 August
Already ecstatically received in the U.S., where it is being billed as the "thinking person's *Ghost*", the home-grown British, BBC-financed *Truly, Madly, Deeply* has its London release. Marking an accomplished feature debut by its writer-director, Anthony Minghella, the film's resemblance to *Ghost* begins and ends with the fact that the dead (of sudden but natural causes) lover of the grief-stricken girl he has left behind reappears in her life as a ghost. After that, despite much humor, the film is about coming to terms with pain and loss. It's charming, tender, tearjerking and, as cast and played (Juliet Stevenson and Alan Rickman star), truly, madly English.

Miscarriage of justice brilliantly filmed

The appalling moment when preparations are made to hang Derek Bentley.

London, 4 October
In the bleak postwar London of the early 50s, Derek Bentley, an 18-year-old youth of low IQ, subject to epilepsy, became friendly with 16-year-old Chris Craig, a delinquent on the fringes of the petty criminal underworld. The liaison led to an attempted robbery, in the course of which the boys were apprehended and Craig shot a policeman. Before he fired, Bentley, reportedly, shouted "Let him have it", meaning, give the gun to the cop. The jury found both boys guilty of murder, but recommended mercy for Bentley. However, since Craig was too young to hang, the recommendation was ignored and, despite repeated protests from the public and crusading members of parliament, Bentley went to the gallows. The attempts to clear Bentley still go on, and this unequivocal and appalling miscarriage of British justice is recounted in Peter Medak's *Let Him Have It*. A brilliant cast plays out the drama in a faultless period re-creation of the time and, if the film is harrowing, it is also thoroughly gripping and certainly to be applauded.

Jacques Rivette demonstrates the mystery of the creative process

Paris, 4 September
Just as Henri-Georges Clouzot once did with *The Picasso Mystery* (1956), in which he filmed the Spanish master in the process of painting, so Jacques Rivette, in his latest film *la Belle Noiseuse*, has attempted to capture the mystery of creation by observing an artist at work. Rivette has concentrated on a fictional painter, whom Michel Piccoli portrays with great conviction. The film reveals the ambivalent sado-masochistic relationship existing between Piccoli and his model, Emmanuelle Béart, and the manner in which nudity is used in painting, and by extension, on screen. The best scene is the meticulous preparation the artist goes through before brush touches canvas.

Jane Birkin and Michel Piccoli as the artist and his wife in Rivette's film.

Liz (Birkin) tries to understand.

Christopher Eccleston is Bentley.

France, U.S. and China divide lion's share

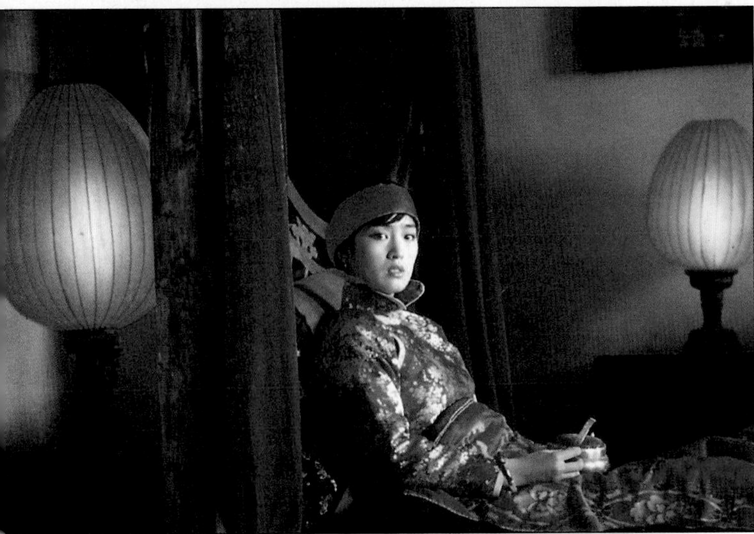

Gong Li, the arresting star of Zhang Yimou's **Raise the Red Lantern**.

Robin Williams (left) and Jeff Bridges in Terry Gilliam's **The Fisher King**.

An imposing visual moment from the Russian Nikita Mikhalkov's **Urga**.

Venice, 14 September
The televised award ceremony at the close of the 48th Venice Film Festival was held on a temporary platform set up in Saint Mark's Square, on which stood a huge plywood Golden Lion. The actual Golden Lion, made of gilded bronze, was awarded to the Russian director Nikita Mikhalkov for *Urga*, a visually stunning film from the USSR made mostly with French money. It is an enjoyably boisterous folk comedy set on the Mongolian Steppes, with a simple birth control message. The Silver Lion was shared by three pictures from different corners of the world: Philippe Garrel's poetic *J'entends plus la guitare* from France; Zhang Yimou's *Raise the Red Lantern*, a remarkable tale of female rivalry from China, and Terry Gilliam's haunting *The Fisher King* from the U.S. This last is set in contemporary New York, but adopts a medieval quest theme, with two down-and-outs (Jeff Bridges, Robin Williams) as a modern knight and his fool. Gus Van Sant's *My Own Private Idaho*, in which 20-year-old River Phoenix won the best actor prize for his poignant portrait of a lonely, narcoleptic gay hustler, is tenuously based on Shakespeare's *Henry IV* plays. Adding to the range of nations which left Venice with prizes was Great Britain, whose Tilda Swinton won the best actress award for her role as Queen Isabella in Derek Jarman's version of Christopher Marlowe's classical tragedy, *Edward II*.

Mike (River Phoenix, left) and Scott (Keanu Reeves): **My Own Private Idaho**.

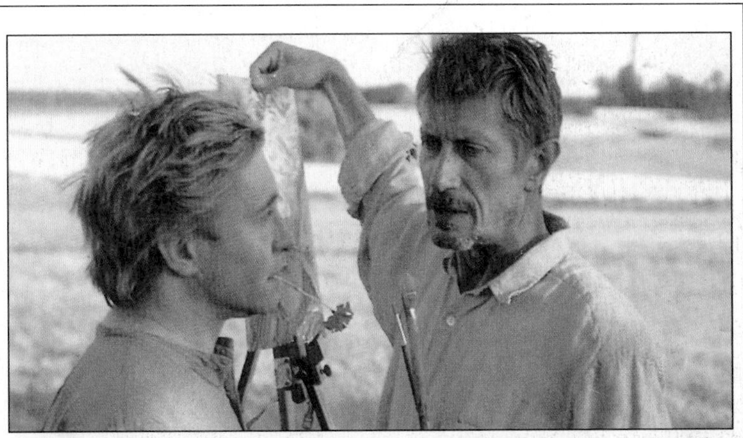

In his new film, *Van Gogh*, Maurice Pialat has scrupulously respected the truth of the great Dutch painter's final years. The ex-pop singer Jacques Dutronc (r) impresses, playing Van Gogh neither as saint nor visionary, but as a man with a secret pain that led him to paint but also to despair.

▷

Tale of love and folly overcomes problems

Juliette Binoche minus her lover but with her friend (Klaus Michael Gruber).

Paris, 8 October

It seems miraculous that Leos Carax's *les Amants du Pont Neuf* has finally seen the light of day, after all the problems that beset it. They began when the leading actor Denis Lavant sprained his wrist. Then it was found that there was no possibility of shooting the picture on the Pont Neuf, so it had to be rebuilt elsewhere. When the budget swelled enormously, the original producer retreated. Finally, the film was completed at a cost of 200 million francs. This richly romantic and spectacular movie tells of two outsiders, who have sought refuge on this famous Parisian landmark. The stars of Carax's previous film, *The Night is Young* (1986), Denis Lavant, as a young vagrant, and Juliette Binoche, as a painter trying to cope with encroaching blindness, make a splendidly passionate couple.

Yves Montand plays out his own death

Paris, 9 November

Yves Montand has died of cardiac arrest a few days after he had acted out a scene in which his on-screen character dies of cardiac arrest in Jean-Jacques Beineix's *IP5*. It has been suggested that the great 70-year-old actor-singer's death was hastened by what he had to endure during the shooting, such as having to dive into a cold lake. On his way to the hospital, Montand said, "I know I'm a goner, but it's not serious. I've had a terrific life."

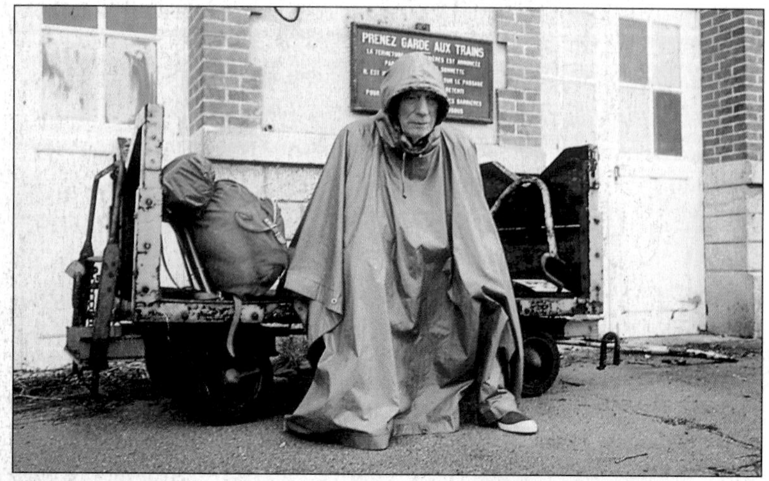
PRENEZ GARDE AUX TRAINS

*Beineix's film, **IP5**, was made in great secrecy with Yves Montand.*

Disney's latest film a treat for all ages

© Walt Disney

Beauty with her Beast and her array of talking, singing artifact-friends.

Hollywood, 17 November

It took Walt Disney studios 30 year to venture back into the territory of the classic fairy tale with *The Little Mermaid*. Its success convinced Walt's heirs to put even more effort and money into *Beauty and the Beast*. Derived from the story by Madame Leprince de Beaumont, the animated feature is a throwback in the best sense of the word – its melodious score alone is reminiscent of the golden age of musicals – but it is also very much a product of the 90s. For example, the ballroom sequence features the first computer-generated color background to be both animated and fully dimensional. The characters also have depth, especially the gutsy Belle and the poignant Beast.

© Walt Disney

Classic Disney, sheer enchantment.

Scorsese remake both stylish and repellent

De Niro: terrifyingly tattooed.

New York, 13 November
Martin Scorsese's surprising remake of the 1962 *Cape Fear* affords a masterly demonstration of his technical virtuosity, but eschews the creepy realism of the original to play to contemporary taste for overwrought horror. The result is stylistically brilliant and harrowing. The basic plot remains the same: vengeful ex-con (Robert De Niro) mounts a terror campaign against the lawyer (Nick Nolte) he blames for his imprisonment, targeting the man's wife and daughter (Jessica Lange, and remarkable newcomer Juliette Lewis). J. Lee Thompson's film was simple good vs. bad; Scorsese opts for more complex themes of guilt and sin, with a dysfunctional family playing into the con's hands. De Niro's tattooed wacko, in contrast to Robert Mitchum's easy menace, goes spectacularly over the top en route to the finale, but the performances and psychology are as mesmerizing as they are repugnant. Nice touches are cameos from the original stars, Mitchum and Gregory Peck, and Bernard Herrmann's memorable score, rearranged by Elmer Bernstein.

Stone and the Kennedy assassination

New York, 20 December
After taking on the war in Vietnam in *Platoon* and capitalism in *Wall Street*, Oliver Stone's new film, *JFK*, is likely to have more of an impact on American political life. In a brilliant three-hour mixture of real and fictionalized documentary, stylish thriller and courtroom drama, Stone sets out to prove that the assassination of John F. Kennedy was not the work of Lee Harvey Oswald, but an attempt at a *coup d'état* by members of the "military-industrial complex". Whatever the flaws in the argument – Pierre Salinger, the White House spokesman under Kennedy, has called the film "a tissue of lies" – it is put over in an extremely persuasive manner, strong enough to have put the Warren Commission Report into question, and to have created pressure for the reopening of the investigation. The case is put by Kevin Costner as the idealistic District Attorney Jim Garrison, who uncovers a nest of vipers during his quest for the truth. Sissy Spacek plays his long-suffering wife, Gary Oldman is Oswald, and Tommy Lee Jones and Joe Pesci are homosexual villains involved with anti-Castro Cubans.

Costner as lawyer Jim Garrison.

Ambitious Barbra films 'Prince of Tides'

New York, 25 December
Following on *Yentl*, a film of mixed merits which failed at the box office, Barbra Streisand, undaunted, has chosen for her second directing venture material so sprawling and complex as to be considered unfilmable by some. Pat Conroy's best-selling novel, *The Prince of Tides*, a dark, episodic and epic family saga, concerns the traumatic childhood of a sister and brother, and its effects. She ends up catatonic and hospitalized in New York; he, seemingly happily married, journeys to meet her psychiatrist, also married, and they fall in love. That's the précis version. Streisand plays the shrink, Nick Nolte the unhappy brother. It's a lush, romantic melodrama which, despite faults, succeeds as well as it could have done.

The Whistle Stop Cafe worth a detour

New York, 27 December
Producer Jon Avnet directs *Fried Green Tomatoes at the Whistle Stop Cafe*, from Fannie Flagg's novel. Set in the deepest South, the story uses a long, detailed trip down memory lane by octogenarian Ninny Threadgoode (Jessica Tandy), to change life in the present for plump, anxious housewife Evelyn Couch (Kathy Bates), who befriends her while visiting an old people's home. Ninny's past, concerning one Idgie Threadgoode (marvelously played by Mary Stuart Masterson), is jam-packed with drama, melodrama, humor and sadness. The movie, best described as heartwarming, is a testament to the indomitability of womenfolk, played out in a rich period atmosphere, with terrific landscape, photography and performances.

Director and star Barbra Streisand with Nick Nolte in ***The Prince of Tides.***

Kathy Bates, Jessica Tandy: ***Fried Green Tomatoes at the Whistle Stop Cafe.***

*Jean-Pierre Jeunet and Marc Caro's bizarre **Delicatessen** was a surprise hit.*

*Val Kilmer as musician Jim Morrison in Oliver Stone's **The Doors**.*

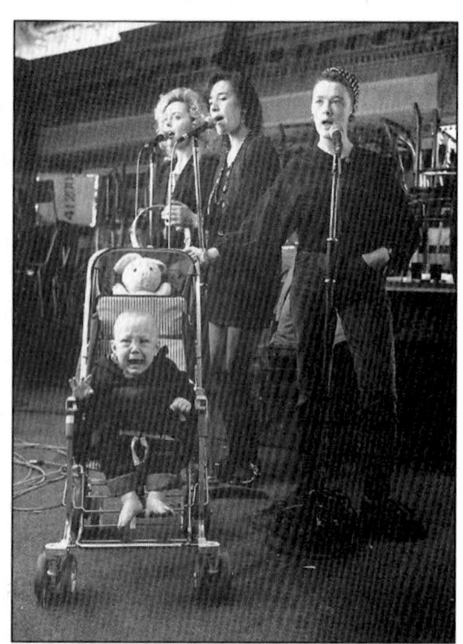

*Three of the band in Alan Parker's **The Commitments** (Ireland).*

*Dustin Hoffman as Spielberg's **Hook**, which cost over $60 million to make.*

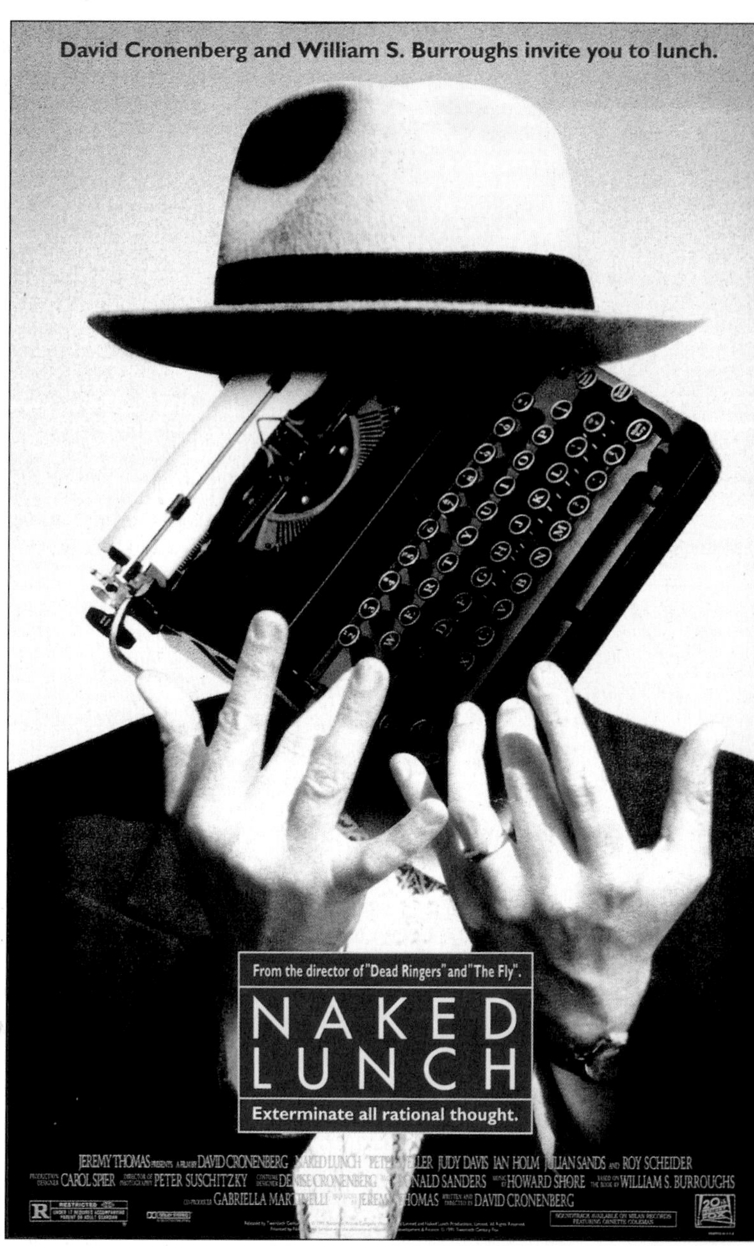

David Cronenberg and William S. Burroughs invite you to lunch.
From the director of "Dead Ringers" and "The Fly".
NAKED LUNCH
Exterminate all rational thought.
JEREMY THOMAS DAVID CRONENBERG JUDY DAVIS IAN HOLM ROY SCHEIDER
CAROL SPIER PETER SUSCHITZKY HOWARD SHORE WILLIAM S. BURROUGHS
GABRIELLA DAVID CRONENBERG
RESTRICTED

Director David Cronenberg attempted the impossible and partly succeeded.

***The Addams Family**: Morticia (Anjelica Huston), Fester (Christopher Lloyd).*

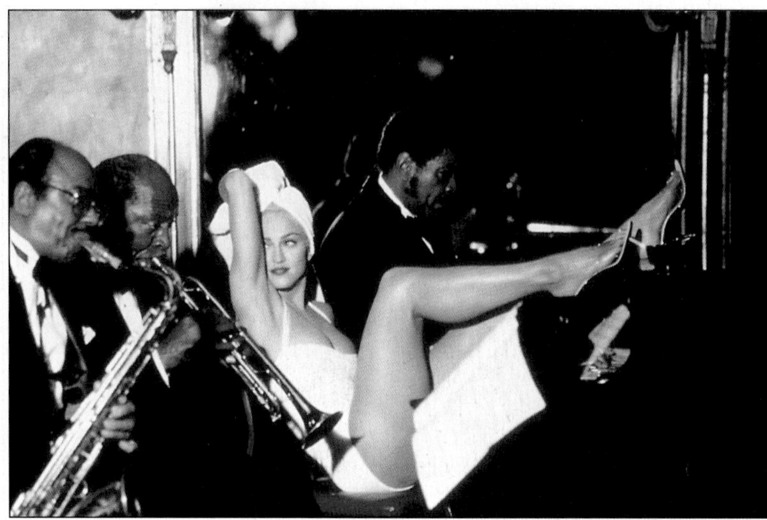
Outrageous star in a scene from ***In Bed with Madonna*** *(aka* ***Truth or Dare****).*

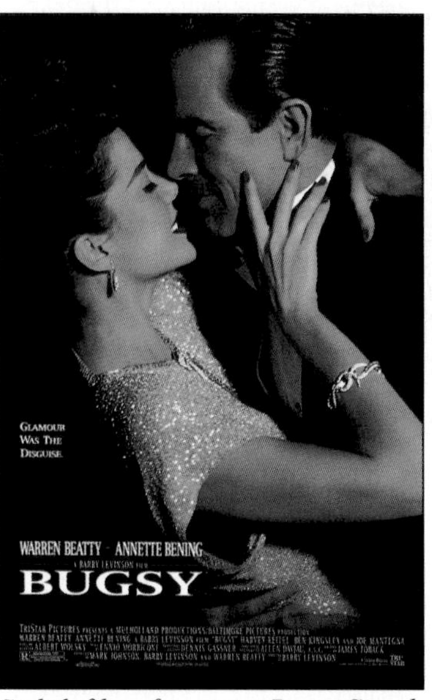
Glamour Was The Disguise
WARREN BEATTY ANNETTE BENING
BUGSY
Stylish film of gangster Bugsy Siegel.

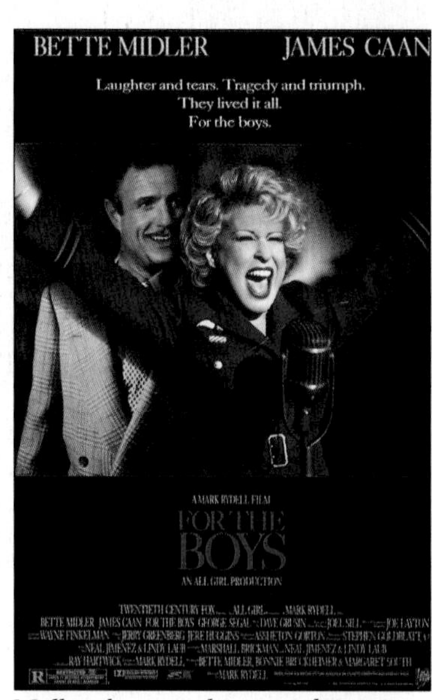
BETTE MIDLER JAMES CAAN
Laughter and tears. Tragedy and triumph.
They lived it all.
For the boys.
A MARK RYDELL FILM
FOR THE BOYS
AN ALL GIRL PRODUCTION
Midler showcased in nostalgia trip.

Danny DeVito as aggressive Larry the Liquidator in ***Other People's Money****.*

Hugo Weaving, the blind photographer in ***Proof****, a stunner from Australia.*

Trail-boss Jack Palance with townie Billy Crystal, one of three ***City Slickers****.*

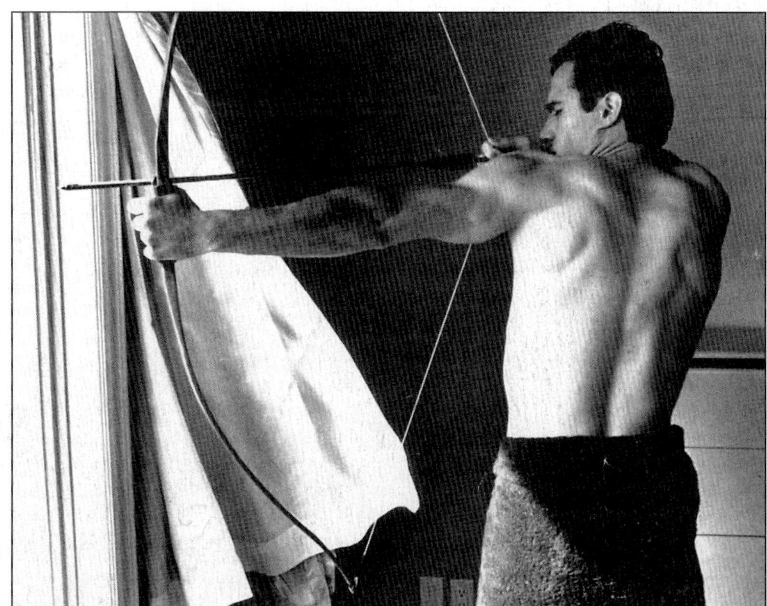
Elias Koteas in his role as ***The Adjuster*** *in Atom Egoyan's compelling film.*

★ ★ ★ ★ ★ ★ ★ ★ ★ 1992 ★

1991 Academy Awards, Dorothy Chandler Pavilion, 30 Mar.

Best Film:	*The Silence of the Lambs* (dir: Jonathan Demme)
Best Director:	Jonathan Demme
Best Actor:	Anthony Hopkins *(The Silence of the Lambs)*
Best Actress:	Jodie Foster *(The Silence of the Lambs)*
Best Supp. Actor:	Jack Palance *(City Slickers)*
Best Supp. Actress:	Mercedes Ruehl *(The Fisher King)*

New York, 6 January
British director Mike Leigh's *Life is Sweet* was named best film of the year yesterday by the National Society of Film Critics. Best actor went to River Phoenix for his performance as the family-seeking gay hustler in *My Own Private Idaho*, while best actress was won by Alison Steadman for *Life is Sweet*. Krzysztof Kieslowski's *The Double Life of Véronique* was voted best foreign film and Jennie Livingston's *Paris is Burning* won best documentary.

London, 2 February
The House of Lords has taken the BBC to task for deciding to screen Martin Scorsese's *The Last Temptation of Christ*. The film is judged highly offensive to Christians.

London, 13 February
Dirk Bogarde was knighted today at Buckingham Palace. Bogarde said it was "a great surprise and a great honor" as he had left England for France 22 years ago, never expecting to return. In 1982 he was made a Chevalier de l'Ordre des Lettres.

Los Angeles, 4 March
Death of Art Babbitt, the master of character animation whose career spanned the early days of sound animation at Terrytoons and Disney. Although he was best known for developing the personality of Goofy, he also worked on such landmark features as Disney's *Snow White*, *Pinocchio* and *Dumbo*.

New York, 4 March
Nestor Almendros, the internationally renowned award-winning cinematographer, has died.

Paris, 25 March
Steven Soderbergh, the winner of the Golden Palm at Cannes in 1989 for his debut picture *sex, lies, and videotape*, is in Paris for the French release of his second feature, *Kafka*, with Jeremy Irons, Theresa Russell and Alec Guinness.

New York, 7 April
Ted Turner and Jane Fonda were among the plethora of celebrities present at yesterday's kickoff festivities for the new "50th anniversary" edition of *Casablanca* at the Museum of Modern Art. All present felt that the film has never looked so good except, perhaps, when it was first shown on 26 November 1942.

Lisbon, 10 April
Release of *The Divine Comedy* (*A Divina Comedia*), a very free adaptation of Dante directed by Manoel de Oliveira, with Maria de Medeiros and Luis Miguel Cintra.

Hollywood, 30 April
After *Bram Stoker's Dracula*, due for U.S. release in August, Francis Ford Coppola is planning to make a new version of Pinocchio, mixing live-action with cartoon characters.

Hollywood, 2 July
Universal has decided to change the title and defer the release of Walter Hill's film *Looters*, with the rappers from the groups Ice-T and Ice Cube. The studio wants to avoid any connection with the riots which have just shaken Los Angeles.

Arizona, 1 August
Veteran movie poster artist Robert Peak, who created key art for films such as *West Side Story* and *My Fair Lady*, died of a brain hemorrhage at his home yesterday.

New York, 2 August
Ephraim Katz, the sole author of the colossal critical-historical reference book, *The Encyclopedia of Film* (1979), died today.

California, 12 September
Death of Hans F. Koenekamp, a pioneer in the field of special effects photography who was responsible for many technical innovations, including a synchronized motor connection between a background projector and a camera.

New York, 14 September
Bill Cosby is America's top-paid entertainer. His expected $98 million in earnings for 1991-92 combined knocks the teeny-bop sensation New Kids on the Block off the top spot.

Hollywood, 16 September
Democratic presidential candidate Bill Clinton is reported to have told a group of 1,200 Hollywood supporters at a fundraising event ("Voices of Change '92") that he "always aspired to be in the cultural elite."

Tokyo, 24 September
The Tokyo Festival, opening today, has reneged on showing Belgium's violent Cannes Critics' Prize winner, *Man Bites Dog*.

Amsterdam, 29 September
The Dutch Film Museum has unearthed what it believes to be the only surviving copies of six early Walt Disney silents made between 1923 and 1927. The films will be shown at next month's Pordenone silent film festival in Italy.

Los Angeles, 5 October
A suit brought against Spike Lee in the U.S. District Court here last month by George Halliday, concerning Lee's usage of Halliday's Rodney King footage in *Malcolm X*, has been settled out of court.

South Korea, 5 October
More than 120,000 Koreans have seen Chung Ji-Yoing's *White Badge* since its January opening. The film, which depicts South Korea's participation in the Vietnam War, is the first overtly anti-war film to be permitted by Seoul's censors.

Berlin, 12 October
A court has ordered the destruction of the gory post-mortem sex movie *Necromantic 2*, from Jörg Buttgereit, without a trial or a hearing. The court holds it breaks a German law forbidding graphic violence in films.

Rome, 4 November
According to a poll compiled by AGIS (General Association of Italian Spectacles), *Last Tango in Paris* is the biggest grosser ever released here over the last 40 years. *La Dolce Vita* only gains fifth place after a trio of Spaghetti Westerns, *Trinity is Still My Name*, *For a Few Dollars More* and *A Fistful of Dollars* in that order.

New York, 6 November
A U.N. agency is sending a delegation of Writers Guild of America members to visit refugee camps in Somalia, Kenya, Croatia and Bosnia with the hope of generating scripts which will convey the immense gravity of the situation in these war-torn and troubled zones.

Hollywood, 11 December
The Jack Nicholson-Tom Cruise starrer *A Few Good Men*, directed by Rob Reiner, is the first Hollywood movie ever to have premiered simultaneously in the U.S. and 50 other countries.

DEATHS

Santa Barbara, 3 January
Judith Anderson

Florida, 23 January
Freddie Bartholomew

Florida, 26 January
José Ferrer

Connecticut, 2 March
Sandy Dennis

Hollywood, 11 March
Richard Brooks

Los Angeles, 18 March
Vilma Banky

Los Angeles, 29 March
Paul Henreid

Calcutta, 23 April
Satyajit Ray

Paris, 6 May
Marlene Dietrich

England, 3 June
Robert Morley

Hollywood, 12 September
Anthony Perkins

Spain, 6 October
Denholm Elliott

California, 17 December
Dana Andrews

Hollywood's newest blonde bombshell and sex symbol, Sharon Stone, with her 'victim' Michael Douglas in ***Basic Instinct****. The film is hugely successful and very controversial.*

XVIIth century musician intrigues in 1992

*Carole Richert, J.-P. Marielle, Anne Brochet: **Tous les matins du monde**.*

Paris, 10 January
Who would have thought that an elegant and intelligent film such as *Tous les matins du monde*, about two scarcely known 17th-century musicians, should have attracted such large audiences? There are a number of reasons for the success: the sheer joy of the music-making, the gorgeous costumes and decor, the theme of the striving for perfection, and the performances both musical (by the talented violist Jordi Savall) and dramatic. Jean-Pierre Marielle plays Sainte Colombe, a virtuoso of the viol da gamba, and two Depardieus (Guillaume, young; Gérard, old) are his pupil Marin Marais.

Clean sweep for 'Silence of the Lambs'

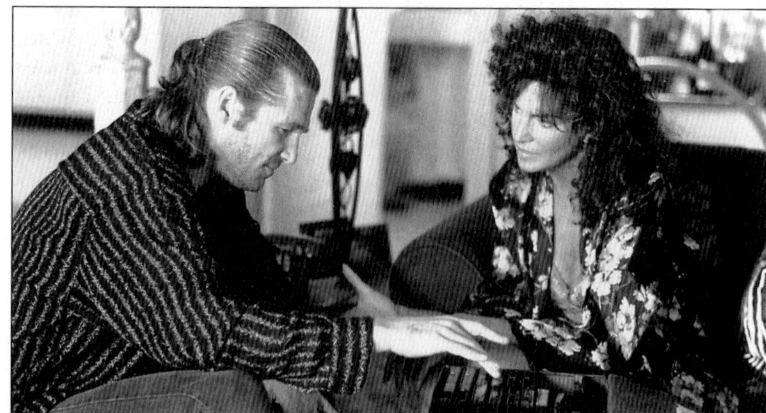

*Best Supporting Actress Mercedes Ruehl and Jeff Bridges in **The Fisher King**.*

Los Angeles, 30 March
Following directly on the year of the "Wolves", this was the year of the "Lambs", *The Silence of the Lambs* to be exact, which won five of the main awards, including Best Film. It was a popular winner, especially the Best Actor prize, which was presented to Anthony Hopkins, even though he was the third British star in succession to win it (after Daniel Day Lewis and Jeremy Irons), and the role was, strictly speaking, a supporting one. But his few scenes as Dr. Hannibal "the Cannibal" Lecter were so powerful and unsettling, that he dominated the whole film. His co-star Jodie Foster (Best Actress), in her most mature role yet as an FBI agent seeking his help in tracing a serial killer, revealed toughness without attempting to hide the character's sensitivity. The film also provided a first Oscar for director Jonathan Demme, who has been up-and-coming for years.

Blockbusting appeal to baser instincts

Hollywood, 10 February
Although the director Paul Verhoeven had to cut certain scenes from *Basic Instinct* which were considered too violent or erotic for a wide audience, this sexual thriller has reawakened arguments about censorship. *Basic Instinct*, showing with an R certificate which allows adolescents to see it only if accompanied by an adult, has been violently opposed by lesbians, who are depicted as dangerously malicious, while other women object to the uneasy presence of sex-as-violence. However, stars Michael Douglas and Sharon Stone provide a riveting double act in a gripping film.

Michael Douglas and Sharon Stone in Paul Verhoeven's disturbing film.

WAYNE'S
WORLD

With *Wayne's World*, Mike Myers and Dana Carvey re-create the goofy metalheads Wayne and Garth so beloved of TV's *Saturday Night Live* viewers, and expand their regular sketches as presenters of a homemade TV chat show into a guided tour of American junk culture. This absurd revel in Heavy Metaldom is haphazardly directed by Penelope Spheeris.

Altman takes satirical swipe at Tinseltown

Tim Robbins, star of ***The Player***.

Los Angeles, 10 April

"Hollywood is afraid of me, I guess. I can't make the kind of films they want to make, and the kind of films I make, they just don't want to make," said Robert Altman in the 1980s. After being in the commercial doldrums for some time, Altman has now made a scintillating critical and box-office comeback with *The Player*, his revenge on Tinsel Town. This brilliantly crafted and wickedly funny movie is a mordant satire on the Hollywood film industry, firing alike on studio executives, spoiled stars, hustling writers, shark-like agents and power players. At its center is Tim Robbins as a bland yet thrusting young studio executive, who reveals the palpable edginess behind the Hollywood smile. Comic asides, acid wit and celebrity cameos thread their way through the enjoyable proceedings.

Disneyland opens its doors in Europe

Paris, 12 April

The original agreement to build a Disney theme park in Europe was signed in 1987, but it has taken almost five years to complete this ambitious project. Conceived during the heady days of the late Eighties boom years, the $4.5 billion version of the American Disneyworld, built 25 miles east of Paris, will start off with a heavy burden of debt, though only a fraction of the costs will be carried by the Disney company itself. It is uncertain whether the formula that works so well in sunny California (where the first Disneyland opened in 1955) and Florida, will be equally successful in Europe. The new theme park will include some unique experiences (e.g. a castle with a roaring dragon in its dungeon), but will mostly offer American rides in Gallic disguise, like "Dumbo, l'Éléphant Volant".

The merry opening ceremony.

'Indochine': an epic wallow in French Vietnam, stars Deneuve

Paris, 15 April

Following on the heels of *The Lover* and *Dien Bien Phu*, comes *Indochine*, the best of the recent films dealing with the colonial experience of the French in Vietnam. All three films, which took advantage of being able to shoot in Vietnam, play on a certain nostalgia for the period, while not being uncritical of French rule. *The Lover*, based on an autobiographical novel by Marguerite Duras, told of the passionate love affair between a young French girl and a seductive Chinese man. *Dien Bien Phu* dealt more overtly with the politics, reconstructing the decisive battle in the struggle for Vietnamese independence. *Indochine* falls between the two other epics, in being the story of a love affair disrupted by political events. The film, which cost 120 million francs, was conceived as a vehicle for the talents of Catherine Deneuve as a powerful colonial landowner who falls for a young officer, but loses him to her young adopted daughter. The indomitable Deneuve, never better, fights to preserve her love and save her land from destruction, and gradually comes to understand the Vietnamese point of view. Director Régis Wargnier has made splendid use of the exotic landscapes of the country as a setting for the romance.

Vincent Perez and Catherine Deneuve in Régis Wargnier's ***Indochine***.

Pierre Schoendoerffer's ***Dien Bien Phu*** *bore vivid witness to history.*

Marlene laid to rest in her fatherland

Berlin, 16 May

Marlene Dietrich, who died a week ago at her Paris apartment, has been buried in Berlin, the city where she was born 93 years ago. At the funeral, a small but vociferous group of Germans protested because they considered her a traitor. The screen legend had not left her apartment since 1980, although the reclusive star allowed Maximilian Schell to enter in order to interview her for a documentary called *Marlene* in 1983. However, she refused point blank to appear before the camera. The last time Marlene was seen on screen was in the disastrous *Just a Gigolo* (1978), opposite David Bowie. She will be remembered in the cinema mainly for the seven films directed by Josef von Sternberg between 1930 and 1935, in which she played an exotic, sensuous and mysterious character. The iconographic figure of Marlene, the illusory vision of Woman, the eternal *femme fatale* appeared in different guises as Lola-Lola (*The Blue Angel*), Amy Jolly (*Morocco*), Helen Faraday (*Blonde Venus*), Spy X27 (*Dishonored*), Shanghai Lily (*Shanghai Express*), Catherine the Great (*The Scarlet Empress*) and Concho Perez (*The Devil is a Woman*).

Batman's return visit hits record box office

*Catwoman Michelle Pfeiffer and Penguin Danny De Vito in **Batman Returns**.*

New York, 22 June
Exactly three years since *Batman* topped the U.S. box office, *Batman Returns* has opened here and is already set to be one of the major hits of this year. With Tim Burton again directing and Michael Keaton reprising the title role, the stunts, sets and spectacular effects look to outdo those of the earlier film, and have had the benefit of a budget estimated at well over $50 million. An additional $20 million is being spent on advertising, including merchandising and licensing deals, notably with Coca-Cola and McDonalds. As with the first movie, the real stars are the villains, especially Danny De Vito's Penguin and Michelle Pfeiffer's irresistibly sexy Cat Woman.

Lundgren, Van Damme in head-on collision

*Jean-Claude Van Damme (left) and Dolph Lundgren in **Universal Soldier**.*

Los Angeles, 10 July
Muscles from Brussels Jean-Claude Van Damme and Swedish Meatball Dolph Lundgren meet as adversaries in *Universal Soldier*, a surprisingly enjoyable mix of sci-fi, martial arts and mayhem. The twosome are among U.S. soldiers killed in Vietnam but revived years later as genetically altered zombie warriors in a secret program to create elite commandos. Naturally, it all goes wrong, memories return, and Van Damme's sensitive good guy is on the run from psychopathic Lundgren, once his nemesis in 'Nam. This drivel is a strong pointer to what sells right now, but it does make agreeably hunky hokum for a bloodthirsty Saturday night.

Welcome to the living dead of Beverly Hills

Los Angeles, 31 July
"I don't want to become one of the living dead in Beverly Hills," says plastic surgeon Bruce Willis in Robert Zemeckis' new film, *Death Becomes Her*. Using elements of the Zombie movie and camp melodrama – the rivalry between two ambitious women – the picture is an attempt to satirize the West Coast craze for youth and beauty. The rivals are novelist Goldie Hawn and actress Meryl Streep, who each take a magic rejuvenation potion supplied to them by Isabella Rossellini with bizarre results. The special effects win the day, but Streep and Hawn are deliciously bitchy.

*Goldie Hawn coming back to life after being killed in **Death Becomes Her**.*

Actor-director Eastwood's majestic Western

New York, 7 August
If *Unforgiven* really proves to be the last Western from the man who can be credited with keeping the genre alive, Clint Eastwood, it's a grand one on which to ride out. The film is dark, gripping, and embraces complex themes, with Eastwood playing a weathered, reformed killer reluctantly going after the bounty offered by a town's whores in order to avenge a woman's mutilation by drunken cowboys. The film is at its most fascinating in its revisionist approach to the myths of the Old West, contrasting its glorification in penny dreadful novellas with its ugly realities. Superbly shot and uniformly well-acted by a splendid cast (including Richard Harris), it's a fine piece of craftsmanship from Eastwood the director, with Gene Hackman taking performance honors as a brutal sheriff. Ironically, the element that gives pause is Eastwood's own enigmatic character, his professed loss of appetite for killing not ringing *quite* true. When eventually he is roused, the result is precisely what one has been awaiting with dubious anticipation: Clint's William Munny becomes an amalgam of all the violent, avenging riders he has portrayed in many a horrific showdown. Nevertheless, a richly satisfying achievement.

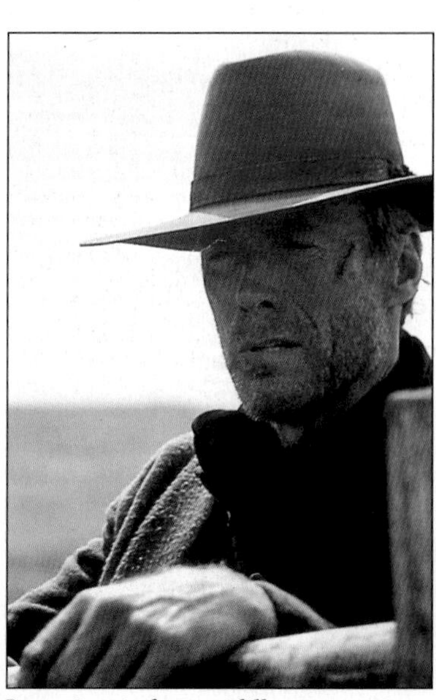

Imposing in late middle age.

Woody and Mia: custody battle rages

New York, 28 August
Court hearings have been resumed in Manhattan in the continuing battle between Woody Allen and Mia Farrow over the custody of their children. Woody has accused his long-time lover of trying to blackmail him over allegations that he had sexually abused two of the three children he shares with the actress. Allen has rejected as "totally false and outrageous" allegations that he had molested either their seven-year-old adopted daughter Dylan or their four-year-old biological son, Satchel. He stated that Farrow's lawyers had demanded $7 million to stop them making the allegations public. Farrow's lawyers deny this. They showed the judge sexually explicit nude photographs of Soon Yi Previn, the adopted daughter of Farrow with whom Woody had an affair, which sparked the whole row, to provide "a good indication of the mental stability and condition of the man who is seeking custody of these children." But Allen has stated, "The only thing I have been guilty of is falling in love with Mia Farrow's adult daughter at the end of our own years together."

'Husbands and Wives' close to the bone

Judy Davis, Sydney Pollack: at the heart of disturbance in Woody Allen's film.

New York, 18 September
Because of the wall-to-wall press coverage of the continuing battle between Woody Allen and Mia Farrow over their children, the release of *Husbands and Wives* has been brought forward. This (presumably) last Allen picture with Farrow creates some uncomfortable analogies with real life, as novelist-lecturer Woody, married to Mia, has an affair with one of his young students (Juliette Lewis). Farrow, unmade up, naturalistically lit to look her age, is characterized as "a passive aggressor". A second couple, philanderer Sydney Pollack and neurotic wife Judy Davis, also play a part in this painfully funny and tragic look at sex, love and marriage, the director's habitual themes but made even more profound than in his previous films by Allen's recent personal experiences.

'1492' the best of a poor bunch

New York, 9 October
The plethora of Columbus enterprises marking the 500th anniversary of his voyage of discovery has ranged from the merely tedious *Christopher Columbus: The Discovery*, to a German animated feature about a cute talking woodworm on board the explorer's ship, the "Santa Maria". But it was always assumed that Ridley Scott's epic, with Gérard Depardieu as the obstinate navigator, *1492: Conquest of Paradise* would be the Big One, so it is all the more disappointing that it, too, misses the boat. Scott employs handsome spectacle, a large and sometimes incomprehensible Euro cast (Sigourney Weaver's Queen Isabella is a notable exception) and moody Olde Worlde atmosphere, but there is no disguising the confusion in a two-and-a-half-hour film, heavily cut but still sagging, that can't make up its mind about its central character. Depardieu imposes humanity by sheer force of presence, but audience indifference to things Columbus (the British are contributing *Carry on Columbus*) suggests the movie began with the wind taken out of its sales.

Versatile Dan makes a striking Mohican

Los Angeles, 25 September
James Fennimore Cooper's 1826 novel, *The Last of the Mohicans*, is an entertaining mixture of colonial history, romance, and the sort of myth-making that laid the groundwork for the Western. In the role of Hawkeye, the free-spirited trapper who wanders the forests with his Mohican friends Chingachgook (Russell Means) and Uncas (Eric Schweig), Daniel Day Lewis is a worthy successor to Randolph Scott in the 1936 screen version. Hawkeye is sent to protect the British woman Cora (Madeleine Stowe) from Magua (Wes Studi), a vengeance-crazed Huron. Aside from a lively performance from Day Lewis, most of the characters are rather cardboard, sacrificed to the action. Michael Mann directs the movie as an old-fashioned adventure, only paying lip-service to the doomed nobility of the Native American. Yet the series of attacks, escapes, sieges, fights, deaths and triumphs are spectacularly handled. An outstanding moment is when a distant fireworks display turns out to be a nocturnal battle.

Day Lewis: a magnificent figure.

Redford and the gentle art of fly-fishing

Chicago, 9 October
Robert Redford should direct more often. His third feature, *A River Runs Through It*, sensitively adapted and superbly crafted from Norman MacLean's autobiographical novella, is a heartachingly graceful film of warmth and great beauty. It spans the early decades of this century and explores the deep love in a Montana minister's family who are not given to communicating well with each other. The men – Tom Skerritt as father, Craig Sheffer as solid young Norman (voiced in maturity by Redford as narrator) and Brad Pitt (as radiant as the young Redford) as wild, self-destructive golden boy brother, Paul – find mutual understanding in one common bond: fishing for trout on the Big Blackfoot River, where life, religion and self-expression become a joyous unity and make surprisingly compelling cinema. It's really all about the tragedy of being unable to save a lost soul who will have none of it, but it does much to promote fly-fishing as an artful pastime, courtesy of Philippe Rousselot's stunning camera and Redford's loving direction.

Brad Pitt catches the big one.

Australian talents bring delirious delight with 'Strictly Ballroom'

Tara Morice, Paul Mercurio dance in the grand finale of ***Strictly Ballroom.***

London, 16 October
From Australia comes the year's most original, irresistible and joyous film, *Strictly Ballroom.* Adored at the Cannes Festival and garlanded with eight awards in its own country, the movie started life as an improvised stage production in Oz, co-written by Baz Luhrman. He has now made his film directing debut with it – so successfully, that it can only be a matter of time before he joins the international filmmaking scene. The story concerns a young ballroom dancer (Paul Mercurio) with ambitions to become champion. His unorthodox approach, however, incenses the conventional ballroom dancing establishment, his partner departs, and he ends up with a seemingly plain novice (Tara Morice). The plot cannot convey the imagination, humor and originality of the piece, performed by an amazing cast in which newcomers Mercurio and Morice are totally enchanting. It has style, exuberance and heart – on no account miss it.

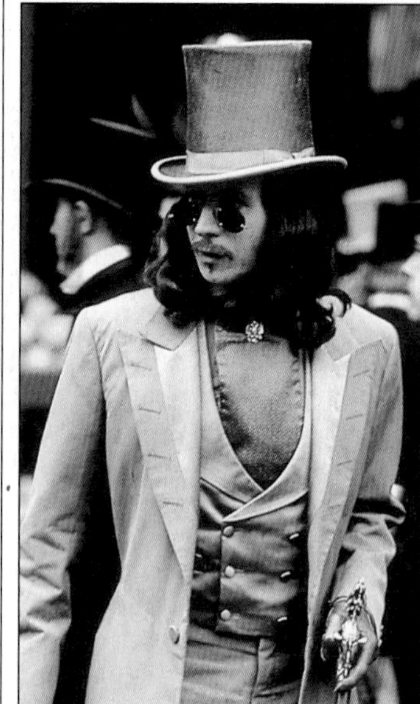
The versatile British actor Gary Oldman in the title role of the visually stunning *Bram Stoker's Dracula*, so named by its director Francis Coppola, because of its fidelity to the famous Gothic novel. Among an all-star cast, Oldman is a more seductive vampire than is usual in the part.

French director faces his own savage illness

Paris, 21 October
Although Cyril Collard's *Savage Nights* (*les Nuits fauves*), adapted from his own novel, is not overtly autobiographical, the story of Jean, a young photographer (played by Collard), who discovers he is HIV positive, is based on reality. Collard was one of the first well-known people in France to talk openly about his illness, and it is impossible not to make a connection between the director-writer and the promiscuous bisexual character he plays. Filmed in a vivid semi-documentary style, it follows the activities of the irresponsible Jean who continues to have unsafe sex, and threatens a gang with his infected blood. But the character and the film gradually gain our sympathy, leading to greater understanding.

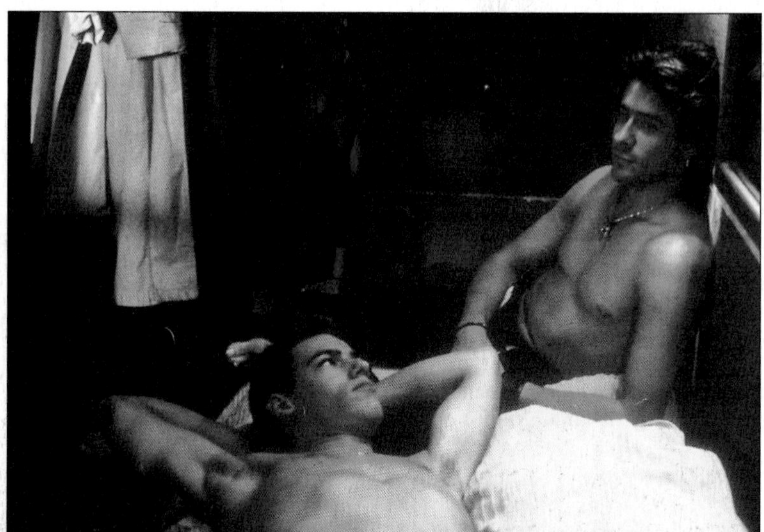
Cyril Collard (right), with Carlos Lopez, in his autobiographical film.

'Reservoir Dogs' is a bravura bloodbath

New York, 23 October
Directorial debuts don't come much more sensationally than that of writer and director Quentin Tarantino. *Reservoir Dogs* is sickeningly violent, appallingly funny and arrestingly accomplished – clearly the work of a movie brat intelligently versed in Scorsese, Hong Kong action flicks and pulp fiction. A testosterone-heavy ensemble headed by Harvey Keitel (who co-produced) are the Dogs, a team of professional thieves assembled for a job. The cleverly structured script begins at the aftermath of their bungled heist, flashing back and forth between the hoods' individual recollections and their present efforts to unmask the informer in their midst. Michael Madsen, Steve Buscemi and Tim Roth all score in brutish moments.

Freddy alias Mr. Orange (Tim Roth), bleeding to death in Tarantino's film.

Williams' genial genie helps socko B.O.

© Walt Disney

Aladdin with the Princess Jasmine in Disney's latest magical blockbuster.

Los Angeles, 11 November
After the overwhelming success of *Beauty and the Beast*, Walt Disney's newest animated feature, *Aladdin*, looks like being an even greater hit. The statistics behind its production are as impressive as the film – over three years in the making, nearly 600 artists, over a million drawings, and computer-generated imagery that create the illusion of three-dimensional space. The characters have more depth, too, with a hunky hero and a spunky heroine, and a hilarious genie, a vocal tour de force performed by Robin Williams.

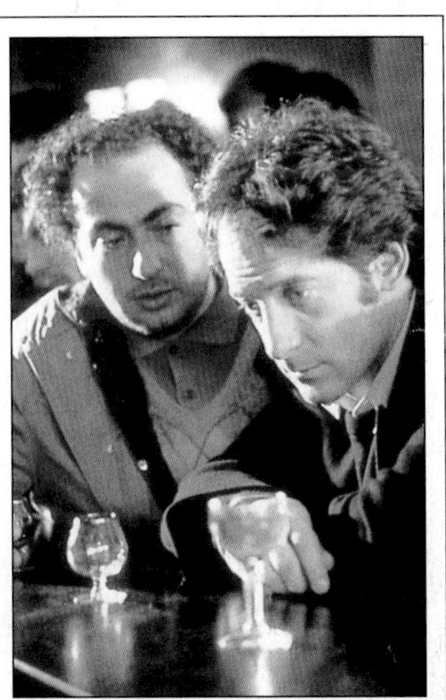

Vincent Lindon (l) with Patrick Timsit in Coline Serreau's fourth feature, *la Crise*. It's a hectic and caustic comedy about the crumbling world of a man who loses his wife, his mistress and his job.

Whitney Houston makes her debut as a singer who hires an ex-CIA man to guard her against threats to her life. The movie is *The Bodyguard*, he's Kevin Costner, the public loves it.

Washington is a persuasive Malcolm X

Delroy Lindo (l) with star Denzel Washington in Spike Lee's ***Malcolm X****.*

New York, 18 November
There have been complaints that Spike Lee's *Malcolm X* is "inflammatory", mainly due to the use of the notorious videotape of the Rodney King police beating that led to the recent L.A. riots. It seems unlikely, however, that this sober and meticulous biography of the charismatic 1960s civil rights leader could create further violence. The picture's main strength lies in the remarkable performance of Denzel Washington in the title role.

Chaplin lives again in Robert Downey Jr.

London, 18 December
Sir Richard Attenborough has continued his exploration of the lives of great 20th-century figures with *Chaplin*, in which he has attempted to make narrative sense of the long life of the most famous screen comic, within the limits of the conventional biopic. More difficult, however, was the casting of Charlie. He had to be handsome, but not tall; he had to age from 18 to 83; he had to be a superb mime and acrobat, and he had to start with a Cockney accent and finish with a polished English voice of the later years. The director found him in Robert Downey Jr., who has succeeded in being almost entirely convincing in all these departments.

An uncanny reincarnation.

Geraldine Chaplin plays his mother. ▷

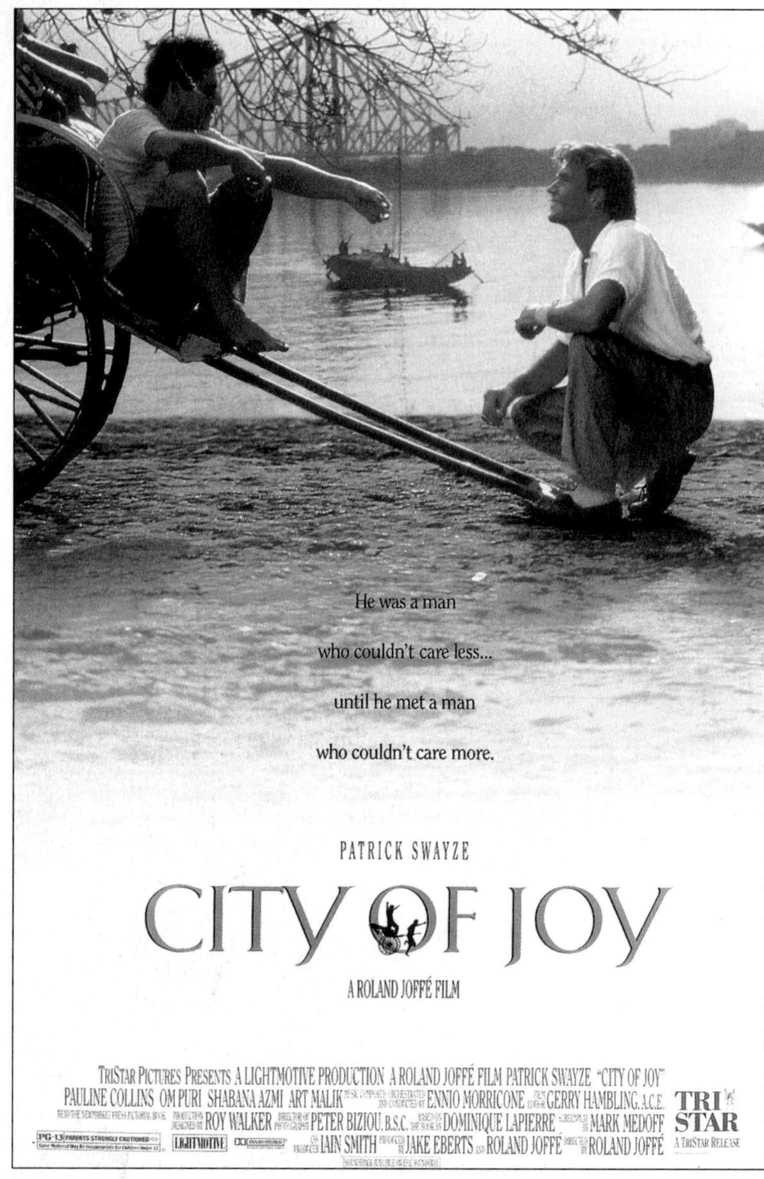
He was a man
who couldn't care less...
until he met a man
who couldn't care more.
PATRICK SWAYZE
CITY OF JOY
A ROLAND JOFFÉ FILM
TRISTAR PICTURES PRESENTS A LIGHTMOTIVE PRODUCTION A ROLAND JOFFÉ FILM PATRICK SWAYZE "CITY OF JOY"
PAULINE COLLINS OM PURI SHABANA AZMI ART MALIK ENNIO MORRICONE GERRY HAMBLING, A.C.E.
ROY WALKER PETER BIZIOU, B.S.C. DOMINIQUE LAPIERRE MARK MEDOFF
IAIN SMITH JAKE EBERTS ROLAND JOFFÉ ROLAND JOFFÉ
PG-13 PARENTS STRONGLY CAUTIONED
LIGHTMOTIVE
TRI STAR
A TRISTAR RELEASE
Patrick Swayze plays a well-meaning medic in India, for Roland Joffe.

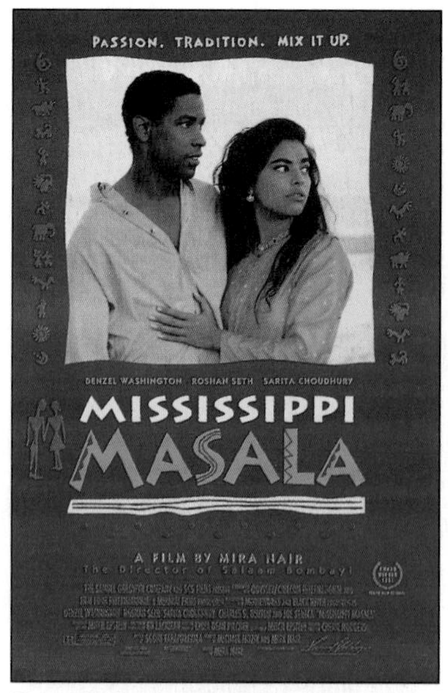
PASSION. TRADITION. MIX IT UP.
DENZEL WASHINGTON ROSHAN SETH SARITA CHOUDHURY
MISSISSIPPI MASALA
A FILM BY MIRA NAIR
The Director of Salaam Bombay!
From **Salaam Bombay**'s Mira Nair.

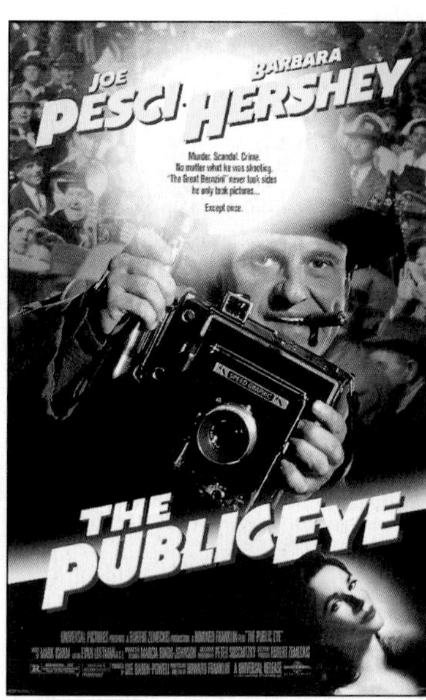
JOE PESCI · BARBARA HERSHEY
Murder. Scandal. Crime.
No matter what he was shooting,
"The Great Bernzini" never took sides
he only took pictures...
Except once.
THE PUBLIC EYE
Tabloid photographer's sleazy world.

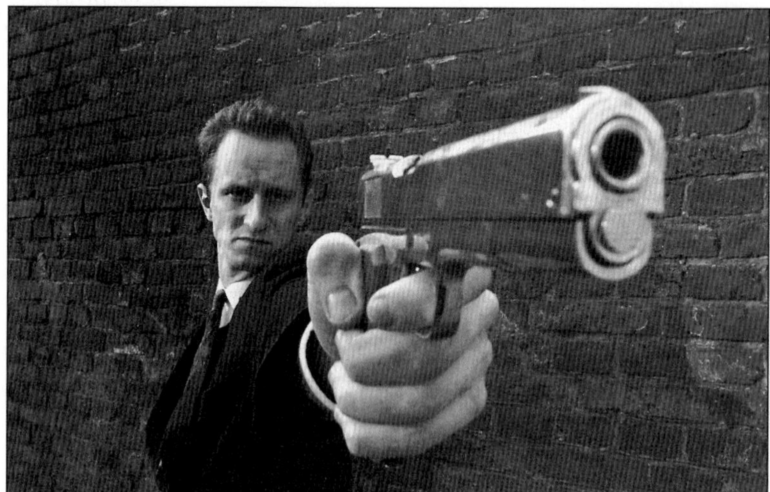
A trio of first-time Belgian directors made **Man Bites Dog**, a repellent but original serial-killer comedy with Benoit Poelvoorde (above).

Mother Superior Maggie Smith and 'nun' Whoopie Goldberg in **Sister Act**.

Harrison Ford, the former CIA agent in **Patriot Games**, with Anne Archer.

FROM THE DIRECTOR OF 'BEVERLY HILLS COP'
PACINO
SCENT OF A WOMAN

Al Pacino impressed as a blind man in this remake of an Italian film.

Tim Robbins in ***Bob Roberts****, which also marks his directorial debut.*

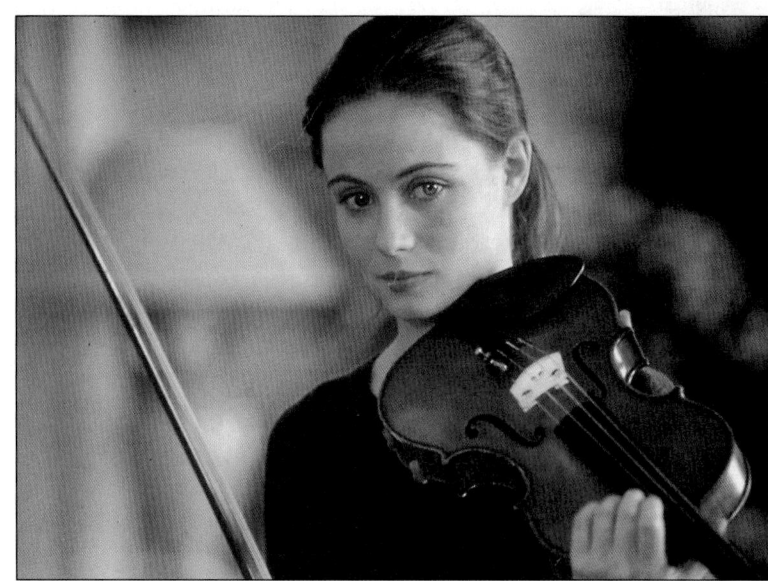

Emmanuelle Béart, violinist caught between two men in ***Un coeur en hiver****.*

Tom Cruise and Demi Moore in Rob Reiner's slick drama ***A Few Good Men****.*

Mesmerisingly beautiful: ***The Story of Qiu Ju*** *from China's Zhang Yimou.*

Geena Davis scores well as one of the team girls in ***A League of Their Own****.*

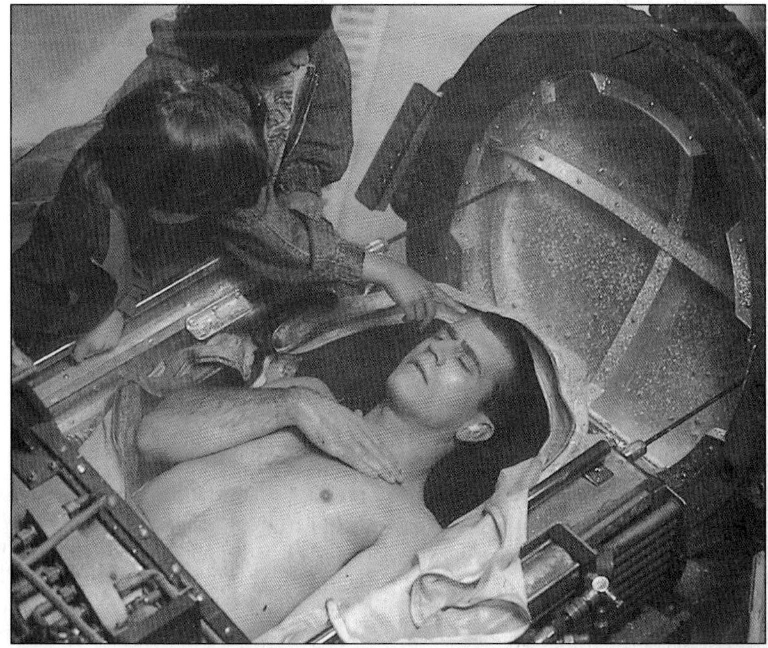

Mel Gibson, a pilot kept frozen since 1939, about to wake in ***Forever Young****.*

1993

1992 Academy Awards, Dorothy Chandler Pavilion, 28 Mar.

Best Film:	*Unforgiven* (dir: Clint Eastwood)
Best Director:	Clint Eastwood
Best Actor:	Al Pacino *(Scent of a Woman)*
Best Actress:	Emma Thompson *(Howard's End)*
Best Supp. Actor:	Gene Hackman *(Unforgiven)*
Best Supp. Actress:	Marisa Tomei *(My Cousin Vinny)*

Hollywood, 23 January
At the 50th annual Golden Globe awards, *Scent of a Woman* was voted best film. Its writer, Bo Goldman, won for the best screenplay and its star Al Pacino was best actor. Clint Eastwood was best director for *Unforgiven* and Emma Thompson best actress for *Howard's End.*

Hollywood, 25 January
Paramount has announced that out-take footage from its films over the last 70 years is available to be hired for use in other films.

Paris, 5 March
Cyril Collard, who directed and starred in the semi-autobiographical *les Nuits fauves* (*Savage Nights*), about a young man with AIDS, has died of the disease.

London, 23 April
The former manager of the Scala Cinema was convicted of breach of copyright for screening Stanley Kubrick's *A Clockwork Orange* this month. Since 1973, following a public outcry over its violence and supposed corrupting influence, Kubrick ordered the film to be withheld from British theaters.

Los Angeles, 30 April
Disney's Buena Vista Pictures Distribution today announced a deal by which they acquire Miramax Films, America's leading distributor of art-house films. Founded by Bob and Harvey Weinstein, it will become an autonomous division of Buena Vista continuing to distribute films under its own label.

London, 17 May
A host of Hollywood's top stars have flown in for today's opening at the London Planet Hollywood burger restaurant. More than 4 million pounds has been spent on the interior of the restaurant, strategically situated at the corner of Coventry and Rupert Streets, where the rent alone costs 650,000 pounds a year.

New York, 7 June
After a long series of acrimonious court hearings, the custody battle between Woody Allen and Mia Farrow has come to an end. The judge has decided in Mia's favor: Dylan, Moses and Satchel will remain with their mother.

Hollywood, 19 July
Despite the growing anxiety in the industry about dwindling profits, six major studios, Fox Inc., Walt Disney Co., Warner Bros., Paramount Pictures, Sony Pictures and Universal, are spending $1 billion to turn their studios into high-tech production palaces of the future in the biggest Hollywood building boom since the advent of sound.

New York, 16 August
Costume designer Irene Sharaff has died, aged 83. During her 50-year career she designed costumes for dozens of top screen and stage stars including Elizabeth Taylor for her roles in *Cleopatra* (1963) and *Who's Afraid of Virginia Woolf?* She was nominated for 15 Oscars, winning eight times.

Paris, 10 September
The French box-office sensation for the year is Jean-Marie Poiré's time-travel comedy *les Visiteurs.* Already France's highest grosser, with a total take of $65 million (unadjusted for inflation), the movie has moved into the French all-time admissions top 10, with over 10.74 million viewers.

Washington D.C., 17 October
Actress Jane Alexander, Broadway star and four-times Oscar nominee (for *The Great White Hope*, *All the President's Men*, *Kramer vs. Kramer* and *Testament*) was sworn in today as chairman of the National Endowment for the Arts under the Clinton administration. Miss Alexander will be in charge of the government arts subsidy, and is the first performing artist ever to hold this challenging and prestigious position.

Los Angeles, 22 October
Disney Pictures has released an edited version of *The Program.* The costly cuts were made after a teenager was killed and two others critically injured while imitating a scene in which a group of drunken college footballers lie down on a busy road to prove their toughness.

New York, 26 October
The new Warner Bros. Fifth Avenue store opened today. The store, complete with multi movie screens and a 15-foot wingspan Bat Jet which descends from the ceiling to engage in laser-beamed battle with videotaped bad guys, sells items from a $1.50 key ring to $10,000 individual motion picture frames produced by Warner cartoon artists.

Los Angeles, 4 November
Producer Sherry Lansing, appointed to the newly created position of chairman of the Motion Picture Group of Paramount Pictures, becomes the highest-ranking woman in the film industry. Lansing, aged 48, has signed a five-year contract, and she intends to push through projects already in development including *The Coneheads*, *The Firm*, and *Indecent Proposal.*

New York, 12 November
American Multi-Cinema, part of the AMC and Sony-owned Loew's Theaters, are launching a 20-theater chain to exhibit "cinematic games", interactive feature films from Inter Film Inc.

New York, 1 December
Vincent Canby has stepped down after nearly 25 years as the *New York Times*' leading film critic. Janet Maslin takes over his column.

Los Angeles, 5 December
President Clinton set aside his prepared speech at a Democratic party fund-raiser here last night and made an impassioned plea to the 500 entertainment industry guests to be more sensitive to the impact of popular culture on young people growing up without jobs or a stable family life.

New York, 15 December
Vivien Leigh's Oscar for Scarlett O'Hara in *Gone With the Wind* was auctioned at Sotheby's today and fetched a massive $510,000 from an anonymous telephone bidder.

London, 17 December
Charlie Chaplin's legendary hat and cane were sold for 55,000 pounds at Christie's today. The sale ranged from silent movie memorabilia to a piece of "Kryptonite" from the 1978 production of *Superman.*

Hollywood, 30 December
The legendary agent Irving 'Swifty' Lazar has died, aged 86.

DEATHS

Switzerland, 20 January
Audrey Hepburn

New York, 5 February
Joseph L. Mankiewicz

Manhattan, 27 February
Lillian Gish

California, 28 February
Ruby Keeler

New York, 17 March
Helen Hayes

London, 6 May
Ann Todd

Los Angeles, 6 June
James Bridges

Los Angeles, 9 June
Alexis Smith

Spain, 18 July
Jean Negulesco

Los Angeles, 16 August
Stewart Granger

Hollywood, 25 October
Vincent Price

Hollywood, 31 October
River Phoenix

Rome, 31 October
Federico Fellini

Arizona, 6 December
Don Ameche

New York, 14 December
Myrna Loy

***Schindler's List**, Steven Spielberg's impressive screen version of the best-selling novel by Thomas Kenneally, has proved massively successful for its director and its studio.*

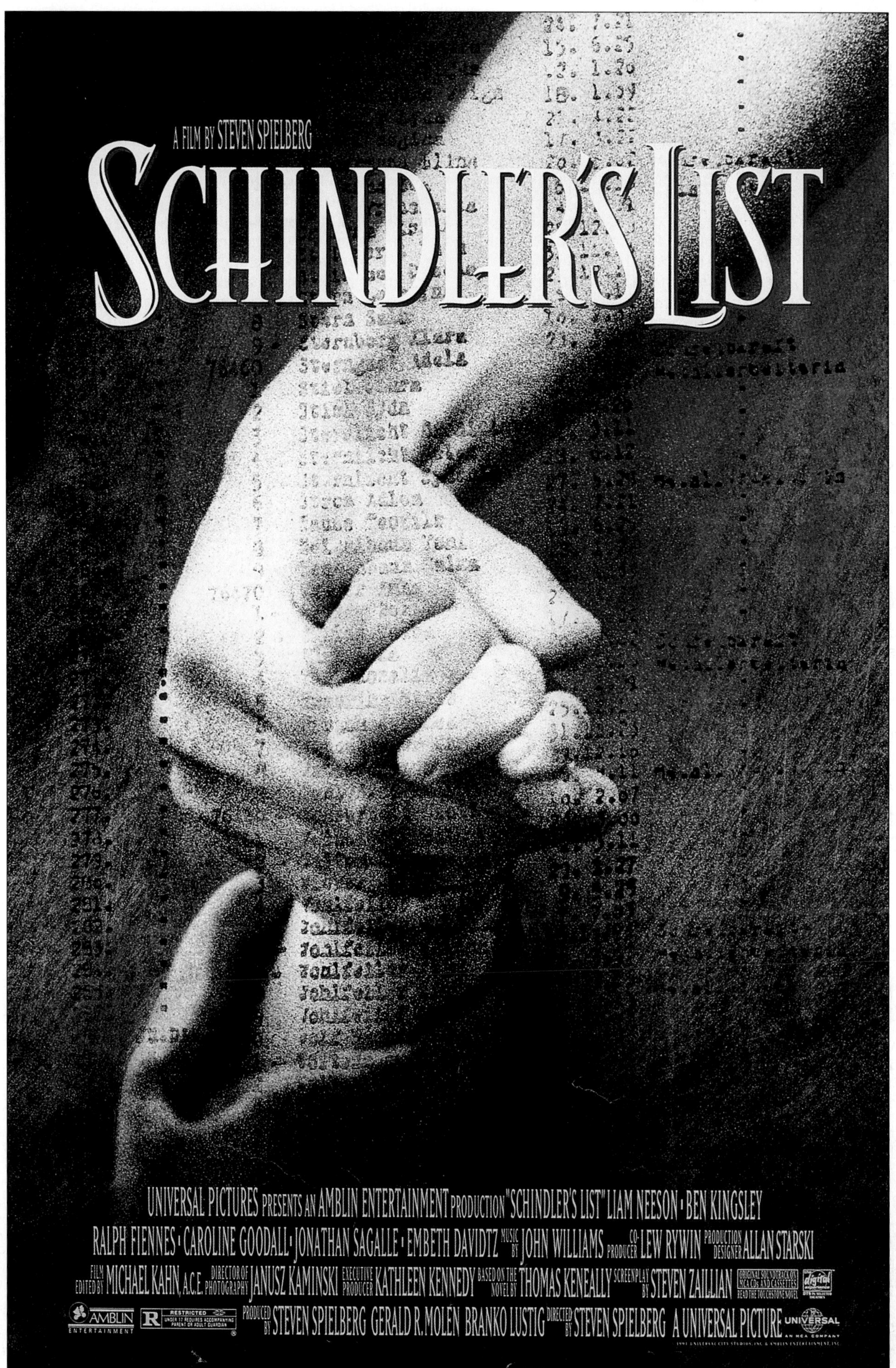
A FILM BY STEVEN SPIELBERG
SCHINDLER'S LIST
UNIVERSAL PICTURES PRESENTS AN AMBLIN ENTERTAINMENT PRODUCTION "SCHINDLER'S LIST" LIAM NEESON · BEN KINGSLEY
RALPH FIENNES · CAROLINE GOODALL · JONATHAN SAGALLE · EMBETH DAVIDTZ MUSIC BY JOHN WILLIAMS CO-PRODUCER LEW RYWIN PRODUCTION DESIGNER ALLAN STARSKI
FILM EDITED BY MICHAEL KAHN, A.C.E. DIRECTOR OF PHOTOGRAPHY JANUSZ KAMINSKI EXECUTIVE PRODUCER KATHLEEN KENNEDY BASED ON THE NOVEL BY THOMAS KENEALLY SCREENPLAY BY STEVEN ZAILLIAN
ORIGINAL SOUNDTRACK ON MCA CDs AND CASSETTES
READ THE TOUCHSTONE NOVEL
AMBLIN ENTERTAINMENT
R RESTRICTED UNDER 17 REQUIRES ACCOMPANYING PARENT OR ADULT GUARDIAN
PRODUCED BY STEVEN SPIELBERG GERALD R. MOLEN BRANKO LUSTIG DIRECTED BY STEVEN SPIELBERG A UNIVERSAL PICTURE
UNIVERSAL AN MCA COMPANY

'El Mariachi' shines sweetly at Sundance

Carlos Gallardo is the musician.

Utah, 31 January
Founded by Robert Redford's Sundance Institute in 1985 to showcase independent American Films, the Sundance Festival has consistently mined emerging talents, discovering films such as *Blood Simple* and *sex, lies and videotape*. One of this year's gems is *El Mariachi*, made South of the Border by 24-year-old Robert Rodriguez for a derisory $7,000. It's a remarkably assured and ingenious thriller of mistaken identity, in which a black-clad guitarist (Carlos Gallardo as the mariachi) in a small Mexican town is mistaken for an identically dressed hit man who carries weapons in a guitar case. The consequences make for a film that is full of panache and wit.

Would you really like your life over again?

New York, 12 February
A new and intriguing comedy directed by Harold Ramis, *Groundhog Day*, is about repeating the past. Bill Murray brilliantly takes the role of a cynical TV weatherman, sent for the fifth year running to the small town of Punxsutawney to cover the Groundhog ceremony held every February 2nd. He wakes up next morning to find it's February 2nd again, and he has to relive the day over and over, until forced to examine his attitudes and turn himself into a nicer person. In this he has help from Andie MacDowell as the romantic interest. This inventive and entertaining comedy-drama is reminiscent of Frank Capra's *It's a Wonderful Life*.

Phil (Bill Murray) with groundhog.

There's not much point in this 'Return'

Los Angeles, 19 March
Bridget Fonda stars as a killer druggie punk, transformed by a government agency program into a classy political assassin. Sound familiar? *Point of No Return* is a virtual shot-by-shot remake of Luc Besson's *Nikita*, with a few Hollywood frills muting the stylish force of the original. Americanizing foreign hits is not new: in 1932 the French *Monsieur Topaz* was snapped up for John Barrymore, while *The Magnificent Seven* originates in Kurosawa's masterpiece, *Seven Samurai*. Now this approach – cheaper than developing an original idea – is becoming an epidemic since Disney's 1987 remake of *Trois hommes et un couffin* into the $250 million-grossing *Three Men and a Baby*. Others among many include *Cousins*, *Three Fugitives* and *The Woman in Red*. Italy's 1976 *Scent of a Woman* won Al Pacino his Oscar, while the classy *Sommersby* was fashioned from *The Return of Martin Guerre*. The trend shows no signs of slowing: Depardieu will reprise his French role in *My Father the Hero*, and *les Choix de la vie* becomes *Intersection* for Richard Gere and Sharon Stone.

The L.A. court rules against Kim Basinger

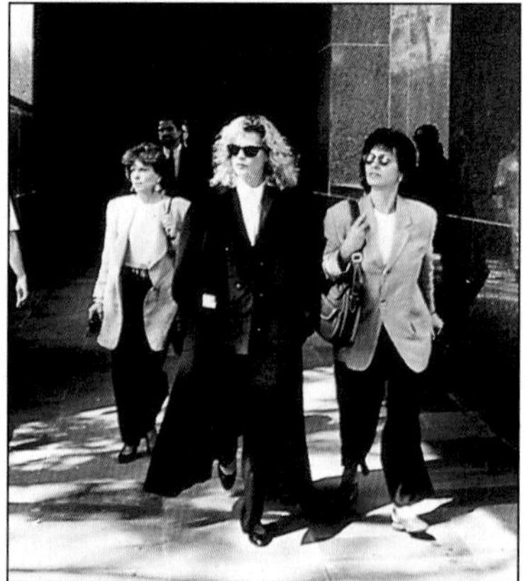
Kim Basinger leaving the court.

Los Angeles, 25 March
The law has ruled in favor of Carl Mazzocone and Main Line Pictures in their case against actress Kim Basinger. Miss Basinger backed out of *Boxing Helena* (directing debut of David Lynch's daughter, Jennifer), the tale of a man who severs the limbs of a beautiful woman in order to keep her to himself. Although sexy blonde Basinger, who was replaced by Sherilyn Fenn, argued that she had not signed a contract, the judge ordered her to pay a massive $8.9 million in damages for the loss of her advantageous presence.

Jodie Foster and Richard Gere in the reasonably successful ***Sommersby****.*

'Falling Down' provokes copy-cat unrest

Los Angeles, 3 April
With violence all too distressingly frequent here, the mindless shooting of at least six Asian grocers in the few weeks since *Falling Down* opened cannot be blamed on the film, but its reception has disquieted many. Michael Douglas, a stressed-out urban Everyman, snaps his spring and pitches into a Korean store owner, a fast food restaurant's staff, and anyone else who irritates him, using assorted weapons in a murderous spree that panders to the rage of self-pitying, middle-class white males who think themselves oppressed. The film takes a blackly comic stance on a screwed-up society, yet has provoked disturbing cheers of encouragement.

Michael Douglas in ***Falling Down****.*

Academy Award choices run the gamut

Anthony Hopkins and Emma Thompson in James Ivory's ***Howard's End.***

Hollywood, 30 March
Clint Eastwood, after 30 years in the movie business, has finally gained his first Oscar as Best Director for the Best Picture, *Unforgiven*. This "revisionist" Western is striking for its willingness to confront the effects of violence, and for the characters' realization of their own mortality. It took 25 years and eight nominations for Al Pacino to be honored with a Best Actor prize as the embittered blind ex-army colonel in *Scent of a Woman*. Pacino was completely convincing as a blind man, shifting seamlessly from comedy to pathos. The Best Actress award went to Emma Thompson for her nicely shaded performance as Margaret Schlegel in *Howard's End*, one of the most subtle and least showy winners in this category. The surprise of the evening was the Best Supporting Actress winner, the hardly known Marisa Tomei for her hilarious gum-chewing motor-mechanic in *My Cousin Vinny*. In contrast, the Best Supporting Actor recipient was veteran Gene Hackman, the brutal sheriff in *Unforgiven*.

Best Supporting Actress Tomei.

Al Pacino and Gabrielle Anwar.

Jaye Davidson in ***The Crying Game.***

Intelligent suspenser on Italian corruption

A car is blown up by a bomb in this vivid sequence from ***The Escort.***

Rome, 18 April
Ricky Tognazzi (son of actor-director Ugo) typifies a heartening return by a new generation of Italian filmmakers to social themes. *La Scorta* (*The Escort*), a fictional but grimly realistic political thriller, is derived from incidents in a brutal war on prosecutors by the Sicilian Mafia. The tale of four incorruptible young *carabinieri* assigned to protect a new judge (Carlo Cecchi) determined to root out corruption, is grippingly well-told, and an intelligent tribute to the bravery of decent men. It should travel well.

The Ken and Emma Shakespeare show

New York, 7 May
"This play is *youthful*," explained Kenneth Branagh, the director of the all-star *Much Ado About Nothing*. "There's a lot of sex in it. I felt it should be surrounded by nature and grapes and sweat and horses and just that kind of lusty, bawdy thing." Shot in the summer of 1992 in a 14th-century villa in the center of the Chianti wine region, this is a gorgeous, exuberant and sensuous movie, though it sometimes strives too strenuously to prove to a wide audience that "Shakespeare can be fun". Enjoying themselves thoroughly are Michael Keaton, Keanu Reeves, Denzel Washington, and Branagh as Benedick opposite his wife Emma Thompson as Beatrice.

Benedick and Beatrice (Branagh, Thompson) in ***Much Ado About Nothing.*** ▷

'The Piano' strikes the right chord for Campion

Best actor David Thewlis in ***Naked***.

Holly Hunter and Anna Paquin in Jane Campion's award-winning ***The Piano***.

The Scent of Green Papaya.

Cannes, 24 May
Jane Campion's *The Piano* and Chen Kaige's *Farewell My Concubine* shared the Golden Palm at this year's Cannes Film Festival. This decision represents a number of firsts for Cannes – Campion is the first woman director to have won the top prize, and the two films were the first productions from either Australia or Hong Kong to gain this accolade. (Although set and shot in Beijing, *Farewell My Concubine* was financed from Hong Kong.) The American Holly Hunter won the best actress prize for her role in *The Piano* as a mysteriously mute 19th-century Scottish woman sent by her father to New Zealand with her young daughter, to marry a man she has not seen. It is only through playing the piano that she can find her voice and liberation. Another English-language film that did particularly well was the cruelly comic *Naked* for which Mike Leigh won the best director award and David Thewlis was voted best actor.

A triumph of technology for Steven Spielberg with 'Jurassic Park'

Jurassic Park: *based on Michael Crichton's best-selling novel about dinosaurs.*

New York, 11 June
Steven Spielberg's uncanny insight into what the public, especially the young, will flock to, has continued unabated with *Jurassic Park*, which looks like topping even his earlier commercial triumphs. The tale of an entrepreneur who develops genetically produced dinosaurs to place in the world's most fantastic amusement park, lends itself to animatronic and special effects wizardry. The excitement builds when the Tyrannosaurus Rex and other prehistoric monsters run amok, terrorizing some visiting scientists and two little kids. Though it might frighten younger children in the audience, older ones and adults will thrill to the extraordinary lifelike creatures, created by the Matsushita workshops. Rather less lifelike are the human cast, including Sam Neill (both William Hurt and Tim Robbins turned down the role) and Laura Dern as paleontologists who head for an obscure Central American island where tycoon Richard Attenborough, and Jeff Goldblum as his gene-splicing genius, have recreated the Age of Giants.

The battle of the summer blockbusters starts here, with Stallone in *Cliffhanger*. A snow-strewn romp full of stunts, death and dumb one-liners, with mountain-rescue hero Sly pumped up to alarming proportions for his return from flop comedies.

Mexican melodrama tickles U.S. taste buds

Marco Leonardi is Pedro and Lumi Cavazos is Tita in Alfonso Arau's film.

New York, 12 June
Mexico has made news with Alfonso Arau's *Like Water for Chocolate*, adapted from his wife Laura Esquivel's international bestseller. The film is hot property, breaking out of the art house circuit to become the highest-grossing Latin American movie ever. A captivating tragicomic fairy tale of romance, revolution and recipes, it recounts the fate of three sisters in audacious "magic realism" style, and Lumi Cavazos as a radiant culinary heroine.

Tailor-made star role for Clint Eastwood

New York, 9 July
Clint Eastwood follows his triumph in *Unforgiven* with a straight acting job in Wolfgang Petersen's *In the Line of Fire*, gracing it with a great performance. Amid slick, pacy suspense, Eastwood's aging, tired, soon-to-retire Secret Service agent, haunted by his inability to have saved Kennedy, finds himself engaged in a cat-and-mouse game with John Malkovich's cunning psycho, a rogue who taunts the bodyguard with his plans to assassinate the incumbent President. The latest computer techniques put the actors into real news footage from the Clinton and Bush campaigns for credible tension. Roundly entertaining, with that something extra, a real Star.

Secret Service agents Lilly Raines (Rene Russo) and Frank Horrigan.

'Sleepless in Seattle' a romantic throwback

Meg Ryan, Ross Malinger and Tom Hanks in Nora Ephron's directing debut.

Seattle, 25 June
Writer Nora Ephron makes her directing debut with *Sleepless in Seattle*, starring Meg Ryan and Tom Hanks. This out-and-out romantic fantasy is of the gloriously old-fashioned school which has given us *Working Girl*, *Pretty Woman* and *When Harry Met Sally* (written by Ephron). It's unusual in that the couple don't meet until the final frame; it's also witty, very sentimental, and rich in deliberate iconic references to a Hollywood cinematic past in its soundtrack and, especially, its use of *An Affair to Remember* from which it self-consciously borrows. Welcome too, to a refreshingly uncutesy and attractive child, Ross Malinger.

Luck for Wayne Wang, joy for audiences

San Francisco, 8 September
Amy Tan has adapted her novel, *The Joy Luck Club*, and director Wayne Wang skillfully interweaves the tale's dramatic pasts in pre-Revolutionary China with funny, tearful psychodrama in contemporary America. An unconventional epic of women's lives and family relationships across generations, it is superbly acted by a large ensemble and directed with clarity and affection by Wang, making his biggest-budget venture to date.

Mother Tsai Chin and daughter Tamlyn Tomita in ***The Joy Luck Club****.*

'Short Cuts' shares the Golden Lion with 'Three Colors Blue'

*Anne Archer as Claire the housewife who works as a clown in **Short Cuts**.*

***Three Colors Blue**: Juliette Binoche.*

Venice, 11 September
The jury at the 50th Venice Film Festival diplomatically divided the Golden Lion between the USA and Europe, with Robert Altman's *Short Cuts* and Krzysztof Kieslowski's *Three Colors Blue* sharing the top prize. Altman's impressive three-hour movie expertly interweaves nine of John Carver's minimalist short stories and a narrative poem, and 22 disparate characters, whose lives occasionally cross. *Short Cuts* also received a merited special prize for the entire cast. Kieslowski's film is the first part of a Red, White and Blue trilogy, dealing with freedom, fraternity and equality. *Blue* is the freedom story, about how a woman (Juliette Binoche, best actress winner) tries to adapt to life after her husband, a celebrated composer, is suddenly killed in a car crash. It is an intricate and brilliantly shot film, though rather overloaded with symbols. A film from Tadjikhistan, *Kosh ba Kosh*, won the Silver Lion.

'The Age of Innocence' a triumphant departure for Martin Scorsese

New York, 17 September
The film version of Edith Wharton's 19th-century novel of New York manners, *The Age of Innocence*, has opened to enthusiastic acclaim. Miss Wharton nailed her characters firmly to the cross of convention and hypocrisy that dictated the behavior of the rich and fashionable, and which prevents her protagonist, Newland Archer, from following his heart to the Countess Ellen Olenska, an enigmatic woman with a "past". The film is wonderfully lavish, with loving attention to period detail – the credits even boast a food consultant – and the cast superb. Daniel Day Lewis is Archer, Michelle Pfeiffer Ellen, and Winona Ryder (her best performance), is the "suitable" girl Archer marries. But it is Scorsese's achievement which gives most cause for comment. The industry was agog with the news that he would direct the film, but he has conclusively revealed that his gifts go deeper than the streetwise.

Newland Archer (Day Lewis) and his wife May (Winona Ryder) in London.

With Countess Olenska (Pfeiffer).

Zola classic opens at monumental cost

Gérard Depardieu is Maheu.

Paris, 29 September
Claude Berri's *Germinal* cost 175 million francs, thus becoming the most expensive movie ever made by a European company in Europe. The monumental set took seven months to build on location near Valenciennes. Zola's novel is a literary beacon casting its light on the dark social and economic conditions of the coal miners in the north of France in the late 19th century. Berri has risen splendidly to the challenge of transposing this bleak tale to the screen. The film does not idealize working people, among whom Gérard Depardieu, Miou-Miou and the singer Renaud give towering performances, neither has it ignored the fact that Zola sometimes stretches the physical to the point of nausea.

Renaud is Etienne Lantier.

Director Robert De Niro tells 'A Bronx Tale'

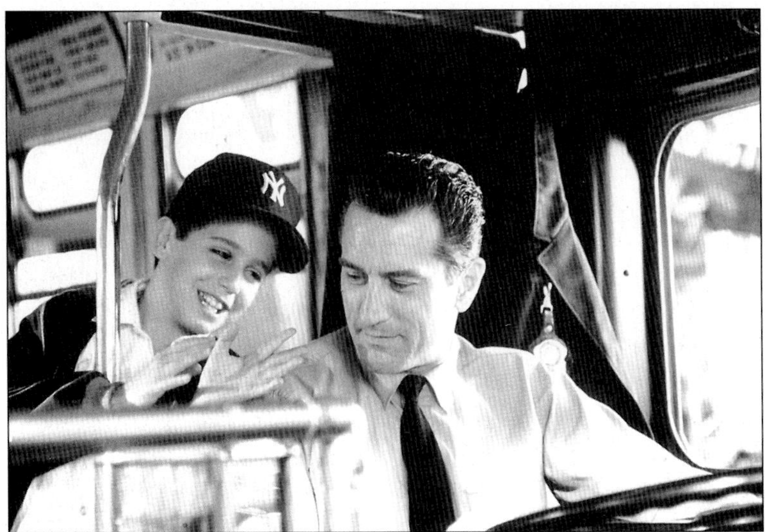

Bus driver Lorenzo (Robert De Niro) and his young son (Francis Capra).

New York, 29 September
With his New York-based TriBeca company having already been home to several directors, actor Robert De Niro joins their ranks, proving with his directing debut that he paid attention when working with Scorsese. Adapted by Chazz Palminteri (who plays the local hood) from his one-man show about a boy's torn loyalties and transition to manhood in Brooklyn, *A Bronx Tale* has De Niro as a poor but honest bus driver, struggling for his son's respect when the boy (teenage De Niro look-alike Lillo Brancato taking over from child Francis Capra) falls prey to the hood's blandishments. Both tough and sentimental, this father-son tale is gutsy and engaging.

Sudden and terrible death of River Phoenix

Los Angeles, 1 November
River Phoenix died yesterday after collapsing on the sidewalk outside of the West Hollywood nightclub owned by his friend Johnny Depp.

River Phoenix: a tragic end.

He had been drinking heavily while on drugs. His brother Leaf, who was with him, called an ambulance, but it was too late. What shocked and surprised fans most was that the actor was known to be a vegetarian teetotaller. Although he was only 22, he seemed much younger, as if he were strongly resisting the coming of manhood. He had little of the show business ambition of his contemporaries. This might have had something to do with his unconventional upbringing, which his curious name reflected. He was born in a log cabin in Oregon, the son of nature-and-peace-loving hippie parents. His two best performances reflected his early peripatetic existence: in Sidney Lumet's *Running on Empty* and Gus Van Sant's *My Own Private Idaho.* In the latter, there was a gravity and fragility in his role as a gay hustler that made audiences feel protective of him. River Phoenix will be remembered as an actor of looks and talent who endured the rites of passage without being able to enjoy the rewards that seemed certain.

Stallone paired with super-villain Snipes

Los Angeles, 8 October
Sylvester Stallone and Wesley Snipes make a dynamite team as, respectively, the titular destructive cop, *Demolition Man*, and his nemesis, a bleached blond maniac with one blue eye and a fiendish way with a one-liner. This spiffy futuristic action caper may not be the most memorably intelligent movie ever made, but it has panache and humor, and proves that Snipes' continuing rise in the echelons of black actors is no accident. Debut director Marco Brambilla has Stallone delightfully spoofing his own personality as he comes up against Snipes in the 21st century when they both thaw out, having been cryogenically frozen for "attitude adjustment".

Wesley Snipes in ***Demolition Man.***

Chen Kaige's 'Concubine' seduces the West

New York, 15 October
Banned in its native China, Chen Kaige's beguiling *Farewell My Concubine*, having changed its country of origin to Hong Kong, is now showing successfully in the USA. Kaige's fifth film is a sumptuously detailed panorama of Chinese history seen through the eyes of two dedicated star actors in the Peking Opera. Cheng Dieyi and Duan Xialou are inextricably linked from 1925, a time of warlords' rule, to the Japanese invasion, the rise of communism and the Cultural Revolution. The unrequited love that Dieyi has for Xialou is mirrored in their nightly performance of a traditional opera that gives the film its title, with Xialou as the King, and Dieyi as the self-sacrificing concubine. When Xialou marries his real-life concubine, tragedy ensues. Kaige uses the relationship to develop themes rarely explored in Chinese cinema such as homosexuality, and the individual's plight in a society given over to the masses.

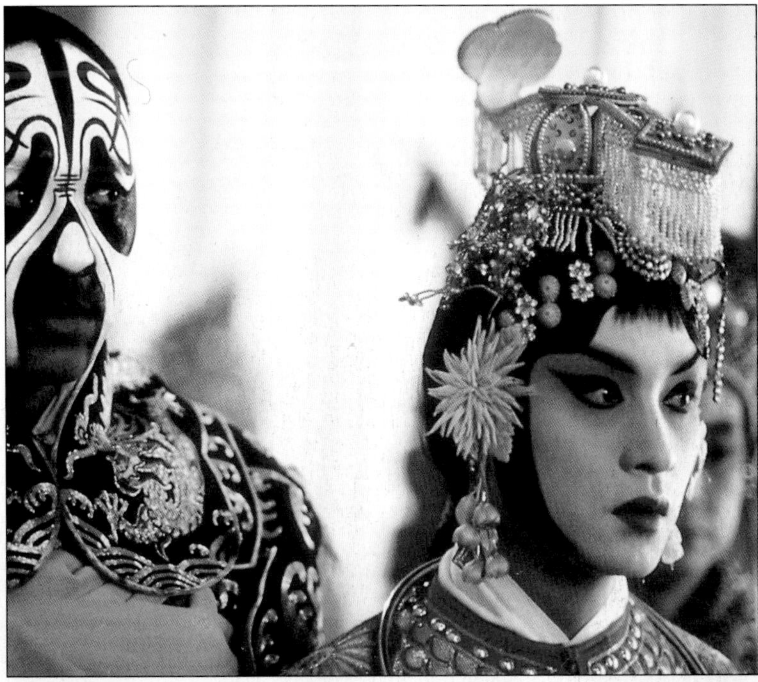

Zhang Fengyi (King Chu), Leslie Cheung (concubine) in Chen Kaige's film. ▷

They have passed on but have left a rich legacy

With Rex Harrison.

Director Joseph L. Mankiewicz.

*Gish, Davis in **Whales of August**.*

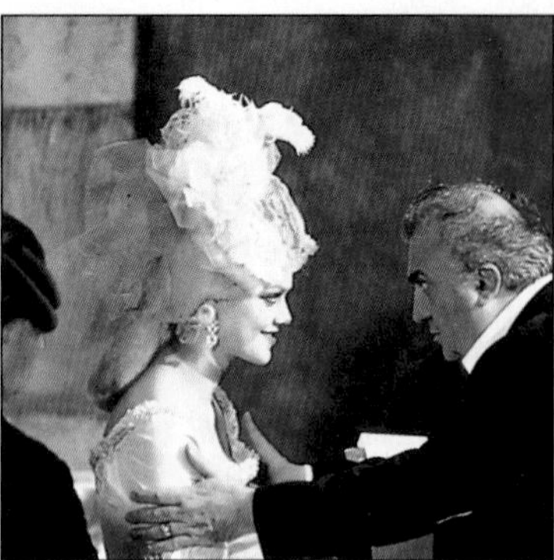

*Fellini at work on **Casanova**.*

Rome, 1 November
Italy's Federico Fellini, one of the most unique and influential creative geniuses in cinema history, died yesterday, following a stroke last August. Several of his 20 films were drawn from his own inner life, notably *8½*, about a film director, played by Marcello Mastroianni, the director's frequent alter ego. Even the least successful of his films were innovative, but he will be best remembered for the poignant *La Strada*, starring his wife Giulietta Masina (now herself ill), the controversial *La Dolce Vita*, and the delightful odyssey of youth, *Amarcord*.

Fellini is the most recent of many deaths this year. The first tragic loss was that of the graceful, gamine and glorious Audrey Hepburn at her Swiss home on 20 January. This daughter of a Dutch aristocrat mother and a British father, who spent the war years starving and hiding from the Nazis in Occupied Holland, took the world by storm in *Roman Holiday*, which won her the Best Actress Oscar. With her huge expressive eyes and magic smile, she went on to many further successes, including *Sabrina*, *Funny Face*, *Breakfast at Tiffany's*, *Charade*, *My Fair Lady*, and *Robin and Marian*. Twice married and the mother of two sons, she made a second career as a dedicated high-profile ambassador for UNICEF. She was adored on screen and off, and her death from cancer at the age of 63 left a gap which will not easily be filled.

Joseph L. Mankiewicz, the highly respected director whose interesting and varied career included *All About Eve* and the notorious Taylor-Burton *Cleopatra*, died of a heart attack in New York on 7 February, just before his 84th birthday. Twenty days later, the remarkable Lillian Gish died at 96. A great pioneer of the silent cinema and the leading lady for D.W. Griffith in many memorable films, she was a beauty and a fine actress who had the longest career in movie history. In 1960, she played Audrey Hepburn's mother in *The Unforgiven*; in 1969 she published her autobiography, *The Movies, Mr. Griffith and Me*; in 1978, after a 10-year absence, she appeared in Robert Altman's *A Wedding*. Her last film was *The Whales of August* in 1987, which co-starred Bette Davis.

'The Remains of the Day' is proving a winner for Merchant-Ivory

London, 12 November
The latest Merchant-Ivory offering, *The Remains of the Day*, was adapted from Anglo-Japanese writer Kazuo Ishigura's prizewinning novel about an English butler and his ambiguous relationships with his employer and housekeeper. The film carries all the hallmarks audiences expect from James Ivory: an elegiac camera, period detail and atmosphere, an authoritative cast, and finely balanced emotion. Ivory's technique, however, has seldom been put to better use. Anthony Hopkins is impeccable as the butler whose personal happiness is subsumed to the notion of service and, with Hannibal Lecter behind him and C.S. Lewis in *Shadowlands* to come, proves himself the outstanding actor of our time in his age range. Emma Thompson's housekeeper is almost a match for him, and James Fox perfect as the effete, politically suspect landowner. There is little doubt that English audiences will echo the enthusiastic American response.

Anthony Hopkins is the perfect butler, Emma Thompson is the housekeeper.

GATT agreements in sight for films

New York, 15 December
The United States and Europe have agreed to put aside their unresolved differences in a number of key areas, including freer access to films and TV, so as to pave the way for a new and far-reaching GATT agreement, aimed at lowering tariffs and reducing other restrictions on world trade. This decision is a victory for the French in particular, who feel very strongly about maintaining their system of domestic subsidies and taxes designed to encourage French and European production, while restricting outside (mainly U.S.) access to French markets. They have recently rallied to support Claude Berri's new film version of *Germinal*, an example of the kind of film which would not have been made without generous government assistance, though it is hardly typical of French production with its $25 million budget making it one of the most expensive French films ever.

'Schindler's List' a triumphant personal journey

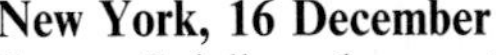

Oskar Schindler (Liam Neeson) arguing with a guard at Auschwitz.

A group of terrified Jewish women await their appalling fate in the camp.

New York, 16 December
Steven Spielberg has made a radical departure from popular escapist entertainment, putting himself on the line with *Schindler's List*. Himself a Jew, a personal concern with his people's history and a desire to help ensure that the Holocaust is never forgotten, resulted in the film. There were some problems at the start, when the World Jewish Congress forbade him to shoot inside the Auschwitz death camp, though they allowed him to build a replica outside the main gates. The 185-minute film is based on Thomas Keneally's novel about Oskar Schindler, the real-life German businessman who rescued more than a thousand Jews from the gas chambers by employing them in his munitions factory. Schindler, a member of the Nazi Party, learned how to manipulate the corrupt and cruel system to his own purposes. With an intelligent script (by Steven Zaillian), a superb cast (headed by Irish actor Liam Neeson taking the title role), and telling black-and-white images (photographed by Janusz Kaminski), Spielberg pays an unforgettable homage to survival, re-creating history with power and restraint. Perhaps the most moving sequence in the film is the epilogue, featuring actual survivors and their families, as well as Schindler's widow, filing past this complex man's grave in Israel. The film sees the culmination of its maker's 10-year-long ambition.

Jonathan Demme and Tom Hanks tackle AIDS issue on screen

Denzel Washington the lawyer, with his client Tom Hanks in ***Philadelphia****.*

Hollywood, 22 December
Director Jonathan (*Silence of the Lambs*) Demme and screenwriter Ron Nyswaner, basing their story on a true case, have made Hollywood's first mainstream movie concerning AIDS. Tom Hanks, in a truthful performance commendably devoid of histrionic flourishes, is Andy Becker, high-flying lawyer and favorite of boss Jason Robards, until it is learnt that he is gay and has AIDS. Sacked, he decides to sue, defended by an intially reluctant and conventionally prejudiced Denzel Washington. Gay rights groups are complaining that the film is sanitized; this is to miss the point that it is an unashamedly commercial movie and is thus able to get across its message about discrimination and groundless fear. Well-acted, thought-provoking and poignant, it deserves audiences and respect.

What's Love Got to Do With It **is based on Tina Turner autobiography. Angela Bassett is Tina, Laurence Fishburne is Ike. Lots of straight-ahead realism, dozens of songs.**

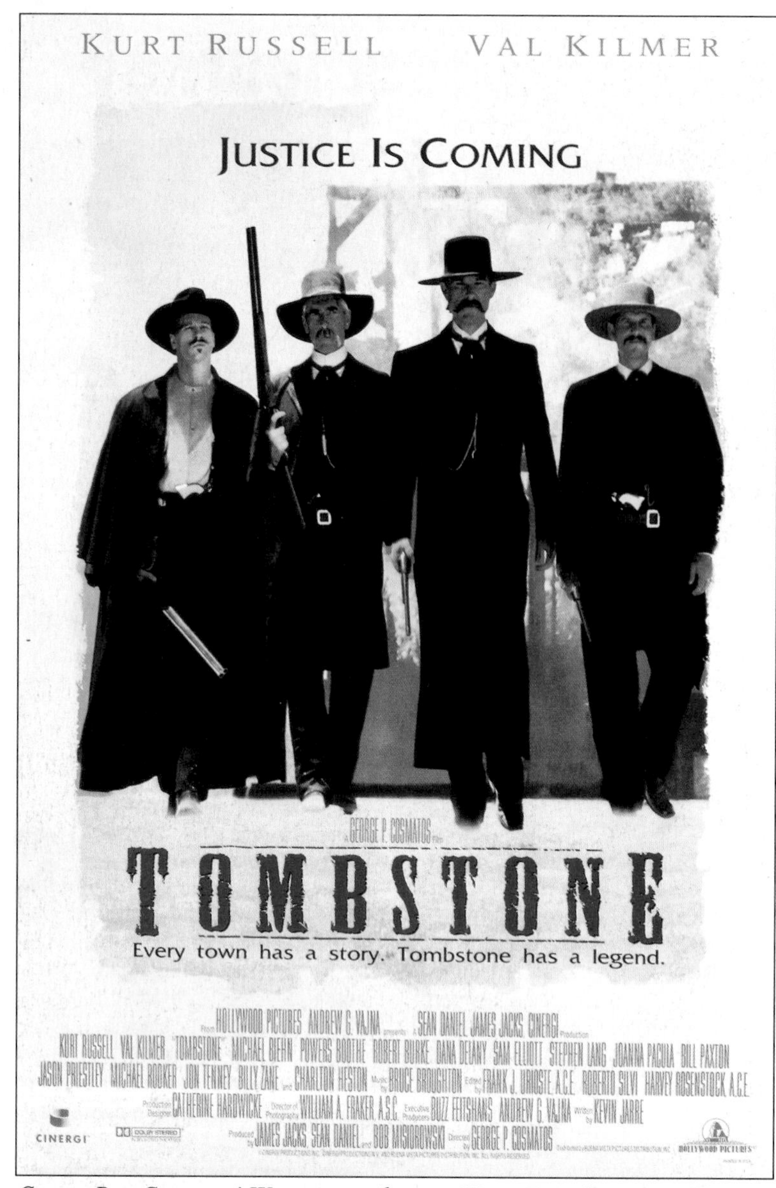
KURT RUSSELL VAL KILMER
JUSTICE IS COMING
GEORGE P. COSMATOS
TOMBSTONE
Every town has a story. Tombstone has a legend.
From HOLLYWOOD PICTURES ANDREW G. VAJNA presents A SEAN DANIEL JAMES JACKS CINERGI Production
KURT RUSSELL VAL KILMER "TOMBSTONE" MICHAEL BIEHN POWERS BOOTHE ROBERT BURKE DANA DELANY SAM ELLIOTT STEPHEN LANG JOANNA PACULA BILL PAXTON
JASON PRIESTLEY MICHAEL ROOKER JON TENNEY BILLY ZANE and CHARLTON HESTON Music by BRUCE BROUGHTON Edited by FRANK J. URIOSTE A.C.E. ROBERTO SILVI HARVEY ROSENSTOCK A.C.E.
Production Designer CATHERINE HARDWICKE Director of Photography WILLIAM A. FRAKER A.S.C. Executive Producers BUZZ FEITSHANS ANDREW G. VAJNA Written by KEVIN JARRE
Produced by JAMES JACKS SEAN DANIEL and BOB MISIOROWSKI Directed by GEORGE P. COSMATOS
CINERGI
DOLBY STEREO
HOLLYWOOD PICTURES

George Pan Cosmatos' Western: a tribute to Wyatt Earp (Kurt Russell).

Mexican Guillermo del Toro's stylish vampire variation ***Cronos****.*

Bruce Jones in Ken Loach's highly acclaimed ***Raining Stones*** *(G.B.).*

l to r: Leon, Rawle D. Lewis, Malik Yoba, Doug E. Doug in ***Cool Runnings****.*

Juliette Lewis, Brad Pitt in road movie ***Kalifornia****: yet another serial-killer.*

Writer, director, actor 'Beat' Takeshi Kitano in ***Sonatine****, his fourth feature.*

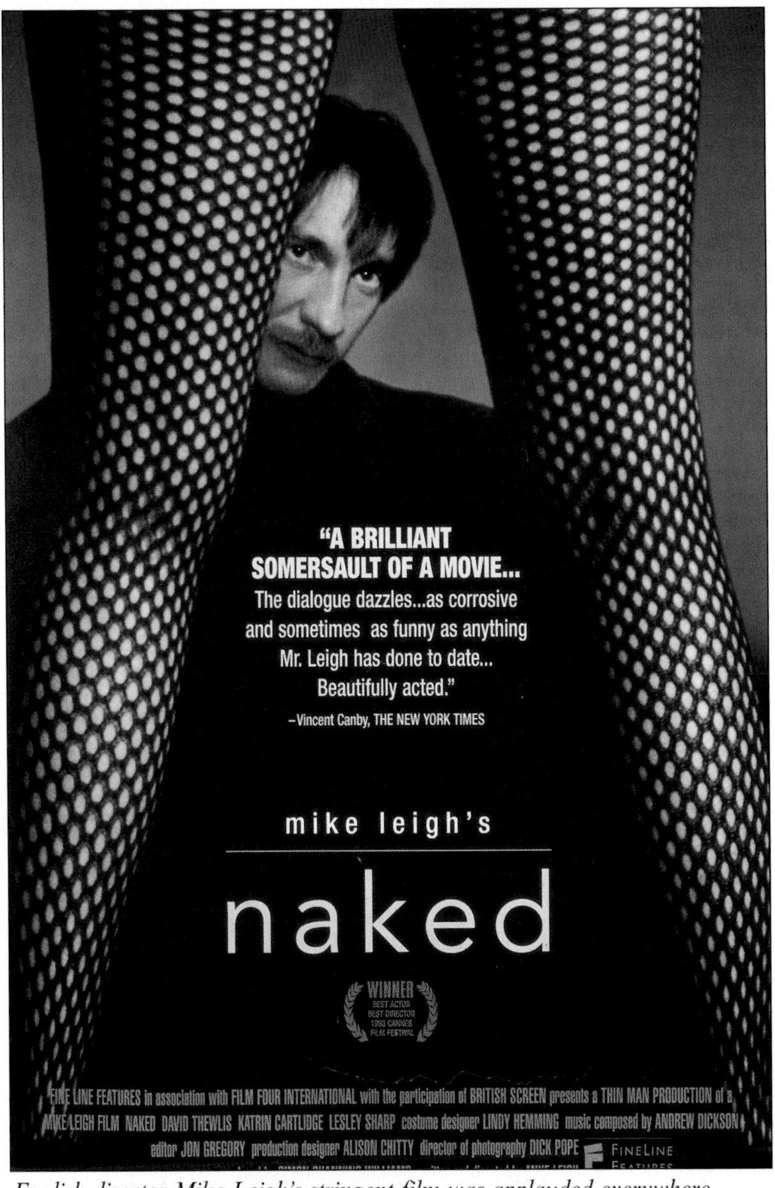
"A BRILLIANT
SOMERSAULT OF A MOVIE...
The dialogue dazzles...as corrosive
and sometimes as funny as anything
Mr. Leigh has done to date...
Beautifully acted."
–Vincent Canby, THE NEW YORK TIMES
mike leigh's
naked
WINNER
BEST ACTOR
BEST DIRECTOR
1993 CANNES
FILM FESTIVAL
FINE LINE FEATURES in association with FILM FOUR INTERNATIONAL with the participation of BRITISH SCREEN presents a THIN MAN PRODUCTION of a
MIKE LEIGH FILM NAKED DAVID THEWLIS KATRIN CARTLIDGE LESLEY SHARP costume designer LINDY HEMMING music composed by ANDREW DICKSON
editor JON GREGORY production designer ALISON CHITTY director of photography DICK POPE
FINELINE
FEATURES

English director Mike Leigh's stringent film was applauded everywhere.

al St 華 華

***Manhattan Murder Mystery**: Diane Keaton and Woody Allen re-united.*

*Sally Field's 'housekeeper' **Mrs Doubtfire** (Robin Williams).*

*Tyrin Turner threatens Martin Davis in L.A. urban drama **Menace II Society**.*

*Jason Scott, Lauren Holly: Bruce and Linda in **Dragon: The Bruce Lee Story**.*

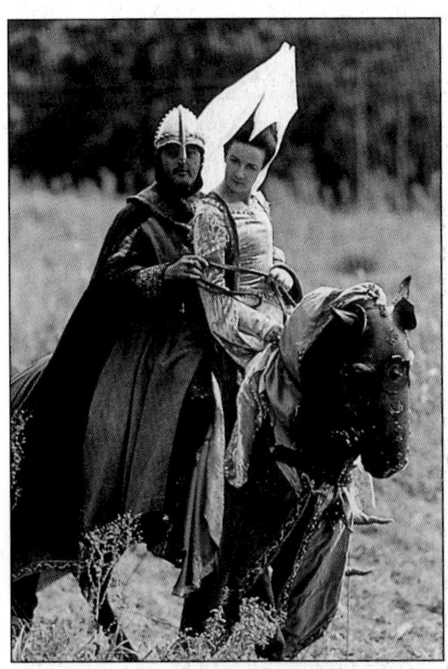

*Time-travel fantasy **Les Visiteurs**, a mega-hit for the French industry.*

*Yi Tian, the star of **The Blue Kite** from China's Tian Zhuang-Zhuang.*

1994

1993 Academy Awards, Dorothy Chandler Pavilion, 21 Mar.

Best Film:	*Schindler's List* (dir: Steven Spielberg)
Best Director:	Steven Spielberg
Best Actor:	Tom Hanks *(Philadelphia)*
Best Actress:	Holly Hunter *(The Piano)*
Best Supp. Actor:	Tommy Lee Jones *(The Fugitive)*
Best Supp. Actress:	Anna Paquin *(The Piano)*

Los Angeles, 7 January
Mike Medavoy, chairman of Tristar Pictures, has announced his resignation. Sony have named Columbia's Mark Canton to fill the post.

Berlin, 21 February
Jim Sheridan's *In the Name of the Father* has won the Golden Bear at the Berlin Festival. Krzysztof Kieslowski was voted best director for *Three Colours: White*, Tom Hanks and Britain's Crissy Rock were best actor and actress for *Philadelphia* and *Ladybird, Ladybird* respectively, while *Strawberry and Chocolate* (*Fresa y Chocolate*), Cuba's international breakthrough film, captured the jury's special prize.

Hollywood, 4 March
Jack Nicholson last night became the 22nd and youngest recipient of the American Film Institute Life Achievement Award. A second award, given to Elizabeth Taylor, makes her only the fourth woman to receive the honor, following Lillian Gish, Bette Davis and Barbara Stanwyck. Miss Taylor, who has made 54 films, now devotes her time to campaigning for AIDS research.

Durango, 4 March
Actor John Candy, aged 43, has died of a sudden heart attack while filming *Wagons West* here. Candy's *Cool Running* grossed $68.8 million.

Los Angeles, 11 March
Jack Cardiff has been honored by the Los Angeles Society of Cinematographers with its International Award for Outstanding Achievement. Cardiff is the only person ever to receive Oscars for both cinematography (*Black Narcissus*) and direction (*Sons and Lovers*).

Los Angeles, 28 March
Lana Turner, who was diagnosed as having throat cancer two years ago, is due to be discharged today from Cedars-Sinai Medical Center where she has been undergoing tests.

Los Angeles, 4 April
The film community is in mourning for Frank Wells, who died yesterday in a helicopter accident in Nevada. Wells, aged 62, the universally admired president of the Walt Disney Co., revitalised the Disney studio alongside chief executive Michael Eisner, propelling revenues from $1.5 to $8.5 billion with hits such as *Pretty Woman, Beauty and the Beast* and *Aladdin*, and developing the company's theme-park, real estate and merchandising concerns.

Berlin, 5 April
In a worldwide survey, 456 film critics and historians, named the top five German films of all time: *M* (1933), *The Cabinet of Dr Caligari* (1919), *Berlin, Symphony of a Great City* (1927), *Nosferatu* (1922), *People on Sunday* (1929).

London, 19 May
Ex-Beatle George Harrison has sold his production company, HandMade Films, to Paragon Entertainment of Toronto for $8.5 million cash. Among HandMade's biggest hits were *Monty Python's Life of Brian* and Neil Jordan's *Mona Lisa*.

New York, 3 June
HarperCollins today publishes the long-awaited, expanded second edition of Ephraim Katz's Film Encyclopedia, regarded as the bible of reference books. Katz, who died aged 60 in 1992, completed the original tome in 1979.

London, 5 June
For the first time in years, Britain's two major studios, Pinewood and Shepperton, are playing host to Hollywood features. Shooting has begun on *Mary Reilly*, starring Julia Roberts, Sylvester Stallone's *Judge Dredd* will be underway next month, and Kenneth Branagh's *Frankenstein* is already in post-production at Shepperton. The favorable pound to dollar exchange rate has fuelled this welcome trend.

London, 9 June
At a press conference here yesterday, it was announced that Pierce Brosnan will take over from Timothy Dalton to become the fifth 007, in the 17th James Bond movie.

London, 20 June
Quentin Tarantino's *Reservoir Dogs* (1991), still awaiting British censor approval for video release, has re-entered the U.K.'s Top 10. Box-office receipts here are now almost triple those of the U.S.

New York, 19 August
Hollywood kingpin Michael Ovitz, chief of Creative Artists Agency (CAA), will be teaming up with three regional telephone giants to create a 'cyberstudio' for the acquisition, production and distribution of virtual reality, CD-ROM and other interactive programming.This offers a major financial opportunity for talent agencies, who are barred from feature film investment.

Los Angeles, 28 August
Shock announcement of the year: Disney supremo Jeffrey Katzenberg has quit the studio amid acrimony.

Los Angeles, 6 October
Carolco Pictures, the independent studio whose blockbusters included *Cliffhanger* and *Total Recall*, faces financial disaster owing to severe liquidity problems. In July, Arnold Schwarzenegger defected with his new epic *Crusade*, while star Michael Douglas quit *Cut-Throat Island* two weeks before commencement of shooting.

Rome, 10 October
Michelangelo Antonioni, in poor health since a stroke in 1984, will co-direct *Lies* with Wim Wenders. Antonioni's first feature in 13 years, it will begin shooting in Portofino next month with a cast that includes Jeremy Irons, Fanny Ardant and Marcello Mastroianni.

France, 11 November
The controversial debut feature, *le Demon au feminin* (*The Demon in Women*), from Algeria's first woman director, Hafsa Zinai Koudil, had its first public showing in Amiens last night. Made two years ago, the film's anti-fundamentalist stance has brought Koudil death threats and an attempted kidnapping.

New York, 28 November
The National Endowment for the Arts, suffering financial cuts, is withdrawing all funds for the preservation of film. The decision affects thousands of films and millions of feet of newsreel footage.

Toronto, 8 December
The unique talent of director Atom Egoyan has finally been rewarded with eight Genie awards (Canada's Oscar) for *Exotica*, his brooding sexually charged drama.

DEATHS

Paris, 22 January
Jean-Louis Barrault

Los Angeles, 6 February
Joseph Cotten

New York, 6 March
Melina Mercouri

Madrid, 9 March
Fernando Rey

London, 17 March
Mai Zetterling

Rome, 23 March
Giulietta Masina

Los Angeles, 8 May
George Peppard

Los Angeles, 14 June
Henry Mancini

Canterbury, England, 11 August
Peter Cushing

France, 30 August
Lindsay Anderson

Connecticut, 11 September
Jessica Tandy

California, 1 November
Noah Beery Jr

Greece, 6 December
Gian Maria Volonte

Rome, 24 December
Rossano Brazzi

This charming comedy, which shot to instant success on both sides of the Atlantic, was a British-made film which seemed to discover the secret of the commercial American market.

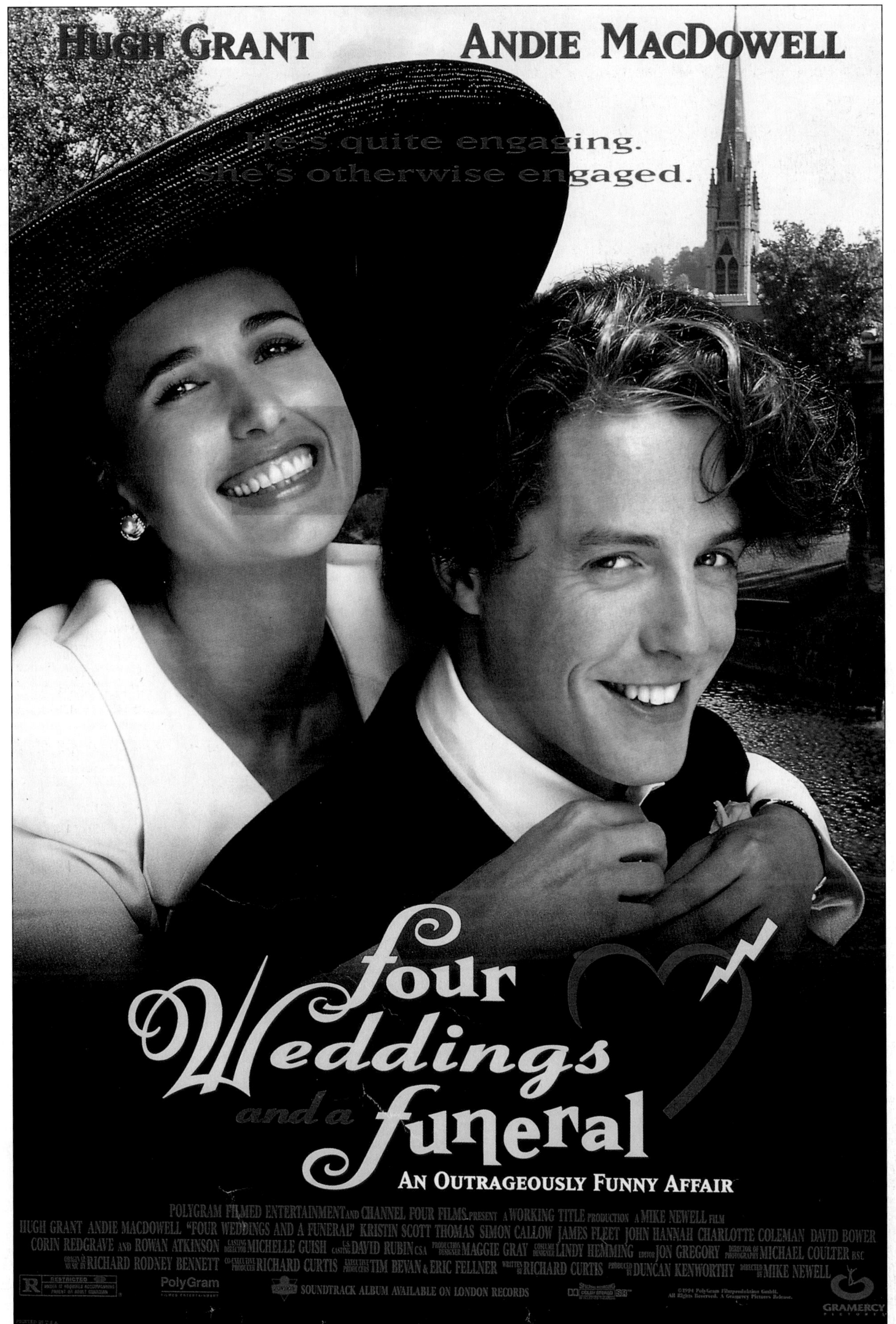
HUGH GRANT
ANDIE MACDOWELL
He's quite engaging.
She's otherwise engaged.
four Weddings and a funeral
AN OUTRAGEOUSLY FUNNY AFFAIR
POLYGRAM FILMED ENTERTAINMENT AND CHANNEL FOUR FILMS PRESENT A WORKING TITLE PRODUCTION A MIKE NEWELL FILM
HUGH GRANT ANDIE MACDOWELL "FOUR WEDDINGS AND A FUNERAL" KRISTIN SCOTT THOMAS SIMON CALLOW JAMES FLEET JOHN HANNAH CHARLOTTE COLEMAN DAVID BOWER
CORIN REDGRAVE AND ROWAN ATKINSON CASTING DIRECTOR MICHELLE GUISH U.S. CASTING DAVID RUBIN CSA PRODUCTION DESIGNER MAGGIE GRAY COSTUME DESIGNER LINDY HEMMING EDITOR JON GREGORY DIRECTOR OF PHOTOGRAPHY MICHAEL COULTER BSC
ORIGINAL MUSIC BY RICHARD RODNEY BENNETT CO-EXECUTIVE PRODUCER RICHARD CURTIS EXECUTIVE PRODUCERS TIM BEVAN & ERIC FELLNER WRITTEN BY RICHARD CURTIS PRODUCED BY DUNCAN KENWORTHY DIRECTED BY MIKE NEWELL
R RESTRICTED
PolyGram
SOUNDTRACK ALBUM AVAILABLE ON LONDON RECORDS
GRAMERCY

Gilbert Grape reveals new depths to Depp

Gilbert Grape (Johnny Depp) comforts his brother Arnie (Leonardo DiCaprio).

Los Angeles, 9 February
Swedish director Lasse (*My Life as a Dog*) Hallström, the latest foreign import to Hollywood, observes American life with heightened reality but tenderness in *What's Eating Gilbert Grape?* Quirky and sweetly offbeat, the movie reveals as odd and funny a collection of cares as ever beset a youthful protagonist. As rueful narrator hero Gilbert, a vastly charming and sympathetic Johnny Depp copes with exasperating responsibilities that include his retarded brother, given a stand-out performance by Leonardo DiCaprio.

AIDS claims the life of filmmaker Jarman

London. 19 February
Derek Jarman, one of British cinema's most controversial and independent directors, has died of AIDS complications at the age of 52. The openly gay Jarman was an active spokesman for AIDS research, after having gained a cult following with his innovative films, many of which are of a homo-erotic nature. Making the most of shoestring budgets, they included *Sebastiane*, in Latin; *The Tempest*, which contained a rendition of "Stormy Weather"; *Jubilee*, a punk vision of England; *Caravaggio*, a stylized biography of the painter, and finally *Blue*, which consisted of a personal commentary on the progress of his illness, spoken over an unvarying blue image.

*Singer Elizabeth Welch in Derek Jarman's reworking of **The Tempest**.*

Controversial IRA drama opens in London

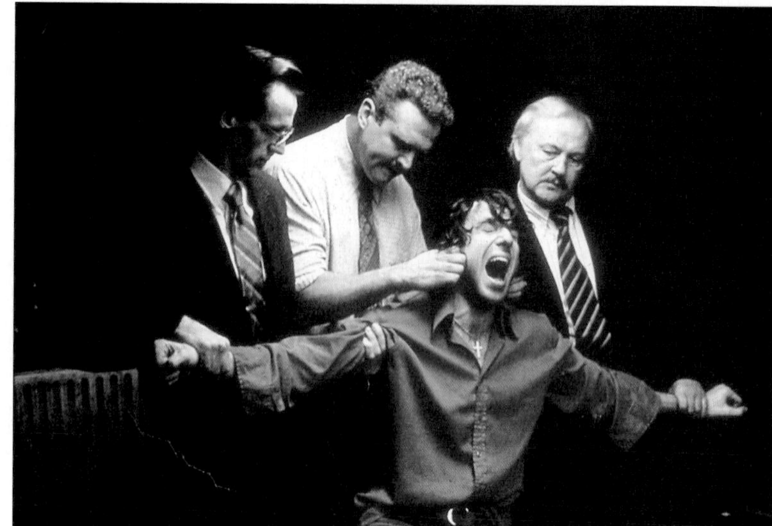

Daniel Day Lewis as wrongfully arrested IRA suspect Gerard Conlon.

London, 11 February
There is no more controversial subject in Great Britain than the situation in Northern Ireland, and the activities of the IRA. It was therefore extremely bold of Jim Sheridan, the Irish director of *My Left Foot*, to bring *In the Name of the Father* to the screen. But although this compelling drama attacks the British judicial system over wrongfully convicting the Guildford Four – those men imprisoned for many years for pub bombings, and only recently released – it focuses on one particular poignant father-son relationship. Daniel Day Lewis, again revealing his wide acting range, is Gerry Conlon, the troubled Belfast youth, whose father (Pete Postlethwaite) is also imprisoned when he comes to his son's aid. Emma Thompson plays Gareth Pierce, the lawyer who finally gets them exonerated.

Major studio now owned by Viacom

New York, 16 February
The hard-fought 125-day battle for Paramount has now ended. This means success for Sumner Redstone and Viacom Inc., owner of the MTV and Nickelodeon cable networks, the Showtime pay-TV stations, five other TV stations, and a major program syndicator. Main loser is QVC, the home shopping television service company and former Fox and Paramount studio boss Barry Diller, who conceded defeat with the simple statement, "They won. We lost." The ongoing saga began last September with the Viacom tender of an initial offer at $8.2 billion, then was forced to raise the stakes, supported by Blockbuster Entertainment, the world's largest home video retailer. Viacom ended up paying around $10 billion, but now emerges as a media giant with $12 billion annual revenues, second only in size to Time-Warner.

Joys and sorrows of a long friendship

Paris, 2 March
Mina Tannenbaum is an impressive first feature by Martine Dugowson about the 25-year-long friendship between two Jewish girls in Paris that stretches from 1968 to 1993. The story beautifully captures the awkward, unspoken rivalry between Mina, an idealistic painter, and the more opportunistic Ethel, nicely played by Romane Bohringer and Elsa Zylberstein. Their love/hate relationship reflects their emotional and professional attitudes.

Bohringher and Zylberstein (right).

Hopkins, Winger excel in 'Shadowlands'

Debra Winger and Anthony Hopkins as Joy Davidman and C.S. Lewis.

London, 4 March
Set in Oxford in the early 1950s, *Shadowlands* is the beautifully crafted account of fantasy author and academic C.S. Lewis' love affair with prickly New York poet Joy Davidman (Gresham). Lewis can't quite commit to her, though he marries her so that she and her young son can stay in England. Then she gets cancer... Following his disappointing *Chaplin*, Richard Attenborough has subtly avoided the trap of sentimentality, making an inspiring, moving film with two great central performances. Anthony Hopkins as the Catholic Lewis and Debra Winger as the Jewish Gresham make the chalk-and-cheese love affair into something rare and wonderful.

The unfortunate fate of the fifth Beatle

London, 1 April
The early days of The Beatles in Hamburg provide a colorful backdrop for the story of Stuart Sutcliffe (Stephen Dorff), the Fifth Beatle, who died of a brain hemorrhage in 1962. *Backbeat* centers on artist Stu's intense affair with style-setting photographer Astrid Kirchherr (Sheryl Lee). The film's major asset, though, is the charismatic performance of Ian Hart as a sardonic, angry young Lennon, loving, envying and influenced by Stu and Astrid. A nicely timed film to tap into the current Beatles revival.

Beatle Stuart Sutcliffe (Stephen Dorff) with girlfriend Astrid (Sheryl Lee).

Spielberg's 20-year Oscar wait is over

An Oscar for Tommy Lee Jones.

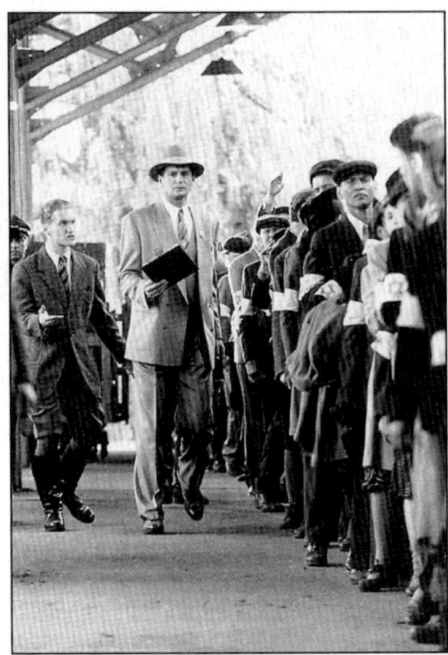

Schindler: garlanded with awards.

Los Angeles, 21 March
Steven Spielberg must have been wondering what he had to do to win one of the top Academy Awards in 20 years of trying. Evidently, the answer was to make *Schindler's List*, though only a cynic would suggest that in choosing the subject of the Holocaust, he had the Best Picture and Best Director Oscars in mind. The long (185 minutes) and ambitious black-and-white movie was one of the hottest favorites ever to enter the Oscar race. To add to Spielberg's satisfaction, *Schindler's List* garnered a further five awards, for art direction, cinematography, editing and screenplay adaptation. In his restrained rendering of the story of Oskar Schindler, the German businessman who rescued more than a thousand Jews from the gas chambers, Spielberg has probably come closer than most directors to filming the impossible. As if to prove there were other films around, the acting awards went elsewhere. Tom Hanks won Best Actor for *Philadelphia*. As an AIDS-stricken gay lawyer, not only fighting the disease, but prejudice, Hanks displayed hitherto untapped tragic resources. The Best Actress winner was Holly Hunter for her splendid portrayal of the self-imposed mute woman sent from Scotland to 19th-century New Zealand in *The Piano*. Best Supporting Actress was the amazing 11-year-old Anna Paquin, who played Hunter's daughter, while the Best Supporting Actor was Tommy Lee Jones, long deserving of the honor, for his splendid pursuing cop in *The Fugitive*.

Killer Kathleen in John Waters territory

New York, 15 April
In *Serial Mom*, bad taste maestro John Waters trashes motherhood, family and middle-class suburbia in grotesque, hilarious style, with an energetic Kathleen Turner to relish. She is a perfect all-American Baltimore homemaker who develops a taste for terrorizing, then hideously murdering, people who dare slight any of her adoring family – dentist husband Sam Waterston and two perky teenage kids. Mom's feting by the media once she's busted might be satirical, or just evidence of the wicked Waters' eccentricity, but it's not far off the mark!

Kathleen Turner, Suzanne Somers.

Temporary life after death for Brandon Lee

*The late Brandon Lee as the avenging Eric Draven given life by **The Crow**.*

Los Angeles, 11 May
Bruce Lee's son Brandon, tragically killed last year in a shooting accident on the set of *The Crow*, is a handsome and brooding presence in the film, a certain hit. A dark-avenger fantasy from a comic, it is, despite a cartoonish script, a somber, exciting and visually stunning story of, ironically, a murdered rock star who returns from the dead to settle the score. The film was completed with the latest in sophisticated digital compositing techniques, creating new scenes from available footage of Lee (an excellent performance) whose death at 28 undeniably adds to the macabre lure.

Keanu gets up speed as bus-chasing hero

Los Angeles, 10 June
Preview audiences have been screaming with delight at *Die Hard* cinematographer Jan De Bont's directorial debut, *Speed*, a Die Hard-On-Wheels of wild non-stop action which should rocket Keanu Reeves from teen heart-throb to major leading man status. Butchly shorn Reeves is the L.A. cop hero scampering up, down, atop and under a city bus, booby-trapped to explode by crazed extortionist Dennis Hopper should it slow below 55 mph. Sandra Bullock's the plucky passenger who grabs the wheel. This summer's big guns will be hard-pressed to top this for entertainment value.

*Keanu Reeves follows as Sandra Bullock mans the runaway bus in **Speed**.*

Wedding circuit makes star of bachelor boy

London, 14 May
It is extremely rare for a British film to reach number one at the U.S. box office, and also arrive in England on the back of an American triumph. *Four Weddings and a Funeral*, made on a budget of just 3 million pounds, is an immensely charming romantic comedy, which took Richard Curtis three years to write, and director Mike Newell 36 days to shoot. The very "Englishness" of the picture has been an asset in the United States, but so too is the strikingly handsome Hugh Grant, delightful in the part that has made him a star. The film's title sums up the episodic tale of an accident-prone young man who, alone among his friends, seems unable to get himself hitched.

Hugh Grant, a big new star.

Cheers and jeers greet violent winner

Cannes, 23 May
The announcement that Quentin Tarantino's *Pulp Fiction* had won the Golden Palm at this year's Cannes Film Festival was greeted with as many catcalls as cheers. The award especially surprised because Krzysztof Kieslowski's *Three Colors Red*, the favorite, came away empty-handed. The main objection to *Pulp Fiction* was the film's excessive violence, the thrust of most of the criticism behind Tarantino's previous (well-received) film, *Reservoir Dogs*. Violent it is, but, as the title suggests, it is also a witty and brilliantly inventive thriller, drawing on cheap novels of the 50s and 60s. It was thought that the choice of *Pulp Fiction* over the Kieslowski derived from the influence of Clint Eastwood, the president of the jury. Perhaps Catherine Deneuve was behind the best actress award given to the Italian actress Virna Lisa, brought out of retirement to play a devastating Catherine of Medici in the expensive French costume drama, *la Reine Margot*, directed by Patrice Chereau. The best actor was Ge You as a man who survives the fluctuations of modern Chinese history in Zhang Yimou's *To Live*, which shared the Grand Jury prize with Nikita Mikhalkov's superb *Burnt by the Sun*. The latter is about a hero of the Soviet revolution pursued by Stalin's secret police, which contains a fine performance from the director himself. Nanni Moretti, winner of the best director for *Dear Diary*, stars in his own richly amusing film, subtitled "Events from the life of a splendid forty-year-old."

*Irene Jacob in **Three Colors Red**.*

*Uma Thurman in **Pulp Fiction**.*

Bertolucci provides a magnificent visual journey to wisdom

Bernardo Bertolucci's ***Little Buddha*** *is an astonishing visual feast. Keanu Reeves (right) plays the legendary Siddartha.*

Seattle, 25 May
After journeying to the exotic climes of China for *The Last Emperor* (1987), and the Moroccan desert for *The Sheltering Sky* (1990), Bernardo Bertolucci has ventured into Bhutan for his latest epic, *Little Buddha*. The moral fable tells of how a Seattle couple (Chris Isaak and Brigitte Fonda) are visited by Buddhist monks claiming their little son might be the reincarnation of one of their most revered lamas. Accompanying the monks back home to their isolated mountain kingdom, the film then flashes back 2,500 years to the beginning of Buddhism and the court of Prince Siddartha, played by Keanu Reeves. Vittorio Storaro's photography makes the rather simplistic trip gloriously worthwhile.

Hollywood's love affair with John Grisham continues to flourish

New York, 27 June
A year ago lawyer-turned-author John Grisham, whose legal thrillers have made him a household name, signed an unprecedented $3.75 million film deal for his uncompleted novel *The Chamber*. Now a best-seller, it was something of a surprise to winning bidders Universal, since it is not in the same thriller mold as his previous work. The deal was made when *The Firm*, starring Tom Cruise, the first of the Grishams on screen, became a smash-hit. It was followed by *The Pelican Brief*, starring Julia Roberts, and *The Client* with Susan Sarandon will soon be released. Clearly Grisham is considered the goose that lays the golden egg, and studios are wooing him with offers rumored to be in the region of $4 million for *A Time to Kill*, his first novel which he has been cagey about selling without script and star approval. He's at work on a new book, *The Rainmaker*, due for completion in the fall when the several contenders anticipate the rights will be theirs for something like a record-setting $6 million.

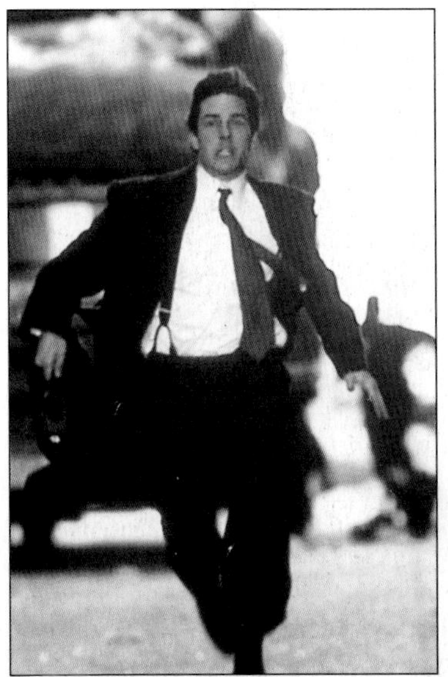

Denzel Washington and Julia Roberts star in Grisham's ***The Pelican Brief***.

Tom Cruise in ***The Firm***.

History through the eyes of Gump

New York, 8 July
Tom Hanks plays the eponymous *Forrest Gump*, a dim-witted but sweet-hearted innocent whose path through 30 turbulent years of American history accidentally makes him a sports star, war hero and tycoon, while remaining true to his elusive lifelong love (Robin Wright). Director Robert Zemeckis' agility with great special effects sees Gump "interact" with presidents (JFK, LBJ, Nixon), pop stars and TV celebrities in his touching and hilarious adventures. The film is too long to sustain its dramatic thrust, but Hanks' unpatronizing, enchanting performance will enthrall.

Tom Hanks is Forrest Gump.

Lots of effects, loads of money

Hollywood, 15 July
Arnold Schwarzenegger and James Cameron have tried too hard to top *Terminator 2*, with a reputed $100 million plus spent on making *True Lies* the most outrageously stunt-packed, techno-gadgeted adventure yet. There *are* muscular thrills and good laughs in the overblown, overlong but entertaining caper of a secret agent's complicated double life, as he tries to save his marriage, with wife Jamie Lee Curtis having to put up with a lot. But making back the film's cost will be as tough as the action – and that's the truth. ▷

'Lion King' roars out hat-trick for Disney

© Walt Disney

The King of the jungle, his family and friends, in Disney's latest family treat.

Los Angeles, 26 July
Disney has another clear winner as *The Lion King* hits $200 million after 41 days on release. The story of Simba the cub's journey to manhood and future kingship is presented against a stunning African landscape, in which fearful, funny and tender incidents unfold. A superior voicing team includes Rowan Atkinson, hilarious as Zazu the Hornbill, Whoopi Goldberg's strident Shenzy the Hyena, and, most brilliantly, Jeremy Irons as the murderous villain, Simba's uncle Scar. Elton John and Tim Rice's songs delight.

Tim Burton's *Ed Wood*, starring Johnny Depp (above), brilliantly reconstructs the sleazy side of 50s Hollywood, and is a sympathetic tribute to the director of such gems of the awful as *Glen or Glenda* and *Plan 9 From Outer Space*. A chronicle of sad dreams and disappointments, with Martin Landau outstanding as washed-up horror star Bela Lugosi.

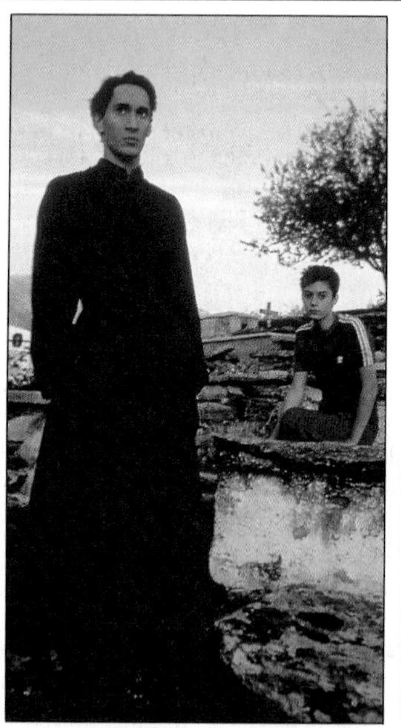

At the 51st Venice Film Festival, a deadlocked jury chaired by David Lynch emulated the international critics in awarding a tie for the Golden Lion. The winners were Taiwan's *Vive l'Amour* and *Before the Rain* (illustrated). The latter is an impressive first feature about the Balkan war, made in three parts by director Milcho Manchevski from Macedonia.

Brain scam reveals cool winner for Redford

GERITOL

Christopher McDonald with contestants Ralph Fiennes (l), John Turturro (r).

New York, 16 September
Robert Redford's *Quiz Show* opens nationwide today. A literate screenplay and A-grade production and cast unveil the insidious corruption at the heart of *Twenty One*, the nation's favorite 50s TV show, capturing the look and atmosphere of the time. MC Jack Barry (Christopher McDonald) is the Svengali to competing "contestants", brash Jewish Herbie Stempel (John Turturro) and WASP intellectual Charles Van Doren (Ralph Fiennes), Rob Morrow the legal eagle who uncovers the scam. A class act.

Woody Allen firing shots on all cylinders

New York, 21 October
Woody Allen is on top form with *Bullets Over Broadway*, an 18-carat combined side-swipe and affectionate homage to the shenanigans of ego-obsessed theater folk. The plot charts the consequences for aspiring playwright-director John Cusack when his production is financed by a mobster as a vehicle for his talentless girlfriend Jennifer Tilly. Her minder, Chazz Palminteri, sorts out the script, while grand dame Dianne Wiest, making a comeback, causes other havoc. *Bullets* is rich in originality, cruelly accurate characters and humor. Woody's always brilliant casting has never been better, and his sparkling ensemble should contend heavily for Oscars.

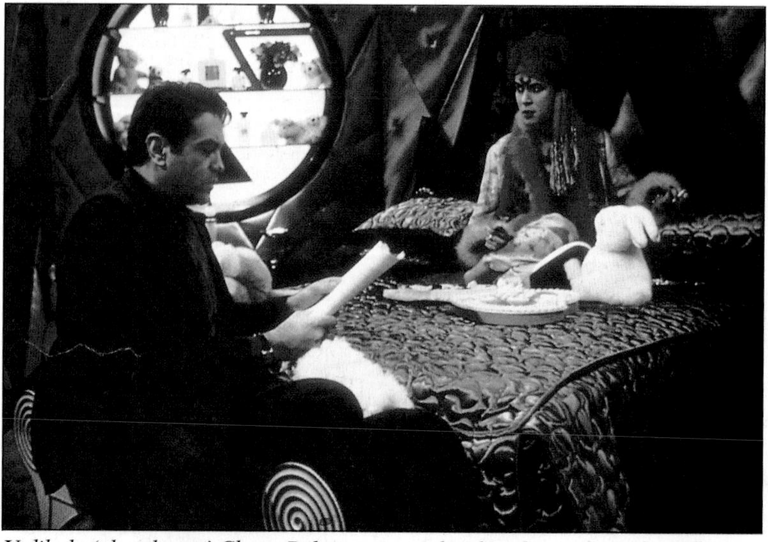

Unlikely 'play-doctor' Chazz Palminteri coaches his charge Jennifer Tilly.

The lights go out for Burt, Raul and Sergei

Burt Lancaster in **Trapeze** (1956).

New York, 25 October
Following the deaths of Burt Lancaster in L.A. and actor-director Sergei Bondarchuk in Moscow, both on 20 October, the much-loved Puerto Rican-born actor Raul Julia died yesterday at the age of 54, following a stroke. Julia came to the U.S. in 1964, studied acting, and made his New York stage debut in a Spanish production. A long association with Joe Papp and the Public Theater began in 1964, and he went on to prove his versatility in musicals, and in plays by Shakespeare, Chekhov and Pinter. A four-time Tony nominee, his first films were *The Organization* and *Panic in Needle Park* (1971), but his film career only blossomed in the 80s, receiving a big boost from his co-starring role in *The Kiss of the Spider Woman* (1986), while he gained widespread popularity for his manic Gomez in *The Addams Family* (1991).

Burt Lancaster, the tough street-kid who loved literature and opera and became a circus acrobat, only entered movies at age 32, became an overnight star with his debut film, *The Killers* (1946), and made 77 more. In danger of becoming typecast as a knuckleheaded *noir* patsy, he formed a production company with his agent, Harold Hecht, scoring a huge success with two swashbucklers, *The Flame and the Arrow* (1950) and *The Crimson Pirate* (1952). With his god-like physique, graceful athleticism and flashing white teeth, Burt remained at the top for three decades, through good movies and bad. Oscar-nominated for *From Here to Eternity*(1953), he won for his barnstorming Elmer Gantry (1961), but is perhaps most acclaimed for his vicious J.J. Hunsecker in *Sweet Smell of Success* (1958), the aristocrat of Visconti's *The Leopard* (1963) and his ageing has-been in *Atlantic City* (1983). A compelling, often dignified screen presence disguised a volatile temperament and tough-minded ambition. At 76 he made a last appearance in *Field of Dreams* (1989).

Sergei Bondarchuk was a great actor in the heroic mold and an epic-style director. He will be internationally remembered for his portrayal of Othello (1956) and his finest directing achievement, the authentic, 507-minute, Oscar-winning *War and Peace* (1967).

Raul Julia as the secret police chief in **Moon over Parador** (1988).

Sergei Bondarchuk: Russian great.

A schoolgirl journey from heaven to hell

Mother (Sarah Peirse, l), daughter (Melanie Lynskey), friend (Kate Winslet).

New York, 16 November
New Zealand's *Heavenly Creatures* are set to transport American audiences into their secret world. Peter Jackson's film is fluent, imaginative and, given the subject, surprisingly humorous. It deals with the true case of two Wellington schoolgirls, Pauline (Melanie Lynskey) and Juliet (Kate Winslet), who, when their bizarre and intense friendship is put under threat, plan to murder Pauline's mother (Sarah Peirse) whom they hold responsible for their imminent separation. Shocking, compelling, engaging, and very well acted.

National Registry adds twenty-five

Washington, 27 November
The Library of Congress has announced 25 new titles for preservation in the National Film Registry, bringing to 150 the number of films being protected for their cultural and historic significance. Librarian James H. Billington also announced that next year will see a nine-city tour of selected titles from the Registry, with future plans to tour countrywide. "We will", he said, "put into practice our firmly held belief that films, once preserved, must not be forever locked away in a remote vault or made available only on video or TV screens." The new titles range widely, in time and subject, from D.W. Griffith's *A Corner in Wheat*(1909) to Spielberg's *E.T.* (1982). Among others are Disney's *Pinocchio* (1940), Minnelli's *Meet Me in St. Louis* (1944), Huston's *The African Queen* (1951), Wilder's *The Apartment* (1960), Scorsese's *Taxi Driver* (1976) and Abraham Zapruder's 20-second amateur footage of the Kennedy assassination.

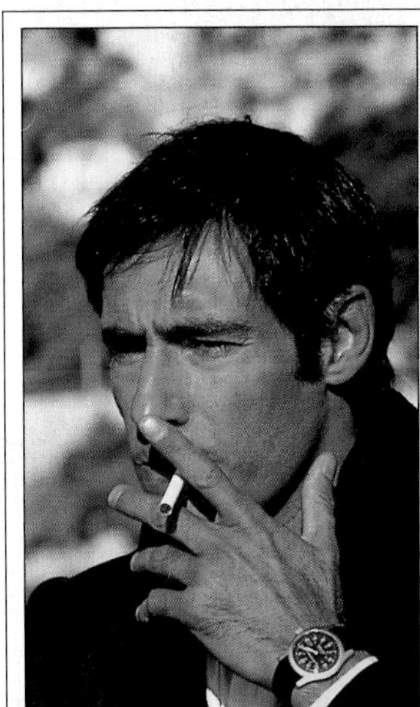

Le Fils préferé **marks the directing debut of actress Nicole Garcia. She accurately captures the family tensions in a sensitive, authentically photographed account of the relationship between three very different French brothers (Gérard Lanvin, Jean-Marc Barr, Bernard Giraudeau) and their Italian immigrant father. As the brother in trouble, Lanvin (above) is superb.**

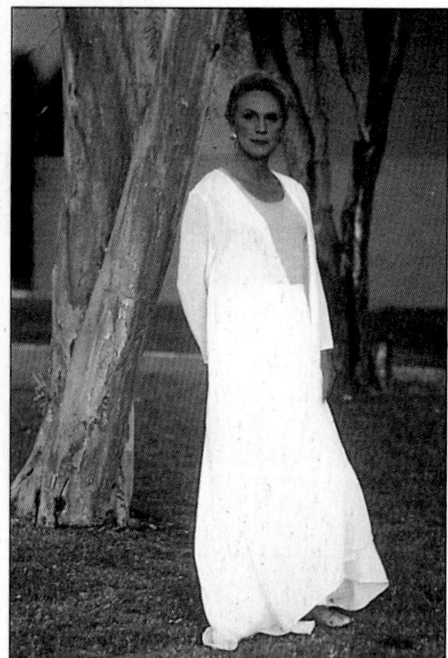

The Adventures of Priscilla, Queen of the Desert: *Terence Stamp.*

Lived in our hearts
For generations,
Now comes to the screen
For the holidays.
WINONA RYDER
LITTLE WOMEN
CHRISTMAS DAY

Gillian Armstrong's successful remake of the much-loved classic.

The Arnold Schwarzenegger-James Cameron team's ***True Lies****.*

Gary Oldman portrays a passionate Beethoven in ***Immortal Beloved****.*

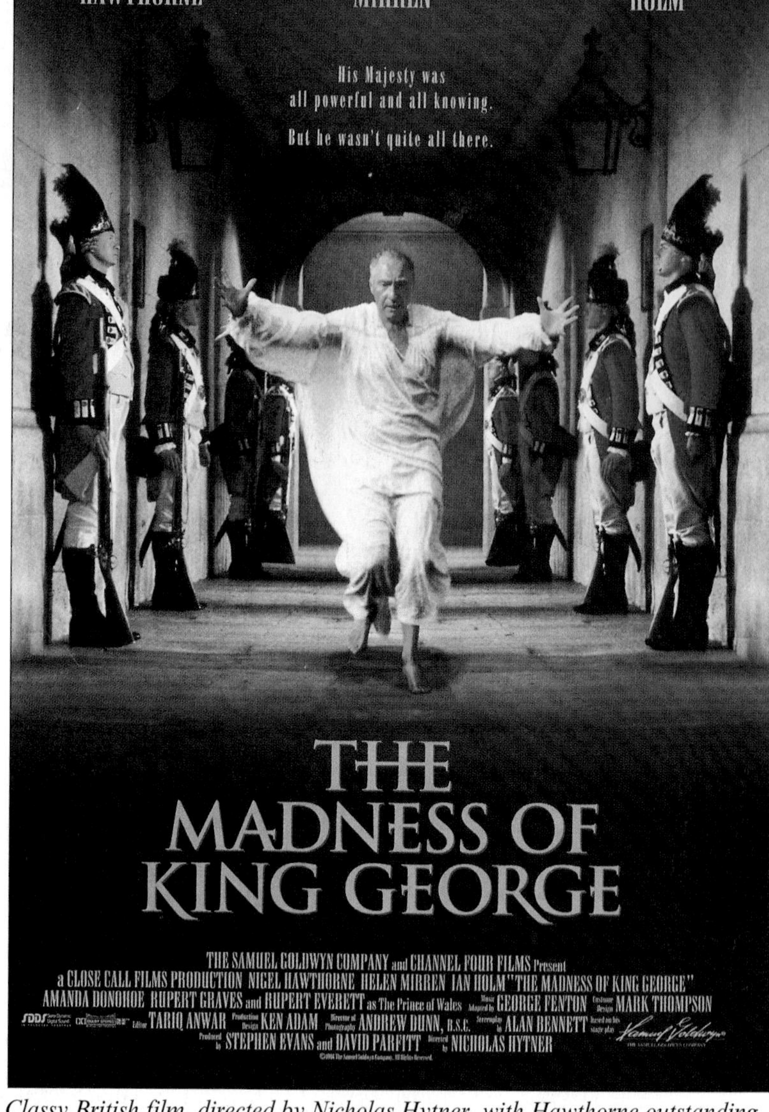
NIGEL HAWTHORNE
HELEN MIRREN
IAN HOLM
His Majesty was all powerful and all knowing.
But he wasn't quite all there.
THE MADNESS OF KING GEORGE
THE SAMUEL GOLDWYN COMPANY and CHANNEL FOUR FILMS Present
a CLOSE CALL FILMS PRODUCTION NIGEL HAWTHORNE HELEN MIRREN IAN HOLM "THE MADNESS OF KING GEORGE"
AMANDA DONOHOE RUPERT GRAVES and RUPERT EVERETT as The Prince of Wales Music Adapted by GEORGE FENTON Costume Design MARK THOMPSON
Editor TARIQ ANWAR Production Design KEN ADAM Director of Photography ANDREW DUNN, B.S.C. Screenplay by ALAN BENNETT based on his stage play
Produced by STEPHEN EVANS and DAVID PARFITT Directed by NICHOLAS HYTNER

Classy British film, directed by Nicholas Hytner, with Hawthorne outstanding.

Linda Fiorentino, a ***noir*** *'heroine' for the 90s, in* ***The Last Seduction****.*

Ace Ventura's Jim Carrey hit higher with ***The Mask****, Chuck Russell directed.*

Jack Nicholson and Michelle Pfeiffer in Mike Nichols' atmospheric ***Wolf***.

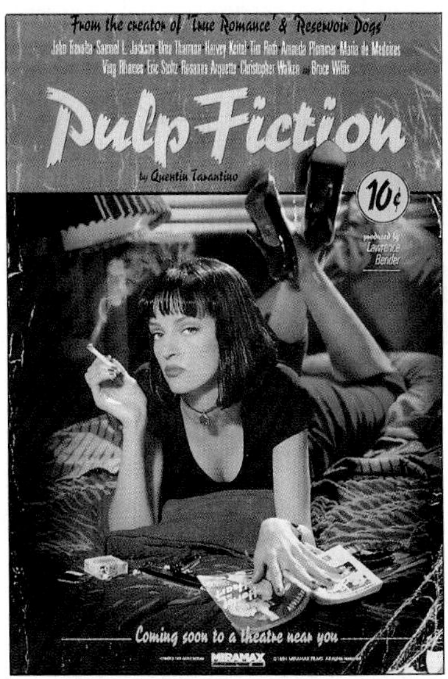
From the creator of 'True Romance' & 'Reservoir Dogs'
Pulp Fiction
by Quentin Tarantino
10¢
Coming soon to a theatre near you
A brilliant satire from Tarantino.

MICHAEL DOUGLAS
DEMI MOORE
sex is power
DISCLOSURE
Poster provoked scandal in Europe.

Liam Neeson comes to the rescue of Jodie Foster's 'wild girl' in ***Nell***.

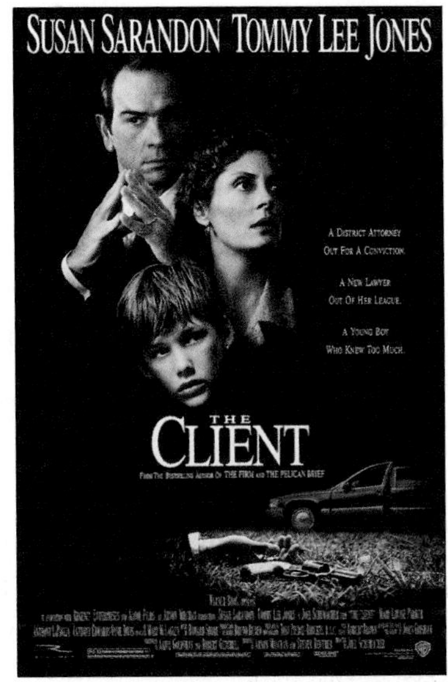
SUSAN SARANDON TOMMY LEE JONES
A District Attorney Out For A Conviction.
A New Lawyer Out Of Her League.
A Young Boy Who Knew Too Much.
THE CLIENT
Great cast in more from Grisham.

*Paul Newman is **Nobody's Fool**.*

***The Shawshank Redemption**: Morgan Freeman (left), with Tim Robbins.*

*Jorge Perugorria (r) as Diego, Vladimir Cruz as David, in the internationally successful Cuban movie **Strawberry and Chocolate**.*

1995

1994 Academy Awards, Shrine Auditorium, 27 March

Best Film: *Forrest Gump* (dir: Robert Zemeckis)
Best Director: Robert Zemeckis
Best Actor: Tom Hanks *(Forrest Gump)*
Best Actress: Jessica Lange *(Blue Sky)*
Best Supp. Actor: Martin Landau *(Ed Wood)*
Best Supp. Actress: Dianne Wiest *(Bullets Over Broadway)*

New York, 4 January
Quentin Tarantino's *Pulp Fiction* yesterday emerged as the overwhelming critical favorite of 1994, scooping up best film, director and screenplay honors at the National Society of Film Critics' annual award ceremony. Voting at the Algonquin Hotel, where Dorothy Parker and her literary set convened during the swinging 20s and 30s, the 42 critics appropriately named Jennifer Jason Leigh best actress for her portrayal of the caustic writer in *Mrs Parker and the Vicious Circle*. Paul Newman was chosen as best actor for *Nobody's Fool*.

Paris, 4 January
Suspending a strike which has lasted since mid-October 1994, France's dubbing artists yesterday returned to work pending the outcome of a new round of negotiations. The dispute centers on a claim by some 600 performers that they should be paid residual fees. Apparently, 90% of French audiences prefer dubbed rather than subtitled versions of foreign films.

Los Angeles, 10 January
John Dahl's icy *noir* drama, *The Last Seduction*, and its star, Linda Fiorentino, are the latest casualties in disputes over the coming Oscars. An LA Superior Court judge yesterday upheld a previous ruling that the film is ineligible for nomination because it had its initial screening on HBO cable TV.

Hollywood, 1 February
The Walt Disney Co. yesterday announced a revamped version of *Fantasia*, to comprise four segments of the original 1940 classic plus five new segments. Release is planned for 1998 but, meanwhile, according to Disney executives, 100,000 New Yorkers will catch a preview glimpse in June of the latest animated musical, *Pocahontas*, to be shown on four eight-storey-tall screens on the Great Lawn in Central Park.

Miami Beach, 2 February
Broadway's legendary George Abbott has died of a stroke at the age of 107. Last night at 8 p.m. the lights of theaterland were dimmed for a full minute in tribute. Abbott's uniquely productive career included variously writing, directing or producing movies, notably comedies such as *Three Men on a Horse* (1934) and musicals such as the *Pajama Game* (1957) and *Damn Yankees* (1958). Stage director Hal Prince, choreographer Bob Fosse and the multitalented Gene Kelly were among his countless proteges.

Sweden, 3 February
Ingmar Bergman, who retired from film-making after *Fanny and Alexander* (1981), has chosen 11 of his favorite films by other directors to be shown at the Gothenberg Festival, which begins today. Among them are: Tarkovsky's *Andrei Rublev*, Fellini's *La Strada*, Kurosawa's *Rashomon*, Wilder's *Sunset Boulevard*, Carné's *Quai des brumes*, Dreyer's *The Passion of Joan of Arc* and Chaplin's *The Circus*.

Los Angeles, 13 February
Martin Scorsese's *Casino*, a 70s Mob tale starring Robert De Niro and Sharon Stone has wrapped in Las Vegas after an indulgent 100-day shoot. However, this was less than half the time taken on Kevin Jackson's troubled *Waterworld*, still in production. The budget for this 26th-century aquatic adventure starring Kevin Costner is nearing an other-worldly $175 million.

London, 17 February
Banned in India, Shekhar Kapur's *Bandit Queen* opens here today, the story of Phoolan Devi, married at 11, gang-raped by high-caste Thakurs and subsequently accused of murdering 22 Thakur men. Devi, released after 10 years in jail, cooperated on the making of the film, but is now denouncing the violence as misrepresentation.

Los Angeles, 17 February
Gene Kelly, 81-year-old actor, dancer, choreographer and director, who suffered a stroke last July, is recovering from another stroke at Cedars-Sinai Medical Center.

Los Angeles, 21 February
The spirited homage to television's sudsiest family of the early 1970's, *The Brady Bunch Movie*, grossed $414,827,066 over the four-day holiday weekend.

Berlin, 21 February
Festival audiences were surprised that Bertrand Tavernier's *l'Appât* (*The Bait*) won the Golden Bear for best film over Wayne Wang's *Smoke*. The latter had to be content with the special jury prize, and a special mention for Harvey Keitel's performance. However, Paul Newman was a popular choice as best actor for *Nobody's Fool*, Josephine Siao was best actress for *Summer Snow* and Richard Linklater was best director for *Before Sunrise*. Vladimir Abdrashitov's *Play for a Passenger* won the Silver Bear.

California, 24 February
With over a decade elapsed since his *Star Wars* trilogy, producer, director and technology wizard George Lucas is taking off a year to write a three-part sequel to the series. Lucas may have to sell part or all of his empire, including the Industrial Light and Magic Company, said to be worth $350 million, to finance the state-of-the-art technology needed to realize his vision.

London, 4 March
Barry Levinson's *Disclosure*, from the novel by Michael Crichton, in which Demi Moore sexually harasses her office subordinate Michael Douglas, is causing a storm under bus shelters throughout the U.K. Reason for all the excitement is the movie's provocative poster, that includes hands on Demi's rear and the slogan 'Sex is Power'. In the U.S. the ad featured a benign close-up of the stars' faces.

Los Angeles, 7 March
The Walt Disney Co. yesterday announced record-breaking sales in excess of 20 million copies of the video of *The Lion King*. The film has so far grossed a stratospheric $740 million in theaters worldwide.

New York, 13 March
Before Val Kilmer flies into 2000 theaters in June as the new Batman, he will appear in Jean-Jacques Annaud's *Wings of Courage*, the first filmed drama to use IMAX 3-D technology. The 40-minute, $15 million-plus story about French aviators opens 21 April at New York's Sony Lincoln Square, one of only 120 theaters worldwide capable of screening the process.

Chicago, 14 March
Steve James' 170-minute documentary, *Hoop Dreams*, about teenage pro basketball aspirants, superseded its category yesterday to be named best film of 1994 by the Chicago film critics. This follows its Golden Globe win as best documentary, a special Producers Guild award, and the National Critics' documentary vote. All of which serves to emphasize the snub to this $6 million grosser when it failed to gain an Oscar nomination. Protests by outraged filmmakers have brought an Academy pledge to re-examine documentary nomination procedure.

Hamburg, 15 March
Designer Karl Lagerfeld has won a temporary injunction against the Berlin-based distributor of Altman's *Prêt-à-Porter*, a week before its German release. A character in the film refers to him as a 'thief'.

Hollywood, 20 March
TV writer-producer Diane English is scripting her first major theatrical feature, New Line's remake of the 1939 classic, *The Women*. Julia Roberts and Meg Ryan are slated to head the cast of this updated version, due for release in 1966.

DEATHS

France, 2 February
Donald Pleasence

England, 20 February
Robert Bolt

England, 25 February
Jack Clayton

The summer welcomes ***Batman Forever*** *with Val Kilmer replacing Michael Keaton, Joel Schumacher replacing Tim Burton, and, best of all, Jim Carrey acting The Riddler.*

JUNE 16

Lion leads Forrest in Variety Top Ten

Los Angeles, 3 January
With the average cost of a movie now at some $30 million, *Variety*'s year-end figures for 1994 make interesting reading. With a gross of $298,879,911 at 31 December, *The Lion King* leads *Forrest Gump* by a short head. Thereafter the figures take a noticeable drop, with *True Lies* in at No. 3 and a $146,260,993 take, followed by *The Santa Clause*, grossing some $12 million less. But the latter, starring *Home Improvements*' Tim Allen, only hit the circuit towards the end of the year and could be a contender for stratospheric box-office. The rest, in order: *The Flintstones*, *Clear and Present Danger*, *Speed*, *The Mask*, *Mrs. Doubtfire* and *Maverick*, with Tom Cruise's Vampire sneaking in at 11.

Ghouls and style from Scotland

London, 6 January
Danny Boyle's impressive debut feature, the award-winning *Shallow Grave*, gives British (actually Scottish) cinema a lift with its uncharacteristic venture into *noir* territory. A journalist (Ewan McGregor), an accountant (Christopher Eccleston) and a doctor (Kerry Fox), twenty-something flat-sharing friends in Edinburgh, get into dark concealment and bloody corpse dismemberment with great style. A sharp-edged, talented black comedy that promises international appeal.

Christopher Eccleston in the film.

Neil Jordan's vampire epic finally arrives on English screens

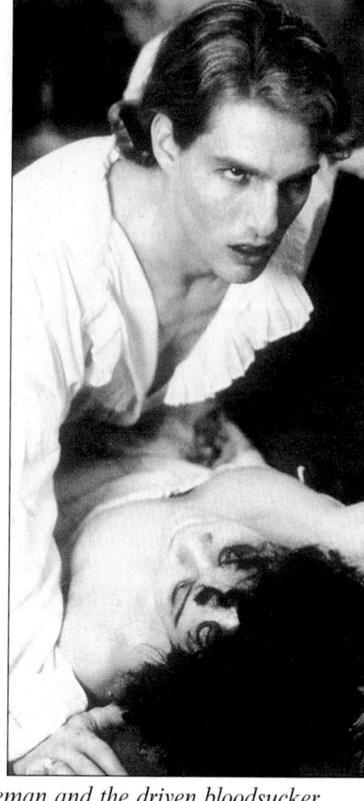

Anne Rice's master vampire Lestat (Tom Cruise) in two guises, the elegant gentleman and the driven bloodsucker.

London, 21 January
After countless attempts to make a film of Anne Rice's *Interview with the Vampire*, Hollywood has succeeded, with British director Neil Jordan at the helm. It opens here on the back of huge hype and success in the U.S. where, on its opening weekend last November, it took the fifth biggest ever gross in box-office history. This could be partly explained by America's enthusiasm for Rice's book, and the starry casting of Tom Cruise and Brad Pitt as, respectively, the aristocratic and immortal vampire Lestat, and his chosen acolyte, Louis. Rice initially denounced the choice of Cruise, then published a fulsome change of heart in *Variety*, declaring "the charm, the humor and invincible innocence which I cherish in my beloved hero Lestat, are all alive in Tom Cruise's courageous performance." This "courageous" performance is reputed to be worth over $10 million in salary and bonuses to Cruise, *plus* a percentage, a statistic in itself bound to attract admiration in the U.S. In the event, the undeniably stylish film lacks emotional depth, suffers noticeable longeurs, and offers some horrific bloodsucking sequences.

'Legends of the Fall' hits theaters as year's first major release

Chicago, 13 January
Released nationwide today, director Edward Zwick's film of Jim Harrison's novella, *Legends of the Fall*, was seen in L.A. and New York last month so as to enable an Oscar bid. Whether or no honors come its way, it's a handsomely mounted, engrossingly entertaining epic of complex emotions and disintegration in the ranching Ludlow family as World War I approaches. A mite sprawling and melodramatic perhaps, but performances are terrific, with Anthony Hopkins as father to brothers Henry Thomas, Aidan Quinn and heart-throb Brad Pitt, a charismatic hero figure whose star rating is still clearly on the rise.

A charismatic Brad Pitt as Tristan Ludlow in Edward Zwick's family saga.

Not-so-dumb Jim Carrey brings audiences a $7 million laugh

Los Angeles, 27 January
Following on his hat-trick of blockbusters that started 12 months ago with *Ace Ventura: Pet Detective*, took in *The Mask*, and culminated in *Dumb and Dumber* which has hit the $100 million mark in its first 43 days of release, the industry is dubbing the actor with the cosmic grin "Cash and Carrey". Peter Farrelly's *Dumb and Dumber*, the latest vehicle for the unstoppable Jim, is scatologically inspired and unapologetic in its celebration of stupidity. The goofy, good-natured road movie is driven by the infectious chemistry of Carrey, who seems to have cornered the market in wholesome zaniness (here aided by co-star Jeff Daniels). A Canadian who conquered the comedy circuit by the age of 19, Carrey moved to the movie capital in 1981, playing a number of zesty bit parts (*Peggy Sue Got Married*, *Earth Girls are Easy*) over 13 years, as well as outrageous head-turners on TV's *In Living Color*, before his rubbery, cartoonesque features became a national phenomenon – most notably in the hilarious marriage of effects both digital and human in *The Mask*. New Line originally offered Carrey $750,000 for *Dumb*, before *Ace Ventura* opened. As the movie climbed the charts, joined by *The Mask*, so did the actor's asking price, forcing New Line to capitulate to $7 million. It looks as though they won't regret the investment. Meanwhile, audiences eagerly await *Ace Ventura Goes to Africa* later in the year. Before that, however, they are anticipating the sight of the much-loved grin twisted to menacing effect as The Riddler in *Batman Forever* this summer.

Jim Carrey (l), a modern comic screwball phenomenon, with Jeff Daniels.

Mega-bucks fulfill SKG studio dream

Los Angeles, 1 February
Since announcing their plans to found a new studio, latter-day moguls Stephen Spielberg, Jeffrey Katzenberg and David Geffen, predictably dubbed the Dream Team, look set to realize their ambitions. Challenging the old-established majors, Dreamworks SKG aims to be a multimedia empire, equipped with the latest digital technology and servicing the TV, video, music and CD-ROM markets, as well as making 24 features by the year 2000. The massive financial resources needed far outstrip the personal $33.3 million stake from each partner that billionaire Geffen and multimillionaire Spielberg can well afford, but which puts Katzenberg, Disney's former production genius, at serious risk. But the skepticism which greeted their initially vague statements is disappearing as they reveal details, and promises of backing, notably from Paul Allen of the Microsoft empire. While many wish them well, others fear the threat.

Sundance Festival creeps into mainstream

Park City, 2 February
Twenty-five percent of the 100 films at this year's Sundance Festival came with distribution deals, and featuring such actors as Ethan Hawke, Hugh Grant and Sarah Jessica Parker. The limited facilities were stretched by distributors and agents crowding in to snap up saleable products, both in and out of the competition (won by Edward Burns' very low-budget drama, *The Brothers McMullen*). There are complaints that the raw-talent spirit of America's most significant showcase has been lost in favor of more mainstream polish, but who can argue when Robert Redford's vision and commitment have advanced the likes of Quentin Tarantino?

Besson's Léon: a new kind of hit man

London, 3 February
The French company Gaumont, the oldest in the world, celebrates the 100 years of cinema with an English-language movie, made in New York by one of its top commercial assets, Luc Besson (*The Big Blue*, *Nikita*). Successful in the U.S., where it was shown as *The Professional*, *Léon* arrives to divide British audiences. An orgy of over-the-top bloodletting, in the center of which reclusive hit man Jean Reno develops a close relationship with 12-year-old Natalie Portman, whose sleazy family has been murdered, the movie is as hollow and ambiguous as it is breathtakingly stylish and original – all the usual Besson trademarks. Reno is superb, Portman uncomfortably beguiling.

*Sundance's guiding light Robert Redford directing **A River Runs Through It**.*

Hitman Jean Reno instructs nubile Natalie Portman in the art of guns.

British censors let Stone's 'Killers' loose

Repellent yet disturbingly glamorous: Woody Harrelson and Juliette Lewis.

London, 24 February
Slick, intriguing, repellent and, thanks to the lurid media it implicitly criticizes, ludicrously over-hyped, Oliver Stone's *Natural Born Killers* has opened. Its single showing at the London Film Festival in November was the season's hottest ticket, but the British censors then turned squeamish and considered a total ban. The controversial saga of a couple (Woody Harrelson, Juliette Lewis) whose cross-country killing spree makes them media darlings and role models, intended by Stone as a satire on the horrors of tabloid culture, misses the mark. Instead, it comes across as a morally dubious excursion into grotesque violence, filmed with breathtaking expertise.

Paris to see Altman's vision of fashion

Marcello Mastroianni and Sophia Loren, a pair of delicious veterans.

Paris, 1 March
Film and fashion fans, not to mention anxious Miramax execs, are awaiting reaction to *Ready to Wear* (*Pret-à-Porter*), opening here today after a critical lambasting in the U.S. What the world's fashion capital will make of the much talked-about nude grand finale is anybody's guess, though the French might get the joke. But the shallow characterizations in which Robert Altman's huge, glitzy, international cast are trapped, the risible threads of story that pass for plot, and the undisguised contempt visited upon the denizens of the showroom are likely to be less well received. The movie looks good, though, and has atmosphere and some fun moments.

'Four Weddings' wins best foreign César

Paris, 26 February
At the 20th annual César Awards, the jury voted *Four Weddings and a Funeral* the best foreign film, echoing American enthusiasm for this British hit comedy. The homegrown winners, important to the French industry, saw the matchless Isabelle Adjani receive her fourth Cesar for best actress in Patrice Chéreau's upmarket bodice-ripper, *La Reine Margot*, while Gérard Lanvin was voted best actor for Nicole Garcia's *Le Fils préfere* (*The Favorite Son*). The best director, screenplay and film awards were swept up by André Techiné for *Les Roseaux sauvages* (*Wild Reeds*), a sensitive account of adolescent relationships at the time of the Algerian war.

Gael Morel, ***Les Roseaux sauvages***.

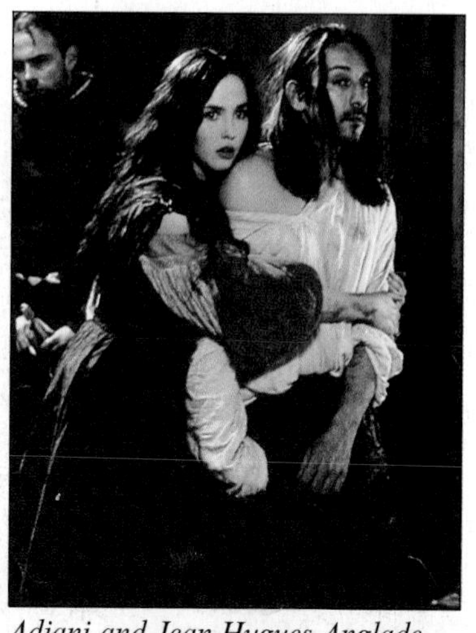
Adjani and Jean-Hugues Anglade.

Parting bells chime for Gong and Zhang

Hong Kong, 24 February
After another run-in, this time over *Shanghai Triad*, with the Beijing authorities who announced a ban on him last October, Zhang Yimou has wrapped the shoot - and his association with Gong Li. The eight-year collaboration between this distinguished 44-year-old director and the luminous 29-year-old actress yielded seven memorable films, including *Raise the Red Lantern* and *To Live*, and made Gong Li the first Chinese actress to become an international star. Off-screen, too, it was an intimate relationship that, with Yang until recently married, scandalized conservative China. He is to film *Empress Wu* for the French company Ciby 2000, and it is not known whether Gong Li, who is to make another with Chen (*Farewell My Concubine*) Kaige, will star. Zhang's series of troubles began when his recent masterwork, *To Live*, about life in the Communist Revolution seen through the eyes of a village family, was shown at Cannes against the wishes of the authorities.

Gong Li and Ge You in ***To Live***.

Oscar's 67th year in a century of moving pictures

Smiles for the fortunate winners ... ... disappointment for the unlucky losers

Tom Hanks as innocent Gump, with his troubled life-long love Robin Wright.

Mad George (Hawthorne) and his queen (Helen Mirren), both nominated.

Cherishable Wiest, John Cusack.

Landau: magnificent as Lugosi.

Winner Lange, Tommy Lee Jones.

Los Angeles, 28 March

Although coinciding with the international fervor for the 100 years of cinema, last night's Oscar ceremony disappointed. All the usual suspects were present, and the Academy's Arthur Hiller made a welcome plea for film preservation in light of funding cuts, but the only surprise was TV's David Letterman replacing Tinseltown's Billy Crystal to underwhelm as MC. The evening's theme, comedy, misfired in a series of clumsy, lackluster compilations, while the winners were predictable to the point of anti-climax. Academy members clearly shared the nation's enthusiasm for Best Picture winner *Forrest Gump*, also crediting Robert Zemeckis as Best Director, but it is hard to swallow the second win in a row for Tom Hanks in view of the quality competition. He accepted his trophy with another embarrassingly lachrymose display. Jessica Lange's anticipated Best Actress Oscar for the barely seen *Blue Sky*, the late Tony Richardson's last film made three years ago, was well-deserved, while the supporting awards to Martin Landau for his brilliant Bela Lugosi in *Ed Wood* and Dianne Wiest for her skillfully funny egomaniac actress in *Bullets Over Broadway* were genuinely popular and accurate choices. The night's grace note came from Italy's veteran director Michelangelo Antonioni, accepting his honorary statuette with a simple "grazie".

Los Angeles, 28 March

There can have been few Academy Award ceremonies to present as many undeserving losers as this year witnessed. Indeed, the difficulty of choosing between British Nigel Hawthorne's unhappy monarch in *The Madness of King George*, a portrayal of depth and distinction, and John Travolta's striking Vincent Vega in *Pulp Fiction*, combining casual thuggery with unnerving niceness, might account for the favoring of Hanks - and there was always a chance that the marvellously aged-in-the-wood Paul Newman would steal away with the Best Actor trophy for *Nobody's Fool*. *The Shawshank Redemption* got less than its due: at least the splendid Tim Robbins could have expected joint nomination with his co-star Morgan Freeman, who lost the Best Supporting Oscar to Landau. Relief that Quentin Tarantino's *Pulp Fiction*, which, in another year, could have swept the board, at least won for its screenplay. And spare a thought for Winona Ryder (*Little Women*) and Susan Sarandon (*The Client*), losing but worthy contenders for Best Actress honors. In the always badly neglected foreign category, Nikita Mikhalkov's *Burnt by the Sun* unaccountably ousted the highly popular *Eat Drink Man Woman*.

A new lease of life for John Travolta, here with Samuel L. Jackson.

▷

Special Effects: Tricks of the Trade

The origins of the many types of photographic tricks which can be accomplished with a movie camera can be traced back to the very beginnings of the cinema. Georges Méliès, the pioneering French director, stands out as the most imaginative and innovative creator of effects, which he used in his many fantasy films from 1897 to 1912, including *Voyage to the Moon* (1902), *20,000 Leagues Under the Sea* and *The Conquest of the Pole* (1912). From the days of Méliès onwards, the term 'special effects' is most often associated with fantasy, science fiction and horror on the screen. Yet remarkable effects have often been accomplished in other types of films ranging from the Buster Keaton comedy *Sherlock Jr.* (1924) to *The Wizard of Oz* (1939) and Woody Allen's *Zelig* (1982). And that great classic of the cinema, *Citizen Kane* (1941) makes far more extensive use of special effects photography (models, mattes, false perspectives) than was ever realized at the time of the film's first release. During the early years, special effects were most often achieved quite simply and cheaply *in* the movie camera by literally winding the film back and re-exposing it to get a dissolve, double exposure or split-screen effect, or in making use of models or miniatures. But by the 20s the growth of the large studios in the U.S. and Germany (notably UFA) led to major technical advances such as the development of the Schüfftan process, a sophisticated method of combining live action with models, which can be seen in Fritz Lang's *Metropolis* (1926). Back projection, mattes (background paintings on glass) and traveling mattes also came into use at that time. Special effects departments demonstrated their expertise in such films as MGM's *San Francisco* (1936) with its climactic earthquake, RKO's *King Kong* (1933), the horror cycle at Universal, and Korda's *Things to Come* (1936) and *The Thief of Bagdad* (1940) in Britain. But it was the 50s boom in sci-fi fantasy and horror which set the trend. There were some notable landmarks in the 60s such as *Fantastic Voyage* (1966) and *2001*, in which Kubrick pioneered the new computer technology. (His innovative use of front projection techniques was further developed in the later *Superman* movies.) But it was the spectacular success of such 'effects' pictures as *The Exorcist*, *Jaws*, *Close Encounters of the Third Kind* and, most notably, *Star Wars* in the 70s which led to ever larger budgets and greater technical resources. This change in emphasis resulted in 'morphing' – the computerized creation of special effects – resulting in even more amazing images for such films as *Ghostbusters* (1984), *Who Framed Roger Rabbit* (1988, combining animation with live action), *The Abyss* (1989, underwater effects), *Terminator 2* (1991, simulated liquid metal transformations) and *Jurassic Park* (1993), which combined full-size dinosaur robotics with the latest in computer-generated imagery. By the mid-90s, effects were in danger of swamping other areas of creativity.

Meryl Streep, the victim of grotesque and brilliant special effects in Robert Zemeckis' ***Death Becomes Her*** *(1992).*

Terminator 2: Judgment Day *(1991): Schwarzenegger morphs into metal man.*

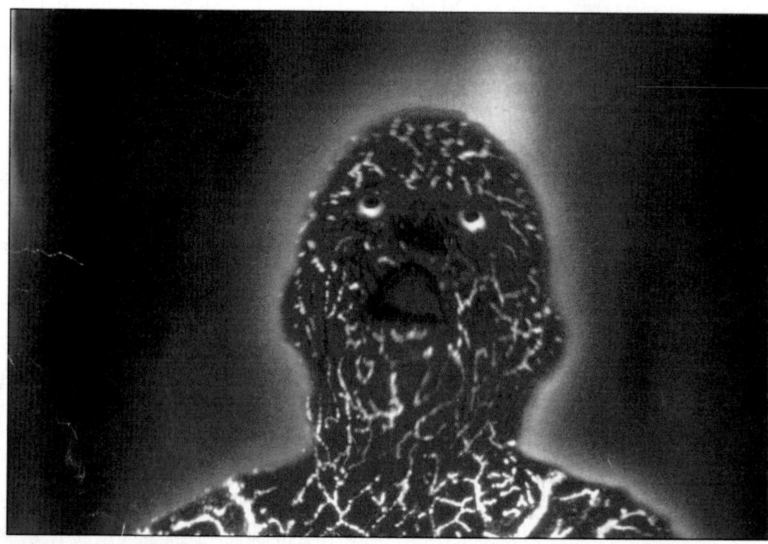

A bizarre, psychedelic image from Ken Russell's ***Altered States*** *(1980).*

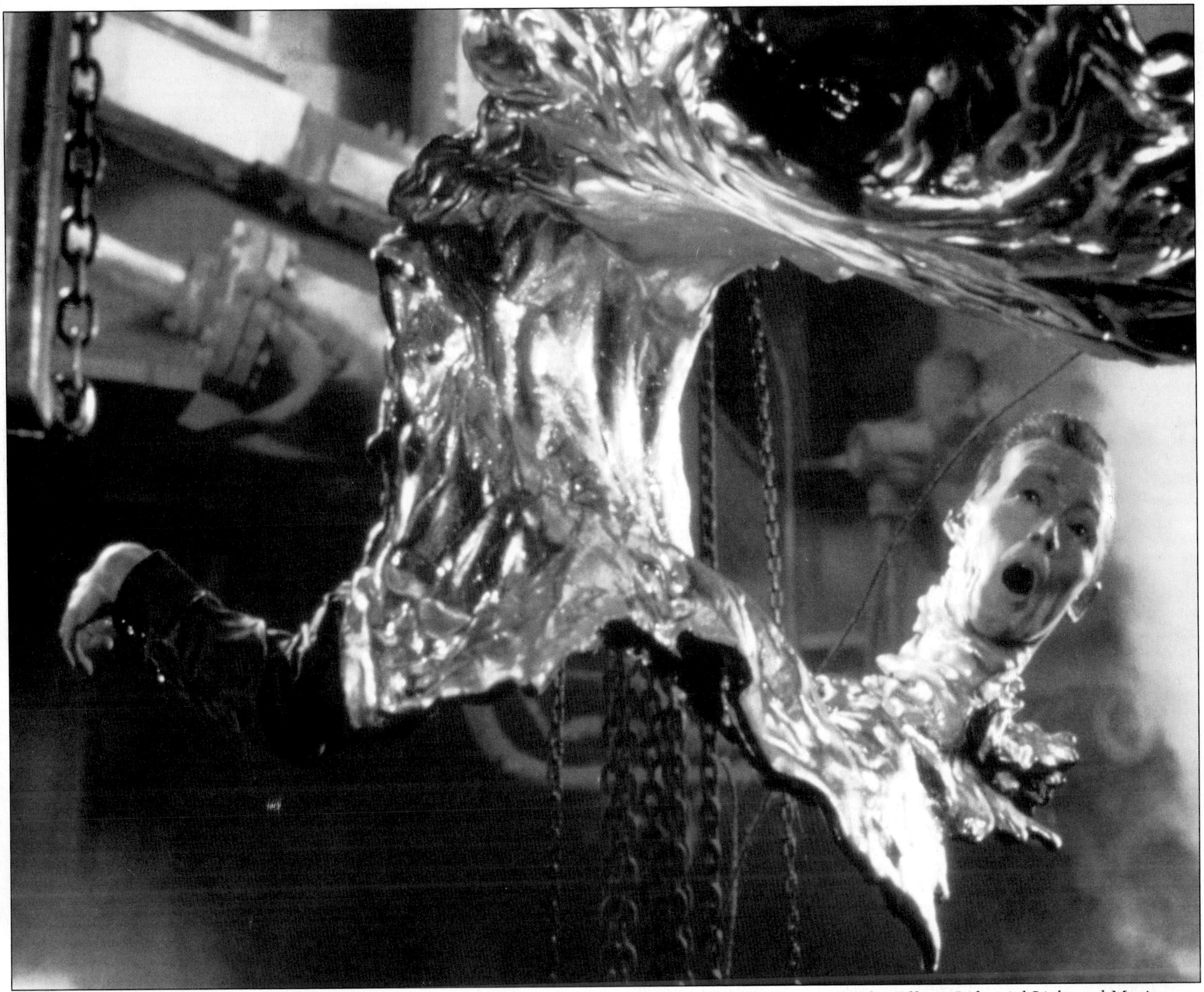

***Terminator 2**: designers Dennis Murren, Stan Winstone, Gene Warren Jr., Robert Skotak. Made by Fantasy II Film Effects, Industrial Light and Magic.*

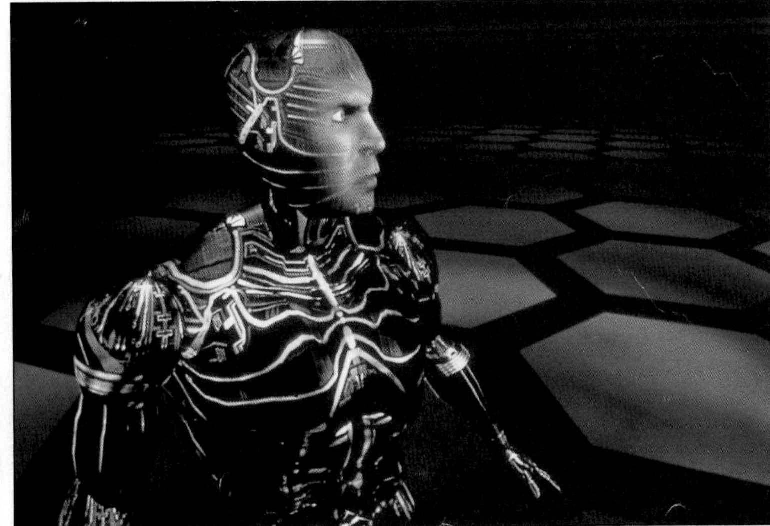

*Impressive simulations of 'virtual reality' enlivened **The Lawnmower Man**.*

*Steven Spielberg (left) and George Lucas, the **Indiana Jones** team at work.*

General Index

A

- *Monsieur Vincent* wins major French cinema award **07/01/48** 376
- Armand Tallier Prize **09/03/50** 596
- Arthur Freed receives the Irving G. Thalberg Memorial Award **20/03/52** 417
- Alfred Hitchcock wins the Thalberg Award **10/04/67** 564
- Jean Vigo Prize **20/03/69** 586
- John Ford receives Life Achievement Award **31/03/73** 624
- James Cagney receives Life Achievement Award **13/03/74** 634
- Louis Malle receives National Society of Film Critics award **04/01/82** 716
- Frank Capra receives Life Achievement Award **04/03/82** 716
- Rouben Mamoulian receives the D.W. Griffith award **16/08/82** 716
- Emmy Awards **18/02/87** 766
- Barbara Stanwyck receives Life Achievement Award **10/04/87** 766
- Victoires de la musique award for Eric Serra **19/11/88** 776
- National Critics Association awards **06/01/91** 810, **06/01/92** 822
- Golden Globe awards **23/01/93** 832

Axel, Gabriel
- Born in Denmark **08/04/17** 128
- Foreign Film Award for *Babette's Feast* **11/04/88** 778

Axelrod, George 06/06/55 444
Axton, Hoyt
- *Gremlins* **08/06/84** 740

Aykroyd, Dan
- Born in Canada **01/07/52** 414
- *Trading Places* **08/06/83** 730
- *Ghostbusters* **08/06/84** 740
- *My Stepmother is an Alien* **1988** 785
- *Driving Miss Daisy* **26/03/90** 802

Aylesworth, Merlin
- To become new president of RKO **20/01/32** 232

Ayme, Jean
- *Vampire* series **30/06/16** 119

Ayres, Agnes 23/08/26 184
Ayres, Lemuel 28/11/44 345
Ayres, Lew
- *All Quiet on the Western Front* **23/05/30** 218
- *Advise and Consent* **06/06/62** 518

Azema, Sabine
- César award for *Sunday in the Country* **02/03/85** 749
- *Melo* **1986** 765

Aznavour, Charles
- Born in France **22/05/24** 168
- *Shoot the Piano Player* **1960** 503
- *Candy* **29/08/70** 596

B

B. and C. Company
- *Florence Nightingale* **11/03/15** 112

Babbitt, Art 04/03/92 822
Babenco, Hector
- *Pixote* **11/09/81** 711
- *Kiss of the Spider Woman* **20/05/85** 750
- Academy Award nomination **24/03/86** 759

Bacall, Lauren
- Born in U.S. **16/09/24** 168
- *To Have and Have Not* **11/10/44** 344
- *The Big Sleep* **23/08/46** 360
- *Dark Passage* **05/09/47** 366
- *Key Largo* **16/07/48** 376
- Has first child with Humphrey Bogart **06/01/49** 384
- *How to Marry a Millionaire* **10/11/53** 429
- Humphrey Bogart dies of cancer **17/01/57** 462
- Marries Jason Robards **04/07/61** 504
- *Murder on the Orient Express* **1974** 643
- Publishes autobiography **30/09/79** 682

Bach, Steve 17/09/78 674
Bachau, Patrick
- *La Collectionneuse* **02/03/67** 566

Baclanova, Olga
- *The Docks of New York* **29/09/28** 198
- *Freaks* **31/08/32** 236

Bacon, Kevin
- Born in U.S. **08/07/58** 470
- *Diner* **14/05/82** 720

Bacon, Lloyd
- *42nd Street* **09/03/33** 240

Badger, Clarence
- *It* **05/02/27** 189

Badham, John
- *Saturday Night Fever* **15/12/77** 670
- *War Games* **1983** 735

Badham, Mary 25/12/62 523
Bailey, David 18/08/65 546
Bainter, Fay
- Academy Award for *Jezebel* **23/02/39** 298
- *The Secret Life of Walter Mitty* **14/08/47** 371
- Dies in Hollywood **16/04/68** 574

Baka, Miroslaw
- *A Short Film About Killing* **23/05/88** 780

Baker, Caroll
- Born in U.S. **28/05/31** 224
- *Baby Doll* **18/12/56** 457
- *Easy to Love* **18/12/56** 457
- *Giant* **18/12/56** 457

Baker, Chet
- *Let's Get Lost* **1990** 809

Baker, Joe Don
- *Walking Tall* **1973** 632

Baker, Rick 18/12/76 661
Bakshi, Ralph (animator)
- *Fritz the Cat* **1972** 623

Balaban, Barney 19/10/66 560
Balasko, Josiane
- Born in France **15/04/52** 414
- *Trop belle pour toi!* **31/10/88** 776

Balazsovits, Lajos
- *Private Lives and Public Virtues* **1975** 653

Balcon, Michael
- Head of British Gaumont **10/09/34** 253
- Produces Hitchcock thrillers **06/06/37** 262
- Head of Ealing studios **07/03/49** 386

Baldwin, Alec 03/04/58 470
Baldwin, William
- *Internal Affairs* **12/01/91** 800

Bale, Christian
- *Empire of the Sun* **09/12/87** 772

Balfour, Betty
- *Le Diable au cœur* **25/01/27** 186

Balin, Mireille
- Born in Monte Carlo **20/07/11** 86
- *Pépé-le-Moko* **29/01/37** 279
- *Macao, l'enfer du jeu* **1939** 305

Balint, Andras
- *Father* **1966** 562

Balint, Eszter
- *Stranger Than Paradise* **1984** 744

Balk, Fairuza
- *Valmont* **1989** 795

Ball, Lucille 10/10/57 460, **26/04/89** 786
Ballard, Lucien 01/10/88 776
Balsam, Martin
- Academy Award for *A Thousand Clowns* **18/04/66** 557
- *Catch 22* **24/06/70** 602

Ban, Junzaburo
- *Dodes' kaden* **31/10/70** 596

Bancroft, Anne
- Born in U.S. **17/09/31** 224
- Academy Award for *The Miracle Worker* **08/04/63** 530
- Marries Mel Brooks **05/08/64** 536
- *The Graduate* **21/12/67** 571

Bancroft, George
- *The Docks of New York* **29/09/28** 198
- *Stagecoach* **02/03/39** 298

Banderas, Antonio
- *Tie Me Up, Tie Me Down* **20/06/90** 798

Bankhead, Tallulah
- Born in U.S. **31/01/03** 46
- *Lifeboat* **12/01/44** 340
- Dies in New York **12/12/68** 574

Banks, Leslie
- *The Man Who Knew Too Much* **06/06/37** 262

Banky, Vilma
- *The Son of the Sheik* **23/08/26** 184
- Dies in Los Angeles **18/03/92** 822

Bannerjee, Subir
- *Pather Panchali* **11/05/56** 453

Bara, Theda
- *A Fool There Was* **12/03/15** 112
- *Cleopatra* **17/10/17** 126
- Dies in Los Angeles **07/04/55** 440

Barakat, Henry
- *The Sin* **03/03/65** 546

Barattolo, Guiseppe
- Founds UCI **09/01/19** 136
- Signs agreement with UFA **09/03/20** 144
- Withdraws backing from *Napoleon* **30/01/24** 168
- Reinstates backing for Abel Gance's *Napoleon* **07/04/27** 190

Barbera, Joe (animator)
- *Puss Gets the Boot* **10/02/40** 310

Bardot, Brigitte
- Born in U.S. **28/09/34** 250
- Marries Roger Vadim **21/12/52** 414
- *And God Created Woman* **28/11/56** 457
- *La Chatte* **19/02/57** 460
- *Love is My Profession* **17/09/58** 476
- Sues Bruno Coquatrix **18/12/58** 470
- *La Femme et le pantin* **13/02/59** 482
- Marries Jacques Charrier **29/03/59** 480
- *La Vérité* **01/05/60** 494
- *Vie privée* **31/01/62** 514
- *Repos du Guerrier* **05/02/62** 514
- Divorces Jacques Charrier **20/11/62** 514
- *Contempt* **20/12/63** 533
- *Viva Maria!* **22/11/65** 551
- *The Bear and the Doll* **1969** 593
- Announces her retirement **25/10/73** 631
- Sues Roger Vadim **22/09/86** 756
- Sells dresses and souvenirs at auction **18/06/87** 766
- Agrees to return to the screen in TV program **19/05/89** 786
- Denies planning to play Elena Ceausescu **20/03/90** 798

Bardou, Camille
- *The Lion of the Moguls* **15/04/24** 168

Barker, Lex 07/09/53 422
Barkin, Ellen
- Born in U.S. **16/04/54** 432
- *Diner* **14/05/82** 720
- *The Big Easy* **21/08/87** 771
- *Sea of Love* **15/09/89** 791

Barnes, Binnie
- *The Private Life of Henry VIII* **17/08/33** 245

Barnet, Boris
- Born in Russia **16/06/02** 42
- Co-directs *Miss Mend* **26/10/26** 180
- Directs *Girl with the Hatbox* **13/12/27** 193

Baron, Auguste
- Obtains patent for new sound system **04/04/1898** 28
- Patents Graphonoscope **16/11/1899** 32

Baroncelli, Jacques de
- *The Secret of the Lone Star* **20/09/19** 134
- René Clair to be assistant director **08/07/22** 160
- *The Legend of Sister Beatrix* **28/12/23** 162
- *The Woman and the Puppet* **31/10/28** 194
- *Le Père Goriot* **31/10/37** 282

Barr, Jean-Marc
- *The Big Blue* **11/05/88** 779
- *Le Fils Préféré* 851

Barrault, Jean-Louis
- Born in France **08/09/10** 80
- *Jenny* **16/09/36** 272
- *The Puritan* **16/02/38** 288
- Marries Madeleine Renaud **05/09/40** 308
- *Hélène* **05/09/40** 308
- *Montmartre-sur-Seine* **1941** 322
- *La Symphonie fantastique* **01/04/42** 327
- *Children of Paradise* **09/03/45** 351
- *Man to Men* **1948** 382
- *La Ronde* **17/06/50** 401
- Death of **22/01/94** 844

Barrault, Marie-Christine
- *Cousin, Cousine* **08/01/76** 656

Barreto, Bruno
- *Dona Flor and her Two Husbands* **1978** 680

Barreto, Lima
- *The Bandit* **29/04/53** 426

Barry, Iris 12/10/58 476
Barry, Joan
- Contract cancelled by Chaplin **23/12/42** 324
- Loses paternity suit against Chaplin **06/06/45** 348

Barrymore, Drew 22/2/75 644
Barrymore, Ethel 18/06/59 480
Barrymore, John
- Born in U.S. **15/02/1882** 33
- *Dr. Jekyll and Mr. Hyde* **02/04/20** 147
- *Don Juan* **06/08/26** 183
- *General Crack* **1929** 209
- *Grand Hotel* **12/04/32** 235
- *A Bill of Divorcement* **02/11/32** 232
- *Twentieth Century* **03/05/34** 250
- Dies in Hollywood **29/05/42** 324

Barrymore, Lionel
- *Fighting Blood* **01/10/11** 90
- *The New York Hat* **05/12/12** 92
- *Mysteries of New York* **03/12/15** 115
- *Sadie Thompson* **1928** 194
- *His Glorious Night* **28/09/29** 200
- Academy Award **10/11/31** 228
- *A Free Soul* **10/11/31** 228
- *Grand Hotel* **12/04/32** 235
- *Duel in the Sun* **12/47** 369
- *Key Largo* **16/07/48** 376
- Dies in California **15/11/54** 432

Bartel, Paul
- In and directs *Eating Raoul* **1982** 724

Barthélémy, René 07/10/30 214
Barthelmess, Richard
- *Way Down East* **20/09/20** 149
- Sets up Inspiration Pictures in partnership with Henry King **21/09/21** 154
- *Tol'able David* **21/09/21** 154
- *The Dawn Patrol* **10/07/30** 219
- *Only Angels Have Wings* **11/05/39** 296
- Dies in New York **17/08/63** 526

Bartholomew, Freddie
- *David Copperfield* **18/01/35** 260
- *Captains Courageous* **10/03/38** 289
- Dies in Florida **23/01/92** 822

Barwood, Hal 24/05/74 638
Basehart, Richard
- *La Strada* **07/09/54** 436
- Dies in Los Angeles **17/09/84** 736

Basevi, James 26/06/36 270
Basinger, Kim
- Born in U.S. **08/12/53** 422
- *My Stepmother is an Alien* **1988** 785
- *Batman* **31/12/89** 792
- Backs out of *Boxing Helena* and loses court case **25/03/93** 834

Bass, Saul
- Poster design for *Saint Joan* **1957** 469
- Title for *Vertigo* **28/05/58** 473
- Poster design for *One, Two, Three* **1961** 512
- Poster design for *Walk on the Wild Side* **1962** 525
- Directs *Phase IV* **1974** 643

Bassett, Angela
- *What's Love Got to Do With It* **1993** 841

Bassey, Shirley 01/08/64 536
Batalov, Alexei
- *The Cranes Are Flying* **18/05/58** 474

Bates, Alan
- Born in England **17/02/34** 250
- *A Kind of Loving* **21/05/61** 517
- *Zorba the Greek* **05/04/65** 549
- *The Go-Between* **24/09/71** 611
- *An Unmarried Woman* **1978** 680
- *The Rose* **07/11/79** 682

Bates, Kathy
- Academy Award for *Misery* **25/03/91** 813
- *Fried Green Tomatoes at the Whistle Stop Cafe* **27/12/91** 819

Bates, Norman
- *Psycho II* **1983** 735

Bauer, Evgeni
- *The Child from the Big City* **05/03/14** 104
- *The Revolutionary* **30/03/17** 122
- *Song of Triumphant Love* **27/04/18** 131
- *Children of the Age* **27/04/18** 131
- *Beauty Should rule the World* **27/04/18** 131
- *A Life for a Life* **27/04/18** 131

Baumann, Charles
- Founds Bison Life Films **14/04/09** 72
- Founds the New York Motion Picture Company **14/04/09** 76
- Founds the Keystone Picture Corporation **23/09/12** 96
- Founds Kay Bee Motion Pictures **01/10/12** 92

Baur, Harry
- *The Legend of the Good Knight* **14/11/09** 72
- *The Clairvoyant* **31/10/24** 168
- *Redhead* **07/12/32** 232
- *Les Misérables* **03/02/34** 252
- *The Life and Loves of Beethoven* **07/12/36** 266
- *Dance Card* **07/09/37** 281
- *Volpone* **23/03/40** 308

Baxter, Anne
- *Swamp Water* **28/10/41** 316
- *Five Graves to Cairo* **26/05/43** 335
- Academy Award for *The Razor's Edge* **13/03/47** 369
- *All About Eve* **22/10/50** 402
- *The Ten Commandments* **05/10/56** 450
- Dies in New York **04/12/85** 746

Baxter, Warner
- *Such Men Are Dangerous* **09/03/30** 217
- Academy Award for *In Old Arizona* **05/11/30** 220
- Dies in Hollywood **07/05/51** 406

Baye, Nathalie
- *Everyman for Himself* **1980** 704
- *The Return of Martin Guerre* **12/05/82** 719
- César award for *la Balance* **27/02/83** 729

Bazin, André
- Born in France **18/04/17** 128
- Jury at Brussels World Fair **12/10/58** 476
- Dies of Leukemia **11/11/58** 477

Beals, Jennifer
- *Flashdance* **1983** 734

Béart, Emmanuelle
- Born in France **14/08/65** 546
- *La Belle Noiseuse* **04/09/91** 814
- *Un cœur en hiver* **1992** 831

Beatles, The
- *A Hard Day's Night* **31/08/64** 540

Beaton, Cecil
- Designer for *Gigi* **15/05/58** 473
- Costume Design Award for *Gigi* **07/04/59** 483
- *My Fair Lady* **21/10/64** 542
- Academy Award for *My Fair Lady* **05/04/65** 549

Beatty, Ned
- *Deliverance* **1972** 622
- *The Big Easy* **21/08/87** 771

Beatty, Warren
- Born in U.S. **30/03/37** 276
- *Splendor in the Grass* **11/10/61** 509
- *The Roman Spring of Mrs. Stone* **08/07/67** 569
- Produces and stars in *Bonnie and Clyde* **14/08/67** 569
- *McCabe and Mrs. Miller* **24/06/71** 610
- *Shampoo* **11/02/74** 646
- *The Parallax View* **19/06/74** 639
- Directs and stars in *Reds* **04/12/81** 713
- Academy Award **29/03/82** 719
- *Ishtar* **07/12/88** 782
- Produces, directs and stars in *Dick Tracy* **15/06/90** 803

Beauregard, Georges de 15/04/66 557
Beauvais, Henri 30/10/40 308
Becker, Jacques
- Born in France **15/09/06** 58
- *Falbalas* **17/10/45** 352
- Cannes award for *Antoine and Antoinette* **25/09/47** 372
- *Rendez-vous de juillet* **06/12/49** 390

Folsey, George
- Cameraman for *Meet Me in St. Louis* **28/11/44** 345

Fonda, Bridget
- *Scandal* **1989** 795
- *Point of No Return* **19/03/93** 834
- *Little Buddha* **25/05/94** 849

Fonda, Henry
- Born in U.S. **17/05/05** 54
- *The Trail of the Lonesome Pine* **13/03/36** 269
- *Jezebel* **10/03/38** 289
- *The Grapes of Wrath* **24/01/40** 310
- *The Lady Eve* **25/03/41** 319
- *My Darling Clementine* **03/12/46** 356
- *The Fugitive* **27/03/48** 376
- *Mister Roberts* **1955** 449
- *War and Peace* **21/08/56** 455
- *Twelve Angry Men* **05/07/57** 465
- *Warlock* **1959** 491
- *Advise and Consent* **06/06/62** 518
- *The Longest Day* **10/10/62** 520
- *Once Upon a Time in the West* **28/05/69** 588
- *On Golden Pond* **04/12/81** 713
- Academy Award **29/03/82** 719
- Dies in Los Angeles **12/08/82** 716

Fonda, Jane
- Born in U.S. **21/12/37** 276
- *Tall Story* **17/04/60** 494
- Marries Roger Vadim **18/08/65** 546
- *La Curée* **22/11/65** 546
- *Barbarella* **25/12/67** 571
- Defends American Indians **21/11/68** 574
- Protests against Vietnam war **16/04/70** 596
- Arrested for possessing drugs **09/11/70** 596
- *Klute* **23/06/71** 610
- Goes to North Vietnam **14/07/72** 616
- *A Doll's House* **1973** 633
- Marries Tom Hayden **19/01/73** 624
- Academy Award **10/04/75** 620
- Co-directs *Introduction to the Enemy* **18/06/75** 644
- *Julia* **1977** 673
- *Coming Home* **15/02/78** 676
- *The China Syndrome* **28/03/79** 685
- Academy Award for *Coming Home* **09/04/79** 685
- *Nine to Five* **1980** 705
- *On Golden Pond* **04/12/81** 713
- Publishes fitness book **30/11/82** 716
- Divorces Tom Hayden **16/02/89** 786
- Present at screening of new edition of *Casablanca* **07/04/92** 822

Fonda, Peter
- Born in U.S. **23/02/39** 296
- *The Wild Angels* **1966** 554
- *Easy Rider* **14/07/69** 589

Fontaine, Joan
- Born in Japan **22/10/17** 122
- *Rebecca* **28/03/40** 311
- *Suspicion* **16/11/41** 321
- Academy Award **26/02/42** 326
- *Beyond a Reasonable Doubt* **1956** 458
- *Island in the Sun* **18/07/57** 460

Forbes, Brian
- *The Madwoman of Chaillot* **24/05/73** 629

Forbes-Robertson, Johnston
- *Hamlet* **29/10/13** 102

Ford, Aleksander
- *Sabra* **31/12/33** 240
- *Street of the Young* banned **02/01/36** 266
- Creates Avant-Garde cinema company **01/01/43** 332
- *Majdanek* **01/01/44** 340

Ford, Glenn
- Born in Canada **01/05/16** 116
- *Gilda* **27/07/46** 360
- *Affair in Trinidad* **26/01/53** 424
- *The Big Heat* **05/08/53** 428
- *The Blackboard Jungle* **20/03/55** 442
- Divorces **25/11/59** 480
- *Is Paris Burning?* **13/10/66** 559

Ford, Harrison
- Born in U.S. **13/07/42** 324
- *American Graffiti* **05/08/73** 629
- *Star Wars* **25/03/77** 668
- *Raiders of the Lost Ark* **12/06/81** 710
- *Blade Runner* **25/06/82** 721
- *Witness* **08/02/85** 748
- *Working Girl* **21/12/88** 783
- *Indiana Jones and the Last Crusade* **24/06/89** 789
- *Patriot Games* **1992** 830

Ford, John
- Born in U.S. **01/02/1895** 33
- *The Tornado* (as Jack Ford) **03/03/17** 122
- *Hell Bent* (as Jack Ford) **06/07/18** 132
- *The Iron Horse* **09/09/24** 171
- *Four Sons* **13/02/28** 194
- *The Informer* **09/05/35** 261
- *The Whole Town's Talking* **09/05/35** 261
- *The Lost Patrol* **09/05/35** 261
- Academy Award **05/03/36** 269
- *Stagecoach* **02/03/39** 298
- *The Grapes of Wrath* **24/01/40** 310
- 14 Academy Award nominations for *The Grapes of Wrath* **27/02/41** 316
- *How Green Was My Valley* **28/10/41** 320
- Academy Award **26/02/42** 326
- *My Darling Clementine* **03/12/46** 356
- *The Fugitive* **27/03/48** 376
- Academy Award for *The Quiet Man* **19/03/53** 425
- *Mogambo* **31/10/53** 428
- *The Searchers* **22/05/55** 454
- *The Man Who Shot Liberty Valance* **11/04/62** 517
- *How the West Was Won* **01/11/62** 521
- *Up the River* **11/06/67** 568
- A.F.I.'s Lifetime Achievement Award **31/03/73** 624
- Dies of cancer **31/08/73** 630

Ford, Reginald 07/02/34 252

Foreman, Carl 26/06/84 736

Forman, Milos
- *Peter and Pavla* **17/04/64** 536
- *Black Peter* **18/11/66** 560
- *Loves of a Blonde* **18/11/66** 560
- *The Firemen's Ball* withdrawn from Cannes Festival **18/05/68** 579
- *Taking Off* **29/03/71** 608
- *One Flew Over the Cuckoo's Nest* **20/11/75** 651
- *Hair* **14/03/79** 685
- *Ragtime* **23/10/80** 702
- *Amadeus* **19/09/84** 742
- Academy Award **25/03/85** 749
- *Valmont* **06/12/89** 786

Formby, George 06/03/61 504

Forrest, Frederic
- Born in U.S. **23/12/36** 266
- *The Rose* **07/11/79** 682

Forsyth, Bill
- *Local Hero* **1983** 734

Fortenski, Larry
- Marries Elizabeth Taylor **06/10/91** 810

Fortier, Robert
- *Three Women* **1977** 672

Fosse, Bob
- *Cabaret* **14/02/72** 618
- Academy Award **27/03/73** 627
- *All That Jazz* **19/12/79** 690
- Shared Golden Palm for *All That Jazz* **23/05/80** 700

Fossey, Brigitte
- *Forbidden Games* **09/05/52** 418

Foster, Barry
- *Frenzy* **1972** 623

Foster, Jodie
- Born in U.S. **19/11/62** 514
- *The Accused* **14/10/88** 781
- Academy Award **29/03/89** 789
- *Silence of the Lambs* **14/02/91** 813
- Academy Award **30/03/92** 824
- *Sommersby* **19/03/93** 834
- *Nell* **1994** *853*

Foster, Norman
- Co-directs *Journey Into Fear* **1943** 339

Foster, R. Lewis
- *Double Whoopee* **18/05/28** 205

Fouché, André
- *Fanny* **23/01/37** 278

Fox, Edward
- *The Day of the Jackal* **1973** 632

Fox, James
- Born in England **19/05/39** 296
- *The Loneliness of the Long Distance Runner* **1962** 524
- *The Servant* **10/02/64** 538
- *Performance* **05/01/71** 608

Fox, John
- *The Covered Wagon* **25/03/23** 164

Fox, Kerry 06/01/95 856

Fox, Michael J.
- Born in U.S. **09/06/61** 504
- *Back to the Future* **26/11/84** 736, **03/07/85** 752
- *Casualties of War* **18/08/89** 791

Fox, William
- Purchases the "Automat" **19/06/04** 52
- Opens projection room **05/06** 58
- Founds Fox Film Corporation **01/02/15** 110
- *A Fool There Was* **12/03/15** 112
- Produces *A Daughter of the Gods* **30/10/16** 121
- Asks F.W. Murnau to work **29/11/27** 193
- To absorb Loew's Incorporation **03/03/29** 200
- Dismissed from his company **05/04/30** 214
- Dies in New York **08/05/52** 414

Fox-Europa
- Company run by Erich Pommer **15/12/33** 240
- *Liliom* **15/12/33** 240

Fox Film Corporation
- Founding **01/02/15** 110
- *Cleopatra* **17/10/17** 126
- Continues to grow **17/10/17** 126
- *The Iron Horse* **09/09/24** 171
- *The Air Circus* **31/12/28** 194
- Filming of *Such Men are Dangerous* ends in tragedy **09/03/30** 217
- *The Big Trail* **24/10/30** 219
- Opening of Movietone City Studios **26/06/32** 232
- *Cavalcade* **09/10/33** 245
- Signs contract with Monroe **31/12/55** 447

Foy, Brian
- *Lights of New York* **06/07/28** 194

Francen, Victor
- *The End of the World* **24/01/31** 226
- *The King* **05/10/36** 266

***France Soir* 08/07/58** 470

Franciosa, Anthony
- *A Face in the Crowd* **28/05/57** 464

Francis, Freddie (cameraman)
- *The Elephant Man* **19/01/81** 708

Francis, Kay
- *The Cocoanuts* **03/08/29** 205
- *Trouble in Paradise* **08/11/32** 232
- Dies in New York **26/08/68** 574

Franco-Film 30/09/27 186, **02/10/29** 200

Franju, Georges
- Born in France **12/04/12** 92
- Founds FIAF **15/07/38** 291
- *Le Grand Méliès* **15/10/52** 414
- *Yeux sans visage* **03/03/60** 494
- Resigns from Cinémathèque **30/03/81** 706

Frank, Charles
- *The Right Stuff* **21/10/83** 732

Frank, Fredric M. 15/12/61 511

Frank, Melvin
- Co-directs and co-writes *The Court Jester* **01/02/56** 452

Frankenheimer, John
- Born in U.S. **19/02/30** 214
- *The Manchurian Candidate* **23/10/62** 521
- *The Iceman Cometh* **31/10/73** 624

Frankeur, Paul
- *Jour de fête* **04/05/49** 387

Fraser, John
- *Repulsion* **10/06/65** 550

Frazee, Jane 1944 347

Frears, Stephen
- Born in England **20/06/41** 316
- *My Beautiful Laundrette* **16/11/85** 753
- *The Grifters* **25/01/91** 812

Frechette, Mark
- *Zabriskie Point* **05/08/68** 574

Freda, Riccardo 24/02/09 72

Freed, Arthur
- Songs for *The Broadway Melody* **02/02/29** 202
- Produces *Meet Me in St. Louis* **28/11/44** 345
- Produces *On the Town* **08/12/49** 390
- Produces *An American in Paris* **04/10/51** 410
- Receives the Irving G. Thalberg Memorial Award **20/03/52** 417
- Songs for *Singin' in the Rain* **27/03/52** 417
- Produces *Gigi* **15/05/58** 473

Freeland, Thornton
- *Flying Down to Rio* **22/12/33** 240

Freeman, Morgan
- *Driving Miss Daisy* **26/03/90** 802
- *Robin Hood: Prince of Thieves* **14/06/91** 815
- *The Shawshank Redemption***1994** *853*, **28/03/95** 859

Fregoli, Leopoldo 18/01/1898 28

Freleng, Friz
- *I Haven't Got a Hat* **02/03/35** 258
- *Life With Feathers* **24/03/45** 348

Frend, Charles
- *Scott of the Antarctic* **07/03/49** 386

Fresnay, Pierre
- *Marius* **17/10/31** 224
- *Fanny* **23/01/37** 278
- *The Grand Illusion* **08/06/37** 280
- *The Puritan* **16/02/38** 288
- *The Murderer Lives at No. 21* **07/08/42** 324
- Venice award for *Monsieur Vincent* **25/09/47** 372

Freuler, John R.
- Founds Western Film Exchange **23/07/06** 58
- Founds the Majestic Motion Picture Company **12/01/11** 86

Frey, Hugues Eugène 15/11/01 38

Frey, Sammy
- Born in France **13/10/37** 276
- *La Vérité* **01/05/60** 494
- *Pourquoi pas?* **1977** 672

Freykowsky, Voyteck 09/08/69 589

Fric, Martin
- Directs *Father Vojtech* **01/03/29** 200
- *Hej Rup!* **26/10/34** 250
- *Svet patri nam* **30/07/37** 276

Fricker, Brenda
- *My Left Foot* **26/03/90** 802

Friedhofer, Hugo
- Academy Award for score of *The Best Years of Our Lives* **13/03/47** 369
- Score for *The Young Lions* **02/04/58** 472

Friedkin, David 24/04/65 549

Friedkin, William
- *The French Connection* **08/10/71** 612
- *The Exorcist* **1973** 633, **26/12/73** 631
- Academy Award **10/04/75** 620
- Marries Jeanne Moreau **30/01/77** 664
- *Cruising* **12/02/80** 696

Friedman, Dave 08/07/82 716

Fritsch, Willy 22/03/28 194, **15/09/30** 219

Frobe, Gert (Froebe)
- Born in Germany **25/02/13** 98
- *The Longest Day* **10/10/62** 520
- *Is Paris Burning?* **13/10/66** 559 aaFroelich, Carl
- *The Refuge* **31/08/28** 194
- *La Nuit est à nous* **01/02/30** 216
- *Das Schonheitsfleckchen* **30/06/36** 266

Frohman, Daniel
- Founds Famous Players Film Company **12/07/12** 95

Fuji, Tatsuya 15/09/76 659

Fujita, Susumu 19/03/43 332

Fukaya, K. 14/06/00 34

Fuller, Mary 18/03/10 82

Fuller, Samuel (Sam)
- *Merril's Marauders* **1962** 525
- *Shock Corridor* **12/09/63** 526
- *The Big Red One* **18/07/80** 696
- *White Dog* **09/12/83** 726

Funakoshi, Eiji
- *Fires on the Plain* **1959** 490

Funès, Louis de
- Born in France **11/07/14** 104
- Special César award **13/02/80** 696

Funt, Alex
- *What Do You Say to a Naked Lady?* **23/06/71** 610

Furse, Robert 05/09/48 380

Furst, Anton
- Academy Award for art direction of *Batman* **25/11/91** 810
- Dies in Los Angeles **25/11/91** 810

Furthman, Jules
- Screenplay for *The Big Sleep* **23/08/46** 360

G

Gabin, Jean
- Born in France **17/05/04** 48
- *Chacun sa chance* **19/12/30** 221
- Marries Jeanne Mauchain **23/11/33** 240
- *Maria Chapdelaine* **19/12/34** 250
- *La Bandera* **20/09/35** 258
- *The Lower Depths* **22/12/36** 273
- *Pépé-le-Moko* **29/01/37** 279
- *The Grand Illusion* **08/06/37** 280
- *Gueule d'amour* **29/09/37** 281
- *Quai des brumes* **18/05/38** 291
- *Hôtel du Nord* **16/12/38** 293
- *La Bête humaine* **21/12/38** 293
- *Daybreak* **09/06/39** 300
- *Moontide* **1942** 331
- *The Imposter* **31/12/42** 329
- *The Walls of Malapaga* **1949** 392
- Marries Christiane Fournier **28/03/49** 384
- *La Marie du port* **25/02/50** 398
- *La Vérité sur Bébé Donge* **13/02/52** 414
- *French Cancan* **271954** 443
- *Honor Among Thieves* **17/03/54** 434
- *Love is My Profession* **17/09/58** 476
- *A Monkey in Winter* **11/05/62** 518
- *L'Année Sainte* **19/11/76** 660
- Dies in Paris **19/11/76** 660
- Creation of a Jean Gabin Museum in France **10/12/90** 798

Gable, Clark
- Born in U.S. **01/02/01** 38
- Marries Josephine Dillon **13/12/24** 168
- *Susan Lennox* **1931** 230
- *Strange Interlude* **1932** 239
- *Red Dust* **22/10/32** 237
- *The Painted Desert* **22/10/32** 237
- *It Happened One Night* **22/02/34** 252
- *China Seas* **1935** 264
- Academy Award for *It Happened One Night* **27/02/35** 260
- *Mutiny on the Bounty* **08/11/35** 258
- Academy Award nomination **05/03/36** 269
- *San Francisco* **26/06/36** 270
- *Saratoga* **07/06/37** 280
- To star in *Gone With the Wind* **25/08/38** 286
- Marries Carole Lombard **23/04/39** 299
- *Gone With the Wind* **14/12/39** 303
- Academy Award nomination **29/02/40** 310
- Carole Lombard killed in aircrash **17/01/42** 326
- Marries Sylvia Hawkes **21/12/49** 390
- *Mogambo* **09/10/53** 422
- Leaves MGM **02/03/54** 432
- *The Tall Men* **1955** 448
- *The Misfits* **16/11/60** 501
- Dies aged 60 **17/11/60** 501

Gabor, Zsa Zsa
- *Moulin Rouge* **04/09/53** 427

Gabriel de Gavrone
- *La Roue* **17/02/23** 164

Gabrio, Gabriel
- *Les Misérables* **25/12/25** 174
- *Harvest* **28/10/37** 282

Gad, Urban
- Marries Asta Nielsen **30/04/12** 92
- *Little Angel* **31/01/14** 104

Gade, Sven
- *Hamlet* to be banned in France **19/08/24** 168

H

Hayward, Susan
- *With a Song in My Heart* **04/04/52** 418
- *Smash-Up, The Story of a Woman* **21/12/55** 446
- *My Foolish Heart* **21/12/55** 446
- *I'll Cry Tomorrow* **21/12/55** 446
- Academy Award for *I Want to Live* **07/04/59** 483
- Dies in Los Angeles **14/03/75** 644

Hayworth, Rita
- Born in U.S. **17/10/17** 128
- *Criminals of the Air* **30/06/37** 276
- *Only Angels Have Wings* **11/05/39** 296
- *Blood and Sand* **1941** 323
- *The Strawberry Blonde* **21/02/41** 316
- Divorces Edward Judson **22/05/42** 324
- *My Gal Sal* **22/05/42** 324
- *You Were Never Lovelier* **19/11/42** 328
- Marries Orson Welles **07/09/43** 337
- *Cover Girl* **1944** 342
- *Gilda* **27/07/46** 360
- *The Lady from Shanghai* **08/04/48** 379
- Divorces Orson Welles **30/11/48** 376
- Marries Prince Aly Khan **27/05/49** 384
- Divorces Prince Aly Khan **26/01/53** 424
- *Affair in Trinidad* **26/01/53** 424
- Court action against Columbia **27/12/55** 447
- Dies of Alzheimer's disease **14/05/87** 769

Heacock, Linnea
- *Taking Off* **29/03/71** 608

Head, Edith (costume designer)
- *Vertigo* **28/05/58** 473
- Dies in Hollywood **24/10/81** 706

Head, Murray
- *Sunday, Bloody Sunday* **01/07/71** 611

Headly, Glenne
- *Dick Tracy* **15/06/90** 803

Heard, John
- *Between the Lines* **1977** 673

Hearst, William Randolph
- Collaborates with cinema **31/03/14** 106
- Suspected of shooting Thomas Harper Ince **21/11/24** 172
- Forbids Hearst press to mention *Citizen Kane* **10/01/41** 316
- Dies **14/08/51** 406

Hecht, Ben
- *Nothing Sacred* **26/09/37** 283
- Dies in New York **18/04/64** 536

Hecht, Harold
- Produces *Marty* **11/04/54** 442
- *The Bachelor Party* **09/04/57** 463

Heckart, Eileen
- Academy Award for *Butterflies Are Free* **27/03/73** 627

Hedren, Tippi
- *The Birds* **29/03/63** 529
- *Marnie* **01/06/64** 540

Heflin, Van
- *The Strange Love of Martha Ivers* **24/07/46** 359
- *The Prowler* **1951** 412
- *Airport* **05/03/70** 599
- Dies in Hollywood **23/07/71** 606

Helm, Brigitte
- Born in Germany **17/03/08** 66
- *Metropolis* **10/01/27** 188

Helmond, Katharine
- *Brazil* **29/06/85** 748

Hemblen, David
- *Family Viewing* **1987** 775

Hemingway, Mariel
- Born in U.S. **22/11/61** 504
- *Manhattan* **28/04/79** 682

Hemmings, David
- Born in England **18/11/42** 324
- *Blow Up* **18/12/66** 561
- *Camelot* **1967** 570
- *The Charge of the Light Brigade* **1968** 583

Henabery, Joseph
- *The Birth of a Nation* **10/04/15** 113
- *His Majesty, The American* **01/09/19** 138

Henie, Sonja 08/04/12 92, **13/10/69** 584

Hennessy, Ruth 1914 141

Henning, Uno 14/09/31 224

Henreid, Paul
- *Casablanca* **1942** 330
- *Now, Voyager* **31/10/42** 328
- *The Spanish Main* **30/12/45** 348
- Dies in Los Angeles **29/03/92** 822

Henrey, Bobby
- *The Fallen Idols* **1948** 382

Henriksen, Lance
- *The Right Stuff* **21/10/83** 732

Henry, Buck
- *Catch 22* **24/06/70** 602
- *Taking Off* **29/03/71** 608

Henry, Justin
- *Kramer vs. Kramer* **19/12/79** 690

Henson, Jim
- Avoriaz Grand Prix for *Dark Crystal* **23/01/83** 728

Henze, Hans Werner 22/02/84 738

Hepburn, Audrey
- Born in Belgium **04/05/29** 200
- *Roman Holiday* **27/08/53** 427
- *Sabrina* **1954** 438
- Academy Award for *Roman Holiday* **25/03/54** 434
- *War and Peace* **21/08/56** 455
- *Funny Face* **28/03/57** 463
- *A Nun's Story* **18/06/59** 485
- *The Unforgiven* **07/04/60** 494
- Birth of first child **17/07/60** 494
- *Breakfast at Tiffany's* **05/11/61** 509
- *Charade* **05/12/63** 533
- *My Fair Lady* **21/10/64** 542
- Snubbed at Academy Awards **05/04/65** 549
- Returns to films after 9-year absence with *Robin and Marian* **11/03/76** 656
- Opens first Festival of French Films in Sarasota **19/11/89** 786
- Ambassador to UNICEF **01/11/93** 840
- Dies of cancer **01/11/93** 840

Hepburn, Dee
- *Gregory's Girl* **1981** 714

Hepburn, Katharine
- Born in U.S. **08/11/07** 62
- *A Bill of Divorcement* **02/11/32** 232
- *Christopher Strong* **1933** 249
- *Little Women* **11/11/33** 240
- Venice award for *Little Women* **01/08/34** 253
- Academy Award for *Morning Glory* **01/08/34** 253
- *Sylvia Scarlett* **15/05/36** 266
- *Quality Street* **1937** 285
- *Bringing Up Baby* **03/03/38** 286
- *The Philadelphia Story* **27/12/40** 313
- *Woman of the Year* **15/04/42** 327
- *Keeper of the Flame* **18/03/43** 332
- *Undercurrent* **1946** 364
- *The Sea of Grass* **1946** 365
- *Adam's Rib* **25/12/49** 384
- *The African Queen* **26/12/51** 411
- *Summer Madness* **29/05/54** 443
- *Woman of the Year* **11/06/67** 568
- *Adam's Rib* **11/06/67** 568
- *Guess Who's Coming to Dinner* **11/12/67** 570
- Academy Award **10/04/68** 577
- Academy Award for *The Lion in Winter* **14/04/69** 586
- *On Golden Pond* **04/12/81** 713
- Academy Award **29/03/82** 719

Hepworth, Cecil
- Films Queen Victoria's funeral **04/02/01** 39
- *Rescued By Rover* **03/07/05** 56
- *Oliver Twist* **24/12/12** 92
- *Hamlet* **29/10/13** 102

Herman, Pee Wee (Paul Rubens)
- Born in U.S. **27/08/52** 414
- *Pee Wee's Big Adventure* **27/08/85** 746
- Arrested for indecent behavior **28/07/91** 810

Hernandez, Juano
- *Intruder in the Dust* **03/02/50** 398

Herrand, Marcel
- *Children of Paradise* **09/03/45** 351

Herrmann, Bernard (composer)
- *Vertigo* **28/05/58** 473
- *The Bride Wore Black* **17/04/68** 578
- Dies in Hollywood **25/12/75** 644

Hershey, Barbara
- *Hannah and Her Sisters* **07/02/86** 758

Hersholt, Jean
- *Greed* **26/01/25** 176
- *The Country Doctor* **1936** 275
- Dies in California **02/06/56** 450

Hertz, Alexander 31/12/12 92, **31/12/15** 110

Hervil, René 14/11/17 122, **22/03/18** 128

Herzog, Werner
- *Aguirre, the Wrath of God* **05/01/73** 626
- Cannes award for *Every Man for Himself and God Against All* **23/05/75** 647
- *Woyzeck* **1978** 680
- *Nosferatu the Vampire* **22/09/79** 688
- Cannes award for *Fitzcarraldo* **26/05/82** 720

Hessling, Catherine
- *Une vie sans joie* **09/11/27** 186
- Husband Jean Renoir wanted her in *la Chienne* **19/11/31** 229
- *Nana* **22/07/34** 250

Heston, Charlton
- Born in U.S. **04/10/23** 162
- *The Greatest Show on Earth* **02/01/52** 416
- *The Ten Commandments* **05/10/56** 450
- *Touch of Evil* **08/06/58** 474
- *Ben-Hur* **18/11/59** 487
- Academy Award **05/04/60** 497
- *El Cid* **15/12/61** 511
- *Major Dundee* **1965** 552
- *Planet of the Apes* **09/02/68** 576
- *Earthquake* **01/11/74** 634
- Re-elected chairman of American Film Institute **28/10/75** 644

Heuzé, André 15/04/05 54, **27/02/14** 104

Higgins, Anthony
- *The Draughtman's Contract* **1982** 725

Higgins, Colin 20/12/71 613
- *Nine to Five* **1980** 705

Hildyard, Jack
- Cinematography Award for *The Bridge on the River Kwai* **26/03/58** 472

Hill, George Roy
- *Butch Cassidy and the Sundance Kid* **23/09/69** 590
- *The Sting* **1973** 624
- Academy Award **02/04/74** 637

Hill, Walter
- *The Warriors* **16/02/79** 682
- *48 HRS* **08/12/82** 722
- Universal to change title of film *The Looters* **02/07/92** 822

Hiller, Arthur
- *The Hospital* **1971** 614
- *Love Story* **22/01/71** 606

Hiller, Wendy
- *Pygmalion* **02/12/38** 292
- Academy Award for *Separate Tables* **07/04/59** 483

Hines, Gregory
- *The Cotton Club* **14/12/84** 736

Hirsch, Judd
- *Ordinary People* **19/09/80** 701

Hirsch, Robert
- *Notre-Dame de Paris* **1956** 459

Hirschfield, Alan
- President of Columbia Pictures Industries **25/07/73** 624
- Fired as president and CEO of Columbia **20/07/78** 677
- Made head of 20th-Century Fox **18/12/79** 689
- Removed as head of 20th-Century Fox **01/10/84** 736

Hitchcock, Alfred
- Born in England **13/08/1899** 33
- *The Lodger* **14/02/26** 182
- First solo directing credit *The Pleasure Garden* **01/03/26** 180
- First sound film *Blackmail* **25/11/29** 207
- *The Thirty-Nine Steps* **06/06/37** 262
- *The Waltzes of Vienna* **06/06/37** 262
- *The Man Who Knew Too Much* **06/06/37** 262
- Arrives in New York **22/08/37** 276
- *The Lady Vanishes* **25/08/38** 286
- *Rebecca* **28/03/40** 311
- *Foreign Correspondent* **16/08/40** 311
- *Mr. and Mrs. Smith* **31/01/41** 316
- *Suspicion* **16/11/41** 321
- *Saboteur* **16/11/41** 321
- *Shadow of a Doubt* **20/01/43** 334
- *Lifeboat* **12/01/44** 340
- *Spellbound* **01/11/45** 348
- *Notorious* **22/07/46** 359
- *Rope* **26/08/48** 380
- Signs contract with Warner Bros. **03/01/49** 384
- *Under Capricorn* **06/08/49** 388
- Buys rights of novel *Strangers on a Train* **20/04/50** 396
- *Strangers on a Train* **28/08/51** 409
- *I Confess* **21/08/52** 414
- *Dial M for Murder* **25/09/53** 422
- *Rear Window* **04/08/54** 435
- Remake of *The Man Who Knew Too Much* **16/05/56** 450
- *Vertigo* **28/05/58** 473
- *North by Northwest* **06/08/59** 486
- *Psycho* **10/08/60** 499
- *The Birds* **29/03/63** 529
- *Marnie* **01/06/64** 540
- Book project with Truffaut **13/08/65** 551
- Biography by Truffaut published **05/01/66** 554
- *Torn Curtain* **27/07/66** 554
- Wins the Thalberg Award **10/04/67** 564
- *Frenzy* **17/06/71** 606
- Receives Life Achievement award **07/03/79** 684
- Receives knighthood **03/01/80** 696
- *Family Plot* **29/04/80** 699
- Dies in Hollywood **29/04/80** 699

Hoag, Judith
- *Teenage Mutant Ninja Turtles* **30/03/90** 802

Hobson, Valerie
- *The Werewolf of London* **13/05/37** 262
- *Knave of Hearts* **09/04/54** 435

Hoch, Winton (cinematographer)
- *She Wore a Yellow Ribbon* **1949** 393

Hodgkinson, William Wadsworth
- Creates Paramount Pictures Corporation **15/07/14** 108

Hodiak, John
- *Lifeboat* **12/01/44** 340

Hoff, Halvard 09/02/20 144

Hoffman, Dustin
- Born in U.S. **08/08/37** 276
- *The Graduate* **21/12/67** 571
- *Midnight Cowboy* **25/05/69** 587
- *Little Big Man* **14/12/70** 603
- *Papillon* **17/12/73** 631
- *Lenny* **1974** 642
- *All the President's Men* **08/04/76** 658
- *Marathon Man* **23/09/76** 654
- *Kramer vs. Kramer* **19/12/79** 690
- Academy Award **14/04/80** 699
- *Tootsie* **17/12/82** 723
- *Ishtar* **07/12/88** 782
- *Rain Man* **16/12/88** 783
- Academy Award **29/03/89** 789
- *Hook* **1991** 820
- Signs three-year contract with Columbia TriStar **12/08/91** 810

Hoffman, Günther
- *The Bridge* **1959** 491

Hofschneider, Marco
- *Europa, Europa* **1990** 809

Hogan, Paul
- *Crocodile Dundee* **26/09/86** 762

Holden, William
- *Sunset Boulevard* **10/08/50** 402
- *Born Yesterday* **26/12/50** 403
- *The Moon is Blue* **04/06/53** 425
- Academy Award for *Stalag 17* **25/03/54** 434
- *The Country Girl* **30/03/54** 442
- *The Bridge on the River Kwai* **29/11/57** 467
- *The Wild Bunch* **18/06/69** 588
- *The Towering Inferno* **18/12/74** 641
- *Network* **14/11/76** 660
- Dies in California **16/08/81** 706

Holger-Madsen, Forest
- *Opium Dreams* **24/04/14** 104
- *Put down Your Arms* **18/09/15** 110
- *400 Million Leagues under the Earth* **22/02/18** 128

Holland, Agnieszka
- *Europa, Europa* **1990** 809

Holliday, Judy
- *Adam's Rib* **25/12/49** 384
- *Born Yesterday* **26/12/50** 403
- Academy Award **29/03/51** 408
- *Bells Are Ringing* **1960** 503
- Dies in New York **07/06/65** 546

Holloway, Stanley
- *Hamlet* **05/09/48** 380
- *Passport to Pimlico* **01/04/49** 386
- *The Lavender Hill Mob* **1951** 412
- *My Fair Lady* **21/10/64** 542

Holly, Lauren
- *Dragon: The Bruce Lee Story* **1993** 843

Hollywood
- *The Count of Monte Cristo* first movie filmed in California **02/02/08** 68
- Opening of first studio in Hollywood by Selig Company **01/11/09** 76
- David Horsley builds studio in Hollywood **02/10/11** 86
- Keystone cameras come to Hollywood **23/09/12** 96
- Cecil B. DeMille begins shooting Western *The Squaw Man* **29/12/13** 103
- Founding of Columbia Pictures **10/01/24** 168
- Norma Talmadge makes first footprints at Grauman's Chinese **19/05/27** 191
- Screen Writers Guild call for strike **16/01/60** 494
- "Disaster" films a new Hollywood genre **18/12/74** 641
- Hollywood acknowledges Vietnam War in Academy Awards **09/04/79** 685
- Sylvester Stallone is the most highly paid actor **01/08/86** 761
- Centenary celebration **27/02/87** 766
- Harvey Wilcox registers land subdivision as Hollywood Ranch **27/02/87** 766
- Movie profession worried by series of helicopter accidents **07/07/89** 786
- Growth in movie attendance **31/12/89** 792
- Six major studios undergo high-tech renovations **19/07/93** 832
- *Philadelphia* first mainstream movie about AIDS **22/12/93** 841

Hollywood General Studios
- Bought by Francis Ford Coppola **11/03/80** 696

***Hollywood Reporter* 10/02/70** 598

***Hollywood Story, The* 22/04/88** 776

Hollywood Ten
- Directors, producers and writers blacklisted by HUAC **26/11/47** 373
- Supreme court refuses to hear appeal of two of Hollywood Ten **10/04/50** 396

Holm, Astrid
- *Master of the House* **05/10/25** 174

Holm, Celeste
- Academy Award for *Gentlemen's Agreement* **20/03/48** 378

Holmes, Phillips
- *An American Tragedy* **22/08/31** 228

Holt, Janny 07/12/36 266

Holt, Tim
- *The Magnificent Ambersons* **01/07/42** 328

Holton, Mark
- *Pee Wee's Big Adventure* **1985** 755

Homolka, Oscar 27/01/78 674

Hooper, Tobe
- *The Texas Chainsaw Massacre* **18/10/74** 641

Hope, Bob
- Born in England **29/05/03** 46
- *Road to Singapore* **13/03/40** 308
- *Road to Zanzibar* **11/04/41** 319
- *Road to Morocco* **1942** 330
- *The Greatest Show on Earth* **02/01/52** 416
- *Paris Holiday* **26/02/71** 608

N

- To co-produce *Popeye* **22/12/79** 682
- Lansing and Jaffe sign five-year rights agreement **03/01/83** 726
- *Trading Places* **08/06/83** 730
- Barry Diller resigns **01/10/84** 736
- *Terms of Endearment* **09/11/84** 740
- *Beverly Hills Cop* **05/12/84** 743
- *Clue* **13/12/85** 746
- Accounts for 20% of total distribution takings for the year **31/12/87** 766
- *Ghost* **22/08/90** 798
- Out-take footage available for hire **25/01/93** 832
- Studios undergo high-tech renovations **19/07/93** 832
- Sherry Lansing appointed chairman of Motion Picture Group **04/11/93** 832
- Acquired by Viacom Inc. **16/02/94** 846

Paramount-Publix 17/06/35 258

Parillaud, Anne
- Born in France **06/05/60** 494
- *Pour la peau d'un flic* **09/09/81** 706
- *Nikita* **21/02/90** 800
- César award **13/03/91** 813

Paris
- First public film projection by the Lumière brothers **22/03/1895** 16
- Fifth Lumière Cinematograph opens **03/1897** 24
- Clément Maurice opens Phono-Cinéma-Théâtre **01/11/00** 34
- Henri Langlois founds *La Cinémathographique Française* **02/09/36** 271
- Henri Langlois founds the FIAF **15/07/38** 291
- Henri Langlois inaugurates first cinema museum **26/10/48** 376
- Opening of Video Library **07/02/88** 776
- Disneyland opens **12/04/92** 825

***Paris-Match* 30/09/64** 541

Paris Video Library
- Opening **07/02/88** 776

Parisy, Andréa
- *Youthful Sinners* **10/10/58** 476
- *Greed in the Sun* **1964** 544

Parker, Alan
- Born in England **14/02/44** 340
- *Bugsy Malone* **10/08/78** 678
- *Midnight Express* **10/08/78** 678
- *Birdy* **20/05/85** 750
- *Mississippi Burning* **09/12/88** 782
- *The Commitments* **1991** 820

Parker, Albert
- *The Black Pirate* **08/03/26** 183

Parker, Dorothy 26/09/37 283

Parker, Eleanor
- Venice award for *Caged* **10/09/50** 396

Parker, Jean
- *The Ghost Goes West* **17/11/35** 258

Parker, Sarah Jessica
- *L.A. Story* **08/02/91** 812

Parks, Gordon
- *Shaft* **23/06/71** 610

Parks, Larry
- *The Jolson Story* **10/10/46** 362
- Admits membership of Communist Party **21/03/51** 406
- Dies in California **13/04/75** 644

Parlo, Dita
- *L'Atalante* **05/10/34** 254

Parnaland, François
- Inventor of Photothéagraph **08/04/00** 34

Parretti, Giancarlo
- Buys MGM/UA **01/11/90** 805

Parrot, James 21/08/131 224

Parsons, Estelle
- *Bonnie and Clyde* **14/08/67** 569

Parsons, Louella 09/12/72 616

Parton, Dolly
- *Nine to Five* **1980** 705
- *The Best Little Whorehouse in Texas* **1982** 724

Parvo, Elli 09/08/46 356

Pascal, Gabriel
- Co-directs *Pygmalion* **02/12/38** 292

Pasolini, Pier Paolo
- Born in Italy **05/03/22** 156
- Expelled from Communist Party **26/10/49** 384
- *Accatone* **23/11/61** 511
- *Mama Roma* **22/09/62** 514
- Taken to court for filming *La Ricotta* **01/03/63** 529
- Collective film *RoGoPaG* **01/03/63** 529
- Venice award for *The Gospel According to Saint Matthew* **10/09/64** 541
- Venice award for *Theorem* **18/09/68** 580
- *Decameron* **13/11/71** 606
- Directs and acts in *The Canterbury Tales* **07/10/72** 616
- Cannes award for *The Arabian Nights* **24/05/74** 638
- *Salo or the 120 days of Sodom* **01/11/75** 650
- Found murdered **01/11/75** 650
- Release of *Comizi d'Amore* **16/03/77** 664

Passer, Ivan
- *Intimate Lighting* **18/11/66** 560

Pasternak, Joe
- *The Great Caruso* **10/05/51** 409
- Dies in Los Angeles **13/09/91** 810

Pastrone, Giovanni
- To work with Carlo Rossi **04/07** 62
- Founds Itala Film **15/09/08** 66
- *The Fall of Troy* **07/04/11** 86
- Patents the Carello **05/08/12** 95
- *Cabiria* **18/04/14** 107
- *Il Fuoco* **01/04/16** 116
- To retire from cinema **27/02/17** 122

Pasztoory, Miklos 31/12/17 122

Pathé, Charles
- Gives demonstration of Edison phonograph **09/09/1894** 14
- Buys copy of Edison's Kinetoscope **02/1895** 16
- Patents a chronophotographic machine **26/08/1895** 16
- Founds Pathé Frères **01/10/1896** 20
- Founding of General Company of Cinematographs **28/12/1897** 26
- Opens studio at Vincennes **06/1898** 29
- *The Dreyfus Affair* **11/1899** 31
- Increases production **01/01** 38
- Takes on Ferdinand Zecca as head of production **19/10/01** 41
- Builds new studio at Vincennes **10/10/03** 48
- *Fire in the Chicago Theater* **01/03/04** 48
- Has international ambitions **31/07/04** 53
- Opens showroom at Vincennes **16/02/05** 54
- Signs exclusive contract with Benoît-Lévy **12/07/07** 65
- Opens branches overseas **08/07** 62
- Refuses to take part in meeting against Edison **09/03/08** 66
- Principal shareholder in SCAGL **01/10/08** 70
- Attends International Congress of Film Producers **04/02/09** 74
- Competes with George Eastman **16/03/09** 75
- Builds large factory in Vincennes **31/08/10** 84
- Distributes Georges Méliès film **11/11/11** 91
- *Napoléon: Du sacre à Sainte-Hélène* **17/01/14** 104
- Reorganizes U.S. branch Pathé Exchange **31/10/14** 104
- Impressed by Abel Gance **12/10/17** 126
- Rapid Film merges with Pathé **03/07/29** 200
- Dies in Monte Carlo **25/12/57** 460

Pathé, Emile
- Founds Pathé Frères **01/10/1896** 20
- Founding of General Company of Cinematographs **28/12/1897** 26

Pathé-American (see Pathé)

Pathé-Cinéma (see Pathé)

Pathé Consortium (see also Pathé Frères)
- Opens new film studio **14/06/21** 152

Pathé-Exchange (U.S.)
- Reorganization of U.S. branch by Charles Pathé **31/10/14** 104
- To export American films **05/15** 110
- *Mysteries of New York* **03/12/15** 115
- *The Exploits of Elaine* **03/12/15** 115

Pathé Frères (France)
- Founding of company **01/10/1896** 20
- Founding of General Company of Cinematographs **28/12/1897** 26
- A thriving concern **13/07/1899** 30
- *Episodes of the Transvaal War* **01/01/00** 34
- Makes Maltese Cross camera **10/09/00** 34
- Takes over Bünzli and Continsouza's precision camera factory **10/09/00** 34
- *The Czar in France* **21/09/01** 38
- Has produced 70 films in the year **31/12/01** 38
- *The President in Russia* **31/05/02** 42
- *The King of Spain's Coronation* **31/05/02** 42
- *The Marvellous Doll* **31/05/02** 42
- *The Victims of Alcoholism* **31/05/02** 42
- *La Vie d'un joueur* **05/04/03** 46
- *Métamorphoses d'un Papillon* **11/06/04** 48
- Expanding abroad **31/07/04** 53
- *The Apaches of Paris* **1905** 54
- Opening of salon **1905** 57
- Releases *Ten Women for One Husband* **15/04/05** 54
- *The Life and Passion of Jesus Christ* **28/07/05** 57
- *A Schoolboy's First Day Out* **05/08/05** 54
- *La Course à la perruque* **15/08/06** 58
- Opens first venue in Paris **15/12/06** 61
- *Aladdin and his Magic Lamp* **01/01/07** 62
- *The Life and Passion of Christ* **01/04/07** 62
- *Struggle for Life* **01/06/07** 62
- Setting up monopoly **15/04/08** 68
- Puts *L'Arlésienne* on sale **01/10/08** 70
- *A Man Who Follows Women* **13/11/08** 66
- Joins Edison trust **04/02/09** 74
- Launches weekly newsreel **31/03/09** 75
- *The Death of Ivan the Terrible* **10/10/09** 72
- To hire out films only **28/02/10** 80
- *The Girl from Montana* **16/05/10** 80
- *The Secret Adventure of Marie Antoinette* **10/06/10** 83
- *The Samurai's Punishment* **27/08/10** 80
- Improves on 'Pathécolor' process **28/08/10** 84
- Builds large factory in Vincennes **31/08/10** 84
- *The Tragic Adventure of Robert the Taciturn* **01/10/10** 80
- *Rigadin goes into the Wide World* **29/10/10** 80
- *The Inventor* **26/11/10** 80
- *Anna Karenina* **04/03/11** 86
- *The Victims of Alcohol* **20/05/11** 86
- *Max and his Mother-in-Law* **17/06/11** 89
- *Nick Winter contre Nick Winter* **08/11** 89
- Distributes Georges Méliès film **11/11/11** 91
- *Little Moritz Hunts Big Game* **29/12/11** 86
- *The Paris Mysteries* **28/06/12** 92
- *The Amazing Waltz* **06/09/12** 92
- Méliès films unsuccessful **31/12/12** 97
- *A Curse on War* **23/05/14** 104
- Signs contract with André Antoine **01/07/14** 104
- Pathé-Exchange to export American films **05/15** 110
- *The Exploits of Elaine* **11/08/16** 116
- *Clubs are Trump* **12/07/17** 128
- *The Sea Workers* **03/03/18** 128
- Pathé Consortium opens new film studio **14/06/21** 152
- *The Three Musketeers* **01/01/22** 156
- Finances *la Roue* **17/02/23** 164
- Finances *Napoleon* **07/04/27** 190
- Pathé-Natan declared bankrupt **17/02/36** 266
- *Children of Paradise* **09/03/45** 351

Patinkin, Mandy
- *Yentl* **18/11/83** 732

Patric, Jason
- *The Lost Boys* **1987** 774

Paul, Robert William
- Intends to make the Kinetoscope **10/1894** 14
- Gives first public projection with Theatograph **24/03/1896** 20
- Founds the Paul Animatograph Company **04/1897** 24
- Invents the Cinematograph **04/1897** 24, **09/1899** 32

Paulin, Jean-Paul
- *Trois de Saint-Cyr* **25/01/39** 296

Paulin, Scott
- *The Right Stuff* **21/10/83** 732

Paull, Lawrence G 25/06/82 721

Paulvé, André
- *Children of Paradise* **09/03/45** 351

Pawle, Lennox
- *David Copperfield* **18/01/35** 260

Peak, Robert 01/08/92 822

Pech, Antonin 01/05/11 86

Peck, Gregory
- Born in U.S. **05/04/16** 116
- *Days of Glory* **16/06/44** 343
- *Spellbound* **01/11/45** 348
- *Gentleman's Agreement* **11/11/47** 373
- *Duel in the Sun* **12/47** 369
- Academy Award nomination **20/03/48** 378
- *Twelve O'Clock High* **1949** 393
- *The Gunfighter* **1950** 405
- Production shut down on *Quo Vadis?* **08/11/51** 411
- *Roman Holiday* **27/08/53** 427
- *The Guns of Navarone* **1961** 513
- *Cape Fear* **12/04/62** 517
- *To Kill a Mockingbird* **25/12/62** 523
- Academy Award **08/04/63** 530
- Wins Jean Hersholt Award **10/04/67** 564
- *The Omen* **1976** 663

Peckinpah, Sam
- *Major Dundee* **18/06/69** 588
- *The Wild Bunch* **18/06/69** 588
- *Cross of Iron* **1977** 673
- Dies in California **28/12/84** 736

Peerce, Larry
- *Goodbye, Columbus* **1969** 592

Peirse, Sarah 16/11/94 851

Pellonpää, Matti 18/10/86 756

Pendleton, Austin
- *Catch 22* **24/06/70** 602

Penn, Arthur
- *Bonnie and Clyde* **14/08/67** 569
- *Little Big Man* **14/12/70** 603
- *Night Moves* **1975** 652

Penn, Christopher
- *Rumble Fish* **09/10/83** 732

Penn, Sean
- Born in U.S. **17/08/60** 494
- Marries Madonna **16/08/85** 746
- *Casualties of War* **18/08/89** 791

Pens Rode, Nina
- *Gertrud* **01/01/65** 546

Peploe, Mark (screenwriter)
- Academy Award for *The Last Emperor* **11/04/88** 778

Peppard, George
- *Breakfast at Tiffany's* **05/11/61** 509
- Dies in Los Angeles **08/05/94** 844

Pera, Marilia
- *Pixote* **11/09/81** 711

Pereira dos Santos, Nelson
- Born in Brazil **22/10/28** 194
- *Vidas Secas* **24/08/63** 526

Perelman, S.J. 18/10/56 456

Pérès, Marcel
- *Children of Paradise* **09/03/45** 351

Perestiani, Ivan 25/10/23 162

Perez, Vincent
- *Cyrano de Bergerac* **28/03/90** 801
- *Indochine* **15/04/92** 825

Périer, François
- Born in France **10/11/19** 134
- *Silence is Golden* **29/06/47** 370

Périnal, Georges 10/03/41 319

Perkins, Anthony
- Born in U.S. **04/04/32** 232
- *Tall Story* **17/04/60** 494
- *Psycho* **10/08/60** 499
- *Is Paris Burning?* **13/10/66** 559
- Directs and stars in *Psycho II* **30/06/82** 716
- Dies in Hollywood **12/09/92** 822

Perkins, Elizabeth
- Born in U.S. **18/11/60** 494
- *Big* **03/06/88** 779

Perkins, Millie
- *The Diary of Anne Frank* **18/03/58** 482

Pernet, André 24/08/39 296

Perret, Léonce
- *Molière* **10/09/10** 84
- Directs and stars in *In the Midst of Life* **04/02/11** 86
- *Lest We Forget* **22/09/18** 128
- *Madame Sans-Gêne* **20/04/25** 177

Perrin, Jacques
- Born in France **13/07/41** 316
- *Family Diary* **08/09/62** 519
- *The Young Girls of Rochefort* **08/03/67** 566
- *Crabe-Tambour* **09/11/77** 664

Perugorria, Jorge 1994 *853*

Pesci, Joe
- *GoodFellas* **19/09/90** 805
- Academy Award **25/03/91** 813
- *JFK* **20/12/91** 819

Peters, Bernadette
- *Pennies From Heaven* **1981** 714

Peters, Brock
- *To Kill a Mockingbird* **25/12/62** 523

Peters, Jon
- To head Japanese-owned Columbia Pictures **25/11/89** 786
- *Batman* **31/12/89** 792

Petersen, Axel 11/06/28 194

Petersen, Wolfgang
- *Das Boot* **15/09/81** 711
- *In the Line of Fire* **09/07/93** 837

Peterson, Oscar 10/10/58 476

Petit, Pascale
- *Youthful Sinners* **10/10/58** 476

Petit-Demange, Charles 29/10/10 80

Petri, Elio
- Born in Italy **29/01/29** 200
- Cannes award for *Investigation of a Citizen Above Suspicion* **16/05/70** 601
- Academy Award **15/04/71** 609
- Cannes award for *Lulu the Tool* **19/05/72** 620

Petrov, Vladimir
- *Peter the Great* Part II **07/03/39** 296
- *Peter the Great* Part I wins award at Karlovy-Vary Festival **07/08/49** 388

Pfeiffer, Michelle
- Born in U.S. **29/04/59** 480
- *Scarface* **09/12/83** 733
- *Married to the Mob* **29/08/88** 776
- *Dangerous Liaisons* **21/12/88** 783
- *The Fabulous Baker Boys* **13/09/89** 791
- *Batman Returns* **22/06/92** 826
- *The Age of Innocence* **17/09/93** 838
- *Wolf* **1994** *853*

Phalke, D.G. (Dhundiraj Govind)
- *Raja Harishchandra* **05/05/13** 100

Phantascope
- Invented by Thomas Armat **25/03/1895** 16

Philbin, Mary
- *The Phantom of the Opera* **15/11/25** 179

Philipe, Gérard
- Born in France **04/12/22** 156
- *Devil in the Flesh* **29/06/47** 370
- *Riptide* **20/01/49** 384
- *La Ronde* **17/06/50** 401
- *Fanfan the Tulip* **20/03/52** 416
- *Les Orgueilleux* **03/04/53** 422
- *Monsieur Ripois* **08/07/53** 422, **1954** 438
- Cannes award for *Knave of Hearts* **09/04/54** 435
- *Modigliani of Montparnasse* **04/04/58** 473
- Dies in Paris **25/11/59** 480
- Release of *Republic of Sin* **06/01/60** 496

Protazanov, Yakov
- *Anfissa* **24/01/12** 92
- *Father Sergius* **31/05/18** 131
- *Aelita* **25/10/24** 168
- *The Forty First* **13/12/27** 193
Provine, Dorothy
- *It's a Mad, Mad, Mad, Mad World* **07/11/63** 532
Pryce, Jonathan
- *Brazil* **29/06/85** 748
Pryor, Richard
- Born in U.S. **01/12/40** 308
- *Car Wash* **1976** 662
Pszoniak, Wojtek
- *Korczak* **09/01/91** 812
Ptouchko, Alexander
- Silver Lion award for *Sadko* **04/09/53** 427
Publicité Animé 08/02/08 66
Pudovkin, Vsevolod
- Born in Russia **16/02/1893** 33
- *Chess Fever* **21/11/25** 174
- *Mother* **04/10/26** 180
- *The End of St. Petersburg* **13/12/27** 193
- Publishes manifesto *The Advent of Sound Film* **19/07/28** 197
- *Storm over Asia* **05/11/28** 194
- *Life is Beautiful* **05/01/31** 224
- *A Simple Case* **03/12/32** 232
Puenzo, Luis
- *The Official Story* **04/04/85** 746
Pujol, René
- Co-directs *Chacun sa chance* **19/12/30** 221
Pullman, Bill
- *Ruthless People* **27/06/86** 760
Pulver, Lilo (Liselotte)
- *One, Two, Three* **15/12/61** 511
- *La Religieuse* **15/04/66** 557
Purviance, Edna
- Co-stars in with Chaplin in *Work* **21/06/15** 114
- *The Floorwalker)* **15/05/16** 116
- *The Rink* **04/12/16** 121
- *The Adventurer* **20/10/17** 122
- *Sunnyside* **1919** 141
- Title role in *A Woman of Paris* **01/10/23** 166
- *The Sea Gull* **03/26** 180
- *The Education of Prince* **18/01/27** 186
- Small part in *Monsieur Verdoux* **01/05/46** 359
- Brief appearance in *Limelight* **23/10/52** 419
- Dies in California **13/01/58** 470
Puttnam, David
- Academy Award for *Chariots of Fire* **29/03/82** 719
- *The Killing Fields* **02/09/84** 743
- Appointed chairman of Columbia Pictures **01/09/86** 756
- Resigns as chairman of Columbia Pictures **18/09/87** 766
Puzo, Mario 08/04/75 646

Q

Quadflieg, Will
- *Lola Montès* **22/12/55** 447
Quaid, Dennis
- Born in U.S. **09/04/54** 432
- *Breaking Away* **1979** 693
- *The Right Stuff* **21/10/83** 732
- *The Big Easy* **21/08/87** 771
Quaid, Randy
- *The Last Detail* **1973** 633
Quellien, Georges 27/02/14 104
Queseda, Enrique Diaz 06/08/13 98
Quigley, Martin 17/02/30 216
Quimby, Fred (animator)
- *Puss Gets the Boot* **10/02/40** 310
Quinn, Aidan 08/03/59 480
Quinn, Anthony
- *La Strada* **07/09/54** 436
- *Heller in Pink Tights* **17/04/60** 494
- *The Guns of Navarone* **1961** 513
- *Zorba the Greek* **05/04/65** 549
Quintina, Rosita
- *Susana* **11/04/51** 406

R

Rabal, Francisco
- *Nazarin* **04/06/59** 485
- *Viridiana* **16/03/77** 664
Rabier, Benjamin
- *The Adventures of Clémentine* **15/06/17** 122
Radios Society
- Signs contract with aviator Wilbur Wright **22/03/09** 75
Radziwilowicz, Jerzy
- *Man of Marble* **25/02/77** 667
Rafelson, Bob
- *Head* **1968** 582
- *Five Easy Pieces* **12/09/70** 602
- *Stay Hungry* **1976** 663
- *Brubaker* **09/04/79** 682
- *The Postman Always Rings Twice* **20/01/81** 709
- *Mountains of the Moon* **20/04/90** 802
Raff, Charles
- Opens first Kinetoscope Parlor with Frank Gammon **14/04/1894** 14
- Buys Vitascope **15/01/1896** 20
Raft, George
- *I Am a Fugitive from a Chain Gang* **11/10/32** 237
- *Scarface* **11/10/32** 237
- *The Bowery* **04/10/33** 240
- *Bolero* **1934** 256
- Turns down part in *Double Indemnity* **06/09/44** 343
- *Around the World in 80 Days* **18/10/56** 456
- *Some Like It Hot* **29/03/59** 483
- Dies in New York **24/11/80** 696
Rahn, Bruno
- *The Tragedy of the Streets* **15/06/28** 194
Raimondi, Ruggero
- *Don Giovanni* **14/11/79** 689
- *Carmen* **14/03/84** 739
Raimu
- Born in France **17/12/1883** 33
- *Marius* **17/10/31** 224
- *Fanny* **23/01/37** 278
- *César* **23/01/37** 278
- *Gribouille* **08/06/37** 276
- *Dance Card* **07/09/37** 281
- *The Strange Mr. Victor* **13/05/38** 286
- *The Baker's Wife* **08/09/38** 292
- *L'Assassinat du Père Noël* **31/12/41** 321
- Dies in France **20/09/46** 356
Rainer, Luise
- Academy Award for *The Great Ziegfeld* **04/03/37** 279
- Academy Award for *The Good Earth* **10/03/38** 289
Rainous, William
- Founds Independent Motion Pictures (IMP) **12/03/09** 72
Rains, Claude
- *The Invisible Man* **13/05/37** 262
- *Casablanca* **1942** 330, **23/01/43** 334
- *Notorious* **22/07/46** 359
- *The Passionate Friends* **26/01/49** 384
- Dies in New Hampshire **30/05/67** 564
Raizman, Yuli (also Yuri)
- *The Last Night* **02/02/37** 276
- *Dream of a Cossack* **29/07/51** 406
Ralston, Gilbert A. 18/06/71 610
Ralston, Jobyna
- *Why Worry* **02/09/23** 165
Rambaldi, Carlo
- Creator of *E.T.* **131982** 721
Rambova, Natasha 21/04/22 160
Ramis, Harold
- *National Lampoon's Animal House* **28/07/78** 677
- *Caddyshack* **1980** 704
- *Ghostbusters* **08/06/84** 740
- *Groundhog Day* **12/02/93** 834
Rampling, Charlotte
- Born in England **05/02/46** 356
- *The Damned* **28/05/69** 588
- *The Flesh of the Orchid* **29/01/75** 644
- *Stardust Memories* **26/09/80** 696
- *The Verdict* **08/12/82** 722
Rand, Ayn 08/07/49 388
Randall, Tony
- *Will Success Spoil Rock Hunter?* **08/02/57** 462
Rank, J. Arthur
- Finances *Henry V* **30/11/44** 345
- *Great Expectations* **27/01/46** 358
Rankin, Caroline
- *Be My Wife* **06/12/21** 150
Rank Organisation
- Founds J. Arthur Rank Productions Ltd. **18/01/45** 348
Ransohoff, Martin
- *The Americanization of Emily* **18/03/64** 536
Raphael, Frederic 03/08/65 550
Rapid Film 03/07/29 200
Rappe, Virginia
- Fatty Arbuckle charged with death **10/09/21** 153
- Fatty Arbuckle cleared **18/04/22** 159
Rappeneau, Jean-Paul
- Screenwriter for *Zazie dans le métro* **28/10/60** 500
- Directs *Cyrano de Bergerac* **28/03/90** 801
- César awards for *Cyrano de Bergerac* **13/03/91** 813
Rapper, Irving
- *Now, Voyager* **31/10/42** 328
Ratcliffe, Sandy
- *Family Life* **1972** 622
Rathbone, Basil
- *David Copperfield* **18/01/35** 260
- *The Garden of Allah* **1936** 274
- *The Adventures of Marco Polo* **07/04/38** 286
- *The Adventures of Robin Hood* **12/05/38** 290
- *The Hound of the Baskervilles* **11/09/39** 302
- *The Court Jester* **01/02/56** 452
- Dies in New York **21/07/67** 564
Ratoff, Gregory
- *Intermezzo: A Love Story* **05/10/39** 302
Ray, Aldo 27/03/91 810
Ray, Nicholas
- Born in U.S. **07/08/11** 86
- *They Live by Night* **04/11/49** 384
- Interruption of filming of *Rebel Without a Cause* **04/04/55** 440
- *Rebel Without a Cause* **01/10/55** 445
- *55 Days at Peking* **1963** 534
- Dies in New York **02/06/79** 682
Ray, Satyajit
- Born in India **02/05/21** 150
- *Pather Panchali* **11/05/56** 453
- Venice award for *Aparajito* **09/09/57** 466
- *The Music Room* **1958** 479
- *The World of Apu* **14/09/59** 486
- *Charulata* **1965** 553
- Presides at Indian Film Festival **30/12/74** 634
- *The Chess Player* **12/02/78** 674
- Dies in Calcutta **23/04/92** 822
Raye, Martha
- *Monsieur Verdoux* **11/04/47** 369
Rea, Steven
- *Prêt à Porter* **10/03/94** 844
Read, Dolly
- *Beyond the Valley of the Dolls* **17/06/70** 601
Reagan, Nancy
- *Hellcats of the Navy* **07/09/60** 494
Reagan, Ronald
- Born in U.S. **06/02/11** 86
- Signs 7-year contract with Warner Bros. **30/06/37** 276
- *King's Row* **24/12/41** 321
- President of Screen Actor's Guild **13/03/47** 368
- *Bedtime for Bonzo* **1951** 413
- Marries Nancy Davis **04/03/52** 416
- *Hellcats of the Navy* **07/09/60** 494
- Elected Republican governor **09/11/66** 560
- Elected President of the United States **04/11/80** 696
Rebot, Saddy 22/09/62 520
Redd, Mary Robin
- *The Group* **1966** 563
Redford, Robert
- Born in U.S. **18/08/37** 276
- Opens ski resort **31/08/68** 574
- *Butch Cassidy and the Sundance Kid* **23/09/69** 590
- *The Candidate* **29/06/72** 621
- *The Sting* **1973** 624
- *The Great Gatsby* **06/06/73** 624
- *The Way We Were* **17/10/73** 630
- Acquires rights of *All the President's Men* **07/03/74** 634
- *The Great Waldo Pepper* **1975** 652
- *All the President's Men* **08/04/76** 658
- Directs *Ordinary People* **19/09/80** 701
- Academy Award **31/03/81** 709
- *The Natural* **1984** 745
- Directs *A River Runs Through It* **09/10/92** 827
- Creates Sundance Institute in 1985 **31/01/93** 834
- Sundance Institute founds the Sundance Festival **31/01/93** 834
- Directs *Quiz Show* **16/09/94** 850
- Sundance Festival **02/02/95** 857
Redgrave, Michael
- *The Lady Vanishes* **1938** 294
- Cannes award for *The Browning Version* **20/04/51** 409
- *Oh! What a Lovely War* **10/04/69** 586
- *The Go-Between* **24/09/71** 611
- Dies in England **02/03/85** 746
Redgrave, Vanessa
- Born in England **30/01/37** 276
- *Blow Up* **18/12/66** 561
- *Camelot* **1967** 570
- *Oh! What a Lovely War* **10/04/69** 586
- Cannes award for *Isadora* **23/05/69** 587
- Academy Award for *Julia* **03/04/78** 676
- *The Palestinian* **15/06/78** 674
Reed, Angela
- *The Picture of Dorian Gray* **01/03/45** 348
Reed, Carol
- *Odd Man Out* **06/02/47** 368
- Cannes award **17/09/49** 389
- Starts filming *Mutiny on the Bounty* **28/11/60** 494
- Leaves *Mutiny on the Bounty* **25/02/61** 504
- Academy Awards for *Oliver!* **14/04/69** 586
- Dies in London **25/04/76** 654
Reed, Donna
- *They Were Expendable* **1945** 355
- Academy Award for *From Here to Eternity* **25/03/54** 434
Reed, Luther 06/10/29 206
Reeve, Christopher
- Born in U.S. **25/09/52** 414
- *Superman* **15/12/78** 679
Reeves, Keanu
- Born in Lebanon **02/09/64** 536
- *Bill and Ted's Excellent Adventure* **1989** 794
- *My Own Private Idaho* **14/09/91** 817
- *Much Ado About Nothing* **07/05/93** 835
- *Little Buddha* **25/05/94** 849
- *Speed* **10/06/94** 848
Reggiani, Serge
- Born in Italy **05/03/22** 156
- *The Lovers of Verona* **07/03/49** 386
- *La Ronde* **17/06/50** 401
- *Casque-d'or* **24/09/51** 406
Reggio, Godfrey
- *Koyaanisqatsi* **27/04/82** 716
Rei, Geraldo del
- *Mudar de Vida* **20/04/67** 564
Reichhardt, Paul 26/12/45 348
Reid, Wallace
- *Carmen* **01/10/15** 110
- *The Affairs of Anatol* **18/09/21** 154
- Dies of drug addiction **19/01/22** 164
Reiner, Carl
- *The Jerk* **1979** 693
- *All of Me* **21/09/84** 742
Reiner, Rob
- *This is Spinal Tap* **1984** 744
- *When Harry Met Sally* **12/07/89** 791
- *A Few Good Men* **11/12/92** 822
Reinhardt, Max
- *The Island of Happiness* **03/10/13** 98
- *Sumurun* **01/09/20** 144
Reinhardt, Wolfgang
- *Freud* **13/12/62** 522
Reinhold, Judge
- *Ruthless People* **27/06/86** 760
Reisz, Karel
- *Isadora* **23/05/69** 587
- *Who'll Stop the Rain?* **1978** 681
- *The French Lieutenant's Woman* **18/09/81** 712
- *Sweet Dreams* **1985** 755
Reitman, Ivan
- *Ghostbusters* **08/06/84** 740
Réjane, Gabrielle
- *Madame Sans-Gêne* **10/11/11** 91
- Dies in Paris **29/10/20** 149
Rellys
- *Manon des Sources* **16/01/53** 422
Remick, Lee
- Born in U.S. **14/12/35** 258
- *A Face in the Crowd* **28/05/57** 464
- *Anatomy of a Murder* **06/07/59** 486
- *Days of Wine and Roses* **26/12/62** 523
- Dies in California **02/07/91** 810
Renant, Simone
- *Quai des Orfèvres* **03/10/47** 372
Renard, Jules
- *Redhead* **07/12/32** 232
Renaud
- *Germinal* **29/09/93** 838
Renaud, Madeleine
- Born in France **21/02/03** 46
- *John of the Moon* **10/11/30** 214
- *Maria Chapdelaine* **19/12/34** 250
- *The Strange Mr. Victor* **13/05/38** 286
- Marries Jean-Louis Barrault **05/09/40** 308
- *Hélène* **05/09/40** 308
- *Le Dialogue des Carmélites* **10/06/60** 494
Renault-Decker, G 15/02/39 296
Rennie, James 13/07/20 148
Reno, Jean
- *The Big Blue* **11/05/88** 779
- *Léon (The Professional)* **03/02/95** 857
Renoir, Jean
- Born in France **15/09/1894** 33
- Marries Andrée Heuschling **24/01/20** 144
- *Nana* starring wife now called Catherine Hessling **14/08/26** 180
- *Voyage to the Congo* **31/03/27** 186
- Has bad car accident **31/05/27** 186
- *La Chienne* **19/11/31** 229
- *Boudu Saved from Drowning* **11/11/32** 232
- *Madame Bovary* **03/02/34** 252
- *A Day in the Country* **20/08/36** 271
- *The Lower Depths* **20/08/36** 271
- Louis Delluc prize for *The Lower Depths* **22/12/36** 273
- *The Grand Illusion* **08/06/37** 280
- Venice award for *The Grand Illusion* **03/09/37** 281
- *The Crime of Monsieur Lange* **24/01/38** 268
- *La Marseillaise* **09/02/38** 288
- *La Bête humaine* **21/12/38** 293
- *The Rules of the Game* **22/07/39** 300
- Goes to America **20/12/40** 308
- Signs contract with 20th Century-Fox **15/01/41** 316
- *Swamp Water* **28/10/41** 316
- *This Land is Mine* **27/05/43** 336
- *Vivre Libre* **06/02/44** 340
- Venice award for *The Southerner* **01/09/46** 362
- *French Cancan* **271954** 443
- *Eléna et les hommes* **12/09/56** 455
- *The Vanishing Corporal* **20/04/67** 564
- Receives Legion of Honor **02/01/76** 656
- Dies in Beverly Hills **13/02/79** 684
Renoir, Pierre
- *Madame Bovary* **03/02/34** 252
- *La Marseillaise* **09/02/38** 288
- *Macao, l'enfer du jeu* **16/12/42** 324
- *Children of Paradise* **09/03/45** 351
Resnais, Alain
- Born in France **03/06/22** 156
- *Hiroshima mon amour* **16/05/59** 484
- Withdraws film from Cannes Festival **18/05/68** 579

S

W

XYZ

Film Index

In this index, dates are followed by pages numbers in roman or italic. Those in italic refer to illustrated films with no text.

C

D

G

H

IJK

L

M

N

O

P

T

UV

W

XYZ

Picture credits

Whilst every effort has been made to trace the Copyright of the photographs and illustrations used in this publication, there may be a possibility where an inadvertent error has been made in the picture credit. If this is the case, we apologize for the mistake and ask the copyright holder to contact the publisher so that it can be rectified.

The position of the pictures are indicated by letters: b=bottom, t=top, r=right, l=left, m=middle, x=middle left, y=middle right, sp=spread.

The following agency names have been abbreviated. Full names are:

BFI: BFI Stills, Posters and Design
Carson: The Carson Collection (Richard Allen)
Cinémathèque: Cinémathèque Française
Columbia: Columbia Pictures
Disney: The Walt Disney Company
Ent. Film Dist.: Entertainment Film Distributors
Finler: Joel Finler
Fox: 20th Century-Fox
Grant: Ronald Grant Archive
Kharbine: Kharbine-Tapabor
Kipa: Kipa-Interpress
Kobal: The Kobal Collection
Sipa: Sipa-Press
UA: United Artists
Warners: Warner Bros

1 – Finler, sp
12 – Fox, courtesy Kobal, sp
14 – RR/Cinémagence, tr, br – RR/Coll. Pierre Lherminier, mr
15 – All RR/Cinémagence
16 – RR/Cinémagence, bm – RR/Coll. Pierre Lherminier, tr
17 – RR/Cinémagence, br – RR/Coll. Larousse, tm – RR/Coll. Maurice Gianati, bl – RR/Coll. Pierre Lherminier, tr – RR/Kharbine, tl
18 – All RR/Coll. Maurice Gianati
19 – RR/Cinémagence, mr, bl – RR/Coll. Cinémathèque, br – RR/Coll. Pierre Lherminier, tm – RR/Kharbine, tl
20 – All RR/Cinémagence
21 – RR/Archives L'Avant-Scène, bl – RR/Cinémagence, tl, br
22 – RR/De Selva-Tapabor
23 – RR/Coll. Maurice Gianati, br
24 – Sygma/L'Illustration, br
25 – RR/Coll. Pierre Lherminier, mm – Sygma/L'Illustration, tl, bl, br
26 – RR/Cinémagence, bl – RR/Cinémagence, mr – RR/Coll. André Marinie, tr
27 – All RR/Ciné-Plus
28 – RR/Cinémagence, mr
29 – RR/Coll. Maurice Gianati, br – Sygma/L'Illustration, tl, tm, tr
30 – RR/Cinémagence, br
31 – RR/Ciné-Plus, bl – RR/Coll. Cinémathèque, tr
32 – Archives du film/C.N.C., tr – RR/Cinémagence, bm
34 – Finler, bm
35 – RR/Cinémagence, sp
36 – RR/Ciné-Plus, tl, br – RR/Kharbine, bl
37 – RR/Cinémagence, tl – RR/Coll. Cinémathèque, r – RR/Coll. Pierre Lherminier, mm
38 – RR/Ciné-Plus, bm
39 – RR/Coll. Cinémathèque, sp
40 – BFI, tm – RR/Ciné-Plus, br
41 – BFI, bl – RR/Cinémagence, tl – RR/Coll. Cinémathèque, br
42 and 43 – All RR/Ciné-Plus
44 – RR/Cinémagence, br – RR/Cinémagence, tr
45 – RR/Ciné-Plus, bl – RR/Cinémagence, tr
46 – Finler, br
47 – RR/Cinémagence, sp
48 – BFI, bl – RR/Ciné-Plus, br – RR/Cinémagence, tr
49 – RR/Ciné-Plus, bl – RR/Cinémagence, tr – RR/DITE, br
50 – RR/Ciné-Plus,
51 – RR/Cinémagence, sp
52 – RR/Ciné-Plus, bl – RR/Coll. Maurice Gianati, br – Finler, tr
53 – RR/Ciné-Plus, bl – RR/Cinémagence, br – RR/Coll. Maurice Gianati, tr
54 and 55 – All RR/Cinémagence
56 – Finler, tr
57 – RR/Ciné-Plus, tr – RR/Coll. Maurice Gianati, br
58 – Finler
59 – RR/Cinémagence, sp
60 – RR/Ciné-Plus, bl – RR/Cinémagence, br – RR/Roger Viollet, tm, tr
61 – BFI, br – RR/Cinémagence, tl, tr
63 – RR/Cinémagence, sp
64 – BFI, br – RR/Ciné-Plus, ml, tr
65 – BFI, bm – RR/Cinémagence, ml, mr
67 – RR/Cinémagence, sp
68 – RR/Ciné-Plus, tr – RR/Coll. Maurice Gianati, bl, br
69 – RR/Cinémagence, br – RR/Coll. Maurice Gianati, tr
70 – RR/Ciné-Plus, bl – RR/Cinémagence, br – Sygma/L'Illustration, tr
71 – RR/Cinémagence, br – RR/Coll. Pierre Lherminier, tr
73 – RR/Cinémagence, sp
74 – BFI, br – RR/Coll. Maurice Gianati, tl
75 – RR/Ciné-Plus, tm – RR/Cinémagence, br – RR/Coll. Maurice Gianati, tr
76 – BFI, bl – RR/Coll. Chemel, ml – RR/Coll. Pierre Lherminier, tr, br
77 – BFI, tl, bl – RR/Coll. Cinémathèque, br – RR/Coll. Maurice Gianati, tr
78 and 79 – All Finler
81 – BFI, sp
82 – RR/Archives Gaumont, mm – Finler, br
83 – RR/Ciné-Plus, tl – RR/Cinémagence, tr – RR/Coll. Cinémathèque, mr – Finler, bl
84 – BFI, br – RR/Coll. Pierre Lherminier, tr – Finler, bl
85 – RR/Archives Gaumont, br – RR/Ciné-Plus, mr – RR/Cinémagence, bl – Finler, tl
87 – Finler, sp
88 – Finler, br – Vitagraph, courtesy Kobal, tr
89 – RR/Ciné-Plus, tr – RR/Cinémagence, br – Sipa, ml
90 – All RR/Ciné-Plus
91 – RR/Archives Gaumont, tr – RR/Cinémagence, bm
93 – RR/Ciné-Images, sp
94 – All RR/Cinémagence
95 – RR/Coll. Pierre Lherminier, tm – Finler, bl
96 – All RR/Coll. Pierre Lherminier
97 – RR/Archives Gaumont, ml – RR/Cinémagence, tr, br
99 – Finler, sp
100 – RR/Coll. Maurice Gianati, br – RR/Coll. Pierre Lherminier, tr – Finler, bl
101 – RR/Archives Gaumont, tm – RR/Ciné-Plus, bl – Finler, br
102 – BFI, tr – RR/Ciné-Plus, bl – Finler, br
103 – BFI, tr – RR/Coll. Pierre Lherminier, bl
105 – Finler, sp
106 – BFI, tl – RR/Cinémagence, ml – RR/Coll. Pierre Lherminier, mr
107 – RR/Ciné-Plus, tr – RR/Det Danske Filmmuseum, bl
108 – BFI, tl – Finler, tr, br
109 – BFI, bm – RR/Ciné-Plus, tm
111 – RR/Ciné-Plus, sp
112 – All BFI
113 – All RR/Ciné-Plus
114 – RR/Ciné-Plus, tr, bm – Finler, ml
115 – RR/Ciné-Plus, tr – RR/Cinémagence, tm – RR/Coll. André Bernard, tl – Paramount, courtesy Kobal, bl
117 – Carson, sp
118 – All RR/Ciné-Plus
119 – Bubbles Inc., 1994, bl – RR/Archives Gaumont, tr, br
120 – RR/Ciné-Plus, br, tl – RR/Cinémagence, tr
121 – Bubbles Inc., 1994, bl – RR/Ciné-Plus, br – RR/Coll. Pierre Lherminier, tm
123 – Finler, sp
124 – RR/Ciné-Plus, tr, br – RR/Coll. Cinémathèque, tl
125 – Bubbles Inc., 1994, br – RR/Archives Gaumont, tm, ml
126 – RR/Cinémagence, bl, bm – Finler, tl, tm, br
127 – RR/Ciné-Plus, tl – Finler, br
129 – Finler, sp
130 – RR/Cinémagence, tr – Finler, tl – Sipa, br
131 – BFI, br, bm – RR/Ciné-Plus, tl, tm
132 – BFI, tr – RR/Coll. Pierre Lherminier, mr – RR/Gosfilmofond, bl – Universal, courtesy Kobal, tl
133 – BFI, tl, tm – RR/Coll. Pierre Lherminier, br – Finler, bl
135 – Finler, sp
136 – RR/Ciné-Plus, bl – Finler, tr
137 – RR/Ciné-Plus, br – RR/Cinémagence, bm – Finler, tl
138 – RR/Ciné-Plus, bm – RR/Coll. Cinémathèque, bl – Finler, tm
139 – BFI, bm – RR/Ciné-Plus, tr – Finler, tl
140 – RR/Ciné-Images, ml, tm, tr, bl, br – Carson, tl, mr, bm
141 – RR/Ciné-Images, br – Carson, tl, ml, tm, tr, mr, bl, bx, by
142 and 143 – All Finler
145 – RR/Ciné-Plus, sp
146 – RR/Coll. Cinémathèque, tl – RR/Coll. Pierre Lherminier, bm – Finler, tr
147 – BFI, tm – RR/Ciné-Plus, br – Sygma/L'Illustration, bm
148 – BFI, tl, bm – RR/Cinémagence, mr – RR/Coll. Larousse, tr
149 – BFI, br – Bubbles Inc., 1994, bl – RR/Ciné-Plus, mr – Finler, ml
151 – RR/Ciné-Plus, sp
152 – BFI, bl – Bubbles Inc., 1994, tl, tm – RR/Cinémagence, tr – Sipa, bm
153 – RR/Ciné-Plus, tl – RR/Coll. Pierre Lherminier, bl – Sygma/L'Illustration, tr
154 – RR/Coll. Cinémathèque, tr – Finler, ml, bm
155 – RR/DITE, bl – Finler, tm, tr
157 – Finler, sp
158 – RR/Coll. Pierre Lherminier, tl – RR/Kharbine, mr
159 – RR/Cinémagence, tl – RR/Coll. Pierre Lherminier, br – Finler, mr
160 – RR/Archives Gaumont, tr – RR/Ciné-Plus, bl, br – Finler, tl
161 – BFI, bm – RR/Ciné-Plus, br – Finler, tl
163 – RR/Cinémagence, sp
164 – BFI, br – RR/Coll. Cinémathèque, tm – Finler, bl
165 – All Finler
166 – Bubbles Inc., 1994, tr – RR/Cinémagence, bl – RR/Coll. Cinémathèque, tl – Finler, br
167 – RR/Coll. Pierre Lherminier, tl – Finler, mr, bm – Sygma/L'Illustration, tm
169 – Finler, sp
170 – RR/Coll. Cinémathèque, tm – Finler, bm
171 – Finler, tl, br – Kobal, bl
172 – RR/Cinémagence, ml – RR/Coll. Cinémathèque, bm – Finler, mr
173 – BFI, tr, br – Finler, bl
175 – Carson
176 – RR/Ciné-Plus, mr – RR/Cinémagence, bm – Finler, tl, tm
177 – All RR/Cinémagence
178 – Bubbles Inc., 1994, tm, mm, bl – Finler, br
179 – BFI, tr – RR/Ciné-Plus, bl – Finler, tl, br
181 – Carson, sp
182 – RR/Cinémagence, tr – RR/Coll. Cinémathèque, tl – Kobal, br
183 – RR/Ciné-Plus, bm – Finler, tr
184 – RR/Cinémagence, mm – RR/Coll. Pierre Lherminier, tr, bm – Finler, tl, br
185 – RR/Coll. Pierre Lherminier, bm – Finler, tl, tr, br
187 – RR/Cinémagence, sp
188 – RR/Cinémagence, tr, bl, br – RR/Coll. Cinémathèque, mm – RR/De Selva-Tapabor, tm
189 – RR/Cinémagence, mr – Finler, tl, bm
190 – RR/Ciné-Plus, tl – RR/Cinémagence, tr, bm – RR/Coll. Cinémathèque, tm – Finler, mm
191 – BFI, tl – Bubbles Inc., 1994, bm – RR/Coll. Pierre Lherminier, bl
192 – RR/Cinémagence, tm, tr – Finler, bl
193 – RR/Cinémagence, tl, br – Finler, bl
195 – Finler, sp
196 – Bubbles Inc., 1994, ty, tr – RR/Cinémagence, ml, bm, bl
197 – RR/Kharbine, br – Finler, tl, tr
198 – RR/Cinémagence, tr, mm – RR/Kharbine, mr – Finler, tl
199 – BFI, mm – Finler, tr, bm
201 – Carson, sp
202 – RR/Cinémagence, tl – RR/Gosfilmofond, bm – Finler, tm, tr
203 – RR/Archives L'Avant-Scène, tm – RR/Cinémagence, bl, bm – Finler, mr
204 – RR/Cinémagence, tl, tr, mm – Finler, tm – Photo X/RR, bm
205 – RR/Cinémagence, tr – RR/DITE, bm – TM(C),L. Harmon Pict Corp, ml
206 – BFI, tr – Finler, tl, bl
207 – Finler, bm – Keystone, tl
208 – RR/Ciné-Images, ml – Carson, tl, tm, tr, mr, bl, bx, by, br
209 – RR/Ciné-Images, bl, bm – Carson, tl, ml, tm, tr, mr, br
210 – BFI, tr – RR/Cinémagence, tl, tx, ty, ml, mx, mr, by – Finler, my, bl, bx, br
211 – Jacques Legrand SA, tl – Finler, tr, bl – Sygma/L'Illustration, br
212 and 213 – All Finler
215 – RR/Cinémagence,
216 – RR/Archives L'Avant-Scène, bl – RR/Ciné-Plus, tl – RR/Cinémagence, mr
217 – BFI, bl – RR/Cinémagence, tr – Finler, tl, br
218 – RR/Ciné-Plus, tr, br, bm – RR/Cinémagence, bl – Finler, tl
219 – RR/Ciné-Plus, br – RR/Cinémagence, bl – Finler, tl, tr
220 – RR/Ciné-Plus, tm, bl, bm – RR/Cinémagence, br – Turner Entertainment, tr
221 – RR/Ciné-Plus, tr, br – RR/Cinémagence, bm – RR/Kharbine, tl
222 and 223 – All Carson
225 – Finler, sp
226 – RR/Cinémagence, tm, tr, br – RR/Kharbine, tl, bl
227 – RR/Cinémagence, bm, bl – Finler, tl, tm – Keystone, mr
228 – RR/Ciné-Plus, br – RR/Cinémagence, tl, bl – Finler, tr
229 – RR/Ciné-Plus, ml, tr, bm – RR/Cinémagence, tm, br
230 – RR/Ciné-Images, tm, tr – Carson, tl, bl, bm, br
231 – RR/Ciné-Images, br – Carson, tl, tm, tr, bl, bm
233 – Disney, sp
234 – RR/Ciné-Plus, ml – RR/Cinémagence, mr – Finler, br, bl
235 – BFI, br – RR/Cinémagence, tl – Finler, bl, tr
236 – RR/Ciné-Plus, tl, br – RR/Cinémagence, tm, bl, tr
237 – BFI, bm – RR/Ciné-Images, tl – Finler, tr
238 – All Carson
239 – RR/Ciné-Images, tl, br, LX, LY – Carson, bl, bm, tr
241 – Carson, sp
242 – RR/Cinémagence, tm – RR/Coll. Pierre Lherminier, bl – Finler, br
243 – RR/Cinémagence, tl, tm, bm – Finler, br
244 – RR/Archives Gaumont, tr – RR/Ciné-Plus, bm – RR/Cinémagence, br – RR/Coll. Pierre Lherminier, tm
245 – RR/Ciné-Images, tl – RR/Cinémagence, tr – Finler, bm
246 – All RR/Cinémagence

247 – RR/Ciné-Images, bl – RR/Ciné-Plus, bm, br – Finler, tl, mr
248 – RR/Ciné-Images, tr – Carson, tl, ml, tm, mr, bl, bx, by, br
249 – RR/Ciné-Images, bm, br – Carson, tl, tm, tr, bl
251 – Carson, sp
252 – RR/Ciné-Plus, tm, bl – RR/Cinémagence, tr – Sygma/L'Illustration, bm
253 – RR/Cinémagence, tm, mm – RR/Coll. Cinémathèque, tl – Finler, bm – Keystone, mr
254 – RR/Ciné-Images, bm – RR/Coll. Pierre Lherminier, br – Finler, tl, tr
255 – RR/Cinémagence, br – Finler, tl, bl, tr
256 – RR/Ciné-Images, ml – Carson, tl, tm, tr, mr, bl, bx, by, br
257 – RR/Ciné-Images, tl, ml – Carson, tr, bl, bx, by
259 – Carson, sp
260 – RR/Cinémagence, bl, bm – RR/Coll. Larousse, tl – Finler, tr, mm
261 – BFI, bl – RR/Cinémagence, tm, br – Finler, tl
262 – RR/Cinémagence, bm, br – Finler, tr, tl, tm, bm, bl
263 – BFI, bl – Finler, tm, br, tr
264 – RR/Ciné-Images, tr, mr, bl, bx – Carson, tl, by, br
265 – RR/Ciné-Images, ml – Carson, tl, tm, tr, mr, bl, bx, by, br
267 – Carson, sp
268 – Bubbles Inc., 1994, tm, tr – RR/Ciné-Plus, bm – RR/Cinémagence, ml
269 – RR/Cinémagence, tl, bl – Finler, tm, tr, br
270 – RR/Ciné-Plus, tl – RR/Cinémagence, tm – Finler, tr, bm
271 – RR/Cinémagence, bm, br – RR/Kharbine, tl, tr
272 – RR/Cinémagence, br – RR/Coll. Pierre Lherminier, bl – Finler, tl, tr
273 – RR/Ciné-Plus, tl – RR/Kharbine, tm – Finler, mr – TM(C),L. Harmon Pict Corp, bl, bm
274 – RR/Ciné-Images, tr, bl, bm, br – Carson, tl, mr
275 – All Carson
277 – Finler, sp
278 – RR/Cinémagence, br – RR/Coll. André Marinie, tr – RR/Coll. Pierre Lherminier, bm – Finler, tl, bl
279 – RR/Cinémagence, br – RR/Kharbine, tl – Finler, bl
280 – All RR/Cinémagence
281 – RR/Ciné-Plus, tr – RR/Cinémagence, tl, bm, bl, br
282 – RR/Ciné-Plus, bm, br – RR/Cinémagence, tl, tr
283 – Finler, tr, tl, tm, bl – Disney, bm, br
284 – All Carson
285 – RR/Ciné-Images, tl, ml, bl – Carson, tr, mm, bm, br
287 – Carson, sp
288 – RR/Ciné-Plus, br – RR/Kharbine, tr – Kobal, bl
289 – All RR/Cinémagence
290 – Finler, bm – Keystone, tr – Roger Corbeau, tl
291 – RR/Ciné-Plus, tl, mr – RR/Cinémagence, tm, ml, bm
292 – RR/Ciné-Plus, tr – Finler, br – Roger Corbeau, tl
293 – RR/Ciné-Plus, bl – RR/Cinémagence, bm – Finler, tl – Les Films du Carosse, tr
294 – RR/Ciné-Images, br, tl, ml – Carson, tr, bl, bm
295 – RR/Ciné-Images, mr, tm – Carson, tr, bm, br, tl, bl
297 – Carson, sp
298 – RR/Ciné-Plus, tl – RR/Cinémagence, tm, bl, bm – Finler, tr
299 – RR/Cinémagence, tl, bm – PH X/RR, br – Warners, courtesy Kobal, tr
300 – RR/Ciné-Plus, bl – RR/Cinémagence, tl, tm – Paramount, courtesy Kobal, br
301 – BFI, bm – Finler, tm
302 – BFI, br – Finler, bl, tl – Sygma/L'Illustration, tr
303 – RR/Ciné-Plus, tr, ml, br – RR/Kipa, tl
304 – RR/Ciné-Images, ml, bl – Carson, tl, tm, tr, bm, br
305 – RR/Ciné-Images, mr – Edgar Rice Burroughs 1994, tr – Carson, tl, tm, bl, bx, by, br
306 and 307 – All Finler
309 – Bubbles Inc., 1994, sp
310 – RR/Ciné-Images, tl – RR/Cinémagence, tm, br – Finler, bl
311 – RR/Cinémagence, tl – Finler, tr, bm
312 – Bubbles Inc., 1994, tm, br – RR/Cinémagence, bl – Finler, tr
313 – RR/Ciné-Images, bl – Finler, br – Disney, tm, tr
314 – RR/Ciné-Images, bl – Carson, tl, tm, tr, br
315 – RR/Ciné-Images, ml, mr, bm – Carson, tl, tm, tr, bl, br
317 – RR/Cinémagence, sp
318 – RR/Cinémagence, tr – Finler, bl, br
319 – BFI, bl – Finler, tl, tr – Warners, courtesy Kobal, br
320 – RR/Ciné-Images, tr – RR/Ciné-Plus, bl – RR/Cinémagence, br – RKO/Samuel Goldwyn, courtesy Kobal, tl
321 – RR/Ciné-Plus, br – RR/Cinémagence, tl, bl – Finler, tr
322 – RR/Ciné-Images, ml – MGM, courtesy Kobal, br – Carson, tr, bl, bm, tl, tm
323 – RR/Ciné-Images, tl, ml – Carson, tr, by, br, bl, bx
325 – Carson, sp
326 – All Finler
327 – RR/Ciné-Plus, tl – RR/Cinémagence, bm – Finler, tr
328 – RR/Cinémagence, tl, tr – Finler, br – Warners, courtesy Kobal, bl
329 – BFI, tl, br – RR/Cinémagence, tr – Finler, ml
330 – RR/Ciné-Images, br, tl, tm, ml – Carson, tr, bl, bm
331 – RR/Ciné-Images, ml – Carson, tr, bl, bm, br, tl, tm
333 – Carson, sp
334 – RR/Cinémagence, br – Finler, tm, bl
335 – RR/Cinémagence, bm, br – Finler, tr – Carson, tl
336 – RR/Cinémagence, br – RR/Kharbine, tr – Finler, tl, ml
337 – BFI, bl – RR/Ciné-Plus, br – Finler, tl, tm
338 – Finler, bl – Carson, tl, br, tm, tr
339 – RR/Ciné-Images, tl – Carson, tr, bm, br, bl, tm
341 – Grant, sp
342 – BFI, bl – RR/Ciné-Plus, tl – RR/Cinémagence, tr – Finler, br
343 – BFI, tl, tr – RR/Cinémagence, bm
344 – BFI, tl – RR/Archives L'Avant-Scène, br – RR/Ciné-Plus, bm – RR/Coll. Larousse, tr – Finler, bl
345 – All Finler
346 – RR/Ciné-Images, tl, tr, mr, bl, br – Carson, ml, tm
347 – RR/Ciné-Images, mr, bl – Finler, br – Carson, tl, ml, tm, tr, bm
349 – RR/Ciné-Images, sp
350 – RR/Ciné-Plus, tm – Keystone, bl, br
351 – RR/Cinémagence, tl, br – Finler, tr, bl
352 – BFI, tl – RR/Cinémagence, tr, bl – Finler, br
353 – All Finler
354 – RR/Ciné-Images, ml, bl – Finler, br – Carson, tl, tm, tr, mr, bm
355 – RR/Ciné-Images, ml, bl – Finler, tl, br – Carson, tr
357 – Carson, sp
358 – BFI, tr – RR/Cinémagence, bm – Finler, tl
359 – BFI, bl, br – Finler, tm
360 – RR/Aero/Sipa-Press, tl, tm – RR/Ciné-Plus, bl – RR/Cinémagence, br
361 – Denis Huisman, tm, tr – RR/Cinémagence, bl – RR/Kharbine, br – Roger Corbeau, mm
362 – RR/Ciné-Plus, bl – RR/Cinémagence, tl – RR/Cinémathèque de Prague, mr – RR/Sygma/L'Illustration, ml – Finler, br
363 – RR/Cinémagence, bm – Finler, tl, tr
364 – RR/Ciné-Images, bl, ml, tl, bm, br – Carson, tr
365 – RR/Ciné-Images, by, br, tm, ml, bl – Carson, tr, tl, bx
367 – Bubbles Inc., 1994, sp
368 – BFI, tl – Finler, tr, bm
369 – RR/Ciné-Plus, tr – RR/Cinémagence, tl, bl – Finler, bm
370 – RR/Cinémagence, tl, ml, br – Finler, tr – Sygma/L'Illustration, bl
371 – RR/Coll. André Marinie, mr – Finler, tm, bl
372 – BFI, tl – RR/Ciné-Plus, br, bl, bm – RR/Cinémagence, tr
373 – BFI, br – Finler, tm, bl
374 – RR/Ciné-Images, tr, br, bl – Finler, tl – Carson, ml, mm
375 – RR/Ciné-Images, by, br, ml, bm, tl, tm – Carson, tr, bm, tm
377 – RR/Ciné-Images, sp
378 – BFI, tr – RR/Ciné-Plus, tl – Photo RR/Ciné-Images, bm
379 – BFI, tl, br – RR/Cinémagence, bl – Finler, tr
380 – RR/Cinémagence, bl – RR/Kharbine, br – Finler, tl, tr
381 – RR/Cinémagence, mr – Finler, tl, bm
382 – RR/Ciné-Images, tr, bm, br, mt, mb – Finler, bl – Carson, tl, mm
383 – RR/Ciné-Images, tr, mr – Finler, bl, tm – Carson, tl, bm, br
385 – RR/Ciné-Images, sp
386 – RR/Cinémagence, tm, mr – Finler, bl, br
387 – BFI, mm – RR/Cinémagence, tr – Finler, tl, bl, br
388 – RR/Cinémagence, tr – Finler, tl, bl – Novosti, bl
389 – RR/Cinémagence, ml, tr – RR/Kharbine, bl – Traverso, tl
390 – RR/Cinémagence, bl – Finler, tl, tr
391 – All Finler
392 – All RR/Ciné-Images
393 – RR/Ciné-Images, bl – Finler, tl – Carson, tr, bm, br, mm, ml
394 – Finler, mm
395 – Universal, courtesy Kobal, mm
397 – Carson, sp
398 – RR/Cinémagence, tl, bl – Finler, tr, br
399 – BFI, bl – RR/Cinémagence, tr, mr – RR/Kharbine, br – Finler, tl
400 – BFI, tl – RR/Ciné-Plus, br, bl – RR/Kipa, bm – Finler, tr
401 – All Finler
402 – BFI, bm – RR/Kharbine, tl – Photofest, tr
403 – RR/Kharbine, tl, bm – Finler, tr
404 – RR/Ciné-Images, bl, tr, ml, mr – Carson, tl, bm, br
405 – RR/Ciné-Images, tm, mr – Carson, tr, tl, bm, br – Roger Corbeau, bl
407 – Carson, sp
408 – RR/Ciné-Images, tl – Finler, bl, br – Roger Corbeau, tm
409 – RR/Ciné-Plus, tl – Finler, bm – Photofest, tr
410 – BFI, tr – RR/Kharbine, tl – Finler, br, bl
411 – BFI, br – RR/Kharbine, bl – MGM, courtesy Kobal, tl, tr
412 – RR/Ciné-Images, bl, tm, tr, mr – Finler, br – Carson, bm
413 – RR/Ciné-Images, tm, tr, mr, bm, br – Estate of Marilyn Monroe, 1994, bl – Carson, tl
415 – Carson, sp
416 – BFI, bm – RR/Ciné-Plus, tr – Finler, tl – Léo Mirkine, tm
417 – Finler, br – MGM, courtesy Kobal, tl, tr
418 – 2Oth Century Fox, courtesy Kobal, tl – Franco Civirani, br – Robert Tomatis, bl – Stanley Kramer/UA, courtesy Kobal, tr
419 – BFI, bl, br – Bubbles Inc., 1994, tr, tl
420 – Finler, bl, tm – Carson, tl, br, tr
421 – RR/Ciné-Images, tr – R. Forster/R. Poutrel, bl – Carson, tl, br
423 – RR/Ciné-Plus, sp
424 – André Dino, bm – RR/Ciné-Plus, tr – Finler, tl
425 – BFI, tl – RR/Kharbine, tr – Finler, bl, br
426 – RR/Ciné-Plus, mm – RR/Coll. Larousse, bl, br – Keystone, tr – Lucienne Chevert, tl
427 – RR/Ciné-Plus, br – Finler, tm, bl
428 – RR/Ciné-Plus, tl – Finler, br – Photofest, tl
429 – Finler, tl, tr, mm – Sipa, br – Warners, courtesy Kobal, bl
430 – RR/Ciné-Images, tr, br – Finler, bl, mr – Carson, tl
431 – RR/Ciné-Images, br, ml – Carson, tr, tl, tm, bl, bm
433 – Carson, sp
434 – Finler, tr, bm – Marcel Bouguereau, tl
435 – BFI, tr – RR/Ciné-Plus, bm – RR/Cinémagence, tl – Finler, br
436 – RR/Ciné-Images, bl – RR/Cinémagence, tl – RR/Coll. Larousse, tr – RR/Kharbine, br
437 – RR/Ciné-Plus, bl, tm – Paramount, courtesy Kobal, br
438 – Cyril Stanburough, bm – RR/Ciné-Images, mm, tr, mr, ml, bl – Carson, tl, br
439 – Estate of Marilyn Monroe, 1994, bl – Finler, br – Carson, tl, tm, tr
441 – Carson, sp
442 – BFI, bl – Finler, tr, br – L. Mirkine/R. Joffres, tl
443 – Finler, bl, br – Raymond Bègue, tl – Serge Beauvarlet, tr
444 – RR/Kharbine, br – Estate of Marilyn Monroe, 1994, tl – Popperphoto, bl
445 – RR/Cinémagence, tl, bl – RR/DITE, tr – RR/Sunset/Kipa, br
446 – BFI, br – Finler, bl – MGM/Samuel Goldwyn, courtesy Kobal, tl
447 – Estate of Marilyn Monroe, 1994, bl – Raymond Voinquel, tr
448 – RR/Ciné-Images, bl, tm, tr, mr – Carson, tl
449 – RR/Ciné-Images, tr, bm, br – Finler, bl – Carson, tl, tm, ml, mm
451 – Carson, sp
452 – All Finler
453 – RR/Ciné-Plus, bl, – RR/Kipa, ml – Finler, tr
454 – Fox, courtesy Kobal, bl – Finler, tr – MGM, courtesy Kobal, br – Warners, courtesy Kobal, tl
455 – Emmanuel Lowenthal, bm – Finler, tr, ml
456 – BFI, br – RR/Kipa, tm – Finler, ml, bl
457 – RR/Ciné-Plus, tl, br – Emmanuel Lowenthal, bl – Léo Mirkine, tr
458 – RR/Ciné-Images, tl, bl, mr – Léo Mirkine, mm – Carson, tm, tr, br
459 – BFI, mr – RR/Ciné-Images, bl – Carson, tl, tm, tr, bm, br
461 – Carson, sp
462 – RR/Cinémagence, mr – Keystone, bl – PH X/RR, tl
463 – BFI, tr – RR/Cinémagence, tl – Finler, bl – UA, courtesy Kobal, br
464 – BFI, br – RR/Cinémagence, tm – Finler, bl
465 – Fox, courtesy Kobal, mr – BFI, tl, bl
466 – BFI, bl – RR/Cinémagence, tm, tr – RR/Kharbine, tl – Finler, br
467 – BFI, br – RR/Ciné-Plus, tl – Finler, bl
468 – All Carson
469 – RR/Ciné-Images, mr – Finler, bl – Carson, tl, tm, tr, mm – Roger Corbeau, br
471 – Carson,
472 – BFI, br – RR/Cinémagence, bl – Jean-Louis Castelli, tl, tm
473 – Henri Thibault, tr, tm – Finler, br – MGM, courtesy Kobal, M, bm
474 – André Dino, bl – RR/Cinémagence, tl, mr
475 – RR/Cinémagence, bm, tr – Paramount, courtesy Kobal, tl
476 – Finler, bl – Walter Limot, tl, tm, br
477 – Finler, bm – Vincent Russel, tl, tm
478 – RR/Ciné-Images, tl, bl, bm, br, tr – Carson, mr
479 – RR/Ciné-Images, tl – Finler, br – Carson, tr, ml, bl, bx, by
481 – Carson, sp
482 – Finler, tr, bm – Roger Corbeau, tl
483 – André Dino, bl – Finler, tm – PH X/RR, br
484 – André Dino, tm, tr – RR/Cinémagence, bl, bm – RR/Kipa, ml
485 – BFI, bl – Finler, tl, tr, br
486 – BFI, br – RR/Sunset/Kipa, tl – Finler, tr, bl
487 – RR/Cinémagence, tr – Finler, br, bl
488 and 489 – All Finler
490 – RR/Ciné-Images, tl, bl, tr – Finler, mr – Carson, bm, br
491 – BFI, bl – RR/Ciné-Images, bm, br – Estate of Marilyn Monroe, 1994, tr – Carson, tl
492 and 493 – All UA, courtesy Kobal
495 – Carson, sp
496 – RR/Cinémagence, tl – Henri Thibault, tr – Production Georges De Beauregard, bm – Raymond Cauchetier, br
497 – BFI, bm – RR/Cinémagence, tl – Finler, tr, mr
498 – RR/Cinémagence, tm – Finler, tl, bm
499 – Finler, tl, tr – Paramount, courtesy Kobal, bm
500 – Jean-Louis Castelli, br – Finler, ml, tr – UA, courtesy Kobal, bl
501 – Estate of Marilyn Monroe, 1994 tl, tm – Finler, bl, br
502 – RR/Ciné-Images, mm, bl – Finler, tm, tr – Carson, tl, br – Universal, courtesy Kobal, mr
503 – RR/Ciné-Images, mm, mr – Finler, tr – Paramount, courtesy Kobal, bl – Carson, tl, br
505 – Carson, sp
506 – RR/Ciné-Plus, bl – Estate of Marilyn Monroe, 1994, tl – Finler, tr – Carson, br
507 – RR/Cinémagence, tr, bl, br – PH X/RR, tl
508 – All Finler
509 – BFI, tl, tr – Warners, courtesy Kobal, bm
510 – BFI, bm – RR/Cinémagence, tl, mr
511 – RR/Cinémagence, tl, bm – Finler, tr
512 – RR/Ciné-Images, tl, tm, tr, bm, br – Production Georges De Beauregard, bl – Carson, mr
513 – RR/Ciné-Images, br, bl – Finler, ml – Carson, tr, tl, tm
515 – Carson, sp
516 – RR/Cinémagence, bl – Les Films du Carosse, tl – Les Films du Carosse/SEDIF, courtesy Kobal, tm – Production Georges De Beauregard, br
517 – BFI, tl – RR/Coll. Pierre Lherminier, br – Finler, bl – Grant, tr
518 – BFI, bl – RR/Cinémagence, tr, br – RR/Kipa, tl
519 – Fox, courtesy Kobal, ml – Keystone, tr, mr
520 – RR/Cinémagence, tm, tr, br – RR/Kharbine, bl
521 – All Finler
522 – RR/Cinémagence, br, bl – RR/Kharbine, tr – Finler, tl
523 – BFI, bl – Finler, tl, tr
524 – RR/Ciné-Images, bl – Finler, br, tr, mr – Carson, tl – Grant, bm
525 – RR/Ciné-Images, bl, br, tm – Carson, tl, mr, tr
527 – Carson, sp
528 – RR/Cinémagence, tr, mr – Finler, tl – Production Georges De Beauregard, bl
529 – RR/Cinémagence, tl – RR/Kipa, tr – PH X/RR, ml – Photo RR/Ciné-Images, br
530 – RR/Kharbine, br – RR/Kipa, tr – Kobal, bl – Photo RR/Ciné-Images, tl
531 – BFI, br – RR/Cinémagence, bl – Finler, tm
532 – Finler, tl – Grant, tr – UA, courtesy Kobal, bm
533 – Finler, tl, bm – Photo RR/Cinémagence, tr
534 – RR/Ciné-Images, tl, ml, mr, br – MGM, courtesy Kobal, bm – Carson, tr, bl
535 – RR/Ciné-Images, tr, mr – Finler, bm – Carson, tl, br, bl
537 – Carson, sp
538 – RR/Cinémagence, tl – Jean-Louis Castelli, bm – Finler, tr
539 – RR/Ciné-Plus, tl – RR/Kharbine, bl – Les Films du Carosse, mr
540 – BFI, bl – RR/Cinémagence, tr, br – RR/Kharbine, tl
541 – RR/Cinémagence, tr – Finler, tm – Disney, bm
542 – RR/Cinémagence, tr – RR/Kipa, br – Warners, courtesy Kobal, tl, bl
543 – RR/Cinémagence, tl – RR/Kipa, tr, br – Finler, bl
544 – RR/Ciné-Images, tr, bl, bm, mm, br – Carson, tl, mr
545 – RR/Ciné-Images, br, tl – RR/Kipa, mm – Finler, bl – Carson, tr, ml
547 – Carson, sp
548 – Claude Schwartz, mr – RR/Cinémagence, tl, tr – Finler, bm
549 – BFI, bl, tr – Finler, tl, br
550 – BFI, tr – RR/Ciné-Plus, ml – RR/Cinémagence, tl – Finler, bl, br
551 – RR/Cinémagence, bl – Georges Pierre, tr – Finler, br
552 – RR/Ciné-Images, bl, br, mr, tm – RR/Kipa, tr – Carson, tl
553 – RR/Kipa, tm – Finler, br, bl, tl – Carson, tr, mm, ml
555 – Carson, sp
556 – BFI, tr – RR/Kipa, br – Finler, ml
557 – BFI, tm – Pierre Zucca, bm
558 – RR/Ciné-Plus, br – RR/Cinémagence, tl, tm – Finler, bl
559 – RR/Cinémagence, br – RR/Kharbine, tr – Les Films du Carosse, tl, ml
560 – RR/Cinémagence, tr, mm, bm – RR/Kharbine, br
561 – RR/Cinémagence, bl, mr – RR/Coll. Abbas Fahdel, br – RR/Kipa, mm
562 – BFI, tr – RR/Ciné-Images, mm, bl – Finler, br – Carson, tl, tm, mr
563 – BFI, mm, br – RR/Ciné-Images, bl – Finler, tr – Carson, tl, tm, mr
565 – Carson, sp
566 – RR/Ciné-Plus, tl – Les Films du Losange, br
567 – BFI, br – RR/Ciné-Plus, tr – RR/Cinémagence, tl – Finler, bl
568 – RR/Kharbine, tr – RR/Kipa, tm – Finler, bm
569 – RR/Ciné-Plus, bm, br – Finler, tr – Warners/Seven Arts, courtesy Kobal, tl
570 – BFI, tr, bl – RR/Cinémagence, tl – Warners, courtesy Kobal, br
571 – RR/Archives Gaumont, tr – RR/Cinémagence, br, bl – Finler, tl
572 – RR/Ciné-Images, tl, mr, br – Finler, bm – Carson, bl
573 – Columbia, courtesy Kobal, ml – RR/Ciné-Images, tr – Finler, tl, bl – Carson, br
575 – Carson, sp
576 – Fox, courtesy Kobal, tm – BFI, ml – Finler, br
577 – All RR/Ciné-Plus
578 – BFI, tl, bl – Sygma, tr – U. Josephsson/Cahier du Cinéma, br
579 – RR/Christophe L., tr – RR/Sunset/Kipa, bm – Sygma, tl
580 – RR/Cinémagence, tr – RR/Kipa, bl – Finler, br – UA, courtesy Kobal, tl
581 – BFI, bl – Kobal, mr – Carson, br – Warners, courtesy Kobal, tl
582 – Columbia, courtesy Kobal, bl – RR/Ciné-Images, tr – Finler, br – Carson, tl, mm, mr
583 – RR/Ciné-Images, bl, br, mm, mr, tr – Carson, tl
585 – Carson, sp
586 – RR/Cinémagence, bl – Finler, br – Paramount, courtesy Kobal, tl, tr
587 – RR/Cinémagence, tr, mr – RR/Kipa, tl – Finler, bm

588 – RR/Ciné-Images, tl – RR/Kipa, tr – Pegaso-Italnoleggio-Praesidens-Eichberg, courtesy Kobal, bl, bm – Warners/Seven Arts, courtesy Kobal, br
589 – RR/Ciné-Plus, bl – RR/Cinémagence, br – Finler, tm, tr – MGM, courtesy Kobal, tl
590 – Fox, courtesy Kobal, tl – Finler, mr, bl – Grant, bm
591 – RR/Ciné-Plus, tl – RR/Cinémagence, tm – Finler, br
592 – RR/Ciné-Images, tr, mr, bl, br – Finler, tl – Carson, ml, mm
593 – RR/Ciné-Images, tr, mr, ml – Finler, br, bl – Carson, tl
594 – Warners, courtesy Kobal, mm
595 – Finler, mm
597 – Carson, sp
598 – RR/Ciné-Plus, bm – RR/Cinémagence, tl, tr, bl – Georges Pierre/Sygma, tm
599 – Finler, bl, br – Pierre Zucca, tl, tm
600 – RR/Ciné-Plus, tl – RR/Kipa, br – Finler, tr, mr, bl
601 – RR/Kipa, tl, tm – Finler, bl, mr
602 – Fox, courtesy Kobal, bl – RR/Coll. Abbas Fahdel, br – Finler, tr – Paramount/Filmways, courtesy Kobal, tl
603 – RR/Cinémagence, bl – RR/Kipa, tl – Finler, tr, br
604 – BFI, bl – RR/Ciné-Images, tl, mr – Finler, ml, tm, tr, br
605 – RR/Ciné-Images, br – Carson, tr, tl, tm – Grant, bl
607 – Carson, sp
608 – RR/Cinémagence, ml, mr – Finler, tl, tr
609 – RR/Cinémagence, tm – RR/Kipa, br – Warners, courtesy Kobal, bl
610 – All Finler
611 – Avco Embassy, courtesy Kobal, tl – Finler, tr, bl, br
612 – BFI, bl – RR/Cinémagence, tl – Etienne George, tr – Finler, br
613 – RR/Cinémagence, bl – Finler, tl, br – Paramount, courtesy Kobal, tr
614 – RR/Ciné-Images, br – Finler, bl, tr, mr – Carson, tl
615 – RR/Ciné-Images, mr, ml, mm, bl – Etienne George/Sygma, tr – Carson, tl, br
617 – Carson, sp
618 – BFI, br – RR/Cinémagence, tm – Finler, bl
619 – RR/Cinémagence, tm, tr, bl – RR/Kharbine, bm
620 – Bubbles Inc., 1994, tm – RR/Cinémagence, mm, br – RR/Kipa, ml
621 – BFI, br – RR/Kharbine, tr – Finler, tl, bl
622 – RR/Ciné-Images, bl, ml, my – RR/Kipa, tr – Finler, br, mx, tl – Carson, mr
623 – RR/Ciné-Images, bl, tl, tr, mm – Finler, ml, mr, br
625 – Carson, sp
626 – RR/Ciné-Plus, tl, bm – RR/Kipa, tr
627 – RR/Ciné-Plus, ml – RR/Cinémagence, tm – RR/Kipa, tr – Finler, br
628 – RR/Cinémagence, tr – RR/Kipa, tl, mm – Keystone, br – Topor, bl
629 – RR/Kipa, bl – Finler, tl – Pierre Zucca, tr, br
630 – RR/Cinémagence, br – Finler, ml, tr, tl
631 – RR/Ciné-Plus, tl – RR/Kipa, bl – Finler, tm, tr, br
632 – Concord/Warners, courtesy Kobal, mr – RR/Ciné-Images, br – RR/Kipa, bl – Finler, tl, tm, tr – Topor, ml
633 – BFI, ml – RR/Ciné-Images, tm, tr, mr, br, bl – Finler, tl
635 – Carson, sp
636 – Etienne George, tl – Finler, tr, br – Pierre Zucca, bl
637 – RR/Ciné-Plus, tl, tm – RR/Kipa, br – Julian Wasser/Gamma, bm – Warners, courtesy Kobal, bl
638 – RR/Ciné-Plus, bl, br – RR/Cinémagence, tl, tr
639 – RR/Cinémagence, bl – RR/Coll. Abbas Fahdel, br – Finler, tl, tr
640 – RR/Ciné-Plus, ml, mm, bm – RR/Cinémagence, tr – RR/Kipa, tl, br
641 – RR/Cinémagence, br – Finler, tr, bl
642 – RR/Ciné-Images, tl, br, bl, mr – Finler, ml, tr – Pierre Zucca, tm
643 – RR/Ciné-Images, tm, tr, bl, ml – Finler, br, mr, tl
645 – Carson, sp
646 – RR/Cinémagence, tr, br – Finler, tl, bl
647 – RR/Cinémagence, br – RR/Kipa, ml, bl – Finler, tm
648 – BFI, bl – Finler, tl, tr, bm, br
649 – RR/Cinémagence, tl – Finler, tr – Les Films du Carosse, bm, br
650 – RR/Ciné-Plus, bl – RR/Cinémagence, tm, br – Georges Pierre/Sygma, bm – Sygma, tr
651 – RR/Cinémagence, bm, br – Finler, tl, tr, bl
652 – RR/Ciné-Images, ml, bl, bm, br, tl – Finler, tr, mr
653 – RR/Ciné-Images, mr, bl, br, tl – Finler, ml, mm, tm, tr
655 – Carson, sp
656 – RR/Archives Gaumont, tm, tr – RR/Cinémagence, bl – Finler, br
657 – Claude Schwartz, br – RR/Cinémagence, ml – Georges Pierre/Sygma, tl – Finler, tr
658 – RR/Ciné-Images, tl – RR/Cinémagence, tr, bl
659 – RR/Cinémagence, tl – Finler, tr, bm
660 – James Andanson/Sygma, tr – Finler, tl, bl, br
661 – RR/Ciné-Plus, br – RR/Cinémagence, bl, tr – Carson, tl
662 – BFI, tl – RR/Ciné-Images, mr, ml, bl – RR/Kipa, tr – Finler, tm, br – Carson, mm
663 – RR/Ciné-Images, tr, ml, bl, br – Finler, tm, mr, tl
665 – Carson, sp
666 – RR/Cinémagence, bl – RR/Kipa, tl, tr
667 – RR/Cinémagence, tr – RR/Kipa, tl, bm
668 – RR/Kipa, br – Finler, tl, tm, bl
669 – RR/Ciné-Plus, tr – RR/Kipa, tl – Sunshine/Sipa-Press, bm
670 – All Finler
671 – D. Hennings/Sygma, bm – James Andanson/Sygma, br – Finler, tr, bl
672 – RR/Ciné-Images, br, mm – RR/Kipa, bl – Finler, ml, tl – Carson, tr
673 – BFI, br, tl – RR/Ciné-Images, bl, tm – RR/Kipa, mr – Eva Sereny/Sygma, tr – Finler, ml
675 – Carson, sp
676 – RR/Ciné-Plus, tl – RR/Cinémagence, tr – Finler, br – UA, courtesy Kobal, bl
677 – RR/Kipa, bl – Finler, tm – Universal, courtesy Kobal, br
678 – Finler, tm, bl, br – Grant, tr
679 – RR/Ciné-Plus, bl – Falcon International, courtesy Kobal, tl – Finler, tr
680 – RR/Kipa, tr, ml – Finler, tl, tm, mr, bl, br – Roger Corbeau, mm
681 – RR/Ciné-Images, tr, br – Finler, tl, ml, mr, bl
683 – Carson, sp
684 – RR/Kipa, tl, tr – Finler, bm
685 – Finler, tr, bl – Moune Jamet/Sygma, br – T. Korody/Sygma, tl, ml
686 – RR/Ciné-Plus, tr, br – RR/Cinémagence, tl – RR/Kipa, ml, tm
687 – RR/Kipa, tl, bl – Finler, br – N.S.W. Film Corp., courtesy Kobal, mr
688 – RR/Cinémagence, tm, mr, bl, bm – RR/Kipa, tr – Eva Sereny/Sygma, ml
689 – C. Simonpietri/Sygma, tr – RR/Archives Gaumont, bm – Finler, ml
690 – Finler, br – Lacombe/Sygma, bl – Schapiro/Sygma, tl – UA, courtesy Kobal, tr
691 – Finler, mm
692 – Finler, bl, br, tr, mr – Carson, tl
693 – BFI, tr – Finler, bl, bm, br, mr – Carson, tl
694 – Fox, courtesy Kobal, mm
695 – RENN/Films AZ/RAIZ/AMLF, courtesy Kobal, mm
697 – Carson, sp
698 – All Finler
699 – Deborah Beer/Sygma, tl – RR/Cinémagence, tr – RR/Kipa, bl – Sygma, mr, br
700 – RR/Ciné-Plus, br – RR/Kipa, tl, bl, bm, tr
701 – C. Simonpietri/Sygma, bl – Finler, tl, br
702 – RR/Kipa, br – Finler, tm, tr, bl
703 – RR/Cinémagence, br – Finler, tl, tr – L. De Raemy/Sygma, bl
704 – BFI, bl – RR/Archives Gaumont, bm – RR/Kipa, tl, br – Paul Grimault, ml – Carson, tr
705 – courtesy CIBY, ml – Finler, tl, mm, br – Carson, tr, bl, bm
707 – Carson, sp
708 – Dominique Le Strat, br – RR/Cinémagence, tr – RR/Kipa, tm – Morgan Renard/Sygma, bl
709 – RR/Cinémagence, tl, tr, bm – Finler, bl – John Bryson/Sygma, br
710 – RR/Kipa, ml – G. Ranciman/Sygma, tm – Sygma/Lucas Production, br
711 – All Finler
712 – Finler, tl, bl, bm – Paramount, courtesy Kobal, tr
713 – J.P. Naffony/Sygma, br – Finler, tr – Carson, bl
714 – RR/Ciné-Images, tx, tl – Finler, bl, ty, tr, ml – Carson, br
715 – RR/Ciné-Images, bl – Finler, br, ml, tr – K. Heyman/Sygma, tm – Carson, tl
717 – Carson, sp
718 – Dominique Le Strat, br – RR/Kipa, tl, tm – Finler, bl
719 – RR/Kipa, tr, ml – Finler, bm, br
720 – RR/Kipa, tm, tr – Finler, bl, br – Sygma, tl
721 – RR/Ciné-Plus, tm – Finler, bl, br – Sygma, tr
722 – RR/Kipa, ml – Finler, tr, bl, br
723 – RR/Kipa, tr – Finler, tl, br, bl
724 – BFI, bl – RR/Ciné-Images, mm – RR/Kipa, tr, mr – Finler, br – Carson, tl
725 – BFI, mr – RR/Kipa, tr – Finler, bl, bm – Carson, tl, br
727 – Carson, sp
728 – G. Schachmes/Sygma, tr – Finler, tl – Sygma, bl, br
729 – Etienne George/Sygma, bl – Finler, tl, tm, br
730 – RR/Kipa, tl, tm – Finler, bm – Carson, tr
731 – BFI, br – RR/Kipa, tr, bl – Sygma, tl
732 and 733 – All Finler
734 – BFI, ml – RR/Ciné-Images, mr – RR/Kipa, br – Finler, bl – Carson, tl, tx, ty, tr
735 – BFI, mr – RR/Ciné-Images, bl – RR/Kipa, tl, br – Finler, bm, ml – Carson, tr
737 – Carson, sp
738 – Georges Pierre/Sygma, bm – Finler, tl – William Karel/Sygma, tr
739 – RR/Cinémagence, tm – RR/Kipa, tl – Finler, bl, br – Jonathan Levine/Sygma, tr
740 – RR/Kipa, bl – Finler, tl, tr, br
741 – Etienne George/Sygma, bl – John Bryson/Sygma, mm – Sygma, tm, br
742 – Finler, ml, tr, bl – Les Films du Carosse, br
743 – All Finler
744 – RR/Ciné-Images, tr – Finler, bl, mr – Carson, tl, bm, br
745 – Finler, tl, tm, ml – Carson, tr, br, bl
747 – Carson, sp
748 – 20th Century-Fox Film, bl – Finler, tl, tr – Paramount, courtesy Kobal, ml
749 – Etienne George/Sygma, bm – Finler, tr – Orion, courtesy Kobal, tl – TriStar, courtesy Kobal, tm – William Karel/Sygma, bl
750 – RR/Kipa, bl, ml – Finler, tr – Mafilm/Mokep/ZDF, courtesy Kobal, tl
751 – Finler, bl, bm – Matsumo/Sygma, tm – Warners, courtesy Kobal, br
752 – Amblin/Universal, courtesy Kobal, bl – Finler, tl, tr, br
753 – Finler, tl, tm, tr – Svensk Filmindistri/AB Filmteknik, courtesy Kobal, br – Working Title/Channel 4, courtesy Kobal, bl
754 – Andy Schwartz/Sygma, ml – BFI, mr – RR/Ciné-Images, tl – RR/Kipa, tm, bl – Finler, tr, br
755 – RR/Ciné-Images, tr – Finler, bm, tl, mr, ml – Carson, br, bl
757 – Carson, sp
758 – Fabian Cevalo/Sygma, tl, tm – Finler, mr, bl – Merchant-Ivory/Goldcrest, courtesy Kobal, br
759 – Fox, courtesy Kobal, tl – Island Alive, courtesy Kobal, tr – J. Jacques Beineix/Gaumont, bm, br – Finler, tm
760 – All Finler
761 – Island Films, courtesy Kobal, br – Jérôme Minet/Kipa, tr – Finler, bl – Les Films du Losange, tm
762 – De Laurentiis, courtesy Kobal, tl – Finler, bl, tr, br
763 – RR/Cinémagence, br – Finler, tl, bl – Richard Melloul/Sygma, tr
764 – David James/Sygma, tm – RR/Ciné-Images, tr – RR/Kipa, br – Jérôme Minet/Kipa, mr – Finler, bl – Carson, tl
765 – Bernard Fau/Sipa Press, tr – Cannon, courtesy Kobal, bm – De Laurentiis, courtesy Kobal, bl – RR/Kipa, br – Etienne George/Sygma, mr – Carson, tl
767 – Carson, sp
768 – RR/Kipa, tm, bm, br – Finler, bl
769 – BFI, bl – RR/Kipa, tr – E. Lari/Sygma, mr – Finler, br – S. Legrand/Kipa, tm
770 – RR/Kipa, br – Finler, tl, bl – RENN/Films AZ/RAIZ/AMLF, courtesy Kobal, tr
771 – Columbia, courtesy Kobal, bl – Jeanne L. Bulliard/Sygma, tr – Finler, br – Vestron, courtesy Kobal, tl
772 – Columbia, courtesy Kobal, mr – RR/Kipa, ml – Fabian/Sygma, bm – Finler, mm, bl, br
773 – RR/Kipa, bl – Finler, tl, tr, br
774 – Fox, courtesy Kobal, tr – Finler, ml, mm – Carson, br, tl, tm, bl
775 – RR/Kipa, ml – Finler, tr, tl – Marcia Reed/Sygma, bl – Carson, br
777 – Carson, sp
778 – Finler, tr – Moune Jamet/Sygma, tl – Sygma, bm, br, bl
779 – RR/Ciné-Images, br – Finler, bl – Patrick Camboulive, tm
780 – Fox, courtesy Kobal, br – BFI, tr – RR/Kipa, mr – Finler, tl, ml, bl
781 – Fox, courtesy Kobal, tl – RR/Ciné-Images, tr – Finler, bl – Paramount, courtesy Kobal, mr
782 – Benoît Barbier/Sygma, bl – Finler, tr – Orion, courtesy Kobal, br – Sygma, tl
783 – RR/Kipa, br – Finler, bl – UA, courtesy Kobal, tl – Warners, courtesy Kobal, tr
784 – BFI, bl – RR/Ciné-Images, tr, bm – Finler, mr – Carson, tl, br – Valérie Blier/Sygma, tm
785 – RR/Kipa, bl, bm, ml – Carson, tl, tx, ty, tr – Sygma, br – Warners, courtesy Kobal, mr
787 – Carson, sp
788 – El Desea/Lauren, courtesy Kobal, ml – Finler, tl, tr, br
789 – RR/Kipa, tr – Gordon/Universal, courtesy Kobal, bl – Lucasfilm Ltd/Paramount, courtesy Kobal, br – Orion, courtesy Kobal, ml – Warners, courtesy Kobal, tl
790 – RR/Kipa, tm, br – Finler, tr – Outlaw, courtesy Kobal, bl – Valérie Blier/Sygma, tl
791 – Finler, tl, tr, br – Columbia TriStar, courtesy Kobal, bl
792 – Finler, tl, bl, bm – Muray Close/Sygma, br – Renaissance Films/BBC/Curzon Films, courtesy Kobal, tr
793 – Finler, bl – Kobal, tr
794 – David Doyle, bl – Finler, br, tl, tm, ml – Carson, tr
795 – Cinemarque-New World, courtesy Kobal, bl – courtesy Mainline Pictures, tr – Finler, tm, tl, mr, ml – Richard Melloul/Sygma, br
796 – Finler, mr – Paramount, courtesy Kobal, mm
797 – First Independent, mm
799 – Carson, sp
800 – Jeanne L. Bulliard/Sygma, bl – Paramount, courtesy Kobal, mm – Warners, courtesy Kobal, br
801 – Artificial Eye, br – Benoît Barbier/Sygma, bm – Finler, tl – Patrick Camboulive/Sygma, bl – Touchstone/Warners, courtesy Kobal, tr
802 – RR/Kipa, tm – Finler, bl, br – MO/Kipa, tl
803 – Carolco/TriStar, courtesy Kobal, bl – Finler, br – Nikolai Ejevski, tm – Sygma, tr
804 – Columbia, courtesy Kobal, br – Hollywood Pictures/Amblin, courtesy Kobal, bl – Finler, tr – Warners, courtesy Kobal, tl
805 – RR/Ciné-Images, br – Jerôme Prébois/Sygma, bl – Paramount, courtesy Kobal, tl
806 – RR/Kipa, bm – Finler, tm, bl, br – Orion, courtesy Kobal, tr
807 – Finler, mm
808 – David Doyle, bl – Electric Pictures, bm – Film Workshop, courtesy Kobal, tr – Finler, tm – Carson, tl, br – Vestron/MGM/UA, courtesy Kobal, mr
809 – courtesy Electric Pictures, tr – courtesy Mainline Pictures, bm – RR/Kipa, bl – Erre Prods/Sovereign Pictures/Reteitalia, courtesy Kobal, br – Finler, mr – Carson, tl
811 – Carson, sp
812 – Cineplex Odeon, courtesy Kobal, bl – RR/Kipa, tl – Finler, br – Paramount, courtesy Kobal, tr
813 – RR/Kipa, tl – E.D.R. Pressman/Shochiku Fuji/Sovereign Pictures, courtesy Kobal, mm – James Andanson/Sygma, br – P. Ramey/Sygma, bl – Carson, tr
814 – CEH, br – David Doyle, bl – RR/Kipa, tr – Finler, tl
815 – CEH, br – RR/Kipa, tr – Reitalia/Scena Film, courtesy Kobal, bl – Warners, courtesy Kobal, tl
816 – BBC Films, courtesy Kobal, tl – Moune Jamet/Sygma, bl, bm – Vivid/Canal Plus/British Screen, courtesy Kobal, tr, br
817 – CEH, tr – Electric Pictures, tl – Finler, bl – Luc Roux/Sygma, br – Sygma, ml
818 – Benoît Barbier/Sygma, tl – J. Jacques Beineix/Sygma, bl – Disney, tr, br
819 – Columbia, courtesy Kobal, bl – Finler, br – Universal, courtesy Kobal, tl – Warners, courtesy Kobal, tr
820 – CEH, bl – David Doyle, br, ml – RR/Kipa, tl – Finler, mm – Carson, tr
821 – BFI, bl – courtesy Artificial Eye, mr – De Laurentiis/Propaganda/Boy Toy, courtesy Kobal, tl – Finler, br – Carson, tr, tm – Warners, courtesy Kobal, ml
823 – Photofest, sp
824 – CEH, tr – David Doyle, br – RR/Kipa, bl – Lux Roux/Sygma, tl
825 – David Doyle, tl – RR/Kipa, tr – Jean Marie Leroy/Sygma, mm – Patrick Chauvel/Sygma, bm
826 – Finler, bl – Sygma, tl – TriStar, courtesy Kobal, tr – Warners, courtesy Kobal, br
827 – 2Oth Century Fox/Morgan Creek, courtesy Kobal, bl – CEH, tm, br
828 – Artificial Eye, bl – CEH, tr, tl – Finler, br
829 – Carolco/Canal Plus/RCS Video, courtesy Kobal, by, br – CEH, tr – Electric Pictures, bl – Finler, bx – Disney, tl
830 – courtesy Metro Tartan Pictures, mr – Finler, bl – Paramount, courtesy Kobal, br – Carson, tl, tm, tr
831 – CEH, ml, bl – courtesy Artificial Eye, tr – courtesy Electric Pictures, mr – David Doyle, tm – Carson, tl – Warners, br
833 – Carson, sp
834 – CEH, br – Finler, tr – Los Hooligans/Columbia, courtesy Kobal, tl – Sipa, mm – Warners/Regency/Canal Plus, courtesy Kobal, bl
835 – Fox, courtesy Kobal, ml – CEH, tl, bm, bl – courtesy Ent. film dist., br – courtesy Metro Tartan Pictures, tr
836 – Artificial Eye, tr – CEH, br, bl – Ent. film dist., tm – Film 4 Int/British Screen/Thin Man Prods, courtesy Kobal, tl
837 – Arau/Cinevista/Aviacsa, courtesy Kobal, tl – Buena Vista/Hollywood, courtesy Kobal, br – CEH, tr, bl
838 – Artificial Eye, tl, tm – CEH, bl, bm – RR/Sygma-Finler, tr, br
839 – courtesy Artificial Eye, br – courtesy Electric Pictures, bl – Finler, tl – Silver Pix/Warners, courtesy Kobal, tr
840 – Merchant-Ivory/Columbia, courtesy Kobal, bm – Sipa, tl, tx, ty, tr
841 – courtesy © TriStar Pictures, bl – courtesy © Touchstone Pictures, br – David Doyle, tl, tr
842 – courtesy First Independent Films, tr – courtesy ICA Projects, br – Finler, bl, mr – Metro Tartan Pictures, tm – Carson, tl
843 – CEH, tm – Anita Weber/Sipa Press, tr – courtesy Arrow Films, bm – courtesy First Independent FILMS, mr – courtesy ICA Projects, br – Finler, bl – Carson, tl
845 – Carson, sp
846 – CEH, tl – Columbia, courtesy Kobal, bl – Sipa, br – Universal, courtesy Kobal, tr
847 – CEH, tr, tl – David Doyle, tm – Finler, bl – Photofest, br
848 – Artificial Eye, bm – Ent. film dist., tl, tr – Photofest, bl, br
849 – CEH, tm, bm – courtesy © CIBY, tl – Finler, bl – Photofest, mr
850 – Disney, tl – courtesy © Hollywood pictures, tr – courtesy Polygram Filmed Entertainment (UK), tl – Photofest, bl, bm, br
851 – Universal courtesy Kobal, ml – courtesy Kobal, bl – Sipa Press, tl – Sygma, br – © Miramax, courtesy McDonald & Rutter, tr
852 – courtesy Polygram Filmed Entertainment (UK), tl – Ent. film dist., br – Photofest, ml – Carson, tm, tr – courtesy Ent. film Dist., mr – courtesy Metro Tartan Pictures, bl
853 – courtesy © Columbia, tl – Carson, tm, tr, mm – Photofest, mr, bl – courtesy Metro Tartan Pictures, br – courtesy Polygram Filmed Entertainment, ml
855 – Carson, sp
856 – courtesy McDonald & Rutter, bl – Geffen Pictures courtesy Kobal, tm – Sipa Press, tr – courtesy © Tristar Pictures, br
857 – courtesy © First Independent Films, t – Photofest, br – © Columbia Pictures courtesy Kobal, bl
858 – courtesy Kobal, tl – courtesy McDonald & Rutter, bm – courtesy Electric Pictures, br – courtesy Gala Film Distributors, bl – © Miramax Films, tr
859 – Photofest, tr, ml, bml, bl – Sipa Press, tl – courtesy © Miramax Buena Vista, br
860 – Carolco, courtesy Kobal, bl – Universal, courtesy Kobal, tr – Warners, courtesy Kobal, br
861 – Carolco, courtesy Kobal, t – First Independent, bl – Finler, br

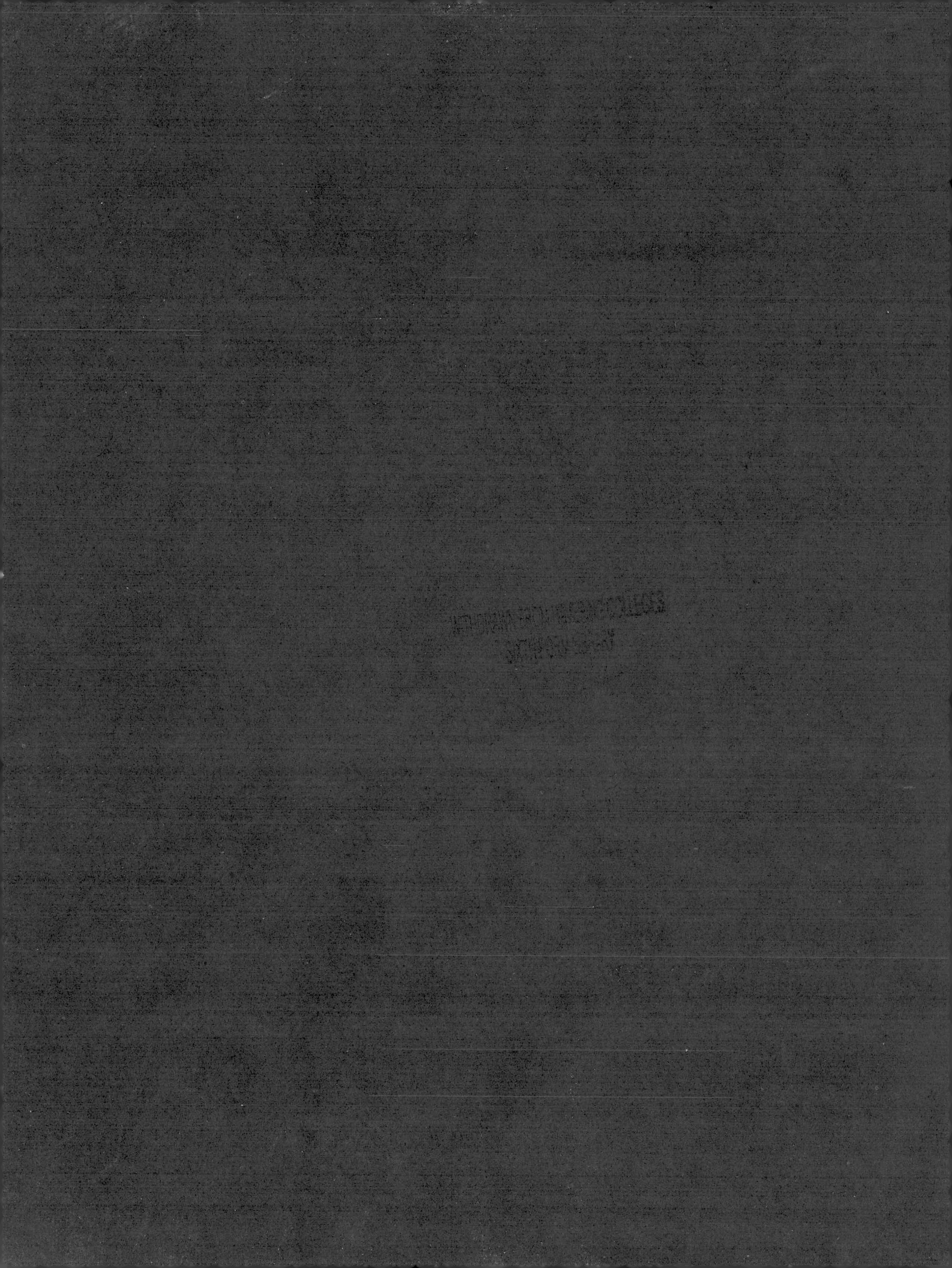